Europe

this edition researched and updated by

David Abram, Rob Andrews, Jon Bousfield, Lance Chilton,
Belinda Dixon, Marc Dubin, Nick Edwards, John Fisher, Simon
Foster, Paul Gray, Patrick Graham, Lucia Graves, Rob Humphreys,
Daniel Jacobs, Fran Kellett, Phil Lee, Chris Lloyd, Norm Longley,
Lucy Mallows, James McConnachie, Patrick McConnell, Jose
Navarro, Catherine Phillips, James Proctor, Donald Reid, Paul
Sentobe, Laura Stone, Matthew Teller, Sam Thorne, Geoff Wallis,
Greg Ward and Paul Whitfield.

ROUGH GUIDES

NEW YORK • LONDON • DELHI
www.roughguides.com

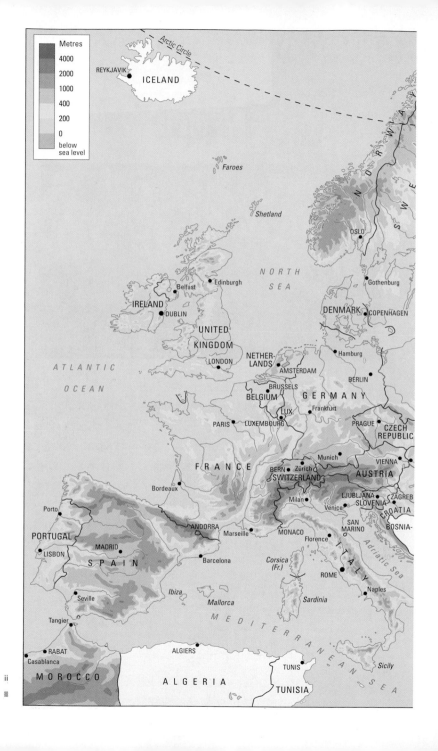

iii

▽ Santorini, Greece

Introduction to
Europe

Ongoing expansion of the European Union, and ever-closer ties among its member states, have contributed to a feeling that Europe is increasingly becoming a single entity. In part, this is a superficial analysis, but although true European unity remains a long way off, developments such as the introduction of the euro, the creation of the frontier-free Schengen Group and the opening of the Channel Tunnel have done much in recent years to bring it closer.

Conventionally, the **geographical boundaries** of Europe are the Ural Mountains in the east, the Atlantic Coast in the north and west, and the Mediterranean in the south. However, within these rough parameters Europe is massively diverse. The environment changes radically within very short distances, with bleak mountain ranges never far from broad, fertile plains, and deep, ancient forests close to scattered lake systems or river gorges. Politically and ethnically, too, it is an extraordinary patchwork: Slavic peoples are scattered through central Europe from Poland in the north to Serbia and Bulgaria in the south; the Finnish and Estonian languages bear no resemblance to the tongues of their Baltic and Scandinavian neighbours, but more to that of Hungary, over 1000km south; meanwhile Romansch, akin to ancient Latin, is spoken in the valleys of southeastern Switzerland, while the Basques of the western Pyrenees have a language unrelated to any others known. These differences have become more political of late with the rise of nationalism that coincided with the fall of Communism, and borders are even now being redrawn, not always peacefully, and usually along lines of language, race or religion.

This book is a little eccentric in its **definition of Europe**. We have excluded countries such as Albania, Belarus, Moldova and Ukraine, which are too far off the beaten track to be on most people's European "grand tour", while of the war-torn and strife-riven republics that have been carved out of the former Yugoslavia, only Slovenia and Croatia have been included as easily accessible and currently safe to visit. On the other hand, we cover countries such as Morocco and Turkey that are not strictly part of Europe, in the main because they are easy to reach on a European tour and are included by the InterRail pass. We also have chapters on Russia, Estonia, Latvia and Lithuania, though these countries are *not* covered by the InterRail pass.

Where to go

here you head for obviously depends on your tastes and the kind of vacation you want: you can sample mountain air and winter sports in the Alps of France, Austria or Switzerland, lie on a beach in the swanky resorts of the south of France or Italy, or view architecture and works of art in the great cities of London, Paris, Florence and Amsterdam. Suffice to say, the lifting of restrictions on travel in eastern Europe, with only a handful of countries still requiring visas and nothing like the bureaucratic regulations there were before, means that the

▽ Trevi Fountain, Rome

Working in Europe

There are plenty of ways of supplementing your travel budget in Europe. Bar- and restaurant-work is fine, so long as you speak the local language, but grape-picking is the perennial favourite with travellers.

Help is needed from August to October – and in far more countries than you may at first think, from Germany in the north, by way of eastern European countries such as Hungary, to the more familiar vineyards of France, Italy and Spain.

Continent really is there for the travelling – something manifest in the increasingly good-value rail passes (see pp.20–29) that cover most of the countries in this book. Although you may want to make a long hop or two by air, rail is *the* way to see the Continent, highlighting the diversity of the place when you travel in a few hours from the cool temperatures of northern Europe to the rich and sultry climes of the Mediterranean. In fact, with the richness and diversity of its culture, climate, landscapes and peoples, there is no more exciting place to travel.

The European Union

The European Economic Community (EEC), formed by the Treaty of Rome in 1957, had six members: France, Germany, Italy, Belgium, the Netherlands and Luxembourg. By the time the Maastricht Treaty came into force in 1993, changing the organization's name to the **European Union (EU)**, the original six had been joined by Denmark, Ireland and the UK (1973), Greece (1981), Portugal and Spain (1986), and Austria, Finland and Sweden (1995), making a total of fifteen member states. Norway voted in a 1972 referendum to stay out. In 2004, ten more states will join: Cyprus, the Czech Republic, Estonia, Hungary, Latvia, Lithuania, Malta, Poland, Slovakia and Slovenia, bringing the number to 25. Twelve of the original fifteen (all bar the UK, Denmark and Sweden) already use a single currency, the **euro**, and all of the new ten are expected to follow suit when they join.

Whether this vast union, headed by a Council of Ministers and a directly elected European Parliament, should move towards becoming a fully fledged United States of Europe, or confine itself to being just a trading bloc, is a matter of some controversy. The original six members tend to favour further political union, leading to a federal Europe, whereas the UK and Denmark are the countries most consistently opposed to moves towards federalism. Only time will tell.

When to go

Europe's **climate** is as variable as everything else about the Continent. In **northwestern Europe** – Benelux, Denmark, southwestern Norway, most of France and parts of Germany, as well as the British Isles – the climate is basically a cool temperate one, with the chance of rain all year round and no great extremes of either cold or hot weather. There is no bad time to travel in most of this part of Europe, although the winter months (Nov–March) can be damp and miserable – especially in the upland regions – and obviously the summer period (May–Sept) sees the most reliable and driest weather.

In **eastern Europe** – to the right of a north–south line drawn roughly through the heart of Germany and extending down as far as the western edge of Bulgaria (taking in eastern Germany, Poland, central Russia, the Baltic states, southern Sweden, the Czech and Slovak republics, Austria, Switzerland, Hungary and Romania) – the climatic conditions are more extreme, with freezing winters and sometimes sweltering summers. Here the transitional spring and autumn seasons are the most pleasant time to travel; deep midwinter, especially, can be very unpleasant, although it doesn't have the dampness associated with the northwestern European climate.

Southern Europe, principally the countries that border the Mediterranean and associated seas – southern France, Italy, Spain, Portugal, Greece

Festivals

Wherever you find yourself in Europe, you'll not be far away from some annual event or other. From Venice's extravagant **Carnival** (Feb) to Munich's boozy **Oktoberfest** (Sept–Oct), by way of the **Pamplona Bull Run** (July) and the **Edinburgh Arts Festival** (Aug), you can be sure of coinciding your trip with at least one of Europe's big events. Be sure to always book your accommodation in advance at these times – rooms can fill up months in advance for the bigger events.

▽ Pamplona, Spain

and western Turkey – has the most hospitable climate in Europe, with a general pattern of warm, dry summers and mild winters. Travel is possible at any time of year here, although the peak summer months can be very hot and very busy and the deep winter ones can see some rain.

There are, too, marked regional variations within these three broad groupings. As they're such large countries, inland Spain and France can, for example, see a **continental** type of weather as extreme as any in central Europe, and the Alpine areas of Italy, Austria and Switzerland – and other **mountain areas** such as the Pyrenees, Apennines and parts of the Balkans – have a climate mainly influenced by altitude, which means short summers and long winters that always see snow. There are also, of course, the northern regions of Russia and Scandinavia, which have an **Arctic climate** – again, bitterly cold, though with some surprisingly warm weather during the short summer when much of the region is warmed by the Gulf Stream. Winter sees the sun barely rise at all in these areas, while high summer can mean almost constant daylight.

There are obviously **other considerations** when deciding when to go. If you're planning to visit fairly touristed areas, especially beach resorts in the Mediterranean, avoid July and August, when the weather can be too hot and the resorts at their most congested. Bear in mind, also, that in a number of countries in Europe everyone takes their vacation at the same time (this is certainly true in France, Spain and Italy, where everyone goes away in August). Find out the holiday month beforehand for the countries where you intend to travel, since you can expect the crush to be especially bad in the resorts; meanwhile, in the cities the only other people around will be fellow tourists, which can be miserable. In northern Scandinavia the climatic extremes are such that you'll find opening times severely restricted, and even road and rail lines closed, outside the May to September period, making travel futile if not impossible. In mountainous areas, things stay open for the winter sports season (Dec–April), though outside the main resorts you'll again find many things closed. On the other hand, mid-April to mid-June can be a quiet period in many mountain resorts, when you may have much of the place to yourself.

△ Temperature map

Average daily maximum temperatures in °C/°F

	Jan	Feb	Mar	Apr	May	June	July	Aug	Sept	Oct	Nov	Dec
Amsterdam	4/40	5/42	9/49	13/56	18/64	21/70	22/72	22/71	19/67	14/57	9/48	6/42
Ankara	4/40	6/42	11/51	17/63	23/73	26/78	30/86	31/87	26/78	21/69	14/57	6/43
Athens	13/55	14/57	16/60	20/68	25/77	30/86	33/92	33/92	29/84	24/75	19/66	15/58
Berlin	2/35	3/37	8/46	13/56	19/66	22/72	24/75	23/74	20/68	13/56	7/45	3/38
Brussels	4/40	7/42	10/51	14/58	18/65	22/72	23/73	22/72	21/69	15/60	9/48	6/42
Bratislava	-1/30	0/30	5/41	10/50	13/58	12/54	20/68	19/67	16/61	10/50	4/40	0/32
Bucharest	1/34	4/40	10/50	18/64	23/74	27/81	30/86	30/85	25/78	18/65	10/49	4/40
Budapest	1/34	4/40	10/50	17/62	22/71	26/78	28/82	27/81	23/74	16/61	8/47	4/40
Copenhagen	2/36	2/36	5/41	10/51	16/61	19/67	22/71	21/70	18/64	12/54	7/45	4/40
Dublin	8/46	8/47	10/50	13/55	15/60	18/65	20/67	19/67	17/63	14/57	10/51	8/47
Helsinki	-3/26	-4/25	0/32	6/44	14/56	19/66	22/71	20/68	15/59	8/47	3/37	-1/31
İstanbul	8/46	9/47	11/51	16/60	21/69	25/77	28/82	28/82	24/76	20/68	15/59	11/51
Lisbon	14/57	15/59	17/63	20/67	21/71	25/77	27/81	28/82	26/79	22/72	17/63	15/58
London	6/43	7/44	10/50	13/56	17/62	20/69	22/71	22/71	19/65	14/58	10/50	7/45
Luxembourg	3/37	4/40	10/49	14/57	18/65	21/70	23/73	22/71	19/66	13/56	7/44	4/40
Madrid	9/47	11/52	15/59	18/65	21/70	27/80	31/87	30/85	25/77	19/65	13/55	9/48
Moscow	-9/15	-6/22	0/32	10/50	19/66	21/70	23/73	22/72	16/61	9/48	2/35	-5/24
Oslo	-2/28	-1/30	4/40	10/50	16/61	20/68	22/72	21/70	16/60	9/48	3/38	0/32
Paris	6/43	7/44	12/54	16/60	20/68	23/73	25/76	24/75	21/70	16/60	10/50	7/44
Prague	0/31	1/34	7/44	12/54	18/64	21/70	23/73	22/72	18/65	12/53	5/42	1/34
Rabat	17/63	18/65	20/68	22/71	23/73	26/78	28/82	30/83	27/81	25/77	21/70	18/65
Rīga	-4/25	-3/27	2/35	10/50	16/61	21/69	22/71	21/70	17/63	11/52	4/40	-2/29
Rome	11/52	13/55	15/59	19/66	23/74	28/82	30/87	30/86	26/79	22/71	16/61	13/55
Sofia	2/35	4/40	10/50	16/60	21/69	24/76	27/81	26/79	22/70	17/63	9/48	4/40
Stockholm	-1/30	-1/30	3/37	8/47	14/58	19/67	22/71	20/68	15/60	9/49	5/40	2/35
Tallinn	-4/25	-4/25	0/32	7/45	14/57	19/66	20/68	19/66	15/59	10/50	3/38	-1/30
Vienna	1/34	3/38	8/47	15/58	19/67	23/73	25/76	24/75	20/68	14/56	7/45	3/37
Vilnius	-5/25	-3/26	1/34	12/54	18/65	21/71	23/74	22/71	17/62	11/52	4/40	-3/26
Warsaw	0/32	0/32	6/42	12/53	20/67	23/73	24/75	23/73	19/66	13/55	6/42	2/35
Zürich	2/36	5/41	10/51	15/59	19/67	23/73	25/76	24/75	20/69	14/57	7/45	3/39

32

things not to miss

It's not possible to see everything that Europe has to offer in one trip – and we don't suggest you try. What follows is a selective and subjective taste of the continent's highlights: outstanding natural features, spectacular cities, festivals, history and beautiful architecture. They're arranged in five colour-coded categories to help you find the very best things to see, do and experience. All entries have a page reference to take you straight into the guide, where you can find out more.

01 Carnevale, Venice Page **548** • Don a costume, get a mask and join the crowds congregating in the squares for this pre-Lent festival.

02 **Cordoba, Spain** Page **883** • Nothing can prepare you for the breathtaking beauty of Cordoba's Grand Mosque (Mezquita).

04 **Ljublijana, Slovenia** Page **814** • Stunning architecture, a hilltop castle and leafy riverside cafés.

03 **The Edinburgh Festival** Page **171** • Europe's biggest arts festival.

05 **Oktoberfest, Germany** Page **423** • An orgy of beer drinking – festival-goers down 400,000 litres of beer every day, for sixteen days.

06 **Cappadocia, Turkey** Page **982** • Water and wind have created a land of fantastic forms from the soft tufa rock, including forests of cones, table mountains and canyon-like valleys.

07 Belgian chocolates Page 85 • Many would say that Belgium's chocolates are the finest in Europe.

08 Diocletian's Palace, Split Page 217 • Extraordinary 1700-year-old palace housing shops, restaurants and bars.

09 Avignon, Provence Page 359 • The great city of the popes and for centuries one of the major artistic centres of France.

10 **Adventure sports, Switzerland** Page **943** • Try anything from paragliding to zorbing, or face up to the world's longest bungee-jump, a 220m knee-trembler.

11 **London, Britain** Page **113** • Behind the grandeur, London isn't a city so much as a collection of villages – expensive, crowded and endlessly fascinating.

12 **Amsterdam's canals** Page **665** • The Venice of the north? Maybe not, but definitely an experience in their own right.

13 **The Kremlin, Russia** Page **782** • Evocative complex of political, architectural and artistic associations.

14 **Kaffee und Kuchen** Page **68** • Have a Viennese coffee and a fabulously gooey cake in one of Central Europe's great coffee houses.

15 **Island hopping, Greece** Page **452–471** • Old-town charm, deserted beaches or full-on party-town atmosphere – whatever you're looking for, you'll find a Greek island that suits you.

16 **Nyhavn, Copenhagen** Page **259** • Canalside bars and cafés in this district are *the* place to be seen in summer.

17 **Barcelona, Spain** Page **869** ● Enjoy a drink or some tapas in a *fin-de-siècle* bar in Spain's city of cool.

18 **Surfing, England** Page **140** ● Test your mettle against the Atlantic rollers off England's Cornwall coast.

19 **Rome, Italy** Page **572** • Just as languorous, chic and visually striking as you imagine.

20 **Paris, France** Page **311** • Europe's most romantic capital, easily living up to all your expectations – and more.

21 **Atlas Mountains, Morocco** Page **638** • Get away from it all on a hiking trip into these world-famous mountains. Any tourist office can give you details of organized trips.

22 **Food, France** Page **309** • French food is amongst the finest in the world and the range of cheeses alone gives an idea of the quality on offer.

23 **Athens, Greece** Page **433** • The iconic Parthenon stands in the heart of the Acropolis, high above the Greek capital.

24 **April Feria, Sevilla, Spain**
Page **884** • A week-long party of flamenco, parades and bullfights.

25 **Trekking in Lapland, Finland** Page **304** • Trek across the tundra of Lapland, where, if you're lucky, you might even see reindeer grazing.

26 **Prague** Page **233** • One of Europe's most beautiful cities; an unmissable stop on any trip.

Sidebar: ACTIVITIES | CONSUME | EVENTS | NATURE | SIGHTS

27 **Kraków, Poland** Page **720** •
Buy wonderful handcrafted gifts in
characterful surroundings at the heart of one
of Europe's most beautiful squares.

28 **Ibiza, Spain** Page **870** • Party
the night away on Europe's most
famous clubbing island.

29 **Király Baths, Budapest** Page **482** • Relax in the steamy healing waters to
enjoy this typically Hungarian experience.

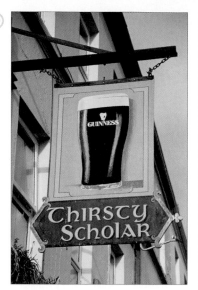

31 **Northern Lights, Sweden** Page **912** • One of the natural wonders of the world.

30 **Guinness, Ireland** Page **502** • All over Europe you'll find Irish theme-bars offering draft Guinness, but none can compare to the stuff served back home.

32 **Tatra mountains, Poland/Slovakia** Page **723/803** • Fantastic hiking opportunities in these towering peaks that form the border between Slovakia and Poland.

Contents

Using this Rough Guide

We've tried to make this Rough Guide a good read and easy to use. The book is divided into five main sections, and you should be able to find whatever you want in one of them.

Colour section

The front colour section offers a quick survey of Europe. The **introduction** aims to give you a feel for the place, with suggestions on where to go and when. Next, our authors round up their favourite aspects of Europe in the **things not to miss** section – whether it's great food, amazing sights or a spectacular festival. Right after this comes a contents list.

Basics

The Basics section covers all the **pre-departure** nitty-gritty to help you plan your trip. This is where to find out about getting to Europe by air, sea and land, the various rail passes and routes that cover the continent, what paperwork you'll need, what to do about money and insurance, how to find accommodation, opportunities for working – in fact just about every piece of **general practical information** you might need.

Guide

This is the heart of the Rough Guide, divided into user-friendly chapters, each of which covers a specific country. Every chapter starts with a list of **highlights** and an **introduction** that helps you to decide where to go,

depending on your time and budget. The introduction prefaces the mini **basics** section, covering country-specific practicalities like public transport and food and drink. Chapters then move on to **detailed coverage** of your destination. We start most **town accounts** with information on arrival and accommodation, followed by a tour of the sights, and finally reviews of places to eat and drink, and details of nightlife. Longer accounts also have a directory of practical **listings**. Each chapter concludes with details of **public transport** routes for the country.

Language

Here you'll find lists of all the essential **words and phrases** you might need on your trip, arranged by language.

Index + small print

Apart from a **full index**, which includes maps as well as places, this section covers publishing information, credits and acknowledgements, and also has our contact details in case you want to send in updates and corrections to the book – or suggestions as to how we might improve it.

Map and chapter list

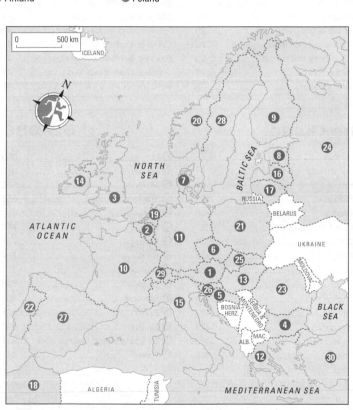

Contents

Colour section

Basics

The Guide

Language

987–997

Index and small print

999–1012

CONTENTS

Map symbols

maps are listed in the full index using coloured text

-------	International boundary	✡	Synagogue
——— ··	Province boundary	🕌	Mosque
——■——	Railway	⊞	Hospital
﹖﹖﹖﹖﹖	Funicular	⊠	Post office
●- - -●	Cable car	ⓘ	Information office
▬▬▬	Motorway	ⓒ	Telephone office
▬▬▬	Tolled motorway	@	Internet access
═══	Road	★	Bus stop
═══	Pedestrianized street	Ⓜ	Metro station
▥▥▥	Steps	Ⓡ	RER station
- - - - -	Path	Ⓢ	S-Bahn
— — —	Ferry route	Ⓣ	Tram stop
———	Waterway	Ⓤ	U-Bahn
▬▬▬	Wall	⊖	London Underground Station
峠	Mountains	⊜	FGC station
▲	Peak	🅿	Parking
☼	Hill	⊠	Gate
ꞒꞒꞒꞒꞒ	Rocks	⊛	Swimming pool
∴	Ruins	⊙	Statue
⌂	Cave	▬	Building
🜄	Waterfall	⊞	Church (town)
⚱	Fountain	⬭	Stadium
⤋	Viewpoint	▦	Park
⚐	Lighthouse	⊡	Christian cemetery
◆	Point of interest	⊡	Muslim cemetery
⚑	Museum	⊡	Jewish cemetery
🏛	Stately house	▦	Beach
⛪	Monastery	⊡	Glacier
⚶	Church (regional)	▦	Forest

Basics

Basics

Getting there

Airfares always depend on the season, with the highest being roughly mid-June to early September and over the Christmas period, with cheaper deals available for the rest of the year, particularly during the winter months (Nov–March), when fewer people are travelling. Note also that flying on weekends can sometimes add $20–60/£15–50 to the round-trip fare; price ranges quoted below assume midweek travel.

Barring special offers, the cheapest of the **airlines' published fares** are usually subject to an advance purchase of two to three weeks, and certain restrictions, such as heavy penalties if you change your schedule. These tickets sometimes go under names like "Apex" or "Super-Apex". Many airlines offer youth or student fares to **under-26s**; a passport or driving licence is sufficient proof of age, though these tickets are subject to availability and can have eccentric booking conditions. It's worth remembering that most cheap return fares will only give a percentage refund, if any, should you need to cancel or alter your journey, so make sure you check the restrictions carefully before buying a ticket.

You can often cut costs by going through a **specialist flight agent** – either a consolidator, who buys up blocks of tickets from the airlines and sells them at a discount, or a **discount agent**, who in addition to dealing with discounted flights may also offer special student and youth fares and a range of other travel-related services such as travel insurance, rail passes and tours. Some agents specialize in **charter flights**, which may be cheaper than anything available on a scheduled flight, but again departure dates are fixed and withdrawal penalties are high. Be advised, however, that the pool of travel companies is swimming with sharks – exercise caution, especially when dealing with small firms that are not well-established, and never deal with a company that demands cash up front or refuses to accept credit cards.

If Europe is only one stop on a longer journey, and especially if you are based in Australia or New Zealand, you might want to consider buying a **Round-the-World (RTW) ticket**. Some travel agents can sell you an "off-the-shelf" RTW ticket that will have you touching down in about half a dozen cities (London, Paris, Amsterdam, Rome, Athens and Moscow are on many off-the-shelf itineraries); others will have to assemble one for you, which can be tailored to your needs but is apt to be more expensive. Figure on US$1800/Aus$2000 for a RTW ticket including one or two European stopovers.

Booking flights online

Many airlines and discount travel websites offer you the opportunity to book your tickets online, cutting out the costs of agents and middlemen. Good deals can often be found through discount or auction sites, as well as through the airlines' own websites.

Useful websites

ⓦ **www.airfares.co.uk** Easy-to-use flight search and booking from Britain and Ireland only.
ⓦ **www.cheapflight.com** (in US);
ⓦ **www.cheapflights.ca** (in Canada);
ⓦ **www.cheapflights.com** (in UK and Ireland);
ⓦ **www.cheapflights.com.au** (in Australia). Flight deals, travel agents, plus links to other travel sites.
ⓦ **www.cheaptickets.com** Discount flight specialists (US only).
ⓦ **www.etn.nl/discount.htm** International hub for online consolidators, discount agents and bucket shops, maintained by the non-profit European Travel Network.
ⓦ **www.etntelephone.com/discountflights** One of the best sites for discount fares from the USA.
ⓦ **www.expedia.com** (in US);
ⓦ **www.expedia.ca** (in Canada);
ⓦ **www.expedia.co.uk** (in UK). Discount airfares, all-airline search engine and daily deals.
ⓦ **www.flyaow.com** Online air travel info and reservations site.

ⓦ **www.geocities.com/thavery2000** An extensive list of airline toll-free numbers (from the US) and websites.

ⓦ **www.hotwire.com** Bookings from the US only. Last-minute savings of up to forty percent on regular published fares. Travellers must be at least 18 and there are no refunds, transfers or changes allowed. Log-in required.

ⓦ **www.lastminute.com** (in UK);

ⓦ **www.lastminute.com.au** (in Australia). Offers good last-minute holiday package and flight-only deals.

ⓦ **www.priceline.com** (in US);

ⓦ **www.priceline.co.uk** (in UK). Name-your-own-price website that has deals at around forty percent off standard fares. You cannot specify flight times (although you do specify dates) and the tickets are non-refundable, non-transferable and non-changeable.

ⓦ **www.skyauction.com** Bookings from the US only. Auctions tickets and travel packages using a "second bid" scheme. The best strategy is to bid the maximum you're willing to pay, since if you win you'll pay just enough to beat the runner-up regardless of your maximum bid.

ⓦ **www.smilinjack.com/airlines.htm** Lists an up-to-date compilation of airline website addresses.

ⓦ **www.travelocity.com** Destination guides, hot web fares and best deals for car rental, accommodation and lodging as well as fares. Provides access to the travel agent system SABRE, the most comprehensive central reservations system in the US.

ⓦ **www.travelshop.com.au** Australian website offering discounted flights, packages, insurance, and online bookings.

ⓦ **travel.yahoo.com** Incorporates a lot of Rough Guide material in its coverage of destination countries and cities across the world, with information about places to eat, sleep, etc.

From North America

The airspace between **North America** and Europe is one of the most heavily travelled in the world. It is served by literally dozens of airlines, both US carriers and the national airlines of almost every European country, and there is consequently a huge range of seats at a huge range of prices. It all depends on when and from where you're travelling, and, of course, where you want to go. There are, however, a number of "gateway" cities into which you'll find a greater – and cheaper – choice of flights. You'll often find the lowest fare by leaving from the airline's "hub" – New York, Atlanta, Dallas, Chicago, Los Angeles, San Francisco, Seattle, Vancouver, Toronto and Montreal are the main ones. Hub cities also tend to have nonstop flights. You do, however, need to be flexible: London, Paris, and Amsterdam are usually the cheapest gateway cities in Europe, simply because they are served by more flights; Milan, Rome and Frankfurt run a close second in some cases. Flying mid-week rather than at the weekend is also a few dollars cheaper.

Flights from eastern and central US

There are lots of options from most of the **eastern** hub cities, though the best deals are generally out of New York and Chicago to London. Official round-trip fares bought in advance from New York to London with the major carriers, such as Virgin Atlantic (the best in terms of service), British Airways or American, are around $200–600 in low season, $400–800 in high season (plus fees and taxes of around $100). You should, however, be able to find discounted fares, without the need to book three months in advance, for around $290/$480, especially if you're a student or under 26. From Chicago, official advance-purchase fares to London are around $300/$500 depending on the season, with more flexible discounted tickets at around $370/$530. To give an idea of other alternatives, discounted tickets from New York can be found for $340/700 to Paris, $350/700 to Frankfurt, $370/725 to Madrid, or $410/850 to Athens; flying from Chicago, discounted tickets can be had at $410/760 to Paris, $400/810 to Frankfurt, $365/740 to Madrid, or $455/930 to Athens. There may also be special limited promotional offers which appear from time to time, especially in the off-peak seasons; Virgin Atlantic, for example, usually have New York–London fares in late winter for $99 each way, with no advance purchase necessary.

Flights from the US west coast

From the **west coast** it's much the same story. The big airlines fly at least three times a week (sometimes daily) from Los Angeles, San Francisco and Seattle to the main

European cities, with round-trip advance-purchase tickets from LA to London at around $330/530, depending on season. Again, you can avoid the three-month advance booking and length of stay restrictions and still find a comparatively inexpensive fare by going to a discount agent or youth travel specialist, where tickets can be had for $410/680 (depending on the time of year) for a round trip to London, $410/790 to Paris, $540/460 to Frankfurt, $510/970 to Madrid, or $540/1010 to Athens.

Flights from Canada

Most of the big airlines fly to the major European hubs from **Montréal** and **Toronto** at least once daily (three times a week for the smaller airlines). From Toronto, London is your cheapest option, with the lowest round-trip fares, direct from the airline, costing around C$375/550 (depending on the season). From Montréal to Paris you can expect to pay C$1200/1300. Once again, a discount/student specialist should be able to find a fare that's more flexible and, possibly, less expensive; current examples of discounted fares include C$220/235 from Toronto to London and C$800/1200 from Montréal to Paris. **Vancouver** has daily flights to several European cities, with round-trip fares to London on offer for around C$470/680, depending on the season.

Airlines in North America

Aer Lingus (Irish) ☎1-800/223-6537, ⊛www.aerlingus.ie.
Aeroflot (Russian) US ☎1-888/340-6400, Canada 416/642-1653, ⊛www.aeroflot.com.
Air Canada ☎1-888/247-2262, ⊛www.aircanada.ca.
Air France US ☎1-800/237-2747, Canada ☎1-800/667-2747, ⊛www.airfrance.com.
Alitalia US ☎1-800/223-5730, Canada ☎1-800/361-8336, ⊛www.alitalia.com.
American Airlines ☎1-800/433-7300, ⊛www.aa.com.
Austrian ☎1-800/843-0002, ⊛www.aua.com.
BMI British Midland ☎1-800/788-0555, ⊛www.flybmi.com.
British Airways ☎1-800/247-9297, ⊛www.ba.com.
Continental ☎1-800/231-0856, ⊛www.continental.com.

Czech US ☎1-800/223-2365, Canada 416/363-3174, ⊛www.czechairlines.com.
Delta ☎1-800/241-4141, ⊛www.delta.com.
Finnair ☎1-800/950-5000, ⊛www.finnair.com.
Iberia (Spanish) ☎1-800/772-4642, ⊛www.iberia.com.
KLM/Northwest ☎1-800/447-4747, wwww.klm.com.
Lauda Air (Austrian) ☎1-800/843-0002, ⊛www.laudaair.com.
LOT (Polish) US ☎1-800/223-0593 or 718/264-6480, Canada ☎1-800/668-5928, ⊛www.lot.com.
Lufthansa (German) US ☎1-800/645-3880, Canada ☎1-800/563-5954, ⊛www.lufthansa.com.
Malev (Hungarian) ☎1-800/223-6884 or 212/566-9944, ⊛www.hungarianairlines.com.
Martinair (Dutch) ☎1-800/627-8462, ⊛www.martinairusa.com.
Olympic (Greek) ☎1-800/223-1226 or 718/896-7393, ⊛www.olympic-airways.gr.
Royal Air Maroc ☎1-800/344-6726, ⊛www.royalairmaroc.com.
SAS (Scandinavian) ☎1-800/221-2350, ⊛www.scandinavian.net.
Swiss ☎1-877/359-7947, ⊛www.swiss.com.
TAP Air Portugal ☎1-800/221-7370, ⊛www.tap-airportugal.pt.
Tarom Romanian Air ☎212/560-0840, ⊛www.tarom.ro.
Turkish ☎1-800/874-8875 or 212/339-9650, ⊛www.thy.com.
United ☎1-800/538-2929, ⊛www.ual.com.
US Airways ☎1-800/622-1015, ⊛www.usair.com.
Virgin Atlantic ☎1-800/862-8621, ⊛www.virgin.com.

Discount agents in North America

Air Brokers International ☎1-800/883-3273, ⊛www.airbrokers.com. Consolidator and specialist in RTW tickets.
Airtreks ☎1-877/AIRTREKS or 415/912-5600, ⊛www.airtreks.com. RTW specialists: the website lets you build and price your own itinerary.
Council Travel ☎1-800/2COUNCIL, ⊛www.counciltravel.com. Specializes in student/budget travel. Flights from the US only.
Educational Travel Center ☎1-800/747-5551 or 608/256-5551, ⊛www.edtrav.com. Student/youth discount agent.
New Frontiers ☎1-800/677-0720 or 310/670-7318, ⊛www.newfrontiers.com. Discount-travel firm.

SkyLink US ☎1-800/AIR-ONLY or 212/573-8980, Canada ☎1-800/SKY-LINK, ⊛www.skylinkus.com. Consolidator.

STA Travel US ☎1-800/781-4040, Canada 1-888/427-5639, ⊛www.sta-travel.com. Worldwide specialists in independent travel; also student IDs, travel insurance, car rental, rail passes, etc.

Student Flights ☎1-800/255-8000 or 480/951-1177, ⊛www.isecard.com. Student/youth fares, student IDs.

TFI Tours ☎1-800/745-8000 or 212/736-1140, ⊛www.lowestairprice.com. Consolidator.

Travac ☎1-800/TRAV-800, ⊛www.thetravelsite.com. Consolidator and charter broker.

Travelers Advantage ☎1-877/259-2691, ⊛www.travelersadvantage.com. Discount travel club; annual membership fee required (currently $1 for 3 months' trial).

Travel Avenue ☎1-800/333-3335, ⊛www.travelavenue.com. Full-service travel agent that offers discounts in the form of rebates.

Travel Cuts Canada ☎1-800/667-2887, US ☎1-866/246-9762, ⊛www.travelcuts.com. Canadian student-travel organization.

Worldtek Travel ☎1-800/243-1723, ⊛www.worldtek.com. Discount travel agency.

From Britain

Heading **from Britain** to destinations in northwestern Europe, train, long-distance bus and crossing the Channel by ferry tend to be best value for money, but the further you go the cheaper air travel becomes, and it's normally cheaper to fly than take the train to most parts of southern Europe, although special deals on rail passes can bring prices down considerably.

Flights from Britain

As ever, the best way to find the cheapest **flight** is to shop around: air travel in Europe is still highly regulated, which means that the prices quoted by the airlines can usually be undercut considerably, even on Apex fares, by going to an agent. During the summer you can reach most of the countries of southern Europe – Portugal, Spain, Italy, Greece – on **charter flights**, block-booked by package holiday firms and usually having a few seats left over which they sell off cheaply through selected **agents** which are sometimes known as "bucket shops".

Though these tickets are inevitably rather restricted, with fixed return dates, a maximum validity of a month, and no chance of cancelling or changing after purchase, they can be very cheap – so much so in some cases that it's actually worth just using the outward portion if the return date doesn't suit. "**No frills**" **airlines** such as easyJet, bmibaby and Ryanair, best booked online, offer low-cost tickets to airports around Europe (though not always the most convenient ones), and they often have some outstandingly cheap special offers in winter. They also have by far the cheapest flights if you only want to go one-way, as they charge for each leg of the journey separately, but some of them do have a reputation for leaving passengers in the lurch if anything goes wrong or if flights have to be cancelled. It's also worth checking with flight agents who specialize in low-cost, discounted flights (charter and scheduled), some of them – like STA Travel or Trailfinders – concentrating on deals for young people and students, though they can be a good source of bargains for everyone. In addition, there are agents specializing in offers to a specific country or group of countries on both charters and regular scheduled departures. Excellent deals can also be found on Teletext and the Internet (see p.9).

London is predictably Britain's main hub for air travel, offering the highest frequency of flights and widest choice of destinations from all five airports (Heathrow, Gatwick, Stansted, Luton and City), but **Manchester** has flights to most parts of Europe, and there are also regular flights to the Continent from Birmingham, Bristol, Cardiff, Glasgow, Edinburgh, Leeds/Bradford and Newcastle. Failing that, you can get a BA or BMI British Midland flight from most UK airports (but not from Birmingham) to London, and take an onward flight from there, or fly to Paris with Air France, or Amsterdam with KLM, and change there.

To give a rough idea of prices booked through agents on scheduled flights in high season, reckon on paying, not including departure taxes, £45–100 to Paris, Brussels or Amsterdam; £80–200 to Scandinavia; £90–200 to the major cities of Spain or Italy; £110–280 to Athens; £150–300 to Istanbul;

or £90–300 to the major cities of eastern Europe. Many agents also do "open jaw" tickets, flying you into one city and out from another, not necessarily even in the same country.

Airlines in Britain

Adria (Slovenian) ☎020/7734 4630, ⊛www.adria.si.
Aer Arann ☎0800/587 2324, ⊛www.aerarann.ie.
Aer Lingus ☎0845/084 4444, ⊛www.aerlingus.ie.
Aeroflot ☎020/7355 2233, ⊛www.aeroflot.co.uk.
Air France ☎0845/084 5111, ⊛www.airfrance.co.uk.
Alitalia ☎0870/544 8259, ⊛www.alitalia.co.uk.
Austrian ☎0845/601 0948, ⊛www.aua.com.
BMI British Midland ☎0870/607 0555, ⊛www.flybmi.com.
bmibaby ☎0870/264 2229, ⊛www.bmibaby.com.
Britannia ☎01582/424 155, ⊛www.britanniaairways.com.
British Airways ☎0845/773 3377, ⊛www.ba.com.
British European ☎0870/567 6676, ⊛www.flybe.com.
Croatian ☎020/8563 0022, ⊛www.croatiaairlines.hr.
Czech ☎0870/444 3747, ⊛www.csa.cz.
easyJet ☎0870/600 0000, ⊛www.easyjet.com.
Estonian ☎020/7333 0196, ⊛www.estonian-air.ee.
Finnair ☎0870/241 4411, ⊛www.finnair.com.
Iberia ☎0845/601 2854, ⊛www.iberiaairlines.co.uk.
KLM ☎0870/507 4074, ⊛www.klmuk.com.
Lauda Air ☎0845/601 0948, ⊛www.aua.com.
LOT (Polish) ☎020/7580 5037, ⊛www.lot.com.
Lufthansa ☎0845/773 7747, ⊛www.lufthansa.co.uk.
Malev (Hungarian) ☎020/7439 0577, ⊛www.malev.hu.
Olympic (Greek) ☎0870/606 0460, ⊛www.olympic-airways.co.uk.
Royal Air Maroc ☎020/7439 4361, ⊛www.royalairmaroc.com.
Ryanair ☎0871/246 0000, ⊛www.ryanair.com.
SAS (Scandinavian) ☎0845/607 2772, ⊛www.scandinavian.net.
SN Brussels ☎0870/735 2345, ⊛www.brussels-airlines.com.
Swiss ☎0845/601 0956, ⊛www.swiss.com.

TAP Air Portugal ☎020/7630 0900, ⊛www.tap-airportugal.pt.
Tarom (Romanian) ☎020/7224 3693, ⊛www.tarom.ro.
Turkish ☎020/7766 9300, ⊛www.turkishairlines.com.
Virgin Express ☎020/7744 0004, ⊛www.virgin-express.com.

Discount agents in Britain

Bridge the World ☎0870/444 7474, ⊛www.bridgetheworld.com. Specializing in RTW tickets, with good backpacker deals.
Flightbookers ☎0870/010 7000, ⊛www.ebookers.com. Low scheduled fares.
Flights4Less ☎0871/222 3432, ⊛www.flights4less.co.uk. Good discount airfares.
Flynow ☎0870/444 0045, ⊛www.flynow.com. Large range of discounted tickets.
North South Travel ☎01245/608 291, ⊛www.northsouthtravel.co.uk. Friendly, competitive travel agency, offering discounted fares worldwide. Profits are used to support projects in the developing world, especially the promotion of sustainable tourism.
STA Travel ☎0870/160 0599, ⊛www.statravel.co.uk. Worldwide specialists in low-cost flights and tours for students and under-26s, though other customers are welcome.
Top Deck ☎020/7244 8000, ⊛www.topdecktravel.co.uk. Long-established agent dealing in discount flights.
Trailfinders ☎020/7628 7628, ⊛www.trailfinders.co.uk. One of the best-informed and most efficient agents for independent travellers; produce a very useful quarterly magazine worth checking for RTW routes.
Travelcare ☎0870/112 0085, ⊛www.travelcare.co.uk. Discount charter flights.
Travel Cuts ☎020/7255 2082, ⊛www.travelcuts.co.uk. British branch of Canada's main youth and student travel specialist.

By train from Britain

Direct **trains** through the Channel Tunnel from London to Paris (14 daily, 3hr) and Brussels (8 daily, 3hr 40min) are operated by Eurostar. Tickets for under-26s start at £50 one-way, £79 return. For over-26s, the cheapest ticket is a weekend day return which, at £70, costs less than a single fare. Through-ticket combinations including onward connections from Brussels and Paris can be booked through Trainseurope, International Rail and Rail Europe.

Other rail journeys from Britain involve some kind of **sea crossing**, by ferry or, sometimes, catamaran. Current rail–sea–rail return fares from London (which include the crossing) are £67 to Paris, £70 to Brussels, £79 to Amsterdam, and £157 to Berlin. They can be bought from International Rail or Trainseurope, and from some major rail stations (in London, at Charing Cross if routed via France or Belgium, or from Anglia Railways at Liverpool Street if routed via the Hook of Holland). For some destinations, there are cheaper Apex and SuperApex fares (£50 and £60 to Amsterdam, for example) requiring advance booking and subject to greater restrictions. Five-day return tickets to Paris and Brussels are also available, at £56. Otherwise, international tickets are valid for two months and allow for stopovers on the way, providing you stick to the prescribed route (there may be a choice, with different fares applicable). One-way fares are generally around two-thirds the price of a return fare. If you're **under 26** you're entitled to all sorts of special deals, not least cut-price youth fares. Also issued by International Rail and Trainseurope, these tickets are also valid for two months with stopovers permitted en route. Examples of under-26 return ticket prices are £58 to Paris, £46 to Brussels, £64 to Amsterdam and £138 to Berlin.

Whatever your age and whether you cross the Channel by ferry or through the tunnel, **through tickets** to European destinations beyond France and Germany are becoming harder to find, largely because most intercity routes in Europe are now covered by superfast, deluxe train services with "special" (high, in other words) fares which cannot be had as part of a through ticket. You could, for example, buy a ticket from London to Rome for £167 return (over-26s £175), but you wouldn't be able to use it on any through train from Paris to Italy, so you'd have to travel by local services, changing along the way. Trainseurope and International Rail are the best people to contact for through tickets.

During the summer, especially if you're travelling at night or a long distance, it's best to make reservations wherever you can; on some trains (most French TGV services, for example) it is compulsory. At night,

couchettes in six-berth compartments cost around £10–15 per person; sleeper cars cost around £20–60, depending on the train, and may be two-, three- or four-bed.

For **rail passes** and other types of discounted rail travel, see "Getting around", p.27.

Rail contacts in Britain
European Rail ℡ 020/7387 0444, ⓦ www.europeanrail.com.
Eurostar ℡ 0870/160 6600, ⓦ www.eurostar.com.
Eurotunnel ℡ 0870/535 3535, ⓦ www.eurotunnel.com.
International Rail ℡ 0870/120 1606, ⓦ www.international-rail.com.
The Man in Seat 61 ⓦ www.seat61.com.
Rail Europe ℡ 0870/584 8848, ⓦ www.raileurope.co.uk.
Trainseurope ℡ 0900/195 0101, ⓦ www.trainseurope.co.uk.

By bus from Britain

A long-distance **bus**, although much less comfortable than the train, is at least a little cheaper. The main operator based in Britain is **Eurolines**, which has a network of routes spanning the continent – north as far as Scandinavia, east to Poland and the Baltic states, and south to Spain, Portugal and Morocco. Prices can be up to a third less than the equivalent train fare, and there are marginally cheaper fares on most services for those under 26, which undercut youth rail rates for the same journey. Current Eurolines fares from London's Victoria Coach Station to Paris or Amsterdam are £36 one-way, £49 return (£40/52 without a youth reduction). Brussels is £34/46 (£37/50), Berlin £67/87 (£70/94), Nice £73/98 (£79/105), Madrid £92/122 (£99/132), and Stockholm £102/165 (£112/183). There is usually a discount of £4–10 if you buy your ticket at least two days in advance, and bigger discounts for return journeys booked two weeks or a month in advance. Slightly higher fares apply at Easter, in July and August, and from mid-December to the beginning of January, when reductions for two-week and one-month advance purchases do not apply. Add-on fares of £10–14 one-way, £13–18 return, are available for connecting services from elsewhere in England and Wales, or £18 one-way, £23 return, from Scotland. The German-based firm **Gullivers** offers an alternative service to Amsterdam, Brussels, Berlin, Hamburg and Hannover via the Channel Tunnel, and **Anglia International** serves all of those plus Prague, Kosice (Slovakia), Copenhagen, Oslo, Gothenburg (Sweden) and Moscow.

Eurolines also has **Minipass** return tickets from London to two or more European cities, valid for ninety days: London-Paris-Brussels-London costs £58, London-Amsterdam-Paris-London is £69, London-Amsterdam-Brussels-Paris-London £72, London-Cologne-Paris-London £75. Alternatively, you might consider Eurolines's fifteen-, thirty- and sixty-day passes, or one of the various passes offered by **Busabout** for their services around the continent (see "Getting around", p.37).

Bus contacts in Britain

Anglia Lines ☎0870/608 8806, ⊛www.anglia-lines.co.uk.
Busabout ☎020/7950 1661, ⊛www.busabout.com.
Eurolines ☎0870/514 3219, ⊛www.eurolines.co.uk. Tickets can also be purchased from any Eurolines or National Express agent, at ☎0870/580 8080, ⊛www.nationalexpress.com.
Gullivers ☎00800/4855 4837, ⊛www.gullivers.de.

By ferry from Britain

There are numerous **ferry services** between Britain and Ireland, and between the British Isles and the European mainland. Which service you use will depend on where exactly you are coming from and which part of Europe you are aiming for. Ferries from the southeast of Ireland and the south coast of England connect with northern France and Spain; those from Kent in the southeast of England reach northern France and Belgium; those from the east coast and northeast of England cross the North Sea to the Netherlands, Germany and Scandinavia.

Brittany Ferries ☎0870/366 5333, ⊛www.brittanyferries.co.uk. Portsmouth to Caen and St Malo; Poole to Cherbourg; Plymouth to Roscoff and Santander.

Condor Ferries ☎0845/245 2000, ⊛www.condorferries.co.uk. Poole to Cherbourg and St Malo; Weymouth to St Malo via Guernsey; Portsmouth to Cherbourg; Poole, Portsmouth, Weymouth and St Malo to Jersey and Guernsey.
DFDS Seaways ☎0870/533 3000, ⊛www.dfdsseaways.co.uk. Harwich to Esbjerg and Cuxhaven; Newcastle to Amsterdam, Gothenburg and Kristiansand.
Fjord Line ☎0191/296 1313, ⊛www.fjordline.co.uk. Newcastle to Stavanger, Haugesund and Bergen.
Hoverspeed ☎0870/240 8070, ⊛www.hoverspeed.com. Dover to Calais; Newhaven to Dieppe.
Norfolk Line ☎0870/870 1020, ⊛www.norfolkline.com. Dover to Dunkerque.
P&O Ferries ☎0870/242 4999, ⊛www.poferries.com. Hull to Zeebrugge and Rotterdam; Dover to Calais; Portsmouth to Bilbao, Cherbourg and Le Havre.
SeaFrance ☎0870/571 1711, ⊛www.seafrance.com. Dover to Calais.
Smyril Line ☎01595/690 845, ⊛www.smyril-line.fo. Lerwick (Scotland) to Bergen, with connecting P&O Scottish service from Aberdeen.
Stena Line ☎0870/570 7070, ⊛www.stenaline.co.uk. Harwich to Hook of Holland.
Transmanche Ferries ☎0800/917 1201, ⊛www.transmancheferries.com. Newhaven to Dieppe.

From Ireland

There are direct flights **from Dublin** to most major cities in mainland Europe, and connections from those or from London to practically any airport you want to fly to. There are also one or two direct flights to the Continent **from Shannon** and **from Cork**. You may save a little money travelling by land, sea or even air to London and buying your flight there, but the small amount you'd save hardly makes it worthwhile, and if you're going to London by surface routes, you may as well go the whole hog and carry on that way into Europe. **From Belfast**, there are direct flights with easyJet to Amsterdam and British European to Brussels and Toulouse. For other destinations, you'll have to change at one of those, or at London (served by easyJet, British Midland and BA) or Manchester (served by BA).

Airlines in Ireland

Adria ☎ 01/631 1111, ⊛ www.adria.si.
Aer Arann ☎ 1890/462726, ⊛ www.aerarann.ie.
Aer Lingus ☎ 0818/365 000, ⊛ www.aerlingus.ie.
Aeroflot ☎ 01/844 6166, ⊛ www.aeroflot.co.uk.
Air France ☎ 01/605 0383,
⊛ www.airfrance.com/ie.
Alitalia ☎ 01/677 5171, ⊛ www.alitalia.ie.
BMI British Midland ☎ 01/407 3036, UK
☎ 0870/607 0555, ⊛ www.flybmi.com.
bmibaby ☎ 01/236 6130 ⊛ www.bmibaby.com.
British Airways ☎ 1800/626 747, UK
☎ 0845/773 3377, ⊛ www.ba.com.
British European ☎ 1890/925 532, UK
☎ 0870/567 6676, ⊛ www.flybe.com.
Czech ☎ 01/814 4626, ⊛ www.csa.cz.
easyJet UK ☎ 0870/600 0000,
⊛ www.easyjet.com.
Finnair ☎ 01/844 6565, ⊛ www.finnair.com.
Iberia ☎ 01/407 3017,
⊛ www.iberiaairlines.co.uk.
Lufthansa ☎ 01/844 5544,
⊛ www.lufthansa.com.
Ryanair ☎ 0818/303 030, ⊛ www.ryanair.com.
SAS ☎ 01/844 5440, ⊛ www.scandinavian.net.
Skynet ☎ 061/234400, ⊛ www.skynetair.net.
Swiss ☎ 1890/200 515, ⊛ www.swiss.com.
TAP Air Portugal ☎ 01/679 8844, ⊛ www.tap-airportugal.pt.

Discount agents in Ireland

Aran Travel International ☎ 091/562 595,
⊛ homepages.iol.ie/~arantvl/aranmain.htm. Good-value flights.
CIE Tours ☎ 01/703 1888, ⊛ www.cietours.ie.
General flight and tour agent.
Go Holidays ☎ 01/874 4126,
⊛ www.goholidays.ie. Package tour specialists.
Joe Walsh Tours ☎ 01/676 0991, ⊛ www.joewalshtours.ie. General budget fares agent.
Lee Travel ☎ 021/277 111, ⊛ www.leetravel.ie.
Flights and holidays.
McCarthy's Travel ☎ 021/427 0127,
⊛ www.mccarthystravel.ie. General flight agent.
Neenan Travel ☎ 01/607 9900,
⊛ www.neenantrav.ie. Specialists in European travel.
Student & Group Travel ☎ 01/677 7834. Student and group specialists.
Trailfinders ☎ 01/677 7888, ⊛ www.trailfinders.ie. Excellent agent for independent travel.
USIT Republic ☎ 01/602 1600, Northern Ireland ☎ 028/9032 7111, ⊛ www.usitnow.ie. Ireland's main student and youth travel specialists.

By train from Ireland

From Ireland, direct **rail** tickets to Europe via Britain generally include both boat connections, and are available from Iarnród Éireann's Continental Rail Desk in the Republic, or Northern Ireland Railways in the North, with discounted under-26 tickets available from these and from USIT.

Iarnród Éireann ☎ 01/836 6222,
⊛ www.irishrail.ie.
Northern Ireland Railways ☎ 028/9024 2420,
⊛ www.translink.co.uk.

Ferry operators in Ireland

Brittany Ferries ☎ 021/427 7801,
⊛ www.brittanyferries.ie. Cork to Roscoff (March–Oct only).
Irish Ferries Republic ☎ 1890/313131, UK ☎ 0800/018 2211, ⊛ www.irishferries.com. Dublin to Holyhead; Rosslare to Pembroke, Cherbourg and Roscoff.
NorseMerchant Ferries Republic ☎ 01/819 2999, UK ☎ 0870/600 4321,
⊛ www.norsemerchant.com. Belfast to Liverpool.
P&O Irish Sea Republic ☎ 1800/406049, UK ☎ 0870/242 4777, ⊛ www.poirishsea.com. Larne to Cairnryan, Fleetwood and Troon; Dublin to Liverpool and Mostyn; Dublin and Rosslare to Cherbourg.
SeaCat Republic ☎ 1800/805055, UK ☎ 0870/552 3523, ⊛ www.steam-packet.com. Belfast to Heysham, Troon and Isle of Man; Dublin to Liverpool and Isle of Man; Liverpool and Heysham to Isle of Man.
Stena Line Republic ☎ 01/204 7777, UK ☎ 028/9074 7747, ⊛ www.stenaline.co.uk. Rosslare to Fishguard; Dun Laoghaire and Dublin to Holyhead; Belfast to Stranraer.
Swansea–Cork Ferries Republic ☎ 021/427 1166, UK ☎ 01792/456116, ⊛ www.swansea-cork.ie. Cork to Swansea.

From Australia and New Zealand

There are **flights** from Melbourne, Sydney, Adelaide, Brisbane and Perth to most European capitals, and there really is not a great deal of difference in the fares to the busiest destinations: a scheduled return fare from Sydney to London, Paris, Rome, Madrid, Athens or Frankfurt should be available through travel agents for around

A$1550 in low season. A one-way ticket costs slightly more than half that, while a return flight from Auckland to Europe is approximately NZ$2000 in low season. Asian airlines often work out cheapest, and may throw in a stopover, while there are often bargain deals to be had from Melbourne to Athens on Olympic Airways – ring around first. For RTW deals and other **low-price tickets**, the most reliable operator is STA Travel, who also supply packages with companies such as Contiki and Busabout and can issue rail passes. STA can also advise on visa regulations for Australian and New Zealand citizens – and for a fee will do all the paperwork for you.

Airlines in Australia & NZ

Aer Lingus Australia ☎02/9244 2123, NZ ☎09/308 3351, ⓦwww.aerlingus.ie.
Aeroflot Australia ☎02/9262 2233, ⓦwww.aeroflot.com.au.
Air France Australia ☎02/9244 2100, NZ ☎09/308 3352, ⓦwww.airfrance.com.au.
Air New Zealand Australia ☎13 24 76, ⓦwww.airnz.com.au, NZ ☎0800/737 000, ⓦwww.airnz.co.nz.
Alitalia Australia ☎02/9244 2445, NZ ☎09/308 3357, ⓦwww.alitalia.com.
British Airways Australia ☎1300/767 177, NZ ☎0800/274 847 or 09/356 8690, ⓦwww.ba.com.
Cathay Pacific Australia ☎13 17 47, NZ ☎09/379 0861 or 0508/800 454, ⓦwww.cathaypacific.com.
Czech Australia ☎02/9247 7706, ⓦwww.csa.cz.
EgyptAir Australia ☎02/9232 6677, ⓦwww.egyptair.com.eg.
Emirates Australia ☎02/9290 9700 or 1300/303 777, NZ ☎09/377 6004, ⓦwww.emirates.com.
Finnair Australia ☎02/9244 2299, NZ ☎09/308 3365, ⓦwww.finnair.com.
Garuda Australia ☎02/9334 9970, NZ ☎09/366 1862, ⓦwww.garuda-indonesia.com.
Gulf Air Australia ☎02/9244 2199, NZ ☎09/308 3366, ⓦwww.gulfairco.com.
Japan Airlines Australia ☎02/9272 1111, NZ ☎09/379 9906, ⓦwww.japanair.com.
KLM Australia ☎1300/303 747, NZ ☎09/309 1782, ⓦwww.klm.com.
Lauda Air Australia ☎1800/642 438 or 02/9251 6155, NZ ☎09/522 5948, ⓦwww.aua.com.

LOT Polish Airlines Australia ☎02/9244 2466, NZ ☎09/308 3369, ⓦwww.lot.com.
Lufthansa Australia ☎1300/655 727, NZ ☎09/303 1529, ⓦwww.lufthansa.com.
Malaysia Airlines Australia ☎13 26 27, NZ ☎0800/777 747, ⓦwww.malaysiaairlines.com.my.
Olympic (Greek) Australia ☎1800/221 663, ⓦwww.olympic-airways.gr.
Qantas Australia ☎13 13 13, NZ ☎0800/808 767, ⓦwww.qantas.com.
Royal Jordanian Australia ☎02/9244 2701, NZ ☎03/365 3910, ⓦwww.rja.com.jo.
SAS (Scandinavian) Australia ☎1300/727 707, NZ agent: Air New Zealand ☎09/357 3000, ⓦwww.scandinavian.net.
Singapore Airlines Australia ☎13 10 11, NZ ☎0800/808 909, ⓦwww.singaporeair.com.
Swiss Australia ☎1300/724 666, ⓦwww.swiss.com.
TAP Air Portugal Australia ☎02/9244 2344, NZ ☎09/308 3373, ⓦwww.tap-airportugal.pt.
Tarom (Romanian) Australia ☎02/9262 1144, ⓦwww.tarom.ro.
Thai Australia ☎1300/651 960, NZ ☎09/377 0268, ⓦwww.thaiair.com.
Turkish Australia ☎02/9299 8400, ⓦwww.turkishairlines.com.
Virgin Atlantic Australia ☎02/9244 2747, NZ ☎09/308 3377, ⓦwww.virgin-atlantic.com.

Discount agents in Australia & NZ

Anywhere Travel Australia ☎02/9663 0411, ⓦwww.anywheretravel.com.au.
Destinations Unlimited NZ ☎09/414 1685 ⓦwww.holiday.co.nz.
Flight Centre Australia ☎13 31 33 or 02/9235 3522, ⓦwww.flightcentre.com.au, NZ ☎0800 243 544 or 09/358 4310, ⓦwww.flightcentre.co.nz.
Holiday Shoppe NZ ☎0800/808 480, ⓦwww.holidayshoppe.co.nz.
Northern Gateway Australia ☎1800/174 800, ⓦwww.northerngateway.com.au.
STA Travel Australia ☎1300/733 035, NZ ☎0508/782 872, ⓦwww.statravel.com.
Student Uni Travel (SUT) Australia ☎02/9232 8444, ⓦwww.sut.com.au, NZ ☎09/379 4224, ⓦwww.sut.co.nz.
Travel.com Australia ☎1300/130 482 or 02/9249 5444, ⓦwww.travel.com.au, NZ ☎0800/468 332, ⓦwww.travel.co.nz.
Trailfinders Australia ☎02/9247 7666, ⓦwww.trailfinders.com.au.

Red tape and visas

Since the lifting of many immigration restrictions for European Union member countries in 1993, border-crossing for most EU nationals has become an informal procedure, with holders of most passports just having to wave their documents at border officials.

Border controls between most EU countries are virtually nonexistent. In addition, fifteen countries (Austria, Belgium, Denmark, Finland, France, Germany, Greece, Iceland, Italy, Luxembourg, the Netherlands, Norway, Portugal, Spain and Sweden), known as the Schengen Group, now have joint visas which are valid for travel in all of them; in theory, there are also no immigration controls between these countries – but, in practice, often more ID spot-checks within their borders.

Citizens of the UK (but not other British passport holders), Ireland, Australia, New Zealand, Canada and the US do not need a **visa** to enter most European countries (current exceptions are listed in the next paragraph), and can usually stay for one to three months, depending on nationality; for some countries, passports must be valid at least six months beyond the end of stay. Always check visa requirements before travelling, as they can and do change; this especially applies to Canadian, Australian and New Zealand citizens intending to visit eastern European countries, though EU countries never require visas from British or Irish citizens.

Everyone needs a visa to visit Russia. **American**, **British** and **Irish citizens** need a visa for Turkey (available at the border). **Canadians** need visas for the Czech Republic, Estonia, Poland and Turkey (last one available at the border). **Australians** need visas to visit the Czech Republic, Hungary, Poland, Romania and Turkey (last one available at the border). **New Zealanders** need visas for Poland and Romania. The Baltic states of Estonia, Latvia and Lithuania allow entry to certain nationalities holding a valid visa for any one of them. You will need a transit visa if crossing Ukraine or Belarus (when travelling, for example, from Poland, Slovakia, Hungary or Romania to Moscow).

Finally, don't leave it too late to get a passport before leaving home, since this can take four weeks or longer by post in the summer, and is either irksome or impossible to do in person.

Customs

Customs and duty-free restrictions vary throughout Europe, but are standard for travellers arriving in the EU at one litre of spirits, plus two litres of table wine, plus 200 cigarettes (or 250g tobacco, or fifty cigars). There is no duty-free allowance for travel within the EU, but travellers between EU countries can – in effect – carry as much in the way of duty-paid goods as they want (so long as they are for personal use). Remember that carrying contraband such as controlled drugs, banned pornography or firearms is illegal, not to mention foolhardy in the extreme. If you are carrying prescribed drugs of any kind, it might be a good idea to have a copy of the prescription to show to suspicious customs officers.

Passport offices

Australia ☎ 13 12 32, ✆ www.passports.gov.au. Applications can be made at most post offices.
Canada ☎ 1-800/567-6868, ✆ www.ppt.gc.ca. Walk-in offices in 29 cities.
Ireland ☎ 1890/426888, ✆ www.irlgov.ie/iveagh.
New Zealand ☎ 0800/225 050, ✆ www.passports.govt.nz.
UK ☎ 0870/521 0410, ✆ www.passport.gov.uk. Applications can be made at any post office.
US ☎ 202/647-0518, ✆ travel.state.gov.

European embassies

Austrian US ☎ 202/895-6700, Canada ☎ 613/789-1444, UK ☎ 020/7235 3731, Ireland ☎ 01/269 4577, Australia ☎ 02/6295 1533, NZ ☎ 04/499 6393.

Belgian US ☎202/333-6900, Canada ☎613/236-7267, UK ☎020/7470 3700, Ireland ☎01/269 2082, Australia ☎02/6273 2501, NZ ☎04/472 9558.

British US ☎202/588-6500, Canada ☎613/237-1530, Ireland ☎01/205 3700, Australia ☎02/6270 6666, NZ ☎04/942 2888.

Bulgarian US ☎202/387-7969, Canada ☎613/789-3215, UK ☎020/7584 9400, Ireland ☎01/660 3293, Australia ☎02/9327 7581.

Croatian US ☎202/588-5899, Canada ☎613/562-7820, UK ☎020/7387 2022, Australia ☎02/6286 6988, NZ ☎09/836 5581.

Czech US ☎202/274-9100, Canada ☎613/562-3875, UK ☎020/7243 1115, Ireland ☎01/668 1135, Australia ☎02/6290 1386.

Danish US ☎202/234-4300, Canada ☎613/562-1811, UK ☎020/7333 0200, Ireland ☎01/475 6404, Australia ☎02/6273 2195, NZ ☎04/471 0520.

Dutch US ☎202/244-5300, Canada ☎613/237-5030, UK ☎020/7590 3200, Ireland ☎01/269 3444, Australia ☎02/6273 3111, NZ ☎04/471 6390.

Estonian US ☎202/588-0101, Canada ☎416/461-0764, UK ☎020/7589 3428, Ireland ☎01/269 1552, Australia ☎02/9810 7468.

Finnish US ☎202/298-5800, Canada ☎613/236-2389, UK ☎020/7838 6200, Ireland ☎01/478 1344, Australia ☎02/6273 3800, NZ ☎04/499 4599.

French US ☎202/944-6000, Canada ☎613/789-1795, UK ☎020/7201 1000, Ireland ☎01/260 1666, Australia ☎02/6216 0100, NZ ☎04/802 7787.

German US ☎202/298-4000, Canada ☎613/232-1101, UK ☎020/7824 1300, Ireland ☎01/269 3011, Australia ☎02/6270 1911, NZ ☎04/473 6063.

Greek US ☎202/939-5800, Canada ☎613/238-6271, UK ☎020/7229 3850, Ireland ☎01/676 7254, Australia ☎02/6273 3011, NZ ☎04/473 7775.

Hungarian US ☎202/362-6730, Canada ☎613/230-2717, UK ☎020/7235 5218, Ireland ☎01/661 2902, Australia ☎02/6282 3226, NZ ☎09/376 3609.

Irish US ☎202/462-3939, Canada ☎613/233-6281, UK ☎020/7235 2171, Australia ☎02/6273 3022.

Italian US ☎202/328-5500, Canada ☎613/232-2401, UK ☎020/7312 2200, Ireland ☎01/660 1744, Australia ☎02/6273 3333, NZ ☎04/473 5339.

Latvian US ☎202/726-8213, Canada ☎613/238-6014, UK ☎020/7312 0040, Australia ☎02/9745 5981.

Lithuanian US ☎202/234-5860, Canada ☎613/567-5458, UK ☎020/7486 6401, Australia ☎02/9498 2571.

Luxembourg US ☎202/265-4171, UK ☎020/7235 6961.

Moroccan US ☎202/462-7979, Canada ☎613/236-7391, UK ☎020/7581 5001, Ireland ☎01/660 9449, Australia ☎02/9957 6717.

Norwegian US ☎202/333-6000, Canada ☎613/238-6571, UK ☎020/7591 5500, Ireland ☎01/662 1800, Australia ☎02/6273 3444, NZ ☎09/355 1830.

Polish US ☎202/234-3800, Canada ☎613/789-0468, UK ☎0870/774 2700, Ireland ☎01/283 0855, Australia ☎02/6273 1208, NZ ☎04/475 9453.

Portuguese US ☎202/328-8610, Canada ☎613/729-0883, UK ☎020/7235 5331, Ireland ☎01/289 4416, Australia ☎02/6290 1733.

Romanian US ☎202/232-3694, Canada ☎613/789-3709, UK ☎020/7937 9666, Ireland ☎01/269 2852, Australia ☎02/6286 2343.

Russian US ☎202/298-5700, Canada ☎613/235-4341, visa section ☎613/236-7220, UK ☎020/7229 3628, Ireland ☎01/492 2048, Australia ☎02/6295 9033, NZ ☎04/476 6113.

Slovakian US ☎202/965-5160, Canada ☎613/749-4442, UK ☎020/7313 6470, Ireland ☎01/660 0012, Australia ☎02/6290 1516.

Slovenian US ☎202/667 5363, Canada ☎613/565-5781, UK ☎020/7495 7775, Australia ☎02/6243 4830.

Spanish US ☎202/452-0100, Canada ☎613/747-2252, UK ☎020/7235 5555, visa section ☎0906/550 8970, Ireland ☎01/269 1640, Australia ☎02/6273 3555.

Swedish US ☎202/467-2600, Canada ☎613/241-8553, UK ☎020/7917 6400, Ireland ☎01/671 5822, Australia ☎02/6270 2700, NZ ☎09/373 5332.

Swiss US ☎202/745-7900, Canada ☎613/235-1837, UK ☎020/7616 6000, Ireland ☎01/218 6382, Australia ☎02/6273 3977, NZ ☎04/472 1593.

Turkish US ☎202/612-6700, Canada ☎613/789-4044, UK ☎020/7393 0202, visa section ☎020/7589 0949, Ireland ☎01/668 5240, Australia ☎02/6295 0227, NZ ☎04/472 1292.

Information and maps

Before you leave, it's worth contacting the tourist offices of the countries you're intending to visit for free leaflets, maps and brochures, some of which can be quite useful for planning your trip and when travelling.

This is especially true in parts of central and eastern Europe, where up-to-date maps can be harder to find within the country than in tourist offices abroad. Estonia, Latvia, Lithuania and Russia do not have official tourist offices, so it may help to contact their embassies for more information. Go easy, though: much of the information these places pump out can be picked up just as easily on your travels, and it can weigh a ton. As some tourist offices in the UK charge premium rates for phone enquiries (numbers beginning ☎09), if you're based in the UK you'll find it cheaper to call the office in the US instead.

Once you're in Europe, on-the-spot information is easy enough to pick up. Most countries have a network of tourist offices that answer queries, dole out a range of (sometimes free) maps and brochures, and can often book accommodation, or at least advise you on it. As you might expect, they are better organized in northern Europe – Scandinavia, the Netherlands, France, Switzerland – with branches in all but the smallest village, and mounds of information; in Greece, Turkey and eastern Europe you'll find fewer tourist offices and they'll be less helpful on the whole, sometimes offering no more than a couple of dog-eared brochures and a photocopied map. We've given further details, including a broad idea of opening hours, in "Practicalities" for each country.

Tourist information websites and offices

If there is no office in your home country, apply to the embassy instead.

Austria ⓦ www.austria-tourism.at. US ☎212/944-6885; Canada ☎416/967-4867; UK ☎020/7629 0461; Australia ☎02/9299 3621.
Belgium ⓦ www.visitbelgium.com. US ☎212/758-8130; Canada ☎514/457-2888; UK: office for Brussels & Wallonia ☎020/7531 0390,

office for Brussels & Flanders ☎0906/302 0245 (premium rate).
Britain ⓦ www.visitbritain.com. US ☎1-800/462-2748; Canada ☎1-888/VISIT-UK; Ireland ☎01/670 8000; Australia ☎02/9021 4400 or 1300/858589; New Zealand ☎09/377 6965.
Croatia ⓦ www.croatia.hr. US ☎212/279-8672; UK ☎020/8563 7979.
Czech Republic ⓦ www.visitczech.cz. US ☎212/288-0830; Canada ☎416/363-9928; UK ☎020/7631 0427.
Denmark ⓦ www.visitdenmark.com. US ☎212/885-9700; UK ☎020/7259 5959.
Estonia ⓦ www.visitestonia.com.
Finland ⓦ www.finland-tourism.com. US & Canada ☎1-800/FIN-INFO; UK ☎020/7365 2512; Ireland ☎01/407 3362.
France ⓦ www.franceguide.com. US ☎410/286-8310; Canada ☎514/876-9881; UK ☎0906/824 4123 (premium rate); Ireland ☎1560/235 235; Australia ☎02/9231 5244.
Germany ⓦ www.germany-tourism.de. US ☎212/661-7200; Canada ☎1-877/315-6237; UK ☎020/7317 0908; Australia ☎02/8286 0488.
Greece ⓦ www.gnto.gr. US ☎212/421-5777; Canada ☎416/968-2220; UK ☎020/7495 9300; Australia ☎02/9241 1663.
Hungary ⓦ www.hungarytourism.hu. US ☎212/355-0240; UK ☎020/7823 1055.
Ireland ⓦ www.ireland.travel.ie. US ☎1-800/223-6470; Canada ☎1-800/223-6470; UK ☎0800/039 7000; Australia ☎02/9299 6177; New Zealand ☎09/379 8720.
Italy ⓦ www.enit.it. US ☎212/245-4822; Canada ☎416/925-4882; UK ☎020/7399 3562; Australia ☎02/9262 1666.
Latvia ⓦ www.latviatourism.lv.
Lithuania ⓦ www.tourism.lt. US ☎718/423-6161.
Luxembourg ⓦ www.ont.lu. US ☎212/935-8888; UK ☎020/7434 2800.
Morocco ⓦ www.tourism-in-morocco.com. US ☎212/557-2520; Canada ☎514/842-8111; UK ☎020/7437 0073; Australia ☎02/9922 4999.
Netherlands ⓦ www.holland.com. US ☎1-888/GO-HOLLAND; Canada ☎416/363-1577; UK ☎0906/871 7777 (premium rate).

Norway ⓦ www.visitnorway.com. US ⓣ 212/885-9700; UK ⓣ 020/7839 2650.

Poland ⓦ www.polandtour.org. US ⓣ 212/338-9412; UK ⓣ 020/7580 8811.

Portugal ⓦ www.portugal-insite.pt. US ⓣ 212/719-3985; Canada ⓣ 416/921-7376; UK ⓣ 0906/364 0610 (premium rate); Ireland ⓣ 01/670 9133.

Romania ⓦ www.romaniatourism.com. US ⓣ 212/545-8484; UK ⓣ 020/7224 3692.

Russia ⓦ www.russia-travel.com. US ⓣ 1-877/221-7120.

Slovenia ⓦ www.slovenia-tourism.si. US ⓣ 212/358-9686; UK ⓣ 0870/225 5305.

Spain ⓦ www.tourspain.es. US ⓣ 212/265-8822; Canada ⓣ 416/961-3131; UK ⓣ 020/7486 8077.

Sweden ⓦ www.visit-sweden.com. US ⓣ 212/885-9700; UK ⓣ 020/7870 5601; worldwide toll-free ⓣ +800/3080 3080.

Switzerland ⓦ www.myswitzerland.com. US ⓣ 1-877/SWITZERLAND; UK toll-free ⓣ 00800/1002 0030; worldwide toll-free ⓣ +800/1002 0030.

Turkey ⓦ www.turizm.gov.tr. US ⓣ 212/687-2194; Canada ⓣ 613/230-8654; UK ⓣ 020/7629 7771; Australia ⓣ 02/9223 3055.

Maps

Whether you're doing a grand tour or confining yourself to one or two countries, you will need a decent **map**. Though you can often buy maps on the spot, you may want to get them in advance to plan your trip – if you know what you want, the best advice is to contact Stanfords in London (arguably the world's best map shop) or Rand McNally in the US; both sell maps by mail order.

We've recommended the best maps of individual countries throughout the book. In general, the best series are Bartholomew/RV, Kümmerley & Frey and Hallwag; and, in North America, those published by Rand McNally. With plans of over fifty European cities, the Falk series of detailed, indexed maps are excellent, and easy to use. Geo-Center's 1:1,250,000 double-sided Europe map is one of the best covering the entire continent – clear, with a large scale, showing roads, railways and relief. Other good road maps covering the whole of Europe include Michelin (1:3,000,000), Hallwag (1:3,600,000), Freytag & Berndt (1:3,500,000), and Philip's (1:3,500,000), all of which show the road networks pretty well, though they omit most

of Turkey and Morocco. Of the four, only Hallwag and Freytag & Berndt show railways, and not very clearly. Kümmerley and Frey's map (1:5,000,000) includes Turkey and Morocco but omits road numbers. On a similar scale, Collins (1:5,000,000) and Penguin (1:5,500,000) both show the main road and rail routes pretty clearly. For extensive motoring, it is better to get a large-page road atlas such as Michelin's Tourist and Motoring Atlas. If you intend to travel mainly by rail, it might be worth getting the Thomas Cook Rail Map of Europe.

Map outlets

In the US and Canada

Adventurous Traveler.com US ⓣ 1-800/282-3963, ⓦ adventuroustraveler.com.

Book Passage 51 Tamal Vista Blvd, Corte Madera, CA 94925 ⓣ 1-800/999-7909, ⓦ www.bookpassage.com.

Distant Lands 56 S Raymond Ave, Pasadena, CA 91105 ⓣ 1-800/310-3220, ⓦ www.distantlands.com.

Elliot Bay Book Company 101 S Main St, Seattle, WA 98104 ⓣ 1-800/962-5311, ⓦ www.elliotbaybook.com.

Globe Corner Bookstore 28 Church St, Cambridge, MA 02138 ⓣ 1-800/358-6013, ⓦ www.globecorner.com.

Map Link 30 S La Patera Lane #5, Santa Barbara, CA 93117 ⓣ 1-800/962-1394, ⓦ www.maplink.com.

Rand McNally US ⓣ 1-800/333-0136, ⓦ www.randmcnally.com. Around thirty stores across the US.

The Travel Bug Bookstore 2667 W Broadway, Vancouver, BC V6K 2G2 ⓣ 604/737-1122, ⓦ www.swifty.com/tbug.

World of Maps 1235 Wellington St, Ottawa, ON, K1Y 3A3 ⓣ 1-800/214-8524, ⓦ www.worldofmaps.com.

In the UK and Ireland

Blackwell's Map and Travel Shop 50 Broad St, Oxford OX1 3BQ ⓣ 01865/793 550, ⓦ maps.blackwell.co.uk.

Easons 40 O'Connell St, Dublin 1 ⓣ 01/858 3881, ⓦ www.eason.ie.

Heffers Map and Travel 20 Trinity St, Cambridge CB2 1TJ ⓣ 01865/792 792, ⓦ www.heffers.co.uk.

Hodges Figgis Bookshop 56 Dawson St, Dublin 2 ⓣ 01/677 4754.

The Map Shop 30a Belvoir St, Leicester LE1 6QH
℡0116/247 1400,
ⓦwww.mapshopleicester.co.uk.
National Map Centre 22 Caxton St, London
SW1H 0QU ℡020/7222 2466,
ⓦwww.mapsnmc.co.uk.
Newcastle Map Centre 55 Grey St, Newcastle
NE1 6EF ℡0191/261 5622.
Stanfords 12 Long Acre, London WC2E 9LP
℡020/7836 1321, ⓦwww.stanfords.co.uk.
The Travel Bookshop 13 Blenheim Crescent,
London W11 2EE ℡020/7229 5260,
ⓦwww.thetravelbookshop.co.uk.

In Australia and New Zealand
The Map Shop 6 Peel St, Adelaide, SA 5000
℡08/8231 2033, ⓦwww.mapshop.net.au.
Mapland 372 Little Bourke St, Melbourne, VIC
3000 ℡03/9670 4383, ⓦwww.mapland.com.au.
MapWorld 173 Gloucester St, Christchurch, NZ
℡0800/627 967, ⓦwww.mapworld.co.nz.
Perth Map Centre 900 Hay St, Perth, WA 6000
℡08/9322 5733, ⓦwww.perthmap.com.au.
Specialty Maps 46 Albert St, Auckland, NZ
℡09/307 2217, ⓦwww.specialtymaps.co.nz.

Insurance and health

Wherever you're travelling from, it's a very good idea to have some kind of travel insurance. Before paying for a new policy, however, it's worth checking whether you're already covered: some all-risks home insurance policies may cover your possessions when overseas, and many private medical schemes include cover when abroad.

In Canada, provincial health plans usually provide partial cover for medical mishaps overseas, while holders of official student/teacher/youth cards in Canada and the US are entitled to meagre accident coverage and hospital in-patient benefits. Students will often find that their student health coverage extends during the vacations and for one term beyond the date of last enrolment.

After exhausting these possibilities, you might want to contact a specialist travel insurance company, or consider Rough Guides' own travel insurance deal (see box). A typical **travel insurance policy** usually provides cover for the loss of baggage, tickets and – up to a certain limit – cash or cheques, as well as cancellation or curtailment of your journey. Most of them exclude

Rough Guides travel insurance

Rough Guides offers its own low-cost travel insurance, especially customized for our statistically low-risk readers by a leading British broker, provided by the American International Group (AIG) and registered with the British regulatory body, GISC (the General Insurance Standards Council).

There are five main Rough Guides insurance plans: **No Frills** for the bare minimum for secure travel; **Essential**, which provides decent all-round cover; **Premier** for comprehensive cover with a wide range of benefits; **Extended Stay** for cover lasting two months to a year; and **Annual multi-trip**, a cost-effective way of getting Premier cover if you travel more than once a year. Premier, Annual Multi-Trip and Extended Stay policies can be supplemented by a "Hazardous Pursuits Extension" if you plan to indulge in sports considered dangerous, such as scuba-diving or trekking.

For a policy quote, call the Rough Guide Insurance Line: toll-free in the UK ℡0800/015 09 06 or ℡+44 1392 314 665 from elsewhere. Alternatively, get an online quote at ⓦ**www.roughguides.com/insurance**.

so-called **dangerous sports** unless an extra premium is paid: in Europe this can mean anything from scuba-diving to mountaineering, skiing and even bungee-jumping. Many policies can be chopped and changed to exclude coverage you don't need; for example, sickness and accident benefits can often be excluded or included at will. If you do take **medical coverage**, ascertain whether benefits will be paid as treatment proceeds or only after you return home, and whether there is a 24-hour medical emergency number. When securing baggage cover, make sure that the per-article limit – typically under $800/£500 – will cover your most valuable possession. If you need to make a claim, you should keep receipts for medicines and medical treatment, and in the event you have anything stolen, you must obtain an official statement from the police.

Health

There aren't many particular health problems you'll encounter travelling in Europe. You don't need to have any inoculations for any of the countries covered in this book, although for Morocco and Turkey typhoid jabs are advised, and in southeastern Turkey malaria pills are a good idea for much of the year. Check @www.cdc.gov for full details. When travelling, remember to be up-to-date with your polio and tetanus boosters.

EU citizens resident in the UK or Ireland are covered by reciprocal health agreements for free or reduced-cost emergency treatment in many of the countries in this book (main exceptions are the Baltic states, Switzerland, Slovenia, Morocco and Turkey). To claim this,

you will often need only your passport, but you may also be asked for your NHS card or proof of residence. In EU countries plus Norway, Switzerland and Liechtenstein you'll also need **form E111**, available in Britain from post offices and at @www.doh.gov.uk /traveladvice. Without an E111 you won't be turned away from hospitals but you will almost certainly have to pay for any treatment or medicines. Also, in practice, some countries' doctors and hospitals charge anyway and it's up to you to claim reimbursement when you return home. Make sure you are insured for potential medical expenses, and keep copies of receipts and prescriptions.

Tap water in most countries is drinkable. You may prefer the taste of bottled water, but you only need to avoid tap water altogether in southern Morocco and parts of Turkey. **Unfamiliar food** may well give you a small dose of the runs, but this is usually nothing to worry about, and is normally over in a couple of days; you shouldn't go plugging yourself up with anti-diarrhoea pills in the meantime. **AIDS** is of course as much of a problem in Europe as in the rest of the world, and it hardly needs saying that unprotected casual sex is extremely dangerous; members of both sexes should carry condoms and, if it comes down to it, insist on using them.

For minor health problems it's easiest to go to the local **pharmacy**. You'll find these pretty much everywhere and we've detailed out-of-hours ones in the text. In more serious cases contact your nearest consulate, which will have a list of English-speaking doctors, as will the local tourist office. In the accounts of larger cities we've listed the most convenient hospital casualty units/emergency rooms.

Costs, money and banks

It's hard to generalize about what you're likely to spend travelling around Europe. Some countries – Norway, Switzerland, the UK – are among the most expensive in the world, while in others (Turkey, for example) you can live like a lord on next to nothing. In general, countries in the north and west of Europe are more expensive than those in the south and east.

Prices and exchange rates

We've quoted **prices** in local currency wherever possible, except in those countries where the weakness of the currency and the inflation rate combine to make this a meaningless exercise. In these cases – parts of eastern Europe and Turkey – we've resorted to either US dollars, British pounds or euros, depending on which hard currency is most commonly used within that country.

The current **exchange rates** are given in the "Basics" section at the beginning of each country chapter, but bear in mind that in the case of less stable currencies, the approximate rates quoted may fluctuate considerably. You can find the latest market rates (bank rates will not be as good) at ⓦ www.oanda.com – click on "Cheat Sheet" to get a printable table comparing two currencies.

For **accommodation** prices, we've used a standard coding system throughout this book: see p.38 for details.

Accommodation will be your largest single expense, and can really determine where you decide to travel. For example, it's hard to find a double hotel room anywhere in Scandinavia – perhaps the most expensive part of the continent – for much under £45/$70 a night, whereas in most parts of southern Europe, and even in France, you might be paying under half that on average. Everywhere, though, even in Scandinavia, there is some form of bottom-line accommodation available, and there's nearly always a hostel on hand. In general, reckon on a minimum budget of around £10/$15 a night per person in most parts of Europe.

Food and drink costs also vary wildly, although again in most parts of Europe you can assume that a cheap restaurant meal will cost £5–10/$8–15 a head, with prices nearer the top end of the scale in Scandinavia, at the bottom end in eastern and southern Europe, and below that in Turkey and Morocco. **Transport** costs are something you can pin down more exactly if you have a rail pass. Nowhere, though, are transport costs a major burden, except perhaps in Britain where public transport is less heavily subsidized than elsewhere. Local city transport, too, is usually good, clean and efficient, and is normally fairly cheap, even in the pricier countries of northern Europe. It's hard to pinpoint an average daily budget for touring the continent, but a bottom-line survival figure – camping, self-catering, hitching, etc – might be around £15/$25 a day per person; building in an investment for a rail pass, staying in hostels and eating out occasionally would bring this up to perhaps £20/$30 a day; while staying in private

rooms or hotels and eating out once a day would mean a personal daily budget of at least £25/$40. Obviously in the more expensive countries of northern Europe you might be spending more than this, but on a wide tour this would be balanced out by spending less in southern and eastern Europe, where everything is much cheaper.

When you are travelling also makes a difference. Accommodation rates tend to go up across the board in July and August, when everyone is on vacation – although paradoxically there are good deals in Scandinavia during these months. Also bear in mind that in capital cities and major resorts in the peak season everything will be a grade more expensive than anywhere else, especially if you're there when something special is going on, for example in Munich during the Beer Festival, Pamplona for the running of the bulls or Siena during the Palio. These are, in any case, times when you'd be lucky to find a room at all without having booked.

As for ways of **cutting costs**, there are plenty. It makes sense, obviously, to spend less on transport by investing in some kind of rail pass. Always try to plan in advance. Although it's good to be flexible, buying one-off rail tickets can add a huge amount to your travel budget. The most obvious way to save on accommodation is to use hostels; you can also save by planning to make some of your longer trips at night, if you're able to sleep easily on trains or buses. It's best not to be too spartan when it comes to food costs, but doing a certain amount of self-catering, especially at lunchtime when it's just as easy (and probably nicer) to have a picnic lunch rather than eat in a restaurant or café, will save money.

Youth and student discounts

If you're a student, an **ISIC card** is well worth investing in. It can get you reduced (usually half-price, sometimes free) entry to museums and other sights – costs which can eat their way into your budget alarmingly if you're doing a lot of sightseeing – as well as qualifying you for other discounts in certain cities; it can also save you money on some transport costs, notably ferries, and especially if you are over 26. For Americans there's also a health benefit, providing up to $3000 in emergency medical coverage and $100 a day for sixty days in hospital, plus a 24-hour hotline to call in the event of a medical, legal or financial emergency. The card costs $22 in the US, $16 in Canada, £7 in the UK, €12.70 in Ireland, $16.50 in Australia and $20 in New Zealand. If you are not a student but under 26, get an **International Youth Travel Card**, which costs the same and can in some countries give much the same sort of reductions. Teachers qualify for the **International Teacher Identity Card**, offering similar discounts. All these cards are available from youth travel specialists such as Council Travel, STA and Travel Cuts; full information is at ⓦ**www.isic.org**. Basically, it's worth flashing whichever card you've got at every opportunity – you never know what you might get.

Carrying your money

The easiest way to carry your money is in the form of plastic. Hotels, shops and restaurants across Europe accept major **credit and debit cards**, although cheaper places may not take them. More importantly, you can use them 24/7 to get cash out of ATMs throughout Europe, including Morocco, as long as they are affiliated to an international network (such as Visa, Mastercard or Cirrus). If you're not sure whether your card will work in the countries you intend to visit, check with the issuer before you leave home. With credit cards (but not debit cards), cash withdrawals will be subject to a transaction fee, usually a percentage of the total withdrawn with a minimum fee per transaction; both credit and debit cards may also impose a limit on the amount you can draw at one time, or in one day – check with your card issuer. In the case of credit cards, of course, if you're away for more than a month, you'll need to have someone back home taking care of the bills.

Cash and travellers' cheques

As well as carrying a **cash back-up**, you may also want to consider **travellers' cheques**, in either dollars, euros or pounds sterling. These are available for a small commission from any bank, or direct from offices of the issuing companies; the most commonly accepted brands are Thomas Cook/Mastercard, American Express and

The euro

The **euro** (€) – made up of 100 cents – is the currency of twelve EU countries at the time of writing: Austria, Belgium, Finland, France, Germany, Greece, Ireland, Italy, Luxembourg, the Netherlands, Portugal and Spain. Pending the result of national referendums in 2003, Cyprus, the Czech Republic, Estonia, Hungary, Latvia, Lithuania, Malta, Poland, Slovenia and Slovakia are due to adopt the euro when they join the EU in 2004. The remaining three EU countries (the UK, Denmark and Sweden) are expected to join the euro zone eventually, though their politicians may have a hard time convincing voters that it is a good idea. The British government has promised a referendum before joining; Denmark had one and voted against.

Euro **coins** come as 1c, 2c, 5c, 10c, 20c, 50c, €1 and €2. One side of the coin states the denomination, and is the same everywhere, while the other side has a design unique to the issuing country. Euro **notes** come as €5, €10, €20, €50, €100, €200 and €500. All euro notes and coins are legal tender throughout the euro zone, regardless of their country of issue.

Visa. Travellers' cheques have the major advantage over cash of being refundable if lost or stolen, but the downside is that they're expensive: you'll usually have to pay a commission fee again when you cash each cheque. It pays to get a selection of denominations, and you should keep the purchase agreement and a record of cheque serial numbers safe and separate from the cheques themselves. If cheques are lost or stolen, the issuing company will expect you to report the loss forthwith to their local office; most companies claim to replace lost or stolen cheques within 24 hours. Keep a record of the cheques as you cash them, as you can get the value of all uncashed cheques refunded immediately if you lose them.

In some countries **banks** are the only places where you can legally change money, and they often offer the best exchange rates and lowest commission. Local banking hours are given throughout this book. Outside normal hours you can normally resort to **bureaux de change**, often located at train stations and airports, though their rates and/or commissions may well be less favourable (common practice is either to impose a high commission fee in the small print – sometimes as much as ten percent – or to charge no commission at all but offer a poor exchange rate). You'll also come across automatic money-changing machines. You'd do best to avoid changing money or cheques in hotels, where the exchange rates are generally very poor.

Visa TravelMoney

A compromise between the security of travellers' cheques and the convenience of plastic is **Visa TravelMoney**, a disposable prepaid debit card charged up before you leave home with whatever amount you like, separate from your normal banking or credit accounts. You can then access these dedicated travel funds from any ATM that accepts Visa worldwide, with a PIN that you can choose. Travelex/Interpayment outlets sell the card worldwide (see ⓦwww .travelex.com for locations). When your money runs out, you just throw the card

away. Since you can buy up to nine cards to access the same funds – useful for couples or families travelling together – it's recommended that you buy at least one extra card as a back-up in case your first is lost or stolen. Full details are at ⓦwww.international.visa.com (click on "Get A Card"). While you're travelling, the 24-hour Visa global customer service line can be accessed from most countries with a toll-free local number, all of which are listed on the website; alternatively, you can call collect (reverse-charge) to the USA at ☏410/581-9091.

Wiring money

Having **money wired** from home is not cheap, and should be considered as a last resort. Funds can be sent to most countries via MoneyGram and Western Union. Both companies' fees depend on the amount being transferred, but as an example, wiring £700/$1000 will cost around £40/$60. The funds should be available for collection (usually in local currency) from the company's local agent within minutes of being sent; you can do this in person at the company's nearest office (in the UK all post offices are agents for MoneyGram), or over the phone using your credit card with Western Union. It's also possible, and slightly cheaper, to have money wired from a bank in your home country to one in Europe, but this is much slower (two working days is the norm, but a couple of weeks is not unheard of) and less reliable; if you go down this route, the person wiring the funds will need to know the routing number of the destination bank.

If you have no money in your account, and there is no one you can persuade to send you any, then the options are inevitably limited. The best option is to find some casual, cash-in-hand work (see p.48) or develop a talent for street-performance that could bag you some change. In some European countries you can sell your blood. As a last resort, you can throw yourself on the mercy of your nearest consulate; they won't be sympathetic or even helpful, but they may cash a cheque drawn on a home bank and supported by a cheque card. They might, if there's absolutely no other possibility, repatriate you, though if they do, your passport will be confiscated as soon as you set foot in your home country and you will have to pay back all costs incurred (at top-whack rates). Consulates never lend money.

Money-wiring companies

MoneyGram US ☏1-800/955-7777, Canada ☏1-800/933-3278, UK ☏0800/018 0104, Ireland ☏1850/205 800, Australia ☏1800/230 100, NZ ☏0800/262 263, ☏www.moneygram.com. **Thomas Cook** US ☏1-800/287-7362, Canada ☏1-888/823-4732, UK ☏01733/318 922, Ireland ☏01/677 1721, ☏www.thomascook.com. **Western Union** US & Canada ☏1-800/325-6000, UK ☏0800/833 833, Ireland ☏1800/395 395, Australia ☏1800/501 500, NZ ☏0800/270 000, ☏www.westernunion.com.

Getting around

It's easy enough to travel in Europe, and a number of special deals and passes can make it fairly economical too. Air links are extensive, but also expensive – give or take the odd charter deal in season. In any case, you really appreciate the diversity of Europe best at ground level, by way of its enormous and generally efficient web of rail, road and ferry connections.

By train

Though to some extent it depends on where you intend to spend most of your time, **train** is the best way to make a tour of Europe. The rail network in most countries is comprehensive and the continent boasts some of the most scenic rail journeys you could make anywhere in the world. Train travel is relatively cheap, too, even in the richer parts of northwest Europe, where – apart from Britain (whose rail system is in a state of virtual collapse following privatization) – trains are heavily subsidized, and prices are brought down further by the multiplicity of passes and discount cards available, both Europe-wide (**InterRail** for those based in Europe or the British Isles, **Eurail** for anyone based elsewhere) and on an individual country basis. We've covered the various passes here, as well as the most important international routes and most useful addresses; supplementary details, including frequencies and journey times of domestic services, are given throughout the guide in each country's "Travel details" section.

If you intend to do a lot of rail travel, the *Thomas Cook European Timetable* is an essential investment, detailing the main lines throughout Europe, as well as ferry connections, and is updated monthly. Thomas Cook also publishes a rail map of Europe, which may be a good supplement to our own train map on pp.28–29.

Finally, whenever you board an international train in Europe, check the route of the car you are in, since trains frequently split, with different carriages going to different destinations.

Europe-wide rail passes

InterRail

For young Europeans, probably the most popular of all the ways of travelling around the continent is the **InterRail pass**, a ticket for unlimited travel on rail lines the length and breadth of Europe (but you pay half fares in the country where you bought the card). InterRail passes are available from main stations and international rail agents in all countries covered by the scheme. For contacts in Britain and Ireland, see pp.14 & 16. A zoning system applies for the European countries valid under the pass, as follows:

Zone A Britain, Ireland
Zone B Sweden, Norway, Finland
Zone C Denmark, Germany, Switzerland, Austria
Zone D Poland, Czech Republic, Slovakia, Hungary, Croatia

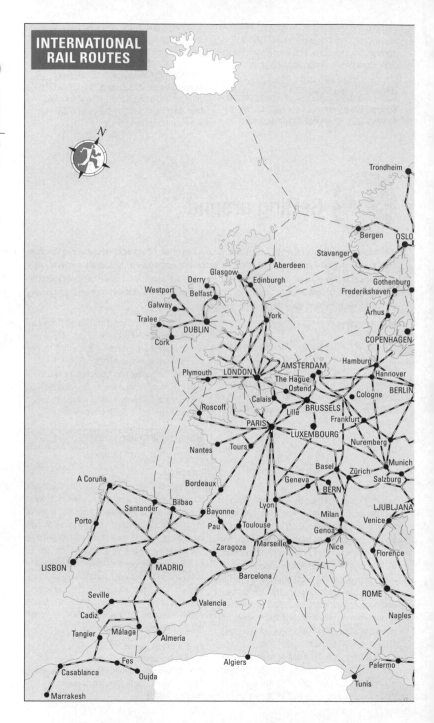

INTERNATIONAL RAIL ROUTES

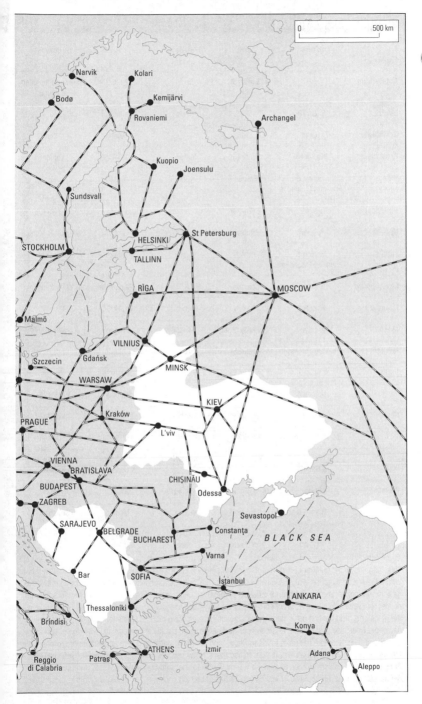

International rail routes

TO / FROM	Amsterdam	Berlin	Bratislava	Brussels	Bucharest
Amsterdam	—	3 (6hr15)	Berlin	22 (2hr30)	Frankfurt Flughafen & Vienna
Berlin	3 (6hr20)	—	1 (10hr)	1 (8hr30)	Prague
Bratislava	Berlin	1 (10hr)	—	Vienna	1 (17hr35)
Brussels	22 (2hr40)	1 (8hr45)	Vienna	—	Vienna
Bucharest	Vienna & Frankfurt Flughafen	Prague	1 (18hr05)	Vienna	—
Budapest	Berlin	2 (2hr20)	6 (2hr20)[2]	Vienna	6 (14hr10)
Copenhagen	Duisberg	Hamburg	Hamburg & Břeclav	Hamburg	Budapest & Munich
Ljubljana	Munich & Frankfurt Flughafen	Munich	Vienna	Munich	Budapest
Luxembourg	Brussels	Cologne	Zurich & Vienna	22 (2hr40)	Zurich & Budapest
Milan	Frankfurt	Munich	Vienna	1 (11hr35)	Vienna
Moscow	Hannover[b]	3–7 weekly (28hr)[b]	1 (34hr05)[b]	Cologne[b]	1 (47hr05)[u]
Munich	Frankfurt Flughafen	7 (6hr35)	Vienna	1 (9hr45)	Budapest
Paris	7 (4hr10)	1 (11hr35)	Vienna	28 (1hr25)	Vienna
Prague	Duisberg	5 (5hr20)	6 (4hr25)	Frankfurt	1 (23hr25)
Rome	Basel	Munich	Vienna	Milan	Vienna
Vienna	Frankfurt Flughafen	2 (9hr50)	18 (1hr)[2]	1 (14hr40)	1 (17hr45)
Vilnius	Warsaw & Berlin[1]	Warsaw[1]	Warsaw[1]	Warsaw & Cologne[1]	Warsaw & Krakow[1]
Warsaw	Berlin	4–5 (5hr45)	2 (7hr45)	Cologne	Krakow
Zagreb	Munich & Frankfurt Flughafen	Munich	Vienna	Munich	Budapest
Zurich	1 (12hr)	1 (11hr45)	Vienna	2 (7hr45)	Vienna

This chart shows the number of **direct daily trains** between European capitals, and the fastest scheduled time. Where there is no direct service, a suggested **interchange point** is given instead, but note that you may have to pick up your connecting service from a different terminal, and that you may have to wait several hours for your connection: you could take it as an opportunity to wander round town, with your bags at the left luggage deposit in the meantime, or to freshen up – many major stations have washing facilities. Depending on the time of day, or day of the week, you may be able to get to your destination more quickly or conveniently with one or two extra changes of train. Note too that most trains to Russia and the Baltic states pass through Belarus or Ukraine, and that you may therefore need a **transit visa** to use them. Many services to Athens, Istanbul and Sofia pass through Belgrade and sometimes Skopje, so you may wish to check on the current political situation in Serbia–Montenegro, the Republic of Macedonia and neighbouring countries before deciding to use these trains.

Budapest	Copenhagen	Ljubljana	Luxembourg	Milan
Berlin	Duisberg	Frankfurt Flughafen & Munich	Brussels	Frankfurt
2 (12hr)	Hamburg	Munich	Cologne	Munich
6 (2hr20)[2]	Břeclav & Hamburg	Vienna	Vienna & Zurich	Vienna
Vienna	Hamburg	Munich	22 (2hr40)	1 (12hr25)
7 (14hr)	Munich & Budapest	Budapest	Budapest & Zurich	Vienna
—	Munich	3 (8hr25)	Zurich	Venice (Mestre)
Munich	—	Munich	Cologne	Munich
3 (8hr40)	Munich	—	Zurich	Venice (Mestre)
Zurich	Cologne	Zurich	—	1 (8hr40)
Venice (Mestre)	Munich	Venice (Mestre)	1 (9hr25)	—
1 (39hr10)[u]	Hannover & Hamburg[b]	Budapest[u]	Cologne[b]	Vienna[4,b]
2 (7hr35)	1 (15hr)	3 (6hr15)	Strasbourg	2 (7hr20)
Munich	Hamburg	Munich	5 (3hr45)	3 (6hr50)
4 (6hr50)	Hamburg	Munich	Frankfurt & Cologne	Munich
Trieste	Munich	Venice (Mestre)	Milan	27 (4hr30)
7 (2hr45)[2]	Munich	1 (6hr15)	Zurich	1 (13hr25)
Warsaw[1]	Warsaw, Berlin & Hamburg[1]	Warsaw & Vienna[1]	Warsaw & Cologne[1]	Warsaw & Vienna[1]
2 (10hr55)	Berlin & Hamburg	Vienna	Cologne	Vienna
4 (5hr05)	Munich	8 (2hr15)	Zurich	Venice (Mestre)
1 (13hr10)	Cologne	1 (10hr55)	2 (5hr)	8 (3hr40)

[1] The Warsaw–Vilnius train should not be routed via Belarus, but check before travelling. On days when there is no direct connection, change (also) at Šeštokai.
[2] There is also a hydrofoil service in summer.
[3] Through cars are available three days a week; on other days, change cars between Kiev and Budapest.
[4] On days when there is no direct service between Vienna and Moscow, change (also) at Warsaw.
[b] Runs via Belarus – transit visa needed.
[u] Runs via Ukraine – transit visa needed.

International rail routes (continuation)

TO FROM	Moscow	Munich	Paris	Prague	Rome
Amsterdam	Hannover[b]	Frankfurt Flughafen	7 (4hr10)	Duisberg	Basel
Berlin	3–7 weekly (28hr50)[b]	7 (6hr40)	1 (11hr35)	5 (5hr15)	Munich
Bratislava	1 (33hr20)[b]	Vienna	Vienna	6 (4hr30)	Vienna
Brussels	Cologne[b]	1 (10hr50)	28 (1hr25)	Frankfurt	Milan
Bucharest	1 (46hr)[u]	Budapest	Vienna	1 (23hr45)	Vienna
Budapest	1 (37hr35)[u]	2 (7hr25)	Munich	4 (6hr50)	Trieste
Copenhagen	Hamburg & Hannover[b]	1 (14hr15)	Hamburg	Hamburg	Munich
Ljubljana	Budapest[u]	3 (6hr30)	Munich	Munich	Trieste
Luxembourg	Cologne[b]	Strasbourg	5 (3hr15)	Cologne & Frankfurt	Milan
Milan	Vienna[4b]	2 (7hr20)	3 (6hr50)	Munich	27 (4hr30)
Moscow	—	Prague[b]	Cologne[b]	1 (34hr50)[b]	Vienna[4b]
Munich	Prague[b]	—	4 (8hr30)	1 (9hr25)	2 (10hr30)
Paris	Cologne[b]	4 (8hr30)	—	Frankfurt	2 (15hr10)
Prague	1 (31hr40)[b]	1 (9hr)	Frankfurt	—	Munich
Rome	Vienna[4b]	2 (10hr40)	2 (15hr10)	Munich	—
Vienna	4–7 weekly (34hr10)[4b]	6 (4hr35)	2 (13hr50)	4 (4hr35)	1 (13hr25)
Vilnius	2–3 (14hr50)[b]	Warsaw & Prague[1]	Warsaw & Cologne[1]	Warsaw[1]	Warsaw & Vienna[1]
Warsaw	2–3 (20hr40)[b]	Prague	Cologne	3 (9hr10)	Vienna
Zagreb	1 (50hr50)[3u]	3 (8hr40)	Munich	Munich	Trieste
Zurich	Prague[b]	4 (4hr15)	3 (6hr)	1 (12hr20)	1 (11hr30)

This chart shows the number of **direct daily trains** between European capitals, and the fastest scheduled time. Where there is no direct service, a suggested **interchange point** is given instead, but note that you may have to pick up your connecting service from a different terminal, and that you may have to wait several hours for your connection: you could take it as an opportunity to wander round town, with your bags at the left luggage deposit in the meantime, or to freshen up – many major stations have washing facilities. Depending on the time of day, or day of the week, you may be able to get to your destination more quickly or conveniently with one or two extra changes of train. Note too that most trains to Russia and the Baltic states pass through Belarus or Ukraine, and that you may therefore need a **transit visa** to use them. Many services to Athens, Istanbul and Sofia pass through Belgrade and sometimes Skopje, so you may wish to check on the current political situation in Serbia–Montenegro, the Republic of Macedonia and neighbouring countries before deciding to use these trains.

Vienna	Vilnius	Warsaw	Zagreb	Zurich
Frankfurt Flughafen	Berlin & Warsaw[1]	Berlin	Frankfurt Flughafen & Munich	1 (11hr50)
2 (10hr05)	Warsaw[1]	4–5 (5hr45)	Munich	1 (11hr50)
18 (1hr)[2]	Warsaw[1]	2 (7hr40)	Vienna	Vienna
1 (15hr50)	Cologne & Warsaw[1]	Cologne	Munich	2 (7hr45)
1 (17hr50)	Krakow & Warsaw[1]	Krakow	Budapest	Vienna
7 (2hr40)[2]	Warsaw[1]	2 (10hr40)	4 (5hr)	1 (12hr40)
Munich	Hamburg, Berlin & Warsaw[1]	Hamburg & Berlin	Munich	Munich
1 (6hr15)	Vienna & Warsaw[1]	Vienna	7 (2hr10)	1 (11hr55)
Zurich	Cologne & Warsaw[1]	Cologne	Zurich	2 (5hr)
1 (12hr30)	Vienna & Warsaw[1]	Vienna	Venice (Mestre)	8 (3hr40)
4–7 weekly (33hr40)[4b]	2–3 (14hr50)[b]	2–3 (18hr30)[b]	1 (51hr)[3u]	Prague[b]
6 (4hr40)	Prague & Warsaw[1]	Prague	3 (8hr40)	4 (4hr15)
2 (14hr40)	Cologne & Warsaw[1]	Cologne	Munich	3 (6hr)
4 (4hr40)	Warsaw[1]	3 (9hr)	Munich	1 (12hr30)
1 (13hr)	Vienna & Warsaw[1]	Vienna	Venice (Mestre)	1 (13hr)
—	Warsaw[1]	2 (7hr45)	2 (6hr35)	3 (9hr)
Warsaw[1]	—	every 2 days (10hr55)[1]	Warsaw & Vienna[1]	Warsaw & Vienna[1]
2 (7hr35)	every 2 days (9hr50)[1]	—	Vienna	Vienna
2 (6hr30)	Vienna & Warsaw[1]	Vienna	—	1 (14hr25)
3 (9hr)	Vienna & Warsaw[1]	Vienna	1 (13hr15)	—

[1] The Warsaw–Vilnius train should not be routed via Belarus, but check before travelling. On days when there is no direct connection, change (also) at Šeštokai.
[2] There is also a hydrofoil service in summer.
[3] Through cars are available three days a week; on other days, change cars between Kiev and Budapest.
[4] On days when there is no direct service between Vienna and Moscow, change (also) at Warsaw.
[b] Runs via Belarus – transit visa needed.
[u] Runs via Ukraine – transit visa needed.

Zone E France, Belgium, the Netherlands, Luxembourg
Zone F Spain, Portugal, Morocco
Zone G Italy, Slovenia, Greece, Turkey
Zone H Bulgaria, Romania, Serbia–Montenegro, Republic of Macedonia

The zones you want to travel in determine the price, which starts at £125 for those under 26 (£182 for over-26s) for a one-zone card valid for twelve days, £149/219 for 22 days. Cards for more than one zone are valid for a month and cost £195/275 for two zones, £225/320 for three zones and £265/379 for all the zones. To qualify, you need to have been resident in one of the participating countries for six months or more; you also need a valid passport. For further details, price updates and online purchasing, see ☻www.inter-rail.co.uk.

In fact, unlimited free travel is a bit of a myth. Increasingly with InterRail passes, you need to pay **supplements** on most European express trains – all of them on some routes, and certainly all the most convenient ones. Even where there is in theory no supplement, there is often a compulsory reservation fee, which may cost you double if you only find out about it once you're on the train.

Eurail

Non-European residents aren't eligible for InterRail passes, though many agents don't check residential qualifications. For them, a **Eurail pass**, which should be bought outside Europe (but can be obtained from Rail Europe in London by non-residents who were unable to get it at home), gives unlimited travel in seventeen countries – Austria, Belgium, Denmark, Finland, France, Germany, Greece, Hungary, Ireland, Italy, Luxembourg, the Netherlands, Norway, Portugal, Spain, Sweden and Switzerland – fewer than InterRail, but valid for more express trains, thus saving money on supplements. The **Eurailpass Youth** (for under-26s) costs US$414 for fifteen days, US$534 for 21 days, US$664 for one month, US$938 for two months, and US$1160 for three months; if you're 26 or over you'll have to buy a first-class pass, also available for fifteen days (US$588), 21 days (US$762), one

month (US$946), two months (US$1338) and three months (US$1654). If there are between two and five of you travelling together, the **Eurailpass Saver** (first class only) knocks about fifteen percent off the cost of the standard Eurail offerings.

You stand a better chance of getting your money's worth out of a **Eurailpass Flexi**, which is good for a certain number of travel days in a two-month period. This, too, comes in under-26 and first-class versions: ten days costs US$488 for under-26s (US$694 for first-class travel); and fifteen days costs US$642/914. There's also a **Eurailpass Saver Flexi** for two to five people travelling together.

If you only want to travel in a small number of adjoining countries, the **Eurail Selectpass** allows travel in 3–5 countries linked to each other by rail or boat on 5, 6, 8, 10 or 15 days in two months; overnight journeys starting after 7pm count as part of the next day, and Belgium, the Netherlands and Luxembourg ("Benelux") count as a single country. Prices for under-26s and over-26s range from US$249/356 for five days in three countries to US$556/794 for fifteen days in five countries (fifteen-day tickets are not available for less than five countries). There's also a **Eurail Selectpass Saver** version for people travelling together. All Eurail passes are available from the agents listed on pp.14 & 37. For full details, price updates and online purchasing, see ☻www.eurail .com.

National rail passes

Some European countries provide a **national rail pass**, which can be good value if you're doing a lot of travelling within one country, or a 3- to 8-day **EuroDomino** (also called a **Freedom Pass**), which you buy before you leave. Main second-class options are listed below; there are, in addition, first-class versions of most EuroDominos, Railpasses and Flexipasses, plus first-class passes for Bulgaria, Hungary, Portugal, Romania and the Balkans. In general, those passes quoted in pounds or dollars need to be bought before you leave home from the country's rail company or national tourist office, or from a general sales agent such as

RailEurope (some prices may vary between agents, and some agents may offer passes which others do not). There is no pass as such for Estonia, Latvia or Lithuania.

Austria The VORTEILSCard rail pass gives a 45 percent discount throughout Austria for a year for €18.10 (€93.70 for over-26s). A EuroDomino pass costs from £55 (over-26s £71) for three days up to £89/115 for eight days. An Austrian Railpass gives three days' free travel in a fifteen-day period for $107, plus up to five additional days at $15 each. Also see "Eastern Europe".

Belgium A Belgian Tourrail gives five days' unlimited travel within a one-month period for €68. The Go Pass allows under-26s ten single journeys of any length in six months for €40 (the over-26 version, Rail Pass, costs €60), but on weekdays it is only valid after 9am. A EuroDomino pass costs from £28 (£37 for over-26s) for three days up to £45/64 for eight days. Also see "Benelux".

Benelux (Belgium, Netherlands & Luxembourg) A Benelux Tourrail card gives five days' travel in a month on all three countries' networks for $109 ($163 for over-26s, $244 for two people travelling together). The one-person card is available in the Benelux countries for €92 under-26, €122 over-26.

Britain The BritRail pass, available from agents outside Britain, gives unlimited rail travel throughout England, Wales and Scotland for four days at $155 ($189 for over-26s), eight days at $219 ($269), fifteen days at $285 ($405), 22 days at $359 ($515), or a month at $429 ($609). It also gives a discount on some Eurostar (Channel Tunnel) fares. Alternatively, the BritRail Flexipass gives unlimited travel on any four days in two months for $189 ($239 for over-26s), eight days for $245 ($349) or fifteen days for $369 ($525). Other options include the Freedom of Scotland Pass, giving four days' travel in Scotland in an eight-day period at $139, eight days in fifteen at $179; and the Freedom of Wales pass, which gives unlimited bus travel in Wales for eight days with unlimited rail travel on any four of them for $89, or unlimited bus travel for fifteen days with unlimited rail travel on any eight of them for $149. With a BritRail Pass Plus Ireland, you get five days' travel in a month throughout Britain and Ireland (plus a round trip on Stena Line Irish Sea ferries) for $359, or ten days for $545. The Young Person's Railcard – buyable in Britain for £18 – gives a 33-percent reduction on standard fares for full-time students and under-26s for a year.

Bulgaria A EuroDomino pass costs from £22 (£28 for over-26s) for three days up to £43/55 for eight days.

Croatia A EuroDomino pass costs from £29 (£38 for over-26s) for three days up to £53/69 for eight days.

Czech Republic A EuroDomino pass costs from £24 (£32 for over-26s) for three days up to £55/70 for eight days. A Czech Flexipass gives three days' free travel in a fifteen-day period for $48, plus up to five additional days at $6 each. Also see "Eastern Europe".

Denmark A EuroDomino pass costs from £43 (£56 for over-26s) for three days up to £87/111 for eight days. For ScanRail passes see "Scandinavia".

Eastern Europe A European East Pass gives five days' free travel in a month in Austria, the Czech Republic, Hungary, Poland and Slovakia for $158, plus up to five additional days at $18 each.

Finland Finnrail passes are valid for unlimited rail travel on three, five or ten days in a month and cost $138, $182 and $248 respectively; add-on round-trips to Tallinn (Estonia) or St Petersburg (Russia) are available. A EuroDomino pass costs from £61 (£81 for over-26s) for three days up to £112/145 for eight days. For ScanRail passes see "Scandinavia".

France A EuroDomino pass costs from £88 (£122 for over-26s) for three days up to £173/231 for eight days. The France Railpass costs $218 for any four days' travel in a month, with up to six additional rail days at $28 each. For under-26s, the France Youthpass gives four days' travel in a month for $164, with up to six additional days at $21 each. A France'n'Italy Pass gives four days' free travel in two months throughout France and Italy for $199 (over-26s $239), with up to six additional days at $21 ($25) each. A France'n'Spain Pass gives four days' free travel in two months throughout France and Spain for $189 (over-26s $252), with up to six additional days at $21 ($28) each. "Saver" versions of the France Railpass and the over-26 France'n'Italy and France'n'Spain passes exist, giving discounts for 2–5 people travelling together.

Germany The German Rail BahnCard gives a 25 percent discount on all trains in Germany for €60. A EuroDomino pass costs from £92 (£123 for over-26s) for three days up to £137/184 for eight days. A German Rail Pass costs $142 ($180 for over-26s, $270 for two travelling together) for any four days' travel in a month, rising to $216 ($316, $474) for ten (with prices in between for five to nine days). Länder tickets give free travel on local trains in any one German state from 9am on any weekday until 3am next morning for €21.

Greece A EuroDomino pass costs from £32 (£41 for over-26s) for three days up to £60/79 for eight days.

Hungary A EuroDomino pass costs from £26 (£33 for over-26s) for three days up to £56/77 for eight days. Also see "Eastern Europe".

Ireland Irish Rail's Rover ticket buys unlimited rail travel in the Republic and the North on any five days out of fifteen for €130, with an Irish Explorer Rail Ticket (the same deal in the Republic only) at €105. The Emerald Card covers rail and bus travel in the Republic and the North, at €180 for eight days in fifteen and €310 for fifteen days in thirty. The Irish Explorer Rail and Bus Ticket is valid for eight days in fifteen in the Republic only at €160. A EuroDomino pass costs from £44 sterling (£48 for over-26s) for three days up to £85/96 for eight days and is valid only in the Republic. See "Britain" for details of the BritRail Pass Plus Ireland (not available in Britain or Ireland).

Italy A EuroDomino pass costs from £89 (£118 for over-26s) for three days up to £140/186 for eight days. A Flexi Rail Card gives four days in a month for $160 ($191 for over-26s, $326 for two travelling together), plus up to six additional days for $16 ($19, $34) each. A France'n'Italy Pass gives four days' free travel in two months throughout France and Italy for $199 ($239), with up to six additional days at $21 ($25) each.

Luxembourg One-day rail passes are €4.40 each, €17.60 for a book of five. A EuroDomino pass costs from £11 (£15 for over-26s) for three days up to £15/22 for eight days. Between Easter and the end of October, a Luxembourg Card that also covers buses costs €9 for one day, €16 for any two days in two weeks, and €22 for any three days in two weeks, with free entry to numerous sights as well. See also "Benelux".

Morocco A EuroDomino pass costs from £23 (£24 for over-26s) for three days up to £50/55 for eight days.

Netherlands A Dagkaart (Day Card) gives a day's unlimited travel for €37.10 (an OV Dagkaart, covering buses, trams and metro too, is €41.60). A Zomertoer (Summer Tour) ticket giving free travel on any three days in ten during July and August costs €45 for one person, €59 for two travelling together (€55/73 covering bus services too). A HollandRail Pass gives three days' free travel in a month at $68, or five days for $103. A EuroDomino pass costs from £28 (£37 for over-26s) for three days up to £69/88 for eight days. Also see "Benelux".

Norway A Norway Railpass gives either three days' free travel in a month for $148 (over-26s $194), plus up to 5 additional days for $25 ($33) each, or (from other agents) three days in a month (over- or under-26) for $146, four days for $182, five days for $202. A EuroDomino pass costs from £88 (£116 for over-26s) for three days up to £166/218 for eight days. For ScanRail passes see "Scandinavia".

Poland Polrail passes cost £54 (£76 for over-26s) for eight days travel, £63/89 for fifteen, £69/99 for 21 days, and £89/128 for a month. A EuroDomino pass costs from £33 (£39 for over-26s) for three

days up to £67/79 for eight days. Also see "Eastern Europe".

Portugal A Bilhete Turistico pass, which costs €100 for a week's rail travel, €170 for two weeks, and €250 for three, is really only worthwhile for first-class travel, which it allows. A EuroDomino pass costs from £31 (£45 for over-26s) for three days up to £65 (£79) for eight days.

Romania A EuroDomino pass costs from £28 (£37 for over-26s) for three days up to £65/88 for eight days.

Russia A EuroDomino pass costs from £31 (£41 for over-26s) for three days up to £58/75 for eight days.

Scandinavia The ScanRail pass is valid on the rail networks of Denmark, Norway, Sweden and Finland, and costs £105 (£151 for over-26s) for five days' travel in two months, £141 (£202) for ten days in two months, and £163 (£234) for 21 days unlimited.

Slovakia A EuroDomino pass costs from £21 (£27 for over-26s) for three days up to £41/51 for eight days. Also see "Eastern Europe".

Slovenia A EuroDomino pass costs from £26 (£35 for over-26s) for three days up to £43/55 for eight days.

Spain A EuroDomino pass costs from £65 (£75 for over-26s) for three days up to £150/177 for eight days. The Spain Flexipass gives three days' free travel in a two-month period for $165, plus $30 each for up to seven additional days.

Sweden EuroDomino passes for Sweden cost from £90 (£112 for over-26s) for three days up to £148/183 for eight days. The Sweden Railpass gives three days' free travel in a month for $155, four days for $175, five for $195. ScanRail passes are also valid (see "Scandinavia").

Switzerland A Swiss Pass, valid for unlimited travel on rail, bus and ferry routes, costs $120 for four days ($160 for over-26s, $136 each for two or more people travelling together), $169 ($225/192) for eight days, $203 ($270/230) for fifteen days, $237 ($315/268) for 22 days, and $263 ($350/298) for a month. Alternatives are the Swiss Flexi Pass (giving three to eight days in a month at $156–282, or $132–240 each for two or more travelling together), the Half-Fare Card (fifty percent discount on rail travel for a month for SFr.150 – buyable only in Switzerland), and the Swiss Card (one free return journey from the border or airport to any town plus fifty percent discount on other tickets for a month at $116; buyable in Switzerland for SFr.170). A EuroDomino pass costs from £55 (£73 for over-26s) for three days up to £86/113 for eight days.

Turkey A EuroDomino pass costs from £14 (£18 for over-26s) for three days up to £31/42 for eight days.

Rail contacts

See p.14 for the UK and p.16 for Ireland.

In North America

Armchair World Travel ☎310/477-8960, ⒲www.armchair.com. European and many individual country passes.

BritRail Travel ☎1-877/677 1066, ⒲www.britrail.com. British passes.

CIE Tours International ☎1-800/CIE-TOUR or 973/292-3438, ⒲www.cietours.com. Irish passes.

CIT Rail US ☎1-800/CIT-RAIL or 212/730-2400, Canada ☎1-800/361-7799, ⒲www.cit-rail.com. Eurail passes, BritRail and others.

DER Travel ☎1-888/337-7350, ⒲www.dertravel.com/rail. European and many individual country passes.

Europrail International Canada ☎1-888/667-9734, ⒲www.europrail.net. European and many individual country passes.

Online Travel ☎1-800/660-5300, ⒲www.eurorail.com. European and many individual country passes.

Orbis Polish Travel Bureau ☎1-800/TO-POLAND, ⒲www.orbistravel.com. Passes for Poland.

Rail Europe US ☎1-800/438-7245, Canada ☎1-800/361-7245, ⒲www.raileurope.com. Official Eurail agent, with the widest range of regional and one-country passes.

ScanTours ☎1-800/223-7226 or 310/636-4656, ⒲www.scantours.com. Eurail, Scandinavian and other European country passes.

Switzerland Tourism ☎1-877/SWITZERLAND, ⒲www.myswitzerland.com. Eurail and all Swiss passes.

In Australia and New Zealand

Bentours Australia ☎02/9241 1353, ⒲www.bentours.com.au. Scandinavian rail and bus passes.

CIT World Travel Australia ☎02/9267 1255 or 03/9650 5510, ⒲www.cittravel.com.au. Eurail and Italian rail passes.

Rail Plus Australia ☎1300/555 003 or 03/9642 8644, ⒲www.railplus.com.au, NZ ☎09/303 2484, ⒲www.railplus.co.nz. Eurail and BritRail passes.

Trailfinders Australia ☎02/9247 7666, ⒲www.trailfinder.com.au. All Europe passes.

By bus

On the whole, you'll find yourself using **buses** only for the odd local trip, since long-distance journeys between major European cities are generally slow and uncomfortable and not particularly cheap, especially if you have a rail pass. If you have a limited itinerary, however, a **bus pass** or **circular bus ticket** can undercut a rail pass, especially for over-26s. The **Eurolines** pass is valid for unlimited travel between 31 cities in Europe and the British Isles (though, with certain exceptions, it is not supposed to be used for journeys that do not cross international frontiers). It costs £113 (£135 for over-26s) for fifteen days in low season and £145/174 in high season; for one month it's £153/189 and £209/259 and for two months it's £189/239 and £229/299. Alternatively, **Busabout** run services for their own pass holders every two to four days in summer, covering London and the major cities of nine European countries, with add-on connections to more. Two-week Busabout passes are £199 for youth or student cardholders, £219 for others, rising to £259/289 for 21 days, £319/359 for a month, £459/509 for two months, £559/629 for three and £659/739 for the whole season (April–Oct). Busabout also has Flexipasses for any seven days in a month (£199/219), twelve days in two months (£309/349), sixteen days in three months (£389/439), twenty days in four months (£459/509), and 24 days in five months (£519/579), with additional days at £30. There are small "early bird" discounts on passes bought before the end of January. Major youth/student travel agents in Britain, North America, Australia and New Zealand sell Busabout passes; for more information, and prices, see ⒲www.busabout.com.

By ferry

Travelling by **ferry** is often the most practical way to get from one part of Europe to another, the obvious routes being from the mainland to the Mediterranean islands, as well as moving between the countries bordering the Baltic and Adriatic seas. There are countless routes serving a huge range of destinations, too numerous to outline here; where possible we've given the details of ferries to other countries within each chapter. For further details of schedules and operators, see the *Thomas Cook European Timetable*, or see ⒲www.ex.ac.uk/~mspunter/ifg.

Accommodation

Although accommodation is one of the more crucial costs to consider when planning your trip, it needn't be a stumbling block to a budget-conscious tour of Europe. Indeed, even in Europe's pricier reaches the hostel system means there is always an affordable place to stay, and if you're prepared to camp you can get by on very little while staying at some excellently equipped sites.

The one thing you should bear in mind is that in the more popular cities and resorts – Florence, Venice, Amsterdam, Prague, Barcelona, the Algarve, and so on – things can get chock-a-block during the peak summer months, and even if you've got plenty of money to throw around you should **book in advance**.

Hostels

The cheapest way to travel around Europe is by using the extensive network of hostels that covers the continent. Some of these are **private** places, but by far the majority are **official hostels**, members of Hostelling International (**HI**), which incorporates the national youth hostel associations of each country in the world. Youth hostelling isn't the hearty, up-at-the-crack-of-dawn and early-to-bed business it once was; indeed, hostels have been keen to shed this image of late and now appeal to a wider public. In many countries they simply represent the best-value overnight accommodation available. Most are clean, well-run places, always offering dormitory accommodation, some – especially in Scandinavia and other parts of northern Europe – offering a range of private single and double rooms, or rooms with four to six beds. Many hostels also either have self-catering facilities or provide low-cost meals, and the larger ones have a range of other facilities – a swimming pool, games room, common room, etc. There is no age limit (except in Bavaria, in southern Germany), but where there is limited space, priority can be given to those under 26.

Strictly speaking, to use an HI hostel you have to be a member, although if there is room you can stay at most hostels by simply paying a bit extra – and you can often join the HI on the spot. If you do intend to do a lot of hostelling, however, it is certainly worth joining, which you can do by becoming a member of your home country's hostelling association. Annual **membership** costs are low everywhere. We've detailed the hostelling situation in each country in the text, as well as giving the name and address of the relevant national hostelling organization if you want further information. HI hostels can usually be booked through their country's hostelling association website, almost always over-the-counter at other hostels in the same country, and often through the international HI website at ⓦwww.iyhf.org. The *HI Guide to Europe*, available from bookstores and national hostelling associations, is a good investment at £8.50/$13.95, detailing every official hostel in Europe (but not Morocco, which is

Accommodation price codes

Throughout this guide, accommodation is coded on a scale of ❶ to ❾, the code indicating the lowest price per night for a double room in each establishment in high season. The prices indicated by the codes are as follows:

❶ up to £10/$16 (€15)
❷ £10–20/$16–32 (€15–29)
❸ £20–30/$32–48 (€29–44)
❹ £30–40/$48–64 (€44–58)
❺ £40–50/$64–80 (€58–72)

❻ £50–60/$80–96 (€72–87)
❼ £60–70/$96–112 (€87–102)
❽ £70–80/$112–128 (€102–116)
❾ over £80/$128 (€116)

covered by the *HI Guide to Africa, the Americas, Asia and the Pacific*).

Youth hostel associations

Australia ☎02/9565 1699, ✆www.yha.com.au. Annual membership A$52, renewal A$32.
Canada ☎1-800/663-5777, ✆www.hihostels.ca. Sells membership valid from 16 to 28 months, depending on when you buy it, for C$35, life membership costs C$175 (both plus tax).
England & Wales ☎0870/870 8808, ✆www.yha.org.uk. Annual membership £13.50, life membership £195.
Ireland ☎01/830 4555, ✆www.irelandyha.org. Annual membership €25, life membership €100.
New Zealand ☎03/379 9970, ✆www.yha.co.nz. Annual membership NZ$40, renewal NZ$40; life membership NZ$300.
Northern Ireland ☎028/9031 5435, ✆www.hini.org.uk. Annual membership £10, life membership £75.
Scotland ☎01786/891 400, ✆www.syha.org.uk. Annual membership £6, life membership £60.
USA ☎202/783-6161, ✆www.hiayh.org. Annual membership $28, life membership $250.

Hotels and pensions

If you've got a bit more money to spend, you may want to upgrade from hostel accommodation to something a little more comfortable and private. With **hotels** you can really spend as much or as little as you like. Most hotels in Europe are graded on some kind of star system. One- and two-star category hotels are plain and simple on the whole, usually family-run, with a number of rooms without private facilities; sometimes breakfast won't be included. In three-star hotels all the rooms will have private facilities, prices will normally include breakfast and there may well be a phone or TV in the room; while four- and five-star places will certainly have all these, perhaps on a plusher, roomier basis, perhaps also including access to other facilities – sauna, swimming pool, etc. In the really top-level places breakfast, oddly enough, isn't always included. When it is, in the Netherlands, Britain or Germany, it's fairly sumptuous; in France it wouldn't amount to much anyway and it's no hardship to grab a croissant and coffee in the nearest café.

Obviously **prices** vary greatly, but you're rarely going to be paying less than £15/$25 for a double room even in southern Europe, while in the Netherlands the average price is around £30/$45, and in Scandinavia and the British Isles somewhat higher than that. In some countries a *pension* or **B&B** (variously known as a guest house, *pensão*, Gasthaus or numerous other names) – smaller, simpler affairs, usually with just a few rooms, that is sometimes part of a larger family house – is a cheaper alternative. In some countries these advertise with a sign in the window; in others they can be booked through the tourist office, which may demand a small fee. There are various other kinds of accommodation – apartments, farmhouses, cottages, *paradores* in Spain, *gîtes* in France, and more – but most are geared to longer-term stays and we have detailed them only where relevant.

Camping

The cheapest form of accommodation is, of course, a **campsite**, either pitching your own tent or parking your caravan or camper van. Most sites make a charge per person, plus a charge per plot and another per vehicle. Obviously you'll pay less if you're travelling on foot – maybe just a couple of pounds per night between two people – but parking a car or camper van doesn't add a lot to the cost. Bear in mind also, especially in countries like France where camping is very popular, that facilities can be excellent (though the better the facilities, the pricier the site). If you're on foot you should add in the cost and inconvenience of getting to the site, since most are on the outskirts of towns, sometimes further. Some sites have **cabins**, which you can stay in for a little extra, although these are usually fairly basic affairs, only really worth considering in regions like Scandinavia where budget options are thin on the ground. In Britain, the AA issues *Camping and Caravanning in Europe* (£10), which provides a **list of campsites** in eleven west European countries. Alternatively, **tourist offices** can recommend well-equipped and conveniently located sites.

If you're planning to do a lot of camping, an **international camping carnet** is a good investment. The carnet gives discounts at member sites, serves as useful identification, and is obligatory on some sites in Portugal and some Scandinavian countries. Many campsites will take it instead of making you surrender your passport during your stay, and it covers you for third-party insurance when camping. However, the carnet is not recognized in Sweden, where you may have to join their own carnet scheme. In the **US and Canada**, the carnet is available from Family Campers and RVers (FCRV) at ☎1-800/245-9755 or 718/668 6242, ⓦwww.fcrv.org; their annual membership is $25, and the carnet is an additional $10. In the **UK and Ireland**, the carnet is available to members of the Camping and Caravanning Club, at ☎024/7669 4995,

ⓦwww.campingandcaravanningclub.co.uk (membership £32.50, carnet £4.50); Carefree Travel Service (☎024/7642 2024), the foreign touring arm of the same company, provides the carnet free if you take out insurance with them.

As for **camping rough**, it's a fine idea if you can get away with it – though perhaps an entire trip of rough camping is in reality too gruelling to be truly enjoyable. In some countries it's easy – in parts of Scandinavia it is a legal right, and in Greece and other southern European countries you can usually find a bit of beach to pitch down on – but in others it's almost a non-starter and can get you into trouble with the law.

Communications

Communications throughout northern and western Europe are generally excellent: public phones are readily available and normally work, and the postal system is reasonably efficient and easy to use. In southern Europe, services are sometimes less impressive, notably in Italy and Spain, where the post is not overly reliable; while in eastern Europe the infrastructure is poor and services consequently unpredictable.

Mail

For buying stamps and, sometimes, making phone calls, we've listed the **central post offices** in major cities and given an idea of opening hours. Bear in mind, though, that throughout much of Europe you can avoid the queues in post offices by buying **stamps** from newsagents and the like. If you know in advance where you're going to be and when, it is possible to receive mail through the **poste restante** (general delivery) system, whereby letters addressed to you, marked "poste restante" and sent to the main post office in any town or city will be kept under your name – for at least two weeks and usually for a month – for collection at the relevant counter. When collecting mail, make sure you take your passport for identification, and bear in mind that there's a possibility of letters being misfiled by someone unfamiliar with your language; try looking under your first name as well as your surname.

Phones

It is often possible, especially in western Europe, to make **international calls** from a public call box; this can often be more trouble than it's worth from a coin phone due to the constant need to feed in change, although most countries now have phone cards, making the whole process much easier. Otherwise, you can go to a **post office**, or a special **phone bureau**, where you can make a call from a private booth and pay afterwards. Most countries have these in one form or another, and the local tourist office will point you in the right direction. Wherever possible, avoid using the phone in your **hotel room** – it costs the earth.

To **call any country** in this book from Britain, Ireland or New Zealand, dial ☎00, then the country code (see box), then the city/area code (if there is one) without the initial zero – except for Italy and Moscow, where the initial zero must be dialled, and Latvia and

Country codes

Andorra ☏376	Gibraltar ☏350	Norway ☏47
Australia ☏61	Greece ☏30	Poland ☏48
Austria ☏43	Hungary ☏36	Portugal ☏351
Belgium ☏32	Ireland ☏353	Romania ☏40
Bulgaria ☏359	Italy ☏39	Russia ☏7
Canada ☏1	Latvia ☏371	Slovakia ☏421
Croatia ☏385	Liechtenstein ☏423	Slovenia ☏386
Czech Republic ☏420	Lithuania ☏370	Spain ☏34
Denmark ☏45	Luxembourg ☏352	Sweden ☏46
Estonia ☏372	Monaco ☏377	Switzerland ☏41
Finland ☏358	Morocco ☏212	Turkey ☏90
France ☏33	Netherlands ☏31	UK ☏44
Germany ☏49	New Zealand ☏64	USA ☏1

Lithuania, where the initial 8 must be dialled – then the local number. From the US and most of Canada, the international access code is ☏011, from Australia it's ☏0011; otherwise the procedure is the same.

To **call home** from almost all European countries, dial ☏00, then the country code, then the city/area code (without the initial zero if there is one), then the local number. The exception is Russia, where you dial ☏8, wait for a continuous dialling tone and then dial ☏10, followed by the country code, area code and number.

For **collect calls**, "Home Country Direct" services are available in most of the places covered in this book. In the UK and some other countries, international calling cards available from newsagents enable you to call North America, Australia and New Zealand very cheaply. Most North American, British, Irish and Australasian phone companies either allow you to call home from abroad on a **credit card**, or billed to your home number (contact your company's customer services before you leave to find out their toll-free access codes from the countries you'll be visiting), or else will issue an **international calling card** which can be used worldwide, and for which you will be billed on your return. If you want a calling card and do not already have one, leave yourself a few weeks to arrange it before leaving.

Mobile phones from North America are unlikely to work in Europe – for details of which phones will work outside the US and Canada, contact your provider. Mobiles from the British Isles, Australia and New Zealand can be used in most parts of Europe, and a lot of countries – certainly in western Europe – have nearly universal coverage, but for all bar the very top-of-the-range packages, you'll have to inform your provider before leaving home to get international access switched on, and you will be charged for receiving calls. Also note that it will not always be possible to charge up or replace your **pre-paid cards**, so again check beforehand and if necessary remember to bring enough credit with you. A standard two-pin socket is used on the continent so you may need an **adaptor** for charging up.

The most useful resource for information on phone codes and electrical systems around the world is the encyclopedic website ⓦ www.kropla.com.

Internet and email

Europe still lags some way behind the US in terms of **Internet** access, and surfing the web can be more expensive due to the high rates charged for local phone calls. Nonetheless, things are improving all the time: more and more Internet cafés are opening up, and it is becoming increasingly easy to access the web and send and receive **email**. That being the case, a good way to keep in touch is to open up an account with one of the free **Internet email sites** that can be accessed from anywhere, for example Yahoo Mail (ⓦmail.yahoo.com) and Hotmail (ⓦwww.hotmail.com), so that you can receive emails while on the road.

The media

British newspapers and magazines are fairly widely available in Europe, sometimes on the day of publication, more often the day after. They do, however, cost around three times as much as they do at home.

Exceptions to this rule are the *Guardian* and *Financial Times*, which print European editions that are cheaper and available on the day of issue. You can also find the *International Herald Tribune* and *USA Today* just about everywhere. If you're lucky you may come across the odd *New York Times* or *Washington Post*, while *Time*, *Newsweek* and *The Economist* are widely available.

It's cheaper to get your news by tuning a **radio** into the BBC World Service (considered to have the most reliable news of all the media), the Voice of America, Radio Canada, or one of the many local news broadcasts in English. The easiest way to pick up BBC World Service is on medium wave, at 648kHz (western Europe) or 1323kHz (southeastern Europe); short wave frequencies include 6.195, 9.410, 12.095, 15.485 and 15.565MHz. In addition, FM stations in cities from Gibraltar to Helsinki slot the BBC news and/or some programming into their schedules; ⓦwww.bbc.co.uk has details. In northern France, the Netherlands and Belgium you can pick up BBC domestic services on medium and long wave. Voice of America (ⓦwww.voa.gov) can be found during the day on 1197kHz medium wave, and at night on 6.040, 9.760 or 15.205MHz short wave, among other frequencies. Radio Canada (ⓦwww.rcinet.ca) broadcasts on short wave on 5.850 and sometimes 6.045 and 9.770MHz between 8pm and 10pm GMT.

With the advent of cable and satellite channels, **television** has become more of a pan-European medium than radio. CNN, Eurosport and MTV Europe are all popular and normally available in pricier hotels. In many parts of Europe there is, in any case, a reasonably wide choice of terrestrial channels, since a border is never far away and you can often pick up at least one other country's TV stations. For instance, in Belgium and the southern Netherlands, you can pick up all the satellite and cable channels, plus Dutch and Belgian TV, French TV, British BBC1 and BBC2, all the German stations, and even the state Italian channel.

Festivals and annual events

There's always some annual event or other happening in Europe, and the bigger shindigs can be reason enough for visiting a place – some are even worth planning your entire trip around. Be warned, though, that if you're intending to visit a place during its annual festival you need to plan well in advance, since accommodation can be booked up months beforehand, especially for the larger, more internationally known events.

Religious and traditional festivals

Many of the festivals and annual events you'll come across were – and in many cases still are – **religion-inspired affairs**, centring on a local miracle or saint's day. **Easter** is celebrated throughout Europe, with most verve and ceremony in Catholic and Orthodox Europe, where Easter Sunday or Monday is usually marked with some sort of procession; it's especially enthusiastically celebrated in Greece, where it is more important than Christmas (though be aware that the Orthodox Church's Easter can fall a week or two either side of the Western festival). Earlier in the year, traditionally at the beginning of Lent in February, **Carnival** (or Mardi Gras) is celebrated most conspicuously (and perhaps most stagily) in **Venice**, which explodes in a riot of posing and colour to become one of Italy's major tourist draws at this time of year. There are smaller, perhaps more authentic carnivals around Europe at this time, most notably in **Viareggio** in Italy, **Luzern** and **Basel** in Switzerland, **Cologne** in Germany, **Maastricht** in the Netherlands and tiny **Binche** in the Belgian Ardennes, where you can view some 1500 costumed *Gilles* or dancers in the streets.

Also in Belgium, in mid-Lent, catch if you can the procession of white-clad *Blanc Moussis* through the streets of **Stavelot** in the Ardennes – one of Europe's oddest sights. Other religious festivals you might base a trip around include the Festa di San Gennaro three times a year in **Naples**, when the dried blood of the city's patron saint is supposed to liquefy to prevent disaster befalling the place (it rarely fails); the Ommegang procession through the heart of **Brussels** city centre to commemorate a medieval miracle; the Heilig Bloed procession in **Bruges**, when a much-venerated relic of Christ's blood is carried shoulder-high through the town; and, in Italy, the annual procession across **Venice**'s Grand Canal to the church of the Madonna della Salute to recall the deliverance of the city from a seventeenth-century plague.

In Morocco and Turkey, where the predominant religion is Islam, and in the Muslim areas of Bulgaria, **Ramadan**, commemorating the revelation of the Koran to the Prophet Muhammad, is observed. The most important time of the year for Muslims, it lasts a month, during which time the observant fast from sunrise until sunset – although otherwise, as far as is possible, life carries on as normal.

There are, of course, other, equally long-established events that have a less obvious foundation. One of the best-known is the

April *Feria* in **Seville**, a week's worth of flamenco music and dancing, parades and bullfights, in a frenziedly enthusiastic atmosphere. Also in Spain, for a week in early July, the San Fermín festival in **Pamplona** is if anything even more famous, its centrepiece – the running of the bulls, along with local macho men, through the streets of the city – drawing tourists from all over the world, though there is much more to the festival than that. Also in July, at the beginning of the month (and again in mid-August), the Palio in **Siena** is perhaps the most spectacular annual event in Italy, a bareback horse race between representatives of the different quarters of the city around the main square, its origins dating back to medieval times. It's a brutal affair, with few rules and a great sense of deeply felt rivalry, and, although there are other Palio events in Italy, it's like no other horse race you'll ever see. At least as big a deal as these is the **Munich** Oktoberfest, a huge beer festival and fair in the last two weeks in September. Unlike most events of its size in Europe it's less than two hundred years old, but it attracts vast numbers of people to consume gluttonous quantities of beer and food. **London**'s Notting Hill Carnival, held at the end of August, is also a recent phenomenon, a predominantly Black British and Caribbean celebration that's become the world's second biggest street carnival after Rio. Other, smaller events include the great **Venice** Regata Storica each September, a trial of skill for the city's gondoliers, and the gorgeous annual displays and processions of flowers in the **Dutch bulbfield towns** in April and May.

Arts festivals

Festivals celebrating all or one specific aspect of the **arts** are held all over Europe throughout the year, though particularly in summer, when the weather is better suited to outdoor events. Of general international arts festivals, the **Edinburgh Arts Festival** held every August is perhaps the best known and most enjoyable, not to mention one of the most innovative, with a mass of top-notch and fringe events in every medium, from rock to cabaret to modern experimental music, dance and drama. For three weeks every year the whole city is given over to the festival and it's a wonderful time to be around if you don't mind the crowds and have booked somewhere to stay in advance. The Festival dei Due Mondi in **Spoleto** is Italy's leading international arts festival, held over two months each summer but on a somewhat smaller scale than Edinburgh, while the midsummer **Avignon** festival in southern France is slanted towards drama but hosts plenty of other events besides and is again a great time to be in town. Smaller general arts festivals, though still attracting a variety of international names, include the **Holland Festival** in Amsterdam in June; the **Flanders Festival**, an umbrella title for all sorts of dramatic and musical events held mainly in the medieval buildings of Bruges and Ghent in July and August; and the **Dubrovnik Summer Festival**, with a host of musical events and theatre performances against the backdrop of the Croatian town's beautiful Renaissance centre.

As regards more specialist gatherings, the **Montreux Jazz Festival** in July is these days only loosely committed to jazz, and takes in everything from folk to breakbeats, while the **North Sea Jazz Festival** in The Hague in mid-July sticks closer to its orthodox roots. The same month sees the beginning of the **Salzburg Music Festival**, perhaps the foremost – if also the most conservative – serious music festival in Europe, though London's **Proms** season (July–Sept) maintains very high standards at egalitarian prices. Florence's **Maggio Musicale** is also worth catching, a festival of opera and classical music that runs from late April until early July. Less highbrow musical forms – rock, folk, etc – are celebrated most conspicuously at the huge **Glastonbury festival** in Britain; at the **Pink Pop Festival** near Maastricht in the Netherlands; and the **Roskilde Festival** in Denmark. Look out also for the **WOMAD** get-togethers, a number of which are usually held each year at a variety of sites all over Europe, celebrating world music, and the excellent and still relatively small **Cambridge Folk Festival** in England in late July. For **films**, there is, of course, **Cannes**, though this is more of an industry affair than anything else; the **Venice**, **Berlin** and **Locarno** film festivals are more geared to the general public.

Crime and personal safety

Travelling around Europe should be relatively trouble-free, but, as in any part of the world, there is always the chance of petty theft. However, conditions do vary greatly from, say, Scandinavia, where you're unlikely to encounter much trouble of any kind, to the inner-city areas of metropolises such as London, Paris or Barcelona, where the crime-rate is higher, and poorer regions such as Morocco, Turkey and southern Italy, where street crime is low but tourists are an obvious target.

In order to minimize the risks, you should take some basic **precautions**. First and perhaps most important, you should try not to look too much like a tourist. Appearing lost, even if you are, is to be avoided, and it's not a good idea – especially in southern Europe – to walk around showing off the latest handheld camcorder or flashing an obviously expensive camera: the professional bag-snatchers who tour train stations can have your valuables off you in seconds. Be discreet about using a mobile phone, and be sure to put it back into a secure pocket as soon as you've finished. If you're waiting for a train, keep your eyes (and hands if necessary) on your bags at all times; if you want to sleep, put everything valuable under your head as a pillow. You should be cautious when choosing a train compartment and avoid any situation that makes you feel uncomfortable. Padlocking your bags to the luggage rack if you're on an overnight train means that they're more likely to still be there in the morning. If you're staying in a hostel, take your valuables out with you unless there's a very secure store for them on the premises; you might even want to make photocopies of your passport and ID and leave them at home. Storing a copy of your address book with friends or family can be a good idea. If you're driving, don't leave anything valuable in your parked car.

If the worst happens and you do have something stolen, inform the **police** immediately (we've included details of the main city police stations in the text); the priority is to get a statement from them detailing exactly what has been lost, which you'll need for your insurance claim back home. Generally you'll find the police sympathetic enough, sometimes able to speak English, though they'll often be unwilling to do much more than make out a report for you.

As for **offences** you might commit, it's hardly necessary to state that **drugs** such as amphetamines, cocaine, heroin, LSD and ecstasy are illegal all over Europe, and although use of cannabis is widespread in most countries, and legally tolerated in some (famously in the Netherlands, for example), you are never allowed to possess more than a tiny amount for personal use. Unlicensed sale remains illegal. Penalties for possession of hard drugs and psychedelics can be severe; in certain countries, such as Turkey, even possession of cannabis can result in a hefty prison sentence, and your consulate is most unlikely to plead any kind of case for you. Other, more minor, misdemeanours you should be wary of committing include **sleeping rough**, which is more tolerated in some parts of Europe than others and should be undertaken everywhere with a certain amount of circumspection, and **topless sunbathing**, which is now fairly common throughout southern Europe but still often frowned upon, especially in parts of Greece, Turkey and Italy. As always, be sensitive, and err on the side of caution. It's also worth remembering that, in theory, it is illegal to be on the streets without an official **ID card or passport** throughout most of mainland Europe (except the Netherlands and Scandinavia). Finally, although this is much less of an issue than it once was, avoid photography around sensitive military sites or installations: you may be arrested as a spy.

Sexual harassment

One of the major irritants for women travelling through Europe is **sexual harassment**, which in Italy, Greece, Turkey, Spain and Morocco especially can be almost constant for women travelling alone or with another woman, and can put certain areas completely out of bounds. Southern European coastal areas, especially, can be a real problem, where women tourists are often regarded as being on the lookout for sex. By far the most common kind of harassment you'll come across simply consists of street whistles and cat-calls; occasionally it's more sinister and very occasionally it can be dangerous. Indifference is often the best policy, avoiding eye contact with men and at the same time appearing as confident and purposeful as possible. If this doesn't make you feel any more comfortable, shouting a few choice phrases in the local language is a good idea; don't, however, shout in English, which often seems to encourage them. You may also come across gropers on crowded buses and trains, in which case you should complain as loudly as possible in any language – the ensuing scene should be enough to deter your assailant. The best way of avoiding more dangerous situations is to simply be as suspicious as possible: don't ever get yourself into a situation where you're alone with a man you don't know.

Gay and lesbian travellers

Gay men and lesbians will find most of Europe a tolerant part of the world in which to travel, the west rather more so than the east. Gay sex is no longer a criminal offence in any country covered by this book, but some still have measures that discriminate against gay men (a higher age of consent for example). Lesbianism would seem not to officially exist, so it is not generally subject to such laws.

In general, the Netherlands and Scandinavia (except Finland) are the most tolerant parts of the continent, with anti-discrimination legislation and official recognition of lesbian and gay partnerships. Homophobic laws against "public scandal" and "luring into perversion" still exist in Romania and Bulgaria. For further information, check the International Lesbian and Gay Association's European region website at ⓦ www.ilga-europe.org.

Most cities of any size, at least in northern Europe, have a few bars or cafés frequented by **gay men**, and it's not hard to make contact with other gay people. In the major northern capitals, certainly, the gay scene is usually fairly sophisticated, with any number of bars, bookshops, clubs and gay organizations and switchboards, though things are usually firmly slanted towards gay men. The gay capital of Europe is Amsterdam, but there is plenty of interest for gay men in London, Paris, Copenhagen, and, to a lesser extent, Madrid, Barcelona, Ibiza and the Greek island of Mykonos. In southern Europe, things are less developed: the main cities may have the odd gay bar, but it may not advertise itself as such, and outside the capitals there may not be many obvious places to meet at all. **Lesbians** can likewise usually find somewhere to meet with other gay women in northern Europe, albeit on a much smaller scale than gay men, while elsewhere, in southern and eastern Europe, word-of-mouth is about the only course open. We've detailed the best of the gay scenes of the major cities in the guide; for further information, contact the organizations listed below.

Contacts for gay and lesbian travellers

Spartacus Gay Guide Bruno Gmünder Verlag, PO Box 610104, 10921 Berlin ☎ +4930/6100 1120. US: at Bookazine Co, 75 Hook Rd, Bayonne, NJ 07002 ☎ 1-800/548 3855; UK: at Turnaround, Unit 3, Olympia Trading Estate, Coburg Rd, London N22 6TZ ☎ 020/8829 3000; Australia: at Bulldog Books, PO Box 300, Beaconsfield, NSW 2014 ☎ 02/9699 3507. International gay guide with information on meeting and cruising spots for gay men, but nothing much for lesbians.

In the US and Canada

Damron Company ☎ 1-800/462-6654 or 415/255-0404, ⓦ www.damron.com. Publishes a men's and a women's guide, and an accommodation guide and gay road atlas, all mainly on North America but covering major European cities too.

Gay Travel ⓦ www.gaytravel.com. Gay online travel agent, offering accommodation, cruises, tours and more.

International Gay & Lesbian Travel Association ☎ 1-800/448-8550 or 954/776-2626, ⓦ www.iglta.org. Trade group that can provide a list of gay- and lesbian-owned or -friendly travel agents, accommodation and other travel businesses.

In the UK

ⓦ www.gaytravel.co.uk Gay and lesbian travel agent, offering good deals on all types of holiday. Also lists gay- and lesbian-friendly hotels in several European cities and resorts.

Madison Travel ☎ 01273/202532, ⓦ www.madisontravel.co.uk. Established travel agents specializing in packages to gay- and lesbian-friendly mainstream destinations, and also to gay/lesbian destinations.

Respect Holidays ☎ 0870/770 0169, ⓦ www.respect-holidays.co.uk. Offers exclusively gay packages to all popular European resorts.

In Australia and NZ

Gay and Lesbian Tourism Australia
ⓦ www.galta.com.au. Directory and links for gay and lesbian travel worldwide.
New Zealand Gay and Lesbian Tourism Association ⓦ www.nzglta.org.nz. Organization devoted to enhancing the NZ travel experience for gay, lesbian and bisexual visitors.
Parkside Travel Australia ☏ 08/8274 1222,

ⓔ parkside@herveyworld.com.au. Gay travel agent associated with local branch of Hervey World Travel; all aspects of gay and lesbian travel worldwide.
Silke's Travel Australia ☏ 02/8347 2000 or 1800/807860, ⓦ www.silkes.com.au. Long-established gay and lesbian specialist, with the emphasis on women's travel.
Tearaway Travel Australia ☏ 1800/664 440 or 03/9510 6644, ⓦ www.tearaway.com. Gay-specific business dealing with international and domestic travel.

Travellers with disabilities

Unsurprisingly, northern Europe is easier for diasbled travellers than the south and east, but the gradual enforcement of EU accessibility regulations is making life easier within the European Union at least.

Wheelchair access to public buildings nonetheless remains far from easy in many countries, as is wheelchair accessibility to public transport – indeed, the only big-city underground systems that are accessible are those in Berlin, Amsterdam, Stockholm and Helsinki, with the rest lagging far behind. Most buses are still inaccessible to wheelchair users, but airport facilities are improving, as are those on cross-Channel ferries. As for rail services, these vary greatly: France, for example, has very good facilities for disabled passengers, as have Belgium, Denmark, Switzerland and Austria, but many other countries make little if any provision, though things are improving.

Your particular disability may govern whether you decide to see Europe on a **package tour** or **independently**. There are any number of specialist tour-operators, mostly catering for physically disabled travellers, and the number of non-specialist operators who cater for disabled clients is increasing.

Pressure on space means that it is impossible for us to detail wheelchair-access arrangements for everywhere we list; neither can we detail the best and worst of the operators. For more **information on disabled travel abroad** you should get in touch with the organizations listed below. As well as their publications, look out for *Access London* and *Access Paris,* with information specific to those cities, published by Access Project in the UK.

Contacts for travellers with disabilities

In the US and Canada

Access-Able ⓦ www.access-able.com. Online resource for travellers with disabilities.
Directions Unlimited 123 Green Lane, Bedford Hills, NY 10507 ☏ 1-800/533-5343 or 914/241-1700. Tour operator specializing in custom tours for people with disabilities.
Mobility International US 451 Broadway, Eugene, OR 97401, voice and TDD ☏ 541/343-1284, ⓦ www.miusa.org. Information and referral services, access guides, tours and exchange programmes. Annual membership $35 (includes quarterly newsletter).
Society for the Advancement of Travelers with Handicaps (SATH) 347 5th Ave, New York, NY 10016 ☏ 212/447-7284, ⓦ www.sath.org. Non-profit educational organization that passes queries on to its members as appropriate; allow plenty of time for a response.
Wheels Up! ☏ 1-888/38-WHEELS, ⓦ www.wheelsup.com. Provides discounted airfare, tour and cruise prices for disabled travellers, also publishes a free monthly newsletter and has a comprehensive website.

In the UK and Ireland

Access Travel 6 The Hillock, Astley M29 7GW ☎01942/888844, ⓦwww.access-travel.co.uk. Small tour operator that can arrange flights, transfer and accommodation in France, Spain, Portugal and parts of Greece.

Disability Action Portside Business Park, 189 Airport Rd W, Belfast BT3 9ED ☎028/9029 7880, ⓦwww.disabilityaction.org. Information about access for disabled travellers abroad.

Holiday Care 2nd floor, Imperial Building, Victoria Rd, Horley RH6 7PZ ☎0845/124 9971, Minicom ☎0845/124 9976, ⓦwww.holidaycare.org.uk. Provides free lists of accessible accommodation abroad. Information on financial help for holidays available.

Irish Wheelchair Association Blackheath Drive, Clontarf, Dublin 3 ☎01/818 6400, ⓦwww.iwa.ie. Useful information provided about travelling abroad with a wheelchair.

Tripscope Alexandra House, Albany Rd, Brentford TW8 0NE ☎0845/758 5641, ⓦwww.justmobility.co.uk/tripscope. This registered charity provides a national telephone information service offering free transport and travel advice for people with a mobility problem.

In Australia and NZ

ACROD (Australian Council for Rehabilitation of the Disabled) PO Box 60, Curtin ACT 2605; Suite 103, 1st floor, 1–5 Commercial Rd, Kings Grove 2208; ☎02/6282 4333, TTY ☎02/6282 4333, ⓦwww.acrod.org.au. Provides lists of travel agencies and tour operators for people with disabilities.

Disabled Persons Assembly 4/173–175 Victoria St, Wellington ☎04/801 9100 (also TTY). Resource centre with lists of travel agencies and tour operators for people with disabilities.

Work and study

The opportunities for working or studying your way around Europe are almost unlimited, especially for EU citizens, who can legally work in any EU state. You can fix something up before you leave home and build your trip around it, or look out for casual labour on your travels as a way of topping up your vacation cash.

The best way of discovering a country properly is to **work** there, learning the language if you can and discovering something about the culture. **Study** opportunities are also a good way of absorbing yourself in the local culture, but they invariably need to be fixed up in advance; check the newspapers for ads or contact one of the main organizations (listed on p.49) direct.

There are any number of jobs you can pick up on the road to supplement your spending money. It's normally not hard to find **bar or restaurant work**, especially in large resort areas during the summer, and your chances will be greater if you can speak the local language – although being able to speak English may be your greatest asset in the more touristy areas. In EU countries, British and Irish citizens do not need work permits (though other bureaucratic hurdles may be thrown in your path instead if you choose to go by the book). Don't be afraid to march straight in and ask, or check the noticeboards in local bars, hostels or colleges, or the local newspapers, particularly the English-language ones. Cleaning jobs, nannying and **au pair** work are also common, if not spectacularly well paid, often just providing room and board plus pocket money. Some of them can be fixed up on the spot, while others need to be organized before you leave home. If staying in a place for a while, you can place ads offering your services. The other big casual earner is farmwork, particularly **grape-picking**, an option from August to October when the vines are being harvested. The best country for this is France, but there's sometimes work in Germany too, and you're unlikely to be asked for documentation. Also in France, along the Côte d'Azur, and in other yacht-havens in Greece and parts of southern Spain, there is sometimes **crewing** work available, though you'll obviously need some sailing experience. Or try tour operators, who are often on the lookout for **travel couriers**, though this is better arranged from home. If you're really serious, get in touch with the companies that run bus tours for young people around Europe, who are often keen to take on new blood.

Rather better paid, and equally wide-spread, if only during the September to June period, is **teaching English as a foreign language** (TEFL), though it is becoming harder to find English-teaching jobs without a TEFL qualification. You'll normally be paid a liveable local salary, sometimes with somewhere to live thrown in, and you can often supplement your income with more lucrative private lessons. The TEFL teaching season is reversed in Britain and to a lesser extent Ireland, with plenty of work available during the summer in London and on the English south coast (but again, some kind of TEFL qualification is pretty well indispensable).

If you want to know more about working in Europe, get hold of one of several handy **publications**. The publishers Vacation Work (ⓦwww.vacationwork.co.uk) produce the useful *Work your Way around the World* by Sue Griffiths, and *Summer Jobs Abroad* by David Woodworth and Ian Collier, which has details of places you could try before leaving home; for more on TEFL possibilities, check out Sue Griffiths' *Teaching English Abroad*. For voluntary work, the place to look is *International Voluntary Work* by Victoria Pybus. Travel magazines such as *Wanderlust* (every two months; £3.50) have a job section that often advertises opportunities with tour companies.

Studying abroad invariably means learning a language, doing an intensive course that lasts between two weeks and three months and staying with a local family. There are plenty of places you can do this, and you should reckon on paying around £200/$300 a week including room and board. If you know a language well, you could also apply to do a short course in another subject at a local university; scan the classified sections of the newspapers back home, and keep an eye out when you're on the spot. The EU runs a programme called **Erasmus** (part of a wider project called Socrates) in which university students from Britain and Ireland can obtain mobility grants to study in one of 26 European countries (including the other EU countries, plus Bulgaria, the Czech Republic, Estonia, Hungary, Latvia, Lithuania, Norway, Poland, Romania, Slovakia and Slovenia) for three months to a full academic year if their university participates in the programme. Check with your university's international relations office, or at ⓦeuropa.eu.int/comm/education/erasmus.html.

AFS Intercultural Programs ⓦwww.afs.org. US ☎1-800/AFS-INFO or 212/299-9000, Canada ☎1-800/361-7248 or 514/288-3282, UK ☎0113/242 6136, Australia ☎1300/13 17 16, NZ ☎0800/600 300 or 04/494 6020. Global UN-recognized organization running summer experiential programmes to foster international understanding.

American Institute for Foreign Study ⓦwww.aifs.com. US ☎1-800/727-AIFS, UK ☎020/7581 7300. Language study and cultural immersion for the summer or school year in Austria, Britain, the Czech Republic, France, Italy, Russia and Spain.

ASSE International ⓦwww.asse.com. US ☎1-800/333-3802, Canada ☎1-800/361-3214, UK ☎01255/506 347, Australia ☎03/9775 4711. International student exchanges to Scandinavia, Germany, Switzerland, the Netherlands, France, Spain, Italy, the Czech Republic, Slovakia, Poland and the UK; also offers summer language programmes in most of those.

Association for International Practical Training ⓦwww.aipt.org. US ☎410/997-2200. Summer internships in various European countries for students who have completed at least two years of college in science, agriculture, engineering or architecture.

Australians Studying Abroad ⓦwww.asatravinfo.com.au. Australia ☎03/9509 1955. Study tours focusing on art and culture.

British Council ⓦwww.britishcouncil.org. UK ☎020/7930 8466. Produces a free leaflet which details study opportunities abroad. The Council's Central Management Direct Teaching (☎020/7389 4931) recruits TEFL teachers for posts worldwide (check the website for a list of current vacancies), and its Central Bureau for International Educational and Training (☎020/7389 4004, ⓦwww.centralbureau.org.uk) enables those who already work as educators to find out about teacher development programmes abroad. It also publishes a book, *Year Between*, aimed principally at gap-year students detailing volunteer programmes, and schemes abroad.

Council on International Educational Exchange (CIEE) ⓦwww.ciee.org/study. US ☎1-800/40-STUDY, UK ☎020/7478 2000, Australia ☎02/8235 7000, ⓦwww.councilexchanges.org .au. An international organization worth contacting for advice on studying, working and volunteering in Europe. They run summer-semester and one-year study programmes, and volunteer projects, in Belgium, the Czech Republic, France, Hungary, Ireland, Italy, the Netherlands, Poland, Romania,

Russia, Spain, Turkey and the UK.

World Learning ⓦwww.usexperiment.org. US ☎1-800/345-2929 or 802/257-7751. The Experiment in International Living has summer programmes for high-school students in France, Germany, Ireland, Italy, Poland, Spain, Switzerland, Turkey and the UK, while the School for International Training (www.sit.edu/studyabroad) offers accredited college semesters abroad, with language and cultural studies, homestay and other academic work, in Croatia, the Czech Republic, France, Germany, Ireland, Morocco, the Netherlands, Russia, Spain and Switzerland.

Directory

Bargaining The only places where you need really do any bargaining when shopping are in Turkey – in the bazaars and carpet shops – and in the souks of Morocco. Everywhere else, even in the less developed parts of southern Italy and Greece, people would think it odd if you tried to haggle.

Contraceptives Condoms are available everywhere, and are normally reliable international brands such as Durex, at least in northwestern Europe; the condoms in eastern European countries, Morocco and Turkey are of uncertain quality, however, so it's best to stock up in advance. The pill is available everywhere, too, though often only on prescription; again, bring a sufficient supply with you.

Electric current The supply in Europe is 220v (240v in the British Isles), which means that

anything on North American voltage (110v) normally needs a transformer. However, one or two countries (notably Spain and Morocco) still have a few places on 110v or 120v, so check before plugging in. Continental, Moroccan and Turkish sockets take two round pins, British and Irish ones take three square pins. A travel plug which adapts to all these systems is useful to carry. See ⓦwww.kropla.com for more.

Left luggage (Baggage deposit) Almost every train station of any size has facilities for "left luggage", either lockers or a desk that's open long hours every day. We've given details in the accounts of major capitals.

Tampons In western and southern Europe you can buy tampons in all chemists and supermarkets, although in parts of eastern Europe

Metric conversions

All figures are approximate.

1 centimetre = 0.39 inches; 1 inch = 2.5cm; 1 foot = 30cm.
1 metre = 1.09 yards or 39 inches; 1 yard = 0.91m.
1 hectare = 2.47 acres; 1 acre = 0.41 ha.
1 kilometre = 0.62 miles; 1 mile = 1.61km; 5 miles = 8km.
1 kilo = 2.2lb; 1lb = 45g/0.45kg; 1oz = 28g.
1 litre = 2.11 US pints; 1 US pint = 0.47 litres; 1 US quart = 0.95 litres.
1 litre = 0.26 US gallons; 1 US gallon = 3.79 litres.
1 litre = 1.76 UK pints; 1 UK pint = 0.57 litres; 1 UK gallon = 4.54 litres.
1 US pint = 0.83 UK pint; 1 UK pint = 1.2 US pints; 6 US pints = 5 UK pints.

Temperatures

°C	-5	0	5	10	15	20	25	30	35
°F	23	32	41	50	59	68	77	86	95

they can still be hard to come by. If you're travelling in the east for any length of time, it's best to bring your own supply.

Time The places covered in this book are in four time zones. Britain, Ireland, Portugal and Morocco are in principle on GMT (or UTC), which is five hours ahead of Eastern Standard Time, eight hours ahead of Pacific Standard Time, eight hours behind western Australia, ten hours behind eastern Australia, and twelve hours behind New Zealand. Most of the continent is on GMT+1, with Finland, Estonia, Latvia, Lithuania, Romania, Bulgaria, Greece and Turkey on GMT+2, and Moscow and St Petersburg on GMT+3. All of these (except Morocco) have daylight saving time from March to October; thankfully, they usually manage to all change over at the same time nowadays, but this change, along with daylight saving in North America, Australia and New Zealand, can mean a further hour or two's difference.

Tipping Although it varies from one country to the next, tipping is not really the serious business it is in North America. In many countries it is customary to leave at least something in most restaurants and cafés, if only rounding the bill up to the next major denomination. Even in swankier establishments, a ten percent tip is sufficient, and you shouldn't feel obliged to tip at all if the service was bad, especially if service has been included in the bill. In smarter hotels you should tip hall porters, etc. Cab drivers expect a tip in Britain and Ireland, but not necessarily on the Continent. The opposite is true of bartenders (but if you want to tip a bartender in Britain or Ireland, buy them a drink).

Guide

Guide

Austria

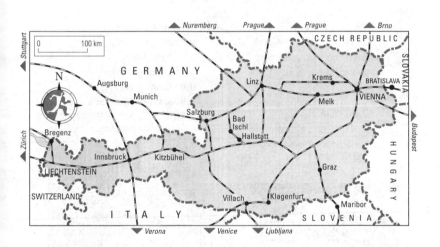

Austria highlights

✳ **Schönbrunn Palace, Vienna** The epitome of opulence. **See p.67**

✳ **Coffee and cake, Vienna** An unmissable part of any trip: get your *Kaffee und Kuchen*, sit back and watch the world go by. **See p.68**

✳ **Staatsoper, Vienna** Drink in a performance at Vienna's ornate opera house from just €2. **See p.69**

✳ **Melk** Over-the-top Baroque decor at this Benedictine monastery. **See p.70**

✳ **The Sound of Music tour, Salzburg** Cheesy but fun, whether you're into Julie Andrews or not. **See p.75**

✳ **Hallstatt** Picture-postcard village in the lovely Salzkammergut region. **See p.77**

✳ **Adventure sports, Innsbruck** Hiking, mountain-biking, canyoning and more in the stunning setting of the Austrian Alps. **See p.78**

Introduction and basics

Long the heart of the Habsburg Empire, with a pivotal role in the political and cultural destiny of Europe, **Austria** underwent decades of change and uncertainty in the twentieth century. The interwar state, shorn of its empire and racked by economic problems and political strife, fell prey to the promises of Nazi Germany. After World War II, denazification was pretty desultory, since most Austrians preferred to forget their wartime role. Postwar economic stability encouraged an emphasis on social policy as the guiding principle of national life, and the growth of a low-key patriotism. With the end of the Cold War, the country returned to the heart of Europe, finally joining the EU in 1995. From time to time, however, Austria's reactionary past has come back to haunt it, most notably in recent years with the rise of Jörg Haider and the far-right Freedom Party (FPÖ); the persistence of xenophobic attitudes and their exploitation by the populist right continue to be a source of concern.

Politics aside, Austria is primarily known for two contrasting attractions – the fading imperial glories of the capital, and the stunning beauty of its Alpine hinterland. **Vienna** is the gateway to much of central Europe and a good place to soak up the culture of *Mitteleuropa* before heading towards the Magyar and Slav lands over which the city once held sway. Less renowned provincial capitals such as **Graz** and **Linz** provide a similar level of culture and vitality. The most dramatic of Austria's Alpine scenery is west of here, in and around the **Tyrol**, whose capital, **Innsbruck**, provides the best base for exploration. **Salzburg**, between Innsbruck and Vienna, represents urban Austria at its most picturesque, an intoxicating Baroque city within easy striking distance of the mountains and lakes of the **Salzkammergut**.

Information & maps

Tourist offices (usually *Information, Tourismusverband, Verkehrsamt, Fremdenverkehrsverein* or other variants) are plentiful, often hand out free maps and almost always book accommodation, sometimes for a small fee and/or deposit. They are open all day, every day, in the larger cities during the summer; in other seasons, and in smaller towns and remote areas, times may be restricted to a few hours on weekday mornings and afternoons. There are plenty of good general **maps**, including the 1:500,000 Freytag & Berndt. The 1:200,000 Generalkarte series of regional maps are useful for lengthier touring, as are the 1:50,000 Freytag & Berndt Wanderkarten and rival Kompass Wanderkarten.

Money and banks

Austria's currency, in common with many EU countries, is the **euro** (€). **Banking** hours tend to be Mon–Fri 8am–12.30pm & 1.30–3pm; in Vienna they're mostly Mon–Fri 8am–3pm, Thurs until 5.30pm. Post offices charge slightly less commission on **exchange** than banks, and in larger cities are open longer hours.

Austria on the net

- ⓦ**www.austria-tourism.at** Austrian Tourist Board website.
- ⓦ**www.austriatoday.at** Website version of the monthly English-language newspaper.
- ⓦ**www.info.wien.at** Vienna's Tourist Board site.
- ⓦ**www.oebb.at** Train site, including excellent English-language journey planner.
- ⓦ**www.austrosearch.at** Search engine for all things Austrian.
- ⓦ**www.tiscover.com** Detailed information on all regions of the country.

Communications

Most **post offices** are open Mon–Fri 8am–noon & 2–6pm; in larger cities they do without the lunch break and also open Sat 8–10am; some are open 24hr. Stamps can also be bought at tobacconists (*Tabak-Trafik*). The smallest coin accepted in **public phones** is €0.20; two should suffice for a local call. Insert €0.50 and upwards if calling long distance, or buy a phone card (*Telefonkarte*; €3.60 or €6.90), available from tobacconists. You can make international calls from all public phones, but it's easier to do so from larger post offices, which have booths. The operator number is ☎1611 (domestic), ☎1616 (international). **Internet access** is widespread in the big cities, less so in rural areas; expect to pay around €5/hr.

Getting around

Austria's public transport system is fast, efficient and comprehensive. Austrian Federal Railways (ÖBB; ⊛www.oebb.at) runs a punctual, clean and comfortable network, which includes most towns of any size. **Trains** marked EC or EN (EuroCity and EuroNight international expresses), ICE or IC (Austrian InterCity expresses) are the fastest. Those designated D (*Schnellzug*) or E (*Eilzug*) are next, stopping at most intermediate points, while the *Regionalzug* (R) is the slowest service, stopping at all stations. InterRail and Eurail are valid. The national timetable (*Kursbuch*) costs €8.

The **Bahnbus** and **Postbus** system serves remoter villages and Alpine valleys; fares are around €9.50 per 100km. As a general rule, *Bahnbus* services, operated by ÖBB, depart from outside train stations; the *Postbus* tends to stop outside the post office. Daily and weekly regional **travelcards** (*Netzkarte*), covering both trains and buses, are available in many regions.

Austria is bike-friendly, with **cycle lanes** in all major towns. Many train stations rent bikes for €13 per day (€8.70 with a valid rail ticket). You can return them to any station for an extra fee of €6.50/€3.30.

Accommodation

Outside popular tourist spots such as Vienna and Salzburg, **accommodation** need not be too expensive. Most tourist offices book accommodation with little fuss, usually for a fee (€2–3) and/or a deposit.

A high standard of cleanliness and comfort can usually be taken for granted in Austrian **hotels**. Outside Vienna, expect to pay a minimum of €45 for a double with bathroom, less for rooms with shared facilities. Good-value **B&B** is usually available in the many small family-run hotels known as *Gasthöfe* and *Gasthaüser*, with prices starting at €40 for a double. In the larger towns and cities a **pension** or *Frühstuckspension* will offer similar prices. Most tourist offices also have a stock of **private rooms**, although in well-travelled rural areas, roadside signs offering *Zimmer Frei* are fairly ubiquitous anyway. Prices for a double room are usually €30–45.

There are around 100 **HI hostels** (*Jugendherberge* or *Jugendgästehaus*), run by either the ÖJHV (☎1/533 5353, ⊛www.oejhv.or.at) or the ÖJHW (☎1/533 1833, ⊛www.oejhw.or.at). **Rates** are €10–18, normally including a nominal breakfast. Sheet sleeping bags are obligatory, although the cost of renting one is often included in the charge. Many hostels also serve lunch and dinner for an additional €3.50–5.50. There are also a number of excellent independent hostels.

Austria's high standards are reflected in the country's **campsites**, most of which have laundry facilities, shops and snack bars. Most are open May–Sept, although in the winter-sports resorts many open year-round. In general, you can expect to pay €4–6 per person, €3–9 per pitch.

Food and drink

Eating out in Austria is marginally cheaper than self-catering, but both will take a large chunk out of your daily expenses. By contrast, **drinking** is remarkably affordable, especially wine, and the country's bars and cafés are among its real joys.

For ready-made snacks, try a bakery (*Bäckerei*) or confectioner's (*Konditorei*), which sell sweet pastries and cakes, as well as sandwiches. **Fast food** centres on the *Würstelstand*, which sells hot dogs, *Bratwurst* (grilled sausage), *Käsekrainer* (spicy sausage with cheese), *Bosna* (spicy, thin Balkan sausage) and *Currywurst*, usually chopped up and served with a *Semmel* or bread roll, along with a dollop of *Senf* (mustard) and *Dose* (can) of beer. Most places offer **snacks and meals** of some kind. Similarly, it's possible just to have a drink in most restaurants. Food served up in town-centre *Kaffeehäuser* or cafés and bars can be great value, with light meals and snacks starting at about €5; most restaurant and café menus have filling stand-bys such as spicy *Serbische Bohnensuppe* (Serbian bean soup) and *Gulaschsuppe* (goulash soup) for less than €4. Main dishes (*Hauptspeisen*) are dominated by *Schnitzel* (tenderized veal) often accompanied by potatoes and a vegetable or salad: *Wienerschnitzel* is fried in breadcrumbs, *Pariser* in batter, *Natur* served on its own or with a creamy sauce. In general you can expect to pay €6.50–9.50 for a standard main course, though set lunchtime menus (*Mittagsmenü*) always offer a wide range of cheaper dishes. Desserts (*Mehlspeisen*) include sweets and pastries: various types of Torte (including the famous rich chocolate *Sachertorte*); strudel, cheesecake; and *Palatschinken* (pancake, with various nut or jam fillings) are all common.

Drink

For urban Austrians, daytime drinking traditionally centres on the **Kaffeehaus**, relaxed places furnished with a stock of the day's newspapers and serving alcoholic and soft drinks, snacks and cakes, alongside a wide range of different coffees: a *Schwarzer* is small and black, a *Brauner* comes with a little milk, while a *Melange* is half-coffee and half-milk; a *Kurzer* is a small espresso; an *Einspönner* a glass of black coffee topped with *Schlag*, the ubiquitous whipped cream that is offered with most pastries and cakes. A cup of coffee in one of these places is pricey at around €2.50–3 and numerous stand-up **coffee bars** are a much cheaper alternative at €1.50 a cup. Also commonplace is the **Café-Konditorei**, or **Kaffee-Konditorei** where a tempting array of freshly baked Austrian cakes and pastries are usually on offer. *Apfelstrudel* is apple and raisins wrapped in pastry and

topped with icing sugar. *Mohnstrudel* has a poppyseed and raisin filling. *Topfenstrudel* has a sweet curd cheese filling while *Linzertorte* is a jam tart with almond pastry.

Night-time drinking centres on **bars** and cafés, although more traditional *Bierstuben* and *Weinstuben* are still thick on the ground. Austrian **beers** are good quality. Most places serve the local brew on tap, either by the *Krügerl* (half-litre, €2.90–3), *Seidel* (third-litre, €1.80) or *Pfiff* (fifth-litre, €0.80–1.30). Wine, drunk by the *Viertel* (25cl mug) or the *Achterl* (12.5cl glass), is widely consumed. The *Weinkeller* is the place to go for this or, in the vine-producing areas, a *Heuriger* or *Buschenshenk* – a traditional tavern, customarily serving cold food as well.

Opening hours

Traditionally, **opening hours** for shops are Mon–Fri 9am–noon & 2–6pm, with late opening on Thurs till 7.30/8pm & Sat 8am–noon (1st Sat of month 8am–5pm). It's increasingly common for shops to open all day every Sat and some also stay open at lunchtimes. The only shops open outside these hours are the small general stores at main train stations and airports. Many **cafés** and **restaurants** also have a weekly *Ruhetag* (closing day). Shops and banks close, and most museums have reduced hours, on **public holidays**: Jan 1; Jan 6; Easter Mon; May 1; Ascension Day; Whit Mon; Corpus Christi; Aug 15; Oct 26; Nov 1; Dec 8; Dec 25 & 26.

Emergencies

Austria is law-abiding and reasonably safe. **Police** are armed, and are not renowned for their friendliness. As for **health**, city hospital casualty departments will treat you and ask questions later. For prescriptions, **pharmacies** (*Apotheke*) tend to follow normal shopping hours. A rota system covers night-time and weekend opening; each pharmacy has details posted in the window.

Emergency numbers
Police ☎133; Ambulance ☎144; Fire ☎122.

Vienna (Wien)

Most people visit **VIENNA** (Wien in German) with a vivid image in their minds: a romantic place full of Habsburg nostalgia and musical resonances. Visually it's unlikely to disappoint: an eclectic feast of architectural styles, from High Baroque, through the monumental imperial projects of the late nineteenth century, to Modernist experiments and enlightened municipal planning. However, the capital often seems aloof from the rest of the country; Alpine Austrians look on it as an alien eastern metropolis with an impenetrable dialect, staffed by an army of fund-draining bureaucrats.

It was only with the rise of the Babenberg dynasty in the tenth century that Vienna became an important centre. In 1278 the city fell to **Rudolf of Habsburg**, but had to compete for centuries with Prague, Linz and Graz as the imperial residence on account of its vulnerability to attack from the Turks, who first laid siege to it in 1529. It was only with the removal of the Turkish threat in 1683 that the court based itself here permanently. The great aristocratic families, grown fat on the profits of the Turkish wars, flooded in to build palaces and summer residences in a frenzy of construction that gave Vienna its Baroque character. **Imperial** Vienna was never a wholly German city; as the capital of a cosmopolitan empire, it attracted great minds from all over central Europe. By the end of the Habsburg era it had become a breeding-ground for the ideological movements of the age: nationalism, socialism, Zionism and anti-Semitism all flourished here. This turbulence was reflected in the cultural sphere, and the ghosts of Freud, Klimt, Schiele, Mahler and Schönberg are nowadays bigger tourist draws than old stand-bys such as the Lipizzaner horses and the Vienna Boys' Choir. There is more to Vienna than *fin-de-siècle* decadence, however; a strong, home-grown, youthful culture, together with influences from former Eastern Bloc neighbours, has once more placed the city at the heart of European cultural life.

Vienna is divided into **numbered districts** (*Bezirke*). District 1 is the Innere Stadt, the area enclosed by the Ringstrasse (a sweeping boulevard-cum-ringroad); districts 2–9 are arranged clockwise around it; beyond here, districts 10–23 are a fair way out. All Viennese **addresses** begin with the number of the district, followed by the name of the street, and then the number of the house or building, followed where relevant by the number of the apartment.

Arrival, information and city transport

Trains from the west and from Hungary terminate at the **Westbahnhof**, five U-Bahn stops from the city centre; services from eastern Europe, Italy and the Balkans arrive at the **Südbahnhof**, south of the city centre (U-Bahn Südtiroler Platz, or tram #D); services from Lower Austria and the odd train from Prague arrive at **Franz-Josefs-Bahnhof**, north of the centre (tram #D). Long-distance **buses** arrive at Marxergasse on the corner of Invalidenstrasse, east of the city centre (U-Bahn Wien-Mitte/Landstrasse); while DDSG **boats** (@www.ddsg-blue-danube.at) from further up the Danube, or from Bratislava or Budapest, dock at the Schiffahrtszentrum by the Reichsbrücke, some way northeast of the city centre – the nearest station (U-Bahn Vorgartenstrasse) is five minutes' walk away, one block west of Mexicoplatz. The **airport**, Flughafen Wien-Schwechat (@www.viennaairport.com) lies around 20km southeast of the centre by S-Bahn line S7; trains (every 30min 5am–10pm; takes 30min; €3 single) run to Wien-Mitte. Buses (every 20min 5am–1am; takes 20min; €5.80 single) run to the City Air Terminal beside Wien-Mitte station. There are also hourly buses (5.30am–midnight) to the Südbahnhof and Westbahnhof.

Note that the city **phone code** for Vienna is ☎1 when dialling from abroad, but ☎0222 when dialling from elsewhere in Austria.

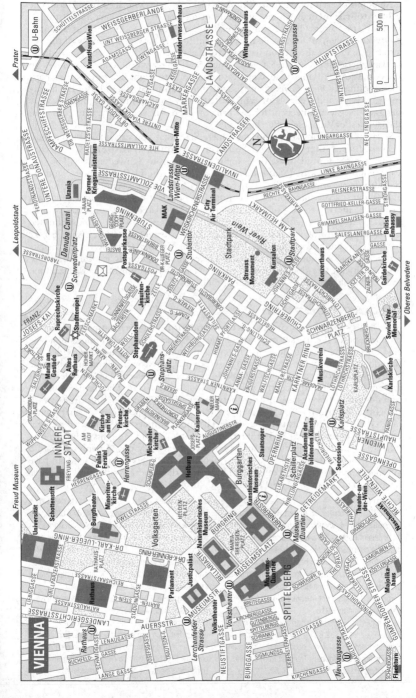

VIENNA

Vienna (Wien)

▲ Prater
Ⓤ U-Bahn

WEISSGERBERLÄNDE

LANDSTRASSE

KunstHausWien
Hundertwasserhaus
Wittgensteinhaus

Ⓤ Rochusgasse

HAUPTSTRASSE

Ⓤ Wien-Mitte

Landstrasse
Wien-Mitte

City Air Terminal

UNGARGASSE

Urania

Former Kriegsministerium

J-RAAB PLATZ

GEORG COCH PLATZ

MAK

STUBENRING

Danube Canal

LINKE BAHNGASSE

RECHTE BAHNGASSE

REISNERSTRASSE

GOTTFRIED-KELLER-GASSE

GRIMMELSHAUSEN-GASSE

SALESIANERGASSE

British Embassy

Gardekirche

Ⓤ Schwedenplatz

Postsparkasse

Stadttempel

Ruprechtskirche

Stadtpark

River Wien

Stadtpark

Strauss Monument

Kursalon

Konzerthaus

Jesuiten-kirche

Stephansdom

Stephans platz

Soviet War Memorial

▲ Oberes Belvedere

SCHWARZENBERG-PLATZ

SCHUBERTRING

Maria am Gestade

Altes Rathaus

Kirche am Hof

Peters-kirche

Kaisergruft

Michaeler-kirche

Ⓘ

Musikverein

Karlskirche

Karlsplatz

Ⓤ Karlsplatz

Akademie der bildenden Künste

Secession

Freud Museum

Universität

Schottenstift

Burgtheater

Minoriten-kirche

Palais Ferstel

Herrengasse

Hofburg

Staatsoper

OPERNRING

Schillerplatz

Theater an-der-Wien

Naschmarkt

OPERNGASSE

WIEDNER HAUPTSTRASSE

Ⓤ Rathaus

Rathaus

Parlament

Justizpalast

Volksgarten

Heldenplatz

Kunsthistorisches Museum

Burggarten

Ⓘ

BURGRING

Naturhistorisches Museum

MARIA-THERESIEN-PLATZ

Museums Quartier

GETREIDEMARKT

Ⓤ Volkstheater

Volkstheater

Bellariastr.

MUSEUMSPLATZ

Museums-Quartier

SPITTELBERG

Majolika-haus

Ⓤ

INNERE STADT

DR.-KARL-LUEGER-RING

DR.-KARL-RENNER-RING

500 m

61

All points of arrival have tourist kiosks which can help with accommodation. The central **tourist office**, which can hand out maps and arrange accommodation, is behind the opera house on Albertinaplatz (daily 9am–7pm; ☎24 555, ⊛www.info.wien.at). Its excellent website, in English, has links to many of the key attractions. There's also a good **information centre** for young people, Jugendinfo, at Babenbergerstr. 1 (Mon–Sat noon–7pm; ☎1799, ⊛www.jugendinfowien.at), on the corner of the Ringstrasse. **Gay** visitors and others might like to pick up a copy of the official *Queer Guide* from tourist information or Jugendinfo. It's highly informative – with details of which of the city's monumental buildings were designed by gay architects or for gay princes – and also very witty, with plenty on the campest of Viennese coffee houses.

So many attractions are within the Innere Stadt that you can do and see a great deal on foot. Otherwise, you'll be reliant on **public transport**, which runs 5am–midnight (outside these times night buses run from Schwedenplatz). The network consists of **trams** (*Strassenbahn* or *Bim*), **buses**, the **U-Bahn** (metro) and the **S-Bahn** (fast commuter trains). Buy your ticket from the ticket booths or machines at U-Bahn stations and from tobacconists, and punch it on-board buses and trams or before entering the U- or S-Bahn. **Fares** are calculated on a zonal basis: tickets for the central zone (covering most of Vienna) cost €1.50 and allow unlimited changes on any mode of transport. On offer are a **travel pass** (*Netzkarte*; €5/12 for 24/72hr) and the much-touted *Wien-Karte* or **Vienna Card** (€16.90); the latter includes a 72-hour travel pass and also gives minor discounts at local attractions. The penalty for fare-dodging is €40, plus the fare. **Taxis** run from the ranks around town; to book, call ☎31330, ☎40100 or ☎60160.

Accommodation

There's no shortage of expensive **accommodation**, but extreme pressure on the cheaper end of the market means booking ahead is essential in summer and advisable during the rest of the year. The city has some excellent **hostels**, which are friendly, clean and efficient but also very popular; it's worth calling ahead. These aside, it's hard to find anything affordable and central: the cheapest double rooms within easy reach of the centre will set you back at least €56. The likeliest hunting grounds are in the western districts between the Ring and the outer orbital road, the Gürtel (districts 5–9); places here are often on the upper floors of characterful nineteenth-century apartment buildings. The tourist offices have a limited number of **private rooms** (☎24 555; from €50 for a double; min. 3 nights), but these go quickly and are often in distant suburbs. You could also try the Mitwohnzentrale, 8 Laudongasse 7 (Mon–Fri 10am–2pm & 3–6pm; ☎402 60 61), which tends to offer cheaper properties and also offers weekly rates; or the nearby youth travel specialists STA, at 9 Türkenstr. 6 (Mon–Fri 9am–5.30pm, ☎401 48).

Hostels

Hostel Ruthensteiner 15 Robert Hamerlinggasse 24 ☎893 4202, ⊛www.hostelruthensteiner.com. An excellent hostel with a good atmosphere, set around a courtyard, within easy walking distance of the Westbahnhof. Dorm beds, doubles and triples. Internet, and laundry facilities, plus the use of musical instruments, a (small) kitchen and barbecue. Breakfast not included. No curfew. U-Bahn Westbahnhof. €10.

Jugendgästehaus Wien-Brigittenau 20 Friedrich-Engels-Platz 24 ☎332 8294, ⊛www.oejhv.or.at. Huge, modern HI hostel in a dour suburb. Dorms and en-suite bunk-bed doubles. Tram #N from U-Bahn Schwedenplatz or Dresdnerstr. €14.50.

Jugendgästehaus der Stadt Wien Hütteldorf-Hacking 13 Schlossberggasse 8 ☎877 0263, ⊛www.hostel.at. A 285-bed hostel with dorms plus some double and triple rooms. Out in the sticks, but convenient if you want to explore the wilds of the Lainzer Tiergarten and Schönbrunn. S- and U-Bahn Hütteldorf. €14.50 (inc breakfast).

Jugendherberge Wien-Myrthengasse/ Neustiftgasse 7 Myrthengasse 7 & Neustiftgasse 85 ☎523 6316, ⊛www.oejhv.or.at. Most central of the official hostels; 270 beds (some doubles), divided between two nearby addresses. Book well in advance and go to the Myrthengasse reception on arrival. A short walk up Neustiftgasse from U-Bahn Volkstheater. €14.50 (inc breakfast).

Kolpingfamilie Jugend-gastehaus Wien-Miedling 12 Bendlgasse 10–12 ☏ 813 5487, ⓦ www.kolpinghaus-wien12.at. Large, institutional hostel, easily reached from the city centre. No curfew. U-Bahn Niederhofstr. Breakfast not included. €11.50.

Westend City Hostel 15 Fugergasse 3 ☏ 597 67 29, ⓦ www.westendhostel.at. 211-bed hostel a few minutes' walk from the Westbahnhof, with friendly staff. Pleasant enough, but a bit institutional. Patio, left-luggage and laundry. Dorm beds €16, en-suite doubles €23, breakfast included.

Wombat's 15 Grangasse 6 ☏ 897 2336, ⓦ www.wombats.at. Excellent hostel option, with dorm beds, bunk-bed doubles and a party atmosphere (you get a free welcome drink at the bar). Within easy walking distance of U-Bahn Westbahnhof. Internet access, laundry facilities and nightly movies. No curfew. Dorm beds €15, doubles €38, breakfast not included.

Hotels and pensions

Pension Kraml 6 Brauergasse 5 ☏ 587 8588, ⓦ www.pensionkraml.at. Clean, reliable pension off Mariahilferstr. All rooms en-suite. U-Bahn Zieglergasse/Neubaugasse. **⓻**

Hotel Kugel 7 Siebensterngasse 43 ☏ 523 3355, ⓦ www.hotelkugel.at. Close to Spittelberg's numerous restaurants and bars. Plain but clean rooms; continental breakfast. On the corner of Siebensterngasse and Neubaugasse. U-Bahn Neubaugasse. **⓹**

Pension Lindenhof 7 Lindengasse 4 ☏ 523 0498, ⓔ pensionlindenhof@yahoo.com. Appealing rooms with creaky parquet flooring in a lugubrious

building off Mariahilferstr. U-Bahn Neubaugasse. Includes breakfast. **⓹**

Hotel Post 1 Fleischmarkt 24 ☏ 515 830, ⓦ www.hotel-post-wien.at. A civilized, very large central hotel with big old rooms and modern furnishings. U-Bahn Schwedenplatz. Some rooms with shared facilities. **⓻**

Schweizer Pension Solderer 1 Heinrichsgasse 2 ☏ 533 8156. Bright, clean modern rooms in a friendly 4th-floor pension. Excellent location, near the central sights and nightlife. Some en suites. U-Bahn Schwedenplatz. Includes breakfast. **⓺**

Pension Wild 8 Lange Gasse 10 ☏ 406 5174, ⓦ www.pension-wild.com. Pleasant location a short walk from the Ring; popular with backpackers. The more expensive rooms are positively plush, the cheaper ones functional but clean. U-Bahn Lerchenfelderstr. **⓹–⓽**

Campsites

Aktiv Camping Neue Donau 23 Am Kaisermuhlendamm 119 ☏ 202 4010, ⓦ www.wiencamping.at. 4km east of the centre, near the Danube. All the mod cons, including beach volleyball. U-Bahn 1 to Uno City, then bus #91a.

Camping Rodaun 23 An der Au 2 ☏ 888 4154. By a stream in the southwestern outskirts, near the Wienerwald (Vienna Woods). Tram #60 from U-Bahn Hietzing to its terminus, then 5-min walk. Closed mid-Nov to early April.

Wien West 14 Hüttelbergstr. 80 ☏ 914 2314, ⓦ www.wiencamping.at. In the plush far-western suburbs of Vienna, close to the Wienerwald, with four-bed bungalows to rent (€25). Bus #148 or #152 from U-Bahn Hütteldorf.

The City

Central Vienna may well bowl you over with its grandiosity, but for all that, it's surprisingly compact: the historical centre or **Innere Stadt**, bound to the northeast by the Danube canal and surrounded on all other sides by the majestic ribbon of the **Ringstrasse**, is just 1km wide at its broadest point. Most of the important sights are concentrated in the central district and along the Ring. One of the best ways to grasp its grand sweep is to board tram #1 or #2 from outside the Staatsoper (opera house); these circle the boulevard, letting you get a taste for which areas you'd like to explore at a more leisurely pace. Important outlying sights include the imperial palace at **Schönbrunn** and the funfair and parklands of the **Prater**. Judicious use of public transport enables you to travel from one side of the city to the other in less than thirty minutes, so you should be able see a great deal in a couple of days.

Stephansplatz

The obvious place to begin a tour of the city is **Stephansplatz**, the lively pedestrianized central square dominated by the hoary Gothic bulk of the **Stephansdom** (Mon–Sat 9am–noon & 1–5pm, Sun 12.30–5pm; free). The first thing that strikes you as you enter the gloomy, high-vaulted interior is that, despite the tourists, Stephansdom is still very much a place of worship. The highlight in the nave is the early sixteenth-century carved stone pulpit with portraits of the four fathers of the Christian church, and a self-portrait by the sculptor who peers from a window below the pulpit stairs. The area beyond the transepts is roped off, so to get a good look at the **Wiener Neustädter Altar**, a masterpiece of late Gothic art, and, to its right, the tomb of the Holy Roman Emperor Friedrich III, you must sign up for a guided tour (English tours April–Oct daily 3.45pm; €4). Other features include the **catacombs** (Mon–Sat 10–11.30am & 1.30–4.30pm, Sun 1.30–4.30pm; €4), where, among other macabre remains, the entrails of illustrious Habsburgs are housed in bronze caskets; and the north or Eagle Tower, which can be ascended by lift (daily 8.30am–5/5.30/6pm; €4) for a look at the *Pummerin* (Great Bell). The more energetic might choose to climb up to the spire, 137m high and nicknamed *Steffl* or "Little Stephen" (daily 9am–5.30pm; €3), reached via a blind scramble up internal stairways; it has better views than the north tower.

East of Stephansplatz

The warren of alleyways north and east of the cathedral preserve something of the medieval character of the city, although the architecture reflects centuries of continuous rebuilding. The medieval house on Raubensteingasse 8 where **Mozart** died while at work on his *Requiem* has long since disappeared, but is commemorated by a small memorial on the ground floor of the Steffl department store that now occupies the site. The only one of the composer's residences to survive is the so-called **Figarohaus**, immediately east of the cathedral at Domgasse 5 (Tues–Sun 9am–6pm; €1.80, free on Fri morn), though there's little to see inside. A more intriguing find is the **Treasury of the Order of Teutonic Knights**, around the corner at Singerstr. 7 (Mon, Thurs & Sat 10am–noon, plus Wed, Fri and Sat 3–5pm; €4) where you can view ceremonial regalia and domestic trinkets assembled by seven centuries of Grand Masters.

North of Stephansdom, **Judenplatz**, one of the prettiest little squares in Vienna, is dominated by a bleak concrete **Holocaust Memorial**, designed by British sculptor Rachel Whiteread. Judenplatz stands on the site of the medieval Jewish ghetto and you can view the foundations of an old synagogue at the excellent **Museum Judenplatz** at no. 8 (Mon–Thurs & Sun 10am–6pm, Fri 10am–2pm, closed Sat; €3; joint ticket with Jüdisches Museum €7), which has an interactive multimedia exhibition on Jewish life in the ghetto. Further east, the seventeenth-century **Jesuitenkirche** on Dr.-Ignaz-Seipel-Platz is by far the most awesome High Baroque church in Vienna. Inside, the most striking features are the red and green barley-sugar spiral columns, the exquisitely carved pews and the clever trompe l'oeil dome. Nearby, on the far side of Stubenring, is Vienna's most enjoyable museum, known as the **MAK** (Tues 10am–midnight, Wed–Sun 10am–6pm; €7.90; free on Sat; ⑩www.mak.at). The highlights of its superlative, eclectic collection, dating from the Romanesque period to the twentieth century, are Klimt's *Stoclet Frieze* and the unrivalled collection of Wiener Werkstätte products.

Kärntnerstrasse, Graben and Kohlmarkt

From Stephansplatz, **Kärntnerstrasse** leads off southwest, a continuous pedestrianized ribbon lined with street entertainers and elegant shops that ends at the city's illustrious **Staatsoper** (Opera House; ⑩www.wiener-staatsoper.at), opened in 1869 as the first phase of the development of the Ringstrasse. You can tour the venue (times vary – for details check at the arcades under the opera house; €4.50) but a more unusual tribute to the city's musical genius can be found down Annagasse at the new **Haus der Musik**, Seilerstatte 30 (daily 10am–10pm; €8.50), a hugely enjoyable, state-of-the-art exhibition on the nature of sound. At the southwest exit of Neuer Markt square is the **Kaisergruft** (daily 9.30am–4pm; €3.60), where Habsburg family members were interred from 1633. Maria Theresia reputedly came here on the eighteenth of every month to commune with the remains of her late husband Franz Stephan, and was eventually placed beside him in a riotously ornamented sarcophagus of stunning proportions – a stark contrast to the humble, unadorned coffin of her enlightened successor, Josef II.

The prime shopping streets of **Graben** and **Kohlmarkt** lead northwest off Stephansplatz; just off Graben, at Dorotheergasse 11, is the intriguing **Jüdisches Museum** (Mon–Fri & Sun 10am–6pm, Thurs till 8pm; €5; joint ticket with the Museum Judenplatz €7; ✆www.jmw.at). The emphasis of the museum's excellent exhibitions on the first floor is on contemporary Jewish life, while on the second floor, visitors are confronted with a series of freestanding glass panels imprinted with holograms, ghostly images of the city's once vast Jewish population. At the far end of Kohlmarkt is Michaelerplatz, site of the **Looshaus**. Built as a department store in 1911 by pioneering Modernist Adolf Loos, it marked a total break with the Jugendstil confections of Otto Wagner. Its initial unpopularity was largely due to the fact that it was constructed directly opposite the statue-laden nineteenth-century Michaelertor, entrance to the Habsburgs' city residence, the Hofburg.

The Hofburg

The **Hofburg** (✆www.hofburg.at) is a swathe of immense, highly ornate buildings that house many of Vienna's key sights. Apart from being the seat of the Austrian president, it now contains a range of museums with imperial connections, which begin with the rather dull parade of **Kaiserappartements** (daily 9am–5pm; €7.50) on the north side of the main courtyard. To the southeast is the brightly painted entrance to the Schweizerhof, a smaller courtyard where you'll find the much more impressive **Schatzkammer** (daily except Tues 10am–6pm; €7), which holds some of the finest medieval craftsmanship and jewellery in Europe, including the imperial regalia and relics of the Holy Roman Empire as well as the Habsburgs' own crown jewels. Steps beside the Schatzkammer lead up to the **Burgkapelle** (Jan–June & mid-Sept to Dec Mon–Thurs 11am–3pm, Fri 11am–1pm; €1.10), primarily known as the venue for Mass with the **Vienna Boys' Choir** (mid-Sept to June Sun 9.15am; ✆www.wsk.at), for which you can obtain free, standing-room only tickets from 8.30am. Another monument to the Habsburgs' hoarding instincts is the ornate Baroque **Prunksaal** (mid-May to Oct daily 10am–4pm, Thurs till 7pm; Nov to mid-May daily 10am–2pm; closed Sept; €5), overlooking Josefsplatz and worth a glimpse for its frescoes, globes and gold-bound volumes. On the other side of Josefsplatz, a door leads to the imperial stables, home to the performing white horses of the **Spanish Riding School** (performances March–June & Sept–Dec times vary; €24 standing, €35–105 sitting. Training sessions same months Tues–Sat 10am–noon; €7.30; ✆www.spanische-reitschule.com). Tickets for performances are hard to come by, but training sessions tickets are sold at the museum entrance in advance, or at the Josefsplatz entrance box office on the day. The queue is at its worst early on, but by 11am it's usually easy enough to get in. South of Josefsplatz, down Augustinerstrasse, lies the **Albertina** (daily 10am–6pm, Wed till 9pm; €7.50; ✆www.albertina.at) home to one of the largest collections of **graphic arts** in the world, with works by the likes of Raphael, Rembrandt, Dürer, Leonardo, Michelangelo, Rubens, Bosch, Picasso, Klimt, Schiele and Kokoschka. With regular visiting exhibitions, it's definitely worth a look.

West of the Hofburg are still more museums, with some interesting features. Across the Ring in Maria-Theresien-Platz is the **Naturhistorisches Museum** (Mon & Wed–Sun 9am–6.30pm, Wed till 9pm; €3.60), where you'll find Celtic grave finds from the Salzkammergut village of Hallstatt, and a copy of the *Venus of Willendorf*, a curvy stone figure carved by Paleolithic inhabitants of the Danube valley 25,000 years ago. Another highlight is one of the richest museums in the world, the **Kunsthistorisches Museum** (Tues–Sun 10am–6pm; €9). Here you'll find Egyptian, Greek and Roman artefacts as well as Gothic-infused canvases of Danubian painters such as Altdorfer and the two Cranachs. However, it's the unparalleled collection of Pieter Bruegel the Elder that attracts most visitors: pictures such as *The Meeting of Lent and Carnival* and the famous winter scenery of the *Return of the Hunters*. Nearby is Vienna's **MuseumsQuartier** (@www.mqw.at); housed in the former imperial stables, it hopes to do for Vienna what the Tate Modern has done for London. It's the new home to the city's chief permanent collection of Modern Art and to the Leopold Museum (Mon & Wed–Sun 10am–7pm, Fri till 9pm; €9); the world's biggest collection of works by Egon Schiele.

Rathausplatz and the Freud Museum

By now you will have crossed the **Ringstrasse**, built to fill the gap created when the last of the city's fortifications were demolished in 1857 and subsequently lined with monumental civic buildings – "Ringstrasse Historicism" became a byword for the bombastic taste of the late Habsburg bourgeoisie. The broad sweep of the Ring wasn't just a symbol of imperial and municipal prestige: it was designed to ease the mobility of cannons in the event of any rebellious incursions from the proletarian districts beyond. **Rathausplatz**, northwest of the Hofburg, is the Ringstrasse's showpiece square, framed by four monumental public buildings: the Rathaus (City Hall), the Burgtheater, Parliament and the University – all completed in the 1880s. The most imposing is the cathedralesque **Rathaus**, parts of which are accessible only as part of a guided tour (Mon, Wed & Fri 1pm; free). Directly opposite stands the **Burgtheater**, flanked by two grandiose staircases decorated with frescoes by, among others, Gustav Klimt (guided tours only: daily 3pm, Sun also 11am; €4.50). The **Parliament** is an imposing affair fronted by a monumental statue of Pallas Athene (guided tours only: July to mid-Sept Mon–Fri hourly 9am–3pm, except noon; mid-Sept to June Mon–Fri 11am & 3pm, Fri also 2pm; free). Not far north is the former home of Sigmund Freud, who moved to the second floor of Berggasse 19, six blocks north of the Ring, in 1891 and stayed there until June 4, 1938, when he and his family fled to London. His apartment, now the **Freud Museum** (daily 9am–5/6pm; €5; @www.freud-museum.at; tram #D to Schlickgasse), is a place of pilgrimage, even though Freud took almost all his possessions with him into exile. His hat, coat and walking stick are still here, and there's home-movie footage from the 1930s, but the only room with any original decor is the waiting room.

Karlsplatz

South of the Hofburg in **Karlsplatz**, traffic interchanges and seedy subways dominate, but you can still see examples of Vienna's Art Nouveau, or Jugendstil (literally "Youth Style") movement. On the west side of the square is the **Secession** building (Tues–Sun 10am–6pm, Thurs till 8pm; €5.50; @www.secession.at) completed in 1898 as the headquarters of the movement in the city. Led by Gustav Klimt, this younger generation rebelled against academic historicism in favour of something more modern. Look out for the so-called "gilded cabbage" that crowns it. One of Klimt's most characteristic works, the Beethoven Frieze, created for an exhibition of 1902, remains on permanent display in the basement. There's more Jugendstil on offer in the form of Otto Wagner's elegant **Station Karlsplatz** pavilions, now used as a café (daily 10am–7pm) and exhibition space (April–Oct Tues–Sun 1–4.30pm; €1.80). Rising majestically above everything around it, the **Karlskirche** (Mon–Sat 9–noon & 1–6pm, Sun 1–6pm; €4), designed by Fischer von Erlach, is one of the city's finest Baroque churches; a huge Italianate dome with a Neoclassical portico, flanked by two giant pillars.

South of the Ring

Immediately south of the Ring, beyond the Soviet war memorial and fountain on Schwarzenbergplatz, near Karlsplatz, is the **Belvedere** (tram #D from the opera house), one of Vienna's finest palace complexes. Two magnificent Baroque mansions, designed for Prince Eugene of Savoy, face each other across a sloping formal garden, commanding a superb view. Today, the loftier of the two palaces, the

Oberes Belvedere (Tues–Sun 10am–6pm; €10; ⓦwww.belvedere.at) has the best concentration of paintings by **Klimt** in the city, plus some choice works by Schiele and Kokoschka. The same ticket lets you into the **Unteres Belvedere**, which preserves more of its original, lavish decor; for that reason it's worth exploring the Barock-Museum (same hours and ticket) now installed in its rooms.

Beyond the Belvedere, the area around the **Südbahnhof** has a distinctly Balkan feel, with scattered bars and restaurants providing a meeting-place for emigrants from the former Yugoslavia and Turkey. Heading southeast from the Südbahnhof through the Schweizer Garten brings you to the former **Arsenal**, a huge barracks complex that also houses the **Heeresgeschichtliches Museum** (daily except Fri 9am–5pm; €5.10), built in 1856 to glorify the imperial army. Among the exhibits is the Gräf & Stift open-top car in which Archduke Ferdinand and his wife Sophie Chotek were assassinated in Sarajevo in June 1914; his bloodstained uniform lies nearby.

Ten minutes' walk from here (or tram #71 from Schwarzenbergplatz) is the **St Marxer Friedhof**, on Leberstrasse (daily 7am–dusk), Vienna's principal cemetery from 1784 to 1874. Planted with a rather lovely selection of trees, the cemetery today gives little indication of the bleak and forbidding place it must have been when, on a rainy night in December 1791, Wolfgang Amadeus **Mozart** was given a pauper's burial in an unmarked mass grave with no one present but the grave-diggers. A memorial marking the area in which the composer was interred – a broken column accompanied by a cherub – was first raised in 1859. The original, however, now stands in Vienna's greatest necropolis, the **Zentralfriedhof** on Simmeringer Hauptstrasse – penultimate stop on tram #71 (daily 7/8am–5/7pm), in which graves of eminent Viennese are grouped by profession. The musicians, principally Mozart, Beethoven, Schubert, Brahms and the Strauss family, lie a short way beyond Gate 2, to the left of the central avenue.

East of the Ring

One of Vienna's most popular tourist attractions, the kitsch **Hundertwasserhaus** (no public access), lies in the unassuming residential area of Landstrasse, east of the Ring; take tram #N from Schwedenplatz U-Bahn to Hetzgasse. Following his philosophy that "the straight line is godless", the Austrian artist Friedensreich Hundertwasser (1928–2000) transformed some dour council housing on the corner of Löwengasse and Kegelgasse into a brightly coloured, higgledy-piggledy ensemble that caught the popular imagination. Understandably, the residents were none too happy when hordes of pilgrims began ringing on their doorbells, asking to be shown round; Hundertwasser obliged with a shopping arcade opposite, called **Kalke Village**, the most disconcerting aspect of which is his penchant for uneven floors. There's another of Hundertwasser's Gaudí-esque conversions, **KunstHausWien** (daily 10am–7pm; €8; ⓦwww.kunsthauswien.com) three blocks north up Untere Weissgerberstrasse.

On the other side of the Danube canal, which runs east of the centre, is **Leopoldstadt**, home to a thriving Jewish community until the Nazi Holocaust. The district's main attraction is the **Prater** (U-Bahn Praterstern), a large expanse of parkland that stretches for miles between the Danube canal and the river itself – formerly the royal hunting grounds. The public were allowed access to the Prater by Josef II, who often walked here himself, quixotically ordering passing members of the public not to salute him. The funfair at the northern end near the U-Bahn stop is renowned for the **Riesenrad** (daily: March–Oct 9/10am–10pm/midnight; Nov–Feb 10am–8pm; €7.50), the giant Ferris wheel featured in Carol Reed's film *The Third Man*. You can take U1 east from Praterstern to the **Donauinsel**, an island in the middle of the Danube crisscrossed with cycle paths and the city's most popular summer bathing area.

Schönbrunn

The biggest attraction in the west of the city is the imperial summer palace of **Schönbrunn**, reachable by U4 to Schönbrunn or Hietzing. This was originally a royal hunting lodge until Leopold I commissioned Fischer von Erlach to draw up plans for a palace on the model of residences like Versailles. The plans proved too expensive, however, and what was eventually completed during the reign of Maria Theresa, was, for all its size and elegance, far more modest. To visit the palace rooms or **Prunkräume** (daily 8.30am–4.30/5pm; July & Aug till 6pm) there's a choice of two tours: the "Imperial Tour" (€8), which takes in 22 state rooms, and the "Grand Tour" (€10.50), which includes all 40 rooms. However, the shorter tour misses out the best rooms – such as the Millions Room, a rosewood-panelled chamber covered from floor to ceiling with wildly irregular Rococo cartouches, each holding a Persian miniature watercolour. There are coaches and carriages to see in the **Wagenburg** (April–Oct daily 9am–6pm; Nov–March Tues–Sun 10am–4pm; €4.50) in the right wing, but it's better to concentrate on strolling through the **Schlosspark** (daily 6am–dusk; free), with its frolicking fountain statuary, its maze (April–Oct daily 9am–4.30/7pm) and Gloriette – a hilltop colonnaded monument, now a café (daily 9am–dusk), from which you can enjoy splendid views back towards the city. The park also holds Vienna's Tiergarten or **Zoo** (daily 9am–dusk; €10) and **Palmenhaus** (daily 9.30am–4.30/5.30pm; €3.30), a glasshouse full of tropical ferns.

Eating and drinking

Vienna has a wide range of **cuisines**, from Balkan to South American, and is, of course, also the home of the *Kaffeehaus*. In summer a visit to a wine tavern (*Heuriger*), to sample their produce along with traditional fare, is extremely popular; you'll find *Heurigen* in Vienna's outlying districts such as Grinzing (tram #38) or Stammersdorf (tram #31). For **snacks**, head for a *Wurstelstand* or one of the lunchtime stand-up snack bars selling bite-size open-topped sandwiches (*Brötchen*) in the city centre. The Naschmarkt – the city's main fruit and veg **market** off Karlsplatz – is a great place to assemble a picnic or grab a take-away. Other budget options are the student dining-halls, or Mensas, which serve subsidized three-course lunches; ask for details from the tourist office.

Cafés

Aera 1 Gonzagagasse 11. Relaxing café upstairs serving tasty food; live bands in dimly lit cellar downstairs. Open till 2am. U-Bahn Schwedenplatz.

Alt Wien 1 Bäckerstr. 9. Dark, smoky *Kaffeehaus*. Good food, if you can find a table. Open till 2am. U-Bahn Stephansplatz.

Berg 9 Berggasse 8. Trendy modern café, with good food and relaxed, mostly gay, clientele. Open till 1am. U-Bahn Schottentor.

Central 1 Herrengasse 14. Traditional meeting place of Vienna's intelligentsia, and Trotsky's favourite café, this is probably the most ornate of Vienna's cafés. Open Mon–Sat till 10pm, Sun till 6pm. U-Bahn Herrengasse.

Demel 1 Kohlmarkt 14. Vienna's most prestigious and priciest café. U-Bahn Herrengasse.

Diglas 1 Fleischmarkt 14. Homely café offering a mellow respite from the outside world. Piano music every Wed 5–8pm. U-Bahn Stephansplatz.

Drechsler 6 Linke Wienzeile 22. Opens at 3am for the stallholders of the Naschmarkt. A good place for breakfast after the bars and clubs have closed. Closed Sun. U-Bahn Kettenbrückengasse.

Europa 7 Zollergasse 8. Lively, spacious café that attracts a trendy crowd; food is a tasty mixture of Viennese and Italian. Open till 5am. U-Bahn Neubaugasse.

Hawelka 1 Dorotheegasse 6. Famed for its smoky, Bohemian atmosphere, this is a popular drinking venue. Open till 2am. Closed Tues. U-Bahn Stephansplatz.

Landtmann 1 Dr-Karl-Lueger-Ring 4. One of the poshest of the *Kaffeehäuser*, it was a favourite with Freud; other famous visitors include Marlene Dietrich. Today's clientele is a mixture of politicians, actors, regulars and tourists. U-Bahn Herrengasse/Schottentor.

Palmenhaus 1 Burggarten. Stylish modern café set amidst the palms of the greenhouse in the Burggarten behind the Hofburg. Open till 2am. U-Bahn Karlsplatz.

Prückel 1 Stubenring 24. Great original 1950s decor; opposite the MAK. U-Bahn Stubentor. Daily till 10pm.

Savoy 6 Linke Wienzeile 36. Wonderfully scruffy, but ornate decor, packed with boho bargain-hunters during the Saturday fleamarket. Closed Sun. U-Bahn Kettenbrückengasse.

Sperl 6 Gumpendorferstr. 11. The *fin-de-siècle*

interior is one of the finest of the city's coffee-house scene. July & Aug closed Sun. U-Bahn Karlsplatz/Babenbergerstr.

Stein 9 Währingerstr. 6 ⊛www.café-stein.com. Big, trendy, designer café, with funky music, online facilities and decent food. Open till 1am. U-Bahn Schottentor.

Restaurants

Beim Czaak 1 Postgasse 15. Cosy and smart with traditional food and lovely dark green wood panelling and low-lighting. Closed Sun. U-Bahn Schwedenplatz.

Figlmüller 1 Wollzeile 5. In an little side alley, very popular; famous for its Wienerschnitzel. U-Bahn Stephansplatz. Daily noon–midnight.

Fischerbräu 19 Billrothstr. 17. Civilized microbrewery near the Gürtel, serving lots of tasty food. Open till 1am. U-Bahn Nussdorferstr.

Osteria Veneziana 3 Rennweg 11/corner of Marokkanergasse. Delicious Venetian menu in this small, attractive restaurant, just round the corner from the Unteres Belvedere. Tram #71.

Regina Margherita 1 Wallnerstr. 4. Smart, bustling Neapolitan pizza and pasta joint in the inner court of the Palais Esterházy. Closed Sun. U-Bahn Herrengasse.

Schnitzelwirt 7 Neubaugasse 52. Another great place to eat Wienerschnitzel – and cheaper than *Figlmüller*. Closed Sun. Tram #49.

Schweizerhaus 2 Str. des 1 Mai 116. Czech-owned restaurant in the Prater; known for its draught beer and grilled pigs' trotters (Steltzen). Closed Nov–Feb. U-Bahn Praterstern.

Siebenstern Bräu 7 Siebensterngasse 19. Popular modern *Bierkeller* that brews its own beer and serves solid Viennese food. U-Bahn Volkstheater/Neubaugasse.

Wrenkh 1 Bauernmarkt 10. Fashionable vegetarian restaurant just north of Stephansplatz.

Nightlife

Vienna's late-night **bars** are concentrated in three main areas: the central district (dubbed the Bermuda Triangle) of Rabensteig, Seitenstetten-gasse and Ruprechtsplatz just north of Stephansplatz, where you're bound to find somewhere that appeals; the Naschmarkt, where late-night licences abound; and the Spittelberg, between Burggasse and Siebensterngasse. At **clubs**, you may have to pay admission, though it's rarely more than €7.50; for the latest information, visit ⊛www.viennahype.at. The local **listings** magazine *Falter* (⊛www.falter.at) has comprehensive details of the week's cultural pro-gramme and is pretty easy to decipher. The tourist office also publishes the free month-ly *Programm*. You can catch high-class international **opera** and **ballet** at the Staatsoper, 1 Opernring 2 (⊛www.wiener-staatsoper.at). Seats often sell out weeks in advance and can cost up to €250, but hundreds of standing tickets go on sale each night 80 minutes before a performance from just €2. Ask at the ticket office under the arcades at the opera house for details. Opera and operetta are also staged at the Volksoper, 9 Währingerstr. 78 (⊛www.volksoper.at). The principal **classical music** venues are the Musikverein, 1 Karlsplatz 6 (⊛www.musikverein-wien.at), home of the Vienna Philharmonic, and the Konzerthaus, 3 Lothringerstr. 20 (⊛www.konzerthaus.at). Bookings for all these can be made at Bundestheaterkassen, 1 Hanuschgasse 3 (☎01/51444 2960) – though, again, you can usually get cheap standing-room tickets by queuing up an hour before a performance.

Musikcafés, live venues and clubs

American Bar 1 Kärntnerstr. 59. Small, dark late-night bar with a rich interior designed by Adolf Loos. Open till 2am. U-Bahn Stephansplatz.

B72 8 Stadtbahnbögen 72, Hernalser Gürtel. Dark, designer club underneath the U-Bahn arches, features a mixture of DJs and live indie bands. Open till 4am. U-Bahn Alserstr.

Blue Box 7 Richtergasse 8. *Musikcafé* with resident DJs and a good snack menu. Open till 2am or later. U-Bahn Neubaugasse.

Chelsea 8 U-Bahnbögen 29–31, Lerchenfelder Gürtel. Favourite venue with up-and-coming Brit guitar bands. Situated underneath the U-Bahn. U-Bahn Thaliastr.

Flex 1 Donaukanal ⊛www.flex.at. Devotees claim it has the best sound system in Austria, popular with the indie crowd. Live bands and an open space beside the canal. Open till 4am. U-Bahn Schottenring.

Porgy & Bess 1 Riemergasse 11 ⊛www.porgy.at. A converted porn cinema, now the new home for Vienna's top jazz venue, attracting acts from all over the world. U-Bahn Stubentor.

Rhiz 8 Stadtbahnbögen 37–38, Lerchenfelder Gürtel ⊛www.rhiz.org. Bar/café/club, with several DJs spinning everything from dance to trance.

Open until 4am. U-Bahn Josefstadterstr.
Rosa-Lila-Villa 6 Linke Wienzeile 102. Gay and lesbian centre housing a café/restaurant with a nice leafy courtyard. A good place to pick up information about events. Open till 2am. U-Bahn Pilgramgasse.
Shultz 7 Siebensterngasse 31. Large, trendy bar with outdoor seating and good cocktails. Open till 2am or later.
U4 12 Schönbrunnerstr. 222 ☻www.u4club.com. Dark, cavernous disco, mostly break beats and house, with frequent gigs; a favourite with the alternative crowd. Gay and lesbian night on Thurs. Open till 5am. U-Bahn Meidling-Hauptstr.
Volksgarten 1 Burgring 1 ☻www.volksgarten.at. Situated in the park of the same name, Vienna's longest-running club. Popular with the dance crowd. Open till 5am. U-Bahn Volkstheater.
w.u.k. 9 Währingerstr. 59 ☻www.wuk.at. Old school now an arts venue run by a sprinkling of anarchists and others. Café, live music and much more. Open till 2am. U-Bahn Währingerstr.-Volksoper.

Listings

Bike rental Pedal Power, 2 Ausstellungstr. 3 ☎729 7234, ☻www.pedalpower.at (€32/day).
Embassies Australia, 4 Mattiellistr. 2–4 ☎512 85 80; Canada, 1 Laurenzerberg 2 ☎531 38 3000; Ireland, 1 Rotenturmstr. 16–18 ☎715 42 46; UK, 3 Jauresgasse 10 ☎716 13 5151; US, 9 Boltzmanngasse 16 ☎313 39.
Exchange Outside banking hours try the offices at the Westbahnhof (daily 7am–10pm) or the Südbahnhof (daily 6.30am–9pm), or around the Stephansdom.

Hospital Allegemeines Krankenhaus, 9 Währinger Gürtel 18–20; U-Bahn Michelbeuern-AKH.
Internet Bignet, at 1 Mariahilferstr. 27 (daily 8am–2am), 1 Kartnerstr. 61 & 1 Hoher Markt 8 (both daily 10am–midnight); Surfland.c@fe, 1 Krugerstr. 10 (daily 10am–11pm).
Laundry Karlberter, 3 Schlachthaukasse 19 (Mon–Fri 7.30am–6.30pm, Sat 7am–1pm).
Pharmacy Alte Feldapotheke, opposite the Stephansdom and at the Westbahnhof.
Post office 1 Fleischmarkt 19; Westbahnhof; Südbahnhof (all 24hr).

The Danube Valley

Heading west from Vienna, there are two alternative routes for onward travel: to Salzburg, around three hours away, and then on to Munich or Innsbruck; or a more leisurely route following the Danube through the **Wachau**, a winding stretch of water where vine-bearing, ruin-encrusted hills roll down to the river from the north. This is an Austria decidedly different from either cosmopolitan Vienna or the Alpine southwest; at **Melk** is a superb Benedictine monastery overlooking the river. Transport to Salzburg from Melk is pretty straightforward, although the industrialized, but culturally vibrant, northern city of **Linz** has enough of interest to make a further stopoff worthwhile. Melk is reached on the main line from Vienna's Westbahnhof. The most stylish way to travel is **by boat**. DDSG (☻www.ddsg-blue-danube.at) operates boats at weekends between Vienna, Linz and Passau during the summer, with year-round services on the most scenic stretch between the historic town of Krems and Melk. The journey takes about three hours upstream, two downstream, and costs about €15.50 each way. Making your way along the river by shorter hops will work out more expensive. Eurailers travel free; InterRailers go half-price.

Melk

For real High Baroque excess, head for the Benedictine monastery at **MELK** – a pilgrimage centre associated with the Irish missionary St Coloman – designed by local architect Jakob Prandtauer in the first half of the eighteenth century. The monumental coffee-cake **monastery**, perched on a bluff over the river, dominates the town. Highlights of the interior (mid-April to mid-Nov daily 9am–6pm; rest of year guided tours only: 11am & 2pm; €6.90, €8.50 with guided tour; ☻www .stiftmelk.at) are the exquisite library, with a cherub-infested ceiling by Troger, and the monastery church, with similarly impressive work by Rottmayr. Melk's **river** station is about ten minutes' walk north of town; the **train station** is at the head of Bahnhofstrasse, which leads directly into the old quarter. The **tourist office**, Babenbergstr. 1 (April–June, Sept & Oct Mon–Fri 9am–noon & 2–5/6pm, Sat 10am–2pm; July & Aug Mon–Sat 9am–7pm, Sun 10am–2pm; ☏02752/52307, ⓦwww.tiscover.com/melk), has a substantial stock of private rooms, though most are out of the centre. The **HI hostel** is ten minutes' walk from the tourist office, at Abt Karlstr. 42 (☏02752/52681, ⓦwww.oejhv.or.at; April–Oct; €14.80). A similar distance in the opposite direction is the town's **campsite**, *Melker Camping* (☏02752/53291, ⓔfaehrhaus-jensch@melker.net; March–Nov), by the river station.

Linz

Away from its industrial suburbs, **LINZ** is a pleasant Baroque city straddling the Danube, even though its greatest claim to fame is as the childhood home of Adolf Hitler, something about which the local tourist board is understandably coy. The heart of the city is the rectangular expanse of the main square, **Hauptplatz**, with its pastel-coloured facades and central Trinity Column, crowned by a gilded sunburst. In the nearby **Pfarrkirche**, a gargantuan marble slab contains Emperor Friedrich III's heart (the rest of him is in Vienna's Stephansdom); he made Linz the imperial capital for four years from 1489. A decidedly modern addition to the city's cultural scene nestles beside the Danube: the shimmering, hangar-like steel and glass **Lentos Kunstmuseum Linz** (Mon & Wed–Sun 10am–6pm, Thurs till 10pm; €6.50) shows contemporary and modern art, including Klimt, Kokoschka, and Schiele. Beside it is the Nibelungen bridge which links Linz to its northern suburb of Urfahr. To the right is the **Ars Electronica Center**, Hauptstr. 2 (Wed–Sun 10am–6pm; €6; ⓦwww.aec.at), a fun museum dedicated to new technology; most of the instructions are in German, but the helpful staff speak English. You can play around with various pieces of state-of-the-art computer equipment, but the highlight is a visit to the "CAVE", a virtual reality room with 3D projections on the walls and floor – get there early to book for it. Also from Urfahr you can take a ride on the **Pöstlingbergbahn**, a narrow-gauge railway which climbs to the eighteenth-century pilgrimage church of Pöstlingberg. Trains leave from a twee station at the end of the #3 tram line (daily 5.40am–8.20pm; every 20min; €3.20).

Practicalities

Linz's **train station** is 2km south of the centre, on the far side of the city's main artery, Landstrasse; tram #3 runs to Hauptplatz. There's a **tourist office** in the Altes Rathaus, Hauptplatz 1 (Mon–Fri 8am–6/7pm, Sat & Sun 9/10am–6/7pm; ☏070/7070 1777). Affordable **accommodation** is rare: the *Wilder Mann*, ten minutes' walk from the station at Goethestr. 14 (☏070/65 60 78, ⓔwilder-mann@aon.at; ❹), has en-suite showers but shared hallway WCs; the similarly equipped but more pleasant *Goldenes Dachl*, Hafnerstr. 27 (☏070/77 58 97; ❸), is one block south of the cathedral. The **hostel**, *Jugendgastehaus Linz*, is at Stanglhofweg 3 (☏070/66 44 34, ⓦwww.oejhv.or.at; closed mid-Dec to mid-Jan; bus #17 from the station; €16). The best **campsite** is on the Pleschinger See, 3km northeast of the centre on the Danube at Seeweg 11 (☏070/24 78 70, ⓔkolmer@ione.at; bus #33 from Rudfrasse in Urfahr). There are plenty of central **bars and restaurants** around Hauptplatz. *Mangolds* at no. 6 is a self-service vegetarian café with cheap but tasty food, while the former monastery *Klosterhof*, Landstr. 30, serves solid Austrian fare and boasts a large beer garden. The traditional coffee house *Traxlmayr*, Promenade 16, is a good place to treat yourself to a slice of *Linzer Torte*, the local chocolate cake. *Alte Welt*, Hauptplatz 4 (closed Sun), is a trendy **wine bar**, and there are *Weinkellers* along the riverfront in Urfahr. The characterful *Café Ex-Blatt*, Waltherstr. 15, is a studenty pub decked out with nostalgic posters. A welter of **nightclubs** line the Hofberg, between the Landhaus and the Danube, while *Posthof*, 2km east at Posthofgasse 43 (ⓦwww.posthof.at; bus #21), organizes regular gigs and **club nights**.

Southeast Austria

Austria's **southeastern** corner, with the subalpine terrain of the province of Styria and the sun-baked plains of the Burgenland, is bypassed by most visitors. The area's wealth of diffuse attractions demand leisurely exploration, although the obvious focus of concentrated interest is the provincial capital of **Graz**.

Graz

European City of Culture for 2003 and Austria's second-largest city, **GRAZ** owes its importance to the defence of central Europe against the Turks. From the fifteenth century, it was constantly under arms, rendering it more secure than Vienna and leading to a modest seventeenth-century flowering of the arts (the Baroque style appeared first in Graz). The city's former reputation as a conservative place full of pensioners has been superseded, thanks to a clutch of architectural adventures: modern buildings of glass and steel sit surprisingly well in a city that recently won UNESCO's coveted World Heritage status. A large student population also feeds some varied nightlife.

Graz is compact and easy to explore, most sights being within striking distance of the broad **Hauptplatz** square. The easiest way to get your bearings is to take a trip up the **Schlossberg**, a wooded hill overlooking the town: either walk up a balustraded stone staircase which zigzags from Schlossbergplatz to the summit, or take the lift or funicular, a little further along Sackstrasse (both daily: April–Sept 9am–11pm; Oct–March 10am–10pm; €1.60) The Schloss, or fortress, was destroyed by Napoleon in 1809; only two prominent features survive – the sixteenth-century **Uhrturm** (clock tower), and more distant **Glockenturm** (bell tower), whose bell "Liesl" is said to be cast from 101 Turkish cannonballs.

From Hauptplatz, it's a few steps to the river Mur and two examples of Graz's architectural renaissance. The Kunsthaus, due for completion in late 2003, looks not unlike a futuristic porcupine, while the "Island in the Mur" is an ultra-modern floating bridge-cum-meeting place linking the two banks, inspired by an opened mussel shell. Nearby, the galleries of the **Landeszeughaus**, Herrengasse 16 (Tues–Sun 10am–6pm, Thurs till 8pm; €4.30), bristle with weapons used to keep the Turks at bay. West of Herrengasse is the **Landesmuseum Joanneum**, a vast collection housed in different locations: one, the **Alte Galerie** at Neutorgasse 45 (Tues–Sun 10am–6pm, Thurs till 8pm; €4.30), houses Gothic devotional paintings, including a fifteenth-century altarpiece depicting the martyrdom of Thomas à Becket and a macabre *Triumph of Death* by Bruegel. On the other side of Herrengasse, Stempfergasse leads into a neighbourhood of narrow alleyways that dog-leg their way up the hill towards the **Mausoleum of Ferdinand II** (currently undergoing renovation; check opening hours with the tourist office). It's a fine example of the early Baroque style, begun in 1614 when its intended incumbent was a healthy 36-year-old. The **Burg** is nearby, a former imperial residence; peer through the archway at the end of the first courtyard to view the unique double spiral of a fifteenth-century Gothic staircase. A short way north of Hauptplatz, down Sackstrasse, the **Neue Galerie** (Tues–Sun 10am–6pm, Thurs till 8pm; €4.30), displays nineteenth- and twentieth-century painting.

Practicalities

Graz's **train station** is on the western edge of town, a fifteen-minute walk or short tram ride (#1, #3 #6 or #7) from Hauptplatz. There's a **tourist office** at the station (Mon–Sat 9am–6pm, Sun 10am–6pm; ☎0316/80750, ⊛www.graztourismus.at) and a bigger one at Herrengasse 16 (same hours). **Accommodation** can be found at the comfortable *Hotel Alter Telegraf*, Grabenstr. 12 (☎0316/686 558, ⓔalter.telegraf@aon.at; ❺), and *Pension Rückert*, Rückertgasse 4 (☎316/32 30 31; closed June; ❺), 2km east of the centre; take tram #1 from the train station to

Teggethofplatz, then walk 10min north. The **HI hostel** is four blocks south of the station at Idlhofgasse 74 (☎0316/71 48 76, ⓦwww.oejhv.or.at; €14.20) and offers dorms and en-suite doubles; it's justifiably popular so book ahead. **Camping** *Central* is south at Martinhofstr. 3 (☎0676/378 5102, ⓦwww.tiscover.com/campingcentral; bus #32 from Jakominiplatz). There's **Internet** access at *Sit 'n' Surf*, Hans-Sachs-Gasse 10 (daily 8am–11pm) and a coin-op **laundry** on Jakominmistrasse, corner of Grazbackgasse (Mon–Fri 8am–5pm, Sat 8am–noon; tram #4 or #5).

Graz is foremost among Austria's provincial cities in preserving the culture of the **Kaffeehaus**. *Hofcafé Edegger Tax*, Hofgasse 8, is a sedate refuge; modern *Operncafé*, Opernring 22, attracts a youthful crowd and is equally popular in the evening; *Café Promenade*, Erzherzog-Johann-Allee 1 (daily 8am–midnight), is an attractive pavilion in the Stadtpark. *Gambrinuskeller*, Farbergasse 6–8 (closed Sun), has a wide choice of **food**, including kebabs, stuffed peppers and other Balkan dishes; *Glockenspielkeller*, Mehlplatz 3, has more standard Austrian fare and pleasant outdoor seating. *Zu den 3 goldenen Kugeln*, east of the centre in the university district, on the corner of Goethestrasse and Heinrichstrasse, doles out Schnitzel-and-chips fare. Many of the best places to **drink** are in the alleys around Hauptplatz: *MI*, Färberplatz, is a swish designer bar, while *Flann O'Brien's*, Paradiesgasse, is the best of the Irish pubs. It's also worth venturing out to the university, east of the Stadtpark: *Café Harrach*, Harrachgasse 26, is good, and *Bier Baron*, Heinrichstr. 56, is a student favourite, serving inexpensive food. *Park House*, a pavilion in the Stadtpark, is a late bar with resident DJs. Other **clubs** include the *Kulturhauskeller*, a studenty dive at Elisabethstr. 31, and *Arcadium*, Griesgasse 25 (ⓦwww.arcadium.at), which pulls in guest DJs. Graz is also something of a **festival** city: events (June–Sept) range from story-telling through classical and jazz to street theatre.

Salzburg and the Salzkammergut

Salzburg, hugging the border with Germany, is Austria's most heavily touristed city after Vienna – a magnet for those seeking the best of the country's Baroque heritage and a taste of subalpine scenery. The most accessible and popular of these mountain areas is the **Salzkammergut**, a peaceful region of glacier-carved lakes and craggy peaks a couple of hours east by bus or train.

Salzburg

For many visitors, **SALZBURG** represents the quintessential Austria, offering ornate architecture, mountain air, and a musical heritage provided by the city's most famous son, Wolfgang Amadeus **Mozart**, whose bright-eyed visage peers from every box of the city's ubiquitous chocolate delicacy, the *Mozartkügel*. The city, once home to the renowned singing Von Trapp family (immortalized in the movie **The Sound of Music**), wastes no time in cashing in on the connection via a variety of tours and shows.

The City

Salzburg's compact centre straddles the River Salzach. The city and surrounding area used to be ruled by a series of prince-archbishops and the resulting collection of episcopal buildings on the **west bank** forms a tight-knit network of alleys and squares, overlooked by the brooding presence of the medieval Hohensalzburg castle. From here it's a short hop over the river to a narrow ribbon of essential sights on the **east bank**.

From the Staatsbrücke, the main bridge, tourists are funneled along Judengasse and up into **Mozartplatz**, home to a statue of the composer and overlooked by the **Glockenspiel**, a seventeenth-century musical clock whose chimes attract crowds at 7am, 11am and 6pm. The complex of Baroque buildings on the right exudes the ecclesiastical and temporal power wielded by Salzburg's archbishops, whose erstwhile living quarters – the **Residenz** – dominate the west side of Residenzplatz. You can make a self-guided audio-tour of the lavish state rooms, then visit the **Residenzgalerie,** one floor above (daily 10am–5pm; closed the 2 weeks before Easter; joint ticket €7.30), which includes works by Rembrandt and Caravaggio. From here arches lead through to Domplatz, dominated by the pale marble facade of the **Dom**; an impressively cavernous Renaissance structure with dazzling ceiling frescoes. Across Domplatz, an archway leads through to the Gothic **Franziskanerkirche**, which houses a fine Baroque altar around an earlier Madonna and Child. The altar is enclosed by an arc of nine chapels, adorned in a frenzy of stucco ornamentation. Look out also for the twelfth-century marble lion that guards the stairway to the pulpit. Northwest of here, the **Museum Carolino-Augusteum**, Museumplatz 1 (daily 9am–5pm, Thurs until 8pm; €3.50) contains Roman finds, including reconstructed mosaics retrieved from beneath Mozartplatz. Getreidegasse leads back to the centre, lined with opulent boutiques, painted facades and wrought-iron shop signs. At no. 9 is **Mozarts Geburtshaus** (daily 9am–5.30/6.30pm; ⓦ www.mozarteum.at; €5.50; joint ticket with Wohnhaus €9), where the musical prodigy was born (in 1756) and lived till the age of 17. Between the waves of tour parties it can be an evocative place, housing some fascinating period instruments, including a baby-sized violin used by Wolfgang Amadeus as a child. The fortified **Höhensalzburg** (daily 9am–5/6/8pm; ⓦ www.salzburg-burgen .at), is a key landmark, looming over the city from the rocky Mönchberg. You can get up there by funicular (daily 9am–10pm; every 10min; closed early Jan & Feb; €8.50 return, €5.60 one-way; includes admission to castle grounds) from Kapitelplatz behind the cathedral. Begun around 1070 to provide the city's archbishops with a refuge, the fortress was gradually trans-formed into a more salubrious courtly seat. You can visit the state rooms with an audioguide, although a roam around the ram-parts and passageways is enough to gain a feel for the place. The hike up on foot isn't as hard as it looks, but to get into the castle you'll still have to pay €3.60.

Streets on the eastern bank of the river radiate out from Platzl, a small square at the foot of the **Kapuzinerberg**, named after a

SALZBURG

Pedestrianized Area

Schloss Mirabell
BERGSTRASSE
MAKART PLATZ
Dreifaltigkeitskirch
THEATERGASSE
DREIFALTIG.-GTSGASSE
SCHWARZSTR
LINZERGASSE
ELIZABETHKAI
ZWEIT. WEG
Mozart-Wohnhaus
PLATZL
Kapuzinerberg
Train Station
STAATSBRÜCKE
IMBERGSTR
Salzach
GISELAKAI
H A N U S C H P L A T Z
GETREIDEGASSE
JUDENGASSE
N
Mozarts Geburtshaus
ALTER MARKT
BROGGASSE
GOLDGASSE
Kollegienkirche
WIENER-PHILHARMONIKER G.
SIGMUND-HAFNER-
CHURFÜRSTSTR.
MOZARTPLATZ
ⓘ
Residenz
RESIDENZ-PLATZ
Franziskaner-kirche
FRANZISKANERG.
DOMPLATZ
Rupertinum
Dom
KAPITELPLATZ
Mönchsberg Lift
HERRENGASSE
BIERJODLGASSE
FESTUNGSGASSE
Mönchsberg
Funicular Railway
0   100 m
Hohensalzburg

Capuchin monastery at the summit. It can be scaled in five minutes for excellent views of Salzburg's domes and spires. Linzergasse heads east from Platzl towards the **Sebastianskirche** and its fascinating graveyard, resting-place of the Renaissance humanist and alchemist Paracelsus and home to the tiled mausoleum of the seventeenth-century archbishop Wolf Dietrich. Two blocks northwest of Platzl, on Makartplatz, is **Mozarts Wohnhaus**, the family home from 1773 to 1787 (daily 9am–5.30/6.30pm; €5.50; joint ticket with Geburtshaus €9), containing an engrossing multimedia history of the composer and his times. The **Dreifaltigkeitskirche** stands nearby, notable for the elegant curve of its exterior and murky frescoes inside. Dreifaltigkeitsgasse leads north to **Schloss Mirabell**, on the site of a previous palace built by Archbishop Wolf Dietrich for his mistress Salome, with whom the energetic prelate was rumoured to have sired a dozen children. Rebuilt in the early eighteenth century, and reconstructed after a fire in the nineteenth, it features a Baroque, cherub-lined staircase and ornate gardens – the rose-filled high ground of the adjoining Kurgarten, which offers a much-photographed view back across the city.

Practicalities

Salzburg's **train station** is 1km west of town, with regular buses (#2, #5, #6, #51 & #55) to the central Ferdinand-Hanusch-Platz. A 24hr travel pass (*Tageskarte*) costs €3.20. There's a tourist kiosk at the train station (platform 2a; daily 9.10am–5.45pm), and a larger **tourist office** at Mozartplatz 5 (daily 9am–6/7pm; ☎0662/889 870, ⊛www.salzburginfo.at). Both offices have accommodation details and book rooms; they also sell the Salzburg card (€20/28 for 24/48hr), which grants unlimited use of public transport and free admission to many of the sights. Panorama Tours on Mirabellplatz (☎0662/874 029, ⊛www.panoramatours.com) runs what they dub "**The Original** *Sound of Music* **Tour**" (daily 9.30am & 2pm; €33) on which you're bussed to the key locations of the film, played the soundtrack and sent away with a free packet of edelweiss seeds. You'll either love the singalong trip, or feel a bit herded through your "doh-a-deer" experience. Salzburg can also serve as a base for a day trip into the **mountains**: Crocodile Sports, Gaisbergstr. 34a (☎0662/642 907, ⊛www.crocodile-sports.com) runs rafting, canyoning and canoeing from around €40.

One of the most conveniently placed **hostels** is the *Yo-Ho International Youth Hotel*, Paracelsusstr. 9 (☎0662/87 96 49, ⊛www.yoho.at; €14), between the train station and main sights – it has a party atmosphere, with no curfew, no lock-out and daily screenings of *The Sound of Music* in the bar. The HI-affiliated *Haunspergstrasse* hostel is three blocks west of the train station at Haunspergstr. 27 (☎0662/87 50 30, ⊛www.oehw.or.at; €14; July & Aug only; midnight curfew). **Hotel** rooms fill quickly in summer and can be pricey. Spartan but clean *Pension Junger Fuchs*, Linzergasse 54 (☎0662/875 496; ❸; no breakfast) is a bargain, in a good location. Nearby is the wonderful, creaky old *Schwarzes Rössl*, Priesterhausgasse 6 (☎0662/87 44 26, ⊛www.academia-hotels.at; July–Sept only; ❹). *Goldene Krone*, also on the left bank at Linzergasse 48 (☎0662/87 23 00; ❺), is an old-fashioned place with some en suites. *Camping Nord-Sam*, Samstr. 22a, is the most convenient **campsite** (☎0662/64 04 94, ⊛www.camping-nord-sam.com; mid-May to mid-Oct; bus #33).

Plenty of outlets offer sandwiches and **snacks**; riverside *Fischkrieg*, Ferdinand-Hanusch-Platz 4, serves up everything from fishburgers to grilled squid. Of Salzburg's elegant **cafés**, the most renowned are *Tomasselli*, Alte Markt 9, and *Bazar*, Schwarzstr. 3, with a nice river-view terrace. *Resch & Lieblich* **restaurant**, next to the Festspielhaus at Toscaninihof 1, offers good-value Austrian cuisine in dining rooms carved out of the Hohensalzburg cliffs. *Gablerbräu*, Linzergasse 9, serves good Austrian grub (from €7 for a main meal) and has several vegetarian options, as does *Stieglkeller*, Festungsgasse 10 – also a good place for drinking beer on warm evenings. There are many raucous night-time **drinking** venues along Rudolfskai.

Zwettlers Gastwirtschaft, Kaigasse 3, is a relaxing pub with good food and blues music. *Augustiner Bräu,* Augustinerstr. 4–6, is an open-air courtyard fifteen minutes northeast of the centre serving huge mugs of locally brewed beer.

The city hosts dozens of **concerts** – many of them Mozart-related – all year round; check with Salzburg Ticket Service (Ⓦwww.salzburgticket.com), inside the tourist office on Mozartplatz. The **Salzburg Festival** (end-July to end-Aug; Ⓦwww.salzburgfestival.at) is one of Europe's premier festivals of classical music, opera and theatre. Some standing places for outdoor performances are available on a stand-by basis; check with the box office on Hofstallgasse (Ⓣ0662/804 5500).

Listings

Consulates UK, Alte Markt 4 Ⓣ0662/848133; US, Alte Markt 1 Ⓣ0662/848776.

Exchange Outside banking hours try at the main station (daily 7/7.30am–8.30/9pm).

Hospital Müllner, Hauptstr. 48 Ⓣ0662/4482.

Internet access Bignet, Judengasse 5–7;

Piterfun, opposite the train station.

Laundry Wolf Dietrichstr. 19 (Mon–Fri 7.30am–6pm, Sat 8am–noon).

Left luggage 24hr lockers at the main station.

Pharmacy Elisabethstr. 1.

Post office Residenzplatz 9.

The Salzkammergut

The peaks of the **Salzkammergut** may not be as lofty as those further south, but the lakes that fill the glacier-carved troughs separating them make for some spectacular scenery. Most of the settlements here are modest, quiet until the annual summer influx of visitors. The hub is the nineteenth-century spa town of **Bad Ischl**, 60km east of Salzburg, near two of the most scenic lakes – the **Wolfgangersee** and **Hallstättersee**. You can reach Bad Ischl by train, either branching off the main Salzburg–Vienna route at Attnang-Puchheim, or leaving the Salzburg–Graz line at Stainach-Irdning to the south. Once in Bad Ischl you're just a half-hour train ride from dramatic **Hallstatt**.

St Wolfgang

Hourly buses between Salzburg and Bad Ischl run east along the southern shores of the Wolfgangersee, though they bypass the lake's main attraction, the village of **ST WOLFGANG**, on the opposite shore: get off at Strobl, at the lake's eastern end, and pick up a connecting bus from there. St Wolfgang can be crowded in summer, but is worth visiting, if only to see the **Pfarrkirche**, just above the lake shore; its high altar, an extravagantly pinnacled structure 12m high, was completed between 1471 and 1481, and features brightly gilded scenes of the *Coronation of the Virgin* in the centrepiece flanked by scenes from the life of St Wolfgang. From Ash Wednesday to the day before Palm Sunday the wings are opened further to allow a glimpse of eight richly coloured paintings from the life of Christ. Little trains climb the local **Schafberg** peak (May–Oct; €22 return; InterRail/Eurail discounts) from a station on the western edge of town. The **tourist office** (May–Oct Mon–Fri 9am–7pm, Sat 9am–noon & 2–7pm; Nov–April Mon–Fri 9am–noon & 2–5pm, Sat 9am–noon; Ⓣ06138/2239, Ⓦwww.wolfgangsee.org) is at the eastern entrance to the road tunnel, and can help arrange accommodation.

Bad Ischl

The elegant town houses, fountains and gardens of **BAD ISCHL** have an air of bourgeois repose. The soothing properties of the waters here prompted the penultimate Habsburg emperor, Franz Josef, to summer in the **Kaiservilla** (April Sat & Sun 9–11.45am & 1–5.15pm; May to mid-Oct daily same hours; €9.50; park only €3.60) across the River Ischl from the centre. Beyond the villa (which is crammed with victims of the emperor's hunting expeditions) stretches a park containing the **Marmorschlössel** (April–Oct daily 9.30am–5pm; €1.50), an exquisite neo-Gothic garden retreat built for the Empress Elizabeth; it now houses a small muse-

Bad gastein + Youth Hotel town 1½ hr S of Salzburg built around waterfall.

um of photography. Both the **bus** and **train stations** are on the eastern fringe of the centre, a few steps from the **tourist office**, Bahnhofstr. 6 (May–Oct Mon–Fri 9am–7pm, Sat 9am–3pm, Sun 10am–1pm; Nov–April Mon–Fri 9am–5pm, Sat 9am–noon; ☎06132/27757, ⓦwww.badischl.at). There's a modern, functional **HI hostel** near the swimming pool at Am Rechensteg 5 (☎06132/26577, ⓦwww.oejhv.or.at; €14) and the clean and characterful *Gasthof Sandwirt*, Eglmoosgasse 4 (☎06132/26403; ❹), with en suite rooms.

Hallstatt

The jewel of the Salzkammergut is the UNESCO World Heritage Site of **HALL-STATT**, which clings to the base of precipitous cliffs on the shores of the Hallstättersee, 20km south of Bad Ischl. With towering peaks and a pristine lake, this is a stunning setting in which to hike, swim or rent a boat. Look out for the local sharp-prowed boats, known as *Fuhr*, propelled by a single paddle at the stern rather like a punt; before the road was built, these were the main local form of transport. Arriving **by train** is a highly evocative experience; the station is on the opposite side of the lake, and the ferry which meets all incoming trains gives truly dramatic views. (Note that after 6pm, trains don't stop here and instead continue to Obertraun, 5km away on the lakeshore.) Buses stop in the suburb of Lahn, a ten-minute lakeside walk away.

Hallstatt gave its name to a distinct period of Iron Age culture after Celtic remains were discovered in the salt mines above the town. Many of the finds date back to the ninth century BC, and can now be seen in the **World Heritage Hallstatt Museum** (daily 9/10am–4/6pm; €6; ⓦwww.museum-hallstatt.at); they include wooden mining implements, pit props and hide rucksacks used by Iron Age miners, alongside ornamental objects such as jewellery and crafted dagger handles. The **Pfarrkirche** has a south portal adorned with sixteenth-century Calvary scenes and, inside, a Gothic winged altar on the right with heavily gilded statuettes of the Madonna and Child flanked by St Catherine (the patron of woodcutters, on the left) and St Barbara (the patron of miners). In the graveyard outside is a small stone structure known as the **Beinhaus** (May–Oct daily 10am–4pm; €1), traditionally the repository for the skulls of villagers: rows and rows of empty eye sockets stare back at you, with bones neatly stacked below. The skulls, some of them quite recent, are inscribed with the names of the deceased and dates of their death, and are often decorated with finely painted floral patterns. Steep paths behind the graveyard lead up to a highland valley, the Salzachtal (1hr 30min of hard hiking), where the **salt mines** that provided the area's prosperity can be viewed (guided tour only: May–Oct daily 9.30am–3/4.30pm; €14.50). You can also take the **funicular** (daily May–Oct 9am–4.30/6pm; €7.90 return) from the nearby suburb of Lahn.

Hallstatt's **tourist office** is in the centre of town (April–Oct Mon–Fri 9am–noon & 2–5pm, Sat & Sun 10am–2pm; Nov–March Mon–Fri 9am–1pm; ☎06134/8208, ⓦwww.hallstatt.net). The friendly *Gasthaus zur Mühle*, set back from the landing-stage at Kirchenweg 36 (☎06134/8318; ❸), has doubles and dorms (€12.50). *Jugendherberge Lahn*, Salzbergstr. 50 (☎06134/8212; €8.50; closed Nov–April), is a more institutional hostel. Friendly *Pension Seethaler*, Dr F. Mortonweg 22 (☎06134/8421, ⓦwww.dement.com; ❸) is a great place to stay – each room has a lake-view balcony. The **campsite** *Klausner-Holl* is in Lahn by the petrol station on Lahnstrasse (☎06134/8322, closed Nov–March), a short walk from the landing stage. **Canoes** can be rented from the boatshed beside the landing stage (€7/hr). The tourist office can advise on a route for the four-hour **hike** up to the *Wiesberghaus* mountain hut (☎06134/20620, ⓦwww.wiesberghaus.at; closed Oct–Christmas; €14.50), and also sell you a hiking guide in English (€5). There are plenty of **places to eat**: *Bräugasthof*, Seestr. 120, does excellent Austrian food, with a lakeside terrace and competitively priced fresh fish. For **drinking**, the bar in the *Gasthaus zur Mühle* offers a warm welcome, while the one at Marktplatz 59 is popular with locals.

Western Austria

West towards the mountain province of the **Tyrol**, the grandiose scenery of Austria's Alpine heartland begins to unfold in earnest. Most trains from Vienna and Salzburg travel through a corner of Bavaria in Germany before joining the Inn valley and climbing back into Austria to the Tyrolean capital, **Innsbruck**. A less direct but more scenic route (more likely if you're coming from Graz) cuts by the majestic **Hoher Tauern** – site of Austria's highest peak, the Grossglockner – before joining the Inn valley at Wörgl. The exclusive resort-town of **Kitzbühel** provides a potential stopoff, although it's Innsbruck that offers the most convenient mix of urban sights and Alpine splendour. Further west, **Bregenz**, on the shores of Lake Constance, makes for a tranquil stop before pressing on into Germany or Switzerland.

Innsbruck

High in the Alps, with ski resorts within easy reach, **INNSBRUCK** is a compact city encircled by towering mountains. It has a rich history: Maximilian I based the imperial court here in the 1490s, placing this provincial Alpine town at the heart of European politics and culture for a century and a half. Most attractions are confined to the central Altstadt, bounded by the river and the Graben, following the course of the moat which used to surround the medieval town. Leading up to this, Innsbruck's main artery is **Maria-Theresien-Strasse**, famed for the view north towards the great rock wall of the Nordkette, the mountain that dominates the city. At its southern end the triumphal arch, **Triumphpforte**, was built for the marriage of Maria Theresia's son Leopold in 1756. Halfway along, the **Annasäule**, a column supporting a statue of the Virgin, was erected to commemorate the retreat of the Bavarians, who had been menacing the Tyrol, on St Anne's day (July 26), 1703. Herzog-Friedrich-Strasse leads on into the centre, opening out into a plaza lined with arcaded medieval buildings. At the plaza's southern end is the **Goldenes Dachl**, or Golden Roof (though the tiles are actually copper), built in the 1490s to cover an oriel window from which the court of Emperor Maximilian could observe the square below. Inside is the **Maximilianeum** (May–Oct daily 10am–6pm; Nov–April Tues–Sun 10am–12.30pm & 2–5pm; €3.60; ✆www.tiroler-landesmuseum.at), a flashy museum that includes an entertaining video-style documentary about the emperor. An alley to the right leads down to Domplatz and the **Domkirche St Jakob**, home to a valuable *Madonna and Child* by German master Lucas Cranach the Elder, although it is buried in the fussy Baroque detail of the altar. The adjacent **Hofburg**, entered around the corner, has late-medieval roots but was remodelled in the eighteenth century, its Rococo state apartments crammed with opulent furniture (daily 9am–5pm; €5.45). At the head of Rennweg, entered through the Tiroler Volkskunstmuseum (see below), is the **Hofkirche**, which contains the Cenotaph of Emperor Maximilian (Mon–Sat 9am–5pm; €3) This extraordinary project was originally envisaged as a series of 40 larger-than-life statues, 100 statuettes and 32 busts of Roman emperors, representing both the real and the spiritual ancestors of Maximilian, but in the end only 32 of the statuettes and 20 of the busts were completed. The resulting ensemble is still hugely impressive. Upstairs is the Silberkapelle or silver chapel, named after the silver Madonna that adorns the far wall. The same complex houses the **Tiroler Volkskunstmuseum** (Mon–Sat 9am–5pm, Sun 9am–noon; €5) which features recreations of traditional wood-panelled Tyrolean peasant interiors. The **Tiroler Landesmuseum Ferdinandeum**, a short walk south at Museumstr. 15 (May–Sept daily 10am–5pm; Oct–April Tues–Sat 10am–noon & 2–5pm, Sun 9am–1pm; €8), contains one of the best collections of Gothic paintings in Austria; most originate from the churches of the South Tyrol (now the Italian region of Alto-Adige). Also worth a visit is **Schloss Ambras** (April–Oct daily 10am–5pm; closed Nov; Dec–March closed Tues;

€7.50), 2km southeast on tram #6; this was the home of Archduke Ferdinand of Tyrol and still houses his wide-ranging collection of artworks and objects from around the globe.

The quickest route to higher altitudes is the **Hungerburgbahn** (daily 8/8.30am–5/6pm; €4.20 return), which runs from the end of Rennweg (end of tram #1) up to the Hungerburg plateau, a good base for hikes. A two-stage sequence of cable cars continues from here to just below the summit of the Nordkette, where you can enjoy stupendous views of the high Alps.

Practicalities

Innsbruck's **train station** has a tourist kiosk (daily June–Sept 8am–10pm, Oct–May 9am–9pm), while the main **tourist office** is at Burggraben 3 (daily 9am–6pm; ☎0512/535617, ⊛www.innsbruck.at). Both sell the "Innsbruck Card" (€19/24/29 for 24/48/72hr), which allows free travel in the centre and admission to all the sights. A 24hr transport pass costs €3.30. A Club Innsbruck Card (given free on hotel check-in) gives free guided hikes, reduced cable-car fares and free lake bathing. The basic *St Nikolaus* **hostel**, Innstr. 95 (☎0512/286 515, ⊜innsbruck@hostelnikolaus .at; €14.80), has a basement bar and no curfew; it's a ten-minute walk into town. The HI *Jugendherberge Innsbruck*, is 4km east at Reichenauerstr. 147 (☎0512/346179, ⊛www.oejhw.or.at; €13); bus O from Museumstrasse trundles past. *Paula*, Weiherburggasse 15 (☎0512/29 22 62, ⊛www.pensionpaula.at; ❹), is a friendly **pension** on a hillside north of the river – ask for a room with balcony and mountain views. More central options are the pleasant *Gasthof Innrain*, Innrain 38 (☎0512/58 89 81, ⊛www.gasthof-innrain.com; ❹), and *Gasthof Innbrucker*, Innstr. 1 (☎0512/281 934, ⊜innbruecke@nextra.at; ❹) just over the bridge from the old town. The only **campsite** is *Innsbruck Kranebitten*, 5km west at Kranebittner Allee 214 (☎0512/28 41 80, ⊜campinginnsbruck@hotmail.com; bus O towards Allerheilgenhofe, get off at the technical university, then take bus LK to the site).

The streets around the Goldenes Dachl are packed with old coaching inns transformed into **restaurants**; one of the more atmospheric is the *Ottoburg*, Herzog-Friedrich-Str. 1, with solid Austrian fare and veggie options. The slightly cheaper *Stiftskeller*, is at Stiftgasse 1, offering a good choice of fresh fish; and the cheaper-still *La Cucina*, Museumstr. 26, has a wide range of pizza and pasta. *Café Central*, Gilmstr. 5, is a venerable old coffeehouse serving up excellent pastries and cakes as well as decent breakfasts. There are plenty of convivial **drinking venues**: *Elferhaus*, on Herzog-Friedrich-Strasse, is a popular beer bar that also does good food. *Weli*, under the railway arches just east of the centre at Ing-Etzelstr. 26, is an informal café/bar with decent food. *Innkeller*, Innstr. 1, is another late-night haunt.

The Innsbruck Alpine School runs a programme of guided **hikes** (June–Oct; free with a Club Innsbruck Card), including sunrise and lantern-lit ones; the tourist office has details. **Bikes** can be rented from Sport Neuner (☎0512/56 15 01; from €10/day). As befits such a stunning setting, there's a range of **adventure sports** on offer. Snow stays on the nearby Stubai Glacier all year, making summer skiing possible: the tourist office organizes day trips, from €47 including equipment, bus transfer and lift passes. Trips to see the glacier cost €23. Adrenaline junkies can shoot down the 1000m **bobsleigh run** in just over a minute (May–Sept Thurs & Fri 4pm & 6pm; ☎05275/5386, ⊛www.sommerbobrunning.at; €22) There's **whitewater rafting** (☎05234/68 100; from €40) and **paragliding** through *Flugschule Parafly* (☎05226/3344; from €95).

Listings

Consulates UK, Kaiserjaegerstr. 2 ☎0512/58 83 20.
Hospital Universitätklinik, Anichstr. 35 ☎0512/504.
Internet access *Moderne*, Maria-Theresien-Str. 14.
Laundry *Bubble Point*, Andreas-Hoferstr. 37 &

Brixnerstr. 1 (Mon–Fri 8am–11pm, Sat & Sun 8am–8pm).
Left luggage At the station (June–Sept 24hr; Oct–May 6.30am–midnight).
Post office Maximilianstr. 2.

Bregenz

On the eastern tip of the Bodensee (Lake Constance), **BREGENZ** is an obvious staging post on journeys into neighbouring Germany, Liechtenstein or Switzerland. The Vorarlbergers who live here speak a dialect close to Swiss German, and have always considered themselves separate from the rest of Austria. At first sight Bregenz is curiously disjointed, the tranquil lakeside parks cut off from town by the main road and rail links along the lakeshore. Most points of interest are in the old town, up the hill from the lake, around **St Martinsturm**, an early seventeenth-century tower crowned by a bulbous wooden dome. Up the street from here is the seventeenth-century **town hall**, an immense half-timbered construction with a steeply inclined roof. Down in the modern town near the lake on Kornmarkt, the **Kunsthaus Bregenz** (Tues–Sun 10am–6pm, Thurs till 9pm; €6; @www .kunsthaus-bregenz.at), known as the KUB, is a coolly modernist green cube that hosts high-profile modern art exhibitions. The **Vorarlberger Landesmuseum**, Kornmarkt 1 (Tues–Sun 9am–noon & 2–5pm; €2) has some outstanding paintings by Angelika Kauffmann, a local painter who achieved success in eighteenth-century London. Beyond here, leafy parks line the lake to the **Festspielhaus**, a modern concert hall built to accommodate the Bregenz Festival (mid-July to mid-Aug; @www.bregenzerfestspiele.com), which draws hundreds of thousands of opera lovers every year. A cable car rises from a station at the eastern end of town to the **Pfänder** (daily 9am–7pm; €9.80), a wooded hill with excellent views; alternatively, you can follow the worthwhile Pfänderweg on foot to the top (1hr 30min).

Practicalities

The **tourist office** is at Bahnhofstr. 14 (Mon–Fri 9am–noon & 1–5/6pm, Sat 9am–noon; during the festival Mon–Sat 9am–7pm; ☎05574/49590, @www .bregenz.at). *Gästehaus Tannenbach*, Im Gehren 1 (☎05574/44174; closed Oct–April; ❸), is a friendly place with a lovely garden east of the centre; *Pension Sonne*, Kaiserstr. 8 (☎05574/642572, @www.bbn.at/sonne; ❹) is a good place in the centre that hikes its rates steeply during the festival. The HI **hostel** west of the train station at Mehrerauerstr. 5 (☎05574/42867, @www.jgh.at; €17.20) offers dorms as well as swanky doubles, while *Seecamping*, Bodangasse 7, is a large **campsite** by the lake, 2km west (☎05574/71896, @www.seecamping.at). *Günz*, Anton-Schneider-Str. 38, serves low-priced traditional Austrian **food**; *Zum Goldener Hirschen*, Kirchstr. 8, is a more atmospheric, pub-like venue with slightly more expensive eats. Amongst the good central **bars** are *1 Akt*, Kornmarktstr. 24, and the stylish but cosy *Flexibel*, Rathausgasse 27.

Travel details

Trains
Bad Ischl to: Hallstatt (10 daily; 30min).
Graz to: Innsbruck (7 daily; 6hr); Linz (every 2hr; 3hr 30min); Salzburg (8 daily; 4hr 30min).
Innsbruck to: Bregenz (10 daily; 3hr).
Salzburg to: Innsbruck (8 daily; 2hr 30min); Linz (hourly; 1hr 20min).
Vienna to: Bregenz (8 daily; 10hr); Graz (every 2hr; 2hr 40min); Innsbruck (every 2hr; 5hr 20min); Krems (hourly; 1hr 15min); Linz (1–2 hourly; 2hr); Melk (every 1–2hr; 1hr); Salzburg (every 1–2hr; 3hr 20min).

Buses
Bad Ischl to: Hallstatt (5–7 daily; 40min); Salzburg (hourly; 1hr 40min); St Wolfgang (hourly; 45min).
Krems to: Melk (3–4 daily; 1hr).
Linz to: St Florian (Mon–Fri every 2hr; 35min).

Belgium and Luxembourg

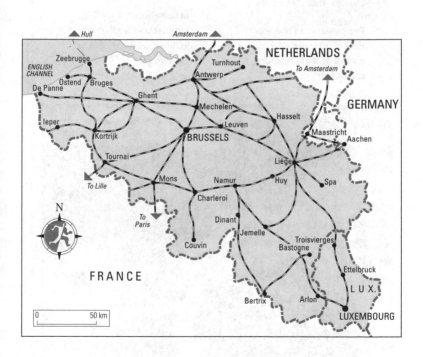

Belgium and Luxembourg highlights

* **Grand-Place, Brussels** Wonderfully preserved square with beautiful guildhouses, in the heart of the city. See p.89

* **Het Gravensteen, Ghent** This stern, formidable castle dominates the old town. See p.98

* **Procession of the Holy Blood, Bruges** A colourful but solemn religious procession each Ascension Day. See p.100

* **Canoeing** Great opportunities, mostly along the River Lesse, in the wooded, hilly landscape of the Ardennes. See p.103

* **Luxembourg City** The spectacular setting alone justifies a visit to this tiny capital. See p.104

Introduction and basics

A federal country, with three official languages and an intense regional rivalry, **Belgium** has a cultural diversity that belies its rather dull reputation. Its population of around ten million is divided between Flemish-speakers (about sixty percent) and French-speaking Walloons (forty percent), with a few pockets of German-speakers in the east. Prosperity has shifted back and forth between the two leading communities over the centuries, and relations have long been acrimonious. The constitution was redrawn in 1980, with three separate entities: the Flemish north, Walloon south, and Brussels, which is officially bilingual.

The north and south of **Belgium** are visually very different. Marking the meeting of the two, **Brussels**, the capital, is a culturally varied city at the heart of the European Union. The **north**, made up of the provinces of West and East Flanders, Antwerp, Limburg and much of Brabant, is mainly flat, with a landscape and architecture not unlike Holland. **Antwerp** is the principal Flemish city, a bustling old port with doses of high art, redolent of its sixteenth-century golden age. Further west lie the great historic cities of **Bruges** and **Ghent**, each with a stunning concentration of Flemish art and architecture. By contrast, Belgium's most scenically rewarding region, the **Ardennes**, an area of deep, wooded valleys, high elevations and dark caverns, sprawls across the south of the country with the attractive town of **Namur** the obvious gateway.

The Ardennes reach across the border into the northern part of the Grand Duchy of **Luxembourg**, a verdant landscape of rushing rivers and high hills topped with crumbling castles. The best base for rural expeditions is **Luxembourg City**, a pleasant town with a splendid rugged setting. The city has a population of around 80,000, which makes it one of Europe's smallest capitals.

Information & maps

Both Belgium and Luxembourg have **tourist offices** in all but the smallest of villages.

They usually provide free local maps, and in the larger towns offer a free accommodation-booking service too. The best general road **map** is the easy-to-use Baedeker & AA Belgium and Luxembourg (1:250,000) map.

Money and banks

Belgium and Luxembourg both use the **euro** (€). **Banks** are the best places to change money and are generally open Mon–Fri 9am–4/4.30pm in both countries, though some have a one-hour lunch break between noon and 2pm. **ATMs** are commonplace.

Communications

Post offices are usually open Mon–Fri 9am–noon & 2–5pm. Some urban post offices also open on Saturday mornings. Many public **phones** take only phonecards, which are available from newsagents and post offices. There are no area codes in either country. The international operator numbers are ☎1324 in Belgium, ☎010 in Luxembourg. **Mobile phone** coverage is good. **Internet** access is increasingly widespread, with at least one or two cybercafés in all the larger cities; libraries are often a good bet where all else fails.

Getting around

Travelling around Belgium is rarely a problem. Distances are short, and efficient, reasonably priced trains link all the major centres. Luxembourg, on the other hand, can be problematic: the train network is not extensive and bus timetables demand careful study.

Belgium's railways (@www.sncb.be) are comprehensive and efficient, and fares are comparatively low. InterRail and Eurail passes are valid throughout the network, as are a number of other regional passes – see p.35 for further details. SNCB also publishes information on offers and services in their comprehensive timetable book, which has an English-language section and is available at major train stations. **Buses** are only really used for travelling short distances, or in parts of the Ardennes where rail lines fizzle out.

Luxembourg's railways (@www.cfl.lu) comprise one main north–south route down the middle of the country, with a handful of branch lines fanning out from the capital, but most of the country can only be reached by **bus**. Fares are comparable with those in Belgium, and there are a number of passes available, giving unlimited train and bus travel.

The modest distances and flat terrain make **cycling in Belgium** an attractive proposition. That said, cycling in most big cities and on the majority of trunk roads is still rather precarious and only in the countryside is there a decent network of signposted cycle routes. You can take your own bike on a train for a small fee or rent one from any of around thirty train stations during the summer at about €8.50 per day; note also that some train excursion tickets include the cost of **bike rental**. Full details, with a list of stations offering bike rental, are on the SNCB website and in the *Train & Vélo* leaflet. In **Luxembourg** you can rent bikes for around €10 a day, and take your own bike on trains (not buses) for €1.10 per journey. The Luxembourg Tourist Office has leaflets showing cycle routes and also sells cycling guides.

Accommodation

Hotel **accommodation** is one of the major expenses you will incur on a trip to Belgium or Luxembourg – indeed, if you're after a degree of comfort, it's going to be the costliest item by far. There are, however, budget alternatives, principally the no-frills end of the hotel market, private rooms arranged via the local tourist office and hostels.

In both countries prices begin at around €30–50 for a double room in the cheapest one-star **hotel** and climb to €70–120 for a comfortable double in a mid-range establishment. Breakfast is normally (but not always) included in the room rate. During the summer you'd be well advised to book ahead. Hotel **reservations** can be made for free through most tourist offices on the day itself – the deposit they require is subtracted from your final hotel bill. **Private rooms** can be booked through local tourist offices too. Expect to pay €40–60 a night for a double, but be aware that they're often inconveniently situated on the outskirts of cities and towns. An exception is in Bruges, where rooms can be booked direct and many are in the centre.

Hostels and student rooms

Belgium has around 25 **HI hostels**, run by two separate organizations. In Flanders (northern Belgium), this is Vlaamse Jeugdherbergcentrale (☏032 32 72 18, @www.vjh.be), in Wallonia (southern Belgium) it's Les Auberges de Jeunesse de Wallonie (☏022 19 56 76, @www.laj.be). Most charge a flat rate per person of between €12.50–14.50 for a bed in a dormitory, non-members a little more, and breakfast is included. Many also offer meals for €5–10. During the summer you should book ahead wherever possible. Some of the larger cities – Bruges, Antwerp and Brussels, for example – have **privately run hostels**. These normally charge about €15 for a dorm bed and are often just as comfortable as their HI counterparts. You'll also find some universities offering **student rooms** for rent during the summer vacation, Ghent being a good example. Rooms are basic – reckon on about €15 per person per night.

There are eleven HI hostels in **Luxembourg**, all of which are members of the Centrale des Auberges de Jeunesse Luxembourgeoises (☏26 29 35 00,

@www.youthhostels.lu). Dorm-bed rates for HI members are €14–16, with non-members paying an extra €3–5. Breakfast is always included; lunch or dinner is €6–7.

Camping

Camping is a popular pastime in both Belgium and Luxembourg, though many sites can only be reached by car or bike. In **Belgium**, there are literally hundreds of sites, anything from a field with a few tent pitches through to extensive complexes with all mod cons. Campsites are regulated by three governmental agencies – one for Flanders, one for Brussels and one for Wallonia – and each produces its own **camping booklet**. All three do, however, apply the same one- to five-star grading system. The vast majority are one- and two-star establishments, for which two adults with a car and a tent can expect to pay €10–15 per night. Surprisingly, most four-star sites don't cost much more – add about €2.50 – though the occasional five-star campsite can reach €35. All **Luxembourg's** campsites are detailed in the free tourist office booklet. They're classified into three broad bands: the majority are in Category 1, the best-equipped and most expensive classification. Prices vary considerably, but are usually €3–5 per person, plus €3–5 for a pitch. In both countries, it's a good idea to **reserve ahead** during peak season; phone numbers are listed in the free camping booklets, and in Luxembourg the national tourist board (☎42 82 82 10) will make a reservation on your behalf.

Food and drink

Belgian cuisine is held in high regard, second only to French; the country also offers a wide range of ethnic food. **Luxembourg's** food is less varied and more Germanic – but you can still eat out extremely well. As for drink, **beer** is one of the real delights of Belgium, and Luxembourg produces some very drinkable white **wines** along its side of the River Moselle.

Food

Southern Belgian cuisine is not unlike traditional French, retaining its neighbour's fondness for rich sauces and ingredients. In **Flanders** the food is more akin to that of the Netherlands, with many traditional dishes. Pork, beef, game, fish and seafood, especially mussels, are staple items, often cooked with butter, cream and herbs, or sometimes in beer. Soups, too, are common: hearty affairs, especially in the south and the **Ardennes**, a region also renowned for its smoked ham and pâté.

In both countries, many **bars** offer inexpensive meals, at least at lunchtimes, and a host of **cafés** serve basic dishes too: omelettes, steak or mussels with chips (the last of these virtually the Belgian national dish). The distinction between cafés and bars is increasingly blurred, with **café/bars** often the most fashionable place to be, especially in the cities. Most places have a dish of the day for €10–15. **Restaurants** are almost always more expensive, but the food they offer is almost always excellent; a main course will rarely cost under €12.

Belgium is also renowned for its **chocolate**. The big chocolatiers, Godiva and Leonidas, have shops in all the main towns and cities, and their pralines and truffles are almost worth the trip by themselves. Of the two, Leonidas is the cheaper; reckon on spending €17 or so for 500g.

Drink

Drinking **beer** in Belgium is a real treat. The most common brands are Stella Artois, Jupiler and Maes, but this merely scrapes the surface. There are several hundred **speciality beers**, usually served by the bottle but occasionally on draught, from dark stouts to fruit beers, wheat beers and brown ales – something to suit any palate and enough to overwhelm the hardiest of livers. The most famous are the strong ales brewed by the country's five Trappist monasteries, of which the most widely available is Chimay. Luxembourg doesn't really compete, but its three most popular brews – Diekirch, Mousel and Bofferding – are pleasant enough lagers. Bar prices don't vary greatly: in both countries you'll pay around €1.50 for a glass of beer and from €3.50 for a bottle.

French **wines** are the most commonly available, although Luxembourg's wines, produced along the north bank of the Moselle, are very drinkable. In the shops, you'll pay

9–12 for a bottle of local sparkling ...r ordinary white. Restaurants ...wo or three times as much. You'll ...utch-style **jenever** (a local gin) in most ...rs in the north of Belgium, and in Luxembourg home-produced, super-strong **eau-de-vie**, distilled from various fruits.

Emergency numbers

Belgium
Police ☎101; fire & ambulance ☎100.

Luxembourg
Police ☎113; fire & ambulance ☎112.

Opening hours and holidays

In both countries, the weekend fades painlessly into the week with some shops staying closed on Monday morning, even in major cities. Nonetheless, normal **shopping hours** are Mon–Sat 9/10am–6/7pm with many urban supermarkets staying open until 8/9pm on Fridays and many smaller places shutting early on Saturday. In the big cities, a smattering of convenience stores (*magasins de nuit/avondwinkels*) stay open either all night or until around 1/2am daily, and some souvenir shops open late or on Sundays too. At the other extreme, some shops close for a half-day (Wed or Thurs am), though this tradition has died out in all but the smaller towns and villages. Shops, banks and many museums are closed on the following **public holidays**: Jan 1; Easter Monday; May 1; Ascension Day (40 days after Easter); Whit Monday; Assumption (mid-Aug); Nov 1; Nov 11 (Belgium only);

and Dec 25. In addition, the Luxembourg national day is June 23, Belgium's is July 21.

Emergencies

You shouldn't have much cause to come into contact with the police, although all the cities have rough neighbourhoods, which should be avoided at night. If you are unlucky enough to have something stolen, report it immediately to the nearest police station and get a report number, or better still a copy of the statement itself, for your insurance claim when you get home. With regard to medical emergencies, if you're reliant on free treatment within the EU health scheme, try to remember to make this clear to the ambulance staff and any medics. EU citizens need to have a completed form E111 to be treated within the EU scheme. Non-EU citizens need private insurance. Outside working hours, all pharmacies display a list of open alternatives. Weekend rotas are also listed in local newspapers.

BELGIUM AND LUXEMBOURG | Basics

Brussels (Bruxelles, Brussel)

Wherever else you go in Belgium, at some point you'll wind up in **BRUSSELS**, a capital boasting architecture and museums to rank with the best of Europe, a well-preserved medieval centre and an energetic nightlife. It's also very much an international city, with European civil servants and business folk, plus immigrants from Africa, Turkey and the Mediterranean, making up a quarter of the population. Brussels airport is a major European gateway and Eurostar trains arrive here direct from London.

The city takes its name from Broekzele, or "village of the marsh", which grew up in the sixth century on the trade route between Cologne and the towns of Bruges and Ghent. Under the Habsburgs, the town flourished, eventually becoming capital of the Spanish Netherlands. In the nineteenth century it became the capital of the newly independent Belgium, and was kitted out with all the attributes of a modern European capital. Since World War II, the city's appointment as headquarters of both NATO and the EU has brought major developments, including a metro.

Arrival, information and transport

Brussels has three main **train stations** – Bruxelles-Nord, Bruxelles-Centrale and Bruxelles-Midi, each a few minutes apart; almost all domestic trains stop at all three. The majority of **international** trains, including expresses from London, Amsterdam, Paris and Cologne, stop only at Bruxelles-Midi (Brussel-Zuid). **Bruxelles-Centrale** is a five-minute walk from Grand-Place; **Bruxelles-Nord** lies in the business area just north of the main ring road; and **Bruxelles-Midi** is south of the city centre. To transfer from one of the three main stations to another, simply jump on the next available mainline train. Eurolines **buses** arrive at the Gare du Nord complex. The **airport** is in Zaventem, 13km northeast of the centre, served by regular trains to the city's three main stations (30min; €2.40).

There are two **tourist offices** in the centre. The main one is the BI-TC, on the Grand-Place (Mon–Sat 9am–6pm; May–Sept Sun 9am–6pm, Oct–Dec Sun 10am–2pm; ☎025 13 89 40, ☜www.tib.be). The Belgian tourist information centre, nearby at rue du Marché aux Herbes 63 (Mon–Fri 9am–6/7pm, Sat & Sun 9am–1pm & 2–6/7pm; ☎025 04 03 90; ☜www.belgique-tourisme.net), has information on the rest of Belgium.

City transport

The easiest way to get around central Brussels is to **walk**, but to reach some of the more widely dispersed attractions you'll need to use **public transport**. The system (☜www.stib.be) runs on a mixture of bus, tram, premetro (underground tram) and metro lines. A single flat-fare **ticket** costs €1.40, a strip of five €6.30, and a strip of ten €9.20 – all available from tram and bus drivers, metro kiosks and ticket machines, plus STIB information offices in the Port de Namur, Midi and Rogier stations. A **day-pass**, allowing unlimited travel for 24hr, costs €3.70. Spot fines for fare-dodging are heavy. Services run from 6am until midnight; route maps are available free from the tourist office and from STIB information kiosks. **Taxis** can be picked up from ranks around the city – notably on Bourse and place De Brouckère; to book, phone Taxis Verts (☎023 49 49 49) or Taxis Orange (☎023 49 43 43).

> In Brussels, the languages of the French- and Flemish-speaking communities have parity. This means that every instance of the written word, from road signs to the Yellow Pages, must appear in both languages. Visitors soon adjust, but on arrival this can be confusing, especially in the names of the city's three main train stations: Bruxelles-Nord (in Flemish it's Brussel-Noord), Bruxelles-Centrale (Brussel-Centraal), and, bewilderingly, Bruxelles-Midi (Brussel-Zuid). Note that for simplicity we've used the French versions throughout this account.

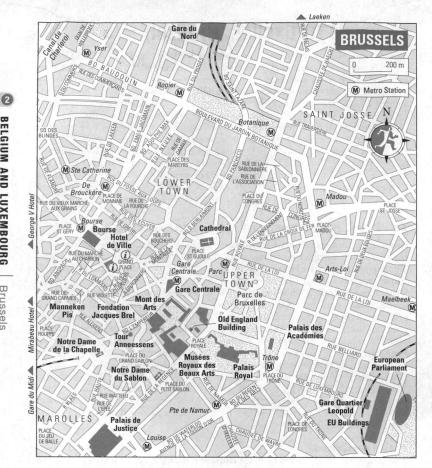

Accommodation

Brussels has no shortage of **places to stay**, but given the number of visitors, finding a room can be hard, particularly in summer, and it's best to book ahead at least for your first night. There are several inexpensive places near the Grand-Place and these put you at the centre of the action. The tourist office offers a reservation service, as does BTR (Belgium Tourist Reservation; ☏02 513 74 84, 🖷02 513 92 77, 🖃btr@horeca.be).

Hostels

Bruegel rue du Saint Esprit 2 ☏025 11 04 36, 🆆www.vjh.be. This HI hostel, housed in a smart and modern building, has 135 beds. It's fairly central and a basic breakfast is included. Dorms sleep six to twelve, double and quadruple rooms also available. Curfew 1am. Métro Gare Centrale. Dorms €13. Doubles ❸

CHAB rue Traversière 8 ☏022 17 01 58, 🆆www.ping.be/chab. A rambling, spacious hostel

with a good reputation, though it can seem chaotic. Sinks in all rooms, but shared showers and toilets. No curfew. Breakfast included. Sheet rental €3.50. One-, two- and four-bed rooms. Métro Botanique. Dorms €14. Doubles ❸

Jacques Brel rue de la Sablonnière 30 ☏022 18 01 87, 🆆www.planet.be/aubjeun. HI hostel – modern and comfortable, and with a hotel-like atmosphere. Showers in every room; bar, restaurant and meeting room. Beds in two- to twelve-bedded dorms. Métro Madou or Botanique. €13.

New Sleep Well rue du Damier 23 ☎ 022 18 50 50, ⓦ www.sleepwell.be. Bright and breezy hostel in a recently refurbished building, a five-minute walk from place Rogier. Hotel-style facilities including a bar; good disabled access. Sheet rental €3.50. Advance booking essential. One-, two-, three- and four-bed rooms. Métro Rogier. Dorms €13. Doubles ❸

Hotels

Les Bluets rue Berckmans 124, Saint Gilles ☎ 025 34 39 83, ⓔ bluets@swing.be. Charming, family-run hotel with ten en-suite rooms in a handsome terrace house one block south of the petit ring. Immaculate *fin de siècle* decor. Advance reservations recommended. Métro Hôtel des Monnaies. ❹

George V rue 't Kint 23 ☎ 025 13 50 93, ⓦ www.george5.com. A ramshackle old hotel in an atmospheric if somewhat down-at-heel neighbourhood of big, balconied tenement blocks. Rooms are plain and modern, but with clean and well-appointed en suites. Prémétro Bourse. ❺

Mirabeau pl Fontainas 18 ☎ 025 11 19 72, ⓔ hotel.mirabeau@skynet.be. Welcoming hotel with thirty neat, modern en-suite rooms. Occupies a good-looking, early twentieth-century, seven-storey block and overlooks a busy square bordering bld Anspach. Prémétro Anneessens. ❺

Résidence Rembrandt rue de la Concorde 42, Ixelles ☎ 025 12 71 39, ⓔ rembrandt@brutele.be. Popular, pleasant pension-style hotel. 13 clean and comfortable rooms – six en suite – and kitsch bygones in the foyer. Located on a dispiriting street off avenue Louise, near place Stéphanie. Trams #93 and #94 run along ave Louise. ❻

Sabina rue du Nord 78 ☎ 022 18 26 37, ⓦ www.hotelsabina.com. 24 workaday, en-suite rooms in a late nineteenth-century terrace town house. Located in an appealing residential area that was once a favourite haunt of the city's Victorian bourgeoisie. Métro Madou. ❺

Saint-Michel Grand-Place 15 ☎ 025 11 09 56, ⓔ hotelsaintmichel@hotmail.com. One of the city's most distinctive hotels and the only one that looks out over the Grand-Place. It occupies an old guildhouse on the east side of the square, but the grandness of the facade isn't universally matched by the rooms inside – which range from the basic and small at the back of the building to more elegant period rooms at the front. If you're a light sleeper, revellers on the Grand-Place may well disturb your slumbers. Prémétro Bourse. ❺

La Tasse d'Argent rue du Congrès 48 ☎ 022 18 83 75. A popular, family-run hotel with just eight modest, modern rooms in a good-looking, *fin de siècle* mansion about five minutes' walk north of the cathedral. Métro Madou. ❺

The City

Central Brussels is enclosed within a rough pentagon of boulevards – the **petit ring** – which follows the course of the medieval city walls. The centre is also divided between the Upper and Lower Towns, the neighbourhoods generally becoming smarter the higher you go. Of the two, the **Lower Town** is much the larger and it's here you'll find the **Grand-Place**, perhaps the best-preserved city square in Europe. South of the Grand-Place, the centre fades into the old working-class streets of the Marolles district and Gare du Midi, now a relatively depressed, predominantly immigrant area; north, the shopping street of rue Neuve leads up to place Rogier and the office blocks that surround the Gare du Nord. The **Upper Town** is quite different in feel from the rest of the centre, with statuesque buildings lining wide, classical boulevards and squares. Beyond the petit ring, several places are worth a visit, particularly the Musée Victor Horta.

The Lower Town

The obvious place to begin any tour of the **Lower Town** is the **Grand-Place**, the commercial hub of the city since the Middle Ages. With its stupendous tower, the **Hôtel de Ville** (tours in English: April–Sept Tues & Wed 3.15pm, Sun 12.15pm; Oct–March Tues only 3.15pm; €2.50) dominates the square, and inside you can view various official rooms. The most dazzling is the sixteenth-century council chamber, decorated with gilt moulding, faded tapestries and an oak floor inlaid with ebony. But the real glory of the Grand-Place lies in its **guildhouses**, built in the early eighteenth century, their slender facades swirling with exuberant carving and sculpture. At the end of the row, on the west side of the square at no. 1, the

Roi d'Espagne was once the headquarters of the guild of bakers and is named after its bust of Charles II, the last of the Spanish Habsburgs. Moorish and Native American prisoners flank Charles, symbolizing his mastery of a vast empire. At no. 4 is the **Maison de Sac**, the headquarters of the carpenters and coopers; the upper storeys, appropriately designed by a cabinet-maker, feature pilasters and caryatids resembling the ornate legs of Baroque furniture. Next door, the **Maison de la Louve** was once the home of the influential archers' guild and its elegant pilastered facade is studded with pious representations of concepts like Peace and Discord. Adjoining it, at no. 6, the **Maison du Cornet** was the headquarters of the boatsmen's guild, a fanciful creation of 1697 whose top storey resembles the stern of a ship. The adjacent **Maison du Renard** was the house of the haberdashers' guild; on the ground floor animated cherubs in bas-relief play at haberdashery, while a scrawny, gilded fox – after which the house is named – squats above the door.

Most of the northern side of the square is taken up by the sturdy neo-Gothic **Maison du Roi**, a reconstruction of a sixteenth-century building that now houses the **Musée de la Ville de Bruxelles** (Tues–Fri 10am–5pm, Sat & Sun 10am–1pm; €2.50). Here you'll find an eclectic mix of locally manufactured tapestries, ceramics, pewterware and porcelain.

South to the Marolles quarter

Rue de l'Etuve leads south from the Grand-Place down to the **Manneken Pis**, a diminutive statue of a little boy pissing that's supposed to embody the "irreverent spirit" of the city and is today one of Brussels' biggest tourist draws. Jerome Duquesnoy cast the original statue in the 1600s, but it was stolen several times and the current one is a copy. From here it's another short hop to place de la Vieille-Halle aux Blés and the **Fondation internationale Jacques Brel** (Tues–Sat 11am–6pm; July & Aug also Sun 11am–6pm; €5), a small but inventive museum celebrating the life and times of the Belgian singer Jacques Brel (1933-78). Brel became famous in the 1960s as a singer of mournful *chansons*. Suitably quirky, the museum begins with a false lift that actually doesn't move at all – despite the sounds – and beyond you can hear Brel pouring out his feelings on a mock-up stage and in a replica bar with juke box. From here, it's a short walk south to boulevard de l'Empereur, a busy carriageway that disfigures this part of the centre. Across the boulevard, you'll spy the crumbling brickwork of **La Tour Anneessens**, a chunky remnant of the medieval city wall, while to the south gleams the recently restored **Notre Dame de la Chapelle** (June–Sept Mon–Sat 9am–5pm & Sun 11.30am–4.30pm; Oct–May daily 12.30–4.30pm; free), a sprawling Gothic structure founded in 1134 that is the city's oldest church. Running south from the church, rue Haute and parallel rue Blaes form the spine of the **Quartier Marolles** – an earthy neighbourhood of cheap restaurants, shops and bars that grew up in the seventeenth century as a centre for artisans working on the nearby mansions of Sablon. Today, gentrification is creeping in, but it's got some way to go, and **place du Jeu de Balle**, the heart of Marolles, is still the scene of the city's best **flea market** (daily from 7am), at its busiest on Sundays.

The Upper Town

The steep slope that marks the start of the **Upper Town** rises just a couple of minutes' walk from the Grand-Place at the east end of rue d'Arenberg. Here you'll find the city's **Cathedral** (daily 8am–6pm; free), a splendid Brabantine-Gothic building begun in 1220 and sporting a striking twin-towered, whitestone facade. Inside, the triple-aisled nave is an airy affair supported by plain, heavy-duty columns and displaying a massive oak pulpit featuring Adam and Eve. Look out also for the gorgeous sixteenth-century **stained glass** windows in the transepts and above the main doors.

Five minutes' walk south of the cathedral, the so-called **Mont des Arts** also occupies the slopes of the Upper Town, its collection of severe geometric buildings given over to a variety of government- and arts-related activities. In the middle, a wide stairway climbs up towards **place Royale** and **rue Royale**, the dead-straight backbone of the Upper Town. To the left of the top of the stairway is the **Old England building**, one of the finest examples of Art Nouveau in the city. It now holds the **Musée des Instruments de Musique**, rue Montagne de la Cour 2 (Tues–Fri 9.30am–5pm, Thurs until 8pm, Sat & Sun 10am–5pm; €5), which contains around 1500 instruments and a string of interactive displays. Around the corner, the **Palais Royal** (late July to Sept Tues–Sun 10.30am–4.30pm; free) is something of a disappointment, a sombre conversion of some eighteenth-century town houses that together serve as the official residence of the Belgian royals.

Just off place Royale, at the start of rue de la Régence, the **Musées Royaux des Beaux Arts** (Tues–Sun 10am–5pm; €5 for both museums) comprise two museums: the Musée d'Art Moderne and the Musée d'Art Ancien. Together they make up Belgium's most satisfying all-round collection of fine art, with marvellous collections of work by the likes of Pieter Bruegel the Elder, Rubens and the surrealists Paul Delvaux and René Magritte. The permanent collection is vast, but a system of colour-coded zones makes it easy to negotiate your way around. In the **Musée d'Art Ancien**, the **blue zone** takes in paintings of the fifteenth and sixteenth centuries, including works by Lucas Cranach, Quentin Matsys, Rogier van der Weyden and Pieter Bruegel the Elder's haunting *The Fall of Icarus*. The **brown zone** concentrates on work of the seventeenth and eighteenth centuries, notably some glorious canvases by Rubens and his contemporaries Jacob Jordaens and Anthony van Dyck. Moving on into the **Musée d'Art Moderne**, the **yellow zone** begins with the Social Realism of Charles de Groux and Constantin Meunier and continues with a collection of Neoclassical paintings, most notably by Jacques-Louis David, whose famous *Death of Marat* is displayed here. Then come the Symbolists, including several works by Fernand Khnopff, and a separate section devoted to the disconcerting canvases of James Ensor. The **green zone** boasts an extremely varied collection of modern art and sculpture, laid out on six subterranean levels. There are fine examples of Fauvism, Cubism, Futurism, Expressionism, and, above all, Surrealism, with the oddly erotic works of Paul Delvaux and a small show of paintings by Magritte.

From the Beaux Arts it's a short stroll south to the **place du Petit Sablon**, decorated with 48 statues representing the medieval guilds, and a fountain surmounted by the Counts Egmont and Hoorn, beheaded on the Grand-Place for their opposition to Spanish tyranny in the 1500s. On the opposite side of rue de la Régence stands the fifteenth-century church of **Notre Dame du Sablon**, built after a statue of Mary with powers of healing was brought by boat from Antwerp, an event still celebrated each July by the Ommegang procession. Behind the church, the sloping wedge of **place du Grand Sablon** is the centre of one of the city's wealthiest districts and scene of a lively weekend antiques market.

Nearby, at the southern end of rue de la Régence, is the immense – and immensely ugly – **Palais de Justice**. Built in 1883, it is actually larger than St Peter's in Rome.

Outside the petit ring: the parks and outer boroughs

Brussels by no means ends with the petit ring. To the east of the ring road, the **Quartier Leopold** has been colonized by the huge concrete and glass high-rises of the EU, notably the winged **Berlaymont** building beside Métro Schuman. The latest addition to the sprawling EU complex is the lavish **European Union Parliament building** (free guided tours: usually Mon–Thurs 10am & 3pm, Fri 10am; ☎022 84 34 57), an imposing structure topped off by a spectacular curved glass roof. It's a couple of minutes' walk from place du Luxembourg, behind the Gare Quartier Leopold train station.

Just south of the petit ring is **St Gilles**, a gritty multiracial borough that stretches from the refinement of avenue Louise in the east to the solidly immigrant quarters around the Gare du Midi. The main reason to trek out here is the **Musée Victor Horta**, the former home of the Belgian Art Nouveau architect at rue Américaine 25 (Tues–Sun 2–5.30pm; €5); take tram #91 or #92 from place Louise. The exterior is modest, but inside are all the architect's trademarks: crisp, bright rooms spiralling around a superbly worked staircase, stained glass, sculpture and ornate furniture and panelling.

Some 3km north of the ring road, **Laeken** is the royal suburb of Brussels. Its large public **park** is best known for the **Atomium** (daily 9/10am–5.30/7.30pm; €5.45), a model of a molecule expanded 165 billion times, which was built for the 1958 World Fair. Poking its very distinctive head into the sky, the structure has become something of a symbol of the city, but its interior can only muster up an unremarkable exhibition on the construction of – and the concepts behind – itself.

Eating and drinking

Brussels has an international reputation for the quality of its cuisine, and even at the dowdiest snack bar you'll find that the food is well-prepared and generously seasoned – and then there are the city's **restaurants**, many of which equal any in Paris. Traditional Bruxellois dishes are canny amalgamations of Walloon and Flemish ingredients and cooking styles. In addition, the city is among Europe's best for sampling a wide range of different cuisines – from the Turkish restaurants of St Josse to Spanish, Vietnamese and Japanese. You can also eat magnificent fish and seafood, especially around the fashionable district of Ste Catherine.

Eating out is rarely cheap, but **prices** are usually justified by the quality. It's also hard to distinguish between the less expensive restaurants and the city's **cafés**, some of which provide the tastiest food in town, as do many **bars**. For **fast food**, there are plenty of stands and kebab places around the Grand-Place.

For **drinking**, the enormous variety of bars and cafés is one of the city's real joys – sumptuous Art Nouveau cafés, speciality-beer bars with literally hundreds of different varieties of ale, and, of course, more modern hangouts. Many of the centrally located bars are much frequented by tourists and expats, but many aren't, and even tucked away off the Grand-Place, there are places that remain refreshingly local. Bars stay open late – most until 2 or 3am, some until dawn.

Restaurants and cafés

On and around the Grand-Place

Le Cirio rue de la Bourse 18. One of Brussels' oldest café-bars, sumptuously decorated in *fin de siècle* style, though now somewhat frayed round the edges. Once frequented, they say, by Jacques Brel.

Le Falstaff rue Henri Maus 17–23. Art Nouveau café opposite the Bourse, attracting a mixed bag of tourists, gays and bourgeois Bruxellois. Full of atmosphere, and so crowded in the evenings that you're unlikely to find a seat. Inexpensive beer and workaday sandwiches, but pastries to swoon for.

't Kelderke Grand-Place 15 ☎025 13 73 44. Busy cellar restaurant specializing in traditional Bruxellois dishes. Serves an excellent *lapin à la gueuze* (rabbit cooked in gueuze) and a superb *carbonnades flamandes à la bière* (beef in beer).

Totem rue de la Grande Île 42. Tucked away down a sidestreet off boulevard Anspach, this friendly, fashionable restaurant is a hit with veggies, who come here for the organic soups, fresh salads and a delicious selection of cakes and pastries. Has a good choice of organic wines and serves meat dishes too. Closed Mon; no credit cards.

On and around place Ste Catherine

Bij den Boer quai aux Briques 60 ☎025 12 61 22. There's nothing pretentious here in this good old neighbourhood café/bar with its tiled floor and bygones on the wall. A great place for a drink or a meal, though the service can be slow. The seafood is delicious and reasonably priced. Closed Sun.

Iberica rue de Flandre 8 ☎025 11 79 36. Agreeable Spanish restaurant offering all the classics. Tapas around €6. Closed Wed.

Kasbah rue Antoine Dansaert 20. Popular with a youthful crowd, this Moroccan eatery is famous for serving enormous portions of couscous and other North African specialities. Vibrant and fashionable.

La Marée rue du Flandre 99 ☎025 11 00 40. Outstanding, pocket-sized restaurant, and not to be confused with its namesake on rue au Beurre. The speciality is seafood, always fresh and always prepared in a simple, direct manner. Frugal decor that somehow manages to feel quite cosy. Closed Sun eve & Mon.

La Papaye Verte rue Antoine Dansaert 53. First-rate Vietnamese food at bargain basement prices. Good range of vegetarian options. Smart, authentically Vietnamese interior.

Le Pré Salé rue de Flandre 16 ☎025 13 43 23. Friendly, old-fashioned neighbourhood restaurant providing a nice alternative to the swankier eateries of the district. Very Bruxellois. Great mussels, fish and other Belgian specialities. Closed Mon.

Bars

On and around the Grand-Place

À la Bécasse, rue de Tabora 11. This old-fashioned bar has long wooden benches, ancient blue and white tiles on the walls and serves beer in earthenware jugs.

Au Bon Vieux Temps rue du Marché aux Herbes 12. Cosy old place tucked down an alley. Has tile-inlaid tables and a handsome seventeenth-century chimney piece. Popular with British servicemen just after the end of World War II, the bar still has comforting old-fashioned signs advertising Mackenzies' Port and Bass pale ale. A great place for a quiet drink.

La Fleur en Papier Doré rue des Alexiens 53. Cluttered, cosy locals' bar whose walls are covered with doodles and poems. Was once one of the chosen drinking places of René Magritte.

Le Greenwich rue des Chartreux 7. Brussels' traditional chess café with a lovely old wood-panelled and mirrored interior. Laid-back atmosphere.

À l'Imaige de Nostre-Dame rue du Marché aux Herbes 6. A welcoming, quirky little bar situated at the end of a long, narrow alley. Decorated like an old Dutch kitchen. Good range of speciality beers.

À la Mort Subite rue Montagne aux Herbes Potagères 7. Twenties bar just northeast of the square that loaned its name to a widely available bottled beer. A long, narrow room with nicotine-stained walls and mirrors, a dissolute-arty clientele and an animated atmosphere. Snacks served.

Au Soleil rue Marché au Charbon 86. Popular bar with a wide choice of beers, crowded nightly till late with a young, trendy crowd.

Toone Impasse Schuddeveld 6, off Petite rue des Bouchers. Bar belonging to the Toone puppet theatre. Two small rooms with old posters on rough plaster walls, a reasonably priced beer list, a modest selection of snacks, and a soundtrack of classical and jazz, make it one of the centre's more congenial watering-holes.

Nightlife

Although it's not as lively a scene as in some European capitals, Brussels is a reasonably good place to catch **live bands**. **Club** culture has also made some headway in the city and, although it's hardly cutting edge stuff, there are several good venues in the centre. As a general rule, clubs **open** Thursday to Saturday from 11pm to 5/6am and entry **prices** are low – rarely more than €10 and many of the smaller clubs have no cover at all, though you should tip the bouncer (€2 or so) on the way out. For **listings** of concerts and events, check the *What's On* section of the weekly *Bulletin*, the city's English-language magazine. **Tickets** for most things are available from Fnac in the City 2 complex, rue Neuve (☎022 09 22 11).

Live music venues

AB bd Anspach 110 ☎025 48 24 24. One of the capital's premier rock venues. Has a reputation for showcasing prime local bands. Prémétro Bourse. Closed July & Aug.

Le Cercle rue Ste Anne 20 ☎025 14 03 53. Small, unremarkable venue, but the live music is a real attraction – everything from jazz and Latino to *chanson* three or four times a week. Just off place du Grand Sablon.

Forest National ave du Globe 36 ☎090 00 09 91. The main arena for big-name international acts. Tram #18.

Magazin 4 rue du Magasin 4 ☎022 23 34 74. In an old warehouse off bld d'Anvers, this is a favourite venue for up-and-coming local indie bands. Open only when there's a gig – call for details. Métro Yser.

VK rue de l'Ecole 76 ☎024 14 29 7. Regularly features top-class hip-hop, ragga, rock and indie acts and occasionally puts on the odd punk band too – it's probably the best cutting-edge "alternative" venue in the capital. Just to the west of Métro Comte de Flandre – an area with a bad reputation: take a taxi.

Clubs

Le Bazaar rue des Capucins 63. Split-level club with a competent restaurant upstairs and a dance-floor below, offering funk, soul, rock and indie. In the Marolles, off rue Haute – and below the Palais de Justice. Closed Sun.

The Fuse rue Blaes 208. Large, young, and vibrant techno, jungle and house club in the Marolles district. Big-name, international DJs a regular feature. Chill-out rooms and visuals. Métro

Porte de Hal. Sat only.
Le Pacha rue de l'Écuyer 41. Much vaunted Ibiza import. Spectacular stuff, with all the fury and action you might expect. Fri is funk, '60s and '70s rock, soul and house, Sat is house music, Sun is gay night. Closed Mon–Thurs.

Who's Who Land rue du Poinçon 17. A short walk east of Prémétro Annessens, this is one of the capital's runaway success stories. A trendy house club, it's always packed with legions of revellers. Classic techno and house anthems are blasted out until the wee hours. Sat only.

Listings

Embassies Australia, rue Guimard 6–8 ☎ 022 86 05 00; Canada, ave de Tervuren 2 ☎ 027 41 06 11; Ireland, rue Froissart 89 ☎ 022 30 53 37; New Zealand, bd du Régent 47–48 ☎ 025 12 10 40; UK, rue d'Arlon 85 ☎ 022 87 62 11; US, bld du Régent 27 ☎ 025 08 21 11.

Internet easyEverything, place De Brouckère 9.
Laundry Wash Club, place St Géry 25.
Left luggage At the train stations.
Pharmacy Multipharma, rue du Marché aux Poulets 37.
Post office First floor, Centre Monnaie, pl de la Monnaie.

Northern Belgium

The region north of Brussels is **Flemish-speaking** and possesses a distinctive and vibrant cultural identity. It's dull countryside on the whole, but a string of fine historic cities more than compensates, beginning with **Antwerp**, a large old port located due north of Brussels and dotted with many reminders of its sixteenth-century golden age. To the west, in Flanders, lie two more fascinating cities – **Ghent** and **Bruges** – which became prosperous during the Middle Ages on the back of the cloth trade. Both possess lovely ancient centres, graced by a medley of early Flemish art and architecture. All three cities have great bars and fine restaurants too.

Belgium's only international ferry port is **Zeebrugge**, with ferries from Hull and Rosyth. Ferries dock out on a mole 2km from the train station, so check with the ferry company to make sure they provide onward bus connections.

Antwerp

ANTWERP, Belgium's second city, fans out from the east bank of the Scheldt about 50km north of Brussels. Many people prefer it to the capital and indeed it does have a denser concentration of things to see, not least some fine churches and distinguished museums – reminders of its auspicious past as centre of a wide trading empire. In recent years, the city has also become the effective capital of Flemish Belgium, a lively cultural centre with a spirited nightlife. On the surface it doesn't appear wealthy, but its diamond industry (centred on Centraal Station) is the world's largest. There is also the enormous legacy of Rubens, some of whose finest works adorn Antwerp's galleries and churches.

Arrival, information and accommodation

Antwerp has two mainline train stations, Antwerp Berchem and **Centraal Station**; the latter, 2km east of the main square, Grote Markt, is the one you want for the city centre. **Trams** #2 and #15 (direction Linkeroever) run from the Diamant prémétro (underground tram) station beside Centraal Station to the centre; get off at Groenplaats. **Transport information** is available from the Diamant station (Mon–Fri 8am–12.30pm & 1.30–4pm), and they also sell several sorts of **ticket**. A single fare costs €1, a ten-strip *Rittenkaart* €7.50 and a 24-hour pass (*dagpas*) €2.90. Single tickets can also be bought direct from bus and tram drivers, and every type of ticket is on sale at every prémétro station. The **tourist office** is at Grote Markt 15 (Mon–Sat 9am–6pm, Sun 9am–5pm; ☎ 032 32 01 03, ⓦ www.visitantwerpen.be).

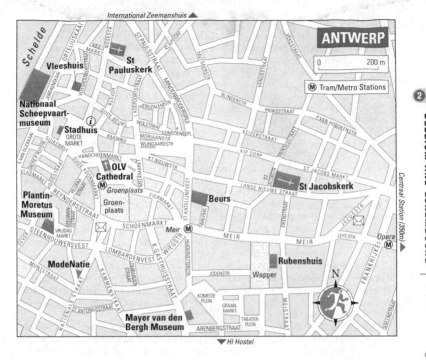

Finding **accommodation** is rarely difficult, although there are surprisingly few places in the centre. Many mid-priced and budget places are clustered in the scruffy area around Centraal Station, where you should exercise caution at night, particularly if travelling alone. The tourist office has a comprehensive list of places and will make bookings for you.

Hostels

Jeugdherberg Op Sinjoorke HI Hostel Eric Sasselaan 2 ☎032 38 02 73, ⓦwww.vjh.be. HI hostel close to the ring road, 5km south of the centre. Around 130 beds in four-, six- and eight-bedded rooms. Canteen, self-catering facilities and a laundry room. Tram #2 from Centraal Station. Dorms €13.

New International Youth Hotel Provinciestraat 256 ☎032 30 05 22, ⓦwww.niyh.be. Hotel-cum-hostel with spick-and-span singles and doubles just ten minutes' walk from Centraal Station. To get here head south down Pelikaanstraat, turn left along Plantin en Moretuslei, and take the third right. Doubles **④**

Scoutel Jeugdverblijfcentrum Stoomstraat 3 ☎032 26 46 06, ⓦwww.vvksm.be. Spick-and-span hostel-cum-hotel offering frugal but perfectly adequate doubles and triples with breakfast. It's about five minutes' walk from Centraal Station. No curfew (guests have their own keys), but reception closes 6pm. Reservations are advised. Discounts for the under-26s. Doubles **④**

Hotels

Cammerpoorte Nationalestraat 38 ☎032 31 97 36. Budget, two-star hotel with forty plain modern rooms. Close to the Grote Markt. **⑤**

Eden Lange Herentalsestraat 25 ☎032 33 06 08, ⓦwww.diamond-hotels.com. Chain hotel in the diamond district. The modern rooms are perfectly adequate but quite plain – and stand by for attack in the mosquito season. Breakfasts are very good. **⑥**

Ibis Antwerpen Centrum Meistraat 39 ☎032 31 88 30 www.ibishotel.com. Chain hotel with routine modern rooms hidden behind a ghastly concrete exterior; all is compensated for by a decent location, close to the Rubenshuis. **⑥**

Internationaal Zeemanshuis Falconrui 21 ☎032 27 54 33, ⓦwww.zeemanshuis.be. Spartan but perfectly acceptable en-suite doubles ten minutes' walk north of the Grote Markt. **③**

Tourist Hotel Pelikaanstraat 20 ☎032 32 58 70, ⓦwww.demahotels.be. Straightforward, modern rooms near Centraal Station – OK for a night or two, though Pelikaanstraat can be noisy. **④**

The City

The centre of Antwerp is the spacious **Grote Markt**, at the heart of which stands the **Brabo fountain**, a haphazard pile of rocks surmounted by a bronze of Silvius Brabo, the city's first hero, depicted flinging the hand of the giant Antigonus – who terrorized passing ships – into the Scheldt. The north side of Grote Markt is lined with daintily restored sixteenth-century **guildhouses**, though they are overshadowed by the **Stadhuis** (tours Mon, Tues, Thurs & Fri 11am, 2pm & 3pm, Sat 2pm & 3pm; €1), completed in 1566, and one of the most important buildings of the Northern Renaissance. Among rooms you can visit are the Leys Room, named after Baron Hendrik Leys, who painted the frescoes in the 1860s, and the Wedding Room, which has a chimney piece decorated with two caryatids carved by the architect Cornelius Floris.

Southeast of Grote Markt, the **Onze Lieve Vrouwe Cathedral** (Mon–Fri 10am–5pm, Sat 10am–3pm, Sun 1–4pm; €2) is one of the finest Gothic churches in Belgium, mostly the work of Jan and Pieter Appelmans in the middle of the fifteenth century. Inside, the seven-aisled nave is breathtaking, if only because of its sense of space, an impression that's reinforced by the bright, light stonework revealed by a recent refurbishment. Four early paintings by **Rubens** are displayed here, the most beautiful of which is the *Descent from the Cross*, a triptych painted after the artist's return from Italy.

It takes about five minutes to walk southwest from the cathedral to the **Plantin-Moretus Museum**, on Vrijdagmarkt (Tues–Sun 10am–5pm; €4), which occupies the grand old mansion of Rubens' father-in-law, the printer Christopher Plantin. One of Antwerp's most interesting museums, it provides a marvellous insight into how Plantin and his family conducted their business.

From here it's a brief stroll to the riverfront and the **Nationaal Scheepvaartmuseum** (Tues–Sun 10am–5pm; €4) – the maritime museum in the Steen, the remaining gatehouse of what was once an impressive medieval fortress, at the end of Suikerrui. Inside, the cramped rooms feature exhibits on inland navigation, shipbuilding and waterfront life, while the open-air section has a long line of tugs and barges under a rickety corrugated roof. Crossing Jordaenskaai, it's a short walk east to the impressively gabled **Vleeshuis** (Tues–Sun 10am–5pm; €2.50), built for the guild of butchers in 1503 and now used to display a substantial but incoherent collection of applied arts – everything from antique musical instruments to medieval woodcarvings.

Just north of here, along Vleeshouwersstraat, **St Pauluskerk** (May–Sept daily 2–5pm; free) is a dignified late Gothic church built for the Dominicans in the early sixteenth century. Inside, the airy and elegant nave is decorated by a series of paintings depicting the Fifteen Mysteries of the Rosary, including Rubens' exquisite *Scourging at the Pillar* of 1617.

Ten minutes' walk east from the OLV Cathedral is the **Rubenshuis**, Wapper 9 (Tues–Sun 10am–5pm; €5), the former home and studio of Rubens, now restored as a (very popular) museum. Unfortunately, there are only one or two of his less distinguished paintings here, but the restoration of the rooms is very convincing. Rubens died in 1640 and was buried in **St Jacobskerk**, just to the north at Lange Nieuwstraat 73 (April–Oct daily 2–5pm; €2). The artist and his immediate family are buried in the chapel behind the high altar, where, in one of his last works, *Our Lady Surrounded by Saints*, he painted himself as St George, his two wives as Martha and Mary, and his father as St Jerome.

South of the Grote Markt

Heading south from the Groenplaats along Nationalestraat, it takes about five minutes to reach the new **ModeNatie** (@www.modenatie.com), an ambitious complex spread over several floors that showcases the work of local fashion designers. Part of the building contains **MoMu** (Mode Museum; Tues–Sun 10am–5pm; €5), which has some great contemporary fashion displays; other sections hold a brasserie and a specialist bookshop. The success of Antwerp's fashion designers has left the city with dozens of excellent designer shops and stores. The tourist office booklet *Antwerp Fashion Walk* (€3) takes you past all the best shops, but there's a particular concentration around ModeNatie, including Modepaleis, Nationalestraat 16, and Alamode opposite at no. 27. On Kammenstraat are the contemporary jewellery of Anne Zellien, at no. 47, and the secondhand clothes of Naughty–I, at no. 65. Arguably the best secondhand clothes shop in town is Francis, Steenhouwersvest 14.

About fifteen minutes' walk south of ModeNatie is the **Museum voor Schone Kunsten** (Tues–Sun 10am–5pm; €5) which has one of the country's better fine art collections. Its early Flemish section features paintings by Jan van Eyck, Memling, Rogier van der Weyden and Quentin Matsys. **Rubens** has two large rooms to himself, in which one very large canvas stands out: the *Adoration of the Magi*, a beautifully human work apparently completed in a fortnight. The museum also displays a comprehensive collection of modern Belgian art with Paul Delvaux and James Ensor being particularly well-represented.

Eating and drinking

Antwerp is an enjoyable and inexpensive place to **eat**, full of informal café–restaurants that excel at combining traditional Flemish, Mediterranean and French cuisines. Several of the best are clustered on Suikerrui and Grote Pieter Potstraat near the Grote Markt, and there's another concentration in the vicinity of Hendrik Conscienceplein. For **fast food**, try the kebab and falafel places on Oude Koornmarkt. Antwerp is also a fine place to **drink**, the narrow lanes of its centre dotted with small and atmospheric bars.

Cafés and restaurants

Het Dagelijks Brood Steenhouwersvest 48. An enjoyable and distinctively artsy café serving wholesome soups and light meals.

Facade Hendrik Conscienceplein 18. A laid-back, funky café with good music and inexpensive vegetarian, meat and fish dishes.

De Matelote Haarstraat 9 ☎032 31 32 07. Modish, pastel-painted fish restaurant off Grote Pieter Potstraat, near the Grote Markt. Closed Sun.

Pizzeria Da Antonio Grote Markt 6. Tasty and swiftly served pasta and pizza at reasonable prices.

De Stoemppot Vlasmarkt 12. *Stoemp* is a traditional Flemish dish consisting of puréed meat and vegetables – and this is the best place in town to eat it. Closed Wed.

Bars

Café de Muze Melkmarkt 15. With its bare brick walls and retro film posters, this laid-back and central café-bar is a popular spot. Frequent live music – mainly jazz and blues.

Het Elfde Gebod Torfbrug 10. On one of the tiny squares fronting the north side of the cathedral, this bar is something of a tourist trap, but it's still worth visiting for the kitsch religious statues which cram the interior; avoid the food.

Den Engel Grote Markt 3. Traditional, very Flemish bar bang in the centre of town.

Kulminator Vleminckveld 32–34. This long-established, laid-back bar lays claim to a stock of 500 beers.

De Vagant Reyndersstraat 21. Specialist gin bar serving an extravagant range of Belgian and Dutch jenevers in spruce, modern surroundings.

De Volle Maan Oude Koornmarkt 7. Lively, likeable and offbeat bar close to the Grote Markt.

Ghent (Gent)

The largest town in western Europe during the thirteenth and fourteenth centuries, **GHENT** was once at the heart of the medieval Flemish cloth trade. By 1350, the city boasted a population of 50,000, of whom no less than 5000 were directly involved in the industry, a prodigious concentration of labour in an overwhelmingly rural continent. However, the cloth trade began to decline in the early sixteenth century and Ghent decayed – until better times finally returned in the nineteenth century when the city was industrialized. It is now the third largest city in Belgium.

▼ S.M.A.K & Musuem voor Schone Kunsten

The best place to start exploring is at the mainly Gothic **St Baaf's Cathedral**, squeezed into the corner of St Baafsplein, bang in the centre of town (daily: 8.30am–5/6pm). Inside, a small chapel (April–Oct Mon–Sat 9.30–5pm & Sun 1–5pm; Nov–March Mon–Sat 10.30am–4pm, Sun 2–5pm; €2.50) holds Ghent's greatest treasure, the altarpiece of the *Adoration of the Mystic Lamb*, a wonderful early fifteenth-century painting by Jan van Eyck. The inside panels reveal God the Father, the Virgin and John the Baptist on the upper level, while down below the Lamb of God is depicted in a sort of earthly paradise, approached by saints, popes, patriarchs and godly knights.

On the west side of St Baafsplein lurks the medieval **Lakenhalle**, a gloomy hunk of a building whose first-floor entrance leads to the adjoining **Belfry** (mid-March to mid-Nov 10am–1 & 2–6pm; €3), a much-amended edifice dating from the fourteenth century. A glass-sided lift climbs up to the roof for excellent views over the city centre. From the belfry, it's a few strides north to the **Stadhuis** (tours: May–Oct Mon–Thurs; check tourist office for latest times; €3), which possesses a long stone facade that was erected in two distinct phases: the earlier, fancier carving reflects the city in its pomp, but the money ran out and the building had to be completed in a much plainer style.

A short walk west of the Stadhuis, **Graslei** forms the eastern side of the old city harbour and is home to a splendid series of gabled **guildhouses** dating from medieval times. From here, it's another short haul to the sinister-looking **Het Gravensteen** (daily 9am–5/6pm; €6.20), the Castle of the Counts of Flanders, where a self-guided tour leads through a labyrinth of cold, stark rooms and chambers. Nearby, just to the east, are the narrow cobbled lanes and alleys of the **Patershol**, a pocket-sized district that was formerly home to the city's weavers, but is now Ghent's main restaurant quarter. Here you'll find the **Huis van Alijn**, Kraanlei 65 (Tues–Sun 11am–5pm; €2.50), a folk museum sited in a series of restored almshouses and boasting a delightful chain of period rooms depicting local life and work in the eighteenth and nineteenth centuries.

Strolling south from the centre along Ghent's main shopping street, Veldstraat, it takes about twenty minutes to reach the **Museum voor Schone Kunsten** at Nicolaas de Liemaeckereplein 3 (Tues–Sun 10am–5pm; €2.50). The museum displays a first-rate sample of Flemish paintings, including two exquisite works by Hieronymus Bosch, along with work by the likes of Pieter Bruegel the Younger, Jordaens and Van Dyck. Opposite, the old casino has been turned into **SMAK** (Tues–Sun 10am–6pm; ⌨www.smak.be; €5), a museum of contemporary art that is well-known for its adventurous programme of temporary exhibitions.

Practicalities

Of Ghent's two **train stations**, the most useful is **St Pieters**, 2km south of the centre and connected to it by **trams** #1, #10, #11, #12 and #13. The **tourist office** is in the crypt of the Lakenhalle, right in the centre on the Botermarkt (daily: April–Oct 9.30am–6.30pm; Nov–March 9.30am–4.30pm; ☎092 26 52 32, ⓦwww.gent.be). The best way of seeing the sights is on **foot**, but Ghent is a large city and you may find you have to use a **tram** or **bus** at some point. Standard single fares cost €1, a ten-journey *Rittenkaart* €7.50 and a day pass €2.90. Single tickets can be bought direct from the driver; passes are sold at shops and kiosks all over town.

Ghent has around twenty **hotels**, ranging from the delightful to the mundanely modern, as well as a bright, cheerful and centrally located **HI hostel**. As for **eating out**, Ghent's numerous **cafés** and **restaurants** offer the very best of Flemish and French cuisines, with a sprinkling of Italian, Chinese and Arab places. The fancier restaurants are concentrated in and around the Patershol, while less expensive spots, including a rash of fast food joints, cluster the Korenmarkt. Ghent has lots of great **bars** too.

Hostels and student rooms

Jeugdherberg De Draecke HI Hostel St Widostraat 11 ☎092 33 70 50, ⓔyouthhostel.gent@skynet.be. Excellent, well-equipped hostel in the city centre, five minutes' walk north of the Korenmarkt. Over a hundred beds, in two-, three-, four-, five- and six-bed rooms. Facilities include lockers, currency exchange, bike rental and a bar. Breakfast included, and lunch and dinner offered.Advance reservations advised. Dorm beds €13. ❸

Universitaire Homes ☎092 64 71 2. Offers student rooms at several sites across the south of town. Mid-July to late Sept only. ❷

Private rooms

Brooderie Jan Breydelstraat 8 ☎092 25 06 23. The *Brooderie* is an appealing café (see opposite) handily located near the Korenmarkt and its owners rent out three neat and trim little rooms above it. Breakfast is excellent. ❺

Hotels

Boatel Voorhuitkaai 29a ☎092 67 10 30, ⓦwww.theboatel.com. Certainly the most distinctive of the city's hotels – as its name implies, it's a converted boat, and an imaginatively and immaculately refurbished canal barge to be precise. The seven bedrooms are decked out in crisp, modern style and breakfasts, taken on the poop deck, are first rate. Moored in one of the outer canals, a fifteen-minute walk east from the centre. ❻

Flandria Centrum Barrestraat 3 ☎092 23 06 26, ⓦwww.flandria-centrum.be. Somewhat dishevelled hotel in the narrow sidestreets off the Reep, five minutes' walk northeast of the cathedral. After the youth hostel, these are the least expensive rooms in the centre. All sixteen (modest) rooms are en suite. ❹

Poortackere Monasterium Oude Houtlei 58 ☎092 69 22 10 ⓦwww.poortackere.com. This unusual hotel-cum-guesthouse occupies a rambling former monastery dating from the nineteenth century. Guests have a choice between en suites in the hotel section and the more authentic monastic-cell experience in the guest house, either en suite or shared facilities. Located five minutes' walk west of Veldstraat. ❻

Cafés and restaurants

Avalon Geldmunt 32. Vegetarian restaurant offering a wide range of well-prepared food served in several rooms and on the terrace in summer. Mon–Sat noon–2pm.

Brooderie Jan Breydelstraat 8. Pleasant and informal café with a health-food slant. Wholesome breakfasts, lunches, sandwiches and salads. Centrally located, near the castle. B&B above the café too (see opposite). Closed Mon.

Malatesta Korenmarkt 35. Informal, fashionable café/restaurant; modern decor and good pizza and pasta dishes at very affordable prices. Closed Tues.

Pakhuis Schuurkenstraat 4. A lively bistro-brasserie occupying an old warehouse down a narrow alley near St Michielsbrug with acres of glass and metal. Offers an extensive menu – Flemish and French and beyond. Good for just a drink too. Closed Sun.

Bars and clubs

Bardot Oude Beestenmarkt 8. This new hip venue is one of the top places in town. Regular DJs offer house, techno and plenty of the newest sounds. Wed–Sat 8pm–5am.

't Dreupelkot Groentenmarkt 10. Cosy bar specializing in jenever, of which it stocks more than 100 brands. Down a little alley, next door to the famous *Het Waterhuis* (see p.100).

Pink Flamingos Onderstraat 55. Weird, wonderful and the height of kitsch – film stars, religion, Barbie-dolls; if it's cheesy it's somewhere in the decor. Great place for an aperitif or one of their large selection of cocktails.

De Tap en de Tepel Gewad 7. Charming, candlelit bar with an open fire and a clutter of antique furnishings. Wine is the main deal here, served with a good selection of cheeses. Wed–Sat from noon.

Het Waterhuis aan de Bierkant Groentenmarkt 9. More than 100 types of beer are available in this engaging, canal-side bar near the castle. Popular with tourists and locals alike.

Bruges (Brugge)

BRUGES's reputation as one of the most perfectly preserved medieval cities in Europe has made it the most popular tourist destination in Belgium, packed with visitors throughout the summer. Inevitably, the crowds tend to overwhelm the city's charms, but you would be mad to come to Flanders and miss the place – its intimate, winding streets, woven around a pattern of narrow canals and lined with ancient buildings, live up to even the most inflated hype.

Bruges boomed throughout the Middle Ages, sharing effective control of the **cloth trade** with its two great rivals, Ghent and Ieper (Ypres), its weavers turning English wool into items of clothing that were exported all over the world. It was an immensely profitable business and at its height the town was one of the richest in Europe. By the end of the fifteenth century, though, Bruges was in decline, partly because of a recession in the cloth trade, but principally because the Zwin river – the city's vital link to the North Sea – was silting up. By the 1530s its sea trade had collapsed completely, and Bruges simply withered away. Frozen in time, the city escaped damage in both world wars.

The City

The older sections of Bruges fan out from two central squares, Markt and Burg. **Markt**, edged on three sides by nineteenth-century gabled buildings, is the larger of the two, an impressive open space flanked on its south side by the mighty **Belfort** (Belfry; Tues–Sun 9.30am–5pm; €5), built in the thirteenth century when the town was at its richest and most extravagant. The belfry is attached to the rectangular **Hallen**, a much-restored edifice dating from the thirteenth century, its style and structure modelled on the cloth hall at Ieper. Entry to the Belfry is via the Hallen and inside a tapering staircase leads up to the roof after a very long haul.

From the Markt, Breidelstraat leads through to **Burg**, whose southern half is fringed by the city's finest group of buildings. One of the best is the **Heilig Bloed Basiliek** (Basilica of the Holy Blood; April–Sept daily 9.30am–noon & 2–6pm; Oct–March daily 10am–noon & 2–4pm, Wed 10am–noon only; free), named after a phial of the blood of Christ brought back here from Jerusalem by the Crusaders, and one of the holiest relics in medieval Christendom. The basilica divides into a shadowy Lower Chapel, built to house another relic, that of St Basil, and an Upper Chapel where the phial is stored in a grandiose silver tabernacle. The Holy Blood is still venerated on Ascension Day, when it is carried through the town in a colourful but solemn procession.

To the left of the basilica, the **Stadhuis** has a beautiful, turreted sandstone facade, a much-copied exterior that dates from 1376. Inside, the magnificent **Gothic Hall** of 1400 (Tues–Sun 9.30am–5pm; €2.50) is well worth a look for its ornate decoration. The price of admission covers entry to the former alderman's mansion, the **Renaissancezaal 't Brugse Vrije** (Tues–Sun 9.30am–12.30pm & 1.30–5pm), also on the square; it has just one exhibit: an enormous sixteenth-century marble and oak chimney piece carved in honour of the ruling Habsburgs.

A €15 **combined ticket** for six of Bruges' central museums – the Arentshuis, Groeninge, Gruuthuse, Memling, Renaissancezaal 't Brugse Vrije, and Stadhuis – is available at any of them, as well as from the tourist office.

Heading south from the Burg, through the archway next to the Stadhuis, it's a brief walk to both the eighteenth-century **Vismarkt** and the huddle of picturesque houses that make up **Huidenvettersplein**. Close by, Dijver follows the canal to the **Groeninge Museum** at no. 12 (Tues–Sun 9.30am–5pm; €7), which houses a superb sample of Flemish paintings from the fourteenth to twentieth centuries. The best section is the early Flemish work, including several canvases by Jan van Eyck, who lived and worked in Bruges from 1430 until his death eleven years later. There's also work by Hieronymus Bosch and Gerard David. Further along, at no. 17, the **Gruuthuse Museum** (Tues–Sun 9.30am–5pm; €5), sited in a rambling fifteenth-century mansion, has a varied collection of fine and applied art, including intricately carved altar pieces and many different types of antique furniture. Beyond, the **Onze Lieve Vrouwekerk** (Tues–Sat 9.30am–12.30pm & 1.30–5pm, Sun 1.30–5pm; free) is a massive shambles of different dates and styles, among whose treasures is a delicate marble *Madonna and Child* by Michelangelo, an influential early work brought from Tuscany by a Flemish merchant. The chancel (€2.50) is home to the **mausoleums** of Charles the Bold and

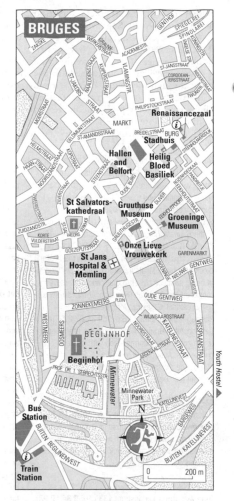

his daughter Mary of Burgundy, both striking examples of Renaissance carving.

Opposite the church, the large medieval ward of **St Jans Hospitaal** (Tues–Sun 9.30am–5pm; €7) has been turned into a lavish museum celebrating the city's history in general and St John's hospital in particular. In addition, the old hospital chapel displays a small but exquisite collection of paintings by **Hans Memling**. Born near Frankfurt in 1433, Memling spent most of his working life in Bruges, producing serene but warmly coloured and stunningly beautiful paintings. From St Jans, it's a quick stroll down to the **Begijnhof** (daily 9am–6pm), a circle of whitewashed houses around a tidy green. Nearby, the picturesque **Minnewater** was once used as a town harbour, and still has a little lock gate.

Practicalities

Bruges **train station** adjoins the **bus station** about 2km southwest of the centre. Local **buses** leave from outside the train station for the main square, the Markt. Inside the train station is a tourist office (Mon–Sat 10am–6pm; ☎050 44 86 86) which concentrates on hotel reservations. The main **tourist office** is in the centre at Burg 11 (April–Sept Mon–Fri 9.30am–6.30pm, Sat & Sun 10am–noon & 2–6.30pm; Oct–March Mon–Fri 9.30am–5pm, Sat & Sun 9.30am–1pm & 2–5.30pm; ☎050 44 86 86, ⊛www.brugge.be); it, too, offers an accommodation-booking service. If you're arriving in July or August, be sure to **book ahead** or, at a pinch, make sure you get here in the morning. Given the crush, many visitors book through the tourist office – it only costs a few euros and can save you a lot of hassle. Most of the city's **restaurants** and **cafés** are geared up for tourists, churning out some pretty mediocre stuff. Exceptions, including the places we recommend below, are well worth seeking out. There's also a very good range of **bars**, the pick of which sell a wide range of Belgian beers.

Hostels

Bauhaus International Youth Hotel Langestraat 135 ☎050 34 10 93, ⊛www.bauhaus.be. Laid-back hostel with dorms sleeping up to eight and a mishmash of doubles and triples. There's bike rental, currency exchange and coin-operated lockers. Situated fifteen minutes' walk east of the Burg, next to the *Bauhaus Hotel* (see below). Dorm beds €15.

Charlie Rockets Hoogstraat 19 ☎050 33 06 60, ⊛www.charlierockets.com. New kid on the hostel block, this place steals a march on its rivals by dint of being so much closer to the Markt. Has eleven rooms on two floors above a busy American-style bar. Breakfast €2 extra. Dorm beds from €14.

Passage Dweersstraat 26 ☎050 34 02 32. The best hostel in Bruges. Accommodates fifty people in ten comfortable rooms, each with shared bathrooms. About ten minutes' walk west of the Markt. The *Passage Hotel* next door is also a bargain (see below). Dorms €14.

Private rooms

Salvators Korte Vulderstraat 7 ☎050 33 19 21, ⊛www.hotelsalvators.be. This smart place offers three rooms, two en suite, in an attractive, well-maintained, three-storey brick house. Central location. ❼

Hotels

Bauhaus Hotel Langestraat 133 ☎050 34 10 93, ⊛www.bauhaus.be. Twenty rooms with shared facilities, plus one en suite. Don't expect too much in the way of creature comforts, but the atmosphere is usually agreeable and the clientele friendly. ❸

Cordoeanier Cordoeaniersstraat 18 ☎050 33 90 51, ⊛www.cordoeanier.be. Medium-sized, family-run hotel handily located in the narrow side streets a couple of minutes north of the Burg. Mosquitoes can be a problem here, but the small rooms are clean and pleasant. ❺

Jacobs Baliestraat 1 ☎050 33 98 31, ⊛www.hoteljacobs.be. Pleasant hotel in a creatively modernized old brick building complete with a precipitous crowstep gable. Occupies a quiet location in one of the more attractive parts of the centre, a ten-minute walk to the northeast of the Markt. ❺

Passage Hotel Dweersstraat 28 ☎050 34 02 32. Ten simple but well-maintained rooms – four en suite – ten minutes' stroll west of the Markt. It's a very popular spot, so advance booking is essential. Also has a busy bar that's a favourite with backpackers. ❸

Cafés and restaurants

Het Dagelijks Brood Philipstockstraat 21. Excellent bread shop which doubles as a wholefood café. Mouth-watering homemade soup and bread makes a meal in itself for just €7, or you can chomp away on a range of snacks and cakes. Handy location, just off the Burg. Closed Tues.

Gran Kaffee de Passage Dweersstraat 26. This lively café is extremely popular with backpackers, many of whom have bunked down in the nearby *Passage Hostel* (see above). Serves up a good and filling line in Flemish food with many dishes cooked in beer. Mussels are featured, too, along with vegetarian options.

Lokkedize Korte Vulderstraat 33. Sympathetic bar/café, all subdued lighting, fresh flowers and jazz music, serving up a good line in Mediterranean food. Closed Sun & Mon.

De Vlaamsche Pot Helmstraat 3–5. Informal and friendly, this restaurant, with its cosy furnishings and fittings, is justifiably popular. The menu is confined to a few traditional Flemish dishes, each competently prepared; excellent value.

Bars

Het Brugs Beertje Kemelstraat 5. Small and friendly speciality beer bar that claims a stock of 300 beers. Five minutes' walk southwest of the Markt, off Steenstraat. Closed Wed.

Cohiba Zilverstraat 38. Idiosyncratic bar popular with a fashionable, thirty-something crew. Closed Sun & Mon.

Het Dreupelhuisje Kemelstraat 9. Tiny and eminently agreeable, laid-back bar specializing in jenevers and advocaats, of which it has an outstanding range. Closed Tues.
Oud Vlissinghe Blekerstraat 2. With its wood panelling, antique paintings and long wooden tables, this is one of the oldest and most distinctive bars in Bruges. Relaxed and easy-going atmosphere with the emphasis on quiet conversation. Five minutes' walk from Jan van Eyckplein. Closed Mon & Tues.

De Republiek Sint-Jacobsstraat 38. Arguably one of the most fashionable and certainly one of the most popular café/bars in town with an arty, sometimes alternative crew. Filling snacks, including vegetarian and pastas.
De Vuurmolen Kraanplein 5. Not far from the Markt, this crowded bar is a lively spot with a reasonably wide range of beers and some of the best DJs in town – techno through house and beyond.

Southern Belgium

South of Brussels lies **French-speaking** Belgium, where a belt of heavy industry interrupts the rolling farmland that itself precedes the high wooded hills of the **Ardennes**. The latter spreads over three provinces – Namur in the west, Luxembourg in the south and Liège in the east – and is a great place for hiking and canoeing. The best gateway town for the Ardennes is the lively provincial centre of **Namur**, an hour from Brussels by train.

Namur

NAMUR is a pleasant and appealing town straddling the confluence of the rivers Sambre and Meuse, with the narrow streets of its antique centre dotted with elegant, eighteenth-century mansions, its nightlife lent vigour by the university. Occupying an important strategic location, it has been fought over time and again, the main result being the massive, rambling **Citadel**, which rolls along the top of the steep bluff overlooking the south bank of the Sambre. Originally constructed in medieval times, the citadel has been remodelled on several occasions and its assorted redoubts, underground passages, artillery emplacements and barracks span several centuries – and can take a couple of days to explore, though you can speed things up by taking a guided tour on the **miniature train** (June–Sept daily 11am–7pm; €6).

Cutting through the old town centre is **rue de l'Ange** and its continuation **rue de Fer**, which together comprise the main shopping street. A few metres east of here, the **Trésor du Prieuré d'Oignies**, rue Julie Billiart 17 (Treasury of the Oignies Priory; Tues–Sat 10am–noon & 2–5pm, Sun 2–5pm; €1.25), is Namur's best – and smallest – museum. Located in a nunnery, it holds a spellbinding collection of reliquaries and devotional pieces created by local craftsman Hugo d'Oignies in the first half of the thirteenth century; the nuns give the guided tour in English

Practicalities

Namur's **train** and **bus stations** are on the northern edge of the city centre, place de la Station. Close by is the **tourist office** on square Léopold, *ar.be);* end of rue de Fer (daily 9.30am–6pm; ☎081 24 64 49, ⓦwwŵ̟ʷ⁴), *There's* here, you can get advice on cycling, walking and canoeing in ʷ. *Namur has a* also a seasonal tourist information chalet (April–Sept dày *restaurants has a small sup-* utes' walk away, over the Sambre bridge on the far *quaint, pedestrianized* and a couple of budget **accommodation** options *of rue de Fer – on and* place Chanoine Descamps. ply of **private rooms** (❸). There's an ☎ *namur@laj.be. This 100-bed hostel* good supply of lively **bars**, many of *pies a big old house on the southern edge of* squares just west of rue de l'Anɡ̥ around place Marché-aux-P̟

Hostel
Auberge de Jeunesse ave F

103

town on the banks of the Meuse past the casino. There's no lock-out and the hostel has a kitchen, laundry and self-service restaurant. It's 3km from the train station; buses #3 or #4 run here from the centre. Dorm beds €13.

Hotel

Beauregard ave Baron de Moreau 1 ☎081 23 00 28. Part of Namur's casino complex, this hotel has attractive, large and modern rooms, some with a river-view and balcony. It's a ten-minute walk south of the centre, on the banks of the Meuse below the citadel. An excellent breakfast is included in the price. ⑥

Grand Hôtel de Flandre pl de la Station 14 ☎081 23 18 68. Competent if slightly dog-eared hotel directly opposite the station. ④

Opera Parisien rue Emile Cuvelier 16 ☎081 22 63 79. Adequate if uninspiring hotel in a routine modern building close to the town centre on the corner of rue Emile Cuvelier and rue Pépin. ④

Restaurants

La Bonne Fourchette rue Notre Dame 112. Pint-sized, informal and family-run restaurant down below the citadel on the way to the casino. A little off the beaten track, so the prices are very reasonable and the food is delicious. Closed Wed.

La Fondue rue St Jean 19. Medium-sized restaurant serving excellent fondues and steaks. Just off place Marché-aux-Légumes.

Le Moulin à Poivre rue Bas de la Place 23. Cosy little restaurant offering tasty French food from premises just off place d'Armes.

Bars

Le Chapitre rue du Séminaire 4. Unassuming, sedate little bar with an extensive beer list. Behind the cathedral.

Henry's Bar pl St Aubain 3. Right by the cathedral, this is a big loud brasserie in the best tradition.

Le Monde à L'Envers rue Lelièvre 28. Lively, fashionable bar just up from the cathedral. A favourite spot for university students.

Piano Bar pl Marché-aux-Légumes. One of Namur's most popular bars. Live jazz Fri & Sat from 10pm.

Luxembourg

Some 100km southeast of Namur, across the border from the Belgian province of Luxembourg, the **Grand Duchy of Luxembourg** is one of Europe's smallest sovereign states, a tiny principality with a population of around 430,000. Many travellers tend to write it off as a dull and expensive financial centre, but this is a mistake. The northern part boasts charming scenery in the green forested hills of the Ardennes and is within easy reach – by road, rail and bus – of **Luxembourg City**, the country's agreeable and dramatically sited capital, well worth one or two nights' stay. After exploring the city, the place to head for is the village of **Vianden** with its clifftop castle. Every native speaks the indigenous language, Letzebuergesch – a dialect of German that sounds a bit like Dutch – but most also speak French and German and many speak English too.

Luxembourg City

LUXEMBOURG CITY is one of the most spectacularly sited capitals in Europe. The valleys of the rivers Alzette and Pétrusse, which meet here, cut a green swathe in the city, their deep canyons once key to the city's defences, but now providing a beautiful setting. It's a tiny place, and divides into three distinct sections. The **old town**, appealing of the northern side of the Pétrusse valley, is not noticeably ancient, but is very appealing: a tight grid of streets holds most of the city's sights. On the opposite side of the train station, accessible by the **modern city** – less attractive and of interest only for its parkland, banks and hotels. The **valleys** themselves, far below and most easily The **Old Town**, fringed with Esprit, are a curious mixture of houses, allotments and d'Armes, mainly along G... e massive bastions that secure the old town. shops, ... to the larger pl... uares, the more important of which is **place** through to the larger pl... rants. To the north lie the city's principal market (Wed & Fri am). ...n the southern side a small alley cuts ... ue of Luxembourg's main general

Not far away, a group of patrician mansions on Marché aux Poissons holds the city's largest museum, the **Musée National d'Histoire et d'Art** (Tues–Sun 10am–5pm; €5), where there's an enjoyable sample of fifteenth- and sixteenth-century Dutch and Flemish paintings. East of the museum lie the **Casements du Bock** (daily March–Oct 10am–5pm; €1.75), underground fortifications built by the Spaniards in the eighteenth century. The city occupies an ideal defensive position and its defences were reinforced on many occasions – hence the massive bastions and subterranean artillery galleries of today. These particular casements are the most diverting to visit – though several others are also open throughout the summer – and afterwards you can follow the dramatic **chemin de la Corniche**, which tracks along the side of the cliff with great views of the slate-roofed houses of **Grund** down below. It leads to the gigantic **Citadelle du St-Esprit**, whose top has been levelled off and part turned into a leafy park.

LUXEMBOURG CITY

Practicalities

The **train station**, fifteen minutes' walk south of the centre, is the hub of all city **bus** lines and close to many of the city's cheapest (but plainest) hotels. There is a branch of the national **tourist office** inside the station (June–Sept Mon–Sat 9am–7pm, Sun 9am–12.30pm & 2–6pm; Oct–May daily 9.15am–12.30pm & 1.45–6pm; ☎42 82 82 20; ⊛www.ont.lu). It sells the **Luxembourg Card**, which entitles you to unlimited use of public transport throughout the Grand Duchy and admission to selected museums and attractions from Easter to October (1/2/3 days for €9/16/22). The central **tourist office**, on place d'Armes (April–Sept Mon–Sat 9am–7pm, Sun 10am–6pm; Oct–March Mon–Sat 9am–6pm, Sun 10am–6pm; ☎22 28 09; ⊛www.luxembourg-city.lu/touristinfo) deals only with the city. Walking is the best way of getting around.

Most **hotels** are clustered near the train station, which is the least interesting part of town. You're much better off staying in the Old Town and won't necessarily pay much more to do so, though you're limited to just a handful of places. The Old Town is crowded with inexpensive **cafés** and **restaurants**. French cuisine is popular here, but traditional Luxembourgish dishes are found on many menus too, mostly meaty affairs such as neck of pork with broad beans (*judd mat gaardebounen*) or black sausage (*blutwurst*). Keep an eye out also for *Gromperenkichelchen* (potato cakes usually served with apple sauce) – and, in winter, stalls and cafés selling *Glühwein* (mulled wine). As for **nightlife**, there's a lively bar and club scene, with bars in the Old Town and Grund, and clubs mostly west of the train station in Hollerich.

Hostel
Luxembourg Auberge de Jeunesse rue du Fort Olisy 2 ☎ 22 68 89, ✆ luxembourg@youthhostels.lu. This barracks-like HI hostel is 3km northeast of the station on the edge of the centre in the Alzette valley; take bus #9. It has a laundry and cooking facilities and breakfast is included. Dorms €16.

Hotels
Francais place d'Armes 14 ☎ 47 45 34 ✆ hfinfo@pt.lu. This attractive place has smart and spotless rooms furnished in a crisp modern style. Great location, too, on the Old Town's main square. ❽
Schintgen rue Notre Dame 6 ☎ 22 28 44, ✆ schintgen@pt.lu. Bang in the middle of the Old Town, this simple, unassuming hotel is short on accessories, but it is reasonably priced. ❻

Cafés and restaurants
Brasserie Chimay rue Chimay 15. Small, pleasantly old-fashioned café/restaurant off place d'Armes. Traditional, straightforward dishes at inexpensive prices.
Francais pl d'Armes 14. The pavement café of the *Hotel Francais* offers tasty salads and a wide-ranging menu including several Luxembourgish favourites. Excellent value daily specials.
Giorgio's Pizzeria rue du Nord 11. A sociable and eminently fashionable place tucked away off côte d'Eich in the Old Town. Closed Sun.
Maison des Brasseurs Grande Rue 48. On a modern shopping street just to the north of place d'Armes, this long-established and smartly decorated restaurant sells delicious Luxembourgish dishes. Sauerkraut is the house speciality. Closed Sun.

Nightlife
Chiggeri rue du Nord 15. Groovy bar in the Old Town that has a great atmosphere, funky decor and a mixed straight and gay clientele.
Conquest rue du Palais de Justice 7. Gay club in the Old Town. House music. Closed Sun.
Sodaz Café Bar rue de la Boucherie 16. Small and crowded bar featuring cocktails plus soul and rock.

Listings
Bike rental rue Bisserwé 8, Grund (☎ 47 96 23 83; €10/day, discounts for under-26s; advance booking advised).
Internet Chiggeri, rue du Nord 15.
Laundry Quick-Wash, rue de Strasbourg 31 (☎ 48 78 33).

Left luggage At the train station.
Pharmacies Goedert, pl d'Armes 5; Mortier, ave de la Gare 11.
Post office pl E. Hamilius (Mon–Fri 7am–7pm, Sat 7am–5pm).

Travel details

Trains

Antwerp to: Bruges (hourly; 1hr 20min); Brussels (every 30min; 40min); Ghent (every 30min; 50min); Ostend (hourly; 1hr 40min).
Bruges to: Antwerp (hourly; 1hr 20min); Brussels (every 30min; 1hr); Ostend (every 20min; 15min); Zeebrugge (hourly; 15min).
Brussels to: Antwerp (every 30min; 40min); Bruges (every 30min; 1hr); Ghent (every 30min; 40min); Luxembourg City (every 2hr; 2hr 30min); Namur (hourly; 50min); Ostend (hourly; 1hr 20min).
Ghent Antwerp (every 30min; 50min); Bruges (every 20min; 25min); Brussels (every 30min; 40min); Ostend (every 30min; 50min).
Luxembourg City to: Brussels (hourly; 2hr 30min); Namur (hourly; 1hr 40min).
Namur to: Brussels (hourly; 50min); Luxembourg City (hourly; 1hr 40min).
Ostend to: Antwerp (hourly; 1hr 40min); Bruges (every 20min; 15min); Brussels (hourly; 1hr 20min); Ghent (every 30min; 50min).

Ferries

For information, see p.15.

Britain

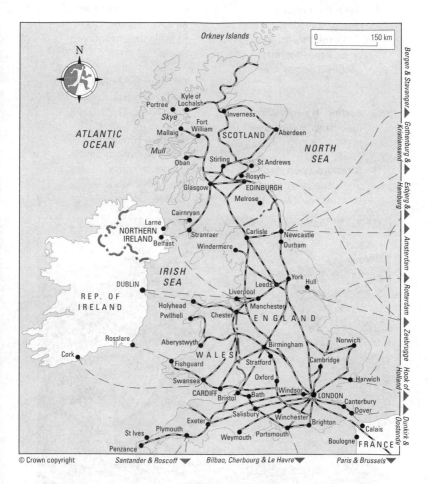

Orkney Islands

0   150 km

ATLANTIC
OCEAN

Portree   Kyle of Lochalsh
Skye   Inverness
Mallaig   Fort William
Mull   SCOTLAND   Aberdeen
Oban   Stirling   St Andrews
  Rosyth
Glasgow   EDINBURGH
  Melrose
Cairnryan

NORTH SEA

NORTHERN IRELAND
Larne
Stranraer   Carlisle   Newcastle
Belfast   Windermere   Durham

IRISH SEA

DUBLIN
REP. OF IRELAND
Holyhead   Leeds   York   Hull
Pwllheli   Liverpool
  Chester   Manchester
  E N G L A N D
Rosslare   Aberystwyth   Birmingham   Norwich
Cork   W A L E S
Fishguard   Stratford   Cambridge
Swansea   Oxford   Harwich
CARDIFF   Bath   Windsor   LONDON
Bristol   Canterbury
Exeter   Salisbury   Winchester   Brighton   Dover
St Ives   Plymouth   Weymouth   Portsmouth   Calais
Penzance   Boulogne   F R A N C E

Bergen & Stavanger ▶
Gothenburg & Kristiansand ▶
Esbjerg & Hamburg ▶
Amsterdam ▶ Rotterdam ▶ Zeebrugge ▶ Hook of Holland ▶
Dunkirk & Oostende ▶

© Crown copyright   Santander & Roscoff ▼   Bilbao, Cherbourg & Le Havre ▼   Paris & Brussels ▼

Britain highlights

Tate Modern London's new modern-art gallery, spectacularly housed in a former power station. See p.121

Eden Project Disused clay pit turned hothouse, with exotic plants and crops housed in vast geodesic domes. See p.138

Surfing, Newquay Test the Atlantic rollers. See p.140

Stratford-upon-Avon Shakespeare's home town and host to the world-renowned RSC. See p.143

Snowdonia Craggy Welsh range that offers hiking and climbing opportunities, including an ascent of the country's highest mountain. See p.164

Edinburgh Festival The world's biggest arts festival. See p.171

Scottish Highlands Dramatic, moody landscapes in some of the last wildernesses in Europe. See p.177

Introduction and basics

The single most important thing to remember when travelling round **Britain*** is that you're visiting not one country, but three: England, Wales and Scotland. That means contending with three capital cities (London, Cardiff and Edinburgh) and three sets of national identity – not to mention the myriad accent shifts as you move between them.

England remains the dominant and most urbanized member of the British partnership, but crossing the border into predominantly rural **Wales** brings you into an unmistakably Celtic land, while in **Scotland** (a nation whose absorption into the state was rather more recent) the presence of a profoundly non-English world view is striking.

For cultural sightseeing as for nightlife, **London** is a ceaselessly entertaining city, and is the one place that features on everyone's itinerary. Within the heavily built-up southeast, **Brighton** and **Canterbury** offer contrasting diversions – the former an appealing seaside resort, the latter one of Britain's finest medieval cities. The southwest of England, with the rugged moorlands of **Devon** and the rocky coastline of **Cornwall**, is an altogether wilder region, albeit one that pulls in droves of visitors in the height of summer. The chief attractions of central England are the university cities of **Oxford** and **Cambridge**, and Shakespeare's home town, **Stratford-upon-Avon**. Further north, the former industrial cities of **Manchester**, **Liverpool** and **Newcastle** are lively places, and **York** has splendid historical treasures, but the landscape is again the real magnet, especially the uplands of the **Lake District**. For true wilderness, however, you're better off heading to the **Welsh mountains** or **Scottish Highlands**. The

finest of Scotland's lochs, glens and peaks, and the magnificent scenery of the west coast islands, can be reached easily from the contrasting cities of **Glasgow** and **Edinburgh** – the latter perhaps Britain's most attractive urban landscape.

Information & maps

Tourist information centres (TICs) exist in virtually every British town, offering a basic range of maps and information. In many cases this is free, but a growing number make a small charge for an accommodation list or a town guide. Some have also switched to using very expensive ☏09-prefixed phone numbers; in these cases, it's cheaper to look for information online. National Parks also have their own information centres, which are better for guidance on outdoor pursuits. The most comprehensive series of **maps** is produced by the Ordnance Survey (⊛www.ordnancesurvey.co.uk), who cover the whole country at 1:50,000 and 1:25,000.

Money and banks

Britain is one of the few EU countries *not* to have embraced the euro: the **pound** (£) ster-

---

Britain on the net

⊛**www.visitbritain.com** Tourist board site with links to regional sites.
⊛**www.pti.org.uk** Information on public transport.
⊛**www.backpackers.co.uk** The low-down on independent hostels.
⊛**www.knowhere.co.uk** Irreverent local knowledge.
⊛**www.multimap.com** Town plans and area maps.

---

* "Britain" is a geographical term, referring to the largest of the British Isles. "United Kingdom" is a political term, referring to a state comprising England, Scotland, Wales and Northern Ireland. Northern Ireland is covered with the rest of the island of Ireland in Chapter 14.

ling, divided into 100 pence, remains the national currency. There are coins of 1p, 2p, 5p, 10p, 20p, 50p, £1 and £2; and notes of £5, £10, £20 and £50; notes issued by Scottish banks (including a £1 note) are legal tender throughout the UK. Normal **banking hours** are Mon–Fri 9.30am–4.30pm, but some branches open on Sat. Most banks have **ATMs** that accept a wide range of debit and credit cards.

Communications

Post offices are usually open Mon–Fri 9am–5.30pm, Sat 9am–12.30/1pm, though some town-centre offices may have extended hours. Most public **phones** are operated by BT, though you'll also see other companies' boxes in a variety of designs. Most BT phones take all coins from 10p upwards (minimum charge 20p), as well as £5, £10 or £20 **phonecards**, available from post offices and newsagents. An increasing number accept credit cards too. Newsagents can sell you good-value cards from other phone companies for making **international** calls. **Domestic** calls are cheapest from 6pm to 8am and at weekends; calls to numbers starting ☎084 are charged at local rate; ☎087 at long-distance rate; those starting ☎080 are free; ☎07 and ☎09 are very expensive. For the operator, call ☎100 (domestic) or ☎155 (international); of several directory enquiry lines, BT's is ☎118500. **Internet cafés** are common, and you'll also find access at some hostels and some public phones. Prices vary, but £1 should be enough for you to reply to your email.

Getting around

Public transport has been shaken up by large-scale privatization in recent years, but most places are still accessible by **train** and/or **coach** (as long-distance buses are known), though costs are among the highest in Europe. **Traveline** (☎0870/608 2608, daily 8am–8pm; ☻www.traveline.org.uk) is a national service that can advise about trains, coaches, ferries and, most usefully, local buses.

Trains

Following privatization, standard train **fares** have become extremely expensive. Britain is in **InterRail** Zone A, but **Eurail** passes aren't valid here; for details of other passes, see p.35. Cheap deals for train travel do exist, but the bafflingly complicated pricing system makes them hard to find. Generally speaking, avoid rush hours (especially Fri eve), and book your ticket as far in advance as you can to get the best deals, often **saver**, **supersaver**, **apex** or **superapex** tickets. Always ask the person selling you your ticket to specify the cheapest options open to you; if you don't, there's a good chance you'll end up paying the so-called "**standard fare**", which allows more flexibility as to when you can travel but is often twice the price of other tickets on the same route. If you're travelling on routes between major cities at busy times, especially during public holidays or around Christmas, you should **book a seat**. Reservations are usually free if made at the same time as ticket purchase, although on some routes you'll have to pay an extra £1. National Rail (☎0845/748 4950, ☻www.nationalrail.co.uk) has details of all train services; or you can buy online at ☻www.thetrainline.com.

Coaches and buses

The **coach** services run by **National Express** (☎0870/580 8080, ☻www.nationalexpress.com) duplicate many intercity rail routes, very often at half the price or less. The frequency of service is often comparable to rail, though the journey time is generally longer. If you're a student, under 26 or over 50 you can buy a National Express Coachcard (£10), which gives up to thirty percent off standard fares. Their Tourist Trail Pass offers unlimited travel for two days in three (£49; £39 with a Coachcard), or five (£85/£69), eight (£135/£99) or fifteen (£190/£145) days in thirty, or fifteen days in sixty (£205/£160). Both the Coachcard and Pass are valid on National Express through-routes to Scotland, but not on services within Scotland itself. These are provided by the sister company **Scottish Citylink** (☎0870/550 5050, ☻www.citylink.co.uk), which has its own Explorer Pass for three consecutive days (£39), five days in ten (£59) or eight days in sixteen (£85); their discount card for students, under-26s and over-50s (£7) gives up to twenty percent off standard fares. **Local bus** services are run by a bewildering array of companies, some private, some not. As a rule, the further away from urban areas you get, the less frequent bus services become, but there are very few rural areas which aren't served by at least the occasional minibus.

Accommodation

Budget **accommodation** isn't hard to come by in Britain. Many tourist offices will book rooms for you, whether in the locality or in other towns (the "Book a Bed Ahead" service), but you should generally expect to pay a small fee for this service, as well as putting down a ten-percent deposit on your first night's stay.

Hotels in Britain are generally of a high quality but are also expensive – in tourist cities it's hard to find a double for less than £50 a night. Fortunately, there's a wide range of budget accommodation in the form of **guest houses** and **B&Bs** – often a comfortable room in a family home, plus a substantial breakfast, from around £15 a head (a bit more in the affluent south, and a lot more in London).

Britain has an extensive network of **HI hostels** (see p.39 for their websites). In Scotland, a bed for the night can cost as little as £4, except in the cities, where you might pay more than twice that. In England and Wales charges start at around £8. **Privately run hostels** are generally of a comparable standard and can be several pounds cheaper. There are more than 750 official **campsites** in Britain, charging from around £5 per tent per night. In the countryside farmers will let you camp in a field if you ask, sometimes charging a couple of pounds. Camping rough is illegal in designated parkland and nature reserves.

Food and drink

British **food** has long had a poor reputation, but things have been changing in recent years, thanks chiefly to the inspiration of Britain's ethnic communities. Social life,

however, has always focused more on **drinking** than eating, and a pub is often the best introduction to the life of a town.

Food

In many B&Bs you'll be offered an "**English breakfast**" – basically sausage, bacon and fried eggs – although most places will give you the option of cereal, toast and fruit as well. Every major town will have upmarket restaurants, but for most visitors the quintessential British meal is **fish and chips**, a dish that can vary from the succulently fresh to the indigestibly greasy. However, the once ubiquitous fish-and-chip shop ("chippy") is now outnumbered on Britain's high streets by pizza, kebab and burger joints. Less threatened is the so-called "**greasy spoon**", generally a down-at-heel diner where the average menu will include high-cholesterol variations on sausages, fried eggs, bacon and chips.

Many **pubs** also serve food, often at lunchtime only; menus may consist of dishes such as steak-and-kidney pie, shepherd's pie (minced lamb topped with potato), chops or steaks, accompanied by potatoes and veg, but the range and quality is improving and some so-called **gastro-pubs** can offer menus to rival any restaurant. There's also an increasing number of **vegetarian** restaurants, especially in the larger towns, but most places – including pubs – will make some attempt to cater for vegetarians.

For sit-down dining, though, the innumerable outlets for **non-British cuisine** offer the best-value meals. In every town of any size you'll find Chinese, Indian (the "curry house" has become a national institution to rival the chippy) and Italian eateries, and more – from Caribbean to Thai – with London and the industrial cities of the north holding the widest choice and the finest quality.

Drink

Drinking traditionally takes place in the **pub**, where a standard range of draught **beers** – sold by the pint or half-pint – generates most of the business, although imported bottled beers are also popular. Beers fall into two distinct groups: cold, blond, fizzy lager and the very different darker ale, or bitter, which is flat, served at room temperature and varies in taste from brewer to brewer. In England, pubs are generally open Mon–Sat 11am–11pm, Sun noon–10.30pm (though some close daily 3–5.30pm); hours are often longer in Scotland, while Sun closing is common in Wales. In bigger towns there's an increasing number of wine bars and European-style cafés, which also serve food.

In Scotland, the national drink is of course **whisky**, a spirit of far greater subtlety than bland mass-marketed blended whiskies might lead you to believe. The best are the single malts, produced by often very small distilleries from local spring water.

Opening hours and holidays

General **shop hours** are Mon–Sat 9am–5.30/6pm, although an increasing number of places in big towns are also open Sun (usually 10am–4pm) and till 7/8pm at least once a week. Many small towns still have an "early closing day" when shops close at 1pm (often Wed or Thurs). In England and Wales, **public holidays** ("bank holidays") are: Jan 1; Good Fri; Easter Mon; first Mon in May; last Mon in May; last Mon in Aug; Christmas Day and Boxing Day (Dec 25 & 26). In Scotland, Jan 1, Jan 2 & Dec 25 are the only fixed public holidays – otherwise towns are left to pick their own holidays.

Museums and monuments

Many of Britain's national **museums** are free, but stately homes and monuments are often administered by the state-run **English Heritage** (given as **EH** in opening times through this chapter; ®www.english-heritage.org.uk) and **Historic Scotland** (**HS**; ®www.historic-scotland.gov.uk); while in Wales **CADW** (®www.cadw.wales .gov.uk) owns several dramatic ruins. The trio run a joint membership scheme – if you join one, admission to sites run by the other two is half-price for the first year – good value if you intend to visit more than

half-a-dozen. The annual fee for EH is £34 (£15 if you're under 19 or a student), for HS £30 (£23 if you're a full-time student). CADW's Explorer Pass (3 days £9.50, 7 days £15.50) is more likely to be useful than annual membership. The privately run **National Trust** (**NT**; ®www.nationaltrust .org.uk) and **National Trust for Scotland** (**NTS**; ®www.nts.org.uk) also run a large number of gardens and stately homes nationwide; annual membership of NT/NTS costs £34/£32 (£15.50/£12 for under-26s), and each pass is recognized by the other. All these let you join at any of their properties. The **Great British Heritage Pass**, which covers sites administered by all the organizations above and many others too, is worth considering; it's available from the British Visitor Centre, Lower Regent St, London, and selected tourist information centres (7/15/30 days £35/46/60; ®www.visitbritain.com for details), as well as worldwide agents. All but the biggest **churches** are free, although most charge for access to towers, museums, cloisters and the like, and nearly all request donations.

Emergencies

Police remain approachable and helpful. Tourists aren't a particular target for criminals except perhaps in the crowds of central London, where you should be on your guard against pickpockets. Britain's bigger conurbations all contain inner-city areas where you may feel uneasy after dark, but these are usually away from tourist sights. **Pharmacists** can dispense only a limited range of drugs without a doctor's prescription. Most are open standard shop hours, though in large towns some may stay open as late as 10pm. Local newspapers carry lists of **late-opening** pharmacies. For complaints that require immediate attention, go to the accident and emergency (A&E) department of a local **hospital**.

Emergency numbers

Police, fire & ambulance ☎999.

London

With a population of just under eight million, **LONDON** is Europe's biggest city, spreading over an area of more than 1500sq km from its core on the River Thames. This is where the country's news and money are made, and if Londoners' sense of superiority causes some resentment in the regions, it's undeniable that the city has a unique aura of excitement and success. However, all this comes at a price; with high accommodation and transport costs, this is one of the most expensive cities in the world.

London is a thrilling place to visit. Thanks to the national lottery and the millennium-oriented funding frenzy of the last few years, virtually every one of London's world-class museums, galleries and institutions has been reinvented, from the British Museum to the Tate Modern, and the vast majority are free of charge. London also boasts the world's largest observation wheel and the first new bridge to cross the Thames for over a hundred years. Of course, the traditional sights – from Big Ben to the Tower of London – continue to draw in millions of tourists every year. Yet there's also much enjoyment to be had from the city's Georgian squares, riverside walks and its sizeable, very central parks: Hyde Park, Green Park and St James's – not to mention Hampstead Heath, Greenwich and Kew on the periphery.

The **Romans** founded the town of Londinium on the north bank of the Thames soon after invading Britain in 43 AD, but the city's expansion didn't really begin until the eleventh century, when the last successful invader of Britain, **William of Normandy**, became in 1066 the first king of England to be crowned in Westminster Abbey. Subsequent monarchs left their imprint, but many of the city's finest structures were destroyed in a few days in 1666, when the **Great Fire of London** razed over 13,000 houses and nearly ninety churches. Christopher Wren was commissioned to replace much of the lost architecture, and rose to the challenge by designing such masterpieces as St Paul's Cathedral. Unfortunately, only a portion of the post-Fire splendours has survived, due partly to the bombing raids of the **Blitz** in World War II and partly to some equally disfiguring postwar development. However, the special atmosphere comes less from the look of the streets than from the life on its streets. This has been a multicultural city since at least the seventeenth century, when it was a haven for Huguenot (French Protestant) refugees. Today, London is by far Europe's most **multicultural city**, continuing to absorb immigrant communities from all over the world.

Arrival and information

Flying into London, you'll arrive at one of the capital's five **international airports**: Heathrow, Gatwick or Stansted (@www.baa.com), Luton (@www.london-luton.com) or City (@www.londoncityairport.com). From **Heathrow**, fifteen miles west, the Piccadilly Line underground runs to central London in about an hour (£3.70), or there are Heathrow Express trains to Paddington Station (every 15min; 15min; £13 single, £23 return). There's also National Express coach service to Victoria Coach Station (every 30min; 45min; £7) or Airbus #2 which goes to several central destinations terminating at Euston (every 30min; 1hr 30min; £8 single, £12 return). After midnight, night bus #N9 runs to Trafalgar Square (every 30min; 55min; £1). **Gatwick**, thirty miles south, is connected by several train companies: the Gatwick Express speeds to Victoria Station (every 15–30min; 35min; £11), although South Central trains on the same route are cheaper (every 15–30min; 40min; £8.20), and Thameslink trains run to Blackfriars and King's Cross (Mon–Sat every 15–30min; 45min; around £10). **Stansted**, 34 miles northeast, is served by Stansted Express trains to Liverpool Street Station (every 15–30min; 45min; £13 single, £23 return). Airbus #6 runs to Victoria Coach Station (every 30min; 1hr 30min; £8 single, £12 return). From **Luton**, 37 miles north, free buses shuttle to Luton Airport Parkway station, from where there are Thameslink trains to King's

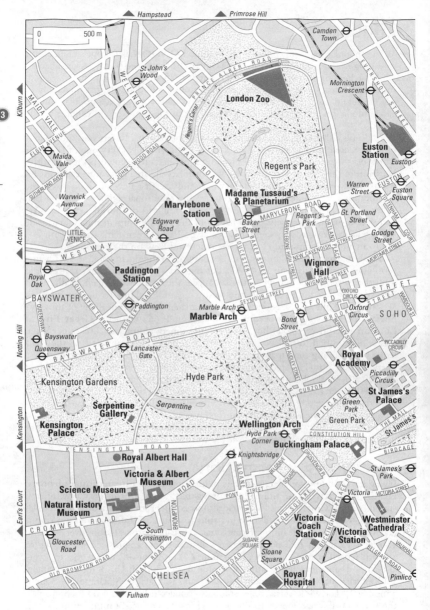

Cross and Blackfriars stations and Midland Mainline trains to St Pancras Station (every 15min; 25–50min; £11 single, £20 return). Green Line bus #757 runs from the airport terminal into central London (every 30min; 1hr 15min; £8). From **London City**, ten miles east, there's a green shuttle bus (£2.50) to Canning Town underground station, or a blue shuttle bus to Liverpool Street Station (£6).

Eurostar **trains** from Paris or Brussels through the Channel Tunnel terminate at

Waterloo. Trains from the English Channel ports arrive at Victoria, Liverpool Street or Charing Cross stations, while those from elsewhere in Britain come into one of London's numerous mainline termini (most important are Paddington or Waterloo from the west, Euston or King's Cross from the north, Liverpool Street from the east), all of which have tube stations. **Buses** from around Britain and continental Europe arrive at Victoria Coach Station, 500m walk south of Victoria Station.

London is divided up by area **postcodes**, used by everyone to locate addresses. It's an arcane system that's difficult for first-time visitors to pick up, but here are a few central districts: W1 is the "West End", comprising Soho, Mayfair and Marylebone; WC1 is Bloomsbury; WC2 covers Leicester Square and Covent Garden.

Information

London Tourist Board (LTB, ⊛www.londontown.com) has a desk in the "Heathrow Terminals 1, 2 & 3" tube station (daily 8am–6pm), but the main central office is near Piccadilly in the **British Visitor Centre**, 1 Regent St (Mon–Fri 9/9.30am–6.30pm, Sat & Sun 10am–4pm; Aug & Sept same times except Sat 9am–5pm; ⊛www.visitbritain.com). There are also offices at Waterloo International (daily 8.30am–10.30pm), Liverpool Street tube station (daily 8am–6/7pm), and in Victoria Station (Mon–Sat 8/9am–7/9pm, Sun 8am–6.15pm). None of these offices accepts phone queries but LTB's well-designed website is crammed with useful material.

City transport

The **London Transport information office** at Piccadilly Circus tube station (daily 8.45am–6pm; ⊛www.londontransport.co.uk) will provide free transport maps, with other desks at Euston, Heathrow Terminals 1, 2 & 3, King's Cross, Liverpool Street and Victoria. There's also a 24–hour phone line for information on all bus, tube and boat services (☏020/7222 1234). The quickest way to get around London is by **Underground**, or **tube**, as it's known to all Londoners (daily 5.30/7.30am–midnight). Tickets must be bought in advance from the machines or booths in station entrance halls; if you cannot produce a valid ticket on demand, you'll be charged an on-the-spot Penalty Fare of £10. A one-way journey in central Zone 1 costs £1.60, or you can buy a Carnet of ten tickets for £11.50. Better value is a **Travelcard**, valid for buses, suburban trains and the tube. Day Travelcards come in two varieties: Off-Peak – which are valid after 9.30am on weekdays and all day during the weekend – and Peak. A Day Travelcard (Off-Peak), costs £4.10 for the central zones 1 and 2, rising to £5.10 for zones 1–6 (including Heathrow); the Day Travelcard (Peak) starts at £5.10 for zones 1 and 2. A bargain Weekend Travelcard costs £6.10 for Zones 1–2. Visitor Travelcards, which come packaged with discount vouchers for city attractions, are only available outside the UK (see website).

Without a travelcard, any bus journey in the central zone costs £1; normally you pay the driver on entering, although older buses with an open rear platform are staffed by a fare-collecting conductor. A lot of bus stops are **request stops**, so if you don't hold your arm out the bus will drive past. A **One-Day Bus Pass** (zones 1–4) costs £2 and can be used before 9.30am. After midnight, **night buses** prefixed with the letter "N" take over; fares are £1 (Travelcards are valid).

River-boat services on the Thames are fairly limited and expensive. Westminster Pier, beside Westminster Bridge, Embankment Pier and Waterloo Pier near the London Eye are the main central embarkation points. Among the many routings are boats east to the Tower of London (every 40min; 30min; £5.20) and Greenwich (50min; £6.30), and west to Kew (3 daily; 1hr 30min; £9) and Hampton Court (3 daily; 3hr 30min; £12). Return fares are much better value than singles. Travelcards get you a 33-percent discount.

If you're in a group of three or more, London's metered **black cabs** (taxis) can be an economical way of riding across the centre; from Euston to Victoria should cost around £10. However, after 8pm fares go sky high and you're best off using the tube. A yellow light over the windscreen tells you if the cab is available – just wave to hail it. To book in advance, call ☏020/7272 0272. **Minicabs** look just like regular cars and are considerably cheaper than black cabs, but they are a bit of a law unto themselves. There are hundreds of minicab firms all over London: you'd do best to get the number of a local outfit from the pub or club you're at. For women drivers, call Ladycabs on ☏020/7254 3501; for gay/lesbian drivers call Freedom Cars ☏020/7734 1313. Most minicabs are not metered, so check the fare before you get going.

Accommodation

London is extremely expensive, and budget **accommodation** in the centre tends to be poor quality. However, the sheer size of the city means you'll have little trouble finding a room, even in midsummer, and the tube network makes staying outside the centre a feasible option. All the LTB offices listed above operate a **room booking service**, which costs £5, or you can book by phone with a credit card through the LTB (☏020/7932 2020) or via ⌨www.londontown.com. To book a **hostel bed**, contact the individual hostels, or for HI hostels, the YHA (☏020/7373 3400, ⌨www.yha.org.uk). A good **website** for booking independent hostels is ⌨www.hostellondon.com. **Student rooms** are also available over Easter and from July to September: contact Imperial College (☏020/7594 9507, ⌨www.ad.ic.ac.uk) or the LSE (☏020/7955 7370, ⌨www.lse.ac.uk).

Hostels

HI hostels

City of London 36 Carter Lane, EC4 ☏020/7236 4965. 200-bed hostel in the City – a desolate area at night – with crowded dorms or private rooms. St Paul's or Blackfriars tube. ❺

Earl's Court 38 Bolton Gardens, SW5 ☏020/7373 7083. Dorms only, but comfortable and fairly capacious, with good-value meals. Earl's Court tube. ❺

Hampstead Heath 4 Wellgarth Rd, NW1 ☏020/8458 9054. One of the biggest and best-appointed, near the wilds of Hampstead Heath. Golders Green tube. ❺

Holland House Holland Walk, W8 ☏020/7937 0748. Fairly convenient for the centre, with a nice location overlooking parkland, and large dorms. Holland Park or High St Kensington tube. ❺

Oxford Street 14 Noel St, W1 ☏020/7734 1618. In the heart of the West End, but with only 75 beds, it fills up very fast. Discounts for weekly stays. Oxford Circus or Tottenham Court Rd tube. ❺

Rotherhithe Island Yard, Salter Rd, SE16 ☏020/7232 2114. Rather far out to the east, but a viable option in peak season, with 320 beds. Canada Water tube or bus #381 from Waterloo. ❺

St Pancras 79 Euston Rd, NW1 ☏020/7388 9998. Sparkling new hostel in a good location opposite St Pancras station and within walking distance of both the West End and Camden Town, with small dorms and twins. King's Cross tube. ❺

Other hostels

Generator Compton Place, W1 ☏020/7388 7666, ⌨www.the-generator.co.uk. Neon-lit post-industrial decor, and a youthful clientele. No sharing with strangers, so prices get cheaper the

more you have in your posse. Russell Sq or Euston tube. ❹

Leinster Inn 7–12 Leinster Sq, W2 ☏020/7229 9641, ⌨www.astorhotels.com. The biggest and liveliest of the Astor hostels, close to Notting Hill, with a variety of rooms from singles to dorms. Under 30s only. Queensway or Notting Hill Gate tube. ❺

Museum Inn 27 Montague St, W1 ☏020/7580 5360, ⌨www.astorhotels.com. The quietest of the Astor hostels, near the British Museum, with the usual friendly young crowd. Russell Sq tube. ❹

St Christopher's Village 121 Borough High St, SE1 ☏020/7407 1856, ⌨www.st-christophers.co.uk. Upbeat and cheerful hostel in a series of buildings near London Bridge, with a café and late bar onsite and cosmopolitan clientele. London Bridge tube. ❻

Hotels and B&Bs

Abbey House 11 Vicarage Gate, W8 ☏020/7727 2594, ⌨www.abbeyhousekensington.com. Victorian B&B, with large, bright rooms with shared facilities. High St Kensington tube. ❽

Cavendish 75 Gower St, WC1 ☏020/7636 9079, ⌨www.hotelcavendish.com. Clean, tastefully decorated guest house, one of the best in Bloomsbury. Goodge St tube. ❻

Crescent 49–50 Cartwright Gardens, WC1 ☏020/7387 1515, ⌨www.crescenthoteloflondon.com. En-suite doubles and a few bargain singles in a beautiful Regency house that are a cut above the rest. Euston or Russell Sq tube. ❽

Garden Court 30–31 Kensington Gardens Sq, W2 ☏020/7229 2553, ⌨www.gardencourthotel.co.uk. Presentable, family-run hotel near Portobello Market. Bayswater tube. ❻

Melbourne House 79 Belgrave Rd, SW1 ☎020/
7828 3516, ⓦwww.melbournehousehotel.com. One
of the best B&Bs in the area; all doubles en suite. ❽
Oxford House 92–94 Cambridge St, SW1
☎020/7834 6467. Very friendly B&B with pristine
rooms and shared facilities; booking essential.
Victoria tube. ❺
Philbeach 30–31 Philbeach Gardens, SW5
☎020/7373 1244,
ⓦwww.philbeachhotel.freeserve.co.uk. London's
busiest gay hotel, with a popular restaurant
attached. Earl's Court tube. ❼
Ridgemount 65–67 Gower St, WC1 ☎020/7636
1141, ⓦwww.ridgemounthotel.co.uk. Old-
fashioned family-run Bloomsbury hotel with a
garden and a laundry service. Goodge St tube. ❻
Rushmore Hotel 11 Trebovir Rd, SW5
☎020/7370 3839, ⓦwww.rushmore.activehotels

.com. A cut above the average in this often dreary
Earl's Court area. Earl's Court tube. ❽
Woodville House and **Morgan House** 107 &
120 Ebury St, SW1 ☎020/7730 1048,
ⓦwww.woodvillehouse.co.uk. Jointly run above-
average B&Bs, some en-suite rooms. Patio
gardens and great breakfasts. Victoria tube. ❼

Campsites
Abbey Wood Federation Rd, SE2 ☎020/8311
7708. Enormous, well-equipped Caravan Club site
east of Greenwich. Open all year. Train from
Charing Cross to Abbey Wood.
Crystal Palace Crystal Palace Parade
☎020/8778 7155. All-year Caravan Club site,
maximum two weeks' stay in summer, three
weeks in winter. Train from Victoria or London
Bridge to Crystal Palace.

The City

The majority of sights are north of the **River Thames**, but there's no single focus of
interest. One of the few areas that's manageable on foot is the area around Whitehall,
with **Trafalgar Square** at one end and Parliament Square at the other, with
Buckingham Palace to the west. The busiest, most popular area for visitors and
Londoners alike is the **West End**, centred on Leicester Square and Piccadilly Circus,
and home to the majority of the city's theatres and cinemas. The financial district
lies a mile or so to the east, and is known, confusingly, as the **City of London**, at
once the most ancient and most modern part of London. Over on the other side of
the river, the **South Bank** has become a prime tourist destination thanks to, among
others, the London Eye, the Tate Modern and Shakespeare's Globe. Further afield,
Greenwich makes for a great day out, as do the Royal Botanic Gardens at **Kew**,
and the outlying royal palaces of **Hampton Court** and **Windsor Castle**.

Trafalgar Square and the National Gallery
Despite being little more than a glorified traffic island, **Trafalgar Square** is still
one of London's grandest architectural set-pieces. The square's focal point is
Nelson's Column, featuring the one-eyed admiral who died whilst defeating the
French at the 1805 Battle of Trafalgar. Four lions (and innumerable pigeons) guard
the column's base, and two adjacent fountains are a magnet for overheating sightseers during the summer.

Extending across the north side of the square is the bulk of the **National Gallery**
(daily 10am–6pm, Wed till 9pm; free; ⓦwww.nationalgallery.org.uk), one of the
world's great art collections. A quick tally of the National's Italian masterpieces
includes works by Piero della Francesca, Raphael, Botticelli, Michelangelo,
Leonardo da Vinci, Caravaggio, Titian and Veronese. From Spain there are dazzling
pieces by Velázquez (including the *Rokeby Venus*), El Greco and Goya. From the
Low Countries there's Memlinck, van Eyck (the *Arnolfini Marriage*), Rubens, and
some of Rembrandt's most searching portraits. The collection also includes several
very famous Impressionist and Post-Impressionist works by the likes of Seurat,
Cézanne, Van Gogh and Monet. If you want to take the art chronologically, you
should start in the Sainsbury Wing, a mildly postmodern annexe on the west side.
Round the side of the National Gallery, in St Martin's Place, is the **National
Portrait Gallery** (daily 10am–6pm, Thurs & Fri till 9pm; free; ⓦwww.npg.org.uk),
which houses portraits of the great and good from Hans Holbein's larger-than-life
drawing of Henry VIII, to photographs of the latest pop stars and footballers.

The Mall and Buckingham Palace

The tree-lined sweep of **The Mall** runs from Trafalgar Square through the imposing Admiralty Arch, and on to **Buckingham Palace** (Aug & Sept daily 9.30am–4.15pm; £11.50; ⓦwww.royal.gov.uk). Popularly known as "Buck House", the palace has served as the monarch's permanent residence only since the accession of Queen Victoria in 1837. The building's exterior, last remodelled in 1913, is as bland as could be; inside, it's all suitably lavish, but only worth a visit to view the van Dycks and Rembrandts on the walls. There's more high-class art on display in the newly revamped **Queen's Gallery** (daily 10am–5.30pm; £6.50), on the south side of the palace. When Buckingham Palace is closed, most folk simply mill about outside the gates, with the largest crowds assembling for the **Changing of the Guard** (April–Aug daily 11.30am; Sept–March alternate days; no ceremony if it rains). However, you're better off heading for the **Horse Guards** building on Whitehall (see below), where a more elaborate equestrian ceremony takes place (Mon–Sat 11am, Sun 10am). Wherever you watch the Changing of the Guard, you can relax afterwards in nearby **St James's Park**, immaculately laid out south of the Mall, its lake providing an inner-city reserve for wildfowl and a recreation area for the employees of Whitehall.

Whitehall

Heading south from Trafalgar Square is the broad sweep of **Whitehall**, lined with government buildings and civil service offices. The original Whitehall was a palace built for King Henry VIII and subsequently extended, but virtually the only bit to survive a fire in 1698 is the supremely elegant **Banqueting House** (Mon–Sat 10am–5pm; £3.90; ⓦwww.hrp.org.uk), begun by Inigo Jones in the Palladian style in 1619 and decorated with vast ceiling paintings by Rubens, glorifying the Stuart dynasty. They were commissioned by James's son Charles I – who on January 30, 1649, stepped onto the executioner's scaffold from one of the building's front windows. Further down this west side of Whitehall is London's most famous address, **10 Downing St**, residence of the Prime Minister since 1732. During World War II, the Cabinet was forced to vacate Downing St in favour of a bunker in nearby King Charles St. The **Cabinet War Rooms** (daily 9.30/10am–6pm; £5.80; ⓦwww.iwm.org.uk) – left

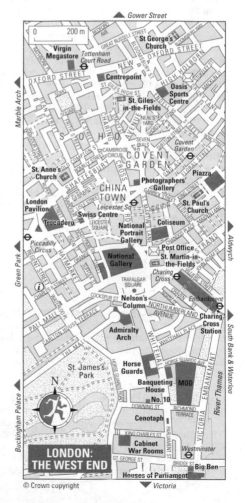

© Crown copyright

more or less as they were in 1945 – provide a glimpse of the claustrophobic suites from which Winston Churchill directed wartime operations.

The Houses of Parliament and Westminster Abbey

Clearly visible at the south end of Whitehall is one of London's best-known buildings, the Palace of Westminster, better known as the **Houses of Parliament**. The city's finest Gothic Revival building and symbol of a nation once confident of its place at the centre of the world, it's distinguished above all by the ornate, gilded clock tower popularly known as **Big Ben**, after the thirteen-ton bell that it houses. The original royal palace, built by Edward the Confessor in the eleventh century, burnt down in 1834. The only relic of the medieval palace to survive is the magnificent Westminster Hall, which can be glimpsed en route to the **public galleries** from which you can watch parliament's proceedings. The public are let in slowly from about 4pm onwards on Mondays, from 1pm Tuesday to Thursday, and from 10am on Fridays; security checks are very tight, and the whole procedure can take an hour or more. To avoid the queues, turn up after 6pm, when most tourists have disappeared. In the summer, it's also possible to go on a **guided tour** of the building (Aug & Sept Mon, Tues, Fri & Sat 9.15am–4.30pm, Wed & Thurs 1.15–4.30pm; £7).

The Houses of Parliament dwarf their much older neighbour, **Westminster Abbey** (Mon–Fri 9.30am–4.45pm, Wed also 6–7pm, Sat 9.30am–2.45pm; £6; ⊕www.westminster-abbey.org), yet this single building embodies much of the history of England: it has been the venue for all but two coronations since the time of William the Conqueror, and the site of more or less every royal burial for five hundred years until George II. Many of the nation's most celebrated citizens are honoured here, too, and the interior is crowded with monuments, reliefs and statuary. Entry is currently via the north door, and the highlights include the **Lady Chapel**, with its wonderful fan vaulting, the much venerated Shrine of Edward the Confessor, which you can now only peek into, and **Poets' Corner**, where the likes of Chaucer, Tennyson, T.S. Eliot and many others are buried, and still more, like Shakespeare, are honoured. On your way out, don't miss the Great Cloister, which gives access to the **Chapter House** (daily 9.30/10am–4/5pm; £1) with its thirteenth-century paving stones and the Norman **Undercroft Museum** (daily 10.30am–4pm; free), in which several generations of royal death-masks are displayed.

From Parliament Square, Millbank runs south to the **Tate Britain** (daily 10am–5.50pm; free; ⊕www.tate.org.uk; Pimlico tube). Displaying British art from 1500 onwards, plus a whole wing devoted to Turner, it also showcases contemporary British artists. The galleries are rehung more or less annually, but always include a fair selection of works by Hogarth, Constable, Gainsborough, Reynolds, Blake, Spencer, Bacon, Hockney and others. The gallery also runs contemporary art's prestigious, and often controversial, Turner prize. Every autumn, the finalists' work is displayed for a month or two prior to the prize-giving.

Covent Garden and the British Museum

Northeast of Trafalgar Square lies the attractive area of **Covent Garden**, centred on the Piazza, London's oldest planned square, laid out in the 1630s, and now centred on the nineteenth-century market hall that housed London's principal fruit and vegetable market until the 1970s. The structure now shelters a gaggle of tasteful shops and arty stalls. On the western side, by Jones's classical St Paul's Church, is a semi-institutionalized venue for buskers and more ambitious street performers. In the Piazza's southeast corner is the **London Transport Museum** (daily 10am–6pm, Fri from 11am; £5.95; ⊕www.ltmuseum.co.uk), a fun scamper through the history – and possible future – of public transport in the city.

From here it's a short walk northwards up fashionable Neal St and across New Oxford St into the district of Bloomsbury, home to the **British Museum** on Great Russell St (daily 10am–5.30pm, Thurs & Fri till 8.30pm; free; ⊕www.british-museum .ac.uk), one of the great museums of the world and Britain's most popular tourist attraction (after Blackpool). The building itself is the grandest of London's Greek Revival edifices, and is now even more amazing, thanks to Norman Foster's glass-and-steel covered Great Court, at the centre of which stands the **Round Reading Room**, where Karl Marx penned *Das Kapital*. With over four million exhibits, the BM is far too big to be seen in one go – head for the two or three displays that interest you most. The museum's Roman and Greek antiquities are second to none, but the exhibits that steal the headlines are the **Elgin Marbles**, taken from the Parthenon in Athens by Lord Elgin in 1801 and still the cause of discord between the British and Greek governments. Upstairs, there's a vast Egyptian mummy collection, the 2000-year-old Lindow Man, preserved in a Cheshire bog after his sacrificial death, and the famous twelfth-century Lewis Chessmen, carved from walrus ivory. Two of the most remarkable treasure troves on this floor were found in East Anglia: Saxon pieces from Sutton Hoo, and the Roman silverwork known as the Mildenhall Treasure.

The South Bank

The **South Bank** of the Thames is home to one of London's most prominent landmarks, the **London Eye** (daily: April–Sept 9.30am–10pm; Oct–March 9am–8pm; £10.50; ☎0800/500 0600; ✪www.ba-londoneye.com), a 135m-tall observation wheel that revolves slowly and silently over the Thames. A full-circle "flight" in one of its pods takes thirty minutes and lifts you high above the city. From the Eye, a riverside footpath heads east past the **South Bank Centre** (✪www.sbc.org.uk), London's concrete "culture bunker", for a mile or so before reaching Bankside, the old entertainment district of Tudor and Stuart London. Contemporary Bankside is dominated by the austere power station, which has been transformed into the **Tate Modern** (daily 10am–6pm, Fri & Sat till 10pm; free; ✪www.tate.org.uk). The collection is arranged thematically, and minor rehangs take place every six months or so, but you're pretty much guaranteed to see works by Monet, Bonnard, Matisse, Picasso, Dalí, Mondrian, Warhol, Beuys and Rothko. Directly outside Tate Modern is Norman Foster's **Millennium Bridge**, London's famous bouncing bridge, which wobbled so worryingly when it first opened in 2000 that it was closed for repairs for almost two years. It's open again now and will take you effortlessly over to St Paul's Cathedral (see below). Seriously dwarfed by the Tate Modern is the equally spectacular **Shakespeare's Globe Theatre** (✪www.shakespeares-globe.org), a reconstruction of the polygonal playhouse where most of the Bard's later works were first performed. The Globe's pricey but stylish exhibition (daily: May–Sept 9am–noon & 12.30–4pm; Oct–April 10am–5pm; £8) is well worth a visit, and includes a guided tour of the theatre, except in the afternoooons during the summer – at this time, however, you'd be better off watching a show.

One other national institution on the south bank worth seeking out is the **Imperial War Museum**, on Lambeth Rd, half a mile south of Waterloo Station (daily 10am–6pm; £5.50; free after 4.30pm; ✪www.iwm.org.uk; Lambeth North tube). This is by far the best military museum in the country, its treatment of the subject wide-ranging and fairly sober. The museum also contains the nation's only permanent **Holocaust Exhibition**, which pulls few punches and has made a valiant attempt to avoid depicting the victims of the Holocaust as nameless masses by focusing on individual cases, interspersing the archive footage with eyewitness accounts from survivors.

The City of London

Once the fortified heart of the capital, the **City of London**, also known as the Square Mile, is now its financial district. Few people actually live here, making it a desolate place after nightfall and at the weekend. Postwar redevelopment and the 1666 Fire of London destroyed most of the old City, but the area's finest structure, **St Paul's Cathedral** (Mon–Sat 8.30am–5pm; £6; ✪www.stpauls.co.uk; St Paul's tube), was designed by Christopher Wren. The most distinctive feature of this Baroque edifice is the dome, second in size only to St Peter's in Rome, and still a dominating presence on the London skyline. The interior of the church is filled with dull imperialist funerary monuments, for the most part, but a staircase in the south transept leads up to a series of galleries in the dome. The internal **Whispering Gallery** is the first, so called because of its acoustic properties – words whispered to the wall on one side are distinctly audible on the other. The broad exterior Stone Gallery and the uppermost Golden Gallery both offer good panoramas over London. The **crypt** is the resting place of Wren himself, along with Turner, Reynolds and other artists, but the most imposing sarcophagi are the twin black monstrosities occupied by the Duke of Wellington and Lord Nelson.

The eastern extent of the City is marked by the **Tower of London** (March–Oct Mon–Sat 9am–6pm, Sun 10am–6pm; Nov–Feb Mon & Sun 10am–5pm, Tues–Sat 9am–5pm; £11.50; @www.hrp.org.uk), on the river a mile southeast of St Paul's. Despite all the hype and heritage claptrap, it remains one of London's most remarkable buildings, site of some of the goriest events in the nation's history, and somewhere all visitors should explore. For a start, the Tower is the most perfectly preserved (albeit heavily restored) medieval fortress in the country, begun by William the Conqueror, and pretty much completed by the end of the thirteenth century. Before you set off exploring, take one of the free tours given by the "Beefeaters", ex-servicemen in Tudor costume. The central White Tower holds part of the **Royal Armouries** collection (the rest resides in Leeds), and, on the second floor, the Norman Chapel of St John, London's oldest church. Close by is Tower Green, where the likes of Lady Jane Grey, Anne Boleyn and Catherine Howard were beheaded. The Waterloo Barracks house the **Crown Jewels**, among which are the three largest cut diamonds in the world. On the south side of the complex, the **Bloody Tower** is where the murder of the "Princes in the Tower", Edward V and his brother, is thought to have taken place. Below lies **Traitor's Gate**, through which prisoners arrived after having been ferried down the Thames from the courts of justice at Westminster. River views from here are dominated by the twin towers of **Tower Bridge**, completed in 1894 and now one of London's most famous landmarks. The raising of the bascules to allow tall ships through remains an impressive sight. Sadly, though, you can only visit the walkways linking the summits of the towers by joining a guided tour dubbed the "Tower Bridge Experience" (daily 9.30am–6pm; £4.50; @www.towerbridge.org.uk).

Hyde Park and west to Notting Hill

The best way to approach **Hyde Park**, London's largest central green space, is from the southeastern corner known as Hyde Park Corner. Here, in the middle of the traffic interchange, stands the **Wellington Arch** (Wed–Sun 10am–4/6pm; £2.50), erected in 1828 to commemorate Wellington's victories in the Napoleonic Wars. The arch now houses a small exhibition on London's outdoor memorials. Wellington himself used to live at **Apsley House** (Tues–Sun 11am–5pm; £4.50; @www.apsleyhouse.org.uk), overlooking the arch, and now home to the Wellington Museum, which holds works by Velázquez, Goya, Rubens and Canova. In the middle of Hyde Park is the **Serpentine** lake, with a popular lido towards its centre; the nearby Serpentine Gallery (daily 10am–6pm; free; @www.serpentine-gallery.org) hosts excellent contemporary art exhibitions. Nearby stands the **Albert Memorial**, an over-decorated Gothic canopy covering a gilded statue of Queen Victoria's much-mourned consort, who died in 1861. To the west the park merges into Kensington Gardens, leading to **Kensington Palace** daily 10am–5/6pm; £10; @www.hrp.org.uk), a modestly proportioned Jacobean brick mansion that was Princess Diana's London residence following her separation from Prince Charles. The highlights of the sparsely furnished state apartments are the *trompe l'oeil* ceiling paintings by William Kent, and the oil paintings in the King's Gallery.

South Kensington museums

London's richest concentration of free museums lies to the south of Hyde Park. In terms of sheer variety and scale, the **Victoria and Albert Museum** (daily 10am–5.45pm; Wed & last Fri of month until 10pm; free; @www.vam.ac.uk), on

Cromwell Rd, is the greatest museum of applied arts in the world. The most celebrated of the V&A's numerous exhibits are the Raphael Cartoons, seven vast biblical paintings that served as templates for a set of tapestries destined for the Sistine Chapel. Other highlights include the largest collection of Indian art outside India, the new British Galleries, plaster casts of European art's greatest sculptures, twentieth-century *objets d'art*, more Constable paintings than the Tate and a decent collection of Rodin sculptures.

Established as a technological counterpart to the V&A, the **Science Museum** on Exhibition Rd (daily 10am–6pm; free; ⊕www.nmsi.ac.uk) is undeniably impressive. First off, visit the Making of the Modern World, a display of inventions such as *Puffing Billy*, the world's oldest surviving steam train, and a Ford Model T, the world's first mass-produced car. From here, the darkened, ultra-purple Wellcome Wing beckons you on, its ground floor dominated by the floating, sloping underbelly of the museum's IMAX cinema (£6.95). The four floors of the Wellcome Wing are filled with high-tech hands-on gadgetry, which makes some of the galleries in the rest of the museum look decidedly dated.

The nearby **Natural History Museum**, back on Cromwell Rd (Mon–Sat 10am–5.50pm, Sun 11am–5.50pm; free; ⊕www.nhm.ac.uk), is London's most handsome museum. Most folk come here with the kids to see the Dinosaur gallery, and wince at the Creepy-Crawlies. Even more stunning, however, are the new Earth Galleries, a visually exciting romp through the earth's evolution. The most popular sections are the slightly tasteless Kobe earthquake simulator, and the spectacular display of gems and crystals in the Earth's Treasury.

North London: Regent's Park to Hampstead

As with almost all of London's royal parks, Londoners have Henry VIII to thank for **Regent's Park**, which he confiscated from the Church for yet more hunting grounds. Flanked by some of the city's most elegant residential buildings, the park is best known for **London Zoo** (daily 10am–4/5.30pm; £11; ⊕www.londonzoo.co.uk), one of the world's oldest and most varied collections of animals, which hides in the northeastern corner. A short stroll from the southwestern corner of the park, on busy Marylebone Rd, is one of London's most enduring tourist traps, **Madame Tussaud's** (daily 9.30/10am–5.30pm; £14.95; ⊕www.madame-tussauds.com), which has been pulling in the crowds since the good lady arrived in 1802 with the sculpted heads of guillotined aristocrats. The entrance fee might be extortionate, the likenesses risible, but you can still rely on finding some of London's biggest queues here. Tickets to Madame Tussaud's include entry into the neighbouring **London Planetarium** (Mon–Fri 10/11.30am–5pm; shows every 30min; Planetarium only £2.45), which features a standard romp through the basics of astronomy accompanied by high-tech visuals and cosmic astro-babble.

Five minutes' walk from the north side of the park lies bustling **Camden Town**, host to a vast weekend market that sprawls around the canal, spilling over several locations either side of the main street. Camden gets so crowded that the tube station is deemed exit-only on Sunday afternoons. Further north still is the affluent suburb of **Hampstead**, which gives access to Hampstead Heath, one of the few genuinely wild areas left within reach of central London. One major attraction east of Hampstead is **Highgate Cemetery**, ranged on both sides of Swains Lane (Highgate or Archway tube). Highgate's most famous corpse is Karl Marx, who lies in the East Cemetery (daily 10/11am–4/5pm; £2); more intriguing and atmospheric is the overgrown West Cemetery (guided tours only: March–Nov Mon–Fri noon, 2pm & 4pm, Sat & Sun hourly 11am–4pm; Dec–Feb Sat & Sun hourly 11am–3pm; £3), with its spooky Egyptian Avenue and terraced catacombs.

Greenwich

Some nine miles east of central London, **Greenwich** (pronounced "gren-itch") is one of London's most beguiling spots. At its heart is the architectural set-piece of the former Royal Naval College overlooking the Thames; nearby are two prime tourist sights: the Royal Observatory and the National Maritime Museum. Transport links are good: boats run regularly from Westminster Pier, trains run from Charing Cross, and the Docklands Light Railway scoots east from the Bank or Tower Gateway in the City via the redeveloped Docklands, south to the **Cutty Sark**, which stands in a dry dock next to Greenwich pier (daily 10am–5pm; £3.90; ✪ www.cuttysark.org.uk). This majestic vessel was one of the last of the clippers, sail-powered cargo ships built for speed and used on long-distance routes to bring wool, tea and other produce to London from the far-flung corners of the Empire. Hugging the riverfront to the east is Wren's beautifully symmetrical Baroque ensemble of the **Old Royal Naval College** (daily 10am–5pm; £3; ✪ www.greenwichfoundation.org.uk). Across the road the **National Maritime Museum** (daily 10am–5/6pm; free; ✪ www.nmm.ac.uk) exhibits model ships, charts and globes, and has been wonderfully rejuvenated with some inventive new galleries under an enormous glazed roof. Inigo Jones's adjacent **Queen's House**, Britain's first Neoclassical building, also forms part of the museum. From here Greenwich Park stretches up the hill, crowned by the Wren-inspired **Royal Observatory** (daily 10am–6pm; free), home of Greenwich Mean Time and Zero Longitude. As well as housing numerous timepieces, telescopes and navigational equipment, the museum also has a fascinating exhibition on the search for longitude and displays four of the marine clocks designed by John Harrison. Clearly visible from the vantage point of Greenwich Park is the **Millennium Dome**, designed by Richard Rogers for the one-year only millennium extravaganza.

Out west: Kew to Windsor

Boats ply westwards from Westminster Pier upstream to **Kew** where you'll find the **Royal Botanic Gardens** (daily 9.30am–dusk; £7.50; Kew Gardens tube; ✪ www.kew.org), established in 1759, and now home to over 50,000 species grown in the plantations and glasshouses of a beautiful 300-acre site. Further upstream, thirteen miles southwest of the centre and also served by riverboat, is the finest of England's royal mansions, **Hampton Court Palace** (April–Oct Mon 10.15am–6pm, Tues–Sun 9.30am–6pm; Nov–March closes 4.30pm; £11; ✪ www.hrp.org.uk). Built in 1516 by the upwardly mobile Cardinal Wolsey, it was purloined enlarged and improved by Henry VIII, and later rebuilt by William III who hired Wren to remodel the buildings. The palace is laid out into six thematic walking tours, with costumed guided tours available at no extra charge. If your energy is lacking, the most rewarding sections are Henry VIII's State Apartments, which feature the glorious double hammerbeamed Great Hall, the King's Apartments, and the Tudor Kitchens. There's plenty more to see in the grounds: the Great Vine, the Lower Orangery, which houses Mantegna's *The Triumphs of Caesar*, and, of course, the famous **Maze**, laid out in 1714, lies just north of the palace.

WINDSOR, 21 miles west of central London, is dominated by **Windsor Castle** (daily 9.45am–4.15/5.15pm; £11.50; train from Waterloo; ✪ www.royal.gov.uk). The castle began its days as a wooden fortress built by William the Conqueror, with numerous later monarchs having had a hand in its evolution. It's an undeniably awesome sight, but the small selection of rooms open to the public are relatively unexciting; the only exception is the Perpendicular Gothic glory of St George's Chapel, resting place of numerous monarchs.

Eating and drinking

London is a great place in which to **eat out**. You can sample more or less any kind of cuisine here, and wherever you come from, you should find something new and quite possibly unique. The only drawback is that eating out can also be very expensive. For those on a budget, however, there are still plenty of options: London has some of the best Cantonese restaurants in Europe, top Indian and Bangladeshi food, and numerous French, Greek, Italian, Japanese, Spanish and Thai restaurants. The city's great period of **pub** building took place in the Victorian era, to which many taverns still pay homage; genuine Victorian interiors are increasingly difficult to find, as are genuinely individual pubs – chain pubs are as ubiquitous in London as elsewhere in the country. As for modern **bars**, there are countless numbers of them, with more opening and closing as each year goes by, and an eternally young, hip clientele seemingly oblivious to the sky high prices.

Snacks and quick meals

Bar Italia 22 Frith St, W1. Open 24hr except Sun 3-6am. Tiny café serving coffee, croissants and sandwiches.

Café Delancey 3 Delancey St, NW1. Excellent brasserie-style café near Camden Town, serving snacks, coffee and full meals.

Café in the Crypt St Martin-in-the-Fields church, Trafalgar Sq. The self-service buffet food is nothing special, but there are regular veggie dishes and the handy location makes this an ideal refuelling spot. Charing Cross tube.

Centrale 16 Moor St, W1. Tiny, friendly Italian café that serves up huge plates of steaming, garlicky pasta, as well as omelettes, chicken and chops for around £5. Leicester Square tube.

Food For Thought 31 Neal St, WC2. Very small vegetarian restaurant – the inexpensive food is delicious, but don't expect to linger. Covent Garden tube.

Gaby's 30 Charing Cross Rd, WC2. Busy café serving a wide range of home-cooked veggie and Middle Eastern specialities. Hard to beat for value, choice and location. Leicester Sq tube.

Lee Ho Fook 4 Macclesfield St, cnr Dansey Place, Chinatown, W1. No English sign. An authentic Chinese barbecue house, tiny, bright and fast-paced. Leicester Sq tube.

Mô 25 Heddon St, W1. The ultimate Arabic pastiche, and a successful one at that. This tearoom, just off Regent St, serves delicious snacks from mid-morning and is a great place to hang out. Piccadilly Circus tube.

Saucebarorganicdiner 214 Camden High St, NW1. Organic fast food – burgers, wraps and sandwiches – with a juice and cocktail bar attached. Camden Town tube.

Stockpot 18 Old Compton St, W1. Chain of cafés serving filling bistro-style stews and such like at rock-bottom prices. Soho Leicester Sq tube. Branches all across town.

Wagamama 4 Streatham St, Bloomsbury WC1. Austere, minimalist canteen-style place where the diners share long benches and slurp huge bowls of noodle soup and stir-fry plates. Expect to queue and don't expect to linger. Tottenham Court Rd tube. Branches all across town.

Restaurants

Al Waha 75 Westbourne Grove, W2. One of London's best Lebanese restaurants. Queensway or Bayswater tube.

Belgo Centraal 50 Earlham St, WC2. Hugely popular Belgian restaurant serving heaps of mussels and other hearty fare, as well as beer, of course. The lunchtime deals are hard to beat. Covent Garden tube.

China City White Bear Yard, 25 Lisle St, WC2. Large restaurant with *dim sum* that's up there with the best, and service that is Chinatown brusque. Leicester Sq tube.

Chowki 2–3 Denman St, W1. Large, cheap Indian restaurant serving authentic food. Piccadilly Circus tube.

Ikkyu 67a Tottenham Court Rd, W1. Busy, basic basement Japanese restaurant with reasonable prices. Goodge St tube.

Mandalay 444 Edgware Rd, W2. Small, non-smoking restaurant that serves pure, freshly cooked, unexpurgated Burmese cuisine. Closed Sun. Edgware Rd tube.

The Providores 109 Marylebone High St, W1. Outstanding fusion restaurant run by New Zealanders. Tapas bar downstairs and restaurant upstairs. Baker St or Bond St tube.

RSJ 13a Coin St, SE1. Good Anglo-French cooking, in an excellent spot for a meal before or after a show on the South Bank. Waterloo tube.

Spiga 84–86 Wardour St, W1 A pleasant Italian venue with wood-fired oven. Leicester Square tube.

Pubs and bars

Albert 52 Victoria St, SW1. Handily situated pub serving good food, including hearty breakfasts in the upstairs restaurant. St James's Park tube.

Anchor Bankside 34 Park St, SE1. Old Bankside inn, with tables overlooking the river – handy for the Tate Modern. London Bridge, Southwark or Blackfriars tube.

Blackfriars 174 Queen Victoria St, City. Art Nouveau landmark, handy for the City sights. Closed Sat & Sun. Blackfriars tube.

Bunch of Grapes 207 Brompton Rd, SW3. Popular High Victorian pub that is the perfect place for a post-V&A pint, pie and chips. South Kensington tube.

Cutty Sark Ballast Quay off Lassell St, Greenwich. Ancient riverside pub with a nautical theme, outside tables and fine views of Docklands and the Dome. Cutty Sark DLR, then walk downstream.

Dog & Duck 18 Bateman St, Soho. Tiny pub that retains much of its old character and a loyal clientele. Leicester Sq tube.

Flask 14 Flask Walk, NW3. Convivial local, close to the station and serving good food and real ale. Hampstead tube.

George Inn 77 Borough High St. Half a magnificent seventeenth-century coaching inn, now owned by the National Trust. Borough or London Bridge tube.

Lamb 94 Lamb's Conduit St, Bloomsbury. Pleasant pub with a well-preserved Victorian interior. Russell Sq tube.

Lamb & Flag 33 Rose St, WC2. Busy, atmospheric pub tucked away down an alley between Garrick and Floral streets. Covent Garden tube.

Museum Tavern 49 Great Russell St, WC1. Large old pub, right opposite the main entrance to the British Museum, once Marx's favourite. Tottenham Court Rd tube.

Paviour's Arms Page St, SW1. Untouched Art Deco pub, close to Tate Britain with cheap Thai food. Pimlico tube.

Salisbury 90 St Martin's Lane, WC2. One of the most beautifully preserved Victorian pubs in the centre. Leicester Sq tube.

The Social 5 Little Portland St, W1. Bacchanalian, industrial club/bar, with great DJs playing everything from rock to rap, a truly hedonistic-cum-alcoholic crowd. Oxford Circus tube. Closed Sun.

Two Floors 3 Kingly St, W1. Relaxed, modernist Soho bar attracting a mixed straight/gay crowd, with pumping music. Closed Sun. Oxford Circus or Piccadilly Circus tube.

Nightlife

On any night of the week London offers a bewildering range of things to do after dark, ranging from top-flight opera and theatre to clubs. The **listings magazine** *Time Out* (every Tues), is essential if you want to get the most out of this city, giving full details of prices and access, plus previews and reviews. If you're looking for **dance music**, then welcome to Europe's party capital, with everything from hip-hop to house, techno to trance, samba to soca. The **gay and lesbian** scenes in London are also livelier than almost anywhere else in Europe, with a vast range of venues from quiet pubs to cruisy bars and frenetic clubs. London's **theatre** scene is dominated by big musicals, but there's plenty of other stuff on offer, too. Cut-price stand-by tickets can sometimes be had on the day; otherwise head for the large booth in Leicester Square selling **half-price theatre tickets** (Mon–Sat 10am–7pm, Sun noon–3pm) for that day's performances at all West End theatres (note that they specialize in the top end of the price range). An even better bargain are the standing tickets for around £4 for the **Proms** (July–Sept), the annual classical music festival held at the Royal Albert Hall, or the free classical concerts that take place during weekday lunchtimes in the City's churches.

Live music venues

100 Club 100 Oxford St, W1. The 100 Club is an unpretentious and inexpensive jazz venue – in a very central location. Tottenham Court Rd tube.

Astoria 157 Charing Cross Rd, WC2. One of London's best-used venues – a large balconied theatre that has live bands and clubs. Tottenham Court Rd tube.

Borderline Orange Yard, Manette St, W1. Intimate venue with diverse musical policy, and a good place to catch new bands. Also has club nights. Tottenham Court Rd tube.

Forum 9–17 Highgate Rd, NW5. Perhaps the capital's best medium-sized venue – large enough to attract established bands, but also a prime spot for newer talent. Kentish Town tube.

Jazz Café 5 Parkway, NW1. Futuristic, white-walled venue with an adventurous booking policy exploring Latin, rap, funk, hip-hop and musical fusions. Camden Town tube.

Ronnie Scott's 47 Frith St, W1. The most famous jazz club in London, small, smoky and rather precious, but featuring top-line names. Leicester Sq tube.

Subterania 12 Acklam Rd, W10. One of the original live music/club crossover venues in an arch under a bridge. The crowd is as trendy as the music, which is often dance-oriented. Ladbroke Grove tube.

Underworld 174 Camden High St, NW1. This labyrinthine venue is good for new bands and has sporadic club nights. Camden Town tube.

Clubs and discos

Bagley's Studios King's Cross Freight Depot, off York Way, N1. Vast warehouse-style venue with a different DJ in each of the three rooms, and a chill-out bar complete with sofas. King's Cross tube.

Bar Rumba 36 Shaftesbury Ave, W1. Small West End venue with a programme of Latin, jazz-based and funk dance. Piccadilly Circus tube.

Café de Paris 3 Coventry St, W1. Elegantly restored ballroom that plays house, garage and disco. No jeans or trainers. Leicester Square tube.
Camden Palace 1a Camden High St, NW1. Most often home to Balearic beats; great lights, great sound, heaving crowds. Mornington Crescent tube.
The End 16a West Central St, WC1. A club designed by clubbers for clubbers – large spacious with chrome minimalist decor. Tottenham Court Rd tube.
Fabric 77a Charterhouse St, EC1. If you're seriously into dance music then there really isn't a better weekend venue in London. Get there early. Farringdon tube.
Ministry of Sound 103 Gaunt St, SE1. Vast, state-of-the-art club with an exceptional sound system. Corporate clubbing, but it still draws the top talent. Elephant & Castle tube.
The Scala 278 Pentonvlle Rd, N1. One of London's best clubs, holding unusual and multi-faceted nights that take in film, live bands and music from hip hop to deep house. King's Cross tube.

Gay and lesbian nightlife

Black Cap 171 Camden High St, NW1. Drag and cabaret acts of wildly varying quality almost every night; upstairs bar is quieter, and opens onto a lush and lovely summer roof garden. Camden Town tube.
Brief Encounter 41–43 St Martin's Lane, WC2. A popular pre-*Heaven* or post-opera hangout; the front bar is light, the back bar dark, and both are busy. Leicester Square tube.
Candy Bar 4 Carlisle St, W1. Britain's first seven-day all-girl bar offers a retro-style cocktail bar-cum-pool room upstairs; a noisy, beery ground level cruising bar. Tottenham Court Rd tube.
First Out 52 St Giles High St, WC2. The West End's original gay café/bar, and still permanently packed, serving good veggie food at reasonable prices. *Girl Friday* is a busy women-only Fri night pre-club session. Tottenham Court Rd tube.
Freedom 60 Wardour St, Soho, W1. Hip, busy café/bar attracting a mixed gay/straight crowd. Leicester Sq tube.
G.A.Y. at *The Astoria*, 157 Charing Cross Rd, WC2. Huge, unpretentious and fun-loving dance nights for a young crowd on Fri & Sat. Tottenham Court Rd tube.
Heaven under the Arches Villiers St, WC2. Britain's most popular gay club, this legendary, 2000-capacity club continues to reign supreme. Charing Cross tube.
Vespa Lounge Under Centrepoint House, St. Giles High St, WC1. London's newest girl bar sets up shop at weekends, and it gets busy. Pool table, video screen, and a mostly young crowd. Tottenham Court Rd tube.

Theatre, cinema and the arts

Barbican Centre Silk St, EC2 (@www.barbican .org.uk). Home of the London Symphony Orchestra and venue for a wide range of concerts from classical to world music. Barbican or Moorgate tube.
BFI London IMAX Centre South Bank, SE1 (@www .bfi.org.uk). Remarkable state-of-the-art building showing the usual IMAX fodder. Waterloo tube.
Donmar Warehouse Earlham St, WC2 (@www.donmar-warehouse.com). Formerly the spiritual home of Sam Mendes, and the best bet for a central off-West End show. Covent Garden tube.
English National Opera Coliseum, St Martin's Lane, WC2 (@www.eno.org). More radical and democratic than the ROH, with opera (in English) and ballet. Leicester Sq tube.
ICA Nash House, The Mall, SW1 (@www.ica.org.uk). Theatre, dance, films and art at London's enduringly avant-garde HQ. Charing Cross tube.
National Film Theatre South Bank, SE1. London's only really serious arts cinema, with six different films shown each day on two screens. Waterloo tube.
National Theatre South Bank Centre, South Bank, SE1 (@www.nationaltheatre.org.uk). The NT has three separate theatres, and consistently good productions – some sell out months in advance, but discounted dayseats available from 10am. Waterloo tube.
Open Air Theatre Regent's Park, Inner Circle, NW1. If the weather's good, there's nothing quite like a dose of al fresco Shakespeare, or a musical, play or concert. Regent's Park tube.
Prince Charles 2–7 Leicester Place, WC2 (@www .princecharlescinema.com). The bargain basement of London's cinemas, with a programme of new movies, classics and cult favourites. Leicester Sq tube.
Royal Opera House Bow St, WC2 (@www.royaloperahouse.org). Newly refurbished, but still as expensive as ever. 44 discounted day seats available. Covent Garden tube.
Sadler's Wells Rosebery Avenue, EC1 (@www.sadlers-wells.com). London's biggest dance venue puts on a mixed bag of the best contemporary dance, kids' shows and ballet. Angel tube.
Shakespeare's Globe New Globe Walk, SE1 (@www.shakespeares-globe.org.uk). Replica open-air Elizabethan theatre that puts on shows from mid-May to mid-Sept, with standing tickets for £5. London Bridge, Blackfriars or Southwark tube.
Wigmore Hall 36 Wigmore St, W1 (@www.wigmore-hall.org.uk). Intimate and elegant classical recital venue, just off Oxford St, that remains many Londoners' favourite. Bond St or Oxford Circus tube.

Listings

Embassies Australia, Australia House, Strand, WC2 ☎020/7379 4334, ⊛www.australia.org.uk; Canada, MacDonald House, 1 Grosvenor Square, W1 ☎020/7258 6600, ⊛www.canada.org.uk; Ireland, 17 Grosvenor Place, SW1 ☎020/7235 2171; New Zealand, New Zealand House, 80 Haymarket, SW1 ☎020/7930 8422, ⊛www.nzembassy.com; South Africa, South Africa House, Trafalgar Square, WC2 ☎020/7451 7299, ⊛www.southafricahouse.com; US, 24 Grosvenor Square, W1 ☎020/7499 9000, ⊛www.usembassy.org.uk.

Exchange Shopping areas such as Oxford St and Covent Garden are littered with private exchange offices, and there are 24hr booths at the biggest central tube stations, but their rates are always worse than the banks. You'll find branches of all major banks around Oxford St, Regent St and Piccadilly.

Hospital St Mary's Hospital, Praed St, W2, Paddington tube ☎020/7886 6666; University College Hospital, Grafton Way, WC1, Euston Square tube; ☎020/7387 9300.

Internet access easyEverything: 9 Tottenham Court Rd (Tottenham Court Rd tube), 358 Oxford St (Bond St tube), 7 The Strand (Charing Cross tube) and across the city.

Left luggage At all airport terminals and major train stations.

Lost property On a bus or tube, call ☎020/7486 2496; on a train ☎0845/748 4950; in a black taxi ☎020/7918 2000.

Pharmacies Bliss, 5 Marble Arch, W1 (daily 9am–midnight).

Police 10 Vine St, W1 ☎020/7437 1212.

Post office 24–28 William IV St, WC2N 4DL (Leicester Sq or Charing Cross tube). Mon–Fri 8.30am–6.30pm, Sat 9am–5.30pm.

Southeast England

Nestling in self-satisfied prosperity, **southeast England** is the richest part of the country, due to its agricultural wealth and proximity to the capital. Swift, frequent rail and coach services make it ideal for day-trips from London. Medieval ecclesiastical power-bases such as **Canterbury** and **Winchester** offer an introduction to the nation's history; while on the coast is the upbeat, hedonistic resort of **Brighton**, London's playground by the sea.

DOVER is the main port of entry along this stretch of coast, and the country's busiest. It's not a particularly inspiring town, and its famous White Cliffs are best enjoyed from a boat several miles out. Ferries (Calais and Zeebrugge) use the Eastern Docks, while Hoverspeed (Calais and Ostend) uses the Hoverport, south of the centre. The main **train station**, for services to Canterbury and London (last one around 10pm), is Dover Priory, ten minutes' walk west of the centre and served by free shuttle buses from both docks. **Coaches** to London (last one around 8.20pm) pick up from both docks and the town-centre **bus station** on Pencester Rd. The **tourist office** is on Biggin St (daily 9/10am–4/5.30pm; Sept–May closed Sun; ☎01304/205108, ⊛www.whitecliffscountry.org.uk).

Canterbury

CANTERBURY, one of England's oldest centres of Christianity, was home to the country's most famous martyr, Archbishop Thomas à Becket, who fell victim to Church–State rivalry in 1170. It became one of northern Europe's great pilgrimage sites, as Chaucer's *Canterbury Tales* attest, until Henry VIII had the martyr's shrine demolished in 1538. The cathedral remains the focal point of a compact centre, which is enclosed on three sides by medieval walls. Today, as well as hosting a sizeable student population, it's thronged with visitors, but remains relatively unspoilt.

Built in stages from 1070 onwards, the vast **Cathedral** (Mon–Sat 9am–5/6.30pm, Sun 12.30–2.30pm & 4.30–5.30pm; £4, free on Sun; ⊛www.canterbury -cathedral.org) derives its distinctive presence from the perpendicular thrust of the late Gothic towers, dominated by the central, sixteenth-century Bell Harry tower. Notable features of the high vaulted interior are the tombs of Henry IV and his wife, and a gilded effigy of the Black Prince, both in the Trinity Chapel behind the main altar. The site of Becket's murder is marked by a modern shrine in the northwest transept, with a crude sculpture of the supposed weapons suspended above. Steps descend from here to the Romanesque arches of the **crypt**, one of the few remaining visible relics of the Norman cathedral. East of the cathedral, across the ring road, are the evocative ruins of **St Augustine's Abbey** (daily 10am–4/6pm; £3; EH), on the site of a church founded by St Augustine, who began the conversion of the English in 597. Most of the town's other sights are located on or near High St. The **Eastbridge Hospital** (Mon–Sat 10am–4.45pm; £1), opposite the library, was founded in the twelfth century to provide poor pilgrims with shelter, and a thirteenth-century wall painting of Christ is still faintly visible in the upstairs refectory. The **West Gate**, at the far end of St Peter's St (a continuation of High St), is the city's last remaining medieval gate, housing a small museum (Mon–Sat 11am–12.30pm & 1.30–3.30pm; £1; @www.canterbury-museums.co.uk) featuring weaponry used by the medieval city guard. The best exposition of local history is provided by the interactive **Museum of Canterbury**, on Stour St (Mon–Sat 10.30am–5pm, Sun 1.30–5pm; Nov–May closed Sun; £3; @www.canterbury-museums.co.uk).

Practicalities

Canterbury has two **train stations**, Canterbury East for most services from London Victoria and Dover Priory, and Canterbury West for services from London Charing Cross – the stations are ten minutes south and northwest of the centre respectively. The **bus station** is on St George's Lane; just below the High St. The **tourist office** is opposite the entrance to the cathedral at 13 Sun St (daily 9.30/10am–4/6pm; Jan–Easter closed Sun; ☎01227/378 100, @www .canterbury.co.uk); it will book a room for you for a small fee, a service which is often necessary in the summer months.

Hostels

YHA 54 New Dover Rd ☎0870/770 5744, @www.yha.org.uk. Victorian villa a mile southeast of the centre. Closed Jan. ③

KiPPS hostel 40 Nunnery Fields ☎01227/786121, @www.kipps-hostel.com. A short walk south of the centre. ③

Guest houses

Ann's House 63 London Rd ☎01227/768767. Traditional Victorian villa offering comfortable rooms, most en suite. ⑥

St Stephen's Guest House 100 St Stephen's Rd ☎01227/767644. Ten minutes' walk north along the river Stour, this place has excellent value en suites. ⑥

Wincheap Guest House 94 Wincheap ☎01227/762309. Good-value Victorian B&B near East station. ④

Eating and drinking

Bell & Crown 10 Palace St. A friendly medieval pub with excellent home-cooked food.

Café des Amis du Mexique 95 St Dunstan's St. Serves popular Mexican fare.

Casey's 5 Butchery Lane. Irish pub serving Irish stew and soda bread, with live folk music.

Chaopraya River 2 Dover St. Serves tasty, affordable Thai food.

Oranges Bar 14 St Peter's St. Friendly pub serving delicious veggie dishes until 4pm.

Simple Simon's 3 Church Lane. Old hostelry popular with students, with regular live blues and jazz.

Tapas en Las Trece 13 Palace St. Tasty tapas from around £5 a dish, and occasional live music.

Brighton

BRIGHTON has been a prime target for day-tripping Londoners since the Prince Regent (later George IV) started holidaying here in the 1770s with his mistress, launching a trend for the "dirty weekend". This is one of Britain's most entertaining seaside resorts, and has emerged from seediness to embrace a new, fashionable hedonism which is turning the heads of London's style gurus. The wide range of nightlife owes much to the large student population, and there's a colourful music and arts festival (@www.brighton-festival.org.uk), which runs for three weeks in May.

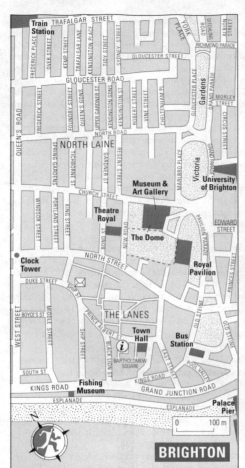

Train Station TRAFALGAR STREET
YORK PLACE
DITCHING ROAD
AUBREY ROAD
FREDERICK PLACE
DYER STREET
KEMP STREET
TRAFALGAR LANE
KENSINGTON PLACE
FOUNDRY STREET
SYDNEY STREET
RICHMOND PARADE
GLOUCESTER STREET
GLOUCESTER ROAD
RICHMOND PLACE
GRAND PARADE
MORLEY STREET
QUEEN'S ROAD
FREDERICK STREET
FOUNDRY STREET
QUEEN'S GDNS
UPPER GARDNER ST
KENSINGTON GDNS
ROBERT STREET
VINE STREET
CHELTENHAM PL
Gardens
CIRCUS STREET
NORTH ROAD
NORTH LAINE
MARLBRO PLACE
Victoria
University of Brighton
SPRING GARDENS
TICHBORNE ST
GARDNER ST
REGENT STREET
Museum & Art Gallery
GRAND PARADE
CHURCH STREET
WINDSOR STREET
PORTLAND STREET
KING STREET
Theatre Royal
NEW ROAD
The Dome
PAVILION PARADE
EDWARD STREET
Clock Tower
NORTH STREET
Royal Pavilion
PRINCES STREET
DUKE STREET
SHIP ST
OLD STEINE
WEST STREET
BOYCE'S ST
MIDDLE STREET
THE LANES
PRINCE ALBERT ST
SHIP STREET
BLACK LION ST
Town Hall
Bus Station
OLD STEINE
EAST STREET
SOUTH ST
BARTHOLOMEW SQUARE
KINGS ROAD
POOL VALLEY
Fishing Museum
KINGS ROAD
GRAND JUNCTION ROAD
ESPLANADE
ESPLANADE
Palace Pier
0   100 m

BRIGHTON

© Crown copyright

From the train station on Queen's Rd it's a ten-minute stroll straight down to the seafront, a four-mile-long pebble beach bordered by a balustered promenade. (Coaches arrive at the Pool Valley **bus station**, very near the front.) The wonderfully tacky **Palace Pier** is an obligatory call, basically a half-mile amusement arcade lined with booths selling fish and chips, candyfloss and assorted tat. Near here the antiquated locomotives of **Volk's Railway** (Easter to mid-Sept daily 11am–5/6pm; £2.40 return), the first electric train in the country, run eastward towards the Marina and the nudist beach. On the western seafront you can see – but not enter – the brooding **West Pier**, damaged in World War II, severed from the mainland following a hurricane in 1987, and gutted by fire in 2003. A block back from the seafront are **The Lanes**, a shopping area of narrow alleys preserving the layout, but little of the ambience, of the fishing port that Brighton once was. Inland from here, overlooking the traffic-heavy Old Steine, is the distinctive **Royal Pavilion** (daily 10am–5.15/5.45pm; £5.80; @www.royalpavilion.org.uk), a wedding-cake confection of pagodas, minarets and domes built in 1817 as a pleasure palace for the Prince Regent. Just around the corner on Church St is Brighton's **Museum and Art Gallery** (Mon–Sat 10am–5/7pm, Sun 2–5pm; free), with displays of Art Nouveau and Art Deco furniture and Dalí's surreal sofa based on Mae West's lips. North of Church St is one of the main draws of Brighton – the arty, bohemian quarter of **North Laine**, with secondhand clothes-, record- and junk-shops interspersed with stylish boutiques and co-op coffee houses.

Practicalities

Brighton has a fast and frequent **train** service from London (Victoria, King's Cross, Blackfriars and London Bridge) and from Gatwick and Luton airports. The **tourist office** is at 10 Bartholomew Sq in The Lanes (daily 9/10am–4/5pm, closed Sun in winter; ☎0906/711 2255, @www.visitbrighton.com). Note that many of the B&Bs in town require a minimum two nights' stay at weekends and in August. **Cafés** and **restaurants** abound, with a particularly good selection in North Laine. Many also offer student discounts. For drinking, the **pubs** around The Lanes are the place to head for. Brighton has a frenetic **nightlife** scene, livelier than just about anywhere outside London. We've listed a few of the most highly rated places below, but for full listings, pick up a copy of the free magazines *This is Brighton* or *Insight*, available from the tourist office. Brighton also has a lively **gay scene**; for full details check out the free listings magazine *3Sixty* or ⓦwww.gay.brighton.co.uk.

Hostels

Baggies Backpackers 33 Oriental Place ☎01273/733740. Just beyond the West Pier and more spacious than *Brighton Backpackers*. ❸

Brighton Backpackers 75 Middle St ☎01273/777717, ⓦwww.brightonbackpackers.com. Just off the seafront and a much livelier option than the YHA place; has a quieter annexe around the corner. ❸

YHA Patcham Place ☎0870/770 5724, ⓦwww.yha.org.uk. Sixteenth-century manor house four miles north of Brighton on the A23 London Rd; take bus #5 or #5a. ❸

Guest houses

The Aquarium 13 Madeira Place ☎01273/605761, ⓔtherese_cahill2000 @yahoo.com. Central, good-value B&B with bright yellow facade. No smoking. ❺

Lichfield House 30 Waterloo St, Hove ☎01273/777740, ⓦwww.lichfieldhouse .freeserve.co.uk. Stylish place just off the seafront. No smoking in rooms. ❻

Cafés and restaurants

Bamboo 10 Kensington Gardens. Trip-hoppy place in North Laine with a balcony upstairs.

Bombay Aloo 39 Ship St. In The Lanes; check out the £5 eat-all-you-can buffet.

Food for Friends 17 Prince Albert St. A classy budget wholefood veggie eatery.

Wai Kika Moo Kau 11 Kensington Gardens. Funky global veggie café-restaurant in North Laine, with low prices.

Pubs

The Aquarium 6 Steine St. Popular, central gay pub.

Dr Brighton's 16 Kings Rd. Another popular gay haunt, this one on the seafront.

Hector's Grand Parade. A favourite student hangout.

Prince Albert 48 Trafalgar St. Pre-club venue near the station.

Clubs and live music venues

Concorde 2 Madeira Drive. Live music venue with club nights at weekends.

Escape 10 Marine Parade. Brighton's trendiest club, specializing in funk and house.

Honey Club 214 Kings Rd Arches. Garage, house and hip-hop.

Revenge 32 Old Steine. Predominantly gay venue. Cabaret on Mon night.

Winchester

WINCHESTER's rural tranquillity betrays little of its former role as the political and ecclesiastical power base of southern England. A town of Roman foundation fifty miles southwest of London, Winchester rose to prominence in the ninth century as King Alfred the Great's capital, and remained influential well into the Middle Ages. The shrine of St Swithin, Alfred's tutor and Bishop of Winchester, made the town an important destination for pilgrims.

Alfred's statue stands at the eastern end of the Broadway, the town's main thoroughfare, which becomes High St as it progresses west towards the train station. To the south of here is the **Cathedral** (daily 8.30am–6pm; £3.50 donation; ⓦwww.winchester-cathedral.org.uk); much of its exterior is twelfth century, although there's some Norman stonework visible in the south transept. Above the high altar are mortuary chests holding the remains of the pre-Conquest kings of England. The Angel chapel contains sixteenth-century wall paintings of the miracles of the Virgin Mary, although a modern protective replica now covers the originals. Jane Austen is buried on the south side of the nave; the inscription on the floor slab remembers her merely as the daughter of a local clergyman, ignoring her renown as a novelist. Immediately outside are traces of the original Saxon cathedral, built by Cenwalh, king of Wessex, in the mid-seventh century. The true grandeur of this structure is shown by a model in the **City Museum** (daily 10am/noon–4/5pm; Oct–March closed Mon; free) on the western side of the cathedral close; other exhibits include mosaics and pottery from Roman Winchester. Further west along

High St is the thirteenth-century **Great Hall** (daily 10am–4/5pm; free), a banqueting chamber used by successive kings of England and renowned for what is alleged to be King Arthur's Round Table – but the piece, which now hangs from the wall, is probably fourteenth-century (and so about 500 years too young). It seems to have been repainted with portraits and the names of King Arthur's knights for the visit of Emperor Charles V, who was entertained here by Henry VIII in 1522. South of the Cathedral is the fourteenth-century Pilgrims Hall, from where a signposted route leads through a medieval quarter to **Winchester College**, the oldest of Britain's public schools. It's then a half-hour stroll across the Water Meadow to the almshouse of **St Cross** (Mon–Sat 9.30/10.30am–3.30/5pm; £2), founded in 1136, whose church contains a triptych by the Flemish painter Mabuse. Continuing a medieval tradition, needy wayfarers may still apply for the "dole" here – a tiny portion of bread and beer.

Practicalities

Winchester's **train station** is about a mile northwest of the cathedral on Stockbridge Rd. The **bus terminal** is on Broadway, just opposite the Guildhall, in which the **tourist office** is situated (Mon–Sat 9.30/10am–5/5.30pm, Sun 11am–4pm; Oct–April closed Sun; ☏01962/840500, ⊛www.visitwinchester.com). Winchester's affluence is reflected in both the style and prices of its **B&Bs**, most of which cluster in the streets between St Cross and Christchurch roads, south of town. *The Farrells*, 5 Ranelagh Rd (☏01962/869555, ✉thefarrells@easicom.com; ⑤), is a good central option, or try *Sullivans*, 29 Stockbridge Rd, beside the train station (☏01962/862027, ✉sullivans_bandb@amserve.net; ④). There's also a lovely **hostel** in the *City Mill*, 1 Water Lane, just east of Alfred's statue (☏0870/770 6092, ⊛www.yha.org.uk; closed Nov–Feb; ③). For **food**, *Forte's Tea Rooms*, 78 Parchment St, offers snacks, full meals and a buzzy atmosphere, while the cool, modern *Alcatraz*, Jewry St, provides pizzas and pastas.

England's West Country

England's "**West Country**" has never been a precise geographical term, and there will always be a certain amount of argument as to where it actually starts. But as a broad generalization, the cosmopolitan feel of the southeast begins to fade into a slower, rural pace of life from **Salisbury** onwards, becoming more pronounced the further west you travel. In Neolithic times a rich and powerful culture evolved here, as shown by monuments such as **Stonehenge** and **Avebury**, and the isolated moorland sites of inland **Cornwall**. Urban attractions of western England include **Bristol** and the well-preserved Regency spa town of **Bath**; those in search of rural peace and quiet should head for the compelling bleakness of **Dartmoor**. The southwestern extremities of Britain include some of the most beautiful stretches of coastline, its rugged, rocky shores battered by the Atlantic, although the excellent sandy beaches make it one of the country's busiest corners over the summer. All of the region's major centres can be reached fairly easily by train or coach from London. Local bus services cover most areas, although in the rural depths of Dartmoor they can be very sparse indeed. Check the tourist office website ⊛www.westcountrynow.com.

Salisbury and around

SALISBURY's central feature is the elegant spire of its **Cathedral** (daily 7.15am–6.15/8.15pm; £3.80 donation; ⊛www.salisburycathedral.org.uk), the tallest in the country, rising over 400ft. With the exception of the spire, the cathedral was almost entirely completed in the thirteenth century, and is one of the few great English churches that is not a hotch-potch of different styles. Prominent among the features of the interior are the fourteenth-century clock just inside the north porch, one of the oldest working timepieces in the country, and an exceptional Tudor memorial to the Earl of Hertford, Lady Jane Grey's brother-in-law, in the Lady Chapel at the eastern end of the church. An octagonal **chapterhouse**, approached via the extensive **cloisters** (Mon–Sat 9.30/10am–5.30/6.45pm, Sun noon–5.30pm; free), holds a collection of precious manuscripts, among which is one of the four original copies of the Magna Carta. Most of Salisbury's remaining sights are grouped in a sequence of historic houses around The Close, the old walled inner town around the cathedral. The **Salisbury and South Wiltshire Museum**, opposite the main portal of the cathedral on West Walk (Mon–Sat 10am–5pm; July & Aug also Sun 2–5pm; £3.50), is a good place to bone up on the Neolithic history of Wessex before heading out to Stonehenge and Avebury. The **Mompesson House** on The Close's North Walk (April–Sept Mon–Wed, Sat & Sun 11am–5pm; £3.90) is a fine eighteenth-century house complete with Georgian furniture and fittings. For the postcard view of the cathedral immortalized by John Constable, wander across the meadows and over the River Avon to **HARNHAM**, where you can have lunch or a drink at the *Old Mill* pub. A ten-minute hop on any Andover- or Amesbury-bound bus takes you to the ruins of **OLD SARUM** (daily 9/10am–4/6pm; £2.50), abandoned in the fourteenth century when the bishopric moved to Salisbury. Traces of the medieval town are visible in the outlines of its Norman cathedral and castle mound, but the ditch-encircled site is far older, populated in Iron Age, Roman and Saxon times.

Practicalities

It's a short walk southeast from Salisbury's **train station** (services from London Waterloo) across the River Avon into town. **Buses** from nearby Winchester and elsewhere terminate behind Endless St, a block south of which is the **tourist office**, just off Market Square (daily 9.30/10.30am–4.30/6pm; closed Sun in winter; ☏01722/334956, ⊛www.visitsalisbury.com).

Hostels

Matt & Tiggy's Salt Lane ☏01722/327443. Small, privately run hostel near the bus station. ❸
YHA Milford Hill House, Milford Hill ☏0870/770 6018, ⊛www.yha.org.uk. Excellent, secluded hostel five minutes east of the city centre. ❸

Guest houses

Glen Lyn 6 Bellamy Lane ☏01722/327880, ⊛www.glenlynbandbatsalisbury.co.uk. Elegant Victorian house ten minutes' walk from the centre. No smoking. ❺
Leena's 50 Castle St ☏01722/335419. Good-value basic B&B with shared or private bathrooms. No smoking in rooms. ❺

Wyndham Park Lodge 51 Wyndham Rd ☏01722/416517, ⊛www.wyndhamparklodge .co.uk. Solid Victorian house in a quiet street, with all rooms en suite. No smoking. ❺

Eating and drinking

Bishop's Mill Bridge St. Popular pub offering outdoor seating and bar meals.
Haunch of Venison Minster St. Atmospheric old pub serving good food.
Michael Snell's Tea Rooms St Thomas's Square. Traditional tearooms, serving snacks and delicious buns. Closed Sun.
Moloko 5 Bridge St. Cool café and cocktail bar, serving croissants, panini and salads.

Stonehenge

The uplands northwest of Salisbury were a thriving centre of Neolithic civilization, the greatest legacy of which is **STONEHENGE** (daily 9/9.30am–4/7pm; £5). It is served by buses from Salisbury. You can also take a tour – ask at the bus station for details – or get an Explorer (£5.70) or Wiltshire Rover (£6) pass, which are valid all day and include travel to Avebury and Bath. The monument's age is being constantly revised as research progresses, but it's known that it was built in several distinct stages and adapted to the needs of successive cultures. The first Stonehenge probably consisted of a circular ditch dug in around 3000 BC. This was followed by the erection within the ditch of around forty bluestones, which were transported here from the Preseli area of Wales. Shortly after 2500 BC, these were replaced by a circle and inner horseshoe of trilithons, made up of local Wiltshire sarsen stones up to 21ft in height and topped by horizontal slabs; the smaller bluestones were later arranged in various patterns within the outer circle. The way in which the sun's rays penetrate the central enclosure at dawn on midsummer's day has led to speculation about Stonehenge's role as either an astronomical observatory or a place of sun worship, but knowledge of the cultures responsible for building it is too scanty to reach any firm conclusions. The stones themselves are controversially fenced off to prevent the erosion caused by thousands of visitors, but it makes the visit a slightly disappointing experience. The only way to enter the circle itself is to take a **guided tour** (apply on ☎01980/626267 or at ⍾www.english-heritage.org.uk; £10).

Avebury

Salisbury also serves as a base for visiting the equally important – and much more atmospheric – Neolithic site at **AVEBURY**. Buses #5 and #6 run here daily from Salisbury. The Avebury monoliths were probably erected soon after 2500 BC, and the main circle – with a diameter of some 400m – easily beats Stonehenge in terms of scale, even if it is not as impressive for its architectural sophistication. The atmosphere here is far more relaxed, however, and you can contemplate the grassy site armed with a pint or two from the *Red Lion* village pub, set right beside the main stone circle. Avebury's **Alexander Keiller Museum** (daily 10am–4/6pm; £4) has displays on the monoliths as well as other ancient sites in the vicinity, while the **Barn Gallery** (same times, same ticket) favours a more interactive approach. Both places are worth visiting before or after exploring the cluster of archeological sites to the south of Avebury, best approached along the (signposted) **West Kennet Avenue**, two lines of standing stones thought to have been a processional way. Originally this ran two miles south to the so-called **Sanctuary**, possibly a gathering place of religious significance from around 3000 BC, of which little remains today. More compelling is the enormous conical mound of **Silbury Hill** just west of here, Europe's largest Neolithic construction, dating from around 2600 BC. Signposted up a track on the other side of the A4, **West Kennet Long Barrow** is an impressive stone passage grave in use for over 1500 years from about 3700 BC. From the Sanctuary at Overton Hill, hikers can loop northeast on a section of the **Ridgeway**, a 4000-year-old prehistoric highway which may once have run the breadth of Britain; it can still be walked or cycled as far as Tring, in the Chilterns. Get details from Avebury's **tourist office** on Green St (daily 10/10.30am–4.30/5.30pm; ☎01672/539425, ⍾www.kennet.gov.uk).

Bath

BATH is an ancient Roman spa revived in the eighteenth century for the tastes of the wealthy upper classes. Extensive reconstruction put into effect by Neoclassicist architects John Wood and his son, John Wood the Younger, gives the town its distinctive appearance, with terraces of weathered sandstone fringed by spindly black railings. The hot spring that gave the city its name was dedicated to Sulis, the Celtic goddess of the waters, and provided the centrepiece of an extensive **Roman Baths** complex, now restored and holding a fascinating museum (daily 9/9.30am–5.30/6pm; July–Aug till 10pm; ⍾www.romanbaths.co.uk; £8.50). The pools, pipes and underfloor heating are remarkable demonstrations of the ingenuity of Roman engineering. The **Pump Room** (free), built above the Roman site in the eighteenth century, is now a restaurant and tea room where you can sample the waters while listening to genteel tunes from the resident chamber ensemble. You can also bathe or receive any number of health treatments in the modern **Thermae Bath Spa** (daily 9am–10pm) on nearby Hot Bath St. Next to the Roman Baths, **Bath Abbey** (daily 9am–4.30/6pm; £2.50 donation) is renowned for the lofty fifteenth-century vault of its choir and the dense carpet of gravestones and memorials that cover the floor. The Abbey's **Heritage Vaults** (Mon–Sat 10am–4pm; £2.50) house Saxon and Norman sculpture and a reconstruction of the original building.

The best of Bath's eighteenth-century architecture is on the high ground to the north of the town centre, where the well-proportioned urban planning of the Woods is best showcased by the elegant Circus and the adjacent **Royal Crescent**. The house at 1 Royal Crescent is now a museum (Tues–Sun 10.30am–4/5pm; closed Dec to mid-Feb; £4), showing how the Crescent's houses would have looked in the Regency period. The social calendar of Bath's elite centred on John Wood the Younger's **Assembly Rooms** (daily 10am–5pm; free), just east of the Circus; recently renovated, it includes the interesting **Museum of Costume** in the basement (daily: 10am–5pm; ⊛www.museumofcostume.co.uk; £5.50; joint ticket with Roman Baths £11). The triple arches of Pulteney Bridge lead northeast from the town centre across the River Avon and up Great Pulteney St to the **Holburne Museum** (Tues–Sat 10am–5pm, Sun 2.30–5.30pm; closed mid-Dec to mid-Feb; ⊛www.bath.ac.uk/holburne; £4), which contains silver, porcelain and furniture from the Regency period, as well as some fine art, including works by Gainsborough.

Practicalities

The **train** and **bus stations** are both on Manvers St, five minutes south of the centre. The **tourist office** is just off the Abbey churchyard (Mon–Sat 9.30am–5/6pm, Sun 10am–4pm; ☏0906/711 2000, ⊛www.visitbath.co.uk). The main tourist thoroughfares and neighbouring backstreets provide more **tearooms** than you can handle. We've listed some of the best, along with the best **restaurants** and **pubs**, below. Bath also hosts the eclectic *International Music Festival* (⊛www.bathmusicfest.org.uk) in May and June. For **Internet** access and coffee try the *Green Park Brasserie* at Old Green Park Station, off James St (☏01225/338565; £3/hr).

Hostels

Backpackers' Hostel 13 Pierrepoint St ☏01225/446787, ⊛www.hostels.co.uk. Relaxed and centrally located, just five minutes' walk north of the train and bus stations. ❸

YHA Bathwick Hill ☏0870/770 5688, ⊛www.yha .org.uk. A hillside villa a mile east of town; bus #18. ❸

Guest houses

Henry 6 Henry St ☏01225/424052, ⊛www .thehenry.com. Near the Abbey, with more rooms than most, but still books up quickly. No en suites. ❺

Holly Villa 14 Pulteney Gardens ☏01225/310331, ⊛www.hollyvilla.com. Friendly place close to the Kennet and Avon canal, with six rooms, all with showers, and a nice garden. No smoking. No credit cards. ❻

Cafés and restaurants

Café Retro 18 York St. Popular café and bistro with an inventive international menu.

Demuth's 2 North Parade Passage off Abbey Green. Stylish vegetarian restaurant.

Walrus and Carpenter Barton St. Friendly place behind the theatre, serving steaks and burgers as well as veggie dishes.

Pubs

The Bell Walcot St. Grungy pub with garden and live music Mon and Wed eve, plus Sun lunch.

Pig & Fiddle Saracen St. Real ales, outside terraces, table football and food. Very popular.

The Porter 15 George St. Cheap meals at lunchtime and a pre-club crowd in the evenings.

Bristol

Situated on a succession of lumpy hills twelve miles beyond Bath and just inland from the mouth of the Avon, the city of **BRISTOL** grew rich on transatlantic trade – slaving, in particular – in the early part of the nineteenth century. It has moved on since then, while remaining a wealthy, commercial centre, now home to computer and aviation industries, a major university and a thriving cultural scene.

The city centre – in so much as there is one – is an elongated traffic interchange, **The Centre**. Its southern end gives onto the **Floating Harbour**, an area of waterways that formed the hub of the old port and now the location of numerous bars and restaurants as well as two of Bristol's best contemporary arts venues, housed in converted warehouses on either side of the water: the **Arnolfini** (⊛www.arnolfini

.demon.co.uk) and the **Watershed Arts Centre** (@www.watershed.co.uk); both have pleasant, reasonably priced cafés which serve food and stay open late. Behind the Watershed lies the "at-Bristol" complex (@www.at-bristol.org.uk), where two interactive centres – **Explore** (daily 10am–6pm; £7.50), a hands-on technology park, and **Wildwalk** (same times; £6.50), a hi-tech wildlife museum – are over-shadowed by a giant **IMAX cinema** (screenings 11.15am–4.30/7.15pm; £6.50); a ticket for all three costs £15.50 or £16.50. From the Arnolfini, on Prince's Wharf, a swing bridge leads to the quayside **Bristol Industrial Museum** (Mon–Wed, Sat & Sun 10am–5pm; Nov–March Sat & Sun only; free), with cars and ship models. Just east of here rises the **Church of St Mary Redcliffe** (Mon–Sat 9am–4/5pm, Sun 8am–8pm), a glorious Gothic confection begun in the thirteenth century. A brief walk further east from here along the busy Redcliffe Way will bring you to the **British Empire and Commonwealth Museum**, attached to the main train station (daily 10am–5pm; £4.95), which reviews Britain's colonial empire and the trading network that succeeded it. To the west of the Industrial Museum, ten min-utes' walk or a brief ride on the harbour ferry brings you to the **Maritime Heritage Centre** (daily 10am–4.30/5.30pm; £6.25), celebrating Bristol's ship-building past and providing access to Brunel's **SS Great Britain** (@www.ss-great-britain.com), the first propeller-driven iron ship, launched from this dock in 1843, and to a replica of the **Matthew**, which carried John Cabot to America in 1497.

The rest of your time is best spent wandering around the suburb of **CLIFTON**, whose airy terraces are reminiscent of the Georgian splendours of nearby Bath. It's a somewhat genteel quarter, but full of enticing pubs and with a spectacular focus in the **Clifton Suspension Bridge** (@www.clifton-suspension-bridge.org.uk), the cre-ation of the indefatigable engineer and railway builder Isambard Kingdom Brunel, spanning the limestone abyss of the Avon Gorge. An interpretive Visitor Centre is due to open here in 2004. On a height above the bridge, the diminutive **Observatory** (daily 11am/noon–4/5pm; closed when cloudy; £1), holds a Victorian *camera obscura* which encompasses views of the gorge and bridge, and provides access to a steep tun-nel ending at Giant's Cave, a ledge on the side of the gorge (same hours; £1).

Practicalities

Bristol's main Temple Meads **train station** is a five-minute bus ride southeast of the centre, or a fifteen-minute walk. The **bus station** is close to the Broadmead shopping centre on Marlborough St. There's a **tourist office** in the at-Bristol complex on Harbourside (daily 10/11am–4/6pm; ☎0906/711 2191, @www.visitbristol.co.uk). For **food and drink**, the stretch between Clifton and the city centre offers a vast choice of ethnic eats and late bars. For nightlife **listings** galore check out the magazine *Venue* (@www.venue.co.uk) available at any newsagent. Arnolfini and Watershed both have arts **cinemas**, and there's a renowned **theatre** company at the Old Vic on King St. Bristol's vibrant **music** scene has produced a host of influential names (Tricky, Massive Attack, Portishead); top **clubs** are listed below.

Hostels

Bristol Backpackers 17 St Stephen's St ☎0117/925 7900, @www.bristolbackpackers .co.uk. Friendly place in the heart of the pub district, with bar and Internet access. ❸

YHA 14 Narrow Quay ☎0870/770 5726. Splendidly situated HI hostel in an old wharfside building next to the Arnolfini. Breakfast included. ❹

Hotels and guest houses

Oakfield Hotel 52 Oakfield Rd ☎0117/973 5556. A mile from the centre in Clifton; the public rooms are gloomy but the rooms are fine. No en suites. No smoking in rooms. No credit cards. ❺

St Michael's Guest House 145 St Michael's Hill ☎0117/907 7820. Simple rooms over one of Cotham's most popular cafés. No en suites. ❺

Eating and drinking

Mud Dock Café The Grove. In the harbourside area, this funky restaurant/bar also has regular DJs most nights.

Riverstation The Grove. A good-value deli/bar with a classier restaurant upstairs.

Tantric Jazz Café 39 St Nicholas St. Serves up middle-eastern cuisine, live music and a bohemian atmosphere.

Academy Frogmore St. Live bands and international DJs. Open Thurs–Sat.

Thekla The Grove. Great riverboat venue staging

eclectic events until 2am or later.

Vibes 3 Frog Lane, Frogmore St. Central gay club with two bars and dance areas and themed nights. Thurs is student night.

Wells and Glastonbury

A small market town possessed of an extraordinary cathedral, **WELLS** is served by shoals of buses from Bristol and Bath, all arriving at Princes Rd bus station, five minutes from the centre. Follow Market St eastwards from here to the picturesque inn-lined Market Place, and the **tourist office** in the Town Hall (daily 9.30/10am–4/5.30pm; ☎01749/672552). From here a gateway leads through to The Close, bringing you face to face with an intoxicating array of Gothic statuary, mostly from the 1230s and 1240s. Inside the majestic **Cathedral** (Mon–Sat 9.30am–6/7pm, Sun 12.30–2.30pm; ☎www.wellscathedral.org.uk; £4.50 donation), the great interlacing "scissor-arches" at the crossing were devised to support the unstable tower; in the north transept a fourteenth-century clock strikes the quarter-hours. North of the cathedral are **Vicar's Close**, a row of fourteenth-century terraced houses, and the **town museum** (Easter–Oct daily 10am–4/5.30, Aug till 8pm; Nov–Easter Mon & Wed–Sun 11am–4pm; £2.50). The nearest **hostel** (☎0870/770 5760, ☎www.yha.org.uk; closed Jan; ❸) is six miles northwest in the village of **CHEDDAR**, reached on bus #126 or #826, walking distance from the dramatic **Cheddar Gorge**, formed by the collapse of a cave system.

Twice-hourly buses head southeast from Wells to **GLASTONBURY**, a small rural town whose associations with the Holy Grail and King Arthur have made it a magnet for those with a taste for the mystical – the **Tor**, a natural mound overlooking the town, is identified with the Isle of Avalon. Joseph of Arimathea, a relation of the Virgin Mary, is also said to have owned land nearby, and to have brought Mary and Jesus here; William Blake's poem *Jerusalem* replays the legend: "And did those feet in ancient time / Walk upon England's mountains green?" Around the Market Cross, Glastonbury's High St is overrun by New Age cafés and shops. The impressive ruins of the **Abbey** are approached from nearby Magdalene St (daily 9.30/10am–4.30/6pm; £3.50; ☎www.glastonburyabbey.com); this was the oldest Christian establishment in continuous use in England until Henry VIII ordered its near-destruction. The choir is alleged to hold the tomb of King Arthur and Guinevere. A mile to the east is the Tor, at the base of which stands the natural spring known as **Chalice Well** (daily 10/11am–4/6pm; ☎www.chalicewell.org.uk; £2.50). The ferrous waters that flow from the hillside here were popularly thought to have gained their colour from the blood of Christ, supposedly flowing from the Holy Grail, buried here by Joseph of Arimathea. On top of the Tor stands the remains of a fourteenth-century church; the views from here are spectacular and it is a popular place from which to see the sunrise on the summer solstice.

By nightfall Glastonbury reverts to sleepy rural stillness – except over the summer solstice and during the **Glastonbury Festival**, which is held on a nearby farm over a weekend in mid-June and draws 80,000 people to its binge of music, drugs and events. The **tourist office**, housed in the Tribunal on High St, sells tickets (daily 10am–4/5.30pm; ☎01458/832954, ☎www.glastonburytic.co.uk). There's a friendly crowd at the *Glastonbury Backpackers* **hostel** on Market Place (☎01458/833353, ☎www.glastonburybackpackers.com; ❸), while the *Isle of Avalon* **campsite** is a short walk up Northload St from the centre (☎01458/833618). For **food and drink**, the *Backpackers* has cheap, filling meals and a lively bar with events; you'll also find well-priced veggie food at *Rainbow's End* on the High St.

Exeter

EXETER is the first stop for travellers to England's westernmost counties of Devon and Cornwall, and makes a feasible base for visiting a clutch of attractions within an easy bus-ride, including Dartmoor. The most distinctive feature of the skyline, **St Peter's Cathedral** (daily 8am–5/7.30pm; £3.50 donation; ⓦwww.exeter-cathedral .org.uk), is a stately monument made conspicuous by the two great Norman towers flanking the nave. The facade's ornate Gothic screen, made up of three tiers of sculpted (and very weathered) figures – including various medieval kings – was begun around 1360, part of a rebuilding programme which left only the Norman towers from the original construction. Inside, you can admire the longest unbroken Gothic ceiling in the world, intricately rib-vaulted, and the thirteenth-century Lady Chapel and Chapter House. Elsewhere in town, the **Royal Albert Memorial Museum** on Queen St (Mon–Sat 10am–5pm; free) is worth a visit for its imaginative review of the city's various building styles, and the old **Quayside** area, on the banks of the River Exe, is the place to head for cafés, pubs and clubs.

Exeter has two **train stations**, Central and St David's, the latter a little way out from the centre of town. **Buses** stop at the station on Paris St, right across from the **tourist office** (July & Aug Mon–Sat 9am–5pm, Sun 10am–4pm; rest of year Mon–Sat 9am–1pm & 2–5pm; ☎01392/265700, ⓦwww.exeter.gov.uk). *Globe Backpackers*, 71 Holloway St (☎01392/215521, ⓦwww.globebackpackers .freeserve.co.uk; ❸), is a clean and central independent **hostel**; the **YHA hostel** lies two miles south of the city centre on Countess Wear Rd (☎0870/770 5826; closed Jan–Feb; ❸). *Herbie's,* 15 North St (closed all Sun & Mon eve), is a good wholefood **restaurant**, and there are cheap eats at the Quayside. Two of the best **clubs** are in the centre: the *Cavern Club*, in Gandy St and the *Timepiece*, Little Castle St. Saddles & Paddles **rents bikes** and **canoes** (☎01392/424241, ⓦwww.saddlepaddle.co.uk), good for exploring the Exeter Canal, which runs for five miles from the Quayside area to Topsham and beyond.

Dartmoor

Dartmoor (ⓦwww.dartmoor-npa.gov.uk) is one of England's most beautiful wilderness areas, an expanse of wild uplands some 75 miles southwest of Bristol. It's home to an indigenous breed of wild pony and dotted with **tors**, characteristic wind-eroded pillars of granite. The main focus for visitors in the middle of the park is **POSTBRIDGE**, reached by local bus from Exeter and Plymouth on the #82 Transmoor service (daily in summer, weekends only in winter). Famous for its medieval bridge over the East Dart river, this is a good starting point for walks in the woodlands surrounding Bellever Tor to the south. Postbridge's **tourist office**, on the main road through the village (daily Easter–Oct daily 10am–5pm, Nov–Dec weekends 10am–4pm; ☎01822/880272, ⓦwww.dartmoor-npa.gov.uk), can supply information on the national park. The nearest **hostel** is at Bellever, one mile south (☎0870/770 5692, ⓦwww.yha.org.uk; closed Nov–Feb; ❸).

The wildest parts of the moor, around its highest points of High Willhays and Yes Tor, are south of the market town of **OKEHAMPTON** – served by regular buses from Plymouth and Exeter. Despite the stark beauty of the terrain, this part of the moor is used by the Ministry of Defence as a firing range: details of times when it's safe to walk the moor are available from the **tourist office** on Fore St (April to late July & mid-Sept to Oct Mon–Sat 10am–4.30pm; late July to mid-Sept daily 10am–4.30pm; Nov–Easter Mon, Fri & Sat 10am–4.30pm; ☎01837/53020, ⓦwww.okehamptondevon.co.uk). Surrounded by woods one mile southwest of town is the now crumbling Norman keep of **Okehampton Castle** (April–Oct daily 10am–5/6pm; £2.60). There's a **YHA hostel** in a converted goods shed at the station (☎0870/770 5978, ⓦwww.yha.org.uk; closed Dec & Jan; ❸).

The Eden Project

In the heart of Cornwall, England's most southwesterly county, is one of the newest and highest-profile attractions in the country; the **Eden Project** (daily 10am–6pm or dusk; £10; ⓦwww.edenproject.com) lies four miles northeast of St Austell (bus

#T9 from St Austell train station or #T10 from Newquay). Occupying a 160-foot-deep disused clay pit, the centre showcases the diversity of the planet's plant-life in an imaginative, sometimes wacky, but refreshingly ungimmicky style. At centre stage of the stunningly landscaped site are two vast geodesic "biomes", or conservatories: one holding groves of olive and citrus trees, cacti and other plants more usually found in the warm, temperate zones of the Mediterranean, southern Africa and southwestern USA; the larger of the two recreates a tropical zone, with teak and mahogany trees, and has a waterfall and river gushing through it. Equally impressive are the external grounds, where plantations of bamboo, tea, hops, hemp and tobacco are interspersed with brilliant swathes of flowers. The whole "living theatre" presents a constantly changing spectacle, and should ideally be visited in different seasons. Allow at least half a day for a full exploration, but arrive early to avoid congestion. There are timed "story-telling" sessions, a lawn-carpeted arena where Celtic and other music is played, and good food on hand.

Penzance and around

The busy port of **PENZANCE** forms the natural gateway to the westernmost extremity of Cornwall – and, indeed, England – the Penwith Peninsula, and all the major sights of the region can be reached on day-trips from here. From the **train station**, at the northern end of town, Market Jew St threads its way through the town centre, culminating in the Neoclassical facade of Market House, fronted by a statue of local-born chemist and inventor Humphry Davy. West of here, a series of parks and gardens punctuate the quiet residential streets overlooking the promenade. The **Penlee House Gallery and Museum**, off Morrab Rd (Mon–Sat 10/10.30am–4.30/5pm; £2, free on Sat), features works by members of the Newlyn school, late nineteenth-century painters of local land- and seascapes. The view east across the bay is dominated by **St Michael's Mount**, site of a fortified medieval monastery perched on an offshore pinnacle of rock. At low tide, the Mount is joined by a cobbled causeway to the mainland village of Marazion (regular buses from Penzance); at high tide, a boat can ferry you over (£1). You can amble around part of the Mount's shoreline, but most of the rock lies within the grounds of the **castle**, now a stately home belonging to Lord St Levan (April–Oct Mon–Fri 10.30am–5.30pm, plus most weekends; Nov–March in good weather only; £4.80).

The other obvious excursion is to **LAND'S END**, the cliffy extremity of the Penwith Peninsula, accessible on frequent buses from Penzance. Despite the hold it exerts over the popular imagination, the site may fail to live up to expectations – especially now that a small theme park has been built here – and it's worthwhile using the coastal path to explore some of the less frequented spots of the peninsula. A mile and a half south of Land's End you'll find rugged beauty at **Mill Bay**, while there are acres of beaches the same distance north at **Whitesand Bay**, and more spectacular headlands around **Cape Cornwall**, four miles north of Land's End.

Practicalities

Penzance **train** and **bus stations** are at the northeastern end of town, a step away from Market Jew St. The **tourist office** (May–Sept Mon–Sat 9am–5pm, Sun 10am–1pm; Oct–April Mon–Fri 9am–5pm, Sat 10am–1pm; ☎01736/362207, ⊛www.go-cornwall.com) is by the bus station. **B&Bs** congregate at the western end of town around Morrab Rd. The **YHA hostel**, Castle Horneck, Alverton (☎0870/770 5992, ⊛www.yha.org.uk; closed Jan; ❸), is a about a mile from the centre off the Land's End road and has **camping** facilities, or there's *Penzance Backpackers*, Alexandra Rd (☎01736/363 836, ⊛www.penzancebackpackers.ndirect.co.uk; ❸). Near Whitesand Bay and Land's End, the excellent *Whitesands Lodge* offers dorms, private rooms and camping (☎01736/871776, ⊛www.whitesandslodge.co.uk; ❸). *Co-Co's Tapas Bar*, Chapel St, has **snacks** and cakes as well as coffee and beer; *Dandelions*, on Causeway, is a veggie café. Town-centre **pubs** include the *Star* on Market Jew St, or the more touristy *Admiral Benbow* on Chapel St, a seventeenth-century house with maritime fittings. Look out for live music and other performances at the *Acorn Theatre*, Parade St.

St Ives and the north Cornwall coast

Across the peninsula from Penzance, the fishing village of **ST IVES** is the quintessential Cornish resort, featuring a maze of narrow streets lined with whitewashed cottages, sandy beaches and lush subtropical flora. The village's erstwhile tranquillity attracted several major artists throughout the twentieth century – Ben Nicholson, Barbara Hepworth and Naum Gabo among them. You can see examples of the work of these and others of the various St Ives schools at the **Tate Gallery**, overlooking Porthmeor Beach (daily 10am–4.30/5.30pm; Nov–Feb closed Mon; £4.25; ☺www.tate.org.uk/stives). A combined ticket (£6.95) admits you to the **Barbara Hepworth Museum** on Barnoon Hill (same hours), which preserves the studio of the modernist sculptor. Her photos of Cornwall quoits and landscapes provide clues to the inspiration behind her sleek monoliths, many splendid examples of which are displayed in the garden. Of the town's three beaches, the north-facing Porthmeor occasionally has good surf, and boards can be rented at the beach.

The **train station** is at Porthminster Beach, just north of the **bus station** on Station Hill. The **tourist office** in the Guildhall, St An Pol (May–Sept Mon–Sat 9am–6pm, Sun 10am–1/4pm; Oct–April Mon–Fri 9am–5pm, Sat 10am–2pm; ☎01736/796297, ☺www.go-cornwall.com), is a couple of minutes from both stations. Nearby is the *St Ives Backpackers* **hostel**, in a restored Wesleyan chapel on The Stennack (☎01736/799444, ☺www.backpackers.co.uk/st-ives; ❸).

Newquay, Padstow and Tintagel

Buffeted by Atlantic currents, Cornwall's cliffy north coast has a harsh grandeur, and is the area of the West Country most favoured by the **surfing** set. King of the surf resorts is **NEWQUAY**, whose somewhat tacky centre is surrounded by seven miles of golden sands, including Fistral Beach, the venue for surfing championships. There's a **tourist office** at Marcus Hill (mid-May to mid-Sept Mon–Sat 9.30am–5.30pm, Sun 9.30am–1pm; rest of year Mon–Fri 9.30am–4.30pm, Sat 9.30am–12.30pm; ☎01637/854020, ☺www.newquay.co.uk), and numerous campsites and **hostels**, including *Newquay International Backpackers*, 69 Tower Rd (☎01637/879366, ☺www.backpackers.co.uk/newquay; ❸), and *Matt's Surf Lodge*, 110 Mount Wise (☎01637/874651, ☺www.matts-surf-lodge.co.uk; ❸).

However, unless you're dedicated to sand and surf, or drawn by the clubbing scene – Newquay's hectic nightlife is legendary – you could plump for less packed resorts nearby. Ten miles north, **PADSTOW** makes a more appealing base for some first-class beaches, such as Constantine Bay, four miles west, and Polzeath, on the eastern side of the Camel estuary. Primarily a fishing port, Padstow is renowned for its fish restaurants, not least those belonging to celebrity chef Rick Stein; dodge the expensive *Seafood Restaurant* and *St Petroc's Bistro* in favour of the more casual *Rick Stein's Café*, 10 Middle St, which serves lunchtime snacks and moderately priced evening meals, and his *Seafood Deli* on South Quay for take-aways (all ☺www.rickstein.com). Across the Camel estuary, twelve miles northwest, the village of **TINTAGEL** trades on its associations with King Arthur. Even if you're bored by all the hocus-pocus surrounding the legend, **Tintagel Castle** (daily 10am–4/7pm; £3.20), supposedly Arthur's birthplace, merits a visit, its black and tattered Norman ruins straddling an outcrop above the sea. It's an evocative spot, with splendidly craggy coastline to either side, the coast path running along the cliff-top. Padstow **tourist office** is on the harbourside (daily 9.30am–4/5pm; Nov–March closed weekends; ☎01841/533449, ☺www.padstow.uk.com). Two **YHA hostels** in the region enjoy superb locations: just off the beach at Constantine Bay, near Padstow (℡0870/770 6076; closed Nov to March; ❸), and about a mile south of Tintagel at Dunderhole Point (℡0870/770 6068; closed Nov to mid-April; ❸).

Central England

Central England was the powerhouse of the Industrial Revolution and is still predominantly a region of gritty manufacturing towns. Birmingham, at the hub of the industrial sprawl, may boast one of the best concert halls and orchestras in the country, but is still unlikely to feature on a quickstop national tour. The university town of **Oxford**, and **Stratford-upon-Avon**, the birthplace of William Shakespeare, are the main draws here – and, in the east of the region, the other university town of **Cambridge**.

Oxford

Think of **OXFORD** and inevitably you think of its university, revered as one of the world's great academic institutions, inhabiting honeystone buildings set around ivy-clad quadrangles. Much of this is accurate enough, but although the university dominates central Oxford, the wider city has an entirely different character, its economy built on the car plants of Cowley. The **university** has long operated a collegiate system in which many students and tutors live, work and take their meals together in the same complex of buildings – usually a couple of quadrangles ("quads") with a chapel, library and dining hall. Taken together, the colleges form a dense maze of historic buildings in the heart of the city. Access may be restricted during examinations – especially in May and June – conferences and functions.

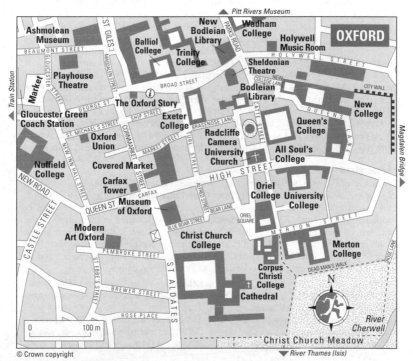

© Crown copyright

The City

The main point of reference is **Carfax**, a central crossroads overlooked by the chunky **Carfax Tower** (daily 10am–3.30/5.15pm; £1.20), one of many opportunities to enjoy a panorama of Oxford's "dreaming spires". From here, head south down St Aldates to the biggest of Oxford's colleges, **Christ Church** (Mon–Sat 9am–5.30pm, Sun noon–5.30pm; £4). The main entrance passes underneath the dome of Tom Tower, built in 1681 by Christopher Wren, before opening onto the vast expanse of Tom Quad, mostly dating from the college's foundation in the sixteenth century. An indication of the prestige and wealth of the college is that the city's late Norman **cathedral** also serves as the college chapel. The complex also holds the college's **Picture Gallery**, with a strong collection of Italian Renaissance paintings and prints (Mon–Sat 10.30am–1pm & 2–4.30/5.30pm, Sun 2–4.30/5.30pm; £2), while across the road from Tom Tower and down Pembroke St lies **Modern Art Oxford** (Tues–Sat 10am–5pm, Sun noon–5pm; free; ⊛www.modernartoxford.org.uk), one of England's most vibrant regional museums of contemporary art, with a fine basement café. South of the college, **Christ Church Meadow** offers gentle walks – either east to the River Cherwell or south to the Thames (perversely referred to hereabouts as the Isis). From the north side of the meadows, a path off Dead Man's Walk will bring you through to **Merton** (Mon–Fri 2–4pm, Sat & Sun 10am–4pm; free), perhaps the prettiest college, founded in the thirteenth century. Continuing east, Dead Man's Walk joins Rose Lane, which emerges at the eastern end of the High St beside the River Cherwell, where you can rent punts in summer. Opposite is the fifteenth-century bell tower of **Magdalen College** (pronounced "maudlin"; daily noon/1–6pm or dusk; £3).

Many of the university's most important and imposing buildings lie just north of the High St. The most dramatic is the Italianate **Radcliffe Camera**. Built in the 1730s by James Gibbs, it is now used as a reading room for the **Bodleian Library**, whose main building is immediately to the north in the Old Schools Quad. Most of the library is closed to the general public, but you can see part of the collection of ancient manuscripts on an hour-long guided tour (Mon–Fri 9am–5pm, Sat 9am–12.30pm; £4). The adjacent **Sheldonian Theatre** (Mon–Sat 10am–12.30pm & 2–3.30/4.30pm; £1.50), a copy of the Theatre of Marcellus in Rome, was designed by Christopher Wren and is now a venue for concerts and university functions. A couple of hundred yards north along Parks Rd lies the **Pitt Rivers Museum** (Mon–Sat noon–4.30pm, Sun 2–4.30pm; free), a fascinating anthropological hoard, while five minutes west of the Sheldonian is the mammoth **Ashmolean Museum** (Tues–Sat 10am–5pm, Sun 2–5pm; June–Aug Thurs till 7.30pm; free; ⊛www.ashmol.ox.ac.uk). Highlights include the Egyptian rooms with their well-preserved mummies and sarcophagi; the Islamic and Chinese art sections, which both hold superb ceramics; and the rich collections of French and Italian paintings.

Practicalities

From Oxford's **train station**, it's a ten-minute walk to the centre. Long-distance buses terminate at the central Gloucester Green **bus station**. The **tourist office** is at 15–16 Broad St (Mon–Sat 9.30am–5pm, Easter–Oct also Sun 10am–1pm & 1.30–3.30pm; ☎01865/726871, ⊛www.visitoxford.org), with a branch office at the train station (daily: April–Oct 9.30am–5.45pm; Nov–March 9.30am–3.45pm). Bike Zone at 6 Market St (☎01865/728877), is the best place for **bike rental**. For **listings** of gigs and other events, consult *Daily Info*, a poster put up in colleges and all around town (daily term-time, otherwise weekly; ⊛www.dailyinfo.co.uk).

Hostels

Oxford Backpackers Hostel 9a Hythe Bridge St ☎01865/721761, ⊛www.hostels.co.uk. Independent hostel, with ten bunkrooms holding a maximum of ten people each. Fully equipped kitchen, laundry, bar and Internet facilities. Handy location, between the train station and the centre. Advance booking recommended. No curfew. From £13 per person.

YHA 2a Botley Rd ☎01865/727275, ⊛www.yha.org.uk. Next door to the train station, this popular HI hostel has 184 beds divided up into two-, four-

and six-bedded en-suite rooms. Inexpensive meals available plus self-catering facilities, Internet access and laundry. Advance booking recommended. No curfew. £18.75 per person B&B.

Guest houses and B&Bs

Becket Guest House 5 Becket St ☎ & ℱ 01865/ 724675. Modest but well-run bay-windowed, non-smoking guest house in a plain terrace close to the train station. Most rooms are en suite. **❺**

Isis Guest House 45–53 Iffley Rd ☎ 01865/248894, ✉ isis@herald.ox.ac.uk. Large college house with some en-suite rooms, just across Magdalen Bridge. Good value, but spartan. July–Sept only. **❹**

St Michael's Guest House 26 St Michael's St ☎ 01865/242101. Often full, this friendly, well-kept B&B, in a cosy three-storey terrace house, has unsurprising furnishings and fittings, but a very central location. **❺**

Cafés and restaurants

Chiang Mai Kitchen Kemp Hall Passage, 130A High St ☎ 01865/202233. Best Oriental restaurant in town, with superb Thai food – including a vegetarian menu – and excellent service, in a timber-framed seventeenth-century building off the west end of High St.

Heroes 8 Ship St. Oxford's best sandwich bar, with a huge range of hot and cold fillings to eat in or take away, as well as breakfasts, cakes, salads and soups.

News Café 1 Ship St. A wide range of salads and daily-special hot dishes offered at this good-value

and very central day-and-night café, plus plenty of newspapers and satellite news channels on TV.

Pizza Express 8 Golden Cross, Cornmarket ☎ 01865/790442. In an imaginatively renovated Tudor building, this reliable chain offers the best-value pizzas in central Oxford. Expect a long wait at weekends.

Pubs, bars and clubs

Beat Café Little Clarendon St, off St Giles. Bohemian bar with fancy decor and stained glass windows selling a good line in cocktails. Evenings only.

Eagle & Child 49 St Giles. This pub was once the haunt of J.R.R. Tolkien, C.S. Lewis and other literary types, and still attracts a comparatively genteel mix of professionals and academics.

Freud Walton St ☎ 01865/311171. Classy café-bar – pizzas a speciality – in an imposing Neoclassical former church, with live jazz, blues, Latin and funk every night till late.

Turf Tavern Off Holywell St. This atmospheric pub, tucked down a winding alleyway (which also connects with New College Lane), offers good food, fine ales and ample outdoor seating.

White Horse 52 Broad St. A tiny, old pub with a coveted "crow's nest" snug, pictures of old university sports teams on the walls and real ales. It was used as a set for the *Inspector Morse* series.

Zodiac 190 Cowley Rd ☎ 01865/420042, ⒲ www.thezodiac.co.uk. Oxford's most respected live music and dance venue, with bands and club nights throughout the week.

Stratford-upon-Avon

STRATFORD-UPON-AVON makes the most of its association with William Shakespeare, who was born here on April 23, 1564. There are five restored properties recalling the Bard, three in the town itself and two on the outskirts. If you've time to visit them all, it's worth considering a **combined ticket** (£9/three town properties, £13/all five); otherwise save your money and go and watch the excellent Royal Shakespeare Company (see box). Top of everyone's Bardic itinerary is **Shakespeare's Birthplace** (daily 9/9.30/10/10.30am–4/5pm; £6.50), comprising an ugly modern visitor centre attached to the heavily restored half-timbered building on Henley St where the great man was born. A short walk away is **Nash's House**, Chapel St (daily 9.30/10/11am–4/5pm; £3.50), once the property of Thomas Nash, first husband of Shakespeare's granddaughter, Elizabeth Hall. Kitted

The Royal Shakespeare Company, or **RSC** (ⓦ www.rsc.org.uk), works on a repertory system, which means you could see four or five different **plays** in a visit of a few days. Tickets start at around £5 for standing room and a restricted view, rising to £40 for the best seats in the house. However, very popular shows get booked up months in advance. There are two adjoining theatres – the Swan and the Royal Shakespeare – and one **box office** (Mon–Sat from 9am, Sun from 11.30am; ☎ 01789/403403).

out with period furnishings, the house features displays on the history of Stratford and the attractive Elizabethan-style Knot Garden. Chapel St continues south as Church St. At the end, turn left along Old Town St for the impressive medieval **Hall's Croft** (daily 9.30/10/11am–4/5pm; £3.50), former home of Shakespeare's elder daughter, Susanna, and her doctor husband, John Hall. Immaculately maintained, with its creaking wooden floors, beamed ceilings and fine kitchen range, it holds a fascinating display on Elizabethan medicine. Beyond, Old Town St steers right to reach the handsome **Holy Trinity Church** (Mon–Sat 8.30/9am–4/6pm, Sun 2–5pm; free), whose mellow, honey-coloured stonework is enhanced by its riverside setting. Shakespeare lies buried here in the chancel (£1). About a mile west of the town centre in Shottery is **Anne Hathaway's Cottage** (daily 9/9.30/10/10.30am–4/5pm; £5), whose wooden beams and thatching were home to Anne before she married Shakespeare. **Mary Arden's House**, four miles north of the centre in Wilmcote (daily 9.30/10/10/30am–4/5pm; £5.50), was the home of Shakespeare's mother and is now a well-furnished example of an Elizabethan farmhouse, attached to the **Shakespeare Countryside Museum**.

Practicalities

Stratford's **train station** is on the northwestern edge of town, ten minutes' walk from the centre, served by roughly hourly shuttles from Birmingham and frequent trains from Oxford and London Paddington, via Leamington Spa. Long-distance **buses** pull into the Riverside station on the northeast side of town, off Bridgeway. The **tourist office** (Mon–Sat 9.30am–4.30/5.30pm, Sun 10/10.30am–3/4.30pm; ☎01789/293127, ⓦwww.shakespeare-country.co.uk), a couple of minutes' walk from the bus station by the bridge at the junction of Bridgeway and Bridgefoot, operates an efficient accommodation booking hotline. **Bike rental** is available at Pashley on Guild St (☎01789/205057).

Hostel

YHA Hemmingford House, Alveston
☎01789/297093, ⓦwww.yha.org.uk. HI hostel occupying a rambling Georgian mansion on the edge of the pretty village of Alveston, two miles east of the town centre on the B4086. Has dormitories, doubles and family rooms, some en suite. Laundry, Internet access, cafeteria and self-catering. Regular buses from Stratford's Riverside bus station. From £16.50 for a dorm bed.

Guest houses

Chadwyns Guest House 6 Broad Walk
☎01789/269077, ⓦwww.chadwyns.co.uk. Just off Evesham Place, this well-maintained, most agreeable guest house occupies pleasant Victorian premises and offers en-suite rooms. Great breakfasts with vegetarian options. ❺
Parkfield Guest House 3 Broad Walk
☎01789/293313, ⓦwww.parkfieldbandb.co.uk. Very pleasant, non-smoking B&B in a rambling Victorian house down a residential street off Evesham Place. Most of the rooms are en suite. Less than ten minutes' walk from the centre. ❺
Woodstock Guest House 30 Grove Rd
☎01789/299881, ⓔwoodstockhouse @compuserve.com. A smart, non-smoking B&B ten minutes' walk from the centre, by the start of the path to Anne Hathaway's Cottage. It has five extremely comfortable bedrooms, most of them en suite. No credit cards. ❻

Campsite

Stratford Racecourse Luddington Rd ☎01789 /201063, ⓦwww.stratfordracecourse.net. Well-equipped camping and caravan site one mile southwest of the town centre. Regular buses into town (not Sun). Closed Oct–March. Tent pitches from £4.

Restaurants and cafés

Kingfisher Fish Bar 13 Ely St. The best fish-and-chip shop in the town centre, with a dining room. Closed Sun.
Lamb's Café Bistro 12 Sheep St
☎01789/292554. Smart restaurant in a sixteenth-century building serving a wide range of stylish dishes, including plenty for veggies; lunch and pre-theatre set menus.
Russons 8 Church St ☎01789/268822. Excellent but good-value cuisine, featuring interesting meat and vegetarian dishes on the main menu and an extensive blackboard of seafood reflecting the catch of the day; cheaper lunch and pre-theatre menus.

Pubs

The Dirty Duck (aka *The Black Swan*) 53 Waterside. The archetypal actors' pub, stuffed to the gunwales every night with a vocal entourage of RSC employees and hangers-on. Essential viewing, plus good food.

Cambridge

Tradition has it that the University of **CAMBRIDGE** was founded by refugees from Oxford, who fled the town after one of their number was lynched by hostile townsfolk in the 1220s; there's been rivalry between the two institutions ever since. What distinguishes Cambridge is "**the Backs**", the green swathe of land straddling the River Cam, which overlooks the backs of the old colleges, and provides the town's most enduring image of grand academic architecture. Note that, as in Oxford, access to the colleges may be restricted during examinations – especially in May and June – conferences and functions.

A logical place to begin a tour is **King's College**, whose much celebrated **chapel** (term time Mon–Fri 9.30am–3.30pm, Sat 9.30am–3.15pm, Sun 1.15–2.15pm; rest of year Mon–Sat 9.30am–4.30pm, Sun 10am–5/5.30pm; £4) is an extraordinarily beautiful building, home to an almost equally vaunted choir (term-time choral services Mon–Sat 5.30pm, Sun 10.30am & 3.30pm). King's flanks King's Parade, originally the medieval High St, at the northern end of which is the **Senate House**, the

BRITAIN | Central England

3

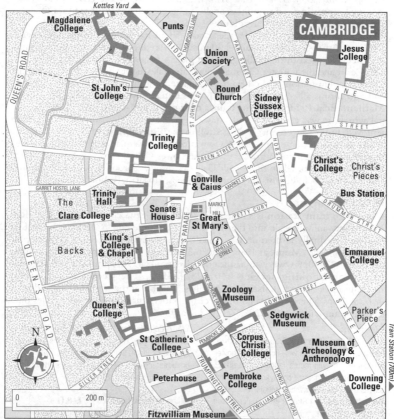

© Crown copyright

145

scene of graduation ceremonies on the last Saturday in June, when champagne corks fly. Nearby Trinity St holds the main entrance to **Gonville and Caius College**, known simply as Caius (pronounced "keys"), whose two adjoining courts boast three fancy gates representing a different stage on the path to academic enlightenment. On the south side, the "Gate of Honour" leads into Senate House Passage, which itself heads west to **Clare College** (April–Sept daily 10am–4.30pm; £2; reduced hours in winter, admission free). One of seven colleges founded by women, Clare's plain period-piece courtyard leads to one of the most picturesque of all the bridges over the Cam, **Clare Bridge**. Beyond lies the Fellows' Garden, one of the loveliest college gardens open to the public (times as college). Just north of Caius, **Trinity College** (March–Oct daily 10am–5pm; £2; reduced hours in winter, admission free) is the largest of the Cambridge colleges. A statue of Henry VIII, who founded the college in 1546, sits in majesty over Trinity's Great Gate, his sceptre replaced with a chair leg by a student wit. Beyond lies the vast asymmetrical expanse of Great Court, which displays a fine range of Tudor buildings, the oldest of which is the fifteenth-century clock tower – the annual race against its midnight chimes is now common currency thanks to the film *Chariots of Fire*. To get through to Nevile's Court – where Newton first calculated the speed of sound – you must pass through "the screens", a passage separating the Hall from the kitchens, a common feature of Oxbridge colleges. The west end of Nevile's Court is enclosed by the beautiful Wren Library (term time Mon–Fri noon–2pm, Sat 10.30am–12.30pm; rest of year Mon–Fri only; free). Back outside Trinity, it's a short hop to the River Cam, where you can go **punting** – the quintessential Cambridge activity. **Punt rental** (£8/hr) is available at the bridge on Garret Hostel Lane.

Doubling back along King's Parade, it takes about five minutes to reach **Queens' College** (April–Sept daily 10am–4.30pm; £1.20; reduced hours in winter, admission free), accessed through the gate on Queen's Lane, just off Silver St. Here, the Old Court and the Cloister Court are twin fairy-tale Tudor courtyards, with the first the perfect illustration of the original collegiate ideal with kitchens, library, chapel, hall and rooms all set around a tiny green. Equally eye-catching is the wooden **Mathematical Bridge** over the Cam, a copy of the mid-eighteenth-century original which, it was claimed, would stay in place even if the nuts and bolts were removed. From Queens', it's a short stroll to the **Fitzwilliam Museum** (Tues–Sat 10am–5pm, Sun 2.15–5pm; free; ⓦ www.fitzmuseum.cam.ac.uk). Of all the museums in Cambridge, this is the best, with the Lower Galleries containing a wealth of classical antiquities, while the Upper Galleries display European painting, sculpture and furniture, including masterpieces by Rubens, Hogarth, Renoir and Picasso.

Practicalities

Cambridge **train station** is a mile or so southeast of the city centre, off Hills Rd. It's a twenty-minute walk into the centre, or take shuttle bus #C1 or #C3. The **bus station** is centrally located on Drummer St. The **tourist office** is on Wheeler St, off King's Parade (Mon–Sat 10am–5.30/6.30pm, plus Easter–Sept Sun 11am–4pm; ☏01223/322640, ⓦ www.tourismcambridge.com), and operates a useful **accommodation booking service** (☏01223/457581). The weekly *Real City* and monthly *Explorer* are free **listings** magazines, available at the tourist office and larger bookshops. There are several **bike rental** outlets, including Station Cycles outside the train station (☏01223/307125; £8/day).

Hostels

YHA 97 Tenison Rd ☏01223/354601, ⓦ www.yha.org.uk. This well-equipped HI hostel has dorms and twin rooms, laundry and self-catering facilities, a small courtyard garden, and serves breakfast and evening meals. It's close to the train station – off Station Rd. £16 per person, including breakfast.

YMCA Gonville Place ☏01223/356998, ⓦ www.theymca.org.uk. Central location on the south side of Parker's Piece. Singles and doubles, with breakfast included. Very busy during summer; book well in advance. ❹

Guest houses and B&Bs

Benson House 24 Huntingdon Rd ☏ &

⊕01223/311594. Pleasant, well-kept, non-smoking accommodation in a demure brick house, north of Magdalene Bridge near New Hall College. Five rooms, three en suite. ❺

Netley Lodge 112 Chesterton Rd ⊕01223/363845. Cosy, non-smoking B&B in a Victorian town house a long but manageable walk from the centre. Three attractively furnished bedrooms, one en suite. No credit cards. ❺

Sleeperz Hotel Station Rd ⊕01223/304050, ⊛www.sleeperz.com. This popular hotel is in an imaginatively converted granary warehouse, right outside the train station. Most of the rooms are bunk-style affairs done out in the manner of a ship's cabin, and there are a few doubles too. All are en suite, with shower and TV. ❺

Restaurants and cafés

Clowns 54 King St. Licensed, day-and-night Italian café with a roof garden, serving cakes, sandwiches, all-day breakfasts, pasta and daily specials.

Efes 80 King St ⊕01223/350491. Intimate Turkish restaurant, with chargrilled meats prepared under your nose and a decent *meze* selection.

Eraina Taverna 2 Free School Lane ⊕01223/

368786. Packed Greek taverna near the tourist office that satisfies the hungry hordes with huge platefuls of stews and grills, as well as pizzas, curries and a whole host of other menu madness.

Rainbow Vegetarian Bistro 9a King's Parade ⊕01223/321551. Vegetarian restaurant opposite King's College with main courses – ranging from salads to lasagne and enchilladas – all under £8. Organic wines, beers and ciders served with meals. Closed Sun.

Pubs, bars and clubs

Eagle Bene't St. An ancient inn with good food, and a cobbled courtyard where Crick and Watson sought inspiration in the 1950s, at the time of their discovery of DNA. It's been tarted up since and gets horribly crowded, but is still worth a pint of anyone's time.

Light 66 Regent St (continuation of St Andrew's St) ⊕01223/308100. Hip café-bar with DJ nights Thurs–Sun, serving reasonably priced European and Asian dishes. Closed Sun lunchtime.

Junction Clifton Rd ⊕01223/511511, ⊛www.junction.co.uk. Live bands, club nights, comedy, drama, dance, performance and digital art at this popular and eclectic venue.

Northern England

The main draw of **northern England** is the **Lake District**, a scenic region just thirty miles across, taking in stone-built villages, sixteen major lakes and the steeply pitched faces of England's highest mountains. However, to restrict yourself purely to the outdoors would be to do a disservice to cities such as **Manchester** and **Liverpool** on the northwest coast, and **Newcastle** on the northeast, whose centres are alive with the ostentatious civic architecture of nineteenth-century capitalism and twenty-first-century renewal. An entirely different angle on northern history is provided by the great ecclesiastical centres of **Durham** and **York**, where famous cathedrals provide a focus for extensive medieval remains.

Manchester

Few cities in the world have embraced social change so heartily as **MANCHESTER**. From engine of the Industrial Revolution to test-bed of contemporary urban design, the city has no realistic provincial rival in England. After a massive IRA bomb destroyed much of the centre in 1996, rebuilding has transformed the city, and with a huge student population, a lively Gay Village, and a venerable history of churning out talent for the twin glories of British culture – music and football – Manchester today hosts one of the country's most vibrant social and cultural scenes. From the main Piccadilly train station, it's a few minutes' walk northwest to **Piccadilly Gardens** (hub of the local tram and bus network). North of the gardens is what's been dubbed the **Northern Quarter**, an edgy old wholesale district full of boutiques, music stores, bars and cafés. West of the gardens, **St Ann's Square** has been transformed into a pedestrianized shopping area, and is home to the **Royal Exchange** building, which houses the famous Royal Exchange Theatre. New Cathedral St runs through the landscaped expanse of Exchange Square to the demure fifteenth-century **Cathedral**, and beyond to **Urbis** in Cathedral Gardens (daily 10am–6pm, Sat until 8pm; £5; www.urbis.org.uk), a spectacular glass building with interactive displays exploring life in different world cities. South down Deansgate and right into Liverpool Rd is a celebration of the triumphs of industrialization at the superb **Museum of Science and Industry** (daily 10am–5pm; free; ®www.msim.org.uk), where exhibits include working steam engines, textile machinery, a hands-on science centre and a glimpse of the Manchester sewer system. Fifteen minutes' walk northeast, on Albert Square, stands the city's finest Victorian Gothic building, its **Town Hall** ; a block to the east is the **Manchester Art Gallery** on Mosley St (Tues–Sun 10am–5pm; free; ®www.manchestergalleries .org), which includes a fine collection of Pre-Raphaelite works.

Metrolink trams run from Mosley St to **Salford Quays**, scene of a massive urban renewal scheme in the old dock area. Centrepiece is the spectacular waterfront **Lowry Centre** (daily from 10am; free; ®www.thelowry.com), where – as well as theatres and galleries – room is always made for the work of the artist L.S. Lowry, best known for his "matchstick men" scenes. To reach it, take the tram to Broadway, or walk down the docks from the Salford Quays stop. A footbridge runs across the docks to the **Imperial War Museum North** (daily 10am–6pm; free; ®www.iwm.org.uk), a striking aluminium-clad building designed by Daniel Libeskind, where imaginative exhibits explore the effects of war since 1900. It's as resonant in its way as the other great building that looms in the near distance, Old Trafford, home of **Manchester United Football Club**, whose museum is sited in the North Stand (daily 9.30am–5pm; museum and tour £8.50, museum only £5.50; Metrolink to Old Trafford; advance booking essential for tours, ☎0870/442 1994, ®www.manutd.com).

Practicalities

Most **trains** arrive at Piccadilly station, on the city's east side. **Coaches** stop at Chorlton St, just west of Piccadilly. The **airport** is ten miles south, with a direct 24-hour train service to Piccadilly. The **Manchester Visitor Centre** is in the town hall extension on Lloyd St, at St Peter's Square (Mon–Sat 10am–5.30pm, Sun 10.30am–4.30pm; ☎0161/234 3157, ®www.manchester.gov.uk/visitorcentre), with branches in both airport terminals. For cheap **eating**, head a couple of blocks east of the visitor centre to Chinatown. Alternatively, the scores of restaurants along Wilmslow Rd in Rusholme (buses #40–49), otherwise known as "Curry Mile", feature some of Britain's best (and cheapest) Asian cooking. The trendiest places to **drink** are in the Castlefield area around Liverpool Rd; under the railway arches along Deansgate Locks (Whitworth St West); in the Northern Quarter around Oldham St; and the Gay Village around Canal St.

For details of **nightlife**, consult the weekly magazine *City Life* or Friday's *Manchester Evening News*; top **clubs** of the moment are *Music Box*, 65 Oxford St (☎0161/273 3435), and *Sankey's Soap*, Beehive Mill, Jersey St, Ancoats (☎0161/237 5606). Up-and-coming bands play *The Roadhouse*, Newton St; bigger acts play the *Academy* on Oxford Rd. The Cornerhouse, 70 Oxford St (☎0161/200 1500, ®www.cornerhouse.org), is a centre for contemporary arts, with cinemas, galleries, café and bar.

Accommodation

Jury's Inn 56 Great Bridgewater St ☎0161/953 8888, ®www.bookajurysinn.com. Very handy location for this large, budget, three-star hotel. Rates, which are room only, are particularly good value at weekends. ➐ Weekends ➎
Manchester Backpackers' Hostel 64 Cromwell Rd, Stretford ☎0161/865 9296. Two miles out of the centre, with dorms and twins/doubles, kitchen and bike rental. Metrolink to Stretford. From £14 per person.

The Ox 71 Liverpool Rd ☎0161/839 7740, ®www.theox.co.uk. Nine rooms above a classy bar-restaurant opposite the Science and Industry Museum. ➎
YHA Potato Wharf, Castlefield ☎0161/839 9960, ®www.yha.org.uk. Opposite the Science and Industry Museum. Well-designed HI hostel (all dorm rooms have private bathroom), which comes with all mod cons. £19 per person, including breakfast.

Cafés and restaurants

Dimitri's 1 Campfield Arcade, Deansgate. Pick and mix from the Greek/Spanish/Italian menu, or grab an arcade table and sip a drink.

Earth 16–20 Turner St. Gourmet veggie food – curries, pies, salads and juices – in a stylish Northern Quarter café in the Manchester Buddhist Centre. Closed Sun & Mon.

Eighth Day 107–111 Oxford Rd ☎0161/273 1850. Manchester's oldest vegetarian and vegan café, a workers' co-operative, with a shop, takeaway and juice bar, and a café/restaurant. Closed Sun.

Shere Khan 52 Wilmslow Rd, Rusholme ☎0161/256 2624. Popular Indian brasserie, serving marvellous kebabs, and great *karahi* and *biryani* dishes.

Wong Chu 63 Faulkner St. The best of the budget Chinatown eateries, this no-frills joint serves up enormous portions of Cantonese staples.

Bars and pubs

Britons Protection 50 Great Bridgewater St. Elegantly decorated traditional pub, with good home-made food, comedy nights and other events, and a beer garden.

Dry Bar 28–30 Oldham St. The first of the designer café-bars on the scene, and catalyst for much of what goes on in the Northern Quarter.

Dukes '92 Castle St, Castlefield. Former stableblock for canal horses, now a large, sociable pub with terrace seating and a great-value range of pâtés and cheeses.

Mr Thomas' Chop House 52 Cross St. Victorian pub with a Dickensian feel to its nooks and crannies, serving Lancashire hotpot and other good-value traditional dishes.

Mumbo 35a King St. The city's first tea-bar, with sipping and eating on three floors and a roof terrace.

Via Fossa 28 Canal St. This elaborate mock-Gothic bar packs in a high-energy (largely gay) crowd.

Liverpool

Once Britain's main transatlantic port and the empire's second city, **LIVERPOOL** spent too many of the twentieth-century postwar years struggling against adversity. Things are looking up at last, as economic and social regeneration brightens the centre and the old docks on the River Mersey. Acerbic wit and loyalty to one of the city's two great football teams are the linchpins of Liverpudlian "Scouse" culture, along with an underlying pride in the local musical heritage – fair enough from the city that produced The Beatles. Just north of the main **Lime Street station**, on William Brown St, is the renowned **Walker Art Gallery** (Mon–Sat 10am–5pm, Sun noon–5pm; free), including a representative jaunt through British art history, with Hogarth, Gainsborough, Stubbs and Hockney all well represented. From here it's a fifteen-minute walk west to the **Pier Head** and Liverpool's waterfront, where it's worth taking a "Ferry 'cross the Mersey" (*à la* Gerry and the Pacemakers) to Birkenhead for the views back towards the city; ferries serve commuters during morning and evening rush hours (£2 return), but in between operate extended hourly cruises with commentary (£4.50). A short stroll south is the **Albert Dock**, showpiece of the renovated docks area, whose main focus is **Tate Liverpool** (Tues–Sun 10am–5.50pm; free; ⊛www.tate.org.uk), northern home of the national collection of modern art; there's a great café here, too. Occupying the other side of the dock is the **Maritime Museum** (daily 10am–5pm; free), housing – amongst other highlights – a shocking exhibition detailing Liverpool's key role in the slave trade. The Albert Dock is also home to **The Beatles Story** (daily 10am–5/6pm; £7.95), a multimedia attempt to capture the essence of the Fab Four's rise. Continuing the theme, the area back in the city centre around Mathew St has been designated the "**Cavern Quarter**", its pubs and shops providing an excuse to wallow in nostalgia, especially at the rebuilt version of the original **Cavern Club** (hosting live bands Thurs–Sun), where The Beatles played in the 1960s. You can take a two-hour "Magical Mystery Tour" of other sites associated with the band, such as Penny Lane and Strawberry Fields, on a bus that departs from The Beatles Story and ends up at the *Cavern Club* (daily tours; book on ☎0871/222 1967, or at The Beatles Story or tourist offices; £10.95) – and join in with moptops galore at the **International Beatles Festival** in the last week of August. Ten minutes' walk southeast of Mathew St at 88 Wood St is **FACT** (⊛www.fact.co.uk). This imposing modern edifice shelters two galleries showing film, video and new media projects (Tues & Wed 11am–6pm, Thurs–Sat noon–9pm, Sun noon–5pm; free), three more traditional arthouse cinemas, and a cool café and bar. To the east, at either end of Hope St, stand the city's two eye-catching twentieth-century cathedrals: the Roman Catholic **Metropolitan Cathedral** (daily 7.30am–5/6pm; suggested £2.50 donation), ten minutes' walk up Mount Pleasant, is a vast inverted funnel of a building, while the pale red neo-Gothic Anglican **Liverpool Cathedral** (daily 8am–6pm; suggested £2.50 donation), largest in the country, although designed by Sir Giles Gilbert Scott in 1903, wasn't completed until 1978.

Practicalities

Trains arrive at Lime St station, on the eastern edge of the city centre; **coaches** stop on Norton St, northeast of the station. John Lennon **airport** is eight miles southeast (take bus #80/80A, or the pricier express bus #500 into the centre). **Ferry** arrivals – including from Dublin and Belfast – dock just north of Pier Head, close to Albert Dock. **Tourist information** (℡0151/709 5111, ✆www.visitliverpool.com) is available from two downtown offices: one centrally located in Queen Square (Mon–Sat 9/10am–5.30pm, Sun 10.30am–4.30pm), the other at Albert Dock at the Atlantic Pavilion (daily 10am–5.30pm); both can book accommodation (℡0845/601 1125). Budget **accommodation** includes, from mid-June to early September, self-catering **student halls** at John Moores University (℡0151/709 3197) and the University of Liverpool (℡0151/794 6402).

There's a wide range of inexpensive ethnic **food** found around Mount Pleasant and Hardman and Bold streets, while Berry and Nelson streets to the south form the heart of **Chinatown**. As for **pubs and bars**, Fleet St, Slater St, Wood St and Concert Square (off Bold St) are where all the action is. *The Picket*, 24 Hardman St (℡0151/708 5318), and the *Lomax*, 11–13 Hotham St (℡0151/236 4443), are the best **live music venues**, while the *Royal Court Theatre*, Roe St (℡0151/709 4321), gets the major touring bands. Hottest **club nights** at the moment come courtesy of Chibuku Shake Shake, at various venues including *Lemon Lounge*, 21 Berry St, *Beige* at Albert Dock, and *The Masque*, Seel St. The **Bluecoat Arts Centre** on School Lane (℡0151/709 5297, ✆www.bluecoatartscentre.com) is always worth a look for drama, dance, poetry, music and art. The evening paper, the *Liverpool Echo*, has what's-on **listings**.

Accommodation

Aachen 89–91 Mount Pleasant ℡0151/709 3477, ✆www.aachenhotel.co.uk. The most popular and central budget hotel, with value-for-money rooms and big "eat-as-much-as-you-like" breakfasts. ❺

Embassie Hostel 1 Falkner Square ℡0151/707 1089, ✆www.embassie.com. Twenty minutes' walk from Lime St station (bus #80), east of the Anglican cathedral; kitchen and laundry; free tea, toast and coffee. £13.50 1st night, £12.50 thereafter.

International Inn 4 South Hunter St, off Hardman St ℡0151/709 8135, ✆www.internationalinn.co.uk. Large, new, central hostel in a converted Victorian warehouse near the Catholic cathedral. En-suite dorms for 2–10 people, café, kitchen, laundry and Internet access. From £15 per person.

YHA Wapping ℡0151/709 8888, ✆www.yha.org.uk. One of the best HI hostels, with all the mod cons, just south of Albert Dock. Smart three-, four- or six-bed rooms, all with private bathroom. £19 per person, including breakfast.

Eating and drinking

60 Hope St ℡0151/707 6060. Stylish café-bar under a smart restaurant, serving interesting salads, sandwiches and modern European main courses at reasonable prices. Closed Sun.

The Baltic Fleet 33a Wapping St. Restored maritime pub with real ales and a great period feel.

Bluecoat Café Bar Bluecoat Arts Centre, School Lane. Good-value, mostly veggie, food – salad bar, quiches, hot specials and great cakes – served throughout the day. Closed Sun.

Far East 27–35 Berry St ℡0151/709 6072. One of the longest-serving and most reliable of Liverpool's Cantonese eating houses, with authentic *dim sum* (noon–6pm).

Green Fish Café 11 Upper Newington. Cool and very cheap vegetarian café off Renshaw St. Closed Sun.

Life Café 1a Bold St. The eighteenth-century Lyceum Library makes a grand backdrop for this late-opening café-bar.

Number Seven Deli & Coffee Shop 13 Falkner St. Great sandwiches, salads, soups and cakes to eat inside or out at the streetside tables, or to take away.

The Philharmonic 36 Hope St. Huge, ornate pub boasting mosaic floors, gilded wrought-iron gates and marble decor in the gents.
Tabac 126 Bold St. Contemporary café-bar, serving a wide-ranging menu.

The Lake District

The site of England's highest peaks and its biggest concentration of lakes, the glacier-carved **Lake District** is the nation's most popular walking area. The weather changes quickly here, but the sudden shifts of light on the bracken and moorland grasses, and on the slate of the local buildings, are part of the area's appeal. The most direct access is via the mainline **train** route from London Euston towards Glasgow, disembarking at Lancaster, from where bus #555 runs right through the area, calling at Kendal, Windermere, Ambleside, Grasmere, Keswick and Carlisle. Alternatively, you could get off at Oxenholme, connecting with a branch line service to Windermere; or take a direct train from Manchester to Windermere. A National Express **coach** service runs daily from London Victoria to the Lake District, while local Stagecoach **buses** go everywhere in the region – an **Explorer Ticket** (£7.50/day, £17/four days), valid on their entire network and available on the bus, is just one of many local passes, including bus-and-boat tickets. The region boasts dozens of **campsites**, covering all the towns described below (see Ⓦwww.golakes.co.uk) – or as a compromise between that and hostelling, you might want to check out the plentiful **camping barns** (Ⓦwww.lakelandcamping-barns.co.uk).

Windermere, Bowness, Ambleside and around

Lake Windermere is the largest and southernmost of the lakes, and also one of the most crowded in summer. The town of **WINDERMERE** (where the train stops) is set a mile or so back from the lake and, other than the short climb up to the viewpoint of Orrest Head, offers little to do. Instead, stroll down (or catch the #599 or Windermere Shuttle Bus from outside the station) to the prettier sister town of **BOWNESS** on the lakeshore. Windermere's **tourist office** is just outside the train station (daily 9am–5/6.30pm; ☎015394/46499), steps from the cosy *Lake District Backpackers Hostel* (☎015394/46374, Ⓦwww.lakedistrictbackpackers.co.uk; £12.50 including breakfast). A top B&B choice is *Brendan Chase*, 1–3 College Rd (☎ & ☎015394/45638; ❹). **Bikes** can be rented from Country Lanes Cycle Centre at the train station (☎015394/44544, Ⓦwww.countrylanes.co.uk). The nearest HI hostel is at **Troutbeck**, two miles northwest of Windermere (☎015394/43543, Ⓦwww.yha.org.uk; £11.50 per person); they have a shuttle-bus, which meets trains at Windermere.

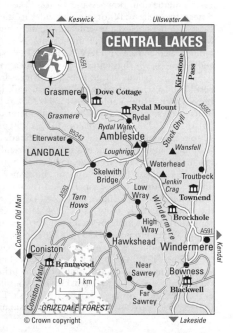

CENTRAL LAKES

© Crown copyright

Accommodation in Bowness tends to be more expensive; but don't miss a drink in *The Hole in't Wall* pub, behind the church, the town's oldest hostelry. Lake **ferries** (℡015395/31188, ⊛www.windermere-lakecruises.co.uk) run to Lakeside at the southern tip (£6.60 return) or to Waterhead (for Ambleside) at the northern end (£6.40 return). A 24-hour Freedom-of-the-Lake ticket costs £11.50. There are also boats to the excellent **Lake District National Park Visitor Centre** (April–Oct daily 10am–5pm; free; ℡015394/46601, ⊛www.lake-district.gov.uk) at Brockhole, also reached on the #555 or #599 buses from Windermere.

From Waterhead, it's a mile north to **AMBLESIDE** – or take bus #555 or #599 from Windermere and Bowness. Stroll along Rydal Rd to the **Ambleside Museum** (daily 10am–4.30pm; £2.50; ⊛www.armitt.com) for the lowdown on lakeland writers and artists, and make time too for a more unusual gallery, **The Homes of Football**, 100 Lake Rd (daily 10am–5/7pm; Oct–March closed Tues; free), a permanent archive of over 60,000 images of stadiums and fans around the world. The **tourist office** is in the Central Buildings by the Market Cross (daily 9am–5pm; ℡015394/32582). One of the Lake District's best-sited HI **hostels** fronts the lake at Waterhead (℡015394/32304, ⊛www.yha.org.uk; ❸), and there's the independent *Ambleside Backpackers* in a refurbished nineteenth-century cottage on Old Lake Rd (℡015394/32340, ⊛www.englishlakesbackpackers.co.uk; from £12 including breakfast), while B&Bs line central Ambleside streets. *Zeffirelli's*, a cinema on Compston Rd, also specializes in inexpensive vegetarian **food**, either in the daytime *Garden Room Café* or upstairs in the night-time pizza-and-pasta restaurant. The #516 bus from Ambleside runs four miles west to the hamlet of **ELTERWATER**, centred on a tiny green and boasting another HI hostel, *Elterwater Langdale* (℡015394/37245, ⊛www.yha.org.uk; £10.25 per person), as well as the fantastic *Britannia Inn* (℡015394/37210, ⊛www.britinn.co.uk; ❽), an old lakeland pub with tasty food. The hikes around here, and three miles further up the valley in **Langdale** (also on the #516 route), are famously good.

Hawkshead and Coniston

Ferries shuttle from Bowness piers across Lake Windermere to Sawrey, from where it's a steep two-mile walk (or minibus ride) to the hamlet of **NEAR SAWREY** and Beatrix Potter's beloved seventeenth-century house and garden, Hill Top (April–Oct Mon–Wed, Sat & Sun 10.30am–4.30pm; NT; £4.50). It's another two miles to the whitewashed cottages of **HAWKSHEAD** (also served by bus #505 from Ambleside and Bowness), which is refreshingly peaceful after the hurly-burly of Windermere and has some marvellous village pubs (the *King's Arms*, which serves decent food, is the best). The **tourist office** at the main car park (daily: April–Oct 9.30am–5.30/6pm; Nov–March 10am–3.30pm; ℡015394/36525) handles a range of B&Bs and farmhouse stays; check out the family-oriented **HI hostel**, *Esthwaite Lodge* (℡015394/36293, ⊛www.yha.org.uk; £11.50 per person), a mile south of town.

From Hawkshead, walking through **Grizedale Forest**, with its startling outdoor sculptures, and descending towards the graceful **Coniston Water** is a good way of reaching **CONISTON** village, a cluster of houses nestling beneath the craggy Old Man of Coniston (which you can climb in 2hr). Bus #505 comes this way too. There's a **tourist office** on Ruskin Avenue (daily: April–Oct 9.30am–5.30pm; Nov–March 10am–3.30pm; ℡015394/41533), as well as an **HI hostel** just north of the village at Holly How (℡015394/41323, ⊛www.yha.org.uk; £10.25 per person), and another more peaceful one above Coniston on the slopes of Old Man, at Coppermines House (℡015394/41261; £10.25 per person). The central *Beech Tree Guesthouse*, a fine eighteenth-century house with attractive gardens on Yewdale Rd (℡015394/41717; ❺), is pick of the B&Bs; best **pub** is the *Sun Hotel*, an old inn serving filling meals 200m uphill from the bridge in the centre. The most popular walk from Coniston is to **Tarn Hows**, two miles northeast, a serene lake with several vantage points across the hills. The wooden Coniston Launch (℡015394/36216, ⊛www.conistonlaunch.co.uk) operates a year-round lake service on two routes, north and south (£3.80 & £5.80 return). This, along with the Steam Yacht Gondola (April–Oct; £5 return), is the best means of reaching the elegant lakeside villa, **Brantwood** (mid-March to mid-Nov daily 11am–5.30pm; rest of year Wed–Sun 11am–4.30pm; £4.75, gardens only £3; ⊛www.brantwood .org.uk). Once inhabited by the artist and critic John Ruskin, whose work provided the theoretical substance for that of the Pre-Raphaelites, the house is full of Ruskin's own drawings and sketches, as well as items relating to the painters he inspired; there are also no less than eight beautiful gardens, as well as a good café.

Rydal and Grasmere

From Windermere and Ambleside, the trusty #555 bus connects to **RYDAL**, three miles northwest of Ambleside, where Wordsworth made his home from 1813 until his death in 1850; his house, **Rydal Mount** (daily 9.30/10am–4/5pm; Nov–Feb closed Tues; £4, gardens only £1.75), is famous largely for the gardens laid out by Wordsworth himself. Paths on either side of Rydal Water cover the two miles to **GRASMERE**, site of Wordsworth's more famous abode, **Dove Cottage** (daily 9.30am–5.30pm; closed Jan; £5, museum only £2.50; ⊛www.wordsworth.org.uk). The adjoining museum has portraits and manuscripts relating to Wordsworth, Coleridge – who regularly hiked over from Keswick to visit him here – and De Quincey, author of *Confessions of an English Opium-Eater*. Wordsworth and his sister Dorothy lie in simple graves in the churchyard of St Oswald's, in the village. Grasmere's **tourist office** is on Redbank Rd, by the main car park (April–Oct daily 9.30am–5.30pm; Nov–March Fri–Sun 10am–3.30pm; ☏015394/35245). The *Dove Cottage Tea Rooms and Restaurant* is the nicest spot for **tearoom** favourites (at night, prices shoot up for fashionable dinners; ☏015394/35268). The **HI hostel** choices are *Butterlip How* (£13 per person), 150 yards north of the green on Easedale Rd, and simpler *Thorney How* (£10.25 per person), under a mile further along the unlit road (both ☏015394/35316, ⊛www.yha.org.uk). There's also the excellent *Grasmere Independent Hostel* at Broadrayne Farm (☏015394/35055, ⊛www.grasmerehostel.co.uk; from £12.50), just north of town on the A591, near the *Travellers' Rest* **pub** (which serves bar meals).

Keswick and Derwent Water

Principal centre for the northern lakes, **KESWICK** (pronounced "kez-ick") lies on the northern fringes of **Derwent Water**, one of the few stretches of water in the area which can be walked all the way around – although the **Keswick Launch** (mid-March to Nov daily; Dec to mid-March Sat & Sun; £5.80 round trip, 85p per stage; ☏017687/72263, ⊛www.keswick-launch.co.uk) runs right around the lake too. The easiest hike is up **Latrigg Fell** to the north (2–3hr), giving splendid views; the trek up **Skiddaw** (5hr) is more demanding, but the easiest of the many true mountain hikes around and about. Otherwise, the best thing to do is to hike a mile and a half eastwards to **Castlerigg Stone Circle**, a Neolithic monument commanding a spectacular view, or take the #77/77A/79 bus ride down into **Borrowdale**, south of town, perhaps the most beautiful valley in England. **Buses** use the terminal behind Lakes Foodstore, off Main St. Keswick's **tourist office** is in the Moot Hall, Market Sq (daily 9.30am–5.30/6pm; ☏017687/72645, ⊛www.keswick.org). The local **HI hostel** is on Station Rd by the river (☏017687/72484; ⊛www.yha.org.uk; £11.50 per person); there's another on the eastern shores of Derwentwater, two miles south, in Barrow House (☏017687/77246, ⊛www.yha.org.uk; £11.50 per person); buses #77/77a/79 and the Keswick Launch come this way. *Bluestones*, 7 Southey St (☏017687/74237, ⊛www.members.tripod.com/bluestoneskeswick; ❹), a welcoming **guest house** that offers big buffet breakfasts, is particularly good value. Keswick's most agreeable **café** is the *Lakeland Pedlar*, Henderson's Yard, off Main St, serving breakfasts and inventive veggie food, and there are fine **pub** meals and good beer at the *Four In Hand* on Lake Rd. Theatre by the Lake (☏017687/74411, ⊛www .theatrebythelake.com) hosts drama, dance and music, and has a pleasant bar and café.

York

It's the spectacular Gothic Minster, alleyways and ancient walls that draw tourists to **YORK**, but the city's character-forming experiences go back a lot further than that. It was the principal northern headquarters of the Romans, while the city's position as the north's spiritual capital dates from 627, when Edwin of Northumbria adopted Christianity. Northumbrian power crumbled in the face of a Danish invasion that swept through York in 866, and by 876 one of the Danish leaders, Halfdan, had settled here with half the Viking army, beginning a century of Scandinavian rule.

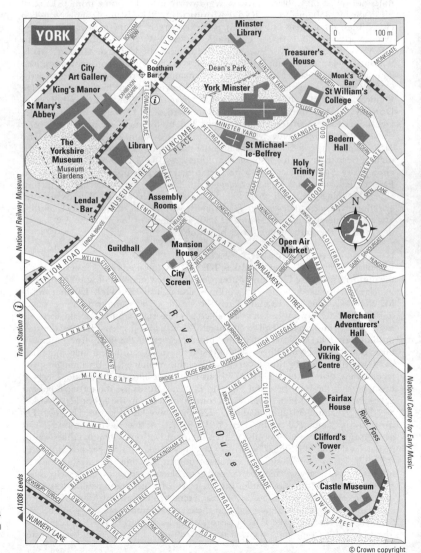

Best introduction to York is a stroll around the **city walls** (daily till dusk), a three-mile circuit – two miles of it on the walls themselves – that takes in the various medieval Bars, or gates, and grants fine views of the Minster, amongst other buildings. **Guided walks**, from evening ghost walks to historical rambles, include a free, daily, two-hour tour (at 10.15am) by the York Association of Voluntary Guides, plus additional tours in summer (April–Oct 2.15pm; June–Aug also 6.45pm), departing from outside the art gallery in Exhibition Square; just turn up. Ever since Edwin built a wooden chapel on the site, **York Minster** (Mon–Sat 7am–6/8.30pm, Sun 1–6/8.30pm; £3.50 donation requested; ❻www.yorkminster.org) has been the centre of religious authority for the north of England. Most of what's visible now was built in stages between the 1220s and the 1470s, and today it ranks as the country's largest Gothic building. Inside, the apocalyptic scenes of the East Window, completed in 1405, and the abstract thirteenth-century *Five Sisters* window represent the finest collection of stained glass in the country. Various parts of the Minster have separate admission charges and opening hours (which change by the month), including the crypt and undercroft (£3.80), which hold remnants and artefacts from the previous Roman and Norman buildings, though best use of a limited budget is to climb the central tower (£3), which gives views over the medieval pattern of narrow streets to the south, known as the **Shambles**. Southwest of the Minster, just outside the city walls, Museum Gardens lead to the ruins of the Benedictine abbey of St Mary and the **Yorkshire Museum** (daily 10am–5pm; £4), which contains much of the abbey's medieval sculpture, and a selection of Roman, Saxon and Viking finds. The shopping streets spread south and east from here, focusing eventually on Coppergate, former site of the city's Viking settlement. The blockbuster experience that is **Jorvik** (daily 10am–4/5pm; £7.20; ❻www.vikingjorvik.com) provides a taste of the period through a recreation of Viking streets, complete with appropriate smells and recorded sounds, to the accompaniment of an informative commentary. Further south, the superb **Castle Museum** (daily 9.30am–5pm; £6) indulges in full-scale recreations of life in bygone times, with evocative street scenes of the Victorian and Edwardian periods. Another museum worth a call is the excellent **National Railway Museum**, ten minutes' walk from the station on Leeman Rd (daily 10am–6pm; free; ❻www.nrm.org.uk), which includes the nation's finest collection of steam locomotives.

Practicalities

York's **train** station lies just outside the city walls, with services from Manchester, as well as fast trains from London and Edinburgh; long-distance **coaches** also drop off and pick up here. There's a **tourist office** at the train station (Mon–Sat 9am–5/6pm, Sun 9.30/10am–4/4.30pm), though the main office is over Lendal Bridge, in the **De Grey Rooms**, on Exhibition Square (Mon–Sat 9am–5/6pm, Sun 10am–4/5pm; ☎01904/621756, ❻www.york-tourism.co.uk).

There's some good hostel **accommodation**, and the University of York offers good-value B&B rooms year-round (☎01904/430000). Cultural entertainment is wide and varied, including the **National Centre for Early Music** in St Margaret's Church, Walmgate (❻www.ncem.co.uk), which hosts a prestigious early music festival in July, and delivers much more than it promises, with world, jazz, folk and "late" music. The famous **York Mystery Plays**, held every four years, will be performed in 2004 – details from the tourist office. As well as being an arthouse cinema, **City Screen**, 13 Coney St (☎01904/541155, ❻www.picturehouses.co.uk), has a fine riverside café-bar and hosts comedy, poetry, live music and DJ nights.

Accommodation

The Bar Convent 17 Blossom St
☎01904/643238, ❻www.bar-convent.org.uk.
Working convent in a grand Georgian building, just south of the train station next to Micklegate Bar, offering good-value B&B with self-catering kitchens and a café. ❺

York Backpackers Hostel Micklegate House, 88–90 Micklegate ☎01904/627720, ❻www.yorkbackpackers.co.uk. Dorm space, doubles and family rooms in a rather grand building, former home of the High Sheriff of Yorkshire. There's a café, kitchen, laundry and bar, plus Internet access. From £12 per person.

York YHA Water End, Clifton ☎01904/653147, ⓦwww.yha.org.uk. HI hostel in large mansion, twenty minutes' walk along Bootham from the tourist office. Four-bedded dorms and some private rooms (book in advance), a licensed café, laundry, self-catering facilities, Internet access, bike rental and large garden. From £16.50 per person.

York Youth Hotel 11–13 Bishophill Senior, off Micklegate ☎01904/625904, ⓦwww.yorkyouthhotel.com. Dorms, singles and twin/double rooms in characterful city-centre hostel, with a kitchen, laundry and bar; bike rental and meals available. From £11 per person.

Cafés and restaurants

Betty's 6–8 St Helen's Square. If there are tea shops in heaven they'll be like *Betty's*, a York institution which also serves main courses, to the accompaniment of a pianist, until 9pm.

Blake Head Vegetarian Café 104 Micklegate. Bookstore/café with patio for freshly baked cakes, breakfasts, quiches, salads and soups – a favoured student hangout.

El Piano 15 Grape Lane. Bohemian café-restaurant decorated with Spanish rugs and ceramics (for sale), serving good coffee and cakes,

and vegetarian and vegan tapas; bring your own alcohol; live music Fri and Sat eves. Closed Sun.

Pizza Express River House, 17 Museum St. Grand old riverside club rooms with sought-after balcony, the venue for this chain's usual menu of good-quality pizzas.

The Rubicon 5–7 Little Stonegate ☎01904/676076. Contemporary style and vegetarian world flavours, so there's moussaka and lasagne but also Thai curries and burritos on offer.

Pubs

Black Swan Southeast of the minster on Peasholme Green. York's oldest (sixteenth-century) pub with some superb stone flagging and wood panelling, and regular singer-songwriter and folk nights.

Judge's Lodging Cellar Bar 9 Lendal. Lively drinking hole in the eighteenth-century cellars of a smart hotel, with a large outdoor terrace and regular DJ nights.

The Three-Legged Mare 15 High Petergate. York Brewery's cosy outlet for its own quality beer and definitely a pub for grown-ups – no jukebox, no video games and no kids.

Durham

Seen from the train, **DURHAM** presents a magnificent sight, with cathedral and castle perched atop a bluff enclosed by a loop of the River Wear (pronounced "weer"), and linked to the suburbs by a series of sturdy bridges. Nowadays a quiet provincial town with a strong student presence, Durham was once one of northern England's power bases: the Bishops of Durham were virtual royal agents in the north for much of the medieval era, responsible for defending a crucial border province frequently menaced by the Scots. The town initially owed its reputation to the possession of the remains of St Cuthbert, which were evacuated to Durham in the ninth century because of Viking raids. Since then, his shrine has dominated the eastern end of the spectacular **cathedral** (Mon–Sat 9.30am–6.15/8pm, Sun 12.30–5pm; £3 donation requested; ⓦwww.durhamcathedral.co.uk). The cathedral itself is the finest example of Norman architecture in England, with the nave, completed in 1128, the first to use pointed arches, raising the interior dimensions to dizzying heights. Medieval frescoes depicting St Cuthbert are just visible in the Galilee Chapel, which also contains the tomb of the Venerable Bede, England's first historian. The Treasures of St Cuthbert exhibition is in the undercroft (Mon–Sat 10am–4.30pm, Sun 2–4.15/4.30pm; £2), while the tower gives breathtaking views (Mon–Sat 9.30/10am–3/4pm; £2). On the opposite side of Palace Green is the **castle** (mid-March to mid-April & July–Sept daily 10am–12.30pm & 2–4.30pm; Jan to mid-March, May, June & Oct–Dec Mon, Wed, Sat & Sun 2–4pm; £3; ⓦwww.durhamcastle.com), a much-refurbished Norman edifice that's now a university hall of residence. A half-hour stroll follows a pathway on the wooded river bank below the cathedral and castle, all the way around the peninsula, passing a succession of elegant bridges.

Durham **train station** is ten minutes' walk from the centre, via either of two river bridges. The **bus station** is just south on North Rd. The **tourist office** is in the Gala Theatre, at Millennium Place (Mon–Sat 9.30am–5.30pm, Sun 11am–4pm; ☎0191/384 3720, ⓦwww.durhamtourism.co.uk). Good **B&Bs** include *Green*

Grove, 99 Gilesgate (℡0191/384 4361, ⓦwww.smoothhound.co.uk/hotels/green-gro.html; ❹), and *Castle View Guest House*, 4 Crossgate (℡0191/386 8852, ⓔcastle_view@hotmail.com; ❻). For good-value **food**, *Vennel's Café*, Saddler's Yard, serves everything from cakes to pasta in a lovely little hidden courtyard off Saddler St, while the *Almshouse* on Palace Green, near the cathedral, conjures up tasty dishes for around £5 (till 8pm in summer). For a traditional **pub**, try the *Half Moon* by Elvet Bridge, which has good ales and a riverside beer garden. *Cathedrals*, in the old police station on Court Lane, has something for everyone – restaurant, bar, and coffee house which turns into a good-value Italian bistro at night. The **Gala Theatre** at Millennium Place is focus of the latest in drama and the arts (ⓦwww.galadurham.co.uk).

Newcastle-upon-Tyne

Once a tough, industrial city with a proud shipbuilding heritage, **NEWCASTLE** has retained its undeniable raw vigour, most conspicuously in its famously high-spirited nightlife. These days, it is streets ahead of its rivals in the northeast, and has a slew of good galleries and arts venues. It also serves as a good base for explorations of **Hadrian's Wall**, a Roman-era barricade that stretched from coast to coast. Arriving by train, your first view is of the River Tyne and its redeveloped quaysides, along with the Norman keep of the castle itself and the many bridges that join Newcastle to Gateshead. The single steel arch of the **Tyne Bridge**, built in 1929, and the high-tech "winking" **Millennium Bridge**, completed in 2001, are world-renowned landmarks. Newcastle's centre owes a lot of its character to John Dobson, who remodelled the city along Neoclassical lines in the early nineteenth century. His most imposing legacy is the sweep of **Grey St** to the east of the station, curving down from the lofty Grecian column of **Grey's Monument**, the city's central landmark, towards the Quayside. The northeast's main art collection is housed in the splendidly organized **Laing Art Gallery** on New Bridge St, east of the monument (Mon–Sat 10am–5pm, Sun 2–5pm; free), but it has been dwarfed

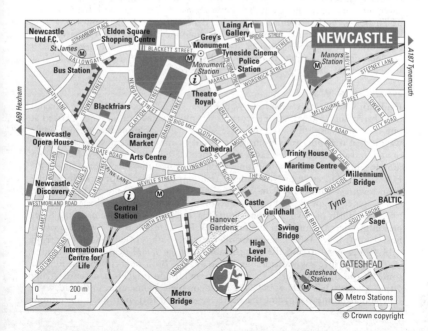

by the opening of the **Baltic Centre for Contemporary Art** (Mon–Wed, Fri & Sat 10am–7pm, Thurs 10am–10pm, Sun 10am–5pm; free; ℠www.balticmill.com), on the southern banks of the Tyne next to the Millennium Bridge. The converted former Baltic Flour Mill is second only in scale to London's Tate Modern and, as well as galleries for temporary exhibitions, it accommodates artists' studios, a cinema and a lofty viewing platform, plus a bar and two restaurants. The Baltic will be joined by the similarly ambitious **Sage** in 2004 (℠www.musicnorth.org), a billowing steel, aluminium and glass structure that will be a centre for music and home to the Northern Sinfonia. The best museum in the area is on this side of the Tyne too, five miles east in Jarrow (Metro to Bede station): **Bede's World** (Mon–Sat 10am–4.30/5.30pm, Sun noon–4.30/5.30pm; £4.50; ℠www.bedesworld.co.uk) imaginatively evokes the life and times of the great early Christian scholar, alongside a reconstructed Anglo-Saxon farm and the remains of Bede's monastery.

Newcastle's **train station** is five minutes' walk south of Grey's Monument; the **coach station**, on Gallowgate, a couple of minutes west. The **ferry port** (for crossings from Amsterdam and Scandinavia) is in North Shields, seven miles east, with connecting buses running to the centre, and the **airport** is six miles north, served by the Metro. There are **tourist offices** in Central Station (Mon–Fri 9.30am–5pm, Sat 9am–5pm; ℡0191/277 8000, ℠www.newcastle.gov.uk) and at 132 Grainger St (Mon–Sat 9.30am–5.30pm, Thurs till 7.30pm, plus June–Sept Sun 10am–4pm; same number). The **HI hostel** is at 107 Jesmond Rd (℡0191/281 2570, ℠www.yha.org.uk; dorms from £8.50). Jesmond – a mile north of the centre and on the Metro – is also the main location for **B&Bs**; try the *George*, 88 Osborne Rd (℡0191/281 4442; ❺), or the *Minerva* at no. 105 (℡0191/281 0190; ❹). The University of Northumbria (℡0191/227 4024) and Newcastle University (℡0191/222 6296) offer good-value, summertime B&B (mostly single rooms) in their halls of residence.

Local institutions for cheap **eats** are the *Side Café Bistro,* near the Quayside at 1–3 The Side, and *Pani's,* an Italian café-restaurant at 61 High Bridge St, off Grey St (closed Sun); nearby at 1 Market Lane, *Paradiso* is a mellow restaurant with great food (℡0191/221 1240; closed Sun). City-centre **pubs** and bars are clustered around Bigg Market, a block west of Grey St, and down on the Quayside. In the latter area, be sure to check out the *Crown Posada,* 31 The Side, and *The Cooperage,* 32 The Close, both of them cosy drinking dens, or by the Millennium Bridge, the sleek and stylish *Pitcher & Piano* which has fine views of the river. The city's foremost **club** venues are *Foundation,* 57 Melbourne St, and *World Headquarters,* 9 Marlborough Crescent; the free monthly **listings** magazine, *The Crack,* is the best way to find out about gigs, clubs and other entertainment.

Hadrian's Wall

Hadrian's Wall (℠www.hadrianswallcountry.org), separating Roman England from barbarian Scotland, was punctuated by "mile castles", strong points spaced at one-mile intervals, and by sixteen more substantially garrisoned forts. An 84-mile waymarked trail now runs from coast to coast, linking the substantial remains, though a day-trip from Newcastle will suffice to see a little of the wall. The best jumping-off point and base for longer exploration is the abbey town of **HEXHAM**, 45 minutes west of Newcastle by train or bus. It has a **tourist office**, in the main town car park (daily 9am–5/6pm; Nov–Easter closed Sun; ℡01434/65220, ℠www.tynedale.gov.uk) and plenty of accommodation including a basic HI **hostel** two miles north of town in Acomb (℡01434/602864, ℠www.yha.org.uk; £8 per person). Other accommodation along the Wall is available at the *Once Brewed* HI hostel (℡01434/344360, ℠www.oncebrewed.co.uk; closed Dec & Jan; from £11.40 per person) and the comfortable *Hadrian Lodge* near Haydon Bridge (℡01434/684867, ℠www.hadrianlodge.co.uk; ❻). Both of these options lie near some of the finest preserved sections of wall, including **Housesteads** (daily 10am–4/6pm; £3.10; EH & NT), the most complete Roman fort in Britain, set in spectacular countryside, and the partly re-created fort and lively museum at

Vindolanda (Feb–Nov daily 10am–4/5.30pm; £4.10; ☎www.vindolanda.com). A **bus service** (late May to mid-Sept, plus various weekend services; #AD122; day rover ticket £6) runs between Hexham and Carlisle via all the main sites; at least once a day it links through to Newcastle and Wallsend. The year-round #185 bus runs from Carlisle to Housesteads via Haltwhistle (on the Newcastle–Carlisle train line).

Wales

The relationship between England and **Wales** (Cymru in Welsh) has never been entirely easy. Impatient with constant demarcation disputes, the eighth-century Mercian king Offa constructed a dyke to separate the two countries; today, the 177-mile **Offa's Dyke Path** follows its route from near Chepstow in the south to Prestatyn in the north, still marking the border to this day. During Edward I's reign the last of the Welsh native princes, Llywelyn ap Gruffudd, was killed, and Wales passed uneasily under English rule. Trouble flared again with the rebellion of Owain Glyndŵr in the fifteenth century, but the Welsh prince Henry Tudor's defeat of Richard III at the Battle of Bosworth crowned him King Henry VII of England and paved the way for the 1536 Act of Union, which joined the English and Welsh in restless but perpetual partnership. The arrival of the 1999 National Assembly for Wales, the first all-Wales tier of government for nearly six hundred years, may well indicate that power is shifting back, though so far it is a slow trickle. Indigenous Welsh culture survives largely through language and song. The **Eisteddfod festivals** of Welsh music, poetry and dance still take place throughout the country in summer – the annual *Royal National Eisteddfod* (☎www.eisteddfod.org.uk), a very Welsh affair that breaks out in a different location during the first week of August, and the *Llangollen International Musical Eisteddfod* (☎www.international-eisteddfod.co.uk), held on the first full week in July, being the best-known examples. The Welsh language is undergoing a revival and you'll see it on bilingual road signs all over the country, although you're most likely to hear it spoken in the north, west and mid-Wales. Some Welsh place-names have never been anglicized, but where alternative names do exist, we've given them in the text.

Much of the country, particularly the **Brecon Beacons** in the south and **Snowdonia** in the north, is relentlessly mountainous and offers wonderful walking and climbing terrain. **Pembrokeshire** to the west boasts a spectacular rugged coastline, dotted with offshore island nature reserves. The biggest towns, including the capital **Cardiff** in the south, **Aberystwyth** in the west, and **Caernarfon** in the north, all cling to the coastal lowlands, but even then the mountains are no more than a bus-ride away. **Holyhead**, on the island of **Anglesey**, is the main British port for ferry sailings to the Irish capital, Dublin.

Cardiff

Though once shackled to the fortunes of the coal-mining industry, Wales's largest city, **CARDIFF** (Caerdydd), 150 miles west of London, has made its mark as the vibrant Welsh capital, and since 1999 has been the home of the Welsh Assembly. The city's narrow Victorian arcades are interspersed with new shopping centres and wide pedestrian precincts. Long-distance coaches, and buses from the airport, arrive at the **bus terminal**, right beside Cardiff Central **train station**, south of the city centre off Penarth Rd (local trains use Queen Street station instead, east of the centre). There's a **tourist office** at 16 Wood St (Mon–Sat 9am–5pm, Sun 10am–2pm; ☎029/2022 7281, ☎enquiries@cardifftic.co.uk).

The geographical and historical heart of the city is **Cardiff Castle** (tours daily 9.30am–4.30/6pm; £5.25, winter tours £3.15, grounds only £2.60). Standing on a Roman site developed by the Normans, the castle was embellished by William

Burges in the 1860s, and each room is now a wonderful example of Victorian "medieval" decoration; best of all are the Chaucer Room, the Banqueting Hall, the Arab Room and the Fairy-tale Nursery. Five minutes' walk northeast, the **National Museum and Gallery** in Cathays Park (Tues–Sun 10am–5pm; free; ⓦwww.nmgw.ac.uk/nmgc) houses a fine collection of Impressionist paintings, and natural history and archeological exhibits. A half-hour walk south of the centre is the **Cardiff Bay** area, also reached by bus #8 from Central Station, or a train from Queen St. Once known as Tiger Bay, the long-derelict area (birthplace of singer Shirley Bassey) has seen massive redevelopment since the opening of the Welsh Assembly; now you'll find waterfront walks, glittering new architecture and an old Norwegian seamen's chapel, converted into a cosy café. The **Museum of Welsh Life** is at St Fagans, four miles west of the centre on bus #320. This 100-acre open-air museum is packed with reconstructed rural and industrial heritage buildings (daily 10am–5pm; free; ⓦwww.nmgw.ac.uk/mwl). Fans of William Burges' elaborate interiors shouldn't miss the fairy-tale **Castell Coch** at Tongwynlais, five miles north of town on bus #26 (April–Oct daily 9.30am–5/6pm; Nov–March Mon–Sat 9.30am–4pm, Sun 11am–4pm; £2.50). Perched dramatically on a steep, forested hillside, Burges' lavish Victorian showpiece was commissioned by the third Lord Bute as a country retreat, complete with turrets.

Cardiff's **HI hostel** is a couple of miles north of the centre at 2 Wedal Rd (☎0870/770 5750, ⓔcardiff@yha.org.uk; £14.50), or you could try the excellent *Cardiff International Backpacker*, just west of the centre across the River Taff at 98 Neville St (☎029/2034 5577, ⓦwww.cardiffbackpacker.com; dorms £14.50; rooms ❹). **B&Bs** include *Acorn Lodge*, 182 Cathedral Rd, Pontcanna (☎029/2022 1373; ❹), fifteen minutes' walk west of the centre; the best budget hotel is the trendy **Big Sleep Hotel**, Bute Terrace (☎029/2063 6363, ⓦwww.thebigsleephotel.com; ❺), opposite the Cardiff International Arena. To **eat** laver bread and other Welsh delicacies, head for *Celtic Cauldron* in the shopping arcade opposite the castle. *Cibo*, 83 Pontcanna St (☎029/2023 2226), is a small Italian trattoria serving sandwiches and more substantial fare, while the café in the Norwegian church by Cardiff Bay is great for salads and snacks. Ale-lovers can sample the local bitter surrounded by rugby memorabilia in the *Old Arcade* pub, Church St.

South Wales

The region's most spectacular historic monument is accessible from the old market town of **CHEPSTOW** (Cas-Gwent), itself ringed on three sides by thirteenth-century walls and on the fourth by the River Wye. Within the town, the Wye bridge gives stunning views of cliff-faces soaring above the river and of the first stone **castle** in Britain, built by the Normans in 1067, a year after William the Conqueror's victory at Hastings (April–Oct daily 9.30am–5/6pm; Nov–March Mon–Sat 9.30am–4pm, Sun 11am–4pm; £3). Nothing within the town can match the six-mile stroll north along the Wye to the romantic ruins of **Tintern Abbey**, built in 1131, rebuilt 150 years later and now in a state of majestic disrepair (same hours as castle; £2.50). The nave walls rise to such a height that, from a distance, you might think the magnificent Gothic church still stood intact beneath the overhang of the wooded cliff – only when you get close do you find the roof is long gone. If you don't fancy walking, catch bus #69 (every 2hr), which runs from Chepstow to Tintern and on to Monmouth, eight miles north. You can top up for the return journey in the fourteenth-century *Moon and Sixpence* **pub** – almost a mile north of the Abbey by the river – which does excellent food. For information on Chepstow and the popular **Offa's Dyke Path** contact the **tourist office** on Bridge St (daily 10am–4/6pm; ☎01291/623772, ⓔchepstow.tic@monmouthshire.gov.uk). The *Coach and Horses Inn* on Welsh St offers **B&B** (☎01291/622626; ❺). The cheapest options are some way out of town: the superb St Briavels Castle HI **hostel** (☎0870/770 6040, ⓔstbriavels@yha.org.uk; dorms £11.25), is set in a moated

Norman castle seven miles northeast of Chepstow, reached by bus #69; and the St Pierre Caravan & **Camping**, at Portskewett (℡01291/425114) is four miles west, reached on the Caldicot and Newport bus.

Newport and around

First stop in Wales for mainline trains from Bristol and London is **NEWPORT** (Casnewydd), also served by buses and local trains from Chepstow. An unexciting town, Newport nevertheless does have its claim to fame: the legendary *TJ's* pub music venue, 14 Clarence Place (just over the river from the station), was where Kurt Cobain proposed to Courtney Love. Three miles northeast, and almost contiguous, is **CAERLEON**, a small, traffic-bedevilled town that preserves the extensive remains of its important Roman forebear, Isca. The state-of-the-art **Legionary Museum**, High St (Mon–Sat 10am–4.30/6pm, Sun 2–4.30/6pm; free; ⓦwww.nmgw.ac.uk/rlm), contains finds from all the adjacent sites. The museum stands opposite the road leading to the less dramatic remains of the barracks and grassed-over amphitheatre (free). Beside the museum is the **tourist office** (daily 10am–4.30/6pm; ℡01633/422656), while further down the High St are the **Fortress Baths**, built on the site of a 75 AD bath-house (April–Oct daily 9.30am–5pm; Nov–March Mon–Sat 9.30am–5pm, Sun 1–4pm; £2). Caerleon is more amenable to stay in than Newport, and has three good **B&Bs**, including *Pendragon House*, 18 Cross St (℡01633/430871; ⑤).

Bus #X23 from Newport runs fourteen miles north to **BLAENAFON**, a town recently awarded the status of UNESCO World Heritage Site for its place in the Industrial Revolution. It is home to both a vast ironworks museum and, housed in a defunct coal-mine a mile west of town, the **Big Pit Mining Museum** (mid-Feb to Nov daily 9.30am–5pm; free; ⓦwww.nmgw.ac.uk/bigpit), which gives a revealing glimpse of working life in the South Wales valleys. The mine closed in 1980, and former miners are now employed as guides. The full tour (last 3.30pm) involves descending 294ft in a miners' cage to inspect coalfaces, underground roadways and haulage engines that are almost 200 years old.

The Brecon Beacons

The **Brecon Beacons National Park** occupies a swathe of rocky uplands that are perfect walking territory. The Beacons themselves, a pair of hills 2900ft high accessed from Brecon town, share the limelight with the **Black Mountains** north of Crickhowell. Bus #21 (every 2hr, not Sun) runs from Newport to Brecon, passing through Abergavenny and Crickhowell, but trains from Newport veer off into England after Abergavenny.

The market town of **ABERGAVENNY** (Y Fenni) sits in a fold between seven green hills at the eastern edge of the park, about fifteen miles north of Newport. Before setting out for the mountains, pick up maps from the combined **tourist office** and **national park information office** (daily 9.30/10am–4.30/6pm; ℡01873/857588, ✉abergavenny.tic@monmouthshire.gov.uk) at Swan Meadow beside the bus station – and check what sort of weather you can expect, as conditions change rapidly. The most accessible walking areas are the **Sugar Loaf** (1955ft), four miles northwest, and **Holy Mountain** (Skirrid Fawr; 1595ft), three miles north. The *Black Sheep* **hostel** opposite the train station has dorm beds (℡01873/859125, ⓦwww.blacksheepbackpackers.com; £10). Plenty of **B&Bs** line Monmouth Rd on the five-minute walk between the train station and the town centre; *Maes Glas* on Raglan Terrace is best (℡01873/854494, ✉maesglasbb @amserve.com; ④). For good value **eating** try the *Greyhound Vaults* on Market St or the upmarket *Trading Post*, 14 Neville St. **CRICKHOWELL** (Crughywel), a friendly village with a fine seventeenth-century bridge five miles west of Abergavenny, is more picturesque. A six-mile hike into the Black Mountains from here takes you through remote countryside to tiny **Partrishow Church**; inside, you'll find a rare carved fifteenth-century rood screen complete with dragon, and an ancient mural of the grim reaper. Beaufort St in Crickhowell holds both the **tourist office** (April–Oct daily 9am–1pm & 2–5pm; ℡01873/812105, ⓦwww.crickhowell.co.uk), and *Greenhill Villas* **B&B** (℡01873/811177; ❹).

The largest of the central Brecon Beacons rise just south of **BRECON** (Aberhonddu), a lively little town eight miles west of Crickhowell that springs to life in mid-August for the huge international Brecon Jazz Festival (ⓦwww.brecon-jazz.co.uk). For details of the numerous trekking routes and an extensive programme of guided walks, call in at the park's **information office**, which shares premises with the **tourist office** in the Cattle Market car park beside Safeway (daily 9/10am–5/6pm; ℡01874/622485, ⓦwww.brecon.co.uk). **B&Bs** abound; both *Pickwick House*, St John's Rd (℡01874/624322, ⓦwww.pickwick-house.brecon.co.uk; ❹), and *Beacons*, in a rambling town house at 16 Bridge St (℡01874/623339, ⓦwww.beacons.brecon.co.uk; ❹), also cook excellent evening meals. The *Ty'n-y-Caeau* HI **hostel** is two miles east of Brecon at Groesfford (℡0870/770 5718, Ⓔtynycaeau@yha.org.uk; £10.25), a mile off the Abergavenny bus route, while the *Held Bunkhouse* hostel is in Cantref (℡01874/624646, ⓦwww.heldbunkhouse.co.uk; £9.50), a mile southwest of town.

Pembroke and the southwest

PEMBROKE (Penfro), birthplace of Henry VII, is a sleepy town, easily accessible by train from Cardiff. Centrepiece is the magnificent water-girt **castle** (daily 9.30/10am–4/6pm; £3.50), whose circular keep, dating from 1200, offers fine views of the countryside. The castle overshadows the high street where shops are shoehorned into an assortment of Tudor and Georgian buildings, one of them housing the **Museum of the Home** (May–Sept Mon–Thurs 11am–5pm; £1.20), an eclectic mix of exhibits ranging from toys and games to fashion accessories. The Visitor Centre on Commons Rd includes the tourist office (Easter–Oct daily 10am–5.30pm; ℡01646/622388). *Beech House* is the best-value **B&B** in town, 78 Main St (℡01646/683740; ❹). The nearest **HI hostel** is six miles east at Manorbier (℡0870/770 5954; £11.25), accessible by train. Regular **ferries** to Rosslare in Ireland (4hr) leave from Pembroke Dock, two miles north of the town.

The **Pembrokeshire Coast National Park** sweeps all the way around the edge of the southwestern peninsula of Wales, and the coastal path includes some of the country's most stunning and remote scenery, offering sheer cliff-faces, panoramic sea views and excellent seabird-watching. From Pembroke, bus #349/359 runs north to Haverfordwest where you can catch bus #411 sixteen miles west to **ST DAVID'S** (Tyddewi), one of the most enchanting spots in Britain, where a breathtakingly beautiful **cathedral**, delicately tinted purple, green and yellow by a combination of lichen and geology, hides in a dip below the High St. Constructed between 1180 and 1522, but heavily restored in the nineteenth century, it hosts a prestigious classical music festival in late May or early June. Across a thin trickle of river thousands of jackdaws congregate around the extensive remains of the magnificent fourteenth-century **Bishop's Palace** (Easter–Oct daily 9.30am–5/6pm; Nov–Easter Mon–Sat 9.30am–4pm, Sun 11am–4pm; £2.20), which adds to the beauty of the setting. Bus 411 runs two miles northwest to the St David's **HI hostel** at Llaethdy (℡0870/770 6042; £8.75), and seven miles southeast to the Penycwm HI hostel, near the attractive little village of Solva (℡01437/721940; £11.50). *Pen Albro*, 18 Goat St (℡01437/721865; ❹) is a central **B&B**. The **tourist office** is at the top of the High St (Easter–Oct daily 9.30am–5.30pm; Nov–Easter Mon–Sat 10am–4pm; ℡01437/720392, ⓦwww.stdavids.co.uk).

About 17 miles further north on bus #411 – at the end of the main train line from Cardiff and London – is **FISHGUARD** (Abergwaun), an attractive fishing port that's another embarkation point for Rosslare, with ferries and catamarans departing daily from alongside the train station. *Hamilton Backpackers Lodge*, a **hostel** near the tourist office at 21 Hamilton St (℡01348/874797, ⓦwww.fishguard-backpackers.com; £10) is a good option.

Mid-Wales

Mid-Wales, an area of wild mountain roads, hidden valleys and genteel ex-spa towns, is the least visited part of the country, perhaps because access is a little trickier than elsewhere. Nevertheless, it's worth making the effort, because it's here that you'll discover the traditional rural Wales, in quiet towns where the pub conversation takes place in Welsh rather than English. But this is also Wales at its most "alternative": look out for healthfood shops and trendy bookshops, their owners often escapees from England's industrial Midlands' sprawl.

Trains run from Shrewsbury, accessible on the main line north from Cardiff. Three miles inside Wales is **WELSHPOOL** (Y Trallwng), a market town full of the distinctive black-and-white half-timbered houses typical of the Marches, the Welsh–English borders. It's worth a stop simply to visit the thirteenth-century **Powis Castle**, a gorgeous red limestone building that's been continuously inhabited for five hundred years (April–Oct Wed–Sun 1–5pm; July & Aug also Tues; NT; £7.50). The castle houses a fine collection of furniture, tapestries and pictures, as well as the Clive of India collection of Indian treasures. Capability Brown designed the lovely terraced **gardens** (same days 11am–6pm; free with castle ticket, or £5). The **tourist office** is on Church St (daily 9.30am–5pm; ☎01938/552043). One of the many **B&Bs** is *Montgomery House* on Salop Rd (☎01938/552693; ❹).

Trains terminate at **ABERYSTWYTH**, a lively, thoroughly Welsh seaside resort of neat Victorian terraces and a thriving student culture. The train station is ten minutes' south of the seafront, reached by walking up Terrace Rd past the **tourist office** (July & Aug daily 10am–6pm, Sept–June Mon–Sat 10am–5pm; ☎01970/612125, ⓔaberystwythtic@ceredigion.gov.uk). Upstairs, the **Ceredigion Museum** (free) contains coracles once used by local fishermen as well as a reconstructed cottage interior. The flavour of the town is best appreciated on the seafront, where one of Edward I's castles bestrides a windy headland to the south. There's also a Victorian *camera obscura* further north, which can be reached via the clanking cliff railway (Easter–Oct daily 10am–5pm; £2.25 return). For a more extended rail trip, you could take the very popular **Vale of Rheidol** narrow-gauge steam train to **Devil's Bridge**, a canyon where three bridges span a dramatic waterfall (April–Oct; 3hr return trip, 1hr to Devil's Bridge; £11). The town seafront is lined with genteel **guest houses**; try *Yr Hafod*, 1 South Marine Terrace (☎01970/617579; ❹). Out of term-time, contact University of Wales about beds in **student halls** (☎01970/621960; £11). *The Treehouse*, on Eastgate, is a great daytime vegetarian cafe. Check out the university's Arts Centre on Penglais Hill for films, plays, exhibitions and other events.

North of Aberystwyth the train passes through a succession of seaside resorts before reaching **HARLECH**, where one of the best of Edward I's great castles, later Owen Glyndŵr's residence, towers above everything else on a rocky crag overlooking the sea (April–Oct daily 9.30am–5/6pm; Nov–March Mon–Sat 9.30am–4pm, Sun 11am–4pm; £3); the ramparts offer panoramic views over the mountains of Snowdonia on one side and Tremadog Bay on the other. The town huddles apologetically behind the castle; if you want **to stay**, try the *Arundel B&B*, High St (☎01766/780637; ❸), or the *Plas Newydd* HI **hostel**, three miles south by bus #38 or train in Llanbedr (☎01341/241287, ⓔllanbedr@yha.org.uk; £10.25). Midway between Aberystwyth and Harlech is down-at-heel **Barmouth**, from where you can catch bus #94 inland to **DOLGELLAU**, a base for exploring **Cadair Idris** (2930ft). The mountain looms over the southern side of town, its summit accessible via a tough six-mile, five-hour trek along the Pony Path starting three miles south of Dolgellau at Ty Nant – just one of the many walks in the area. Dolgellau **tourist office** is on central Eldon Sq, right by the bus stop (Easter–Oct daily 10am–5/6pm; Nov–Easter closed Tues–Thurs; ☎01341/422888, ⓔticdolgellau@hotmail.com). There's handy camping and B&B at *Tan-y-Fron* (☎01341/422638), half a mile east along Arran Rd, or you could make for *Kings* HI **hostel** at Penmaenpool, four miles west, off the #28 bus route (☎01341/422392; £10.25).

North Wales

Snowdonia National Park is the glory of **North Wales**, with some of the most dramatic mountain scenery Britain has to offer – jagged peaks, towering waterfalls and glacial lakes decorating every roadside. Walkers congregate here in large numbers, and the villages around the area's highest peak, Snowdon (3650ft), see steady tourist traffic even in the bleakest months of the year. Whatever season you're here, make sure you're equipped with suitable shoes, warm clothing, and food and drink to see you through any unexpected hitches. There are two main access routes. From Porthmadog, a few miles north of Harlech, **buses** skirt the base of Snowdon west to Caernarfon and Llanberis, and east to Blaenau Ffestiniog; while mainline **trains** from Crewe and Chester hug the north coast through Conwy and Bangor to Holyhead, with a branch line heading south to Betws-y-Coed and Blaenau Ffestiniog.

Blaenau Ffestiniog and Betws-y-Coed

The narrow-gauge **Ffestiniog Railway** (call for times; ☎01766/516006, ⒲www.festrail.co.uk) loops inland from Porthmadog for 14 miles up to the slate-quarrying town of **BLAENAU FFESTINIOG**. On a grey day, Blaenau Ffestiniog can look particularly desolate, but it's worth a call for the **Llechwedd Slate Caverns** a mile north, reached by bus. One train tour takes visitors into the side of the mountain, while the Deep Mine tour visits an underground lake and spectacular caverns on Britain's steepest train incline (daily 10am–5/6pm; one tour £7.50, both £11.50; ⒲llechwedd.co.uk). Should the brooding scenery have cast its spell over you, **B&B** can be had at *Afallon*, Manod Rd (☎01766/830468; ❸).

Most people push on to **BETWS-Y-COED**, ten miles northeast by ordinary train. A popular base for Snowdonia National Park – though no serious walks start here – the town has one of the prettiest settings in Wales but is overrun with visitors in summer, many coming here just to see the **Swallow Falls** in the wooded Llugwy Valley, two miles west of town. Mountain biking in the nearby Gwydyr Forest Park may be more tempting. A new HI **hostel** (☎01690/710796, Ⓔbetwsycoed@yha.org.uk; ❸) is due to open in 2003 at the *Swallow Falls Hotel*, two miles west of Betws-y-Coed on the A5, and there's another hostel at Capel Curig (☎01690/720225, Ⓔcapelcurig@yha.org.uk) a further four miles west. In Betws-y-Coed try the **B&B** above the *Riverside Restaurant*, Holyhead Rd (☎01690/710650; ❹). The *Royal Oak Hotel* and *Three Gables*, both on Holyhead Rd, do meals and the *Royal Oak* is the liveliest place to drink. Beside the station sits the **tourist office** (daily 9.30/10am–4/6pm; ☎01690/710426, Ⓔticbetws@hotmail.com). From Betws-y-Coed there are trains and buses to Llandudno Junction, on the main Chester–Holyhead line.

Conwy and Caernarfon

A couple of miles west of Llandudno Junction is **CONWY**, where Edward I's magnificent **castle** (April–Oct daily 9.30am–5/6pm; Nov–March Mon–Sat 9.30am–4pm, Sun 11am–4pm; £3.50) and the town walls are a UNESCO World Heritage Site. The entrance contains the **tourist office** (same hours; ☎01492/592248). The ramparts offer fine views of Thomas Telford's recently restored 1826 suspension bridge (April–Oct daily except Tues 10am–5pm; July & Aug also Tues; £1) over the River Conwy. For **B&B** try the popular *Gwynedd Guesthouse*, 10 Upper Gate St (☎01492/596537, Ⓔabs.conwy@virgin.net; ❹). Otherwise, there's Conwy **HI hostel**, *Lark Hill*, just west of the centre (☎0870/770 5774, Ⓔconwy@yha.org.uk; £13). West of Conwy, trains pass through **Bangor** on the way to Holyhead. To get to **CAERNARFON** – the springboard for trips into Snowdonia from the north – you'll need bus #88 from the bus station off Bangor High St. **Caernarfon Castle** (daily: April–Oct 9.30am–5/6pm; Nov–March 9.30/11am–4pm; £4.50), built in 1283, is arguably the most splendid castle in Britain. Little of the interior has survived, however, and the three-acre space is largely grassed over; it is here that the Princes of Wales are invested. Buses stop on

Penllyn, just across Castle Square from the **tourist office**, Castle St (daily 10am–4.30/6pm; Nov–Easter closed Wed; ☎01286/672232, ⓔcaernarfon.tic @gwynedd.gov.uk). In town, the cheapest place **to stay** is *Totters*, an excellent backpacker hostel at 2 High St (☎01286/672963, ⓦwww.applemaps.co.uk/totters; £9.50); *Isfryn Guesthouse*, 11 Church St (☎01286/675628; ④) is another good bet.

Llanberis and Snowdon

Regular buses run the seven miles northeast from Caernarfon to **LLANBERIS**, a lakeside village bursting to grow into a town in the shadow of **Snowdon**, at 3560ft the highest mountain in England and Wales. With the biggest concentration of guest houses, hostels and restaurants close to the mountains, Llanberis offers the perfect base for even the most tentative Snowdonian exploration. The longest but easiest ascent of the mountain is the Llanberis Path, a signposted five-mile hike (3hr) that is manageable by anyone reasonably fit. Alternatively, you can cop out and take the generally steam-hauled **Snowdon Mountain Railway** (daily mid-March to October; £18), which operates from Llanberis to the summit café, pub and post office, weather permitting (note that in adverse conditions trains may terminate at Clogwyn, three-quarters of the way up the mountain). Return tickets permit half an hour's viewing from the summit. The slate quarries that seared Llanberis's surroundings now lie idle, with the **Welsh Slate Museum** (Easter–Oct daily 10am–5pm; Nov–Easter daily except Sat 10am–4pm; free; ⓦwww.nmgw.ac.uk/wsm) remaining as a memorial to the workers' tough lives. Nearby, the Dinorwig Pumped Storage Hydro Station is carved out of the mountain and can be visited on underground tours (£5) starting at the **Electric Mountain Museum** (daily 9.30/10.30am–4.30/5.30pm; Feb–Easter Thurs–Sun only; Jan closed; free), which has a good café and interesting displays on ancient wooden boats recovered locally.

Buses stop near the **tourist office**, 41 High St (Easter–Oct daily 10am–6pm; Nov–Easter Wed & Fri–Sun 11am–4pm; ☎01286/870765, ⓔllanberis.tic @gwynedd.gov.uk). Walkers have a good choice of **accommodation**. The Sherpa Bus services (£2.50 all day) collectively encircle Snowdon providing access to several **HI hostels**, each at the base of a footpath up Snowdon: *Llanberis*, Llwyn Celyn (☎0870/770 5932, ⓔllanberis@yha.org.uk; £11.50); *Snowdon Ranger*, Rhyd Ddu (☎0870/770 6038, ⓔsnowdon@yha.org.uk; £10.25); *Bryn Gwynant*, Nantgwynant (☎0870/770 5732, ⓔbryngwynant@yha.org.uk; £10.25); and *Pen-y-Pass*, Nantgwynant (☎0870/770 5990, ⓔpenypass@yha.org.uk; £11.50). Llanberis's High St is lined with small **hotels**: try *The Heights* at no. 74 (☎01286/871179, ⓦwww.heightshotel.co.uk; ⑤), which also has eight-bed dorms (£12), or *Dolafon*, another pleasant B&B (☎01286/870933, ⓦwww.dolafon.com; ⑤). The enduringly popular *Pete's Eats*, 40 High St, satisfies walkers' appetites.

Anglesey – and boats to Dublin

The Menai Bridge was built by Thomas Telford in 1826 to connect North Wales with the island of **Anglesey** (Ynys Môn) across the Menai Straits, and it's one of the two chief sights on the little island, even though it's been superseded by a newer rival alongside. The other draw is the last of Edward I's masterpieces, **Beaumaris Castle** (April–Oct daily 9.30am–5/6pm; Nov–March Mon–Sat 9.30am–4pm, Sun 11am–4pm; £3), reached by bus #53, #57 or #58 from Bangor. The giant castle was built in 1295 to guard the straits and has a fairy-tale moat enclosing its twelve sturdy towers. Nonetheless, most tourist traffic in this direction speeds past to **HOLYHEAD** (Caergybi), the busiest Welsh **ferry-port**, with several daily ferry and catamaran sailings leaving for Dublin. **B&Bs** galore are within a few minutes' walk of the combined bus, train and ferry terminal, including *Orotavia*, 66 Walthew Ave (☎01407/760259; ④) and others on nearby Newry St. The **tourist office** (daily 8.30am–6pm; ☎01407/762622, ⓔholyhead.tic@virgin.net), is inside the ferry terminal.

Scotland

Scotland is a model example of how a small nation can retain its identity within the confines of a larger one. Down the centuries the Scots, unlike the Welsh, successfully repulsed the expansionist designs of England, and when the "old enemies" first formed a union in 1603, it was because King James VI of Scotland inherited the English throne, rather than the other way around. Although the two countries' parliaments merged 100 years later, Scotland retained many of its own institutions, notably distinctive legal and educational systems. However, the most significant reawakening of Scottish political nationalism since then has been in the last few years, with a separate parliament looking after most of Scotland's day-to-day affairs being re-established in Edinburgh in 1999. The most recent election for this parliament was in 2003.

Most of the population clusters in the narrow "central belt" between the two principal cities: stately **Edinburgh**, the national capital, with its magnificent architecture and imperious natural setting, and earthy **Glasgow**, a powerhouse of the Industrial Revolution but now as well known for its cultural core as its rough edges. Although the third city, **Aberdeen**, perched on the North Sea coast, has grown wealthy on the proceeds of offshore oil, Scotland is overwhelmingly rural outwith the Central Belt. Only pockets of the land are particularly fertile, yet in the **Highlands and Islands**, which comprise over two-thirds of the total area, the harsh, mountainous landscape is spectacularly beautiful, its rugged landscapes enhanced by the volatile climate, producing an extraordinary variety of moods and colours. It's a terrific place for those keen on outdoor activities such as hiking and mountain biking, though even the highest mountain, **Ben Nevis**, is an uncomplicated ascent for the average walker and much of the scenery – such as the famous **Loch Lomond** and **Loch Ness** – is easily accessible.

Edinburgh

EDINBURGH, the showcase capital of Scotland, is a historic, cosmopolitan and cultured city. Its stone-built houses, historic buildings and fairy-tale castle, perched on a rocky crag right in the heart of the city, make it visually stunning and it is little surprise that this city is the most popular draw for tourists in Scotland. The 430,000 population swells massively in high season, peaking in mid-August during the **Edinburgh Festival**, by far the biggest arts event in Europe. Yet despite this annual invasion, the city is still emphatically Scottish in character and atmosphere, mixing rich history with fast-moving current affairs which have seen the re-establishment of a Scottish parliament and the consequent reaffirmation of Edinburgh as a dynamic European capital.

The centre has two distinct parts. The castle rock is the core of the medieval city, where nobles and servants lived side by side for centuries within tight defensive walls. Edinburgh earned the nickname "Auld Reekie" for the smog and smell generated by the cramped inhabitants of this **Old Town**, where the streets flowed with sewage tipped out of tenement windows and disease was rife. The riddle of medieval streets and alleyways remained a rundown slum well into the last century. The **New Town** was begun in the late 1700s on farmland lying to the north of the Castle. Edinburgh's wealthier residents speculated profitably on tracts of this land and engaged the services of eminent architects in their development. The result is an outstanding example of Georgian town planning, still largely intact.

Arrival, information and accommodation

Edinburgh **airport** is seven miles west of the centre; there are bus connections around the clock to the city. **Trains** pull into Waverley Station, bang in the centre; the New Town and Princes St lie to the north, the Old Town and the castle to the south. The **bus** terminal is on St Andrew Square, just north of Princes St. The best way to **get around** the city centre is on foot. There's also a good local bus service;

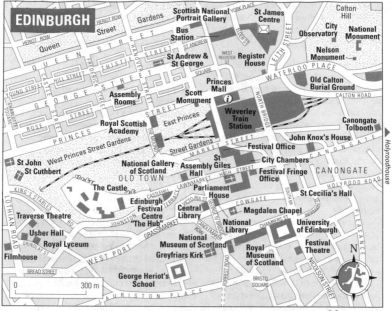

© Crown copyright

day passes (£2.50; off-peak £1.80) are available on board. The main **tourist office** is at 3 Princes St, above the station on the top level of Princes Mall (July & Aug Mon–Sat 9am–8pm, Sun 10am–8pm; rest of year Mon–Sat 9am–5/7pm, Sun 10am–5/7pm; ☎0845/225 5121; ✆www.edinburgh.org). The tourist office has full listings of **accommodation**, and will book rooms for a £3 fee. Central hotels and hostels book up quickly in peak season, but **B&B** is easier to come by, with prices starting from £15 per person. In addition, you can get **student rooms** over the summer, though they're not cheap; try Napier University (☎0131/455 4427; ❾) or Pollock Hall, Edinburgh University (☎0131/651 2007; ❽). **Campsites** are on the fringes of the city. If you want to stay **during the Festival** (early Aug to early Sept), you'll need to book months in advance.

Hostels

Argyle 14 Argyle Place, Marchmont ☎0131/667 9991, ✆www.argyle-backpackers.com. Quieter hostel, with small dorms and a dozen double/twin rooms. Pleasant location in studenty Marchmont. £17.

Brodies 12 High St, Old Town ☎0131/556 6770, ✆www.brodieshostels.co.uk. Tucked down a typical Old Town close, it's cosier than many others, but with limited communal areas. £18.

Bruntsfield 7 Bruntsfield Crescent, Bruntsfield ☎0131/447 2994, ✆www.syha.org.uk. Large HI hostel a mile south of Princes Street. £13.50.

Castle Rock 15 Johnston Terrace, Old Town ☎0131/225 9666, ✆www.scotlands-top-hostels.com. Busy 200-bed hostel tucked below the castle ramparts. £13.

Edinburgh Backpackers 65 Cockburn St, Old Town ☎0131/220 2200, ✆www.hoppo.com. Big hostel with a great central location in a side street off the Royal Mile. £14.50.

Eglinton Hostel 18 Eglinton Crescent, Haymarket ☎0871/330 8516, ✆www.syha.org.uk. The more central of the two HI hostels, in a characterful town house west of the centre. £13.50.

High Street Hostel 8 Blackfriars St, Old Town ☎0131/557 3984, ✆www.scotlands-top-hostels.com. Large but lively and well known hostel in a sixteenth-century building just off the Royal Mile. £13.

Royal Mile Backpackers 105 High St, Old Town ☎0131/557 6120, ✆www.scotlands-top-hostels.com. Small hostel popular with longer-term residents; shares facilities with the nearby *High Street Hostel*. £13.

St Christopher's Inns 9–13 Market St, Old Town ☎0131/226 1446, ⓦ www.st-christophers.co.uk. Edinburgh's first mega-hostel; 110 beds (all bunks) with smaller rooms as well as dorms. £15

Hotels and B&Bs

Ardenlee Guest House 9 Eyre Place ☎0131/556 2838. Welcoming, non-smoking guest house near the Royal Botanic Garden, with spacious rooms. **❼**

Bar Java 48–50 Constitution St, Leith ☎0131/553 2020. Simple but brightly designed rooms above one of Leith's funkiest bars. Food and drink available till late in the bar itself. **❻**

Cluaran House 47 Leamington Terrace, Viewforth ☎0131/221 0047, ⓦ www.cluaran-house-edinburgh .co.uk. Pleasant B&B in a nicely decorated, non-smoking house near Brunstfield serving wholefood breakfasts. **❾**

The Greenhouse 14 Hartington Gardens, Viewforth ☎0131/622 7634, ⓦ www.greenhouse -edinburgh.com. A fully vegetarian/vegan guest house, where a relaxed atmosphere prevails. **❼**

International Guest House 37 Mayfield Gardens, Mayfield ☎0131/667 2511, ⓦ www .accommodation-edinburgh.com. One of the best Southside guest houses, with comfortable well equipped rooms. **❽**

Six Mary's Place Raeburn Place ☎0131/332 8965, ⓦ www.sixmarysplace.co.uk. Collectively run "alternative" guest house; has a no-smoking policy and offers excellent home-cooked vegetarian meals. **❼**

Stuart House 12 E Claremont St ☎0131/557 9030, ⓦ www.stuartguesthouse.co.uk. Cosy, bright Georgian house in the Broughton area. No smoking. **❽**

Teviotdale House Hotel 53 Grange Loan, Grange ☎0131/667 4376, ⓔ teviotdale.house@btinternet .com. Peaceful non-smoking hotel, offering luxurious standards at reasonable prices. Particularly good (and huge) home-cooked Scottish breakfasts. **❽**

Campsites

Edinburgh Caravan Club Marine Drive, Silverknowes ☎0131/312 6874. Pleasantly located close to the shore in the northwestern suburbs, 30min from the centre on bus #28.

Mortonhall Caravan Park 38 Mortonhall Gate, Frogston Rd ☎0131/664 1533. A good site, five miles south of the centre, near the Braid Hills; take bus #11(marked Captain's Rd) or #31 from the centre of town. Closed Jan–March.

The Old Town

The cobbled **Royal Mile** – composed of Castlehill, Lawnmarket, High St and Canongate – is the central thoroughfare of the **Old Town**, running down a prominent ridge to the Palace of Holyroodhouse (see below) from the **Castle** (daily 9.30am–5/6pm; £8.50). The castle is thought to have evolved from an Iron Age fort, the sheer volcanic rock on which it stands providing formidable defence on three sides. Within its precincts are St Margaret's Chapel, probably the oldest building in the city, the ancient crown jewels of Scotland and the even older Stone of Destiny – coronation stone of the kings of Scotland that was returned north of the border in 1996 after a 700-year stay in London. There's a large military museum here, too, and the castle esplanade provides a dramatic setting for the world-famous Military Tattoo, an unashamed display of martial pomp staged during the Festival. Year round, at 1pm (not Sun) a cannon shot is fired from the battlements.

Descending Castlehill from the Esplanade you'll pass the **Scotch Whisky Heritage Centre** (daily 10am–6pm, longer hours in summer; £7.50), which offers an informative and entertaining introduction to Scotland's national beverage. A little further down in an imposing black Gothic church building is **The Hub** (daily 9.30am–late; free), permanent home of the Edinburgh International Festival, where you'll find a pleasant café/bistro, a bookshop and various quirky art installations. A little further down, leading off the far side of Lawnmarket, Lady Stair's Close is home to the **Writers' Museum** (Mon–Sat 10am–5pm; during Festival also Sun 2–5pm; free), dedicated to Sir Walter Scott, Robert Burns and Robert Louis Stevenson.

At the southern end of Lawnmarket, George IV Bridge leads south from the Royal Mile to Chambers St; here the important **Museum of Scotland** (Mon–Sat 10am–5pm, Tues till 8pm, Sun noon–5pm; free; ⓦ www.nms.ac.uk), housed in an imaginatively designed modern sandstone building, is home to many of the nation's principal historical treasures, ranging from Celtic pieces to twentieth-century icons.

Immediately next door is the **Royal Museum** (same times), a soaring Victorian pile housing a rich collection of colonial acquisitions. The area south of here is dominated by **Edinburgh University**, Scotland's largest with over 15,000 students.

Back on the Royal Mile, High St starts at Parliament Square, dominated by the **High Kirk of St Giles** (daily 9am–5/7pm), whose beautiful crown-shaped spire is an Edinburgh landmark. Inside, the Thistle Chapel (1911) is an amazing display of mock-Gothic woodcarving. Outside, near the west door, the heart-shaped cobble pattern set in the cobbles is the Heart of Midlothian – traditionally, passers-by spit on it for luck. On the south side of Parliament Square are the Neoclassical law courts, incorporating the seventeenth-century **Parliament House**, under whose spectacular hammerbeam roof the Scottish parliament met until the 1707 Union. This stretch of the Royal Mile is the starting point for entertaining **ghost tours** which prowl around the spookiest of the medieval nooks and crannies, including some underground streets. Look out for information boards on the street or contact Auld Reekie (℡0131/557 4700) or Mercat Tours (℡0131/557 6464).

The final section of the Royal Mile, Canongate, starts just beyond medieval **John Knox's House** (July & Aug Mon–Sat 10am–5pm, Sun noon–5pm; rest of year closed Sun; £2), which juts out into the street. Reputedly the home of the city's famously fierce Calvinist cleric, its bare interiors give a good idea of the labyrinthine layout of Old Town houses. The final section of Canongate is dominated by the new Scottish **Parliament**, a costly and controversial but undoubtedly striking piece of contemporary architecture which is set to open in 2004. In complete contrast is the **Palace of Holyroodhouse** (daily 9.30am–3.45/5.15pm; £7.50), the Royal Family's official Scottish residence, which principally dates from the seventeenth century. The public are admitted to the sumptuous state rooms and historic apartments unless the royals are in residence. The palace looks out over Holyrood Park, 650 acres of wilderness in the heart of the city, where fine walks lead along the dramatic **Salisbury Crags** and up **Arthur's Seat** beyond; a fairly stiff climb is rewarded by magnificent views over the city and out to the Firth of Forth.

The New Town

The clear divide between the Old and **New Town** is the wide grassy valley of Princes Street Gardens, along the north side of which runs **Princes St**, the main shopping area, with chain stores crammed in cheek-by-jowl. Splitting the gardens halfway along is the **National Gallery of Scotland** (daily 10am–5pm, Thurs till 7pm; free), an Athenian-style sandstone building. One of the best small collections of pre-twentieth century art in Europe, it includes works by major European artists including Botticelli, Raphael, Titian, Rembrandt, Vermeer, Degas, Gauguin and Van Gogh. The Scottish collection is relatively limited, though it's worth looking out for the charming *Reverend Robert Walker Skating* by Henry Raeburn – a postcard favourite. The National Gallery is currently undergoing a major upgrade, during which sections of its exterior will be hidden by scaffolding until at least 2005; the gallery remains open throughout.

East of the National Gallery the peculiar Gothic spire of the **Scott Monument** (Mon–Sat 9am–3/6pm, Sun 10am–3/6pm; £2.50), a tribute to Sir Walter Scott, stands out. You can climb the tightly winding internal spiral staircase for heady views of the city below and hills beyond. Nearby George St, which runs parallel to Princes St, is fast becoming the domain of designer-label shops; but suave Charlotte Sq, at its western end, remains the most elegant square in the New Town. North of George St is the broad avenue of Queen St, at whose eastern end stands the **Scottish National Portrait Gallery** (daily noon–5pm, Thurs till 7pm; free). The remarkable red sandstone building is modelled on the Doge's Palace in Venice; inside the collection of portraits offers an engaging procession through Scottish history with famous Scots such as Bonnie Prince Charlie and Mary, Queen of Scots on display alongside contemporary heroes such as Sean Connery and Alex Ferguson.

East of here, best approached along Waterloo Place (an extension of Princes St), **Calton Hill** rises up above the New Town and is worth heading for both for the views you'll get to all parts of the city, and for an odd collection of Neoclassical buildings including the **National Monument**, perched on the very top of the hill. It was begun in 1822 to imitate the Parthenon in Athens, but funds quickly ran out and only twelve of its massive columns were built, earning it the nickname "Edinburgh's Disgrace".

In the northwest corner of the New Town lies **Stockbridge**, a smart residential suburb with bohemian pretensions – especially noticeable around the huddle of old mill buildings known as Dean Village. From here Belford Rd leads up to the **Scottish National Gallery of Modern Art** and the **Dean Gallery** extension opposite (both daily 10am–5pm, Thurs till 7pm; free); the two offer an accessible introduction to all the notable movements of twentieth century art, displaying work by the likes of Matisse, Picasso, Giacometti and Mondrian, as well as modern Scottish artists such as the Colourists and industrial sculptor Sir Eduardo Paolozzi.

Eating, drinking and nightlife

Edinburgh is well served with **restaurants** and bistros, while its **cafés** are among the most enjoyable spots in the city – serving coffee, food and often alcohol too, and sometimes doubling as exhibition and performance spaces during the Festival. The city's many **pubs** and **bars** are among the most congenial in the country; live music a frequent bonus and you'll easily find places open after midnight. The city has a lively **nightlife**, and venues change name and location with such speed that the only way to keep up with what's going on is to get hold of *The List*, a comprehensive **listings** magazine published fortnightly. The best **theatre** is the *Traverse*, 10 Cambridge St, and there's an excellent art-house **cinema**, *The Filmhouse*, nearby at 88 Lothian Road. **Gay nightlife** is centred on the top of Leith Walk, notably at *C.C. Bloom's* and *Planet Out*, next to the Playhouse on Greenside Place.

Cafés and restaurants

Blue Moon 36 Broughton St. Coffee, snacks and filling meals at this friendly lesbian/gay café; all welcome.

Café Mediterraneo 73 Broughton St ☏0131/557 6900. Deli with a small dining space serving good quality Italian food at great prices.

Elephant House 21 George IV Bridge. Popular café near the university with a cavernous back room.

Favorit Teviot Pl and 30–32 Leven St, Bruntsfield. Modern café/diner open till the wee small hours.

Henderson's 94 Hanover St. Self-service restaurant with a lively atmosphere, good-value vegetarian food and occasional live music.

Kalpna 2 St Patrick Sq ☏0131/667 9890. Prize-winning vegetarian Indian; great prices for superb food.

Lost Sock Diner 11 East London St, Broughton. Burgers, wraps and blackboard specials at low prices in this quirky laundrette-cum-diner.

Mamma's American Pizza Company 30 Grassmarket. Good pizzas and a lively atmosphere that often spills out onto the Grassmarket cobbles.

Mussel Inn 61–65 Rose St ☏0131/225 5979. Owned by two Scottish shellfish farmers, you can feast on a kilo of mussels and a basket of chips for under £10.

The Outsider 15–16 George IV Bridge ☏0131/226 3131. Stylish, vibrant restaurant in the Old Town. Modern, filling and affordable food.

Le Sept 7 Old Fishmarket Close ☏0131/225 5428. Long established French brasserie serving filling savoury crepes and good fish dishes.

Susie's Diner 51 West Nicolson St. Popular student veggie/vegan café.

Pubs and bars

City Café 19 Blair St. A stylish yet inviting café/bar that is popular with the pre-club crowd.

Garibaldi's 97a Hanover St. A basement Mexican bar serving authentic dishes and cocktails alongside a dancefloor.

Human Be-In 2–8 West Crosscauseway. Super-trendy student bar serving excellent food.

Last Drop Tavern 74 Grassmarket. A late-closing studenty pub.

Malt Shovel 11 Cockburn St. Good beer, plenty of local colour and a wide choice of single malt whiskies; live jazz some evenings.

The Outhouse 12a Broughton St Lane. Pre-club bar and beer garden.

Live music venues and clubs

Cabaret Voltaire 36–38 Blair St. Features eclectic beats and the occasional live band.

Ego 14 Picardy Pl. Popular club playing anything from house to swing to a mixed crowd.
Liquid Room 9c Victoria St. Holds house and indie nights; also a popular live venue.
Massa 36–39 Market St. Dressy club that grooves to house and pop.

Royal Oak Infirmary St. Venue for Scottish folk music.
Venue 15 Calton Rd. Features up-and-coming indie bands as well as a range of club nights.
Whistlebinkies 4–6 South Bridge. Late night rock and folk venue.

The Edinburgh Festival

The city's essential cultural event is the **Edinburgh Festival** (ⓦwww.edinburgh -festivals.com), by far the world's largest arts jamboree, which was founded in 1947 and now attracts thousands of artists from August to early September. The event is, in fact, several different festivals taking place at around the same time: the Edinburgh International Festival traditionally presents highbrow fare; but it's the frenetic **Fringe** (ⓦwww.edfringe.com) that gives the city its unique buzz during August, with all sorts of unlikely venues turned into performance spaces for a bewildering array of artists. In addition, there's a Film Festival focusing on the latest movies, a Jazz Festival, and a Book Festival. **Tickets** are available at the venues and from the International Festival Office, The Hub, Castlehill (☏0131/473 2000), or the Fringe Office, 180 High St (☏0131/226 0026).

Listings

Banks and exchange Several big branches on and around Andrew, Hanover and George squares.
Bike rental Biketrax, 11 Lochrin Place ☏0131/228 6333; Edinburgh Cycle Hire, 29 Blackfriars St ☏0131/556 5560, ⓦwww.cyclescotland.co.uk.
Consulates Australia, 69 George St ☏0131/624 3333; Canada, 30 Lothian Rd ☏0131/220 4333; USA, 3 Regent Terrace ☏0131/556 8315.
Hospitals Royal Infirmary, Old Dalkieth Rd

☏0131/536 1000.
Laundry Sundial, 7 East London St; Tarvit Launderette, 7 Tarvit St.
Left luggage At Waverley Station and in lockers by St Andrew Sq bus station.
Pharmacy Boots, 40–44 North Bridge.
Police Fettes Ave ☏0131/311 3131.
Post office St James' Shopping Centre, near the east end of Princes St.

Glasgow

GLASGOW is the largest city in Scotland, home to 750,000 people. It once thrived on the tobacco trade with the American colonies, on cotton production and, most famously, on the shipbuilding on the River Clyde. The civic architecture of Victorian Glasgow was as grand as any in Britain, and the West End suburbs were regarded as among the best designed in the country. Since this heyday, however, it has not enjoyed the best of reputations. The Gorbals area became notorious as one of the worst slums in Europe, and the city's association with violence and heavy drinking stuck to it like a curse. However, like many British cities, rejuvenated Glasgow has undergone another change of image, symbolized by its selection as the European City of Culture in 1990 and City of Architecture and Design in 1999, titles which recognize that the city has broken the industrial shackles of the past and evolved into a city of stature and confidence.

The City

Glasgow's centre lies on the north bank of the Clyde, around the grandiose **George Square**, a little way east of Central Station. Just south of the square, down Queen St, is the **Gallery of Modern Art** (Mon–Wed & Sat 10am–5pm, Thurs 10am–8pm, Fri & Sun 11am–5pm; free). Formerly a "temple of commerce" built by one of the eighteenth-century tobacco lords, it now houses an exciting collection of contemporary Scots art, notably works by Peter Howson and John Bellany. A short way west on Mitchell Lane, just off Buchanan St, **The Lighthouse** (Mon–Sat 10.30am–5.30pm, Tues from 11am, Sun noon–5pm; £3) was the first commission of Glasgow's famous architect Charles Rennie Mackintosh, whose distinctively streamlined Art Nouveau designs appear in shops all over the city; inside is an exhibition devoted to the man. Northeast of George Sq is the **cathedral** on Castle St (Mon–Sat 9.30am–4/6pm, Sun 1–4/5pm). Built in 1136, destroyed in 1192 and rebuilt soon after, it's the only Scottish mainland cathedral to have escaped the hands of the country's sixteenth-century religious reformers, whose hatred of anything that smacked of idolatry wrecked many of Scotland's ancient churches. Just as interesting as the cathedral is the adjacent **Necropolis**, a hilltop cemetery for the magnates who made Glasgow rich; there are great views across the city from here.

North and west of George Square, on Glasgow's most famous thoroughfare, Sauchiehall St (pronounced "socky-hall"), the **McLellan Galleries** (Mon–Thurs & Sat 10am–5pm, Fri & Sun 11am–5pm; free) are a temporary home for some of the best pieces from the Glasgow Art Gallery and Museum, which is currently undergoing renovation. The collection has notable pieces by Rembrandt, Degas, Millet, Van Gogh and Monet, as well as an impressive body of Scottish painting. Just off Sauchiehall St is the **Glasgow School of Art**, 167 Renfrew St, a remarkable building designed by Mackintosh that is a fusion of Scottish manor house solidity and modernist refinement. The interior, making maximum use of natural light, was also furnished and fitted entirely by the architect, and can be seen on a guided tour (Mon–Fri 11am & 2pm, Sat 10.30am & 11.30am; July–Sept also Sun 10.30am & 11.30am; £5; ☎0141/353 4526). A short distance north is the **Tenement House**, 145 Buccleuch St (March–Oct daily 1–5pm; £3.50), an intriguing if sanitized vision of working-class life.

About four miles south of the centre, in **Pollok Country Park** (bus #45, #48 or #57 from Union St, or train to Pollokshaws West), is the astonishing **Burrell Collection**, housed in a custom-built gallery (Mon–Thurs & Sat 10am–5pm, Fri & Sun 11am–5pm; free). Sir William Burrell began collecting at the age of 15 and kept going until his death at 96, buying an average of two pieces a week. Works by Memling, Cézanne, Degas, Bellini and Géricault feature among the paintings, while in adjoining galleries there are pieces from ancient Rome and Greece, medieval European arts and crafts, and a massive selection of Chinese artefacts, with outstanding ceramics, jades and bronzes.

Practicalities

Glasgow International airport (☎0141/887 1111) is eight miles west of the city, with regular buses shuttling to Buchanan St bus station; **Glasgow Prestwick airport** (☎01292/479822), thirty miles south, is connected to the city centre by train. Glasgow has two main **train stations**: Central serves all points south and west, Queen St serves Edinburgh and the north. It's an easy city to explore on foot – the grid pattern of the centre makes navigation relatively simple. The **Underground** is cheap and easy, operating on a circular chain of fifteen stations with a flat fare of 90p (day-pass £1.70). The **Strathclyde Travel Centre**, above St Enoch underground station (Mon–Sat 8.30am–5.30pm), has information on all public transport, as well as discount passes. The helpful **tourist office** is on the south side of George Sq, near the top of Queen St (Mon–Sat 9am–6/8pm, Sun 10am–6pm; Oct–April closed Sun; ☎0141/204 4400, ◎www.seeglasgow.com); there's a smaller office at the airport (Mon–Sat 7.30am–5pm; April–Sept Sun 7.30am–5pm, Oct–March Sun 8am–3.30pm; ☎0141/848 4440). During summer, the universities of Glasgow (☎0141/330 5385) and Strathclyde (☎0141/553 4148) let out **rooms** (❺).

There are plenty of inexpensive **eating** options in the city centre and a huge number of **pubs** in which to down a pint. As for **nightlife**, the fortnightly magazine *The List* is the best source of club listings, but pick of the crop are *The Arches*, on Midland St, and *The Tunnel*, 84 Mitchell St. You can often find innovative, challenging theatre at the Citizens' or Tramway theatres, both on the south side of the river, pop gigs at the Barrowland (244 Gallowgate) and the Carling Academy (121 Eglinton St) while the **Centre for Contemporary Arts** or CCA, 346 Sauchiehall

St, has a reputation for a programme of controversial performances and exhibitions. The wonderful Glasgow Film Theatre, Rose St, shows art films and old favourites.

Hostels and B&Bs

Adelaide's 209 Bath St ☎0141/248 4970, ⓦwww.adelaides.co.uk. Simple but decent rooms attached to a city-centre church. ⑤

Alamo 46 Gray St ☎0141/339 2395, ⓦwww.alamoguesthouse.com. Attractive B&B near Kelvingrove. ⑥

Euro Hostel 318 Clyde St ☎0141/222 2828, ⓦwww.euro-hostels.com. Very central, 360-bed hostel. £13.75.

Glasgow SYHA 7 Park Terrace ☎0141/332 3004, ⓦwww.syha.org.uk. Attractive location, near Kelvingrove Park; due to reopen in March 2004. £12.75.

Campsite

Craigendmuir Park Campsie View ☎0141/779 4159. Four miles northeast of the centre; take a train to Stepps, from where it's a fifteen-minute walk.

Cafés and restaurants

Ashoka Ashton Lane. Excellent-value Indian restaurant.

Corinthian 191 Ingram Rd, Ultra-ornate if pricey bar and restaurant, worth a visit for the decor alone.

Grassroots Café 97 St George's Rd. Innovative organic food in bright and airy surroundings.

Grosvenor Café 31 Ashton Lane. Just off Byres Rd in the West End, this is one of the best places in town for inexpensive snacks.

Sleepless on Sauchiehall 415 Sauchiehall St. Burgers and coffees through the night, packed with a post-club crowd in the wee hours.

University Café Byres Rd. A period piece where you can fill up on basic but filling fare.

Willow Tea Rooms 217 Sauchiehall St. Mackintosh-designed place, good for a light meal.

Pubs and live music venues

Bar 10 10 Mitchell St. A good example of a traditional Glasgow style bar.

Bargo Albion St. A trendy pre-club DJ-bar in fashionable Merchant city.

Del Monica's 68 Virginia St. The liveliest gay bar in town.

The Horseshoe Bar 17 Drury St. Has the longest bar in the UK and plenty of atmosphere.

King Tut's Wah Wah Hut 272a Vincent St. Famous as the place where Oasis were discovered, and still hosts excellent gigs.

Scotia 112 Stockwell St. Has live folk music.

Listings

Bike rental Dales, 150 Dobbies Loan ☎0141/332 2705; West End Cycles, 16 Chancellor St ☎0141/357 1344.

Hospitals Royal Infirmary, 84 Castle St ☎0141/211 4000.

Laundry Bank Street Laundry, 39–41 Bank St; Majestic Launderette, 1110 Argyle St.

Pharmacy Boots, Buchanan Galleries.

Police Pitt St ☎0141/532 2000.

Post office 47 St Vincent St.

Melrose

If you've only time to visit one town in the Scottish Borders, the upland region lying between England and Scotland, then **MELROSE**, 37 miles south of Edinburgh, is the obvious choice. Tucked in between the River Tweed and the gorse-backed Eildon Hills, this is the most beguiling of towns, its narrow streets trimmed by a harmonious ensemble of styles, from pretty little cottages and tweedy shops to high-standing Georgian and Victorian facades. Its chief draw is its ruined **abbey** (April–Sept daily 9.30am–6.30pm; Oct–March Mon–Sat 9.30am–4.30pm, Sun 2–4.30pm; £3.50). It's best seen on a bright morning, with the sun streaming through the tracery of the exquisite east and south windows and illuminating the richly sculpted capitals and cornices of the nave. The Scots Baronial house of **Abbotsford** (June–Sept daily 9.30am–5pm; mid-March to May & Oct Mon–Sat 9.30am–5pm, Sun 2–5pm; £4), three miles west of Melrose, was designed to satisfy the Romantic inclinations of **Sir Walter Scott**, who lived here from 1812 until his death twenty years later. Despite all the exterior pomp, the interior is surprisingly small and poky, with just six rooms open for viewing, starting with the wood-panelled study where Scott banged out the Waverley novels at a furious rate to try and pay off his debts. Even more aesthetically pleasing is Scott's burial place, **Dryburgh Abbey** (hours as for Melrose Abbey; £2.80), five miles southeast of Melrose. The romantic setting is second to none, though the abbey ruins are much less substantial than at Melrose. Virtually nothing survives of the nave, but the transepts have fared better and now serve as a burial ground for Scott, and Field Marshal Haig, the World War I commander responsible for needless slaughter of millions.

Buses to Melrose stop in Market Sq, from where it's a short walk north to the abbey ruins and the **tourist office**, opposite (Mon–Sat 9.30/10am–5/6.30pm; ☎0870/608 0404). The **HI hostel** is in an old Victorian villa overlooking the abbey (☎01896/822521; £10–12). There's a plentiful supply of **B&Bs**, most notable of which is *Braidwood*, on Buccleuch St (☎01896/822488; ❸). The old coaching inns in the village offer quality **food**: *Burt's* does good bar meals, as does *The Ship*.

St Andrews

Well-groomed **ST ANDREWS**, on the coast 56 miles northeast of Edinburgh, has the air of a place of importance. Retaining memories of its days as medieval Scotland's metropolis, it is the country's oldest university town, the Scottish answer to Oxford or Cambridge with a snob-appeal to match. The upper-class English accents that you hear everywhere in term time certainly haven't diminished now that the university is playing host to Prince William's undergraduate years. St Andrews has an exalted place in Scottish sporting history too. Entering the town from the Edinburgh road, you pass no fewer than four golf links, the last of which is the **Old Course**, the most famous and – in the opinion of Jack Nicklaus – the best in the world. At the southern end of the Old Course, down towards the waterfront, is the award-winning **British Golf Museum** (April–Oct daily 9.30am–5.30pm; Nov–March Mon & Thurs–Sun 11am–3pm; £4); if you want to step onto the famous fairways, head to the **Himalayas** putting green, located right by the first hole and only 90p per round. Sweeping north from the Old Course is a great swathe of sandy beach; immediately south of the Old Course begins North St, one of St Andrews' two main arteries. Much of it is taken up by university buildings, with the tower of **St Salvator's College** rising proudly above all else. Together with the adjoining chapel, this dates from 1450 and is the earliest surviving part of the university. Further east, you can reach the ruined **castle** on North Castle St (April–Sept daily 9.30am–6.30pm; Oct–March daily 9.30am–4.30pm; £3, or combined ticket with cathedral £4). A short distance further along the coast is the equally ruined Gothic **cathedral** (same hours; £2.50), the mother church of medieval Scotland and the largest and grandest ever built in the country. Even though little more than the cemetery survives, the intact east wall and the exposed foundations give an idea of the vast scale of what has been lost. With the cathedral entrance ticket you can get a token to ascend the austere Romanesque **St Rule's Tower** – part of the priory that the cathedral replaced – for superb views over the sea and town.

Practicalities

You can reach St Andrews by **bus** on a day-trip from Edinburgh or Stirling. There are no direct trains, though frequent buses connect with the train station five miles away in Leuchars (where the parish church incorporates the most beautiful and intact piece of Norman architecture in Scotland). St Andrews' **tourist office**, 70 Market St (Mon–Sat 9.30am–7pm, Sun 10.30am–5pm; shorter hours and closed Sun in winter; ☎01334/472021, ⊛www.standrews.com/fife), will book **rooms** for a ten percent deposit – worth paying in the summer and during big golf tournaments, when **accommodation** is in short supply. The only **hostel** in the area is *St Andrews Tourist Hostel* on St Mary's Pl (☎01334/479911; £16). *Doune House*, 5 Murray Place (☎01334/475195; ⊛www.dounehouse.co.uk; ❸), and *Craigmore*, 3 Murray Park (☎01334/472142; ⊛www.standrewscraigmore.com; ❼), are two options of the many on those streets. For **eating**, student favourites are *The Inn on North Street*, 127 North St, and the Mexican *La Pasada* on St Mary's Place; for a more stylish contemporary bistro try *The Doll's House* at 3 Church Sq (☎01334/477422). Most **pubs** are concen-

trated on Market St and South St; best of the bunch are *Central*, 1 Market St, *Ma Belle's*,
40 The Scores, both popular student joints, while *Broons Bistro and Bar* beside the New
Picture House cinema on North St is a trendier spot with live music sessions.

Stirling

Occupying a key strategic position between the Highlands and Lowlands at the
easiest crossing of the River Forth, **STIRLING** has played a major role throughout
Scottish history. With its castle and steep, cobbled streets, it can appear like a smaller
version of Edinburgh. Imperiously set on a rocky crag, the atmospheric and
explorable **castle** (daily 9.30am–5/6pm; £7, includes Argyll's Lodging) combined
the functions of a fortress with those of a royal palace. Highlights within the complex are the **Royal Palace**, dating from the late Renaissance, and the earlier **Great
Hall**, where recent restoration, including a complete rebuilding of the vast hammerbeam roof, has revealed the original form and scale. The oldest part of Stirling is
grouped around the streets leading up to the castle. Look out for the Gothic
Church of the Holy Rude (daily 10am–5pm), with its fine timber roof, where
the infant James VI – later James I of the United Kingdom – was crowned King of
Scotland in 1567. From here, Broad St slopes down to the lower town, passing the
Tolbooth, the city's newly restored arts and cultural centre. Stirling is famous as
the scene of Sir William Wallace's battlefield victory over the English in 1297, a crucial episode in the Wars of Independence (as portrayed in the film *Braveheart*). The
Scottish hero was commemorated in Victorian times by the **Wallace Monument**
(daily 9.30am–6pm, shorter hours in winter; £5), about a mile north near the university. Though the refurbished building seems ugly close up, compensation comes
in the stupendous views – finer even than those from the castle.

The train and bus stations are both five minutes' walk from the **tourist office**, 41
Dumbarton Rd, in the lower part of town (July & Aug daily 9am–7pm; rest of year
Mon–Sat 9/10am–5/6pm; ☎01786/475019, ◍www.scottish.heartlands.org). The
HI hostel, St John St, is a little characterless but occupies a great setting at the top
of town in a converted church (☎01786/473442; £12.75), while *Willy Wallace
Independent Hostel*, 77 Murray Place, is a lively, welcoming backpacker **hostel**
(☎01786/446773; £11). Of the many guest houses, *No. 10*, 10 Gladstone Place, is
especially friendly (☎01786/472681; ◍www.cameron-10.co.uk; ❺). The pictur-
esque *Witches' Craig* **campsite** is three miles east of town on bus #62, off the St
Andrews road (☎01786/474947; closed Nov–March). Try the lively *Barnton Bar and
Bistro*, Barton St, or the cafe/bar or restaurant in the *Tolbooth Arts Centre* on Broad
St for decent **meals** and relaxed drinking.

Loch Lomond and the Trossachs

Loch Lomond – the largest stretch of fresh water in Britain – is the epitome of
Scottish scenic splendour, thanks in large part to the ballad that fondly recalls its
"bonnie, bonnie banks". The easiest way to get to the loch is to take one of the frequent trains from Glasgow Queen St Station to **BALLOCH** at its southwestern
tip, from where you can take a cruise around the 33 islands nearby. The **western
shore** is very developed, with the upgraded A82 zipping along its banks. The only
place to find any peace and quiet now is on the **eastern shore**, large sections of
which are only accessible via the footpath which forms part of the West Highland
Way. The easiest access to the graceful peak of **Ben Lomond** (3192ft) is from
Rowardennan, from which it's a straightforward three-hour hike to the summit; in
summer you can reach Rowardennan by ferry from Inverbeg on the western shore.

Loch Lomond is at the heart of the **Trossachs National Park**, Scotland's first
national park, opened in 2002. A huge development called Lomond Shores incorporating shops, information points and cafés has been built at Balloch; the Gateway
Centre here is the best place for information (daily 9/10.30am–4.30/7pm;

☎01389/722199) and a taste of the park if you're not able to explore further. A couple of miles northwest of Balloch is Scotland's most beautiful **HI hostel**, complete with resident ghost (☎01389/850226; March–Oct; £11.50); and there's another alluringly sited HI hostel at Rowardennan (☎01360/870259; March–Oct; £11.50). There are **campsites** and plenty of **B&Bs** in all the villages.

The isles of Mull and Iona

The **ISLE OF MULL** is the most accessible of all the Hebridean islands off the west coast of Scotland: just forty minutes by ferry from **Oban**, which is linked by train to Glasgow. The chief appeal of the island is its remarkably undulating coastline – three hundred miles of it in total. Despite its proximity to the mainland, the slower pace of life is clearly apparent: most roads are single lane, with only a handful of buses linking the main settlements. **CRAIGNURE**, the ferry terminal for boats from Oban (4–6 daily; 45min; £3.75 single), is little more than a smattering of cottages. It does, however, have the island's main **tourist office** (daily 8.30/10.30am–5/7pm; ☎01680/812377), a decent pub, bike rental and a campsite. On its way into Craignure, the ferry passes the dramatic **Duart Castle** (April to mid-Oct daily 10.30/11am–4/6pm; £4); two miles' walk along the bay. The stronghold of the MacLean clan from the thirteenth century, it was restored earlier last century – you can peek in the dungeons and ascend to the rooftops. Mull's "capital", **TOBERMORY**, 22 miles northwest of Craignure, is easily the most attractive fishing port on the west coast of Scotland, its clusters of brightly coloured houses and boats sheltering in a bay backed by a steep bluff. For a list of the local **B&Bs** head for the **tourist office** (April–Oct daily 9/10am–5/6pm; ☎01688/302182), in the Cal-Mac ferry ticket office at the northern end of the harbour. The **HI hostel** (☎01688/302481; £11; closed Nov–Feb) is on Main St, near *Harbour House*, an inexpensive guest house (☎01688/302209; ❺; closed Nov–Feb). Also on Main St is the *Mishnish Hotel* **pub**, popular for the live folk music at the weekends.

At the opposite end of Mull, 35 miles west of Craignure, is the **ISLE OF IONA**. Just three miles long and not much more than a mile wide, Iona has been a place of pilgrimage for several centuries: it was to this flat Hebridean island that St Columba fled from Ireland in 563 and established a monastery that was responsible for the conversion of more or less all of pagan Scotland. No buildings remain from Columba's time: the present **Abbey** (daily 9.30am–4/6pm; £3), which dominates all views of the island, dates from a re-establishment of monasticism here by the Benedictines in around 1200; it was extensively rebuilt in the fifteenth and sixteenth centuries, and restored wholesale last century. Iona's oldest building, **St Oran's Chapel**, lies south of the abbey, and boasts an eleventh-century door. It stands at the centre of the sacred burial ground, Reilig Odhrain, which is said to contain the graves of sixty kings of Norway, Ireland, France and Scotland, including the two immortalized by Shakespeare – Duncan and Macbeth. In front stand three delicately carved **crosses** from the eighth and ninth centuries, among the masterpieces of European sculpture of the Dark Ages. Iona is a very popular day-trip in summer, reached in a few minutes by regular ferry from **Fionnphort** at the western tip of Mull. To appreciate its special atmosphere, it's best to stay the night on Iona. Camping is not permitted, but there is a **hostel** (☎01681/700642; £12.50), a mile or so from the ferry, past the abbey; for **B&B**, try *Sithean House* (☎01681/700331; ❺; April–Oct), a mile from the ferry on the west side of the island; the better of the two **hotels** is the *Argyll* (☎01681/700334; ❻).

A basaltic mass rising direct from the sea, the **Isle of Staffa** is the northern end of the Giant's Causeway (the southern end of which reaches the Irish coast), and is the most romantic and dramatic of Scotland's many uninhabited islands. On one side, its perpendicular rockface has been cut into caverns of cathedral-like dimensions, notably **Fingal's Cave**, whose haunting noises inspired Mendelssohn's

Hebrides Overture. To get to Staffa, jump aboard the Iolaire (℡01681/700358; £12.50), which sails out of Fionnphort and Iona.

The Isle of Skye

Jutting out from the mainland, the bare and bony promontories of the **ISLE OF SKYE** fringe a deeply indented coastline. The most popular destination on the island is the **Cuillin ridge**, whose jagged peaks dominate the island during clear weather; equally dramatic in their own way are the rock formations of the Trotternish peninsula in the north. The easiest way to reach Skye is either to catch a **ferry** from the train terminus of Mallaig, or by **bus** (via the Skye Bridge) from the train terminus of Kyle of Lochalsh. Either way, you'll end up in the southeast corner of the island, where there's a concentration of hostels. From Mallaig, you disembark in **ARMADALE**, where there's an HI hostel (℡01471/844260; £9; closed Oct–mid March) along the shore from the harbour. From Kyle of Lochalsh, you arrive in **KYLEAKIN**, which has an HI hostel a few minutes' walk from the dock (℡01599/534585; £11) with the laid-back *Skye Backpackers* nearby (℡01599/534510; ❸). Further up the road at **KILMORE** the *Flora MacDonald Hostel* is open all year (℡01471/844440; ❸). These places are preferable to **BROADFORD**, a charmless village, which does, however, have a small **tourist office** (April–Oct Mon–Sat 9.30am–5/5.30pm; June–Sept also Sun 10am–2pm; ℡01471/822361).

The best approach to the **Cuillin**, whose sharp snowcapped peaks rise mirage-like from the flatness of the surrounding terrain, is via **ELGOL**, fourteen miles southwest of Broadford at the end of the most dramatic road in Skye. From here there are **boat trips** on the *Bella Jane* (℡0800/731 3089) to Loch Coruisk, after which you can walk the eight miles up gentle Glen Sligachan to the welcoming *Sligachan Hotel* (℡01478/650204; ❸) and adjacent campsite (closed Nov–March). Serious hikers head for **GLENBRITTLE**, ten miles southwest of Sligachan and north of the Cuillin, where there's an HI hostel (℡01478/640278; ❷; closed Oct–Feb) and a campsite not far away by the sandy beach (℡01478/640404; closed Nov–March). The only real town on Skye is the "capital", **PORTREE**, an attractive fishing port in the north of the island. Here you'll find the island's main **tourist office** just off Bridge St (Mon–Sat 9am–5.30/7pm; April–Oct also Sun 10am–4pm; ℡01478/612137). The town has several **hostels**, smartest of which is the *Portree Independent Hostel* (℡01478/613737; £10), housed in the Old Post Office on the Green. Of the dozens of **B&Bs**, try *Conusg* (℡01478/612426; ❺; closed Oct–Easter), in a quiet spot by the *Cuillin Hills Hotel*. **Food** in Portree can be pricey, but the fish and chips down by the harbour are excellent.

From Portree, head north up the east coast of the **Trotternish** peninsula. Some nine miles from Portree, at the edge of the Storr ridge, is a distinctive 165-foot obelisk known as the **Old Man of Storr**, while a further ten miles north, rising above Staffin Bay, are the **Quiraing** – a spectacular forest of mighty pinnacles and savage rock formations, including the Needle, the Prison and the Table, where the locals used to play shinty. The straggling village of **UIG**, on the west coast, has ferries to the islands of the Outer Hebrides, including Harris and North Uist, as well as an HI hostel (℡01470/542211; £10; closed Oct–March), high up above the harbour, a mile or so from the ferry terminal.

Inverness and the Highlands

Capital of the Highlands, **INVERNESS** is 160 miles north of Edinburgh, the train line between the two traversing the gentle countryside of Perthshire before skirting the stark Cairngorm mountains. Approaching from Skye in the west, there's the magnificent eighty-mile train journey from Kyle of Lochalsh. Inverness **airport** (℡01667/464000) is seven miles east. The town has a fine setting astride the River Ness at the head of the Beauly Firth, but despite having been a place of importance for a millennium – it was probably the capital of the Pictish kingdom and the site of Macbeth's castle – there's nothing remarkable to see, nor any particularly strong sense of character. The chief attractions of historical interest lie some six miles east of town, reached by regular buses. **Culloden Moor** was the scene in 1746 of the last pitched battle on British soil, when the troops of "Butcher" Cumberland crushed Bonnie Prince Charlie's Jacobite army in just forty minutes. This ended forever Stuart ambitions of maintaining the monarchy, and marked the beginning of the break-up of the clan system which had ruled Highland society for centuries. A **visitor centre** (daily 9/10am–4/7pm; closed Jan; £5) has displays describing the action.

As well as the only big choice of shops, restaurants and nightlife in the Highlands, you'll find **B&Bs** by the score in Inverness. These tend to fill up in summer, and the **tourist office** on Castle Wynd (March–Sept Mon–Fri 9am–7pm, Sat 9am–6pm, Sun 9.30am–5pm; rest of year Mon–Fri 9am–5pm, Sat 10am–4pm; ℡01463/234353, 𝕎www.host.co.uk) charges £3 to find a room. The modern **HI hostel** is on Victoria Drive, off Milburn Rd (℡01463/231771; £11.50); there are plenty of independent hostels, including the non-smoking *Bazpackers*, at the top of Castle St (℡01463/717663; £11). Also try the *Eastgate Backpackers*, 38 Eastgate (℡01463/718756; £10.50), which has a wide range of facilities including Internet access and bike rental. There are **campsites** at Culloden (closed Nov–Feb), on the road to Loch Ness, and within Inverness at Bught Park, west of the river. Inverness and around is best explored by bike: contact *Barney's*, 35 Castle St (℡01463/232249).

Loch Ness

Loch Ness forms part of the natural fault line known as the Great Glen, which slices across the Highlands between Inverness and Fort William. In the early 1800s, Thomas Telford linked the glen's lochs by means of the **Caledonian Canal**, enabling ships to pass between the North Sea and the Atlantic without having to navigate Scotland's treacherous northern coast. Today, pleasure-craft galore ply the route, with **cruises** from Inverness (summer only; book at tourist office) providing the most straightforward way of seeing the terrain. Most visitors are eager to catch a glimpse of the elusive Loch Ness **Monster**: tales of "Nessie" date back at least as far as the seventh century, when the monster came out second best in an altercation with St Columba. However, the possibility that a mysterious prehistoric creature might be living in the loch only attracted worldwide attention in the 1930s, when sightings were reported during the construction of the road along its western shore. Numerous appearances have been reported since, but even the most hi-tech surveys of the loch have failed to come up with conclusive evidence. To find out the whole story, take a bus to **DRUMNADROCHIT**, fourteen miles southwest of Inverness, where the most informative displays are at the **Loch Ness 2000 Exhibition** (daily: July & Aug 9am–8pm; shorter hours at other times; £5.95). Most photographs allegedly showing the monster have been taken around the ruined **Castle Urquhart** (daily 9.30am–4/6/8.30pm; £3.80), one of Scotland's most beautifully sited fortresses, a couple of miles further south.

Into the Highlands

With its beguiling mix of bare hills, green glens and silvery lochs and rivers, the spectacular scenery of the **Highlands** (which covers most of Scotland north of the Central Belt and west of Aberdeen) is a major draw. The distances involved, however, as well as poor public transport, mean that you really need a few days to explore any one part of it properly. Coachloads of sightseers take in what they can from carefully positioned viewpoints on the main roads, but **outdoor activities** are a major reason to visit: most tourist information centres and backpacker hostels carry information on good local hiking routes, bike rental and adventure sports. While you can get a taste of the Highlands as far south as Loch Lomond and the Trossachs

National Park, barely an hour from Edinburgh or Glasgow, any trip to Inverness, Mull or Skye will take you through some magnificent upland country. Obvious stopping-points for further exploration include **AVIEMORE**, at the foot of the looming Cairngorm range, which offers challenging hiking, ancient pine forests, and skiing and other winter sports in season. On the west coast, the town of **FORT WILLIAM** is a great base for draws such as Ben Nevis, the West Highland Way long-distance footpath and Glen Coe, where soaring scenery and poignant history combine like nowhere else in the country.

Getting around the Highlands without a car does require patience, although good-value travel passes are available on Scotrail's **train** network (Ⓦwww.scotrail.co.uk), which has some superbly scenic stretches including the famous **West Highland Line** from Glasgow to Oban, Fort William and Mallaig. Alternatively, a couple of rival companies offer lively **minibus tours** designed specifically for backpackers: Haggis (Ⓣ0131/557 9393, Ⓦwww.haggisadventures .com) and Macbackpackers (Ⓣ0131/558 9900; Ⓦwww.macbackpackers.com) depart from Edinburgh on trips lasting between one and seven days; you can also buy a jump-on/jump-off ticket allowing you to cover their circuits (which generally take in Inverness, Skye, Oban and Stirling) at your own pace.

Aberdeen

On the east coast 120 miles north of Edinburgh, **ABERDEEN** is the third city of Scotland. Solid and hard-wearing like the distinctive silver-grey granite used for so many of its buildings, it has been nicknamed the "Silver City", although its wealth is built on black gold – North Sea oil. Until a hundred years ago, Aberdeen was two separate towns a couple of miles apart, based around the mouths of the rivers Dee and Don. While Old Aberdeen slumbered in academic and ecclesiastical tranquillity, the newer town became a major port and commercial centre, and was subject to grandiose planning schemes. The most ambitious of these, in the early nineteenth century, included the layout of spacious **Union St**, a block north of the bus and train stations, which runs for more than a mile east–west across the centre. Despite the grand buildings, Union St today is fairly tawdry, with uninspiring shops and the continual drone of traffic. Best of the sights is down Shiprow, near the eastern end of Union St, where Provost Ross's House, a sixteenth-century mansion, now abuts the award-winning **Maritime Museum** (Mon–Sat 10am–5pm, Sun noon–3pm; free). The collection here describes Aberdeen's relationship with the sea through imaginative displays, films and models, including a thirty-foot oil rig. A further short walk downhill is the bustling **harbour** area, seen at its best in the early morning, before the daily fish market winds down at 8am. Across Union St from Shiprow is Broad St, dominated by **Marischal College**, the younger half of Aberdeen University. Its facade, a century-old historicist extravaganza, is probably the most spectacular piece of granite architecture in existence. Less than a mile east of Union St is the best **beach** to be found in any British city, a great two-mile sweep of clean sand, very popular in summer.

Aberdeen **airport** is seven miles northwest; the **bus** and **train** stations are on Guild St, 200m south of Union St. The **tourist office**, 23 Union St (June–Sept Mon–Sat 9am–7pm, Sun 10am–4pm; Oct–May Mon–Sat 9.30am–5.30pm; Ⓣ01224/288828), can help with finding B&B. The **HI hostel** is at 8 Queen's Rd (Ⓣ01224/646988; ❸); take buses #14, #15, #23 or #27. One of Aberdeen's perennially popular spots for **eating** is the *Ashvale*, 46 Great Western Rd, long rated as one of Britain's best fish-and-chip shops. Cheap meals can also be found at *Café 52*, on The Green near Union St, and at the café at the *Lemon Tree Arts Centre*, 5 West North St. For **drinking**, the *Prince of Wales* on St Nicholas Lane is Aberdeen's most colourful real ale pub, while Cameron's Inn, 6 Little Beaumont St, is a popular hangout.

Travel details

Trains

Bristol to: Bath (1–3 hourly; 15min); Cardiff (every 30min; 50min); Manchester (2 daily; 3hr 30min–4hr); Salisbury (hourly; 1hr 10min); York (hourly; 4hr).

Edinburgh to: Aberdeen (hourly; 2hr 30min); Durham (hourly; 2hr); Glasgow (every 15min; 50min); Inverness (6 daily; 3hr 30min); Newcastle (hourly; 1hr 30min); Leuchars for St Andrews (hourly; 1hr 20min); Stirling (every 30min; 50min); York (hourly; 2hr 30min).

Glasgow to: Aberdeen (hourly; 2hr 20min); Inverness (some change at Perth; 4hr); Mallaig for Skye (Mon–Sat 3 daily; Sun 1 daily; 5hr 15min); Oban for Mull (2–4 daily; 3hr); Preston for Liverpool & Manchester (13 daily; 1hr 30min); Newcastle (every 2hr; 2hr 30min); Stirling (every 30min; 40min).

Inverness to: Aberdeen (10 daily; 2hr 15min); Kyle of Lochalsh for Skye (Mon–Sat 3 daily; Sun 1 daily; 2hr 30min); Stirling (some change at Perth; 9 daily; 2hr 30min).

Liverpool to: Cardiff (some change at Crewe; 13 daily; 4hr); Manchester (every 20min; 50min); Preston for Glasgow (hourly; 1hr); York (hourly; 2hr 20min).

London to: Aberdeen (6 daily; 7hr 30min); Aberystwyth (change at Birmingham; 14 daily; 5hr); Bath (every 15min; 1hr 20min); Brighton (every 15min; 50min); Bristol (every 30min; 1hr 45min); Cambridge (every 15min; 45min); Canterbury (every 30min; 1hr 20min–1hr 50min); Cardiff (hourly; 2hr–2hr 20min); Dover (every 30min; 1hr 45min); Durham (hourly; 2hr 45min); (hourly; 4hr 30min–5hr); Glasgow (hourly; 5hr 30min); Liverpool (hourly; 2hr 50min); Manchester (20 daily; 2hr 40min); Newcastle (every 30min; 3hr); Newport (every 30min; 1hr 45min); Oxford (every 20–30min; 1hr); Penzance (8 daily; 5hr 30min–6hr); Stratford-upon-Avon (5 daily; 2hr 15min); Winchester (every 15min; 1hr); York (every 30min; 2hr 15min).

Manchester to: Newcastle (12 daily; 3hr); Preston for Glasgow (every 20min; 1hr); Windermere (5 daily; 1hr 45min); York (every 30min; 1hr 40min).

Buses

Bristol to: Bath (every 30min; 50min); Cardiff (2 daily; 1hr 10min); Manchester (3 daily; 3hr 10min–5hr); Oxford (1 daily; 2hr 40min); Salisbury (1 daily; 2hr); Wells (hourly; 50min).

Edinburgh to: Aberdeen (change at Perth or Dundee; hourly; 3hr 20min); Durham (1 daily; 4hr 30min); Glasgow (every 20min; 1hr 10min); Inverness (hourly; 4hr); Kyle of Lochalsh for Skye (2 daily 7hr); Manchester (3 daily; 5hr 30min); Melrose (hourly; 1hr); Newcastle (3 daily; 3hr); St Andrews (every 30min; 2hr–3hr); Stirling (every 30min; 1hr 15min).

Glasgow to: Aberdeen (hourly; 3hr 30min); Inverness (hourly; 4hr); Liverpool (2 daily; 4hr 40min–5hr 15min); Manchester (3 daily; 5hr 30min); Newcastle (every 2hr; 2hr 30min); Oban for Mull (3 daily; 3hr); St Andrews (12 daily; 2hr 20min); Stirling (every 30min; 30min).

Inverness to: Aberdeen (10 daily; 2hr 15min); Stirling (2 daily; 3hr 20min).

Liverpool to: Cardiff (4 daily; 5hr 40min–6hr 40min); Manchester (hourly; 50min); Newcastle (3 daily; 4hr 30min–7hr 30min); Oxford (4 daily; 5hr 30min); York (2 daily; 3hr 40min–5hr).

London to: Aberdeen (2 daily; 12hr); Aberystwyth (1 daily; 6hr 45min); Bangor (for Holyhead; 1 daily; 8hr 30min); Bath (13 daily; 2hr 20min); Brighton (hourly; 2hr); Bristol (hourly; 2hr 50min); Cambridge (hourly; 1hr 50min); Canterbury (hourly; 1hr 50min); Cardiff (6 daily; 3hr 10min); Dover (hourly; 2hr 15min–2hr 45min); Durham (5 daily; 5hr 30min); Edinburgh (4 daily; 8hr 30min–9hr 10min); Glasgow (5 daily; 7hr 45min–8hr 50 min); Inverness (2 daily; 12hr 20min–13hr 10min); Liverpool (5 daily; 4hr 45min); Manchester (7 daily; 4hr 35min); Newcastle (5 daily; 6hr); Newport (6 daily; 2hr 45min); Oxford (every 15min; 1hr 40min); Penzance (5 daily; 7hr 45min–9hr 15min); Salisbury (2–3 daily; 2hr 45min); Stirling (2 daily; 9hr); Stratford (3 daily; 2hr 45min–3hr 15min); Winchester (9 daily; 2hr); York (3 daily; 4hr 30min).

Manchester to: Durham (3 daily; 4hr 15min–4hr 45min); Glasgow (2 daily; 4hr 30min–5hr); Newcastle (5 daily; 4hr 50min); York (3 daily; 3hr 20min).

Bulgaria

BULGARIA

Bucharest

ROMANIA

0   100 km

SERBIA &
MONTENEGRO

N

Belgrade

Ruse

Pleven

Varna

Gorna Oryahovitsa
Veliko Târnovo

SOFIA

Koprivshtitsa

Nesebâr

BLACK
SEA

Burgas

Sozopol

MACEDONIA

Dupnitsa

Rila
Monastery

Septemvri

Stara Zagora

Blagoevgrad

Plovdiv

Bansko

Bachkovo
Monastery

Svilengrad

İstanbul

Sandanski

GREECE

TURKEY

Athens

Bulgaria highlights

✱ **Aleksandâr Nevski Cathedral, Sofia** One of the most awe-inspiring buildings in the Balkans. See p.190

✱ **Rila Monastery** Bulgaria's largest and most beautiful monastery, in the mountains south of Sofia. See p.192

✱ **Old Quarter, Plovdiv** A wealth of brightly painted National Revival houses, art galleries and Roman remains. See p.194

✱ **Koprivshtitsa** This picturesque village boasts Bulgaria's finest ensemble of National Revival architecture. See p.196

✱ **Archeology Museum, Varna** A treasure trove of Neolithic and Roman antiquities. See p.198

✱ **Nesebâr** The Black Sea Coast's prettiest resort, with several fine medieval churches. See p.199

Introduction and basics

If Westerners have an image of **Bulgaria**, it tends to be coloured by the murky intrigues of Balkan politics, with tales of poisoned umbrellas and plots to kill the pope. The nation has come a long way, though, since it threw off the 500-year yoke of the Ottoman Empire in the 1870s, and is now struggling to cope with the aftermath of Communist misrule. The Socialists retained power through the early 1990s, and moves towards free-market reforms were slow. The election of a right-of-centre government in 1997 brought some measure of economic stability, and in 2001, the former king, Simeon II, was democratically elected as prime minister; his party has pledged to fight institutional corruption, speed up the privatization process and prepare the country for membership of both NATO and the EU (slated for 2004 and 2007 respectively). In the meantime, low wages and high unemployment remain ever-present features of life, and recent war in neighbouring Serbia and unrest in Macedonia have also taken their toll.

Independent travel here is not common, but it is perfectly possible, the costs are low, and for the committed there is much to take in. The main attractions are the mountainous scenery and the web of towns and villages with a crafts tradition, where you'll find the wonderfully romantic architecture of the National Revival era. Foremost among these are **Koprivshtitsa** in the Sredna Gora range, **Bansko** in the Pirin mountains and **Plovdiv**, the second largest city. The monasteries are stunning, too – the finest, **Rila**, should be on every itinerary. For city life, the bustling, if rather faded capital, **Sofia**, and the cosmopolitan coastal resort of **Varna** are the places to aim for.

Information & maps

There are few publicly funded **tourist offices** in Bulgaria, and those that do exist are fairly undeveloped. Most main towns have agencies, working on commission, who will book accommodation and transport for you, but are of little use for other information. Hotel and travel agency staff in Sofia and the larger towns generally speak some English, but

knowledge of foreign languages elsewhere in the country is patchy; younger people are more likely to know a few words of English, but German is the preferred second language in the coastal resorts. Most street signs, menus and so on are written in the **Cyrillic** alphabet, but an increasing number have English translations. The best **maps** of Bulgaria and of Sofia are produced by Datamap. They are widely available.

Money and banks

The Bulgarian currency is the **lev** (Lv), which is divided into 100 stotinki (st) and pegged to the euro. There are notes of 1Lv, 2Lv, 5Lv, 10Lv, 20Lv and 50Lv, and coins of 1st, 2st, 5st, 10st, 20st and 50st, and 1Lv. Since it was revalued in 1999, the lev has been stable, although hotels, travel agencies and the like frequently quote prices in euros or US dollars; the latter form has been followed in the text. Nonetheless, you can always pay in the local currency, and many places prefer it. Museums and galleries charge in leva, and foreigners are required to pay more for entry than Bulgarians. Producing a student ID

Bulgaria on the net

ⓦ**www.bulgaria.com** Comprehensive travel information.
ⓦ**www.hotelsbulgaria.com** Online hotel-booking facility.
ⓦ**www.onlinebg.com** News site.
ⓦ**www.travel-bulgaria.com** Information on history and culture, as well as travel.

card will often get you a discount. Be sure to keep a ready supply of coins for small purchases, as shops are often unable to change larger denomination notes.

Banks are open Mon–Fri 9am–4pm, and there are ATMs in all big towns. Private exchange bureaux, offering variable rates, are widespread – but beware of hidden commission charges. Also watch out for black market moneychangers who approach unwary foreigners with offers of better rates; if they sound too good to be true, they are. Many smaller banks and offices won't accept **travellers' cheques**, and while Visa and Mastercard are gaining greater acceptance, **credit cards** are generally usable only at the more expensive shops and hotels.

Communications

Post offices (*poshta*) are usually open Mon–Sat 8.30am–5.30pm, longer in big towns. The main office will have a poste restante facility, but postal officers tend to return mail to sender if it's not claimed immediately.

Card-operated **public phones** are on the whole reliable and can be used to make international calls. **Phonecards** (*fonkarta*) are available from post offices and many street kiosks and shops. The operator number for domestic calls is ☏121, for international calls ☏0123.

You'll find at least one or two **Internet cafés** in the cities, and often in smaller towns, too, though connection times can be slow. You'll rarely pay more than 1.50Lv per hour.

Body language

Bulgarians shake their heads when they mean "yes" and nod when they mean "no". Sometimes they reverse these gestures if they know they're speaking to foreigners, thereby complicating the issue further. Emphatic use of the words *da* (yes) and *ne* (no) should avoid misunderstandings.

Getting around

Public transport in Bulgaria is inexpensive but notoriously slow and not always clean or

comfortable. Travelling by bus is usually the quickest way of getting between major towns and cities, and an ever-growing number of privately run bus companies ply these routes; these are generally faster and more comfortable, though you'll pay slightly more.

Bulgarian State Railways (BDZh; ⊛www.bdz.bg) can get you to most towns; trains are punctual and fares low; it is always worth paying the extra thirty percent or so to travel first class (*purva klassa*) – if nothing else, you'll have more room. Express services (*Ekspresen*) are restricted to main routes, but on all except the humblest branch lines you'll find so-called Rapid (*bârz vlak*) trains. Where possible, use these rather than the snail-like *pâtnicheski* services. Long-distance/overnight trains have reasonably priced couchettes (*kushet*) and/or sleepers (*spalen vagon*). For these, on all expresses and many rapids, you need seat **reservations** (*zapazeni mesta*) as well as **tickets** (*bileti*). To ensure a seat in a non-smoking carriage (*myasto nepooshachi*), you will have to specify this when booking. In large towns, it's usually easier to obtain tickets and reservations from **railway booking offices** (*byuro za bileti*) rather than at the station, and wise to book a day in advance at weekends and in summer. Tickets can only be bought on the day of travel at the station. Advance bookings are required for **international tickets** and are bought through the Rila Agency; branches can be found in all major cities. Most stations have **left-luggage offices** (*garderob*). InterRail and Eurail are valid.

Most places are accessible by **bus** (*avtobus*), though in more remote areas there may only be one or two services a day. Generally, you can buy a ticket at the bus **station** (*avtogara*) at least an hour in advance when travelling between towns, but on some routes they're only sold when the bus arrives. On rural routes, tickets are often sold by the driver.

Accommodation

Although foreigners are required to pay around double the rate charged to Bulgarians, **accommodation** is still cheap by Western standards, and the quality is generally improving. Prices are often quoted in euros or US dollars, but many places now prefer that you pay in leva. Most one- and two-star **hotels** (for the most part uninspiring high-rise blocks) rent double rooms from around £20/$32, a little more in Sofia and Plovdiv. Cosier family-run hotels are common on the coast and in village resorts such as Koprivshtitsa and Bansko.

Private rooms (*chastni kvartiri*) are available in most large towns, and are usually administered by accommodation agencies, although in the smaller resorts you can usually find a room by asking around; expect to pay around £10–15/$16–24 for a double, more in Sofia and Plovdiv. Single travellers usually get a small reduction on the price of a double. The quality varies enormously, and it's rarely possible to inspect the place first, but as a rule, private rooms in big cities will be in large residential blocks, while those in village resorts can often be in atmospheric, traditional houses.

Hostels (*turisticheska spalnya*) are thin on the ground, although those that exist (in Sofia or Plovdiv, for example) are well run and accustomed to foreigners. Some towns of interest have a **campsite** (*kamping*; usually summer only) on the outskirts, although these are few and far between, and can be unkempt affairs with poor connections to the town centre. Many also feature two-person chalets (£5–10/$8–16 per night). **Camping rough** is illegal and punishable with a fine.

Food and drink

Fresh fruit and vegetables have long formed the basis of **Bulgarian cuisine**, a tradition rarely reflected in restaurants, where menus have become pretty standardized and uninspiring. Grilled meats are the focus of most restaurant meals, although you'll sometimes find more traditional roasted or stewed dishes.

Sit-down meals are eaten in either a **restorant** (restaurant) or a **mehana** (taverna). There's little difference between the two, save for the fact that a *mehana* is likely to offer folksy decor and a wider range of traditional Bulgarian dishes. Wherever you go, you're unlikely to spend more than 15Lv for a main course, salad and drink. The most characteristic **traditional Bulgarian dishes** are those baked and served in earthenware pots. The best-known dish is *gyuvech* (which literally means "earthenware dish"), a

rich stew comprising peppers, aubergines and beans, to which is added either meat or meat stock. *Kavarma*, a spicy meat stew (either pork or chicken), is prepared in a similar fashion. Fish dishes (*riba*) are most common on the coast. **Vegetarian meals** (*yastia bez meso*) are hard to obtain, although *gyuveche* (a variety of *gyuvech* featuring baked vegetables) and *kachkaval pane* (cheese fried in breadcrumbs) are worth trying, as is *tarator*, a traditional cold summer soup, made with cucumber and yoghurt.

Foremost among **snacks** are *kebapcheta* (grilled sausages), or variations such as *shishche* (shish kebab) or *kiofteta* (meatballs). Another favourite is the *banitsa*, a flaky-pastry envelope with a filling – usually cheese; it's sold by street vendors in the morning and evening, to people going to and from work. Elsewhere, *sandvichi* (sandwiches) and *pitsi* (pizzas) dominate the fast-food repertoire. Pork (*svinsko*), veal (*teleshko*), chicken (*pile*) and offal, in various forms, all make a strong appearance on restaurant menus, usually accompanied by potatoes (*kartofi*) and a couple of vegetables, as well as bread. Bulgarians consider their **yoghurt** (*kiselo mlyako*) the world's finest, and hardly miss a day without consuming a glass.

Drink

The quality of Bulgarian **wines** is constantly improving, and the industry now exports worldwide. Among the best reds are the heavy, mellow Melnik, and rich, dark Mavrud. Dimyat is a good, dry white wine. If you prefer the sweeter variety, try Karlovski Misket (Muscatel) or Tramminer. Cheap native **spirits** are highly potent, and should be drunk diluted with water in the case of *mastika* (like ouzo in Greece) or downed in one, Balkan-style, in the case of *rakiya* – brandy made from either plums (*slivova*) or grapes (*grozdova*). Bulgarian **beer** is as good as any, and brands such as Kamenitza and Zagorka are much preferable to pricey imported alternatives.

Coffee (*kafe*) usually comes *espresso* style, though you will also encounter forms of *kapuchino*. Tea (*chai*) is nearly always herbal – ask for *cheren chai* (literally "black tea") if you want the real stuff, normally served with lemon.

Opening hours and holidays

Big-city **shops and supermarkets** are generally open Mon–Fri 8.30am–6pm or later; on Sat they close at 2pm. In rural areas and small towns, an unofficial siesta may prevail between noon and 3pm. Many shops, offices, banks and museums are closed on the following **public holidays**: Jan 1; March 3; Easter Sun; Easter Mon; May 1; May 24; Sept 6; Sept 22; Dec 25 & Dec 31. Additional public holidays may occasionally be called by the government.

Emergencies

Petty theft is a danger on the coast, and the Bulgarian **police** can be slow in filling out insurance reports unless you're insistent. **Consulates** may be helpful in some respects, but they never lend cash to nationals who've run out or been robbed. Foreign tourists are no longer a novelty in much of the country, but **women** travelling alone can expect to encounter stares, comments and sometimes worse from macho types, and discos on the coast are pretty much seen as cattle-markets. A firm rebuff should be enough to cope with most situations. Note that everyone is required to carry some form of **ID** at all times.

If you need a **doctor** (*lekar*) or dentist (*zâbolekar*), go to the nearest *poliklinika* (health centre), whose staff might well speak English or German. Emergency treatment is free of charge although you must pay for **medicines** – larger towns will have at least one 24-hour pharmacy.

Emergency numbers

Police ☎166; Ambulance ☎150; Fire ☎160.

Sofia

One of Europe's least known and least glamorous capital cities, **SOFIA** can appear an uninspiring place to first-time visitors, with its drab suburbs and crumbling old buildings. However, much has been done in recent years to revitalize the heart of the city, and once you've settled in and begun to explore, you'll find it a surprisingly laid-back place, especially on fine spring days, when its lush public gardens and pavement cafés buzz with life. Urban pursuits can be combined with the outdoor possibilities offered by verdant **Mount Vitosha**, just 12km to the south.

Sofia was founded by a Thracian tribe some 3000 years ago, and various **Roman ruins** attest to its zenith as the regional imperial capital of Serdica in the fourth century. The Bulgars didn't arrive on the scene until the ninth century, and with the notable exception of the thirteenth-century Boyana Church, their cultural monuments largely disappeared during the Turkish occupation (1381–1878), of which the sole visible legacy is a couple of stately **mosques**. The finest architecture postdates Bulgaria's liberation from the Turks: handsome public buildings and parks, and the magnificent **Aleksandâr Nevski Cathedral**.

Arrival, information and city transport

Trains arrive at **Central Station** (*Tsentralna Gara*), a dingy concrete hangar harbouring a couple of exchange bureaux and snack bars, but little else to welcome the visitor. Five minutes' ride along bul Knyaginya Mariya Luiza (tram #1 or #7) is pl Sveta Nedelya, within walking distance of several hotels and the main accommodation bureaux (see below). Most national **buses** arrive in the various bus parks situated around the *Hotel Princess*, just opposite the train station, although some Bansko services and Blagoevgrad buses (for connections to Rila monastery) use the Ovcha Kupel terminal, 5km southwest of the centre along bul Tsar Boris III (tram #5 from behind the Law Courts). International buses (daily connections with Istanbul, Thessaloniki, Athens and Skopje) also arrive near the *Hotel Princess*. The

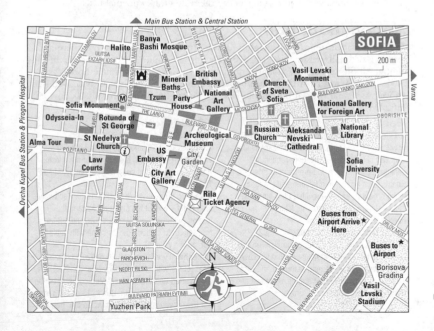

best way to get into town from **Sofia airport** is to catch minibus #30, which runs until around 10pm (every 15–30min), and operates like a shared taxi; it will take you to the city centre for 1Lv. Bus #84 (every 10–20min, until around 11.30pm), takes a more tortuous route and drops you, rather inconveniently, outside Borisova Gradina, at the eastern edge of the city centre. Taxis might well try to charge you an exorbitant $20 or more, so be sure to negotiate a reasonable price first ($10).

Sofia does have an official **tourist office**, the National Information and Advertising Centre on Sveta Nedelya (Mon–Fri 9am–5pm; ☎02/987-9778, ⓦwww.bulgariatravel.org), but a better bet is the friendly travel agent Odysseia-In, at bul Stamboliiski 20 (entrance on ul Lavele; Mon–Fri 9am–6.30pm; ☎02/989-0538, ⓦwww.newtravel.com), which charges a 5Lv consultancy fee, deductible from any accommodation you book through them. The free quarterly *Sofia Inside & Out* and the monthly *Sofia City Guide*, available from some hotel reception desks, contain general information and **listings**, while the English-language weekly *Sofia Echo*, sold at newsstands around Tzum, is a good source for local news and events.

City transport

The **public transport** network – consisting of buses (*avtobus*), trolleybuses (*troleibus*), a one-line metro system, and trams (*tramvai*) – runs between 5am and midnight and is cheap and efficient. There's a **flat fare** of 50st on all urban routes; tickets (*bileti*) are sold from street kiosks, and, occasionally, on board, and must be punched as you enter the vehicle (inspections are frequent and there are spot fines of 4Lv for fare-dodgers). Kiosks at the main tram stops sell one-day tickets (*karta za edin den*; 2Lv) and five-day tickets (*karta za pet dena*; 9Lv). Metro tickets must be bought from the station; a "combination ticket" (*kombiniran bilet*) costs 80st and is valid for one metro and one bus or tram journey. **Taxis** should charge about 40st per kilometre until nightfall, after which rates double; make sure the driver has his meter running. Additionally, there's a fleet of private **minibuses** (*marshrutka*), acting like shared taxis and covering around forty different routes across the city for a flat fare of 1Lv. Destinations and routes are displayed on the front of the vehicles – in the Cyrillic alphabet – and passengers flag them down like normal taxis.

Accommodation

Accommodation tends to be slightly dearer than in other towns, but there are a number of small, reasonably priced **hotels** and a couple of good **hostels** in the centre. All fill up quickly, though, especially in summer, and advance bookings are advisable. **Private rooms** (❷) can be booked by agencies such as Odysseia-In (see above) and Alma Tour, at bul Stamboliiski 27 (Mon–Fri 9am–6pm, Sat 10am–4pm; ☎02/987-7233, ⓦwww.almatour.net).

Hostels

Art Hostel Angel Kânchev 21a ☎02/987-0545, ⓦwww.art-hostel.com. Sofia's trendiest hostel, with two six-bed dorms, hosting frequent art exhibitions, live music and drama performances. Guests have access to a kitchen and tea room, while breakfast can be provided for a small extra charge. Internet and laundry facilities are also on hand. $10 per person.

Hostel Sofia Pozitano 16 ☎02/989-8582, ⓦwww.hostelsofia.com. Clean and well-run two-dorm, fourteen-bed hostel, just behind the Law Courts, with shared kitchen, bathroom and cable TV. Discounts available for groups. Breakfast and drinks included. $10 per person.

Hotels

Baldzhieva Tsar Asen 23 ☎02/981-1257, ⓔbaldjievahotel@yahoo.com. Small hotel in a smart town house one block west of bul Vitosha. Rooms are clean and cosy, all with phone, fridge, TV and WC. ❹

Enny Pop Bogomil 46 ☎02/983-1649. Good-value little hotel – one of the cheapest in central Sofia – just off bul Knyaginya Mariya Luiza, and not far from the train station. Rooms come with cable TV but shared WCs. ❷

Ganesha Al von Humboldt 26 ☎02/971-9228. Neat rooms with en-suite shower and cable TV, in a converted apartment block. Midway between the city centre and the airport. Bus #213 or #313 from the train station, bus #84 or minibus #30 from the

airport to the *Hotel Pliska* stop. ❸
Lyulin Serdika 8 ☎02/940-2147. Well-located, if
somewhat characterless hotel, offering small en-
suite rooms in an anonymous apartment block
right behind Tzum. ❹
Maya Trapezitsa 4 ☎02/980-2796. Large, homely

rooms, some with great views over Sveta Nedelya
Square, in an apartment block just off the Largo.
Shared bathrooms. ❷
Tsar Asen Tsar Asen 68 ☎02/547-801. Basic
family-run pension, offering small en-suite rooms
with cable TV. ❸

The City

At the heart of Sofia is **Ploshtad Sveta Nedelya**, a pedestrianized square dominated by the Sveta Nedelya church, built after the liberation as the successor to a number of churches that have stood here since medieval times. Running south of the
square is **Bulevard Vitosha**, Sofia's main shopping street, which leads to **Yuzhen
Park**. Heading north from pl Sveta Nedelya, you'll come to the **Largo**, an elongated plaza flanked on three sides by severe monumental buildings, the most arresting
of which is the towering monolith of the former **Party House**, originally the
home of the Communist hierarchy, and now serving as government offices.

An underpass gives access from pl Sveta Nedelya to a sunken shop-lined plaza,
with the tiny **Church of Sveta Petka Samardzhiiska** (Mon–Sat 9am–7pm, Sun
9am–2pm; 5Lv) at its centre. Dating back to the fourteenth century, the church
contains fragmentary and much-restored frescoes. The plaza extends westwards to
the Serdika metro station, watched over by the **Sofia Monument**, representing the
eponymous Goddess of Wisdom – the city's new symbol. On the northern side of
the Largo is the Council of Ministers (Bulgaria's cabinet) and Sofia's upmarket
shopping mall, **Tzum**.

Just beyond, on Bulevard Knyaginya Mariya Luiza, you'll find the **Banya Bashi
Mosque**, built in 1576 by Hadzhi Mimar Sonah, who also designed the great
mosque at Edirne in Turkey. Behind stand Sofia's **mineral baths**, housed in a yellow and red-striped *fin-de-siècle* building, which is largely derelict and currently
being restored. Locals gather daily to bottle the hot, sulphurous water, which gushes
into long stone troughs outside. Opposite the mosque is the **Halite**, an elegant
building dating from the early 1900s, housing the city's central food hall, with three
floors of shops and restaurants.

On the southern flank of the Largo, the *Sheraton Hotel*'s sombre wings run round a
courtyard containing Sofia's oldest church, the fourth-century **Rotunda of St
George**. It houses frescoes from the eighth century onwards, although most eyes are
drawn to the fourteenth-century Christ Pantokrator, surrounded by a frieze of 22
prophets, in the dome. Alongside is the **Presidency**, guarded by soldiers in colourful
nineteenth-century garb (Changing of the Guard hourly). Immediately to the east, a
fifteenth-century mosque now holds the **Archeological Museum** (Tues–Sun
10.30am–4.30pm; 3Lv), whose prize exhibit is a magnificent gold cauldron and cups
of the Thracian Vâlchitrân treasure. Also on show is a collection of Thracian armour,
medieval church wall paintings and numerous Roman tombstones.

A little further along is **Ploshtad Aleksandâr Battenberg**, named after the
German aristocrat chosen to be the newly independent country's first monarch in
1878. The square, surfaced with attractive yellow bricks, was once the scene of
Communist rallies and, until its demolition in 1999, was dominated by the mausoleum of Georgi Dimitrov, first leader of the People's Republic of Bulgaria. On
the northern side of the square is the dilapidated former **Royal Palace**, today
home to the National Art Gallery and Ethnographic Museum, though these are of
little note; instead, try the **City Art Gallery** (Tues–Sat 11am–7pm, Sun
11am–5pm; free) in the City Garden, immediately to the south, which stages
monthly exhibitions of contemporary Bulgarian art.

Follow the yellowbrick Bulevard Tsar Osvoboditel east, and you'll see the
Russian Church, a stunning golden-domed confection, with an emerald spire and
an exuberant mosaic-tiled exterior, concealing a dark, candle-scented interior. Just

beyond is a particularly busy road junction; turn left, up ul Rakovski, where a glint of gold betrays the proximity of the **Aleksandâr Nevski Cathedral**, one of the finest pieces of architecture in the Balkans. Financed by public subscription and built between 1882 and 1924 to honour the 200,000 Russian casualties of the 1877–78 War of Liberation, it's a magnificent structure, bulging with domes and semi-domes and glittering with gold leaf. Within the gloomy interior, a beardless Christ sits enthroned above the altar, and numerous scenes from his life, painted in a humanistic style, adorn the walls. Many other frescoes have peeled and darkened considerably over the years, and the whole building is currently undergoing major restoration. The crypt, entered from outside (Mon & Wed–Sun 10.30am–6pm; 3Lv), contains a superb collection of icons from all over the country. Pride of place goes to a fifteenth-century double-sided icon from Sozopol, carrying an image of the Virgin and Child on one side and the Crucifixion on the other.

On the northeastern edge of the cathedral square, an imposing white building houses the **National Gallery for Foreign Art** (Mon & Wed–Sun 11am–6.30pm; 1.50Lv), which devotes a lot of space to Indian wood-carvings and second-division French and Russian artists, though there are a few minor works by the likes of Rodin, Chagall and Kandinsky. Heading west across the square, you'll pass two recumbent lions flanking the Tomb of the Unknown Soldier, set beside the wall of the plain, brown-brick **Church of Sveta Sofia**. Originally raised during the sixth century, it has been much restored since. The best route from here is to cut down past the **Parliament** building onto pl Narodno Sâbranie, watched over by an equestrian statue of the Russian Tsar Alexander II, known as the "Liberator" (*Osvoboditel*). From here, it's a brief stroll along bul Tsar Osvoboditel, past Sofia University, to **Borisova Gradina**, named after Bulgaria's interwar monarch, Boris III. The park – the largest in Sofia – has a rich variety of flowers and trees, outdoor bars, two football stadiums and two huge Communist monuments, still impressive despite the graffiti and rubbish scattered around them.

Mount Vitosha

A wooded granite mass 20km long and 16km wide, **Mount Vitosha** is where Sofians come for picnics and skiing – and the ascent of its highest peak, the 2290m **Cherni Vrâh**, has become a traditional test of stamina. Getting here on public transport is straightforward, although there are fewer buses on weekdays than at weekends. One approach is to take tram #5 from behind the Law Courts to Ovcha Kupel bus station, then change to bus #61, which climbs through the forests towards **ZLATNI MOSTOVE**, a beauty spot on the western shoulder of Mount Vitosha beside the so-called **Stone River**. Beneath the large boulders running down the mountainside is a rivulet, which once attracted gold-panners. Trails lead up beside the rivulet towards the mountain's upper reaches: Cherni Vrâh is about two to three hours' walk from here.

Another route is on tram #9 from the train station or #14 from Graf Ignatiev to the Hladilnika terminus on bul Cherni Vrâh, and then bus #66 to the resort centre of **ALEKO**. Aleko can also be reached by taking bus #64 or #93 from Hladilnika to the suburb of **Dragalevtsi**, where there's a chairlift (*lifta*; daily in winter; rest of year weekends only); or taking bus #122 from Hladilnika to **Simeonovo**, starting point for the Aleko-bound gondola (daily). Aleko is a thriving winter sports centre, with pistes to suit all and a couple of ski schools that also rent out gear; outside the ski season, there are plenty of walking trails to explore (Cherni Vrâh is an easy forty-minute walk from here). The resort is well-served with snack bars and restaurants throughout the year.

Eating, drinking and nightlife

Eating and drinking in Sofia can be remarkably cheap and quite varied, with new **restaurants** and **bars** opening all the time. Numerous fast-food outlets serve up the usual range of burgers, sandwiches and kebabs, while pizza parlours and restaurants offering grilled meats, salads and chips are also common. In addition, there are plenty of pricier restaurants offering a range of international cuisine, but don't expect total authenticity. The cheapest places to grab a beer or a coffee are the many cafés and kiosks around bul Vitosha or in the city's public gardens, while for night-time entertainment, there's an ever-growing number of **clubs**, most playing a mix of pop and the ubiquitous local "folk pop" (*chalga*). Jazz and Latino music are also popular.

Restaurants

Baalbek Dyakon Ignati 4. Highly regarded Lebanese establishment, with sit-down restaurant upstairs and fast-food counter offering kebabs, shawarma and falafel on the ground floor.

Chen Rakovski 86. Popular Chinese with authentic food, opposite the opera house.

Divaka Gladston 54. Bright and busy restaurant, just west of Graf Ignatiev, serving excellent, meat-heavy Bulgarian dishes.

Friends Corner of Graf Ignatiev & Rakovski. Large self-service restaurant offering a range of Bulgarian specialities. Also has a bar and takeout kebab counter.

Happy Bar and Grill Sveta Nedelya 4. Popular home-grown diner chain, with a fair range of dishes, mostly of the salad, grilled meat and chips variety.

Perfect In the sunken plaza beneath Tzum. Spacious, modern place, offering reasonably priced Bulgarian and international dishes, including grills, salads and pizzas.

Pizza Troll Vitosha 27. One of the better pizza and pasta restaurants in the centre, with vaguely Art Nouveau decor. There's another branch on Graf Ignatiev.

Ramayana Hristo Botev 17. Recently relocated but long-running Indian restaurant, with a range of vegetarian options.

Trops-kâshta Graf Ignatiev 12. Good-value buffet-style chain restaurant, with several branches around town, offering tasty – if invariably luke-warm – Bulgarian standards.

Cafés, bars and clubs

Art Club Museum Café Cnr of Sâborna & Lege. Chic café with a pleasant patio set amid Thracian tombstones next to the Archeological Museum. Serves a variety of drinks, light meals and desserts.

Bibliotekata Vasil Levski 88. Glitzy, recently renovated nightclub beneath the National Library building, drawing in a moneyed young crowd.

Blaze Slavyanska 36. Lively bar and club near the University, with a good sound system and trendy clientele.

Caramba Tsar Osvoboditel 4. Sofia's premier Latino club, featuring different Latin rhythms nightly.

Chervilo Tsar Osvoboditel 8. Bar and disco with a different style of music every night, and a resident DJ.

Club Lavazza Vitosha 13. Smart place for coffee and cakes, which also offers light meals and an excellent-value English breakfast.

J.J. Murphy's Kârnigradska 6. Sofia's top Irish bar, offering filling pub grub, big-screen sports and live music at the weekends.

Pri Kmeta Parizhka 3. Roomy basement beer hall, serving good food, and with a nightly disco or live music.

Schveik Vitosha 1A. Basement beer hall just off Vitosha, serving up meaty snacks and frequent live music.

Swingin' Hall Dragan Tsankov 8. Cheap, cheerful and crowded bar, with live music (usually pop/rock or jazz) on two stages.

Listings

Embassies & consulates Australia, Trakia 37 ☏02/946-1334; Canada, Asen Zlatarov 11 ☏02/943-3704; UK, Moskovska 9 ☏02/933-9222; US, Sâborna 1 ☏02/937-5100.

Gay Sofia Bulgarian Gay Organization, bul Vasil Levski 3 (☏02/987-6872, ⊛www.bgogemini.org); *Spartacus*, a gay club, can be found in the underpass below the university.

Internet access Infocafe, Graf Ignatiev 32 (daily 9am–10pm); Ultima Internet Centre, Lavele 16 (daily 9am–11pm).

Hospital Pirogov hospital, bul General Totleben 21 ☏02/51531.

Pharmacy No. 7, pl Sveta Nedelya 5.

Post office Ul General Gurko 6 (daily 7am–8.30pm).

Southern Bulgaria

Trains heading from Bulgaria to Greece follow the Struma Valley south from Sofia, skirting some of the country's most grandiose mountains on the way. Formerly noted for their bandits and hermits, the Rila and Pirin Mountains contain Bulgaria's highest peaks, swathed in forests and dotted with alpine lakes. If time is short, the place to head for is the most revered of Bulgarian monasteries, **Rila**, lying some 30km east of the main southbound route. **Bansko**, on the eastern side of the Pirin range, is a small detour from the main north–south route, and boasts a wealth of traditional architecture, as well as being a burgeoning **ski** resort and a good base for **hiking**. Another much-travelled route heads southeast from Sofia towards Istanbul, through the Plain of Thrace, a fertile region that was the heartland of the ancient Thracians, whose origins date back to the third millennium BC. The main road and rail lines now linking Istanbul and Sofia essentially follow the course of the Roman Serdica–Constantinople road, past towns ruled by the Ottomans for so long that foreigners used to call this "European Turkey". Of these, the most important is **Plovdiv**, Bulgaria's second city, whose old quarter is a wonderful mixture of National Revival mansions and classical remains. Some 30km south of Plovdiv is **Bachkovo Monastery**, containing Bulgaria's most vivid frescoes.

Rila monastery

As the most celebrated of Bulgaria's religious sites, famed for its fine architecture and mountainous setting – and declared a world heritage monument by UNESCO – the **RILA MONASTERY** receives a steady stream of visitors, many of them day-trippers from Sofia. Joining one of these one-day tours from the capital is the simplest way of getting there, but can work out expensive (most tours cost around $60). Far cheaper is to travel by public transport, though realistically you'll have to stay the night. There is a twice-daily bus service from Sofia's Ovcha Kupel terminal to **Rila village**, from where four buses a day make the 27km run up to the monastery. Otherwise, you'll need to catch a bus or train to Dupnitsa or Blagoevgrad in the Struma Valley, and then change to a local bus for Rila village.

The road from Rila village to the monastery runs above the foaming River Rilska, fed by springs from the surrounding pine-clad mountains. Even today there's a palpable sense of isolation, and it's easy to see why **Ivan Rilski** chose this valley to escape the savagery of feudal life and the laxity of the established monasteries at the end of the ninth century. The current foundation, 4km from Ivan's original hermitage, was plundered during the eighteenth century and repairs had hardly begun when the whole structure burned down in 1833. Its resurrection was presented as a religious and patriotic duty: public donations poured in throughout the nineteenth century, and the east wing was built as recently as 1961 to display the treasury.

Ringed by mighty walls, the monastery has the outward appearance of a fortress, but this impression is negated by the beauty of the interior, which even the crowds can't mar. Graceful arches above the flagstoned courtyard support tiers of monastic cells, and stairways ascend to wooden balconies. Bold red stripes and black-and-white check patterns enliven the facade, contrasting with the sombre mountains behind and creating a harmony between the cloisters and the **church**. Richly coloured frescoes shelter beneath the church porch and cover much of its interior. The iconostasis is particularly splendid, almost 10m wide and covered by a mass of intricate carvings and gold leaf. Beside the church is **Hrelyo's Tower**, the sole remaining building from the fourteenth century. Cauldrons, which were once used to prepare food for pilgrims, occupy the soot-encrusted kitchen on the ground floor of the north wing, while on the floors above you can inspect the spartan refectory and panelled guest rooms. Beneath the east wing is the **treasury** (daily 8.30am–4.30pm; 5Lv), where, amongst other things, you can view a wooden cross carved with more than 1500 miniature human figures by the monk Raphael during the 1790s.

It's possible to **stay** in the monastery cells, if you don't mind the lack of hot water and the curfew (summer 8pm; winter 5pm; $10 per person). Otherwise, try the cheaper *Turisticheska spalnya* ($5 per person), just outside the monastery's eastern gate, the comfortable *Hotel Tsarev Vrah* nearby (☎07054/2280; ❸), or the older

Hotel Rilets (☏07054/2106; ❷), a few hundred metres up the valley. Near the *Rilets*, the primitive *Bor* **campsite** occupies an attractive riverside spot. For **snacks**, delicious bread can be obtained at a bakery run by monks outside the monastery's east gate. The **restaurants** at the hotels *Tsarev Vrah* and *Rilets* are preferable to the outlets near the monastery gates, which sometimes overcharge stray foreigners.

Bansko

Lying some 40km east of the main Struma Valley route, **BANSKO** is the main centre for walking and skiing on the eastern slopes of the Pirin mountains. It's a traditional agricultural centre and a rapidly growing tourist resort, boasting a wealth of stone-built nineteenth-century farmhouses and numerous small hotels. Though connected to Sofia and other towns by bus, Bansko can also be reached by a **narrow-gauge railway**, which leaves the main Sofia–Plovdiv line at **Septemvri** and forges its way across the highlands. It's one of the most scenic trips in the Balkans, but also one of the slowest, taking five hours to cover just over 100km.

Bansko centres on the modern pedestrianized pl Nikola Vaptsarov, where the **Nikola Vaptsarov Museum** (Mon–Fri 8am–6pm, Sat & Sun 8am–noon & 2–6pm; 2Lv) contains a display relating to the local-born poet and socialist martyr, as well as housing a crafts exhibition where you can purchase distinctive local rugs. Immediately north of here, pl Vâzrazhdane is watched over by the solid stone tower of the **Church of Sveta Troitsa**, whose interior contains exquisite nineteenth-century frescoes and icons. On the opposite side of the square, the **Rilski Convent** contains an icon museum (Mon–Fri 9am–noon & 2–5pm; 2Lv) devoted to the achievements of Bansko's nineteenth-century icon painters. The easiest way of getting into the **Pirin mountains** from Bansko is to head west – on foot or by taxi – via a steep fourteen-kilometre uphill climb to the Vihren hut, where cheap dorm accommodation is available. This is the main trail-head for hikes towards the 2914m summit of **Mt Vihren** (Bulgaria's second-highest peak), or gentler rambles around the meadows and lakes nearby.

There are ten buses a day to Bansko from Sofia, although if you're approaching the area from Rila, it's far easier to head for **Blagoevgrad** and change buses there. In Blagoevgrad is the **Pirin Tourist Forum**, Stefan Milenkov 3 (Mon–Fri 8.30am–6.30pm; ☏073/81458, ⊛www.pirin-tourism.bg), which is the best source of information on hiking and accommodation in the region.

At Bansko, the **bus and train stations** are on the northern fringes of town, ten minutes' walk from pl Vaptsarov, where you'll find the main **tourist office** (irregular hours; ☏07443/5048). Best of the family-run **hotels** are the friendly and cosy *Yatse*, in a quiet area five minutes' walk from the centre at Gotse Delchev 21 (☏07443/3538; ❷), and *Dzhangal*, close by at Gotse Delchev 24 (☏07443/2661; ❷), which features a sauna. *Georgi's*, a little further up the hill at Pirin 69 (☏07443/3162; ❷), is a good fall-back option. For **eating** and entertainment, there are over forty *mehanas* offering traditional specialities and folk music at weekends: *Sirleshtova Kâshta*, *Momini Dvori* and *Dyado Pene*, all around the main two squares, are among the most atmospheric.

Plovdiv and around

Bulgaria's second largest city, **PLOVDIV**, has more obvious charms than Sofia, which locals tend to look down on. The old town embodies Plovdiv's long history – Thracian fortifications subsumed by Macedonian masonry, overlaid with Roman and Byzantine walls, and by great timber-framed mansions erected during the Bulgarian renaissance, symbolically looking down upon the derelict Ottoman mosques and artisans' dwellings of the lower town. But Plovdiv isn't just another museum town: the city's arts festivals and trade fairs are the biggest in the country, and its restaurants and bars are equal to those of the capital.

There's a nightly **train** to Istanbul, which leaves Plovdiv at 9pm; Turkish visas can be bought at the Kapikule frontier (UK citizens £10; US citizens US$100; Canadian citizens US$45; Australian and New Zealand citizens US$20) – have the exact sum ready in cash, as they don't always have change and won't let you in without the visa. Other nationals should contact the Turkish consulate at ul Filip Makedonski 10 in Plovdiv (☎032/632309) for current visa prices. Several agencies at the Yug bus station sell tickets for **international buses**; Hebros Bus (daily 7.30am-7pm; ☎032/626916), a Eurolines agent, can book seats on buses to Greece, Turkey and Western Europe.

The City

Plovdiv centres on the large **Ploshtad Tsentralen**, dominated by the monolithic *Hotel Trimontium Princess*. Heading north from here, the pedestrianized ul Knyaz Aleksandâr I Battenberg, lined with shops, cafés and bars, leads onto the attractive **Ploshtad Dzhumaya**, where stallholders gather to sell a range of touristy knick-knacks, including paintings, jewellery and icons. The ruins of a **Roman Stadium**, visible in a pit beneath the square, are just a fragment of the arena where up to 30,000 spectators watched gladiatorial spectacles. Among the variously styled buildings here, the **Dzhumaya Mosque**, with its diamond-patterned minaret and lead-sheathed domes, steals the show; it's believed that the mosque, sadly now looking a little dilapidated, dates back to the reign of Sultan Murad II (1359–85). From the square, ul Raiko Daskalov continues north to meet bul 6 Septemvri; turning westwards you'll find ploshtad Sâedinenie and two small museums. The **Historical Museum** (Mon–Fri 9am–noon & 1–5pm; 2Lv) holds the usual patriotic exhibitions, while next door, the **Archeological Museum** (Mon–Fri 9am–12.30pm & 1–5.30pm; 2Lv) has a rather more interesting display of Thracian and Roman artefacts, including a curious plaque depicting a three-headed Thracian Rider.

With its cobbled streets and colourful mansions covering one of Plovdiv's three hills, the **Old Quarter** is a painter's dream and a cartographer's nightmare. As good a route as any is to start from pl Dzhumaya and head east up ul Sâborna. Blackened fortress walls dating from Byzantine times can be seen around Sâborna and other streets, sometimes incorporated into the dozens of timber-framed National Revival houses that are Plovdiv's speciality. Outside and within, the walls are frequently decorated with niches, floral motifs or false columns, painted in the style known as *alafranga*. Turn right, up steps beside the Church of Sveta Bogoroditsa, and continue, along twisting cobbled lanes, to the **Roman Theatre** (daily 9am–5pm; 3Lv), the best preserved in the country, and still an impressive venue for regular concerts and plays. Back on Sâborna, the **State Gallery of Fine Arts** (Mon–Fri 9am–12.30pm & 1–5.30pm, Sat 10am–5.30pm; 2Lv) holds an extensive collection of nineteenth- and twentieth-century Bulgarian paintings, including some fine portraits by Stanislav Dospevski. Further along, the **Church of SS Constantine and Elena** contains a fine gilt iconostasis, partly decorated by the prolific nineteenth-century artist Zahari Zograf, whose work also appears in the adjacent **Museum of Icons** (Mon–Fri 9am–12.30pm & 1–5.30pm, Sat 10am–5.30pm; 2Lv). A little further uphill is the richly decorated **Kuyumdzhioglu House**, now home to the **Ethnographic Museum** (Tues–Thurs, Sat & Sun 9am–noon & 2–5pm, Fri 2–5pm; 3Lv). Folk costumes and crafts are on display on the ground floor, while upstairs, the elegantly furnished rooms reflect the former owner's taste for Viennese and French Baroque. Heading west from the Hisar Gate, a road leads downhill to ul Artin Gidikov, where, at no. 4, the **Hindlian House** (daily 9.30am–5pm; 3Lv), former home of an Armenian merchant, harbours some of Plovdiv's most evocative nineteenth-century interiors.

Practicalities

Plovdiv's **train station** is on the southern fringe of the centre, on bul Hristo Botev, and the two **bus stations** are nearby: Rodopi, serving the mountain resorts to the south, is just on the other side of the tracks; while Yug, serving Sofia and the rest of the country, is one block east. Private **rooms** (❷) can be booked through Esperansa, Ivan Vazov 14 (☎032/260653 or 265127). Basic **hostel** accommodation and twin rooms are available in the atmospheric *Turisticheski Dom* (☎032/633211; $11 per person) in the old town at ul Slaveikov 5. **Hotel** prices are relatively high, but you can get decent-value rooms at the ageing, high-rise *Leipzig*, bul Ruski 70 (☎032/632250, ✆www.leipzig-bg.com; ❷), and the smaller *Trakia*, near the train station at ul Ivan Vazov 84 (☎032/624101; ❸), both of which have their own restaurants. Closer to the old town, try the pleasant *Elit* at ul Daskalov 53 (☎032/624537; ❸). The *Gorski Kat* **campsite** (☎032/551360) is located some 4km west, reached by bus #222 from outside the train station.

The best **restaurants** are in the old town, many occupying elegant old houses and serving good, traditional Bulgarian food; try *Apoloniya*, ul Vasil Kânchev 1, *Ulpia*, ul 4 Yanuari 17, or the excellent *Philipopol*, ul Konstantin Stoilov 56B. In the new town, ul Knyaz Aleksandâr I is awash with cheaper fast-food outlets, though better quality can be found away from the main drag; the *Red Dragon*, on the corner of bul Ruski and ul Filip Makedonski, is a good Chinese restaurant, serving generous portions, while *Malâk Bunardzhik*, ul Volga 1, at the foot of the Hill of the Liberators, is a smart but surprisingly cheap restaurant serving excellent Bulgarian cuisine. **Drinking** takes place in the pavement cafés of ul Knyaz Aleksandâr I. *Dreams*, at Knyaz Aleksandâr I 42, is a popular spot for coffee, cocktails and cakes, while *Dzhumayata*, built into the side of the Dzhumaya mosque, serves authentic Turkish coffee and sweets, such as baklava. The *Caligula Club*, Knyaz Aleksandâr I 30, is a good central spot for an alfresco beer, and has a late night disco. *Morris*, north of the river at bul Maritsa 122, is a trendy nightclub with regular live music. For **Internet** access, try Royal, ul Naiden Gerov 6 (just off ul Knyaz Aleksandâr I), or Fantasy, ul Knyaz Aleksandâr I 31.

Bachkovo Monastery

The most attractive destination south of Plovdiv is **BACHKOVO MONASTERY**, around 30km away and an easy day-trip from the city (hourly buses from Rodopi station to Smolyan). Founded in 1038 by two Georgians in the service of the Byzantine Empire, this is Bulgaria's second-largest monastery and, like Rila, has been declared a UNESCO World Heritage Site.

A great iron-studded door admits visitors to the cobbled courtyard, surrounded by wooden galleries and adorned with colourful frescoes. Along one wall is a pictorial narrative of the monastery's history, showing Bachkovo roughly as it appears today, and watched over by the Madonna and Child. Beneath the vaulted porch of Bachkovo's principal church, **Sveta Bogoroditsa**, are frescoes depicting the horrors in store for sinners; the entrance itself is more optimistic, overseen as it is by the Holy Trinity. Floral motifs in a naive style decorate the beams of the interior, where you can view a fourteenth-century Georgian icon of the Virgin, though legend claims it to be the original handiwork of St Luke. The church of **St Nicholas**, originally founded during the nineteenth century, features a fine *Last Judgement* covering the porch exterior, which includes a portrait of the artist, Zahari Zograf. Finally, not far from the main gate is the recently restored **Ossuary**, which dates from the eleventh century and contains a number of early medieval frescoes, but sadly, it's rarely open to visitors. It's possible to **stay** in recently refurbished rooms in the monastery (☎03327/277; $5 per person), and you can eat at three **restaurants** just outside; *Vodopada*, with its mini-waterfall, is the best.

Northern Bulgaria

Routes from Sofia to the Black Sea coast take you through the mountainous terrain of central and northern Bulgaria – a gruelling eight- or nine-hour ride that's worth interrupting to savour something of the country's heartland. For over a thousand years, Stara Planina – known to foreigners as the **Balkan range** – has been the cradle of the Bulgarian nation. It was here that the Khans established the First Kingdom, and here, too, after a period of Byzantine control, that the Boyars proclaimed the Second Kingdom and created a magnificent capital at **Veliko Târnovo**. Closer by, the **Sredna Gora** (Central Range) was inhabited as early as the fifth millennium BC, but for Bulgarians this forested region is best known as the Land of the April Rising, the nineteenth-century rebellion for which the picturesque town of **Koprivshtitsa** will always be remembered.

Although they lie a little way off the main rail lines from Sofia, neither Veliko Târnovo nor Koprivshtitsa is difficult to reach. The former lies just south of Gorna Oryahovitsa, a major rail junction midway between Varna and Sofia, from where you can pick up a local train or bus; the latter is served by a stop on the Sofia–Burgas line, whose four daily trains in each direction are met by local buses to ferry you the 12km to the village itself.

Koprivshtitsa

Seen from a distance, **KOPRIVSHTITSA** looks almost too lovely to be real, its half-timbered houses lying in a valley amid wooded hills. It would be an oasis of rural calm if not for the tourists drawn by the superb architecture and Bulgarians paying homage to a landmark in their nation's history. From the Bridge of the First Shot to the Place of the Scimitar Charge, there's hardly a part of Koprivshtitsa that isn't named for an episode or participant in the **April Rising of 1876**. As neighbouring towns were burned by the Bashibazouks – the irregular troops recruited by the Turks to put the rebels in their place – refugees flooded into Koprivshtitsa, spreading panic. The rebels eventually took to the hills while local traders bribed the Bashibazouks to spare the village – and so Koprivshtitsa survived unscathed, to be admired by subsequent generations as a symbol of heroism.

Buses arrive at a small station 200m south of the main square, where you'll find a **museum centre** (irregular hours; ☎07184/2191) selling tickets for Koprivshtitsa's six house museums. The entry fee for each museum is 3Lv, but you can buy a combined ticket covering entry to all six for 5Lv; if the centre is closed, you can buy the combined ticket at any of the museums, and it's also possible to hire an English-speaking guide for a two-hour tour (15Lv).

A street running off to the west of the main square leads to the **Oslekov House** (Tues–Sun 9.30am–5.30pm), where pillars of cedar wood support a facade decorated with scenes of Italian cities. Its Summer Guest Room is particularly impressive, with a vast wooden ceiling carved with geometric motifs. Further along, the street joins ul Debelyanov, which straddles a hill between two bridges and boasts some more lovely buildings. Near the Surlya Bridge is the birthplace of the poet **Dimcho Debelyanov** (Tues–Sun 9.30am–5.30pm), who is buried in the grounds of the hilltop **Church of the Holy Virgin**, just to the south. Built in 1817 and partly sunk into the ground to comply with Ottoman restrictions, the church contains icons by nineteenth-century artist Zahari Zograf. A gate at the rear of the churchyard leads to the birthplace of **Todor Kableshkov** (Tues–Sun 9.30am–5.30pm), leader of the local rebels. Kableshkov's house now displays weapons used in the Uprising and features a wonderful circular vestibule. Continuing south, cross the **Bridge of the First Shot**, which spans the Byala Reka stream, and head up ul Nikola Belodezhdov, and you'll come to the **Lyutov House** (Mon & Wed–Sun 9.30am–5.30pm), once home to a wealthy yoghurt merchant and today housing some of Koprivshtitsa's most sumptuous interiors. The house is especially notable for its colourful murals depicting palaces, temples and world cities. On the opposite side of the River Topolnitsa at the southern end of the village, steps lead up to the birthplace of another major figure in the uprising, **Georgi Benkovski** (Mon & Wed–Sun 9.30am–5.30pm). A tailor by profession, he made the insurgents' uniforms and famous silk banner embroidered with the Bulgarian Lion and "Liberty or Death!" as well as commanding a rebel band on Mount Eledzhik, which fought its way north until it was wiped out near Teteven. Returning towards the main square along the eastern bank of the river, you'll find the birthplace of **Lyuben Karavelov** (Mon & Wed–Sun 9.30am–5.30pm), who published émigré newspapers from exile in Bucharest, advocating armed struggle against the Ottomans. His printing press and other oddments are on display.

A **tourist office** (irregular hours; ☎07184/2191, ✆www.kopriv.com) on the main square books private **rooms** in charming village houses (❶). The nearby *Trayanova Kâshta* (☎07184/2250; ❷), just up the street from the Oslekov House, has delightful rooms in the National Revival style, while *Zdravets*, near the Lyutov House at ul Nikola Belovezhdov 3 (☎07184/2286; ❷), has neat modern rooms in an attractive wooden house with a large garden. For **eating and drinking**, the best places to sample traditional food are the *Dyado Liben Inn*, in a fine nineteenth-century mansion opposite the main square, and *Lomeva Kâshta*, a folk-style restaurant just north of the square.

Veliko Târnovo

With its dramatic medieval fortifications and huddles of antique houses teetering over the lovely River Yantra, **VELIKO TÂRNOVO** holds a uniquely important place in the minds of Bulgarians. When the National Assembly met here to draft Bulgaria's first constitution in 1879, it did so in the former capital of the Second Kingdom (1185–1396), whose civilization was snuffed out by the Turks. It was here, too, that the Communists chose to proclaim the People's Republic in 1944.

Modern Târnovo centres on **Ploshtad Mayka Bâlgariya**: from here bul Nezavisimost (which becomes ul Stefan Stambolov after a few hundred metres) heads northeast into a network of narrow streets, which curve above the River Yantra and mark out the old town, with its photogenic houses. Alleyways climb from Stefan Stambolov to the peaceful old **Varosh Quarter**, where you'll find a couple of nineteenth-century churches. Continuing along Stefan Stambolov, you'll notice steps leading downhill to ul General Gurko; don't miss the **Sarafina House** at no. 88 (Mon–Fri 9am–noon & 1–6pm; 4Lv), whose elegant restored interior is notable for its splendid octagonal vestibule and a panelled rosette ceiling. Rejoining Stefan Stambolov and continuing downhill, you'll find the blue-and-white building where the first Bulgarian parliament assembled in 1879. It's now home to the **Museum of the Bulgarian Renaissance and Constituent Assembly** (Mon & Wed–Sun 8am–noon & 1–6pm; 4Lv), where you can see a reconstruction of the original assembly hall, and a collection of icons. From here, Ivan Vazov leads directly to the medieval fortress, **Tsarevets** (daily 8am–7pm; 4Lv). The boyars Petâr and Asen led a successful rebellion against Byzantium from this citadel in 1185, and Tsarevets remained the centre of Bulgarian power until 1393, when, after a three-month siege, it fell to the Turks. The partially restored fortress is entered via the **Asenova Gate** halfway along the western ramparts. To the right, paths lead round to **Baldwin's Tower**, where Baldwin of Flanders, the so-called Latin Emperor of Byzantium, was incarcerated by Tsar Kaloyan. Above lie the ruins of the royal palace and a reconstruction of the thirteenth-century Church of the Blessed Saviour.

All **trains** between Sofia and Varna stop at Gorna Oryahovitsa, from where local trains and frequent buses cover the remaining 13km to Veliko Târnovo. From Târnovo train station, 2km south of the city centre, buses #4 and #13 run to pl Mayka Bâlgariya, where you'll find a **tourist office** (Mon–Fri 9am–6pm; ☎062/22148) and 24-hour **Internet** access nearby at Bezanata on ul Hadji Dimitar. The *Comfort* **hotel**, in the Varosh quarter at ul Paneyot Tipografov 5 (☏062/28728; ❷), is a basic, family-run place, with splendid views of the Tsarevets. Down near the Sarafina House, at ul Stefan Denchev 14, is the more eccentric *Rose* pension (❶), with two small rooms and a shared bathroom. The *Bolyarski Stan* **campsite** can be found on the western outskirts of the town, and is served by bus #110. The best **restaurants** are the traditional *mehanas* off Stefan Stambolov – try *Mecha Dupka*, which serves authentic Bulgarian fare in a cellar below ul Rakovski, often with music and dancing. A good cheap option – with a great view – is the *Rich* restaurant, down some steps off Stefan Stambolov at ul Yantra 1. For **drinking**, there are numerous cafés and bars around town; *Yasna*, on pl Slaveykov, is a good spot for coffee or cocktails.

The Black Sea coast

Bulgaria's **Black Sea** resorts have been popular holiday haunts for more than a century, though it wasn't until the 1960s that the coastline was developed for mass tourism, with Communist party officials from across the former Eastern Bloc descending on the beaches each year for a spot of socialist fun in the sun. Since then, the **resorts** have mushroomed, growing increasingly sophisticated as the prototype mega-complexes have been followed by holiday villages. With fine weather practically guaranteed, the selling of the coast has been a success in economic terms, but with the exception of ancient **Sozopol** and touristy **Nesebâr**, there's little to please the eye. Of the coast's two cities – **Varna** and Burgas – the former is by far preferable as a base for getting to the less-developed spots.

Varna

VARNA's origins date back almost five millennia, but it wasn't until seafaring Greeks founded a colony here in 585 BC that the town became a port. The modern city is a port both for commercial freighters and the navy, as well as being a popular tourist resort in its own right. It's a cosmopolitan place, and nice to stroll through: Baroque, nineteenth-century and contemporary architecture are pleasantly blended with shady promenades and a handsome seaside park.

Social life revolves around **Ploshtad Nezavisimost**, where the opera house and theatre provide a backdrop for restaurants and cafés. The square is the starting point of Varna's evening promenade, which flows eastward from here along bul Knyaz Boris I and towards bul Slivnitsa and the seaside gardens. Beyond the opera house, Varna's main lateral boulevard cuts through pl Mitropolit Simeon to the domed **Cathedral of the Assumption**. Constructed in 1886, it contains a splendid iconostasis and bishop's throne, with armrests carved in the form of magnificent winged panthers. The **Archeology Museum** on the corner of Mariya Luiza and Slivnitsa (Tues–Sun 10am–5pm; winter closed Sun; 4Lv) houses one of Bulgaria's finest collections of antiquities. Most impressive are the skeletons and gold jewellery, some dating back almost 6000 years, recovered from a Neolithic necropolis on the outskirts of town. There's also an array of Greek and Roman artefacts, including an extensive display of funerary sculpture, and a gallery of icons.

South of the centre, on ul Han Krum, are the extensive remains of the third-century **Roman baths** (Mon–Sat 10am–5pm; winter closed Mon; 3Lv), which played a central role in the social life of the city. It's still possible to discern the various bathing areas and the once huge exercise hall. Ten minutes west of here on ul Panagyurishte is the **Ethnographic Museum** (Tues–Sun 10am–5pm; 2Lv), where you can see displays illustrating traditional local crafts, folk costumes and reconstructions of nineteenth-century interiors. At the southern edge of the Sea Gardens, the **Navy Museum** (Mon–Fri 10am–5.30pm; 2Lv) houses a musty collection of naval relics, with some rusting armaments, including a couple of helicopters, in the gardens. Meanwhile, the boat responsible for the Bulgarian Navy's only victory – the *Drazki* – is embedded on the waterfront outside; it sank the Turkish cruiser *Hamidie* off Cape Kaliakra in 1912.

Practicalities

Each of the main points of arrival has good bus connections with the centre. The **bus terminal** (bus #1, #22 or #41) is a ten-minute journey northwest of the centre on bul Vladislav Varnenchik; Varna **airport** is about a 50-minute ride (#409) in the same direction; and the **train station** is ten minutes' walk south of the centre along ul Tsar Simeon.

  Private rooms in central Varna (●) can be obtained from the Isak accommodation bureau, inside the train station (summer daily 5.30am–10.30pm; winter Mon–Fri 8am–6pm, Sat 8am–noon; ☎052/602318), or from Victorina, across the road at Tsar Simeon 36V (daily 9am–5pm; winter closed Sat & Sun; ☎052/603541, ✉victorina_m@top.bg), which also sells a good city map. Best of the cheap **hotels** are the *Voennomorski Klub*, opposite the cathedral at bul Varnenchik 2 (☎052/238312; ❷), and the *Three Dolphins*, near the train station at ul Gabrovo 27 (☎052/600911; ❸), which has a pleasant café downstairs. Closer to the beach, at ul Slivnitsa 33, is the glitzier high-rise *Cherno More* (☎052/232110; ❹).

  Varna has no shortage of **eating and drinking** venues. For authentic Bulgarian standards, try *Arkitekt*, a traditionally furnished wooden town house with a pleasant courtyard garden at ul Musala 10, while for pizzas and other light meals, the *Red Fox Pub* at M Koloni 4, is a reasonable bet; as the name suggests, it also has an English-style bar. There are plenty of other **bars** to choose from along bul Knyaz Boris I, while in summer, the **beach**, reached by steps from the Sea Gardens, is lined with open-air bars and fish restaurants, such as *Tonga* and *Zhatra*, and a seemingly unending strip of nightclubs. Outside high season, though, it's pretty dismal. For **Internet access**, try Doom, ul 27 July 13, or Cyber X, Knyaz Boris I 53, both open 24 hours.

Burgas and around

The south coast's prime urban centre and transport hub, **BURGAS**, can be reached by train from Sofia and Plovdiv, or by bus from Varna, and provides easy access to the picture-postcard town of Nesebâr to the north and Sozopol to the south. Burgas's train and bus stations are both located at the southern edge of town, near the port. Bypassed by most tourists, the pedestrianized city centre, lined with smart boutiques, bars and cafés, is pleasant enough, though its best feature is the **Sea Gardens**, overlooking the beach at the eastern end of town. More attractive and better cared for than Varna's, they are laid out with pristine flowerbeds, statues and a wide variety of plant life. If you want to stay, contact Dimant, ul Tsar Simeon 15 (daily: summer 8.30am-8.30pm; winter 8.30am–6.30pm; ☎056/840779, ✉dimant91@abv.bg), which can book **private rooms** (●). The city's few **hotels** are pricey; the towering *Bulgaria* is just north of the train station at ul Alexandrovska 21 (☎056/842820, ⊛www.bulgaria-hotel.com; ❹).

Nesebâr

Founded by Greek colonists from Megara, **NESEBÂR** – 35km northeast of Burgas and served by buses every twenty minutes – grew into a thriving port during the Byzantine era, and ownership alternated between Bulgaria and Byzantium until the Ottomans captured it in 1453. The town remained an important centre of Greek culture and the seat of a bishop under Turkish rule, which left Nesebâr's **Byzantine churches** reasonably intact. Nowadays the town depends on them for its tourist appeal, demonstrated by the often overwhelming stream of summer visitors crossing the man-made isthmus that connects the old town with the mainland. Outside the hectic summer season, the place seems eerily deserted, with little open other than a few sleepy cafés.

Buses arrive at the harbour at the western end of town, above which stands the **Archeological Museum** (summer daily 8am–8pm; winter Mon–Fri 9am–5pm; 2.50Lv). There's an array of Greek tombstones and medieval icons on display, as well as an intriguing small Hellenistic statue showing a triple image of Hecate, goddess of witches. Immediately beyond the museum is **Christ Pantokrator**, the first of Nesebâr's churches, currently in use as an art shop. Dating from the fourteenth century, its ceramic inlays and red brick motifs are characteristic of late Byzantine architecture, and it features an unusual frieze of swastikas – an ancient symbol of the sun and continual change. Downhill on ul Mitropolitska is the eleventh-century church of **St John the Baptist** (now an art gallery), only one of whose frescoes – a seventeenth-century depiction of St Marina – still survives. Overhung by half-timbered houses, ul Aheloi branches off from ul Mitropolitska towards the **Church of Sveti Spas** (summer only: Mon–Fri 10am–1.30pm & 2–5.30pm, Sat & Sun 10am–1.30pm; 2Lv), outwardly unremarkable but filled with seventeenth-century frescoes. Down an alley from here are the now ruined **Church of the Archangels Michael and Gabriel** and the **Church of Sveta Paraskeva**, patterned with green ceramic inlays. A few steps to the east lies the ruined **Old Metropolitan Church**, dominating a plaza filled with pavement cafés and street traders. The church itself dates back to the sixth century, and it was here that bishops officiated during the city's heyday. South of the town's main street, down ul Ribarska, lies the **New Metropolitan Church** (*Sveti Stefan*; daily 9am–1pm & 2–6pm; 2Lv), whose interior fresco of the Forty Martyrs, on the west wall, gives pride of place to the patron who financed the church's enlargement during the fifteenth century. Downhill from here is the ruined **Church of St John Aliturgetos**, standing in splendid isolation beside the shore and representing the zenith of Byzantine architecture in Bulgaria. Its exterior employs limestone, red bricks, crosses, mussel shells and ceramic plaques for decoration.

Accommodation can be hard to come by during the busy summer season, and advance bookings are advisable. **Private rooms** (❷), many in fine old houses, can be booked through Suvet Tourism at ul Tervel 7, opposite the Church of Sveti Spas (irregular hours; ☎0554/42199). The unsigned *Hotel Tony*, at ul Kraybrezhna 20 (☎0554/42329; ❷), and the nearby, summer-only *Hotel Rai*, at ul Sadala 7 (☎0554/46094; ❷), are small and comfortable family-run pensions on the northern side of the peninsula. There are plenty of places to **eat**, although most restaurants are aimed at the passing tourist crowd, serving predictably mediocre food. Two of the better restaurants are the *Kapetanska Sreshta,* overlooking the harbour, and the sea-facing *Neptun*, towards the far end of town. Snacks are available from summertime kiosks along the waterfront.

Sozopol

SOZOPOL, the oldest settlement on the coast, was founded in the seventh century BC by Greek colonists from Miletus, who called the town Apollonia and prospered by trading textiles and wine for honey and corn. Today it's a busy fishing port and holiday resort, especially popular with East European tourists. The **Archeological Museum** (closed for restoration at the time of writing), hidden behind the library, holds an extensive collection of amphorae and barnacle-encrusted stone anchors, dredged from the surrounding waters, as well as a display of exquisitely decorated Greek vases. There's little else in the way of specific sights, though Sozopol's charm owes much to its old wooden houses. With space at a premium, their upper storeys project so far out that houses on opposite sides of the narrow, cobbled streets almost meet. Half-hourly **buses** from Burgas arrive at the southern edge of the old town. **Accommodation** can be even harder to find during summer than in Nesebâr, and most places shut down for the rest of the year. The Amon-Ra bureau at ul Republikanska 1 (irregular hours; ☎05514/2208) can arrange rooms (❷). Most **hotels** are located in the new part of town; *Alfa-Beta*, ul

Republikanska 9 (℡05514/3614; ❷), is a small pension with a pleasant breakfast garden, while uphill from here at ul Vihren 28 is the modern *Orion* (℡05514/3193; ❷), whose en-suite rooms have TV and balconies. The *Poseidon*, ul Apoloniya 7, and the *Vyatarna Melnitsa*, ul Morski Skali 27, are a couple of good, if touristy **restaurants**.

Travel details

Trains

Gorna Oryahovitsa to: Veliko Târnovo (10 daily; 20min).
Plovdiv to: Burgas (4–6 daily; 4–5hr); Sofia (14 daily; 2hr–3hr 30min); Varna (3 daily; 5hr).
Septemvri to: Bansko (3 daily; 5hr).
Sofia to: Blagoevgrad (6 daily; 2hr 30min–3hr 30min); Burgas (6 daily; 6–8hr); Gorna Oryahovitsa (10 daily; 4hr 30min); Koprivshtitsa (5 daily; 1hr 50min); Plovdiv (12 daily; 2hr–3hr 30min); Septemvri (17 daily; 1hr 30min–2hr 15min); Varna (6 daily; 8–9hr).

Buses

Blagoevgrad to: Bansko (hourly; 1hr 20min); Rila village (hourly; 40min).
Burgas to: Nesebâr (every 20min; 50min); Sozopol (every 30min; 40min); Varna (hourly; 3hr).
Gorna Oryahovitsa to: Veliko Târnovo (every 15min; 30min).
Plovdiv to: Bachkovo (hourly; 40min); Sofia (hourly; 2hr).
Rila village to: Rila monastery (4 daily; 30min).
Sofia to: Bansko (10 daily; 3hr); Burgas (8 daily; 7hr); Koprivshtitsa (1–2 daily; 2hr); Plovdiv (hourly; 2hr); Rila village (2 daily; 2hr); Varna (hourly; 6hr); Veliko Târnovo (every 30min; 3hr).

Croatia

Croatia highlights

✳ **Amphitheatre, Pula** This magnificent arena is the sixth largest in the world. See p.214

✳ **Windsurfing, Bol** The Adriatic's most attractive beaches also provide the best windsurfing opportunities. See p.219

✳ **Diocletian's Palace, Split** This extraordinary 1700-year-old palace houses shops, restaurants and bars, as well as some fascinating remains. See p.217

✳ **Vis Island** One of the coast's lushest and most peaceful islands. See p.220

✳ **City Walls, Dubrovnik** Sensational views of the Old Town and the Adriatic from the 25m high city walls. See p.224

✳ **Dubrovnik Summer Festival** Classical concerts and theatre at Croatia's most prestigious festival. See p.223

Introduction and basics

Croatia (Hrvatska) has come a long way since 1991, when foreign tourists fled from a region standing on the verge of war. Now that stability has returned, visitors are flooding back to a country which boasts one of Europe's finest stretches of coastline. Croatia was an independent kingdom in the tenth century, but was subsequently absorbed by the Austro-Hungarian Empire before becoming part of the new state of Yugoslavia in 1918. Local aspirations were frustrated by a Yugoslav state which was initially dominated by Serbs, and then (after 1945) ruled by Communists. Croatia's declaration of independence on June 25, 1991, was fiercely contested by a Serb-dominated Yugoslav army eager to preserve their control over areas in which groups of ethnic Serbs lived. The period of war – and fragile, UN-supervised ceasefire that followed – was finally brought to a close in 1995.

The capital, **Zagreb**, is a typical central European metropolis, combining elegant nineteenth-century architecture with plenty of cultural diversions and a vibrant café scene. At the northern end of the Adriatic coast, the peninsula of **Istria** contains many of the country's most developed resorts, with old Venetian towns like **Rovinj** rubbing shoulders with the raffish port of **Pula**. Further south lies **Dalmatia**, a dramatic, mountain-fringed stretch of coastline studded with islands. Dalmatia's main towns are **Zadar**, an Italianate peninsula town, and **Split**, an ancient Roman settlement and modern port which provides a jumping-off point to a series of enchanting **islands**. It's on Brač, Hvar, Vis and Korčula that you'll find the best of the beaches, as well as some lively fishing villages. South of Split lies the medieval walled city of **Dubrovnik**, site of an important festival in the summer and a magical place to be, whatever the season.

Information & maps

Most towns of any size have a **tourist office** (*turistički ured*) run by the local authority, which will happily give out brochures and local maps; English is widely spoken in these places. Few offices book private rooms, but they will at least direct you to an agency that does. Freytag & Berndt produce a good 1:600,000 **map** of Croatia, Slovenia and Bosnia-Herzegovina, as well as 1:100,000 regional maps of Istria and the Dalmatian coast.

Money and banks

The local currency is the **kuna** (kn), which is divided into 100 lipa. There are coins of 1, 2, 5, 10, 20 and 50 lipa, and 1kn, 2kn and 5kn; and notes of 5kn, 10kn, 20kn, 50kn, 100kn, 200kn, 500kn and 1000kn. Accommodation and ferry prices are often quoted in euros, but you still pay in kuna. **Banks** (*banka*) are open Mon–Fri 9am–5pm (sometimes with longer hours in the summer), Sat 7.30am–1pm. Money can also be changed in post offices, travel agencies and **exchange bureaux** (*mjenjačnica*), which have more flexible hours. Credit cards are accepted in a large number of hotels and restaurants, and you can use them to get cash from ATMs and the bigger banks.

Croatia on the net

- ⓦ**www.adriatica.net** General info about the Adriatic resorts, and an online booking service with wide range of apartments, villas and hotels.
- ⓦ**www.croatia.hr** Croatia's tourist board site.
- ⓦ**www.zagreb-touristinfo.hr** Zagreb's main website.
- ⓦ**www.istra.com** One of the better regional sites.
- ⓦ**www.dalmacija.net** Comprehensive coverage of the Dalmatian islands.
- ⓦ**www.dubrovnik.online.com** Excellent city site, including message board.

Communications

Post offices (*pošta* or HPT) are open Mon–Fri 7/8am–8pm, Sat 8am–1pm. In big towns and resorts, some are open daily and until 10pm. Stamps (*marke*) can also be bought at newsstands.

Public **phones** use magnetic cards (*telekarta*), which come in denominations of 13kn, 24kn, 38kn and 67kn; you can buy these from post offices or newspaper kiosks. When making long-distance and international calls, it's usually easier to go to the post office, where you're assigned a cabin and given the bill afterwards.

Internet access is readily available in the capital and most towns and cities; expect to pay around 20kn per hour.

Getting around

Trains are of limited value in a country with such a small rail network, although they do connect Zagreb with the coastal towns of Rijeka and Split. Elsewhere, Croatia is well served by an extensive and reliable **bus** network. **Ferries** offer a leisurely way of getting up and down the coast, and provide the only transport to Croatia's many Adriatic islands.

Croatian Railways (Hrvatske željeznice; ⊛www.hznet.hr) runs a smooth and efficient service. Trains (*vlak*, plural *vlakovi*) are divided into *putnički* (slow ones which stop at every halt) and *IC* (intercity trains which are faster and more expensive). There's an overnight service from Zagreb to Split, for which places in couchettes (*kušet*) and sleeping cars (*spalnica*) are best booked in advance. Timetables (*vozni red*) are usually displayed on boards in stations – *odlazak* means departure, *dolazak* arrival.

The **bus** network is run by a confusing array of small local companies, but services are well integrated and bus stations tend to be well-organized affairs with clearly listed departure times and efficient booking facilities. If you're at a big city bus station, tickets (*karta*) must be obtained from ticket windows before boarding the bus. Elsewhere, they can be bought from the driver. You'll be charged around 5kn for items of baggage to be stored in the hold.

Jadrolinija (⊛www.jadrolinija.hr) operates **ferry** services down the coast on the Rijeka-Zadar-Split-Korčula-Dubrovnik route at least once a day in both directions between June and August, and two or three times weekly for the rest of the year. Rijeka to Dubrovnik is a 22-hour journey, involving one night on the boat. In addition, ferries link Split with the islands of Brač, Hvar, Vis and Korčula. Ferries are also a good way of moving on from Croatia, with connections to Italy (Split and Zadar to Ancona, Pula and Brioni to Trieste, Dubrovnik to Bari) and Greece (Dubrovnik to Igoumenitsa). Fares (often quoted in dollars or euros, but payable in kuna) are reasonable for short trips: Split to Hvar costs around $4. For longer journeys, prices vary greatly according to the level of comfort you require. The cheapest Rijeka–Dubrovnik fare, in high season, is $29, while you'll pay double that for a couchette-style bunk bed, and three times more for a bed in a well-appointed cabin (breakfast included); bicycles travel free of charge. Book in advance for longer journeys wherever possible; addresses and phone numbers are provided in the text where relevant.

Accommodation

Private rooms have long been the mainstay of Croatian tourism, especially on the coast, and represent an inexpensive way of finding a bed for the night. There are well-appointed **campsites** all along the Adriatic coast.

Croatian **hotels** are generally modern multi-storey affairs providing modern comforts but little atmosphere. Most have now been classified according to the international five-star grading system, although some of the grades awarded might seem a little generous. Generally speaking, one-star hotels have rooms with shared WC and bathroom; two-star hotels have rooms with en-suite facilities; three-star hotels have slightly larger en-suite rooms and, most probably, a TV; while four- and five-star are in the international luxury bracket. One-star establishments are in short supply, however, and in most places you'll be dependent on two-star hotels, where you should expect to pay £35–50/$50–70 for a double room. In addition to hotels, there's a growing number of family-run **pensions**, offering 2- or 3-star comforts at a slightly cheaper price – £30/$42 a double being the average.

Private rooms (*privatne sobe*) are available just about everywhere. Bookings are made through the local tourist office or private travel agencies. Agencies are usually open daily 8am–8/9pm in summer, although they may take a long break on Sunday afternoons. Prices are around £8/$12 per person for a simple double sharing a WC and bathroom, £10/$14 for a double with en-suite facilities; stays of less than three nights are often subject to a surcharge of thirty percent or over. Places fill up quickly in July and August, when it's a good idea to arrive early or book ahead. Single travellers will sometimes find it difficult to get a room at all at this time, unless they're prepared to pay the price of a double; at other times, you could expect to get a thirty percent discount on the room rate. It is very likely that you will be offered rooms by elderly ladies waiting outside train, bus and ferry stations, particularly in southern Dalmatia. Whilst they can be alarmingly persistent, don't be afraid to take a room offered in this manner, but be sure to establish the location of the room and agree a price before setting off. If taking a room this way expect to pay around twenty percent less than you would with an agency. However you find a room, you can usually examine it before committing to paying for it.

Hostels and campsites

HI **hostels** are thin on the ground, although those that exist – mostly in the big cities – are generally clean and well run. You can get details, and make reservations, from Hrvatski Ferijalni i Hostelski Savez, Dežmanova 9, Zagreb (℡01/48-47-474, ❼www.hfhs.hr). In addition, **student rooms** are often let out cheap to travellers during the summer vacation (usually mid-July to Aug). For both, expect to pay £8–10/$12–$14 for a bed. **Campsites** (most open May–Sept) abound on the Adriatic coast, and tend to be large-scale, well-appointed affairs with plentiful facilities, restaurants and shops. Two people travelling with a tent can expect to pay roughly £8/$12 each.

Food and drink

There's a varied and distinctive range of **cuisine** on offer, largely because Croatia straddles two culinary cultures: the fish- and seafood-dominated cuisine of the Mediterranean and the hearty meat-oriented fare of central Europe.

Basic **self-catering** and picnic ingredients such as cheese (*sir*), vegetables (*povrće*) and fruit (*voće*) can be bought at a supermarket (*samoposluga*) or open-air market (*tržnica*). Bread (*kruh*) is bought from either a supermarket or a *pekarna* (bakery). For breakfasts and fast food, look out for street stalls or snack-food outlets selling *burek*, a flaky pastry filled with cheese; or grilled meats such as *ćevapčići* (rissoles of minced beef, pork or lamb), and *pljeskavica* (a hamburger-like mixture of the same meats).

For a more relaxed, sit-down meal, a **restaurant** menu (*jelovnik*) will usually include speciality starters such as *pršut* (home-cured ham) and *paški sir* (piquant hard cheese), as well as a range of soups (*juha*). Typical main courses include *punjene paprike* (peppers stuffed with rice and meat), *gulaš* (goulash) or some kind of *odrezak* (fillet of meat, often pan-fried), usually either *svinjski* (pork) or *teleški* (veal). *Mješano meso* is a mixed grill. Lamb, often roasted, is *janjetina*. Traditional dishes from the area around Zagreb include *purica z mlincima* (turkey with pasta noodles) and *štrukli* (ravioli-like blobs of pasta dough with a cheese filling). One typically Dalmatian dish is *pašticada* (beef and bacon cooked in vinegar and wine). On the coast, you'll be regaled with every kind of seafood. *Riba* (fish) can come either *na žaru* (grilled) or *u pečnici* (baked). *Brodet* is a hot peppery fish stew. Otherwise, the main menu items to look out for on the coast are *lignje* (squid), *škampi* (unpeeled prawns eaten with the fingers), *rakovica* (crab), *oštrige* (oysters), *kalamari* (squid), *školjke* (mussels) and *jastog* (lobster); *crni rizoto* is risotto with squid. No town is without at least one pizzeria, often the cheapest place to eat and the easiest, if not the most imaginative, source of a **vegetarian** meal. Typical **desserts** include *palačinke* (pancakes), *voćna salata* (fruit salad) and *sladoled* (ice cream).

Drink

Daytime **drinking** takes place in a *kavana* (café) or a *slastičarnica* (patisserie). Coffee (*kava*) is usually served black unless specified otherwise – ask for *mlijeko* (milk) or *šlag* (cream). Tea (*čaj*) is widely available, but is drunk without milk. Night-time drinking takes place in a growing number of small *kafići* or café/bars. Croatian **beer** (*pivo*) is of the light lager variety; Karlovačko and Ožujsko are two good local brands to look out for. The local wine (*vino*) is consistently good and reasonably cheap. In Dalmatia there are some pleasant whites, crisp dry wines such as Kastelet, Grk and Posip, as well as reds such as the dark heady Dingač and Babić. In Istria, Semion is a bone-dry white, and Teran a light fresh red. Local spirits include *loza*, a clear grape-based spirit; *travarica*, herbal brandy; *vinjak*, locally produced cognac, and *Maraskino*, a cherry liqueur from Dalmatia.

Opening hours and holidays

Most **shops** open Mon–Fri 8am–8pm, Sat 8am–1pm, although many supermarkets, outdoor markets and the like are open daily 7am–7pm. **Museum and gallery** times vary from place to place, although most are closed Mon. All shops and banks are closed on the following **public holidays**: Jan 1; Jan 6; Easter Mon; May 1; Corpus Christi; June 22; June 24; Aug 5; Aug 15; Oct 8; Nov 1; & Dec 25 & 26.

Emergencies

The crime rate is low by European standards. **Police** (*policija*) are generally helpful when dealing with holiday-makers, although they can be slow when filling out reports. They also often make routine checks on identity cards and other documents; always carry your passport. **Hospital** treatment is free to EU citizens. **Pharmacies** (*ljekarna*) tend to follow normal shopping hours, and a rota system covers night-time and weekend opening; details are posted in the window of each pharmacy.

Emergency numbers

Police ☎92; Fire ☎93; Ambulance ☎94; Sea rescue and diving alert ☎9155.

Zagreb

Capital of an independent state since 1991, **ZAGREB** has served as the cultural and political focus of Croatia since the Middle Ages. The city grew out of two medieval communities, **Kaptol**, to the east, and **Gradec**, to the west, each sited on a hill and divided by a river long since dried up but nowadays marked by a street known as Tkalčićeva. Zagreb grew rapidly in the nineteenth century, and the majority of its buildings are relatively well-preserved, grand, peach-coloured monuments to the self-esteem of the Austro-Hungarian Empire. Nowadays, with a population topping one million, Zagreb is the boisterous capital of a newly self-confident nation. A handful of good museums and a vibrant nightlife ensure that a few days here will be well spent.

Arrival, information and city transport

Zagreb's central **train station** is on Tomislavov Trg, on the southern edge of the city centre, a ten-minute walk from Trg bana Jelačića, the main square. The main **bus station** is a fifteen-minute walk east of the train station, at the junction of Branimirova and Držićeva – trams #2, #3 and #6 run between the two stations, with #6 continuing to the main square. Zagreb **airport** is 10km southeast of the city; Croatia Airlines buses run to the main bus station (6am–8pm, every 30min; 25kn). There are two **tourist offices** in central Zagreb; the main one is at Trg bana

Jelačića 11 (Mon–Fri 8.30am–8pm, Sat 9am–5pm, Sun 10am–2pm; ☎01/48-14-051, ⍉www.zagreb-touristinfo.hr), the other is at Trg N. Zrinskog 14 (Mon–Fri 8am–8pm, Sat & Sun 9am–6pm; ☎01/49-21-645). Both sell the **Zagreb Card** (72hr, 60kn), which gives unlimited city transport and good discounts in museums and restaurants. The superb *Zagreb In Your Pocket* (20kn), available from the tourist offices, hotels and shops, is by far the best source of information on the city.

Zagreb has an efficient and comprehensive **tram** network and, to a lesser extent, bus network, though much of the city centre can easily be seen on foot. Flat-fare tram and bus **tickets** (*karte*) are sold from cigarette and newspaper kiosks (6.50kn) or from the driver (8kn). Day tickets (*dnevne karte*) cost 18kn. Validate your ticket by punching it in the machines on board the trams. The train station and Trg bana Jelačića are the two main hubs of the city transport system.

Accommodation

Zagreb has very little in the way of budget **accommodation**. **Private rooms** (❸) can be arranged through the Evistas agency at Šenoina 28, midway between the train and bus stations (Mon–Fri 9am–8pm, Sat 9am–5pm; ☎01/48-39-546, ⍉evistas@zg.tel.hr). In addition to the hostels listed below, some **student rooms** are available (mid-July to late Sept only; ❹). The two main locations are at Cvijetno naselje, Odranska 8 (☎01/61-91-245; tram #14 or #17 from Trg bana Jelačića), and Stjepan Radić, Jarunska 2 (☎01/36-34-255; tram #17 from Trg bana Jelačića). The nearest **campsite** (☎01/65-30-444) is 10km southwest of town at the *Plitvice Motel* beside the main Zagreb–Ljubljana motorway; there's no public transport to it.

Hostels

HI hostel Petrinjska 77 ☎01/48-41-261. Grotty 200-bed hostel five minutes' walk from the train station, due to close in winter 2003 for much-needed renovation – so call in advance. 120kn per person.

Ravnice hostel 1. Ravnice 38b ☎23-32-325, ⍉www.ravnice-youth-hostel.hr. Fabulous and welcoming new hostel east of the centre. Tram #4, #11 or #12 to the Ravnice stop, then ten minutes' walk south along 1. Ravnice. 110kn per person.

Hotels

Astoria Petrinjska 71 ☎01/48-41-222, ⍉hotel-astoria@zg.tel.hr. Slightly careworn though clean en suites; all rooms have TV, too. Convenient for the train and bus stations. ❺

Dora Trnjanska 11f ☎01/63-11-900, ⍉www.zeljeznicko-ugostiteljstvo.hr. This simple but cheery place, ten-minutes' walk south of the train station (via the subway), has clean, wood-furnished rooms. Breakfast not included. ❺

Ilica Ilica 102 ☎01/37-77-522, ⍉www.hotel-ilica.hr. Modern, smart and friendly B&B with en-suite rooms 1.5km west of the main square. Popular, so book in advance. ❺

Jadran Vlaška 50 ☎01/45-53-777. Cheapest of the central hotels, with en-suite rooms. Just east of the city centre and fifteen minutes' walk from the train station at the top end of Draskovićeva. ❺

Sliško Supilova 13 ☎01/61-84-777, ⍉www.slisko.hr. Clean, comfortable and welcoming hotel 300m east of the main bus station. ❺

The City

Modern Zagreb falls neatly into three parts. **Donji Grad** or "Lower Town", which extends north from the train station to Trg bana Jelačića, the main square, is the bustling centre of the modern city. Uphill from here, to the northeast and the northwest, are the older quarters of **Kaptol** (the "Cathedral Chapter") and **Gradec** (the "Upper Town"), both peaceful districts of ancient mansions, quiet squares and leafy parks.

Donji Grad

Tomislavov Trg, opposite the train station, is the first in a series of three shady, green squares which form the backbone of the lower town. Its main attraction is the **Art Pavilion** (Mon–Sat 11am–7pm, Sun 10am–1pm; 20kn, free Mon;

@www.umjetnicki-paviljon), built in 1898 and now hosting art exhibitions in its gilded stucco and mock-marble interior. There's little to divert you in the second of the squares, but beyond, in the last of the three – **Trg Nikole Zrinskog** – lies the **Archeological Museum** (Tues–Fri 10am–5pm, Sat & Sun 10am–1pm; 20kn; @www.amz.hr); the museum has pieces from prehistoric times to the Middle Ages, including pottery fragments from the fourth century BC Vučedol culture, ancient Roman and Greek artefacts and Egyptian antiquities.

Walk up from here and you're on **Trg bana Jelačića**, flanked by cafés, hotels and department stores, and hectic with the whizz of trams and hurrying pedestrians. The statue in the centre is of the nineteenth-century governor of Croatia, Josip Jelačić. Running west from the square, below Gradec hill, is **Ilica**, the city's main shopping street. A little way along it and off to the right, you can take a **funicular** (daily 6.30am–9pm, every 10min; 2.5kn) up to Strossmayerovo Šetaliste; alternatively, cut down via **Preradovićev Trg**, a small lively square where there's a flower market, to **Trg maršala Tita**. This is a grandiose open space, centred on the late nineteenth-century **National Theatre**, a solid ochre-coloured pile behind a piece by Ivan Meštrović, the strangely erotic *Well of Life*. Across the square, the **Museum of Arts and Crafts** (Tues–Fri 10am–6pm, Sat & Sun 10am–1pm; 20kn; @www.muo.hr) boasts an impressive display of furniture, ceramics, clothes and textiles from the Renaissance to the present day. On the southern side of the square, on Trg Ivana Mažuranića, the **Ethnographic Museum** (Tues–Thurs 10am–6pm, Fri–Sun 10am–1pm; 15kn) has a collection of costumes from every corner of the country, as well as an engaging heap of artefacts brought back from the South Pacific, Asia and Africa.

A couple of minutes west, on Rooseveltov Trg, lies Zagreb's most prestigious art collection, the **Mimara Museum** (Tues–Sat 10am–7pm, Thurs closes 2pm; 25kn; @www.mimara.hr), housing the art and archeological collection of Ante Topić Mimara, a native of Zagreb who spent much of his life in Austria. Ground-floor exhibits include ancient glass from Egypt, Greece, Syria and the Roman Empire, and Chinese art from the Shang through to the Song dynasty. Upstairs, there's a fine collection of European paintings, including works by Rembrandt, Rubens and Renoir.

Kaptol and Gradec

Behind Trg bana Jelačića, the filigree spires of Zagreb's **Cathedral** mark the edge of the district (and street) known as **Kaptol**, ringed by the ivy-cloaked turrets of the eighteenth-century **Archbishop's Palace** – a "southern Kremlin" fancied the archeologist Arthur Evans before its decimation by an earthquake in 1880. After the disaster, the cathedral was rebuilt in neo-Gothic style, a high, bare structure inside, with very little left from the years before the earthquake. Behind the altar lies a shrine to Archbishop Stepinac, head of the Croat church in the 1940s, imprisoned by the Communists after World War II, and beatified by the Pope in 1998.

Immediately west of Kaptol, **Gradec** is the most ancient and atmospheric part of Zagreb, a leafy, tranquil backwater of tiny streets, small squares and Baroque palaces, whose mottled brown roofs peek out from the hill to the west. From Trg bana Jelačića, make your way to the **Dolac** market, which occupies several tiers immediately beyond the square; this is the city's main food-market, a feast of fruit, vegetables, meat and fish held every morning. From the far side of Dolac market, **Tkalčićeva** spears north, following the course of the river which once formed the boundary between Kaptol and Gradec. Entry to Gradec proper from here is by way of **Krvavi Most**, which connects the street with Radićeva. On the far side of Radićeva, the **Kamenita Vrata** is a gloomy tunnel with a small shrine that formed part of Gradec's original fortifications. Close by, the fourteenth-century **Kula Lotrščak** (May–Oct: Tues–Sun 11am–8pm; 5kn) marks the top station of the funicular (see above). There are fantastic views from here over the rest of the city and the plains beyond. North of the tower, the **Gallery of Naive Art**,

Ćirilometodska 3 (Tues–Fri 10am–6pm, Sat & Sun 10am–1pm; 20kn; @www.hmnu.org), is an impressive collection of work by peasant artists. At the northern end of Ćirilometodska, **Markov Trg** marks the centre of Gradec – fringed by government offices, the square's focus is the squat **Church of St Mark**, a much renovated place whose tiled roof displays the coats-of-arms of the constituent parts of Croatia.

Just north of Markov Trg, at Mletačka 8, is the **Meštrović Atelier** (Tues–Fri 9am–2pm, Sat 10am–6pm; 10kn), an exhibition dedicated to Croatia's most famous twentieth-century artist – in the sculptor's former home and studio. On display are sketches, photographs, memorabilia from exhibitions worldwide, and small-scale studies of his more familiar public creations. Left off Markov Trg, the **Historical Museum of Croatia**, at Matoševa 9 (Mon–Fri 10am–5pm, Sat & Sun 10am–1pm; 10kn; @www.hismus.hr), is the venue for prestigious temporary exhibitions. The **Museum of Zagreb**, at Opatička 20 (Tues–Fri 10am–6pm, Sat & Sun 10am–1pm; 20kn), close to the thirteenth-century **Popov Toranj**, is perhaps more appealing, telling the tale of Zagreb's development from medieval times to the early twentieth century with the help of paintings and lumber from the city's wealthier households, and the original seventeenth-century statues that once adorned the portals of the city's cathedral.

Eating and drinking

Whilst not outstanding, Zagreb's **restaurant** scene is becoming more varied, and there's no shortage of budget places to eat. There's a wide range of Croatian cuisine, including several superb seafood restaurants, and any number of pizzerias. Expect to pay 50–70kn for a decent meal in any of the places listed below. For **snack food**, head to the area around Dolac market. There's a 24-hour bakery, *Pekarna Dora*, between the train station and the centre at Strossmayerov Trg 8 and **picnic supplies** can be purchased from Dolac, or from the supermarkets in the subterranean Importanne shopping centre in front of the train station. Zagreb has a wealth of **cafés and bars** offering outdoor seating in the pedestrian area around Gajeva and Bogovićeva – particularly along Tkalčićeva, just north of Trg bana Jelačića.

Restaurants

Boban Gajeva 9. Popular and central pasta place in the vaulted basement of the stylish café of the same name.

Cantinetta Teslina 14. Good-quality Croatian and Italian food just south of the main square. Chic, but not too expensive. Closed Sun.

Club Havana Perkovčeva 2. This brilliant Cuban restaurant, located under the *Press Club*, has high-class food, sophisticated decor and attentive waiting staff, making it the most engaging place in town to eat. Closed Sun.

Kerempuh Dolac bb. Hidden away behind the main fruit-and-veg market, this is one of the best places in town to fill up on traditional Croatian pork-based favourites. Cheap lunchtime specials.

Nokturno Skalinska 4. In a side street just off Tkalčićeva, offering serviceable pizzas, varied lasagnes, and good salads.

Pivnica Medvedgrad Savska 56. Located 1.5km southwest of the centre, this huge beer hall serves up large, cheap portions of grilled meats; the beer, brewed on the premises, is excellent, too.

Pod Gričkim Topom Zakmardijeve stube. Good Croatian food in a cosy restaurant on the steps leading down from Strossmayerovo Šetalište to Trg bana Jelačića.

Rubelj Frankopanska 2 & Dolac market. Cheapest central place for simple but tasty grilled-meat standards.

Stari Fijaker Mesnička 6. A dimly lit, intimate restaurant serving local cuisine.

Zdravljak Nova Ilica 72. A friendly, unfussy vegetarian restaurant in a cramped but cosy upstairs room, sharing the same building as Zagreb's premier health food shop.

Cafés and bars

Bulldog Bogovićeva 6. A typically elegant Zagreb bar and pavement café, this is one of the most popular meeting places in the town centre.

Dobar Zvuk Gajeva 18. Popular café-bar with cheap drinks and a moderately bohemian clientele.

Hemingway Dežmanova. Funky cocktail bar, popular with Zagreb's smart set. West of the main square and off Ilica.

Kolding Berislavićeva 8. Civilized cellar bar with turn-of-the-century furnishings. Good place for an intimate drink.
Londoner Pub Kaptol Centar, Nova Ves 11. Roomy basement bar north of the Cathedral, packed with party animals at the weekends.

Occasional live music.
Melin Košarska 19. This energetic pub is a terrific alternative to the posier establishments nearby.
Tolkien's Katarinin Trg. Funky, *Lord of the Rings* inspired place on a quiet square In Gradec.

Nightlife

Zagreb offers a rich and varied diet of high culture, with the **National Theatre**, Trg maršala Tita 15 (ticket office Mon–Fri 10am–1pm & 5–7.30pm, Sat 10am–1pm & 1hr 30min before each performance, Sun 30min before each performance; ☎01/48-28-532, ⌨www.hnk.hr), providing the focus for serious, Croatian-language drama, as well as opera and ballet. The city's main orchestral-music venue is the **Lisinski Concert Hall** south of the train station at Trg Stjepana Radića 4 (ticket office Mon–Fri 9am–8pm, Sat 9am–2pm; ☎01/61-21-166, ⌨www.lisinski.hr). Intimate chamber-music concerts take place at the **Croatian Musical Institute**, Gundulićeva 6 (☎01/48-30-922). The free monthly pamphlet *Events and Performances*, available from the Zagreb tourist office, contains **listings** in English of all forthcoming events. Nightlife centres on a clutch of established, and reasonably varied, **discos** and **clubs**, many presenting the best opportunities for catching live rock and jazz – check the posters plastered liberally around the city centre or pick up flyers from record shops for an idea of what's on.

Discos and clubs

Aquarius Aleja Mira bb. At the eastern end of Lake Jarun, 4km southwest of the centre, the place specializes in techno and drum 'n' bass. Occasional host to live bands. Thurs–Sun.
BP Club Teslina 7. Established jazz club and relaxed late-night drinking haunt.
Močvara Tvornica Jedinstvo building, Trnjanski nasip. Unpretentious cultural centre in an old factory on the banks of the River Sava. Live gigs (usually alternative rock), film shows and club nights – something happening every night. Take

any bus heading for Novi Zagreb and alight just before the bridge – the club is on your right.
Saloon Tuškanac 1a. Legendary meeting place in a leafy corner of town, 500m west of the centre. Music is an enjoyable mish-mash of commercial disco. Tues–Sat.
Sax Palmotićeva 22. Large, comfortable basement club, two blocks east of Trg N. Zrinskog, with live music (with a jazz bias) most nights.
Tvornica Šubićeva 1. Former ballroom just north of the bus station, now hosting live rock, club nights and theatre.

Listings

Embassies Australia, Nova Ves 11 ☎01/48-91-200; Canada, Prilaz Gjure Deželića 4 ☎01/48-81-200; UK, Ivana Lučića 4 ☎01/60-09-100; US, Hebrangova 2 ☎01/66-12-200.
Exchange In the main post office.
Hospital Draskovićeva 19 ☎01/46-10-011.
Internet access Aquarius, Kralja Držislavova 4; Art Net Club, Preradovičeva 25; Mama, Preradovićeva 18; Sublink, Teslina 12.

Laundry Predom, Draškovičeva 31 (Mon–Fri 7am–7pm, Sat 8am–noon).
Left luggage At the train and bus stations (both 24hr).
Pharmacy Ilica 43 (24hr).
Police Petrinjska 30.
Post offices Branimirova 4 (24hr); Jurišićeva 13 (Mon–Fri 7am–9pm, Sat 7am–7pm, Sun 8am–2pm).

Istria

A large peninsula jutting into the northern Adriatic, **Istria** hosts Croatian tourism at its most developed. Many of the towns here were tourist resorts in the nineteenth century, and in recent years their proximity to northern Europe has ensured an annual influx of sun-seekers from Germany, Austria and the Netherlands. Yet the

Travelling on from Istria towards Zagreb or Dalmatia, most routes lead through the brusque port city of **RIJEKA**, hardly worth a stopoff in its own right but an important transport hub for onward travel: regular **buses** run from here to Zagreb, Zadar, Split and Dubrovnik, and it's the starting point for the Jadrolinija coastal **ferry**, which calls in at Zadar, Split and Dubrovnik on its way south. Rijeka's train and bus stations are about 400m apart; the former at the western end of Trpimirova, the latter at the eastern end of the same street on Trg Žabica. The Jadrolinija ferry office (daily 7am–6/9pm; ☏051/211-444) is along the waterfront from the bus station at Riva 16.

⑤

growth of modern hotel complexes, sprawling campsites and (mainly concrete) beaches has done little to detract from the essential charm of the region. This stretch of the coast was under Venetian rule for 400 years and there's still a fair-sized Italian community, with Italian very much the second language. Istria's largest centre is the port city of **Pula**, which, with its Roman amphitheatre and other relics of Roman occupation, is a rewarding place to spend a couple of days. On the western side of the peninsula, the resort town of **Rovinj**, with its cobbled piazzas and shuttered houses, is almost overwhelmingly pretty.

Pula

Once the chief port of the Austro-Hungarian Empire, **PULA** is an engaging combination of working port, naval base and brash riviera town. The Romans put the city squarely on the map when they arrived in 177 BC, transforming it into an important commercial centre. The most obvious relic of their rule is the first century BC **Amphitheatre** (daily: June–Sept 8am–8pm; Oct–May 9am–5pm; 30kn) just north of the centre, a great grey elliptical skein of connecting arches, silhouetted against the skyline from wherever you stand in the city. It's the sixth largest in the world, and once had space for over 23,000 spectators. The outer shell is fairly complete, as is one of the towers, up which a slightly hair-raising climb gives a good sense of the enormity of the structure and a view of Pula's industrious harbour. The cavernous rooms underneath, which would have been used for keeping wild animals and Christians before they met their death, are now given over to piles of crusty amphorae and reconstructed olive presses.

South of the amphitheatre, central Pula circles a pyramidal hill, scaled by secluded streets and topped with a star-shaped Venetian fortress. On the eastern side of the hill, Istarska – which later becomes Giardini – leads down to the first-century BC **Triumphal Arch of the Sergians**, through which ul Sergijevaca, a lively pedestrianized thoroughfare, leads in turn to a square known as **Forum** – site of the ancient Roman forum and now the centre of Pula's old quarter. On the far side of here, the slim form of the **Temple of Augustus** was built between 2 BC and 14 AD to celebrate the cult of the emperor; its imposing Corinthian columns, still intact, make it one of the best examples of a Roman temple outside Italy.

Heading north from Forum along Kandlerova leads to Pula's **Cathedral** (daily 7am–noon & 4–6pm), a broad, simple and very spacious structure that is another mixture of periods and styles: a fifteenth-century renovation of a Romanesque basilica built on the foundations of a Roman temple. From the cathedral, you can follow streets up to the top of the hill, the site of the original Roman Capitol and now the home of a mossy seventeenth-century **fortress**, built by the Venetians and housing a pretty inessential local museum. You're better off following tracks to the far side of the fortress where there are the remains of a small **Roman Theatre** and the **Archeological Museum** (May–Sept Mon–Sat 9am–8pm, Sun 10am–3pm; Oct–April Mon–Fri 9am–2pm; 20kn), which has pillars and toga-clad statues mingling haphazardly with ceramics, jewellery and trinkets from all over Istria, some dating back to prehistoric times.

Pula's **train station** is a ten-minute walk north of the centre, at the far end of Kolodvorska; the **bus station** is along Istarska, just south of the amphitheatre. The **tourist office** is in the Forum (June–Sept daily 9am–10pm; Oct–May Mon–Fri 9am–7pm; ☏052/219-197, ⊛www.pulainfo.hr). **Private rooms** (❷) can be booked through Arenatours, Splitska Ulica 1 (☏052/529-400, ⊛www .arenaturist.hr), or Atlas, Ulica Starih Statuta 1 (☏052/214-172). There's an **HI hostel** at Valsaline bay, 4km south of the centre (☏052/391-133, ⓔhfhs-pula@pu.hinet.hr; 85kn per person); take bus #2 or #7 from Giardini to Vila Idola and then bear right towards the bay. Cheapest of the **hotels** is the *Omir*, slightly uphill from Giardini at Sergia Dobrića 6 (☏052/213-944; ❹). The plush *Scaletta*, just north of the amphitheatre at Flavijevska 26 (☏052/541-599; ❻), is one of the best family-run hotels in Croatia. The nearest **campsite** is *Stoja*, on a rocky wooded peninsula 3km southeast of town (☏052/387-144); take bus #1 from Giardini.

The vast **market** on Narodni Trg will yield all the provisions you'll need. Most **eating out** options are around the arena, Forum and Kandlerova: *Dva Ferala*, near the cathedral at Kandlerova 14, offers inexpensive grilled meats and fish; *Jupiter*, below the fortress at Castropola 38, is easily the best of the pizzerias; and *Pompei*, just off Sergijevaca at Clarissova 1, does good pasta dishes and salads. Best of the **drinking** haunts are *Ulix*, an elegant bar next to the triumphal arch; *Bounty Pub*, an animated place with plenty of outdoor seating two blocks east of the arch at Veronska 8; and *Uljanik*, Dobrilna 2, a counter-cultural club of many years' standing that has DJ nights at weekends and live music in summer. During the summer, the liveliest party venues are in Verudela, 3km south of town.

Rovinj

ROVINJ lies 40km north of Pula, its harbour a likeable mix of fishing boats and swanky yachts, its quaysides a blend of sunshaded café-tables and the thick orange of fishermen's nets. From the main square, **Trg maršala Tita**, the Baroque **Vrata svetog Križa** leads up to Grisia Ulica, lined with galleries selling local art. It climbs steeply through the heart of the old town to **St Euphemia's Church** (daily 10am–noon & 4–7pm), dominating Rovinj from the top of its peninsula. This eighteenth-century church, Baroque in style, has the sixth-century sarcophagus of the saint inside; you can climb its 58-metre-high tower (same times; 10kn). Back on maršala Tita, the **Town Museum** (May–Sept Mon–Sat 9am–12.30pm & 6–9pm; Oct–April Tues–Sat 10.30am–1.30pm; 10kn) has the usual collection of archeological oddments, antique furniture and Croatian art. North of here is **Trg Valdibora**, home to a small fruit and vegetable market. Paths on the south side of Rovinj's busy harbour lead south towards **Zlatni rt**, a densely forested cape, crisscrossed by tracks and fringed by rocky **beaches**. Other spots for bathing can be found on the two islands just offshore from Rovinj – **Sveta Katarina**, the nearer of the two, and **Crveni otok**, just outside Rovinj's bay; both are linked by boats from the harbour (every 30min).

Rovinj's **bus station** is five minutes' walk southeast of its centre, just off Trg na lokvi, at the junction of Carrera and Carducci. The **tourist office** is located at Obula Pina Budicin 12 (June–Sept daily 8am–9pm; rest of year Mon–Sat 8am–3pm; ☏052/811-566, ⊛www.tzgrovinj.hr). **Private rooms** (❷) can be obtained from Natale, opposite the bus station at Carducci 4 (☏052/813-365, ⊛www.natale.hr), and Kompas-Istra, Trg maršala Tita 5 (☏052/813-211). The only reasonably priced **hotel** in town is the *Rovinj*, Svetoga Križa 59 (☏052/910-751, ⓔhotel-rovinj@pu.hinet.hr; ❻). The nearest **campsite** is the *Porton Biondi* (☏052/813-557, ⊛www.cel.hr/porton-biondi), which occupies a pine-shaded site right by the sea 1km north of town. The harbourfront area is teeming with places to **eat and drink**. Away from here, *da Sergio*, at Grisia 11, is the best place for pizza; while *Konoba Veli Jože*, at Svetog Križa 1, has top-notch seafood.

Dalmatia

Stretching from Zadar in the north to the Montenegrin border in the south, **Dalmatia** possesses one of Europe's most dramatic shorelines, the sheer wall of Croatia's mountain ranges sweeping down to the sea from stark, grey heights, scattering islands in their path. For centuries, the region was ruled by Venice, spawning towns, churches and an architecture that wouldn't look out of place on the other side of the water. All along, well-preserved medieval towns sit on tiny islands or just above the sea on slim peninsulas, beneath a grizzled karst landscape that drops precipitously into some of the clearest – and cleanest – water in the Mediterranean. In northern Dalmatia, the busy port city of **Zadar** provides a vivacious introduction to the region. Otherwise, the main attractions are in the south: the provincial capital **Split** is served by trains from Zagreb and provides onward bus connections with the walled city of **Dubrovnik**. Ferry connections to the best of the islands – **Brač**, **Hvar**, **Vis** and **Korčula** – are also from Split.

Zadar

A bustling town of around 100,000 people, **ZADAR** boasts a compact historic centre crowded onto a tapered peninsula jutting northwest into the Adriatic. It displays a pleasant muddle of architectural styles, with Romanesque churches competing for space with café-bars. Near the northwestern end of the peninsula, Zadar's main square or **Forum** is dominated by the ninth-century **St Donat's Church** (summer only: daily 9am–10pm; 5kn), a hulking cylinder of stone built – according to tradition – by St Donat himself, an Irishman who was bishop here for a time. The cavernous, bare interior makes the perfect venue for summer chamber concerts. Opposite, the **Archeological Museum** (Mon–Sat 9am–1pm; summer also Mon–Sat 6–9.30pm, Sun 6–9.30pm; 10kn) has an absorbing collection of Neolithic, Roman and medieval Croatian artefacts. The adjacent **Permanent Exhibition of Church Art** (Mon–Sat 10am–1pm; summer also Mon–Sat 6–8pm, Sun 10am–1pm; 20kn) is a storehouse of Zadar's finest church treasures. On the northwestern side of the Forum, the twelfth- and thirteenth-century **Cathedral of St Anastasia** has an arcaded west front reminiscent of Tuscan churches. Around the door frame stretches a frieze of twisting acanthus leaves, from which various beasts emerge – look for the rodent and bird fighting over a bunch of grapes. Southeast of the Forum is **Narodni trg**, an attractive Renaissance square overlooked by the clock tower of the sixteenth-century **Guard House**. A little further southeast, on Trg Petra Zoranića, the Baroque **St Simeon's Church** houses the exuberantly decorated reliquary of St Simeon, ordered by Queen Elizabeth of Hungary in 1377 and fashioned from 250kg of silver by local artisans.

Practicalities

Ferries arrive on Liburnska obala, from where the town centre is a five-minute walk uphill. Zadar's **train** and **bus stations** are about 1km east of the town centre, a fifteen-minute walk or a quick hop on municipal bus #5 – tickets cost 6kn from the driver or 8kn (valid for two journeys) from kiosks. The **tourist office** is near St Simeon's Church at Ilije Smiljanića 5 (summer daily 8am–10pm; winter Mon–Fri 8am–3pm; ☎023/212-412, ✆tz-zadar@zd.tel.hr). **Private rooms** (❷) in the old town are available from Aquarius, Nova Vrata bb (☎023/212-919, ⊛www.jureskoaquarius.com); and Miatours, Vrata sv. Krševana (☎023/254-400, ⊛www.miatours.hr), both near the ferry quays. *Verona*, Šime Ljubića 4a (☎023/370-264; ❹) is an old-town **pension** offering minuscule but neat en suites. About 4km northwest at the beach resort of Borik (bus #5 from the bus and train stations) is a big, friendly **hostel** at Obala kneza Trpimira 76 (☎023/331-145; 90kn per person), and the well-equipped *Borik* **campsite** (☎023/332-074). In Zadar, old-town **eating** opportunities include *Konoba Martinac*, A. Papavije 7, which offers excellent grilled fish and scampi; and *Dva Ribara*, Borelli 7, with more of the same plus tasty pizzas. Atmospheric café-bars are tucked into the alleys off Narodni trg – head down Klaiča and its continuation Varoška to find them.

Split

The largest city in the region, and its major transit hub, **SPLIT** is one of the most enticing spots on the Dalmatian coast; a hectic city, full of shouting stall-owners and travellers on the move. At the heart of all this, hemmed in by the sprawling estates and a modern harbour, lies a crumbling old town built within the precincts of **Diocletian's Palace**, one of the most outstanding classical remains in Europe. Built as a retirement home by Dalmatian-born Roman Emperor Diocletian in 305 AD, it has been modified over the centuries, but has remained the core of Split. The best place to start a tour of the palace area is on the seaward side, through the **Bronze Gate**, a functional gateway giving access to the sea that once came right up to the palace itself. Inside, you find yourself in a vaulted hall, from which imposing steps lead through the now domeless vestibule to the **Peristyle**. Once the central court-yard of the palace complex, these days the Peristyle serves as the main town square, crowded with cafés and surrounded by remnants of the stately arches that once framed the square. At the southern end, steps lead up to the **vestibule**, a round, for-merly domed building that is the only part of the imperial apartments to be left anything like intact. You can get some idea of the grandeur of the old apartments by visiting the **subterranean halls** (daily: July & Aug 8am–8pm; Sept–June 8am–noon & 4–7pm; 10kn) beneath the houses which now stand on the site; the entrance is to the left of the Bronze Gate.

On the east side of the Peristyle stands one of two black granite Egyptian sphinx-es, dating from around 15 BC, that flanked the entrance to Diocletian's mausoleum; the octagonal building, surrounded by an arcade of Corinthian columns, has since been converted into Split's **cathedral** (Mon–Sat 7am–noon & 4–7pm). On the right of the entrance is the **campanile** (same hours; 5kn), a Romanesque structure much restored in the late nineteenth century – from the top, the views across the city are splendid. As for the cathedral itself, the walnut and oak main **doorway** is one of its most impressive features – carved in 1214 with an inspired comic strip showing scenes from the life of Christ. Inside is a hotchpotch of styles, the dome ringed by two series of decorative Corinthian columns and a frieze that contains portraits of Diocletian and his wife. The **pulpit** is a beautifully proportioned exam-ple of Romanesque art, sitting on capitals tangled with snakes, strange beasts and foliage. But the church's finest feature is on the Altar of St Anastasius – a cruelly realistic *Flagellation of Christ*, completed by local artist Juraj Dalmatinac in 1448.

North of the cathedral and reached by following Dioklecijanova is the grandest and best preserved of the palace gates, the **Golden Gate**. Just outside there's a piece by Meštrović, a gigantic statue of the fourth-century Bishop **Grgur Ninski**. Fifteen minutes' walk northwest of here, the **Archeological Museum** at Zrinsko Frankopanska 25 (June–Sept Tues–Sat 9am–1pm & 5–8pm, Sun 10am–noon; Oct–May Tues–Fri 9am–2pm, Sat & Sun 10am–1pm; 20kn) contains comprehen-sive displays of Illyrian, Greek, medieval and Roman artefacts. Outside, the arcaded courtyard is crammed with a wonderful array of Greek, Roman and early Christian gravestones, sarcophagi and decorative sculpture.

If you want some peace and quiet, head for the woods of the **Marjan peninsula** west of the old town. It's accessible from Obala hrvatskog narodnog preporoda via Sperun and then Senjska, which cuts up through the slopes of the **Varoš** district. Most of Marjan's visitors stick to the road around the edge of the promontory with its scattering of tiny rocky **beaches**; the Bene beach, on the far northern side, is especially popular. From the road, tracks lead up into the heart of the Marjan Park, which is thickly wooded with pines. The main historical attractions of Marjan are on the lower, southern edge, along Šetalište Ivana Meštrovića. Highlight of these lies some fifteen minutes west of the centre (bus #12 from the seafront). The

Meštrović Gallery, Ivana Meštrovića 46 (Tues–Sat 11am–6pm, Sun 10am–3pm; 20kn, includes entrance to Kaštelet), is another Croatian shrine, housed in the ostentatious Neoclassical building that was built – and lived in – by Croatia's most famous twentieth-century artist, the sculptor Ivan Meštrović (1883–1962). This fabulous collection consists largely of boldly fashioned bodies curled into elegant poses. Mestrović's former workshop, **Kaštelet** (same times and ticket), is 300m up the same road, and contains a chapel decorated with one of Meštrović's most important set-piece works: a series of wood-carved reliefs showing scenes from the Stations of the Cross.

Practicalities

Split's main **bus and train stations** are next to each other on Obala Kneza Domagoja, five minutes' walk round the harbour from the centre; the **ferry terminal** for both domestic and international ferries – and the Jadrolinija booking office – is a few hundred metres south of here. Split **airport** is 16km west of town; Croatia Airlines buses connect with scheduled flights and run to the waterfront Riva (25kn); alternatively the #37 Split–Trogir bus runs from the main road outside the airport to the suburban bus station (13.50kn). The **tourist office** is in the Peristyle of the Palace (June–Sept Mon–Sat 9am–9pm, Sun 9am–1pm; Oct–May Mon–Fri 9am–7.30pm, Sat 9am–1pm; ☎021/355-088, ⓦwww.visitsplit.com). **Private rooms** (②) can be booked through Turist Biro, on the waterfront at Obala narodnog preporoda 12 (☎021/342-544, ⓔturist-biro-split@st.hinet.hr). Cheapest of the **hotels** are the *Slavija* at Buvinova 3 in the old town (☎021/347-053; ③), which has basic rooms, some with shower; and the slightly more comfortable *Bellevue* on the western fringes of the old town at bana Jelačića 2 (☎021/585-701; ④).

The daily **market** at the eastern edge of the old town is the place to shop for fruit, veg and local cheeses. Most **restaurants** are just outside the old town: *Ponoćno sunce*, Teutina 15, has a good range of meat and fish dishes as well as excellent salads. Further afield, *Konoba kod Joe* at Sredmanuška 4, ten minutes northeast of the old town, is an atmospheric place specializing in seafood; while *Konoba Varoš*, up behind the *Bellevue Hotel* at ban Mladenova 7, is another traditional Dalmatian restaurant. *Buffet Fife*, 500m west of the old town at Trumbićeva obala 11, offers enormous portions of cheap home cooking. For **cafés**, the busy waterfront Riva is a good spot, as is the old town, whose many small squares yield clusters of options: on Mihovilova Širina, *Song* and *Shook* are fairly upbeat places, whilst just around the corner, at Dosud 10, is the *Getto Club*, a welcome alternative to the posier establishments round about. For quieter, more reflective options, head to Majstora Jurja and, in particular, *Teak Caffe*. Other places worth trying are *Planet Jazz*, a bohemian hangout on Grgura Ninskog, and the similar *Jazz III* on Vukičovićeva. The beach at Bačvice, a few minutes' walk south past the railway station, is a popular party place in summer. For **Internet access** head to *Issa*, Dobrić 12 in the old town.

The island of Brač

BRAČ is famous for its milk-white marble, which has been used in places as diverse as Berlin's Reichstag, the high altar of Liverpool's Metropolitan Cathedral, the White House in Washington – and, of course, Diocletian's Palace. In addition to the marble, once great many islanders were once dependent on the grape harvest, though the phylloxera (vine lice) epidemics of the late nineteenth century and early twentieth century forced many of them to emigrate. Even today, as you cross Brač's interior, the signs of this depopulation are all around in the tumbledown walls and overgrown fields. The easiest way to reach Brač is by **ferry** from Split to **Supetar**, an engagingly laid-back fishing port on the north side of the island, from where it's a straightforward bus journey to **Bol**, a major windsurfing centre on the island's south coast and site of one of the Adriatic's most beautiful beaches.

Supetar

Though the largest town on the island, **SUPETAR** is a rather sleepy village onto which package tourism has been painlessly grafted. There's little of specific interest, save for several attractive shingle **beaches** which stretch west from the harbour, and the **Petrinović Mausoleum**, a neo-Byzantine confection on a wooded promontory 1km west of town, built by sculptor Toma Rosandić to honour a local businessman. Supetar's **tourist office** beside the ferry dock at Porat 1 (July & Aug daily 8am–10pm; June & Sept daily 9am–4pm; Oct–May Mon–Fri 9am–1pm; ☎021/630-551, ⓦwww.supetar.hr) has information on the whole island. **Private rooms** (②) are available from Brač Tours (☎021/757-316, ⓔbractours @hi.hinet.hr), and Atlas (☎021/631-105) on the harbourfront. The *Palute,* 1.5km west of the harbour at Put pašike 16 (☎021/631-541; ③), is a friendly **pension**, but soon fills up. The *Supetar* **campsite** is 1.5km east of the ferry dock. Best of the places to **eat** on the harbourfront is *Palute* at Porat 4, which serves good grilled fish. *Vinotoka,* just inland from the harbour at Dobova 6, has a wide range of traditional Croatian food and an extensive choice of local wines. The clear waters around Supetar are perfect for **scuba diving**; the Dive Center Kaktus in the *Kaktus Hotel* complex (☎021/630-421; closed Nov–March) rents out gear and arranges scuba and snorkelling courses (from 220kn), as well as renting out mountain bikes (110kn/day).

Bol

Stranded on the far side of the Vidova Gora mountains, there's no denying the beauty of **BOL**'s setting, or the charm of its old stone houses. However, the main attraction of the village is its beach, **Zlatni rat**, which lies to the west of the centre along the wooded shoreline. The pebbly cape juts into the sea like an extended finger, changing shape from season to season as the wind plays across it. Unsurprisingly, it does get very crowded during summer. While you're here, look in at the late-fifteenth-century **Dominican Monastery** (daily 10am–noon & 5–9pm; 10kn), dramatically perched on a bluff just east of central Bol. **Buses** from Supetar stop just west of Bol's harbour, at the far end of which stands the **tourist office** (June–Aug daily 8.30am–10pm; Sept–May Mon–Fri 8.30am–3pm; ☎021/635-638, ⓦwww.bol.hr). **Private rooms** (②) can be booked through Boltours, 100m west of the bus stop at Vladimira Nazora 18 (☎021/635-693, ⓦwww.boltours.com), or Adria, just beyond it at Vladimira Nazora 28 (☎021/635-966). There are a couple of **campsites**, the *Ranč* (☎021/635-635) and the *Meteor* (☎021/635-630), on Hrvatskih Domobrana uphill from the centre. For **eating**, there are numerous places along the waterfront, although *Gust,* above the harbour at F. Radića 14, has the widest range of traditional food. Big Blue (☎021/306-222, ⓦwww.big-blue-sport.hr), on the path leading to Zlatni rat, is the best of several **windsurfing** centres; as well as board rental (60kn/hr) and a range of courses for beginners, they also rent out sea kayaks (25kn/hr) and **mountain bikes** (110kn/day).

The island of Hvar

One of the most hyped of all the Croatian islands, **HVAR** is undeniably beautiful – a slim, green slice of land punctured by jagged inlets and cloaked with hills of spongy lavender. Tourist development hasn't been too crass, and the island's main centre, **Hvar Town**, retains much of its old Venetian charm. At least one daily **ferry** from Split arrives at Hvar Town itself; numerous others head for Stari Grad, 4km east, from where buses run into Hvar Town.

The best view of **HVAR TOWN** is from the sea, the tiny town hugging the bay, grainy-white and brown with green splashes of palms and pines bursting from every crack and cranny. At the centre, the main square is flanked to the south by the arcaded bulk of the Venetian arsenal, the upper storey of which was added in 1612 to house a **theatre** (daily: summer 9am–1pm & 5–11pm; winter 11am–noon; 10kn), the oldest in Croatia and one of the first in Europe. The theatre has since been converted to a cinema, but its painted Baroque interior has survived pretty much intact. At the eastern end of the square is Hvar's **cathedral** (usually open mornings), a sixteenth-century construction with an eighteenth-century facade that's a characteristic mixture of Gothic and Renaissance styles. Inside is routine enough, but the **Bishop's Treasury** (daily: summer 9am–noon & 5–7pm; winter 10am–noon; 10kn) is worth the entry fee for its small but fine selection of chalices and reliquaries. The rest of the old town stretches back from the piazza in an elegant confusion of twisting lanes and alleys. Up above, the **fortress** (daily: May–Sept daily 8am–dusk; 10kn) is a good example of sixteenth-century military architecture. The views over Hvar and the islands beyond are well worth the trek to the top. From the fort you can pick out the fifteenth-century **Franciscan Monastery** (summer Mon–Fri 10am–noon & 5–7pm; winter 10am–noon; 10kn), to the left of the harbour; next door, the monastic **church** is pleasingly simple, with beautifully carved choir stalls.

The **beaches** nearest to town are rocky and crowded, and it's best to make your way towards the **Pakleni otoci**, just to the west. Easily reached by water taxi from the harbour (about 15kn each way), the Pakleni are a chain of eleven wooded islands, three of which cater for tourists with simple bars and restaurants: Jerolim island is the nearest; next is Marinkovac; then Sv Klement, the largest of the islands. Bear in mind that camping is forbidden throughout Pakleni.

Practicalities

Hvar Town's **tourist office** (July & Aug daily 8am–2pm & 3–10pm; June & Sept Mon–Sat 8am–1pm & 4–9pm, Sun 10am–noon & 6–8pm; Oct–May Mon–Sat 8am–1pm; ☏021/741-059, ⊛www.hvar.hr) is on the waterfront below the theatre. For **private rooms** (❸), head for the Mengola agency, also on the harbour (☏021/742-099, ⊛www.mengola.hr), or Pelegrin, by the ferry dock (☏021/742-743, ⊜pelegrin@inet.hr). The **hotels** *Dalmacija*, on the eastern side of the harbour (☏021/741-120, ⊛www.suncanihvar.hr; ❻), and the *Delfin*, over on the western side (☏021/741-168; ❻), are as reasonable as you'll get here. The *Milna* **campsite** (☏021/745-027) is 3km southeast of town on Milna Bay – most Hvar Town–Stari Grad buses drop off nearby. There are dozens of **restaurants** in Hvar Town, none of which is too expensive. *Marinero*, behind the Mengola travel agency at Vinka Pribojevića bb, next to the *Delfin hotel*, dishes up cheap seafood in a candlelit courtyard; while *Hanibal*, on the main square, has a slightly pricier, but wider ranging menu. *Macondo*, signposted in a backstreet uphill from the harbour, is the best place for meat and fish. For **drinking**, there are several cafés and bars around the harbour: *Loco*, *Gromit* and *Carpe Diem* are three of the best.

The island of Vis

Compact, humpy, and at first glance a little forbidding, **VIS** is situated further offshore than any other of Croatia's inhabited Adriatic islands. Closed to foreigners for military reasons until 1989, the island has never been overrun by tourists, and even now depends much more heavily on independent tourism than its package-oriented neighbours. Croatia's bohemian youth seem to have fallen in love with the place over the last decade, drawn by its wild mountainous scenery, two good-looking towns, **Vis Town** and **Komiža**, and a brace of fine wines, including the white Vugava and the red Viški plavac. Ferries and, in summer, hydrofoils from Split arrive at Vis Town, from where buses depart for Komiža on the western side of the island.

Vis Town

VIS TOWN is attractively sited, a sedate arc of grey-brown houses on a deeply indented bay, above which looms a steep escarpment covered with the remains of abandoned agricultural terraces. The most attractive parts of town are east of the ferry landing in the suburb of **Kut**, a largely sixteenth-century tangle of narrow cobbled streets overlooked by the summer houses built by nobles from Hvar. A kilometre further on lies a small British war cemetery, and just behind it, a wonderful pebbly **beach**. Heading west around the bay soon brings you to a small peninsula, from which the campanile of the Franciscan **monastery of St Hieronymous** rises gracefully alongside a huddle of cypresses. The **tourist office** (May–Sept Mon–Sat 9am–1pm & 6–9pm; Oct–April Mon–Fri 9am–1pm; ☎021/717-114, ⊛www .tz-vis.hr) is just to the right of the ferry dock. **Private rooms** (❷) can be booked through Ionios, Obala Sv Jurja 37 (☎021/711-531, ✉ionios@st.hinet.hr). Best of the **hotels** are the stately turn-of-the-century *Tamaris*, on the waterfront at Obala Sv Jurja 20 (☎021/711-350; ❺), and the smaller, pension-like *Paula*, at Petra Hektorovića 2 (☎021/711-362, ✉paula_hotel@st.tel.hr; ❹) in Kut. *Pizzeria Katerina* near the ferry dock is good for a quick bite; while *Pojoda* and *Vatrica*, both in Kut, are worth splashing out on for sumptuous seafood.

Komiža

KOMIŽA, 10km from Vis Town, is the island's main fishing port – a compact town with a palm-fringed seafront on one side and a ring of mountains on the other. Dominating the southern end of the harbour is the **Kaštel**, a stubby sixteenth-century fortress which now holds a **Fishing Museum** (June–Sept Mon–Sat 10am–noon & 7–10pm, Sun 7–10pm; 10kn). Komiža's nicest **beaches** are a further ten minutes south of the museum, where you'll find a sequence of pebbly coves. Each morning small boats leave Komiža harbour for the nearby island of Biševo in order to visit the so-called **Blue Cave**. A grotto filled with eery shimmering light, it's well worth seeing – expect to pay 100–120kn for the trip. **Buses** from Vis Town terminate about 100m behind the harbour, from where it's a short walk southwards to the **tourist office** (July & Aug Mon–Sat 8am–noon & 6–10pm; rest of year Mon–Fri 8am–1pm; ☎021/713-455), on the Riva just beyond the Kaštel. The town's **hotel**, the *Biševo* (☎021/713-095; ❺), is at the northern end of the bay, and there are **private rooms** (❷) available through Darlić & Darlić, on the harbourfront (☎021/717 205, ⊛www.darlic-travel.hr), and Srebrnatours at Ribarska 4 (☎021/713 668, ✉sandra.vitaljic@st.tel.hr). There are a couple of pizzerias on the harbour, and one very good seafood **restaurant**, *Bako*, just off Ribarska. For **drinking**, head for the tiny main square, Škor, which is ringed by lively café-bars.

The island of Korčula

Like so many islands along this coast, **KORČULA** was first settled by the Greeks, who gave it the name Korkyra Melaina or "Black Corfu" for its dark and densely wooded appearance. Even now, it's one of the greenest of the Adriatic islands, and one of the most popular. The island's main settlement is **Korčula Town**, and the rest of the island, although beautifully wild, lacks any real centres. The main coastal **ferry** docks at Korčula Town harbour. In addition, local ferries travel daily between Split and Vela Luka at the western end of Korčula island, from where there's a connecting bus service to Korčula Town. There's also a **bus service** from Dubrovnik, which crosses the narrow stretch of water dividing the island from the mainland by ferry from Orebić.

KORČULA TOWN sits on a beetle-shaped hump of land, a medieval walled city ribbed with a series of narrow streets that branch off the spine of the main street like the veins of a leaf. The Venetians first arrived here in the eleventh century, and stayed, on and off, for nearly eight centuries. Their influence is particularly evident in Korčula's old town, which huddles around the **Cathedral of St Mark**, squeezed into a space between the buildings that roughly passes for a main square. The cathedral facade is decorated with a gorgeous fluted rose window and a bizarre cornice frilled with strange gargoyles. The interior, reached through a door framed by statues of Adam and Eve, is one of the loveliest in the region – a curious mixture of styles, ranging from the Gothic forms of the nave to the Renaissance northern aisle, tacked on in the sixteenth century. The best of the church's treasures have been removed to the **Bishop's Treasury** (July & August: daily 10am–noon & 5–7pm; at other times enquire at the tourist office; 10kn), a couple of doors down. This small collection of fine and sacral art is one of the best in the country, with an exquisite set of paintings, including a striking *Portrait of a Man* by Carpaccio and a Leonardo da Vinci sketch of a soldier wearing a costume bearing a striking resemblance to that of the Moreška dancers (see below). Opposite the treasury, a former Venetian palace holds the **Town Museum** (July & August daily 9am–1pm & 5–7pm; rest of year Mon–Sat 9am–1pm; 10kn), whose more modest display contains a plaster cast of a fourth-century BC Greek tablet from Lumbarda – the earliest evidence of civilization on Korčula. Close by the main square, down a turning to the right, is another remnant from Venetian times, the so-called **House of Marco Polo** (summer daily 10am–1pm & 5–7pm; 10kn). Korčula claims to be the birthplace of Marco Polo, although it seems unlikely that he had any connection with this seventeenth-century house, which these days is little more than an empty shell with some terrible twentieth-century prints.

Your best bet for **beaches** is to head off by **water taxi** from the old harbour to one of the **Skoji** islands just offshore. The largest and nearest of these is **Badija**, where there are some secluded rocky beaches, a couple of snack bars and a naturist section. There's also a sandy beach just beyond the village of **Lumbarda**, 8km south of Korčula (reached by hourly bus in the summer).

Practicalities

Korčula's **bus station** is 400m southeast of the old town. Work your way round to the northwestern side of the peninsula to find the **tourist office** (June–Sept Mon–Sat 8am–8pm, Sun 8am–3pm; Oct–May Mon–Sat 8am–noon & 5–8pm; ☎021/715-701; ⓦwww.korcula.net). **Private rooms** (❸) are handled by Marko Polo (☎020/715-400, ⓔmarko-polo-tours@du.tel.hr), whose office is between the bus station and the entrance to the old town. Cheapest of the **hotels** is the *Badija*, accessible by taxi boat from the harbour (☎020/711-115; ❸), a spartan but idyllically situated place in a former Franciscan monastery on Badija. The *Park* is a package-tour-oriented place in a bay southeast of the centre (☎020/726-004; ❻). The nearest **campsite** is *Autocamp Kalac* (☎020/711-182), about 3km southeast of town and reached by hourly buses for Lumbarda. Not surprisingly, most **restaurants** in the old town tend to be expensive. One exception is the excellent *Adio Mare*, near Marco Polo's House and justifiably popular; arrive early to get a table. Another good choice is *Gradski Podrum*, just inside the main gate of the old town. A cheaper and more functional alternative is *Planjak* at Plokata 21. Wherever you eat, do try some of the excellent **local wines**: the delicious dry white Grk from Lumbarda, Posip from Smokvica, or the headache-inducing red Dingač from Postup on Peljesac. Performances of Korčula's famous **folk dance**, the Moreška, take place outside the main gate to the old town in summer every Thursday evening (tickets from Marko Polo; 50kn). This frantic, sword-based dance is the story of a conflict between the Christians (in red) and the Moors (in black): the heroine, Bula, is kidnapped by the evil foreign king and his army, and her betrothed tries to win her back in a ritualized sword fight which takes place within a shifting circle of dancers.

Dubrovnik

DUBROVNIK is a beautifully preserved medieval fortified city. First settled by Roman refugees in the early seventh century and given the name Ragusa, the town soon exploited its favourable position on the Adriatic with a maritime and commercial genius unmatched anywhere else in Europe. By the mid-fourteenth century, having shaken off the yoke of first the Byzantines and then the Venetians, it had become a successful and self-contained city state, its merchants trading far and wide. Dubrovnik fended off the attentions of the Ottoman Empire and continued to

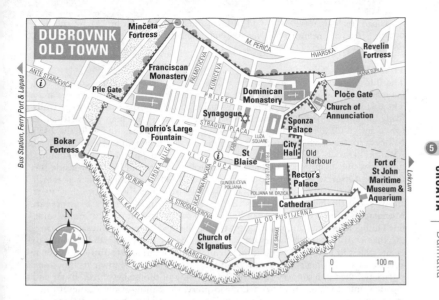

prosper until 1667, when an earthquake devastated the city. Though the city-state survived, it fell into decline and, in 1808, was formally dissolved by Napoleon. An eight-month siege by Yugoslav forces in the early 1990s caused much destruction, but the city swiftly recovered. The prestigious **Summer Festival** (July 10 to Aug 25; ☎020/412-288, ⊛www.dubrovnik-festival.hr) is a good, if crowded, time to be around, with classical concerts and theatre performances in most of the city's court-yards, squares and bastions. Book tickets well in advance.

Arrival, information and accommodation

The **ferry and bus terminals** are located in the port suburb of Gruž, 3km west of town. The main western entrance to the old town, the Pile Gate, is a thirty-minute slog along ul Ante Starčevića; you'd be better off catching a bus – #1a and #3 from the ferry terminal; #1a, #3 or #6 from behind the bus station. Tickets for local buses are bought from the driver (10kn; exact change only) or from newspaper kiosks (7kn). The main **tourist office** is in the old town at Miha Pracata bb (daily: summer 8am–8pm; winter 9am–4pm; ☎020/323-587, ⊛www.tzdubrovnik.hr), although there are branches just up from Pile Gate at Ante Starčevića 7 (same hours), and opposite the ferry terminal in Gruž (same hours). **Private rooms** (③) can be booked through Gulliver, opposite the ferry terminal at Obala Stjepana Radića 32 (☎020/313-300, ⊛www.gulliver.hr); and Dubrovnikturist, 100m east of the bus station at put Republike 7 (☎020/356-959, ⊛www.dubrovnikturist.hr). There's a basic, well-run **HI hostel** at bana Jelačića 15/17 (☎020/423-241, ✉dubrovnik@hfhs.hr; 90kn per person) – head up Ante Starčevića from the bus station and turn uphill to the right after five minutes. *Vila Micika*, Mata Vodopica 10, Lapad (bus #6 to Lapad post office; ☎020/437-332, ✉booking-vila-micika@email.hinet.hr; ③) is a family-run **pension** offering hostel-style arrangements (a bed in a clean and comfortable 2- or 3-person room) as well as bright en-suite doubles. Affordable **hotels** are in short supply: the *Petka*, opposite the ferry terminal at Obala Stjepan Radića 38 (☎020/418-008, ✉hotel-petka@du.hinet.hr; ⑤); the *Lero*, 1.5km west of Pile Gate at Iva Vojnovića 14 (☎020/332-122, ⊛www.hotel-lero.hr; ⑥), and the *Zagreb*, Šetalište kralja Zvonimira

31, Lapad (bus #6; ☎020/431-011, ✉hot-sumratin@du.hinet.hr; ✆) are the best options. The free, monthly *DubrovnikGuide*, available from hotels and the tourist office, lists bus and ferry timetables as well as forthcoming events.

The City

The **Pile Gate**, main entrance to the old town, is a fifteenth-century construction complete with a statue of St Blaise, the city's protector, set in a niche above the arch. The best way to get your bearings is by making a tour of the fabulous **city walls** (daily: summer 9am–7.30pm; winter 10am–3pm; 15kn), 25m high and with all its towers intact. Of the various towers and bastions that punctuate the walls, the 1455 **Minčeta fortress**, which marks the northeastern side, is by far the most imposing.

Within the walls, Dubrovnik is a sea of roofs faded into a pastel patchwork, punctured now and then by a sculpted dome or tower. At ground level, just inside the Pile Gate, **Onofrio's Large Fountain**, built in 1444, is a domed affair at which visitors to this hygiene-conscious city had to wash themselves before they were allowed any further. Across the street is the fourteenth-century **Franciscan Monastery** complex (free access); its treasury (daily 9am–4pm; 5kn) holds some fine Gothic reliquaries and manuscripts tracing the development of musical scoring, together with relics from the apothecary's shop, dating from 1317 and claiming to be the oldest in Europe. From outside the monastery church, **Stradun** (also known as Placa), the city's main street, runs dead straight across the old town, its limestone surface polished to a slippery shine by the tramping of thousands of feet. Its far end broadens into the pigeon-choked **Luža Square**, the centre of the medieval town and even today hub of much of its activity. On the left, the **Sponza Palace** was once the customs house and mint, with a facade that's an elegant weld of florid Venetian Gothic and more sedate Renaissance forms; its majestic courtyard is given over to contemporary art exhibitions. Across the square, the Baroque-style **Church of St Blaise**, built in 1714 to replace an earlier church, serves as a graceful counterpoint to the palace. Outside the church stands the carved figure of an armoured knight, known as **Orlando's Column** and once the focal point of the city-state. On the eastern side of the square a Gothic arch leads through to an alley which winds past the **Dominican monastery**. Here, an arcaded courtyard filled with palms and orange trees leads to a small **museum** (daily 9am–5pm; 10kn), with outstanding examples of local sixteenth-century religious art. Back on Luža, a street leads round the back of St Blaise towards the fifteenth-century **Rector's Palace**, the seat of the Ragusan government, in which the incumbent Rector sat out his month's term of office. Today it's given over to the **City Museum** (summer daily 9am–7pm; winter Mon–Sat 9am–1pm; 15kn), though for the most part it's a rather paltry collection, with mediocre sixteenth-century paintings and dull furniture.

Immediately south of the Rector's Palace, Dubrovnik's seventeenth-century **cathedral** is a rather plain building, although there's an impressive Titian polyptych of *The Assumption* inside. The **Treasury** (Mon–Sat 8am–5pm, Sun 11am–5pm; 5kn) boasts a twelfth-century reliquary containing the skull of St Blaise; an exquisite piece in the shape of a Byzantine crown, the reliquary is stuck with portraits of saints and frosted with delicate gold and enamel filigree work. From the cathedral, it's a short walk through to the small harbour, dominated by the monolithic hulk of the **Fort of St John**, which now houses a downstairs **aquarium** (summer: daily 10am–8pm; winter: Mon–Sat 10am–1pm; 15kn); upstairs is the **maritime museum** (summer daily 9am–7pm; winter Tues–Sun 9am–1pm; 15kn), which traces the history of Ragusan sea power through a display of naval artefacts and model boats. Walking back east from here, you skirt one of the city's oldest quarters, **Pustijerna**, much of which predates the seventeenth-century earthquake. On the far side, the **Church of St Ignatius**, Dubrovnik's largest, is a Jesuit confection, modelled, like most Jesuit places of worship, on the enormous church of Gesù in Rome. The steps that lead down from here also had a Roman model – the Spanish Steps – and they sweep down to **Gunduliceva Poljana**, the square behind the cathedral which is the site of the city's morning fruit and vegetable market.

The noisy and crowded main city **beach** is a short walk east of the old town; a better bet is to head for the less crowded, and somewhat cleaner, beach on the Lapad peninsula, 5km to the west, or to catch one of the **boats** from the old city jetty (April–Oct 9am–6pm, every 30min, journey time 10min; 30kn return) to the wooded island of **Lokrum**. Crisscrossed by shady paths overhung by pines, Lokrum has some extensive rocky beaches running along the eastern end of the island, and there's a nudist section (FKK) at the far eastern tip.

Eating and drinking

For self-catering, there are morning fruit-and-vegetable **markets** (not Sun) on Gundulićeva Poljana. For **snacks**, try the sandwich bars lining the alleys running uphill from Stradun, the best of which is *Kaktus* on Vetranovićeva. *Express Restaurant*, Kaboge 1, is a decent self-service canteen with vegetarian options. There's no shortage of **restaurants** in the old town, though many on Prijeko, the street running parallel to Stradun to the north, make too much of a hard sell, which is generally offputting: head instead for *Kamenica*, at Gundulićeva poljana 8, a simple place serving up cheap portions of *girice* (tiny deep-fried fish) and *kamenice* (oysters); or *Ekvinocijo*, a family-run seafood eatery at Ilije Sarake 10; alternatively, there's *Konoba Posat*, uz Posat 1, a large garden terrace just outside the Pile Gate which is good for grilled meats.

The pavement cafés at the eastern end of Stradun are popular spots for daytime and evening drinking, but for something with a bit more character, head for the smaller **café-bars** in the backstreets: *Hard Jazz Café Troubadur*, on Bunićeva Poljana, has live jazz most nights; *Buža*, Iza Mira, is an atmospheric outdoor bar perched on rocks beside the city walls; and *Irish Pub Karaka*, Između polača 5, will satisfy those seeking a more beery evening. Outside the centre, ulica bana Jelačića, just above the bus station, is lined with bars buzzing until late on summer evenings. For **clubbing**, *Latino Club Fuego*, outside the Pile Gate, and *Esperanza*, near the bus station at Put Republike 30, are mainstream places. Live music and themed disco nights take place at the Karantena, a cultural centre just beyond Pile Gate on Frana Supila.

Listings

Consulates UK, Petilovrijenci 2 ☏311-466.
Exchange Dubrovačka Banka, Stradun (Mon–Fri 7.30am–1pm & 2–7pm, Sat 7.30am–1pm); Gospodarsko-Kreditna Banka, Pile Gate (daily 8am–8pm).
Hospital Roka Mišetiča bb ☏431-777.
Internet access Dubrovnik Internet Centar, Brsalje 1 (daily 10am–10pm; 20kn/hr); Internet, Prijeko 15 (Mon–Sat 10am–10pm; 20kn/hr).
Left luggage At the bus station (daily 5am–9.30pm).
Pharmacy Kod Zvonika, Stradun (24hr).
Post office A. Starčevića 2 (Mon–Fri 7am–9pm, Sat 7am–7pm, Sun 9am–2pm).

Travel details

Trains

Pula to: Zagreb (2 daily; 6hr 40min).
Zagreb to: Pula (2 daily; 6hr 40min); Rijeka (6 daily; 4hr); Split (July & Aug 2 daily; Sept–June 1 daily; 9hr).

Hvar Town to: Starigrad (7 daily; 35min).
Poreč to: Rijeka (5 daily; 2hr 30min); Pula (9 daily; 2hr); Zagreb (7 daily; 7hr).
Pula to: Dubrovnik (1 daily; 14hr); Poreč (8 daily; 2hr); Rijeka (hourly; 2hr 30min); Rovinj (12 daily; 1hr); Split (3 daily; 10hr); Zagreb (12 daily; 6hr).
Rijeka to: Dubrovnik (4 daily; 13hr); Pula (hourly; 2hr 30min); Split (4 daily; 8hr); Zagreb (hourly; 4hr).
Rovinj to: Poreč (8 daily; 45min); Pula (12 daily; 1hr); Rijeka (8 daily; 5hr).

Buses

Dubrovnik to: Korčula (1 daily; 3hr 30min); Rijeka (6 daily); Split (15 daily; 4hr 30min); Zagreb (8 daily; 11hr).

Split to: Dubrovnik (hourly; 4hr 30min); Pula (3 daily; 10hr); Rijeka (12 daily; 8hr); Zagreb (hourly; 7-9hr).

Supetar to: Bol (5 daily; 1hr).

Vis Town to: Komiža (5 daily; 25min).

Zadar to: Dubrovnik (9 daily; 8hr 30min); Pula (4 daily; 6hr); Rijeka (13 daily; 4hr 30min); Split (hourly; 3hr 30min); Zagreb (hourly; 5hr).

Zagreb to: Dubrovnik (6 daily; 11hr); Poreč (8 daily; 5hr); Pula (12 daily; 6hr); Rijeka (hourly; 4hr); Rovinj (5 daily; 9hr); Split (hourly; 7–9hr).

Ferries

Services from Dubrovnik and Rijeka run daily in summer and twice weekly at other times.

Brač to: Split (7 daily; 1hr).

Dubrovnik to: Korčula (4hr); Hvar Stari Grad (7hr); Rijeka (21hr); Split (9hr); Zadar (15hr).

Hvar Town to: Korčula (2 weekly; 45min); Split (1 daily; 2hr); Vis (1 weekly; 1hr 15min).

Hvar Stari Grad to: Split (3–5 daily; 2hr).

Korčula to: Hvar (2 weekly; 45min); Split (1–2 daily; 3hr).

Rijeka to: Split (12hr); Hvar Stari Grad (14hr); Korčula (18hr); Dubrovnik (20hr); Zadar (6hr).

Split to: Dubrovnik (1 daily; 9hr); Hvar Town (1 daily; 2hr); Hvar Stari Grad: (3–5 daily; 2hr); Korčula (1–2 daily; 3hr); Rijeka (1 daily; 12hr); Supetar (7 daily; 1hr); Vis (1–2 daily; 2hr 30min); Zadar (summer 1 daily; winter 2 weekly; 5hr 15min).

Vis to: Hvar (1 weekly; 1hr 15min); Split (1–2 daily; 2hr 30min).

Czech Republic

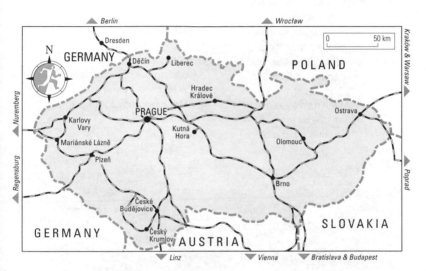

Czech Republic highlights

* **Prague Castle** Home to the cathedral, royal palace and numerous art galleries, with great views across the city. See p.237

* **Obecní dům, Prague** The city's finest Art Nouveau building, housing two restaurants, a café, bar, art gallery and concert hall. See p.240

* **Český Krumlov** A gem of a medieval town, tucked into a bend of the River Vltava. See p.243

* **Brewery, Plzeň** Take a tour of the Pilsner Urquell brewery, home of the world's first lager. See p.244

* **Moravian karst region** Limestone region of caves, chasms and underground rivers, easily reached from the Moravian capital, Brno. See p.248

Introduction and basics

Czechoslovakia's "Velvet Revolution" of 1989 was the most unequivocally positive of Eastern Europe's anti-Communist upheavals, as the Czechs and Slovaks shrugged off 41 years of Communist rule without a shot being fired. But the euphoria and unity of those first few months evaporated more quickly than anyone could have imagined. Just three years on, the country split into two separate states: the **Czech Republic** and Slovakia. The Czechs – always the most urbane, agnostic and liberal of the Slav nations – have fared well, although they have had to contend with rising crime and an increasing cost of living. The country is due to accede to the European Union in May 2004. For coverage of Slovakia, see Chapter 25.

Almost untouched by the wars of the twentieth century, the Czech capital **Prague** is justifiably one of the most popular destinations in Europe. An incredibly beautiful city with a wealth of architecture, from Gothic cathedrals and Baroque palaces to Art Nouveau cafés and Cubist villas, it's also a lively meeting place for young people from all over Europe. The rolling countryside of **Bohemia** is swathed in forests and studded with well-preserved medieval towns and castles, especially in the south around **České Budějovice**. In the west, you'll find the old watering holes of the European aristocracy, the spa towns of **Karlovy Vary** and **Mariánské Lázně**. The country's eastern province, **Moravia**, is every bit as beautiful, only less touristed. **Olomouc** is the most attractive town here, but **Brno**, the regional capital, has its own pleasures and lies within easy reach of Moravia's spectacular **karst region**.

Information & maps

Most cities and towns have their own **tourist offices** (*informační centrum*), where you should find at least one English-speaker. A comprehensive range of **maps** is available.

You can buy them, often very cheaply, from bookshops, petrol stations and some hotels – ask for a *plán města* (town plan) or *mapa okolí* (regional map). For hiking, Shocart produces a 1:50,000 *turistická mapa* series detailing the country's complex network of marked footpaths, as well as a 1:75,000 *cykloturistické* series, and a 1:100,000 series.

Money and banks

The local currency is the Czech **crown**, or *koruna česká* (Kč), which is divided into one hundred hellers or *haléř* (h). There are coins of 10h, 20h and 50h, plus 1Kč, 2Kč, 5Kč, 10Kč, 20Kč and 50Kč; and notes of 20Kč, 50Kč, 100Kč, 200Kč, 500Kč, 1000Kč and 2000Kč (less frequently 5000Kč). The crown is fully convertible, though you may still find problems getting hold of any in foreign banks. **Banks** are the best places to change money and are normally open Mon–Fri 8am–5pm. Given the abundance of **ATMs**, credit and debit cards are a cheaper and more convenient way of carrying funds than **travellers' cheques**, though it's a good idea to keep some hard currency in cash for emergencies.

The Czech Republic on the net

ⓦ **www.czech.cz** Basic information on the whole country.

ⓦ **www.pis.cz** Prague's tourist office site.

ⓦ **www.praguepost.com** Online version of the capital's own English-language paper.

ⓦ **www.radio.cz/english** Updated news and cultural features.

ⓦ **www.ticketpro.cz**, ⓦ **www.ticketstream.cz**, ⓦ **www.ticketsbti.cz** Three good sites for finding out what's on in Prague and booking tickets online.

Communications

Most **post offices** (*pošta*) are open Mon–Fri 8am–5pm, Sat 8am–noon. Look for the right sign to avoid queuing unnecessarily: *známky* (stamps), *dopisy* (letters) or *balky* (parcels). You can buy stamps from newsagents, tobacconists and kiosks, as well as at post offices. The majority of public **phones** only take phonecards (*telefonní karty*), available from post offices, tobacconists and some shops. You can make local and international calls from all card phones, all of which have instructions in English. You'll find at least one **Internet café** in almost every major Czech town; charges are usually 50–100Kč/hr.

Getting around

The most pleasant way of travelling around the Czech Republic is by **train** (*vlak*) – it's scenic, safe and inexpensive, although fares are gradually creeping up. If you're in a hurry, however, **buses** (*autobusy*) are nearly always quicker and more frequent. A useful **website** for times and information is ⓦwww.vlak.cz.

The Czech Republic has one of the most comprehensive **rail** networks in Europe. Czech Railways (České dráhy or ČD; ⓦwww.cd.cz) runs two main types of **trains**: *rychlík* (R) or *spěšný* (Sp) trains are the faster ones which stop only at major towns, while *osobní* trains stop at just about every station, averaging as little as 30kph. Fast trains are further divided into SuperCity (SC), which are first class only, EuroCity (EC) or InterCity (IC), for which you need to pay a supplement, and Expres (Ex), for which you don't. **Tickets** (*jízdenky*) for domestic journeys can be bought at the station (*nádraží*) before or on the day of departure. ČD runs reasonably priced **sleepers** to and from a number of cities in neighbouring countries, for which you must book as far in advance as possible and in any case no later than six hours before departure. **InterRail** and **EuroDomino** passes are valid in the Czech Republic; **Eurail** passes are not.

Regional **buses** – mostly run by the state bus company, Česká státní automobilová doprava (ČSAD) – travel to most destinations, with private companies such as

ČEBUS providing an alternative on popular intercity routes. Bus stations are usually next to the train station, and if there's no separate terminal you'll have to buy your ticket from the driver. It's essential to book your ticket at least a day in advance if you're travelling at the weekend, on a public holiday or early in the morning on one of the main routes.

Accommodation

Accommodation remains the most expensive aspect of travelling in the Czech Republic. There is no organized hostel system, as such, though some places are now affiliated with Hostelling International (HI). Private rooms are available all over the country, and more often than not the local tourist office will help to book a room. To book accommodation **online**, try ⓦwww.avetravel .cz or ⓦwww.marys.cz.

Hotels are still occasionally priced up for foreigners and are in any case fairly expensive, especially in Prague. Most old state hotels have been refurbished by their new owners, and many new hotels and pensions have opened, particularly in the more heavily touristed areas. In the newer places, continental or buffet-style breakfast is normally included. Ignore the star system as it is no guarantee of quality, service or atmosphere. With ongoing privatization, refurbishment and renovation work, make it a rule to check hotel prices before you book.

Private rooms are available in Prague, Brno and several other towns on the tourist trail, and are a good bet, though not as widespread as they used to be. Elsewhere, just keep your eyes peeled for signs saying *Zimmer Frei*. Prices start at around 300Kč per person per night, but expect to pay more in Prague.

Prague now has a number of **hostels**, which offer varying degrees of discomfort. The student travel organization CKM at Mánesova 77 in Prague (☏222 721 595, ⓦwww.ckm.cz) can arrange cheap **student accommodation** in the big university towns during July and August and usually charge from 250Kč per person for dorm beds. The KMC (Club of Young Travellers), at Karolíny Světlé 30 in Prague (☏222 220 347,

6

CZECH REPUBLIC | Basics

www.kmc.cz), is an umbrella organization for youth hostels throughout the Republic who can help organize accommodation for you.

Campsites, known as *autokemp*, are plentiful all over the Republic; the facilities are often basic and the ones known as *tábořiště* are even more rudimentary. Most have simple **chalets** (*chaty* or *bungolovy*) for anything upwards of 500Kč for two people. Very few sites remain open all year, and most don't open until May, closing sometime in September. Although prices are sometimes inflated for foreigners, camping charges remain minimal.

Food and drink

The good news is that you can eat and drink very cheaply in the Czech Republic. The bad news is that forty years of culinary isolation and centralization under the Communists introduced few innovations to **Czech cuisine**, with its predilection for pork, gravy, dumplings and pickled cabbage. Still, washed down with divine Czech beer, anything tastes good.

Despite the recent arrival of cereals into Czech homes, the whole concept of **breakfast** (*snídaně*) as such is alien to the Czechs, though in hotels and pensions you'll probably get the standard coffee, roll and cheese or salami. Popular street **snacks** include *bramborák*, a potato pancake with flecks of bacon, *párek*, a frankfurter dipped in mustard or ketchup and shoved in a white roll, and *smažený sýr* – a slab of melted cheese fried in breadcrumbs and served in a roll (*v housce*) with tartar sauce. More and more Czech cafés have proper espresso machines serving half-decent **coffee** (*káva*); elsewhere, the Czechs drink Turkish-style or *turecká*, with grains at the bottom of the cup. The **cake shop** (*cukrárna*) is an important part of the country's social life, particularly on Sundays when it's often the only place that's open, although the cakes aren't up to Austrian standards.

Restaurants (*restaurace*) are on the whole inexpensive and always display their menus and prices outside. They serve hot meals from about 11am until 11pm. Most **pubs** (*pivnice*) also serve a menu of basic hot dishes, as do **wine cellars** (*vinárna*) – often the most stylish places around. Most lunchtime menus start with **soup** (*polévka*), one of the country's culinary strong points. **Main courses** are overwhelmingly based on pork (*vepřový*) or beef (*hovězí*), but one treat is carp (*kapr*), traditional at Christmas and cheaply and widely offered just about everywhere, along with trout (*pstruh*). Goose (*husa*), duck (*kachna*) and wild boar (*kančí maso*) dishes are also generally delicious. Main courses are served with different varieties of **dumpling** (*knedlíky*) or **vegetables**, most commonly potatoes (*brambory*) and sauerkraut (*zelí*). With the exception of *palačinky* (pancakes), filled with chocolate or fruit and cream, fruit dumplings (*ovocné knedlíky*) and ice cream, **desserts** can be pretty uninspiring.

Drink

Even the simplest *bufet* (self-service cafeteria) in the Czech Republic almost invariably has beer (*pivo*) on draught. The **pub** (*pivnice*), most of which close around 11pm, is still a predominantly male affair, with heavy drinking the norm; **wine bars** (*vinárna*) and restaurants are generally far more upmarket, and **cocktail bars** have opened up in most main towns.

The Czech Republic tops the world league table of **beer** consumption, even beating the Germans – hardly surprising since its beer ranks among the best in the world. The most natural starting point for any beer tour is the Bohemian city of **Plzeň** (Pilsen), whose local lager is the original Pils. The other big brewing town is **České Budějovice** (Budweis), home to Budvar, a mild beer by Bohemian standards but still leagues ahead of the American Budweiser. The burgeoning in-house breweries offer some great brews, as do the hundreds of small breweries dotted around the country. There's also a modest selection of medium-quality **wines**; the largest wine-producing region is southern Moravia. The home-production of firewater is a national pastime, resulting in some almost terminally strong concoctions, most famously a plum brandy called *slivovice*. The best-known Czech **spirit** is Becherovka, a medicinal herbal tipple from Karlovy Vary, known as a *beton* when ordered with ice and tonic.

Opening hours and holidays

Shops are open Mon–Fri 9am–5pm, with some, especially in Prague, and most supermarkets, staying open till 6pm or later. Smaller shops close for lunch between noon and 2pm, while others stay open late on Thurs. In larger towns, some shops stay open all day at weekends, and the **corner shop** (*večerka*) stays open daily till 11pm. **Public holidays** include Jan 1; Easter Mon; May 1; May 8; July 5 & 6; Sept 28; Oct 28; Nov 17; Dec 24, 25 & 26.

Emergencies

In the last decade, public confidence in the **police** (*policie*) has declined as the crime level has risen. For tourists, theft from cars is the biggest worry, although pickpockets are as rife in the centre of Prague as in any European capital, particularly in the Old Town Square, on the #22 tram, in the metro and in the main railway stations. Although everyone is obliged to carry some form of ID and you should theoretically carry your **passport** with you at all times, you're highly unlikely to get stopped unless you're driving a car bearing foreign plates or if you are non-white, so you may choose to leave your ID in the hotel safe.

Minor ailments can be easily dealt with at a **pharmacy** (*lékárna*), but language is likely to be a problem outside the capital. If it's a repeat prescription you want, take any empty bottles or remaining pills along with you. If the pharmacist can't help, they'll be able to direct you to a **hospital** (*nemocnice*). If you have to pay for any medication, keep the receipts for claiming on your insurance once you're home.

Emergency numbers

Police ☎158; fire ☎150; ambulance ☎155.

Prague (Praha)

PRAGUE (Praha) is one of the least "eastern" European cities you could imagine. Architecturally it is a revelation: few other cities anywhere in Europe look so good, and no other European capital can present six hundred years of architecture so untouched by war or – until severe floods hit the city in 2002 – natural disaster. Fortunately, the floods seem not to have inflicted any lasting damage.

Prague rose to prominence in the ninth century under Prince Bořivoj, its first Christian ruler and founder of the Přemyslid dynasty. His grandson, Prince Václav, became the **Good "King" Wenceslas** of the Christmas carol and the country's patron saint. The city prospered from its position on the central European trade routes, but it was after the dynasty died out in 1306 that Prague enjoyed its **golden age**. In just thirty years Holy Roman Emperor Charles IV transformed it into one of the most important cities in fourteenth-century Europe, founding an entire new town, Nové Město, to accommodate the influx of students. Following the execution of the reformist preacher Jan Hus in 1415, the country became engulfed in **religious wars**, and trouble broke out again between the Protestant nobles and the Catholic Habsburgs in 1618. The full force of the Counter-Reformation was brought to bear on the city's people, though the spurt of Baroque rebuilding that went with it gave Prague its most striking architectural aspect.

After two centuries as little more than a provincial town in the Habsburg Empire, Prague was dragged out of the doldrums by the **Industrial Revolution** and the **národní obrození**, the Czech national revival that led to the foundation of the **First Republic** in 1918. Shortly after World War II, which it survived substantially unscathed, Prague disappeared completely behind the Iron Curtain. The city briefly re-emerged onto the world stage during the **Prague Spring** in 1968, but the decisive break came in November 1989, when a peaceful student demonstration, brutally broken up by the police, triggered off the **Velvet Revolution**, which eventually toppled the Communist government. The popular unity of that period is now history, but there is still a great sense of new-found potential in the capital, which has been transformed by restorations since 1989.

Arrival, information and city transport

Prague's **airport**, Ruzyně, is 10km northwest of the city. The cheapest way of getting into town is by taking local bus #119 (every 7–15min) for the 20-minute ride to Dejvická metro station. Alternatively, there's the ČEDAZ **express minibus** (every 30min), which stops first at Dejvická metro station, and ends up at náměstí Republiky (90Kč). The express minibuses will also take you straight to your hotel for around 360Kč per drop-off – a bargain if there's a few of you. "Fixed-price" taxis are best avoided, at around 700Kč to the centre. Arriving by **train** from the west, you're most likely to end up at **Praha Hlavní nádraží** (station). It's only a short walk to Wenceslas Square from here (though inadvisable at night), and there's also a metro station inside the station. International expresses, passing through Prague, usually stop only at **Praha Holešovice** station, north of the city centre (metro Nádraží Holešovice). Some trains from Moravia and Slovakia wind up at the central **Praha Masarykovo** station (metro Náměstí Republiky); and trains from the south at **Praha Smíchov** station (metro

---

If you want to see the interior of a building, you'll often be forced to go on a **guided tour** that will last at least 45 minutes; the last tour usually leaves an hour before the advertised closing time. Ask for an *anglický* text, an often unintentionally hilarious English résumé. **Entrance tickets** to most sights of interest throughout the Czech Republic rarely cost more than 50–100Kč, so prices are only quoted in this chapter where the admission fee is prohibitively high.

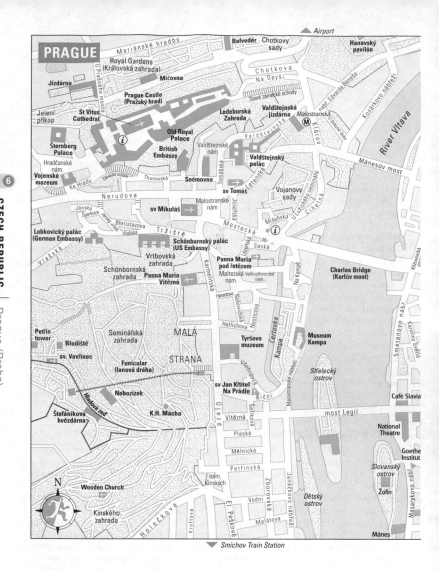

Smíchov Train Station

Smíchovské nádraží). There are lockers and left-luggage offices (open 24hr) at all these stations. The main **bus station** is Praha-Florenc, on the eastern edge of Nové Město (metro Florenc). Busabout buses arrive at the *A&O Hostel* (see p.236).

The best place to go for information is the **Prague Information Service**, or PIS (Pražská informační služba), which has several branches around town; the main office is at Na příkopě 20 (Mon–Fri 9am–6/7pm, Sat & Sun 9am–3/5pm; Ⓦwww.pis.cz). The staff speak English, but their helpfulness varies; they can usually answer most enquiries, and can organize accommodation, sell maps, guides and theatre tickets. As for listings, it's worth getting hold of the English-language monthly *Culture in Prague/Česká kultura*. The English-language newspaper *Prague Post* (every Wed) also has a good listings section.

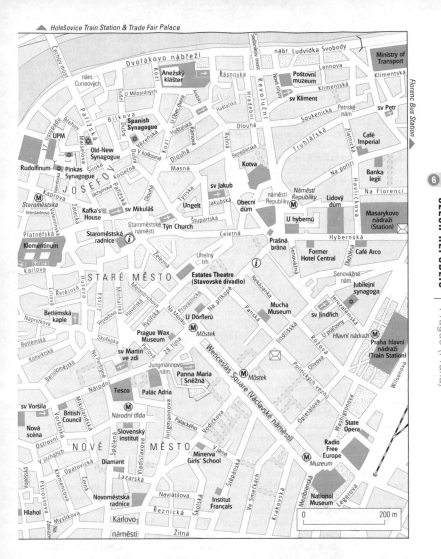

City transport

Prague's city centre is reasonably small and best explored on foot, but to cross the city quickly, or reach some of the more widely dispersed attractions, you'll need to use the public transport system (*dopravní podnik* or *DP*). There are two main types of **ticket**: the 12Kč *přestupní jízdenka*, which is valid for an hour (1hr 30min off-peak), during which time you may change metro lines, trams and buses as often as you like, and the 8Kč *nepřestupní jízdenka*, which allows you to travel for up to fifteen minutes on a single tram or bus, or up to four stops on the metro (not including the one you start at). Tickets must be bought in advance from a tobacconist, kiosk or from one of the ticket machines inside all metro stations and at some tram stops; basically, you want to hit the "8" or "12" button and then put your money in. You must validate your ticket on board or at the metro entrance. If you're going to be using the public transport system a lot, it's worth getting hold of a **travel pass** (*časová jízdenka*; 100Kč/24hr, 200Kč/72hr, 250Kč/week); write your name and date of birth on the reverse of the ticket and validate it when you first use it. Plain-clothes inspectors (*revizoři*) check tickets – it's a fine of 400Kč on the spot if it's not valid.

The fast, Soviet-built **metro** (daily 5am–midnight) is the most useful form of city transport. The **trams** (every 10–20min) navigate Prague's hills and cobbles with remarkable dexterity. Tram #22, whose run includes Vinohrady and Hradčany, is a good way to sightsee, though beware of pickpockets. Night trams #51–58 (midnight–4.30am; every 30min) all pass by Lazarská in Nové Město. The horror stories about Prague **taxi** drivers ripping off tourists are too numerous to mention, so your best bet is to flag a taxi down or call the English-speaking AAA (☎221 111 111), rather than go to the mafia-controlled ranks on Wenceslas Square, Národní and outside Obecní dům.

Accommodation

Prague's **hotels** are exorbitant for what you get, and booking ahead is essential. As a result, most tourists on a budget now stay in private rooms or **hostels**, both of which are easy to organize on arrival. At both the main international train stations and at the airport, there are numerous **accommodation agencies** dealing with private rooms (from ❷): the largest and best is AVE (☎251 553 402, ⊛www .avetravel.cz), which also has over 350 hotels and pensions on its books. Prague's university, the Karolinum, rents out over a thousand **student rooms** in summer; contact the booking office at Voršilská 1, Nové Město (Mon–Fri only; ☎224 913 692; beds available June to mid-Sept; from 220Kč).

Hostels

A&O Hostel U Výstaviště 1, Holešovice ☎220 870 252, ⊛www.arenahostel.com. Clean, well-run place with a bar, Internet access and lockers in the dorms. Metro Nádraží Holešovice or tram #5 to Výstaviště from nám. Republiky. 330Kč.

Clown and Bard Bořivojova 102, Žižkov ☎222 716 453, ⊛www.clownandbard.com. Clean hostel with laid-back atmosphere and loads of staged events. Laundry service and Internet access. Doubles as well as dorms. Tram #5, #9 or #26 to Lipanská from metro Hlavní nádraží. 250Kč.

Hostel Týn Týnská 19, Staré Město ☎222 734 590. The most centrally located hostel, offering four- and five-bed dorms and simple doubles. Metro Náměstí Republiky. 400Kč.

Klub Habitat Na Zderaze 10, Nové Město ☎224 921 706, ⊜hostel@iol.cz. The best of Prague's hostels, located a short walk from Karlovo náměstí. Rates include breakfast. Book ahead. Metro Karlovo náměstí. 450Kč.

Sokol Nosticova 2, Malá Strana ☎257 007 397. Friendly student hostel in sports centre in a great location. Tram #12 or #22 from metro Malostranská. 300Kč.

Travellers' Hostel Dlouhá 33, Staré Město ☎224 826 662, ⊛www.travellers.cz. Centrally located hostel, which can also arrange summer-only dorms. There's a bar and Internet access in the main hostel. Metro Náměstí Republiky. 370Kč.

Hotels and pensions

Avalon-Tara Havelská 15, Staré Město ☎224 228 083, ⊜avalon-tara@volny.cz. Perfect location right over the market on Havelská, though the eight rooms are pretty spartan. Metro Můstek. ❹

City Belgická 10, Vinohrady ☎222 521 606, ⊛www.hotelcity.cz. Reasonable-value hotel in a quiet location within walking distance of Wenceslas Square, offering en-suite rooms and cheaper rooms with shared facilities. Metro Náměstí Míru. ❹

Dum U velké boty Vlašská 30, Malá Strana ☎257 311 107. If you can afford to splash out, try this delightful, tastefully decorated pension, run by a very welcoming couple. Metro Malostranská. ❾

Expres Skořepka 5, Staré Město ☎224 211 801, ⊛www.hotelexpres.wz.cz. Smart, central hotel with friendly staff and breakfast included. Metro Národní třída. ❼

Imperial Na Poříčí 15, Nové Město ☎222 316 012, ⊛www.hotelimperial.cz. Atmospheric and spotless rooms with shared facilities in an Art Nouveau hotel on the edge of the old town, with a great café below. Metro Náměstí Republiky. ❻

Pension Unitas Bartolomějská 9, Staré Město ☎224 221 802, ⊛www.unitas.cz. Hotel-cum-hostel in a centrally located former nunnery; rooms range from the clean and bright to claustrophobic converted secret-police prison cells (where the former Czech president Václav Havel was once detained). Breakfast included. Metro Národní třída. ❹

U medvídků Na Perštýně 7 ☎ 224 211 916, ⓦ www.umedvidku.cz. Plainly furnished rooms above a famous Prague pub. Metro Národní třída. ❽

The City

The River Vltava divides the capital into two unequal halves: the steeply inclined left bank, which accommodates the castle district of Hradčany and Malá Strana, and the gentler, sprawling right bank, which includes Staré Město, Josefov and Nové Město. **Hradčany**, on the hill, contains the most obvious sights – the castle, the cathedral and the old royal palace. Below Hradčany, **Malá Strana** (Little Quarter), with its narrow eighteenth-century streets, is the city's ministerial and diplomatic quarter, though its Baroque gardens are there for all to enjoy. Over the river, on the right bank, **Staré Město** (Old Town) is a web of alleys and passageways centred on the city's most beautiful square, Staroměstské náměstí. Enclosed within the boundaries of Staré Město is **Josefov**, the old Jewish quarter, now down to a handful of synagogues and a cemetery. **Nové Město** (New Town), the focus of the modern city, covers the largest area, laid out in long wide boulevards – most famously Wenceslas Square – stretching south and east of the old town.

Hradčany

Hradčany is wholly dominated by the city's omnipresent landmark, **Prague Castle**, or Pražský hrad (daily 5/6am–11pm/midnight; sights 9am–4/5pm, unless otherwise stated; ⓦ www.hrad.cz), the vast hilltop complex that looks out over the city centre from the west bank of the River Vltava. Viewed from the Charles Bridge, the castle stands aloof from the rest of the city, protected by a rather austere palatial facade that's breached only by the great mass of **St Vitus Cathedral**. Building started under Charles IV, who summoned the precocious 23-year-old German mason **Peter Parler** to work on the church. But only the choir and the south transept were finished when Charles died in 1399, and the whole structure wasn't completed until 1929. The eastern section recalls the building's authentic Gothic roots and the south door, or **Golden Gate** (Zlatá brána), is also pure Parler in style.

The Cathedral is the country's largest church, and, once inside, it's difficult not to be impressed by its sheer height. The grand chapel of **sv Václav**, by the south door, is easily the main attraction. Built by Parler, its rich decoration resembles the inside of a jewel casket: the gilded walls are inlaid with over 1300 semiprecious stones, set around ethereal fourteenth-century Biblical frescoes, while above, the tragedy of Wenceslas unfolds in later paintings. A door in the south wall leads to the coronation chamber, which houses the Bohemian crown jewels, including the gold crown of St Wenceslas. At the centre of the choir, within a fine Renaissance grill, cherubs lark about on the sixteenth-century marble **Imperial Mausoleum**, commissioned by Rudolf II for his grandfather, Ferdinand I, and father, Maximilian II.

If you want to see the choir, crypt or tower you'll need to buy a **ticket** (220Kč), which also gives you entry into a handful of other sights in the castle, including the **Old Royal Palace** (Starý královský palác), just across the courtyard from the south door of the cathedral, and home to the princes and kings of Bohemia from the eleventh to the seventeenth centuries. It's a sandwich of royal apartments built by successive generations – these days you enter at the third floor, built at the end of the fifteenth century. The massive Vladislav Hall (Vladislavský sál) is where the early Bohemian kings were elected, and where every president since Masaryk has been sworn into office – including Václav Havel on December 29, 1989.

Don't be fooled by the uninspiring red facade of the **Basilica of St George** (Bazilika sv Jiří) – this is Prague's most beautiful Romanesque monument (and a popular venue for events), its inside meticulously restored to re-create the honey-coloured basilica which replaced the original tenth-century church in 1173. Next door, the **Convent of St George** (Jiřský klášter), founded in 973, now houses the

National Gallery's **Rudolfine and Baroque art collection** (Tues–Sun 10am–6pm; ℗www.ngprague.cz), mostly of specialist interest only, though including a brief taste of the overtly sensual and erotic Mannerist paintings from the reign of Rudolf II (1576–1612). Round the corner from the convent is the **Golden Lane** (Zlatá ulička), a blind and crowded alley of miniature sixteenth-century cottages in dolly-mixture colours. A plaque at no. 22 commemorates Franz Kafka's brief sojourn here during World War I.

North of the castle walls, across the Powder Bridge (Prasný most), is the entrance to the **Royal Gardens** (Královská zahrada; April–Oct daily 10am–6pm), founded by Ferdinand I and still the best-kept gardens in the country, with fountains and immaculately cropped lawns. At the end of the gardens is Prague's most celebrated Renaissance legacy, the **Belvedér**, a delicately arcaded summer house.

Hradčanské náměstí fans out from the castle's main gates, surrounded by the oversized palaces of the old nobility. A passage down the side of the Archbishop's Palace leads to the early eighteenth-century **Šternberg Palace** (Tues–Sun 10am–6pm; ℗www.ngprague.cz), housing the National Gallery's relatively modest **Old European art collection** (ie non-Czech), which primarily consists of works from the fifteenth to eighteenth centuries, the most significant of which is the *Festival of the Rosary* by Dürer.

Malá Strana

More than anywhere else, **Malá Strana** conforms to the image of Prague as the quintessential Baroque city. Its focus is the sloping, cobbled **Malostranské náměstí**, a busy square split in two by the former Jesuit seminary and church of **sv Mikuláš** (daily 9am–4.30pm; tower: April–Oct daily 10am–6pm; Nov–March Sat & Sun 10am–5pm), possibly the most magnificent Baroque building in the city. Nothing of the plain west facade prepares you for the overwhelming High Baroque interior – the fresco in the nave alone covers over 1500 square metres, and portrays some of the more fanciful feats of St Nicholas.

Follow Tomášská north from the square and you'll enter Vladštejnská, flanked on one side by the gargantuan Valdštejn Palace, and on the other by the **Ledeburská zahrada** (May–Oct daily 10am–6pm). These terraced gardens, which connect higher up with the Zahrada na valech beneath the Castle, are one of the chief joys of Malá Strana. This is where the royal vineyards used to be, and the gardens command superb views over Prague.

South of the main square, a continuation of Karmelitská brings you to the funicular railway up **Petřín** hill (daily 9am–11.30pm; every 10–15min), a better green space than most in Prague, and a good place for a picnic and views from **Petřín tower** (March–May, Sept & Oct daily 10am–6/7pm; June–Aug daily 10am–10pm; Nov–Feb Sat & Sun 10am–5pm).

Staré Město

Staré Město, founded in the early thirteenth century, is where most of the capital's shops, restaurants and pubs are located. It is linked to Malá Strana by the city's most familiar monument, the **Charles Bridge** (Karlův most), begun in 1357. The statues that line it – brilliant pieces of Jesuit propaganda added during the Counter-Reformation – have made it renowned throughout Europe and choked with tourists throughout the year. Cross to Staré Město and head down the narrow, crowded **Karlova**, which winds past the massive **Klementinum** (April–Oct Mon–Fri 2–7pm, Sat & Sun 10am–7pm; Nov–March Sat & Sun 10am–7pm), the former Jesuit College, completed just before the order was turfed out of the country in 1773. It now serves as the national library and state technical library, though you can visit the spectacular Baroque library and the astronomical tower on a guided tour.

At the end of the street lies **Staroměstské náměstí**, the most spectacular square in Prague and the city's main marketplace from the eleventh century. At its centre is the dramatic Art Nouveau **Jan Hus Monument**, featuring the great fifteen-century religious reformer. The best-known sight on the square, however, is the **Astronomical Clock** (chimes hourly 8am–8pm), which features a mechanical performance by Christ and the Apostles. The clock is an integral part of **Staroměstská radnice**, the town hall, inside which you can view a few chambers (Mon 11am–5.30pm, Tues–Sun 9am–5.30pm), climb the tower and get a close-up view of the aforementioned mechanical figures. Staré Město's most impressive Gothic structure is the mighty **Týn Church**, whose towers rise above the two arcaded houses which otherwise obscure its facade. Behind, at the end of Týnská, lies the **Ungelt**, a stunning fortified courtyard where customs used to be collected; it houses the Renaissance Granovský Palace plus some upmarket shops and cafés.

Josefov

Within Staré Město lies **Josefov**, the Jewish quarter of the city until the end of the nineteenth century, when this ghetto area was demolished in order to create a beautiful bourgeois district on Parisian lines. The writer **Franz Kafka** spent most of his life in and around Josefov, and the destruction of the Jewish quarter, which continued throughout his childhood, had a profound effect on his psyche; a small exhibition (Tues–Fri 10am–6pm, Sat 10am–5pm) on the site of his birthplace at náměstí Franze Kafky 5 tells the story of his life.

The "sights" of Josefov are covered by one ticket, available from any of the quarter's box offices (daily except Sat & Jewish holidays 9am–4.30/6pm; ⊛www.jewishmuseum .cz; 250Kč, plus another 200Kč for the Old-New Synagogue). Unfortunately, the quarter was one of the worst affected by the 2002 floods, and at the time of writing, a couple of sites were partially or completely closed for repair work.

The best place to begin is the **Pinkas Synagogue** on Široká, which contains a chilling memorial to the 77,297 Czechoslovak Jews who were killed during the Holocaust – the names of all the victims cover the walls, while children's drawings from the Theresienstadt (Terezín) camp are displayed in the women's gallery. From here, you enter the **Old Jewish Cemetery** (Starý Židovský hřbitov), established in the fifteenth century and in use until 1787, by which time there were some 100,000 graves here piled on top of one another. The jumble of 12,000 Gothic, Renaissance and Baroque tombstones are a poignant reminder of the ghetto, its inhabitants subjected to overcrowding even in death. By the exit to the cemetery on U Starého hřbitová is the Baroque **Klaus Synagogue**, which, along with the neo-Gothic **Maisel Synagogue** on Maiselova, displays some beautiful religious objects and portrays the history of the Jews in the Czech lands until the eighteenth century.

Halfway down **Pařížská**, Prague's most glamorous shopping street, is the steep brick gable of the **Old-New Synagogue**, completed in the fourteenth century and still the religious centre of Prague's Jewish community. Originally it was known simply as the New Synagogue, but after several fires gutted the ghetto it became the oldest synagogue building in the quarter – hence its name. Opposite the synagogue is the **Židovská radnice**, the old Jewish town hall founded in the sixteenth century and later turned into a creamy-pink Baroque house crowned by a wooden clocktower. In addition to the four main clocks, there's one on the north gable, which (like the Hebrew script) goes "backwards". A couple of blocks east of Pařížská, at Vězeňská 1, is the highly ornate neo-Byzantine **Spanish Synagogue**, which contains an exhibition on the history of the city's Jewish community from 1781.

Nové Město

Nové Město, now a sprawling quarter of late nineteenth-century bourgeois dwellings, was actually founded in 1348 by Charles IV. The borderline between Staré and Nové Město is made up by the continuous boulevards of **Národní** and **Na příkopě**, a boomerang curve that follows the course of the old moat. The former was the unlikely setting for the November 17 demonstration that sparked off the Velvet Revolution.

At the river end of Národní is the gold-crested **National Theatre**, a proud symbol of the Czech nation. Refused money by the Austrian state, Czechs of all classes dug deep into their pockets to raise funds for the venture themselves. Halfway along Na příkopě, you can visit the **Mucha Museum**, at Panská 7 (daily 10am–6pm; ⊛www.mucha.cz; 120Kč), dedicated to the country's best-known artist, Alfons Mucha.

At the far end of Na příkopě, on náměstí Republiky, stands the **Obecní dům**, where you can see more of Mucha's work. Begun in 1903, it was decorated inside and out with the help of almost every artist connected with the Czech Secession. The easiest way of soaking up the dramatic interior, covered with Art Nouveau mosaics and pendulous chandeliers, is to have a reasonably pricey but delicious meal in the French restaurant to the right of the entrance or a coffee in the equally dazzling café to the left. Alternatively, you can go on a guided tour of the interior on weekends; tickets are available from the information centre inside (daily 10am–6pm; ⊛www.obecni-dum.cz; 150Kč).

Cross the boulevard at its central point and you're into the pivot of modern Prague and the political focus of the events of 1989 – the wide, gently sloping **Wenceslas Square** (Václavské náměstí). The square's history of protest goes back to the Prague Spring of 1968: towards the top end, there's a small memorial to the victims of Communism, the most famous of whom, the 21-year-old student Jan Palach, set himself alight on this very spot in 1969 in protest against the Soviet occupation. A six-lane freeway effectively cuts off the square from the **National Museum** (daily 9/10am–5/6pm), one of the great symbols of the nineteenth-century Czech national revival, with its monumental glass cupola, sculptural decoration and frescoes from Czech history. However, unless you're a geologist or a zoologist you're likely to remain unmoved by the exhibits.

Trade Fair Palace: The Museum of Modern Art

One reason to hop on a tram is to visit the city's modern-art museum, housed in a vast functionalist 1920s building known as the **Trade Fair Palace** (Veletržní palác; Tues–Sun 10am–6pm; ⊛www.ngprague.cz; 150–300Kč, depending on number of floors visited), on Dukelských hrdinu 47 (tram #5 from nám. Republiky). The museum's *raison d'être* is its unrivalled permanent collection of nineteenth- and twentieth-century Czech art, but it also houses the National Gallery's modest collection of nineteenth- and twentieth-century European art, including works by Klimt, Schiele, Picasso and the French Impressionists, as well as temporary exhibitions of contemporary Czech and foreign art.

Eating

While traditional Czech food still predominates in the city's pubs, Prague now has a wide range of **restaurants** offering anything from French to Japanese cuisine. Steer clear of places in the main tourist areas, such as either side of the Charles Bridge, which tend to be overpriced and of indifferent quality.

Bar Bar Všehrdova 17, Malá Strana. Arty crêperie with big, cheap salads and sweet and savoury pancakes.

Dynamo Pštrossova 29, Nové Město. Eye-catching retro 1960s designer decor, competent fish, chicken, steak and pasta dishes make this place a popular, trendy little spot.

Jarmark Vodičkova 30, Nové Město. Popular, inexpensive self-service steak and salad buffet in the Lucerna pasáž, where the chef prepares your food in front of you; a few veggie dishes on offer, too.

Klub Architektů Betlémské nám. 5, Staré Město ☎224 401 214. Attractive, lively cellar restaurant serving tasty Czech and international cuisine. Booking recommended.

Lotos Platnéřská 13, Staré Město. Veggie wholefood versions of Czech cuisine – this is your chance to have a meat-free pork and dumplings. No smoking but there is alcohol.

Pizzeria Kmotra V jirchářích 12, Nové Město. Hugely popular basement pizza place in the backstreets behind Národní.

Radost FX Café Bělehradská 120, Vinohrady.

Outstanding veggie food attracts ultra-fashionable crowd; open till very late, brunch at weekends.
Tulip Café Opatovická 3, Nové Město. Sleek, minimalist decor and delicious designer cooking

available at this resolutely expat café/restaurant.
U sádlů Klimentská 2. Deliberately over-the-top themed medieval banqueting hall serving inexpensive hearty fare and lashings of frothing ale.

Drinking

The choice of Prague **cafés** is pretty varied – from Art Nouveau relics and swish espresso bars (both of which are called *kavárna* and are licensed), to simple sugar and caffeine joints (*cukrárna*). For no-nonsense boozing you need to head for a **pub** (*pivnice*), which invariably serves excellent beer by the half-litre, but many of which close around 11pm. For late-night drinking, head for one of the clubs or all-night bars.

Café Imperial Na poříčí 15, Nové Město. An endearingly shabby yet grand Habsburg-era *Kaffeehaus*, which has retained its original, tiled decor.

Café Louvre Národní 20, Nové Město. Resurrected Habsburg-era *Kaffeehaus* with high ceiling, mirrors, daily papers and a billiard hall.

Café Slavia Národní 1, Nové Město. Famous café opposite the National Theatre, with great riverside views and Manet's *Absinthe Drinker* on the wall.

Dahab Dlouhá 33, Staré Město. The mother of all Prague teahouses, a vast Bedouin tent of a place serving tasty Middle Eastern snacks, couscous and hookahs to a background of funky world music.

Globe Pštrossova 6, Nové Město. Large, buzzing café, at the back of the English-language

bookstore of the same name, that's a serious expat hangout, but enjoyable nevertheless.

Jo's Bar Malostranské náměstí 7, Malá Strana. A narrow bar in Malá Strana that is the original expat/backpacker hangout. Tex-Mex food served all day, bottled beer only and a heaving crowd guaranteed most evenings. Downstairs is *Jo's Garáž* disco.

Obecní dům Nám. Republiky 5, Nové Město. Glorious Art Nouveau decor, impeccable service and a good cake trolley.

Pivovarskýdům Lipova 15, Nové Město. In-house brewery offering everything from wheat- to banana-beer – along with excellent Czech pub grub and good service.

Velryba Opatovická 24, Nové Město. Smoky and studenty café, with cheap Czech food and an art gallery in the basement.

Nightlife

As far as live music is concerned, the classical scene still has the edge in Prague, though some good jazz clubs, discos and **nightclubs** have sprouted up in recent years. Predictably enough, with a playwright as president until recently, **theatre** in Prague is thriving; without knowing the language, however, your scope is limited, though there's a tradition of innovative mime, puppetry and "black light" theatre in the city. **Tickets** are cheap and available from various agencies around town, including Ticketpro, as well as from tourist offices and the venues themselves.

Classical concerts take place throughout the year in concert halls and churches, the biggest event being the Prague Spring **international music festival** (Ⓦ www.festival.cz), which traditionally begins on May 12, the day of Smetana's death, with a performance of *Má vlast*, and finishes on June 2 with a rendition of Beethoven's Ninth. Watch out for concerts in the churches and palaces, as well as in the main venues (listed below), and in the summer for the many open-air concerts and plays held at Hradčany.

Classical music and opera

Estates Theatre (Stavovské divadlo) Ovocný trh 1, Staré Město Ⓦ www.narodni-divadlo.cz. Prague's main opera house, which witnessed the première of Mozart's *Don Giovanni*.

Rudolfinum Alsovo nábřeží 12, Staré Město Ⓦ www.rudolfinum.cz. Stunning Neo-Renaissance concert hall and home to the Czech Philharmonic.

Smetana Hall Obecní dům, náměstí Republiky 5, Nové Město. Fantastically ornate and recently renovated Art Nouveau concert hall, which is home to the excellent Prague Symphony Orchestra.

State Opera Prague Wilsonova 4, Nové Město Ⓦ www.opera.cz. The former German opera house and the city's second-choice venue for opera and ballet.

Clubs and live venues

AghaRTA Jazz Centrum Krakovská 5, Nové Město ⓦ www.agharta.cz. Prague's best jazz club, with a good mix of top-name foreigners and locals.

Akropolis Kubelíkova 27, Žižkov ⓦ www
.palacakropolis.cz. Decent live arts/world music venue in the backstreets of Žižkov, renowned for Romany and other ethnic music festivals. Tram #5, #9 or #26.

Karlovy lázně Novotného lávka 1, Staré Město ⓦ www.karlovylazne.cz. Mega, high-tech club by the Charles Bridge; techno on the top floor, progressively more retro as you descend to the

Internet café on the ground floor.

Lucerna Music Bar Vodičkova 36, Nové Město ⓦ www.musicbar.cz. Central, small dance space, with live music.

Radost FX Bělehradská 120, Vinohrady ⓦ www.radostfx.cz. Still the slickest (and longest-running) all-round dance club venue in Prague, with a great veggie café attached.

Roxy Dlouhá 33, Staré Město ⓦ www.roxy.cz. Laid-back, rambling old theatre with an interesting programme of events from arty films and exhibitions to live acts and DJ nights.

Listings

Embassies and consulates Australia, Klimentská 10, Nové Město ☎ 251 018 350; Canada, Muchova 6, Hradčany ☎ 272 101 800; New Zealand, Dykova 19, Vinohrady ☎ 222 514 672; Ireland, Tržiště 13, Malá Strana ☎ 257 530 061; UK, Thunovská 14, Malá Strana ☎ 257 402 111; US, Tržiště 15, Malá Strana ☎ 257 530 663.

Gay & lesbian Prague The city doesn't have a large or very upfront gay and lesbian scene, but there are a few bars and clubs worth checking out: *Friends*, Náprstkova 1, Staré Město, is a friendly, laid-back gay/lesbian cellar bar in the centre of the old town, while *Gejzee…r*, Vinohradská 40 (closed

Sun & Mon), is the largest and most popular gay club, with dance floor, DJs and darkroom.

Internet access *Globe* (see p.241) has several fast terminals; *Tiscali iCafe*, Újezd 16, Malá Strana, also serves great bagels.

Laundry Laundryland, Na příkopě 12, Nové Město (Mon–Fri 9am–8pm, Sat 9am–7pm, Sun 11am–7pm; ⓦ www.laundryland.cz); plus several other locations around town.

Pharmacy Palackého 5, Nové Město ☎ 224 946 982 (Mon–Fri 7am–7pm, Sat 8am–noon).

Post office Jindřišská 14, Nové Město (daily 2am–midnight).

Bohemia

Prague is the natural centre and capital of Bohemia; the rest divides easily into four geographical districts. South Bohemia, bordered by the Šumava Mountains, is the least spoilt; its largest town by far is the brewing centre of **České Budějovice**, and its chief attraction, aside from the thickly forested hills, is a series of well-preserved medieval towns, whose undisputed gem is **Český Krumlov**. Neighbouring West Bohemia has a similar mix of rolling woods and hills, despite the industrial nature of its capital **Plzeň**, home of Pilsen beer and the Škoda empire. Beyond here, as you approach the German border, Bohemia's famous spa region unfolds, with magnificent resorts such as **Mariánské Lázně** and **Karlovy Vary** enjoying sparkling reputations. North Bohemia has real problems: devastated by industrialization, many parts are virtually uninhabitable. East Bohemia has suffered indirectly from the polluting industries of its neighbour, but remains relatively blight-free. There's some great walking and climbing country here, but the only essential stop on a quick tour is the silver-mining centre of **Kutná Hora**.

České Budějovice

Since its foundation in 1265, **ČESKÉ BUDĚJOVICE** has been a self-assured place, convinced of its own importance. Its wealth, based on medieval silver mines and its position on the salt route from Linz to Prague, was wiped out in the seventeenth century by war and fire, but the Habsburgs lavishly reconstructed most of the town in the eighteenth century. české Budějovice's real renown, however, is for its local **beer**, Budvar, better known abroad under its original German name, Budweiser.

České Budějovice has a compact old town that's only a five-minute walk from the **train** and **bus stations**, both situated to the east of the city centre, along the pedestrianized Lannova třída. The medieval grid plan leads inevitably to the magnificent central **náměstí Přemysla Otakara II**, one of Europe's largest market squares. Its buildings are elegant enough, but it's the arcades and the octagonal **Samson's Fountain** – once the only tap in town – that make the greatest impression. The 72-metre status symbol, the **Black Tower** (černá věž), one of the few survivors of the 1641 fire, leans gently to one side of the square; its roof gallery (April–Oct Tues–Sun 10am–6pm; July & Aug also Mon 10am–6pm) provides superb views. The **Budvar brewery** is 2.5km up the road to Prague, on Karolíny Světlé (bus #2), and has a modern *pivnice* inside the nasty titanium-blue headquarters (☎387 705 341, ⑩www.budvar.cz for information on guided tours).

There's a friendly **tourist office** at no. 2 on the main square (June–Sept Mon–Fri 8.30am–6pm, Sat 8.30am–5pm, Sun 10am–noon & 12.30–4pm; Oct–May Mon–Fri 9am–noon & 12.30–5pm, Sat 9am–noon & 12.30–3pm; ☎386 359 480, ⑩www.c-budejovice.cz). České Budějovice's popularity means that **hotels** tend to be expensive. The best-value options in the old-town are the canal-side *Hotel Klika*, Zátkovo nábřeží 17 (☎387 318 360, ⑩www.hotelklika.cz; ④), and *Hotel Malý pivovar*, Karla IV 8–10 (☎386 360 471, ⑩www.budvar.cz; ⑥). From July to September rooms are available in **student halls**, located at Studentská 15 (☎387 774 201; ②). There's also a good **campsite**, *Dlouhá louka*, at Stromovka 8 (☎387 210 601; bus #16 from station). The most famous **pub** in town, the *Masné krámy* at Krajinská 29, was damaged by floods in 2002 and was still closed at the time of writing. The Budvar-run *Malý pivovar* serves great pub **food** and beer, as does the *Hotel Zvon* on the main square – head for the pub section, rather than the more expensive restaurant.

Český Krumlov

Squeezed into a tight S-bend of the River Vltava, **ČESKÝ KRUMLOV** is one of the most picturesque towns in the country, having hardly changed in the last three hundred years. This, however, is no secret, and the crowds are getting increasingly thick throughout the summer. The **train station** is twenty minutes' walk north of the old town, up a precipitous set of steps, while the **bus station** is just outside the old town. The twisting River Vltava divides the town into two: the circular Staré Město on the right bank and the Latrán quarter on the hillier left. For centuries, the focal point has been the **Castle** (April–Oct Tues–Sun 8.45am–5/6pm; 150Kč English-language tour) in the Latrán quarter, where there's a choice of two hour-long guided tours: one concentrating on feudal opulence, the other peaking at the castle's eighteenth-century Rococo ballroom. Another covered walkway puts you high above the town in the unexpectedly expansive **terraced gardens**. The houses leaning in on Latrán lead to a wooden, ramp-like bridge which connects with the Staré Město. Head straight up the soft incline of Radniční to the main square, náměstí Svornosti, where a long, white Renaissance entablature connects two-and-a-half Gothic houses to create the **town hall**. On the other side, the high lancet windows of the church of **St Vitus** rise above the ramshackle rooftops. Continuing east off the square, down Horní, the beautiful sixteenth-century Jesuit college now provides space for the town's grandest hotel, the *Hotel Růže*. Opposite, the local **museum** (Tues–Fri 9am–4pm, Sat & Sun 1–4pm) includes a reconstructed seventeenth-century shop interior among its exhibits. West of the square, on Široká, the excellent **Egon Schiele Art Centrum** (daily 10am–6pm; ⑩www.schieleartcentrum.org; 180Kč) has a series of galleries and exhibition halls housed in a fifteenth-century former brewery, devoted in part to the Austrian painter Egon Schiele, who lived here briefly in 1911.

The helpful **tourist office** (Mon–Fri 9am–6pm, Sat & Sun 9am–noon & 1–6pm; ☎380 704 622, ⑩www.ckrumlov.cz) is situated on the main square. For **accommodation**, the friendly pub/pension *Na louži*, Kájovská 66 (☎380 711 280, ⑩www.nalouzi.cz; ③), is a good bet. There are lots of **hostels** in Český Krumlov, including the central HI *Travellers' Hostel* at Soukenická 43 (☎380 711 345; 300Kč per person) and the more attractive *Merlin*, down by the river at Kájovská 59 (☎606 256 145; 250Kč per person), both of which offer Internet access. There are also several reasonable **campsites** south of town along the road to Rožmberk. As far as **eating** goes, there's a wide choice: *Papa's Living Restaurant*, Latrán 13, offers funky Mexican, Italian and veggie dishes, while the fish restaurant *Rybařská bašta*, off Široká, is good value. **Drinking** is best done at the *Eggenberg*, the brewery tap, on the eastern edge of the Latrán quarter, or at the aforementioned *Na louži*.

Plzeň

PLZEŇ (Pilsen) is Bohemia's second city, with a population of around 175,000. Despite its industrial character, there are compensations – eclectic architecture and an unending supply of (probably) the best **beer** in the world. Plzeň's **train stations** are works of art in themselves: your likeliest point of arrival is the Hlavní nádraží, just a little east of the city centre. The **bus terminal** is on the west side of town. From both stations, the city centre is only a short walk away. The main square, **náměstí Republiky**, presents a full range of architectural styles, starting with the exalted heights of the Gothic cathedral of **sv Bartoloměj**, its green spire (daily 10am–6pm) reaching up almost 103m. Over the way rises the sgraffitoed Renaissance **Old Town Hall**, self-importantly one storey higher than the rest of the square. Here and there other old buildings survive, but the vast majority of Plzeň's buildings hail from the city's heyday during the industrial expansion around the turn of the twentieth century.

The reason most people come to Plzeň, however, is to sample its famous 12° Plzeňský Prazdroj, or **Pilsner Urquell** (its Germanized export name). Beer has been brewed in the town since it was founded in 1295, but it wasn't until 1842 that the famous Bürgerliches Brauhaus was built, after a near-riot by the townsfolk over the declining quality of their brew. For a guided tour of the **brewery** (☎377 062 888, ⓦwww.beerworld.cz; 120Kč), you can either book in advance or simply show up at 12.30pm or 2pm for tours in English. You could, of course, just settle for a half-litre of the stuff at the vast *Na Spilce* pub (daily 11am–10/11pm), just inside the brewery's triumphal arch.

The **tourist office** (daily 9am–6pm; ☎378 032 750, ⓦwww.plzen-city.cz), at nám. Republiky 41, can arrange **private rooms**. Finding a vacancy in one of Plzeň's **hotels** presents few problems, though they don't come cheap. The best-value rooms in town are the three at *Pension V Solní*, Solní 8 (☎377 236 652, ⓔpension.solni@post.cz; ❸), just off the main square; alternatively, try the *U Salzmannů* pub at Pražská 8 (☎377 235 855, ⓦwww.usalzmannu.cz; ❸). There are a handful of **hostels** in town, including *Zahradní*, 2km southeast of the centre at Zahradní 21 (☎377 443 262; 180Kč per person; tram #1). Bus #20 from the train station will drop you at the *Bílá hora* **campsite** (☎377 562 225; closed Oct–March) on 28 Října in the northern suburb of the same name. For cheap meals you might as well combine your **eating** with your **drinking**. Apart from *Na Spilce*, you can get cheap, hearty grub at the wood-panelled *U Salzmannů* (see above), while Gambrinus, Plzeň's other main beer, is best at *Žumbera* at Bezručova 14.

Mariánské Lázně

Once one of the most fashionable European spas, **MARIÁNSKÉ LÁZNĚ** is far less exclusive today. The riotous *fin-de-siècle* architecture is gradually being restored, and the spa now surveys busloads of elderly Germans getting the full works. Buses and trains stop 3km from the spa, from where trolleybus #5 runs up Hlavní třída to the centre. Sumptuous, regal buildings, most dating from the second half of the nineteenth century, rise up from the pine-clad surroundings – an appropriate backdrop for the genteel classical music festivals hosted annually here. The focal point of the spa is the **Kolonáda**. This beautiful wrought-iron colonnade gently curves like a whale-ribbed railway station, the atmosphere relentlessly genteel and sober, although the view has been marred by a functionless concrete splat left by Communist developers. The spa's first and foremost **spring**, Křížový pramen, has its own adjoining Neoclassical colonnade, and its life-giving faucets are accessible daily from 6am to 6pm. Mariánské Lázně's altitude lends an almost subalpine freshness to the air, and **walking** is as important to "the cure" as the various specialized treatments; maps showing marked walks in the area are available in hotels and shops.

The **tourist office** at Hlavní 47 (summer daily 9am–noon & 1–6pm; winter Mon–Fri 9am–noon & 1–4pm; ☎354 622 474, ⊛www.marienbad.cz) has its own Internet café, plus seven **private rooms** (❷) with shared facilities, which are the cheapest in town. **Hotels** are getting increasingly pricey, but the *Zlatý zámek*, Klíčová 4 (☎354 623 924; ❷), offers exceptional value for its central locale. The *Kossuth/Suvurov*, Ruská 77 (☎354 622 861, ⊜kossut@iol.cz; ❷), parallel to the main street, is pretty basic, while the *fin-de-siècle Polonia*, Hlavní třída 50 (☎354 622 451, ⊛www.orea.cz; ❸), has rooms overlooking the spa gardens – the *Café Polonia* here is probably Mariánské Lázně's most opulent **café**, offering stucco decoration as rich as its cakes. A little way down the street from the *Polonia*, past the *Hotel Excelsior*, is the *Classic* **restaurant**, specially recommended for vegetarians.

Karlovy Vary

KARLOVY VARY, undisputed king of the Bohemian spas, is one of the most cosmopolitan Czech towns. Its international clientele – largely Russians – annually doubles the local population, which is further supplemented by thousands of able-bodied tourists in summer, mostly German. There are two **train stations**, one by the bus station and one by the River Ohře. Don't get off from the Prague bus at the **bus station** on Varšavská; along with almost everyone else, hop off at Tržnice, one stop before, which is far more central. Half a kilometre south, the pedestrianized **spa quarter** stretches along the winding Teplá Valley. Unfortunately, many visitors' first impressions are marred by the inexcusable concrete scab of the **Thermal** sanatorium, for whose sake a large slice of the old town bit the dust. However, its open-air spring-water **swimming pool** is superb and offers unbeatable views. As the valley narrows, the river disappears under a wide terrace in front of the graceful **Mlýnská kolonáda**, each of whose four springs is more scalding than the last. Most powerful of the town's twelve springs is the **Vřídlo**, which belches out over 2500 gallons every hour. The smooth marble floor of the modern **Vřídelní kolonáda** (the old fountain was melted down for armaments by the Nazis) allows patients to shuffle up and down contentedly, while inside the glass rotunda the geyser shoots hot water forty feet upwards. Clouds of steam obscure a view of Dientzenhofer's Baroque masterpiece, the **church of sv Maria Magdalána**, pitched nearby on a precipitous site. South of the Sprudel is Karlovy Vary's most famous shopping street, the **Stará louka**. Its shops are beginning once more to exude the snobbery of former days – there's even a branch of Versace at the far end of the street. At Stará louka 30 is the **Grand Hotel Pupp**, which was founded in 1701 as the greatest hotel in the world and still has a certain snooty grandeur.

Karlovy Vary's **tourist office** is located next to the Mlýnská kolonáda at Lázeňská 1 (Mon–Fri 8am–6pm, Sat & Sun 10am–6pm; ☎353 224 097, ⊛www.karlovyvary.cz). It's best to start looking for **accommodation** early in the day – Karlovy Vary is a very fashionable spa town so nothing comes dirt cheap. W Privat, an office on náměstí Republiky (Mon–Fri 8.30am–5pm, Sat & Sun 9am–1pm; ☎353 227 768, ⊜wprivat@volny.cz), can organize **private rooms** (❷). Moderately priced **hotels** include the central *Pension Kučera*, Stará louka 2 (☎353 235 053, ⊛www.pensionkucera.cz; ❸), and *Clara*, Na kopečku 23 (☏353 449 983; ❸), which is more comfortable but located out of town beyond the railway station. Karlovy Vary's most central **campsite** is at *Motel Gejzír* (☏353 225 101; closed Nov–March), on Slovenská; take bus #7 from the bus station. For **eating**, head for the *Zámecký vrch*, an intimate restaurant up at no. 14 on the street of the same name, the Moravian wine cellar at *Promenáda*, Tržíště 31, or *Embassy*, Nová louka 21. The *Elefant Café* on Stará louka is the nearest Karlovy Vary comes to an elegant Habsburg-style **café**.

Kutná Hora

KUTNÁ HORA, 60km east of Prague, was once one of the most important towns in this neck of the Habsburg Empire. In 1308 Václav II founded the royal mint here, and the town's sudden wealth allowed it to underwrite the construction of one of the most magnificent churches in central Europe, plus a number of other prestigious monuments. By the late Middle Ages its population was equal to that of London, its shantytown suburbs straggling across what are now green fields. When the silver mines dried up at the end of the sixteenth century, Kutná Hora's importance came to an abrupt end.

The easiest way to get here from Prague is by bus, as the main train station is several kilometres from the centre, whereas the buses stop just across the ring road. The small houses that line the town's medieval lanes give little idea of its former glories, and the same goes for **Palackého náměstí**, nominally the main square, though it's no showpiece. A narrow alleyway on the south side of the square leads to the leafy Havlíčkovo náměstí, off which the **Italian Court**, where Florentine workers produced Prague's silver *Groschen*, a coin used throughout central Europe until the nineteenth century. Better still, head for the **Mining Museum** (April–Oct Tues–Sun 9/10am–5/6pm), the other side of sv Jakub, the town's oldest church. Here, you can visit some of the medieval mines that were discovered beneath an old fort in the 1960s. The Jesuits arrived too late to exploit the town's silver stocks, but with their own funds they built a **Jesuit College** on the ridge to the southwest of town. With its gallery of saints and holy men, it was a crude attempt to eclipse the astounding achievement of the neighbouring Gothic **Cathedral of sv Barbora** (Tues–Sun: May–Sept 9am–5.30pm; Oct–April 9am–noon & 1/2–3/4pm). Not to be outdone by St Vitus Cathedral in Prague, the miners of Kutná Hora financed the construction of a great cathedral of their own, dedicated to Barbara, the patron saint of miners and gunners. The foundations were probably laid by Peter Parler in the 1380s, but the church remained unfinished until the late nineteenth century. From the outside it's an incredible sight, bristling with pinnacles, finials and flying buttresses supporting a roof of three tent-like towers and unequal needle-sharp spires. Inside, light streams through the plain glass, illuminating a vaulted nave whose ribs form branches and petals stamped with coats of arms belonging to Václav II and the miners' guilds.

While you're in Kutná Hora, don't miss the weird subterranean *kostnice* or **ossuary** (daily: April–Sept 8am–6pm; Oct–March 9am–noon & 1–4/5pm), overflowing with 40,000 complete sets of bones, moulded into sculptures and decorations by František Rint in the nineteenth century. To get there, take bus #1 or #4 to the giant tobacco factory 3km northeast of the centre; you'll find the ossuary behind a Baroque church.

The **tourist office** at Palackeho náměstí 377 (Mon–Fri 9am–5/6.30pm; April–Oct also Sat & Sun 9am–5pm; ☏327 512 378, ⓦwww.kutnohorsko.cz) can book **private rooms**. *U rytířů*, on Rejskovo náměstí (☏327 512 256; ❷), is a simple inexpensive pension, while *Hotel Anna*, Vladislavova 372 (☏327 516 315, ⓦsweb.cz/hotel.anna; ❸), is a bit more upmarket. The nearest **campsite** is the unlikely sounding *Santa Barbara* on česká (☏327 512 051; closed Nov–March), 800m from the cathedral, with hot showers and a restaurant.

Moravia

Wedged between Bohemia and Slovakia, **Moravia** is the smallest of the three provinces that once made up Czechoslovakia, but perhaps the prettiest, friendliest and most bucolic. Although the North Moravian corridor is heavily industrialized and has suffered from increasingly high unemployment over the past decade, much of the region is rural and the folk roots, traditions and religion here are strongly felt. The Moravian capital, **Brno**, a once-grand nineteenth-century city, is within easy striking distance of Moravia's spectacular **karst region**. In the northern half of the province, the Baroque riches of the Moravian prince-bishopric have left their mark on the old capital, **Olomouc**, now a thriving university town and one of the region's main attractions.

Brno

As the second-largest city in the Czech Republic, with a couple of really good museums and galleries plus a fair bit of nightlife, **BRNO** is worth a day of anyone's time. The city was a late developer, the first cloth factory being founded in 1766, but by the end of the nineteenth century it was easily the largest city in Moravia. Between the wars Brno enjoyed a cultural boom, heralded by the 1928 Exhibition of Contemporary Culture, which provided an impetus for much of the city's modernist architecture. After the war, Brno's German-speakers (one quarter of the population) were sent packing on foot to Vienna. Capital fled with the capitalists and centralized state funds were diverted to Prague and Bratislava.

A steady stream of people plough up and down **Masarykova**, the main shopping route, which is lined with five-storey mansions, some embellished with fantastic decorations. Follow the flow north and you'll end up at **náměstí Svobody** – where most of Brno comes to shop. To the left, halfway up Masarykova, is **Zelný trh**, a low-key vegetable market on a sloping cobbled square, with a huge fountain in its centre. At the top of the square, the plain mass of the Dietrichstein Palace contains the **Moravian Museum** (Tues–Sat 9am–5pm), a worthy collection of ancient and medieval artefacts. Much more interesting, if only for its macabre value, is the **Capuchin Crypt** (Tues–Sat 9am–noon & 2–4.30pm, Sun 11–11.45am & 2–4.30pm) to the far south of the square, a gruesome collection of dead monks and top nobs mummified in the crypt of the Capuchin church. Clearly visible from Zelný trh is the **Old Town Hall**. Anton Pilgram's Gothic doorway is its best feature, the thistly pinnacle above the statue of Justice symbolically twisted – Pilgram's revenge on the town aldermen who shortchanged him for his work. Inside, the courtyards and passageways are jam-packed with tour groups, most of them here to see the so-called Brno dragon (actually a stuffed crocodile) and the Brno Wheel, made in 1636 by a cartwright from nearby Lednice. If you're still hazy on the geography of the town, the **tower** (daily 9am–5pm) is worth a climb for the panorama across the red-tiled rooftops.

Southwest of the square, the Petrov hill – on which the **Cathedral of SS Peter and Paul** stands – is one of the best places to escape from the choked streets below. The cathedral's needle-sharp Gothic spires dominate the skyline for miles around, but close up, the crude nineteenth-century rebuilding has made it a lukewarm affair. On the western edge of the city centre, the **UPM** at Husova 14 (Wed–Sun 10am–6/7pm) contains one of the country's best collections of applied art, displaying everything from medieval textiles to swirling Art Nouveau vases; it also has excellent temporary shows. At the **Pražák Palace** (Wed–Sun 10am–6/7pm), a little further down the road, there's a very good cross-section of twentieth-century Czech art on display. Skulking in the woods above the gallery is the barely visible **Špilberk Castle**, one of the worst prisons in the Habsburg Empire, and later the Brno Gestapo jail; the dungeons (*kasematy*; July & Aug daily 9am–6pm; Sept–June Tues–Sun 9am–5/6pm) are open to the public, while the city museum (Tues–Sun 9am–5/6pm; Nov–March closed Tues) occupies the upper floors.

Practicalities

Brno's main **train** and **bus station** sit closely together, on the edge of the city centre; the train station has lockers and a 24-hour left-luggage office. Most of Brno's sights are within easy walking distance, although **trams** will take you almost anywhere in the city within minutes. You need to buy either a 7Kč ticket for ten minutes' travel or a 12Kč ticket, valid for forty minutes and allowing changes between trams or buses. Tickets must be bought beforehand from kiosks, hotel lobbies or yellow ticket machines, and validated on board. The main **tourist office** is in the Old Town Hall at Radnická 8 (Mon–Fri 8am–6pm, Sat & Sun 9am–5pm; ☎542 211 090, ⊛www.kultura-brno.cz). Brno hosts many trade fairs, so it's wise to book **accommodation** ahead. One of the cheapest **hotels** is the *Amphone*, třída. kpt. Jaroše 29 (☎545 428 310; ❹), a short walk from the old town; *Pegas*, Jakubská 4 (☎542 210 104; ❹), just off česká, is more central and above a microbrewery. Best of Brno's **campsites** is the *Radka* (☎546 215 821; closed Sept–May; tram #1, #3 or #11), 10km northwest of the city on the shores of the Brno dam, at Brneňska prehrada-kninia. The **eating and drinking** scene has improved enormously in the last decade. The most popular café around is the Italian-run *Arca di Adria*, at Masarykova 31, which serves great ice cream and pizzas. If you want to sup beer Czech-style, try *Špalíček*, at the top of Zelný trh, which has tables outside in summer and lashings of the local Starobrno beer, or the replica functionalist café, *Zemanova kavárna*, near the Janáček Theatre. The microbrewery, *Pegas*, on Jakubská, is deservedly popular, or you could swing by *Elektra*, a cellar pub with decent food at Běhounská 7. **Internet cafés** include *Internet Centrum Coffee* at Masarykova 22–24 and @ *Internet Café* at Lidická 17.

The Moravian karst region

Well worth a visit is the limestone **karst region** just over 25km northeast of Brno. To get there by public transport, you need to catch a morning train from Brno out to Blansko, from where buses depart for Skalní Mlýn, location of the main ticket office and information centre for the caves – the Brno tourist office will give you a list of connection times. The **Punkevní cave** (Tues–Sun 8.20am–2/3.50pm; ⊛www.cavemk.cz) is the cave to head for – it's the biggest and best and includes an underground boat trip. To reach the cave, walk or catch the Eko-Train from Skalní Mlýn, where there are also bikes for rent. Alternatively, it's a very nice walk (8km) through the woods from Blansko; follow the green waymarkers.

Olomouc

Occupying the crucial Morava crossing-point on the road to Kraków, **OLOMOUC** (pronounced "olla-moats") was the capital of Moravia from the Middle Ages to the mid-seventeenth century and the seat of the bishopric for even longer. All this attracted the destructive attention of Swedish troops in the Thirty Years War, though the wealth of the Church and its strategic trading position kept the place going. And with a well-preserved old town, sloping cobbled squares and a plethora of Baroque fountains, not to mention a healthy quota of university students and a few interesting festivals, Olomouc has a great deal going for it.

The **Staré Město** is a strange contorted shape, squeezed in the middle by an arm of the Morava. The train station is 1.5km east, so on arrival take any tram heading west up Masarykova and get off after three or four stops; the bus station is even further out, and connected to the centre by tram #4. In the western half of the old town, all roads lead to the city's two central cobbled main squares, which are hinged to one another at right angles. At the centre of the upper square, the irregular **Horní náměstí**, stands the amalgamation of buildings that collectively make up the **town hall**. From its creamy rendering the occasional late Gothic or Renaissance gesture emerges – notably the handsome lanterned tower soaring to its conclusion of baubles and pinnacles. On the north side, next to the arcade of shops, is an astronomical clock, which was destroyed in the war. The remake chimes all right, but the hourly mechanical show is disappointing. Big enough to be a chapel, the **Holy Trinity Column** to the west of the town hall is the country's largest plague column; many such monuments were erected as thanksgiving for deliverance from the forces of Protestantism, but few are left standing. Set into the west facade of the square is the **Moravian Theatre**, where Mahler arrived as the newly appointed *Kapellmeister* in 1883; the local press took an instant dislike to him, and he lasted just three months. **Fountains** grace each of Olomouc's six ancient market squares. Horní náměstí boasts two: Hercules, looking unusually athletic for his years, and a vigorous depiction of Julius Caesar bucking on a steed that coughs water from its mouth.

Two of the city's best-looking backstreets, Školní and Michalská, lead southeast from Horní náměstí up to the **church of sv Micháł**, plain on the outside but inside clad in a masterly excess of Baroque. Firmly wedged between the two sections of the old town is the Jesuit church of **Panna Maria Sněžná**, deemed particularly necessary in a city where Protestantism had spread like wildfire in the sixteenth century. Jutting out into the road, it signals the gateway to the less hectic part of town. The great mass of the former Jesuit College, now the **Palacký University**, dominates the first square, náměstí Republiky, opposite which is the dull town museum and, next door, the vastly superior **Museum of Art** (Tues–Sun 10am–6pm); the top floor houses a fascinating selection of twentieth-century works by local-born artists and features a viewing tower. Three blocks east of náměstí Republiky, the **Cathedral**, or Dóm, of sv Václav comes into view. Though it started life as a Romanesque basilica, the current structure is mostly nineteenth-century neo-Gothic. However, the walls and pillars of the nave are prettily painted in Romanesque style, and the **crypt** (Tues & Thurs–Sat 9am–2pm, Wed 9am–4pm, Sun 11am–5pm) has a wonderful display of gory reliquaries and priestly sartorial wealth.

Practicalities

The **tourist office** in the town hall (daily 9am–7pm; ☎585 513 392, ⊛www .olomoucko.cz), will book **private rooms** for you. Of the town's **hotels**, the *Sigma* (☎585 232 076, ⊛www.sigmahotel.cz; ❸) is conveniently located opposite the train station at Jeremenkova 36; a much better option, however, is *Na hradbách*, Hrnčířská 3 (☎585 233 243; ✉nahradbach@quick.cz; ❷), a spotless, three-room **pension** hidden away in one of the city's prettiest backstreets. For real budget accommodation head down Ztracená to the student travel agency CKM (Mon–Fri 9am–5.30pm) at Denisova 4. Note that rooms can be hard to come by in May when the spring **Music Festival** follows the **Flora Festival**.

For **restaurants**, *U červeného volka* on Dolní náměstí is a cheap place with a wide range of veggie dishes, while *Caesar* in the cobbled vaults under the town hall is the most popular joint in town. A good range of cakes can be found in *Maruška* on 28 Října or the *Café Mahler*, at Horní náměstí 11. In the evenings, head for a backstreet **pub** like the reasonably priced *U bakaláre*, on Žerotinovo náměstí. The *U-Klub*, at the Studentcentrum at the far end of Křížovského, has occasional DJs and bands.

Travel details

Trains

Brno to: Olomouc (6 daily; 1hr 30min).
České Budějovice to: Brno (4–5 daily; 4hr 20min); Český Krumlov (9 daily; 1hr); Plzeň (hourly;

1hr 50min–3hr 15min).
Mariánské Lázně to: Karlovy Vary (6–7 daily; 1hr 40min); Plzeň (every 2hr; 1hr–1hr 15min).
Plzeň to: Brno (4 daily; 5hr–6hr 30min).
Prague to: Brno (hourly; 3hr–3hr 30min); České

Budějovice (8–9 daily; 2hr 15min–3hr); Karlovy Vary (3 daily; 3hr 20min–4hr); Mariánské Lázně (every 2hr; 2hr); Olomouc (every 1–2hr; 3hr–3hr 30min); Plzeň (hourly; 1hr 40min–2hr 15min).

Buses

Prague to: Brno (hourly; 2hr); České Budějovice (hourly; 2hr 20min–3hr 45min); Český Krumlov (up to 14 daily; 3hr–5hr); Karlovy Vary (hourly; 2hr 30min); Kutná Hora (every 30min; 55min–1hr 40min); Olomouc (2 daily; 4hr).

Denmark

Denmark highlights

* **Fireworks at Tivoli** A perfect end to an evening in Copenhagen. See p.258

* **Ny Carlsberg Glyptotek, Copenhagen** The city's finest gallery, with the biggest collection of Etruscan art outside Italy. See p.258

* **Christiana, Copenhagen** Hang out with the hippies in Denmark's "free city", a 1970s commune which is home to all things weird and wonderful. See p.261

* **Louisiana, Humlebæk** A magnificent modern art museum, whose sculpture garden overlooks the Øresund to Sweden. See p.264

* **Frederiksborg Slot, Hillerød** Frederik II's dramatic castle, impressively situated on three islands and complete with lake and gardens. See p.264

* **Viking Ship Museum, Roskilde** Five excellent specimens of Viking shipbuilding. See p.265

Introduction and basics

Between Scandinavia proper and mainland Europe, *Denmark* is a difficult country to pin down. In many ways it shares the characteristics of both regions: it's an EU member, and has prices and drinking laws that are broadly in line with those in the rest of Europe. But Denmark's social policies and its style of government are distinctly Scandinavian: social benefits and the standard of living are high, and its politics are very much that of consensus.

Denmark is the easiest Scandinavian country in which to travel, but its **landscape** is the least dramatic: very green and flat, largely farmland interrupted by pretty villages. Apart from a scattering of small islands, three main landmasses make up the country – the islands of Zealand and Funen and the peninsula of Jutland, which extends northwards from Germany. Most visitors make for **Zealand** (Sjælland), and, more specifically, **Copenhagen**, an exciting focal point with a beautiful old centre, a good array of museums and a boisterous nightlife. **Funen** (Fyn) has only one real urban draw, **Odense**; otherwise, it's renowned for cute villages and sandy beaches. **Jutland** (Jylland) has, as well as some varied scenery, ranging from soft green hills to desolate heathlands, **Århus** and **Aalborg**, two of the liveliest Danish cities.

Information & maps

Most places have a **tourist office**; staff can sometimes help with accommodation and change money. They're open daily, with long hours, in the most popular spots, but have reduced hours from October to March. All airports and many train stations also offer a hotel booking service. The best general **map** is by *Hallwag*, but the HI Association map is excellent, available free at ⓦwww.danhostel.dk.

Money and banks

Currency is the **krone** (plural *kroner*), made up of 100 øre. It comes in notes of 50kr, 100kr, 200kr, 500kr and 1000kr, and coins of 25øre, 50øre, 1kr, 2kr, 5kr, 10kr and 20kr. **Banking hours** are Mon–Fri 10am–4pm, Thurs till 6pm; and banks are generally the best places to **exchange cash** and travellers' cheques, charging 25kr per transaction. Forex bureaux charge only 20kr per transaction, but they're rarer. Most airports and ferry terminals have late-opening exchange facilities. ATMs are everywhere.

Communications

Post offices are open Mon–Fri 9.30/10am–5/5.30pm, Sat 9.30/10am–noon/1pm, with reduced hours in smaller communities. You can also buy stamps from most newsagents. Coin-operated **phones** are white and require a minimum of 2 x 1kr for a local call (they swallow one of the coins if the number is engaged), and 5kr for international calls; **phonecards** for the blue phones (which are a little cheaper) come as 30kr, 50kr and 100kr. The operator number is ☎118 (domestic), ☎113 (international) – both 7kr/min. **Internet access** is free at most libraries and tourist offices; most towns have cybercafés.

Denmark on the net

ⓦ*www.visitdenmark.com* Official Danish Tourist Board site
ⓦ*www.useit.dk* For budget travellers; focuses mainly on Copenhagen
ⓦ*www.aok.dk* Covering most of Zealand
ⓦ*www.visitcopenhagen.dk* Official Copenhagen tourist site
ⓦ*www.rejseplanen.dk* Public transport journey planner

Getting around

Denmark has swift and easy-to-use **public transport**. Danish State Railways (Danske Statsbaner or DSB; ⓦwww.dsb.dk) runs an exhaustive and reliable **rail** network. Train types range from the large inter-city expresses (*Lyntog*) to smaller local trains (*regionaltog*). **InterRail** and **Eurail** passes are valid on all DSB trains, as is the ScanRail pass (see p.36). Everywhere not served by train can be easily reached by **buses**, which often supplement the train timetable – some operated privately, some by DSB itself – and on these, railcards are valid. DSB's **timetable** or *Køreplan* (free) details all train, bus and ferry services, including the S-train system in Copenhagen.

Ferries link all the Danish islands. Where applicable, train and bus fares include the cost of crossings (although you can also pay at the terminal and walk on). Routes and prices are covered on the very useful HI map.

Cycling is the best way to appreciate Denmark's flat landscape, which is crisscrossed by cycle routes (maps and information at ⓦwww.dcf.dk). Most country roads have sparse traffic and all large towns have cycle tracks. Bikes can be rented at hostels, tourist offices and some train stations, as well as from bike shops (from 50kr/day, 200–250kr/week; 200–500kr deposit). All trains and most long-distance buses accept bikes, but you'll have to pay according to the zonal system used to calculate passenger tickets – 50kr to take your bike from Copenhagen to Århus by train with 20kr on top if you want to reserve a space in advance; 70kr by bus.

Accommodation

Accommodation is a major expense. Hotels, however, are by no means off-limits if you are prepared to seek out the better offers. Expect to pay around 500kr for an ensuite double **hotel** room, although most large towns have hotels offering rooms without bathrooms for as little as 400kr for a double. Hotels offer an inclusive all-you-can-eat breakfast – so large you won't need to buy lunch. It's a good idea to book in advance, especially in peak season, which you can do through tourist-office websites. Tourist offices can also supply details of **private rooms**, which cost 300–400kr a double. **Farmstays** (*Bondegårdsferie*) are becoming increasingly popular; see ⓦwww.bondegaardsferie .dk.

Hostels are the cheapest option. Every town has one and they have a high degree of comfort, most offering a choice of **private rooms**, often with en-suite toilets and showers, as well as dorm accommodation; nearly all have cooking facilities. Rates are around 100kr per person for a dorm bed; non-HI members pay an extra 30kr a night. Danhostel Danmarks Vandrerhjem (☎33.31.36.12, ⓦwww.danhostel.dk) produce a free hostel guide. Cheaper still are **sleep-ins**, chiefly found in major towns and often open only in summer (May–Aug). You need your own sleeping bag, sometimes only one night's stay is permitted and there is sometimes an age restriction. Local tourist offices have the latest details.

If you don't already have an International Camping Card, you'll need to get hold of a **Camping Card Scandinavia** (80kr) if you plan to camp, which is available at official campsites and is valid on all sites in Scandinavia until the year's end. A Transit Pass (20kr) can be used for a single overnight stay. All sites are open at least from June to August, many from April to September, while a few stay open all year. There's a rigid **grading system**: one-star sites have drinking water and toilets; two-stars also have showers, laundry and a food shop within 1km; three-stars, by far the majority, include a TV-room, shop, cafeteria, etc. Prices vary only slightly, three-stars charging 52–62kr per person, others a few kroner less. **Camping rough** without permission is illegal, and an on-the-spot fine may be imposed. Many campsites also have **cabin accommodation**, usually with cooking facilities, for 2000kr–4000kr per week for a six-berth place, although they are often fully booked in summer. Tourist offices have a free leaflet listing all sites.

Food and drink

Traditional Danish **food** centres on meat and fish, served with potatoes and another, usually boiled, vegetable. **Breakfast** (*morgenmad*) can be the tastiest Danish meal, and almost all hotels and hostels offer a sumptuous breakfast: a table laden with cereals, bread, cheese, ham, fruit juice, milk, coffee and tea, for around 50kr. Brunch, served in most cafes from 11am until mid-afternoon, is a popular and filling option for late starters and costs 40–90kr.

For daytime **snacks**, you can buy *smørrebrød* – open sandwiches heaped with meat, fish or cheese, and assorted trimmings – for 9–25kr. There are also **fast-food stands** (*pølsevogn*) in all main streets and at train stations, serving hot sausages (*pølser*) and hot dogs, toasted sandwiches (*parisertoast*) and chips (*pommes frites*). Cafés sell **Danish pastries** (*wienerbrød*), tastier and much less sweet than the imitations sold elsewhere, and you can usually get a generous sandwich or filling portion of salad (usually served with fresh bread) for around 50kr. You can find an excellent-value set **lunch** (*frokost*) at restaurants and bodegas (bars that sell no-frills food). *Tilbud* is the "special", *dagens ret* the "dish of the day", and you can expect to pay around 40kr for these, 80–100kr for a three-course set lunch. Open **buffets**, where you help yourself to as much as you like, will set you back 60–80kr. Kebabs and Chinese food are easy to find in most larger towns; a filling snack will cost around 25kr. You can also get a filling but ordinary self-service meat, fish or omelette lunch in a supermarket cafeteria for 50–90kr. Restaurants that are promising for lunch turn into expense-account affairs at night, although many still will have good-value buffets for **dinner** (*aftensmad*). Many hostels serve filling evening meals for 50–65kr. If you plan to save money by **self-catering**, head for Netto or Fakta supermarkets, where the food and drink are cheap and of excellent quality.

The most sociable places to **drink** are pubs and cafés, where the emphasis is on beer. As a general rule, bars and bodegas tends to favour wines and spirits. The cheapest **beer** is bottled, the so-called gold beer (*Guldøl* or *Elefantøl*; 20–30kr/bottle) is the strongest. Draught beer (*Fadøl*) is more expensive (15–30kr/250ml, 30–45kr/500ml) and a touch weaker, but tastes fresher. The most common brands are Carlsberg and Tuborg; Lys Pilsner is a very low alcohol lager. Most international **wines** (from 25kr) and **spirits** (15–35kr) are widely available. There are many varieties of the schnapps-like **Akvavit**; a tasty relative is the hot and strong **Gammel Dansk Bitter Dram** – drunk occasionally at breakfast time.

Opening hours and holidays

Standard **shop hours** are Mon–Fri 9.30/10am–5.30/7pm, Sat 9/9.30am–2 /5pm. All shops and banks are closed, and public transport and many museums run to Sun schedules on **public holidays**: Jan 1; Maundy Thurs to Easter Mon; Prayer Day (4th Fri after Easter); Ascension (40th day after Easter); Whit Sun & Mon; Constitution Day (June 5); Dec 24 (pm only); Dec 25 & Dec 26. On **International Workers' Day**, May 1, many offices and shops close at noon.

Emergencies

You're unlikely to have little direct contact with **police**, as street crime and hassle are minimal; however, they're helpful and likely to speak English. For prescriptions, doctors' consultations and dental work – but not **hospital** visits – you have to pay on the spot; to get a full refund, take your receipt, E111 and passport to the local health office.

Emergency numbers
All emergencies ☏112.

Copenhagen (København)

COPENHAGEN is Scandinavia's most affordable capital, and one of Europe's most user-friendly cities: welcoming and compact, with a centre largely given over to pedestrians. It is the seat of all national institutions – politics, finance and the arts – and dominates any visit to Denmark; its first-rate galleries, museums and summertime street entertainers fill your days, while by night its live music and an intimate bar and club scene is rivalled only by that on offer in Århus. There was no more than a tiny fishing settlement here until the twelfth century, when **Bishop Absalon** built a castle on Christiansborg's present site. Prosperity and trade flourished with the introduction of the Sound Toll on vessels in the Øresund, and after the demise of the Hanseatic ports, the city became the Baltic's principal harbour, earning the name **København** ("merchant's port"), and in 1443 it was made the Danish capital. A century later, Christian IV created Rosenborg Slot, Rundetårn and the districts of Nyboder and Christianshavn, and in 1669 Frederik III graced the city with its first royal palace, Amalienborg.

Arrival, information and city transport

Kastrup **airport** is 8km from the centre, connected to it by train (6 hourly 5am–midnight; hourly overnight; takes 13min; 22.50kr), which pull into Københavns Hovedbanegård (**Central Station**), near Vesterbrogade; **long-distance buses** from elsewhere in Denmark stop either here or a short bus or S-train ride from the centre. **Ferries** and catamarans dock close to Nyhavn, a few minutes' walk from the centre. The **tourist office**, opposite the station at Bernstorffsgade 1 (May–Aug Mon–Sat 9am–6/8pm; July & Aug also Sun 10am–6pm; rest of year Mon–Fri 9am–4pm, Sat 9am–2pm; ☎70.22.24.42, ⊛www.visitcopenhagen.dk), can arrange your accommodation for a 60kr fee. Far better for youth and budget-oriented information, however, is **Use-It**, centrally located in the Huset complex at Rådhusstræde 13 (mid-June to mid-Sept daily 9am–7pm; rest of year Mon–Wed 11am–4pm, Thurs 11am–6pm, Fri 11am–2pm; ☎33.73.06.20, ⊛www.useit.dk). Its friendly staff provide poste restante and free email, luggage storage facilities and the very useful free magazine, *Playtime*. If you're sightseeing on a very tight schedule, consider the **Copenhagen Card** (215/375/495kr for 24/48/72hr), which is valid for the entire public transport network (including much of eastern Zealand) and gives entry to most museums in the area. It's available at tourist offices, hotels, travel agents and the train station.

An integrated network of **buses**, electric **S-trains** (S-tog) and a new **metro** covers the city (5.30am–12.30am); overnight, a night bus (*Natbus*) network takes over. You can get a free route map from stations. InterRail or Eurail cards are valid on the S-trains. Otherwise, the best option is a Copenhagen Card (see above); the **24-timer ticket** (85kr), which covers the same area, but doesn't include admission to museums; or the **Klippekort** (90/120kr for two/three zones), which consists of ten stamps, each giving unlimited transfers for one hour within the designated zones (make sure you validate your ticket when boarding the bus or in machines on station platforms). For a single journey, get a **Billet** (14kr), valid for unlimited transfers in one hour within two zones. *Billets* can be bought on board buses or at train stations; *Klippekort* and *24-timers* at stations, HT Kortsalg kiosks and newsagents. Travelling without a ticket leaves you open to an instant fine of 500kr. In summertime, under the **City Bike scheme** (⊛www.citybike.dk), you can borrow bikes from racks across the city for a deposit of 20kr, which is returned when the bike is locked back into any other city rack after use. You'll be fined if you use the bikes outside the city limits (the old rampart lakes mark the border) and you'll need to get yourself some lights if you want to cycle at night, as you'll be fined if you're caught without any.

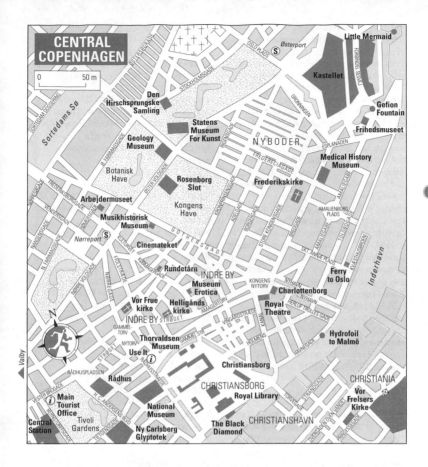

CENTRAL COPENHAGEN

0   50 m

Østerport (S)

Little Mermaid

Kastellet

Gefion Fountain

Den Hirschsprungske Samling

Frihedsmuseet

Statens Museum For Kunst

Geology Museum

NYBODER

Medical History Museum

Botanisk Have

Rosenborg Slot

Frederikskirke

Arbejdermuseet

Kongens Have

Musikhistorisk Museum

AMALIENBORG PLADS

Nørreport (S)

Cinemateket

Rundetårn

INDRE BY

Museum Erotica

KONGENS NYTORV

Charlottenborg

Ferry to Oslo

Vor Frue kirke

Helligånds kirke

INDRE BY STRØGET

Royal Theatre

Hydrofoil to Malmö

Thorvaldsens Museum

Use It (i)

Christiansborg

RÅDHUSPLADSEN

Rådhus

CHRISTIANSBORG

CHRISTIANIA

Main Tourist Office (i)

National Museum

Royal Library

Vor Frelsers Kirke

Central Station

Tivoli Gardens

Ny Carlsberg Glyptotek

The Black Diamond

CHRISTIANSHAVN

Valby

N

Accommodation

Accommodation is not easy to come by, especially if you arrive late, or during July and August, when it's essential to book in advance. Most of the cheaper **hotels** are around Istedgade, a slightly seedy area on the far side of the train station, and there's a good range of mid-priced hotels around Nyhavn, on the opposite side of the Indre By. Check with the tourist office early in the day and they may find you a double room for as little as 450kr; **private rooms** (❸) will be an S-train ride away from the centre. There's a great, though less central, selection of **hostels**; space is only likely to be a problem in the peak summer months, when you should call ahead or turn up as early as possible to be sure of a place (*Use-It* keeps a daily list of availability). Breakfast is not included in the prices given, unless otherwise stated.

Hostels and sleep-ins

Bellahøj Vandrehjem Herbergsvejen 8, Brønshøj ☎38.28.97.15, ⊛www.danhostel.dk/bellahoej. HI hostel with large dorms, but more cosy than its rivals, and just fifteen minutes from the city centre on buses #2a and #8, nightbus #82N. No curfew. Closed mid-Jan to March. 95kr.

City Public Hostel Absalonsgade 8, Vesterbro ☎32.31.20.70, ⊛www.city-public-hostel.dk. Noisy sixty-bed dorm on the lower floor, less crowded conditions on other levels. Just ten minutes' walk from the train station. Buses #6 and #28 stop close by. No curfew. Breakfast 20kr. May to mid-Aug. 120kr.

Hotel Jørgensens Rømersgade 11
☎33.13.81.86, ⊛www.hoteljoergensen.dk. A stone's throw from Nørreport station on Israels Plads. Mostly dorms of six, nine and twelve beds, with a few basic doubles. Popular with gay travellers. Age limit 35. Dorms 125kr.

Sleep In Blegdamsvej 132, Østerbro
☎35.26.50.59, ⊛www.sleep-in.dk. North of the centre, next to Fælledparken and within walking distance of lively Sankt Hans Torv. Basic but adequate four- and six-bed dorms. Bus #1, #6 or #14, nightbus #85N or #95N. July & Aug only. 90kr.

Sleep-In-Fact Valdemarsgade 14 ☎33.79.67.79, ⊛www.sleep-in-fact.dk. In the heart of Vesterbro, this is a sports centre out of season. Fifteen minutes' walk from the Central Station or bus #6. Late June to Aug. Small breakfast included. 120kr.

Sleep In Green Ravnsborggade 18, Nørrebro
☎35.37.77.77, ⊛www.sleep-in-green.dk. Close to Sankt Hans Torv's café- and bar-life, this place has 68 dorm beds. Bus #5 or #16, nightbus #81N or 84N. Organic breakfast 30kr. June–Sept. 95kr.

Sleep in Heaven Struensegade 7, Nørrebro
☎35.35.46.48, ⊛www.sleepinheaven.com. Two vast halls, the largest with 76 beds divided into four- and eight-bed compartments. Pleasant atmosphere, with youthful staff and occasional free gigs. Ten minutes from the centre by bus #8, #12 or #13, nightbus #92N. No curfew. 110kr.

Hotels

Bertrams Hotel Vesterbrogade 107a
☎33.25.04.05. Relaxed and cosy, modelled on Agatha Christie's *Bertrams* in London, a quiet haven in lively Vesterbro. Large rooms, some

en suite. Bus #6 or #28. Breakfast buffet included. ➏

Hotel Cab Inn Scandinavia Vodroffsvej 55, Frederiksberg ☎35.36.11.11, ⊛www.cab-inn.dk. Inspired by the Oslo ferry, 200 small en-suite cabins. Breakfast 50kr. ➏

Saga Hotel Colbjørnsensgade 18–20
☎33.24.49.44, ⊛www.sagahotel.dk. Cheap, central hotel, a stone's throw from Central Station (head out the back exit). On the edge of the red light district. Shared bathrooms. Breakfast included. ➍

Campsites

Absalon Korsdalsvej 132, Rødovre ☎36.41.06.00, ⊛www.camping-absalon.dk. Reasonable site 9km southwest of the city. S-train line B to Brøndbyøster, then fifteen minutes' walk or bus #550S, nightbus #93N. Open all year.

Bellahøj Camping Hvidkildevej 66
☎38.10.11.50. Near the hostel of the same name. Central but grim, with long queues for the showers. Bus #11 or S-train F or M to Fuglebakken, nightbus #82N. June–Aug.

Charlottenlund Strandpark Strandvejen 144, Charlottenlund ☎39.62.36.88,
⊛www.campingcopenhagen.dk. Beautifully situated at Charlottenlund Beach. Bus #6 or nightbus #85N. Mid-May to mid-Sept.

FDM Camping Tangloppen, Ishøj Havn, Ishøj
☎43.54.07.67, ⊛www.fdmcamping.dk. Near the Ishøj hostel, 14km from the centre, but a fantastic location near both a beach and a plethora of watersports facilities. S-train A or E, then a ten-minute walk. May to mid-Sept.

The City

Just off hectic Vesterbrogade outside the station is perhaps Copenhagen's most famous attraction, the **Tivoli Gardens** (mid-April to Sept daily 11am–11pm/1am; 55kr), whose opening each year marks the beginning of summer. Throughout the season, the gardens feature fairground rides, fireworks, fountains, and a variety of nightly entertainment in the central arena, including live music on Fridays. It's rather overrated and expensive, but you can still have an enjoyable evening wandering among the revellers of all ages. On the south side of Tietgensgade, the **Ny Carlsberg Glyptotek** (Tues–Sun 10am–4pm; 30kr, Wed & Sun free; ⊛www.glyptoteket.dk) is Copenhagen's finest gallery, with an array of Greek, Roman and Egyptian art and artefacts, as well as what is considered the biggest and best collection of Etruscan art outside Italy. There are also excellent examples of modern European art, including a collection of Degas casts, Manet's *Absinthe Drinker* and works by Man Ray, Chagall and Picasso.

Directly behind the train station begins **Vesterbro** proper, the former red light district, currently undergoing a bit of a gentrification process as a home to Copenhagen's wealthiest students and young families. In the narrow streets between Vesterbrogade and Istedgade, a few porno shops remain as evidence of the area's former role. At Vesterbrogade 59, the **City Museum** (Mon & Wed–Sun

10am/1pm–4pm; 20kr, free on Fri) contains reconstructed ramshackle house fronts and tradesmen's signs from early Copenhagen, a large room recording the form Christian IV gave the city, and a collection of memorabilia concerning the nineteenth-century Danish philosopher Søren Kierkegaard. Further along Vesterbrogade, down Pile Allé and along Gamle Carlsberg Vej (buses #6 and #18), the exhibition at **Carlsberg Brewery Visitors Center** (Tues–Sun 10am–4pm; free) is well worth seeing, if only for the free booze provided at the end.

Indre By

Indre By forms the city's inner core, an intricate maze of streets, squares and alleys. The main way in is from the buzzing open space of Rådhuspladsen on the north side of the Tivoli Gardens, where you'll find the **Rådhus** (tours: Mon–Fri 3pm, Sat 10am & 11am; 30kr), which has an elegant *fin-de-siècle* hall and a **bell tower** (separate tours: Mon–Sat noon, June–Sept also Mon–Fri 10am & 2pm; 20kr) that gives wonderful views over the city. Jens Olsen's World Clock (10kr), in a room close to the entrance, took 27 years to perfect; it contains a 570,000-year calendar, plotting solar and lunar eclipses and various planetary orbits, as well as telling the local time – all with astounding accuracy.

Beyond Rådhuspladsen, **Strøget**, a busy pedestrianized street, leads into the heart of the city. The liveliest part is around Gammeltorv and Nytorv, squares on either side of Strøget, where there's a morning fruit and vegetable market, and jewellery and bric-a-brac stalls. A few minutes further on is the **Helligånds Kirke** (daily noon–4pm), founded in the fourteenth century and largely rebuilt from 1728 onwards, it is one of the oldest churches in the city. Strøget ends at **Kongens Nytorv**, the city's largest square, with an equestrian statue of its creator, Christian V, in the centre and a couple of grandly ageing structures around two of its shallow angles, most notably the Danish Royal Theatre and Charlottenborg – finished in 1683, at the same time as the square itself, for a son of Frederik III. Since 1754 Charlottenborg has been the home of the **Royal Academy of Art** (daily 10am–5pm, Wed till 7pm; 20kr; ❀www.charlottenborg-art.dk), which hosts decidedly eclectic art exhibitions in its spacious rooms.

There's more to see among the tangle of buildings and streets **west of Strøget**, not least the old university area, sometimes called the Latin Quarter, where the **Vor Frue Kirke** (Mon–Sat 8.30am–5pm, Sun noon–3/5pm), Copenhagen's cathedral, dates from 1829. The figure of Christ behind the altar and the solemn statues of the Apostles, crafted by Bertel Thorvaldsen and his pupils, merit a quick call. Northeast, the **Rundetårn** (Mon–Sat 10am–5/8pm, Sun noon–5/8pm; 20kr), whose summit is reached by a spiral ramp, was built by Christian IV as an observatory. Close by, the **Musikhistorisk Museum**, just off Kultorvet at Åbenrå 30 (daily except Thurs 1–3.50pm; 30kr), holds an impressive collection of musical instruments and sound-making devices, spanning the globe and the last thousand years. Over Nørre Voldgade, the **Arbejdermuseet** (Workers Museum) at Rømersgade 22 (daily 10am–4pm; Nov–June closed Mon; 50kr) is an engrossing guide to working-class life in Copenhagen from 1930 to 1959. **Nørrebro**, northwest of the train station, has shed its crime-related reputation and is now a lively, young area that houses an increasing number of trendy fashion shops and buzzes right through the night.

North of Indre By

There's a profound change of mood once you cross Gothersgade: the congenial alleys of the old city give way to long, broad streets and proud, aristocratic structures. At no. 55, **Cinemateket** (Tues–Fri 9.30am–10pm, Sat & Sun 12.30–10pm; free, movies 50kr; ❀www.cinemateket.dk), houses a three screen art-house cinema, a *videotek* section with free film showings, and a museum and library with exhibits on the city's early film industry. Running from Kongens Nytorv, a slender canal divides the two sides of **Nyhavn**, picturesquely lined by colourful eighteenth-century houses – now bars and cafés, which are a lovely spot for a beer in summer. Just north, the cobbled **Amalienborg Plads** centres on a statue of Frederik V flanked by four identical Rococo palaces. Two serve as royal residences, and there's a changing of the guard at noon, if the monarch is at home. Between the square and the harbour are the lavish gardens of Amaliehaven; in the opposite direction is the great marble dome of **Frederikskirke**, also known as "Marmorkirken" or marble church (Mon–Thurs 10am–5pm, Wed till 6pm, Fri–Sun noon–5pm), which was modelled on St Peter's in Rome. Begun in 1749, it remained unfinished until a century and a half later because of the enormous costs involved. Further along Bredgade, a German armoured car commandeered by Danes to bring news of the Nazi surrender marks the entrance to the **Frihedsmuseet** (Museum of the Danish Resistance Movement; Tues–Sat 10/11am–3/4pm, Sun 10/11am–4/5pm; 40kr, free on Wed). The road behind the museum crosses into the grounds of the **Kastellet** (daily 6am–sunset; free), a fortress built by Christian IV and expanded by his successors through the seventeenth century. It's now occupied by the Danish army and closed to the public, but on a nearby corner, the diminutive **Little Mermaid** has, since its unveiling in 1913, been a magnet for tourists to the city, despite overlooking a ferry port. A bronze statue of a Hans Christian Andersen character, it was sculpted by Edvard Erichsen and paid for by the founder of the Carlsberg brewery. A short walk to the south, the spectacular **Gefion Fountain** shows the goddess Gefion with her four sons, whom she's turned into oxen having been promised, in return, as much land as she can plough in a single night.

West of here lies **Nyboder**, a curious area of narrow streets lined with rows of compact yellow dwellings, originally built by Christian IV to encourage his sailors to live in the city. The oldest (and cutest) houses can be found along Skt. Pauls Gade. Across Sølvgade from Nyboder is the main entrance to **Rosenborg Slot** (May–Oct daily 10/11am–3/5pm; Nov–April Tues–Sun 11am–2pm; 60kr). This Dutch-Renaissance-style palace served as the main residence of Christian IV and, until the end of the nineteenth century, of the monarchs who succeeded him. The main building displays the rooms and furnishings used by the regal occupants, although the highlight is the downstairs treasury, which displays the crown jewels and rich accessories worn by Christian IV. Adjacent to Rosenborg Slot is **Kongens Have**, the city's oldest public park and a popular place for picnics, while on the west side is the **Botanical Garden** (daily 8.30am–4/6pm; winter closed Mon; free). The neighbouring **Statens Museum for Kunst** (daily 10am–5pm, Wed till 8pm; 40kr, free on Wed; ⊛www.smk.dk) holds a mammoth collection of art, from minor Picassos to major pieces by Matisse and Braque, Cranach, El Greco, Titian, Rubens, Poussin and Claude Lorrain – although it's the grotesque pieces by Emil Nolde that steal the show. The Skagen artists (see p.272), known for their interesting use of light, are amongst a nearby collection of twentieth-century Danish art across the park, at **Den Hirschsprungske Samling** on Stockholmsgade (Mon & Wed–Sun 11am–4pm, Wed till 9pm; 25kr, free on Wed; ⊛www.hirschsprung.dk).

Christiansborg

Christiansborg sits on the island of Slotsholmen, with several short bridges tenuously connecting it to Indre By. It was here, in the twelfth century, that Bishop Absalon built the castle that instigated the city. The drab royal palace completed in 1916 that now occupies the site is primarily given over to government offices and the state parliament, or **Folketinget** (guided tours July–Sept daily 2pm; rest of year Sun 2pm; free). Close to the bus stop on Christiansborg Slotsplads is the doorway to the **Ruins under Christiansborg** (daily 9.30am–3.30pm; Oct–April closed Mon, Wed & Fri; 20kr), where a staircase leads down to the remains of Absalon's original building; it's surprisingly absorbing, the mood enhanced by the semi-darkness and lack of external noise. The Royal Reception Rooms (guided tours: May–Sept daily 11am, 1pm & 3pm; Oct–April Tues, Thurs & Sat 3pm; 45kr), in the palace's north wing and used by the royal family to entertain important visitors, are worth a peek. On the north side of Slotsholmen, the **Thorvaldsens Museum**

(Tues–Sun 10am–5pm; 20kr, Wed free) is the home of an enormous collection of work and memorabilia (and the body) of Denmark's most famous sculptor, who lived from 1770 to 1844. There's another major collection a short walk away over the Slotsholmen moat, in the **National Museum** (same hours; 40kr, free on Wed; ⓦ www.natmus.dk), which has excellent displays on Denmark's prehistory and Viking days – jewellery, sacrificial gifts, and even bodies, all remarkably well preserved by Danish peat bogs.

Christianshavn and Christiania

From Christiansborg, a bridge crosses to **Christianshavn**, built by Christian IV as an autonomous new town in the early sixteenth century as housing for shipbuilding workers. It was given features more common to Dutch ports of the time, even down to small canals, and in parts is more redolent of Amsterdam than Copenhagen. Reaching skywards on the far side of Torvegade is the blue-and-gold spire of **Vor Frelsers Kirke** (daily 11am–3.30/4.30pm; tower April–Aug only; free, tower 20kr), whose helter-skelter outside staircase was added to the otherwise plain church in the mid-eighteenth century, making it one of the city's most recognizable features. A few streets from Vor Frelsers Kirke, **Christiania** is a former barracks area that was colonized by hippies after declaring itself a "free city" in 1971. A pseudo-Statue of Liberty greets visitors as they pass under the little arched entrance and head for the open hash market, known as *Puscherstreet*, where smoking is tolerated by the government. Bob Marley and John Lennon blare out from the bars and the area is awash with psychedelic painting. Residents ask visitors not to camp or take photos. Beyond the touristy entrance, you'll find plenty of buildings, art and inhabitants of interest. There are guided tours of the area (daily 3pm; 30kr; ☎ 32.95.65.07, ⓦ www.christiania.org); but it's more fun to just turn up and wander.

Eating and drinking

There's a wide choice of **eating** options in the city centre; the areas around Kultorvet and along Studiestræde are loaded with great places to eat. Farther afield, Nørrebro across Peblinge Søen draws the trendy set, and Vesterbrogade turns up a number of lower-key places, better the further you venture. An almost unchartable network of **cafés** and bars serving drinks and snacks covers Copenhagen. The best are in or close to Indre By, though bear in mind that on Fridays and Saturdays you'll probably need to queue. If you're **self-catering**, there are numerous *smørrebrød* outlets – Domhusets Smørrebrød, Kattesundet 18, and Centrum Smørrebrød, Vesterbrogade 6C, are two of the most central – and there's a Netto at Nørre Voldgade 94, Fiolstræde 9, Landemærket 11 and Store Kongensgade 47. Fakta is on Nørrebrogade 14–16 and on Borgergade 27.

Brunches, snacks and fast food

Amokka Dag Hammerskjölds Allé 38–40. A coffee temple near Østerport station serving more varieties of coffee than you can imagine. Also sells sandwiches, etc. Outdoor seating in summer.

Bang & Jensen Istedgade 130. Popular café at the quieter end of Istedgade, serving a renowned brunch until 4pm and sandwiches all day.

Café Europa Amagertorv 1. Its coffee is said to be the best in town, and it also sells fabulous cakes, sandwiches and light meals. Outdoor seating on Strøget.

Café Sommersko Kronprinsensgade 6. A popular café, whose filling Sunday brunch (veggie options available) is particularly recommended.

Den Sorte Gryde, Istedgade 108. Legendary huge burgers, but also good traditional Danish fare.

Front Page Sortedams Dosseringen 21. Overlooking one of the city's finest lakes, this is a perfect spot for a quiet coffee or beer and light snacks.

Husets Café Rådhusstræde 13. Sandwich spot located in the Huset complex, which doubles as a jazz venue in the evenings. Closed Sun.

La Galette Larsbjørnstræde 9. Authentic Breton pancakes made with organic buckwheat and an array of fillings – from smoked salmon to chocolate and chestnut mousse.

Morgenstedet Langgade, in Christiania. Tasty and mostly organic vegan and vegetarian salads, snacks and meals at very affordable prices. No smoking, No alcohol. Closed Tues.

Pussy Galore's Flying Circus Sankt Hans Torv 30. Trendy brunch spot with outdoor seating on the square. Brunch served till 4pm. Also popular in the evening, when beer and wine take priority.
The Taco Shop Nørre Farimagsgade 57. The best taco spot in town; no tables.

Restaurants

Ankara Vesterbrogade 35. Popular Turkish restaurant with all-you-can-eat buffets for 49/69kr (lunch/eve).
Atlas Bar Larsbjørnstræde 18. Eco-restaurant/café serving tasty Asian and South American dishes. The portions are enormous, with main courses from 100kr. Closed Sun.
Den Grønne Kælder Pilestræde 48. A simple tiled-floor vegetarian eatery. Closed Sun.
Delicatessen Vesterbrogade 120. Cosy basement restaurant serving outstanding international dishes, tapas from 20kr a plate. Take out available.
Hackenbusch Vesterbrogade 124. Colourful café/bar with an inventive blackboard menu.
Nyhavns Færgekro Nyhavn 5. Slightly pricey, but the lunchtime fish-laden buffet (89kr) cannot be surpassed. Outdoor seating in summer.
RizRaz Kompagnistræde 20. Excellent-value Mediterranean food; buffets are 49/59kr (lunch/eve).
Shezan Viktoriagarde 22. The first Pakistani restaurant in Copenhagen and still going strong. Main courses from 50kr, with plenty of vegetarian dishes.
Spiseloppen Christiania. It's won culinary accolades, and hiked up its prices, but the *Spiseloppen* is still great and the portions generous. Meals from 140kr. Closed Mon.

Thai Esan Lille Istedgade 7. Bargain Thai food in a very popular restaurant.

Bars

Café Louise Nørrebrogade 5. Open 1–7am every night (weekends until 9am), this is a legendary last stop after a big night out. Ring a door bell to get in.
Charlie's Bar Pilestræde 33. Award-winning Real Ale pub.
Dan Turell Store Regnegade 3. Something of an institution with the artier student crowd, this place is packed at weekends, when it's open till 4am.
Drop Inn Kompagnistræde 34. Easy going and unpretentious place near Huset with live blues or rock almost every night. Cheap beer and late opening hours.
Hviids Vinstue Kongens Nytorv 19. Old-fashioned bar with crowded rooms patrolled by uniformed waiters. Outdoor seating in summer.
Krasnapolsky Vestergade 10. Danish avant-garde art on the wall reflects the trend-setting reputation of this ultramodern watering hole. DJs Thurs, Fri & Sat. Tasty food too.
Kulkafeen Teglgårdsstræde 5. Cosy café that gets going in the evening and has live music on Sat.
Peder Hvitfeldt P. Hvitfeldtsstræde 15. Immensely popular spit-and-sawdust place. Come early if you want a seat.
Sebastopol Sankt Hans Torv 2. Trendy spot on the Sankt Hans Torv square that catches the last rays of sun and therefore gathers large crowds in summer. Good brunches too.
Universitetscaféen Fiolstræde 2. A prime location, long hours (until 5am), outdoor seating in summer and live blues or rock every Thurs.

Nightlife

Copenhagen is a pretty good place for **live music**. Major international names visit regularly, and there are always plenty of minor gigs in cafés and bars, often free during the week. For **listings** of what's on, pick up the free *Nat & Dag* or *Gaffa*, from cafés and music shops. Clubs and discos are busy from midnight and 5am, with fairly easy-going dress codes; drinks are seldom expensive and admission is fairly cheap (from 40kr).

Live music, clubs and discos

Barfly & Britannia Løvstræde 4. A multistorey temple of entertainment. The bottom half plays music from the 70s and 80s, the top two floors techno and mainstream pop. Pool tables and pinball machines too. Wed–Sat till 5/6am.
Bombay Club Nørregade 41. This large oriental-style club plays soul, R&B, and Latino house. Admission 60kr.
Copenhagen JazzHouse Niels Hemmingsensgade 10 ⓦ www.jazzhouse.dk. Laid-

back jazz venue, followed by a jazz, funk or mainstream disco.
JazzHuset Vognporten Rådhusstræde 13. In the same building as Use-It, with regular live bands. Mon–Thurs bebop, Fri & Sat jazz.
Klaptræet Kultorvet 11. A café/bar during the week, at weekends it hosts DJs with a dancefloor out back. Closes 5am.
Loppen Bådsmandsstræde 43, Christiania. Regular rock, jazz and performance artists. Discos follow live music events on Fri & Sat. Closes 5am.

Mojo Løngangstræde 21 ⓦ www.mojo.dk.
Renowned jazz and blues evenings – live music
every night. Happy hour 8–10pm.
Park Café Østerbrogade 79 ⓦ www.parkcafe.dk.
Popular café/music venue. Thurs–Sat, it's home to
Kitty Club, with mainstream disco upstairs, live
music downstairs.
Pumpehuset Studiestræde 52
ⓦ www.pumpwhuset.dk. Venue for mainstream
rock, hip-hop and funk from around the world.
Rust Guldbergsgade 8, Nørrebro ⓦ www.rust.dk.
Huge complex hosting rock bands on a main
stage, and three dancefloors playing everything
from Break Beat to Latin jazz. Closed Mon.

Sabor Latino Vester Voldgade 85. Popular Latin
dance venue. Free Salsa lessons Thurs–Sat
10–11pm.
Stengade 30 Stengade 18 ⓦ www.stengade30
.dk. Mixed bag of live music and dance events,
and a popular hardcore metal venue. Techno
Thurs. Closed Mon.
Stereo Bar Linnésgade 16A. Once-trendy bar
that's mellowed with age, with a dancefloor in the
basement playing mostly house. Closes 3am.
Vega Enghavevej 40 ⓦ www.vega.dk. Two concert
halls, Lille Vega and Store Vega, with international
acts, a nightclub, lounge and chill-out bar. Popular
with everyone, and an excellent night out. Free
admission 11pm–1am. Over-20s only.

Listings

Bike rental Københavns Cykelbørs, Gothersgade
157; Københavns Cykler, Reventlowsgade 11;
Østerport Cykler, Oslo Plads 9.
Embassies Australia, Strandboulevarden 122
☏ 39.29.20.77; Canada, Kristen Bernikowsgade 1
☏ 33.48.32.00; Ireland, Østbanegade 21
☏ 35.42.32.33; Netherlands, Toldbodgade 33
☏ 33.70.72.02; New Zealand, use UK; UK,
Kastelsvej 40 ☏ 35.44.52.00; US, Dag
Hammerskjölds Allé 24 ☏ 35.55.31.44.
Exchange Arbejdernes Landsbank, Vestrebrogade
5 (24hr); Den Danske Bank at the Airport (daily
6am–10pm); Forex at the Central Station (daily
8am–9pm). Kontanten ATMs everywhere.
Gay and lesbian Copenhagen The city has a
lively gay scene. For information, contact the
National Organization for Gay Men and Women,
Teglgårdstræde 13 (☏ 33.13.19.48, ⓦ www.lbl.dk),
or get hold of Pan magazine. The Cosy Bar,
Studiestræde 24, is popular with gay men of all

ages, while Sebastian, Hyskenstræde 10, draws a
predominantly young trendy crowd. Pan Club,
Knabrostræde 3, part of the largest gay centre in
the country, has a great disco (Thurs is Carma
Club for women only). Masken, Studiestræde 33,
has a great bar and disco (women only Thurs
9pm–2am). Of primarily lesbian places,
Kvindehuset, Gothersgade 37, has a café and the
XXBar disco every 1st & 3rd Fri of the month, as
well as other regular events.
Hospital Rigshospitalet, Blegdamsvej 9
☏ 35.45.35.45.
Left luggage Free for a day at Use-It,
Rådhusstræde 13. Otherwise, lockers at Central
Station, from 25kr for 24hr.
Pharmacies Steno Apotek, Vesterbrogade 6C;
Sønderbro Apotek, Amagerbrogade 158. Both 24hr.
Police ☏ 33.25.14.48.
Post office Tietgensgade 37; also at Central
Station.

Short trips from Copenhagen

If the weather's good, take a trip to the Amager **beaches** on bus #9, #12, #13 or
#19 along Øresundsvej. On the other side of the airport from the beaches lies
DRAGØR, an atmospheric cobbled fishing village which has good local history
collections in the harbourside Dragør Museum (May–Sept Tues–Sun noon–4pm;
20kr), and the Amager Museum (same hours, plus Oct–April Wed & Sat
noon–4pm), just off the Copenhagen road at the western edge of the village. From
the city, take bus #30 or #34. If you're in the mood for an amusement park but can't
afford Tivoli, venture out to **BAKKEN** (late March to Aug daily noon/2pm–midnight; free; 199kr day pass; ⓦ www.bakken.dk), close to the Klampenborg stop at the
end of lines C and F on the S-train. Besides swings and rollercoasters it offers pleasant woods of oak and beech, which were once royal hunting grounds.

Two more attractions are on Zealand's eastern coast. Fifteen minutes' walk from
Rungsted Kyst train station, the simple **Karen Blixen Museum** (May–Sept
Tues–Sun 10am–5pm; Oct–April Wed–Sun 11am/1pm–4pm; 35kr) presents a
moving testament of this remarkable woman's life, best known as the author of Out

of Africa. In **HUMLEBÆK**, 10km further north and a short walk from its train station, is **Louisiana**, an excellent modern art gallery, at Gammel Strandvej 13 (daily 10am–5pm, Wed till 10pm; 68kr); its setting alone is worth the journey, harmoniously combining art, architecture and the natural landscape.

The rest of Zealand

As home to the capital, **Zealand** is Denmark's most important and most visited region, and, with a swift metropolitan transport network covering almost half of the island, you can always make it back to the capital in time for an evening drink. North of Copenhagen, **Helsingør**, the departure point for ferries to Sweden, is the site of the Kronborg Slot – given a run for its money by nearby Frederiksborg Slot at **Hillerød**. West of Copenhagen, and on the main route to Funen, is **Roskilde**, its extravagant cathedral the resting place for Danish monarchs, and with a gorgeous location on the Roskilde fjord – from where five Viking boats were salvaged and are now restored and displayed in a specially built museum.

Hillerød

Last stop on lines A and E of the S-train, or 30 minutes by train from Helsingør, **HILLERØD**'s highlight is the lovely **Frederiksborg Slot** (daily 10/11am–3/5pm; 60kr) which lies decorously across three small islands on an artificial lake. The Frederiksborg ferry does a half hour trip on the castle lake in summer (20kr). Buses #701, #702 and #703 run from the train station to the castle, but it's only a twenty-minute signposted walk. The castle was rebuilt at the turn of the seventeenth century in Dutch Renaissance style and the unusual design – prolific use of towers and spires, pointed Gothic arches and flowery window ornamentation – still dominates. There's an illustrated guide to the interior (60kr), but most rooms have detailed descriptions in English pasted up on the walls. Two rooms deserve special mention: the exquisite chapel, where monarchs were anointed between 1671 and 1840, and the Great Hall above, bare but for the staggering wall- and ceiling-decorations: tapestries, wall-reliefs, portraits and a glistening black marble fireplace. The *Spisestedet Leonora*, in one of the castle's gatehouses, serves fantastic *smørrebrød* (from 37kr a piece), should you get peckish.

Helsingør

First impressions of **HELSINGØR** are none too enticing, but away from the hustle of its train and ferry terminals it is a quiet and likeable town. Its position on the four-kilometre strip of water linking the North Sea and the Baltic brought the town prosperity when, in 1429, the Sound Toll was imposed on passing vessels. Today, it's once again an important waterway, with ferries across it to Swedish Helsingborg, accounting for most of Helsingør's through-traffic and innumerable cheap booze shops. The town's great tourist draw is **Kronborg Slot** (May–Sept daily 10.30am–5pm; rest of year Tues–Sun 11am–3/4pm; 40kr, 60kr joint ticket with the Maritime Museum; Copenhagen Card not valid), principally because of its literary associations as Elsinore Castle, whose ramparts Shakespeare's Prince Hamlet supposedly strode. The playwright never actually visited Helsingør, and the tenth-century character Amleth on whom his

Three *ferry* lines make the twenty-minute crossing from Helsingør to *Helsingborg* in Sweden. Scandlines is the main one (every 20min; 34kr return), leaving from the main terminal by the train station. Otherwise, there's Sundbusserne (every 30min; 32kr), and HH Ferries (30kr), the latter docking a good walk from central Helsingborg. Rail passes are valid on all three and the Copenhagen Card gives a fifty percent discount.

hero was based long predates the castle, but nevertheless there's a thriving Hamlet souvenir business. The present castle dates from the sixteenth century and though various bits have been destroyed and rebuilt since, it remains a grand affair, enhanced immeasurably by its setting; the interior, particularly the royal chapel, is spectacularly ornate. The castle also houses the national **Maritime Museum** (30kr, 60kr joint ticket with the castle itself), a motely collection of model ships and nautical knick-knacks.

The **tourist office,** opposite the train station at Havnepladsen 3 (Mon–Fri 9am–4/5/6pm, Sat 10am–1/3pm; ☎49.21.13.33, ⊛www.helsingorturist.dk), leads into Helsingør's well-preserved medieval quarter. **Stengade** is the main pedestrianized street, linked by a number of narrow alleyways to Axeltorv, the town's small market square and a good spot for a beer. Near the corner of Stengade and Skt. Annagade, the newly renovated spired **Skt. Olai's Kirke** (Mon–Fri 10am–2/4pm) is now Helsingør's cathedral. Just beyond is Skt. Mariæ Kirke, whose **Karmeliterklostret**, built circa 1400 is now the best-preserved medieval monastic complex in Scandinavia (mid-May to mid-Sept, Mon–Fri 10am–2/3pm; 20kr). Its former hospital contains the **Town Museum** (daily noon–4pm; 10kr), which prided itself on brain operations – the unnerving tools of which are still here, together with diagrams of the corrective procedures used. For **food**, *Rådmands Davids Hus*, Strandgade 70, is a prime lunchtime spot for its daily specials; *Møllers Conditori*, Stengade 39, Denmark's oldest bakery, has sizeable sit-down sandwiches and Danish pastries to follow; or try the varied delights in the courtyard at Stengade 26, including *Biocafeen* which has live music in the evenings.

Roskilde

ROSKILDE, also an enjoyable day-trip from Copenhagen, was the base of the Danish church in the twelfth century and as a consequence became the nation's capital. Its importance waned after the Reformation, but its ancient centre is one of Denmark's most appealing – well worth a look on your way west. Showpiece is the fabulous **Roskilde Domkirke** (Mon–Sat 9/10am–3.45/4.45pm, Sun 12.30–3.45/4.45pm; 15kr), founded in 1170 and largely completed by the fourteenth century, although bits have been added since. Four royal chapels house a claustrophobic collection of regal remains: twenty kings and seventeen queens. The most richly endowed chapel is that of Christian IV, a previously austere resting place jazzed up in the early nineteenth century with bronze statues, frescoes and vast paintings of scenes from his reign. A roofed passageway, the Arch of Absalon, runs from the Cathedral into the **Roskilde Palace**, housing the **Palace Collections** (mid-May to mid-Sept daily 11am–4pm; rest of the year Sat noon–4pm; 25kr): paintings, furniture and other artefacts belonging to the wealthiest Roskilde families of the eighteenth and nineteenth centuries. In the same building is the **Museum of Contemporary Art** (Tues–Fri 11am–5pm, Sat & Sun noon–4pm; 20kr, Wed free), hosting temporary exhibitions and including a charming sculpture garden. The town's history is recorded in the **Roskilde Museum** at Skt. Ols Gade 18 (daily 11am–4pm; 25kr), with strong sections on medieval pottery and toys, although more absorbing is the modern **Viking Ship Museum** (daily 10am–5pm; 60kr; ⊛www.vikingeskibsmuseet.dk), at Vindeboder 12 on the banks of the fjord. Inside, five excellent specimens of Viking shipbuilding are proudly displayed: a deep-sea trader, a merchant ship, a warship, a ferry and a longship, each one retrieved from the fjord where they had been sunk to block invading forces.

The **tourist office** (Mon–Fri 9am–4/5/6pm, Sat 10am–1/2pm; ☎46.31.65.65, ⊛www.visitroskilde.dk) is at Gullandsstræde 15, a short walk from the main square. For **lunch**, head to *Café Satchmo*, down a passageway between the *Hotel Prindsen* and Bryggergården on Algade. Contact the tourist office well in advance if you wish to stay during the **Roskilde Festival** (⊛www.roskilde-festival.dk), one of the largest open-air rock events in Europe, attracting almost 100,000 people annually. The festival takes place late June/early July and there's a special free camping ground beside the festival site, to which shuttle buses run from the train station every ten minutes.

Funen

Known as the "Garden of Denmark", partly for the lawn-like neatness of its fields, partly for the fruit and vegetables grown in them, **Funen** is the smaller of the two main Danish islands. The pastoral outlook of the place and the coastline draw many visitors, but its attractions are low-profile cultural sights, such as the collections of the "Funen painters" and the birthplaces of writer Hans Christian Andersen and composer Carl Nielsen. **Odense**, Denmark's third city, is the island's main urban attraction, while nearby is the laid-back former fishing town of **Kerteminde**, and the picturesque Hindsholm peninsula.

Odense

ODENSE loves to remind you it's the birthplace of Denmark's best-loved writer, Hans Christian Andersen, as well as the childhood home of composer Carl Nielsen. Named after Odin, chief of the pagan gods, this is one of the oldest settlements in the country. The inner core of the city is pedestrianized with a range of good museums to visit; the nightlife is surprisingly lively, with a focus on live music and jazz.

The city's major attraction is the **Hans Christian Andersen Hus** at Hans Jensen Stræde 37–45 (mid-June to Aug daily 9am–7pm; rest of year Tues–Sun 10am–4pm; ⊛www.odmus.dk; 40kr), in the house where the writer was born in 1805. Currently undergoing renovation to celebrate his bicentenary in 2005, parts of the museum will be temporarily closed during 2004, but it will include a library of Andersen's works, audio collections of his best-known works and the intriguing paraphernalia of his life, including school reports, manuscripts and drawings from his travels. For some local history, head to **Bymuseet Møntergården** a few streets away at Overgade 48–50 (Tues–Sun 10am–4pm; ⊛www.odmus.dk; 25kr), where there's an engrossing assemblage of artefacts dating from the city's earliest settlements to the Nazi occupation. There's more about Andersen at Munkemøllestræde 3–5, between Skt. Knud Kirkestræde and Horsetorvet, in the tiny **Hans Christian Andersen's Barndomshjem** (Childhood Home; daily 10/11am–3/4pm; 10kr), where Andersen lived from 1807 to 1819. Nearby, the crypt of **Skt. Knud's Kirke** (Mon–Sat 9/10am–4/5pm, Sun noon–3pm; free), holds the remains of King Knud II (aka Canute) and his brother Benedikt, both murdered at the altar of nearby Skt. Albani Kirke in 1086. The cathedral is the only example of pure Gothic church architecture in the country; its enormous and finely detailed sixteenth-century altarpiece, coated in 23 carat gold leaf, is one of the greatest works of the Lübeck master, Claus Berg.

At Jernbanegade 13, the **Fyns Kunstmuseum** (Funen Art Gallery; Tues–Sun 10am–4pm; ⊛www.odmus.dk; 30kr), just a few minutes' walk from Skt. Knud's, gives a good indication of the region's importance to the Danish art world during the late nineteenth century; this collection contains some stirring works by Vilhelm Hammershøi, P.S. Krøyer, Michael and Anne Ancher, and H.A. Brendekilde's emotive *Udslidt*. A short walk east, at Claus Bergs Gade 11, is the **Carl Nielsen Museet** (Thurs & Fri 4–8pm, Sun noon–4pm; ⊛www.odmus.dk; 25kr). Born in a village just outside Odense, Nielsen is best remembered in Denmark for his popular songs, though it was his operas, choral pieces and symphonies that established him as a major international composer. The exhibits, detailing Nielsen's life and achievements, are enlivened by the accomplished sculptures of his wife, Anne Marie, and you can listen to some of his work on headphones.

West of the centre and well worth a visit is the **Brandts Klædefabrik**, on Brandts Passage just off Vestergade, a large former textile factory now given over to an art school, a cinema, a music library, several cafés and restaurants, and four museums (July & Aug daily 10am–5pm; rest of year Tues–Sun 10am–5pm; 50kr combined ticket; ⊛www.brandts.dk). In the large halls that once housed the huge machinery are the **Brandts Kunsthallen** (30kr), which displays work of high-flying new talent in art and design, and the **Museet for Fotokunst** (25kr), featuring changing exhibitions of photography. On the third floor the **Danmarks Grafiske Museum** (25kr), with its bulky machines and devices, chronicles the development of printing, book binding and illustrating from the Middle Ages to the present. Further down Brandts Passage, upstairs at no. 29, the titchy **Tidens Samling** (daily 10am–5pm; ⊛www.tidenssamling.dk; 30kr) gives an intimate insight into the changing fashions of sitting-rooms and clothing since the turn of the last century.

South of the centre at Sejerskovvej 20 is **Den Fynske Landsby** (Funen Village; April–Oct Tues–Sun 10am–5pm; mid-June to mid-Aug daily 9.30am–7pm; Nov–March Sun only 11am–3pm; ⊛www.odmus.dk; 55kr), a reconstructed nineteenth-century village made up of buildings from all over Funen. In summer, some of the old trades are revived in the former workshops and crafthouses, and free shows are staged at the open-air theatre. Buses #21, #22 and #42 run to the village from the city centre.

Practicalities

Odense **train station** is a ten-minute walk from the city centre, and is also the terminus for all long-distance **buses**. The **tourist office** (mid-June to Aug Mon–Fri 9.30am–7pm, Sat & Sun 10am–4pm; rest of year Mon–Fri 9.30am–4.30pm, Sat 10am–1pm; ☎66.12.75.20, ⊛www.visitodense.com) is on the Vestergade side of the Rådhus – follow the signs. They sell the useful **Adventure Pass** (110/150kr for 24/48hr), which gives free entry to the most interesting museums and unlimited travel on all local buses.

The only reasonable **hotels**, both of which include breakfast, are *Det Lille Hotel*, Dronningensgade 5 (☎66.12.28.21; ⊛www.lillehotel.dk; ❹), and *Ydes*, Hans Tausens Gade 11 (☎66.12.11.31, ⊛www.ydes.dk; ❺). There are two **hostels**: one alongside the train station at Østre Stationsvej 31 (☎66.11.04.25, ⊛www.cityhostel.dk; 115kr); and a quieter one at Kragsbjergvej 121 (☎66.13.04.25, ⊛www.odense-danhostel.dk; 100kr; closed Dec to mid-Feb) – take bus #61 south to Tornbjerg or Fraugde and get out along Munkebjergvej at the junction with Vissenbjergvej. The closest **campsite** (☎66.11.47.02) is due south at Odensevej 102, near Den Fynske Landsby, and has cabins as well as tent space; take buses #21, #22 or #23 from the Rådhus or train station to Højby. There's free **Internet** access in the library in the train station.

There are plenty of **restaurants** and **snack bars** in the city centre. *Den Gyldne ovn* on Fisketorvet is a reliable spot for freshly made sandwiches, while the best pizzeria is *Italiano*, Vesterbro 9. *Tortilla Flat*, Frederiksgade 38 is a popular Mexican restaurant, or you could try the inexpensive café in the Badstuen cultural centre, Østre Stationsvej 26. Vegetarians should make for *Kærnehuset*, Nedergade 6, where at 6pm (Tues–Fri) you can eat as much as you like for a bargain 40kr. For a **drink**, try *Carlsen's Kvarter*, an inexpensive pub with fruity Belgian beers and English ales that sometimes hosts Danish folk music, on the corner of Hunderupvej and Læssøgade, or the fashionable *Café Biografen* in Brandts Passage. As for **nightlife**, Jazzhus Dexter, Vindegade 65 (⊛www.dexter.dk), is the place to head for jazz, while the Badstuen cultural centre (⊛www.badstuen.dk) and Rytmeposten, across the road at Østre Stationsvej 35 (⊛www.rytmeposten.dk), host raucous live bands.

Kerteminde

A thirty-minute bus ride (#890) northeast from Odense takes you to **KERTE-MINDE**, a sailing and holiday centre that has a prettily preserved nucleus of shops and houses around its fifteenth-century Skt. Laurentius Kirke. Just down the street at Strandgade 1B is the **tourist office** (mid-June to Aug Mon–Sat 9am–5pm; rest of year Mon–Fri 9am–4pm, Sat 9.30am–noon; ☎65.32.11.21, ⊛www.kerteminde-turist.dk), who can provide a cycling route and information on the lovely Hindsholm peninsula north of town. Across the road from the bus station on Magrethes Plads 1, **Fjord & Bæltcentret** (mid-Feb to Nov daily 10am–4/6pm;

75kr; @www.gounderwater.com) is a state-of-the-art aquarium with a fifty-metre long underwater tunnel from where you can see seals and porpoises in their natural sea environment. At Langegade 8, the **Kerteminde Museum Farvergården** (Tues–Sun 10am–4pm; 15kr) is crammed with relics from ways of life over the centuries, including seven reconstructed craft workshops, a peasant's living room and a collection of local fishing equipment.

Jutland

Long ago, the Jutes, the people of **Jutland**, were a separate tribe from the more warlike Danes who occupied the eastern islands. In pagan times, the peninsula had its own rulers and much power, and it was here that the ninth-century monarch Harald Bluetooth began the process that turned the two tribes into a unified Christian nation. By the Viking era, however, the battling Danes had spread west, absorbing the Jutes, and real power gradually shifted towards Zealand, where it has largely stayed ever since. Unhurried lifestyles and rural calm are thus the overriding impression of Jutland for most visitors; indeed, its distance from Copenhagen makes it the most distinct and interesting area in the country. In the south, Schleswig is a territory long battled over by Denmark and Germany, though beyond the immaculately restored **Ribe** town, it holds little of abiding interest. **Århus**, halfway up the eastern coast, is Jutland's main urban centre and Denmark's second city. Further inland, the countryside is the country's most dramatic – stark heather-clad moors, dense forests and swooping gorges. North of vibrant **Aalborg**, sited on the bank of the Limfjord, the landscape reaches a crescendo of storm-lashed savagery around **Skagen**, on the very tip of the peninsula.

Ribe

Exquisitely preserved **RIBE** was once a major stopover point for pilgrims on their way to Rome, as well as a significant port, until thwarted by the Reformation and the silting-up of the harbour in the Middle Ages. Since then, not much appears to have changed, making it a delight to wander around. From the train station, Dagmarsgade leads to Torvet and the towering **Domkirke** (daily 10am/noon–4/5.30pm; 12kr), begun around 1150. Only the "Cat's Head Door" on the south side remains from the original construction; much more modern are the interior's colourful mosaics, stained glass windows and paintings, completed by CoBRA member Carl-Henning Pedersen in 1984. You can normally climb the red-brick tower and peer out over the town and beyond to the Wadden Sea. Behind the cathedral, the **Weis' Stue** is a tiny inn built around 1600, from which the nightwatchman of Ribe makes his rounds – a throwback to the days when Danish towns were patrolled by guards looking for unattended candles, though these days he stops at points of interest to explain the town's history to tourists

There are two international *ferry ports* in Jutland. *ESBJERG* (30min by train north of Ribe), has boats to Britain; the passenger harbour is twenty minutes' walk from the centre, but trains to and from Copenhagen connect directly with ferries at the harbour. The main train station is at the end of Skolegade, where, at no. 33, you'll find the tourist office (Mon–Fri 9/10am–5pm, Sat 9.30/10am–1/3.30pm; ☎75.12.55.99, @www.esbjerg-tourist.dk). *FREDERIKSHAVN*, in the far north of the region (2hr 40min by train from Århus), has boats to Sweden and Norway. Its ferry terminal is near Havnepladsen, not far from the centre. All buses and most trains terminate at the central train station, a short walk from the town centre; some continue to the ferry terminal itself. The tourist office is close by at Skandiatorv 1 (mid-June to Aug daily 8.30am–5/7pm; rest of year Mon–Fri 9am–4pm, Sat 11am–2pm; ☎98.42.32.66, @www.frederikshavn-tourist.dk).

(May to mid-Sept 10pm; June–Aug also 8pm; free).

The **tourist office** (Mon–Fri 9/9.30am–4/5.30pm, Sat 10am–1/5pm; ☎75.42.15.00, ⓦwww.ribetourist.dk) is behind the cathedral, opposite the Weis' Stue; it has a full list of **private homes** with rooms to rent (❹). For 15kr you can get a map and directions for a wonderfully quiet and relaxing bicycle ride to the nearby Wadden Sea and island of Mandø; you can rent a bike for 57kr per day from the **hostel** (☎75.42.06.20, ⓦwww.danhostel.dk/ribe; 105kr; closed Dec & Jan). To get there from the station follow Skt. Nicolai Gade onto Saltgade, then turn left in Skt. Peders Gade. If it's full, make your way to Torvet and try *Weis' Stue* (☎75.42.07.00; ❻), opposite the atmospheric but expensive *Hotel Dagmar*, the oldest hotel in Denmark. The nearest **campsite** is *Ribe Camping*, which is 1.5km from Ribe along Farupvej, and also has cabins (☎75.41.07.77; bus #715 on weekdays; closed Nov to Easter). For **food**, try *Restaurant Backhaus*, Grydergade 12, with good value portions of steaks or burgers. *Kolvig Café and Restaurant*, next to Skibroen, offers filling salads and sandwiches at reasonable prices with relaxed riverside seating. There's excellent coffee in *Valdemar Sejr* next to the art gallery on Skt. Nicolaj Gade, which is also a good spot for **drinks** and **music** in the evening. *Stenbohus*, at Stenbogade 1, has live blues, folk or rock bands at least once a week.

Århus

Tempted by the shelter of the River Å, Vikings first settled here in Aros ("river mouth" in old Nordic), over a thousand years ago. **ÅRHUS** (or Aarhus) is now Denmark's second-largest city, an instantly likeable assortment of intimate cobbled streets, sleek modern architecture, brightly painted houses and laid-back students. It's small enough to get to grips with in a few hours, but lively enough to make you linger for days – its excellent music scene, interesting art, pavement cafés and energetic nightlife all earn it the unofficial title of Denmark's culture capital.

Arrival, information and accommodation

Trains, **buses** and **ferries** all stop on the southern edge of the city centre. Frequent buses from the **airport** run to the train station (45min; 60kr). The **tourist office** is a short walk from the stations, in Park Allé (Mon–Fri 9am–4/6pm, Sat 10am–1/5pm; mid-June to mid-Sept also Sun 9.30am–1pm; ☎89.40.67.00, ⓦwww .visitaarhus.com), on the first floor of the city's Rådhus, and can arrange private rooms (❷) for a 25kr booking fee. Pick up a city map plus film, music and theatre listings for free. Buses form the city's **public transport system**, which is divided into four zones: one and two cover the centre; three and four reach into the country; a basic ticket costs 15kr from machines on board and is valid for any number of journeys for two hours from the time stamped on it. And while it's easy to get around on foot – you'll need buses only to get to the beaches or woods on the outskirts – it might be worth considering the **Århus Pass** (97/121kr for 24/48hr),

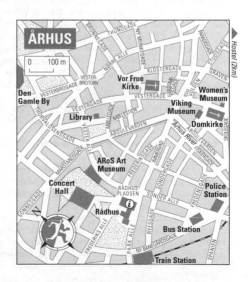

which, along with unlimited bus travel, covers entrance to most museums and sightseeing tours (book these at the tourist office first).

There's a **hostel** 3km from the centre at Marienlundsvej 10 (℡86.16.72.98, ⓦwww .hostel-aarhus.dk; 105kr; bus #1, #6, #8, #9, #16, #56 or #58), in the middle of Risskov wood and close to Den Permanente beach, to which locals flock in summer. Much more central (and fun) is the *Århus City Sleep-In*, Havnegade 20 (℡86.19.20.55, ⓦwww.citysleep-in.dk; 105kr), with picnic tables in the courtyard, a barbecue, no curfew and TV/pool rooms among its impressive range of facilities. There are just two reasonably priced central **hotels**: *Hotel Guldsmeden* at Guldsmedegade 40 (℡86.13.45.56; ⓦwww.hotelguldsmeden.dk; ➐) and *Hotel Cab Inn Århus*, Kannikegade 14 (℡86.75.70.00, ⓦwww.cab-inn.dk; ➏). To the northwest there's a good B&B: *Get In*, Jens Baggesensvej 43 (℡86.10.86.14, ⓦwww.get-in.dk; ➍; bus #4 or #7). Of a number of **campsites**, the two most useful are *Blommehaven* (ⓦwww.blommehaven.dk; closed early Sept to March; bus #6 or #19), overlooking the bay 3km south of the city centre, and *Århus Nord* 8km north (ⓦwww.dk-camping .dk/aarhusnord; bus #117 or #118 from the bus station); both have cabins.

The City

Søndergade is the main street, a pedestrianized strip that leads down into Bispetorvet and the old centre, the streets of which form a web around the **Domkirke** (Mon–Sat 10am–3/4pm), a massive Gothic church, most of which dates from the fifteenth century. The area to the north, known as the Latin Quarter, is crammed with browsable shops, galleries and enticing cafés. Across the road from the cathedral, the basement in Nordea houses the **Viking Museum** (Mon–Fri 10am–4pm, Thurs till 6pm; free) with a skeleton and a reconstructed "sunk pit" house. West along Vestergade, the thirteenth-century **Vor Frue Kirke** (Mon–Fri 10am–2pm, Sat 10am–noon) has some interesting medieval frescoes, depicting local workers rather than biblical scenes, and an atmospheric eleventh-century crypt church below. The **Rådhus**, home to the tourist office and one of the modern city's major sites, is a controversial 1940s building clad in sickly Norwegian marble. Above the entrance hangs Hagedorn Olsen's huge mural, *A Human Society*, symbolically depicting the city emerging from World War II. You can wander in and investigate this for yourself, but to see Albert Naur's subversive murals in the civic room and to enjoy a view over the city and bay from the bell tower, you'll need to take a guided tour (mid-June to Aug Mon–Fri 11am; 10kr). It's a short walk from here to the city's best-known attraction, **Den Gamle By**, on Viborgvej (daily: June–Aug 9am–6pm; rest of year 10/11am–3/5pm; 75kr; ⓦwww.dengamleby.dk), an open-air museum of traditional Danish life, with seventy-odd half-timbered town houses taken from across the country. Many of the craftsmen's buildings are used for their original purpose, the overall aim of the place being to give an impression of an old Danish market town, something it does very effectively. The Århus Art Museum is currently relocating from Vennelystparken to opposite the Rådhus, in astonishing new premises designed by the same architects as the "Black Diamond" extension to the Royal Library in Copenhagen. The new museum, to be called **ARoS** (Tues–Sun 10am–5pm, Wed till 8pm; 40kr; ⓦwww.aarhuskunstmuseum.dk), is scheduled to open in March 2004.

Eating, drinking and nightlife

Many of the old-town **cafés** and **restaurants** offer lunchtime specials for around 55kr; try theatrical *Pind's Café* at Skolegade 11, which does excellent *smørrebrød*. *Café Jorden* is a popular brunch hangout, with pavement seating overlooking Rosengade. *Athena*, on the first floor on Storetorv, is also good value, as are the highly rated **vegetarian** meals at *Restaurant Gyngen*, Mejlgade 53, and *Under Engle*, Mejlgade 28. The classy architecture of Åboulevarden, overlooking the recently uncovered River Å, towers above a string of trendy eating and drinking venues; try *Cross Café* for their generous brunch platters. The sun-drenched steps outside are a popular picnic spot. For superb Danish pastry, head to *Emmerys*, Guldsmedegade 24–26, the city's oldest patisserie; the bakery is organic, the coffee freshly ground and the cakes to die for. For **self-catering**, there's a late-opening supermarket (8am–midnight) at the train station. Århus and Aalborg, further north, are the only places in Denmark with a **nightlife** to match that of Copenhagen. The city has particularly good **bars**, many situated in the streets close to the cathedral, including the movie-themed *Casablanca* at Rosensgade 12, *Den Smagløse* at Klostertorv 7, and *Englen* on Studsgade (which also does good food). The cream of Danish and international rock acts can be found at *Voxhall*, Vester Allé 15, and *Train*, Toldbogade 6; *Fatter Eskil*, Skolegade 25, and *Kulturgyngen*, Fronthuset, Mejlgade 53, have more run-of-the-mill blues bands. The leading **jazz** venue is the smoky, atmospheric *Bent J*, at Nèrre Allé 66.

Aalborg

The main city of north Jutland, **AALBORG** hugs the southern bank of the Limfjord and boasts a nightlife and music scene to rival Copenhagen's. The most obvious place to spend a night or two before venturing into the wilder countryside beyond, Aalborg is the main transport terminus for the region, and boasts a well-preserved centre dating from its seventeenth-century trading heyday. The era is perhaps best exemplified by the Jens Bangs Stenhus opposite the tourist office, a grandiose five-storey affair in the Dutch Renaissance style. The commercial roots of the city are further evidenced by the collection of portraits of the town's merchants that hang inside the **Budolfi Domkirke** (Mon–Fri 9am–3/4pm, Sat 9am–noon/2pm), behind. The cathedral is a small but elegant specimen of the Gothic style, built on the site of an eleventh-century wooden church, from which a few tombs remain, embedded in the walls close to the altar. In July and August it also hosts small **concerts**. Outside, across the square, the **Aalborg Historical Museum** at Algade 48 (Tues–Sun 10am–5pm, 20kr; ⊛www.aahm.dk) has an impressive glasswork collection.

On the other side of Østerågade, the sixteenth-century **Aalborghus Slot** is worth a visit for its **dungeon** (May–Oct Mon–Fri 8am–3pm; free) and the underground passages (till 9pm). Fifteen minutes' walk southwest out of the centre on Kong Christians Allé, the **North Jutland Art Museum** (Tues–Sun 10am–5pm, 30kr; ⊛www.nordjyllandskunstmusem.dk; buses #5, #8, #10 or #11) is one of the country's best modern art collections, featuring works by Max Ernst, Andy Warhol, Le Corbusier and Claes Oldenburg, alongside many Danish contributions.

The **tourist office** is centrally placed at Østerågade 8 (Mon–Fri 9am–4.30/ 5.30pm, Sat 10am–1/4pm; ☎98.12.60.22, ⊛www.visitaalborg.com). There are no cheap **hotels**, just the basic *Aalborg Sømandshjem*, Østerbro 27 (☎98.12.19.00, ⊛www.hotel-aalborg.com; ❼) and cosy *Hotel Krogen*, Skibstedsvej 4 (☎98.12.17.05, ⊛www.krogen.dk; ❻). There's a large **hostel**, *Fjordparken* (☎98.11.60.44, ⊛www.danhostelnord.dk/aalborg; reservations necessary; 115kr), 3km west of the town on the Limfjord bank beside the marina – take bus #8 from the centre to the end of its route. In the same direction is a **campsite**: *Strandparken* (☎89.12.76.29, ⊛www.strandparken.dk; closed mid-Sept to mid-April). For a little more adventure, catch the half-hourly **ferry** (☎98.11.78.23; 6.30am–11.15pm; 13kr) from near the campsite to Egholm, an island in Limfjord with free camping under open-sided shelters. For **food and drink**, head for Jomfru Ane Gade, a small street off Bispensgade which is crammed with eateries and pubs, try the medieval-looking *Fyrtøjet* at no.7. Aalborg Kongres & Kultur Center at Europa Pads 4 (☎99.35.55.55, ⊛www.akkc.dk) is the city's new **theatre** and **concert venue**. For smaller gigs head for *Skråen*, Standvejen 19 (☎98.12.21.89, ⊛www.skraaen.dk).

Skagen

About 100km north of Aalborg, **SKAGEN** perches at the very top of Jutland amid a breathtaking landscape of heather-topped sand dunes. It can be reached by private bus or train (Eurail not valid, Scanrail and InterRail fifty percent reduction on both) roughly once an hour. The bus is the best choice if you're planning to stay at the Skagen hostel, as it stops right outside. Sunlight seems to gain extra brightness as it bounces off the two seas which collide off Skagen's coast, something which attracted the **Skagen artists** in the late nineteenth century. They arrived in the small fishing community during 1873 and 1874 and often met in the bar of *Brøndum's Hotel*, off Brøndumsvej, the grounds of which now house the **Skagen Museum** (April & Oct Tues–Sun 11am–4pm; May–Sept daily 10am–5/6pm; Nov–March Wed–Fri 1–4pm, Sat & Sun 11am–3pm; 60kr). Many of the canvases depict local scenes, using the town's strong natural light to capture subtleties of colour. Nearby, at Markvej 2–4, **Michael and Anna Anchers' Hus** (April–Oct daily 10/11am–3/6pm; Nov–March Sat & Sun 11am–3pm; 40kr), home to one of the group's leading lights and his wife, herself a skilful painter, evokes the atmosphere of the time through an assortment of used tubes of paint, piles of canvases, paintings, sketches, books and ornaments.

The artists made Skagen fashionable, and the town continues to be a popular holiday destination. But it still bears many marks (and smells) of its tough past as a fishing community. The impressive new **Skagen Odde Naturcenter** (daily 10am–4/6pm; 65kr) is designed by Jørn Utzon, architect of the Sydney Opera House, and centred on the themes of sand, water, wind and light. The forces of nature can be further appreciated at Grenen, 4km north of Skagen (hourly bus #79 in summer), along Skt. Laurentii Vej, Fyrvej and the beach, where two seas – the Kattegat and Skagerrak – meet, sometimes with a powerful clashing of waves. You can get to the tip by a tractor-drawn bus (mid-April to mid-Oct; 15kr return) – although it's an enjoyable walk as the scenery is beautiful.

Handily, the **bus and train station** on Skt. Laurentii Vej also incorporates the **tourist office** (June–Aug Mon–Sat 9am–5/6pm, Sun 10am–2/4pm; rest of year Mon–Fri 9am–3/5pm, Sat 10am–1pm; ☎98.44.13.77, ⊛www.skagen-tourist.dk). If you can afford it, *Brøndum's Hotel*, Anchervej 3 (☎98.44.15.55, ⊛www.broendumshotel.dk; ❽), is by far the most atmospheric spot to stay – book well ahead in summer. A little cheaper is *Clausens Hotel*, Skt. Laurentii Vej 35 (☎98.45.01.66, ⊛www.clausenshotel.dk; ❻). There are two **hostels**: one at Rolighedsvej 2 (☎98.44.22.00, ⊛www.danhostelnord.dk/skagen; no dorms; 115kr), the other at Højensvej 32 in Gammel Skagen (☎98.44.13.56, ⊛www.skaw.dk/hostel; ❹; closed mid-Oct to Easter), 3km west of Skagen; take bus #79. Of a number of **campsites**, the most accessible are *Grenen* (☎98.44.25.46, ⊛www.grenencamping.dk; closed early Sept to May), to the north along Fyrvej, which has cabins, and *Poul Eeg's* (☎98.44.14.70; closed Sept to mid-May), on Batterivej, left off Oddenvej just before the town centre.

Travel details

Trains

Århus to: Aalborg (32 daily; 1hr 25min); Ribe (2 hourly; 2hr 40min); Viborg (hourly; 1hr 10min).
Copenhagen to: Aalborg (hourly; 4hr 40min, last at 8pm); Århus (36 daily; 2hr 45min–3hr 10min); Frederikshavn (every 2hr; 5hr 50min); Helsingør (every 20min; 50min); Odense (58 daily; 1hr 30min); Roskilde (8 hourly; 22min).
Frederikshavn to: Skagen (hourly; 45min).

Helsingør to: Hillerød (hourly; 30min).
Odense to: Århus (38 daily; 1hr 30min).
Ribe to: Odense (hourly; 1hr 45min–2hr 20min).
Roskilde to: Odense (43 daily; 1hr 10min).

Buses

Copenhagen to: Aalborg (3 daily; 4hr 45min); Århus (7 daily; 3hr–3hr 30min).
Odense to: Kerteminde (5 an hour; 40min).

Estonia

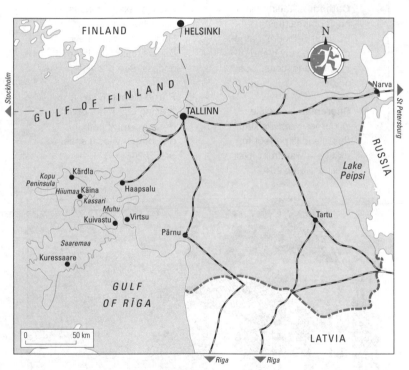

Estonia highlights

* **Tallinn's Old Town**
Within medieval turreted
walls, this ancient corner
of the city is beautifully
preserved. See p.279

* **Alexander Nevsky
Cathedral, Tallinn** High
on Toompea, this
Russian Orthodox cathe-
dral is a heady blend of
incense and icons. See
p.280

* **Saaremaa** If you like
wilderness and walking,
this island is perfect for
that get-away-from-it-all
feeling. See p.284

* **Kuressaare Castle,
Saaremaa Island** The
best-preserved medieval
castle in the region. See
p.284

* **Café Wilde, Tartu** A
calm, relaxed tea house
in the heart of Estonia.
Huge pots of tea, news-
papers, cake and Internet
access. See p.286

* **Pärnu Beach** Enjoy a
bracing dip in the Baltic
or take a mud bath in
one of many local spas.
See p.286

Introduction and basics

It's a tribute to the resilience of the people of **Estonia** that, since independence in 1991, they've transformed their country from a dour outpost of the Soviet Union into a viable nation with the Baltic region's most stable economy. A Finno-Ugric people related to the Finns, the Estonians have had the misfortune to be surrounded by powerful, warlike neighbours. Conquered by the Danes in the thirteenth century, then German crusading knights, then Swedes and Russians, the country snatched independence at the end of World War I. This brief freedom was extinguished by the Soviets in 1940 and the country disappeared from view again only to emerge from the Soviet shadow in 1991.

Estonia's capital, **Tallinn**, is an atmospheric city with a magnificent medieval centre and lively nightlife. Two other major cities, **Tartu**, a historic university town, and **Pärnu**, a major seaside resort, are worth a day or so each. Estonia's small population means that the countryside – almost half of which is covered by forest and much of the rest by lakes – is generally empty and unspoiled. To get a feel for it at its best, head for the island of **Saaremaa**: the island capital **Kuressaare** is home to one of the finest castles in the Baltics.

Information & maps

The national tourist association operates **tourist offices** in all the places covered in this chapter, which can be useful for booking B&Bs and hotel rooms. The Kümmerly & Frey 1:1,000,000 **map** of the Baltic States covers Estonia and includes a rudimentary street plan of central Tallinn. The best detailed street map of Tallinn is the *Falk Plan*, which includes enlarged Inner and Old Town sections and also covers public transport routes. **Addresses** often include *mantee* (mnt.), meaning road; *puiestee* (pst.), avenue; *tänav* (tn.), street.

Money and banks

Currency is the **Eesti kroon** (Estonian Crown), pegged to the euro at €1 = 15.65EEK, and divided into 100 sents. Notes come as 1, 2, 5, 10, 25, 50, 100 and 500 EEK and coins as 0.05, 0.10, 0.20, 0.50, 1 and 5 EEK. **Bank** (*pank*) opening hours are Mon–Fri 9am–4pm, many staying open in larger towns tilll 6pm and most also opening Sat 9am–2/4pm. ATMs are widely available. **Credit cards** can be used in most hotels, restaurants and stores, but outside urban areas cash is preferred.

Communications

Post offices (*postkontor*) open Mon–Fri 9am–6pm & Sat 9am–3pm. You can buy stamps here and at some shops, hotels and kiosks. Most **public phones** take phonecards (of 30, 50 and 100EEK) for local and long-distance calls. You'll find **Internet cafés** in most towns; expect to pay from 50EEK/hr.

Getting around

Places covered in this chapter are all reached easily by **bus**. Tickets can be

---

Estonia on the net

ⓦ **www.visitestonia.com** Tourist board site.
ⓦ **www.ee** Search engine and good starting point.
ⓦ **www.estica.org** General information from the Estonian Institute.
ⓦ **www.weekend.ee** Entertainment listings.
ⓦ **www.baltictimes.com** English-language weekly newspaper.

bought either from the bus station ticket office or direct from the driver. It's best to buy long-distance tickets in advance if you're travelling at the height of summer or at weekends, especially to the islands. Opt for an express (*ekspress*) bus if possible. Normally luggage is taken on board: if you have a large bag you may have to pay a nominal fee to have it stowed in the luggage compartment. Buses are also the best method for travelling to the other Baltic countries, with services linking Tallinn, Vilnius and Riga.

The **rail** network has been cut back drastically; you're unlikely to use it, save perhaps for international services. Ticket windows at stations are marked *linnalähedanel* for suburban lines; *piletite müük* for national services; and *rahvusvaheline* for international lines. Tickets for the last need to be bought 45min in advance. Long-distance services are divided either *reisirong* (passenger) or *kiir* (fast). Both are slow, but the latter, usually requiring a reservation, stop only at every other village. Both train and bus information is available from station timetable boards – departure is *väljub*, arrival is *saabub*.

Accommodation

Though cheaper than in Western Europe, **accommodation** in Estonia will still take a large chunk out of most budgets. Booking a **private room** is often the cheapest option (usually 200–400EEK per person). This can be arranged through tourist offices or private agencies. You should be able to find plain but clean **hotel** rooms for 300–500EEK per person, often in converted student hostels or apartment buildings, and better value than the purpose-built Soviet-era places. There's a growing number of small **guest houses** and mid-range pension-type establishments in the more popular destinations; expect to pay between 200–350EEK per night. Prices for mid-range places usually include breakfast, and many places accept credit cards. In all but the very cheapest hotels there will usually be at least one English-speaking member of staff. **Hostels** are often just student dorms converted for the summer; the Estonian Youth Hostel Association in Tallinn

(☏372/6461 455, ✆www.baltichostels.net) has details. Beds cost 100–200EEK per person. An ex-Soviet phenomenon is the cabin **campsite** (*kämping*), usually offering accommodation in three- to four-bed cabins (shared facilities) for 180–260EEK per person; many of them will also let you pitch a tent, which works out slightly cheaper than sleeping under a roof.

Food and drink

Not many people come to Estonia for the **food**. The national cuisine consists mainly of pig by-products teamed with potatoes and other vegetable-patch produce. You're likely to encounter indigenous recipes in restaurants, where stodgy meat-and-two-veg dishes dominate menus. Soup (*supp*), dark bread (*leib*), sour cream (*hapukoor*) and herring (*heeringas*) figure prominently, a culinary legacy of the country's largely peasant past. A typical **national dish** is *verevorst* and *mulgikapsad* (blood sausage and sauerkraut), and you're also likely to encounter various kinds of smoked fish, particularly eel (*angerjas*), perch (*ahven*) and pike (*haug*). You'd have to be invited into a local home to enjoy Estonian food at its best, as the average **restaurant** (*restoran*) tends to serve up hearty international meat dishes, the most common of which is *karbonaad* – pork chop (sometimes fried in batter) – with potatoes and seasonal vegetables. You might occasionally encounter game, and several ethnic restaurants break the culinary monotony in Tallinn. **Vegetarianism** is not a widely understood concept.

When eating out you're best off heading for bars and cafés, many of which serve snack dishes and even full meals, and where the bill is likely to be less than in a restaurant. You should be able to have two courses and a drink for less than 150EEK; you'd have to really push the boat out to spend more than 200EEK. If you really want to keep costs down then try one of the various **fast-food** options. Some places going under the name of café (*kohvik*) are canteen-style restaurants where you can pick up main courses and dishes-of-the-day for as little as 30EEK, as well as basic soups, salads and sweets. There's also a growing number of pizzerias, many of which offer pasta dishes. **Self-catering** poses no major problems: supermarket staples such as bread, cheese, smoked meat and tinned fish can be supplemented by fruit and vegetables from markets.

Drink

Estonians are enthusiastic drinkers, with **beer** (*õlu*) being the most popular tipple. The principal local brands are *Saku* and *A. Le Coq*, both of which are rather tame light lager-style brews, although both companies also produce stronger, dark beers – the strongest are found on the islands (*Saaremaa õlu* is the best known). In bars a lot of people favour **vodka** (*viin*) with mixers which, thanks to generous measures, is a more cost-effective route to oblivion. Local alcoholic specialities include **hõõgvein** (mulled wine) and *Vana Tallinn*, a pungent dark liqueur which some suicidal souls mix with vodka. Pubs and bars – most of which imitate Irish or American models – are beginning to take over, especially in Tallinn; if you're not boozing, head for a *kohvik* (café), where alcohol is still served but getting drunk is not a priority. **Coffee** (*kohv*) is usually of the filter variety, and **tea** (*tee*) is served without milk.

Opening hours and holidays

Most **shops** open Mon–Fri 9/10am–6/7pm & Sat 10am–2/3pm. Some food shops stay open till 10pm or later and are also open Sun. **Public holidays**, when most shops and all banks are closed, are: Jan 1; Feb 24; Good Fri; Easter Mon; May 1; Whitsun; June 23 & 24; Aug 20; Dec 25 & 26.

Emergencies

While theft and street crime are probably on the rise, they're still at lower levels than in most other European cities, and if you keep your wits about you and avoid staggering around the backstreets drunk after dark you should come to no harm. The **police** (*politsei*) are mostly very young and some may speak a little English, but don't bank on it. Emergency **health** care is free, but hospitals are under-equipped and if you fall seriously ill it's best to head for home if possible.

Emergency numbers

Police ☏110; fire & ambulance ☏112.

Tallinn

The port city of **TALLINN**, Estonia's compact capital, has been shaped by nearly a millennium of outside influence. Its name, derived from the Estonian for "Danish Fort" (*taani linnus*), is a reminder of the fact that the city was founded by the Danes at the beginning of the thirteenth century, and since that time political control has nearly always been in the hands of foreigners. The **Germans** have undoubtedly had the most lasting influence on the city; Tallinn was one of the leading cities of the Hanseatic League, the German-dominated association of Baltic trading cities, and for centuries it was known to the outside world by its German name, Reval. Even when Estonia was ruled by the kings of **Sweden** and the tsars of **Russia**, the city's public life was controlled by the German nobility, and its commerce run by German merchants. Today reminders of foreign rule abound in the streets of Tallinn, where each of the city's one-time rulers have left their mark.

Arrival, information and city transport

Tallinn's international **train station** is at Toompuiestee 35, just northwest of the Old Town, while the city's **bus terminal** is at Lastekodu 46, 2km southeast of the centre – trams #2 and #4 run from nearby Tartu mnt. to Viru väljak at the eastern entrance to the Old Town. Arriving by **sea**, the passenger port is just northeast of the centre at

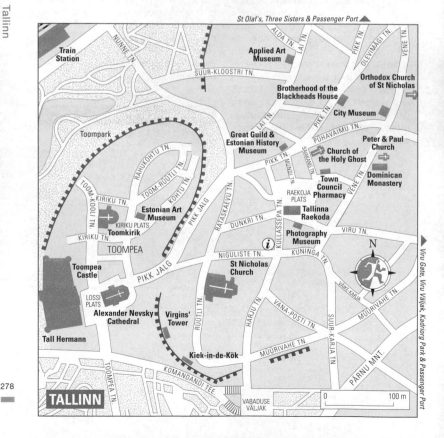

Sadama 25. The **airport** is 3km southeast of the city centre and linked to Viru väljak by bus #2 (every 30min; 15EEK). The **tourist office**, in the Old Town at Kullasseppa 4 (April–Oct Mon–Fri 9am–6pm, Sat & Sun 10am–4pm; Nov–March Mon–Fri 9am–5pm, Sat 10am–4pm; ☎0/645 7777, ⊛www.tourism.tallinn.ee), sells various maps and city guides. You can also buy a **Tallinn Card** here (205/275/325EEK for 24/48/72hr) which gives unlimited use of public transport, discounts and savings at museums and other sights. The widely available free paper *Tallinn This Week*, the *City Paper*, and the informative *Tallinn In Your Pocket* city guide have what's-on listings.

Though most of the sights can be covered on foot, Tallinn has an extensive **tram**, **bus** and **trolleybus** network. Services are frequent and cheap, with tickets (*talongid*) common to all three systems available from kiosks near stops for 10EEK or from the driver for 15EEK. Validate your ticket using the on-board punches. **Taxis** are reasonably cheap (around 10EEK/km, slightly more after 10pm) though as a foreigner you may occasionally find your meter running faster than it should. Most companies have a minimum charge of 25EEK, but a taxi from one point in the city centre to another rarely exceeds 50EEK.

Accommodation

There's a shortage of cheap and mid-range hotels in central Tallinn, making **private rooms** the best value for money if you want to be close to the heart of things. Bed & Breakfast Rasastra, a few steps north of Viru väljak at Mere 4 (daily 9.30am–6pm; ☎0/661 6291, ⊛www.bedbreakfast.ee), offers rooms (❷) in family homes throughout the Baltics and private apartments for longer stays.

Hostels

Hostel Uus 26 ☎0/641 1281. Rambling old-town house with a handful of cosy doubles (❹) and a single cramped dorm with beds at 240EEK.
Merevaik Sõpruse 182 ☎0/655 3767. Faded but clean singles, doubles and triples in a red-brick block 3km southwest of the Old Town. Trolleybus #2 or #3 from Vabaduse väljak to the Linnu stop. Ten percent discount for HI and ISIC cardholders. ❷
Vana Tom Väike-Karja 1 ☎0/631 3252. In the Old Town, this place has clean dorms doubles. Discounts for HI, Peace Corps members and those who bring their own sleeping bag. Dorms ❷

Guest house and B&Bs

Dorell Karu 39 ☎0/626 1200. A ten-minute walk from the Old Town, this place offers comfy rooms with TV, some with shared facilities, others en suite. Entrance via a passage on Narva mnt. ❸–❹
Hotell G9 Gonsiori 9 ☎0/626 7100, ⊛www.hotelg9.ee. Sparsely-furnished but comfy en suites on the third floor of an apartment building, nicely poised between the Old Town and

the bus station. Breakfast costs 50EEK extra. ❸
Kristiine Luha 16 ☎0/646 4600, ⊛www.kristiine.ee. Quiet, friendly place on two floors of a grey office block, around 15min from the centre. Rooms are plain but en suite and have TV. Bus #5, #18, #36 from Vabaduse väljak or tram #3, #4 from Pärnu mnt. to the Luha stop. ❸
Old House Bed & Breakfast Uus 22 ☎0/641 1464, ⊛www.oldhouse.ee. Small and friendly five-room guest house in the Old Town; all rooms with shared facilities. ❸
PÄÄSU Sõpruse 182 ☎0/654 2013, ⓔpaasu@mail.ee. Unpretentious place occupying the same building as the *Merevaik* hostel (see above). Rooms have dated furnishings, but all are clean and with TV. Shared facilities. ❷
TTK Üliõpilashotell Nõmme tee 47 ☎0/655 2679, ⓔttkhotell@hot.ee. Hotel attached to a student hostel some 3km southwest of the centre, offering plain, cheap rooms. One bathroom for every two rooms. No breakfast. Bus #17 or #17a from Vabaduse väljak to Koolimaja, or trolleybus #4 from the train station to Tedre. ❷

The City

The heart of Tallinn is the **Old Town**, once enclosed by the city's medieval walls. At its centre is the **Raekoja plats**, the medieval marketplace, above which looms **Toompea**, the hilltop stronghold of the German Knights who controlled the city during the Middle Ages. Outside the city centre, **Kadriorg Park**, a peaceful wooded area to the east with a cluster of historic buildings and a view of the sea, and the **Open Air Museum**, to the west, are both worth a visit.

Around Raekoja plats

Raekoja plats, the cobbled and gently sloping market square at the heart of the Old Town, is as old as the city itself. On its southern side stands an imposing reminder of the Hanseatic past: the fifteenth-century **Town Hall** (Tallinna Raekoda), which boasts an elegant arcade of gothic arches at ground level, and a delicate, slender steeple at its northern end. Near the summit of the slender steeple, Vana Toomas, a sixteenth-century weather vane depicting a medieval town guard, has become Tallinn's city emblem. Of the other old buildings that line the square, the most venerable is the **Town Council Pharmacy** in the northeastern corner, whose blinding white facade dates from the seventeenth century, though the building is known to have existed in 1422 and may be much older. If the tiny museum inside (daily 9am–5pm; free) leaves you underwhelmed, head for the former Town Gaol behind the town hall at Raekoja 4/6, which now houses the **Museum of Photography** (April–Oct Mon & Thurs–Sun 11am–5pm; Nov–March Thurs–Tues 10.30am–6pm 10EEK), an entertaining little collection with English captions.

Close to Raekoja plats are a couple of churches that neatly underline the social divisions of medieval Tallinn. The fourteenth-century **Church of the Holy Ghost** (daily 10am–4pm; 10EEK), tucked away on Pühavaimu and reached via a small passage called Saiakang tänav next to the Raeapteek, is the city's most appealing church, a small Gothic building with stuccoed limestone walls, stepped gables and a tall, verdigris-coated spire. Originally the Town Hall chapel, it later became the place where the native Estonian population worshipped, and in 1535 priests here compiled an Estonian-language Lutheran catechism, an important affirmation of identity at a time when most Estonians had been reduced to serf status. The ornate clock set in the wall above the entrance dates from 1680 and is the oldest in Tallinn. Contrasting sharply is the late Gothic **St Nicholas Church**, sitting on raised open ground just southwest of Raekoja plats. These days the church serves as a museum and concert hall (Wed–Sun 10am–6pm; 35EEK) displaying a stunning collection of medieval altarpieces. It also hosts organ music recitals (Sat & Sun 4pm; usually 100EEK).

Toompea

Toompea is the hill where the Danes built their fortress after conquering what is now Tallinn in 1219. According to legend, it is also the grave of Kalev, the mythical ancestor of the Estonians. The most atmospheric approach is through the sturdy gate tower – built by the Teutonic Knights to contain the Old Town's inhabitants in times of unrest – at the foot of Pikk jalg. This is the cobbled continuation of Pikk, the Old Town's main street, and climbs up to Lossi plats, dominated by the incongruous-looking **Alexander Nevsky Cathedral** (daily 8am–7pm). This gaudy, onion-domed concoction, complete with souvenir shop, was built at the end of the nineteenth century for the city's Orthodox population; it is an enduring reminder of the two centuries Tallinn spent under tsarist rule.

At the head of Lossi plats is **Toompea Castle**, on the site of the original Danish fortification. Today's castle is the descendant of a stone fortress built by the Knights of the Sword, the Germanic crusaders who kicked out the Danes in 1227 and controlled the city until 1238 (when the Danes returned). The castle has been altered by every conqueror who raised their flag above it since then; these days it wears a shocking-pink Baroque facade, the result of an eighteenth-century rebuild for Catherine the Great. The northern and western walls are the most original part of the castle, and include three defensive towers, the most impressive of which is the fifty-metre **Tall Hermann** at the southwestern corner, dating from 1371. Toompea Castle is now home to the Riigikogu, Estonia's parliament, and is therefore out of bounds to the public, but nearby a couple of towers that formed part of the Old Town fortifications are accessible. A narrow archway in the medieval walls just south of the Alexander Nevsky Cathedral leads to the ironically named **Virgins' Tower**, which was once a prison for prostitutes and is now home to a café/bar. A little south of here on Komandandi tee is the imposing **Kiek-in-de-Kök tower** dating from 1475; it now contains a **museum** (Tues–Fri 10.30am–6pm, Sat & Sun 11am–4.30pm; 20EEK) devoted to the history of Tallinn fortifications, with all exhibits labelled in English.

From Lossi plats, Toom Kooli leads north to the **Toomkirik** (Tues–Sun 9am–4pm), the city's outwardly understated Lutheran cathedral, boasting an interior spectacularly covered with elaborately carved heraldic emblems. A stone's throw from the Toomkirik, in a peppermint green neo-Renaissance palace, is the **Estonian Art Museum**, Kiriku plats 1 (Wed–Sun 11am–6pm; 15EEK), housed here temporarily, pending the construction of a new building in Kadriorg park. This small museum displays a range of works that includes everything from nineteenth-century studies of Tallinn and portraits of peasants in traditional costume to twentieth-century paintings heavily influenced by European artistic trends like Expressionism.

Elsewhere in the Old Town

The remainder of the Old Town contains the commercial streets of medieval Tallinn, lined by merchants' residences and warehouses. Pikk tänav, running north-east from Pikk jalg gate and linking Toompea with the port area, has some of the city's most important secular buildings from the Hanseatic period, kicking off with the **Great Guild** at Pikk 17. Completed in 1430 this was the city's main guild, meeting place of the German merchants who controlled the city's wealth. Its gloomy Gothic facade now fronts the **Estonian History Museum** (11am–6pm; closed Wed; 10EEK) where a predictable array of weaponry, domestic objects and jewellery offers an uninspiring history of Estonia from the Stone Age to the eighteenth century. If the appearance of their headquarters is anything to go by, the guild who occupied the **Brotherhood of the Blackheads House**, Pikk 26, were a more exuberant bunch than the merchants of the Great Guild. The Renaissance facade of this building, inset with an elaborate stone portal and richly decorated door, cuts a bit of dash amid the stolidity of Pikk. The Brotherhood moved here in 1531 and remained until the guild was abolished by the Soviets in 1940. A short detour eastwards to the parallel street of Vene brings you to the **City Museum** at no. 17 (Mon & Wed–Sun 11am–6pm; 20EEK), recounting the history of Tallinn in imaginative multimedia style.

Continuing north along Pikk brings you to **St Olaf's Church**, first mentioned in 1267 and named in honour of King Olaf II of Norway, who was canonized for battling against pagans in Scandinavia. Were it not for its size, this slab-towered Gothic structure would not be particularly eye-catching, and extensive renovation between 1829 and 1840 has left it with an unexceptional nineteenth-century interior. The church is chiefly famous for its 124-metre spire. According to local legend the citizens of Tallinn wanted the church to have the highest spire in the world to attract passing ships and trade. Whether Tallinn's prosperity during the Middle Ages had anything to do with the church spire is not known, but between 1625 and 1820 the church burned down eight times as a result of lightning striking the tower. Bearing witness to the city's medieval wealth are the Old Town's merchants' houses. The best examples are the **Three Sisters**, a gabled group at Pikk 71. Supremely functional with loading hatches and winch-arms set into their facades, these would have served as combined dwelling places, warehouses and offices, and are among the city's best-preserved Hanseatic buildings. At its far end Pikk is straddled by the **Great Coast Gate**, a sixteenth-century city gate flanked by two towers. The larger of these, the aptly named Fat Margaret Tower, has walls four-metres thick and now houses the **Estonian Maritime Museum** (Wed–Sun 10am–6pm; 25EEK; some English captions), a surprisingly diverting collection of model boats and nautical ephemera.

West of Lai is one of the longest-surviving sections of Tallinn's medieval **city wall**; to reach it, head down Suur-Kloostri. The walls that surrounded the Old Town were mostly constructed during the fourteenth century, and enhanced over succeeding centuries. Today, 2km of them survives, along with eighteen towers.

Out of the centre

Kadriorg Park, a heavily wooded area 2km east of the Old Town, was laid out according to the instructions of Russian tsar Peter the Great, who first visited Tallinn in 1711, the year after the Russian conquest. The main entrance to the park is at the junction of Weizenbergi tänav and J. Poska (tram #1 or #3 from Viru väljak). Weizenbergi cuts through the park, running straight past **Kadriorg Palace**, a Baroque residence designed by the Italian architect Niccolò Michetti, which Peter had built for his wife Catherine. These days the palace houses the **Museum of Foreign Art** (Tues–Sun 10am–5pm; 35EEK), with a fine collection. The smaller palace behind it is now home to Estonia's president. While waiting for the palace to be completed, Peter lived in a small cottage in the park grounds, at the junction of Weizenbergi and Mäekalda. Today this houses the **Peter the Great House Museum** (mid-May to Sept Wed–Sun 10.30am–6pm, 10EEK) with furniture from the time Peter lived there, along with a few objects from the palace.

The path down Mäekalda from Peter's cottage leads, after around fifteen minutes, to Narva mnt. On the other side of this busy road is the **Lauluväljak**, a vast amphitheatre that's the venue for Estonia's Song Festivals. These gatherings, featuring massed choirs thousands strong, have been an important form of national expression since the first all-Estonia Song Festival was held in Tartu in 1869, and are held every two years. The present structure, which can accommodate 15,000 singers (with room for a further 30,000 or so on the platform in front of the stage), went up in 1960. The grounds were filled to capacity for the 1988 festival – a significant public expression of longing for independence from Soviet rule, which gave rise to the epithet "Singing Revolution". A tree-lined avenue heads downhill from the amphitheatre to Pirita tee, which runs along the seashore. Turn right here and continue north for 750m to reach **Maarjamäe Palace**, a neo-Gothic residence built for a Russian count in the 1870s, which looks out over Tallinn Bay. The building now houses a branch of the **History Museum** (March–Oct Wed–Sun 11am–6pm; Nov–Feb Wed–Sun 10am–5pm 10EEK), covering the mid-nineteenth century onwards, and is far more interesting and imaginative than its city-centre counterpart.

At the other end of Tallinn, on the western outskirts, is the **Open-Air Museum** (daily: May–Aug 10am–8pm; Sept & Oct 10am–6pm; Nov–April 10am–4pm; 25EEK; bus #21 from the train station), a collection of eighteenth- and nineteenth-century village buildings gathered here from around the country and illustrating how Estonian farms developed. You can also view a wooden church and a windmill, though for many the biggest attraction is the Kolu Kõrts café which serves up traditional bean soup and beer. The museum site slopes down to the sea.

Eating, drinking and nightlife

Meat and potatoes figure heavily on most **restaurant** menus in Tallinn, with alternatives available in a handful of ethnic places. Vegetarians are not well catered for, though a few places make a token effort. Many **cafés** and **bars** also offer snacks and full meals, and are usually a cheaper option; many feature live music or dancing. Most of Tallinn's **clubs** cater for a mainstream crowd. More underground, cutting-edge dance music events change location frequently and are advertised by fly-posters, or try asking around in the city's hipper bars; expect to pay 50–150EEK admission.

Cafés and snacks

Apollo Bookstore café Viru 23. Above the book shop there's a comfortable little café with strong coffee, organic tea and wicked chocolate cake. Three swift Internet terminals.

Balti Sepik Süda 1. Café with its own bakery and eight computer terminals provided by Internetti.

Coffer Vanaturu Kael 8. Good place for a breakfast pastry or a pasta-based lunch, just off the main square.

Kompressor Rataskaevu 3. Roomy café-bar popular with a youngish crowd, and famous for its Estonian pancakes – wonderfully stodgy and filling.

Maiasmokk Pikk 16. Tallinn's most venerable café – founded in 1864 – with a beautiful wood-panelled interior. Queue up for your coffee and pastry, then, like the regulars, take your used dishes back when you're done.

Mocha Vene 1. Quiet café with good coffee, pastries and salads.

Stockmann Department Store Liivalaia 53, 5th floor. Self-service restaurant with excellent sandwiches and salads; also has Internet access.

Tristan ja Isolde Raekoja plats 1. Dark, atmospheric café in the town hall with a full range of drinks and tasty salads and cakes.

Restaurants

Beer House Dunkri 5. Engaging, roomy beer cellar which brews its own ales and serves up hearty pork-and-potatoes meals.

Buon Giorno Müürivahe 17. Good place for soups, pasta dishes and cheap specials.

Café Anglais Raekoja plats 14. Excellent coffee and hot chocolate, and sumptuous range of salads and sweets. More expensive than average, but worth the price for fresh vegetables.

China White Väike-Karja 1. Highly recommended Chinese place with a large variety of vegetarian options, and an all-you-can-eat lunchtime buffet.

Elevant Vene 5. Chic Indian restaurant with affordable range of dishes, including plenty of vegetarian choices.

Kuldse Notsu Kõrts Dunkri 8. Serves Estonian country dishes in rustic bare-boards surrounds. Folk music in the evenings.

Pizza Americana Müürivahe 2. Excellent deep-pan pizzas and a range of inexpensive pasta dishes.

Pudru ja Pasta Pikk 35. Cellar bar/restaurant with small but imaginative range of inexpensive pasta and meat-and-potato standards.

Bars

Kloostri Ait Vene 14. With its enormous open fire and intellectual-ish crowd this is quieter than most beer-swilling places. Cheap buffet meals, plus live folk or jazz.

Levist Väljas Olevimägi 12. Laid-back cellar bar offering cheap drinks and strictly non-top 40 music to an engaging arty-alternative crowd. There's no sign – look for a low door with a pastiche of the Levi Jeans logo stuck to it.

Molly Malone's Möndi 2. Large pub just off Raekoja plats – a blend of ex-pat haunt, tourist pub and local yuppy meeting-place. Frequent live music by cover bands and pub-grub menu.

Nimega Baar Suur-Karja 13. Bar and disco opened by a Scottish football fan. DJs and live music at weekends.

Nimeta Baar Suur-Karja 4/6. Sister venture of the *Nimega Baar*, offering curry and kebabs. International soccer matches screened live.

VS Pärnu mnt. 28. Industrial decor, late-night DJs, hip clientele, and great food.

Woodstock Tatari 4. Hippy-retro bar with psychedelic murals, cheap meals, and occasional live bands.

X-Baar Sauna 1. Relaxed gay bar with bright pink decor.

Live music and clubs

Café Amigo In the Viru Hotel, Viru väljak 4. Heaving but likeable place playing mainstream dance music for locals and tourists into the early hours. Frequent appearances by Estonian bands.

Club Privé Harju 6. Style-conscious temple to cutting-edge dance culture, attracting big-name DJs and live bands. Dress up in club gear or risk being left out in the cold.

Guitar Safari Muurivahe 22. Popular venue for live cover-bands and dancing.

Hollywood Club Vana-Posti 8. Popular Old Town dance club specializing in commercial techno. Trendy and busy. No trainers. Wed–Fri only.

Terrarium Sadama 6. Filling up rapidly with the dance crowd. Visiting international DJs and beautiful young things in this minimalist club by the port. Closed Sun–Tues.

Von Krahli Bar Rataskaevu 10/12. Hip hangout that's always packed with a bohemian crowd. Frequent live music and dancing.

Listings

Embassies Canada, Toom-Kooli 13 (☎0/627 3311); Ireland, 2nd floor, Viru 2 (☎0/681 1888); UK, Wismari 6 ☎0/667 4700; US, Kentmanni 20 ☎0/668 8100.

Exchange Outside banking hours, try the Monex exchange offices in the ferry dock, or the Kaubamaja or Stockmann department stores (all daily 9am–8pm).

Hospital Ravi 18 ☎0/602 7000; 24hr information ☎0/620 7015, ⊛www.keskhaigla.ee.

Internet access Escape, Tatari 4; @5, in the Kaubamaja department store, Gonsiori 2.

Laundry Sauberland, Maakri 23; Seebimull, Liivalaia 7.

Left luggage At the bus station (Mon–Sat 6.30am–10.20pm, Sun 7.45am–8.20pm).

Pharmacies Tonismae Apteek, Tõnismägi 5; Tallinna Linna Apteek, Pä Apteek, Pärnu mnt. 10.

Police Pärnu mnt. 11 ☎0/6123 523.

Post office Narva mnt. 1, opposite the *Viru Hotel*.

The rest of Estonia

The island of **Saaremaa**, off the west coast of Estonia, is easily reached from Tallinn yet under-exploited as a holiday destination, its forests and coastline ripe for exploration. On the mainland some 190km southeast of Tallinn, **Tartu**, the former Hansa city of Dorpat, is regarded by many Estonians as the spiritual capital of Estonia, thanks to its role in the nineteenth-century National Awakening. These days it's a laid-back university town with a population of 100,000 and a small and easily walkable Old Town. **Pärnu**, Estonia's fifth-largest city, lies west of Tartu. There are a handful of sights in its Old Town, but the city's main claim to fame is as the country's main resort, its sandy beach drawing thousands of visitors every summer – especially in July, for its jazz festival.

The island of Saaremaa

Cloaked with pine trees and juniper bushes, and littered with glacial boulders, the island of **SAAREMAA** is a tranquil place. It was the last part of Estonia to come under foreign control (when the Knights of the Sword captured it in 1227) and the locals have always maintained a strong-minded indifference to the influence of foreign occupiers – a fact that has led many to claim that the island is one of the most authentically Estonian parts of the country. To get here, take a ferry from Virtsu on the mainland to Kuivastu on nearby Muhu island, which is linked to Saaremaa by a causeway.

Approaching **KURESSAARE**, Saaremaa's main town, don't be put off by the ugly Soviet-era industrial zone that surrounds it – the centre remains much as it was before World War II and is home to one of the finest castles in the Baltic region. From the bus station on Pihtla turn left onto Tallinna in order to reach **Kesk väljak**, the main square. Here you'll find Kuressaare's second oldest building (after the castle), the yellow-painted **Town Hall**, dating from 1670, its door guarded by stone lions; facing it is the **Weigh House**, another yellow building with a stepped gable. From the square, Lossi runs south past a monument to the dead of the 1918–20 War of Independence, past the eighteenth-century **Nikolai kirik**, a white Orthodox church with green onion domes, and on to the magnificent **Kuressaare Castle**, a vast fortress built from locally quarried dolomite. Set on an artificial island surrounded by a moat, the castle was founded during the 1260s as a stronghold for the bishop of Ösel-Wiek who controlled western Estonia from his base at Haapsalu on the mainland. What you see today dates largely from the fourteenth century and is a formidable structure, protected by huge seventeenth-century ramparts. The labyrinthine keep houses the **Saaremaa Regional Museum** (daily 11am–7pm; Oct–April closed Mon & Tues; 30EEK), an interesting but confusingly laid-out collection covering the history and culture of the island from prehistoric times. The various sections are summarized in English. It's also possible to view the spartan living quarters of the bishops on the ground floor and climb the watchtowers. **Tall Hermann**, the eastern (and thinner) corner tower, is linked to the rest of the keep only by a wooden drawbridge.

The **tourist office** is in the town hall (June–Aug daily 9am–7pm; rest of year Mon–Fri 9am–5pm; ☎45/33120, ✆www.saaremaa.ee), and will book **private rooms** across the island for around 150EEK per person. About the cheapest **place to stay** in town is the *Guesthouse Mardi*, Vallimaa 5a (☎45/24633; ❸); its hostel beds, available from May to August, are in double and triple rooms, with bathrooms shared between two rooms. The *Arabella Guesthouse*, Tomi 12 (☎45/55885, ✉aara@hot.ee; ❸), is also more of an upmarket hostel with around fifty double rooms, each en suite. On the outskirts of town at Piibelehe 4, *Piibelehe Holiday Home* (☎45/36206, ✉piibilehe@saaremaa.ee; ❷) has two guest rooms with shared bathroom/toilet; traditional Saaremaa breakfasts are included. Alternatively, try the *Ovelia Majutus* at Suve 8 (☎45/55732; ❷), another family-run B&B. For **food**, the *Classic* kohvik, Lossi 9, has an excellent selection of pasta, salads, omelettes and pancakes, or pour your own coffee and select from a tempting array of pastries at the *Vannalinna Kohvipood* café at Kauba 10. Be sure to sample *Saaremaa*, the locally brewed beer, which packs a punch. To sample it in situ, head for *Veski*, Pärnu 19, a pub in an old windmill, which also dishes up basic food (pork and potato variations). *Budweiser Pub*, Kauba 6, has Czech and German beers on tap, a pool table and pub grub, Estonian-style. **Internet** access is at the gloomy *Piljardisaal* Billiard Hall, Raekoja 1.

Around the island

There's not much public transport on the island, although the odd daily bus from Kuressaare to outlying villages ensures that several places are within day-trip distance. Thanks to its largely flat terrain, exploring Saaremaa by bike is also a viable option. **KAARMA**, just over 10km north of Kuressaare, is the location of the thirteenth-century Kaarma kirik, a large, red-roofed church containing a christening stone from the same period. The church's graveyard is littered with ancient stone crosses – the oldest are the so-called "sun crosses", set within a circle carved in stone. In woods at the edge of the village of **KAALI**, 10km northeast of Kaarma, is a murky green pool about 100m in diameter, created by the impact of a meteorite during the eighth century BC. Though not particularly spectacular, it is one of the world's few easily accessible meteorite craters, and the locals are very proud of it. Around 15km north of Kaali is **ANGLA**, with five much-photographed wooden windmills by the roadside. A right turn just past the windmills leads to the thirteenth-century Karja kirik, a plain white village church with an unusual crucifixion carving above its side door. Inside the church are more stone carvings, depicting religious figures and scenes from village life.

Tartu

The main sights of **TARTU**, less than three hours from Tallinn by bus, lie between Cathedral Hill, right in the centre, and the River Emajõgi. The train station is about 500m southwest of the centre at Vaksali 6, and the bus station is just east of the centre at Turu 2. The city's focal point is its cobbled **Town Hall Square**, lined by prim Neoclassical buildings, the most eye-catching of which is the **Town Hall**, a toytown edifice at the head of the square, painted lilac and purple and topped by a spire. The Neoclassical theme continues in the yellow and white stucco facade of the main **Tartu University** building at Ülikooli 18, a couple of hundred metres north of the square. About 100m beyond the university is the red-brick shell of the Gothic **St John's Church**, founded in 1330, bombed out in 1944 and now undergoing restoration. The building is inaccessible, but from the street you can admire the unusual terracotta sculptures in niches that surround the main entrance. From behind the Town Hall, Lossi climbs **Cathedral Hill**, now a pleasant park with a few historic buildings dotted among its trees. On the way up, the street passes beneath **Inglisild**, a brightly painted wooden bridge dating from the nineteenth century. At the top of the hill you'll find the remains of the red-brick **Cathedral**, built by the Knights of the Sword in the thirteenth century. Tacked onto the end of the cathedral is a new building housing the **University History Museum** (Wed–Sun 11am–5pm; 20EEK), with three floors of ancient-looking textbooks, and the sabres and flags brandished by nineteenth-century student fraternities. Within a few minutes' walk of Cathedral Hill is the **Estonian National Museum**, J. Kuperjanovi 9 (Wed–Sun 11am–6pm; 20EEK). Devoted to peasant life and the development of agriculture, it includes some imaginatively recreated farmhouse interiors and a detailed display of folk costume from all over the country; there's good English labelling, too.

Practicalities

Tartu's **tourist office** is at Raekoja plats 14 (Mon–Fri 10am–6pm, Sat 10am–3pm; ☎7/432 141, ✇www.tartu.ee). There are a number of small **guest houses** (❷) in the suburbs offering accommodation, although few of the hosts speak English and you're best off making reservations through the tourist office. They will also advise on which of the university **hostels** have vacancies; the student dorm at Pepleri 14 (☎7/420 676; ✉mty-tyk@ut.ee; 250EEK per person) is only ten minutes' from the centre and usually has rooms in summer. The only affordable central **hotel** is the *Park* at Vallikraavi 23 (℡7/427 000, ✆www.parkhotell.ee; ❸). The nearby *Oru Villa* B&B, Oru 1 (℡7/422 894, ✆www.oruvilla.ee; ❸), provides rooms with atmosphere and a sense of history. For **food** try the fast and cheap *Pronto Pizzeria* at Küütri 3; or *Tsink Plekk Pang*, Küütri 6, which serves Chinese food in an arty café ambience. For a **drink**, the superb *Wilde*, Vallikraavi 4, offers tea, coffee, alcohol and atmosphere. Alternatively, head to *Zavood*, a bohemian dive just north of the centre at Lai 30. *Atlantis*, on the opposite bank of the river from the centre at Narva mnt 2, is a large and lively mainstream **disco**; although *Club Tallinn*, Narva mnt 27, attracts more in the way of big-name DJs. **Club** nights also take place at *Varjend 2000*, a graffiti-covered bunker 500m south of the centre on Pargi; and at the more mainstream *Pattaya*, just beyond the bus station at Turu 21. There's an **Internet café**, *Virtuaal* (daily 11am–midnight; 30EEK/hr), at Pikk 40, on the opposite side of the Emajõgi from the centre.

Pärnu

The main town on Estonia's southwestern coast, **PÄRNU** comes into its own in summer, when the faded beach resort fills with visitors intent on making the most of the brief good weather. The sandy beaches are popular with young families, but the festivals cater to an alternative, cultural crowd and the mud baths of the many sanatorium spas are a must. The historic sights are mostly clustered in its **Old Town**. The bus station is on Pikk at the northeastern edge of the Old Town (information & ticket office at Ringi 3, round the corner), and the **train station** is about 5km east of the centre at Riia mnt. 116. **Rüütli**, lined with two-storey wooden houses, is the Old Town's main thoroughfare, cutting east–west through the centre. Near the junction with Aia is the **Pärnu Museum**, Rüütli 53 (Wed–Sun 10am–6pm, 30EEK), devoted to local history, and housing some of Estonia's oldest archeological finds as well as examples of local traditional costume. The oldest building in town is the **Red Tower**, a fifteenth-century remnant of the medieval city walls on Hommiku, running north from Rüütli a few blocks west of the museum. Despite its name the tower is white – only the roof and window frames are red – and it now houses an antiques shop. **Pühavaimu**, a few blocks to the west, has a pair of respectable-looking seventeenth-century houses near the junction with Malms, one in lemon yellow, the other in washed-out green with a large gabled vestibule. Moving west from Pühavaimu along Uus leads to the **Catherine Church**, a green-domed and multi-spired Orthodox church dating from 1760 and named after the Russian empress Catherine the Great. The interior is abundantly furnished with icons but is open for services only. From here, Vee runs down to **Kuninga**, the Old Town's other major street, at the western end of which is the seventeenth-century **Tallinn Gate**, an elegant relic of the Swedish occupation set into the remains of the city ramparts and now home to a bar. Kuninga heads east to the Lutheran **Elizabeth Church** (Mon–Fri 10am–2pm) dating from 1747, with a maroon and ochre Baroque exterior and plain, wood-panelled interior. From here, Nikolai leads south to Esplanaadi, where the **Chaplin Centre** (daily 9am–9pm; 15EEK) occupies the former Communist party HQ at no. 10. Taken over by local artists in the post-independence years, it holds regular shows, film festivals and a collection of contemporary Estonian paintings and other works donated by international artists, including Yoko Ono. South of here Nikolai joins Supeluse, which runs down to the city's **resort area**, passing beneath the trees of the Rannapark, a shady park separating the town from the beach. At the southern end of Supeluse are the grand, colonnaded Neoclassical **Pärnu Mud-Baths**, built in 1926, and painted in the familiar ochre. Nearby is Pärnu's sandy, white beach, packed at weekends and on public holidays.

Practicalities

The **tourist office** is at Rüütli 16 (June–Aug Mon–Sat 9am–6pm, Sun 10am–3pm; rest of year Mon–Fri 9am–5pm; ℡44/73000, ✆www.parnu.ee).

Private rooms (❶) are available from *Majutusbüroo*, a block east of the bus station at Hommiku 5 (☎44/31070, ✉tanni@online.ee). The best **hotels** lie between the town centre and the beach: try the *Leharu*, offering neat en suites on one floor of a high-rise sanatorium at Pärna 12 (☎44/25700, ✉leharu@hot.ee; ❸) or the snazzier *Vesiroos*, Esplanaadi 42a (☎44/30940; ❹), which has the only outdoor pool in town. Alternatively, try the **hostel** *Lõuna*, centrally located at Lõuna 2 (☎44/30943; beds from 250EEK), which is well-situated and can provide breakfast. *Linnakamping Green*, 3km east at Suur-Jõe 50b (closed Oct–April), has cabins as well as tent pitches. For **food**, try *Kohvik Georg*, Rüütli 43, an inexpensive self-service restaurant open until 7.30pm; *Steffani*, Nikolai 24, which has a big choice of pizza and pasta dishes; or *Mõnus Margarita*, Akadeemia 5 – a lively Tex-Mex joint with reasonable prices. The best of the **drinking** venues also do good food – try *Viies Villem*, a pub-style venue at Kuninga 11 with a meaty Estonian menu. *Sunset Club*, Ranna pst 3, on the Baltic shore, hosts beach-side music events. For **Internet** access, head to the Chaplin Centre (see above; 30EEK/hr).

Travel details

Trains

Tallinn to: Pärnu (2 daily; 3hr); Tartu (3 daily; 3hr 20min).

Tallinn to: Kuressaare (6 daily; 4hr 30min); Pärnu (every 30min; 2hr); Tartu (every 30min; 2hr 30min).
Tartu to: Kuressaare (2 daily; 5hr); Pärnu (4 daily; 2hr 45min); Tallinn (every 30min; 2hr 30min).

Buses

Kuressaare to: Tallinn (6 daily; 4hr 30min).
Pärnu to: Kuressaare (3 daily; 2hr 45min); Tallinn (every 30min; 2hr); Tartu (4 daily; 2hr 45min).

Ferries

Virtsu to: Kuivastu for Saaremaa (12–20 daily; 30min).

How to make a call

Dial the Access Number for the country you are in - see list below.

Enter your Account Number

and press #

Followed by your PIN

and press #

You are now in the main menu. Please follow the voice prompts.

Fold Here

To make a call press ②

then dial the country code (1 for the US, 44 for the UK), the area code and phone number.

To listen to messages press ①

To speak to 24-hour Customer Service or to recharge press ⓞ

Follow the voice prompts for other services.

Use any touch-tone phone globally.

$10 bonus talk time expires February 2006. Account expires 9 months after date of last call.

Access Number list

To get the latest Rough Guides Phonecard Access Numbers for over 55 countries and tips on making calls visit www.roughguides.ekit.com or speak to a Customer Service Consultant.

Belgium 0800-77888	Portugal§ 800-812-993
Canada 1800-808-5773	Spain¶ 800-099-665
Denmark § 8088-3550	Sweden¶ 0200-888-074
France¶ 0805-113-721	Switzerland» 0800-837-798
Germany 0800-634-8086	United Kingdom» 0800-376-2366
Ireland¶ 1800-992-363	UK alternate number . . . 0800-731-5664
Italy§ 800-985-675	London economy* 0207-943-2772
Netherlands § 0800-023-3971	United States (48 States)§. 1-800-706-1333

¶ Higher charges may be incurred from mobiles and payphone.
* Use economy numbers where available for cheaper calls. May incur local call charges.
§ Unavailable from mobile phones in some cases. » Unavailable from payphones in some cases.

Fold Here

RGU014 Aug03

Additional services

Your Rough Guides Phonecard also gives you access to many additional services designed specifically for travelers, including:

- **Voicemail** - family and friends can leave you messages for FREE!
- **Travel Vault** - store your travel document details securely online
- **Email** - a personalized account, you can even listen to email over the phone

For information on all additional services visit
www.roughguides.ekit.com

Recharge - 24 hours a day via the phone or web

Visit www.roughguides.ekit.com to recharge your card or dial the Access Number for the country you are in and press ⓞ # to speak with a Customer Service Consultant.

Joined? Need more ContactMe Cards?

Visit www.roughguides.ekit.com
and log-in to your account.
Click 'My Contact Details' and follow the easy steps.

Rough Guides Phonecard

To join over the web:
visit
www.roughguides. ekit.com & click 'Join eKit'

To join over the phone:

In the US dial
1-800-706-1333

In the UK dial
0800-731-5664

then press

ⓞ #

to speak to a Customer Service Consultant.

Visit the web for Access Numbers in other countries.

Quote reference code
RGEURBC1
when joining to receive your $10 bonus*

For assistance and information about our additional services, contact Customer Service or visit www.roughguides. ekit.com

*$10 Bonus applies to an initial charge of US$20 or more. Correct at August 2003

9

Finland

Finland highlights

* **Senate square, Helsinki** The capital's main square, dominated by the awe-inspring Lutheran cathedral, Tuomiokirkko. See p.296

* **Aura river, Turku** Sip a cool beer on board a boat-café, moored in the heart of the former capital. See p.300

* **Lenin museum, Tampere** Fascinating collection delving into the long, mutually respectful relationship between Lenin and Finland. See p.301

* **Olavinlinna castle, Savonlinna** The best preserved medieval castle in Finland. See p.301

* **Crossing the Arctic Circle, Rovaniemi** The trip everybody wants to make – and visit Father Christmas. See p.303

* **Pielpajärvi wilderness church, Inari** Trek across the tundra of Lapland to reach this former Saami outpost. See p.304

Introduction and basics

Scandinavia's most culturally isolated and least understood country, **Finland** has been independent only since 1917, having been ruled for hundreds of years by first the Swedes and then the Tsarist Russians. Much of its history involves a struggle for recognition and survival, and so modern-day Finns have a well-developed sense of their own culture, manifest in the popular Golden Age paintings of Gallen-Kallela and others, the music of Sibelius, the National Romantic style of architecture, and the ingrained values of rural life.

Finland is mostly flat and punctuated by huge forests and lakes, but has wide regional variations. The south contains the least dramatic scenery, but the capital, **Helsinki**, more than compensates, with its brilliant architecture and superb collections of national history and art. Stretching from the Russian border in the east to the industrial city of Tampere, the vast waters of the **Lake Region** provide a natural means of transport for the timber industry – indeed, water here is a more common sight than land. Towns lie on narrow ridges between lakes. North of here, Finland ranges from the flat western coast of **Ostrobothnia** to the thickly forested heartland of **Kainuu** and gradually rising fells of **Lapland**, Finland's most alluring terrain and home to the Saami, semi-nomadic reindeer herders.

Information & maps

Most towns have a **tourist office**, which sometimes book accommodation. In summer they generally open daily 9am–7pm in more popular centres; in winter, hours are much reduced and some don't open at all. The best general **map** is by *Freytag & Berndt*; there's also an excellent map in the *Finland: Budget Accommodation* booklet, available from tourist offices.

Money and banks

Finland's currency is the **euro** (€). **Banks** are open Mon–Fri 9.15am–4.15pm. Some banks have exchange desks at transport terminals, and ATMs are widely available. You can also change money at hotels, but the rates are generally poor.

Communications

Communications are dependable and quick. **Post offices** are generally open 9am–5pm, with later hours in Helsinki. **Public phones** are ubiquitous; you'll need a phone card (*puhelukortti*; €5–20), available at post offices and tourist offices. Some phones also accept credit cards. International calls are cheapest between 10pm and 8am. Operator numbers are ☎118 (domestic) and ☎92020 (international). Free **Internet access** is readily available, even in the most out-of-the-way places – most likely at the local library (though you may need to book a few hours in advance) or the tourist office.

Getting around

For the most part **trains** and **buses** integrate well, and you'll only need to plan with care when travelling through the remoter areas of the far north and east. **Trains** are operated by Finnish State Railways (VR; ⌨www.vr.fi).

Finland on the net

⌨**www.finland-tourism.com** The Finnish tourist board site
⌨**www.finland.org** General facts about Finland
⌨**www.sauna.fi** The Finnish Sauna Society
⌨**www.srmnet.org** Finnish Youth Hostel Association

Comfortable Express and InterCity trains, plus tilting Pendolino trains, serve the principal cities several times a day. Elsewhere, especially on east–west hauls through sparsely populated regions, trains are often tiny or replaced by buses on which rail passes are still valid. **InterRail** and **ScanRail** passes (see p.36) are valid on all trains. The best timetable is the *Rail Pocket Guide* published by VR and available from all train stations and tourist offices. **Buses** – privately run, but with a common ticket system – cover the whole country, but are most useful in the north. Tickets can be purchased at bus stations and most travel agents; only ordinary one-way tickets can be bought on board. The timetable (*Pikavuoroaikataulut*), available at all main bus stations, lists all bus routes.

Domestic flights can be comparatively cheap as well as time-saving, especially if you're planning to visit Lapland and the far north. Finnair (⊛www.finnair.com) offers a range of discounts aimed at under-26s. For budget flights from Helsinki to Rovaniemi and Kittilä in the far north check out Flying Finn (⊛www.flyfi.net).

Accommodation

Hotels are expensive. Special offers in summer mean that you'll be able to sleep well on a budget in high season, but may have difficulty finding anything affordable out of season; the reverse of the norm. You can **book** through Hotel Booking Centre (☎09/22881400), inside the train station in Helsinki. The free *Finland: Budget Accommodation* booklet, available from any tourist office, contains a comprehensive list of hostels and campsites.

Most **hotels** come with TV, phone and private bathrooms, and all-you-can-eat buffet breakfasts. Taking advantage of discount schemes and summer reductions, such as the **Finncheque**, can cut prices to around €35 per person for double rooms. Finncheque must be arranged through the Finnish Tourist Board or a specialist travel agent before arriving in Finland; it entitles the holder to an unlimited number of vouchers for hotel rooms in participating chains, for use between mid-May and Sept; there's often a surcharge (€13.50) in more expensive hotels, but in other places lunch is thrown in. The **Scanhotel** chain offers a similar system, which works out to about €75 for a double room, including breakfast, but once again look out for surcharges. In many towns you'll also find **tourist hotels** (*matkustajakoti*), offering less frills for €35–50 per person, although they are often full during summer. **Summer hotels** (*kesähotelli*; June–Aug only) are another option, offering decent accommodation in student blocks for €25–45 per person, normally with breakfast thrown in.

HI hostels (*retkeilymajat*; ⊛www.srmnet .org) are the cheapest option and always spotlessly clean. Each city has at least one. It's always advisable to book ahead, especially between June and August. Note that many close altogether from mid-August till June. Hostels range from the basic dormitory type to those with two-bedded rooms and a bathroom between three. Bed linen, if not included, costs an extra €3.50–5; Finnish health regulations prohibit the use of sleeping bags in hostels. HI cards reduce overnight charges by €2.50.

Official **campsites** (*leirintäalue*) are plentiful. Most open from May or June until August or September, although some stay open longer and a few all year. Many three-star sites also have **camping cottages**, often with TV, sauna and kitchen. Two people sharing a tent pay €5–15, depending on site facilities; cabins cost €100–500 per week (book cabins as far ahead as possible in July & Aug). You'll need either an International Camping Card or a National Camping Card; the latter (€3.40), available at all sites, is valid for a year.

Food and drink

Restaurants can be pricey; take advantage of special lunchtime deals and self-catering. Though tempered by many regulations, **alcohol** is more widely available and considerably less expensive than in the rest of Scandinavia.

Though it may at first seem a stodgy, unsophisticated cuisine, **Finnish food** is an interesting mix of Western and Eastern influences, with Scandinavian-style fish specialities and exotic meats such as reindeer and elk alongside dishes that bear a Russian stamp – pastries, and casseroles strong on cabbage and pork. **Breakfasts** (*aamiainen*) are sumptuous buffets of herring, eggs, cereals, cheese, salami and bread. You can lunch on the economical **snacks** sold in market halls (*kauppahalli*) or adjoining cafés. Most train stations and some bus stations and supermarkets also have cafeterias offering a selection of snacks and light meals, and the Grilli and Nakkikioski street stands turn out burgers and hot dogs for €2.50–3.50. Otherwise, campus **mensas** are the cheapest places to get a hot dish (€2–4). Theoretically, you have to be a student, but you're unlikely to be asked for ID. In regular restaurants or *ravintola*, **lunch** (*lounas*) deals are good value, with many places offering a lunchtime buffet table (*voileipäpöytä* or *seisova pöytä*) stacked with a choice of traditional goodies for a set price of €8.50–13. Pizzerias are another good bet, serving lunch specials for €6–9. For **evening meals**, a cheap pizzeria or *ravintola* will serve up standard plates of meat and two veg. In Helsinki and the big towns there's usually a good range of options, including Chinese and Thai. Prices run from €6 for a cheap pizza to €50 for a substantial meal plus drinks in a smart restaurant.

Drink

Whilst the attitude to **drinking** can seem austere, Finland has a huge problem with alcoholism: bars in smaller towns can be quite depressing. In Helsinki and the bigger towns, however, the drinking culture is more sophisticated and appealing. Most restaurants are fully licensed, and many are frequented more for drinking than eating. **Bars** are usually open till midnight or 1am and service stops half an hour before closing. You have to be 18 to buy beer and wine, 20 to buy spirits. Expect to queue to get into popular bars, as there's no standing allowed, so you'll only be let in if there's a seat free. Remember to tip the doorman (*portsari*; €1), if there is one, on leaving; if there isn't, then there'll almost certainly be an obligatory

cloakroom fee (also €1). The main – and cheapest – outlets for alcohol are the ubiquitous government-run **ALKO** shops (Mon–Thurs 10am–5pm, Fri 10am–6pm; Oct–April also Sat 9am–2pm).

Beer (*olut*) falls into three categories: "light beer" (I-Olut), like a soft drink; "medium strength beer" (*Keskiolut*, III-Olut), perceptibly alcoholic, sold in supermarkets and cafés; and "strong beer" (A-Olut or IV-Olut), on a par with the stronger European beers, and only available at licensed restaurants, clubs and ALKO shops. Strong beers, such as Lapin Kulta and Koff, cost about €1.35 per 300ml bottle. Imported beers go for €1.50–2 per bottle. Finlandia **vodka** is €27 a litre; Koskenkorva, a rougher vodka, is €25.

Opening hours and holidays

Shops open Mon–Fri 9am–6pm, Sat 9am–4pm. Along with banks, they close on **public holidays**, when most public transport and museums run to a Sun schedule: Jan 1; Jan 6 (Epiphany); Good Fri & Easter Mon; May 1; June 21; Nov 1; Dec 6; Dec 24, 25 & 26.

Emergencies

You won't have much cause to come into contact with the Finnish **police**, though if you do they are likely to speak English. As for **health problems**, if you're insured, you'll save time by seeing a doctor at a private health centre (*lääkäriasema*) rather than queuing at a national health centre (*terveyskeskus*). Medicines must be paid for at a **pharmacy** (*apteekki*), generally open daily 9am–6pm; outside these times, a phone number for emergency help is displayed on every pharmacy's front door.

Emergency numbers

All emergencies ☏112.

Helsinki

The southern coast of Finland is the most populated, industrialized and richest part of the country, with the densest concentration, not surprisingly, around the capital, **HELSINKI**. A city of 560,000 people, Helsinki is quite different from the other Scandinavian capitals, closer both in mood and looks to the major cities of eastern Europe. For a century an outpost of the Russian Empire, its very shape and form is derived from its powerful neighbour. Yet through the twentieth century it has become a showcase of independent Finland, much of its impressive architecture drawing inspiration from the dawning of Finnish nationalism and the rise of the republic. The streets have a youthful buzz, the short summer bringing crowds along the boulevards and at outdoor cafés and restaurants. At night the pace picks up, with a great selection of pubs and clubs and free rock concerts in the numerous parks.

Arrival, information and city transport

All points of arrival are close to the city centre: the **ferry** terminals are less than 1km from the centre; the **train station** is in the heart of the city; the **long-distance bus station** is a short way up Simonkatu; and the **airport**, Vantaa, is 20km to the north, connected by Finnair buses to the central train station (every 15–30min; €4.90).

The **City Tourist Office** at Pohjoisesplanadi 19 (Mon–Fri 9am–6/8pm, Sat & Sun 9/10am–4/6pm; ☎09/169 3757, ⊛www.hel.fi/tourism), stocks the useful, free listings magazines *Helsinki This Week*, *City* and *Helsinki Happens*. If you're staying a while, consider purchasing a **Helsinki Card** (€24/34 for 24/48hr), giving unlimited travel on public transport and free entry to more than forty museums. For information on the rest of the country, use the **Finnish Tourist Board** across the road at Eteläesplanadi 4 (Mon–Fri 9am–5pm; May–Sept also Sat & Sun 11am–3pm; ☎09/4176 9300, ⊛www.finland-tourism.com).

Most sights are within easy walking distance of each other. However, quick hops across the centre are easily done on the efficient **public transport** system (trams, buses and a small metro). One-way tickets can be bought on board (€2) or from the bus station, tourist office or kiosks around the centre (€1.70), while a **tourist ticket** (€4.80/9.60/14.40 for one/three/five days) permits unlimited use of the whole network for the period covered. **Tram** #3T follows a useful figure-of-eight route around the centre.

Accommodation

There's plenty of **accommodation**, the bulk of it mid-range **hotels**. However, there are a number of cheaper, if less luxurious, **tourist hotels**, providing basic accommodation in private rooms without bathrooms, and a few **hostels**, though space can be tight in summer. You can book hotel rooms and hostel beds at the **Hotel Booking Centre** at the train station for a fee of €5 in person or for free by email or phone (June–Aug Mon–Fri 9am–7pm, Sat 9am–6pm, Sun 10am–6pm; rest of year Mon–Fri 9am–6pm, Sat 9am–5pm; ☎09/2288 1400, ⊕hotel@helsinkiexpert.fi).

Hostels and tourist hotels

Hostel Academica Hietaniemenkatu 14 ☎09/1311 4334. On the fringes of the city centre with dorms and double rooms. HI and student card discounts. June to Aug only. €16.

Erottajanpuisto Uudenmaankatu 9 ☎09/642 169. Conveniently positioned for the buses, with singles to quadruples. €17.

Eurohostel Linnankatu 9 ☎09/622 0470. The biggest hostel in Finland, close to the ferry terminals and with a free sauna. €19.50.

Omapohja Itäinen teatterikuja 3 ☎09/666 211. Dorms and smaller rooms, some en suite. ❺

Stadion Hostel in the Olympic Stadium ☎09/477 8480. Out of the centre by 2km and often crowded, but cheap and open all year. Trams #3T, #7A, #7B and #10 to stadium, then follow the signs. €14.50.

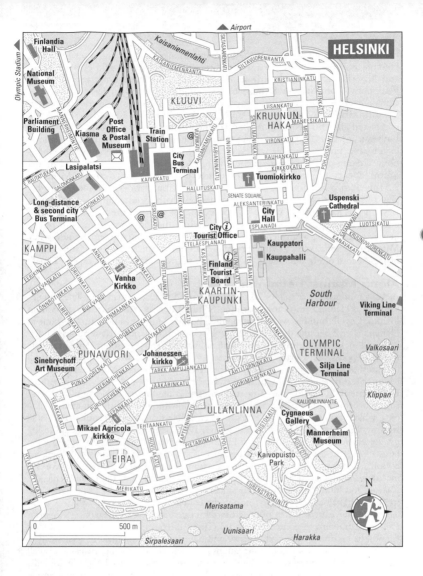

Summer Hotel Satakunta Lapinrinne 1
☎09/6958 5231. Centrally located, doubles as an
HI hostel. June–Aug only. €17.

Hotels

Anna Annankatu 1 ☎09/616621. Small and
central, with a cosy atmosphere. ⑧
Arthur Vuorikatu 19 ☎09/173441. Good-quality
hotel, with some en-suite rooms. ⑧
Finn Kalevankatu 3b ☎09/6844 360. A peaceful,

modern place, virtually in the city centre. ⑤
Kongressikoti Snellmaninkatu 15a
☎09/1356839. Clean and cosy place close to
Senate square. Discounts for longer stays. ④

Campsite

Rastila Karavaanikatu 4 ☎09/321 6551. Located
13km east of the city centre, at the end of the
metro line and served by night buses #90N and
#93N till 1.30am. Also has cabins (③).

The City

Following a devastating fire and the city's appointment as Finland's capital in 1812, Helsinki was totally rebuilt in a style befitting its new status: a grid of wide streets and Neoclassical brick buildings modelled on the then Russian capital, St Petersburg. From **Senate Square** to **Esplanadi** the grandeur has endured. The square itself is dominated by the exquisite form of the recently renovated **Tuomiokirkko** (Mon–Sat 9am–6pm, Sun noon–6pm), designed by Engel and completed after his death in 1852. After the elegance of the exterior, the spartan Lutheran interior comes as a disappointment; better is the gloomily atmospheric **crypt** (same times as cathedral; entrance on Kirkkokatu), now often used for exhibitions. Walking east, the square at the end of Aleksanterinkatu is overlooked by the onion domes of the Russian Orthodox **Uspenski Cathedral** (Mon–Sat 9.30am–4pm, Sun noon–3pm, Oct–April closed Mon; tram #3). Inside, a rich display of icons glitters while incense mingles with the sound of Slavonic choirs. Beyond is Katajanokka, a wedge of land extending between the harbours, where a dockland development programme is converting the old warehouses into pricey new restaurants and apartments. Just a block south of Senate Square, the new **City Museum** at Sofiankatu 4 (Mon–Fri 9am–5pm, Sat & Sun 11am–5pm; €3) offers a hi-tech record of Helsinki life in an impressive permanent exhibition called "Time".

Along Mannerheimintie

Across a mishmash of tramlines from the harbour is Esplanadi, a wide tree-lined boulevard that is Helsinki at its most charming. South of here, on Annankatu, is the **Vanha kirkko**, Engel's humble wooden structure, the first Lutheran church to be built in Helsinki after it became the capital. A few blocks from the end of Kasarminkatu is the large and rocky **Kaivopuisto** park, where nobility from St Petersburg came to sample the waters at its 1830s spa house. However, it's beyond the northern end of Bulevardi that most of the city's attractions can be found. On the corner of Aleksanterinkatu and Mannerheimintie is the Constructivist brick exterior of the **Stockmann Department Store**. Europe's largest, it sells everything from bubble gum to Persian rugs. Further along Mannerheimintie, steps head down to the **Tunneli** shopping complex, which leads to one of the city's most enjoyable structures, **Helsinki train station**, a solid yet graceful building dating from 1914. Beside the station is the imposing granite **National Theatre**, home of Finnish drama since 1872. Directly opposite the bus station is the **Atheneum Art Museum**, Kaivokatu 2 (Tues–Fri 9am–6/8pm, Sat & Sun 11am–5pm; €7.50). Its stirring selection of late-nineteenth-century works – including Akseli Gallén-Kallela and Albert Edelfelt's scenes from the Finnish epic, the *Kalevala*, and Juho Rissanen's moody studies of peasant life – recalls a time when the spirit of nationalism was surging through the country.

Mannerheimintie spears north from the city centre, past the striking **Kiasma**, Helsinki's museum of contemporary art (Tues 9am–5pm, Wed–Sun 10am–8.30pm; €7.50). Its gleaming steel-clad exterior and high-tech interior make it well worth a visit, and its collection includes installations in which sound, moving images and smell add a sensory dimension to the experience. Opposite is the **Lasipalatsi**, a multimedia complex situated in a recently renovated 1930s classic Functionalist building, inside which are trendy shops and cafés. Further along on the left, the **Parliament Building** (guided tours Sat 11am & noon, Sun noon & 1pm; July & Aug also Mon–Fri 2pm; free), with its pompous columns and choking air of solemnity, was completed in 1931. North of here is the **National Museum** (Tues–Sun 11am–6/8pm; €4), its design drawing on the country's medieval churches and granite castles. The exhibits, from prehistory to the present, are exhaustive; it's best to concentrate on a few specific sections, such as the marvellously restored seventeenth-century manor house interior and the ethnographic displays from the nation's varied regions.

Directly opposite the National Museum, **Finlandia Hall** (guided tours by appointment; ☏09/402 4246; free) was designed in the 1970s by the country's premier architect, Alvar Aalto. Inside, Aalto's characteristic asymmetry and wave pattern (his surname means "wave") are everywhere, from the walls and ceilings through to the lamps and vases. A little further up Mannerheimintie, the **Olympic Stadium** is clearly visible; originally intended for the 1940 Olympics, it hosted the second postwar games in 1952. Its **tower** (Mon–Fri 9am–8pm, Sat & Sun 9am–6pm; €2) gives an unsurpassed view over the city and a chunk of the southern coast. Back towards the city centre, the **Hietaniemi Cemetery** houses the graves of some of the big names of Finnish history – Mannerheim, Engel and Alvar Aalto, whose witty little tombstone, with its chopped Neoclassical column, stands beside the main entrance. East of here, at Lutherinkatu 3, is the late-1960s **Temppeliaukio kirkko** (Mon–Fri 10am–8pm, Sat till 6pm, Sun noon–1.45pm & 3.15–5.45pm; closed Tues 1–2pm and during services; tram #3B). Blasted from a single lump of granite beneath a domed copper roof, it's a thrill to be inside.

Suomenlinna

Built by the Swedes in 1748 to protect Helsinki from seaborne attack, the fortress of **Suomenlinna** stands on five interconnected islands and is the biggest sea fortress in the world. It's reachable by ferry (every 30min) from the harbour: you can either visit independently, or take one of the hour-long summer **guided walking tours**, beginning close to the ferry stage and conducted in English (June–Aug daily 10.30am, 1pm & 3pm; €5). Suomenlinna has a few museums, none particularly riveting. The best of the lot is **Suomenlinna Museum** (daily 10/11am–4/6pm; Oct–April closed Mon; €5) which contains a permanent exhibition on the island, but it is the views from the island back across the water towards the capital that are truly superb.

Eating and drinking

Many places offer good-value **lunchtime** deals, and there are plenty of affordable ethnic **restaurants** and fastfood *grillis* for the evenings. At the end of Eteläesplanadi the old market hall, Kauppahalli (Mon–Fri 8am–7pm, Sat 8am–4pm), is good for snacks and reindeer kebabs. Helsinki has several **student mensas**, two of which are centrally located at Aleksanterinkatu 5 and Yliopistonkatu 3; both are open during term time, and one or the other will be open through summer. **Drinking** can be enjoyed in the city's many pub-like restaurants; on Fridays and Saturdays it's best to arrive as early as possible to get a seat. Most places also serve food, although the grub is seldom at its best in the evening. There are ALKO shops at Fabianinkatu 9–11 and Kaivokatu 10.

Restaurants and cafés

Café Ekberg Bulevardi 9. Nineteenth-century fixtures and a *fin-de-siècle* atmosphere, with starched waitresses bringing expensive sandwiches and pastries to marble tables.

Café Fazer Kluuvikatu 3. Owned by Finland's biggest chocolate company, with justly celebrated pastries.

Kasakka Meritullinkatu 13. Great atmosphere and food in this old-style Russian restaurant.

Lappi Annankatu 22. Great Lapland food in a restaurant done out in tacky log cabin style. Lunchtime specials are good value, but prices escalate in the evenings.

Lasipalatsi Mannerheimintie 22–24. Decent modern Finnish food served in a classic Functionalist style building with great views of Kiasma and the street life below.

Mamma Rosa Runeberginkatu 55. A classic pizzeria also serving fish steaks and pasta.

Namaskar Bulevardi 6 & Mannerheimintie 100. Popular evening buffet and plenty of vegetarian options.

Saslik Neitystpolku 12. Pricey but delicious authentic Russian grub.

Strindberg Pohjoisesplanadi 33. The upstairs restaurant serves contemporary Scandinavian cuisine, while the street level café is one of *the* places in town to see and be seen.

Bars

Ateljee Bar on the roof of *Hotel Torni*, Yrjönkatu 26. The best views of Helsinki in a stylish atmosphere.

Bar N°9 Uudenmaankatu 9. A popular hangout for professionals at lunchtime and bohos in the evening, it has a beer list and menu as cosmopolitan as its staff. Food is reasonably cheap and filling and there is always a vegetarian option.

Bulevardia Bulevardi 34. Art Deco fittings and reasonably priced lunchtime specials.

Elite Eteläinen Hesperiankatu 22. Once the haunt of the city's artists, many of whom settled their bill with the paintings that line the walls. Especially good in summer, when you can drink on the terrace. **St Urho's Pub** Museokatu 10. One of the most popular student pubs. Guitars, a piano, etc available for jam sessions. **Wanha** Mannerheimintie 3. Self-service and

comparatively cheap café/bar. Arrive early for a seat on the balcony overlooking the streets below. The cellar is given over to a smoky beerhall, whilst other parts of the building serve as an indie/rock concert venue.

Nightlife

Helsinki has a vibrant night scene, with several venues putting on a steady diet of **live music** and free gigs almost every summer Sunday in Kaivopuisto park. There is also a wide range of **clubs and discos**, which charge a small admission fee (around €5). For details of **what's on**, read the entertainments page of *Helsingin Sanomat*, or the free fortnightly paper, *City*, found in record shops, bookshops, department stores and tourist offices. **Tickets** can be booked at Tiketti, Yrjönkatu 29c (Mon–Fri 9am–5pm; ☏0600/11 616, premium-rate call).

Botta Museokatu 10. Vibrant dance music of various hues most nights.
Kerma Erottaja 7. One of the grooviest places in town. Seventies-style decor and funky Latin rhythms abound. Open till 4am at weekends.
KY-Exit Pohjoinen Rautatiekatu 21. Sometimes has international bands; more often lively disco nights.

Saunabar Eerikinkatu 27. With a sauna attached and a legendary Sun night DJ spot, this is one of the most idiosyncratic places in town.
Soda Uudenmaankatu 16–20. Losing its edge a little, but still a good night out. Dance music downstairs; bar and guest DJs upstairs.
Storyville Museokatu 8. Popular venue for nightly live jazz. Good food, too.

Gay Helsinki

Finland decriminalized homosexuality in 1971 and introduced partnership laws in 2001. In recent years the gay scene in Helsinki has flourished and there's an impressive number of exclusively gay and gay-friendly establishments. For the latest details, pick up a copy of the monthly *Z* **magazine** – in Finnish only but with a useful listings section – widely available in larger newsagents, or drop into the state-supported gay organization SETA, Hietalahdenkatu 2b 16 (☏09/6123233, ⌗www.seta.fi).

Con Hombres Eerikinkatu 14. The most popular bar in Helsinki and one of the oldest in the country. If it's quiet elsewhere, the chances are there'll be people here. Very cruisy at weekends.
DTM (Don't Tell Mamma) Annankatu 32 ⌗www.dtm.fi. The capital's legendary night club and *the* place to go, with occasional drag shows and house music most nights.
Hercules Lönnrotinkatu 4b. Not quite as trendy as *DTM*, this club plays varied music, including some

of Finland's best offerings.
Hideaway Annankatu 6. Two bars on two floors, with a small dancefloor downstairs. Very popular at weekends with a mixed crowd.
Mann's Street Mannerheimintie 12 (upstairs). If you're looking for karaoke, Finnish music and older gay men, you'll find generous helpings here.
Room Erottajankatu 5. Next to *Lost and Found* and one of Helsinki's better neighbourhood bars; attracts the young and beautiful.

Listings

Embassies Canada, Pohjoisesplanadi 25b ☏09/228 530; Ireland, Erottajankatu 7A ☏09/646 006; UK, Itäinen Puistotie 17 ☏09/2286 5100; US, Itäinen Puistotie 14a ☏09/171 931. Australia, contact Stockholm embassy (see p.904).
Exchange Other than the banks, try Travelex at the airport (5.30am–11.30pm) or Forex at the train station (daily 8am–9pm).
Hospital Marian Hospital, Lapinlahdenkatu 16 ☏09/4711.
Internet Akateeminen Kirjakauppa (Micronia department), Keskuskatu 2; Netcup,

Aleksanterinkatu 52; mbar and Book Cable in the Lasipalatsi, Mannerheimintie 22–24.
Laundry Rööperin pesulapalvelut, Punavuorenkatu 3 and Easywash, Runeberginkatu 47.
Left luggage At the train station.
Pharmacies Yliopiston Apteekki, Mannerheimintie 96 (24hr).
Police Pieni Roobertinkatu 1–3 ☏1891.
Post office Elielaukio 2F.
Sauna Kotiharjun sauna (Tues–Fri 2–8pm, Sat 1–7pm), Harjutorinkatu, near the Sörnäinen metro station.

Around Helsinki: Porvoo

About 50km east of Helsinki, **PORVOO** is one of the oldest towns on the south coast and one of Finland's most charming. Its narrow cobbled streets, lined by small wooden buildings, give a sense of the Finnish life which predated the capital's bold squares and Neoclassical geometry. Close to the station, the **Johan Ludwig Runeberg House**, Aleksanterinkatu 3 (Mon–Sat 10am–4pm, Sun 11am–5pm; Sept–April closed Mon & Tues; €4), is where the famed Finnish poet lived from 1852 while a teacher at the town school; despite writing in Swedish, one of his poems provided the lyrics for the Finnish national anthem. The old town is built around the hill on the other side of Mannerheimkatu, crowned by the fifteenth-century **Tuomiokirkko** (May–Sept Mon–Fri 10am–6pm, Sat 10am–2pm, Sun 2–5pm; Oct–April Tues–Sat 10am–2pm, Sun 2–4pm), where Alexander I proclaimed Finland a Russian Grand Duchy and convened the first Finnish Diet. This, and other aspects of the town's past, can be explored in the **Porvoo Museum** (daily 10am/noon–4pm; Sept–April closed Mon & Tues; €5) at the foot of the hill in the main square; the collection of furnishings, musical instruments and oddities mostly date from the days of Russian rule.

Buses run daily from Helsinki to Porvoo (€8 one-way), arriving opposite the **tourist office**, which is at Rihkamakatu 4 (Mon–Fri 9.30am–4.30/6pm, Sat & Sun 10am–2/4pm; Sept to mid-June closed Sun; ☎019/520 2316, ⊛www.porvoo.fi). There's a **hostel** at Linnankoskenkatu 1–3 (☎019/523 0012; €13), and a **campsite** (☎019/581 967; June to Aug), 1.5km from the town centre. The cheapest place **to eat** is *Rosso* at Piispankatu 21.

Southwest Finland

The area west of Helsinki is probably the blandest section of the country – endless forests interrupted only by modest-sized patches of water and virtually identical villages and small towns. The far **southwestern** corner is more interesting, with islands and inlets around a jagged shoreline and some of the country's distinctive Finnish-Swedish coastal communities. The former capital **Turku** is historically and visually one of Finland's most enticing cities.

Turku

TURKU was once the national capital, but lost its status in 1812 and most of its buildings in a ferocious fire in 1827. These days it's a small and sociable city, bristling with history and culture and with a sparkling nightlife, thanks to the students from its two universities.

To get to grips with Turku and its pivotal place in Finnish history, cut through the centre to the river. This tree-framed space was, before the great fire of 1827, the bustling heart of the community, and is overlooked by Turku's **Tuomiokirkko** (daily 9am–7/8pm except during services), erected in the thirteenth century and still the centre of the Finnish Church. Despite repeated fires, a number of features survive, notably the ornate seventeenth-century tomb of Torsten Stålhandske, commander of the Finnish cavalry during the Thirty Years War. On top of a small hill near the cathedral, you'll see the wooden dome of the **Engel Observatory**, which currently houses the **Turku Art Museum** (Tues–Thurs 11am–6/7pm, Fri–Sun 10am–4pm; €5.50–7, according to the exhibition). The museum contains one of the better collections of Finnish art, with works by all the great names of the country's golden age plus a commendable stock of moderns. Retrace your steps to the riverbank to find Turku's newest and most splendid museum, the combined **Aboa Vetus and Ars Nova** (daily 11am–7pm; mid-Sept to mid-April closed Mon–Wed; €7). Digging the foundations of the modern art gallery revealed a warren of medieval lanes, now on view beneath the glass floor of the building. The gallery comprises 350 striking works plus temporary exhibits, and there's a great café too.

Just north of the cathedral is the sleek, low form of the **Sibelius Museum** (Tues–Sun 11am–4pm, Wed also 6–8pm; €3), which – although Sibelius had no direct connection with Turku – displays family photo albums and manuscripts, the great man's hat, walking stick and even his final half-smoked cigar. A short walk away, on the southern bank of the river at Itäinen Rantakatu 38, the **Wäinö Aaltonen Museum** (Tues–Sun 11am–7pm; €3–5.50, depending on exhibition) is devoted to the best-known modern Finnish sculptor, who grew up close to Turku and studied at the local art school – his imaginative and sensitive work turns up in every major Finnish town. Crossing back over Aurajoki and down Linnankatu and then towards the mouth of the river will bring you to **Turku Castle** (daily 10am–3/6pm; mid-Sept to mid-April closed Mon; €6.50). The featureless exterior conceals a maze of cobbled courtyards, corridors and staircases, with a bewildering array of finds and displays. The castle probably went up around 1280; its gradual expansion accounts for the patchwork architecture.

Practicalities

The river Aura splits the city, its tree-lined banks forming a natural promenade as well as a useful landmark. On the northern side of the river is Turku's central grid, where you'll find the **tourist office** at Aurakatu 4 (Mon–Fri 8.30am–6pm; also Sat & Sun: May–Sept 9am–4pm, rest of year 10am–3pm ; ℡02/262 7444, ⓦwww.turkutouring.fi). Both the **train** and **bus station** are within easy walking distance of the river, just north of the centre; for the Stockholm ferry, stay on the train for the terminal, 2km west, or catch bus #1 on Linnankatu.

There are some good deals to be had at Turku's mid-range **hotels**, especially if you make an early reservation and pick a weekend. Try *Hotel Julia*, Eerikinkatu 4 (℡02/336 311; ➏), or for a real slice of luxury and character try *Park Hotel*, Rauhankatu 1 (℡02/273 2555; ➑). Alvar Aalto fans should stay at *Quality Hotel Ateljee* (℡02/336 111; ➏), Humalistonkatu 7, housed in a building designed by Finland's most famous architect; ask for room no. 422 or 534. The excellent **hostel**, *Hostel Turku*, is by the river at Linnankatu 39 (℡02/262 7680; €17); take bus #1 or #30. The nearest **campsite** (℡050/559 0139; June to mid-Aug; bus #8) is on the island of Ruissalo, which has two sandy beaches and overlooks Turku harbour.

For excellent **food** at sensible prices, it's worth trekking out to *Alabama Datacity* restaurant in the Data Centre, close to Turku hospital (take the train one stop to Kupittaa; 5min); run by the catering college, the food and service are excellent. In the centre, *Gadolinia*, a **student mensa**, part of Åbo Akademi on Porthaninkatu, offers the cheapest food; or there's *Pizzeria Dennis*, Linnankatu 17, for affordably priced pizza. Near the tourist office **Market Square** (*Kauppatori*) sells fresh produce, and in summer is full of open-air cafés; nearby, the effervescent market hall or **Kauppahalli** (Mon–Fri 8am–5pm, Sat 8am–2pm) offers a slightly more upmarket choice of delis and other eateries. Top-notch food can be had at *Herman*, Läntinen Rantakatu 37, in a bright, airy storehouse dating from 1849, with excellent lunches (€7.10). Floating bar-restaurants change each summer, but look out for *Papa Joe*, *Svarte Rudolph* and *Donna*. Otherwise, the most popular **drinking** venue is *Uusi Apteekki*, Kaskenkatu 1, which, true to its name, is an old pharmacy complete with ancient fittings.

Finland's Lake Region

About a third of Finland is consumed by the **Lake Region**, a huge area of bays, inlets and islands interspersed with dense forests. Despite holding much of Finland's industry, it's a tranquil, verdant area, and even **Tampere**, the major industrial city, enjoys a peaceful lakeside setting. The eastern part of the region is the most atmospheric, slender ridges furred with conifers linking the few sizeable landmasses. The regional centre, **Savonlinna**, stretches delectably across several islands and boasts a superb medieval castle.

Tampere

TAMPERE, a leafy place of parks and lakes, is Scandinavia's largest inland city. Its rapid growth began just over a century ago, when the Scot James Finlayson opened a textile factory, drawing labour from rural areas where traditional crafts were in decline. Metalwork and shoe factories soon followed, their owners paternally promoting a vigorous local arts scene for the workforce. Free outdoor concerts, lavish theatrical productions and one of the best modern art collections in Finland maintain such traditions to this day. Almost everything of consequence is within the central section, a thin strip of land bordered on two sides by lakes Näsijärvi and Pyhäjärvi. The main streets run off either side of Hämeenkatu, which leads directly from the train station across Hämeensilta bridge. Left off Hämeenkatu, up slender Hämeenpuisto, the **Lenin Museum** at no.28 (Mon–Fri 9am–6pm, Sat & Sun 11am–4pm; €4) remembers the time when Lenin lived in Finland and attended the Tampere conferences, held in what is now the museum. Nearby, at Puutarhakatu 34, the **Art Museum of Tampere** (Tues–Sun 10am–6pm; €4/6) holds temporary exhibitions, but if you're looking for Finnish art you might be better off visiting the **Hiekka Art Gallery**, a few minutes' walk away at Pirkankatu 6 (Tues–Thurs 3–6pm, Sun noon–3pm; €4), which has sketches by Gallen-Kallela and Helene Schjerfbeck. Better still is the tremendous **Sara Hildén Art Museum** (daily 11am–6pm, closed Mon Oct-Apr; €4), built on the shores of Näsijärvi, a quirky collection of Finnish and foreign modern works; take bus #16 from the centre.

Tampere's **tourist office** is by the river, 500m from the **train station** at Verkatehtaankatu 2 (Mon–Fri 8.30am–5/8pm; June–Sept also Sat & Sun 10am–5pm; ☎03/3146 6800, ⊛www.tampere.fi), and a similar distance along Hatanpään from the **bus station**. Central, moderately priced **hotels** include the *Victoria*, Itsenäisyydenkatu 1 (☎03/242 5111; ❻), and *Sokos Hotel Villa*, Sumeliuksenkatu 14 (☎03/262 6267; ❻). There are various **hostels**, the best being the *Uimahallin maja*, an HI hostel centrally located at Pirkankatu 10–12 (☎03/222 9460; €19.50), and the *NNKY* opposite the cathedral at Tuomiokirkonkatu 12a (☎03/252 4020; June–Aug; €13.50). The nearest **campsite** is *Härmälä*, 5km south (☎03/2651355; mid-May to late Aug; bus #1), which also has cabins (❸).

The cheapest places to eat are the **student mensas** at the university at the end of Yliopistonkatu; the usual pizza joints such as *Paprilla* on the second floor of the *Hostel Uimahallion Maja*, Pirkankatu 10–12; and, for relaxed posing, *Café Strindberg*, opposite the train station. For a local speciality, try *mustamakkara*, a type of black sausage, at the Laukontori open-air **market** by the rapids. For **drinking**, the busiest and trendiest place is *Cafe Europa* at Aleksanterinkatu, which, despite its name, is more bar than café. Also worth a look is *Plevna*, a German-style beer hall in Finlayson's converted factory on Kuninkaankatu, which is especially busy at weekends; for live music, head for *Tullikammari*, a **nightclub** in an old customs house on Itsenäisyydenkatu behind the train station.

Savonlinna and around

SAVONLINNA is one of the most relaxed towns in Finland, a woodworking centre that also makes a decent living from tourism and its renowned **opera festival** (⊛www.operafestival.fi) in July. It's packed throughout summer, so book well ahead if you're visiting at this time. Out of peak season, its streets and beaches are uncluttered, and the town's easy-going mood makes it a pleasant place to linger. The best locations for soaking up the atmosphere are the **harbour** and **market square** at the end of Olavinkatu, where you can cast an eye over the grand *Seurahuone Hotel*, with its Art Nouveau fripperies. Follow the harbour around Linnankatu, or better still around the sandy edge of Pihlajavesi, which brings you to atmospheric and surprisingly well-preserved **Olavinlinna Castle** (guided tours daily 10am–3/5pm; €5), perched on a small island. Founded in 1475, the castle witnessed a series of bloody conflicts until the Russians claimed possession of it in 1743 and relegated it to the status of town jail. Nearby is the **Savonlinna Regional Museum** in Riihisaari (July to mid-Aug daily 11am–5/8pm; rest of the year closed Mon; €3), which occupies an old granary and displays an intriguing account of the evolution of local life, with rock paintings and ancient amber carved with human figures.

There are two **train stations**; be sure to get off at Savonlinna-Kauppatori, just across the main bridge from the **tourist office**, Puistokatu 1 (June & Aug daily 8am–6pm, till 10pm during July; rest of year, Mon–Fri 9am–5pm; ☎015/517 510, ⌨www .savonlinnatravel.com). The **bus station** is off the main island, but within easy walking distance of the town centre. **Bikes** can be rented at several places on Olavinkatu, including at Koponen, no. 19–21 (☎015/533977); for **canoes** and **rowing boats** try Saimaan Vuokravenko at Kivrunkatu 15. For information and tickets for the **festival** visit the opera office, Olavinkatu 27 (☎015/476 7515, ⌨www.operafestival.fi). The most central **accommodation** is at the *Perehotelli Hospitz*, Linnankatu 20 (☎015/515661; ⑥). Another good choice, *Malakias*, Pihlajavedenkatu 6 (☎015/533 283; ⑨) is 2km west of the centre along Tulliportinkatu and then Savontie. The best place in town is the summer hotel (June-Aug) *Vuorilinna*, on Kasinosaari (☎015/739 5494; ⑤), five minutes over the bridge from the marketplace. The nearest **campsite** is 7km from the centre at Vuohimäki (☎015/537 353; June–Aug; bus #4). Good, cheap **food** is available at the pizza joints along Olavinkatu and Tulliportinkatu. *Majakka*, Satamakatu 11, offers good Finnish nosh at lunchtime.

Around Savonlinna

Savonlinna boasts beautiful scenery all around, and the place to sample it is **Punkaharju Ridge**, a narrow strip of land between the Puruvesi and Pihlajavesi lakes, 28km from town. Locals say it has the healthiest air in the world, super-oxygenated by abundant conifers. This is the Lake Region at its most breathtakingly beautiful. The ridge is traversable by road and rail, both running into the town of Punkaharju and passing the incredible **Retretti Arts Centre** (June–Aug daily 10am–5pm/6pm; €15), set in caves and with a large sculpture park. Trains and buses make the short journey between Savonlinna and Retretti.

Northern Finland

The northern regions take up a vast portion of Finland: one third of the country lies north of the Arctic Circle. It is sparsely populated, with small communities often separated by long distances. The coast of **Ostrobothnia** is affluent due to the adjacent flat and fertile farmland; busy and expanding **Oulu** is the region's major city as well as a centre of high-tech expertise, though it maintains a pleasing small-town atmosphere. Further north, **Lapland** is a remote and wild territory whose wide open spaces are home to several thousand Saami, who have lived in harmony with this harsh environment for millennia. Here, though the long winters are eerily dark, summer days are long and bright with the midnight sun. There is an extensive bus service and regular flights from Helsinki. Make sure you try Lappish cuisine, too – fresh cloudberries, smoked reindeer and wild salmon are highlights. **Rovaniemi** is the rather bland gateway to the Arctic North; from here a road leads on towards and **Inari**, both convenient bases, and on to Norway.

Oulu

OULU, with its renowned university, is a leading light in Finland's burgeoning computing and microchip industries. During the nineteenth century it was the centre of the world's tar industry and the city's affluence and vibrant cultural scene date from that time. In the centre of town on Kirkkokatu, the **City Hall** retains some of the grandeur of the late nineteenth century, when it was a luxury hotel, and you can peek in at the wall paintings and enclosed gardens. Further along

Kirkkokatu, the copper-domed and stuccoed **Tuomiokirkko** (daily: June–Aug 11am–8/9pm; rest of year Mon–Fri noon–1pm), seems anachronistic amid the bulky blocks of modern Oulu. Across the small canal just to the north, the **North Ostrobothnia Museum** (daily 10/11am–6/7pm; closed Mon; €3) has a large regional collection with a good Saami section.

The connected **train and bus stations** are linked to the city centre by several parallel streets feeding to the *kauppatori* and *kauppahalli* (**markets**) by the water beyond. The **tourist office** is at Torikatu 10 (Mon–Fri 9am–4pm; mid-June to mid-Aug also Sat 10am–3pm; ☎08/5584 1330, ⊛www.oulutourism.fi). Low-cost **accommodation** in the centre is available at the *Hotel Turisti*, opposite the train station at Rautatienkatu 9 (☎08/563 6100; ❺), which provides good value accommodation during summer. Alternatively *Hotelli Oppimästäri* (☎018/8848 527; ❹) at Nahkatahtaankatu 3 offers more no-nonsense hostel-style rooms. There's a **campsite** (☎08/5586 1350) with cabins on Hietasaari Island, 4km from town; take bus #5 from outside the tourist office. Oulu boasts some charming **cafés** including *Sokeri Jussi* in an old salt warehouse on Pikisaari just over the bridge from the mainland, while *Katri Antell* on Rotuaari (Mon–Fri 8.30am–5pm, Sat 9am–2.30pm) is justly famed for its luscious, but expensive, cakes. Cheapest **meals** are at the pizzerias – *Fantasia* serves the best and also has a selection of Finnish dishes; *Oskarin Kellari*, opposite the train station, also serves a stuff-your-face lunch buffet for about €7.50. For **nightlife** try the eclectic *Panimo*, Kappurienkatu 13, a pub that is generally stuffed with Oulu's young and trendy.

Rovaniemi

Easily reached by train, **ROVANIEMI** is touted as the capital of Lapland, though its administrative buildings and busy shopping streets are a far cry from the surrounding rural hinterland. The elegant wooden houses of old Rovaniemi were razed by departing Nazis at the close of World War II, and the town was completely rebuilt during the late 1940s. Aside from eating reindeer in the local restaurants, the best way to prepare yourself for what lies further north is to visit the 172m long glass tunnel of **Arktikum**, Pohjoisranta 4 (daily 9/10am–5/7pm; Sept to mid–May closed Mon; €10; ⊛www.arktikum.fi). Subterranean galleries along one side house the **Provincial Museum of Lapland** with genuine Saami crafts and costumes alongside the imitations sold in souvenir shops to emphasize the romanticization of their culture. Across the corridor is the **Arctic Centre**, which gives a thorough treatment of all things circumpolar. For a couple of weeks either side of midsummer, the **midnight sun** is visible from Rovaniemi, the best vantage points being either the striking bridge over the Ounaskoski or atop the forested and mosquito-infested hill, Ounasvaara, across the bridge. The remaining sight is on the south side of town near the bus and train stations, where pristine Aalto-designed civic buildings line Hallituskatu. The city **library** (Mon–Thurs 11am–8pm, Fri 11am–5pm, Sat 11am–4pm) has a Lapland Department with a staggering hoard of books in many languages covering every Saami-related subject. Most other things of interest are outside town, not least the **Arctic Circle**, 8km north and connected by the hourly bus #8 from the railway station. On the circle is the **Santa Claus Village** (daily 9/10am–5/7pm; free), a large log cabin where you can meet Father Christmas all year round and leave your name for a Christmas card from Santa himself.

The main **tourist office** is at Rovakatu 21 (Mon–Fri 8am–4/6pm; June–Aug also Sat & Sun 10am–4pm; ☎016/346270, ⊛www.rovaniemi.fi). The **hostel**, *Tervashonka* at Hallituskatu 16 (☎016/344644; ❸), is always crowded in summer – try to book in advance. Otherwise you can fall back on the **guest houses**, the best of which are within five minutes' walk of the train station: *Matka Borealis* is nearest at Asemieskatu 1 (☎016/3420130; ❹), whilst *Matka Outa*, Ukkoherrantie 16 (☎016/312474; ❹), is towards the town centre. The only other budget accommodation is the **campsite** (☎016/345 304; June–Aug) on the far bank of Ounaskoski, facing town, a thirty-minute walk from the station. For filling **food** at very reasonable prices try *Café Kisälli*, Korkalonkatu 35 (Mon–Fri 8.30am–5pm), or *Martina*, Koskikatu 11, for good value pizzas and pasta dishes.

Inari

A half-day bus ride north of Rovaniemi, **INARI** lies along the fringes of Inarijärvi, one of Finland's largest lakes, and makes an attractive base from which to further explore this part of Lapland. The **bus** stops outside the **tourist office** (Mon–Fri 9/10am–4/7pm; June–Sept also Sat & Sun 10am–3pm; ☎016/661 666, ⍟www.inarilapland.org), on the main street, Inarintie, before continuing to Karasjok in Norway and – from June to late August only – the North Cape. Staff here have information on guided snow scooter trips in winter and fishing trips around the lake in summer. Close by is the excellent "Siida", the **Saami Museum** (daily 9/10am–5/8pm; Oct–May closed Mon; €7). An excellent outdoor section gives you an idea of how the Saami survived in Arctic conditions in their tepees, or *kota*, while the indoor section has a well-laid-out exhibition on all aspects of life in the Arctic. Towards the northern end of the village, summer boat tours (€12) depart from under the bridge to the ancient Saami holy site on the island of **Ukonkivi**; a plaque marks an ancient site of worship rumoured to have been a place of sacrifice. If walking's your thing then check out the pretty **Pielpajärvi Wilderness Church**, a two-hour well-signposted 7km hike from the village. There was a church on this site as far back as 1646, and the present one dates from 1754.

Accommodation should not be too problematic, though Inari does get very busy during the summer. The *Inarin Kultahovi* (☎016/671221; ⓔinarin .kultahovi@co.inet.fi; ⓖ) at Saarikoskentie 2 is a basic hotel with a decent **restaurant**. The *Uruniemi* **campsite** (☎016/671331, ⓔpentti.kangasniemi @uruniemi.inet.fi; Oct–April advanced booking obligatory) is about 3km south of the village in a lovely location right by the lake.

Travel details

Trains

Helsinki to: Jyväskylä (12 daily; 3hr 30min); Oulu (8 daily; 7hr); Rovaniemi (5 daily; 9hr 45min); Tampere (hourly; 2hr); Turku (12 daily; 2hr).
Oulu to: Rovaniemi (5 daily; 3hr).
Rovaniemi to: Helsinki (5 daily, 9hr 45min); Oulu (5 daily; 3hr).
Savonlinna to: Parikkala for Helsinki (2 daily; 50min).
Tampere to: Helsinki (hourly; 2hr); Oulu (7 daily; 5hr); Savonlinna (2 daily; 5hr); Turku (8 daily; 2hr).
Turku to: Tampere (8 daily; 2hr).

Flights

Helsinki to: Ivalo for Inari (2–3 daily; 1hr 40min); Oulu (10–15 daily; 1hr); Rovaniemi (5–7 daily; 1hr 20min).

Buses

Helsinki to: Porvoo (15 daily; 1hr).
Inari to: North Cape (June to late Aug 1 daily; 5hr 30min); Rovaniemi (4 daily; 5hr 30min).
Rovaniemi to: Sodankylä (5 daily; 1hr 45min); Inari (4 daily; 5hr 30min); North Cape (June to late Aug 1 daily; 10hr 30min).
Sodankylä to: Inari (4 daily; 3hr 30min).

Ferries

Helsinki to: Rostock, Germany (June to early Sept 3 weekly; 24hr); Stockholm, Sweden (2 daily; 17hr); Tallinn, Estonia (15–25 daily; 1hr 40 min–4hr).
Turku to: Stockholm (4 daily; 10–11hr).

France

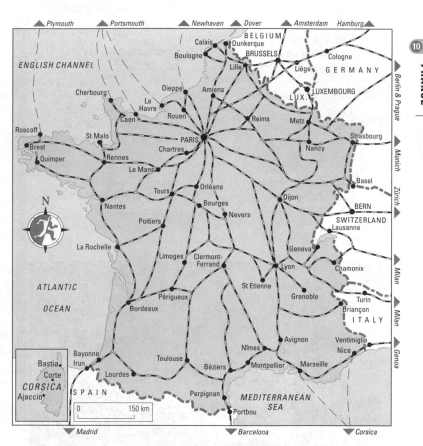

France highlights

* **Food and wine** Pamper your tastebuds – from humble coffee-and-croissant breakfasts to the highest of *haute cuisine*, via 265 kinds of cheese. See p.309

* **The Louvre, Paris** Vast, fascinating and inspiring museum. See p.316

* **Jardin du Luxembourg, Paris** The city's most beautiful park, ideal for picnics and people-watching. See p.319

* **Chartres cathedral** A gem of Gothic architecture. See p.325

* **Reims** The heart of the Champagne region. See p.327

* **The Loire Valley** Studded with châteaux, a fine area for wine-tasting. See p.334

* **Carcassonne** A fairy-tale medieval city. See p.346

* **Avignon** Stunning architecture, great cafés and a summer festival. See p.359

* **Nice** Take a stroll on the chic Promenade des Anglais. See p.365

Introduction and basics

Straddling the continent, **France** is a core country on any European tour. It would be hard to exhaust its diversity in a lifetime of visits. Each area looks different, feels different, has its own style of architecture and food and often its own *patois* or dialect. There is an astonishing variety of things to see, from the Gothic cathedrals of the north, through the boulevards and museums of Paris, to the Roman monuments of the south and the beaches of the Mediterranean and Atlantic coasts.

Budget restaurants and hotels proliferate, the rail and road networks are efficient, and the tourist information service is highly organized. As for where to go, it's hard to know where to begin. If you arrive from the north, you may pass through the Channel ports – Calais or Boulogne – or **Normandy**, to **Paris**, one of Europe's most elegant and compelling capitals. To the west lie the rocky coasts of **Brittany** and, further south, the châteaux of the **Loire**, although most people push on south to the limestone hills of **Provence**, the canyons of the **Pyrenees** mountains on the Spanish border, or the glorious Riviera coastline of the **Côte d'Azur** heading into Italy. There are good reasons, however, for taking things more slowly, not least the Germanic towns of **Alsace** in the east, the gorgeous hills and valleys of the **Lot** and the **Dordogne**, and, more adventurously, the high and rugged heartland of the **Massif Central**.

months. The best **map** is the Michelin no. 989 (1:1,000,000); the Michelin yellow series (scale 1:200,000) is better for regional detail. If you're planning to walk or cycle, check out the IGN green (1:100,000 and 1:50,000) and blue (1:25,000) maps.

Money and banks

Currency is the **euro** (€). Standard **banking hours** are Mon–Fri 9am–noon & 2–4.30pm; some also open on Sat. The Banque Nationale de Paris often gives the best rate for the least commission. **Exchange** counters – at the train stations of all big cities and usually one or two in the town centre as well – have longer opening hours, though normally offer a much worse deal. You can also change money at post offices and some tourist offices, and draw cash direct from ubiquitous **ATMs**.

Information & maps

Most towns and villages have a Syndicat d'Initiative (SI) or Office de Tourisme, giving out local **information** and free maps. Some can book accommodation anywhere in France. In larger cities and resorts offices will be open every day during the high season, often without a break, although times are greatly cut back in most places in the winter

Communications

Post offices *(la Poste)* are generally open Mon–Fri 8.30am–6.30pm, Sat 8.30am–noon. You can also buy **stamps** *(timbres)* from *tabacs*. International **phone calls** can be made from any box *(cabine)*. They take **phonecards** *(télécartes)*, available from post offices, *tabacs* and train station ticket counters. For calls within France – local or long

France on the net

ⓦ **www.tourisme.fr** French Tourist Board
ⓦ **www.franceguide.com** Excellent resource, with links to many tourist offices
ⓦ **www.discoverfrance.net** Useful tourist information, with links to other sites
ⓦ **www.viafrance.com** Information on festivals, expos, events and concerts
ⓦ **www.monum.fr** Information on major historical monuments

distance – you must dial all ten digits. Directory enquiries is ☎12. To phone via an operator call ☎3123. To call Monaco, prefix the eight-digit number with ☎00377. All towns have cybercafés offering **Internet access** for around €4/hr. Post offices also offer access; to use their terminals you need a prepaid card – *Carte Cyberposte* – costing €7 for the first hour and €4 for each subsequent hour. Street-side kiosks in major cities are operated by France Telecom *télécartes*.

Getting around

France has the most extensive **rail** network in western Europe, run by SNCF (⑩www .sncf.com). The only areas not well served are the mountains, where rail routes are replaced by SNCF **buses**. Private bus services tend to be uncoordinated.

SNCF **trains** are clean, fast and frequent. Fares are reasonable. InterRail, Eurail and EuroDomino are valid, though high-speed **TGV**s *(Trains à Grande Vitesse)* require compulsory reservation (€1.5–3), plus a supplement at peak times. The slowest trains are those marked *Autorail* in the timetable, stopping at all stations. All tickets (not passes) must be stamped in the orange machines in the foyer of the train station (**gare SNCF**). Rail journeys may be broken any time, anywhere, for up to 24hr. On night trains, a couchette costs an extra €14. Regional rail maps and timetables are on sale at *tabacs*, and leaflet timetables are available free. All but the smallest stations have an information desk and most have *consignes automatiques* – coin-operated left-luggage lockers.

The designation *Autocar* at the top of a timetable column means it's an **SNCF bus service**, on which rail tickets and passes are valid. Apart from these, the only time you'll need to take a **bus** is in cities. Indeed the most frustrating thing about buses is that they rarely serve regions outside the SNCF network.

Cyclists are much admired. Traffic keeps at a respectful distance (except in the big cities) and restaurants and hotels go out of their way to find a safe place for your bike. Bikes go free on some SNCF trains, though the standard charge is €10. Some SNCF stations

and tourist offices also **rent bikes** for around €10–15 per day (you might be required to leave a deposit or a credit card number).

Accommodation

For most of the year it's possible to turn up in any town and find **accommodation**. However, booking in advance is essential from mid-July to mid-Aug, when the French take their holidays. The first weekend of August is the busiest time of all.

All **hotels** are officially graded, and prices are relatively uniform. Ungraded and single-star hotels cost €15–30 per double room, two-stars €23–45; breakfast is sometimes extra, but you will nearly always do better at a café. It is illegal for hotels to insist on your taking meals, but they sometimes do, and in busy resorts you may not find a room unless you agree. In country areas you'll find **chambres d'hôtes** – B&B in a house or on a farm. These vary in standard and usually cost the equivalent of a two-star hotel. Full lists of accommodation for each province are available from any tourist office. It's worth getting hold of these, together with a handbook for the **Logis de France** – independent hotels, promoted for their consistently good food and reasonably priced rooms, and recognizable by their green and yellow logo.

There's a wide network of official **hostels** *(auberges de jeunesse)*, and most are of a high standard. However, at €7–13 for a dorm bed (more in Paris), they are sometimes no less expensive for a couple than the cheapest hotel room. There are two associations: ⑩www.fuaj.org and ⑩www.auberges-de-jeunesse.com. HI membership covers both, though only those of the former are detailed in the HI handbook. A few large towns provide a more luxurious hostel accommodation in **Foyers des Jeunes Travailleurs/-euses**, residential hostels for young workers and students, charging around €11 for a room. Most also have a good canteen. In rural areas, **gîtes d'étape** – often run by the local village or municipality and less formal than the hostels – provide bunkbeds and simple kitchen facilities. Tourist offices provide listings and sell guides to *gîtes* and *chambres d'hôte*.

Practically every town and village has at least one **campsite**. The cheapest – starting at €4 per person per night – is usually the *Camping Municipal*, normally clean, well-equipped and in a prime location. Never **camp rough** without permission: farmers have been known to shoot first and ask questions later. Lists of sites are available from tourist offices and at ⓦwww.campingfrance.com.

Food and drink

Food in France has art status: the top chefs are stars, and dining out is a national pastime, whether it's at the local brasserie or a famed house of *haute cuisine*. Eating out isn't particularly cheap, but as long as you avoid tourist hotspots, you should be able to get decent *plats du jour* with wine for less than €15.

Generally the best place to eat **breakfast** is in a bar or café. Most serve *baguettes* (French bread) and have a basket of croissants on the counter to which you can help yourself. **Coffee** is invariably espresso and strong. *Un café* or *un express* is black; *un crème* is with milk; *un grand café* is a large cup; *un café au lait* is a large cup with plenty of hot milk. **Tea** *(thé)* is less popular, though most cafés and restaurants serve it. Hot chocolate *(chocolat chaud)* is also widely available. Every establishment displays a full price list for drinks taken at the bar *(au comptoir)*, sitting inside *(la salle)*, or outside *(la terrasse)* – the last can work out surprisingly expensive.

Cafés are often the best option for a light **lunch** as well, serving omelettes, sandwiches (generally half-baguettes filled with cheese or meat), and *croque-monsieur* and *-madame* (variations on the grilled cheese sandwich). On street stalls you'll also find *frites* (chips/french fries), *crêpes*, *galettes* (wholewheat pancakes) and *gaufres* (waffles). For **takeaway**, there's nothing to beat the salads and fully prepared main courses from a *charcuterie* (delicatessen), which are also available at supermarket *charcuterie* counters. Buy by weight, or ask for *une tranche* (a slice), *une barquette* (a carton) or *une part* (a portion).

You can also eat lunch at a **brasserie** – like a restaurant, but open all day and geared to quicker meals. **Restaurants** tend to stick to the traditional meal times of noon–2pm & 7–9/9.30pm. City-centre brasseries often serve until 11pm or midnight. Prices at both are posted outside. Normally there is a choice between one or more *menus fixes* as well as *à la carte*; the latter is more expensive, but often the only option after 9pm. Look out, at lunchtime and in the evening, for the **plat du jour** (daily special), which for as little as €10–15 will often be the most interesting and best-value thing on the menu. *Service compris* means the service is included; if not, you need to add fifteen percent. Wine *(vin)* or a drink *(boisson)* may be included in a *menu fixe*, but when ordering your own wine ask for *un quart*, *un demi-litre* or *une carafe* (a litre) – it'll be house wine unless you specify otherwise.

Drink

Where you can eat you can usually **drink**, and vice versa. Drinking is done most often at a café and at a leisurely pace, whether taken as an *apéritif* before eating, a *digestif* after eating, or as a meal's accompaniment. **Wine** *(vin)* is drunk at just about every meal or social occasion. *Vin de table* or *vin ordinaire* (table wine) is cheap and generally drinkable, and in wine-producing areas can be very good indeed. Wines marked AOC *(Appellation d'Origine Contrôlée)* can be excellent value at the lower end of the scale – just €1.50 or so a bottle – but serious wines command serious prices. In a café, a glass of wine is simply *un rouge* or *un blanc*. If you select an AOC wine you may have the choice of a round glass *(un ballon)* or a smaller glass *(un verre)*.

Most of the **beers** you'll find comprise the familiar Belgian and German names, plus home-grown brands. Beer on tap *(à la pression)* is France's cheapest alcoholic drink, alongside wine – just ask for *une pression*. Stronger alcohol is drunk by some folk from 5am as a pre-work fortifier, right through the day: **cognac** or **armagnac** brandies, dozens of *eaux-de-vie* (spirits distilled from fruit) and **liqueurs**. Measures are generous, but don't come cheap. **Pastis** is a refreshing and inexpensive aniseed-flavoured liquor (popular brands are Pernod and Ricard), drunk diluted with water and ice *(glaçons)*.

Common **soft drinks** include fresh orange/lemon juice *(orange pressée/citron pressé)*, while bottled **spring water** *(eau minérale)* – either sparkling *(gazeuse)* or still *(eau plate)* – is everywhere, but you can ask for tap water *(l'eau du robinet)*, which is free.

Opening hours and holidays

Basic **working hours** are 9am–noon/1pm & 2/3–6.30/7.30pm. Sun and/or Mon are the standard **closing days**, though you'll always find at least one *boulangerie* (bakery) open. **Museums** open at around 9/10am and close 5/6pm, with reduced hours outside the mid-May to mid-Sept season, sometimes even outside July and Aug; they also tend to close on Mon or Tues, usually the latter. All shops, museums and offices are closed on the following **national holidays**: Jan 1; Easter Sun & Mon; Ascension Day; Pentecost; May 1; May 8; July 14; Aug 15; Nov 1; Nov 11; Dec 25.

Emergencies

There are two main types of **police**, the Police Nationale and the Gendarmerie Nationale. You can report a theft, or other incident, to either. You can be stopped at any time and asked to produce ID, so always carry your passport. Every **hospital** visit, doctor's consultation and prescribed medicine is charged, though in an emergency not upfront. In **emergencies** you'll always be admitted to the local hospital *(hôpital)*, whether under your own power or by ambulance. To find a **doctor**, stop at any *pharmacie* and ask for an address. Consultation fees for a visit should be €20–25 and in any case you'll be given a *Feuille de Soins* (Statement of Treatment) for your insurance claims. Prescriptions should be taken to a *pharmacie*, which is also equipped – and obliged – to give first aid (for a fee). For minor illnesses **pharmacists** will dispense free advice and a wide range of medication.

Emergency numbers

Police ☎17; Ambulance ☎15; Fire ☎18.

Paris

PARIS is the paragon of style – perhaps the most captivating city in Europe. It is an artistic and intellectual pacesetter, and yet at the same time a deeply traditional and village-like metropolis. Neighbourhood shops stand alongside famous fashion boutiques, and old-fashioned cafés next to trendy nightspots.

Even the city's history is glamorous, a long tale of extravagant monarchs and world-shaking revolutions. From a shaky start, the kings of France gradually extended their control from Paris over their feudal rivals, centralizing administrative, legal, financial and political power as they did so. The supremely autocratic Louis XIV made the city into a glorious symbol of the pre-eminence of the state, a tradition his successors have been happy to follow. Napoleon I added to the Louvre and built the Arc de Triomphe, the Madeleine and the Arc du Carrousel, while Napoleon III had Baron Haussmann redraw the city centre. The habit of breaking architectural moulds has continued with the Pompidou Centre's luridly coloured tubing, the landmark steel-and-glass Louvre Pyramide and the enormous hollow cube of the Grande Arche de la Défense.

The most tangible pleasures of Paris are to be found in its **street life** and along the lively banks of the River Seine. Few cities can compete with the cafés, bars and restaurants – trendy and traditional, local and cosmopolitan, humble and pretentious – that line every street and boulevard. And the city's compact size makes it possible to experience the individual feel of the different *quartiers*. You can move easily, even on foot, from the calm, almost small-town atmosphere of **Montmartre** and the **Latin Quarter** to the busy commercial centres of the **Bourse** and **Opéra** or the relaxed chic of the **Marais**. An imposing backdrop is provided by the monumental architecture of the **Arc de Triomphe**, the **Louvre** and the **Eiffel Tower**, and by the endless parade of bridges over the river. As for entertainment, Paris is a world **cinema** capital and has a **club** scene renowned across Europe, incorporating the continent's most vibrant African music scene.

Paris is divided into twenty postal districts, known as **arrondissements**, which are used by everyone to locate addresses. The first, or *premier* (abbreviated as 1er), is centred on the Louvre, with the rest (abbreviated as 2e, 3e, 4e) spiralling outwards in a clockwise direction. The inner hub of the city, where most of the major sights and museums are located, is covered by the first six *arrondissements*.

Arrival, information and city transport

Paris has two main **airports**: Roissy-Charles de Gaulle and Orly. **Charles de Gaulle** (CDG), is 23km northeast and connected to the Gare du Nord by Roissyrail, on the RER train line B (every 15min 5am–midnight; 30min; €7.70). You can pick it up direct from terminal 2, but from CDG 1 you have to take the free shuttle bus to the station. There's also the Roissybus, which departs from both terminals and terminates at métro Opéra (every 15min 5.45am–11pm; 45min; €8), or two Air France bus lines, which depart from both terminals to métro Charles-de-Gaulle-Étoile and Porte Maillot (every 15min 5.45am–11pm; €10), or to Gare Montparnasse and Gare de Lyon (every 30min 7am–9.30pm; €11.50). **Orly** (ORY), 14km south of Paris, has two bus–rail links: Orly-Rail, a shuttle bus then RER line C to the Gare d'Austerlitz and other Left Bank stops (every 20min 5.50am–10.50pm; 35min; €5.15); and Orlyval, a fast train shuttle link to RER line B station Antony then connection to the métro stations Denfert-Rochereau, St-Michel and Châtelet (every 4–8min 6.30/7am–10.30/11pm; 35min; €8.65). Air France buses go to the Gare des Invalides via Montparnasse (every 15min 6am–11.30pm; 30min; €7.50), Orlybus goes to métro Denfert-Rochereau (every 15min 6am–11.30pm; 30min; €5.50) and Jetbus (every 15min; 6.15am–10.15pm, 15min; €4.80) goes to the métro station Villejuif-Louis Aragon at the end of line 7. If you call 48 hours in advance, you can book Blue Vans' door-to-door **minibus** service from either airport (☎01.30.11.13.00, ⊛www .airportshuttle.fr; €14.50 per head for two or more people, €22 for a single person).

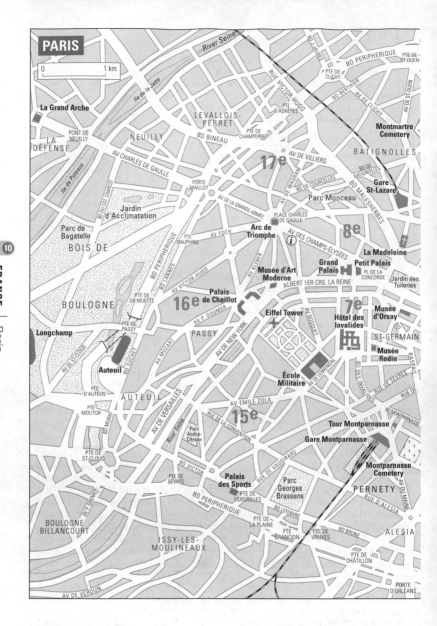

Paris has six mainline **train** stations, all of which are served by the métro. You can buy national and international tickets at any of them. Eurostar trains from London, as well as trains from northern France, Belgium, the Netherlands, northern Germany and Scandinavia, arrive at the **Gare du Nord**; Eurostar have their own booking offices at one side of the station. The **Gare de l'Est** serves eastern France, Luxembourg, southern Germany, northern Switzerland, Austria and eastern

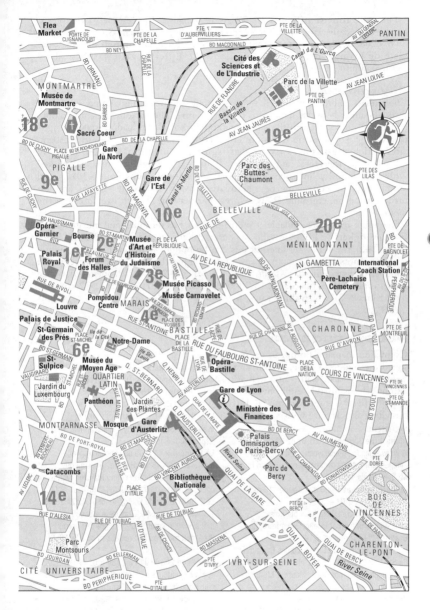

Europe; **Gare St-Lazare** serves the Normandy coast; **Gare de Lyon** serves the
south, the Alps, western Switzerland, Italy, Greece and TGV lines to southeast
France; **Gare Montparnasse** serves Chartres, Brittany, the Atlantic coast and TGV
lines to southwest France; **Gare d'Austerlitz** serves the Loire Valley, the southwest
and Spain. Most long-distance **buses** use the main *gare routière* (International Coach
Station) at Bagnolet in eastern Paris (métro Gallieni, last stop on line #3).

The main **tourist office** is at 127 av des Champs-Élysées, métro Georges V (April–Sept daily 9am–8pm; Oct–March Mon–Sat 9am–8pm, Sun 11am–7pm; ☏08.92.68.31.12, ⊛www.paris-touristoffice.com). There are **branch offices** at the Gare de Lyon (Mon–Sat 8am–8pm) and the Eiffel Tower (May–Sept daily 11am–6.40pm).

City transport

The **métro** (abbreviated as M°) is the simplest way of getting around, with only short distances between stations in the city centre. The various lines are colour-coded and numbered, and the name of the train's final destination is always sign-posted to let you know its direction. The métro operates from 5.30am to 12.30am, after which **night buses** *(Noctambus)* run on eighteen routes from place du Châtelet near the Hôtel de Ville (every 30min–1hr). Nightbus stops are marked with a black and yellow owl. The regular bus network runs from 6.30am until around 8.30pm. Longer journeys across the city, or out to the suburbs, are best made on the underground **RER** express rail network, which overlaps with the métro.

Free route **maps** are available at métro stations, bus terminals and tourist offices. Flat-fare **tickets** (€1.30) are valid on buses, the métro and, within the city limits (zones 1–2), the RER rail lines; tickets can be bought individually or, for slightly less, in **carnets** of ten (€9.60). If you plan on using the network extensively, then consider buying a one-day *Mobilis* pass (€5/zones 1–2, €11.70/zones 1–5), or the *Paris Visites* (€8.35/one day, €13.70/two days, €18.25/three days, €26.65/five days; zones 1–3), which throws in a few minor discounts on admission to monuments.

Accommodation

Compared to many European capitals, Paris is a relatively inexpensive place to spend the night – a double room in a decent and centrally located **hotel** can be found for less than €40 – although you should always book in advance. There are also numerous **hostels**, either independent or belonging to one of three organizations: MIJE (⊛www.mije.com), UCRIF (⊛www.ucrif.asso.fr) and the official FUAJ hostelling association (⊛www.fuaj.fr), which is open to HI members only.

Hostels

Aloha 1 rue Borromé, 15e ☏01.42.73.03.03, ⊛www.aloha.fr. Popular, young and noisy independent with its own bar serving cheap beer. M° Volontaires. €21.

Auberge Internationale des Jeunes 10 rue Trousseau, 11e ☏01.47.00.62.00, ⊛www.aijparis.com. Laid-back but noisy independent in a great location 5min from the Bastille. M° Ledru-Rollin. €14.

BVJ Paris Quartier Latin 44 rue des Bernardins, 5e ☏01.43.29.34.80 Central, efficient and slightly institutional UCRIF hostel. M° Maubert-Mutualité. €25.

D'Artagnan 80 rue Vitruve, 20e ☏01.40.32.34.55. Enormous, colourful FUAJ hostel with good facilities, but it's a fair way out on the eastern fringes of the city. M° Porte de Bagnolet. €21.

Jules Ferry 8 bd Jules-Ferry, 11e ☏01.43.57.55.60, ⊛www.fuaj.org. The smaller and more central of the two FUAJ hostels, in a lively area. Get there early – it fills up fast. M° République. €19.

Le Fauconnier 11 rue du Fauconnier, 4e ☏01.42.74.23.45. MIJE hostel in a superbly renovated seventeenth-century mansion with a courtyard. Breakfast included. M° St-Paul. €24.

Le Fourcy 6 rue de Fourcy, 4e ☏01.42.74.23.45, ⊛www.mije.com. MIJE hostel in a beautiful mansion with small, four- to eight-bed dorms. Breakfast included and restaurant on site. M° St-Paul. €24.

Le Village 20 rue d'Orsel, 18e ☏01.42.64.22.02, ⊛www.villagehostel.fr. Attractive new independent with good facilities and a terrace with a Montmartre view. M° Anvers. €20.

Maubuisson 12 rue des Barres, 4e ☏01.42.74.23.45. MIJE hostel in a magnificent medieval building in a quiet street. Breakfast included. M° Pont-Marie. €24.

Three Ducks 6 place Étienne-Pernet, 15e ☏01.48.42.04.05, ⊛www.3ducks.fr. Lively independent with bar, beer and use of kitchen.

Book ahead May–Oct. M° Félix Faure. €22.
Woodstock 48 rue Rodier, 9e ☏01.48.78.87.76,
🕸www.woodstock.fr. Independent in the heart of
Montmartre. Friendly staff, cheap bar, courtyard
and a lively atmosphere. M° Anvers. €22.

Hotels

Bonséjour 11 rue Burq, 18e ☏01.42.54.22.53.
Friendly place with clean, good-value rooms on a
quiet street in the centre of Montmartre. M°
Abbesses. ❸
Grand Hôtel du Loiret 8 rue des Mauvais-
Garçons, 4e ☏01.48.87.77.00. Simple place but
good value. M° Hotel-de-Ville. ❹
Henri IV 25 place Dauphine, 1er
☏01.43.54.44.53. Well-known cheapie in the
beautiful place Dauphine on the Île de la Cité.

Breakfast included. Booking essential. M° Pont-
Neuf. ❷
Hôtel du Marais 16 rue de Beauce, 3e
☏01.42.72.30.26. Primitive but clean and
characterful. M° Arts-et-Métiers. ❸
Le Central 6 rue Descartes, 5e ☏01.46.33.57.93.
Clean and decent accommodation above a Latin
Quarter café-restaurant. M° Maubert-Mutualité. ❸
Marignan 13 rue du Sommerard, 5e
☏01.43.54.63.81. One of the best backpacker
bargains in town, with free laundry and self-
catering facilities. Book a month ahead in summer.
M° Maubert-Mutualité. ❹
Tiquetonne 6 rue Tiquetonne, 2e
☏01.42.36.94.58. Good-value, old-fashioned
place on a small, attractive street. Closed Aug. M°
Étienne-Marcel. ❸

The City

Paris is split into two halves by the Seine. On the north of the river, the **Right Bank**
(rive droite) is home to the grand boulevards and most monumental buildings, many
dating from Haussmann's nineteenth-century redevelopment, and is where you'll
probably spend most time, during the day at least. The top museums are here – the
Louvre and the Pompidou Centre, to name just two – as well as the city's widest range
of shops around rue de Rivoli and Les Halles; and there are also fashionable quarters
like the Marais for strolling. The **Left Bank** *(rive gauche)* has a noticeably different feel,
its very name conjuring Bohemians and intellectuals, and something of this atmosphere survives in the city's best range of bars and restaurants, and its most wanderable
streets: the areas around St-Germain and St-Michel are full of nooks and crannies to
explore. Parts of Paris, of course, don't sit easily in either category. **Montmartre**, rising
up to the north of the centre, has managed to retain a village-like atmosphere despite
the daily influx of tourists, while the dilapidated quarters of **eastern Paris**, undisturbed by tourism, offer a rich, ethnically diverse slice of Parisian streetlife.

The Arc de Triomphe, Champs-Élysées and around

The **Voie Triomphale** (Triumphal Way) stretches in a straight line from the Louvre
to the corporate skyscrapers at La Défense, 9km northwest, and has some of the city's
most famous landmarks. The best view is from the top of the **Arc de Triomphe**,
Napoleon's homage to the armies of France and himself (daily 10am–10.30/11pm;
€7, €4.50 for under-25s; métro Charles-de-Gaulle-Étoile), at the centre of place
Charles-de-Gaulle – popularly known as place de l'Étoile – where traffic swarms from
the twelve avenues leading into it. From here, Paris's most famous street, the **Champs-
Élysées**, sweeps gracefully southeast to the equally traffic-bound **place de la
Concorde**, whose centrepiece, an obelisk from the temple of Luxor, was given to the
city by the viceroy of Egypt in 1829. The symmetry continues beyond the square in
the formal layout of the **Jardin des Tuileries** (daily 8/9am–7/8pm; métro Concorde),
which stretches down to the Louvre. Towards the river, the **Orangerie** (currently
undergoing renovation; due for completion summer 2004) displays Monet's largest
water-lily paintings, as well as works by Cézanne, Matisse, Utrillo and Modigliani.

If you plan to see more than a few museums, it's a good idea to invest in a **museum
pass** (€15/30/45 for one/three/five days), available at participating museums, tourist
offices and larger métro stations. Note that many museums offer discounted entry to
the under-25s and have reduced fees for all on Sundays – and are often free on the
first Sunday of every month. Most are closed on Mondays or Tuesdays.

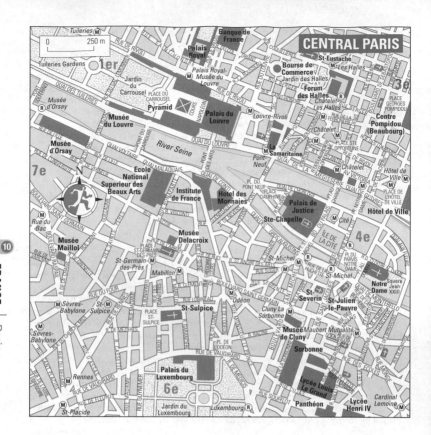

A short walk south of the Arc de Triomphe is the **Musée d'Art Moderne de la Ville de Paris** in the Palais de Tokyo, 11 av du Président-Wilson (Tues–Sun 10am–5.45/6.45pm; €7; métro Iéna). Major early twentieth-century artists, particularly those working in France – Braque, Chagall, Delaunay, Derain, Léger, Picasso and many others – are well represented, but the centrepieces are the leaping figures of Matisse's *La Danse* and Dufy's enormous mural, *La Fée Électricité*, illustrating the story of electricity from Aristotle to the modern power station in 250 colourful panels. Located in the semi-derelict western wing of the palace is the **Site de Création Contemporaine** (Tues–Sun noon–midnight; cost varies according to exhibitions; métro Iéna), given over to cutting-edge contemporary art exhibitions. A short walk down the river, at **Trocadéro**, the terrace of the Palais de Chaillot gives splendid vistas across the river to the Eiffel Tower.

The Louvre

On the east side of the Jardin des Tuileries is the home of the *Mona Lisa*, the mighty **Louvre** (Mon & Wed 9am–9.45pm, Thurs–Sun 9am–6pm; €7.50; after 3pm and all day Sun €5; métro Palais Royal-Musée du Louvre/Louvre-Rivoli; ⓦwww.louvre.com). The building was first opened to the public in 1793, during the Revolution, and within a decade Napoleon had made it the largest art collection on earth with the takings from his empire. It's a vast collection that would take months to see in detail.

I.M. Pei's stunning glass pyramid is the main entrance, with an alternative entrance at the Portes des Lions. **Oriental Antiquities** covers the Sumerian, Babylonian, Assyrian and Phoenician civilizations, plus the art of ancient Persia and the Islamic collection. **Egyptian Antiquities** comprises a wealth of jewellery, domestic objects, sarcophagi and statues like the pink granite *Mastaba Sphinx*. **Greek and Roman Antiquities**, divided between the Denon and Sully wings, is mostly nude statuary, notably the famous *Venus de Milo*. The **Objets d'Art** collection is a chronology of the finest tapestries, ceramics, jewellery and furniture commissioned by France's wealthiest patrons, from medieval times to the nineteenth century. **Sculpture** covers the entire development of the art in France from Romanesque to Rodin, all in the Richelieu wing, plus Italian and northern European sculpture in Denon, including Michelangelo's *Slaves*, designed for the tomb of Pope Julius II.

The largest and busiest section is **Painting**. French from the year dot to mid-nineteenth century – notably works by Poussin – is covered in the Richelieu wing, which also houses the Dutch, German and Flemish collections – look out for Rembrandt's masterful *Supper at Emmaus* and two exquisite Vermeers. Over in the Denon wing, the Italians attract the biggest crowds, Leonardo's *Mona Lisa* most of all. Other Leonardos hang more peacefully in the nearby Grande Galerie, along with an amazing parade of works by Giotto, Botticelli, Titian, Tintoretto and Mantegna, including, most strikingly, Paolo Veronese's huge *Marriage at Cana*. Two rooms behind house giant canvases by the great nineteenth-century artists David, Ingres and Delacroix, as well as Géricault's harrowing *Raft of the Medusa*.

The Opéra, Les Halles and the Pompidou Centre

A short walk north of the Louvre is the preposterously ornate **Opéra-Garnier**, on place de l'Opéra. Built in 1875 as the venue for opera, since the completion of the Opéra-Bastille in 1989 it has been used chiefly for ballet. You can see the splendid interior (daily 10am–5pm; €6; métro Opéra), including the auditorium, where the domed ceiling is the work of Chagall. South of here is the area around the former **Les Halles** (a covered market), which was redeveloped in the 1970s amid widespread opposition. A young, international crowd shops and hangs out in the pedestrianized streets, but the shopping precinct at the area's core, the **Forum des Halles**, is a tacky affair, and it can be unsafe, too, especially at night. During the day the main flow of feet is from here a little way east to the **Pompidou Centre** (métro Rambuteau; ⓦ www.centrepompidou.fr). This seminal design by Renzo Piano and Richard Rogers was the first public structure to manifest the hi-tech notion of displaying its services on the outside, the tubing colour-coded according to function, leaving maximum space for the interior. Inside, the **Multimedia Library** (daily 11am/noon–10pm) remains hugely popular, as does the **Musée National d'Art Moderne** (11am–9pm, closed Tues; €5.50, €3.50 for under-25s), with a superb collection that ranges from Fauvism and Cubism through Pop Art to the present day.

The Marais, the Bastille and Île St-Louis

Just east of Beaubourg, the **Marais** was a fashionable aristocratic district that became one of the city's poorer quarters. Regentrification has since turned the renovated mansions into museums, offices and chic apartments flanked by designer clothes shops and cafés for brunching media types. A little way down the main drag, rue des Francs-Bourgeois, one of the grandest Marais mansions houses the **Musée Carnavalet** (entrance around the corner at 23 rue de Sévigné; Tues–Sun 10am–6pm; free; métro St-Paul), which presents the history of Paris from the reign of François I to the early twentieth century, with models, maps and plans, reconstructions of interiors and mementoes of the 1789 Revolution. Slightly further north, at 71 rue du Temple, the **Musée d'Art et d'Histoire du Judaïsme** (Mon–Fri 11am–6pm, Sun 10am–6pm; €6.10, €3.81 for under 26s; métro Rambuteau) has a fascinating display of Jewish artefacts and historical documents as well as paintings by Chagall and Soutine. A short walk east, another mansion, the proud seventeenth-century Hôtel Juigné Salé at 5 rue de Thorigny, is home to the **Musée Picasso** (9.30am–5.30/6pm, closed Tues; €5.50, €4 on Sun and for under-25s; métro St-Paul). It is an overwhelming collection, much of which was the artist's personal property, and comprises the largest number of his works anywhere.

At the far end of rue des Francs-Bourgeois, off to the right, **place des Vosges** is a masterpiece of aristocratic urban planning, a vast square of stone and brick symmetry built for Henri IV and Louis XIII. At no. 6, the **Maison Victor Hugo** (Tues–Sun 10am–6pm; free; métro Bastille) is the former home of the writer of *Les Misérables*; not surprisingly, a whole room is devoted to posters of the various musical productions.

A short walk southeast, heading for the landmark column with the gilded "Spirit of Liberty", is **place de la Bastille**, the site of the Bastille that was famously stormed in 1789. The column was erected not to commemorate the surrender of the prison, which was subsequently demolished, but the July Revolution of 1830 – although it is the 1789 Bastille Day that France celebrates every July 14. The Bicentennial in 1989 was marked by the inauguration of the **Opéra-Bastille**, on the far side of the square, a bloated building that caused great controversy when it went up – a "hippopotamus in a bathtub", one critic called it.

Just south of here, across Henri IV bridge, the **Île St-Louis** is one of the centre's swankier quarters, with no monuments or museums, just high houses on single-lane streets. It's a peaceful and atmospheric route through to the Île de la Cité, either strolling down the centre along the shop-filled rue Île-St-Louis – a real weekend promenade with pedestrians taking over the street, many queuing for an ice-cream at the famous *Berthillon* – or along the tree-lined *quais* down by the Seine.

Île de la Cité

Île de la Cité is where Paris began. It is the original site of the Roman garrison and later the palace of the Merovingian kings and the counts of Paris, who in 987 became kings of France. Nowadays the main lure is the astounding **Cathédrale de Notre-Dame** (daily 8am–6.45/7.45pm, closed Sat 12.30–2pm; métro Cité), begun in 1163 under the auspices of Bishop de Sully and completed around 1345. In the nineteenth century, Viollet-le-Duc carried out extensive renovation work, remaking most of the statuary and adding the steeple and baleful-looking gargoyles, which you can see close up if you brave the 387-step ascent of the **towers** (daily 9/10am–5/9pm; €5.50). The sculpture of the west front portals is amazingly detailed, dating mainly from the twelfth and thirteenth centuries, while inside, the immediately striking feature is the dramatic contrast between the darkness of the nave and the light falling on the first great clustered pillars of the choir. In front of the cathedral, the **crypte archéologique** (Tues–Sun 10am–6pm; €3.30) holds the remains of the original cathedral, as well as of streets and houses of the Cité back as far as the Roman era.

At the western end of the island, the dull mass of the **Palais de Justice** swallowed up the palace that was home to the French kings until the bloody revolt of 1358 frightened them into the greater security of the Louvre. The only part of the older complex that remains in its entirety is Louis IX's **Ste-Chapelle** at 4 blvd du Palais (daily 9.30/10am–5/6.30pm; €5.50, €8 joint ticket with the Conciergerie; métro Cité). This was built to house a collection of holy relics and is one of the finest achievements of French Gothic style, lent a fragility by its height and huge expanses of glorious stained glass, most of which is original. You should also visit the **Conciergerie**, Paris's oldest prison, whose entrance is around the corner facing the river on quai de l'Horloge (same times and prices). This was where Marie-Antoinette and, in their turn, the leading figures of the Revolution were incarcerated before execution. Its chief interest is the enormous late-Gothic Salle des Gens d'Armes (canteen and recreation room of the royal household staff), as well as Marie-Antoinette's cell and various macabre mementoes of the guillotine's victims. Outside the Conciergerie is Paris's first public clock, the **Tour de l'Horloge**, built in 1370.

The Eiffel Tower, Les Invalides and the Musée d'Orsay

Though no conventional beauty, the **Eiffel Tower** is nonetheless an amazing structure, at 300m the tallest building in the world when it was completed by Gustave Eiffel in 1889. Reactions to it were violent, but it stole the show at the 1889 Exposition, for which it had been constructed. Lifts take you straight to the top (daily 9/9.30am–11pm/midnight; €9.90; métro Bir Hakeim/RER Champ de Mars; ⊛www.tour-eiffel.fr); if you're fit enough, you can save money by walking up as far as the second level (704 stairs; €3), from where you can join the lift for the final leg (€3). The queues can be dispiriting on clear summer days, so think about going at night, when the views can be even more impressive.

To the east, the **Esplanade des Invalides** strikes south from the river to the wide facade of the **Hôtel des Invalides**, built as a home for invalided soldiers on the orders of Louis XIV and topped by a distinctive gilded dome which is a real Paris landmark. It now houses the giant **Musée de l'Armée** (daily 10am–5/6pm; €6), with a vast collection of armour, uniforms, weapons and Napoleonic relics, and a more rewarding wing devoted to World War II. One of the building's two pompous churches now contains the mortal remains of Napoleon. Immediately east, the **Musée Rodin** at no. 77 (Tues–Sun 9.30am–4.45/5.45pm; €5, €3 for under-25s; métro Varenne; ⊛www.musee-rodin.fr), on the corner of rue de Varenne, houses many of the sculptor's best-known works, including *The Kiss*, in a beautiful eighteenth-century mansion.

A little way northeast along the river, on the quai d'Orsay, the **Musée d'Orsay** (Tues–Sun 9/10am–6pm, Thurs till 9.45pm; €8.50, €6.50 after 4.15pm & Thurs after 8pm, €5 on Sun and for under-25s; free on 1st Sun of month; RER Musée d'Orsay/métro Solférino; ⊛www.musee-orsay.fr), converted from a disused train station in the 1980s, houses an outstanding collection of painting and sculpture from the pre-modern period (1848–1914). On the ground floor are works by the likes of Ingres, Delacroix, Degas, Daumier, Corot and Millet; in the top floor attics are the Impressionists and post-Impressionists, ranging from Manet, Renoir, Pissarro and Monet through to Cézanne, Van Gogh, Gauguin and Toulouse-Lautrec. The middle floor is dominated by sculpture, with some amazing works by Rodin.

The Latin Quarter, St-Germain and Montparnasse

The quarter around the broad boulevards St-Michel and St-Germain has been known as the **Quartier Latin** since medieval times, because it was the home of the Latin-speaking universities. It is still a student-dominated area, its pivotal point being **place St-Michel**, whose cafés and shops are jammed with people – mainly young and, in summer, largely foreign. The warren of streets around Rue de la Huchette, gathering-place of beatniks and bums in the 1950s, is now a tacky tourist trap. Close to the St-Michel/St-Germain junction, the walls of the third-century Roman baths are visible in the garden of the Hôtel de Cluny on place Paul-Poinlevé. This sixteenth-century mansion, built by the abbots of the powerful Cluny monastery as their Paris pied-à-terre, now houses the **Musée National du Moyen Age – Thermes de Cluny** (Mon & Wed–Sun 9.15am–5.45pm; €5.50, €4 on Sun and for under-25s; métro Cluny-La Sorbonne), a treasure-house of medieval art that includes some wonderful tapestries. The real masterpieces are the six fifteenth-century panels depicting *The Lady with the Unicorn*, which symbolize the five senses and the Christian virtue in resisting them.

Immediately south of here, the Montagne Ste-Geneviève slopes up to the domed **Panthéon**, Louis XIV's thankyou to Geneviève, patron saint of Paris, for curing him of illness, which was transformed during the Revolution into a mausoleum for the great: its incumbents include Voltaire, Rousseau, Zola and Hugo (daily 10am–6/6.30pm; €7, €4.50 for under-25s; métro Cardinal Lemoine/RER Luxembourg). Down rue Soufflot, across blvd St-Michel, you might prefer to while away a few hours in the elegant surrounds of the **Jardin du Luxembourg** (daily dawn to dusk; métro Luxembourg), laid out by Marie de Médici, Henri IV's widow, to remind her of the Palazzo Pitti and Giardino di Bóboli of her native Florence. They are the chief recreation grounds of the Left Bank, with tennis courts, a *boules* pitch, toy yachts to rent on the pond and wooded and grassy areas much used by students for sun-bathing and socializing.

Beyond the Luxembourg gardens, the northern half of the 6e *arrondissement* is one of the most attractive parts of the city, full of bookshops, art galleries, antique shops, cafés and restaurants. It is also, perhaps, its most culturally historic: Picasso painted *Guernica* in rue des Grands-Augustins; in rue Visconti, Delacroix painted and Balzac's printing business went bust; and in parallel rue des Beaux-Arts, Oscar Wilde died and the crazy poet Gérard de Nerval went walking with a lobster on a blue ribbon. **Place St-Germain-des-Prés**, the hub of the *quartier*, is the site of the *Deux Magots* café, renowned for the number of politico-literary backsides that have shined its seats.

On the southern side of the Luxembourg gardens, **Montparnasse** also trades on its association with the colourful characters of the interwar years, many of whom were habitués of the cafés *Select, Coupole, Dôme* and *Rotonde* on blvd du Montparnasse. Close by, the colossal 59-storey skyscraper **Tour Montparnasse**, av du Maine, has become one of the city's principal landmarks since its construction in 1973; it can be climbed for less than the Eiffel Tower, but it is more than 100m shorter (daily 9.30am–10.30/11.30pm; €7.60; métro Montparnasse-Bienvenue). A short walk down blvd Edgar-Quinet, the **Montparnasse cemetery** (daily 8/9am–5.30/6pm; free; métro Raspail) has plenty of illustrious names, from Baudelaire to Sartre and André Citroën to Serge Gainsbourg.

Montmartre and eastern Paris

Montmartre lies in the middle of the largely working-class 18e *arrondissement*, a mixture of depressing slums towards the Gare du Nord and Gare de l'Est, and respectable, almost countrified pockets around its main focus on the hill, the **Butte Montmartre**. You can get up here by funicular from place Suzanne-Valadon (ordinary métro tickets and passes are valid) or, for a quieter and prettier approach climb the steep stairs via place des Abbesses. The **place du Tertre** is the heart of touristic Montmartre, photogenic but totally bogus, jammed with day-trippers, overpriced restaurants and "artists" painting garish Eiffel Towers from memory. Crowning the hill is the nineteenth-century **Sacré-Cœur** (daily 6am–10.30pm; free; métro Anvers/Abbesses), a classic of the Paris skyline; you can climb to the top of the pimply dome (daily 8.40am–6pm; €5) for a wonderful view.

Off the curving rue Lepic, the **Moulin de la Galette** is the only survivor of Montmartre's forty-odd windmills, which were immortalized by Renoir. Down the hill on blvd de Clichy, the notorious Moulin Rouge was never a windmill; these days it's a mere shadow of its former self. The stretch of road around it, known as **Pigalle**, has always been a sleazy neighbourhood of peepshows and transvestite prostitution. At the western end of Pigalle, a little way up rue Caulaincourt, the **Montmartre cemetery** (daily 8/9am–5.30/6pm; métro Place de Clichy) holds the graves of Zola, Stendhal, Berlioz, Degas, Offenbach and François Truffaut among others.

East of Montmartre, the **Bassin de la Villette** and the **canals** at the northeastern gate of the city were for generations the centre of a densely populated working-class district but have recently become the subject of yet another big Paris redevelopment. The area's major extravagance is the **Cité des Sciences et de l'Industrie** (Tues–Sun 10am–6/7pm; €7.50; métro Porte de la Villette; ⊛ www.cite-sciences.fr) in the **Parc de la Villette**, built into the concrete hulk of the abandoned abattoirs on the north side of the canal de l'Ourcq. Three times the size of the Pompidou Centre, this is the most astounding monument to be added to the capital in the last two decades, and is worth visiting for the interior alone – all glass and stainless steel, cantilevered platforms and suspended walkways. Its permanent exhibition, Explora, on the top two floors, is the science museum to end all science museums, covering everything from microbes to outer space.

South of La Villette, Paris' **eastern** districts – Belleville and Ménilmontant – are among the poorest of the city and not on most visitors' itineraries. However, the **Père-Lachaise cemetery**, on blvd de Ménilmontant, draws a fair number of tourists (daily 8/9am–5.30/6pm; métro Père-Lachaise), most of them heading for Jim Morrison's small, guarded grave in the east of the cemetery and Oscar Wilde's more extravagant tomb. There are countless famous others buried here – Edith Piaf, Modigliani, Abélard and Héloïse, Sarah Bernhardt, Ingres and Corot, Delacroix and Balzac, to name only a few.

The Beaux Quartiers, Bois de Boulogne and La Défense

South and west of the Arc de Triomphe lie the so-called **Beaux Quartiers**, the 16e and 17e *arrondissements*, in turns aristocratic and rich, bourgeois and staid, which hold little of interest save the wonderful **Musée Marmottan**, 2 rue Louis-Boilly (Tues–Sun 10am–6pm; €6.50; métro La Muette), whose Monet paintings were bequeathed by the artist's son. Among them is the canvas entitled *Impression, Soleil Levant*, an 1872 rendering of a misty sunrise over Le Havre, whose title unwittingly gave the Impressionist movement its name. Beyond the museum, the **Bois de Boulogne**, running down the west side of the 16e, is the city's largest open space, supposedly modelled on London's Hyde Park.

La Défense has been elevated to one of the top places of pilgrimage for visitors to Paris by the breathtaking **Grande Arche** (métro Grande-Arche-de-la-Défense), a 112m high hollow cube clad in white marble. Suspended within its hollow are open lift shafts and a "cloud canopy". You can ride up to the roof (daily 10am–7pm; €7), but the views – right down the Voie Triomphale 6km to the Arc de Triomphe – are no more impressive than those gained from the series of steps which lead up to the Arch. Between here and the river is the business complex of La Défense, a perfect monument to capitalism that lacks any formal pattern to its dizzying arrangement of towers.

Eating

Eating out in Paris need not be an enormous extravagance. There are numerous fixed-price menus from €12, providing simple but well-cooked French fare, and a wide range of ethnic restaurants – North and West African, Chinese, Japanese, Vietnamese, Greek and lots more, though they are not necessarily any cheaper. Being vegetarian in Paris is not always easy, but there are a handful of vegetarian restaurants; Indian, Jewish and Italian restaurants are also a good bet for non-meat dishes. Anyone in possession of an ISIC card is eligible to apply for tickets for the **university restaurants** run by CROUS, 39 av Georges-Bernanos, 5e (☏01.40.55.55.55); CROUS can provide a list of addresses, but you must buy your tickets from the restaurants themselves.

Snacks, sandwiches, cakes and ice cream

Berthillon 31 rue St-Louis-en-l'Île, 4e. Long queues for superb ice creams and sorbets. Closed Mon & Tues. M° Pont Marie.

Café de la Mosquée 39 rue Geoffroy St Hilaire, 5e. Mint tea and Middle Eastern cakes in this oasis of calm, popular with women. M° Jussieu.

La Samaritaine 19 rue de la Monnaie, 1er. Wonderful views over the Pont Neuf, la Monnaie and the Conciergerie from the inexpensive self-service rooftop café of this Art Deco department store. M° Pont Neuf.

La Sancerre 35 rue des Abbesses, 18e. Daily 7am–2am. Hangout for the young and trendy

under the southern slope of Montmartre. M° Abbesses.

Le Loir dans la Théière 3 rue des Rosiers, 4e. Peaceful, sometimes quirky retreat with leather armchairs and a laid-back atmosphere. Sun brunch, midday *tartes* and omelettes, fruit teas and cakes served all day. M° St-Paul.

Taverne Henri IV 13 pl du Pont-Neuf, Île de la Cité, 1er. Old-style wine bar serving generous plates of meats and cheeses. M° Pont-Neuf.

Restaurants and brasseries

Au Virage Lepic 61 rue Lepic, 18e. Simple, good-quality meaty fare served in a noisy, friendly, old-fashioned bistro. M° Abbesses.

Bistro de la Sorbonne 4 rue Toullier, 5e. Large portions of traditional French and North African dishes in a noisy, friendly ambience. M° Place Monge.

Café du Commerce 51 rue du Commerce, 15e. Long-established place serving nourishing, inexpensive food. M° Commerce.

Chardenoux 1 rue Jules-Vallès, 11e. An authentic oldie that still serves solid meaty fare at moderate prices. Closed Sun & Aug. M° Charonne.

Chartier 7 rue du Faubourg-Montmartre, 9e. Good inexpensive food in an original and splendid turn-of-the-century soup kitchen. Expect to queue. M° Le Peletier.

Chez Gladines 30 rue des Cinq-Diamants, 13e. Tiny, welcoming corner bistro serving hearty Basque dishes. Close to the cool bars of the Butte-aux-Cailles. M° Corvisart.

Flo 7 cours des Petites-Écuries, 10e. Handsome old-school brasserie, where you eat elbow-to-elbow at long tables. Excellent food and thoroughly enjoyable atmosphere. M° Château d'Eau.

Goldenberg 7 rue des Rosiers, 4e. Paris's best-known Jewish restaurant. Its borscht, blinis, strudels and other central European dishes are a real treat. M° St-Paul.

La Fresque 100 rue Rambuteau, 1er. Good-value traditional French food served in an ex snail-merchant's hall. M° Les Halles.

La Petite Légume 36 rue des Boulangers, 5e. Tiny, homely vegetarian café with an organic approach. Closed Sun. M° Jussieu.

Le Petit St-Benoît 4 rue St-Benoît, 6e. A simple, genuine and very appealing local serving solid traditional fare. M° Mabillon.

Les Philosophes 28 rue Vieille-du-Temple, 4e. Stylish Marais bistro serving trendy but not overpriced cuisine. M° Hôtel-de-Ville.

Le Potager du Marais 22 rue Rambuteau, 3e. Light, modern and all-organic vegetarian and fish dishes, served at a long communal table. Closed Sun. M° Rambuteau.

Le Temps des Cerises 18–20 rue de la Butte-aux-Cailles, 13e. A well-established and excellent-value workers' co-op restaurant with convivial packed-in seating. M° Corvisart.

Perraudin 157 rue St-Jacques, 5e. Well-known traditional bistro with good-value lunchtime menus. M° Cluny La Sorbonne.

Polidor 41 rue Monsieur-le-Prince, 6e. Traditional bistro packed with noisy regulars tucking into well-made French standards till late. M° Odéon.

Thoumieux 79 rue St-Dominique, 7e. Cavernous and deeply old-fashioned brasserie in a rather smart district. M° Invalides.

Drinking

Most squares and boulevards have **cafés** spreading out onto the pavements and, although these are usually the priciest places to drink, it can be worth shelling out for a coffee if only for the streetlife. The Left Bank has some of the city's best-known and longest-established cafés and **bars**, especially around the university quarter and near St-Germain-des-Près. The Bastille is trendier and livelier than ever, while the Marais offers small crowded café-bars and some upbeat gay establishments. For old-fashioned **wine bars**, often serving food, Montmartre is a good bet, while bars and **pubs** inspired by Belgian or British watering holes can be found throughout the city. Places listed below are open all day until 2am unless otherwise stated.

Café Charbon 109 rue Oberkampf, 11e. Hugely successful revival of a *fin-de-siècle* café, packed in the evenings with a young pre-club clientele, relaxed during the day. Daily 9am–2am. M° St-Maur/Parmentier.

Café de l'Industrie corner of rue Sedaine and rue St-Sabin, 11e. One of the best and most packed-out Bastille cafés, with rugs on the floor around solid old wooden tables, and a young, unpretentious crowd. Open till 2am. M° Bastille.

Café de la Mairie 8 place St-Sulpice, 6e. Famous yet unpretentious café in an enviably sunny spot overlooking St Sulpice church. M° St-Sulpice.

Chez Georges 11 rue des Canettes. Old-fashioned, tobacco-stained wine bar upstairs, lively cellar-bar below. Tues–Sat noon–2am; closed Aug.

M° Mabillon.

La Folie en Tête 33 rue Butte-aux-Cailles, 13e. Alternative-spirited, laid-back bar on a lively street, serving cheap drinks and daytime snacks. Mon–Sat 5pm–2am. M° Place-d'Italie.

La Fourmi Café 74 rue des Martyrs, 18e. High-ceilinged café-bar full of trendy young Parisians. Mon–Thurs 8am–2am, Fri & Sat 8am–4am, Sun 10am–2am. M° Pigalle/Abbesses.

Le Rubis 10 rue du Marché-St-Honoré, 1er. One of the oldest wine bars in Paris, with excellent snacks and *plats du jour*. Mon–Fri 7.30am–10pm, Sat 9am–3pm; closed mid-Aug. M° Tuileries.

Le Sélect 99 blvd du Montparnasse, 6e. The least spoilt of the swanky Montparnasse cafés, still thriving since its 1920s heyday. Open till 3/4am. M° Vavin.

Le Violon Dingue 46 rue de la Montagne-Ste-Geneviève, 5e. A noisy, friendly student pub that's also popular with travellers, partly for its inexpensive drinks. Daily 6pm–2.30/4.30am; happy hour 8–10pm. M° Maubert-Mutualité.

Web Bar 32 rue de Picardie, 3e. This Internet café is very Marais-chic, a multimedia centre with comfy couches and films and arty events on its menu. Mon–Fri 8.30am–2am, Sat & Sun 11am–2am. M° Temple.

Nightlife

Paris's reputation for **live music** is impeccable: its world music is second to none, live jazz continues to be excellent, and there's an almost limitless choice of classical music and opera. **Clubs** come and go as rapidly as in any other large city, but there are one or two long-established places that won't let you down; most clubs open around 11pm and get going from around 1am; some stay open until dawn and beyond. For **what's on** listings, the best weekly guide is *Pariscope* (🌐www.pariscope.fr; €0.40), which comes out on Wednesdays and has a small *Time Out* section in English. The best places to buy **tickets** are FNAC, Forum des Halles, 1–5 rue Pierre-Lescot, level 3 (métro Les Halles), and the Virgin Megastore, 56–60 av des Champs-Élysées (métro Franklin Roosevelt).

There are over 350 **films** showing in Paris in any one week. Tickets cost around €8, €5 for students. Almost all of the huge selection of foreign films will be shown at some cinemas in their original language – *v.o.* in the listings (as opposed to *v.f.*, which means it's dubbed into French). Committed film freaks should head to the small *cinémathèques*, which show a choice of over fifty movies a week; tickets are only €4.75. The Forum des Images in the Forum des Halles, 2 Grande Galerie, Porte Eustache (métro Les Halles), is an excellent-value venue for the bizarre or obscure on celluloid, with themed repertoires and a *vidéothèque* where you can call up a huge range of films for private viewing on video.

Live music venues

Le Bataclan 50 bd Voltaire, 11e. Classic ex-theatre venue with one of the best and most eclectic line-ups of any venue, covering anything from international and local dance and rock musicians to opera, comedy and techno nights. M° Oberkampf.

La Cigale 120 bd de Rochechouart, 18e. An eclectic programming policy in an old-fashioned converted theatre. M° Pigalle.

Le Divan du Monde 75 rue des Martyrs, 18e. Café with one of the city's most eclectic, exciting programmes, ranging from techno to Congolese rumba, with dancing till dawn on weekend nights. M° Pigalle.

La Guinguette Pirate Quai François Mauriac, 13e. Beautiful Chinese barge, moored alongside the quay in front of the Bibliothèque Nationale, hosting relaxed but up-beat world music nights from Tuesday to Sunday. M° Quai-de-la-Gare.

Le Petit Journal 71 bd St-Michel, 5e. Small, smoky bar-restaurant with good, mainly French, traditional and mainstream sounds. RER Luxembourg.

Péniche Makara Quai François Mauriac, 13e. Barge moored to the banks of the Seine, this time with a chilled-out reggae and world flavour. M° Quai-de-la-Gare.

Clubs

Batofar Quai de la Gare, 13e. A good bet for a not-too-expensive club night out, with a cool setting in an old lighthouse boat outside the Bibliothèque Nationale. M° Quai-de-la-Gare.

Les Bains 7 rue du Bourg-l'Abbé, 3e. As posey as they come, set in an old Turkish bathhouse with a plunge pool. Mostly house, hip hop and garage. Daily midnight–dawn. M° Étienne-Marcel.

La Fabrique 53 rue du Faubourg-St-Antoine, 11e. Hyper-trendy club-bar heaving with Bastille trendies partying well into the morning. M° Bastille.

La Locomotive 90 bd de Clichy, 18e. High-tech monster club with three dance floors. M° Blanche.

Nouveau Casino 109 rue Oberkampf, 11e. Eclectic, innovative mix of musical styles played at this large, trendy club. M° Parmentier.

Rex Club 5 bd Poissonnière, 2e. The clubbers' club: spacious and serious about its music, which is strictly electronic. Big-name DJs. M° Grands-Boulevards.

Classical music, opera and ballet

Opéra-Bastille 120 rue de Lyon, 12e ☎08.36.69.78.68. Paris's ultra-modern opera house. Tickets cost €10 to €105, with the cheapest seats only available to personal callers; unfilled seats are sold at a discount to students five minutes before the curtain goes up. M° Bastille.

Opéra-Garnier place de l'Opéra, 9e ☏08.92.89.90.90. The original opera house now stages smaller operas and ballet productions. M° Opéra.
Salle des Concerts 221 av Jean-Jaurès, 19e ☏01.44.84.44.84. Adjustable concert hall with seating for 800–1200 listeners. The programme covers ancient music, contemporary works, jazz, chansons and world music. M° Porte-de-Pantin.
Salle Pleyel 252 rue du Faubourg-St-Honoré, 8e ☏08.25.00.02.52. The Orchestre de Paris performs here most frequently along with visiting international orchestras. M° Ternes.
Théâtre des Champs-Élysées 15 av Montaigne, 8e ☏01.49.52.50.50. Home to the Orchestre National de France, but also hosts international superstar conductors, ballet troups and operas. M° Alma-Marceau.
Théâtre Musical de Paris (Châtelet) 1 place du Châtelet, 1er ☏01.40.28.28.40. As well as operas, the programme includes visiting ballets, concerts and solo recitals. M° Châtelet.

Gay and lesbian Paris

Paris has a well-established **gay scene** concentrated mainly in the Halles, Marais and Bastille areas, and there are numerous gay organizations. For information, check out *Têtu*, France's main gay monthly magazine, which is full of contact details, addresses and reviews, or visit the main gay and lesbian bookshop, Les Mots à la Bouche, 6 rue Ste-Croix-de-la-Bretonnerie, 4e (☏01.42.78.88.30, ⓦwww .motsbouche.com; métro Hôtel de Ville).

Amnesia Café 42 rue Vieille-du-Temple. 4e. Fashionably dressed young things pack in to this classic, relaxed gay bar, with its sofas and basement club. M° St-Paul.
Banana Café 13 rue de la Ferronnerie, 1e. Seriously hedonistic club-bar, packing in the punters with up-tempo clubby tunes. M° Châtelet.
Boobsburg 26 rue de Montmorency, 3e. Fashionable, mainly lesbian bar, with good food, classy decor and a chic young clientele. M° Rambuteau.
Le Piano Zinc 49 rue des Blancs-Manteaux, 4e.

On Thurs, Fri and Sat nights, this bar becomes a happy riot of *chanson* music, music-hall acts and dance. M° Rambuteau/Hôtel-de-Ville.
Les Scandaleuses 8 rue des Ecouffes, 4e ☏01.48.87.39.26; M° Hôtel-de-Ville. Trendy and high-profile lesbian bar in the Marais – men are welcome if accompanied. Lively atmosphere guaranteed, with DJs at weekends. Daily 5pm–5am.
Le Tango 13 rue au-Maire, 3e. Gay and lesbian dance-hall with a traditional *bal* until midnight, then house and mainstream dance later on. M° Arts-et-Métiers.

Listings

Bike rental From about €13 a day. Paris Vélo, 4 rue du Fer-à-Moulin, 5e ☏01.43.37.59.22 (M° Censier Daubenton); Paris à Vélo C'est Sympa, 37 blvd Bourdon, 4e ☏01.48.87.60.01 (M° Bastille).
Embassies Australia, 4 rue Jean-Rey, 15e ☏01.40.59.33.00 (M° Bir Hakeim); Canada, 35 av Montaigne, 8e ☏01.44.43.29.00 (M° Franklin Roosevelt); Ireland, 4 rue Rude, 16e ☏01.44.17.67.00 (M° Charles-de-Gaulle-Étoile); New Zealand, 7 rue Léonard-de-Vinci, 16e ☏01.45.01.43.43 (M° Victor Hugo); UK, 35 rue Faubourg-St-Honoré, 8e ☏01.44.51.31.00 (M°
Concorde); US, 2 rue St Florentin, 1er ☏01.43.12.22.22 (M° Concorde).
Hospital 24hr medical help from SOS-Médecins ☏01.43.37.77.77; ☏18 for emergencies.
Left luggage Lockers at all train stations and *consignes* for bigger items.
Pharmacies Dérhy, 84 av des Champs-Élysées, 8e (M° Georges V).
Police ☏17 in emergencies; for thefts, report to the *commissariat de police* of the *arrondissement* in which the theft took place.
Post office 52 rue du Louvre, 1er (M° Les Halles).

Day-trips near Paris

Around 32km east of the city is **Disneyland Paris** (daily 9/10am–8/11pm; €39; RER line A to Marne-la-Vallée; ⓦwww.disneylandparis.com), a 5000-acre slice of the US beamed down to the Paris region. It's predictably commercial, but with enough thrill and technology-based rides to make it Europe's leading theme park. Aside from this, the most popular day-trip is to **Versailles**, but the most rewarding is the cathedral at **Chartres**.

Versailles

The **Palace of Versailles** (Tues–Sun 9am–5.30/6.30pm; €7.50, €5.30 after 3.30pm; ⓦwww.chateauversailles.com) is one of the three most visited monuments in France. The palace, 16km west of Paris, is the apotheosis of French regal indulgence, its decor an unrestrained homage to two of the greatest of all self-propagandists, Louis XIV (the "Sun King") and Napoleon. It's more impressive for its size than anything else, which, by any standards, is incredible. The most amazing room is perhaps the **Hall of Mirrors**, although the mirrors are not the originals; this is, more importantly, the room in which the Treaty of Versailles was signed, so bringing World War I to an end. You can also visit the state apartments of the king and queen, and the **royal chapel**, a grand structure that ranks among France's finest Baroque creations. Outside, the **park** is something of a relief, and you could wander for hours through its vast extent. It is inevitably a very ordered affair, but the scenery becomes less formal the further you go from the palace, especially around the **Grand** and **Petit Trianons** (Tues–Sun noon–5.30/6.30pm; €5 for both). Beyond is **Le Hameau**, an area of thatched cottages, a mill and a dairy set around a lake where Marie Antoinette played at being a shepherdess. The easiest way to get to Versailles is the half-hourly RER line C5 from Gare d'Austerlitz to Versailles-Rive Gauche (35min; €4.75 return).

Chartres

About 35km southwest of Versailles, an hour by train from Paris-Montparnasse, **CHARTRES** is a pretty but undistinguished town. However, its **Cathédrale Notre-Dame** (daily 8am–7.15/8pm) is one of the finest examples of Gothic architecture in Europe. The heart-lifting space is unique in being almost unaltered since its consecration, lit by 130 stunning and mostly original stained-glass windows. The stonework is just as wonderful, with a Renaissance choir screen and a host of sculpted figures above each door. There's also a treasury and crypt, and you can climb the north **tower** (€4). Though the cathedral is the main reason for visiting, Chartres town is not entirely without appeal, with a small old quarter and a picturesque district of bridges and old houses down by the River Eure. The **Musée des Beaux-Arts** in the former episcopal palace just north of the cathedral (Mon & Wed–Sat 10am–noon & 2–5/6pm, Sun 2–5/6pm; €1.50) has some beautiful tapestries, a room full of Vlaminck paintings, and Zurbarán's *St Lucy*, as well as good temporary exhibitions. The **tourist office** is in front of the cathedral, at place de la Cathédrale (Mon–Sat 9/10am–6/7pm, Sun 9.30/10am–1pm & 2.30–4.30/5.30pm; ☎02.37.18.26.26, ⓦwww.ville-chartres.fr), and can help with accommodation. Rue du Cygne is the place to look for **restaurants**.

Northern France

Northern France includes some of the most industrial and densely populated parts of the country. However, it is possible that you'll both arrive and leave France via this region, and there are curiosities within easy reach of the Channel ports – of which only **Boulogne** is worth a visit. Further south, the *maisons* and vineyards of the **Champagne** region are the main draw, for which the best base is **Reims**, which also has a fine cathedral.

The main port of entry is **CALAIS**, France's busiest passenger port with the shortest and most frequent connections to Dover, England. There's a **free bus** service during the day from the ferry dock alongside Calais-Maritime train station to place d'Armes and on to the central Calais-Ville **train station** in Calais-Sud. The **tourist office** is at 12 blvd Clémenceau (Easter–Aug Mon–Sat 9am–7pm, Sun 10am–1pm; rest of year Mon–Sat 10am–1pm & 2-6.30pm; ☎03.21.96.62.40, ⓦwww.ot-calais.fr); it can book accommodation for a small charge.

Boulogne

BOULOGNE is the one northern Channel port that might tempt you to stay. Its **Ville Basse**, centring on place Dalton, is home to some of the best *charcuteries* and *pâtisseries* in the north, as well as an impressive array of fish restaurants. Rising above, the **Ville Haute** is one of the gems of the northeast coast, flanked by grassy ramparts that give impressive views over the town and port. Inside the walls, the **Basilique Notre-Dame** is something of an oddity, raised by the town's vicar in the nineteenth century without any architectural knowledge or advice. Its crypt (Tues–Sun 2–5pm; €2) has frescoed remains of the previous Romanesque building and relics of a Roman temple to Diana, while the main part of the church has a curious statue of the Virgin and Child on a boat-chariot, drawn here on its own wheels from Lourdes. The **tourist office** (July & Aug daily 9am–7pm; rest of the year Mon–Sat 9am–12.30pm & 1.30–6pm, Sun 10.15am–1pm; ☎03.21.10.88.10, ⊛www.tourisme-boulognesurmer .com), over the bridge as you leave the ferry terminal, can advise on availability of rooms, which in summer fill early. Your best bet is the friendly **hostel** in front of the train station, 56 place Rouget de Lisle (☎03.21.99.15.30; €12.70). Most of the budget **hotels** are around the port area: try *Alexandra*, 93 rue Thiers (☎03.21.30.52.22, ℻03.21.30.20.03; ❹), or *Hôtel des Arts*, 102 blvd Gambetta (☎03.21.31.53.31, ℻03.21.33.69.05; ❸). For **eating**, there are dozens of possibilities around place Dalton and the cathedral, but you need to be selective. The brasserie *Chez Jules*, 8 place Dalton, is always a good bet and serves food all day. Opposite the cathedral on rue de Lille, *Estaminet du Château* offers inexpensive menus in a pleasant setting. Near place Dalton is the *Hamiot* restaurant, 1 rue Faidherbe, a decent alternative, while *La Houblonnière*, 8 rue Monsigny, has a vast international selection of brews to wash down its plats du jour.

Lille

LILLE is the very symbol of French industry and working-class politics, but suffers from some of the country's worst poverty and racial conflict, and a crime rate rivalled only by Paris and Marseille. Though hardly a prime destination, the city is a stop for Eurostar trains between London and Paris, and is worth at least a night for its lovely old quarter, along with some vibrant and prosperous commerce. It's also a place that takes its culture and its restaurants very seriously. Marking the southern boundary of the old quarter, the **Grand Place**, also known as place du Général de Gaulle (he was born here in 1890), is a busy square dominated by the old exchange building, the lavishly ornate Ancienne Bourse. A few minutes' walk north is the **Hospice Comtesse**, 32 rue de la Monnaie, a former hospital now containing a selection of Dutch, Flemish and French paintings on loan from the Palais des Beaux-Arts in its old ward, the **Salle des Malades** (Mon 2–6pm, Wed–Sun 10am–12.30pm & 2–6pm; €2.30). South of the old quarter lies the modern place Rihour, beyond which the stylish rue de Béthune leads into café-lined place Béthune, and on to blvd de la Liberté and the city's **Palais**

des Beaux-Arts on place de la République (Mon 2–6pm, Wed–Sun noon–6pm, Fri till 7pm; €4.60).

The **train station** is only a few minutes' walk from the old town. The **tourist office** is in the old Palais Rihour on place Rihour (Mon–Sat 9.30am–6.30pm, Sun 10am–noon & 2–5pm; ☎03.21.21.94.21, ⊛www.lille.cci.fr). The *Hôtel Flandre Angleterre*, at 13 place de la Gare (☎03.20.06.04.12, ⊛www.hotel-flandre-angleterre.fr; ❺), is a reasonable and pleasant place to stay; you could also try the *Hôtel de France* at 10 rue de Béthune (☎03.20.57.14.78, ℱ03.20.57.06.01; ❸), which is right in the centre. The **hostel is** near the Hôtel de Ville at 12 rue Malpart (☎03.20.57.08.94; dorm bed €12.70). The main area for **restaurants** is around place Rihour and place Béthune. For mussels – a local speciality – the brasseries around the station are as good as any in town, and *La Galetière*, 4 place Louise-de-Bettignies, is a pleasant crêperie. For **drinking**, monied local students hang around *Café Imaginaire* on place Louise-de-Bettignies.

Reims

Laid flat by World War I artillery, **REIMS** is not the most inspiring of cities, although there are two good reasons for visiting: it's the best centre (along with Épernay) for the Champagne region, and it's home to one of the country's most impressive Gothic cathedrals, once scene of the coronations of French monarchs. The battered west front of the **Cathédrale** is still a rare delight, with an array of restored and remarkably expressive statuary – although many of the originals have been removed to the former bishop's palace. Inside, the stained glass includes stunning designs by Marc Chagall in the east chapel and glorifications of the champagne-making process in the south transept. Next door to the cathedral, the **Palais du Tau** (May–Aug Tues–Sun 9.30am–6.30pm; rest of year Tues–Sun 9.30–12.30pm & 2–5.30pm; €5.50), the former bishop's palace, is worth a visit to see some of the dislodged west-front figures: there are grinning angels, friendly looking gargoyles and a superb Eve. The building also preserves the paraphernalia of Charles X's coronation in 1824. Most of the early kings were buried in Reims's oldest building, sited 1km east of the cathedral – the eleventh-century **Basilique St-Rémi** (daily 8am–dusk/7pm; free). Part of a former Benedictine abbey, it's an immensely spacious building that preserves its Romanesque transept walls and ambulatory chapels.

If you're in town for the **Champagne**, head to place des Droits-de-l'Homme and place St-Niçaise, around which are most of the Reims *maisons*; most charge a small fee for their tours. If you're limiting yourself to one, the **Maison Veuve Clicquot**, 1 place des Droits-de-l'Homme (April–Oct Mon–Sat; rest of the year Mon–Fri; 7 visits a day by appointment only; €7; ☎03.26.89.53.90, ⊛www.veuve-clicquot.com), is one of the least pompous. There's also **Pommery**, 5 place du Général Gouraud (April–Nov 14 daily 9.30am–6pm; rest of year Mon–Fri 10am–6pm; by appointment only; €7.50/10/12.50; ☎03.26.61.62.56, ⊛www.pommery.com), and **Taittinger**, 9 place St-Nicaise (Mon–Fri 9.30–1pm & 2–5.30pm, Sat & Sun 9–noon & 2–6pm; Dec–Feb closed Sat & Sun; €5.50; ☎03.26.85.45.35, ⊛www.taittinger.com).

Reims **train station** is on the northwest edge of the town centre, on Square Colbert. It's a five-minute walk to the **tourist office**, which is at 2 rue Guillaume de Machault (Mon–Sat 9am–6/7pm, Sun 10/11am–5/6pm; ☎03.26.77.45.25, ⊛www.tourisme.fr/reims). Among central **hotels**, the *Thillois*, 17 rue de Thillois (☎03.26.40.65.65; ❷), and the *Alsace*, 6 rue Général Sarrail (☎03.26.47.44.08, ℱ03.26.47.44.52; ❸), are the most affordable, and there's a *Centre Internationa de Séjour* with **dorm beds** south of the centre at Parc Léo Lagrange (☎03.26.40.52.60, ⊛www.cis-reims.com; €10–26), fifteen minutes' walk from the station. For **food**, place Drouet d'Erlon is lined with cafés and restaurants: try *A Casa Mia* at no. 84 or the more upmarket *l'Apostrophe* at no. 59. There's **Internet** access at *Clique et Croque*, 27 rue de Vesle.

Normandy

To the French, the essence of **Normandy** is its produce: this is the land of butter and cream, cheeses and seafood, cider and calvados. Yet parts of Normandy are among the most economically depressed of the whole country. The Normans themselves have a reputation for being insular and conservative, with a hatred of Parisians with weekend homes in the region. Along the coast, there are occasional surprises, notably the picturesque harbour at **Honfleur**. Inland, it's hard to pin down specific highlights; the pleasures lie in the feel of particular landscapes – lush meadows and orchards, half-timbered houses, and the food and drink for which the region is famous. Of urban centres, **Rouen**, the Norman capital, is by far the most compelling.

The main ports of entry along this stretch of coast are Le Havre, Cherbourg and Dieppe, of which **DIEPPE** is the most enjoyable, with a good market, a castle and some nice restaurants. Its **tourist office** is beside the ferry terminal on Pont Ango (Mon–Sat 9am–noon/1pm & 2–6/8pm; summer also Sun 10am–1pm & 3–6pm; ☎02 .35.84.11.77, ⊛www.dieppetourisme.com); the **train station** is about 800m southwest.

Honfleur

HONFLEUR is the best-preserved of the Normandy ports and a near-perfect seaside town. The ancient port still functions and although only pleasure craft now make use of the moorings in the harbour basin, fishing boats tie up alongside the pier close by, and there are usually freshly caught fish for sale either directly from the boats or from stands on the pier. It's all highly picturesque, and not so different from the town that had such appeal for artists in the late nineteenth century.

It's this artistic past – and a present-day concentration of galleries – which dominates Honfleur. The town owes most to Eugène Boudin, forerunner of Impressionism, who was born and worked here, trained the eighteen-year-old Monet, and was joined for various periods by Pissarro, Renoir and Cézanne. There's a good selection of his work in the **Musée Eugène Boudin**, west of the port on pl Erik-Satie (mid-March to Sept Mon & Wed–Sun 10am–noon & 2–6pm; Oct–Dec & mid-Feb to mid-March Mon & Wed–Fri 2.30–5pm, Sat & Sun 10am–noon & 2.30–5pm; closed Jan to mid-Feb; €5), along with an impressive set of works by Dufy and Monet. The composer, musician, artist and author Erik Satie was also born in Honfleur, and the rooms of his childhood home have been converted into an exhibition of his life and works. **Les Maisons Satie**, 76 bd Charles V (Mon & Wed–Sun 10/11am–6/7pm; closed Jan to late Feb; €5), is no conventional museum, however. Visitors are conducted through a series of innovative "stage sets" by the man himself – or rather his words and music – by way of an infra-red controlled headset. Expect flying giant pears and indoor rain showers, rather than dusty artefacts – all very entertaining and insightful, like a walk through the mind of the artist.

Honfleur is on the direct **bus** route between Caen and Le Havre (4 buses daily); the town's nearest **train station** is at Deauville, connected by bus #20 (takes 20min). The **tourist office** is on quai Le Paulmier (July & Aug Mon–Sat 10am–7pm, Sun 10am–5pm; rest of year Mon–Sat 10am–noon & 2–5.30pm; ☎02.31.89.23.30, ⊛www.ot-honfleur.fr). None of Honfleur's **hotels** is very affordable – the *Cascades*, 17 place Thiers (☎02.31.89.05.83; ❸), is the best bet, or there's a **campsite**, *Du Phare*, at the west end of blvd Charles V on place Jean de Vienne (☎02.31.89.10.26; closed Oct–March). The most reasonable **restaurants** and **bars** are on rue Haute, on the way up to the Boudin museum: try *Au P'tit Mareyeur* at no. 4. At the harbour itself, it's hard to beat *Le Vieux Honfleur*, 13 quai St Étienne.

Bayeux

BAYEUX's magnificent cathedral and world-famous tapestry depicting the 1066 invasion of England by William the Conqueror make it one of the high points of Normandy. However, it receives an influx of summer tourists that can make its charms pall somewhat. The **Bayeux Tapestry** is housed in the **Centre Guillaume le Conquérant**, clearly signposted on rue de Nesmond (daily 9/9.30am–6/7pm; Nov to mid-March closed 12.30–2pm; €6.40). Visits begin with a projection of slides on swathes of canvas, before moving on to an almost full-length reproduction of the original, complete with photographic extracts and detailed commentary. Beyond this lies the tapestry itself, a 70m strip of linen embroidered over nine centuries ago with coloured wools. It records scenes from the Norman Conquest, as well as incidental details of domestic and daily life, which run along the bottom as a counterpoint. The tapestry was commissioned for the consecration of the nearby **Cathédrale Notre-Dame** in 1077 where, despite some eighteenth-century vandalism, the Romanesque plan of the church is still intact. The crypt, entirely unaltered, is a beauty, its columns graced with frescoes of angels playing trumpets and bagpipes. Also well worth a visit is the **Memorial Museum to the Battle of Normandy** on bd Fabian Ware (daily 9.30/10am–6/6.30pm; Oct–April closed 12.30–2pm; €5.40). The numerous original documents, life-sized models, equipment and videos dramatically capture the most decisive chapter in the 1944 Allied invasion of Europe.

Bayeux's **train station** is on the southern side of town, on bd Sadi Carnot. The **tourist office**, at Pont St Jean (Mon–Sat 9am–7pm, Sun 9am–12.30pm & 2–6.30pm; Oct–June closed Mon–Sat 12.30–2pm & all Sun; ☎02.31.51.28.28, ⓦwww.bayeux-tourism.com), might be able to help you find reasonable **accommodation**. Most affordable of the **hotels** are the *Maupassant*, 19 rue St-Martin (☎02.31.92.28.53; ❸), and *la Gare*, 26 pl de la Gare (☎02.31.92.10.70; ❷). The *Family Home* at 39 rue du Général de Dais (☎02.31.92.15.22; €16.50), north of the cathedral, functions as a friendly and decent **hostel**, and serves good food too. The nearest **campsite** is on bd d'Eindhoven, a fifteen-minute walk from the centre (☎02.31.92.08.43; closed Oct–April). Most of the **restaurants** are on the pedestrianized rue St-Jean – *La Fringale* at no. 43 is the most popular, while *La Table du Terroir* at no. 42 serves good French cuisine.

Mont St-Michel

The island of **Mont St-Michel**, site of a marvellous **Gothic abbey** (tours daily 9/9.30am–6/7pm; €7), on the far western edge of Normandy, is a big draw. The abbey church, long known as the Merveille, is visible from all around the bay, and it becomes more awe-inspiring the closer you get. The granite structure was sculpted to match the contours of the hill, and though space was always limited, the building has grown through the centuries in ever more ingenious uses of geometry. However, the current dour state of the stone walls is a far cry from the way the monastery would have looked in medieval times, brightly painted and festooned with tapestries. **To stay** on the island, head up the one twisting street to the *du Guesclin* (☎02.33.60.14.10; ❹), with excellent rooms and a run-of-the-mill **restaurant**. There's a **campsite** (☎02.33.60.22.10; closed mid-Nov to mid-Feb) near the causeway to the island. The nearest **train station** is at Pontorson, 6km south, from where you can rent a bike or take the expensive bus to the Mont.

Rouen

ROUEN was flattened during World War II, although a flood of money was spent on restoring it to an attractive, if in parts fake, medieval centre complete with half-timbered houses, cobbled streets and impressive churches. A prominent point in the centre, between place du Vieux-Marché and the cathedral, is the Gros Horloge, a colourful one-handed clock that spans the street named after it. Just off here is the **Cathédrale de Notre-Dame** (Mon 2–6pm, Tues–Sun 8am–6pm; free), a Gothic masterpiece built in the twelfth and thirteenth centuries. The west facade, intricately sculpted like the rest of the exterior, was Monet's subject for his series of celebrated studies of changing light. The church of **St-Ouen**, in a park a short walk northeast, is larger than the cathedral and has far less decoration, so that the Gothic proportions have a more instant impact. Close by, the church of St-Maclou is more flamboyant, although perhaps the real interest is in its adjacent **Aître St-Maclou**, once a cemetery for plague victims, which still has its original macabre decorations. Also worth a visit is the **Musée Flaubert et d'Histoire de la Médicine** in the Hôpital Hôtel-Dieu on the corner of rue de Lecat and rue du Contrat-Social (Tues 10am–6pm, Wed–Sat 10am–noon & 2–6pm; €2), dedicated to Rouen's most famous novelist, Gustave Flaubert, whose father was chief surgeon at the medical school here.

The main **train station**, Rouen Rive-Droite, is a ten-minute walk or one metro stop from the centre. The **bus station** is just off the southern end of the main rue Jeanne d'Arc. The **tourist office** is opposite the cathedral at 25 pl de la Cathédrale (Mon–Sat 9am–6/7pm, Sun 9.30/10am–12.30/1pm & 2–6pm; Oct–April closed Sun afternoon; ☎02.32.08.32.40, ⓦwww.rouen.fr). Inexpensive **hotels** include: the bare-bones *Sphinx*, 130 rue Beauvoisine (☎02.35.71.35.86; ❷); *des Carmes*, 33 pl des Carmes (☎02.35.71.92.31; ❹); and *Le Palais*, 12 rue du Tambour (☎02.35.71.41.40; ❸). The town's **campsite** is 5km northwest on rue Jules-Ferry in Déville-lès-Rouen (☎02.35.74.07.59; bus #2 from Théâtre des Arts). Rouen has a reputation for good **food**, and its most famous dish, duckling (*caneton*), can be enjoyed quite affordably at *Pascaline*, 5 rue de la Poterne. For good basic meals, the south side of place du Vieux-Marché and the north side of St-Maclou church are both lined with good-quality restaurants. There's **Internet** access at Cybernetics, 59 pl du Vieux-Marché.

Giverny

GIVERNY is famous for **Monet's house and gardens**, complete with water-lily pond (April–Oct Tues–Sun 10am–6pm; €5.50, €4 gardens only; ⓦwww.fondation-monet.com). Monet lived here from 1883 until his death in 1926 and the gardens that he laid out were considered by many of his friends to be his masterpiece; the best months to visit are May and June, when the rhododendrons flower around the lily pond and the wisteria hangs over the Japanese bridge, but it is overwhelmingly beautiful at any time of year. There aren't any original paintings on show, however; the house is filled with Monet's collection of Japanese prints. The easiest way to get to Giverny is to take a train to nearby **VERNON**, then either rent a bike or take the *Gisor* bus from the station (not Mon). Giverny's only **hotel** is the small *Auberge La Musardiere*, 123 rue Claude Monet (☎02.32.21.03.18; ❹).

Brittany

For generations the people of **Brittany** risked their lives fishing and trading on the violent seas or struggling with the arid soil of the interior, and their resilience is tinged with Celtic culture: mystical, musical, sometimes morbid, sometimes vital and inspired. Unified with France in 1532, the Bretons have seen their language steadily eradicated, and the interior severely depopulated. Today, the people still tend to think of France as a separate country, even if few of them actively support Breton nationalism. The recent economic resurgence, helped partly by summer tourism, has largely been due to local initiatives. At the same time, a Celtic artistic identity has been revived at festivals of traditional Breton music, poetry and dance. For most visitors to Brittany, the **coast** is the dominant feature. After the Côte d'Azur, this is the most popular summer resort area in France, and the attractions are obvious – white sand beaches, towering cliffs and offshore islands. Whether you approach across the Channel by ferry, or along the coast from Normandy, the River Rance, guarded by **St-Malo** on its estuary and **Dinan** 20km upstream, makes a spectacular introduction to Brittany. Brittany's southern coast takes in France's most famous prehistoric site, the alignments of **Carnac**, and although the beaches are not as spectacular as Finistère's, the water is warmer. Of the cities, **Vannes** has one of the liveliest medieval town centres.

Brittany's main port apart from St-Malo is **ROSCOFF**, close to the north-western tip. Follow the signs from the **ferry terminal** to the town centre; the **train station** is 100m south of the town on rue Ropartz Morvan. The **tourist office** is at 46 rue Gambetta (July & Aug Mon–Sat 9am–12.30pm & 1.30–7pm, Sun 10am–12.30pm; rest of year Mon–Sat 9/10am–noon & 2–5/6pm; ☎02.98.61.12.13, ⊛www.sb-roscoff.fr/Roscoff).

St-Malo

ST-MALO, walled and built with the same grey granite as Mont St-Michel, presents its best face to the River Rance and the sea. Once within the old ramparts it can seem a little grim and squat, and overrun by summer tourists, but away from the thoroughfares of the tiny **citadel**, with its high seventeenth-century houses, random exploration is fun. The **town museum**, in the castle to the right as you enter Porte St-Vincent (daily 10am–noon/12.30pm & 2–6pm; winter closed Mon; €4.40), glorifies, on several exhausting floors, St-Malo's sources of wealth and fame – colonialism, slave-trading and privateering among them. **Buses** drop you at the main city gate, the Porte St-Vincent, while **trains** stop on the other side of the docks, a ten-minute walk away. The **tourist office** is on the Esplanade St-Vincent, right in front of the gate (July & Aug Mon–Sat 8.30am–8pm, Sun 10am–7pm; April–June & Sept Mon–Sat 9am–12.30pm & 1.30–7pm, Sun 10am–12.30pm & 2.30–6pm; rest of year closed Sun; ☎02.99.56.64.48, ⊛www.saint-malo -tourisme.com). It's always hard to find **accommodation** in the old city, despite the extraordinary number of hotels, but rooms at *Le Nautilus*, 9 rue de la Corne de Cerf (☎02.99.40.42.27; ❸), and *Le Louvre*, 2 rue des Marins (☎02.99.40.86.62; ❸), are worth trying. Otherwise, there's an array of places near the train station. In the suburb of Paramé, 2km northeast of the station, is an often-crowded hostel at 37 av R.P. Umbricht (☎02.99.40.29.80; 1; €15; bus #2 or #5). There's a municipal **campsite**, *Cité d'Aleth*, on allée Gaston Buy (☎02.99.81.60.91), near some shops and the beach. Most of the citadel's **restaurants** are pricey tourist traps, so you're better off at the *crêperies* and *mouleries* such as *La Brigantine*, 13 rue du Dinan, and *Le Brick*, 5 rue Jacques-Cartier. **Internet** access is at Cop Imprim, 39 bd des Talards.

Dinan

A short distance from St-Malo along the River Rance lies **DINAN**, one of the most enjoyable towns in Brittany. Its **citadel** has been preserved almost intact within a three-kilometre circuit of walls, inside which lies a warren of beautiful late-medieval houses. It's almost too good to be true and time is easily spent rambling from *crêperie* to café, admiring the houses on the way. Unfortunately, there's only one small stretch of the **ramparts** that you can walk along – from the gardens behind St-Sauveur to just short of the Tour Sillon – but you get a good general overview from the **Tour de l'Horloge** (April & May daily 2–6pm; June–Sept daily 10am–7pm; €2.50). Another good view can be had from the **Château Duchesse Anne** (June–Sept daily 10am–6.30pm; rest of year closed noon–2pm & Tues; closed Jan; €4). An inevitable target of any Dinan wanderings is the church of **St-Sauveur**, a real mix of styles, with a Romanesque porch and eighteenth-century steeple.

Dinan's **train station** is a ten-minute walk away from the central place du Guesclin. The **tourist office** (mid-June to Sept Mon–Sat 9am–7pm, Sun 10am–12.30pm & 2.30–6pm; Oct to mid-June Mon–Sat 9am–12.30pm & 2–6pm; ☎02.96.87.69.76, ⊛www.dinan-tourisme.com) is at the southwest corner of the *place*, at 9 rue du Chateau. The less pricey **hotels** are near the station: *De l'Océan*, 9 pl du 11-Novembre (☎02.96.39.21.51; ❷), is as good as any. Within the walls there's *La Duchesse Anne* at 10 pl du Guesclin (☎02.96.39.09.43; ❸). Dinan's **hostel** (☎02.96.39.10.83; €15; closed

Jan) is attractively set in the Moulin de Méen near the port at Taden, about 3km away, while the closest **campsite** is at 103 rue Châteaubriand (℡02.96.39.11.96; closed late Sept to late May), which runs parallel to the western ramparts. Of the wide choice of **eating places**, one of the best bets is *Crêperie Ahna*, 7 rue de la Poissonerie.

Quimper and around

QUIMPER, capital of the ancient diocese and kingdom of Cornouaille, is the oldest Breton city, founded according to legend by St Corentin, who came here across the channel to the place they named Little Britain some time between the fourth and seventh centuries. It's a laidback town, with old granite buildings, two rivers and the rising woods of Mont Frugy overlooking the centre. Quimper focuses on the enormous Gothic Cathédrale St-Corentin, while the **Musée des Beaux-Arts**, alongside at 40 pl St-Corentin (July & Aug daily 10am–7pm; rest of year closed noon–2pm & Tues; €4), has an amazing collection of drawings by Cocteau, Max Jacob and Gustave Doré (shown in rotation) and nineteenth- and twentieth-century paintings of the famed Pont-Aven school. To see pottery made on an industrial scale, and an exhibition of the changing styles since the first Quimper *ateliers* of the late seventeenth century, head for rue Jean-Baptiste Bosquet, where you'll find the **Faïenceries de Quimper** (guided visits only; €3; ℡02.98.90.09.36) and the **Musée de la Faïence** (April–Oct Mon–Sat 10am–6pm; €5).

The adjacent **train** and **bus stations** are a short walk east along the river from the town centre. The **tourist office** is on the south bank at 7 rue de la Déesse, pl de la Résistance (July–Sept Mon–Sat 9am–7pm, Sun 10am–1pm & 3–6pm; June & Sept closed Sun afternoon; rest of year closed all Sun & Mon–Sat 12.30–1.30pm; ℡02.98.53.04.05). Budget **hotels** include the *Hôtel le Derby*, near the station at 13 av de la Gare (℡02.98.52.06.91; ❷), and *TGV*, nearby at 4 rue de Concarneau (℡02.98.90.54.00; ❸). The **hostel** (℡02.98.64.97.97; €15) and **campsite** (℡02.98.55.61.09; reserved for caravans in winter) are downstream on av des Oiseaux in the Bois du Séminaire – take bus #1 from place de la Résistance. For **food**, a good bet is the *La Krampouzerie*, 9 rue du Sallé, on the lively little place du Beurre north of the cathedral. Note that rooms book up fast for the last full week of July, when the town hosts the **Festival de Cornouaille**, a jamboree of Breton music, costume and dance.

Boats down the Odet to the coast leave from the end of quai de l'Odet, opposite the Faïenceries, making a winding journey to the upmarket resort of **BÉNODET**, where there's a long sheltered beach; for times and prices call ℡02.98.52.98.41. Hotels here are comparatively expensive, but there are several large campsites. There are more **beaches** along the coast between Penmarch and Loctudy and beyond, about an hour by bus from Quimper. Another possibility is a trip to the **Pointe du Raz**, the Land's End of France, a series of plummeting fissures, filling and draining with deafening force, above which you can walk on precarious paths.

Carnac and around

About 30km southeast along the coast from the functional port of Lorient, **CARNAC** is home to one of the most important prehistoric sites in Europe, a congregation of some two thousand or so **menhirs** stretching for more than 4km to the north of the village, long predating the Pyramids or Stonehenge. The stones may have been part of an observatory for the motions of the moon, but no one really knows. The main alignments, fenced from the public, are viewed from a raised platform at one end of the plain. There's plenty of information on them at the **Musée de la Préhistoire**, 10 pl de la Chapelle, near rue du Tumulus in Carnac-Ville (May–Sept Mon–Fri 10am–6.30pm, Sat & Sun 10am–noon & 2–6.30pm, €5; rest of year Mon & Wed–Sun 10am–noon & 2–5pm, €4; ❦www.museedecarnac.com). Carnac itself, made up of Carnac-Ville and the newer seaside resort of Carnac-Plage, is extremely popular. **Buses** arrive at the main **tourist office** at 74 av des Druides in Carnac-Plage (July &

Aug Mon–Sat 9am–7pm, Sun 3–7pm; rest of year Mon–Sat 9am–noon & 2–6pm; ☎02.97.52.13.52, ⊛www.ot-carnac.fr). Among the town's **hotels**, the *Ratelier*, 4 chemin du Douet (☎02.97.52.05.04; ❹; closed Oct–March), is a good deal, as is the central *Chez Nous*, 5 pl de la Chapelle (☎02.97.52.07.28; ❸; closed Nov–March). The best of the many **beaches** is the smallest, the **Men Dû**, just off the road towards La Trinité. For **camping**, by the sea, head for *Men Dû* (☎02.97.52.04.23; ⊛www.camping-du-mendu.com; closed Oct–Easter); the best site, though, is *La Grande Métairie* (☎02.97.52.24.01; closed mid-Sept to March), opposite the stones.

South of Carnac, the town of **QUIBERON** is a lively port and provides a jumping-off point for boats out to the nearby islands or simply a base for the peninsula. The ocean-facing shore, known as the **Côte Sauvage**, is a wild and unswimmable stretch, but the sheltered eastern side has safe and calm sandy beaches, and offers plenty of **campsites**. In Quiberon, **Port Maria**, the fishing harbour, is the most active part of town and has the best concentration of **hotels**, though they're often full in high season – try *Le Neptune* at 4 quai de Houat (☎02.97.50.09.62; ❹), or *Au Bon Accueil*, 6 quai de Houat (☎02.97.50.07.92; ❸; closed Jan), which also has a very good fish restaurant. The spartan **hostel**, *Les Filets Bleus*, 45 rue du Roch-Priol (☎02.97.50.15.54; €15; closed Oct–March), is set back from the sea about 1km southeast of the train station. Fish **restaurants** line the seafront, while the **cafés** by the long bathing beach are also enjoyable. The **train station**, with services in July and August only, is a couple of minutes north of the centre on place de la Gare. The **tourist office** is at 14 rue de Verdun (July & Aug Mon–Sat 9am–7.30pm, Sun 9.30am–12.30pm & 2.30–7pm; rest of year Mon–Sat 9am–12.30pm & 2–6pm; ☎02.97.50.45.12, ⊛www.quiberon.com).

Vannes and the Golfe de Morbihan

VANNES, whose old centre is a chaotic web of streets crammed around the cathedral and enclosed by ramparts and gardens, is one of the most historic towns in Brittany. It was here that the Breton assembly ratified the Act of Union with France in 1532, in the building known as **La Cohue**, opposite the cathedral, which now houses the **Musée de Vannes** (June–Sept daily 10am–6pm; rest of year Mon & Wed–Sat 10am–noon & 2–6pm, Sun 2–6pm; €4). Vannes' harbour is a channelled inlet of the ragged-edged **Golfe de Morbihan**, which lets in the tides through a narrow gap. By popular tradition, the **islands** scattered around this enclosure used to number the days of the year, though for centuries the waters have been rising and there are now fewer than one for each week. Of these, thirty are privately owned, while two – the Île aux Moines and Île d'Arz – have small communities and regular ferry services, and end up being crowded in summer. You can take a **boat tour** around the rest, a compelling trip through a baffling muddle of channels, megalithic ruins, stone circles and solitary menhirs; contact Navix (☎02.97.46.60.00, ⊛www.navix.fr) or Compagnie des Îles (☎02.97.46.18.19, ⊛www.compagniedesiles.com) for details.

It's twenty minutes' walk south from the **train station** to the centre at place de la République. The **tourist office** is at 1 rue Thiers (July & Aug Mon–Sat 9am–7pm, Sun 10am–6pm; rest of year Mon–Sat 9.30am–12.30pm & 2–6pm; ☎02.97.47.24.34, ⊛www.pays-de-vannes.com/tourisme). Vannes has the best choice of **hotels** anywhere around the Golfe de Morbihan: two good ones are *Le Bretagne*, 36 rue du Mené, in the old town (☎02.97.47.20.21, ⊛www.bretagne-hotel.com; ❸), and *Le Marina* overlooking the port at 4 pl Gambetta (☎02.97.47.22.81; ❸). For **food**, the *Crêperie La Cave St-Gwenaël*, 23 rue St-Gwenaël, is good-value, set in a lovely old house facing the cathedral.

Nantes

Though **NANTES**, the former capital, is these days not officially a part of Brittany, it remains to its inhabitants an integral part of the province. Crucial to its self-image is the **Château des Ducs**, subjected to a certain amount of damage over the centuries, but still preserving the form in which it was built by two of the last rulers of independent Brittany, François II and his daughter Duchess Anne, who was born here in 1477. You can walk into the courtyard and up onto the low ramparts for free, and visit temporary exhibitions in the Harnachement building, but the rest of the castle is undergoing a huge renovation in order to become the Museum of the History of Nantes and its Region, due for completion by 2008. In 1800 the castle's arsenal exploded, shattering the stained glass of the **Cathédrale de St-Pierre et St-Paul**, 200m away, just one of many disasters that have befallen the church. Its soaring heights are home to the tomb of François II and his wife, Margaret. Back past the château, the **Île Feydeau**, once an island, was the birthplace of **Jules Verne**; the museum dedicated to him is at 3 rue de l'Hermitage (Mon & Wed–Sat 10am–noon & 2–5pm, Sun 2–5pm; €1.55). The **train station** is a short way east of the castle. For **accommodation**, try the central *Hôtel Rénova*, 11 rue Beauregard (℡02.40.47.57.03; ❷), *Hôtel de l'Océan*, 11 rue du Maréchal-de-Lattre-de-Tassigny (℡02.40.69.73.51, ⓦwww.hotel-nantes.com; ❷), or *Fourcroy*, 11 rue Fourcroy (℡02.40.44.68.00; ❷). The city's **hostel**, at 2 pl de la Manu (℡02.40.29.29.20; €15), is a ten-minute walk east of the train station along the tram tracks, or take tram #1 to Beaujoire. The **tourist office** is on pl du Commerce, in a large FNAC book and music store (Mon–Sat 10am–8pm; ℡02.40.20.60.00, ⓦwww.nantes-tourisme.com) in an appealing, largely pedestrian area that is a good source of **restaurants**. There's **Internet** access at Cyber City, 14 rue de Strasbourg.

The Loire Valley

The sheer density of châteaux can be daunting when choosing where to go in the **Loire**, but if you pick selectively – the best are those at **Chenonceaux** and **Loches** – this can be one of the most enjoyable of all French regions. The Loire itself is known as the last wild river in France, as well as the longest; no one swims in it, nor are any goods carried along it. The stretch above Saumur is the loveliest on the lower reaches, the land to the south planted with vines and sunflowers. Other than the châteaux, the region has few sights; of the towns, **Tours** is good for low-key bustle, while **Saumur** and **Chinon** are perfect for provincial indolence.

Tours and around

The regional capital **TOURS** makes a good base for châteaux-hunting. The city has two main areas, sited either side of the central rue Nationale. To the east loom the extravagantly Gothic twin towers of the **Cathédrale St-Gatien**, with some handsome old streets behind. Adjacent, the **Musée des Beaux-Arts**, on pl François Sicard (9am–12.45pm & 2–6pm, closed Tues; free), has some beauties in its rambling collection, notably Mantegna's *Christ in the Garden of Olives* and *Resurrection*. Tours' **old town** meanwhile crowds around medieval place Plumereau, on the west side of the city. It is crammed with cafés, bars and restaurants, and in the winding streets around the square, the medieval half-timbered houses and bulging stairway towers are the city's showpieces.

The **tourist office** is in front of the **train station** at 78–82 rue Bernard-Palissy (mid-April to mid-Oct Mon–Sat 8.30am–7pm, Sun 10am–12.30pm & 2.30–5pm; mid-Oct to mid-April Mon–Sat 9am–12.30pm & 1.30–6pm, Sun 10am–1pm; ℡02.47.70.37.37, ⓦwww.ligeris.com). There are plenty of reasonably priced **hotels** in the cathedral quarter: the *Regina*, 2 rue Pimbert (℡02.47.05.25.36; ❷), and *Mon Hôtel*, 40 rue de la Préfecture (℡02.47.05.67.53; ❷) are decent places, while the *Hôtel du Musée*, 2 pl François-Sicard (℡02.47.66.63.81; ❸) is attractively ancient. There is no hostel or campsite, but under-25s can stay at *Le Foyer,* 16 rue Bernard-Palissy (℡02.47.60.53.00; €17; closed to new arrivals at weekends). Rue du Grand-Marché and rue de la Rôtisserie, on the periphery of old Tours, and rue Colbert, which runs down to the cathedral, are the most promising streets for **restaurants**. Try *Le Petit Patrimoine* at 58 rue Colbert for good regional cuisine, or *Le Franglais*, 27 rue Colbert, for hearty, inexpensive meals. Top Communication, at 68 rue du Grand Marché, offers **Internet** access.

Villandry, Chenonceaux and Loches

The most popular attraction close to Tours is the **château** of **VILLANDRY**, about 13km west, where there are some extraordinary Renaissance **gardens** set out on several terraces with marvellous views over the river (daily 9am–5/6.30pm; gardens till 5.30/7.30pm; €7.50, €5 gardens only). The handsome château holds Spanish paintings and a Moorish ceiling from Toledo. There's no public transport, but if you rent a bike it's a wonderful ride along the banks of the Cher. Perhaps the finest Loire **château**, however, is that straddling the river at **CHENONCEAUX** (daily 9am–4.30/7pm; €7.60), about 15km from Villandry and accessible by train from Tours. The building went up in the 1520s and was the home of first Diane de Poitiers and then Catherine de Médicis, respectively the lover and wife of Henry II. There are numerous gorgeous rooms of tapestries, paintings and furniture, but the views onto the placid Cher river are the highlight – you can rent boats in summer. The **château** at **LOCHES**, an hour by train southeast of Tours, is visually the most impressive of the Loire fortresses, with ramparts and a huddle of houses below still partly enclosed by the outer wall of the medieval town (daily 9am–5/7pm; Oct–March closed noon–2pm; €5.10). You can climb to the top of the ruined keep, poke around in the dungeons and torture chamber and visit the royal lodgings, where Charles VII had his residence.

Saumur and around

SAUMUR is a peaceful and pretty town, and a good place to base yourself, with Tours and Chinon within easy reach, and the local sparkling wines available everywhere. It has a dramatic **château** (June–Aug daily 9.30am–6pm; Sept–May daily 10am–1pm & 2–5.30pm, except Nov–March closed Tues; €6), where you can visit dungeons and a watchtower, and two museums – the Musée des Arts Décoratifs and the Musée du Cheval. The immense **Abbaye de Fontévraud** (daily: June–Sept 9am–6.30pm; April, May & Oct 10am–6pm; Nov–March 10am–5.30pm; €5.50), 13km southeast of Saumur on bus #16, was founded in 1099 as both a nunnery and a monastery with an abbess in charge. Its chief significance is as the burial ground of the Plantagenet kings and queens, notably Henry II, Eleanor of Aquitaine and Richard the Lionheart. Saumur **train station** is on the north bank of the river; from here cross over the bridge to the island, then over another bridge to the main part of the town on the south bank. The **tourist office** is at the foot of the second bridge, on place de la Bilange (mid-May to mid-Oct Mon–Sat 9.15am–7pm, Sun 10.30am–12.30pm & 2.30–5.30pm; rest of the year Mon–Sat 9.15am–12.30pm & 2–6pm, Sun 10am–noon; ☎02.41.40.20.60, ⊛www.saumur-tourisme.com). The best **hotel** is *Le Cristal*, 10 place de la République (☎02.41.51.09.54; ❹), with river views from most rooms and Internet access; alternatively there's *Le Volney*, 1 rue Volney (☎02.41.51.25.41; ❷), on the south side of town. On the Île d'Offard, connected by bridges to both banks of the town, there's a good **hostel** at the eastern end of rue de Verden (☎02.41.40.30.00; €14.50), and a **campsite** next door. The best area for **eating** is around place St-Pierre: *Auberge St-Pierre*, at no. 6, has a fairly cheap menu, or try *Les Forges de St-Pierre*.

Chinon

The ruined **château** at **CHINON** (daily: April–Sept 9am–7pm; Oct–March 9.30–11.30am & 2–5.30pm; €4.60) was one of the few places in which Charles VII could stay while Henry V of England held Paris and the title to the French throne. Charles' situation changed with the arrival here in 1429 of Joan of Arc, who persuaded him to give her an army in the ruined Grande Salle. More interesting is the **Tour Coudray**, to the west, covered with intricate thirteenth-century graffiti carved by imprisoned and doomed Templar knights. Below the castle, the town suffers from day-trippers, with very few **hotels** and some tacky restaurants. Two good, inexpensive places to stay are the tiny *Hôtel de la Treille*, 4 pl Jeanne d'Arc (℡02.47.93.07.71; ❷), and the *Le Menestrel*, 102 quai Jeanne-d'Arc (℡02.47.93.07.20; ❷). Across the river at Île-Auger, the **campsite** (℡02.47.93.08.35) rents out kayaks on the River Vienne. The **tourist office** is on pl Hofheim (May–Sept daily 10am–7pm; Oct–April Mon–Sat 10am–noon & 2–6pm; ℡02.47.93.17.85, ◍www.chinon.com). The most reasonable **restaurant** is *Les Années 30*, 78 rue Voltaire.

Orléans

Due south of Paris, **ORLÉANS** continually harks back to the glory it enjoyed when Joan of Arc delivered the city from the English in 1429. The north transept of the enormous **Cathédrale Ste-Croix** (daily 9.15am–6.45pm) holds her pedestal, while the late nineteenth-century stained-glass windows in the nave tell the story of her life, with caricatures of the loutish Anglo-Saxons and snooty French nobles; and there's more on her at the **Maison de Jeanne d'Arc** on place Général-de-Gaulle (May–Oct Tues–Sun 10am–12.15pm & 1.30–6pm; Nov–April Tues–Sun 1.30–6pm; €3). If you've had your fill of Joan of Arc, head for the excellent collection of French painting in the **Musée des Beaux-Arts**, opposite the Hôtel de Ville (Tues–Sat 10am–12.15pm & 1.30–6pm, Sun 1.30–6pm; €3).

The **train station** and **tourist office** (Mon 10am–1pm & 2–6/6.30pm, Tues–Sat 9am–1pm & 2–6/6.30pm; ℡02.38.24.05.05, ◍www.ville-orleans.fr) are both on the busy place d'Arc, north of the town centre, connected by rue de la République to the central place du Martroi. There's an annexe to the tourist office near the cathedral at 6 rue Jeanne d'Arc (Mon 2–6pm; Tues–Sun 10am–6pm). Just back from the station there's an inexpensive **hotel**, *Hôtel de Paris*, 29 rue Faubourg-Bannier (℡02.38.53.39.58; ❷), and in the centre, you could try the *Charles Sanglier*, 8 rue Charles Sanglier (℡02.38.53.38.50; ❸). The **hostel** is at 14 rue Faubourg-Madeleine, fifteen minutes' walk to the west of town, and accessible on buses #4 or #8 from the train station (℡02.38.53.60.06; €7.80; closed Dec & Jan). Bus #26 goes to the **campsite** at St-Jean-de-la-Ruelle, 3km out on the Blois road on rue de la Roche (℡02.38.88.39.39). Rue de Bourgogne, parallel to the river, has a good choice of snack bars and **restaurants** of which *La Petite Marmite*, at no. 178, serving traditional French food, is one of the best. Another good bet is the bustling *Brin de Zinc*, at 62 rue Ste-Catherine, just off place du Martroi. **Internet** access is at Odysseus, 32 rue du Colombier.

Poitou-Charente and the Atlantic coast

The summer light, the warmth, the fields of sunflowers and the siesta-silent air of the farmhouses of **Poitou-Charente** give the first exciting promise of the south. The coast has great charm in places – it remains distinctly Atlantic, with dunes, pine forests and misty mud flats, and lacks much of the glitz and glamour of the Côte d'Azur. The principal port, **La Rochelle**, is one of the prettiest and most distinctive towns in France, and the island of **Ré**, out of season at least, is lovely, with kilometres of sandy beaches. **Poitiers** is a likely entry point to the region, a pleasant enough town with an attractive old centre. South of here, the valley of the Charente river, slow and green, epitomizes blue-overalled, peasant France, accessible on boat trips from **Cognac**, famous for its brandy.

Poitiers

POITIERS is a country town with a charm that comes from a long and sometimes influential history as seat of the dukes of Aquitaine, discernible in the winding lines of the streets and the breadth of architectural fashions of its buildings. The tree-lined **place Leclerc**, and **place de Gaulle** just a few streets north, are the two poles of communal life, flanked by cafés and market stalls. Between is a web of streets, with rue Gambetta cutting north past the **Palais de Justice** (daily 8.45am–noon & 1.45–5.30pm; free), whose nineteenth-century façade hides the twelfth-century great Gothic hall of the dukes of Aquitaine. This magnificent room is where Jean, Duc de Berry, held his sumptuous court in the late fourteenth century, seated on the intricately carved dais at the far end of the room. In one corner, stairs give access to the old castle keep and lead out onto the roof with a memorable view over the town. Across from the Palais is one of the most idiosyncratic churches in France, **Notre-Dame-la-Grande** (Mon–Sat 8.30am–7pm, Sun 2–7pm), whose west front is loaded with enthralling sculpture, typical of the Poitou brand of Romanesque. There is another unusual church a little way east, literally in the middle of rue Jean-Jaurès as you head towards the River Clain. This is the mid-fourth-century **Baptistère St-Jean** (April–Oct daily 10/10.30am–12.30pm & 2.30/3–8pm; rest of the year daily 2.30–4.30pm; €0.60), reputedly the oldest Christian building in France and until the seventeenth century the only place in town to conduct a proper baptism; the font was the octagonal pool sunk into the floor. There are also some ancient and faded frescoes on the walls, including one of the Emperor Constantine on horseback.

Poitiers **train station** is at the foot of the hill that forms the kernel of the town, from where it's a ten-minute walk up to the centre. Cheap **hotels** nearby include the *Bistrot de la Gare* at 131 bd du Grand Cerf (℡05.49.58.56.30; ❷), and the *Petite Villette*, 14 bd de l'Abbé de Frémont (℡05.49.41.41.33, ℻05.49.50.09.77 ❸); in the town centre there's the attractive *Plat d'Étain*, 7–9 rue du Plat d'Étain (℡05.49.41.04.80; ℻05.49.52.25.84; ❹). The **hostel** is at 1 allée Roger Tagault (℡05.49.30.09.70; €8.85; bus #3 or #7) and there's a municipal **campsite** on rue du Porteau, 2km north of town (℡05.49.41.44.88, ℻05.49.46.41.91; closed Sept–June; bus #7). The **tourist office** is at 45 Pl Charles de Gaulle (Mon–Sat 9.30/10am–6/7.30pm; April–Oct also Sun 10am–6pm; ℡05.49.41.21.24, ☏www.mairie-poitiers.fr). *Le St-Hubert*, 13 rue Cloche Perse, does regional food at reasonable prices, and *Le Cappuccino*, on 5 rue de l'Université, is one of several good Italian **restaurants**.

La Rochelle

LA ROCHELLE is the most attractive seaside town in France, with a beautiful seventeenth- and eighteenth-century centre and waterfront and a lively, bustling air. Eleanor of Aquitaine gave it a charter in 1199, and it rapidly became a port of major importance, trading in salt and wine, the principal terminus for trade with the French colonies in the West Indies and Canada. Indeed, many of the settlers, especially in Canada, came from this part of France. The heavy Gothic gateway of the **Porte de la Grosse Horloge** straddles the entrance to the old town, dominating the pleasure-boat-filled inner harbour, overlooked by two towers. Through the Grosse Horloge, the main shopping street of **rue du Palais** is lined by eighteenth-century houses and arcaded shop fronts. To the west, especially in **rue de l'Escale**, are the discreet residences of the eighteenth-century ship owners and chandlers, while to the east, rue du Temple leads to the **Hôtel de Ville**, begun in the reign of Henri IV, whose initials, intertwined with those of Marie de Médici, are carved on the ground-floor gallery. It's a beautiful specimen of Frenchified Italian taste, adorned with niches and statues and coffered ceilings. There's more of this rich world in the **Musée du Nouveau Monde**, 10 rue Fleuriau (Mon & Wed–Sat 10.30am–12.30pm & 1.30–6pm, Sun 3–6pm; €3.50), which occupies the former residence of the Fleuriau family, who, like many of their fellow *Rochelais*, made fortunes from slaving and West Indian sugar, spices and coffee. For **beaches**, you're best off crossing over to the **Île de Ré**, a long narrow island immediately west of La Rochelle (buses from place de Verdun or pricey boat trips from the Vieux Port), which is surrounded by sandy strands. Out of season it has a slow, misty charm, with life in its little ports revolving around the cultivation of oysters and mussels, although in the summer you'll find it packed.

From the **train station**, it's ten minutes down av de Gaulle to the town centre. The **tourist office** is by the harbour on pl de la Petite Sirène, Quai de Gabut (Jul & Aug Mon–Sat 9am–8pm, Sun 11am–5pm; June & Sept Mon–Sat 9am–7pm, Sun 11am–1/5pm; rest of the year Mon–Sat 9am–6pm, Sun 10am–1pm; ☎05.46.41.14.68, ☜www.larochelle-tourisme.fr). You should book accommodation in advance in summer. There's a **hostel** in av des Minimes to the west (☎05.46.44.43.11; €12.70; bus #10 from pl de Verdun or the train station) and two **campsites** – the *Soleil* by the hostel (☎05.46.44.42.53; closed mid-Sept to mid-May) and the *Port Neuf*, on the northwestern side of town on bd A. Rondeau (☎05.46.43.81.20; bus #6 from Grosse Horloge). Of the handful of budget **hotels**, the best central bets are the *Bordeaux*, 45 rue St-Nicolas (☎05.46.41.31.22, ☜hbordeaux@wanadoo.fr; ➍), which is atmospheric but a bit noisy, and the friendly *Henri-IV*, 31 rue des Gentilshommes (☎05.46.41.25.79, ☜05.46.41.78.64; ➌). For **food**, try the area around rue du Port and rue St-Sauveur just off the waterfront, and rue St-Nicolas. *À Côté de Chez Fred*, 34 rue St-Nicolas, serves fresh fish in a homely atmosphere, and *Café de la Poste*, pl de l'Hôtel de Ville, also has decent menus. For **Internet** access, aim for Squatt, 63 rue St-Nicolas.

Cognac

COGNAC is a sunny, prosperous little town, best known for its brandy distilleries, which reveal themselves through the heady scent that pervades the air. The **tourist office**, close by the central pl François I, 16 rue du 14 juillet (daily: July & Aug 9am–7pm, otherwise 9.30/10am–5/5.30pm; ☎05.45.82.10.71, ☜www.tourism-cognac.com), has information on visiting the various cognac *chais*, most of which are at the end of Grand-Rue, which winds through the old quarter of town. Perhaps the best for a visit are those of **Hennessy** at 1 rue de la Richonne (March–Dec daily 10am–5/6pm; Jan & Feb Mon–Fri by appointment only; ☎05.45.35.72.68, ☜www.hennessy-cognac.com; €5.30), a seventh-generation family firm of Irish origin, where tours begin with a film explaining what's what in the world of cognac. Hennessy alone keeps 180,000 barrels in stock; all are regularly checked and various blends made from barrel to barrel. Only the best is retained, a choice that depends on the taste buds of the *maître du chais*. The present heir apparent has already been under his father's tutelage for two decades and is still said to not yet be fully qualified. From the **train station**, take rue Mousnier, then rue Bayard, which leads up rue du 14-Juillet to place François I. There are a couple of **cafés** and a reasonable **brasserie** on the square or try the excellent *La Boîte à Sel*, 68 av Victor Hugo. The cheapest **rooms** are at *Le Cheval Blanc*, 6–8 pl Bayard (☎05.45.82.09.55, ☜lechevalblanccognac@free.fr; ➍); while the *Hotel d'Orléans* at 25 rue d'Angoulême (☎05.45.82.01.26, ☜VRBonnin@aol.com; ➌) is slightly more upmarket. Upstream from the bridge, the oak woods of the Parc François I stretch along the riverbank to the town **campsite** (☎05.42.32.13.32; closed mid-Oct to April).

Aquitaine, the Dordogne and the Lot

Steamy, moist and green, the southwest of France can feel like a lower-latitude England. In the **Dordogne** heartlands, the country is certainly beautiful, but the more famous spots, especially in the Dordogne valley, have become oppressively crowded in season. **Bordeaux** is the main entry point to the region, and makes a stimulating base for those interested in wine. East of Bordeaux, the **Périgord Blanc** is named for the light, white colour of its rock outcrops – undulating, fertile, wooded country, rising in the north and east to the edge of the Massif Central. The regional capital is **Périgueux**, which, because of its central position and relative ease of access, makes the best base for the whole region, especially for the cave paintings at **Les Eyzies** and around. The **Périgord Noir** is the stretch of territory from Bergerac to Brive. It's this area that people tend to think of when you say Dordogne – not only picture-book villages, but cuisine at its richest and prices at their highest. To the south lies the drier, poorer and more sparsely populated region through which the **River Lot** flows, an ideal area to hike, bike and camp.

Bordeaux

Famous the world over for the wines of the surrounding countryside, **BORDEAUX** is a bustling city, though with few major sights of interest outside its grand eighteenth-century centre. Wine *aficionados* won't want to miss a wine tour or the biennial **Fête de Vin**, a four day celebration of local viticulture and gastronomy held in June. Although it's the wines, rather than the landscape, that are the draw, within a day trip from Bordeaux you will find the vast pine-covered expanses of Les Landes and wild Atlantic **beaches**. The centre of the city is **place Gambetta**; conceived in the time of Louis XV. In one corner, the eighteenth-century arch of the Porte Dijeaux spans the street. East, cours de l'Intendance, full of chic shops, leads to the impeccably classical 1780 **Grand Théâtre** on place de la Comédie. Cours du 30-juillet leads into **Esplanade des Quinconces**, said to be Europe's largest municipal square, with a memorial to the Girondins, the influential local deputies to the Revolutionary Assembly of 1789, purged by Robespierre as counter-revolutionaries. Rue Ste-Catherine leads down from place de la Comédie towards the best of the city's museums, the **Musée d'Aquitaine** at 20 cours Pasteur (Tues–Sun 11am–6pm; €4), illustrating the history of the region from prehistoric times through to the 1800s. To the east stand the cathedral of **St-André** (Mon–Fri 7.30–11.30am, Sun 8am–12.30pm; free) with its slender twin spires, and the classical **Hôtel de Ville**. Around the corner at 20 cours d'Albret, the **Musée des Beaux-Arts** (Mon & Wed–Sun 11am–6pm; €4) displays works by Rubens, Matisse and Renoir, as well as Lacour's 1804 evocative Bordeaux dockside scene, *Quai des Chartrons*.

Along with Burgundy and Champagne, the **wines** of Bordeaux form the Holy Trinity of French viticulture. The reds in particular – known as claret to the English – have graced the tables of the discerning for centuries, produced from districts such as Médoc, Haut-Médoc, Bourg, Blaye, Pomerol and St-Émilion. South of the city is the domain of the great whites, notably the super-dry Graves and the sweet dessert wines of Sauternes. The **Maison du Vin de Bordeaux**, at 3 cours du 30-Juillet (Mon–Fri 9am–5.30pm; ☎05.56.00.22.66, ✉ecole@vins-bordeaux.fr) has information on châteaux visits and wine-tasting, as does the Bordeaux tourist office, which also organizes half-day **wine tours** (April to mid-Nov daily at 1.30pm; mid-Nov to March Wed & Sat only; €26) and two-hour *dégustations* (mid-July to mid-Aug Thurs & Sat 4.30pm; rest of the year Thurs only; €20, including meal).

Practicalities

Bordeaux **airport**, 12km west, is connected by regular shuttle **bus** (daily 7am–10.45pm; 30–45min; €6) to place Gambetta and the **train station**, the gare St-Jean (from here take bus #7 or #8 to the centre, €1.15). The main **tourist office** is at 12 cours du 30-Juillet, north of place de la Comédie (Mon–Sat 9am–6.30/7.30pm, Sun 9/9.30am–4.30/6.30pm; ☎05.56.00.66.00, ⦿www .Bordeaux-tourisme.com). For **accommodation**, try the *Hôtelière la Terrasse*, 20 rue St-Vincent de Paul (☎05.56.33.46.46, ⦿www.hotellaterrasse.fr; ❹); *Bristol*, on pl Gambetta (☎05.56.81.85.01, ✉bristol@hotel-bordeaux.com; ❸); or *Acanthe*, 12-14 rue St-Rémi (☎05.56.81.66.58, ⦿www.acanthe-hotel-bordeaux.com; ❹). The **hostel** is near the station, on cours Barbey (☎05.56.33.00.71; €16). There are a lot of inexpensive **restaurants** in the station quarter, and along the left bank of the river near the station; try the *Café des Arts* on the corner of rue St-Catherine and cours Victor-Hugo. For typical French cooking there's *Croc-Loup*, 45 rue du Loup.

Rue St-Rémi has a good range of international restaurants, including *Peperoni*, at no. 57. The city's lively **bars** include the *Frog & Rosbif*, a themed "British" pub at 23 rue Ausone, and the Cuban style *Calle Ocho* at 24 rue des Pilliers-de-Tutelle. There's **Internet access** at Cyberstation, 23 cours Pasteur.

Périgueux

PÉRIGUEUX, a busy and prosperous market town, makes a good base for seeing the best of the Dordogne's prehistoric caves. The centre of town focuses on **place Bugeaud**, a ten-minute walk from the train station. Ahead, down rue Taillefer, the **Cathédrale de St-Front** – its square, pineapple-capped belfry surging above the roofs of the surrounding medieval houses – is one of the most distinctive Romanesque churches in France. Outside, place de la Clautre gives on to Périgueux's renovated old quarter, with a number of fine Renaissance houses, particularly along rue Limogeanne. The **Musée du Périgord**, at the end of rue St-Front, at 22 cours de Tourny (Mon & Wed–Fri 10am–5pm, Sat & Sun 1–6pm; €4), has some beautiful Gallo-Roman mosaics from local sites. The **tourist office** is at 26 pl Francheville (Mon–Sat 9am–7pm; June–Sept also Sun 10am–6pm; ☎05.53.53.10.63, ⊛www.ville-perigueux.fr), next to the Tour Mataguerre, the last remnant of the town's medieval defences. There are some good, inexpensive **hotels** in the centre of town, like the riverside *Hôtel des Barris*, 2 rue Pierre Magne (☎05.53.53.04.05, ℻05.53.05.19.08; ❸), which has a great view of the cathedral. Opposite the train station, at 14 rue Denis-Papin, is the more modern *Comfort Hôtel Régina* (☎05.53.08.40.44, ℮comfort.perigueux@wanadoo.fr; ❹). Alternatively, there is a **campsite** on the river, *Barnabé Plage* (☎05.53.53.41.45, ℻05.53.54.16.62). Périgueux isn't greatly blessed with decent **restaurants**, but *Hercule Poireau*, 2 rue de la Nation, and the rather cheaper *L'Amandier*, 12 rue Eguillerie, are good places to try some of the local specialities.

The Vézère valley caves

Half-an-hour or so by train from Périgueux is a luxuriant cliff-cut region riddled with **caves** and subterranean streams. Cro-Magnon skeletons were first unearthed here in 1868, and an incredible wealth of archeological evidence of the life of late Stone Age people has since been found. The paintings that adorn the caves – perhaps to aid fertility or hunting rituals – are remarkable not only for their age, but also for their exquisite colouring and the skill with which they are drawn.

LES EYZIES is the centre of the region, a rambling, unattractive village given over to tourism. **Trains** run daily to Les Eyzies; the Périgueux tourist office issues a sheet detailing how to get there and back in a day. Worth a glance before or after visiting the caves is the **Musée National de la Préhistoire** (July & Aug 9.30am–6.30pm; rest of the year Mon & Wed–Sun 9.30am–12.30pm & 2–5.30pm; €4.50), which exhibits prehistoric artefacts and art objects including copies of one of the most beautiful pieces of Stone Age art – two clay bison from the Tuc d'Audoubert cave in the Pyrenees. Just outside Les Eyzies, off the road to Sarlat, the tunnel-like **Grotte de Font de Gaume** (daily: May to mid-Sept 9.30am–5.30pm; rest of the year 9.30am–12.30pm & 2–5.30pm; €6.10) contains dozens of polychrome paintings, most miraculous of which is a frieze of five bison, the colour remarkably preserved by a protective layer of calcite. Only twenty people are allowed in at any one time and tickets sell out fast; get there at least an hour before opening. Les Eyzies' **tourist office** at 19 rue de la Préhistoire (June–Sept Mon–Sat 9am–7pm, Sun 9/10am–noon & 2–5/6pm; rest of year Mon–Sat 9am–noon & 2–6pm, Sun 10am–noon & 2–5pm; ☎05.53.06.97.05, ⊛www.leseyzies.com) has information on private rooms in the area and rents out bikes.

Abri du Cap Blanc (daily: April–June, Sept & Oct 10am–noon & 2–6pm; July & Aug 10am–7pm; €5.60) is a steep but manageable 7km bike ride from Les

Eyzies. Not a cave but a rock shelter, its 15,000-year-old sculpted frieze of horses and bison is polished and set off against a pockmarked background in extraordinary high relief. Of the ten surviving prehistoric sculptures in France, this is the best. The road up takes you past the **Grotte des Combarelles** (mid-May to mid-Sept daily 9.30am–5.30pm; rest of the year 9.30am–12.30pm & 2–5.30pm; Jan–April closed Sat; €6.10, bookings at Font de Gaume), whose engravings of humans, reindeer and mammoths dating from the Magdalanian period are also worth a visit.

Up the valley of the Vézère river to the northeast, **MONTIGNAC** is more attractive than Les Eyzies but is of prime interest for the cave paintings at nearby **Lascaux** – or, rather, for a tantalizing replica, Lascaux II (Feb–Dec Tues–Sun 10am–noon & 2-5.30pm; July & Aug daily 9am–7pm; closed Jan; €8); the original has been closed since 1963 due to deterioration caused by the breath and body heat of visitors. Executed 17,000 years ago, the paintings are said to be the finest prehistoric works in existence. There are five or six identifiable styles, and subjects include the bison, mammoth and horse, plus the biggest-known prehistoric drawing in existence of a bull with astonishingly expressive head and face. Tickets are available from the **tourist office** on pl Bertran-de-Born (Mon–Sat 10am–1pm & 3–6pm; ☎05.53.51.82.60, ⓦwww.bienvenue-montignac.com); visits last forty minutes, and the commentary is in French, with English translation if requested. Montignac is short on moderately priced **accommodation**, though the *Hôtel de la Grotte*, 63 rue du 4 Septembre (☎05.53.51.80.48, ⓔhoteldelagrotte@wanadoo.fr; ❸), is a rare exception. There is also a **campsite**, *Le Moulin du Bleufond*, a short walk away on the riverbank (☎05.53.51.83.95; closed Nov–March).

Bergerac

Lying on the banks of the Dordogne southeast of Périgueux, **BERGERAC** is the main market centre for the surrounding maize, vine and tobacco farms. Devastated in the Wars of Religion, when most of its Protestant population fled overseas, it is essentially a modern town, yet what's left of the old quarter has a lot of charm. In rue de l'Ancien-Pont the seventeenth-century Maison Peyrarède houses a **tobacco museum** (Tues–Fri 10am–noon & 2–6pm; mid-April to mid-Nov also Sat & Sun 2–6pm; July & Aug also Mon 2–6pm; €3), detailing the history of the weed, with collections of pipes and tools of the trade. The **train station** is on av du 108e Régiment d'Infantrie, a short walk north of the town centre. The **tourist office** is at 97 rue Neuve d'Argenson (July & Aug daily 9.30am–7.30pm; rest of the year Mon–Sat 9.30am–1pm & 2–7pm; ☎05.53.57.03.11, ⓦwww.bergerac-tourisme.com). For **accommodation**, try *Le Colombier de Cyrano et Roxane*, 17 pl de la Myrpe (☎05.53.57.96.70; ⓔbluemoon2@club-Internet.fr; ❹), a lovely small hotel in a renovated sixteenth century house, or for a bit more luxury, the *Hôtel de Bordeaux*, 38 pl Gambetta (☎05.53.57.12.83, ⓦwww.hotel-bordeaux-bergerac.com; ❺), a three-star place with a swimming pool and pleasant garden. There's also a **campsite**, *La Pelouse* (☎ & ⓕ05.53.57.06.67), ten minutes' walk north of the centre, by the river.

The Pyrenees

Basque-speaking and humid in the west, snowy and Occitan-speaking in the middle, dry and Catalan in the east, **the Pyrenees** are physically beautiful, culturally varied and a great deal less developed than the Alps. The whole range is marvellous walking country, especially the central region containing the **Parc National des Pyrénées**, with its 3000-metre-high peaks, streams, forests, flowers and wildlife. If you're a serious hiker, you can walk all the way across from Atlantic to Mediterranean between June and September, following the GR10 or the more difficult *Haute Randonnée Pyrénéenne* (HRP) between well-spaced alpine refuges –

although bear in mind that these are big mountains, and to do any of the trail sections you'll need hiking boots and, despite the southerly latitude, warm and windproof clothing. As for more conventional tourist attractions, the **Basque coast** is lovely but very popular, suffering from seaside sprawl and a surfeit of caravan sites. **St-Jean-de-Luz** is much the prettiest of the resorts, while **Bayonne** is the most attractive town, with an excellent Basque museum and art gallery; **Biarritz** has the best surf. The foothill towns are generally dull, but **Pau** is worth a day or two, while **Lourdes** is a monster of kitsch that has to be seen to be believed.

Biarritz

BIARRITZ is a nineteenth-century resort once patronized by French Emperor Napoleon III – who built a seaside palace for Empress Eugénie here – and an impressive list of European aristocracy and royalty. Today it still has an air of quiet gentility out of season, while crashing waves make Biarritz Europe's premier summer surfing venue, with a prestigious competition held each July. The town's beaches – particularly the central **Grande Plage** – are the main attraction, while there are also a few small museums to provide diversion on a rainy day. The **Musée de la Mer**, on the Esplanade du Rocher de la Vierge (daily: July & Aug 9.30am–midnight; rest of the year 9.30am–12.30pm & 2–6pm; €7) has an interesting collection from the Bay of Biscay in its aquarium, plus a rooftop seal pool. Sweet-toothed visitors may prefer a look round the small **Musée du Chocolat**, 14 av Beaurivage (daily 10am–noon & 2.30–6/7pm; €5), with its gallery of remarkably intricate sculptures, all made out of chocolate. **Asiatica**, at 1 rue Guy Petit (Mon–Fri 10.30am–6.30pm, Sat & Sun 2–7pm; €7), holds one of Europe's most important collections of oriental art, dating from prehistoric to modern times.

Biarritz **train station** lies 3km southeast of the centre in La Negresse district, at the end of av Kennedy. Buses #2 and #9 run from there to square d'Ixelles, where you'll find the **tourist office** (daily: July & Aug 8am–8pm; rest of the year Mon-Sat 9-6pm, Sun 10am-5pm; ☎05.59.22.37.00, ⊛www.biarritz.tm.fr). There's a limited amount of reasonably priced **accommodation** in town, which must be booked weeks in advance during summer. Try *Le Baron de Biarritz*, south of the centre above an affordable Vietnamese restaurant at 13 av Maréchal Joffre (☎05.59.22.08.22; ❷), or the *Rocher de la Vierge*, 13 rue de Port Vieux (☎05.59.24.11.74; ❸), towards the quieter end of this central street leading down to a protected beach. There's a **hostel** at 8 rue Chiquito de Cambo (☎05.59.41.76.00; ❷), 2km southwest of town by Lac Mouriscot. For **food** - specifically grills and seafood for under €25 - head to *Le Surfing*, behind Plage de la Côte des Basques, festooned with antique boards. With Spain just a stone's throw away, tapas bars are much in evidence; longest-lived and most affordable is *Bar Jean* at 5 rue des Halles, beside the market. Start the day at *Salon de Thé L'Orangerie*, 1 rue Gambetta, where juice, cereal and yoghurt-enhanced breakfasts go for under €8.

Bayonne

BAYONNE continues seamlessly inland from Biarritz, though its position 6km from the Atlantic at the junction of the Nive and Adour rivers has protected the city from major touristic exploitation. With the shutters of its older half-timbered houses painted in the Basque tones of green and rust-red, Bayonne remains a distinctive and enjoyable town. The two main medieval quarters line the banks of the Nive, whose quays are home to many bars and restaurants. Close to the confluence of the two rivers, **Place de la Liberté** is the landmark square, with a stop for bus #1 (for Biarritz and the beaches) alongside the Hôtel de Ville. In the area known as "Petit Bayonne" on the Nive's right bank, stands the **Musée Basque** at Quai des Corsaires (Tues–Sun: May–Oct 10am–6.30pm; Nov–April 10am–12.30pm & 2–6pm; €5.50), giving a comprehensive overview of modern

Basque culture (though no English labelling). The city's second museum, the **Musée Bonnat** on nearby rue Jacques Laffitte (daily except Tues & Sun: May–Oct 10am–6.30pm; Nov–April 10am–12.30pm & 2–6pm; €5.50, €9 combo ticket with Musée Basque), is an unexpected treasury of art, with works by, among others, Goya, El Greco, Rubens and Degas. Across the Nive in "Grande Bayonne", the **Cathédrale Ste-Marie** looks best from a distance, its twin spires rising with airy grace above the houses; the **cloister** (daily 9am–12.30pm & 2–5/6pm; free) rewards a visit with a good view of the stained glass and buttresses.

Bayonne's **train station** is in the St-Esprit quarter on the opposite bank of the Adour from the centre, ten minutes' walk over the Pont St-Esprit. The **tourist office** is five minutes' west of the Hôtel de Ville, on pl des Basques (Mon–Sat 9/10am–6.30/7pm; July & Aug also Sun 10am–1pm; ☎05.59.46.01.46, ⊛www.bayonne-tourisme.com). Budget **accommodation** is available at the basic *Hôtel des Basques* at 4 rue des Lisses (☎05.59.59.08.02; ❷). A more comfortable choice is the *Monbar* at 24 rue Pannecau, Petit Bayonne (☎05.59.59.26.80; ❸). The closest **campsite** is well-equipped *La Chêneraie* (☎05.59.55.01.31; closed Oct-Easter), in the St-Frédéric quarter on the north bank of the Adour. Most **cafés** and **restaurants** line the Nive quays; two budget exceptions, where you can eat stylishly for under €20, are *Bar du Marché* at 39 rue des Basques (lunch only), or *Le Bistrot Ste-Cluque* at 9 rue Hughes in St-Esprit. For **live music** three nights weekly and a pint of Guinness, head to *Katie Daly's* on pl de la Liberté.

St-Jean-de-Luz

ST-JEAN-DE-LUZ is by far the most attractive resort on the Basque coast. Although crowded and with an undistinguished seafront, it boasts a long curve of beautiful fine sand while still thriving as a fishing port; the old houses around the harbour, both in St-Jean and across the water in Ciboure (essentially the same town) are very picturesque. At the heart of town is **place Louis XIV**, with its cafés, bandstand and plane trees. The seventeenth-century **Maison Louis XIV** (June–Sept Mon–Sat 10.30am–noon & 2.30–5.30/6.30pm; €5), on the harbour side of the square, was where Louis XIV stayed at the time of his marriage to Maria Theresa in 1660, and the suitably stately building houses a fine array of period furnishings. A short distance up rue Gambetta, on the town side of the square, is the large church of **St-Jean-Baptiste**, where Louis and Maria Theresa were married. The **train station** is on place de Verdun, close to the **tourist office** on pl du Maréchal-Foch (Mon–Sat 9am–12.30pm & 2–7pm, Sun 10am–1pm; July & Aug Mon–Sat 9am–8pm, Sun 10.30am–1pm & 3–7pm; ☎05.59.26.03.16; ⊛www.saint-jean-de-luz.com). Cheapest **hotels** are near the train station: *Le Verdun*, 13 av de Verdun (☎05.59.26.02.55; ❸), is comfortable and has a restaurant attached; alternatively try *Hôtel de Paris* at 1 bd du Commandant Passicot (☎05.59.85.20.20; ❷). There are plenty of **campsites** in the vicinity, all grouped together a few kilometres northwest of the town, including the *Chibau Berria* (☎05.59.26.11.94), off the N10 towards Guéthary.

Pau

Once capital of the viscounty of Béarn, **PAU** has had a turbulent history, suffering atrocities from both sides in the sixteenth-century Wars of Religion, while maintaining its independence from the French crown until being annexed by Louis XIII in 1620; even today many streets are dually signposted in Gascon (the *Béarnais* version of Occitan) as well as French. Pau is an attractive and prosperous university city, occupying a steep scarp overlooking the Gave (River) de Pau, and from **boulevard des Pyrénées** running along the rim of the scarp there are superb views of the higher peaks. Foremost among Pau's own attractions is the **Château** (daily 9.30am–12.15pm & 1.30–5.30pm; 1-hr guided visits €7), at the western end of bd des Pyrénées, now home to a museum with sumptuous eighteenth- and nineteenth-century furniture and tapestries.

From the **train station** down by the river, a free funicular shuttles you up to boulevard des Pyrénées. CITRAM and TPR **buses** to the mountains begin from rue Gachet, just off place Clemenceau. The **tourist office** is at the end of pl Royale (Mon–Sat 9am–6/6.30pm, Sun 9am–1pm; ℡05.59.27.27.08, ⊛www.ville-pau.fr). Pau is one of the best sources of information for the Parc National des Pyrénées Occidentales, which lies just to the south. Stock up on detailed maps at the Librairie des Pyrénées at 14 rue St-Louis, or stop in for advice at the **Club Alpin Français**, 5 rue René Fournets (Mon–Fri 5-7pm). There's a **hostel** in Pau at 30 rue Michel-Houneau (℡05.59.30.45.77; ❷). Among **hotels**, try *Le Matisse*, 17 rue Mathieu-Lalanne (℡05.59.27.73.80; ❸), or the soundproofed *Central* at 15 rue Léon Daran (℡05.5927.72.75; ❸). The best, most convenient local **campsite** is *Base de Plein Air* in Gélos (℡05.59.06.57.37), across the river from the train station. Numerous **restaurants** line the medieval streets near the château; at *Chez Maman*, 6 rue du Château, you can down *crêpes* and cider for under €20 while gazing at the castle. Near the hostel, *Don Quichote* at 30 rue Castetnau has Spanish-flavoured food at budget prices.

Lourdes and the mountains

In 1858 Bernadette Soubirous, 14-year-old daughter of a poor local miller in **LOURDES**, 30km southeast of Pau, had eighteen visions of the Virgin Mary in a spot called the Grotte de Massabielle, by the Gave de Pau. Miraculous cures at the grotto soon followed and Lourdes grew exponentially, now catering for six million Catholic pilgrims a year. Whole streets are devoted to the sale of religious kitsch: Bernadette, in every shape and size, adorning barometers, key rings, bottles and thermometers. At the **grotto** itself – a moisture-blackened overhang by the riverside with a statue of the Virgin inside – long queues of the faithful process through clockwise. Above looms the first, neo-Gothic church built here, in 1871, while nearby a massive subterranean **basilica** has a capacity of 20,000. Lourdes **train station** is on the northeastern edge of town. For the **tourist office** on place Peyramale turn right outside the station, then left down Chaussée Maransin (Mon–Sat 9am–noon & 2–6/7pm; Easter–Oct also Sun 11am–6pm; ℡05.62.42.77.40, ⊛www.lourdes-france.com). There's an abundance of inexpensive **hotels** on av de la Gare, and more en route to the grotto and around the castle. **Hostel** accommodation is near the western edge of town at the *Centre Pax Christi*, route de la Forêt (℡05.62.94.00.66; ❷; closed Nov–March). Closest of several **campsites** is *La Poste*, 26 rue de Langelle (℡05.62.94.40.35; closed Nov–March), between the train station and post office.

From Lourdes train station, several SNCF buses ply daily to Gavarnie and Barèges, two resorts near the heart of the **Parc National des Pyrénées Occidentales**. From either, a few hours on the GR10 or HRP brings you to staffed alpine refuges (rough camping is not generally allowed in the park). **GAVARNIE** is smaller and pricier, but has an incomparable namesake cirque towering above, forming the border with Spain. You can **stay** hostel-style at *Le Gypaète* (℡05.62.92.40.61; ❷), or **camp** at primitive but superbly set *La Bergerie* (℡05.62.92.48.41) towards the cirque. **BARÈGES** is more of a real village, with a good streamside **campsite** – *La Ribère* (℡05.62.92.69.01) – and two high-quality **gîtes** next to each other: *L'Oasis* (℡05.62.92.69.47; ❷) and *L'Hospitalet* (℡05.62.92.68.08; ❷). During mid-July, the Tour de France passes through; in winter, Barèges offers some of the best downhill skiing in the Pyrenees.

Languedoc and Roussillon

Languedoc is more an idea than a geographical entity. The modern region covers only a fraction of the lands that stretched south from Bordeaux and Lyon into Spain and northwest Italy where once *Occitan* or the *langue d'Oc* was spoken. Although things are changing, the sense of being Occitanian remains strong, a regional identity that dates back to the Middle Ages, when the castles and fortified villages were the final refuges of the Cathars, a heretical religious sect. The old Roman town of **Nîmes** is one entry point; beyond, **Montpellier** is a good base, though otherwise the coast is not generally noteworthy, the beaches for the most part windswept and cut off from their hinterland by marshy lakes. The picturesque medieval town of **Carcassonne** is an enjoyable diversion, as is **Toulouse**, the elegant cultural capital. South of Languedoc, **Roussillon**, or French Catalonia, maintains much of its Catalan identity, though there is little support nowadays for political independence or reunification with Spanish Catalunya, of which it was a part until the seventeenth century. Its hills and valleys provide some fine walking, and although the coast is again something of a disappointment, the region's main town, **Perpignan**, is an attractive place.

Nîmes

NÎMES is inescapably linked to two things: Rome – whose influence is manifest in some of the most extensive Roman remains in Europe – and denim, a word corrupted from *de Nîmes*. Denim was first manufactured as *serge* in the city's textile mills and exported by a certain Mr Levi-Strauss to the USA to clothe miners. The old centre of Nîmes spreads northwards from place des Arènes, site of the magnificent first-century **Les Arènes** (daily 9am–noon & 2–5/6.30pm; €4.45), one of the best-preserved Roman arenas in the world, still capable of holding 20,000 spectators. Four centuries after it was built, and with the Roman Empire crumbling away, the arena was turned into a fortress by invading Visigoths. Eventually, it became a slum, home to some two thousand people until the early 1800s, but now it's been restored it hosts bullfights, opera and an international jazz festival every summer. The other Roman survivor is found northeast along boulevard Victor Hugo, where the **Maison Carrée** (daily 9am–noon & 2pm–6/7pm; free) is a compact temple built in 5 AD and celebrated for its harmony of proportion. You can buy a **museum pass** (€9.95) from the Arena, which gives access to all the town's other attractions for three days. These include the **Musée Archéologique** and the **Muséum d'Histoire Naturelle** (Tues–Sun 11am–6pm; €4.45 for both museums), housed in a seventeenth-century chapel on bd Amiral-Courbet, which hold a sizeable collection of Roman artefacts. Further out, across rue de la Libération, the **Musée des Beaux-Arts** on rue Cité Foulc (daily 11am–6pm; €4.45) prides itself on a huge Gallo-Roman mosaic showing the *Marriage of Admetus*. Roman history aside, there's also an excellent **Musée d'Art Contemporain** (Tues–Sun 11am–6pm; €4.45), designed by Norman Foster and home to an impressive collection of post-1960 art.

Nîmes **train station** is at the end of av Feuchères. The main **tourist office** is at 6 rue Auguste, by the Maison Carrée (Mon–Sat 8/9am–7/8pm, Sun 10am–6pm; ☎04.66.58.38.00, ⓦwww.ot-nimes.fr). To stay in the heart of things, try the enticing *Hôtel Lisita*, at 2 bis bd des Arènes (☎04.66.67.66.20; ➋), or nearby *Cat*, 22 bd Amiral-Courbet (☎04.66.67.22.85; ➋). There's a **hostel** 2km northwest of town on Chemin de la Cigale (☎04.66.23.25.04; €9), which also has tent space. The main **campsite** is the *Domaine de la Bastide* on route de Générac (☎04.66.38.09.21), 5km south of the centre. For good regional **food** at reasonable prices, try *La Belle Respire*, 12 rue de l'Étoile. Place du Marché and boulevard Amiral-Courbet are home to several good cafés and brasseries, while bd Victor Hugo has plenty of lively spots for a drink. Netgames offers **Internet** access just behind the temple, at place de la Maison Carrée.

Montpellier

MONTPELLIER is a vibrant city, renowned for its ancient university, once attended by such luminaries as Petrarch and Rabelais. Ruled over by the Kings of Mallorca for almost a hundred and fifty years during the Middle Ages, it's a cosmopolitan place, which today is the regional capital of Languedoc-Roussillon. At the town's hub is **place de la Comédie**, a grand oval square paved with cream-coloured marble and surrounded by cafés. The **Opéra**, an ornate nineteenth-century theatre, presides over one end, while the other end leads onto the pleasant park of the Champs du Mars. Nearby, the much-vaunted **Musée Fabre** is closed until 2006. Behind the Opéra lie the tangled, hilly lanes of Montpellier's **old quarter**, full of seventeenth- and eighteenth-century mansions and small museums. One of the more interesting, at 7 rue Jacques-Coeur, is the **Musée Languedocien** (Mon–Sat 2–5/6pm; €5), which houses an eclectic display of ceramics, furniture and tapestries. At the end of rue Foch, on the western edge of town, are the formal gardens of the Place du Peyrou. The **Jardin des Plantes** (Mon–Sat 8.30/10am–noon & 2-5/6pm; free), just north of here, with its alleys of exotic trees, is France's oldest botanical garden, founded in 1593.

The **train station** is next to the **bus station** on the southern edge of town, a short walk down rue Maguelone. The main **tourist office** is in the passage du Tourisme, at the top end of place de la Comédie (Mon–Fri 9am–6/7.30pm, Sat 10am–6pm, Sun 10am–1pm & 2–5pm; ☎04.67.60.60.60, ⊛www.ot-montpellier.fr); there's also a desk in the train station during July and August. There are numerous **hotels** between the stations and place de la Comédie: the basic *Floride*, 1 rue François-Perrier (☎04.67.65.73.30; ❸), and *des Étuves*, 24 rue des Étuves (☎04.67.60.78.19; ❷), are both worth a try. The **hostel** is on rue des Écoles-Laïques (☎04.67.60.32.22; €12.70), and there's a municipal **campsite** (☎04.67.15.11.61) just south of town on the D21 (bus #28). Of the large number of **restaurants** in town, try *La Diligence*, 2 pl Pétrarque, or *Caves Jean-Jaurès*, 3 rue Callot, for traditional French cuisine. *Tripti Kulai*, 20 rue Jacques-Coeur, is a good vegetarian restaurant. Most of the lively **nightlife** scene is centred on place de la Comédie, place du Marché-aux-Fleurs and place Jean-Jaurès. For **Internet** access, make for Cybersurf, 22 pl du Millénaire.

Carcassonne

CARCASSONNE, on the main Toulouse–Montpellier train link, is one of the most dramatic (if also most commercialized) towns in Languedoc. It owes its division into two separate "towns", the Cité and Ville Basse, to the Cathar wars of the Middle Ages. Following Simon de Montfort's capture of the town in 1209, its people tried to restore their traditional ruling family, the Trencavels, in 1240. In reprisal King Louis IX expelled them, only permitting their return on condition they built on the low ground by the River Aude. The main attraction is the **Cité**, a double-walled and turreted **fortress-town** crowning the hill above the Aude like a scene from a medieval fairy-tale. Viollet-le-Duc rescued it from ruin in 1844, and his rather romantic restoration has been furiously debated ever since. Inevitably, it's become a real tourist trap, with its narrow lanes lined with innumerable souvenir shops and regularly crammed with hordes of day-trippers. There is no charge for admission to the main part of the city, or the grassy *lices* (moat) between the walls. However, to see the inner fortress of the **Château Comtal**, with its small **museum** of medieval sculpture, and to walk along the walls, you have to join a guided tour (daily 9.30am–5/7.30pm; €5.50). In addition to wandering the narrow streets, don't miss the beautiful church of **St-Nazaire** at the end of rue St-Louis (daily 9–noon & 2–5/7pm), a serene combination of Romanesque nave with carved capitals, and Gothic transepts and choir. Especially attractive are the two colourful Rose windows, dating from the thirteenth and fourteenth centuries.

The **tourist office** is at 15 bd Camille-Pelletan, at the end of place Gambetta in the Ville Basse (July & Aug daily 9am–6pm; Sept–June Mon–Sat 9am–12.30pm & 1.30–6pm; ☎04.68.10.24.30, ⊛www.carcassonne.org), with an annexe in the Tours Narbonnaises in the Cité (daily 9am–5/7pm). **Accommodation** in the Cité is pricey, apart from the 120-bed **hostel** on rue du Vicomte Trencavel (☎04.68.25.23.16; €12.70; closed mid-Dec to Jan), and you're better off at a **hotel** in the Ville Basse, such as the faded but comfortable glory of the *Grand Hôtel Terminus*, 2 av de Maréchal Joffre (☎04.68.25.25.00; ❹). The nearest **campsite**, *Camping de la Cité*, is off route de St-Hilaire (☎04.68.25.11.17) just west of the Cité (bus #8). There's an abundance of reasonably priced **restaurants** in the Cité, with several touristy, but very good, brasseries located around place Marcou – try *Auberge de Dame Carcas*, 3 pl du Château, which serves good regional dishes, especially *cassoulet*.

Toulouse

TOULOUSE is one of the most vibrant provincial cities in France, a result of a policy to make it the centre of hi-tech industry. Always an aviation centre – St-Exupéry and Mermoz flew out from here on their pioneering flights over Africa in the 1920s – Toulouse is now home to Aérospatiale, the driving force behind Airbus and the Ariane space rocket. Added zest comes from its large student population, second only to that of Paris. The centre of Toulouse is a rough hexagon clamped around a bend in the wide, brown River Garonne. The **Musée des Augustins**, 21 rue de Metz (Mon & Thurs–Sun 10am–6pm, Wed 10am–9pm; €2.20), incorporates the two cloisters of an Augustinian priory and houses collections of outstanding Romanesque and Gothic sculpture, much of it saved from the now-vanished churches of Toulouse's golden age. Outside the museum, the main shopping street, **rue Alsace-Lorraine**, runs north. West of here are the cobbled streets of the **old city**, lined with the ornate *hôtels* of the merchants who grew rich on the woad trade, the city's economy base until the sixteenth century. The predominant building material is the flat Toulousain brick, whose cheerful rosy colour gives the city its nickname of *ville rose*. Best known of these palaces is the **Hôtel Assézat**, towards the river end of rue de Metz, which houses the marvellous private art collection of the **Fondation Bemberg** (Tues–Sun 10am–6pm, Thurs till 9pm; €4.60), which includes excellent works by Bonnard. Modern art is on display at **Les Abattoirs**, a vaulted nineteenth-century building on the west bank of the Garonne at 76 allées Charles de Fitte (Tues–Sun noon–8pm; €6.10). One highlight is an enormous theatre backdrop painted by Picasso, entitled *La dépouille de Minotaure en costume d'Arlequin*.

The **place du Capitole** is the site of Toulouse's town hall and a great meeting-place, with numerous cafés and a weekday market. Rue du Taur leads northwards to place St-Sernin and the largest Romanesque church in France, the **basilica de St-Sernin**. Begun in 1080 to accommodate the passing hordes of pilgrims, it is one of the loveliest examples of its kind. Inside, the ambulatory (daily 10am–6pm; €1.10) is worth a visit for its succession of richly housed relics and exceptional eleventh-century marble bas-reliefs. Opposite the church is the **Musée St-Raymond** (daily 10am-6/7pm; €2.20), with exhibits charting the history of the Roman town of *Tolosa*, as Toulouse was then known. West of place du Capitole, on rue Lakanal, the church of **Les Jacobins** is another unmissable ecclesiastical building, a huge fortress-like rectangle of unadorned brick, with an interior divided by a central row of slender pillars from whose capitals spring a colourful splay of vaulting ribs. Beneath the altar lie the bones of the philosopher St Thomas Aquinas, while on the north side is a calm cloister (€2.30).

Practicalities

Trains and buses arrive at the **gare Matabiau**, twenty minutes' walk from the centre down allées Jean-Jaurès or a five-minute métro ride. The **tourist office** is just behind place du Capitole, in a restored medieval tower on pl Charles de Gaulle (Mon–Sat 9am–12.30/1pm & 2–6/7pm, Sun 10am–12.30pm & 2–5pm; ☎05.61.11.02.22, ⓦwww.ot-toulouse.fr). Best of the city's central budget **hotels** are the *Castellane*, 17 rue Castellane (☎05.61.62.18.82; ❹), the slightly run-down but classic *Grand Balcon*, 8 rue Romiguières (☎05.61.21.48.08; ❸), *des Ambassadeurs*, 68 rue Bayard (☎05.61.62.65.84; ❷), and *Ours Blanc*, next to the covered market at 25 pl de Victor-Hugo (☎05.61.21.62.40; ❹). The closest **campsite** is on the chemin du Pont de Rupé, just north of the city (☎05.61.70.07.35; bus #59 from pl

Jeanne-d'Arc). There are plenty of very good **restaurants** in town. *Au Chat Deng*, 37 rue Peyrolières, offers a good-value menu in trendy surroundings, while for more classical regional cuisine try *La Bascule*, 14 av Maurice-Hauriou. Pasta-lovers can fill up from the imaginative menu at *Mille et Une Pâtes*, 1 rue Mirepoix. The food market on place Victor Hugo also houses several good, small lunchtime restaurants, while if you're just looking for a snack, try *Jour de Fête*, 43 rue de Taur. *Le Chat d'Oc* at 7 rue de Metz has a wide range of **beers**.

Albi

Though not itself an important centre of Catharism, **ALBI** gave its name to both the heresy and the crusade to suppress it (Albigensian). Today it is a small industrial town an hour's train ride northeast of Toulouse, with two sights of interest. The first, the **Cathédrale Ste-Cécile** (daily 8.30am–noon & 2–5.45/7pm; free), is visible the moment you arrive at the train station, its brutal, fortress-like exterior expressing the power and authority the church once had over the townspeople. Opposite the east end of the cathedral, rue Mariès leads into the shopping streets of the **old town**, but the most interesting sight is next door in the powerful red-brick Palais de la Berbie, which houses the **Musée Toulouse-Lautrec** (daily 9/10am–noon & 2–5/6pm; €4.50). There's a huge collection of the local lad's paintings, drawings, lithographs and posters, from the earliest work to his very last. The **tourist office** is on the corner of Palais de la Berbie and pl Ste-Cécile (Mon–Sat 9am–12.30pm & 2–6/7.30pm, Sun 10am–12.30pm & 2.30–5/6.30pm; ☎05.63.49.48.80). There's a basic *Auberge de Jeunesse* **hostel** at 13 rue de la République (☎05.63.54.53.65; €7.35); inexpensive **hotels** include the *Le Vieil Alby*, 25 rue Toulouse-Lautrec (☎05.63.54.15.69; ❹), and *St-Clair*, 8 rue St-Clair (☎05.63.54.25.66; ❸), both very central. The nearest **campsite** is the *Camping de Caussels*, about 2km east on the D999 (☎05.63.60.37.06; closed Oct–March). For local **cuisine**, try *Moulin de Mothe* on rue de Lamothe or the faintly surreal *La Tête de l'Art*, 7 rue de la Piale.

Perpignan

This far south, climate and geography alone would ensure a palpable Spanish influence, but **PERPIGNAN** is in fact of Spanish origin, being as it is the home of refugees from the Civil War and their descendants. The southern influence is further augmented by a sizeable North African community, including both Arabs and white French settlers repatriated after Algerian independence in 1962. While there are few memorable monuments, this is a pleasant city with a lively street life. Its heyday was the thirteenth and fourteenth centuries, when the kings of Mallorca held their court here, and it wasn't until 1659 that it finally became part of the French state. The centre of Perpignan is marked by the palm trees and smart cafés of **place Arago**. From here rue Alsace-Lorraine and rue de la Loge lead past the massive iron gates of the classical Hôtel de Ville to the tiny **place de la Loge**, the focus of the renovated old core, dominated by the **Loge de Mer**, a late fourteenth-century Gothic building designed to hold the city's stock exchange and a maritime court. North up rue Louis-Blanc is one of the city's few remaining fortifications, the crenellated fourteenth-century gate of **Le Castillet**, now home to the **Casa Païral**, a fascinating museum of Roussillon's Catalan folk culture (Mon & Wed–Sun 10/11am–5.30/7pm; €4.20). In the gloomy nave of the fourteenth-century **Cathédrale St-Jean**, down rue St-Jean and across place Gambetta, are some elaborate Catalan altarpieces, while a side-chapel houses a Rhenish altarpiece dating from around 1400. Through place des Esplanades, crowning the hill that dominates the southern part of the old town, is the **Palais des Rois de Majorque** (daily 9/10am–5/6pm; €3.30). Vauban's walls surround it now, but the two-storey palace and its great, arcaded courtyard date from the late thirteenth century. The Spanish–Moorish influence lends sophistication and finesse to the architecture and detailing, particularly the beautiful marble porch to the lower of the two chapels.

To get to the centre from the **train station**, follow av Général-de-Gaulle to place de la Catalogne, and then continue along boulevard Clemenceau as far as Le Castillet. The **tourist office** is a short stroll from here, in the Palais des Congrès at the end of bd Wilson (Mon–Sat 9am–6/7pm, Sun 9/10am–noon & 2–5/6pm; ☎04.68.66.30.30, ⓦwww.perpignantourisme.com). The **bus station** is by Pont Arago, on av Général-Leclerc. The best place for **accommodation** is around the train station: try the basic but comfortable *Avenir*, 11 rue de l'Avenir (☎04.68.34.20.30; ❷). The **hostel** (☎04.68.34.63.32; €11.60) is about 1km from the train station in Parc de la Pépinière by the river. The **campsite**, *Le Catalan*, is on route de Bompas (☎04.68.63.16.92), north of town. The train station is also a good area for inexpensive **food** - for traditional Catalan fare, try *La Cave*, 3 rue du Puit qui Chante.

The Massif Central

Thickly forested, and sliced by numerous rivers and lakes, the **Massif Central**, occupying a huge swathe of the middle of France, is geologically the oldest part of the country, and culturally one of the most firmly rooted in the past. Industry and tourism have made few inroads here, and the taciturn population has an enduring sense of regional identity. The heart of the region is the **Auvergne**, a wild, inaccessible landscape dotted with extinct volcanic peaks known as *puys*, much of it now incorporated into the **Parc Naturel Régional des Volcans d'Auvergne**. To the southeast are the gentler wooded hills of the **Cévennes** that form part of the **Parc National des Cévennes**. Only a handful of towns have gained a foothold in this rugged terrain. **Le Puy**, spiked with jagged pinnacles of lava and with a majestic cathedral, is the most compelling, but there is appeal, too, in the provincial capital, **Clermont-Ferrand**.

Clermont-Ferrand

CLERMONT-FERRAND is an incongruous capital for rustic Auvergne – a lively, youthful city with a major university and a manufacturing base (it's the HQ of the Michelin organization). Although hardly resplendent with cultural treats, it has a well-preserved historic centre and is an ideal base for this side of the Massif and the nearby spectacle of **Puy de Dôme** and the Parc des Volcans. Clermont and neighbouring Montferrand were united in 1630 to form a single city, but you're likely to spend most of your time in the former, since what is left of Vieux Montferrand stands out on a limb to the east. Clermont's most immediate feature is its *ville-noire* aspect – so-called for the local black volcanic rock used in the construction of many of its buildings. On the edge of old Clermont, the huge and soulless **place de Jaude** is the hub of the city and its main shopping area. In the centre stands a rousing statue of the Gallic chieftain Vercingétorix, who in 52 BC led his people to their only – and indecisive – victory over Julius Caesar. North from place de Jaude, **place St-Pierre** is the site of Clermont's principal market, with a food **market** (Mon-Sat 7am–7.30pm), at its liveliest on Saturdays. The nearby **Musée du Ranquet**, in a sixteenth-century building at 34 rue des Gras (Tues-Sun 10am-6pm; free), is one of the city's best museums, with displays on local history back to Roman times. The streets gather up to the dark and soaring **Cathédrale Notre-Dame**, whose strong volcanic stone made it possible to build vaults and pillars of unheard-of slenderness and height; off the nave, the **Tour de la Bayette** (daily 10am–5.15pm; €1.50) gives extensive views across the city. A short step northeast of the cathedral, on place Delille, stands Clermont's other great church, the **Basilique Notre-Dame du Port**, a beautiful building, pure Auvergnat Romanesque.

Clermont-Ferrand **train station** is on av de l'URSS, east of the centre, and is connected by frequent buses with place de Jaude. The **tourist office** is on pl de la Victoire (Mon–Fri 9am–6/7pm, Sat 10am–1pm & 2–6pm, Sun 9.30/

10am–12.30pm & 2–6pm; ℡04.73.98.65.00, ⓦwww.clermont-fd.com), with lots of information on **hiking** and **mountain-biking** in the area. Clermont's **hostel** is at 55 av de l'URSS (℡04.73.92.26.39; €8.40; closed Nov–March), two minutes' walk right of the station. There's a cluster of **hotels** outside the station, of which the *Grand Hôtel du Midi*, 39 av de l'URSS (℡04.73.92.44.98, ℡04.73.92.29.41; ❸), is one of the least expensive; nearer the centre is the *Foch*, 22 rue Maréchal-Foch (℡04.73.93.48.40, ⓔregina.foch@wanadoo.fr; ❸). The nearest **campsite**, *L'Oclède*, is at Royat to the west (℡04.73.35.97.05, ⓔoclede@camping-indigo.com; closed Nov–March; bus #41). For **food**, the very popular *Crêperie 1513*, 3 rue des Chaussetiers, has a fine setting in a sixteenth century mansion opposite the cathedral, while *Le Café Pascal* and *Le Bar d'O*, both nearby on place de la Victoire, offer excellent value *plats du jour*. **Internet** access is at Internet@Café, 34 rue Ballainvilliers.

Le Puy

LE PUY sprawls across a broad basin in the mountains in a muddle of red roofs barbed with poles of volcanic rock; both landscape and architecture are totally theatrical. In medieval times it was the assembly point for pilgrims heading for Santiago de Compostela in Spain, and amid the cobbled streets of the old town are some of the most richly endowed churches in the land. The surrounding countryside is an added attraction. And the town still produces its famous green Le Puy lentils. The **old town**, reached by climbing the sequence of steep streets and steps that terrace the town's *puy* foundation, is dominated by the **Cathedral** – almost Byzantine in style, striped with alternate layers of light and dark stone and capped with a line of small cupolas. The Black Virgin inside is a copy of a revered original burned during the Revolution, and is still paraded through the town every August 15. Other, lesser treasures are displayed at the back of the church in the sacristy, beyond which is the entrance to the beautiful twelfth-century **cloister** (July & Aug daily 9am–6.30pm; rest of the year daily 9am–noon & 2–5/6.30pm; €4). At the highest point in the town is the giant crimson statue of the **Virgin and Child**, fashioned from the metal of guns captured in the Crimean War; you can pay €3 to climb to the top for some stunning views. The nearby church of **St-Michel** (daily: May–Sept 9am–6.30pm; rest of the year 9.30am–noon & 2–5.30pm; €2.50), sitting on the peak of an even steeper *puy*, the Rocher d'Aiguilhe, is an eleventh-century construction that seems to grow out of the rock itself. It's a tough ascent, but one you should definitely make: St-Michel is a quirky little building decorated with mosaics, arabesques and trefoil arches, its bizarre shape following that of the available flat ground. Back down below, Le Puy's old lanes form a wonderful maze, while in the new part of town, beyond the squat Tour Pannessac, place de Breuil and place Michelet comprise the social hub, where you'll find spacious public gardens and the **Musée Crozatier** (May–Sept daily 10am–noon & 2–4/6pm; Oct–April same hours but closed Tues; €3), with exhibits illustrating the local lace industry.

Buses and trains arrive at place du Maréchal-Leclerc, a ten-minute walk from place de Breuil and the **tourist office** (Easter–Sept daily 8.30am–noon & 1.30–6.15pm; July & Aug daily 8.30am–7.30pm; Oct–Easter Mon–Sat 8.30am–noon & 1.30–6.15pm, Sun 10am–noon; ℡04.71.09.38.41, ⓦwww.ot-lepuyenvelay.fr), and within easy striking distance of some reasonably priced **hotels**, including the *Régional*, 36 bd Maréchal Fayolle (℡04.71.09.37.74; ❸). There's a **hostel** at the *Centre Pierre Cardinal*, 9 rue Jules Vallès (℡04.71.05.52.40; €7.35), and a municipal **campsite**, *Bouthézard*, half-an-hour's walk from the station along chemin de Roderie (℡04.71.09.55.09; bus #6). For inexpensive regional **food**, try *L'Âme des Poètes* or *Comme à la Maison*, both on rue Séguret.

Burgundy

Peaceful, rural **Burgundy** is one of the most prosperous regions of modern France and was for a long time independent from the French state. In the fifteenth century its dukes ruled an empire that embraced much of northeastern France, Belgium and the Netherlands, with revenues equalled only by Venice. Everywhere there is startling evidence of this former wealth and power, both secular and religious. **Dijon**, the capital, is a slick and prosperous town with plenty of remnants of old Burgundy. South, there are the famous **vineyards**, whose produce has been a major money-maker since Louis XIV's doctor prescribed the stuff for the royal dyspepsia. **Beaune** is a good centre for sampling the best of the wine, and be sure to try local specialities such as *escargots à la bourguignonne*, *bœuf bourguignon* and *coq au vin*.

Dijon

DIJON grew out of its strategic position on the merchant route from Britain up the Seine and across the Alps to the Adriatic. But it was as capital of the dukes of Burgundy from 1000 until the late 1400s that it knew its finest hour. The dukes used their tremendous wealth and power to make Dijon one of Europe's greatest centres of art, learning and science. Though it lost some of this status with incorporation into the French kingdom in 1477, it has remained one of the pre-eminent provincial cities, especially since the industrial boom of the mid-nineteenth century. You sense Dijon's former glory more in the lavish houses of its burghers than in the former seat of the dukes, the **Palais des Ducs**, an undistinguished building from the outside and one that has had many alterations, especially in the sixteenth and seventeenth centuries when it became the Parliament of Burgundy. In fact, the only outward reminders of the dukes' building are the fifteenth-century **Tour Philippe le Bon** (April–Nov, 10 tours daily; Dec–March Sat, Sun & Wed afternoon only; €2.30), from whose terrace on the clearest of days you can supposedly see Mont Blanc, and the fourteenth-century **Tour de Bar**. The latter now houses Dijon's wonderful **Musée des Beaux-Arts** (Mon & Wed–Sun 9.30/10am–5/6pm; €3.40, free on Sun), with a collection of paintings representing many different schools and periods from Titian and Rubens to Monet and Manet. The museum ticket also allows you to visit the vast kitchen and magnificent **Salle des Gardes**, richly appointed with panelling, tapestries and a minstrels' gallery, as well as the tombs of the dukes of Burgundy, Philippe le Hardi and Jean sans Peur, and Jean's wife, Marguerite de Bavière. The palace looks onto **place de la Libération**, a gracious semicircular space designed in the late seventeenth century and bordered by houses of honey-coloured stone. Behind it is the tiny, enclosed **place des Ducs** and a maze of lanes flanked by beautiful old houses, best of which are those on **rue des Forges**. Parallel to rue des Forges, **rue de la Chouette** passes the north side of the impressive thirteenth-century Gothic church of **Notre–Dame**, whose north wall holds a small sculpted owl (*chouette*), which people touch for luck and which gives the street its name. At the end of the street is the attractive **place François–Rude**, a favourite summer hangout, crowded with café tables. Just to the south, the **Musée Archéologique**, 5 rue Docteur-Maret (daily except Tues 9am–6pm; Oct–May also closed 12.30–1.30pm; €2.20, free on Sun), has interesting Gallo-Roman funerary bas-reliefs depicting the perennial Gallic preoccupation with food and wine.

Dijon **train station** is at the end of av Maréchal-Foch, beside the **bus station** and five minutes from place Darcy, site of the main **tourist office** (daily: May to mid-Oct 9am–8pm; mid-Oct to April 10am–6pm; ☎03.80.44.11.44, ⊛www.ot-dijon.fr). Another tourist office is at 34 rue des Forges (May to mid-Oct Mon–Sat 9am–1pm & 2–6pm; rest of year Mon–Fri 9am–noon & 2–6pm). The official **hostel** is 4km from the centre at 1 bd Champollion (☎03.80.72.95.20; €15.80) – take bus #5 from place Grangier. As for **hotels**, try the old-fashioned *Chambellan*, at 92 rue Vannerie (☎03.80.67.12.67; ❸) or the *Hostellerie Le Sauvage*, at 64 rue Monge

(☎03.80.41.31.21; **③**), a former coaching inn. The nearest **campsite** is by the lake off bd Chanoine Kir (☎03.80.43.54.72; closed Nov–March; bus #12). There's no problem finding a good **restaurant** in this centre of *haute cuisine*, though locating affordable places is harder. Good bets are bustling rue Berbisey and place Émile Zola, where you could try the lively *Verdi*, for pizzas and grills, or the relatively refined *Le Chabrot*, at 36 rue Monge, for Burgundian cuisine. For a **drink**, there's the studenty *Au Vieux Léon*, 52 rue Jeannin, or the welcoming, alternative-flavoured *Le Chez Nous*, just behind rue Quentin. Multirezo, in the bus station, offers **Internet** access.

Beaune and the Burgundy vineyards

Burgundy's best wines come from a narrow strip of hillside – the **Côte d'Or**, which runs southwest from Dijon to Santenay. Its principal town, rather overrun by wine tourists, is **BEAUNE**, whose chief attraction is the fifteenth-century hospital, the **Hôtel-Dieu** on the corner of place de la Halle (April–Nov daily 9am–6.30pm; Dec–March daily except Tues 9.30am–5pm; €5.10). The vast stone-flagged hall has an impressive painted timber roof and until quite recently continued to serve its original purpose. It is here that the Hospices de Beaune's wines are auctioned during the annual *Trois Glorieuses*, the prices paid setting the pattern for the season. The private residence of the dukes of Burgundy on rue d'Enfer now contains the **Musée du Vin** (daily 9.30am–5/6pm; Dec–March closed Tues; €5.10), with giant winepresses and an interesting collection of tools of the trade. From Beaune **train station**, the town centre is 500m up av du 8 Septembre, across the boulevard and left onto rue des Tonneliers. **Buses** leave from outside the walls at the end of rue Maufoux. The **tourist office** is opposite the Hôtel-Dieu on rue de l'Hôtel-Dieu (Mon–Sat 9.30/10am–6/8pm, Sun 9.30/10am–1pm & 2–5/6pm; ☎03.80.26.21.30, ⊛www.ot-beaune.fr) and has information on wine tours. **Accommodation** is pricey: it's cheaper to make Dijon your base, but you could try *Hôtel Foch* (☎03.80.24.05.65; **②**). There's a **campsite**, *Les Cent Vignes* (☎03.80.22.03.91), 1km out on rue Auguste Dubois off rue du Faubourg-St-Nicolas. **Eating** can also be expensive, though the brasserie *Le Carnot*, 18 rue Carnot, and the tiny *Bistrot Bouguignon*, 8 rue Monge, are both reasonably priced.

The Côte d'Or is divided into two wine regions – **Côte de Nuits** and **Côte de Beaune**. With few exceptions, the reds of the Côte de Nuits are considered the better of the two: they are richer, age better and, consequently, cost more. The villages, strung along the N74 through Beaune and beyond, are sleepy and exceedingly prosperous, full of houses inhabited by well-heeled *vignerons*, and *caves* at which to sample wines before you buy.

Alsace and Lorraine

France's eastern borderlands were a battleground for centuries. Disputed since the Middle Ages, in the twentieth century they became the scene of some of the worst fighting in the two world wars. The democratically minded burghers of **Alsace**, the more beautiful of the two provinces, created a plethora of well-heeled semi-autonomous towns for themselves centuries before their seventeenth-century incorporation into the French state. These are neat, well-ordered places full of Germanic fripperies adorning the houses – but the Alsatian people remain fiercely and proudly French, despite the German dialect spoken by many. The mélange of cultures is at its most vivid in the string of little wine towns that punctuate the *Route du Vin* along the eastern margin of the wet and woody **Vosges** mountains, and in the great cathedral city of **Strasbourg**. By comparison, the province of **Lorraine**, though it has suffered much the same vicissitudes, is rather wan, the elegant eighteenth-century provincial capital of **Nancy** being the main exception.

Nancy

NANCY, capital of Lorraine, is lighter and more southern in feel than its close neighbour Metz, with a relatively untouched eighteenth-century core that was the work of the last of the independent dukes of Lorraine, Stanislas Leczynski, dethroned King of Poland and father-in-law of Louis XV. During the twenty-odd years of his office in the mid-eighteenth century he ordered some of the most successful urban redevelopment of the period in all France. The centre of this is **place Stanislas**, a supremely elegant, partially enclosed square at the far end of rue Stanislas, whose south side is taken up by the **Hôtel de Ville**, its roof line topped by florid urns and lozenge-shaped lanterns dangling from the beaks of gilded cockerels. On the west side of the square, the excellent **Musée des Beaux-Arts** (Mon & Wed–Sun 10am–6pm; €4.57; €7.62 joint ticket with Musée de l'École and Musée Lorrain) boasts work by Bonnard, Dufy, Modigliani and Matisse. A little to the north, at 64 Grande-Rue, is the **Musée Lorrain** (Mon & Wed–Sun 10am–12.30pm & 1.30–6pm; €3.10), devoted to Lorraine's history and with a room of etchings by the seventeenth-century artist, Jacques Callot, whose concern with social issues presaged much nineteenth- and twentieth-century art. It's then a twenty-minute walk to the **Musée de l'École de Nancy**, 36–38 rue Sergent Blandan (Wed–Sun 10.30am–6pm; €4.57), which holds a collection of Art Nouveau furniture and furnishings, arranged as if in a private house.

Nancy **train station** is at the end of rue Stanislas, a five-minute walk from place Stanislas, where you'll find the **tourist office** (Mon–Sat 9am–6/7pm, Sun 10am–1/5pm; ☎03.83.35.22.41, ⊛www.ot-nancy.fr). Among cheap **hotels**, there's the *Poincaré*, 81 rue Raymond Poincaré, west of the train station (☎03.83.40.25.99; ⊛www.hotel-poincare.com; ❸), and the trendy new *4A*, 32 ave du XXe Corps (☎03.83.37.99.66, ⊛www.voyages4a.com; ❷). There's a **hostel** out at the *Centre d'Accueil*, Château de Rémicourt, Villers-lès-Nancy (☎03.83.27.73.67; €8.40; bus #122 to St-Fiacre). *Camping de Brabois* (☎03.83.27.18.28, ⊜campeoles.brabois @wanadoo.fr) is the nearest **campsite**. For reasonably priced **food**, Grande Rue and rue des Ponts offer the best choice. Try *Chez Bagot*, at 45 Grande Rue. The ornate café *L'Excelsior*, across place Thiers from the train station, is a beautiful place for a coffee and a hearty meal. For **Internet** access, head to e-café, 11 rue des Quatre Églises.

Strasbourg

The prosperous and attractive capital of Alsace, **STRASBOURG** is big enough to have a metropolitan air, but with a cheerful cosiness that prevents it from being overwhelming. It has one of the loveliest cathedrals in France, an ancient but active university and is the current seat of the Council of Europe and the European Court of Human Rights, and part-time base of the European Parliament. Even if you're not planning to spend much time in eastern France, Strasbourg is a genuine highlight and well worth a detour.

Strasbourg focuses on two main squares, the busy **place Kléber**, and, to the south, **place Gutenberg**, named after the pioneer of printing type, who lived here in the early fifteenth century. Close by, the **Cathédrale de Notre-Dame** (daily 7/11.30am–12.40/7pm; free) soars from a square of crooked-roofed medieval houses, with a spire of such delicate, flaky lightness it seems the work of confectioners rather than masons. In the south transept the slender triple-tiered thirteenth-century column, the Pilier des Anges, is decorated with some of the most graceful and expressive statuary of its age. Don't miss the tremendously complicated **astrological clock** (open only noon–12.20pm; tickets sold from 11.50am; €0.80), built by Schwilgué of Strasbourg in 1842. Visitors arrive in droves to witness its crowning performance – striking the hour of noon with unerring accuracy at 12.30pm. South of the cathedral the **Musée de l'Oeuvre Notre-Dame**, 3 pl du Château (Tues–Sun 10am–6pm; €3), houses the original sculptures from the cathedral exterior, damaged in the Revolution and replaced today by convincing copies. There's

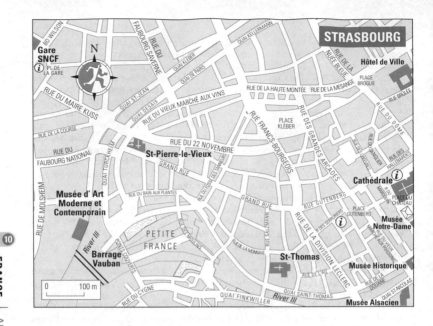

also the eleventh-century *Wissembourg Christ*, perhaps the oldest representation of a human figure in stained glass, retrieved from the previous cathedral. Just north of the old centre, across the river, **place de la République** is surrounded by vast German neo-Gothic edifices erected during the Prussian occupation (1870–1918), a few hundred metres beyond which are the imposing pieces of contemporary architecture that are home to the European Court of Human Rights and the European Parliament. The western edge of the city centre is much more picturesque. Around quai Turckheim, four square towers guard the so-called **Ponts Couverts** over a series of canals. This beautiful area, known as the Petite France, has winding streets bordered by sixteenth- and seventeenth-century houses with carved woodwork and decked with flowers. The **Musée d'Art Moderne et Contemporain**, 1 pl Jean Hans-Arp (Tues–Sun 11am–7pm, Thurs until 10pm; €4.50), stands on the west bank of the river and houses an impressive collection featuring Monet, Klimt, Ernst, Klee and Jean Arp.

Practicalities

From the **train station** take rue du Maire Kuss, cross the Rhine into rue du 22 Novembre and continue to place Kléber, from where rue des Grandes Arcades heads south to place Gutenberg and the **tourist office** at 17 place de la Cathédrale (Mon–Sat 9am–7pm, Sun 9am–6pm; ☏03.88.52.28.28, ⊛www.ot-strasbourg.fr). The tourist office also has annexes in the underground shopping centre in front of the train station and at the Pont de l'Europe, at the German border. **Hotels** are expensive and often fully booked, though excellent value are the *Hôtel de l'Ill*, 8 rue des Bateliers (☏03.88.36.20.01, ☏03.88.35.30.03; ❸), and *Hôtel du Rhin,* 7–8 pl de la Gare (☏03.88.32.35.00, ⊛www.hotel-du-rhin.com; ❹). A little more upmarket, the *Hôtel des Arts* is at 10 pl du Marché-aux-Cochons-de-Lait in the old town (☏03.88.37.98.37, ⊛www.hotel-arts.fr; ❹). The *René Cassin* **hostel** is at 9 rue de l'Auberge-de-Jeunesse (☏03.88.30.26.46; €12.70; closed Jan; bus #2); the HI hostel *Parc du Rhin* is on rue des Cavaliers, close to the Pont de l'Europe (☏03.88.45.54.20; €12.70; bus #2 and #21); and there are more central hostel beds at *CIARUS*, 7 rue de Finkmatt (☎03.88.15.27.88, ⊕www.ciarus.com; ❷) – rates at the latter include meals. The nearest **campsite**, *La Montagne Verte*, is at 2 rue Robert Forrer (☎03.88.30.25.46). For **food**, the *FEC* student canteen on place St-Étienne has rock-bottom prices and good meals. Otherwise, eating out can be pricey. *Flam's*, 1 rue de l'Epine, serves the local speciality, *tarte flambée*, a pizza-like onion tart; and *La Victoire*, 24 quai des Pêcheurs, is a lively studenty place. The city abounds in **wine bars** and **beer halls**: *L'Académie de la Bière*, 17 rue Adolphe-Seyboth, is its most serious beer palace; *La Salamandre*, 3 rue Paul-Janet, is a good place for live music and is open until 1am or later. **Internet** access is at Midi Minuit, 5 pl du Corbeau.

The French Alps

Rousseau wrote in his *Confessions*, "I need torrents, rocks, pine trees, dark forests, mountains, rugged paths to go up and down, precipices at my elbow to give me a good fright." And these are, in essence, the principal joys of the **French Alps**. Along the mountains' western edge, **Grenoble** and **Annecy** are the gateways to the highest parts, although you really need to spend several days here to create time for anything more strenuous than viewing the peaks from your hotel window. There are six **national or regional parks** – Vanoise, Écrins, Bauges, Chartreuse, Queyras (the least busy) and Vercors (the gentlest) – each of which is ideal walking country, as is the professionals' **Route des Grandes Alpes**, which crosses all the major massifs from Lake Geneva to Menton, not far from Nice. But on a quick tour you're best off grabbing a taster at **Chamonix**, principal base for accessing **Mont Blanc** on the French–Italian border, or simply doing day walks from the main centres. All **routes** are clearly marked and equipped with refuge huts and *gîtes d'étape*. The CIMES office in Grenoble can provide detailed information on GR paths, and local tourist offices often produce detailed maps of walks in their areas. Bear in mind that anywhere above 2000m will be free of snow only from early July until mid-September.

Grenoble

The economic and intellectual capital of the French Alps, **GRENOBLE** is a thriving city, beautifully situated on the Drac and Isère rivers. The old centre, south of the Isère, focuses on place Grenette and place Notre Dame, both popular with local students lounging in the many outdoor cafés. The city celebrates local boy Stendhal, author of *The Red and the Black*, in the **Musée Stendhal**, 1 rue Hector Berlioz (mid-July to mid-Sept Tues–Sun 9am–noon & 2–6pm; mid-Sept to Oct & Easter to mid-July Tues–Sun 2–6pm; Nov–Easter Sat & Sun 2–6pm; free). For more of an insight into the region, visit the **Musée Dauphinois**, 30 rue Maurice Gignoux (Mon & Wed–Sun 10am–6/7pm; €3.20; free for under-25s), which occupies the former convent of Ste-Marie-d'en-Haut on rue Maurice-Gignoux. The French Resistance was particularly active in the Vercors Massif near Grenoble during World War II, and is commemorated – along with victims of the Holocaust – in the **Musée de la Résistance et de la Déportation**, 14 rue Hébert (Mon & Wed–Sun 9/10am–6/7pm; €3.20; free for under-25s). Finally, the one thing you shouldn't miss is the trip by *téléférique* from the riverside quai Stéphane Jay up to **Fort de la Bastille** on the steep slopes above the north bank of the Isère (daily 9.30/11am–7.25/11.45pm; €5.50 one-way). It's a hair-raising ride to an otherwise uninteresting fort, but the view over the surrounding mountains and valleys, and down onto the town, is stunning.

The **train station** and **bus station** are on the western edge of the centre, at the end of ave Félix Viallet. The **tourist office** is at 14 rue de la République, near pl Grenette (Mon–Fri 9am–6.30pm, Sun 10am–1pm; April–Sept also Sun 2–5pm; ☎04.76.42.41.41, ⊕www.grenoble-isere.info). The **CIMES** desk in the same office can provide detailed information on hiking and climbing. There are numerous **hotels** near the station, among them the *Alizé* at 1 pl de la Gare (☎04.76.43.12.91,

ⓣ04.76.47.62.79; ❸). The *Bellevue* (ⓣ04.76.46.69.34, ⓕ04.76.85.20.12; ❸), on the corner of quai Stéphane-Jay and rue Belgrade, has simple rooms with river views. There's a **hostel** 4km to the south of town in Échirolles (ⓣ04.76.09.33.52; €8.85; bus #16), and a **campsite**, *Les Trois Pucelles*, 4km to the west, in Seyssins (ⓣ04.76.96.45.73, ⓦwww.camping-trois-pucelles.com). For reasonably priced local food there's a wide selection of **cafés and brasseries** between place St-André and place Notre-Dame; try *Le Valgo* at 2 rue St Hughes. For **Internet** access go to Le New Age Cyber Café, 1 rue Barnabe.

Annecy

ANNECY, busy but undeniably pretty, serves as a transit point for hikers. The most interesting part of the city is a warren of seventeenth-century lanes and passages cut through by branches of the Canal du Thiou. The **train** and **bus** station complex is five minutes' walk northwest of the centre. The **tourist office** is at 1 rue Jean Jaurès (July & Aug Mon–Sat 9am–6.30pm, Sun 9am–noon & 1.45–6.30pm; rest of the year Mon–Sat 9am–12.30pm & 1.45–6pm, Sun 10am–1pm; Nov–March closed Sun; ⓣ04.50.45.00.33, ⓦwww.lac-annecy.com). The local **hostel** is 4 route du Semnoz (ⓣ04.50.45.33.19; €12.70), and **hotels** fill up fast, so it's advisable to book. For rooms close to the centre, try the *Hôtel Pâquier*, 3 rue du Pâquier (ⓣ04.50.45.09.67, ⓕ04.50.45.97.35; ❸); further out, the *Belvédère*, 7 chemin de Belvédère (ⓣ04.50.45.04.90, ⓦwww.belvedere-annecy.com; ❻), has great views over the lake. The **campsite** is off bd de la Corniche, just south of town (ⓣ04.50.45.48.30; closed Oct to mid-March). A clutch of **restaurants** can be found in the old centre; try *Restaurant des Arts*, 4 passage de l'Île.

Chamonix and Mont Blanc

At 4810m, **Mont Blanc** is both Europe's highest mountain and the Alps' biggest draw, but by walking you can soon get away from the worst of the crowds. The two approach routes come together at Le Fayet, where the **tramway du Mont-Blanc** begins its haul to the **Nid d'Aigle** (mid-June to Sept; 1hr 15min; €15.40), a vantage point on the northwest slope. There's more exciting access 30km further on, at the resort of **CHAMONIX**, via the expensive **téléférique** (€33.80 return) to the **Aiguille du Midi** (3842m), a terrifying granite pinnacle on which the *téléférique* station and a restaurant are precariously balanced. The view of Mont Blanc from here is incredible. At your feet is the snowy plateau of the **Col du Midi**, with the glaciers of the Vallée Blanche and Géant crawling off at their millennial pace. To the right, a steep snowfield leads to the "easy" ridge route to the summit with its cap of ice. You must, however, go before 9am, because the summit usually clouds over towards midday and the crowds become intolerable. Be sure also to take warm clothes: even on a summer's day it can be well below zero at the top.

The Chamonix **tourist office** is located near the church at 85 pl du Triangle de l'Amitié (daily 9am–12.30pm & 2–6.30pm; ⓣ04.50.53.00.24, ⓦwww.chamonix .com). From Chamonix there are transport connections on to Switzerland. A fifteen-minute walk south of the tourist office, across the river, takes you to the **train station**, where the spectacular mountain train line **Mont-Blanc Express** starts its precipitous journey to the Swiss town of Martigny (at least 5 daily; 2hr 20min; €35 return; ⓦwww.momc.ch). **Buses** leave the SAT bus station, located at the train station building, for Geneva via Le Fayet (3 daily; 2hr; €32). Finding **accommodation** in the area can be a big problem. There are some budget **hotels**, but you will need to book in advance; try *La Boule de Neige*, 362 rue Vallot (ⓣ04.50.53.04.48, ⓔpostmaster@hotel-labouledeneige.fr; ❹). You might have more luck at the comfortable, welcoming **hostel** just west of Chamonix at 127 Montée Jacques-Balmat in Les Pèlerins en Haut (ⓣ04.50.53.14.52; €12.70); take a bus to Pèlerins-École, from where the hostel is signposted. **Campsites** are numerous: most convenient are *Les Molliases* (ⓣ04.50.53.16.81; closed mid-Sept to May) on the left of the main road, going west from Chamonix towards the Mont Blanc tunnel entrance; and *Les Arolles* (℡04.50.53.14.30; closed Oct to mid-June), on the opposite side of the road, fifteen minutes' walk from the station.

Rhône Valley and Provence

Of all the regions of France, **Provence** is the most irresistible, with attractions that range from the high mountains of the southern Alps to the wild plains of the Camargue. Yet, apart from the coast, large areas remain remarkably unscathed by development. Its complete integration into France dates only from the nineteenth century and, although the Provençal language is rarely heard, the accent is distinctive even to a foreign ear. The main problem is choosing where to go. The **Rhône valley**, north–south route of ancient armies, medieval traders and modern rail and road, is nowadays fairly industrialized, and other than the big city delights of **Lyon** – not strictly in Provence but the main gateway for the region – there's not much to detain you before the old papal stronghold of **Avignon**, which also hosts a wonderful summer festival. Deeper into Provence, on the edge of the flamingo-filled lagoons of the **Camargue**, the ancient settlement of **Arles** boasts an impressive Roman legacy.

Lyon

LYON, France's third-largest city, became a UNESCO World Heritage site in 1998, one of only five urban sites in the world thus honoured. Its charms are manifold, not least its gastronomy: there are more restaurants per square metre here than anywhere

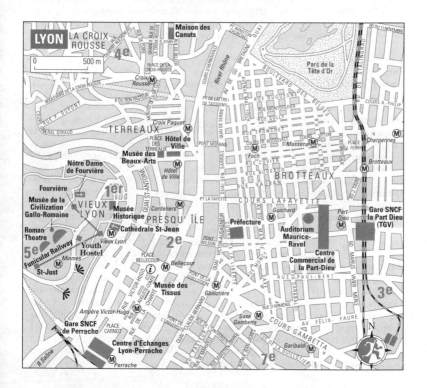

else on earth. It also has a beautifully preserved old quarter and an elegant town centre of grand boulevards and public squares. With a population of more than two million, including over 100,000 university students, there is a vibrant nightlife and cultural scene, boasting one of the few national operas outside Paris and a major summer-long **festival**, *Les Nuits de Fourvière*, celebrating theatre, cinema, music and dance.

Arrival, information and accommodation

Lyon-St-Exupéry **airport** is 45 minutes from the centre by bus (daily 5am–11.20pm, every 20min; €8.20). The TGV train station, **Gare de la Part Dieu**, is on bd Marius Vivier-Merle, in the heart of the commercial district on the east bank of the Rhône, and connected to the centre by a regular métro service. Other **trains** arrive at the **Gare de Perrache**, on what was once the tip of the peninsula. The **tourist office** is on pl Bellecour (daily 9/10am–6/7pm; ☏04.72.77.69.69, ⓦwww.lyon-france.com), where you can pick up local transport maps and book guided tours. Tickets for **city transport** cost a flat €1.40, or you can buy a **carnet** of ten for €11.20; the tourist office's **liberté ticket** gives unlimited travel on trams, buses and métro for a day (€4; under 21s €2.80). The **City Card**, also available at the tourist office, covers entry to all museums, monuments, tours and transport (€15/25/30, for 1, 2 or 3 days respectively). *Le Petit Bulletin* is a very useful, free weekly listings newspaper, available from shops and restaurants. For **accommodation** close to the centre, try the comfortable *Elysée*, 92 rue Edouard Herriot (☏04.78.42.03.15, ⓦwww.elysee-hotel.com; ❹). Nearer the Gare de Perrache is the clean and homely *Vaubecour*, 28 rue Vaubecour (☏04.78.37.44.91, ☏04.78.42.90.17; ❷). The modern *Athéna Part-Dieu*, 45 bd Marius Vivier Merle (☏04.72.68.88.44, ⓦwww.athena-hotel.fr; ❹), next to the TGV station, is a very handy option but consequently often full. Vieux Lyon has a **hostel** at 41–45 montée du Chemin Neuf (☏04.78.15.05.50; €12.70), with great city views. The closest **campsite** is the *Porte de Lyon* at Dardilly (☏04.78.35.64.55, ⓦwww.camping-lyon.com), a ten-minute ride by bus #89 from the bus station in Gare de Vaise, north of the city.

The City

Directly in front of Gare de Perrache is the green square of **place Carnot** which leads to the pedestrian rue Victor-Hugo, in turn opening out onto the vast **place Bellecour**, where even the statue of Louis XIV on horseback looks small. On rue de la Charité, which runs parallel to rue Victor-Hugo on the Rhône side, is the **Musée des Tissus** (Tues–Sun 10am–5.30pm; €4.60; métro Victor Hugo), a surprisingly interesting collection of fabrics, clothes and tapestries dating from ancient Egypt to the present. From here, push straight on up the busy rue de la République, past place Bellecour. Turning left leads to quai St-Antoine, lined in the mornings with a colourful food market; a Sunday book market lies just upriver. Heading north, to **Place des Terreaux**, the centrepiece is an imposing nineteenth-century fountain sculpted by Bartholdi, more famously responsible for New York's Statue of Liberty. The square also features the splendidly ornate **Hôtel de Ville**, as well as the **Musée des Beaux-Arts** (Mon & Wed–Sun 10.30am–6pm; €3.80; métro Hôtel de Ville). This absorbing collection includes ancient Egyptian, Greek and Roman artefacts as well as works by Rubens, Renoir and Picasso.

North of Place des Terreaux, the old silk weavers' district of **La Croix Rousse** is still a working-class area, but today only twenty or so people work on the computerized looms that are kept in business by the restoration and maintenance of the palaces and châteaux. You can watch traditional looms in action at **La Maison des Canuts** at 10 rue d'Ivry, one block north of place de la Croix Rousse (Mon–Sat 9am–noon & 2–6pm; €3.80; métro Croix Rousse). From here, cut through to the river and cross to **Vieux Lyon**. The tangled streets on the left bank of the Saône form an attractive muddle of cobbled lanes and Renaissance facades, riddled with the famous *traboules*, or covered alleyways, running between streets. Originally used to transport silk safely through town, they later served as escape routes and hideouts for the resistance during World War II. The **Musée Historique de Lyon** on pl du Petit Collège (Mon & Wed–Sun 10.45am–6pm; €3.80; métro Vieux Lyon) has a good collection of Nevers ceramics, although the **Musée de la Marionnette** (same hours and ticket) on an upper floor of the same fifteenth-century mansion is more engaging, containing the eighteenth-century Lyonnais creations *Guignol* and *Madelon* (the French Punch and Judy), which you can see in action at **Théâtre Guignol**, 2 rue Louis Carrand (Tues–Fri 9am–noon & 2–6pm; Sat & Sun 2–6pm; €8).

Rue St-Jean ends at the **Cathédrale St-Jean**, and though damaged during World War II, its thirteenth-century stained glass (above the altar and in the rose windows of the transepts) is in perfect condition, as is the magnificent fourteenth-century clock. Just beyond the cathedral, at métro Vieux Lyon on av Adolphe-Max, is a **funicular station**, from which you can ascend to the two **Roman theatres** on rue de l'Antiquaille (daily 7am–7/9pm; free), and the excellent **Musée de la Civilisation Gallo-Romaine** at 17 rue Cléberg (Tues–Sun 10am–5/6pm; €3.80). The drab concrete building houses a wealth of artefacts from the ancient Roman city of *Lugdunum*, as Lyon was then known, including some superb mosaics, and the lower half of the famed "Claudian Table", a large bronze plaque recording a speech made by the locally born Emperor, Claudius. From here, it's a short walk to the late nineteenth-century **Basilique de Notre-Dame** (April–Oct Mon–Sat 10am–noon & 2-7pm, Sun 2–4.30pm; €4), a gaudy showcase of multicoloured marble and mosaic. The belvedere behind the church affords an impressive view of Lyon and its curving rivers. Reminders of the war are never far away in France and this is particularly true of Lyon where the **Centre d'Histoire de la Résistance et de la Déportation** at 14 av Berthelot (Wed–Sun 9am–5.30pm; €3.80) tells of the immense courage and ingenuity of the French resistance, and also serves as a poignant memorial to the city's Jews who were deported to concentration camps.

Eating, drinking and nightlife

Lyon is the self-proclaimed gastronomic capital of France, and not without reason. It has hundreds of **restaurants** offering delicious, if somewhat heavy, Lyonnais fare. Vegetarians will be disappointed, however, as specialities focus on meat and offal, most famously in its *quenelles* (soufflé-like dumplings) and *andouillettes* (hefty tripe sausages). Lyon is crammed with touristy restaurants claiming to be *bouchons*, typical Lyon wine bars serving food. For the real thing, try *Chabert et Fils*, 11 rue des Marronniers, serving excellent local fare; or, opposite at no. 8, *Le Bouchon des Carnivores*, which offers a beef-heavy menu and walls covered with paintings, photos and models of bulls. Other options include the *Café des Fédérations*, 10 rue du Major Martin (closed Sat, Sun & Aug), and *Café 203*, by the Opera House at 9 rue du Garet, which is popular with Lyon's trendy set and offers excellent-value menus. If you just want a light meal or a **drink**, try the *Bar Americain-Café Anglais*, 24 rue de la République. For **Internet** access, there's *Connectik Café*, 19 quai St-Antoine, which has a bar, and *Raconte-moi La Terre*, 38 rue Thomassin (closed Sun), with a bookshop specializing in travel literature. Lyon also boasts a few **gay bars**: head for *La Ruche* at 22 rue Gentil, with 1930s decor; or *Le Village* at 8 rue St-Georges, for women only (not to be mistaken for *Le Village Club* on rue Violi, aimed at a broader gay community).

Avignon

AVIGNON, great city of the popes and for centuries one of the major artistic centres of France, is today one of the country's biggest tourist attractions and always crowded in summer. It is an immaculately preserved medieval town, and it's worth putting up with the inevitable queues and the camcorder-wielding hordes to enjoy its unique stock of monuments, churches and museums. During the drama festival in July, it's the only place to be, though as around 200,000 spectators come here for the show, doing any normal sightseeing becomes virtually impossible.

Central Avignon is enclosed by medieval **walls**, built by one of the nine popes who based themselves here in the fourteenth century, away from the anarchic feuding and rival popes of Rome. Centre of town is **place de l'Horloge**, lined with cafés and market stalls on summer evenings, just beyond which is the enormous **Palais des Papes** (daily 9/9.30am–5.45/6.30pm; July, Aug & Sept open until 8/9pm; €9.50, joint ticket with Pont d'Avignon €11). The denuded interior gives little indication of the richness of the papal court, although the building is impressive for sheer size alone. The nearby **Musée du Petit Palais** (Mon & Wed–Sun 9.30/10am–1pm & 2–5.30/6pm; €6) houses a collection of religious art from the thirteenth to sixteenth centuries, while more modern works are on show at the **Musée Calvet**, 65 rue Joseph Vernet (Mon & Wed–Sun 10am–1pm & 2–6pm; €6) and in the **Collection Lambert**, 5 rue Violette (Tues–Sun 11am–6pm; July daily 11am–7pm; €5.50). Jutting out halfway across the river is the famous **Pont d'Avignon** (same hours as Palais des Papes; €3.50). The struggle to keep the bridge in good repair against the ravages of the Rhône was finally abandoned in 1660, three-and-a-half centuries after it was built, and today just four of the original 22 arches survive.

Practicalities

Avignon's **train station** is by the porte de la République on boulevard St-Roch, on the southern edge of the centre. There's a separate **TGV station** in the Quartier de Courtine, to the west, and reached by regular shuttle bus from the stop just inside the main gate. The **tourist office** is a short walk from the main station at 41 cours Jean-Jaurès (Mon–Sat 9am–6/7pm; Nov–March Sat closes at 5pm; ☎04.32.74.32.74, ⊛www.ot-avignon.fr), and there's another office open daily at the Pont d'Avignon. The free **Discovery Passport**, valid for fifteen days and available from the tourist office, gives reductions of between twenty and fifty percent on entrance fees to all monuments and museums. During Avignon's **festival** (July), theatre dominates, but opera, classical music and film also feature, with the streets given over to the fringe. The **festival headquarters**, open from May to July, is at l'Espace St-Louis, 20 rue du Portail Boquier (☎04.90.14.14.14, ⊛www.festival-avignon.com.

Even outside festival time, finding **accommodation** can be a problem. One of the cheaper options is the *Monclar*, 13 av Monclar (☎04.90.86.20.14, ⊛www .hotel-monclar.fr; ❸), an attractive eighteenth-century house just round the corner from the train station. Other reasonable choices include *Le Parc*, 18 rue Agricol Perdiguier (☎04.90.82.71.55; ⊛wwww.hotelduparc.multimania.com; ❸), and the *Innova*, 100 rue Joseph Vernet (☎04.90.82.54.10, ✉hotel.innova@wanadoo.fr; ❹). There's a **hostel**, the *Auberge Bagatelle* (☎04.90.86.30.39; €10.26), across the river on Île de la Barthelasse, which also has a **campsite**; take bus #10 or #11 to the bridge, from where you can cross to the island. **Eating** on a budget is easy. The touristy brasseries on place de l'Horloge all do well-priced meals and have outdoor seating – try *Les Domaines*. Alternatively, *Maison Nani*, 29 rue Théodore Aubanel, is a lively spot, popular with locals, which does good *plats du jour*. Place de l'Horloge also has plenty of places to sip an early evening **drink**. There's **Internet** access at Cyberdrome, 68 rue Guillaume Puy, and at the tourist office.

Arles

Around 25km south of Avignon, **ARLES** was one of the most important settlements of Gaul, providing grain for most of the western Roman empire, as well as being a crucial port and shipbuilding centre – indeed, in the fourth century it became the capital of Gaul, Britain and Spain. Today, Arles is a picturesque town with a laid-back Mediterranean atmosphere and well-preserved vestiges of its illustrious past – not least a marvellous Roman amphitheatre. Arles' most famous inhabitant, Vincent van Gogh, spent a fruitful, if turbulent, year here, producing some of his most famous works, including *Starry Night* and *Night Café*, yet not one of his paintings remains in the town. **Boulevard des Lices** is the main street, along with rue

Jean Jaurès and its continuation, rue Hôtel de Ville. The most obvious place to start exploring is the central **place de la République**, between rue Jean Jaurès and rue Hôtel de Ville, highlight of which is the **Cathédrale St-Trophime**, whose doorway is one of the most famous bits of twelfth-century Provençal carving, depicting a *Last Judgement* trumpeted by angels playing with the enthusiasm of jazz musicians. The cloister (daily 9/10am–4.30/6.30pm; €3.50), with its mix of Romanesque and Gothic architecture, is also worth a look. Immediately east of the cathedral is the **Théâtre-Antique** (daily: May–Sept 9am–6.30pm; Oct–April 9/10–11.30am & 2–4.30/5.30pm; €3). For a better insight into Roman Arles, head for the **Musée de l'Arles Antique** (daily 9/10am–5/7pm; €5.35), west of the town centre on the spit of land between the Rhône and the Canal du Rhône, where fabulous mosaics, sarcophagi and sculpture illuminate Arles' early history. Through the museum you gain access to the **Cirque Romain**, the town's most impressive Roman structure, built in the first century AD and which originally seated 20,000. Housed in a splendid medieval building once used by the Knights of the Order of Malta, the **Musée Réattu** (March–Oct daily 10am–12.30pm & 2–5.30/7pm; rest of the year daily 1–5.30pm; €4) hosts a fine collection of modern art, including sketches and sculptures by Picasso. Opposite are the remains of the fourth century **Roman baths** (daily: Oct–April 9/10–11.30am & 2–4.30/5.30pm; May–Sept 9am–6.30pm; €3).

Practicalities

The **train station** is a few blocks north of the Cirque Romain, close to the Porte de la Cavalerie. The **tourist office** is opposite rue Jean Jaurès on bd des Lices (April–Sept daily 9am–6.45pm; Oct–March Mon–Sat 9am–4.45/5.45pm, Sun 10am–2.30pm; ☎04.90.18.41.20, ⊛www.tourisme.ville-arles.fr), and provides a hotel booking service. For central **accommodation**, try the *Mirador* at 3 rue Voltaire (☎04.90.96.28.05, ⊛www.hotel-mirador.com; ❸), or *De l'Amphithéâtre* at 5 rue Diderot (☎04.90.96.10.30; ⊛www.hotelamphitheatre.fr; ❹), a wonderfully renovated seventeenth-century mansion with small, neat rooms. There's a **hostel** at 20 av Maréchal-Foch (☎04.90.96.18.25; ❷; closed Jan), a five-minute walk from the tourist office. Of the five **campsites** within easy reach of the city, the most pleasant is *La Bienheureuse* (☎04.90.98.48.04), 7km out on RN453 at Raphèle-les-Arles and with a restaurant and regular bus connections; closer to town is *Camping City*, 67 route de la Crau (☎04.90.93.08.86; ⊛www.camping-city.com). To sample traditional Provençal **cuisine**, try *La Gueule du Loup*, 39 rue des Arènes, or *Lou Peyrou*, 18 bd Georges Clémenceau. **Internet** is available at Hexaworld, on rue du 4 septembre, by the train station.

The Camargue

The flat, marshy delta immediately south of Arles – the **Camargue** – is a unique area that is used as a breeding-ground for the bulls which participate in *corridas* around here, along with the horses that their herdsmen ride. The true wildlife of the area is made up of flamingos, marsh- and seabirds, and a rich flora of reeds, wild flowers and juniper trees. The only town is **SAINTES-MARIES-DE-LA-MER**, best known for the annual **Gypsy Festival** held each May, and which is linked by a regular bus service to Arles. It's a pleasant, though touristy, place, with some fine sandy beaches, while if you're interested in bird-watching or touring the lagoons, your first port of call should be the **tourist office** on 5 av Van Gogh (daily: July & Aug daily 9am–8pm; rest of the year 9am–6/7pm; winter closes 5pm; ☎04.90.97.82.55; ⊛www.saintes-maries.camargue.fr), which has information on a number of organized cycle, horse and boat tours of the Camargue. There are also several places to **rent bicycles** and **hire horses**, if you prefer to explore alone. Reasonably priced **hotels** include *Le Bleu Marine*, 15 av du Docteur Cambon (☎04.90.97.77.00, ⊛www.hotel-bleumarine.com; ❺), and, slightly further from the sea, at 14 rue Camille Pelletan, *Le Mirage* (☎04.90.97.80.43; ⊛www.lemirage.camargue.fr; ❹), which also has a restaurant serving Camarguais specialities.

Marseille and the Côte d'Azur

The **Côte d'Azur**, synonymous with wealth and luxury, is one of the most built-up and expensive stretches of coast anywhere in the world. While its reputation as a pricey playground for the super-rich is still very much intact, that doesn't mean that holidaying here is necessarily more expensive than elsewhere in France, providing you avoid the more obvious tourist traps. The coast's eastern reaches are its most spectacular, the mountains breaking their fall just a few metres before levelling off to the shore. **St-Tropez** is an expensive high spot, though only **Nice** has real substance – a major city with the second busiest airport in the country. At the opposite end of the coast, the vast, cosmopolitan sprawl of **Marseille** is quite different, with its big-city buzz and down-to-earth charm. July and August are the busiest months of the year, when accommodation can be hard to come by; and May can be equally hectic, with both **Monaco**'s Grand Prix and **Cannes**' Film Festival, pulling in the crowds.

Marseille

France's most populous city after Paris, **MARSEILLE** has been a major centre of international maritime trade ever since it was founded by Greek colonists, 2500

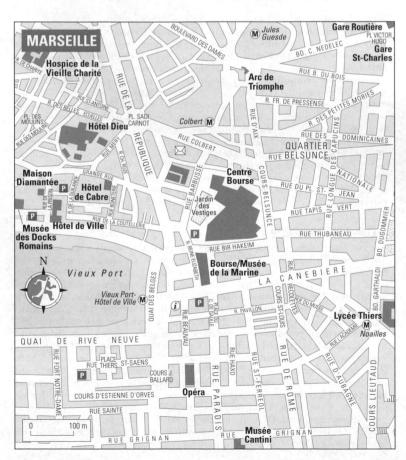

years ago. Like the capital, the city has suffered plagues, religious bigotry, republican and royalist terror and had its own Commune and Bastille-storming. It was the presence of so many revolutionaries from this city marching to Paris in 1792 that gave the name *Marseillaise* to the national anthem. Though this working city has little of the glamour of its ritzy Riviera neighbours, it is nevertheless a vibrant and exciting place, with a cosmopolitan population including large numbers of Italians and North Africans. In addition, it's a world-class diving and sailing centre, and, surprisingly, it's also France's second fashion capital.

The old harbour, or **Vieux Port**, is a good place to indulge in the sedentary pleasures of observing the city's streetlife. Two **fortresses** guard the entrance to the harbour, a little way south of which is the **Abbaye St-Victor** (daily 8.30am–6.30pm), the city's oldest church. It looks and feels like a fortress – the walls of the choir are almost 3m thick – and you can visit the crypt and catacombs (daily 9am–7pm; €2). On the northern side of the harbour is the former old town of Marseille, known as **Le Panier**, a densely populated area that was dynamited by the Nazis, who deported around 20,000 people from here. Nowadays it's a largely working-class quarter, although it's becoming a fashionable area for the young and bohemian. After the war, archeologists reaped the benefits of the destruction by finding remains of the Roman docks equipped with vast storage jars for foodstuffs, now housed in the small **Musée des Docks Romains** on pl Vivaux (Tues–Sun 10/11am–5/6pm; €2). The quarter's main attraction, though, is **La Vieille Charité**, a Baroque seventeenth-century church and hospice complex, on rue de la Charité, which is now home to a couple of museums, including the **Musée d'Archéologie Méditerranéenne** (Tues–Sun 10/11am–5/6pm; €2.70). Of most interest is the excellent Egyptian collection, with its array of mummified animals, while there are also galleries devoted to Greek, Etruscan and Phoenician antiquities.

Leading east from the Vieux Port is **La Canebière**, Marseille's main street. Just off the lower end, on busy cours Belsunce, the **Centre Bourse** is a giant mall, also home to an excellent museum of finds from Roman Marseille, the **Musée d'Histoire de Marseille** (Mon–Sat 10.30am–5.30pm; €1.50), which includes the well-preserved remains of a third-century Roman merchant vessel. There's also a garden, where you can explore the scanty remains of the Roman docks, now some way from the modern seafront. At the far eastern end of La Canebière, the **Palais Longchamp** (bus #81) was the grandiose conclusion of an aqueduct bringing water from the outlying hills to the city. Water is still pumped into the middle of the central colonnade of the building, which houses the **Musée des Beaux-Arts** (Tues–Sun 10/11am–5/6pm; €2). South of La Canebière are Marseille's main shopping streets, rue Paradis, rue St-Ferréol and rue de Rome, and the **Musée Cantini**, 19 rue Grignan (Tues–Sun 10/11am–5/6pm; €3), a collection of twentieth-century art with pieces by Dufy, Léger and Picasso.

A twenty-minute boat ride offshore is the **Château d'If**, the notorious island fortress that figured in Dumas' great adventure story, *The Count of Monte Cristo*. In reality, no one ever escaped, and most prisoners, incarcerated for political or religious reasons, ended their days here. The relatively comfortable cells on the upper floor, with their large fireplaces and windows, held the more distinguished internees, such as the Count of Mirabeau, while the less fortunate were herded into the gloomy dungeons. Hourly boats leave for the island from the Quai des Belges (€7.60 return, plus €3.80 admission to the château).

Practicalities

Marseille's main train station, **gare St-Charles**, is on the northern edge of the 1er *arrondissement*, round the corner from the **bus station** on place Victor-Hugo. The best way of getting around is to walk, although if you need to cover longer distances fast the **public transport** system – bus, tram and métro – is efficient enough, and tickets cost €1.40 from métro stations and on buses. The **tourist office** is at 4 La Canebière, down by the harbour (Mon–Sat 9am–7/7.30pm, Sun 10am–5/6pm; ☎04.91.13.89.00, ⑩www.marseille-tourisme.com) and offers a free accommodation booking service, as well as selling the **Carte Privilèges**, which allows free entry to all museums, as well as the boat ride and visit to the Château d'If (€15/23/30, for one/two/three days). Among the budget **hotels**, *La Maison du petit Canard*, 2 impasse St-Françoise (☎04.91.91.40.31, ⊛www.maison.petit.canard.free.fr; ④), is a small, friendly place in the middle of the Panier district; *Alizé*, 35 quai des Belges (☎04.91.33.66.97, ⊛www.alize-hotel.com; ⑤), is basic, but in a good central position; while the *Béarn*, 63 rue Sylvabelle (☎04.91.37.75.83, ☎04.91.81.54.98; ③), is a few blocks east of the harbour. For a luxury address, try *La Résidence du Vieux Port* at 18 quai du Port (☎04.91.91.91.22, ⊛www.hotelmarseille.com; ⑧). There are two **hostels**, the *Bois Luzy*, allée des Primevères (☎04.91.49.06.18; €8.40; bus #6; 10.30pm curfew), housed in an old château; and the *Bonneveine*, on av Joseph Vidal (☎04.91.17.63.30; €8.85; bus #44), three miles from the city centre.

Marseille's speciality is *bouillabaisse*, a delicious fish stew served in most **restaurants** around the Vieux Port; the finest place to try it is *Le Miramar*, 12 quai du Port, a local institution with high prices that books up fast. The best low-priced brasserie meals can be found on trendy cours d'Estienne d'Orves: *Le plat Provençal* at no. 28 does very good *plats du jour*; while *Les Arcenaulx*, at no. 25 serves light meals, and has a wonderful tea room, surrounded by shelves of books. For **nightlife**, the clubs around cours d'Estienne d'Orves and cours Julien are the places to head for, though prices tend to be high. *Café Julien*, 39 cours Julien, is a popular **bar** with live music at weekends. **Internet** access is at Infocafé, 1 Quai de Rive-Neuve.

St-Tropez and around

The heart of **ST-TROPEZ** is surprisingly village-like, gathered around a port founded by the ancient Greeks and made up of a web of cobbled alleys and butter-coloured houses. Rustic it is not, however: the place was transformed in 1956 after the arrival of Roger Vadim, who filmed Brigitte Bardot in *Et Dieu Créa La Femme (And God Created Woman)*. The road into St-Tropez splits in two as it enters the village, with the bus station between them; a short distance beyond on place Georges Grammont is the **Musée de l'Annonciade** (Mon & Wed–Sun 10am–noon & 2/3–6/7pm; €4.60–5.35) – a reason in itself for coming here, with works by Matisse, Signac and Derain. Beyond the museum, the **Vieux Port** is the centre of the town, a regular promenade for orange-tanned yacht owners and an international crowd of wealthy style-slaves. Up from here, at the end of quai Jean-Jaurès, rue de la Mairie passes the **Hôtel de Ville**, with a street to the left leading down to the rocky **Baie de la Glaye**, and, along rue de la Ponche, to the fishing port with a tiny **beach**. Beyond the fishing port, roads lead up to the sixteenth-century **Citadelle**, which has a drab maritime museum but marvellous views from the ramparts, or along to Les Graniers and further **beaches** on Baie des Canoubiers – accessible by a coastal path and by frequent bus service.

St-Tropez has no train service. **Buses** arrive at the *gare routière* on av Général de Gaulle, a short walk from quai Jean Jaurès, where you'll find the **tourist office** (daily: July & Aug 9.30am–8.30pm; rest of the year 9.30am–12.30pm & 2–6/7pm; ☎04.94.97.45.21, ⊛www.saint-tropez.st). **Hotels** are pricey and regularly full in summer, with few staying open for the winter. *Lou Cagnard*, 18 av Paul Roussel (☎04.94.97.04.24, ☎04.94.97.09.44; ④), is one option, or you could try *La Méditerranée*, 21 bd Louis Blanc (☎04.94.97.00.44, ☎04.94.97.79.79; ⑦), though you'll need to book well in advance. There's a better choice of accommodation in **ST-RAPHAËL**, north of St-Tropez; try *Le Clocher* (☎04.94.19.06.96, ⊛le-clocher@wanadoo.fr; ⑤) at 50 rue de la République, by the train station, or *Maison sous les Pins* on av des Golfs (☎04.94.82.42.10, ☎04.94.44.63.67; ⑤), in the lush Mediterranean pine forests that overlook the town. **Camping** poses similar problems: the two closest sites to St-Tropez are on the plage du Pampelonne and cost a fortune. Better is *Les Tournels* on route de Camarat near Ramatuelle (☎04.94.55.90.90, ⊛www.tournels.com). There are plenty of **restaurants** on rue Clemenceau and place des Lices, but don't expect any bargains: try *La Patate* or *Café des Arts*.

Cannes

Fishing village turned millionaires' playground, **CANNES** is chiefly known for the International Film Festival, held in May, during which time the place is overrun by the denizens of Movieland, their hangers-on, and a small army of paparazzi. The seafront promenade, **La Croisette**, and the **Vieux Port** form the focus of Cannes life, while the old town, **Le Suquet**, on the steep hill overlooking the bay from the west, with its quaint winding streets and eleventh century castle, is a pleasant place to wander. Meanwhile, the attractive **Îles des Lérins**, composed of touristy Ste Marguerite and the quieter St Honorat, home to a Cistercian monastery, are just a fifteen-minute ferry ride from the Vieux Port (€8).

The **train station** is on rue Jean Jaurès, a short walk north of the centre along rue des Serbes. There's a **tourist office** at the train station (Mon–Sat 9am–7pm), with the main office in the Palais des Festivals on the waterfront (daily 9am–7/8pm; ☎04.93.39.24.53, ⓦwww.cannes-on-line.com). Finding accommodation can be a problem during high season, and all but impossible during the Film Festival, when prices are bumped up considerably. There are several budget **hotels** around the train station: try the *Bourgogne*, 11 rue du 24 Août (☎04.93.38.36.73, ⓦwww.hotel-de-bourgogne.com; ❸), or nearby *Little Palace*, at no. 18 (☎04.92.98.18.18, ⓔlittle-palace@wanadoo.fr; ❹). Another option, a little closer to the seafront, is the cosy *Albe*, 31 rue Bivouac Napoléon (☎04.97.06.21.21, ⓦwww.albe-hotel.com; ❸). The nearest **campsite** is *Parc Bellevue*, 67 av Maurice Chevalier (☎04.93.47.28.97, ⓦwww.parcbellevue.com; bus #2 or #9). Le Suquet is full of **restaurants**, which get cheaper as you reach the top. *Au Bec Fin*, 12 rue du 24 Août, has superb traditional cooking and good *plats du jour*; *Le Sevrina*, 3 rue Félix Faure, serves pizza, pasta and fondue; and *Le Bouchon d'Objectif*, 10 rue de Constantine, is an excellent, reasonably priced bistro. Cannes abounds with **nightclubs**, though prices, as you might expect, are high; try *Brummel*, 3 bd de la République, one of the trendiest spots in town. **Internet** access is available at Station-Cyber, 32 rue Jean-Jaurès.

Nice

NICE, capital of the French Riviera and fifth-largest city in the country, grew into a major tourist resort in the nineteenth century, when large numbers of foreign visitors – many of them British – were drawn here by the mild Mediterranean climate. The most obvious legacy of these early holiday-makers is the famous **promenade des Anglais** stretching along the pebble beach, laid out by nineteenth-century English residents to facilitate their afternoon stroll by the sea, while Russian aristocrats erected an **Orthodox Cathedral** at the end of avenue Nicolas II, not far from the train station. These days, Nice is a busy, bustling city with an incredible amount of

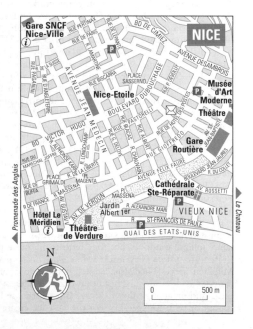

traffic, but it's still a lovely place, with a beautiful location and attractive historical centre. The city also makes the best base for visiting the Riviera coast, which stretches for 30km, east to the Italian border and west to Cannes. **Carnival** (Feb/early March) packs out the town, with parades and music culminating at Mardi Gras, a city-wide party that takes up every street. The old town, **Vieux Nice**, nestles around the hill of Nice's former château, a rambling collection of narrow alleys lined with tall, rust-and-ochre houses, sadly scarred by a bewildering amount of graffiti, and centring on place Rossetti and the Baroque **Cathédrale Ste-Réparate**. Nearby is the entrance to the **Parc du Château** (there's an elevator and stairway by the Tour Bellanda, at the eastern end of quai des États-Unis), decked out in a mock-Grecian style harking back to the original Greek settlement of Nikea. The point of climbing the stairs, apart from enjoying the perfumed greenery, is the view stretching west over the bay. Nearby, on promenade des Arts, is the **Musée d'Art Moderne et d'Art Contemporain** (Tues–Sun 10am–6pm; €4), with a collection of Pop Art and neo-Realist work, including pieces by Andy Warhol and Roy Lichtenstein. The **Musée des Beaux-Arts** (Tues-Sun 10am–6pm; €4), meanwhile, is on the other side of town at 33 av des Baumettes, with a superb collection of works dating from the fifteenth to the twentieth century.

Up above the city centre, **Cimiez**, a posh suburb reached by bus #15 from av Thiers, was the social centre of the town's elite some seventeen centuries ago, when the city was capital of the Roman province of Alpes-Maritimae. Excavations of the Roman baths are housed, along with accompanying archeological finds, in the **Musée d'Archéologie**, 160 av des Arènes (Mon & Wed–Sun 10am–6pm; €4). Overlooking the baths is the wonderful **Musée Matisse** (Mon & Wed–Sun 10am–6pm; €4): Nice was the artist's home for much of his life, and the collection covers every period and includes models for the chapel in Vence, a complete set of the books that he illustrated, and *Fleurs et Fruits*, a large decorative piece created for a Californian villa by Matisse in 1953.

Practicalities

Nice **airport** is 6km southwest, connected to its train station by bus #99 (daily 8am–9pm, every 30min; €3.50) and centre by bus #23 (daily 6/7am–8/8.50pm, every 10/15min; €1.30). The main **train station**, Nice-Ville, is ten minutes' walk northwest from the centre, at the top of av Jean-Médecin. There's a **tourist office** next to the station on av Thiers (daily: June–Sept 7.30am–8pm; rest of the year 8am–7pm) and another one at the airport (June–Sept daily 8am–10pm; rest of the year Mon–Sat 8am–10pm), with the main office at 5 promenade des Anglais (Mon–Sat 8/9am–6/8pm; June–Sept also Sun 9am–6pm; ☏08.92.70.74.07, ⓦwww.nicetourism.com). For **city transport**, single bus tickets (€1.30) can be bought on board, while *carnets* of ten (€8.50) are available from kiosks and *tabacs*, who also sell the one-, five- and seven-day **bus pass** (€4, €13, €17). There are lots of cheap, though not terribly attractive, **hotels** around the train station, including *Les Orangers*, 10bis av Durante (☏04.93.87.51.41, ⓕ04.93.82.57.82; ❸). There's a better choice in the centre, such as the friendly *Carlyna*, 2 rue Sacha Guitry (☏04.93.80.77.21, ⓕ04.93.80.08.80; ❹), and the *Cronstadt*, 3 rue Cronstadt (☏04.93.82.00.30, ⓕ04.93.16.87.40; ❺). The **hostel** is 4km out of town on route Forestière du Mont-Alban (☏04.93.89.23.64; €8.40); take bus #14 from place Masséna. The tourist office has a list of the numerous **campsites** in the area.

The old town stays up late and is full of **restaurants**. Marché aux Fleurs (not to be missed in the mornings for its colourful market) is lined with restaurants, their tables spilling outdoors, but they tend to be quite pricey. *Pasta Basta*, 18 rue de la Préfecture, offers very good value *plats du jour*; while *Chez René Socca*, 2 rue Miralhéti, serves Niçois specialities at busy outdoor tables, including great *socca*, a pancake made from chickpea flour. *Passez à Table*, 30 rue Pertinax, serves vegetarian meals and organic produce. *Wayne's* **bar** on rue de la Préfecture has live music and is popular with backpackers. For the best ice cream in town, head for *Fenocchio* on

10

place Rossetti, where you can sample such novel flavours as lavender, tomato and thyme. *La Florentine*, on the corner of rue de France and rue Meyerbeer, in the new part of town, is a great place for authentic Italian coffee and pastries. For **Internet** access, there's Cyber Point at 10 av Félix Faure.

Monaco

The tiny independent principality of **MONACO** rears up over the rocky Riviera coast like a Mediterranean Hong Kong. The ruling family, the Grimaldis, have held power here for more than seven centuries. The present Prince, Rainier III – who famously married American actress Grace Kelly – has been on the throne since 1949. The three-kilometre-long state consists of the old town of Monaco-Ville; Fontvieille; La Condamine by the harbour; Larvotto – with its artificial beaches of imported sand – and, in the middle, **MONTE CARLO**. There are relatively few conventional sights, best the superb aquarium at the **Musée Océanographique** on av St-Martin (daily 9/10am–7/8pm; €11), which displays a living coral reef, transplanted from the Red Sea into a 40,000-litre tank. Also unmissable is the famous **Casino** (daily noon–dawn; admission €15; over-21s only) – and you'll be refused entry if you don't look enough like a gambler.

The **train station** is on av Prince-Pierre in La Condamine, a short walk from the **bus station** on place d'Armes. Bus #4 (direction Larvotto) takes you from the train station to the Casino-Tourism stop, near the **tourist office** at 2a bd des Moulins (Mon–Sat 9am–7pm, Sun 10am–noon; ☎92.16.61.16, ⊛www.monaco-tourisme.com). The efficient and free lift system spares steep north–south journeys. **Accommodation** is often in short supply, especially when the Grand Prix is in town (end of May/beginning of June). La Condamine is your best bet: try *Helvetia*, 1bis rue Grimaldi (☎93.30.21.71, ⊛hotel-helvetia@monte-carlo.mc; ❹); or *Hôtel de France*, 6 rue de la Turbie (☎93.30.24.64, ⊛hotel-france@monte-carlo.mc; ❻). **Dorm beds** are available at *RIJ Villa Thalassa*, on the coast at Cap d'Ail, 3km from Monte Carlo towards Nice (☎04.93.78.18.58; €14). Regular train services link Cap d'Ail train station, 300m from the hostel, to Monaco – alternatively you can walk there by the sea in about an hour. La Condamine and the old town are the places to look for – usually expensive – **restaurants**; try *Le Pinocchio*, 30 rue Félix Gastaldi.

Corsica (Corse)

Despite nearly two-and-a-half centuries of French rule, the island of **CORSICA** (Corse in French) has more in common culturally with Italy than with its governing country, with which it has for the past three decades been locked in a grim – and often bloody – struggle for autonomy. A history of repeated invasion has strengthened the cultural identity of an island whose reputation for violence and xenophobia has overshadowed the more hospitable nature of its inhabitants. An amazing diversity of landscapes are to be found in Corsica, one third of which is protected as a national park: its magnificent rocky coastline is interspersed with outstanding beaches, while the mountains soar to 2706m at Monte Cinto – one of a string of Pyrenean-scale peaks lining the island's granite spine. The extensive forests and sparkling rivers provide the locals with a rich supply of game and fresh fish: regional specialities include wild boar, chestnut-flour dishes, a soft ewe's cheese called *brocciu* and some of France's most prized *charcuterie* (cured meats).

Two French *départements* divide Corsica, each with its own capital: Napoleon's birthplace, **Ajaccio**, is on the southwest coast, while **Bastia** faces Italy in the north. The old capital of **Corte** dominates the interior, backed by a formidable wall of mountains. Of the coastal resorts, **Calvi** draws tourists with its massive citadel and long sandy beach, while **Bonifacio**, huddled on the southernmost point facing Sardinia, is a tightly

For full details of **ferries to Corsica**, go to ⓦwww.corsicaferries.com, ⓦwww.corsica-marittima.com, ⓦwww.happylines.it, ⓦwww.mobylines.it, ⓦwww.saremar.it or ⓦwww.sncm.fr. The Nice-Calvi and Livorno-Bastia routes are covered by fast NGV hydrofoils, which cost the same as conventional ferries. The cheapest crossings are from Nice (€15–25) and the mainland Italian ports (€15–27).

From France
Marseille to: Ajaccio (3–7 weekly; 4hr 30min–11hr); Bastia (1–3 weekly; 10hr).
Nice to: Ajaccio (1–6 weekly; 12hr); Bastia (3–24 weekly; 6–7hr); Calvi (2–5 weekly; 2hr 45min).
Toulon to: Ajaccio (April–Sept 1–4 weekly; 10hr); Bastia (April–Oct 1–3 weekly; 8hr 30min).

From Italy
Genoa to: Bastia (June–Sept 4–6 weekly; 6–11hr).
La Spezia to: Bastia (May–Sept 5–7 weekly; 5hr).
Livorno to: Bastia (April–Oct 1–6 daily; 2–7hr).
Piombino to: Bastia (July to mid-Sept 1 daily; 3hr 30min).
Santa-Teresa-di-Gallura (Sardinia) to: Bonifacio (2–4 daily; 1hr 30min).
Savona to: Bastia (June–Sept 2–3 weekly; 3hr).

packed grid of Genoan houses perched atop limestone cliffs buffeted by the clearest water in the Mediterranean. The most dramatic of the island's landscapes, though, lie around the **Golfe de Porto** in the far northwest. Corsica's narrow-gauge **train** connects the island's main towns. InterRail and other passes are valid for all services, or you could invest in a dedicated **Carte Zoom** (from any station; €45), which gives unlimited train travel over a seven-day period. Otherwise you're reliant on **buses**, which run regularly between the larger towns but rarely reach the interior villages; services are scaled back drastically between November and May.

Punctuated by refuges offering cheap beds and bivouac-camping space, **trekking routes** penetrate some of the wildest and most dramatic terrain in the entire Mediterranean, though you'll need good footwear, waterproof gear and a lightweight pack to tackle them. On lower altitude **coast-to-coast walks**, accommodation is provided in *gîtes d'étapes* (hikers' hostels) costing around €10 per dorm bed. For further information, contact the Parc Naturel Régional Corse, 2 rue Sergeant-Casalonga, Ajaccio (☎04.95.51.79.00, ⓦwww.parc-naturel-corse.fr).

Ajaccio

Set in a magnificent bay, **AJACCIO** combines all the ingredients of a Riviera-style town with its palm trees, spacious squares, glamorous marina and street cafés. Napoleon was born here in 1769, but did little for the place except to make it the island capital for the brief period of his empire. It is, however, a pleasant spot to spend time, particularly around the harbour and narrow streets inland from the fifteenth-century Genoese citadel. The most rewarding sight is the **Musée Fesch**, halfway down rue Cardinal-Fesch (Mon 1–5.15/6.30pm; Tues–Sun 9.15am–12.15pm & 2.15–5.15/6.30pm; €5.35), home to the country's finest collection of Renaissance paintings outside Paris, including works by Botticelli, Titian and Poussin. As for beaches, avoid the Plage St-François, below the citadel, in favour of the cleaner **Plage Trottel**, ten minutes' further away from the centre along the promenade. Better still, jump on one of the hourly buses that run from the bus station to the beaches beyond the airport and Porticcio, on the far southern side of the gulf: **Plage de Verghia**, at the end of the bus route, is the nicest and has a pleasant campsite, *La Vallée* (☎04.95.25.44.66; closed Nov–April).

The **airport**, Campo dell'Oro, is 8km southeast and connected to town by shuttle bus (€5); taxis cost around €25. The **ferry port** and **bus station** occupy the same building in the town centre, but the **train station** is a ten-minute walk north along the seafront. The **tourist office** (summer Mon–Sat 9am–8.30pm, Sun 9am–1pm; winter Mon–Fri 8am–6pm, Sat 8am–noon & 2–5pm; ☎04.95.51.53.03, ⓦwww.tourisme.fr/ajaccio) is on the place du Marché, directly behind the Hôtel de Ville on place Foch. Budget **accommodation** is thin on the ground and books up fast, especially at weekends. Try *Le Dauphin*, just north of the ferry port/bus station on bd Sampiero (☎04.95.21.12.94; ④), or *Marengo*, twenty minutes' walk from the centre at 2 rue Marengo (☎04.95.21.43.66; ⑤). The most convenient **campsite** is *Le Barbicaja*, 5km west (☎04.95.52.01.17; closed Nov–March); take bus #5 from place de Gaulle.

For location, the **restaurants** along quai de la Citadelle are hard to beat, though the seafood served up tends to be mediocre; stick to pizza and a *pichet* of house red and you'll not go far wrong. Out on the route Sanguinaires (near the *Barbicaja* campsite; bus #5), the *Ariadne* has a much funkier atmosphere, with World cuisine, live salsa or reggae most nights and a terrace right on a little beach. Hanging out in **bars** dressed up to the nines is a favourite pastime in Ajaccio, and cafés, cocktail joints and *glaciers* line most of the pavements and squares. The oldest watering hole in town, and the one with the most authentically Ajaccien atmosphere, is *Le Grand Café Napoleon*, at the south end of the main cours Napoleon. At weekends, *Safari* and its neighbours next to the casino (behind the plage St-François) is where *le beau monde* strut their stuff. Game.net, on the corner of cours Napoleon and place de Gaulle, offers **Internet** access.

Le Golfe de Porto

Corsica's most startling landscapes surround the **Golfe de Porto**, in the northwest of the island. A deep blue bay, enfolded by outlandish red cliffs, the gulf is framed by snow-topped mountains and a vast pine forest. The entire area holds endless possibilities for outdoor enthusiasts, with a superb network of waymarked trails (free maps available from Porto tourist office) and canyoning routes, perfect kayaking bays and some of the finest diving sites in the Mediterranean. Less adventurous visitors can explore the coast on one of the excursion boats that work out of the village of **PORTO** itself, the gulf's main tourist hub, where there's a **tourist office** (☎04.95.26.10.55, ⓦwww.porto-tourisme.com) and a huge range of **accommodation**. Best value among the cheap hotels are the *Panorama* (☎04.95.26.11.05; ③) on the route de la Marine, and *Le Golfe*, opposite the Genoese watchtower (☎04.95.26.13.33; ④). Of the four **campsites**, the *Camping Sol e Vista*, behind the supermarkets just off the main road, is the most pleasant.

Calvi

Seen from the water, the great citadel of **CALVI** resembles a floating island, sharply defined by a hazy backdrop of snowcapped mountains. Home to the Paratroop Regiment of the Foreign Legion, this is the island's third port, a light-hearted holiday town which draws thousands of tourists to its 6km of sandy beach. The **Haute Ville**, a labyrinth of cobbled lanes and stairways, rises from **place Christophe Colomb**, the square which links the two parts of town. The name of the *place* derives from the local belief (hotly disputed by historians) that the "discoverer" of the New World was born here, in a now ruined house on the edge of the citadel. The **Basse Ville** backs onto the marina and to reach the **beach**, keep walking past the boats.

Calvi's **airport** is 8km southeast, with only **taxis** (€14–16) available to get you into town. **Trains** stop behind the marina, and close by is the stop for **buses** from Bastia. The **ferry port** is below the citadel, at the far end of quai Landry. The **tourist office** is at the opposite end of the harbourside, behind the marina (daily

9am–5/7pm; winter closed noon–2pm & all Sun; ☎04.95.65.16.67, ⓦwww
.tourisme.fr/calvi). The most convenient budget **accommodation** is at *BVJ
Corsotel* (☎04.95.65.14.16; €20.60; closed Nov–April), in a grand building overlooking the marina, where rates include breakfast and an evening meal.
Alternatively, there's the *Hôtel du Centre* (☎04.95.65.02.01; ❸), hidden away in the
Basse Ville at 12 rue Alsace-Lorraine. The long pine forest behind the sands shelter a
string of large **campsites**, among which *la Pinède* (☎04.95.65.17.00), 2km out of
town, is one of the smartest; you can reach it on the hourly trains from Calvi station. **Restaurants** cram the streets of the Basse Ville; of the options along quai
Landry, the *Pizzeria Cappuccino* is affordable, while further into the old quarter, *U
San Carlu*, pl St-Charles, serves excellent seafood at reasonable prices. Lively but
touristy *La Santa Maria*, 14 rue Clemenceau, turns out some unusual Corsican specialities such as *stifatu,* a tasty blend of stuffed meats; while the famous piano bar
and restaurant *Chez Tao* is worth a visit for its impressive views of the bay.

Bastia

BASTIA is a charismatic harbour town, its crumbling buildings set against a backdrop of bare hills. Now a thriving commercial port, it was the island capital under
the Genoese and has remained a working town with few concessions to tourism.
However, it has much to recommend it: the dilapidated Vieux Port, a sprinkling of
Baroque churches, the imposing citadel, or bastion, from which the town gets its
name, and the vast place St-Nicolas, lined with trees and cafés open to the sea.

The most appealing area is the **Vieux Port**, the site of the original fishing village
around which the town grew. Dominating the harbour are the twin towers of
Église St-Jean-Baptiste, the largest church in Bastia, which shoulders the place
du Marché, where a lively **market** takes place each morning. A flight of steps leads
from the southern edge of the harbour up through a small park to the citadel, or
Terra Nova. Worth hunting out amid the grid of colour-washed old tenements is
the **Oratoire St-Croix**, a splendidly gaudy Baroque chapel renowned for its mira-
cle-working black crucifix.

Bastia's **airport** is 16km south of town off RN197. Shuttle **buses** to the centre
(€8) terminate opposite the **train station**, located above pl St-Nicolas. Other
buses stop opposite the **tourist office** on the north side of pl St-Nicolas (June–
Sept daily 8am–6/7pm; Oct–May Mon–Sat 8am–6/7pm; ☎04.95.54.20.41,
ⓦwww.bastia-tourisme.com) – only worth dropping into for bus timetables.
Ferries dock a short way north of pl St-Nicolas. Pick of the budget **accommodation** is the *Central*, 3 rue Miot (☎04.95.31.71.12, ⓦwww.centralhotel.fr; ❺), just
off the south side of place St-Nicolas; alternatively, there's the *Riviera*, 1 rue du
Nouveau Port (☎04.95.31.07.16; ❺), or the *Posta-Vecchia*, near the Vieux Port on
the quai des Martyrs (☎04.95.32.32.38, ⓔhotel-postavecchia@wandadoo.fr; ❺).
Top **campsite** is *Camping Casanova* (☎04.95.33.91.42; closed Nov–Feb), 5km
north at Miomo (buses every 30min Mon–Sat, hourly Sun, until 7.30pm from the
top of place St-Nicholas opposite the tourist office). The Vieux Port and nearby
market place are crammed with **restaurants**. For lunch, *La Table du Marché*, on the
east side of place du Marché, has the best deal. In the evening, head for the outdoor
cafés on the harbourside or the quirky *Chez Jo La Braise*. *Le Pub Assunta*, at 5 pl
Fontaine-Neuve (just off the south end of bd Paoli) is a dependably lively **bar**,
hosting live music on Thursdays.

Corte

Set against a spectacular backdrop of craggy mountains, **CORTE**, the island's only
interior town, is regarded as the spiritual capital of Corsica, as this is where Pascal
Paoli had his seat of government during the brief period of independence in the
eighteenth century. Paoli founded a university here which reopened in the early
1980s, and its student population add a much needed bit of life. For outdoor enthu-

siasts, this is also an ideal base for trekking, with two superb gorges stretching west into the heart of the mountains. The main street, cours Paoli, runs the length of town, culminating in **place Paoli**, a pleasant market square lined with cafés. A cobbled ramp leads from there up to the Ville Haute, where you can still see the bullet marks made by Genoese soldiers during the War of Independence in tiny **place Gaffori**. Continuing north you'll come to the gates of the **Citadelle**, behind whose well-preserved ramparts is a museum hosting a collection of old farming implements. Give this a miss, as the best views of the citadel, town and valley are from the **Belvédère**, a platform opposite the tower which you don't have to pay to reach.

Corte's **train station** is 1km east of town at the foot of the hill near the university. **Buses** stop at the south end of cours Paoli. The **tourist office** is within the citadel (Mon–Fri 9am–1pm & 2–6/8pm; ☎04.95.46.26.70, ⓦwww.corte-tourism.com), where there's a desk of the **Parc Naturel Régional Corse** (same hours), providing information for walkers. **Accommodation** is plentiful and inexpensive in comparison with the rest of the island. *Hôtel HR*, near the train station on allée du 9 Septembre (☎04.95.45.11.11; ❷), is a charmless but cheap converted police station; or there's the more characterful *de la Poste*, 2 pl Padoue (☎04.95.46.01.37; ❸), and the smart, friendly and efficient *du Nord et de L'Europe*, halfway along cours Paoli (☎04.95.46.00.68, ⓦwww.hotel-dunord-corte.com; ❸). Of the five **campsites**, much the nicest is the *Ferme Equestre l'Albadu* (☎04.95.46.24.55), fifteen minutes' walk away – follow the main road south down the hill from place Paoli and take the second right after crossing the second river bridge. Of the many **restaurants** around place Gaffori, the *Paglia Orba* on av Xavier Luciani is your best bet, with plenty of vegetarian options. For a more inspiring location try *U Museu*, huddled beneath the citadel's walls and serving a superb goat's cheese salad and tasty wild boar stew.

Bonifacio

BONIFACIO is superbly isolated on a narrow peninsula of dazzling white limestone at Corsica's southernmost point, only minutes by boat from Sardinia. For five hundred years the town was a virtually independent republic, and a sense of detachment from the rest of Corsica persists, with many Bonifaciens still speaking their own dialect. It has become a chic holiday spot and sailing centre, and can be unbearably overcrowded in midsummer. The **Haute Ville** is connected to the marina by a steep flight of steps at the west end of the quay, at the head of which is revealed the glorious view across the straits to Sardinia. Within the massive fortifications of the citadel is packed an alluring maze of cobbled streets. Keep heading west and you'll emerge from the houses at the **Cimetière Marin**, a walled cemetery at the far end of the promontory filled with elaborate mausoleums. From the marina, take a **boat excursion** (€8–10, depending on demand and how well you haggle) round the base of the cliffs and out to the **sea-caves**, grottoes where the rock glitters with rainbow colours and the turquoise sea is deeply translucent. Some outstanding **beaches** lie near Bonifacio, most notably the shell-shaped plage de la Rondinara, 10km north. Further north still, off the main Porto-Vecchio road, the plages de Santa Giulia and Palombaggia wouldn't look outclassed in the Maldives.

Ferries from Sardinia dock at the far end of the quay; **buses** from Ajaccio stop in the car park by the marina. The **tourist office** is in the Haute Ville, at the bottom of rue Fred Scamaroni (May–Oct daily 9am–noon & 2–6/8pm; Nov–April closed Sat afternoon & all Sun; ☎04.95.73.11.88, ⓦwww.bonifacio.com). Most affordable **hotel** is *Étrangers*, 1km out of town from the marina on av Sylver Bohn (☎04.95.73.01.09; ❻). En route to it you pass the campsite, *L'Araguina* (☎04.95.73.02.96). For **food**, head for *Cantina Doria*, up in the Haute Ville on rue Doria, which does affordable Bonifacien specialities such as stuffed aubergine. *Les Kissing Pigs*, on the marina near the ferry dock, is a quirky **bar** that stays open late.

Travel details

Trains

Ajaccio to: Bastia (4 daily; 3hr 15min); Calvi (2 daily; 4hr 25min); Corte (4 daily; 1hr 45min).

Bastia to: Ajaccio (4 daily; 3hr 10min); Calvi (2 daily; 3hr); Corte (2–4 daily; 1hr 30min).

Bergerac to: Sarlat (2–6 daily; 1hr 15min).

Bordeaux to: Bayonne-Biarritz (10 daily; 1hr 45min); Bergerac (10 daily; 1hr 20min); Marseille (5 daily; 6hr 30min); Nice (3 daily; 8hr 30min); Périgueux (19 daily; 1hr 20min); Toulouse (17 daily; 2hr 20min).

Calvi to: Ajaccio (2 daily; 3hr 30min); Bastia (2 daily; 3hr 30min); Corte (2 daily; 2hr 30min).

Clermont-Ferrand to: Marseille (at least 6 daily, most of them changing at Lyon; 4hr 40min–6hr 20min); Nîmes (4 daily; 4hr 50min); Toulouse (at least 6 daily, most of them changing at Lyon; 6–10hr).

Corte to: Ajaccio (4 daily; 2hr); Bastia (4 daily; 2hr); Calvi (2 daily; 2hr 30min).

Dijon to: Beaune (frequent; 25min); Lyon (10–15 daily; 1hr 45min).

Le Puy to: Lyon (2–4 daily; 2hr 30min).

Lyon to: Avignon (14 daily; 2hr 30min); Grenoble (8–10 daily; 1hr 30min); Marseille (4–7 daily; 3hr 30min); Orange (8 daily; 2hr 20min).

Nancy to: Strasbourg (8–13 daily; 1hr 30min).

Nice to: Marseille (every 40min daily; 2hr 45min); St-Raphaël (every 20min; 1hr 15min).

Nîmes to: Arles (7 daily; 20min); Avignon (9 daily; 30min); Clermont-Ferrand (4 daily; 4hr 50min); Marseille (10 daily; 1hr 20min); Montpellier (hourly; 30min); Perpignan (10–15 daily; 2hr 10min).

Paris to: Avignon (6 daily; 4hr); Bayonne (6 daily; 4hr 30min); Besançon (6 daily; 2hr 30min); Bordeaux (hourly; 3hr); Boulogne (4–6 daily; 2hr 40min); Brest (hourly until 7pm; 6hr); Caen (hourly; 2hr–2hr 30min); Calais (1–3 daily; 3hr 30min); Carcassonne (4 daily; 8hr); Cherbourg (roughly every 2hr; 3hr–3hr 30min); Clermont-Ferrand (3–6 daily; 3hr 30min); Dieppe (2 daily; 2hr 15min); Dijon (frequent; 1hr 40min–3hr 15min); Grenoble (6 daily; 3hr 20min); Le Havre (every 2–3hr; 2hr–2hr 30min); Lille (hourly; 1hr); Lyon (half-hourly; 2hr–2hr 30min); Marseille (every 2hr; 3hr 15min); Metz (9 daily; 2hr 30min); Montpellier (10 daily; 3hr 25min); Nancy (11 daily; 2–3hr); Nantes (frequent; 3hr 30min); Nice (10 daily; 5–6hr); Nîmes (10 daily; 3hr); Pau (8 daily; 5hr 30min); Poitiers (every 2hr; 1hr 30min); Reims (8 daily; 1hr 30min); Rennes (hourly; 2hr 30min); Rouen (hourly; 1hr 15min); Strasbourg (every 2 hours; 4hr); Toulouse (10 daily; 5hr 30min–6hr 30min); Tours (7–15 daily; 1hr 10min).

Périgueux to: Les Eyzies (2–5 daily; 30min).

Poitiers to: Bordeaux (3–15 daily; 1hr 45min); La Rochelle (12 daily; 1hr 45min).

Rennes to: Nantes (3–8 daily; 2hr); Quimper (4–10 daily; 2hr 30min); St-Malo (4–10 daily; 1hr 15min).

Sens to: Dijon (3–5 daily; 2hr).

Toulouse to: Albi (9–19 daily; 1hr); Bayonne-Biarritz (5 daily; 3hr); Bordeaux (12 daily; 2hr 20min); Clermont-Ferrand (at least 6 daily, most of them changing at Lyon; 6–10hr); Lourdes (6–10 daily; 2hr 20min); Lyon (9 daily changing at Montpellier; also at least two direct trains daily; 4hr 40min); Marseille (9 daily; 4hr); Pau (5–8 daily; 2hr 30min).

Tours to: Chinon (6–10 daily; 45min–1hr 10min); Loches (6–10 SNCF trains or buses daily; 1hr); Lyon (3 daily; 5hr); Orléans (at least hourly; 1hr 20min); Saumur (10 daily; 30–50min).

Buses

Ajaccio to: Bastia (2 daily; 3hr); Bonifacio (2 daily; 4hr); Corte (2 daily; 1hr 45min).

Corte to: Ajaccio (2 daily; 2hr); Bastia (2 daily; 1hr 15min).

Ferries

For Channel crossings, see p.15; for Corsica crossings, see p.368.

Germany

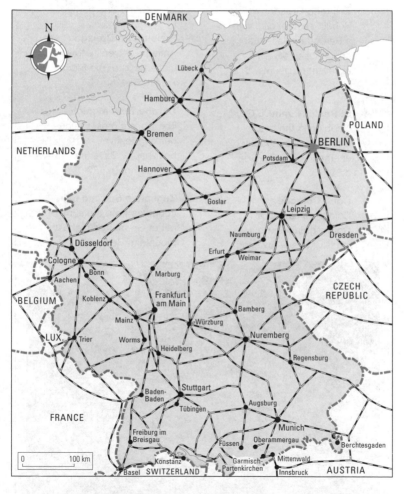

Germany highlights

* **Berlin** Dramatic history and cool modernity combine impressively in this most vibrant of European capitals. See p.378

* **Zwinger, Dresden** Rebuilt eastern city, with a Baroque palace that now houses several excellent museums. See p.389

* **St Pauli, Hamburg** Go clubbing in the buzziest district of this attractive, energetic port city. See p.393

* **Dom, Cologne** Cologne's cathedral is Gothic grandeur on a massive scale, towering above this exciting Rhineside city. See p.399

* **Rhine Gorge** Sit back for a half-day cruise through some spectacular scenery. See p.404

* **Freiburg im Breisgau** Amiable university town in the heart of the Black Forest. See p.417

* **Oktoberfest, Munich** The world's most famous drinking festival, in the beer-happy Bavarian capital. See p.423

* **Zugspitze** See into four countries from the summit of Germany's highest mountain. See p.424

Introduction and basics

The stereotype of **Germany** as a great monolith has always been a long way from the truth. Regional characteristics are a strong feature of German life, and there are many hangovers from the days when the country was a patchwork of independent states. To travel from the ancient ports of the north, across the open fields of the German plain, down through the Ruhr conurbation, and on to the forests, mountains and cosmopolitan cities of the south is to experience a variety as great as any European country can offer.

Several cities have the air of national capitals. **Cologne**, with a spectacular cathedral, is rich in monuments. **Munich** is another star attraction, with great museums and thriving nightlife. **Berlin** has an engaging, and sometimes electrifying, atmosphere, while **Nuremberg** retains more than a trace of its bygone glory. **Hamburg**, burned to the ground in 1943, is now a pleasant city with nightlife comparable to Berlin's. **Frankfurt**, the economic dynamo of postwar reconstruction, vies with the skyscrapers and consumerist buzz of **Stuttgart** for the title of commercial capital. In the east, as well as Berlin, there's the Baroque splendour of **Dresden**. However, in many respects the smaller towns of Germany offer a richer experience. There's nowhere as well loved as the university city of **Heidelberg**, while **Trier**, **Regensburg** and **Rothenburg** in the west and **Potsdam** and **Meissen** in the east are all attractive places that reward exploration.

Among the scenic highlights are the **Bavarian Alps** on Munich's doorstep, the **Bodensee** (Lake Constance) marking the Swiss border, the **Black Forest** and the **Rhine Valley**, whose majestic sweep has spawned a rich fund of legends and folklore.

Information & maps

You'll find a **tourist office** (*Fremdenverkehrsamt*) in virtually every town. Staff are invariably friendly and efficient, providing large amounts of literature and maps. The major cities share the same phone number for information: simply dial the local code followed by ☎19433. The best general **map** is Kümmerly and Frey's 1:500,000. Specialist cycling or hiking maps can be bought in the relevant regions. "Altstadt", widely used in this chapter and on streetsigns, means "Old Town".

Money and banks

German currency is the **euro** (€). **Exchange** facilities are in most banks, post offices and commercial exchange shops called *Wechselstuben*. The Deutsches ReiseBank has branches in the train stations of most main cities (generally open daily, often until 10/11pm). Basic **banking hours** are Mon–Fri 9am–noon & 1.30–3.30pm, on Thurs till 6pm. ATMs are widespread. **Credit cards** are used relatively infrequently.

Communications

Post offices are open Mon–Fri 8am–6pm & Sat 8am–noon. **Poste restante** is available at main post offices: head for the counter marked *Postlagernde Sendungen*. You can **phone** abroad from all payphones except those marked "National"; phonecards (€5)

Germany on the net

ⓦ**www.germany-tourism.de** Official tourist board site.
ⓦ**www.stadtplan.de** City maps.
ⓦ**www.webmuseen.de** Information on the country's museums.
ⓦ**www.galerie.de** Digest of the country's galleries and artists.
ⓦ**www.party.de** Nightlife and events listings.

are widely available. The **operator** is on ☎03. **Internet access** is easy to find in larger towns and cities, and many department stores (notably the Karstadt chain) also offer the facility. Expect to pay €3–4/hr.

Getting around

While it may not be cheap, getting around Germany is quick and easy. **Trains** are operated by Deutsche Bahn (DB; ⊛www.db.de). Fares cost €0.14/km second class, exclusive of supplements, and a return costs the same as two one-way tickets. The most luxurious service is the 280kph InterCityExpress (ICE); otherwise the fastest trains are InterCity (IC) and EuroCity (EC). InterRegio (IR) trains run on less heavily used routes. Major cities often have an **S-Bahn** commuter rail network. InterRail and Eurail are both valid (including on S-Bahn trains). Some also have a **U-Bahn**, or metro. Supplements apply on sleepers, and for InterRailers on fast trains as well. All stations have free pocket timetables for local routes.

Many **buses** are run by regional co-operatives in association with DB, although there are a few privately operated routes on which rail passes cannot be used. You're most likely to need buses in remote rural areas, or along designated "scenic routes" where scheduled services are more luxurious than on standard routes and buses pause at major points of interest.

Cyclists are well catered for: many smaller roads have cycle paths, and bike-only lanes are a common sight in cities. Between April and October, the best place to **rent a bike** is from a railway station participating in the *Fahrrad am Bahnhof* scheme (around €6/day). You can return it to any other participating station; rail pass-holders pay half-price.

Accommodation

Nearly all tourist offices will book **accommodation** for a fee. You're never far away from a large, functional **HI hostel** (*Jugendherberge*) – run by DJH (☎52 31/740 10, ⊛www.djh .de) – but at any time of the year (especially summer weekends) they're liable to be block-

booked by school groups, so reserve as far in advance as possible. Hostels divide into categories according to location and facilities. A bed in the most basic costs around €13; the most luxurious – which go under the title *Jugendgästehaus* (youth guest house) – charge upwards of €20. Except in youth guest houses, HI members over 27 pay around €2 extra per night; non-members, if admitted at all, also pay an extra €2 per night. Note that in the southern province of Bavaria people over 27 cannot use hostels at all, unless they're accompanying children. In larger cities, **"backpacker" hostels** tend to have less stringent rules and more personalized accommodation and service.

Hotels are all graded, clean, comfortable and functional. Just take care not to turn up in a large town or city during a trade fair, or *Messe*, when hotels often double their rates. In country areas, rock-bottom prices start at about €30 for a double room; in cities, add roughly €10. Hotels in eastern Germany are overwhelmingly geared to the business market, but the situation is much better for the budget traveller in holiday areas. **Pensions** are plentiful, either rooms above a bar or restaurant or in a private house. An increasingly prevalent budget option is **B&B** in a private house (look for signs saying *Fremdenzimmer* or *Zimmer frei*). Cheapest rates start around €25 for a double. Particularly plentiful along the main touring routes are **country inns** or **guesthouses** (*Gasthöfe* or *Gasthäuser*). The best budget option in the east is a room in a **private house**, though prices vary widely and may cost as much as €25 per person in the cities.

Even the most basic **campsites** have toilets, washing facilities and a shop, while the grandest have swimming pools and supermarkets. Prices usually comprise a fee per person and per tent (each €2.50–5), plus extra for vehicles. Many sites are full from June to September, so check-in early in the afternoon. Aside from those in popular skiing areas, most close for winter.

Food and drink

German **food** is both good value and high quality, but it helps if you share the national penchant for solid, meat-heavy fare and fresh salads. The majority of hotels and guest houses include **breakfast** in the price of the room – typically, a small platter of cold meats and cheeses, with a selection of breads, marmalades, jams and honey, and sometimes muesli and yoghurt. Elegant **cafés** are a popular institution, serving *Kaffee und Kuchen*, a choice of coffee and cream cakes or pastries. At **butcher's shops** you can generally choose from a variety of freshly roasted meats to make up a hot sandwich, though the easiest option for a snack is to head for the ubiquitous **Imbiss** stands and shops, which serve sausages, meatballs, hamburgers and chips, plus sometimes soups, schnitzels, chops, spit-roasted chickens and salads.

In **restaurants**, hot meals are usually served throughout the day; lunch tends to be treated as the main meal, with good-value menus on offer. Most of the *Gaststätte*, *Gasthaus*, *Gasthof*, *Brauhaus* or *Wirtschaft* establishments belong to a brewery and function as a *gemütlich* (cosy) meeting-point, drinking haven and cheap restaurant. Their cuisine resembles hearty home-cooking, and portions are usually generous. Main courses are overwhelmingly based on pork, served with a variety of sauces. Sausages feature regularly, with distinct regional varieties. **Vegetarians** will find eastern Germany extremely difficult – menus are almost exclusively for carnivores. However, student towns and popular stopover points are slowly becoming more veggie-friendly. Germany's multicultural society is mirrored in its wide variety of **ethnic** eateries: Italian restaurants are the most reliable, but there are also plenty offering Balkan, Greek, Turkish and Chinese cooking.

Drink

For **beer** drinkers, Germany is paradise; around forty percent of the world's breweries are found here, with some eight hundred in Bavaria alone. Munich's beer gardens and beer halls are the most famous drinking dens in the country, offering a wide variety of premier products, from dark lagers through tart *Weizens* to powerful *Bocks*. Cologne holds the world record for the number of city breweries, all of which produce the beer called *Kölsch*. Düsseldorf has its own distinctive brew, the dark *Alt*, but wherever you go you can be fairly sure of getting a locally brewed beer. Most people's knowledge of German **wine** starts and ends with Liebfraumilch, a medium-sweet wine. Sadly, its success has obscured the high quality of other German wines, especially those made from the Riesling grape. **Apfelwein** is a variant of cider beloved in and around Frankfurt. The most popular **spirits** are the fiery *Korn* and after-dinner *Schnapps*, which is usually fruit-based.

Opening hours and holidays

Shops open at 8.30am and close Mon–Sat at 8pm at the latest (more usually 5pm) and all Sun (except for bakers, who may open for a couple of hours between 11am and 3pm). Smaller shops also close noon–2pm. Exceptions are pharmacies and shops in and around train stations, which stay open late and at weekends. **Museums** and **historic monuments** are, with few exceptions (mainly in Bavaria), closed on Mon. Most museums offer half-price entry for students with valid ID and many are free on Sun. **Public holidays** are: Jan 1; Jan 6 (regional); Good Fri; Easter Mon; May 1; Ascension Day; Whit Mon; Corpus Christi (regional); Aug 15 (regional); Oct 3; Nov 1 (regional); Dec 25 & 26.

Emergencies

The **police** (*Polizei*) usually treat foreigners with courtesy. Reporting **thefts** at local police stations is straightforward, but inevitably there'll be a great deal of bureaucracy to wade through. The level of theft in eastern Germany has increased dramatically, but provided you take the normal precautions, there's no real risk. **Doctors** generally speak English. **Pharmacies** (*Apotheken*) can deal with many minor complaints and staff will often speak English. All display a rota of local pharmacies open 24hr. In western Germany you'll find international *Apotheken* in most large towns who'll be able to fill a prescription in English.

| **Emergency numbers** |
| Police ☎110; Fire & Ambulance ☎112. |

Berlin

The speed of change in **BERLIN** in the past few years has been astounding. With a long history of decadence and cultural dynamism, the revived national capital has become a magnet for artists and musicians, who were quick to see the opportunities that the cheap properties of the former East provided. Berlin today is culturally diverse, surprisingly spacious, green and welcoming, and continues to be one of the exciting capitals to visit. Events like August's annual Love Parade – the world's largest techno dance gathering – also ensure that it is in the vanguard of European youth culture.

Berlin is something of a weather-vane of modern European history. It played a dominant role in Imperial Germany, during the Weimar Republic after 1914, and in the Nazis' Third Reich. After 1945, the city was partitioned by the victorious Allies, and as a result was given the frontline of the Cold War. In 1961, its division into two hostile sectors was given a very visible expression by the construction of the notorious Berlin Wall. After the Wall fell in 1989, Berlin's status as national capital was confirmed. These days, parliament sits in the renovated Reichstag, and some of the city's world-class museum collections have been put back together again, housed in buildings at the forefront of architectural design. The central district of **Mitte** – extending either side of the main Unter den Linden boulevard, in what was formerly the Communist East – and the ritzy strip of the Kurfürstendamm, or **Ku'damm**, in the west, are where things are liveliest.

Arrival, information and city transport

From Berlin's **Tegel airport** (TXL; ⊛www.berlin-airport.de), frequent #X9 express or local #109 buses (€2.10) run to Bahnhof Zoologischer Garten (shortened to **Bahnhof Zoo**), the most important train station, located in western Berlin. The same buses also run to the other major train station, **Ostbahnhof**, which lies directly east of Mitte in the suburb of Friedrichshain. The JetExpressBus TXL (€5) runs from Tegel airport to Unter den Linden. From Berlin's **Schönefeld airport** (SXF), S-Bahn trains run to Ostbahnhof, Friedrichstrasse (just off Unter den Linden) and Bahnhof Zoo (€2.10; every 30min; 20–30min). Some trains from Poland and the east terminate at **Bahnhof Lichtenberg**, easily accessible on the S-Bahn. Most international buses stop at the **bus station** near the Fernsehturm, linked to the centre by bus #149 or U-Bahn from Kaiserdamm.

Berlin's **tourist office** is in the Europa Center at Budapester Str. 45 (Mon–Sat 8.30am–8.30pm, Sun 10am–6.30pm; ☎030/25 00 25, ⊛www.berlin-tourism.de), with additional offices at the Brandenburg Gate (daily 10am–6pm) and the Fernsehturm on Alexanderplatz (daily 10am–6pm). Smaller "Info Points" are at Tegel Airport and the KaDeWe department store, Tauentzienstr. 21–24. Berlin has two **listings magazines**, *Zitty* (€2.40; ⊛www.zitty.de) and *Tip* (€2.50; ⊛www.tip-berlin.de), published on alternate weeks.

The **U-Bahn** metro system is efficient and extensive; trains run daily 4am–12.30am (Fri & Sat 1.30am). The **S-Bahn**, whose stops are further apart, travels to the outer suburbs (such as Wannsee) and out of the city boundaries (to Potsdam). The city **bus network** – and the **tram system** in eastern Berlin – covers most of the gaps left by the U-Bahn: night buses run at intervals of around twenty minutes, although the routes often differ from daytime ones; agents in the U-Bahn stations can usually provide a map. **Tickets** can be bought from machines at U-Bahn station entrances, on trams, or from bus drivers; good for any mode of transport, they cost €2.10, allow you to travel in two of the three tariff zones, and are valid for two hours after stamping. Longer trips, from central Berlin to Potsdam for example, cost €2.40. An **Einzelfahrschein Kurzstreckentarif** (short-trip ticket, €1.20) allows you to travel up to three train or six bus stops. A **day ticket** is €6.10 for two tariff zones, €6.30 for all three. There are on-the-spot fines of €30 for those without a valid ticket or pass. The three-day **Welcome Card** (€19) provides free travel in all zones and free entrance to all the major museums.

Accommodation

Accommodation in high season can be hard to find and it's best to call at least a couple of weeks in advance. The tourist office in the Europa Center offers a free **hotel-booking service**; most of the accommodation listed can be booked on their website.

Hostels

Bax Pax Skalitzer Str. 104 ☎030/69 51 83 22. Laid-back with clean, bright-as-a-button rooms, this backpacker outfit offers cooking facilities and a rare chance to sleep in a VW Beetle. Görlitzer Bahnhof U-Bahn. €15.

The Circus Rosa-Luxemburg-Str. 39–41 & Weinbergsweg 1a ☎030/28 39 14 33, ⓦwww.circus-berlin.de. Clean, welcoming and traveller-oriented bases near the action in the east, with Internet access and breakfast service. No curfew. Rosa Luxemburg Platz U-Bahn & Rosenthaler Platz U-Bahn. €15.

Generator Hostel Storkower Str. 160 ☎030/4 17 24 00, ⓦwww.the-generator.co.uk. Truly enormous, with 854 beds in variously sized, rather institutional rooms; large clubby bar and trendy post-modern restaurant. Landsberger Allee S-Bahn. €12.

Jugendherberge JGH Berlin Kluckstr. 3 ☎030/2 61 10 98. Slightly clinical HI-option in a quiet location between the two city centres. Dorms must be booked two weeks ahead. No curfew. Bus #129 to "Gedenkstätte Deutscher Widerstand". €12.

Jugendgästehaus am Zoo Hardenberg Str. 9a ☎030/3 12 94 10. Rough and ready but extremely popular hostel; excellent location in the western side of the city. No curfew. Zoologischer Garten U- and S-Bahn or Ernst-Reuter-Platz U-Bahn. €16.

Mitte's Backpacker Hostel Chausseestr. 102 ☎030/28 39 09 65, ⓦwww.backpacker.de. In a renovated factory building on the city's east side, this welcoming hangout for the party crowd features themed rooms including the "honeymoon suite". No curfew. U-Bahn line #6. €15.

Odyssee Globetrotter Hostel Grunberger Str. 23 ☎030/29 00 00 81, ⓦwww.globetrotterhostel.de. Young, well-organized hostel with individually designed rooms, ideally situated for the Friedrichshain nightlife scene. No curfew. Frankfurter Tor U-Bahn. €16.

Hotels

Acksel Haus Belforter Str. 21 ☎030/44 33 76 33. Small, effortlessly stylish hotel in the midst of the lively Prenzlauer Berg scene. ⑤

Artemisia Brandenburgerischestr. 18 ☎030/8 73 89 05, ⓦwww.artemisia-berlin.com. Women-only hotel with airy pastel-coloured rooms and a pleasant roof terrace. ⑥

Artist Hotelpension Die Loge Friedrichstr. 115 ☎030/2 80 75 13. Seven well-equipped rooms with an earthy, arty charm in this small friendly hotel. ⑤

Bogota Schlüterstr. 45 ☎030/8 81 50 01, ⓦwww.hotelbogota.de. Traditional style, including a dozen four-bed rooms, in a stuffy but comfortable 1911 building. ⑥

Bregenz Bregenzer Str. 5 ☎030/8 81 43 07, ⓦwww.hotelbregenz-berlin.de. Very quiet and cosy family-run set-up only a 5min walk from the Ku'damm. ⑤

Charlot Giesebrechstr. 17 ☎030/3 27 96 60. Neatly restored but impersonal mid-range hotel near Adenauerplatz. Good value for money. ⑤

Merkur Torstr. 156 ☎030/2 82 82 97. Comfortable rooms, including one with five beds, within easy walking distance of city-centre attractions and local nightlife. Most rooms have showers. ⑤

Western Berlin

Bahnhof Zoo (Zoo Station) is at the centre of the city's western side: a short walk south and you're at the eastern end of the Kurfürstendamm, or **Ku'damm**, a 3.5-kilometre strip of ritzy shops, cinemas, bars and cafés. A landmark here is the Kaiser-Wilhelm-Gedächtniskirche, destroyed by British bombing in 1943 and left as a reminder of the horrors of war. There's little to do on the Ku'damm other than stroll, window-shop and spend money; the only cultural attraction nearby is the **Käthe-Kollwitz-Museum** at Fasanenstr. 24 (Mon & Wed–Sun 11am–6pm; €5; ⓦwww.kaethe-kollwitz.de), devoted to the drawings and prints of the left-wing pacifist artist Käthe Kollwitz.

The zoo itself, beside Zoo Station, forms the beginning of the **Tiergarten**, a restful expanse of woodland and a good place to wander along the banks of the

BERLIN

Tegel Airport (2km)

Ⓤ U-Bahn
Ⓢ S-Bahn

Jungfernheide

Belvedere
Mierendorffplatz

Schloss
Charlottenburg

Schinkel-Pavillon

Berggruen-
Sammlung

Ägyptisches
Museum

Westend
Bröhan-
Museum

CHARLOTTENBURG

Richard-
Wagner-Platz

Siegessäule

Tiergarten

Bellevue

Hansaplatz

Deutsche
Oper

Ernst-
Reuter-Platz

Sophie-
Charlotte-Platz

Bahnhof
Zoo

Zoologischer
Garten

Wilmersdorfer
Str.

Charlottenburg

Savignyplatz

Kaiser-
Wilhelm-
Gedächtniskirche

Europa-Center

Westkreuz

Adenauerplatz

Uhlandstr.

Kurfürstendamm

Käthe-Kollwitz-Museum

Wittenbergplatz

Augsburger Str.

Halensee

Spichernstr.

Viktoria-Luise-
Platz

Landwehrkanal. Strasse des 17 Juni heads all the way east to the **Brandenburg Gate**, built as a city gate-cum-triumphal arch in 1791 and now – since it stands at the fulcrum between the city's eastern and western halves, at the head of the Unter den Linden boulevard (see below) – the much-photographed symbol of German reunification. A little way north stands the **Reichstag**, the nineteenth-century home of the German parliament, remodelled by Norman Foster for the resumption of its historic role in 1999. Foster's glass cupola has become a landmark, and a popular trip to the top (daily 8am–midnight; free) affords a stunning view. Immediately behind the Reichstag, it's now only just possible to make out the course of the **Berlin Wall**, which divided the city for 28 years until November 9, 1989. The heart of prewar Berlin used to be to the south of the Brandenburg Gate, its core formed by **Potsdamer Platz**. A huge commercial project here, involving various eateries, theatres and a shopping mall built within the impressive Sony Center, attempts to recreate the area's former liveliness. Just to the east, near the corner of Wilhelmstrasse and An der Kolonnade, lies the site of **Hitler's bunker**, where the Führer spent his last days, issuing meaningless orders as the Battle of Berlin raged above.

West of Potsdamer Platz lies the Kulturforum, a series of museums centred on the unmissable **Gemäldegalerie**, Matthäikirchplatz 8 (Tues–Sun 10am–6pm, Thurs till 10pm; €6, free on 1st Sun of month; ✆www.smpk.de). Inside is a world-class collection of old masters, covering all the main European schools from the Middle Ages to the late eighteenth century. One highlight of the German section is Cranach's tongue-in-cheek *The Fountain of Youth*. The interconnected building to the north houses the **Kunstgewerbemuseum** (Tues–Sun 10/11am–6pm; €3 if

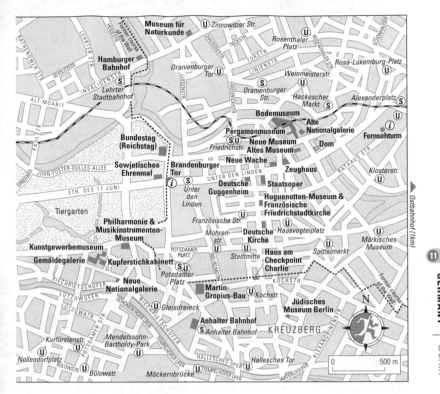

visited separately, free on 1st Sun of month; ⓦwww.smpk.de), a sparkling collection of European arts and crafts from Byzantium to Bauhaus. At Potsdamer Str. 50, a couple of minutes' walk to the south, the **Neue Nationalgalerie** (Tues–Sun 10/11am–6pm, Thurs till 10pm; €6, free on 1st Sun of month; ⓦwww.smpk.de) has a good collection of twentieth-century German paintings, best of which are the Berlin portraits and cityscapes by George Grosz and Otto Dix.

Southeast of here, the **Martin-Gropius-Bau** at Niederkirchner Str. 7 (Mon & Wed–Sun 10am–8/10pm; admission varies; ⓦwww.gropiusbau.de) is now a venue for prestigious art exhibitions. Next door, the open-air exhibition **Topography of Terror** (daily 10am–6pm; free; ⓦwww.topographie.de), occupies the former site of Gestapo and SS headquarters, and documents their history. From here it's a ten-minute walk on Wilhelmstrasse and Kochstrasse to the site of the notorious Checkpoint Charlie, the most infamous crossing-point between East and West Berlin in the old days; evidence of the trauma the Wall caused is still on hand in the popular **Haus am Checkpoint Charlie** at Friedrichstr. 43–45 (daily 9am–10pm; €7.50; ⓦwww.mauer-museum.com), which tells the history of the Wall and the stories of those who tried to break through.

The checkpoint area marks the northern limit of **Kreuzberg**, famed for its large immigrant community, its self-styled "alternative" inhabitants and nightlife. Daniel Libeskind's striking zinc-skinned **Jewish Museum Berlin** (daily 10am–8/10pm; €5; ⓦwww.jmberlin.de) documents the culture, notable achievements, and tragic history of Berlin's Jewish community using a plethora of multimedia exhibits, art installations, religious artefacts and historic manuscripts.

Eastern Berlin

The most atmospheric approach to eastern Berlin starts at the Brandenburg Gate, described above, and leads along **Unter den Linden**, a stately broad boulevard that is rapidly reassuming its prewar role as one of Berlin's most important thoroughfares. You'll pass the **Deutsche Guggenheim Berlin**, Unter den Linden 13–15 (daily 11am–8pm, Thurs till 10pm; €3, free on Mon; ®www.deutsche-guggenheim-berlin.de), which, as well as its collection of contemporary art, hosts three to four major exhibitions per year. Nearby Bebelplatz was the site of the infamous Nazi bookburning of May 10, 1933; an unusual memorial – an underground room visible through a glass panel set in the centre of the square – marks the event. More than anyone, it was Karl Friedrich Schinkel who shaped nineteenth-century Berlin. One of his most famous creations can be found opposite the Staatsoper further along Unter den Linden: the **Neue Wache**, a former royal guardhouse resembling a Roman temple and now a memorial to victims of war and tyranny. Next door is one of Berlin's finest Baroque buildings, the old Prussian Zeughaus (Arsenal).

Following Charlottenstrasse south from Unter den Linden leads to the **Gendarmenmarkt**, much of whose appeal is derived from the **Französische Kirche** on the northern side of the square. Built as a church for Berlin's influential Huguenot community at the beginning of the eighteenth century, it also now houses the **Hugenottenmuseum** (daily 11am/noon–5pm; €1.60), documenting their way of life. Friedrichstrasse, a high-class shopping district with an eclectic mix of modernist architecture, lies a block west of here.

At the eastern end of Unter den Linden lies the **Schlossplatz**, former site of the imperial palace, now home to the abandoned parliament building of the former East Germany. It stands at the midpoint of a city-centre island whose northwestern part, **Museumsinsel**, is the location of some of the best of Berlin's museums (a ticket bought at one gives same-day admission to all Berlin's state-owned museums). An extensive reconstruction programme has closed several of the museums: the Bodemuseum will remain dark until 2005, the Neues Museum until 2008. But there's plenty left, starting with the **Alte Nationalgalerie** (Tues–Sun 10am–6pm, Thurs till 10pm; €6, free on 1st Sun of month; ®www.smpk.de), which houses a collection of nineteenth-century European art. In the **Altes Museum** (Tues–Sun 10am–6pm; €6, free on 1st Sun of month; ®www.smpk.de) are Greek and Roman antiquities, though it's the **Pergamonmuseum** (Tues–Sun 10am–6pm, Thurs till 10pm; €6, free on 1st Sun of month; ®www.smpk.de) that houses the real treasure trove of the German archeologists who plundered the ancient world in the nineteenth century. Two must-sees here are the spectacular Pergamon Altar, which dates from 160 BC, and the huge Processional Way from sixth-century BC Babylon.

To reach **Alexanderplatz**, the commercial hub of eastern Berlin, head along Karl-Liebknecht-Strasse (the continuation of Unter den Linden), past the Neptunbrunnen fountain and the thirteenth-century Marienkirche. Like every other building in the vicinity, the church is overshadowed by the gigantic **Fernsehturm** (TV tower), known locally as "the Alex" (daily 9am–midnight/1am; €6; ®www.berlinerfernsehturm.de), whose observation platform and café offer unbeatable views from 203m. Southwest of here lies the **Nikolaiviertel**, a modern development that attempts to recreate the winding streets and small houses of this part of prewar Berlin, which was razed overnight on June 16, 1944.

Out of the centre

Way over to the northwest of the Tiergarten stretches the district of **Charlottenburg**, its most significant target being the sumptuously restored **Schloss Charlottenburg** (Tues–Sun 9/10am–5pm; €8). Commissioned by the future Queen Sophie Charlotte in 1695, it was added to throughout the eighteenth and early nineteenth centuries. Admission includes a tour of the main state apartments, self-guided visits to the private chambers (where the Prussian crown jewels can be seen), the Knobelsdorff-Flügel with its wonderful array of paintings by Watteau and other eighteenth-century French artists, and the Belvedere and Mausoleum in the park. Just to the south, at Schloss-Str. 70, is the **Ägyptisches Museum** (Tues–Sun 10am–6pm; €6, free on 1st Sun of month; ⓦwww.smpk.de), a fabulous collection of Egyptian antiquities; a famous bust of Nefertiti can be seen on the first floor. Also worth visiting is the **Berggruen Collection: Picasso and His Era** (Tues–Sun 10/11am–6pm; €6, free on 1st Sun of month; ⓦwww.smpk.de) directly opposite, which houses some seventy paintings collected by the former friend of the Spanish artist.

The southwestern suburb of **Dahlem**, reached by U-Bahn line #1 to Dahlem-Dorf, is home to the **Dahlem Museums** (Tues–Sun 10/11am–6pm; €3, free on 1st Sun of month; ⓦwww.smpk.de). Check out the rich and imaginatively laid out Museum of Ethnology, featuring treasures from Asia, the Pacific and South Sea Islands, and the museums of East Asian and Indian Art, the latter featuring a spectacular group of Buddhist cave paintings from the Silk Road.

For a break from the city, head out to the **Grunewald** forest, which boasts some beaches on the Havel lakes. Take S-Bahn #1 or #7 to Nikolassee station, from where it's a ten-minute walk to **Strandbad Wannsee** (April–Sept daily 8/10am–7/8pm; €4), a one-kilometre strip of pale sand that's the largest inland beach in Europe.

⑪

Eating, drinking and nightlife

The range and quality of **restaurants** in Berlin is unmatched in any other German city, and there's a wealth of **bars**, from Bavarian-style beer halls to sleek cocktail lounges. Cheapest way of warding off hunger is to use the *Imbiss* snack stands, or one of the *Mensas*, officially for German students but usually open to anyone who looks the part. Eating out in a restaurant won't break the bank, though, with prices for a main course usually between €6 and €16.

Nightlife is the equal to many European capitals. In **Eastern Berlin** there's a fast-developing scene: Oranienburger Strasse, Rosenthaler Strasse and Gipsstrasse in the Mitte neighbourhood host dozens of new bars and clubs that attract a young professional crowd as well as tourists, while the streets further north around Prenzlauer Berg and to the east around Boxhagener Strasse in Friedrichshain are more alternative. **Western Berlin** has four focal points for drinking: Savignyplatz is for conspicuous good-timers; Kreuzberg drinkers include political activists and the grungy student crowd; the area around Nollendorfplatz (northwestern Schöneberg) and Winterfeldtplatz is the territory of sped-out all-nighters and the pushing-on-forty crew; and central Schöneberg bars are on the whole more mixed and more relaxed. Unless you're into drunken businessmen, avoid the Ku'damm and the rip-off joints around the Europa Center. Don't bother turning up before midnight for the all-night clubs in Kreuzberg and Schöneberg. To find out what's on, buy one of the listings magazines *Tip*, *Zitty* or *Prinz*, get the Berlin *Programm* leaflet, or look for flyers around town.

Snacks

Al Rai Grosse Hamburger Str. 20/21, Mitte. Informal place where you can linger over tea and Arab specialities such as couscous and falafel.

Naan Pizza Zionskirch Str 104, Mitte. With an interesting blend of Asian and Italian that caters mainly for the passing late night trade.

Soup Kultur Kurfürstendamm 224. A closet-sized place that offers a budget-priced selection of ten often exotic and always delicious soups. Closed Sun.

Restaurants

Amrit Oranienburger Str. 45, Mitte. Medium-priced Indian food, a huge outdoor candlelit seating area, and cheap lunchtime deals.

Assel Oranienburger Str. 21, Mitte. A vine-covered restaurant/bar with streetside tables, a bohemian air, and a fast trade in quality breakfasts.

Athener Grill Meinekestr. 22. Kreuzberg. More moderately priced than its appearance suggests, this Greek restaurant serves hearty fare in a quiet spot off the Ku'damm.

Café Aroma Hochkirchstr. 8, Schöneberg

☎030/782 58 21. Well above average, inexpensive Italian. It's advisable to book after 8pm.

Carib Motzstr. 30, Schöneberg. Caribbean cuisine including curried goat, friendly service, lethal rum cocktails.

Casolare Grimmstr. 30, Kreuzberg. A wonderful, always packed Italian restaurant using authentic pizza bases and with a unique line in punk poster interior decor.

Einbogen Simon Dach Str. 1, Friedrichshain. Quintessential modern bar/restaurant serving decent German cuisine, with outdoor seating and a large cocktail bar.

Gugelhof Kollwitzstr. 59, Prenzlauer Berg. Stylish and popular Alsatian restaurant in the trendy Kollwitzplatz neighbourhood; the set meals are the best value.

Kellerrestaurant im Brecht-Haus Chausseestr. 125, Mitte ☎030/28 28 43. Formal restaurant in the basement of Brecht's old house, decorated with Brecht memorabilia and boasting Viennese specialities supposedly dreamt up by Brecht's wife, Helen Weigel. Booking advised.

Merhaba Hasenheide 39, Kreuzberg. Highly rated Turkish restaurant that's usually packed with locals. A selection of the starters here can be more interesting than a main course.

Monsieur Vuong Alte Schönhauser Allee 45, Mitte. This small Vietnamese has been packed since the day it opened. A small changing daily menu ensures prices are low and quality high.

Pasternak Knaackstr. 24. Intimate Russian restaurant in the thick of the bustling scene in Prenzlauer Berg; also open for breakfast.

Preet Boxhagener Str. 17, Friedrichshain. Popular, pukka and cheap Punjabi restaurant in the thick of the bars and clubs of the area.

Restaurant am Wasserturm Knaackstr. 22. Prenzlauer Berg. Favourite old Eastern European dishes with a few surprises from Jewish cuisine.

Tuk-Tuk Grossgörschenstr. 2, Schöneberg. Amiable Indonesian near Kleistpark U-Bahn, with an extensive but expensive vegetarian selection. Enquire about the heat of your dish before ordering.

Bars and cafés

Anderes Ufer Hauptstr. 157, Schöneberg. Cramped, cool yet casual gay café that's slightly kitschy and something of an institution in the city.

Ankerklause Kotthuser Damm 104, Kreuzburg. Cosy, relaxed bar overlooking the riverbank, drawing an unpretentious crowd.

Astro Simon Dach Str. 40, Friedrichshain. Always packed pre-club bar with different DJs nightly. Free entrance.

Begine Potsdamer Str. 139, Schöneberg. Stylishly decorated women-only bar/bistro/gallery with limited choice of inexpensive food.

Café Einstein Kurfürstenstr. 58, Charlottenburg. Housed in a seemingly ancient mansion, this is about as close as you'll get to the formal ambience of the prewar Berlin *Kaffeehaus*, with international newspapers and breakfast served daily till 2pm.

Lurette Boxhagener Str. 105, Friedrichshain. Retro bar/club complete with Sixties wall projections, dishing up cheap cocktails to an upbeat lounge crowd.

Morena Bar Wiener Str 60, Kreuzberg. Studenty, blue tiled bar that opens early for good breakfasts.

The Oscar Wilde Friedrichstr. 112, Mitte. A large pub near Oranienburger Tor U-Bahn, for those who prefer their pints black and with a creamy white head. Live Irish music most weekends.

The Pips Auguststr. 84, Mitte. Packed, welcoming, friendly bar with vibrant designer furnishings; different cocktail offers every day.

Schwarzes Café Kantstr. 148, Charlottenburg. Kantstrasse's best hangout for the young and chic, with a relaxed atmosphere, good music and *Kölsch* on tap. Open Mon till 3am, Tues from noon and Wed–Sun 24hr.

Schwarzsauer Kastanienalle 13/14, Prenzlauer Berg. Large, ragged alternative bar/café that is popular with students sitting out their tuition fees.

VEB OZ Auguststr. 92, Mitte. Hopelessly tacky but fun bar that attracts a loud crowd of punks and their admirers.

Zum Nussbaum Am Nussbaum 3, Mitte. In the heart of the Nikolaiviertel, this is a convincing 1980s replica of a prewar *Kneipe*.

Discos, clubs and live music venues

90 Grad Dennewitzstr. 37, Schöneberg. Practically an institution, this long-lived, predominantly gay club still maintains its cutting edge, although gaining entry past the snooty staff is never a formality.

Cookies Charlotten Str. 44, Mitte. A magnet for many locals from out-of-town, this designer club plays an eclectic mix of house, funk and techno. Cheap entrance but long queues after midnight.

Duncker Dunckerstr. 64, Mitte/Prenzlauer Berg. Indie gigs and frequent club evenings attract a party-hard local crowd. Small but atmospheric venue with deep sofas inside and open-air gigs in the back yard in summer. Cheap entrance.

Junction Bar Gneisenaustr. 18, Kreuzberg. A fixture on the local jazz circuit, with nightly concerts and DJs at the weekends.

Kaffee Burger Tor Str 60, Mitte. Small, meandering bar decorated in deep flushed red, with an attached live music venue next door.
Matrix Warschauer Platz 18. Famous disco that aims to satisfy all tastes across three dance floors. House, soul, rock and more.
Privat Club Pücklerstr. 34, Kreuzberg. Highly intimate basement club with an eclectic and unpredictable lightshow, drawing in a dance orientated crowd of all ages.
SO 36 Oranienstr. 190, kreuzberg. Dark, punky cult club with a mainly gay and lesbian following. Spontaneous outbreaks of belly dancing are not unknown.
WMF Karl Marx Alle 34, Mitte. Housed in an old GDR building, with two dancefloors and a chillout room. Pricey, but queues round the block at weekends nevertheless.

Classical music

Deutsche Oper Bismarckstr. 35 ☎030/3 41 02 49. Good classical concerts, plus opera and ballet in a large, modern venue.
Komische Oper Behrenstr. 55–57 ☎030/47 99 74 00. The house orchestra performs classical and contemporary music, and some very good opera productions are staged here.
Konzerthaus Berlin Schauspielhaus am Gendarmenmarkt, Gendarmenmarkt 2 ☎030/2 03 09 21 01. Home to the Berlin Sinfonie Orchester and host to visiting orchestras.
Philharmonie Herbert-von-Karajan-Str. 1 ☎030/25 48 80. Custom-built home of the world's most celebrated orchestra, the Berlin Philharmonic.
Staatsoper Unter den Linden 7 ☎030/20 35 45 55. Excellent operatic productions in one of central Berlin's most beautiful buildings.

Listings

Bike rental Fahradstation, Friedrichstrasse station ☎030/20 45 45 00; Pedal Power, Grossbeerenstr. 53 ☎030/78 99 19 39. From €10/day, €35/week; deposit, insurance payment and passport required.
Embassies and consulates Australia, Friedrichstr. 200 ☎030/8 80 08 80; Canada, Friedrichstr. 95 ☎030/20 31 20; Ireland, Friedrichstr. 200 ☎030/22 07 20; New Zealand, Friedrichstr. 60 ☎030/20 62 10; UK, Wilhelmstr. 70/71 ☎030/20 45 70; US, Neustädtische Kirchstr. 4–5 ☎030/83 05 0.
Exchange ReiseBank, at the main entrance to the Zoo Station (daily 7.30am–1pm), the Friedrichstrasse station (daily 7am–8pm) and the Ostbahnhof (daily 7am–1pm).
Hospitals Charité University Clinic, Schumannstr. 20/21 ☎030/4 50 50; Prenzlauer Berg Hospital, Fröbelstr. 15 ☎030/4 24 20; Spandau Hospital, Neue Bergstr. 6 ☎030/3 38 70.
Internet easyEverything, corner of Kurfürstendamm and Meinekestr; Surf and Sushi, Oranienburgerstr. 17; Zoon.com within the Sony Center, Potzdamer Platz.
Laundry Rosenthaler Str. 71; Hermannstr. 74–75.
Left luggage At major stations, such as Zoo and Friedrichstrasse.
Pharmacies Europa-Apotheke, Europa Center, Tauentzienstr. 9.
Police Platz der Luftbrücke 6 ☎030/69 95.
Post office Joachimsthaler Str. 7 (daily 8am–midnight).

Eastern Germany

By the time the Communist GDR (German Democratic Republic, or East Germany) was fully incorporated into the Federal Republic (West Germany), one year after the peaceful revolution (or Wende) of 1989, most vestiges of the old political system had been swept away. Yet there remains a long way to go before the two parts of the country achieve parity, and the cities of eastern Germany are still in the process of social and economic change. Berlin stands apart from the rest of the east, but its sense of excitement finds an echo in the two other main cities – **Leipzig**, which provided the vanguard of the revolution, and **Dresden**, the beautiful Saxon capital so ruthlessly destroyed in 1945. Equally enticing are some of the smaller places, notably **Weimar**, the fountainhead of much of European art and culture. The small cathedral town of **Meissen**, and the old Prussian royal seat of **Potsdam**, retain more of the appearance and atmosphere of prewar Germany than anywhere in the west.

Potsdam

POTSDAM is an excellent day-trip from Berlin. From Alexanderplatz,

Friedrichstrasse or Zoo, S-Bahn line #7 will take you directly to Potsdam's main station. This lies on the opposite side of the Havel from the historic centre, whose skyline is dominated by the huge dome of the Nikolaikirche. Stretching for 2km west of the centre is **Park Sanssouci** (daily 9am–dusk; free; joint ticket covering entry to all sights below €15; ⓦwww.spsg.de), the fabled retreat of the Prussian kings. These days it's too often overrun by visitors – to avoid the crowds, visit on a weekday. Frederick the Great worked closely with his court architect on designing **Schloss Sanssouci** (tours Tues–Sun 9am–4/5pm; €8), which was to be a place where the king could escape Berlin and his wife Elizabeth Christine, neither of which he cared for. Begun in 1744, it's a surprisingly modest one-storey Baroque affair, topped by a copper dome and ornamental statues looking out over vine terraces. The most eye-catching chambers are the opulent Marble Hall and the Concert Room, where the flute-playing king had eminent musicians play his own works on concert evenings. West of the palace, overlooking the ornamental Holländischer Garten, is the **Bildergalerie** (mid-May to mid-Oct Tues–Sun 10am–5pm; €3), a restrained Baroque creation that contains paintings by Rubens, Van Dyck and Caravaggio. On the opposite side of the Schloss, steps lead down to the **Neue Kammern** (mid-May to mid-Oct Tues–Sun 10am–5pm; €3), the architectural twin of the Bildergalerie, originally used as an orangery and later as a guest house. Immediately to the west of the Neue Kammern is the prim Sizilianischer Garten, crammed with coniferous trees and subtropical plants, complementing the Nordische Garten just to the north. From the west of the Sizilianischer Garten, Maulbeerallee cuts through the park and ascends to the **Orangerie** (mid-May to mid-Oct Tues–Sun 10am–5pm; €3), an Italianate Renaissance-style structure with belvedere towers. A series of terraces with curved retaining walls sporting water spouts in the shape of lions' heads leads to the sandy-coloured building. To the west through the trees rises the **Neues Palais** (Mon–Thurs, Sat & Sun 9am–4/5pm; €5), another massive Rococo extravaganza from Frederick's time. The interior is predictably opulent, though a couple of highlights stand out: the vast and startling Grottensaal on the ground floor decorated entirely with shells and semi-precious stones to form images of lizards and dragons, and the equally huge Marmorsaal, with its beautiful floor of patterned marble slabs. The southern wing (which these days houses a small café) contains Frederick's apartments and the theatre where the king enjoyed Italian opera and French plays.

Leipzig

LEIPZIG has always been among the most dynamic of German cities. With its influential and respected university, and a tradition of trade fairs dating back to the Middle Ages, there was never the degree of isolation from outside influences experienced by so many cities behind the Iron Curtain. Leipzigers have embraced the challenges of reunification and are set to show off their city during the 2006 World Cup. In the meantime, its imposing monuments, narrow cobbled backstreets and wide-ranging nightlife make for an inviting visit. Most points of interest lie within the old centre. Following Nikolaistrasse due south from the train station brings you to the **Nikolaikirche**, a rallying point during the Wende. Although a sombre medieval structure outside, inside the church is a real eye-grabber. A couple of blocks west is the Markt, whose eastern side is entirely occupied by the **Altes Rathaus** (Tues–Sun 10am–6pm; €2.50, free on 1st Sun in month), built in the grandest German Renaissance style with elaborate gables, an asymmetrical tower and the longest inscription to be found on any building in the world. On the north side of the square is the handsome **Alte Waage**, or weigh house. To the rear of the Altes Rathaus, approached by a graceful double flight of steps, is the **Alte Handelsbörse**, a Baroque gem that was formerly the trade exchange headquarters. The nearby Handelshof at Grimmaische Str. 1–7 is the temporary home of the **Museum der Bildenden Künste** (Tues & Thurs–Sun 10am–6pm, Wed 1–9.30pm; €2.50), a distinguished collection of old masters, including Cranach,

Rubens and Caspar David Fredrich. This is due to move into its new custom-built premises on Sachsenplatz in late 2005. Following Barfussgässchen off the western side of the Markt brings you to Kleine Fleischergasse and the cheerful Baroque **Zum Coffe Baum**. One of the German pioneers of the coffee craze that followed the Turkish invasion of central Europe in the late seventeenth century, it gained further fame courtesy of the composer Robert Schumann, who came here regularly. Klostergasse leads southwards to the **Thomaskirche**, where Johann Sebastian Bach served for the last 27 years of his life. Predominantly Gothic, the church has been altered down the centuries. The most remarkable feature is its musical tradition: the Thomanerchor choir, which Bach once directed, can usually be heard on Fridays (6pm), Saturdays (3pm) and during the Sunday service (9.30am). Directly across from the church is the **Bach-Museum** (daily 10am–5pm; €3; ⓦwww.bach-leipzig .de), with an extensive show of mementos of the great composer. Close by, at Dittrichring 24, is another historically important museum, the Round Corner or **Runde Ecke** (daily 10am–6pm; free), a fascinating trawl through the methods and machinery of the Stasi, East Germany's secret police.

Leipzig's enormous **train station** is at the northeastern end of the Ring, which encircles the old part of the city. The **tourist office**, directly opposite at Richard-Wagner Str. 1 (Mon–Fri 9am–7pm, Sat 9am–4pm, Sun 9am–2pm; ☎0341/710 42 60, ⓦwww.leipzig.de), can book private rooms (❸) and sells the Leipzig Card (€5.90/11.50 for one/three days), which covers public transport costs plus museum admission. Two well-run backpacker **hostels** are the *Hostel Sleepy Lion*, just west of the centre at Käthe Kollwitz-Str. 3 (☎0341/993 94 80, ⓦwww.hostel-leipzig.de; €14) and, three minutes west of the station, the popular *Central Backpackers*, Kurt-Schumacher Str 41 (☎0341/149 89 60; €13). The HI hostel is at Volksgartenstr. 24 (☎0341/245 70 11; €20; tram #1 to Löbauer Strasse); and the **campsite**, *Auensee*, at Gustav-Esche-Str. 5 (☎03 41/4 65 16 00; tram #10).

Three main areas hold the **eating** and nightlife options: the traditional, almost medieval, Barfussgässchen, Gottsched Strasse just to the west, and the student area of Karl-Liebnecht Strasse in Süd Vorstadt. At the start of Barfussgässchen, *Zum Coffe Baum* serves excellent *Kaffee und Kuchen*, though it's often swamped with tour groups during the day. *Varadero*, at no. 8, is a popular Cuban restaurant specializing in grills and cocktails. Nearby, at the southeastern end of the Markt in the Mädler-Passage, is *Auerbachs Keller*, a historic and quite formal restaurant that was the setting for a scene in Goethe's *Faust*. Further west in Gottsched Strasse, *Barcelona* at no. 12, is a popular tapas and cocktail bar with a great Sunday buffet. *Apels Garten*, Kolonnadenstr. 2, is a traditional restaurant which uses recipes from a 300-year-old cookbook. South of the centre in Süd Vorstadt, *Duke* at Münzgasse 3, is a small bar for hip, young art students, while nearby *Ilses Ericka* on Bernardguering 152, is a cultish bar and music venue. Back in the Altstadt, housed beneath the Moritzbastei, is *MB*, a tightly packed collection of bars and clubs where students go to pair off. The city is also famous for its satirical **cabaret**: if your German's up to it, try *Pfeffermühle* in the same building as the Bach-Museum, or *Sanft Wut* in the Mädler-Passage.

Weimar

Despite its modest size, **WEIMAR** has played a role in the development of German culture that is unmatched: Goethe, Schiller, Herder and Nietzsche all made it their home, as did the Cranachs and Bach, and the architects and designers of the Bauhaus school. The town was also chosen as the seat of government of the democratic republic established after World War I, a regime whose failure ended with the Nazi accession. Buchenwald, one of the most notorious concentration camps, was built here, and its preservation is a shocking reminder of the Nazi era. Weimar's laid-back, quietly highbrow atmosphere is worth a day's detour.

Weimar's former seat of power was the **Schloss** (Tues–Sun 10am–4.30/6pm; €3.50; ⓦwww.kunstsammlungen-weimar.de), set by the River Ilm at the eastern edge of the town centre, a Neoclassical complex of a size more appropriate for ruling a mighty empire. On the ground floor is a collection of old masters, including pieces by both Cranachs, and Dürer's portraits of the Nürnberg patrician couple, Hans and Elspeth Tucher. South of nearby Herderplatz is the spacious **Markt**, lined by an unusually disparate jumble of buildings, of which the most eye-catching is the green and white gabled Stadthaus on the eastern side, opposite the neo-Gothic Rathaus. Schillerstrasse snakes away from the southwest corner of the Markt to the **Schillerhaus** (Mon & Wed–Sun 9am–4/6pm; €3.50), the home of the poet and dramatist for the last three years of his life. Beyond lies Theaterplatz, in the centre of which is a large monument to Goethe and Schiller. The **Nationaltheater** on the west side of the square was founded and directed by Goethe, though the present building, for all its stern Neoclassical appearance, is a modern pastiche. On Frauenplan south of the Markt is **Goethewohnhaus und Nationalmuseum** (Tues–Sun 9am–4/6pm; €6), where Goethe lived for some fifty years until his death in 1832. From here, Marienstrasse continues to the **Liszthaus** (Tues–Sun 9am–1pm & 2–4/6pm; €2), home of the Hungarian composer and pianist for the last seventeen years of his life, when he was director of Weimar's orchestra and opera. A few minutes' walk west down Geschwister-Scholl-Strasse is the **Hochschule für Architektur und Bauwesen**, where Walter Gropius established the original Bauhaus in 1919. The **Park an der Ilm** stretches from the Schloss to the southern edge of town on both sides of the river; aim for the southern suburb of Oberweimar, where stands the full-blown summer palace of **Schloss Belvedere** (Tues–Sun 10am–4.30/6pm; €3; ⓦwww.kunstsammlungen-weimar.de), whose light and airy Rococo forms a refreshing contrast to the Neoclassical solemnity of so much of the town. The **Konzentrationslager Buchenwald** (Tues–Sun 8.45/9.45am–5/6pm; free) is situated north of Weimar on the Ettersberg heights, and can be reached by bus (hourly from just south of the train station). Over 240,000 prisoners were incarcerated in this concentration camp, with 65,000 dying here.

Weimar's **train station**, on the Leipzig–Erfurt line, is a twenty-minute walk north of the main sights. One of the **tourist offices** (daily 10am–8pm) is there; another, larger one is in the Stadthaus at Markt 10 (Mon–Fri 9.30/10am–6pm, Sat & Sun 9.30/10am–2/4pm; ☎036 43/2 40 00, ⓦwww.weimar.de). The cheapest and most central **hostel** is the environmentally minded *Hababusch* at Geleit Str. 4 (no phone; €10). There are neat and tidy **HI hostels** at Humboldt Str. 17 (☎03643/85 07 92, ⓦwww.djh.de; €19.50) and Carl-August-Allee 13 (☎03643/85 04 90; €19.50). Reasonably priced **pensions** include the recently refurbished *Savina*, Meyerstr. 60 (☎03643/8 66 90; ❹). Weimar's range of **eating and drinking** spots comes as a surprise, given its relatively small size. Centrally located *Zum Zwiebel*, Zeichgasse 6, is a deservedly popular, cosy and lively restaurant serving local specialities at cheap prices. The *Residenz-Café* on Grüner Markt, though rather plush, has good coffee and cakes; nearby *A.C.C.*, Burgplatz 1, is a more relaxed bar and restaurant with quiet candlelit tables lining a cobbled sidestreet.

Dresden

Generally regarded as Germany's most beautiful and culturally significant city, **DRESDEN** survived World War II largely unscathed until the night of February 13, 1945. Then, in a matter of hours, it was reduced to ruins in saturation bombing – according to official figures at least 35,000 civilians died (though the total was probably considerably higher), as the city was packed with people fleeing the advancing Red Army. With this background, it's all the more remarkable that Dresden is the one city in the former East Germany that has slotted easily into the economic framework of the reunited Germany, and the post-Communist authorities are now brilliantly restoring the historic buildings. With Prague only 150km away, Dresden is developing into a dynamic gateway between eastern and western Europe, and has a vibrant nightlife scene.

Arrival, information and accommodation

Dresden has two main train stations – the **Hauptbahnhof**, south of the Altstadt, and **Neustadt Bahnhof**, at the northwestern corner of the Neustadt, convenient for the backpacker hostels and nightlife. One of the **tourist offices** is in a pavilion at Prager Str. 10 (Mon–Fri 9am–7pm, Sat 9am–4pm; ☎0351/49 19 20, ✆www.dresden-tourist.de), a short walk from the Hauptbahnhof; the other is in the heart of the Altstadt, in the Schinkelwache on Theaterplatz (Mon–Fri 10am–6pm, Sat & Sun 10am–4pm). Both sell the **Dresden Card** (€18/two days), which covers public transport, museum admission and sundry discounts. Otherwise, there's a 24-hour **transport ticket** (€4) and a separate **day ticket** for the museums (€6.10).

The tourist offices can book private rooms and pensions (❸). There are two back-packer **hostels** in Neustadt, well placed for nightlife in the Hechtviertel artists' ghetto: the relaxed *Mondpalast*, Louisenstr. 77 (☎0351/5 63 40 50, ✆www.mondpalast.de; €13.50); and *Die Boofe*, Hechtstr. 10 (☎0351/8 01 33 61, ✆www.boofe.com; €14.50), ten minutes' north of Neustadt Bahnhof, which has its own sauna. The much larger **HI hostel** is just southwest of the Altstadt at Maternistr. 22 (☎0351/49 26 20; €16.50). Budget **hotels** include *Am Birkenhain*, Barbarastr. 76 (☎0351/8 51 40; ❸), which lies close to the Pieschen S-Bahn station. The *Mockritz* **campsite** is at Boderitzghter Str. 30 (☎0351/4 71 52 50; bus #76 from Hauptbahnhof).

The City

If you arrive at the Hauptbahnhof, you see the worst of modern Dresden first: the **Prager Strasse**, a vast Stalinist pedestrian precinct with a few fountains and statues thrown in for relief. At the far end, beyond the inner ring road, is the **Altmarkt**, much extended after its wartime destruction; the only building of note that remains is the **Kreuzkirche**, a church which mixes a Baroque body with a Neoclassical tower. On Saturdays at 6pm, and at the 9.30am Sunday service, it usually hosts the Kreuzchor, one of the world's leading church choirs. North of here, the **Albertinum** (Mon–Wed & Fri–Sun 10am–6pm; €3.50; ✆www.staatl-kunstsammlungen-dresden .de) houses one of the greatest of Romantic paintings, Friedrich's *Cross in the Mountains*. For the time being, the Albertinum is also home to the major part of the **Grünes Gewölbe** or Green Vault, a dazzling array of treasury items including the Baroque fancies created by the Saxon Electors' own jeweller, Johann Melchior Dinglinger. West of the Albertinum is the **Neumarkt**, formerly dominated by the round, domed Frauenkirche. Only a fragment of wall was left standing after the war, and after fierce controversy, the decision was taken in 1991 to rebuild the church completely, with much of the funding coming from the UK and US. The colossal **Residenzschloss** (Tues–Sun 10am–6pm; €2.50) was also wrecked in the war, and the rebuilding programme now under way is a massive task, though the projected completion date of 2006 – the city's 800th anniversary – looks achievable. Sooner or later, the miraculously preserved **Mirror Rooms** (currently closed) will re-house the entire Grünes Gewölbe collection. At the end of nearby Augustusstrasse is the Baroque **Hofkirche**, or Dom. The existence of this Catholic church in a staunchly Protestant province is explained by the fact that the Saxon rulers converted in order to gain the Polish throne.

Baroque Dresden's great glory was the palace known as the **Zwinger**, which faces the Residenzschloss and now contains several museums. Beautifully displayed in the southeastern pavilion, entered from Sophienstrasse, is the **Porzellansammlung** (Tues–Sun 10am–6pm; €2.50); products from the famous Meissen factory are extensively featured. The southwestern pavilion is known as the **Mathematisch-Physikalischer Salon** (10am–6pm, closed Thurs; €1.50), and offers a fascinating array of globes, clocks and scientific instruments. In the nineteenth-century extension is the **Gemäldegalerie Alte Meister** (Tues–Sun 10am–6pm; €3.50), whose collection of old masters ranks among the dozen best in the world, and includes some of the most familiar Italian Renaissance paintings: Raphael's *Sistine Madonna*, Titian's *Christ and the Pharisees* and Veronese's *Marriage at*

Cana. The German section includes Dürer's *Dresden Altarpiece*, Holbein's *Le Sieur de Morette* and Cranach's *Duke Henry the Pious*. Van Eyck's *Madonna and Child* triptych, executed with miniaturist precision, kicks off a distinguished Low Countries section in which Rubens and Rembrandt are extensively featured.

Across the River Elbe, the **Neustadt** was a planned Baroque town and its layout is still obvious, even if few of the original buildings survive. Today it is the focus of the city's gentrification with a burgeoning art scene. In the park overlooking the Elbe is the most esoteric creation of Dresden Baroque, the **Japanisches Palais** (Tues–Sun 10am–6pm; €4), which now contains archeological and ethnographic museums focusing largely on the South Seas. You don't have to pay to see the courtyard, a fantasy inspired by the eighteenth-century infatuation with the Orient.

Eating, drinking and nightlife

There's a wide choice of **restaurants**, and with over 130 **bars and clubs** clustered around a handful of cobbled, narrow streets, the Neustadt provides something for everyone. For up-to-date nightlife **listings**, pick up a copy of *Sax*, *Dresdner* or *Fritz* from kiosks or backpacker hostels.

Cafés and restaurants

Am Thor Hauptstr. 35, Neustadt. A worthy survivor from Communist days, serving traditional fare.

Dürüm Kebap Haus Rothenburger Str 41. A rock-bottom favourite, serving as a cheap takeaway, quick restaurant and general meeting place.

El Perro Borracho Kunsthof alleyway, off Alaunstrasse, Neustadt. A highly regarded Spanish eatery.

Herr Rosso Und Seine Hund Louisen Str. 47, Neustadt. Cosy café and restaurant that's always busy with students.

Kügelgenhaus Hauptstr. 13, Neustadt. Atmospheric restaurant-cum-beer cellar in a fine Baroque building.

Pfund's Bautzner Str. 79, Neustadt. Café/restaurant attached to a wonderful dairy shop, with immaculately restored Jugendstil decor.

Ratskeller Dr-Kulz-Ring 19, Altstadt. Serves hearty local dishes.

Schlemmerland Pragerstr. You'll find plenty of cheap and cheerful fast-food outlets under one roof here.

Szeged Wilsdruffer Str. 4, Altstadt. Offers both Hungarian and German cuisine.

Neustadt bars

Blue Note Görlitzer Str. 2b. Dark, cavernous, smoke-filled blues bar that gets packed to the gills on live music nights.

Bottoms Up Martin Luther Str. 31. Down a quiet backstreet away from the main action, this large easy-going bar and beer garden, is an unpretentious favourite.

El Cubanito Sebnitzer Str. 8b. A cramped, tiny tabled, cosy Cuban tapas and cocktail bar that receives rave reviews.

Groove Station Katherinen Str. 11–13. Situated at the back of a courtyard, this rough-and-ready rock bar and live venue has been a Neustadt cornerstone for years.

Hebeda's Rothenburger Str. 30. A large, crumbling and basic pub that epitomizes the Neustadt alternative scene.

Mona Lisa Corner Louisenstr. & Kamenzerstr. Hip local haunt, serving upmarket cocktails to a largely gay crowd.

Raskolnikov Böhmische Str. 34. A large, rambling, bohemian Russian bar and restaurant.

Scheune Alaunstr. 36–40. Neustadt arts centre with a quiet and welcoming bar, large beer garden, live music, theatre, and gay and lesbian nights.

Meissen

The porcelain-producing town of **MEISSEN** makes an interesting, photogenic excursion from Dresden. Unlike its larger neighbour, it survived World War II almost unscathed. Walking towards the centre from the train station, you see the commandingly sited castle almost immediately. The present building, the **Albrechtsburg** (daily 10am–5/6pm; closed Jan; €3.50; ⊛www.albrechtsburg-meissen.de), is a late fifteenth-century combination of military fortress and residential palace. Cocooned within the castle precinct is the **Dom** (daily 9/10am–4/6pm; €2); inside, look out for the superb brass tomb plates of the Saxon dukes and the rood screen with its colourful altarpiece by Cranach. Between the castle hill and the Elbe lies the atmospheric **Altstadt**, a network of twisting and meandering streets. Centrepiece is the **Markt**, dominated by the Renaissance Rathaus. On its own small square to the side is the Flamboyant Gothic **Frauenkirche**, whose carillon, fashioned from local porcelain, can be heard six times daily. On the terrace just above is the celebrated **Gasthaus Vinzenz Richter**, a half-timbered tavern that preserves an eighteenth-century winepress. The wines served here are said to be the best in eastern Germany. The **Staatliche Porzellan-Manufaktur Meissen** (tours daily 9am–5/6pm; €3), about 1.5km south of the Markt, is most easily reached by going down Fleischer Gasse, then continuing straight down Neugasse; it's also close to the S-Bahn terminus, Meissen-Triebischtal. There's also a city bus from the station (hourly 10am–5pm). This is the latest factory to manufacture Dresden china, whose invention came about when Augustus the Strong imprisoned the alchemist Johann Friedrich Böttger, ordering him to produce some gold. Instead, he invented the first true European porcelain, according to a formula that remains secret. In addition to seeing the works, you can also view the **museum** (same hours; €4.50), which displays many of the factories' finest achievements, most notably some gloriously over-the-top Rococo fripperies made by the most talented artist ever employed here, Joachim Kaendler. Meissen's **tourist office** at Markt 3 (Mon–Fri 9/10am–6pm, Sat & Sun 10am–3/4pm; Jan closed weekends; ☎03521/4 19 40, ✆www.meissen.de) books private rooms (❸). There are also a couple of reasonably priced central **pensions**: *Burkhardt*, Neugasse 29 (☎03521/45 81 98; ❹), and *Schweizerhaus*, Rauheutal Str. 1 (☎03521/45 71 62; ❸). There's a backpacker **hostel** at Wilsdruffer Str. 28 (☎03521/45 30 65; €13). The one unmissable **restaurant** is the *Gasthaus Vinzenz Richter*, which specializes in local and national dishes. Other possibilities include *Domkeller*, Domplatz 9, and the traditional *Bauernhaus'l*, Oberspaarer Str. 20.

Northern Germany

Hamburg, Germany's second city, is infamous for the sleaze of the Reeperbahn strip – its flipside, though, is a sophisticated cultural scene and vibrant nightlife which ranks as some of the best in the country. In this unprepossessing region, another maritime city, **Lübeck**, has the strongest pull, with a similar appeal to the mercantile towns of the Low Countries. To the north, Schleswig-Holstein's mix of dyke-protected marsh, peat bog and farmland holds few rewarding sights on the way to mainland Denmark. To the south lies Lower Saxony, whose capital, **Hannover**, is worth a visit for its museums and gardens. The province's smaller towns present a fascinating contrast – the former silver-mining town of **Goslar**, in particular, is a rare treat. Near the centre of Lower Saxony is **Bremen**, the region's largest city.

Hamburg

Stylish media centre and second-largest port in Europe, **HAMBURG** is undeniably cool – more laid-back than Berlin or Frankfurt, more sophisticated than Munich or Cologne, and with nightlife to rival the lot. Its skyline is dominated by the pale green of its copper spires and domes, but a few houses and the churches are all that's left from older times. The Great Fire of 1842 was a main cause of this loss, plus wartime bombing. Much of the subsequent rebuilding might not be especially beautiful, but the result is an intriguing mix of old and new, coupled with an appealing sense of open space. Two thirds of Hamburg is occupied by parks, lakes or tree-lined canals, adding some much needed leafiness to this major industrial centre.

The best place to begin an exploration is the oldest area, the **harbour**, dominated by the clock tower and green dome of the St Pauli Landungsbrücken. The main tourist draw is a one-hour **boat tour** of the harbour (many companies operate these; prices start at €9), but they are best avoided unless you have a fascination for industrial containers. Far more pleasurable is the late-nineteenth-century **Speicherstadt**

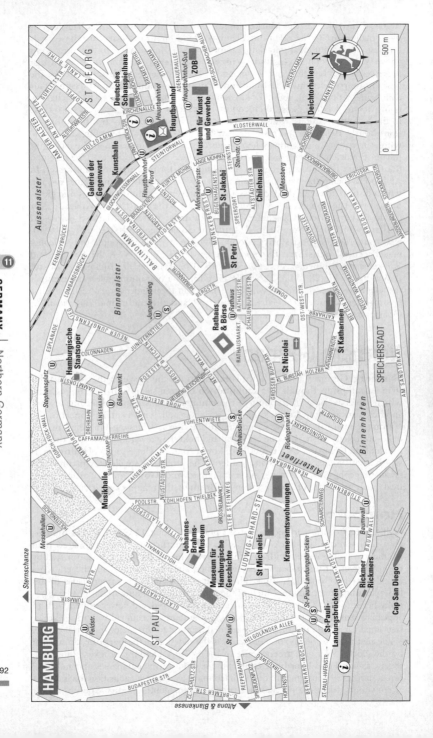

GERMANY | Northern Germany

HAMBURG

◀ Sternschanze

◀ Altona & Blankenese

N

500 m

0

ST GEORG

Deutsches Schauspielhaus

ZOB

Hauptbahnhof

Hauptbahnhof-Süd

Museum für Kunst und Gewerbe

Deichtorhallen

Kunsthalle

Galerie der Gegenwart

Hauptbahnhof-Nord

St Jakobi

St Petri

Chilehaus

Messberg

KLOSTERWALL

Aussenalster

Binnenalster

Jungfernstieg

Rathaus & Börse

Rathaus

St Nicolai

St Katharinen

SPEICHERSTADT

Hamburgische Staatsoper

Stephansplatz

Binnenhafen

Musikhalle

Stadthausbrücke

Alsterfleet

Johannes-Brahms-Museum

Museum für Hamburgische Geschichte

St Michaelis

Krameramtswohnungen

Rickmer Rickmers

St-Pauli-Landungsbrücken

Cap San Diego

ST PAULI

Feldstr.

St Pauli

11

lying a little to the east, whose tall, ornate warehouses are still very much in use. You'll see bundles of oriental carpets being hoisted, and smell spices and coffee wafting on the breeze. The Speicherstadt is within the **Freihafen** (customs-free zone), into which you can walk unrestricted. It's an interesting place to stroll around and criss-cross the bridges (Hamburg has more than Venice or Amsterdam). Just to the north is the nightlife centre of **St Pauli**, whose main artery is the notorious **Reeperbahn** – ugly and unassuming by day, blazing with neon at night. Just north of here runs Grosse Freiheit, the street that famously hosted The Beatles' first gigs. The main road along the waterfront on St Pauli's edge is the Hafenstrasse, which runs west to the trendy suburb of **Altona**. Its reputation for racial tolerance is one of the reasons it grew, and it still has a large Portuguese population – and good, cheap Portuguese restaurants. On the waterfront here, one of the city's main weekly events takes place: the **Fischmarkt**. Come early on Sunday and you'll find yourself in an amazing trading hubbub; everything is in full swing by 6am, and by 11am it's over.

The commercial and shopping district centres on **Binnenalster** lake and the neo-Renaissance **Rathaus**, a magnificently pompous demonstration of the city's power and wealth in the nineteenth century. From the Rathausmarkt, continue up **Poststrasse** to the heart of Hamburg's exclusive shopping area. Just north of the Hauptbahnhof is the **Kunsthalle**, the unmissable art collection (Tues–Sun 10am–6pm, Thurs till 9pm; €7.50; ⓦwww.hamburger-kunsthalle.de). There are three altarpieces by Master Bertram, the first German painter identifiable by name, and a Dutch and Flemish section where two Rembrandts take centre stage, but it is the nineteenth-century German section that is the museum's main strength. Next door is the **Galerie der Gegenwart** (same hours and ticket), showing contemporary art. Nearby is the **Museum für Kunst und Gewerbe** (same hours; €7.20) which hosts exciting exhibitions from graphic design to the latest in furniture.

Practicalities

An Airport Express connects the **airport** to the main train station, the **Hauptbahnhof**, in the eastern end of the city centre (every 15min; 25min; €4.60). **Ferries** from Britain dock at Fischerhafen on Grosse Elbstrasse, from where buses run to **Bahnhof Altona**, west of town. Ferries from elsewhere dock at St Pauli Landungsbrücken. The **tourist office** in the Hauptbahnhof (daily 7am–10pm; ☏040/3005 1351, ⓦwww.hamburg-tourismus.de) has a room-finding service (€4). Pick up the **Hamburg Card** (€7/14.50 for one/three days) here, which gives free or reduced admission to most of the city's museums as well as use of public transport. A one-day travel card (S- and U-Bahn) costs €4.45. Close to Sternschanze station (north of St Pauli; U-Bahn #3, S-Bahn #21 or #31) are two **hostels**: *Backpacker Hostel Instant Sleep*, Max-Brauer-Allee 277 (☏040/4318 2310, ⓦwww.instantsleep.de; €16), and the more comfortable *Schanzenstern*, Bartelsstr. 12 (☏040/439 84 41, ⓦwww.schanzen-stern.de; €17). The cheapest, and most popular, **hotels** are near the train station. *Annenhof*, Lange Reihe 23 (☏040/24 34 26, ⓦwww.hotel-annenhof.de; ❸), is clean and cosy; or there's small but stylish *Sarah Petersen* at no. 50 (☏040/24 98 26; ❹). **B&B** is available through *bed&breakfast*, Müggenkampstr. 35 (☏040/491 56 66; ❸).

Some of the best **places to eat** are northwest of the city centre, in the Univiertel or the Schanzenviertel, around Schulterblatt and Schanzenstrasse (two minutes' walk south of Sternschanze station). For **snacks**, the stalls in front of the Rathaus are pricey but delicious, while most café-bars have food as well as drinks. Hamburg's **nightlife** is outstanding, with several nightlife hubs, a good bar scene and a wide range of excellent clubs. For up-to-the-minute listings, pick up a copy of *Prinz* magazine (€1), or look out for a number of free mags in bars. St Pauli is the city's main venue for clubbing and live music, with big-name DJs and bands playing at weekends. Admission is from about €10. The student bar scene is in Schanzenviertel, while Altona is more popular with young professionals. The best way to find out what's on in the lively **gay scene** is through the free *Eurogay* magazine from the tourist office. They also produce a short gay city guide, *Hamburg's Pride*, in German and English.

Cafés and restaurants

Alt Hamburger Aalspeicher Deichstr. 43. One of the best-known addresses in the city centre for traditional German cuisine and fish dishes.

Bok Schulterblatt 3. An outlet of the excellent local Thai eatery.

Einstein Bahrenfelder Chaussee 45. The place to seek out if an inexpensive fill-up is a priority.

Erika's Eck Sternstr. 98. Best breakfast in the city.

Frank & Frei Schanzenstr. 93. Serves enormous salads, pasta and pizza, like others on the same street.

Petisco Schulterblatt 78. A popular Portuguese restaurant, serving authentic, inexpensive fare.

Presse Susannenstr. 42. Small and trendy place, worth trying for its cheap wraps.

Sagres Vorsetzen 42. Good and inexpensive Portuguese restaurant in the vicinity of the harbour.

Clubs and music venues

Betty Ford Klinik Grosse Freiheit 6. The finest in house and techno. Fri & Sat.

Bunker Feldstrasse 66, Heiligengeistfeld. Swanky venue featuring a VIP lounge, two dance floors and four bars, one of them serving sushi. Fri & Sat.

Echochamber Nobistor 1. Trendy hip-hop venue featuring major guest DJs and live music.

Fabrik Barnerstrasse 36 ⓦwww.fabrik.de. Major live music and party venue in Altona, with an emphasis on world music, jazz and dance.

Grosse Freiheit Grosse Freiheit 36. A tourist attraction in itself, Hamburg's leading live venue books major acts most weekends.

Grünspan Grosse Freiheit 58. Uncompromisingly heavy rock. Wed–Sat.

Gum Hamburger Berg 12–13. The name stands for Global Underground Music; probably the best place for serious techno, trance and house.

Kaiserkeller Grosse Freiheit club basement. Massive subterranean club playing mostly alternative music; famous for hosting the Beatles in the early 1960s.

Logo Grindelallee 1. Hosts mainly English and American underground bands.

Lounge Gerhardstr. 16. Another good hip-hop venue, plus some breakbeat and drum'n'bass nights.

Gay Hamburg

Frauenkneipe Stresemannstrasse 60. The city's leading address for women only. Occasionally organizes lesbian club nights elsewhere.

G-Bar Lange Reihe 81. Well-known bar and club, packed at weekends.

Juice Club Stressemannstr. 206. Hosts the biggest lesbian club nights, with mostly house and disco music; accompanied gay men welcome.

Purgatory Talstr. 14. Relaxed gay and lesbian bar with eccentric decor.

Listings

Bike rental At left luggage in the train station's travel centre.

Consulates UK, Harvestehuder Weg 8a ⓣ040/448 03 20; Ireland, Feldbrunnenstr. 43 ⓣ040/4418 6213; US, Alsterufer 28 ⓣ040/417 11 00.

Hospital Krankenhaus Bethesda, Glindersweg 80 ⓣ040/46 68 0.

Internet access Baff Internetcafe, Schulterblatt 116; Int. Telecom, Kirchenallee 9; also at Hauptbahnhof-Süd station.

Left luggage At the train station.

Pharmacy Bergstr. 26.

Post office At the Kirchenallee exit from the train station.

Lübeck

LÜBECK makes a delightful day-trip, just an hour from Hamburg, and linked by Finn-Lines **ferries** to Helsinki, Finland (3 weekly; ⓣ0451/150 74 43, ⓦwww.finnlines.de). Set on an egg-shaped island surrounded by the water defences of the Trave and the city moat, the fine Altstadt is a five-minute walk from the train station, past the twin-towered **Holstentor**, the city's emblem. On the waterfront to the right of the Holstentor is a row of lovely gabled buildings – the **Salzspeicher**. Straight ahead, over the bridge and up Holstenstrasse, the first church on the right is the Gothic **Petrikirche**; an elevator goes to the top of its spire (daily 10/11am–4/5/6pm, closed Feb; €2) for panoramic views. Back across Holstenstrasse is the Markt and the imposing **Rathaus**. Opposite is **Konditorei-café Niederegger**, renowned for its vast marzipan display; its old-style first-floor café is surprisingly affordable. Behind the north wing of the town hall is the **Marienkirche**, Germany's oldest brick-built Gothic church. The interior makes a light and lofty backdrop for the church's treasures: a magnificent 1518 carved altar, a life-size figure of John the Evangelist dating from 1505, a beautiful Gothic gilded tabernacle and some fourteenth-century murals. The imposing **Katharinenkirche**, on the corner of Königstrasse and Glockengiesserstrasse, boasts three sculptures on its west facade by Ernst Barlach; he was commissioned to make a series of nine in the early 1930s, but had completed only these when his work was banned by the Nazis. To the north at Königstr. 9-11 are the **Behnhaus** and the **Drägerhaus**, two patricians' houses now converted into a museum (Tues–Sun 10am–4/5pm; €3, free first Fri of the month). The former has a good collection of modern paintings, including works by Kirchner and Munch, while the latter's impressive interior contains nineteenth-century furniture and porcelain. Across from the nearby **Jakobikirche**, on Breite Strasse, is a Renaissance house that used to belong to the sailors' guild, the **Haus der Schiffergesellschaft**. A tavern since 1535, it is decked out with all sorts of seagoing paraphernalia. At the opposite end of the Altstadt is the **St-Annen-Museum**, closed at time of writing; a modern extension housing the **Kunsthalle** is due to open soon (check with tourist office for the latest).

Lübeck **train station** is just west of the Altstadt. The main **tourist office** is at Breite Str. 62 (Mon–Fri 9.30am–6pm, Sat 10am–3pm, June–Sept also Sun 10am–2pm; ℡0180/588 22 33, ✆www.luebeck-tourismus.de). The cheapest **hotel** is *Stadt Lübeck*, Am Bahnhof 21 (℡0451/83 8 83; ➎). The best **hostel** is in the Werkhof complex at Kanalstr. 70 (℡0451/70 68 92, ✉rucksack-hotel -luebeck@freenet.de; €24). One HI hostel is at Gertrudenkirchhof 4 (℡0451/3 34 33, ✆ww.djh.de; €16.20); another, more luxurious, HI place is in the historic centre at Mengstr. 33 (℡0451/702 03 99; €17.40). Lübeck has a good choice of **cafés** and restaurants. The excellent *Ratskeller*, Markt 13, offers traditional cuisine; *Schmidt's*, Dr-Julius-Leber-Str. 60–62, has an eclectic menu; *Tipasa*, Schlumacherstr. 12–14, has cheap bistro-type dishes, popular with students. *Café Affenbrot*, part of the Werkhof (Kanalstr. 70), has tasty veggie food and cakes. The Engelsgrube is the best street for bars.

Bremen

BREMEN – home of Becks beer – has a reputation for being the most politically radical part of the country, electing the first Green MPs in 1979. The city has a fiercely independent flavour, mirrored in its unique mix of bland modern shopping streets and comely cobbled lanes of fishermen's cottages. The latter can be found in the Schnoorviertel, part of the Altstadt on the Weser's northeast bank, reached by walking straight ahead from the train station. At the top of Sögestrasse, Bremen's main shopping street, is the **Liebfrauenkirche**, a Gothic hall church engulfed by a flower market. The **Marktplatz** ahead of the church is dominated by the **Rathaus**, one of the most splendid buildings in northern Germany. You can visit the main reception rooms as part of a tour (Mon–Sat 11am, noon, 3pm & 4pm, Sun 11am & noon; €4), which are awash with gilded wallpaper and ornate carving. On a small rise beyond the Rathaus stands the **Dom**, its brooding interior ranging from Romanesque to late Gothic. Off the southeast corner is the **Bleikeller** (Mon–Fri 10am–5pm; €1.40); a macabre attraction is provided by the corpses that were discovered here when the room was opened up, perfectly preserved in the air-free environment. **Böttcherstrasse**, off the south side of Marktplatz, was transformed in the 1920s by the Bremen coffee magnate Ludwig Roselius into a Gothic-cum-Art Nouveau fantasy. Tucked away between the Dom and the river is the city's highlight, the **Schnoorviertel**, a small, well-preserved area of medieval fishing houses. At Wüste Stätte 10 is the multimedia **ZeitRaum Packhaus** (daily 10.30/11am–6/8pm; €6), an interactive museum depicting the history of Bremen, with displays, films and virtual reality aimed mainly at school groups. Just east of the Schnoorviertel at Am Wall 207, the **Kunsthalle** (Wed–Sun 10am–5pm, Tues till 9pm; €5; ✆www.kunsthalle-bremen.de) houses a superb array of nineteenth- and early twentieth-century paintings.

The **train station** is just north of the city centre. Immediately outside is the **tourist office** (Mon–Fri 9.30am–6.30/8pm, Sat & Sun 9.30am–4pm; ☎0180/510 10 30, ⊛www.bremen-tourism.de); there is another small office at the Marktplatz (same hours). The **HI hostel** is in the western part of the Altstadt at Kalkstr. 6 (☎04 21/17 13 69, ⊛www.djh.de; €20) and has a great river view. Of **hotels**, try the excellent *Heinisch*, Wachmannstr. 26 (☎0421/34 29 25, ⊛hotel-heinisch @t-online.de; ❹), north of the train station; *Weltevreden*, Am Dobben 62 (☎0421/780 15; ❹), between the city centre and the Ostertorviertel; or the more central *Am Hillmanplatz 1*, Am Hillmanplatz 1 (☎0421/132 58; ❹). Bremen is known for fish (particularly eel) – best sampled in the *gemütlich* old **restaurants** of the Schnoorviertel, such as the characterful *Ausspann*, Schnoor 1–2. The best areas for **café/bars** is the renovated riverside stretch of Schlachte, to the south of the Altstadt. Try also *Café Engel*, Ostertorsteinweg 31, which offers inexpensive daily specials. Bremen's native Becks **beer** is heavily exported; while in town, go for Haake-Beck beers at, for example, the *Kleiner Ratskeller*, Hinter dem Schütting 11.

Hannover

HANNOVER has a closer relationship with Britain than any other German city, a consequence of the 1701 Act of Settlement, which resulted in Georg Ludwig of Hannover becoming the British King George I in 1714. Anticipating the accession, the court director of music, Georg Friedrich Händel, had established himself in London by the time his employer arrived, and went on to write his finest works there. Hannover's showpiece – refreshingly – is not a great cathedral, palace or town hall, but a series of **gardens**, which are among the most impressive in Europe. Add this to a number of first-class museums and it's worth spending a day here.

Standing at Hannover's most popular rendezvous, the **Kröpcke**, the most imposing building in view is the Neoclassical Opernhaus, perhaps the finest of the city's public buildings. A short distance southwest, a few streets of rebuilt half-timbered buildings convey some impression of the medieval town; most notable is the high-gabled fifteenth-century **Altes Rathaus**, its elaborate brickwork enlivened with colourful glazed tiles. Alongside is the fourteenth-century **Marktkirche**, with some miraculously preserved stained glass. Close by, at Pferdestr. 6, the **Historisches Museum** (Tues 10am–8pm, Wed–Sun 10am–4/6pm; €3; ⊛www.hannover-museum .de) has displays including state coaches. Southwards, across the Friedrichswall, is the **Neues Rathaus**, a Baroque-cum-Neo-Gothic extravaganza whose dome gives the best views of the city (April–Oct daily 9.30/10am–6pm; €2). Next door, the **Kestner-Museum** (Tues–Sun 11am–6pm, Wed till 8pm; €2.60; ⊛www .kestner.org) is a compact and eclectic decorative arts museum. Round the back of the Rathaus on Willy-Brandt-Allee is the **Niedersächsisches Landesmuseum** (Tues–Sun 10am–5pm, Thurs till 7pm; €3; ⊛www.nlmh.de), housing an excellent collection of paintings from the Middle Ages to the early twentieth century. On the first floor, the archeology department's showpieces are the bodies of prehistoric men preserved in the peat bogs of Lower Saxony, along with the contents of several graves and an array of Bronze Age jewellery. A bit further down the road, the **Sprengel-Museum** (Tues–Sun 10am–6/8pm; €3.50; ⊛www.sprengel-museum.de) is one of the most exciting modern art galleries in Germany. Much of the display space is given over to changing exhibitions of photography, graphics and experimental art-forms, but there's also a first-rate permanent display of twentieth-century painting and sculpture.

The royal gardens of **Herrenhausen**, summer residence of the Hannover court, can be reached by U-Bahn #4 or #5 from the Kröpcke. Proceeding north from town along Nienburgerstrasse, head past the Welfengarten on the right. To the left, the dead-straight Herrenhäuser Allee cuts through the **Georgengarten**, an English-style landscaped garden with an artificial lake, created as a foil to the magnificent formal **Grosser Garten** (daily 8am–4.30/8pm; €3, free in winter), the city's pride and joy. If possible, time your visit to coincide with the playing of the fountains (April–Sept daily 11am–noon & 2/3–5pm), when the illuminations are switched on (May–Aug after sunset; €3), or during one of the concerts and fireworks displays (check with tourist office for programme; €15). Just inside the entrance gate is the striking Hedge Theatre, a permanent amphitheatre whose hedges double as scenery and changing rooms. Across Herrenhäuser Strasse north of the Grosser Garten is the **Berggarten** (daily 9/10am–7/8pm; €2), set up to shelter rare and exotic plants.

Practicalities

The **train station** is in the centre of town; behind is the bus station. The **tourist office** is beside the train station in the post office, Ernst-August-Platz 2 (Mon–Fri 9am–6pm, Sat 9am–2pm; ☎0511/1234 5111, ⓦwww.hannover-tourism.de). Pick up a Hannover Card here (€8/12 for one/three days), covering public transport and entrance to the main museums and sights. There's an **HI hostel** at Ferdinand-Wilhelm-Fricke-Weg 1 (☎0511/131 76 74, ⓦwww.djh.de; €19.30); take U-Bahn #3 or #7 to Fischerhof, from where it's a five-minute walk to the left over the bridge, then right. For €6.50 the tourist office will book you into a **hotel**. Hannover charges fancy business prices; the lowest rates in the centre are at the spotless *Flora*, Heinrichstr. 36 (☎0511/38 39 10; ❹), and *Gildehof*, Joachimstr. 6 (☎0511/36 36 80; ❺); or you could try the pricier *Reverey*, Aegidiendamm 8 (☎0511/88 37 11; ❻). For **snacks** head for the Markthalle, where German, Italian, Spanish and Turkish stalls sell great value meals. Alternatively, try the shops around Goetheplatz, or pop into the *Mövenpick* complex, Joachimstr. 1-3, which includes a sit-down restaurant, self-service Italian and all-you-can-eat buffet. Good **cafés** include the *Kröpcke*, while *Fire*, Knochenhauerstr. 30, is a trendy bar serving food, as is the convenient *Cuabar*, Ernst-August-Platz 1, beside the train station. Popular clubs include *Red Orange*, Odeonstr. 13, which offers hip-hop, soul and 80s pop, and *H.De.M.* on Windmühlenstr. 1, more geared towards techno and trance. **Internet access** is at *Surfin*, in the Kaufhof shopping centre, Seilwinderstr. 8.

Goslar

GOSLAR is an absurdly picturesque mining town located at the northern edge of the gentle wooded Harz mountains. Silver was discovered in the nearby Rammelsberg in the tenth century, and Goslar soon became the "treasure chest of the Holy Roman Empire". The presence of a POW hospital during World War II spared it from bombing, and Goslar can claim to have more old houses than any other town in Germany. Although it hosts an attractive market (Tues & Fri mornings), the central **Marktplatz** is best seen empty to fully appreciate its visual variety, with an elegantly Gothic **Rathaus** (daily 11am–4pm; €2) and roofs of bright red tiles and contrasting grey slate. The Huldigungssaal in the Rathaus contains a dazzling array of medieval wall and ceiling paintings, with the most valuable items hidden in altar niches and closets behind the panelling. Just behind the Rathaus is the **Marktkirche**, facing the sixteenth-century **Brusttuch**, with its top storey crammed with satirical carvings. Goslar's half-timbered beauty begins in earnest in the streets behind the church – the Frankenberg Quarter – the oldest houses lying in the Bergstrasse and Schreiberstrasse areas. Down Peterstrasse, past a variety of attractive buildings, lies the remarkable **Kaiserpfalz**, built in the early eleventh century; much of the interior (daily 10am–4/5pm; €4.50) is occupied by the vast Reichssaal, decorated with romantic depictions of the emperors. Below, a car park fills the former site of the **Dom**, pulled down in 1822 due to lack of funds for restoration: only the entrance hall with its facade of thirteenth-century statues survived. A ten-minute walk northwest of Marktplatz brings you to the **Mönchehaus Museum** (Tues–Sat 10am–5pm, Sun 10am–1pm; €3). A black-and-white half-timbered building over 450 years old, it's the curious home to Goslar's modern art collection. East of here, the **Jakobikirche** contains a moving Pietà by the great but elusive sixteenth-century sculptor, Hans Witten.

Goslar's **tourist office** is at Marktplatz 7 (Mon–Fri 9.15am–5/6pm, Sat 9.30am–2/4pm, Sun 9.30am–2pm; Nov–April closed Sun; ☎05321/7 80 60, ⓦwww.goslarinfo.de). A few minutes' walk from the **train station** at the northern end of town is the excellent *Gästehaus Möller*, Schieferweg 6 (☎05321/2 30 98; ❸). The quaint **HI hostel**, Rammelsberger Str. 25 (☎05321/2 22 40, ⓦwww.djh.de; €16.70), is ten minutes' walk from the centre. The eighteenth-century *Zur Börse*, Bergstr. 53 (☎05321/3 45 10; ❹), is one of the prettiest **hotels**. Marktplatz is a good place to pick up **snacks** of sausages and fish rolls (Wed & Fri). For **restaurants**, try *Köpi am Markt*, Worthstr. 10, which does salads and steaks; further down is *Worthmühle*, Worthstr. 4, good for provincial cooking; almost opposite the Rathaus, at Marktkirchhof 3, is *Butterhanne*, serving coffee and cakes as well as full meals.

Central Germany

Central Germany is the most populous region of the country and home to the zone of heaviest industrialization – the **Ruhrgebiet**. Within this conurbation, **Cologne** is the outstanding city, managing to preserve many of the splendours of its long centuries as a free state. Neighbouring **Bonn** is another historic city, renowned for being the birthplace of Beethoven. The other city of top-class historical interest is **Aachen**, the original capital of the Holy Roman Empire. The adjoining province of Rhineland-Palatinate (Rheinland-Pfalz) is the land of the national epic, of the alluring Lorelei, of robber barons and of the traders who used the river routes to make the country rich. Nowadays pleasure cruisers run through the **Rhine gorge**, past a wonderful landscape of rocks, vines, white-painted towns and ruined castles. Industry exists only in isolated pockets, and **Mainz**, the state capital, only just ranks among the forty largest cities in Germany. Its monuments, though, merit more than a passing glance, while **Trier** preserves the finest buildings of classical antiquity this side of the Alps. In the province of Hesse (Hessen), dynamic **Frankfurt** dominates, with its banking and communications industries providing the region's real economic base. Of the historical centres here, the old university town of **Marburg** is of particular interest.

Cologne (Köln)

COLOGNE (Köln) has a population of just over a million, and its huge Gothic Dom is the country's most visited monument. Try and coincide your visit with the annual **Carnival** in early spring – Cologne boasts the largest street parties in Germany and the entire city does little but celebrate for a full four days. In a similar vein, the city ranks high as a **beer** centre, with some two dozen breweries, all of which produce the distinctive **Kölsch**. Another good time to visit is during the **Christmas market**, which attracts visitors from all over Europe.

Founded by the Romans in 33 BC, Cologne acquired the relics of the Three Magi from Milan in the twelfth century, thus increasing its standing as one of the greatest centres of pilgrimage in northern Europe. Situated on the intersection of the Rhine and several major trade routes, medieval Cologne became immensely rich – and the largest city in Germany. Later decline was partially reversed in the eighteenth century with the exploitation of an Italian recipe for distilling flower blossoms into almost pure alcohol. Originally created as an aphrodisiac, it was marketed here as a toilet water, achieving worldwide fame as **eau de Cologne**.

Arrival, information and accommodation

The main train station, the **Hauptbahnhof**, is immediately below the Dom; directly behind is the **bus station**. Coming from the **airport**, bus #170 runs from both terminals (every 15min; takes 20min; €5) to the Hauptbahnhof. The **tourist office**, Unter Fettenhennen 19, in front of the Dom (Mon–Sat 8am–9/10pm, Sun 10am–6pm; ☎0221/2213 0400, ⓦwww.koelntourismus.de), publishes a monthly guide to what's on, *Köln-In* (€1). Far better is *Prinz* (€1.50) available at newsagents. The **public transport** network is a mixture of buses and trams, the latter becoming the U-Bahn around the centre. Fares are high, so it's best to get a pass (€5.15/12.95 for one/three days) or the **Welcome Card** (€9/19 for one/three days), which also covers entrance to some sights. **Accommodation** is mainly geared to trade fairs. For a hotel room, the best advice is to pay the tourist office's €3 search fee; they often offer special discounts.

Hostels

Köln Deutz City Hostel Siegesstr. 5 ☎0221/81 47 11, ⓦwww.djh.de. HI hostel close to Deutz station, directly across the Rhine from the Altstadt. Large and functional with little character. €18.

Köln Riehl City Hostel An der Schanz 14 ☎0221/76 70 81, ⓦwww.djh.de. Large HI hostel tucked away in the quiet northern suburb of Riehl; U-Bahn #15 or #16 to Boltensternstrasse. €21.50.

Station Backpacker's Hostel Marzellenstr. 44–48 ☎0221/912 53 01, ⓔstation@hostel-cologne.de. Best choice in town is this comfortable, privately run hostel with a friendly bar and central location. €15.

Station Hostel and Bar Rheingasse 34–36 ☎0221/23 02 47. A branch of *Station Backpacker's*, set on the river ten minutes' walk from the station. €16.

Hotels and pensions

Das Kleine Stapelhäuschen Fischmarkt 1–3 ☎0221/257 78 62, ⓔstapelhaeuschen @compuserve.com. Characterful hotel/restaurant in the heart of the Altstadt. Rooms overlooking the river are the nicest, although all suffer from street noise. ⑤

Im Kupferkessel Probsteigasse 6 ☎0221/13 53 38, ⓦwww.im-kupferkessel.de. Good-value rooms in a location just far enough from the centre to be peaceful. ⑤

Jansen Richard-Wagner-Str. 18 ☎0221/25 18 75. Friendly, simple six-room pension; all rooms have TV. ⑤

Rossner Jakordenstr. 19 ☎0221/12 27 03. Homely and clean, and looking exactly as it must in the 1950s, this is the pick of the cluster of hotels behind the station. ③

The City

One of the largest Gothic buildings ever constructed, Cologne's **Dom** is built on a scale that reflects its power – the archbishop was one of the seven Electors of the Holy Roman Empire, and the Dom remains the seat of the Primate of Germany. The chancel was completed in 1322, but then the extravagant ambition of the plans began to take its toll. In 1560 the project was abandoned, to be resumed only in the nineteenth century, so what you see today is an act of homage from one age to another. From the west door your eye is immediately drawn down the length of the building to the high altar, with the spectacular golden shrine to the Magi, made in 1181. Other masterpieces include the ninth-century Gero crucifix, the most important monumental sculpture of its period, and the greatest achievement of the fifteenth-century Cologne school of painters, the *Adoration of the Magi* by Stefan Lochner. Then climb the 509 steps to the top of the south tower for a breathtaking panorama over the city and the Rhine (daily 9am–5pm; €2). The **Domschatzkammer** (daily 10am–6pm; €4, joint ticket with

tower €5) in the cellars, entered from the north side of the building, contains a stunning array of treasury items, the original sculptures from the medieval south portal and items excavated from Merovingian royal graves.

In a modern building next to the Dom, the outstanding **Museum Ludwig** (Tues–Sun 10/11am–6/8pm; €5.10; ⒲www.museenkoeln.de) is one of Germany's premier collections of modern art, particularly strong on the German Expressionists. Attached is the Agfa-Foto-Historama, which shows old photographic equipment and a selection of prints from the vast holdings of the local company. The neighbouring **Römisch-Germanisches Museum** (Tues–Sun 10am–5pm; €3.60; ⒲www.museenkoeln.de) has a collection of Roman glass reckoned to be the world's finest, but of more general appeal is the dazzling array of jewellery on the first floor, mostly dating from the Dark Ages. Its star exhibit is the Dionysus Mosaic, the finest work of its kind in northern Europe, created for a patrician villa in about 200 AD.

For nearly 600 years, **Gross St Martin**'s tower, surrounded by four turrets, was the dominant feature of the Cologne skyline. From the cobbled **Alter Markt** just beyond, you can see the irregular octagonal tower of the **Rathaus**, a real fricassee of styles, the highlight being the graceful Renaissance loggia. Just in front of the entrance to the Rathaus, a steel and glass pyramid stands over the **Mikwe** (Mon–Thurs 8am–4.45pm, Fri 8am–noon, Sat 10am–4pm, Sun 11am–1pm; free). This is the only remnant of the Jewish ghetto, which was razed soon after the expulsion order of 1424. Proceeding south, you come to the strikingly angular **Wallraf-Richartz-Museum** (Tues–Sun 10/11am–6/8pm; €5.10; ⒲www.museenkoeln.de), whose holdings centre on the fifteenth-century Cologne school as well as a fine Impressionist collection. The gems of the display are the two large triptychs by the Master of St Bartholomew, from the school's final flowering at the beginning of the sixteenth century. Then go down Rheingasse to see the stepgabled **Overstolzenhaus**, the finest mansion in the city. Further south, on the banks of the Rhine, is the **Schokoladen Museum** (Mon–Fri 10am–6pm, Sat & Sun 11am–5pm; €5.50), a thoroughly enjoyable museum focusing on the history and production of chocolate. Highlight is the "factory", with machines producing milk chocolate tablets, truffles and moulded animal shapes – don't miss the chocolate fountain where white-clad attendants hand out samples.

Eating, drinking and nightlife

Cologne crams over three thousand pubs, bars and cafés into a relatively small area. Their ubiquitous feature is the city's unique beer, **Kölsch**. Light and aromatically bitter, it's served in a small, thin glass (*Stange*), which holds only a fifth of a litre –

hence its rather effete image among other German beer drinkers. Best places to try it are the **Brauhäuser**, brewery-owned beer halls, which, although staffed by horribly matey waiters called *Köbes*, are definitely worth sampling, not least because they serve some of the cheapest and tastiest food in the city. **Nightlife** is concentrated in several distinct quarters. Most obvious of these is the area around Gross St Martin in the Altstadt, which catches the tourists and businessmen, yet manages to create a distinctive atmosphere. The student area focuses on Zülpicher Str. which is lined with cheap restaurants and lively bars, while the area south of Heumarkt has a handful of popular **gay and lesbian** bars.

Beer halls and restaurants

Alt-Köln Trankgasse 7–9. Notable for both the intricate clock mechanism on the outside and the no-nonsense slabs of salmon steak served inside.

Brauhaus Sion Unter Taschenmacher 5. Frequented mainly by locals, despite its proximity to the Dom; the menu concentrates on variations of *Wurst* and knuckles of pork leg.

Das Gaffel Haus Alter Markt. One of the most genuine old-style restaurants serving huge portions of *Schnitzel*; much cosier than most beer halls.

Das Känchen Fischmarkt. 28. The cheapest and least touristy of the riverfront restaurants, serving salads and sausages, coffee and cake.

Früh am Dom Am Hof 12–14. Located opposite the Dom, this heavily touristed *Brauhaus* serves excellent food. Opens for breakfast 8–11am.

Maybach Maybackstr. 11. One of the best beer gardens in town, with a pleasant leafy courtyard lit with fairy lights at night.

Päffgen Friesenstr. 64–68. Less touristy than the places near the Dom with a younger clientele, and brews *Kölsch* on the premises.

Rendevous Zülpicher Str. 11a. One of a handful of good-value Italian restaurants in this area. Big portions and a young, friendly crowd.

Zur Malzmühle Heumarkt 6. Traditional *Hausbrauerei*, which brews its own malty *Malzmühlenkölsch*. Few tourists but always packed out.

Bars and clubs

Apollo Hohenzollernring 79–83. Club spread over two floors, hosting mainly R&B and soul nights.

Biermseum Buttermarkt 39. Small bar tucked away near the river serving eighteen types of beer on tap.

Blue Note Brüsseler Str. 96. Trendy drum'n'bass and hip-hop club, catering to a young, studeny crowd.

Chlodwig-Eck Annostr. 1. Popular Südstadt meeting place, with live sport TV and Mediterranean-flavoured food.

Filmdose Zülpicher Str. 39. Fun pub that's packed with students enjoying a post-lecture *Kölsch*; it has a tiny cabaret stage and also shows films in English.

H90 Hohenzollernring 90. Top techno and house club featuring popular Ibiza-themed nights.

Opera Alteburger Str. 1. Brightly coloured, youth-oriented place with daily specialities on the menu.

Papa Joe's Klimperkasten Alter Markt 50. Deservedly popular Altstadt bar with Twenties decor and live trad jazz.

Quo Vadis Vor St Martin 8-10. Cosy gay bar serving light meals. Hosts popular Eighties themed nights.

Schmelztiegel Luxemburger Str. 34. Located in a former pharmacy, the relaxed "melting pot" now offers eleven varieties of *Kölsch* to combat most ailments.

Listings

Bike rental Rent-a-Bike, Sedanstr. 27 ☎0221/72 36 27.

Hospital Alexianer Krankenhaus, Kölner Str. 64 ☎0221/9 17 00.

Internet Via Phone, Marzellenstr. 3–5.

Laundry Pantaleonsmühlengasse 42.

Left luggage At the train station.

Pharmacy At the station & Neumarkt 2.

Post office At the station & Breitestr. 6.

Bonn

BONN, Cologne's neighbour, served as West Germany's capital from 1949 until the unification of 1990, when Berlin was restored to its former status. Although Bonn's administrative role has all but gone, it remains an important cultural centre, and despite its provincial reputation it is a surprisingly interesting place to visit, not least for its superb museums – and for being the birthplace of Beethoven. The small **Altstadt** is now a pedestrianized shopping area centred on two spacious squares. The square to the east is named after the huge Romanesque **Münster**, whose central octagonal tower with its soaring spire is the city's most prominent landmark. The pink Rococo **Rathaus** adds a touch of colour to the other square, the Markt, which still hosts a market each weekday. A couple of minutes' walk north of here, at Bonngasse 20, is the **Beethoven-Haus** (Mon–Sat 10am–5/6pm, Sun 11am–4pm; €4; @www.beethoven-haus-bonn.de), one of the few old buildings in the centre to have escaped wartime devastation. Beethoven served his musical apprenticeship at the Electoral court, but left the city for good at the age of 22, though this hasn't deterred Bonn from building up the best collection of memorabilia of its favourite son. To the east is the Baroque **Schloss**, an enormously long construction that was formerly the seat of the Archbishop-Electors of Cologne and is now used by the university. Bonn's **government quarter**, a mile south of the centre, was saddled with a temporary status. As a result, nothing was custom-built, but rather government offices utilized existing buildings, such as the Villa Hammerschmidt and the Palais Schaumburg – pompous nineteenth-century buildings now used as conference venues. The **Museumsmeile**, planned as a cultural accompaniment to the government quarter, is home to the superb **Kunstmuseum** (Tues–Sun 10am–6pm, Wed till 9pm; €5, free on Sun), with a fine Expressionism collection. Next door is the **Kunst- und Ausstellungshalle** (Tues–Sun 10am–7/9pm; €5–8; @www.bundeskunsthalle.de), a monumental postmodern arts centre for important temporary exhibitions.

Bonn **train station** lies in the middle of the city; just to the east is the **bus station**, whose local services, along with the **trams** (which become the U-Bahn in the city centre), form part of a system integrated with Cologne's. As the attractions are well spaced out, it's advisable to buy a public transport pass (€5.15/12.25 for one/three days) or the **WelcomeCard** (€9/14 for one/two days), which covers public transport plus museum admission. You can get them from the **tourist office**, Windeckstr. 9 (Mon–Sat 9am–4/6.30pm, Sun 10am–2pm; ☎0228/77 50 00, @www.bonn.de). An **HI hostel** is at Haager Weg 42 (☎0228/28 99 70, @www.djh.de; €21.30) in the suburb of Venusberg; take bus #621. Central **hotels** include the basic *Daufenbach*, Brüdergasse 6 (☎0228/63 79 44; ❸), and hospitable *Deutsches Haus*, 19–21 (☎0228/63 37 77; ❹). For **places to eat** try *Cassius Garten*, Maximilianstr. 28d, which offers a mouthwatering veggie choice; *Don Quijote*, Oxfordstr. 18, the most affordable of many Spanish restaurants; *Em Höttche*, Markt 4, a traditional *Gaststätte* next to the Rathaus; or *Im Bären*, Acherstr. 1–3, an excellent brewery-owned place. Many of the best **bars** are in the Altstadt. *Brauhaus Bönnsch*, Sterntorbrücke 4, produces a distinctive blond ale and does good-value meals, while *Zebulon*, Stockenstr. 19, is a big favourite with arts students, particularly for breakfast.

Aachen

AACHEN – now bordering both Belgium and the Netherlands – was the hub in the eighth century of the great empire of Charlemagne, a choice made partly for strategic reasons but also because of the presence of hot springs: exercising in these waters was one of the emperor's favourite pastimes. Today the town has a pleasant, laid-back atmosphere that reflects its large student population, making it a good day trip from Cologne, or stop-off point between countries: both Maastricht (Netherlands) and Liège (Belgium) are within spitting distance.

Although the surviving architectural legacy of Charlemagne is small, Aachen retains its crowning jewel, the former **Palace chapel**. Now the heart of the **Dom**, the original octagon had to be enlarged by adding the Gothic chancel to accommodate the number of pilgrims that poured in. Adorning the main altar is the Pala d'Oro, an eleventh-century altar front embossed with scenes of the Passion. At the end of the chancel, the gilded shrine of Charlemagne, finished in 1215 after fifty years' work, contains the remains of the emperor. In the gallery is the imperial throne, which you can only see on a tour (daily; €2). Charlemagne's palace once extended across the Katschhof to the site of the fourteenth-century **Rathaus**, which incorporates two of the palace's towers and has a facade lined with the fig-

⑪

ures of 50 Holy Roman Emperors, 31 of whom were crowned in Aachen. The glory of the interior (daily 10am–1pm & 2–5pm; €2) is the much-restored Kaisersaal, repository of the crown jewels – in reproduction. The Rathaus fronts the expansive **Markt**, which boasts the finest of the medieval houses left in the city.

The centre is ten minutes from the **train station** – down Bahnhofstrasse then left into Theaterstrasse. The **tourist office** occupies the Atrium Elisenbrunnen on Friedrich-Wilhelm-Platz (Mon–Fri 9am–6pm, Sat 9am–2pm, April–Dec also Sun 10am–2pm; ☎0241/180 29 60, ⊛www.aachen.de). The **HI hostel** is southwest of the centre, at Maria-Theresia-Allee 260 (☎0241/71 10 10, ⊛www.djh.de; €20.90); take bus #2 as far as Brüsseler Ring or Ronheide. The cheaper **hotels** are near the train station; try *Dura*, Lagerhausstr. 5 (☎0241/40 31 35; ❸), or *Marx*, Hubertusstr 33–35 (☎0241/3 75 41, ⊛www.hotel-marx.de; ❹). A spiced gingerbread called Printen is the main local speciality, and the place to eat it is the old coffee house *Leo van den Daele*, Büchel 18. The most celebrated **bar/restaurant** is *Postwagen*, Markt 40, with a cheerful Baroque exterior and wonderful cramped rooms inside. The student quarter centres on Pontstrasse, which is lined with bars and cheap eateries. The bistro-style *Egmont* at no. 1 is a popular haunt, as is relaxed *Café Kittel*, at no. 37. *Labyrinth* at no. 156 is a large pub serving Greek-style food.

Mainz and beyond

At the confluence of the Rhine and Main rivers, **MAINZ** is an agreeable mixture of old and new, with an attractive restored centre and a jovial populace – it's second only to Cologne in the Carnival stakes. Ecclesiastical power aside, prestige came through Johannes Gutenberg, who revolutionized the art of printing here. Rearing high above the centre of Mainz is the **Dom**, crowded in by eighteenth-century houses. Choirs at both ends of the building indicate its status as an imperial cathedral, with one area for the emperor and one for the clergy. Visit the spacious **Markt**, with its riotously colourful fountain, when it's packed with market stalls (Tues, Fri & Sat mornings). Dominating the adjoining Liebfrauenplatz, is the **Gutenberg Museum** (Tues–Sat 9am–5pm, Sun 11am–3pm; €3; ⊛www.gutenberg.de) – a fitting tribute to one of the greatest inventors of all time, whose pioneering development of movable type led to the mass-scale production of books. In 1978, the museum acquired the last Gutenberg Bible still in private hands – made in the 1450s, it's one of only forty-odd surviving examples. Across Schöfferstrasse from the Dom, Ludwigstrasse runs to Schillerplatz and Schillerstrasse, both lined with Renaissance and Baroque palaces. Up the hill by Gaustrasse is the Gothic **St Stephan** (daily 10am–noon & 2–5pm), whose priest persuaded Marc Chagall to make a series of atmospheric **stained-glass windows**. Symbolizing the reconciliation between France and Germany, Christian and Jew, the nine windows were finished in 1984, a few months before the artist's death.

The **train station** is northwest of the city centre, while the **tourist office** (Mon–Fri 9am–6pm, Sat 10am–3pm; ☎06131/28 62 10, ⊛www.info-mainz.de) is in the Brückenturm am Rathaus at the corner of Rheinstrasse. Near the station are some of the least expensive **hotels**, such as en-suite *Terminus*, Alicenstr. 4 (☎06131/22 98 76, ⊛www.hotel-terminus-mainz.de; ❹). *Stadt Coblenz*, Rheinstr. 49 (☎0 61 31/22 76 02; ❹), is more conveniently located near the Dom, though the rooms suffer from street-noise. The **HI hostel** (☎06131/8 53 32, ⊛www.djh.de; €16.60; buses #61/62) is in the wooded heights of Am Fort Weisenau. Mainz boasts more vineyards than any other German city, and you don't need to stray far for a **wine** crawl. Some *Weinstuben* are open in the evenings only, such as the oldest, *Alt Deutsche Weinstube*, Liebfrauenplatz 7, which offers cheap daily dishes. Even better **food** is available at *Weinhaus Schreiner*, Rheinstr. 38 (closed Sat night & Sun); *Am Fischtor*, Fischtorstr. 1, although rather dark, is also worth a try. Mainz also has an excellent home-brew **pub**, *Eisgrub-Bräu*, Weissliliengasse 4, which serves inexpensive buffet lunches. *Havana*, below the *Stadt Coblenz* hotel at Rheinstr. 49, is a Cuban/Mexican bar and restaurant which gets packed out at weekends.

The Rhine gorge to Koblenz

North of Mainz, the Rhine bends westwards and continues its stately but undramatic journey – then suddenly, at **BINGEN**, the river widens and swings north into the spectacular 80km **Rhine gorge**. This waterway has become one of Europe's major tourist magnets, but the pleasure steamers are still outnumbered by commercial barges – a reminder of the river's crucial role in the German economy. Spring and autumn are the best times to visit, since in summer inexpensive accommodation is scarce and heavily booked. Rail and road lines lie on each side of the river and, although there are no bridges between Bingen and Koblenz, there are fairly frequent ferries, enabling you to hop from one bank to the other. However, it's undeniably most fun by boat. Some **river cruises** (mainly April–Oct) depart from Mainz, where there's a K-D Line office (☎06131/23 28 00, ⓦwww.k-d.com), although more regular through-services start from Bingen. The full one-way boat fare from Bingen to Koblenz is €23.20 (takes 3hr 40min) – though Eurail is valid and other rail passes attract a discount. Ask about bike offers, especially on Tuesdays.

At **BACHARACH**, 10km downstream from Bingen, the chunky castle of Burg Stahleck houses an HI **hostel** (☎06743/12 66, ⓦwww.djh.de; ❷) – it's a steep climb up the hill to get there, but the views are worth it – and there's a **campsite** at Strandbadweg. From **KAUB**, a few kilometres on, you get a great view of the appealing **Pfalz**, a white-walled toll fortress standing on an island that has become a famous Rhineland symbol (Tues–Sun 9am–1pm & 2–5/6pm; €3.60 including ferry). The most famous point along the Rhine is the **Lorelei**, a much-photographed rocky projection a little downstream from Kaub, where, legend has it, a blonde woman would lure passing mariners to their doom with her siren song. The rock can also be spotted from trains heading between Mainz and Koblenz, since the track runs right along the banks of the Rhine as it passes through the gorge.

Quiet **KOBLENZ** stands where the Rhine and Mosel meet. The centre is at its most appealing in the area around the confluence at **Deutsches Eck**, close to which stands the fine Romanesque church of **St Kastor**. However, the most commanding sights are across the Rhine in the district of Ehrenbreitstein, overshadowed by the **Festung**. One of the largest fortresses in the world, it is now home to the **Landesmuseum Koblenz** (mid-March to Nov daily 9.30am–5pm; €2) and one of the best **hostels** in Germany (☎0261/97 28 70, ⓦwww.djh.de; €15.10). The Festung and hostel can be reached by chairlift or a 1.5km walk. Koblenz's main **tourist office** (Mon–Fri 9am–6/8pm, Sat & Sun 10am–4/6/8pm; ☎0261/30 38 80, ⓦwww.koblenz.de) is opposite the **train and bus stations**, a little southwest of the centre. **Hotel** rooms are reasonably priced: try *Sessellift*, Obertal 22 (☎0261/7 52 56; ❸), or *Jan van Werth*, Van-Werth-Str. 9 (☎0261/3 65 00; ❸). The **campsite** (☎0261/8 27 19; closed mid-Oct to March) is opposite Deutsches Eck; a ferry crosses the Mosel here in summer, while another crosses the Rhine further south.

Trier

Birthplace of Karl Marx and the oldest city in Germany, **TRIER** was once the capital of the Western Roman Empire. Nowadays, it has the less exalted role of regional centre for the upper Mosel valley, its relaxed air a world away from the status it formerly held. Despite a turbulent history, an amazing amount of the city's past has been preserved, in particular the most impressive group of Roman monuments north of the Alps.

The centre corresponds roughly to the Roman city and can easily be covered on foot. From the train station, it's a few minutes' walk down Theodor-Heuss-Allee to the **Porta Nigra**, northern gateway to Roman Trier. Nearby, housed in a former monastery, is the **Städtisches Museum Simeonstift** (Tues–Sun 9am–3/5pm; April–Oct also Mon; €2.60), which contains some notable medieval sculptures plus a good Egyptian and Roman ancient history section. From here, Simeonstrasse runs down to the **Hauptmarkt**, a busy pedestrian shopping area, with stalls selling fruit and flowers. At the southern end of the Hauptmarkt a Baroque portal leads to the Gothic **St Gangolf**, built by the burghers of Trier in an attempt to aggravate the archbishops, whose political power they resented. Up Sternstrasse from the Hauptmarkt is the magnificent Romanesque **Dom**, on the site of an original built in the fourth century for Emperor Constantine. The present building dates from 1030, and the facade has not changed significantly since then. Inside, the Schatzkammer (Mon–Sat 10/11am–4/5pm, Sun 1.30–4/5pm; €1.50) has many examples of the work of local goldsmiths, notably a tenth-century portable altar. From here, Liebfrauenstrasse goes past the ritzy Palais Kesselstadt to the **Konstantinbasilika**. Built as Constantine's throne hall, its dimensions are awe-inspiring: 30m high and 75m long, it is completely self-supporting. It became a church for the local Protestant community in the nineteenth century. Next door, the **Rokoko-Palais der Kurfürsten** was built in 1756 for an archbishop who felt that the adjoining old Schloss wasn't good enough for him. Its pink facade overlooks the Palastgarten, setting for the **Rheinisches Landesmuseum** (daily 9.30/10.30am–5pm; Nov–April closed Mon; €5.50). Easily the best of Trier's museums, its collection brings to life the sophistication and complexity of Roman civilization; prize exhibit is the Neumagener Weinschiff, a Roman sculpture of a wine ship. A few minutes further south, the **Kaiserthermen** was once one of the largest bath complexes in the Roman world. The extensive underground heating system has survived, and you can walk around the service channels and passages. From here, the route to the **Amphitheatre,** oldest of Trier's surviving Roman buildings, is well signposted.

Trier's **tourist office**, An der Porta Nigra (Mon–Sat 9/10am–5/6pm, Sun 10am–1/3.30pm; ☎06 51/97 80 80, ⊛www.trier.de), sells the **Trier-Card** (€9/three days), which covers entrance to the museums and other discounts. There's a large **HI hostel** at An der Jugendherberge 4 (☎0651/14 66 20, ⊛www.djh.de; €16.80) on the banks of the Mosel. *Warsberger Hof*, Dietrichstr. 42 (☎0651/97 52 50, ⊛www.warsberger-hof.de; ❸), is the best-value **hotel**, with dorms as well as rooms, and it's ideally situated in the Altstadt. Otherwise, the most central hotel is *Zur Glocke*, Glockenstr. 12 (☎0651/7 31 09; ❸). There's a **campsite**, *Trier City*, Luxemburger Str. 81 (☎0651/8 69 21; closed Dec & Jan), on the western bank of the Mosel. It's easy to get good and inexpensive **food** thanks to the sociable student population: the best bet is *Astarix*, Karl-Marx-Str. 11, a relaxed student bar; or *Zum Domstein*, Hauptmarkt 5, whose eclectic menu includes Roman-style dishes, regional creations and good vegetarian options. Among the many possibilities for tasting the local wines is the late-opening **bar** of the prestigious Reichsgraf von Kesselstatt estates, at Liebfrauenstr. 10. The bright and breezy *InFlagranti*, Viehmarkt 14, is a student favourite serving food, while *Palais* on Stockplatz is a fashionable bar-cum-disco.

Frankfurt

Straddling the River Main just before it meets the Rhine, **FRANKFURT** (often suffixed "am Main") is a city with two faces. The cut-throat financial capital of Germany, with its fulcrum in the Westend district, it's also a civilized place that spends more per year on the arts than any other city in Europe. It has the best range of museums in the country after Berlin, and some excellent (if expensive) nightlife. Over half of the city, including almost all of the centre, was destroyed during the war and the rebuilders opted for innovation rather than restoration. The result is a skyline that smacks more of New York than Germany – hence the nickname "Mainhattan".

Arrival, information and accommodation

Frankfurt **airport** has regular rail links to most German cities, with a frequent service (every 10min) to the main **train station**. The airport is also linked to the train

station by two S-Bahn lines, run by the regional transport company (RMV). Local transport ticket prices vary according to the time of travel, making it better to invest in the one-day ticket (€4.35) or, better still, the **Frankfurt Card** (€7.50/11 for one/two days), which can be bought from tourist offices and allows travel throughout the city, plus reduced entry charges to most museums (though many are free on Wed). From the train station it's a fifteen-minute walk to the centre, or take U-Bahn line #4 or #5, or tram #11. There are two main **tourist offices**: in the train station (Mon–Fri 8am–9pm, Sat & Sun 9am–6pm; ☏069/2123 8800, Ⓦwww.frankfurt-tourismus.de), and at Römerberg 27 (10am–4/5.30pm). Free **listings magazines**, *Fritz* and *Strandgut*, are available at both, although *Prinz* (€1), from newsagents, is more comprehensive.

Accommodation is pricey, thanks to the expense-account clientele. Most reasonably priced options are in the sleazy environs of the train station, close to the Kaiserstrasse red-light district.

Hostel

HI hostel Deutschherrnufer 12, Sachsenhausen ☏069/610 01 50, Ⓦwww.djh.de. The best budget option in town, with 470 places in dorms of up to twelve beds each. Bus #46 from the train station. €18.

Hotels

Atlas Zimmerweg 1 ☏069/72 39 46. Friendly place with bright, airy rooms within walking distance of the station but away from the sleazy side of things. ❺
Backer Mendelssohnstr. 92 ☏069/74 79 92. Pleasant enough place close to the university,

although use of the showers costs €2 a time. U-Bahn line #6 or #7 to Westend. ❸
Glockshuber Mainzer Landstr. 120 ☏069/74 26 28, ©glockshuber@t-online.de. Pleasant budget hotel just north of the train station, away from the sleazier streets. ❹
Gölz Beethovenstr. 44 ☏069/74 61 42, Ⓦwww.hotel-goetz.de. Small, traditionally furnished hotel located on a quiet, tree-lined avenue in the Westend district. ❹
Royal Wallstr. 17 ☏069/62 30 26. Functional but good-value hotel in the heart of Sachsenhausen, close to some of the well-known apple wine taverns. ❺

The City

The city centre is defined by the old city walls, now transformed into a semi-circular stretch of public gardens. **Römerberg** is the historical and geographical centre. Charlemagne built his fort on this low hill to protect the original *frankonovurd* (Ford of the Franks), but the whole quarter was flattened by bombing in 1944. The most significant survivor was the thirteenth-century St Bartholomäus or **Dom**, and even that emerged with only its main walls intact. To the right of the choir is the restored Wahlkapelle, where the seven Electors used to make their final choice of Holy Roman Emperor. To the north, in Domstrasse, is the exceptional **Museum für Moderne Kunst** (Tues–Sun 10am–5pm, Wed till 8pm; €5; ⓦ www.mmk-frank-furt.de), a three-storey slice featuring major modern artists and innovative temporary exhibitions. At the opposite end of the Römerberg is the **Römer**, formerly the Rathaus. Its distinctive facade, with its triple-stepped gables, fronts the Römerplatz market square, home to a twinkling Christmas Market in December. The **Saalhof**, an amalgamation of imperial buildings now housing the Historisches Museum, is nearby on Mainkai, overlooking the river. Its twelfth-century chapel is all that remains of the palace complex, which grew up in the Middle Ages. The **museum** (Tues, Thurs & Sun 10am–4pm, Wed 4–8pm, Fri 10am–2pm, Sat 1pm–5pm; €4) contains a good local history collection, with an eye-opening section on the devastation caused by the bombing. A short distance to the west, on Untermainkai, is the **Jewish Museum** (Tues–Sun 10am–5pm, Wed till 8pm; €2.60; ⓦ www.juedischesmuseum.de), providing an interesting look at the city's Jewish community, which lost 10,000 people to the Nazis.

A little to the northwest of the **Hauptwache** (originally a guard house, now the main shopping area), near the Börse, Frankfurt's stock exchange, are two of the most expensive shopping streets in the city: **Goethestrasse** is all expensive jewellers and designer clothes shops, while **Grosse Bockenheimer Strasse** is home to upmarket delicatessens and smarter restaurants. This area is characterized by gleaming skyscrapers; the **Main Tower** (10am–7/9pm; €4.50) admits the public to its outside viewing platform on the 86th floor, for some unparalleled vistas. East of here, the garden of **Peterskirche** is notable for its unusual and moving memorial to victims of AIDS. Designed by Thomas Fecht, *Verletzte Liebe* ("Wounded Love") is a wall studded with nails, one for each fatality; there are currently over eight hundred nails.

For a laid-back evening out, head for **Sachsenhausen**, the city-within-a-city on the south bank of the Main. The network of streets around Affentorplatz is home to the famous apple wine (*Ebbelwei*) houses, while on Schaumainkai – also known as **Museumsufer** – the Saturday **flea market** is worth a browse. Museumsufer is also lined with excellent musems, pick of the bunch the **Städel** located at no. 63 (Tues–Sun 10am–5pm, Wed till 8pm; €6, ⓦ www.staedelmuseum.de), one of the most comprehensive art galleries in Europe. All the big names in German art are represented, including Dürer, both Holbeins, Cranach and Altdorfer. The **Deutsches Filmmuseum**, at no. 41 (Tues–Sun 10am–5pm, Wed till 8pm, Sat from 2pm; €2.50; ⓦ www.deutsches-filmmuseum.de), has its own cinema and is a popular spot for foreign films and art house screenings. The **Deutsches Architekturmuseum**, no. 43 (Tues–Sun 10am–5pm, Wed till 8pm; €5, free on Wed; ⓦ www.dam-online.de), is also worth a visit, installed in an avant-garde conversion of a nineteenth-century villa; the highpoint is the "house within a house" which dominates the museum like an oversized dolls' house.

Eating, drinking and nightlife

Frankfurt has a wealth of gastronomic possibilities, from the ultra-trendy joints found in the Westend to the cheapo Italian restaurants of Bockenheim, the working-class/boho/student quarter. One of its best-known locales is Kleine Bockenheimer Strasse, aka Jazzgasse, the centre of Frankfurt's jazz scene, while the trendiest bars and clubs can be found around the Salzhaus in the centre, in the Westend district, or the Ostend, around Hanauer Landstrasse.

Apple wine taverns

Adolf Wagner Schweizer Str. 71. One of the best of the taverns, with a lively clientele of all ages and a cosy garden terrace.

Atschel Wallstr. 7. This offers a more extensive menu than many of its counterparts, and has bargain set lunches. Closed Mon.

Zum Eichkatzerl Dreieichstr. 29. An excellent, traditional tavern with a large courtyard and low-priced food. Closed Mon.

Zum Gemalten Haus Schweizer Str. 67. A bit kitsch with its oil-painted facade and stained glass windows, yet quite intimate and lively, with long rows of tables outside. Closed Mon & Tues.

Bars, cafés and café-bars

Café Laumer Bockenheimer Landstr. 67. One of Frankfurt's oldest cafés, halfway up the Westend's main thoroughfare. The all-day breakfasts are a true indulgence.

Club Voltaire Kleine Hochstr. 5. Tasty, good food with a Spanish bias, and a clientele of left-wing political activists, artists and gay people. Frequent events include musical improvisation evenings and political debates. From 6pm.

Dichtung und Wahrheit Am Salzhaus 1. Named after one of Goethe's works, this literary venue is littered with books and newspapers.

Harvey's Bornheimer Landstr. 64. Slick, high-ceilinged colonnaded bar in an appealing end-of-terrace building, which in the evening hosts a mainly gay and lesbian crowd.

Helium Belidenstr. 7. High quality "world" cuisine served to a well-heeled crowd in this fashionable bar. Also popular for after-work drinks.

Lounge Weissadlergasse 15. Popular bar serving cheap lunches, salads and sandwiches to a student crowd.

Pilar Weissadlergasse 2. Good place for lunch in the centre, serving snacks and full meals, turning into a trendy bar in the evenings.

Sansibar Hanauer Landstr. 190. Arabic-styled rooftop bar offering great views and cocktails. Perfect for a quick drink before heading to *190east* (see below) in the basement.

Restaurants

Bistro Rosa Grüneburgweg 25. The walls hung with pictures of pigs lend an element of kitsch, but the very select menu is excellent (if pricey). Closed Mon.

Frankfurter Haus Darmstädter Landstr. 741. Old-style restaurant serving typical Frankfurt dishes

such as *Grüne Sosse* (a green sauce made with at least five types of fresh herbs, served with egg and potatoes) and *Handkäs mit Musik* (a strong cheese smothered with chopped onions, vinegar and oil).

Iwase Vibeler Str. 31. Reasonably priced Japanese, with seating at the counter or the few tables. Closed Mon.

Knoblauch Staufenstr. 39. Friendly, intimate little place where the seasonal dishes come liberally laced with garlic.

Nibelungen-Schänke Nibelungenallee 55. Typical Greek food at very reasonable prices. Attracts a young crowd and is usually open till 1am. U-Bahn line #5.

Stars Bar Friedrich-Ebert-Anlage 49. In the basement of the Messeturm, this American-style restaurant has fantasy decor and good-value set lunches.

Clubs and live music

190east Hanauer Landstr. 190. Top club in Frankfurt's latest hip area. Packed out at weekends, with excellent house, techno and funk nights.

Batschkapp Maybachstr. 24. Grimy, sweaty venue for top-rank indie bands – avoid the school-age club nights though.

Brotfabrik Bachmannstr. 2–4. One of the city's fading stars, featuring live and dance music, plus occasional salsa nights.

Cooky's Am Salzhaus 4. Hip-hop and soul club hosting popular DJ night plus occasional live acts.

Jazzkeller Kleine Bockenheimer Str. 18a. This atmospheric cellar is Frankfurt's premier jazz venue. Closed Sun.

King Kamehameha Hanauer Landstr. 192. Restaurant and club catering to high-maintenance city types. Notable for its pool, which comes into use on wilder nights.

U60311 Rossmarkt Unterführung. Long-standing favourite and one of the best techno clubs in town. Be prepared to queue.

Listings

Bike rental Per Pedale, Leipziger Str. 4 ☎069/70 76 91 10.

Consulates UK, Bockenheimer Landstr. 42 ☎069/1 70 00 20; US, Siesmayerstr. 21 ☎069/7 53 50.

Hospital Bürgerhospital, Nibelungenallee 37–41

☎069/1 50 00.

Laundry Wash World, Moselstr. 17.

Left luggage At the train station.

Pharmacy At the train station.

Post office Goetheplatz 2–4.

Marburg

About 80km north of Frankfurt, the university town of **MARBURG** clusters on the slopes of the Lahn valley in a maze of narrow streets and medieval buildings, crowned by an impressive castle. It has a relaxed and lively atmosphere, and has been touched by war less than almost any other city in the country. The most important building is the **Elisabethkirche** (daily 9/10am–4/5/6pm; chancel €2), the first Gothic church in Germany. It was erected to house the remains of St Elisabeth, who died here in 1231; her thirteenth-century shrine is in the sacristy. Nearby, the Steinweg, a stepped street hemmed in by half-timbered buildings, leads to the **Marktplatz**, centre of the Altstadt and focal point of the lively student nightlife scene. From the Marktplatz make your way up Rittergasse to the thirteenth-century **Marienkirche**, just past which a flight of steps rises to the **Schloss** (Tues–Sun 10/11am–5/6pm; €2.50). Begun by Sophie, the daughter of St Elisabeth, the bulk of what can be seen today dates from the fifteenth and sixteenth centuries. The **train station** is on the right bank of the Lahn at the northern end of town. The **tourist office** is at Am Pilgrimstein 26 (Mon–Fri 9am–6pm; Sat 10am–2pm; ☎06421/9 91 20, ✆www.marburg.de). The **HI hostel** has a pleasant riverside setting at Jahnstr. 1 (☎06421/2 34 61, ✆www.djh.de; €19.70), a ten-minute walk to the south of the Altstadt. Most central **hotels** are a little pricey – *Gästehaus Müller*, Deutschhausstr. 29 (☎06421/6 56 59; ❺), is perhaps the best value. **Camping** is over the river at Trojedamm 47 (☎06421/2 13 31). For **eating and drinking**, two enduring student favourites are *Café Barfuss*, Barfüsserstr. 33, and *Hinkelstein*, Markt 18.

Southern Germany

The southwestern province of **Baden-Württemberg** is the most prosperous part of the country. The motor car was invented here in the late nineteenth century, and the region has stayed at the forefront of world technology ever since, with **Stuttgart** still the home of Mercedes and Porsche. Germany's most famous university city, **Heidelberg**, is here, and the spa resort of **Baden-Baden** remains wonderfully evocative of its nineteenth-century heyday as the playground of Europe's aristocracy. The scenery is wonderful too: its western and southern boundaries are defined by the Rhine and its bulge into Germany's largest lake, the **Bodensee** (Lake Constance). Within the curve of the river lies the **Black Forest**, source of another of the continent's principal waterways, the Danube.

Bavaria (Bayern in German), which occupies the whole southeastern chunk of the country out to the Austrian and Czech frontiers, is the home of all the German clichés: beer-swilling men in Lederhosen, sausage-dogs, sauerkraut and *wurst*. But that's only a small part of the picture, and almost entirely restricted to the Alpine region south of the magnificent state capital **Munich**. In the western parts, around pristine **Augsburg**, the food is less pork and sausages and more pasta and sauces, and the landscape gentle farming country ideal for camping and cycling holidays. To the north lies **Nuremberg**, centre of a region of vineyards and nature parks. Eastern Bavaria – apart from its capital **Regensburg** – is relatively poor; life in its highland forests revolves around logging and workshop industries such as glass production. One practical note: travellers over the age of 27 are barred from using Bavarian hostels – although you'll almost always be able to find a reasonable alternative.

Heidelberg

Home to Germany's oldest university, **HEIDELBERG** is majestically set on the banks of the swift-flowing Neckar between ranges of wooded hills, around 70km south of Frankfurt. Since the days of the Grand Tour it has seduced travellers like no other German city. Centrepiece is the Schloss, a compendium of magnificent buildings, somehow increased in stature by their ruined condition. The rest of the city has some good museums, but the main appeal is its picturesque cobbled streets, crammed with old-style eateries and student pubs. The upbeat, youthful atmosphere is at its most palpable in summer when the streets hum with activity and late-night parties.

The dominating **Schloss** can be reached from the Kornmarkt by funicular (€3.50 return), which continues to the Königstuhl viewpoint; you can also walk up in ten minutes via the Burgweg. At the southeastern corner is the most romantic of the ruins, now generally known as the Gesprengter Turm; a collapsed section lies intact in the moat, leaving a clear view into the interior. The **Schlosshof** (daily 8am–5.30pm; €2.50), holds a group of Renaissance palaces, including the diverting Pharmacy Museum and the Grosses Fass, an enormous wine-barrel built in 1751 capable of holding 220,000 litres. The finest building is the swaggering **Friedrichsbau** (tours only; in English hourly 10.15am–4.15pm; €3.50), which supports a pantheon of the House of Wittelsbach, beginning with Charlemagne. The original statues can be seen inside, along with a number of restored rooms that have been decked out in period style.

The **Altstadt**'s finest surviving buildings are grouped on Marktplatz, in the middle of which is the sandstone **Heiliggeistkirche**. Note the tiny shopping booths between its buttresses, a feature ever since the church was built. The striking Baroque **Alte Brücke** is reached from the Marktplatz down Steingasse; dating from the 1780s, it was blown up in the last war, but has been painstakingly rebuilt. The **Palais Rischer** on Untere Strasse was the most famous venue for the university's *Mensur*, or fencing match; wounds were frequent and prized as badges of courage – for optimum prestige, salt was rubbed into them, leaving scars that remained for life. Universitätsplatz, the heart of the old town, is flanked by the eighteenth-century **Alte Universität** (April–Oct Tues–Sun 10am–4pm; Nov–March Tues–Fri 10am–4pm; €2.50) and the **Neue Universität**, erected with US funds in 1931. The oddest of Heidelberg's traditions was that its students used not to be subject to civil jurisdiction: offenders were dealt with by the university authorities, and could serve their punishment at leisure. Now a protected monument, the **Students' Prison** (same hours and ticket as Alte Universität) is on Augustinergasse; used from 1712 to 1914, the spartan cells are covered with graffiti.

Practicalities

Heidelberg's **train and bus stations** are in an anonymous quarter fifteen minutes' walk west of the centre on the dreary Kurfürsten-Anlage. The **tourist office** is on the square outside (Mon–Sat 9am–6/7pm; April–Sept also Sun 10am–6pm; ☎06221/1 94 33, ⊛www.cvb-heidelberg.de). The **hostel** is on the north bank of the Neckar, about 4km from the centre, at Tiergartenstr. 5 (☎06221/65 11 90, ⊛www.djh.de; €18.60; bus #11). **Hotels** are often booked solid: the chart outside the tourist office details any vacancies. The best budget options are *Jeske*, in the centre at Mittelbadgasse 2 (☎06221/2 37 33; ❹) and *Elite*, a friendly place ten minutes from the centre at Bunsenstr. 15 (☎06221/2 57 34, ⊛www.hotel-elite-heidelberg .de; ❺). The **student taverns** are a must, known for their basic dishes at reasonable prices. At the eastern end of Hauptstrasse are the two most famous: *Zum Sepp'l* at no. 213, popular for its Wiener Schnitzel; and *Roter Ochsen* at no. 217, which serves excellent home-made goulash. Slightly less touristy is the oldest tavern, *Schnookeloch*, at Haspelgasse 8. Among other traditional **restaurants**, try *Essighaus*, Plöck 97. For cheap, filling Thai food there's *Supan's Bistro*, Hauptstr. 133, opposite the Alte Universität. *Café Coyote*, a few doors down at no. 130, has excellent value lunchtime menus for students. Characterful *Destille* is best of the **drinking** spots along Untere Strasse. *Weisser Schwan Biermuseum*, Hauptstr. 143, has 101 types of beer, while *Vetter*, Steingasse 9, has its own small house brewery. The mid-nineteenth-century *Knösel*, Haspelgasse 20, is the oldest of Heidelberg's **cafés**; its speciality is Heidelberger Studentenkuss, a dark chocolate filled with praline and nougat.

Rothenburg ob der Tauber

The **Romantic Road** winds its way along the length of western Bavaria and runs through the most visited – and most beautiful – medieval town in Germany: **ROTHENBURG OB DER TAUBER**, 50km west of Nuremberg and about

80km southeast of Frankfurt. It is connected by a branch railway with Steinach, on the Augsburg–Würzburg line; to reach Nuremberg, you need to change here and again at Ansbach. It takes about an hour to walk around Rothenburg's fourteenth-century walls, the ultimate museum piece. Wandering the cobbled lanes between the half-timbered houses is a delight, and the views from the walls over the surrounding countryside are magnificent. The promontory on the western side of town is the site of the **Burgtor** – the oldest of all the 24 towers – and the **Blasiuskapelle**, with fourteenth-century murals. The sloping **Marktplatz** is dominated by the arcaded front of the Renaissance Rathaus, which supplanted the Gothic building that stands behind it. The sixty-metre tower of the **Gotisches Rathaus** (daily: April–Oct 9.30am–12.30pm & 1–5pm; Dec noon–3pm; €1) provides the best views. The other main attractions on the Marktplatz are the figures on each side of the three clocks of the **Ratsherrntrinkstube**, which seven times daily re-enact an episode that allegedly occurred during the Thirty Years War. The fearsome Johann Tilly agreed that Rothenburg should be spared if one of the councillors could drain in one draught a tankard holding over three litres of wine. A former burgomaster duly sank the contents of the so-called Meistertrunk, then needed three days to sleep off the effects. On the opposite side of the Marktplatz is the Gothic **St Jakob-Kirche** (daily: April–Oct 9am–5.30pm; Nov & Jan–March 10am–noon & 2–4pm; Dec 10am–5pm; €1.50), rising above the sea of red roofs like a great ship; the entrance fee is worth paying purely to see Tilman Riemenschneider's exquisite limewood *Holy Blood Altar*. Of the local museums, the most fascinating is the **Kriminalmuseum** at Burggasse 3 (daily: April–Oct 9.30am–6pm; Nov & Jan–March 2–4pm; Dec 10am–4pm; €3.20), which contains collections of medieval torture instruments and related objects such as the beer barrels that drunks were forced to walk around in.

There are many cheap **pensions** and **inns**; worth trying are the charming old-fashioned *Pöschel*, Wenggasse 22 (☎09861/34 30, ✆pension.poeschel@t-online.de; ❸) and the welcoming *Raidel*, in a medieval house on the same street at no. 3 (☎09861/31 15, ⊛www.romanticroad.com/raidel; ❸). The two **hostels** – *Rossmühle* and its annexe *Spitalhof* (☎09861/9 41 60; both €23.50) – are in beautifully restored houses off the bottom of the Spitalgasse. The highly efficient **tourist office** is on Marktplatz (Mon–Fri 9am–12pm & 1–5/6pm, Sat 10am–1/3pm; ☎09861/4 04 92, ⊛www.rothenburg.de). Local specialities include the *Schneeball* (snowball), a rich pastry dusted with sugar, best washed down with a mug of *Mauerblümchentee* (wallflower tea).

Nuremberg (Nürnberg)

Founded in the eleventh century, **NUREMBERG** (Nürnberg) – halfway between Frankfurt and Munich – was first an economic and political centre, then the national art capital (its most famous inhabitant was Albrecht Dürer), and finally a focal point for the Nazis' most infamous rallies – followed by the war-crimes trials. Today, these images seem a world away from the friendly, bustling town that greets visitors. The town has a relaxed air that makes whiling away a day or two amongst its half-timbered houses, fine museums and beer halls an altogether enjoyable experience.

On January 2, 1945, a storm of bombs reduced ninety percent of Nuremberg's centre to ash and rubble, but you'd never guess it from the meticulous postwar rebuilding. The reconstructed medieval core is surrounded by its ancient city walls and neatly spliced by the River Pegnitz. To walk from one end to the other takes about twenty minutes, but much of the centre, especially the area around the castle – known as the **Burgviertel** – is on a steep hill. One of the highest points of the city is occupied by the **Kaiserburg** (daily 9/10am–4/6pm; €5), whose Sinwellturm, built directly on the rock, can be ascended for the best of all the views. Another survivor of this period is the **Kaiserkapelle**, whose upper level was reserved for the use of the emperor. The area around the **Tiergärtner Tor** next to the Kaiserburg is one

NUREMBERG

Kaiserburg

0   100 m

Stadtmuseum
Fembohaus
Albrecht-
Dürer
Haus   AGNESG.   Pellerhaus

N

St. Sebaldus
Altes Rathaus

Weinstadel
Schöner   *i*
Brunnen   HAUPT-   HANS
           MARKT   SACHS G.
                    Frauenkirche

River Pegnitz

Heilig-
Geist-
Spital

Nassauer
Haus   St. Lorenz

Lorenzkirche   LORENZ

Mauthalle
                St.
                Martha
Germanisches
National-
museum
KOLPINGGASSE   Handwerkerhof

Opernhaus   *i*   Hauptbahnhof
         FRAUENTORGRABEN

Opernhaus   Hauptbahnhof

of the most attractive parts of the old centre, a meeting point for summertime street vendors, artists and musicians. Virtually next door, the **Dürer Haus** (Tues–Sun 10am–5pm, Thurs till 8pm; €4) is where the painter, engraver, scientist, writer, traveller and politician lived from 1509 to 1528, and is one of the very few original houses still standing. There are only copies of his paintings, plus works by other artists. The **Hauptmarkt**, commercial heart of the city and the main venue for weekly markets (and the famous Christmas market), has, on its east side, the **Frauenkirche**, on whose facade a clockwork mechanism, known as the *Männleinlaufen*, tinkles away at noon. South of the Hauptmarkt the Museumsbrücke crosses the river, giving a good view of the Fleischbrücke to the right and the Heilig-Geist-Spital – one of the largest hospitals built in the Middle Ages – on the left. Passing the oldest house in the city, the thirteenth-century Nassauer Haus, you shortly come to the **Lorenzkirche**; the graceful late fifteenth-century tabernacle, some 20m high, was carved by Adam Kraft, who depicted himself as a pensive figure crouching at the base. The **Germanisches Nationalmuseum** (Tues–Sun 10am–6pm, Wed till 9pm; €5) – perhaps the most important collection of the country's arts and crafts – occupies a fourteenth-century monastery on Kornmarkt. On the ground floor the displays follow a roughly chronological layout, beginning with Bronze Age items and moving onto medieval sculptures and carvings. German painting at its Renaissance peak dominates the first floor, while subsequent rooms focus on the Renaissance. The city's leading role in the fast-developing science of geography is exemplified by the first globe of the earth, made by Martin Behaim in 1491 – just before Columbus "discovered" America.

In many minds, Nuremberg conjures up thoughts of **Nazi** rallies and war-crime trials; indeed, the "**Nuremberg Laws**" of 1935, which deprived Jews of their citizenship and forbade relations between Jews and Gentiles, were the device by which the Nazis justified their extermination of six million Jews, 10,000 of whom came from Nuremberg. However, as the city council is eager to point out, the Nazis' choice of Nuremberg had less to do with local support of Nazi ideology, and more to do with what medieval Nuremberg represented in German history. The rallies were held on the **Zeppelin and March fields** in the suburb of Luitpoldhain (tram #9 from the centre). An exhibition documenting the history of the rally grounds and the ruthless misuse of power under National Socialism is now housed in Albert Speer's Congress Hall. **Fascination and Terror** (Mon–Fri 9am–8pm, Sat & Sun 10am–6pm; €5; tram #4 to Dutzendteich) is a multimedia information centre occupying the northernmost wing of this gargantuan but unfinished structure.

Practicalities

The main **tourist office** (Mon–Sat 9am–7pm; ☎0911/233 61 32, ⊛ www.nuernberg.de) is at Königstr. 93, in front of the **train station**, at the entrance to the

⑪

Altstadt. There's a smaller office at Hauptmarkt 18, within the Altstadt (Mon–Sat 9am–6pm; May–Sept also Sun 10am–4pm; ☎0911/233 61 35). The **Nürnberg Card** (€18/two days) covers public transport plus entrance to museums. There's **Internet** access at Flat-S, on the top floor of the train station. The **HI hostel** has a wonderful location within the Kaiserburg, overlooking the Altstadt (☎0911/230 93 60, ☻www.djh.de; €17.70). The popular *Lettem Sleep* hostel at Frauentormauer 42 (☎0911/9 92 81 28, ☻seeyou@backpackers.de; €14) offers free Internet access, and there's another *Jugendhotel* north of the city at Rathsbergstr. 300 (☎0911/5 21 60 92; €21); despite the name, no age restrictions apply. Try to avoid arriving on a Sunday, since many **pensions** are closed for the day. The cheapest central options include *Vater Jahn*, Jahnstr. 13 (☎0911/44 45 07; ❸), and, closer to the castle at Schildgasse 14–16, *Burghotel Stammhaus* (☎0911/20 30 40, ☻www.burghotel-stamm .de; ❻), which has chintzy rooms with large balconies.

Nuremberg is the liveliest Bavarian city after Munich, with a wealth of *Studentenkneipen* and café-bars catering for the students. The cheapest meals in town are to be found in the university **Mensa**, in the northeastern corner of the Altstadt. There are plenty of *Imbiss*-type **snack-joints** in the pedestrian zone around St Lorenz. Good places to eat include *Bratwurst-Häusle*, Rathausplatz 1, the most celebrated of the city's sausage **restaurants**, and the excellent and reasonable *Nassauer Keller*, Karolinerstr. 2, an atmospheric thirteenth-century cellar. At Bergstr. 19 is *Schwarzer Bauer*, the **pub** of the Altstadthof's celebrated house brewery; attached is a small live music venue. Another place that brews its own beer is the *Barfüsser*, which occupies the cavernous cellars of the Mauthalle at Hallplatz 2. Fashionable **café-bars** include *Ruhestörung*, Tetzelgasse 21, and *Zeero* on Prinzregentenufer, while tiny *Meisengeige*, Am Laufer Schlagturm 3, also has a small cinema showing an offbeat selection of films. The trendiest **club** is *Mach 1*, Kaiserstr. 1–9, with four different bars and good lighting (closed Mon & Tues). To find out what else is going on, get *Monatsmagazin* or the trendier *Dopplepunkt* from the tourist office, or *Plärrer* magazine from any kiosk.

Bamberg

The citizens of **BAMBERG**, 60km north of Nuremberg, knock back more **beer** per head than anywhere else in Germany: ten breweries produce thirty different kinds of ale, most notably the distinctive smoky Rauchbier. Today is a simply lovely little town, where most European styles from the Romanesque onwards have left a mark. Heart of the lower town is the **Maximiliansplatz**, dominated by the Neues Rathaus. A daily market is held here and on the adjoining Grüner Markt, which stands in the shadow of the huge Jesuit church of St Martin. On an islet anchoring the Obere Brücke to the Untere Brücke is the picturesque **Altes Rathaus**. Except for the half-timbered section overhanging the rapids, the original Gothic building was transformed into the Rococo style. The famous **Klein-Venedig** (Little Venice) of medieval fishermen's houses is best seen from the Untere Brücke. Uphill, the spacious, sloping **Domplatz** is lined with a superb variety of buildings. The **Kaiserdom** was consecrated in 1012, but the present structure of golden sandstone is the result of a slow rebuilding that continued throughout the thirteenth century. Its most famous feature inside is the enigmatic Bamberg Rider, one of the first equestrian statues to be made since Classical antiquity. Across the square is the huge Baroque **Neue Residenz** (tours only, daily: 9/10am–4/6pm; €3), filled with medieval and Baroque paintings by German masters. From the rose garden behind the Neue Residenz is a view of Michaelsburg, crowned by a huge **Abtei**. Much of the Romanesque shell of the church remains, but the interior is an awesome hotchpotch: lavish Rococo furnishings, tombs of Bamberg bishops and a beautiful ceiling painted with exotic birds and over 600 types of medicinal herbs. The cellars house the **Fränkisches Brauereimuseum** (April–Oct Wed–Sun 1–5pm; €2). Even if you're not interested in the church (or the beer), it's worth heading up here for the excellent views.

Bamberg's **train station** is fifteen minutes' walk northeast of the centre. The **tourist office** (Mon–Fri 9am–6pm, Sat 9.30am–2pm; May–Dec also Sun 9.30am–2pm; ☎0951/297 6200, ⓦwww.bamberg.info) is at Geyerswörthstr. 3, near the Altes Rathaus. Among several inexpensive **hotels** are *Bamberger Weissbierhaus*, Obere Königstr 38 (☎0951/2 55 03; ❸). The **HI hostel** is 2km south of the centre at Oberer Leinritt 70 (☎0951/5 60 02, ⓦwww.djh.de; €16.80), reached by bus #1 from the train station to ZOB Promenade, then bus #18 to Regnitzufer. **Restaurants** worth trying include *Brudermühle*, Schranne 1, which has an unbeatable position by the river overlooking the Altes Rathaus; *Schlenkerla*, Dominikanerstr. 6, famous for its Rauchbier; and *Kaiserdom-Stuben*, Urbanstr. 18, good for vegetarian dishes. One of the best **cafés** is the summer *Rosengarten* in the Neue Residenz. Good places to try the local **beers** include the beer cellar-cum-gardens *Spezial*, Obere Stephansberg 47, and *Greiffenklau*, Laurenziplatz 20.

Regensburg

The undisturbed medieval ensemble of central **REGENSBURG**, stunningly located on the banks of the Danube midway between Nuremberg and Munich, can easily be visited as a day-trip. The main draw here is getting lost in the web of cobbled medieval lanes, or nursing a drink in one of the wide, sunny squares. A good place to start is the twelfth-century **Steinerne Brücke**, which was the only safe crossing along the entire length of the Danube at the time it was built. To the left, the **Historische Wurstküche** (daily 8am–7pm) originally functioned as the bridge workers' kitchen. It's been run by the same family for generations and serves little else but delicious Regensburg sausages. The Gothic **Dom**, begun around 1250, replaced a Romanesque church of which only the Eselsturm remains above ground. Highlights include the fourteenth-century stained-glass windows. Concerts and services are a musical treat here, as the Domspatzen is one of the finest choirs in the country. A short way south is Neupfarrplatz, below which lies a grid of **archeological excavations**, including a Roman camp and the medieval Jewish quarter (entrance with tour only; Thurs, Fri & Sat 2pm; €2.50). Today's Neupfarrkirche occupies the site of the old synagogue, wrecked during the 1519 expulsion. **Schloss Thurn and Taxis** (tours April–Oct Mon–Fri 11am, 2pm, 3pm & 4pm, Sat & Sun also 10am; Nov–March Sat & Sun 10am, 11am, 2pm & 3pm; €8), home of the Prince of Thurn und Taxis, is in the city's southern quarter, in the converted monastic buildings of the abbey of St Emmeram. The former cloisters are fine Gothic, while the nineteenth-century state rooms contain some interesting Brussels tapestries recording the family's illustrious history.

Maximilianstrasse leads straight from the **train station** to the centre. The **tourist office** is in the Altes Rathaus (Mon–Fri 9.15am–6pm, Sat 9am–5pm, Sun 9.30am–4pm; ☎0941/507 44 10, ⓦwww.regensburg.de). The **HI hostel**, Wöhrdstr. 60 (☎0941/5 74 02, ⓦwww.djh.de; €20.20), is about five minutes' walk from the centre, on an island in the Danube. There's only one cheapish **hotel** in the centre, *Am Peterstor*, Fröhliche-Türken-Str. 12 (☎0941/5 45 45; ❸), but the best choice is on the other side of the Steinerne Brücke, on one of the Danube islands, *Spitalgarten*, St Katharinen-Platz 1 (☎0941/8 47 74, ⓦwww.spitalgarten.de; ❸) – conveniently, it also has the best beer garden in town. *Café Prock*, on Kohlenmarkt, serves good breakfasts, light lunches and cakes. As well as the famous *Historische Wurstküche* by the river, there are countless stalls selling fresh Regensburg **sausages** – especially good is *Wurstbraterei* on Neupfarrplatz. For more of a bar-type atmosphere, usually with good music, try *Rote Löwe*, Rote Löwengasse 10, or *Hemingways*, on the corner of Augustinergasse and Obere Bachgasse. *Goldene Ente*, Badstr. 32, is a popular student hangout. Netzblick, Am Römling 9, offers **Internet** access.

Stuttgart

STUTTGART, two hours by train west of Nuremberg, is home to such German success stories as Bosch, Porsche and Daimler-Benz. Founded around 950 as a stud farm (Stutengarten), it became a town only in the fourteenth century. Though certainly not the comeliest of cities, it has a range of superb museums, and a sophisticated cultural scene and nightlife. From the train station, Königstrasse passes the dull modern Dom and enters Schlossplatz, on the south of which is the **Altes Schloss**, home to the **Württembergisches Landesmuseum** (Wed–Sun 10am–5pm, Tues closes 1pm; €2.60). Highlight of this richly varied museum is the Kunstkammer of the House of Württemberg, displayed in one of the corner towers: the first floor has small bronze sculptures of mainly Italian origin, while the second is laid out in the manner of a Renaissance curio cabinet. North of Schlossplatz is the **Staatsgalerie** (Tues–Sun 10am–6pm, Thurs till 9pm; first Sat in month till midnight; €4.50), whose most startling work is the violently expressive *Herrenberg Altar* by Jörg Ratgeb. On the other side of Schlossplatz, the Altes Schloss overlooks **Schillerplatz**, Stuttgart's sole example of an old-world square. Presiding in the middle is a pensive statue of the German poet and playwright Friedrich Schiller, by the Danish sculptor Bertel Thorwaldsen, erected the year after his death. On the western side of Schillerplatz a cutting-edge art museum is being built – check with the tourist office for details.

The **Mercedes-Benz Museum** (Tues–Sun 9am–5pm; free) is an absolute must. Even getting here is an experience – you take S-Bahn #1 to Gottlieb-Daimler-Stadion, from where you're whisked in a sealed minibus to the museum doors. The earliest vehicle on display is the Daimler Reitwagen of 1885, the first ever motorbike, which was capable of 12kph. Daimler's first Mercedes dates from 1902. Other exhibits include fire engines, motorboats, aeroplanes and buses, but it's the luxury cars and the machines specially designed for world record attempts that steal the show. The **Porsche Museum**, Porschestrasse 42 (daily 9am–4/5pm; free), is beside Neuwirtshaus station on S-Bahn line #6. Ferdinand Porsche made his name when Hitler commissioned him to create the original Volkswagen, precursor of the VW Beetle. The vehicles on show illustrate all the company's cars, from the 356 Roadster of 1948 to current models.

Practicalities

Stuttgart **train station** is in the centre of town; immediately behind it is the **bus station**. S-Bahn #2 and #3 link to the **airport** (every 20min). There's a **tourist office** in front of the train station at Königstr. 1a (Mon–Fri 9am–8pm, Sat 9am–6pm, Sun 11am/1pm–6pm; ☎0711/2 22 80, ⊛www.stuttgart-tourist.de). The integrated **public transport** network comprises buses, trams, the U-Bahn, and mainline and S-Bahn trains; a 24-hour ticket costs €4.80. The **StuttCard Plus** (€14/three days) covers public transport, admission to most museums and numerous freebies, including drinks and food; the basic StuttCard (€8.50/three days) gives the same benefits without public transport. The **HI hostel** is a short ride on bus #42 from the train station, at Haussmannstr. 27 (☎0711/24 15 83, ⊛www.djh.de; €16.90); there's also the non-HI *Jugendgästehaus Stuttgart*, Richard-Wagner-Str. 2–4a (☎0711/24 11 32, ⊛www.hostel-stuttgart.de; €15.30). The cheapest **hotel** deals are at the central but scruffy *Museum-Stube*, Hospitalstr. 9 (☎0711/29 68 10; ❹).

Stuttgart is surrounded by vineyards, and the numerous **Weinstuben** are excellent places to try good quality, traditional Swabian dishes and local wines at low cost. *Zur Kiste*, Kanalstr. 2, is the best known of these, but the widest choice of wines is at *Weinhaus Stetter*, Rosenstr. 32. For a **beer hall** try *Ketterer*, Marienstr. 3b. There are **nightlife** details in the tourist office's excellent *Lift Stuttgart*, or buy a copy of *Prinz Stuttgart* (€1) from newsagents. *Schlesinger International*, Schloss Str. 28, is a popular hangout; *Femme*, Theodor-Heuss Str. 15, is a cool bar catering to the city's young and beautiful. Jazz features at *Laboratorium*, Wagenburgstr. 147, while *Lush*, Augustinerstr. 70, has Seventies-inspired decor and funky disco nights. **Internet** access is at California Sidewalk Café, Schellingstr. 7.

Augsburg

Luther's reforms found their earliest support in **AUGSBURG**, on the Stuttgart–Munich train line, and in 1514 the city built the world's first housing estate for the poor, the Fuggerei – an institution still in use today. Heart of the city is the cobbled **Rathausplatz**, which turns into a massive open-air café during the summer and into a glittering market at Christmas. Inside the **Rathaus**, the gold-leaf pillars and marble floor of the Goldener Saal (daily 10am–6pm; €2) recall the period when the Fugger banking dynasty made Augsburg one of Europe's financial centres. To the south, **Maximilianstrasse** is lined by merchants' palaces and punctuated by fountains. At the other end of the town's axis, the **Dom** stands in the grounds of the former Episcopal palace; its Romanesque bronze doors are on view in the **Diocesan Museum St Afra** (Tues–Sat 10am–5pm, Sun 2–5pm, first Fri of the month till 9pm; €2.50) in the cloisters. For a charge of one "Our Father", one "Hail Mary" and one Creed daily, plus €90 per annum, good Catholic paupers can retire to the **Fuggerei** at the age of 55. With an entrance in Jacoberstrasse, it's a town within a town, and compared with modern housing estates is a real idyll, the cloister-like atmosphere disturbed only by the odd ringing doorbell. No. 13 (March–Dec daily 10am–6pm; €1) is one of only two houses from the original foundation; today it's full of furnishings from the sixteenth to the eighteenth century. The **tourist office** (Mon–Fri 9am–6pm; ☎0821/50 20 70, ⊛www.augsburg-tourismus.de) is at Bahnhofstr. 7, a couple of minutes' from the **train station**, with a branch on Rathausplatz (Mon–Sat 9/10am–5/5.30pm; May–Oct also Sun 10am–4pm). Cheapest **pension** is *Jakoberhof*, Jakoberstr. 41 (☎0821/51 00 30, ⊛www.jakoberhof.de; ❸), a friendly place close to the Fuggerei. The central **HI hostel** is at Beim Pfaffenkeller 3 (☎0821/3 39 09, ⊛www.djh.de; €19.80). The cheapest places for **snacks** are the market and meat halls off Annastrasse. For **drinking**, *Kreslesmühle* above the *Helsinki Bar* at Barfüsserstr. 4, is a popular café/bar and cabaret venue.

Tübingen

TÜBINGEN is sited above the willow-lined banks of the Neckar 55km upstream (southwest) from Stuttgart. Over half the population of 70,000 is connected with the university. The old town is a visual treat, a mixture of brightly painted half-timbered and gabled houses grouped into twisting and plunging alleys. **Holzmarkt** is dominated by the **Stiftskirche St Georg** (daily 9am–4/5pm), a gaunt, late-Gothic church with a fine interior. In the chancel (Easter–Oct Fri–Sun 11.30am–5pm; €1) an outstanding series of stained-glass windows casts reflections on the thirteen tombs of the House of Württemberg. Overlooking the banks of the Neckar on Bursagasse is the **Hölderlinturm** (Tues–Fri 10am–noon & 3–5pm, Sat & Sun 2–5pm; €1.50). Originally part of the medieval fortifications, it's named after the poet Friedrich Hölderlin, who lived here in the care of a carpenter's family, hopelessly but harmlessly insane, from 1807 until his death 36 years later. There's a collection of memorabilia – Hölderlin is now regarded as one of the greatest of all German poets. The **Markt**, heart of old Tübingen (markets Mon, Wed & Fri), is a short walk uphill from here. It preserves many of its Renaissance mansions, along with a fountain dedicated to Neptune. Burgsteige, one of the oldest and handsomest streets in town, climbs steeply from one corner to **Schloss Hohentübingen**, within which is the **Schausammlungen der Universität** (Wed–Sun 10am–5/6pm, €3), one of the largest university museums in the world, with archeology, history and ethnology displays. The northwestern part of town, immediately below the Schloss, has some spectacular half-timbered buildings, such as the old municipal **Kornhaus** and **Fruchtschranne**, formerly the storehouse for the yields of the ducal orchards, on Bachgasse.

The adjacent **train and bus stations** are five minutes' walk from the old town. At the edge of Eberhardsbrücke is the **tourist office** (Mon–Fri 9am–7pm, Sat 9am–5pm; May–Oct also Sun 2–5pm; ☎07071/9 13 60, ⊛www.tuebingen-info.de).

Hotels are expensive; the pleasant *Am Schloss*, Burgsteige 18 (℡07071/9 29 40; ❺),
and *Hospiz Tübigen*, a few doors down (℡07071/92 40; ❺), both also offer a couple
of simple, bathless rooms (❸). The **HI hostel** is on the banks of the Neckar, a short
walk from the station at Gartenstr. 22/2 (℡07071/2 30 02, ✉www.djh.de; €19). To
reach the **campsite** (℡07071/4 31 45; closed Nov-Feb), also with a riverside setting
at Rappenberghalde, turn left on leaving the train station and cross at Alleenbrücke.
The best central **restaurant** is *Forelle*, a wine bar at Kronenstr. 8. *Am Schloss* hotel
also has an excellent restaurant specializing in regional *Maultaschen*, large meat-filled
ravioli. *Tangente Jour* on Holzplatz is a popular café serving huge breakfasts, and
Marktschenke, Markt 11, is a lively student bar.

The Black Forest region

Stretching 170km north to south, and up to 60km east to west, the **Black Forest** is
the largest German forest and the most beautiful. As late as the 1920s, much of this
area was an eerie wilderness, a refuge for boars and bandits. Nowadays most of the
villages have been opened up as spa and health resorts, brimming with shops selling
tacky souvenirs, while the old trails have become gravel paths smoothed down for
easier walking. Yet by no means all the modernizations are drawbacks. Railway fans,
for example, will find several of the most spectacular lines in Europe here. It should
be noted, though, that the trains tend to stick to the valleys and that bus services are
much reduced outside the tourist season. Most of the Black Forest is associated with
the Margravate of Baden, whose old capital, **Baden-Baden**, is at the northern fringe
of the forest, in a fertile orchard and vine-growing area. **Freiburg im Breisgau**,
one of the most enticing cities in the country, is surrounded by the forest.

Baden-Baden

The therapeutic value of the town's hot springs, first discovered by the Romans, is
still the main draw in **BADEN-BADEN** – hardly the recipe for a party atmosphere. Nevertheless, it's a pretty town for an afternoon's stroll. South of the original
Kurhaus runs Baden-Baden's most famous thoroughfare, the Lichtentaler Allee,
landscaped with exotic trees and shrubs and flanked by the Parisian-style theatre and
the **Kunsthalle**, which often hosts major exhibitions of twentieth-century art.
North of the Kurhaus is the **Trinkhalle**, whose arcades shelter frescoes illustrating
local legends. Halfway up the Florintinerberg is the **Marktplatz** and the
Stiftskirche, a Gothic hall church containing one of the masterpieces of European
sculpture, an enormous sandstone *Crucifixion* by Nicolaus Gerhaert von Leyden.
Above the Römerbad, just east on Römerplatz, is the **Friedrichsbad** (Mon–Sat
9am–10pm, Sun noon–8pm), begun in 1869 and grand as a Renaissance palace.
Speciality of the house is a three-hour "Roman-Irish Bath", which will set you back
€21 (€29 for soap-brush massage) – or you could opt to pay five cents for a glass of
thermal water. The **train station** – on the fast Karlsruhe–Freiburg line – is 4km
northwest in the suburb of Oos; take bus #201, #205 or #216 into the centre. The
enthusiastic **tourist office** is in the Trinkhalle on Kaiserallee (Mon–Sat 10am–5pm,
Sun 2–5pm; ℡07221/27 52 00, ✉www.baden-baden.de), with details of a few private rooms (❷). An uninspiring **HI hostel** is between the train station and the centre at Hardbergstr. 34 (℡07221/5 22 23, ✉www.djh.de; €17.30); it's signposted from
the Grosse-Dollen-Strasse bus stop. *Münchener Löwenbräu*, Gernsbacher Str. 9, is a
good **place to eat**, with a beer garden. *Leo's*, Luisenstr. 10, is a trendy café-bar, while
for reasonably priced German food, there's *Rathaustglöckel*, Steinstr. 7.

Freiburg im Breisgau

FREIBURG IM BREISGAU – midway between Strasbourg (France) and Basel
(Switzerland) – basks in a laid-back atmosphere that seems completely un-German.
A university town since 1457, its youthful presence is maintained all year round
with the help of a varied programme of festivals. It is a thoroughly enjoyable place

to visit, and makes the perfect base for exploring the surrounding Black Forest. Highlight is the dark red sandstone **Münster**, towering above the main square (which hosts a daily market). Begun in about 1200, the church has a masterly Gothic nave, resplendent with flying buttresses, gargoyles and statues – the magnificent sculptures of the west porch are the most important German works of their time. From the tower (March–Nov Mon–Sat 9.30am–5pm, Sun 1–5pm; €1.50) there's a fine panorama of the city and the surrounding forest-blanketed hills. A local peculiarity is the system of rivulets known as the **Bächle**, which run in deep gulleys all over the city. Formerly used for watering animals and as a fire-fighting provision, they have their purpose even today, helping to keep the city cool. Following the main channel of the Bächle southwards, you come to the **Schwaben Tor**, one of two surviving towers of the medieval fortifications. On Oberlinden, just in front, is *Zum Roten Bären*, generally considered Germany's oldest inn. South of here, on Marienstrasse, the **Museum of Modern Art** (same times; €2) has a good cross-section of twentieth-century German art, including notable sculptures by Ernst Barlach and Herman Scherer. From here, follow Fischerau, the old fishermen's street, and you come to the other thirteenth-century tower, the **Martinstor**, in the middle of Freiburg's central axis, Kaiser-Josef-Strasse.

The **train station**, with the **bus station** on its southern side, is about ten minutes' walk west from the city centre. Following Eisenbahnstrasse, you come to the **tourist office** at Rotteckring 14 (Mon–Fri 9.30am–6/8pm, Sat 9.30am–2/5pm, Sun 10am–noon; ☎0761/3 88 18 80, ⊛www.freiburg.de). For €2.55, they'll find you a room; after closing time, an electronic board (with phone) lists vacancies. The cheapest central **hotel** is *Schemmer*, Eschholzstr. 63 (☎0761/20 74 90, ✉angelavr@t-online.de; ❸). The 443-bed **HI hostel** is at Karthäuserstr. 151 (☎0761/6 76 56, ⊛www.djh.de; €18.60; tram #1 to Hasemannstr.), at the eastern end of the city. Nearby is the *Hirzberg* **campsite** (☎0761/3 50 54); *Mösle-Park* (☎0761/72 39 38; closed Nov–March) is on the opposite riverbank. A pricey but excellent **restaurant** is *Oberkirchs Weinstuben*, Münsterplatz 22, serving Baden specialities, while *Kleiner Meyerhof*, Rathausgasse 27, offers hearty South German cooking. One of the hippest spots is *Uni-café*, Niemensstr. 7, which serves a wide selection of coffees and snacks and is always packed. Also worth trying is the *Art Café* just opposite, which offers a range of *Flammenkuchen*, a type of pizza. Another student favourite is the seafood chain *Nordsee*, for cheap, filling meals – there are outlets on Bertholdstr., Kaiser-Joseph-Str. and Universitätsstr. Freiburg now ranks as one of the leading German cities for **jazz**, thanks to the *Jazzhaus* at Schnewlinstr. 1, which has gigs nightly.

Konstanz and the Bodensee

In the far south, hard up against the Swiss border, **KONSTANZ** lies at the tip of a tongue of land sticking out into the **Bodensee** (Lake Constance). The town itself is split by the water: the **Altstadt** is an enclave on the southern shore. It's a cosy little university town, with a convivial atmosphere in summer, when street cafés invite long pauses and the water is a bustle of sails. The most prominent church is the **Münster**, set on the highest point of the Altstadt, but the regional highlight is the nearby **Insel Mainau** (daily: April–Oct 7am–8pm; Nov–March 9am–6pm; bus #4 from the train station; €5.50), an island occupied by a royal park featuring magnificent floral displays, formal gardens, greenhouses, forests and a handful of well-placed restaurants. Konstanz **tourist office** is beside the **train station** at Bahnhofplatz 13 (Mon–Fri 9.30am–6pm; April–Oct also Sat 9am–4pm & Sun 10am–1pm; ☎07531/13 30 30, ⊛www.konstanz.de); they can book accommodation in private rooms (❷). The **HI hostel** is at Zur Allmannshöhe 18 (☎07531/3 22 60, ⊛www.djh.de; ❷; bus #4 from the train station to Jugendherberge). **Hotel** *Gretel* is at Zollenstr. 6–8 (☎07531/45 58 25; ❸). You can get information on **cruises** and **ferries** from the Bodensee-Schiffsbetriebe at Hafenstr. 6 (☎07531/28 13 98,

@www.bsb-online.com). Ferries depart regularly around the lake, as well as on a scenic trip to the impressive Rhine falls in Switzerland (€17.90), covered in Chapter 29.

Munich (München)

Founded in 1158, **MUNICH** (München) has been the capital of Bavaria since 1503, and as far as the locals are concerned it may as well be the centre of the universe. The city is impossibly energetic, bursting with a good-humoured self-importance that is difficult to dislike. After Berlin, Munich is Germany's most popular city – with its compact and attractive old centre, it is certainly much easier to digest, and it has the added bonus of a great setting, with the mountains and Alpine lakes just an hour's drive away. The best time of year to come here is from June to early October, when the beer gardens, street cafés and bars are in full swing – not least for the world-famous **Oktoberfest** beer festival.

Arrival, information and accommodation

Munich's **airport**, Franz Josef Strauss Flughafen, is connected to the **Hauptbahnhof** by S-Bahn #1 or #8. The **bus station** is a stone's throw from the train station. There are **tourist offices** at Bahnhofplatz 2 (Mon–Sat 9am–8pm, Sun 10am–6pm; ☎089/2339 6500; @www.muenchen-tourist.de) and in the Rathaus on Marienplatz (Mon–Fri 10am–8pm, Sat 10am–4pm), either of which can book rooms. The *Insel* booth on Hauptwache also provides transport information and sells tickets. Day tickets for all **public transport** in the central city area cost €4.50 (€9 for whole system). The **Munich Welcome Card** (€6.50/15.50 for one/three days) covers all public transport and gives big discounts on attractions. Individual

tickets can be bought from the automatic machines in all U–Bahn stations, at some bus and tram stops, and inside trams, but if you're making several journeys it's more economical to invest in a **strip card** (€9/ten), and stamp two strips for every zone crossed – the zones are shown on maps at stations and tram and bus stops. For journeys of up to two S- or U–Bahn stops, or up to four bus or tram stops, only one strip needs to be cancelled. If you travel without a valid ticket, you're liable for an on-the-spot fine of €40. Cheap **accommodation** can be hard to find, especially during the high season in the summer. If you're going to be in town during the Oktoberfest, it's essential to book well in advance; be warned that prices tend to rise during this period. Many pensions offer rooms with three to six beds, a good alternative to the hostels.

Hostels

4you München Hirtenstr. 18 ☎089/5 52 16 60, ✆www.the4you.de. Friendly outfit very close to the main station, with some singles as well as standard dorms. €16.50.

Burg Schwaneck Burgweg 4–6 ☎089/7 44 86 67 0, ✆www.burgschwaneck.de. HI hostel some way from the centre in a beautiful castle on the river, with small, bare rooms. S-Bahn #7 to Pullach, then follow signs to the Jugendherberge. €15.50.

DJH Jugendgästehaus Miesingstr. 4 ☎089/7 23 65 60, ✆www.djh.de. Small, upmarket HI hostel in attractive grounds. U-Bahn to Harras, then tram #16 to Boschetsriederstr. €20.80.

DJH München Wendl-Dietrich-Str. 20 ☎089/13 11 56, ✆www.djh.de. The largest, most central and most basic HI hostel, with 535 beds. U-Bahn to Rotkreuzplatz. €20.80.

Haus International Elisabethstr. 87 ☎089/12 00 60. Centrally located in Schwabing, 186 rooms ranging from five beds to singles. Restaurant and disco, no age limit. U-Bahn to Hohenzollernplatz, then bus #33 or tram #12 to Barbarastrasse. €23.

Hotels and pensions

Acanthus An der Hauptfeuerwache 4 ☎089/2 60 73 64, ✆www.acanthushotel.de. Comfortable hotel near the Sendlinger Tor; friendly staff serve up a huge breakfast buffet. A "family room" with four beds available. ⑥

Eder Zweigstr. 8 ☎089/55 46 60. Cosy hotel in a quiet road between the train station and Marienplatz, offering nicely appointed rooms. ⑥

Frank Schellingstr. 24 ☎089/28 14 51, ✆www.pension-frank.de. A good choice in the student quarter for both price and atmosphere, with homely rooms in a creaky old building. ④

Jedermann Bayerstr. 95 ☎089/54 32 40, ✆www.hotel-jedermann.de. Classy, family-run hotel located well away from any noise and seediness, but just 5min walk from the train station. ④

Am Kaiserplatz Kaiserplatz 12 ☎089/34 91 90. Very friendly place in a good location with big rooms, each done in a different style – from red satin to Bavarian rustic. Six-bed rooms can be arranged. ③

Steinberg Ohmstr. 9 ☎089/33 10 11, ✉pension .steinberg@t-online.de. Friendly and in a good location near Giselastr. U-Bahn station. Some rooms have bathtubs. ④

The City

The central **Marienplatz** is the bustling heart of Munich and always thronged with crowds being entertained by street musicians and artists. At 11am and noon, the square fills with tourists as the tuneless carillon in the Rathaus tower jingles into action. The **Rathaus** itself is a late nineteenth-century neo-Gothic monstrosity whose only redeeming features are the café in its cool and breezy courtyard and the view from the **tower** (by elevator; €2). To the right is the plain Gothic tower of the Altes Rathaus, rebuilt in the fifteenth-century style after being destroyed in the war. It now houses a vast toy collection in the **Spielzeugmuseum** (daily 10am–5pm; €3). Close by, the Peterskirche looks out across the busy **Viktualienmarkt**, a huge open-air food market selling everything from Wiesswurst and beer to fruit and veg. To the west of the Viktualienmarkt is the **Münchener Stadtmuseum** (Tues–Sun 10am–6pm; €2.50; ✆www.stadtmuseum-online.de), the excellent local history museum, which also incorporates a Fashion Museum, Puppet Museum and Film Museum. The latter shows art house films and has a popular café on its ground floor. Southwest of here, at Sendlinger Str. 62, stands the small **Asamkirche**, one of the most splendid Rococo churches in Bavaria.

The pedestrian Kaufingerstrasse, west from Marienplatz, is overlooked by the red-brick Gothic **Dom**, whose twin onion-domed **towers** (April–Oct Mon–Sat 10am–5pm; €3) form the focus of the city's skyline. A little further up Kaufingerstrasse, the Renaissance facade of **St Michael** stands unassumingly in line with the street's other buildings. In the crypt (Mon–Fri 9.30–4.30pm, Sat 9.30am–2.30pm; €2) you'll find the coffins of the Wittelsbach dynasty – a candle is always burning at the foot of mad castle-builder Ludwig II's. North of Marienplatz is the posh end of the city centre. From fashionable **Maximilianstrasse**, the little Kosttor road leads straight to the **Hofbräuhaus**, Munich's largest and most famous drinking hall. Nearby, with its Baroque facade standing proud on the Odeonsplatz, is one of the city's most regal churches, the **Theatinerkirche**, whose golden-yellow towers and green copper dome add a splash of colour to the roofscape.

The palace of the Wittelsbachs, the **Residenz** (daily 9am–4/6pm; €4), stands across the square from the Theatinerkirche. One of Europe's finest Renaissance buildings, it was so badly damaged in the last war that it had to be almost totally rebuilt. To see the whole thing you have to go on two consecutive visits, as parts of the immense complex are shut in the morning and others in the afternoon. On the morning tour you see the Antiquarium, the oldest part of the palace; in the afternoon, the two very contrasting chapels and the Baroque Golden Hall. A separate ticket is necessary to see the fabulous treasures of the **Schatzkammer** (same hours; €4, €7 combined ticket); star piece is the dazzling stone-encrusted statuette of St George, made around 1590.

Munich's most overwhelming museum – the **Deutsches Museum** (daily 9am–5pm; €7.50; ⊛www.deutsches-museum.de) – occupies the mid-stream island of Isarinsel. Covering every conceivable aspect of technical endeavour, from the first flint tools to the research labs of modern industry, this is the most compendious collection of its type in Germany. Another gargantuan collection lies further north – the **Bayerisches Nationalmuseum**, Prinzregentenstr. 3 (Tues–Sun 10am–5pm, Thurs till 8pm; €3, free Sun; ⊛www.bayerisches-nationalmuseum.de), houses a rambling collection of decorative arts. But it is the Pinakothek museums, Barerstr. 27, that are the city's main draw. The **Alte Pinakothek** (Tues–Sun 10am–5pm, Thurs till 10pm; €5, free Sun; ⊛www.alte-pinakothek.de) is one of the largest galleries in Europe, housing the world's finest assembly of German art. The **Neue Pinakothek** (same hours and prices; ⊛www.neue-pinakotheck.de) holds a fine collection of nineteenth-century art; while the **Pinakothek der Moderne** (same hours; €9; ⊛www.pinakothek-der-moderne.de) is worth visiting for its stunning architecture alone. The stark glass and concrete structure presents an impressive collection, from Dali and Picasso to German greats such as Beckman and Polke, and features exhibitions about design, architecture and graphics.

Around Munich: Nymphenburg and Dachau

Schloss Nymphenburg (daily 9am–4/6pm; €3.50, €7.50 combined ticket with pavilions and Marstall), the summer residence of the Wittelsbachs, is reached by tram #17 from the train station. Its kernel is a small Italianate palace begun in 1664 for the Electress Adelaide, who dedicated it to the goddess Flora and her nymphs – hence the name. The **Marstall**, or stables, contain notable collections of historic coaches and porcelain, but more enticing than the palace itself are the wonderful park and its four distinct pavilions. Three were designed by Joseph Effner: the **Magdalenenklause**, built to resemble a ruined hermitage; the **Pagodenburg**, used for the most exclusive parties thrown by the court; and the **Badenburg**, which, like the Pagodenburg, reflects an interest in the art of China. For all their charm, Effner's pavilions are overshadowed by the stunning **Amalienburg**, the hunting lodge built behind the south wing of the Schloss by his successor as court architect, François Cuvilliés. This supreme expression of the Rococo style marries a cunning design – which makes the little building seem like a full-scale palace – with the most extravagant decoration imaginable.

Dachau, now reverted to a picturesque town on the northern edge of Munich, was the site of Germany's first **concentration camp** (Tues–Sun 9am–5pm; free; ⓦwww.kz-gedenkstaette-dachau.de). The motto that greeted arrivals at the gates has taken its chilling place in the history of Third Reich brutality: *Arbeit Macht Frei*, "Work Brings Freedom". Original buildings still standing include this gateway, the administration block, the deeply unsettling Bunker cell-block, two crematoria and the gas chambers, which were never used. However, a replica hut gives an idea of the conditions under which prisoners were forced to live, and the permanent exhibition of photographs speaks volumes. Turn up at 11.30am or 3.30pm and you can also view the short, disturbing documentary *KZ-Dachau* in English. There are also weekend **tours** in English at 1pm. Get there by taking bus #724 or #726 from Dachau S-Bahn station.

Eating and drinking

Mensas are the cheapest places to **eat**; though you're supposed to have a valid student card, no one seems to check. The most central one is at Leopoldstr. 15 (closed Sat & Sun), and there are two more in the main building at Schellingstrasse and at the Technical University, Arcisstr. 17. *Gaststätten* offer filling soups, salads and sandwich-type dishes, too. A more expensive but excellent place to stock up on fresh bread, sausages and fruit is the bustling Viktualienmarkt, which offers an array of outdoor eateries in summer. **Drinking** is central to social life and, apart from the *Gaststätten* and beer gardens, it has a lively café-bar culture, which carries on well into the early hours. The place to head for is Haidhausen, across the river to the southeast of the centre; it has a good mix of bars, cafés and restaurants, a good alternative to glitzy Schwabing.

Cafés, café-bars and wine bars

Alter Simpl Türkenstr. 57. Famous literary café-bar that spawned the satirical magazine *Simplicissimus*, now a favoured student haunt.

Café Kreutzkamm Maffeistr. 4. Airy and elegant, one of the best (and most expensive) *Kaffee und Kuchen* establishments.

Pfälzer Weinprobierstuben Residenzstr. 1. Despite the chandeliers, this is an unpretentious place serving excellent wines from the Palatinate.

Restaurants

Al Mercato Prälat-Zistl-Str 12. No-frills Italian serving cheap pizzas and pasta dishes, just south of the Viktualienmarkt.

Andechser am Dom Behind the Dom, off Kaufinger Str. Typical Munich pub, serving solid Bavarian fare to a cheerful crowd.

Bella Italia Herzog-Wilhelm-Str. 8. One of a small chain of inexpensive Italian restaurants.

Der Kleine Chinese Im Tal 28. Cheap, filling Chinese dishes served all day in this tiny eatery.

Donisl Weinstr. 1. A fine old Munich *Gaststätte* with an ornate gallery, dating back to the early eighteenth century.

Haxnbauer Münzstr. 6. Specializes in the delicious roasted pork knuckles that are such a high point of German cuisine; the lamb version is no less tasty.

Münchner Kartoffelhaus Hochbrücken Str. 3.

Cosy restaurant celebrating the humble potato. Good value selection of carbohydrate-rich dishes.

Prinz Myshkin Hackenstr, 2. Best vegetarian place in the centre, specializing in Italian dishes served beneath a high, vaulted ceiling.

Thai-China Bahnhofplatz 1 (entrance on Schützenstr.). Unbeatable value for Indian food too; also does take-out.

Beer gardens and beer halls

Augustinerbräu Neuhauser Str. 27. One of several beer halls on this central street, with an unusually long menu and wonderfully evocative *fin-de-siècle* decor.

Fraunhofer Fraunhoferstr. 9. Refreshingly tourist-free beer hall serving good Bavarian dishes to a student crowd. Live music some nights and there's a small theatre in the same building.

Hofbräukeller Innere Wiener Str. 19. Nestling under ancient chestnut trees; very popular in the evenings.

Münchner Bier Brotzeitstüberl Viktualien Markt. Popular beer garden in the centre of the market, with wooden trestles set under oak trees. Closes at 7pm.

Weisses Bräuhaus Im Tal 7. Famous for its wheat beer and the favourite Munich *Weisswurt*, a white veal (brain) sausage, best enjoyed with sweet mustard.

Nightlife and entertainment

Munich has a vibrant nightlife scene, ranging from classical concerts and jazz bars to full-on techno clubs. The best sources of **information** are *In München*, a free magazine handed out in bars and restaurants, the monthly *Monatsprogram* from the tourist office, or the English-language *Munich Found*. Munich has three first-rate symphony **orchestras** – the Münchener Philharmoniker, the Bayrisches Rundfunk Sinfonie Orchester and the Staatsorchester – as well as eleven major **theatres** and numerous fringe theatres. Advance tickets for plays and concerts can be bought at the box offices or commercial ticket shops such as the one located in the Marienplatz U-Bahn station. As for clubs, a trendy area is **Kultfabrik** (S- or U-Bahn to Ostbahnhof), a mini-city of clubs and bars housed in a network of old factory buildings that attracts upwards of 30,000 ravers on any given weekend.

The huge **Oktoberfest**, held on the Theresienwiese fairground for sixteen days following the penultimate Saturday in September, is an orgy of beer drinking, spiced up by fairground rides that are so hairy they're banned in the US. The fairgrounds are divided along four main avenues, creating a boisterous city of its own, heaving from morning till night. **Fasching**, Munich's carnival, is an excuse for fancy-dress balls and general shenanigans from mid-January until the beginning of Lent. More sedate is **Auer Dult**, a traditional market that takes place on the Mariahilfplatz during the last weeks of April or May, July and October each year; there are stalls selling food, crafts and antiques, and there's also a fairground.

Clubs and live music venues

Atomic Café Neutrum Str. 5. Retro-style bar and club catering to a fashionable crowd.

Backstage Friedenheimer Brücke 7. Live bands, house and hip-hop nights; popular with students.

Georg Elser Halle Rosenheimer Str. 143. Large-scale dance events spread across three areas, each playing either trance, hip-hop or disco classics.

Keller Club Friedenstr. 20. Indie and nu metal nights for a mix of Goths and trendy types.

Milch und Bar Kunstpark Ost. A long-standing favourite in the Kultfabrik. House, techno and trance, including visiting club nights such as the Ministry of Sound.

Mojos Wilhelm Hale Str. 44. R&B and soul club; occasional hip-hop events.

Muffathalle Zellstr. 4. Live music and regular dance nights including a popular hip-hop night on Fri.

Nachtwerk Landsberger Str. 185. Draws a very young crowd for its chart dance nights on Fri and Sat, and stages occasional up-and-coming live acts.

Night Flight Franz Josef Strauss Flughafen. Despite its bizarre airport setting, this high-tech trance club is proving popular for hectic all-nighters.

Olympiapark Free rock concerts by the lake in summer; they usually get going around 2pm at weekends.

Unterfahrt Einsteinstr. 42. Showcase for avant-garde jazz, with many big names gracing the stage.

Listings

Bike rental From the train station, opposite platform 36.

Consulates UK, Bürkleinstr 10 ☎089/21 10 90; Canada, Tal 29 ☎089/2 19 95 70; Ireland, Denningerstr. 15 ☎089/20 80 59 90; US, Königinstr. 5 ☎089/2 88 80.

Gay Munich Despite Bavaria's deep conservatism, Munich has an active and visible gay scene. *Our Munich* is a gay listings mag, and *Sergej* is a gay guide to the city, available at the tourist office. Cafés that cater predominantly for lesbians are

Inge's Karotte, Baaderstr. 13, *Bei Carla*, Buttermelcherstr. 9, and *Café Glück*, Palmstr. 4. Well-known gay bars include *Colibri*, Utzschneiderstr. 8 and *Juice*, Buttermelcherstr. 2a, while *Soul City*, Maximiliansplatz 5, is one of the most popular gay clubs in town.

Hospital Technische Universität München, Ismaninger Str. 22 ☎089/4 14 00.

Laundry Amalienstr. 61; Paul-Heyse Str. 21.

Pharmacy Bahnhof-Apotheke, Bahnhofplatz 2.

Post office Bahnhofplatz 1.

The Bavarian Alps

It's among the picture-book scenery of the **Alps** that you'll find the Bavarian folklore and customs that are the subjects of so many tourist brochures. The region also encompasses some of the most famous places in the province, such as the Olympic ski resort of **Garmisch-Partenkirchen**, and the fantasy castle of **Neuschwanstein**, just one of the lunatic palaces built for King Ludwig II of Bavaria. The western reaches are generally cheaper and less touristy, partly because they're not so easily accessible to Munich's weekend crowds; much of the eastern region to **Berchtesgaden** is heavily geared to the tourist trade, but if you go outside the high season of July and August, you should have a good chance of avoiding the crowds.

Füssen and around

Lying between the Forggensee reservoir and the Ammer mountains, around 100km by rail from Munich, **FÜSSEN** and the adjacent town of **SCHWANGAU** are the bases for visiting Bavaria's two most popular castles. **Schloss Hohenschwangau** (daily: April–Sept 9am–6pm; Oct–May 10am–4pm; €8), originally built in the twelfth century but heavily restored in the nineteenth, was where Ludwig II spent his youth. A mark of his individualism is left in the bedroom, where he had the ceiling painted with stars that were spot-lit in the evenings. **Schloss Neuschwanstein** (same hours; €8), the ultimate storybook turreted castle, was built by Ludwig a little higher up the mountain. The architectural hotchpotch includes a Byzantine throne hall and an artificial grotto. Left incomplete at Ludwig's death, it's a monument to a very sad and lonely man. The nearest **HI hostel** is in Füssen, at Mariahilferstr. 5 (☏08362/77 54, ☼www.djh.de; €14.60). The **tourist office** at Kaiser-Maximilian-Platz 1 in Füssen (Mon–Fri 8.30am–6pm, Sat 9am–noon; ☏08362/9 38 50, ☼www.fuessen.de) can book accommodation. Füssen is also the end of the much-publicized **Romantic Road** from Würzburg via Augsburg, served by special tour buses in season.

Oberammergau

From Murnau, midway between Munich and Garmisch-Partenkirchen, a branch line runs to **OBERAMMERGAU**, world famous for its Passion Play, first performed in 1633 as thanks for being spared by a plague epidemic. The show takes place every ten years (next in 2010), with a cast of local villagers. Many of Oberammergau's houses have traditional outside frescoes of religious or Alpine scenes, which you can see as either quaint or kitsch – that goes for the wood carvings in the local souvenir shops, too. From here it's a short bus ride to **Schloss Linderhof** (daily 9/10am–4/6pm; €6, €4.50 in winter), one of the architectural fantasies conjured for Ludwig. Though built as a discreet private residence, it has a reception room with intricate gold-painted carvings, stucco ornamentation, and a throne canopy draped in ermine curtains. The real attraction is the delightful **park**: Italianate terraces, cascades and manicured flowerbeds give way to an English garden design that gradually blends into the forests of the mountain beyond. A number of romantic little buildings are dotted around the park, the most remarkable of which is the Venus Grotto. Based on the set for Wagner's opera *Tannhäuser* (Ludwig was the composer's principal patron), it has an illuminated lake supporting a huge floating golden conch in which the king would sometimes take rides.

Garmisch-Partenkirchen and around

GARMISCH-PARTENKIRCHEN is the most famous town in the German Alps, partly because it's at the foot of the highest mountain – the **Zugspitze** (2966m) – and partly because it hosted the 1936 Winter Olympics. It has excellent facilities for skiing, skating and other winter sports, as well as abundant accommodation, a full list of which can be had from the **tourist office** at Richard-Strauss-Platz 2 (Mon–Fri 9am–1pm & 2–7pm, Sat 9am–1pm; ☏08821/18 07 00, ☼www.garmisch-partenkirchen.de). The ascent of Zugspitze by **rack-railway** and cable car (both €42, €33 in winter) is the most memorable local excursion. **MITTENWALD**, which remains a community rather than a resort, is 15km down the road and rail line from Munich. The Karwendl mountain towering above is a popular climb, and the view from the top is exhilarating; a **cable car** goes there (€19 return). The **tourist office**, at Dammkarstr. 3 (Mon–Fri 8am–noon & 1–5pm; July & Aug also Sat 10am–noon; ☎0 88 23/3 30, ⓦwww.mittenwald.de), provides free maps of the area. There are plenty of good **guest houses**, such as *Franziska*, Innsbrucker Str. 24 (☎08823/9 20 30; ❸), and *Schwalbennestle*, Gröblweg 34 (☎08823/80 23; ❷). The nearest **campsite** is 3km north, on the road to Garmisch.

Berchtesgaden

Almost entirely surrounded by mountains at Bavaria's southeastern extremity, the area around **BERCHTESGADEN** has a magical atmosphere, especially in the mornings, when mists rise from the lakes and swirl around lush valleys and rocky mountainsides. The town is just 23km north of Salzburg in Austria, and it is also easily reached by rail from Munich. A star attraction is the stunning **Königssee**, Germany's highest lake, which bends around the foot of the towering Watzmann, 5km south of town – regular buses run out here – and has year-round **cruises** (€13.80 return). You can also take a cable car up the **Jenner**, immediately above the lake (€18 return), used mostly by skiers in the winter months. Berchtesgaden is still indelibly associated with **Adolf Hitler**, who rented a house in the nearby village of Obersalzberg, which he later enlarged into the **Berghof**, a stately retreat where he could meet foreign dignitaries. It was blown up by the Allies, and the ruins are now overgrown. High above the village on the Kehlstein, Hitler's Kehlsteinhaus, or "**Eagle's Nest**", survives as a restaurant, and can be reached by special bus from Obersalzberg (May to mid-Oct; €14). Berchtesgaden has some great **mountain walks** to take you away from the crowds in summer – maps of suggested walking routes can be bought at the **tourist office** opposite the train station (Mon–Fri 8.30am–5/6pm, Sat 8/9am–noon/5pm; late June to mid-Oct also Sun 9am–3pm; ☎08652/96 70, ⓦwww.berchtesgaden.de). Room prices drop dramatically if you stay more than one night; **guest house** options include the friendly *Haus am Hang*, Göllsteinbichl 3 (☎08652/43 5 90; ❷), and *Haus Achental*, Ramsauer Str. 4 (☎08652/45 49; ❸), where all rooms have bathrooms. The tourist office can direct you to any of the five **campsites** in the valley.

Travel details

Trains

Berlin to: Dresden (every 2hr; 2hr 15min); Frankfurt (hourly; 4hr); Hamburg (hourly; 2hr 30min); Hannover (hourly; 2hr); Leipzig (every 20min; 2hr); Munich (every 30min; 7–8hr); Weimar (every 2hr; 3hr).

Cologne to: Aachen (every 30min; 1hr); Frankfurt (hourly; 2hr 15min); Heidelberg (hourly; 2hr 30min); Mainz (every 20min; 1hr 45min); Stuttgart (hourly; 3hr 25min).

Dresden to: Meissen (every 30min; 50min).

Frankfurt to: Baden-Baden (hourly; 1hr 30min); Berlin (hourly; 4–6hr); Cologne (hourly; 2hr 15min); Hamburg (hourly; 3hr 45min); Hannover (hourly; 2hr 20min); Heidelberg (every 30min; 1hr); Munich (hourly; 4hr); Nuremberg (hourly; 2hr).

Hamburg to: Bremen (hourly; 1hr); Hannover (every 30min; 1hr 25min); Lübeck (every 30min; 40min).

Hannover to: Goslar (hourly; 1hr 20min); Heidelberg (every 2hr; 4hr 40min).

Koblenz to: Trier (hourly; 1hr 30min).

Leipzig to: Dresden (hourly; 1hr 40min); Meissen (hourly; 2–3hr); Weimar (hourly; 1hr 25min).

Mainz to: Koblenz (frequent; 50min).

Munich to: Augsburg (every 20min; 30min); Nuremberg (every 30min; 1hr 30min–2hr 30min); Regensburg (hourly; 1hr 30min).

Nuremberg to: Bamberg (every 30min; 45min); Munich (hourly; 1hr 30min); Regensburg (hourly; 1hr).

Stuttgart to: Freiburg (hourly; 2hr); Heidelberg (every 30min; 1hr); Konstanz (hourly; 2hr 40min).

Greece

Greece highlights

Introduction and basics

With 166 inhabited islands and a landscape that ranges from Mediterranean to Balkan, **Greece** has enough appeal to fill months of travel. The country is the sum of an extraordinary diversity of influences. Romans, Arabs, Franks, Venetians, Slavs, Albanians, Turks, Italians, as well as the thousand-year Byzantine Empire, have all been and gone since the time of Alexander the Great. Each has left its mark: the Byzantines through countless churches and monasteries, particularly at the ghost town of Mystra; the Venetians in impregnable fortifications such as Monemvasiá in the Peloponnese; the Franks with crag-top castles, again in the Peloponnese but also in the Dodecanese and east Aegean. Most obvious, perhaps, is the heritage of four hundred years of Ottoman Turkish rule which exercised an inestimable influence on music, cuisine, language and way of life.

The **historic sites** span four millennia of civilization, ranging from the renowned – such as Mycenae, Olympia, Delphi and the Parthenon in **Athens** – to the obscure, where a visit can still seem like a personal discovery. The **beaches** are distributed along a long, convoluted coastline, and they garland cosmopolitan resorts as well as remote islands where the boat may call only once or twice a week. The **landscapes** of Greece encompass the stony deserts of the Máni, the lush Peloponnesian coastal hills, the resin-scented ridges of Skiáthos and Sámos and the wind-blasted rocks of the central Aegean. The simple pleasures of the natural environment, and of the country's **climate** and **food**, are what make Greece special.

Even before the fall of Byzantium, the Greek country people – peasants, fishermen, shepherds – had created one of the most vigorous and truly **popular cultures** in Europe, which endured until quite recently in songs and dances, costumes, embroidery, furniture and the whitewashed houses of popular image. Since the 1970s most of this has disappeared under the impact of Western consumer values, to be largely relegated to museums, but Greek architectural

and musical heritage in particular have undergone a recent renaissance.

Information & maps

The **National Tourist Organization** (**EOT**) publishes an impressive array of free regional pamphlets and maps. There are EOT offices in many larger towns and resorts; in other places, try equally good **municipal tourist offices**. The **tourist police** often has lists of rooms to let, but are there to assist if you have a serious complaint about a hotel or restaurant. The most reliable **maps** are published in Athens. Road Editions (⬉www.road .gr) has the best for mainland regions and islands; maps by Emvelia Editions (⬉www.emvelia.gr) include useful town plans; and Anavasi (⬉www.anavasi.gr) produce the best mountaineering maps.

Money and banks

Greece's **currency** is the euro (€). **Banks** are normally open Mon–Thurs 8am–2.30pm, Fri 8am–2pm. They charge a flat fee (€2–3) to change money, the National Bank usually

---

Greece on the net

⬉**www.culture.gr** Ministry of Culture site; lots of info on ruins and museums.
⬉**www.athensnews.gr** Useful and literate English-language daily.
⬉**www.greekislands.gr** Online reservations for the Cyclades and Crete.
⬉**www.all-hotels.gr** Comprehensive listings of accommodation.
⬉**www.greekferries.gr** Information on ferry and hydrofoil schedules.

being the cheapest; travel agencies and designated money-exchange booths give a poorer rate, but often levy a sliding two-percent commission, which makes them better than banks for changing small amounts. Plenty of **ATMs** accept foreign cards; in isolated areas without ATMs, a small quantity of dollar/sterling notes – *not* travellers' cheques – will prove useful.

Communications

Most **post offices** operate Mon–Fri 7.30am–2pm – into the evening and even weekends in cities and major resorts. **Stamps** can also be bought at designated postal agencies. **Poste restante** is reasonably efficient. **Public phones** are mainly card-operated, though many cafés have counter-top coin-op models. Buy phone cards from newsagents and kiosks. It's possible to make collect (reverse-charge) or charge-card calls from these phones, but you need credit on a Greek phone-card to begin. After recent renumbering, you need to

dial **all ten digits** of every phone number. The **operator** is on ☏151 (domestic) or ☏161 (international). All big towns have several places with **Internet access**, and there's usually at least one place on the more visited islands. Prices are €4.50–6/hr.

Getting around

The **rail** network is limited, and trains are slower than the equivalent buses – except on the showcase IC (intercity) lines, which cost more. However, most trains are cheaper than buses, and some of the routes are highlights in their own right. If you're starting a journey at the initial station of a run you can reserve a seat; at most intermediate points, it's first-come, first-served. **Eurail** and **InterRail** are valid, though passholders must reserve like everyone else.

Buses form the bulk of public transport, and service on the major routes is efficient, with companies organized nationally into a syndicate called the **KTEL**. Larger towns can have several widely spaced termini for

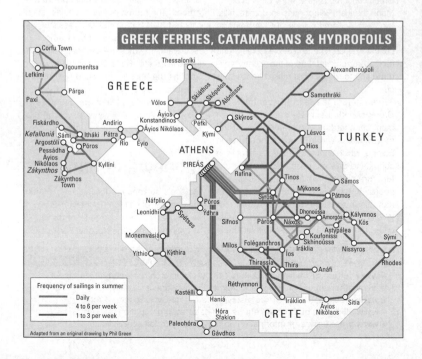

GREEK FERRIES, CATAMARANS & HYDROFOILS

Frequency of sailings in summer
Daily
4 to 6 per week
1 to 3 per week

Adapted from an original drawing by Phil Green

departures in different directions, so ensure you aim for the right station. Ticketing is computerized for major intercity lines, which can get booked-up. On rural routes, tickets are dispensed on the spot, with some standing allowed. On many islands, a bus runs between the port and main town to coincide with ferry arrivals and departures.

Schedules for **sea** transport are notoriously erratic. The most reliable, up-to-date information is available from the local port police (*limenarhío*), at Pireás and on all sizeable islands. Regular ferry tickets are best bought on the day of departure, unless you need to reserve a cabin – although from March 23 to 25, over Easter week and during August it's best to book several days in advance. The cheapest ticket is "deck class". **Hydrofoils** and **high-speed catamarans** are roughly twice as fast and twice as expensive as ordinary ferries. In season, *kaïkia* (caiques) sail to more obscure islets.

Once on the islands, almost everybody rents a **scooter** or a **bike**. Scooters cost from €10 a day, mountain bikes a bit less. To rent a motorbike (over 100cc) you need to show an appropriate licence. You should make sure your travel insurance covers spills and damage to the bike, as bike-agency insurance is usually deficient.

Accommodation

Most of the year you can turn up pretty much anywhere and find a **room**. Only around Easter and during July and August are you likely to experience problems; at these times, it's worth heading off the standard tourist routes, and/or arriving at each new place early in the day.

Hotels are categorized from "Luxury" down to "E-class", but these ratings have more to do with amenities and number of rooms than pricing. In resorts and throughout the islands, you have the additional option of privately let **rooms** *(dhomátia)*. These are divided into three classes (A–C), and are often cheaper than hotels. As often as not, rooms find you: owners descend on ferry or bus arrivals to fill any space they have. Increasingly, rooms are being eclipsed by **self-catering** facilities, which can be

equally good value; if signs or touts are not apparent, ask for studios at travel agencies. There's a handful of **hostels** outside Athens; with few exceptions, they're run-down and not HI-affiliated. Few ever ask for an HI card; charges are around €8 a night.

Official **campsites** range from basic island compounds to highly organized and amenitied complexes, mostly **closed in winter** (Nov–April). Casual places rarely cost much above €3 a night per person; however, at fancier sites it's possible for two people and a tent to pay almost as much as for a basic room. Camping outside authorized sites is forbidden; if you intend to do this, be cautious, especially near seaside resorts and villages – the regulations do get enforced occasionally.

Food and drink

There's no snobbery about **eating out** in Greece; everyone does it, and it's reasonably priced: €11–14 per person for a meal with beer or cheap wine. Greeks generally don't eat breakfast. **Snacks**, however, can be one of the distinctive pleasures of Greek eating. *Tyrópites* and *spanakópites* (cheese and spinach pies respectively) are on sale everywhere, as are *souvlákia* (small kebabs) and *ghýros* (doner kebab), served in *píta* bread with garnish. In choosing a **taverna**, the best strategy is to go where the locals go. Typical **dishes** to try include *moussakás* (aubergine and meat pie), *yígandes* (white haricot beans in red sauce), *tzatzíki* (yoghurt, garlic and cucumber dip), *melitzanosaláta* (aubergine dip), *khtapódhi* (octopus), and *kalamarákia* (fried baby squid). Note that people eat **late**: 2.30–4pm & 9–11.30pm.

The traditional coffee shop or **kafenío** is the central pivot of life in rural villages; like tavernas, these range from the sophisticated to the old-fashioned. Their main business is Greek **coffee**, but they also serves spirits such as aniseed-flavoured **oúzo** and brandy, as well as beer and soft drinks. Islanders take pre-dinner *oúzo* an hour or two before sunset: you'll be served a glass of water alongside, to be tipped into your *oúzo* until it turns a milky white. **Bars** are now ubiquitous in the largest towns and holiday resorts.

They are often housed in buildings of historic interest, with the added enticements of theme parties and hip clientele. Drinks, at €5.50–8, are invariably more expensive than at a *kafenío*. Tavernas offer a better choice of **wines**: Boutari, Tsantali and Calliga are good, low-priced bottles. Otherwise, ask for the local bulk wines – *hýma* or *varelísio* – at around €4.50 per litre.

Opening hours and holidays

Shops generally open at 8.30–9.30am, then take a long break at 2–2.30pm before maybe reopening in the late afternoon. However, tourist areas tend to adopt a more northern timetable, with shops and offices often staying open right through the day. Opening hours for **museums** and **ancient sites** change with exasperating frequency. Smaller sites generally close for a long siesta (even when they're not supposed to), as do monasteries. Many state-owned museums and sites are **free** for students from EU countries (a valid card is required, but not necessarily an ISIC). Non-EU students, and all over-65s, generally pay half-price. There's a vast range of **public holidays** and festivals. The most important, when almost everything will be closed, are: Jan 1 & 6; 1st Mon of Lent; March 25; May 1; Easter Sun & Mon; Pentecost/Whit Mon; Aug 15; Oct 28; Dec 24–27.

Emergencies

The most common causes of a run-in with the **police** are nude (sun)bathing, breaking into archeological sites after-hours, and camping outside an authorized site. Topless bathing is now legal on virtually all Greek beaches but, especially in smaller places, be aware of local sensitivities before stripping off. For minor medical complaints go to the local **pharmacy**. For serious medical attention you'll find English-speaking doctors in all bigger towns or resorts; consult the tourist police for some names. Emergency treatment is free in state **hospitals**, though you'll only get the most basic level of nursing care. Even with an E111 form, you'll have to pay up front for medications.

Emergency numbers

Police ☎110; Ambulance ☎166; Fire ☎199.

Athens

ATHENS has been inhabited continuously for over 7000 years. Its acropolis, protected by a ring of mountains and commanding views of all seagoing approaches, was a natural choice for prehistoric settlement. Its development as a city-state and artistic centre reached its zenith in the fifth century BC with a flourish of art, architecture, literature and philosophy that pervaded Western culture forever after. Since World War II, the city's population has risen from 700,000 to four million – over a third of the country's population. The speed of this process is reflected in Athens' chaotic mix of retro and contemporary: cutting-edge clothes shops and designer bars stand by the remnants of the Ottoman bazaar, while brutalist 1960s apartment blocks dwarf crumbling Neoclassical mansions. The ancient sites are merely the most obvious of Athens' attractions. There are attractive cafés, landscaped stair-streets, and markets; startling views from the hills of Lykavitós and Filopáppou; and, around the foot of the Acropolis, scattered monuments of the Byzantine, medieval and nineteenth-century town. Outside the city, the **Temple of Poseidon** at Sounion is the most popular trip, justified by its dramatic clifftop position.

The port of **PIREÁS**, effectively an extension of Athens, is the main terminus for international and inter-island **ferries**. Get there from Athens by metro: Pireás is the last stop heading southwest from Monastiráki. The other port, **RAFÍNA**, on the east coast of the Attic peninsula, is a useful departure point for many of the Cycladic and north Aegean islands. Frequent buses connects it with central Athens.

Arrival, information and city transport

By mid-2004, a light-rail line should whisk you from Elefthérios Venizelos **airport** to Dhoukíssa Plakendías station, new terminus of the metro network. Tickets into town cost €2.90 and are valid on all Athens public transport for 24hr. Until the rail link opens, take E94 express **bus** (every 15–30min 6am–midnight) from outside arrivals to metro station Ethnikí Ámyna and then continue by metro. Alternatively, take the E95 express bus all the way to central Sýndagma Square (every 25–35min), or the E96 express bus to Pireás port (every 20–40min). International **trains** arrive at the Stathmós Laríssis in the northwest of the city centre, with its own metro station. The nearly adjacent Stathmós Peloponníssou handles traffic to and from the Peloponnese. **Buses** from northern Greece and the Peloponnese arrive at Kifissoú 100, ten minutes from the centre by bus #051. Buses from central Greece (but not Delphi) arrive closer to the centre at Liossíon 260, north of the train stations (bus #024 to Sýndagma). Most international buses drop off at the train station or Kifissoú 100; a few will drop you right in the city centre. Arriving by **boat** at Pireás, the simplest access to the centre is by metro to Monastiráki, Sýndagma or Omónia stations.

The city's main EOT **tourist office** was homeless during 2003; the inconvenient new offices are provisionally at Tsóha 7, Ambelókipi (consult ⦿www.gnto.gr for an update).

All **public transport** operates daily from around 5.30am to midnight. Athens' bus and trolley network is extensive but very crowded at peak times. Line #1 of the **metro** runs from Pireás to Kifissiá, with central stops at Thissío, Monastiráki and Omónia; Line #2 runs from Dháfni to Sepólia via Sýndagma and a station at the foot of the Acropolis; Line #3 heads east from Monastiráki to Ethnikí Ámyna, with extension to Dhoukíssa Plakendías and light-rail continuation to the airport due to open by mid-2004. Tickets are available at all stations from automatic coin-op dispensers or staffed windows. A 24-hr ticket (€2.90) gives you the run of all buses and all metro lines. Tickets for **buses** must be bought in advance from kiosks. **Taxis** can be surprisingly difficult to hail, but are very inexpensive: fares around the city centre should rarely come to more than €4. Taxi drivers will often pick up a whole string of passengers along the way, each passenger paying the full fare for

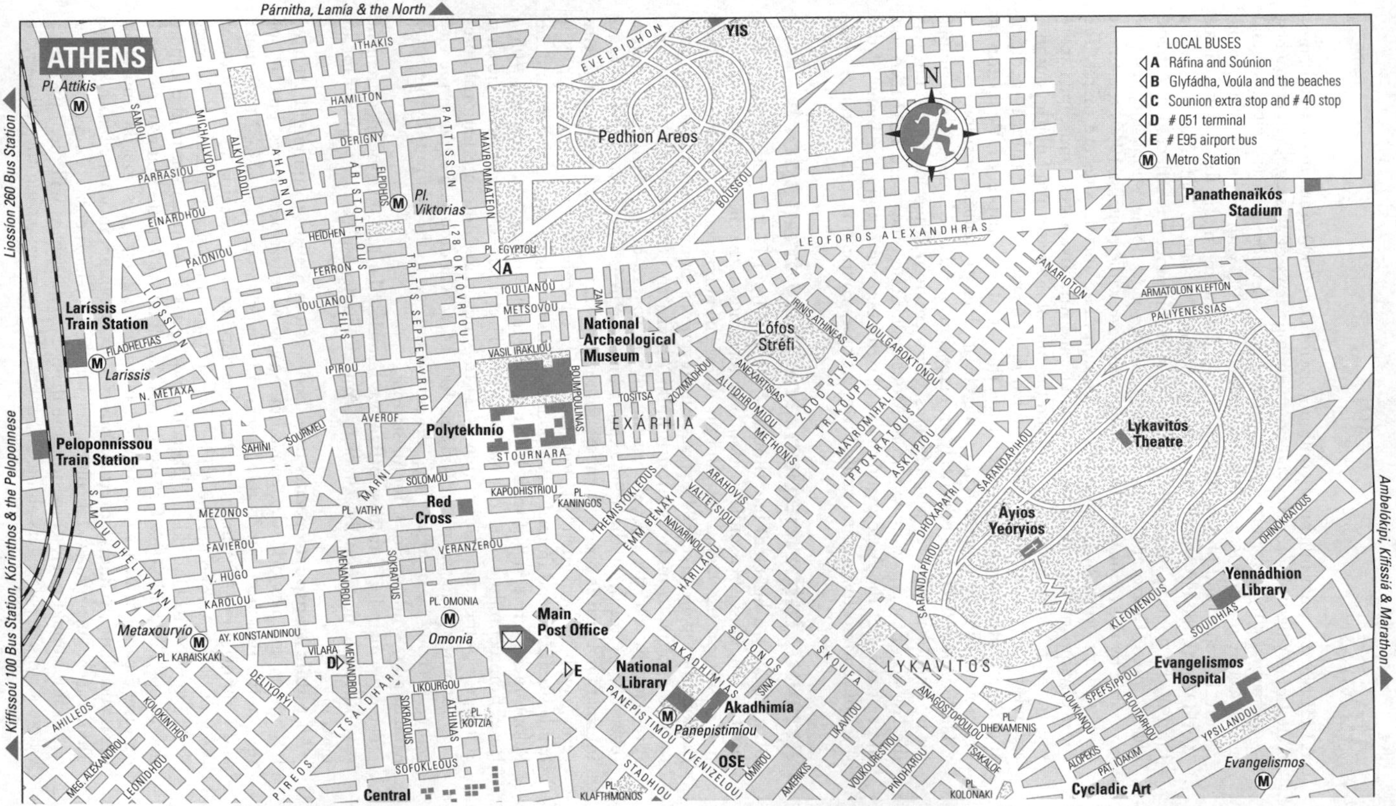

ATHENS
LOCAL BUSES
A Ráfina and Soúnion
B Glyfádha, Voúla and the beaches
C Sounion extra stop and # 40 stop
D # 051 terminal
E # E95 airport bus
Metro Station
N
Párnitha, Lamía & the North
Liossíon 260 Bus Station
Kiffissoú 100 Bus Station, Kórinthos & the Peloponnese
Ambelókipi, Kifissiá & Marathon
Pl. Attikis
Larissis Train Station
Larissis
Peloponníssou Train Station
Metaxouryío
Pl. Viktorias
Pedhion Areos
YIS
Panathenaïkós Stadium
National Archeological Museum
Polytekhnío
Red Cross
Main Post Office
Omonia
National Library
Akadhimía
Panepistimíou
OSE
Central
Lófos Stréfi
EXÁRHIA
Lykavitós Theatre
Áyios Yeóryios
Yennádhion Library
Evangelismos Hospital
Evangelismos
Cycladic Art
LYKAVITOS
LEOFOROS ALEXANDHRAS
PATISSON (28 OKTOVRIOU)
TRITIS SEPTEMVRIOU
ARISTOTELOUS
AHARNON
LIOSSION
SAMOU DHELIYANNI
PANEPISTIMIOU (VENIZELOU)
AKADHIMIAS
SOLONOS
SKOUFA
STADHIOU
PIREOS
(TSALDHARI)
MAVROMMATEON
EVELPIDHON
BOUSGOU
STOURNARA
THEMISTOKLEOUS
EMM BENAKI
SOLOMOU
VERANZEROU
KAPODHISTRIOU
PL. OMONIA
PL. EGYPTOU
PL. KOLONAKI
PL. KLAFTHMONOS
PL. KOTZIA
PL. KARAISKAKI
PL. VATHY
PL. KANINGOS
PL. DHEXAMENIS
SARANDAPIHOU
DHOXAPATRI
SOUIDHIAS
KLEOMENOUS
YPSILANDOU
PLOUTARHOU
SPEFSIPPOU
LOUKIANOU
PAT. IOAKIM
ALOPEKIS
TSAKALOF
ANAGOSTOPOULOU
PINDHAROU
VOUKOURESTIOU
LIKAVITOU
AMERIKIS
OMIROU
SINA
HARILAOU
NAVARINOU
VALTETSIOU
ARAHOVIS
METHONIS
MAVROMIHALI
IPPOKRATOUS
ASKLIPIOU
TRIKOUPI
ZOODOHOU PIYIS
ALLIDHROMIOU
ANEXARTISIAS
ZOZIMADHOU
TOSITSA
BOUMPOULINAS
VASIL IRAKLIOU
ZAIMI
TOULIANOU
METSOVOU
IRINIS ATHINEAS
VOULGAROKTONOU
FANARIOTON
ARMATOLON KLEFTON
PALIYENESSIAS
DHINOKRATOUS
ITHAKIS
HAMILTON
DERIGNY
ELPIDHOS
HEIDHEN
FERRON
IOULIANOU
FILIS
IPIROU
AVEROF
SOURMELI
SAHINI
MARNI
MEZONOS
FAVIEROU
V. HUGO
KAROLOU
AY. KONSTANDINOU
VILARA
MENANDROU
SOKRATOUS
LIKOURGOU
ATHINAS
SOFOKLEOUS
DELIYORYI
KOLOKINTHOS
AHILLEOS
MEG. ALEXANDROU
LEONIDHOU
SAMOU
MICHAILVODA
ALKIVIADOU
PARRASIOU
EINARDHOU
PAIONIOU
FILADHELFIAS
N. METAXA

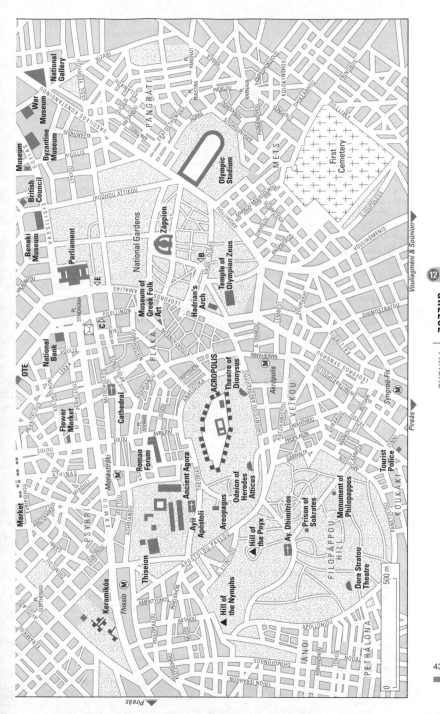

12

Voúliagméni & Soúnion ▶

Pireás ▶

Syngroú-Fix ▶

◀ Pireás

National Gallery

War Museum

Byzantine Museum

Museum

British Council

Benaki Museum

Parliament

National Bank

OTE

Flower Market

Cathedral

Market

National Gardens

Zappion

Museum of Greek Folk Art

Hadrian's Arch

Temple of Olympian Zeus

Olympic Stadium

First Cemetery

METS

PANGRATI

Roman Forum

Ancient Agora

Ayii Apostoli

ACROPOLIS

Theatre of Dionysus

Akropolis Ⓜ

VEIKOU

KOUKAKI

Tourist Police

Thiseion

Keramikós

Areopagus

Odeion of Herodes Atticus

Hill of the Pnyx

Ay. Dhimitrios

Prison of Sokrates

Monument of Philopappos

PILOPÁPPOU HILL

Dora Stratou Theatre

Hill of the Nymphs

PETRALONA

Thissío Ⓜ

Monastiráki Ⓜ

PSYRI

PLAKA

Syndagma

500 m

0

their journey – so if you're picked up by an already occupied taxi, memorize the meter reading; you'll pay from then on, including a €1.50 minimum.

Accommodation

Accommodation can be packed to the gills in midsummer – August especially – but for most of the year there is good availability. In the run-up to the 2004 Olympics, many hotels have hiked their prices unreasonably; the following are some affordable alternatives.

Hostels

Hostel #5 Dhamaréos 75, Pangráti ☎210 75 19 530. In a congenial (if remote) neighbourhood – trolleys #2 or #11 stop nearby – with cooking and laundry facilities, and no curfew. Management can be a bit off-hand, however. ❶

International Youth Hostel Victor Hugo 16, near Metaxouryío metro ☎210 52 34 170. Athens' cheapest option, an official HI hostel with a cheerful atmosphere, well-kept facilities and helpful staff, though the location isn't wonderful. ❶

Student and Travellers' Inn Kydhathinéon 16 ☎210 32 44 808, ✉student-inn@ath.forthnet.gr. Prime location for this popular, clean and well-run hotel-cum-hostel. Singles, doubles, triples and dorms, most with shared bathrooms, as well as luggage storage and Internet access. Dorms ❶ Rooms ❸

Hotels

John's Place Patróöu 5, Pláka ☎210 32 29 719. Dark rooms with baths in the hall, but neat and well-kept. In a peaceful backstreet off Mitropóleos, with a cheap restaurant on the ground floor. ❸

Marble House Cul-de-sac off Anastasíou Zínni 35, Koukáki ☎210 92 28 294, ⊕www.marblehouse

.gr. The best-value outfit south of the Acropolis, this welcoming pension was overhauled in 2001–02; most rooms en suite and with balcony, all rooms with fans and fridge. Reservations essential. ❸

Orion Emm. Benáki 105, corner Anexartisías, Exárhia ☎210 33 02 388. Quiet, well-run budget hotel across from the Lófos Stréfi park – a steep final walk to get there, yet close to many attractions. Rooftop kitchen and common area with an amazing view. ❸

Phaedra Herefóndos 16, Pláka ☎210 32 38 641. All the cheerful, air-con rooms got a face-lift in 2002–03; just over half are en suite. Excellent location on pedestrian street overlooking a Byzantine church and the Acropolis. ❸

Campsites

Nea Kifissia Potamoú 60 Néa Kifissiá ☎210 62 05 646. In a leafy suburb, this year-round place has its own swimming pool. Metro to Kifissiá then bus #528 behind the station.

Várkiza Camping at Km27 on the Athens–Sounion road ☎210 89 73 614. Large year-round site by the beach, 20km south of the centre. Bus #A3 from Amalías Avenue to Glyfáda, then #115 to Várkiza.

The City

Pláka is the best place to begin exploring the city. One of the few parts of Athens with charm and architectural merit, its narrow streets and stepped lanes are flanked by nineteenth-century Neoclassical houses. An attractive approach follows **Odhós Kydhathinéon**, a pedestrian walkway starting on Odhós Filellínon, south of Sýndagma. It continues through café-crowded Platía Filomoússou Eterías to **Odhós Adhrianoú**, which runs nearly the whole east–west length of Pláka from Hadrian's Arch to the Thissíon. From the Roman Forum uphill, Adhrianoú is tattily commercial. But just past the end of Kydhathinéon, there's a quiet and attractive sitting space around the fourth-century-BC **Monument of Lysikratos**, erected to celebrate the success of a prize-winning dramatic chorus. Continuing straight ahead from the Kydhathinéon–Adhriánou intersection up **Odhós Thespídhos**, you reach the edge of the Acropolis precinct. Up to the right, the whitewashed Cycladic houses of Anafiótika cheerfully proclaim an architect-free zone amidst the highest crags of the Acropolis rock.

The Acropolis

A rugged limestone outcrop, watered by springs and rising abruptly from the plain of Attica, the **Acropolis** (daily 8.30am–2.30pm/5pm) was one of the earliest

The **entry ticket** to the Acropolis (€12; non-EU students €6; EU students free) is valid for two days and allows free access to all the other ancient sites in Athens. Otherwise, minor sites charge a €2 separate admission if you haven't visited the Acropolis, and open daily 8.30am–2.30pm.

settlements in Greece, supporting a Neolithic community around 5000 BC. By Mycenaean times it sported a fortified palace and temples where the cult of Athena was introduced. During the ninth century BC, it became the heart of the first Greek city-state, and in the wake of Athenian military supremacy and a peace treaty with the Persians in 449 BC, Pericles had the complex reconstructed under the direction of architect and sculptor Pheidias, producing most of the monuments visible today, including the Parthenon. Having survived more or less intact for over two millennia, the Acropolis finally fell victim to the vagaries of war. In 1687 besieging Venetians ignited a Turkish gunpowder magazine in the Parthenon, blasting off the roof, and in 1801 Lord Elgin removed the frieze (the "Elgin Marbles"), which he later sold to the British Museum. Meanwhile, generations of visitors slowly wore down the Parthenon's surfaces; more recently, smog has been turning the marble to dust. Since 1981, visitors have been barred from the Parthenon's precinct, and a major restoration programme is proceeding sporadically; scaffolding and cranes may obscure the view.

The **Parthenon** was the first great building in Pericles's plan. Designed by Iktinos, it exploits all the refinements available to the Doric order of architecture to achieve an extraordinary and unequalled harmony. Built on the site of earlier temples, it was intended as a new sanctuary for Athena and a house for her cult image, a colossal wooden statue decked in ivory and gold plate that was designed by Pheidias and considered one of the Seven Wonders of the Ancient World; the sculpture was lost in ancient times, but its characteristics are known through later copies. "Parthenon" means "virgins' chamber" and initially referred only to a room at the west end of the temple occupied by the priestesses of Athena.

To the north of the Parthenon stands the **Erechtheion**, the last of the great works of Pericles. Here, in symbolic reconciliation, Athena and the city's previous patron Poseidon-Erechtheus were both worshipped. On the south side, in the Porch of the Caryatids, the Ionic line is transformed into six maidens (caryatids) holding the entablature on their heads.

Placed discreetly on a level below that of the main monuments, the **Acropolis Museum** (Mon 10am–2.30pm, Tues–Sun 8.30am–2.30pm) contains nearly all of the portable objects removed from the Acropolis since 1834. Prize exhibits include the *Moschophoros*, a painted marble statue of a young man carrying a sacrificial calf; the graceful sculpture of Athena Nike adjusting one sandal, known as *Iy Sandalízoussa*. and four caryatids from the Erechtheion, displayed in a vacuum chamber.

Rock-hewn stairs immediately below the entrance to the Acropolis ascend the low hill of the **Areopagus**, site of the court of criminal justice. Following the road or path over the flank of the Acropolis, you come out onto pedestrianized Dhionysíou Areopayítou, just above the Odeion of Herodes Atticus (see below). Turning right, a network of paths leads up **Filopáppou Hill**, its summit capped by a grandiose monument to a Roman consul. Just north of the main path, which follows a line of truncated ancient walls, sits **Áyios Dhimítrios** church, with Byzantine frescoes. North of this rises the **Hill of the Pnyx**, a meeting place in Classical times for the democratic assembly.

The second-century Roman **Odeion of Herodes Atticus**, restored for performances of music and classical drama during the summer festival (the only time it's open), dominates the southern slope of the Acropolis hill. The main interest hereabouts lies in earlier Greek sites to the east, pre-eminent among them the **Theatre of Dionysos**. Masterpieces of Aeschylus, Sophocles, Euripides and Aristophanes were first performed

GREECE | Athens

⑫

here, at one of the most evocative locations in the city. The ruins are impressive; the theatre, rebuilt in the fourth century BC, could hold some 17,000 spectators.

The Agora and Roman Forum

Northwest of the Acropolis, the **Agora** was the nexus of ancient Athenian city life, where acts of administration, commerce and public assembly competed for space. The site is a confused jumble of ruins, dating from various stages between the sixth century BC and the fifth century AD. For some idea of what you are surveying, head for the **museum** in the rebuilt Stoa of Attalos. At the far corner of the agora precinct sits the nearly intact but distinctly clunky Doric **Temple of Hephaistos**, otherwise known as the **Thissíon** from the exploits of Theseus depicted on its friezes.

The **Roman Forum**, or Roman agora, was built as an extension of the Hellenistic agora by Julius Caesar and Augustus. The best-preserved and most intriguing of the ruins, though, is the graceful, octagonal structure known as the **Tower of the Winds**. It was designed in the first century BC by a Syrian astronomer, and served as a compass, sundial, weather vane and water-clock powered by a stream from one of the Acropolis springs. Each face of the tower is adorned with a relief of a figure floating through the air, personifying the eight winds.

Sýndagma Square, National Gardens and Lykavitós

All roads lead to Platía Syndágmatos – **Sýndagma Square** – with its pivotal metro station. Geared to tourism, with a main post office, banks, luxury hotels and travel agents grouped around, it has convenience but little else to recommend it. Behind the parliament buildings on the square, the **National Gardens** provide the most refreshing spot in the city, a shady oasis of trees, shrubs and creepers, whose duck ponds, cafés and sparkling irrigation channels bring relief from the heat and pollution of summer. South of the gardens stands **Hadrian's Arch**, erected by that Roman emperor to mark the edge of the Classical city and the beginning of his own. Directly behind are sixteen surviving columns of the 104 that originally comprised the **Temple of Olympian Zeus** – the largest in Greece, dedicated by Hadrian in 131 AD.

At the northeastern corner of the National Gardens is the fascinating and much-overlooked **Benáki Museum**, Koumbári 1 (Mon & Wed–Sat 9am–5pm, Thurs 9am–midnight, Sun 9am–3pm; €6, free on Thurs), with a well-organized collection that features Mycenaean jewellery, Greek costumes, memorabilia of the Greek War of Independence and historical documents, engravings and paintings.

Taking the second left off Vassilísis Sofías after the Benáki Museum will bring you to the **Museum of Cycladic and Ancient Greek Art**, Neofýtou Dhouká 4 (Mon & Wed–Fri 10am–4pm, Sat 10am–3pm; €3.50), tops both for its subject and the quality of its display methods.

North, past the posh shopping district of Kolonáki, a path through woods begins its ascent to the summit of **Lykavitós**. On top, a chapel of Áyios Yeóryios provides the main focus. A pair of nearby cafés both have views spectacular enough to excuse their high prices.

Eating, drinking and entertainment

Pláka's stepped lanes can still provide a pleasant evening's setting for a meal, despite the touts and tourist hype. But for good-value, good-quality fare, outlying neighbourhoods such as Psyrrí, Koukáki and Exárhia are better. Quintessentially Greek

The fabulous **National Archeological Museum**, Patissíon 44, is closed for major renovation until mid-2004. All of Schliemann's gold finds from the grave circle at Mycenae, including the so-called Mask of Agamemnon, are usually exhibited here, along with an impressive classical art collection and findings from the island of Thíra, dating from around 1450 BC, contemporary with the Minoan civilization on Crete.

ouzerí and mezedhopolía serve filling *mezédhes* (hors d'oeuvres) along with drinks, adding up to a substantial meal. Bars, cinemas, exhibitions and nightlife venues change frequently, so it's useful to have a copy of the English-language weekly *Athens News* (Fri; ⓦwww.athensnews.gr), which has **listings** for clubs, galleries, concerts and films. The summer **Athens Festival** (early June to late Sept) encompasses classical Greek theatre, established and contemporary dance, classical music, big-name jazz, traditional Greek music and a smattering of rock shows. Most performances take place at the Herodes Atticus theatre, which is memorable in itself on a warm summer's evening. There are also special bus excursions to the great ancient theatre at Epidaurus. The main **festival box office** is currently homeless; consult ⓦwww.greekfestival.gr for its future whereabouts and ticket info.

Restaurants

Amvrosia Dhrákou 3, right by Syngroú-Fix metro, Veḯkoú. The best grill on this pedestrian street; always packed. Good takeaway *ghýros*, or enjoy a whole roast chicken at outdoor tables.

Barba Yannis Emmanouíl Benáki 94, Exárhia. Vast menu of inexpensive oven-cooked food, served indoors and out. Food is best at lunch, but open till 1.30am.

Gardhenia Anastasíou Zínni 29, Koukáki. Basic but inexpensive oven-casserole food in a cool, cavernous premises run by a friendly couple. Open 11am–9pm, closes earlier in midsummer.

Iy Ipiros Platía Ayíou Filíppou, Monastiráki. Long-established lunchtime taverna at the heart of the flea market; good value and great for people-watching.

O Kostas Ekális 7, Platía Varnáva, Pangráti. Among the oldest, cheapest tavernas in town; brief, lovingly cooked menu of bean dishes, meatballs and fried fish, accompanied by palatable bulk wine. Indoor/outdoor tables; closed Sun.

Rozalia Valtetsíou 58, Exárhia. The best all-round *mezédhes*-and-grills taverna near the triangular plaza. Garden open in summer; lunch and supper.

Iy Taverna tou Psyrri Eskhýlou 12, Psyrrí. The only straightforward taverna in a zone dominated by *ouzerí*, this excels at grilled/fried seafood, vegetable starters and wine from basement barrels. Arrive early (supper only) or queue for a table.

O Thanasis Mitropóleos 69, Monastiráki. Reckoned the best *souvláki* and Middle Eastern kebab in this district. Always packed with locals at lunchtime; worth the wait. Take out or eat in.

Ouzerí and mezedhopolía

To Athinaïkon Themistokléous 2, cnr Panepistimíou. Long-established *ouzerí* with marble tables and old posters, popular with local workers at lunch; strong on fresh seafood. Closed Sun.

Kafenio Dhioskouri Dhioskoúron, Pláka. Popular, shady bar/café with an unbeatable view of the ancient agora, where cold drinks and coffees take precedence over slightly pricey snacks./

Evvia Yeoryíou Olympíou 8, Koukáki. Fresh dips and seafood titbits, plus good bulk wine or ouzo; sidewalk seating on this pedestrian street. Daily except Aug.

Listings

Bookshops Compendium, Níkis 28 off Sýndagma, has books on Greece, travel guides (including Rough Guides), magazines and a secondhand section. Eleftheroudhakis, Panepistimíou 17 plus other branches, has the largest foreign-language stock in town, plus maps. Iy Folia tou Vivlíou, arcade at Panepistimíou 25, has a good travel guide/map section.

Embassies and consulates Australia, Tsóha 24 ☎210 64 50 404; Canada, Ioánni Yennadhíou 4 ☎210 72 73 400; Ireland, Vassiléos Konstandínou 7 ☎210 72 32 771; New Zealand, Xenías 24 ☎210 77 10 112; UK, Ploutárhou 1, Kolonáki ☎210 72 36 211; US, Vassilísis Sofías 91 ☎210 72 12 951.

Hospital Evangelismós, with its own metro stop, is the most central, but KAT, way out in Maroússi, is the designated Greater Athens emergency ward.

Internet Skynet, corner Voulís and Apóllonos; Museum Internet Café, Patission 46; Sofokleous.com Internet Café, Stadhíou 5 (open Sun noon).

Laundry Angélou Yerónda 10, off Platía Filomoússou Eterías, Pláka.

Pharmacies These are numerous, but unlike other shops open only Mon–Fri until 2pm. Outside these hours, check any pharmacy window for the nearest duty pharmacy.

Post office Main branch Eólou 100, just off Omónia; more convenient one on Mitropóleos, corner Sýndagma.

The Temple of Poseidon at Sounion

The 70km of shoreline south of Athens has good but highly developed beaches. At weekends the sands fill fast, as do innumerable bars, restaurants and clubs. But for most visitors, this coast's attraction is at the end of the road. **Cape Sounion** is among the most imposing spots in Greece, and on it stands the fifth-century BC **Temple of Poseidon** (daily 10am–sunset; €4), built in the time of Pericles as part of a sanctuary to the sea god. In summer you've faint hope of solitude unless you arrive before the tours do, but the temple is as evocative a ruin as Greece can offer. Doric in style, it preserves sixteen of its thirty-four columns, and the view is stunning. Below the promontory lie several coves, the most sheltered of which is a five-minute walk east from the car park and site entrance. The main Sounion **beach** is more crowded, but has a group of tavernas at the far end, which – considering the location – are reasonably priced. There's a single **campsite** about 5km short of the cape, the *Bacchus* (☎22920 39572). Buses to Sounion leave every thirty minutes from the KTEL terminal on Mavromatéon at the southwest corner of the Pédhion Áreos park in central Athens. They alternate between coastal and inland services, the latter slightly longer and more expensive (the coastal route takes around 2hr).

The Peloponnese

The appeal of the **Peloponnese** is hard to overstate. This southern peninsula seems to have the best of almost everything Greek. Its ancient sites include the Homeric palace of Agamemnon at **Mycenae**, the Greek theatre at **Epidaurus** and the sanctuary of **Olympia**, host to the Olympic Games for a millennium. The medieval remains are scarcely less rich, with the fabulous castle at **Acrocorinth**; the strange tower-houses and frescoed churches of the **Máni**; and the extraordinary Byzantine towns of **Mystra** and **Monemvasiá**. The Peloponnesian **beaches**, especially along the west coast, are among the finest and least developed in the country.

The usual approach from Athens is via modern **Kórinthos**; frequent buses and trains run this way. A more attractive route is by hydrofoil, south from Pireás, via the islands of the Argo-Saronic, to Monemvasiá. From Italy and the Adriatic, **PÁTRA** is the **main port** of the Peloponnese. Its EOT office (☎2610 620 353) and tourist police (☎2610 451 833) are at the Italian ferry terminal entrance, with its main bus station (☎2610 273 936) and train station midway along the waterfront. Pátra's *Youth Hostel* (☎2610 427 278; €9) is cheap, but 1.5km from the centre, at Iróön Polytekhníou 62.

Ancient Corinth

Whoever possessed **CORINTH** – the ancient city that displaced Athens as capital of the Greek province in Roman times – controlled both the trade between northern Greece and the Peloponnese, and the short-cut between the Ionian and Aegean seas. It's unsurprising, therefore, that the city's history is a catalogue of invasions and power struggles, until it was razed by the Romans in 146 BC. The site lay in ruins for a century before being rebuilt, on a majestic scale, by Julius Caesar in 44 BC. Nowadays, the remains of the city occupy a rambling site below the acropolis hill of Acrocorinth, itself littered with medieval ruins. To explore both you need a full day, or better still, to stay close by. The modern village of **ARHÉA KÓRINTHOS** spreads around the main archeological zone, where you'll find good **accommodation** at *Hotel Shadow* (☎27410 31481; ❹); there's also a scattering of **rooms** to rent in the backstreets. There are frequent bus and train services from Athens and Pátra to modern Kórinthos, from where you can catch a local bus to the site.

The main excavated site (daily 8am–5/7pm; €6) is dominated by the remains of the Roman city. You enter from the south side, which leads straight into the

Roman agora. The real focus, however, is a survival from the classical Greek era: the fifth-century BC **Temple of Apollo**, whose seven austere Doric columns stand slightly above the level of the forum. Towering 575m above the lower town, **Acrocorinth** (summer daily 8am–7pm; winter Tues–Sun 8.30am–3pm; free) is an amazing mass of rock still largely encircled by 2km of wall. During the Middle Ages this ancient acropolis of Corinth became one of Greece's most powerful fortresses. It's a 4km climb up (about 1hr), but well worth it. Amid the sixty-acre site, you wander through a jumble of semi-ruined chapels, mosques, houses and battlements, erected in turn by Greeks, Romans, Byzantines, Franks, Venetians and Ottomans.

Mykínes (Mycenae)

The ancient site of **MYCENAE** is tucked into a fold of the hills just 2km north-east of the modern village of **MYKÍNES**, near the highway from Kórinthos to Árgos. Agamemnon's citadel, "well-built Mycenae, rich in gold", as Homer wrote, was uncovered in 1874 by the German archeologist Heinrich Schliemann, whose work was impelled by his conviction that there was a factual basis to Homer's epics. Brilliantly crafted gold and sophisticated architecture bore out the accuracy of Homer's epithets. The buildings unearthed by Schliemann show signs of having been occupied from around 1950 BC until 1100 BC, when the town, though still prosperous, was abandoned. No coherent explanation has been found for this event, but war between rival kingdoms was probably a major factor.

You enter the **Citadel of Mycenae** (daily 8am–5/7pm; €6) through the mighty **Lion Gate**. Inside the walls to the right is **Grave Circle A**, the cemetery which Schliemann believed to contain the bodies of Agamemnon and his followers, murdered on their triumphant return from Troy. In fact the burials date from about three centuries before the Trojan war, but they were certainly royal, and the finds (now in Athens' National Archeological Museum) are among the richest yet unearthed. Schliemann took the extensive **South House**, beyond the grave circle, to be the Palace of Agamemnon. But a much grander building, which must have been the **Royal Palace**, was later discovered on the summit of the acropolis. Rebuilt in the thirteenth century BC, probably at the same time as the Lion Gate, it is, like all Mycenaean palaces, centred on a **Great Court**. The small rooms to the north are believed to have been royal apartments and in one of them the remains of a red stuccoed bath have led to its fanciful identification as the place of Agamemnon's murder. Only the ruling elite were permitted to live within the citadel itself; outside the walls lay the main part of the town. The extensive remains of **merchants' houses** have been uncovered near to the road, beside a second grave circle. A few minutes walk down the road from the main site is the astonishing **Treasury of Atreus**, a royal burial vault entered through a majestic fifteen-metre corridor. Set above the chamber doorway is a lintel formed by two immense slabs of stone, one of which – a staggering 9m long – is estimated to weigh 118 tonnes.

There's a **train station** at Fíkhti, 2km west of Mykínes; most long-distance KTEL buses will also drop you off here. There are numerous bus tours here from Athens, making this a popular day-trip destination. **To stay**, try the *Rooms Dassis* (☎27510 76 123; ❸), *Hotel Belle Hélène* (☎27510 76225; ❹), up the hill towards the site, or one of the two fairly central campsites, *Mycenae* (☎27510 76 121) and *Atreus* (☎27510 76 221). The village has plenty of **restaurants**, all aimed at the lunchtime bus-tour trade.

Náfplio and Epidaurus

NÁFPLIO, a lively, beautifully sited town with a faded elegance, inherited from when it was briefly modern Greece's first capital, makes an attractive base for exploring the Argolídha area or for resting up by the sea. The main fort, the **Palamídhi** (daily 8am–7/5pm; €4), is most directly approached by 899 stone-hewn steps up from Polyzoïdhou street, by the side of a Venetian bastion. Within the walls are three self-contained castles, all built by the Venetians in the 1710s. To the west, the **Acronafplía** (Íts Kalé) fortress occupies the ancient acropolis, whose walls were adapted by successive medieval occupants. The third fort, the photogenic **Boúrtzi**, occupies the islet offshore from the harbour and allowed the Venetians to close the shallow shipping channel with a chain. In the town itself, Platía Syndágmatos, the main square, is the focus of most interest and a great place to relax drinking coffee. **Buses** arrive on Syngroú, just south of the interlocking squares Platía Trión Navárhon and Platía Kapodhístria, while the new **train station** is on the waterfront around 600m north. There are also summertime **hydrofoil** connections to the Argo-Saronic islands, and to Pireás and Monemvasiá. The not always reliable EOT **tourist office** is at 25-Martíou 2 (daily 9am–1pm & 4–8pm; ☏27520 24444). **Hotels** are generally overpriced, the most reasonable being *Hotel Economou* (☏27520 23955; ❸) fifteen minutes' walk from the centre at Argonaftón 22, between the roads to Árgos and Toló. Private **rooms**, most of which cluster on the north slope of the Acronafplía, can also be a good deal. For **eating**, try *Kakanarakis*, Vassilísis Ólgas 18, or *Omorfi Tavernaki* at no. 16.

From the sixth century BC to Roman times, **EPIDAURUS**, 30km east of Náfplio, was a major spa and religious centre; its **Sanctuary of Asclepius** was the most famous of all shrines dedicated to the god of healing. The magnificently preserved 14,000-seat theatre (daily 8am–7/5pm; €6), built in the fourth century BC, merged so well into the landscape that it was rediscovered only in the nineteenth century. Constructed with mathematical precision, it has near-perfect acoustics: from the highest of the 54 tiers of seats you can hear coins dropped in the orchestra. Close by is a small **museum** (Mon noon–5/7pm, Tues–Sun 8am–5/7pm; same ticket as theatre) containing various statuary and frieze fragments. The sanctuary itself encompasses hospitals, dwellings for the priest-physicians, and hotels and amusements for the fashionable visitors. Most people take in Epidaurus as a daytrip from Náfplio, but a memorable experience is to catch an evening classical theatre **performance** (June–Aug Fri & Sat; ❀www.greekfestival.gr). You can sometimes camp near the car park, or **stay** in **LYGOURIÓ**, 5km north, at *Hotel Alkyon* (☏27530 22002; ❸). There is an official campsite on the beach at Néa Epídhavros, *Diamantis* (☏27130 31181). The nearest **restaurant** to the campsite is *Oasis* on the Lygourió road, but *Leonides* in the village proper is better.

Mystra

A glorious, airy place, hugging a steep flank of Taïyettos, **MYSTRA** is an astonishingly complete Byzantine city that once sheltered a population of some 20,000. The castle on its summit was built in 1249 by Guillaume II de Villehardouin, fourth Frankish Prince of the Morea (as the Peloponnese was then known), and together with the fortresses of Monemvasiá and the Máni it guarded his territory. In 1262 the Byzantines drove out the Franks and established the Despotate of Mystra. This isolated triangle of land in the southeastern Peloponnese enjoyed considerable autonomy from Constantinople, flowering as a brilliant cultural centre in the fourteenth and early fifteenth centuries and only falling to the Ottomans in 1460, seven years after the Byzantine capital was conquered.

The site of the **Byzantine city** (daily 8/8.30am–3/7pm; €5) has two entrances on the road up from Néos Mystrás: it makes sense to take the bus to the top entrance, then explore a leisurely downhill route. Following this course, the first identifiable building that you come to is the fourteenth century church of **Ayía Sofía**. The chapel's finest feature is its floor, made from polychrome marble. The **Kástro**, reached by a path that climbs directly from the upper gate, maintains the Frankish design of its thirteenth-century construction, though modified by successive occupants. Heading down from Ayía Sofía, there is a choice of routes. The right fork winds past the ruins of a Byzantine mansion, while the left fork is more interesting, passing the massively fortified **Náfplio Gate** and the vast, multi-storeyed complex of the **Despots' Palace**. At the **Monemvasiá Gate**, linking the upper and lower towns, turn right for the **Pandánassa convent**. The church, whose name means "Queen of the World", is perhaps the finest that survives in the town, a perfectly proportioned blend of Byzantine and Gothic. Further down on this side of the lower town make sure you see the diminutive **Perívleptos monastery**, whose single-domed church, partly carved out of the rock, contains Mystra's most complete cycle of frescoes, almost all of which date from the fourteenth century. The **Mitrópolis**, or cathedral, immediately beyond the gateway, ranks as the oldest of Mystra's churches, built from 1270 onward. A marble slab set in its floor is carved with the symbol of the Paleologos dynasty, the double-headed eagle of Byzantium, commemorating the spot where Constantine XI Paleologos, the last emperor, was crowned in 1449.

The modern village, **NÉOS MYSTRÁS**, is a small roadside community whose half-dozen tavernas are crowded with tour buses by day and revert to a low-key life at night. **Accommodation** is limited: there's the *Hotel Byzantion* (☎27310 83309, ✉byzanhtl@otenet.gr; ❹) and *Khristina Vahaviolou* (☎27310 20047; ❸). Nearby **SPÁRTI** (ancient Sparta, though there's little left to see) is a good alternative base, with the friendly *Cecil*, Paleológou 125, near the top of Paleológou (☎27310 24980; ❹), and *Apollon*, Thermopýlon 84 (☎27310 22491; ❹). One **campsite**, 2.5km from Spárti, is *Paleologio Mystras* (☎27410 22724); closer to Mystra itself is *Castle View* (☎27310 83303). There are a number of reasonable **restaurants** in Spárti, including *Averof*, Paleológou 77, and *Diethnes*, Paleológou 105. Spárti's bus station is at the far eastern end of Lykoúrgou, but buses for Mystrá also depart from the corner of Lykoúrgou and Leonídhou, on the west side of the central square.

Monemvasiá

Set impregnably on a great eruption of rock connected to the mainland by a kilometre-long causeway, the Byzantine seaport of **MONEMVASIÁ** is a place of grand, haunted atmosphere. At the start of the thirteenth century it was the Byzantines' sole possession in the Morea, eventually being taken by the Franks in 1249 after three years of siege. Regained by the Byzantines as part of the ransom for the captured Guillaume de Villehardouin, it served as the chief commercial port of the Despotate of the Morea. At its peak in the Byzantine era, Monemvasiá had a population of almost 60,000. You can get there by road or, more enjoyably, by sea. There are more or less daily **hydrofoils** in season, linking it with Pireás and the Argo-Saronic islands, dropping off midway along the causeway. **Buses** connect with Spárti and Athens three times daily, and with Yíthio twice daily in season only, arriving in the village of **YÉFIRA** on the mainland, where most **accommodation** is located. There are several reasonable hotels near the causeway – try the *Monemvassia* (☎27320 61381; ❹) – plus numerous pensions and rooms. The nearest **campsite**, *Kapsis Paradise*, is 3.5km south of Yéfira near a reasonable beach. Rooms on the rock are much more expensive, but worth the splurge: try the long-established *Malvasia* (☎27320 61323; ❺). The best **taverna** in the old town is *Matoula*.

The **Lower Town** once sheltered forty churches and over 800 homes, an incredible mass of building threaded by an intricate network of alleys. A single main street harbours most of the restored houses, plus cafés, tavernas and a scattering of shops. The foremost monument is the **Mitrópolis**, the cathedral built by Emperor Andronikos II Komnenos in 1293, and the largest medieval church in southern Greece. Across the square, the tenth-century domed church of **Áyios Pétros** was transformed by the Ottomans into a mosque and is now a small **museum** of local finds (unpredictable opening hours). Towards the sea is a third church, the **Khrysafítissa**, with its bell hanging from an old acacia tree in the courtyard. It was restored and adapted by the Venetians in the eighteenth century, when for twenty-odd years they took the Peloponnese from the Ottomans. The climb to the **Upper Town** is highly worthwhile, not least for the solitude. Its fortifications, like those of the lower town, are substantially intact; within, the site is a ruin, though infinitely larger than you could imagine from below.

Yíthio and the Máni peninsula

YÍTHIO, Sparta's ancient port, is the gateway to the dramatic Máni peninsula and one of the south's most attractive seaside towns. Its somewhat low-key harbour, with occasional ferries, has a graceful nineteenth-century waterside. Out to sea, tethered by a long narrow causeway, is the islet of **Marathoníssi** (ancient Kranae), where Paris and Helen of Troy spent their first night after her abduction from Sparta. **Buses** drop you close to the centre of town, and finding **accommodation** should be a matter of a stroll along the waterfront Vassiléos Pávlou, where there is, amongst others, the *Kondogiannis* pension, at no. 19 (☎27330 22518; ❹). There are several summer **campsites** (*Meltemi* and *Yíthio Bay* are good choices) along the huge Mavrovoúni beach, which begins 3km south of town off the Areópoli road. For **eating**, try the *Iy Nautila* or *Korali ouzerís* at the head of the port.

The southernmost peninsula of Greece, the **Máni peninsula**, stretches from Yíthio in the east and Kalamáta in the west down to Cape Ténaro, mythical entrance to the underworld. It is a wild and arid landscape with an idiosyncratic culture and history: nowhere in Greece does a region seem so close to its medieval past. The quickest way into it is to take a bus from Yíthio to **AREÓPOLI**, gateway to the so-called Inner Máni. There are **rooms** at a number of tower-houses, including *Pyrgos Tsimova* (☎27330 51301; ❹), or there's the *Hotel Kouris* on the main square (☎27330 51340; ❼). There are regular buses from here north to Stoúpa, Kardhamýli and Kalamáta (a change in Ítylo is usually involved).

More attractions lie to the north of Areópoli, along the eighty-kilometre road to Kalamáta, which has views as dramatic and beautiful as any in Greece. There are numerous cobbled paths for hiking and a series of small **beaches**, beginning at **ÁYIOS NIKÓLAOS**, which has fish tavernas and rooms such as the *Skafidakia* (☎27210 77698; ❹), and extending more or less through to Kardhamýli. **STOÚPA**, which has possibly the best sands, is now geared very much to British tourism, with several small hotels – friendliest and most reasonable of which is *Lefktron* (☎27210 77322; ❹) – a **campsite** five minutes' walk from Kalógria beach, a supermarket and tavernas. **KARDHAMÝLI**, 8km north, remains a beautiful place despite its commercialization and busy road, with a long pebble beach and a restored tower-house quarter. *Lela's* (☎27210 73541; ❸) has some good rooms. If you get as far as **Kalamáta** – the largest city in the area – then ancient **Pýlos**, the impressive medieval fortresses of **Methóni** and **Koróni** and the superb beach at **Finikoúnda** are all close enough to be taken in as day-trips.

Olympia

The historic resonance of **OLYMPIA**, which for over a millennium hosted the Panhellenic Games, is rivalled only by Delphi or Mycenae. Its site, too, ranks with this company, for although the ruins are confusing, the setting is as perfect as could be imagined: a luxuriant valley of wild olive and plane trees beside the twin rivers of Alfiós and Kladhéos, overlooked by the pine-covered hill of Krónos. The contests at Olympia probably began around the eleventh century BC, slowly developing over the next two centuries from a local festival to a major quadrennial celebration attended by states from throughout the Greek world. From the very beginning, the main Olympic events were athletic, but the great gathering of people expanded the games' importance: nobles and ambassadors negotiated treaties here, while merchants chased contacts and sculptors and poets sought commissions. The games eventually fell victim to the Christian Emperor Theodosius's crackdown on pagan festivities in 391–2 AD, and his successor ordered the destruction of the temples, a process completed by invasion, earthquakes and, finally, by the River Alfiós changing its course to cover the sanctuary site. There it remained, covered by seven metres of silt and sand, until the 1870s.

The entrance to the **ancient site** (daily 8/8.30am–3/7pm; €6, joint ticket with museum €9) leads along the west side of the sacred precinct wall past a group of public and official buildings, including a structure adapted as a Byzantine church. This was originally the studio of Pheidias, the fifth-century BC sculptor responsible for the great gold and ivory cult statue in the focus of the precinct, the great Doric **Temple of Zeus**. Built between 470 and 456 BC, it was as large as the Parthenon and its decoration rivalled the finest in Athens. The Pheidias statue was displayed in the *cella*, and here, too, the Olympian flame was kept alight from the time of the games until the following spring – a tradition continued at an altar for the modern games. The smaller **Temple of Hera**, behind, was the first built here; prior to its completion in the seventh century BC, the sanctuary had only open-air altars, dedicated to Zeus and a variety of other cult gods. Rebuilt in the Doric style in the sixth century BC, it's the most complete structure on the site. Finally, is the 200-metre track of the **Stadium** itself that makes sense of Olympia. The start and finish lines are still there, as are the judges' thrones in the middle and seating banked to each side. The tiers accommodated up to 30,000 spectators, with a smaller number on the southern slope overlooking the **Hippodrome** where chariot races were held. Finally, in the **archeological museum** (Mon 11am/noon–5/7pm, Tues–Sun 8/8.30am–5/7pm; €6), the centrepiece is the statuary from the Temple of Zeus, displayed in the vast main hall. Most famous of the individual sculptures is the **Hermes of Praxiteles**, dating from the fourth century BC; one of the best-preserved of all Classical sculptures, it retains traces of its original paint.

Most people arrive at Olympia via Pýrgos, which has frequent buses to the site, plus numerous connections to Pátra and a couple daily to Kalamáta. The modern town of **OLYMBÍA** has developed to serve the excavations and tourist trade. The **tourist office** is on the south side of Praxitélous Kondhýli (Mon–Sat 9am–3pm; ☎26240 23100). Among **hotels**, the least expensive is *Hercules*, by the church (☎26240 22696; ❷). There is also a **hostel** at Praxitélous Kondhýli 18 (☎26240 22580; €9). The closest **campsite**, *Diana*, just off the main road, has a pool and good facilities. For **eating**, most of the tavernas offer standard tourist meals at inflated prices; honourable exceptions include *O Kladhios*, a beautiful and authentic grill near the river.

Central and northern Greece

Central Greece has an indeterminate character, consisting mostly of vast agricultural plains dotted with rather drab market towns and ringed by low hills. The highlights lie at the fringes: **Delphi** and **Ósios Loukás** above all, and further northeast the forested slopes of **Mount Pílion** with magnificent villages and alluring beaches, or northwest at the unworldly rock-monasteries of **Metéora**. Access to these monasteries is through **Kalambáka**, from where the **Katára pass** over the Píndhos Mountains brings you into **Epirus**, the poorest – but most distinctive – region in mainland Greece. En route lies **Métsovo**, perhaps the easiest location for a taste of mountain life, though blatantly commercialized. Nearby **Ioánnina**, once the stronghold of the notorious Ali Pasha, retains some character, and serves as the main transport hub for trips into the relatively unspoilt villages of the **Zagóri**, around the **Víkos gorge**. The northern provinces of Macedonia and Thrace have only been part of the Greek state since 1913 and 1923 respectively. As such, they stand slightly apart from the rest of the nation – an impression reinforced for visitors by scenery and climate that are essentially Balkan. The only areas to draw more than a sprinkling of summer visitors are **Mount Olympus** and **Halkidhikí**, the latter a beach-playground for the Macedonian capital of **Thessaloníki** and also sheltering the "Monks' Republic" of **Mount Áthos**.

IGOUMENÍTSA is Greece's third **passenger port** after Pireás and Pátra, with almost hourly ferries to Corfu; several daily to and from Italy make it a likely arrival point. The tourist office is next to the customs house on the under-used old quay (daily 8am–2pm; ☎26650 22227). There are frequent bus and train services from Thessaloníki on to Bulgaria, Romania or Turkey, though you should get any necessary visas in Athens.

Delphi

Access to the extraordinary site of **DELPHI**, 150km northwest of Athens, is straightforward: six buses arrive from the capital daily, and services are as frequent from **Livádhia**, the nearest rail terminus. With its position on a high terrace overlooking a great gorge, in turn dwarfed by the ominous crags of Parnassós, it's easy to see why the ancients believed Delphi to be the centre of the earth. But what confirmed this status was the discovery of a chasm that exuded strange vapours and reduced all comers to frenzied, incoherent and obviously prophetic mutterings. For over a thousand years a steady stream of pilgrims toiled their way up the dangerous mountain paths to seek divine direction, until the oracle eventually expired with the demise of paganism in the fourth century AD.

You enter the **Sacred Precinct of Apollo** (Tues–Sun 7.30am–6.45pm, Mon 8.30am–2.45pm; €6) by way of a small agora, enclosed by ruins of Roman porticoes and shops for the sale of votive offerings. The paved **Sacred Way** begins after a few stairs, zigzagging uphill between the foundations of memorials and treasuries to the **Temple of Apollo**. Only the foundations stood when it was uncovered in the 1890s; archeologists, however, re-erected six Doric columns, giving a vertical line to the ruins and providing some idea of its former dominance over the sanctuary. In the innermost part of the temple was a dark cell where the priestess would officiate; no sign of cave or chasm has been found, but it was probably closed by earthquakes. The theatre and stadium used for the main events of the Pythian games are on terraces above the temple. The **theatre**, built in the fourth century BC, was closely connected with Dionysos, god of the arts and wine, who reigned in Delphi over the winter months when Apollo was absent and the oracle was silent. A steep path leads up through pine groves to the stadium, which was banked with stone seats in Roman times. The **museum** (daily 8.30am–2.45pm; free until 2005) contains a collection of Archaic sculpture matched only by finds on the Acropolis in Athens. Its most famous exhibit is *The Charioteer*, one of the few surviving bronzes of the fifth century BC, and likely to retain pride of place once the galleries emerge from a lengthy refurbishment. Following the road east of the sanctuary towards Aráhova, you reach a sharp bend. To the left, marked by niches for votive offerings and the remains of an Archaic fountain house, the celebrated **Castalian spring** still flows from a cleft in the cliffs. Visitors to Delphi were obliged to purify themselves in its waters, usually by washing their hair, though murderers had to take the full plunge. Across and below the road from the spring is the **Marmaria** or Sanctuary of Athena Pronoia (same hours as main site; free), the "Guardian of the Temple". The precinct's most conspicuous building is the **Tholos**, a fourth-century BC rotunda whose purpose is a mystery. Outside the precinct on the northwest side, above the Marmaria, is a **gymnasium**, also from the fourth century BC but later enlarged by the Romans.

The modern village of **DHELFÍ** has a quick turnaround of visitors, so **accommodation** should present few problems. There are over twenty hotels and pensions, plus a few rooms to let, though low seasons are brief: in winter, skiers throng the place. Opt for the en-suite *Sivylla* at Pávlou ke Fredheríkis 9 (☎22650 82335; ❷) or the shared-bath *Odysseus* at Iséa 1, corner Fillelínon (☎22650 82235; ❸). The nearest official **campsite** is *Apollon* (☎22650 82750), 1500m west towards Ámfissa. **Restaurant** options aren't brilliant; try *Taverna Vakhos* on Apóllonos street or the cheaper grill *Gargandouas* near the bus stop. The helpful **tourist office** (Mon–Fri 8am–2.30pm; ☎22650 82900), with up-to-date transport schedules, is in the town hall.

Ósios Loukás

The beautifully positioned monastery of **Ósios Loukás** (daily: May to mid-Sept 8am–2pm & 4–7pm; otherwise 8am–5pm; €3), some 32km east of Delphi in a remote valley under Mt Elikónas, is a pain to reach by public transport but worth the effort – even rent a taxi from **DHÍSTOMO**, the nearest village, which has two affordable **hotels**, including the *America* (☎22670 22079; ❸). The eleventh-century church contains superb mosaics, particularly in the narthex (portico), of events from the life of Christ, including the *Washing of the Disciples' Feet*, the *Resurrection* and, high up in the dome, the *Baptism*.

The Pílion peninsula

With its lush fruit orchards and dense broadleaf forests, the **Pílion peninsula** seems decidedly un-Mediterranean. Water tumbles in rivulets beside every road, and summers are rather cooler than in the rest of central Greece. Pílion villages are idiosyncratic too, scattered affairs with sumptuous mansions and barn-like churches lining their cobbled streets. Add to the scenery and architecture a score of excellent beaches, a tiny ski centre, plus easy access from Athens and Thessaloníki, and it's no wonder that this is a well-loved corner of Greece. Avoid July, August, Easter and Christmas unless you're happy to camp out.

The most visited part of Pílion lies just north and east of the industrial city of **Vólos**. The bus station catering for the peninsula's villages is at Grigoríou Lambráki, a short walk south of the train station. If time is limited, the best single targets are the recognized showcases of Makrinítsa and Vyzítsa. **MAKRINÍTSA** has become very commercialized, with eating much better at *Kritsa* in neighbouring Portariá village, though you can stay affordably at *Hotel Theophilos* (☎24280 99435; ❸). Remoter **VYZÍTSA** has equally good bus connections, with budget accommodation in the *Xenon Thetis* (☎24230 86211; ❸), west of the square, and the decent *Taverna O Yiorgaras* on the road east. Generally, you must go to extremes (literally) to save money in Pílion; at the end of the bus lines to the southern peninsula, in the coastal hamlets of **KATIYIÓRYIS** and **PLATANIÁ**, are (respectively) *Flisvos Rooms* (☎24230 71071; ❸), with an excellent ground-floor fish restaurant, and *Hotel Platania* (☎24230 71266; ❸), with more good eats at its restaurant *To Steki*.

The largest village on the Pílion is **ZAGORÁ**, destination of fairly regular buses northeast across the peninsula's summit ridge. Zagorá is more appealing than first impressions suggest, and unlike its seashore neighbours has a life independent of tourism. You're also more likely to find a **room** here in season, for example at *Yiannis Halkias* (☎24260 22159; ❷), than down at **HOREFTÓ** beach, 8km below, where you might try *Hotel Erato* (☎24260 22445; ❸). In Horeftó, eat at all-year *Ta Dhelfinia*, whilst in Zagorá choice is ample, starting with *Venizelos* (under *Rooms Halkias*). Just before Zagorá, a junction funnels traffic southeast to **TSAN-GARÁDHA**, also the terminus of two daily buses from Vólos. Though nearly as extensive as Zagorá, it may not seem so, being divided into four distinct quarters along several kilometres of road. Reasonable accommodation is scarce, though try *Villa ton Rodhon* (☎24260 49340; ❹) in Ayía Paraskeví. Eating out is complicated by poor value and off-season closures; most people do so at **MOÚRESSI**, 3km north-west, where several year-round tavernas dish out Pílion specialities at fairly moderate prices. **KISSÓS**, still further towards Zagorá, is another possibility for lodging and dining, with its inexpensive *Rooms Sofia Gloumi* (☎24260 31267; ❸) and cosy *Makis Taverna*.

Most visitors, however, stay at several nearby beaches, the best on this shore of the peninsula. **ÁYIOS IOÁNNIS**, 6km below Kissós, is an overblown resort with plenty of accommodation – you can try *Hotel Evripidis* (☎24260 31338; ❸), and eat affordable fish at *Posidhonas*. If it's too busy for your tastes, head south along the sand, past the crowded campsite, to **Papá Neró beach** or further still to postcard-perfect **DAMOÚHARI**, with its tiny ruined castle and fishing anchorage. The area's most scenic beach is reached by following a winding 7-km road from the south end of Tsangarádha to **Mylopótamos**, packed out in high season. For more solitude, you can undertake the ninety-minute walk from Damoúhari to **Fakístra beach**, even lovelier, but without facilities.

Kalambáka and Metéora

Few places are more exciting to arrive at than **KALAMBÁKA**. The shabby town itself you hardly notice, for your eye is immediately drawn to the weird grey cylinders of rock overhead. These are the outlying monoliths of the extraordinary valley of **Metéora**. To the right you can make out the monastery of Ayíou Stefánou, firmly planted on a massive pedestal; beyond stretches a chaos of spikes, cones and stubbier, rounded cliffs – river sediment twisted into bizarre shapes as it flowed into the sea that covered the Plain of Thessaly some 25 million years ago. The earliest religious communities in the valley emerged during the late tenth century, when hermits made their homes in the caves that score many of the rocks. In 1336 they were joined by two monks from Mount Áthos, one of whom established the first monastery here. Today, put firmly on the map by films such as the James Bond *For Your Eyes Only*, the four most visited monasteries are essentially museums. Only two others, Ayías Triádhos and Ayíou Stefánou, continue to function with a primarily religious purpose. Each monastery levies an **admission charge** of €2 and operates a strict **dress code**: skirts for women, long trousers for men and covered arms for both sexes.

From Kastráki the road loops between huge outcrops of rock before reaching a path to the left, which winds up a low rock to the fourteenth-century **Ayíou Nikoláou Anápavsa** (9am–3.30pm, closed Fri). A small, 1980s-restored monastery, this has some superb sixteenth-century frescoes in its main chapel. Some 250m past the car park and stairs to Ayíou Nikoláou, a clear path leads up a ravine between assorted monoliths; soon, at a fork, you've the option of bearing left for Megálou Meteórou or right to Varlaám, the two also linked by a higher access road. **Varlaám** (summer 9am–2pm & 3.20–5pm, winter 9am–3pm, closed Thurs, also Fri winter) ranks as one of the oldest and most beautiful monasteries in the valley. It also preserves its old ascent tower; until 1923 the only way of reaching the monasteries was by being hauled up in a net drawn by rope and windlass, or by the equally perilous retractable ladders. Today, however, you reach Varlaám safely, if breathlessly, via steps cut into the side of the rock. From the fork below Varlaám the path system also takes you northwest to **Megálou Meteórou** (9am–5pm, closed Tues). This is the grandest of the monasteries and also the highest, built 400m above the valley floor. Next you follow trails, or the main access road east, ignoring the turning back down for Kastráki, until you reach the signed access path for the tiny, compact convent of **Roussánou** (daily summer 9am–6pm, winter 9am–1pm & 3.20–6pm), approached in the final moment across a dizzying bridge from an adjacent rock. This has perhaps the most extraordinary site of all the monasteries, its walls built right on the edge of a sheer pinnacle. It's less than 30min from Roussánou to the vividly frescoed **Ayías Triádhos** (daily summer 9am–6pm, winter 9am–12.30pm & 3–5pm, closed Thurs), approached up 130 steps carved through a tunnel in the rock. Although Ayías Triádhos teeters above a deep ravine and its little garden ends in a precipitous drop, there is a 3-km, well-marked cobbled trail at the bottom of the monastery's steps back to Kalambáka, which saves a tedious retracing of steps. **Ayíou Stefánou** (9am–2pm & 3.30–6pm, closed Mon), the last of the monasteries, lies a further fifteen minutes' walk east of Ayías Triádhos; bombed in World War II, it's the one to omit if you've run out of time.

Visiting the monasteries demands a full day, which means staying two nights in Kalambáka or at the village of Kastráki, right in the shadow of the rocks. **KALAMBÁKA** is characterless but pleasant enough, with plentiful **accommodation**. Good budget choices in the quieter, upper portion of town towards Kastráki include *Hotel Meteora*, Ploutárhou 13 (☎24320 22367; **③**), and *Koka Roka Rooms*, Kanári 21 (☎24320 24554; ✉kokaroka@yahoo.com; **③**); **eat** at *O Houtos*, 500m out on the Tríkala road. **KASTRÁKI** is twenty minutes' walk out of Kalambáka; there are regular buses in season. Along the way you pass the busy *Vrahos*, the first of two **campsites**, offering rock-climbing lessons (☎24320 22293); the other, *The Cave* (☎24320 24802), is smaller but quieter, grassier and incomparably set under the pinnacles. Kastráki also has hundreds of **rooms** to rent, mostly better value than in Kalambáka (though avoid the main road); good examples include those offered by *The Cave* (**2**), *Ziogas Rooms* (☎24320 24037; **4**) and *Hotel Tsikelli* (☎ 24320 22438; **4**). **Eat** at *Paradhissos* on the through road, for grills and dips, or *Bakalarkaia* below the square and church, for cheap fried hake and house wine.

The Katára pass

West of Kalambáka, the **Katára pass** cuts across the Píndhos mountains to link Thessaly and Epirus. The route is one of the most spectacular in the country, covered by just two buses daily between **Tríkala** and **Ioánnina**. **MÉTSOVO** spreads just west of the Katára pass, a high mountain town built on two sides of a ravine and encircled by a mighty range of peaks. From below the main road, eighteenth- and nineteenth-century stone houses, with their wooden balconies and modern tile roofs, spill down the hillside to the main *platía*, where a few old men still loiter after Sunday Mass, magnificent in full traditional dress. The town **museum** occupies the Arhondikó Tosítsa (tours 9.30am–1.30pm & 4–6pm, closed Thurs; €3), an eighteenth-century mansion restored to full past glory, with panelled rooms, rugs and a fine collection of crafts and costumes. For **eating**, the restaurant of *Hotel Athinai* is excellent for casserole dishes. Métsovo has quite a range of **accommodation** and apart from around July 26, date of the main local **festival**, and during skiing season, you'll have little difficulty getting a room. Try the *Hotel Athinai* (☎26560 41725; **2**), oldest hotel in Epirus but en suite, or *Filoxenia* (☎26560 41021; **3**), below the platía with ravine views from some rooms.

Descending from Métsovo, you approach **IOÁNNINA** through more spectacular folds of the Píndhos Mountains. The fortifications of the old town, former capital of the Albanian Muslim chieftain Ali Pasha, are punctuated by towers and minarets. From this base Ali, "the Lion of Ioannina", prised from the Ottoman Empire a fiefdom encompassing much of western Greece, an act of rebellion that foreshadowed wider defiance in the Greeks' own War of Independence. Disappointingly, most of the city is modern and undistinguished; however, the fortifications of Ali's citadel, the **Kástro**, survive more or less intact. Apart from the Kástro, the most enjoyable quarter is the old **bazaar** area, outside the citadel's main gate.

The island of **Nissí** is served by water-buses (every 30min) from the quay northwest of the Froúrio. Its village, founded during the sixteenth century, is flanked by several beautiful, diminutive monasteries, with the best thirteenth-century frescoes in **Filanthropinón**. You can stay on the island at the basic **rooms** kept by the Dellas family (☎26510 84494; **2**), and **eat** at their *ouzerí* downstairs. In the city itself, budget lodging is in the area between the bazaar and the central plazas; try *Esperia*, Kapláni 3 (☎26510 24111; **3**). The pleasant lakeshore *Limnopoula* **campsite** (☎26510 25265) is 2km out of town on the Pérama/airport road. Besides the Nissí *ouzerí*, more ordinary **tavernas** stand immediately opposite the citadel gate, where two rival grills *Tò Kourmanio* and *Tò Manteio* vie for your custom. The main **bus** station is at Zozimádhon 4, serving most points north and west; a smaller terminal at Bizaníou 19 connects villages south and east. The **tourist office** at Dhodhónis 39, south of the centre, can provide information on the whole Epirus region.

Zagóri and the Víkos Gorge

Few parts of Greece are more surprising, or beguiling, than **Zagóri**, the infertile region to the north of Ioánnina. It's the last place you'd expect to find some of Greece's most imposing architecture, yet the *Zagorohória*, as the region's 46 villages are called, are full of grand stone mansions, enclosed by semi-fortified walls and with deep-eaved gateways opening on to immaculately cobbled streets. In the northwest corner of the region, the awesome trench of the **Víkos Gorge** – its walls nearly 1000m high in places – separates the villages of western and central Zagóri. A hike through or around Víkos is the highlight of any visit to the area, the usual starting point being the handsome village of **MONODHÉNDHRI**. There are twice-daily buses from Ioánnina (Mon, Wed & Fri only); the only real budget option here is *Katerina's Pension* (☎26530 71300; ❷). The most used **path into the gorge**, marked as the long-distance O3, starts beside Áyios Athanásios church; the route is fairly straightforward, and it takes under five hours to reach the point where the gorge begins to open out. From here the best option is to follow the O3 path to **MEGÁLO PÁPINGO**, two hours further on. A hillside village of fifty or so houses along a tributary of the Voïdhomátis river, it offers abundant if pricey **accommodation**; most reasonable are *Xenonas Kalliopi* (☎26530 41081; ❹) and *Pension Koulis* (☎26530 41138; ❹). Around half the size of its neighbour, **MIKRÓ PÁPINGO** just uphill has one main inn, *Xenon O Dhias* (☎26530 41257; ❹). Bus services to Ioánnina are erratic (in theory four weekly in summer). The alternative is to trail-walk west two and a half hours from Pápingo to the village of **Káto Klidhoniá**, where there are regular buses along the Kónitsa–Ioánnina highway.

Thessaloníki

Second city of Greece, **THESSALONÍKI** feels more Balkan-European and modern than Athens. During the Byzantine era, it was the second city after Constantinople, reaching a cultural "Golden Age" until the Ottoman conquest in 1430. As recently as the 1920s, the city's population was as mixed as any in the Balkans: besides the Ottoman Turks, who had been in occupation for close on five centuries, there were Slavs, Albanians and the largest European **Jewish** community of the period – 80,000 at its peak. Today, however, there is little to detain you aside from the excellent archeological museum, and a couple of frescoed/mosaic-ed Byzantine churches. You can also arrange a permit for Mt Áthos here, or make onward connections to the Halkidhikí beaches, and to Bulgaria or Turkey. The **Archeological Museum** (Mon 10.30am/12.30–5/7pm, Tues–Sun 8.30am–3/7pm; €4) is a few paces from the White Tower, the last surviving bastion of the city's medieval walls. The museum contains finds from the tombs of Philip II of Macedon and others at the ancient Macedonian capital of Aegae (modern Veryína). They include startling amounts of gold and silver – masks, crowns, necklaces, earrings, bracelets – all of extraordinary craftsmanship, although the exhibits are now depleted following the transfer of the star items back to a purpose-built subterranean gallery at Veryína itself (see p.451). Among the city's many **churches**, the best three are Áyios Yeóryios, originally a Roman rotunda, decorated with superb mosaics emerging from long restoration; Áyios Dhimítrios, with more seventh-century mosaics of the patron saint in various guises; and still-later Ayía Sofía, with mosaics of the *Ascension* and the *Virgin Enthroned*.

The **train station** on the west side of town is a short walk from the central grid of streets and the waterfront. Except for Halkidhikí services, **buses** use a new joint KTEL terminal 3km southwest of the centre; city bus #1 goes there. From the **airport**, 16km out at Mikrá, bus #78 runs hourly to the train station and KTEL terminal (6am–11pm). The **tourist office** is at Platía Aristotélous 8 (Mon–Sat 7.30am–3pm; ☎2310 271888).

Outside the fair-and-festival season (Sept–Nov), **hotel** vacancies are easy to find, though not, as a rule, attractive or good value. Shun the poor-value "budget" hotels clustered along the noisy beginning of busy Egnatía in favour of *Orestias Kastoria* at Agnóstou Stratiótou 14 (☎2310 276517; ❸); *Nea Mitropolis*, just north of Egnatía at Syngroú 22 (☎2310 525540; ❸); or *Bill*, Syngroú 29 corner Amvrossíou (☎2310 537666; ❹). To **eat**, *Platia Athonos* on Dhragoúmi, an alley off Platía Áthonos, is one of the more dependable of several *ouzerís* in this area; *Koumbarakia*, behind a Byzantine chapel at Egnatía 140, is another option. **Bars** and **clubs** concentrate in the rehabilitated warehouse area southeast of Platía Eleftherías known as Ladhádhika; *Zythos*, Platía Katoúni 5, is the best bar-restaurants, with dozens of well-kept foreign beers. The main indoor **music** venue is the multidisciplinary complex *Mylos*, out in an old flour mill at Andhréou Yeoryíou 56, where you'll find more bars, a summer cinema and exhibition galleries.

Listings

Veryína (Ancient Aegae)

In 1977, archeologists discovered the burial sanctuary of the ancient Macedonian dynasty which culminated in Alexander the Great at the hitherto insignificant village of **VERYÍNA**. The four **Royal Tombs** (Mon 12.30–5/7pm, Tues–Sun 8am–5/7pm; €8) constitute the focus of an unmissable underground museum, featuring delicate gold and silver funerary artefacts, the facades of the tombs, and the bones of the deceased in ornate ossuaries. It's easy to make this a day-trip from Thessaloníki: hourly buses ply to Véria, from where onward buses cover the final 20min to Veryína village.

Mount Olympus

Highest, most magical and most dramatic of all Greek mountains, **Mount Olympus** – the mythical seat of the gods – rears straight up nearly 3000m from the shores of the Thermaïkos gulf, south of Thessaloníki. Dense forests cover its lower slopes and its wild flowers are gorgeous. If you're equipped with decent boots and warm clothing, no special expertise is necessary to reach the top between mid-June and October, though it's a long hard pull, and at any time of year Olympus must be treated with respect: its weather is notoriously fickle and it regularly claims lives. The usual approach is via **LITÓHORO** on the eastern slopes. The train station is 9km from this village, with rare connecting buses; otherwise get a bus direct from Thessaloníki. Cheapest **accommodation** is the plain *Hotel Markesia*, Dhionýsou 5 (℡23520 81831; **②**), just down from main street 28-Oktovríou. Best **eats** are at *Dhamaskinia*, uphill on Vassiléos Konstandínou, or *Psistaria Zeus*, at the start of the road up the mountain. You'd do well to buy a proper **map** of the range in Athens or Thessaloníki (#31 Road Editions 1:50,000 is adequate). Four to five hours' walking along the well-marked, scenic E4 long-distance path up the Mavrólongos canyon brings you to **Priónia**, also the end of the much longer road in. From Priónia there's a sharper three-hour trail-climb to the *Spilios Agapitos* **refuge** (℡23520 81800; **①**; closed mid-Oct to mid–May). It's best to stay overnight here, as you need to make an early start for the three-hour ascent to **Mýtikas**, the highest peak (2917m); the summit frequently clouds up towards midday. The path continues behind the refuge, reaching a signposted fork above the tree line in about an hour; straight on, then right, takes you to Mýtikas via the ridge known as Kakí Skála, while the abrupt right reaches the *Yiosos Apostolidhis* **hut** in one hour (no phone; **①**; closed mid-Sept to July), from where there's an enjoyable loop down to the **Gortsiá** trailhead and from there back down into the Mavrólongos canyon, via the medieval monastery of Ayíou Dhionysíou.

Halkidhikí and Mount Áthos

The squid-shaped peninsula of **Halkidhikí** begins at a perforated edge of lakes east of Thessaloníki and extends into three prongs of land – Kassándhra, Sithonía and Áthos – trailing like tentacles into the Aegean Sea. **Kassándhra** and **Sithonía** are

⑫

GREECE | Central and northern Greece

Thessaloníki's beach-playground, hosting some of the largest holiday resorts in Greece. Both are linked to Thessaloníki by bus, but neither peninsula is easy to travel around on public transport. You really have to pick a spot and stay there, perhaps renting a scooter for local excursions. Áfytos is by far the most attractive place on Kassándhra, while Sithónia is marginally less packaged, with low-key resorts at Kalamítsi, Pórto Koufó and Toróni. **Mount Áthos**, the easternmost peninsula, is in all ways separate: a "Holy Mountain" whose monastic population, semi-autonomous from the Greek state, excludes all women – even as visitors. For men who wish to experience Athonite life, all that's required is a visit to the pilgrims' office in Thessaloníki (detailed above) to arrange the necessary admission paperwork. You need to be over 18, and demonstrate a religious or scholarly interest in Áthos, to be given an entry pass allowing up to four days' stay on the holy mountain, moving to a different monastery each night. A visit is highly recommended, though you can't hope to see more than a fraction of the twenty main monasteries in the time allotted. Choose between the "museum monasteries" of Meyístis Lávras, Vatopedhíou, Ivíron or Dhionysíou with their wealth of treasures and art, or the more modestly endowed cloisters where the brothers will make more time for you, such as Osíou Grigoríou, Pandokrátoros and the Serbian foundation of Hilandharíou.

Both Ierissós and Ouranópoli, villages at the top of the peninsula and the usual gateways to Áthos, are served by several daily buses from Thessaloníki. **IERISSÓS** has many **rooms** to let and the friendly if slightly noisy *Hotel Marcos* (☎23770 22518; ❸); in summer boats sail four days weekly at 8.30am, weather permitting, to the monasteries of Áthos's northeast shore. It's often best to continue to the busy resort of **OURANÓPOLI**, the last settlement before you reach the monastic domains. **Accommodation** is plentiful, with numerous rooms and a few budget hotels, such as *Diana* (☎23770 71052; ❷). From Ouranópoli the most reliable ferries depart for the southwest shore of monastic Áthos, daily at 9.45am. Allow time to queue up at the Grafío Proskynitón (Pilgrims' Bureau) to exchange your reservation from the Thessaloníki office for a full-fledged **pass** (€30, €15 for students) allowing you to stay overnight at any of the major monasteries. From the usual entry port of **DHÁFNI** on the southwest coast, there are more possibilities of moving about by boat and bus, but walking between the religious communities on a dwindling trail network is an integral part of the Athonite experience, so you should be reasonably fit and self-sufficient in dry snack food, as the two meals offered each day tend to be spartan. Most monks pay scant attention to foreigners, so you get more of an idea of the magnificent scenery and architecture than of the religious life, though it's hard to avoid tangling with the disorienting daily schedule, dictated by the hours of sun and darkness. Also, many monasteries have become so visited that you must book a bed by phone in advance; the Pilgrims' Bureau provides a list of contact numbers.

The southern Aegean islands

The **Argo–Saronic** islands are the nearest archipelago to Athens and one of the busiest: more than any other group, these islands are at their best outside peak season. To the east, the **Cyclades** is the most satisfying Greek archipelago for island-hopping. The majority of these islands are arid and rocky, with brilliant-white, cubist architecture. The impact of tourism is haphazard, and though some English is spoken in most places, a slight detour could have you groping for your Greek phrasebook. **Íos**, the original hippie island, is still a backpackers' paradise, while **Mýkonos** – with its teeming old town, nude beaches and highly sophisticated clubs and bars (many of them gay) – is by far the most visited of the group. After these, **Páros**, **Sífnos**, **Náxos** and **Thíra** are currently most popular, their beaches and main towns drastically overcrowded in July and August. The one major ancient site worth making time for is **Delos**, the commercial and religious centre of the classical Greek world. Almost all of the Cyclades are served by boats from Pireás, but there are also ferries from Rafína.

Further east still, the **Dodecanese** islands lie so close to the Turkish coast that some are almost within hailing distance of the shore. They were only included in the modern Greek state in 1948 after centuries of occupation by Crusaders, Ottomans and Italians. Medieval **Rhodes** is the most famous, but almost every one has its classical remains, its Crusaders' castle, its traditional villages and grandiose Art Deco public buildings. The main islands are connected almost daily with each other, and none is hard to reach. Rhodes is the main transport hub, with services to Turkey, Cyprus and Israel, as well as connections with Crete, the northeastern Aegean islands, the Cyclades and the mainland (Thessaloníki and Pireás).

Ídhra

The port and town of **ÍDHRA**, with its tiers of stone mansions and tiled white houses climbing up from a perfect horseshoe harbour, forms a beautiful spectacle. Unfortunately, from Easter to September it's packed to the gills, and the seafront becomes one uninterrupted outdoor café (there are no private cars on Ídhra). Dozens of mansions were built here, mostly during the eighteenth century, on the accumulated wealth of a merchant fleet which traded as far afield as America. There's no lack of expensive cafés and **restaurants** on the waterfront, but better value is to be had inland, for example at *Xeri Elia* and the much-loved *Yeitoniko* (alias *Manolis & Christina's*). **Hotels** and pensions are overpriced; reasonable-value places include *Erofili* (☎22980 54049; ❷) and, up the hill, *Hydra* (☎22980 52102, ✉hydrahotel@aig.forthnet.gr; ❹). As far as **beaches** are concerned, on the opposite side of the harbour a coastal path leads to a pebbly but popular stretch, just before **KAMÍNI**, where there are a pair of reasonable pensions – try *Antonia* (☎22980 52481; ❸) – and a good year-round taverna, *Christina*. Thirty minutes' walk beyond Kamíni (or a boat ride from the port) will bring you to **VLYHÓS**, a small hamlet with pricier rooms and three tavernas. Camping is tolerated here, and the swimming between the pebble shore and an islet is good.

Sífnos

Although **Sífnos** often gets crowded, its modest size means that wherever you stay you can reach the rest of the island by the excellent bus service or on foot over a network of old stone pathways. **KAMÁRES**, the port, is tucked at the base of high bare cliffs in the west. **Accommodation** can be expensive – the best budget option is *Hotel Stavros* (☎22840 31641; ❷), towards the beach from the quay. There are other places like *Mosha Pension* (☎22840 31719; ❸) in Ayía Marína, behind the far end of the beach, which has a mediocre **campsite**. The best **meals** are at the quayside *Meropi*. A steep twenty-minute bus ride takes you up to **APOLLONÍA**, a rambling collage of flagstones, belfries and flowered courtyards. The island bank, post office and tourist police are all here, but rooms, though plentiful, are even more likely to be full than at Kamáres. Outside of high season, there will be vacancies along the road to Fáros; quieter, and pricier, digs are along the stair-street north of the main square, or you can apply to the travel agency Aegean Thesaurus (☎22840 31151, ✉aegean@thesaurus.gr). As an alternative base, head for **KÁSTRO**, a forty-minute trail walk or regular bus ride below Apollonía on the east coast; built on a rocky outcrop with an almost sheer drop to the sea on three sides, this medieval capital of the island retains much of its character. There are many rooms at the lower end of the village, such as *Marianna* (☎22840 33681; ❷). At the southern end of the island, 12km from Apollonía by frequent bus, lies the busy beach resort of **PLATÝS YIALÓS**. It has a poor campsite and numerous rooms to let, as well as tavernas, bakeries and supermarkets. For something more original, ask the driver to drop you off at the bus stop for **Chrissopigí** (from where it's a ten-minute walk down a path), where the beach is less crowded, there is an excellent taverna and a postcard-perfect monastery. Heading northeast to **FÁROS**, you will find a mediocre sandy beach, plenty of rooms and good, cheap tavernas. Perhaps the finest walk is through the hills to **VATHÝ**, around three hours from Apollonía's Katavatí "suburb". A fishing and ex-pottery village on a stunning funnel-shaped bay, Vathý is the most attractive base on the island: there are **rooms** to let, the cheapest being *Manolis* (☎22840 71111; ❷) which is also a **taverna**, as is *To Tsikali,* behind the tiny monastery. An alternative route here is by regular bus from Apollonía.

Mýkonos

Mýkonos has become the most popular and expensive of the Cyclades, visited by nearly a million tourists a year. But if you don't mind the crowds the upscale capital is one of the most beautiful of all island towns. Dazzlingly white, it's the archetypal island-postcard image, with sugar-cube buildings stacked around a cluster of seafront fishermen's dwellings.

The airport is about 3km out of **MÝKONOS TOWN** (also known as **HÓRA**), a short taxi ride away. **Ferries** and cruise ships dock at the northern jetty, where you'll be met by a horde of owners hustling hotels and rooms; you'd do better to proceed to the helpful Mýkonos **accommodation centre** in town (☎22890 23160) – be aware that a private room is likely to be cheaper than staying in a hotel on the nearby beaches. As for **hotels** in town, out of season you might consider *Philippi* at Kaloyéra 25 (☎22890 22294, ☻chrico@otenet.gr; ❹). Otherwise there are very lively official **campsites** at Paradise (☎22890 22852, ☻paradise@paradise .myk.forthnet.gr) and Paránga (☎22890 24578) beaches, of which the latter has a nicer setting. Back in town, the harbour curves around past the dull, central beach, behind which is the **bus station** for Áyios Stéfanos. Continue along

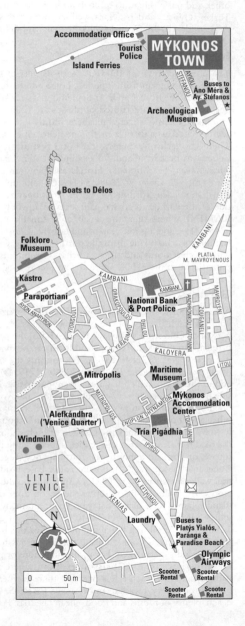

the seafront to the southern jetty for the **tourist police** (☎22890 22482) and kaïkia to Delos. A second **bus terminus**, for beaches to the south of town, is right at the other end of Hóra, beyond the windmills.

Around Kaloyéra is a promising area for **food**. Cheaper eats are at *Nikos*, behind the town hall, and *Yiavroútas* on Mitropóleos. **Drinking** haunts are over in the south of the town (known as "Little Venice"); try *Kástro's* or *Caprice* for an early-evening cocktail, moving on later to *Montparnasse*, which is fairly swanky. The **nightlife** in town is every bit as good – and expensive – as it's cracked up to be. Among the most durable nightspots are *Remezzo*, with sunset views, and *Pierro's*, once the main draw for the island's substantial gay contingent, but now mixed. Just off K. Yiorgoúli, the *Skandinavian Bar-Disco* is a cheap, nonstop party bar, while *Cavo Paradiso* near Paradise camping is the after-hours club for party animals.

The closest decent **beach** is **Áyios Stéfanos** (4km north), connected by a very regular bus service. Better to make for **Platýs Yialós**, 4km south, though you won't be alone there. A kaïki service from Mýkonos town connects almost all the beaches east of Platýs Yialós: gorgeous, pale-sand **Paránga** beach, popular with campers; **Paradise**, well sheltered by its headland, predominantly nudist, with two tavernas; and **Super Paradise**, which has a friendly atmosphere and another taverna and two bars. Probably the island's best beach is **Eliá**: it's a broad sandy stretch with a verdant backdrop, split in two by a rocky area. It boasts a few restaurants, including the excellent *Mattheos*, and an aquatic theme park, Watermania (10am–midnight; €12; free daily bus from Hóra).

Delos

The remains of ancient **DELOS** (Tues–Sun 8.30am–3pm; €5), though skeletal and swarming now with lizards and tourists, give some idea of the past grandeur of this sacred isle a few sea-miles west of Mýkonos. The kaïki trip gives you three hours on the island – barely enough time to take in the main attractions, but it's no longer possible to stay the night. Delos' ancient claim to fame is as the place where Leto gave birth to the divine twins Artemis and Apollo; one of the first things you see on arrival is the **Sanctuary of Apollo**, while three Temples of Apollo stand in a row along the Sacred Way. To the east towards the museum you pass the **Sanctuary of Dionysos** with its marble phalluses' on tall pillars. To the north is the **Sacred Lake** where Leto gave birth: guarding it is a group of lions, masterfully executed in the seventh century BC. Set out in the other direction from the agora and you enter the residential area, known as the **Theatre Quarter**. There are some nice mosaics to be seen: one in the **House of the Trident**, better ones in the **House of the Masks**, including a vigorous portrayal of Dionysos riding on a panther's back. The **Theatre** itself, though much ravaged, offers some fine views.

Páros and Andíparos

With a little of everything – old villages, monasteries, fishing harbour and a labyrinthine capital – **Páros** is a good point to begin your island wanderings, with boat connections to virtually the entire Aegean, though things have become nearly as expensive and commercialized here as on Mýkonos. All ferries dock at **PARIKÍA**, the main town, with its ranks of white houses punctuated by the occasional Venetian-style building and church domes. Just outside the central clutter, the town also has one of the most interesting churches in the Aegean – the **Ekatondapylianí**, or "Church of One Hundred Gates". The original construction was overseen in the sixth century by Isidore of Miletus but the work was carried out by his pupil Ignatius. The **Archeological Museum** (Tues–Sun 8.30am–3pm; €1.50) is just behind the church; its prize exhibit is a portion of the Parian Chronicle, a social and cultural history of Greece up to 264 BC, engraved in marble.

You'll be met off the ferry by locals offering rooms; avoid offers of properties to the north as they're invariably a long walk away, though there is a crowded **campsite**, the *Koula*, at the northern end of the town beach. The better *Krios Camping* (☎22840 21100) is across the bay to the north. Among pensions and hotels not block-booked by tour operators, try the hostel-like *Pension Festos* (☎22840 21635; €12 per bed) and the smart *Hotel Argonauta*, close to the National Bank (☎22840 21440, ⓔhotel@argonauta.gr; ❹), which also has a reliable restaurant. Other **food** options include *Trata* behind the ancient cemetery, which is good for fish. The most popular cocktail bars extend along the seafront, tucked into a series of open squares.

The second village of Páros, **NÁOUSSA** (reached by regular buses leaving from the stop 100m or so to the left off where ferries dock), was until the early 1990s an unspoilt town, but a rash of new concrete hotels has all but swamped its character. Despite this development, there are some pleasant beaches nearby, while rooms are marginally cheaper than in Parikía – track them down with the help of the tourist office just over the bridge, west from the harbour. There are two **campsites**, out of town towards **Kolymbíthres** and **Sánta María** beaches, both better than the mosquito-plagued one in Parikía, and various **tavernas**, all of which are pretty good, specializing in fresh fish and seafood: start with *O Barbarossas* or *Vengera*.

There are boats from Parikía to the island of **ANDÍPAROS** (hourly in high season; 40min), making it a convenient day-trip. There is plenty of **accommodation**, including a campsite. The best beaches are at Psaralíki, Glýfa, Ághios Yeóryios and Kalógeros; kaïkia make daily trips around the island, stopping at them all, as well as the impressive **cave** (daily 10.45am–3.45pm; €3).

Náxos

Náxos is the largest and most fertile of the Cyclades. The Venetian occupation left towers and fortified mansions scattered throughout the island, while medieval Cretan refugees bestowed a singular character upon the eastern settlements. A long causeway protecting the harbour connects **NÁXOS TOWN** with the islet of Palátia, where the huge stone portal of an unfinished **Temple of Apollo** still stands. Most of the town's life goes on down by the port or in the streets just behind it; stepped lanes behind lead up past crumbling balconies and through low arches to the fortified **kástro**, from where the Venetians ruled over the Cyclades. In the same area you will find the **Archeological Museum** (Tues–Sun 8.30am–3pm; €3), with an important early sculpture collection and a Hellenistic mosaic on the roof terrace. Tourism has reached such a level that an annexe of purpose-built **accommodation** extends south of the town centre, since rooms downtown are of a uniformly poor standard and overpriced. The helpful private **tourist office** near the jetty (summer daily 9am–11pm; ☎22850 25201) can book rooms around the island. In-town **hotels** are better on the cooler north slope of the *kástro*: best budget options are the *Dionyssos* youth hostel (☎22850 22331; €15) and the *Pension Katell* (☎22850 24404; ❸). Along the quayside, cafés and **restaurants** are abundant, if a bit expensive; *Iy Kali Kardhia* is worth a visit.

The island's best **beaches** are regularly served by buses in season. **Áyios Yeóryios**, a lengthy sandy bay south of the hotel quarter, lies within walking distance. There are several tavernas here and four mosquito-prone campsites; further south at **Áyios Prokópios** beach you will find the good *Apollon* campsite, or you could follow the tracks a little further – an hour-plus walk from town – to **Ayía Ánna**, a small port where there are plenty of rooms to let and a few modest tavernas. Beyond the headland stretches less-developed **Pláka** beach, a 5km long vegetation-fringed expanse of white sand which comfortably holds the summer crowds of nudists and campers from the two friendly campsites.

Náxos also serves as a convenient entry point to the **Minor Cycladic Islands**, a chain of six small islands still unaffected by mass tourism. In high season local boat *Express Skopelitis* leaves Náxos town at 3pm calling at Koufoníssia, Skhinoússa,

Irakliá and Donoússa, where you will find basic accommodation and good beaches (free camping may be tolerated; check with the locals first). The end point of this journey is the island of **AMORGÓS**, with dramatic mountain scenery and crystal-blue seas. It is best to stay at the port of **Egiáli**, where you will find a friendly campsite and plenty of rooms to let. Make sure that you visit the postcard-pretty village of **Hóra**, and the spectacular monastery of Hozoviótissa, dramatically situated on a cliff high above the sea.

Íos

No other island attracts more crowds than **Íos**, yet the island hasn't been commercialized in quite the same way as, say, Mýkonos, since many visitors are young and impecunious, though the island is being driven steadily more upmarket. You might be tempted to grab a room in **YIALÓS** as you arrive, though it's the most expensive place on the island to stay. A refurbished **campsite** is to the west of the harbour, although there are also two other remoter sites. Yialós beach, five minutes' walk from the harbour, is fringed by hotels and lodgings, but loud music seems to be accepted on the beach and obligatory in the tavernas. Most of the cheaper rooms are in **HÓRA**, a twenty-minute walk (or a short bus ride) up the mountain behind the port, with dorms as well as the usual rooms and hotels. Every evening the streets throb to music from competing **clubs** (mostly free, though drinks tend to be expensive). The *Ios Club* is an antidote to standard techno-pop and a good place to watch the sunset. The most popular stop on the island's bus routes is **MYLOPÓTAS**, site of a magnificent beach and a mini-resort. By day, bodies cover every inch of the bus-stop end of the sand: for a bit more space head the other way, where there are dunes behind the beach. There are two campsites, *The Purple Pig* (☎22860 91302) and *Far Out* (☎22860 91468), which also has bungalows. For rooms, try *Dracos Pension* (☎22860 91281; ❹) to the right of the bus stop, also with a well-respected taverna. From Yialós, daily day-trip boats depart at around 10am to **MANGANÁRI** on the south coast, the beach to go to for serious all-over tans. There's a better atmosphere, though, at **ÁYIOS THEODHÓTIS**, up on the northeast coast, served by daily buses from Yialós.

Santoríni (Thíra)

As the ferry manoeuvres into **Santoríni**, gaunt, sheer cliffs loom hundreds of feet above. Nothing grows to soften the view, and the only colours are the reddish-brown, black and grey pumice striations of the cliff face. As early as 3000 BC Santoríni developed as an outpost of Minoan civilization until, around 1450 BC, the volcano-island erupted; island and settlements were both destroyed and, it is thought, the great Minoan civilizations on Crete went with them.

Some small ferries and excursion boats dock at **Skála Firá**, but most vessels use the somewhat grim port of **Órmos Athiniós**. Half-rebuilt after a devastating earthquake in 1956, the island capital **FIRÁ** lurches dementedly at the cliff's edge. Besieged by day-trippers from cruise-ships, it's become incredibly tacky of late, the most grossly commercialized spot on what can seem a grossly commercialized island. There is no shortage of **rooms**, as well as three **hostels**; the official HI one is at the northern part of town (☎22860 22387; €6 per bed). The **campsite** is well-signposted 500m east of the bus terminal. Firá is not a place to linger, but it is worth having a look at the **Archeological Museum** (Tues–Sun 8.30am–3pm; €3) near the cable car to the north of town, and at the **Museum of Prehistoric Thíra** (Tues–Sun 8.30am-3pm; free), between the cathedral and the bus station. Bus services are plentiful enough between the town and beaches.

Near the northwest tip of the island is one of the most dramatic towns of the Cyclades, **ÍA**, a curious mix of pristine white reconstruction and tumbledown ruins clinging to the cliff face. It's also much the calmest place on Santoríni, and with the presence of a post office, travel agencies and an excellent youth hostel (☏22860 71465; ❶), there's no reason to feel stuck in Firá. **Beaches** on Santoríni are bizarre: long black stretches of volcanic sand which get blisteringly hot in the afternoon sun. There's little to choose between **KAMÁRI** and **PERÍSSA**, the two main resorts: both have long beaches and a mass of restaurants, rooms and apartments; neither is for those seeking solitude. Períssa gets more backpackers, has the better campsite and a well-run hostel, *Anna* (☏22860 82182; ❷). Camping rough is forbidden. Kamári and Períssa are separated by the Mésa Vounó headland, on which stood classical (post-eruption) **Thíra** (Tues–Sun 8.30am–3pm; free); most of the ruins are difficult to place, but the views are awesome. Evidence of the Minoan colony was found at **Akrotíri** (summer Tues–Sat 8.30am–3pm; €15), a town buried under banks of volcanic ash at the southwest tip of the island, and reached by bus from Firá or Períssa. Tunnels through the ash uncovered structures two and three storeys high; lavish frescoes adorned the walls and Cretan pottery was found stored in a chamber. Make sure you have a swim at the spectacular **Kókkini Ámmos beach**, a short walk from the site.

Rhodes

It's no surprise that **Rhodes** is among the most visited of Greek islands. Not only is its east coast lined with sandy beaches, but the core of the capital is a beautiful and remarkably preserved medieval city. **RHODES TOWN** divides into two unequal parts: the compact old walled city, and the new town sprawling around it in three directions. First thing to meet the eye, and dominating the northeast sector of the city's fortifications, is the **Palace of the Grand Masters** (Mon 12.30–7pm, Tues–Sun 8.30am–6pm; €6). Two excellent **museums** occupy the ground floor: one devoted to medieval Rhodes, the other to ancient Rhodes.

The heavily restored **Street of the Knights** (Odhós Ippotón) leads due east from the front of the palace. The "Inns" lining it housed the Knights of St John for two centuries, and at the bottom of the slope the Knights' Hospital has been restored as the **Archeological Museum** (Tues–Sun 8.30am–3/7pm; €3), where the star exhibits are two statues of Aphrodite. Across the way is the **Byzantine Museum** (same hours; €2), housed in the knights' chapel and highlighting the island's icons and frescoes. Leaving the Palace and heading south, it's hard to miss the most conspicuous Ottoman monument in Rhodes, the candy-striped **Süleymaniye Mosque**.

Affordable **accommodation** abounds in the old town and is contained almost entirely in the quad bounded

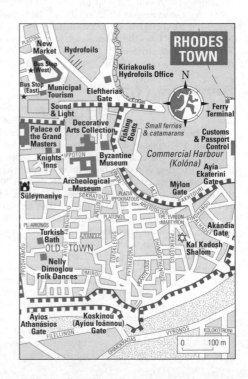

New Market, Hydrofoils, Bus Stop (West), Bus Stop (East), Municipal Tourism, Sound & Light, Palace of the Grand Masters, Decorative Arts Collection, Knights' Inns, Archeological Museum, Süleymaniye, Turkish Bath, OLD TOWN, Nelly Dimoglou Folk Dances, Ayios Athanásios Gate, Koskinoú (Ayíou Ioánnou) Gate, Kiriakoulis Hydrofoils Office, Eleftherías Gate, Fishing Boats, Byzantine Museum, Small ferries & catamarans, Ferry Terminal, Customs & Passport Control, Commercial Harbour (Kolóna), Ayía Ekateríni Gate, Mýlon Gate, Akándia Gate, Kal Kadosh Shalom, 0 100 m by Omírou, Sokrátous, Perikléos and Ippodhámou streets. Quiet, good-value places include *Apollo Rooms*, Omírou 28C (☎22410 63894; **❷**); *Pension Pink Elephant* on Timahídhas, off Irodhótou (☎22410 22469; **❸**), and the modernized, en-suite *Hotel Spot*, Perikleous 21 (☎22410 34737; **❸**). There's a **hostel** at Eryíou 12, just off Ayíou Fanouríou (☎22410 30491; **❶**). **Eating** cheaply can be more of a problem; try the little alleys and backstreets well south of Sokrátous. Here you'll find *Anthony's* on the corner of Pythagóra and Omírou, for fresh *souvláki* in characterful surroundings (eve only). Better value can be had just outside the walls, for instance at *To Steno*, Ayíon Anaryíron 29, 400m southwest of the Ayíou Athanasíou gate, or *Niohori*, Ioánni Kazoúli 29, by the Franciscan monastery. The **post office**, most **banks** (but there are three in the old town), the EOT **tourist office** (Mon–Fri 8am–2.30pm; ☎22410 23255) and the municipal tourist office (June-Sept Mon–Sat 8am–8pm, Sun 8am–3pm) are arrayed around the Italian-built New Market. **Buses** for the rest of the island leave from two terminals within sight of the market. Most central **Internet** café is *Rock Style* at Dhimokratías 7, just southwest of the old town.

Heading down the east coast from Rhodes Town, the giant promontory of **Tsambíka**, 26km south, is the first place to seriously consider stopping – there's an excellent eponymous beach just south of the headland. The best overnight base on this stretch of coast is probably **HARÁKI**, a tiny port with rooms and tavernas overlooked by a ruinous castle. **LÍNDHOS**, Rhodes' number-two tourist attraction, erupts 12km south of Haráki. Like Rhodes Town itself, its charm is undermined by commercialism and crowds, and there are relatively few self-catering units that aren't block-booked through package companies – find vacancies through Pallas Travel (☎22440 31494). On the hill above the town, the Doric **Temple of Athena** and Hellenistic stoa stand inside the inevitable knights' castle (summer Mon 12.30–7pm, Tues–Sun 8am–7pm; €6). Líndhos' beaches are crowded and overrated, but you'll find better ones heading south past Lárdhos, the start of 15km of intermittent coarse-sand beach up to and beyond the growing resort of **Yennádhi**. Inland near here, the late Byzantine frescoes in the village church of **Asklipió** are among the best on Rhodes.

Kós

Kós is the largest and most popular island in the Dodecanese after Rhodes, and there are superficial similarities between the two. Like its rival, the harbour here is also guarded by a castle of the Knights of St John, the streets are lined with grandiose Italian public buildings, and minarets and palm trees punctuate extensive Greek and Roman remains. Except for Kós Town and Mastihári, there aren't many non-package travellers: in high season you'll be lucky to find any sort of bed at all, except perhaps at the far west end of the island. Mostly modern **KÓS TOWN**, levelled by a 1933 earthquake, fans out from the harbour. The helpful municipal **tourist office** (July & Aug daily 8am–9pm; spring & autumn Mon–Fri 9am–8pm, Sat 8am–3pm; winter Mon–Fri 8am–3pm; ☎22420 24460), 500m south of the ferry dock on the shore road, offers maps and ferry schedules. Long-distance **buses** arrive inland 500m west of the tourist office. Among budget **accommodation**, try the clean, friendly *Pension Alexis*, Irodhótou 9 (☎22420 25594; **❷**; closed Dec–Feb), or *Hotel Afendoulis*, 600m southeast at Evripýlou 1 (☎22420 25321; **❸**; closed Dec–March). The official **campsite** (☎22420 23275) is thirty minutes' walk along the scrappy beach to the southeast of town; there are also frequent buses. Avoid the harbourfront **restaurants** in favour of such outfits as *Ambavris*, 1.5km inland in the eponymous hamlet, or *Noufara*, northwest of the port at Kanári 67. Apart from the **castle** (Tues–Sun 8.30am–3pm; €3), the town's main attraction is its wealth of Hellenistic and Roman remains, including mosaics and statues displayed to advantage in the Italian-built **Archeological Museum** (Tues–Sun 8am–2.30pm; €3). Next to the castle, scaffolding props up the branches of the so-called Hippocrates

GREECE | The southern Aegean islands

plane tree, which does have a fair claim to be one of the oldest trees in Europe. Hippocrates is also honoured by the **Asklepion** (Tues–Sun 8am–3/7pm; €3), a temple to Asclepius and renowned centre of Hippocratic teaching, 45 minutes on foot (or a short bus ride) from town. The road to the Asklepion passes through the village of **PLATÁNI**, where the island's ethnic Turkish minority run the *Arap* and *Sherif* tavernas (summer only), serving excellent, affordable food.

For **beaches** you'll need to use long-distance buses, or else rent scooters or pedal-bikes. Around 12km west of Kós town, **Tingáki** is easily accessible and thus oversubscribed. **Mastihári**, 30km from Kos town, has a decent beach and non-package-tour rooms, as well as several daily ferries to Kálymnos. Continuing west, buses run as far as **Kéfalos**, which covers a bluff looking back along the length of Kós. Well before Kéfalos are **Áyios Stéfanos**, where the exquisite remains of a mosaic-floored fifth-century basilica overlook tiny Kastrí islet, and **Kamári**, the package resort just below Kéfalos. Beaches begin at Kamári and extend east past Ayios Stéfanos for 7km, almost without interruption; "Paradise" has the most facilities, but "Magic" (officially Polémi) and Langádha are calmer and more scenic.

Pátmos

St John the Divine reputedly wrote the Book of Revelation in a cave on **Pátmos**, and the monastery which commemorates him, founded here in 1088, dominates the island both physically and politically. While the monks no longer run Pátmos as they did for more than six centuries, their influence has stopped most of the island going the way of Rhodes or Kós. **SKÁLA**, the port and main town, is the chief exception, crowded with day-trippers from Kós and Rhodes or cruise-ship shoppers. **Accommodation** touts meet all ferries and hydrofoils, and their offerings can be a long walk inland – not necessarily a bad thing, as the waterfront is noisy. Less expensive hotels to book in advance include *Australis* in Netiá district (☎22470 31576; ❸), who will refer you to relatives' pensions if they're full. Among **restaurants**, try the reliable seafood *ouzerí To Hiliomodhi*. The next bay north of the main harbour shelters **Méloï Beach**, with a well-run campsite and an excellent taverna, *Stefanos*. For swimming, the next beach north, **Agriolivádhi**, is usually less crowded.

The **Monastery of St John** (daily 8am–1pm; Tues, Thurs & Sun also 4–6pm) shelters behind massive defences in the hilltop capital of **HÓRA**. Buses go up, but the thirty-minute walk by a beautiful old cobbled path puts you in a more appropriate frame of mind. Just over halfway is the **Monastery of the Apocalypse**, built around the cave where St John heard the voice of God issuing from a cleft in the rock. This is merely a foretaste, however, of the main monastery, whose fortifications have guarded a dazzling array of religious treasures dating back to medieval times (museum €5). Hóra itself is a beautiful little town whose antiquated alleys conceal over forty churches and monasteries, plus dozens of shipowners' mansions dating from the island's heyday in the seventeenth and eighteenth centuries. If you're determined to stay in one of the only twenty-odd rooms here, it's best to make morning enquiries at the recommended taverna *Vangelis*, on the inner square. From Hóra a good road runs above the package resort of Gríkou to the isthmus of **Stavrós**, from where a thirty-minute trail leads to the excellent beach, with one seasonal taverna, at **Psilí Ámmos** (summer kaïki from Skála). There are more good beaches in the north of the island, particularly **Livádhi Yeránou**, shaded by tamarisk groves and with a decent taverna, and **Lámbi** with volcanic pebbles and another quality taverna, *Leonidas*.

The northern Aegean islands

The seven scattered islands of the **northeastern Aegean** form a rather arbitrary archipelago. Local tour operators do a thriving business shuttling passengers for absurdly high tariffs between the easternmost islands and the Turkish coast. **Sámos** is the most visited, and was – until a week-long forest fire devastated a fifth of the island in 2000 – perhaps the most verdant and beautiful. **Híos** is culturally fascinating, while **Lésvos** is more of an acquired taste, though once smitten you may find it hard to leave. The **Sporades**, in the northwestern Aegean, are an easier group to island-hop and well connected with Athens by bus and ferry via Áyios Konstandínos or Kými (for Skýros only), and with Vólos.

Sámos

Sámos was the wealthiest island in the Aegean during the seventh century BC, but fell on hard times thereafter; today its economy is heavily dependent on package tourism. Except for express boats, all **ferries** to and from Pireás and the Cyclades call at both Karlóvassi in the west and Vathý in the east; additionally there are services to the Dodecanese out of Pythagório in the south. **VATHÝ**, the capital, lines the steep-sided shore of its namesake bay and is of minimal interest except for its hill quarter of tottering, tile-roofed houses, Áno Vathý, and an excellent **archeological museum** (Tues–Sun 8.30am–3pm; €3) which has a wealth of peculiar votive offerings and a huge, five-metre statue of an idealized youth. **Accommodation** includes the welcoming *Pension Avli*, housed in a former convent at Áreos 2 (☎22730 22939; ❷), and the partly en-suite *Pension Trova*, Manóli Kalomíri 26 (☎22730 27759; ❷). For **food**, head inland to *Ta Kotopoula* grill at Plátanos junction, or just north of the ferry dock to more versatile waterfront *Artemis*, with seafood too. West of Vathý, the busy resort of **Kokkári** is enchantingly set between twin headlands at the base of still partly forested mountains. Nearby beaches are pebbly and exposed, prompting its role as a major windsurfers' resort. Some 13km west is untouristed **ÁYIOS KONSTANDÍNOS**, with several modest pensions and hotels, plus three excellent **tavernas**, the most reliably open being *To Kyma*. Less than an hour's walk west from functional Karlóvassi, **Potámi** is a popular beach ringed by forest and weird rock formations; for more solitude you can continue another hour or so on foot to the two bays of **Mikró Seitáni** (pebbles) and **Megálo Seitáni** (sand). But for an amenitied beach resort in the west of the island, shift south to **ÓRMOS MARATHAKÁMBOU**, adjacent to 2km of sand and pebbles at Votsalákia package resort. In Órmos itself, *Lekatis*, at the east end of the front, does inexpensive seafood; **stay** at *Studios Avra* (☎22730 37221; ❸) above the jetty.

Híos

Increasing numbers of foreigners are discovering **Híos** beyond its port city and single resort strip – fascinating villages, an important Byzantine monument and a healthy complement of beaches. **HÍOS TOWN** is always full of life, with a shambling old bazaar district, some excellent authentic tavernas, and a regular evening promenade along the waterfront. There's relatively cheap **accommodation** along and just behind the waterfront; the helpful **tourist office**, Kanári 18 (daily 7am–2.30/10pm; winter closed Sat & Sun; ☎22710 44389), has comprehensive lists. The best-value include *Rooms Alex*, Mihaíl Livanoú 29 (☎22710 26054; ❸), and *Hios Rooms*, Kokáli 1 (☎22710 20198; ❷). For **eating out** head for *Inomayirio Iakovos*, Ayíou Yeoryíou Frouríou 20, inside the kástro, or *O Hotzas*, well inland at Yeoryíou Kondhýli 3. Green long-distance **buses** run from the terminal south of the central park to most of the villages, though services to the north are sparse. The closest decent beach is **KARFÁS** (7km; frequent blue urban bus), a long if narrow sweep of sand, unfortunately overwhelmed by package tours; the best independent **accommodation** here is *Markos' Place* (☎22710 31990; ❸; closed Dec–March), in a disused monastery. The monastery of **Néa Moní** (daily 8am–1pm & 4–8pm; free), founded by Byzantine emperor Constantine IX in 1042, is the most beautiful and important medieval building on the Greek islands. There are special KTEL bus excursions in summer (Mon, Wed & Fr at 10am; €2), or pricier agency excursions including Anávatos (see below). Once a community of 600 monks, the monastery was pillaged during Ottoman atrocities in 1822 and most of its inmates put to the sword. The deserted medieval village of **Anávatos**, about 9km to the northwest of Néa Moní, is set on a dramatic 300-metre-high rock formation. The hillsides of **southern Híos** are home to the mastic bush, whose resin – for centuries the base of paints and cosmetics – was the source of local wealth before petrochemicals came along. **PYRGÍ**, 24km from the port, is one of the liveliest and most colourful of the "mastic villages", its houses elaborately embossed with geometric patterns cut into the plaster and then outlined with paint. Pyrgí has a handful of rooms and some good beaches nearby, the closest being Emborió, 5km from Pyrgí and served by occasional buses in summer; eating is, however, better at the equally impressive **MESTÁ**, 11km west, with two good tavernas on its square, and more accommodation.

Lésvos

Lésvos, birthplace of Sappho, the ancient world's foremost woman poet, may not at first seem particularly beautiful, but the craggy volcanic landscape of pine and olive groves grows on you. Despite the inroads of tourism, this is still essentially a working island, with few large hotels outside the capital, Mytilíni, and the resorts of Skála Kallonís and Mólyvos. Few people stay in the capital, **MYTILÍNI**, but do pause long enough to **eat** at *Paradhosiako Kalderimi* at Thássou 2, and peek at the new **archeological museum** with its superb Roman mosaics (daily 8am–3/7pm; €3). **MÓLYVOS**, on the northwestern coast, is easily the most attractive spot on Lésvos. Tiers of sturdy, red-tiled houses mount the slopes between the picturesque harbour and the Genoese castle. There are plenty of rooms to let – the **tourist office** by the bus stop (summer daily 8am–3pm & 6.30–8.30pm; ☎22530 71347) can book them – and a campsite east of town. The main lower road, past the tourist office, heads towards the picturesque harbour, where *The Captain's Table* is the best-value taverna. Lésvos' best beach is at **SKÁLA ERESSOÚ** in the far southwest, with **rooms** far outnumbering hotels. Tavernas with wooden terraces line the beach – try *Soulatsos* or *Blue Sardine*. **PLOMÁRI** in the southeast, long the oúzo capital of Greece, is another good base, though beaches lie some distance either side; **stay** at *Pension Lida*, in a restored mansion (☎22520 32507; ❷).

The Sporades

The three northern **Sporades** – package-tourist haven Skiáthos, Alónissos and **Skópelos**, the pick of the trio – have good beaches, transparent waters and thick pine forests. **Skýros**, the fourth Sporade, is isolated from the others and less scenic, but with perhaps the most character; for a relatively uncommercialized island within a day's travel of Athens it's unbeatable.

Skópelos

More rugged yet better cultivated than neighbouring Skiáthos, **Skópelos** is also very much more attractive. **SKÓPELOS TOWN** slopes down one corner of a huge, almost circular bay. There are dozens of rooms to let – take up one of the offers when you land or call the Roomowners Association (☎24240 24576) for vacancies. The most reliable **tavernas** are *Molos*, on the front, and *Alexander*, inland and uphill. Within the town, spread below the oddly whitewashed ruins of a Venetian *kástro*, are an enormous number of churches – 123 reputedly, though some are small enough to be mistaken for houses. **Buses** run along the island's one asphalt road to Loutráki about seven times daily, stopping at the turn-offs to all the main beaches and villages. **Stáfylos** beach, 4km out of town, is the closest, but it's small, rocky and increasingly crowded; the overflow, much of it nudist, flees to **Velanió**, just east. Much more promising, if you're after relative isolation, is sandy **Limonári**, a fifteen-minute road-walk or short kaïki ride from **AGNÓNDAS** (tavernas and rooms). The large resort of **Pánormos** has become overdeveloped, but slightly further on, **Miliá** offers a tremendous 1500m sweep of tiny pebbles beneath a bank of pines.

Skýros

Skýros remained until the 1980s a very traditional and idiosyncratic island. The older men still wear the vaguely Cretan costume of cap, vest, baggy trousers, leggings and clogs, while the women favour yellow scarves and long embroidered skirts. Skýros also has a particularly lively *Apokriatiká* or pre-Lenten **carnival**, featuring the "Goat Dance", performed by masked revellers in the village streets. A **bus** connects Liniariá – a functional little port with a few tourist facilities – to **SKÝROS TOWN**, spread below a high rock rising precipitously from the coast. Traces of Classical walls can still be made out among the ruins of the Venetian *kástro*; within the walls is the crumbling, tenth-century monastery of ** Áyios Yeóryios**. There are several hotels and plenty of **rooms** to let in private houses; you'll be met with offers as you descend from the bus, or Skyros Travel (℡22220 91123) on the main street can help with accommodation. Skyrian **tavernas** have improved considerably of late; choose from among *O Pappous k'Ego*, *Khristina's* and *Maryetis*. The campsite is down the hill at the fishing village of **MAGAZIÁ**, with rooms and tavernas fronting the best beach on the island.

The Ionian islands

The six **Ionian islands** are, both geographically and culturally, a mixture of Greece and Italy. Floating on the haze of the Adriatic, their green silhouettes come as a shock to those more used to the stark outlines of the Aegean. The islands were the Homeric realm of Odysseus and here alone of all modern Greek territory the Ottomans never held sway. After the fall of Byzantium, possession passed to the Venetians, and the islands became a keystone in that city-state's maritime empire from 1386 until its collapse in 1797. Tourism has hit **Corfu** in a big way – so much so that it's one of the few islands known to locals and foreigners by completely different names. None of the other islands has endured anything like Corfu's scale of development, although the process seems well advanced on parts of **Zákynthos**. For a less sullied experience, head for the trio of **Kefalloniá**, **Itháki** and **Lefkádha**.

Corfu (Kérkyra)

Corfu's natural appeal remains an intense experience, if sometimes a beleaguered one, for it has more package hotels and holiday villas than any other Greek island. The commercialism is apparent the moment you step ashore at the ferry dock, or cover the 2km from the airport (local buses #2 and #3 leave from 500m north of the terminal gates). **KÉRKYRA TOWN**, the capital, has a lot more going for it than first exposure to the summer crowds might indicate. The cafés on the Esplanade and in the arcaded Listón have a civilized air, and the **Palace of SS Michael and George** at the north end of the Spianádha is worth visiting for its Asiatic museum (Tues–Sun 8.30am–3pm; €3) and Municipal Art Gallery (daily 9am–9pm; €1.50). The **Byzantine Museum** (Tues–Sun 9am–3pm; €3) and the cathedral are both interesting, as is the **Archeological Museum**, Vraíla 3 (Tues–Sun 8.30am–3pm; €3), where the small but intriguing collection features a 2500-year-old Medusa pediment. The island's patron saint, Spirýdhon, is entombed in a silver-covered coffin in his own church on Vouthrótou, and four times a year, to the accompaniment of much celebration and feasting, the relics are paraded through the streets. Some 5km south of town lies the picturesque convent of **Vlahérna**, which is joined to the plush mainland suburb of Kanóni by a short causeway; the tiny islet of **Pondikoníssi** in the bay can also be visited by a frequent kaïki service(€1.50 return). The best source of independent **accommodation** in Corfu Town and around the island is the Roomowners Association at D. Theotóki 2 (Mon–Fri 9am–1.30pm; Tues, Thurs & Fri also 6–8pm; ℡26610 26133, ✆oitkcrf@otenet.gr); nearby, the **tourist office** on the corner of Vouleftón and

Mantazárou (Mon–Fri 8am–2pm; ☎26610 37520, ⊜E.O.T.corfu@otenet.gr) also has lists of **rooms**. Otherwise, try the least expensive old-town **hotel**, *Europa*, Yitsiáli 10, near the new port (☎26610 39304; ❸). The nearest **campsite** is *Dionysos Camping Village* (☎26610 91417) at Dhassiá, 8km north. For **eating out**, try *Aleko's Beach*, at the jetty below the Palace of St Michael and St George, or the friendly *To Paradosiakon* at Solomoú 20.

The coast north of the port has been remorselessly developed as far as Pyrgí, and much of it is best written off. The best spot is **PEROULÁDHES**, a genuine, somewhat run-down village with a spectacular beach of brick-red sand below wind-eroded cliffs. On the west coast, **PALEOKASTRÍTSA** has gone the way of all package locations, though its coves are on a beautiful stretch of coast. Expensive villas and hotels are present in abundance, plus a few campsites, which are, however, some distance from the town. If you just want a room, search uphill in the villages of Lákones and Makrádhes, 5km away. The tiny village of **VÁTOS**, just inland from west-coast Érmones, is the one place within easy reach of Kérkyra Town that has an easy, relaxed feel to it and reasonable rooms and tavernas. The nearest campsite to picturesque **Myrtiótissa Beach** is *Vatos Camping*, near the village of Vátos. Nearby **PÉLEKAS** is rather busy, but it's a good alternative base, with simple tavernas and rooms – try *Pension Paradise* (☎26610 94530; ❷) – and the excellent *Zanzibar* pub. Further south, **ÁYIOS GÓRDHIS** beach is more remote but that hasn't spared it from the crowds who come to admire the cliff-girt setting or patronize the *Pink Palace* (☎26610 53103; ❷), a youth-oriented holiday village/resort that sprawls from the sand up the hill behind. Beyond Messongí stretches the flat, sandy southern tip of Corfu. **Áyios Yeóryios**, on the southwest coast, consists of a developed area just before its beautiful beach, which extends north alongside the peaceful Korissíon lagoon. **Kávos**, near the cape itself, rates with its many clubs and discos as the nightlife capital of the island; for daytime solitude and swimming, you can walk to beaches beyond the nearby hamlets of Sparterá and Dhragotiná.

Kefalloniá

Kefalloniá is the largest, and at first glance least glamorous, of the Ionian islands; the 1953 earthquake that rocked the archipelago was especially devastating here, with almost every town and village levelled. Couple that with the islanders' legendary eccentricity, and with poor infrastructure, it's no wonder tourism didn't take off until the late 1980s. Already popular with the Italians, the island has, more recently, been attracting large numbers of British tourists, in no small part thanks to the success of Louis de Bernières' novel, *Captain Corelli's Mandolin*, which was set here. There's plenty of interest: beaches to compare with the best on Corfu or Zákynthos, good local wine, and the partly forested mass of Mount Énos (1628m). The island's size, skeletal bus service and shortage of summer accommodation make renting a motorbike or car a must for extensive exploration. **Ferries** mostly dock at **SÁMI** on the east coast, where the main *Corelli* set was built; few people linger here, though there is an excellent campsite, *Karavomilos Beach* (☎26740 22480). **AYÍA EFIMÍA**, 10km north, makes a far more attractive base, with the small but smart *Moustakis* hotel (☎26740 61030; ❸) and highly rated *Dendrinos* taverna. Between the two towns, 3km from Sámi, the **Melissáni cave** (daily 8am–sunset; €4.10), a partly submerged Capri-type "blue grotto", is well worth a stop. Southeast from Sámi you find the resorts of **PÓROS**, with ferries to Kyllíni on the Peloponnese. You may have to continue around the cape, past excellent beaches, to find accommodation in the coastal village of Lourdháta. Just inland, detour to the Venetian castle of **Áyios Yeóryios** (Tues–Sun 8.30am–3/7pm; free). **ARGOSTÓLI**, with occasional ferries to Kyllíni and Zákynthos, is the bustling, inevitably concrete island capital. The waterfront **tourist office** (Mon–Fri 7.30am–2.30pm & in summer only 5pm–10pm, Sat 9am–1pm; ☎26710 22248) keeps comprehensive lists of **accommodation**; you're best off with private rooms as hotels are expensive. The newly refurbished **Archeological Museum** (Tues–Sun 8.30am–3pm; €3) is second only to Corfu's in the archipelago. Heading north, you find the beach of **Mýrtos**, considered the best one on the island, although lacking in facilities; the closest places to **stay** are nearby Dhivaráta and almost bus-less **Ássos**, a beautiful fishing port perched on a narrow isthmus linking it to a castellated headland. At the end of the line, **Fiskárdho**, with its eighteenth-century houses, is the most expensive place on the island; the main reason to come would be for the daily **ferry** to Lefkádha island, and crossings to Itháki.

Itháki

Despite its proximity to Kefalloniá, there's still very little tourist development to spoil **Itháki**, Odysseus's capital. There are no sandy beaches, but the island is good walking country, with a handful of small fishing villages and various coves to swim from. **Ferries** from Pátra and Kefalloniá (and, in peak season, from Corfu) land at the main port and the village-sized capital of **VATHÝ**, at the back of a deep bay within a bay. **Rooms** are fairly easy to come by; they tend, however, to be inconspicuous, and are best sought by nosing around the backstreets south of the ferry dock. There's ample choice for **food**, with seven or eight tavernas, the seafront *To Kohyli* being the best of a remarkably similar bunch. In season the usual small boats shuttle tourists from the harbour to a series of tiny coves along the peninsula northeast of Vathý. The pebble-and-sand **beaches** between Cape Skhinós and Sarakíniko Bay are excellent. Two daily **buses** run north along the main road out of Vathý to **STAVRÓS**, a fair-sized village with a couple of tavernas and some rooms. There's an Homeric site nearby that may be the location for Odysseus's castle. **FRÍKES**, a thirty-minute walk downhill beyond Stavrós, is smaller but has a handful of tavernas, rooms and a pebbly strip of beach. This is where the seasonal **ferries** dock, to and from Lefkádha and Fiskárdho on northern Kefalloniá; the port is linked to Vathý by the same bus as Stavrós.

Zákynthos

Zákynthos was hit hardest by the 1953 earthquake, and the island's grand old capital was completely destroyed. Although some of its beautiful Venetian churches have been restored, it's a town of limited appeal and the attraction for travellers lies more in the thick vineyards, orchards and olive groves of the interior, and some excellent beaches. Under two hours from Kyllíni on the mainland, Zákynthos now gets close to half a million visitors a year. Most tourists, though, are conveniently housed in one place, Laganás, on the south coast; if you avoid July and August, and steer clear of Laganás and the developing villages of Argási and Tsiliví, there is still a peaceful Zákynthos to be found. The most tangible hints of the former glory of **ZÁKYNTHOS TOWN** are in **Platía Solomoú**, the grand and spacious main square. At its waterside corner stands the beautiful fifteenth-century sandstone church of **Áyios Nikólaos**, whose paintings and icons are displayed in the imposing **Byzantine Museum** (Tues–Sun 8am–2.30pm; €3), by the town hall. The large church of **Áyios Dhionýsios** was one of the few buildings left standing after the earthquake, and newly painted murals cover the interior. If you've a couple of hours to fill, walk up the cobbled path to the town's massive **Venetian fortress** (daily 8am–2/7.30pm; €1.50) for great views across the town and sea. The **tourist police** on waterfront Lombárdhou have information about **accommodation** and **bus** services. The Roomowners Association (☎26950 49498) also has vacancies all over the island. Good-value hotels include *Egli* at the corner of Loútzi and Lombárdhou (☎26950 28317; ❷). There are plenty of **eating places**, especially on the seafront on the north side of town; *Taverna Arekia* is excellent and has authentic live music, but it's a twenty-minute walk. To get to the **beaches**, buses depart from the station on Filitá (one block back from the seafront), but since the island is fairly flat, apart from the north and west, this is an ideal place to rent a **bike** – available from Moto-Saki, opposite the phone office. In the summer a number of boats depart from the quay for day-trips around the island, visiting the Blue Caves, Shipwreck Bay and Cape Kerí caves.

Crete

With its flourishing agricultural economy, **CRETE** is one of the few islands that could probably support itself without tourists. Nevertheless, mass tourism is all too evident. Much of the north coast, in particular, is overdeveloped and, though there are coastal areas that have not been spoiled, they are getting harder and harder to find. By contrast, the high mountains of the interior – capped with snow right through to June – are barely touched. Crete is distinguished as the home of the **Minoan** civilization, Europe's earliest, which made the island the centre of a maritime trading empire as early as 2000 BC and produced artworks unsurpassed in the ancient world. The island's strategic position means that it has seen a succession of influences since: control passed from Greeks to Romans to Saracens, through the Byzantine Empire to Venice, and finally to Turkey for more than two centuries before reunion with modern Greece. Almost wherever you go, you'll find some reminder of the island's history. The capital, **Iráklio**, is not somewhere to hang around, although visits to its superb archeological museum and the Minoan palace at nearby **Knossós** are all but compulsory. There are other great Minoan sites at **Mália** on the north coast and at **Festós** in the south. Near the latter are the remains of the Roman capital at **Górtys**. For many people, unexpected highlights also turn out to be Crete's **Venetian forts** and its **Byzantine churches**. Historical heritage apart, the main attractions are that inland this is still a place where traditional rural life continues, and that the island is big enough to ensure that, with a little effort, you can still get away from it all. To do so, head for the far west, the far east or the harder-to-reach places along the south coast. If you want it, there's also a surprisingly sophisticated club scene in the north-coast cities, and plenty of manic, beer-soaked tourist fun in the resorts.

Transport connections are excellent. There are daily ferries from Pireás to Iráklio, Réthimno, Haniá and Áyios Nikólaos, as well as regular connections to Kastélli and Sitía (all on the north coast), a constant stream of buses plying between these places, and onward bus connections from these main centres to much of the rest of the island. Thanks to the tourists, there are also plenty of day-trips available in season, and small boats linking villages on the south coast. Rather than head for Iráklio, you're better off basing yourself initially in the beautiful city of **Haniá** (for the west, the mountains and the famous **Samariá Gorge**), in **Réthimno** (only marginally less attractive, and handy for Iráklio, the major Minoan sites and the south), or **Sitía** to explore the far east.

Iráklio and around

The best way to approach **IRÁKLIO** is by sea; that way you see the city as it should be seen, with Mount Ioúktas rising behind and the Psilorítis range to the west. As you get closer, it's the city walls which first stand out, still dominating and fully encircling the oldest part of town, and finally you sail in past the great fort defending the harbour entrance. Unfortunately, big ships no longer dock in the old port but at great modern concrete wharves alongside – which neatly sums up Iráklio itself: many of the old parts have been restored, but they're of no relevance to the dust and noise which characterize much of the city today. The only real sight of interest is the **Archeological Museum**, just off the north side of the main square, Platía Eleftherías (Mon noon–5/7pm, Tues–Sun 8am–5/7pm; €6). It hosts a collection that includes almost every important prehistoric and Minoan find on Crete (go early or late in the day to avoid tour groups).

Directly opposite the museum is the tiny EOT **tourist office** (Mon–Fri 8.30am–3pm; ☎2810 228 225). You're probably better off treating Iráklio and Knossós as a day-trip – **rooms** are relatively scarce – but if you want to stay try the non-HI hostel at Víronos 5 (☎2810 286 281; dorms only €9) or *Rent Rooms Hellas*, Hándhakos 24 (☎2810 288 851; dorm €9; ❷). The nearest **campsite**, *Creta Camping* at Káto Goúves (☎28970 41400), lies 16km east; Hersónissos-bound buses will drop you there. One thing Iráklio does have going for it is a great **café** life: the pedestrianized alleys off Dedhalou, especially Korai, are crammed with the tables of rival estab-

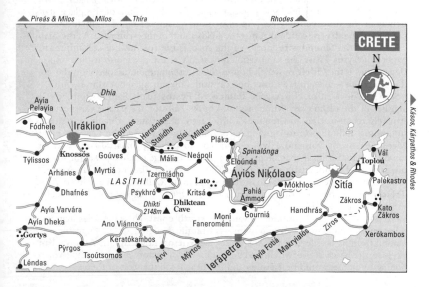

lishments and packed evenings and weekends. Simply to **eat**, you're better off at the fast food places around Fountain Square. One of the few reasonably priced central tavernas is *Ouzeri Mezes Ligeros* at Titou 22, near the back of the church of Áyios Titos. **Internet** access is at Gallery Games, Korái 14. **Buses** for all points along the north-coast highway use two stations on opposite sides of the coast road by the ferry dock; services on inland routes to the south and west (for Festós for example) leave from a terminal outside the city walls at Haniá Gate. For Knossós, city bus #2 sets out from the main bus station, stopping at Fountain Square on the way through town.

Knossós

The largest of the Minoan palaces, **KNOSSÓS** (daily 8am–5/7pm; €6) reached its cultural peak over 3500 years ago, though a town of some importance survived here well into the Roman era. It lies on a low hill some 5km southeast of Iráklio amid country rich in lesser remains spanning twenty-five centuries. As soon as you enter the palace of King Minos through the West Court, the ancient ceremonial entrance, it is clear how the legends of the Labyrinth of the Minotaur grew up around it. Even with a detailed plan, and despite extensive reconstruction by the original excavator, Sir Arthur Evans, it's almost impossible to find your way around the site systematically. Evidence of a luxurious lifestyle is plainest in the **Queen's Suite**, off the grand **Hall of the Colonnades** at the bottom of the stunningly impressive **Grand Staircase**. Going up the Grand Staircase to the floor above the Queen's domain, you come to a set of rooms in a sterner vein, generally regarded as the **King's quarters**. The staircase opens into a grandiose reception chamber known as the **Hall of the Royal Guard**, its walls decorated in repeated shield patterns. Continuing to the top of the staircase you emerge onto the broad **Central Court**, which would once have been enclosed by the walls of the buildings all around. On the far side, in the northwestern corner of the courtyard, is the entrance to one of Knossós' most atmospheric survivals, the **Throne Room**, in all probability the seat of a priestess rather than a ruler.

Górtys, Festós and the south

About 1km west of the village of Áyii Dhéka, where the bus drops you off, **GÓRTYS** (daily 8am–5/7pm; €4) is the ruined capital of the Roman province of Cyrenaica, which included not only Crete but also much of North Africa. If you walk here from Áyii Dhéka you'll get an idea of the huge scale of the place at its height in the third century AD. An enormous variety of remains, including an impressive **theatre**, is scattered across the fields south of the main road. At the main entrance to the **fenced site**, north of the road, is the ruinous but still impressive basilica of **Áyios Títos**, the saint who converted Crete and was also its first bishop. Beyond this is the **Odeion**, which houses the most important discovery on the site, the Law Code – ancient laws inscribed on stones measuring about 10m by 3m.

Some 17km west of Gortys, the **Palace of Festós** (daily 8am–5/7pm; €4) is another of the island's key Minoan sites. Unlike Knossós, the palace was not substantially reconstructed and requires a little more imagination. But the location is stunning, a hillside position giving a commanding view over the Messará plain. Merely following your nose will enable you to find the Theatral Area with an imposing staircase, royal apartments, storerooms with huge ceramic *pithoi* for storing oil, wine and grain, and a magnificent Central Court, the focus of all Minoan palaces. If this fires your imagination, a 45-minute walk will take you to **Ayía Triádha**, a tiny but beautiful and much less crowded site, thought to have been a summer palace or noble's villa.

From here you could continue towards the **south coast**. The easiest destination – some buses from Festós continue there – is **Mátala**, though despite a lingering reputation from its 60s heyday this is a pretty tacky resort nowadays. In **Ayía Galíni**, likewise, the beach is overwhelmed by the number of visitors. A better bet, if you're hoping to escape, would be **Léndas** and the beaches to the west of there.

Eastern Crete

The coast east of Iráklio was the first to be developed, and is still the domain of the package tourist. There are some good beaches, but all of them fully occupied. The heart of the development lies around **HERSÓNISSOS** and **MÁLIA**, which these days form virtually a single resort. If it's the party-holiday spirit you're after, this is the place to come. Hersónissos is perhaps slightly classier, but Mália was a bigger place to start with, which means there's a real town on the south side of the main road, with more chance of reasonably priced food and accommodation. Wherever you go, you'll have no problem finding bars, clubs and English (or Irish or even Dutch) pubs. If you're looking for somewhere **to stay** try the unofficial *Youth Hostel* at the junction of the old and new roads just east of Hersónissos (☏28970 23674; dorm €8), or *Pension Menios*, on Konstantinou Giamboudaki (☏28970 31361; ❸), for basic rooms in Mália old town not far from where the bus drops you. Some of the better beaches stretch east from Mália, and here too are the atmospheric ruins of the **Palace of Mália** (Tues–Sun 8.30am–3pm; €4), much less visited than Knossós or Festós, but with a virtually intact ground plan.

After Mália the road cuts inland, past the turning to the spectacular **Lasíthi Plateau**, before re-emerging on the coast at **ÁYIOS NIKÓLAOS**. The town's beautiful setting, around a supposedly bottomless salt lake now connected to the sea to form an inner harbour, was spotted long ago, and lake and port are surrounded by pricey restaurants and bars. In season, it is also jammed with tourists, many of them staying in hotels on the beaches north and east of town. There's little chance of finding a cheap **room** in season, though at quiet times there are bargains to be had; check at the helpful **tourist office** (April–Oct daily 8am–9.30pm; ☏28410 22357), by the bridge dividing the lake and harbour.

Sleepy **SITÍA**, the port and main town of the relatively unexploited eastern edge of Crete, may be about to wake up. A new airport will bring tourists direct, bypassing the sinuous and spectacular coast road that has discouraged most in the past. For the moment, though, Sitía still offers a plethora of waterside restaurants, a long sandy beach and a lazy lifestyle little affected by the thousands of visitors in peak season. The **tourist office** is on the seafront (summer only Mon–Fri 9am–2.30pm & 5–8.30pm; ☏28430 23300), and there are several **rooms** places around Kondhilaki, a few streets back from the harbour – try *Pension Venus*, Kondhilaki 60 (☏28430 24307; ❷). For **food**, there are inexpensive options in the streets behind the waterfront, such as *Mixos*, Kornárou 117. At the eastern end of the island, **VÁI BEACH** is the most famous on Crete thanks to its ancient grove of palm trees. In season, though, its undoubted charms, now fenced off, are diluted by crowds of day-trippers. Other beaches at nearby Ítanos or Pálekastro are less exotic but emptier. Or head further south – at Káto Zákros the pebbly beach is right by another important Minoan palace, while beyond that you're really off the beaten track (and also beyond the reach of the bus network).

Western Crete

West of Iráklio, the major centres of Réthimno and Haniá are both surrounded by extensive tourist development these days, but they're lively and attractive towns in their own right, and the gateways to less-travelled areas in the south and far west. The old town of **RÉTHIMNO** is a labyrinthine tangle of Venetian and Turkish houses set around an enclosed harbour and wide sandy beach. Medieval minarets lend an exotic air to the skyline, while dominating everything from the west is the superbly preserved outline of the Venetian **fortress** (daily 10am–5/7pm; €2.90). From the **bus station**, head around the inland side of the fortress, to reach the beach and the centre; the **tourist office** (April–Sept Mon–Fri 8am–7pm; ☏28310 56350) is right on the beach. There are plenty of **rooms**; try *Olga's Pension*, Soulíou 57 (☏28310 53206; ❸) or the unofficial **youth hostel**, Tombázi 45 (☏28310 22848; dorm €7). *Camping Elizabeth* (☏28310 28694) is in the hotel strip about

4km east along the beach, served by frequent buses from the main bus station. Much of the pleasure here is just in wandering the streets of the old town; there's an unbroken line of **tavernas**, cafés and cocktail bars right around the waterside and into the area around the old port, but the sea view comes at a price. You'll find an assortment of better-value places around the seventeenth-century Venetian **Rimóndi Fountain**: *Edhodhimo*, on Messologiou at the corner of Salaminos, has good value gyros and pizzas. Just round the corner from here, on Salaminos, a line of clubs make up the heart of Réthimno's **nightlife**.

Réthimno lies at one of the narrower parts of Crete, so it's relatively quick to cut across from here to the south coast. The obvious place to head is **PLAKIÁS**, a growing resort which has managed to retain a small-town atmosphere. There are numerous **rooms** places, very busy in August, as well as a relaxed and friendly Hostel (☎28320 32118; dorm €6) and *Camping Appolonia* on the road into town. Locals can point you in the direction of quieter beaches all around, and there are boat trips to many of them.

Haniá

HANIÁ is the spiritual capital of Crete; for many, it is also the island's most attractive city – especially in spring, when the snowcapped peaks of the Lefká Óri (White Mountains) seem to hover above the roofs. Although it is for the most part modern, the small harbour is surrounded by a jumble of Venetian streets that survived the wartime bombardments. The **bus station** is on Odhós Kydhonías, within easy walking distance of the centre: turn right, then left down the side of Platía 1866 and you'll emerge at a major road junction opposite the top of Halídhon, the main street of the old quarter. The **tourist office** (Mon–Fri 8am–2.30pm; ☎28210 36155), at the time of writing on the ground floor of *Hotel Canea* on Platía 1866, will most likely move in 2004 to Odhós Kydhonías 29; call for the latest information. **Ferries** dock about 10km away at the port of Soúdha: there are frequent city buses which will drop you by the market on the fringes of the old town. The **port area** is the oldest and the most interesting part of town. The little hill that rises behind the landmark domes of the quayside **Mosque of the Janissaries** is called **Kastélli**, site of the earliest habitation and core of the Venetian and Turkish towns. Beneath the hill, on the inner harbour, the arches of sixteenth-century Venetian arsenals survive alongside remains of the outer walls. Behind the harbour lie the less picturesque but more lively sections of the old city. Around the cathedral on Halídhon are some of the more animated shopping areas, particularly leather-dominated **Odhós Skrídhlof**. In the direction of the Spiántza quarter are ancient alleys with tumbledown Venetian stonework and overhanging wooden balconies that appear little touched by modern tourism. Haniá's **beaches** all lie to the west: the packed **city beach** is a ten-minute walk beyond the Maritime Museum, but for good sand you're better off taking the local bus from the east side of Platía 1866 along the coast road to Kalamáki. In between you'll find emptier stretches if you're prepared to walk some of the way.

There are plenty of **rooms** on offer, but in season you may face a long search. *Pension Fidias*, Kalinikoú Sarpáki 8, behind the cathedral (☎28210 52494; ❷, dorm €9), is a friendly place, recently done up but still run along hostel lines. Walk across the old town from here to *Pension Nora*, Theotokopoúlou 60 (☎28210 72265; ❷), near the Maritime Museum and Byzantine Collection, and you'll pass dozens of other options, some in wonderfully chic restored mansions (with prices to match). There's a **campsite**, *Camping Hania* (☎28210 31138), on the coast 4km west, served by city bus from Platía 1866. Both the inner and outer harbours are circled by **cafés**, **tavernas** and **bars**, although you pay for the location. You can stock up on food at the bustling and colourful **market**, three blocks east from the northern end of Platía 1866. The **bars** and **clubs** around the harbour are obvious enough, but you won't find many locals there. Young Haniotes tend to start their evening in the bars and cafés along Akti Miaouli, east of the harbour, and then move on around midnight, either to clubs out of town (beachside places to the west mainly), or to *Daz* (☎28210 72768), beneath the Schiavo bastion, down a narrow alley from the top of Halidhon, or *Premier*, Tsuderon at the back of the market. Haniá is also a good place to catch local Cretan lýra **music**, especially at *Café Kriti*, Kallérgon 22, one block inland from the harbour. **Internet** access is at *Café Vranas*, Isodhion 12, next to *Vranas Studios*, and many others.

Gorges and beaches

The **Gorge of Samariá** – Europe's longest – is an easy day-trip from Haniá (May–Oct only). If you do it, though, be warned that you will not be alone: dozens of coachloads set off before dawn from all over Crete for the dramatic climb into the White Mountains and the long (at least 4hr) walk down. At the bottom is the village of **AYÍA ROÚMELI** from where boats will take you east to **Hóra Sfakíon** and your bus home, or west towards the pleasant resorts of **Soúyia** and **Paleohóra**. The mountains offer endless other **hiking** challenges to help you escape the crowds. Soúyia and Paleohóra are both good starting points, as is **Loutró**, a tiny place halfway to Hóra Sfakíon, accessible only by boat. These places also have decent **beaches**, and from Paleohóra you can reach more at the far west of the island where only **Elafonísi**, an isolated beach with an almost tropical lagoon feel, ever sees crowds.

Travel details

Trains

Athens to: Corinth (12 daily; 1hr 30min–2hr); Kalamáta (3 daily; 7hr); Kalambáka via Paleofársala (2 daily; 5–6hr 30min); Mycenae (5 daily; 2hr 45min); Náfplio (2 daily; 3hr–3hr 30min); Pátra (8 daily; 3hr 30min); Thessaloníki (9 daily, including 1 sleeper; 6–8hr); Vólos (2 daily; 5hr).
Pátra to: Corinth (8 daily; 1hr 30min); Kalamáta (1 daily; 5hr); Pýrgos (7 daily; 2hr).
Thessaloníki to: Litóhoro (6 daily; 1hr 40min); Vólos (2 daily; 3hr).
Vólos to: Athens (2 daily; 5hr); Kalambáka (2 daily; 2hr 45min); Lárissa (13 daily; 1hr).

Buses

Athens to: Corfu (4 daily; 11hr); Corinth (hourly; 1hr 30min); Delphi (6 daily; 3hr); Ioánnina (8 daily; 7hr 30min); Kalamáta (13 daily; 4hr); Kefalloniá (3 daily; 7hr); Kými, for Skýros ferries (3 daily; 3hr 30min); Lárissa (Mt Olympus; 6 daily; 4hr 30min); Mycenae–Fíkhti (hourly; 2hr); Náfplio (hourly; 2hr 30min); Olympia (4 daily; 5hr 30min); Pátra (every 30min; 3hr); Rafína (every 30min; 1hr 30min); Sounion (every 30min; 2hr); Spárti (10 daily; 3hr 30min); Thessaloníki (10 daily; 7hr 30min); Vólos (10 daily; 5hr 20min); Zákynthos (5 daily; 6hr).
Corinth to: Ancient Corinth (hourly; 20min); Árgos (hourly; 1hr); Kalamáta (10 daily; 3hr–4hr); Mycenae–Fíkhti (hourly; 30min); Náfplio (hourly; 1hr 30min); Spárti (8 daily; 3hr–4hr).

Ioánnina to: Igoumenítsa (9 daily; 2hr); Métsovo (2–3 daily, 1hr 30min); Tríkala (2 daily; 4hr).
Kalamáta to: Areópoli (4 daily; 1hr 30min–2hr 30min); Kóroni (8 daily; 1hr 30min); Methóni via Pýlos (5 daily; 1hr 30min); Pátra (2 daily; 4hr); Pýlos (8 daily; 1hr).
Lárissa (Mt Olympus) to: Kalambáka (hourly; 2hr); Litóhoro junction (hourly; 1hr 45min).
Náfplio to: Epidaurus (5 daily; 45min); Mycenae (3 daily; 30min).
Pýrgos to: Kalamáta (2 daily; 2hr); Olympia (hourly; 45min); Pátra (10–11 daily; 2hr).
Thessaloníki to: Ierissós (5–7 daily; 3hr 30min); Ioánnina (5 daily except Tues; 7hr); Kalambáka (7 daily; 4hr 30min); Litóhoro (7 daily; 1hr 30min); Ouranoúpoli (5–7 daily; 3hr 45min); Vólos (4 daily; 4hr).
Vólos to: Áyios Ioánnis (2 daily; 2hr 30min); Kalambáka (4 daily; 3hr); Lárissa (Mt Olympus; hourly; 1hr 15min); Makrinítsa (10 daily; 50min); Miliés (5 daily; 1hr); Tsangarádha (2 daily; 2hr); Vyzítsa (6 daily; 1hr 10min); Zagorá (4 daily; 2hr).

Ferries, catamarans and hydrofoils

Áyios Konstandínos to: Skópelos (2–4 daily; 2hr 20min–3hr 45min).
Híos to: Lésvos (6–10 weekly; 1hr 30min–3hr 30min); Sámos (2–5 weekly; 2hr–5hr).
Íos to: Náxos (2–3 daily; 3hr); Páros (2–3 daily; 5hr); Thíra (1–2 daily; 2hr).
Iráklio to: Pireás (4 daily; 6–12hr); Páros &

Cyclades (1 daily; 7hr); Rhodes (2–3 weekly; 11hr).
Kefalloniá to: Zákynthos (summer 2 daily; 1hr 30min); Itháki (1–3 daily; 45min).
Kós to: Pátmos (2–4 daily; 2hr 30min–5hr); Rhodes (2–4 daily; 2–4hr).
Kyllíni to: Kefalloniá (1 daily; 1hr 45min); Zákynthos (6 daily, 2 in winter; 1hr 30min).
Kými to: Skýros (1–2 daily; 2hr 30min).
Lésvos to: Híos (6–10 weekly; 1hr 30min–3hr 30min); Thessaloníki (2 weekly; 14hr).
Náxos to: Íos (2–3 daily; 3hr); Iráklio (4 weekly; 6hr); Páros (2–3 daily; 1hr); Thíra (2–3 daily; 4hr).
Pátra to: Corfu (3–5 daily; 8–10hr); Igoumenítsa (2–3 daily; 5–8hr); Itháki (2 daily; 4hr); Kefalloniá (2 daily; 2hr 30min).
Pireás to: Crete (2–4 daily; 12hr); Híos (6–9 weekly; 6hr–10hr 30min); Íos (3–6 daily; 5–10hr); Kós (13 weekly; 12hr); Lésvos (6–10 weekly; 8–14hr); Mýkonos (2–3 daily; 2hr30min–5hr); Náxos (4 daily; 4–8hr); Páros (4 daily; 3hr 30min–7hr); Pátmos (2 daily; 11hr); Rhodes (19 weekly; 18–23hr); Sámos (daily; 7hr 30min–14hr); Sífnos (2 daily; 3–5hr); Thíra (2–5 daily; 6–12hr).
Rafína to: Mýkonos, Páros, Náxos, Íos, Thíra (all 1–2 daily; 3–7hr).
Rhodes to: Crete (Sitía/Áyios Nikólaos; 2 weekly; 13hr); Kós (2 daily; 4hr); Pátmos (2 daily; 8hr).
Sámos to: Kós (4–9 weekly; 3hr 45min–4hr 15min); Pátmos (2–11 weekly; 1hr 30min–3hr); Rhodes (1–3 weekly; 6hr 30min–9hr).
Santorini to: Íos (3–4 daily; 1–2hr); Iráklio (5 weekly; 2hr 30min–5hr); Mýkonos (1 daily; 7hr); Náxos (3 daily; 4hr); Páros (3 daily; 5hr).
Thessaloníki to: Híos (1–2 weekly; 18hr 30min); Iráklio (2–5 weekly; 21hr); Lésvos (1–2 weekly; 15hr); Sámos (1 weekly; 19hr); Skópelos (summer daily; 5hr).
Vólos to: Skópelos (4–6 daily; 2hr–3hr 30min); Lésvos (1 weekly; 12hr).

Hungary

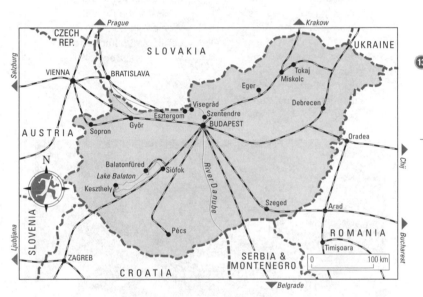

Hungary highlights

＊ **Communist Statue Park, Budapest** Graveyard for statues of old dictators, an ironic open-air museum. **See p.482**

＊ **Széchenyi Baths, Budapest** Relax in the steamy, healing waters. **See p.483**

＊ **Hévíz** A genuine Hungarian health experience at Europe's largest thermal-lake spa. **See p.488**

＊ **Pécs** Terrace cafés, brightly coloured buildings and laid-back attitude; a young, fun destination. **See p.489**

＊ **Szépasszony Valley, near Eger**. No trip to Eger should omit the "Valley of the Beautiful Woman", a horseshoe of cellars and paradise for wine lovers. **See p.491**

Introduction and basics

Visitors who refer to **Hungary** as a Balkan country risk getting a lecture on how this small, landlocked nation of ten million people differs from "all those Slavs": locals are strongly conscious of themselves as Magyar – a race that transplanted itself from Central Asia into the heart of Europe over a thousand years ago.

The magnificent capital **Budapest** (split into historic Buda and vibrant Pest), with its coffee houses, Turkish baths and fad for Habsburg bric-a-brac, has a strong whiff of Mitteleuropa – that ambient culture that welcomed Beethoven in Budapest and Hungarian-born Liszt in Vienna, and continues with a new wave of writers, film directors, artists and other media figures. But there is also an eager modern feel to the place, with international fashions snapped up and adapted to local tastes. Outside the capital, there is much to explore. **Lake Balaton**, in the west, with its string of brash resorts, styles itself as the "Nation's Playground", while other highlights of the region include historic **Sopron**, within spitting distance of Vienna, and Turkish-flavoured **Pécs**. The forested **Northern Uplands** in the far northeast towards Ukraine envelop the famous wine centre of **Eger**.

Information & maps

You'll find branches of **Tourinform**, the Hungarian National Tourist Office, in the capital and in larger towns across the country; branches are open Mon–Fri 9am–5/8pm; summer also open Sat & Sun. They do not book accommodation, but do have information on where rooms and beds are available, including the booklets *Hungarian Hotel Guide* and *Camping*. There are also **local tourist offices** in larger towns (Savariatourist, Balatontourist, etc, according to the region), where you can **book rooms**; opening hours are Mon–Fri 9am–4/6pm;

summer also Sat 8am–1pm. It's cheapest to buy your **maps** in Hungary: the best is Cartographia's full-country fold-out sheet (1:450,000).

Money and banks

The Hungarian currency is the **forint** (Ft), which comes in notes of 200Ft, 500Ft, 1000Ft, 2000Ft, 5000Ft, 10,000Ft and 20,000Ft, and in coins of 1Ft, 2Ft, 5Ft, 10Ft, 20Ft, 50Ft and 100Ft (the 50Ft coin is easily confused with the 10Ft coin). The best rates of exchange are offered by regional tourist offices and the banks. Standard **banking hours** are Mon–Thurs 8am–4pm, Fri 8am–3pm. Budapest has many **ATMs**, and more are appearing in other large towns. You can use a **credit card** to pay in many hotels, restaurants and tourist shops, but otherwise they're of little use.

Communications

Larger **post offices** (*posta*) are usually open Mon–Fri 8am–6pm, Sat 8am–1pm. Smaller branches close at 3pm and don't always open on Sat. Address **poste restante** mail "Poste restante, Posta", followed by the name of the town. You can make local calls from **public phones**, where 20Ft is the minimum charge (40Ft if you're calling a mobile phone), or, better, from **cardphones** – they're increasingly common, and you have less chance of losing your money; cards come in

Hungary on the net

- ⓦ **www.tourinform.hu** National tourist office.
- ⓦ **www.travelport.hu** Excellent general site.
- ⓦ **www.budapestsun.com** Entertainment listings and weekly news.
- ⓦ **www.elvira.hu** Train timetables and information.
- ⓦ **www.pecs.hu** A young, fun site with loads of info.

50 and 120 units and can be bought from post offices and newsstands. To make **national calls**, dial ℗06, wait for the buzzing tone, then dial the area code and number. You can make **international calls** from most public phones: dial ℗00, wait for the buzzing tone, then dial the country code as usual. **Internet access** is widely available (usually 500–700Ft/hr) in larger towns.

Getting around

Public transport reaches most parts of Hungary, and fares are very low. The only problem is getting information, for staff rarely speak anything but Hungarian, although German is spoken around Lake Balaton.

The centralization of the MÁV **rail network** means that many cross-country journeys are easier if you travel via Budapest. Intercity **trains** are the fastest way of getting to the major towns, though seat reservations, made at any MÁV office, are compulsory and cost an extra 440Ft; *személyvonat* trains, which stop at every hamlet en route, do not incur the reservation fee. You can buy tickets *(jegy)* for domestic services at the station *(pályaud-var* or *vasútállomás)* on the day of departure, but it's best to buy tickets for international trains *(nemzetközi gyorsvonat)* at least 36hr in advance. You're permitted to break your journey once. When buying your ticket, specify whether you want a one-way ticket *(egy útra)*, or a return *(retur* or *oda-vissza)*. **InterRail** and **Eurail** passes are valid.

Volán runs the bulk of Hungary's **buses**, which are often the quickest way to travel between the smaller towns. Arrive early to confirm the departure bay and get a seat. For **long-distance services** from Budapest and the major towns, you can buy tickets with a seat booking up to 30min before departure; after that, you get them from the driver (and risk standing). In rural areas, tickets are only available on board and there may be only one bus a day.

Accommodation

Accommodation costs have risen dramatically in recent years. More upmarket places tend to quote prices in euros (they'll usually accept US dollars or pounds sterling too); private rooms and hostels charge in forints. The cheapest places tend to fill up during high season, so it's wise to book ahead.

Outside Budapest and Lake Balaton (where prices are thirty percent higher), a three-star hotel *(szálló* or *szálloda)* will charge from around 12000Ft (€48) for a double room with bath and TV; solo travellers often have to pay this too, since singles are rare. A similar rating system is used for **inns** *(fogadó)* and **pensions** *(panzió)*, which charge a little less than hotels.

Hostels go under various names: in provincial towns they're called *turistaszálló*, but in the highland areas they go by the name of *turistaház*. Local tourist offices can provide details and make bookings; check ⊛www.backpackers.hu. They can also guide you to **student dormitories**, which are usually even cheaper: rooms are rented out in July and August, and are often available at weekends year-round.

Private rooms *(fizet ővendégszoba)* – B&B-style in a private home – are an inexpensive way of staying near town centres. Such accommodation can be arranged through local tourist offices for a small fee, or look for signs saying *szoba kiadó* or *Zimmer Frei*. Doubles range from 2500Ft in provincial towns to around 4500Ft in Budapest and around the Balaton. Rooms in a town's *belváros* (inner sector) are likely to be much better than those in outlying zones.

Bungalows *(faház)* proliferate around resorts and on the larger campsites. The first-class bungalows – with kitchens, hot water and a sitting room or terrace – are excellent, and will cost a few thousand forints, while the most primitive at least have clean bedding and don't leak. **Campsites** (usually signposted *Kemping*) likewise range from de luxe to third class. In high season, expect to pay anything up to 3000Ft, more around Lake Balaton.

Food and drink

For foreigners, the archetypal **Hungarian dish** is goulash – historically a soup made of potatoes and meat, which was later flavoured with

HUNGARY | Basics

paprika. Hungarians like a calorific **breakfast** *(reggeli)* that includes cheese, eggs or salami, plus bread and jam. **Coffee houses** *(kávéház)* are coming back into fashion. You'll find many serving breakfast and a coffee with milk *(tejeskávé)* or whipped cream *(tejszínhabbal)*. Most Hungarians take their coffee short and strong *(eszpresszó)*. A whole range of places sell **snacks**, including bakeries and delicatessens *(csemege)*. Numerous **patisseries** *(cukrászda)* pander to the Magyar fondness for sweet things. Pancakes *(palacsinta)* with fillings are very popular, as are strudels *(rétes)*. On the streets you can buy, in summer, corn-on-the-cob *(kukorica)* and in winter, roasted chestnuts *(gesztenye)*; while stalls selling fried fish *(sült hal)* are common in towns near rivers or lakes.

In theory an *étterem* is a proper restaurant, while a *vendéglő* approximates to the Western notion of a bistro; however, these distinctions are thin. The old word for a roadside inn, *csárda*, is often used by folksy, touristy restaurants. The main meal of the day is **lunch**, when some places offer set menus *(napi menü)*, a basic meal at moderate prices. There are plenty of places where you can eat well and sink a few beers for under 1600Ft. Always check your bill carefully as foreigners are a common target for being ripped off. **Starters** *(előételek)* range from soup *(leves)* to the popular *Hortobágyi palacsinta* (pancakes stuffed with mince and doused in a creamy paprika sauce), though nobody will mind if you just have a **main course** *(főételek)*. Hungarians like most things fried in breadcrumbs, such as *rántott csirkecomb* (chicken drumstick), but they also have a taste for *marhapörkölt* (beef stew). In traditional places the only choice for **vegetarians** will be breaded and fried cheese, mushrooms or cauliflower (*rántott sajt/gomba/karfiol*). In the countryside, pork and lard still rules.

Hungary's mild climate and diversity of soils is perfect for **wine** *(bor)*, which is perennially cheap, whether you buy it by the bottle *(üveg)* or the glass *(pohár)*. Wine bars *(borozó)* are ubiquitous, while true grape devotees make pilgrimages to the wine cellars *(borpince)*

around Pécs and Eger. The best-known types of brandy *(pálinka)* are distilled from apricots *(barack)* and plums *(szilva)*, the latter often available in private homes in a mouth-scorching home-distilled version. **Beer** *(sör)* of the lager type *(világos)* predominates, although you can also find **brown ale** *(barna)*: these come in draught form *(csapolt sör)* or in bottles *(üveges sör)*. Local brands to look out for are Pécsi Szalon sör and Soproni Ászok.

Opening hours and holidays

Shops are generally open Mon–Fri 10am–6pm, Sat 10am–1pm. Most things close down for the following **public holidays**: Jan 1; March 15; Easter Mon; May 1; Whit Mon; Aug 20; Oct 23; Dec 25 & 26.

Emergencies

Tourists are treated with respect by the **police** *(rendörség)* – unless they're suspected of black-marketeering, drug smuggling or driving under the influence of alcohol. Most have a smattering of German, but rarely any other foreign language. Be sure to always carry your passport or a photocopy.

All towns and some villages have a **pharmacy** *(gyógyszertár or patika)*, with staff – often German-speaking – authorized to issue a wide range of drugs. Opening hours are generally Mon–Fri 9am–6pm, Sat 9am–noon or 1pm; signs in the window give the location of all-night pharmacies *(ügyeletes gyógyszertár)*. Tourist offices can direct you to local **medical centres** or **doctors' surgeries** *(orvosi rendelő)*; these will probably be in private *(magán)* practice, so be sure to carry health insurance.

Emergency numbers

Police ☎107; Ambulance ☎104; Fire ☎105.

Budapest

The importance of **BUDAPEST** to Hungary is difficult to overestimate. Around two million people – one-fifth of the population – live in the city, and everything converges here: wealth, political power, cultural life and transport. Surveying the city from Castle Hill, it's obvious why Budapest was dubbed the "Pearl of the Danube". Its grand buildings and sweeping bridges look magnificent, especially when floodlit or illuminated by the barrage of fireworks launched from **Gellért Hill** on St Stephen's Day.

Castle Hill (Várhegy) is the most prominent feature of the **Buda** district, a plateau one mile long laden with old mansions and a huge palace, commanding the **Watertown**. Buda and its twin, **Pest**, have a surfeit of other fine sights, including museums and galleries, restaurants, bars and a wide variety of entertainments, accessible by efficient, inexpensive public transport. A host of new nightclubs show that the city is making up for its dreary postwar past, though it is still true to say that many people get up early and then slope off at around 10pm, interrupting work with breaks in patisseries and *eszpresszó* bars. Ease yourself into Budapest life by wallowing away an afternoon in one of the city's **thermal baths** (*gyógyfürdő*). A basic ticket covers three hours in the pools, sauna and steamrooms (*gőzfürdő*), while supplementary tickets are available for such delights as the mud baths (*iszapfürdő*) and massages (*masszázs*).

Each of Budapest's 23 districts (*kerületek*) is designated on maps, street signs and addresses by a Roman numeral; "V" is Belváros, on the Pest side; "I" is the Castle district in Buda.

Arrival, information and city transport

There are three main **train stations**, all of which are directly connected by **metro** with the central **Deák tér** metro station in the Belváros, in the city-centre district of Pest: Keleti station handles most international trains, including those from Vienna (Südbahnhof), Belgrade, Bucharest, Zagreb and Bratislava, as well as domestic arrivals from Sopron and Eger; Nyugati station handles trains from Prague and Bratislava, some from Bucharest, and domestic ones from the Danube Bend; and Déli station has one train a day from Vienna (Westbahnhof), the odd train from Zagreb, and domestic services from Pécs and Lake Balaton. From Ferihegy **airport**, an Airport Minibus will take you to wherever you're staying (2100Ft; book it in the terminal building). The airport taxi-drivers are notorious sharks. The central **bus station** is at Népliget (blue metro 3), serving international destinations and routes to Transdanubia. Also in Pest, Népstadion bus station (red metro) serves areas east of the Danube; and Árpád híd bus station (blue metro) serves the Danube Bend. **Hydrofoils** from Vienna dock alongside the Belváros embankment.

The best source of information is the friendly **Tourinform** (daily 8am–8pm; ☎1/438-8080, ✆www.tourinform.hu), just around the corner from Deák tér metro at Sütő utca 2, behind the big yellow Lutheran church; other branches are on Vörösmarty tér (open 24hr; ☎1/438-8080); on Liszt Ferenc tér; at Nyugati train station; and in the Castle District on Szentháromság tér. Other useful offices include the **Vista Tourist Center**, Paulay Ede utca 7 (Mon–Fri 9am–8pm, Sat & Sun 10am–6pm; ☎1/267-8603, ✆www.vista.hu), the **IBUSZ tourist office**, Ferenciek tere 10 (Mon–Fri 8.15am–5pm; ☎1/485-2700, ✆www.ibusz.hu), and **Budapest Tourist**, in the subway in front of Nyugati train station (Mon–Fri 9am–4pm; ☎1/342-6521). *The Budapest Sun* weekly has what's-on **listings**, as does *In Your Pocket Budapest* and the free monthly *Where Budapest*, found in hotel foyers. A **Budapest Card** (3950/4950Ft for two/three days), available at tourist offices, hotels and major metro stations, gives unlimited travel on public transport, free museum admission, reductions on the airport minibus (buying single tickets with the card gets you a bigger reduction than buying a return) and other discounts. Tourist offices supply free **maps**, but far better is the wirebound 1:25,000 Budapest Atlas (1500Ft), from newsstands, bookshops and Tourinform offices.

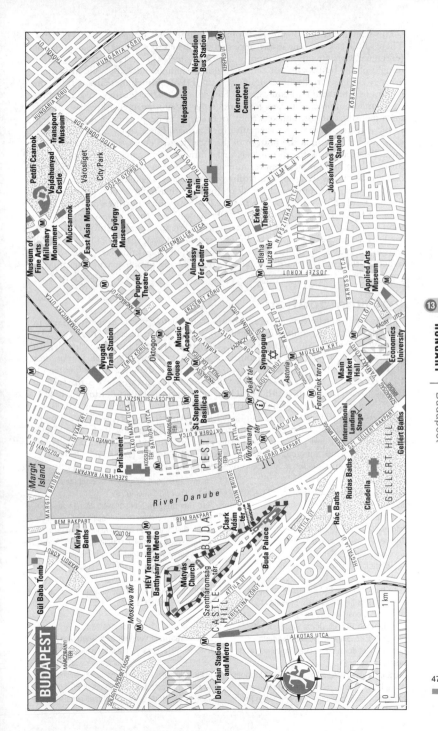

The **metro** (daily 4.30am–11.15pm) has three lines intersecting at Deák tér. There's little risk of going astray once you've learned to recognize the signs: *bejárat* (entrance), *kijárat* (exit), *vonal* (line) and *felé* (towards). A basic 120Ft ticket (140Ft if bought on the bus) is valid for a journey along one line, and is also valid for a single journey on buses, trolleybuses, trams and the **HÉV suburban train** as far as the city limits. On the metro you can also buy 80Ft tickets for journeys of up to three stops, and combination tickets for transferring to another metro line. Buy tickets from metro stations or (quicker) from street stands or newsagents, and punch them in the machines at the station entrance (or on board buses, trolleybuses and trams): inspectors often wait at the bottom of the escalators to check tickets and hand out fines. **Buses** (*busz*) with red numbers make limited stops, while those with the red suffix "E" go nonstop between termini; all run every ten minutes or so during the day – as do **trams** (*villamos*) and **trolleybuses** (*trolibusz*) – and every thirty to sixty minutes between 11pm and dawn along routes with a night service (denoted with the black suffix "É"). Either get a **pass** (925/1850Ft for one/three days), or buy a book of tickets (ten 1070Ft, twenty 2100Ft) – don't tear them out, as they are only valid if kept in the book. **Taxis** are inexpensive, but are also a common rip-off. Go for Fötaxi (☏1/222-2222) or the English-speaking Citytaxi (☏1/211-1111): both charge a basic fee of up to 200Ft plus up to 200Ft per kilometre. They can be hailed in the street, but are cheapest if you order by phone, giving the number you're calling from.

Accommodation

Hotels are generally expensive, and many of the better places expect payment in euros. For bookings, contact HungarHotels, Petöfi Sándor utca 16 (☏1/318-3393, ⊛www.danubiusgroup.com); IBUSZ, V, Vörösmarty tér 6, facing the British Embassy (☏1/317-0532, ⊛www.ibusz.hu); American Express, V, Deák Ferenc utca 10 (☏1/235-4330), which charges a $20 service fee; or the Vista Visitor Center, VI, Paulay Ede utca 7 (☏1/267-8603, ⊛www.vista.hu). You can book a **hostel** bed through the Hungarian Youth Hostel Association near Keleti Station (☏1/413-2065, ⊛www.youthhostels.hu). **Private rooms** downtown cost from 4500Ft a night, rising to 10,000Ft or more in high season. **Apartments**, rented out per night from 8500Ft (12,500Ft high season) are good value for groups. Preferable locales are districts V, VI and VII in Pest, and the parts of Buda nearest Castle Hill. Tribus Non-Stop Hotel Service, V, Apáczai Csere János utca 1 (24hr; ☏1/266-8042, ⊛www.tribus.hu), books private rooms and apartments.

Hostels

Back Pack XI, Takács Menyhért utca 33 ☏1/385-8946. Charming, clean, with a shaded garden, and only 20min from the centre. Lots of city information, plus rock climbing and cave trips. Tram #49 or bus #7 to Tétényi út stop in Buda. Rooms ❸ Dorms ❶

Citadella I, Citadella sétány ☏1/466-5794. Breathtaking views of the city; get there early to get a bunk, but note that the neighbouring nightclub sets the whole place shaking at weekends. Rooms ❹ Dorms ❶

Diáksport Szálló XIII, Dózsa György út 152 ☏1/340-8585. Singles, doubles and dorms in a clean but run-down hostel near the centre, with Internet access. ❷

Museum Guest House VIII, Mikszáth Kálmán tér 4, 1st floor ☏1/318-9508. Behind the National Museum, handy for central bars and cafés. Three clean dorms, each with seven or eight mattresses on the floor. Free Internet. ❷

Red Bus Hostel V, Semmelweis utca 14 ☏1/266-0136. Clean, quiet hostel with basic facilities but a great, central location behind Astoria. Run by a young English/Hungarian couple. ❷

Strawberry Youth Hostel IX, Kinizsi utca 2–6 ☏1/217-3033. The newer of two hostels of the same name, with basic furniture in rooms with two, three or four beds. June to Sept only. Blue metro line to Kálvin tér. ❷

Hotels and pensions

ELTE Peregrinus Vendégház V, Szerb utca 3 ☏1/266-4911. Located in a quiet backstreet in central Pest, this friendly, elegant place is attached to the university; 25 rooms, available year round. ❼

Jager-Trio Panzió XI, Ördögorom út 20 ☏1/246-4558, ✉jagertrio@axelero.hu. Small pension on the edge of the city in the Buda hills, close to the end of the bus #8 route. ⑤

Medosz VI, Jókai tér 9 ☎1/374-3000. Comfortable lodging in an ugly but well located building near the Oktogon. ⑥

San Marcó Panzió III, San Marcó utca 6 ☎1/388-9997, ✉saiban@elender.hu. Small, friendly pension in northern Buda, five rooms, three with private bathrooms. Famous for its hearty breakfasts. ⑤

The City

The **River Danube** (Duna) determines basic orientation, with **Pest** sprawled across the eastern plain and **Buda** reclining on the hilly west bank. Castle Hill is the historic focal point of Buda, home of the Royal Palace and for many years the government. Across the water, Pest has always been the commercial focus, with its hub around the old city centre or Belváros. Construction of the first permanent bridge between the two in 1849 led to rapid expansion, then unification in 1873.

Buda

Seen from the embankments, **Buda** looks irresistibly romantic with its palatial buildings, archaic spires and outsize statues rising from rugged hills. Its centre, **Castle Hill**, is easily reached via the **Chain Bridge**, opened in 1849 and the first permanent bridge between Buda and Pest. From the busy square on its western side, Clark Ádám tér, you can ride up Castle Hill by the nineteenth-century funicular or **Sikló** (daily 7.30am–10pm; 450Ft up, 350Ft down). Alternatively, take the red metro to Moszkva tér and the *Várbusz* from there.

By midday, **Szentháromság tér**, the square at the heart of the district, is crammed with tourists, buskers, handicraft vendors and other entrepreneurs, a multilingual spectacle played out against the backdrop of the wildly asymmetrical **Mátyás Church** (Mon–Fri 9am–5pm, Sat 9am–1pm, Sun 1–5pm; 500Ft). The church is a riotous nineteenth-century re-creation of the medieval spirit, grafted onto those portions of the thirteenth-century structure that survived 150 years of Ottoman rule – when the church was turned into a mosque – and the siege of 1686, which brought the Ottoman occupation to an end. An equestrian statue of **King Stephen** stands just outside the church, commemorating the ruler who forced Catholicism onto his subjects, thus aligning Hungary with the culture of Western Europe. The **Fishermen's Bastion** or Halászbástya (daily 24hr; mid-March to Oct 8.30am–11pm; 300Ft; otherwise free) is a white rampart with cloisters and seven turrets, framing the view of Parliament across the river. Medieval architectural features have survived along **Országház utca**, at the northern end of which the quasi-Gothic **Mary Magdalene Tower** still dominates Kapisztrán tér, albeit gutted and transformed into an art gallery. To the south of Szentháromság tér the street widens as it approaches the **Buda Palace**. The fortifications and dwellings built by Béla III after the thirteenth-century Mongol invasion were replaced by ever more luxurious palaces; the most recent reconstruction dates from after the devastation wrought in World War II. The northern Wing houses the **Museum of Contemporary Art (Ludwig Collection)** (Tues–Sun 10am–6pm; 500Ft), which has pieces by the likes of Picasso, Hockney and Lichtenstein as well as by younger Hungarian artists such as Attila Szücs. The **National Gallery** (Tues–Sun 10am–4/6pm; 700Ft), occupying the central wings B, C and D, contains Hungarian art since the Middle Ages. Gothic stone-carvings, altars and painted panels fill the ground floor, while nineteenth-century painting, including major Hungarian artists such as Csontváry, Rippl-Rónai and Munkácsy, dominates upstairs. On the far side of the Lion Courtyard, the **Budapest History Museum** in Wing E (Wed–Mon 10am–4/6pm; 700Ft) gives the history of the territory that makes up the city, from prehistoric finds on display on the top floor down to the marbled and flagstoned halls of the Renaissance palace deep underground.

Watertown (Víziváros), a wedge-shaped tangle of narrow streets between Castle Hill and the river to the north of the Chain Bridge, was once the poor quarter housing fishermen, craftsmen and their families. Today it's a reclusive neighbour-hood of old mansions meeting at odd angles on the hillside, reached by alleys which mostly consist of steps rising from the main street, Fő utca. North along Fő utca stand the **Király baths** (men only Mon, Wed & Fri 9am–9pm; women only Tues & Thurs 6.30am–7pm, Sat 6.30am–1pm; 1000Ft), distinguishable by four cop-per cupolas.

South of Watertown rises **Gellért Hill** (Gellérthegy), crowned by the **Liberation Monument**, one of the few Soviet monuments to survive the fall of the Iron Curtain, and the **Citadella**, a low fortress built by the Habsburgs to cow the popu-lation after the 1848–49 revolution. Nowadays the fort contains nothing more sin-ister than a few exhibits, a tourist hostel, a new terrace bar and an overpriced restaurant. Descending the southern slopes of the hill through the playgrounds of Jubileumi Park, you'll come to the **Gellért baths**, at the side of *Hotel Gellért*. The best publicized of the city's baths, they were built in 1913, and the grandeur of the entrance hall is continued in the main pool (Mon–Fri 6am–7pm, Sat & Sun 6am–5/7pm; 2000Ft). You can get cheaper tickets just for the stunning thermal baths (which close earlier at weekends; separate baths for men and women), but it's worth paying to enjoy the beauty of the whole complex. Further north, by the Erzsébet Bridge, are the men-only **Rudas baths** (Mon–Fri 6am–7pm, Sat & Sun 6am–1pm; 650Ft, 900Ft for steam bath), Budapest's most atmospheric Turkish baths, whose interior has hardly changed since it was constructed in 1556.

Budapest's ironically nostalgic **Communist Statue Park** (Szoborpark; daily 10am–sunset; 600Ft; ⓦwww.szoborpark.hu) also lies on this side of the river and is well worth a detour to see the monumental statues of Marx, Engels and Lenin. It's stuck out in district XXII; take the direct bus from Deák tér (daily: July & Aug 10am, 11am, 3pm, 4pm; March–June, Sept & Oct 11am & 3pm; Nov–Feb 11am; 1950Ft return).

Pest

Pest, busier and more vital than Buda, is the place where things are decided, made and sold. Much of the architecture and general layout dates from the late nineteenth century, when boulevards, public buildings and apartment houses were built on a scale appropriate to the Habsburg Empire's second city and the capital of Hungary, which celebrated its 1000th anniversary in 1896. The **Belváros** revels in its cos-mopolitanism, with shops selling the latest fashions and French perfumes, posters proclaiming the arrival of Hollywood films and international rock groups, and streets noisy with the sound of foreign cars and languages. The main square, **Vörösmarty tér**, busy with portraitists, conjurers, violinists and other performers, is dominated by crowded café terraces. The most venerable institution here is the **Gerbeaud** patis-serie, the favourite of Budapest's high society since the late nineteenth century, and now packed with tourists. The city's most chic shopping street, **Váci utca**, runs south from the square, parallel to the river and thronged with people. Passing the Pesti Theatre, where 12-year-old Liszt made his concert debut, the crowds flow down to **Ferenciek tere**, overlooking which is a slab of gilt-and-gingerbread archi-tecture, the **Párizsi udvar**, home to an ice-cream parlour and IBUSZ office, but chiefly known for its "Parisian arcade", adorned with arabesques and stained glass. Váci utca continues south to the **Main Market Hall**, with its fancy ironwork, porcelain tiles and stalls festooned with strings of paprika and garlic.

Peering over the rooftops to the north of Vörösmarty tér is the dome of **St Stephen's Basilica**, from the top of which there's a good view over the city (dome: April–Oct daily 10am–5/7pm; 500Ft). On his name day, August 20, St Stephen's mummified hand and other holy relics are paraded round the building; the rest of the year, the hand is on show in a side chapel. Just north of the Basilica, dominating the banks of the Danube, is the large dome of the **Parliament**, a stu-pendous nineteenth-century creation befitting a small country with old longings for grandeur. In 1999 the old **Coronation Regalia** were transferred from the

National Museum to the Parliament. Reputedly the very crown, orb and sceptre used by King Stephen, the regalia are now thought to be a combination of two crowns used by Stephen's successors; nevertheless they are still seen as a symbol of Hungarian statehood. There are daily **tours** of the building – in English – if parliamentary business allows (10am, noon & 2pm; 2000Ft; tickets from Gate X, half way along the east front).

To the east of the Basilica, **Andrássy út** runs dead straight for 2.5km, a parade of grand buildings laden with gold leaf, dryads and colonnades, including the magnificent Opera House at no. 22. Its shops and sidewalk cafés retain some of the style that made the avenue so fashionable in the 1890s. The boulevard culminates at **Hősök tere**, built to mark the 1000th anniversary of the Magyar conquest. Its centrepiece is the **Millennary Monument**, portraying Prince Árpád and his chieftains grouped around a 36m-high column topped by the Archangel Gabriel, and half-encircled by a colonnade displaying statues of Hungary's most illustrious leaders, from King Stephen to Kossuth. Also on the square, the **Museum of Fine Arts** (Tues–Sun 10am–6pm; 800Ft) contains Egyptian funerary relics, Greek and Roman ceramics, and paintings and drawings by European masters from the thirteenth to twentieth centuries – including Dürer, El Greco, Velázquez and Bronzino. Behind the museum lies **Budapest Zoo** (daily 9am–4/7pm; 1800Ft), worth a visit for the architecture alone – the Palm House, the Elephant House and the Aviary in particular. Opposite the zoo, the yellow neo-Baroque walls of the **Széchenyi baths** (daily 6am–6pm; 1800Ft) contain one of Europe's largest spa complexes. Watch locals play chess on floating boards while wallowing in the steam.

Back towards the centre of the Belváros, on the corner of Wesselényi and Dohány utca, stands the dramatic main **Synagogue**, whose Byzantine-Moorish architecture has been undergoing much-needed restoration; the interior is now complete and utterly magnificent. In the **National Jewish Museum** next door (Mon–Thurs 10am–3pm, Fri 10am–2pm, Sun 10am–2pm; 600Ft), exhibits dating back to the Middle Ages are opposed by a harrowing Holocaust exhibition, which casts a chill over the third section, portraying Jewish cultural life today. In the streets behind the synagogue lies Pest's main **Jewish quarter**. In recent years the small Jewish community that survived the Holocaust has become much more visible in the city, although even here, where the community is strongest, it keeps a low profile. Along Dob utca there is the *Fröhlich* kosher coffee shop at no. 22, a wigmaker at no. 31, and at no. 35, by the entrance to the orthodox community buildings, a kosher butcher's, while further along in Klauzál tér you can buy excellent kosher *slivovitz* in the cellar of no. 16 (Thurs 2.30–4.30pm, Fri 11.30am–2pm).

Eating and drinking

Magyar cooking has been overtaken in Budapest's **restaurants** by scores of places devoted to international cuisine. Prices by Western European standards are very reasonable, and your budget should stretch to at least one binge in a top-flight place. The following categories – *cukrászdas* (patisseries) for sweet pastries and coffee, restaurants (for eating), and bars and beer halls (for drinking) – are to an extent arbitrary, since all restaurants serve alcohol and all bars serve some food, while *eszpresszós* (cafés) feature both, plus coffee and pastries.

Patisseries

Angelika I, Batthyány tér 7. The former convent has been modernized with techno soundtrack and a lively terrace, though elderly locals are still hanging in there.

Centrál V, Károlyi Mihály utca 9. Large old coffee house restored to its former glory, with a broad menu ranging from cheap to very expensive.

Eckermann VI, Andrássy út 24. Big coffees and

Internet access (from 2pm) in this popular café next to the Goethe Institute. Closed Sun.

Fröhlich VII, Dob utca 22. A kosher patisserie five minutes' walk from the Dohány utca synagogue, presided over by the Fröhlich family. Specialities include *flódni* (an apple, walnut and poppy-seed cake). Closed Sat & Jewish holidays.

Gerbeaud V, Vörösmarty tér 7. A popular, very grand place in central Pest. A coffee and a torte will set you back around 1000Ft; the same rich pastries are cheaper in *Kis Gerbeaud* around the corner.

Müvész VI, Andrássy út 29. Grand old coffee house that's less touristy and cheaper than *Gerbeaud.*

Múzeum Cukrászda VIII, Múzeum körút 10. Friendly hangout by the National Museum. Fresh pastries arrive at dawn.

Ruszwurm I, Szentháromság utca 7. Excellent cakes, served production-line fashion to those taking a break from sightseeing on Castle Hill.

Fast food, self-service and snack bars

Duran Sandwich Bar V, Október 6 utca 15. A sandwich and coffee bar – still, oddly enough, a rare combination in Budapest. Closed Sun.

Falafel Faloda VI, Paulay Ede utca 53. Best of the city's falafel joints. Closed Sat & Sun.

Karma Café VI, Liszt Ferenc tér 11. Beautifully decorated café with excellent tapas, situated on Pest's trendiest square.

Marie Kristensen Sandwich Bar IX, Ráday utca 7. A decent sandwich bar behind Kálvin tér. Closed Sun.

Nobu VI, Teréz körút 46. Friendly noodle bar with baguettes and coffee too.

Restaurants

Abszint VI, Andrássy út 34. Reasonably priced Provençal cuisine in a fun setting. Budding visionary poets can taste a Bulgarian version of absinthe.

Al-Amir VII, Király utca 17. Syrian restaurant serving excellent salads and hummus, making it a haven for vegetarians in a city of carnivores. No alcohol.

Art Café Alhambra VI, Jókai tér 3. Gorgeous interior, heavenly tapas, exhibitions and Moroccan teas to aid chilling out in style.

Café Kör V, Sas utca 17 ☎1/311-0053. Popular place near the Basilica with excellent food and fine wines. Menu supplemented by specials written up on the wall. Booking essential. Closed Sun.

Gandhi V, Vigyázó Ferenc utca 4. An oasis of spiritual calm in the city serving a range of international vegetarian dishes.

Gundel XIV, Állatkerti út 2 ☎1/468-4040. Prides itself as the flagship of Hungarian cuisine and has correspondingly high prices. On Sunday, though, you can eat your fill for 4700Ft at their bargain brunch. Booking essential. Closed Sun eve.

Kádár étkezde VII, Klauzál tér 9. Jewish home cooking in the old quarter, where friendly staff serve lunches of boiled beef in fruit sauces. Closed Sun.

Márkus Vendéglő II, Lövőház utca 17. Welcoming, inexpensive Hungarian restaurant near Moszkva tér.

Papageno V, Semmelweis utca 19. Small, friendly establishment with top chefs specializing in French and Italian cuisine. Closed Sun.

Bars, wine bars and beer halls

Bambi I, Bem tér. Wonderful old bar from the socialist era serving breakfast, snack lunches, dry-looking cakes and alcohol.

Buena Vista VI, Liszt Ferenc tér 5. Popular bar near the Music Academy on a square where cafés all spill out under the trees. Good restaurant upstairs, plus their own beer in the cellar bar.

Café Miro I, Úri utca 30. A trendy bar in the Castle district, which often has live music.

Castro IX, Ráday utca 35. A lively place on Ráday utca, a street popular with students and lined with cafés and bars. Internet access too.

Darshan Udvar VIII, Krúdy Gyula utca 7. The largest bar in a growing complex of bars, cafés and shops. Set at the back of the courtyard, with oriental/hippie decorations, good food, world music and leisurely service.

Eklektika V, Semmelweis utca 21. Arty, gay-friendly bar with 1960s furniture, art exhibitions, a pasta/salad menu and women-only evenings on the second Sat of the month.

Gusto's II, Frankel Leó út 12. Tiny bar near Buda side of Margit Bridge, serving the best tiramisù in town. Closed Sun.

Old Man's Music Pub VII, Akácfa utca 13. Popular Pest joint with live local acts and good food.

Zöld Pardon XI, by the Buda end of Petőfi Bridge. Large outdoor bar with live music sprawling across the grass near the university quarter, popular with students. Closed Nov–Feb.

Entertainment, nightlife and festivals

The four main venues for **alternative concerts**, **folk music** and **modern dance** events are the Petőfi Csarnok in the Városliget (◉www.petoficsarnok.hu); the Almássy tér Cultural Centre at VII, Almássy tér 6 (◉www.almassy.hu); the Trafó, a revamped transformer station in Pest, at IX, Liliom utca 41 (◉www.trafo.hu); and the Fonó in Buda at XI, Sztregova utca 3 (◉www.fono.hu). **Tickets** for most events can be had through Ticket Express for classical and pop, VI, Andrássy út 18 (☎1/312-0000); or Publika for rock and jazz, VII, Károly körút 9 (☎1/322-2010). New **clubs** are opening all the time, and the rave and floating party scene is growing constantly: check flyers and posters around town, or look in the "Könnyű" section of *Pesti Est*, the free listings magazine in cinema foyers. There's also a variety of cheap **student clubs**, and keep an eye out for the steamy parties organized in the thermal spas by the Cinetrip crew.

Star events in the cultural year are the **Budapest Spring Festival** (two weeks in March or April) and the **Autumn Music Weeks** (late Sept to late Oct), both of which attract top international acts. There are also scores of classical and popular concerts during the summer. On **St Stephen's Day** (Aug 20) the area around the Royal Palace becomes one big folk and crafts fair, and in the evening people line the embankments to watch the fireworks.

Clubs

Angyal VII, Szövetség utca 33. Budapest's premier gay club: looks like an airport lounge but has an interesting crowd. Sat is men only. Closed Mon–Wed.

Capella V, Belgrád rakpart 23. Drag queens, jungle music and lots of tat: just the place for a night on the town.

Cha Cha Cha IX, Kálvin tér subway. Despite its strange location, this place attracts a big crowd spilling out into the concourse, and has DJs at weekends. Closed Sun.

Közgáz Fővám tér 8, behind the Economics University. Liveliest of the student clubs.

Romkert I, Döbrentei tér 9. Outside bar attracting a wealthy young crowd, that's one of the few places you can dance outside until the early hours. Good bar food; worth booking a table if you're eating. Closed Nov-Feb.

Süss Fel Nap V, Honvéd utca 40. Heaving, lively place attracting a young crowd.

Trocadero Café V, Szent István körút 15. Excellent Latin music and dancing just up from Nyugáti Station. Closed Sun & Mon.

Listings

Embassies and consulates Australia, XII, Királyhágó tér 8–9 ☎1/457-9777; Canada, XII, Budakeszi út 32 ☎1/392-3360; Ireland, V, Szabadság tér 7, 7th floor, Bank Center ☎1/302-9600; New Zealand, VI, Teréz körút 38, 4th floor ☎1/428-2208; UK, V, Harmincad utca 6 ☎1/266-2888; US, V, Szabadság tér 12 ☎1/475-4400.

Exchange Gönc Szövetkezeti Takarékpénztár at V, Rákóczi út 5; Magyar Külkereskedelmi Bank at Türr István utca at the top of Váci utca, Pest; Tribus tourist office V, Apáczai Csere János utca 1.

Hospital V, Hold utca 19, behind the US embassy ☎1/311-6816; II, Ganz utca 13–15 ☎1/202-1370.

Internet Ami Internet Coffee, Váci utca 40 (daily 9am-2am); Eckermann Café, VI, Andrássy út 24, near the Opera House (closed Sun); Enternet at V, Deák Ferenc utca 15, corner of Vörösmarty tér; Libri Könyvpalota, VII, Rákóczi út 12 (closed Sun); Vista Visitor Center, VI, Paulay Ede utca 7.

Pharmacy Alkotás utca 1B, opposite Déli station; Teréz körút 41, near Oktogon.

Police Tourinform, on Vörösmarty tér (open 24hr; ☎1/438-8080), has a police information office for reporting crime.

Post office V, Petőfi utca 13.

Around Budapest: Szentendre

To escape Budapest's humid summers, many people flock north of the city to the **Danube Bend**, one of the grandest stretches of the river. The historic town of **SZENTENDRE** on the west bank is the most popular day-trip from the capital (40min by HÉV train from Batthyány tér; 1hr 30min by boat from Vigadó tér pier), a friendly maze of houses painted in autumn colours, secret gardens, and alleys leading to hilltop churches – the perfect spot for an artists' colony, which is what it became in the 1920s, when artists moved out from the city to make the most of the superb natural light. Szentendre's original character was largely shaped by Serbs seeking refuge from the Ottomans. Their townhouses – now converted into galleries, shops and cafés – form a set piece around **Fő tér**, now a stage for musicians and mime-artists. On the north side of the square is **Blagovestenska Church** (Tues–Sun 10am–5pm; winter open for worship only; 100Ft) – whose

HUNGARY | Budapest

iconostasis, painted by Mikhail Zivkovic (1776–1824), suggests the richness of the Serbs' artistry and faith. Just around the corner at Vastagh György utca 1 stands the wonderful **Margit Kovács Museum** (daily 10am–5/6pm; closed Mon in winter; 500Ft), displaying the lifetime work of Hungary's best-known ceramicist, born in 1902. Above Fő tér there's a fine view over Szentendre's steeply banked rooftops and gardens from the hilltop **Templom tér**, where frequent craft fairs help finance the restoration of the Catholic parish church there. Opposite the church, paintings whose fierce brush strokes and sketching were a challenge to the canons of classicism during the 1890s hang in the **Béla Czóbel Museum** (April–Oct Tues–Sun 10am–6pm; 300Ft), beyond which the spire of the **Serbian Orthodox Cathedral** pokes above a walled garden; tourists are generally not admitted, but you can see the cathedral iconostasis and treasury in the adjacent **museum** (March–Oct Tues–Sun 10am–4/6pm; Jan & Feb Fri–Sun only, Nov–Dec closed; 200Ft). An hourly bus runs from the HÉV terminal out along Szabadságforrás út to Szentendre's fascinating **Village Museum** (April–Nov daily 9am–5/7pm; 700Ft; ⊛ www.skanzen.hu), which has reconstructed villages from five regions of Hungary (more are planned). During the summer, on alternate weekends, there are demonstrations of traditional craft techniques, including pottery, baking and basket-making.

For **information**, both on the town and the Danube Bend, head to the branch of Tourinform at Dumtsa Jenő utca 22 (Mon–Fri 9am–4.30pm, Sat & Sun 10am–2pm; ☎26/317-965, ✉szentendre@tourinform.hu). For **accommodation**, the best budget options are the *Horváth fogadó*, Daru piac 2 (☎26/313-950; ❷), to the north of the centre; and *Ilona Panzió*, Rákóczi F. utca 11 (☎26/313-599; ❷), in a pleasant location in the heart of the old quarter. IBUSZ, Bogdányi utca 11 (Mon–Fri 10am–4/6pm; summer also Sat & Sun 10am–1pm; ☎26/500-172) can arrange **private rooms**. A lot of people end up camping rough on Szentendre Island or at the **official campsite**, presently being renovated and expanded on Pap Island (☎26/310-697; closed Oct-April) – accessible by ferry or bus respectively. Most **restaurants** are concentrated in and around Fő tér; the *Aranysárkány*, Alkotmány utca 1/a is a gay-friendly venue, and *Rab Ráby*, Kucsera Ferenc utca 1 offers traditional dishes. *Palapa*, Dumtsa J 14/a, is an excellent Mexican bar/restaurant. **Café terraces** line up along the Danube – you can stay at the *Corner Panzió*, Dunakorzó 4, if you over-indulge in the Balkan food and wine.

Western Hungary

The major tourist attraction to the west of the capital is **Lake Balaton**, over-romantically labelled the "Hungarian sea". Despite the fact that rising prices are pushing out natives in favour of Austrians and Germans, this is still very much the nation's playground, with vacation resorts lining both shores. On the northern bank, development has been limited to some extent by reedbanks and cooler, deeper water, giving tourism a different slant – the spa town of **Balatonfüred** is the main draw here. Historic **Tihany** offers fine sightseeing, while anyone whose social life doesn't take off in **Keszthely** can go soak themselves in the thermal lake at **Hévíz**.

More than other regions in Hungary, the western region of **Transdanubia** is a patchwork land, an ethnic and social hybrid. Its valleys and hills, forests and mud flats have been a melting pot since Roman times: settled by Magyars, Serbs, Slovaks and Germans; torn asunder and occupied by Ottomans and Habsburgs; transformed from a state of near-feudalism into brutal collectives; and now operating under modern capitalism. All the main towns display evidence of this evolution, especially **Sopron**, with its well-preserved medieval centre, and **Pécs**, which boasts an Ottoman mosque and minaret.

Balatonfüred

The Romans were the first to imbibe the curative waters of **BALATONFÜRED**, and nowadays some 30,000 people come every year for treatment in its sanatoriums. A busy harbour and skyscraper hotels dominate approaches to the town, but the centre has a sedate, convalescent atmosphere, typified by the embankment promenade, Rabindranath Tagore sétány, named after the Bengali poet who came here in 1926. Above the tree-lined promenade lies **Gyógy tér**, where you can drink the Kossuth spring's carbonic water at a pagoda-like structure.

The **bus and train stations** are next door to each other on Castricum tér, midway between the old town and the lake. **Ferries** from Tihany dock at the pier at the western end of the promenade. For **information** on the town and region, head to the Tourinform office by the Balatonarács train station – the stop before Balatonfüred – at Petőfi utca 68 off the main Tihany road (Mon–Fri 9am–5/7pm; summer also Sat 9am–1pm; ℡87/580-480, ✉balatonfured@tourinform.hu), or the Balatontourist office at the *Füred* campsite (May–Aug 6/7am–7/10pm; ℡87/482-577). Of the **accommodation** available, best bets are: the *Korona Panzió*, Vörösmarty utca 4 (℡87/343-278, ⊛www.hotels.hu/korona_panzio; ❺), a decent pension; lakeside *Tagore*, Deák Ferenc utca 56 (℡87/343-173; closed Nov–April; ❹); *Blaha Lujza*, Blaha Lujza utca 4 (℡87/581-210, ⊛www.hotelblaha.hu; ❹), with an elegant restaurant in actress Lujza Blaha's former summer villa; and *Fortuna*, Honvéd utca 3 (℡87/343-037; closed Oct–April; ❹). Alternatively, you can arrange **private rooms** through Balatontourist, or IBUSZ in the Arany Csillag store, Zsigmond utca 2 (℡87/482-248). There are **dorms** at Széchenyi Ferenc Kollégium in Iskola utca, though those in the old town can be a long way from the lake. The big lakeside *Füred* **campsite**, Széchenyi utca 24 (℡87/343-823), is west of town, beyond the *Füred* and *Marina* hotels. **Restaurants** and **snack bars** line up along Tagore sétány. There's a clutch of over-priced tourist traps on Vitorlás tér near the Mahart ferry pier; better to head east to the friendly *Borcsa Restaurant* in front of the *Tagore* hotel, or walk uphill to the *Hotel Park Restaurant*, Jókai Mór utca 24, with an open-air grill and substantial three-course menu for under 1000Ft.

Tihany

The historic centre of **TIHANY**, self-proclaimed "Pearl of the Balaton", sits above the harbour where the **ferries** from Balatonfüred dock; you'll find it by following the winding steps up between a screen of trees, and you'll know you've arrived by the mass of tourist boutiques and stalls crowding the streets. Tihany's **Benedictine Abbey**, 2km north of the docks, on top of the hill, was established in 1055 at the request of Andrew I, whose body now lies in the crypt. A few paces north from the abbey brings you to the **Open-Air Folk Museum** (May–Sept Tues–Sun 10am–6pm; 300Ft), a collection of old cottages giving a feel of life in the village in the early twentieth century. Around Petőfi and Csokonai streets, houses are built of grey basalt tufa, with windows and doors outlined in white, and porticoed terraces. Even without a map it's easy to stumble upon the **Inner Lake** (Belső-tó), whose sunlit surface is visible from the abbey. From its southern bank, a path runs through vineyards, orchards and lavender fields past the Aranyház geyser cones and down to Tihanyi-rév. Since trains bypass the peninsula, your alternative method of arrival – other than the ferry – is by **bus** from Balatonfüred. There's a **Tourinform** office up by the abbey at Kossuth utca 20 (℡87/448-804, ✉tihany@tourinform.hu). Hotel prices, like everything else in Tihany, are exorbitant by Hungarian standards. The neighbouring **campsite** or **private rooms** are the only affordable options: book at Balatontourist, Kossuth utca 12 (April–Oct Mon–Sat 8am–6.30pm, Sun 8am–1pm; Nov–March Mon–Fri 8am–4.30pm, Sat 8am–1pm; ℡87/448-519), or Tihany Tourist, Kossuth utca 11 (April–Oct daily 9am–4/8pm; ℡87/448-481, ✉tihany.tourist@axelero.hu). The *Oazis* **restaurant**, Major utca 47 (closed Nov–March), has good food and friendly staff, or try *Két Fazék*, Kossuth utca 23, with traditional food, very friendly staff and a vociferous mynah bird.

Keszthely and Hévíz

Absorbing thousands of visitors gracefully, **KESZTHELY**, Balaton's best hangout, has some good bars and restaurants, a thermal lake at nearby Hévíz, and a university to give it some life of its own. Keszthely's waterfront has two bays (one for swimming, the other for ferries) formed by man-made piers, a slew of parkland backed by plush hotels and miniature golf courses, and dozens of fast-food joints and bars. In the evenings, action shifts from the water to the centre, where the bars and restaurants work at full steam. Walking up from the train station along Martírok útja, you'll pass the **Balaton Museum** at the junction with Kossuth Lajos utca (Tues–Sat 9am–5pm; 300Ft), with exhibits on the region's history and wildlife. From Fő tér onwards, with its much-remodelled Gothic church, Kossuth utca is given over to cafés, vendors, buskers and strollers and leads up towards the **Festetics Palace**, founded in 1745 by Count György Festetics (July & Aug daily 9am–6pm; rest of year Tues–Sun 10am–5pm; 1700Ft), which attracted the leading lights of Magyar literature from the nineteenth century onwards. The building's highlights are its gilt, mirrored ballroom and the Helikon Library, a masterpiece of joinery and carving. It stages regular summer concerts.

The **dock** and the **train station** are roughly ten minutes' walk south of the centre along Erzsébet királyné útja. The train station is five minutes' walk southwest of the cluster of lakeside hotels along Kazinczy utca, where some intercity buses also terminate. Most **buses**, however, drop off on Fő tér, halfway along Kossuth utca, the main drag. There's a **Tourinform** office at Kossuth utca 28 (June to mid-Sept Mon–Fri 9am–8pm, Sat & Sun 9am–6pm; rest of year Mon–Fri 9am–5pm, Sat 10am–1pm; ☎83/314-144). For budget **accommodation**, private rooms are your best bet and are available from Keszthely Tourist, Kossuth utca 25 (Oct–April Mon–Sat 8am–5pm, May–Sept daily 9am–8/9pm; ☎83/312-031, ⊛www.keszthe-lytourist.hu). For information on rooms in college **dorms** (July & Aug daily; rest of year weekends only), ask at either tourist office. There are two **campsites** just south of the train station and the big, expensive *CastrumCamping* (☎83/312-120), 1500m along the shore in the opposite direction. For food, the friendly *Oázis* **restaurant**, down Szalasztó utca from the palace at Rákóczi tér 3 (Mon–Fri 11am–4pm), has an excellent salad and vegetarian self-service bar, while the *Eldorado Étterem*, Kossuth utca 14, by the Festetics Palace gates has a good range of fish dishes. Local student hangouts are the trio of **bars** opposite the post office on Kossuth Lajos utca, whilst the smart *Pelzo Café*, next to the Gothic parish church on Fő tér, is ideal for a coffee stop.

Half-hourly buses from Keszthely train station run to **HÉVÍZ**, a spa based around Europe's largest thermal lake, **Hévízi Gyógy-tó**. The wooden terraces surrounding the **Tófürdő** (daily 8.30am/9am–4/5pm; 3hr 600Ft, all day 1200Ft) have a vaguely *fin-de-siècle* appearance, but the ambience is contemporary, with people sipping beer while bobbing on the murky, egg-scented lake in rented inner-tubes. Otherwise, Hévíz seems to consist of rest homes and costly hotels, with a late-night **bar** and **casino** in the *Hotel Thermál*. An inexpensive **place to stay** is *Pannon*, Széchenyi utca 23 (☎83/340-482, ⊜pannonhotels@axelero.hu; ❸), near the centre of town, or you could try the slightly smarter *Piroska Panzió*, Kossuth utca 10 (☎83/342-698; ❷). Hévíz Tourist, Rákóczi utca 2 (Mon–Fri 8.30am–4.30pm, Sat 9am–1pm; ☎83/341-348, ⊜heviztour@axelero.hu), is an accommodation-booking agency.

Sopron and around

SOPRON – the nearest big Hungarian town to Vienna and consequently a popular destination – has 240 listed buildings, which allow it to claim to be "the most historic town in Hungary". The horseshoe-shaped Belváros (old town) is north of Széchenyi tér and the main train station. At the southern end, **Orsolya tér** features Renaissance edifices dripping with loggias and carved protrusions, and a Gothic church. Heading north towards the main square, **Új utca** (New Street – one of the town's oldest thoroughfares) is a gentle curve of arched dwellings painted in red, yellow and pink, with chunky cobblestones and pavements. At no. 22 stands one of the **synagogues** that flourished when the street was known as Zsidó utca (Jewish Street); Sopron's Jewish community survived the expulsion of 1526 only to be all-but-annihilated during World War II. The main source of interest is up ahead on Fő tér, a parade of Gothic and Baroque architecture partly overshadowed by the **Goat Church** – so called, so legend has it, because its construction was financed by a goatherd whose flock unearthed a cache of loot. The Renaissance **Storno House**, once visited by King Mátyás and Count Széchenyi, now exhibits Roman, Celtic and Avar relics, plus mementoes of Liszt. North of the square rises Sopron's symbol, the **Firewatch Tower** (April–Oct Tues–Sat 10am–6pm; 400Ft), founded upon the stones of a fortress originally laid out by the Romans. From the top there's a stunning view of the town's narrow streets and weathered rooftops. The "Gate of Loyalty" at the base of the tower commemorates the townfolk's decision, when offered the choice of Austrian citizenship in 1921, to remain Magyar subjects. Walk through it and you'll emerge onto Előkapu, a short street where the houses are laid out in a saw-toothed pattern.

The **train station** is on Mátyás Király utca, 500m south of Széchenyi tér and the old town; Sopron is linked to Vienna by a fast intercity service, though it's not on the main Budapest–Vienna route. The **bus station** is to the northwest of the old town, five minutes' walk along Lackner Kristóf utca from Ógabona tér. There's a **Tourinform** at Előkapu 11 (June–Oct Mon–Fri 9am–5pm, Sat 9am–noon; Nov–May Mon–Fri 9am–4pm; ☎99/338-892, ⓔsopron@tourinform.hu). **Private rooms** and student accommodation can be arranged through Ciklámen Tourist, Ógabona tér 8 (Mon–Fri 8am–4pm, Sat 8am–1pm; ☎99/312-040). For **accommodation**, try *Bástya Panzió*, Patak utca 40 (☎99/325-325; ❸), or *Jégverem Panzió*, Jégverem utca 1 (☎99/312-004; ❸), both good-value pensions just across the Ikva Stream to the northeast of town. The *Lővér* **campsite** is 4km south of town – take bus #12 from Deák tér; you'll need to book in advance through Ciklámen Tourist. There are some terrific **restaurants**, including *Várkerület Söröző*, Várkerület 83, serving Hungarian dishes, and *Rókalyukhoz*, opposite, with an extensive and eclectic international menu. Up on Fövényverem utca, *Ameli* at no. 15 serves superb fish dishes (closed Mon), or try *Fekete Bárány* opposite. *Café Dakar*, Várkerület 86, is the place to go for cakes and coffees. To sample the local **wines**, head for the atmospheric *Cézár* cellar, Hátsókapu utca 2, or *Gyógygödör Borozó*, Fő tér 4; both are open daily until 10pm.

Esterházy Palace

Some 27km east of Sopron (hourly buses) lies a monument to one of the country's most famous dynasties: the **Esterházy Palace** at Fertőd (Tues–Sun 10am–6pm; 1000Ft). Originally minor nobility, the Esterházy family began its rise thanks to Miklós Esterházy I (1583–1645), who married two rich widows, sided with the Habsburgs, and got himself elevated to count. The palace itself was begun by his grandson, Miklós the Ostentatious, who inherited 600,000 acres and a dukedom in 1762. With its 126 rooms, fronted by a vast horseshoe courtyard where Hussars once pranced to the music of Haydn – Esterházy's resident maestro for many years – the palace was intended to rival Versailles. Climb the tower (200Ft) for a view of the manicured gardens. You can **stay** in the palace – though the accommodation is all Socialist Realist: rooms with two, three, four or more beds and shared showers are available in the east wing (booking essential; ☎99/537-649; ❷).

Pécs

The town of **PÉCS** is one of Transdanubia's largest and most attractive towns; indeed, it lays claim to being the finest town in the country, with its tiled rooftops climbing the vine-laden slopes of the Mecsek range. Besides some good museums, the fifth-oldest university in Europe (founded in 1367) and a great market, Pécs contains Hungary's best examples of **Islamic architecture**, a legacy of the long Ottoman occupation. Heading up Bajcsy-Zsilinszky út from the bus terminal, or by bus #30 from the train station towards the centre, you'll pass Kossuth tér and Pécs's **synagogue** (May–Oct Mon–Fri & Sun 10am–5pm; 200Ft). The beautiful nineteenth-century interior is a haunting place, with Romantic frescoes swirling around a space emptied by the murder of almost 4000 Jews – ten times the number that live in Pécs today. During the Ottoman occupation (1543–1686), a similar fate befell the Christian population, whose principal church was converted into the **Mosque of Gázi Kászim Pasha** (mid-April to mid-Oct Mon–Sat 10am–noon/4pm, Sun 11.30am–2/4pm; donations) to the north on Széchenyi tér. In a twist of history, the mosque has changed sides again and operates as the City Centre Catholic Parish Church. Also on the square is a gallery of contemporary work by local artists and an **Archeological Museum** (Tues–Sun 10am–2pm; 150Ft) displaying items testifying to a Roman presence between the first and fifth centuries. From here you can follow either Káptalan or Janus Pannonius utca towards the **cathedral** (Mon–Fri 10am–6pm, Sat 10am–4pm, Sun 1–4pm; 500Ft, which includes a bonus glass of wine at the Bishop's Wine Cellar just around the corner from the main entrance). Though its architects have incorporated a crypt and side-chapels from eleventh- to fourteenth-century churches, the cathedral is predominantly nineteenth-century neo-Romanesque.

Pécs Fair, held on the morning of the first Sunday of each month – and the Friday and Saturday immediately before – sees some hard bargaining and hard drinking, and there are smaller markets on the same site every Sunday. Bus #50 carries local shoppers from outside the Konzum store in Rákóczi utca to the brand new Pécs Plaza mall opposite the fair; get a ticket from a newsstand or the train station before boarding. Pécs is also an excellent starting-point for heading to the nearby **wine region** of Villány to the south – ask at Tourinform for further information.

Pécs train and bus stations are roughly twenty minutes' walk from the centre: the **train station** is south of the centre on Indoház tér, the **bus station** northeast of here on Zsolyom utca. There's a branch of **Tourinform** at Széchenyi tér 9 (June–Sept Mon–Fri 8am–7pm, Sat & Sun 9am–6pm; rest of year Mon–Fri 8am–4pm; ☎72/213-315, ✉baranya-m@tourinform.hu). Most of the central **hotels** are expensive – the best-value option is *Főnix Hotel* just off Széchenyi tér, Hunyádi út 2 (☎72/311-680; ❷). Convenient for the station is the good-value *Víg Apát Hotel*, Mártírok utca 14 (☎72/313-340; ❷). The renovated and extended *Hotel Laterum*, 3km west of the centre at Hajnóczi utca 37 (☎72/252-113; ❷), has a restaurant, beer hall, gym and laundry amongst its many facilities, while *Familia Privát Camping*, 3km east at Gyöngyösi utca 6 (☎72/327-034, ❷), has a more homely atmosphere. For inexpensive, central accommodation, book a **private room** or **student hostel bed** through Mecsek Tours, Széchenyi tér 1 (☎72/513-370, ✉utir@mecsektours.hu), or IBUSZ, Apáca utca 1 (☎72/212-157). *Mandulás* **campsite**, Ángyán János utca 2 (☎72/515-655; closed mid-Oct to mid-April; bus #34), is just 2km north of the centre, but up a steep, winding hill. When it comes to **eating**, *Aranykacsa*, Teréz utca 4, is excellent, while wholesome Hungarian food is the order of the day at the magnificently decorated *Dóm Étterem*, Király utca 3. Similarly top-notch Hungarian cuisine is served at the classy *Fortuna Étterem*, Ferencesek utcája 32. The *Morik* café, on Jokai tér, is the place for coffee, while Király utca abounds with pizzerias and cafés. In summer, the **beer garden** of *Rózsakert* on Janus Pannonius utca is very pleasant; **bars** are more numerous in the western part of the Belváros, south of the centre. Pécs has its own brewery in Rókusalja utca, and the local beer is served up in the *Kiskorsó* pub. **Internet** access is available in the café next to the *Fortuna* restaurant.

Eastern Hungary

The hilly and forested northern region of **eastern Hungary** will not feature prominently in any hurried tour of the country, but nobody should overlook the famous wine-producing town of **Eger**, where the "Valley of the Beautiful Woman" attracts wine-lovers from all over Europe.

Eger

Its colourful architecture suffused by sunshine, **EGER** seems a fitting place of origin for Egri Bikavér, the famous red wine marketed abroad as "Bull's Blood", which brings hordes of visitors to the town. Despite occasional problems with accommodation, it's a fine place to hangout and wander around, not to mention all the opportunities for drinking. The Neoclassical **cathedral**, designed by József Hild and constructed between 1831 and 1836, is five minutes' walk southwest from Dobó István tér, the main square. The florid **Lyceum** directly opposite the cathedral is worth visiting for its library (April–Sept Tues–Sun 9.30am–3pm; Oct–March Sat & Sun 9.30am–1.30pm; 350Ft), whose beautiful floor and fittings are made of polished oak. While in the building, check out the **observatory**, at the top of the tower in the east wing (same hours and ticket), where a nineteenth-century *camera obscura* projects a view of the entire town. Close by, facing Széchenyi utca, stands the **Archbishop's Palace** (April–Oct Tues–Sat 9am–5pm; Nov–March Mon–Fri 8am–4pm; 200Ft), a U-shaped Baroque pile with fancy wrought-iron gates; in its right wing you'll find the treasury and a history of the bishopric of Eger. Heading back towards the centre along Bajcsy-Zsilinsky utca you'll come out on the pleasant **Dobó István tér**. Cross the bridge and head to the left to find Eger's most photographed structure, a slender fourteen-sided **minaret** (April–Oct 9am–5pm; 200Ft), looking rather lonely without its mosque, which was demolished during a nineteenth-century building boom. Alternatively, head uphill from the square to the gates of the **Castle** (daily 8/9am–5/8pm, 600Ft, limited access Mon 500Ft). From the bastion overlooking the main gate, a path leads up to the ticket office and the fifteenth-century **Bishop's Palace**. Here, tapestries, ceramics, Turkish handicrafts and weaponry fill the museum upstairs, while downstairs are temporary exhibits and a Hall of Heroes, where a life-size marble István Dobó lies amid a bodyguard of heroes of the 1552 siege in which 2000 soldiers and Eger's women repulsed a Turkish force six times their number.

Just west of town, in the Szépasszony Valley, local **vineyards** produce four types of wine – Muskotály (Muscatel), Bikavér (Bull's Blood), Leányka (medium-dry white with a hint of herbs) and Medoc Noir (rich, dark and sweet red) – and it's possible to sample all of them in the cellars there. Finding the right cellar is a matter of luck and taste, but you could try Auntie Anci's Olaszrizling at no. 28 or the Medoc Noir in Sándor Arvai's at no. 31. Cellars tend to close by 8pm. Take a **taxi** (around 800Ft; ☎36/411-222) or attempt the twenty-minute walk back uphill to town.

Trains from Budapest-Keleti arrive at the station on Állomás tér; to reach the centre, walk up the road to Deák Ferenc út, catch bus #10 or #12, and get off when you see the cupola of the cathedral. There's a **Tourinform/Eger Tourist** office at Bajcsy-Zsilinszky utca 9 (mid-June to Aug Mon–Fri 9am–6pm, Sat & Sun 9am–1pm; rest of year Mon–Fri 9am–5pm, Sat 9am–1pm; ☎36/517-715, ⓦwww.egertourist.hu). For **student hostels** and **private rooms** contact IBUSZ, Széchenyi utca 9 (☎36/311-451, Ⓔed eger@iroda.ibusz.hu), or Express, Széchenyi utca 28 (☎36/427-757). Alternatively, along from the castle, there's the *Tourist Motel*, Mekcsey utca 2 (☎36/429-014; ❶); the *Hotel Minaret*, Harangöntő utca 5 (☎36/410-020, Ⓔhotelminaret@axelero.hu; ❷); or the classier *Senator Ház Hotel*, Dobó István tér 11 (☎36/320-466, ⓦwww.hotels.hu/senatorhaz; ❸). There are two **campsites**: *Autós Caraván Camping* to the north, Rákóczi út 79 (☎36/410-558; closed mid-Oct to mid-April; bus #10/#11), and *Tulipán* in the Szépasszony Valley

(☎36/410-580). Two of the best **restaurants** are *Efendi*, Kossuth utca 19, and *Fehér szarvas Vadásztanya*, Klapka utca 8.

Travel details

Trains

Budapest to: Balatonfüred (every 1–2hr; 2hr 15min); Pécs (10 daily; 2hr 30min–3hr); Sopron (8 daily; 2hr 50min); Szentendre (every 15–30min; 45min); Eger (6 daily; 1hr 30min–2hr 30min).

Buses

Badacsony to: Keszthely (hourly).
Balatonfüred to: Tihany (hourly).
Budapest to: Balatonfüred (2 daily); Eger (hourly); Esztergom (every 30min–1hr); Hévíz (2 daily); Keszthely (2 daily); Sopron (4 daily); Szeged (5 daily); Szentendre (every 30min–1hr); Visegrád (hourly).
Esztergom to: Visegrád (hourly).
Keszthely to: Hévíz (every 30min).
Szentendre to: Esztergom & Visegrád (hourly).
Visegrád to: Esztergom (hourly).

Ferries

Usually operating April–Oct/Nov, weather permitting

Budapest to: Esztergom (1–2 daily; 5hr 20min); Szentendre (1–3 daily; 1hr 40min); Visegrád (2–4 daily; 3hr 20min).
Esztergom to: Budapest (1–2 daily; 4hr); Szentendre (2 daily; 3hr).

Hydrofoils

Usually operating April–Oct/Nov, weather permitting

Budapest to: Esztergom (2 at weekends; 1hr 20min); Vienna (1–2 daily; 6hr 20min); Visegrád (1 at weekends; 50min).

Ireland

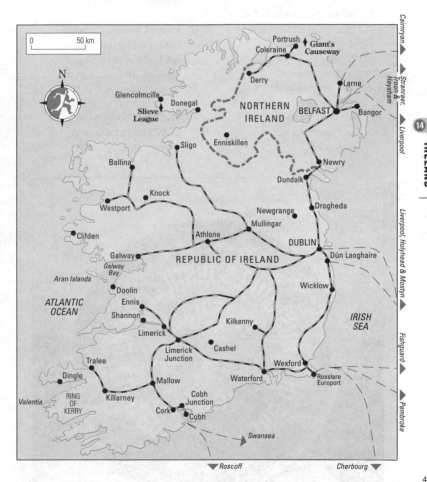

Ireland highlights

✳ **The Guinness Storehouse, Dublin** High-tech temple to Ireland's national brew. See p.502

✳ **St Anne, Shandon** The chance of a lifetime to ring those bells. See p.508

✳ **The Aran Islands** Spectacular setting for some of Ireland's finest archeological remains. See p.514

✳ **Traditional music, Ennis** High-quality pub sessions abound in Ennis and the County Clare countryside. See p.512

✳ **Slieve League, Donegal** Europe's highest sea cliffs offer astounding views of the west coast. See p.517

✳ **The Giant's Causeway** 37,000 basalt columns of wonder! See p.521

Introduction and basics

Ireland's lures are its landscape and people – both in the **Republic** and **Northern Ireland** – the rain-hazed loughs and wild coastlines, the talent for conversation and wealth of traditional music. While economic growth has transformed Ireland's cities, the rural landscape remains relatively unchanged.

Especially in the Irish-speaking areas, there's a strong and enduring **oral tradition**. The speech of the country, moulded by the rhythms of the ancient tongue, inspired such literary greats as Yeats, Joyce and Beckett. **Traditional music**, too, is thriving, with sessions in many pubs.

Ireland's **west** draws most visitors; its coastline and islands – especially **Aran** – combine vertiginous cliffs, boulder-strewn wastes and violent mountains. The interior is less spectacular, but the southern pastures and low wooded hills, and the wide peat bogs of the midlands, are the classic landscapes of Ireland. Northern Ireland's principal draws are the bizarre basalt formation of the **Giant's Causeway** and the alluring, island-studded **Lough Erne**.

Dublin is an extraordinary mix of youthfulness and tradition, of rejuvenated Georgian squares and vibrant pubs. **Belfast**, victim of a perennial bad press, has a lively nightlife, while the cities of **Cork** and **Galway**, in particular, sparkle with newfound energy.

No introduction can cope with the complexities of Ireland's **politics**, which permeate most aspects of daily life, especially in the North. However, regardless of partisan politics, Irish hospitality is as warm as the brochures say, on both sides of the border.

Information & maps

Bord Fáilte provides tourist information in the Republic, and the **Northern Ireland Tourist Board** in the North, with branches in many towns able to help in finding accommodation. The best **maps** are the Michelin 1:400,000 (#405) and the AA 1:350,000. The Ordnance Survey's four 1:250,000 regional Holiday Maps are useful; its 1:50,000 Discovery series is the best option for walkers.

Money and banks

Currency in the Republic is the **euro** (€), in Northern Ireland the **pound sterling** (£). Standard **bank hours** are Mon–Fri 10am–4pm (Republic) and Mon–Fri 9.30am–4.30pm (Northern Ireland). In less populated areas banks may close for lunch and only open on certain weekdays, so it's wise to change money in the large towns. There are **ATMs** throughout Ireland – though not in all villages – and most accept a variety of cards.

Communications

Main **post offices** are open Mon–Fri 9am–5.30pm, Sat 9am–1pm. Stamps and phonecards are often available in newsagents. **Public phones** are everywhere (carry a **phonecard**, as coin-operated phones are rare in rural areas). International calls are cheaper at weekends or after 6pm (Mon–Fri). For the **operator** in the Republic call ☏10 (domestic) or ☏114 (international); in Northern Ireland ☏100 or ☏155. To call the Republic from Northern Ireland dial

Ireland on the net

- ⓦ**www.ireland.travel.ie** Irish Tourist Board.
- ⓦ**www.discovernorthernireland.com** Northern Ireland Tourist Board.
- ⓦ**www.ireland.com** Irish Times site with up-to-date info on Dublin.
- ⓦ**www.local.ie** Region-by-region breakdown.
- ⓦ**www.heritageireland.ie** Official site for monuments and cultural institutions.

☎00353 followed by the area code (without the initial 0) and the local number. To call the North from the Republic use the special code ☎048, followed by the eight-digit local number. **Internet access** is widely available. Most cities and some towns have cyber-cafés, while smaller places may have Internet booths in post offices, hostels and even a few pubs. Rates are around €7.50/hr or £5/hr.

Getting around

Public transport is generally reliable, though sometimes slow and infrequent in rural areas (which often have no Sunday services).

In the Republic, Iarnród Éireann (⊛www.irishrail.ie) operates **trains** to most major towns and cities. Few routes run north–south across the country, so, although you can get to the west coast easily by train, you can't use the railways to explore. The Dublin–Belfast line is the only **cross-border service**. NI Railways (⊛www.translink.co.uk) operates just a few routes in Northern Ireland. It's worth enquiring about off-peak fares and special deals. With the **InterRail** pass, visitors travel free in the Republic while Irish citizens travel half-price; with InterRail in Northern Ireland, all visitors (including Irish citizens) travel free, and UK citizens get a 75-percent discount.

The express **buses** of the Republic's Bus Éireann cover most of the island, including some cross-border services. Fares are generally cheaper than trains, especially mid-week. Major bus stations stock free timetables; remote villages may only have a couple of buses a week, so knowing their times is essential. Private buses operate on major routes throughout the Republic and are often cheaper than Bus Éireann. In the North, Ulsterbus runs regular and reliable services, particularly to towns not served by the rail network.

Cycling is an enjoyable way to see Ireland. In the Republic, bikes can be **rented** in most towns. Raleigh is the biggest operator (€20/day, €80/week; €50–€100 deposit; ☎01/465 9659, ⊛www.raleigh.ie); local dealers (including some hostels) are often cheaper. It costs an extra €8 to carry

a bike on a bus, and €3–8 on a train, though not all buses or trains can carry bikes; check in advance. In the North, bike rental (around £10/day) is more limited; tourist offices have lists of local operators. Taking a bike on a bus costs half the adult single fare (up to a maximum of £5) and, on a train, a quarter of the adult single fare (with no upper limit).

Accommodation

Hostels run by **An Óige** (the Irish Youth Hostel Association) and **HINI** (Hostelling International Northern Ireland) are affiliated to Hostelling International. Some close during the daytime and have evening curfews. HI membership is required at most of these hostels; overnight fees start at €10 in the Republic, €17 in Dublin; and £8–12 in the North. Independent hostels are very often cosy and informal; they don't have curfews, though some cram people in to the point of discomfort. They usually belong to either **Independent Holiday Hostels** (☎01/836 4700, ⊛www.hostels-ireland.com) or the **Independent Hostels Owners** network (☎073/30130, ⊛www.hostellingireland .com). There's a small number of disreputable hostels around, so it's a good idea to enquire locally before booking in at a non-approved hostel. In the Republic, expect to pay €10–15 for a dorm bed (more in Galway, Cork and Dublin), €14–20 per person for private rooms where available; in the North, it's £8–12/£14–18.

B&Bs vary enormously, but most are welcoming, warm and clean. Expect to pay from around €25/£17 per person; en-suite facilities are usually a little more and most **hotels** are generally pricier. For an extra €4 (Republic) or £2 (Northern Ireland), you can book through tourist offices or by phoning the international toll-free line ☎+800/668 668 66. Booking ahead is always advisable during high season and major festivals.

Camping usually costs around €8 a night in the Republic, £6 in the North. In out-of-the-way places nobody minds where you pitch. Farmers in popular tourist areas may ask for a small fee to use their land, but other than this you can expect to camp for free in areas where there's no official site. Some **hostels** also let you camp on their land for around €8/£5 per person.

Food and drink

Irish **food** is meat-orientated. B&Bs usually provide a "traditional" **Irish breakfast** of sausages, bacon and eggs, although many now offer vegetarian alternatives. **Pub lunch** staples are usually meat or fish and two veg, sometimes with a few veggie options. Vegetarian restaurants and cafés are sparse outside major cities and popular tourist areas. All towns have **fast-food** outlets, but old-fashioned fish-and-chips are a better bet, especially on the coast. For the occasional binge, there are some very good **seafood** restaurants, particularly along the southwest and west coasts. Most towns have daytime **cafés** serving a selection of hot dishes, salads, soups, sandwiches and cakes.

Especially in rural areas, the **pub** is the social heart of the community and the focus for the proverbial **craic** ("crack"), a particular blend of Irish fun involving good company, witty conversation and laughter, frequently against a backdrop of music. The classic Irish drink is **Guinness**, best in Dublin, home of the brewery, while the Cork stouts Beamish and Murphy's have their devotees. For English-style keg **bitter**, try Smithwicks, while **lager** brands include Carlsberg, Harp and Budweiser. The price of a pint starts at around €3.20, rising to €4.50 in Dublin. Irish **whiskeys** may seem expensive, but the measures are large: try Paddy, Jameson's, Powers or Bushmills.

Opening hours and holidays

Opening hours are roughly Mon–Sat 9am–6pm, with some late openings (usually Thurs or Fri), half-days and Sunday opening. In rural areas, hours can be more flexible, with later closing times. The main **museums** and attractions will normally be open regular shop hours, though, outside the cities, many will only be open during the summer months. Possession of a valid **student card** can often entitle visitors to significantly discounted entrance charges. **Public holidays** in the **Republic** are: Jan 1; St Patrick's Day (March 17); Good Fri, Easter Mon; May 5; June 2; Aug 4; Oct 27; Dec 25 & 26. In the **North**: Jan 1; St Patrick's Day (March 17); Easter Mon; May 5 & 26; July 12; Aug 25; Dec 25 & 26.

Emergencies

The Republic's **police** are known as the **Gardaí** (pronounced "gar-dee"), while the **PSNI** (Police Service of Northern Ireland) operates in the North. **Hospitals** and medical facilities are high-quality; you'll rarely be far from a hospital, and both Northern Ireland and the Republic are within the E111 scheme. Even the most remote rural areas will have a local doctor on 24-hour call. Most **pharmacies** are open standard shop hours, though in large towns some may stay open as late as 10pm; they dispense only a limited range of drugs without a doctor's prescription.

Emergency numbers

All emergencies in the Republic and Northern Ireland ☏112.

Dublin

Set on the banks of the River Liffey, **DUBLIN** is splendidly monumental, but also a youthful city with a lively nightlife. Ireland's vibrant economy has brought extensive urban regeneration, but there's still much deprivation here. It's this collision of the old and the new, the slick and the shabby, which make Dublin the exciting, aggravating, energetic place it is.

Dublin began as the Viking trading post Dubh Linn (Dark Pool), which soon amalgamated with the Celtic settlement of **Baile Átha Cliath** (Town of the Hurdle Ford) – still the Irish name for the city. Most early buildings were wooden, so only the two cathedrals, part of the castle and several churches date from before the seventeenth century. The city's fabric is essentially **Georgian**, when the Anglo-Irish gentry began to invest their income in new townhouses. After the 1801 Act of Union Dublin entered a long economic decline, but remained the focus of much of the agitation that eventually led to independence. The 1829 Emancipation Act secured a limited role for Catholics in the administration of the city, and Dublin was later the birthplace of the Gaelic League which helped catalyse an Irish national consciousness by nurturing the native language and culture. The long struggle for independence reached a head during the **Easter Rising** of 1916, a rebellion commemorated by a host of monuments in Dublin.

Arrival, information and city transport

Trains arrive at either **Heuston Station** on the city's Southside, or **Connolly Station** on the Northside. All Bus Éireann **buses** arrive at **Busáras**, the central bus station off Beresford Place, just behind the Customs House; private buses terminate at a variety of city centre locations. From the **airport**, six miles north, Airlink buses #747 and #748 run to Busáras (every 10min; €5; 30min), and the Aircoach serves the main shopping areas and hotels (every 15min; €6), or there are regular Citybus services #16A & #41 (every 10–20 min; €1.60). **Boats** dock at either **Dún Laoghaire**, nine miles south, connected to the centre by the **DART** railway (€1.45; 20min), or at the closer **Dublin Port** (bus #53; every 20min; €1.40); through-coaches from Britain usually drop you at Busáras.

The main **tourist office** is on Suffolk St, off College Green (Mon–Sat 9am–5.30pm; July & Aug also Sun 10.30am–3pm; ⑩www.visitdublin.com) with other branches at 14 Upper O'Connell St, the Dún Laoghaire ferry terminal and the airport. Their accommodation service costs €4 per booking. The **USITNow** office on Aston Quay, near O'Connell Bridge (Mon–Fri 9.30am–6.30pm, Thurs till 8pm, Sat 9.30am–5pm; ☎01/602 1600, ⑩www.usitnow.ie), also books B&Bs during the summer, and has its own hostel and a travel agency offering student discounts. For what's-on **listings**, see the free *Event Guide* or *In Dublin* (€2.48), or, for music events, *Hot Press* (€3.95).

Dublin has an extensive **bus** network – but note that all buses are exact-fare-only. Fares are €0.40–1.80, a one-day bus pass is €5, though a pack of five one-day passes costs only €15, or there are bus and rail passes (including DART) for one day/three days (€7.70/€15). Students pay €14.50 for a seven-day bus pass. Free bus timetables are available from Dublin Bus, 59 Upper O'Connell St. The **DART** links Howth and Malahide to the north of the city with Bray to the south (maximum fare €2.50). **Nitelink** buses cost €4–6, depending on your destination.

Accommodation

Although Dublin has lots of **accommodation**, anywhere central is liable to be full at weekends, around St Patrick's Day (March 17), during Easter week and in high summer, so it's always wise to **book ahead**. **Hotels** are generally expensive, and often no more comfortable than good **B&Bs**, but out-of-season reductions can be

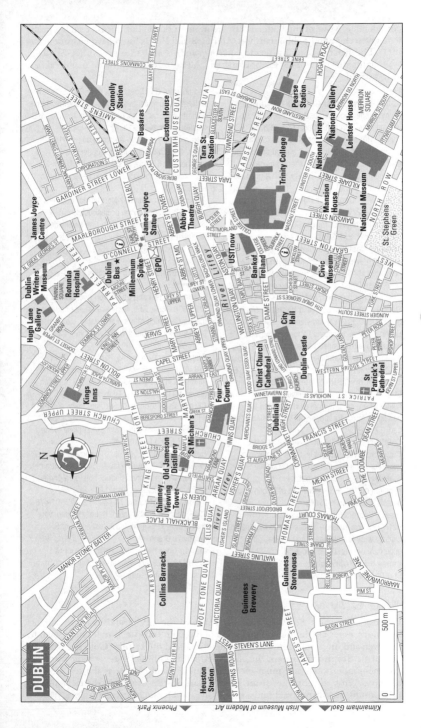

DUBLIN

considerable. Most of the better B&Bs are in the suburbs, but this isn't such a problem, given the good public transport. All hotels and B&Bs listed have en-suite facilities. The **hostel** booking service, *Irelandfound*, is at 10 Lower Abbey St (daily 9am–9pm; ☎01/888 0888; €2 booking fee). All hostels listed provide free breakfast, unless stated.

Hostels

Abbey Court 29 Bachelors Walk ☎01/878 0700, ⓦwww.abbey-court.com. By O'Connell Bridge, with all rooms en suite. Dorm bed €26. **7**

Avalon House 55 Aungier St ☎01/475 0001, ⓦwww.avalon-house.com. Cramped dorms and twin or four-bedded rooms, sharing unisex bathrooms, but friendly, if noisy, with a good café. Dorm bed €20. **6**

Barnacles Temple Bar House 19 Temple Lane ☎01/671 6277, ⓦwww.barnacles.ie. Modern place in the heart of Temple Bar. All rooms en suite. Dorm bed €23. **6**

Brewery Hostel 22-23 Thomas St ☎01/473 8600, ⓔbreweryh@indigo.ie. Housed in a fine converted library near the Guinness Brewery this small hostel often has space when others are full. Breakfast not provided. Dorm bed €21. **5**

Dublin International Youth Hostel 61 Mountjoy St ☎01/830 1766, ⓦwww.anoige.ie. An Óige's Dublin flagship, occupying a former convent, this massive, well-equipped hostel houses 379 beds in a rather dreary Northside location. Dorm bed €17, €19 for non HI members; €3 surcharge Fri & Sat. **Globetrotters Tourist Hotel** 46 Lower Gardiner St ☎01/873 5893, ⓔgtrotter@indigo.ie. Upmarket hostel where security-locked dorms and individual bed lights make for a peaceful night's sleep. Dorm bed €25. **9**

Goin' My Way 15 Talbot St ☎01/878 8484 ⓔgoinmyway@esatclear.ie. Small, family-run, value-for-money hostel close to O'Connell St. Breakfast is not included, but there is a kitchen. Its midnight curfew makes this one of Dublin's quieter hostels. Dorm bed €13. **3**

Isaacs Hostel 26 Frenchman's Lane ☎01/855 6215, ⓦwww.isaacs.ie. Housed in an eighteenth century wine warehouse – no breakfast, but a good café on site. Dorm bed €18. **5**

Kinlay House Christchurch 2–12 Lord Edward St ☎01/679 6644, ⓦwww.kinlayhouse.ie. Bright and cheerful USITNow hostel near Christ Church Cathedral. Doubles, quadruples and six-bed dorms with en-suite facilities. Café, laundry facilities and kitchen. Dorm bed €18. **5**

Litton Lane Hostel 2–4 Litton Lane ☎01/872 8389, ⓔlitton@indigo.ie. This converted warehouse off Bachelor's Walk on the Northside has excellent showers and good security. Dorm bed €25. **8**

Mount Eccles Court 42 North Great George's St ☎01/873 0826, ⓦwww.eccleshostel.com. A splendid converted house in a fine Northside Georgian street. Great kitchen and helpful staff. Dorm bed €30. **6**

Guest houses, B&Bs and hotels

8 Dromard Terrace Off Seafort Ave, Sandymount ☎01/668 3861. Fine, family-run guest house near the beach, which offers comfortable, clean rooms, good breakfasts and a warm welcome. Closed Nov–March. **5**

Anchor Guest House 49 Gardiner St Lower ☎01/878 6913, ⓦwww.anchorguesthouse.com. All rooms in this tastefully refurbished Georgian house are en suite with TV and phone. **7**

Clifden Guesthouse 32 Gardiner Place ☎01/874 6364, ⓦwww.clifdenhouse.com. Friendly guest house in a slightly run-down street close to the city centre and Busáras. **9**

Harding Hotel Copper Alley, Fishamble St ☎01/679 6500, ⓦwww.hardinghotel.ie. Extremely popular, well-furnished budget hotel in a prime Christchurch location. Breakfast extra. **7**

Kilronan Guesthouse 70 Adelaide Rd ☎01/475 5266, ⓦwww.dublinn.com. Handily placed, very comfortable Georgian house just south of St Stephen's Green. **9**

Marian Guesthouse 21 Upper Gardiner St ☎01/874 4129. Friendly, good-value guest house close to the city centre. **5**

The City

Dublin's fashionable **Southside** can lay claim to the city's trendy bars, restaurants and shops, especially in the cobbled alleys of buzzing **Temple Bar** leading down to the river, and most of its historic monuments, centred on **Trinity College**, **Grafton St** and **St Stephen's Green**. But the **Northside**, with its long-standing working-class neighbourhoods and inner-city communities, vaunts itself as the real heart of the city. Across the bridges from Temple Bar are the shopping districts around **O'Connell St**, where you'll find a taste of the old Dublin, particularly along **Moore**

St where traders ply their wares in melodic tones. You'll also find here a fair amount of graceful – if slightly shabby – residential streets and squares, with plenty of interest in the museums and cultural centres around **Parnell Square**. In the Northside in particular, you should be wary of straying off the main streets after dark.

The Southside

The Vikings sited their assembly and burial ground near what is now **College Green**, where **Trinity College** is the most famous landmark. Founded in 1592, it played a major role in the development of a Protestant Anglo-Irish tradition: right up to 1966, Catholics had to obtain a special dispensation to study here, though nowadays make up roughly seventy percent of the students. The stern grey- and mellow red-brick buildings are ranged around cobbled quadrangles in a grander version of the quads at Oxford and Cambridge. **The Old Library** (Mon–Sat 9.30am–5pm, Sun 9.30am/noon–4.30pm; €7) owns numerous Irish manuscripts. Pride of place goes to the ninth-century **Book of Kells**, which totals 680 pages but was rebound in the 1950s into four volumes, of which two are on show at any one time, one open at a completely illuminated page, the other at a text page, itself adorned with patterns and fantastic animals intertwined with the capitals. The **Book of Durrow** is equally interesting: it is the first of the great Irish illuminated manuscripts, dating from between 650 and 680, and has, unusually, a whole page given over to abstract ornament. In the Arts block, the **Dublin Experience** (late May to early Oct daily 10am–5pm; €4.20) provides an audiovisual account of the city's history.

Just south of here, the streets around pedestrianized **Grafton St** frame Dublin's quality shopping area – chic, sophisticated and expensive. After spotting the statue of Molly Malone, drop into **Bewley's** coffee house, whose dark wood and marble-tabled interior is a great place to sit and observe; there's even a small **museum** tracing the history of this Dublin institution. Continuing south you'll arrive at the northwest corner of **St Stephen's Green**, whose pleasant gardens and pools are the focus of Georgian city planning. Running off beside the swanky *Shelbourne Hotel*, Kildare St harbours the imposing Leinster House, built in 1745 as the Duke of Leinster's townhouse, and now the seat of the Irish parliament, the **Dáil**. Alongside are the rotundas of the **National Library** and the **National Museum** (Tues–Sat 10am–5pm, Sun 2–5pm; free; ⓦ www.museum.ie), the repository of the treasures of ancient Ireland. Much of its prehistoric gold was found in peat-bogs, as were a sacrificed human and the Lurgan Longboat. The Treasury and the Viking exhibition display such masterpieces as the Ardagh Chalice and Tara Brooch, St Patrick's Bell and the Cross of Cong. The brooch is perhaps the greatest piece of Irish metalwork and is decorated both on the front and the back, where only the wearer could see the intricate filigree.

Around the block, the other side of Leinster House overlooks **Merrion Square**, the finest Georgian plaza in Dublin. No. 1 was once the home of Oscar Wilde, and a flamboyant statue in the green opposite shows the writer draped insouciantly over a rock; on Sundays, the square's railings are used by artists flogging their wares. Here, the **National Gallery** (Mon–Sat 9.30am–5.30pm, Thurs until 8.30pm, Sun noon–5pm; free; ⓦ www.nationalgallery.ie) owns a fair spread of European old masters and French Impressionists, but the real draw is the trove of Irish paintings, ranging from formal portraits and landscape paintings of the Anglo-Irish era to the modernist creations of Evie Hone and Roderic O'Conor. Best of all is the permanent exhibition devoted to the work of Ireland's best-known painter, Jack B. Yeats, tracing his development from Dublin illustrator to expressionist interpreter of Connemara sea- and landscapes.

Temple bar and west to Kilmainham

Dame St, leading west from College Green, marks the southern edge of the redeveloped **Temple Bar** quarter, whose fashionable restaurants, pubs, boutiques and arts centres make this one of the liveliest parts of town.

IRELAND | Dublin

Uphill, tucked away behind City Hall, **Dublin Castle** (Mon–Fri 10am–5pm, Sat & Sun 2–5pm; €4.50) was founded by the Normans, and symbolized British power over Ireland for 700 years. Though parts date back to 1207, it was largely rebuilt in the eighteenth century. Tours of the State Apartments reveal much about the tastes and foibles of the viceroys and while you can see the lovely Chapel Royal, the real highlights are the excavations of Norman and Viking fortifications in the Undercroft. The Clock Tower building now houses the **Chester Beatty Library** (Mon–Fri 10am–5pm, Sat 11am–5pm, Sun 1–5pm; Oct–April closed Mon; free; ⓦwww.cbl.ie), a sumptuous and massive collection of books, manuscripts, objects and paintings amassed by Sir Arthur Chester Beatty on his travels around Europe and Asia. Over the brow of Dublin Hill, **Christ Church Cathedral** (daily 9.45/10am–5pm; €3 donation; ⓦwww.cccdub.ie) is a resonant monument built between 1172 and 1240 and heavily restored in the 1870s. The north wall of the nave has leaned eighteen inches outwards since the roof collapsed in 1562. The crypt now houses a small museum (€3) of the Cathedral's treasures. The former Synod Hall, connected to Christ Church by an overhead bridge, contains **Dublinia** (daily 10/11am–4/5pm; €5.75; ⓦwww.dublinia.ie), an array of presentations, models and tableaux depicting Dublin's medieval past and Viking and Norman artefacts excavated at nearby Wood Quay. Five minutes' walk south from Christ Church is Dublin's other great Norman edifice, **St Patrick's Cathedral** (daily 9am–5/6pm; Nov–Feb Sun closes 3pm; €4; ⓦwww.stpatrickscathedral.ie). Founded in 1191, this is replete with relics of Jonathan Swift, its dean from 1713 to 1747. Near the entrance are memorials to both him and Esther Johnson, the "Stella" with whom he had a passionate though apparently platonic relationship, while the north pulpit contains Swift's writing table, chair, portrait and death mask. Handel's *Messiah* received its first performance here in 1742.

A mile west of Christ Church, the **Guinness Brewery** covers 64 acres on either side of James's St. Founded in 1759, Guinness has the distinction of being the world's largest single beer-exporting company, dispatching some 300 million pints a year. Set in the centre of the brewery, the **Guinness Storehouse** (daily 9.30am–5pm; €13.50; ⓦwww.guinness-storehouse.com) presents a comprehensive account of the history and manufacture of this famous stout, visits ending with reputedly the best pint of Guinness in Dublin, in the panoramic *Gravity* bar with superb views over the city.

Regular buses (#78A, #79 and #90) ply the road out to Heuston Station and the **Royal Hospital Kilmainham**, Ireland's first Neoclassical building, dating from 1680, which now houses the **Irish Museum of Modern Art** (Tues–Sat 10am–5.30pm, Sun noon–5.30pm; free; ⓦwww.modernart.ie), with excellent permanent and visiting exhibitions. Exiting via the west wing and heading towards the gateway at the end of the avenue, you'll emerge near **Kilmainham Gaol** (April–Sept daily 9.30/10am–4/5pm; €5; ⓦwww.heritageireland.ie), where the British incarcerated patriots such as Charles Stewart Parnell, Pádraig Pearse and James Connolly (the last two were executed here). A superb museum on both crime and political history sets the tone for guided tours of the gaol.

The Northside

Crossing O'Connell Bridge, the view of the Georgian Custom House downstream is marred by a railway viaduct, and many of the handsome buildings on **O'Connell St**, the main avenue on the Northside, have – with the exception of the General Post Office – been spoiled by tacky facades. Halfway up O'Connell St looms the **General Post Office** (Mon–Sat 8am–8pm, Sun 10am–6.30pm; free), the insurgents' headquarters in the 1916 Easter Rising; only the facade survived the fighting, and its pillars are still scarred by bullets. Across the road on the corner of Essex St North is a **statue of James Joyce**. At the same junction, on the site of what was the city's most famous landmark, Nelson's Pillar (it was destroyed in an explosion in 1966), stands a huge, illuminated stainless-steel spike – the **Monument of Light** – representing the city's hopes for the new millennium.

At the northern end of O'Connell St lies Parnell Square, one of the first of Dublin's Georgian squares. Its plain red-brick houses are broken by the grey stone **Hugh Lane Municipal Art Gallery** (Tues–Sat 9.30am–5/6pm, Sun 11am–5pm; free; ⊛www.hughlane.ie), originally the townhouse of the Earl of Charlemont and the focus of fashionable Dublin before the city centre moved south of the river. The gallery exhibits work by nineteenth- and twentieth-century Irish and international masters, and features a reconstruction of Francis Bacon's working studio (€7). Nearby at nos. 18–19, the **Dublin Writers Museum** (Mon–Sat 10am–5/6pm, Sun noon–5pm; €5) whisks you through Irish literary history from early Christian writings up to Samuel Beckett and Brendan Behan. Two blocks east of Parnell Square, at 35 North Great George's St, the **James Joyce Centre** (Mon–Sat 9.30am–5pm, Sun noon–5pm; €4.50; ⊛www.jamesjoyce.ie) runs intriguing walking tours of the novelist's haunts (☎01/878 8547).

Half-a-mile west of O'Connell St, on Church St, stands **St Michan's Church** (March–Oct Mon–Fri 10am–12.30pm & 2–4.30pm, Sat 10am–12.45pm; rest of year Mon–Fri 12.30–3.30pm, Sat 10am–12.45pm; €3.50), the oldest on the Northside, founded in 1095. The crypt is famous for its "mummified" bodies, preserved by the constant temperature and dry air pervaded by methane gas. The oldest – thought to have been a Crusader – dates back 700 years. At the bottom of Church St, on the Liffey bank, stands the **Four Courts**. Like the Custom House down river, it's a grand eighteenth-century edifice by James Gandon that was restored after serious damage during the Civil War, which followed the 1921 treaty.

One block west on Bow St is the **Old Jameson Distillery** (daily 9.30am–6pm; €7); tours cover the history and method of distilling what the Irish called *uisce beatha* ("water of life", anglicized to whiskey) – which differs from Scotch whisky by being thrice-distilled and lacking a peaty undertone – and end with a tasting session involving different types of whiskey, Scotch and bourbon. Outside, lifts convey you to the top of the old distillery **chimney** (Mon–Sat 10am–5.30pm, Sun 11am–5.30pm; €5), where an observation platform provides panoramic views of the city.

Further west along The Quays is the **Collins Barracks** (Tues–Sat 10am–5pm, Sun 2–5pm; free), an annexe of the National Museum housing its decorative arts collection and occasional special exhibitions. Finally, there's **Phoenix Park**, one of the world's largest urban parks (bus #10 from O'Connell St or #37 from Abbey St Lower); originally priory land, it's now home to the Presidential Lodge, and attractions such as **Dublin Zoo** (Mon–Sat 9.30am–4/6pm, Sun 10.30am–4/6pm; €10.10; ⊛www.dublinzoo.ie). The visitor centre (daily 10am–5/6pm; €2.75; ⊛www.heritageireland.ie) has displays on the park's history and wildlife and tickets include a tour of the adjacent **Ashtown Castle**, a seventeenth-century tower house.

Eating, drinking and entertainment

Most kinds of **food** are widely available in Dublin, especially in the eateries of Temple Bar. Many **cafés** and **restaurants** serve lunch at much lower prices than they'll charge in the evening (when it's wise to reserve a table); while Dublin's 800 **pubs** offer anything from soup and sandwiches to a full carvery at lunchtime. The **music** scene – much of which is based in the pubs – is volatile, so it's always best to check listings is the *Event Guide* or *Hot Press*. The best **clubs** can be found around Temple Bar and on Harcourt St, off St Stephen's Green. Dublin's **theatres** are among the best in Europe.

Restaurants and cafés

Alpha Café 37 Wicklow St. A well-kept secret just off Grafton St with old-fashioned homely menu at great prices. Closed Sun.

Bewley's 78 Grafton St; 11–12 Westmoreland St; 40 Mary St. An essential food experience in Dublin, serving everything from a sticky bun to a full meal. Check out the lunchtime theatre programme in Grafton St, with combined lunch and show ticket from €10–€13. Open from 7.30am (Sun 8am); closes Grafton St 11pm; Westmoreland St 7.30pm; Mary St 6pm.

Cornucopia 21 Wicklow St. One of the city's few vegetarian cafés and highly popular too. Closed Sun.

Elephant and Castle 18 Temple Bar ☎01/679 3121. Busy diner-cum-brasserie with burgers and Cajun-Creole dishes; classy without being posey.

Fresh 2nd floor, Powerscourt Townhouse Centre, off Grafton St. Delicious vegetarian food, at tables overlooking the atrium. Closed Sun.

The Gotham Café 8 South Anne St. Lively place, off Grafton St, offering an extensive and reasonably priced global menu.

Govinda's 4 Aungier St. Huge helpings of dhal and rice and tasty vegetarian curries plus daily veggie specials, served by a very friendly team.

Irish Film Centre 6 Eustace St, Temple Bar ☎01/677 8788. Delicious, inventive food in elegantly minimal surroundings. Watch a film or just soak up the atmosphere.

Leo Burdock's 2 Werburgh St. Dublin's best fish-and-chips – takeaway only. Closed Sun.

Nude 21 Suffolk St. Canteen-style café serving hot and cold wraps, panini, soups and salads.

Probe Café Market Arcade, South Great George's St. Excellent, reasonably priced café offering everything from Irish stew to fajitas. Reductions for students. Closed Sun.

The Steps of Rome 1 Chatham Court. Limited seating area, though has great slabs of highly original pizza available to take away also. Good vegetarian options.

Wagamama South King St. Japanese-style noodle dishes served in a near-clinical atmosphere, but great soups, dumplings and juices.

The Winding Stair 40 Lower Ormond Quay. Quaint bookshop downstairs, wholefood café and coffee shop upstairs with great-value hearty lunches.

Pubs

Davy Byrne's 21 Duke St. An object of pilgrimage for *Ulysses* fans, since Leopold Bloom stopped by here for a snack. Despite the pastel-toned refit, it's still a good pub, and serves oysters at lunchtime.

The Globe South Great George's St. Trendy hangout with loud music. Backs onto *RíRá*, an intimate but very lively club.

Kehoe's South Anne St. Wonderful snugs for privacy to sip your pint.

The Long Hall South Great George's St. Victorian pub encrusted with mirrors and antique clocks.

McDaid's 3 Harry St. Excellent Guinness in Brendan Behan's former local.

Mulligan's 8 Poolbeg St. Shabby and smoky, but always packed in the evenings; many claim that it serves the best Guinness in Dublin.

Neary's 1 Chatham St. Plenty of bevelled glass and shiny wood, plus Liberty-print curtains to show some style appropriate for its theatrical clientele.

Stag's Head Dame Court, Dame St, almost opposite the Central Bank. Wonderfully intimate pub, all mahogany, stained glass and mirrors. Good lunches, too.

Music pubs and venues

The Brazen Head 20 Lower Bridge St. The oldest pub in Dublin, with traditional music nightly from 9.30pm.

The Cobblestone 77 North King St, Smithfield. Popular old-fashioned bar with nightly traditional music downstairs and more formal gigs upstairs.

International Bar 23 Wicklow St. Large, smoke-filled saloon with rock bands and a comedy club upstairs.

The Isaac Butt Store St. Everything from the latest Coldplay clones to Ramones revivalists.

J.J. Smyth's 12 Aungier St. One of the few places to catch local jazz and blues talent.

The Village 26 Wexford St. Excellent new venue with an eclectic schedule and a late club (Fri & Sat).

Whelans 25 Wexford St. Very lively venue with nightly gigs and frequent bar extensions.

Clubs

Red Box and POD 35 Harcourt St. Two hugely popular clubs, housed in an old railway station, offering a variety of different regular nights and events.

Spy Powerscourt Townhouse Centre, Clarendon St. Stylishly designed, ultra-cool club spanning three floors.

Switch 23 Eustace St, Temple Bar. DJs nightly, both downstairs and in the bar of this sometimes frenzied venue.

Tivoli Theatre 135–138 Francis St. The latest "in" venue – reckoned to have the best sound system in Dublin.

Theatres

Abbey Theatre Lower Abbey St ☎01/878 7222, ⊛www.abbeytheatre.ie. Founded in 1904 by W.B. Yeats and Lady Gregory, the Abbey's golden era featured Yeats, J.M. Synge and later Sean O'Casey as house playwrights. The building also contains the Peacock Theatre, which stages more experimental shows.

Gate Theatre Cavendish Row, Parnell Square ☎01/874 4045, ⊛www.gate-theatre.ie. Another of Dublin's literary institutions, staging classic and modern Irish theatre.

Project 39 Essex St East, Temple Bar ☎01/679 6622. This long-standing arts venue continues to mount experimental and politically sensitive theatre.

Listings

Bike rental Cycle Ways, 185 Parnell St ☎01/873 4748.

Embassies Australia, Fitzwilton House, Wilton Terrace ☎01/676 1517; Canada, 64–65 St Stephen's Green ☎01/478 1988; UK, 31–33 Merrion Rd ☎01/205 3700; US, 42 Elgin Rd, Ballsbridge ☎01/668 8777.

Exchange Thomas Cook, 118 Grafton St; General Post Office; most city-centre banks.

Hospital Southside: St James's, James St

☎01/453 7941; Northside: Mater Misericordae, Eccles St ☎01/830 1122.

Laundry All American Launderette, Wicklow Court, South Great George's St.

Left luggage Busáras, Heuston and Connolly stations.

Pharmacies Dame Street Pharmacy, 16 Dame St; O'Connell's, 55 O'Connell St.

Police Harcourt Terrace ☎01/666 6666.

Post offices O'Connell St; St Andrew's St.

North from Dublin

The main N1 Belfast road and the railway pass through **Drogheda**, from where it's a short bus hop to the great **NEWGRANGE** tumulus (daily 9/9.30am–5/7pm; €5; ⓦwww.heritageireland.ie); enter by the Brú na Bóinne visitor centre, and, since it's very popular, you may have a long wait. Raised around 5000 years ago and completely restored, the mound of earth and loose stone covers the chambers of a remarkable passage grave. The outer ring of **standing stones**, of which only twelve uprights now remain, was unique among passage grave tombs. Perhaps the most important feature is the unique **roof-box** several feet in from the tunnel mouth. This contains a slit through which, at the **winter solstice**, the light of the rising sun fills the chamber with a sudden blaze of orange light. The entry passage, about three feet wide, leads into the **central chamber**, where the stones are carved with intricate decoration.

Also easily accessible by bus from Drogheda are the monastic ruins of **Monasterboice**, six miles to the north (dawn–dusk; free). Here stands Ireland's tallest **round tower**, 110 feet high, and two of the country's finest high crosses. Both the east cross, known as **St Muiredach's**, and its western counterpart are decorated with a range of Biblical stories and part of the fun lies in trying to determine their meaning.

DROGHEDA itself is a lively town whose layout reflects its medieval origins and is best viewed from the summit of **Millmount** hill, south of the River Boyne. The **Millmount Museum** (Tues–Sat 10am–5.30pm, Sun 3–4.30pm; €3; ⓦwww.millmount.net), is one of Ireland's finest town museums and contains a wealth of exhibits and artefacts recounting the area's history. The **tourist office** (Mon–Sat 10am–1pm & 2–5pm; March–Oct also Sun 11.45am–5pm; ☎041/983 7070; ⓦwww.drogheda-tourism.com) is in the **bus station** on Donore Rd – the **train station** is ten minutes' walk to the east, off Dublin Rd. A good central **place to stay** is the *Green Door* hostel, 47 John St (☎041/983 4422, ⓦwww .greendoorhostel.com; dorm bed €13.50; ❹). Plenty of **eating** choices are available in the centre, especially along West Street where *Weavers* offers economically-priced meals and *Jalapeno* serves filling sandwiches. The most atmospheric **pub** is *Carbery's* on North Strand while *Peter Matthews* on Laurence Street is frequented by a younger crowd and has music most nights.

From Wexford to Cork

The southeast is often Ireland's sunniest and driest corner, and the region's medieval and Anglo-Norman history is richly concentrated in **Kilkenny**, a bustling, quaint inland town, while to the west, at the heart of County Tipperary is the **Rock of Cashel**, a spectacular natural formation topped with Christian buildings from virtually every period. In the southwest, **Cork** is both relaxed and spirited, the perfect place to ease you into the exhilarations of the west coast.

Ferries from Wales (Fishguard and Pembroke) and France (Cherbourg and Roscoff) arrive at **ROSSLARE HARBOUR**, on the southeastern tip of Ireland. Trains depart daily from here for Wexford, Waterford and Dublin, and there's also daily bus services to Dublin and the west. There's a **tourist desk** in the terminal open for incoming sailings (May–Sept, except early mornings; ☎053/33622); otherwise, try the Kilrane tourist office, just over a mile from the dock along the N25 (May–Sept daily 11am–8pm; Oct–April Tues–Sun 2–8pm; ☎053/33232). The An Óige **hostel** is a short walk from the ferry in Goulding St (☎053/33399, ⊛www.anoige.ie; €12.50), though *Kirwan House Hostel*, 13 miles away in **WEXFORD**, 3 Mary St (☎053/21208, ⊜kirwanhostel@eircom.net; dorm bed €14.50, ❸), is a more appealing place to spend your first night in Ireland.

Kilkenny

KILKENNY is Ireland's finest medieval city, its castle set above the broad sweep of the River Nore and its narrow streets laced with carefully maintained buildings. In 1641, the city became virtually the capital of Ireland, with the founding of a parliament known as the Confederation of Kilkenny. The power of this short-lived attempt to unite the resistance to English persecution of Catholicism had greatly diminished by the time Cromwell's wreckers arrived in 1650. Kilkenny never recovered its prosperity, but enough remains to attest to its former importance.

The **bus and train stations** are just north of the city off John St. Following this road over the river and climbing Rose Inn St leads to the **tourist office** (Mon–Sat 9am–5/7pm, July & Aug also Sun 11am–1pm & 2–5pm; ☎056/775 1500, ⊛www.southeastourism.ie), housed in the sixteenth-century **Shee Alms House**. At the top of Rose Inn St to the left is the broad **Parade**, which leads up to the castle. To the right, the High St passes the eighteenth-century **Tholsel**, once the centre of the city's financial dealings and now the town hall. Beyond is **Parliament St**, the main thoroughfare, where the **Rothe House** (Mon–Sat 10am/1pm–5/6pm, Sun 3–5pm; €3) provides a unique example of an Irish Tudor merchant's home, comprising three separate houses linked by cobbled courtyards. The highlight of this end of town is the thirteenth-century **St Canice's Cathedral** (Mon–Sat 9/10am–1pm & 2–4/6pm, Sun 2–4/6pm; €3). Rich in carvings, it has a fine array of sixteenth-century monuments, many in black Kilkenny limestone (which looks remarkably like marble). The **round tower** next to the church (same hours; €1.90) is all that remains of the monastic settlement reputedly founded by St Canice in the sixth century; there are superb views from the top. It's the imposing **Castle**, though, which defines Kilkenny (tours daily: April–Sept 9.30/10.30am–5/7pm; rest of year 10.30–12.45pm & 2–5pm; €4.40; ⊛www .heritageireland.ie). Seat of the Butler family, the castle was founded in the twelfth century and radically altered by the nineteenth century. Its library, drawing room, bedrooms and Long Gallery of family portraits are open for viewing, as well as the **Butler Gallery**, housing exhibitions of modern art.

Practicalities

Kilkenny is well served by **B&Bs**, although in the summer and especially during festival weeks in June and August you'll need to book in advance. *Bregagh* on Dean St (☎056/772 2315; ❺) is very central; also near the centre is *Celtic House*, 18 Michael St (☎056/776 2249; ❺). *Banville's*, 49 Walkin St (☎056/777 0182, ⊜mbanville@eircom.net; ❺), is also good. The *Kilkenny Tourist* **hostel**, 35 Parliament St (☎056/776 3541, ⊜kilkennyhostel@eircom.net; dorm bed €14, ❸), is an excellent budget option and there's **camping** at *Tree Grove* (☎056/777 0302), a mile south of the city on the R700. An influx of artists and craftspeople to the area in pursuit of the good life has boosted the town's restaurants and pubs. Among popular **eating-places** are *Café Sol* (closed Sun) on William St, great for lazy breakfasts and wholesome lunches, and *M.L. Dore*, 65 High St, serving inexpensive sandwiches and full meals. Good spots for **bar food** include *Kyteler's Inn*, St Kieran St, providing meals in medieval surroundings, while *Lenehan's* on Barrack St has traditional Irish cooking. For **traditional music** try *Cleere's* on Parliament St or *Ryan's* on Friary St. *Tynan's* on the Bridge is worth a visit for its cosy Victorian interior. The weekly *Kilkenny People* has information about what's on. The town is renowned for The Cat Laughs comedy **festival** in June (⊛www.thecatlaughs.com), and its Arts Festival in August (⊛www.kilkennyarts.ie).

The Rock of Cashel

Approached from north or west, the **Rock of Cashel** (daily 9am–4.30/7.30pm; €4.40; ⊛www.heritageireland.ie) appears as a mirage of crenellations rising bolt upright from the vast encircling plain. The rock, less than a quarter of a mile wide, is one of Ireland's most extraordinary architectural sites and is also where St Patrick reputedly used a shamrock to explain the doctrine of the Trinity.

Approached from **CASHEL**, a ten-minute walk to the east, the first thing you'll encounter on the Rock is the fifteenth-century **Hall of the Vicars**, whose vaulted undercroft contains the original **St Patrick's Cross**. Tradition has it that the cross's huge plinth was the coronation stone of the High Kings of Munster. **Cormac's Chapel**, built in the 1130s, is the earliest and most beautiful of Ireland's Romanesque churches; both north and south doors feature intricate carving, while inside, the alleged sarcophagus of King Cormac has an exquisite design of interlacing serpents and ribbon decoration. The graceful limestone **Cathedral**, begun a century after Cormac's chapel, is Anglo-Norman in conception, with its Gothic arches and lancet windows; a door in the south transept gives access to the tower, and in the north transept some panels from sixteenth-century altar-tombs survive, one with an intricately carved retinue of saints. The tapering **Round Tower** is the earliest building on the Rock, dating from the early twelfth century. Cashel's **tourist office** (Mon–Sat 9.15am–6pm; July & Aug also Sun 11am–5pm; ☎062/61333) is on Main St alongside the **Cashel of the Kings Heritage Centre** (9.30am–5.30/8pm; Sept–March closed Sat & Sun; free), where a small exhibition covers the history of the town. The **Bolton Library** (June–Sept daily 11am–4.30pm; €2.50), on John St houses a fine collection of early manuscripts and rare maps. Cashel has two excellent **hostels**, both near the centre: *O'Brien's Holiday Lodge*, off the Dundrun Rd (☎062/61003; dorm bed €15, ❹; also with camping), and *Cashel Holiday Hostel*, 6 John St (☎062/62330; dorm bed €13, ❸). For **B&B**, try *Abbey House*, 1 Dominic St (☎062/61104, ⓔteachnamainstreach@eircom.net; ❺), or *Rockside House*, Rock Villas (☎062/63813, ⓔmaryville@iol.ie; ❺), both very near the Rock.

Cork

Everywhere in **CORK** there's evidence of the city's history as a great mercantile centre, with grey stone quaysides, old warehouses, and elegant, quirky bridges spanning the River Lee to each side of the island core – but the city's lively atmosphere and large student population, combined with a vibrant social and cultural scene, are equally powerful draws. **St Finbarre** founded an abbey here in the seventh century, but the Vikings wrecked it in 820 before building a new settlement on one of the islands in the marshes, and eventually integrating with the native Celts. Massive stone walls built by invading Normans in the twelfth century were destroyed by Williamite forces at the **Siege of Cork** in 1690, after which waterborne trade brought increasing prosperity, as witnessed by the city's fine eighteenth-century bow-fronted houses and ostentatious nineteenth-century churches.

The graceful arc of **St Patrick's St** – which with **Grand Parade** forms the commercial heart of the centre – is crammed with major chain stores and modest traditional businesses. Just off St Patrick's St on Princes St, the sumptuous **English Market** offers the chance to sample the local delicacies tripe and drisheen (a peppered sausage made from a sheep's stomach lining and blood). On the far side of St

Patrick's St, chic Paul St is a gateway to the bijou environs of French Church St and Carey's Lane. The downstream end of the island, where many of the quays are still in use, gives the clearest sense of the old port city. In the west the island is predominantly residential, though Fitzgerald Park is the home of the **Cork Public Museum** (Mon–Sat 11am–1pm & 2.15–5/6pm, Sun 3–5pm; free), which focuses on Republican history with side exhibits on the city trades and guilds, silver and glassware and local natural history.

North of the River Lee is **Shandon**, a reminder of Cork's eighteenth-century status as the most important port in Europe for dairy products. The most striking survival is the **Cork Butter Exchange**, stout nineteenth-century Neoclassical buildings recently given over to craft workshops. The old butter market itself, now renovated to house a theatre, sits in a cobbled square. To the rear is the pleasant Georgian church of **St Anne Shandon** (Mon–Sat 9am–6pm; €5 ⓦwww .shandonsteeple.com), easily recognizable from all over the city by its weather vane – an eleven-foot salmon. The church tower gives excellent views and an opportunity to ring the famous bells: a good stock of sheet tunes is provided. West of here in Sunday's Well is the nineteenth-century **Cork City Gaol** (daily 9.30/10am–5/6pm; €5), with an excellent taped tour focusing on social history. From here, you can walk back to the town centre via the Shaky Bridge and Fitzgerald Park.

Practicalities

The **bus station** is at Parnell Place alongside Merchant's Quay, while the **train station** is about one mile out of the city centre on Lower Glanmire Rd. **Ferries** from Swansea and Roscoff arrive at Ringaskiddy, some ten miles out, from where there's a bus into the centre. The **tourist office** is on Grand Parade (Mon–Sat 9/9.15am–4.30/6pm; July & Aug also Sun 10am–5pm; ☎021/427 3251, ⓦwww.cork-kerry.travel.ie). For **B&B**, try *Number Forty Eight*, 48 Lower Glanmire Rd (☎ & ℱ021/450 5790; ❺); *Westbourne House*, 2 Westbourne Villas, Western Rd (☎021/427 6153; ❺); or the many along Western Rd, near the university, and Lower Glanmire Rd. **Hostels** include *Sheila's*, 4 Belgrave Place, Wellington Rd (☎021/450 5562, ⓦwww.sheilashostel.ie; dorm bed €17.50, ❺); *Kelly's Hostel*, 25 Summerhill South (☎021/472 2124, ⓦwww.kellyshostel.com; dorm bed €12, ❸); and the many An Óige place, at 1 Redclyffe, Western Rd (☎021/454 3289, ⓦwww.anoige.ie; €12.50), fifteen-minutes' walk from the centre or bus #8 to University College Cork). *Internet Exchange* on Wood St offers **Internet** access. For **food**, *The Quay Co-op*, 24 Sullivan's Quay, and *Café Paradiso*, on Lancaster Quay, are excellent vegetarian restaurants serving local produce; *Gino's* on Winthrop St is the spot for tasty pizzas; *Oz Cork*, Grand Parade, offers everything from pasta to panini at economical prices. There's plenty of **traditional Irish music**: the best spots are the *Corner Bar* on Coburg St; *An Spailpín Fánach*, South Main St; *Gable's,* Douglas St; and *The Lobby*, Union Quay (which has rock and indie too). Cork's best **club** is *The Savoy* on Patrick St, with DJs and live music; *The Bodega* on Coal Quay is a popular late café-bar with regular DJs; and there's an international **jazz festival** in late October (ⓦwww.corkjazzfestival.com). For **theatre**, the Triskel Arts Centre in Tobin St (☎021/427 2022) is a lively spot with also a cinema, exhibitions, readings and concerts. The Kino Cinema on Washington St screens independent films and is part-host for the excellent **film festival** in October (ⓦwww.corkfilmfest.org). For **listings** of what's on get the free *Whazon?* or the *Evening Echo*.

The west coast

If you've come to Ireland for mountainous scenery, sea and remoteness, you'll find them all in County Kerry. By far the most visited areas are the town of **Killarney** and a scenic route around the perimeter of the Iveragh Peninsula known as the

Ring of Kerry. Ennis and the more tourist-ridden **Doolin** in County Clare are marvellous spots for **traditional music. Galway** is an exceptionally enjoyable, free-spirited sort of place, and a gathering point for young travellers. To its west lies **Connemara**, a magnificently wild coastal terrain of wind, rock and water, with the nearby, elementally beautiful **Aran Islands**, in the mouth of Galway Bay. Up the coast the landscape softens around the historic town of **Westport**, while further north, **Sligo** has plenty of associations with the poet Yeats and a lively, bustling feel. In the far northwest **County Donegal**'s scenery is especially rich with a spectacular two-hundred-mile folded coastline whose highlight is **Slieve League** with its awesome sea cliffs, the highest in Europe. There are plenty of international flights directly into the region, to Shannon airport near Limerick or the smaller Knock airport near Westport.

Killarney and around

Although **KILLARNEY** has been commercialized to saturation point and has little of architectural interest, its location amid some of the best lakes, mountains and woodland in Ireland more than compensates. Pony traps and jaunting cars line up while their owners talk visitors into taking trips through the surrounding country. It's all done with bags of charm, true to Killarney's long tradition of profitably hosting the visiting masses since its establishment as a resort in the mid-eighteenth century. Around the town, three spectacular lakes – Lough Leane, Muckross Lake and the Upper Lake – form an appetizer for MacGillycuddy's Reeks, the highest mountains in Ireland. **Cycling** is a great way of seeing the terrain, and makes good sense because local transport is sparse (Trailways Outdoor Centre on College St and O'Sullivan's in Bishop's Lane both offer **bike rental**). The entrance gates to the **Knockreer Estate**, part of the Killarney National Park, are just over the road from Killarney's cathedral. A short walk through the grounds takes you to the banks of **Lough Leane**, where tall wooded hills plunge into the water, with the peaks rising behind to the highest, **Carrauntoohill** (3414ft). The main path through the estate leads to the restored fifteenth-century tower of **Ross Castle** (April–Sept daily 9am–5/6.30pm; Oct Tues–Sat 10am–5pm; €3.80; gardens free; ⍟www.heritageireland.ie), the last place in the area to succumb to Cromwell's forces in 1652.

A mile or so south of Killarney is the **Muckross Estate**; aim first for **Muckross Abbey**, for both the ruin itself and its calm, contemplative location. Founded by the Franciscans in the mid-fifteenth century, it was suppressed by Henry VIII; the friars returned, but were finally driven out by Cromwell in 1652. Back at the main road, signposts point to **Muckross House** (daily 9am–5.30/7pm; €5 or €7.50 joint ticket with farm; ⍟www.heritageireland.ie), a solid nineteenth-century neo-Elizabethan mansion with wonderful gardens and also a traditional working farm. The estate gives access to well-trodden paths along the shores of the Muckross Lake where you can see one of Killarney's celebrated beauty spots, the **Meeting of the Waters**. Actually a parting, it has a profusion of indigenous and flowering subtropical plants on the left of the Old Weir Bridge. Close by is the massive shoulder of Torc Mountain, shrugging off **Torc Waterfall**. The Upper Lake is beautiful, too, but still firmly on the tourist trail, with the main road running along one side up to Ladies' View, from where the view is truly amazing.

West of Killarney lies the **Gap of Dunloe**, a natural defile formed by glacial overflow that cuts the mountains in two. Rather than joining the continual stream of expensive jaunting cars, you'd do better to walk the four miles in the late afternoon, when the cars have gone home and the light is at its most magical. **Kate Kearney's Cottage**, a pub located six miles from Killarney at the foot of the track leading up to the Gap, is the last place before **Lord Brandon's Cottage**, a summer tearoom (June–Aug), seven miles away on the other side of the valley. The track winds its way up the desolate valley between high rock cliffs and waterfalls, past a chain of icy loughs and tarns, to the top, where you find yourself in what feels like one of the remotest places in the world: the **Black Valley**. Named after its entire population perished during the famine (1845–49), it's now inhabited by a mere handful of families, and was the very last valley in Ireland to get electricity. There's a wonderfully isolated An Óige **hostel** here too (March–Nov; ⓣ064/34712, ⓦwww.anoige.ie; dorm bed €11). From here, the quickest way to Killarney is to carry on down to Lord Brandon's Cottage and take the boat back across the Upper Lake.

Practicalities

B&Bs abound in Killarney, though in high season it's worth booking ahead through the **tourist office**, on Beech Rd off New St (Mon–Sat 9/10am–5.30/6pm; June–Sept also Sun 10am–1pm & 2–6pm; ⓣ064/31633, ⓦwww.cork-kerry.travel.ie). The An Óige **hostel** (ⓣ064/31240, ⓦwww.anoige.ie; dorm bed €12) is three miles west of town along the Killorglin road at Aghadoe, but there are several alternatives in Killarney itself: *Killarney Railway Hostel* is opposite the station (ⓣ064/35299, ⓦwww.railwayhostel.com; dorm bed €11.50, ❸); *The Súgan Hostel* is minutes away on Lewis Rd (ⓣ064/33104; dorm bed €12, ❷); bustling *Neptune's Town Hostel* is in the middle of town on New St (ⓣ064/35255, ⓦwww.neptuneshostel.com; dorm bed €16, ❸); and *Park Hostel* is up the hill off Cork Rd, opposite the petrol station (ⓣ064/32119; dorm bed €10, ❷). **Camping** is available at *Flesk Muckross Caravan and Camping Park* (April–Sept; ⓣ064/31704), a mile south on the N71 Kenmare road. Places to **eat and drink** are thick on the ground: one of the best is *Bricín*, on High St, along with *The Caragh* on New St; or try *Cronin's* on College St, all serving hearty food. *Café Internet* on New St provides **Internet** access. Evening **entertainment** is everywhere as you walk the streets; pick up *The Kerryman* for listings.

The Ring of Kerry

Most tourists view the spectacular scenery of the 110-mile **Ring of Kerry**, west of Killarney, without ever leaving their tour bus or car. So, anyone straying from the road or waiting until the buses stop running in the afternoon will experience the slow twilights of the Atlantic seaboard in perfect seclusion. **Cycling** the Ring takes three days, and a bike will let you get onto the largely deserted mountain roads. Buses from Killarney go right around the Ring in summer (May–Sept 2 daily); for the rest of the year they travel along the northern coast as far as Caherciveen.

Valentia Island to Waterville

Heading anticlockwise on the main N70 around the Ring of Kerry, at **Kells Bay** the road veers inland towards **CAHERCIVEEN**, a long, narrow street of a town and also the main shopping centre for the western part of the peninsula. It has an independent **hostel**, *Sive*, 15 East End (ⓣ066/947 2717, ⓔsivehostel@oceanfree.net; dorm bed €15, ❸), with camping facilities. Beyond here, lanes lead out to **VALENTIA ISLAND**, Europe's most westerly harbour, its position on the Gulf Stream giving it a mild, balmy climate. Access to the island is easiest by **ferry** (single €1.50, return €2) from Reenard Point (two-and-a-half miles from Caherciveen) to **Knightstown**. Its main street has a few shops, a post office offering free maps of the island, and a couple of bars. The much-touted **Grotto** – Valentia's highest point – is a gaping slate cavern with a crude statue of the Virgin perched two hundred feet up amid dripping icy water. More exciting is the spectacular cliff scenery to the northwest. You should book ahead for **accommodation** during the summer season. The Knightstown An Óige **hostel** (June–Sept; ⓣ066/947 6154; dorm bed €10.50) has space for thirty, though facilities are spartan. The *Royal Pier Bar* runs an independent hostel in the village (ⓣ066/947 6144, ⓔroyalpier-val@ireland.com; dorm bed €14.50, ❸), or for **B&B** try *Spring Acre* (ⓣ066/947 6141, ⓔrforan@indigo.ie; ❺).

The stretch of coast south of Valentia is wild and almost deserted, apart from a scattering of farms and fishing villages. Sweet-smelling, tussocky grass dotted with wild flowers is raked by Atlantic winds, ending in abrupt cliffs or sandy beaches. The An Óige **hostel** (June–Sept; ☎066/947 9229, ⓦwww.anoige.ie; dorm bed €10) in **BALLINSKELLIGS** is pretty basic but sells supplies. Monks from the Skellig Islands retreated to Ballinskelligs Abbey in the thirteenth century; today, the village is a focus of the Kerry *Gaeltacht* (Irish-speaking area), busy in summer with schoolchildren and students learning Irish. **WATERVILLE** may be touristy, but it does have a certain grace. Formerly a popular resort, it has an air of consequence that contrasts with the wild Atlantic views and is the best base on the Ring for exploring the coast and the mountainous country inland. For **B&B** try *Klondyke House*, New Line Rd (☎066/947 4119, ⓦhomepage.eircom.net/~klondykehouse; ❺), or *Ashling House*, Main St (mid-March to mid-Oct; ☎066/947 4247; ❺); and there's the *Bru na Domoda* **hostel** at Maistir Gaoithe, seven miles up the Inny Valley (mid May–Oct; ☎066/947 4782, ✉maistirgaoithe@eircom.net; dorm bed €17, ❹).

The Dingle Peninsula

The **Dingle Peninsula** is a place of intense, shifting beauty. Spectacular mountains, long sandy beaches and the splinter-slatted mass of rocks that defines the extraordinary coast at Slea Head all conspire to ensure that, remote though it is, the peninsula is firmly on the tourist trail. Here is one of the greatest concentrations of Celtic ruins in Ireland, and the now uninhabited Blasket Islands once generated a wealth of Irish literature. **DINGLE** makes the best base for exploring the peninsula. Now little more than a few streets by the side of **Dingle Bay**, Dingle was Kerry's leading port in medieval times, later becoming a centre for smuggling. There's no shortage of **accommodation**, and the **tourist office** in Strand St (Mon–Fri 9/10am–5/7pm; July & Aug also Sat 9am–7pm, Sun 10am–6pm; ☎066/915 1188) will book places. Although many of Dingle's **B&Bs** are fairly expensive, the central *Connor's*, Dykegate St (☎066/915 1598; ❺), is comfortable and reasonably priced. *Boland's* on Goat St (☎066/915 1426, ⓦhomepage.eircom.net/~bolanddingle; ❻) is another reliable option. For **hostels**, try the *Grapevine*, Dykegate St (☎066/915 1434; dorm bed €15, ❸); or *Ballintaggart House*, one mile before Dingle Town (☎066/915 1454, ✉info@dingleaccommodation.com; dorm bed €14, ❹; closed Nov to mid-March). Dingle's top **restaurants** serve excellent seafood, landed just a few hundred yards away. Try *Doyle's* or the *Half Door* on John St for a good, if pricey, meal. *Greaney's*, on the corner of Dykegate and Strand streets, offers good cheap lunches and dinners. **Internet** access is at *Dingle Internet Café* on Main St. The best **pubs** for traditional music are *An Droichead Beag* on Main St (nightly) and *O'Flaherty's* on Bridge St (Fri & Sat).

West of Dingle town

Cycling is the best way to explore the peninsula; there are bikes available at Foxy John's on Main St. Public transport in the west of the peninsula amounts to a **bus** from Dingle to Dunquin. The Irish-speaking area west of Dingle is rich with relics of the ancient Gaelic and early Christian cultures and the main concentration of monuments lies between Ventry and Slea Head. First off there's the spectacular **Dún Beag** (daily 9am–6/8pm; €2), about four miles west of Ventry. A promontory fort, its defences include four earthen rings, with an underground escape route by the main entrance. West of here, the hillside above the road is studded with stone beehive huts, cave dwellings, souterrains, forts, churches, standing stones and crosses – over 500 of them in all. The beehive huts were being built and used for storage until the late nineteenth century, but among ancient buildings like the **Fahan group** you're looking over a landscape that's remained essentially unchanged for centuries.

At **Slea Head** the view encompasses the desolate, splintered masses of the **Blasket Islands**, uninhabited since 1953, though there are some summer residents.

In the summer, boats bound for **Great Blasket** depart daily from the pier just south of Dunquin (June–Aug every half hour, Easter–May & Sept to mid-Oct hourly; ☎066/915 6422, ⊛www.blasketferries.com; €20 return). Great Blasket's delights are simple ones: tramping the footpaths that crisscross the island, sitting on the beaches watching the seals and dolphins, or savouring the amazing sunsets. The only accommodation is provided by the *Great Blasket Hostel* (April–Sept; ☎086/852 2321, ⊛www.greatblasketisland.com; dorm bed €18), though you can camp for free and there's a café serving good, cheap vegetarian meals. At **DUNQUIN**, there's an An Óige **hostel** (☎066/915 6121, ⊛www.anoige.ie; dorm bed €9.50), and **B&B** in *Kruger's* pub (☎066/915 6127; ❺).

A couple of miles north around the headland from Dunquin stands **BALLYFER-RITER** where little northward lanes lead to the 500-foot cliffs at Sybil Head or to Smerwick Harbour and **Dún an Óir** (Golden Fort). The single most impressive early Christian monument on the peninsula is the **Gallarus oratory** (April–Oct daily 9am–8pm; €2.50) three miles further east, built sometime between the ninth and twelfth centuries of unmortared stone and still watertight. It's the best-preserved example of around twenty such oratories in Ireland, and represents a transition between the round beehive huts and the later rectangular churches, an example of which is to be found a mile to the north at **KILMALKEDAR**, with a nave dating from the mid-twelfth century and a corbelled stone roof.

County Clare

County Clare is one of the best spots in Ireland to catch a traditional music session and a good place to start is its county town, **ENNIS**. In daytime hours there's little of interest in the town's narrow bustling streets, though the **Clare Museum** on Arthur's Row (June–Sept daily 9.30am–5.30pm; rest of year closed lunchtimes 1–2pm; also Jan & Feb closed Sat & Sun, May closed Sun, Oct–Dec closed Sun & Mon; €3.50) offers a detailed account of local history from Bronze Age times onwards. Ennis has a superb, recently constructed **traditional music** centre, **Glór** on Friar's Walk (⊛www.glor.ie), hosting evening concerts, but it's the **pub sessions** which remain the local music scene's lifeblood. Safe bets for high-standard sessions include: *Cruise's*, Abbey St (nightly); *Ciarán's*, Francis St (Weds–Sun); and *Kelly's*, Carmody St (Sat & Sun) – The Knotted Chord CD store on Cook's Lane is an excellent source of information. Additionally, the town hosts a couple of festivals: *Fleadh Nua* at the end of May; and the *Ennis Trad Festival* in early November.

The **bus** and **train stations** sit alongside one another, a ten-minute walk from the town centre down Station Rd. The **tourist office** (☎065/682 8366) shares both the same building and opening hours as the Clare Museum. **Hostel** accommodation is provided by the *Abbey Tourist Hostel*, Harmony Row (☎065/682 2620, ⊛www.abbeytouristhostel.com; dorm bed €14, ❸). **B&Bs** near the centre include *Railway View House*, Tulla Rd (☎065/682 1646; ❺) and the equally welcoming *Cloneen*, Clon Rd (April–Oct; ☎065/6829681; ❺). **Eating** options include: the *Punjab*, 59 Parnell St, a superb value Indian restaurant; and *Numero Uno*, 3 Barrack St, a cheery pizza place.

Some 25 miles northwest of Ennis is the seaside village of **DOOLIN**, famed for a steady, year-round supply of **traditional music** in its three pubs, though these can often be crowded with tourists. There's plenty of **accommodation** including *Paddy's Doolin Hostel* (☎065/707 4006, ✉doolinhostel@eircom.net; ❷; closed Dec & Jan); *Rainbow Hostel* (☎065/707 4415, ✉rainbowhostel@eircom.net; ❷); *Flanagan's Village Hostel* (☎065/707 4564; ❷); and *Aille River Hostel* (☎065/707 4260, ✉ailleriver @esatclear.ie; ❷), which offers **camping** as well. All of Doolin's pubs serve excellent **food**; the *Lazy Lobster* and *Doolin Café* are two of the best restaurants. By the pier, from which a ferry runs to the **Aran Islands**, bold shelves of limestone pavement step into the sea. The **Cliffs of Moher**, four miles south of Doolin, are the area's most famous tourist spot, their great bands of shale and sandstone rising 660 feet above the waves.

Galway and around

The city of **GALWAY** continues to justify its reputation as the party capital of Ireland. University College Galway guarantees a high number of young people in term-time, but the energy is most evident during Galway's **festivals**, especially the Arts Festival in the last two weeks in July (@www.galwayartsfestival.ie). For locals, however, the most important event is the **Galway Races**, usually held in the last week of July. You'll have to pre-book accommodation during these weeks. Galway began as a crossing point on the River Corrib, and developed as a strong Anglo-Norman colony. Granted city status in 1484, it developed a flourishing trade with the Continent, especially Spain. When Cromwellian forces arrived in 1652, however-er, the city was besieged for ninety days and went into a decline from which it has only recently recovered. The prosperity of maritime Galway was expressed in the distinctive townhouses of the merchant class, remnants of which are littered around the city, even though recent development has destroyed some of its character. The **Browne doorway** in Eyre Square is one such monument, a bay window and doorway with the coats of arms of the Browne and Lynch families, dated 1627. Just about the finest medieval townhouse in Ireland is fifteenth century **Lynch's Castle** in Shop St – along with Quay St, the social hub of Galway. Now housing the Allied Irish Bank, it has a stone facade decorated with carved panels, gargoyles and a lion devouring another animal. Down by the River Corrib stands the **Spanish Arch**: more evocative in name than in reality, it's a sixteenth-century structure that was used to protect galleons unloading wine and rum. Across the river lies the **Claddagh** district, the old fishing village that once stood outside the city walls and gave the world the Claddagh ring as a symbol of love and fidelity. Past the Claddagh the river widens out into **Galway Bay**; for a pleasant sea walk follow the road until it reaches **Salthill**, the city's seaside resort. There are several beaches along the prom, though for the best you'll have to leave the city behind and head two miles from Salthill to **Silverstrand** on the Barna road. Once past Barna and into Connemara the beaches become quieter and more idyllic.

Practicalities

The **bus and train stations** are off Eyre Square, on the northern edge of the city centre. The **tourist office** (July & Aug daily 8.30am–7.45pm; rest of year Mon–Sat 9am–5.45/6.45pm, Nov–March Sat closing at 12.45pm; ☎091/537700, @www.irelandwest.travel.ie) is a short stroll down Forster St. The best budget **accommodation** includes *Kinlay House Galway*, Merchant's Rd (☎091/565244, @www.kinlayhouse.ie; dorm bed €19.50, ④), and *Barnacles Quay Street House*, 10 Quay St (☎091/568644, @www.barnacles.ie; dorm bed €19.50, ④). For **B&B** head for *Ardawn House*, 31 College Rd (☎091/568833, @ardawn@iol.ie; ⑤), or *St Martin's*, 2 Nuns Island Rd (☎091/568286; ⑤), both near the centre. There are **campsites** at *Ballyloughnane Caravan Park* on Dublin Rd (May–Sept), and several in Salthill, the most pleasant being *Hunter's* at Silverstrand, four miles west on the coast road (Easter–Sept). The *Celtel e.centre* on Merchant's Rd offers discounted international calls and **Internet** access.

The **bars** are the lungs of this city, and even the most abstemious travellers are going to find themselves sucked in. Good-value **pub food** is served around midday at *The Quays*, Quay St, *Busker Browne's*, Cross St, and *McSwiggan's* in Eyre St; for a more adventurous menu with a Latin influence, head for *BarCuba* on Eyre Square. In Quay St, *McDonagh's Seafood Bar* is a must for seafood at any time of day, while on Cross St, *Food for Thought*, Lower Abbeygate St, offers wholefood and vegetarian snacks. *Fat Freddy's*, Quay St, is a busy pizza place and excellent noodle dishes can be enjoyed at *Da Tang Noodle House*, Middle St. The Quay St area leading down to the river is known as the "**left bank**" due to the proliferation of popular pubs, restaurants and cafés. *The Quays* bar is one of the city's best loved, along with the nearby *Front Door* on Cross St. Among the best places to hear **traditional music** are *Taaffes* on Shop St, the old-fashioned *Tigh Neachtain* on Cross St and *The Crane* bar across the river on William St West (all nightly). For varied live music gigs, *Róisín Dubh* in Dominick St attracts leading Irish and international names. Galway also has its fair share of **clubs**: *Cuba*, Eyre Square, is a huge draw while other popular venues include *GPO*, Eglinton St, and *Le Metro* in the Radisson Hotel, Lough Atalia Rd. For **listings**, see the weekly *Galway Advertiser*.

The Aran Islands

The **Aran Islands** – Inishmore, Inishmaan and Inisheer, lying thirty miles out across the mouth of Galway Bay – are spectacular settings for a wealth of early remains and some of the finest archeological sites in Europe. The isolation of the Irish-speaking islands prolonged the continuation of a unique, ancient culture into the early twentieth century. There are daily **ferries** to Inishmore year-round, but less frequently to the other islands, departing from Galway city, Rossaveal (20 miles west by bus) and Doolin in County Clare – the cost of a return trip ranges from €15 to €32, depending on the season, with some student reductions and good-value accommodation packages. Book through Island Ferries, Victoria Place (☎091/568903); Inismór Ferries (☎091/568903) or O'Brien Shipping (☎091/567676), both in the tourist office; or Doolin Ferry Company (☎065/707 4455). You can also **fly** with Aer Árann (☎091/593034, ✆www.aerarann.ie); book at Galway tourist office.

Although **INISHMORE** is very tourist-orientated, its wealth of dramatic ancient sites overrides such considerations. It's a long strip of an island, a great tilted plateau of limestone with a scattering of villages along the sheltered northerly coast. The land slants up to the southern edge, where tremendous cliffs rip along the entire shoreline. As far as the eye can see is a tremendous patterning of stone, some of it bare pavements of grey rock split in bold diagonal grooves, latticed by dry-stone walls. The ferry docks at **Kilronan**, where the cheapest place to stay is the *Kilronan Hostel* (☎099/61255, ✆kilronanhostel@ireland.com; dorm bed €13), though the island's tranquillity is best enjoyed at the relaxing *Mainistir House Hostel* (☎099/61318, ✆mainistirhouse@eircom.net; dorm bed €14, ❸), twenty minutes' walk from the pier. **B&Bs** can be booked through the Kilronan **tourist office** (daily 10am–4/6.30pm; ☎099/61263), or when you buy your ferry ticket. Seafood is the island's great speciality, with most of the popular restaurants located in Kilronan: *Dún Aonghasa* has a varied and somewhat pricey menu; more budget-conscious meals are available at *The Pier House* while *Joe Watty's* bar serves good soups and stews. For **bike rental**, there's Aran Bicycle Hire beside the pier. Alternatively, take the minibus up through the island's villages and walk back from any point.

Most of Inishmore's sights are to the northwest of Kilronan; the first hamlet in this direction is Mainistir, from where it's a short signposted walk to the twelfth-century church of **Teampall Chiaráin**, the most interesting of the ecclesiastical sites on Inishmore. Three miles or so down the main road is Kilmurvey, a fifteen-minute walk from the most spectacular of Aran's prehistoric sites, **Dún Aengus**. Accessed via the **visitor centre** (daily 10am–4/6pm; €1.20; ✆www .heritageireland.ie), this massive ring fort, lodged on the edge of three hundred foot sea cliffs, has an inner citadel of precise blocks of grey stone, their symmetry echoing the almost geometric regularity of the land's limestone pavementing. Nearby **Dún Eoghanachta** is a huge drum of a stone fort, set in a lonely field with the Connemara mountains as a backdrop. It's accessible by tiny lanes from Dún Aengus with a detailed map; otherwise retrace your steps to Kilmurvey and follow the road west for just over a mile. At the **seven churches**, just east of Eoghannacht, there are ancient slabs commemorating seven Romans who died here, testifying to the far-reaching influence of Aran's monasteries. The site is, in fact, that of two churches and several domestic buildings, dating from the eighth to the thirteenth centuries, and includes St Brendan's grave, adorned by an early cross with interlaced patterns.

From Inishmore, it's an easy hop by boat to the other two islands; all the ferry companies run daily services. In comparison with Inishmore, **INISHMAAN** is lush, its stone walls forming a maze that chequers off tiny fields of grass and clover. The island's main sight is **Dún Chonchubhair**: built some time between the first and seventh centuries, its massive oval wall is almost intact and commands great views. Inishmaan's indifference to tourism means that amenities for visitors are minimal; if you arrive on spec ask at the pub for information (☎099/73003) – it's a warm and friendly place that also serves snacks in summer. For **B&B** try *Ard Álainn* (April–Sept; ☎099/73027; ➎); or *An Dún* (☎099/73047, ✉anduninismeain @eircom.net; ➎).

INISHEER, at just less than two miles across, is the smallest of the Aran Islands. Tourism has a key role here; Inisheer doesn't have the archeological wealth of Inishmore or the wild solitude of Inishmaan. A great plug of rock dominates the island, its rough, pale-grey stone dripping with greenery, topped by the fifteenth-century **O'Brien's Castle**, standing inside an ancient ring fort. Set around it are low fields, a small community of pubs and houses, and windswept sand dunes. The **Inisheer Island Co-operative** hut by the pier (June–Sept daily 10am–7pm; ☎099/75008) will give you a map and a list of **B&Bs**; try *Radharc an Chláir* (☎ & ☎099/75019; ➎) by the castle. There's also a **hostel**, *Brú Radharc na Mara* (March–Oct; ☎099/75024, ✉maire.searraigh@oceanfree.net; dorm bed €12, ➌) and a **campsite** near the pier. Meals are available at the *Óstán Inis Oírr* hotel. For **music**, head for *Tigh Ned's* bar.

Connemara

CLIFDEN, capital of the beautiful region of Connemara, is perched above the boulder-strewn estuary of the Owenglin River, with the circling jumble of the Twelve Bens providing a magnificent backdrop. The town tries hard to cultivate Galway's cosmopolitan atmosphere and attracts a fair number of young Dubliners, too. The **tourist office** on Galway Rd (Mon–Sat 9.30/10am–5/6.45pm; also July & Aug Sun 10am–6.45pm; ☎095/21163, ⊛www.irelandwest.travel.ie) has lists of the plentiful **B&Bs** around Clifden, though these can be very busy in high season. Try the good value *Ben View House*, Bridge St (☎095/21256, ⊛www.connemara-tourism.org; ➎), or the larger *Clifden House*, further down the same street (☎095/21187, ⊛www.clifden.info; ➏). The best **hostel** is the excellent *Clifden Town Hostel*, Market St (☎095/21076, ✉seancth @eircom.net; dorm bed €12, ➌). Two of the nicest **bars** for drink, **food** and music are *Mannion's* and *E.J. King's* on Market St. *Mitchell's* has a varied, reasonably priced menu, while for evening meals at €15 and upwards, try *Derryclare Seafood Restaurant*. Clifden is a good base for getting out into the Connemara countryside, and to do this you really need your own transport – John Mannion on Bridge St offers **bike rental**.

Westport

Set on the shores of Clew Bay, **WESTPORT** is one of the west's liveliest spots. Planned by the eighteenth-century architect James Wyatt, its formal layout comes as quite a surprise in the midst of its rural surrounds. The craggy **Croagh Patrick** makes an imposing background to the town, standing at 2510 feet above the bay; the climb is a strenuous one, but rewarded by spectacular views. St Patrick reputedly prayed on the mountain for forty days for the conversion of the Irish to Christianity, and on the last Sunday of July many tackle the pilgrimage to the summit barefoot. Another attraction is **Westport House** (April & May Sun 2–5pm; June & Sept daily 1.30–5.30pm; July & Aug Mon–Fri 11.30am–5.30pm, Sat & Sun 1.30–5.30pm; €15; ⊛www.westporthouse.ie), a mile or so out of town towards the bay. The beautifully designed house dates from 1730 and is privately owned: the present family are direct descendants of legendary pirate Grace O'Malley of Clew Bay. Inside the house is a *Holy Family* by Rubens and an upstairs room with intricate Chinese wallpaper dating from 1780.

Buses drop off on Mill St in the centre; the **train** station is on Altamount St, ten minutes north of the centre. Westport's **hostels** include the enormous *Club Atlantic* on Altamount St (March–Oct; ☎098/26644, ✉aran@ainu.ie; dorm bed €10, ❸) and the *Old Mill* on James St (☎098/25657, ⓦwww.oldmill-hostel.com; dorm bed €14, ❸). There are plenty of **B&Bs** – check for availability at the **tourist office** on James St (Mon–Sat 9am–5.45pm; June–Aug also Sun; ☎098/25711, ⓦwww.irelandwest.ie). On Bridge St *McCormack's* is a popular daytime **eating** choice while the Mediterranean-style *Sol Rios* is a good lunch option. The restaurant at *Quay Cottage*, the entrance to Westport House, serves enormous salmon salads and plenty of vegetarian food; the nearby complex of refurbished waterside buildings brims with people, pubs and more expensive restaurants. The best **music** pubs are on Bridge St – *The West* is hugely popular and *Matt Molloy's Bar*, owned by the eponymous Chieftains' flute player, occasionally features visiting celebrities and is a hive of activity during Westport's **Arts Festival** (ⓦwww.westportartsfestival.com) at the end of September.

Sligo and around

SLIGO is, after Derry, the biggest town in the northwest of Ireland. The legacy of W.B. Yeats – perhaps Ireland's best-loved poet – is still strongly felt here: the **Yeats Memorial Building** on Hyde Bridge (Mon–Sat 10am–4.30pm; €4) features a photographic exhibition and film on his life, while the poet's Nobel Prize for Literature and other memorabilia are on show in the **Sligo County Museum** on Stephen St (June–Sept Mon–Sat 10am–noon & 2–5pm; rest of year 2–5pm only; free). The **Model Arts Centre** on The Mall (Tues–Sat 10am–5.30pm; also April–Oct Sun noon–5.30pm; free; ⓦwww.modelart.ie) houses works by the poet's brother Jack B. Yeats and also displays a broad representation of modern Irish art. Across the River Garavogue on Abbey St stands the thirteenth-century **Dominican Friary** whose visitor centre (April–Oct daily 10am–6pm; €1.90; ⓦwww.heritageireland.ie) provides an informative introduction to many of its existing features, including the last remaining sculptured high altar in the country and an impressive cloistered arcade.

Buses and **trains** arrive at the stations on Lord Edward St and Union St respectively, five minutes west of the centre. The **tourist office** is on Temple St (June–Aug daily 9/10am–6/7pm; rest of year Mon–Fri 9am–5pm; ☎071/916 1201, ⓦwww.sligotourism.ie). For **bike rental**, try Flanagan's, Market Yard. The most central **B&B** is *Renaté House*, 9 Upper John St (☎071/916 2014; ❺); or try *St Anne's*, Pearse Rd (☎071/914 3188; ❻) or *Tree Tops*, Cleveragh Rd (☎071/916 0160, ⓦwww.sligobandb.com; ❺). **Hostels** include the well-equipped *Eden Hill*, Pearse Rd (☎071/914 3204, ✉edenhillhostel@eircom.net; dorm bed €12.50, ❸) and the central and popular *White House* on Markievicz Rd (☎071/914 5160; dorm bed €10). There are **camp-sites** five miles from town at Rosses Point to the north (bus #473) and Strandhill to the west (bus #472); both have fine beaches and Strandhill, while unsafe for swimming, attracts plenty of surfers. Most pubs in Sligo serve decent **bar lunches**: *Hargadon's* on O'Connell St has fine old traditional snugs; the *Garavogue* on Stephen St offers excellent international food and bar snacks all day. For top pizza head for *Bistro Bianconni* restaurant on O'Connell St; *The Loft* on Lord Edward St has an extensive menu of world cuisine. Sligo does well for **pubs** – tiny *Shoot the Crows* on Grattan St is popular with the arty set – and the best for **traditional music** are *Sheela na Gig* (nightly) on Bridge St, owned by local stars Dervish, and *Earley's* bar (Thurs) across the road. Popular **clubs** include *Delicious*, in the *Clarence Hotel*, Wine St, and *Toff's* on Kennedy Parade. Check the weekly *Sligo Champion* for listings.

Donegal Town

DONEGAL town is a bustling place focused around its old marketplace, The Diamond, and a fine base for exploring the stunning coastal countryside and inland hills and loughs. However, just about the only sight in the town itself is the well-preserved shell of **O'Donnell's Castle** on Tírchonaill St by The Diamond (Easter–Oct daily 10am–6pm; €3.80; ⊛www.heritageireland.ie), a fine example of Jacobean architecture. On the left bank of the River Eske stand the few ruined remains of **Donegal Friary**, while on the opposite bank a woodland path known as Bank Walk offers wonderful views of **Donegal Bay** and towards the **Blue Stack Mountains**, which rise at the northern end of Lough Eske.

There are dozens of **B&Bs** here, and to avoid a lot of walking it's simplest to call at the **tourist office** on The Quay (Easter–Sept Mon–Sat 9am–5/8pm July & Aug also Sun 9am–8pm; ☎074/972 1148, ⊛www.irelandnorthwest.ie). There are two **hostels** off the Killybegs road just outside town: the nearest is *Donegal Town Independent Hostel* (☎074/972 2805, ⊜lincunn8@eircom.net; dorm bed €11.50, ❷), while An Óige's *Ball Hill Hostel* is three miles out on the north side of Donegal Bay (April–Sept; ☎074/972 1174, ⊛www.anoige.ie; dorm bed €10.50). **Eating-places** are plentiful, including excellent burgers and pizza at the *Harbour*, opposite the tourist office, and substantial cheap meals at the *Atlantic Café*, Main St. Many **pubs** serve lunches and are good evening watering holes. The *Olde Castle Bar*, next to the castle, is fine for a quiet daytime drink; *McGroarty's* on The Diamond has a good bar menu; while *The Scotsman* on Bridge St has regular traditional sessions. The *Abbey Hotel* on The Diamond hosts a popular **disco** on Saturday and Sunday nights. For **bike rental** head for the Bike Shop on Waterloo St.

Slieve League and Glencolmcille

To the west of Donegal town lies one of the most stupendous landscapes in Ireland – the stark and beautiful **Teelin Bay** and the majestic Slieve League cliffs. An ideal base for exploring the region is one of the country's best independent **hostels**, the busy *Derrylahan Independent Hostel* (☎074/973 8079, ⊛homepage.eircom.net/~derrylahan; dorm bed €10, ❷), on the seaside road between **KILCAR** and **CARRICK**.

There are two routes up to the ridge of **Slieve League**: a back way following the signpost to Baile Mór just before Teelin, and the road route from Teelin to Bunglass, a thousand sheer feet above the sea. The former path has you looking up continually at the ridge known as One Man's Pass, on which walkers seem the size of pins, while the frontal approach swings you up to one of the most thrilling cliff scenes in the world, the **Amharc Mór**. On a good day you can see a third of Ireland from the summit.

One Man's Pass across the summit, only a few feet wide in places and dangerous in windy weather, leads via Malinbeg and Malinmore to **GLENCOLMCILLE** – the Glen of St Columbcille, the name by which Columba was known after his conversion. A place of pilgrimage since the seventh century, following Columba's stay in the valley, every June 9 at midnight the locals commence a three-hour barefoot itinerary of the cross-inscribed slabs that stud the valley basin, finishing up with Mass at 3am in the small church. If you want to attempt *Turas Cholmcille* ("Columba's Journey") yourself, get a map of the route from the **Folk Village Museum** (Easter–Sept Mon–Sat 10am–6pm, Sun noon–6pm; €2.75; ⊛www.infowing.ie/donegal/ad/fr), a cluster of replica, period-furnished thatched cottages, including a National School and a Shebeen house. A path up to the left from here leads to the wonderfully positioned *Dooey Hostel* (☎074/973 0130, ⊛www.dooeyhostel.com; dorm bed €10, ❷). The best **food** in Glencolmcille is at *An Cistín*, part of the Foras Cultúir Uladh complex, or there's the *Lace House Restaurant* on the main street above the **tourist office** (June–Aug daily 10am–6pm; ☎074/973 0116). **B&Bs** include *Corner House* (April–Sept; ☎074/973 0021; ❺), near *Biddy's Bar* in the village centre.

Northern Ireland

Both the pace of political change and the uncertainty of its future continue to characterize **Northern Ireland**. In 1998, after thirty years of "The Troubles", its people overwhelmingly voted in support of a political settlement and, it was hoped, an end to political and sectarian violence. Since then the political process has gradually inched forwards, hampered by deep mistrust and suspicion on both sides, with issues such as the decommissioning of IRA weaponry paramount, and inter-community tensions still rife in parts of Belfast. Despite the political instability the North remains a pretty safe place for tourists. **Belfast** and **Derry** – two lively and attractive cities – have no obvious security presence beyond the occasional hovering army helicopter. The northern coastline – especially the weird geometry of the **Giant's Causeway** – is as spectacular as anything in Ireland. Over to the southwest is the great **Lough Erne**, a huge lake complex dotted with islands and surrounded by richly beautiful countryside, and **Enniskillen**, a town resonant with history.

Belfast

A quarter of Northern Ireland's population lives in the capital, **BELFAST**. While the legacy of "The Troubles" is clearly visible in the landscape of areas like West Belfast – the peace walls, derelict buildings and political murals – security measures have been considerably eased, though there are certain flashpoints such as the Short Strand and the Ardoyne which are inadvisable to visit.

Belfast began life as a cluster of forts guarding a ford across the River Farset, which nowadays runs beneath High St. However, its history doesn't really begin until 1604, when Sir Arthur Chichester was "planted" in the area by James I. By the eighteenth century the cloth trade and shipbuilding had expanded tremendously, and the population increased ten-fold in a century. It was then noted for its liberalism, but in the nineteenth century the sectarian divide became wider and increasingly violent. Although Partition and the creation of Northern Ireland with Belfast as its capital inevitably boosted the city's status, the Troubles exacerbated the industrial decline which hit much of the British Isles during the 1980s. However, a massive programme of regeneration commenced in the 1990s at the first signs of peace, fuelled by the billions of pounds pumped in from Britain, the European Union and the International Fund for Ireland in the hope of ensuing political stability. This economic rejuvenation coupled with optimism generated by the early years of the peace process brought a new zest to the city, particularly in terms of the regeneration of areas such as the Docklands. However, some areas of the city now evince obvious economic decline, most notably North Belfast and the once-thriving, now-tarnished Golden Mile, where restaurants that appeared during the boom years during the second half of the 1990s have closed and remain boarded up. On weekday nights the city centre can resemble a ghost town, though there's no doubt that Belfast continues to thrive culturally. Music, theatre and the visual arts are all flourishing and traditional Irish culture is rapidly being rediscovered.

Arrival, information and accommodation

Flights arrive at **Belfast International Airport**, nineteen miles west of town (buses every 30min to Europa bus station; £5 single, £8 return), or **Belfast City Airport**, three miles northeast (bus #600 every 40min to city centre; £2). **Ferries** from Heysham and Troon dock at Donegall Quay (15min walk to centre, £3.50 taxi); those from Stranraer dock a little further north at Corry Rd (taxi £5); and those from Liverpool further north again on West Bank Rd (taxi £6); while ferries from Cairnryan dock 20 miles north at Larne (bus or train into centre). Most **trains** call at the central Great Victoria St Station, though those from Dublin and Larne terminate at Central Station on East Bridge St. **Buses** from Derry, the Republic, the airports and ferry docks arrive at Europa bus station beside Great Victoria St train station; buses from the north coast use Laganside Buscentre in Queen's Square. A regular Centrelink bus connects all bus and train stations. The excellent **Citybus** company covers nearly everywhere you'll want to go; it's worth buying a multi-journey ticket (£3.20) for four rides, available from newsagents and the Citybus kiosk in Donegall Square West, which can also provide a free bus map. **Ulsterbus** serves the outlying areas; and there are special weekend **late-night buses** from Donegall Square West (Fri & Sat 1–2am; £3). Information on all buses and trains is available at ⓦwww.translink.co.uk.

The **Belfast Welcome Centre**, 47 Donegall Place (Mon–Sat 9am–5.30pm; ☎028/9024 6609, ⓦwww.gotobelfast.com), provides information and an accommodation booking service as well as left-luggage facilities and an Internet café. **Bord Fáilte**, for information about the Republic, is at 53 Castle St (Mon–Fri 9am–5pm; March–Sept also Sat 9am–12.30pm; ☎028/9032 7888).

Most of Belfast's numerous **B&Bs** are on the south side of the city in the university area, and there are several budget options.

Hostels

The Ark 18 University St ☎028/9032 9626, ⓦwww.arkhostel.com. Friendly, comfortable hostel close to the university. Dorm bed £8.50. ❸

Arnie's Backpackers 63 Fitzwilliam St ☎028/9024 2867, ⓦwww.arniesbackpackers.co.uk. Cheerful and relaxed independent hostel, also near the university. Dorm bed £9.50. ❸

Belfast International Youth Hostel 22–32 Donegall Rd ☎028/9031 5435, ⓦwww.hini.org.uk. Large, well-equipped but characterless modern HINI hostel. Dorm bed £8.50. ❸

The Linen House Hostel 18 Kent St ☎028/9058 6400, ⓦwww.belfasthostel.com. Large, but welcoming, centrally located hostel. Dorm bed £10. ❸

Hotels and B&Bs

Botanic Lodge 87 Botanic Ave ☎ & ☎028/9032 7682. Popular, family-run B&B; 16 rooms, but only two en suite. ❺

Camera Guest House 44 Wellington Park ☎028/9066 0026, ⓔpauldrumm@hotmail.com. Very luxurious and elegantly decorated town house offering en-suite and standard accommodation. ❽

Eglantine Guest House 21 Eglantine Ave ☎028/9066 7585. Eight cosy B&B rooms in a Victorian house. ❺

Marine House 30 Eglantine Ave ☎028/9066 2828, ⓦwww.marineguesthouse3star.com. A large Victorian guest house in a quiet setting offering attractive, spacious rooms. ❺

Pearl Court House 11 Malone Rd ☎028/9066 6145, ⓦwww.pearlcourtguesthouse.com. Large house with spacious bedrooms, including some triple rooms, offering a fine breakfast. ❼

The City

Belfast **City Hall**, presiding over central **Donegall Square**, is an austere building (tours June–Sept Mon–Fri 11am, 2pm & 3pm, Sat 2.30pm; rest of year Mon–Fri 11am & 2pm, Sat 2.30pm; free; ⓦwww.belfastcitygov.uk), its civic purpose almost subservient to its role in propagating the ethics of Presbyterian power. At the northwest corner of the square stands **The Linen Hall Library** (Mon–Fri 9.30am–5.30pm, Sat 9.30am–4pm; ⓦwww.linenhall.com), entered on Fountain St, where the Political Collection houses over 80,000 publications dealing with every aspect of Northern Ireland's political life since 1966. The streets leading north off Donegall Square North lead to the main shopping area. Towards the river, either side of Ann St, you're in the narrow alleyways known as **The Entries**, where you'll find some great old saloon bars. At the end of High St the clock tower is a good position from which to view the world's second- and third-largest cranes, Goliath and Samson, across the river in the Harland & Wolff shipyard where the **Titanic** was built. North of the clock tower is a series of grand edifices which grew out of a similar civic vanity to that invested in the City Hall. The restored **Customs House**, a Corinthian-style building, is the first you'll see, but the most monolithic is the Protestant **St Anne's Cathedral** at the junction of Donegall and Talbot streets, a neo-Romanesque basilica started in 1899 (Mon–Sat 10am–4pm, Sun noon–3pm; free; ⓦwww.belfastcathedral.org). Across the river from the Customs House is the face of a new Belfast, the ambitious **Odyssey** complex housing a sports stadium, IMAX cinema, W5 science discovery centre (Mon–Fri 10am–5pm, Sat & Sun noon–5pm; last admission 5pm; adults £5.50; ⓦwww.w5online.co.uk)

and Ireland's first *Hard Rock Café*. Further along the waterside is the impressive Waterfront Hall concert venue (℠www.waterfront.co.uk).

The area of **South Belfast** known as "The Golden Mile", stretches from the **Grand Opera House** on Great Victoria St down to the university, and has plenty of eating-places, pubs and bars at each end. Its attractions include the **Crown Liquor Saloon**, one of the greatest of the old Victorian gin palaces. Further south on University Rd, **Queen's University** is the architectural centrepiece, flanked by the most satisfying Georgian terrace in Belfast, University Square. Just south of the university are the verdant **Botanic Gardens** whose Palm House (Mon–Fri 10am–4/5pm, Sat & Sun 2–4/5pm; free) was the first of its kind in the world. Also in the Botanic Gardens is the **Ulster Museum** (Mon–Fri 10am–5pm, Sat 1–5pm, Sun 2–5pm; free; ℠www.ulstermuseum.org.uk), with its collection of Irish art, history and natural sciences exhibits, and treasures salvaged from the Spanish Armada ships which foundered off the Giant's Causeway in 1588.

Eating, drinking and entertainment

Many of the best places to **eat** and the liveliest **pubs** can be found around Great Victoria St and in the university area, and Belfast's best entertainment is **music** in the pubs. There's also a vibrant **club** scene and plenty of DJ bars. Good sources of information are *The Big List*, available free in pubs and record shops, and the *Belfast Evening Telegraph*.

Restaurants and cafés

Archana 53 Dublin Rd ☎028/9032 3713. Indian Balti house with *Little India*, a fine Indian vegetarian restaurant offering extremely cheap lunchtime specials, downstairs.

Ba Soba 38 Hill St. Belfast's first and immensely popular noodle bar, packed even at lunchtime.

Bewley's Donegall Arcade. Branch of the famous Dublin coffee house serving good-value breakfasts, lunches and snacks.

Café Conor 11a Stranmillis Rd. Stylish café beside the Botanic Gardens with hot food specials and breakfasts.

Café Vincents 78 Botanic Ave. Known to all as *Vincents*, this place does excellent breakfasts, value-for-money high teas and plenty of pizzas.

Delaney's 19 Lombard St. Economical, wholesome food from a restaurant handily placed in the main shopping area. Mon–Sat 9am–5pm, Thurs until 9pm.

Maggie May's 45 Botanic Ave. Huge, economically priced portions in this cosy café with lots of veggie choices.

Red Panda 60 Great Victoria St & The Odyssey Pavilion. Very pleasant establishments specializing in dim sum and other authentic Chinese dishes.

Pubs and live music

Crown Liquor Saloon 46 Great Victoria St. The city's most famous pub, decked out like a spa bath, with a good range of Ulster food and Strangford oysters in season.

The Empire 42 Botanic Ave. Music hall and cellar bar in converted church with regular live bands (Thurs, Fri & Sun) and a "pre-club strut" (Sat).

The John Hewitt Donegall St. Owned by Belfast Unemployed Resource Centre, this popular bar has some of Belfast's best traditional sessions (Mon–Wed & Sun 9.30pm, Sat 5pm).

Kelly's Cellars 30 Bank St. One of the city's oldest and finest traditional bars.

The Kitchen Bar 16 Victoria Sq. Fine old bar, tucked away behind Ann St – great value lunches and traditional sessions (Fri & Sun).

Madden's Smithfield. Unpretentious and atmospheric pub, with regular traditional sessions (Fri & Sat).

The Morning Star 17 Pottinger's Entry. Old-fashioned bar serving great food in the restaurant upstairs, with a very cheap lunchtime buffet downstairs.

The Rotterdam 54 Pilot St. Names big and small play in this docklands venue. First-class sounds.

Wetherspoon's 35–37 Bedford St. Belfast's cheapest pint of stout and a range of economically priced meals on offer all day.

Clubs and DJ bars

Apartment 2 Donegall Square. Swish, newly renovated bar and *the* place for bright young Belfast to be seen; DJs most nights.

East 2–14 East Bridge St. Highly rated, European-flavoured bar hosting great club nights.

The Limelight 17 Ormeau Ave. A serious dance club with various club nights.

Milk Bar Club Tomb St. Ever-popular and ever-packed club offering dance music to suit all tastes every night of the week.

Northern Whig 2–10 Bridge St. Massive new bar in the premises of the old newspaper, featuring

The Reliable Airline

Why stretch your journey?

pre-club DJs every night except Wed.
Orpheus & the Underworld University St. Hugely
popular with students, thanks to its low prices, and
Tuesday night retro club; more DJs and live acts

on Fri & Sat.
Thompson's Garage 3 Pattersons Place, Arthur
St. Hosts a variety of club nights – the US house
night (Sat) being the big draw.

Listings

Exchange Thomas Cook, 11 Donegall Place
(☎028/9055 0030); and the Belfast Welcome
Centre.
Hospitals Belfast City Hospital, Lisburn Rd
☎028/9032 9241; Royal Victoria, Grosvenor Rd
☎028/9024 0503.

Internet Broncos Web, 122 Great Victoria St.
Left luggage Belfast Welcome Centre, 47
Donegall Place.
Police North Queen St ☎028/9065 0222.
Post office Castle Place.

The Giant's Causeway and around

Since 1693, when the Royal Society publicized it as one of the great wonders of the
natural world, the **Giant's Causeway**, 65 miles north of Belfast on the coast, has been
a major tourist attraction. Consisting of an estimated 37,000 polygonal basalt columns,
it's the result of a massive subterranean explosion some sixty million years ago which
spewed out a huge mass of molten basalt onto the surface and, as it cooled, solidified
into what are, essentially, massive polygonal crystals. Public transport is well organized
in summer. **Trains** from Belfast go to **COLERAINE**, and some go on to
PORTRUSH; from either, you can catch the "**open-topper**" bus (July & Aug 4
daily) to the Causeway, or from Portrush there's bus #172, both running via
Bushmills. The Antrim Coaster coach (Goldline Express #252) runs from Larne
direct to the Causeway (June–Sept twice daily), taking in the gorgeous scenery of the
Antrim Glens and stunning seascapes as it goes. The Causeway's **visitor centre** (daily
10am–5/7pm; ☎028/2073 1855; free; car parking £5) has information and a small
exhibition. Taking the path down the cliffs from the visitor centre (or the shuttle bus;
every 15min; £1.20 return) brings you to the most spectacular of the blocks where
many people linger, but if you push on, you'll be rewarded with relative solitude and
views of some of the more impressive formations high in the cliffs. One of these,
Chimney Point, has an appearance so bizarre that it persuaded the ships of the
Spanish Armada to open fire on it, believing that they were attacking Dunluce Castle, a
few miles further west. An alternative two-mile circuit follows the spectacular clifftop
path from the visitor centre, with views across to Scotland, to a flight of 162 steps leading down the cliff to a set of 40ft basalt columns known as the **Organ Pipes**, from
where paths lead round to the shuttle-bus stop alongside the Causeway proper.

A restored **narrow-gauge railway** runs between Bushmills and the Causeway
(mid-May to Sept 3–5 times daily plus some days in other months; 20min; single
£2.50, return £4.50). **BUSHMILLS** makes a reasonable base, as there's a new
HINI **hostel**, *Mill Rest*, at 49 Main St (☎028/2073 1222, ☎www.hini.org.uk; dorm
bed £11) and several B&B options. While here you could tour the **Old Bushmills
Distillery** (April–Oct Mon–Sat 9.30am–4pm, Sun noon–4pm; Nov–March call
☎028/2073 1521 for tour times; £3.95; ☎www.whiskeytours.ie) and sample
whiskeys from the world's oldest licit distillery.

Derry

DERRY lies at the foot of Lough Foyle, less than three miles from the border with
the Republic. The city presents a beguiling picture, its two hillsides terraced with
pastel-shaded houses punctuated by stone spires, and, being two-thirds Catholic, has
a very different atmosphere from Belfast. However, from Partition in 1921 until the
late 1980s Derry's Catholic majority was denied its civil rights by gerrymandering,
which ensured that the Protestant minority maintained control of all important
local institutions. The situation came to a head after the Protestant Apprentice Boys'

March in August 1969, when the police attempted to storm the Catholic estates of the Bogside. In the ensuing tension, British troops were widely deployed for the first time in Northern Ireland. On January 31, 1972, the crisis deepened when British paratroopers opened fire on civilians, killing thirteen unarmed demonstrators in what became known as **Bloody Sunday**. Derry is now greatly changed: tensions eased considerably here long before Belfast, thanks in part to a determinedly even-handed local council, although defiant murals remain and marching is still a contentious issue. The city centre has undergone much regeneration too, while Derry has gained a justifiable reputation for innovation in the arts.

The City

You can walk the entire mile-long circuit of Derry's **city walls** – some of the best-preserved defences left standing in Europe. Reinforced by bulwarks, bastions and a parapeted earth rampart, the walls encircle the original medieval street pattern with four gateways – Shipquay, Butcher, Bishop and Ferryquay – surviving from the first construction, in slightly revised form.

The best starting point is the **Guildhall Square**, once the old quay, where most of the city's cannon are lined up, between Shipquay and Magazine gates, their noses peering out above the ramparts. A reconstruction of the medieval **O'Doherty Tower** (June–Sept Mon–Sat 10am–5pm, Sun 2–5pm; rest of year closed Sun & Mon; ⊛www.derry.net/tower; £3.65) houses splendid displays outlining the turbulent historic development of the city. Turning left at **Shipquay Gate**, the promenade doglegs at Water Bastion where the River Foyle once lapped the walls at high tide. Continue on to Newgate Bastion and **Ferryquay Gate**, where you can look out across the river to the Waterside area, once primarily Protestant, now almost half Catholic – further evidence of the lessening of the city's political tensions. Between Ferryquay and Bishop's Gate the major sight is the Protestant **St Columb's Cathedral** (Mon–Sat 9am–1pm & 2–4/5pm; £1.20), just within the south section of the walls; it overlooks the Fountain, the Protestant enclave immediately outside the same stretch of walls, and offers one of the best views of the city. Built in 1633, this was the first post-Reformation cathedral to be constructed in the British Isles. In 1688/89 Derry played a key part in the Williamite victory over the Catholic King James II by holding out against a fifteen-week siege that cost the lives of one-quarter of the city's population. The cathedral was used as a battery during the siege, and in the entrance porch you'll find the cannonball shot into the grounds by the besieging army with proposals for the city's surrender.

Back on the walls, pass the white sandstone **courthouse** next to Bishop's Gate and you'll see, downhill to the left, the only remaining tower of the old Derry jail. At the **Double Bastion** sits the Roaring Meg cannon, used during the siege, while down in the valley below are the streets of the Bogside. These were once the undisputed preserve of the IRA, and **Free Derry Corner** marks the site of the original barricades erected against the British army at the height of the Troubles. Nearby are the Bloody Sunday and Hunger Strikers' memorials, while several large murals commemorate events that took place during the Troubles. Further along the city wall is the **Royal Bastion**, former site of the Rev. George Walker statue which was blown up in 1973. It is in Walker's and their predecessors' memory that the Protestant Apprentice Boys march round the walls every August 12.

Practicalities

Trains from Belfast arrive on the east bank of the Foyle with a free connecting bus service to the **bus station** on Foyle St beside Guildhall Square. City of Derry **airport** (☎028/7181 0784, ⓦwww.cityofderryairport.com) is seven miles northeast, connected to the centre by bus. The **tourist office** is at 44 Foyle St (July–Sept daily 9/10am–5/7pm; rest of year Mon–Fri 9am–5pm, also mid-March to June Sat 10am–5pm; ☎028/7126 7284, ⓦwww.derryvisitor.com) and contains branches of both the Northern Ireland Tourist Board and Bord Fáilte as well as a **bureau de change**. **Hostel** accommodation includes the *Derry City Independent Hostel* at 4 Asylum Rd, half-a-mile down Strand Rd (☎028/7137 7989, ⓦwww.derry-hostel .co.uk; dorm bed £9, ❸). For **B&Bs** try the excellent-value *The Saddler's House*, 36 Great James St (☎028/7126 9691, ⓦwww.thesaddlershouse.com; ❺), or *Clarence House*, 15 Northland Rd (☎028/7126 5342; ❺). Places for **eating out** include *The Leprechaun*, 23 Strand Rd, for delicious home-baking and hot meals, and the stylish *Mange 2* on Clarendon St, offering a variety of meat and fish dishes; *Badger's Bar*, 16 Orchard St, is another good option. **Internet** access is available at *Bean-There.Com*, 20 The Diamond. The **pubs** host most entertainment and Waterloo St just outside the northern walls, is the best bet for **traditional music** venues, including the *Dungloe Bar*, *The Rocking Chair* and *Peadar O'Donnell's*. Students congregate at *Le Roc* where Rock and Strand roads meet; upstairs *Earth Niteclub* is hugely popular. *Downey's*, on Shipquay St, claims it is "Ireland's largest R&B club" and has music most nights while other **clubs** to try include *Fusion* and DJ bars such as the *Strand Bar* and *The Carraig*, all on Strand Rd. Check the bi-weekly *Derry Journal* for listings.

Enniskillen

ENNISKILLEN sits on a lake island, a narrow ribbon of water passing each side of the town between the Lower and Upper **Lough Erne**. The water loops its way around the core of the town, its glassy surface lending Enniskillen a sense of calm and reflecting the mini-turrets of **Enniskillen Castle**. Rebuilt by William Cole, to whom the British gave Enniskillen in 1609, the castle houses the **Watergate History and Heritage Centre** and the **Regimental Museum of the Royal Inniskilling Fusiliers** in the keep (July & Aug Mon 2–5pm, Tues–Fri 10am–5pm, Sat & Sun 2–5pm; May, June & Sept closed Sun; rest of year closed Sat & Sun; £2.25; ⓦwww.enniskillencastle.co.uk), a proud, polished display of the uniforms, flags and paraphernalia of the town's historic regiments. A mile along the Belfast road stands **Castle Coole** (July & Aug daily noon–6pm; June Mon & Wed–Sun same times; mid-March to May & Sept Sat & Sun only same times; £4). A perfect Palladian building of Portland stone, with an interior of fine plasterwork and superb furnishings, it sits in a beautiful landscaped garden (daily 10am–4/8pm; car £2, pedestrians free).

Opposite the **bus station** on Wellington Rd is the **tourist office** (Mon–Fri 9am–5.30/7pm; Easter–Sept also Sat & Sun 10/11am–5/6pm; ☎028/6632 3110, ⓦwww.fermanaghlakelands.com), which can help finding **B&Bs**, most of which are some distance from the town centre. A new HINI **hostel**, *The Bridges*, is on Belmore St by the war memorial (☎028/6634 0110, ⓦwww.hini.org.uk; dorm bed £12). For **eating out**, try *Oscar's* in Belmore St or *Franco's* in Queen Elizabeth Rd. Several **bars** along High St and its continuation, Townhall St, provide pub food, particularly *The Linen Hall* and *Pat's Bar*. You'll find occasional **traditional sessions** at *Blakes of the Hollow* on Townhall St. The *Fort Lodge Hotel* and *Railway Hotel* on Forthill St both have live music and DJs at weekends.

Lough Erne

The earliest people to settle in this region lived on and around the two lakes of **Lough Erne** which features many *crannogs* (Celtic artificial islands). The maze of waterways protected the settlers from invaders and created an enduring cultural isolation. Stone carvings suggest that Christianity was accepted far more slowly here than elsewhere: several pagan idols have been found on Christian sites, and the early Christian remains on the islands reveal the influence of pagan culture.

The easiest place to visit is **Devenish Island**, two miles northwest of Enniskillen. St Molaise founded a monastic settlement here in the sixth century and it remained an important religious centre up until the Plantations. It's a delightful setting and the considerable ruins span the entire medieval period. There are regular **ferries** (Easter–Sept Mon–Sat 10am–6pm, Sun 2–6pm; £2.25) from Trory Point, four miles north of Enniskillen on the A32 road. Four miles further north along the Kesh road lies **Castle Archdale** forest park from which ferries (April–June Sat & Sun 11am–1pm, July & Aug daily 11am–6pm; £3) depart to **White Island** whose ruined abbey bears early Christian carvings that look eerily pagan. The most disconcerting is the lewd female figure known as a Sheila-na-Gig, with bulging cheeks, a big grin, open legs and arms pointing to her genitals. Back in the forest park, there's an excellent HINI **hostel** (March–Oct; ☎028/6862 8118, ⊛www.hini.org.uk; dorm bed £9).

Travel details

Trains

Details are for weekday services; extra services may run on Mondays and Fridays, fewer on Sundays.

Belfast to: Derry (8 daily; 2hr 05min); Dublin (8 daily; 2hr); Larne Harbour (14 daily; 55min).

Coleraine to: Portrush, for Giant's Causeway (21 daily; 15min).

Cork to: Dublin (9 daily; 2hr 40min–3hr 20min); Killarney (5 daily; 2hr).

Derry to: Belfast (7 daily; 2hr 05min); Coleraine (8 daily; 40min).

Dublin (Connolly) to: Belfast (8 daily; 2hr); Rosslare (3 daily; 3hr 10min).

Dublin (Heuston) to: Cork (9 daily; 2hr 40min–3hr 20min); Ennis (2 daily; 3hr 15min–3hr 40min); Galway (5 daily; 2hr 45min); Killarney (6 daily; 3hr 40min); Limerick (11 daily; 2hr 20min–3hr); Sligo (3 daily; 3hr 15min); Westport (3 daily; 3hr 50min).

Ennis to: Dublin (2 daily; 3hr15min–3hr40min).

Galway to: Dublin (4 daily; 2hr 45min).

Killarney to: Cork (4 daily; 2hr); Dublin (4 daily; 4hr).

Sligo to: Dublin (4 daily; 3hr 20min).

Westport to: Dublin (3 daily; 3hr 50min).

Buses

Details below cover Bus Éireann or Ulsterbus services on summer weekdays; extra services may run on Fridays, fewer in winter and on Sundays.

Belfast to: Derry (15 daily; 1hr 40min); Dublin (7 daily; 2hr 55min); Enniskillen (10 daily; 2hr 15min).

Cork to: Dublin (6 daily; 4hr 30min); Galway (12 daily; 3hr 15min); Killarney (12 daily; 2hr).

Derry to: Donegal (5 daily; 1hr 30min); Dublin (5 daily; 4hr 30min); Enniskillen (7 daily; 1hr 30min); Sligo (5 daily; 2hr 30min).

Donegal town to: Derry (4 daily; 1hr 30min); Dublin (5 daily; 4hr 15min); Glencolmcille (3 daily; 1hr 25min); Sligo (5 daily; 1hr).

Dublin to: Belfast (7 daily; 2hr 55min); Cashel (6 daily; 2hr 50min); Cork (6 daily; 4hr 30min); Derry (5 daily; 4hr 30min); Donegal town (5 daily; 4hr 15min); Ennis (12 daily; 4hr 20min); Enniskillen (5 daily; 3hr 40min); Galway (5 daily; 3hr 30min); Killarney (5 daily; 6hr); Kilkenny (6 daily; 2hr); Sligo (4 daily; 4hr); Westport (3 daily; 5hr).

Ennis to: Doolin (3 daily; 1hr 25min); Dublin (12 daily; 4hr 20min).

Enniskillen to: Belfast (8 daily; 2hr 35min); Derry (7 daily; 1hr 30min); Dublin (5 daily; 3hr 40min).

Galway to: Clifden (4 daily; 1hr 30min); Cork (12 daily, 3hr 15min); Doolin (4 daily; 1hr 30min); Dublin (15 daily; 3hr 30min); Killarney (6 daily; 4hr 35min); Westport (2 daily; 1hr 50min).

Killarney to: Cork (12 daily; 2hr); Dingle (2–5 daily; 1hr 45min–2hr 30min); Waterville via Caherciveen (1–3 daily; 1hr 45min); Dublin (5 daily; 6hr).

Sligo to: Derry (5 daily; 2hr 30min); Dublin (4 daily; 4hr); Enniskillen (3 daily; 1hr 25min); Galway (7 daily; 2hr 30min).

Westport to: Dublin (3 daily; 5hr); Galway (2 daily; 1hr 50min).

Italy

Italy highlights

* **Waterfront, Genoa** Lose yourself in the tangle of multiethnic alleys in this eclectic, vibrant port city. See p.537

* **Grand Canal, Venice** Catch an ordinary water-bus – at night, for maximum effect. See p.543

* **Tripe-stalls, Florence** Join the locals for traditional Tuscan street food at its best. See p.560

* **The Palio, Siena** The event of the year, a frenetic horse race in this wonderfully preserved medieval town centre. See p.564

* **Palatine Hill, Rome** Huge, tranquil archeological garden in the heart of the capital. See p.577

* **Pompeii** The excavations of this Roman town, buried by volcanic ash in 79 AD, are hauntingly evocative. See p.589

* **Valle dei Templi, Agrigento, Sicily** Some say these Greek temples are better than any in Greece. See p.598

Introduction and basics

Of all the countries in Europe, **Italy** is perhaps the hardest to classify. It is a modern, industrialized nation; it is the harbinger of style, its designers leading the way with each season's fashions. But it is also a Mediterranean country, with all that that implies. Agricultural land covers much of the country, a lot of it, especially in the south, still owned under almost feudal conditions. In towns and villages all over the country, life stops during the middle of the day for a siesta. It remains strongly family-oriented, with an emphasis on the traditions and rituals of the Catholic Church, and it is not unusual to find people living with their parents until their early thirties.

If there is a single national characteristic, it's to embrace life to the full, manifest in the hundreds of local **festivals** taking place on any given day, and the importance placed on good **food**. Italy is also a very sociable society and Italians spend a lot of time in public places, whether during the collective evening stroll (the **passeggiata**) or out in the piazza of a evening. There is also, of course, the country's enormous cultural legacy: Tuscany alone has more classified historical monuments than any country in the world and every region retains its own relics of an artistic tradition generally acknowledged to be the world's richest.

Italy wasn't unified until 1861, a fact that's borne out by the regional nature of the place today. The country breaks down into nineteen distinct *regione*, but the sharpest division is between north and south. The north is one of the most advanced industrial societies in the world; the south is by contrast one of the most economically depressed areas in Europe. In the northwest, the regions of Piemonte and Lombardy – and the two main centres of **Turin** and **Milan** – epitomize the wealthy north. Liguria, the small coastal province to the south, has long been known as the "Italian Riviera" and is accordingly crowded with sun-seeking holidaymakers. But it's a beautiful stretch of coast, whose provincial capital, **Genoa**, is a bustling port with a long seafaring tradition. The interest of

the northeastern regions of the Veneto and Friuli-Venezia Giulia is of course **Venice** itself – a unique city, and every bit as beautiful as its reputation would suggest, though you won't be alone in appreciating it. If the crowds are too much, aim for the arc of historic towns nearby – **Verona**, **Padua** and **Vicenza**. To the south, the region of Emilia-Romagna has been at the heart of Italy's postwar industrial boom. Its coast is popular, especially brash **Rimini**, and there are also the ancient centres of **Ravenna**, **Parma** and **Bologna**, the latter one of Italy's liveliest but least appreciated cities.

The centre of the country, specifically **Tuscany**, with its classic rolling countryside and the art-packed towns of **Florence**, **Pisa** and **Siena**, represents the most commonly perceived image of Italy. Neighbouring Umbria is similar but quieter, though visitors flock into towns such as **Perugia** and **Assisi** – and unspoilt **Urbino** nearby. Lazio, to the south, is a poor and desolate region whose focal point is **Rome**, the national capital. South of here in Campania, **Naples**, a petulant, unforgettable city, is the spiritual heart of the Italian south, and is close to the fine ancient sites of **Pompeii** and **Herculaneum**, not to mention the spectacular stretch of coast around **Amalfi**. Puglia, the "heel" of Italy, has underrated pleasures – the souk-like quality of its capital, **Bari**, and more notably **Lecce**, a Baroque gem of a city. The

15

ITALY | Basics

Italy on the net

- Ⓦ **www.enit.it** Official Tourist Board site.
- Ⓦ **www.virgilio.it** Search engine with good travel and tourism links.
- Ⓦ **www.paginegialle.it** Italian Yellow Pages.
- Ⓦ **www.beniculturali.it** Listings of national monuments and information on festivals.

island of **Sicily** is a law unto itself, with attractions ranging from Hellenic remains to the drama of Mount Etna. **Sardinia**, too, feels far removed from the mainland, especially in its relatively undiscovered interior.

Information & maps

Most towns, major train stations and airports have a **tourist office** (*ufficio turistico*) and/or a **Pro Loco** information service. Most tourist offices will give out **maps** for free, but if you want an indexed town plan, get Studio FMB's or Falk's. The clearest and best-value large-scale road maps are by Michelin: a 1:1,000,000 map, or 1:400,000 maps of the north and south, Sicily and Sardinia.

Money and banks

Italy's currency is the **euro** (€). **Banking hours** are Mon–Fri 8.30am–1.30pm & 3.30–7.30pm. ATMs are widespread. To change cash or travellers' cheques, **exchange bureaux** are a better choice than the banks. Otherwise, larger hotels will change money and travellers' cheques; in towns and cities the rate is invariably better at the train station exchange bureau.

Communications

Post office opening hours are Mon–Fri 8am–6.30pm, with branches in towns and cities also open on Sat. Stamps can also be bought at *tabacchi* – ask for *posta prioritaria* if you want letters to arrive home before you do. Public **phones** are card-operated; get a phone card (*scheda telefonica*) from *tabacchi* and newsstands for €2.50/5/7.50. Bars will often have a phone you can use, and there are offices at larger train stations where you can make a metered call from a kiosk. For all landline calls – local and long-distance – dial all digits, including the area code. To call home, one of the cheapest options is the *Europa* phone card (€5 or €10). For expensive **directory enquiries**, call ☏176 (international) or ☏412 then 3 (domestic). You'll find at least one place for

Internet access in most towns. Hourly rates vary from €3 in the south to €10 in big cities.

Getting around

Apart from a few private lines, **trains** are operated by Italian State Railways (*Ferrovie dello Stato* or FS; ◍ www.trenitalia.it). For most journeys you'll have a choice between Eurostar/Intercity – for which you have to pay a supplement of thirty percent (and reserve for Eurostar) – and ordinary trains. Some ordinary trains, denoted as Regionale, can be extremely slow – check before boarding. InterRail, Eurail and Italian **passes** are valid on the whole FS network, though you'll have to pay a supplement on the fast trains. Almost everywhere has some kind of **bus** service, but schedules can be sketchy, and are drastically reduced – sometimes nonexistent – at weekends and during school holidays. Buy tickets at *tabacchi* or the bus terminal rather than on board.

Accommodation

Most tourist offices have details of **hotel** rates. Book ahead in the major cities and resorts, especially in summer: many hotels fill up quickly. Hotels in Italy come with a confusing variety of names (*locanda*, *pensione*, *albergo*) but all are star-rated. Rates vary greatly between the poor south and the wealthy north, and between cities and countryside, but on average you can expect to pay €40 for a double without private bathroom in a one-star hotel, and a minimum of €75 for a double in a three-star. In very busy places you might have to stay a minimum of three nights, and many proprietors will add the price of breakfast to your bill whether you want it or not; try to resist this – you can eat more cheaply in a bar. Whatever happens, establish the full price of your room before you accept it.

There is a growing number of **B&Bs**, sometimes in spectacular locations. Many cost as much as a hotel, but it is worth asking the tourist office for a list, if for no other reason than to experience Italian family life first-hand. There are around sixty **hostels,** charging €12–26 per person for a dorm bed for HI members; for two people travelling together, this doesn't represent a massive saving on the cheapest hotel room. You'll need to book ahead in the summer months. You can get a full list from the Associazione Italiana Alberghi per la Gioventù (ⓦwww.ostellionline.org). In some cities it's also possible to stay in **student accommodation** during the summer, generally in individual rooms. This can work out cheaper than a hotel, but again you'll need to book in advance. Convents and monasteries often have cheap rooms, the only disadvantage being a curfew.

There are plenty of **campsites**, most of them well equipped. However they're expensive, not always much cheaper than staying in a hostel. Daily prices are around €5–9 per person, plus the same for a tent and around €5 for a vehicle. Check out ⓦwww.camping.it.

Food and drink

There are few places in the world where you can eat and drink as well as you can in Italy. If you eat only pizza and *panini*, you'll be missing out on the distinct regional cuisines; don't be afraid to ask what the *piatti tipici* (local dishes) are. Most Italians start their day in a bar, with a **breakfast** of a cappuccino and a *cornetto* (croissant), perhaps *con crema* (with cream). At **lunchtime**, bars sell *tramezzini*, sandwiches on white bread that can be toasted, and *panini*. Another stopgap is *arancini,* fried meat- or cheese-filled rice balls. Markets are also a good source of cheap food. However, you'll have to master the art of eating and drinking standing up: many places have no seating and some bars charge more if you sit down. Italian **ice cream** (*gelato*) is justifiably famous: a cone (*un cono*) is an indispensable accessory to the evening *passeggiata*. For the best choice go to a *gelateria*.

For sit-down food, the cheapest thing you can eat is **pizza** – if you're lucky, cooked in the traditional way in wood-fired ovens. There are also stand-up counters selling slices (*pizza al taglio*) and folded-over pizza

(*calzone*). Although a **trattoria** or a **ristorante** often does a fixed-price *menu turistico*, it's not always very good. Traditionally, a trattoria is cheaper than a restaurant, offering *cucina casalinga* (home-style cooking). But in either, pasta dishes go for around €5–8, and although pasta is considered to be a starter there's usually no problem just having this; the main fish or meat courses will normally be €6–10. Almost everywhere you'll pay about €1.50 per person extra for bread (*pane*), which is brought to your table automatically. Fish is served whole or by weight. Order vegetables (*contorni*) separately; salads (*insalate*) are either green (*verde*) or mixed (*mista*). Afterwards there's fruit (*frutta*) and desserts (*dolci*). Note that as well as the **cover charge** (*coperto*), service (*servizio*) will often be added, generally about ten percent (if it isn't, you should tip the same amount).

Drink

Bars are less social centres than functional places for a quick coffee or beer. You pay first at the cash desk (*la cassa*), present your receipt (*scontrino*) and give your order. In the south it's customary to leave a small tip on the counter, though no one will object if you don't. Bear in mind that sitting down sometimes costs twice as much, especially if you sit outside. **Coffee** comes small and black (*espresso*, or just *caffè*), with a dash of milk (*macchiato*) or cream (*con panna*), or white and frothy (*cappuccino*); try a *granita* – cold coffee with crushed ice, usually topped with cream. **Tea** (*te*) comes with lemon (*con limone*) unless you ask for milk (*con latte*); there are usually several types, and it's also served cold (*te freddo*). A *spremuta* is a fresh fruit **juice**; there's also crushed-ice fruit *granitas*. In winter, try a hot punch – *punch alla livornese*, an alcoholic coffee drink found in Tuscany, is one of the best. **Wine** is invariably drunk with meals, and is very cheap. Go for the local stuff: ask for *un mezzo* (a half litre) or *un quarto* (a quarter), sometimes served straight from the barrel. Bottles are pricier but still good value; expect to pay around €12 a bottle in a restaurant. **Beer** (*birra*) usually comes in bottles of one-third or two-thirds of a litre. Cheapest and most common are the Italian brands Peroni and Dreher, or you could choose draught beer (*alla spina*). A generous shot of **spirits** costs from about €3. There's also fiery **grappa**, made from grape pips and stalks. Of the **liqueurs**, Amaro is a bitter after-dinner drink, Amaretto sweeter with a strong taste of marzipan, and Sambuca a sticky-sweet aniseed concoction.

Opening hours and holidays

Most **shops and businesses** open Mon–Sat 8/9am–1pm & 4–7/8pm, though in the north, offices work a 9am–5pm day. Just about everything except bars and restaurants closes on Sunday. Most **churches** keep shop hours. **Museums** traditionally open Tues–Sat 9am–2pm, Sun 9am–1pm, and are closed on Mon; but some have extended hours. Most **archeological sites** open daily from 9am until late – usually one hour before sunset. Everything closes for **national holidays**: Jan 1; Jan 6; Easter Mon; April 25; May 1; Aug 15; Nov 1; Dec 8; Dec 25 & 26.

Emergencies

Most of the **crime** you're likely to come across is small-time: gangs of *scippatori* operate in the major cities and the south, snatching valuables on the street. You can minimize the risk of this by being discreet, not flashing anything of value (including a phone), keeping a firm hand on your camera and bag, and never leaving anything valuable in your car. The **police** come in many forms: the *Polizia Urbana/Vigili Urbani* deal with traffic offences; the *Polizia Stradale* patrol highways; the *Carabinieri* deal with general crime, public order and drug control; but you should report thefts to the *Polizia Statale*. **Pharmacies** (*farmacia*) can give advice and dispense prescriptions; there's one open all night in towns and cities (find the address of the nearest on any pharmacy door). For serious ailments, go to the *Pronto Soccorso* (casualty) section of the nearest **hospital** (*ospedale*).

Emergency numbers

Police ☎112; Ambulance ☎113; Fire ☎115.

Northwest Italy

The northwest of Italy is many people's first experience of the country, and in many ways represents its least "Italian" aspect, at least in the regions of **Piemonte** and **Val d'Aosta**, where French is still spoken by some as a first language. **Turin**, on the main rail and road route from France to Milan, is the obvious initial stop, the first capital of Italy after the Unification in 1860 and a grand city with many reminders of its past. To the east, **Lombardy** was long viewed by northerners as the heart of Italy – emperors from Charlemagne to Napoleon came here to be crowned – and northern European business magnates continue to take its upbeat capital, **Milan**, more seriously than Rome. The region's landscape has paid the price for economic success: industry chokes the peripheries of towns and spreads its tentacles into the northern lakes and mountain valleys. Nonetheless, Lombardy has its attractions, notably **Mantua**, which flourished during the Middle Ages and Renaissance. The region of **Liguria** to the south has perhaps the country's most spectacular stretch of coastline. Chief town of the province is the sprawling port of **Genoa**, while southeast, towards Tuscany, the mix of mountains and fishing villages "discovered" by the Romantics in the late eighteenth century prepared the way for the first package tourists in the early twentieth century. Now the whole area explodes every July and August, with people coming to resorts like **Portofino** strictly for pose value – although stretches like the **Cinque Terre** are still well worth discovering.

Turin (Torino)

After a recent clean up, **TURIN** (Torino) – a virtual Fiat company town - has emerged resplendent with gracious avenues, opulent palaces and splendid galleries. It is a lively, bustling place with cafés and nightlife to rival any European city. The grid plan of the Baroque centre makes finding your way around easy. **Via Roma** is the central spine, a grand affair lined with designer shops and ritzy cafés and punctuated by the city's most elegant piazzas, most notably **Piazza San Carlo**. Around the corner, the **Museo Egizio** (Tues–Sun 8.30am–7.30pm; €6.50; ⓦwww.museoegizio.org) holds a superb collection of Egyptian antiquities, including gorgeously decorated mummy cases, erotic papyri, and the Tomb of Kha, the burial chamber of a 1400–BC architect and his wife, Merit. Above the museum, the **Galleria Sabauda** (Tues–Sun 8.30am–7.30pm; €4) was built around the Savoy dukes' private collection and is still firmly stamped with their taste – a miscellany of Italian paintings, supplemented by a fine Dutch and Flemish collection, including works by Memling, Brueghel, David Teniers Jnr and Van Dyck. Around the corner, the fifteenth-century **Duomo** houses the **Turin Shroud**, which is usually kept under wraps and only shown to the public during holy years, though a copy is on display by the altar. This piece of cloth,

imprinted with the image of a man's body, had long been claimed as the shroud in which Christ was wrapped after his crucifixion. However, in 1989 carbon-dating tests showed it to be a medieval fake, made between 1260 and 1390. Beyond the Duomo is the elegant Piazza della Repubblica, containing the **Palazzo Madama**, whose Baroque exterior conceals its origins as a Roman fortress. The porticoes of Via Po lead down to the river, past the Mole Antonelliana, Via Montebello 20, which houses Turin's **Museo Nazionale del Cinema** (Tues–Sun 9am–8pm, Sat till 11pm; €5.20, €6.80 with lift to top of the Mole). Turin was the birthplace of Italian cinema in the 1910s and 1920s, and the museum houses a magnificent collection including a huge series of magic lanterns. Via Po ends in the vast arcaded **Piazza Vittorio Veneto**. Along the river from here, **Parco del Valentino** is one of Italy's largest parks, home to the **Borgo e Rocca Medioevale** (Tues–Sun 9am–8pm; €3), a fake medieval village and castle, built for the General Italian exhibition of 1884. Further south still, the **Museo dell'Automobile** at Corso Unità d'Italia 40 (Tues–Sun 10am–6.30pm, Thurs till 10pm, Sun till 8.30pm; €5.50; bus #34 from Piazza Marconi) traces the development of the motor car. There's one of the first Fiats on show, a bulky 1899 model, and, the pride of the collection, the 1907 Itala which won the Peking to Paris race in the same year.

Practicalities

Turin's main **train station**, Porta Nuova, is on Corso Vittorio Emanuele, at the foot of Via Roma, convenient for the city centre and hotels. There are two **tourist offices** – the main one at Piazza Castello 161 (Mon–Sat 9.30am–7pm, Sun 9.30am–3pm; ☎011.535.181, ⊛www.turismotorino.org) and a smaller one at the train station (same hours). The **Torino Card** (€15/two days) gives free transport on buses, entrance to all museums and discounts on theatre and concert tickets. **Internet access** is at Internet Train, Via Carlo Alberto 18. Many of Turin's budget **hotels** are in the sleazy quarter off Via Nizza, convenient enough but not an advisable choice. Somewhat safer, but more expensive, are the streets opposite Porta Nuova, close to Piazza Carlo Felice. There are also a number of fairly reasonably priced hotels west of Piazza Castello.

There are **snack bars** on Via Nizza, some tempting delis on Via Lagrange and a superb *rosticceria* on Corso Vittorio Emanuele. Reasonably priced **restaurants** include the *Vecchio Piemonte*, Corso Vinzaglio 21, *Cucco*, Corso Casale 89, and the popular *Porto di Savona*, Piazza Vittorio Veneto 2. Make sure you look in on one of the city's *fin-de-siècle* **cafés**, most of which have an atmosphere that more than compensates for the steep prices. In *Baratti e Milano*, Piazza Castello 29, genteel Torinese sip tea in a rarefied ambience of mirrors, chandeliers and carved wood. The glitzy *Caffè San Carlo*, Piazza San Carlo 156, is a favoured haunt of politicians and industrialists, while *Fiorio*, Via Po 8, is now visited mostly for its ice cream. Later on in the evening, Via Carlo Alberto, Via San Quintino and the Quadrilatero Romano are the areas to check out. Of specific **bars**, *Bar Elena* in Piazza Vittorio is popular, or for **live music**, try *Doctor Sax*, Murazzi di Lungo Po Cadorna 4, or *Doks Dora* on Lungo Dora.

Hostel

Ostello Torino Via Alby 1 ☎011.660.2939.
Friendly HI place with small rooms and Internet access; 30min walk from Porta Nuova or take bus #52. €13.

Hotels

Canelli Via San Dalmazzo 7 ☎011.546.078. Close to the pedestrian area of Via Garibaldi – the cheapest hotel and very central. ❸

Mobledor Via Accademia Albertina 1 ☎011.812.5805. A small friendly one-star hotel in an excellent location. ❹

Paradiso Via Berthollet 3 ☎011.669.8678. Extremely clean one-star hotel with friendly proprietors. ❸

Milan (Milano)

The dynamo behind the country's economic miracle, **MILAN** (Milano) is the capital of Italy's fashion and design industry, a fast-paced business city in which con-

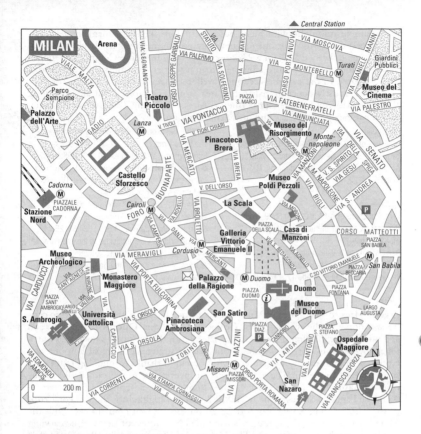

sumerism and the work ethic rule. The swanky shops and nightlife are a big draw, but Milan is also a historic city, and a monument to the prestige-building of the Viscontis and their successors, the Sforzas, who ruled here in Renaissance times. The Gothic cathedral has few peers in Italy, while paintings in the Pinacoteca di Brera and Leonardo da Vinci's iconic fresco of the *Last Supper*, on show in a Milan church, are unmissable treats.

Arrival, information and accommodation

Most international **trains** pull in at the monumental Stazione Centrale, northeast of the centre on Piazza Duca d'Aosta (metro lines MM2 or MM3). **Buses** arrive at and depart from Piazza Castello, in front of the Castello Sforzesco. Of Milan's two **airports**, Linate is the closer, 7km from the city centre and connected by the airport bus to Stazione Centrale (every 20min, 5.40am–10pm; journey time 20min; €2). There are also ordinary city buses (#73; €1) until around midnight from Linate to Piazza San Babila. The other airport, Malpensa, is 50km away towards Lago Maggiore, connected by train to Cadorna station (every 30min; €9) and by bus with Stazione Centrale (until 10.30pm; €5.50). The main **tourist offices** are at the Stazione Centrale (Mon–Sat 9am–1.30pm & 3–6pm; ☎02.8645.4033; ⓦwww.milaninfotourist.com) and Via Marconi 1, off Piazza Duomo (Mon–Fri 8.45am–1pm & 2–6pm, Sat & Sun 9am–1pm & 2/3–6/7pm; same number). Both have the free **listings** guide, *Milan is Milan*. **Public transport** consists of an efficient network of trams, buses and metro (stations denoted below as MM) that runs from 6am to midnight, with night buses until 1am. Tickets (normally valid 1hr 15min; €1) can be used for one journey only on the metro; alternatively buy a *blochetto* of ten tickets (€9.20), or a 24-hour ticket (€3) from the Centrale or Duomo metro stations. Milan is more a business than a tourist city, and its **accommodation** is geared to the expense-account traveller. However, there are plenty of one-star hotels, mostly concentrated in the area around Stazione Centrale, and along Viale Vittorio Veneto and Corso Buenos Aires. Avoid the *Piero Rotta* HI hostel, which can be a rather sleazy and unwelcoming joint.

Hostel

ACISJF Corso Garibaldi 121 ⊕02.290.00164. Run by nuns and open to women under 25 only. Accommodation in four-bedded rooms. MM Moscova. €22.

Hotels

Arno Via Lazzaretto 17 ⊕02.670.5509. Modest one-star place near the station. Gets packed from March to July. ⑤

Casa Mia Viale V. Veneto 30 ⊕02.657.5249. The best option near the station. ⑨

Pensione Eva Via Lazzaretto 17 ⊕02.670.6093.

Another basic one-star option near the station, similar to *Arno*. ⑥

San Tomaso at Viale Tunisia 6 ⊕02.295.14747, ⓦwww.italiaabc.it/hotelsantomaso. Popular hotel in the commercial centre. Rooms have TV, phone and there's Internet access. ⑥

Siena Via P. Castaldi 17 (entrance on Via Lazzaretto) ⊕02.295.16108. Small and clean. ⑧

Speronari Via Speronari 4 ⊕02.864.61125. Friendly and very central, close to the cathedral. ⑥

Hotel Trieste Via M. Polo 13 ⊕02.65.54405, ⓦwww.htrieste.it. Two-star hotel in tranquil area of town, near the centre. ⑨

The City

A good place to start a tour of Milan is **Piazza del Duomo**, the city's historic centre and home to the world's largest Gothic cathedral, the **Duomo**, begun in 1386 and not finished till almost five centuries later. From the outside it's notable as much for its decoration as its size, with a front that's a strange mixture of Baroque and Gothic – though much of this is currently obscured thanks to ongoing restoration work (due to end 2005). The gloomy interior gives access to the cathedral's fourth-century **baptistery** (Tues–Sun 9.45am–12.45pm & 2–5.45pm; €1.50) where St Ambrose baptized St Augustine in AD 387. But the highlight is the cathedral **roof** (9am–4.15/5.45pm; €5 by elevator, €3.50 on foot, €7 combined ticket with the Museo del Duomo), where you are surrounded by a forest of lacy Gothic carving, and have superb views of the city. The **Museo del Duomo** (daily 10am–1.15pm & 3–6pm; €6), on the southern side of the piazza, holds casts of a good many of the three thousand or so statues and gargoyles that spike the cathedral. On the opposite side of the piazza is the opulent **Galleria Vittorio Emanuele**, a cruciform glass-domed gallery designed in 1865 by Giuseppe Mengoni, who was killed when he fell from the roof a few days before the inaugural ceremony. The circular mosaic beneath the cupola is composed of the symbols of the cities of the then newly unified Italy – it's considered good luck to spin round on the testicles of the bull (which represents Turin). The Galleria leads through to the world-famous eighteenth-century **La Scala** opera house, expected to be open again in 2004 after restoration. Its small museum contains composers' death masks, plaster casts of conductors' hands and a statue of Puccini in a capacious overcoat.

The shopping quarter to the northeast of La Scala – the so-called **Quadrilatero d'Oro** – is home to all the big designer names, along with design studios and contemporary art galleries. The area is worth a stroll, if only to observe the better-heeled Milanese searching out the perfect *objet d'art* for their designer pads. A couple of blocks east, **Via Brera** sets the tone for the city's arty quarter with its fancy galleries and art shops, and, at its far end, Milan's most prestigious gallery, the **Pinacoteca di Brera** (Tues–Sun 8.30am–7pm; €4.14), filled with works looted from the churches and aristocratic collections of French-occupied Italy. Venetian painters are well represented, with works by Paolo Veronese, Tintoretto and Giovanni Bellini whose *Pietà* is deemed one of the most moving paintings in the history of art. However, it's Piero della Francesca's *Pala Montefeltro* that is perhaps the most famous painting here.

To the west, the **Castello Sforzesco** rises imperiously from the mayhem of Foro Buonaparte, laid out by Napoleon as part of a grand plan for the city. An arena and triumphal arch remain from the scheme, behind the castle in the **Parco Sempione** (a notorious hangout for junkies and prostitutes), but otherwise the red-brick castle is the main focus of interest, with its crenellated towers and fortified walls. Begun by the Viscontis and rebuilt by their successors, the Sforzas, whose court was one of the most powerful and cultured of the Renaissance, the castle houses the **Museo d'Arte Antica** and **Pinacoteca** (both Tues–Sun 9am–5.30pm; free) – the former including Michelangelo's *Rondanini Pietà*, the latter a cycle of monochrome frescoes illustrating the Griselda story from Boccaccio's *Decameron* and paintings by Vincenzo Foppa, the leading Milanese artist before Leonardo da Vinci. South of the castle, the church of **Santa Maria delle Grazie** is the main attraction. A Gothic pile, partially rebuilt by Bramante (who added the massive dome), it is famous for its fresco of the **Last Supper** by Leonardo da Vinci, which covers one wall of the refectory. Advance booking is essential (call ℡02.894.21146; viewing Tues–Sun 8.15am–6.45pm; €6.50, plus €1 booking fee).

Eating, drinking and nightlife

Food in workaholic Milan, at lunchtime at least, is more of a necessity than a pleasure, with the city centre dominated by *paninoteche* and fast-food outlets. Milan's **nightlife** centres on two areas – the streets around the Brera gallery and the Navigli and Ticinese quarters, clustered around Milan's thirteenth-century canals. Foreign students can often get free admission to clubs, while there's a day-by-day schedule of concerts and events in the *Milan is Milan* booklet. The season at **La Scala** (℡02.860.775; ⊛www.teatroallascala.org), one of the world's most prestigious opera houses, runs from December to July. Although seats are expensive and can sell out months in advance, there is a reasonable chance of picking up a seat in the gods an hour or so before a performance.

Snacks, sandwiches and pizzas

Crota Piemunteisa Piazza Beccaria 10. A vast array of chunky sandwiches for around €2.60, and a few tables.

Grand Italia Via Palermo 5. Cheaper for pizza than *La Bruschetta* and just as good.

La Bruschetta Piazza Beccaria 12. One of the best-known city-centre pizzerias, though you'll have to wait for a table.

Lo Smeraldo Via Baracchini 9, Città Studi. Serves thirty types of pizza.

Luini Via S. Radegonda 16. Just east of the Duomo, justifiably popular for delicious *panzerotti*.

Restaurants

Circolo del Liberty Via Savona 20. Eccentric, intimate restaurant run by a talkative Neapolitan.

Cozzeria Via Muratori Lodovico 7. Mussels by the kilo; also does a delicious lemon and *peperoncino* sorbet.

Da Abele Via della Temperanza 5. A long-established, cosy and very popular haunt that specializes in risotto. MM Pasteur.

Il Cantinone Via Agnello 19. Famous old trattoria and bar, with homemade pasta and some choice wines.

Giulio pane e ojo Via Muratori Lodovico 10. Trendy but inexpensive trattoria.

Trattoria Toscana Corso di Porta Ticinese 58. Very trendy club-style restaurant, which gets packed at aperitif time, but also does excellent food.

Bars and clubs

Bar Magenta Via Carducci 13. Liberty-style bar, timelessly posey and usually packed.

Hollywood Corso Como 15. Long-established club with an airport theme.

La Banque Via Porrone 6. Fasionable bar and nightspot that used to be a bank.

Loolapaloosa Corso Corno 15. Popular student hangout.

Old Fashion Viale Alemagna 6. Has an outdoor disco in summer.

One Way Club Via F.Cavalotti 204. Well-known gay club (Fri & Sat).

Rolling Stone Corso XXII Marzo. Plays a wide range of music and is an enormous place that sometimes hosts big-name rock bands.

Scimmie Via Ascanio Sforza 49. A popular stage, small and buzzy and mainly hosting jazz.

Tunnel Via Sammartini. Right by Stazione Centrale, puts on alternative rock.

Listings

Mantua (Mantova)

MANTUA (Mantova) is undeniably evocative – the birthplace of Vergil, scene of Verdi's *Rigoletto* and with a history of equally operatic plots, most of them perpetrated by the Gonzagas, who ruled the town for three centuries and left two splendid palaces. The town centres on four interlinking squares. **Piazza Mantegna** is dominated by the church of **Sant'Andrea**, inside which are wall-paintings designed by Mantegna and executed by his students, one of whom was Correggio. Opposite Sant'Andrea, sunk below the present level of the busy **Piazza dell'Erbe**, is Mantua's oldest church, the beautiful eleventh-century **Rotonda**, still containing traces of its early medieval frescoes. The dark underpassage beneath the red-brick **Broletto**, the medieval town hall, leads into Piazza Broletto, beyond which the sombre Piazza Sordello is flanked by the Baroque Duomo and the **Palazzo Ducale** (Tues–Sun 8.45am–7.15pm; €6.50, bookings essential on ☎0376.382.150), an enormous complex that was once the largest palace in Europe. When it was sacked by the Habsburgs in 1630 eighty carriages were needed to carry the two thousand works of art contained in its five hundred rooms. In the Salone del Fiume there's a *trompe l'oeil* garden complete with painted creepers and two fountains; while the Sala degli Specchi has a notice outside signed by Monteverdi, who worked as court musician to Vincenzo I. Vincenzo also employed Rubens, whose *Adoration della Trinita* in the Salone degli Arcieri shows the Gonzaga family of 1604. However, the palace's real treasure is in the **Castello di San Giorgio** beyond, where you can see Mantegna's frescoes of the Gonzaga family, splendidly restored in the so-called Camera degli Sposi. Mantua's other main sight, the **Palazzo Tè**, on the opposite side of town (Mon 1–6pm, Tues–Sun 9am–6pm; €8), was designed for Federico Gonzaga and his mistress, Isabella Boschetta, by Giulio Romano, and a tour of it is like a voyage around Giulio's imagination, a sumptuous world where very little is what it seems. In the Sala dei Cavalli, horses stand before an illusionistic background in which simulated marble, fake pilasters and mock reliefs reveal distant landscapes. The function of the Salotta di Psiche, further on, is undocumented, but the sultry frescoes, and its proximity to Federico's bedroom, might give a few clues. Beyond, the extraordinary Sala dei Giganti shows the destruction of the giants by the gods, with cracking pillars, toppling brickwork and screaming giants appearing to crash down into the room.

The city centre is a ten-minute walk from the **train station** down Via Solferino. The **tourist office** (Mon–Sat 8.30am–12.30pm & 3–6pm, Sun 9am–12.30; ☎0376.328.253, ⓦ www.aptmantova.it) is around the corner from Sant'Andrea. Budget **accommodation** is almost non-existent in Mantua. Of the less expensive hotels, you could try the *ABC*, Piazza Don Leoni 25 (☎0376.323.347; ❼), or the *Bianchi Stazione*, next door (☎0376.326.465; ❽), both opposite the station, or the *Broletto* (☎0376.223.678; ❾), a good value three-star at Via Accademia 1. Otherwise, you'll have to stay outside the town – the *Marago* 3km away in Virgiliana has cheap doubles (☎0376.370.313, ⓦ www.ristorante.marago.com; ❹; bus #25). For inexpensive **food**, you eat well at *Il Punto* self-service at Via Solferino 36, near the train station. For really good local fare, try the economical *I Due Cavallini*, Vicolo Salnitro 5 (it's wise to book on ☎0376.322.084). Failing that, the *Bella Napoli*, Piazza Cavalotti 14, serves good pizza, or there's the atmospheric *Leoncino Rosso*, Via Giustiziati 33, off Piazza Broletto. *Osteria dei Canossa*, Vicolo Albergo 3, has excellent pasta.

Genoa (Genova)

GENOA (Genova) is a marvellously eclectic city of Renaissance palaces and old-town streets. It was one of the five Italian maritime republics, and reached the height of its power in the fifteenth and sixteenth centuries; later, during the Unification era, the city was a base for radical thought. After a long period of economic decline, Genoa has been gradually cleaned up – with the city's architect son, Renzo Piano, playing a leading role. But the planners have neither sanitized the slightly menacing air of the narrow alleys around the seafront, nor eradicated the characteristic port smells – brine and fish – that permeate the lower town.

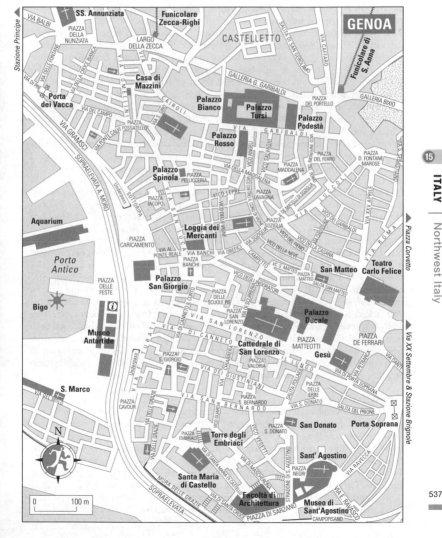

The City

Genoa spreads outwards from its **old town** around the port in a confusion of tiny alleyways and old palaces; its people speak an impenetrable dialect – a mixture of Neapolitan, Calabrese and Portuguese. From 1384 to 1515, except for brief periods of foreign domination, the doges ruled the city from the ornate stuccoed **Palazzo Ducale** in Piazza Matteotti (Tues–Sun 9am–9pm; price varies; ⊛www.palazzoducale.genova.it), across from which the dour **Gesù** church, designed by Pellegrino Tibaldi at the end of the sixteenth century, contains Guido Reni's *Assumption* and two paintings by Rubens. Close by, the Gothic **Cattedrale di San Lorenzo** is home to the Renaissance chapel of St John the Baptist, whose remains once rested in the thirteenth-century sarcophagus. After a particularly bad storm, priests carried his casket through the city to placate the sea, and a commemorative procession takes place each June 24 to honour him. His reliquary is in the **treasury** (tours Mon–Sat 9am–noon & 3–6pm; €5.50), along with a polished quartz plate on which, legend says, Salome received his severed head. East from the adjacent Piazza Ferrari, **Via XX Settembre**, Genoa's commercial nucleus, has big chain stores and pavement cafés in the arcades. South across Via San Bernardo, the mosaic spire of the church of Sant'Agostino marks the adjacent **Museo dell'Architettura e Scultura Ligure** (Tues–Fri 9am–7pm, Sat & Sun 10am–7pm; €3.10), built around the cloister of a thirteenth-century monastery, with a collection of Roman and Romanesque fragments from other churches, as well as wood carvings and ancient maps of Genoa.

Down on the waterfront, ruined by a hideous concrete over-pass, the sea once came up to the vaulted arcades of **Piazza Caricamento**, a hive of activity, fringed by African and Middle Eastern cafés and market stalls. Customs inspectors, and subsequently the city's elected governors, set up in the **Palazzo San Giorgio** on the edge of the square, some rooms of which are open to the public (Sat only 10am–6pm; free). Beyond, the waterfront has been the subject of a massive restoration project, manifest most obviously in the huge **Aquarium** (Mon–Fri 9.30am–6.30pm, Sat & Sun 9.30am–8pm; Oct–March closed Mon; €11.60; ⊛www.acquariodigenova.it). Behind Piazza Caricamento is a thriving commercial zone centred on **Piazza Banchi**, formerly the heart of the medieval city, off which the long Via San Luca leads to the **Galleria Nazionale di Palazzo Spinola** (Tues–Sat 9am–7pm, Sun 2–7pm; €4), with work by the Sicilian master Antonello da Messina. North of here, **Via Garibaldi** is lined with frescoed and stuccoed Renaissance palaces; two are now museums and if you peek into courtyards and buildings you will catch a glimpse of the rest. The **Palazzo Bianco** (Tues–Fri 9am–7pm, Sat & Sun 10am–7pm; joint ticket with Palazzo Rosso €5.16) holds paintings by Genoese artists and others, including Van Dyck and Rubens, while **Palazzo Rosso** across the road (same hours and ticket) has works by Titian, Caravaggio and Dürer, but it's the decor here that really impresses - fantastic chandeliers, mirrors, an excess of gilding and frescoed ceilings. Behind, Genoa heads up the hill like the steps of an amphitheatre, a part of town best seen by way of the **funicular** (bus tickets valid) from Piazza del Portello up to Sant'Anna. The view from the top is much hyped, but the trip is more absorbing than anything you'll see when you arrive.

Practicalities

Trains from Ventimiglia and points west arrive at Stazione Principe in Piazza Acquaverde, just above the port; trains from La Spezia, Rome and points south arrive at Stazione Brignole in Piazza Verdi, on the east side of the city centre; trains from Milan and Turin usually stop at both, but if you have to travel between the two, take bus #18 or #37 (tickets available from *tabacchi* or newspaper stands). **Ferries** arrive at the Stazione Marittima, ten minutes' walk downhill from Stazione Principe. There is a **tourist office** at Stazione Principe (Mon–Sat 9.30am–1pm & 2.30–6pm; ☎010.246.2633, ⊛www.apt.genova.it) and another at Porto Antico, Palazzina S. Maria (Mon–Sat 9am–1pm & 2–6pm, Sun 9am–noon; ☎010.248.711,

ⓦ www.comune.genova.it). Both have *Passport*, a free **listings** guide. If you plan to visit several museums and other tourist attractions, get a **Museum Card** (€12/three days) from the train station or tourist office. There are plenty of one-star **hotels** in the city centre, but many are grim and depressing. Good areas to try are the roads bordering the old town, and Piazza Colombo and Via XX Settembre, near Stazione Brignole.

For cheap lunches, snacks and picnic ingredients, try the Via de Pre near the station and the covered **Mercato Orientale**, halfway down Via XX Settembre in the old cloisters of an Augustinian monastery. Late night, young people congregate at the **bars** around Piazza delle Erbe, while popular **clubs** include *Estoril*, Corso Italia 7d, and the *Matilda Caffe*, Via D'Annunzio 19. The *Louisiana Jazz Club*, Via S. Sebastiano 36R, *Cezanne*, Via Cecchi 7R, and *Mako*, Corso Italia 28R, all have **live music**.

Hostel

Genova Via Costanzi 120 ☏010.242.2457. Friendly, clean and well-run HI place with great views over the port, and Internet access; take bus #40 from Stazione Brignole. €13.

Hotels

Cairoli Via Cairoli 14/4 ☏010.246.1454, ⓦ www.hotelcairoligenova.com. A very pleasant two-star, handy for the old town and Stazione Principe. ❼
Carletto Via Colombo 16/4 ☏010.588.412. Central and quiet, a good fallback option if the *Soana* is full. ❺
Nettuno Via Mercantini 16 ☏010.362.8106. On the seaview walkway on Corso Italia. ❺
Soana Via XX Settembre 23/8/a ☏010.562.814, ⓦ www.hotelsoana.it. Friendly two-star place ten minutes' walk from Stazione Brignole. ❻

Campsite

Villa Doria Via Al Campeggio Villa Doria 15, Pegli ☏010.696.9600, ⓦ www.camping.it/liguria /villadoria. Set in parkland, 8km from Genoa, with its own café, shop and solarium. Take a train to Pegli and then bus #93.

Restaurants

Da Vittorio Opposite Piazza Caricamento, on Sottoripa. A hectic fish restaurant where it can be difficult to get a table.
Ostaja do Castello Salita Santa Maria di Castello 32. Family-run trattoria.
Sâ Pesta Via Giustiniani 16. Well-known source of good local cooking, including *farinata*, a thin chickpea-based pancake, but it closes early.
Trattoria da Maria Via Testadoro 14/b, just off Via XXV Aprile. No-nonsense, endearingly chaotic place which serves up simple Ligurian cooking at rock-bottom prices.

The Riviera di Levante

The stretch of coast east from Genoa, the **Riviera di Levante**, is not the place to come for a relaxing beach holiday. The ports that once survived on navigation, fishing and coral diving have now experienced thirty years of tourism; the coastline is still wild and beautiful in parts, but the sense of remoteness has gone. **PORTOFINO**, at the extremity of the Monte Portofino headland, manages to be both attractive and off-putting at the same time, a wealthy resort but a beautiful one. It's well worth making the two-and-a-half-hour walk to the beach and thirteenth-century **abbey** (June–Sept Mon–Fri 10am–6pm, Sat & Sun 10am–3.45pm; Oct–May closed Mon; €6) at **San Fruttuoso**; boats run there, too. On the corniche road 3km out of Portofino, the sparkling cove at **PARAGGI** is a good place for a swim, with a couple of bars set back from the beach. Or take the bus to Ruta, from where you can either slog on foot to the summit of **Monte Portofino** or catch another bus to Portofino Vetta, from where it's twenty minutes' walk to the top. On very clear days the views are fantastic.

SANTA MARGHERITA LIGURE is a small, thoroughly attractive resort, with palm trees along its front and a minuscule pebble beach and concrete jetties to swim from. If you'd like to stay, try *Albergo Annabella*, Via Costasecca 10, just off Piazza Mazzini (☏0185.286.531; ❻), or *Albergo Fasce*, a little further up the road at Via L. Bozzo 3 (☏0185.286.435; ❼), which has a dozen bikes that guests can use free of charge. For good local **food**, try *Il Faro*, Via Merigliano, or the long-established *Da Pezzi*, at Via Cavour 21, a canteen-like locals' hangout serving pasta and grills, and takeaway snacks for lunch. The **tourist office** is on Via XXV Aprile (daily 9.30am–12.30pm & 2.30–5.30pm; ☎0185.287.485, ⌖www.apttigullio .liguria.it). **RAPALLO** is a highly developed, though still attractive, resort that used to be patronized by a number of writers: Max Beerbohm lived in Rapallo, attracting a vast coterie, and Ezra Pound wrote the first thirty of his Cantos here between 1925 and 1930. There's decent **accommodation** in the town centre, most notably *Pensione Bandoni*, Via Marsala 24/3 (☎0185.50.423, ⌖www.bandoni.supereva.it; ❹); alternatively, try the *Fernanda*, along the front at Via Milite Ignoto 9 (☎0185.50.244; ❻), cosy enough, but more expensive for less pleasant rooms. There are a couple of **campsites**, *Rapallo* at Via San Lazzaro 4 (☎0185.262.018) and the *Miraflores* at Via Savagna 10 (☎0185.263.000, ⌖www.campingmiraflores.it). Perhaps the least expensive and most authentic place to **eat** is *Bansin* at Via Venezia 49, in the heart of the old town; while *Da Mario*, Piazza Garibaldi 23, is a good, moderately priced fish restaurant.

   LEVANTO, further east still, is one of the most pleasant resorts in this area, with a long stretch of sandy beach, plentiful accommodation and a decent campsite, the *Aquadolce*, in the centre of town. It's a good base from which to explore the **CINQUE TERRE**, five small villages perched on tiny cliff-bound inlets to the west. Levanto's **tourist office** is in Piazza Cavour (Mon–Sat 9am–1pm & 2–5pm, Sun 9am–12.45pm; ☎0187.808.125, ⌖wwwaptcinqueterre.sp.it). For **accommodation**, try *Pensione Garden*, right by the sea at Corso Italia 8 (☎0187.808.173; ❸); if that's full, or you have a little more money, there's the slightly cosier atmosphere of the *Europa*, up the street at Via Dante 41 (☎0187.808.126; ❼). For **food** and late-night drinks, the *Caffè Roma*, on the square round the corner from the *Garden*, has a small, reasonably priced restaurant out the back.

Northeast Italy

The appeal of **Venice** hardly needs stating: it's one of Europe's truly unique urban landscapes, and is an unmissable part of any European tour. The region around Venice – the **Veneto** – is a prosperous one, where virtually every acre still bears the imprint of Venetian rule. **Padua** and **Verona** are the main attractions, with their masterpieces by Giotto, Donatello and Mantegna, and a profusion of great buildings from Roman times to the Renaissance. Much of the countryside is dull and flat, only perking up to the north with the high peaks of the Dolomite range. East, on the former Yugoslav border, **Trieste** is capital of the partly Slav region of Friuli-Venezia Giulia, a Habsburg city only united with Italy after World War II. South, between Lombardy and Tuscany, stretching from the Adriatic coast almost to the shores of the Mediterranean, **Emilia-Romagna** is the heartland of northern Italy, a patchwork of ducal territories formerly ruled by a handful of families, whose castles and fortresses remain in well-preserved medieval towns. Carving a straight route through the heart of the region, from Milan to Rimini on the coast, the Via Emilia is a Roman military road, constructed in 187 BC, that was part of the medieval pilgrim's route to Rome and the way east for crusaders to Ravenna and Venice. **Bologna**, the region's capital, is one of Italy's largest cities, but despite having one of the most beautifully preserved centres in the country, it's relatively neglected by tourists. North of Bologna is **Ferrara**, a Renaissance town run for hundreds of years by the Este family, and these days Italy's premier bicycle city. Nearby is **Parma**, a wealthy provincial town that is worth visiting for its paintings by Parmigianino and Correggio. The coast is less interesting, and the water polluted, but just south of the Po delta, **Ravenna** boasts probably the finest set of Byzantine mosaics in the world.

Verona

The easygoing city of **VERONA**, with its Roman sites and streets of pink-hued medieval buildings, stands midway between Milan and Venice at a rail junction for the long trans-Alpine line from Innsbruck (Austria). It reached its zenith as an independent city-state in the thirteenth century under the Scaligeri family. Ruthless in the exercise of power, the Scaligeri were at the same time energetic patrons of the arts, and many of Verona's finest buildings date from the century of their rule.

The city centre clusters in a deep bend in the River Adige, the main sight of its southern reaches the central hub of **Piazza Brà** and its mighty Roman **Arena** (Mon 1.30-6.30pm, Tues–Sun 8.30am–7.30pm; July & Aug closes 3.30pm; €3.10). Dating from the first century AD, and originally with seating for some 20,000, this is the third-largest surviving Roman amphitheatre, and offers a tremendous panorama from the topmost of the 44 marble tiers. Nowadays it is used as an opera venue (ticket information ☎045.800.5151, ⓦwww.arena.it) for big summer productions. To the north, **Via Mazzini**, a narrow traffic-free street lined with expensive shops, leads to a group of squares, most noteworthy of which is the Piazza dei Signori, flanked by the medieval **Palazzo degli Scaligeri** – the residence of the Scaligeri. At right angles to this is the fifteenth-century **Loggia del Consiglio**, the former assembly hall of the city council and Verona's outstanding early Renaissance building, while, close by, the twelfth-century **Torre dei Lamberti** (same hours as Arena; €2.10 by elevator, €1.50 on foot) gives dizzying views of the city. Beyond the square, in front of the Romanesque church of Santa Maria Antica, the **Arche Scaligere** are the elaborate Gothic funerary monuments of Verona's first family, in a wrought-iron palisade decorated with ladder motifs, the emblem of the Scaligeri. Mastino I ("Mastiff"), founder of the dynasty, is buried in the simple tomb against the wall of the church; Mastino II is to the left of the entrance, opposite the most florid of the tombs, that of **Cansignorio** ("Top Dog"); while over the side entrance of the church is an equestrian statue of **Cangrande I** ("Big Dog"). Towards the river from here is the church of **Sant'Anastasia** (Tues–Sat 9/10am–4/6pm, Sun 1–5/6pm; €2, €5 combined ticket for all Verona churches), a mainly Gothic church, completed in the late fifteenth century, with Pisanello's delicately coloured fresco of *St George and the Princess* in the sacristy. Verona's **Duomo** (Tues–Sat 10am–5.30pm, Sun 1.30–5.30pm; €2) lies just around the river's bend, a mixture of Romanesque and Gothic styles that houses an *Assumption* by Titian. In the opposite direction, off Piazza delle Erbe at Via Cappello 23, is the **Casa di Giulietta** (Tues–Sun 9am–7pm; €3.10), a well-preserved fourteenth-century structure, though there's no connection between this house and the historical character to whom Shakespeare's Juliet is distantly related. West of here, at the junction of Via Diaz and Corso Porta Borsari, the **Porta dei Borsari** is a fine Roman monument, with an inscription that dates it to 265 AD, though it's almost certainly older than that. Some way down Corso Cavour from here, the **Arco dei Gavi** is a first-century Roman triumphal arch, beyond which the **Castelvecchio** (same hours as Arena; €3.10) houses a collection of paintings, jewellery and weapons. A kilometre or so to the northwest, the **Basilica di San Zeno Maggiore** (Mon–Sat 8.30am–6pm, Sun 1–6pm; €2) is one of the most significant Romanesque churches in northern Italy. Its rose window, representing the Wheel of Fortune, dates from the twelfth century, as does the magnificent portal, while the door has bronze panels depicting scenes from the Bible and the miracles of San Zeno. The simple interior is covered with frescoes, but the most compulsive image is the altar's luminous *Madonna and saints* by Mantegna.

Practicalities

The **train station** is twenty minutes outside the city centre, connected with Piazza Brà by bus #11, #12, #13 or #14. There's a **tourist office** at the train station (Mon–Sat 9am–6pm, Sun 9am–3pm; winter closed Sun; ☎045.800.0861,

ITALY | Northeast Italy

www.tourism.verona.it) and at the Cortile del Tribunale, close to the Arche Scaligere (Tues–Sun 10am–7pm). For **hotels**, try the *Al Castello*, Corso Cavour 43 (℡045.800.4403; ❼), or *Catullo*, Via Catullo 1 (℡045.800.2786; ❹), in a central position just off Via Mazzini. Verona's excellent **HI hostel** is at Via Fontana del Ferro 15 (℡045.590.360; €12.50 including breakfast), on the north side of the river behind the Teatro Romano (bus #73 or #90), close to which there's a pleasant summer **campsite**. There's also the *Casa della Giovane*, Via Pigna 7 (℡045.596.880; €11.50), in the old centre, for women under 26 only. Among **eating** options, *Alla Costa*, Via della Costa 2, has good pizzas, as does *Pizzeria Arena*, Vicolo Tre Marchetti. *Pero d'Oro*, Via Ponte Pignolo 25, serves inexpensive but genuine Veronese dishes. For evening **drinks**, the ultra-friendly but pricey *Bottega del Vino* in Vicolo Scudo di Francia, just off the north end of Via Mazzini, is an old bar with a selection of wines from all over Italy. For a less touristy ambience, try *Al Carro Armato*, Vicolo Gatto 2a, or *Osteria Al Duomo*, Via Duomo 7a.

Padua (Padova)

Extensively rebuilt after World War II bomb damage, and hemmed in by industrial sprawl, **PADUA** (Padova) is not the most alluring city in northern Italy. However, it is one of the most ancient, and makes a good base for seeing Venice (35min away by frequent trains). A former Roman settlement, the city was a place of pilgrimage following the death of St Anthony here, and it later became an artistic and intellectual centre: Donatello and Mantegna both worked here, and in the seventeenth century Galileo researched at the university. Just outside the city centre, through a gap in the Renaissance walls off Corso Garibaldi, the Giotto frescoes in the **Cappella degli Scrovegni** (daily 9am–6/7pm; appointment only, book at least 72hr in advance; €11 for joint ticket with Musei Civici; ℡049.20.100.20, www.cappelladegliscrovegni.it) are the main reason for coming to Padua, although you get just ten minutes to see them. Commissioned in 1303 by Enrico Scrovegni in atonement for his father's usury, the chapel's walls are covered with illustrations of the life of Mary, Jesus and the story of the Passion – one of the high points in the development of European art in its innovative attention to the inner nature of its subjects. The adjacent **Musei Civici** (Tues–Sun 9am–5pm; €9) contains an assembly of fourteenth- to nineteenth-century art from the Veneto and further afield, the high point being a *Crucifixion* by Giotto that was once in the Scrovegni chapel. South of here, on the other side of the centre, the main sight of the Piazza del Santo is Donatello's **Monument to Gattamelata** of 1453, the earliest large bronze sculpture of the Renaissance. On one side of the square, the basilica of San Antonio or **Il Santo** was built to house the body of St Anthony. The Cappella del Santo has a sequence of panels showing scenes from his life, while the Cappella del Tesoro (daily 8am–noon & 2.30–7pm) houses the saint's tongue and chin in a head-shaped reliquary. From the basilica, Via Umberto leads back towards the **University**, established in 1221, and older than any other in Italy except Bologna. The main block is the **Palazzo del Bò**, where Galileo taught physics from 1592 to 1610, declaiming from a lectern that is still on show, though the major sight is the sixteenth-century **anatomy theatre** (March–Oct, tours Mon, Wed & Fri at 3pm, 4pm & 5pm; Tues, Thurs & Sat at 9am, 10am & 11am; €5). Although Padua's **Duomo** is an unlovely church whose design was cribbed from drawings by Michelangelo, the adjacent Romanesque **Baptistery** is one of the unproclaimed delights of the city, lined with fourteenth-century frescoes by Giusto de'Menabuoi – a cycle which makes a fascinating comparison with Giotto's in the Cappella degli Scrovegni.

Padua **train station** is at the far end of Corso del Popolo, a few minutes' walk north of the city walls. There's a **tourist office** at the station (Mon–Sat 9am–6pm, Sun 9am–noon), but the main office is in Galleria Pedrocchi, just off Via 8 Febbraio (Mon–Sat 9am–12.30pm & 3–7pm; ℡049.876.7927, www.turismopadova.it). It sells the 48-hour **Padova Card** (€13), which buys museum access, free bus travel and a parking space. Of many affordable **hotels**, a good budget option is *Junior*, Via L.

Faggin 2 (☎049.611.756; ❹), just behind the station, or try the clean and pleasant Catholic-run *Casa del Pellegrino*, near Il Santo basilica at Via Cesarotti 21 (☎049.823.9711; ❹). The **HI hostel** is at Via A. Aleardi 30 (☎049.875.2219; €14; curfew 11pm), an easy 2km walk or bus #3, #8, or #18 from the station. The nearest **campsite** is 15km away at Via Roma 123 in Montegrotto Terme, served by frequent trains (15min). For **food**, try the excellent, inexpensive *Osteria l'Anfora*, Via dei Soncin 13; or the restaurant at the *Casa del Pellegrino*, which serves good local fare. On Piazza Cavour, *Pe Pen* (closed Sun) has a wonderful range of pizzas, with seats on the square in summer. *Dotto*, Via Randaccio 23, is a superb mid-range restaurant. In the summer evenings, the best place to hang out are the **bars** around Prato della Valle or near the university, including *Miniera*, Via S. Francesco 144, a fashionable late-night bar.

Venice (Venezia)

The first-time visitor to **VENICE** (Venezia) arrives with a heavy burden of expectations, most of them well founded. It is an extraordinarily beautiful city, and the major sights are all they are cracked up to be. The downside is that Venice is deluged with tourists and it is expensive. At the height of its prosperity in the fifteenth century the city had a huge mainland empire. It later found new popularity as a destination on the Grand Tour and in the nineteenth century John Ruskin's book "The Stones of Venice" made her architecture famous around the world. Today, nearly twenty million visitors come here each year, most seduced by the famous motifs – carnival time, glass ornaments, singing gondoliers and the fabulously pricey cafés – but others in search of the quieter quarters of a city that always has the capacity to surprise.

Arrival, information and accommodation

The city's **Marco Polo** airport is on the edge of the lagoon, linked to the city centre by ACTV bus #5 (€1) or ATVO bus (€2), or the more expensive waterbus (from €10). All road traffic comes into the city at **Piazzale Roma**, at the head of the Canal Grande, from where waterbus services run to the San Marco area, stopping off at Santa Lucia **train station**, the next stop along the Canal Grande. The main **tourist office** is at San Marco 71/f, a couple of minutes' walk east of the square (daily 9.40am–3.20pm; ☎041.529.8711, ⓦwww.turismovenezia.it & ⓦwww.comune.venezia.it). There are also desks at the train station and airport. Pick up the free English-language listings magazines, *Leo* and *Un Ospite di Venezia* (ⓦwww.aguestinvenice.com), from any of them; you can also buy the **Museum Pass** (€15.50), which gives entry to the main museums (but not the Accademia or Guggenheim), and the **Chorus Pass** (€8), which gives entry to fourteen churches. The **Venezia Card** (€47/68 for 3/7 days) covers the waterbuses and most museums.

Walking is the fastest way of getting around and you can cross the whole city in an hour. Tickets for the **waterbus** (*vaporetto*) are available from most landing stages. Flat-rate fares are €5 for any one continuous journey including the Canal Grande, or €3.50 excluding it. There are also one-day (€10.50) and three-day (€22) tickets available. The **traghetti** that cross the Canal Grande (€0.45 a trip) are a cheap way of getting a ride on a gondola. Otherwise, **gondolas** are ludicrously expensive: the official tariff is €62 for 50 minutes but you may be quoted up to €100 for 45 minutes and an extra €100 for a singer.

Accommodation is the major expense in Venice and you should always book ahead. The cheapest option is staying in a **hostel**, most owned by religious foundations, or you may want to sleep in nearby Padua or Trieste. There are **booking offices** (all open daily 9am–8pm) at the station, the Tronchetto, Piazzale Roma, airport and at the autostrada's Venice exit.

Hostels
Domus Civica Calle Campazzo, San Polo 3082 ☎041.721.103. A student house in winter, open to women travellers only from June-Sept. Curfew

11.30pm. €28.50. Rooms ❸
Foresteria Valdese Santa Maria Formosa, Castello 5170 ☎041.528.6797. Three large dorms, and a few rooms for two to four people. Difficult to

find – go from Campo Santa Maria Formosa along Calle Lunga, and it's at the foot of the bridge at the far end. ④

Ostello Santa Fosca, S. Maria dei Servi, Cannaregio 2372, ☎041.715.775 Student-run hostel in an atmospheric former Servite convent. €20.

Ostello Venezia Fondemente delle Zitelle, Giudecca 86 ☎041.523.8211. The official HI hostel, in a superb location looking at San Marco from the island of Giudecca. Curfew 11pm. Waterbus #82 from the station. €16.50.

Suore Canossiane Fondemente del Ponte Piccolo, Giudecca 428 ☎041.522.2157. Women only, no booking. €15.

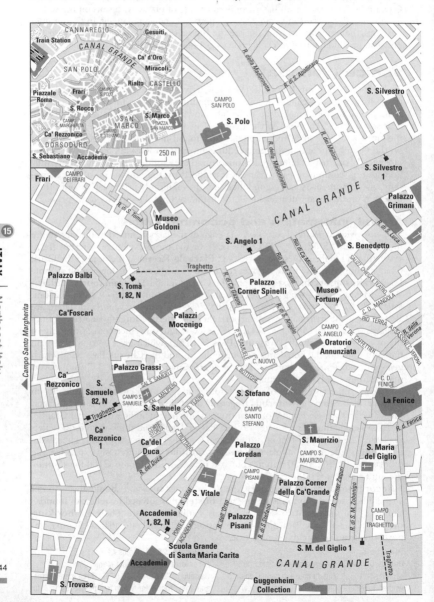

Hotels

Alex Rio Terra Frari San Polo 2606, ℡041.523.1341. A recently refurbished one-star hotel. **5**

Antico Capon Campo S. Margherita, Dorsoduro 3004/B ℡041.528.5292. Situated on one of the city's most atmospheric squares, in the heart of the student district. **7**

Bernardi Semenzato Calle dell'Oca, Cannaregio 4366 ℡041.522.7257. Two-star place with welcoming and helpful English-speaking owners. **5**

Ca' Fóscari Calle della Frescada, Dorsoduro 3887B ℡041.710.401. Quiet, well-decorated and relaxed place, tucked away in a tiny alley near San Tomà. **6**

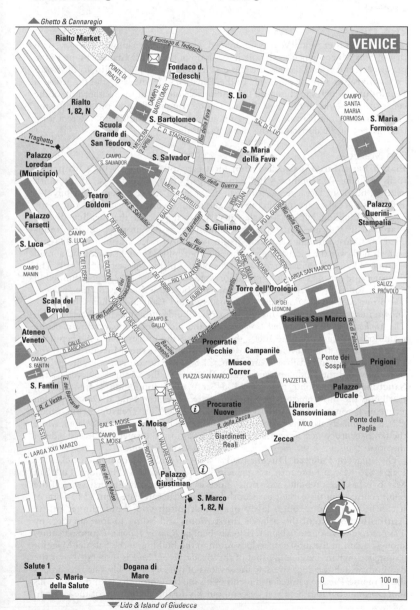

ITALY | Northeast Italy

15

Caneva Ramo della Fava, Castello 5515
☎041.522.8118. Overlooking the Rio della Fava
on the approach to the busy Campo San
Bartolomeo, yet very peaceful. ⑤
Casa Gerotto Calderan Campo S. Geremia 283,
Cannaregio ☎041.715.361. Welcoming place not
far from the train station. Dorm beds sometimes
available. ⑥

Casa Petrarca Calle delle Colonne, San Marco
4394 ☎041.520.0430. Friendly place with just six
rooms. The cheapest near the Piazza. ⑤
Domus Cavanis Rio Terrà Foscarini, Dorsoduro
896 ☎041.522.2826. Clean and central Catholic-
run place. ⑦

The City

The 118 islands of central Venice are divided into six districts known as *sestieri*, with that of **San Marco** (enclosed by the lower loop of the Canal Grande) home to the majority of the essential sights. On the east it's bordered by **Castello**, to the north by **Cannaregio**. On the other side of the Canal Grande, the largest of the *sestieri* is **Dorsoduro**, which stretches from the fashionable quarter at the southern tip of the canal to the docks in the west. **Santa Croce** roughly follows the curve of the Canal Grande from Piazzale Roma to a point just short of the Rialto, where it joins the smartest of the districts on this bank, **San Polo**.

San Marco

Piazza San Marco is signalled from most parts of the city by the **Campanile** (daily 9.30am–4.15/6pm; €4.10), which began life as a lighthouse in the ninth century, but is in fact a reconstruction: the original tower collapsed on July 14, 1902. It is the tallest structure in the city, and from the top you can make out virtually every building, but not a single canal. Across the piazza, the **Basilica di San Marco** (daily 9.45am–5pm; €1.50) is the most exotic of Europe's cathedrals, modelled on Constantinople's Church of the Twelve Apostles, finished in 1094 and embellished over the succeeding centuries with trophies brought back from abroad – proof of Venice's secular might and thus of the spiritual power of St Mark. The Romanesque carvings of the central door were begun around 1225 and finished in the early fourteenth century, while the mosaic above the doorway on the far left – *The Arrival of the Body of St Mark* – was made around 1260 and includes the oldest-known image of the basilica. Inside, the narthex holds more mosaics, together with *The Madonna with Apostles and Evangelists* in the niches of the bay in front of the main door – dating from the 1060s, the oldest mosaics in San Marco. A steep staircase goes from the church's main door up to the **Museo Marciano** and the **Loggia dei Cavalli** (daily 9.45am–5pm; €1.50), where you can enjoy fine views of the city and the Gothic carvings along the apex of the facade. However, it's the **Sanctuary**, off the south transept (Mon–Sat 10am–5.30pm, Sun 2–4pm; €1.50), that holds the most precious of San Marco's treasures, the **Pala d'Oro** or golden altar panel, commissioned in 976 in Constantinople. The **Treasury** (same times; €2), is a similarly dazzling warehouse of chalices, reliquaries and candelabra, while the tenth-century *Icon of the Madonna of Nicopeia* (in the chapel on the east side of the north transept) is the most revered religious image in Venice.

The adjacent **Palazzo Ducale** (daily 9am–5/7pm; €11 combined ticket for Piazza San Marco museums) was principally the residence of the doge. Like San Marco, it has been rebuilt many times since its foundation in the first years of the ninth century, but the earliest parts of the current structure date from 1340. Parts of it can be marched through fairly briskly, although you should linger in the **Anticollegio**, one of the palace's finest rooms and home to four pictures by Tintoretto and Veronese's characteristically benign *Rape of Europa*. Veronese features strongly again in the most stupendous room in the building – the Sala del Maggior Consiglio - where his ceiling panel of the *Apotheosis of Venice* is suspended over the dais from which the doge oversaw the sessions of the city assembly. The backdrop is the immense *Paradiso* painted at the end of his life by Tintoretto, with the aid of his son, Domenico. From here you descend quickly to the underbelly of the Venetian state, crossing the **Ponte dei Sospiri** (Bridge of Sighs) to the prisons, and then back over the water to the Pozzi, the cells for the most hardened malefactors.

West of San Marco: Dorsoduro

Some of the finest architecture in Venice is to be found in **Dorsoduro**, but few visitors wander off the strip that runs between the main sights of the area, the first of which is the **Galleria dell'Accademia** (Mon 8.15am–2pm, Tues–Sun 8.15am–7.15pm; €6.50). This has one of the finest collections of European art, following the history of Venetian painting from the fourteenth to the eighteenth centuries. Five minutes' walk from the Accademia is the unfinished Palazzo Venier dei Leoni, home of the **Guggenheim Collection** (10am–6pm, closed Tues; €8), and of Peggy Guggenheim for thirty years until her death in 1979. Her private collection is an eclectic mix of pieces from her favourite modernist movements and artists, including works by Brancusi, De Chirico, Max Ernst and Malevich. Continuing along the line of the Canal Grande, you'll come to the church of **Santa Maria della Salute**, which houses a hoard of Titian paintings in the sacristy (€2), along with the *Marriage at Cana* by Tintoretto, featuring portraits of some of the artist's friends.

Northwest of San Marco: San Polo and Cannaregio

On the northeastern edge of **San Polo** is the former trading district of **Rialto**. It still hosts the Rialto market on the far side of the Rialto Bridge, a lively affair and one of the few places in the city where it's possible to hear nothing but Italian spoken. The main reason people visit San Polo, however, is to see the mountainous brick church, **Santa Maria Gloriosa dei Frari**, west of here (Mon–Sat 9am–6pm, Sun 1–6pm; €2), whose collection of artworks includes a rare couple of paintings by Titian – most notably his *Assumption*, painted in 1518, a swirling piece of compositional bravura for which there was no precedent in Venetian art. Titian is also buried in the church. At the rear of the Frari is the **Scuola Grande di San Rocco** (daily 9am–4/5.30pm; €5.16), home to a cycle of more than fifty major paintings by Tintoretto – including, in the main hall, three large ceiling panels featuring Old Testament references to the alleviation of physical suffering (coded declarations of the Scuola's charitable activities), while around the walls are New Testament themes.

In the northernmost section of Venice, **Cannaregio**, you can go from the bustle of the train station to some of the quietest and prettiest parts of the city in a matter of minutes. The district boasts one of the most beautiful palazzi in Venice, the **Ca D'Oro** or Golden House (Mon 8.15am–2pm, Tues–Sun 8.15am–6pm; €5), whose facade once glowed with gold leaf; and what is arguably the finest Gothic church in Venice, the **Madonna dell'Orto** (€2), which contains Tintoretto's tomb and two of his paintings. Cannaregio also has the dubious distinction of containing the world's first **ghetto**: in 1516, all the city's Jews were ordered to move to the island of the Ghetto Nuovo, an enclave which was sealed at night by Christian curfew guards. Even now it looks quite different from the rest of Venice, many of its buildings relatively high-rise due to the restrictions on the growth of the area. The **Jewish Museum** in Campo Ghetto Nuovo organizes interesting tours of the area that leave on the half-hour (museum Mon–Fri & Sun 10am–5.30/7pm; tours till 4.30pm; museum €3, tours €8), and the Campo's cafés are worth visiting too.

Northeast of San Marco: Castello

Castello is home among other things to the **Miracoli** church (€2), built in the 1480s to house a painting of the Madonna that was believed to have performed a number of miracles, such as reviving a man who had spent half an hour lying at the bottom of the Giudecca canal. East of here, **Campo San Zanipolo** is the most impressive open space in Venice after Piazza San Marco, dominated by the huge brick church of **San Zanipolo**, founded by the Dominicans in 1246 and best known for its funeral monuments to 25 doges. The other essential sight in this area is to the east of San Marco – the **Scuola di San Giorgio degli Schiavoni** (Tues–Sat 9.30am–12.30pm & 3.30–6.30pm, Sun 9.30am–12.30pm; €3), set up by Venice's Slav population in 1451. The building has a superb cycle by Vittore Carpaccio on the ground floor.

Venice's other islands

Immediately south of the Palazzo Ducale, Palladio's church of **San Giorgio Maggiore** stands on the island of the same name and has two pictures by Tintoretto in the chancel – *The Fall of Manna* and *The Last Supper*, perhaps the most famous of all his images, painted as a pair in the last years of the artist's life. On the left of the choir a corridor leads to the **Campanile** (€3), rebuilt in 1791 after the collapse of its predecessor and one of the best vantage points in the city. The long island of **La Giudecca**, to the west, was where the wealthiest aristocrats of early Renaissance Venice built their villas. The main reason to come is the Franciscan church of the **Redentore** (€2), designed by Palladio in 1577 in thanks for Venice's deliverance from a plague that killed a third of the population. You can see its best paintings in the sacristy, as well as a curious gallery of eighteenth-century wax heads of illustrious Franciscans.

Sheltering Venice from the open sea, the thin strand of the **Lido** used to be the focus of the annual hullaballoo of Venice's "Marriage to the Sea", when the doge went out to the Porto di Lido to drop a gold ring into the brine and then disembarked for mass at San Nicolò al Lido. Later it became the smartest bathing resort in Italy, and although it's no longer as chic as it was when Thomas Mann set *Death in Venice* here, you won't even be allowed to get on the Lido sand unless you're staying at one of the flashy hotels on the seafront or are prepared to pay a ludicrous fee to rent a beach hut. Of the major islands lying to the north of Venice, **Murano** is chiefly famed as the home of Venice's glass-blowing industry. The nearby island of **Burano**, on the other hand, is still largely a fishing community, although there is also a thriving trade in lace-making here.

Eating, drinking and entertainment

Venice is awash with places to eat seafood, and there are also plenty of cheapish pizzerias and **bars and pubs** for the student population. In the evenings, young people tend to hang out in the bars around **Campo Santa Margherita**, while the city's best-known (and some say only) club is *Casanova* on Lista di Spagna, near the station. Venice's **opera house**, La Fenice, is currently being rebuilt after a calamitous fire, but the season continues in a temporary marquee, the Palafenice (☎041.786.511, ✆www.teatrolafenice.it). The city's most famous annual event is **Carnevale**, which occupies the ten days leading up to Lent, finishing on Shrove Tuesday with a masked ball for the glitterati, dancing in the Piazza for the plebs, plus other various pageants and performances. It's also a time to see and be seen: people don costumes and in the evening congregate in the squares. Masks are on sale throughout the year in Venice, but new mask- and costume-shops suddenly appear during Carnevale, and Campo San Maurizio sprouts a marquee with maskmaking demonstrations.

Bars, cafés and pasticcerie

Bar Paolin Campo Santo Stefano, San Marco. Reputed to make the best ice cream in Venice, with outside tables with one of the finest settings in the city. Closed Fri.

Cantinone gia Schiavi Fondamenta Maravegie, Dorsoduro. Great wine shop and bar opposite San Trovaso church. Closed Sun.

Do Mori Calle do Mori, San Polo. Narrow, standing-only bar, catering for the Rialto traders and locals and serving delicious snacks. Closed Wed afternoon & all Sun.

Enoteca Al Volto Calle Cavalli (near Campo S. Luca), San Marco. Stocks 1300 wines from Italy and elsewhere, some cheap, many not; good snacks, too. Closed Sun.

Gelateria Nico Záttere ai Gesuati, Dorsoduro. Celebrated for an artery-clogging creation called a *gianduiotto* – a block of praline ice cream in whipped cream. Closed Thurs.

Marchini Ponte San Maurizio, San Marco. The most delicious and expensive Venetian pasticcerie.

Restaurants

Al Cugnai Piscina del Forner, Dorsoduro. Good-value trattoria close to the Accademia. Get there by 8pm or be prepared to queue. Closed Mon.

Alle Oche Calle del Tintor (south side of Campo S. Giacomo dell'Orio), San Polo. Eighty-odd varieties of inexpensive pizza.

Antico Mola Fondamenta degli Ormesini, Cannaregio. Originally a family-run, local place, but becoming trendier by the year. Still good food and good value. Closed Wed.

Paradiso Perduto Fondamenta della Misericordia, Cannaregio. Fronted by a popular bar, with a lively relaxed atmosphere and occasional live music. Closed Wed.

Rosticceria San Bartolomeo Calle della Bissa, San Marco. Glorified snack bar serving superb seafood.

Trattoria Altanella Calle dell'Erbe, Giudecca. Succulent fish dishes, and a terrace overlooking the island's central canal. Good for a treat. Closed Mon & Tues.

Trattoria Pizzeria Casa Mia Calle dell'Oca, Cannaregio. Very popular trattoria-pizzeria close to St Apostoli Chuch. Closed Tues.

Listings

Exchange American Express, Salizzada San Moisè, San Marco.

Hospital Ospedale Civili Riunti di Venezia, Campo Santi Giovanni e Paolo ☎041.523.0000.

Laundry Ai Tre Ponti, Santa Croce 274; Salizzada del Pistor, Cannaregio 4553, near Santi Apostoli.

Left luggage At the train station.

Pharmacies Farmacia Baldiserotto, Via Garibaldi 1778; or consult *Un Ospite di Venezia* for full list.

Police Via Nicoldi 24, Marghera ☎041.271.5511.

Post office Fondaco dei Tedeschi, by the Rialto Bridge.

Trieste

Backed by a white limestone plateau and facing the blue Adriatic, **TRIESTE** – east of Venice on the Slovenian border – is in a potentially idyllic setting, but until quite recently the town itself, dominated by monumental Neoclassical architecture, had a grey and neglected air. Now it has spruced itself up and is worth a visit, not least for its old-fashioned Viennese-style cafés, small bars and Italo-Slav gastronomy. Trieste has long been a city of political extremes. Yugoslavia and the Allies fought over it until 1954, when the city and a connecting strip of coast were secured for Italy. The neo-Fascist MSI party has always done well here, and there's even a local anti-Slav party, Lista per Trieste. But Trieste is a literary town, once home to James Joyce and Italo Svevo, and it has a more liberal side that it shows to visitors. The social centre is the huge **Piazza dell'Unità d'Italia**, opening onto the harbour and flanked by the vast bulks of the **Palazzo del Comune** and **Palazzo di Governo**. The focal point of the city's history is the hill of San Giusto, with its castle and cathedral, accessible on bus #24. The **Castello** (Tues–Sun 9am–sunset; €1.55 with museum) is a fifteenth-century Venetian fortress, built near the site of the Roman forum, whose ramparts are worth a walk and whose museum (Tues–Sun 9am–1pm) houses a collection of antique weaponry. The **Cattedrale di San Giusto** (daily 8am–noon & 3.30–7.30pm) is a typically Triestine synthesis of styles, with a predominantly Romanesque facade including five Roman columns and a Gothic rose window. Inside, between Byzantine pillars, there are fine thirteenth-century frescoes of St Justus, a Christian martyr killed during the persecutions of Diocletian. On the southern side of the city, the **Risiera di San Sabba** at Rattodella Pileria 43 (Tues–Sun 9am–1pm; April & May till 7pm; free), on the #10 bus route, was one of Italy's two concentration camps. A permanent exhibition serves as a reminder of Fascist crimes in the region.

The **train station** is on Piazza Libertà, on the northern edge of the city centre. There's a tourist information desk here, but the main **tourist office** is at Piazza dell'Unità d'Italia 4b (Mon–Sat 9am–7pm, Sun 10am–1pm & 4–7pm; ☎040.347.8312, ☻www.triestetourism.it). There are many reasonable **hotels**, nicest of which are the *Centro*, Via Roma 13 (☎040.371.116; ❸), the *Blaue Krone*, Via XXX Ottobre 12 (☎040.631.882; ❸), and the *Istria*, Via Timeus 5 (☎040.371.343; ❺). The **HI hostel** is 8km out of the city at Viale Miramare 331 (☎040.224.102;

€12), and has superb views of the Adriatic, although the hostel itself is basic – take bus #36. The nearest **campsite** is in nearby Obelisco, on the #4 bus route. *Pepi Sciavo* in Via Cassa di Risparmio is a favourite student **lunch-stop**, with excellent sausages and sauerkraut. Another student hangout is *Notorious* in Via del Bosco – sandwiches and salads on the ground floor and a cheap trattoria upstairs. Decent **pizzas** can be had at *Il Barattolo* in Piazza Sant'Antonio Nuovo. For more substantial food, try the excellent *Da Giovanni*, at Via Lazzaro 14, or the popular *Galleria Fabris* at Piazza Dalmazia 4, which serves cheap pizzas and fish. The city's favourite **café** is the *Caffè San Marco*, which has occupied its premises on Via G. Battisti for more than eighty years. The *Caffè Tommaseo* on Piazza Tommaseo was a rendezvous for Italian nationalists in the last century and makes a pleasant, if pricey refuge in the summer heat. *Caffè Walter*, Via San Niccolo 31, has *fin-de-siècle* decor and free nibbles in the afternoon, while among the **bars**, *Public House*, Via San Lazzaro 9, and *Osteria de Libero*, Via Risorta 8, are both atmospheric places. In the summer take a trip out of town to one of the *osmizze*, temporary bars run by local farmers serving young wines and simple food; one of the best is *Contovello*, which has stunning sea views.

Bologna

BOLOGNA is the oldest university town in Europe and teems with students and bookshops. Up until the last elections, when it fell to the right, "Red Bologna" had been the Italian Communist Party's stronghold and spiritual home since World War II. It also boasts some of the richest food in Italy, a busy cultural life and a café and bar scene that is one of the most convivial in northern Italy.

The compact, colonnaded city centre is still startlingly medieval in plan, and has enough curiosities to warrant several days' exploration. Buzzing **Piazza Maggiore** is the obvious place to make for first, dominated by the city's cathedral, **San Petronio**, intended originally to have been larger than St Peter's in Rome. You can see the beginnings of the planned side aisle on the left of the building and there are models of what the church was supposed to look like in the **museum** (Mon–Sat 9.30am–12.30pm, Sun 2.30-6pm); otherwise the most intriguing feature is the astronomical clock – a long brass meridian line set at an angle across the floor, with a hole left in the roof for the sun to shine through on the right spot. Bologna's university – the **Archiginnasio** – was founded at more or less the same time as the Piazza Maggiore was laid out, predating the rest of Europe's universities, though it didn't get a special building until 1565. The most interesting part is the **Teatro Anatomico** (Mon–Sat 9am–1pm; free), the original medical faculty dissection theatre, whose tiers of seats surround a professor's chair, covered with a canopy supported by figures known as *gli spellati* – the skinned ones. South, down Via Garibaldi, Piazza San Domenico is the site of the church of **San Domenico**, built in 1251 to house the relics of St Dominic. The saint's bones rest in the Arca di San Domenico, a fifteenth-century work that was principally the creation of Nicola Pisano, though the angel and figures of saints Proculus and Petronius were the work of a very young Michelangelo. North of here, the eastern section of Bologna's *centro storico* preserves many of the older university departments, housed in large seventeenth- and eighteenth-century palaces. At Piazza di Porta Ravegnana, the **Torre degli Asinelli** (daily 9am–6pm; €3) and perilously leaning **Torre Garisenda** are together known as the *Due Torri*, the only survivors of literally hundreds of towers that were scattered across the city during the Middle Ages. From here, Via San Stefano leads down past a complex of four churches, collectively known as **Santo Stefano**. The striking polygonal church of San Sepolcro, reached through the church of Crocifisso, is the most interesting: the basin in its courtyard is by tradition the one used by Pilate to wash his hands after he condemned Christ to death. A doorway leads through to San Vitale e Agricola, Bologna's oldest church, built from discarded Roman fragments in the fifth century; while the fourth church, the

Trinitá, lies across the courtyard. Further east, on Via delle Belle Arti, is the city's most important art collection in the **Pinacoteca Nazionale** (Tues-Sun 9-7pm; €4), a body of paintings from 1300-1700, particularly strong on the Riminese and Romagnolo schools, and featuring some lovely works by Vitale de Bologna.

Practicalities

Bologna's **airport** is northwest of the centre, linked by Airbus (€4.50) to the **train station** on Piazza delle Medaglie d'Oro, at the end of Via dell'Indipendenza. There are **tourist information** booths at the airport (Mon–Sat 8am–8pm) and at the train station (daily 8.30am–7.30pm), and a main office at Piazza Maggiore 6 (daily 9am–8pm); a call centre (☎051.246.541, ⊛www.comune.bologna.it/bolognaturismo) can make hotel bookings. Bologna is not geared up for tourists, least of all for those on a tight budget, and the trade fairs during high season make booking ahead imperative. The least expensive place to stay is either of the **HI hostels**, *Due Torri* and *San Sisto*, 6km outside the centre at Via Viadagola 5 and 14 (☎051.501.810; €13.50; midnight curfew); take bus #93 from Via Irnerio. Among the few affordable **hotels** are the centrally positioned *Garisenda*, Via Rizzoli 9, Galleria del Leone 1 (☎051.224.369; ❺), *Minerva*, Via de Monari 3 (☎051.239.652; ❹), and the *Panorama*, Via Livraghi 1 (☎051.221.802; ❺). More expensive is the *Accademia*, nicely situated at Via delle Belli Arti 6 (☎051.232.318; ❼). For **camping**, the *Camping Hotel and Residence*, Via Romita 12/4a (☎051.325.016, ⊛www.hotelcamping.com), near the exhibition centre, has a swimming pool.

Biggest and liveliest of the city's **markets** is Mercato delle Erbe, Via Ugo Bassi 2; there's a smaller market on Via Draperie. For **snacks**, *Altero*, at Via Indipendenza 33 or Via Ugo Bassi 10, is best for pizza by the slice; *La Torinese*, under the vaults of Palazzo del Podestà in Piazza Maggiore, does daily quiches and stuffed vegetables. *Centro*, Via Indipendenza 45, and *Bassotto*, Via Ugo Bassi 8 (lunchtimes only), serve quality fast food in comfortable surroundings. *Nino's*, Via Volturno 9 (off Via dell'Indipendenza), has inexpensive **pizza and pasta**; and the self-service *Lazzarini*, Via Clavature 1 (closed Sun), is cheap but more stylish than most. There are plenty of good **bars** on Via Pratello and in the student quarter, and late-opening *osterie* all over town that have been the mainstay of Bolognese **nightlife** for a few hundred years. *Matusel*, Via Bertolini 2, close to the university, is a lively and noisy example, with reasonably priced full meals; *Osteria Senzanome*, Via Senzanome 42, serves good meals and has a wide choice of beers and wines; and *Marieina*, Via San Felice 137, close to the city gate, is old and dark, with good wine and snacks. The English-language **listings** magazine *Talkabout* (⊛www.talkabout.it) has details of what's on.

Ferrara

The civilized air and bicycle-filled streets make **FERRARA**, half-an-hour by train north of Bologna, one of the more relaxing places to stay in northern Italy. The town's Renaissance centre is one of the key legacies of the Este family, who ruled the city for over 500 years. Modern Ferrara planners are equally forward looking, and the town is fast establishing a reputation as the most disability-accessible town in Europe. The best times to visit are during its annual **palio**, a horse race held in May (⊛www.paliodiferrara.it) and the lively **buskers' festival** (⊛www.ferrarabuskers.com) during the last week of August. In Ferrara's main square, the magisterial **Castello d'Estense** (9.30am–5pm, closed Mon; €6, €1 supplement to visit Torre dei Leoni) rises from a toy-town moat. The fortress was built in 1385 by Duke Niccolo II to defend the Este family from the people of Ferrara. Later the Este, in another seigneurial move, built a walkway that allowed them to walk unobserved in fragrant gardens all around the city. Of most interest are the dungeons, where prisoners have left sad signatures in candle smoke, and the kitchens, once home to Cristoforo de Messibugo, a celebrity chef in his day and author of grandiose banquets that saw fountains running with wine. A short walk down the Corso Ercole i d'Este is the **Palazzo dei Diamanti**, a stone building ridged with pyramid-shaped blocks. Inside are four museums, of which the **Pinacoteca Nazionale** (Tues–Sun 9am–1/2pm, Thurs till 7pm; €4) is the one to spend your money on. On the other side of the Castello is the thirteenth-century **Duomo** (daily 7.30am–noon & 3.30–6.30pm), whose magnificent facade has a carved portal portraying the Last Judgement. East of here is the **Museo Ebraico** (tours Mon–Thurs & Sun 10am, 11am & noon; €4), which remembers the Jewish community that lived here until World War II – the main synagogue was destroyed by Italian Fascists in 1944. Further east is the **Palazzo Schifanoia**, Via Scandiana 23 (Tues–Sun 9am–6pm; €4.20), another Renaissance palace built by the Estense, with marvellous frescoes.

It's a ten-minute walk along Viale Cavour from the **train station** to the centre. There's a tourist office just inside the station (daily 9am–1pm & 2–6pm), but the main **tourist office** is in the castle courtyard (same hours; ☎0532.209.370); there's a **bicycle rental** point next door (closed Sun; €8/day). A **Card Musei** (€12.40), available from the tourist office, gives access to most museums. Ferrara's **HI hostel** *Ostello Estense*, Corso Biagio Rossetti 24 (☎0532.204.227; €13), is housed in an historic building with frescoed ceilings near Palazzo dei Diamanti. Among **hotels and B&Bs** try *Casa degli Artisti*, Via Vittoria 66 (☎0532.761.038; ❸); the *Daniela*, Via Arginone 198, a twenty-minute walk west of the station (☎0532.773.104; ❻); or *San Paolo*, Via Baluardi 9 (☎0532.762.040; ❻). The closest **campsite**, *Estense*, is at Via Gramicia 5 (☎0532.752.396; closed Oct–April); take bus #1 from the station to Piazzale San Giovanni, and it is ten minutes' walk from there. In **restaurants**, it is difficult to avoid Ferrara's *Salama da Sugo*, a pungent, salty sausage that the locals swear by. Try *Trattoria Volano* on Via Volano, dating from the seventeenth century; *Hostaria Savonarola*, off Piazza Savonarola; *l'Osteria*, Via de Romei 51; or *L'Oca Giuliva*, Via Boccacanale di Santo Stefano – the latter an *enoteca* that does good food. There are two atmospheric **bars** in Via Adelardi by the Duomo – *Due Gobbi* and the historic *Al Brindisi*, one of the oldest in Italy and much frequented by students. There's also *Enoteca*, Via Contrari 52, a very trendy bar with buzzing music and outside tables.

Parma

PARMA, about 80km northwest of Bologna, is about as comfortable a town as you could wish for. The measured pace of its streets, the abundance and quality of its restaurants, and the general air of provincial affluence are almost cloyingly pleasant. There is also plenty to see, not least the works of two key late Renaissance artists – Correggio and Parmigianino. **Piazza Garibaldi** is the fulcrum of Parma; its cafés and surrounding alleyways are home to much of the town's nightlife. The mustard-coloured **Palazzo del Governatore** flanks the square, behind which stands the Renaissance church of **Madonna della Steccata**. Inside there are frescoes by a number of sixteenth-century painters, notably Parmigianino, who spent the last ten years of his life on this work, and was eventually sacked for breach of contract by the disgruntled church authorities. Nearby in the Romanesque **Duomo**, one of Correggio's most famous works, a 1534 fresco of the *Assumption*, can be seen in the central cupola. You should also visit the Duomo's octagonal **Baptistery** (€2.70), considered to be Benedetto Antelami's finest work, built in 1196. Antelami sculpted the frieze that surrounds the building, and was also responsible for the reliefs inside, including a series of fourteen statues representing the months and seasons. More Correggio frescoes can be seen in the **Camera di San Paolo** (Tues-Sun 8.30am–2pm; €2) of the former Benedictine convent off Via Melloni, a few minutes' walk north. East of the cathedral square, it's hard to miss Parma's biggest monument, the **Palazzo della Pilotta**, begun for Alessandro Farnese in the sixteenth century and rebuilt after World War II bombing. It now houses the city's main art gallery, the **Galleria Nazionale** (Tues–Sun 8.30am–1.45pm; €10,), whose massive collection, rich in fifteenth- and sixteenth-century works, includes more paintings by Correggio and Parmigianino.

Parma's **train station** is fifteen minutes' walk from Piazza Garibaldi, or a short ride on bus #7, #8, #9 or #10. The main **tourist office** is on Strada Melloni (Mon–Sat 9am–7pm, Sun 9am–1pm; ☏0521.218.889, ⚲www.turismo.comune .parma.it/turismo), and has an *Informagiovani* point next door where you can sign up for free **Internet access**; or try Libreria Fiaccadori, Via Duomo 8. Finding **accommodation** can be tricky. There's the spartan **HI hostel** with **campsite** at Parco Cittadella 5 (☏0521.961.434; €9; closed Oct–March; curfew 11pm); take bus #19 from the station. Otherwise, among **hotels** near the station, try the *Leon d'Oro* at Viale A. Fratti 4 (☏0521.773.182; ❹) or *Lazzaro*, Via XX Marzo 14 (☏0521.208.944; ❺). One superb but inexpensive **restaurant** is *Il Gallo D'Oro*, Borgo Salina 3. At night, a young clientele drinks at *Bottiglia Azzura*, Borgo Felino 63; another good *enoteca* is *Ombre Rosse*, Vicolo Giandemaria 4; both also do food. There's an annual Verdi **festival** in May/June; the Teatro Regio on Via Garibaldi (☏0521.039.300) is renowned for its **opera**.

Ravenna

RAVENNA's colourful sixth century mosaics are acknowledged to be one of the crowning achievements of Byzantine art – they are the sole reason for visiting the town, these days a pretty but provincial backwater. The mosaics are the legacy of a quirk of fate 1500 years ago, when Ravenna briefly became capital of the Roman Empire, and the best of them can be seen in a day. Aim for the basilica of **San Vitale**, ten minutes northwest of the centre, completed in 548 AD. The mosaics are in the apse, arranged in a rigid hierarchy, with Old Testament scenes across the semicircular lunettes of the choir, Christ, the Apostles and sons of San Vitale on the arch, and, on the semidome of the apse, a beardless Christ presenting a model of the church to San Vitale and Bishop Ecclesius. On the side walls of the apse are portraits of the Emperor Justinian and his wife Theodora, Justinian's foot resting on that of his general, Belisarius, who reclaimed the city from the Goths, while Theodora looks on, her expression giving some hint of the cruelty for which she was apparently notorious. Across from the basilica is the tiny **Mausoleo di Galla Placidia**, whose mosaics glow with a deep blue lustre, most in an earlier style than San Vitale's, full of Roman and naturalistic motifs. Adjacent to San Vitale, the **National Museum of Antiquities** (Tues–Sun 8.30am–7pm; €4.10) displays a sixth-century statue of Hercules capturing a stag, and the so-called "Veil of Classis", decorated with portraits of Veronese bishops of the eighth and ninth centuries. East of here, on the busy Via di Roma, in the sixth-century basilica of **Sant'Apollinare Nuovo**, mosaics run the length of the nave, depicting processions of martyrs bearing gifts for an enthroned Christ and Virgin through an avenue of date palms. Five minutes' walk up Via di Roma, the **Arian Baptistery**, also known as the Basilica dello Spirito Santo, has a fine mosaic ceiling showing the twelve Apostles and the baptism of Christ.

It's only a short walk from the **train station** on Piazza Farini, along Viale Farini and Via A. Diaz, to the central Piazza del Popolo. The **tourist office**, Via Salara 8/12 (daily 8.30am–8/7pm; ☏0544.35.404, ⚲www.turismo.ravenna.it), stocks maps and guides. There's an **HI hostel**, the *Ostello Dante*, at Via Aurelio Nicolodi 12 (☏0544.421.164; €13), ten minutes' walk out of town or bus #1 from outside the

There is a **combined ticket** (€6.50) covering most of Ravenna's sights, including San Vitale, the Mausoleo di Galla Placidia, Sant'Apollinare Nuovo, the Arian Baptistery and more. Available from any of the participating museums, it is valid for one visit to each for a year. **Opening times** for all are daily 9am–7pm.

station. A more central alternative is the *Residenza Galletti Abbiosi*, Via di Roma 140 (☎0544.215.127; ❺), which is run by monks, has some frescoed rooms and no curfew. The best places to **eat** include *Ca' De Ven*, Via C. Ricci 24, *Da Renato* on Via Mentana and its sister restaurant next door, *Guidarello*, on Via R. Gessi.

Central Italy

The Italian heartland of Tuscany represents the archetypal image of the country – its walled towns and rolling, vineyard-covered hills the classic backdrops of Renaissance art. **Florence** is the first port of call, from the Uffizi gallery's masterpieces to the great fresco cycles in the churches. **Siena** is one of the great medieval cities of Europe and also the scene of Tuscany's one unmissable festival – the Palio – which sees bareback horse riders careering around the cobbled central square. The other major cities, **Pisa** and **Lucca**, both have medieval splendours – Pisa its Leaning Tower and cathedral ensemble, Lucca a string of Romanesque churches – and there are, of course, the smaller hill towns, of which **San Gimignano**, the "city of the towers", is the best known. The provincial capital of the upper Arno region, **Arezzo**, an hour's train ride from Florence, is also worth a stop, if only for its marvellous series of paintings by Piero della Francesca. To the east lies Umbria (⊛www.umbria2000.it), a beautiful region of rolling hills, woods and valleys; most visitors head for the capital, **Perugia**, for **Assisi** – with its extraordinary frescoes by Giotto in the Basilica di San Francesco – or **Orvieto**, where the Duomo is one of the greatest Gothic buildings in the country, though lesser-known places like **Spoleto** are worth taking in too. Further east still, in the Marche region, is **Urbino**, with its superb Renaissance ducal palace. **Ancona** is the mid-Adriatic's largest port, a bland, modern place, though useful for ferry connections to Greece and Croatia.

Florence (Firenze)

Ever since the nineteenth-century revival of interest in Renaissance art, **FLORENCE** (Firenze) has been a shrine to the cult of the beautiful. It is a city of incomparable indoor pleasures, its chapels, galleries and museums embodying the complex, exhilarating and often elusive spirit of the Renaissance more fully than any other town in the country. The city became the centre of artistic patronage in Italy under the Medici family, who ruled Florence as an independent state for three centuries, most auspiciously during the years of Lorenzo de' Medici, dubbed "Lorenzo Il Magnifico". On display here are some of the most famous pieces in Western art, including Michelangelo's *David* in the **Accademia** and Botticelli's *Birth of Venus* in the **Uffizi** – but note that these and other big attractions can get very overcrowded; in high summer, you could easily wait in line for two or three hours to enter the Uffizi or the **Duomo**. You may find visiting some lesser-known (but just as high-quality) museums more enjoyable: the **Bargello** and **Museo dell'Opera del Duomo** have a miscellany (the former with a memorably camp *David* by Donatello), the **Cappelle Medicee** house superb Michelangelo sculptures, and the **Cappella Brancacci** is lined with breathtakingly vivid frescoes by Masaccio. For a taste of Florentine life, head for the Mercato Centrale food hall and adjacent street markets, or window-shop on classy Via de' Tornabuoni. Yet exploring Florence can be a stressful business: the sheer number of tourists is overwhelming for much of the year, many of the pavements are too narrow to cope with the flow of people, and traffic still chokes much of the city centre. Roaming the streets isn't always the pleasure you might have anticipated.

Arrival, information and accommodation

Pisa's international **airport** is connected by a regular train service (1hr) with Florence's central Santa Maria Novella **train station** (given on timetables as

"Firenze SMN"). Flights also come into Florence's tiny Perètola airport, 5km out of the city and connected by bus to the main **bus station**, alongside Santa Maria Novella. The main **tourist office** is at Via Cavour 7r, just north of the Duomo (Mon–Sat 8.30am–6.30pm, Sun 8.30am–1pm; ☎055.290.832, ⊕www.firenzeturismo.it), with a branch opposite the train station. **Walking** is the best way of getting around, but if you want to cover a long distance in a hurry, take one of the orange ATAF **buses**; tickets (€1) are valid for one hour and can be bought from *tabacchi*. Alternatively, rent a **bicycle** using the council's "Mille e una bici" scheme (€1.50/hr, €8/day)- there's a pick-up/drop-off point at the train station or ask the tourist office. Florence's most affordable **hotels** are close to the station, in particular along and around Via Faenza and the parallel Via Fiume, and along Via della Scala and Piazza Santa Maria Novella; you could also try Via Cavour, north of the Duomo, or the Oltrarno district on the south bank. Advance booking is advisable, but for help try the Informazioni Turistiche Alberghiere **accommodation office** at the train station (daily 8.45am–8pm; ☎055.282.893), which can make last-minute reservations for a fee.

Hostels

Istituto Gould Via dei Serragli 49, Oltrarno ☎055.212.576. With all the comforts of a hotel, so book in advance. €19–38.

Ostello Villa Camerata Viale Righi 2 ☎055.601.451. HI hostel in a beautiful park, 30min out of town on bus #17 from the train station. Popular, so book in advance. €16.

Santa Monaca Via Santa Monaca 6, Oltrarno ☎055.268.338, ⊕www.ostello.it. Very popular hostel in a converted fifteenth-century convent, though with 1am curfew. €16.

Suore Oblate dell'Assunzione Via Borgo Pinti 15 ☎055.248.0582. Not far from the Duomo, and run by missionaries. Use of kitchen and common room. Singles and doubles only. Midnight curfew. €35 single, €70 double.

Suore Oblate dello Spirito Santo Via Nazionale 8 ☎055.239.8202. Very clean and pleasant women-only place, a few steps from the station. Single, double and triple rooms; 11pm curfew; two-night minimum stay. Closed Nov to mid-June.

Campsite

Michelangelo Piazzale Michelangelo, Viale Michelangelo 80 ☎055.681.197. Centrally located campsite.

Hotels

Ausonia e Rimini Via Nazionale 24 ☎055.496.547, ⊕www.kursonia.com. Halfway between the train station and the market, this welcoming place has some en suites and Internet access. ❽

Azzi/Locanda degli Artisti Via Faenza 56 ☎055.213.806. Probably the most pleasant of six reasonably priced *pensioni* on the upper floors of this building. ❺

Brunetta Borgo Pinti 5 ☎055.247.8134. Friendly place in the historic centre, just east of the Duomo. ❻

Elite Via della Scala 12 ☎055.215.395. Two-star hotel near Santa Maria Novella. ❼

Firenze Piazza dei Donati 4 ☎055.214203. Clean and comfortable en-suite rooms. ❻

Maxim Via Dei Calzaiuoli 11 ☎055.217.474. ⊕www.hotelmaximfirenze.it. A small, friendly one-star hotel near Duomo, some rooms en suite. ❾

The City

Florence's major sights are contained within an area that can be crossed on foot in a little over half an hour. From the train station, all first-time visitors gravitate towards **Piazza del Duomo**, beckoned by the pinnacle of the dome, which lords it over the whole cityscape. Via dei Calzaiuoli, which runs south from the Duomo, is the main catwalk of the Florentine *passeggiata*, a broad pedestrianized avenue lined with shops and activity. It ends at Florence's other main square, **Piazza della Signoria**, fringed on one side by the graceful late-fourteenth-century Loggia della Signoria and dotted with statuary, most famously a copy of Michelangelo's *David*. The streets west of the square retain their medieval character.

The Duomo

The **Duomo** (Mon–Sat 8.30am–7.30pm) was built between the late thirteenth and mid-fifteenth centuries to an ambitious design, originally the brainchild of Arnolfo di Cambio and realized finally by Filippo Brunelleschi, who completed the

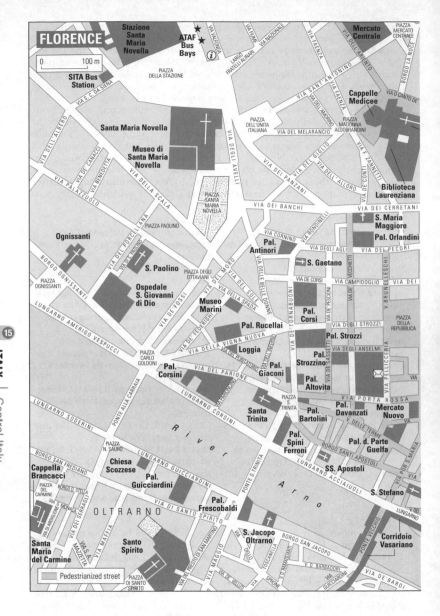

majestic dome. The fourth largest church in the world, its ambience is more that of a great assembly hall than of a devotional building, its most conspicuous pieces of decoration being the two memorials to *condottieri* – Uccello's monument to Sir John Hawkwood, painted in 1436, and Castagno's monument to Niccolò da Tolentino, created twenty years later – and seven stained-glass roundels designed by Uccello, Ghiberti, Castagno and Donatello. These are best inspected from a gallery

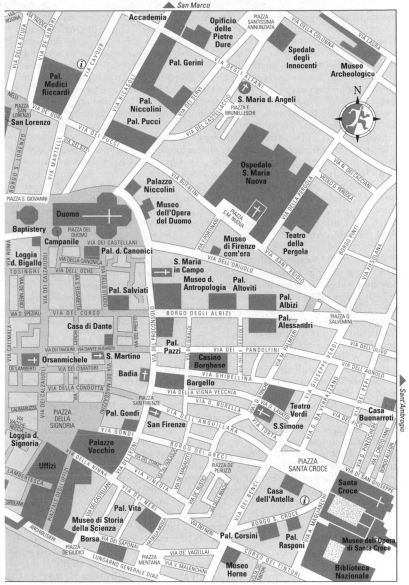

that forms part of the route to the top of the dome (€6), from where the views are stupendous. Next door to the Duomo, the **Campanile** (daily 8.30am–7.30pm; €6) was begun in 1334 by Giotto and continued after his death by Andrea Pisano and Francesco Talenti. The only part of the tower built exactly as Giotto designed it is the lower storey, studded with two rows of remarkable bas-reliefs, the lower one illustrating the *Creation of Man and the Arts and Industries* carved by Pisano. Opposite, the **Baptistery** (Mon–Sat noon–6.30pm; Sun 8.30am–2pm; €6), generally thought to date from the sixth or seventh century, is the oldest building in the city. Its most famous embellishments, the gilded bronze doors, were cast in the early fifteenth century by Lorenzo Ghiberti, and were described by Michelangelo as "so beautiful they are worthy to be the gates of Paradise". They're a primer of early Renaissance art, innovatively using perspective, gesture and sophisticated grouping of subjects to convey the human drama of each scene. Ghiberti included a self-portrait in the frame of the left-hand door – his is the fourth head from the top of the right-hand band. Inside, the Baptistery is equally stunning, with a thirteenth-century mosaic floor and ceiling and the tomb of Pope John XXIII, draped by a superb marble canopy, the work of Donatello and his pupil Michelozzo.

Since the early fifteenth century the maintenance of the Duomo has been supervised from the building at Piazza del Duomo 9, which nowadays houses the **Museo dell'Opera del Duomo** (Mon–Sat 9am–7.30pm, Sun 9am–2pm; €6), the repository of the most precious and fragile works of art from the buildings around. Pieces include Brunelleschi's death mask; models of the dome and a variety of tools and machines devised by the architect; Michelangelo's anguished late *Pietà*; Pisano's bas-reliefs and Donatello's figures for the campanile; and four of Ghiberti's door panels from the Baptistery.

The Palazzo Vecchio, Uffizi and Bargello

The tourist-thronged Piazza della Signoria is dominated by the colossal **Palazzo Vecchio**, Florence's fortress-like town hall (Mon–Sun 9am–7pm, Thurs closes 2pm; €5.70), begun in the last year of the thirteenth century as the home of the *Signoria*, the highest tier of the city's republican government. The huge Salone dei Cinquecento, built at the end of the fifteenth century, is full of heroic murals by Vasari, though it is redeemed by the presence of Michelangelo's *Victory*, facing the entrance door, originally sculpted for Pope Julius II's tomb but donated to the Medici by the artist's nephew.

Immediately south of the piazza, the **Galleria degli Uffizi** (Tues–Sun 8.15am–6.50pm; summer Sat till 10pm; booking advisable on ☏055.294.883; €8.50) is the greatest picture gallery in Italy, with a collection of masterpieces that is impossible to take in on a single visit. Works from the early Renaissance include three altarpieces of the *Madonna Enthroned* by Cimabue, Duccio and Giotto, though it's Filippo Lippi's *Madonna and Child with Two Angels* that's one of the best-known Renaissance images of the Madonna. Some of Botticelli's most famous works are here too, notably *Primavera* and the *Birth of Venus*, and while the Uffizi doesn't own a finished painting that's entirely by Leonardo da Vinci, there's a celebrated *Annunciation* that's mainly by him, as well as the angel in profile that he painted in Verrocchio's *Baptism*. Room 18 houses the most important of the Medici sculptures, first among which is the *Medici Venus*, while Michelangelo's *Doni Tondo* is his only completed easel painting, its contorted gestures and vivid colours later imitated by the Mannerist painters of the sixteenth century. The Uffizi also has a number of compositions by Raphael and Titian, while later rooms include some large works by Rubens, Van Dyck, Caravaggio and Rembrandt.

The **Bargello** museum (Tues–Sat 8.15am–1.50pm; €4) lies just north of the Uffizi in Via del Proconsolo. The first part of the collection focuses on Michelangelo. Beyond, the more flamboyant art of Cellini and Giambologna is exhibited, including Giambologna's best-known creation, the nimble figure of *Mercury*. Out in the courtyard, at the top of its external staircase, the first-floor loggia has been turned into an aviary for Giambologna's bronze birds, imported from the Medici villa at Castello, while a nearby room displays work by Donatello. His sexually ambiguous bronze *David*, the first freestanding nude figure since classical times, was cast in the early 1430s. Upstairs, the Sala dei Bronzetti has Italy's best assembly of small Renaissance bronzes, with plentiful evidence of Giambologna's virtuosity, and a further room holds Renaissance portrait busts.

North: San Lorenzo and around

The church of **San Lorenzo**, north of Piazza del Duomo, has good claim to be the oldest church in Florence, and for the best part of three hundred years was the city's cathedral. At the top of the left aisle and through the cloisters, the **Biblioteca Medicea-Laurenziana** (Mon–Sat 9am–1pm; free) was designed by Michelangelo in 1524; its most startling feature is the vestibule, a room almost filled by a flight of steps resembling a solidified lava flow. Michelangelo's most celebrated contribution to the San Lorenzo buildings, however, is the Sagrestia Nuova, part of the **Cappelle Medicee** (Tues–Sun 8.15am–5pm; €5; separate entrance behind church), which contains the fabulous Medici tombs, carved between 1524 and 1533. To the left is the tomb of Lorenzo, duke of Urbino, the grandson of Lorenzo il Magnifico, bearing figures of *Dawn and Dusk* to sum up his contemplative nature. Opposite is the tomb of Lorenzo il Magnifico's youngest son, Giuliano, his supposedly more active character symbolized by *Day and Night*. Just east of here, the **Accademia** (Tues–Sun 8.15am–6.50pm; summer Sat till 10pm; €6.50), Europe's first school of drawing, is swamped by people come to view **Michelangelo's *David***. Finished in 1504, when the artist was just 29, and carved from a gigantic block of marble, it's an incomparable show of technical bravura. The gallery also houses his remarkable unfinished *Slaves*.

East: Santa Croce

Down by the river, the church of **Santa Croce** (Mon–Sat 9.30am–noon & 3–5.30pm, Sun 3–5.30pm), begun in 1294, is full of tombstones and commemorative monuments, including Vasari's monument to Michelangelo and, on the opposite side of the church, is the tomb of Galileo, built in 1737 when it was finally agreed to give the great scientist a Christian burial. Most visitors, however, come to see the frescoes by Giotto in the Cappella Peruzzi and the Cappella Bardi (on the right of the chancel), which show scenes from the lives of St John the Baptist and St John the Evangelist. The **Museo dell'Opera di Santa Croce**, off the first cloister (10am–5pm, closed Wed; €4.13), houses a miscellany of works of art, the best of which are Cimabue's flood-damaged *Crucifixion* and Donatello's enormous gilded *St Louis of Toulouse*. Brunelleschi's harmonious Cappella dei Pazzi, at the end of the first cloister, was designed in the 1430s and completed in the 1470s, several years after the architect's death; it features decorations by Luca della Robbia.

South: Oltrarno and beyond

The photogenic thirteenth-century **Ponte Vecchio**, loaded with jewellers' shops overhanging the water, leads from the city centre across the river to the district of Oltrarno. Head west, past the relaxed, café-lined square of Santo Spirito, to the church of Santa Maria del Carmine – an essential visit for the superbly restored frescoes by Masaccio in its **Cappella Brancacci** (Mon & Wed–Sat 10am–5pm, Sun 1–5pm; €3.10), including an iconic *Expulsion of Adam & Eve* on the left of the entrance arch: Adam presses his hands to his face in despair, Eve raises her head and screams. St Peter is the focus of all the other scenes; the most famous, the *Tribute Money*, on the upper left wall, shows three separate events within a single frame – in the centre is Christ at Capernaum, being asked to pay a tribute to the city; on the left, St Peter fetches coins from the mouth of a fish on the left, and on the right, he pays the tax official.

South of Santo Spirito is the massive bulk of the **Palazzo Pitti**. Nowadays the fifteenth-century palace contains six separate museums, of which the best is the **Galleria Palatina** (Tues–Sun 8.15am–6.50pm; summer Sat till 10pm; €6.50), which features superb displays of the art of Raphael and Titian, including a number of Titian's most trenchant portraits. Much of the rest of the first floor comprises the state rooms of the Appartamenti Monumentali (included in the Galleria Palatina ticket). The Pitti's enormous formal garden, the delightful **Giardino di Bóboli** (Tues–Sun 8.15am–4.30/7.30pm; €6.50), is full of Mannerist embellishments, including the Grotta del Buontalenti – among its fake stalactites are shepherds and sheep and replicas of Michelangelo's *Slaves*. Beyond here, the multicoloured facade of **San Miniato al Monte** (daily 8am–12.30pm & 2.30–7.30pm) lures troupes of visitors up the hill. The interior is like no other in the city, and its general form has changed little since the mid-eleventh century. In the lower part of the church, don't overlook the intricately patterned panels of the pavement, from 1207, and the tabernacle between the choir stairs, designed in 1448 by Michelozzo.

Out of the centre: Fiesole

A long-established retreat from the summer heat and crowds, the town of **Fiesole** spreads over a cluster of hilltops 8km northeast of Florence (ATAF bus #7 from Florence's train station every 15min; takes 20min). Fiesole's main square is home to the **Duomo**, from where Via San Francesco leads up to a terrace that gives a remarkable panorama of Florence. Around the back of the Duomo, in Via Marini, is the entrance to the **Teatro Romano** and **Museo Archeologico** (daily 9.30am–7pm; €6.50), built in the first century BC, but still used for performances during the *Estate Fiesolana* festival. Narrow Via Vecchia Fiesolana leads from just west of the main square to the hamlet of **San Domenico**, 1.5km southwest, where Fra Angelico was once prior of the Dominican monastery; the church retains a *Madonna and Angels* by him, and the chapterhouse also has a Fra Angelico fresco of *The Crucifixion*.

Eating, drinking and nightlife

The best place to find picnic food and snacks is the **Mercato Centrale**, just east of the train station, which also has bars charging prices lower than elsewhere in the city. Otherwise, try a **vinaio**, a wine cellar/snack bar that serves *crostini* and other snacks. A Florentine speciality, though not for the faint-hearted, is the **trippai**, or tripe-stall, selling tripe-filled rolls – there's one at Mercato Centrale and a stall at Piazza de' Nerli. For **what's-on** information, call in at Box Office, Via Alamanni 39 (☎055.210.804), or consult the listings magazines *Firenze Spettacolo* and *Informa Città*. As for **festivals**, in May there's the *Maggio Musicale* (⊛www.maggiofiorentino.com), while the *Festa di San Giovanni* on 24 June, Florence's saint's day, sees a massive fireworks display.

Cafés and snacks

Antico Noê Volta di San Piero 6. Burgers and salads, with a restaurant next door.
Fiaschetteria Balducci Via de' Neri 17. For classy snacks, *panini* and pasta.
Vinaio I Fratellini Via Cimatori 38. A perfect example of the Florentine *vinaio*.
Vivoli Via Isola delle Stinche 7r, near Santa Croce. Leader of the pack for ice cream; closed Mon.

Restaurants

Antica Mescita San Niccolo Via San Niccolo 60/r. Unrivalled cheese and wine selection, plus superb Tuscan soups.
Benvenuto Via Mosca 16/r, off Via de' Neri. Looks more like a delicatessen than a trattoria from the street; the *gnocchi* and *arista* are delicious.
Da Mario Via Rosina 2r. Popular with students and market workers – be prepared to queue and share a table. Closed evenings.
Osteria Belle Donne Via delle Belle Donne 16/r. Flowers and fruit drip from the walls of this lovely *osteria*; blackboard menu featuring local dishes.
Al Tranvai Piazza T. Tasso 14/r. Good, inexpensive Florentine specialities.

Trattoria Borgo Antico Piazza Santo Spirito 6r. Busy trattoria on a quiet Oltrarno square, with excellent seafood, homemade pasta and tables outside in summer.
Za-Za Piazza del Mercato Centrale 26r. A few tables on ground level, but a bigger canteen below.

Bars and clubs

Dolce Vita Piazza del Carmine. Trendy late-night hangout that also stages small-scale art exhibitions.
Porfirio Rubirosa Viale Strozzi 38r. Where the *bella gente* drop in before heading for a late dinner or club.
Rex Via Fiesolana 25r, Santa Croce. Good music, a varied clientele, and serves snacks and cocktails.
Space Electronic Via Palazzuolo 37. The favourite club for young foreigners, open nightly.
Tenax Via Pratese 47. The city's biggest club and one of its leading venues for new and established bands.
Yab Yum Via de' Sassetti 5r. City-centre club playing the best of new dance music.
Zoe Via dei Renail 13/r, Oltrarno. Atmospheric cocktail bar for poseurs.

Listings

Consulates UK, Lungarno Corsini 2
℡ 055.284.133; US, Lungarno Vespucci 38
℡ 055.239.8276.
Hospital Santa Maria Nuova, Piazza Santa Maria
Nuova 1 ℡ 055.27.581. English-speaking doctors
on 24-hour call at the Tourist Medical Service, Via
Lorenzo il Magnifico 59 ℡ 055.475.411.
Internet access Internet Train, Via Guelfa 24a, Via

dell'Oriuolo 40r, Borgo San Jacopo 30r.
Laundry Onda Blu, Via degli Alfani 24r; Wash &
Dry, Via della Scala 52–54r.
Pharmacies All-night pharmacy at the train
station; Molteni, Via dei Calzaiuoli 7r; All' Insegna
del Moro, Piazza San Giovanni 20r.
Police Via Zara 2 ℡ 055.49.771.
Post office Via Pelliceria 3.

Pisa

There's no escaping the Leaning Tower in **PISA**. The medieval bell tower is one of the world's most familiar images and yet its beauty still comes as a surprise. It is set in chessboard formation alongside the Duomo and Baptistery on the manicured grass of the **Campo dei Miracoli**, where most buildings belong to the city's "Golden Age" – the twelfth and thirteenth centuries, when Pisa was one of the great Mediterranean powers. Perhaps the strangest thing about the **Leaning Tower** (daily 8/9am–5/8pm), begun in 1173, is that it has always tilted; subsidence disrupted the foundations when it had reached just three of its eight storeys. For the next 180 years a succession of architects were brought in to try to correct the tilt, until 1350 when the angle was accepted and the tower completed. Eight centuries on, it was thought to be nearing its limit: the overhang is over 5m, and the tower, supported by steel wires, was closed to the public in the 1990s – though it's open for visits once again now that the tilt has been successfully halted. The **Duomo** (Mon–Sat 10am–4.30/7.30pm, Sun 1–4.30/7.30pm) was begun a century earlier, its facade – with its delicate balance of black and white marble, and tiers of arcades – setting the model for Pisa's highly distinctive brand of Romanesque. The interior continues the use of black and white marble, and with its long arcades of columns has an almost oriental aspect. Its acknowledged highlight is the astonishingly detailed Gothic pulpit by Giovanni Pisano. The third building of the Miracoli ensemble, the circular **Baptistery** (daily 8/9am–4.30/7.30pm), is a slightly bizarre mix of Romanesque and Gothic, embellished with statuary (now displayed in the museum) by Giovanni Pisano and his father Nicola. Along the north side of the Campo is the **Camposanto** (same hours), a cloistered cemetery built towards the end of the thirteenth century. Most of the cloister's frescoes were destroyed by Allied bombing in World War II, but two masterpieces survived relatively unscathed – a fourteenth-century *Triumph of Death* and *Last Judgement* in the Cappella Ammanati, a ruthless catalogue of horrors painted around the time of the Black Death. At the southeast corner of the Campo, a vast array of pieces from the Duomo and Baptistery are displayed in the **Museo dell'Opera del Duomo**, a huge collection that includes statuary by each of the Pisano family.

Away from the Campo dei Miracoli, Pisa takes on a very different character, as tourists give way to students at the still-thriving university. It's nonetheless a quiet

⑮

ITALY | Central Italy

The **ticket office** for the Campo dei Miracoli is next to the tourist office. The best deal is a **joint ticket** (€10.50) which gives admission to the Duomo, the Baptistery, the Camposanto, the Museo dell'Opera del Duomo and less interesting Museo delle Sinopie. Otherwise, you can buy a ticket for the Duomo alone (€2); for one of the other sites alone (€5); for the Duomo plus any two others (€8); or for any four sites (€8.50). The Duomo has free entry from November to March. There's a separate ticket (€15) for guided tours of the Leaning Tower, which depart every 35–40min; expect long queues. For an extra €2 you can pre-book your visit online at ⑳www.opapisa.it – this circumvents the queues but you still need to arrive on site at least one hour prior to the scheduled tour.

place, eerily so at night, set around a series of erratic squares and arcaded streets, and with clusters of Romanesque churches and, along the banks of the Arno, a number of fine palazzi. The **Piazza dei Cavalieri** is an obvious first stop, a large square that was the centre of medieval Pisa, before being remodelled by Vasari as the headquarters of the Knights of St Stephen, whose palace, the curving **Palazzo dei Cavalieri**, topped with busts of the Medici, faces the order's church of **San Stefano**. A short walk east along the river, the **Museo Nazionale di San Matteo** (Tues–Sat 8.30am–7.30pm, Sun 8.30am–1.30pm; €4) is housed in a twelfth-century convent.

Practicalities

Pisa's **train station** is south of the centre on Piazza della Stazione, a ten-minute walk (or bus #3) to Campo dei Miracoli. From the **airport**, take the hourly Florence train for the five-minute journey. There are two **tourist offices**: one to the left of the station (Mon–Fri 8.30am–5.30/7pm, Sat & Sun 9am–5pm; ☎050.422.91, ✆www.opapisa.it) and another in the northeast corner of Campo dei Miracoli (Mon–Sat 8.30am–5.30/7pm, Sun 10.30am–4.30pm; ☎050.560.464). The most attractive budget **hotels** are grouped around Campo dei Miracoli, and the best of the lot is the elegant old *Albergo Gronchi* in Piazza Arcivescovado (☎050.561.823; ❸). Others include the *Locanda Galileo*, Via Santa Maria (☎050.40.621; ❹); *Pensione Helvetia*, Via G. Boschi 31, off Piazza Arcivescovado (☎050.553.084; ❹); and *La Torre*, Via C. Battisti 17 (☎050.252.20; ❹). A good women-only alternative, five minutes' walk from the station (first right), is the *Casa della Giovane*, Via Corridoni 31 (☎050.43.061; ❸). The nearest **hostel** is at Via Pietrasantina 15 (☎050.890.622; €21); take bus #3 from the station or Campo dei Miracoli. The city **campsite**, *Campeggio Torre Pendente*, is 1km west of Campo dei Miracoli at Viale delle Cascine 86 (☎050.561.704; closed Nov–March) – a large, well-maintained site, with a restaurant and shop.

There are some good-value **places to eat** a few blocks south of the tower, around the market on Piazza delle Vettovaglie. One of the best is *Vineria di Piazza*, Piazza delle Vettovaglie 13, which does good soups; or there's the slightly dearer trattoria *La Mescita*, Via Cavalca 2, on the corner of the piazza. Over to the west, *Pizzeria da Cassio*, Piazza Cavallotti 14, is a good *tavola calda*, and the university building on Via Martiri, off Piazza Cavalieri, has a *mensa* (closed mid-July to mid-Sept). Pisa is known for its **Gioco del Ponte**, held on the last Sunday in June, when teams from the north and south banks of the city stage a series of "battles", including pushing a seven-tonne carriage over the Ponte di Mezzo. But the town's most magical event is the **Luminara** on June 16, when buildings along the river are festooned with candles to celebrate San Ranieri, the city's patron saint.

Lucca

LUCCA is as graceful a provincial capital as they come, set inside a thick swathe of Renaissance walls, and with a quiet, almost entirely medieval street plan. Palaces and the odd tower dot the streets, at intervals overlooked by a brilliantly decorated Romanesque church facade. The most enjoyable way to get your bearings is to follow the path around the top of the **walls** – nearly 4km in extent and built with genuine defensive capability in the early sixteenth century, before being transformed to their present, garden aspect by the Bourbon ruler, Marie Louise. In the centre of town, just east of the main Piazza Napoleone on Piazza San Martino, the cathedral of **San Martino** houses Jacopo della Quercia's famous **Tomb of Ilaria del Carretto** (Mon–Sat 9.30am–5.45pm, Sun 11am–noon & 1–4.45pm; €2), which has been restored so vigorously that one expert declared it had been ruined – prompting a libel action from the restorer. Lucca's finest sculptor, however, was Matteo Civitali, whose *Tempietto* in the north aisle was sculpted to house the city's most famous relic, the *Volto Santo* – said to be the "true effigy of Christ" and the focus for international pilgrimage. Northwest across Via Fillungo, the facade of **San**

Michele in Foro (daily 7.30am–8pm) is a triumph of eccentricity, each of its loggia columns different, some twisted, others sculpted or candy-striped. Giacomo Puccini was born almost opposite at Via di Poggio 30, and his home, the **Casa di Puccini** (Tues–Sun 10am–1pm & 3–7pm; €3), is now a school of music with a small museum, featuring the Steinway piano on which he composed *Turandot*. At the end of the street in Via Galli Tassi is the seventeenth-century, Rococo **Palazzo Mansi**, which houses an indifferent art collection (Tues–Sat 8.30am–7pm; €4), but some splendid rooms – particularly the spectacularly gilded bridal suite. Be sure to visit the remarkable **Piazza Anfiteatro**, a circuit of medieval buildings whose foundations are the arches of the Roman amphitheatre. But perhaps the strangest sight in Lucca is the **Casa-Torre Guinigi** (daily 9am–7.30pm; €3.50), the fifteenth-century home of Lucca's leading family, with a battlemented tower surmounted by holm oaks whose roots have grown into the room below. Much of it is being restored, but from Via San Andrea you can climb it for one of the best views over the city. Across the narrow canal on Via della Quarquonia, the fifteenth-century **Villa Guinigi** is now the home to Lucca's major museum of art and sculpture, the **Museo Nazionale Guinigi** (Tues–Sat 9am–7pm, Sun 9am–2pm; €4), with a good deal of lively Romanesque sculpture from the city and some work by the cathedral's maestro, Matteo Civitali.

Lucca's **train station** is just south of the city walls, an easy walk or short bus ride from the centre. One of the most pleasant ways of exploring Lucca is to **rent a bike** (€2.50/hr); the **tourist office** on the north side of Piazza Verdi (daily: summer 9am–7pm; winter 9.30am–5.30pm; ☎0583.442.944, ⊛www.in-lucca.it) has details. Finding accommodation is a problem at almost any time of year, but of the **hotels**, the *Melecchi* at Via Romana 37 (☎0583.950.234; ❹), *Stipino* at Via Romana 95 (☎0583.495.077; ❺), and *Diana* at Via del Molinetto 11 (☎0583.492.202; ❹) are all worth a try. After these the best bet is the *Moderno*, Via Civitali 38 (☎0583.558.40; ❹). The **HI hostel**, *San Frediano*, is at Via della Cavallerizza 12 (☎0583.469.957; €16), next to the church of San Frediano in the centre of town. For **food**, try the *Trattoria da Guido*, Via C. Battisti 28; *Trattoria da Leo*, Via Tegrimi 1; *Trattoria da Giulio*, Via delle Conce 47; or *Ristorante all'Olivo*, Piazza S. Quirico 1. For excellent pizza, with good **beer**, there's the *Gli Orti di Via Elisa*, Via Elisa 17.

Arezzo

AREZZO, southeast of Florence on the main line to Rome, is a quiet, charming town, the backdrop for Roberto Benigni's hit film *La Vita e Bella* (Life is Beautiful). It was once one of the most important settlements of the Etruscan federation and a prosperous independent republic in the Middle Ages, later falling under the sway of Florence. During the Renaissance, Petrarch, Pietro Aretino and Vasari brought lasting prestige to the city, yet it was an outsider – Piero della Francesca – who gave Arezzo its permanent Renaissance monument, the glorious frescoed choir in the Basilica of **San Francesco** (Mon–Sat 9am–5.30pm, Sun 1–5.30pm; advance booking necessary, ☎0575.352.727, ⊛www.pierodellafrancesca.it; €5.03). Don't despair if it's fully booked, as much of the cycle is visible from outside the enclosure. The church (off Corso Italia) was built in the early fourteenth century, and a century later Piero della Francesca was commissioned to paint the choir with a cycle depicting *The Legend of the True Cross*, one of the most radiant creations of the period. Corso Italia leads from the **lower town** to the more interesting **older quarter** at the top of the hill. The twelfth-century **Pieve di Santa Maria** is one of the finest Romanesque structures in Tuscany, with some wonderful early-thirteenth-century carvings of the months over the portal. The fourteenth-century campanile, known locally as "the tower of the hundred holes", has become the emblem of the town. On the other side of the church, the dramatically sloping Piazza Grande is bordered by the tiered facade of the **Palazzetto della Fraternità dei Laci**, with a Gothic ground floor and fifteenth-century upper storeys, and Vasari's **loggia**, occupied by shops that in some instances still have their original stone counters. At the highest point of the town, the large unfussy **Duomo**, begun in the late thirteenth century, has stained-glass windows from around 1520, terracottas by the della Robbia family, and a tiny fresco of the *Magdalene* by Piero della Francesca. A short distance in the opposite direction from the Duomo, the church of **San Domenico** has a dolorous *Crucifix* by Cimabue. Signs point the way to the nearby **Casa di Giorgio Vasari** at Via XX Settembre 55 (Mon & Wed–Sat 9am–7pm, Sun 9am–1pm; €2), designed by the celebrated biographer-architect-painter for himself and coated with his own lurid frescoes.

The **train station** is a short walk from the centre along Via Monaco. The **tourist office** is outside the station at Piazza della Repubblica 28 (Mon–Sat 9.30am–1pm & 3–7pm, Sun 9am–1pm; ☎0575.377.678, ⍟www.apt.arezzo.it). Accommodation is hard to come by on the first weekend of every month (because of the massive antiques fair), and at the end of August and beginning of September. The most convenient, affordable **hotel** is *La Toscana*, Via M. Perennio 56 (☎0575.21.692, ❹), on the main road coming in from the west. Alternatively, try the *Cecco*, at Corso Italia 215 (☎0575.20.986; ⍟www.hotelcecco.com; ❺). The nearest **hostel**, *Ostello Villa Severi*, is some way out of town at Via Redi 13 (☎0575.299.047; €13); take bus #4 from the train station. For **restaurants**, *Da Guido*, Via Madonna del Prato 85, is a basic local trattoria, while for more pricey but high-quality Tuscan cuisine, try *La Buca di San Francesco*, by San Francesco.

Siena

SIENA, 78km south of Florence, is the perfect antidote to its better-known neighbour. Self-contained and still rural in parts behind medieval walls, its great attraction is the cityscape – a majestic Gothic whole that you can roam around and enjoy without venturing into a single museum. It is also a lively university town, so there is no shortage of places to go in the evening. To get the most from it you'll need to stay, especially if you want to see its spectacular horse race, the **Palio** – though you'll definitely need to book during this time (see box). During the Middle Ages Siena was one of the major cities of Europe. The size of Paris, it controlled most of southern Tuscany and its flourishing wool industry dominated the trade routes from France to Rome. The city developed a highly sophisticated civic life, with its own written constitution and a quasi-democratic government.

The City

The Campo is the centre of Siena in every sense: the main streets lead into it, the Palio takes place around its café-lined perimeter, and it's the natural place to gravitate towards. It's been called the most beautiful square in the world – an assessment

---

The Siena Palio

The Siena **Palio** is the most spectacular festival event in Italy, a bareback horse-race around the Campo contested twice a year (July 2 at 7.45pm; and Aug 16 at 7pm) between the ancient wards – or *contrade* – of the city. Each of the seventeen *contrade* has its own church, social centre and museum, and a heraldic animal motif. There's a big build-up, with trials and processions for days before the big event, even though the race itself lasts little more than ninety seconds – a hectic and violent spectacle with few rules: each *contrada* has a traditional rival, and ensuring it loses is as important as winning yourself (and it's the horse that wins the prize, whether or not a jockey is on board). Most spectators crowd into the centre of the Campo; for the best view, you need to have found a position on the inner rail by 2pm and to keep it for the next seven hours. Beware that toilet, shade and refreshments are minimal, the swell of the crowd can be overwhelming, and you won't be able to leave the Campo for at least two hours after the race. If you come to town for the Palio but haven't booked a hotel room, reckon on staying up all night.

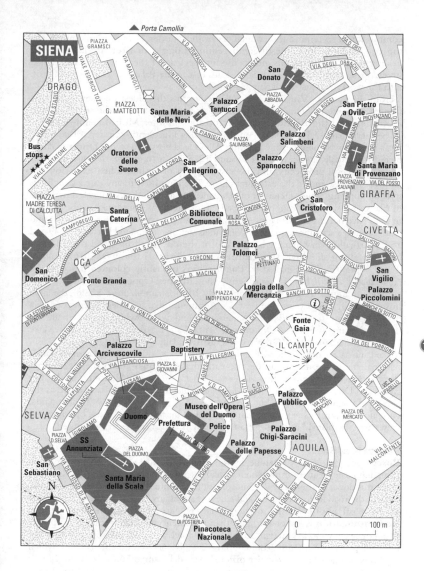

that seems pretty fair; taking a picnic onto the stones to watch the shadows move around the square while topping up your tan is as authentic a Sienese experience as any. The **Palazzo Comunale** (daily 10am–5.30/7pm; tower and museum combined ticket €9.50) – with its 107m bell-tower, the **Torre del Mangia** (€5.50) – occupies virtually the entire south side, and although it's still in use as Siena's town hall, its principal rooms have been converted into a **museum** (€6.50), frescoed with themes integral to the secular life of the medieval city. Best of these are the Sala del Mappamondo, on the wall of which is the fabulous *Maestà* of Simone Martini (1315), an acknowledged masterpiece of Sienese art, and the Sala della Pace, decorated with Lorenzetti's *Allegories of Good and Bad Government* (1377), commissioned to remind the councillors of their duties. Between buildings at the top end of the Campo, the fifteenth-century **Loggia di Mercanzia**, built as a dealing room for merchants, marks the intersection of the city centre's principal streets. From here Via Banchi di Sotto leads east to the Palazzo Piccolomini and on into the workaday quarter of San Martino.

From the Campo, **Via di Città** cuts west across the oldest quarter of the city, fronted by some of Siena's finest private palazzi. At the end of the street, Via San Pietro leads to the **Pinacoteca Nazionale** (summer Mon 8.30am–1.30pm, Tues–Sat 8.15am–7.15pm, Sun 8am–1pm; €4), a fourteenth-century palace housing a rollcall of Sienese Gothic painting. Alleys lead north up to the **Duomo**, completed to virtually its present size around 1215; plans to enlarge it withered with Siena's medieval prosperity, and the vast skeleton of an unfinished extension still stands at the east end of the cathedral square. The Duomo is in any case a delight, its style an amazing conglomeration of Romanesque and Gothic, delineated by bands of black and white marble on its facade. This theme is continued in the *sgraffito* marble pavement, which begins with geometric patterns outside the church and takes off into a startling sequence of 56 panels within, completed between 1349 and 1547; virtually every artist who worked in the city tried his hand on a design. Midway along the nave, the **Libreria Piccolomini** (daily 9/10am–1pm & 2–5/7.30pm; €1.50), signalled by Pinturicchio's brilliantly coloured fresco of the *Coronation of Pius II*, has further superbly vivid frescoes. Opposite the Duomo is the complex of **Santa Maria della Scala** (daily 10/10.30am–4/6pm; €5.20), the city's hospital for over 800 years, and now a vast museum that includes the frescoed Sala del Pellegrinaio (once used as a hospital ward) and, way down in the basement, the dark and strangely spooky Oratorio di Santa Caterina della Notte chapel. Make time for the **Museo dell'Opera del Duomo** (daily 9am–1.30/7.30pm; €5.50), tucked into a corner of the abandoned Duomo extension; on display are Pisano's original statues from the facade; the cathedral's original altarpiece, a haunting Byzantine icon known as the *Madonna dagli Occhi Grossi* (Madonna of the Big Eyes); and Duccio's glittering gold *Maestà*, completed in 1311 and acclaimed as the climax of the Sienese style – but the best reason to visit is to follow "Panorama dal Facciatone" signs to steep spiral stairs that climb up to the top of the building; the views are sensational but the topmost walkway is narrow and scarily exposed.

Practicalities

Buses stop along Viale Curtatone, by the Basilica of San Domenico, and are much faster and more frequent from Florence than the trains (change at Empoli). The **train station** is down in the valley 2km northeast; to get into town, either tackle the walk or cross the road from the station and take just about any city bus heading left, which all drop off about 100m north of Piazza Matteotti near the city centre. **Accommodation** is less of a struggle than in Florence, though it still pays to phone ahead or make your way straight to the Siena Hotels Promotion booth opposite San Domenico (Mon–Sat 9am–7/8pm; ☏0577.288.084, ✆www.hotelsiena.com), which can book rooms; or to the **tourist office**, Piazza del Campo 56 (daily 10am–1pm & 3–7pm; ☏0577.280.551, ✆www.siena.turismo.toscana.it), which provides an accommodation list. Otherwise, try *Tre Donzelle*, Via Donzelle 5 (☏0577.280.358; ❹), which has good clean rooms right in the heart of town; the small, smart *Piccolo Hotel Etruria* at no. 3 (☏0577.288.088; ❺); *La Perla*, Via delle Terme 25 (☏0577.471.44; ❻), a *pensione* in a very central location, two blocks north of the Campo; or the *Bernini* at Via della Sapienza 15 (☏0577.289.047, ✆www.albergobernini.com; ❻), which has stunning views to the Duomo. The comfortable **HI hostel** is at Via Fiorentina 89 (☏0577.522.12; €13), 2km northwest of the centre; take bus #10 from the train station or Piazza Gramsci, or if you're coming from Florence, ask the bus driver to let you off at "Lo Stellino". The well-maintained **campsite** *Campeggio Siena Colleverde*, Strada di Scacciapensieri 47, is 2km north (☏0577.280.044; closed mid-Nov to mid-March; bus #3 from Piazza Gramsci).

There's **pizza** by weight at Via delle Terme 10, and an extravagantly stocked **deli**, the *Pizzicheria Morbidi*, at Via Banchi di Sotto 27. The cheapest sit-down alternative is the *Mensa Universitaria*, Via Sant'Agata 1 (closed Sun & all Aug); there's another *mensa* at Via Bandini 47 or try the unpretentious café *Carla e Franca*, Via di Pantaneto 138, which serves pizza and pasta. **Restaurants** cost a bit over the odds in Siena, especially if you want to eat out in the Campo. *Gallo Nero*, Via del Porrione 65–67, serves meals that follow medieval recipes; or for more conventional local fare try *Osteria Le Logge*, in an old pharmacy along the street at no. 33. Out towards San Lorenzo at Corso San Antonio 4, *Osteria Chiacchieria* is a rustic and welcoming option. For delectable **ice cream**, there's *Nannini Gelateria*, at the Piazza Matteotti end of Banchi di Sopra, or *La Costarella*, just off the Campo near the corner of Via di Città and Via dei Pellegrini. **Internet** access is at Internet Train, Via di Città 121.

San Gimignano

SAN GIMIGNANO is one of the best-known villages in Tuscany. Its skyline of towers, framed against classic Tuscan countryside, has caught the tourist imagination. From May to October, it is very busy and to really get a feel for the place you should come out of season. If you can't, aim to spend the night here – in the evenings the town takes on a very different pace and atmosphere. A **combined ticket** (€7.50) covers all the town's civic museums, available at any of the participating sites. The village was a force to be reckoned with in the Middle Ages, with a population of fifteen thousand (twice the present number). Nowadays you could walk across it in fifteen minutes, and around the walls in an hour. The main entrance gate, facing the bus terminal on the south side of town, is **Porta San Giovanni**, from where Via San Giovanni leads to the town's interlocking main squares, **Piazza della Cisterna** and Piazza del Duomo. You enter the Piazza della Cisterna through another majestic gateway, the **Arco dei Becci**, part of the original fortifications before the town expanded in the twelfth century. The more austere **Piazza Duomo**, off to the left, is flanked by the **Collegiata** cathedral (Mon–Sat 9.30am–5/7.30pm, Sun 1–5pm; €3.50), frescoed with Old and New Testament scenes – best, though, is the superb fresco cycle by Ghirlandaio in the Cappella di Santa Fina, depicting the trials of a local saint. There's more work by Ghirlandaio to the left of the cathedral – a fresco of the Annunciation on the courtyard loggia – while the **Palazzo del Popolo**, next door (daily 9.30am–7pm; €5), gives you the chance to climb the **Torre Grossa** (€4.10), the town's highest surviving tower and the only one you can ascend. The same building is home to a number of rooms given over to the **Museo Civico**, the first of which, frescoed with hunting scenes, is known as the Sala di Dante and houses Lippo Memmi's *Maestà*, modelled on that of Simone Martini in Siena. North from Piazza Duomo, **Via San Matteo** is one of the grandest and best preserved of the city streets, with quiet alleyways running down to the walls. At the **Museo Criminale Medioevale** (daily 10am–5.30/7pm; €8; not covered by combined ticket) at Via del Castello 1, you get a no-holds-barred exploration of the medieval torturer's mind.

The nearest **train station** is Poggibonsi, on the Siena–Empoli line, from where **buses** run to San Gimignano every hour (€1.60). Accommodation lists are available from the **tourist office** on Piazza del Duomo (daily 9am–1pm & 2/3–6/7pm; ☎0577.940.008, ⊛www.sangimignano.com), but from May to September you'll save a lot of frustration by using the Associazione Extralberghiere at Piazza della Cisterna 6 (daily 9.30am–7.30pm; ☎0577.943.111), which can arrange **private rooms** (❺–❻) without commission, or the Pro Loco Association, Piazza del Duomo 1 (daily 9am–7pm; ☎0577.940.809), which offers a similar service for hotel accommodation. One of the cheapest **hotels** is the three-star *Da Graziano*, Via Matteotti 39/a (☎0577.940.101, ⊛www.hoteldagraziano.it; ❺). The nearest **campsite** is *Il Boschetto*, 3km downhill at Santa Lucia (☎0577.940.352). Probably the most authentic Tuscan **restaurant** in town is the *Mandragola*, Via Berignano 58.

Perugia and around

PERUGIA, the Umbrian capital, is an attractive medieval university town that buzzes with young people of every nationality, many of them students at the *Universita per Stranieri* (Foreigner's University). Buitoni, the pasta people, are based here, and it's also where Italy's best chocolate, Perugini, is made. Perugia hinges on a single street, **Corso Vannucci**, a broad pedestrian thoroughfare, at the far end of which the austere Piazza Quattro Novembre is backed by the plain-faced **Duomo San Lorenzo** (daily 8am–noon & 4pm–sunset). The interior – home to the so-called Virgin's "wedding ring", an unwieldy piece of agate that changes colour according to the character of the person wearing it – isn't especially interesting, and the ring is kept locked up in fifteen boxes fitted into one another like Russian dolls, each opened with a key held by a different person; it's brought out for public viewing every July 30. The centrepiece of the piazza is the **Fontana Maggiore**, sculpted by the father-and-son team Nicola and Giovanni Pisano and describing episodes from the Old Testament, classical myth, Aesop's fables and the twelve months of the year. Opposite rises the gaunt mass of the **Palazzo dei Priori**, worth a glance inside for its frescoed **Sala dei Notari** (Tues–Sun 9am–1pm & 3–7pm; free). A few doors down at Corso Vannucci 25 is the **Collegio di Cambio** (March–Oct Mon–Sat 9am–12.30pm & 2.30–5.30pm, Sun 9am–12.30pm; Nov–Feb Tues–Sat 8am–2pm, Sun 9am–12.30pm; €2.60), the town's medieval money-exchange, frescoed by Perugino and said to be the most beautiful bank in the world. The palace also houses the **Galleria Nazionale di Umbria** (Mon–Sat 8.30am–7.30pm, Sun 9am–1pm; closed first Mon of each month; €6.50), one of central Italy's best galleries – a twelve-room romp through the history of Umbrian painting, with works by Perugino and Pinturrichio along with one or two stunning Tuscan masterpieces. The best streets to wander around to get a feel of the old city are either side of the Duomo. **Via dei Priori** is the most characteristic, leading down to Agostino di Duccio's colourful **Oratorio di San Bernardino**, whose richly embellished facade is by far the best piece of sculpture in the city. From here you can wander through the northern part of the centre, along Via A. Pascoli, to the **Arco di Augusto**, whose lowest section is now one of the few remaining monuments of Etruscan Perugia. On the other side of town, along **Corso Cavour**, is the large church of **San Domenico**, one of whose chapels holds a superb carved arch by Agostino di Duccio, and, to the right of the altar, the tomb of Pope Benedict XI. In the church's cloisters, the **Museo Archeologico Nazionale dell'Umbria** (Mon 2.30–7.30pm, Tues–Sun 8.30am–7.30pm; €2) has one of the most extensive Etruscan collections around. Further down Corso Cavour, the esoteric **Orto Medievale** (daily 10am–6.30pm; free) is a unique window into the significance of the medieval garden.

   Trains arrive well away from the centre of Perugia on Piazza V. Veneto; buses #6, #7, #9, #11, #13d, #13s or #15 make the fifteen-minute journey to Piazza Italia or Piazza Matteotti. The **tourist office** is on Piazza IV Novembre 3 (Mon–Sat 8.30am–1.30pm & 3.30–6.30pm, Sun 9am–1pm; ☎075.573.6458). There are two **HI hostels**: *Spagnoli*, near the station on Via Cortonese 4 (☎075.501.1366; €14), and *Torri Baldelli Mombelli* at Via Manicomi (☎075.591.3991; €14; bus #8 or #16). As for **hotels**, try *Rosalba*, at Via del Circo 7 (☎075.572.0626; ❺); *Etruria*, just off the Corso at Via della Luna 21 (☎075.572.3730; ❸); or *Anna*, centrally placed at Via dei Priori 48 (☎075.573.6304; ❹). On the **food** front, *Osteria del Gambero*, Via Baldeschi 17 (closed Mon), has Umbrian specialities, and *La Botte*, Via Volte della Pace 33 (closed Sun), is a decent pizzeria. *Papaya*, Via dei Priori 7, is a good bar with plenty of seating and decent *panini*. The reasonably priced *Dal mi' Cocco*, Corso Garibaldi 12 (closed Mon), with a student clientele, offers traditional cuisine. *Bratislava*, Via Fiorenzuola 12, near Corso Cavour, whch has **live music** on selected nights, and *Caffè Morlacchi*, Piazza Morlacchi 6–8, features live jazz. There's **Internet access** at Internet Point, Via Ulisse Rocchi 4.

Gubbio

For a day-trip from Perugia, take the bus (about ten a day, last 8pm; €4) to **GUBBIO**, the most thoroughly medieval of Umbrian towns, holding onto its charm despite an ever-increasing influx of tourists. Centre-stage on the windswept Piazza della Signoria is the immense fourteenth-century **Palazzo dei Consoli** (daily 10am–1pm & 2/3–5/6pm), whose crenellated outline and campanile command your attention for miles around. Council officials and leading citizens met to discuss business here in the cavernous Salone dell'Arengo, from which the word "harangue" is derived. The building holds the **Museo Civico** (Tues–Sun same times; €4.50), unremarkable except for the famous Eugubine Tablets, Umbria's most important archeological find and the only extant record of the ancient Umbrian language. On the hillside above town, the **Basilica of Sant'Ubaldo** is the place Gubbians drive to on Sunday mornings, a pleasant spot with a handy bar and great views, connected with the town's Porta Romana by a slightly scary **funicular** (€5 return). Both *Locanda del Duca*, Via Piccardi 3, and *Grotta dell'Angelo*, Via Gioia 47, have excellent **restaurants**, though to eat outdoors, try the popular *Trattoria di San Martino*, Via dei Consoli 8 (closed Tues).

Assisi

Thanks to St Francis, Italy's premier saint and founder of the Franciscan order, **ASSISI** is Umbria's best-known town, crammed with people for ten months of the year. But it has a medieval hill-town charm and quietens down in the evening. An earthquake in 1997 caused extensive damage to parts of the town, most notably to the Basilica di San Francesco, but restoration is now complete and the basilica is, mercifully, almost back to its original splendour. The **Basilica di San Francesco** at the end of Via San Francesco (daily 6.30am–7.30pm; ⓦ www.sanfrancescoassisi.org) is justly famed as Umbria's single greatest glory, and one of the most overwhelming collections of art outside a gallery anywhere in the world. Begun in 1228, two years after the saint's death, it was financed by donations that flooded in from all over the world. The sombre **Lower Church** is the earlier of the two churches that make up the basilica, its complicated floor plan and claustrophobic vaults intended to create a mood of meditative introspection. Francis lies under the floor in a crypt only brought to light in 1818. Frescoes cover almost every available space, and span a century of continuous artistic development, from the anonymous early works above the altar, through Cimabue's *Madonna, Child and Angels with St Francis* in the right transept to work by the Sienese School painters, Simone Martini and Pietro Lorenzetti. The **Upper Church**, built to a light and airy Gothic plan, is richly decorated, too, with dazzling frescoes on the life of St Francis, some of which at least are considered to be the work of Giotto. There's not a great deal else to see in Assisi's small centre, though a short trek up the steep Via di San Rufino leads to the thirteenth-century **Duomo**, which has the font used to baptize St Francis and St Clare. Close by is the **Basilica di Santa Chiara**, a virtual facsimile of the basilica up the road and home to the macabre blackened body of Clare herself.

Assisi's **train station** is 5km south of town, connected to it by half-hourly buses. The **tourist office**, Piazza del Comune 12 (Mon–Sat 8am–6.30pm, Sun 10am–1pm & 2–5pm; ⓣ075.812.450), has details of **private rooms**. Otherwise, the functional *Italia*, off the central Piazza del Comune at Vicolo della Fortezza 2 (ⓣ075.812.625; ❸; closed Dec–Feb), is about the cheapest place to stay, while *La Rocca*, Via Porta Perlici 27 (ⓣ075.812.284; ❹), and the *Anfiteatro Romano*, close by at Via Anfiteatro Romano 4 (ⓣ075.813.025; ❸), are also fair bets for **hotels**. There are pilgrim **hostels** (*Case Religiose di Ospitalità*) all over town: the *Suore del Giglio*, Via San Francesco 13 (ⓣ075.816.258; ❸), is the best for location. There's a big **campsite** and **hostel** at Fontemaggio (ⓣ075.813.636; €18;

bus #20 or #34l), 3km out on the road to the monastery of Eremo delle Carceriis ; and the official **HI hostel**, *Ostello della Pace*, at Via di Valecchie (☎075.816.767; €14). For **food**, try the reasonably priced pizzeria, *Il Pozzo Romano*, on Via Sant'Agnese near Santa Chiara (closed Thurs); *Pallotta*, Via San Rufino 4 (closed Tues); or *I Monaci*, Via A Fortini 10, off Via Fontebella on the Scaletti del Metastasio (closed Wed). Otherwise, the *La Rocca* hotel (see above) has a good no-frills restaurant.

Spoleto

SPOLETO is Umbria's most compelling town, remarkable for its extremely pretty position and several of Italy's most ancient Romanesque churches. The lower town, where you arrive, was badly damaged by World War II bombing, and doesn't hold much of interest, so it's best to take a bus straight to the upper town. There's no single, central piazza, but the place to head for is **Piazza Libertà**, site of a much-restored first-century **Roman Theatre**, visible at all times, but also visitable more closely in conjunction with the **Museo Archeologico** (Mon–Sat 9am–7pm, Sun 9am–1pm; €2). The adjoining **Piazza della Fontana** has more Roman remains, best of which is the **Arco di Druso**, built to honour the minor campaign victories of Drusus, son of Tiberius. The homely **Piazza del Mercato**, beyond, is a fine opportunity to take in some streetlife, and from there it's a short walk to the **Duomo**, whose facade of restrained elegance is one of the most memorable in the region. Inside, various Baroque embellishments are eclipsed by the superlative apse frescoes of the fifteenth-century Florentine artist Fra Lippo Lippi, dominated by his final masterpiece, a *Coronation of the Virgin*. He died shortly after their completion (amid rumours that he was poisoned for seducing the daughter of a local noble family) and was interred here in a tomb designed by his son, Filippino. You should also take the short walk out to the **Ponte delle Torri**, a picture-postcard favourite, and an astonishing piece of medieval engineering, best seen as part of a circular walk around the base of the **Rocca** – everyone's idea of a cartoon castle, with towers, crenellations and sheer walls.

Spoleto's **train station** is 1km north of the town centre, with the **tourist office** on central Piazza della Libertà (daily 9/10am–1pm & 4–7pm; ☎0743.238.920). For **accommodation**, best budget choice is the central and reasonably priced *Pensione dell'Angelo*, Via Arco del Druso 25 (☎0743.222.385; ❹). If that's full, then the only other vaguely affordable place in the upper town is the *Pensione Aurora*, off Piazza Libertà at Via dell'Apollinare 3 (☎0743.220.315; ❻). The lower town is very much a second choice, although its hotel-like **hostel**, *Villa Redenta*, Via di Villa Redenta 1, in the converted stables of a seventeenth century villa (☎0743.22.49.36; €13–25), is a real bargain. The closest **campsite** is the tiny but very pleasant *Camping Monteluco*, behind San Pietro (☎0743.220.358; closed Oct–March). Best basic **trattoria** is *Trattoria del Festival*, Via Brignone 8 (closed Fri); *Il Panciolle*, Via del Duomo 3–4 (closed Wed), is also a popular choice. If you are staying in the lower town, head for *Dei Pini*, Via 3 Settembre (closed Mon), near the hostel, for authentic home cooking at bargain prices.

Orvieto

Out on a limb from the rest of Umbria, **ORVIETO** is flooded with tourists in summer, most of whom are drawn by its **Duomo**, one of the greatest Gothic buildings in Italy. It was built, according to tradition, to celebrate the so-called Miracle of Bolsena (1263), in which a doubting priest celebrating Mass in a church on the nearby Lago di Bolsena noticed real blood dripping from the Host onto the altar cloth. The stained linen was whisked off to Pope Urban IV, who was in Orvieto to escape the heat and political hassle of Rome, and the building was constructed over the ensuing three centuries, in a surprisingly unified example of the Romanesque-Gothic style. The star turn is the facade, a riot of columns, spires, bas-reliefs, sculptures and dazzling colour, just about held together by four enormous fluted columns, the work of the master mason Lorenzo Maitini and his pupils, describing episodes from the Old and New Testaments in staggering detail. Inside, the church is surprisingly plain by comparison, mainly distinguished by the **Cappella di San Brizio** (Mon–Sat 10am–12.45pm & 2.30–6/7.15pm, Sun 2.30–5.45pm; €3; tickets from the tourist office), which holds Luca Signorelli's fresco of the *Last Judgement*, a realistic yet grotesque work, full of beautifully observed muscular figures that greatly influenced Michelangelo's celebrated cycle in the Vatican's Sistine Chapel. Signorelli, suitably clad in black, includes himself with Fra Angelico in the lower left-hand corner of *The Sermon of the Antichrist*, both calmly looking on as someone is garrotted at their feet. The twin Cappella del Corporale contains the sacred *corporale* (altar cloth) itself, locked away in a massive, jewel-encrusted casket (an accurate facsimile of the facade). Moving north up Via del Duomo, you come to **Corso Cavour**, the town's pedestrianized main drag, at the far end of which, across Piazza Cahen, is **Il Pozzo di San Patrizio** (daily 10am–6.45pm; €3.50), the novelty act of the town, a huge cylindrical well, commissioned in 1527 by Pope Clement VII to guarantee the town's water supply during an expected siege by the imperial army. It's a dank but striking piece of engineering, named after its alleged similarity to the Irish cave where St Patrick died in 493, supposedly aged 133.

Bus #1 makes a regular trip from the distant **train station** to Piazza XXIX Marzo, a short way north of the Duomo. A more charming alternative is the **funicular** up to Piazza Cahen, from where minibuses wind through the twisting streets to Piazza del Duomo. The **tourist office** is at Piazza del Duomo 24 (Mon–Fri 8.15am–2pm & 4–7pm, Sat & Sun 10am–6pm; ☎0763.341.772, ⊛www.comune .orvieto.tr.it). Of **hotels**, try the pleasant *Posta*, Via Luca Signorelli 18 (☎0763.341.909; ❹). Orvieto also has several religious foundations that rent out rooms, including the *Istituto SS Salvatore*, Via del Popolo 1 (☎0763.342.910; ❹), and *Villa Mercede* at Via Soliana 2 (☎0763.341.766; ❹). The central **hostel**, *Porziuncola*, is very small and located at Loc. Cappuccini 8 (☎0763.341.387; €11). There's a group of cheap **restaurants** at the bottom of Corso Cavour, though the best-value eating is close to the Duomo, at Via Maitani 15, a canteen affair run by a co-operative, offering a choice between a restaurant and self-service trattoria (closed Sun). *La Grotta*, Via Signorelli 5, off Via del Duomo (closed Mon), is a standard, friendly trattoria, and the *Antico Bucchero*, Via de' Cartari 4, is a popular restaurant with reasonable prices (closed Wed). The *Bottega del Buon Vino*, Via della Cave 26, is a wine **bar** that's good for staples and has a few outside tables.

Urbino

For the second half of the fifteenth century, **URBINO** was one of the most prestigious courts in Europe, ruled by the remarkable Federico da Montefeltro, who employed a number of the greatest artists and architects of the time to build and decorate his palace in the town. These days, however, it is notable mainly for its excellent museums; the best time to go is mid-week when the university students are around. In the centre of town, the **Palazzo Ducale** is a fitting monument to

Federico, home now to the **Galleria Nazionale delle Marche** (Mon 8.30am–2pm, Tues–Sun 8.30am–7.15pm; €4), although it's the building itself that makes the biggest impression. Among the paintings in the Appartamento del Duca are Piero della Francesca's strange *Flagellation*, and the *Ideal City*, a famous perspective painting of a symmetrical and deserted cityscape long attributed to Piero but now thought to be by one of his followers. The most interesting and best preserved of the palazzo's rooms is Federico's **Studiolo**, a triumph of illusory perspective created by intarsia (wood inlaid as mosaic) - shelves appear to protrude from the walls, cupboard doors seem to swing open to reveal lines of books, a letter lies in an apparently half-open drawer. Even more remarkable are the delicately hued landscapes of Urbino as it might appear from one of the surrounding hills, and the life-like squirrel perching next to a bowl of fruit. Urbino's pleasant jumble of Renaissance and medieval houses is a welcome antidote to the rarefied atmosphere of the Palazzo Ducale. You can wind down in one of the many bars and trattorias, or take a picnic up to the gardens within the **Fortezza Albornoz**, from where you'll get great views of the town and the countryside, out to **San Bernardino**, a fine Renaissance church 2km away that is the resting place of the Montefeltros.

Urbino is notoriously difficult to reach – the best approach is by **bus** from Pésaro, about 30km away on the coast (last around 8pm; €2). Buses stop in Borgo Mercatale, at the foot of the Palazzo Ducale, which is reached either by lift or by Francesco di Giorgio Martini's spiral staircase. For accommodation, the cheapest options are **private rooms**, most of which are on Via Budassi – lists are available from the **tourist office** on Piazza Rinascimento (Mon–Sat 9am–1pm & 3–6pm, Sun 9am–1pm; ☎0722.2613, ⊛www.comune.urbino.ps.it). The most convenient **hotels** are the *Italia*, Corso Garibaldi 32 (☎0722.2701; ❺), and the slightly dingy *San Giovanni*, Via Barocci 13 (☎0722.2827; ❸; closed July). The best deals for **food** are at the university mensa on Piazza San Filippo, or the *Bar Caffe degli Angeli*, Borgo Mercenate 21/22, which does great *panini* and nibbles. For **restaurants** try the friendly *Il Cantuccio*, Via Budassi 64, where the *strozzapreti* pasta is delicious, or, if your budget's not too tight, *La Taverna degli Artisti*, Via Bramante 52, which serves tasty local dishes. At aperitif time the most popular haunts are the **cafés** around Piazza della Repubblica: *Cocktail & Drink* has a buzzing upstairs lounge and lively music. Later on try the friendly bar *L'Isola*, Via dei Veterani 18, for a quiet drink. Urbino's beautiful people can be found in the disco-pub *Bus Bar*, Via Nazionale Bocca Trabaria 6, a half-hour walk out of the centre.

Rome (Roma)

Of all Italy's historic cities, **ROME** (Roma) exerts the most compelling fascination. For the traveller, it is the sheer weight of history in the city that is most evident, its various eras crowding in on each other to an almost breathtaking degree. There are the classical features – the Colosseum, the Forum and spectacular Palatine Hill – and relics from the early Christian period in ancient basilicas; while the fountains and churches of the Baroque period go a long way to determining the look of the city centre. But there are also swathes of Fascist-era concrete palaces, and even the occasional modern masterpiece such as Renzo Piano's acclaimed new Auditorium. Rome has a vibrant, chaotic life of its own, the crowded streets thronged with traffic, locals, tourists and students. The city has also become much more multicultural in recent years, and different areas have taken on particular ethnic characters. And whether you join in the various social and cultural events, attend the free music festivals, or socialize outdoors during the evening *passeggiata* along Via del Corso, around Campo dei Fiori and on the Spanish Steps, there's always the city to provide a seamlessly beautiful backdrop.

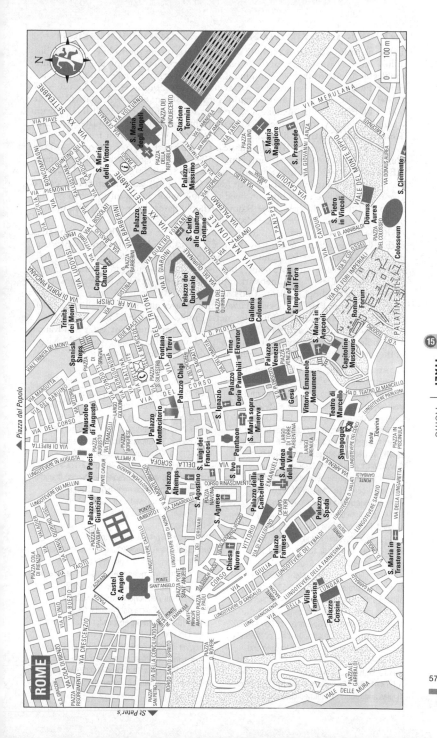

ROME

N

▲ Piazza del Popolo

VIA XX SETTEMBRE
VIA PIAVE
VIA VENETO
S. Maria degli Angeli
PIAZZA DEI CINQUECENTO
Stazione Termini
S. Maria della Vittoria
i
Palazzo Massimo
S. Maria Maggiore
S. Prassede
S. Clemente
Palazzo Barberini
Capuchin Church
S. Carlo alle Quattro Fontane
Domus Aurea
S. Pietro in Vincoli
Palazzo del Quirinale
VIA NAZIONALE
VIA CAVOUR
Colosseum
Trinità dei Monti
Fontana di Trevi
Galleria Colonna
Forum of Trajan & Imperial Fora
Roman Forum
PALATINE HILL
Spanish Steps
Palazzo Chigi
Time Elevator
Palazzo Doria Pamphilj
S. Maria in Aracoeli
Capitoline Museums
Mausoleo di Augusto
Palazzo Montecitorio
S. Ignazio
Palazzo Venezia
Gesù
Vittorio Emanuele Monument
Ara Pacis
S. Maria sopra Minerva
Pantheon
Teatro di Marcello
Palazzo di Giustizia
Palazzo Altemps
S. Luigi dei Francesi
S. Ivo
Synagogue
Isola Tiberina
S. Agostino
S. Agnese
Palazzo della Cancelleria
S. Andrea della Valle
Castel S. Angelo
Chiesa Nuova
CORSO VITTORIO EMANUELE
Palazzo Farnese
Palazzo Spada
CAMPO DE' FIORI
S. Maria in Trastevere
Villa Farnesina
Palazzo Corsini

0 100 m

▲ St Peter's

15

ITALY | Rome

573

Arrival, information and accommodation

The main **train station** is Termini, meeting-point of the metro lines and city bus routes. Rome has two **airports**: Leonardo da Vinci, better known as Fiumicino, handles all scheduled flights; Ciampino is for charter services only. Two train services link Fiumicino to Rome: one to Termini (every 30min; €8.80), the other to Trastevere, Ostiense and Tiburtina stations (every 20min; €4.70). A taxi will cost at least €40. From Ciampino, take a Cotral bus to Anagnina on metro line A, from where it's a twenty-minute metro ride to Termini. Information is available from the **Tourist Call Centre** (daily 9am–7pm; ☎06.3600.4399), which has up-to-the-minute information in five languages; the **tourist information** booth at Fiumicino airport (Mon–Sat 8am–7pm; ☎06.6595.4471); and the **main tourist office** at Via Parigi 5 (Mon–Sat 9am–7pm; ☎06.4889.9200). There are also information kiosks dotted around the city (daily 9am–6pm.) Various **museum cards** give reduced or free entry, but you need to know what you want to see to get the best out of them – the best is the Roma Archeologia card, for ancient sites including the Colosseum and Palatine (€20/7 days).

The best way to get around Rome is to **walk**. That said, **public transport** is both reliable and cheap. A day pass (BIG; €3.10) can be bought from any newspaper stall or *tabaccaio*, or from the ATAC booth on Piazza dei Cinquecento, where they also sell decent transport maps. The buses and the metro stop around 11.30pm (Sat 12.30pm), after which a network of **night buses** takes over, serving most parts of the city until about 5.30am. **Taxis** are costly; hail one in the street, or try the ranks at Termini, Piazza Venezia, Piazza San Silvestro; alternatively call ☎06.3570, 06.5551 or 06.6645 to book one. The meter should start at €2.33.

In summer Rome is very crowded, so book **accommodation** as far in advance as possible. If you can't, make straight for the tourist office to save your legs. Many of the city's cheaper hotels are handily located close to Termini station.

Hostels & religious houses

Alessandro Via Vicenza 42 ☎06.446.1958, ⓦ www.hostelalessandro.com. Friendly, international staff, full use of kitchen. No curfew. €20–27.

Colors Via Boezio 31 ☎06.687.4030, ⓦ www.colorshotel.com. In Prati, near St Peter's. Clean, friendly, good value, use of kitchen. €20.

Fawlty Towers Via Magenta 39 ☎06.445.4802, ⓦ www.fawltytowers.org. Near the station, efficient, clean, with all amenities, including Internet, kitchen use, satellite TV. €20–25.

Hotel Ottaviano Via Ottaviano 6 ☎06.3973.7253, ⓦ www.pensioneottaviano.com. Excellently situated, friendly private hotel/hostel, just outside the Vatican walls. Metro line Ottaviano. €20.

Hotel Sandy Via Cavour 136 ☎06.488.4585, ⓦ www.sandyhostel.com. Good-value, central young people's hotel/hostel. Metro Cavour. €18.

Marello Via Urbana 50 ☎06.482.5361. Run by the oblates of St Joseph, this place has singles and doubles, many en suite. Very central. €27.

M&J Place Hostel Via Solferino 9 ☎06.446.2802, ⓦ www.mejplacehostel.com. Just out of the station and to the right; facilities include kitchen and Internet access. €20–24.

Nostra Signora di Lourdes Via Sistina 113 ☎06.474.5324. Convent near the Spanish Steps, singles and rooms for married couples; 10.30

curfew. €30–36.

Ostello del Foro Italico Viale delle Olimpiadi 61 ☎06.324.2571, ⓦ www.hostelbooking.com. Rome's vast HI hostel. Breakfast included. Midnight curfew. Metro Ottaviano, then bus #32. €16.

Suore Pie Operaie Via di Torre Argentina 76 ☎06.686.1254. Superbly located convent, though with 10.30pm curfew. Closed Aug. €24.

YWCA Via C. Balbo 4 ☎06.488.3917. For all travellers, and more conveniently situated than the HI hostel; 10min walk from Termini. Breakfast included (not Sun). Midnight curfew. €26–74.

Hotels

Campo de' Fiori Via del Biscione 6 ☎06.6880.6865, ⓦ www.hotelcampodefiori.com. Friendly, clean, colourful place, beautiful views over the medieval quarter from its roof terrace. ❼

Davos Via degli Scipioni 239, ☎06.321.7012. Simple, clean *pensione*. Metro Lepanto. ❻

Della Lunetta Piazza del Paradiso 68 ☎06.686.1080. An unspectacular hotel but in a great location. ❻

Katty Via Palestro 35 ☎06.490.079. One of the cheaper, more pleasant options east of the station. ❹

Monaco Via Flavia 84 ☎06.474.4335. Very welcoming and clean; between the station and Via Veneto. ❻

Perugia Via del Colosseo 7 ☎ 06.679.7200. On a peaceful but central street. Breakfast included. Metro Colosseo. **7**
Rosetta Via Cavour 295 ☎ 06.4782.3069. Nice location close to the Colosseum. Metro Colosseo. **6**

Trastevere Via Luciano Manara 24a ☎ 06.581.4713, ⓦ www.hoteltrastevere.com. Handily located for the nightlife of Trastevere – ask for "camere esterne" which are basic but much cheaper than the main hotel. **5**

The City

Rome's city centre is divided neatly into distinct blocks. The warren of streets that makes up the **centro storico** (historic centre) occupies the hook of land on the east bank of the River Tiber, bordered to the east by Via del Corso and to the north and south by water. From here, Rome's central core spreads east: across Via del Corso to the major shopping streets and alleys around the **Spanish Steps** and on down to the main artery of Via Nazionale; and south to the major sites of the **Roman Forum** and **Palatine Hill**. The west bank of the river is oddly distanced from the main hum of the city, home to the **Vatican** and **St Peter's** and, to the south of these, **Trastevere** – even in ancient times a distinct entity from the city proper, as well as nowadays a focus of nightlife.

The Capitoline Hill and around

The best place to start a tour of Rome is the **Capitoline Hill**, formerly the spiritual and political centre of the Roman Empire, which hides beind the Neoclassical Vittorio Emmanuele Monument on the traffic-choked Piazza Venezia. The Capitoline is home to one of Rome's most elegant squares, **Piazza del Campidoglio**, designed by Michelangelo in the 1550s for Pope Paul III, and flanked by the two branches of one of the city's most important museums of antique art – the **Capitoline Museums** (Tues–Sun 9am–8pm; €6.20). On the left, the **Palazzo Nuovo** concentrates on some of the best of the city's Roman and Greek sculpture, and on Renaissance painting, including Caravaggio's *St John the Baptist*. Behind the square, a road skirts the Forum down to the small church of **San Giuseppe dei Falegnami**, built above the prison where St Peter is said to have been held – you can see the bars to which he was chained, along with the spring the saint is said to have created in which to baptize other prisoners. At the top of the staircase is an imprint claimed to be of St Peter's head as he was tumbled down the stairs.

Via del Plebiscito forges west from Piazza Venezia past the church of **Gesù**, a high, wide Baroque church of the Jesuit order, notable for the richness of its interior. Crossing over, streets wind down to **Piazza di Campo dei Fiori**, home to a morning market and surrounded by bars. South of the Campo, at the end of Via dei Balestrari, the **Galleria Spada** (Tues–Sun 8.30am–7.30pm; €5) is decorated in the manner of a Roman noble family and displays a small collection of paintings, best of which are a couple of portraits by Reni. To the left off the courtyard is a crafty *trompe l'oeil* tunnel by Borromini, whose trick perspective makes it appear four times its actual length. Across Via Arenula, through and beyond the Jewish Ghetto, the broad open space of **Piazza della Bocca di Verità** is home to two of the city's better-preserved Roman temples, the **Temple of Fortuna Virilis** and the circular **Temple of Hercules Victor**, both of which date from the end of the second century BC. However, the church of **Santa Maria in Cosmedin**, on the far side of the square, is more interesting, a typically Roman medieval basilica with a huge marble altar and an ingenious Cosmati mosaic floor – one of the city's finest. Outside in the portico, the Bocca di Verità gives the square its name, an ancient Roman drain cover in the shape of an enormous face that tradition says will swallow the hand of anyone who doesn't tell the truth.

The Centro Storico

You need to walk a little way northwest from the Capitoline Hill to find the real city centre of Rome, the **Centro Storico**, circled by a bend in the Tiber, above

Corso Vittorio Emanuele. The old Campus Martius of Roman times, it later became the heart of the Renaissance city, and is now an unruly knot of narrow streets holding some of the best of Rome's classical and Baroque heritage, as well as much of its nightlife.

The boundary of the historic centre to the east, **Via del Corso**, is Rome's main shopping street. Walking north from Piazza Venezia, the first building on the left is the **Galleria Doria Pamphili** (10am–5pm; closed Thurs & last half of Aug; €7.30), one of many galleries housed in palaces belonging to Roman patrician families. Its collection includes Rome's best cache of Dutch and Flemish paintings, canvases by Caravaggio and Velázquez's painting of Pope Innocent X. Five minutes from here is the **Pantheon** (daily 8.30/9am–6.30pm; free) on Piazza della Rotonda, the most complete ancient Roman structure in the city, finished around 125 AD. Inside, the diameter of the dome and height of the building are precisely equal, and the hole in the dome's centre is a full 9m across; there are no visible arches or vaults to hold the whole thing up; instead, they're sunk into the concrete of the walls of the building. It would have been richly decorated – the coffered ceiling was covered in solid bronze until the seventeenth century, and the niches were filled with statues of the gods. There's more artistic splendour on view behind the Pantheon in **Santa Maria sopra Minerva**, one of the city's art-treasure churches, crammed with the tombs and gifts of wealthy Roman families. Of these, the Carafa chapel, in the south transept, is the best known, holding Filippino Lippi's fresco of *The Assumption*. You should look, too, at the figure of *Christ Bearing the Cross*, on the left-hand side of the main altar, a serene work painted for the church by Michelangelo in 1521.

In the opposite direction from the Pantheon, **Piazza Navona** is the most appealing square in Rome, and follows the lines of the Emperor Domitian's chariot arena. Pope Innocent X built most of the grandiose palaces that surround it in the seventeenth century and commissioned Borromini to design the church of **Sant'Agnese** on the west side. The church, typically squeezed into the tightest of spaces by Borromini, supposedly stands on the spot where St Agnes, exposed naked to the public in the stadium, miraculously grew hair to cover herself. The **Fontana dei Quattro Fiumi** opposite, one of three that punctuate the square, is by Borromini's arch-rival, Bernini; each figure represents one of the four great rivers of the world – the Nile, Danube, Ganges and Plate – though only the horse, symbolizing the Danube, was actually carved by Bernini himself.

Just out of the north end, you'll find **Palazzo Altemps** (Tues–Sun 9am–7pm; €5), functioning as part of the Museo Nazionale Romano and featuring the unmissable ancient statuary collected by the Ludovisi family. The highlight is the original fifth-century-BC Greek throne, embellished with a delicate relief of the birth of Aphrodite. Down Via della Scrofa, in the French national church of **San Luigi dei Francesi**, there's early work by Caravaggio describing the life and martyrdom of St Matthew – Matthew is the dissolute-looking youth on the far left, illuminated by a shaft of sunlight. A little way up Via della Ripetta from here, the **Ara Pacis Augustae** (closed for restoration) was built in 13 BC to celebrate Augustus' victory over Spain and Gaul. It supports a fragmented frieze showing Augustus himself, his wife Livia, Tiberius, Agrippa, and various children clutching the togas of the elders, the last of whom is said to be the young Claudius.

At the far end of Via di Ripetta the **Piazza del Popolo** provides an impressive entrance to the city, all symmetry and grand vistas, although its real attraction is the church of **Santa Maria del Popolo**, which holds some of the best Renaissance art of any Roman church. Two pictures by Caravaggio get most attention – the *Conversion of St Paul* and the *Crucifixion of St Peter*.

The Spanish Steps, Palazzo Barberini and Trevi fountain

The area immediately southeast of Piazza del Popolo is travellers' Rome, historically the artistic quarter of the city, with a distinctly cosmopolitan air. At the centre of the district, **Piazza di Spagna** is a long, thin square centring on the distinctive boat-shaped Barcaccia fountain, the last work of Bernini's father. The **Spanish Steps** – a venue for international posing – sweep up from the piazza to the **Trinità dei Monti**, a sixteenth-century church that holds a couple of works by Daniel da Volterra, notably a soft flowing fresco of *The Assumption* in the third chapel on the right, which includes a portrait of his teacher Michelangelo.

From the church, follow Via Sistina to **Piazza Barberini**, a busy traffic junction, in the centre of which is Bernini's Fontana del Tritone. Via Veneto bends north from here, its pricey bars and restaurants once the haunt of Rome's "beautiful people" but now the home of high-class tack. A little way up, the Capuchin **Church of the Immaculate Conception** is worth visiting for its cemetery (9am–noon & 3–6pm, closed Thurs; donation requested); the bones of four thousand monks line the walls of a series of chapels in rococo patterns or as fully clothed skeletons, their faces peering out of their cowls in expressions of agony.

Back across Piazza Barberini, the **Palazzo Barberini** contains the **Galleria d'Arte Antica** (Tues–Sun 9am–7pm; closed winter; €5; book on ☏06.328.101), which displays a rich patchwork of mainly Italian art from the early Renaissance to late Baroque period. In addition to canvases by Tintoretto, Titian and El Greco, highlights include Filippo Lippi's warmly maternal *Madonna and Child*, painted in 1437, and Raphael's beguiling *Fornarina*. But perhaps the most impressive feature of the gallery is the building itself, the epitome of Baroque grandeur worked on at different times by the most favoured architects of the day: Bernini, Borromini and Maderno. West down Via del Tritone from Piazza Barberini, hidden among a tight web of narrow, apparently aimless streets, is one of Rome's more surprising sights – the **Fontane di Trevi**, a huge Baroque gush of water over statues and rocks built onto the back of a Renaissance palace, that can barely be seen for the crowds.

Piazza della Repubblica and Museo Nazionale Romano

Via Nazionale, one of Rome's main shopping streets, lined with boutiques, leads up to **Piazza della Repubblica**, a stern but rather tawdry semicircle of buildings that occupies part of the site of Diocletian's Baths, the scanty remains of which lie across the square in the church of **Santa Maria degli Angeli**. Michelangelo is also said to have had a hand in modifying another part of the baths, the courtyard that makes up part of the **Museo Nazionale Romano** behind the church (Tues–Sun 9am-7.45pm; €9). The museum's collection of Greek and Roman antiquities is second only to the Vatican's and is now partly housed in the Palazzo Altemps, Palazzo Braschi and the Palazzo Massimo across the square at Piazza dei Cinquecento 68, a recently restored building featuring a series of Roman busts, mosaics and fresco fragments. The top floor gallery contains stunning, sylvan frescoes from a country villa that belonged to the emperor Augustus's wife Livia, and some of the best examples of mosaics from Roman villas around the world.

The Forum, Palatine Hill, Colosseum and around

In ancient times, the **Roman Forum, Palatine Hill and Colosseum** (Tues–Sun 9am–6pm/1hr before sunset; forum free, rest €8) formed the centre of what was a very large city. Following the downfall of the city to various barbarian invaders, the area was left in ruin, its relics quarried for construction in other parts of Rome during medieval and Renaissance times.

Running through the core of the Forum, the **Via Sacra** was the best-known street of ancient Rome. At the bottom of the Capitoline Hill, the **Arch of Septimus Severus** was built in the early third century AD to commemorate the emperor's tenth anniversary in power, and the grassy, wide-open scatter of paving and beached columns in front of it was the place where most of the life of the city took place. At the nearby **Curia** - begun in 80 BC, restored by Julius Caesar, and rebuilt by Diocletian in the third century AD - the Senate met during the

Republican period, and augurs would come to announce the wishes of the gods. On the opposite side is the **House of the Vestal Virgins**, where lived the six women charged with the responsibility of keeping the sacred flame of Vesta alight. On the far side of the site, the **Basilica of Constantine and Maxentius** is probably the Forum's most impressive remains. It's said that Michelangelo studied the hexagonal coffered arches here when grappling with the dome of St Peter's. From the basilica, the Via Sacra climbs to the **Arch of Titus** on a low arm of the Palatine Hill – its reliefs showing the spoils of the sacking of Jerusalem being carried off by eager Romans.

Turning right at the Arch of Titus takes you up to the **Palatine Hill**, now a stunningly beautiful archeological garden. In the days of the Republic, the Palatine was the most desirable address in Rome (from it is derived our word "palace"). The gargantuan **Domus Augustana** spreads to the far brink of the hill and you can look down from here onto its vast central courtyard and maze-like fountain, and wander through a handful of its bare rooms. From close by, steps lead down to the **Cryptoporticus**, a passage built by Nero to link the Palatine with his palace on the far side of the Colosseum, and decorated along part of its length with well-preserved Roman stuccowork. A left turn leads to the **House of Livia**, originally believed to have been the residence of the wife of Augustus, whose courtyard and rooms are decorated with scanty frescoes. Turn right down the passage and up some steps and you're in the **Farnese Gardens**, laid out by Alessandro Farnese in the mid-sixteenth century and now a tidily planted refuge from the exposed heat of the ruins. The terrace here looks back over the Forum, while the terrace at the opposite end looks down on the real centre of Rome's ancient beginning – an Iron Age hut, known as the **House of Romulus**, the best preserved part of a ninth-century village, and the so-called **Lupercal**, beyond, which tradition says was the cave where Romulus and Remus were suckled by the she-wolf.

Immediately outside the Forum, the fourth-century **Arch of Constantine** marks the end of the Via Sacra. Across from here, the **Colosseum** is Rome's most awe-inspiring ancient monument, begun by the Emperor Vespasian around 72 AD and finished by his son Titus about eight years later – an event celebrated by 100 days of games. The Romans flocked here for gladiatorial contests and cruel spectacles - they even had mock sea battles, as the arena could be flooded in minutes. After the games were outlawed in the fifth century, the Colosseum was pillaged for building material, and is now little more than a shell. The structure of the place is still easy to see, however, and has served as a model for stadia around the world ever since.

Close by is Nero's **Domus Aurea** (daily 9am–8pm, €5; booking fee €1 ⊕06.3996.7700), whose entrance is opposite the Colosseum, off Via Labicana, a short walk up some steps on the Oppian Hill. Built by Nero as his private house, the palace covered a full square mile and its extravagant halls were decorated in the most lavish style, though little remains today. Stripped of its marble decor and filled with rubble after Nero's death, when the site was first rediscovered hundreds of years later it was thought to be some sort of mystical cave or grotto. It's a short walk from here down to the church of **San Clemente**, a light, twelfth-century basilica that encapsulates the continuity of history in the city. The ground-floor church is a superb example of a medieval basilica, with some fine mosaics; downstairs (€3), there's the nave of an earlier church, dated back to 392 AD; and at the eastern end and down another level are the remains of a Roman apartment building – a labyrinthine set of rooms including a Mithraic temple of the late second century. The same street leads to the basilica of **San Giovanni in Laterano**, Rome's cathedral and the seat of the pope until the Unification of Italy. There has been a church on this site since the fourth century, and the present building, reworked by Borromini in the mid-seventeenth century, evokes Rome's staggering wealth of history. The doors were taken from the Curia of the Roman Forum. Inside, the first pillar on the left of the right-hand aisle shows a fragment of Giotto's fresco of Boniface VIII, proclaiming the first Holy Year in 1300, while further on, a monument commemorating Sylvester I (bishop of Rome during much of Constantine's reign) incorporates part of his original tomb, said to sweat and rattle its bones when a pope is about to die. Behind the papal altar are the reliquaries for the heads of saints Peter and Paul, though the relics themselves were stolen in the early 1800s. The **Baptistery** is the oldest surviving in the Christian world, an octagonal structure built by Constantine, rebuilt during the fifth century, and now carefully restored after a 1993 car bomb damaged the stonework and some of the frescoes. On the other side of the church the **Scala Santa** is claimed to be the staircase from Pontius Pilate's house down which Christ walked after his trial. The 28 steps are protected by boards, and the only way you're allowed to climb them is on your knees.

On the far side of the road from the Colosseum, the main feature of interest on the Esquiline Hill is the church of **San Pietro in Vincoli**, built to house the chains of St Peter from his imprisonment in Jerusalem, along with those that bound him when a prisoner in Rome. These can still be seen in the glass case on the altar, but most people come for Michelangelo's unfinished Tomb of Pope Julius II in the southern aisle. The figure of Moses, pictured as descended from Sinai to find the Israelites worshipping the golden calf, and flanked by the gentle figures of Leah and Rachel, is one of the artist's most arresting works.

On the southern side of the Palatine Hill is the **Circo Massimo**, a long green expanse that was ancient Rome's chariot racing track. The arena once held a crowd of 200,000, but now a litter of stones at the Viale Aventino end is all that remains. Across the far side of Piazza di Porta Capena, the **Baths of Caracalla** (Mon 9am–1pm, Tues–Sun 9am–1hr before sunset; €5) are better preserved, and give a much better sense of the scale of Roman architecture.

Trastevere

Across the Tiber from the centre of town, **Trastevere** is a small, tightly knit neighbourhood that was once the artisan quarter of the city and has since become gentrified. It is now home to much of the city's most vibrant and youthful nightlife – and some of Rome's best restaurants. The best time to come is on Sunday morning, when the **Porta Portese** flea market stretches down Via Portuense to Trastevere station in a congested medley of junk, antiques and clothing. Afterwards, stroll north up Via Anicia to the church of **Santa Cecilia in Trastevere**, built over the site of the second-century home of the patron saint of music. Locked in the hot chamber of her own baths for several days, she sang her way through the ordeal until her head was hacked half off with an axe. If you get the chance, have a peek at the Singing Gallery's beautifully coloured and tender late-thirteenth-century **frescoes** by Piero Cavallini (Tues–Thurs 10am–noon, Sun 11.30am–12.15pm; donation expected). Santa Cecilia is situated in the quieter part of Trastevere, on the southern side of Viale Trastevere, the wide boulevard that cuts through the centre of the district. There's more life on the other side centred on Piazza Santa Maria in Trastevere, named after the church of **Santa Maria in Trastevere** – held to be the first official church in Rome, built on a site where a fountain of oil is said to have sprung on the day of Christ's birth. North towards the Tiber, the **Villa Farnesina** is known for its Renaissance murals, including a Raphael-designed painting of *Cupid and Psyche*, completed in 1517 by the artist's assistants. Raphael did, however, manage to finish the *Galatea* next door. The other paintings in the room are by Sebastiano del Piombo and the architect of the building, Peruzzi, who also decorated the upstairs Salone delle Prospettive, which shows *trompe l'oeil* galleries with views of contemporary Rome – one of the earliest examples of the technique.

St Peter's and the Vatican

Across the Tiber is the **Vatican City**, a tiny territory surrounded by high walls on its far side and on the near side opening its doors to the rest of the city and its pilgrims in the form of Bernini's **Piazza San Pietro**. The basilica of **St Peter's** (daily 7am–6/7pm; free) is the replacement of a basilica built during the time of Constantine, to a plan initially conceived at the turn of the fifteenth century by

Bramante and finished off over a century later by Carlo Maderno, bridging the Renaissance and Baroque eras. The inside is full of features from the Baroque period, although the first thing you see, on the right, is Michelangelo's *Pietà*, completed when he was just 24 and, following an attack in 1972, displayed behind glass. On the right-hand side of the nave, the bronze statue of St Peter was cast in the thirteenth century by Arnolfo di Cambio. Bronze was also the material used in Bernini's massive 28m high baldachino, the centrepiece of the sculptor's embellishment of the interior. Bernini's feverish sculpting decorates the apse, too, his *cattedra* enclosing the supposed chair of St Peter in a curvy marble and stucco throne. An entrance off the aisle leads to the **treasury** (daily 9am–5/6pm; €4.20), while back at the central crossing, steps lead down to the **Vatican Grottoes** (daily 7/8am–5/6pm), where a number of popes are buried in grandiose tombs – in the main, those not distinguished enough to be buried up above. Under the portico, to the right of the main doors, you can ascend by lift to the **roof and dome** (€4.20), from where the views over the city are glorious.

A five-minute walk out of the northern side of Piazza San Pietro takes you up to the only part of the Vatican City you can visit independently, the **Vatican Museums** (Mon–Sat 8.45am–4.45pm, last Sun of month 8.45am–1.45pm; €10, free last Sun of the month) – quite simply the largest, richest museum complex in the world, stuffed with booty from every period of the city's history. If you have little time, start off at the **Raphael Stanze**, at the opposite end of the building to the entrance, a set of rooms decorated for Pope Julius II by Raphael among others. Of these, the **Stanza Eliodoro** is home to the *Expulsion of Heliodorus from the Temple*, an allusion to the military success of Julius II, depicted on the left in portrait. Not to be outdone, Leo X, Julius's successor, in the *Meeting of Attila and St Leo* opposite, ordered Raphael to substitute his head for that of Julius II, turning the painting into an allegory of the Battle of Ravenna at which he was present; thus he appears twice, as pope and as the equally portly Medici cardinal just behind. From here it is impossible to miss the **Sistine Chapel**, built for Pope Sixtus IV in 1481, which serves as the pope's private chapel and hosts the conclaves of cardinals for the election of each new pontiff. The paintings down each side wall are contemporary with the building, depictions of scenes from the lives of Moses and Christ by Perugino, Botticelli and Ghirlandaio among others. But it's the ceiling frescoes of Ghirlandaio's pupil, Michelangelo, depicting the *Creation*, that everyone comes to see, executed almost single-handed over a period of about four years, again for Pope Julius II. Whether the ceiling has been improved by the controversial recent restoration is a moot point. The *Last Judgement*, on the west wall of the chapel, was painted by Michelangelo over twenty years later. The nudity caused controversy from the start, and the pope's zealous successor, Pius IV, would have had the painting removed had not Michelangelo's pupil, Daniele da Volterra, carefully added coverings – some of which have been left by the restorers – to the more obvious nudes, earning himself the nickname of the "breeches-maker".

San Paolo, Via Appia and the catacombs

San Paolo fuori le Mura, 2km south of the city centre, is one of the four patriarchal basilicas of Rome, occupying the supposed site of St Paul's tomb. Of the four, it has fared least well over the years, and the church you see is largely a nineteenth-century reconstruction after a devastating fire. It is a huge, impressive building, and home to a handful of ancient features: in the south transept, the Paschal Candlestick is a remarkable piece of Romanesque carving, supported by half-human beasts and rising through entwined tendrils and strangely human limbs and bodies to scenes from Christ's life; the bronze aisle doors date from 1070, and the Cosmati cloister, just behind here, is probably Rome's finest, its spiralling, mosaic-encrusted columns enclosing a peaceful rose garden.

Further south still, on the edge of the city, the **Via Appia** was the most important of all the Roman trade routes. Its sides are lined with the underground burial cemeteries or **Catacombs** of the first Christians. There are five complexes in all, dating from the first to the fourth centuries, almost entirely emptied of bodies now but still decorated with the primitive signs and frescoes that were the hallmark of the then-burgeoning Christian movement. You can get to the main grouping on bus #218 from the Colosseum (Via San Gregorio in Laterano), but the only ones of any significance are the catacombs of **San Callisto** (8.30am–noon & 2.30–5pm; closed Wed & all Feb; €5), burial place of all the third-century popes and the site of some well-preserved seventh- and eighth-century frescoes; and those of **San Sebastiano** 500m further on (9am–noon & 2.30–5pm; closed Sun & mid-Nov to mid-Dec; €5), under a basilica that was originally built by Constantine. Tours take in paintings of doves and fish, a contemporary carved oil lamp and inscriptions dating the tombs themselves – although the most striking features are three pagan tombs discovered when archeologists were burrowing beneath the floor of the basilica upstairs. Nearby graffiti records the fact that this was indeed, albeit temporarily, where the Apostles Peter and Paul rested.

Eating, drinking and nightlife

You can eat cheaply and well in Rome. **Restaurants** cluster near Campo dei Fiori and Piazza Navona, but Trastevere is Rome's traditional restaurant ghetto and home to some fine, reasonably priced eateries.

The two main areas to go for **bars and clubs** are Monte Testaccio and Trastevere, although there is a good sprinkling of places in the city centre. If you are looking for English-speaking company there are also plenty of **pubs** all over Rome. Clubs run the gamut from vast glittering palaces with stunning lights and sound systems, to the down-to-earth student-run **centri sociali** in the suburbs, many of which first opened in abandoned public buildings in the 1990s; they offer a cheap, alternative programme of concerts, films and parties – some have evolved to be as slick and professional as the commercial alternatives, although others are little more than dope-filled dives. Rome's **rock scene** is a fairly limp affair, and the city is much more in its element with **jazz**. Most clubs close during July and August, or move to locations on the coast, but **Estate Romana** organizes outdoor concerts, discos, bars and cinemas all over Rome - a more appealing option than the clubs on a hot summer's night. The city's best source of **listings** is *Roma C'è* (issued on Friday with a section in English). There's also the *TrovaRoma* supplement published with the Thursday edition of *La Repubblica*.

Snacks, cakes and ice cream

Al Settimo Gelo Via Vodice 21. On the corner with via Oslavia and worth the hike for their *cioccolato al peperoncino*, or their heavenly cardamom-flavoured ice. Metro Lepanto.

Ciampini Piazza San Lorenzo in Lucina. Expensive, but it's so popular, and the ice cream here is so good, that they don't even need to put it out on display.

Il Delfino Corso V. Emanuele 67. Central and very busy cafeteria with a huge choice of snacks and full meals.

Il Forno del Ghetto Via del Portico d'Ottavia 1. Unmarked Jewish bakery with marvellous ricotta- and dried fruit-filled cakes. Closed Sat.

Il Gelato di San Crispino Via della Panetteria 42. Close to the Trevi fountain and considered Rome's best ice cream. Closed Tues.

Giolitti Via Offici Uffici del Vicaro 40. An Italian institution with a choice of seventy ice-cream flavours. Closed Mon.

Pascucci Via di Torre Argentina 20. Just the thing after hours of sightseeing – a Roman *frullato*, the local version of a milkshake.

Sciam Via del Pellegrino 56. A Middle Eastern-style tea room, done up in truly lavish style, offering exotic teas and treats.

Tre Scalini Piazza Navona. Renowned for its absolutely remarkable *tartufo*. Closed Wed.

Restaurants

Ai Marmi Viale Trastevere 53–59. Rome's most traditional pizzeria, with regional extras such as deep-fried stuffed olives and batter-fried cod. Closed Wed.

Antico Falcone Via Trionfale 60. This fifteenth-century posting house near St Peter's appears drab but the food is so good you'll weep; try the *carbonara*.

Da Alfredo e Ada Via dei Banchi Nuovi 14. Genuine home cooking at great prices. Closed Sat and Sun.

Enoteca Cavour Via del Gesu. Lunch only, but great home cooking and good wines, with well-stocked wine shop next door.

Grappola d'Oro Piazza della Cancelleria 80. Curiously untouched place with genuine Roman cuisine and a timeless trattoria feel. Closed Sun.

Da Giggetto Via del Portico d'Ottavia 21a. Much pricier than most, but worth it for great Romano–Jewish cooking. Closed Mon.

Osteria Dell' Angelo Via Bettolo 24 ☎06.372.9470. A short walk from St Peter's and off the tourist trail. Good, basic Italian cooking, with an excellent value set menu in the evening. Book, or get there by 8pm for a seat.

Osteria Della Frezza Via della Frezza 16. New *osteria* in traditional style, with huge selection of cheeses and casked wine.

Pizzeria Dar Poeta Vicolo del Bologna 45, Trastevere. One of the best pizzerias in Rome, so expect to queue. Closed Mon.

Silvio Via Urbana 67–69. Classic Italian cooking at this unpretentious restaurant, near Metro Cavour. Closed Mon.

Sora Margherita Piazza delle Cinque Scole 30. Acclaimed traditional Roman cooking. Open Tues–Fri lunch, & Sat & Sun evening.

Tram Tram Via dei Reti 44–46. San Lorenzo district's top student favourite, featuring regional Pugliese cooking. Closed Mon.

Da Vittorio Via San Cosimato 14a. Neapolitan pizza in the heart of Trastevere. Closed Mon.

Bars and birrerias

Bar della Pace Via della Pace 5. Just off Piazza Navona, this is the summer bar to be seen in, with outside tables full of Rome's self-consciously beautiful people.

Enoteca Cavour Via Cavour 313. At the Forum end of Via Cavour, a handy retreat with an easy-going studenty feel, lots of wine and bottled beers.

Il Fico Piazza del Fico. Late at night the piazza thrums with young Romans; escape inside for a cocktail-bar atmosphere.

Izgud Via Mastro Giorgio 19, Testaccio. For one of the latest trends - aperitifs served with club-style music and a buffet – get here on Sunday by 9pm. It's a restaurant the rest of the week.

Jonathan's Angels Via della Fossa 18, next door to *Il Fico*. This colourful bar presents an explosion of kitsch decor.

La Locandiera Via di Sora, 21. Tiny, friendly *vineria* serving good *bruschetta* and *ciambelle*, with a roaring fire in winter.

Ombre Rosse Piazza Sant'Egidio 12. Trastevere's liveliest venue, offering a huge menu of drinks and good light snacks, plus newspapers in several languages.

La Scala Piazza della Scala. The most popular Trastevere *birreria* – big, bustling and crowded.

Vineria Campo dei Fiori 15. Fashionable *vineria* that spills out into the square during the summer; if this is packed, try the elegant wine bar *Nolano*, a couple of doors to the left.

Centri sociali

Brancaleone Via Levanna 11 ⓦwww.brancaleone.it. In a mansion on Montesacro, the Brancaleone stages concerts, films and political events; one of the best *centri sociali*.

Forte Prenestino Via F. del Pino. ⓦwww.forteprenestino.net/index2.html. Situated in an abandoned nineteenth-century fortress. Two big arenas for concerts and a beehive of smaller spaces used for exhibitions, cinema, a disco and a bar.

Villaggio Globale Ex-Mattatoio, Testaccio ⓦwww.ecn.org/villaggioglobale/pages/campo_boario.htm. In an old slaughterhouse, partly run by the Senegalese community in Rome, which organizes concerts, parties and exhibitions.

Discos and clubs

L'Alibi Via Monte Testaccio 44. Predominantly but not exclusively male venue that's one of Rome's best gay clubs. Downstairs cellar disco and upstairs open-air bar.

Art Cafe Via del Galoppatoio, 33 ☎06.3600.6578. In an underground car park at Villa Borghese, and possibly the trendiest club in Rome. Great music, dancers, occasional art and fashion events. Book, or expect to queue.

Black Out Club Via Saturnia 18. Popular disco playing a mix of house, punk and grunge.

Goa Via Libetta 13. An ethnic feel to accentuate the house, techno and trance high-energy dance atmosphere.

Groove Vicolo Savelli 10. Cool bar, great music, informal dancing. Clientele mostly 30s and upwards.

Grottapinta Lounge Via di Grotta Pinta 12. A mostly foreign crowd. Very fashionable, standard disco music.

Il Locale Vicolo del Fico 3. Local bands, packed with students, dancing usually starts after midnight.

La Maison Vicolo da Granari 4, near Piazza Navona ☎06.6833.312. Very glossy disco, home to Rome's gilded youth and minor celebs. Book or queue.

Qube Via di Portonaccio 212. Popular place with solid rock, soul and ethnic music.

Live music: rock, jazz and Latin

Alexanderplatz Via Ostia 9 ☎06.3974.2171.
Rome's foremost jazz club-restaurant.
Reservations recommended.
Alpheus Via del Commercio 36–38. A four-roomed
venue with concerts, a disco, theatrical
performances and a bar.
Berimbau Via dei Fienaroli 30/b. Live Latin-
American music and Brazilian drinks.
Big Mama Vicolo San Francesco a Ripa 18.
Trastevere-based jazz/blues club of long standing.
Closed July–Sept.
Blue Knight Via delle Fornaci 8–10. Bar and
gelateria on the ground floor; downstairs there's
live music Thurs–Sat.
Caffè Latino Via di Monte Testaccio 96. Multi-
event club in the hip area near the Protestant
cemetery. Best at weekends when it's crowded
and more atmospheric.
Charity Café Via Panisperna 68. Tiny club with
live jazz music and great ambience.
Circolo degli Artisti Via Casilina Vecchia 42.
Huge bar and disco with more alternative live
music. Cheap and fun.
Fonclea Via Crescenzio 82a. Long running
jazz/salsa outfit, with live music most nights.
Metro Ottaviano.

Culture, arts and festivals

For **classical music**, the city's churches host a wide range of choral, chamber and organ recitals, many of them free. International names appear at Rome's snail-shell shaped **Auditorium** (☎800.90.70.80), while the opera scene concentrates on the **Teatro dell'Opera**, Via Firenze, Piazza B. Gigli in winter (box office Mon–Sat 9am–5pm; ☎06.481.601) and at various outdoor venues in summer. Purists should be prepared for a carnival atmosphere and plenty of unscheduled intervals. Rome's two **English-language cinemas** are the Pasquino, Piazza Sant'Egidio 10, Vicolo del Piede in Trastevere, and the Quirinetta at Via Minghetti 4. Other cinemas occasionally showing English-language films are the Nuovo Sacher, Largo Ascianghi 1, and Alcazar, Via Cardinal Merry del Val 14.

Festivals

La Festa di Noantri Viale Trastevere and around.
Medieval Trastevere's traditional summer festival in
honour of the Virgin, with street stalls selling snacks
and trinkets, and a grand finale of fireworks. Main
event is the Virgin's effigy being hauled joyously
from the church of Santa Agata to that of San
Crisogono, and back again. Last two weeks of July.
La Festa dell'Unità Venues change annually;
check *Roma C'è* for details. Throughout the
summer, this cheery hotchpotch of music, film,
eateries, games and other attractions – much of it
free – is the re-founded Communist Party's way of
reminding people of what fun the Left can be.
Fiesta Capannelle Via Appia Nuova 1245. Based
at Rome's racecourse in the southeast of the city,
with a Latin American flavour. Metro A to
Subagosto, then bus #354 to Ippodromo
Capannelle. Mid-June to Aug.
Testaccio Village Viale del Campo Boario. Just
behind the old Testaccio slaughterhouse, this
nightly festival draws a young crowd for the bars
and stalls, live bands and DJs. Metro B to
Piramide, then bus #40N back. June–Sept.
Tevere Expo Tiber Embankment, main entrance
by Castel Sant'Angelo. Atmospheric annual
handicrafts fair along the river; nighttime stalls,
bars and live entertainment. Mid-June to July.

Listings

Embassies Australia, Via Alessandria 215
☎06.852.721; Canada, Via G.B. de Rossi 27
☎06.445.981; New Zealand, Via Zara 28
☎06.441.7171; UK, Via XX Settembre 80
☎06.4220.0001; US, Via V. Veneto 121
☎06.46.741.
Exchange Two offices at Termini station operate
out of banking hours; also Cambio Rosati, Via
Nazionale 186 ☎06.488.5498.
Hospital ☎06.884.0113 for 24-hour assistance.
Most central hospital: Santo Spirito, Lungotevere in
Sassia 1 ☎06.68.351; International Medical
Centre ☎06.488.2371.
Left luggage At Termini station.
Pharmacies PIRAM, Via Nazionale 228; at
Stazione Termini. Rota posted on pharmacy doors.
Police Questura, Via S. Vitale ☎06.4686.
Post office Piazza San Silvestro 18–20.

Day-trips from Rome: Tivoli and Ostia Antica

Two easy day-trips from Rome are to the Roman and Renaissance villas of Tivoli, 40km east, and the excavations of Ostia Antica, a similar distance to the west, near the sea. At **TIVOLI** (bus from Rebibbia metro station), the **Villa Adriana** (daily 8.30am–6.30pm; €6.50) was probably the largest and most sumptuous villa in the Roman Empire, the retirement home of the Emperor Hadrian from 135AD. Highlights include the Canopus, on the far side of the site and the **Teatro Marittimo**, with its island in the middle of a circular pond, to which it's thought Hadrian retired at siesta time. Tivoli's Renaissance villas, **Villa d'Este** (Tues–Sun 8.30am–7.30pm/1hr before sunset; €6.50), and the **Villa Gregoriana** (currently closed for restoration) are worth seeing mainly for their marvellous gardens.

The excavations of the Roman town of **OSTIA ANTICA** (Tues–Sun 8.30am–7pm/1hr before sunset; €4; train from Rome's Piramide station) centre on **Piazzale di Corporazione** with the remains of shops and trading offices still fringing it, the mosaics in front of which denote their trade. Flanking one side of the square, the theatre has been much restored but is nonetheless impressive, enlarged in the second century to hold up to four thousand people. On the left of the square, the **House of Apulius** preserves mosaic floors and, beyond, a dark aisled mithraeum with more mosaics illustrating the cult. Behind here, the **Casa di Diana** is probably the best-preserved private house in Ostia, with a dark set of rooms around a central courtyard, and again with a mithraeum at the back. You can climb up to its roof for a fine view of the rest of the site, afterwards crossing the road to the **Thermopolium** – an ancient Roman café, complete with seats, counter, display shelves and even wall paintings of parts of the menu. North of the Casa di Diana, the **museum** (Tues–Sat 9am–4.30pm, Sun 9am–1pm; same ticket) holds a variety of articles from the site, including frescoes, and some fine sarcophagi and statuary. Left from here, the Forum centres on the Capitol building, reached by a wide flight of steps.

Southern Italy

The Italian **south** or *mezzogiorno* is quite a different experience from the north; indeed, few countries are more tangibly divided into two distinct, often antagonistic, regions. While the north is rich, the south is among the poorest areas in Europe, with a rate of unemployment around twice that of the north. The dialect down here is different, too, sounding almost Arabic sometimes. For most people, **Naples** is the obvious focus, an utterly compelling city just a couple of hours south of Rome. In the **Bay of Naples**, apart from the resort of **Sorrento**, the highlight is the island of **Cápri**, swarmed over by tourists these days but still so beautiful to be worth your time; while the ancient sites of **Pompeii** and **Herculaneum** are Italy's best-preserved and most revealing Roman remains. South of Naples, the **Amalfi Coast** is probably Europe's most dramatic stretch of coastline, harbouring some enticing – if crowded – beach resorts. Puglia – the long strip of land that makes up the "heel" of Italy – was for centuries a strategic province, invaded and colonized by just about every major power of the day. However, apart from the Baroque wonders of **Lecce**, Puglia is really a province you pass through on the way elsewhere – not least by sea to Greece or Croatia.

Ferries from Greece and Croatia to **BARI** dock at the Stazione Maríttima, next to the old city. From here, it is a short bus ride or 45-minute walk to the tourist office on Piazza Aldo Moro (Mon–Fri 8am–2pm, Tues & Thurs till 5.30pm; ☎080.524.2361, ⊛www.pugliaturismo.com/aptbari) and the nearby train station. **BRÍNDISI**, 100km southeast of Bari, has ferries to Greece from the Stazione Maríttima on Via del Mare; from here it's a few minutes' walk to the bottom of Corso Garibaldi, and another twenty minutes on foot (or a short bus ride) to Bríndisi's train station in Piazza Crispi. The tourist office is at Viale Regina Margherita 43 (daily Mon–Fri 8am–8pm; Sat 8am–1pm; ☎0831.523.072, ⊛www.pugliaturismo.com/aptbrindisi).

Naples (Napoli)

Wherever else you travel south of Rome, the chances are that you'll wind up in **NAPLES** (Napoli). It's the kind of city people visit with preconceptions, and it rarely disappoints: it is filthy, large and overbearing; it is crime-infested; and it is most definitely like nowhere else in Italy – something the inhabitants will be keener than anyone to tell you. One thing, though, is certain: a couple of days here and you're likely to be as staunch a defender of the place as its most devoted inhabitants. Few cities on earth excite such fierce loyalties.

Arrival, information and accommodation

Naples' **Capodochino Airport** is northwest of the centre at Viale Umberto Maddalena, connected with Piazza Garibaldi by buses #14 and #15 (every 15min; journey time 30min). There's also a blue official airport bus (6am–midnight, every 30min), which takes you straight to the port, Piazza Municipio and Piazza Garibaldi. **Trains** arrive at Napoli Centrale on Piazza Garibaldi, the main hub of all transport services. There's tourist information at the train station (Mon–Sat 9am–8pm, Sun 9am–1.30pm) and the airport (daily 9am–7pm), but the **main**

15

tourist office is at Piazza Gesù Nuovo dei Martiri 58 (Mon–Sat 9am–8pm, Sun 9am–2.30pm; ☎081.551.2701, ⊛www.inaples.it). Pick up the free **listings** booklet *Qui Napoli*, handy for ferry and bus times.

The only way to get around Naples and stay sane is to walk. However, this is a large, sprawling city, so you'll need to use public transport sooner or later. For city **buses**, buy tickets in advance from tobacconists or the booth on Piazza Garibaldi. There is also the **metropolitana**, an efficient underground network, and **funiculars** scaling the hill of the Vómero from stations at piazzas Montesanto, Amedeo and Augusto. For **trips around the bay** there are three rail systems, the most useful of which is the **Circumvesuviana**, which runs from its station on Corso Garibaldi around the Bay of Naples as far as Sorrento in about an hour. A more entertaining way to travel is the **Metro di Mare** ferry network from Molo Beverello, which goes to Cápri and south as far as Amalfi and is probably the cheapest way to get a sea trip. If you are around for more than a day, invest in the **Artecard** (from €13), which provides various combinations of free transport, including a return trip on the Metro di Mare ferries, along with museum entrance.

Many of the city's cheaper **hotels** are situated around Piazza Garibaldi, within spitting distance of the train station and not badly placed for the rest of town. A word of warning: don't go with any of the touts in the station.

Hostels

Hostel Pensione Mancini Via Mancini 33 ☎081.553.6731, ⊛www.hostelpensionemancini.com. Small, welcoming place right across the piazza from the station. Dorms, singles and doubles. Breakfast included. No curfew. €16–18.

Ostello Mergellina Salita della Grotta 23 ☎081.761.2346. Popular HI site with a view of the bay; 12.30am curfew. Breakfast included. Metro or train to Mergellina, or bus #152 from Piazza Garibaldi. €14–16.

Six Small Rooms Via Diodato Lioy 18 ☎081.7901.378, ⊛www.at6smallrooms.com. Small, friendly hostel with kitchen, run by an Australian; good breakfast. Metro to Montesanto. €18.

Hotels

Bella Cápri Via Melisurgo 4 ☎081.552.9494, ⊛www.bellacápri.it. At the main port, on the top floor of a modern building, with great views of Mt Vesuvius and Cápri. ⑤

Casanova Corso Garibaldi 333 ☎081.268.287, ⊛hcasanova@tin.it. Close to Piazza Garibaldi, with its own roof garden. ④

Hotel Eden Corso Novara 9 ☎081.285.690, ⊛hotel-eden-napoli@libero.it. Sizeable and friendly, on right as you leave the station. ④

Hotel Garibaldi Via Mancini 11 ☎081.563.0656. Two-star place with good facilities, two minutes from the station. ③

Hotel Ginevra Via Genova 116 ☎081.554.1757, ⊛www.hotelginevra.it. Family-run one-star, friendly and helpful. ②

Soggiorno Imperia Piazza Luigi Miraglia 386 ☎081.459.347. Homely, clean hotel, offering kitchen and laundry facilities right in the *centro storico*. Breakfast included. ④

Campsite

Vulcano Solfatara Via Solfatara 161, Pozzuoli ☎081.526.7413. Well-equipped site, with swimming pool, restaurant and Internet access. Bus #152 from Piazza Garibaldi, or metro to Pozzuoli then ten-minute walk uphill. Closed Nov–March.

The City

The area between the vast and busy Piazza Garibaldi, where you will arrive, and Via Toledo, the main street a mile or so west, makes up the old part of the city – the **centro storico**. Buildings rise high on either side of the narrow, crowded streets; there's little light, not even much sense of the rest of the city outside – certainly not of the proximity of the sea. The two main drags here are Via dei Tribunali and Via San Biagio dei Librai, both a maelstrom of hurrying pedestrians, revving cars and buzzing scooters. Via dei Tribunali cuts through to Via Duomo, where you'll find the tucked-away **Duomo**, a Gothic building from the early thirteenth century dedicated to San Gennaro, the patron saint of the city. San Gennaro was martyred in 305 AD. Two phials of his blood miraculously liquefy three times a year – on the first Saturday in May (when a procession leads from the church of Santa Chiara to the cathedral) and on September 19 and December 16. If the blood refuses to liquefy – which luckily is rare – disaster is supposed to befall the city. The first chapel on the right as you walk into the cathedral holds the precious phials and Gennaro's skull in a silver bust-reliquary from 1305. Downstairs, the **Crypt of San Gennaro** is one of the finest examples of Renaissance art in Naples, founded by Cardinal Carafa and holding the tombs of both San Gennaro and Pope Innocent IV.

Across Via Duomo, Via dei Tribunali continues on into the heart of the old city: the **Spaccanapoli**, the city's busiest and architecturally richest quarter. Cut down to its other main axis, Via San Biagio dei Librai, which leads west to Piazza San Domenico Maggiore, marked by the **Guglia di San Domenico** – built in 1737, it is one of many whimsical Baroque obelisks that pop up all over the city. The **church** of the same name flanks the north side of the square, an originally Gothic building from 1289, one of whose chapels holds a miraculous painting of the *Crucifixion* which is said to have spoken to St Thomas Aquinas during his time at the adjacent monastery. North, Via de Sanctis leads off right to one of the city's odder monuments, the **Cappella Sansevero** (Mon & Wed–Sat 10am–5/7pm, Sun 10am–1.30pm; €5), the tomb-chapel of the di Sangro family, decorated by the sculptor Giuseppe Sammartino in the mid-eighteenth century with some remarkable carving including a starkly realistic dead *Christ*. The chapel downstairs, commissioned by alchemist Prince Raimondo, contains the gruesome results of some of his experiments: two bodies under glass, their capillaries and organs preserved by a mysterious liquid developed by the prince. Continuing west, the **Gesù Nuovo** church is most notable for its lava-stone facade, prickled with pyramids that give it an impregnable, prison-like air. Facing the Gesù church, the church of **Santa Chiara** is quite different, a Provençal–Gothic structure built in 1328 (and rebuilt after World War II). The attached **cloister** (Mon–Sat 9.30am–1pm & 2.30–5.30pm, Sun 9.30–11am; €4), covered with colourful majolica tiles depicting bucolic scenes of life outside, is one of the gems of the city.

Piazza del Municipio is a busy traffic junction that stretches down to the waterfront, dominated by the brooding hulk of the **Castel Nuovo**. Built in 1282 by the Angevins and later the royal residence of the Aragon monarchs, it now contains the **Museo Civico** (Mon–Sat 9am–7pm; €5), which holds periodic exhibitions in a series of elaborate Gothic rooms. The entrance of the Castel incorporates a triumphal arch built in 1454 to commemorate the taking of the city by Alfonso I, the first Aragon ruler. Just beyond the castle, on the left, **Teatro San Carlo** (☎081.797.2331; ⊛www.teatrosancarlo.it) is still the largest opera house in Italy, and one of the most distinguished in the world. Beyond, at the bottom of the main shopping street of Via Toledo, the dignified **Palazzo Reale** (9am–8pm, closed Wed; €4) was built in 1602 to accommodate a visit by Philip III of Spain. Upstairs, the palace's first-floor rooms are decorated with gilded furniture, *trompe l'oeil* ceilings, overbearing tapestries and lots of undistinguished seventeenth- and eighteenth-century paintings.

Via Toledo leads north from Piazza Trieste e Trento to the **Museo Archeologico Nazionale** (9am–8pm, closed Tues; €6.50) – Naples' most essential sight, home to the best of the finds from the nearby Roman sites of Pompeii and Herculaneum. The ground floor concentrates on sculpture, including the *Farnese Bull* and *Farnese Hercules* from the Baths of Caracalla in Rome. The mezzanine floor at the back houses the museum's collection of mosaics, remarkably preserved works giving a superb insight into ordinary Roman customs, beliefs and humour. Upstairs, the wall paintings from the villas of Pompeii and Herculaneum are the museum's other major draw, rich in colour and invention; and don't miss the "secret" room of erotic Roman pictures and sculptures, once thought to be a hazard to public morality and only recently opened. The other side of the first floor has sculptures in bronze from the Villa dei Papiri in Herculaneum, including a superb *Hermes at Rest*, a languid *Resting Satyr* and a convincingly woozy *Drunken Silenus*. At the top of the hill is the city's other major museum, the **Museo Nazionale di Capodimonte** (Tues–Sun

8.30am–7.30pm; €7.50; bus #24 from Piazza Dante), the former residence of the Bourbon King Charles III, built in 1738. This has a superb collection of Renaissance paintings, including a couple of Brueghels, *The Misanthrope* and *The Blind*, canvases by Perugino and Pinturicchio, an elegant *Madonna and Child with Angels* by Botticelli and Lippi's soft, sensitive *Annunciation*.

Vómero, the district topping the hill immediately above the old city, can be reached on the Montesanto funicular. Go up to the star-shaped fortress of **Castel Sant'Elmo** (daily 8.30am–7.30pm; €1), occupying Naples' highest point. Built in the fourteenth century, it now hosts exhibitions and concerts, and boasts the very best views of Naples.

Eating, drinking and nightlife

If you're just after a snack, you can pick something up from the city's **street markets** – the Forcella quarter market on the far side of Piazza Garibaldi or the fish market at Porta Nolana, off to the left. Naples, however, is the home of **pizza**, while **restaurants** are best in the historic centre. The beautiful Piazza Bellini is a trendy drinking spot, where tables spill out from the surrounding **bars**. A quieter place for an evening *passeggiata* and supper is the seafront around Castel dell'Ovo, lit up at night and clustered with bars and trattorias. As for **clubs**, one of the trendiest places is *Ahiahi*, Via Discesa Cordoglio 146, a dressy disco-restaurant that has a sea view and often live music; or in the summer try the popular outdoor disco *Virgilio Club*, Via Lucrezio Caro 6.

Cafés, pizzerias and restaurants

Bellini Via Santa Maria di Constantinopoli 80. One of the city's longest-established restaurants, good for a splurge. Closed Sun eve.

Brandi Salita Sant'Anna di Palazzo 1–2, off Via Chiaia. Possibly Naples' most famous pizzeria – very friendly, and serving pasta too. Closed Mon.

Da Antonio Via de Pretis 143. An unpretentious place near the port, serving great regional specialities at moderate prices. Closed Sat.

Da Matteo Via Tribunali 94. Superb for pizza and also offers a risky deep-fried ricotta-filled alternative.

Da Tonino Via Santa Teresa e Chiara 47. An excellent historic trattoria, and cheap.

Intra Moenia, Piazza Bellini 70. A left-wing literary café and publishing house, that also offers Internet access.

L'Antica Pizzeria Da Michele Via Cesare Sersale 1–3, corner of Via Colletta. The cheapest pizza in town and possibly the most authentic. Closed Sun.

Zi Carmela Via Nicolò Tommaseo 11–12. Along the seafront, close to the City Park; special pizzas and inventive seafood pastas. Closed Mon.

Listings

Consulates UK, Via dei Mille 40 ☎081.423.8911; US, Piazza della Repubblica ☎081.583.8111.

Exchange At Stazione Centrale (daily 7am–9pm).

Hospital Ospedale Nuovo Pellegrini, Via FM Briganti 255 ☎081.254.5291.

Laundry Bolle Blu, Corso Novara 62 (closed Sun).

Pharmacy At Stazione Centrale (24hr).

Police Via Medina 75 ☎081.794.1111.

Post office Piazza Matteotti, off Via Toledo.

The Bay of Naples

For the Romans, the **Bay of Naples** was the land of plenty, a blessed region with a mild climate, gorgeous scenery and hence a favourite vacation and retirement area for the city's nobility. Later, when Naples became the final stop on the Grand Tour, the relics of its heady Roman period only added to the charm. However, these days it's hard to tell where Naples ends and the countryside begins, the city sprawling around the Bay in an industrial and residential mess that is quite at odds with the region's popular image. It's only when you reach **Sorrento** in the east, or the islands that dot the bay, that you really feel free of it all. Of the islands, **Cápri** is the best place to visit if you're here for a short time. There's also, of course, the ever-brooding presence of **Vesuvius**, and the incomparable Roman sites of **Herculaneum** and **Pompeii**.

Herculaneum and Vesuvius

The town of **ERCOLANO** is the modern offshoot of the ancient site of **Herculaneum**, which was destroyed by the eruption of Vesuvius on August 2, 79 AD. It's worth stopping here for two reasons: to see the excavations and to climb to the summit of **Vesuvius** – to which buses run from outside the train station. If you're planning to visit both in one day, be sure to see Vesuvius first, and set off reasonably early – buses stop running up the mountain at lunchtime, leaving you the afternoon free to wander around the site.

Situated at the seaward end of Ercolano's main street, **HERCULANEUM** (daily 8.30am–7.30pm, last entry 6.30pm; €10, €18 including Pompeii) was a residential town in Roman times, much smaller than Pompeii, and as such it's a more manageable site – less architecturally impressive, but with better preserved buildings and more easily taken in on a single visit. Because it wasn't a commercial town, there is no central open space or forum, just streets of villas and shops, cut as usual by two very straight main streets. The **House of the Mosaic Atrium** retains its mosaic-laid courtyard, corrugated by the force of the tufa, behind which the **House of the Deer** contains corridors decorated with richly coloured still lifes and a bawdy statue of a drunken Hercules seemingly about to piss all over the visitors. There's also a large **thermae** or bath complex with a domed *frigidarium* decorated with frescoes of fish and a *caldarium* containing a plunge bath at one end and a scallop-shell apse complete with washbasin and water pipes. Opposite, the **House of Neptune and Amphitrite**, holding a sparklingly preserved wall mosaic of the god and goddess, and frescoes of flowers and vegetables, served in lieu of a garden. Under the house is a wine shop, stocked with amphorae in wooden racks, left as they lay when disaster struck. Close by in the **Casa del Bel Cortile** are some skeletons poignantly lying in the same attitude as they were in 79 AD. Further down on the opposite side of the road in the **House of the Wooden Partition**, there's a room with the marital bed still intact, and in the house nearby a perfectly preserved coiled rope. However, the rest of the contents are in Naples' archeological museum.

Since its first eruption in 79 AD, when it buried the towns and inhabitants of Pompeii and Herculaneum, **VESUVIUS** has dominated the lives of those who live on the Bay of Naples. It's still an active volcano, the only one on mainland Europe, and there have been hundreds of eruptions over the years, but only two of real significance: one in December 1631 that engulfed many nearby towns and killed 3000 people; and the last, in March 1944, which caused widespread devastation, though no one was actually killed. The people who live here still fear the reawakening of Vesuvius, and with good reason – scientists calculate it should erupt every thirty years or so, and it hasn't since 1944. Trasporti Vesuviani run bus services from Ercolano train station to a car park and huddle of souvenir shops and cafés close to **the crater**; don't listen to the taxi drivers at the station who will try and persuade you there is no bus. The walk up to the crater from the car park where the bus stops takes about half an hour, across barren gravel on marked-out paths. At the top (admission €6), the crater is a deep, wide, jagged ashtray of red rock emitting the odd plume of smoke, though since the last eruption effectively sealed up the main crevice, this is much less evident than it once was. You can walk most of the way around, but take it easy – the fences are old and rickety.

Pompeii

The other Roman town destroyed by Vesuvius, **POMPEII** (daily 8.30am–5/7.30pm; €10; ☎081.857.5347, ⊛www.pompeiisites.org) was one of Campania's most important commercial centres. Out of a total population of 20,000, it's thought that 2000 perished, asphyxiated by the toxic fumes of the volcanic debris, their homes buried in several metres of volcanic ash and pumice. In effect, the eruption froze Pompeii in time, and the excavations here have probably yielded more information about the life of Roman citizens during the imperial era than any other site. The full horror of their way of death is apparent in plaster casts made from the shapes their bodies left in the volcanic ash. Again, though, most of the best mosaics and murals have found their way to the archeological museum in Naples.

The site covers a wide area, and seeing it properly takes half a day at least. Entering the site from the Pompeii-Villa dei Misteri side, the **Forum** is the first real feature of significance, a slim open space surrounded by the ruins of what would have been some of the town's most important official buildings. North from here, the **House of the Tragic Poet** is named after its mosaics of a theatrical production and a poet inside, though the "Cave Canem" (Beware of the Dog) mosaic by the main entrance is more eye-catching. Close by, the residents of the **House of the Faun** must have been a friendlier lot, its "Ave" (Welcome) mosaic outside beckoning you in to view the atrium and the copy of a tiny bronze, dancing faun that gives the villa its name. On the street behind, the **House of the Vettii** is one of the most delightful houses in Pompeii, a merchant's villa ranged around a lovely central peristyle that gives the best possible impression of the domestic environment of the city's upper middle classes. The first room on the right off the peristyle holds the best of Pompeii's murals viewable in situ: the one on the left shows the young Hercules struggling with serpents, while, through the villa's kitchen, a small room that's normally kept locked has erotic works showing various techniques of lovemaking, together with a potent-looking statue of Priapus from which women were supposed to drink to ensure fertility.

On the other side of the site, the **Grand Theatre** is very well preserved and still used for performances, as is the **Little Theatre** on its far left side. Walk up to the **Amphitheatre**, one of Italy's most intact and also its oldest, dating from 80 BC. Next door, the **Palestra** is a vast parade ground that was used by Pompeii's youth for sport and exercise. One last place you shouldn't miss is the **Villa dei Misteri** (4 tours daily; free; book on ☎081.861.9003, ⊛www.arethusa.net) outside the main site, a short walk from the Porta Ercolano, but accessible on the same ticket. This is probably the best preserved of all Pompeii's palatial houses, and it derives its name from a series of excellently preserved paintings in one of its larger chambers: depictions of the initiation rites of a young woman into the Dionysiac Mysteries, an orgiastic cult transplanted to Italy from Greece in the Republican era and at times partially outlawed for its excesses.

To **reach Pompeii from Naples**, take the Circumvesuviana to Pompeii-Villa dei Misteri (direction Sorrento; journey time roughly 30min); this leaves you right outside the western entrance to the site. The Circumvesuviana also runs to Pompeii-Santuario, outside the site's eastern entrance (direction Sarno), or you can take the main-line train (direction Salerno) to the main Pompeii FS station, on the south side of the modern town. It makes most sense to see the site from Naples, but there is an **HI hostel**, *Casa del Pellegrino*, at Via Duca d'Aosta 4 (☎081.850.8644; ❷), 200m from Pompeii-Santuario station on the Circumvesuviana line, and a large and well-equipped **campsite**, *Zeus*, right outside the Pompeii-Villa dei Misteri station.

Sorrento

Topping the rocky cliffs close to the end of its peninsula, **SORRENTO** is unashamedly a resort, its inspired location and mild climate having drawn foreigners from all over Europe for two hundred years. Nowadays it caters mostly to the package-tour industry, but is none the worse for it – a bright, lively place that retains its southern Italian roots. Cheap restaurants aren't hard to find; neither is reasonably priced accommodation; and there's no better place outside Naples from which to explore the rugged Amalfi shore and the islands of the Bay. Sorrento's centre is **Piazza Tasso**, five minutes from the train station along the busy Corso Italia, the streets around which are pedestrianized for the lively evening *passeggiata*. Strange as it may seem, Sorrento isn't particularly well provided with beaches: most people make do with the rocks and a tiny, crowded strip of sand at **Marina Grande** – fifteen minutes' walk or a short bus ride from Piazza Tasso – or simply use the wooden jetties. If you don't fancy this, try the beaches further along, such as the tiny

Regina Giovanna at Punta del Capo, again connected by bus from Piazza Tasso, where the ruins of the Roman Villa Pollio Felix make a unique place to bathe.

The **tourist office** in the large yellow Circolo dei Foresteri building at Via de Maio 35, just off Piazza Sant'Antonino (Mon–Sat 8.30am–7pm; ☎081.807.4033, ⍟www.sorrentotourism.com) can help with accommodation. There's a **hostel**, *Le Sirene*, close to the station at Via degli Aranci 160 (☎081.807.2925; €18); walk out of the station, turn left on the main road and it's a little way down on your left. Among a number of centrally placed **hotels**, try the *City*, Corso Italia 221 (☎081.877.2210; ⑤), or the *Astoria*, Via Santa Maria delle Grazie 24 (☎081.807.4030; ⑥, including breakfast). The cheapest and closest **campsite** is *Nube d'Argento*, Via del Capo 12 (closed Nov–March), ten minutes' walk from Piazza Tasso in the direction of Marina Grande. For **eating**, the *Ristorante Sant'Antonino*, off Piazza Antonino, is good value; or call Peppe at *Mami Camilla*, Via Cocomella 4 (☎081.878.2067, ⍟www.mamicamilla.com; food from €10; B&B ⑤) whose family-run cookery school doubles as an informal restaurant. For late-night boozing and **nightlife**, there's the lively disco-bar *Matilda* on Piazza Sant'Antonino, or the refined live-music joint *Artis Domus*, Via S. Nicola 56; otherwise Sorrento is rife with English-style **pubs**.

The island of Cápri

Rising from the sea off the far end of the Sorrentine peninsula, the island of **CÁPRI** has long been the most sought-after part of the Bay of Naples. During Roman times the emperor Tiberius retreated here to indulge in legendary debauchery until his death in 37 AD. Later, the discovery of the Blue Grotto and the island's remarkable natural landscape coincided with the rise of tourism; the island has attracted a steady flow of artists, writers and tourists ever since. Inevitably, Cápri is a crowded and expensive place, and in July and August it's sensible to give it a miss. But it would be hard to find a place with more inspiring views, and it's easy enough to visit on a day-trip. There are regular **ferries** to Cápri from Naples' Molo Beverello, at the bottom of Piazza Municipio, and regular **hydrofoils** from the Mergellina jetty a couple of miles north of here (€12 one-way) – and also from Sorrento. For more information, consult the daily newspaper, *Il Mattino*.

Ferries and hydrofoils dock at Marina Grande, the waterside extension of **CÁPRI TOWN**, which perches on the hill above, connected by funicular. Cápri town is a very pretty place, with winding, hilly alleyways converging on the titchy main square of Piazza Umberto. The **Certosa San Giacomo** (Tues–Sat 9am–2pm, Sun 9am–1pm; free) on the far side of the town is a run-down old monastery with a handful of paintings, and the Giardini Augustos next door give tremendous views of the coast below and the towering jagged cliffs above. From here you can wind down to **MARINA PICCOLA**, a huddle of houses and restaurants around a few patches of pebble beach – pleasantly uncrowded out of season, though in season it's heaving. You can also reach the ruins of Tiberius' villa, the **Villa Jovis**, from Cápri town (daily 9am–1hr before sunset; €2), a steep thirty-minute trek east. The site is among Cápri's most exhilarating, with incredible vistas of the bay, although there's not much left of the villa. The island's other main settlement, **ANACÁPRI**, is less picturesque than Cápri town, its tacky main square flanked by souvenir shops, boutiques and touristy restaurants. But during the season, a chair-lift operates up **Monte Solaro** (596m), the island's highest point, and you can also get to the island's most famous attraction, the **Blue Grotto**, from here – a good 45-minute trek down Via Lo Pozzo or reachable by bus from the main square. At €8, with tip expected, it's a bit of a rip-off, with boatmen whisking visitors through the grotto in five minutes flat, but in the evening, after the tourists have gone, you may be able to swim into the cave for nothing – change at the bar next to the entrance. Time is better spent at Axel Munthe's **Villa San Michele** (daily 9am–6pm; €5), a light, airy house with enviable views that was home to the Swedish writer for a number of years, and is filled with his furniture and knick-knacks, as well as Roman artefacts pillaged from a villa on the site.

The main **tourist office** is on Piazza Umberto in Cápri town (Mon–Sat 9am–8.30pm, Sun 9am–1pm & 3.30–6.45pm; ☎081.837.0686), with another useful branch on Via G. Orlandi in Anacápri (same times; ☎081.837.1524). If you're on a tight budget, **accommodation** is prohibitively expensive, though you could try *Stella Maris*, Via Roma 27 (☎081.837.0452; ❻), or the family-run *Villa Eva* in Anacápri, Via La Fabbrica 8 (☎081.837.1549; ❼), a garden paradise with pool, breakfast included. **Eating** is an expense, too, and you may do best with a picnic; for sit-down food try *Di Giorgio* in Via Roma.

The Amalfi Coast

Occupying the southern side of Sorrento's peninsula, the **Amalfi Coast** lays claim to being Europe's most beautiful stretch of coast, its corniche road winding around the towering cliffs. There are no trains; the bus from Sorrento joins the coast road a little west of Positano for the incredible ride east through a handful of villages to Amalfi. If the road is closed due to forest fires or landslides, it takes an alternative route, zigzagging up over a crest and down again in a series of crazy hairpins to Amalfi.

AMALFI has been an established seaside resort since Edwardian times, when the British upper classes spent their winters here. An independent republic in Byzantine times, Amalfi was one of the great naval powers with a population of some seventy thousand. Vanquished by the Normans in 1131, it was devastated by an earthquake in 1343. A few remnants of Amalfi's past glories survive, and the town has a crumbly attractiveness that makes it fun to wander through. The **Duomo**, at the top of a steep flight of steps, dominates the main piazza, its decorated, almost gaudy facade topped by a glazed tiled cupola that's typical of the region. The body of St Andrew is buried in its crypt, though the most appealing part of the building is the cloister (daily 9am–9pm; €2.50) – oddly Arabic in feel, with its whitewashed arches and palms. Close by, the **Museo Civico** (Mon–Fri 9am-2pm; free) displays the original *Tavoliere Amalfitane* – the book of maritime laws which governed the republic, and the rest of the Mediterranean, until 1570. Beyond these, the focus is along the busy seafront, where there's a crowded **beach**. The **tourist office** is at Corso delle Repubbliche Marinare 27–29 (Mon–Fri 8am-2pm & 3–8pm, Sat 8.30am-1pm & 3-10pm; ☎089.871.107, ⓦwww.amalficoast.it), next door to the post office. The cheapest **hotels** are the *Proto*, off Via Genova down Salita dei Curiali 4 (☎089.871.003; ❼), and the *Lidomare*, just off the main square at Via Piccolomini 9 (☎089.871.332, ⓦwww.lidomare.it; ❽); both include breakfast. The popular **hostel-cum-hotel** *A' Scalinatella*, is out of town at Piazza Umberto I 5–6, Atrani (☎089.871.492, ⓦwww.hostelscalinatella.com; hostel ❷), with a beach close by. For **eating**, try *La Taverna del Duca*, Piazza Spirito Santo 26 (closed Thurs; *Trattoria da Gemma* (closed Wed), opposite; or *Il Mulino* further up the hill on Via delle Cartiere.

The best views of the coast can be had inland from Amalfi, in **RAVELLO**. This was also an independent republic for a while, and for a time an outpost of the Amalfi city-state; now it's not much more than a large village, but its unrivalled location, spread across the top of one of the coast's mountains, makes it more than worth the thirty-minute bus ride up from Amalfi. Buses drop off on the main Piazza Vescovado, outside the **Duomo**. It's an eleventh-century church dedicated to St Pantaleone, a fourth-century saint whose blood – kept in a chapel on the left-hand side – is supposed to liquefy like that of Naples' San Gennaro, twice a year on May 19 and August 27. Ten minutes away, the gardens of the **Villa Cimbrone** (daily 9am–8pm; €5) spread across the furthest tip of Ravello's ridge. Most of the villa itself is not open to visitors, though it's worth peeking into the crumbly, flower-hung cloister as you go in, and the open crypt down the steps from here. Best bit of the gardens is the belvedere at the far end of the main path, giving marvellous views over the sea below. **Tourist information** is available at Piazza Duomo 10 (daily 8am–8pm; ☎089.857.096, ⓦwww.ravelloarts.org).

Lecce

LECCE, 40km south of Bríndisi port, has been called the "Baroque Florence" of the south; walking its alleys, there's still a sense of jaw-dropping excitement at discovering its buildings, with forests of vines, flowers and statues enveloping the stonework. Carved from a soft sandstone, the buildings are one of the high-points in Italian architecture, and very different from the heavy Baroque of Rome. Built for wealthy families, churchmen and merchants during the fifteenth to seventeenth centuries, when Lecce was at the height of its power, these buildings are some of the most beautiful examples of the style – some of the most impressive were designed by Giuseppe Zimbale, known as Lo Zingarello. A short walk from the central Piazza Sant'Oronzo is **Santa Croce** (daily 8am–noon & 5–7pm), most famous of the Lecce churches, where delicate engravings and a riot of putti and grotesques soften the Baroque outline of the building. Inside, the excess continues with a riot of stars, flowers and foliage covering everything from the top of columns to chapel altarpieces. Next door, the yellow stone **Palazzo del Governo**, a former Celestine monastery, is another Zingarello building. On **Piazza del Duomo**, a harmonious square surrounded by Baroque palazzi, is the **Duomo** itself (daily 8am–noon & 5–7pm), an explosion of Baroque detail – although its main entrance, on the Piazza Vescovile, is much more restrained. The **train station** is 1km south of the centre on Via Oronze Quarta. The **tourist office** is at Corso Vittorio Emanuele 24, near the Duomo (summer daily 9am–1pm & 3–8pm; winter Mon–Fri 9am–1pm; ☎0832.248.092, ⊛www.pugliaturismo.it/lecce). The cheapest **hotel** is the two-star *Cappello*, in Via Montegrappa near the station (☎0832.308.881; ❹); alternatively, there are **B&Bs** – try Andreina Goffredo, Viale Marche 15 (☎0832.231.724; ❹). Lecce's nearest **campsite** is *Torre Rinalda* at Litoranea Salentina 152 (☎0832.382.161; closed Oct–May; bus from Piazza Sant'Oronzo. For **food** try the cheap student haunt *Osteria da Angiulino*, hidden along Via Principe di Savoia 24; or the popular old-fashioned *Trattoria Casareccia*, via Costadura 9. In the evening follow the crowd to one of the many bars in the area around Via Vittorio Emanuele where the evening *passaggiata* takes place. **Internet access** is at Chatwin Netcafé, Via Isabella Catriota 8.

Sicily (Sicilia)

Coming from the Italian mainland, **SICILY** (Sicilia) feels socially and culturally separate from Europe. Occupying a strategically vital position, the largest island in the Mediterranean has a history and outlook that has less in common with its modern parent than of its erstwhile rulers – from the Greeks who first settled the east coast in the eighth century BC, through a dazzling array of Romans, Arabs, Normans, French and Spanish, to the Bourbons, seen off by Garibaldi in 1860. Substantial relics of these ages remain – temples, theatres and churches are scattered across the island. And there are other, more immediate hints of Sicily's unique past – a hybrid Sicilian language is still widely spoken in the countryside, the food is noticeably spicier, and its sweets (candied fruits and marzipan), have a Middle-Eastern flavour. The capital, **Palermo**, is a bustling city with an unrivalled display of Norman art and architecture and Baroque churches. The most obvious other target is the chic eastern resort of **Taormina,** although if you are looking for fewer people and cleaner water you'd be advised to go to the west or south coasts. Near

---

To get to Sicily, you simply take a **train** from the mainland – they travel across the Straits of Messina on the ferries from Villa San Giovanni and continue on the other side. First stop is Messina, after which services either run west to Palermo (change for Agrigento) or south to Taormina and Siracusa.

ITALY | Sicily (Sicilia)

Taormina you can skirt around the foothills and even up to the craters of **Mount Etna**, or travel south to the ancient Greek centre of **Siracusa**, with its wonderful architecture and ancient remains. To the west, the greatest draw is the grouping of temples at **Agrigento**, the biggest concentration of the island's Greek remnants.

Palermo and around

In its own wide bay underneath the limestone bulk of Monte Pellegrino, **PALERMO** is stupendously sited. Originally a Phoenician, then a Carthaginian colony, this remarkable city was long considered a prize worth capturing, and under Saracen and Norman rule in the ninth to twelfth centuries it became the greatest city in Europe, famed for the wealth of its court and peerless as a centre of learning. Nowadays it's a brash, exciting city, whose lively markets, unique series of Baroque and Arabo-Norman churches, mosaic work and museums are the equal of anything on the mainland. The heart of the old city is the Baroque **Quattro Canti** crossroads, with **Piazza Pretoria** and its racy fountain just around the corner. In nearby Piazza Bellini, the church of **La Martorana** (Mon–Sat 8am–1pm & 3.30–5.30pm, Sun 8.30am–1pm) is one of the finest survivors of the medieval city. Its slim twelfth-century campanile and series of spectacular mosaics make a marked contrast to the adjacent squat chapel of **San Cataldo**, with its little Saracenic red golfball domes. In the district of Albergheria, a warren of tiny streets to the southwest, you'll find the deconsecrated church of **San Giovanni degli Eremiti** (Mon–Fri 8.30am–noon & 2.30–6pm; €4.50), built in 1148 and the most obviously Arabic of the city's Norman relics, with five ochre domes topping a small church that was built upon the remains of an earlier mosque. A path leads up through citrus trees to the church, behind which are its celebrated late-thirteenth-century cloisters. From here it's a few paces north to the **Palazzo dei Normanni**, seat of the Sicilian regional parliament; entrance on Piazza Indipendenza. It was originally built by the Saracens and was enlarged considerably by the Normans, under whom it housed the most magnificent of medieval European courts. The beautiful **Cappella Palatina** (Mon–Fri 9–11.45am & 3–4.45pm, Sat 9–11.45am, Sun 9–10am & noon–1pm; free), the private royal chapel of Roger II, built between 1132 and 1143, is almost entirely covered in glorious twelfth-century mosaics. Down Corso Vittorio Emanuele from the palace, the **Cattedrale** (Mon–Sat 7am–7pm, Sun 8am–1.30pm & 4–7pm) is a more substantial Norman relic, though much restored in the eighteenth century. Still, the triple-apsed eastern end and the lovely matching towers are all original; the interior is cold and Neoclassical, the only items of interest the fine portal and wooden doors and the royal tombs, containing the remains of some of Sicily's most famous monarchs. Away to the northeast, off Via Roma, the **Museo Archeologico Regionale** (daily 9am–1pm, Tues, Wed & Fri also 3–6.15pm; €4.13) is a magnificent collection of artefacts, mainly from the island's Greek and Roman sites. Two cloisters hold anchors and other retrieved hardware from the sea off the Sicilian coast, and there are rich stone carvings from the temple site of Selinunte. Be sure to walk south through the sprawling **Vuccira market** area (daily from 8am) for a glimpse of old Palermo, before making your way to Sicily's **Galleria Regionale** (Mon–Sat 9am–2pm, Tues & Thurs also 3–8.30pm, Sun 9am–12.30pm; €4.13), on Via Alloro in the rough-and-ready La Kalsa district. It's a stunning medieval art collection that includes a magnificent fifteenth-century fresco of the *Triumph of Death*, work by the fifteenth-century sculptor Francesco Laurana and paintings by Antonello da Messina. Near here, at Via Butera 1, is the engaging **Museo delle Marionette** (Mon–Fri 9am–1pm & 4–7pm, Sat 9am–1pm; €3), the definitive collection of traditional Sicilian puppets — in summer, there are free shows (currently Fri 5.30pm), centring on the swashbuckling exploits of Orlando in his battles against the Saracens.

   Trains arrive at Stazione Centrale, at the southern end of Via Roma, from where buses #101 and #102 run to the centre. **Ferry and hydrofoil** services dock just off Via Francesco Crispi, from where it's a ten-minute walk up Via E. Amari to

Piazza Castelnuovo. There are **tourist offices** inside the train station (Mon–Fri 8.30am–2pm & 3–6pm; ⑩www.palermotourism.com) and at Piazza Castelnuovo 34 (same hours; ☎091.583.847). For **Internet** access try Accademia Internet, Via Cala 64 (☎091.611.8483) or Internet Shop, Via Napoli 32/34. Most of the budget hotel **accommodation** is on and around the southern ends of Via Maqueda and Via Roma, near the train station. The welcoming *Olimpia*, just before Corso Vittorio Emanuele (☎091.616.1276; ❸), has clean rooms overlooking Piazza Cassa di Risparmio and a great breakfast; or try *Vittoria*, Via Maqueda 8 (☎091.616.2437; ❸); or the atmospheric *Orientale* at no. 26 (☎091.616.5727; ❺). For authentic Sicilian **fast food**, the old-style *Antica Focacceria*, Via A. Paternostro 58, off Corso Vittorio Emanuele, is the place to go, while best for **pizzas** is *Pizzeria Italia*, Via Orologio 54, off Via Maqueda (eves only). The city's cheapest sit-down **restaurant** is *Trattoria-Pizzeria Enzo*, Via Maurolico 17/19, close to the station, while the *Trattoria Primavera* on Piazza Bologni, near the cathedral (closed Mon), is great for homestyle cooking. On warm evenings a young crowd flocks to the **bars and cafés** around Via dei Candelai, while a favourite late-night student haunt is the *Fuso Orario*, Piazza Bara all'Olivella 2, open until 4am. *Kursaal Kalesa* is a summer **club** by the Foro Italico, near the sea front, partly open-air, though the most fashionable club is currently the pricey *La Cuba*, on Via Scaduto. There's a major theatrical and puppetry tradition in Sicily and Palermo has five **puppet theatres**, with regular performances at *Cuticchio*, Via Bara all'Olivella 95. Look out, too, for *Lapis Palermo*, a fortnightly **listings** guide.

Monreale and the beaches

Sicily's most extraordinary medieval mosaics are to be seen at **MONREALE**, a small hill town 8km southwest of Palermo (bus #389 from Piazza dell'Indipendenza, 20min). The mosaics in the Norman **cathedral** (daily 8am–6pm) represent the apex of Sicilian-Norman art, and were almost certainly executed by Greek and Byzantine craftsmen, revealing a unitary plan and inspiration: your eyes are drawn to the all-embracing figure of Christ in the central apse – an awesome and pivotal mosaic, the head and shoulders alone almost 20m high. Underneath sit an enthroned Virgin and Child, attendant angels and ranks of saints. No less remarkable are the nave mosaics, an animated series starting with the Creation to the right of the altar and running around the entire church. Ask at the desk by the entrance to climb the **tower** (€2) – an unusual and precarious vantage point. The **cloisters** (Mon–Sat 9am–7pm, Sun 9am–1pm; €4.50), part of the original Benedictine monastery, form an elegant arcaded quadrangle, with some 216 twin columns that are a riot of detail and imagination.

To escape to the beach, you need to run out to **MONDELLO** (bus #806 or #833 from Viale della Liberta), 11km from the city, which has a nice sandy stretch, seafood snack bars and restaurants; or take the train an hour west to the resort of **CEFALÙ**. This has another fantastic cathedral with medieval mosaics, and a long sandy beach. It's packed in summer, though the tourist office here or Palermo might be able to find you somewhere to stay.

Taormina and around

On Sicily's eastern coast, and dominating two grand sweeping bays, **TAORMINA** is the island's best-known resort. The outstanding remains of its classical theatre, with Mount Etna as an unparalleled backdrop, arrested passing travellers when Taormina was no more than a medieval hill village, and these days it's virtually impossible to find anywhere to stay between June and August. Despite this, Taormina retains all of its romantic small-town charm, the main traffic-free street, Corso V. Emanuele, lined with fifteenth- to nineteenth-century palazzi interspersed with small, intimate piazzas. The **Teatro Greco** (daily 9am–1hr before sunset; €4.50), however – signposted from just about everywhere – is the only real sight, founded by Greeks in the third century BC, though most of what's left is a Roman rebuilding from the first century

AD, when the stage and lower seats were cut back to provide room and a deep trench dug in the orchestra to accommodate the animals and fighters used in gladiatorial contests. These days it has a summer season of Greek plays (in Italian). The **train station** is way below town, from where it's a steep thirty-minute walk up or a short bus ride to the centre. There is a **tourist office** at the station (Mon–Sat 8am–12pm & 4–7pm) but the main office is in Palazzo Corvaja, Piazza Santa Caterina (same hours; ☏0942.23.243, ⓦwww.taormina-ol.it). There are good **accommodation** possibilities along Via Bagnoli Croce – try *Il Leone* at no. 124–126 (☏0942.23.878; ❸); alternatively, there's the tiny but cheap *Diana* at Via di Giovanni 6, nearby (☏0942.23.898; ❸). There is also a small, friendly **HI Hostel**, *Ulisse*, Vico San Francesco de Paola 9 (☏0942.23.193; €15), which offers superb home-cooked evening meals; its rival, *Taormina's Odyssey*, Travessa A, on Via G.Martino (☏0942.245.33; €15), has mixed rooms. **Eating** in Taormina is relatively pricey compared to the rest of Sicily – if money is tight, try the good **rosticceria** just up from Porta Messina, on the corner of Via Timeo and Via Patrizio. Among the less expensive **trattorias** are *La Botte*, Piazza Santa Domenica 4, and *Il Baccanale* in Piazza Filea, which has outdoor tables and similar prices – both close to Via Bagnoli Croce – or try *Trattoria Siciliana*, a quieter place outside Porta Catania at Salita Ospedale 9.

The closest beach to town is at **MAZZARÓ**, with its much-photographed islet. It's about a thirty-minute descent on foot, but the preferable option is to use the cable car (every 15min; €2) from Via Pirandello. The beach-bars and restaurants at **SPISONE**, 1km or so further north, are also reachable by path from Taormina, this time from below the cemetery in town. Roomier and better for swimming are the sands south of Taormina at **GIARDINI-NAXOS**, which is an excellent alternative source of accommodation and food. Prices tend to be a good bit cheaper than in Taormina and in high season it's worth trying here first. The **tourist office** at Taormina's station and Immobiliare Naxos, Via V. Emanuele 58, in Giardini-Naxos (☏0942.51.184) can help find you **accommodation**. For **eating**, good pizzas and fresh fish can be had at *Fratelli Marano*, Via Naxos 181. *Da Angelina*, on Via Euboea by the pier, serves well-priced pizzas and homemade pasta and has great views. Also good is *La Conchiglia*, Via Naxos 221, specializing in Sicilian meat dishes.

Mount Etna

Mount Etna's massive bulk looms over much of the coastal route south of Taormina. If you don't have the time to reach the summit, the **Circumetnea rail service** (€5.16 one way, InterRail passes not valid) provides alternative volcanic thrills in a ride around the base of the volcano from **GIARRE-RIPOSTO**, thirty minutes by train or bus from Taormina; if you make the entire trip to Catania, allow four hours. However, the **ascent** is a spectacular trip, worth every effort to make. At 3323m, Etna is a fairly substantial mountain; the fact that it's also one of the world's biggest volcanoes (and still active) only adds to the draw. On **public transport**, you'll need to come via Catania by bus, one of which (8am from Catania train station) continues on up to a huddle of souvenir shops and restaurants; arriving on this bus, you'll have enough time to make it to the top and back for the return bus to Catania (4pm). If it is considered safe, a **guide** can take you further up the mountain by jeep or minibus (April–Oct; approximately €30 return); if you are given the go-ahead to walk, take warm clothes, good shoes and glasses to keep the flying grit out of your eyes. In any case you will not be allowed beyond 2,900m, marked off by a rope slung across the track. A **tourist office** in Catania train station can help with accommodation, though if you are travelling alone the cheapest option is the easygoing **hostel**, *Agora*, Piazza Curro 6, near the cathedral (☏095.723.3010; dorms €15.50, rooms ❸).

Siracusa

Further down Sicily's eastern seaboard, **SIRACUSA** (ancient Syracuse) was first colonized by Greeks in 733 BC and grew to become their main power base in Sicily.

Today the city boasts some of the best Greek archeological remains anywhere, and also has a strong Baroque character in its old town, squeezed onto the island of **Ortygia**, by the harbour. At the centre of the island, the most obvious attraction is the **Duomo**, set in a conch-shaped piazza studded with Baroque architecture, and itself incorporating twelve fluted columns belonging to the temple that originally stood here. Round the corner, the severe thirteenth-century Palazzo Bellomo houses the **Museo di Palazzo Bellomo** (Tues–Sun 9am–1.30pm, Wed also 3am–6pm; €2.50), an outstanding collection of medieval art. North of the train station, the city is mainly new and commercial, though there are also the best of Siracusa's archeological sights here. It's a short walk, or take a bus from Piazza della Posta (#1, #3, #6, #8, #12, or #25) as far as Viale Teocrito, from where you walk east for the **Museo Archeologico** (Tues–Sun 9am–2pm; €4.50), which holds a wealth of material from the early Greek colonies. Round the corner, the ruined church of **San Giovanni Evangelista** has interesting catacombs (Tues–Sun 9am–12.30pm & 2.30–4.30pm; €3.50); an earthquake in 1693 destroyed the church, which was never rebuilt.

Siracusa's extensive **Parco Archeologico** (daily 9am–2hr before sunset; €4.50) is a twenty-minute walk west of the Museo Archeologico (or bus #15 from Largo XXV Luglio). Here, the **Ara di Ierone II**, an enormous altar of the third century BC, is the first thing you see, but the main highlight of the park is the **Teatro Greco**, cut out of the rock and looking down towards the sea. It's much bigger than the one at Taormina, capable of holding around 15,000 people (though is less impressive, scenically), and also has a summer season of Greek plays. Nearby, the **Latomia del Paradiso**, a leafy quarry, is best known for the **Orecchio di Dionigi**, an S-shaped cave, 65m long, that Dionysius is supposed to have used as a prison: Caravaggio, a visitor in 1586, coined the name after the shape of the entrance, but the acoustic properties are such that it's not impossible to imagine Dionysius eavesdropping on his prisoners from a vantage point above. The other large cave down here – though you can't go into it – is known as the **Ropemaker's cave**, because its damp conditions made it ideal for the craft. The last section of the park contains the neglected-looking **Roman amphitheatre**. This has a central rectangular-shaped construction, which was probably used for water fights, and just below the small church at the top of the path down to the Parco Archeologico is the Roman water storage tank that would have supplied water for this; the tank was converted into a church in the sixth century.

A good **day-trip** out of Siracusa is the half-hour train ride to the tumbledown town of **NOTO**, whose deserted station and crumbling suburbs give way to a lovely Baroque town centre that was recently nominated as one of UNESCO's world heritage sites.

Practicalities

Siracusa's **train station** is on the mainland, a twenty-minute walk from Ortygia. AST **buses** arrive either in Piazza della Poste, just over the bridge on Ortygia, or else in Piazzale Marconi, in the modern town; SAIS buses stop in Via Trieste, close by Piazza della Poste. There's a privately run tourist point, *Syrako*, in Ortygia at Via Ruggero Settimo 19 (Mon–Sat 9am-6/8pm; ☎0931.24.133); the **main tourist office** is in the new town at Via San Sebastiano 43, opposite the church of San Giovanni Evangelista (Mon–Sat 8.30am–1.30pm & 3.30–6.15pm, Sun 9am-1pm; ☎0931.481.200, ⓦwww.apt-siracusa.it).

In high season you'll need to book **accommodation** in advance. Try the clean but unspectacular *Aretusa* by the station at Via Francesco Crispi 75 (☎0931.24.211; ❹), or the *Centrale*, Corso Umberto 141 (☎0931.60.528; 3), in the modern part of Siracusa just off Piazzale Marconi. Staying in Ortygia is prohibitively expensive although if you are travelling in a group, ask at the tourist office about "residence", self-catering apartments that can be rented by the day. There's a fine **hostel** in Noto, *Il Castello* on Via Fratelli Bandiera (☎0931.571.334; €14.50). The nearest **campsite**, *Agriturist Rinaura* (☎0931.721.224), is 5km away – bus #21, #22 or #23 from Corso Umberto or Piazza delle Poste. As for **restaurants**, *La Siciliana*, Via Savoia 17, does superb value pizzas, and the *Trattoria Archimede*, Via Gemmellaro 8, frequented by locals, is inexpensive and good for fish. *Spaghetteria do Scogghiu*, Via Scina 11, has a huge selection of cheap pasta and is popular at night. And *Da Antonio*, Via Gimillaro 34, is a trattoria with good home cooking. One of the best **bars**, the *Bar Del Ponte*, at the end of the Ponte Nuovo on Ortygia, serves good breakfasts.

Agrigento

Halfway along Sicily's southern littoral, **AGRIGENTO** is primarily of interest for the substantial remains of Pindar's "most beautiful city of mortals", strung out along a ridge facing the sea a few kilometres below town. The series of Doric temples here, mostly dating from the fifth century BC, are the most evocative of Sicilian remains. They are also the focus of a constant procession of tour buses, so budget accommodation should be booked in advance (though Agrigento is a possible day trip from Palermo). A road winds down from the modern city to the **Valle dei Templi**, buses #1, #2 or #3 dropping you at a car park between the two separate zones of **archeological remains** (daily 8.30am–5/7pm; €4.50, or €6 with the museum). The eastern zone is home to the scattered remains of the oldest of the temples, the **Tempio di Ercole**, probably begun in the last decades of the sixth century BC, and the better-preserved **Tempio della Concordia**, dated to around 430 BC, with fine views of the city and sea. There's also the **Tempio di Giunone**, an engaging half-ruin standing at the very edge of the ridge. The western zone, back along the path and beyond the car park, is less impressive but it's fun to wander around the vast tangle of stone and fallen masonry from a variety of temples – get a little off the path and you'll easily lose the other tourists. Most notable is the mammoth construction that was the **Tempio di Giove**, or Temple of Olympian Zeus, the largest Doric temple ever known, though never completed, left in ruins by the Carthaginians and further damaged by earthquakes. The small piece that is standing is a nineteenth-century reconstruction. Around the site there are also some early Christian and Byzantine tombs. Via dei Templi leads back to the town from the car park via the excellent **Museo Nazionale Archeologico** (daily 9am–1.30pm, Wed–Sat also 2–6.30pm; €4.50) – an extraordinarily rich collection devoted to finds from the city and the surrounding area.

    Trains arrive at the edge of the old town, outside which – on Piazza Marconi – buses leave for the temples. The **tourist office** is nearby at Via Cesare Battisti 15 (Mon–Fri 8am–1pm & 3pm–dusk; ☎0922.204.54), at the eastern end of Via Atenea. There's also an information box at the Valle dei Templi site. Among **hotels** worth trying are the *Amici*, in Via Acrone next to the station (☎0922.402.831; ❻); *Concordia*, at Piazza San Francesco 11 (☎0922.596.266; ❹); and the *Bella Napoli*, Piazza Lena 6 (☎0922.20.435; ❺). You can camp 5km away at the coastal resort of San Leone; take bus #2 or #2/ from outside the train station. You can **eat** cheaply and well at *Trattoria Atenea*, Via Ficani 12, an alley above Via Atenea, while best **pizza** in town is at *Chez Jean 2*, Via Cicerone.

Sardinia (Sardegna)

A little under 200km from the Italian mainland, **SARDINIA** (Sardegna) is way off most tourist itineraries, although it boasts some of the country's loveliest beaches and holds fascinating vestiges of the various civilizations that have passed through. In addition to Roman and Carthaginian ruins, Genoan fortresses and a string of lovely Pisan churches, there are striking remnants of Sardinia's only significant native culture, known as the nuraghic civilization after the 7000 *nuraghi*, tower-like stone constructions, that litter the landscape. On the whole, Sardinia's coasts and mountains are the biggest draw, but the capital, **Cágliari** – for many the arrival point – shouldn't be written off as it makes a useful base for exploring the southern third of the island. The other main ferry port and airport is **Olbia** in the north, little more than a transit town for visitors from the mainland, while **Alghero**, in the northwest, is a lively package resort with a third major airport. In the interior, **Nuoro** makes a useful stopover for visiting some of the more remote mountain areas, where you can find what remains of the island's traditional culture, best embodied in the numerous village **festivals**.

Cágliari

Rising up from its port and crowned by an old citadel squeezed within a protective ring of fortifications, **CÁGLIARI** has been Sardinia's capital at least since Roman times and is still the island's biggest town. Nonetheless, its centre is easily explored on foot, with almost all the wandering you will want to do encompassed within the citadel. The most evocative entry to this is from the monumental **Bastione San Remy** on Piazza Costituzione. It's worth the haul up the grandiose flight of steps inside for the views over the port and the lagoons beyond – especially at sunset. From the bastion, wander off in any direction to enter the intricate maze of Cágliari's citadel, traditionally the seat of the administration, aristocracy and highest ecclesiastical offices. It has been little altered since the Middle Ages, though the tidy Romanesque facade on the mainly thirteenth-century **Cattedrale** (Mon–Sat 8am–12.30pm & 4–7pm, Sun 8am–1pm & 4–8pm) in Piazza Palazzo is in fact a fake, added in the twentieth century in the old Pisan style. At the opposite end of Piazza Palazzo a road leads into the smaller Piazza dell'Arsenale, site of the **Museo Archeologico Nazionale** (Tues–Sun 9am–8pm; €4), a must for anyone interested in Sardinia's past. The island's most important Phoenician, Carthaginian and Roman finds are gathered here, but everything pales beside the museum's greatest pieces, from Sardinia's **nuraghic** culture. Of these, the most eye-catching is a series of bronze statuettes, ranging from about 15cm to 45cm in height, spindly and highly stylized, but packed with invention and quirky humour. Off the piazza stands the **Torre San Pancrazio**, from which it's only a short walk to Via dell'Università and the **Torre dell'Elefante** (Tues–Sun 9am–4.30; €2), named after the small carving of an elephant on one side; the towers were erected by Pisa after it had wrested the city from the Genoans in 1305 and formed the main bulwarks of the city's defences. Climb to the top for stupendous views over the city and coast. Nearby, Viale Buon Cammino leads to the **Anfiteatro Romano** (Tues–Sun: April–Oct 9am–1pm & 3–7pm; Nov–March 9am–4pm; free). Cut out of solid rock in the second century AD, the amphitheatre could hold the entire city's population of twenty thousand.

Cágliari's **port** lies in the heart of the town, opposite Via Roma. The **airport** sits beside the Stagno di Cágliari, the city's largest lagoon, fifteen minutes' bus ride west of town. There are **tourist offices** at the port, and opposite the **train and bus stations** on Piazza Matteotti (April–Sept Mon–Sat 8am–8pm; Oct–March Mon–Fri 9am–6pm; ☏070.669.255), but the main office covering the whole of

Sardinia is at Via Mameli 97 (daily 8.30am–1pm & 3–6pm; ☎070.60.231, ⓦwww.esit.net). There's a good selection of budget **hotels**, but book ahead in high season. Via Sardegna has several basic choices, including *Palmas* at no. 14 (☎070.651.679; ❸) and *La Perla* at no. 18 (☎070.669.446; ❸). Just off Piaza Yenne, try *Aurora* at Salita S. Chiara 19 (☎070.658.625; ❸). Right on the seafront, *AeR Bundes Jack*, Via Roma 75 (☎070.667.970, ⓔhotel.aerbundesjack@libero.it; ❻) is clean and friendly. Most of Cágliari's **restaurants** are clustered around Via Sardegna. *Da Serafino*, at Via Sardegna 109, pulls in the locals for its Sardinian specialities. *Da Fabio* at Via Sardegna 90 offers good tourist menus and has an English-speaking boss. Seafood-lovers will do well at the *Ristorante Italia*, Via Sardegna 30, though prices are relatively high. Away from the port area, try *La Damigiana*, a simple trattoria with low prices at Corso Vittorio Emanuele 115. Piazza Yenne has numerous outdoor cafés for a **snack** and a beer, and there's a great gelateria, *L'Isola del Gelato*. *De Candia*, a bar on Bastione San Remy, has open-air **music** on summer nights, while the bars on Via Roma make good breakfast stops.

Su Nuraxi

If you have no time to see any other of Sardinia's ancient stone *nuraghi*, make a point of visiting **Su Nuraxi**, the biggest and most famous of them and a good taste of the primitive grandeur of the island's only indigenous civilization. The snag is access: the site lies 1km outside the village of **BARÚMINI**, 50km north of Cágliari, to which there are only two daily buses, which stop here en route to Désulo and Samugheo. At Barúmini, turn left at the main crossroads and walk the last leg to Su Nuraxi (daily 9am–4/7pm; €4.20). Its dialect name means simply "the *nuragh*" and not only is it the biggest *nuraghic* complex on the island, but it's also thought to be the oldest, dating probably from around 1500 BC. Comprising a bulky fortress surrounded by the remains of a village, Su Nuraxi was a palace complex at the very least – possibly a capital city. The central tower once reached 21m (now reduced to less than 15m), and its outer defences and inner chambers are connected by passageways and stairs. The whole complex is thought to have been covered with earth by Sards and Carthaginians at the time of the Roman conquest, which may account for its excellent state of preservation.

Nuoro

Superbly sited beneath the soaring peak of Monte Ortobene, opposite the stark heights of Sopramonte, **NUORO** is the only one of Sardinia's provincial centres that expresses the island's mountain culture. Much of the town has been disfigured by modern construction, however, and there is little tourist infrastructure, though it can boast some first-class museums. Nuoro's old quarter is the most compelling part of town, spread around the pedestrianized hub of **Corso Garibaldi**. The town's chief attraction is the **Museo del Costume** (daily: mid-June to Sept 9am–8pm; Oct to mid-June 9am–1pm & 3–7pm; €5) on Via Mereu, a ten-minute walk from the Corso south of Piazza Vittorio Emanuele, which contains Sardinia's most comprehensive range of local costumes, jewellery, masks, carpets and other handicrafts. For a more contemporary perspective, drop in at the **Museo d'Arte Nuorese**, just off the Corso (Tues–Sun 10am–1pm & 4.30–8.30pm; €2.58), which displays modern art from the whole island. Nearby on Via Deledda, you can view a typical Nuorese home at the **Casa di Grazia Deledda** (same hours as Museo del Costume; €5), the restored family house of the author Grazia Deledda, who won the Nobel Prize for Literature in 1927. Nuoro's biggest annual festival, the **Festa del Redentore**, takes place on the penultimate Sunday of August, featuring elaborately costumed participants from all over the island. The religious festivities are held on August 29, when a procession from town weaves up to the 955m summit of **Monte Ortobene**, 8km away, where a bronze statue of the Redeemer stands poised above the gorge separating Nuoro from the Sopramonte.

Nuoro's **train station** is a twenty-minute walk from the centre of town along Via Lamármora, and the **bus station** lies a further ten minutes south of here on Via Sardegna. Nuoro's **tourist office** is on Piazza Italia (Mon–Fri 9am–1pm & 3.30–6.30pm; ☎0784.30.083, ⊛www.nuoro.com) and is useful for a street-map. The few **hotels** in town are mostly for business travellers, for example the characterless *Sandalia*, near the train station on Via Einaudi (☎0784.38.353; ❺). However, the best accommodation is on Monte Ortobene, where there are a couple of **B&Bs** enjoying lofty hilltop views: *Casa Solotti* (☎0784.33.954; ❹) and *Su Redentore* (☎328.022.5518; ❹) – for both, ring ahead to be met. Nuoro's **restaurants** offer good-quality, meaty fare at reasonable prices, as at *Tascusi*, near the top end of the the Corso at Via Aspromonte 13, where local dishes are served in simple white rooms decorated with Sard art, and the livelier *Il Rifugio*, Via Mereu 28, a good trattoria-pizzeria.

Alghero

In the northwest of Sardinia, **ALGHERO** owes its predominantly Catalan flavour to a wholesale Hispanicization that followed the overthrow of the Genoan Doria family by Pedro IV of Aragon in 1354. The traces are still strong in the old town today, with its flamboyant churches, wrought-iron balconies and narrow cobbled streets named in both Italian and Catalan. A walk around the old town should include the seven defensive **towers** that dominate Alghero's centre and surrounding walls. From the **Giardino Púbblico**, the **Porta Terra** is the first of these massive bulwarks, erected at the expense of the prosperous Jewish community before their expulsion in 1492. Via Roma runs down from here through the old town's puzzle of lanes to the pedestrianized Via Carlo Alberto, holding most of the bars and shops. Turn right to reach **Piazza Cívica**, the old town's main square, at one end of which rises the grand Neoclassical facade of Alghero's mainly sixteenth-century **Cattedrale**. Inside, the lofty nave's alternating pillars and columns are topped by an impressive octagonal dome. The best excursions you can make are west along the coast past the long bay of Porto Conte as far as the point of **Capo Caccia**, where the spectacular sheer cliffs are riddled by deep marine caves. The most impressive of these is the **Grotta di Nettuno**, or Neptune's Grotto (daily 9/10am–1/7pm; €8), a long snaking passage delving far into the rock, into which hourly tours are led, single-file, past dramatically lit and fantastical stalagmites and stalactites. The return boat trip from the port costs €10, or take the bus from the Giardino Pubblico to Capo Caccia (June–Sept; 1–3 daily), from where it's a 654-step descent.

Trains arrive 3km north of the centre and are connected to the port by regular local buses. Long-distance **buses** arrive in Via Catalogna, on the Giardino Púbblico. Alghero's **tourist office** is on the corner of the Giardino Púbblico (April–Sept Mon–Sat 8am–8pm, Sun 9am–1pm; Nov–March Mon–Sat 8am–2pm; ☎079.979.054, ⊛www.infoalghero.it). There are two good **accommodation** options in the heart of the old town: *Mamjuana*, a B&B at Vicolo Adami 12 (☎339.136.9791; ❺), and the *San Francesco* hotel (☎079.980.330, ⊜hotsfran@tin.it; ❻), Via Machin 2, where each of the clean, quiet rooms has a bathroom. There's a cheaper alternative in the newer part of town: the *Normandie*, on Via Enrico Mattei, at the end of Via Kennedy (☎079.975.302, ⊜hotelnormandie@excite.it; ❹). *La Mariposa* **campsite** (☎079.950.480; April to mid-Oct), 2km north of town, has direct access to the beach; while the **hostel** (☎079.930.478, ⊛www.iyhf.org; ❸) lies 6km along the coast at Fertília, reachable by local bus. Alghero's **restaurants** are renowned for seafood, at its best in spring and winter. *La Lépanto* on Via Carlo Alberto, off Piazza Sulis, is one of the finest fish restaurants, though expensive. *Trattoria Maristella* at Via Kennedy 9 is a cheaper alternative popular with locals, who also flock to *Casablanca*, a more casual pizzeria at Via Umberto 76. For **snacks**, the fast-food joints by the port aren't bad. In the evenings, you can catch live music at *Poco Loco*, Via Gramsci, which also has an **Internet point**.

Travel details

Trains

Bari to: Bríndisi (hourly; 1hr 30min).

Bologna to: Ferrara (every 30min; 30min); Florence (every 30 min; 1hr); Milan (every 30 min; 2hr); Ravenna (hourly; 1hr 20min); Rimini (every 30 min; 1–2hr).

Cágliari to: Macomer (6 daily; 2hr 45min); Olbia (4 daily; 4hr–4hr 40min); Oristano (hourly; 1hr 10min–2hr); Sássari (5 daily; 3hr 20min–4hr 15min).

Ferrara to: Rimini (hourly via Bologna; 2hr).

Florence to: Arezzo (every 30min; 1hr); Bologna (every 30min; 1hr); Genoa (hourly; 3–4hr); Lucca (every 30 min; 1hr 30min); Milan (every 30min; 3hr); Naples (every 30min; 4hr); Perugia (hourly; 2hr); Pisa (every 15min; 1hr); Rome (every 30 min; 1hr 40min–2hr 30min); Venice (hourly; 2hr 50); Verona (hourly; 3hr).

Genoa to: Bologna (hourly; 3hr 30min); Milan (every 30min; 1hr 30min); Naples (10 daily; 8hr); Pisa (hourly; 2–3hr); Rome (hourly; 5hr 20min).

Milan to: Bologna (every 20min; 2hr); Rome (hourly; 4hr 30min); Venice (every 30min; 3hr).

Naples to: Bríndisi (9 daily; 5hr); Palermo (5 daily; 9hr); Siracusa (5 daily; 9hr).

Padua to: Bologna (every 30min; 1hr 20min); Milan (every 30min; 2hr 30min); Verona (every 20min; 1hr).

Palermo to: Agrigento (13 daily; 2hr); Catania (6 daily; 3–5hr).

Perugia to: Assisi (hourly; 20min); Florence (hourly; 2hr); Rome (hourly; 2hr).

Pisa to: Florence (every 15min; 1hr); Lucca (every 15min; 20min).

Rome to: Bologna (every 15min; 2hr 40min); Florence (every 15min; 1hr 30min); Milan (every 30min; 4–5hr); Naples (every 15min; 2–3hr).

Sássari to: Alghero (hourly; 30min); Cágliari (5 daily; 3hr 40min); Macomer (5 daily; 1hr 30min); Olbia (5 daily; 2hr); Oristano (5 daily; 2hr 30min).

Turin to: Genoa (every 30min; 1hr 50min); Milan (every 30min; 1hr 50min).

Venice to: Bologna (every 30min; 2hr); Florence (hourly; 3hr); Milan (every 30min; 3hr); Padua (every 10min; 30min); Trieste (every 30min; 2hr); Verona (every 30min; 1hr 30min).

Verona to: Milan (every 30min; 1hr 30min); Padua (every 30min; 55min); Rome (hourly; 5hr); Venice (every 30min; 1hr 30min).

Buses

Cágliari to: Macomer (4 daily; 2hr 30min); Nuoro (4 daily; 3hr 30min); Oristano (4 daily; 1hr 35min); Sássari (7 daily; 3hr 15min–4hr).

Ferries

Cágliari to: Civitavécchia (1 daily; 14hr 30min–16hr 30min); Genoa (mid-July to Aug 2 weekly; 20hr); Livorno (1 weekly; 7hr); Naples (1–2 weekly; 16hr); Palermo (1 weekly; 13hr 30min); Trápani (1 weekly; 11hr).

Genoa to: Bastia (1 weekly; 9hr); Cágliari (2 weekly in summer; 20hr); Olbia (at least 7 weekly in summer; 13 hr); Palermo (6 weekly; 20hr); Porto Torres (7 weekly; 12hr).

Naples to: Cápri (6 daily; 1hr 15min); Palermo (daily; 9hr); Sorrento (daily; 1hr 15min); Aeolian Islands (2–3 per week; 9hr overnight to Strómboli).

Olbia to: Civitavécchia (1–3 daily; 8hr); Genoa (3–22 weekly; 8–13hr); Livorno (1–4 daily; 10–13hr).

Porto Torres to: Genoa (6–14 weekly; 11hr); Marseille, France (2–4 weekly; 12–16hr).

Reggio di Calabria to: Messina (12 daily; 20min).

Santa Teresa di Gallura to: Bonifacio, Corsica (2–14 daily; 55min).

Sorrento to: Cápri (4 daily; 50min).

Villa San Giovanni to: Messina (every 15min; 45min).

Hydrofoils and fast ferries

Naples to: Cápri (17 daily; 40min); Sorrento (7 daily; 40min); Aeolian Islands (2–4 per day; 4hr to Strombóli).

Olbia to: Civitavécchia (June to early Sept 1–4 daily; 4–6 hr).

Palermo to: Naples (daily; 4hr).

Reggio di Calabria to: Messina (12 daily; 20min); Naples (summer 1 daily; 6hr).

Sorrento to: Cápri (12 daily; 20min).

Latvia

Latvia highlights

* **Milda, the freedom monument, Rīga** A stylized female figure holds aloft three stars; Latvia's symbol of independence. See p.611

* **Central food market, Rīga** Sights, sounds and pungent smells in gigantic former Zeppelin hangars. See p.611

* **Art Nouveau architecture, Rīga** The Latvian capital contains one of Europe's finest arrays of *fin-de-siècle* architecture. See p.611

* **Jūrmala coastline** Fresh air, sand dunes, pine forests and faded elegance, all just forty minutes from Rīga. See p.613

* **Rundāle Palace** Spectacular Baroque palace, highlight of southern Latvia. See p.613

Introduction and basics

The history of **Latvia**, like that of its neighbour Estonia, is largely one of foreign occupation. The indigenous Balts were overwhelmed at the start of the thirteenth century by German crusading knights, who massacred and enslaved them in the name of Christianity. The Germans continued to dominate both land and trade even after political control passed to the Polish-Lithuanian Commonwealth, then Sweden and finally Russia. Latvian independence after a 1918–20 war against the Soviets and the Germans was extinguished by Soviet annexation in 1940. As conditions in the Soviet Union relaxed during the late 1980s demands for increased autonomy turned into calls for independence, and on August 21, 1991, as the attempted coup against Gorbachev disintegrated in Moscow, Latvia declared its independence for the second time.

These days Latvia is engaged in turning over the economy to private ownership and struggling to reverse Soviet-era stagnation and neglect. Environmental damage aside, the most enduring legacy of Soviet occupation is a Russian minority population of thirty percent. The most obvious destination is the capital, **Rīga**, a city whose architectural treasures have largely survived five decades of isolation. Places within easy reach include the palace of **Rundāle**, the resort area of **Jūrmala**, and the gently scenic **Gauja Valley** with the attractive small towns of Sigulda and Cēsis. Latvia also has hundreds of miles of unspoilt **coast** as well as endless **forests** inland.

Information & maps

Tourist information centres run by the Latvian tourist board (⑩www.latviatravel .com) are in major centres. The Kümmerly & Frey 1:1,000,000 **map** of the Baltic States includes Latvia, and has a basic street plan of Rīga. Jāņa Sēta, Elizabetes 83–85, Rīga, is well-stocked with guides, and publishes its own maps. The Falk Plan of Rīga includes enlarged sections and public transport routes. *Rīga in your Pocket* is an excellent English-language **listings** guide.

Money and banks

Latvia's currency is the **lat** (plural lati) – normally abbreviated to Ls – which is divided into 100 santimi. Coins come in 0.01, 0.02, 0.05, 0.10, 0.20, 0.50, 1 and 2Ls and notes in 5, 10, 20, 50, 100 and 500Ls. **Bank** (*banka*) hours vary, but in Rīga there should be some open Mon–Fri 10am–5pm, Sat 10am–3pm. Outside the capital many close at 1pm and all are closed on Saturday and Sunday. Most major banks like the Hansa Banka, Rīgas Komercbanka and Unibank will cash **travellers' cheques** (Thomas Cook and American Express preferred) and some give advances on major credit cards. In Rīga some major hotels will also cash travellers' cheques and accept credit cards. **Exchanging cash** presents few problems, even outside banking hours, as Rīga is full of currency exchange offices (*valūtas apmaiņa*), often little more than kiosks in unlikely locations like food shops. ATMs are nationwide. **Credit cards** are only useful in Rīga's more

16

LATVIA | Basics

expensive restaurants and stores, and in some petrol stations.

Communications

Post offices (*pasts*) generally open Mon–Fri 8am–7pm, Sat 8am–4pm. There are modern digital public **phones** operated using magnetic cards (*telekarte*) which come in 2, 3, 5 and 10Ls denominations and can be bought at post offices and most stores. There are no area codes: you must always dial the full number. Rīga – though nowhere else – has **Internet** cafés; prices are around 1Ls/hr.

Getting around

Buy **train** tickets in advance: stations have separate windows for long-distance (*starpilsetu*) and suburban (*pirpilsetu*) trains. Long-distance services are divided into "passenger" (*pasažieru vilciens*) and "fast" (*ātrs*) – both are painfully slow but the latter, usually requiring a reservation, stops at fewer places. On timetable boards, look for *atiet* (departure) or *pienāk* (arrival).

Buses are slightly quicker, but more expensive, than trains; buy long-distance tickets in advance. Opt for an express (*ekspresis*) bus if possible to avoid frequent stops. Luggage is usually taken on board; if you have a particularly large bag you may have to pay extra to stow it in the luggage compartment. Buses are also useful for travelling to Latvia's neighbours: services link Rīga with Tallinn (Estonia) and Vilnius (Lithuania).

Accommodation

Outside Rīga and Jūrmala, **accommodation** is limited: even in tourist areas towns will often only have a couple of hotels and perhaps a campsite.

Latvia has many hundred-dollars-a-night business **hotels**. Budget travellers will often be restricted to older establishments which haven't been renovated since Soviet times – they're perfectly habitable if you can put up with the dingy decor. A number of small-sized, good-value hotels and guest houses are emerging to fill the gap, but rooms are often in short supply and advance reservations are required in summer. In Rīga and Jūrmala, a number of agencies now offer **private rooms**, although many of these are in gloomy flats.

There's **hostel** accommodation in Rīga (check ⓦ www.hostellinglatvia.com), where it's also possible to find rooms in student halls of residence during college vacations – although staff invariably don't understand English. Elsewhere, the only choice open for budget travellers is generally to head for a campsite (*kempings*), which offers basic cabins with shared toilets and washing facilities, and usually space for tents.

Food and drink

Latvian cooking is based around meat, fish, potatoes and dairy products, plus basic vegetables that people can grow on their own plots. Popular **starters** include cabbage soup (*svaigu kāpostu zupa*) – often almost a meal in itself – and sprats with onions (*šprotes ar sīpoliem*). Most **main courses** are meat- or fish-based – try *cūkas galerts* (pork in aspic) or *rasols* (potato salad with herring, beetroot and apple). Popular fish dishes include herring (*siļķe*) and fried, smoked or salted eel (*zutis*). **Desserts** are normally based around forest berries, such as *debess manna* (creamed wheat, cranberries and vanilla sauce). Eating out, particularly in Rīga, is often **expensive**; two people can easily run up a bill of 20Ls. Keep costs down by dining in fast-food places serving indigenous snacks such as *pīrāgi* (blobs of dough with various stuffings) or *pelmeņi* (East-European ravioli). In Rīga you'll also find a few ethnic restaurants offering vegetarian options. Eating in cafés and bars is another cheap option, and self-catering should be no problem as food shops are well stocked with picnic staples.

Rīga has excellent **bars**, though some are expensive. A lot of places serve imported **beer** (*alus*), but the local brews are fine, and usually cheaper – the most common brand is Aldaris. Worth trying once (and probably only once) is Rīgas Melnais Balzāms, or Rīga black balsam, a kind of bitter made from a secret recipe combining various roots and herbs. Outside the capital most towns will have at least one bar, café or restaurant. **Coffee** (*kafija*) and **tea** (*tēja*) are usually served black – if you want milk (*piens*) and/or sugar (*cukurs*) you'll have to ask.

Opening hours and holidays

Shops usually open Mon–Fri 8/10am–6/8pm, though some close for an hour at lunchtime. A few food shops open until 10pm and also open Sunday. Most shops and all banks close on the following **public holidays**: Jan 1; Good Fri; Easter Day; May 1; 2nd Sun in May; June 23 & 24; Nov 18; Dec 25, 26 & 31.

Emergencies

Latvian organized crime – though a major problem – is unlikely to affect the average visitor. **Theft** is the biggest hazard, and if you're staying in a cheap hotel it's best not to leave valuables in your room. Muggings and casual violence are not unknown in Rīga; avoid the backstreets after dark. **Police** (*policija*) are unlikely to speak much, if any, English. Emergency **medical** care is free, though if you fall ill you'd do best to head for home: Latvian medical facilities are run-down.

Emergency numbers

Police ☏02; Ambulance ☏03; Fire ☏01.

Rīga

RĪGA is the undisputed Baltic metropolis, a major port and industrial centre of nearly a million people. The city was founded by Albert von Buxhoeveden, a German canon who arrived in 1201 with twenty shiploads of crusaders to convert the Latvian tribes to Christianity. The main Hanseatic outpost in the region, Rīga was run by German nobles and merchants even when wider political control passed to other powers, starting with the Polish-Lithuanian Commonwealth in the late sixteenth century. After a subsequent period of Swedish rule Rīga became part of the Russian Empire in 1710 and during the second half of the nineteenth century it developed into a major manufacturing centre. Badly damaged during World War I, the city made a comeback during the first Latvian independence and remained a major centre after the country was swallowed up by the Soviet Union in 1940. Under the Soviets, the influx of Russian immigrants reduced the Latvians to a minority in their own capital – thirty percent of the city's population is now Russian, with a further sixteen percent made up of other non-Latvian nationalities. These days Rīga has a boom-town feel with a small but conspicuous section of the population making big bucks from the get-rich-quick opportunities thrown up by the switch to full-blown market economics.

Arrival, information and accommodation

Rīga's main **train station** (Centrālā Stacija) and **bus station** (Autoosta) are just south of Old Rīga and within easy walking distance of the centre. The sea passenger terminal (Jūras pasažieru stacija) is to the north of the centre. **Trams** #5, #7 or #9 run from the stop in front of the terminal on Ausekļa iela into the centre of town (two stops). There are **tourist offices** at the airport (daily 9am–9pm; ☎720 7800) and on the Old Town's main square, Rātslaukums (daily 10am–7pm; ☎704 4377, ✆www.rigatourism.com), both of which have leaflets and hotel lists. They also sell the **Rīga Card** (8/12/16Ls for 24/48/72hr) which gives unlimited use of public transport and museum discounts, but it's worth doing a few sums to see whether it will save you any money on your planned itinerary. The excellent English-language guide *Rīga in Your Pocket* (1.20Ls; ✆www.inyourpocket.com) is available from kiosks and bookshops. Old Rīga is easily walkable, and you can also cover the New Town on foot. Outlying attractions are reached by bus, tram or trolleybus: flat-fare single-journey **tickets** cost 0.20Ls, bought from the conductor. **Taxis** should cost 0.30Ls per kilometre during the day and 0.40Ls between 10pm and 6am, but watch out for rip-offs or non-functioning meters. Rīga Taxi (☎800 1010) is usually reliable. Rīga has no shortage of expensive **hotels** as well as some very basic budget places. Comfortable, reasonably priced options do exist, but should be reserved in advance in summer. The one **campsite** in the city is ABC, 6km southwest of the centre at Šampētera 139a (☎789 2728, ✆kempingabc@appollo.lv; buses #22 and #22A pass by), with space for tents as well as well-appointed cabins (❸).

Hostels

Latvijas Universitātes dienesta viesnīca Basteja 10 ☎721 6221. Hostel on the edge of the old town, with doubles or triples from 8Ls per person. Fills up quickly.

Placis Laimdotas 2a ☎755 1824. Beds from 5Ls per person. Located 5km northeast of the centre; take bus #1, #14 or #23 to the Teika stop.

Hotels

Homestay Stokholmas 1 ☎755 3016, ✆www.homestay.lv. Three rooms (one double, one single, one suite), in a friendly family home. Take tram 11 to Vizbijas prospekts. ❸

Jūrnieks Sofijas 8 ☎739 2350, ✆www.jurnieks.lv. Civilised cheapie with neat en suites with TV, 6km north of the centre in the Sarkandaugava suburb. Tram #5 or #9 from the Opera to Allažu iela. ❷

Laine Skolas 11 ☎728 8816, ✆www.laine.lv. A friendly and comfortable mid-range hotel, ten minutes' walk northeast of the old town. En suites ❻ Rooms with shared bath ❸

Radi un Draugi Mārstaļu 1/3 ☎724 2239, ✆www.draugi.lv. One of the few affordable places in the old town, offering cosy en suites with TV.

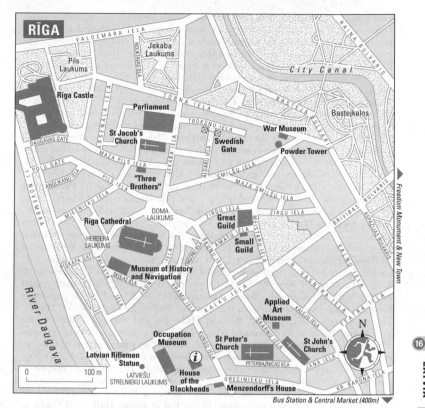

RĪGA

VALDEMĀRA IELA

Jēkaba
Laukums

Pils
Laukums

City Canal

Rīga Castle

Parliament

Bastejkalns

St Jacob's
Church

War Museum

Swedish
Gate

Powder Tower

"Three
Brothers"

DOMA
LAUKUMS

Rīga Cathedral

Great
Guild

HERDERA
LAUKUMS

Small
Guild

Museum of History
and Navigation

River Daugava

Applied
Art
Museum

Occupation
Museum

St Peter's
Church

St John's
Church

Latvian Riflemen
Statue

0   100 m

LATVIEŠU
STRELNIEKU LAUKUMS

House
of the
Blackheads

Menzendorff's House

Freedom Monument & New Town

N

Bus Station & Central Market (400m)

Very popular, so ring in advance. ⑤
Saulīte Merķeļa 12 ☎722 4546. Basic place
opposite the train station. Some renovated rooms
have en-suite WC and showers, but are more
expensive than standard doubles. ②
Tia Valdemāra 63 ☎733 3918, ⓦwww.tia.lv.
Modern hotel with sparsely-furnished but neat

en suites, a 15-min walk northeast of the
centre. ④
Valdemārs Valdemāra 23 ☎733 4462,
ⓦwww.valdemars.lv. En-suite rooms in this Art
Nouveau building have dull brown colour schemes
but are spacious and clean. A 10-min walk
northeast of the centre. ③

The City

Vecrīga or **Old Rīga**, centred on Cathedral Square and neatly cut in two from east
to west by Kaļķu iela, forms the city's nucleus and is home to most of its historic
buildings. To the east Old Rīga is bordered by Bastejkalns Park, beyond which lies
the **New Town**, the nineteenth- and early twentieth-century extension of the city
which contains some remarkable Jugendstil architecture.

Old Rīga

Cathedral Square (Doma laukums) is edged by government offices and a sprinkling of
cafés, and dominated by the red-brick **Rīga Cathedral** (Tues–Fri 1–5pm, Sat
10am–2pm; 0.50Ls), a towering agglomeration of Romanesque, Gothic and Baroque
architecture. The cathedral was established in 1211 by Albert von Buxhoeveden, the
founder of Rīga, who became its first bishop. The interior is relatively unadorned, the

most eye-catching features being a florid pulpit from 1641 and a magnificent nine-teenth-century organ with 6768 pipes. The east wing of the cathedral was once a monastery but now houses the **Rīga Museum of History and Navigation** (Rīgas vestures un kuģniecības muzejs), Palasta 4 (May–Sept Wed–Sun 10am–5pm, Oct–April Wed–Sun 11am–5pm; 1.20Ls), a collection of nautical ephemera and archeological finds. The ticket also gives admission to the Cross Gallery of the Cathedral.

From the Cathedral Square Pils iela runs down to leafy **Castle Square** (Pils laukums) and the nondescript **Rīga Castle** (Rīgas pils), built in 1515 by the Livonian Order (the organization of crusading knights who conquered the region), and recent-ly restored as a residence for the Latvian president. Heading along Mazā Pils iela from Pils laukums takes you past the **Three Brothers** (Trīs brāli), three plain medieval houses, one of which dates from the fifteenth century and is thought to be the oldest surviving house in Latvia. A left turn into Jēkaba iela at the end of Mazā Pils iela leads to the thirteenth-century red-brick **St Jacob's Church** (Jēkaba baznīca), the seat of Rīga's Roman Catholic archbishop. Next door at Jēkaba 11 is Latvia's **Parliament** (Latvijas augstākā padome), housed in a pompous Renaissance-style building dating from the late nineteenth century. Nearby on Torņa iela you'll find the seventeenth-century **Swedish Gate** (Zviedru vārti). This simple archway beneath a three-storey town house was built when Rīga was ruled by the Swedes, and is the sole surviving city gate. A more impressive relic can be found at the end of Torņa iela in the shape of the **Powder Tower** (Pulvertornis), a vast, fourteenth-century bastion whose red-brick walls are still embedded with cannonballs from various sieges. Today, it's home to the **Museum Of War** (Wed–Sun 10am–5pm; 0.50Ls; English-language leaflet 0.40Ls) with sections on the War of Liberation (1918–20), and on the volunteer Latvian Legion who served with the German Waffen SS during World War II. Though it's not readily apparent, **Bastion Hill** – the park that slopes down to the city canal on the eastern edge of Old Rīga – is actually a vast earthworks built as part of the city's outer defences. It's also a reminder of Rīga's more recent history: on January 20, 1991 four people were killed here by sniper fire as Soviet OMON troops stormed the Latvian Ministry of the Interior on nearby Raiņa bulvaris during an attempted crackdown on Latvia's independence drive. Stones bearing the names of the victims mark where they fell near the Bastejas bulvaris entrance. From the Swedish Gate Meistaru iela runs down to the **Great Guild Hall** (Lielā Ģilde) at Amatu 6, once the centre of commercial life in Hanseatic Rīga. Though it dates from the fourteenth century the building owes its present neo-Gothic appearance to a nineteenth-century facelift and now houses the Latvia State Philharmonic. South of Kaļķu iela on Skārņu iela is **St Peter's Church** (Pēterbaznīca; Tues–Sun 10am–5.30pm); a large red-brick structure with a graceful three-tiered spire, it's dedi-cated to the city's patron saint. A lift (same times; 1.60Ls) takes visitors to the church's gallery and observation platform, affording panoramic views over the city.

Before World War II the late-Gothic **House of the Blackheads** (Melngalvju nams, Tues–Sun 10am–5pm, 1Ls), headquarters of a guild of bachelor merchants and one of Rīga's most famous medieval buildings, stood to the west of St Peter's on what used to be the town hall square (Rātslaukums), which was destroyed in 1941, then totally rebuilt in celebration of Rīga's 800-year anniversary in 2001. These days the square, bereft of any other historic buildings, is known as **Latvian Riflemen's Square** (Latviešu Strēlnieku Laukums) in honour of the Latvian sol-diers who fought with the Imperial Russian army during World War I, and then with the Bolsheviks, as the Latvian Red Riflemen, during the Russian Civil War. They are commemorated by a red marble statue depicting three stern figures clad in greatcoats and caps near the bridge at the western end of the square. Also on the square is the **Occupation Museum** of Latvia (Latvijas okupācijas muzejs; ⓦ www.occupationmuseum.lv; May–Sept daily 11am–5pm, Oct–April Tues–Sun 11am–5pm; donations), formerly the Latvian Riflemen's Museum, but now devoted to Latvia's occupation by the Bolsheviks, Nazis and Soviets. Well presented and with some English-language texts, the display is an ideal introduction to Latvian contemporary history. Nearby at Grēcinieku 18 is **Menzendorff's House** (Mencendorfa nams; Wed–Sun 10am–5pm; 0.75Ls), an impeccably restored late-seventeenth-century merchant's house.

The New Town and the Central Market

The boulevards of the **New Town**, rolling east from Old Rīga, bear witness to a period of rapid urban expansion that began in 1857, when the city's medieval walls were demolished, and lasted right up until World War I. As Rīga grew into a major industrial centre and country-dwellers flocked to the city, four- and five-storey apartment buildings – many of them decorated with extravagant Jugendstil motifs – were erected to house the expanding middle class. As you head east out along Kaļķu, which widens out and becomes Brīvības bulvāris, the defiantly modernist **Freedom Monument** (Brīvības piemineklis) dominates the view. This stylized female figure, placed here in 1935 and known as "Milda", holds aloft three stars symbolizing the three regions of Latvia. Incredibly, the monument survived the Soviet era, and nowadays two soldiers stand guard here in symbolic protection of Latvia's independence. Running north from Brīvības bulvāris to the east of the Freedom Monument is the formal **Esplanade Park** with the **Cathedral of Christ's Nativity** (Kristus dzimsanas katedrāle) just inside its grounds. This late nineteenth-century mock-Byzantine creation was recently returned to the city's Orthodox community after serving as a planetarium during the Soviet period. At the far end of the park is the **State Museum of Latvian Art** (Valsts mākslas muzejs), Valdemāra iela 10 (Wed–Mon 11am–5pm, Thurs 11am–7pm; 1.20Ls), housed in a grandiose Neoclassical building. Among the numerous nineteenth- and twentieth-century Latvian works inside, the odd street scenes and portraits of Jānis Tīdemanis (1897–1964) make the most lasting impression. Beyond the park it's worth continuing along Brīvības bulvāris as far as the **Alexander Nevsky Church** (Aleksandra Nevska Baznīca) at no. 56, an attractive little Orthodox church from the 1820s, partly concealed by trees on the southern side of the street.

Jugendstil architectural embellishments – florid stucco swirls surrounding door-ways, stylized human faces incorporated into facades, and towers fancifully placed on top of buildings – can be seen on virtually every street of the New Town. One of the most famous examples is at **Elizabetes 10a and 10b**, an apartment building designed by Mikhail Eisenstein, the father of film director Sergei. Adorned with plaster flourishes and gargoyles, it is topped by two vast impassive faces. An even more impressive ensemble of buildings can be seen a block north of here on **Alberta iela**. Eisenstein designed almost all the apartment blocks on the even num-bered side of the street, emloying a slightly different architectural style for each one. To get an idea of what these *fin-de-siècle* homes were like on the inside, visit the **Janis Rosentāls Museum** at Alberta 12 (Wed–Sun 11am–6pm; 0.60Ls), occupying the flat where Latvia's most famous artist lived in the years prior to World War I.

On the southeastern side of Old Rīga, just beyond the bus and train stations, the bustling **Central Market** (Centrālais tirgus) is housed in a row of hulking 1930s former Zeppelin hangars. As well as being a useful source of fruit and vegetables, the market is an interesting place to wander round – but keep an eye on your pos-sessions.

Eating, drinking and nightlife

Many bars and cafés do **food** that is less expensive and often just as good as restau-rant dishes. There are also plenty of inexpensive fast-food places. Many places have English-language menus. For **drinking**, most of the Old Town bars, particularly those around Cathedral Square, tend to be expensive and geared towards tourists and rich locals. A number of cheaper and more off-beat places can be found in the New Town. The majority of locals can't afford Rīga bar prices so they buy beer from kiosks and wander the streets.

Cafés and snacks

Café Opera Aspazijas 3. Even if you don't have time to catch a production, the marble and wood interior of the Opera House (🕸www.opera.lv) coffee house is worth a visit. Daily 9am–6pm.

Coffee Nation Valdemāra 21. First of a predicted chain of Latvian espresso bars. Excellent cappuccino, cakes and pastries. Popular with film school students and intellectuals. Daily 8am–10pm.

Lido–Staburags Čaka 55. Point and pile your plate up for 2Ls. Traditional Latvian food served amidst old-fashioned oak rooms. Daily noon–1am.

Lido–Vērmanītis Elizabetes 65. All manner of tasty Baltic meat-and-potato dishes, plus salads and fruit bars on the ground floor, pizza and fast food in the cellar. Daily 8am–11pm.

Monte Kristo Ģertrūdes 27. Great coffee house serving pastries. Sun–Fri 9am–9pm, Sat noon–9pm.

Pelmeņi XL Kaļķu 7. Popular fast-food joint on the old town's main street offering Slavic ravioli: blobs of dough (*pelmeņi*) filled with meat or cheese. Mon–Sat 8am–9pm.

Pizza Lulū Ģertrūdes 27. Fashionable little pizzeria with reasonable prices. 24hr.

Šefpavārs Vilhelms Sķūņu 6. Self-service, create your own pancake place near the Cathedral Square. Mon–Thurs 9am–10pm, Fri 9am–11pm, Sat 10am–11pm, Sun 10am–10pm.

Sievasmātes Pīrādziņi Kaļķu 10. Cheap and cheerful canteen specializing in traditional Latvian pasties stuffed with all manner of fillings. Closes 9pm.

Restaurants

Lidojošā Varde Elizabetes 31a. A New Town basement restaurant serving an eclectic international menu in Jugendstil-pastiche decor. Main courses from around 3Ls. Daily 10am–1am.

Pūt Vējiņ! Jauniela 18/22. Cheap burgers and pasta dishes on the ground floor, moderately priced Latvian specialities in the restaurant *Blow Little Winds!* upstairs. Daily noon–midnight.

Rāma Barona 56. Hare-Krishna-run veggie place in the New Town with a tasty range of dirt-cheap Asian dishes. One of the few places in the city for vegans. Daily 9am–9pm.

Salt 'n' Pepper 13. Janvāra 33. Laid-back bar-restaurant with a bit of everything, from hearty breakfasts through lunchtime soups to an international array of main meals. Closes midnight

Vecemeita ar kaķi Māza pils 1. Chic but cheap basement café-restaurant serving up a tasty mix of Latvian and Mediterranean cuisine. Closes 11pm.

Zelta Krogs Citadeles 12. Mixed European-Latvian cuisine in a bright, relaxing spot just north of the Old Town. Plenty of salads, pasta and vegeterian pancakes, all at reasonable prices. Closes 10pm.

Bars

Alus Sēta Tirgotu iela 6. Sample good, cheap Latvian ales accompanied by the national beer-snack – peas (*zirņi*) sprinkled with bacon bits. Outdoor seating in warm months. Daily 11am–1am.

A. Suns Elizabetes 83–85. Named after Dalí and Buñuel's collaboration *Un Chien Andalou*, this arty café/bar has an eclectic menu, with dishes from around 3Ls and some good vegetarian options. Mon–Wed 8am–1am, Thurs & Fri 8am–3am, Sat 11am–3am, Sun 11am–1am.

DECO Bars Dzirnavu 84. Snacks, great cocktails, music, dancing and excellent service. Sun–Thur 11am–1am, Fri & Sat 11am–5am.

Dickens Grēcinieku 11. Brit-pub with wide range of international beers, heaving with expats and locals every weekend. Top-notch pub grub in the restaurant section at the back. Daily 11am–1am.

Paddy Whelan's Bar Grēcinieku 4. Big, lively Irish pub, popular with young locals and expats alike. Mon–Thurs 10am–midnight, Fri 10am–1am, Sat 11am–1am, Sun 11am–midnight.

Pulkvedim Neviens Neraksta Peldu 26/28. Hip bar with industrial-chic decor and alternative-leaning crowd. Serves meat and pasta during the day, becomes a club at night (when there's an admission charge). Frequent live bands. Sun–Thurs noon–2am, Fri & Sat noon–5am.

Rīgas Balzams Torņa 4. Roomy, chic cellar bar serving up Rīga's favourite firewater – the black, syrupy *balzams* – either on its own or in a mind-boggling number of mixer combinations. Closes midnight.

Sarkans Stabu iela 10. Designer bar on three floors attracting a trend-conscious but laid-back crowd. The international food menu has plenty of vegeterian choices. Sun–Thur closes midnight, Fri & Sat closes 4am.

Spalvas pa gaisu Grēcinieku 2. Snazzy and spacious café-bar with loungey corners, loud music and good cocktails. Full menu of food, including some delicious sweets

Vīna Pagrabs Pils 22. Cheap drinks, bench seating and alternative background music in friendly brick-lined cellar. Closes 11pm.

Live music and clubs

Bites Blūzs Klubs Dzirnavu 34a. Laid-back, unpretentious blues pub with regular gigs and a decent food menu. Mon–Thurs till 1am, Fri & Sat till 2am, Sun till midnight.

Četri Balti Krekli Vecpilsētas 12. Large upmarket cellar bar known for its Latvian-only music policy. Regular gigs by domestic rock-pop acts. Daily noon–5am.

Depo Vaļņu 32. Post-industrial cellar space with

alternative DJ nights and live bands. Functions as a laid-back café during the day. 2Ls.

Karakums Lāčplēša 18. A popular café/bar with acoustic bands playing on the ground floor, and a dance floor upstairs with live bands or DJs providing the sounds. Daily 2pm–3am.

M-808 Lāčplēša 5. Small and friendly cellar club 15min walk northeast of the centre, offering a much more cutting-edge menu of dance music than the bigger downtown clubs. Thurs–Sat 9am–6pm. 2Ls.

Roxy Kaļķu 24. Popular with Russian speakers, expats and beautiful young things. Bar, billiards and dancing. Daily 9pm–6am; 5Ls.

Purvs Matīsa 60. Stylish gay club whose name means "Swamp". Erotic performances, sometimes with audience participation. Wed–Sun 8pm till late. 1–3Ls.

Roxy Kaļķu 24. Popular with Russian speakers, expats and beautiful young things. Bar, billiards and dancing. Daily 9pm–6am; 5Ls.

Saksofons Stabu 43. Small rock, jazz and blues venue with a bohemian clientele. The cocktails are cheap and potent. Daily 2pm–2am.

XXL Kalniņa 4. Gay club and restaurant attracting a mixed, dance-oriented crowd. Good food and wild decor. Daily 4pm–6am; cover charge Tues–Sat 1–5Ls.

Listings

Bike rental Gandrs Kalnciema 28 ☏ 7614 775.
Embassies Canada, Doma laukums 4 ☏ 783 0141; UK, Alunāna 5 ☏ 733 8126; US, Raiņa bulvaris 7 ☏ 721 0005.
Exchange Marika: Basteja 14, Brīvības 30, Marijas 5, Merķeļa 10 (all 24hr).
Hospital Ars, Skolas 5 ☏ 720 1001. Some English-speaking doctors.

Internet access Internet Kafejnīca, Elizabetes 75; Internet Klubs, Kalku 10 (24hr).
Left luggage At the bus station (daily 6.30am–11pm). Lockers at the left-luggage office (Rokas Bagāīas) in the train station basement (0.50–1Ls per day, 4.30am–midnight).
Pharmacy Rudens aptieka, Ģertrūdes 105 ☏ 724 4322 (24hr).
Post office Brīvības bulvāris 19 (24hr).

Day-trips from Rīga

JŪRMALA or "Seashore" is the collective name for a string of small seaside resorts that line the Baltic coast for about 20km west of Rīga. Originally favoured by the tsarist nobility, it became the haunt of Latvian intellectuals between the wars. Today, its sandy beaches backed by dunes and pine woods seethe with people at weekends and on public holidays. Trains for Jūrmala leave the suburban terminus of Rīga's central station from platforms 3 and 4; **Majori**, about 10km beyond Rīga city limits, is the main stop. Here you'll find a number of restaurants and cafés along Jomas iela, the pedestrianized main street running east from the station square. Head north from here to Jūras iela, from where a few paths lead to the beach. The **tourist office** at Jomas 42 (June–Aug daily 11am–9pm; Sept–May Mon–Fri 9am–5pm; ☏ 776 4276, @ www.jurmala.lv) can arrange accommodation.

The concentration camp at **SALASPILS**, 22km southeast of Rīga, is where most of Rīga's Jewish population perished during World War II. Around 100,000 people died here, including Jews from other countries who had been herded into the Rīga Ghetto after most of the indigenous Jewish population had been wiped out. Today the site is marked by monumental sculptures and a memorial, with the former locations of the barrack buildings outlined by white stones. To get there take a suburban train in the direction of Ogre and alight at Dārziņi station (little more than a halt in the middle of a forest, it's easy to miss) from where a clearly signposted path leads to the memorial, a walk of about fifteen minutes.

RUNDĀLE PALACE or Rundāles Pils (daily 10am–5/6pm; 1.50Ls), 77km south of Rīga, is one of the architectural wonders of Latvia. This 138-room Baroque palace, built in two phases during the 1730s and 1760s, was designed by Bartolomeo Rastrelli, the architect who created the Winter Palace in St Petersburg. It was privately owned until 1920 when it fell into disrepair, but meticulous restoration, begun in 1973, has largely returned it to its former glory. To get there take the bus to **Bauska** (@ www.bauska.lv) and then a local service to Pilsrundāle, where the palace stands on the other side of the hedge from the bus stop. Should you want to stay overnight, try the *Viesnīca Bauska*, Slimnīcas 7, Bauska (☎3924705; ②) by the bus station.

Sigulda and Cēsis

SIGULDA, dotted with parks and clustered above the southern bank of the River Gauja around 50km northeast of Rīga, is the **Gauja National Park**'s main centre and a good jumping-off point for exploring the rest of the Gauja Valley. From the train station Raiņa iela runs north into town, passing the bus station on the way. After about 800m a right turn into Baznīca iela brings you to **Sigulda Church** (Siguldas Baznīca), built over seven hundred years ago, though much altered since. A left turn after the church leads, by way of **Sigulda New Castle** (Siguldas Jaunā Pils), a nineteenth-century manor house masquerading as a medieval castle, to the ruins of Sigulda Castle (Siguldas Pilsdrupas), a former stronghold of the Knights of the Sword. From here you can admire **Turaida Castle** (Turaidas Pils), perched on a bluff 3km away. To get there, catch one of the Turaida or Krimulda buses from Sigulda bus station, or walk there in about 45 minutes. Begin the walk by taking J. Poruka iela northwest from Sigulda church, and descending the wooden staircase at the end to the bridge across the Gauja river. On the far side of the bridge an asphalt path slopes down to the left, and runs past several sandstone caves before rejoining the main road just short of Turaida itself. Built on the site of an earlier stronghold by the bishop of Rīga in 1214, Turaida Castle was destroyed when lightning hit its gunpowder magazine in the eighteenth century. Extensively restored, these days it houses a local history **museum** (Tues–Sun 10am–5/6pm; 0.80Ls). Just before the castle is the eighteenth-century **Turaidas Church** (Turaidas Baznīcas), an appealing little wooden church with a Baroque tower that's one of the best-preserved examples of Latvian native architecture in the country. Sigulda is also the centre for a range of activities from bobsledding and bungee jumping to bike rental – pick up information from the Sigulda **tourist office** at Pils 6 (Mon–Fri 10am–5pm; ☎797 1335, ⊛www.sigulda.lv).

The well-preserved little town of **CĒSIS**, 35km northeast of Sigulda, is considered by many Latvians to have an atmosphere as close to that of prewar small-town Latvia as it's possible to get. One of the oldest towns in the country, it's the former seat of the master of the Livonian order and was also a member of the Hanseatic League. More recently Cēsis was the site of a crucial battle during the War of Independence, when a combined Latvian/Estonian force defeated the Iron Division of the German *Landeswehr* in June 1919. From the **train** and **bus** stations walk down Raunas iela to Vienības Laukums, the town's main square. The attractive but run-down old town – a few narrow streets lined with flaking wooden buildings – lies to the south of here. On Rīgas iela just south of the square the remains of the old town gates have been excavated. Nearby, on Skolas iela, is the thirteenth-century **St John's Church** (Svēta Jāņa Baznīca), which contains the tombs of several masters of the Livonian order. East of the square are the remains of **Cēsis Castle** (Cēsu Pils) founded by the Knights of the Sword in 1209.

Travel details

Trains

Rīga to: Majori-Jūrmala (every 30min; 40min); Cēsis (7 daily; 1hr 30min); Moscow, Russia (1 daily; 17hr 30min); Sigulda (10 daily; 1hr); St Petersburg, Russia (1 daily; 14hr); Vilnius, Lithuania (3 weekly; 6hr).

Buses

Rīga to: Bauska (every 30min; 1hr 10min–1hr 30min); Cēsis (20 daily; 2hr); Kaunas, Lithuania (3 daily; 4hr 30min); Klaipēda, Lithuania (1 daily; 5hr); Pärnu, Estonia (3 daily; 3hr 30min); Sigulda (hourly; 1hr); Tallinn, Estonia (7 daily; 5hr 30min); Tartu, Estonia (1 daily; 5hr); Vilnius, Lithuania (5 daily; 6hr).
Sigulda to: Turaida (12 daily; 10min).

Lithuania

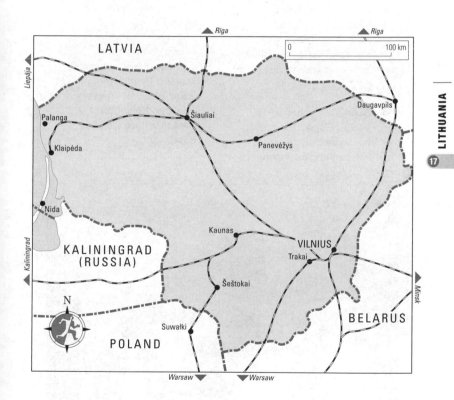

Lithuania highlights

* **St Anne's church, Vilnius** Napoleon wanted to take this little late-Gothic masterpiece home to Paris. **See p.621**

* **Genocide museum, Vilnius** In the former KGB HQ, this museum is a shocking reminder of man's inhumanity. **See p.623**

* **Skonis ir Kvapas, Vilnius** Elegant tea house with gorgeous interiors and an impressive range of teas and coffees. **See p.623**

* **Trakai** A fairy-tale medieval castle sitting on its own little island amongst lush green countryside a little west of Vilnius. **See p.625**

* **Couronian Spit** The wild, beautiful Couronian National Park on the Baltic coast was recently added to UNESCO's World Heritage List. **See p.628**

Introduction and basics

Unlike its Baltic neighbours, **Lithuania** once enjoyed a period of sustained independence, emerging as a unified state in the fourteenth century. In 1569, it united with Poland, but the Great Northern War of 1700–21, in which Poland-Lithuania, Russia and Sweden battled for control of the Baltics, left the country devastated. By the end of the eighteenth century most of Lithuania had fallen into Russian hands, but Russia's collapse in World War I enabled the Lithuanians to re-establish their independence – until effective annexation by the USSR in 1940. The country declared its independence on March 11, 1990, way ahead of the other Baltic States.

Travel in Lithuania presents no real hardships, and even in well-trodden destinations the volume of visitors is low, leaving you with the feeling that there's still much to discover here. **Vilnius**, with its Baroque old town, is the most architecturally beautiful of the Baltic capitals, while the second city, **Kaunas**, also has an attractive centre and a couple of unique museums, along with a handful of surprisingly good restaurants and bars. The port city of **Klaipėda** has a restored old town, and is a stopping-off point en route to the resorts of **Neringa**, a unique spit of sand dunes and forest that shields Lithuania from the Baltic.

Information & maps

Most major towns have **tourist offices** (ⓦ www.tourism.lt), often offering accommodation listings and events calendars in English. *Vilnius In Your Pocket* guide (available from bookshops, newsstands, tourist offices and some hotels; 8Lt) is an indispensable source of practical information. Regional maps and detailed street plans of Vilnius are available in bookshops and kiosks.

Money and banks

Lithuania's currency is the **litas** (usually abbreviated to Lt), which is divided into 100 centai.

Coins come as 0.01, 0.02, 0.05, 0.10, 0.20, 0.50Lt, with notes of 1, 2, 5, 10, 20, 50, 100 and 200Lt. The litas is pegged to the euro (€1 = 3.45Lt). **Bank** (*bankas*) opening hours vary, though branches of the Vilniaus Bankas usually open Mon–Fri 8am–3/4pm. They generally give advances on Visa/Mastercard/AmEx cards and cash travellers' cheques (commission 2–3 percent). Outside banking hours, find an exchange office (*valiutos keitykla*). Credit cards are most likely to be accepted in Vilnius.

Communications

In major towns, **post offices** (*paštas*) are open Mon–Fri 8am–6pm, Sat 8am–3pm; in smaller places hours are more restricted. Stamps are also available at some kiosks and tourist offices. Public **phones** operate with cards (*telefono kortele*; 9Lt, 13Lt, 16Lt and 30Lt) from post offices and kiosks. To make a long-distance call, dial ☎8 before the area code. When calling Lithuania from abroad, omit the initial 8. For international calls, dial ☎8, wait for the tone, then dial 10, then the country code as usual. There's a good choice of **Internet** cafés in Vilnius and a few in Kaunas.

Getting around

Buses are slightly quicker and slightly more

Lithuania on the net

ⓦ **www.tourism.lt** National tourist board site with useful information.
ⓦ **www.exploringvilnius.lt** Attractive city guide with photographs and listings.
ⓦ **www.search.lt** Lithuanian search engine.
ⓦ **www.lietuva.lt** General information about the country.

expensive than trains, though both are desperately slow. You should buy **train** tickets in advance – stations have separate windows for long-distance and suburban (*priemiestinis* or *vietinis*) trains. Long-distance services are divided into "passenger" (*keleivinis traukinys*) and "fast" (*greitas*); the latter usually require a reservation. On timetable boards, look for *išvyksta* (departure) or *atvyksta* (arrival).

It's best to buy long-distance **bus** tickets in advance, and opt for an express (*ekspresas*) if possible, to avoid frequent stops. You can also pay for your ticket on board, although this doesn't guarantee you a seat. Normally luggage is taken on board, though large bags may have to go in the luggage compartment for a small charge. Buses are also useful for travelling to Lithuania's Baltic neighbours.

Accommodation

The best way to keep **accommodation** costs down is by staying in **private rooms**, as budget hotels tend to be pretty grim. The most reliable agency is Litinterp, with offices in Vilnius, Klaipėda and Kaunas. Spartan double rooms in Soviet-era budget hotels cost as little as 40Lt. Smaller, mid-range places charge upwards of 280Lt a double. In Vilnius and Kaunas you'll find many international business hotels charging 400Lt and upwards.

There are a few **hostels**, charging 24–32Lt per night. Space is limited and it's best to try and ring individual establishments in advance. An ex-Soviet phenomenon is the cabin **campsite** (*kempingas*), offering accommodation in three to four-bed cabins (usually primitive facilities are shared with other cabins) for around 20Lt per person. Many will also let you pitch a tent for slightly less. The downside is that they're often located a long way out of town. You can also camp wild in the countryside, subject to the approval of the landowner.

Food and drink

Lithuanian **cuisine**, based on traditional peasant dishes, is less bland than that of its Baltic neighbours, partly as a result of Polish influence. Typical **starters** include marinated mushrooms (*marinuoti grybai*), herring (*silkė*)

and smoked sausage (*rukyta dešra*) along with cold beetroot soup (*šaltibarščiai*). Potatoes play a major role; one of the most common dishes is *cepelinai*, or zeppelins – cylindrical potato dumplings stuffed with meat, mushrooms or cheese. Also popular are potato pancakes (*bulviniai blynai*), and cabbage leaves stuffed with minced meat (*balandėliai* or "*pigeons*"). **Desserts** include stewed fruit (*kompotas*), sweet fruit sauce (*kisielius*), and innumerable varieties of pancakes (*blynai, blyneliai* or *lietiniai* are synonyms for more or less the same thing). Western fast food is making inroads, and Vilnius has a few ethnic places. It's possible to find meat-free options on menus. Most cafés and bars do reasonably priced food.

Beer (*alus*) is popular, while the leading local fire-waters are Starka, Trejos devynerios and Medziotoju – invigorating spirits flavoured with herbs. Lively **bars** sprout up daily in Vilnius and Kaunas. Many ape American or Irish models, although there are also plenty of folksy Lithuanian places, while cafés (*kavine*) come in all shapes and sizes. **Coffee** (*kava*) and **tea** (*arbata*) are usually served black.

Opening hours

Opening hours for shops are 9/10am–6/7pm. Outside Vilnius, some places take an hour off for lunch; most usually close on Sun (though some food shops stay open). Most shops and all banks will be closed on the following **public holidays**: Jan 1; Feb 16; March 11; Easter Sun; Easter Mon; May 1; July 6; Aug 15; Nov 1; Dec 25 & 26.

Emergencies

You're unlikely to meet trouble; car theft and late-night mugging are the most common crimes. The cash-starved **police** expect to be taken seriously – be polite if you have dealings with them. A few of the younger ones may speak a little English. Emergency **health care** is free but if you get seriously ill, head home.

Emergency numbers

Police ☎02; Ambulance ☎03; Fire ☎01.

Vilnius

"Narrow cobblestone streets and an orgy of Baroque: almost like a Jesuit city somewhere in the middle of Latin America," wrote the author Czesław Milosz of prewar **VILNIUS**. Soviet-era satellite suburbs aside, it's a description which still rings true today. Despite being the capital of the medieval Lithuanian state, Vilnius was occupied by Poland between the wars, and was inhabited mainly by Poles and Jews, who played such a prominent role in the city's life that it was known as the "Northern Jerusalem". Vilnius is still a cosmopolitan place – around twenty percent of its population is Polish and another twenty percent is Russian – though with just 543,000 inhabitants it has an almost village-like atmosphere, making it an easy place to get to know.

Arrival, information and accommodation

The main **train station** is at Geležinkelio 16, just south of the Old Town, and the main **bus station** is just across the road. There are exchange facilities at both, although you'll get a better rate at banks in the town centre. Trolleybus #2 takes you from the train station to the main Cathedral Square. Walking into the Old Town is feasible too. The **tourist offices** at Vilniaus 22 (Mon–Thurs 9am–6pm Fri 9am–5pm; ☎5/262 9660, ✉turizm.info@vilnius.lt) and the town hall (Mon–Fri 10am–5pm) offer maps, tours and information on hotels and museums, but your best bet is the excellent *Vilnius in Your Pocket* city guide (✇www.inyourpocket.com), costing 8Lt from newspaper kiosks. Vilnius is well served by **public transport** with buses and trolleybuses covering most of the city. Tickets cost 0.80Lt from newspaper kiosks or 1Lt from the driver; validate your ticket by punching it in the machine on board. Alternatively, hail a minibus at any bus stop in the direction you're going, pay the driver 2Lt and you'll be dropped off at the stop you require. **Taxi** prices are usually reasonable and fares should cost no more than around 1–2Lt per kilometre. Phoning for a taxi is one way of ensuring a fair rate; try Vilniaus Taxi (☎5/212 8888).

Best-value accommodation is in **private rooms**. *Litinterp*, Bernardinų 7/2 (Mon–Fri 8.30am–5.30pm, Sat 9am–3.30pm; ☎5/212 3850, ✇www.litinterp.lt), is the longest-established agency, offering rooms in the Old Town – either with a host family or in *Litinterp's* own self-contained guest house – with singles from 80Lt and doubles from 140Lt. Similar deals are offered by the two Vilnius tourist offices.

Hostels

Filaretai Filaretų 17 ☎5/215 4627. HI-affiliated hostel, with kitchen, common room and washing machine. Fifteen minutes' walk east of the Old Town, or bus #34 from the train station. 28–32Lt.

JNN Hostel Ukmergės 25 ☎5/272 2270, ✉jnn@lvjc.lt. A slightly more upmarket place north of the river. Take bus #2 from the airport or trolleybus #5 from the train station to Žaliasis Tiltas followed by bus #2 or #46. 40–75Lt.

Old Town Hostel Aušros Vartų 20–10 ☎5/262 5357. HI-affiliated hostel near the train and bus stations; reservations essential. Cramped, rowdy but comfortable. 32Lt.

Teacher's University Hotel Vivulskio 36 ☎5/213 0509. A choice of 68 rooms, located 20mins' walk west of the Old Town in a dull neighbourhood. From 28Lt.

Hotels

Apia Šv Ignoto 12 ☎5/212 3426, ✇www.apia.lt. Friendly, five-room guest house in superb Old Town location. ❺

Mikotel Pylimo 63 ☎5/260 9626, ✉mikotel@takas.lt. Small-size hotel a few steps away from the train and bus stations, with pristine modern en suites and quirky decor. ❹

Rūdninkų Vartai Rūdninkų 15/46 ☎5/261 3916. Neat and tasteful, medium-sized place on the fringe of the Old Town, rooms arranged around a central courtyard. ❼

Runmis Panevėžio 8a ☎5/265 6816. Simple but comfortable en suites in a residential street just south of the train station (cross the footbridge and bear right). ❸

Žemaitės Žemaitės 15 ☎5/213 5453, ✇www.hotelzemaites.lt. Modern block 2km southwest of the centre offering sparsely furnished but cosy rooms with TV. Trolleybus #15 or #16 from the train and bus stations. ❹

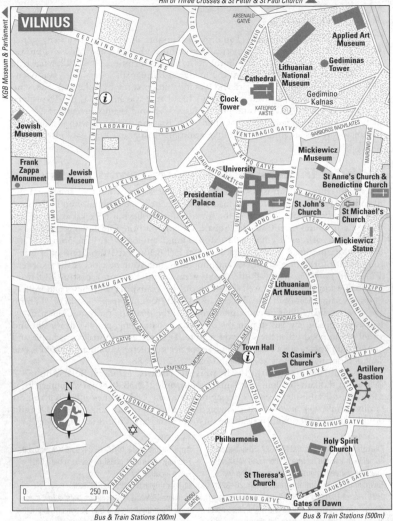

Hill of Three Crosses & St Peter & St Paul Church ▲

VILNIUS

ARSENALO GATVĖ

Applied Art Museum

Gediminas Tower

Lithuanian National Museum

Cathedral

Gedimino Kalnas

GEDIMINO PROSPEKTAS

Clock Tower

KATEDROS AIKŠTĖ

SVENTARAGIO GATVĖ

BARBOROS RADVILAITĖS

Jewish Museum

LABDARIŲ G.

ODMINIŲ GATVĖ

SKAPO GATVĖ

Mickiewicz Museum

Frank Zappa Monument

Jewish Museum

University

St Anne's Church & Benedictine Church

LIELYKLOS G.

Presidential Palace

SV. MYKOLO G.

St John's Church

St Michael's Church

BENEDIKTINŲ G.

SV. IGNOTO

LITERATŲ G.

VILNIAUS G.

SV. JONO G.

Mickiewicz Statue

DOMINIKONŲ G.

ŠVARCO G.

TRAKŲ GATVĖ

Lithuanian Art Museum

UŽUPIO

LYDOS GATVĖ

ŽYDŲ G.

SAVIČIAUS G.

DIDŽIOJI GATVĖ

Town Hall

St Casimir's Church

Artillery Bastion

AŠMENOS

DIDŽIOJI G.

UŽUPIO

N

LIGONINĖS GATVĖ

SUBAČIAUS GATVĖ

PYLIMO GATVĖ

RŪDNINKŲ GATVĖ

Philharmonia

Holy Spirit Church

0   250 m

St Theresa's Church

M. DAUKŠOS GATVĖ

BAZILIJONŲ GATVĖ

Gates of Dawn

Bus & Train Stations (200m) ▼   ▼ Bus & Train Stations (500m)

LITHUANIA | Vilnius

620

17

The City

At the centre of Vilnius, poised between the medieval and nineteenth-century parts of the city, is **Cathedral Square** (Katedros aikstė). To the south of here along Pilies gatvė and Didžioji gatvė is the **Old Town**, containing perhaps the most impressive concentration of Baroque architecture in northern Europe. West of the square in the New Town is **Gedimino prospektas**, a nineteenth-century boulevard and the focus of the city's commercial and administrative life. Wedged between the Old Town and the Gedimino prospektas areas, the traditionally **Jewish areas** of Vilnius were shorn of their populations in the 1941–45 period, but retain some sights.

Cathedral Square and around

Cathedral Square is dominated by the Neoclassical **Cathedral** (daily 7am–7pm), its origins going back to the thirteenth century, when a wooden church is thought to have been built here on the site of a temple dedicated to Perkūnas, the god of thunder. The highlight of the airy, vaulted interior is the opulent **Chapel of St Kazimieras**, dedicated to the patron saint of Lithuania, whose remains lie in a silver casket in the chapel's main altar. Next to the cathedral on the square is the white **belfry**, once part of the fortifications of the vanished Lower Castle but now looking like a stranded Baroque lighthouse. Between the Cathedral and the belfry, locals can often be seen spinning round on a small coloured tile with the word *stebuklas* (miracle) written on it. This marks the spot from where, in 1989, two million people from the Baltic states formed a protest chain which stretched all the way to Tallinn in Estonia. Rising behind the cathedral is the tree-clad **Gediminas Hill**, its summit crowned by the red-brick octagon of **Gediminas Tower**, one of the city's best-known landmarks. The first substantial fortification here was founded by Grand Duke Gediminas, the Lithuanian ruler who consolidated the country's independence. According to legend Gediminas dreamt of an iron wolf howling on a hill overlooking the River Vilnia and was told by a pagan priest to build a castle on the spot. The tower houses the **Upper Castle Museum** (Tues–Sun 11am–5/7pm; 4Lt, free on Wed in winter), showing the former extent of the Vilnius fortifications. About 100m north of the cathedral in a former arsenal building is the **Lithuanian National Museum**, Arsenalo 1 (Wed–Sun 11am–5pm; 4Lt; free Wed in winter; ⊛www.lnm.lt), covering the history of Lithuania from prehistoric times to 1940 but with mostly Lithuanian and Russian labelling. A little further north on Arsenalo, a separate department of the museum houses the much snazzier **Prehistoric Lithuania exhibition** (same times; 4Lt) which, despite its title, covers the story of the Lithuanians up to the Middle Ages. Nearby is the **Applied Art Museum**, Arsenalo 3 (Tues–Sun 11am–5/6pm; 8Lt, free Wed in winter), home to a glittering array of ecclesiastical treasures.

The Old Town

The **Old Town**, just south of Cathedral Square, is a network of narrow, often cobbled streets that forms the Baroque heart of Vilnius, with the pedestrianized **Pilies gatvė** cutting into it from the southeastern corner of the square. To the west of this street is **Vilnius University**, a jumble of buildings constructed between the sixteenth and eighteenth centuries around nine linked courtyards that extend west as far as Universiteto gatvė. Within its precincts is the beautiful, ornate **St John's Church** – access from Šv Jono gatvė. Founded during the fourteenth century, St John's was taken over by the Jesuits in 1561 and given to the university in 1737. Reconstruction after a fire in the same year has left it with its present Baroque facade, and a no-holds-barred Baroque altar inside.

The **Presidential Palace**, just west of the university on **Daukanto aikstė**, was originally built during the sixteenth century as a merchant's residence and remodelled into its present Neoclassical form at the end of the eighteenth century, going on to serve as the residence of the Russian governor-general during the Tsarist period. Napoleon Bonaparte stayed here briefly during his ill-fated campaign against Russia in 1812. The emperor is said to have been so impressed by **St Anne's Church** (Tues–Sat 10am–3pm & 5.30–9pm, Sun 8am–1pm & 5–7pm) on Maironio gatvė, to the east of Pilies gatvė, that he wanted to take it back to Paris on the palm of his hand. Studded with skeletal, finger-like towers, and its facade overlaid with intricate brick traceries and fluting, this late-sixteenth-century structure is the finest Gothic building in Vilnius. Rising behind St Anne's is the Gothic facade of the much larger **Bernardine Church** from 1520. Its once fine Baroque interior suffered during its Soviet-era incarnation as home to the Vilnius Art Academy, and the building is now undergoing a much-needed renovation.

Just south of St Anne's and the Bernardine church is a statue commemorating the Polish Romantic poet Adam Mickiewicz (1798–1855), author of *Pan Tadeusz*, the

Polish national epic. Nearby Bernardinų gatvė is one of the Old Town's more appealing back streets, a narrow lane lined by seventeenth- and eighteenth-century houses. Heading south Pilies becomes Main Street (Didžioji gatvė), with the restored Baroque palace at no. 4 housing the **Lithuanian Art Museum** (Tues–Sat noon–6pm, Sun noon–5pm; 5Lt; free on Wed in winter), a marvellous collection of sixteenth- to nineteenth-century paintings and sculptures from around the country. The colonnaded Neoclassical building standing at the end of **Town Hall Square** (Rotušės aikštė) has recently been restored to its original function as the town hall. The modern building behind it houses the **Contemporary Art Centre** (Tues–Sun 11am–6.30pm; 4Lt; free on Wed in winter), which hosts changing exhibitions of works by modern artists.

Just east of the square, **St Casimir's Church** (Mon–Fri 4–6.30pm, Sun 8am–2pm), dating from 1604 and the oldest Baroque church in the city, remains a striking building – its central cupola topped by an elaborate crown and cross symbolizing the royal ancestry of St Casimir, the son of King Casimir IV of Poland. South of here, Didžioji becomes **Aušros Vartų gatvė**, a short distance along which a gateway on the left-hand side leads to the seventeenth-century **Church of the Holy Spirit**, Lithuania's main Orthodox church, a Baroque structure built on a low hill in the grounds of a monastery. In front of the large iconostasis, the bodies of three fourteenth-century martyred saints are displayed in a glass case, their faces swathed in cloth. A little further along Aušros Vartų gatvė the seventeenth-century **St Theresa's Church** rises to the left of the street, another soaring testimony to the city's dominating architectural style. The end of the street is marked by the **Gates of Dawn**, the sole survivor of nine city gates that once studded the walls of Vilnius. A chapel above the gate houses the city's most celebrated religious monument, the **Madonna of the Gates of Dawn**, an image of the Virgin Mary said to have miraculous powers and revered by Polish Catholics. East of Aušros Vartų gatvė on Boksto 20/18 is the **Artillery Bastion**, a seventeenth-century bastion that was once part of the city's outer fortification ring and which now houses a **museum** (Wed–Sun 10am–5pm; 2Lt, free on Wed in winter) of weapons and armour, though the setting is more interesting than the contents.

Jewish Vilnius

Before World War II Vilnius was one of the most important centres of Jewish life in eastern Europe. The Jews – first invited to settle in 1410 by Grand Duke Vytautas – made up around a third of the city's population, mainly concentrated in the eastern fringes of the Old Town around present-day Vokiečių gatvė, Žydų gatvė and Antokolskio gatvė. The **Great Synagogue** was located just off Žydų gatvė, on a site now occupied by a kindergarten. Massacres of the Jewish population began soon after the Germans occupied Vilnius on June 24, 1941, and those who survived the initial killings found themselves herded into two **ghettos**. The smaller of these ghettos centred around Žydų, Antokolskio, Stiklių and Gaono streets and was liquidated in October 1941, while the larger occupied an area between Pylimo, Vokiečių, Lydos, Mikalojaus, Karmelitų and Arklių streets and was liquidated in September 1943. Most of the Jews of Vilnius perished in Paneriai forest on the southwestern edge of the city (see p.624).

Today, the Jewish population of Vilnius numbers only a few thousand. The city has one surviving **synagogue** at Pylimo 39 (Mon–Thurs 8–10am, Sun 7–9pm), out of the 96 that once existed. To find out about the history of Jewish Vilnius head for the **Lithuanian State Jewish Museum**, housed in various parts of the labyrinthine Jewish community offices at Pylimo 4 (Mon–Thurs 9am–5pm, Fri 9am–4pm; 2Lt, free on Wed in winter). The display includes items salvaged from the Great Synagogue and some of the exhibits are captioned in English. A second branch of the museum, the Catastrophe Exhibition, occupies a small green house nearby at Pamenkalnio 12 (Mon–Thurs 9am–5pm, Fri 9am–4pm; donations), and contains a harrowing display about the fate of Vilnius Jews during the war. The museum can also arrange "history of Jewish Vilnius" tours (℡5/262 0730).

Nearby, the otherwise nondescript Kalinausko street is worth a visit to see the bronze head of rocker **Frank Zappa** perched on a column. Civil servant, Saulis

Paukstys, founded the local Zappa fan club and commissioned the socialist realist sculptor Konstantinas Bogdanas, more accustomed to forging likenesses of Lenin, to create this unique tribute to Zappa.

Gedimino prospektas

Gedimino prospektas, named after the founder of the city, runs west from Cathedral Square, and was, in the past, named after St George, Mickiewicz, Stalin and Lenin, reflecting the succession of foreign powers that controlled the city. It was the main thoroughfare of nineteenth-century Vilnius, and remains the most important commercial street. **Lukiškių aikštė**, around 600m west of Cathedral Square, is the former location of the city's Lenin statue, removed after the failed 1991 coup which precipitated the final break-up of the Soviet Union. The square has long played an infamous role in city history. After the 1863–64 uprising against the Russians, a number of rebels were publicly hanged here, while Gedimino 40, on the southern side of the square, was Lithuania's **KGB headquarters**. The building also served as Gestapo headquarters during the German occupation and more recently the Soviets incarcerated political prisoners in the basement. It's now the **Genocide Museum** (entrance at Aukų 2a; Tues–Sun 10am–4/6pm; 2Lt), with dank green cells and the courtyard where prisoners were tortured and executed preserved in their pre-1991 state. The English-language cassette-tape commentary (8Lt) provides detailed background on the prison and its inmates.

At the far end of Gedimino prospektas stands Lithuania's graceless modern **Parliament Building**. Thousands gathered here on January 13, 1991, when Soviet troops threatened to occupy it following the killing of a dozen people at the TV Tower. Facing the river some of the barricades built to defend the building have been preserved, complete with anti-Soviet graffiti; there's also a moving memorial commemorating those who died at the TV Tower and the seven border guards killed by Soviet special forces in July 1991. The 326-metre **TV Tower** (10am–9pm; 15Lt) itself is around 3km west of the centre in the Karoliniškės district – trolleybus #16 from the train station or #11 from Lukiškių aikštė; alight at the Televizijos bokštas stop on Sausio 13-Osios gatvė. At the tower's base, wooden crosses commemorate those killed here in the bloodiest event of the struggle for Baltic independence.

Eating, drinking and nightlife

There's a fast-growing range of **eateries** in Vilnius offering everything from Lithuanian to Lebanese cuisine – although the majority of places serve the standard meat-and-potatoes. There's little difference between eating and drinking venues: **bars** and **cafés** invariably serve snacks and meals and often represent better value for money than restaurants. Vilnius has a few **clubs** and **discos**, though you may have a better (and cheaper) time in some of the bars mentioned below.

Cafés and snack bars

Afrika Pilies 28. Popular lunchtime stop-off on the Old Town's main street, offering a tasty range of salads, sandwiches and soups.

Bar Italia Gedimino 3a. Strong coffee and excellent sandwich and cake selection.

Greitai Corner of Gedimino and Totorių. Classy cafeteria with cheap main courses (peruse the choice at the counter and point to what you want) and good-ish cakes.

Mano Kavinė Bokšto 7. Stylish place in the Old Town with chic, modernist decor, trendy young clientele, a wide range of snacks and speciality teas.

Pilies Menė Pilies 8. Flash modern café/bar with extensive pancake menu. Good place for a daytime coffee or night-time drink.

Presto Gedimino 32a. Bright modern coffee bar with an impressive range of brews, as well as salads and sumptuous cakes.

Skonis ir Kvapas Trakų 8. The most beautiful vaulted interior in town. Big pots of tea, excellent coffee, and an affordable range of hot meals.

Užupio Kavinė Užupio 2. Relaxed, mildly Bohemian place on the eastern fringes of the Old Town, with lime-tree-shaded outdoor terrace overlooking the Vilnia River.

Restaurants

Balti Drambliai Vilniaus 41. Vegetarian restaurant with friendly service, unusual non-smoking policy

in the cellar and lively beer garden.
Čili Didžioji 5. Popular place for an inexpensive bite, with thin-crust and deep-pan pizzas. Six more branches, one at Gedimino 23.
Finjan Vokiečių 18. Middle-eastern place that looks like a fast-food café but charges restaurant prices. Good kebabs, shawarma and falafel and large portions.
Freskos Didžioji 31. Imaginative, well-presented modern European cuisine behind the Town Hall. Good value lunchtime salad buffet.
Lokys Stiklių 8/10. Reasonably priced Lithuanian cellar restaurant serving boar, elk and beaver meat alongside more traditional meat-and-potato favourites.
Po Saule Labdarių 7. French bistro with superb food at reasonable prices. Great place for a quick *tarte à l'oignon* or a more leisurely three-course meal.
Ritos Slėptuvė Goštauto 8. Excellent pizzas plus quiche, spaghetti and a few vegetarian options. Order local beer to keep your bill manageable. Good for breakfasts and dancing in the evening.
Savas Kampas Vokiečių 4. A cosy wood-furnished interior and extensive list of alcohol, with good pizzas too.
Žemaičių Smuklė Vokiečių 24. The top place for traditional Lithuanian cuisine. An excellent place to try *cepelinai* (potato dumplings stuffed with meat), or *žemaičių blynai* (potato pancakes). Warren of cellar rooms in winter, outdoor courtyard seating in summer.

Bars

Bix Etmonų 6. Great bar with industrial decor, karaoke nights and an enjoyable disco in the cellar – run by members of local rock band Bix. Food available.

Brodvėjaus Pubas Mėsinių 4. Popular drinking/dancing venue with live bands (Thurs–Sun) and DJs. Full menu of snacks and hot meals; lunchtime specials.
Prie Parlamento Gedimino 46. Big, popular café/bar with restaurant-standard food (excellent veggie options) and pub-style bar.
Prie Universiteto Dominikonų 9. British bar with dark interior and covered courtyard. Frequent live music, big-screen sport and extensive food menu.
Šuolaikinio Meno Centras In the Contemporary Art Centre at Vokiečių 2. Dark, minimalist café/bar which has long been a meeting place for arty types and nonconformists.

Clubs and live music

Džiazo Klubas (Jazz Club) Vilniaus 22. Brick-lined cellar bar with decent jazz and blues bands at weekends. Also does decent food.
Gero Viskio Baras Pilies 34. Eternally popular Old-Town drinking joint both day and night. Aside from the main ground-floor bar there's a cocktail bar upstairs; cellar disco after 8pm.
Gravity Jasinskio 16. Ultra-cool joint dedicated to the best in cutting-edge dance culture. Attracts the best of the big-star DJs. Thurs–Sat.
Men's Factory Žygimantų 1. Gay bar and disco found at the north end of the Old Town, beside the river. Bar Wed & Thurs, disco Fri & Sat.
Ministerija Gedimino 46. In the cellar below *Prie Parlamento*, playing newish dance stuff as well as popular classics. Popular with ex-pats and beautiful young things.
Ultra Imperiale Goštauto 12. Trendy place catering for a younger age group. Pop during the week and techno on Sat. Thurs–Sat.

Listings

Embassies and consulates Australia, Vilniaus 23 ☎5/212 3369; Canada, Gedimino 64 ☎5/249 6853; US, Akmenų 6 ☎5/266 5500; UK, Antakalnio 2 ☎5/212 2070.
Exchange Gelezinkelio 6 (24hr).
Hospital Vilnius University Emergency Hospital, Šiltnamių 29 ☎5/216 9140.

Internet access Bazė, Gedimino 50 (entrance round the corner on Rotundo); Collegium, Pilies 22; Netcafe, Antakalnio 36.
Pharmacies Gedimino Vaistinė, Gedimino 27.
Police Jogailos 3 ☎5/261 6208.
Post office Gedimino prospektas 7.

Day-trips from Vilnius

Beyond Vilnius, several places merit a day-trip. **PANERIAI**, the site where the Nazis and their Lithuanian accomplices murdered one hundred thousand people during World War II, lies within Vilnius city limits in a forest at the edge of a suburb, 10km southwest of the centre. Seventy thousand of those killed at Paneriai were Jews from Vilnius, who were systematically exterminated from the time the Germans arrived in June 1941 until they were driven out by the Soviet army in 1944. To get to Paneriai take a southwest-bound suburban train from Vilnius station and alight at Paneriai. From the station platform descend onto Agrastų gatvė, turn right and follow the road through the woods for about a kilometre. The entrance to the site is marked by the **Paneriai Memorial** – two stone slabs with Russian and Lithuanian inscriptions commemorating the murdered "Soviet citizens", flanking a central slab with an inscription in Hebrew commemorating "seventy thousand Jewish men, women and children". From the memorial a path leads to the **Paneriai Museum**, Agrastų 15 (Mon & Wed–Sun 9am–5pm; call to check ☎5/260 2001; donations), with a small display detailing what happened here. Paths lead to the pits in the woods where the Nazis burnt the bodies of their victims and to another eight-metre pit where the bones of the dead were crushed.

    TRAKAI, 25km west of Vilnius, is the former capital of the Grand Duchy of Lithuania. Founded during the fourteenth century and standing on a peninsula jutting out between two lakes, it's the site of two medieval castles. From the **train** and **bus stations** follow Vytauto gatvė to reach the main sights. After about 500m turn right down Kęstučio gatvė to the remains of the **Peninsula Castle**, thought to have been built by Duke Kęstutis, son of Gediminas and father of Vytautas. Trakai is home to the **Karaites**, members of a Judaic sect whose ancestors were brought here from the Crimea by Grand Duke Vytautas to serve him as bodyguards, and whose distinctive wooden cottages line Karaimų gatvė, the northern continuation of Vytauto gatvė. Around two hundred inhabitants of Trakai are Karaites; Lithuania's smallest ethnic minority, they recognize only the laws of the Old Testament. The **Karaim Ethnographic Exhibition**, down the street at no. 22 (Wed–Sun 10am–6pm; 2Lt), holds a small but fascinating display of costumes and furnishings. A hundred metres or so beyond the Kenessa two wooden footbridges lead to the **Island Castle**, a cluster of red-brick towers built around 1400 on a small offshore island and one of Lithuania's most famous monuments. Built by Grand Duke Vytautas, under whom Lithuania reached the pinnacle of its power during the fifteenth century, it fell into ruin from the seventeenth century until a 1960s restoration returned it to its former glory. It now houses a **museum** (daily: May–Sept 10am–7pm; Oct–April 10am–5pm; 8Lt). The main **tower**, built around a galleried courtyard, is separated from the outer buildings by a moat – you cross a footbridge to enter. Within are exhibits covering the history of the castle, plus examples of medieval weaponry and wooden carvings. Trakai's great culinary claim to fame is the *kibinas*, a mincemeat pasty served up at speciality **cafés** like *Kibinine*, Karaimų 65, and *Kybynlar*, Karaimų 29.

The rest of Lithuania

Lithuania is predominantly rural – a gently undulating, densely forested landscape scattered with lakes. However, it does boast at least one more major city in **Kaunas**, a genuine rival to Vilnius in terms of its historical importance. Further west, the main highlight of the coast is the holiday village of **Nida**, whose dramatic dunescapes and traditional timber architecture are reachable by ferry and bus from **Klaipėda**, the country's major port.

Kaunas

KAUNAS, 80km west of Vilnius and easily reached by bus or rail, is Lithuania's second city and seen by many Lithuanians as the true heart of their country. It served as provisional capital during the interwar period when Vilnius was part of Poland, and remains a major commercial and industrial centre. Nevertheless it's an attractive, easygoing city, with enough sights to merit a full day's visit.

    The most interesting part of town is predictably the **Old Town**, or **Senamiestis**, centred around **Town Hall Square** (Rotušės aikstė), on a spur of land between the Neris and Nemunas rivers. The square is lined with fifteenth- and sixteenth-century merchants' houses in pastel stucco shades, but the overpowering feature is the magnificent **Town Hall**, its tiered Baroque facade rising to a graceful 53-metre tower. The other most eye-catching structure on the square is the seventeenth century **Jesuit Church** on the southern side. Originally part of a larger college and monastery complex, the church was built in 1666. In 1825 the Russians handed it over to the Orthodox church, and later the Soviets turned it into a trade school, but the Baroque interior remains intact.

Northeast of the square, the red-brick tower of Kaunas' austere **Cathedral** can be seen at the start of Vilniaus gatvė. Dating back to the reign of Vytautas the Great, the cathedral was much added to in subsequent centuries. After the plain exterior, the lavish gilt and marble interior comes as a surprise. There are nine altars in total, though the large, statue-adorned Baroque high altar (1775) steals the limelight. Predating the cathedral by several centuries is **Kaunas Castle**, whose scant remains survive just northwest of the square. Little more than a restored tower and a couple of sections of wall are left, the rest washed away by the Neris, but in its day the fortification was a major obstacle to the Teutonic Knights. South of the town square, the **Perkūnas House** at Aleksoto 6 is an elaborately gabled red-brick structure, thought to have been built as a Hansa office or possibly a Jesuit chapel, standing on the reputed site of a temple to Perkūnas, the pagan god of thunder. From here Aleksoto descends to the banks of the Nemunas and the glowering Vytautas Church, built by Vytautas the Great in around 1399.

The main thoroughfare of Kaunas' **New Town** is Freedom Avenue (Laisvės alėja), a broad pedestrianized shopping street running east from the Old Town, which, bizarrely, was declared a no-smoking zone during the 1990s. At the junction with L. Sapiegos the street is enlivened by a bronze statue of Vytautas the Great, which faces the **City Garden** where, on May 14, 1972, the 19-year-old student Romas Kalanta immolated himself in protest against Soviet rule. Kalanta's death sparked anti-Soviet rioting, and he is commemorated by a memorial stone in the gardens. Towards the eastern end of Freedom Avenue the silver-domed **Church of St Michael the Archangel** looms over Independence Square (Nepriklausomybės aikštė), while the striking modern building in the northeast corner is one of the best art galleries in the country, the **Mykolas Žilinskas Art Museum** (Tues–Sun 11am–5pm; closed last Tues of every month; 3Lt), with a fine collection of Egyptian artefacts, Chinese porcelain and Lithuania's only Rubens.

Kaunas celebrates its role in sustaining Lithuanian national identity on **Unity Square** (Vienybės aikštė), at the junction of S. Daukanto and K. Donelaičio, a block north of Laisvės. Here a **monument** depicting liberty as a female figure faces an eternal flame flanked by traditional wooden crosses, with busts of prominent nineteenth century Lithuanians between the two. Just north of the square, Kaunas has a unique art collection in the **A. Žmuidzinavičius Art Museum**, Putvinskio 64 (Tues–Sun 11am–5pm; closed last Tues of every month; 5Lt). Better known as the **Devil's Museum**, this houses a vast collection of devil figures put together by the artist Antanas Žmuidzinavičius. Though most of the images are comic, there's also a sinister representation of Hitler and Stalin as devils dancing on a Lithuania composed of skulls. Heading east down Putvinskio brings you to the 1930s **funicular railway** (0.50Lt) which climbs up to the **Žaliakalnis** district to the north of the city centre, giving panoramic views. Near the upper terminal is the **Church of Christ's Resurrection**, a 1930s modernist edifice with a very tall white tower.

Before World War II Kaunas, like Vilnius, had a large Jewish population, but nearly all were killed during the war and little remains to remind of their presence, except the city's sole surviving **synagogue** at Ožeskienės 17 in the New Town, which sports a wonderful sky-blue interior (daily 6–6.30pm). To find out about the fate of the Jews of Kaunas head out of town to the **Ninth Fort Museum**, Žemaičių plentas 73 (Wed–Sun 10am–4pm; 4Lt), housed in the tsarist-era fortress where the Jews were kept while awaiting execution. Take any westbound inter-city bus from Kaunas bus station and get off at the IX Fortas stop.

Practicalities

Kaunas' **train** and **bus stations** are at the southeastern end of the centre, a fifteen-minute walk from Laisvės alėja; a thirty-five minute walk (or short ride on trolleybus #1, #3,# 5 or #7) to the Old Town. There's a helpful **tourist office** at Laisvės 40 (Mon–Thur 9am–6pm, Fri 9am–5pm; ☎37/323 436, ✉turizmas@takas.lt) doling out English-language leaflets and a free map. You can also pick up a copy of *Kaunas and Klaipeda in Your Pocket* here (☉www.inyourpocket.com; 8Lt). For **accommodation** the ever-reliable *Litinterp*, Gedimino 28–7 (☎37/228 718, ☉www.litinterp.lt), can sort you out with a room in the centre for 70Lt single, 110Lt double. Central **hotels** include the unrenovated but tolerable *Monela*, Laisvės 35 (☎37/221 791; ➌); the gloomy but charmingly olde-worlde *Lietuva I*, Daukanto 21 (☎37/225 992, ✉metropol@takas.lt; ➌); and the hulking concrete *Takijoji Neris*, off Laisvės to the north at Donelaičio 27 (☎37/204 224, takneris@takas.lt; ➍). For quick cheap **eating** head for *Viva Blynai, Viva Koldųnai*, Laisvės 53, a snazzy self-service buffet specializing in pancakes. For something more substantial try the *Berneliu Uzeiga*, Valančiaus 9, where you can dine on meaty Lithuanian staples in an attractive rustic interior. *Pizza Jazz*, Laisvės alėja 68, does delicious thin-crust pizzas while *Dviese*, Vilniaus 8, offers deep-fried meat pies and groovy pop-art decor. **Cafés** and **bars** are often a good bet for eating too: *Avilys*, Vilniaus 34, is a chic establishment with a full range of meals and its own beer; *Miesto Sodas*, Laisvės 93, offers drinking and dining in an elegant park-side pavilion. The *Skliautas*, Rotušės aikštė 26, and the nearby *B.O.*, Muitinės 9, are the best places to hook up with a young, arty crowd. *Los Patrankos*, Savanorių 124, is the newest, biggest and friendliest of the techno-oriented **clubs**. You can access the **Internet** at Kavinė Internetas, Vilniaus 24 (6Lt/hr).

Klaipėda

KLAIPĖDA, Lithuania's third largest city and most important port, lies on the Baltic coast, a long and tedious 275km by road or rail northwest of Vilnius. Though it has a handful of sights the city is of more interest as a staging post en route to **Neringa**, the Lithuanian name for the Couronian Spit which shields much of Lithuania's coast from the open Baltic. Until 1919 a part of Germany known as Memel, Klaipėda is bisected by the River Danė. The main sights are in the **Old Town** on its southern bank, an area of half-timbered buildings and cobbled streets, at the heart of which is **Theatre Square** named after the ornate Neoclassical **Theatre** building on its northern side. In front of the theatre is **Anna's Fountain**, a replica of a famous prewar monument to the German poet Simon Dach (1605–1659), which depicts the heroine of his folksong *Ännchen von Tharau*. Southeast of the square, the **History Museum of Lithuania Minor**, Didžioji vandens 6 (Tues–Sat 10am–5.30pm; 3Lt), has local archeological finds, national costumes and ancient domestic implements. In the **New Town**, on the northern side of the Danė, at Liepų 16, is Klaipėda's splendid red-brick Gothic-revival post office. Built between 1883 and 1893, it is a vivid reminder of imperial German civic pride.

Klaipėda's **tourist office** is just off Teatro aikštė at Tomo 2 (July & Aug: Mon–Fri 9am–7pm, Sat 9am–2pm; Sept–June: Mon–Fri 9am–5pm; ☎46/412186, ✉kltic@takas.lt). *Kaunas and Klaipeda in Your Pocket* (8Lt, from the tourist office or bookstores) is your best source of information. *Litinterp*, Šimkaus 21/4 (Mon–Fri 8.30am–5.30pm; summer also Sat 10am–3pm; ☎46/310 296, ☉www.litinterp.lt), has central **private rooms** (➋), and they can also help with rooms in Nida. *Klaipeda Travellers' Guesthouse*, Butkų Juzės 7–4 (☎46/211 879, ✉oldtown@takas.lt; 35Lt), is a centrally located, friendly hostel. Reasonable mid-range **hotels** include the *Fortųna*, Poilsio 64 (☎46/348 028; ➌), a small pension 4km south of the centre best booked in advance. Nearer the centre is the family-run pension *Prųsija*, Šimkaus 6 (☎46/412 081; ➍). There's an unofficial free **campsite** with no facilities at Giruliai, 8km north of Klaipėda next to the *Pajuris* sanatorium on Slaito (shuttle bus #8 from the centre). Good places to **eat** in the Old Town are *Galerija Peda*,

Turgaus 10, whose tasty food looks as arty as the gallery it occupies; and *Bņru Uzeiga*, Kepėjų 17, which serves up Lithuanian meat-and-potato favourites in homely surroundings. For **drinking**, *Bohema*, Aukštoji 3, is a cosy little bar with animated courtyard seating in summer; while *Kurpiai*, Kurpių 1, is a traditional woody pub that also functions as the best jazz bar in the Baltics.

Neringa

Neringa, or the Kuršių Nerija, is the Lithuanian section of the Couronian Spit, a 97-kilometre spit of land characterized by vast sand dunes and pine forests. Much of the area can be seen as a day-trip from Klaipėda, though you need to stay a day or two to soak up the unique atmosphere. Ferries from the quayside towards the end of Žvejų gatvė in Klaipėda (every 30min, 5am–3am; free) sail to **Smiltyne** on the northern tip of the spit. From the landing stage, frequent minibuses (7.50Lt) run south towards the scenic, dune-dominated parts of the spit, terminating at Nida, 35km south.

NIDA is the most famous village on the spit – a small fishing community boasting several streets of attractive wooden houses, although there's some lumpen Soviet resort architecture at its heart. To get a feel for the old fishing settlement head for **Naglių gatvė** and **Lotmiškio gatvė** (5min south of the village centre bus stop). The roads are lined with single-storey blue- and brown-painted wooden houses, many with traditional thatched roofs. The **Fisherman's House**, Naglių 4 (May–Sept Tues–Sun 11am–5pm; 3Lt), is a re-created nineteenth-century cottage with simple wooden furnishings. From the end of Naglių a shore path runs to a flight of wooden steps leading up to the top of the **dunes** south of the village. From the summit you can gaze out across a Saharan sandscape to the Kaliningrad province, part of German East Prussia until 1945 but now belonging to the Russian Federation. Nida's long, luxuriant beach stretches along the opposite, western side of the spit, a 20min walk through the forest from the village. The **tourist office**, in the centre of the village at Taikos 4 (June–Aug: daily 9am–8pm; Sept–May: Mon–Fri 9am–6pm, Sat 10am–3pm; ☎469/52345), will find you a **private room** (❶). Litinterp in Klaipėda can book rooms in advance, but for a slightly higher fee. Best of the numerous small **hotels** in town is the *Rasyte*, Lotmiškio 11 (☎469/52592; ❹), a wooden house in the heart of the old fishing settlement, although it's essential to book in advance. The larger and less atmospheric *Nidos Smilte*, Skruzdynės 2 (☎469/52221; ❸), offers simple doubles with shared facilities and spartan cabins in the Nidos Pušynas holiday settlement nearby. For **food** head for *Seklycia*, Lotmiškio 1, which does simple dishes like *cepelinai* as well as more sophisticated meat and fish dishes. *Reidas*, just behind the bus station at Naglių 20, is a good place to try the delicious, locally smoked fish *rukyta zuvis*. It turns into a lively **bar** with rock music at night.

Travel details

Trains	Buses
Kaunas to: Klaipėda (2 daily; 3hr 30min); Rīga (3 weekly; 7hr); Vilnius (12 daily; 1hr 15min–2hr).	**Kaunas** to: Klaipėda (10 daily; 3hr); Rīga (2 daily; 4hr 30min); Vilnius (every 20–30min; 1hr 30min–2hr).
Klaipėda to: Kaunas (2 daily; 3hr 30min); Vilnius (3 daily; 5hr).	**Klaipėda** to: Kaunas (10 daily; 3hr); Nida (departures from Smiltynė; 8 daily; 50min); Vilnius (10–12 daily; 5hr).
Vilnius to: Kaunas (12 daily; 1hr 15min–2hr); Klaipėda (3 daily; 5hr); Rīga (3 weekly; 9hr); Šeštokai (2 daily; 3hr 30min); Warsaw (3 weekly; 10hr).	**Vilnius** to: Kaunas (every 20–30min; 1hr 30min–2hr); Klaipėda (10–12 daily; 4hr); Rīga (5 daily; 5hr–5hr 30min); Tallinn (2 daily; 11hr 40min); Warsaw (4 daily; 12hr).

Morocco

SPAIN

Tarifa
Málaga

Algeciras
Gibraltar (UK)

Tangier
Ceuta (Sp.)

MEDITERRANEAN
SEA

Asilah
Tetouan

ATLANTIC OCEAN

Chefchaouen
THE RIF

Volubilis
Oujda

RABAT
Salé

Casablanca
Meknes
Fes

MIDDLE ATLAS

HIGH ATLAS

Essaouira

Marrakesh

Agadir

ALGERIA

N

Note: This chapter covers only
the most easily accessible
towns in northern Morocco.
The map therefore shows
only the northern regions,
not the whole of the country

0   250 km

Morocco highlights

* **Chefchaouen** Beautiful and very friendly little town in the Rif mountains, where the houses look like they're made of blue meringue. See p.638

* **Medina, Fes** An incredible labyrinth of alleys, sights and smells in the world's best-preserved medieval city. See p.642

* **Djemaa el Fna, Marrakesh** A spontaneous live circus in a large square in the middle of town, featuring everything from snake charmers to tooth pullers. See p.650

* **Essaouira** Arty, laidback seaside and surfing resort where Jimi Hendrix once played impromptu concerts on the beach. See p.652

Introduction and basics

Just an hour's ferry ride from Spain, **Morocco** seems very far from Europe, with a deeply traditional Islamic culture. Throughout the country, despite its 44 years of French and Spanish colonial rule, a more distant past constantly makes its presence felt. Travel here is, if not always easy, an intense and rewarding experience.

Berbers, the indigenous population, make up over half of Morocco's population. Only around ten percent of Moroccans claim to be "pure" **Arabs**, though with a population shift to the industrialized cities, such distinctions are becoming less significant. More telling is the legacy of the **colonial** period: until independence in 1956, the country was divided into Spanish and French zones. The French, who ruled the larger and more heavily populated area, had the most lasting effect, building **Villes Nouvelles** (new towns) alongside the long-standing **Medinas** (old towns) in all the country's main cities, and created Casablanca in the image of Marseille. Today French is spoken alongside Arabic and the three Berber languages.

Most visitors' introduction to Morocco is **Tangier** in the north, still shaped by its heyday of "international" port status in the 1950s. To its south, in the Rif mountains, the town of **Chefchaouen** is a small-scale and enjoyably laid-back place, while inland lies the enthralling city of **Fes**, the greatest of the four imperial capitals (the others are Meknes, Rabat and Marrakesh), and unique in the Arab world for the chance to witness a city life that remains largely medieval. The sprawl of **Meknes**, with its ancient walls, and nearby Roman site of **Volubilis**, makes an easy day-trip from Fes, but justifies a day or two of exploration on its own.

The power axis of the nation lies on the coast in **Rabat** and **Casablanca**, respectively the seats of government and of industry and commerce. They've acquired their pre-eminence only in the last sixty years, so French and post-colonial influences are dominant: "Casa" looks more like Marseille than anything Moroccan, while the elegant, orderly capital, Rabat, houses some gems of Moroccan architecture. Further south, **Marrakesh** is an enduring fantasy that won't disappoint. The country's loveliest resort, **Essaouira**, a charming walled seaside town, lies within easy reach of Marrakesh and Casablanca.

Information, guides and maps

There's a **tourist office** (Délégation du Tourisme) run by the Office National Marocain du Tourisme (**ONMT**) in every major city, and sometimes also a locally funded Syndicat d'Initiative. They stock leaflets and maps, and can put you in touch with official guides. In addition to the guides trained by the government, there are scores of young Moroccans offering their services. Some of these "**unofficial guides**" are genuine students, while others are out-and-out hustlers (though these have been clamped down on). If they do find you, be polite but firm, and don't be intimidated. Note that it's illegal to harass tourists. Good **maps** of Moroccan cities are hard to obtain locally or abroad. The most functional are those in the *Rough Guide to Morocco*.

18

Morocco on the net

ⓦ**www.tourism-in-morocco.com** Tourist office info.
ⓦ**www.geocities.com/TheTropics/4896/morocco.html** Information and links.
ⓦ**www.lexicorient.com/morocco** Destinations.
ⓦ**www.arab.net/morocco** History, culture and general information.
ⓦ**www.morocco.com/news** News and information.

Money and banks

The unit of currency is the **dirham** (dh), divided into 100 centimes; in markets, prices may well be in centimes rather than dirhams. There are coins of 10c, 20c, 50c, 1dh, 5dh and 10dh, and notes of 10dh, 20dh, 50dh, 100dh and 200dh. You can get dirhams in Algeciras (Spain) and Gibraltar, and can usually change foreign notes on arrival at major sea- and airports. It can be difficult to change travellers' cheques anywhere but a bank. For **exchange** purposes, the most useful and efficient chain of banks is the **BMCE** (Banque Marocaine du Commerce Extérieur), which often has a separate *bureau de change* open longer hours and at weekends. **Travellers' cheques** incur a 10.70dh commission except at the state-run Bank al-Maghrib. Many banks give cash advances on credit cards, which can also be used in tourist hotels (but not cheap unclassified ones) and the **ATMs** of major banks. **Banking hours** are: summer Mon–Fri 8am–2pm; winter Mon–Thurs 8.15–11.30am & 2.15–4.30pm, Fri 8.15–11.15am & 2.45–4.45pm. During the holy month of Ramadan, banks open Mon–Fri 9am–2pm. In major resorts there's usually one bank with flexible hours and large hotels may also change money. Morocco is inexpensive but poor, and **tips** can make a lot of difference; it's customary to tip café waiters.

Communications

Post offices (PTT) open Mon–Thurs 8.30am–12.15pm & 2.30–6.30pm, Fri 8.30–11.30am & 3–6.30pm. Central post offices in large cities will be open longer hours, except in summer and Ramadan. In addition to the post offices, you can buy **stamps** at postcard shops and sometimes at tobacconists (look for three interlocking blue circles). Always post items at a PTT. International **phone calls** are best made with a phonecard (from post offices and some tobacconists). Alternatively, there are privately run téléboutiques, open late. Calls through hotels usually cost a lot more. Coin-operated pay phones accept 50c and 1dh coins; a short local call costs around 50c, and a few dirhams is enough for a long-distance one. You must dial all nine digits of Moroccan phone numbers. **Internet** access is available pretty much everywhere, and at low rates: 10dh/hr is typical.

Getting around

The **train** network is limited, but for travel between the major cities, trains are the best option. Major stations have free timetables, printed by ONCF (@www.oncf.org.ma), the national train company. Second-class fares are comparable to what you'd pay for buses. In addition, there are couchettes (90dh extra) available in summer on trains from Tangier to Marrakesh (9hr 30min) and Fes (4hr 30min); these are worth the money for extra comfort and security.

Collective **grands taxis** are usually big Peugeots or Mercedes, plying set routes for a set fare and are much quicker than buses, though the drivers can be reckless. Make clear you only want *une place* (one seat), otherwise drivers may assume you want to charter the whole car. Within towns **petits taxis** do short trips, carrying up to three people, with luggage on the roof. They queue in central locations and at stations and can be hailed on streets when they're empty. Payment – usually no more than 15dh – relates to distance travelled.

Buses are marginally cheaper than grands taxis, and cover longer distances, but are much slower. Buses run by CTM (the national company) are most reliable, with numbered seats and fixed schedules. An additional express service is run by Supratours, and is fast and comfortable. On small private-line buses, you generally have to pay a standard 5dh for your bags to go on the roof (this also covers unloading at your destination).

Accommodation

Accommodation is inexpensive, generally good value and usually pretty easy to find, although it's more difficult in main cities and resorts in the peak seasons (August, Christmas and Aïd el Kebir). Cheap, unclassified **hotels** and *pensions* (charging about

100–150dh for a double) are mainly to be found in each town's Medina (old town), while hotels with stars tend to concentrate in the Ville Nouvelle (new town). At their best, **unclassified** Medina hotels are beautiful, traditional houses with whitewashed rooms grouped around a central patio. The worst can be extremely dirty, and many have problems with water. Few have en-suite bathrooms, though a *hammam* (public Turkish bath) is usually close at hand. **Classified** hotels' star-ratings are fairly self-explanatory and prices are reasonable for all except five-star places. Except in Marrakesh, most hotels do not include breakfast in their room price. HI **hostels** (*auberges de jeunesse*), often bright, breezy and friendly, offer an alternative to cheap hotels, but generally have strict rules requiring you to be in by 10pm and out by 10am daily. **Campsites** usually suffer the disadvantage of being well out of town. They tend to charge around 15dh per person plus the same again for your tent.

Food and drink

If your funds are limited, you'll probably be **eating** mainly in cheap local diners. Fancier restaurants, definitely worth an occasional splurge, are mostly to be found in the Ville Nouvelle, which is where you'll also find any bars. Moroccan **cooking** is good and filling. The main dish is usually a **tajine**, essentially a stew. Classic *tajines* include chicken with lemon and olives, and lamb with prunes and almonds. The most famous Moroccan dish – Berber rather than Arab in origin – is **couscous**, a huge bowl of steamed semolina piled with vegetables, mutton, chicken or fish. Restaurant **starters** include *salade marocaine*, a finely chopped salad of tomato and cucumber, or soup, most often the spicy, bean-based *harira*, followed by couscous, *tajine*, kebab (*brochettes*), or something like a Western meat-and-two-veg main course. **Dessert** will probably be fruit, yoghurt or a pastry. Restaurants at all levels may offer a set menu, often a bargain at 60–100dh in even quite fancy places. **Vegetarianism** is not really understood, and meat stock may be added even

to vegetable dishes. If you're fussy about such things, you will probably have to avoid main courses and all soups – bar the filling bean-and-olive-oil *baisara*. If **invited** to a home, you're unlikely to use a knife and fork; copy your hosts and eat only with your **right hand**.

The national drink is **thé à la menthe** – green tea with a large bunch of mint and a massive amount of sugar. If you want them to hold back on the sugar, ask for it with *shweeya sukar* (a little) or *blé sukar* (none). Coffee (*café* in French; *qahwa* in Arabic) is best in French-style cafés. Many cafés and street stalls sell fresh-squeezed orange juice and, though water is generally safe to drink, **mineral water** is readily available. As an Islamic nation, Morocco gives **alcohol** a low profile, and it's generally impossible to buy any in the Medinas. Moroccan **wines**, usually red, can be very good, while the best **beer** is Flag Speciale. **Bars** are totally male domains, except in tourist hotels – but even then they can be a bit rowdy.

Opening hours and holidays

Shops and stalls in the *souk* (bazaar) areas open roughly 9am–1pm & 3–6pm. Ville Nouvelle shops are also likely to close for lunch, and also once a week, usually Sunday. Islamic **religious holidays** are calculated on the lunar calendar and change each year. In 2004 they fall (provisionally) as follows: Feb 1 is **Aïd el Kebir** (when Abraham offered to sacrifice his son for God); Feb 22 is the Muslim New Year; May 2 is **Mouloud** (the birthday of Muhammad); **Ramadan** (when all Muslims fast from sunrise to sunset) falls roughly Oct 14 to Nov 13. Non-Muslims are not expected to observe Ramadan, but should be sensitive about not breaking the fast in public. The end of Ramadan is celebrated with **Aïd es Seghir** (aka Aïd el Fitr), a two-day holiday. **Secular holidays** are considered less important, with most public services (except banks and offices) operating normally even during the two biggest ones – the Feast of the Throne (July 30), and Independence Day (Nov 18).

Emergencies

Street **robbery** is rare but not unknown, especially in Casablanca. Hotels are generally secure for depositing money; campsites considerably less so. There are two main types of **police** – grey-clad gendarmes, with authority outside city limits; and the navy-clad sûreté in towns. There's sometimes a brigade of "tourist police" too. Moroccan **pharmacists** are well trained and dispense a wide range of drugs. In most cities there is a night pharmacy, often at the town hall, and a rota of *pharmacies de garde* which stay open till late and at weekends. You can get a list of English-speaking **doctors** in major cities from consulates. Steer clear of **marijuana** (kif) and **hashish** – it's illegal, and buying it leaves you vulnerable to scams, as well as potentially large fines and prison sentences, though the police normally expect to be paid off.

Emergency numbers

Police – Sûreté ☏19, Gendarmes ☏177
Fire and ambulance ☏15

Northern Morocco

The northern tip of Morocco contains enough on its own to justify the short ferry ride over from Spain: in three days or so you could check out the delightfully seedy city of **Tangier** and the picturesque, extremely laid-back little mountain town of **Chefchaouen** in the Rif mountains. There are two crossings from Algeciras: direct to Tangier, which is the easiest way, and takes you straight to a place that is an interesting city in its own right with direct transport connections nationwide; or to the Spanish enclave of **Ceuta**, from which you still have to reach and cross the border.

Tangier

For the first half of the twentieth century **TANGIER** (Tanja in Arabic; Tanger in French) was an "International City" with its own laws and administration, plus an eclectic community of expats and refugees. With independence in 1956, this special status was removed and the expat colony dwindled. Today Tangier is a major port, halfway to becoming a mainstream tourist resort, but with hints of its decadent past.

The **Grand Socco**, or Zoco Grande – once the main market square (and, since Independence, officially Place du 9 avril 1947) – offers the most straightforward approach to the **Medina**. The arch at the northwest corner opens onto Rue d'Italie, which leads up to the Kasbah. To the right, Rue es Siaghin leads to the atmospheric but seedy **Petit Socco**, or Zoco Chico, the Medina's principal landmark. From here, though not easy to follow, Rue des Almohades (aka Rue des Chrétiens) and Rue Ben Raisouli lead to the lower gate of the Kasbah. The **Kasbah** (citadel), walled off from the Medina on the highest rise of the coast, has been the palace and administrative quarter since Roman times. The main point of interest is the former Sultanate Palace, or **Dar el Makhzen** (closed for repairs at time of writing; formerly Mon & Wed–Sun 9am–1pm & 3–6pm; 10dh), now converted into an excellent museum of crafts and antiquities. If you leave by Rue Riad Sultan and Bab el Kasbah, you pass under the **Café-Restaurant Detroit** (up the stairs through a doorway in the tunnel), set up in the 1960s by Beat writer Brion Gysin, and now an overpriced tourist spot but worth the price of a mint tea for the views.

Practicalities

Ferries dock at the terminal immediately below the Medina. The **CTM bus terminal** is at the port entrance, but the *gare routière* **bus station** used by private bus companies and *grands taxis* is 1.5km inland on Av Youssef Ben Tachfine. All **trains** terminate at Tanger Morora (or Moghogha) station, 4km out on the Tetouan road (bus #13 from the port). The **tourist office** is at 29 Bd Pasteur (Mon–Thurs 8.30am–noon & 2.30–6.30pm, Fri 8.30–11.30am & 3–6.30pm; sometimes open lunch and weekends in July & Aug; ℡039 94 80 50), just down from Place de France.

There are dozens of **hotels** and **pensions**, but the city does get crowded in summer, when some places double their prices. In the **Medina**, *Mauretania*, 2 Rue des Almohades, aka Rue des Chrétiens (℡039 93 46 77; ❶), has shared cold showers and toilets, but is clean. *Olid*, 12 Rue Mokhtar Ahardane, aka Rue des Postes (℡039 93 13 10; ❶), has seen better days, but is good value for money, while *Palace*, 2 Rue Mokhtar Ahardane (℡039 93 61 28; ❶), is more attractive with hot running water, balconies and a lovely courtyard. A good-value option in a slightly higher price bracket is *Mamora*, 19 Rue Mokhtar Ahardane (℡039 93 41 05; ❷). In the **Ville Nouvelle** are *Magellan*, 16 Rue Magellan (℡039 37 23 19; ❶), and *El Muniria* or *Tanger Inn*, 1 Rue Magellan (℡039 93 53 37; ❶), the latter now a quiet, family-run *pension*, where William Burroughs wrote his most famous book, *The Naked Lunch*. On the main street opposite the tourist office is *Hôtel de Paris*, 42 Bd Pasteur (℡039 93 18 77; ❷), best value in the area. Top choice on the seafront are *Miramar*, 168 Av des FAR (℡039 94 17 15; ❷), friendly, old and a little shabby with a bar and restaurant; and *Marco Polo*, on the corner of Av d'Espagne and Rue El Antaki (℡039 94

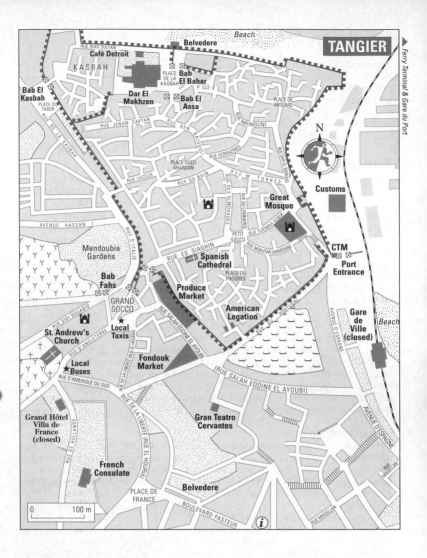

11 24; ❷), well established, with a bar and good restaurant. The **HI hostel**, 8 Rue El Antaki (☎039 94 61 27; ❶; closed 10am–noon and 3–6pm), near the seafront, is clean and well run. The nearest **campsite**, *Tingis* (☎039 32 30 65), is 6km east, beside the Oued Moghogha lagoon.

Eating, drinking and nightlife

As with most Moroccan cities, the cheapest places to **eat** are in the **Medina**, and an authentic Tangier experience is people-watching over a mint tea at one of the Petit Socco **cafés**. Of the Medina's **restaurants**, the small and simple *Andalus*, 7 Rue du Commerce, off the Petit Socco, has excellent, low-priced swordfish steak or fried shrimps. *Ahlen*, 8 Rue des Postes, serves traditional Moroccan dishes. The cheap diners in the Grand Socco are worth a look too; most stay open until midnight or later. Alcoholic drinks are not served in the Medina or Grand Socco. In the **Ville Nouvelle**, *Africa*, 83 Rue Salah Eddine el Ayoubi (aka Rue de la Plage), has a 50dh set menu and is licensed to serve beer and wine with meals, while *Hassi Baida* next door offers a traditional Moroccan menu (without alcohol). *Agadir*, 21 Rue Prince Héretier Sidi Mohammed, uphill from Place de France, is small and friendly, serving French and Moroccan dishes, and *San Remo*, 15 Rue Ahmed Chaouki, specializes in Italian dishes and runs a takeaway pizzeria opposite. For Spanish seafood, including vast portions of fine paella, try the pricier *Romero*, 12 Rue Prince Moulay Abdallah, around the corner from the tourist office. On the **seafront**, many hotels have reliable European restaurants, including *Marco Polo* whose generous servings come at a fair price. As an alternative, try *L'Marsa*, 92 Av d'Espagne, with a roof terrace and offering excellent pasta and pizzas, with home-made ice cream too. Finally, back in town, the long-established *Rubis Grill*, at 3 Rue Ibn Rochd, off Rue Prince Moulay Abdallah, serves European dishes; the candlelit hacienda decor is a bit over the top but the food and service are exemplary.

For **drinking**, the *Tanger Inn*, the bar of the *Hôtel el Muniria* at 1 Rue Magellan (daily 9pm–1am), has been an institution since the days of the International Zone, decorated with photos of the Beat Generation authors who stayed at the hotel, but quiet midweek off-season. *Hôtel Miramar* on Av des FAR is a hard-drinking seafront spot. *Scott's* on Rue El Moutanabi, traditionally a gay disco, is worth a look for its decor, although nothing much happens here before midnight; take care leaving late at night – the best idea is to tip the doorman 5dh to order you a taxi. *Morocco Palace*, Av du Prince Moulay Abdallah, is a strange, sometimes slightly manic place with traditional Moroccan music and a belly-dancing floorshow.

Listings

American Express Voyages Schwartz, 54 Bd Pasteur ☎039 33 03 72.

Consulates UK, 41 Bd Mohammed V ☎039 94 15 57.

Exchange BMCE, 19 Bd Pasteur is the most efficient with a bureau de change and ATM.

Internet Best place is Cybercafé Adam, 4 Rue Ibn Rochd (off Bd Pasteur).

Pharmacies There are several English-speaking pharmacies on Place de France and Bd Pasteur.

Post office Main PTT, 33 Bd Mohammed V.

Police Rue Ibn Toumert near the Prefecture; also at the old Gare de Ville train station and 22 Rue Mountanabi.

Ceuta and Tetouan

A Spanish enclave which dates back to the sixteenth century, the port of **CEUTA** (Sebta in Arabic) is politically and culturally part of Spain. As the crossing here from Algeciras is quicker than to Tangier, this drab outpost has become a popular point of entry. Try to arrive early in the day so that you have plenty of time to move on. The Moroccan border is 3km south of town, reached by local bus from the seafront. Once across, there are shared taxis for the 2km to **FNIDEQ**, where there are buses and shared *grands taxis* to Tetouan and Tangier. There are cash-only exchange places at the frontier. If you get stuck in Ceuta, *Pensión Charito*, c/Arrabal 5 (☎956 513 982; ❷), is cheap, as are others nearby. The **tourist offices** at Muelle Cañonero Dato, the road into town from the ferry dock (in theory daily 9am–8pm; ☎956 501 410, ⓦ www.turiceuta.com), and opposite the town hall (*ayuntamiento*) off Plaza de Africa (same hours; ☎956 528 146), and with a branch in the ferry station itself, keep a list of hotels.

Coming from Ceuta, you usually need to pick up onward transport at **TETOUAN**, a town with a walled Medina and a reputation for having the worst hustlers in Morocco – but a *grand taxi* from Fnideq will leave you close enough to Tetouan's bus station to head straight out again. There are regular **buses** to Meknes, Fes and destinations nationwide. For Tangier, Chefchaouen or Ceuta it's easiest to travel by **grand taxi**; those for Fnideq (Ceuta) leave from Boulevard de Mouquaouama, a stone's throw from the bus station, but those for Tangier and Chefchaouen leave from a stand some 2km west, up Boulevard de Mouquaouama to Place Moulay el Mehdi, then west along Av Mohammed V to the end and ask someone. The ONCF office on Av 10 Mai, alongside Place Al Adala, sells **train** tickets that include a shuttle bus to the station at Tnine Sidi Lyamani. If you're stuck in Tetouan, cheap hotels near the bus station include the friendly *Principe*, 20 Av Youssef Ibn Tachfine (℡066 55 38 20; ❶), on the corner of Boulevard de Mouquaouama midway between the bus station and Place Moulay el Mehdi. Tetouan has a **tourist office**, a few metres east of Place Moulay el Mehdi at 30 Bd Mohammed V (Mon–Thurs 8.30am–noon & 2.30–6.30pm, Fri 8.30–11.30am & 3–6.30pm; ℡039 96 19 16).

Chefchaouen

Shut in by a fold of the Rif mountains, **CHEFCHAOUEN** (sometimes abbreviated to Chaouen or Xaouen) had, until the arrival of Spanish troops in 1920, been visited by just three Europeans. It's a town of extraordinary light and colour, its whitewash tinted with blue and edged by golden stone walls. *Pensions* are friendly and cheap and a few days here is one of the best introductions to Morocco. Buses and grands taxis drop you outside the town walls; the main entrance to the Medina is a tiny arched entrance, **Bab el Ain**. Through the gate a dominant but narrow lane winds up to the main square, the elongated **Place Outa el Hammam**. This is where most of the town's evening life takes place, while by day the town's focus is the **Kasbah** (Mon & Wed–Sun 9am–1pm & 3–6pm; 10dh), a quiet ruin with shady gardens and a small museum, which occupies one side of the square. Beyond, the smaller **Place El Makhzen** is an elegant clearing with an old fountain and tourist pottery stalls.

Along and just off the main route through the Medina is a series of small **hotels**, the quietest of which is *Abie Khancha*, 75 Rue Lala el Hora (℡039 98 68 79; ❶), a converted house with a courtyard and terrace. Outside the Medina, nearer to transport, is the immaculate *Madrid*, Av Hassan II (℡039 98 74 96 or 97; ❸), and nearby is the cosy *Sevilla*, Av Allal Ben Abdallah (℡039 98 72 85; ❷). The **campsite** (℡039 98 69 79), up on the hill above town, by the modern *Hôtel Asma*, is inexpensive and can be crowded in summer. A very inexpensive but basic and inconveniently located **HI hostel** adjoins the campsite (call via the campsite; ❶). **Café-restaurants** in the Place Outa el Hammam serve good-value Moroccan meals; one of the best is the *Ali Baba*. Slightly pricier is *Tissemlal* (aka *Casa Hassan*), 22 Rue Targui, just up from Place Outa el Hammam, which serves delicious food in elegant surroundings. Outside the Medina, on Rue Moulay Ali Ben Rachid, are *Moulay Ali Ben Rachid* and *Al Jazira*, popular with local residents. **Buses** to Fes and Meknes are quite often full, so buy tickets a day in advance. Buses to Tetouan are very frequent, or you can share a *grand taxi*.

Central Morocco

Between the mountain ranges of the Rif to the north and the Atlas to the south lie the great cities that form Morocco's heart: the great imperial cities of **Meknes** and **Fes**, the modern capital, **Rabat**, and the country's largest city and commercial capital, **Casablanca**.

Meknes

More than any other Moroccan town, **MEKNES** is associated with a single figure, the Sultan Moulay Ismail, in whose reign (1672–1727) the city went from provincial centre to spectacular capital with over fifty palaces and fifteen miles of exterior walls. A prosperous city today, its monuments reward a day's exploration.

Place El Hedim originally formed the western corner of the Medina, but Moulay Ismail had the houses here demolished to provide a grand approach to his palace quarter. The **Dar Jamai** (Mon & Wed–Sun 9am–noon & 3–6.30pm; 10dh),

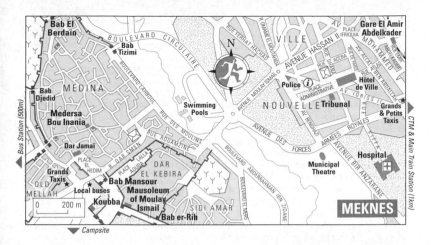

at the back of the square, is one of the best examples of a nineteenth-century Moroccan palace, and the museum inside is one of the best in Morocco, with a fantastic display of Middle Atlas carpets. The lane immediately to the left of the Dar Jamaï takes you to the Medina's major market street: on your left is **Souk en Nejjarin**, the carpet souk; on your right, leading to the Great Mosque and Bou Inania Medersa, are the fancier goods offered in the **Souk es Sebbat**. The **Bou Inania Medersa** (daily 9am–noon & 3–6pm; 10dh), constructed around 1340–50, has an unusual ribbed dome over the entrance hall and from the roof you can look out to the tiled pyramids of the Great Mosque. Behind the magnificent **Bab Mansour** (open for occasional exhibitions) is Place Lalla Aouda. Straight ahead bearing left, you come into another open square, on the right of which is the green-tiled dome of the **Koubba el Khayatine**, once a reception hall for ambassadors to the imperial court (daily 9am–noon & 3–6.30pm; 10dh). Below it, a stairway descends into a vast series of subterranean vaults, known as the **Prison of Christian Slaves**, though it was probably a storehouse or granary. Ahead of the Koubba, within the wall and at right angles to it, are two modest gates. The one on the left opens onto a corridor of walls and, a few metres down, the entrance to **Moulay Ismail's Mausoleum** (daily 9am–noon & 3–6pm, closed Fri am; 10dh donation expected), where you can approach the sanctuary. Past the mausoleum, a long-walled corridor leads to the **Heri as-Souani**, a series of storerooms and granaries once filled with provisions for siege or drought. From the roof garden café, you can gaze out across much of the Dar el Makhzen (Royal Palace) and the wonderfully still **Agdal Basin**, built as an irrigation reservoir and pleasure lake.

Practicalities

Meknes has two **train stations**, both in the Ville Nouvelle. All trains stop at both stations, but **Gare Amir Abdelkader** is more central than **Gare de Ville**. Private **buses** and most **grands taxis** arrive west of the Medina by Bab el Khemis; **CTM buses** arrive at their terminal on Av de Fès, near the Gare de Ville, and some *grands taxis* from Fes also drop you there. The **tourist office** is at 27 Place Administrative (Mon–Thurs 8.30am–noon & 2.30–6.30pm, Fri 8.30–11.30am & 3–6.30pm; ☎055 52 44 26). Pick of the **Medina hotels** is *Maroc*, 7 Rue Rouamzine (☎055 53 00 75; ❶). Budget choices in the **Ville Nouvelle** include the *Bordeaux*, 64 Av de la Gare (☎055 52 25 63; ❶), with a shaded garden, near the Gare de Ville and CTM bus station, and *Touring*, 34 Av Allal Ben Abdallah (☎055 52 23 51; ❶). A good one-star is the *Majestic*, 19 Av Mohammed V (☎055 52 20 35; ❷), handy for the Gare El

Amir Abdelkader. The **HI hostel**, Av Okba Ben Nafi (☎055 52 46 98; ❶), is an easy 1.5km walk northwest of the city centre. Arguably the best **campsite** in Morocco is *Aguedal* (☎055 55 53 96), south of the Imperial City, a twenty-minute walk from Place El Hedim, opposite the Heri as-Souani.

For straight Moroccan **food** the *Economique*, 123 Rue Dar Smen, opposite Bab Mansour, is a top Medina café/restaurant. Budget eats in the Ville Nouvelle include excellent, cheap fried fish at *Casse-Croute Driss*, 34 Rue Emir Abdelkader, and the *Lorraine* next door, which specializes in roast rabbit. Not so cheap but still reasonable are *Pizzeria Le Four* (pasta and pizzas) on Rue Atlas, near the *Hôtel Majestic*, and *La Coupole*, on the corner of Av Hassan II and Rue Ghana, serving Moroccan and European food (with a bar and nightclub). *Collier de la Colombe*, 67 Rue Driba, in an ornate mansion on the edge of the Medina, offers outstanding international cuisine and moderate prices. For a not too expensive splurge, the lovely *Riad*, in a section of original palace at 79 Ksar Chaacha in the Medina, serves well-prepared Moroccan dishes in beautifully restored rooms or outdoors beside a sunken garden. In the Ville Nouvelle, *Diafa* has great home cooking in what looks like a private house at 12 Rue Badr el Kobra (off Av Hassan II at its western end). There are plenty of **bars**, several in Ville Nouvelle hotels, including the 1930s-style bar of the Art Deco *Hôtel Volubilis* at 45 Av des FAR.

Volubilis

Visible for miles, **VOLUBILIS** occupies the ledge of a long, high plateau and was the Roman Empire's most remote city. Direct Roman rule lasted little more than two centuries – the garrison withdrew in 285 AD to ease pressure elsewhere – but the city remained active well into the eighteenth century, when its marble was carried away for the building of Meknes. What you see today, well-excavated and maintained, are largely the ruins of second- and third-century AD buildings. The **entrance** (daily 9am–6pm; 20dh) is through a minor gate set into the city wall, built in 168 AD following a series of Berber insurrections. Just inside are the ticket office, a café/bar and a small **museum** of sculpture. The best of the finds made here – including a superb collection of bronzes – are in the Rabat museum. Volubilis has, however, retained the great majority of its **mosaics**, some thirty or so in a good state of preservation. **Getting there** from Meknes is easy enough – take a collective grand taxi for Moulay Idris and ask to be set down en route. The problem is getting back: if you're not prepared to hitch, or walk the 3km to Moulay Idriss, you'll have to wait for a passing bus from Ouezzane, which could easily be a couple of hours. Alternatively, charter a *grand taxi* from Meknes – about 300dh for the round trip including waiting time.

Fes (Fez)

The most ancient of the imperial capitals, **FES** (Fès in French, Fez in English) stimulates the senses and seems to exist somewhere between the Middle Ages and the modern world. Some 200,000 of the city's half-million inhabitants live in the oldest part of the Medina, **Fes el Bali**, which has a culture and atmosphere quite different from anywhere in mainland Europe.

Arrival, information and accommodation

The **train station** is in the Ville Nouvelle, fifteen minutes' walk from the hotels around Place Mohammed V. If you prefer to stay in the Medina, take a *petit taxi*, or walk down to Place de la Résistance (aka La Fiat) and pick up bus #9 to Dar Batha/Place de l'Istiqlal, near the western gate to Fes el Bali, Bab Boujeloud. The *gare routière* **bus station** is just outside the walls near Bab Boujeloud. The new terminal for CTM buses is off Rue Atlas, which links the far end of Av Mohammed V with Place d'Atlas. **Grands taxis** mostly operate from the *gare routière*; exceptions include those serving Meknes (from the train station). The **tourist office** is on

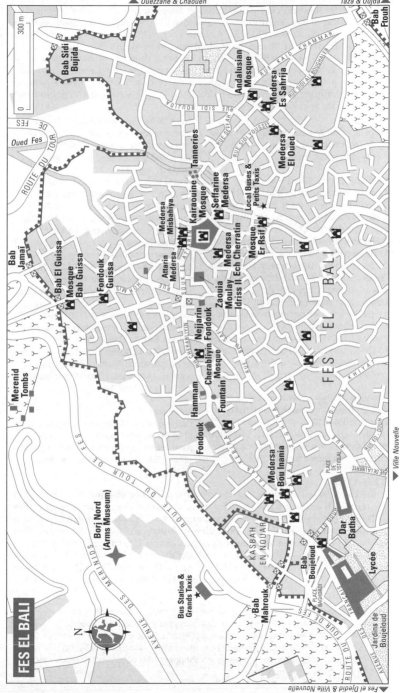

FES EL BALI

▲ *Ouezzane & Chaouen*

Taza & Oujda ▲

Bab Ftouh

Bab Sidi Bujida

Oued Fes

DE FES

Oued Fes

ROUTE DU TOUR

RUE SIDI BOUJIDA

RUE SEFLAH

RUE KAID KHAMMAR

RUE SIDI AL BOUGHALEB

RUE SIDI YOUSSEF

Andalusian Mosque

Medersa Es Sahrija

Medersa El Oued

Tanneries

Kairaouine Mosque

Seffarine Medersa

Local Buses & Petits Taxis

Medersa Misbahiya

Medersa El Ech Cherratin

Mosque Er Rsif

Bab Jamaï

Bab El Guissa

Mosque Bab Guissa

Fondouk Guissa

HOR MASS

Attarin Medersa

SOUK EL ATTARIN

RUE CHERABLIYIN

Zaouia Moulay Idriss II

Neijarin Fondouk

Cherabliyin Mosque

Fountain

FES EL BALI

RUE CHIYATA

RUE SIDI EL DOUH

RUE DE DOUH

RUE DE LA LIBERTÉ

Hammam

Fondouk

RUE YEBBA SEGHIRA

Medersa Bou Inania

PLACE DE L'ISTIQLAL

▶ *Ville Nouvelle*

ROUTE DU TOUR DE FES

AVENUE DES MERINIDS

Merenid Tombs

Borj Nord (Arms Museum)

KASBAH EN NOUAR

Bus Station & Grands Taxis

Bab Mahrouk

Bab Boujeloud

Dar Batha

Lycée

PLACE BAGHDADI

AVENUE DES FRANÇAIS

ROUTE DU TOUR DE FES

Jardins de Boujeloud

N

300 m

0

Place de la Résistance (Mon–Thurs 8.30am–noon & 2.30–6.30pm, Fri 8.30–11.30am & 3–6.30pm; ☎055 62 34 60), with a Syndicat d'Initiative on Place Mohammed V (same hours plus Sat 8.30am–noon). Both can tell you about June's seven-day **Festival of World Sacred Music**; more details from the secretariat (☎055 74 05 35, ◉www.fesfestival.com). There's a shortage of **hotel** space in all categories, so be prepared for higher-than-usual prices; booking ahead is advisable. For atmosphere and character, the Medina is the place to be, though you'll need an easy-going attitude towards size and cleanliness. The less engaging Ville Nouvelle has a wider choice of hotels.

Hostel

HI hostel 18 Rue Abdeslam Seghrini ☎055 62 40 85. One of Morocco's best hostels – well-kept, friendly and spotlessly clean. **①**

Hotels in the Medina

Cascade Just inside Bab Boujeloud, Fes el Bali ☎055 63 84 42. An old building, with a useful public *hammam* (bath house) behind. Small rooms, but clean and friendly. **①**

Du Commerce Place des Alaouites, Fes el Djedid, facing the doors of the royal palace ☎055 62 22 31. Still owned by a Jewish family in what was the Jewish quarter; old, but comfortable and friendly, with a lively café at street level. **①**

Lamrani Talâa Seghira, Fes el Bali ☎055 63 44 11. Friendly with small but spotless rooms, mostly doubles, opposite a *hammam*. **①**

Pension Talaa 14 Talâa Seghira, Fes el Bali ☎055 63 33 59. A small place and slightly pricier than the other Medina cheapies, but slightly more comfortable. **①**

Hotels in the Ville Nouvelle

Amor 31 Rue Arabie Saoudite, formerly Rue du Pakistan ☎055 62 27 24. One block from Av Hassan II, behind the Bank al-Maghrib. Comfortable though sombre rooms with good bathroom but hot water mornings and evenings only. **②**

Grand Bd Abdallah Chefchaounei ☎055 93 20 26, ◉grandhotel@fesnet.net.ma. Old colonial hotel opposite the sunken park on Place Mohammed V. Refurbished, en-suite rooms, some very large. **③**

Mounia 60 Rue Asilah ☎055 65 07 71. Modern hotel with friendly management, plus restaurant and a popular bar (which can be noisy). **③**

Nouzha 7 Av Hassan Dkhissi ☎055 64 00 02 or 12. Splendidly decorated public areas and comfortable rooms, slightly out-of-centre but convenient for the CTM terminal. **②**

De la Paix 44 Av Hassan II ☎055 62 50 72, ◉hoteldelapaix@iam.net.ma. Tour-group hotel, nicely refurbished, with a good seafood restaurant and a bar. **②**

Rex 32 Place Atlas ☎055 64 21 33. Small, congenial hotel built in 1910, but clean, pleasant and near the CTM terminal. **①**

Royal 36 Rue es Soudan ☎055 62 46 56. Handy for the train station. All rooms have a shower (some have toilets too), but they vary in quality; look before you book. **①**

Campsite

Camping International Route de Sefrou ☎055 61 80 61. Some 4km south of town, this site is pricey but has good facilities, including a pool in summer. Take bus #38 from Place de l'Atlas.

The City

The Medina is actually two cities: the newer section, **Fes el Djedid**, established in the thirteenth century, is mostly taken up by the Royal Palace. The older part, **Fes el Bali**, founded in the eighth century on the River Fes, was populated by refugees from Tunisia on one bank – the **Kairouine quarter** – and from Spain on the other bank – the **Andalusian quarter**. In practice, almost everything you will want to see is in the Kairouine quarter. For a view over the whole city, take a hike up to the **Arms Museum** in the fort above the bus station (Mon & Wed–Sun 8.30am–noon & 2.30–6pm; 10dh), from which the whole of Fes el Bali is laid out at your feet.

Getting lost is one of the great joys of the Fes Medina, and a **guide** is not really necessary; if you get in difficulties, you can always ask people for directions to Bab Boujeloud, Place Nejjarine or the Medersa el Attarin. Should you want to engage one, official guides wear a medallion to identify themselves, unofficial guides do not; both can be found at Bab Boujeloud. Never go shopping with either kind of guide however, as prices are liable to double.

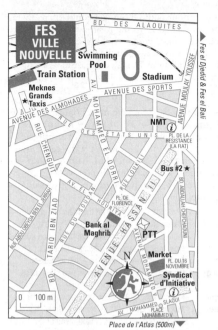

Place de l'Atlas (500m) ▼

Talaa Kebira, the Medina's main artery, can be accessed by entering Bab Boujeloud, taking the first left and then turning right. About 100m down is the most brilliant of Fes's monuments, the **Medersa Bou Inania**, which comes close to perfection in every aspect of its construction, with beautiful carved wood, stucco and *zellij* tilework. Closed some years now for restoration, it should soon reopen, and will most definitely warrant a visit when it does. Continuing down Talâa Kebira you reach the entrance to the **Souk el Attarin** (Souk of the Spice Vendors), the formal heart of the city. To the right, a street leads past the charming **Souk el Henna** – a tree-shaded square where traditional cosmetics are sold – to Place Nejjarin (Carpenters' Square). Here, next to the geometric tilework of the **Nejjarin Fountain**, is the imposing eighteenth-century **Nejjarin Fondouk**, now a woodwork museum (daily 10am–5pm, during Ramadan closes 4.30pm; 20dh), though the building is rather more interesting than its exhibits. Immediately to the right of the fountain, Talâa Seghira is an alternative route back to Bab Boujeloud, while the alley to the right of that is the aromatic **carpenters' souk**, ripe with the scent of sawn cedar, and top on the list of great Medina smells.

The street opposite the Nejjarin Fountain leads to the **Zaouia Moulay Idriss II**, one of the holiest buildings in the city. Buried here is the son and successor of Fes's founder, who continued his father's work. Only Muslims may enter to check out the *zellij* tilework, original wooden *minbar* (pulpit) and the tomb itself. Beyond it is the **Kissaria**, where fine fabrics are traded. Meanwhile, over to your left (on the other side of the Kissaria), Souk el Attarin comes to an end opposite the fourteenth-century **Attarin Medersa** (daily 9am–6pm; during Ramadan closes 4pm; 10dh), the finest of the city's medieval colleges after the Bou Inania. To the right of the Medersa, a narrow street runs along the north side of the **Kairaouine Mosque**. Founded in 857 AD by a refugee from Kairouan in Tunisia, the Kairouine is one of the oldest universities in the world, and the fountainhead of Moroccan religious life. Its present dimensions, with sixteen aisles and room for 20,000 worshippers, are essentially the product of tenth- and twelfth-century reconstructions. Non-Muslims can look into the courtyard through the main door.

The street emerges in **Place Seffarine**, almost wilfully picturesque with its faience fountain, gnarled fig trees and metalworkers hammering away. On the west side of the square, the thirteenth-century **Seffarine Medersa** is still in use as a hostel for students at the Kairaouine (visitors may enter for a look at any reasonable hour without paying). If you're beginning to find the medieval prettiness of the central *souks* and *medersas* slightly unreal, then the area beyond the square should provide the antidote. The dyers' market – **Souk Sabbighin** – is directly south of the Seffarine Medersa, and is draped with fantastically coloured yarn and cloth drying in the heat. Below, workers in grey toil over cauldrons of multicoloured dyes. Place er Rsif, nearby, has buses and taxis to the Ville Nouvelle. The street to the left (north) of the Seffarine Medersa leads to the **tanneries**, constantly visited by tour groups with whom you could discreetly tag along if you get lost. Inside the tanneries (pay a tip to the *gardien*, usually 10dh, to enter), water deluges through holes that were once windows of houses, and hundreds of skins lie spread out on the rooftops, above vats of dye and the pigeon dung used to treat the leather, reminiscent of the pits of hell from Dante's *Inferno*. Straight on, the road eventually leads back round to the Attarin Medersa.

Eating and drinking

Cafés are plentiful in the Ville Nouvelle, with some of the most popular along Av Mohammed es Slaoui and Av Mohammed V. Fes el Bali has two main areas for **budget eating**: around Bab Boujeloud and along Rue Hormis (running from Souk el Attarin towards Bab Guissa), and in the Ville Nouvelle, try the café/restaurants near the municipal market, on the left-hand side of Av Mohammed V as you walk from the post office. For **bars**, you have to look a little harder. *Café Chope*, 55 Av Mohammed V, south of Place Mohammed V, with its 1930s mock-classical interior, does good bar snacks, or try the hotel bars.

Bouanania Talâa Kebira, behind Bab Boujeloud. Rooftop or indoor eating, with *tajines* and other good food in large portions.

Chamonix 5 Rue Moukhtar Soussi, off Av Mohammed V. A reliable restaurant serving Moroccan and European dishes. Attracts a young crowd, and stays open late in summer.

La Cheminée 6 Av Lalla Asma (aka Rue Chenguit). Small and friendly licensed restaurant, moderate prices.

Chez Vittorio Pizzeria 21 Rue du Nador, opposite *Hôtel Central*. Pizza and pasta; reliable and good value, but not very exciting.

Fish Friture 138 Av Mohammed V, at the far end of a short passageway off the main street. Fish dishes are the mainstay (the paella's great), but there is much else on offer. Courteous and quick.

Des Jeunes (aka *Chez Hamid*), inside Bab Boujeloud. Cheap and basic – soups, kebabs, couscous and *pastilla* (poultry-filled pie – a Fes speciality).

Marrakesh 11 Rue Abes Tazi (between *Hôtel Mounia* and the old CTM terminal). Small, but good and inexpensive, with a limited menu of tasty food.

Zagora 5 Av Mohammed V in a small arcade, behind the Derby shoe shop. New and a little pretentious, but the food and service are well above average.

Listings

Exchange BMCE, Place Mohammed V, Place de l'Atlas and Place Florence (all with ATMs).

Internet Cyber Club, 70 Rue Bou Khessissat, Fes el Djedid; 2 Rue el Houria; Av Mohammed V opposite *Hôtel Central*.

Pharmacies Night pharmacy in the *baladiya* (town hall) on Av Moulay Youssef (daily 9pm–8.30am).

Police Commissariat Central is on Av Mohammed V behind the post office.

Post office Corner of avenues Mohammed V and Hassan II.

Rabat

Capital of Morocco since 1912, **RABAT** is elegant, slightly self-conscious in its modern ways, and a little bit dull. However, its monuments punctuate the span of Moroccan history, and are among the country's most picturesque.

Arrival and accommodation

Rabat Ville **train station** is at the heart of the Ville Nouvelle, with most classified hotels situated only a few minutes' walk away (don't get off at the smaller Rabat Agdal train station, 2km from the centre). The main **bus terminal** is 5km west of the centre, served by local bus #30 and *petits taxis*. It's easier, if you're arriving by bus from the north, to get off in Salé across the river, and take a *grand taxi* from there into Rabat. **Grands taxis** for non-local destinations operate from outside the main bus station; those to Casa cost only a couple of dirhams more than the bus and leave more or less continuously. **Local bus services** radiate from the corner of Rue Nador and Bd Hassan II, where *petits taxis* and local *grands taxis* can be found. **Accommodation** can fill up in midsummer and during festivals; it's best to phone ahead.

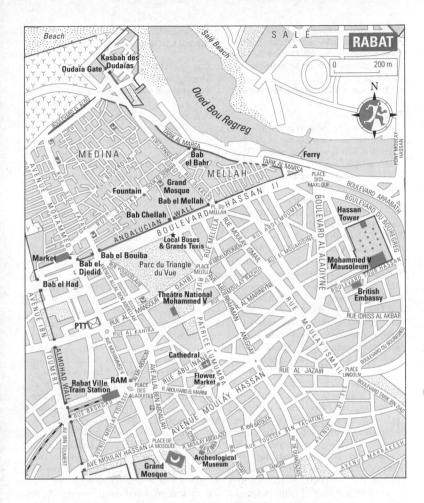

Hostel

HI hostel 43 Rue Marrassa ☏037 72 57 69. Just outside the Medina walls north of Bd Hassan II. Closed 10am–noon. ❶

Hotels

Berlin 261 Av Mohammed V ☏037 72 34 35. Small hotel with hot showers. Centrally located above the Chinese restaurant *Hong Kong*. ❶

Central 2 Rue Al Basra ☏037 70 73 56. Central position near train station and alongside better-known *Hôtel Balima* on Av Mohammed V. A good budget choice and, with 34 rooms, likely to have space. ❶

Dorhmi 313 Av Mohammed V, Medina, just inside Bab Djedid ☏037 72 38 98. Above *Café Essalem*

and Banque Populaire. Well furnished and maintained. ❶

Gaulois Corner of Rue Hims and Av Mohammed V ☏037 72 30 22. One of a cluster of budget hotels around the bottom end of Av Mohammed V. ❶

Majestic 121 Av Hassan II ☏037 72 29 97, ℮majestic@welcom.net.ma. Popular and good value, with bright, spotless rooms, some overlooking the Medina. ❷

D'Orsay 11 Av Moulay Youssef, on Place de la Gare ☏037 70 13 19. Convenient for train station and café/restaurants, this is a friendly, helpful and efficient hotel. ❷

Splendid 8 Rue Ghazza ☏037 72 32 83. Nice place whose best rooms overlook a courtyard. *Café-Restaurant Ghazza* opposite is good for

breakfast and a snack any time. **②**
Terminus 384 Av Mohammed V ☎037 70 52 67.
A good alternative to the *D'Orsay* round the corner.
A large, featureless block, but the interior has been
updated. **③**
Des Voyageurs 8 Souk Semarine, Medina, near

Bab Djedid ☎037 72 37 20. Inexpensive, popular
and often full. Clean, airy rooms but no showers. **①**

Campsites
Camping de la Plage ☎063 59 36 63. Across
the river at Salé. Basic but well-managed.

The City

Rabat's compact **Medina** – the whole city until the French arrived in 1912 – is
wedged on two sides by the sea and the river, on the others by the twelfth-century
Almohad and fifteenth-century Andalusian walls. Laid out in a simple grid, its
streets are very easy to navigate. North lies the **Kasbah des Oudaïas**, a charming
and evocative quarter whose principal gateway – **Bab el Kasbah** or Oudaïa Gate,
built around 1195 – is one of the most ornate in the Moorish world. Its interior is
now used for art exhibitions. Down the steps outside the gate, a lower, horseshoe
arch leads directly to Moulay Ismail's palace, housing a **Museum of Moroccan
Arts** (provisionally daily 9am–5pm; 10dh), which features Berber and Arab jewellery and traditional costumes from most regions of Morocco. The adjoining
Andalusian Garden – one of the most delightful spots in the city – was actually
constructed by the French in the last century, though true to Arab Andalusian tradition, with deep, sunken beds of shrubs and flowering annuals.

The most ambitious of all Almohad buildings, the **Hassan Mosque** (daily
8.30am–6.30pm; free), with its vast minaret, dominates almost every view of the
city. Designed by the Almohad ruler Yacoub el Mansour as the centrepiece of the
new capital, the mosque seems to have been more or less abandoned at his death in
1199. The minaret, despite its apparent simplicity, is among the most complex of all
Almohad structures: each facade is different, with a distinct combination of patterning, yet the whole intricacy of blind arcades and interlacing curves is based on just
two formal designs. Facing the tower are the **Mosque and Mausoleum of
Mohammed V**, begun on the sultan's death in 1961 and dedicated six years later.
On the opposite side of the Ville Nouvelle from the mausoleum is the
Archeological Museum, Rue Brihi (Mon & Wed–Sun 9am–noon & 2.30–6pm;
10dh), the most important in Morocco. Although small, it has an exceptional and
beautiful collection of Roman-era bronzes, found mainly at Volubilis. The most
beautiful of Moroccan ruins, the royal burial ground called the **Chellah** (daily
8.30am–6pm; 10dh), is a startling sight as you emerge from the long avenues of the
Ville Nouvelle, with its circuit of fourteenth-century walls, legacy of **Abou el
Hassan** (1331–51), the greatest of Merenid rulers. Off to the left of the main gate
are the partly excavated ruins of the Roman city that preceded the necropolis. A set
of Islamic ruins are further down to the right, situated within a second inner sanctuary, approached along a broad path through half-wild gardens.

Eating and drinking

Rabat has a wide range of good **restaurants** serving both Moroccan and international dishes. As ever, the cheapest ones are to be found in the **Medina**. Just on the
edge of the quarter, down Rue Mohammed V and along Rue Souika, there is a
string of good everyday café/restaurants, with *Jeunesse*, 305 Av Mohammed V, and
Taghazoute, round the corner at 7 Rue Sebbahi, among the better choices, the latter
a good place for breakfast. In the **Ville Nouvelle**, restaurants are grouped around
the train station, Place de la Gare and Av Moulay Youssef. Try *Brasserie Française*, 3 Av
Moulay Youssef, with an upstairs restaurant that is one of the best places to eat
around the train station. *La Clef*, alongside *Hôtel d'Orsay* on Rue Hatim, serves good
French and Moroccan dishes upstairs, and has a small bar downstairs. Worthwhile,
but more expensive, choices include *Saïdoune*, in the mall at 467 Av Mohammed V,
opposite *Hôtel Terminus*, a good Iraqi-run Lebanese restaurant. *Hong Kong*, 261 Av
Mohammed V, does a tasty range of Chinese and Vietnamese dishes. *La Bamba* on

18

Rue Tanta, behind *Hôtel Balima*, offers a choice of tourist, gastronomic and Moroccan set menus. For Italian specialities, go to *La Mamma* (with takeaway and home-delivery options), or the trendy *Equinox*, both also on Rue Tanta and with set and *à-la-carte* menus. Most of these serve beer and wine with meals. Better suited for lunch is the alcohol-free *Café-Restaurant El Bahia*, set into the Andalusian wall on Bd Hassan II, with reasonably priced Moroccan dishes served in a pleasant courtyard, upstairs or on the street outside. If you're looking for a treat, try the more expensive *Restaurant de la Plage* on the beach below the Kasbah des Oudaïas (℡037 20 29 28), which specializes in fish. Avenues Mohammed V and Allal Ben Abdallah have some good **cafés**, but **bars** are few and far between outside the main hotels. The one at the *Hôtel Balima* is as good a place as any. Late-night options include a string of disco-bars around Place de Melilla and on Rue Patrice Lumumba.

Listings

Embassies Australia represented by Canada; Canada, 13bis Rue Jaafar as Sadiq, Agdal ℡037 67 28 80; New Zealand represented by the UK; UK, 17 Bd Tour Hassan ℡037 72 09 05 or 06; USA, 2 Av Mohammed el Fassi ℡037 76 22 65. Irish citizens covered by their embassy in Lisbon, but may get help from the UK embassy.

Exchange Along Av Allal Ben Abdallah and Av Mohammed V. BMCE also has a *bureau de change* in Ville train station.

Internet Student Cyber, 83 Av Hassan II; Cybercountry, 2nd floor, 2 Rue du Caire; ETSI Net, 12 Av Prince Moulay Abdellah.

Police Av Tripoli, near the Cathedral. Police post at Bab Djedid.

Post office Halfway down Av Mohammed V.

Casablanca

Morocco's main city and economic capital, **CASABLANCA** (or "Casa") is also North Africa's largest port. Its Westernized image – with fancy beach clubs and almost no women wearing the veil – masks what is still substantially a "first-generation" city with some of Morocco's most intense social problems. Film buffs will be disappointed to learn that Bogart's *Casablanca* wasn't shot here – the *Bar Casablanca* commemorates it as a gimmick in the luxury *Hyatt Regency* hotel on Place des Nations-Unies, with T-shirts and baseball caps available. The city's main monument, the **Grande Mosquée Hassan II** (tours daily except Fri 9am, 10am, 11am & 2pm; 100dh, students 50dh), opened in 1993, is the world's second largest mosque, with space for 100,000 worshippers, and a minaret that soars to a record 172m. Commissioned by the last king, who named it after himself, it cost an estimated £320m/US$500m, raised by not wholly voluntary public subscription. It's a twenty-minute walk northwest from the centre. The French colonial buildings grouped around **Place Mohammed V** are built in a style called Mauresque, a French idealization of Moorish design, heavily influenced by Art Deco. The **Medina**, above the port and recently gentrified, is largely the product of the late nineteenth century, when Casa began its modest growth as a commercial centre.

Practicalities

Some trains stop only at the **Gare des Voyageurs** (2km southeast of the centre) rather than continuing to the better-situated **Gare du Port**, between the town centre and the port. Bus #30 runs into town from the Voyageurs; otherwise, it's a twenty-minute walk or a *petit taxi* ride. Coming by **bus**, take the CTM if possible as it drops you downtown on Rue Léon l'Africain, behind *Hôtel Safir* on Av des FAR; other buses arrive at the *gare routière*, southeast of town on Route des Ouled Ziane. **Grands taxis** from Rabat arrive a block east of the CTM terminal, while those from points south come into a station south of town on the Route de Jadida in Beauséjour. The **tourist office** is inconveniently located south of the centre at 55 Rue Omar Slaoui (Mon–Thur 8.30am–noon & 2.30–6.30pm, Fri 8.30–11.30am 3–6.30pm; ℡022 27 11 77); more convenient is the **Syndicat d'Initiative**, 98 Bd Mohammed V (Mon–Fri 8.30am–noon & 3–6.30pm, Sat 8.30am–noon & 3–5pm, Sun 9am–noon; ℡022 22 15 24).

Hotels are plentiful, though often near capacity. *Mon Rêve*, 7 Rue Chaouia (☎022 31 14 39; ❶), is the best option in an area of cheap hotels, but often fills up, with *Colbert*, 38 Rue Chaouia (☎022 31 42 41; ❶), a good fall-back option. *Du Centre*, 1 Rue Sidi Belyout, corner of Av des FAR (☎022 44 61 80 or 81; ❷), is another golden oldie, cheered up with a splash of paint and new en-suite bathrooms. *Terminus*, 184 Bd Ba Hamad (☎022 24 00 25; ❶), is handy for the Gare des Voyageurs, and for eating places nearby. *Foucauld*, 52 Rue Araibi Jilali (☎022 22 26 66; ❶), is great value, with en-suite rooms, and is near several good café/restaurants. Very central is *Plaza*, 18 Bd Houphouët Boigny (☎022 29 78 22; ❸), which has good facilities. The **HI hostel**, 6 Place Ahmed Bidaoui (☎022 22 05 51; ❶; closed 10am–noon), is a friendly, well-maintained place just inside the Medina and sign-posted from the nearby Gare du Port. The **campsite**, *Oasis*, is on Av Jean Mermoz, 4km from the centre in the Beauséjour district (☎022 23 42 57; bus #31).

Casa has the reputation of being the best place to **eat** in Morocco, and if you can afford the fancier restaurant prices, this is certainly true. For those on a budget, some of the best possibilities lie in the smaller streets off Bd Mohammed V. A very cheap place is *Snack Bab Rkha* on Rue Bab Rkha, where it meets Rue Sidi Bou Smara and Bd Houphouët Boigny at the edge of the Medina. *Snack Amine* at 32 Rue Chaouia (aka Rue Colbert) has low-priced fish dishes including paella. Of slightly pricier places offering reasonable set menus, *Le Buffet* at 99 Bd Mohammed V is good value, and *L'Étoile Marocaine*, 107 Rue Allal Ben Abdallah, has a decent menu and a good atmosphere. Quite expensive by local standards is *Centre 2000*, by Casa Port station, with three good restaurants serving French, Italian and Moroccan food. *Le Dauphin*, 115 Bd Houphouët Boigny, is a long-established and popular fish restaurant, worth queuing for, and the stylish *Petit Poucet*, 86 Bd Mohammed V, has a cheaper snack bar next door – one of the best places for some serious drinking.

Marrakesh

MARRAKESH (Marrakech in French) is a city of immense beauty, low, pink and tent-like before a great shaft of mountains. It's an immediately exciting place, espe-cially around the vast space of its central square, the **Djemaa el Fna**, the stage for a long-established ritual in which shifting circles of onlookers gather around groups of acrobats, drummers, pipe musicians, dancers, storytellers and comedians. Unlike Fes, for so long its rival as the nation's capital but these days stagnating, Marrakesh's population is growing and it has a thriving industrial area; the city remains the most important market and administrative centre of southern Morocco.

The Djemaa el Fna (referred to simply as "el Djemaa", or even "la Place") lies right at the heart of the Medina, and almost everything of interest is concentrated in the web of alleyways around it. Just to the west of the Djemaa, an unmistakable landmark is the minaret of the great **Koutoubia Mosque** (enchanting under floodlights at night), in the shadow of which begins Avenue Mohammed V, leading out of the Medina and up the length of the new city, **Gueliz**. It's a fairly long walk between Gueliz and the Medina, but there are plenty of taxis and the regular buses #1 and #16 between the two.

Arrival, information and accommodation

From the **train station**, by Gueliz, cross the street and take bus #3/#10 or a *petit taxi* (10–15dh) for the Djemaa. The **bus terminal** is just outside the northwestern walls of the Medina by Bab Doukkala; from here it's a 20-minute walk to the Djemaa, or bus #3/#8/#10/#14 (opposite Bab Doukkala), or a *petit taxi* (8–10dh). CTM buses take you to their office in Gueliz. The **airport**, 5km southwest, is served by the erratic bus #11 (supposedly every half-hour to the Djemaa) – *petits* or *grands taxis* (40–50dh by day, 70–80dh at night) are a better option. The **tourist office** is on Place Abdelmoumen Ben Ali (Mon–Fri 8.30am–noon &

18

MARRAKESH

▲ Bab Aylen   ▲ Bab Aghmat

Tanneries

Bab Debbagh

Bab el Khemis

RUE DE BAB KHEMIS

PLACE EL MOUKEF

Ben Youssef Medersa
& Marrakesh Museum

Dar Si Said
Palace

Palais el
Bahia

Mosque
Ben Youssef

Chrob ou Chouf
Fountain

RUE ASSOUEL

PLACE BEN
SALAH

Zaouia Sidi
Ben Salah

Maison
Tiskiwin

El Badi
Palace

DERB DEBBACHI

RUE BAB TAGHZOUT

Almoravid
Koubba

SOUK SMARINE

M E D I N A

RUE ZITOUN EL QDIM

Kasbah
Mosque

Bab Er
Robb

RUE ZITOUN EL KEDIM

Zaouia Sidi
Mohammed
Ben Slimane

RUE EL BIA

Dar El
Glaoui

RUE BAB DOUKKALA

Mouassin
Mosque

DJEMAA
EL FNA

BMCE

RUE DE LA KASBAH

HOUMAN EL TOUJJAK

RUE MOULAY ISMAIL

RUE BANI MARINE

AVENUE HOUMAN EL TOUJJAK

RUE DE BAB AGNAOU

Bab
Agnaou

Bab
Doukkala
Mosque

RUE BAB DOUKKALA

RUE AL YAMAN

Ensemble
Artisanal

Koutoubia

PL YOUSSEF
BEN TACHFINE

Bab
Doukkala

Bus
Station

Bab Er
Raha

Swimming
Pool

Bab El
Makhzen

Bab El
Djedid

EL HAMMAM

EL FEDOUAK

PLACE
MOURABITON

Bab
Nkob

BOULEVARD

Y A R M O U K

BOULEVARD
DE SAFI

PLACE
DE LA LIBERTÉ
EL KOUBBA

AVENUE ECHOHADA

AVENUE DE LA MENARA

Crédit
du Maroc

AVENUE DES NATIONS UNIES

AVENUE YACOUB EL MARINI

AVENUE DU 16 NOVEMBRE

PARC DES
SPORTS

HIVERNAGE

AVENUE MOULAY EL HASSAN

AVENUE EL KADISSIA

Market

Post
Office

BMCE

AV.
MOHAMMED

AVENUE MOHAMMED II

BOULEVARD
MOHAMMED
V

RUE SOURIYA

RUE ABDELKRIM EL KATTABI

RUE MAURITANIA

RUE DE YOUGOSLAVIE

AVENUE DU PRESIDENT KENNEDY

AVENUE DE FRANCE

CTM
Office

PLACE ZERKTOUNI

ABDELMOUMEN
BEN ALI

RUE DE YOUGOSLAVIE

AV.
MOHAMMED

BOULEVARD MOHAMMED EL BEKAL

AVENUE EL KADISSIA

AVENUE DE FRANCE

AV. MOHAMMED

BOULEVARD
DE
FRANCE

GUELIZ

PLACE DU 11
JANVIER

RUE
EL
MASSIRA

AVENUE HASSAN II

RUE IBN EL MANSUR

AVENUE HASSAN II

AVENUE DE FRANCE

Train Station

Youth
Hostel

N

MARRAKESH

0   500 m

MOROCCO | Marrakesh

18

649

2.30–6.30pm, & sometimes Sat; ☏044 43 62 39) keeps current details of services you might need. There's a branch office at Place Venus by the Koutoubia (same hours). The Medina, as ever, has the main concentration of cheap **accommodation** – most places quite pleasant – and, unusually, has a fair number of classified hotels too. Given the attractions of the Djemaa el Fna and the *souks*, this is the first choice. Booking in advance is advisable. All our recommendations are in the Medina unless stated otherwise.

Hostel

HI hostel Rue El Jahid, Gueliz ☏044 44 77 13. Immaculate, refurbished and close to the train station. Closed 9am–2pm. 40dh.

Hotels

Ali Rue Moulay Ismail ☏044 44 49 79, ⓔhotelali@hotmail.com. Popular with overlanders and High Atlas trekkers (guides can be found here). Rooms have showers, and there's cheap dorm accommodation. ❷

CTM Djemaa el Fna ☏044 44 23 25. Above the old bus station, with decent-sized rooms, though a little glum; rooms 28–32 overlook the square, as does the roof terrace. ❶

Essaouira 3 Derb Sidi Bouloukat ☏044 44 38 05, ⓔhotelessaouira@hotmail.com). Well-run, popular cheapie, with laundry service, baggage deposit and rooftop café. ❶

Farouk 66 Av Hassan II, on the corner with Rue Mauretania, Gueliz ☏044 43 19 89, ⓔhotelfarouk@hotmail.com. Excellent hotel with en-suite rooms and a popular restaurant, within walking distance of the train station. ❶

De France 197 Rue Zitoun el Kedim ☏044 44 30 67. One of the oldest Medina cheapies, nothing special but friendly with decent rooms. ❶

Gallia 30 Rue de la Recette ☏044 44 59 13, ⓦwww.ilove-marrakesh.com/hotelgallia. Pleasant building in a quiet road; airy and spotless rooms (all en suite and with air-con) off two tiled courtyards. Highly recommended – reserve by fax well ahead if possible. ❸

Islane 279 Av Mohammed V, facing the Koutoubia minaret ☏044 44 00 81 or 83. Views of the Koutoubia and comfortable modern rooms (en suite, a/c and satellite TV) compensate for the traffic noise. ❷

Jnane Mogador Derb Sidi Bouloukat, by 116 Riad Zitoun Kadem ☏044 42 63 23, ⓦwww.jnanemogador.com. Beautifully restored old house with charming but fully equipped rooms around a lovely patio. ❸

Medina 1 Derb Sidi Bouloukat ☏044 44 29 97. A real gem: low-priced, clean, friendly and good value, with an English-speaking proprietor and breakfast on the roof terrace. ❶

Souria 17 Rue de la Recette ☏061 55 22 11, ⓔhotelsouria@yahoo.fr. Deservedly popular family-run *pension*, spotless and very homely. ❶

Des Voyageurs 40 Bd. Mohammed Zerktouni ☏044 44 72 18. Pleasant, old-fashioned hotel, with big, clean rooms and a nice little garden. ❶

The City

There's nowhere in the world like the **Djemaa el Fna**: by day it's basically a market, with a few snake charmers and an occasional troupe of acrobats; in the late afternoon it becomes a whole carnival of musicians, storytellers and other entertainers; and in the evening dozens of stalls set up to dispense hot food to crowds of locals, while the musicians and performers continue. If you get tired of the spectacle, or if things slow down, you can move over to the rooftop terraces of the *Café de France* or the *Restaurant Argana* to gaze at it all from above. The absence of any architectural feature in the Djemaa serves to emphasize the drama of the **Koutoubia Minaret**. Nearly 70m high and visible for miles, it was begun shortly after the Almohad conquest of the city, around 1150, and displays many features that were to become widespread in Moroccan architecture – the wide band of ceramic inlay, the pyramid-shaped merlons, and the alternation of patterning on the facades.

The northern Medina

A lane opposite the *Café de France* on the Djemaa el Fna leads to a stuccowork arch that marks the beginning of the crowded **Souk Smarine**, an important thoroughfare traditionally dominated by textiles. Just before the red ochre arch at its end, Souk Smarine narrows and you get a glimpse through the passageways to its right of the **Rahba Kedima**, a small and fairly ramshackle square whose most interesting features are its apothecary stalls. At the end of Rahba Kedima, a passageway to the left gives access to another, smaller square – a bustling, carpet-draped area known as la **Criée Berbère**, which is where slave auctions used to be held.

Cutting back to **Souk el Kebir**, which by now has taken over from the Smarine, you emerge at the **kissarias**, the covered markets at the heart of the *souks*. Kissarias traditionally sell more expensive products, which today means a predominance of Western designs and imports. Off to their right is **Souk des Bijoutiers**, a modest jewellers' lane, while at the north end is a convoluted web of alleys comprising the **Souk Cherratin**, essentially a leatherworkers' market.

If you bear left through this area and then turn right, you should arrive at the open space in front of the Ben Youssef Mosque. The originally fourteenth-century **Ben Youssef Medersa** (daily 9am–6pm; 20dh) – the annexe for students taking courses in the mosque – stands off a side street just to the east. It was almost completely rebuilt in the sixteenth century under the Saadians, with a strong Andalusian influence. Parts have exact parallels in the Alhambra Palace in Granada, and it seems likely that Muslim Spanish architects were employed in its construction. Next door, the **Marrakesh Museum** (daily 9.30am–6pm; 30dh) exhibits jewellery, art and sculpture, both old and new, in a beautifully restored nineteenth century palace. Almost facing it, just south of the Ben Youssef Mosque, the small **Almoravid Koubba** (daily 9am–1pm & 2.30–6pm; 10dh) is easy to pass by, but it is the only building in the whole of Morocco from the eleventh century Almoravid dynasty still intact, and at the root of all Moroccan architecture. The motifs you've just seen in the *medersa* – the pine cones, palms and acanthus leaves – were all carved here first.

If you're keen to buy the best in the *souks*, you should study the more-or-less fixed prices of the range of crafts in the excellent **Ensemble Artesenal** (Mon–Sat 9am–1pm & 2.30–7pm, Sun 9am–1pm), just inside the ramparts on Av Mohammed V.

The southern Medina

South of Djemaa el Fna there are two places not to be missed: the Saadian Tombs and El Badi Palace, the ruined palace of Ahmed el Mansour. For the tombs, the simplest route from the Djemaa is to follow Rue Bab Agnaou outside the ramparts, then aim for the conspicuous minaret of the **Kasbah Mosque** – the minaret looks gaudy and modern but is in fact contemporary with the Koutoubia, and was restored to its original state in the 1960s. The narrow passageway to the tombs is well signposted from the right-hand corner of the mosque.

Sealed up by Moulay Ismail after he had destroyed the adjoining El Badi Palace, the sixteenth-century **Saadian Tombs** (daily 8.30–11.45am & 2.30–5.45pm; 10dh) lay half-ruined and half-forgotten for centuries but are now restored to their full glory. There are two main mausoleums in the enclosure. The finer is on the left as you come in, a beautiful group of three rooms built to house El Mansour's own tomb and completed within his lifetime. The tombs of over a hundred more Saadian princes and royal household members are scattered around the garden and courtyard, their gravestones likewise brilliantly tiled and often elaborately inscribed.

Though substantially in ruins, enough remains of Ahmed el Mansour's **El Badi Palace** (daily 8.30–11.45am & 2.30–5.45pm; 10dh) to suggest that its name – "The Incomparable" – was not entirely immodest. It took a later ruler, Moulay Ismail, over ten years of systematic work to strip the palace of everything movable or of value, and, even so, there's a lingering sense of luxury. What you see today is essentially the ceremonial part of the palace complex, planned for the reception of ambassadors. To the rear extends the central court, over 130m long and nearly as wide, and built on a substructure of vaults in order to allow the circulation of water through the pools and gardens. In the southwest corner of the complex is an ancient *minbar* (pulpit) from the Dwiria, or Koutoubia mosque; both mosque and *minbar* have been lovingly restored (admission is an extra 10dh).

Heading north from El Badi Palace, **Rue Zitoun el Djedid** leads back to the Djemaa, flanked by various nineteenth-century mansions. Many of these have been converted into carpet shops or tourist restaurants, but one of them has been kept as a museum, the **Palais El Bahia** (daily 8.30–11.45am & 2.30/3–5.45pm; 10dh; guided tour compulsory, with a tip of at least 10dh expected), former residence of a grand vizier. The palace is still used by the royal family (usually over the Western New Year) and there is no public admission at these times. The name of the building means "The Brilliance", but after the guided tour around the rambling palace courts and apartments you might feel this a somewhat tall claim. Also on this route is the **Dar Si Said** palace, which houses the **Museum of Moroccan Arts** (Mon & Wed–Sun 9am–12.15pm & 3–6.15pm; 20dh). A further superb collection of Moroccan and Saharan artefacts is housed in the **Maison Tiskiwin** (daily 10am–12.30pm & 3–6pm; 15dh), which lies between the El Bahia and Dar Si Said palaces at 8 Rue de la Bahia.

Eating and drinking

The most atmospheric place to **eat** is the Djemaa el Fna, where foodstalls set up around sunset and serve up everything from *harira* soup and couscous or *tajine* to stewed snails and sheep's heads, all eaten at trestle tables. For tea with a view, the terrace cafés of the *Hôtel CTM* and neighbouring *Café le Grand Balcon* overlook the Djemaa el Fna, as do two relatively reasonable rooftop restaurants: *Argana* and *Hôtel Café de France*. As usual in Morocco, cheap restaurants tend to gather in the Medina, with posher places uptown in Gueliz, along with French-style cafés and virtually all the city's bars.

Hotel Ali Rue Moulay Ismail. The eat-all-you-like buffet here, served 7–11pm, is justifiably popular and great value at 60dh. There are also lunchtime menus.

Café Snack Le Sindibad 216 Av Mohammed V, near the post office, Gueliz. Couscous, *tajine* or brochettes at 25–35dh a plate. Open 24hr.

Chez Bahia Riad Zitoun Kadim, 50m from Djemaa el Fna. Café/diner offering *pastilla, tajine,* breakfast and snacks at low prices.

Chez Jack'line 63 Av Mohammed V, Gueliz. Italian, French and Moroccan dishes at moderate prices, with an 80dh set menu.

Hotel Farouk 66 Av Hassan II, Gueliz. The restaurant here offers an excellent-value set menu with soup, salad, couscous, *tajine* or brochettes, followed by fruit, ice-cream or home-made yoghurt, for 50dh.

Le Progrès 20 Rue Bani Marine. The best of several decent choices in a street of cheap eateries.

Listings

Doctor Dr Abdelmajid Ben Tbib, 171 Av Mohammed V ☎ 044 43 10 30.

Exchange BMCE has branches with adjoining *bureaux de change* and ATMs in the Medina (Rue Moulay Ismail, facing Place de Foucauld) and Gueliz (114 Av Mohammed V).

Internet Super Cyber de la Place in an arcade off Rue Bani Marine by the *Hôtel Ichbilia*.

Pharmacies Place Djemaa el Fna at the top of Rue Bab Agnaou; Pharmacie de la Liberté, just off Place de la Liberté (or Houria).

Post office Place du 16 Novembre, midway along Av Mohammed V, and on the Djemaa el Fna.

Essaouira

ESSAOUIRA, the nearest beach resort to Marrakesh, is a lovely eighteenth-century walled seaside town. A favourite with the likes of Frank Zappa and Jimi Hendrix back in the 1960s, its tradition of hippie tourism has created a much more laid-back relationship between local residents and foreign visitors than you'll find in the rest of Morocco, and made Essaouira a centre for arts and crafts in addition to being the country's top surfing and windsurfing spot. Still largely contained within its ramparts, Essaouira is a simple place to get to grips with. At the northeast end of town is the **Bab Doukkala**; at the southwest is the town's pedestrianized main square, **Place Prince Moulay el Hassan**, and the fishing **harbour**. Between them run two main parallel streets: Av de l'Istiqlal/Av Mohammed Zerktouni and Rue Sidi Mohammed Ben Abdallah.

Essaouira is a great place just to walk around and the **ramparts** are the obvious place to start. Heading north along the lane at the end of Place Prince Moulay el Hassan, you can access the **Skala de la Ville**, the great sea bastion topped by a row of cannons, which runs along the northern cliffs. At the end is the circular **North Bastion**, with panoramic views (closes at sunset). Along the Rue de Skala, built into the ramparts, are the **wood-carving workshops**, where artisans use thuja, a distinctive local hardwood. Marquetry and other woodwork, past and present, is displayed at the **Musée Sidi Mohammed Ben Abdallah** (closed at last check), on Rue Derb Laâlouj, the road running down from the ramparts to Av de l'Istiqlal (daily 8.30am–6pm; 10dh). The town's other **souks** spread around and to the south of two arcades, on either side of Rue Mohammed Zerktouni, and up towards the Mellah (former Jewish ghetto), in the northwest corner of the ramparts. Worth particular attention are the **Marché d'Épices** (spice market) and **Souk des Bijoutiers** (jewellers' market). Art studios and hippie-style clothing shops centre around Place Chefchaouni by the clocktower. By the harbour is another impressive sea bastion, the **Skala du Port** (daily 8.30am–6pm; 10dh). The southern **beach** (the northern one is less attractive) extends for miles, past the Oued Ksob riverbed and the ruins of an old fort known as the **Bordj el Berod** – the inspiration for Jimi Hendrix's *Castles Made of Sand*.

The helpful **tourist office** is on Av du Caire (Mon–Fri 9am–noon & 3–6.30pm, June to mid-Sept Mon–Sat 9am–1pm & 3–7pm; ☎044 78 35 32). **Buses** arrive at a new bus station, about 500m (ten minutes' walk) northeast of Bab Doukkala. Especially at night, it's worth taking a *petit taxi* (about 5dh) or horse-drawn calèche (about 10dh). **Grands taxis** also operate from the bus station, though they will drop arrivals at Bab Doukkala or Place Prince Moulay el Hassan. **Accommodation** can be tight over Easter and in summer, when advance booking is recommended. Local residents may approach you with offers of rooms, and Jack's Kiosk, a newspaper shop on Place Prince Moulay el Hassan, displays ads for apartments. Of **hotels**, *Majestic*, opposite the museum, 40 Rue Laâlouj (☎044 47 49 09; ❶), has good, clean rooms, though a little cheerless; *Souiri*, 37 Rue El Attarine (☎044 47 53 39; ❶), is a popular, colourful hotel in the Medina, and the *Tafraout*, 7 Rue Marrakech (☎044 47 62 76; ❶), is clean and friendly with some en-suite rooms. *Shahrazed*, 1 Rue Youssef el Fassi (☎044 47 29 77; ❷), is new, spacious and very comfortable; *Sahara*, Av Okba Ibn Nafia (☎044 47 52 92; ❶), has big rooms around a central well, with en-suite hot showers, and *Beau Rivage* (☎044 47 59 25; ❶), newly refurbished, has spotless en-suite rooms right on the main square. There's also a **campsite**, *Sidi Magdoul*, 1km south of town behind the lighthouse (☎044 47 21 96).

For an informal **meal**, you can do no better than eat at the line of grills down at the port, an Essaouira institution. A couple of snack bars on Av de l'Istiqlal offer the cheapest eats in town. Among the regular restaurants, try the budget *Essalam*, on Place Prince Moulay el Hassan, or the pricier *Petite Perle*, just off the clocktower square, with well-prepared dishes in a traditional setting. For a seafood splurge, you can't beat the two fish restaurants by the port, the long-established *Chez Sam's* and upmarket newcomer *Le Coquillage*, which is the first you come to.

Leaving for **Marrakesh**, there is a twice daily nonstop Supratours bus which leaves from Av Lalla Aicha, opposite Bab Marrakesh, at 6am and 4pm, arriving at Marrakesh train station; buy tickets from the kiosk here the day before. The best buses direct to **Casablanca** are the CTM Mumtaz Express (leaves Essaouira bus station daily at 1am, arrives 6am), or the cheaper 11.15am service; both are fast, comfortable and take you to the centre of Casa.

Travel details

Trains

Only direct trains are listed here; for connections, consult ⊛www.oncf.org.ma. Any station ticket office will issue a table of direct and connecting services to any other station.

Casablanca Port to: Rabat (half-hourly 6.30am–8.30pm; 1hr).

Casablanca Voyageurs to: Fes (8 daily; 4hr); Marrakesh (8 daily; 3hr 10min); Meknes (8 daily; 3hr 15min); Mohammed V airport (hourly 6am–10pm; 35min); Rabat (13 daily; 1hr); Tangier (3 daily; 5hr 40min).

Fes to: Casablanca Voyageurs (8 daily; 4hr); Marrakesh (5 daily; 7hr 30min); Meknes (9 daily; 50min); Rabat (8 daily; 3hr); Tangier (1 daily; 5hr 15min).

Marrakesh to: Casablanca Voyageurs (8 daily; 3hr 10min); Fes (5 daily; 7hr 30min); Meknes (5 daily; 6hr 45min); Rabat (8 daily; 4hr 20min); Tangier (1 daily; 9hr).

Meknes to: Casablanca Voyageurs (8 daily; 3hr 15min); Marrakesh (5 daily; 6hr 45min); Fes (9 daily; 50min); Rabat (8 daily; 2hr 20min); Tangier (1 daily; 4hr 15min).

Rabat to: Casablanca Voyageurs (13 daily; 1hr); Casablanca Port (half-hourly 6.30am–8.30pm; 1hr); Fes (8 daily; 3hr); Marrakesh (8 daily; 4hr 15min); Meknes (8 daily; 2hr 20min); Tangier (3 daily; 4hr 30min).

Tangier Moghogha to: Casablanca Voyageurs (3 daily; 5hr 10min–5hr 40min); Fes (1 daily; 5hr 10min); Meknes (1 daily; 4hr); Marrakesh (1 daily; 9hr); Rabat (3 daily; 4hr 15min).

Buses

Casablanca to: Essaouira (48 daily; 7hr); Fes (32 daily; 5hr 30min); Fnideq (for Ceuta) (15 daily; 7hr); Marrakesh (half-hourly; 4hr); Meknes (20 daily; 4hr 30min); Mohammed V airport (12 daily; 1hr); Rabat (frequent; 1hr 20min); Tetouan (26 daily; 6hr); Tangier (35 daily; 6hr 30min).

Chefchaouen to: Fes (8 daily; 5hr); Meknes (2 daily; 5hr 30min); Rabat (5 daily; 8hr 30min); Tangier (8 daily; 3hr 30min); Tetouan (26 daily; 2hr).

Essaouira to: Casablanca (48 daily; 7hr); Rabat (12 daily; 8hr 30min); Marrakesh (15 daily; 3hr 30min); Tangier (1 daily; 14hr).

Fes to: Casablanca (32 daily; 5hr 30min); Chefchaouen (8 daily; 5hr); Marrakesh (12 daily; 10hr); Meknes (frequent; 1hr); Rabat (21 daily; 4hr); Tangier (10 daily; 5hr 45min); Tetouan (7 daily; 5hr 20min).

Marrakesh to: Casablanca (half-hourly 4am–9pm; 4hr); Essaouira (15 daily; 3hr 30min); Fes (12 daily; 10hr); Meknes (6 daily; 9hr); Rabat (33 daily; 5hr 30min); Tangier (2 daily; 10hr).

Meknes to: Casablanca (20 daily; 4hr 30min); Chefchaouen (2 daily; 5hr 30min); Fes (frequent; 1hr); Marrakesh (6 daily; 9hr); Rabat (10 daily; 3hr); Tangier (9 daily; 8hr); Tetouan (7 daily; 6hr).

Rabat to: Casablanca (frequent; 1hr 20min); Essaouira (12 daily; 8hr 30min); Fes (21 daily; 4hr); Marrakesh (33 daily; 5hr 30min); Meknes (10 daily; 3hr); Salé (frequent; 15min); Tangier (35 daily; 5hr).

Tangier to: Casablanca (35 daily; 6hr 30min); Chefchaouen (8 daily; 3hr 30min); Essaouira (1 daily; 14hr); Fes (10 daily; 5hr 45min); Fnideq (for Ceuta) (12 daily; 1hr); Marrakesh (2 daily; 10hr); Meknes (9 daily; 8hr); Rabat (35 daily; 5hr); Tetouan (50 daily; 1hr 30min).

Tetouan to: Casablanca (26 daily; 6hr); Chefchaouen (22 daily; 2hr); Fnideq (for Ceuta) (12 daily; 1hr); Fes (7 daily; 5hr 20min); Marrakesh (8 daily; 10hr); Meknes (7 daily; 6hr); Rabat (21 daily; 5hr); Tangier (50 daily; 1hr 30min).

Ferries and hydrofoils

Ceuta to: Algeciras, Spain (20–36 daily; 35min–1hr 30min).

Tangier to: Algeciras, Spain (12–24 daily; 1hr 30min–2hr 30min); Tarifa, Spain (2 daily; 35min); Gibraltar (2 weekly; 1hr 15min).

The Netherlands

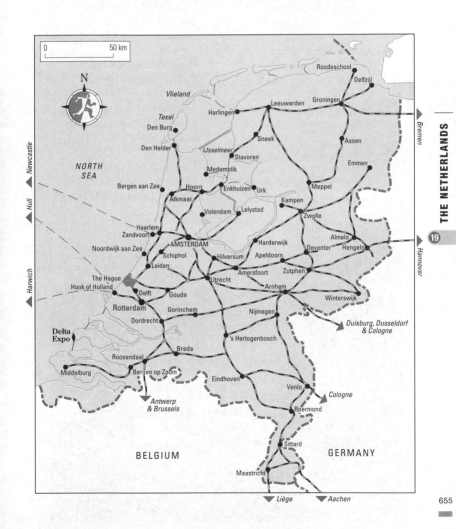

Netherlands highlights

* **Cannabis coffeeshops**
Every Dutch city has a
choice of "coffeeshops",
where you can buy mari-
juana and hash. See
p.659

* **Amsterdam's canals**
Cruise your way to
famous art venues such
as the Rijksmuseum and
Van Gogh Museum. See
p.665

* **Delft** Enjoy wonderful
applecake at the *Kobus
Koch Café*, beside the
old market square in this
picturesque town. See
p.674

* **Groningen**
Cosmopolitan northern
city that takes its bikes
seriously. See p.677

* **Hoge Veluwe National
Park** Spend the day on
a free bike, picnicking
and checking out a
world-class Van Gogh
museum. See p.678

* **Maastricht** Dynamic
border town with a lovely
old quarter. See p.678

Introduction and basics

The Netherlands is a country partly reclaimed from the waters of the North Sea, and around half of it lies at or below sea level. Land reclamation has been the dominant motif of its history, with the result a country of unique images – flat, fertile landscapes punctuated by windmills and church spires; ornately gabled terraces flanking peaceful canals; and mile upon mile of grassy dunes, backing onto stretches of pristine sandy beach.

Most people travel only to the uniquely atmospheric capital, **Amsterdam**. Nearby is a group of towns known collectively as the **Randstad** (literally "rim town"), including **Haarlem** and **Delft** with their old canal-girded centres, and **Den Haag** (The Hague), a stately city with fine museums and easy beach access. Outside the Randstad, life moves more slowly. In the north, **Groningen** is a busy cultural centre, lent verve by its large student population. To the south, the landscape undulates into heathy moorland, best experienced in the **Hoge Veluwe National Park**. Further south still lies the compelling city of **Maastricht**, squeezed between the German and Belgian borders.

Information & maps

"VVV" **tourist offices** are usually in town centres – often on the main square or **Grote Markt** – or by train stations, and have information in English, including maps and accommodation lists (a fee is payable); they will also book rooms, again for a small charge. The best general **map** is Kümmerley and Frey's. The Dutch motoring organization ANWB publishes an excellent series covering the whole country.

Money and banks

Dutch currency is the **euro** (€). **Banking hours** are Mon 1–4/5pm, Tues–Fri 9am–4/5pm; in larger cities some banks also open Thurs 7–9pm and occasionally on Sat mornings. GWK **exchange offices** at train stations open late daily; they change money and travellers' cheques, and give cash advances. You can also change money at most VVV tourist offices, post offices and *bureaux de change*, though rates are worse. **ATMs** are widespread. Smaller places (including B&Bs) may not accept cards.

Communications

Post offices open Mon–Fri 9am–5pm, Sat 9am–noon. Post international items in the "Overige" slot. Most public **phones** take phonecards (buyable from post offices and VVVs) or credit cards. The operator is on ☎0800/0410 (free). Many cafés and public libraries offer **Internet** access.

Getting around

Trains (✆www.ns.nl) are fast, fares relatively low, and the network comprehensive. Various passes cut costs – ask at a station (passport needed for ID). With any ticket, you're free to stop off en route and continue later that day. Stations usually have a reasonably priced restaurant, left-luggage lockers (around €2.70 for 24hr), and a GWK change office. The NS **treintaxi** scheme (not valid in Amsterdam, Rotterdam or The Hague) means you pay €3.80 for a taxi to

THE NETHERLANDS | Basics

19

The Netherlands on the net

- ✇ **www.holland.com** National tourist board.
- ✇ **www.ns.nl** Train information.
- ✇ **www.bookings.nl** Online hotel bookings.
- ✇ **www.museumjaarkaart.nl** Museum guide.

take you anywhere within the city limits, up to 15min away from your destination train station – very useful for smaller towns. Buy vouchers for *treintaxis* when you buy your train ticket.

Urban **buses** and **trams** are very efficient. You only need one kind of ticket: a **strippenkaart**. The whole country is divided up into zones; cancel one strip on your *strippenkaart* for yourself plus one for each of the zones you travel through. On trams you fold the *strippenkaart* over to the right place and insert it into the date-stamping machines; you only need to stamp the last of your strips. On buses, hand the *strippenkaart* to the driver. You can buy 2- and 3-strip *strippenkaarts* from bus drivers, or better-value 15-strip (€6.20) or 45-strip (€18.30) *strippenkaarts* in advance from train stations, tobacconists and public transport offices. One *strippenkaart* can be used by any number of people, cancelling the requisite number of strips each.

There's a nationwide system of **cycle** paths, which often divert away into the countryside; bookshops sell maps. You can rent bikes cheaply from main train stations and also from outlets in almost any town and village. Theft is rife: never leave your bike unlocked, and don't leave it on the street overnight – most stations have a storage area.

Accommodation

Accommodation can be a little pricey, especially in places like Amsterdam and Haarlem. Book ahead during the summer and over holiday periods, especially Easter. The cheapest one- or two-star **hotel** double room, not en suite, starts at around €50. Three-star hotel rooms average out at around €80. Prices usually include a reasonable breakfast. You can reserve for free through the Netherlands Reservation Centre (⊛www.hotelres.nl), or at VVV offices (for a small charge). There are 30 excellent HI **hostels** nationwide (⊛www.stayokay.com), charging €20–25 per person including breakfast (HI members pay €2.50 less), more for singles and doubles. Hostels often serve meals; some have kitchens where you

can self-cater. Larger cities often have independent hostels with similar prices, though standards are sometimes not as reliable. There are plenty of well-equipped **campsites**. Generally expect to pay around €3 per person, plus €2–4 for a tent. Some sites also have cabins for up to four people, for around €35 a night; book in advance.

Food, drink and drugs

Dutch **food** tends to be plain, mainly steak, chicken or fish, along with soups and stews, but thanks to colonial history, the Netherlands boasts the best **Indonesian** food outside Indonesia. *Nasi goreng* and *bami goreng* (rice or noodles with meat) are good basic dishes; chicken or beef in peanut sauce (*sateh*) is always available. A *rijsttafel* is rice or noodles served with a huge range of tasty side-dishes.

Breakfast (*ontbijt*) is filling, made up of rolls, cheese, ham, eggs, jam and honey, chocolate spread or peanut butter. **Fast food** includes chips – *frites* or *patat* – smothered with mayonnaise, curry, satay or tomato sauce, *kroketten* (bite-size chunks of meat goulash coated in breadcrumbs and deep fried) and *fricandel* (a frankfurter-like sausage). **Fish** specialities sold from street kiosks include salted raw herrings, smoked eel (*gerookte paling*), mackerel in a roll (*broodje makreel*) and mussels. The nationwide chain *Noordzee* serves good-value fish-based sandwiches and light fish lunches. Other common snacks are **shoarma** (kebab) and **falafel**. Most bars serve sandwiches and rolls (*boterham* and *broodjes* – *stokbrood* if made with baguette) and, in winter, *erwtensoep*, a thick pea soup with smoked sausage, and *uitsmijters*, fried eggs on buttered bread, topped with ham or roast beef. In **restaurants**, stick to the dish of the day (*dagschotel*). Train station restaurants serve good meals for €7, student places for under €9. Many places have at least one meat-free item, and you'll find veggie restaurants in most towns. At the many **Surinamese** places try *roti*, flat bread with spicy curry.

Sampling the Dutch and Belgian **beers** in every region is a real pleasure, often done in a cosy brown café (*bruine kroeg*, named because of the colour of the tobacco-stained walls); the big brands Heineken, Amstel, Oranjeboom and Grolsch are the tip of the iceberg. A standard, small glass (*een pils*) costs about €1.50; a bigger glass is *een vaasje*. You may also come across *proeflokalen* or tasting houses, small, old-fashioned bars that close around 8pm, and specialize in **jenever**, Dutch gin, drunk straight; *oud* (old) is smooth, *jong* (young) packs more of a punch. **Coffee** is normally good and strong, while **tea** generally comes with lemon. **Chocolate** is also popular, served hot or cold.

Drugs

Purchases of up to 5g of **cannabis**, and possession of up to 30g (the legal limit) are tolerated; in practice, many "**coffeeshops**" offer discounted bulk purchases of 50g with impunity. No one will ever call the police on you in the big cities for discreet, personal dope-smoking, but if in doubt ask somebody. Coffeeshops in city centres – plasticky, neon-lit dives, pumping out mainstream rock, reggae or techno – are worth avoiding: the dope is limited and low-grade, and quite often the deals are rigged. Less touristy districts house more congenial, high-quality outlets. When you walk in, ask to see the **menu**. This will list all the different hashes and grasses on offer, along with exactly how many grammes you get for your money. The in-house dealer can answer queries. Take care with spacecakes (cakes or biscuits baked with hash), mainly because you can never be sure what's in them, and don't ever buy from street dealers. All other narcotics are illegal.

Opening hours and holidays

Many **shops** stay closed on Mon morning, although markets open early. Otherwise, opening hours tend to be 9am–5.30/6pm, though certain shops open late on Thurs or Fri. Night shops (*avondwinkels*) in major cities open 4pm–1/2am. **Museum** times are generally Tues–Sat 10am–5pm, Sun 1–5pm. Shops and banks are closed, and museums adopt Sunday hours, on **public holidays**: Jan 1; Good Fri; Easter Sun & Mon; April 30; May 5; May 13; Whitsun & Mon; Dec 25 & Dec 26.

Emergencies

Be wary of pickpockets and badly lit streets at night. You're unlikely to come into contact with the police. **Pharmacies** (*apotheek*) open Mon–Fri 8.30am–5.30pm; there'll be a note of the nearest open pharmacy on the door. Duty doctors at the Centrale Doktorsdienst (☎0900/503 2042) offer advice; otherwise head for any hospital (*ziekenhuis*).

Emergency numbers

Police, fire and ambulance ☎112.

THE NETHERLANDS | Basics

19

Amsterdam

AMSTERDAM is a beguiling capital, a compact mix of the provincial and the cosmopolitan. It has a welcoming attitude towards visitors and a uniquely youthful orientation. For many, its world-class museums and galleries – notably the **Rijksmuseum**, with its collection of seventeenth-century Dutch paintings, and the

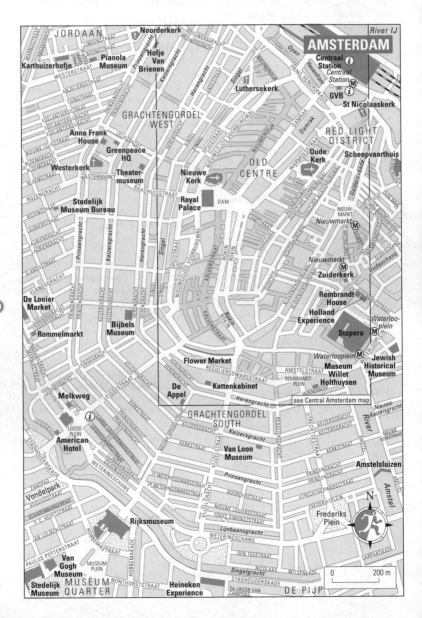

Van Gogh Museum – are reason enough to visit. Amsterdam was founded on a dam on the river Amstel in the thirteenth century. During the Reformation it rose in stature, taking trade away from Antwerp and becoming a haven for its religious refugees. The city went from strength to strength in the seventeenth century, becoming the centre of a vast trading empire with colonies in Southeast Asia. Amsterdam accommodated its expansion with the cobweb of **canals** that gives the city its distinctive and elegant shape today. By the eighteenth century, Amsterdam was in gentle decline, re-emerging as a fashionable focus for the alternative movements of the 1960s. Despite a backlash in the 1980s, the city still takes a progressive approach to social issues and culture, with a buzz of open-air summer events, intimate clubs and bars, and relaxed attitude to soft drugs.

Arrival, information and accommodation

Schiphol **airport** is connected by train with the main **Centraal Station** (every 15min; hourly at night), which is at the hub of all **bus** and **tram** routes and just five minutes' walk from central Dam Square. International buses arrive at Amstel Station, ten minutes south of Centraal Station by metro. For **information**, the main VVV is outside Centraal Station, Stationsplein 10 (daily 9am–5pm; ☏0900/400 4040, ⊛www.visitamsterdam.nl); there's another inside the station (Mon–Sat 8am–8pm, Sun 9am–5pm), a smaller kiosk on the Leidseplein corner of Leidsestraat (daily 9am–5pm), and an office in the airport (daily 7am–10pm). Any of these can sell you an **Amsterdam Pass** (€26/36/46 for one/two/three days), which gives free or reduced entry to major attractions as well as free public transport and restaurant discounts. The VVV has a monthly **listings** guide, *Day by Day – What's On in Amsterdam* (€1.50).

The excellent network of **trams**, **buses** and the **metro** (all daily 6/7am–midnight) isn't expensive. The GVB public transport office in front of Centraal Station (Mon–Fri 7am–9pm, Sat & Sun 8am–9pm; winter closes 7pm; ☏0900/9292) has free route maps and an English guide to the *strippenkaart* ticketing system (see "Getting around"). After midnight, **night buses** take over, running roughly hourly from Centraal Station to most parts of the city. **Bikes** can be rented from Centraal Station or from a number of firms around town (see "Listings").

Hostels

Bob's Youth Hostel Nieuwezijds Voorburgwal 92 ☏020/623 0063. An old favourite of backpackers; lively and smoky, with small dorms, cheap meals and Internet access. Ten minutes from Centraal Station. €17.

Bulldog Low-Budget Hotel Oudezijds Voorburgwal 220 ☏020/620 3822, ⊛www.bulldog.nl. Part of the Bulldog coffeeshop chain with bar and DVD lounge, dorms with TV and showers, doubles and apartments. Tram #4, #9, #16 or #24 to Dam, then a 3min walk. €26.

Durty Nelly's Warmoesstraat 115–117 ☏020/638 0125, ✉nellys@xs4all.nl. Good-quality dorms above packed Irish pub. 5min from Centraal Station. €22–25.

Flying Pig Downtown Nieuwendijk 100 ☏020/420 6822, ⊛www.flyingpig.nl. Clean, large and well run by ex-backpackers. Free kitchen facilities and Internet access, no curfew, all-night bar. Not for faint-hearted anti-smokers. Five-minute walk from Centraal Station. €19.

Flying Pig Palace Vondelpark Vossiusstraat 46 ☏020/400 4187, ⊛www.flyingpig.nl. Tram #1/#2/#5 to Leidseplein, then walk. On the edge of the city's big park; clean and well maintained. Free kitchen facilities and Internet access, no curfew, good tourist information. €18.

Hans Brinker Kerkstraat 136 ☏020/622 0687, ⊛www.brinker.nl. Well-established and raucously popular cheapie, though a little more upmarket than some. Café with cheap dishes available. Tram #1/#2/#5 to Prinsengracht. €21.

International Budget Hostel Leidsegracht 76 ☏020/624 2784. Excellent budget option on a peaceful little canal in the heart of the city. Tram #1/#2/#5 to Prinsengracht. €30.

The Shelter City Barndesteeg 21 ☏020/625 3230, ⊛www.shelter.nl. Non-evangelical Christian hostel smack in the middle of the red-light district: single-sex dorms, lockers, midnight curfew (1am weekends). Sizeable breakfast included. Metro Nieuwmarkt. €15.50.

The Shelter Jordaan Bloemstraat 179 ☏020/624 4717, ⊛www.shelter.nl. Another easy-going Christian hostel in the Jordaan district, with very cheap beds. No smoking. Tram #13/#17 to Marnixstraat. €15.50.

Stadsdoelen Kloveniersburgwal 97 ☎020/624 6832, ⓦwww.stayokay.com. The more accessible of the two HI hostels, with clean semi-private dorm rooms. HI members have priority in high season. Tram #4/#9/#16/#24/#25 to Muntplein. €20.65.

Vondelpark Zandpad 5 ☎020/589 8993, ⓦwww.stayokay.com. For facilities, the better of the two HI hostels, with bar, restaurant, TV lounge and kitchen; also well located on the edge of the park. Secure lockers and a lift. Tram #1/#2/#5 to Leidseplein, then walk. €21.

Hotels

Abba Overtoom 120 ☎020/618 3058. Conveniently located for the big art museums, Concertgebouw and Leidesplein. Rooms have showers and are quiet at the back of the hotel. Breakfast included in the price. Tram #1. ⑤

Arena 's-Gravesandestraat 51 ☎020/850 2410, ⓦwww.hotelarena.nl. East of the centre, this hip and minimalist 3 star hotel has a lively bar, intimate restaurant and late-night club. All rooms are en suite. Metro Weesperplein then walk or tram #9. ⑨

Asterisk Den Texstraat 16 ☎020/626 2396, ⓦwww.asteriskhotel.nl. Good-value budget hotel, just across the canal from the Heineken Brewery. Tram #16/#24/#25 to Weteringcircuit. ⑤

Bema Concertgebouwplein 19b ☎020/679 1396, ⓦwww.hotel-bema.demon.nl. Small place, kept very clean by the English-speaking manager. The rooms are not modern, but are full of character. Handier for concerts and museums than nightlife. Tram /#5/#16 to Museumplein. ⑤

Clemens Raadhuisstraat 39 ☎020/624 6089, ⓦwww.clemenshotel.nl. One of many options on this hotel strip. Clean, neat and value for money.

Ask for a room at the back. Tram #13/#17 to Westermarkt. ⑤

Euphemia Fokke Simonszstraat 1 ☎020/622 9045, ⓦwww.euphemiahotel.com. A likeable, laid-back atmosphere: rooms are big and basic, with free showers and TVs. Very reasonable prices, which means it's usually full. Tram #16/#24/#25 to Weteringcircuit. ⑥

King Leidsekade 85–86 ☎020/624 9603. Clean but very small rooms in a small hotel. Breakfast included. Minimum three nights during summer. Tram #1/#2/#5 to Leidseplein. ⑤

Quentin Leidsekade 89 ☎020/626 2187. Friendly small hotel, often a stopover for bands performing at the Melkweg. Well regarded among gay and lesbian visitors. Tram #1/#2/#5 to Leidseplein. ⑦

Rokin Rokin 73 ☎020/626 7456, ⓦwww.bookings.nl/hotels/rokin. Something of a bargain considering the location. 5min walk from Centraal Station, or tram #4/#9/#16/#24/#25 to Dam or Spui. ⑥

St Nicolaas Spuistraat 1a ☎020/626 1384. Very pleasant, well-run little hotel housed in a former mattress factory (with a king-size lift to prove it). ⑧

Van Onna Bloemgracht 104 ☎020/626 5801. A quiet, comfortable, family-run place on a tranquil canal in the Jordaan. Tram #13/#17 to Westermarkt. ⑥

Campsites

Vliegenbos Meeuwenlaan 138 ☎020/636 8855, ⓦwww.vliegenbos.com. In Amsterdam North, a ten-minute ride on bus #32 or #36 from Centraal Station. Closed Oct–March.

Zeeburg Zuiderzeeweg 20 ☎020/694 4430, ⓦwww.campingzeeburg.nl. Bus #22 to Kramatweg or tram #14 from Dam Square.

The City

Amsterdam's compact centre contains most of the city's leading attractions but it takes only about forty minutes to stroll from one end to the other. **Centraal Station**, where you're most likely to arrive, lies on the centre's northern edge, its back to the River IJ, and from here the city fans south in a web of concentric canals, surrounded by expanding suburbs. Just wandering around to get the flavour of the place is often the most enjoyable way to proceed.

At the heart of the city is the vivacious **Old Centre**, an oval-shaped area featuring a jumble of antique streets and beautiful, narrow little canals. This is the unlikely setting for the sleazy, infamous **Red-Light District**. Forming a ring around it is the first of the major canals, the Singel, followed closely by the Herengracht, Keizersgracht and Prinsengracht. This is the Amsterdam you see in the brochures: still, dreamy canals, crisp reflections of seventeenth-century town houses, cobbled streets, railings with chained bicycles. To the south is the city's main square, **Leidseplein**, with the world-class trio of the **Rijksmuseum**, the **Van Gogh Museum** and the **Stedelijk Museum** just beyond, forming a prelude to the lovely

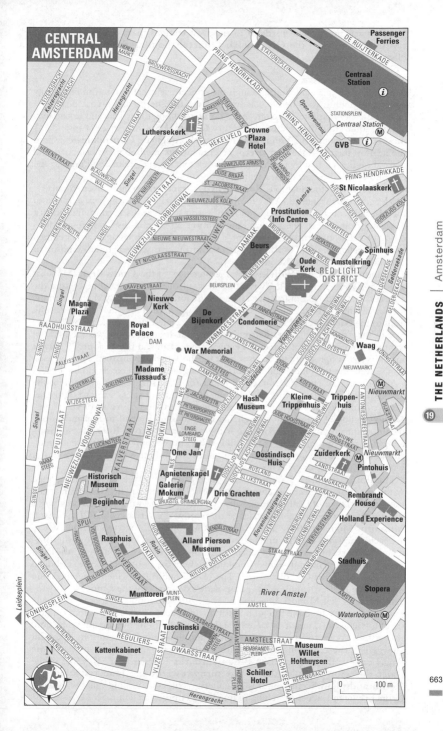

CENTRAL AMSTERDAM

Passenger Ferries

DE RUIJTERKADE

Centraal Station ⓘ

STATIONSPLEIN

HERENMARKT

BROUWERSGRACHT

PRINS HENDRIKKADE

STATIONSPLEIN

STATIONSPLEIN

Centraal Station Ⓜ

GVB ⓘ

KEIZERSGRACHT

HERENGRACHT

LANGESTRAAT

SINGEL

SMAKSTEEG

NIEUWENDIJK

KATTENGAT

HEKELVELD

PRINS HENDRIKKADE

Lutherseker

TEERKETELSTEEG

Crowne Plaza Hotel

PRINS HENDRIKKADE

HERENSTRAAT

BLAUWBURG. WAL

Singel

OUDE NIEUWESTR.

SPUISTRAAT

NIEUWEZIJDS ARMSTG.

OUDE BRAAK

ST. JACOBSSTRAAT

NIEUWEZIJDS KOLK

HASSELSTEEG

HARING PAKKERSTEEG

Open Havenfront

Damrak

NIEUWE BRUGSTG

St Nicolaaskerk ✝

HERENGRACHT

HERENGRACHT

HERENSTR.

SINGEL

SINGEL

NIEUWEZIJDS VOORBURGWAL

O. VAN HASSELTSSTEEG

NIEUWE NIEUWESTRAAT

NIEUWENDIJK

Prostitution Info Centre

OUDE ARMSTEEG

OUDEZIJDS KOLK

ST. NICOLAASSTRAAT

BRUGSTEEG

Beurs

H. HOEKSTEEG

LANGE NIEZEL

Spinhuis

GELDERSEKADE

GELDERSEKADE

Magna Plaza

GRAVENSTRAAT

Nieuwe Kerk

DAMRAK

BEURSSTRAAT

BEURSPLEIN

Oude Kerk

RED LIGHT DISTRICT

Amstelkring

ZEEDIJK

RAADHUISSTRAAT

SINGEL

SINGEL

SINGEL

PALEISSTRAAT

De Bijenkorf

ST ANNENSTRAAT

Condomerie

VOORBURGWAL

OUDEZIJDS ACHTERBURGWAL

MONNIKENSTR.

Waag

KONINGSSTRAAT

Royal Palace

DAM

WARMOESSTRAAT

ST. JANSSTRAAT

OUDEZIJDS

OUDEZIJDS VOORBURGWAL

OUDEZIJDS BLOEDSTR.

BARNDESTEEG

NIEUWMARKT

KEIZERRIJK

J. ROELENSTEEG

War Memorial

SERVETSTEEG

STOOFSTEEG

KOESTRAAT

NIEUWMARKT Ⓜ

WIJDESTEEG

Madame Tussaud's

PIJLSTEEG

DAMSTRAAT

PIETERSPOORTSTG

Hash Museum

Kleine Trippenhuis

Trippenhuis

ST ANTONIESBREESTRAAT

Nieuwmarkt

SPUISTRAAT

SINGEL

NES

N.P. JACOBSZSTR.

ST. PIETERSHALSTG

NIEUWE HOOGSTRAAT

DIJKSTRAAT

NIEUWEZIJDS VOORBURGWAL

ROKIN

ROKIN

ENGE LOMBARD STEEG

'Ome Jan'

OUDEZIJDS ACHTERBURGWAL

OUDE HOOGSTRAAT

Oostindisch Huis

Zuiderkerk Ⓜ

ZANDSTRAAT

Nieuwmarkt

Pintohuis

Historisch Museum

KALVERSTRAAT

ST. LUCIENSTEEG

Agnietenkapel ✝

Galerie Mokum

BRUGSTG. GRIMBURGWAL

Drie Grachten

RUSLAND

SLIJKSTRAAT

RAAMGRACHT

RAAMGRACHT

Rembrandt House

Begijnhof

SPUI

VOETBOOGSTRAAT

HANDBOOGSTRAAT

OUDEZIJDS VOORBURGWAL

KLOVENIERSBURGWAL

GROENBURGWAL

Holland Experience

Rasphuis

HEILIGEWEG

KALVERSTRAAT

ROKIN

Allard Pierson Museum

NIEUWE DOELENSTRAAT

KLOVENIERSBURGWAL

VERVERSTRAAT

Stadhuis

Stopera

SINGEL

SINGEL

OUDE TURFMARKT

Munttoren

MUNT-PLEIN

River Amstel

AMSTEL

STAALSTRAAT

ZWANENBURGWAL

AMSTEL

Waterlooplein Ⓜ

KONINGSPLEIN

SINGEL

SINGEL

Flower Market

REGULIERSBREESTRAAT

HALVEMAANSTEEG

AMSTEL

AMSTELSTRAAT

UTRECHTSESTRAAT

AMSTEL

HERENGRACHT

REGULIERS-

Tuschinski

REMBRANDT-PLEIN

Kattenkabinet

VIJZELSTRAAT

DWARSSTRAAT

Museum Willet Holthuysen

N

Schiller Hotel

THORBECKE PLEIN

Herengracht

0   100 m

▲ Leidseplein

THE NETHERLANDS | Amsterdam

19

Vondelpark nearby. The **Jordaan** to the west features mazy streets and narrow canals. To the east is the **Old Jewish Quarter**, housing the first-rate Jewish Historical Museum.

The Old Centre

Amsterdam is a small city, and, although the concentric canal system can be initially confusing, finding your bearings is straightforward. The medieval core boasts the best of the city's bustling streetlife and is home to shops, many bars and restaurants, fanning south from the nineteenth-century **Centraal Station**, one of Amsterdam's most resonant landmarks. From here, the busy thoroughfare **Damrak** marches into the heart of the city, lined with overpriced restaurants and bobbing canal boats, and flanked on the left first by the Modernist stock exchange or Beurs, and then by the enormous De Bijenkorf department store.

East of Damrak, the infamous **Red-Light District**, stretching across two canals – Oudezijds (abbreviated to O.Z.) Voorburgwal and O.Z. Achterburgwal – is one of the real sights of the city, thronged in high season with visitors keen to discover just how shocking it all is. The legalized prostitution on flagrant display here is world-renowned. The two canals, with their narrow connecting passages, are crammed with neon-lit "window brothels", where scantily clad women often stand or sit behind glass for up to twelve hours a day.

Behind the Beurs, off Warmoesstraat, the precincts of the **Oude Kerk** (Mon–Sat 11am–5pm, Sun 1–5pm; €4; ⓦ www.oudekerk.nl) offer a reverential peace after the excesses of the red-light district; it's a bare, mostly fourteenth-century church with the memorial tablet of Rembrandt's first wife, Saskia van Uylenburg. Just beyond, Zeedijk leads to the **Nieuwmarkt** square, centred on the turreted **Waag** building, an original part of the city's fortifications. **Kloveniersburgwal**, heading south, was the outer of the three eastern canals of sixteenth-century Amsterdam and boasts, at no. 29, one of the city's most impressive canal houses, built for the Trip family in 1662. Further along on the west side, the Oudemanhuispoort passage is filled with secondhand bookstalls.

At the southern end of Damrak, the **Dam** (or Dam square), is the centre of the city, its War Memorial serving as a meeting place for tourists. On the western side, the **Koninklijk Paleis** (Royal Palace; open for guided tours and exhibitions; ⓦ www.koninklijkhuis.nl) was originally built as the city hall in the mid-seventeenth century. Vying for importance is the adjacent **Nieuwe Kerk** (open during exhibitions; ⓦ www.nieuwekerk.nl), a fifteenth-century church rebuilt several times, and now exhibiting works from the Rijksmuseum and Stedelijk Museum, both of which are currently under renovation.

South of Dam square, **Rokin** follows the old course of the Amstel River, lined with grandiose nineteenth-century mansions. Running parallel, Kalverstraat is a monotonous strip of clothes shops, halfway down which, at no. 92, a gateway forms the entrance to the former orphanage that's now the **Amsterdams Historisch Museum** (Mon–Fri 10am–5pm, Sat & Sun 11–5pm; €6; ⓦ www.ahm.nl), where artefacts, paintings and documents survey the city's development from the thirteenth century. Just around the corner, off Sint Luciensteeg, the **Begijnhof** is a small court of seventeenth-century buildings where the poor and elderly celebrated Mass in a concealed Catholic church. The plain English Reformed Church, taking up one side of the Begijnhof, has pulpit panels designed by the famous twentieth-century artist Piet Mondriaan. Close by, the **Spui** (pronounced "spow") is a lively corner of town whose mixture of bookshops and packed bars centres around a statue of a young boy known as *'t Lieverdje* (Little Darling). In the opposite direction, Kalverstraat comes to an end at **Muntplein** and the Munttoren – originally a mint and part of the city walls, topped with a seventeenth-century spire. Across the Singel canal is the fragrant daily **Bloemenmarkt** (Flower Market), while in the other direction Reguliersbreestraat turns towards the loud restaurants of **Rembrandtplein**. To the south is Reguliersgracht, an appealing canal with seven distinctive steep bridges stretching in line from Thorbeckeplein.

The main canals around Leidseplein

Amsterdam's expansion in the seventeenth century was designed around three new canals, **Herengracht**, **Keizersgracht** and **Prinsengracht**, which formed a distinctive cobweb shape around the centre. Development was strictly controlled, resulting in the tall, very narrow residences with decorative gables you see today. The appeal lies in wandering along, taking in the calm of the tree-lined waterways, while looking into people's windows (Amsterdammers tend not to bother with curtains, a habit which lends the city an open and cosy atmosphere). For shops, bars and restaurants, you're better off exploring the crossing-streets which connect the canals.

From the Spui, trams and pedestrians cross Koningsplein onto Amsterdam's main drag, **Leidsestraat** – a long, slender shopping street that cuts across the main canals. On the corner with Keizersgracht, the designer department store Metz & Co has a top-floor café with one of the best views of the city. Leidsestraat broadens at its southern end into **Leidseplein**, the bustling hub of Amsterdam's nightlife, a cluttered and disorderly open space criss-crossed by tram lines. The square has a frenetic feel, and is flanked by dozens of bars, restaurants and clubs, a bright jumble of jutting signs and neon lights. On the far corner, the **Stadsschouwburg** is the city's prime performance space after the Muziektheater, while behind, the fairy-castle *American Hotel* has a bar whose carefully co-ordinated furnishings are a fine example of Art Nouveau.

However if you head straight here, you'll miss out on the grand canal frontages of Herengracht, especially between Leidsestraat and Vijzelstraat, a stretch known as the "Golden Curve". To see the interior of one of the canal houses, head for the **Museum Willet-Holthuysen**, Herengracht 605 (Mon–Fri 10am–5pm, Sat & Sun 11am–5pm; €4; ⊛www.willetholthuysen.nl), splendidly decorated in Rococo style and containing a collection of glass and ceramics and a seventeenth-century kitchen.

One of the city's loveliest neighbourhoods lies on and around Prinsengracht, focused on the gracious 1631 tower of the **Westerkerk** – north of Leidseplein, and a short stroll west of Dam square. Directly outside, a statue of Anne Frank by the sculptor Marie Andriessen signals the fact that the **Anne Frank House** (daily: April–Aug 9am–9pm; Sept–March 9am–7pm; closed Yom Kippur; €6.50; ⊛www.annefrank.nl), where the young diarist lived, is just a few steps away at Prinsengracht 263. It's deservedly one of the most popular tourist attractions in town, so arrive before 9am (or at the end of the day) and be prepared to queue. Anne, her family and friends went into hiding from the Nazis in 1942, staying in the house for two years until they were betrayed and taken away to labour camps, an experience which only Anne's father survived. Anne Frank's diary was among the few things left behind, and was published in 1947, since when it has sold over thirteen million copies worldwide. The rooms the Franks lived in are left much as they were, even down to the movie-star pin-ups in Anne's bedroom and the marks on the wall recording the children's heights.

Across Prinsengracht to the west, the **Jordaan** is a beguiling area of narrow canals, narrower streets and architecturally varied houses. With some of the city's best bars and restaurants, alternative clothes shops and good outdoor markets, especially those on the square outside the Noorderkerk (which hosts an antique and household goods market on Mondays and a popular farmers' market on Saturdays), it's a wonderful area to wander through. The hottest contemporary artists show work at the **Stedelijk Museum Bureau Amsterdam** gallery, Rozenstraat 59 (Tues–Sun 11am–5pm; ⊛www.smba.nl).

The Museum Quarter and south

Immediately south of Leidseplein begins the **Vondelpark**, the city's most enticing park, a regular forum for drama and other performance arts on summer weekends, when young Amsterdam flocks here to meet friends, laze by the lake and listen to music; in June, July and August there are free concerts every Sunday at 2pm. Southeast of the park is a residential district, with designer shops and delis along chic **P.C. Hooftstraat** and **Van Baerlestraat** and some of the city's major museums grouped around the grassy wedge of **Museumplein**.

The **Rijksmuseum**, Stadhouderskade 42 (currently daily 10am–5pm but undergoing major renovation; €9; ⓦwww.rijksmuseum.nl), has fine collections of medieval and Renaissance applied art, displays on Dutch history, a fine Asian collection and, most importantly, an array of seventeenth-century Dutch paintings that is among the best in the world. Most people head straight for one of the museum's great treasures, Rembrandt's *The Night Watch*, but there are many other examples of his work, along with portraits by Frans Hals, landscapes by Jan van Goyen and Jacob van Ruisdael, the riotous scenes of Jan Steen and the peaceful interiors of Vermeer and Pieter de Hooch. Just south is the **Vincent Van Gogh Museum**, Paulus Potterstraat 7 (daily 10am–6pm; €7; ⓦwww.vangoghmuseum.nl). Long queues can be a feature in high season so arrive early. The collection includes the early years in Holland, to the brighter works he painted after moving to Paris and then Arles, where he produced vivid canvases like *The Yellow House* and the *Sunflowers* series. Along the street at Paulus Potterstraat 13 is the modern-art **Stedelijk Museum** (daily 11am–5pm; €5; ⓦwww.stedelijk.nl), which will be undergoing refurbishment until late 2005. Its permanent collection, including works by Picasso, Matisse, Van Gogh, Chagall, Kandinsky and Braque, has been dispersed to other museums in the city and the Nieuwe Kerk.

Further along Stadhouderskade from the Rijksmuseum, the **Heineken Experience** at no. 78 (Tues–Sun 10am–6pm; €7.50; ⓦwww.heinekenexperience.nl) provides an overview of Heineken's history and the brewing process; afterwards you're given snacks and **free beer**. South of here is the neighbourhood known as **De Pijp** ("The Pipe") after its long, sombre canyons of brick tenements. This has always been one of the city's closest-knit communities, and one of its liveliest, with numerous inexpensive Surinamese and Turkish restaurants and a cheerful hub in the long slim thoroughfare of **Albert Cuypstraat**, whose food and clothes **market** is the largest in the city.

East of the centre

East of Rembrandtplein across the Amstel, the large, squat **Muziektheater** and **Stadhuis** flank **Waterlooplein**, home to the city's excellent flea market (Mon–Sat). Behind, Jodenbreestraat was once the main street of the Jewish quarter (emptied by the Nazis in the 1940s); no. 6 is **Het Rembrandthuis** (Rembrandt House; Mon-Sat 10am–5pm, Sun 1–5pm; €7; ⓦwww.rembrandthuis.nl), which the painter bought at the height of his fame, living here for over twenty years. The interior displays a large number of the artist's engravings. Across the way, the excellent, award-winning **Joods Historisch Museum** (Jewish Historical Museum; daily 11am–5pm; closed Yom Kippur; €5; ⓦwww.jhm.nl) is cleverly housed in a complex of Ashkenazi synagogues dating from the late seventeenth century and gives an imaginative introduction to Jewish life and beliefs.

Down Muiderstraat from here, the prim **Hortus Botanicus**, Plantage Middenlaan 2 (Mon–Fri 9am–4/5pm, Sat & Sun 11am–4/5pm; €3.40), is a pocket-sized botanical garden whose 8000 plant species make for a wonderfully relaxed break; stop off for coffee and cakes in the orangery. The eye-catching Plancius Building at Plantage Kerklaan 61 houses the excellent **Verzetsmuseum** (Dutch Resistance Museum; Tues–Fri 10am–5pm, Sat–Mon noon–5pm; €4.50), where a variety of exhibits depict the ways in which the Dutch people opposed Nazi oppression. A short walk north brings you to Kattenburgerplein and the **Nederlands Scheepvaartmuseum** (Maritime Museum; Tues–Sun 10am–5pm; mid-June to mid-Sept also Mon 10am–5pm; €7; ⓦwww.generali.nl /scheepvaartmuseum), which is housed in a seventeenth-century arsenal, crammed with maps, weapons and large models of sailing ships.

Eating and drinking

Amsterdam has an extensive supply of ethnic **restaurants**, especially Indonesian and Chinese, as well as *eetcafés* and bars which serve decent, well-priced food in an unpretentious setting. We've also listed a handful of places to get a snack, as well as the best of the city's so-called **coffeeshops**, where smoking dope is the primary pastime (ask to see "the menu"). You must be 18 or over to enter these, and don't expect alcohol to be served. Most open at 9am and close at 1am (2/3am at weekends). Check out the widely available *Smokers Guide* (€4.50; ⓦwww.smokersguide.com).

Cafés and snacks

Café Esprit Spui 10a. Swish modern café, with wonderful sandwiches and superb salads.

Gary's Muffins Prinsengracht 454, near Leidseplein; also Reguliersdwarsstraat 53. The best muffins and bagels in town, with big cups of coffee (and half-price refills).

Lunchcafé Winkel Noordermarkt 43, opposite the Noorderkerk. Popular local hangout on Saturday mornings during the farmers' market. Excellent apple pie.

Maoz Falafel Leidsestraat 85, near Leidsesplein; also Regulierbreestraat 45 and Muntplein 1. The best street-food in the city – falafel and as much salad as you can eat for €4.

Mr Hot Potato Leidsestraat 44. Baked potatoes for €2.50 enlivened by Marilyn Monroe decor. Daily 10am–8pm.

The Pancake Bakery Prinsengracht 191. A large selection of pancakes from €5. Quite touristy.

Puccini Staalstraat 17–21, near Waterlooplein. Dreamy cakes, pastries and chocolates, all handmade.

Restaurants

Asmara Jonas Daniel Meijerplein 8. Small and very popular Ethiopian restaurant next to the Jewish Historical Museum. Look for the Coca-Cola sign.

Centra Lange Niezel 29. Wonderful Spanish food and genial atmosphere in this cantina near the Oude Kerk. One of Amsterdam's best.

De Eettuin 2e Tuindwarsstraat 10, Jordaan. Hefty portions of Dutch food with DIY salad.

Golden Temple Utrechtsstraat 126 ☏020/626 8560. Laid-back lacto-vegetarian joint south of Remdbrandtplein. No smoking and no alcohol.

Japan-Inn Leidsekruisstraat 4. Cheap and cheerful Japanese restaurant near the busy Leidseplein. Open until midnight.

Mensa Atrium Oudezijds Achterburgwal 237. Amsterdam University's self-service cafeteria with meals under €5. Open to all; extra discounts for students.

Piet de Leeuw Noorderstraat 11. Superb steakhouse off Vijzelgracht, dating from the 1940s. Good desserts too.

Shiva Reguliersdwarsstraat 72. Outstanding Indian restaurant, with well-priced, expertly prepared food, including veggie.

Sie Joe Gravenstraat 24. Small Indonesian café-restaurant with a limited menu but well-made *gado gado*, *sateh* and *rending*. Great value for money.

Top Thai Herenstraat 22. Some of the best-value authentic Thai food in Amsterdam. Popular, with a friendly atmosphere.

Bars

't Arendsnest Herengracht 90. Dutch beers on tap, all eight of them enthusiastically selected and poured for you by the owner from 4pm onwards.

De Buurvrouw St Pieterspoortsteeg 29. Dark, noisy bar near the Allard Pierson Museum with a wildly eclectic crowd.

De Drie Fleschjes Gravenstraat 16, near Dam Square. Tasting house for spirits and liqueurs. No beer, and no seats either. Closes 8pm.

De Duivel Reguliersdwarsstraat 87. Amsterdam's only hip-hop café, near the Rembrandtplein. Opposite the hip-hop coffeeshop *Free I*.

De Engelbewaarder Kloveniersburgwal 59. Relaxed and informal haunt of Amsterdam's bookish types, with live jazz on Sunday afternoons.

De Jaren Nieuwe Doelenstraat 20–22, near Muntplein. Grand café overlooking the river – one of the best places to peruse the Sunday paper.

Het Molenpad Prinsengracht 653. One of the city's most atmospheric brown cafés, with remarkably good food. Fills with young professionals after 6pm.

't Smackzeyl Brouwersgracht 101. Uninhibited drinking den on the corner of Prinsengracht in north Jordaan. Guinness on tap and inexpensive food.

Spanjer & van Twist Leliegracht 60. Perfect for laid-back summer afternoons, with chairs looking out over the quietest canal in Jordaan.

De Twee Zwaantjes Prinsengracht 114. Tiny oddball Jordaan bar where locals sing along raucously to accordion music – you'll either love it or hate it.

De Zotte Proeflokaal Raamstraat 29. Belgian hangout just north of Leidseplein with food, liqueurs and hundreds of different kinds of beers.

Smoking coffeeshops

The Bulldog Leidseplein 15 and other central outlets. One of the oldest and biggest coffeehouses. It also can be the noisiest – not the place for a thoughtful smoke.

De Dampkring Handboogstraat 29. One of the best koffiehuises in town with nice decor and a refined menu. Favoured by tourists and locals, it can get busy.

Global Chillage Kerkstraat 51. Celebrated slice of tie-dyed dope culture, with friendly staff.

Homegrown Fantasy Nieuwezijds Voorburgwal 87a. Part of the Dutch Passion seed company, selling the widest range of (mostly Dutch) marijuana in Amsterdam.

Kadinsky Zoutsteeg 9 & Rosmarijnsteeg 9, both in the old centre. Sensational chocolate chip cookies, scrupulously accurate deals and a background of jazz dance.

Paradox 1e Bloemdwarsstraat 2, Jordaan. Satisfies the munchies with outstanding natural food, including spectacular fresh-fruit concoctions. Closes 8pm.

Rusland Rusland 16. A cramped but vibrant place just north of Muntplein, serving up 43 different kinds of tea. A cut above the rest.

Siberië Brouwersgracht 11. Relaxed, long-standing place that's worth a visit whether you want to smoke or not.

Nightlife

Amsterdam is a gathering spot for fringe performances, and buzzes with places offering a wide and inventive range of **entertainment**. Drinks prices are normally fifty percent or so more than what you pay in a bar, but entry prices are low and there's rarely any kind of door policy. Most places open around 10pm and close around 4am or slightly later. **Cinemas** screen English-language movies, subtitled in Dutch, and rarely show foreign-language films without English subtitles. Check out the lavish Art-Deco interior of the Tuschinski, Reguliersbreestraat 26, or cult and classic flicks at The Movies, Haarlemmerdijk 161, and Kriterion, Roeterstraat 170. "Boom Chicago" is a hugely popular rapid-fire **comedy** troupe, performing nightly in English at Korte Leidsedwarsstraat 12. The best source of information is the **Uitburo**, or **AUB**, in the Stadsschouwburg theatre on the corner of Marnixstraat and Leidseplein (daily 10am–6pm, Thurs until 9pm; ☎0900/0191). Wednesday's *Het Parool* newspaper has a good entertainment supplement, *Uit en Thuis*.

Rock, jazz and world music venues

Akhnaton Nieuwezijds Kolk 25 ☎020/624 3396, ⓦwww.akhnaton.nl. A "Centre for World Culture", specializing in African and Latin American music and dance parties.

Café Alto Korte Leidsedwarsstraat 115, ☎020/626 3249, ⓦww.jazz-cafe-alto.nl. Legendary jazz café-bar, with free live music every night from 10pm until 3am. Big on atmosphere, not space. Near Leidseplein.

Arena 's-Gravesandestraat 51 ☎020/694 7444, ⓦwww.hotelarena.nl. Multimedia centre featuring live music every weekend, cultural events, a bar, coffeeshop and restaurant. Near Oosterpark.

Bimhuis Oude Schans 73–77 ☎020/623 1361, ⓦwww.bimhuis.nl. Premier jazz venue with excellent auditorium and modern bar. Big name concerts Thurs–Sat. Free sessions Mon–Wed.

Hof van Holland Rembrandtplein 7. Traditional brown café with live performances of Dutch music throughout the week.

Melkweg Lijnbaansgracht 234a ☎020/624 1777, ⓦwww.melkweg.nl. Amsterdam's most famous entertainment venue, with a young, hip clientele. Live music from reggae to rock, as well as excellent DJs at the weekend, a monthly film programme, theatre, gallery, bar and restaurant. Near Leidseplein.

Paradiso Weteringschans 6–8 ☎020/626 4521, ⓦwww.paradiso.nl. Set in a lovely old church, this atmospheric haunt of musos features both biggish names and up-and-coming bands. Near Leidseplein.

Winston Kingdom Warmoesstraat 123 ☎020/623 1380, ⓦwww.winston.nl. Small renovated venue with rock, jazz-poetry, R&B and punk/noise nights.

Clubs

Escape Rembrandtplein 11. Huge place packed at weekends, with several floors and top DJs. Closed Sun.

iT Amstelstraat 24, near Rembrandtplein. Large disco with popular and glamorous gay nights, attracting a dressed-up, uninhibited crowd. Friday is mixed gay/straight night.

Mazzo Rozengracht 114, Jordaan. Perhaps the city's hippest and most laid-back club, with a choice of music to appeal to all tastes.

Melkweg Lijnbaansgracht 234a, near Leidseplein. After the bands, this multimedia centre hosts theme nights from African dance parties to experimental jazz-trance.

Ministry Reguliersdwarsstraat 12. A flourishing club near Rembrandtplein which features quality DJs playing speed garage, house and R&B to party people. Monday night jam session with the local jazz talent.

Panama Oostelijke Handelskade 4. Hosts a wide variety of funky gigs and themed club nights. Well out from the centre in the Oosterdok.

Paradiso Weteringschans 6–8. One of the principal venues in the city, which on Fridays hosts an unmissable club night, from midnight onwards. Check listings for one-off events. Near Leidseplein.

Classical music and opera

Beurs van Berlage Damrak 213, city centre. The splendid interior of the former stock exchange hosts a wide selection of music from the Dutch Philharmonic and Dutch Chamber orchestras.

Concertgebouw Concertgebouwplein 2–6 ☎020/ 671 8345. Home to the Borodin Quartet. Catch world-renowned orchestras playing amid wonderful acoustics for just €20. Summer concerts and free lunchtime performances on Wednesdays from Sept to May.

Engelse Kerk Begijnhof 48. Three to four performances a week, lunchtime, afternoon and evening, with the emphasis on period instruments.

Muziektheater Waterlooplein. Full and reasonably priced opera programme. Tickets sell quickly.

Stadsschouwburg Leidseplein 26. Somewhat overshadowed by the Muziektheater, but still a significant stage for opera and dance.

Gay Amsterdam

Amsterdam has one of the biggest and best-established **gay** scenes in Europe: attitudes are tolerant and facilities unequalled. The nationwide organization COC, Rozenstraat 14 (☎020/626 3087, ☁www.cocamsterdam.nl), can provide on-the-spot **information**, and has a café and popular discos (Sat: women under 24 only). For further advice contact the English-speaking Gay & Lesbian Switchboard (daily 2–10pm; ☎020/623 6565, ☁www.switchboard.nl) or check ☁www.gayamsterdam.com. The gay and lesbian bookshop **Vrolijk** is just behind Dam square at Paleisstraat 135.

Gay hotels

Golden Bear Kerkstraat 37 ☎020/624 4785. Clean and spacious rooms, not far from the busy Leidseplein. Trams #1, #2 & #5. ⑤

ITC Hotel Prinsengracht 1051 ☎020/632 0230, ☁www.itc-hotel.com. Friendly hotel in lovely old house, not far from Rembrandtsplein and main gay areas. Tram #4 to Prinsengracht. ⑤

Orfeo Leidsekruisstraat 14 ☎020/623 1347, ☁www.hotelorfeo.com. Very pleasant gay and lesbian hotel behind Leidseplein. Decent breakfasts served until midday. Tram #1, #2 or #5 to Prinsengracht. ⑥

Gay cafés and bars

Amstel Taveerne Amstel 54. Perhaps the best-established bar, at its most vivacious in summer when the guys spill out onto the street.

April Reguliersdwarsstraat 37. Large and trendy, with newspapers, coffee and cakes as well as booze.

Camp Café Kerkstraat 45. Agreeable mix of tourists and locals, with tasty dishes on offer.

Downtown Reguliersdwarsstraat 31, off Rembrandtplein. A favourite with visitors. Relaxed and friendly, with inexpensive meals.

Le Shako 's-Gravelandseveer 2. Friendly bar in a quiet street on the Amstel.

The Web St Jacobsstraat 6. Strict rubber, leather and denim bar with a dance floor, darkrooms and a pool table. From 2pm.

Listings

Bike rental Cheapest from main train stations. Also try: Bike City, Bloemgracht 70 ☎020/626 3721; Damstraat Rent-a-Bike at Damstraat 20 ☎020/625 5029; or MacBike, Mr Visserplein 2 ☎020/620 0985 and Marnixstraat 220 ☎020/626 6964. All charge around €5.50 a day plus €100 deposit with ID.

Bike tours Yellow Bike, Nieuwezijds Kolk 29 ☎020 620 6940, ☁www.yellowbike.nl (€17/person).

Embassies and consulates Note that most of the following are in Den Haag, not Amsterdam. Australia, Carnegielaan 4, Den Haag ☎070/310 8200; Canada, Sophialaan 7, Den Haag ☎070/311 1600; Ireland, Dr Kuyperstraat 9, Den Haag ☎070/363 0993; New Zealand, Carnegielaan 10, Den Haag ☎070/346 9324; UK, Koningslaan 44, Amsterdam ☎020/676 4343; US, Museumplein 19, Amsterdam ☎020/575 5309.

Exchange GWK in Centraal Station and Leidseplein;
Thomas Cook at Dam 23, Damrak 1–5 and
Leidseplein31a; American Express at Damrak 66.
Hospital De Boelelaan 1117 ☎020/444 444.
Laundry The Clean Brothers, Kerkstraat 56 and

Jacob van Lennepkade 179.
Left luggage Centraal Station.
Police Elandsgracht 117 ☎020/559 9111.
Post office Singel 250 (Mon–Fri 9am–6pm, Thurs
until 8pm, Sat 10am–1.30pm).

The Randstad towns

The string of towns known as the **Randstad**, or "rim town", situated amid a typically Dutch landscape of flat fields cut by canals, form the country's most populated region and recall the seventeenth-century heyday of the provinces. Much of the area is easily visited as day-trips from Amsterdam, but it's easy and more rewarding to make a proper tour. **Haarlem** is worth a look, while to the south, the university centre of **Leiden** makes a pleasant detour before you reach the refined tranquillity of **Den Haag** and the busy urban centre of **Rotterdam**. Nearby **Delft** and **Gouda** repay visits too, the former with one of the best-preserved centres in the region.

Haarlem

Just over fifteen minutes from Amsterdam by train, **HAARLEM** is a handsome, mid-sized city that sees itself as a cut above its neighbours. It makes a good alternative base for exploring North Holland, or even Amsterdam itself. The core of the city is **Grote Markt** and the adjoining Riviervischmarkt, flanked by the gabled, originally fourteenth-century **Stadhuis** and the impressive bulk of the **Grote Kerk** or **Sint Bavokerk** (Mon–Sat 10am–3.30/4pm; €2). Inside, the mighty Christian Müller organ of 1738 is said to have been played by Handel and Mozart. The town's main attraction is the outstanding **Frans Hals Museum**, Groot Heiligland 62 (Tues–Sat 11am–5pm, Sun noon–5pm; €5.40; ⓦwww.franshalsmuseum), a five-minute stroll from Grote Markt in the Oudemannhuis almshouse. It houses a number of his lifelike seventeenth-century portraits, including the "Civic Guard" series which established his reputation.

Haarlem **train station**, connected to Amsterdam and to Leiden by four trains an hour, is on the north side of the city, about ten minutes' walk from the Grote Markt; **buses** stop right outside. The **VVV**, attached to the station (Mon–Fri 9am–5.30pm, Sat 9.30am–3.30pm; ☎0900/616 1600, ⓦwww.vvvzk.nl), has maps and can book private rooms for a small fee. Haarlem has a few reasonably priced and central **hotels**, including *Amadeus*, Grote Markt 10 (☎023/532 4530; ❻), and *Carillon*, Grote Markt 27 (☎023/531 0591, ⓦwww.hotelcarillon.com; ❺), both in the central square. Further out there's a **HI hostel** at Jan Gijzenpad 3 (☎023/537 3793, ⓦwww.stayokay.com; €23.20; 10min on bus #2 from the station), and **campsites** among the dunes west of town (bus #81 from the station, including *Bloemendaal*, Zeeweg 72, in Bloemendaal-aan-Zee (☎023/573 2178; closed Nov–March) and the sprawling *De Lakens*, Zeeweg 60 (☎0900/384 6226, ⓦwww.kennemerduincampings.nl; closed Nov–March). For **eating**, the eccentric *Haarlem aan Zee*, Oude Groenmarkt 10 (☎023/531 4884) serves splendid seafood surrounded by beach decor, while the popular and affordable *Restaurant La Plume*, Lange Veerstraat 1 (☎023/531 3202) dishes up pastas and traditional Dutch food. Slightly more upmarket, *Applause* at Grote Markt 23a (☎023/531 1425) is a chic Italian bistro with main courses around €20. The long-standingly popular *Café 1900*, Barteljorisstraat 100, serves drinks and light meals in an attractive setting, while the *Grand Café Fortuyn*, Grote Markt 21 is quieter, with charming 1930s decor. *Ze Crack*, at the junction of Lange Veerstraat and Kleine Houtstraat, is a dim, smoky **bar** with good music and beer by the pint, or for a little traditional character, try the *proeflokaal* (a spirit-tasting room turned bar) *In den Uiver*, Riviervischmarkt 13 or the intimate and typically Dutch *Proeflokaal Sliterij* at Lange Veerstraat 7.

Leiden and around

The charm of **LEIDEN** lies in the peace and prettiness of its gabled streets and canals, though the town's museums are varied and comprehensive enough to merit a visit in themselves. Its most appealing quarter is Rapenburg, a peaceful area of narrow pedestrian streets and canals that is home to the city's best-known attraction at no. 28, the **Rijksmuseum Van Oudheden** (National Museum of Antiquities; Tues–Fri 10am–5pm, Sat & Sun noon–5pm; €6), the country's principal archeological museum. Outside sits the first-century AD Temple of Teffeh while inside are more Egyptian artefacts, along with classical Greek and Roman sculpture and exhibits from prehistoric, Roman and medieval times. Across Rapenburg, a network of narrow streets converges on the Gothic **Pieterskerk** (daily 1.30–4pm; free). East of here, **Breestraat** marks the site of a vigorous **market** (Wed & Sat), which sprawls right over the sequence of bridges into Haarlemmerstraat, the town's major shopping street. Close by, the **Burcht** (daily 10am–10pm; free) is a shell of a fort, whose battlements you can clamber up for the views. Leiden's municipal museum, **Lakenhal**, Oude Singel 28–32 (Tues–Fri 10am–5pm, Sat & Sun noon–5pm; €4), has mixed rooms of furniture, tiles, glass and ceramics and a collection of paintings by Rembrandt and others. Around the corner on Molenwerf, the **Molenmuseum de Valk**, 2e Binnenvestgracht 1 (Tues–Sat 10am–5pm, Sun 1–5pm; €2.50), displays the history of windmills.

Leiden's **train** and **bus stations** are no more than ten minutes' walk from the centre. The **VVV**, a short walk from the stations at Stationsweg 2d (Mon–Fri 11am–7pm, Sat 11am–3pm; ☏0900/222 2333, ⊛www.leiden.nl), can book private rooms. Central **accommodation** includes *The Rose*, Beestenmarkt 14 (☏071/514 6630; ⑥); much more appealing is *Nieuw Minerva*, a cosy and central canalside hotel at Boommarkt 23 (☏071/512 6358, ⊛www.nieuwminerva.nl; ❽). The closest **campsite** is *Koningshof* (☏071/402 6051), 6km north of Leiden (bus #40). For **eating**, *M'n Broer*, by the Pieterskerk at Kloksteeg 7, has a reasonable Dutch menu, while *Barrera*, on Rapenburg, has good sandwiches. In the evening, the studenty *La Bota*, Herensteeg 11, by the Pieterskerk, has great-value food and beers, while *Jazzcafé The Duke* on the corner of Oude Singel and Nieuwe Beestenmarkt has a busy bar and live jazz most nights.

The bulbfields

Along with Haarlem to the north, Leiden and Delft are the best bases for seeing the Dutch **bulbfields** which flourish here in spring. The view from the train can be sufficient in itself as the line cuts directly through the main growing areas, the fields divided into stark geometric blocks of pure colour. Should you want to get closer, make a bee-line for **LISSE**, home to the **Keukenhof Gardens** (late-March to late-May daily 8am–7.30pm; €11.50; ⊛www.keukenhof.nl), the largest flower gardens in the world. Some six million blooms are on show for their full flowering period, complemented by 5000 square metres of greenhouses. Special buses (#54) run daily to the Keukenhof from Leiden bus station twice an hour.

Den Haag (The Hague)

With its urbane atmosphere, **DEN HAAG** (**The Hague**) is different from any other Dutch city. Since the sixteenth century it's been the Netherlands' political capital though its older buildings are a rather subdued collection with little of Amsterdam's flamboyance. Diplomats and multinational businesses ensure that many of the city's hotels and restaurants are in the expense-account category, and the nightlife is similar-

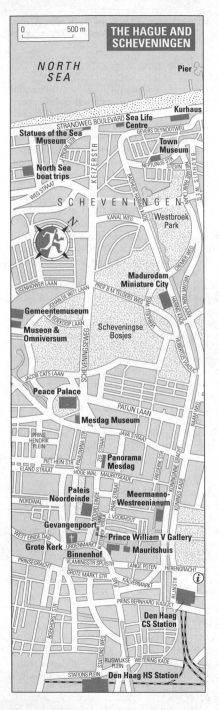

ly packaged. But, away from this, Den Haag does have cheaper and livelier bars and restaurants, as well as some excellent museums. Right in the centre, the **Binnenhof** is the home of the Dutch parliament with roots in the thirteenth-century castle. The present complex is a rather mundane affair, the small **Hof Vijver** lake mirroring the symmetry of the facade; inside there's little to see except the **Ridderzaal**, a slender-turreted structure that can be viewed on regular guided tours from the information office at Binnenhof 8a (Mon–Sat 10am–3.45pm; €3). Immediately east, the **Mauritshuis** picture gallery, Korte Vijverberg 8 (Tues–Sat 10am–5pm, Sun 11am–5pm; €7; @www.mauritshuis.nl), located in a magnificent seventeenth-century mansion, is of more interest, famous for its extensive range of Flemish and Dutch paintings including work by Vermeer, Rubens, Bruegel the Elder and Van Dyck. Down the street at Buitenhof 35, the **Galerij Prins Willem V** (Tues–Sun 11am–4pm; €1.50, free with Mauritshuis ticket) has paintings by Rembrandt, Jordaens and Paulus Potter in a reconstructed eighteenth-century gallery. About fifteen minutes' walk from the Mauritshuis, **Panorama Mesdag** at Zeestraat 65 (Mon–Sat 10am–5pm, Sun noon–5pm; @www.panorama-mesdag.com; €4) has an astonishing 360-degree painting of seaside scenes from the 1880s. North, the **Gemeentemuseum**, Stadhouderslaan 41 (Tues–Sun 11am–5pm; €7; bus #4/#14 from Centraal Station), contains superb collections of musical instruments and Islamic ceramics, and an array of modern art tracing the development of Dutch painting, with the world's largest collection of Mondriaan paintings. Halfway between Den Haag and its adjacent beach resort of **SCHEVENINGEN** is one of the city's most hyped attractions, the mildly interesting **Madurodam Miniature City** (daily 9am–6/8/10pm; €11; @www.madurodam.nl;

tram #1/#9), a scale model of a Dutch town.

Practicalities

The city has two **train stations** – "Den Haag HS" (short for Hollands Spoor) and, about 1km to the north, "Den Haag CS" (Centraal Station). Trains stop at one or the other and sometimes both; the latter is the more convenient, being next to the **VVV** (Mon–Sat 10am–5.30pm, July & Aug also Sun 11am–3pm; ☎0900/340 3505, ⓦwww.denhaag.com). **Accommodation** is quite expensive. The VVV has a small stock of private rooms, or there's a cluster of seedy but reasonably priced hotels just outside Den Haag HS station including *Aristo*, Stationsweg 164–166 (☎070/389 0847; ❹), and *Astoria*, Stationsweg 139 (☎070/384 0401; ❹). About 500m to the east is the smart **HI hostel** at Scheepmakerstraat 27 (☎070/315 7888, ⓦwww.stayokay.com; €22). You might get a better deal on accommodation 4km north of Den Haag at the busy and developed beach resort of **Scheveningen**; ask at the VVV on the seafront at Gevers Deynootweg 1134 (Mon–Sat 9/10am–5/5.30pm; April–Sept also Sun 1–5pm; ☎0900/340 3505).

There are plenty of cheap places to **eat** around Denneweg and Frederikstraat, just north of Lange Voorhout, amongst them the coolly decorated cafe-restaurant *De Dekxels*, Denneweg 130, with international and Dutch dishes for around €10–12, and *Malienkolder*, Maliestraat 9, an inexpensive French/Dutch bistro. South of the Paleis Noordeinde at Molenstraat 21, *HNM* has tasty Dutch, Indonesian, French and Italian daily specials for just €7. For **drinking**, aim for the studenty bar *Zwarte Ruiter* (also with good food) in the busy square south of Den Haag's Grote Kerk, or nearby *De Boterwaag*, Grote Markt 8a, an appealing brick-vaulted café-bar. Near Denneweg, the canalside *Le Café Hathor*, Maliestraat 22, has a convivial atmosphere, as does *De Oude Mol*, a traditional bar tucked down a narrow sidestreet further north on Oude Molenstraat.

Delft

DELFT, 2km inland from Den Haag, has considerable charm, with its gabled red-roofed houses standing beside tree-lined canals. The pastel colours of the pavements, brickwork and bridges give the town a faded tranquillity – though one that can suffer beneath the tourist onslaught during summer. A good starting point is to follow the Historic Walk around the old town with a map from the VVV. The town is perhaps best known for Delftware, the delicate blue and white ceramics to which the town gave its name in the seventeenth century. **Koninklijke Porceleyne Fles**, a factory producing Delftware at Rotterdamsweg 196, is open for visits (daily 9am–5pm; Oct–April closed Sun; €2.50; ⓦwww.royaldelft.com), and the **Huis Lambert van Meerten Museum**, Oude Delft 199 (Tues–Sat 10am–5pm, Sun 1–5pm; €3.50), has a large collection of Delft and other tiles. **Markt** is also a useful place to start exploring, with the **Nieuwe Kerk** (Mon–Fri 9/11am–4/6pm, Sat 9/11–5/6pm; €2.50) at one end and the Renaissance **Stadhuis** opposite. William the Silent – leader of the struggle for Dutch independence in the seventeenth century – is buried in this fine old church and you can climb the 370 steps of the tower for spectacular views. West of here, **Wynhaven**, an old canal, leads to Hippolytusbuurt and the Gothic **Oude Kerk** (same hours and price as Nieuwe Kerk), perhaps the town's finest building, with an unhealthily leaning tower. The nearby **Prinsenhof,** William the Silent's base for his revolt against the Spanish and also where he was assassinated, has a decent collection of early Dutch art.

From Delft's train station, aim for the big steeple you see on exit and it's a ten-minute walk north to the Markt. Delft's VVV is currently closed, but when it reopens it will almost certainly be on the Markt. The town has some delightful family **B&Bs**: warmly recommended is friendly and welcoming *Oosteinde*, at Oosteinde 156 (☎015/213 4238; ❺), with lovely rooms. At the cheaper end, try *Hotel Restaurant Radethuys*, Markt 38-40 (☎015/212 5115; ❸). The **campsite**,

Delftse Hout, is at Kortftlaan 5 (☎015/213 0040; bus #64 from station). The least expensive **eating** is at a number of student mensas (term-time only) such as *De Koornbeurs* near the main square and *Jansbrug*, Kornmarkt 50–52; *Ladera* on Oosteinde also has good-value food. *Kobus Koch* is a gem of a café/restaurant on the Beestenmarkt; sampling the tasty *appeltart met slagroom* (apple cake with cream) is a must. *Willem Van Oranje*, centrally located on Markt, has pancakes, *uitsmijters* (ham or cheese with eggs), light meals for around €4.50 and three-course menus for €9. *Locus Publicus*, Brabantse Turfmarkt 67, is a popular local bar, serving a staggering array of beers as well as sandwiches. Further nightlife is provided by the nearby club *Speakers*, which often features live music, and a jazz bar, *The Piano Bar*.

Rotterdam

Just beyond Delft lies **ROTTERDAM**, at the heart of a maze of rivers and artificial waterways that together form the outlet of the rivers Rijn (Rhine) and Maas (Meuse). After devastating damage during World War II, Rotterdam has grown into a vibrant, forceful city dotted with first-division cultural attractions. Redevelopment also hasn't obliterated the city's earthy character: its tough grittiness is part of its appeal, as are its boisterous bars and clubs. A nice feel for the city can be had by walking from the station (or taking #5 tram from just outside) down to the Museumpark. Here, the **Boymans-Van Beuningen Museum**, Mathenesserlaan 18–20 (Tues–Sat 10am–5pm, Sun 11am–5pm; €6; ⊛www.boijmans .nl), is enormous, with a superb collection. The first floor contains works by Monet, Van Gogh, Picasso, Gauguin and Cézanne, while among the earlier canvases are several by Bosch, Bruegel the Elder and Rembrandt. A stroll through the Museumpark brings you to the **Kunsthal** (Tues–Sat 10am–5pm, Sun 11am–5pm; €6.50), which showcases first-rate exhibitions of contemporary art, photography and design. Water taxis leave the Veerhaven and the Leuvehaven for the splendid *Hotel New York*, occupying the building where transatlantic cruise liners once docked. From here you can walk back to the centre over the futuristic bridge, the Erasmusbrug, an ideal spot for photos. Ten minutes' walk away is the entertaining **Maritiem Museum** (Maritime Museum; Tues–Fri 10am–5pm, Sat

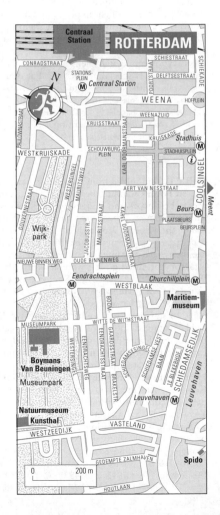

19

& Sun 11am–5pm; €3.50) at the Leuvehaven. Close by is the seventeenth-century mansion at Korte Hoogstraat 31 that houses the **Museum Het Schielandshuis** (Tues–Sat 10am–5pm, Sun 11am–5pm; €3.50), with displays on the city's history. Another short walk away is Blaak, a pocket-sized area that was levelled in World War II, but has since been rebuilt. The architectural highlight is a remarkable series of cube-shaped houses, the *kubuswoningen*, completed in 1984. One of them, the **Kijk-Kubus** (Show Cube; March–Dec daily 11am–5pm; Jan & Feb Fri–Sun same hours; €1.75; ⓦwww.kubuswoning.nl), at Overblaak 70, near Blaak train and metro station, is open to visitors, offering a somewhat disorientating tour of what amounts to an upside-down house.

If little in Rotterdam city centre can exactly be called picturesque, **DELFS-HAVEN**, a couple of kilometres southwest of Centraal Station, makes up for it – to get there, catch tram #4 or #6 (direction Schiedam, tram stop Spanjaardstraat), or take the metro to Delfshaven. Once the harbour that served Delft, it was from here that the Pilgrim Fathers set sail for the New World in 1620. Most of the buildings lining the district's two narrow canals are eighteenth- and nineteenth-century warehouses. At Voorhaven 12 is the **Museum de Dubbelde Palmboom** (Tues–Fri 10am–5pm, Sat & Sun 11am–5pm; €2.70), once a jenever distillery and now a wide-ranging historical museum.

Practicalities

Rotterdam's large centre is bordered by its main rail terminal, **Centraal Station**, also the hub of a useful **tram** and **metro** system, though best avoided late at night. The main **VVV** office is a ten-minute walk away at Coolsingel 67 (Mon–Thurs 9am–6pm, Fri 9.30am–9pm, Sat 9.30am–5pm; ☏010/414 0000, ⓦwww.vvvrotterdam .nl), where you can pick up a comprehensive city brochure (€2). There are plenty of central, reasonably priced **hotels**. Southwest of the station is *Wilgenhof*, Heemraadssingel 92–94 (☏010/425 4892; ❺; tram #1/#7 from Centraal Station). Near the Museumpark, the lively and agreeable *Bazar*, Witte de Withstraat 16 (☏010/206 5151 ⓦwww.bazarhotel.com; ❻) also has a great cafe-restaurant. A five-minute walk from Wilhelminaplein metro, on the south bank of the Nieuwe Maas, is the *New York*, Koninginnenhoofd 1 (☏010/439 0500; ❼), with a great atmosphere and excellent restaurant. The **HI hostel** is a 25-minute walk from the station, Rochussenstraat 107 (☏010/436 5763, ⓦwww.stayokay.com; €22.45; tram #4 or metro stop Dijkzigt). The nearest **campsite**, *Stadscamping* (☏010/415 9772), is north of the station at Kanaalweg 84 (bus #33).

Oude and Nieuwe Binnenweg host a number of affordable and tasty **eating** options, including *Rotown*, Nieuwe Binnenweg 19, *Siff* at Oude Binnenweg 115 and *De Vijgeboon* at Oude Binnenweg 146a. Witte de Withstraat is also worth wandering along: *The Bazar* at no. 16 does excellent kebabs and vegetarian food, while *Witte de With* at no. 92 is a popular **coffeeshop**. Rotterdam has a lively **club** scene; two current hotspots are *Off Corso*, near Centraal Station at Kruiskade 22, with top DJs, and *De Blauwe Vis*, in a disused underpass at the north end of the Lijnbaan. Tickets for rock gigs and concerts are on sale at the main post office, Coolsingel 42 (☏0900/300 1250, ⓦwww.ticketservice.nl).

From the Leuvehaven, there are numerous **boat trips** through the harbour (year-round; 1hr 15min; €8). From April to September, there are also trips to Dordrecht, the array of windmills at Kinderdijk, and the Delta Project from €15–30 per person; contact the VVV or Spido for details (☏010/275 9988, ⓦwww.spido.nl).

Gouda

A pretty little place some 25km northeast of Rotterdam, **GOUDA** is almost everything you'd expect of a Dutch country town: a ring of quiet canals encircling ancient buildings and old quays. Its **Markt** is the largest in Holland, a reminder of the town's prominence as a centre of the medieval cloth trade, and later of the manufacture of cheeses and clay pipes. A touristy **cheese market** is held here every Thursday morning from June to August. Slap bang in the middle, the elegant Gothic **Stadhuis** dates from 1450; on the north side is the **Waag**, a tidy seventeenth-century building whose top two floors house a cheese museum (April–Oct Tues–Sun 1–5pm, Thurs 10am–5pm; €2). South, off the Markt, **St Janskerk** (Mon–Sat 9/10am–4/5pm; €2) was built in the sixteenth century and is famous for its magnificent stained-glass windows.

Gouda's **train** and **bus stations** are north of the centre, ten minutes from the **VVV**, Markt 27 (Mon–Fri 9am–5pm, Sat 10am–4pm; June–Aug also Sun noon–3pm; ☏0900/468 32888, ⊛www.vvvgouda.nl), which offers a limited supply of private rooms. The most reasonably priced **hotel** is *De Utrechtsche Dom*, fifteen minutes' walk from the train station at Geuzenstraat 6 (☏0182/528 833, ⊛www.hotelgouda.nl; ❺); otherwise, try *De Keizerskroon*, Keizerstraat 11–13 (☏0182/528 096; ❺). For **food**, there are plenty of cafés catering to the swarms of summer day-trippers. You can eat cheaply at '*t Groot Stedelijk*, Markt 44, among other places; '*t Goudse Winkeltje*, Achter de Kerk 9a, has good pancakes; and there's good-quality Dutch food at the attractive *Eetcafé De Beursklok*, Hoge Gouwe 19. For a **drink**, find your way to the excellent *Eetcafé Vidocq*, Koster Gijzenstraat 8, or check out *Café Central*, Markt 23.

Utrecht

"I groaned with the idea of living all winter in so shocking a place," wrote Boswell in 1763, and **UTRECHT**, surrounded by shopping centres and industrial developments, still promises little as you approach. But the centre, with its distinctive sunken canals – whose brick cellar warehouses have been converted into chic cafés and restaurants – is one of the country's most pleasant. The focal point is the **Dom Tower**, built between 1321 and 1382, which at over 110m is the highest church tower in the country, soaring to a delicate octagonal lantern. A guided tour (Mon–Sat 10am–5pm, Sun noon–5pm; last entry 4pm; €3.40) takes you unnervingly close to the top, from where you can see Rotterdam and Amsterdam on a clear day. Below is the Gothic **Dom Kerk**; only the eastern part of the cathedral remains today after the nave collapsed in 1674, but it's worth peering inside (Mon–Fri 10/11am–4/5pm, Sat 10am–3.30pm, Sun 2–4pm; free) and wandering through the Kloostergang, the fourteenth-century cloisters that link the cathedral to the chapterhouse. South of the church at Nieuwe Gracht 63, the national collection of ecclesiastical art, the **Catharijne Convent Museum** (Tues–Fri 10am–5pm, Sat & Sun 11am–5pm; €4.50; ⊛www.catharijneconvent.nl), has wonderful paintings, manuscripts and church ornaments from the ninth century on.

Utrecht's **train** and **bus stations** both lead into the Hoog Catharijne shopping centre. The main **VVV** office is a short walk away at Vinkenburgstraat 19 (Mon–Fri 9.30am–6.30pm, Sat 9.30am–5pm; ☏0900/128 8732, ⊛www.utrechtstad.com). For **accommodation**, the pleasant HI hostel (☏030/656 1277, ⊛www.stayokay.com; €20) lies 5km southeast, in an old country manor house at Rhijnauwenselaan 14, Bunnik – take bus #40/#41 from the train station. More central is the friendly seventeenth-century *Strowis*, Boothstraat 8 (☏030/238 0280, ⊛www.strowis.nl; €12; ❹), a fifteen-minute walk from Centraal Station or a short ride on bus #3/#4/#8/#11 to the Janskerkhof stop, plus a two-minute walk. The well-equipped **campsite**, *De Berenkuil*, Ariënslaan 5 (☏030/271 3870), is served by bus #57. **Restaurants** are mainly situated along Oude Gracht; best is the moderately priced *Stadskasteel Oudaen* at no. 99, the oldest house in town, which serves beer from its own brewery downstairs. *De Oude Muntkelder* at no. 112 has inexpensive pancakes, while vegetarians should seek out *De Werfkring* at no. 123, or *Milky*, a more upmarket restaurant off the canal at Zakkerdragssteeg 22. The city's best **bars** cluster around the junction of Oude Gracht and the Lijnmarkt; one to visit on a weekend is *Winkel van Sinkel* at Oude Gracht 158, with regular dance nights and a chill-out room downstairs.

Beyond the Randstad

Outside the Randstad towns, the Netherlands is relatively unknown territory to visitors. To the north, there's superb cycling and hiking to be had through scenic **dune reserves** and delightful villages, with easy access to pristine beaches. The island of **Texel** offers the country's most complete beach experience, with plenty of birdlife. In the northeast, the main draw is **Groningen**, a lively, cosmopolitan town with a buzzing nightlife and a museum and art gallery. To the south, the countryside grows steadily more rolling as you head towards Germany. The **Hoge Veluwe National Park**, near Arnhem, boasts one of the country's best modern art museums and has cycle paths through a delightful landscape. Further south, in the provinces of North Brabant and Limburg, the landscape slowly fills out, rolling into a rougher countryside of farmland and forests and eventually into the hills around **Maastricht**, a city with a vibrant, pan-European air.

The island of Texel

The largest of the islands off the north coast – and the easiest to get to (2hr from Amsterdam) – **TEXEL** (pronounced *tessel*) is diverse and pretty, and one of Europe's most important bird breeding-grounds. **Ferries** from the town of Den Helder on the mainland depart every hour (€4; coming from Amsterdam, ask for an all-in discounted "Waddenbiljet"). Once there, Texel's main settlement, **DEN BURG**, makes a convenient base and has bike rental outlets. On the coast 3km southeast of Den Burg is **OUDESCHILD**, home to the **Maritiem en Juttersmuseum** (Beachcombers' Museum; Tues–Sat 10am–5pm, July & Aug also Mon 10am–5pm; €4.10), a fascinating collection of marine junk from wrecks, while in the opposite direction is **DE KOOG**, with a good sandy beach and the **EcoMare** nature centre, Ruijslaan 92 (daily 9am–5pm; €7), a refuge for lost birds, where you can also take an excursion to the Wad, the banks of sand and mud to the east of the island, a gathering-place for seals and birds. Den Burg's **VVV** is at Emmalaan 66 (Mon–Fri 9am–6pm, Sat 9am–5pm, July & Aug also Sun 10am–1.30pm; ☎0222/314 741, ⊛www.texel.net). The cheapest **hotel** is in Den Burg: *'t Koogerend*, Kogerstraat 94 (☎0222/313 301; ❷), while there's a **HI hostel** on the road to Oudeschild, at Schanseweg 7 (☎0222/315 441, ⊛www.stayokay.com; €22). **Campers** are spoilt for choice: close to Den Burg is the small, well-run *De Koorn Aar*, Grensweg 388 (☎0222/312 931; closed Nov–March); among the beachside dunes in De Koog is *Kogerstrand*, Badweg 33 (☎0222/317 208; closed Nov–March) and there's *De Krim*, Roggeslootweg 6, in De Cocksdorp, a hamlet at the island's north tip (☎0222/390 111). The best **food** in Den Burg is *De Worsteltent*, Smitweg 6, while in De Koog plump for *Vogelhuis Oranjerie*, Dorpsstraat 204 (☎0222/317 279), where main courses are around €16.

Groningen

The northern city of **GRONINGEN** comes as something of a surprise in the midst of quiet, rural surroundings. Hip, streetwise fashions, a cosmopolitan feel and thriving student life imbue the city with vigour. Competitively priced restaurants dish up exotic curries and fresh falafel alongside the standard Dutch staples, and the arts scene is vibrant, particularly during the academic year. Virtually destroyed in 1945, Groningen is now a jumble of arts and architectures: from traditional canalside townhouses to colourful Art-Deco tilework parading along the upper facades of the shopping streets. This eclecticism culminates in the innovative **Groninger Museum** (Tues–Sun 10am–5pm, July & Aug also Mon 1pm–5pm; €6; ⊛www.groninger-museum.nl), resplendent in acid-greens and golds on its own little island across from the train station; its controversial design encases a superb collection of contemporary art, set off by numerous and varied exhibitions. The west pavilion is given over to travelling exhibitions but also houses the permanent art collection, including Rubens, Hague school paintings, and a number of late works by the Expressionists.

Groningen's **bus** and **train stations** are on the south side of town, fifteen minutes' walk from the **VVV** at Grote Markt 25 (Mon–Fri 9am–6pm, Sat 10am–5pm; ℡0900/202 3050, ⊛www.groningen.nl); they'll give you a short list of private rooms, though few are near the city centre. Otherwise, the cheapest **accommodation** is in the dorms of *Simplon Jongerenhotel*, north of the centre at Boterdiep 73 (℡050/313 5221; €11.60). Reasonably priced **hotels** include *Garni Friesland*, Kleine Pelsterstraat 4 (℡050/312 1307; ❹), just south of the Grote Markt. Bus #2 from Grote Markt runs via Peizerweg on a ten-minute ride to the **campsite** *Stadspark* (℡050/525 1624; closed mid-Oct to mid-March). For Groningen's cheapest **food**, head for *Maoz Falafel*, Gedempte Zuiderdiep 23. Best of the rest are concentrated around Poelestraat: *Café d'Opera* at no. 17 has good Dutch food; *'t Pakhuis*, Peperstraat 8, has Dutch snacks and a lively **bar** in an atmospheric building, while to the west at A-Kerkstraat 24 is high-quality, moderately priced fish and vegetarian food in *Brussels Lof*. On the south side of Grote Markt is a flank of outdoor **cafés**, best of which are the old-style brown café *De Witz*, no. 47, and *Hooghoudt*, no. 42, which serves food until 4am at weekends. Thanks to its large student population, Groningen has good **nightlife**. For **live music** try *Vera*, in the basement at Oosterstraat 44; or *Troubadour*, Peperstraat 19. *De Spieghel*, Peperstraat 11, has live jazz most nights, while *Palace*, Gelkingestraat 1, is a lively club which occasionally hosts live bands.

The Hoge Veluwe National Park

Some 70km southeast of Amsterdam, and just north of the town of Arnhem, is the huge and scenic **Hoge Veluwe National Park** (daily: April–Aug 8am–8/10pm; rest of year 9am–5.30/7pm; ⊛www.hogeveluwe.nl; €5, or €10 combined ticket to park and Kröller-Müller museum). Formerly the estate of wealthy local couple Anton and Helene Kröller-Müller, it has three entrances – one near the village of **Otterlo** on the northwest perimeter, another near **Hoenderloo** on the northeast edge, and a third to the south at **Rijzenburg**, near the village of Schaarsbergen. The easiest way to get here is by bus #107 from Arnhem's train station, then change at Otterlo to bus #110 which runs direct to the **Bezoekerscentrum** (Visitors' Centre; daily 10am–5pm). The Centre is one of the five signposted places from where you can pick up **white bicycles** which are available free to all visitors and which are by far the best way to explore the park. At the centre sits a terraced café/restaurant, *De Koperen Kop*. Also within the park is the **Museonder** (daily 10am–5pm), an underground natural history museum, and the **St Hubertus Hunting Lodge** (daily 10am–5pm), the former Art Deco home of the Kröller-Müllers, with free guided tours on offer. The park's unmissable highlight is the **Kröller-Müller Museum** (Tues–Sun 10am–5pm; ⊛www.krollermuseum.nl; free with park admission), a superb collection of fine art with paintings by Van Gogh, as well as Picasso, Seurat, Léger and Mondriaan. Behind the museum is a lovely and imaginative **sculpture garden** (Tues–Sun 10am–4.30pm; same ticket), the largest in Europe.

Trains run from Amsterdam to nearby **ARNHEM**, from where you can catch the bus to the park. Arnhem's VVV office is near the station, Willemsplein 8 (℡0900/202 4075, ⊛www.vvvarnhem.nl); staff can help you find **accommodation** in the area. There's an **HI hostel** at Diepenbrocklaan 27 (℡026/442 0114, ⊛www.stayokay.com), just north of town towards the park (bus #3). You can **camp** by the park's northeastern Hoenderloo entrance (℡055/378 2232; closed Nov–March).

Maastricht

Squashed between the Belgian and German borders, **MAASTRICHT** is one of the most delightful cities in the Netherlands. A cosmopolitan place, where three languages happily coexist, it's also one of the oldest towns in the country. The busiest of

Maastricht's many squares is **Markt**, at its most crowded during the Wednesday and Friday morning **market**. At the centre is the mid-seventeenth-century **Stadhuis** (Mon–Fri 8.30am–12.30pm & 2–5.30pm; free). Just west, **Vrijthof** is a grander open space flanked by a line of café terraces on one side and on the other by **St Servaaskerk** (daily 10am–5/6pm; €2), a tenth-century church. Next door is **St Janskerk** (Easter–Oct Mon–Sat 11am–4pm; free), with its high fifteenth-century Gothic tower (€1.15 donation). Maastricht's other main church, the **Onze Lieve Vrouwe Basiliek**, is a short walk south of Vrijthof, down Bredestraat, in a small, shady square crammed with café tables. On the other side of the square lies the appealing district of **Stokstraat Kwartier**, with narrow streets winding out to the fast-flowing River Jeker and the **Helpoort** of 1229. Continuing south, the case-mates in the **Waldeck Park** (guided tours: July–Sept daily 12.30pm & 2pm; rest of year Sun 2pm; €3) are further evidence of Maastricht's once-impressive fortifications. Fifteen minutes' walk further south is the 110m hill of **St Pietersberg**. Of the two ancient defensive tunnel systems under the hill, the **Zonneberg** is probably the better, situated on the far side of the hill at Casino Slavante (guided tours: July & Aug daily 2.45pm; €3). Just outside the city lies the busy tourist town of **VALKEN-BURG,** which provides a base for walking the nearby hills and forests.

Practicalities

The centre of Maastricht is on the west bank of the river. You're likely to arrive, however, on the east bank, in the district known as Wijk, home to the **train** and **bus stations** and many of the city's hotels. The **VVV** is in the centre at Kleine Straat 1, at the end of the main shopping street (Mon–Sat 9am–5/6pm, Sun 11am–3pm; Nov–March closed Sun; ☎043/325 2121, ⓦwww.visitmaastricht.nl); it has copies of *Uit In Maastricht* and a tourist guide with map and a list of private rooms. There are several good central **hotels**, including *La Cloche*, Bredestraat 41 (☎043/321 2407, ⓦwww.lacloche.com; ❺). The *Botel Maastricht* (☎043/321 9023; ❸) is moored on the river on Maasboulevard, not far from the Helpoort, and does an excellent breakfast. For **camping**, the large and well-equipped *De Dousberg* site (☎043/343 2171; closed Nov–March) is a ten-minute ride from the station on bus #11 (after 6.25pm, take bus #28 towards Pottenburg and ask the driver). The same bus also takes you to the **HI hostel** at Dousbergweg 4 (☎043/346 6777, ⓦwww.stayokay.com; €17.05), which has access to open-air and indoor swimming pools.

For cheap **food**, head for Koestraat; elsewhere, *Pizzeria Napoli* at Markt 71 gives a 20 percent student discount, while *Il Giardino della Mamma*, Onze Lieve Vrouweplein 15 offers pizzas and pasta from €10 with a view of the church. Late-night snack attacks can be assuaged at *'t Witte Bruudsje*, Platielstraat 12, which serves baguettes and hot meals until 2am (3am on Fri & Sat). The **bars** on the east side of Vrijthof are packed in summer; *In den Ouden Vogelstruys*, on the corner of Platielstraat, is one of the nicest. Away from Vrijthof, *De Bóbbel*, on Wolfstraat just off Onze Lieve Vrouweplein, is a bareboards bar, lively in the early evening; in the student area around Tongesestraat both *Van Sloun* at no. 3 and *Tribunal* opposite are excellent. For **live music** all year round try *D'n Awwestiene*, Kesselskade 43 (Wed–Sun 10pm–5am). **Internet** access is at the *Centre Céramique*, five minutes from the station.

⑲

Travel details

Amsterdam to: Arnhem (for Hoge Veluwe National Park; every 30min; 1hr 10min); Groningen (every 30min; 2hr 20min); Haarlem (every 10min; 15min); Den Haag (every 15min; 50min); Leiden (every 15min; 35min); Maastricht (hourly; 2hr 30min); Rotterdam (every 30min; 1hr 10min); Schiphol Airport (every 15min; 20min); Texel (via Den Helder; every 30min; 1hr 10min); Utrecht (every 30min; 30min).

Arnhem (for Hoge Veluwe National Park) to:

Amsterdam (every 30min; 1hr 10min); Utrecht (every 15min; 30min).

Groningen to: Amsterdam (every 30min; 2hr 20min).

Den Haag to: Delft (every 15min; 15min); Gouda (every 20min; 20min); Rotterdam (every 15min; 25min); Utrecht (every 20min; 40min).

Leiden to: Amsterdam (every 30min; 35min); Den Haag (every 30min; 35min).

Maastricht to: Amsterdam (every 30min; 2hr 30min).

Rotterdam to: Gouda (every 20min; 20min); Utrecht (every 20min; 45min).

Utrecht to: Arnhem (every 15min; 30min).

Norway

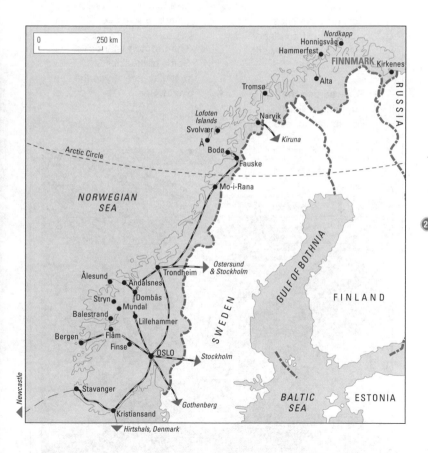

Norway highlights

* **Viking Ships Museum, Oslo** A must on any tourist itinerary. See p.689

* **Vigeland Sculpture Park, Oslo** Scandinavia's finest – and most extraordinary – open-air sculpture park. See p.690

* **Ferry across the Sognefjord** To Balestrand, for example, for the quintessential fjordland experience. See p.695

* **The Jostedalsbreen glacier** Magnificent – hike to it or view it near Mundal See p.696

* **The Lofoten Islands** Some of the finest mountain scenery in the world. See p.701

20

Introduction and basics

In many ways **Norway** is still a land of unknowns. Comparatively quiet for a thousand years since the Vikings stamped their mark on Europe, the country can often seem more than just geographically distant even today. Beyond Oslo and the famous fjords the rest of the country might as well be blank for all many visitors know – and, in a manner of speaking, large parts of it are. Vast stretches in the north and east are sparsely populated, and here it's possible to travel for hours without seeing a soul.

Beyond **Oslo**, one of the world's most prettily sited capitals, the major cities of interest are historic **Trondheim**, **Bergen**, on the edge of the fjords, and hilly, northern **Tromsø**. All are likeable, imminently walkable cities, worth time for themselves as well as being good bases for exploring the startlingly handsome countryside. The perennial draw is, however, the **western fjords** – every bit as scenically stunning as they're cracked up to be. Dip into the region from Bergen or **Åndalsnes**, both accessible by train from Oslo, or take more time and appreciate the subtleties of the innumerable waterside towns and villages. Further north, the stunning **Lofoten Islands** are well worth the effort for their calm atmosphere and sheer beauty. To the north of here, Norway grows increasingly barren, and the tourist trail focuses on the long journey to the North Cape or **Nordkapp** – the northernmost accessible point of mainland Europe. The route leads through the province of **Finnmark**, a vast, eerily bleak wilderness where the Arctic tundra rolls as far as the eye can see, one of the last strongholds of the Sami and their herds of reindeer.

Information & maps

Every town has a **tourist office**, usually with a stock of free maps and timetables. Many book private rooms and hotel beds and some rent out bikes and change money. During the high season – late June to August – they nor-mally open daily for long hours, while in the shoulder season they mostly adopt shop hours; many close down altogether in winter. The *Hallwag* **map** (1:1,000,000) comes with an index, although in Norway, the Statens Kartverk maps – at several scales – are best.

Money and banks

Currency is the **krone** (kr), divided into 100 øre. Coins are 50 øre, 1kr, 5kr, 10kr and 20kr; notes are 50kr, 100kr, 200kr, 500kr and 1000kr. **Banking hours** are Mon–Fri 9am–3.30pm, Thurs till 5pm, though many close half an hour earlier in summer. Most airports and some train stations have exchange offices, open evenings and weekends, and some tourist offices also change money, though at worse rates than banks and post offices. ATMs are in even the smaller towns.

Communications

Post office opening hours are usually Mon–Fri 8/8.30am–4/5pm, Sat 8/9am–1pm. Stamps are available from post offices, kiosks and most bookstores. Many public **phones** (minimum charge 5kr) take 1kr, 5kr, 10kr and 20kr coins. There are phonecards of 40kr, 90kr and 140kr. There are no area codes. Directory enquiries is ☏180 within Scandinavia, ☏181 international. The international operator is on ☏115. Many hotels have **Internet** access, and most libraries offer free access.

NORWAY | Basics

20

Norway on the net

ⓦ**www.visitnorway.no** Official Norwegian Tourist Board site.
ⓦ**www.odin.dep.no** Government site with good information links.
ⓦ**www.museumnett.no** Comprehensive details of museums and exhibitions.

Getting around

Public transport is extraordinarily reliable. In the winter (especially in the north), services can be cut back severely, but no part of the country is isolated for long. A synopsis of all the main air, train, bus and ferry services is given in the free *NRI Guide to Transport and Accommodation* brochure, available in advance from the Norwegian Tourist Board; and all local tourist offices have detailed regional public transport timetables. There are four main **train** routes. These link Oslo to Stockholm in the east, to Kristiansand and Stavanger in the southwest, to Bergen in the west and to Trondheim and on to Fauske and Bodø in the north. The nature of the country makes most of the routes worth a trip in their own right. The tiny Flåm branch line, and sweeping Rauma run to Åndalsnes, are exciting examples, as is the journey from Oslo to Bergen, an impressive six-and-a-half-hour cross-country ride. InterRail and Eurail passes are valid, as is the ScanRail pass. ScanRail and InterRail and, to a lesser extent, Eurail provide large discounts on major ferry crossings and long-distance buses. You'll need to use **buses** principally in the western fjords and the far north. Tickets aren't expensive and are usually bought on board, although bus stations sell advance tickets too. Information on specific routes and timetables is available from local tourist offices; Nor-Way Bussekspress (ⓦwww.nor-way.no) sells several passes.

Travelling by **ferry** is one of the real pleasures of a trip to Norway. Rates are fixed nationally on a sliding scale, with a ten- to fifteen-minute ride costing 18–24kr for foot passengers. Bus fares include the cost of any ferry journey made en route. Some of the busier ferry routes have a control kiosk, where you pay on arrival, but for the most part a crew member comes round to collect fares either on the quayside or on board. The **Hurtigrute** ("rapid route") boat shuttles up and down the coast, linking Bergen with Kirkenes and stopping off at over thirty ports on the way. Short hops are more expensive than buses – a six-hour jaunt, for instance, costs around 470kr per passenger, 790kr for car and driver. Sleeping in the lounges or on deck is allowed – and you can use a shower on the lower corridors. Each ship has a 24-hour cafeteria and restaurants. Bikes travel at ten percent of the standard car tariff.

Accommodation

For budget travellers as well as hikers, climbers and skiers, **hostels** provide the accommodation mainstay – there are about a hundred in total, spread right across the country and run by Norske Vandrerhjem (ⓦwww.vandrerhjem.no). Prices vary greatly (100–180kr), although the more expensive ones nearly always include a first-rate breakfast. Most places also have a supply of doubles for 250–450kr. Non-members pay an extra 25kr a night. Between June and mid-September you should call ahead to check on space. Most hostels close 11am–4pm, and there's often an 11pm/midnight curfew.

There are hundreds of official **campsites**, plenty of them easily reached by public transport. On average expect to pay 80–160kr per night for two people using a tent. The tourist board lists 400 in their free *Camping* brochure (ⓦwww.camping .no). Sites also often have **cabins** (*hytter*), usually four-bedded affairs with kitchen facilities and sometimes a bathroom, for upwards of 400kr. You can camp rough in open areas as long as you are at least 150m away from houses or cabins or otherwise have permission from the landowner.

Hotels are generally too pricey for travellers on a budget – the cheapest double room costs around 700kr. Still, there are bargains to be found, particularly during summer, when most hotels have discounts of between twenty and forty percent. **Guest houses** (*pensjonater*) in the more touristy towns are about 500kr a double; breakfast is usually extra. Tourist offices in larger towns can often fix you up with a **private room** in someone's house for around 300–350kr a double, though there's a booking fee (15–25kr) on top and rooms are frequently out of the centre.

Food and drink

Norwegian **food** can be excellent: fish is plentiful, as are reindeer steak and elk. However, eating well on a tight budget can de difficult. **Breakfast** (*frokost*) – a self-service affair of bread, cheese, eggs, preserves, cold meat and fish, washed down with unlimited tea and coffee – is usually excellent at hostels, and memorable in hotels. Almost everywhere breakfast is included in the price of a room; where it isn't, reckon on an extra 50–70kr. **Picnic** food is the best stand-by during the day, although there are **fast-food** alternatives. The indigenous Norwegian variety, served up at street stalls (*gatekjøkken*), consists mainly of rather unappetizing hot dogs (*varm pølse*), pizza slices and chicken and chips. A much better choice, and often no more expensive, is simply to get a *smørbrød*, a huge open sandwich heaped with a variety of garnishes. You'll see them in most cafés and bakeries. Good **coffee** is available everywhere and in cafeterias is usually half-price after the first cup. **Tea** is usually served with lemon – if you want milk, ask for it. The best deals for sit-down food are at **lunchtime** (*lunsj*), when self-service *kafeterias* offer a limited range of daily specials (*dagens rett*) costing 80–100kr. These include a fish or meat dish with vegetables or salad, often a drink, sometimes bread, and occasionally coffee, too. In the larger towns, you'll also find more original cafés called *kaffistovas*, which serve high-quality Norwegian food at quite reasonable prices. **Restaurants**, serving dinner (*middag*), are out of the range of most budgets – main courses average 200–220kr – but the seafood can be superb. Again, the best deals are at lunchtime, when some restaurants put out a *koldtbord* (the Norwegian *smörgåsbord*), where, for a fixed price (100–200kr), you can eat as much as you like for the three to four hours it's served. There are also a sizeable number of café/bars where a substantial main course and a couple of small beers will cost about 180kr.

Alcohol prices are among the highest in Europe. Buying from the supermarkets and Vinmonopolet (the state off-licences) is often the only way you'll afford a tipple: in a bar, **beer** costs 40kr/500ml. It comes in three strengths: class I is light, class II is what you get in supermarkets and is the most widely served in pubs, while class III is the strongest and only available at Vinmonopolet. In the cities bars stay open until at least 1am; in the smaller towns, they tend to close at around 11pm. **Wines** and **spirits** can only be purchased from Vinmonopolet – *aquavit*, served ice-cold in little glasses is, at forty percent proof, real headache stuff. There's generally at least one Vinmonopolet in each town, more in the cities; opening hours are usually Mon–Wed 10am–4/5pm, Thurs 10am–5/6pm, Fri 9am–4/6pm, Sat 9am–1/3pm.

Opening hours and holidays

Opening hours are usually Mon–Wed & Fri 9am–5pm, Thurs 9am–6/8pm, Sat 9am–1/3pm. Almost everything – including the supermarkets – is closed on Sunday, the main exceptions being newspaper kiosks (*Narvesen*) and takeaway food stalls, which stay open every evening until 10 or 11pm. Most businesses are closed on **public holidays**: Jan 1; Maundy Thurs; Good Fri; Easter Sun & Mon; May 1; Ascension Day (mid-May); May 17; Whit Sun & Mon; Dec 25 & 26.

Emergencies

Norway is safe; the people are friendly and helpful, and petty crime is unusual. The **police** are amiable and can normally speak English. Most good hotels as well as pharmacies and tourist offices have lists of local **doctors** and dentists. Norway is not in the EU, but operates reciprocal health agreements with all EU countries. This means that EU citizens get free hospital treatment with an E111. Pharmacies (*apotek*) – should they be closed – mostly carry a rota in the window advising of the nearest one that's open.

> ### Emergency numbers
>
> Police ☎112; Ambulance ☎113; Fire ☎110.

Oslo

OSLO retains a low profile among European cities. Yet the city is definitely worth seeing. It has some of Europe's best museums, fields a street life that surprises most first-time visitors, and provides lots of opportunities for outdoor pursuits, everything from swimming to skiing. Oslo is the oldest of the Scandinavian capital cities, founded around 1048 by Harald Hardrada. Several decimating fires and 600 years later, Oslo upped sticks and shifted west to its present site, abandoning its old name in favour of **Christiania** – after the seventeenth-century Danish king Christian IV responsible for the move. The new city prospered and by the time of the break with Denmark (and union with Sweden) in 1814, Christiania – indeed Norway as a whole – was clamouring for independence, something it finally achieved in 1905, though the city didn't revert to its original name for another twenty years. Today's city centre is largely the work of the late nineteenth and early twentieth centuries, an era reflected in the wide streets, dignified parks and gardens, solid buildings and long, consciously classical vistas. Its half a million inhabitants have room to spare in a city whose vast boundaries encompass forests, sand and sea.

Arrival, information and accommodation

All **trains** arrive at Oslo Sentralstasjon, known as **Oslo S**, at the eastern end of the city centre. The central **bus terminal** is handily placed a short walk to the northeast of Oslo S, beneath the Galleriet shopping centre; it handles most of the bus services within the city as well as those to and from the airport. Long-distance buses arrive and depart here too, but note that some services terminate on the south side of Oslo S at the bus stands beside Havnegata. **Ferries** arrive at either the Vippetangen quays, a fifteen-minute walk south of Oslo S, or at Hjortneskaia, some 3km west of the city centre; take bus #56 to the centre – an infrequent service, though it's mostly linked to ferry arrival times. The main **tourist office** is in the centre, behind the Rådhus at Fridtjof Nansens plass 5 (May & Sept Mon–Sat 9am–5pm; June–Aug daily 9am–7pm; Oct–April Mon–Fri 9am–5pm; ☏24 14 77 00, ⓦ www.visitoslo.com). They have a full range of information, issue free city maps, make reservations on guided tours, and operate an accommodation booking service. They also supply the excellent and very thorough *Oslo Official Guide* and *What's On in Oslo*. There's another tourist office inside Oslo S (May–Sept daily 8am–11pm; Oct–April Mon–Sat 8am–5pm) with similar services. Both offices sell the useful **Oslo Card** (190/280/370kr for one/two/three days), which gives free museum admission, discounts in shops and restaurants and free transport. Den Norske Turistforening (DNT), Storgata 3 (Mon–Fri 10am–4pm, Thurs 10am–6pm, Sat 10am–2pm; ☏22 82 28 00, ⓦ www.turistforeningen.no/codeland), sells **hiking maps** and gives general advice and information on route planning nationwide for walkers.

The city transport **Trafikanten information office** is on Jernbanetorget, the pedestrianized square outside Oslo S (Mon–Fri 7am–8pm, Sat 8am–6pm; ☏177, ⓦ www.trafikanten.no). They supply a useful free transit map and a free timetable booklet, *Rutebok for Oslo*, which details every transport schedule in the city. The **trams** run on eight lines, crossing the centre from east to west. There are also **buses** and an underground Tunnelbanen (**T-bane**), which has eight lines, all of which converge to share a common slice of track that crosses the city centre from Majorstuen in the west to Tøyen in the east. Numerous **local ferries** cross the Oslofjord to the south of the centre, connecting the city with its outlying districts and archipelagos. **Tickets** cost a flat-fare of 22kr; there's an eight-journey card (135kr) and the 24hr-travel pass (50kr) available from Trafikanten.

You're best off **staying** on or near the western reaches of Karl Johans gate, between the Stortinget and the Nationaltheatret. Many of the least expensive places are in the vicinity of Oslo S. It is always worth calling ahead to check on space, but you can cut the hassle by using the tourist office accommodation service. A good budget alternative to the hostels listed below is a **private room**, also booked by the tourist office and with a standard tariff of 170kr single, 300kr double; the supply rarely dries up, but there's often a minimum two-night stay.

Hostels

Oslo Ekeberg Vandrerhjem Kongsveien 82 ☎22 74 18 90, ©oslo.ekeberg.hostel@vandrerhjem.no. Small, simple HI hostel occupying part of a school complex 4km southeast of Oslo S. Take tram #19 or the less frequent #18 from the centre and it is 100m from the Holtet tram stop. June to mid-Aug only. Dorm beds 175kr. ❸

Oslo Haraldsheim Vandrerhjem

Haraldsheimveien 4, Grefsen ☎22 22 29 65, ⓦwww.haraldsheim.oslo.no. The best of the three HI hostels, 4km northeast of the centre, with 71 rooms, mostly in four-bed dorms, the majority en suite. Take tram #15 or #17 from the bottom of Storgata to the Sinsenkrysset stop, from where it's a signposted five- to ten-minute walk along a

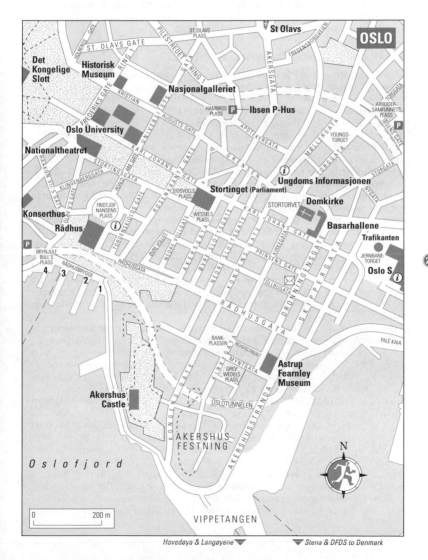

footpath. Advance booking necessary in summer. Dorm beds 170–190kr. ➍

Oslo Vandrerhjem Holtekilen Michelets vei 55, 1320 Stabekk ☎67 51 80 40, Ⓔoslo.holtekilen .hostel@vandrerhjem.no. Located 10km west of the city centre, this place has both dorm beds and one- to four-bedded rooms. Also has kitchen, laundry facilities and restaurant. From Bussterminalen, take bus #151 to the Kveldsroveien bus stop; the hostel is 100m away on the right. Dorm beds 180kr. ➍

Hotels

Bondeheimen Rosenkrantz gate 8 ☎23 21 41 00, Ⓦwww.bondeheimen.com. One of Oslo's most delightful hotels, tastefully decorated with polished pine everywhere. It's a short walk north of Karl Johans gate – and the buffet breakfast, included in the price, is excellent. ➒

City Skippergaten 19 ☎22 41 36 10, Ⓦwww.cityhotel.no. This modest but pleasant hotel, a long-time favourite with budget travellers, is located above shops and offices in a typical Oslo apartment block near Oslo S. The surroundings are a little seedy, but the hotel is cheerful enough, with small but perfectly adequate rooms. ➏

Cochs Pensjonat Parkveien 25 ☎22 33 24 00, Ⓦwww.cochs.no. Reasonable guest house with good deals on triples and quads. Mostly shared facilities. Pleasant location to the west of the royal palace. ➍

The city centre and around

Oslo's main street, **Karl Johans gate**, leads west up the slope from Oslo S train station. It begins unpromisingly with a clutter of tacky shops and hang-around junkies, but steps away at the corner of Dronningens gate is the curious **Basarhallene**, a circular building of two tiers, whose brick cloisters once housed the city's food market. The adjacent **Domkirke** (daily 10am–4pm; free) dates from the late seventeenth century, though its heavyweight tower was remodelled in 1850; plain and dour from the outside, the cathedral boasts an elegantly restored interior, its nave and transepts awash with maroon, green and gold paintwork. It's a brief stroll further up Karl Johans gate to the **Stortinget**, the parliament building, an imposing chunk of neo-Romanesque architecture that was completed in 1866. In front of the parliament, a narrow park-piazza flanks Karl Johans gate; in summer it teems with promenading city folk, while in winter people flock to its floodlit open-air skating rinks. Lurking at the western end of the park is the Neoclassical **Nationaltheatret**, built in 1899 and fronted by a stodgy statue of playwright Henrik Ibsen. Beyond, up the hill, **Det Kongelige Slott** (Royal Palace) is a mon- ument to Norwegian openness; built between 1825 and 1848, when other monar- chies were nervously counting their friends, it still stands without railings and walls, and the grounds – **Slottsparken** – are open to the public. The daily chang- ing of the guard (1.30pm) is a snappy affair, well worth a look. An equestrian stat- ue of the king who built the palace, Karl XIV Johan, stands in front of the main facade.

Back on Karl Johans Gate, the nineteenth-century buildings of the **University** fit well into this monumental end of the city centre. Among them, at Universitetsgata 13, you will find the **Nasjonalgalleriet** (Mon, Wed & Fri 10am–6pm, Thurs 10am–8pm, Sat 10am–4pm, Sun 11am–4pm, Tues closed; free; Ⓦwww.nasjonalgal- leriet.no), which boasts Norway's largest and best collection of fine art. Highlights include some wonderfully romantic, nineteenth-century landscapes by the likes of Johan Christian Dahl and Thomas Fearnley, and two rooms devoted to Edvard Munch, featuring the original version of the famous *Scream*. Heading south from the University buildings, you can't miss the monolithic brickwork of the **Rådhus** (daily 9am–4/5pm; free: guided tours June & July daily at 10am, noon & 2pm; Aug– May Mon-Fri at 10am, noon & 2pm; 30kr), the massive City Hall, opened in 1950 to celebrate the city's 900th anniversary. Few people had a good word to say about the place when it was first built, but the Rådhus has worn well, its twin towers a grandiose but somehow rather amiable statement of civic pride. The interior – best seen on one of the guided tours – celebrates all things Norwegian; the main hall or Rådhushallen is decorated with vast murals by several of the country's leading artists.

The Bygdøy peninsula

The most enjoyable way to reach the leafy **Bygdøy peninsula**, southwest of the city centre, is by **ferry**. These leave from the Rådhusbrygge (pier 3) behind the Rådhus (May–Aug every 40min Mon–Fri 7.45am–9.05pm, Sat & Sun from 9.05am; late April & Sept every 40min 9.05am–6.25pm), departing and returning to a similar schedule. They have two ports of call on the peninsula – first at the Dronningen (15min from Rådhusbrygge) and then the Bygdøynes piers (20min); note that they only go in that direction. The two most popular attractions – the Viking Ships and Folk museums – are within easy walking distance of the Dronningen pier, the others – the Kon-Tiki, the Maritime and the Fram museums – are beside Bygdøynes. If you decide to walk between the two groups of museums, allow about fifteen minutes: the route is well signposted but dull. The alternative to the ferry is **bus #30** (every 15min), which runs all year from Jernbanetorget to the Folk Museum and Viking Ships, and, when the ferry isn't running, to the other three museums as well.

The entertaining **Norsk Folkemuseum**, at Museumsveien 10 (Norwegian Folk Museum; mid-May to mid-Sept daily 10am–6pm; 70kr: mid-Sept to mid-May Mon–Fri 11am–3pm, Sat & Sun 11am–4pm; 50kr; ⓦwww.norskfolke.museum.no), combines indoor collections of furniture, china and silverware with an intriguing open-air display of reassembled period farms, houses and other buildings. From here, it's a few minutes' walk to the **Vikingskipshuset** (Viking Ships Museum; daily: May–Sept 9am–6pm; Oct–April 11am–4pm; 40kr; ⓦwww.ukm.uio.no/vikingskipsmuseet), which occupies a large hall, specially constructed to house a trio of ninth-century Viking ships, with viewing platforms to enable you to see inside the hulls. The three oak vessels were retrieved from ritual burial mounds in southern Norway towards the end of the nineteenth century, each embalmed in a subsoil of clay – hence their excellent state of preservation. The star exhibit is the **Oseberg ship**, thought to be the burial ship of a Viking chieftain's wife. Its ornately carved prow and stern rise high above the hull, where thirty oar-holes indicate the size of the crew. Treasure buried with the boat is on display at the back of the museum. Down by Bygdøynes pier, the **Kon-Tiki museet** (daily: April–May & Sept 10.30am–5pm; Oct–March 10.30am–4pm; June–Aug 9.30am–5.45pm; 35kr; ⓦwww.kon-tiki.no) displays the balsawood raft on which Thor Heyerdahl made his now legendary 1947 journey across the Pacific to prove that the first Polynesian settlers could have sailed from pre-Inca Peru. Over the road, in front of the **Frammuseet** (March–April daily 11am–3.45pm; early May & Sept daily 10am–4.45pm; mid-May to mid-June daily 9am–4.45pm; mid-June to Aug daily 9am–6.45pm; Oct daily 10am–3.45pm; Nov–Feb Mon–Fri 11am-2.45pm, Sat & Sun 11am-3.45pm; 30kr), is the *Gjøa*, the one-time sealing ship in which Roald Amundsen made the first complete sailing of the Northwest Passage in 1906. Another of Amundsen's ships, the polar vessel *Fram*, is displayed inside – this was the vessel that carried him to within striking distance of the South Pole in 1911. Complete with most of its original fittings, the interior gives a superb insight into the life and times of these early Arctic explorers. Next door, the **Sjøfartsmuseum** (Norwegian Maritime Museum; mid-May to Sept daily 10am–6pm; Oct to mid-May Mon-Wed & Fri-Sun 10.30am–4pm, Thurs 10.30am–6pm; 30kr) is held within a good-looking new building that accommodates a fairly pedestrian collection of maritime artefacts. You'll probably be more taken with the café, a handy vantage point overlooking the bay.

The Munch Museum and Vigeland Sculpture Park

Also out of the centre but without question a major attraction, the **Munch-museet**, Tøyengata 53 (June to mid-Sept daily 10am–6pm; mid-Sept to May Tues–Fri 10am–4pm, Sat & Sun 11am-5pm; 60kr; ⓦwww.munch.museum.no), is reachable by T-bane: get off at Tøyen and it's a signposted five-minute walk. Born in 1863, **Edvard Munch** is Norway's most famous painter. His lithographs and woodcuts, a dark catalogue of swirls and fog, are shown in one half of the gallery, and in the main gallery there are early paintings along with the great, signature works of the 1890s. The museum also owns no less than fifty versions of *The Scream*. On the other side of the city and reachable on tram #12 and #15 from the centre (get off at Vigelandsparken), **Frogner Park** holds one of Oslo's most striking cultural targets in the **Vigeland Sculpture Park** (free access), which commemorates another modern Norwegian artist of world renown, **Gustav Vigeland**. The open-air sculptures, which Vigeland started in 1924 and was still working on when he died in 1943, are simply fantastic. A long series of life-size figures frowning, fighting and posing lead up to the central fountain, an enormous bowl representing the burden of life, supported by straining, sinewy bronze Goliaths while, underneath water tumbles out around clusters of playing and standing figures. The 20m obelisk up on the stepped embankment behind, and the grouped granite sculptures around it, comprise the summation of the work, a writhing mass that depicts the cycle of life as Vigeland saw it. The park comes to life in summer when the city's inhabitants come out to play and enjoy the green space.

The islands of the inner Oslofjord

The archipelago of low-lying, lightly forested **islands** in the **inner Oslofjord** is the city's summer playground. Although most of the islets are cluttered with summer homes, the least populated are favourite party venues for the city's preening youth. **Ferries** to the islands leave from the Vippetangen quay, at the foot of Akershusstranda – a twenty-minute walk, or a five-minute ride on bus #60, south from Jernbanetorget. Conveniently, **Hovedøya** (ferry #92; mid-March to Sept 7.30am–7pm, every hour or 90min; Oct to mid-March 3 daily; 10min), the nearest island, is also the most interesting, its rolling hills incorporating both farmland and deciduous woods as well as the overgrown ruins of a twelfth-century Cistercian monastery. There are plenty of footpaths to wander, you can swim from the shingle beaches on the south shore, and there's a seasonal café opposite the monastery ruins. Camping is not permitted, however, as Hovedøya is a protected area – that's why there are no summer homes. The pick of the other islands is wooded **Langøyene** (ferry #94; June–Aug hourly 9am–7pm; 30min), the most southerly of the archipelago and the one with the best beaches. The H-shaped island has a **campsite**, *Langøyene Camping* (☎22 11 53 21; June to mid-Aug), and at night the ferries are full of people armed with sleeping bags and bottles, on their way to join swimming parties.

Eating, drinking and nightlife

Oslo boasts scores of **eating places**. Those carefully counting the kroner will find it easy to buy bread, fruit, snacks and sandwiches from stalls, shops and kiosks across the city centre, while fast-food joints offering hamburgers and hot dogs (*pølser*) are legion. Far more interesting are the city's **cafés**. These run the gamut from cosy family places to student haunts and ultra-fashionable hangouts, but nearly all of them serve inexpensive lunches and sometimes bargain evening meals too. **Restaurants** are more expensive and frequently rather formal, but even here it's possible to find some excellent deals, especially if you stick to pizza and pasta at one of the many Italian places. The principal open-air **market** is on Youngstorget (Mon–Sat 7am–2pm), a brief stroll north of the Domkirke along Torggata. The city centre is also dotted with **supermarkets** – Rimi is the biggest name.

Downtown Oslo has a vibrant **bar** scene, at its most frenetic on summer weekends. The busiest mainstream bars are concentrated in the side streets near the Rådhus and down along the Aker Brygge, while other popular but less assertively heterosexual bars are clustered around Universitetsgata and on Rosenkrantz gate. Karl Johans gate also weighs in with a string of bars, but the coolest places are to the east of the centre in newly fashionable Grønland and Grünerløkka. **Jazz** fans are well served, with several first-rate nightspots dotted round the city centre. The busiest **clubs** are on and around Karl Johans gate, although lately some good places have opened up in the

Grønland and Grünerløkka districts. Entry will set you back 50–100kr – though drinks prices are the same as anywhere else. Nothing gets going much before 11pm; closing times are generally 3–4am. For **entertainment listings** check *Natt & Dag*, a monthly Norwegian-language broadsheet available free from cafés, bars and shops.

Cafés and restaurants

Arakataka Mariboes gate 7. Gourmet food, especially seafood, at extremely reasonable prices. On the east side of central Oslo.

Ett Glass Karl Johans gate 33, entrance round the corner on Rosenkrantz gate. Trendy, candlelit café/bar. Imaginative inexpensive menu focuses on Mediterranean-influenced light meals and lunches and provides some curious, often mouthwatering delights.

Kaffistova Rosenkrantz gate 8. Part of the Bondeheimen hotel, this spick-and-span self-service café serves tasty, traditional Norwegian cooking at very fair prices. There's usually a vegetarian option, too.

Krishna Cuisine Kirkeveien 59B. In the middle of busy Majorstukrysset, this is the city's best vegetarian option. Closed Sat & Sun.

Sult Thv Meyers gate 26. Serves innovative dishes using seasonal ingredients, at surprisingly low prices. The attached bar *Tørst* is one of Oslo's most popular spots.

Tullins cafe Tullins gate 2. Close to the National Gallery, this fashionable spot serves light meals, snacks and coffee in the daytime and turns into a café/bar at night. Reasonably priced.

Zoolounge Kristian August gate 7B. Stylish modern café/bar with nice snack/meal options, tasty coffee and posh drinks in the evening. Hip young crowd and DJ sessions at night.

Bars and pubs

Bar Boca Thorvald Meyers gate 30. Tiny Fifties-retro bar, with the best dry Martinis in Norway. Get there early. Grünerløkka.

Cafe con Bar Brugata 11. As hip as you like, with retro interior and a long bar that can, however, make buying a drink hard work. Good atmosphere, loungy decor.

Dattera til Hagen Grønland 10. This trendy Grønland spot is a café during the day and a lively bar at night, sometimes with a DJ on the small first-floor dance-floor.

Mono Pløens gate 4 ⊛www.cafemono.no. Dark interior with plush old couches and retro 1970s fixtures and fittings. Attracts mostly students and music business types, and hosts live acts – mainly indie – several nights a week with diverse DJ sounds, too.

Savoy Bar Universitetsgata 11. With its stained-glass windows and wood-panelled walls, this small, intimate bar is an agreeably low-key spot to nurse a beer. Part of the *Savoy* hotel.

Clubs and music venues

Blå Brenneriveien 9C ⊛www.blx.no. Creative, cultural nightspot in Grünerløkka, featuring everything from live jazz and cabaret through to public debates and poetry readings. Also features some of the best DJs in town, keeping the crowd moving until 3.30am at the weekend. In summer, there's a pleasant riverside terrace and the food is pretty good too.

Herr Nilsen C.J. Hambros plass 5. Great spot for live jazz and blues.

So What? Grensen 9. Indie music on the ground floor, live acts and dance-floor in the blacker than black basement. Brings out the student club-hoppers.

Rockerfeller Music Hall Torggata 16. This former bathhouse is now one of Oslo's major concert venues, hosting well-known and up-and-coming bands – mostly rock or alternative.

Listings

Embassies and consulates Australia, Jernbanetorget 2 ⊕22 47 91 70; Canada, Wergelandveien 7 ⊕22 99 53 00; Ireland, c/o *Radisson SAS Scandinavia Hotel*, Holbergs gate 30 ⊕22 20 43 70; UK, Thomas Heftyes gate 8 ⊕23 13 27 00; USA, Drammensveien 18 ⊕22 44 85 50.

Laundry Mr Clean, Parkveien 6, entrance on Welhavens gate (daily 7am–11pm).

Pharmacy 24hr pharmacy near Oslo S – Jernbanetorgets Apotek, Jernbanetorget 4b.

Bergen and the fjords

The **fjords** are the most familiar and alluring image of Norway: huge clefts in the landscape which occur along the west coast right up to the Russian border, though the most beguiling portion lies between Bergen and Ålesund. Wild, rugged and peaceful, this part of the country elicits inordinate amounts of purple prose from tourist office handouts, and for once it's rarely overstated. In the summer, the fjords are, it's true, patrolled by a steady flotilla of cruise ships, and the hills heave with hikers, but the crowds are rarely oppressive and what little development there has been is seldom intrusive. **Bergen**, Norway's second largest city, is a handy springboard for the fjords, notably the **Flåm valley** and its inspiring mountain railway, which trundles down to the Aurlandsfjord, a tiny arm of the mighty **Sognefjord**, Norway's longest and deepest. North of the Sognefjord, there is the smaller but less stimulating **Nordfjord**, though there's superb compensation in the **Jostedalsbreen** glacier, which nudges the fjord from the east. The tiny S-shaped **Geirangerfjord**, further north again, is magnificent too – narrow, sheer and rugged – while the northernmost **Romsdalsfjord** and its many branches and inlets reach pinnacles of isolation in the **Trollstigen** mountain highway.

By rail, you can only reach Bergen and Flåm in the south and Åndalsnes in the north. For everything in between – including most of the Sognefjord, Nordfjord and the Jostedalsbreen glacier – **buses** and **ferries** together comprise a complicated but fully integrated system. It's a good idea to pick up full bus and ferry **timetables** from the local tourist office whenever you can. Catamarans and ferries are considered an extension of the train system, and holders of rail passes often qualify for fifty-percent discounts.

Bergen

Although it's one of the rainiest places in rainy Norway, **BERGEN** does benefit from a spectacular setting among seven hills and is one of the country's most enjoyable cities. There's plenty to see, from fine old buildings to a series of good museums, and Bergen is also within easy reach of some of Norway's most spectacular scenic attractions, both around the city and further north. Founded in 1070, the city was the largest and most important town in medieval Norway, a regular residence of the country's kings and queens, and later a Hanseatic port and religious centre, though precious little of that era survives today. Nowadays, the city centre divides into two main parts: the wharf area, **Bryggen**, adjacent to the Bergenhus fortress, once the working centre of the Hanseatic merchants and now the oldest part of Bergen; and the **modern centre**, which stretches inland from the head of the harbour and down along the Nordnes peninsula, taking in the best of Bergen's museums, cafés and bars.

The obvious place to start a visit is the **Torget**, an appealing harbourside plaza that's home to a colourful fish- and fresh-produce market. From here, it's a short stroll round to the **Bryggen**, where a string of distinctive wooden buildings line up along the waterfront. These once housed the city's merchants and now hold a string of shops, restaurants and bars. Although none of these structures was actually built by the Hanseatic Germans – most of the originals were destroyed by fire in 1702 – they carefully follow the original building line. Among them, the **Hanseatic Museum** (June–Aug daily 9am–5pm; Sept–May daily 11am–2pm; 40kr) is the most diverting, an early eighteenth-century merchant's dwelling kitted out in late-Hansa style. Also worth visiting is the **Bryggens Museum** (May–Aug daily 10am–5pm; Sept–April Mon–Fri 11am–3pm, Sat noon–3pm, Sun noon–4pm; 30kr), just along the harbourfront, where a series of imaginative exhibitions attempts a complete reassembly of local medieval life – from domestic implements, handicrafts and maritime objects through to trading items. These are all set in context by a set of twelfth-century foundations, which were unearthed during the first archaeological dig here in the 1950s. A few steps from the museum, slender **Øvregaten** has long marked the boundary of the Bryggen. By walking along its length you'll soon reach the terminal of the **Fløibanen**, a dinky funicular railway (May–Aug Mon–Fri 7.30am–midnight, Sat 8am–midnight, Sun 9am–midnight;

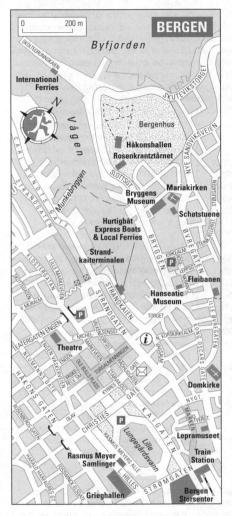

BERGEN

0 — 200 m

Byfjorden

SKOLTEGRUNNSKAIEN

International Ferries

Vågen

SKUTEVIKSTORGET

Bergenhus

Håkonshallen
Rosenkrantztårnet

NYE SANDVIKSVEIEN

CARL SUNDTS GATE

SLOTTSGT

Munkebryggen

Mariakirken

Bryggens Museum

Schøtstuene

STØLEGATEN

ØVREGATEN

STEINKJELLER

Hurtigbåt Express Boats & Local Ferries

BRYGGEN

Strand-kaiterminalen

KIRKEALM

LEPPSGT

STRANDGATEN

LILLE MARKEVEIEN

KLOSTERGATEN

Fløibanen

Hanseatic Museum

TORGET

LILLE ØVREGATEN

V MURALM

STRANDKAIEN

VÅGSALM

KONG OSCARS GATE

TEATERGATEN

ENGEN

ENGEN

VASKERELVEN

C. MICHEL

MARKEVEIEN

SENSGT

N. KORSKIRKEALM

VAAGSMG

Theatre

OLE BULLS PLASS

TORGALMENNINGEN

RÅDHUSGT

NEUMANNS GATE

VASKE RELV. SM.

KYRRE GATE

STRØMG

KAIGATEN

Domkirke

NYGT

HÅKONS GATE

ROSENBERGSGATEN

OLAV

CHRISTIES

RASMUS MEYERS ALLE

K A I G A T E N

VEVERG.

 MARKEN

NYGATEN

Lepramuseet

Rasmus Meyer Samlinger

Lille Lungegårdsvann

Train Station

HARALD HÅRFAGRES GT

FOSSVINCKELSG ATE

HILLES

STRØMGATEN

Grieghallen

Bergen Storsenter

Sept–April Mon–Fri 7.30am–11pm, Sat 8am–11pm, Sun 9am–11pm; departures every 30 min; return fare 50kr), which runs up to the top of 320m Mount Fløyen, from where there are panoramic views over the city. About five minutes' walk from the funicular, in the modern centre, Bergen's four main **art museums** are on the south side of a pleasant, artificial lake. The pick of these is the **Rasmus Meyer Samlinger**, Rasmus Meyers Allé 7 (mid-May to mid-Sept daily 11am–5pm; mid-Sept to mid-May Tues–Sun 11am–5pm; 50kr), which holds an extensive collection of Norwegian painting, including several works by Edvard Munch.

Practicalities

Bergen is a busy international port and may well be your first stop in Norway. **International ferries** arrive at Skoltegrunnskaien, the quay just beyond Bergenhus fortress, on the east side of the harbour; **domestic ferries** line up on the opposite side of the harbour at the Strandkaiterminalen. The **train** and **bus stations** face Strømgaten, a five-minute walk east of the head of the harbour. The **airport**, 20km south of the city, is connected to the bus station by regular *flybussen* (Mon–Fri & Sun 5am–9pm, Sat 5am–4pm, every 15–20min; 45min; 60kr). The city is also the southern terminus of the **Hurtigrute coastal boat**, which leaves from the Frieleneskaien quay behind the university, about 1.5km south of the train station. The **tourist office** is a few metres from the head of the harbour at Vågsallmenning 1 (May & Sept daily 9am–8pm; June–Aug daily 8.30am–10pm; Oct–April Mon–Sat 9am–4pm; ☎55 55 20 00; ⊛www.visitbergen.com). It issues free copies of the *Bergen Guide*, an exhaustive consumer's guide to the city, and also sells the **Bergen Card** (165kr/day, 245kr/two days), which allows travel on all the city's buses and free entrance to, or discounts on, most of the city's sights, including sightseeing trips. Flat-rate fare on public transport is otherwise 20kr per journey.

Accommodation is no great problem. As well as the places listed below, there are plenty of **private rooms** (➍) available; book through the tourist office. Bergen has a good supply of first-rate **restaurants** concentrated in the Bryggen, with seafood a particular speciality. Less expensive – and more fashionable – are the city's café/restaurants, which often double up as lively **bars**. Several of the best are located to the southwest of Ole Bulls plass, the main pedestrianized square, just a couple of minutes' walk from the head of the harbour. The largest annual event is the **Bergen International Festival** (ⓦwww.festspillene.no), which presents an extensive programme of music, ballet, folklore and drama. The festival lasts for twelve days at the end of May, and is supplemented by **Nattjazz** (ⓦwww.nattjazz.no), a prestigious international jazz festival held at the same time in the city's contemporary arts centre, the Kulturhuset USF, down on Georgernes Verft on the Nordnes peninsula (ⓦwww.kulturhuset-usf.no).

Hostels

Bergen Vandrerhjem YMCA Nedre Korskirkealmenning 4 ☎55 60 60 55, ⓔbergen.ymca.hostel@vandrerhjem.no. Close to Torget, a five- to ten-minute walk from the train station. HI hostel with 175 beds – dorms, singles and doubles - but fills quickly. Facilities include showers, kitchen and laundry. Closed mid-Sept to April. Dorm beds 100kr. ❸

Bergen Vandrerhjem Montana Johan Blyttsveien 30, Landås ☎55 20 80 70, ⓦwww.montana.no. This large and comfortable hostel occupies lodge-like premises in the hills 6km east of the centre, with good views over the city. Bus #31 from Nygaten. Dorms 185kr. ❹

Intermission Kalfarveien 8 ☎55 30 04 00. Trim Christian-run hostel close to the train station. Closed mid-Aug to mid-June. Dorm beds 100kr.

Guest houses and hotels

Crowded House Travel Lodge Håkonsgaten 27 ☎55 90 72 00, ⓦwww.crowded-house.com. Lively, appealing place with bright and airy, if spartan, bedrooms. Self-catering facilities too. Halfway along traffic-clogged Håkonsgaten, five minutes' walk from the city centre. ❹

Golden Tulip Rainbow Hotel Rosenkrantz Rosenkrantzgaten 7 ☎55 30 14 00, ⓦwww

.rainbow-hotels.no. Efficient mid-range hotel in an old building just behind the Bryggen with very comfortable rooms and discounts in the summer. ❾

Skansen Pensjonat Vetrlidsallmenningen 29 ☎55 31 90 80, ⓔmail@skansen-pensjonat.no. Simple little place in a nineteenth-century stone house of elegant proportions just above – and up the steps from – the Fløibanen terminus, near Torget. Has eight rooms, one en suite. ❹

Cafés, restaurants and bars

Bryggeloftet & Stuene Bryggen 11. Slightly staid and expensive restaurant, but it does serve the best and widest range of seafood in town.

Café Opera Engen 24. White wooden building near Ole Bulls plass, bustling with a fashionable crew drinking beer and good coffee. Tasty, filling snacks including some good veggie options. Crowded club-like venue in the evening.

Kafe Kippers Kulturhuset USF, Georgernes verft. Ultra groovy café/bar in an imaginatively recycled old herring factory, with delicious, inexpensive food and a prime seashore location; the terrace is *the* place to be on sunny summer days.

Naboen Restaurant Neumannsgate 20. Excellent, moderately priced meals at this easy-going restaurant, which features Swedish specialities. A student favourite.

Listings

Exchange The main post office offers competitive exchange rates for foreign currency and travellers' cheques, with longer opening hours (Mon–Fri 8am–6pm & Sat 9am–3pm) than those of banks. The tourist office will also change foreign currency and travellers' cheques but their rates are poor, as are rates at the city's big hotels. There are ATMs dotted all over the city centre.

Hiking The DNT-affiliated Bergen Turlag, Tverrgaten 4–6 (Mon–Wed & Fri 10am–4pm, Thurs 10am–6pm; ☎55 32 22 30), can advise on hiking trails in the region and sells hiking maps.

Internet and email The *Cyberhouse Internet Café*, just below the funicular at Vetrlidsalmenning 30 (ⓦwww.cyberhouse.no), open daily until late, charges 20kr for 30min.

Laundry Jarlens Vaskoteque, Lille Øvregate 17, near the funicular.

Pharmacy Apoteket Nordstjernen, at the bus station (Mon–Sat 8am–midnight, Sun 9.30am–midnight).

Post office On Olav Kyrres gate, corner Rådhusgaten (Mon–Fri 8am–6pm, Sat 9am–3pm).

Around Bergen

There is more to Bergen than the city centre, not least a number of sights just outside the city limits, most notably Edvard Grieg's old lakeside home, **Troldhaugen**, which is – along with several other sights – readily reached on the special "**Attractions**" **bus** from outside the tourist office (hourly June–Aug daily 10am–5pm); a day-long, hop-on, hop-off ticket costs 40kr. Further out, but still within day-tripping distance, are some of the fjords. If you're not journeying through the fjord region – the better option – you can get a taste by taking the train to Myrdal, at the head of the remarkable branch line down the valley to **Flåm** and the **Aurlandsfjord** – one of the most popular of all fjord trips. Pick up transport timetables from the tourist office or at the train station before you set out.

Troldhaugen

Troldhaugen (Hill of the Trolls; May–Sept daily 9am–6pm; Oct & Nov Mon–Fri 10am–2pm, Sat & Sun noon–4pm; mid-Jan to April Mon–Fri 10am–2pm; 50kr) was Edvard Grieg's home for the last 22 years of his life. A visit begins at the **museum** where Grieg's life and times are exhaustively chronicled. The **house** itself is a pleasant and unassuming villa built in 1885, and still much as Grieg left it, with a jumble of photos, manuscripts and period furniture; the obligatory guided tour is very entertaining. Grieg didn't, in fact, compose much at home, but preferred to walk round to a tiny **hut** he had built just along the shore. The hut survives beside a modern concert hall, the **Troldsalen**, where there are Grieg recitals from late June through to October: tickets for these, which include transport, are available from Bergen tourist office. To get there by public transport, either take the "Attractions" bus (see above) or any bus from platforms 19, 20 or 21 at the city bus station. Thereafter, get off at the Hopsbroen stop, walk back along the road for about 200m and then turn left up Troldhaugsveien for a stiff twenty-minute walk.

Flåm

If you're short on time, but want to sample a goodly slice of fjord scenery, then make the train journey east from Bergen, through Voss, to **Myrdal**, a lonely railway junction, from where specially built trains squeak down a branch line that plummets 900m into the **Flåm valley**. The track took four years to lay and is one of the steepest anywhere in the world, making a wonderously dramatic journey. With a little more time, you might also consider the "Norway in a Nutshell" trip, which, as well as the magnificent train ride, includes a cruise on two of the narrowest "arms" of the Sognefjord from Flåm to Gudvangen and the spectacular bus ride from Gudvangen back to Voss and Bergen. The round-trip takes seven hours from Bergen and costs 630kr (420kr from Voss); tickets can be bought at any train station. **FLÅM village**, the train's destination, lies alongside meadows and orchards on the Aurlandsfjord, a matchstick-thin branch of the Sognefjord. Hikers can get off the train at **Berekvam** station, the halfway point, and stroll down the winding country road from there. Flåm is a tiny village that can be packed with tourists on summer days, but out of season – or on summer evening, when the day-trippers have gone – it can be a pleasantly restful place. There are two good places **to stay**: the homely *Heimly Pensjonat* (☎57 63 23 00, ⓦ www.heimly.no; ⑥), which provides simple but adequate lodgings in a modern block about 450m along the shore from the train station; and the excellent *Flåm Camping* (☎57 63 21 21, ⓔ flaam.hostel@vandrerhjem.no; closed Oct–April), a combined **campsite** and **hostel** (dorms 115kr; ❸) 200m from the train station. The **tourist office** is at the ferry dock (May, June & Sept daily 8.30am–3.30pm & 4-8pm; July–Aug daily 8.30am–8pm; ☎57 63 21 06), by the train station, and has information on local hikes.

The Sognefjord and the Jostedalsbreen glacier

With the exception of Flåm, the southern shore of the **Sognefjord** remains sparsely populated and relatively inaccessible, whereas the north shore boasts a couple of very appealing places. Top-of-the-list **BALESTRAND** is the prettiest base, a tourist destination since the mid-nineteenth century when it was discovered by

20

European travellers in search of cool, clear air and mountain scenery. Buses (and express boats from Bergen and Flåm) arrive at the minuscule harbourfront, near which you'll find the **tourist office** (early June & late Aug to Sept Mon–Fri 7.30am–1pm & 3.30–6pm, Sat 7.30am–1pm & 3.30–6.30pm & Sun 8am–12.30pm & 3.30–5.30pm; late June to late Aug Mon–Fri 7.30am–1pm & 3.30–9pm, Sat 7.30am–1pm & 3.30–6.30pm & Sun 8am–12.30pm & 3.30–6.30pm; Oct–May Mon–Fri 9am–3pm; ☎57 69 12 55, ⊕www.sognefjorden.no). The comfortable and very appealing *Kringsjå Hotel*, 100m from the tourist office, incorporates the local **HI hostel** (☎57 69 13 03; ⊕balestrand.hostel@vandrerhjem.no; hotel ❻, hostel ❹, dorms 180kr; late June to mid-Aug only). Another good choice is the relaxing *Midtnes Pensjonat* (☎57 69 11 33, ⊕www.midtnes.no; ❻), about 300m from the dock behind the little wooden church.

There's not too much to see in Balestrand itself, but several lovely places are within in easy striking distance, particularly the delightful village of **MUNDAL**, on the Fjærlandsfjord. Mundal can be reached direct by ferry from Balestrand from late May to early September (2 daily; 1hr 25min; passengers 140kr; car & driver 245kr), and by bus throughout the rest of the year (change at Sogndal). Formerly one of the most isolated spots on the Sognefjord, Mundal is now connected to the road system, but it retains its old-fashioned atmosphere and appearance, with a string of handsome clapboard buildings in a wildly beautiful location. Mundal is also Norway's self-styled book town, and there are various **literature events** held here in the summer (⊕www.bokbyen.no or ⊕www.booktown.net). Mundal's **tourist office** is in the centre of the village metres from the ferry dock (late May to early Sept daily 9.30am–5.30pm; ☎57 69 32 33). **Accommodation** is limited. Choose from the splendid *Hotel Mundal* (☎57 69 31 01, ⊕www.fjordinfo.no/mundal; ❾; closed Oct–April), a quirky, old-fashioned sort of place, and the *Fjærland Fjordstue Hotell* (☎57 69 32 00, ⊕www.home.sol.no; ❻), a well-tended family hotel with smart modern furnishings. A third option is *Bøyum Camping* (☎57 69 32 52) on the edge of the village near the Bremuseum (glacier museum); they have huts (❸) as well as spaces for tents. Both hotels offer good, wholesome food. Mundal's other advantage is its proximity to the southern edge of the **Jostedalsbreen glacier**, a vast ice plateau that dominates the whole of the inner Nordfjord region – Nordfjord being the next fjord system to the north. The glacier's 24 arms – or nodules – melt down into the nearby valleys, giving the local rivers and glacial lakes their distinctive blue-green colouring. In 1991, the glacier was placed within the **Jostedalsbreen Nasjonalpark** in order to co-ordinate its conservation. The main benefit of this for tourists has been to provide **guided glacier walks** (May–Sept; from around 250kr) on its various arms, ranging from two-hour excursions to all-day, fully equipped hikes. Equipment is provided, though you'll need good boots, warm clothes, gloves and hat, sunglasses and (usually) your own food and drink. One of the many places that takes bookings is the Mundal tourist office; glacier walks booked here mostly start at the Øygarden car park, about 7km from Mundal – transport from the village is included. If all this sounds too strenuous (and expensive), you can reach an arm of the glacier under your own steam – and without too much sweat – by strolling north from Mundal on Highway 5; about 10km north of the village, just before the tunnel, a signed side road leads the 200m to the **Bøyabreen** glacier arm; note, however, that you're not allowed to walk on it – gawpers only.

The Geirangerfjord

On the north side of the Jostedalsbreen glacier is the **Nordfjord**, but this fjord system does not have the scenic lustre of its more famous neighbours and you're much better off pressing on to the S-shaped **Geirangerfjord**, one of the region's smallest and most breathtaking fjords. A convoluted branch of the Storfjord, it cuts well inland, marked by impressive waterfalls and with a village at either end of its snake-like profile. You can reach the Geirangerfjord in dramatic style by bus from the north or south, but you'd do best to approach from the north if you can. From this direction, the journey begins in Åndalsnes (see below), from where Highway 63 wriggles over the mountains via the wonderful **Trollstigen Highway**, which climbs through some of the country's highest peaks before sweeping down to the tiny Norddalsfjord. From here, it's a quick ferry ride and dramatic journey along the Ørnevegen, the Eagle's Highway, for a first view of the Geirangerfjord and the village that bears its name glinting in the distance. There is little as stunning anywhere in western Norway, and from mid-June to August it can all be seen on a twice-daily bus following this so-called "Golden Route". **GEIRANGER** village enjoys a commanding position at one end of the fjord. However, it's hopelessly overdeveloped and your best bet, especially in high season, is to pass straight through, taking the ferry on to the hamlet of **HELLESYLT**, an hour's boat ride away through the double bend of the fjord. There's nothing much to the place, but by nightfall Hellesylt makes for a quiet and peaceful **overnight stay**. The ferry terminal is a few steps from the *Grand Hotel* (℡70 26 51 00; ⊛www.grand-hotelhellesylt .no; ❻), a local landmark since its construction in 1871, though patchily renovated and enlarged – guests are put up in the modern annexe next door. The hotel's main competitor is the **HI hostel** (℡70 26 51 28; dorm beds ❷, doubles ❸; closed Sept–May), set on the hillside just above the village – just follow the signs. Alternatively, *Hellesylt Camping* (℡70 26 51 88) occupies the shadeless field beside the fjord about 400m from the quay. Usefully, Hellesylt is also on the main Bergen to Loen, Stryn and Ålesund bus route; **buses** stop near the jetty.

Åndalsnes and Ålesund

Travelling north from Oslo by train, the line forks at Dombås – the Dovre line continuing northwards over the fells to Trondheim (see p.698), the Rauma line beginning a thrilling, roller-coaster rattle west down through the mountains to the **Isfjord** at Åndalsnes (1hr 30min). Apart from the Aurlandsfjord, an arm of the Sognefjord, reached from Bergen, the Isfjord is the only Norwegian fjord accessible by train, which explains the number of backpackers wandering its principal town of **ÅNDALSNES**, many people's first – sometimes only – contact with fjord country. Despite a wonderful setting between lofty peaks and looking-glass water, the town is unexciting, but it does make a convenient base for further explorations. Åndalsnes has an outstanding **HI hostel** (℡71 22 13 82; ⓔaandalsnes.hostel@vandrerhjem.no; dorm beds ❷, doubles ❹; closed mid-Sept to late May), which occupies a group of charming wooden buildings in a rural setting 2.5km along the E136 towards Ålesund. Another very good option is the riverside *Åndalsnes Camping og Motell* (℡71 22 16 29), with cabins (❹), rowboats and bikes for rent, a 25-minute walk from the train station – take the first left after the river on the road out to the hostel. The **tourist office** is at the train station (late June to Aug Mon–Sat 10am–7pm, Sun 1–7pm; Sept to late June Mon–Fri 9am–5pm; ℡71 22 16 22; ⊛www.andalsnes .net), and has a free and comprehensive guide to local hikes as well as bus, boat and train timetables.

At the end of the E136, some 120km west of Åndalsnes, the fishing and ferry port of **ÅLESUND** is immediately – and obviously – different from any other Norwegian town. In 1904, a disastrous fire left 10,000 people homeless and the town centre destroyed. A hectic reconstruction programme saw almost the entire area speedily rebuilt in a style that borrowed heavily from the German Jugendstil movement. Kaiser Wilhelm II, who used to holiday hereabouts, gave assistance, and the architects ended up creating a strange but fetching hybrid of up-to-date foreign influences and folksy local elements, with dragons, faces, flowers and even a decorative pharaoh or two. The finest buildings are concentrated on the main street, **Kongensgate**, and around the slender, central harbour, the **Brosundet**. Ålesund **bus station** is situated on the waterfront a few metres south of the Brosundet and across from the **tourist office** in the Rådhus (June–Aug Mon–Fri 8.30am–7pm, Sat 9am–5pm, Sun 11am–5pm; Sept–May Mon–Fri 8.30am–4pm; ℡70 15 76 00,

@www.visitalesund.com). The pick of the town's **hotels** are the *Comfort Home Hotel Bryggen*, an elegantly converted waterside warehouse at Apotekergata 1 (⌀70 12 64 00; @www.bryggen-hotel.no; ❾), and the similar *Brosundet Gjestehus* along the street at no. 5 (⌀70 12 10 00, @www.brosundet.no; ❽). There's also a small and central **HI hostel** at Parkgata 14, at the top of Rådstuggata (⌀70 11 58 30, @aalesund.hostel@vandrerhjem.no; dorm beds ❷, doubles ❹; closed Oct–April). For **eating**, the *Sjøbua Fiskerestaurant*, Brunholmgata 1, is an expensive but first-rate seafood restaurant, which comes complete with its own lobster tank. A cheaper if much more mundane option is *Metz*, a café/restaurant overlooking the Brosundet; everyone flocks to its terrace in fine weather.

Northern Norway

The long, thin counties of **Trøndelag** and **Nordland** mark the transition from rural southern to blustery northern Norway. The main town of Trøndelag, appealing **Trondheim**, is easily accessible from Oslo by train, but north of here travelling becomes more of a slog as the distances between places grow ever greater. In **Nordland** things get wilder still, though save the scenery there's little of interest until you reach the steel town of **Mo-i-Rana**. Just north of here lies the **Arctic Circle**, beyond which the land becomes ever more spectacular, not least on the offshore chain of the **Lofoten Islands**, whose idyllic fishing villages (and cheap accommodation) richly merit a stop. Back on the mainland, **Narvik** is a modern port handling vast quantities of iron-ore amid some startling rocky surroundings. Further north still, the provinces of **Troms** and **Finnmark** are subtle in their appeal, but the travelling can be harder still, with **Tromsø**, a lively urban centre and university town, making the obvious stopping point. As for Finnmark, most visitors head straight for **Nordkapp**, from where the Midnight Sun is visible between early May and the end of July.

The **train** network reaches as far north as Fauske and Bodø, buses making the link to Narvik, from where a separate rail line runs to the border and then south through Sweden. Further north, access is either by the **Hurtigrute coastal boat** or bus. The boat takes just over two days to sail from Trondheim to Tromsø, two more to circumnavigate the huge fjords between Tromsø and Kirkenes, hard by the Russian border. Bus transport throughout the summer (and some of the winter) is efficient and regular, using the windswept E6 Arctic Highway as far as Kirkenes, with the E69 branching off to Nordkapp on the way.

Trondheim

TRONDHEIM, an atmospheric city with much of its eighteenth-century centre still intact, has been an important Norwegian power base for centuries, its success guaranteed by the excellence of its harbour and its position at the head of a wide and fertile valley. The early Norse parliament, or Ting, met here, and the city was once a major pilgrimage centre. The city centre sits on a small triangle of land, a pocket-sized area where the main sights – bar the marvellous cathedral – have an amiable low-key quality. Trondheim also possesses a clutch of good restaurants and a string of busy bars.

The colossal **Nidaros Domkirke**, Scandinavia's largest medieval building, gloriously restored following the ravages of the Reformation and several fires, remains the focal point of the city centre (May to mid-June & late Aug to mid-Sept Mon–Fri 9am–3pm, Sat 9am–2pm, Sun 1–4pm; late June to late Aug Mon–Fri 9am–6pm, Sat 9am–2pm, Sun 1–4pm; mid-Sept to April Mon–Fri noon–2.30pm, Sat 11.30am–2pm, Sun 1–3pm; 35kr). Taking Trondheim's former name (Nidaros means "mouth of the River Nid"), the cathedral is dedicated to King Olav, Norway's first Christian ruler, who was killed at the nearby battle of Stiklestad in 1030. After the battle, Olav's body was spirited away and buried here, his resting place marked by the erection of a chapel, which was altered and enlarged over the years to accommodate the growing bands of pilgrims, achieving cathedral status in 1152. Thereafter, it became the traditional burial place of Norwegian royalty and, since 1814, it has also been the place where Norwegian monarchs are crowned. The stonework of the early Gothic choir is especially fine, with the flying buttresses and pointed arches decorated with all manner of tiny heads and gargoyles. Inside, the gloomy half-light hides much of the lofty decorative work, but it is possible to examine the striking choir screen and font, both the work of the Norwegian sculptor Gustav Vigeland (1869–1943). If possible, visit in the early morning to avoid the tour-bus crowds. Behind the Domkirke lies the heavily restored archbishop's palace, the **Erkebispegården**, a courtyard complex flanked by stone and brick wings of medieval provenance. The archbishops were kicked out during the Reformation and the palace was subsequently used as the city armoury. Some of the old weapons are now displayed in the west wing, which has been turned into the **Army and Resistance Museum** (March–Nov Sat & Sun 11am–4pm; June–Aug also Mon–Fri 9am–3pm; free). Its most interesting section, on the top floor, recalls the German occupation during World War II, dealing honestly with the sensitive issue of collaboration. Near at hand is **Torvet**, the main city square, a spacious open area anchored by a statue of Olav Tryggvason, perched on a stone pillar like some medieval Nelson. The broad and pleasant avenues of Trondheim's centre radiate out from here; they date from the late seventeenth century, when they doubled as fire breaks. They were originally flanked by long rows of wooden buildings, now mostly replaced by uninspiring modern structures. One conspicuous survivor is the **Stiftsgården** (guided tours hourly on the hour till 1hr before closing: early to mid-June Mon–Sat 10am–3pm, Sun noon–5pm; late June to late Aug Mon–Sat 10am–5pm, Sun noon–5pm; 50kr), the yellow creation just north of Torvet on Munkegata. Built in 1774–1778 as the home of a provincial governor, it's now an official royal residence.

Practicalities

Trondheim is the first major northbound stop of the Bergen–Kirkenes **Hurtigrute coastal boat**, which docks about 600m behind and to the north of **Sentralstasjon**, the combined **bus and train terminal**. Sentralstasjon is situated just over the bridge from the town centre, which occupies a small island at the mouth of the River Nid. The **tourist office** is bang in the middle of town on the main square, the Torvet (mid-May to early June & late Aug Mon–Fri 8.30am–6pm, Sat & Sun 10am–4pm; mid- to late June & mid-Aug Mon–Fri 8.30am–8pm, Sat & Sun 10am–6pm; early Aug Mon–Fri 8.30am–10pm, Sat & Sun 10am–8pm; Sept to mid-May Mon–Fri 9am–4pm; ☎73 80 76 60, ⊛www.trondheim.com). They can book **private rooms** at a fixed rate of 400–440kr per double (250–320kr single), plus a 20kr booking fee and a 30kr deposit. Alternatively, there's a large and well-equipped **HI hostel** at Weidemannsvei 41 (☎73 87 44 50, ⊛www.trondheim-vandrerhjem .no; dorm beds ❷, doubles ❺), a steep twenty minutes' hike east from the centre out over the Bakkebru bridge. More convenient alternatives include *Pensjonat Jarlen*, Kongensgate 40 (☎73 51 32 18; ❹), with frugal rooms at bargain prices, and the *Tulip Inn Rainbow Trondheim*, Kongensgate 15 (☎73 50 50 50, ⊛www.rainbow-hotels .no;❼), a big and popular **hotel** offering well-maintained modern double rooms at reasonable rates. The city centre is best seen on foot, but if you're staying on the edge of town, take advantage of the brightly coloured **municipal bicycles** that are available from bike racks all over the centre; they are free, but you need 20kr to unlock them – as per a supermarket trolley. For **eating**, the cafés and restaurants in the area of Bakklandet are a good choice. Try the *Dromedar*, Nedre Bakklandet 3, a fashionable café/bar offering tasty snacks and meals with a wholefood slant, or *Credo*, Ørjaveita 4, which has a very good ground-floor restaurant serving innovative seasonal food, and a bar above. The town has an active **nightlife**; one good place to be is *Brukbar* Munkegata 26, a lively bar catering for everyone from business folk dropping in after work, to hardcore student boozers.

The Arctic Circle, Mo-i-Rana and Bodø

North of Trondheim, it's a long haul up the coast to the next major places of interest: Bodø, which is the main ferry port for the Lofoten Islands, and the gritty but likeable town of Narvik, respectively 730km and 908km away. You can cover most of the ground by train, a rattling good journey with the scenery becoming wilder and bleaker the further north you go. Departing Trondheim, it takes nine hours to reach Fauske, where the railway reaches its northern limit and turns west for the final 65km dash across to Bodø. On the way you cross the **Arctic Circle**, which, considering the amount of effort it takes to get there, is something of an anticlimax. The landscape, uninhabited for the most part, is, undeniably impressive – bare and bleak – but the gleaming **Polarsirkelsenteret** (Arctic Circle Centre; daily: May to early June & Aug 9am–8pm, late June to July 8am–10pm & early Sept 10am–6pm; ⍟www.polarsirkelsenteret.no) disfigures the scene – a giant lampshade of a building plonked by the E6 highway and stuffed with every sort of tourist bauble imaginable, from "Polarsirkelen" certificates to specially stamped postcards. If you don't fancy making the long journey between Trondheim and Bodø in one hop, stop at **MO-I-RANA**, or simply "Mo", just south of the Arctic Circle. Formerly a grimy steel town, Mo has recently cleaned itself up and its leafy centre holds a pretty eighteenth-century church with a dinky onion dome. Mo has an excellent **hotel**, the *Meyergården* (⍟75 13 40 00, ⍟www.meyergarden.no; ❽), an extremely comfortable establishment on Ole Tobias Olsensgate, about 300m from the train station. For the adventurous, there are two great options for cave-walking here – one fairly straightforward tour to Grønligrotta and a more advanced trip into Setergrotta. Information on these tours is available from the **tourist office**, about 300m from the bus and train stations, also on Ole Tobias Olsens gate (mid-June to mid-Aug Mon–Fri 9am–8pm, Sat 9am–4pm & Sun 1–7pm; mid-Aug to mid-June Mon–Fri 9am–4pm; ⍟75 13 92 00, ⍟www.arctic-circle.no).

Further north, **FAUSKE** is, along with Bodø, an important transport hub and one of the departure points of the Nord-Norgeekspressen bus service that complements the trains by carrying passengers as far as Alta. These buses leave one to three times daily from beside Fauske train station, and tickets are purchased from the driver. There's a fifty-percent discount for InterRail and ScanRail pass holders on the first step of the route, to Narvik, a gorgeous five-hour run past fjords and snowy peaks. In Fauske, Storgata – also the E6 – accommodates the handful of shops that pass for a town centre. It's actually much better to stay in Bodø (see below), but Fauske does have a couple of useful **accommodation** options. At Storgata 82, you'll find the modern *Fauske Hotel* (⍟75 60 20 00, ⍟firmapost@fauskehotell.no; ❽), and there's also the *Lundhøgda* **campsite** (⍟75 64 39 66, ⍟lundhogda@c2i.net; May-Sept; cabins ❸), in a splendid location about 3km west of the town centre along the E80, overlooking the mountains and the fjord. In both cases, advance booking is advised.

An hour west of Fauske, **BODØ** is where trains terminate. It's also a stop on the Hurtigrute coastal-boat route and the main port of departure for the Lofoten Islands. Bodø **train station** is midway between the Lofoten Island (Moskenes, Værøy and Røst) and Hurtigrute **ferry docks**, respectively 500m and 700m to the northeast, and the Sentrumsterminalen, at Sjøgata 3, which is home to the **bus station**. The Sentrumsterminalen also holds the **catamaran** (*Hurtigbåt*) quay for Svolvær, on the Lofoten, and Bodø **tourist office** (June–Aug Mon–Fri 9am–8pm, Sat 10am–8pm, Sun noon–8pm; Sept–May Mon–Wed & Fri 9am–4pm, Thurs 9am–6pm, Sat 10am–3pm; ⍟75 54 80 00, ⍟www.bodoe.com). If you're heading further north, note that the same half-price bus deal for rail pass holders travelling from Fauske to Narvik operates from Bodø to Narvik. Bodø offers plenty of choice of **accommodation**. The tourist office has a small supply of **private rooms** both in the town and its environs (❸) and there's a no-frills **HI hostel** next door to the train station at Sjøgata 55 (⍟75 52 11 22, ⍟bodo.hostel@vandrerhjem.no; dorm beds 150kr, ❸; closed Oct–April). Among several central hotels, the pick is the *Comfort Home Hotel Grand*, at Storgata 3 (☎75 54 61 00, 🕸www.grand-bodo.no; ❾), whose handsome public rooms boast elegant Art Deco flourishes. There are one or two competent **cafés** and **restaurants**, kicking off with the traditional and inexpensive *Løvolds Kafé* (closed Sun), down by the quay at Tollbugata 9: its Norwegian menu features local ingredients, with main courses averaging around 100kr. More upmarket, the first-rate, waterfront *Molostua Fiskerestaurant og Kafé*, Moloveien 9, is a café in the daytime and restaurant at night, serving tasty seafood and classic Norwegian dishes jazzed up with French-style sauces.

The Lofoten Islands

Stretched out in a skeletal curve across the Norwegian Sea, the **Lofoten Islands** are perfect for a simple, uncluttered few days. For somewhere so far north the weather is exceptionally mild, and there's plentiful **accommodation** (🕸www.lofoten-tourist .no; from 450kr) in *rorbuer*, originally fishermen's shacks, but now usually well-equipped huts designed to accommodate from two to six people. In addition, the Lofotens have five hostels and plentiful campsites. The **Hurtigrute coastal boat** calls at two ports, Stamsund and Svolvær, while the southern Lofoten ferry leaves Bodø for Moskenes, Værøy and Røst. There are also **passenger express boats**, which work out slightly cheaper than the Hurtigrute, linking both Bodø and Narvik with Svolvær. By **bus** the main long-distance services from the mainland to the Lofotens are from Bodø to Svolvær via Fauske and from Narvik to Svolvær.

The main town on **Austvågøy**, the largest and northernmost island of the group, is **SVOLVÆR**, a rather disappointingly modest and modern place, although it is a hub of island bus routes. **Ferries** from Bodø dock about 1km west of the town centre, whereas the Hurtigrute docks in the centre, a brief walk from the **bus station** and the busy **tourist office**, where you can pick up island-wide information and bus schedules (late May to mid-June Mon–Fri 9am–4pm & Sat 10am–2pm; mid-June to mid-Aug Mon–Fri 9am–4pm & 5–7.30/9.30pm, Sat 9/10am–2/4pm, Sun 4–7pm; mid-Aug to late Aug Mon–Fri 9am–7pm, Sat 10am–2pm; Sept to mid-May Mon–Fri 9am–4pm; ☎76 06 98 00). One of the most pleasant **places to stay** in Svolvær is the long-established *Svolvær Sjøhus*, by the seashore at the foot of Parkgata (☎76 07 03 36, 🕸www.svolver-sjohuscamp.no; ❹), five minutes' walk from the square. The accommodation here is in old boathouses and the price includes use of a well-equipped kitchen. Alternatively, at the east end of the harbour, a causeway leads out to the slender islet of Svinøya, where accommodation at *Svinøya Rorbuer* (☎76 06 99 30, 🕸www.svinoya.no) ranges from plain and simple *rorbuer* (❹) through to deluxe en-suite cabins (❼). Reachable by bus from Svolvær, **HENNINGSVÆR**, 23km to the southwest, is a much more beguiling village, its cramped and twisting lanes of brightly painted wooden houses lining a postcard-pretty harbour. It's well worth an **overnight stay**: try the centrally located *Den siste Viking*, Misværveien 10 (☎76 07 49 11, 📧postmaster@nordnorskklatreskole.no; ❸), which provides unadorned lodging right in the centre.

It's the next large island to the southwest, **Vestvågøy**, which captivates many travellers, due in no small part to the laid-back charm of **STAMSUND**, whose older buildings are strung along a rocky, fretted seashore. This is the first port of call for the **Hurtigrute coastal boat** as it heads north from Bodø, and is much the best place to stay on the island. Getting there by **bus** from Austvågøy is reasonably easy, too, with several buses making the trip daily, though you do have to change at Leknes, 16km away to the west. In Stamsund, the first place to head for is the friendly, very informal **hostel** (☎76 08 93 34; ❷; closed late Oct to Dec), made up of several *rorbuer* perched over a pint-sized bay, about 1km down the road from the port and 200m from the Leknes bus stop. Fishing around here is first-class: the hostel rents out rowing boats and lines or you can go on an organized trip (200kr); afterwards, you can cook your catch on the hostel's wood-burning stoves.

By any standard the next two Lofoten islands, **Flakstadøya** and **Moskenesøya**, are extraordinarily beautiful. As the Lofotens taper towards their southerly conclusion, rearing peaks crimp a sea-shredded coastline studded with a string of fishing villages. Remarkably, the E10 travels along almost all of this dramatic shoreline, by way of tunnels and bridges, to **MOSKENES**, the **ferry port** midway between Bodø and the remote, southernmost bird islands of Værøy and Røst. Some 6km further on, the E10 ends at the tersely named **Å**, one of the Lofotens' most delightful villages, its huddle of old buildings rambling over a foreshore that's wedged in tight between the grey-green mountains and the surging sea. The same family owns the assortment of smart *rorbuer* (❹) that surround the dock, the adjacent **hostel** (❷), the bar and the only restaurant, where the seafood is very good; all **accommodation** can be reserved on ☎76 09 11 21, ⊛www.lofotenrorbu.com. **Local buses** run along the length of the E10 from Leknes to Å once or twice daily from late June to late August, less frequently the rest of the year. Buses do not, however, tend to coincide with sailings to and from Moskenes. Consequently, if you're heading from the Moskenes ferry port to Å, you'll either have to walk – it's an easy 6km – or take a taxi.

Narvik and beyond

NARVIK was established less than a century ago as an ice-free port to handle the iron ore brought by train from northern Sweden, and the **iron ore docks** are still immediately conspicuous upon arrival, the rust-coloured machinery overwhelming the whole waterfront. Try and devote an hour or so to the **Krigsminne Museum** (March to early June & late Aug to Sept daily 10am–4pm; early June to late Aug daily 10am–10pm; 35kr), in the main square close to the docks. Run by the Red Cross, it documents the wartime German saturation bombing and bitter sea and air battles for control of the ore supplies, in which hundreds of foreign servicemen died alongside many locals. The **train station** is at the north end of the town and from here it's a five- to ten-minute walk along the main drag, Kongens gate, to the **bus station**, in the basement of the Amfi shopping centre on the west side of the street. The **tourist office**, a few metres further along Kongens gate on the main square (June to mid-Aug Mon–Fri 9am–5pm, Sat 10am–5pm & Sun 11am–5pm; late August Mon–Fri 9am–5pm, Sat 10am–3pm; Sept–May Mon–Fri 8.30am–3.30pm; ☎76 94 33 09; wwww.narvikinfo.no), has the full range of bus and ferry timetables and provides lots of information on outdoor pursuits; it can also assist with ferry and activity reservations. The best place **to stay** is the *Briedablikk Gjestehus*, Tore Hundsgate 41 (☎76 94 14 18, ⊛www.narviknett.no/breida; ❹), a well-tended guest house, a short, stiff walk from the tourist office at the top of Kinobakken.

There's a choice of several routes on from Narvik. The **rail link**, cut through the mountains a century ago, runs east and then south into **Sweden**, reaching Kiruna in three and Stockholm in eighteen hours. It's a beautiful journey, but **bus** travellers, heading north on the *Nord-Norgeekspressen* to **Tromsø** and **Alta**, do no worse with a succession of switchback roads, lakeside forests, high peaks, gentle valleys and plunging, black-blue fjords. In summer, cut grass dries everywhere, stretched over wooden poles forming long lines on the hillsides like so much washing. Narvik is also connected to Svolvær, on the Lofotens, by bus and catamaran. Note that on all these buses and the catamaran InterRail and ScanRail pass holders get a fifty-percent discount.

Tromsø

TROMSØ was once known, rather preposterously, as the "Paris of the North", and the city still likes to think of itself as the capital of northern Norway, with two cathedrals, a clutch of reasonably interesting museums and an above-average (and affordable) nightlife, patronized by its high-profile student population. Certainly, as a base for this part of the country, it's hard to beat, set in magnificent landscape – dramatic mountains and craggy shoreline. In the centre of town, the **Domkirke** (Tues–Sat 10am–4pm, Sun 10am–2pm; free) reflects the town's nineteenth-century prosperity, the result of its barter trade with Russia. From the church, it's a short walk north along the harbourfront to the most diverting of the city's museums, the **Polar Museum** (daily: mid-May to mid-June & mid-Aug to mid-Sept 11am–5pm; mid-June to mid-Aug 10am–7pm; mid-Sept to mid-May 11am–3pm; ⓦwww.polarmuseum.no; 40kr), whose varied displays include skeletons retrieved from the permafrost of Svalbard and a detailed section on the polar explorer Roald Amundsen. On the other side of the water, over the spindly Tromsø Bridge, the white and ultramodern **Arctic Cathedral** (mid April to May daily 3–6pm; June to mid-Aug Mon–Sat 10am–8pm, Sun 1–8pm; mid-Aug to Sept daily 3–6pm; 20kr) is spectacular, made up of eleven immense triangular concrete sections representing the eleven Apostles left after the betrayal.

The **Hurtigrute coastal boat** docks in the centre of town at the foot of Kirkegata. Long-distance **buses** arrive and leave from the adjacent car park. The **tourist office** is at Storgata 61, near the Domkirke (mid- to late May & mid-Aug to mid-Sept Mon–Fri 8.30am–4pm, Sat & Sun 10.30am–2pm; June to mid-Aug Mon–Fri 8.30am–6pm, Sat 10am–5pm, Sun 10.30am–5pm; mid-Sept to mid-May Mon–Fri 8.30am–4pm, Sat 10.30am–2pm; ☎77 61 00 00; ⓦwww.destinasjontromsoe.no). They have a small supply of **private rooms** (❹). The frugal **HI hostel**, *Tromsø Vandrerhjem*, Åsgårdsveien 9, Elverhøy (☎77 65 76 28, Ⓔtromso.hostel @vandrerhejm.no; late June to late Aug only; dorm beds ❷), is some 2km west of the quay; several city buses go near there – ask at the bus station - or else it's a stiff thirty-minute walk. Alternatively, try the much more appealing *Ami Hotel*, on the hillside behind the city centre at Skolegata 24 (☎77 68 22 08, ⓦwww.amihotel.no; ❹), or the *Pensjonat Nord*, nearby at Parkgata 4 (☎77 66 83 00, ⓦwww.hotellnord .no; ❹). The nearest **campsite**, the all-year *Tromsdalen Camping* (☎77 63 80 37), lies over the bridge on the mainland, about 1800m beyond the Arctic Cathedral. Tromsø has a varied selection of **restaurants**, **cafés** and **pubs**. For excellent coffee, pastries and light snacks try *Kaffebønna*, Strandtorvet 1. *Aunegården*, at Sjøgata 29, has everything from coffee and mouth-watering cheese cake to traditional Norwegian dishes. The *Sjømatrestauranten Arctandria* offers magnificent seafood with main courses averaging around 200kr. In the evening, *Blå Rock Café*, Strandgata 14, is a lively spot with a jukebox and a rock-n-roll crowd.

Honningsvåg and Nordkapp

The bleak and treeless island of Magerøya is connected to the northern tip of the mainland by an ambitious combination of tunnels and bridges. The only settlement of any size here is **HONNINGSVÅG**, a crusty fishing village that makes a steady income from accommodating the hundreds of summertime tourists bent on visiting Nordkapp, just 34km away. Amongst several **hotels**, one of the more appealing is the *Rica Bryggen*, which occupies a plain but well-kept concrete high-rise down at the head of the harbour (☎78 47 28 88; ⓦwww.rica.no; ❾). Alternatively, much cheaper and plainer accommodation is available at *NAF Nordkapp Camping* (☎78 47 33 77, Ⓔnordkapp.camping@nordkapp.com; late May to mid-Sept), which comprises a **campsite** and cabins (❹); the complex is located about 8km from Honningsvåg on the road to Nordkapp. Long-distance buses arrive in the centre of Honningsvåg and there's a limited bus service on to Nordkapp (late June to mid-Aug 1–2 daily; 50min). When the buses aren't running, the only option is a taxi (900kr return) – though note that the road is closed throughout the winter and often in spring too. Travellers northbound with the **Hurtigrute coastal boat**, which puts in at Honningsvåg, should note that there's a special coach on to Nordkapp and back within the two-and-a-half-hour stop. For **food** in Honningsvåg, there are a couple of takeaway kiosks along Storgata and a very good seafood restaurant at the *Honningsvåg Brygge Hotel*.

NORDKAPP is only a cliff, 307m high, with an arguable claim to being the northernmost point of Europe. But there is something exhilarating about this bleak, wind-battered promontory. Originally a Sami sacrificial site, it was actually named by the English explorer Richard Chancellor in 1553, but it was not until the late nineteenth century that a visit by King Oscar II opened the tourist floodgates. These days the headland is occupied by **Nordkapphallen** (North Cape Hall; daily: April to late May & Sept to early Oct noon–5pm; late May to mid-June noon–1am; mid-June to early Aug 9am–2am; early Aug to end Aug noon–midnight; 185kr for 48hr, including parking), an extremely flashy complex that contains souvenir shops, cafés, restaurants and huge windows from where you can survey the surging ocean below. The complex also has a **post office**, where you can get your letters specially stamped. Tourists gather here in numbers to watch the **Midnight Sun** (between early May and end of July).

Travel details

Trains

Åndalsnes to: Dombås (2–3 daily; 1hr 30min); Oslo (2 daily; 6hr 30min).
Dombås to: Trondheim (3–4 daily; 2hr 30min).
Myrdal to: Flåm (June–Sept 11–12 daily; Oct–May 4 daily; 50min).
Oslo to: Åndalsnes (2–3 daily; 6hr 30min); Bergen (4–5 daily; 6hr 30min); Trondheim (3–4 daily; 8hr 15min); Voss (4–5 daily; 5hr 40min).
Trondheim to: Bodø (2–3 daily; 10hr); Dombås (3–4 daily; 2hr 30min); Fauske (2–3 daily; 9hr 20min); Mo-i-Rana (2–3 daily; 7hr); Oslo (3–4 daily; 7hr); Stockholm (2 daily; 12hr).

Buses

Ålesund to: Bergen (1–2 daily; 10hr); Hellesylt (1–2 daily except Sat; 2hr 40min); Stryn (1–2 daily except Sat; 4hr); Trondheim (1–2 daily; 8hr 10min).
Alta to: Hammerfest (1–2 daily except Sat; 3hr); Honningsvåg (late June to mid-Aug 1–2 daily; 5hr); Tromsø (April to late Oct 1–2 daily; 7hr).
Åndalsnes to: Geiranger (mid-June to late Aug 2 daily; 3–4hr); Ålesund (3–4 daily; 2hr 20min).
Balestrand to: Sogndal (2 daily; 1hr 10min).
Bergen to: Ålesund (1–2 daily; 10hr); Trondheim (1 daily; 14hr); Voss (4 daily; 1hr 45min).

Fauske to: Bodø (2–3 daily; 1hr 10min); Narvik (2 daily; 7hr).
Hammerfest to: Alta (1–2 daily except Sat; 3hr); Skaidi (1–2 daily except Sat; 1hr 15min).
Honningsvåg to: Nordkapp (late June to mid-Aug 1–2 daily; 50min).
Narvik to: Alta (1 daily; 14hr); Tromsø (1–2 daily; 4hr 40min).
Oslo to: Bergen (4–5 daily; 10hr).
Stryn to: Bergen (2 daily; 7hr); Oslo (1 daily; 8hr 30min).
Tromsø to: Alta (April to late Oct 1–2 daily; 7hr); Narvik (2 daily; 7hr); Nordkapp (late June to mid-Aug 1 daily except Sat; 14hr).
Trondheim to: Ålesund (2–3 daily; 8hr); Bergen (2 daily; 14hr); Stryn (2 daily; 7hr 20min).
Voss to: Bergen (4 daily; 1hr 45min); Sogndal (2 daily; 3hr).

Catamaran ferries

Bergen to: Balestrand (1–2 daily; 4hr); Flåm (1–2 daily; 5hr 30min).
Bodø to: Svolvær (1 daily except Sat; 5hr 30min).
Narvik to: Svolvær (1 daily except Sat; 4hr).

Poland

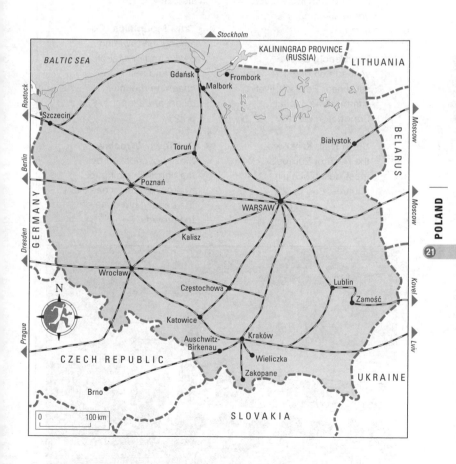

Poland highlights

✳ **Old Town, Warsaw**
Rebuilt from rubble after
World War II, this monu-
ment to Polish suffering
and recovery is also well
stocked with lively cafés
and restaurants. See
p.711

✳ **The beach, Sopot** A
vast stretch of white
sand near Poland's lively
summertime capital,
Sopot. See p.716

✳ **Cloth Hall, Kraków** At
the heart of Europe's
most beautiful main
squares. See p.720

✳ **Auschwitz-Birkenau
camps** Fifty years on,
the Nazis' most infa-
mous death camps still
make a haunting impres-
sion. See p.722

✳ **Tatra Mountains** Hike
among the towering
peaks and crystal-clear
lakes and rest in the
charming mountain
resort of Zakopane. See
p.723

✳ **Old Town, Wrocław**
Mostly overlooked by
the hordes heading for
Kraków, Wrocław has all
the beauty, but none of
the crowds. See p.724

Introduction and basics

Images of **Poland** flooded the world media throughout the 1980s: strikes at the shipyards of Gdańsk were the harbingers of the disintegration of communism in Eastern Europe. The decade's end saw the establishment of a government led by the Solidarity trade union. Poland joined NATO in 1999, and is due to join the EU in 2004. The rebirth of democratic Poland was a uniquely Catholic revolution. The Church has always been the principal defender of the nation's identity, and its physical presence is inescapable in Baroque buildings, roadside shrines and images of the national icon, the Black Madonna.

Much of **Warsaw**, the capital, plumb in the centre of the country, conforms to the stereotype of Eastern European greyness, but its historic centre, beautiful parks and vibrant nightlife are diverting enough. **Kraków** in the south, the ancient royal capital, is the real crowd puller, rivalling the elegance of Prague and Vienna. **Gdańsk** in the north offers a dynamic brew of politics and commerce, while nearby **Sopot** features golden beaches. German influences abound in the north and southwest of the country, in Gdańsk itself, in the austere castles and fortified settlements along the River Wisła (Vistula) and in the divided province of Silesia. Yet, to the north of Silesia, quintessentially Polish **Poznań** is revered as the cradle of the nation. Of the many regions of unspoilt natural beauty, the alpine **Tatras** on the Slovak border offer the most exhilarating walking terrain in the country.

Information & maps

Most towns and cities have a **tourist office** (known as IT or *informacja turystyczna*); sometimes these are run by the local municipality and are rather good; elsewhere, they're privately run travel agencies using the label to sell tours and tickets. Two long-established tourist organizations which may be of help are **PTTK** specializing in hiking tourism, and **Almatur**, a student travel bureau. In Poland, EMPiK stores (on most high streets) are well stocked with regional and city **maps**, most with tram and bus routes marked.

Money and banks

Currency is the **złoty** (zł), divided into 100 groszy. Coins come as 1, 2, 5, 10, 20 and 50 groszy, and 1, 2 and 5 złoty; notes as 10, 20, 50, 100 and 200 złoty. **Banks** (usually open Mon–Fri 7.30am–5pm, Sat 7.30am–2pm) and exchange offices (*kantors*) offer similar exchange rates. Most kantors will not change travellers' cheques. Hotels offer poor exchange rates. Major **credit cards** are accepted by most hotels and restaurants, and an increasing number of shops take plastic. ATMs are widespread.

Communications

Post offices are identified by the name Urząd Pocztowy (Poczta for short). Theoretically, each city's head office has a **poste restante** facility: make sure that anyone addressing mail to you adds "No. 1" after the city's name. Head office opening hours are usually Mon–Sat 7/8am–8pm; branches close at 6pm or earlier. For public **phones** you'll need a phone card from a post office or newsagent kiosk – 25, 50 or 100 units (12.5zł, 25zł &

40zł). You'll find at least one decent, central **Internet café** in the larger towns (4–10zł/hr).

Getting around

Polish State Railways (PKP) runs three main types of **trains**. Express services (*ekspresowy*), particularly IC (intercity) or EC (Eurocity), stop at the main cities only; seat reservations, for a small charge, are compulsory. "Fast" trains (*pośpieszny*) have more stops, and reservations are optional. The grubby normal services (*osobowy*) are best avoided: in rural areas they stop at every haystack. It's sometimes worth paying the fifty percent extra to travel first-class or make a reservation (*miejscówka*), as sardine-like conditions are fairly common. Some long journeys are best done overnight; second-class sleepers are a bargain at around £7/$11 per person. For journeys of over 100km and for international trips you can buy tickets in advance at Orbis travel agencies (branches in all towns and cities). InterRail passes are valid.

Intercity **buses** operated by PKS, the national bus company, may be cheaper than trains, but are slow and often overcrowded. In rural areas, notably the mountain regions, there's greater choice and convenience, and here the bus may be faster than the train. Main bus stations are usually alongside the train station. The private company **Polski Express** (✆www.polskiexpress.pl) offers slightly pricier intercity journeys in rather more comfortable and faster buses – they're particularly useful if you're travelling out from Warsaw, but are still much slower than trains. Many stations cannot allocate seats for services starting from another town – in such cases you have to buy a ticket from the driver. Orbis offices are the best place to go to book on an international route.

Accommodation

Most Polish towns have at least one budget **hotel** offering spartan but habitable rooms with toilet and shower in the hallway, usually costing less than £8/$12 per person. Hotels in this category often include three- or four-person rooms, which work out very cheaply indeed if you're travelling as a group. Establishments offering additional comforts such as en-suite shower, TV and a decent breakfast need not cost a great deal more (reckon on £10–18/$14–25 per person), although standards can be unpredictable: some rooms have fittings that haven't changed for decades.

There are some 200 **hostels** (*schroniska młodzieżowe*). Many are only open at the height of summer and are liable to be booked solid, while most of the year-round hostels have lockouts and curfews. Prices are rarely more than £4/$6 a head, and many hostels are located close to town centres. For a complete list, check ✆www.ptsm.pl. Alternatively you can ask the tourist offices about summer accommodation in **university hostels**; charges (including breakfast) are around £3/$4.50 for ISIC card-holding students and £5–7/$7.50–12 for others (no age limit), depending on whether they wish to share a room. They are often the best bet in summer, being as cheap as hostels without the restrictions, although they tend to be located in the suburbs.

You can get a **room** in a private house (*kwatery prywatne*) almost anywhere in the country. Those in the cities are often pretty shabby, although in mountain resorts they can be extremely comfortable. Several major cities have a **room-finding service**, usually known as the Biuro Zakwaterowania, and most tourist information offices will also help. Charges are around £8/$12 per person, £12/$18 in Warsaw. You'll be given a choice of location and category. Many houses in rural holiday areas hang out signs saying *noclegi* (lodging) or *pokoje* (rooms). It's up to you to bargain: £3/$4.50 is the least you can expect to pay. Individuals with rooms to let may approach you at train stations – this can be the way to a bargain, but carries all the usual risks of an unofficial deal.

There are hundreds of **campsites**; for a complete list see the *Campingi w Polsce* map, available from EMPiK and other bookshops. Most open May–Sept only. Charges usually work out at less than £2/$3 a head. Many sites have chalets to rent which, though spartan, are good value at around £4/$6 per head. Camping rough, outside of the national parks, is fine so long as you're discreet.

Food and drink

Poles take their **food** seriously, providing meals of feast-like proportions for the most casual visitors. The cuisine is a complex mix of influences: Russian, German, Ukrainian, Lithuanian and Jewish traditions have all left their mark. Hotel **breakfasts** might include fried eggs with ham, mild frankfurters, a selection of cold meats and cheese, rolls and jam. If you need to find your own breakfast you could do worse than head for a **milk bar** (*bar mleczny*; usually open from early morning until 5/6pm), the traditional place for cheap and filling Polish snacks. Traditional Polish **takeaway stands** usually sell *zapiekanki*, baguette-like pieces of bread topped with melted cheese, while some sell chips (*frytki*) with sausage (*kiełbasa*) or chicken (*kurczak*). Many **restaurants** close late, but the older tradition of closing at 9 or 10pm persists in some places. First on the menu in most places are **soups**, varying from delicate dishes to concoctions that are virtually meals in themselves. Best known are *barszcz*, a spicy beetroot broth, and *żurek*, a soup made of fermented rye that tastes much better than it looks. The basis of most **main courses** is fried or grilled meat, such as *kotlet schabowy* (a pork cutlet). Two inexpensive specialities you'll find everywhere are *bigos* (cabbage stewed with meat) and *pierogi*, dumplings stuffed with meat and mushrooms, or with cottage cheese, onion and spices (*pierogi ruskie*). Pancakes (*naleśniki*) often come as a main course, stuffed with cottage cheese (*ze serem*). Fried potato pancakes (*placki ziemniaczane*) are particularly good, served in sour cream or spicy paprika sauce. The **cakes, pastries and other sweets** that can be found in cake shops (*cukiernia*) – even in small villages – are as good as any in Central Europe. *Sernik* (cheesecake) is a national favourite, as are *makowiec* (poppyseed cake), *drożdżówka* (a sponge cake, often topped with plums), and *babka piaskowa* (marble cake).

Drinking is a national pursuit. Poles can't compete with their Czech neighbours in the production and consumption of **beer** (*piwo*), but there are a number of fairly drinkable local brands. It's with **vodka** (*wódka*) that Poles really get into their stride. Ideally it is served neat, well chilled, in measures of 25 or 50 grams and knocked back in one go. Best of the clear vodkas are *Żytnia* and *Wyborowa*. Of the flavoured varieties, first on most people's list is *żubrówka*, infused with bison grass.

Opening hours and holidays

Most **shops** open on weekdays, around 10am–6pm, except food stores which may open as early as 6am and stay open well into the evening. Many shops close on Sat afternoons and all day Sun. RUCH kiosks, where you buy newspapers and municipal transport tickets, generally open at about 6am. Increasing numbers of street traders do business well into the evening, and you can find shops in major cities (particularly the EMPiK stores) offering late-night opening throughout the week. **Museums** and **historic monuments** almost invariably close one day per week, usually Monday. Entrance tends to cost very little, and is often free on one day of the week. **Public holidays** are: Jan 1; Easter Mon; May 1; May 3; Corpus Christi (May/June); Aug 15; Nov 1; Nov 11; Dec 25 & 26.

Emergencies

The biggest potential hassles are hotel room thefts, pickpocketing and car break-ins. Safely store your valuables when travelling by night train; on international trains it's wise to book a couchette compartment with a lockable door. Polish **police** (*policja*) are courteous and helpful but may not speak English. In a medical emergency most foreigners tend to rely on the pricey private medical centres run by **Medicover** (☎022/570 11 11, ⊛www.medicover.com).

> **Emergency numbers**
>
> Police ☎997; fire ☎998; ambulance ☎999.

POLAND | Basics

21

Warsaw (Warszawa)

First impressions of **WARSAW** (Warszawa) are all too often negative. The years of Communist rule did little for the city aesthetically, and there's sometimes a hollowness to the faithful reconstructions of earlier eras. On the plus side, the city is one of the fastest growing of Eastern Europe capitals and for visitors the best reflection of this is its vibrant bar, club and restaurant scene.

Warsaw became the capital of Poland in 1596, when **King Zygmunt III** moved his court here from Kraków. The city was badly damaged by the Swedes during the invasion of 1655 and then extensively reconstructed in the late seventeenth century. The **Partitions** abruptly terminated this golden age, as Warsaw was absorbed into Prussia in 1795. Napoleon's arrival in 1806 gave Varsovians brief hopes of liberation, but following the 1815 Congress of Vienna, the city was integrated into the Russian-controlled Congress the **Kingdom of Poland**. It was only with the outbreak of World War I that Russian control began to crumble, and with the restoration of Polish independence in 1918, Warsaw reverted to its position as capital. Then, with the outbreak of World War II, came the progressive annihilation of the city. Hitler, infuriated by the 1943 Ghetto Uprising and the 1944 **Warsaw Uprising**, ordered the elimination of Warsaw; by the end of the war 850,000 Varsovians – two-thirds of the city's 1939 population – were dead or missing. The task of rebuilding took ten years.

Arrival, information and accommodation

Okęcie **airport** is 8km southwest of the Old Town: avoid the rip-off taxi drivers and take bus #175 (#611 at night) into town, which passes the main **train station**, Warszawa Centralna, in the modern centre, before arriving in the Old Town. The main **bus station**, Międzynarodowa Dworzec PKS, is located right next to the Warszawa Zachodnia suburban train station, 3km west of Centralna station. To get into town from here catch any eastbound train or bus #127, #130, #508, #517 or #E5. Polski Express **intercity buses** arrive at and depart from the bus stop on al Jana Pawla II, just outside the western entrance of Centralna train station. The best source of **information** is the helpful IT office in the main hall of Centralna station (daily: May–Sept 8am–8pm; Oct-April 8am-6pm; ☏022/9431, ⊛www.warsaw-tour.pl), which has excellent free city maps and brochures. There's another IT office on the corner of Plac Zamkowy at Krakowskie Przedmieście 89 (same times), as well as information booths at the airport arrivals hall and main bus station.

Buses and **trams** are the main forms of transport and run until a little after 11pm; after that, night buses (with a slightly dodgy reputation) leave every thirty minutes from the new stop beside the Dworzec Centralny train station. There is also one **metro** line running through the centre of town (as far north as Ratusz station on Plac Bankowy). **Tickets** for trams, buses and the metro (2.4zł/single trip, 3.6zł/1hr) are bought from green RUCH kiosks or from automatic ticket machines. You need three tickets for night buses and an extra ticket for bulky luggage. Punch your tickets in the machines on board – Warsaw's zealous inspectors are merciless. Day (7.2zł), three-day (12zł) and week (24zł) **passes** are also available from some kiosks and should be punched the first time you use them. **Taxis** cost as little as 1.3zł per kilometre, but to avoid being ripped off take only taxis that have the price per kilometre, the name and the telephone number clearly marked. Don't get a taxi from outside the Centralna Station – go to the nearby ul. Emilii Plater, or better still, book one by phone; try Partner (☏022/9669), Bayer (☏022/9667) or Wawa (☏022/9644) – English spoken at all three.

Warsaw has a paltry collection of **hostels**, although during July and August the **student hostels** are another possibility, without those nasty lockouts and curfews – ask at the Centralna Station information centre. The best bet for help with hotel bookings are the Centralna station and Old Town IT offices (see above). Advance booking is essential in summer.

Hostels

Agrykola ul. Myśliwiecka 9 ☎ 022/622 91 10, ℮ recepcja@hotelagrykola.pl. The city's best hostel, with clean modern rooms, friendly staff, no curfew, sauna, solarium, tennis courts etc. Near Łazienki park; bus #151 from the station to the Rozbrat stop on the bridge. 47zł.

Przy Rynku ul. Rynek Nowego Miasta 4 ☎ 022/831 50 33. The best of the summer hostels. 40zł.

Syrenka ul. Karolkowa 53a ☎ 022/632 88 29. Big, basic but cheap rooms, plus Internet access. Lockout 5–10pm; curfew 11pm. Tram #12 or #24 from Centralna station for six stops, Ochota direction (get off near the Wola department store). 35zł.

Ul. Smolna 30 ul. Smolna 30 ☎ 022/827 89 52. Barrack-like conditions but central location and reductions for HI members. A five-minute bus ride along al Jerozolimskie from the main station – any bus heading towards Nowy Świat will drop you at the corner of the street. Reception 4–9pm; curfew 11pm. 27zł.

Hotels

Harctour Niemcewicza 17 ☎ 022/659 00 11, ℮ hharctur@beph.pl. Spartan but tolerable, 500m east of the main bus station, weekend reductions. ❸

Ibis Centrum al Solidarności 165 ☎ 022/520 30 00, ℮ h2894@accor-hotels.com. Fairly central, good standard mid-range chain hotel. ❻

Mazowiecki ul. Mazowiecka 10 ☎ 022/827 23 65, ℮ www.mazowiecki.com.pl. Renovated budget hotel, bang in the centre. Some en suites. ❹

Metalowcy ul. Długa 29 ☎ 022/831 40 21. Slightly grubby basic rooms with shared bathrooms on the top floor of a building just west of the Old Town. ❷

Na Wodzie Wybrzeże Kościuszkowski ☎ 022/628 58 83. A central "boatel" with clean rooms, moored right next to Poniatowskiego bridge. Take any tram from Centralna station towards Praga and get off at the fourth stop, on the bridge. Closed Nov–April. ❷

Praski al Solidarności 61 ☎ 022/818 49 89. Clean, simple rooms, just across the river from the Old Town. The tram drops you right outside the hotel. ❹

The City

Most of what you'll want to see in Warsaw lies on the western bank of the **Wisła** (Vistula) river. It's here that you'll find the central business and shopping district, **Śródmiescie**, grouped around Centralna station and the nearby Palace of Culture, with the more picturesque and tourist-friendly **Old Town** (Stare Miasto) just to the north.

The Old Town, New Town and Ghetto

The title "Old Town" – *Stare Miasto* – is in some respects a misnomer for the historic nucleus of Warsaw. After World War II this compact network of streets and alleyways lay in rubble, only to be painstakingly reconstructed in the decades afterwards. **Plac Zamkowy** (Castle Square), on the south side of the Old Town, is the obvious place to start a tour. On the east side of the square is the former **Royal Castle** (℮ www.zamek-krolewski.art.pl), once home of the royal family and seat of the Polish parliament, now the **Castle Museum** (daily 10/11am–6pm; 15zł). Though the structure is a replica, many of its furnishings are the originals, scooted into hiding during the first bombing raids. After passing the most lavish section of the castle, the Royal Apartments of King Stanisław August, you come to the magnificent Canaletto Room, with its views of Warsaw by Bernardo Bellotto, nephew of the famous Canaletto – whose name he appropriated to make his pictures sell better. Marvellous in their detail, these cityscapes provided important information for the architects rebuilding the city after the war. On Świętojańska, north of the castle, stands **St John's Cathedral**, the oldest church in Warsaw. A few yards away, the Old Town Square is one of the most remarkable bits of postwar reconstruction anywhere in Europe. Flattened during the Warsaw Uprising, its three-storey merchants' houses have been rebuilt to their seventeenth- and eighteenth-century designs. The **Warsaw Historical Museum** (Tues & Thurs 11am–5pm, Wed & Fri 10.30am–3pm, Sat & Sun 10.30am–4pm; 5zł, free Sun) has an important section about the resistance to the Nazis and an impressive English-language film (shown Tues–Sat at noon) with footage of the city in ruins immediately after the war. The nearby sixteenth-century **Barbakan** used to guard the Nowomiejska Gate, the

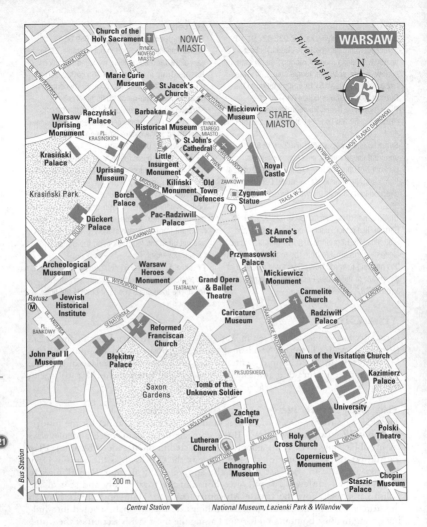

northern entrance to the city. The fortress is part of the old town defences, which run all the way around from Plac Zamkowy to the northeastern edge of the district.

Cross the ramparts from the Barbakan and you're into the **New Town** (Nowe Miasto) district, which despite its name dates from the early fifteenth century, but was formally joined to Warsaw only at the end of the eighteenth. The heart of the district is the **Rynek Nowego Miasta**, once a commercial hub, now a soothing change from the bustle of the Old Town. Tucked into the eastern corner is the **Church of the Holy Sacrament**, commissioned by Queen Maria Sobieska in memory of her husband Jan's victory over the Turks at Vienna in 1683. West from the square, near the Warsaw Uprising monument, is the majestic **Krasiński Palace**, its facade bearing fine sculptures by Andreas Schlüter. To the south of the palace gardens stands the former Stock Exchange, now housing the extensive **John Paul II Collection** (Tues–Sun 10am–4pm; 8zł), featuring paintings from all periods between the Renaissance and the Impressionists.

West of here is the former **Ghetto** area. In 1939 there were an estimated 380,000 Jews living in and around Warsaw – one-third of the total population. By May 1945, the ghetto had been razed to the ground and around 300 Jews were left. The **Nożyk Synagogue** on ul. Twarda is the only one of the Ghetto's three synagogues still standing. To the north of the Ghetto area, the **Ghetto Heroes Monument** was made from materials ordered by Hitler for a monument to the Reich's anticipated victory. You can get an idea of what most of Jewish Warsaw looked like in the miraculously untouched **ul. Próżna**.

Śródmieście

The area stretching from the Old Town down towards Łazienki Park – **Śródmieście** – is the increasingly fast-paced heart of Warsaw, bisected by the Royal Way thoroughfare, which runs almost uninterrupted from Plac Zamkowy to the palace of Wilanów. **Krakowskie Przedmieście**, the first part of the Royal Way, is lined with historic buildings. Even in a city not lacking in Baroque churches, the **Church of the Nuns of the Visitation** stands out, with its columned, statue-topped facade; it's also one of the very few buildings in central Warsaw to have come through World War II unscathed. Most of the rest of Krakowskie Przedmieście is taken up by **Warsaw University**. On the main campus courtyard stands the seventeenth-century **Kazimierz Palace**, once a royal summer residence, while across the street from the gates is the **Czapski Palace**, now home of the Academy of Fine Arts. Just south is the Baroque **Holy Cross Church**, wrecked in a two-week battle during the Warsaw Uprising; photographs of the distinctive figure of Christ left standing among the ruins became poignant emblems of Warsaw's suffering. On a pillar to the left side of the nave there's an urn containing Chopin's heart.

Biggest among Warsaw's palaces is the early-nineteenth-century **Staszic Palace**, now the headquarters of the Polish Academy of Sciences. South of here, the main street becomes **Nowy Świat** (New World), with some of Warsaw's most expensive shopping and a good selection of cafés. West along al Jerozolimskie is the **National Museum** (Tues, Wed & Fri-Sun 10am–4pm, Thurs 10pm–6pm; 15zł, free Sat), an impressive compendium of archeology and European paintings and sculptures – Caravaggio, Bellini, Brueghel and Rodin included. Further west lies the commercial heart of the city. Marszałkowska, the main north-south road cutting across Jerozolimskie, is lined with stores and boutiques. Towering over everything is the **Palace of Culture and Science**, a gift from Stalin that the Polish people could hardly refuse. The interior contains a vast conference hall, offices, theatres, nightclubs, cinemas, swimming pools and a casino. Outside are the city's most popular summer basketball courts which turn into a free-to-all ice rink in the winter. The platform on the thirtieth floor (daily 9am–6pm, summer until midnight; 15zł) of the palace offers an impressive bird's eye view of the city.

Out of the centre

South of the commercial district, on the eastern side of al Ujazdowskie, is the attractive **Łazienki Park**. Once a hunting ground, the area was bought in the 1760s by King Stanisław August, who turned it into an English-style park and built the slender Neoclassical **Łazienki Palace** (Tues-Sun 9am–4pm; 11zł) across the park lake. Oak-lined paths lead from the park entrance and the ponderous **Chopin Monument** to the palace. Most of the lavish furnishings, paintings and sculptures survived the war intact, having been hidden during the occupation, and the stuccoed ballroom is lined with a tasteful collection of busts and sculptures.

The one must-see on the eastern **Praga** side of the river is the **Stadion Dziesięciu-lecia**, the largest outdoor market in Europe, based in Poland's former national football and athletics stadium. You can buy anything from life rafts to machine guns here – though most people come for the vast range of cheap pirate CDs (10zł each) and the sharp contrast to the rapidly westernizing Warsaw on the other side of the river. To see the market at its best, get there by 11am at the latest.

Get off at the first stop after the river, going from Centralna station.

The grandest of Warsaw's palaces, **Wilanów** (9.15am–2.30pm, closed Tues; 18zł) makes an easy excursion from the city centre: take bus #180 south from anywhere along Krakowskie Przedmieście or Nowy Świat to its terminus. King Jan Sobieski purchased the existing manor house and estate in 1677 and spent nearly twenty years turning it into the "Polish Versailles" and the sixty-odd rooms provide a vast range of decorative styles. The gate on the left side beyond the main entrance opens onto the stately **palace gardens** (daily 9am–sunset; 4zł, free Thurs), while to the right before you enter is the **Poster Museum** (Tues–Sun 10am–4pm; 8zł, free Wed), a mishmash of the inspired and the bizarre.

Eating, drinking and entertainment

For basic snacks, **milk bars** and **fast-food** joints provide a good fill for under £3/$5. Although service is often bad and prices are higher than elsewhere in Poland, the **restaurant and bar** scene in Warsaw has really taken off in the last few years. The city is now genuinely a great night out and detailed English-language tips on the vast range of places to go can be found in the *Warsaw Insider* and *Warsaw In Your Pocket*. Warsaw **festivals** include the excellent Jazz Jamboree (Oct) and Festival of Contemporary Music (Sept). **Films** at the city's numerous modern multiplexes are in the original language with Polish subtitles. For **what's on** listings in English the best source is the monthly *Warsaw Insider* (ⓦwww.warsawinsider.com; 6zł) or the bi-monthly *Warsaw in Your Pocket* guide (ⓦwww.inyourpocket.com; 10zł). Both are available at information centres, in most bigger hotels and at the central EMPiK opposite the Palace of Culture on ul. Marszałkowska.

Cafés and snack bars

Belle Epoque ul. Freta 18. Sip tea amongst a wonderful collection of antiques – all for sale.

Brama Nowy Świat 60/ul. Krucza 16/22. Cheapish Warsaw chain of cafés with good sandwiches, omelettes and coffee.

Coffeeheaven Nowy Świat 46. Chain operation sandwiches, cakes and good coffee.

Marak ul. Świętokrzyska 18. Excellent, affordable and trendy soup kitchen.

Pod Barbakanem ul. Mostowa 29. Milk bar with prime location overlooking the Barbakan.

Uniwersytecki Krakowskie Przedmieście 20. Milk bar frequented by students.

Restaurants

Kompania Piwna ul. Podwale 25. Rowdy cellar restaurant, with live traditional music, huge portions of country-style food and Czech beer.

Le Cedre al Solidarności 61. Excellent Lebanese cuisine just across the river from the Old Town. Choose the set meal.

Manufaktura ul. Bednarska 28/30. Cheap and central medieval-style pancake restaurant.

Pod Samsonem ul. Freta 3/5. Good, cheap Jewish food in simple surroundings.

Qchnia Artystyczna al Ujazdowskie 6. In Ujazdowski Castle, with a wonderful view of Łazienki Park from the terrace. Good vegetarian selection.

Venezia ul. Marzałkowska 10/16. Excellent Italian food at reasonable prices.

Warsaw Tortilla Factory ul. Wilcza 46. A lively expat favourite with affordable Tex-Mex food and great homemade lemonade.

Bars

Browar Soma ul. Foksal 19. Busy central bar with minimalist decor, a cool crowd, good home-brewed beer (9zł) and DJs spinning alternative dance discs at weekends.

Chimera ul. Podwale 29. Wackily decorated cellar bar that attracts a fun-minded crowd.

Lolek ul. Rokitnicka 20. Popular beer hall and terrace in the middle of a park, with grilled food, beer and live music. Metro: Pole Mokotowskie.

Między Nami ul. Bracka 20. Relaxed gay-friendly café-bar with good salads and an excellent atmosphere.

Organza ul. Sienkewicza 4. Large bar and restaurant with good pastas and a lively, (very) beautiful people crowd.

Paparazzi ul. Mazowiecki 12. Upmarket Warsaw edition of a Kraków institution, where the new middle class come after work.

Szparka pl Trzech Krzyży 16a. One of a row of three comfy late night openers. Decent food.

Utopia ul. Jasna 1. Camp gay bar with comfy couches and decent snacks.

Clubs, discos and live music

Jadłodajnia Filozoficzna ul. Dobra 33/35. Cheap, friendly bar-club filled with students and reggae/hip-hop sounds; in the cool Powisle district. **Jazzgot** pl Defilad 1. Grungy jazz club inside the Palace of Culture (eastern entrance) with regular gigs. Bad beer though. **Labo** ul. Mazowiecka 11a. The most relaxed and modern of the city centre clubs. Young crowd, nice sofas and they don't just play house. **Paradise** ul. Wawelska 5. The main gay club, southwest of the centre. Closed Sun-Wed.

Piekarnia ul. Młocinska 11. Prides itself on being at the forefront of musical fashion. Closed Sun-Wed. **Proxima** ul. Zwirki i Wigury 99a. Prime student venue offering a wide range of crowd-pleasing club nights. Closed Sun. **Tygmont** ul. Mazowiecka 6/8. Warsaw's top jazz club, with regular gigs, good food and a smoke-free environment.

Listings

Embassies Australia, ul. Nowogrodzka 11 ☏022/521 34 44; Canada, al Matejki 1/5 ☏022/584 31 00; Ireland, ul. Humańska 10 ☏022/849 66 55; New Zealand – matters handled by the UK embassy; UK, al Róż 1 ☏022/628 10 01; US, al Ujazdowskie 29 ☏022/628 30 41. **Internet access** Casablanca, ul. Krakowskie Przedmieście 4/6; EMPiK Megastore, Marszałkowska 116/122; plus numerous small cafés in the tunnels under Centralny train station. **Laundry** Alba, ul. Chmielna 26 (closed Sun).

Left luggage There's a 24hr left-luggage office at Warszawa Centralna, as well as lockers where you can store luggage for up to ten days. **Medical services** IMC Damian Hospital ☏022/853 62 34 (8am–8pm; after hours ☏0602183733); CM Medical Centre ☏022/458 70 00. **Pharmacies** 24hr *apteka* on top floor of Centralny Station in main hall, or opposite KFC at corner of al. Jerozolimskie/ul. Marszałkowska. **Post office** ul. Świętokrzyska 31/33 (24hr).

Northern Poland

Even in a country accustomed to shifting borders, northern Poland presents an unusually tortuous historical puzzle. Successively the domain of a Germanic crusading order, of the Hansa merchants and of the Prussians, it's only in the last fifty years that the region has really become Polish. **Gdańsk**, **Sopot** and **Gdynia** – the **Tri-City**, as their conurbation is known – dominate the area from their coastal vantage point. The most enjoyable excursions from Gdańsk are to the medieval centres of **Malbork** and **Toruń**.

Gdańsk

Both the starting point of World War II and the birthplace of the Solidarity movement, Gdańsk has played more than a fleeting role on the world stage. Traces of its past can be seen in the steel skeletons of derelict shipyard cranes and the Hanseatic and Prussian-influenced architecture of the beautifully restored old town. After all the political and social upheavals of the last century the city is now busy reinventing itself as a popular student and tourist hub.

The **Główne Miasto** (Main Town) is the obvious starting point and is within easy walking distance of the train station. Entering it is like walking straight into a Hansa merchants' settlement, but its ancient appearance is deceptive: by May 1945 war had reduced the core of Gdańsk to ruins, leaving the city facing a laborious rebuilding programme. Huge stone gateways guard both entrances to **ul. Długa**, the main thoroughfare. Start from the sixteenth-century gate at the top, **Brama Wyznna**, and you'll soon come across the huge tower of the Town Hall, which houses the **Historical Museum** (Tues, Thurs, Fri, Sat 10am–5pm, Sun 11am–5pm; 5zł, Wed free 10am–4pm). Past the Town Hall, the street opens onto the wide expanse of **Długi Targ**, where **Arthur's Court** (Dwór Artusa) stands out in a square filled with fine mansions. At the end of the street the archways of the **Brama Zielona** (Green Gate) open directly onto the waterfront. From the bridge over the Motława Canal you get a good view of the granaries on Spichlerze Island and along the old harbour quay.

Halfway down is the largely original fifteenth-century **Gdańsk Crane**, the biggest in medieval Europe (May–Sept Tues–Sun 10am–6pm; Oct–April Sat & Sun only 10am–4pm; 4zł). A little further on is the **Central Maritime Museum** (May–Sept Tues–Sun 10am–6pm; Oct–April Tues–Fri 9.30am–4pm; 12zł), with its exhibition of primitive boats and photographs illustrating the life of Polish writer Józef Korzeniowski, better known as Joseph Conrad. All the streets back into the town from the waterfront are worth exploring, especially **Mariacka**, brimming with amber traders and cafés. Next up from the Brama Zielona is ul. Chlebnicka, which ends at the gigantic **St Mary's Church**. Inside, the Chapel of 11,000 Virgins has a tortured Gothic crucifix, for which the artist apparently nailed his son-in-law to a cross as a model. Dominating the waterside here is the seven-storey **Great Mill**, the biggest mill in medieval Europe. To the right of the crossway is the fourteenth-century **St Catherine's Church**, one of the city's nicest with a well-preserved interior. The most interesting part of the district is west along the canal from the mill, centred on the **Old Town Hall**, on the corner of ul. Bielanska and Korzenna. Looming large are the cranes of the famous **Gdańsk shipyards**, the crucible of the political strife of the 1980s. Outside the gates is the famous anchor-topped **monument** to the workers killed during the 1970s riots, while the nearby **Roads to Freedom** exhibition on ul. Doki 1 (Tues–Sun 10am–5pm; 5zł) details the bloody struggle to topple communism.

Gdańsk's main **tourist office** (PTTK Gdańsk Tourist) is opposite the Town Hall at ul. Długa 45 (Mon–Fri 10am–6pm; May–Sept also Sat & Sun 10am–6pm; ☎058/301 91 51). *Gdańsk in Your Pocket* (from newsstands) is good for hotel, restaurant and bar listings. The most central **hostel** is at ul. Wałowa 21 (☎058/301 23 13; 16zł) a red-brick building with clean dorms ten minutes' walk from the main station; there's a midnight curfew. The hostel at ul. Grunwaldzka 238/240 (☎058/341 41 08; dorms 30zł, rooms ❶) also has basic doubles. *Willa Złota Plaża* (☎058/553 08 51; ❷; tram #8) is an old wooden villa set right on the beach. Of the cheaper **hotels**, try the central *Dom Harcerza*, ul. Za Murami 2/10 (☎058/301 36 21; dorms 14zł, rooms ❷), though you'll find *Dom Aktora*, ul. Straganiarska 55/6 (☎058/301 59 01; ❺), more comfortable, with snug en suites with TV. The most convenient **campsite** is at ul. Jelitkowska 23 (☎058/553 27 31; closed Oct–May), near the beach at Jelitkowo and a short walk from the terminus for trams #2, #6 or #8 from the train station.

For cheap **meals**, check out *Bar Neptun* at ul. Długa 33/34, one of the city's classic milk bars (open till 6pm, closed Sun). Nearby is *Bar Pod Rybą*, Długi Targ 35/38, a student institution dishing up a variety of jacket potatoes. *Sphinx*, Długi Targ 31/32, serves a reliable menu of Middle-Eastern food, while *Goldwasser Magic*, on the waterfront at ul. Długie Pobrzeże 22, has fresh snacks and light lunches at knockdown prices. The popular *Cocktail Bar Capri*, Długa 74, is the best place for coffee and cakes. For **drinking**, try *Kamiennica*, ul. Mariacka 37/39, a wonderfully intimate bar, or the *Irish Pub*, ul. Korzenna 33/35, frequented by an energetic crowd of young beer monsters. *Gospoda Pod Wielkim Młynem*, Na Piaskach 1, is one of the most picturesque bars in town. Best of the **clubbing** venues is the sprawling *Parlement*, ul. Św. Ducha 2.

PolFerries, ul. Przemysłowa 1 (☎058/343 18 87, ✆www.polferries.com.pl), runs a **ferry service** from Gdańsk to Nynäshavn near Stockholm (June–Sept daily; Oct–May Tues, Thurs and Sun at 6pm), while Stena Line, ul. Kwiatkowskiego 60 (☎058/665 14 14, ✆www.stenaline.pl), sails from Gdynia to Karlskrona (daily at 9am & 9pm, Fri also 7.30pm).

Sopot

Some 15km north of Gdańsk city centre is **SOPOT**, Poland's most upmarket coastal resort, with a famous pier and a vast stretch of sandy beach. Once regarded as the "Monte Carlo of the Baltics", Sopot is becoming a magnet for young Polish party animals. Commuter **trains** run between Gdańsk and Sopot every ten minutes during the day. The breezy main artery, ul. Bohaterów Monte Cassino, packed with year-round bars and restaurants, runs east from the train station towards the seaside gardens and the pier. *Pension Wanda*, 800m south of the pier at ul. Poniatowskiego 7

(☎058/550 30 38; ❹), has comfy en suites. *Chemik*, 1km further south at Bitwy pod Plowcami 61 (☎058/551 12 09; ❷), is a hideous concrete box with surprisingly good-value rooms. *Bar Przystan*, al Wojska Polskiego 11, is one of the area's best known fish **restaurants** (cheap too), while meat-eaters will appreciate the hearty helpings at *Harnaś*, ul. Moniuszki 9. *Greenway*, ul. Bohaterów Monte Cassino 67, has excellent vegetarian food and *Mandarynka*, ul. Bema 6, serves a good mixed bag of cuisine until late evening. Sopot's **nightlife** centres on ul. Bohaterów Monte Cassino. Film buffs might want to check out *Galeria Kiński*, ul. Kościuszki 10, a bar dedicated to local hero, actor Klaus Kinski. The justly famed **club** *Sfinks* – generally accepted as the country's top nightclub – is in the middle of the park off Powstańców Warszawy. *Enzym*, ul. Mamuszki 21, also has a wide range of club nights.

Malbork

Dating from the fourteenth-century, the castle of **MALBORK** is one of Poland's most spectacular fortresses. Built to serve as headquarters for the Teutonic Knights, it casts a threatening shadow over what is an otherwise sleepy town. The **train** and **bus stations** are sited next to each other about ten minutes' walk south of the castle; Malbork is on the main Warsaw line, so there are plenty of trains from Gdańsk (30–40min), as well as a regular bus service. You approach the **fortress** (Tues–Sun: May–Sept 9am–7pm; Oct–April 9am–3pm; 22zł) through the old outer castle, a zone of utility buildings never rebuilt after the war. Passing over the moat and through the daunting main gate, you come to the **Middle Castle**. Spread out around an open courtyard, this part of the complex contains the Grand Master's palace, of which the **Main Refectory** is the highlight. From the Middle Castle a passage rises to the smaller courtyard of the **High Castle**, the oldest section of the fortress, harbouring the focus of the Knights' austere monasticism – the vast **Castle Church**.

Toruń

The biggest and most important of the Hanseatic trading centres along the Wisła, **TORUŃ** miraculously survived the recurrent wars afflicting the region, and the historic centre is a rich assembly of architectural styles. Now it's a very friendly university city, with lots of cheap student bars sprinkled throughout the tight streets. Highlight of the westerly Old Town area is the mansion-lined **Rynek**. Inside the fourteenth-century Town Hall, the **Town Museum** (Tues–Sun 10am–4pm, May–Sept until 6pm; 6zł) has a gorgeous collection of fourteenth-century stained glass, fine sculpture and artefacts from the fifty-odd local guilds. In the western corner of the Rynek stands the impressive medieval **Church of the Blessed Virgin Mary**. South of the Rynek, at ul. Kopernika 15/17, is the **Copernicus Museum** (Tues–Sun 10am–4/6pm; 6zł), installed in the high brick house where the great man was born and containing a collection of Copernicus artefacts and a sound-and-light show of fifteenth-century Toruń (8zł extra). The font in which Copernicus was baptized can be seen in the massive **St John's Cathedral** (May–Sept Mon–Sat 9am–5.30pm; 2zł) at the eastern end of ul. Kopernica. To the northeast lies the **New Town** district with a number of illustrious commercial residences grouped around the Rynek Nowomiejski. Ul. Prosta leads north of the square to a park in which stands the former arsenal, now an **Ethnographic Museum** (May–Sept Mon, Wed & Fri 9am–4pm, Tues, Thurs, Sat & Sun 10am–6pm; Oct–April Tues–Fri 9am–4pm, Sat & Sun 10am–4pm; 8zł), dealing with the customs and crafts of northern Poland, including an outdoor display of wooden buildings.

The principal stations are on opposite sides of the Old Town. Toruń Główny, the main **train station**, is 2km away south of the river; buses #22 and #27 (every 10min; 1.7zł) run to pl. Rapackiego, on the western edge of the Old Town. Exit the station beyond platform 4 and buy tickets from the kiosk beside the bus stop. From the **bus station** on ul. Dabrowskiego it is a short walk south to the centre. The very friendly **tourist office** at Rynek Staromejski 1, in the town hall (Mon & Sat 9am–4pm, Tues–Fri 9am–6pm; May–Sept also Sun 9am–1pm; ☎056/621 09 31, ⊛www.it.torun.pl), hands out free maps and can advise about accommodation. For **hotels**, there's the excellent *Hotelik w Centrum*, just east of the centre at ul. Szumana 2 (☎056/652 22 46; ❷). All rooms have TV and there's a kitchen and Internet access. If this is full, try the simple but clean *Dom Wycieczkowy PTTK*, ul. Legionow 24 (☎056/622 38 55; dorms 30zł, rooms ❷); take bus #27 four stops north from the main station. The two **hostels** are both about 3km from the centre – at ul. Św. Józefa 22/24 to the northwest (☎056/659 61 84; 16zł); and in an old fortress at ul. Chobrego 86 to the northeast (☎056/655 82 36, ⊛fortiv@wp.pl; 15zł; bus #28 or #14). The *Tramp* **campsite** at ul. Kujawska 14 (☎056/654 71 87; closed Oct–April), a short walk west of the train station, also has **bungalows** (sleep 4-6; 75zł).

Best of the cheap **places to eat** in town is the *Bar Mleczny*, on the corner of Rózana and Sw. Ducha, with a branch on ul. Szczytna, offering filling soups and meaty snacks. Popular with students, *Manekin*, north of Rynek Nowomiejski at ul. Wysoka 5, serves 53 varieties of excellent pancakes. Head for the vaulted rooms of *Staromiejska* at ul. Szcytna 2–4 for cheap pasta dishes and pizzas, or to *U Sołtysa*, ul. Mostowa 17, for Polish fare in folksy surroundings. Riverbank **cafés** provide numerous outdoor drinking opportunities. Otherwise, best of the regular **bars** is *Pod Aniołem*, a cellar under the town hall which sometimes hosts DJs and dancing. Other good choices are *Metropolis*, a lively restaurant, bar and club at ul. Podmurna 28, and *Pod Krzywà Wiezą*, a tremendous bar in the Old Town battlements on ul. Bankowa. Find the *Jeremi* **Internet café** at Rynek Staromejski 33 (24hr).

Southern Poland

Southern Poland garners more visitors than any other region in the country, and its attractions are clear enough from just a glance at the map. The **Tatra Mountains**, which form the border with Slovakia, are Poland's grandest and most beautiful, snowcapped for much of the year and markedly alpine in feel. **Kraków** ranks with Prague and Vienna as one of the architectural gems of Central Europe, and is the country's intellectual heart. Pope John Paul II was Archbishop of Kraków until his election in 1978 but equally important are the city's Jewish roots: until World War II, this was one of the great European Jewish centres. This past remains clear in the old Jewish area of Kazimierz, and its culmination is starkly enshrined at the death camps of **Auschwitz–Birkenau**, west of the city.

Kraków

KRAKÓW was the only major city in the country to come through World War II essentially undamaged, and its assembly of monuments has now been listed by UNESCO as one of the world's most significant historic sites. Although swarming with visitors in summer, the city's Old Town retains an atmosphere of *fin-de-siècle* stateliness, and its streets are a cavalcade of churches and aristocratic palaces. A university centre, Kraków has a tangible buzz of arty youthfulness and boasts a wealth of nightlife opportunities to match.

Arrival, information and accommodation

Kraków Główny, the central **train station**, and the main **bus station** just opposite, are five minutes' walk northeast of the city's historic centre. Everything there is to see in the city is within walking distance. The **city tourist office** occupies a circular pavilion between the stations and the Old Town at ul. Szpitalna 25 (May–Sept Mon–Fri 8am–8pm, Sat & Sun 9am–5pm; Oct–April Mon–Fri 8am–4pm; ☎012/432 00 60, ⊛www.krakow.pl); they can provide information on accommodation possibilities but won't ring them up on your behalf. Staff at the **regional**

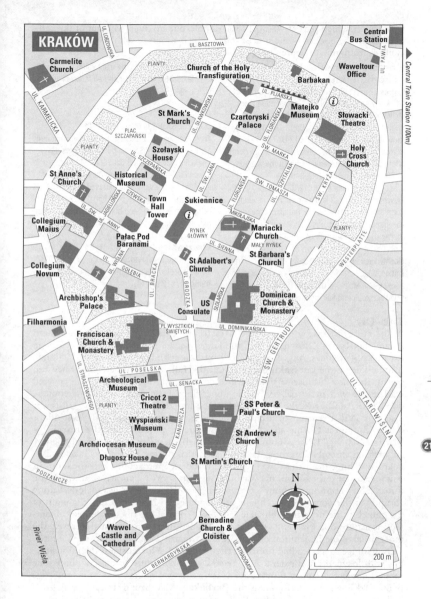

KRAKÓW

Carmelite Church

Church of the Holy Transfiguration

Central Bus Station

Barbakan

Waweltour Office

St Mark's Church

Czartoryski Palace

Matejko Museum

Słowacki Theatre

PLAC SZCZAPAŃSKI

Szołayski House

Holy Cross Church

St Anne's Church

Historical Museum

Town Hall Tower

Sukiennice

Mariacki Church

Collegium Maius

Pałac Pod Baranami

RYNEK GŁÓWNY

St Barbara's Church

MAŁY RYNEK

Collegium Novum

St Adalbert's Church

Archbishop's Palace

US Consulate

Dominican Church & Monastery

Filharmonia

Franciscan Church & Monastery

Archeological Museum

Cricot 2 Theatre

SS Peter & Paul's Church

Wyspiański Museum

St Andrew's Church

Archdiocesan Museum

Długosz House

St Martin's Church

N

Wawel Castle and Cathedral

Bernadine Church & Cloister

River Wisła

0   200 m

tourist office, Rynek Główny 1/3 (Mon–Fri 9am–6pm, Sat 9am–1pm; ☎012/421 77 06, ⬥www.mcit.pol), have a lot of good info on out-of-town sights. Just off the main square at ul. Św. Jana 2, the **Cultural Information Centre** (Mon–Fri 10am–6pm, Sat 10am–4pm; ☎012/421 77 87, ⬥www.karnet .krakow2000.pl) publishes **listings** of cultural events in a monthly booklet called *Karnet* and sells tickets. In English, there's the reliable *Kraków in Your Pocket* (⬥www.inyourpocket.com), available from newsstands. You'll need to book **accommodation** in advance. If you can't, be prepared to try your luck with a **pri-**

vate room, which start at 40–50zł for a double, but are often well out of the centre; they can be booked at the tourist office, which also deals with **student hostels**, available from June to September.

Hostel and student accommodation

Express Hostel ul. Wrocławska 91 ☏ 012/633 88 62, ⊛ www.express91.pl. Well-equipped student complex north of the centre. Bus #130 from the train station (towards Azory). Dorm 29zł, rooms ❷
Nawojka ul. Reymonta 11 ☏ 012/633 58 77, ⊛ www.bratniak.krakow.pl/nawojka. Student dorm offering en-suite doubles throughout the year, as well as cheaper rooms. July–Sept. ❷
Piast ul. Piastowska 47 ☏ 012/637 49 33, ⊛ www.piast.bratniak.krakow.pl. Large university dorm 3km west of the centre. Regular student accommodation plus some higher-grade rooms. ❷
Ul. Oleandry ul. Oleandry ☏ 012/633 88 22. The main hostel, 10min walk west of the centre, is a gloomy, grey place. Tram #15 or #18 from the train station. 20zł.
Żaczek al 3 Maja 5 ☏ 012/633 19 14, ⊛ www.zaczek.bratniak.krakow.pl. Well-placed students' hostel next to the main youth hostel. Simple doubles with either shared facilities or en suites. ❷

Hotels

Mistia ul. Szlak 73a ☏ 012/633 29 26, ⊛ www.mistia.org.pl. Decent budget hotel 5min walk north of the station. Spartan but clean rooms. ❸
Saski ul. Sławkowska 3 ☏ 012/421 42 22, ⊛ www.hotelsaski.com.pl. Central location, great ambience and a wonderful antique lift. ❺
Trzy Kafki al Słowackiego 29 ☏ 012/632 94 18, ⊛ www.trzykafki.pl. Good budget option, with clean rooms, laundry service and an Internet café. ❷

Campsite

Krak Camping ul. Radzikowskiego 99 ☏ 012/637 21 22. Located in the northwest of the city; take trams #4, #12 or #44.

The City

At the heart of Kraków is the **Stare Miasto**, the Old Town, with its great central square, the **Rynek Główny**. It was the largest square in medieval Europe: a huge expanse of flagstones, ringed by magnificent houses and towering spires. Its dominant building is the vast **Sukiennice** or **Cloth Hall**, rebuilt in the Renaissance and one of the most distinctive sights in the country, still housing a bustling covered market and with an art gallery on the upper floor. To its south is the tiny copper-domed **St Adalbert's**, the first church to be founded in Kraków. The tall tower nearby is all that remains of the fourteenth-century town hall. On the east side is one of the finest Gothic structures in the country, the **Mariacki Church** (St Mary's; Mon–Sat 11.30am–6pm, Sun 2–6pm; 4zł), the taller of its towers topped by an amazing ensemble of spires. Legend has it that during one of the Tatar raids, a guard watching from the tower saw the invaders approaching and took up his trumpet to raise the alarm; his warning was cut short by an arrow through the throat. Every hour on the hour a trumpeter plays the sombre *hejnał* melody, halting abruptly at the point the watchman was supposed to have been hit. Highlight of the church is the majestic high altar (1477–89), one of the finest examples of late-Gothic art; at noon (Sun and saints' days excluded) the altar is opened to reveal the inner panel of the Dormition of the Virgin, an amazing tableau of life-sized figures.

Of the three streets leading north off the Rynek, **ul. Floriańska** is the most striking, with fragments of medieval and Renaissance architecture among the shops. The robust fourteenth-century **Floriańska Gate**, at the end of the street, marks the edge of the Old Town proper. Beyond is the **Barbakan** (May–Sept daily 9am–6pm; 4zł) a bulbous, spiky fort, added in 1498. Back through Floriańska Gate, a right turn down the narrow ul. Pijarska brings you to the **Czartoryski Palace**, housing Kraków's finest art collection (Tues & Thurs 9am–3pm, Wed & Fri 11am–5.30pm, Sat & Sun 10am–3pm; 7zł, free Sun), a rich display of works ranging from the thirteenth to the eighteenth century. Most famous pieces here are Rembrandt's brooding *Landscape Before a Storm* and Leonardo da Vinci's *Lady with an Ermine*, though an intriguing highlight is the collection of Turkish trophies from the Battle of Vienna (1683).

West from the Rynek is the **university area**, whose heart is the Gothic Collegium Maius building, at ul. Jagellionska 15. Now the **University Museum**, the Collegium is open for guided tours only (Mon–Fri 10am–2.20pm, Sat 9am–1.20pm; 10zł, Sat free; ☎012/422 05 49) – you need to book places at least a day in advance. Inside, the ground-floor rooms retain the mathematical and geographical murals once used for teaching. In the treasury, the most valued possession is the Jagiellonian globe (1510), featuring the earliest-known map of America.

For over five hundred years, **Wawel Hill** was the seat of Poland's monarchy. The original **Cathedral** (May–Sept Mon–Sat 9am–2.45pm, Sun 12.15–2.45pm; 8zł) was built here around the time King Bolesław the Brave established the Kraków bishopric in 1020, but the present brick-and-sandstone basilica is essentially Gothic. All bar four of Poland's forty-five monarchs are buried in the cathedral, and their tombs and side chapels are like a directory of Central European architecture, art and sculpture of the last six centuries, not least the Gothic **Holy Cross Chapel**. The high spot of the whole cathedral though remains the opulent **Zygmuntowska chapel**. Arrive early or book ahead if you want to visit the various sections of **Wawel Castle** (ticket office Mon–Sat 9am–3pm, Sun 10am–3pm; ☎012/422 16 97) – only a limited number of tickets are sold each day. The **State Rooms** (Tues–Sat 9.30am–3pm, Sun 10am–3pm; 12zł) are furnished with Renaissance paintings, furniture and tapestries, while a tour of the **Royal Private Apartments** (same times; 15zł) reveals the King's private quarters. Although much of the contents had been sold by the time of the Partitions to pay off marriage dowries and debts of state, the **Royal Treasury and Armoury** (Tues–Sat 9.30am–3pm; 12zł) still features some fine items. The **Lost Wawel** exhibition (Mon & Wed–Sat 9.30am–3pm, Sun 10am–3pm; 3zł), beneath the old kitchens south of the cathedral, takes you past the excavated remains of the hill's most ancient buildings, including the foundations of the tenth-century **Rotunda of SS Felix and Adauctus**, the oldest church in Poland. Return to ground level via the **Dragon's Den** (May–Oct daily 10am–5pm; 3zł), a spiral staircase leading to a cavern. Legend has it that Smok the dragon lived here, feeding on a steady diet of children, cattle and unsuccessful knights. A clever peasant boy, Krak, fed him a sheep stuffed with sulphur; to quench the burning Smok drank half the Wisła, causing him to explode.

South from Wawel Hill lies the **Kazimierz** district, which in 1495 became the city's Jewish quarter. Kazimierz grew to become one of the main cultural centres of Polish Jewry, but in March 1941 the entire Jewish population of the city was crammed into a tiny ghetto over the river. Waves of deportations to the camps followed and the ghetto was finally liquidated in March 1943, ending seven centuries of Jewish life in Kraków. Today Kazimierz is a fashionable and bohemian residential district, with much to see. The tiny **Remu'h Synagogue** at ul. Szeroka 40 (Mon–Fri 9am–4pm; 5zł) is one of two still functioning in the quarter. The tombstones of its cemetery were buried and therefore largely saved from Nazi ransacking. Fragments are collaged together to form an impressive wall just inside the entrance. The **Old Synagogue** on ul. Szeroka is the oldest surviving Jewish religious building in Poland. Since the war it's been carefully restored and turned into a **Museum of Kraków Jewry** (Mon 10am–2pm, Wed–Sun 10am–3.30pm; 6zł, Mon free), including a permanent exhibition of traditional art by Polish Jews. The museum provides an excellent English-language introduction to the basic beliefs and rituals of Judaism. Another interesting visit is the refurbished **Synagoga Izaaka** (Isaac Synagogue), at ul. Kupa 18, which has an exhibition of photographs and short silent films illustrating the life of Kazimierz Jews before the war and after the formation of the ghetto (Sun–Thurs 9am–7pm, Fri 9am till sunset; 6zł).

Eating, drinking and nightlife

The *cukiernia* dotted around the city centre provide delicious cakes to most Kraków **cafés**, and Kraków's tourist status has resulted in a fine selection of **bars** and **restaurants**. In the city's **clubs** techno rules.

Cafés, milk bars and snacks

Babcia Malina ul. Sławkowska 17. Good Polish

food in a mountain-hut-style basement milk bar.

Bar Grodzki ul. Grodzka 47. Filling Polish standards

(including excellent potato pancakes or *placki*).

Café Numero Rynek Główny 6. Deliciously glam café serving excellent coffee (try it with syrup).

Chimera ul. Św. Anny 3, off the main square. Atmospheric rooms with a terrace upstairs in summer. Offers cheap, mainly veggie meals.

Kawiarnia u Literatów Kanonicza 7. A courtyard-cum-garden retreat for discerning drinkers.

Tajemnicky Ogród ul. Bracka 3–5. Lively café with a popular courtyard terrace, just of the Rynek.

Unnamed Café ul. Meiselska 20. Relaxed atmosphere and excellent cakes in a trendy Kazimierz café.

Restaurants

Arka Noego ul. Szeroka 2. The best-value Jewish restaurant in Kazimierz, with occasional live music.

Greenway ul. Mikołajska 12. Charming little vegetarian self-service restaurant with Polish and Mexican specialities.

Morskie Oko pl Szczepański 8. Huge piles of meat in a merry Zakopane-type setting with plenty of wood and waitresses in mountain garb.

Szlacheckie Jadło ul. Sławkowski 32. Polish fare at reasonable prices in a medieval decor; the lunch menu is 14zł.

Bars

Alchemia ul. Estery 5. Darkly atmospheric Kazimierz

bar catering for Bohemian regulars, curious tourists and permanently sozzled Cracovians.

Black Gallery ul. Mikołajska 24. Cellar bar with industrial decor, garden courtyard and lively crowd.

C.K. Browar ul. Podwale 6–7. Excellent beer hall that brews on the premises. Also has a good restaurant and disco.

Galaria Cocteau ul. Karmelicka 10. A popular gay-friendly bar.

Pauza ul. Floriańska 18. Lively first floor bar-gallery.

Pod Jemiola ul. Floriańska 20. Cramped but cosy "alternative" bar with cutting-edge dance music on the sound system.

Clubs and live music venues

Jazz Rock Café ul. Sławkowska 12. Techno-oriented bar with a dance floor.

Klub Kulturalny ul. Szewska 35. Trance and house music in a popular student cellar bar. Open till 2am.

Pod Jaszczurami Rynek Główny 8. Buzzing student club.

Prozac pl. Dominikański. For breakbeat, house and drum'n'bass.

Stalowe Magnolia ul. Św. Jana 15. Live music, though drinks don't come cheap.

Strefa 22 Rynek Główny 22. A young crowd parties here at weekends.

U Muniaka ul. Floriańska 3. Jazz sessions, Thurs–Sat at 9.30pm.

Listings

Consulates UK, ul. Św. Anny 9 ☎012/421 70 30; US, ul. Stolarska 9 ☎012/424 51 00.

Internet access Br@cka, above the Tajemnicky

Ogród café at ul. Bracka 3–5; Looz, ul. Mikołajska 13.

Pharmacies Grodzka 26. Rota posted on window.

Post office Ul. Westerplatte 20.

Oświęcim (Auschwitz-Birkenau)

In 1940, **OŚWIĘCIM**, a small town 70km west of Kraków, became the site of the Oświęcim-Brzeźinka concentration camp, better known by its German name of **Auschwitz-Birkenau**. Of the many camps built by the Nazis in Poland and other countries during World War II, this was the largest and most horrific: something approaching two million people, 85–90 percent of them Jews, died here. If you want all the specifics on the camp, you can pick up a detailed guidebook or join a guided group, often led by former inmates. Children under thirteen are not admitted. Get to Auschwitz-Birkenau from Kraków using one of the regular trains or buses to **Oświęcim station** (1hr 30min). From there it's a short bus ride to the gates of Auschwitz, though some buses from Kraków will drop you off at the Auschwitz entrance. There's an hourly **shuttle-bus service** to the Birkenau section from the car park at Auschwitz; taxis are also available, otherwise it's a 3km walk.

Most of the Auschwitz camp buildings have been preserved as the **Museum of Martyrdom** (daily: June–Aug 8am–7pm; May & Sept 8am–6pm; Oct–April 8am–5pm; free; ⊛www.auschwitz-museum.oswiecim.pl). The cinema is a sobering starting point, showing film taken by the Soviet troops who liberated the camp in May 1945. The bulk of the camp consists of the prison cell blocks, with the first section dedicated to "exhibits" found in the camp after liberation – namely rooms full of clothes and suitcases, toothbrushes, glasses, shoes and a huge mound of women's hair. Other barracks are given over to national memorials, and the blocks terminate with the gas chambers and the ovens where the bodies were incinerated. The huge **Birkenau camp** (same hours) is much less visited than Auschwitz, though it was here that the majority of executions were carried out. Birkenau was designed purely as a death camp, and the huge gas chambers at the back of the camp were damaged but not destroyed by the fleeing Nazis in 1945. Victims arrived in closed trains to be driven directly into the gas chambers; railway line, ramp, sidings – they are all still there, just as the Nazis abandoned them.

Zakopane and the Tatras

The **Tatra Mountains** – Tatry in Polish – are the most spectacular and most revered part of the almost unbroken chain of ridges extending along Poland's southern border. Some 80km long, with peaks of up to 2500m, most of the range actually rises in Slovakia. The major Polish resort on the fringes of the mountains is **ZAKOPANE**, a bustling tourist town, which serves as a good base for skiing or hiking, depending on the season. Skiing in particular is cheap, with the premier slopes of **Kasprowy Wierch** just five minutes by taxi from the centre.

Zakopane is easily reached by train (3–4hr) or bus (2hr) from Kraków. Both **stations** are a ten-minute walk east of the bustling pedestrian main street, ul. Krupówki. Uphill, the street merges into ul. Zamoyskiego, which runs on out of town towards the entrance to the Tatra National Park. **Tourist information**, housed in a wooden chalet west of the stations at ul. Kościuszki 17 (daily 8am–6pm; ⓦwww .polskietatry.pl), can book you into private rooms or pensions, and has maps, guidebooks, details on mountain huts and the latest weather. You can hire an English-speaking **mountain guide** here for 200–450zł per person. Near the park entrance, the **Tatra National Park Information Centre** at ul. Chałubińskiego 44 (daily 9am–3pm; ☎018/206 37 99, ⓔkozica@tpn.zakopane.pl) also sells maps and has weather details displayed in the window. There's a **hostel** just north of tourist information at ul. Nowotarska 45 (☎018/201 36 18; dorms 35zł), offering dorms or neat modern en-suite doubles. The more central and similar *Dom Turysty PTTK* is just off the main drag at ul. Zaruskiego 5 (☎018/206 32 81, domturysty@regle.zakopane.pl; dorms 20zł, rooms ❷). The best central **pension** is *Api-2*, north of the tourist office at Kamieniec 13a (☎018/206 29 31; ❸), while about every third house in town has decent **private rooms** (❷). The *Pod Krokwià* **campsite** (☎018/201 22 56) is at the end of ul. Żeromskiego on the south side of town. **Restaurants and cafés** are concentrated on ul. Krupówki. Local favourite *Sabala* (no. 11) offers slightly more expensive traditional fare, outside tables and indoor folk music. *Bąkowo Zohlina*, near the ski slopes at ul. Piłsudskiego 6, is a lively mountain-style restaurant with live music and dancing, serving excellent trout. *Paparazzi*, just off the main street at ul. Galicy 8, is the most convivial place to **drink**. Upstairs, *Widmo* offers 24-hour **Internet** access.

Silesia and Wielkopolska

In Polish it's known as Śląsk, in Czech as Sleszko and in German as Schlesien: all three countries hold part of the disputed province of **Silesia**, but since 1945 it's been almost all Polish, a dominance gained as compensation for the eastern territory incorporated into the USSR in 1939 and never returned. Silesia's main city, **Wrocław**, is one of Central Europe's most enticing cosmopolitan centres. North of Silesia, the region known as **Wielkopolska** formed the core of the original Polish nation, and its chief interest is supplied by the vibrant regional capital of **Poznań**.

Wrocław

WROCŁAW (pronounced "vrots-wav") is a city used to regular rebuilding.

Through centuries of regularly changing ownership it was largely dominated by Germans and generally known as **Breslau**. This all altered after the war, however, when the displaced population of Polish **Lwów** (now L'viv), which was annexed by the Soviets in 1939, were encouraged to take over the severely depopulated Breslau, which in turn had been confiscated from Germany. The multinational influences that shaped the city are reflected in much of its architecture: huge Germanic churches, Flemish-style mansions and Baroque palaces. The latest rebuilding came after a catastrophic flood in the early 1990s, which left most of the centre under several feet of water. Luckily the energy involved in the reconstruction that followed has left the city and its airy Old Town rejuvenated – and without the tourist mobs of Kraków.

The City

Wrocław's centre is delineated by the River Odra to the north and the bow-shaped ul. Podwale – the latter following the former city walls, whose moat, now bordered by a shady park, still largely survives. At the centre of town is the vast **Rynek** with its magnificent fifteenth-century Town Hall. The famous west face and south facade are real show stoppers, while the building itself now serves as the **Historical Museum** (Wed–Sat 11am–5pm, Sun 10am–6pm; 5zł, Wed free). In the northwest corner of the Rynek are two curious Baroque houses known as **Jaś i Małgosia**, linked by a gateway giving access to **St Elizabeth's**, the most impressive of Wrocław's churches. Since the mid-fifteenth century, its huge ninety-metre tower (Mon–Sat 9am–4pm, Sun 1–4pm; 4zł) has been the city's most prominent landmark. Southwest of the Rynek lies the maze-like former **Jewish quarter**, whose inhabitants fled or were driven from their tenements during the Third Reich. One of the largest synagogues in Poland, the **Synagoga pod Białym Bocianem** (Sun–Fri 10am–5pm; 4zł), lies hidden in a courtyard at ul. Włodkowica 9. Immediately to the east stands the monumental Royal Palace, housing the **Ethnographic Museum** (Tues–Sun 10am–4pm, Thurs 9am–4pm; 4zł, free Sat), its main draw a large collection of dolls dressed in traditional Silesian costume.

A specially designed concrete rotunda houses Wrocław's best-known sight, the **Panorama of the Battle of Racławice** (Tues–Sun 9am–6pm; in winter closes at 4pm; shows every 30min; 19zł, includes entrance to the National Museum). This painting, 120m long and 15m high, was commissioned in 1894 for the centenary of the Russian army's defeat by Tadeusz Kościuszko's militia near the village of Racławice, between Kraków and Kielce. At the other end of the park is the **National Museum** (Tues, Wed & Fri 10am–4pm; Thurs 9am–4pm, Sat & Sun 10am–4pm; 10zł, Thurs free), in whose medieval stone sculpture section is the poignant early fourteenth-century *Tomb of Henryk the Righteous*, with its group of weeping mourners.

North of the Rynek, the triangular-shaped university quarter, jam-packed with historic buildings, is bounded by two streets, ul. Uniwersytecka and ul. Grodzka. At the centre of things is the 171-metre-long **Collegium Maximum**, whose **Aula Leopoldina** assembly hall, upstairs at pl. Uniwersytecki 1 (Mon, Tues & Thurs 10.30am–3.30pm, Fri–Sun 11am–5pm; 4zł), is one of the greatest secular interiors of the Baroque epoch, fusing architecture, painting, sculpture and ornament into one bravura whole. From the Market Hall, the Piaskowski Bridge leads to the island of **Wyspa Piasek** and the fourteenth-century hall church of **St Mary of the Sands**, majestically vaulted and featuring a wonderfully kitsch animated children's altar. Two elegant little bridges connect Wyspa Piasek with **Ostrów Tumski**, the city's ecclesiastical heart. Ul. Katedralny leads past several Baroque palaces to the twin-towered **Cathedral of St John the Baptist**. Rebuilt after the war, the gloomy interior features some worthwhile Gothic and Baroque chapels. Take the lift up the tower (Mon–Sat 10am–6pm; 4zł) for good views of the city.

Practicalities

The main **train station**, Wrocław Głowny, faces the broad boulevard of ul. Piłsudskiego, about fifteen minutes' walk south of the Rynek; the main **bus sta-**

tion is behind the train station. The **tourist office** at Rynek 14 (Mon–Fri 9am–5pm, Sat 10am–2pm; ☎071/344 31 11) provides hotel listings, but they won't book rooms. There's a cluster of rather basic **hotels** near the train station – nearest is the *Hotel Piast* at ul. Piłsudskiego 98 (☎071/343 00 34; ❷), which gives 25zł reductions to ISIC holders. Between the stations and the Old Town the *Savoy*, pl. Kościuszki 19 (☎071/340 32 19; ❷), offers cheap, acceptable en suites. Best deal in the Old Town is the *Bursa Nauczycielska* at ul. Kotlarska 42 (☎071/344 37 81; ❷), with simple doubles and triples. The nearest **hostel** is 100m from the train station at ul. Kołłątaja 20, off ul. Piłsudskiego (☎071/343 88 56; 22zł), with nice small rooms with a domestic atmosphere but a 10pm curfew. The hostel occupying half of *Hotel Tumski*, north of the Old Town at Wyspa Słodowa 10 (☎071/322 60 99, ⓦwww.hotel-tumski.com.pl; 30zł), offers better standards but the same curfew. Information on summer **student hostels** (late June to Sept; ❶) is from Almatur, ul. Tadeusza Kościuszki 34 (Mon–Fri 10am–5pm; ☎071/343 41 35). There are bungalow beds at the **campsite** at al Padarewskiego 35 (☎071/348 46 51; 17zł; closed Oct-April) – trams #9, #12, #17 and #32 run nearby – and at ul. Na Grobli 16–18 (☎071/343 44 42; 30zł).

Mis, ul. Kuźnicza 48 (closes 6pm, and all Sun) is a student-packed **canteen**; while *Bar Mleczny Mewa*, ul. Nasypowa 2, *Jacek i Agatka*, pl. Nowy Targ 27, and *Kurna chata*, ul. Odrzańska 7, all provide cheap and good Polish fare. *Vega*, Rynek-Ratusz 27a, has **vegetarian** options daily till 5/7pm. The liveliest student haunt in the university quarter is *Kalogródek* at ul. Kuźnicza 29b. *Gumowa Róza*, entered from the Św. Wita alley, is a relaxed basement **bar** with a bohemian edge, while *Spiź* on the Rynek brews its own beer. For **dancing** try the bars on the Rynek, *Piec Nutek*, Podwale 37/38 (regular live gigs), or the student club *Kolor* on pl. Nowy Targ. There are also a series of new places on pl. Solny.

Poznań

Thanks to its position on the Berlin–Warsaw–Moscow rail line, **POZNAŃ** is many visitors' first taste of Poland. In many ways it's the ideal introduction, as no other city is more closely identified with Polish nationhood. It is a city of great diversity and hosts the country's most important trade fair. For seven centuries the grandiose **Stary Rynek** has been the hub of town life. The turreted Town Hall boasts a vivacious eastern facade, its lime-green pilasters framing a frieze of Polish monarchs. Inside lies the **Museum of the History of Poznań** (Mon & Tues 10am–4pm, Wed noon–6pm, Fri 10am-6pm, Sun 10am–3pm; 5.5zł), worth visiting for the stunning Renaissance **Great Hall** on the first floor, its coffered vault bearing polychrome bas-reliefs with scenes of Samson, King David and Hercules. Many a medieval and Renaissance interior lurks behind the Baroque facades of the **gabled houses** lining the outer sides of the Stary Rynek – the diverting **Museum of Musical Instruments** at no. 45 (Tues–Sat 11am–5pm, Sun 11am–3pm; 5.5zł, free Sat) is one fine example. Just to the west of the Stary Rynek at the end of ul. Zamkowa stands a hill with remnants of the inner circle of the medieval walls. This particular section guarded the **Castle**, which was the seat of the rulers of Wielkopolska. Modified down the centuries, it was almost completely destroyed in 1945, but has been partly restored to house the **Museum of Applied Arts** (Tues, Wed, Fri & Sat 10am–4pm, Sun 10am-3pm; 3.5zł), a collection of crafts from medieval times to the present. Nearby, at al Marcinkowskiego 9, is Plac Wolności, where the excellent **National Museum** (Tues 10am–6pm, Wed 9am–5pm, Thurs, Fri & Sat 10am–5pm, Sun 10am–4pm; 10zł) houses one of the few important displays of old master paintings in Poland. Highlights include Zurbarán's *Madonna of the Rosary* and the *Adoration of the Magi* by Joos van Cleve. East of the Stary Rynek, the Bolesława Chrobrego bridge crosses to the quiet holy island of **Ostrów Tumski**. The first buildings you see are the late-Gothic **Psalteria** and the brick **St Mary's**, while behind that is the **Cathedral of SS Peter and Paul**. Most of this cathedral, Poland's oldest, was restored to its Gothic shape after wartime devastation, but a lack of documentary evidence for the eastern chapels meant that their successors had to be retained, as were the Baroque spires. Inside, the **crypt** has been excavated, uncovering earlier foundations, as well as parts of the sarcophagi of the early Polish monarchs.

Practicalities

The main **train station**, Poznań Główny, is 2km southwest of the historic quarter; tram #5 runs from the western exit beyond platform 7 to the city centre. The **bus station** is five minutes' walk east of the train station, across the bridge. The **city tourist office**, next to the EMPiK store on the corner of Ratajczaka and 27 Grudnia (Mon–Fri 10am–7pm, Sat 10am–5pm; ☏061/851 96 45, ✇www.cim.poznan.pl) hands out free maps and cultural information as well as selling the monthly **listings** guide *Iks*. The **regional tourist office** at Stary Rynek 59 (Mon–Fri 9am–5pm, May–Sept also Sat 10am–2pm; ☏061/852 61 56) has information on the surrounding province and sells the *Poznań in Your Pocket* guide. Poznań **hotel** prices double during trade fairs, which take place throughout the year, July and August excepted. Cheap and decent is *Mini-Hoteli*, al Niepodległości 8 (☏061/863 14 16; ❷). Alternatively, try the *PTTK Dom Turysty* at Rynek 91 (☏061/852 88 93; 50zł). There's one **hostel** 500m southwest of the train station at ul. Berwińskiego 2/4 (☏061/866 40 40; 30zł), while further out is the excellent *Schronisko TPD*, ul. Drzymały 3 (22zł; seventh stop on tram #11 towards Jeżyce). Almatur at Ratajczaka 3 (Mon–Fri 10am–5pm, Sat 10am–2pm; ☏061/855 76 34) arranges accommodation in **student hostels** (June–Sept). **Private rooms** (❷) can be had from the Globtour office in the train station (open 24hr; rooms available until 10pm). The **campsite**, *Malta*, ul. Krańcowa 98 (☏061/876 62 03; tram #8 from train station), is set by a lake 2km east of the centre and has great bungalows (❷) available year-round.

Find cheap Polish food at the *Apetyt* **milk bar**, just off the Rynek on Szkolna, or at *Pod Kuchcikiem* at ul. Św. Marcina 71. *Ali Baba*, ul. Św. Marcin 11, has filling piles of cheapish Middle Eastern food, while *Bar Wegeterianski*, ul. Wrocławska 21, is healthy and cheap (open till 5.30pm, Sat 3pm, closed Sun). The large student population also ensures a lively **nightlife** scene. Danish-owned *Faxe Pub*, Rynek 62, is jam-packed on weekends, while the bars on ul. Nowowiejskiego are great for meeting students: *Pod Minogą* (no. 8) hosts bands on weekends and *W Starym Kinie* shows free art films. Further west on ul. Kościuszki *Blue Note* is a famed jazz bar hosting regular live gigs and club nights. **Internet** access is available at Klik, south of the Rynek on Jaskółca.

Travel details

Trains

Gdańsk to: Kraków (7 daily; 7–10hr overnight); Poznań (7 daily; 4hr); Toruń (6 daily; 3hr); Warsaw (15 daily; 4hr); Wrocław (4 daily; 6–7hr); Zakopane (2 daily; overnight).

Kraków to: Gdańsk (8 daily; 7hr–10hr overnight); Oświęcim/Auschwitz (16 daily; 1hr 30min); Poznań (7 daily; 6–7hr); Toruń (1 daily; overnight); Warsaw (15 daily; 2hr 30min); Wrocław (11 daily; 4hr–4hr 30min); Zakopane (14 daily; 3–4hr).

Poznań to: Gdańsk (7 daily; 4hr); Kraków (6 daily; 6–7hr); Toruń (4 daily; 2–3hr); Warsaw (17 daily; 3hr); Wrocław (20 daily; 2hr).

Toruń to: Gdańsk (5 daily; 3hr); Kraków (2 daily; overnight); Poznań (3 daily; 2hr); Warsaw (5 daily; 3hr); Wrocław (2 daily; 4hr 30min).

Warsaw to: Gdańsk (15 daily; 4hr); Kraków (14 daily; 2hr 30min); Poznań (17 daily; 3hr); Toruń (5 daily; 3hr); Wrocław (10 daily; 5hr); Zakopane (2 daily; 8hr 30min).

Wrocław to: Gdańsk (4 daily; 6–7hr); Kraków (11 daily; 4hr 30min); Poznań (18 daily; 2hr); Toruń (2 daily; 4hr 30min); Warsaw (9 daily; 5hr).

Zakopane to: Kraków (15 daily; 3–4hr).

Buses

Kraków to: Oświęcim/Auschwitz (19 daily; 1hr 30min); Zakopane (56 daily; 2hr 30min).

Portugal

Portugal highlights

* **Alfama, Lisbon**
Traditional village life in
the heart of the capital;
getting lost in the alleys
is half the fun. See p.735

* **A night out in Lisbon**
Great city for clubbing;
have a night in the Bairro
Alto or the club *Lux* to
find out why. See p.737

* **Óbidos** Picturesque village, its dazzling white-
washed houses
enclosed by medieval
walls. See p.741

* **Queima das Fitas,
Coimbra** University town
that celebrates the end
of the academic year big
time every May. See
p.744

* **Port wine lodges, Porto**
Various lodges offer free
tastings. See p.747

* **The Douro rail route**
One of the most beauti-
ful lines in Europe, along
the foot of the steep
Douro river valley. See
p.749

Introduction and basics

Portugal has always been influenced by the sea. The Portuguese are very conscious of themselves as a seafaring race; mariners like Vasco da Gama led the way in the exploration of Africa and the Americas, and until thirty years ago Portugal remained a colonial power. The vibrant capital, Lisbon, has enough going on to please most city devotees, while along the coast nearby, and further south on the well-developed Algarve, there are sophisticated beach resorts. But in its rural areas this is still a conspicuously underdeveloped country, and there are plenty of opportunities to experience a lifestyle that has changed little over the last century.

Roughly north of the River Tagus, or Tejo – which cuts across the country at its midpoint – the people are of predominantly Celtic and Germanic stock. South of the Tagus, where the Moorish and Roman civilizations were most established, people tend to be darker-skinned and maintain more of a "Mediterranean" lifestyle. The 1974 **revolution** came from the south – an area of vast estates, rich landowners and a dependent workforce. More profoundly even than that, **emigration** and **colonial power** have altered people's attitudes and the appearance of the country. Returning emigrants have brought in modern ideas and challenged many traditional rural values, while the colonies brought African and South American strands to the country's culture: in the distinctive music of *fado*, sentimental songs heard in Lisbon and Coimbra, for example, or in the Moorish-influenced architecture.

Scenically, the most interesting parts of the country are in the north: the **Minho**, green, damp, and often startling in its rural customs; and the sensational gorge and valley of the **Douro**, followed along its course by the railway, off which antiquated branch lines edge into remote **Trás-os-Montes**. For contemporary interest, spend some time in both **Lisbon** and **Porto**, the two major cities. And if it's monuments you're after, the centre of the country – above all, **Coimbra** and **Évora** – retains a faded grandeur. The coast is virtually continuous beach, and apart from the **Algarve** and a few pockets around Lisbon and Porto, resorts remain low-key. Perhaps the loveliest are along the northern **Costa Verde** or, for isolation, the wild beaches of **southern Alentejo**.

Information & maps

You'll find a tourist office (**Turismo**) in almost every town. Staff can help you find a room, and often have local maps and leaflets. The best **maps** are put out by the Automóvel Clube de Portugal, GeoCenter or the Michelin #437.

Money and banks

Currency is the **euro** (€). **Banks** open Mon–Fri 8.30am–3pm; in Lisbon and in some of the Algarve resorts banks may open in the evening to change money. ATMs are widespread; commission on travellers' cheques can be high.

㉒

Portugal on the net

- Ⓦ**www.min-cultura.pt** Ministry of Culture, with an agenda of major events.
- Ⓦ**www.portugal.org** Tourist office site, with information and advice.
- Ⓦ**www.portugalvirtual.pt** Comprehensive directory listings.
- Ⓦ**www.algarvenet.com** Detailed site dedicated to the Algarve region.

Communications

Post offices (*correios*) are normally open Mon–Fri 9am–6pm, Sat 9am–noon. For poste restante, look for a counter marked *encomendas*. International **phone calls** can be made direct from any phone booth or post office. Phonecards cost €3, €6 or €9, from post offices, larger newsagents and tobacconists. The operator is on ☎118 (domestic), ☎098 (international). **Internet cafés** are common (€1.20–4/hr). Most major post offices also have Internet booths – just buy a card behind the counter.

Getting around

You can get almost everywhere easily and efficiently by public transport. CP (✪www.cp.pt) operates the **trains**. Most are designated *Regional* and stop at most stations. *Intercidades* are twice as fast and twice as expensive, and must be reserved. The fastest and most luxurious are the *Rápidos* (known as "*Alfa*"), which speed between Lisbon, Coimbra and Porto – sometimes they have only first-class seats. CP sells its own **rail passes** (valid on any train and in first class), but you'd have to do a lot of travelling to make them worthwhile. InterRail and Eurail are valid, though supplements must be paid on *Intercidades* and *Rápidos*. You can buy a complete timetable at ticket offices (€2.50), or check online. **Buses** are often more flexible than trains and fares are usually competitive. On a number of major routes (particularly Lisbon–Algarve) express coaches can knock hours off the standard multiple-stop bus journeys. ✪www.rede-expressos.pt has timetables. There's 24hr national bus information on ☎707 22 33 44. **Cycling** is popular, though there are few facilities and little respect from motorists. Bikes can be transported on any *Regional* or *Interregional* train as long as there is space – check with the baggage office in advance – for around €2 (free if the bike is dismantled).

Accommodation

In almost any town you should be able to find **accommodation** in a single room for under €25 and a double for under €50. Even in high season you shouldn't have many problems finding a bed, except in Lisbon and the Algarve. The main budget stand-bys are **pensions**, or *pensões*. A three-star *pensão* is usually about the same price as a one-star **hotel**. Seaside resorts invariably offer **rooms** (*quartos* or *dormidas*) in private houses. These are sometimes advertised, or just hawked by people at the bus and train stations. They're slightly cheaper than pension rooms – especially if you haggle, as is expected in the main resorts. Tourist offices have lists. At the higher end of the scale are **pousadas**, run by the state and similar to the Spanish *paradores*. These charge at least four-star hotel prices, but they are often converted from old monasteries or castles and well worth a visit even if you can't afford to stay.

There are over 40 **hostels** (*Pousadas de Juventude*; ✪www.pousadasjuventude.pt); most stay open all year and impose a curfew (usually midnight) and all demand a valid HI card. A dormitory bed costs €7.50–15, depending on season and location; doubles cost €19.50–35. Portugal has around 200 **campsites**, most small, low-key and attractively located, and all remarkably inexpensive – you'll rarely pay more than €5 a person. You can get a fairly complete map list from any tourist office, or buy the detailed *Roteiro Campista* booklet (✪www.roteiro-campista.pt) from bookshops. Camping rough is banned; beach areas are especially strict about this.

Food and drink

Portuguese **food** is excellent, cheap and served in quantity. Virtually all cafés will serve you a basic meal, or at least a snack, for under €8, and for a little more you have the run of most of the country's restaurants. You'll often come across a whole range of dishes at a **café**, but classic snacks include *tosta mistas* (cheese and ham toasties); *prego* (steak sandwich), usually served with a fried egg;

Portugal is one hour behind Spain.

biftoque (steak, chips, fried egg); *rissóis de carne* (deep-fried meat patties); *pastéis de bacalhau* (codfish cakes); and *sandes* (sandwiches). **Restaurant** servings tend to be huge. Indeed, you can usually have a substantial meal by ordering a *meia dose* (half portion), or *uma dose* between two. Meals are often listed like this on the menu and it's normal practice. Most restaurants serve an *ementa turística* (set meal) which can be good value, particularly in *pensões* that serve meals, or in the cheaper workers' cafés. It's always worth going for the **prato do dia** (dish of the day) and, if you're on the coast, plumping for fish and seafood. Typical dishes include *sopa de marisco* (shellfish soup), *caldo verde* (finely shredded green kale leaves in broth) and *bacalhau* (dried cod, cooked in a myriad of different ways). *Caldeirada* is a fish stew cooked with onions and tomatoes. Also typical is *carne de porco á Alentejana*, in which fried pork is covered with a clam, tomato and onion sauce or stewed with tomato and onions. Regional **cheeses** are well worth sampling, particularly goat and sheep cheese. **Puddings** include *arroz doce* (rice pudding), *salada da fruta* (fresh fruit salad) and *nuvens* (egg custard). Cakes – *bolos* or *pastéis* – are often at their best in *casas de chá* (tearooms), though you'll also find them in cafés and in *pastelarias* (cake shops). Among the best are custard tarts (*pastéis de nata*), marzipan cakes from the Algarve, and the incredibly sweet egg-based *doces de ovos*.

Portuguese **wines** (*tinto* for red, *branco* for white) are very inexpensive and of high quality – even a standard *vinho da casa* in the humblest of cafés. The fortified **port** (*vinho do Porto*) and **madeira** (*vinho da Madeira*) wines are the best known. The light, slightly sparkling **vinhos verdes** – "green wines", in age not colour – are produced in the Minho, and are excellent and refreshing served chilled. **Brandy** is available in two varieties, Macieiera and Constantino, and like local gin is ridiculously cheap; if you're asking at a bar, always specify "gin nacional", "vodka nacional", etc – it'll save you a fortune. The two most common local **beers** (*cervejas*) are Sagres and Super Bock. Order *um fino* or *um imperial* if you want a small glass; *uma caneca* will get you a half-litre.

Opening hours and holidays

Shop **opening hours** are generally Mon–Fri 9am–12.30/1pm & 2/2.30–6/6.30pm, Sat 9am–12.30/1pm. Larger supermarkets tend to stay open until 8pm. Museums, churches and monuments open from around 10am to 6pm; almost all, however, close on Mondays and at Easter. The main **public holidays** are: Jan 1; Feb carnival; Good Fri; April 25; May 1; Corpus Christi; June 10; June 13 (Lisbon only); Aug 15; Oct 5; Nov 1; Dec 1; Dec 8; Dec 25.

Emergencies

Lisbon and the larger tourist areas have seen increases in petty crime. Possession of any kind of hard or soft drugs no longer constitutes a prisonable offence – although dealing does. **Police**, though relatively easygoing, carry guns and are not to be argued with. For minor health complaints go to a **pharmacy** (*farmácia*), which you'll find in almost any village, normally open Mon–Fri 9am–1pm & 3–7pm, Sat 9am–1pm. A sign at each one will show the nearest 24hr pharmacy. Pharmacists are highly trained and can dispense many drugs without a prescription. You can get the address of an English-speaking **doctor** from a consular office or, with luck, the local police or tourist office.

Emergency numbers

All emergencies ☎112.

Lisbon (Lisboa)

There are few more immediately likeable capitals than **LISBON** (Lisboa). A lively place, it remains in some ways curiously provincial, rooted as much in the 1920s as the 2000s. Wooden trams clank up outrageous gradients, past mosaic pavements, Art Nouveau cafés and the medieval quarter of Alfama, which hangs below the city's São Jorge castle. Modern Lisbon has kept an easy-going, human pace and scale, while boasting a vibrant, cosmopolitan identity. The city invested heavily during the 1990s as disused dockland was reclaimed and communication links improved, and yet more improvements have been made as Lisbon gears up to host the 2004 European Football Championship.

The city has a huge amount of historic interest. The **Great Earthquake** of 1755 (followed by a tidal wave and fire) destroyed most of the grandest buildings, but frantic reconstruction led to many impressive new palaces and churches, as well as the street grid pattern spanning the seven hills of Lisbon. Several buildings from Portugal's golden age survived the quake – notably the Castelo de São Jorge and the Monastery of Jerónimos at **Belém**. Contemporary sights include the **Fundação Calouste Gulbenkian**, with its superb collections of ancient and modern art.

Arrival, information and accommodation

From Portela **airport** the #91 Aerobus (7am–9pm, every 20min; takes 20min; €2.35) runs from outside the arrivals hall to Praça dos Restauradores, Rossio, Praça do Comércio and Cais do Sodré; the ticket is then valid for transport on buses and trams for that day. Local buses #44 and #45 (€1) run from the road outside the airport to Rossio and Cais do Sodré (train station for Cascais). Long-distance **trains** use **Santa Apolónia station**, fifteen minutes' walk from the waterfront Praça do Comércio, or a short ride on buses #9, #39, #46 or #90 to Rossio. Local trains from Sintra arrive at **Rossio station**, while trains from the Algarve terminate at **Barreiro**, on the far bank of the river, from where you catch a ferry (included in price of train ticket) to the **Fluvial** station next to the Praça do Comércio. Most trains from Santa Apolónia also pass through **Oriente** station.

Best place for up-to-date information is the **Lisboa Welcome Centre**, on the corner of Praça do Comércio and Rua do Arsenal (daily 9am–8pm; ☎210 312 700, ⓦwww.atl-turismolisboa.pt). For information on the rest of the country, visit the main **tourist office** on the western side of Praça dos Restauradores in the Palácio da Foz (daily 9am–8pm; ☎213 466 307, ⓦwww.portugalinsite.pt); there's also a small tourist office at the airport (daily 6am–midnight; ☎218 450 660). The **Lisboa Card** (€13/22/27 for one/two/three days), available from any tourist office, gives unlimited travel, entry to 26 museums plus discounts. The best Lisbon **map** is the *Falkplan*, which shows all the minor streets not usually shown on other maps; it's sold in the newsagent next to the tourist office in Praça dos Restauradores.

Most places of interest are within walking distance, while the fast **metro** (ⓦwww.metrolisboa.pt) covers much of the city; tickets cost €0.65 each, €5.10 for ten, or €1.40 for a day pass. The **trams and buses** (ⓦwww.carris.pt) are the most

---

The picture-book **tram #28** is one of Lisbon's greatest rides, though at times it carries more tourists than Lisboetas: you may have to stand. With a travel pass, you can hop on and off where you like. The central section of its route runs from Rua da Conceição in the Baixa, past the Sé and up Rua Augusto Rosa, before rattling through some of Lisbon's steepest and narrowest streets – so close to the shopfronts you could almost take a can of sardines off the shelves. The route is of less interest after you reach Rua de Voz do Operário, from where it's a short walk down to the Feira da Ladra market; or get off at the next stop, in Largo da Graça, for the superb city views.

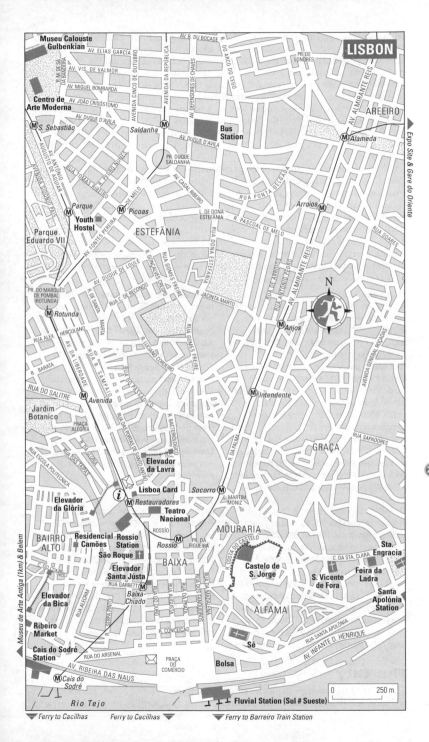

enjoyable way of getting around – tickets (€1, valid on both) can be used for two journeys when purchased in advance from kiosks, or for one journey when bought on board. A one-day **travel pass** (*bilhete turístico*; €2.75) allows unlimited travel on buses, trams and the metro until midnight; alternatively, there are *Passe Turístico* bus/metro/*elevador* **passes**, valid for four days (€9.95) or seven days (€14.10), available from booths. A short hop in a **taxi** shouldn't cost more than €10, but they can be hard to find at night – if you're leaving a bar or club book one by phone from Rádio Táxis de Lisboa (☎218 119 000) or Teletáxis (☎218 111 100). **Ferries** cross the River Tagus (Rio Tejo); most are operated by Transtejo (€0.55–1.55; ⊛www.transtejo.pt) and depart from Belém, Cais do Sodré and Praça do Comércio.

Lisbon has scores of small, cheap **pensions**, most of which are around Rua das Portas de Santo Antão and Rua da Glória. Most of those listed below are one- or two-star; addresses, written as 53-3°, for example, show the street number followed by the floor. The Bairro Alto is the most atmospheric neighbourhood, though rooms can be hard to find and noisy. At Easter and in midsummer, availability is stretched: many single rooms are "converted" to doubles and prices may start as high as €25. However, during the rest of the year you should have little difficulty finding a place, and for maybe a third less than the midsummer prices. For more expensive **hotels**, use the commission-free 24-hour reservation service (☎213 141 562) at the Praça dos Restauradores tourist office or the airport.

Hostels

Casa de Juventude Lisboa Parque das Nações Rua da Moscavide 47–101, Parque das Nações ☎218 920 890. Modern hostel, 20min from the centre but right on the banks of the Tagus. No curfew. Metro to Oriente. ❶

Pousada de Juventude da Catalazete Estrada Marginal, Oeiras ☎214 430 638. Overlooking the beach, 15km outside the city. Take any train from Cais do Sodré and follow signs from Oeiras station. It's small, so phone before setting out. Reception open 6–11pm. ❶

Pousada de Juventude de Lisboa Rua Andrade Corvo 46 ☎213 532 696. Lisbon's main hostel, with good facilities and no curfew. Book in advance. One block south of Picoas metro stop, or take buses #1, #21 or #36 from Restauradores or Rossio. ❷

Pensions and hotels

Residencial Camões Trav. do Poço da Cidade 38-1°, Bairro Alto ☎213 467 510. Brilliant location, though invest in some earplugs for streetside rooms at weekends. Breakfast included in high season, English spoken. ❸

Pensão Coimbra e Madrid Praça da Figueira 3-3°, Baixa ☎213 421 760. Superb views, though the rooms are noisy. Decent proprietors, shabby though clean furnishings and a TV room. ❸

Residencial Florescente Rua das Portas de Santo Antão 99, Baixa ☎213 426 609. One of the

city's best-value establishments, with lots of rooms, some with TV, some without windows, so ask about alternatives. ❹

Pensão Ninho das Águias Costa do Castelo 74, Alfama ☎218 854 070. Bright, light rooms with a lovely garden terrace overlooking the city. ❸

Pensão Prata Rua da Prata 71-3°, Baixa ☎213 468 908. Small rooms, some with showers, up three extremely steep flights of stairs in a welcoming, family-run apartment. Book ahead. ❸

Pensão São João de Praça Rua São João de Praça 97-2°, Alfama ☎218 862 591. Clean, quiet and friendly place in a lovely old town house just below the cathedral. Front rooms have wrought-iron balconies. Half-board compulsory during summer. ❹

Campsites

Camping Obitur-Guincho Lugar da Areia, Guincho ☎214 870 450, ⊛www.orbitur.pt. A well located site some way out of the city in surfer's paradise Guincho, with supermarket, sports facilities and cabins to rent. Train from Cais do Sodré to Cascais, then bus to Guincho.

Parque Municipal de Campismo Parque Florestal Monsanto ☎217 623 100. Main city campsite, 6km west of the centre. The entrance is on Estrada da Circunvalação on the park's west side. Bus #43 from Praça da Figueira.

The City

The heart of the capital is the lower town – the **Baixa** – Europe's first great example of Neoclassical design and urban planning. It's an imposing quarter of rod-straight

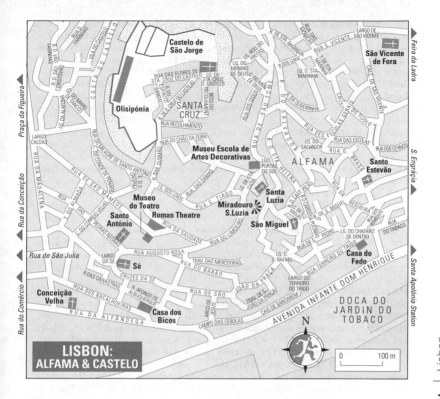

LISBON:
ALFAMA & CASTELO

The map labels include: Castelo de São Jorge, São Vicente de Fora, Olisipónia, SANTA CRUZ, Museu Escola de Artes Decorativas, ALFAMA, Santo Estêvão, Santa Luzia, Miradouro S.Luzia, São Miguel, Museu do Teatro, Roman Theatre, Santo António, Sé, Conceição Velha, Casa dos Bicos, Casa do Fado, DOCA DO JARDIM DO TOBACO, AVENIDA INFANTE DOM HENRIQUE, Praça da Figueira, Rua da Conceição, Rua de São Julia, Rua do Comércio, Feira da Ladra, S. Engrácia, Santa Apolónia Station, 0 100 m, N

streets, cobbled underfoot and either streaming with traffic or turned over to pedestrians and pavement artists. Between the Baixa and the Bairro Alto, halfway up the hill, lies an area known as the **Chiado**, which suffered much damage from a fire in 1988 but has been elegantly rebuilt by Portugal's premier architect Alvaro Siza Viera. It remains the city's most affluent quarter, focused on **Rua Garrett** and its fashionable shops and beautiful old tearooms. **Rossio** square is very much a focus for the city, with a couple of great cafés, though its main concession to grandeur is the **Teatro Nacional**, built along the north side in the 1840s. At the waterfront end of the Baixa lies the city's other main square, the beautiful arcaded **Praça do Comércio**.

A couple of blocks east stands the **Sé** or Cathedral (daily 9am–7pm). Founded in 1147 to commemorate the city's reconquest from the Moors, it occupies the site of the principal mosque of Moorish Lishbuna. Like so many of the country's cathedrals, it is Romanesque and extraordinarily restrained in both size and decoration. You'll need to pay to visit the thirteenth-century cloisters (€1) and the treasury museum (€2.50), including the relics of St Vincent. From the Sé, Rua Augusto Rosa winds up towards the castle, past the **Miradouro de Santa Luzia,** which offers spectacular views over the Tejo. The **Castelo São Jorge** (daily 9am–dusk; free) contains the shell of the Moorish palace that once stood here; now it hosts **Olisipónia** (daily 10am–12.30pm & 2–5pm; €1.50), a multimedia show that makes an excellent introduction to the city. The castle itself is an enjoyable place to spend a couple of hours, wandering amid the ramparts and towers.

The **Alfama** quarter, tumbling from the walls of the Castelo to the banks of the River Tejo, is the oldest part of Lisbon. In Arab times it was the city's grandest district, but with subsequent earthquakes the new Christian nobility moved out, leaving it to the fishing community. Despite some commercialization, the quarter still retains a largely traditional life. The **Feira da Ladra**, Lisbon's rambling flea market, fills the Campo de Santa Clara, at the edge of Alfama, every Tuesday and Saturday. Also take a look inside **Santa Engrácia** (Tues–Sun 10am–5pm; €2), the loftiest and most tortuously built church in the city – begun in 1682, its vast dome was finally completed in 1966. Through the tiled cloisters of nearby **São Vicente de Fora** you can visit the old monastic refectory, since 1855 the pantheon of the Bragança dynasty (Tues–Sun 10am–5.30pm; €2.50). Here, in more or less complete sequence, are the bodies of all Portuguese kings from João IV, who restored the monarchy in 1640, to Manuel II, who lost it and died in exile in England in 1932.

High above and to the west of the Baixa is **Bairro Alto**, the focus of the city's nightlife. The district can be reached by one of two funicular-like trams – the **Elevador da Glória** from the Praça dos Restauradores or the **Elevador da Bica** from Rua de São Paulo/Rua da Moeda (both €1 one-way). The other means of access, the great **Elevador Santa Justa** (€1), built by Eiffel disciple Raul Mésnier de Ponsard, is still being renovated, but you can ride to the top to a café and superb views. Hanging almost directly above the exit of Mésnier's funicular are the ruined Gothic arches of the **Convento do Carmo** (Tues–Sun 10am–5/6pm; €2.50). Once the largest church in the city, this was half-destroyed by the earthquake and is perhaps even more beautiful as a result; its small archeological museum contains treasures from monasteries that were dissolved after the 1834 Liberal revolution.

Parque Eduardo VII and the Gulbenkian

North of Praça dos Restauradores are the city's principal gardens, the **Parque Eduardo VII** (metro Marquês de Pombal). Though there are some pleasant cafés here, the park's big attraction is the **Estufa Fria** (daily 9am–4.30/5.30pm; €1.15), a huge and wonderful glasshouse filled with tropical plants, flamingo pools, and endless varieties of palms and cacti. The **Museu Calouste Gulbenkian** (Tues–Sun 10am–5.45pm; €3, free Sun; joint ticket with Centro de Arte Moderna €5), the great museum of Portugal, is ten minutes' walk north of the Parque Eduardo VII – or take bus #31 or #46 from Restauradores or the metro to São Sebastião or Praça de Espanha. Established by the Armenian oil magnate Calouste Gulbenkian, the Fundação helps finance various aspects of Portugal's cultural life – including an orchestra, three concert halls and two galleries for temporary exhibitions on the site. This showpiece museum is divided into two distinct parts – the first devoted to Egyptian, Greco-Roman, Islamic and Oriental arts, the second to European, including paintings from all the major schools. There's also a stunning room full of Art Nouveau jewellery by René Lalique. Across the gardens, the separate **Centro de Arte Moderna** (same hours; €3) has all the big names from the twentieth-century Portuguese scene.

Museu Nacional de Arte Antiga

The one other museum that stands up to the Gulbenkian is the national art collection, the **Museu Nacional de Arte Antiga** (Tues 2–6pm, Wed–Sun 10am–6pm; €3), situated near the riverfront to the west of the city at Rua das Janelas Verdes 95 (bus #40 or #60 from Praça do Comércio). Its core is formed by fifteenth- and six-teenth-century Portuguese works, the acknowledged masterpiece being Nuno Gonçalves' *St Vincent Altarpiece*, a brilliantly marshalled canvas depicting Lisbon's patron receiving homage from all ranks of its citizens. After Gonçalves and his con-temporaries, the most interesting works are by Flemish and German artists (Cranach, Bosch – a fabulous *Temptation of St Anthony* – and Dürer), and miscella-neous gems by Raphael, Zurbarán and Rodin.

Belém

Even before the Great Earthquake, the **Monastery of Jerónimos** (daily 10am–5/6.30pm, free; cloisters same hours, €3; tram #15 from Praça do Comércio or #14 from Praça da Figueira) at **Belém** was Lisbon's finest monument: since then, it has stood quite without comparison. It was from Belém in 1497 that Vasco da Gama set sail for India, and it was here, too, that he was welcomed home by Dom Manuel. The monastery was funded by a levy on the fruits of his discovery – a five-percent tax on all spices other than pepper, cinnamon and cloves, whose import had become the sole preserve of the Crown. Begun in 1502, this is the most ambitious achievement of Manueline architecture. The main entrance to the church is a shrine-like hierarchy of figures centred around Henry the Navigator. Vaulted throughout and fantastically embellished, the cloister is one of the most original and beautiful pieces of architecture in the country, holding Gothic forms and Renaissance ornamentation in an exuberant balance. The **Torre de Belém** (Tues–Sun 10am–5/6.30pm; €3), guarding the entrance to the port around 500m from the monastery, is a multi-turreted whimsy built over the last five years of Dom Manuel's reign. Back towards the monastery are a number of museums, of which the best are the **Museu de Arte Popular** (Tues–Sun 10am–12.30pm & 2–5pm; €1.75, free Sun morning), a province-by-province display of Portugal's folk arts, and the **Museu do Design** (daily 11am–8pm; €3) in the Centro Cultural de Belém, featuring design classics from the twentieth century. Opposite is the vast concrete **Monument to the Discoveries** (Tues–Sun 9am–5/7pm; free) erected in 1960 to commemorate the 500th anniversary of the death of Henry the Navigator; inside, a small exhibition space has changing displays on the city's history. The lift (€1.90) takes you to the top for spectacular views.

Eating, drinking and nightlife

Lisbon has some great **cafés and restaurants** serving large portions of food at sensible prices. Seafood is widely available – there's an entire central street, Rua das Portas de Santo Antão, as well as a whole enclave of restaurants across the River Tejo at Cacilhas, which specialize in it. Lisbon also has a rich vein of inexpensive foreign restaurants featuring food from the former colonies (including Angola, Goa and Macau). Many restaurants are **closed on Sundays**, while on Saturday nights you may need to book for the more popular places. The best **food market** is Mercado da Ribeira, Avda 24 de Julho, Cais do Sodré (Mon–Sat 5am–2pm).

The densest concentration of designer bars and clubs is in **Bairro Alto** – Lisbon's traditional nightlife centre. Late-night (though pricier) action can also be found out in the **Docas** (Docklands) district, just east of the 25 de Abril bridge (train to Alcântara Mar from Cais do Sodré or tram #15 or #18). Converted warehouses at the **Doca de Santo Amaro** host waterfront bars and cafés, while a little closer to the city centre the **Doca de Alcântara** has emerged as the hangout for Lisbon's chic. Clubs don't really get going until around 2am and tend to stay open till 6am. Admission fees are usually about €10 (usually including one or two drinks), although some clubs leave the cover charge to the doorman's discretion – anything from €5 to €50. To sample local **fado**, a mournful, romantic singing style somewhere between the blues and flamenco, which bemoans lost loves and better times, try clubs in the Bairro Alto or Alfama and expect to pay over €15. If you check out the posters around Restauradores there's a good chance of catching **African music**. What's-on **listings** are in the free *Agenda Cultural*, issued monthly, or in the Friday supplements of the *Independente* or *Diario de Noticias* newspapers.

Cafés

Antiga Confeitaria de Belém Rua de Belém 90, Belém. Historic tiled café famous for its delicious custard tarts or *pastéis de nata*.

Café a Brasileira Rua Garrett 120. The most famous of Rua Garrett's old-style coffee houses. Open until 2am.

Café Nicola Praça Dom Pedro IV 26. On the west side of Rossio, this grand old place is a good stop for breakfast. Closed Sat pm & all Sun.

Café Pastelaria Bernard Rua Garrett 104. Superb cakes and an outdoor terrace on Chiado's most fashionable street.

Café Suiça Praça Dom Pedro IV 96. Famous for cakes and pastries.

Restaurants

Adega Santo Antão Rua das Portas de Santo Antão 42, Baixa. Good value *adega* with local character, offering great grilled meat and fish.

Closed Mon.

Algures na Mouraria Rua das Farinhas 1. Inexpensive place with excellent Angolan dishes such as *moamba de ginguba* (chicken with peanut sauce). Closed Mon.

Arco do Castelo Rua do Chão da Feira 25. Cheerful place by the castle entrance with tempting Goan cooking.

Bota Alta Trav. da Queimada 37, Bairro Alto. Old tavern restaurant that pulls in the punters for its large portions of traditional Portuguese food. Closed Sat lunch & Sun.

Restaurante Calcuta Rua do Norte 17, Bairro Alto. Indian restaurant with chicken, seafood and lamb curries, tandooris, good vegetarian options. Closed Sun.

O Cantinho do Bem Estar Rua do Norte 46, Bairro Alto. Inexpensive Alentejan restaurant that's as friendly and authentic as you can get.

Carvoeiro Rua Vieira Portuense 66–68, Belém. One of many inexpensive fish restaurants near the monastery, with outdoor tables. Closed Mon.

Casa Faz Frio Rua Dom Pedro V 96, Bairro Alto. Beautiful, very traditional restaurant, with tiny cubicles. Around €10 for a full meal and wine.

Casanova Armazém B, Cais da Pedra à Bica do Sapato, Santa Apolónia. Fashionable riverside restaurant serving pizza, pasta and *crostini* with great views from its outside terrace. You can't book, so turn up early. Closed Mon, & Tues lunch.

Cervejaria da Trindade Rua Nova da Trindade 20, Bairro Alto. Wonderful, vaulted beer-hall restaurant, the oldest in the city, with a tiny patio garden. Expensive.

Hell's Kitchen Rua da Atalaia 176, Bairro Alto. Well worth seeking out for a menu of world foods that includes vegetarian dishes. Closed Mon.

Hua Ta Li Rua dos Bacalhoeiros 119. Very good, affordable Chinese/Macau restaurant near the Sé – seafood scores highly. Popular for Sunday lunch.

Mestré André Calçadinha de Santo Estêvão 4–6, Alfama. A fine neighbourhood tavern, with good grills (*churrasco*). Outdoor seating in summer. Closed Sun.

Rei dos Frangos/Bom Jardim Trav. de Santo Antão 11–18, Baixa. Excellent for spit-roast chicken – a whole one with fries for about €8.

São Cristóvão Rua de São Cristóvão 28 ☏218 885 578. Titchy all-day Cape Verdean restaurant which crams in tables, a TV and live music on Fri–Sun eves. Booking advised, because there's not much room.

Teatro Taborda Costa do Costelo 75, Alfama. Fashionable theatre café/restaurant with fine views from the terrace, serving fresh vegetarian dishes and Greek salads. Closed Mon.

Os Tibetanos Rua da Salitre 117, Rato. Fine vegetarian restaurant run by Buddhists serving organic food. Closed Sat & Sun.

Yin-Yang Rua dos Correeiros 14, Baixa. When all the animal protein gets too much, find tofu and fresh juice here.

Bars

Bar Ártis Rua Diário Notícias 95, Bairro Alto. Chill to mellow jazz with a good mix of locals. Closed Mon.

Cena de Copos Rua da Barroca 103–105, Bairro Alto. The place to be if it's after midnight, you're under 25 and bursting with energy.

Instituto do Vinho do Porto Rua de São Pedro de Alcântara 45, Bairro Alto. Over 200 types and vintages of port, from €1 a glass. Closed Sun.

Pavilhão Chinês Rua Dom Pedro V 89, Bairro Alto. Overly decorated bar, completely lined with cabinets of bizarre artefacts. Daily till 2am. Very expensive.

A Tasca Trav. da Quiemada 13–15, Bairro Alto. Cheerful and welcoming tequila bar.

Clubs

Doca de Santo Doca de Santo Amaro, Ponte 25 de Abril. Large palm-fringed club, one of the first and the most popular in this area.

Kapital Avda. 24 de Julho 68, opposite Santos station. Sweaty outmoded dance venue where you can have a laugh until 6am.

Kasino Rua Cozinha Económica 11, Alcântara. Big house/techno spot. Closed Sun-Tues.

Kremlin Escadinhas da Praia 5. One of the city's most snobbish nightspots, packed with flash young Lisboetas. Techno still rules. Closed Sun & Mon.

Lux Cais da Pedra a Santa Apolónia, opposite Santa Apolónia station. Top Portuguese DJs as well as big European names. Closes 6am.

Salsa Latina Gare Marítima de Alcântara, Doca de Santo Amaro. A bar/restaurant and club in a fantastic 1940s cruise-ship terminal, offering salsa (Tues–Sat) and live music at weekends. Closed Sun.

Trumps Rua da Imprensa Nacional 104b, Rato, north of Bairro Alto. The biggest gay disco in Lisbon with a reasonably relaxed door policy. Closed Mon.

WIP Elevador da Bica. Halfway down the hill, this bar has a host of different DJs covering reggae/Afro through soul to drum'n'bass.

Fado and live music

Adega do Ribatejo Rua do Diário de Notícias 23, Bairro Alto. Popular *fado* venue with a lower-than-usual minimum charge. Singers include a couple of professionals, the manager and even the cooks. Closed Sun.

Atlantic Pavilion Parque das Nações. Portugal's largest indoor venue hosting big-name stars.

B.leza Largo do Conde Barão 50, Santos. Live African music most nights in a sixteenth-century building, with space to dance and Cape Verdean food. Closed Sun.

Chafarica Calçada de São Vicente 81, Alfama. Tiny, long-established Brazilian bar with live music every night. Best after midnight, especially after a few *caipirinhas*.

Hot Clube de Portugal Praça da Alegria 39, off Avda. da Liberdade. Tiny basement jazz club, which hosts local and visiting artists. Closed Mon.

Paradise Garage Rua João de Oliveira Miguens 38, Alcântara. Big on the club scene, also hosts regular gigs. It's on a tiny side road off Rua da Cruz à Alcântara. Closed Sun-Wed.

O Senhor Vinho Rua do Meio a Lapa 18, Lapa. Famous Lapa club sporting some of the best *fado* singers in Portugal.

A Severa Rua das Gáveas 51–61, Bairro Alto. A city institution featuring big *fado* names at big prices. Closed Thurs.

Listings

Embassies Australia, Avda. da Liberdade 198–2° ☏213 101 500; Canada, Avda. da Liberdade 196–200 ☏213 164 600; Ireland, Rua da Imprensa à Estrela 1–4° ☏213 929 440; UK, Rua de São Marçal 174 ☏213 929 440; US, Avda. das Forças Armadas ☏217 273 300.

Exchange Main bank branches in the Baixa. Exchange office at the airport (24hr) and at Santa Apolónia station (daily 8.30am–4pm).

Hospital British Hospital, Rua Saraiva de Carvalho 46 ☏213 955 067.

Internet Ask Me Lisboa, above Lisboa Welcome Centre, Praça do Comércio; Web C@fe, Ruo do Diário de Notícias 126, Bairro Alto.

Laundry Lava Neve, Rua de Alegría 37, Bairro Alto (closed Sat pm & all Sun).

Post office Praça dos Restauradores 58.

Day-trips from Lisbon

Half an hour south of Lisbon, dunes stretch along the **Costa da Caparica**, which the quirks of the River Tejo's currents have largely spared from the pollution that plagues the city. Travelling north instead you'll pass the coastal resorts of Estoril and Cascais before reaching the lush wooded heights and royal palaces of **Sintra** and the monastery of **Mafra**, one of the most extraordinary buildings in the country. These places can all be seen on a day-trip from Lisbon, but to do justice to Sintra you'll need to stay overnight.

Caparica

A short journey south of the capital, **CAPARICA** is a thoroughly Portuguese resort, popular with surfers and crammed with restaurants and beach cafés, yet solitude is easy enough to find, thanks to the mini-railway (*transpraia*) that runs along the 8km of dunes in summer. The most enjoyable way to get there is to take a **ferry** from the Fluvial station by Praça do Comércio, or from Cais do Sodré, to Cacilhas, and then pick up the connecting bus. Alternatively, take a **bus** direct to Caparica from Praça de Espanha (metro Praça de Espanha). Buses either stop at a bus park by the beach, or at the station five minutes back from the sands. From the latter, turn right up to the main road, turn right and keep walking until you reach Praça da Liberdade, the main square, where there's a **tourist office** (Mon–Fri 9am–1pm & 2–5.30pm, Sat 9am–1pm; ☏212 900 071), market, cinema and banks. The tourist office can direct you to one of several hotels in Caparica, though buses run back to Lisbon/Cacilhas at regular intervals throughout the day. **Campsites**, which range along the first few kilometres of the beach, are on the whole overcrowded and overpriced, but functional enough. There are dozens of good, relaxed, cheap **fish and seafood** places, as well as beach bars, along the main Rua dos Pescadores, which leads from the square to the beach. Get off at *transpraia* stop 12 to try the excellent food at the *Cabana do Pescador*.

Sintra

SINTRA is one of Portugal's most spectacular sights, cool, deciduous woodland that once attracted Moorish lords and the kings of Portugal from Lisbon during the hot summer months. The layout of Sintra – an amalgamation of three villages – can be confusing, but the extraordinary **Palácio Nacional** (10am–5.30pm, closed Wed; €3), about twenty minutes' walk from the train station, is an obvious landmark. The palace was probably in existence under the Moors, but takes its present form from the rebuilding commissioned by Dom João I and his successor, Dom Manuel, in the fourteenth and fifteenth centuries. Its style is a fusion of Gothic and the latter king's Manueline additions. The chapel and its adjoining chamber – its floor worn by the incessant pacing of the half-mad Afonso VI who was confined here for six years by his brother Pedro I – are well worth seeing.

One of the best local walks leads past the church of Santa Maria and up to the ruined ramparts of the **Moorish Castle** (daily 10am–5/7pm; €3), from where the views are extraordinary. Beyond the castle, a steep ninety-minute walk from town, is the lower entrance to the immense **Pena Park**, at the top end of which rears the fabulous **Palácio de Pena** (Tues–Sun 10am–5/7pm; €5; gardens only €3), a wild nineteenth-century fantasy of domes, towers and a drawbridge that does not draw. The interior has been preserved exactly as left by the royal family on their flight from Portugal in 1910. Another must-see site is **Quinta da Regaleira** (daily 10am–5.30/8pm; €5), one of Sintra's most elaborate private estates, five minutes' walk west out of town on the Seteais-Monserrate road. The palace and its fantastic gardens were built at the turn of the last century by a theatrical set designer for one of the richest industrialists in Portugal. The highlight is the Initiation Well, inspired by the initiation practices of the Knight Templars and Freemasons. Entering via an Indiana Jones-style revolving stone door, you can walk down a moss-covered spiral stairway to the foot of the well and to a tunnel, which eventually resurfaces at the edge of a lake. Beyond Quinta da Regaleira, the road leads past a series of beautiful private estates to **Monserrate** – about an hour's walk - whose vast **gardens** (daily 9am–5/7pm; €3), filled with endless varieties of exotic trees and subtropical shrubs and plants, extend as far as the eye can see.

Trains run here regularly from Rossio station in Lisbon. Finding **accommodation** in summer can be a problem, though if you arrive early in the day you should end up with something. The best-value pension is probably *Adelaide*, Rua Guilherme Gomes Fernandes 11 (☎219 230 873; ❷), midway between the train station and Sintra village. *Pielas* (☎219 241 691; ❸), Rua João de Deus 70–72, near the station, offers superb rooms above a café. A little further out, in São Pedro, *Residencial Sintra*, Travessa dos Alvares (☎219 230 738; ❹), is a fantastic place with a rambling garden, swimming pool and giant rooms which can easily accommodate extra beds. Alternatively, cheap **private rooms** (❷) can be booked through the extremely helpful **Turismo** (daily 9am–7/8pm; ☎219 231 157), just off the central Praça da República. There's also a tourist office at the train station. The **hostel** (☎219 241 210; dorms ❶, rooms ❷; closed noon–6pm) is at Santa Eufemia in the hills above Sintra, 5km from town – take a local bus to São Pedro from outside the train station and walk from there (2km). **Restaurants** are generally poor value, relying heavily on the tour parties. Try *Xentra*, Rua Consiglieri Pedroso 2A, behind the Turismo, or the grilled fish at *Adega de Caves* in the main square.

Mafra

Connected by regular buses from Sintra train station and from outside Campo Grande metro stop in Lisbon, **MAFRA** is dominated by one building: the vast, pink marble **Palace-Convent** (10am–4.30pm, closed Tues; €3), built in emulation of Madrid's El Escorial in 1717 by João V, the wealthiest and most extravagant of all Portuguese monarchs. The convent was initially intended for just thirteen Franciscan friars, but as more gold poured in from Brazil, João expanded it into the world's largest basilica, with two royal wings and monastic quarters for 300 monks and 150 novices. The sheer magnitude of the building is what stands out: there are 5200 doorways, 2500 windows, and two bell towers each containing over 50 bells.

The highlight is the magnificent Rococo library, rivalling that of Coimbra in both design and grandeur. The basilica is no less imposing, with the multicoloured marble designs of its floor mirrored in the ceiling decoration.

Central Portugal

The **Estremadura** region has played a crucial role in each phase of the nation's history – and the monuments are there to prove it. A comparatively small area of fertile rolling hills, it boasts an extraordinary concentration of vivid architecture and engaging towns. **Alcobaça, Batalha, Óbidos** and **Tomar** – home to the most exciting buildings in Portugal – all lie within ninety minutes' bus ride of one another, as does the pilgrimage centre of **Fátima**. North of Estremadura, life on the fertile plain of the **Beira Litoral** has been conditioned over the centuries by the twin threats of floodwaters from Portugal's highest mountains and silting by the restless Atlantic. The highlight here is **Coimbra**, an ancient university town stacked high on the right bank of the Mondego.

Óbidos

ÓBIDOS is a small town of whitewashed houses draped in bougainvillea and encircled by lofty medieval walls. "The Wedding Town" was the traditional bridal gift of the kings of Portugal to their queens, a custom begun in 1282 by Dom Dinis. The town – a couple of hours from Lisbon by train – can hardly have changed in appearance since then: its cobbled streets and steep staircases wind up to the ramparts, from where you can gaze across a fable-like countryside of windmills and vineyards. The parish church, **Igreja de Santa Maria**, in the central Praça, was chosen for the wedding of the ten-year-old child-king Afonso V and his eight-year-old cousin, Isabel, in 1444. The interior, lined with seventeenth-century blue *azulejos*, contains a retable in a side chapel to the right painted by Josefa de Óbidos, one of the finest Portuguese painters and one of the few women artists afforded any reputation by art historians. One corner of the triangular fortifications is occupied by a massively towered **Castle** built by Dom Dinis and now converted into an expensive *pousada*. Other **hotels** in Óbidos also tend to be expensive. Your cheapest option is to consult the list of **private rooms** posted in the **tourist office**, in the main coach park, just south of the town walls (daily 9.30am–6/7pm; ☎262 959 231); there are comfortable rooms at Rua Direita 83 (☎262 959 328; ❷). *Hospedaria Louro*, five minutes' walk south of the coach park, has smart rooms, superb breakfasts, a lovely garden and a pool (☎262 955 100; ❸). One of the better budget places to **eat** is the *Café 1º de Dezembro*, next to the church of São Pedro.

Leiria

With regular bus services to the three big sites of northern Estremadura – Alcobaça, Batalha and Fátima – **LEIRIA** makes a handy centre for excursions. The chief sight here is the **Castle** (daily 9/10am–5.30/6.30pm; €2), incorporating an elegant royal palace with a magnificent balcony high above the River Lis. At the heart of the old town, Praça Rodrigues Lobo is surrounded by beautiful buildings and arcades. The **tourist office** (daily: summer 10am–1pm & 3–7pm; winter 2–6pm; ☎244 814 748) and **bus station** are on opposite sides of a park overlooking the river in the modern city centre. The **train station** is about 4km out of town, with a connecting bus service. For accommodation, check the **pensions**, such as *Pensão Dom Dinis*, Trav. de Tomar 2 (☎244 815 342; ❸), and the restaurants (some offering rooms) around Praça Rodrigues Lobo and on narrow side streets like Rua Mestre Aviz and Rua Miguel Bombarda. There's also a fancy **hostel** with a good atmosphere at Largo Cândido dos Reis 9 (☎244 831 868; ❷). As for **restaurants**, try the seafood at *Jardim*, by the tourist office (closed Mon), or slightly more expensive Portuguese cuisine at *Montecarlo*, Rua Dr Correia Mateus 32–34.

Alcobaça

From the twelfth century until the middle of the nineteenth, the Cistercian **Abbey of Alcobaça** (daily 9am–5/7pm; €3) was one of the greatest in the Christian world. Owning vast tracts of farmland, orchards and vineyards, it held jurisdiction over a dozen towns and three seaports until its ultimate dissolution in 1834. The monastery was originally founded by Dom Afonso Henriques in 1147 in celebration of the liberation of Santarém from the Moors, and is a truly vast complex – its main **Church** (free entry) is the largest in Portugal. The exterior is disappointing, as the Gothic facade has been superseded by unexceptional Baroque additions. Inside, however, all later adornments have been swept away, restoring the narrow soaring aisles to their original vertical simplicity. The only exception to this Gothic purity is the frothy Manueline doorway to the sacristy, hidden behind the high altar. The abbey's most precious treasures are the fourteenth-century **tombs** of Dom Pedro and Dona Inês de Castro, sculpted with phenomenal wealth of detail to show the story of Pedro's love for Inês de Castro, the daughter of a Galician nobleman. Fearing Spanish influence over the Portuguese throne, Pedro's father, Afonso V, forbade their marriage. The ceremony nevertheless took place in secret, whereupon Afonso sanctioned his daughter-in-law's murder. When Pedro succeeded to the throne in 1357 he exhumed the corpse of his lover, forcing the entire royal circle to acknowledge her as queen by kissing her decomposing hand. The tombs – inscribed with the motto "Até o Fim do Mundo" (Until the End of the World) – have been placed foot to foot so that on the Day of Judgement the lovers may rise and immediately feast their eyes on one another. The most amazing room in the building is the **kitchen**, with its cellars and gargantuan conical chimney, supported by eight trunk-like iron columns. A stream tapped from the River Alcôa still runs straight through the room: it was used not merely for cooking and washing but also to provide a constant supply of fresh fish. The **Sala dos Reis** (Kings' Room), off the beautiful **Cloisters of Silence**, displays statues of virtually every king of Portugal down to Dom José, who died in 1777.

Alcobaça's **tourist office** (daily 10am–1pm & 3–6/7pm; ☎262 582 377) is opposite the abbey on Praça 25 de Abril. The best budget **pension** is *Pensão Corações Unidos* (☎262 582 142; ❸), around the corner at Rua Frei António Brandão 39. There's an all-year **campsite** (☎262 582 265), ten minutes north of the bus station along Avenida Professor Vieira Natividade. Good-value **restaurants** include the touristy *Frei Bernado*, Rua D Pedro V 17–19, a huge place serving copious meals, and *Celeiro dos Frades*, atmospherically situated under the arches alongside the abbey.

Batalha

The Mosteiro de Santa Maria da Vitória, better known as the **Mosteiro de Batalha** (daily 9am–5.30/6.30pm; €3), is the finest building in Portugal, an enduring symbol of national pride. It was originally founded to commemorate the Battle of Aljubarrota (1385), which sealed Portugal's independence after decades of Spanish intrigue. It's easily reached on a day-trip from Leiria (4–5 buses daily). The honey-coloured abbey was transformed by Manueline additions in the late fifteenth and early sixteenth centuries, but the bulk was completed between 1388 and 1434 in a profusely ornate version of French Gothic. Within this flamboyant framework there are also strong elements of the English Perpendicular style, an influence explained by the **Capela do Fundador** (Founder's Chapel), directly to the right upon entering the church: beneath the octagonal lantern rests the tomb of Dom João I and Philippa of Lancaster, their hands clasped in the ultimate expression of harmonious relations between Portugal and England. Their four younger sons are buried along the south wall of the Capela do Fundador in a row of recessed arches.

Second from the right is the **Tomb of Prince Henry the Navigator**, who guided the exploration of Madeira, the Azores and the African coast as far as Sierra. The **Claustro Real** (Royal Cloister) dates from this period of burgeoning self-confidence under Manuel I (1495–1521), its intricate stone grilles being added by Diogo de Boitaca, architect of the cloisters at Belém and the prime genius of Manueline art. Off the east side, the early-fifteenth-century **Sala do Capítulo** (Chapter House) is remarkable for the unsupported span of its ceiling. The Church authorities were convinced that the whole chamber would come crashing down and only employed as labourers criminals already condemned to death. The **Capelas Imperfeitas** (Unfinished Chapels) form a separate structure tacked on to the east end of the church and accessible only from outside the main complex. Dom Duarte, eldest son of João and Philippa, commissioned them in 1437 as a royal mausoleum but the original design was transformed beyond all recognition by Dom Manuel's architects. It is unique among examples of Christian architecture in its evocation of the great shrines of Islam and Hinduism: perhaps inspired by the tales of Indian monuments that filtered back along the eastern trade routes.

Fátima

FÁTIMA is one of the most important centres of pilgrimage in the Catholic world, a status deriving from the six **Apparitions of the Virgin Mary**. On May 13 1917, three children from the village were tending their parents' flock when, in a flash of lightning, they were confronted with "a lady brighter than the sun" sitting in the branches of a tree. The vision returned on the thirteenth day of the next five months, culminating in the so-called Miracle of the Sun on October 13, when a swirling ball of fire cured lifelong illnesses. To commemorate these extraordinary events a vast white **Basilica** and gigantic esplanade have been built, more than capable of holding the crowds of 100,000 who congregate here for the main **pilgrimages** (May 12 & 13; Oct 12 & 13). In the church the tombs of two of the children, who died in the European flu epidemic of 1919–20, are the subject of constant attention. Hospices and convents have sprung up in the shadow of the basilica, and inevitably the fame of Fátima has resulted in its commercialization. Pensions and restaurants abound, but there's little reason to stay except during the big pilgrimages to witness the midnight processions. Regular **bus services** to Fátima from Tomar make a day-trip easy.

Tomar

TOMAR, 34km east of Fátima, is famous for the Convento de Cristo, an artistic *tour de force* which entwines the main military, religious and imperial strands in the history of Portugal. However, it's an attractive town in its own right – especially during the Festas dos Tabuleiros, in the first week of July, when the place goes wild – and is worth a day or two.

Built on a simple grid plan, Tomar's old quarters preserve all their traditional charm, with whitewashed cottages lining narrow cobbled streets. On the central Praça da República stands an elegant seventeenth-century town hall, a ring of houses of the same period and the Manueline church of **São João Baptista**, remarkable for its octagonal belfry and elaborate doorway. Nearby, at Rua Joaquim Jacinto 73, you'll find an excellently preserved fourteenth-century Synagogue, now the **Museu Luso-Hebraicoa Abraham Zacuto** (daily 10am–7pm; free); in 1496, Dom Manuel ordered the expulsion or conversion of all Portuguese Jews, and the synagogue at Tomar was one of the few to survive. The **Convento de Cristo** (Tues–Sun: summer 9.15am–12.30pm & 2–6pm; winter 2–5pm; €3) is set among pleasant gardens with splendid views, about a quarter of an hour's walk uphill from the centre of town. Founded in 1162 by Gualdim Pais, first Master of the Knights Templar, it was the headquarters of the Order. The heart of the complex remains the **Charola**, the temple from which the knights drew their moral conviction. It's a strange place, more suggestive of the occult than of Christianity; like almost every circular church, it's based on the Church of the Holy Sepulchre in Jerusalem, for whose protection the Knights Templar were originally founded. The highlight of the convent is the ornamentation of the windows on the main facade of its **Chapter House**, where maritime motifs form a memorial to the sailors who established the Portuguese empire. Later João III (1521–1557) transformed the convent into a thoroughgoing monastic community. The adjoining two-tiered **Great Cloisters** comprise one of the purest examples of the Renaissance style in Portugal. Tomar's **Turismo** (daily 10am–6/7pm; ☎249 322 427) is at the top of Avenida Dr Cândido Madureira. There is a pleasant all-year **campsite** (☎249 322 608) in town and a number of reasonable **pensions**, each with a **restaurant**: *Tomarense*, Avda. Torres Pinheiro 13 (☎249 312 948; ❸), near the bus station; *Luz*, Rua Serpa Pinto 144 (☎249 312 317; ❸), with **Internet** access; and the very popular *Residencial União*, Rua Serpa Pinto 94 (☎249 323 161; ❹), in the centre of town.

Coimbra

COIMBRA was Portugal's capital from 1143 to 1255 and it ranks behind only the cities of Lisbon and Porto in historic importance. Its university, founded in 1290 and finally established here in 1537 after a series of moves back and forth to Lisbon, was the only one existing in Portugal until the beginning of the last century. For a provincial town it has remarkable riches, and it's an enjoyable place to be – lively when the students are in town, sleepy during the holidays. The best time of all to be here is in May, when the students celebrate the end of the academic year in the **Queima das Fitas**, tearing or burning their gowns and faculty ribbons. This is when you're most likely to hear the Coimbra *fado*, distinguished from the Lisbon version by its mournful pace and complex lyrics.

Old Coimbra sits on a hill on the right bank of the River Mondego, with the university crowding its summit. The main buildings of the **Old University**, dating from the sixteenth century, are set around a courtyard dominated by a Baroque clocktower and a statue of João III. The **chapel** (€1.50) is covered with *azulejos* and intricate decoration, but takes second place to the **Library** (daily 9.30am–12.30pm & 2–5.30/7.30pm; €2.50; tickets from the office under the clock tower), a Baroque fantasy presented to the faculty by João V in the early eighteenth century. Below the university, a good first stop is the **Museu Machado de Castro** (Tues–Sun 9.30am–12.30pm & 2–5.15pm; €3), just down from the unprepossessing Sé Nova (New Cathedral). Named after an eighteenth-century sculptor, the museum is housed in the former archbishop's palace and is positively stuffed with sculpture, paintings, furniture and ceramics. The **Sé Velha** (Old Cathedral; Mon–Thurs & Sat 10am–5pm, Fri 10am–2pm), halfway down the hill, is one of the most important Romanesque buildings in Portugal. Solid and square on the outside, it's also stolid and simple within, the decoration confined to a few giant conch shells and some unobtrusive *azulejos*. Restraint and simplicity certainly aren't the chief qualities of the **Igreja de Santa Cruz** (Mon–Sat 9am–noon & 2–5.45pm, Sun 4–6pm; €1 for cloister), at the bottom of the hill past the city gates. Although it was founded before the Old Cathedral, nothing remains that has not been substantially remodelled. In the early sixteenth century, Coimbra was the site of a major sculptural school; the new tombs for Portugal's first kings, Afonso Henriques and Sancho I, and the elaborately carved pulpit, are among its very finest works. The Manueline theme is at its clearest in the airy arches of the Cloister of Silence, its walls decorated with bas-relief scenes from the life of Christ.

Most mainline **trains** stop at Coimbra B, 3km north of the city, from where there are frequent connecting services to Coimbra A, right at the heart of things. The main **bus station** is on Avenida Fernão de Magalhães, fifteen minutes' walk from the centre – turn right out of the bus station and head down the main road. The **tourist office** (Mon–Fri 9am–5/7pm, Sat & Sun 9/10am–1pm & 2–5/5.30pm;

☎239 488 120, ⓦwww.turismo-centro.pt) is opposite the bridge in the Largo da Portagem. Near the station, the sleazy Rua da Sota and its side streets have a few **pensões** that aren't as bad as they look – try the *Pensão Vitória* at Rua da Sota 9 & 19 (☎239 824 049; ❸), or the *Residencial Domus* at Rua Adelino Veiga 62 (☎239 828 584; ❸). Alternatively, there are several options east of the university; beneath the aqueduct, *Antunes*, Rua Castro Matoso 8 (☎239 854 720; ❹) offers good service. The **hostel**, above the park at Rua Henrique Seco 14 (☎239 822 955; ❷), is friendly and immaculately run – it's a twenty-minute walk from Coimbra A, or take bus #7, #29 or #46. For really basic **food**, served up with loads of atmosphere, try the little dives tucked into the alleys between Largo da Portagem, Rua da Sota and Praça do Comércio. *Adega Paço do Conde* on Rua Paço do Conde is a cavernous, locally renowned *churrasqueira*. And don't miss one of the traditional **coffee houses** found along Rua Ferreira Borges – notably *Café Santa Cruz* – and Rua Visconde da Luz.

Northern Portugal

Porto, the country's second largest city, is an attractive and convenient centre from which to begin an exploration of the region. Magnificently set on a rocky cliff astride the River Douro, it is perhaps most famous for the port-producing suburb of **Vila Nova de Gaia**, supplied by vineyards further inland along the river. The **Douro Valley** is traced by a spectacular rail route, with branch lines following valleys north along the River Tâmega to Amarante and along the Corgo to Vila Real – the main centre for transport connections into the ancient, isolated region of **Trás-os-Montes** and its old capital of **Bragança**. In the northwest, the **Minho**, considered by many to be the most beautiful part of the country, is a lush wilderness of rolling mountain forests and rugged coastlines (the Costa Verde), with some of the most unspoilt beaches in Europe. A quietly conservative region, its towns have a special charm and beauty, amongst them the religious centre of **Braga**, and the self-proclaimed birthplace of the nation, **Guimarães**.

Porto (Oporto)

Capital of the north, **PORTO** (sometimes called "Oporto" in English) is very different from Lisbon – unpretentious, inward-looking, unashamedly commercial. As the local saying goes: "Coimbra sings; Braga prays; Lisbon shows off; and Porto works." The attraction of the city lies largely in the contrast between the prosperous business core and the timeless charm of its Ribeira area, where the cobbled warren of steep alleys and passages appears to have changed little in centuries.

Arrival, information and accommodation

Most trains from the south will drop you at the distant **Estação de Campanhã**; change here for a local train to the central **Estação de São Bento** (5min). Trains no longer run to the Minho and the north, although they will eventually be linked by Porto's ambitious new metro system, expected to be operational by 2005. As a general rule, **buses** from the south come in around Rua Alexandre Herculano, and those from the north use the bus station at Rua Dr Alfredo Magalhães 46, about 250m north of the defunct Estação da Trindade. From the Francisco Sá Carneiro **airport**, 10km north of the city, an Aerobus (7.45am–7.15pm, every 30min; €2.60, free for TAP passengers) runs to Avenida dos Aliados, a few yards north of São Bento. The most helpful of three central **tourist offices** is next to the Câmara Municipal on Rua Clube dos Fenianos 25 (Mon–Fri 9am–5.30pm, Sat & Sun 9am–4.30pm; ☎222 393 472). **Internet** access is available a few doors down at PortWeb, and the central **post office** is at Pr. Dom João I. The cheapest **rooms** are on Rua do Loureiro and Rua Cimo do Vila, around the corner from São Bento

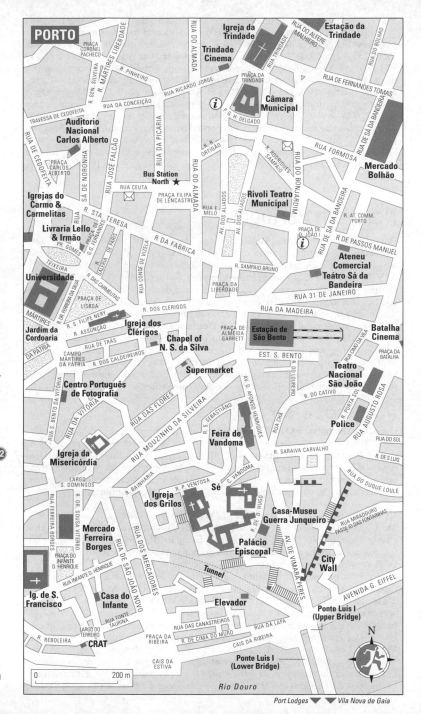

PORTO

Igreja da Trindade

Trindade Cinema

Estação da Trindade

Câmara Municipal

Auditorio Nacional Carlos Alberto

Bus Station North ★

Rivoli Teatro Municipal

Mercado Bolhão

Igrejas do Carmo & Carmelitas

Livraria Lello & Irmão

Universidade

Ateneu Comercial Teátro Sá da Bandeira

Jardim da Cordoaria

Igreja dos Clérigos

Chapel of N. S. da Silva

Estação de São Bento

Batalha Cinema

Supermarket

Teatro Nacional São João

Centro Português de Fotografia

Feira de Vandoma

Police

Igreja da Misericórdia

Igreja dos Grilos

Sé

Casa-Museu Guerra Junqueiro

Mercado Ferreira Borges

Palácio Episcopal

City Wall

Ig. de S. Francisco

Casa do Infante

Elevador

Ponte Luis I (Upper Bridge)

Tunnel

CRAT

Ponte Luis I (Lower Bridge)

Rio Douro

Port Lodges ▼▼   ▼ Vila Nova de Gaia

0   200 m

N

– though this is something of a red-light district. For more salubrious places, your best bet is to head for the areas west or east of Avenida dos Aliados; most of the hotels listed below are to the west. There are also some bargain rooms around lively Praça da Batalha.

Hostel

Pousada de Juventude Rua Paulo Gama 552 ☎226 177 257. Large and clean, with a great view of the mouth of the Douro. Bus #35 from Largo Dos Loios. ❷

Pensions and hotels

Pensão Residencial Duas Nações Praça Guilherme Gomes Fernandes 59 ☎222 081 616, ℮duasnacoes@mail.teleweb.pt. Cheap and dependable, offering en-suite accommodation and free Internet access. Book in advance. ❸
Pensão Estoril Rua de Cedofeita 193 ☎222 002 751. Wonderful value en-suite rooms. ❸
Pensão Monte Sinai Rua Alexandre Herculano 146 ☎222 008 218. Cheapest option in town, although a little dingy and noisy. Not for the fussy. ❷
Pensão Oporto Chique Rua Conde de Vizela 26 ☎222 080 069. Reasonable and near São Bento.

Breakfast included. ❷
Residencial Paris Rua da Fábrica 27–29 ☎222 073 140. Popular old hotel with huge rooms. Breakfast included. ❹
Residencial Porto Novo Rua Alexandre Herculano 185 ☎222 055 739. Clean, modern rooms with TV and bath, back rooms with balconies and great views of the river. Recommended. ❸

Campsites

Marisol Rua Alto das Chaquedas 82 ☎227 135 942. Peaceful location south of the river; Espirito Santo bus from Rua Infante D. Henrique.
Prelada ☎228 312 616. The closest of the campsites; bus #56 or #87 from Cordoaria or the airport (both run until midnight) or #6 from Avda. dos Aliados.

The City

To get your bearings, climb the 250 steps of the Baroque **Igreja e Torre dos Clérigos** (9.30/10am–noon/1pm & 2–5/7pm; €1), once the tallest building in Portugal. To the south, a statue of Porto's most famous son, Henry the Navigator, provides the centrepiece of a square that bears his name. His birthplace is on one of the streets running down from here towards the river. On the west side of the square is the extravagant facade of the glass-domed former Stock Exchange, the **Bolsa,** and behind it, the most extraordinary church in Porto, **Igreja de São Francisco** (daily 9am–6pm; €3 including museum). It's rather plain from the outside, but inside, once your eyes adjust to the gloom, you are greeted by a fabulously opulent eighteenth-century refurbishment, with gold dripping from every corner. Don't miss the church's small **museum**, set in an eerie underground crypt, and containing an *ossário*, a collection of bones dating from before the time of public cemeteries. Tram #1 departs for the **beaches** by the mouth of the Douro every half an hour from in front of the church. The **Museu Nacional Soares dos Reis** at Rua de Dom Manuel II (Tues 2–6pm, Wed–Sun 10am–6pm; €3), over to the west behind the city hospital, was the first national museum in Portugal. Its collection includes glass, ceramics and a formidable array of eighteenth- and nineteenth-century paintings, as well as the late-nineteenth-century sculptures of Soares dos Reis – his *O Desterro* (The Exile) is probably the best-known work in Portugal. Follow the road past the museum, or take any bus from the Cordoaria stop except #6 and #18, and you'll come to the **Jardim do Palácio de Cristal**, a peaceful park dominated by a space-age domed pavilion which now serves as a sports centre. In summer the park is home to a vast funfair. On the far side of the park, below the Museu Romântico, is the **Solar do Vinho do Porto** (Mon–Sat 2pm–midnight), where you can sample one of hundreds of varieties of port on the relaxing river terrace.

Vila Nova de Gaia, essentially a city in its own right, is dominated by the port trade. From the north bank of the river, the names of the various companies (Croft's, Taylor's, Sandeman, Graham's), spelled out in neon letters across the terra-cotta roofs of the lodges, leave you in no doubt as to what awaits you when you cross. You can walk to Gaia across the **Ponte Luís I**: the most direct route to the wine lodges is across the lower level from the Cais da Ribeira, but if you've a head for heights it's an amazing sensation to walk over the upper deck; otherwise, take bus #32, #57 or #91 from Porto's São Bento station. Almost all the companies offer free **tasting and tours** of their lodges, although some of the bigger names like Sandeman charge €2.50, redeemable against the price of a bottle. There's little pressure to buy anything – but do try the dry white ports, which are often unobtainable elsewhere.

Eating, drinking and nightlife

Porto has a strong **café culture**, which includes some elegant rivals to *the fin-de-siècle* places in Lisbon, while the **Cais da Ribeira** waterfront offers a vibrant scene at night with its lively bars and clubs. Most of the city's big nightclubs are in the outlying **Matosinhos** district. Porto's culinary speciality is *Tripas á Modo* (tripe). Don't let this put you off – there's always plenty of choice on the menu, and there are lots of places where you can eat cheaply. At the basic level, there are **workers' cafés** galore, all with wine on tap, and often with a set menu for the day. Prime areas are Rua do Almada and Rua de São Bento da Vitória. All are busy at midday and invariably close around 7.30pm and all Sunday.

Cafés and restaurants

Adega do Olho Rua Alfonso Martins Alho 6. Traditional cheap dive full of local character. Closed Sun.

Café Majestic Rua de Santa Catarina 112. Porto's best café-restaurant with ornate surroundings and delicious breakfasts and teas. Closed Sun.

Casa Filha da Mãe Preta Arcos do Douro 2–3, Cais da Ribeira. Bustling restaurant with excellent views over the river. Dishes cost around €9. Closed Sun.

Churrasqueira de Brasil Campo dos Mártires da Pátria 136, near Torre dos Clerigos. Cheap workers' diner serving ample portions.

Ginjal do Oporto Rua do Bonjardim 724. Bargain local specialities in a no-frills setting. Closed Sun.

Café Restaurant Miradouro Cais da Ribeira, on the arches by the entrance to the bridge. A popular local hangout with great salads and cheap meals.

Regaleira Rua do Bonjardim 87. One of the best places for fish and seafood. English menu can be a little perplexing, but worth persevering. Mains cost €5–12.50.

Bars

Aniki-Bóbó Rua da Fonte Taurinha 36. Upbeat late-night acid jazz/house bar. Occasional alternative happenings (eg theatre). Until 4am. Closed Sun.

Bar da Praia do Ourigo Esplanada do Castelo. Trendy tapas bar frequented by students, also serves good coffee on the beach.

Quando-Quando Avda. do Brasil 60, Foz do Douro. Popular waterfront hotspot with the in-crowd. Closed Sun & Mon.

Taberna da Ribeira Praça da Ribeira. Prime riverside spot with outdoor tables. Open till 2am.

Clubs

Hard Club Cais de Gaia, Vila Nova de Gaia. Porto's main venue for DJs and live music, including a good number of British and Stateside acts. Night bus #91.

Industria Avda. Brasil 843. Like its Lisbon namesake attracts a mixed crowd out for a good time. Open Fri–Sun 11pm–6am.

River Cançada João do Carmo 31. Pricey entrance fee and strict dress code but worth it for the chilled, jazzy atmosphere. Closed Sun-Tues.

Swing Praçeta Enginheiro Amaro da Costa 766. Fun Seventies revival disco. Smart dress code. Daily till 2am.

Tomate Rua Manuel Pinto de Azevedo 15. Current hot spot with a warehouse atmosphere and visiting DJs playing drum'n'bass and trance. Closed Sun.

Braga

BRAGA is Portugal's religious capital – the scene of spectacular **Easter celebrations** with torchlight processions. You won't be able to miss the **Archbishop's Palace**, a great fortress-like building, right at the centre of the old town. Nearby is the **Sé**, which, like the palace, encompasses Gothic, Renaissance and Baroque styles. Founded in 1070, its south doorway is a survival from this earliest building; its most striking element, however, is the intricate ornamentation of the roofline. A guided tour of the interior (daily 9am–1pm & 2–6.30pm; cathedral free, museum and Capela dos Reis €2) takes you through three Gothic chapels, of which the outstanding specimen is the **Capela dos Reis** (King's Chapel), built to house the tombs of Henry of

Burgundy and his wife Teresa, the cathedral's founders. The Art Deco **tourist office** (Mon–Fri 9am–12.30pm & 2–6.30pm, Sat & Sun closes at 5.30pm; ☎253 262 550) is at the corner of Praça da República. A **hotel** offering excellent value is the *Pensão Francfort*, Avda. Central 1–7 (☎253 262 648; ❷). Braga's well-equipped **hostel** is at Rua Santa Margarida 6 (☎253 616 163; ❷), off Avenida Central; the **campsite** (☎253 273 355) is a two-kilometre walk along the Guimarães road, but is very cheap and right next to the municipal swimming pool. *Churrasqueira Lareira do Conde*, Praça Conde de Agrolongo, serves reasonably priced, quality **food** in generous quantities, as does the *Restaurante Moçambicana* at Rua Andrade Corvo 8, one of several excellent cheap restaurants grouped around the Arco da Porta Nova. By far the best of the old **coffee houses** is the mahogany-panelled *Café Astória*, Praça da Republica.

The glorious ornamental stairway of **Bom Jesus**, 3km outside Braga, is one of Portugal's best-known images. Set on a wooded hillside, high above the city, it's a monumental place of pilgrimage created by Braga's archbishop in the early eighteenth century. **Buses** run from in front of the Cristal Farmácia on Avda. da Liberdade in Braga to the foot of the stairway about every thirty minutes at weekends, when half the city piles up there to picnic. If you resist the temptation of the **funicular** (€1) and climb up the **stairway**, Bom Jesus's simple allegory unfolds. Each landing has a fountain: the first symbolizes the wounds of Christ, the next five the Senses, and the final three represent the Virtues. At each corner are chapels with mouldering wooden tableaux of the life of Christ, leading to the Crucifixion at the altar of the church. Beyond are wooded gardens, grottoes and miniature boating pools, and several cheap, lively **restaurants**.

Guimarães

First capital of medieval Portucale, **GUIMARÃES** remains a lively and atmospheric university town. The town's chief attraction is the **Castelo** (daily 9.30am–noon & 2–5pm; free), whose square keep and seven towers are an enduring symbol of the emergent Portuguese nation. Built by the Countess of Mumadona and extended by Henry of Burgundy, it became the stronghold of his son, Afonso Henriques. From here the Reconquest began along with the creation of a kingdom that, within a century of Afonso's death, was to stretch to its present borders. Afonso is said to have been born in the castle, and may have been baptized in the font of the Romanesque chapel of **São Miguel** on the grassy slope below. Guimarães' **bus station** is fifteen minutes' walk west of town in a vast shopping centre. From the **train station** south of town you'll pass one **Turismo** (Mon–Fri 9.30am–12.30pm & 2–6.30pm; ☎253 412 450, ✆www.cm-guimaraes.pt) as you walk up Avenida D. Alfonso Henriques to the centre; the other office is in the centre of the old town in Praça de Santiago (Mon–Fri 9.30am–6.30pm, Sat 10am–6pm, Sun 10am–1pm; ☎253 518 790). For **accommodation** try *Casa dos Pombais*, Avda. de Londres 40 (☎253 412 917; ❺), which has beautiful rooms overlooking attractive gardens. For **food**, *Oriental* on Largo do Toural has very good regional specialities. *El Rei Dom Alfonso*, Praça de Santiago, is worth the moderate rise in price for its location in the heart of the old town. Across the square, *Cinecittá* does excellent soups and salads.

The Douro rail route

The valleys of the **River Douro** and its tributaries are among the most spectacular landscapes in Portugal, and the Douro Valley itself, a narrow, winding gorge for the majority of its long route, is the most beautiful of all. The **Douro rail route**, which joins the river about 60km inland and then sticks to it across the country, is one of those journeys that needs no justification other than the trip itself. There are regular connections along the line as far as Peso da Régua, first capital of the demarcated port-producing region; beyond Régua, there are less frequent connections to Tua and Pocinho, which marks the end of the line.

At **Livração**, about an hour from Porto, the Tâmega line cuts off for the lovely mountain town of **AMARANTE**. The journey is spectacular, the rickety, single-carriage train struggling through pine woods and vineyards on the climb, with the river visible like a piece of lapis lazuli far below. Amarante is a fine place to stop, with much of its history revolving around the thirteenth-century hermit **Gonçalo**, who is credited with a hand in the founding of just about everything in the town. Although it has a nice church and unusual modernist museum, the main attraction is the setting, the peaceful family atmosphere and relaxing old streets. A good cheap **hotel** is *Residencial A Raposeira*, Largo António Cândido 53 (☎255 432 221; ❷), above the restaurant of the same name, which serves huge, if basic, meals. Shortly after Livração, the main line finally reaches the Douro and heads upstream until, at Mesão Frio, the valley broadens into the little plain commanded by **PESO DA RÉGUA**, the depot through which port wine must pass on its way from Pinhão – the centre of production – to Porto. Beyond Peso da Régua begin the terraced slopes where the **port vines** are grown: they look their best in August, with the grapes ripening, and in September when the harvest has begun. The country continues in this vein, craggy and beautiful, with the softer hills of the interior fading dark green into the distance, to Tua (junction for the Corgo line with services to the transport centre of **Vila Real**, the gateway to Tras-os-Montes) and Pocinho, where buses take over for routes east towards Miranda do Douro.

Trás-os-Montes and Bragança

Perhaps more than anywhere else in Portugal, the province of **Trás-os-Montes** – literally "behind the mountains" – still upholds its traditional customs and farming methods.

On a hillock above **BRAGANÇA**, the small and remote provincial capital, stands a pristine circle of walls, the extraordinary **Cidadela**, enclosing a medieval village and castle. The **Domus Municipalis** here, a twelfth-century pentagonal Romanesque civic building, is the only one of its kind in Europe. Next to it is the church of **Santa Maria**, with its eighteenth-century barrel-vaulted, painted ceiling – a feature common to several churches in Bragança. Towering above these two is the **Castle** itself (Mon–Wed & Fri–Sun 9am–noon & 2–5pm; €1.50, free Sun morning), which the Portuguese royal family rejected as a residence in favour of their vast estate in the Alentejo. At its side a curious pillory rises from the back of a prehistoric granite pig, or *porca*, thought to have been a fertility idol of a prehistoric cult. Celtic-inspired medieval tombstones rub shoulders with a menagerie of *porcas* in the gardens of **Museu do Abade de Baçal**, between the citadel and cathedral in Rua Abílio Beça (Tues–Fri 10am–5pm, Sat & Sun 10am–6pm; €1.25, free Sun). The **tourist office** (Mon–Fri 9am–12.30pm & 2–5/7pm; ☎273 381 273, ⓦwww.bragancanet.pt) is on an extension of Avenida Cidade de Zamora, a couple of hundred metres north of the cathedral. The cheapest **pension** in town is the very basic *Hospedaria Brigantina*, next to the post office on Rua Almirante Reis (☎273 324 321; ❷). For somewhere more comfortable pay a little more for the *Residencial Poças*, Rua Combatentes da G. Guerra 200 (☎273 331 428; ❷). The nearest **campsite** (☎273 351 535; closed Nov–April) is 6km out of town on the França road; a better option is the plush, private site *Cepo Verde* (☎273 999 371;

From Bragança the most obvious route **into Spain** is via Quintanilha (34km), the nearest town to the San Martin border post. There are one or two direct buses daily to Quintanilha. You can stay above the *Evaristo*, San Martin's only shop and restaurant. At 7am there's a bus to Zamora, connected to Madrid by road and rail. At Bragança bus station you could also reserve on the Zamora-Valladolid-Madrid **express bus** (Mon, Tues, Thurs & Fri; ⓦwww.alsa.es/internacional). Spain is one hour ahead of Portugal.

closed Nov–April), 8km down the Vinhais road, with good facilities and a pool. As for **restaurants**, two favourites are *Restaurante Poças*, next to the *residencial*, serving big, wholesome meals, and *Restaurante D. Fernando*, Cidadela 197, inside the walled old town. South of Bragança, hugging the border with Spain in the east, is the vast and beautiful wilderness of the newly designated **Parque Natural do Douro Internacional**, home to Europe's largest concentration of Egyptian Vultures and a huge number of other birds of prey. The best place to base yourself for a visit is the town of **MOGADOURO**, site of the park's headquarters and connected by daily weekday bus from Bragança (1hr 40min). Accommodation is plentiful: try the *Pensão Russo* (☎279 342 134; ❷), on Rua das Eiras.

Southern Portugal

The huge, sparsely populated plains of the **Alentejo**, southeast of Lisbon, are over-whelmingly agricultural, dominated by vast cork plantations well suited to the low rainfall, sweltering heat and arid soil. This impoverished province is divided into vast estates that provide nearly half of the world's cork but only a sparse living for its rural inhabitants. Visitors to the Alentejo often head for **Évora**, the province's dominant and most historic city. But the **Alentejo coast**, the Costa Azul, is a breath of fresh air after the stifling plains of the inland landscape.

With its long, sandy beaches and picturesque rocky coves, the southern coast of the **Algarve** is the most visited region in the country. West of **Faro**, the lively capital of the Algarve, you'll find the classic postcard images of the province – a series of tiny bays and coves, broken up by weird rocky outcrops and fantastic grottoes, at their most exotic around the resort of **Lagos**. To the east of Faro lie the less developed sandy offshore islets, **the Ilhas** – which front the coastline for some 25 miles – and the lower-key resorts of **Olhão** and **Tavira**. Or head inland where you'll find a more Portuguese way of life at **Silves**, the impressive former capital of the Moors. Throughout the Algarve, accommodation can be a major problem in summer, with hotels block-booked by package companies and pensions filling up early in the day.

Évora

ÉVORA is one of the most impressive cities in Portugal. The Romans were in occupation for four centuries and the Moors, who settled for just as long, left their stamp in the tangle of narrow alleys which rise steeply among the whitewashed houses. Most of the monuments, however, date from the fourteenth to the sixteenth centuries, when, with royal encouragement, the city was one of the leading centres of Portuguese art and architecture. The **Templo Romano** in the central square is the best-preserved Roman temple in Portugal, its stark remains consisting of a small platform supporting more than a dozen granite columns with a marble entablature. Directly opposite, the former **Convento dos Lóios**, now converted into a luxurious *pousada*, has been partly attributed to Francisco de Arruda, architect of the Tower of Belém in Lisbon. To the left of the *pousada* lies the church of the convent, dedicated to **São João Evangelista**. This is the private property of the ducal Cadaval family, who still occupy a wing or two of the adjacent ancestral palace. Some rooms of the palace, containing *azulejos*, trick paintings and ossuary, are open to visitors (Tues–Sun 9.30am–12.30pm & 2.30–5pm; €3). The Romanesque cathedral, or **Sé** (daily 9am–12.30pm & 2–5pm), was begun in 1186, about twenty years after the reconquest of Évora from the Moors. Adjacent, in the archbishop's palace, is the excellent **Museu de Évora** (Tues–Sun 9.30am–12.30pm & 2–6pm; €1.50), which houses important collections of fifteenth- and sixteenth-century Flemish and Portuguese paintings assembled from the city's churches and convents. However, the most memorable sight in Évora is the **Capela dos Ossos** (daily 9am–1pm &

2.30–5.30pm; €1) in the church of **São Francisco**, just south of Praça do Giraldo. A gruesome reminder of mortality, the walls and pillars of this chilling chamber are entirely covered with the bones of more than 5000 monks; an inscription over the door reads, "Nós ossos que aqui estamos, Pelos vossos esperamos" – We bones here are waiting for your bones.

Évora's **bus station** and **train station** are 1km out of the old town, though there are regular green buses from the bus station that run to **Praça do Giraldo**, centre of Évora's lively student scene. The **tourist office** (daily 9am–12.30pm & 2–5.30/7pm; ☎266 702 671) is sited here, along with a couple of outdoor cafés. Évora's tourist appeal pushes **accommodation** prices way over the norm. Best options are *Residencial Diana*, just east of the Sé at Rua Diogo Cão 2 (☎266 702 008; ❸); *Pensão Invicta*, Rua Romão Ramalho 37a, overlooking São Francisco (☎266 702 047; ❷); and *Pensão Giraldo* at Rua dos Mercadores 15 & 27 (☎266 705 833; ❸). Évora's **hostel** (☎266 744 848; ❸) is just off Praça do Giraldo at Rua Miguel Bombarda 40. If you're stuck for a room, the tourist office will sometimes arrange accommodation in **private homes**. The **campsite** (☎266 705 190) is 2km out of town on the Alcáçovas road; bus #5 goes there ten times daily from Praça do Giraldo (except Sun). For inexpensive **restaurants** try *Adego do Neto*, Rua dos Mercadores 46, or the homely *O Portão*, on Rua do Cano 27 alongside the aqueduct. For slightly more you could sample the outstanding Italian food at the enormously popular *Pane & Vino*, Patio do Salema (entrance on Rua Diogo Focardo). *Oficin@bar*, at Rua da Moeda 27, is an easy-going **bar** that also offers **Internet** access (closed Sun & Mon).

The Alentejo coast

The coast south of Lisbon features towns and beaches as inviting as those of the Algarve. Admittedly, it's exposed to the winds and waves of the Atlantic, and the waters are colder, but it's fine for summer swimming and far quieter. Local bus services and the twice-daily **Zambujeira Express** from Lisbon take you within easy range of the whole coastline, stopping at the beaches of Vila Nova de Milfontes and Zambujeira do Mar. Five buses a day run from Lisbon to Alcacer do Sal, from where there are reasonable connections south to **SANTIAGO DO CACÉM**, a pleasant little town overlooked by a castle. In turn, there are five buses daily (in summer) from Santiago to **Lagoa de Santo André** and the adjoining **Lagoa de Melides**, with two of the best beaches in the country. The **campsites** at both places are of a high standard and there are masses of signs offering **rooms**, chalets and houses to let. Beyond the beach-cafés and ice cream stalls, miles and miles of sand stretch all the way to Comporta in the north and Sines in the south. There are high waves and good surf, but take local advice as the undertow can be fierce. If you'd rather base yourself at Santiago than at the beaches, there's no shortage of good **food and accommodation**. The *Restaurante Covas*, by the bus station at Rua Cidade de Setúbal 10 (☎269 822 675; ❸), is recommended both for its rooms and for its outstanding meals, and there's another great restaurant, *Praceta,* at Largo Zeca Afonso (behind the bus station). Some 40km southwest of Santiago do Cacém lies the popular resort of **PORTO CÔVO**, which, although overdeveloped, has plentiful accommodation, a campsite and beautiful beaches to the south. The larger resort of **VILA NOVA DE MILFONTES** lies a little to the south on the estuary of the River Mira, whose sandy banks gradually expand and merge into the coastline. This is the most popular resort in the Alentejo, with lines of villas and hotels radiating from the centre of the old village. It's still a pretty place, though, with a handsome little castle and an ancient port, reputed to have harboured Hannibal and his Carthaginians during a storm. Finding reasonable **rooms** shouldn't be a problem, and there are a couple of large **campsites** to the north of the village: *Parque de Milfontes* (☎283 996 104) and the more modest *Campiférias* (☎283 996 409). The main inland base is **ODEMIRA**, a quiet, unspoiled country town, connected by eight daily buses to Vila Nova de Milfontes. **Pensions** include *Residencial Rita*,

Largo do Poço Novo (☎283 322 531; ❹), and *Residencial Idálio*, Rua Eng. Arantes Oliveira 28 (☎283 322 156; ❸), just to the left when you come out of the bus station. Of the **restaurants**, try *O Tarro*, near the main road junction. South of Odemira at **ZAMBUJEIRA DO MAR**, a large cliff provides a dramatic backdrop to the beach, more than compensating for the winds. There are only a few small **pensions**, such as the *Mar-e-Sol* (☎283 961 171; ❸), a few *dormidas* and a couple of bars, as well as a reasonable **campsite** (☎283 961 172), about 1km from the cliffs.

Lagos

LAGOS is a thriving fishing port and market centre as well as being one of the most popular tourist destinations in the Algarve, with some superb beaches within walking distance. It was a favoured residence of Henry the Navigator, who used Lagos as a base for the African trade. Europe's first slave market was built here in 1441 in the arches of the **Customs House**, which still stands in the Praça da República near the waterfront. On the waterfront and to the rear of the town are the remains of Lagos's once impregnable fortifications, devastated by the Great Earthquake. One rare and beautiful church which did survive was the **Igreja de Santo António**; decorated around 1715, its gilt and carved interior is wildly obsessive, every inch filled with a private fantasy of cherubic youths struggling with animals and fish. The church forms part of a visit to the adjacent **Museu Municipal** (Tues–Sun 9.30am–12.30pm & 2–5pm; €2), housing an extraordinarily eclectic collection of artefacts including Roman busts and deformed animal foetuses. To the east of Lagos is a splendid sweep of sand – **Meia Praia** – where there's space even at the height of summer. The promontory south is fringed by extravagantly eroded cliff faces, which shelter a series of tiny cove beaches. **Praia de Dona Ana** is considered the most picturesque, though its crowds make the smaller coves of **Praia do Pinhão**, down a track just opposite the fire station, and **Praia Camilo**, a little further along, more appealing.

The **train station** is across the river, fifteen minutes' walk from the centre via a swing bridge in the marina; the **bus station** is a bit closer in, a block back from the main Avenida dos Descobrimentos. The **tourist office** is in the central Largo M. Pombal (July & Aug daily 10am–10pm, Sept–June Mon–Fri 10am–6pm, Sat 10am–2pm; ☎282 764 111) and can help find a room for you, but most economical are the **private rooms** (❷) touted at the bus station. Two of the more convenient and pleasant **pensions** are *Pensão Caravela*, Rua 25 de Abril 16 (☎282 763 361; ❸), and *Residencial Marazul*, at no. 13 (☎282 769 143; ❹). There's a **hostel** at Rua de Lançarote de Freites 50 (☎282 761 970; ❸), which also has **Internet** access. Lagos's **campsite**, *Campismo da Trindade* (☎282 763 893), is on the way to Praia de Dona Ana but gets very crowded. In season a regular bus service marked "D. Ana/Oporto de Mós" connects it to town; on foot, follow the main road beyond the fort. Some of the better **restaurants** are the fish and shellfish places by the market, where Rua das Portas de Portugal meets Avenida dos Descobrimentos. On the latter, the popular *Casa do Zé* is open 24 hours a day. For authentic *piri-piri* chicken try the inexpensive *O Franguinho* at Rua Luís de Azevedo 25 (closed Mon). *Casa Rosa,* Rua do Ferrador 22 (closed Mon), serves substantial €3.50 set meals and is a backpackers' favourite. *Mullens* **bar**, Rua Cândido dos Reis 86, serves meals until 10pm, plays jazz, salsa and soul on the sound system and stays open until 2am. *Hideaway*, Travessa 1° de Maio 9, just off Praça Luís Camões, is a cosily atmospheric bar, also open till 2am. For contemporary **club** sounds, there's *Bon Vivant*, Rua 25 de Abril 105, with its "tropical" roof terrace (till 4am).

Silves

SILVES is the one inland Algarve town that merits a detour. Capital of the Moorish kings of the al-Gharb (now Algarve), it's still an imposing place and has a lively summer beer festival. The **train station** – an easy approach from Lagos or Faro – lies 2km outside the town; there is a connecting bus, but it's worth walking, allowing the town and its fortress to appear slowly as you emerge from the wooded hills. Under the Moors, Silves was a place of grandeur and industry, described in contemporary accounts as being "of shining brightness". In 1189 an army led by Sancho I put an end to this splendour, killing some 6000 Moors in the process. The impressively complete sandstone walls of the Moorish **fortress** (daily 10am–6/7pm; €1.50) retain their towers and elaborate communication system, but inside there's little left of the old citadel. Just below the fortress is Silves' **Cathedral** (daily 8.30am–6.30pm, Sun between masses only), built on the site of the mosque in the thirteenth century. The nearby **Museu Arqueologia** (Mon–Sat 9am–6pm; €1.50) is an engaging museum that romps through the history of Silves from the year dot to the sixteenth century. The **tourist office**, in the heart of the town at Rua 25 de Abril 26 (Mon–Fri 9.30am–1pm & 2–5.30pm; ☎282 442 255), will help you find a **private room**. Recommended are those at Rua Cândido dos Reis 36 (☎282 442 667; ❸), where you share the use of a kitchen and a little outdoor terrace. Another promising option is the *Residencial Sousa* **pension** at Rua Samora Barros 17 (☎282 442 502; ❹).

Faro

FARO is the capital of the Algarve. Excellent beaches are within easy reach, and in summer there's quite a nightlife scene, as thousands of travellers pass through on their way to and from the airport, 6km west of town. Sacked and burned by the Earl of Essex in 1596, and devastated by the Great Earthquake of 1755, the town has few historic buildings. By far the most curious sight is the Baroque **Igreja do Carmo** (Mon–Fri 10am–1pm & 3–5pm, Sat 10am–1pm) near the central post office on Largo do Carmo. A door to the right of the altar leads to a macabre **Capela dos Ossos** (€1), its walls decorated with bones disinterred from the adjacent cemetery. This aside, the most interesting buildings are all in the old, semiwalled quarter on the south side of the harbour, centred around the majestic Largo da Sé and entered through the eighteenth-century town gate, the **Arco da Vila**. The cathedral here was heavily remodelled after the Great Earthquake and more impressive is the nearby **Museu Arqueológico** (Mon & Sat 2/2.30–5.30/6pm, Tues–Fri 9.30/10am–5.30/6pm; €2), installed in a fine sixteenth-century convent. The most striking exhibit is a third-century Roman mosaic of Neptune and the four winds, unearthed near Faro train station.

Taxis from the **airport** to the centre cost around €8, or take bus #16 (daily 8am–8.30/11pm, every 45min; €1), a twenty-minute journey to town. From June to October there is also a free Aerobus service (hourly 9am–8pm; not Tues) for air-ticket holders. The **bus station** is right in the centre, behind the *Hotel Eva*, across from the old town; you'll find the **train station** a few minutes beyond, up Avenida da República. There's a **tourist office** at the airport (daily 10am–midnight; ☎289 818 582), though the main office is near the harbour at Rua da Misericórdia 8 (Mon–Fri 9.30am–5.30/7pm, Sat & Sun 9.30am–12.30pm & 2–5.30/7pm; ☎289 803 604). **Pensions** are concentrated just northeast of the harbour. *Casa de Hóspedes Adelaide* (☎289 802 383; ❹), near the Igreja de São Pedro at Rua Cruz das Mestras 7–9, is the best budget choice – during the summer they also open the roof as a dorm (€10). Otherwise, among the better places are *Pensão Madalena* (☎289 805 806; ❹), Rua C. Bivar 109; *Pensão São Félipe*, Rua Infante Don Henrique 55a (☎289 824 182; ❸); and *Residencial Pinto*, Rua 1° de Maio 27 (☎289 807 417; ❸). The **campsite** (☎289 817 876) is at Praia de Faro, and is always packed in summer – phone ahead; bus #16 from town. There are **restaurants** to meet most budgets: try the characterful *Adega Dois Irmãos*, Largo Terreiro do Bispo 13, or for something less expensive, cram in with locals at *Adega Nova*, Rua Francisco Barreto 24, close to the train station. The town's **nightlife** centres around cobbled Rua do Prior; *Millennium III* is the best club.

Olhão and the islands

OLHÃO, 8km east of Faro, is the largest fishing port on the Algarve and an excellent base for visiting the local sandbank islands. **Train** and **bus** stations are near each other off Avenida da República northeast of town, an easy walk from the **tourist office**, just off Rua do Comércio (Mon–Fri 9.30am–5.30pm; ☎289 713 936). For **accommodation**, try the highly rated *Pensão Bela Vista* (☎289 702 538; ❸), right out of the tourist office then first right; or the *Pensão Boémia*, slightly further out of the centre at Rua da Cerca 20, off Rua 18 de Junho (☎289 714 513; ❸). The nearest **campsite** (☎289 700 300) is at Marim, 3km east – buses hourly till 7pm from the main station. There are clusters of **restaurants** and **bars** around Rua do Comércio and on the seafront: *A Bote*, near the market on Avda. 5 de Outubro, is good (closed Mon), or for something cheaper try *Restaurante Bela Vista*, Rua Dr Teofilio Braga 59 (closed Sun), near the tourist office. **Ferries** leave for the *ilhas* (islands) of Armona and Culatra from the jetty at the far end of Olhão's municipal gardens, five minutes from the market. The service to **Armona** (15min; €0.90 each way) drops you off at a long strip of holiday chalets and huts that stretches right across the island on either side of the main path. The only type of accommodation available here is in chalets (April–Oct only; ☎289 714 173), and you'll be lucky to get one in summer. On the ocean side, the beach disappears into the distance and a short walk will take you to totally deserted stretches of sand and dune. Boats to the more distant **Ilha da Culatra** (35–45min; €1–1.20 each way) call first at unattractive Culatra town, then at **FAROL**, a pretty village of holiday homes edged by beautiful beaches on the ocean side.

Tavira

TAVIRA is a good-looking little town with superb island beaches within easy reach, and despite ever-increasing visitors it continues to make its living as a tuna-fishing port. **Buses** pull up at the terminal by the river, a two-minute walk from the central square, Praça da República; the **train station** is 1km from the centre of town, straight up the Rua da Liberdade. From July to mid-September, boats to the beach on **Ilha de Tavira** depart from the quayside at the town side of the flyover (daily 8am–7.30pm; €1 return). In addition, year-round boats cross from Quatro Águas (every 15min–1hr; €1 return), 2km east of town. The beach is backed by dunes and stretches west almost as far as Fuzeta, 14km away. Despite increasing development – a small chalet settlement, a **campsite** (☎281 324 455; closed Nov–March) a minute from the sands, watersports, beach umbrellas and half a dozen bar/restaurants facing the sea – it's an enjoyable spot in which to hang out. The best **accommodation** in Tavira is the *Residencial Lagoas Bica*, north of the river at Rua Almirante Cândido dos Reis 24 (☎281 322 252; ❸), with the bonus of the budget eatery, *Bica*, below. Alternatives include the smart *Pensão do Castelo* (☎281 320 790; ❺) at Rua da Liberdade 22, the *Residencial Mirante* at Rua da Liberdade 83 (☎281 322 255; ❹, with breakfast) just up the main road (though it can be a bit noisy), and the lovely *Residencial Princesa do Gilão*, across the river on the quayside (☎281 325 171; ❹), whose front rooms have balconies overlooking the river. The **tourist office** just off the main Praça da República (Mon–Fri 9.30am–1pm & 2–5/6pm; ☎281 322 511) might also be able to find you a **private room**. There's **Internet** access at *Café Bela Fria*, Rua das Polanos 1, opposite the bus station. **Bars and restaurants** line the gardens along the bank of the River Gilão, which flows through the centre of town. Best choice is the *Imperial*, which serves seafood at fairly reasonable prices,

Two daily buses (around 9am & 5pm) run from **VILA REAL**, the eastern terminus of the rail line from Faro and Tavira, to Ayamonte in **Spain**, continuing to Huelva for easy connections on to Seville. The same timetable operates in reverse. Spain is one hour ahead of Portugal.

though also good are *Anazu*, Rua Jacques Pessoa 13, a riverfront café, and *Beira Rio*, at Rua Borda da Água de Assêca 44–46, a riverside bar/restaurant with tree-shaded tables serving pizza, pasta and salads. The *Arco*, at Rua Almirante Cândido dos Reis 67, is a laid-back, gay-friendly **bar**. Tavira's only **club**, *UBI* (closed Mon), is reached by following Rua Almirante Cândido dos Reis to the outskirts of town; it's the huge metallic warehouse on the right.

Travel details

Trains

Coimbra to: Aveiro (hourly; 45min–1hr); Lisbon (13 daily; 2–3hr); Porto (12 daily; 1hr 20min–2hr).

Faro to: Lagos (7 daily; 1hr 40min); Lisbon (4 daily; 5hr 30min–6hr); Olhão (16 daily; 10min); Silves (7 daily; 1hr–1hr 15min); Tavira (12–17 daily; 35–45min).

Lagos to: Faro (7 daily; 1hr 40min); Lisbon (4 daily; 5hr 15min); Silves (13 daily; 30–50min).

Lisbon to: Braga (2 daily; 4hr 40min); Coimbra (13 daily; 2–3hr); Évora (2 daily; 3hr); Faro (4 daily; 5hr 30min–6hr); Leiria (5 daily; 2–3hr); Porto (10–13 daily; 3hr 30min–4hr); Sintra (every 15min; 45min); Tavira (4 daily; 6–7hr); Tomar (7 daily; 2hr).

Peso da Régua to: Porto (14–15 daily; 2hr 10min–2hr 30min); Vila Real (5 daily; 1hr).

Porto to: Barcelos (11 daily; 1hr 10min–1hr 40min); Braga (13–16 daily; 1hr–1hr 45min); Coimbra (15–19 daily; 2hr); Lisbon (12 daily; 3–4hr 20min); Madrid, Spain (2 daily; 12hr); Peso da Régua (14–15 daily; 2hr 10min–2hr 30min); Viana do Castelo (7 daily; 1hr 36min–2hr); Vigo, Spain (3 daily; 4hr 30min).

Buses

Braga to: Barcelos (Mon–Fri every 30min, Sat & Sun hourly; 30–50min); Bragança (2 daily; 5hr); Guimarães (every 30min; 30min–1hr); Porto (every 30min; 1hr); Viana do Castelo (4–10 daily; 1hr 40min).

Coimbra to: Fátima (5 daily; 1hr–1hr 30min); Lisbon (16 daily; 2hr 20min); Leiria (10 daily; 1hr); Porto (8–10 daily; 1hr 30min–2hr 45min); Tomar (2 daily; 2hr).

Faro to: Évora (4 daily; 3hr 30min–4hr); Huelva (for connections to Sevilla, Spain; 2 daily; 4hr); Lagos (8 daily, 1hr 45 min); Lisbon (5–10 daily; 4hr 20min); Olhão (every 15min–1hr; 20min); Tavira (7–11 daily; 1hr).

Leiria to: Alcobaça (4 daily; 50min); Batalha (5 daily; 15min); Coimbra (10 daily; 50min); Fátima (9 daily; 25min); Tomar (2 daily; 1hr 10min–2hr).

Lisbon to: Alcobaça (3–4 daily; 2hr); Coimbra (16 daily; 2hr 30min); Évora (6–12 daily; 2hr); Faro (5–10 daily; 4hr 20 min); Fátima (7 daily; 1hr 45min–2hr 15min); Lagos (9 daily; 4hr 20 min); Leiria (9 daily; 1hr–2hr 10min); Mafra (hourly; 1hr 30 min); Óbidos (7 daily; 1hr); Porto (hourly; 3hr); Tomar (2–4 daily; 1hr 45min–2hr); Zambujeira do Mar (1 daily; 4hr 45min).

Porto to: Braga (hourly; 1hr); Bragança (3 daily; 1hr 50min–3hr); Coimbra (8–10 daily; 1hr 30min); Guimarães (12 daily; 2hr); Viana do Castelo (12–14 daily; 2hr); Vila Real (9 daily; 2hr).

Romania

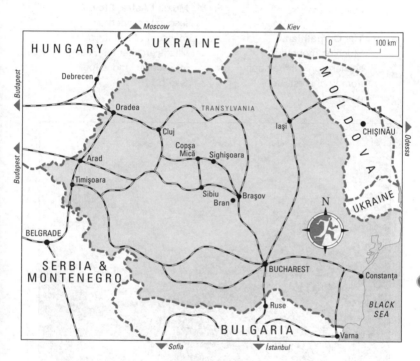

Romania highlights

* **Bucharest** Hectic traffic, Stalinist architecture, pretty residential streets and good dining and nightlife: love it or hate it, Bucharest is unmissable. See p.762

* **The Carpathians** Stunning mountain scenery, only three hours from Bucharest. See p.767

* **Sighişoara** Beautiful medieval citadel in the heart of Transylvania, with authentic Dracula connections. See p.769

* **Muzeul Astra, Sibiu** A fascinating open-air museum of Romanian village architecture, set in a scenic landscape. See p.770

Introduction and basics

Nowhere in Eastern Europe defies preconceptions quite like **Romania**. The country suffers from a poor public image, but don't be put off – the train system is surprisingly efficient, and outstanding landscapes, a huge diversity of wildlife and a bizarre mix of cultures and people await you if you seek them out. However, while pockets of rural Romania appear forgotten by time, life here is changing fast. The dictatorship of Nicolae Ceauşescu left the country on the verge of bankruptcy in the 1990s, but the dysfunctional economy that emerged is now being dragged towards the bright lights of EU membership.

Romanians trace their ancestry back to the Romans, and a mix of Latin and Balkan traits prevails. The people are generally warm, spontaneous, anarchic, and appreciative of style and life's pleasures. In addition to ethnic Romanians, there are communities from half a dozen other races and cultures: Transylvanian Germans (Saxons) live around the fortified towns and churches built to guard the mountain passes during the Middle Ages; so do some one and a half million Magyars (Hungarians), many of whom pursue a traditional lifestyle long since vanished in Hungary; and elsewhere there are Jews, Ukrainians, Serbs, Bulgarians, Gypsies, Turks and Tatars.

The capital, **Bucharest**, is perhaps daunting for the first-time visitor – its savage history is only too evident – but parts of this once-beautiful city retain a voyeuristic appeal. More attractive by far, and easily accessible on public transport, is **Transylvania**, a region steeped in history and legend, offering some of the most beautiful, but least known, mountain scenery in Europe.

Information & maps

Getting hold of **information** is a nightmare. Western-style tourist offices are virtually non-existent, and the authorities don't have a clue about foreign visitors' needs. You're best off going to privately run **tourist agen-**cies, many of which have English-speaking staff. Most bookshops and street vendors selling magazines and books have up-to-date **maps** (*harta*), though it's best to buy them at home.

Money and banks

The currency, the **leu** (plural lei), comes in notes of 2000, 10,000, 50,000, 100,000 and 500,000 lei, with coins of 500, 1000 and 5000 lei. Plastic notes are entering circulation, so when changing money it's best to ask for these. Hotels, rental agencies and other services quote prices in dollars and euros. **Changing money** in most towns is best done at private exchange offices (*casa de schimb*) rather than hotels or banks, as they offer competitive rates. Never change money on the streets. There are plenty of **ATMs** in towns. **Travellers' cheques** are seldom accepted, a hassle to change, and have high commission rates. **Credit cards** are increasingly accepted at hotels and upmarket shops.

Communications

Post offices (*poşta*) in towns are open Mon–Fri 7am–8pm, Sat 8am–noon, and sell **stamps** (*timbru*) and envelopes (*plic*). You can **phone** from the orange cardphones or

ROMANIA | Basics

post offices. **Phonecards** (80,000 or 135,000 lei – you'll need the latter for international calls) are available from post offices and some kiosks. Rates are lower between 11pm and 7am. **Internet access** is available in every town; it's cheap, though not fast.

Getting around

Public transport is cheap and reliable. Allow plenty of time to cover the ground. Of the **train** services available, *InterCity* are the most comfortable; they're followed by *Rapid* and *Acelerat* trains, which stop more often. *Personal* trains stop everywhere and are generally grubby and crowded. Most overnight trains have **sleeping carriages** (*vagon de dormit*) and **couchettes** (*cuşet*) for a modest surcharge. Smoking is allowed in the corridors only. Seat reservations are required for all fast trains, and are automatically included with locally purchased tickets. You'll also need one for travelling on **international trains** that do not require a reservation before entering Romania, so make sure to buy one before departure or face fines. The best place to **buy tickets** and book seats up to ten days in advance is at the local Agenţia SNCFR (offices are generally open Mon–Fri 8am–7pm); at the station you can only book up to one hour in advance. Wasteels – in some major stations – offer discounts of up to 40% on national trains for under-26s. **InterRail** is valid, **Eurail** is not.

Only resort to rural **bus** (*autobuz*) services if a train doesn't serve your destination. Most routes offer only a few buses each day and some don't run to a timetable. A number of new **intercity minibus services** compete – usually departing from near the train station, they depart regularly or when they fill up. Expect to pay half the price of the train ticket. Most **taxis** are now honest, very cheap and therefore an attractive alternative to crowded public transport, particularly in Bucharest. A glaring exception is the taxis at Bucharest's Otopnehi airport, which should be avoided at all costs. On the street, choose a taxi which has a clearly marked company name, phone number and price (in lei per km) on the rear window, and make sure the meter is working.

Accommodation

Accommodation is affordable. Apart from a growing number of four- and five-star hotels offering Western comforts (and prices), **hotel** standards tend to be fairly low. The cheaper hotels will cost £5–8/$8–13 per person per night, for a reasonably clean room and shared shower; breakfast is normally an extra £1.50/$2.50. An alternative is to take a **private room** (*cazare la persoane particulare*), which will probably be the only option in smaller towns and villages. You'll usually come across people offering accommodation at the train or bus station; if approached ask them "*Cât costă pe noapte?*" ("How much per night?"). Expect to pay around £6/$10. **Hostels** (⑳ www.dntcj.ro/yhr) – though still fairly scarce – are proliferating. University towns have **student accommodation** (*caminul de studenţi*) from late June to August, for around £1.50/$2.50 per night. **Campsites** are usually very basic. Expect to pay around £2.25/$3.50 per night for tent space, with little more than a tap and dirty loo. Outside national parks, most officials will turn a blind eye if you are discreet about camping wild in the mountains.

Food and drink

Breakfast (*micul dejun*) is typically a light meal, featuring rolls and butter (*chifle cu unt*) and an *omleta* washed down with a coffee (*cafea*) or tea (*ceai*). The most common **snacks** are flaky pastries (*pateuri*) filled with cheese (*cu brânză*) or meat (*cu carne*); and a variety of spicy grilled sausages and meatballs such as *mici* and *chiftele*. Menus in most Romanian **restaurants** concentrate on grilled meats, or *friptura*. *Cotlet de porc* is the common pork chop, while *muşchi de vacă* is fillet of beef. Dishes usually arrive with a garnish of soggy French fries and a minimalist side salad. At smarter restaurants you can sample traditional **Romanian dishes**, which can be delicious. The best-known of these is *sarmale* – pickled cabbage stuffed with rice, meat and herbs, usually served with sour cream. Stews (*tocană*) and other dishes often feature a combination of meat and dairy products. **Vegetarians** in ordinary restaurants could try asking for *cašcaval pane* (hard cheese fried in breadcrumbs); *ghiveci* (mixed fried veg); *ardei umpluţii* (stuffed peppers) or vegetables and salads. When in doubt, stipulate "*fără carne, vă rog*" (without meat, please). Establishments called **cofetărie** serve coffee and cakes, and sometimes beer and ice cream. Coffee, whether *cafea naturală* (finely ground and cooked Turkish fashion), *filtru* (filtered), or *nes* (instant coffee), is usually drunk black and sweet; ask for it *cu lapte* or *fără zahăr* if you prefer it with milk or without sugar. **Cakes** and **desserts** are sweet and sticky, as throughout the Balkans. Romanians enjoy pancakes (*clătite*) and pies (*plăcintă*) with various fillings; Turkish-influenced *baclava* and *cataif cu frisca*; and the traditional *dulceaţă*, or glass of jam.

Evening **drinking** takes place in outdoor beer gardens, *cramas* (beer cellars), restaurants (where boozers often outnumber the diners), and in a growing number of Western-style cafés and bars. As an aperitif, or at any other time, people like to drink **ţuică**, a powerful plum brandy taken neat; in rural areas, it is home-made and often twice distilled tò yield fearsomely strong *palincă*. Most **beer** (*bere*) is Germanic-style lager. Romania's best **wines** are *Grasa* and *Feteasca Neagră* from the vineyards of Cotnari and Dealul Mare, and the sweet dessert wines of Murfatlar. Expect to pay £1–2.25/$1.60–3.50 for a good quality bottle. Romania has a huge amount of natural springs, and **mineral water** (*apă minerală*) is readily available.

Opening hours and holidays

Shop **opening hours** are Mon–Fri 9am–6pm, with some supermarkets open until 8pm. Museums and castles open at similar times (though most are closed on Mon or Tues); **admission charges** are minimal – we've not quoted them. **National holidays** are: Jan 1 & 2; Easter Monday; May 1; Dec 1; Dec 25 & 26.

Emergencies

Keep an eye on your belongings at all times, and be aware of pickpockets in crowded buses and trams and when getting on or off trains. Do not believe anyone claiming to be a policeman and asking to see your passport and/or the contents of your wallet; keep walking, offer to go to a police station or simply scream *poliţia!* (police!). Make sure you have health insurance. Bucharest's central emergency **hospital** is up to Western standards, while Medicover, Calea Plevnei 96 (☏021/310 4410), also offers Western-standard care, with English-speaking doctors. **Pharmacies** (*farmacie*) are usually well-stocked and open Mon–Sat 9am–6pm; every town has at least one place open 24hr.

Emergency numbers

All emergencies ☏112.

ROMANIA | Basics

Bucharest (Bucureşti)

On arriving in **BUCHAREST** (Bucureşti), most tourists want to leave as soon as possible, but to do so would mean missing the heart of Romania. Bucharest does have its charm and elegance – it's just that it does things in its own way. Added to which, it's a dynamic city, changing quicker than any other in Romania. Old, dusty residential areas with beautiful but crumbling eclectic architecture surround the centre and show what the city was like in a bygone era. Head south and you'll come across unfinished projects from Ceauşescu's reign, frozen in time but still littering the landscape. Seeing the true scale of what a dictatorship can do is something you won't forget. Love it or hate it, Bucharest is a must-see.

Arrival, information and accommodation

The modern **Otopeni Airport** is 16km north; ignore the rip-off taxi drivers and head for the #783 bus stop just outside. Buy your two-ride ticket from the aluminium RATB kiosk, stamp it yourself and don't hand it to the driver. Virtually all **trains** terminate at Gara de Nord. The station has done much to improve its dodgy reputation, though it's still wise to keep a sharp eye on your belongings. Use the ATM or the adjacent currency exchange to get cash and head straight for the **metro station** to get to the centre (reach Piaţa Universitaţii by changing trains at Piaţa Victoriei). Honest taxi drivers can only be found outside the main entrance beyond the Wasteels ticket office – look for the yellow Cristaxi or Cobalcescu cars.

Bucharest has no **tourist office**; the Elvis' Villa Hostel booth at Gara de Nord can give basic directions. The excellent bi-monthly English-language **city guide** *Bucharest In Your Pocket* (Ⓦwww.inyourpocket.com; €2) is essential reading, with maps and witty reviews of accommodation, restaurants, nightlife and sights; buy it at Gara de Nord's Wasteels office, the airport kiosk or from hotels and bookstores. **Public transport**, although crowded, is efficient and cheap. The most useful lines of the strangely lit metro system are the M1 (a near-circle) and the more used M2 (north–south). There's also a strange array of trams, buses and trolleybuses. Buy a **ticket** from the kiosks located near the bus stops and validate it in the machine on board. At night, you'll have to depend on **taxis**; they tend to be honest and are now ludicrously cheap, charging about €0.15/km; try Proftaxi (Ⓣ9422), Mondial (Ⓣ9423) or Cobalcescu (Ⓣ9451), and make sure the driver has the meter running.

Many **budget** hotels have been renovated in recent years, making them good value for hostel-haters. A good alternative, especially if you're in a group, are **private apartments**, which cost from e30 per night and are often better and more spacious than hotel rooms; *Adrian Accommodation* (Ⓣ0723/34 71 92, Ⓦwww.bucharest-accommodation.ro) and *George* (Ⓣ0722/36 75 68, Ⓦwww.for-rent.ro) have good options.

Hostels

Elvis' Villa Str Avram Iancu 5 Ⓣ021/312 1653, Ⓦwww.elvisvilla.ro. Australian-run, luxurious, clean and fun – Elvis is alive, and runs an HI hostel with air-conditioned rooms sleeping 2–8 people. Laundry, breakfast, drinks and Internet are all included, and there's a kitchen and TV room. Their information kiosk at the station will help you get here, otherwise take trolleybus #85 from Piaţa Universitaţii east to the Calea Mosilor stop, and continue on foot past the roundabout, turning right at the Greek church. €12.

Funky Chicken Guesthouse Str Gen. Berthelot 63 Ⓣ021/312 1425. The *Villa Helga*'s little sister, conveniently located just north of Cişmigiu Park, between Gara de Nord and the centre. It has clean communal bathrooms, a TV room, kitchen, laundry service (€2.25) but no longer a chicken. No reservations, but guaranteed accommodation for

Despite Bucharest's reputation for scams, it's safer than it was. Still, never pay anything to anyone in advance, never change money without being aware of the exchange rate, and never hand your passport or wallet to anyone claiming to be a policeman.

BUCHAREST

Amzei Market

CALEA VICTORIEI

STRADA P. AMZEI

STRADA ENESCU

STR. MENDELEEV

B-DUL GENERAL MAGHERU

STR. JULLES MICHELET

British
Embassy

STRADA PICTOR ARTUR VERONA

STR. GEN. BERTHELOT

Gara de Nord ◄

STR. LUTERANĂ

Athénée
Palace

Romanian
Athenaeum

Royal
Palace

STRADA ȘTIRBEI VODA

PIAȚA
REVOLUȚIEI

University
Library

STRADA C. A. ROSETTI

B-DUL N. BĂLCESCU

STRADA TUDOR ARGHEZI

STR. BATIȘTEI

Cișmigiu
Park

PIAȚA
WALTER
MĂRĂCINEANU

STR. ÎN CÎMPINEANU

PIAȚA
REVOLUȚIEI

Senate

Crețulescu
Church

STRADA ACADEMIEI

STR. CÎMPINEANU

Enei
Church

US
Embassy

National
Theatre
of Bucharest

CALEA VICTORIEI

STR. M. MILLO

STRADA EDGAR QUINET

University

PIAȚA
UNIVERSITĂȚII

B-DUL CAROL I

STR. C. MILLE

Cercul Militar

STR. BREZOIANU

Doamnei
Church

B-DUL REGINA ELISABETA

Bucharest
History
Museum

Colțea
Church

B-DUL REGINA ELISABETA

CFR/TAROM

STRADA EFORIE

Police
Headquarters

PASAGIUL
VILACROSSE

STRADA DOAMNEI

Russian
Church

PIAȚA
SF. GHEORGHE

STRADA LIPSCANI

STRADA MIHAI VODĂ

STR. ACADEMIEI

SMÂRDAN

ȘELARI

STR. BLĂNARI

St Gheorghe
Nou Church

CALEA MOȘILOR

Sf Nicolae-
Mihai Vodă
Church

River Dâmbovița

B-DUL LIBERTĂȚII

STR. STAVROPOLEOS

Stavropoleos
Church

National
History Museum

STRADA LIPSCANI

STRADA
COVACI

STR. GABROVENI

STR. I. C. BRĂTIANU

Choral
Temple

Pedestrian
Bridge

B-DUL NAȚIUNILE UNITE

St Apostoli
Church

Domnița Bălașa
Church

STRADA FRANCEZĂ

SPLAIUL INDEPENDENȚEI

Curtea
Veche

Unirea
Market

Hanul Lui
Manuc

Unirea
Department
Store

Piața Unirii

B-DUL UNIRII

◄ Palatul Parlamentului

ROMANIA | Bucharest

23

Arcade
Pedestrianized Street

N

0   100 m

everyone who turns up. From Gara de Nord, follow B-dul Golescu, cross Str Berzei and enter the street next to the pharmacy. €8.

Villa Helga Str Salcâmilor 2 ☏021/610 2214, ⓦwww.rotravel.com/hotels/helga. For years the only hostel in town, *Helga* remains a popular and friendly HI hostel, and a good place to meet up with other travellers. It has new beds in doubles as well as in mixed and female-only dorms, a kitchen, TV room, courtyard with barbecue and free laundry. Take bus #79, #86 or #133 from Gara de Nord to Piaţa Gemeni, two stops after Piaţa Romana; then take the first right off B-dul Dacia into Str Vittorului. €10.

Villa 11 Str Institutul Medico Militar 11 ☏0722/495 900, €vila11bb@hotmail.com. This friendly and quiet family-run twelve-bed hostel offers standard facilities including free laundry and is in a run-down area close to the Gara de Nord. Phone ahead to book and to be picked up from the station or airport. €14.

Hotels

Bucegi Str Witing 2 ☏021/212 71 55, ⓦwww.stalingrad.ro. A cheap and grubby hotel near the station with cramped doubles with shared facilities and larger en suites. ❷

Carpaţi Str Matei Millo 16 ☏021/315 0140, ⓦwww.carpatihotel.compace.ro. Near Cişmigiu park, quiet and with helpful staff. Rooms with shared showers or toilet and some en suites. ❸

Cerna B-dul Golescu 29 ☏021/311 05 35. Opposite the station; rooms are clean and light; more expensive en-suite doubles also include breakfast. ❷

Marna Str Buzeşti 3 ☏021/212 7582. Renovated budget hotel near Gara de Nord with en suites and shared showers. ❷

Muntenia Str Academiei 19–21 ☏021/314 6010, ⓦmuntenia.kappa.ro. Old-fashioned hotel in a central but slightly noisy location, 100m northwest of Piaţa Universăţii. En suites and shared showers. ❷

Campsite

Băneasa ☏021/230 4525. Out towards the airport – take bus #301 from Piaţa Romana and get off at the Casa Alba tourist complex.

The City

"A savage hotch-potch" was Ferdinand Lasalle's verdict on Bucharest between the wars, with its boulevards and nightlife, its slums and beggars, its aristocratic mansions and crumbling Orthodox churches. The extremes of wealth and poverty, once mitigated, have now returned thanks to burgeoning capitalism and profiteers. But among the ruptured roads and disintegrating buildings, you'll find leafy squares, shaded parks and dressed-up Romanian girls adding a touch of glamour to the surroundings. Freezing in winter and hot and dusty in the summer, woodlands and a girdle of lakes freshen Bucharest's northern outskirts, beyond the familiar-looking Arcul de Triumf.

Most inner-city sights are within walking distance of **Calea Victoriei**, an avenue of vivid contrasts, scattered with vestiges of *ancien régime* elegance interspersed with apartment blocks, glass and steel facades and cake shops. Fulcrum of the avenue is **Piaţa Revoluţiei**, created during the 1930s on Carol II's orders to ensure a field of fire around the Royal Palace. The palace now contains the excellent **National Art Museum** (Wed–Sun 10/11am–6/7pm; ⓦart.museum.ro; $3, free on 1st Wed of month) including works by Rembrandt, Monet and Sisley – as well as galleries of modern and ancient Romanian art. North of the palace, the **Athénée Palace Hotel** (now part of the Hilton chain) has always been a hive of intrigue, but was a veritable "intelligence factory" in the 1950s, with bugged rooms, tapped phones and informer prostitutes. Opposite the palace stands the grand **Romanian Atheneum**, the main concert hall, which can be visited by asking the concierge, and the **University Library**, torched, allegedly by the Securitate, in the confused fighting of the 1989 revolution, but now rebuilt and reopened. Just south of here is the former Communist Party HQ, now the Senate, which dominated TV screens worldwide in 1989. The low balcony is where Nicolae Ceauşescu made his last speech on December 21. Minutes into his speech the booing took over and the dictator's disbelief was broadcast to the nation just before the screens went blank. The next day Ceauşescu and his wife Elena escaped by helicopter from the roof, fleeing to their eventual execution on Christmas Day. Opposite, the restored eighteenth-century **Creţulescu Church** fronts a tangle of streets wending west towards **Cişmigiu Park**, Bucharest's oldest, containing a boating lake, playgrounds, summer terrace cafés and animated chess players.

Beyond the grand **Cercul Militar** building on the junction with B-dul Regina Elisabeta, the main east–west boulevard, Calea Victoriei continues southwards past the police headquarters. Directly opposite is the **Pasagiul Vilacrosse** arcade, one of the remnants of the Bucharest that used to be known as the "Paris of the East". Near the river at no. 1, the **Muzeul National de Istorie** (National History Museum; Tues–Sun 10am–6pm), is worth visiting for the cellar vault with superb gold and silverware left by Romania's pre-Christian inhabitants, the Dacians. Currently under renovation, this is one of the few areas still open to the public. Nearby is Bucharest's **historic centre**; a maze of dusty cobblestone streets with decrepit houses and tiny shops, concentrated around the pedestrianized Strada Lipscani. The whole area is slated for a major EU-funded renovation project, urgently necessary to save what's left, but which no doubt will cause the area to lose some of its authenticity. Just south of Strada Lipscani stands the small **Stavropoleos Church**; built in the 1720s, it has gorgeous, almost arabesque, patterns decorating its facade, and an elegant columned portico. Further south are the modest remains of the **Curtea Veche** (Old Court; daily 10am–4pm), Vlad the Impaler's fifteenth century citadel. Dating from 1559, the adjacent Old Court church is Bucharest's oldest church. Inside the large white building opposite the church you'll find the lush courtyard of the **Hanul lui Manuc** inn, now home to an over-priced restaurant and wine cellar. The inn's southern wall forms one side of **Piaţa Unirii**, which is where the old Bucharest makes way for the new.

The Centru Civic, Piaţa Universităţii and north

The infamous **Centru Civic** was Ceauşescu's pet urban project. After an earthquake in 1977 damaged much of the city, Ceauşescu took the opportunity to remodel the entire southern portion of central Bucharest as a monument to Communism. By the early 1980s bulldozers had moved in to clear the way for the Victory of Socialism Boulevard (now **Bulevardul Unirii**), taking with them thousands of architecturally significant houses, churches and monuments. The eastern end of the boulevard is now a banking district, while the other end is dominated by the **Palatul Parlamentului** (Parliament Palace), the second-largest administration building in the world. The structure was started in 1984 and still has not been completed, despite the efforts of 100,000 workers, toiling in shifts. The building which has 1100 rooms and a nuclear shelter now houses the Romanian Parliament and a conference centre. **Guided tours** in English (daily 10am–4pm; $3) start at the northern entrance, to the right-hand side of the building. Returning northwards from Piaţa Unirii along B-dul Brătianu, you'll see the *Hotel Intercontinental* towering above busy **Piaţa Universităţii**. This is where the students pitched their post-revolution City of Peace encampment, which was violently overrun, together with the illusion of true democracy, by the miners that President Iliescu had called in to "restore order" in June 1990. The miners returned to Bucharest in 1991, this time in protest against the government rather than as its storm troopers. When they advanced again in 1999, Bucharest politicians had riot police prevent them from approaching the capital. Just to the east rises Elena Ceauşescu's **Teatrul National** (National Theatre), resembling an Islamicized reworking of the Colosseum. On the corner opposite, **Bucharest University** forecourt is thronged with students, snack stands and book vendors. The bulbous domes of the **Students' Church**, originally a Russian church, appear through a gap in the grand buildings lining the southern side of the boulevard.

Stretching north from Piaţa Victoriei, Şoseaua Kiseleff leads into the more pleasant, leafy suburbs. At no. 3, the **Muzeul Ţăranului Român** (Museum of the Romanian Peasant; Tues–Sun 10am–6pm, last entry 5pm; ⊛ www.itcnet.ro/mtr) is a must-see, giving an insight into the country's varied rural traditions, with exhibits on everything from costume to religious icons, and with excellent souvenir and book shops. At the northern end of the Şoseaua is the **Arcul de Triumf**, commemorating Romania's participation on the side of the Allied victors in World War

I. Just to the north of the arch is **Herăstrău Park**, the city's largest. Inside the park, just off the northern end of Şoseaua Kiseleff, is the **Muzeul Satului** (Village Museum; daily 9am–6pm), boasting wooden houses, churches and windmills from various regions of the country.

Eating, drinking and nightlife

Traditional fresh **snacks**, such as *gogoşi* (Romanian doughnuts) and *covrigi* (pretzels), are sold all over the city. Most Romanians choose to eat at home, but local restaurants can be delicious, and just as cheap as fast-food outlets. Beware, though, that some restaurants still have the nasty habit of charging food by weight – if the menu shows the cost per 100 grams, check the real price with the waiter. **Nightlife** is becoming increasingly good, offering something for pretty much all tastes. The streets around Strada Gabroveni in the historic centre attract many new bars and crowds. In summer, the clubs and restaurants around Herăstrău lake are popular – but don't expect good service. For full **listings**, get hold of the invaluable English-language city guide *Bucharest In Your Pocket*; available at the hostels, hotels, bookstores and online at ⓦwww.inyourpocket.com. The weekly Romanian-language *Şapte Seri* magazine, found free at bars, has events and cinema listings.

Restaurants

Barka Saffron Str Av Sănătescu 1, near Piaţa Domeni on B-dul Mihalache ☎021/224 1004. Trendy, with charming staff and excellent international, Indian and vegetarian food. Worth the trip north of the centre, and the higher prices.

La Belle Epoque Str Beller 6, just off Piaţa Dorobanţi ☎021/230 0770. Traditional Belgian dishes are on offer here, served in a traditional Belgian atmosphere. Hoegaarden and Leffe beer on tap.

La Mama Str Văcărescu 3 ☎021/212 4086. Good-value Romanian food and great wines. Very popular – booking ahead is essential. Metro Ştefan cel Mare.

La 'mpinge Tava Piaţa Rosetti 4. A cheap and popular self-service restaurant serving Romanian food and a few vegetarian options till 6pm. On B-dul Carol I. Closed Sat & Sun.

Nicoreşti Str Maria Rosetti 40. All the traditional Romanian dishes at rock-bottom prices; accompanied with live music. Near *Villa Helga*.

Paradis Str Hristo Botev 10.Unprepossessing, but serves excellent, inexpensive Lebanese food. Just east of Piaţa Universităţii.

Smarts Str Al. Donici 14 ☎211 9035. In a beautifully quiet tree-lined street, this quiet and friendly restaurant serves up French food alongside the more usual local dishes. Nice bar downstairs.

Cafés and bars

Amsterdam Grand Café Str Covaci 22. Heralded as the best new place in Bucharest, this spacious Dutch-run café in the historic centre has a relaxed atmosphere, good service, a reading table, and serves inexpensive food as well as Dutch and Belgian beer.

Jukebox Str Sepcari 22. Opposite Hanul lui Manuc, this cheerful cellar bar comes alive at night with live music and karaoke along with the beer.

Lăptăria lui Enache 4th floor of the National Theatre, Piaţa Universităţii. Justifiably one of Bucharest's most popular bars. Cool and with live music in winter, in summer you can watch free films on the rooftop terrace (*La Motor*). Entrance next to the hotel near the Dominuszart sign.

Planter's Str Mendleev 10. Immensely popular bar with a small dancefloor. South off Piaţa Romana.

Yellow Bar Str E. Quinet 10. Trendy cellar lounge bar with comfortable sofas. Near Piaţa Universităţii.

Clubs

Club A Str Blănari 14. Crowded place catering for students.

Ramirez Str 11 Iunie 51, just north of Parcul Carol. Worth visiting – imports top DJs for a discerning crowd.

Studio Martin B-dul Iancu de Hunedoara 41. Brings in the ravers with its international guest DJs and gay-friendly atmosphere.

Twice Str Sf. Vineri 4. Bucharest's biggest club, heaving and very popular.

Listings

Embassies and consulates Australia, B-dul Unirii 74 ☎021/320 98 02; Canada, Str N. Iorga 36 ☎021/307 5000; UK, Str J. Michelet 24 ☎021/312 0303; US, Str T. Arghezi 7–9

☎021/210 4042.
Gay and lesbian For information, contact Accept,
Str Lirei 10 ☎021/252 1637, ⊛www.accept-romania.ro.
Hospital Spitalul Clinic de Urgenţa, Calea

Floreasca 8 ☎021/230 0106. Medicover, Calea
Plevnei 96 ☎021/310 4410.
Internet Brit C@fe, Calea Dorobanţilor 14; PC-Net
Café, Calea Victoriei 136 and B-dul Carol 1 25.
Post office Str M. Millo 10.

Transylvania

Thanks to Bram Stoker's novel, **Transylvania** is famed abroad as the homeland of Count Dracula, but you'll find there's a lot more to explore here than the story of a bloodthirsty nobleman. Two train lines travel west from Bucharest into Hungary via either Arad or Cluj, carving their way through the spectacular **Carpathian** mountain range, which offers Europe's cheapest skiing in winter and wonderful hiking during the summer. It's well worth setting aside some time to explore the rest of Transylvania's caves, alpine meadows, dense forests sheltering bears, and lowland valleys with quaint villages and buffalo cooling off in the rivers. The population is a mix of Romanians, Magyars, Germans, Gypsies and others, thanks to centuries of migration and colonization. The Trianon Treaty of 1920 placed Transylvania within the Romanian state, but the character of many towns still reflects past patterns of settlement. Most striking are the former seats of Saxon power with their medieval streets, defensive towers and fortified churches. **Sighişoara** is the most picturesque but could be the Saxons' cenotaph: their culture has evaporated here, as it threatens to do in **Braşov**, **Sibiu** and in the old German settlements around.

Braşov

With an eye for trade and invasion routes, the medieval Saxons sited their largest settlements near Transylvania's mountain passes. **BRAŞOV**, which they called Kronstadt, grew prosperous as a result, and for centuries the Saxons constituted an elite whose economic power long outlasted its feudal privileges. The Communist government brought thousands of Moldavian villagers to Braşov to work in the new factories. As a result, there are two parts to Braşov: the quasi-Gothic bit coiled beneath Mount Tâmpa, which looks great, and the surrounding sprawl of flats, which doesn't. The park beside B-dul Eroilor meets the eastern end of the pedestrianized Str Republicii, the hub of Braşov's social life. At the top of Str Republicii, sturdy buildings line Piaţa Sfatului, the main square. The fifteenth-century council house in the centre is now the **History Museum** (Tues–Sun 10am–5pm). The exhibits illustrate the power of the Saxon guilds, whose main hangout was the red **Merchants' Hall** opposite. The Gothic pinnacles of the town's most famous landmark, the **Black Church** (Mon–Sat 10am–3.30pm), stab upwards like a series of daggers. An endearingly monstrous hall-church that took almost a century to complete (1385–1477), it is so called for its soot-blackened walls, the result of being torched by the Austrian army in 1689. Inside, by contrast, the church is startlingly white, with Oriental carpets creating splashes of colour along the walls of the nave. In summer (June–Sept Tues, Thurs & Sat at 6pm), the church's 4000-pipe **organ** is used for concerts. A length of fortress wall runs along the foot of Mount Tâmpa, behind which a **cable car** whisks tourists up to the summit. Of the original seven bastions the best preserved is that of the weavers, on Str Coşbuc. This complex of wooden galleries and bolt-holes now contains the **Museum of the Bârsa Land Fortifications** (Tues–Sun 10am–4pm). Inside are models and weaponry recalling the bad old days when the region was repeatedly attacked by Tatars, Turks and by Dracula, who impaled hundreds of captives to terrorize the townsfolk. The Saxons' widely publicized stories of Dracula's cruelty unwittingly contributed to Transylvania's dark image and eventually caught Bram Stoker's attention.

ROMANIA | Transylvania

㉓

Braşov's **train station** is northeast of the old town, 2km from the centre – take bus #4 into town or spend $1 on a taxi. You'll probably be approached by the legendary Maria Bolea, who offers **private rooms** or apartments (❶) in and around Braşov. Don't be fazed, the rooms are fine and she's a mine of information on the local area. Fun-loving backpackers should look in the station hall for the kiosk of the excellent *Elvis' Hostel*. Located at Str Democraţiei 2B (☎0721/844 940, ⓦwww.elvisvilla.com; €10), just off Piaţa Unirii in the Schei district, it has a barbecue in the garden and many free perks, including Internet access and laundry. Also off Piaţa Unirii is the *Casa Speranţei* at Str Piatra Mare 101 (☎0268/151 501, ⓔmedipal@deuroconsult.ro; ❷), where a portion of the room-rates goes to help cancer victims. Further into town, the *Beke Guesthouse*, Str Cerbului 32 (☎0723/461 888; ❷), is cosy and quiet. Cheapest of the **hotels** is the basic *Aro Sport*, between Str Republicii and Str Mureşenilor at Str Sfântu Ioan 3 (☎0268/478 800; ❶). Campers have the suburban *Dârste* **campsite** to the southeast of town at Calea Bucureşti 285 (☎0268/315 863); it's best reached by taxi. The old town is dotted with affordable **restaurants** and **cafés**. Good Romanian food is served at *Blue Corner*, Piaţa Enescu 13 (☎0268/478 590), through the archway next to the Orthodox church on Piaţa Sfatului. Next door at no. 11, the pricier *Bistro De L'Arte* (☎0268/473 994) has bistro dishes and breakfasts. At Str Republicii 10, *Mando* is a popular spot for people-watching, with very affordable meal deals and take-away ice creams. A great **place to drink** is *Festival 39*, Str Mureşenilor 23, which is full of the strangest things – from badly stuffed animals and fake plastic trophies to a barman from Cuba; a few doors up the street, *Saloon* at no. 11–13 has more seating and bar food. The Romanian-language magazine *Zile şi Nopţi*, free at bars, lists **events**.

Bran, Râşnov and Zărneşti

Cosy little **BRAN**, 28km by bus from Braşov, is situated at the foot of the stunning Bucegi mountains. Despite what you may hear, its **castle** (Tues–Sun 9am–5pm) has only tenuous associations with Dracula – aka Vlad the Impaler, who may have attacked it in 1460. Hyperbole is forgivable, though, as Bran really does look like a vampire count's residence. The castle was built in 1377 by the Saxons of Braşov to safeguard what used to be the main route into Wallachia, and it rises in tiers of towers and ramparts from amongst the woods, against a glorious mountain background. A warren of stairs, nooks and chambers around a small courtyard, the interior is filled with elaborately carved four-poster beds, throne-like chairs and portraits of grim-faced boyars. For a more authentic experience than Bran, jump off the Braşov bus in nearby **RÂŞNOV**, where the hilltop fortress ruins – and the views – are stunning. In between the two is **ZĂRNEŞTI**, whose **Large Carnivore Centre** (daily 10am–5pm; €3; ⓦwww.clcp.ro) is due to open in 2004, housing brown bears, wolves, lynx and wild boar – indigenous inhabitants of the nearby Piatra Craiului range – in 30 hectares; there'll also be exhibits, films and English information on the Carpathians. If you're interested in exploring further, contact **Carpathian Nature Tours** (☎0745/512 096; ⓦwww.cntours.de) an ecotourism outfit which will provide information on hiking in the Piatra Craiului range and can organize **guided walks** tracking the animals (advance booking required), as well as accommodation.

Buses to Bran and Zărneşti leave from bus station #2, 3km west of central Braşov at the end of Str Lungă; take bus #28 from Braşov's central park or bus #10 from the train station, and get off opposite the stadium. There's no shortage of **private rooms** in Bran; Ovi-Tours, Str Bologa 16 (☎0268/236 666; ❷), have some clean and rustic-style rooms or can help book one elsewhere. For a near-medieval mountain escape, spend a night at *Cabana Montana* (☎0744/801 094; ❷), in the picturesque hamlet of **MAGURĂ**, on the flanks of the Piatra Craiului mountains just south of Zărneşti. Be sure to phone ahead and they'll pick you up from Zărneşti's bus station.

Sighişoara

A forbidding silhouette of battlements and needle spires looms over the citadel of **SIGHIŞOARA**, perched on a hill overlooking the Tărnave Mare valley; it seems fitting that this was the birthplace of Vlad Ţepeş, the man known to posterity as **Dracula**. Ill-conceived plans to build a "Dracula-land" theme park nearby were abandoned after widespread protest – yet another illustration of Romania's inability to decide what kind of tourism it wishes to promote. Look out for the Medieval and the Ethnical & Art **festivals** held annually in July and August, when Sighişoara gets overrun by thousands of beer-guzzlers.

The route from the train station to the centre passes the **Romanian Orthodox Cathedral**, its gleaming white, multifaceted facade a striking contrast to the dark interior. Across the Tărnave Mare river, the **Citadel** dominates the town from a hill whose slopes support a jumble of ancient houses. Steps lead up from the lower town's main square, Piaţa Hermann Oberth, to the main gateway, above which rises the mighty **Clock Tower**. The tower was founded in the fourteenth century when Sighişoara became a free town controlled by craft guilds – each of which had to finance the construction of a bastion and defend it during wartime. Sighişoara grew rich on the proceeds of trade with Moldavia and Wallachia, as attested by the regalia and strongboxes in the tower's **museum** (daily 10am–4/6.30pm). The ticket also gives access to the seventeenth century **torture chamber** and the **Museum of Armaments** next door with its small and poorly presented Dracula Exhibition. In 1431 or thereabouts, the child later known as **Dracula** was born in a two-storey house near the clock tower at Str Muzeului 6. At the time his father – Vlad Dracul – was commander of the mountain passes into Wallachia, but the younger Vlad's privileged childhood ended eight years later, when he and his brother Radu were sent to Anatolia as hostages to the Turks. There Vlad observed the Turks' use of terror, which he would later turn against them, earning the nickname of "The Impaler". Nowadays, Vlad's birthplace is a mediocre tourist restaurant.

Sighişoara's **train station** is on the northern edge of town, on Str Libertăţii. Backpackers are met at the station by employees of the excellent *Elvis' Villa* **hostel**, just down the road at Str Libertăţii 10 (☎0265/772 546, ⓦwww.elvisvilla.com; €10), which has all the perks of the other Elvis hostels, including free laundry and Internet access. Less fun but more centrally located is the German-run *Berg Hostel* in the citadel's oldest house at Str Bastionului 4–6 (☎0265/506 087, ⓦwww.ibz.ro; €10), with dorm rooms, doubles, and a dingy bar in the cellar. There's a charming pension run by the Faur family in the citadel at Str Cojocarilor 1 (☎0744/119 211; ②). Romantics will appreciate *Casa cu Cerb* **hotel**, Str Şcolii 1 (☎0265/774 625, ⓦwww.ar-messerschmidt-s.ro; ④) as the bathtubs fit two and the contents of the minibar are included in the price (but breakfast isn't). The friendly *Pensiunea Turistică Hera*, just south of the centre at Str Eminescu 62 (☎0265/778 850; ②), is spacious and cheap, while *Hotel Poienţa*, one valley east of the centre at Str D. Cantemir 24 (☎0265/772739; ②), has a small swimming pool and lovely views. To find it, follow the signs from Str Decembrie 1918. The **restaurant** in the *Casa cu Cerb* hotel and the *Café Wagner*, Piaţa Cetăţii 7, are the best dining options in the citadel, while in the lower town *Jo*, overlooking the field at Str Goga 12, and *Strada*, Str Morii 7, have good pizzas and outdoor seating. *Pani Toya Rom*, Str Morii 11, has tasty Turkish snacks including *baklava*; more filling are the homemade sandwiches and cakes in the *House on the Rock*'s café on Piaţa Cetăţii. *Rustic*, Str 1 Decembrie 1918 5, offers fairly good Romanian food and becomes a popular **bar** at night. The *Culture Pub* in the basement of the *Berg Hostel* has some live music, while *No Limits*, beneath the Clock Tower, is the most central club. The fastest **Internet** access is in the basement of the *House on the Rock*.

Sibiu

The narrow streets and old gabled houses of **SIBIU**'s older quarters look like

ROMANIA | Transylvania

㉓

they've come straight off the page of a fairytale. Sibiu was the Saxons' main town, and nowadays has stronger and more lucrative links with Germany than any Transylvanian town, with many people speaking German. Like Braşov, Sibiu was founded by Germans invited by the Hungarian King Géza II to colonize strategic regions of Transylvania in 1143. Its inhabitants came to dominate trade in Transylvania and Wallachia, forming exclusive guilds under royal charter. Alas for the Saxons, their citadels were no protection against the tide of history, which eroded their influence after the eighteenth century. Within the last decades almost the entire Saxon community has left Romania. Set aside a whole day to explore Sibiu's wonderful open-air **Muzeul Astra** museum of traditional cultures.

To reach the centre from the main train station, cross the square and follow Str Gen. Magheru until you hit **Piaţa Mare**. Traditionally the hub of public life, it's surrounded by the houses of sixteenth- and seventeenth-century merchants. On its western side stands the **Muzeul Brukenthal** (Tues–Sun 9am–5pm), one of the finest in Romania with an evocative collection of works by Transylvanian painters. The city's **Muzeul Istorie** (History Museum, Tues–Sun 9am–5pm) is housed in the impressive Old City Hall, just to the north. On the north side of Piaţa Mare, the huge Catholic church stands next to the **Council Tower** (daily 10am–6pm), which offers fine views over Sibiu's rooftops and the Carpathians. To the north, Piaţa Mică is surrounded by arcaded medieval houses. Just beyond, on Piaţa Huet, the **Evangelical Cathedral** (10am–6pm, Sun from 11am) – a massive hall-church raised during the fourteenth and fifteenth centuries – dominates its neighbours. You can climb the tower (Mon–Sat noon–4pm). The crypt, entered from outside, contains impressive tombstones of local mayors, priests and other notables as well as the tomb of Mihnea the Bad, Dracula's son, who was stabbed to death outside here in 1510. Head down into the rambling **lower town** using one of two staircases behind the cathedral – one overshadowed by arches and the medieval citadel wall. Alternatively use the road from Piaţa Mică, which is spanned by the elegant **Liars' Bridge** – so called because of the legend that no one can stand on it and tell a lie without the structure collapsing – or from the corner of the square via another ancient stairway, pock-marked with medieval windows, doorways and turrets. Easily outclassing that of Bucharest, Sibiu has an outstanding open-air museum, the **Muzeul Astra** (Tues–Sun 9am–5pm) on Calea Răşinari, south of the centre; take trolleybus #1 to the end of the line. Scenically set to a backdrop of mountains, the museum offers a fantastic insight into Romanian rural life, with authentic wooden houses, churches and mills, all of which are lovingly tended to and proudly shown off by an array of old gentlemen. The houses' simple interiors, brightly furnished with traditional rugs, often contain the workshop of a past profession such as candlemaking. The grounds hold a pleasant lake for boating, and a traditional inn serving local food and drink.

Sibiu's **train and bus stations** are next to each other on Piaţa 1 Dec 1918, 400m northeast of the main square. Sibiu's **tourist office**, inside the Schiller bookstore on Piaţa Mare (☎0269/211 110, ✆sibiu.ro), also sells maps and hands out the *Sibiu Live* and *Şapte Seri* **listings magazines**. The best-value **accommodation** is in the lower town at *Hotel Ela*, Str Nova 43 (☎0269/215 197; ❷), which is friendly and family-run, with a pleasant garden, nine spotless en-suite rooms and guest kitchen. From the train station take Strada 9 Mai, turn right onto Str Rebreanu, then first left onto Str Nova. More central, although still in the lower town, is the tiny, family-run *Podul Minciunilor* at Str Azilului 1, by the Liar's Bridge (☎0269/217 259; ❶), with adequate shared-bath doubles. The *Evangelisches Pfarrhaus* next to the cathedral at Piaţs Huet 1 (8am–3pm, or call in advance so a key can be left for you; ☎0269/211 203; €8) has a **hostel** with simple rooms sleeping two to four. *Gasthof Clara*, Str Râului 24 (☎0269/222 914; ❸), is the finest **hotel** in town, with large beds, en-suite bathrooms and breakfasts. Excellent local **food** is served up at *Mara*, Str Bălcescu 21, and at *La Turn*, on Piaţa Mare next to the Council Tower. *Michelangelo* at Str Turnului 3 serves good pizzas. *Gasthof Clara* has pizzas and spaghetti as well as local and German dishes. For something typically Romanian, complete with live folk music, head for the cosy *Crama Sibiu Vechi*, Str Ilarian 3, off Str Bălcescu. Sibiu effectively closes down at 9pm; however, the smoky *Art Café*, Str Filarmonicii 2 (till 2.30am), has occasional **jazz** gigs and is full of arty types, while the *Chill Out Club* at Piaţa Mică 23 holds out till 6am, playing mostly house music. There's an **Internet café** at the side entrance of the Împăratul Romanilor hotel, Str Bălcescu 4.

Timişoara

TIMIŞOARA, 250km west of Sibiu near the Serbian border, and 50km south of the rail junction at Arad, evolved around a Magyar fortress, and from the fourteenth century onwards functioned as the capital of the **Banat** region in the far west of Romania. The Turks conquered the town in 1552, and ruled the surrounding area from here until 1716. The Habsburgs who ejected them proved relatively benign masters, and during the late nineteenth century the municipality rode a wave of progress, becoming one of the first towns in the world to have horse-drawn trams and the first in Europe to install electric street-lighting. Nowadays, Timişoara is one of the most westward-oriented cities of Romania, its good location and multilingual inhabitants attracting many foreign investments. The city's fame abroad rests on its crucial role in the **overthrow** of the Ceauşescu regime. A local Hungarian priest, Lászlo Tökes, took a stand on the rights of his community, and when the police came to turf him out of his house on December 16, 1989, his parishioners barred their way. The five-day battle that ensued provided crucial inspiration for the people of Bucharest, so that Timişoara now regards itself as the guardian of the revolution.

Approaching from the train station, you'll enter the centre at Piaţa Victoriei, Romania's most pleasant pedestrian area, with fountains and flowerbeds along its length. Focal point is the huge **Romanian Orthodox Cathedral**; completed in 1946, it blends neo-Byzantine and Moldavian architectural elements and exhibits a collection of icons (ask at the bookstall) in its basement. At the other end, the plush **Opera House** stands near the **castle** once extended by Iancu de Hunedoara, which now houses the stuffy and very missable Museum of the Banat. Antiquated trams trundle past the Baroque **Town Hall** on the central Piaţa Libertăţii, while two blocks north the marvellous Piaţa Unirii is dominated by the monumental **Roman Catholic and Serbian Orthodox Cathedrals**. Built between 1736 and 1773, the former is a fine example of Viennese Baroque, the latter is roughly contemporaneous and almost as impressive. The huge Baroque palace on the southern side of the square houses the **Museum of Fine Arts**, usually displaying work by minor Italian, German and Flemish masters, but currently undergoing extensive renovation. In 1868, the municipality demolished most of the redundant citadel, leaving two **Bastions** to the east and west of Piaţa Unirii. The part to the east is occupied by an **Ethnographic Museum** (Tues–Sun 10am–5pm; entrance at Str Popa Şapcă 4). Varied folk costumes, painted glass icons and furnished rooms illustrate the region's ethnic diversity effectively, but in an anodyne fashion – for example, there's no mention of the thousands of Serbs deported in 1951 when the Party turned hostile towards Tito's neighbouring Yugoslavia. The museum has a good souvenir shop.

Timişoara Nord **train station** is a fifteen-minute walk east of the centre, along B-dul Republicii. There's no tourist office, but the free **listings magazine** *Timişoara What Where When*, found at some hotels, has a basic map. The **hostel** *Timişoara* is located south of the centre on the third floor of the largely derelict *Casa Tineretului* youth centre at Str Arieş 19 (☎0256/293 960; €7); take trolleybus #15 from near the castle – not an appealing option for solo women. The only other budget option is the recently renovated *Hotel Nord* (☎0256/197 504; ❷), opposite the train station at B-dul Gen. Dragalina 47, whose bright, clean rooms have bathrooms and TV. The central hotels are all mid-range, such as the glamorous and friendly *Central* off Piaţa Victoriei at Str Lenau 6 (☎0256/190 091, ⊛www.hotel-central.ro; ❸) whose en-suite rooms all have air conditioning. The fairly basic **campsite** on Aleea Pădurea Verde (☎0256/208 925) can be reached by trolleybus #11 from the train station. For good Romanian **food**, try *Club XXI*, Piaţa Victoriei 2, which offers large, hearty meals, or *Grizzly*, Str Ungureanu 7, which has good vegetarian options. A concentration of **cafés and bars** can be found west of Piaţa Unirii; *Evolution* on Str Lazăr 5 is a laid-back lounge with a cellar club while *Café Corso* at Str Savoya 24 is a popular new drinking den but also pleasant for morning coffees; both are open round the clock. In the evenings, the canal-side *Jazz Club Pod 16*, behind the Orthodox Cathedral, is great for **live music**. Party animals should head straight for the lively **student area**, just across the Michelangelo bridge, where there are numerous cheap restaurants, terrace cafés as well as **clubs** such as the excellent *The Note*, on Str Fagului 22. Find out what's going on in the weekly *Şapte Seri* **listings magazine**, found free at most bars. *Argus*, south of Piaţa Unirii at Str Mercy 4, has cheap **Internet** access.

Travel details

Trains

Braşov to: Bucharest (15 daily; 3hr); Sibiu (4 daily; 2hr 30min); Sighişoara (12 daily; 1hr 30min); Timişoara (3 daily; 8hr 30min–9hr 30min).
Bucharest to: Braşov (15 daily; 3hr 10min–4hr 15min); Sibiu (3 daily; 6hr); Sighişoara (9 daily; 5hr); Timişoara (9 daily; 8–9hr).
Sibiu to: Braşov (5 daily; 2hr 30min); Bucharest (4 daily; 6–7hr); Sighişoara (change at Copşa Mică; 4 daily; 2hr); Timişoara (1 daily; 6hr).
Sighişoara to: Braşov (11 daily; 1hr 30min); Bucharest (9 daily; 5hr); Sibiu (change at Copşa Mică; 4 daily; 2hr).
Timişoara to: Bucharest (9 daily; 8–9hr); Braşov (1 daily; 9hr 30min); Sibiu (1 daily; 6hr).

Buses

Braşov to: Bran (every 30min 7am–6pm; 45min).

Russia

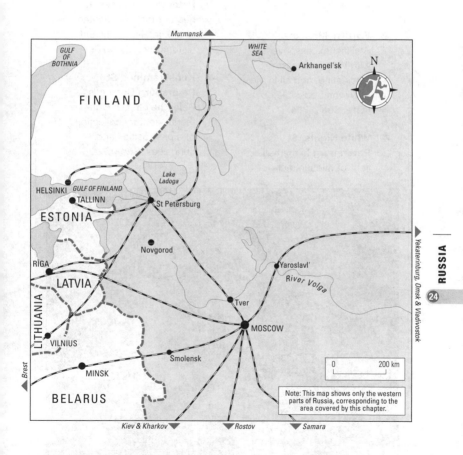

Russia highlights

* **Kremlin, Moscow** A cheat to call this one highlight, of course, as it's a whole complex of political, architectural and artistic associations. See p.782

* **VDNKh, Moscow** Stalinist excess, overlaid with Wild Capitalism – fascinating, and all in the very worst possible taste. See p.784

* **White Nights, St Petersburg** In the half-light of midsummer nights the whole city becomes mirage-like, arising dimly from the waters. See p.786

* **Hermitage, St Petersburg** Defines the heart of the city architec-turally, intellectually and historically. See p.789

* **Kunstkammer, St Petersburg** Don't miss Peter the Great's eigh-teenth-century collection of monstrosities and curiosities. See p.790

Introduction and basics

European **Russia** stretches from the borders of Belarus and Ukraine to the Ural mountains, over 1000km east of Moscow; even without the rest of the vast Russian Federation, it constitutes by far the largest country in Europe. Although visas are obligatory and accommodation often has to be booked in advance, independent travel grows hugely every year. Moscow and St Petersburg are connected to the rest of Europe by fast trains and buses, and remain the easiest places to visit.

Moscow, the capital, is chaotic and not a beautiful city by any means. The central core, however, reflects Russia's fascinating history, whether in the relics of the Communist years, the Kremlin with its palaces and churches of the tsars, the wooden buildings still tucked away in back streets, or in the massive building projects which have radically changed the face of the city in recent years. By contrast, **St Petersburg**, Russia's second city, is Europe at its most gracious, an attempt by the eighteenth-century tsar Peter the Great to re-create the best of Western European elegance in what was then a far-flung outpost. Its position in the delta of the River Neva is unparalleled, full of watery vistas of huge and faded palaces. The city has not been revamped anywhere near as much as Moscow, and it preserves a unity and stability lacking in the capital.

Information & maps

Russia has few **tourist offices**. Most travellers use the information desks at hotels and hostels, but the best resources are English-language newspapers such as the *Moscow Times* (daily) and *St Petersburg Times* (twice weekly), and free quarterly magazines available at leading hotels. High-quality **maps** in English are widely available from bookshops at very low prices; don't waste your money on expensive foreign maps.

Money and banks

Currency is the **ruble**, divided into 100 kopeks. There are coins of 1, 5, 10 and 50 kopeks and 1, 2 and 5 rubles, and notes of 5, 10, 50, 100, 500 and 1000 rubles. Everything is charged and paid for in rubles – it's illegal to pay in foreign currency – but, to give a stable idea of costs amid inflation, we've quoted prices in US dollars. Always **change money** in an official bank or currency exchange. Most **banks** are open Mon–Sat 10am–6/8pm, or later. Avoid the black market: official exchange rates are absolutely fair, and any better-looking deal will involve cheating you. ATMs are plentiful. Both cities can be expensive if you choose familiar shops and brands – or really quite cheap if you look out for the excellent local shops, eateries and clubs.

Communications

Most **post offices** are open Mon–Sat 8am–7pm. All district post offices have poste

---

Russia on the net

ⓦ **www.infoservices.com** Useful listings for Moscow and St Petersburg.

ⓦ **www.themoscowtimes.com** & ⓦ **www.sptimesrussia.com** English-language newspapers, with news, travellers' tips and events.

ⓦ **www.museum.ru** General information on even the most obscure museums.

ⓦ **www.geographia.com/russia** Official site of the Russian National Tourist Office; out of date but good on history and travel outside cities.

ⓦ **www.travel-russia.com** Nota Bene travel agency – excellent for up-to-date information.

restante (*do vostrébovaniya*) services. Both Moscow and St Petersburg have excellent express-letter post companies, such as Post International and Westpost, which despatch mail via Finland or the US for moderate sums. Street **phones** are good for local and international calls – buy a phonecard from kiosks. Phone booths in airports and major hotels aren't always run by the city phone network, and are much more expensive, but usually take Amex or Visa cards. The numerous **Internet** cafés are cheap.

Getting around

The network of trains and buses is extensive and relatively efficient. Buying tickets for long-distance and international **trains** is easy. More than a dozen trains a day in each direction connect the two main cities; the journey takes around eight hours (6hr for the popular day train "Aurora"; 4hr for the evening train). All trains are safe, reliable and cheap. Most of Moscow's and St Petersburg's outlying sights are easily reached by **metro**, suburban buses and efficient minibuses from the end of a metro line. Fares are also low, although transport is often packed. Many Russians **hitch**, especially after the public transport system closes down, when you'll see people flagging down anything that moves. If the driver finds the destination acceptable, he'll state a price, which may or may not be negotiable. However, we do not recommend hitching as a means of transport, and you should certainly never accept lifts from anyone who approaches you outside restaurants and nightclubs.

Accommodation and visas

Anyone travelling on a tourist visa to Russia must (technically) have **accommodation** arranged before arrival, but this is increasingly easy to get round. Hostels can usually provide invitations for a stay of up to a month as long as you spend (or pay for) just one night there. Unless otherwise stated, all hostels and hotels listed can arrange the necessary visa support for you. Note that it's important to register your visa with your hotel or hostel within three days of your arrival, otherwise you face a fine and much inconvenience. You can also apply online for visas at ⦿www.infinity.ru, ⦿www.ostwest.com and ⦿www.visatorussia .com (this last has good info on visa requirements and local embassies).

Hostels are definitely the best-value accommodation, at around $15–25 per person. Safer and cleaner than most hotels offering similar rates, they can help with many of the problems that face budget travellers. You should **reserve** three to four weeks in advance. There is no age restriction. Plenty of agencies offer self-contained **apartments** or **B&B** in Russian households, varying from $15 to $70 per person per night, depending on location and whether you opt for B&B or full board. Russian **hotels** are star-rated from two to five. Two-star **hotels** tend to consist of 1950s low-rises with matchbox-sized rooms; three-star hotels are typically 1960s and 1970s high-rises, equipped with several restaurants, bars and nightclubs. Cheaper hotels often have "improved" rooms which cost a few dollars more but have better bathroom facilities and newer furniture – it's always worth asking. Recent years have seen the appearance of central "family" hotels, with a tiny number of clean, attractive rooms, though these are not cheap (around $70 a night). Most hotels include breakfast in the price.

Food and drink

Moscow and St Petersburg abound in **cafés and restaurants** offering everything from pizza to Indian, French and Chinese dishes. Cheap and mid-range establishments are plentiful and more likely to serve food with a local flavour, but do not accept credit cards. **Menus** in smaller establishments are usually in Russian only, although some have an English version (not always regularly updated). You can always ask what they recommend ("*shto-by vy porekomendovali?*").

First come the all-important **zakuski** – "tasters" or small dishes consumed before a meal with vodka, as a snack or as a light meal. Herring is a firm favourite (try *selyodka pod shuboy*, herring "in a fur coat" of beetroot, carrot, egg and mayonnaise), as are pancakes (*bliny*) with caviar (*ikra*); red caviar is very cheap and a worthy rival to black. Great emphasis is placed on **soup**, a daily dose of which is thought to be vital to a healthy body. Cabbage soup (*shchi*), served with a generous dollop of sour cream (*smetana*), is much tastier than it sounds; try the gourmet version, green (or sorrel) soup (*zelyonye shchi*). In summer try cold *borshch* (beetroot soup). **Vegetarians** often have to get by on *zakuski*, since main courses are overwhelmingly based on meat (*myaso*), which makes its way into *pelmeny*, a Russian version of ravioli. Georgian restaurants always have interesting veggie dishes, such as bean stew or stuffed aubergines. Fresh **fish** – usually salmon, sturgeon or pike-perch – appears as a main course in all self-respecting eateries. Savoury **pies** (*pirozhki*) with cabbage, curd cheese or rice are very popular (never buy from street vendors). Sweet pancakes (*blinchiki*) are restaurant **dessert** (*sladkoe*) perennials, and Russian ice cream is outstanding, eaten outdoors even when the temperature drops to -20°C.

Vodka (*vódka*) is still the national drink, though sales have been overtaken by beer. It's normally served chilled and drunk neat in one gulp, followed by a mouthful of *zakuska*. Flavoured vodkas come and go, but connoisseurs stick to the straight stuff, making an exception only for Pertsovka (hot pepper vodka), whose kick cures all known diseases in seconds. Russians drink **beer** (*pívo*) in the morning to alleviate a hangover, or merely as a thirst quencher. The numerous local brands (in bottles and on tap) have an excellent fresh taste, with fewer preservatives than imports. Russian **wine** (*vinó*) is an acquired taste, so most foreigners avoid it. "Soviet Champagne" (*sovetskaya shampanskoe*), however, is a must at any party, and it's well worth trying Georgian dry and semi-sweet wines (such as Stalin's favourite, Khvanchkara) and the fortified wines of the Crimea (*kheres* or sherry and Madeira). **Tea** (*chay*) is traditionally brewed and stewed for hours, and topped up with boiling water from a samovar (though cafés use teabags).

Russians drink it black. Sadly, traditional cafés offering excellent Turkish **coffee** are rapidly being replaced by the ubiquitous chains of coffee shops. Tea and coffee may have sugar already added unless you specifically ask for them without.

Opening hours and holidays

Most **shops** open Mon–Sat 10am–7pm or later; few close for lunch. Department stores, bars and restaurants stay open on Sundays. **Museum** hours are 10am–5/6pm. They are invariably closed one day a week, with one day in the month set aside as a "cleaning day". Ticket offices always close one hour early. **Churches** are accessible from 8am until the end of the evening service. Official **public holidays** are: Jan 1; Jan 6 & 7; Feb 23; March 8; May 1 & 2; May 9; June 12; Nov 7; Dec 12. Russians also informally celebrate the unofficial Julian New Year's Eve, which falls on 13 Jan.

Emergencies

You won't be bothered by the so-called Russian "mafia", but beware of **petty crime**, particularly pickpocketing. Don't leave valuables in your hotel room, and lock the door before going to sleep. The **police** (*militsia*) wear blue-grey uniforms and are sometimes armed; report a robbery to them ("*Menya obokrali*" means "I've been robbed"). High-street **pharmacies** (*aptéka*) offer many familiar medicines over the counter. Foreigners tend to rely for treatment on **private clinics**, which charge excessively high rates, so travel insurance is essential. St Petersburg water contains the giardia parasite, which can rarely cause severe diarrhoea – metranidazol is the cure, but it's better just to avoid drinking tap water.

RUSSIA | Basics

24

| **Emergency numbers** |
| Police ☏02; ambulance ☏03; fire ☏01. |

Moscow (Moskva)

MOSCOW (Moskva) is all things to all people. For Westerners, the city may look European, but its unruly spirit seems closer to Central Asia. To Muscovites, however, Moscow is both a "Mother City" and a "big village", a tumultuous community which possesses an underlying collective instinct that shows itself in times of trouble. Its beauty and ugliness are inseparable, its sentimentality the obverse of a brutality rooted in centuries of despotism, while private and cultural life in the city are as passionate as business and politics are cynical. Moscow has been imbued with a sense of its own destiny since the fourteenth century, when the principality of Muscovy took the lead in the struggle against the Mongol-Tatars who had reduced the Kievan state to ruins. Under Ivan the Great and Ivan the Terrible its realm came to encompass everything from the White Sea to the Caspian, while after the fall of Constantinople to the Turks, Moscow assumed Byzantium's suzerainty over the Orthodox world. Despite the changes wrought by Peter the Great – not least the transfer of the capital to St Petersburg – Moscow kept its mystique and bided its time until the Bolsheviks made it the fountainhead of a new creed. Since the fall of Communism, Muscovites have given themselves over largely to the "Wild Capitalism" that intoxicates the city, and major building programmes are changing the face of the city more radically than at any time since the Stalin era.

Arrival, information and accommodation

Trains from Warsaw (23hr) arrive at **Belarus Station**, 1km northwest of the Garden Ring. Services from Budapest (40hr) terminate at **Kiev Station**, south of the Moskva River. From St Petersburg, Finland or Estonia, you'll arrive at **Leningrad Station**. To get into the centre from any of these, it's best to take the metro, as taxi drivers are notorious for overcharging. Eurolines **buses** from Germany and eastern Europe terminate near the Leningrad Station. The best place for leaflets, maps and general **information** is the information desk of the *Metropol Hotel*, Teatralniy pr. 1/4 (℡095/927 6000). The *Travellers Guest House* (see below) is also an excellent information centre. Russian-speakers can buy the glossy bi-weekly listings magazine *Afisha* (⊛www.afisha.ru).

Although the city centre is best explored on foot, Moscow is so big you won't get by without its famous **metro** (⊛www.metro.ru). Buy jetons (tokens) or a travel card for a set number of rides. You can travel any distance and change lines as many times as you like for the cost of one ride (around $0.20). Stations are marked with a large neon "M", all signs and maps are in Russian, including "entrance" (*vkhód*), "exit" (*vykhod*) and "passage to another line" (*perekhód*). **Bus** stops are marked with yellow signs and **trolleybus** stops have blue-and-white signs suspended, like those for **tram** stops, from overhead cables. Tickets (*talony*) are available from kiosks or the driver of the vehicle (single tickets or batches of ten for around $2). Some buses and trams have conductors who sell and check tickets. In general, though, overground transport is inefficient and you're best off sticking with the metro. Official taxis come in all shapes and sizes and are viciously expensive, even if the driver uses the meter.

Budget travellers will not have an easy time: **hotels** are overpriced. Most of those listed below are in high-rise buildings, which have the advantage of being in greener parts of town. The best budget options, though, are a **hostel**, or **private accommodation**, which you can arrange in advance through St Petersburg-based *HOFA* (℡812/275 19 92, ✉homestay@yahoo.com).

Hostels

G&R Hostel Asia Zelenodolskaya ul. 3/2 ℡095/378 0001, ✉info@hostels.ru; Ryazainskiy prospect metro. Check in on the 15th floor. Despite its apparent distance from the centre, it's only a

short metro ride away. $18.

Prakash Guest House Profsoyuznaya ul. 83/1 ℡095/334 2598, ✉standkoindo@yahood.com; Belyaevo metro. Indian-run and offering full tourist support. Dorm $20. ❸

Travellers Guest House Bolshaya Pereyaslavskaya ul. 50 ☎095/971 40 59, ©tgh@startravel.ru; Prospekt Mira metro and 10min walk. American-run hostel on the 10th floor, pleasant, clean and fairly central, with a laundry, café and bar. $25.

Hotels

Izmailovo Complex – Alfa Izmailovskoe shosse 71 ☎095/166 0163, ⊛www.alfa-hotel.ru; Izmailovskiy Park metro. Tiny rooms with minimal facilities, but they have their own bathrooms. ❸

Izmailovo Complex – Vega Izmailovskoe shosse 71 ☎095/956 0506, ⊛www.hotel-vega.ru; Izmailovskiy Park metro. Like *Alfa* but fancier with a business centre. ❸

Minsk Hotel Tverskaya ul. 22 ☎095/229 1213, ⒻF095/229 0362; Mayakovskaya or Pushkinskaya metro. Anonymous 1960s high-rise right in the centre, with a business centre and sauna. ❹

Sputnik Leninskiy prospect 38 ☎095/930 2287, ⒻF095/930 6383; Leninskiy Prospect metro. Ideal for budget travellers in price and location, despite a rather gloomy appearance. ❸

Tsentralniy Dom Turista Leninskiyy prospect 146 ☎095/434 3719, ⊛www.tourintel.ru; Yugo-Zapadnaya metro. Way out but offering excellent facilities (even a swimming pool) and service. ❹

Zolotoy Kolos Yaroslavskaya ul. 15 ☎095/217 4355, ⒻF095/217 4356; VDNKh metro. Makes up in service and simple but reliable facilities what it lacks in charm. ❷

The City

Despite the vast size of Moscow, and the inhuman scale of many of its buildings and avenues, the city's general layout is easily grasped – a series of concentric circles and radial lines emanating from the Kremlin – and the centre is compact enough to explore on foot. **Red Square** and the **Kremlin** are the historic nucleus of the city, signifying a great sweep of history that encompasses Ivan the Terrible, Peter the Great, Stalin and Gorbachev. Here you'll find Lenin's Mausoleum and St Basil's Cathedral, the famous GUM department store, and the Kremlin itself, whose splendid cathedrals and Armoury museum head the list of attractions. The Kremlin is ringed by two quarters defined by boulevards built over the original ramparts of medieval times, when Moscow's residential areas were divided into the inner **Beliy Gorod** and the humbler outer **Zemlyanoy Gorod**. The cosy **Zamoskvoreche** area to the south is home to the Tretyakov Gallery of Russian art and Gorky Park. Beyond this core lie some key sites best reached by metro. To the southwest, **Novodevichiy Convent** nestles in the loop of the River Moskva and Moscow State University rises high up on the Sparrow Hills; south is the romantic ex-royal estate of **Kolomenskoe**. In the north sprawls the **VDNKh**, a huge Stalinist exhibition park with amazing statues and pavilions, while in the east lies the **Andrei Rublev Museum of Old Russian Art and Culture**.

Red Square

Every visitor to Moscow is irresistibly drawn to **Red Square**, the historic and spiritual heart of the city, so loaded with associations and drama that it seems to embody all of Russia's triumphs and tragedies. In fact, the name Red Square (Krasnaya ploshchad) has nothing to do with communism, but derives from "krasniy", the old Russian word for "beautiful". On the west side the Lenin Mausoleum squats beneath the ramparts of the Kremlin and on the other sprawls **GUM** – what was during Soviet times the State Department Store – built in 1890–93, and now a hymn to expensive fashion outlets, while St Basil's Cathedral erupts in a profusion of onion domes and spires at the far end. In post-Communist Russia, the **Lenin Mausoleum** (Tues, Wed, Thurs, Sat & Sun 10am–1pm; free) can be seen as either an awkward reminder or a cherished relic of the old days. Although leaving Lenin's embalmed corpse *in situ* seems inappropriate, the Mausoleum itself is a stylish piece of architecture. When Boris Yeltsin suggested closing it, Communist extremists blew up a monument to Nicholas II in protest, and although the subject crops up regularly it always drops after a few weeks of hysteria. Behind the Mausoleum, the **Kremlin wall** – 19m high and 6.5m thick – contains a mass grave of Bolsheviks who perished during the battle for Moscow in 1917 and the ashes of an array of luminaries, including writer Maxim Gorky, first man in space Yuriy Gagarin, and

MOSCOW

Museum of Applied,
Decorative and Folk Art

SADOVAYA-SAMOTYOCHNAYA ULITSA

Tsvetnoy
Bulvar

Hermitage
Gardens

Central
Market Ⓜ

Yury Nikulin
Circus

Museum of
Unique Dolls

Lenkom
Theatre

Mayakovskaya Ⓜ

TRIUMFALNAYA
PLOSHCHAD

Church of the
Nativity of Our
Lady in Putinki

PETROVSKIY BULVAR

Tchaikovsky
Concert Hall

Minsk
Hotel

Upper
Monastery
of St Peter

American
Express

Pushkinskaya Ⓜ

Ⓜ Chekhovskaya

Museum of
Contemporary
Russian History

Tverskaya

Petrovskiy
Passazh

Patriarch's
Ponds

Tsentralnaya
Hotel

TsUM

Zoo Park

Planetarium

Barrikadnaya

Chekhov House-
Museum

Church of the
Resurrection
of Christ in
Jerusalem

Moscow
Art Theatre

Bolshoy
Theatre

Stalin
Skyscraper

Gorky House-
Museum

Museum of
Folk Art

Teatralnaya

House
of Unions

Metropol
Hotel

Chaliapin
House-Museum

House
of Writers

Stanislavsky
House-Museum

Central
Telegraph
Office

State
Duma

US Embassy

Oriental
Arts Museum

National Hotel

Moskva
Hotel

Tsvetaeva
Museum

Moscow
Conservatory

Okhotny Ryad

History
Museum

Kazan

Lermontov
House-Museum

Church of
St Simeon
the Stylite

Moscow
University

Gogol
Memorial
Room

Biblioteka
Imeni Lenina

Manège

Lenin

Scriabin
House-Museum

ULITSA NOVIY ARBAT

ULITSA VOZDVIZHENKA

Kremlin

Church of St
Saviour in Peski

Vakhtangov
Theatre

ARBATSKAYA
PLOSHCHAD

Ⓜ Arbatskaya

Dostoyevsky
Library

Alexand-
rovskiy Sad

Smolenskaya

Melnikov House

ULITSA ZNAMENKA

Borovitskaya

Smolenskaya

Pushkin on
the Arbat
Museum

Pushkin Museum
of Fine Arts

River

Ministry of
Foreign Affairs

Museum of
Private Collections

House on the
Embankment

Pushkin
Museum

Kropotkinskaya

Cathedral of
Christ the Saviour

Church of
St Nicholas

Tolstoy
Literary
Museum

Tretyakov
Gallery

0   500 m

Peter the Great
(monument)

KHAMOVNIKI

John Reed, the American Communist who witnessed the Revolution. Beyond lie
the graves of a select group of Soviet leaders, each with his own bust: a pompous
Brezhnev and a benign-looking Stalin. No description can do justice to **St Basil's
Cathedral** (11am–7pm, closed Tues; $3), silhouetted against the skyline where Red
Square slopes down towards the Moskva River. Commissioned by Ivan the Terrible
to celebrate his capture of the Tatar stronghold of Kazan in 1552, its popular title

commemorates a "holy fool", St Basil the Blessed, who foretold the fire that swept Moscow in 1547. Stalin hated the building, resenting the fact that it prevented his troops from marching out of Red Square en masse. At the other end of the square is the **State History Museum** (11am–7pm, closed Tues; $5), with only a tiny proportion of its varied collection of everything from archeological finds to Soviet badges and textiles on display. Beyond, to the north, is the supreme symbol of

Moscow's exchange of communism for capitalism: in place of the empty space formerly used for parades and displays of military hardware is the vast underground shopping centre, **Okhotniy ryad**, buried beneath a mass of tasteless landscaping.

The Kremlin

Brooding and glittering in the heart of Moscow, the **Kremlin** (10am–5pm, closed Thurs) thrills and tantalizes whenever you see its towers against the skyline, or its cathedrals and palaces arrayed above the Moskva River. Its name is synonymous with Russia's government, and in modern times assumed connotations of a Mecca for believers, and the seat of the Antichrist for foes of communism. The founding of the Kremlin is attributed to Prince Yuriy Dolgorukiy, who erected a wooden fort above the confluence of the Moskva and Neglinna rivers in about 1147. Under Grand Duke Ivan III (1462–1505) this "kremlin" grew to confirm Moscow's stature as the centre of Russia. One **ticket** ($8) admits you to the Kremlin and cathedrals, while separate tickets ($5) are required for the Patriarch's Palace and exhibitions. A couple of visits are needed to do it all justice: one to see the cathedrals, and another for touring the Armoury Palace, which can only be entered at set times.

Roughly two-thirds of the Kremlin is off-limits to tourists, the accessible part beginning around the corner from the Great Kremlin Palace. The **Patriarch's Palace** houses a Museum of Seventeenth-Century Life and Applied Art and incorporates the former Cathedral of the Twelve Apostles. Next, the **Tsar Cannon**, cast in 1586, is one of the largest cannons ever made and was intended to defend the Saviour Gate, but has never been fired. Close by looms the earthbound **Tsar Bell**, the largest bell in the world, cast in 1655. Beyond lies **Cathedral Square**, the historic heart of the Kremlin, dominated by the magnificent, white **Ivan the Great Bell Tower**, the tallest structure within the Kremlin's walls, and with four key churches. The most important is the **Cathedral of the Assumption**, used throughout tsarist times for coronations and solemn acts of state. Its exterior is remarkably plain, while the interior is spacious, light and echoing, its walls, roof and pillars entirely covered with icons and frescoes. Next door is the white **Church of the Deposition of the Robe** while the **Cathedral of the Archangel** houses the tombs of Russia's rulers from Grand Duke Ivan I to Tsar Ivan V (later rulers were buried in St Petersburg). Last comes the golden-domed **Cathedral of the Annunciation**, the private royal church, with some of Russia's finest icons, including works by Theophanes the Greek and Andrei Rublev. Situated between the Great Kremlin Palace and the Borovitskiy Gate, the **Armoury Palace** (by ticket purchased in advance; $13) conceals a staggering array of treasures – among them the tsars' coronation robes, carriages, jewellery, dinner services and armour – well worth the trouble and expense involved in seeing them. The palace also houses the **State Diamond Fund** (20min guided tours; $12), which contains the most valuable gems in Russia.

The Beliy Gorod

The **Beliy Gorod** or "White Town" is the historic name of the residential district that encircled the Kremlin. Multi-domed churches cluster along ulitsa Varvarka, and around Kitay-gorod east of the Kremlin: this was the very heart of the city during the sixteenth century, and even today it has a strongly medieval feel. Its main seventeenth-century thoroughfare, Tverskaya ulitsa, owes its present form to a massive reconstruction programme during the mid-1930s, and yet, despite the scale of some of its gargantuan buildings, the variety of older, often charming side streets gives the avenue a distinctive character. Those interested in Russia's Communist past and turbulent politics should pay a visit to the **Museum of Contemporary Russian History** (Tues–Sun 10am–6pm; $3), at Tverskaya 21, formerly the Museum of the Revolution. Its bold displays of propaganda posters, photographs and state gifts to Lenin and Stalin are fascinating even if you cannot read the Russian labelling. South of Tverskaya, Moscow's **Pushkin Museum of Fine Arts**, Volkhonka ul. 12 (Tues–Sun 10am–7pm; $5), has a rich collection of European painting, from Italian

High Renaissance works to Rembrandt and Poussin, and an outstanding display of Impressionists. It also has charming Egyptian portraits, and of course the magnificent gold of the lost city of Troy, removed from Germany at the end of World War II and still the subject of conflict between the two countries. In 1994, Moscow's Mayor Luzhkov took the populist step of announcing the rebuilding of the **Cathedral of Christ the Redeemer** opposite the museum. The vast original structure had been blown up by the Soviet government in 1934 and a swimming pool built on the site. Financed largely by donations and perceived as a symbol of Moscow's (and Russia's) revival, the cathedral is today a monument to one man's overweening pride and ambition. Luzhkov appears smiling broadly in numerous photographs in the museum recording the history of the building, housed in the crypt (daily 10am–6pm; free).

The Zemlyanoy Gorod

In medieval times, the white-walled Beliy Gorod was encircled by a humbler **Zemlyanoy Gorod** or "Earth Town". Separated from the Beliy Gorod by the tree-lined "boulevard ring", this is one of the best-looking parts of Moscow, with Neoclassical and Art Nouveau mansions on every corner. Admirers of Bulgakov, Chekhov, Lermontov, Gorky and Pushkin will find their former homes preserved as museums in the pretty, leafy back streets around the **Patriarch's Ponds**, southwest of Tverskaya. The Patriarch's Ponds are, in fact, one large pond, which forms the heart of a square surrounded by wrought-iron railings and mature trees. At Bolshaya Sadovaya ul. 10, a plaque attests that Mikhail Bulgakov lived here from 1921 to 1924; his satirical fantasy *The Master and Margarita* is indelibly associated with this area in particular. It's usually possible to visit: go into the courtyard and look for entrance 6, on the left; the apartment (no. 50) is at the top of the stairs. Anton Chekhov lived at Sadovaya-Kudrinskaya ul. 6, in what is now the **Chekhov House-Museum** (Tues, Thurs & Sat 11am–5pm, Wed & Fri 2–6pm; $4), while Maxim **Gorky's House-Museum** (Mon & Thurs 10am–4.30pm, Tues, Wed & Fri noon–6pm; closed last Thurs of month; $4), on the corner of Povarskaya ulitsa and ulitsa Spiridonovka, is worth seeing purely for its amazing Art Nouveau decor, both inside and out. West of here, the **Arbat** once stood for bohemian Moscow in the way that Carnaby Street represented swinging London, and still has a vibrant street life. It retains some of these characteristics today, with its array of cafés and antique shops. It tends to get busier beyond the **Peace Wall** – a cute piece of propaganda against Reagan's Star Wars.

West beyond the Garden Ring

West of the river, patriotic ardour finds an outlet at the immense **Borodino Panorama** at Kutuzovskiy pr. 38 (daily 10am/noon–6pm; $2), housing a painting 115m long and 15m high, with 3000 figures. This monument to the Battle of Borodino, fought against Napoleon in 1812, was completed in 1912. It was dismantled soon after the Revolution, then re-established here thirty years later. South of here, **Moscow State University** occupies the largest of the city's seven 1950s Stalinist-Gothic skyscrapers, dominating the plateau of the **Sparrow Hills** (Vorobyovie gory), overlooking the Moskva River. Besides the university, the attraction is quite simply the panoramic view of Moscow, with Luzhniki stadium and the Novodevichiy Convent in the foreground, the Kremlin in the middle distance, and six more Stalinist skyscrapers ranged across the city. Visible across the loop of the river, a cluster of shining domes above a fortified rampart proclaims the presence of the lovely **Novodevichiy Convent** (daily 8am–7pm for worship). At its heart stands the white Cathedral of the Virgin of Smolensk, with a superb interior. Metro Sportivnaya (ulitsa 10-ti Letiya Oktyabrya exit) brings you to within a ten-minute walk of the convent. Beyond its south wall lies the venerable **Novodevichiy Cemetery** (daily 10am–6pm), burial place of numerous famous writers, musicians and artists, including Gogol, Chekhov, Stanislavsky, Bulgakov and Shostakovich.

Krushchev is also here – he died out of office, and was denied burial in the Kremlin wall. A little nearer to the centre, **Gorky Park** (daily 10am–10pm; $1) is famous abroad from Martin Cruz Smith's classic thriller. Inaugurated in 1928, the Soviet Union's first "Park of Culture and Rest" covers 300 acres and includes funfairs, a large outdoor skating rink and lots of woodland.

Zamoskvoreche and the south

South of the Kremlin lies **Zamoskvoreche** (simply "Across the Moskva River"), an area dating back to medieval times and preserving a host of colourful churches and the mansions of civic-minded merchants. One of the most charming parts of the city, with a strongly residential feel, it can be easily traversed on one of the trams which start from Chistye prudy metro. Founded in 1892 by the financier Pavel Tretyakov, the **Tretyakov Gallery** (Tues–Sun 10am–7.30pm; ⊛www.tretyakov.ru; $5), five minutes' walk from Tretyakovskaya metro, displays an outstanding collection of Russian art before the Revolution. Russian **icons** – which originally came to Russia from Byzantium and were valued for their religious and spiritual content rather than artistic merit – are magnificently displayed on the second floor. The exhibition continues through to the late nineteenth century, with one vast room filled with the nightmare-like, fantastical works of Mikhail Vrubel. Twentieth-century and contemporary art (dominated by Tatlin, Chagall and Malevich) is on show at the **New Tretyakov** opposite the entrance to Gorky Park, at Krymskiy val 10 (Tues–Sun 10am–7.30pm; $4). **Kolomenskoe estate** (grounds daily 9am–7pm, free; museum Tues–Sun 10am–6pm, $2), 10km southeast of the Kremlin, was once a royal summer retreat. Though its legendary wooden palace no longer exists, Kolomenskoe still has one of the finest churches in the whole of Russia, the **Church of the Ascension** (services Sun 8am), and vintage wooden structures such as Peter the Great's cabin, set amid hoary oaks above a great bend in the river. In summer, Muscovites flock here for the fresh air and to sunbathe. Take the metro to Kolomenskaya, fifteen minutes' walk from the site itself.

East and north of the centre

In the northeast of the city is the fourteenth-century **Andronikov Monastery**, on the steep east bank of the Yauza. Its most famous monk was the great icon painter Andrei Rublev, canonized by the Russian Orthodox Church in 1989 and buried in the grounds. At the centre of the monastery stands Moscow's oldest architectural monument, the **Church of the Saviour** (1420s), with wall paintings by Rublev himself (currently undergoing restoration), which now houses the **Andrei Rublev Museum of Old Russian Art and Culture** at Andronyevskaya pl. 10 (11am–6pm, closed Wed; $3; Ploshchad Ilyicha metro). The most famous icons may be in the Tretyakov, but the atmosphere here is something else – you retire from the noise and bustle of the city and enter a peaceful, serene land. Even the fact that until the 1950s the church housed the archive of the Ministry of State Security could do nothing to destroy its romance. A few stops north is the Exhibition of Economic Achievements – or **VDNKh** (daily 10am–7pm) – a permanent trade-fair-cum-shopping-centre housed in the magnificent park and Stalinist architecture of the All-Union Agricultural Exhibition of 1939, a display of the fruits of social-ism. Today, cheap imported goods make the whole thing rather tawdry, but when the sun glints off the gilded fountains it still looks magnificent. It is officially now the **All-Russia Exhibition Centre** (VVTs) – but everyone still calls it VDNKh. Near the main entrance stands one of the best-ever Soviet monuments, the **Space Obelisk**, a rocket blasting nearly 100m into the sky on a stylized plume of energy clad in shining titanium. It was unveiled in 1964, three years after Gagarin orbited the earth, an unabashed expression of pride in this unique feat. On the other side of the entrance is the famous monument of the **Worker and Collective Farm Girl**, colossal twin figures intended to embody Soviet industrial progress, though in fact they were handmade.

Eating, drinking and entertainment

Cafés serve plentiful and excellent food at much lower prices than full-blown **restaurants**, and seldom require bookings. Most places have at least one member of staff with a rudimentary grasp of English. The city's **nightlife** is given over to hundreds of small, intimate clubs, many open all night, and great **live music** of all genres. A full list can be found in the *Moscow Times* supplement, *Metropolis*. There's a busy schedule of **classical music**, **opera** and **ballet** throughout the year, sometimes held in palaces, churches or – in summer – parks and gardens. Puppet and **circus** shows transcend language barriers.

Cafés, bars and fast food

Amalteya Stremyanny per. 28/1; Serpukhovksya metro. Vast range of *meze* served in this cheap Turkish café, which has a singer in the evenings.

Annushka Tsvetnoy bulvar 7; Tsvetnoy Bulvar metro. Have a Russian blow-out for under 300 rubles on a tram running round Chistye prudy.

Donna Clara Malaya Bronnaya ul. 21/13; Mayakovskaya metro. Small café in the heart of literary Moscow with great window seats.

Dzhagannat Express Inside Dom Khudozhnika (House of Artists), ul. Kuznetskiy Most; Kuznetskiy Most metro. Centrally located vegetarian café, offering take away, but with no alcohol.

Khvanchkara Sretenka 16/2; Sukharevskaya metro. The cheapest Georgian food in town. Khvanchkara was Stalin's favourite wine.

Kofe-In (Caffeine) Bolshaya Dmitrovka ul. 16; Teatralnaya metro. A few main meals, but mainly great coffee and desserts.

Kot Begemot Spiridonyevskiy per. 10A; Mayakovskaya metro. Food nearly as good as the location.

Ogonyok Krasnaya Presnaya ul. 36; 1905-goda metro. Russian food that doesn't limit itself to *pelmeni* and beetroot.

PiR O.G.I. Pyatnitskaya ul. 29, Novokuznetskaya metro; also Bolshaya Dmitrovka 12/2, Teatralnaya metro. Great food and beer.

Taras Bulba ul. Petrovka 30/7; Pyatnitskaya ul. 14; Sadovo-Samotechnaya ul. 13; etc. Chain of Ukrainian cafés; their *borshch* is something else.

U Nikitskikh Vorot Bolshaya Nikitskaya ul. 23/9; Okhotny Ryad metro. Cheap Georgian food in a comfortable bar (rather plain restaurant).

Yolki-Palki Bolshaya Dmitrovka ul. 23/8; Klimentovskiy per. 14/1; Novyy Arbat ul. 11; etc. To eat Russian/Ukrainian/Mongolian food at rock-bottom prices, join the queue at one of ten or so branches of this popular eatery.

Restaurants

Petrovich Club Myasnitskaya ul. 24 ☎095/923 0082; Chistye Prudy metro. Russian *nouvelle cuisine* and nostalgia for a Soviet childhood in the 1960s and 1970s.

Raisky Dvor Spiridonovka ul. 25 ☎095/290 13 41; Mayakovskaya metro. Russian and European food, surrounded by *Animal Farm*-inspired decor.

Shesh-Besh Smolenskaya Ploshchad 6a; Smolenskaya metro. Never eaten Azeri (from Azerbaijan) food? This is the place to check it out.

Clubs and live music

B2 Bolshaya Sadovaya ulitsa 8; Mayakovskaya metro. Acid rock, popular with locals and the expat crowd. Open 24hr.

Cult Yauzskaya ulitsa 5; Kitai-gorod metro. Aggressive dance club with the city's best DJs. Open noon to the wee hours.

Dom Bolshoy Ovchinnikovskiy per. 24/4; Novokuznetskaya metro. For the hip "intellectual" crowd. Closed Mon-Wed.

Dom Kukera Lubyansky proyezd 25; Kitai-gorod metro. The "Cooker House" disco dance club. Open 24hr.

Kitayskiy Lyotchik Dzhao Da Lubyanskiy proezd 25; Kitay-gorod metro. Coolest place to be seen and hear the best bands. Open 24hr.

Le Club Verkhnyaya Radishchevskaya ulitsa 21; Taganskaya metro. Moscow's best jazz and blues. Open noon to 2am.

Mesto Vstrechi Maly Gnezdnikovskiy per. 9/8, Building 7; Pushkinskaya metro. The name comes from a cult 1970s TV series and it means "meeting place". Open 24hr.

Project O.G.I. Potapovskiy per. 8/12; Chistiye prudy metro. Hip club, bar and restaurant with sessions for kids in the mornings. Open 24hr.

Svalka Profsoyuznaya ul. 27/1; Profsoyuznaya metro. Best for grunge – *Svalka* does, after all, mean "rubbish dump". Cover charge can be very high, depending on event – and gender. Open noon to early morn.

Woodstock Pokrovsky Bulvar 3; Chistye Prudy metro. Rock – as you might have guessed from the name – but definitely one of the best. Open 24hr.

Opera and ballet

Bolshoy Theatre Teatralnaya pl. 1 ☎095/292 0050; Teatralnaya metro. Fierce rival of Petersburg's Mariinskiy, with some great performances, but the designs can be crushingly vulgar. Foreigners pay from $8 to $80. Performances Tues–Sun at 7pm, matinée on Sun.

Helikon Opera Bolshaya Nikitskaya ul. ☎095/290 0971; Biblioteka im. Lenina metro. Prize-winning theatre offering intimate, small-scale productions.

Film

America Cinema At the *Radisson-Slavyanskaya Hotel* ☎095/941 87 47; Kievskaya metro. One of

several cinemas showing films in their original language. Discount for students.

Circus

Circus on Tsvetnoy Tsvetnoy bul. 13 ☎095/200 06 68; Tsvetnoy bulvar metro. Great atmosphere in this small circus, where clowns are the forte. Performances Thurs–Sun.

New Circus pr. Vernadskovo 7 ☎095/930 28 15; Universitet metro. One of the finest in the world, with lots of animal acts. Performances Wed–Sun.

Listings

Embassies Australia, Kropotkinskiy per. 13 ☎095/956 6070; Canada, Starokonyushenniy per. 23 ☎095/956 6666; Ireland, Grokholskiy per. 5 ☎095/937 5911; New Zealand, Povarskaya ul. 44 ☎095/956 3579; UK, Smolenskaya nab. 10 ☎095/956 7301; US, Novinskiy bulvar 19/23 ☎095/728 5000.
Hospital American Medical Center, Grokholskiy per. 1 ☎095/933 7700, ✆www.amcenters.com; Mediclub Moscow Ltd, Michurinskiy pr. 56 ☎095/931 5018, ✆www.mediclub.ru. Both recognized by international insurance companies.
Internet Cafemax, ul. Pyatnitskaya 25, Novokuznetskaya metro; Internet Club, Kuznetskiy most 12, Kuznetskiy Most metro; Nirvana,

Rozhdestvenka 29, Kuznetskiy most metro; Timeonline, Manezhnyay ploshchad 1.
Laundry California Cleaners, Leninskiy prospect 113/1.
Left luggage Most train stations have lockers and/or a 24hr left-luggage office.
Pharmacy Staryy Arbat, Arbatskaya ul. 25; Multifarma, Turistkaya ul. 27; 24hr pharmacy at pr. Mira 71.
Post office Central Telegraph Office, Tverskaya ul. 7; Main Post Office, Myasnitskaya ul. 26/2, 101000. Express postal services via Westpost ☎095/ 234 9038, ✆www.westpost.ru; Courier Service, Bolshaya Sadovaya 10; Mayakovskaya metro ☎095/209 1735.

St Petersburg (Sankt Peterburg)

ST PETERSBURG, Petrograd, Leningrad and St Petersburg again – the city's succession of names mirrors Russia's turbulent history. Founded in 1703 as a "window on the West" by Peter the Great, the city celebrated its 300th anniversary with great pomp in 2003. For two centuries the capital of the tsarist empire, synonymous with excess and magnificence, the city was the cradle of the revolutions that overthrew the monarchy and brought the Bolsheviks to power in 1917. As Leningrad it epitomized the Soviet Union's heroic sacrifices in the war, withstanding nine hundred days of Nazi siege. Then, in 1991 – the year the USSR collapsed – the change of name back to St Petersburg proved deeply symbolic of the country's mood. St Petersburg's sense of its own identity owes much to its origins and to the interweaving of myth and reality throughout its history. Created by the will of an autocrat, the imperial capital embodied both Peter the Great's rejection of Old Russia – represented by "Asiatic" Moscow, the former capital – and of his embrace of Europe. Intensely proud of itself, of its intellectual – and its workers' revolutionary – past, St Petersburg is an easy and relaxing city. It's also one of contrasts: beautiful yet drab, with beggars and *nouveaux riches* rubbing shoulders on the main street, **Nevskiy prospekt**. The most celebrated time to visit is during the famous "**White**

From May to October all **bridges** across the River Neva in St Petersburg are raised between 2am and 5am – a beautiful sight which draws crowds, but inconvenient if you're on the wrong side of the water.

Nights" of midsummer (mid-June to mid-July), when darkness never falls and the city celebrates with a special festival and weeks of partying.

Arrival, information and accommodation

Trains from Helsinki (6hr) bring you to the famous **Finland Station** (the train on which Lenin arrived to start the Revolution in 1917 stands by the concourse), while those from Europe (including Tallinn) usually terminate at the **Baltic Station**. Trains from Moscow draw into **Moscow Station**. All are on the metro. Eurolines **buses** from Germany and the Baltic States can drop you anywhere in the centre of town. For **information**, pick up *St Petersburg: The Official City Guide* (@www.city-guide.spb.ru), the best of several quarterly English freebies, available in hotels. The Friday *St Petersburg Times* and the monthly *Pulse* are also free and have good listings and reviews. The fullest listings in Russian are to be found in the bi-weekly *Afisha* or *Kalendar*. Major hostels can provide everything from visa support to theatre tickets. The **City Tourist Information Office** at Nevskiy pr. 41 (☎812/311 2843) is crawling up a steep learning curve.

Petersburgers walk everywhere, summer or winter. Yet it is a big city, and you'll need to use its cheap public transport system. Overground transport is more useful in the centre than the fast **metro**. Choose from **trams**, **buses** and **trolleybuses** (tickets from conductor), or efficient commercial **minibuses** (tickets from driver). One of the best ways to see the city is by **boat** (May–Oct) – either a private motorboat from any bridge on Nevskiy prospekt (from $50/hr), or a large tour boat by the Anichkov Bridge ($5 per person).

Centrally located **hotels** are few in number and expensive. **Hostels** are best: reasonably central, with decent facilities and no age restriction. Or try **B&B** with families, arranged via the well-established agencies *HOFA* (☎812/275 1992, @homestay@yahoo.com) and *NotaBene* (@www.travel.spb.ru). *OstWest* (☎812/327 3416, @www.ostwest.com) will book more or less any kind of accommodation. For a small group of people it's even cheaper to rent an **apartment** for several days: try *BedandBreakfast* (☎812/315 1917, @www.bednbreakfast.sp.ru) or *Pulford Estates* (☎812/325 6277, @www.pulford.com). Prices rise dramatically during the White Nights (May–July).

Hostels

Hostel Holiday Arsenalnaya naberezhnaya 9, ☎812/327 1070, @www.hostel.ru; Ploshchad Lenina metro. Good, large, busy hostel with full range of services, including Internet access; some rooms overlook the River Neva. $14.

St Petersburg International Hostel 3-ya Sovetskaya ul. 28 ☎812/329 8018, @www.ryh.ru; Ploshchad Vosstaniya metro. The independent traveller's dream, though book ahead. Can provide invitations even if you are not intending to stay here and has attached student travel agency, Sindbad. $22.

Hotels

Kievskaya Dnepropetrovskaya ul. 49 ☎812/166 8250, @www.kievskaia.spb.ru; Ligovskiy prospect metro. Tucked away by the bus station. Also has cheaper rooms with shared bathroom. ❸

Matisov Domik Naberezhnaya reki Pryazhki 3/1 ☎812/318 5445. Small modern hotel on tree-lined canal, 15min walk west of Mariinsky Theatre. ❻

Mir ul. Gastello 17 ☎812/108 4910; Moskovskaya metro. Clean, modest and very efficient, not central but convenient for the metro. ❺

Neva Chaykovskovo ul. 17 ☎812/278 0504; Chernyshevskaya metro. Old-fashioned, even quaint, and just a hop away from the Summer Garden. ❺

Oktiabrskaya Ligovskiy pr. 10 ☎812/277 6330, @www.oktober-hotel.spb.ru; Ploshchad Vosstaniya/Mayakovskaya metro. Nineteenth-century warren overlooking Moscow Station with gloomy service but indefinable charm. Ask for an "upgraded room" – the plumbing is better. ❺

White Nights Sredneokhtinskiy pr. 18/12 ☎812/224 1750, @info@wnights.spb.ru. Not central, nor pretty, but definitely clean and decent. No visa support. ❷

Campsite

Olgino Camping Primorskoe shossee 59 ☎812/238 3671; bus or local train to Olgino. The air is fresh, the pine forest healthy, the Gulf of Finland not far away. Perfect for summer. ❸

24

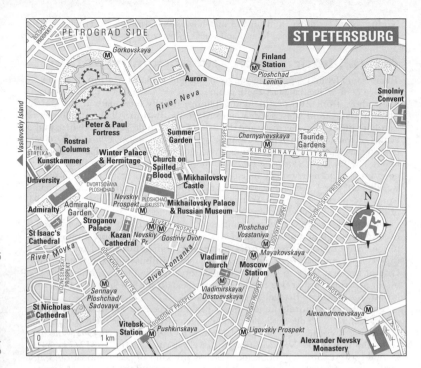

The City

The city is split by the **River Neva** and its tributaries, with further sections delineated by the course of the canalized Moyka and Fontanka rivers, all of which conveniently divide St Petersburg into a series of islands, making it fairly easy to get your bearings. St Petersburg's centre lies on the south bank of the Neva, with the curving **River Fontanka** marking its southern boundary. The area within the **Fontanka** is riven by a series of wide avenues, which fan out from the most visible landmark on the south bank of the Neva, the **Admiralty**. Many of the city's greatest sights and monuments – the Hermitage, the Russian Museum, the Mikhail Castle, the Summer Garden and the St Isaac and Kazan cathedrals – are located on and around **Nevskiy prospekt**, the main avenue. Across the Neva is **Vasilevskiy Island**, largest of the city's islands and on the **Strelka**, the island's eastern tip, are found some of St Petersburg's oldest institutions as well as some fascinating museums. On the north side of the River Neva, the Petrograd Side is home to the **Peter and Paul Fortress**, whose construction is seen as marking the foundation of the city itself. Beyond the River Fontanka, the two most popular destinations are the **Smolniy**, from where the Bolsheviks orchestrated the October Revolution, and the **Alexander Nevsky Monastery**.

Nevskiy prospekt to the Winter Palace

Stretching from the Alexander Nevsky Monastery to Palace Square and the Hermitage, **Nevskiy prospekt** has been the backbone and heart of the city for the last three centuries. Built on an epic scale during the reign of Peter the Great, it manifests every style of architecture from eighteenth-century Baroque to 1950s Stalinist Classicism. Near the striking Dom Knigi bookshop, former emporium of the Singer sewing-machine company, is **Kazan Cathedral**, built between 1801 and 1811 (services daily 9am & 6pm), one of the city's grandest churches, modelled on St Peter's in the Vatican. The cathedral was built to house the venerated icon, Our Lady of Kazan, reputed to have appeared miraculously overnight in Kazan in 1579, and transferred by Peter the Great to St Petersburg, where it resided until its disappearance in 1904. In Soviet times the cathedral housed the Museum of Religion and Atheism.

The two-hundred-metre long Baroque **Winter Palace** at the westernmost end of Nevskiy prospekt is the city's largest, most opulent palace. As loaded with history as it is with gilt and stucco, the palace was the official residence of the tsars, not to mention the court and 1500 servants. The main building was finished in 1762 and later new buildings were added to the east: the Small and Large Hermitages were added by Catherine the Great to enable her to be alone with her friends and her paintings, while the New Hermitage was launched as Russia's first public art museum in 1852. Beyond stands the Hermitage Theatre, Catherine the Great's private theatre, now used for concerts. Together these buildings now form one of the world's greatest museums, the **Hermitage** (Tues–Sun 10.30am–5pm; ⓦwww.hermitagemuseum.org; $10). Of awesome size and diversity, it embraces some three million objects, everything from ancient Scythian gold to Cubism. The Italian art section has works by Leonardo, Botticelli, Michelangelo, Raphael, Titian, Veronese and Tiepolo; the Dutch and Flemish art collection features magnificent selections of paintings by Rembrandt, Rubens and Van Dyck; and there is an impressive collection of seventeenth- and eighteenth-century French art. After the state rooms and the Gold Collection, the most universally popular section is that covering modern European art from the nineteenth and twentieth centuries, which is due to move in the near future to the majestic General Staff Building on the other side of Palace Square. It includes a fine spread of works by Matisse and Picasso, Rodin, Gauguin, Van Gogh, Henri Rousseau, Delacroix, Cézanne, Pissarro, Monet, Degas and Renoir.

North of Nevskiy prospekt

Visible from Nevskiy prospekt is the multicoloured, onion-domed **Church on Spilled Blood** (11am–6pm, closed Wed; $8), begun in 1882 to commemorate Tsar Alexander II, assassinated on the site the previous year. In pseudo-traditional Russian style, stuffed full of thousands of metres of mosaics, it is one of St Petersburg's most striking landmarks, quite unlike the dominant Neoclassical architecture. East of the church stands the vast **Mikhail Palace**, housing the **Russian Museum**, containing the finest collection of Russian art in the world. It encompasses fourteenth-century icons, Russian art's coming of age in the late nineteenth century (see the vast historical canvases of Vasiliy Surikov and the socially conscious realism of Ilya Repin), and the movements of the early twentieth century, from Symbolism to Analytical Art. A little further east is the idiosyncratic and heavily fortified **Mikhail Castle**, built by Paul I in 1801 shortly after he came to the throne, to protect him from the assassination attempt he feared. Indeed, he was murdered in his bedroom there just three weeks after moving in. The **Mikhail Garden** next door (behind the Russian Museum) is much loved by Petersburgers of all ages, who also adore the **Marsovo pole** (Field of Mars) on the other side of the River Moyka, heavy with the scent of lilac in spring. At its northwestern corner stands the **Marble Palace** ($4), designed by Antonio Rinaldi for Catherine the Great's lover, Count Orlov, and now displaying works by foreign artists living in Russia in the eighteenth and nineteenth centuries, and contemporary art. Most popular of all, however, is the **Summer Garden** (daily 8/11am–6/10pm; small admission fee in summer) to the east, commissioned by Peter the Great in 1704 and rebuilt by Catherine the Great in the informal English style that survives today. In the northeastern corner, Domenico Trezzini erected a **Summer Palace** (May–Nov 11am–7pm, closed Tues; $3) for Peter the Great in 1710, a modest two-storey building of brick and stucco – one of the first such structures in the city.

Southwest of Nevskiy prospekt

The **Admiralty** standing at the western end of Nevskiy prospekt is one of the world's most magnificent expressions of naval triumphalism, extending 407m along the waterfront, from Palace Square to Decembrists' Square. Originally founded in 1704 as a fortified shipyard, the Admiralty gradually became purely administrative in function and a suitable building was erected in the early 1820s. Today, the key feature of the building is still its central tower (72.5m high), culminating in a slender spire. The wooded Admiralty Garden leads towards **Decembrists' Square**, named after a group of reformist officers who, in December 1825, marched three thousand soldiers into the square in a doomed attempt to proclaim a constitutional monarchy. Today, the square is dominated by the **Bronze Horseman**, Falconet's renowned statue of Peter the Great and the city's unofficial symbol, against which newlyweds are traditionally photographed. Looming majestically above the square, **St Isaac's Cathedral** (11am–7pm, colonnade till 5pm, closed Wed; $8, colonnade $3) is one of the glories of St Petersburg's skyline, its gilded dome the third largest in Europe. The opulent interior is equally impressive, decorated with fourteen kinds of marble. The cathedral's height (101.5m) and rooftop statues are best appreciated by climbing the 262 steps to the outside colonnade. More intimate in mood is the **St Nicholas Cathedral**, to the south near Theatre Square and the Mariinskiy Theatre. Traditionally the church of naval officers, it is a lovely example of eighteenth-century Russian Baroque – painted ice blue with white Corinthian pilasters, crowned with five gilded onion domes. Its low, vaulted interior is festooned with icons, and during services (6pm) the cathedral resounds with the sonorous Orthodox liturgy, chanted and sung amid clouds of incense.

Vasilevskiy Island

Pear-shaped **Vasilevskiy Island** cleaves the River Neva into its Bolshaya and Malaya branches, forming a strategic wedge whose eastern "spit", or **Strelka**, is as much a part of St Petersburg's waterfront as the Winter Palace or Admiralty. Originally, Peter envisaged making the island the centre of his capital, compelling rich landowners and merchants to settle here but the lack of bridges and hazardous crossing by boat led people to prefer settling on the mainland. Although you can reach the Strelka by numerous buses from Nevskiy prospekt, it's better to walk across **Palace Bridge**, which offers fabulous views of both banks of the Neva (richly illuminated at night). On the Strelka are the weird **Rostral Columns** and Classical **Stock Exchange** building (now housing the Naval Museum), an ensemble created at the beginning of the nineteenth century by Thomas de Thomon, who also designed the granite embankments and cobbled ramps leading down to the Neva – reminders that the city's port and commercial centre were once located here. Not to be missed is the **Kunstkammer** (11am–6pm, closed Mon; $4), founded by Peter the Great in 1714. Its name (meaning "art chamber" in German) dignified Peter's fascination for curiosities and freaks: he offered rewards for "human monsters" and unknown birds and animals, which were preserved in vinegar or vodka. To attract visitors, each received a glass of vodka or a cup of coffee.

The Peter and Paul Fortress

Across the Neva from the Winter Palace, on a small island, stands the **Peter and Paul Fortress**, built to secure Russia's hold on the Neva delta. Forced labourers toiled from dawn to dusk to construct the fortress in just seven months. The day of its foundation, 27 May 1703, is considered to mark the founding of the city. The fortress is permanently open – with no admission charge – but its **cathedral** and numerous **museums** covering the history of the city and Russian life keep regular visiting hours (11am–6pm, closed Wed; $5 for all the museums). The midday gun, fired daily from the roof, resounds across the city centre, making windows shake and setting off nearby car alarms. The Dutch-style **Peter and Paul Cathedral**, completed in 1733, remained the tallest structure in the city until the 1960s. Sited around the nave are the tombs of the Romanov monarchs from Peter the Great onwards – excluding Peter II, Ivan VI and Nicholas II. Nicholas and his family, whose bones were discovered in a mineshaft in the Urals in 1989, were finally buried in a chapel beside the cathedral in 1998.

Beyond the Fontanka

Nestling in a bend of the River Neva, northeast of Nevskiy prospekt, lies the quiet **Smolniy district**, its ice-blue cathedral towering on the eastern horizon. This is the focal point of the former **Smolniy Convent**, founded in the eighteenth century by the Empress Elizabeth. Rastrelli's grandiose Baroque structure hides an austere white interior (10am–5pm, closed Thurs), used to host temporary exhibitions and concerts. The **Smolniy Institute**, now the Governor's Headquarters, was built in 1806–08 to house the Institute for Young Noblewomen. Lenin ran the Revolution from here, and for the 74 years of Communist rule, the word "Smolniy" was synonymous with the Revolution and the Party. At the eastern end of Nevskiy prospekt lies the **Alexander Nevsky Monastery**, founded in 1713 by Peter the Great and one of only four monasteries in the Russian Empire with the rank of *lavra*, the highest in Orthodox monasticism. Two famous cemeteries lie in the monastery grounds: the **Tikhvin Cemetery**, also known as Necropolis for Masters of the Arts, with the graves of Dostoyevsky, Rimsky-Korsakov, Tchaikovsky, Rubinstein and Glinka, and, directly opposite, the smaller **Lazarus Cemetery**, the oldest in the city. **Tickets** are required for entry to both (10.30am–4/6pm, closed Thurs; $3), and foreigners are increasingly asked to make a "contribution" before entering the monastery proper. At the gates of the **monastery** (daily dawn to dusk) is Trezzini's **Church of the Annunciation** (11am–5pm, closed Mon & Thurs; $2), original burial place of Peter III, Catherine the Great's deposed husband.

Eating, drinking and entertainment

In recent years a growing number of modestly priced, intimate **restaurants** have opened up in St Petersburg, serving good food and offering a better feel of local life than those aiming to imitate Western stereotypes and prices. The city also offers plenty of potential for a wild night out. There's a wide range of **clubs** and, for Russians, the city is associated with several legendary homegrown bands and is the hippest place in the country. The city is also famed for its **classical concerts**, **ballet** and **opera**. For ballet, stick to the Mariinskiy (formerly Kirov). For details of what's happening, check the listings papers (see "Arrival").

Cafés and bars

Cynic Goncharnaya ul. 4; Moskovkiy vokzal metro. Grungy student crowds overflow onto the street. Unpredictable, but can be fun.

Green Crest Salad Bar Vladimirskiy pr. 7; Vladimirskaya/Dostoevskaya metro. Salads, salads and more salads – good healthy eating.

Idiot nab. reki Moyki 82; trolleybus #5 or #22, minibus #190 or #169 from Nevskiy prospekt. Vegetarian bar with books and board games, stuffed with foreigners and social-climbing Russians.

Krokodil Galernaya ul. 181; trolleybus #5 or #22, minibus #190 or #169 from Nevskiy prospekt. Café for the in-crowd, particularly good at lunchtime. Original menu, all fresh food.

Layma nab. kanala Griboedova 16; Gostiniy Dvor/Nevskiy Prospekt metro. Excellent fast food, including steaks and salads, plus beer; great for late suppers. Open 24hr.

Russkie bliny ul. Furmanova 13. Ornate, cosy, popular, cheap lunchtime spot, off Liteyniy prospekt. Traditional Russian pancakes, savoury and sweet.

Sunduk Art Cafe Furshtatskaya ul. 42; Chernyshevskaya metro. Great food and cocktails, live jazz most evenings (small cover charge), comfortable decor.

Restaurants

Demyanova Ukha Kronverkskiy pr. 53 ☎812/232 8090; Gorkovskaya metro. Serves fish and nothing else, but a bit touristy. Reservations essential.

Krunk Solyanoy per. 14; Chernyshevskaya metro or a 5min walk from Summer Garden. Armenian food and a friendly atmosphere, opposite the Stieglitz Art School.

Patio Pizza Nevskiy pr. 30; Gostiniy Dvor/Nevskiy Prospekt metro. Best salad bar in town.

Rioni Shpalernaya ul. 24. Excellent Georgian food, tucked away up a side alley. Order lots of different *zakuski*.

Clubs and live music

Amnesia Furshtatskaya 58b; Chernyshevskaya metro. Some of the best DJs in town.

Decadence Admiralteyskaya nab. 12; Nevskiy Prospekt metro. If you can get past the face control (are you beautiful enough?) you'll love both the jazz/blues and the food.

Fish Fabrique Pushkinskaya ul. 10 (entrance from Ligovskiy pr. 53); Mayakovskovo metro. Café-club at the heart of the city's famous artists' colony.

Griboedov Voronezhskaya ul. 2a; Ligovskiy Prospekt metro. Still the coolest of cool dance clubs, in a former bomb shelter.

JFC Jazz Club Shpalernaya ul. 33; Chernyshevskaya metro. The city's most exciting jazz programme. Tucked away in a courtyard.

Jimi Hendrix Blues Club Liteynyy pr. 33; Chernyshevskaya metro. Some of the bands are really bad, but most aren't – the food's good too. Open 24hr.

Moloko Perekupnoy per. 12; Ploshchad Aleksandra Nevskovo metro. Underground rock club with a reputation for discovering great acts.

Money Honey Saloon Apraksin Dvor 13 (in yard); Gostiniy Dvor/Nevskiy Prospekt metro. Russian rockabilly, cheap beer, always packed; don't forget the leather jacket.

Tunnel Bunker on corner of Lyubanskiy per. and Zverinskaya ul.; Sportivnaya metro. The home of techno and electronic dance music. Fri & Sat only.

Classical, opera and ballet

Mariinskiy (formerly Kirov) Theatre Teatralnaya pl. 1 ☎812/114 5264. Prices for foreigners from $5 to $75. Performances at 7pm with Sun matinées at noon. The company is on tour late July to Sept.

Philharmonia Mikhaylovskaya ul. 2 ☎812/311 7333; Nevskiy Prospekt metro. Draws international classical musicians as well as Russia's best. Performances at 7pm.

Listings

Consulates Canada, Malodetskoselsky pr. 32 ☎812/325 8448; UK, pl. Proletarskoy diktatury 5 ☎812/320 3200; US, Furshtadtskaya ul. 15 ☎812/331 2600.

Exchange Best ATM machine (24hr) at Sberbank, Dumskaya ul. 3.

Hospitals International Clinic, Dostoevskovo ul. 19/21 ☎812/320 3870, ✉infor@icspb.com; Euromed, Suvorovskiy pr. 60 ☎812/327 0301, ⊛www.euromed.ru; American Medical Centre, Serpukhovskaya ul. 10 ☎812/326 1730; British-American Family Practice, Grafsky per. 7

☎812/327 6030. All open 24hr and recognized by international insurance companies.

Internet access Quo Vadis, Nevskiy pr. 24 (24hr), or Westpost at Nevskiy pr. 86.

Pharmacy Petropharm, at Nevskiy pr. 22 (24hr). Other branches at nos. 50, 66 & 83.

Post office Pochtamskaya ul. 9, just off St Isaac's Square. Express letter post: Westpost, Nevskiy pr. 86 ☎812/327 3092; City Express, Shpalernaya ul. 24 ☎812/327 3883. Letters can be sent via Finnish post from the *Grand Hotel Europe*.

Day-trips from St Petersburg

You should aim to make at least one day-trip out of St Petersburg – the locals get out of town whenever they can, to swim in the Gulf in summer, or ski or gather mushrooms in winter.

In summer, most visitors opt for **Peterhof**, 29km west, famed for its marvellous fountains and cascades at the **Great Palace** (10.30am–5pm, closed Mon; palace $9, Lower Park $6). Almost unknown is the charming neo-Gothic **Cottage Palace** (May–Oct daily except Fri 10am–5pm; Oct–April Sat & Sun 10am–5pm; $5) in the nearby Alexandria Park. Travel by hydrofoil in summer ($5 each way) from outside the Winter Palace or take one of the frequent minibuses from Avtovo metro station ($0.50). In winter, try **Tsarskoe Selo** (also known as Pushkin), 17km southeast of St Petersburg. The palace (10am–5pm, closed Tues; $10) is a vulgar blue-and-white Baroque structure, set in a richly landscaped park, with Neoclassical additions including Scottish architect Charles Cameron's supremely elegant Gallery, stretching high above the park. The famous Amber Room, stolen by the Germans during World War II and lost, was re-created in time for St Petersburg's 300th anniversary in 2003. To get to Tsarskoe Selo, frequent minibuses ($0.50) run from Moskovskaya metro station. The same minibuses will take you on to Neoclassical **Pavlovsk**, its **Great Palace** (10am–5pm, closed Fri; $8) a monument to the taste and habits of Paul I's wife Maria Fyodorovna. Pavlovsk park is much loved by St Petersburg's inhabitants, who walk here and feed the squirrels in summer, and ski through the grounds in winter.

Slovakia

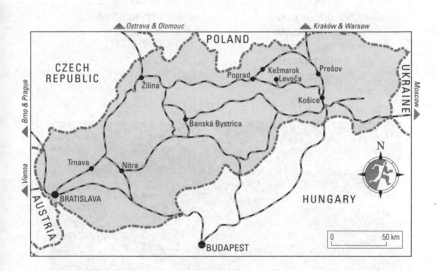

Slovakia highlights

* **Bratislava** The Slovak
capital has a small but
beautifully restored old
town full of Baroque
palaces, leafy squares
and lively pavement
cafés. See p.798

* **High Tatras** These
jagged, granite peaks –
the most spectacular
mountains in Slovakia –
rise dramatically from
the Poprad plain. See
p.803

* **Levoča** An attractive
walled medieval town,
originally settled by
Saxons. See p.805

* **Spišský hrad** This
sprawling medieval cas-
tle in the east of the
country is Slovakia's
most stunning hilltop
ruin. See p.806

Introduction and basics

The republic of **Slovakia** consists of the long, narrow strip of land that stretches from the fertile plains of the Danube basin up to the peaks of the High Tatras, which are celebrated as Europe's most exhilarating mountain range outside the Alps. The country's mountain chains have long formed barriers to industrialization and modernization, and parts of Slovakia remain surprisingly rural and unspoilt, some to the point of neglect.

There was only one independent Slovakia before 1993 – when the Slovaks split from the Czechs in 1938, forming an independent state allied to Nazi Germany, a period in the nation's **history** that remains contentious today. Before 1918, current-day Slovakia was known as Upper Hungary and lay under Magyar rule for roughly a millennium; Bratislava even became the Hungarian capital when the Turks occupied the rest of Hungary. In 1918, however, the Slovaks threw in their lot with their Slav neighbours, the Czechs, forming **Czechoslovakia**, a union that lasted 75 years until the country's "velvet divorce" took place in 1993 (the Czech Republic is covered in Chapter 6). Slovakia is due to join the EU in 2004. **Catholicism** is much stronger here than in the Czech Republic, and the churches are often full to overflowing on Sundays. The republic also has a more diverse population, with over half a million ethnic **Hungarians** in the south, as well as thousands of Romanies (Gypsies), who live a fairly miserable existence throughout the country, and several thousand Ruthenians (Rusyns) in the east.

Bratislava, the capital, has been much maligned in the past but its compact old town has been beautifully restored in the last decade and it's now a rewarding, lively place. **Poprad** provides the transport hub for the **High Tatras**, the most spectacular of Slovakia's many mountain ranges, and is also the starting point for exploring the intriguing medieval towns of the **Spiš** region, east Slovakia's architectural high point.

Further east still, **Prešov** is the cultural centre of the Ruthenian minority, while **Košice**, Slovakia's vibrant second city, boasts a fine Gothic cathedral, ethnic diversity and a lively independence from much of the rest of the country.

Information & maps

Just about every town has some kind of **tourist office** (*informačné centrum*), most with English speakers. In summer they're generally open Mon–Fri 9am–6pm, Sat & Sun 9am–2pm; in winter they tend to close an hour earlier and all day Sun. **Maps** are available, often very cheaply, from bookshops and some hotels (a town plan is *plán mesta* or *orientačná mapa*). The VKÚ's 1:50,000 series details hiking paths.

Money and banks

Currency is the **Slovak crown** or *Slovenská koruna* (Sk), which is divided into 100 heller or *halér* (h). Coins are 10h, 20h, 50h, 1Sk, 2Sk, 5Sk and 10Sk; notes are 20, 50, 100, 200, 500 and 1000Sk (less frequently 5000Sk). The crown is not fully convertible, which theoretically means you can't buy any currency until you arrive. **Credit and debit cards** are accepted in most upmarket hotels and restaurants and some shops, though it's a good idea to keep at least some hard currency in **cash** for emergencies. Exchange

---

Slovakia on the net

ⓦ **www.slovakspectator.sk** English-language weekly, with news and listings.
ⓦ **www.tatry.sk** Excellent guide to the High Tatras, with plenty of travel and accommodation info.
ⓦ **www.sacr.sk** Tourist board site, with basic but useful information.

offices (*zmenáren*) can be found in all major hotels, travel agencies and department stores.

Communications

Most **post offices** (*pošta*) open Mon–Fri 8am–5pm – you can also buy stamps (*známky*) from some tobacconists (*tabák*) and street kiosks. Poste restante is available in major towns; write *Pošta 1* (the main office), followed by the name of the town. Cheap local calls can be made from any **phone**, but for international calls it's best to use a card phone; buy a card (*telefonná karta*) from a tobacconist or post office. **Internet cafés** have appeared in the larger towns; expect to pay 50–120Sk/hr.

Getting around

With two-thirds of the **train** network made up of single-track lines, services are slow, but some of the journeys are worth it for the scenery alone. Slovak Railways (*železnice Slovenskej republiky* or *ŽSR*) runs fast *rýchlik* trains that stop at major towns; the *osobný vlak*, or local train, stops everywhere. You can buy tickets (*lístok*) for domestic journeys at the station (*stanica*) before or on the day of departure. Supplements are payable on all EuroCity (EC) trains, and occasionally for InterCity (IC) and Expres (Ex) trains. ŽSR runs reasonably priced sleepers (*lôžkový vozeň*) and couchettes (*ležadlový vozeň*) – book in advance, no later than six hours before departure. **InterRail** is valid; **Eurail** requires supplements. Travelling by **bus** (*autobus*) is quicker and covers a more extensive network. In most cities the bus and train stations are adjacent. The state bus company is *Slovenská automobilová doprava* or *SAD*. The usual practice is to buy your ticket from the driver, since ticket offices are often closed. Book in advance if you're travelling at the weekend or early in the morning on one of the main routes.

Accommodation

It's always a good idea to arrange **accommodation** as far in advance as possible. Some **hotels** have double pricing, with higher rates for foreigners, but a basic room for £6/$9 per head is not hard to find anywhere outside Bratislava, though probably with an extra £1/$1.50 for breakfast. While the old state hotels and spa complexes are slowly being refurbished, their rooms are usually box-like and overpriced; the new hotels and pensions that have opened up, particularly in the more heavily touristed areas, are often better value for money. **Private rooms** are a good option in many towns – keep your eyes peeled for *Zimmer frei* signs. Prices start at around £5/$7.50 per person per night.

There is no real network of **hostels**, though a few are affiliated to HI and others come under CKM, the student travel agency (ⓦwww.ckm.sk). Bratislava has a few private hostels offering varying degrees of discomfort. Elsewhere, CKM or local tourist offices can give information on cheap **student accommodation** in the university towns during July and August. In the High Tatras, in addition to panel-built spa accommodation, you can find a fair number of chalet-style **refuges** (*chata*) scattered about the hillsides. Some are practically hotels and cost around £10/$15 a bed, while simpler, more isolated wooden shelters cost much less. **Campsites** are plentiful, and many feature simple **bungalows** (*chata* again), often available for upwards of £5/$8 a bed. A few sites remain open year-round, but about half operate May–Sept. Prices are sometimes inflated for foreigners, but are still reasonable.

Food and drink

Slovak **food** is no-nonsense, filling fare; traces of Hungarian, Polish and Ukrainian influences can be found in different regions. The usual mid-morning snack at the **bufet** (stand-up canteen) is *párek*, a hot frankfurter dipped in mustard or horseradish and served inside a white roll. The national dish is *bryndzové halušky* – gnocchi with a thick sheep's cheese sauce and crumbled grilled bacon – but Hungarian influences are strong here, too. Goulash is very popular (although a mild stew rather than the authentic spicy soup), as are *langoše* – deep-fried dough smothered in a variety of toppings. Most menus start with **soup** (*polievka*), served at both midday and evening meals. **Main courses** are based on pork or beef, but trout and carp are usually featured somewhere on the menu, and you may find catfish or pike-perch if you're lucky, and occasionally lamb. Most main courses are served with delicious potatoes (*zemiaky*) – but fresh salads or green vegetables are still a rarity in local restaurants. In addition to *palačinky* (cold pancakes) filled with chocolate, fruit and cream, Slovak **desserts** invariably feature apple or cottage-cheese strudel and ice cream. An increasing number of **restaurants** offering international cuisine have sprouted up, from fast food and pizzerias to Bratislava's many oriental eateries. **Opening times** have been extended too – though in outlying regions closing time will still be 9 or 10pm, the bigger cities have restaurants open till 11pm or later. **Coffee** (*káva*) is drunk black – espresso-style in the big cities, but sometimes simply hot water poured over grounds in towns and villages (described rather hopefully as "Turkish" or *turecká*). The **cake shop** (*cukráreň*) is an important part of social life, particularly on Sunday mornings when it's often the only place that's open in town. Whatever the season, Slovaks love their daily fix of **ice cream** (*zmrzlina*), available at *cukráreň* or dispensed from little window kiosks in the sides of buildings.

Vineyards in the south of Slovakia produce some pretty good white **wines**, which share characteristics with their Hungarian and Austrian neighbours. The most famous local firewater is *slivovice*, a plum **brandy** available just about everywhere. After more than seventy years of close association with the Czechs, the Slovaks have also learnt to love draught **beer**, but the *pivnica*, where most heavy drinking goes on, is still less common in Slovakia than in the Czech Republic. Slovaks tend to head instead for restaurants or **wine bars** (*vináreň*), which usually have slightly later opening hours and often double as nightclubs.

Opening hours and holidays

Opening hours for shops are Mon–Fri 9am–6pm, Sat 8am–noon, with some shops and most supermarkets staying open later. In large towns, supermarkets and out-of-town hypermarkets also open on Sunday. Smaller shops take an hour or so for lunch between noon and 2pm. The basic opening hours for **castles** and **monasteries** are Tues–Sun 9am–5pm. In April and October, opening hours are often restricted to weekends and holidays. Most castles are closed in winter. When visiting a sight, always ask for an *anglický text*, an often unintentionally hilarious English resumé. **Museums** are usually open Tues–Sun year-round, though most close early in winter. Admission rarely costs more than 100Sk – hence we haven't quoted any prices. **Public holidays** include Jan 1; Jan 6; Good Fri; Easter Mon; May 1; May 8; July 5; Aug 29; Sept 1; Sept 15; Nov 1; Dec 24, 25 & 26.

Emergencies

The state **police** (*polícia*) wear khaki-green uniforms, and the local municipal or *mestská polícia* wear a variety of outfits. Theft from cars and hotel rooms is your biggest worry. You should carry your **passport** with you at all times, though you're most unlikely to get stopped. Minor ailments can be easily dealt with by the **pharmacist** (*lekáreň*), but language is likely to be a problem. If the pharmacy can't help, they'll direct you to a **hospital** (*nemocnica*).

Emergency numbers

Police ☎158; Ambulance ☎155; Fire ☎150.

Bratislava

BRATISLAVA – just 60km east of Vienna – has two distinct sides: the old quarter is an attractive slice of Habsburg Baroque, while the rest of the city has the drab, concrete looks of the average East European metropolis. Indeed, more buildings have been destroyed here since World War II than were bombed out during it, including virtually the whole Jewish quarter, which was bulldozed to make way for a colossal suspension bridge and highway. Much has been done recently, however, to spruce the city up, and the paved streets and squares of the old town are now abuzz with cafés and bars. Thanks to its large student population and position at the meeting-point of three nations (Bratislava lies very close to both the Austrian and Hungarian frontiers), the city has a lively, cosmopolitan atmosphere – and with none of the sightseeing crowds of Prague, it makes for a pleasant place to spend a couple of days.

Arrival, information and accommodation

The scruffy main **train station**, Bratislava-Hlavná stanica, is a short distance north of the centre. Once you've arrived, go down to the tram terminus below and, having bought your ticket from one of the machines on the platform, hop on tram #1 into town. Some trains, particularly those heading for west Slovakia, pass through Bratislava Nové Mesto station, 4km northeast of the centre, which is linked by tram #6. **Buses** usually arrive at the main bus station, Bratislava autobusová stanica, on Mlynské nivy, fifteen minutes' walk east of the centre; trolleybus #210 will take you across town to the main train station, while #206 will drop you on Hodžovo námestie. The **tourist office**, BIS, at Klobučnícka 2 (summer Mon–Fri 9am–7pm, Sat & Sun 10am–1pm & 1.30–6pm; rest of year Mon–Fri 9am–6pm, Sat 10am–2pm; ☏02/5443 4415, ⊛www.old.bratislava.sk/bis), is good for general queries and getting hold of a map and the monthly listings magazine, *Kam v Bratislave*; it also books accommodation (50Sk fee). There's another smaller office in the main train station. The weekly *Slovak Spectator*, available from kiosks and hotels, has news and some listings. *C@fe Online*, Hurbanovo nám. 5, has **Internet** access.

Walking is the only way to see the mainly pedestrianized old town, or Staré Mesto. However, if you're staying outside the city centre or visiting the suburbs, you'll need to make use of the inexpensive **transport system**. Buy your ticket (14Sk to the centre) beforehand from newsagents, kiosks, hotel lobbies or ticket machines; validate it as soon as you get on; and use a fresh ticket each time you change. The booth on the left outside the main entrance of the train station, near the bus departure points, sells a one/two-day pass (80/150Sk). Night buses congregate at námestie SNP, every quarter to the hour.

Hotels are more expensive than anywhere else in the country, making **private rooms** the most popular option for most budget travellers. You can book centrally located rooms (❷–❸) through the tourist office; alternatively, try *Gabriel*, Paulinyho 1 (☏0903/783 333; ❷), which has several rooms sleeping up to six people. The tourist office can also help with finding rooms in Bratislava's various student **hostels**, though these are open only in summer.

Hostels

Bernolák Bernolákova 1 ☏02/5249 7724. The liveliest hostel in the city, only a short tram ride northeast of the centre. Breakfast included. Own bar with regular discos and gigs. July & Aug only. Tram #7 or #11 from Kamenné námestie. 340Sk.

Svoradov Svoradova 13 ☏02/5441 5386. Another bustling, youthful hostel, centrally located just two blocks north of the castle. July & Aug only. 270Sk.

Hotels and pensions

Arcus Moskovská 5 ☏02/5557 2522. Small pension within walking distance of the old town, just east of Americké námestie. Clean, quiet, comfortable and affordable. Take any tram heading up Špitalská from Kamenné námestie. ❹

Astra Prievozská 14a ☏02/5341 5816. Inexpensive hotel just over 2km east of the centre, offering decent, recently refurbished rooms; take

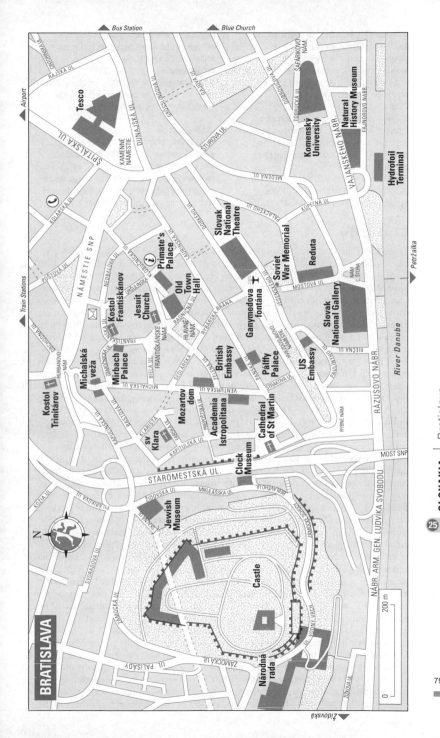

BRATISLAVA

▲ *Bus Station* ▲ *Blue Church*

▲ *Airport*

▲ *Train Stations*

Tesco

Kostol Trinitárov

Michalská veža

Mirbach Palace

Kostol Františkánov

Jesuit Church

Primate's Palace

Old Town Hall

Slovak National Theatre

Komenský University

Natural History Museum

Hydrofoil Terminal

Reduta

Soviet War Memorial

Ganymedova fontána

Slovak National Gallery

British Embassy

Pálffy Palace

US Embassy

Mozartov dom

Academia Istropolitana

sv Klara

Cathedral of St Martin

Clock Museum

Jewish Museum

Castle

Národná rada

NÁMESTIE SNP

STAROMESTSKÁ UL.

MOST SNP

River Danube

RAŽUSOVO NÁBR.

NÁBR. ARM. GEN. LUDVÍKA SVOBODU

N

0   200 m

▼ *Petržalka*

▲ *Židovská*

trolleybus #210 from the train station and walk from the bus station. ❷
Baronka Murdorchova 2 ☎02/4488 2089, ⓦwww.baronka.sk. Comfortable, refurbished hotel with swimming pool, fitness centre and restaurant, outside the city centre on tram #3. ❹
Caribic's Žižkova 1a ☎02/5441 8334, ⓦwww.caribics.sk. Pleasant rooms in an old fisherman's lodge by the busy road just below the Hrad, and, given its proximity to the old town, pretty good value – although noisy thanks to passing trams. ❹
Gremium Gorkého 11 ☎02/5413 1026, ⓔcherrytour@mail.pvt.sk. The only halfway decent, relatively inexpensive option in the old

town. Clean, with extremely basic en-suite bathrooms, plus a café and sports bar on the bottom two floors. ❸
Spirit Vančurova 1 ☎02/5477 7817, ⓦwww.hotelspirit.sk. Welcoming yet bizarre hotel round the back of the train station that offers guests use of its regeneration pyramid. ❸

Campsites
Zlaté Piesky Intercamp ☎02/4445 0592, ⓦwww.intercamp.sk. Two fairly grim campsites, 8km northeast of the city centre, near the swimming lake of the same name. Bungalows on offer all year round; tents May–Sept only. Tram #2 from the main train station or #4 from town.

The City

Trams from the main train station offload behind the *Hotel Fórum* on Obchodná – literally Shop Street – which descends into Hurbanovo námestie, a busy junction on the northern edge of the old town. Here you'll find the hefty mass of the **Kostol trinitárov**, one of the city's finest churches, its exuberant *trompe l'oeil* frescoes creating a magnificent false cupola. Opposite the church, a footbridge crosses a small section of what used to be a moat towards the city's last remaining double gateway. The tower above the gateway's second arch, the **Michalská veža** (Tues–Fri 9.30/10am–4.30/5pm, Sat & Sun 11am–6pm), provides an evocative and impressive entrance to the old town and is now a weapons museum – worth visiting if only for the view from the top. Michalská and Ventúrska, which run into each other, have both been beautifully restored and are lined with some of Bratislava's finest Baroque palaces. There are usually plenty of students milling about amongst the shoppers, as the main university library is on this thoroughfare. The palaces of the Austro-Hungarian aristocracy continue into Panská, starting with the **Pálffy Palace**, at Panská 19, today an **art gallery** (Tues–Sun 10am–5pm), housing a patchy collection of Slovak paintings from the nineteenth and twentieth centuries.

A little northeast of here are the adjoining main squares of the old town – **Hlavné námestie** and **Františkánske námestie** – on the east side of which is the Old Town Hall, a lively hotchpotch of Gothic, Renaissance and nineteenth-century styles containing the main **City Museum** (Tues–Fri 10am–5pm, Sat & Sun 11am–6pm), which features a medieval torture exhibition in the basement dungeons. The Counter-Reformation, which gripped areas not under Turkish occupation, issues forth from the square's **Jesuit Church**, whose best feature is its richly gilded pulpit. Diagonally opposite is the **Mirbach Palace** (Tues–Sun 10am–5pm), arguably the finest of Bratislava's Rococo buildings, preserving much of its original stucco decor. The permanent collection of Rococo and Baroque art and sculpture inside isn't up to much, save for the room of wall-to-wall miniatures set into the wood panelling. Round the back of the Old Town Hall is **Primaciálne námestie**, dominated by the Neoclassical **Primate's Palace** (Tues–Sun 10am–5pm), whose pediment frieze is topped by a cast-iron cardinal's hat. The palace's main claim to fame is its Hall of Mirrors, where Napoleon and the Austrian emperor signed the Peace of Pressburg (as Bratislava was then called) in 1805. You can now visit this, and several other rooms hung with portraits of the Habsburgs and minor works by seventeenth-century Dutch and Italian masters.

The most insensitive of Bratislava's postwar developments took place on the west side of the old town. After the annihilation of the city's Jewish population by the Nazis, the Communist authorities tore down almost all of the Jewish quarter in order to build the brutal showpiece bridge, the SNP Bridge, now known as the

Nový most or New Bridge. The traffic which now tears along Staromestská has seriously undermined the foundations of the **Cathedral of St Martin**, the Gothic coronation church of the kings and queens of Hungary for over 250 years, whose ill-proportioned steeple is topped by a tiny gilded Hungarian crown; the church was closed for restoration at the time of writing. Having passed under the approach road for the Nový most, you'll notice the **Clock Museum** at Židovská 1 (Tues–Fri 9.30/10am–4.30/5pm, Sat & Sun 11am–6pm), with a display of brilliantly kitsch Baroque and Empire clocks. The large prewar Slovak Jewish population is commemorated at the **Jewish Museum** at Židovská 17 (Mon–Fri & Sun 11am–5pm), with a display of Judaica and a brief history of Slovak Jewry. The **castle** (daily 9am–6/8pm) is an unwelcoming giant box built in the fifteenth century by Emperor Sigismund, burnt down by its own drunken soldiers in 1811 and restored in the 1950s and 1960s. It houses the **Slovak Historical Museum** (Tues–Sun 9am–5pm), which features Slovak trades, handicrafts and folk art, and the **Music Museum** (Tues–Sun 9am–5pm), which contains traditional Slovak instruments. The castle's small collection of old clocks is also worth viewing, and you also get the chance to climb to the top of one of the castle's four corner towers, for an incredible view south across the Danube plain and over the river to the Petržalka housing estate, where a third of the city's population lives.

Despite the fast road on the embankment, it is just about possible to enjoy a stroll along the **River Danube** – *Dunaj* in Slovak. In addition to a terminal for boats to Budapest and Vienna, there's a summer ferry service across the river, an alternative to crossing by either of the two bridges, the larger of which is the infamous "Bridge of the Slovak National Uprising" or **Nový most**. Its one support column leans at an alarming angle, topped by a saucer-like, pricey penthouse café reminiscent of the Starship Enterprise. A couple of hundred metres east along the waterfront is the humdrum **Slovak National Gallery** (Tues–Sun 10am–5.30pm), which is gradually being renovated. There are two entrances: the one on the embankment lets you into the main building, a converted naval barracks, while the one on Stúrovo námestie gives access to the Esterházy Palace wing. The permanent collection in the main building features a rundown of Slovak Gothic and Baroque art, while the Esterházy Palace puts on temporary exhibitions, mostly focusing on modern art. Further along the quayside, past the rather tatty **Natural History Museum** (Tues–Sun 9am–5pm) and hidden away behind Safárikovo námestie, is Ödön Lechner's concrete, sky-blue Art Nouveau **Blue Church** at Bezručova 2, a lost monument to this once-Hungarian city, abandoned in the Slovak capital and dedicated to St Elizabeth, the city's one and only famous saint, born in Bratislava in 1207.

Eating, drinking and nightlife

The choice of **places to eat** has improved over the last few years, as have standards. Prices are generally low. The most memorable aspect of the whole experience, however, is often the ambience, and exploring the atmospheric streets of the old town by night is all part of the fun. Bratislava's **nightlife** is heavily biased towards high culture, with **opera** and **ballet** at the Slovak National Theatre (⊛www.snd.sk) and concerts at the Reduta, as well as the varied programme put on at the modern Istropolis complex on Trnavské myto (tram #2 from the station; tram #4 or #6 from the centre). The most prestigious **festival** is a classical music event in October. There are few out-and-out dance **clubs**, but you'll find plenty of late-opening pubs and **bars** helping to fill the gap.

Cafés and restaurants

Caribic's Žižkova 1 ☎02/5441 8334. Popular, reliably good but pricey fish restaurant on the ground floor of a former fisherman's house down by the waterfront below the castle (there's a

posher, more expensive version upstairs). Reservations recommended.
Chez David Zamocka 13 ☎02/5441 3824. Kosher restaurant serving fresh, beautifully prepared Jewish cuisine. Closed Sat.

Hradná vináreň Dubčeka námestie 1. Smart restaurant and bar in the castle grounds, with breathtaking views and serving excellent Slovak specialities and wine.

Kaffee Mayer Hlavné námestie 4. A resurrected century-old café that emulates its Viennese-style ancestor – very popular with the city's older cake-and-coffee fans.

Korzo Hviezdoslavovo námestie 11. Passable shot at a Viennese-style café and a possible breakfast halt, with tables outside overlooking Rybné námestie and the Nový most.

Mekong Palackého 18. Swish restaurant serving slap-up Thai classics.

Pizzeria Park Hviezdoslavovo námestie 21. The best pizza joint in the city, with a good range of moderately priced, thin-base pizzas.

Prašná Bašta Zámočnícka 11. Cosy, low-ceilinged restaurant with a nice summer courtyard, serving up excellent Slovak and international dishes.

Vegetarian Laurinská 8. Plain and simple vegetarian lunch spot, with a short list of salads and soya-based main dishes. Closed Sat & Sun.

Bars and clubs

Charlie Centrum Špitálska 4. Bratislava's longest-serving nightspot, with a multiscreen art-house cinema and a late-night bar/disco in the basement.

Dubliner Sedlárska 6. Very popular, stereotypical Irish bar – complete with cobbled floor – which sometimes stages live music.

Gremium Gorkého 11. Busy sports bar, with a big screen, betting shop and a gallery area, along with a café upstairs.

Hystéria Odbojárov 9. Located behind the ice hockey stadium (tram #4 or #6 from Kamenné námestie), this place is worth the trek for its Tex-Mex food, pool and regular live music.

Stará sladovňa Cintorínska 32. The city's malthouse until 1976, *Mamut*, as it's known, is Bratislava's most famous (and largest) pub. Czech Budvar on tap, big band and country & western music Thurs–Sat, and a bingo hall and slot machine room on site as well.

U-Club Nábrežie arm. gen. L. Svobodu. Cheap, loud and slightly weird club located in an old nuclear bunker underneath the castle.

Slovakia's mountain regions

The great virtue of Slovakia is its mountains, particularly the **High Tatras**, which, in their short span, reach alpine heights and have a bleak, stunning beauty. By far the country's most popular destination, they are, in fact, the least typical of Slovakia's mountains, which are predominantly densely forested, round-topped limestone ranges. In the heart of the mountains is **Banská Bystrica**, one of the many towns in the region originally settled by German miners, and still redolent of those times. Generally, though, the towns in the valley bottoms have been fairly solidly industrialized, and are only good as bases for exploring the surrounding countryside. Rail lines, where they exist, make for some of the most scenic **train** journeys in the country.

Banská Bystrica

Lying at the very heart of Slovakia's mountain ranges, the old German mining town of **BANSKÁ BYSTRICA** is a useful introduction to the area and is also a handsome historic town in its own right – once you've made it through the tangled suburbs of the burgeoning cement and logging industries. **Námestie SNP**, the former medieval marketplace, is still the centre of life here. The black obelisk of the Soviet war memorial and a fountain that enthusiastically chucks water over a pile of mossy rocks form the square's centrepiece. One or two of the burgher houses bear closer inspection, particularly the **Venetian House** at no. 16, with its slender first-floor arcaded loggia. Opposite is a sgraffitoed building that is now an arts and crafts shop. Just a few doors up is the most imposing building on the square, the honey-coloured Thurzo Palace at no. 4, decorated like a piece of embroidery and sporting cute oval portholes, and now housing the **town museum** (Mon–Fri & Sun 8/9am–noon & 1–4pm), with a small selection of folk art and period furniture. At the top end of the square, beyond the leaning clock tower, there's an interesting ensemble of buildings – all that's left of the old castle. The first building in view is the castle's last remaining **barbican**, curving snugly round a Baroque tower. Next door, the former **town hall** (Tues–Fri 10am–5pm, Sat & Sun 10–11.30am & noon–4pm), a boxy little Renaissance structure, is now the town's main art gallery, which puts on temporary exhibitions from its extensive catalogue of modern Slovak art. Behind it is the rouge-red church of **Panna Mária**, which dates back to the thirteenth century; the north side chapel contains the town's greatest art treasure, a carved late-Gothic altarpiece by Master Pavol of Levoča. About 200m southeast of námestie SNP is the **SNP Museum** at Kapitulská 23 (Tues–Sun 9am–6pm), looking like an intergalactic mushroom chopped in half and dating from 1969. The museum deals as best it can with the complex issues raised by the Slovak National Uprising (SNP) against the Nazis (and the Slovak puppet regime), which began on August 29, 1944, in Banská Bystrica and was eventually crushed by the Germans two months later, just a month or so before the town's liberation. Outside, amid the bushes, you'll notice an exhibition of tanks and guns from the uprising and the town's last two surviving medieval bastions.

Banská Bystrica's main **bus** and **train stations** are in the new part of town, ten minutes' walk east of the centre; if you arrive on a slow train, you can alight at Banská Bystrica mesto train station, just five minutes' walk south of the main square. There's a **tourist office** inside the barbican (Mon–Fri 9am–12.30pm & 1.15–5pm; ☎048/16 186), which can help arrange **accommodation**. The late-nineteenth-century *Národný dom* (☎048/412 37 37, ✉narodnydom@slovanet.sk; ❸), at Národná 11, is a central option, with a wonderful café and restaurant. Two cheaper options are the *Penzión Uhlisko* (☎048/414 56 12; ❷), at Lesná 3, across the river from the stations, and the private rooms offered at *Privát Hodžová*, M. Hodžu 5 (☎048/415 31 19; booking essential; ❶), east of the old town – walk to the end of Dolná, cross the bridge and turn right onto J. Kráľa, then left onto M. Hurbana. There's also a **campsite** on Tajovského 180, 1km west of the main square, just by the turn-off to Tajov. There are plenty of cafés, bars and **restaurants** around the main square; try *Starobystrická pivnica* at no. 9 on the square for hearty Bohemian fare, or *Evijo*, just down Národná, for tasty pizzas. *Reštaurácia U Tigra* at Dolná 36 serves wonderful pub grub, while *Zlatý bažant* at nám. SNP 3 is a popular **drinking** spot.

The High Tatras

Rising like a giant granite reef above the patchwork Poprad plain, the **High Tatras** are the main reason for venturing this far into Slovakia. Even after all the tourist-board hype, they are still an inspirational sight. A wilderness, however, they are not; all summer, visitors are shoulder to shoulder in the necklace of resorts which sit at the foot of the mountains. But once you're above the tree line, surrounded by bare primeval scree slopes and icy blue tarns, nothing can take away the exhilaration or the breathtaking views.

The mainline train station for the Tatras is Poprad-Tatry in **POPRAD**, an unprepossessing town on the plain. With its great swathe of off-white high-rise housing encircling a small old centre, it is best viewed (if at all) as a stopover on the way to the mountains proper. Poprad's **tourist office** (Mon–Fri 8.30am–12.30pm & 1–5/6pm, Sat 9am–1pm; ☎052/16 186, ⊛www.poprad.sk), at the western end of námestie sv Egídia, can organize private rooms in town and all types of **accommodation** elsewhere in the Tatras; the *Hotel Garni*, near the train station at Karpatská 11 (☎052/776 38 77, ⊛www.hotelgarni.sk; ❷), is a good inexpensive option. From the high-level platform at Poprad-Tatry, cute red tram-like trains trundle across the fields, linking Poprad with the string of resorts and spas halfway up the Tatras within the **Tatra National Park** or **TANAP**. They range from tasteless new hotels to turreted edifices from the nineteenth century set in civilized spa gardens and pine woods – but it's the mountains to which they give access that make them worth visiting.

The best base for accommodation in the Tatras is the scattered settlement of **STARÝ SMOKOVEC** (30min from Poprad-Tatry), whose nucleus is the stretch of lawn between the half-timbered supermarket and the sandy-yellow *Grand Hotel*. The best place to head for help with **accommodation** is T-Ski (daily 9am–5/6pm; ☎052/442 32 00, ◐www.slovakiatravel.sk), up by the cable car, which can book **mountain chaty**, as well as renting out skis and other equipment. The best **campsite** is *Eurocamp FICC*, just south of **TATRANSKÁ LOMNICA** (get off at Tatranská Lomnica-Eurocamp FICC station, 15min (6km) beyond Starý Smokovec), with bungalows, a restaurant and café, hot showers and many other facilities. Serious climbers and hikers can get information from Horská záchranná služba, the 24-hour **mountain rescue service**, just uphill from Starý Smokovec station (☎052/442 28 20, ◐www.horskasluzba.sk).

If the weather's reasonably good, the most straightforward and rewarding climb is to follow the blue-marked path that leads from behind the *Grand Hotel* in Starý Smokovec to the summit of **Slavkovský štít** (2452m), a return journey of nine hours. Alternatively, a narrow-gauge funicular, again starting from behind the *Grand* (every 30min), climbs 250m to **HREBIENOK** (45min on foot), one of the lesser ski resorts on the edge of the pine forest. The smart wooden *Bilíkova chata* (☎052/442 24 39; ❸) is a five-minute walk from the top of the funicular – even if you don't stay there you should stop for a drink on the balcony. Beyond the chata, the path continues through the wood, joining two others (from Tatranská Lesná and Tatranská Lomnica respectively), before passing the gushing waterfalls of the **Studenovodské vodopády**. Just past the waterfall, a whole variety of trekking possibilities opens up. The right-hand fork takes you up the **Malá Studená dolina** and then zigzags above the tree line to the *Téryho chata*, set in a lunar landscape by the shores of the **Päť Spišských ples**. Following the spectacular trail over the Prieane sedlo to *Zbojnícka chata*, you can return via the **Vejká studená dolina** – an eight-hour round trip from Hrebienok. Another possibility is to take the left-hand fork to the *Zbojnícka chata*, and continue to Zamruznuté pleso, which sits in the shadow of **Východná Vysoká** (2428m); only a thirty-minute hike from the lake, this peak dishes out a fine view of **Gerlachovský štít** (2655m) – the highest peak in the Tatras. If you don't have the time or inclination to hike, you can still enjoy some fabulous views by taking a series of **cable cars** (daily 8am–4/5pm) from Tatranská Lomnica to the summit of **Lomnický štít** (2632m), the second-highest peak.

East Slovakia

Stretching from the High Tatras east to the Ukrainian border, the landscape of **East Slovakia** is decidedly different from the rest of the country. Ethnically, this is probably the most diverse region in the country, with different groups coexisting even within a single valley. The majority of the country's Romanies live here, mostly on the edge of Slovak villages, in shantytowns of almost medieval squalor. In the ribbon-villages of the north and east, the Rusyn minority struggle to preserve their culture and religion, while along the southern border there are large numbers of Hungarians. After spending time in the rural backwaters, **Košice**, Slovakia's second city, can be a welcome though somewhat startling return to city life. Gradually realizing its potential as a diverse and vibrant cosmopolitan centre, it certainly contains enough of interest for at least a day's stopover.

The Spiš region

The land that stretches northeast up the Poprad Valley to the Polish border and east along the River Hornád towards Prešov is known as the **Spiš region**, for centuries a semi-autonomous province within the Hungarian kingdom. After the devastation

25

of the mid-thirteenth-century Tatar invasions, the Hungarian Crown encouraged Saxon families to repopulate the area. The wealthy settlers built some wonderful Gothic churches, and later enriched almost every town and village with the distinctive touch of the Renaissance. Today, with only a few of its ethnic Germans and Hungarians remaining, the Spiš shares the low-living standards of the rest of East Slovakia. But the region's architectural richness offers a glimmer of hope in the growth of tourism – indeed in the high seasons, in towns such as **Levoča**, you can often hardly move for the tour buses.

Kežmarok

Just 14km up the road from Poprad, **KEŽMAROK** is one of the easiest Spiš towns to visit from the High Tatras. It's an odd place, combining the distinctive traits of a Teutonic town with the dozy feel of an oversized Slovak village. Kežmarok is dominated by the giant, gaudy **Lutheran Church** (May–Oct daily 9am–noon & 2–5pm; Nov–April Tues & Fri 9am–noon & 2–4pm), built by Theophil Hansen, the Danish architect responsible for much of late-nineteenth-century Vienna, and funded by the town's merchants. It's a seemingly random fusion of styles – Renaissance campanile, Moorish dome, classical dimensions, all dressed up in grey-green and rouge rendering. Next door is an even more remarkable **wooden Lutheran Church** (same times), a work of great carpentry and artistry whose ornately decorated interior is capable of seating almost 1500 people. The old town itself is little more than two long leafy streets that fork off from the important-looking central town hall. The town's Catholic basilica of **sv Kríž**, tucked away in the tangle of dusty back alleys between the two prongs, was once surrounded by its own line of fortifications. It is now protected by a Renaissance belfry whose uppermost battlements burst into sgraffito life in the best Spiš tradition. The **castle** (May–Sept Tues–Sun 8am–noon & 1–4pm; Oct–April Mon–Fri same hours), at the end of the right-hand fork, is impressively fortified and decorated with Renaissance crenellations, but the interior doesn't really justify signing up for the compulsory hour-long guided tour. A better idea is to head for the **town museum**, back along the street at Hradné námestie 55 (June–Sept Tues–Sun 9am–noon & 1–5pm; Oct–May Mon–Fri 9am–noon & 1–4pm), which contains, among other things, the personal effects of Countess Hedviga Mária Szirmayova-Badányiova. The helpful **tourist office** (Mon–Fri 8.30am–5pm, Sat & Sun 9am–2pm; winter closed Sun; ☎052/452 40 47, ⓦwww.kezmarok.net), on the main square at Hlavné námestie 46, can book cheap **private rooms**; otherwise the best option is the excellent *Hotel Club*, at ulica MUDr Alexandra (☎052/452 40 51, ⓔhotelclub@sinet.sk; ❸), an efficiently run, tastefully modernized place in the old town, with a great restaurant on the ground floor. For budget travellers there's the *Hotel Štart* (☎052/452 2916; ❷), which lies in the woods to the north of the castle, a good twenty-minute walk from the train station. The *Castellan Club* tucked into the side of the castle provides a watering hole late at night.

Levoča

Some 25km east of Poprad, across a broad sweep of Spiš countryside, the ravishingly beautiful walled town of **LEVOČA**, set on a slight incline, has a wonderfully medieval look, and is very much a Gothic and Renaissance haven. The Euclidian efficiency with which the old town is laid out means you'll inevitably end up at the main square, **námestie Majstra Pavla**. To the north is the square's least distinguished but most important building, the municipal weigh-house; a law of 1321 obliged every merchant passing through the region to hole up at Levoča for fourteen days, pay various taxes and allow the locals first refusal on their goods. Of the three freestanding buildings on the main square paid for with these riches, it's the Catholic church of **sv Jakub** (Mon 11/11.30am–4/5pm, Tues–Sat 8.30/9am–4/5pm, Sun 1–4/5pm; Oct–Easter closed Sun & Mon) that has the most valuable booty. The church can be visited only with a guide, and **tours** (every

30min, hourly in winter) leave from the *kassa* opposite the main entrance. Every nook and cranny is crammed with religious art, the star attraction being the magnificent sixteenth-century wooden **altarpiece** by Master Pavol of Levoča, which, at 18.6m, is reputedly the tallest of its kind in the world. A small **museum** (daily 9am–5pm) dedicated to Master Pavol stands opposite the church on the eastern side of the square. South of the church is the **town hall** (daily 9am–5pm), built in a sturdy Renaissance style. On the first floor, there's a museum on the Spiš region, and some fine examples of Spiš handicrafts on the top floor. The last building in the centre of the square is the oddly squat **Lutheran Church**, built in an uncompromisingly Neoclassical style.

Train services to Levoča were suspended at the time of writing, but it is easier anyway to get there by bus, from Poprad, Prešov or Košice. The **bus** and **train stations** are a ten-minute walk southeast of the old town. The **tourist office** (May–Sept Mon–Sat 9am–5pm, Sun 10am–2pm; Oct–April Mon–Fri 9am–4.30pm; ☎053/451 37 63, ⓦwww.levoca.sk) is located in the northwest corner of the main square. Outside the annual Catholic pilgrimage in early July to the church on Marianska Hora, the sacred hill to the north of town, **accommodation** shouldn't be hard to find. A reasonable option is the *Hotel Barbakan* at Košická 15 (☎053/451 43 10, ⓦwww.barbakan.sk; ❸), which includes a buffet breakfast in the price; alternatively, there are several cheaper pensions in town, including the *Penzión pri Košickej bráne* (☎053/451 28 79; ❷), next door to the *Barbakan*. There's also a good **campsite**, *Kováčova vila*, 3km north of Levoča. Authentic Slovak pub **food** can be had from *U Janusa*, Klástorská 22 (Sat & Sun by reservation only), and from the atmospheric *U troch apoštolov*, above a butcher's, on the east side of the main square. There's a self-service lunchtime-only vegetarian restaurant, *Vegeterián*, at Uholná 3 (closed Sat & Sun), northwest of the main square, and the self-explanatory *Pizzeria* nearby on Vetrová.

Spišský hrad

The road east from Levoča takes you to the edge of Spiš territory, clearly defined by the Branisko ridge, which blocks the way to Prešov. Even if you're not going any further east, you should at least take the bus as far as **SPIŠSKÉ PODHRADIE**, for perhaps the most spectacular sight in the whole country – the **Spišský hrad** (daily 8.30am–5/6pm). This pile of chalk-white ruins, strung out on a bleak hill, is irresistibly photogenic and finds its way into almost every tourist brochure. The ruins themselves don't quite live up to expectations, though the view from the top is pretty spectacular. The *Penzión Podzámok* at Podzámková 28 (☎053/454 17 55; ❶) is a good **place to stay**, with superb views up to the castle.

Prešov

Capital of the Slovak Šariš region and a cultural centre for the Rusyn (Ruthenian) minority, **PREŠOV** has been treated to a wonderful face-lift over the last few years. There's not much of interest beyond its main square, but it's a refreshingly youthful and vibrant town, partly due to its university. The lozenge-shaped main square, **Hlavná ulica**, is flanked by creamy, pastel-coloured eighteenth-century facades. At the square's southern tip is the **Greek-Catholic Cathedral**, a wonderful Rococo affair with a huge iconostasis. Further along, on the same side of the square, is Prešov's **town hall**, from whose unsuitably small balcony Béla Kun's Hungarian Red Army declared the short-lived Slovak Socialist Republic in 1919. Further north along the square, the **town museum**, situated in the dogtooth-gabled Rákociho dom at no. 86 (Tues–Fri 9am–noon & 12.30–5/6pm, Sun 1–6pm), offers a thorough retelling of the history of the town and the Šariš region. Prešov's Catholic and Protestant churches vie with each other at the widest point of the square. The fourteenth-century Catholic church of **sv Mikuláš** has the edge, not least for its modern Moravian stained-glass windows and its sumptuous Baroque altarpiece. Behind sv Mikulás, the much plainer **Lutheran Church**, built in the mid-seventeenth century, bears witness to the strength of religious reformism in the outer reaches of Hungary at a time when the rest of the Habsburgs' lands were suffering the full force of the Counter-Reformation. Lastly, the town's ornate *fin-de-siècle* **synagogue** in the northwest corner of the old town – access from Okružná – has been turned into a small **Museum of Judaica** (Tues & Wed 11am–4pm, Thurs 3–6pm, Fri 10am–1pm, Sun 1–5pm), with an exhibition on Judaism and the region's Jewish community, 6000 of whom perished in the Holocaust. The **bus** and **train stations** are opposite each other about 1km south of the main square; the best buses and trolleybuses into town are those which stop at Na Hlavnej. There's a **tourist office** (Mon–Fri 9am–5/6pm, Sat 9am–1pm; ☏051/16 186) near the town hall. The closest cheap **accommodation** to the centre is at the *Šariš*, Sabinovská 1 (☏051/771 63 51; ❷), 300m north of the main square; otherwise there's the smarter *Senator*, at Hlavná 67 (☏051/773 11 86; ❸), above the tourist office. A few **restaurants** spill out onto the square in summer, including the *Melódia* at no. 61, which has a comprehensive menu with some vegetarian dishes. For more traditional fare, try the basement *U richtára*, nearby at no. 71.

Košice

Slovak towns rarely amount to much more than their one long main square, and even **KOŠICE**, the country's second-largest city, is no exception. Rather like Bratislava, Košice was, until relatively recently, a modest little town on the edge of the Hungarian plain. Then, in the 1950s, the Communists established a giant steelworks on the outskirts of the city. Fifty years on, Košice has a population of around 250,000, a number of worthwhile museums, arguably Slovakia's finest cathedral, and a lively cosmopolitanism that can be quite reassuring after a journey in the back-of-beyond. Just 21km north of the Hungarian border, Košice also acts as a magnet for the Hungarian community – to whom the city is known as Kassa – and the underemployed Romanies of the surrounding region, lending it a diversity and vibrancy absent from small-town Slovakia.

Almost everything of interest is situated on Košice's long pedestrianized main square, which is called **Hlavná ulica** at its northern and southern extremities, **Hlavné námestie** to the north of the cathedral, and **námestie Slobody** to the south of the cathedral. Lined with handsome Baroque and Neoclassical palaces, it's dominated by the city's unorthodox Gothic **Cathedral of St Elizabeth**, its charcoal-coloured stone recently sandblasted back to its original honeyed hue. Begun in 1378, it's an unusual building from the outside, with striped roof tiles and two contorted towers. Inside, imposing Gothic furnishings add an impressive touch to an otherwise plain nave, the main gilded altar depicting scenes from the life of the cathedral's patron saint. On the busy north side of the cathedral is the fourteenth-century **Urbanova veža**, the town tower, standing on its own set of mini-arcades. The public park and fountains beyond are a favourite spot for hanging out and make an appropriately graceful approach to the city's grand Austro-Hungarian **theatre**. The peculiar **Vojtech Löffler Museum** at Alžbetina 20 (Tues–Sat 10am–6pm, Sun 1–5pm), west off the main square, features the work and private collections of Košice's most prominent Communist-sanctioned sculptor. Another unusual attraction is the **Mikluš Prison** (Tues–Sat 9am–5pm, Sun 9am–1pm), east off the square down Univerzitna, whose original dimly lit dungeons and claustrophobic cells graphically transport you into its history as the city prison and torture chamber. At the northern tip of the main square, námestie Maratónu mieru is flanked to the east and west by the bulky nineteenth-century **East Slovak Museum** (Tues–Sat 9am–5pm, Sun 10am–1pm). The western building is worth visiting for its basement collection of fifteenth- to seventeenth-century **gold coins** – 2920 in all – minted at Kremnica, but stashed away by city burghers and discovered by accident in 1935. Hidden round the back of the museum is a wooden **Greek-Catholic church**, brought here from the Ukrainian borderlands.

②⑤

The **train** and **bus stations** are opposite each other, ten minutes' walk east of the old town. There's a small but helpful **tourist office** (Mon–Fri 9am–5/6pm, Sat 9am–1/2pm; ☎055/16 186) in the Dargov department store on the corner of Hlavná and Štúrova, which can help with finding **rooms**. Otherwise, try *Atlantic*, Rázusova 1 (☎055/622 65 01; ❷), a small, central pension that's often fully booked, so it's worth calling well in advance. *Ubytovania*, Jesenského 20 (☎055/633 59 12; 200Sk), offers **hostel** accommodation to the east of the main square, and cheap dorm beds are also available at several student hostels, including one at Podhradová 11 (☎055/633 34 37; 100Sk; July & Aug only). The nearest **campsite** (closed Oct to mid-April) is 5km south of the city centre and also rents out bungalows; take tram #4 or bus #52 from the *Slovan* hotel to the flyover, then get off and walk 500m west along Alejová, the road to Rožňava. The best **places to eat** are located in the streets to the east of the main square: *Ajvega*, Orlia 10, is a popular vegetarian place with a summer terrace, and serves soya versions of standard Slovak dishes, washed down with fresh juices. The seafood and fish restaurant *Caravella*, just up the street at Orlia 4, does an admirable job considering its distance from the ocean, while *Sedliacky dvor*, at Biela 3, is a hymn to Slovak folk culture and cuisine. *Kleopatra Pizza Bar*, at Hlavná 24, occupies a fine setting, with outdoor tables overlooking the gardens to the south of the cathedral. Košice's **nightlife** revolves around the main square, where there are plenty of options for drinking: the *Music Pub Diesel* at Hlavná 92, *Keltská Krčma* at no. 80 and *Bernard's Club* at Alžbetina 4 all have frequent live music and a good atmosphere. You can also catch **live jazz** most nights at the city's smoky *Jazz Club*, Kováčska 39. Mainstream culture predominates in Košice, though the city also boasts a **Hungarian theatre**, Thália, on Mojmírova, and Slovakia's one and only **Romany theatre**, Romathan, Štefánikova 4, which puts on a range of events from concerts to plays. The tourist office stocks the free **listings** booklet *Kultúrny informačník*. You can access the **Internet** at *Net Club*, Hlavná 9.

Travel details

Trains

Bratislava to: Banská Bystrica (1 daily; 3hr 45min); Poprad-Tatry (every 2hr; 4hr 40min); Košice (every 2hr; 6hr).
Poprad-Tatry to: Starý Smokovec (hourly; 35min); Košice (hourly; 1hr 15min).

Buses

Levoča to: Spišské Podhradie (up to 10 daily; 30min).
Poprad to: Kežmarok (every 30min; 20min); Levoča (hourly; 30–50min); Spišské Podhradie (up to 6 daily; 30–45min); Prešov (hourly; 2hr).

Slovenia

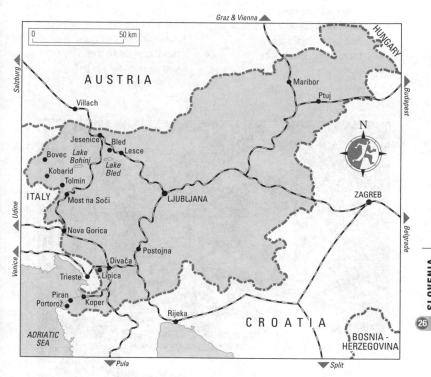

Slovenia highlights

* **Old Town, Ljubljana**
  Stunning architecture, a hilltop castle and leafy riverside cafés adorn the alluring Slovenian capital. **See p.814**

* **Lake Bohinj** Pearl of Slovenian lakes, less visited and more serene than Bled. **See p.821**

* **Kobarid Museum, Soča Valley** Beautiful valley, compelling museum. **See p.822**

* **Ptuj** Slovenia's oldest and prettiest town. **See p.823**

* **Postojna Caves** Subterranean wonderland, highlight of the Karst region. **See p.818**

Introduction and basics

Slovenia is the most stable, prosperous and welcoming of all Europe's erstwhile Communist countries. It was always the richest and most Westernized of the Yugoslav federation, and apart from the Ten-Day War which brought independence in 1991, it managed to avoid much of the strife which plagued the republics to the south. For centuries, Slovenia was administered by German-speaking overlords and was, until 1918, part of the Austro-Hungarian empire. The Slovenes absorbed the culture of their captors during this period while managing to retain a strong sense of ethnic identity through their Slavic language, a close relation of Czech, Serbo-Croat and Slovak.

The landscape is as varied as it is beautiful: along the Austrian border the **Julian Alps** provide stunning mountain scenery, most accessibly at **Lake Bled** and **Lake Bohinj**; further south, the brittle karst scenery is riddled with spectacular caves like those at **Postojna**. Slovenia's capital, **Ljubljana**, is easily the best of the cities, a vital, youthful place, manageably small and cluttered with Baroque and Habsburg buildings, while the short stretch of Slovenian coast, between Italy and Croatia, is punctuated by a couple of towns that were among the most attractive resorts of the former Yugoslavia – **Piran** and **Portorož**. On the main route east towards Budapest, the well-preserved town of **Ptuj** is also worth a visit.

Information & maps

Most towns and resorts have a **tourist information centre**, providing information and maps; some also act as an agency for private rooms. A high standard of English is spoken pretty much everywhere. Freytag & Berndt publishes a good 1:300,000 country **map**, while the Slovene Alpine Association's excellent hiking maps (ⓦ www.pzs.si) are widely available in bookshops.

Money and banks

Currency is the **tolar** (SIT), divided into 100 stotini. There are coins of 50 stotini and 1, 2, 5 and 10SIT; and notes of 10, 20, 50, 100, 200, 500, 1000, 5000 and 10,000SIT. **Banks** (*banka*) generally open Mon–Fri 8.30am–12.30pm & 2–5pm, Sat 8.30am–11am/noon. You can also change money in tourist offices, post offices, travel agencies and exchange bureaux (*menjalnica*), all of which have more flexible hours. Credit cards are accepted in a large number of hotels and restaurants, and ATMs are widespread. Prices for accommodation and tours are sometimes given in euros – although you usually pay in tolars.

Communications

Most **post offices** (*pošta*) are open Mon–Fri 8am–6/7pm and Sat 8am–noon/1pm. Stamps (*znamke*) can also be bought at newsstands. Public **phones** use cards (*telekartice*; 700, 1000, 1700 and 3500SIT), buyable from post offices, kiosks and tobacconists. It's usually easier to make long-distance and international calls at a post office, where you're assigned to a cabin and given the bill afterwards. **Internet** access is quite poor, even in the capital. Where you do find

SLOVENIA | Basics

Slovenia on the net

ⓦ **www.matkurja.com** Comprehensive site.
ⓦ **www.slovenia-tourism.si** Official tourist board site.
ⓦ **www.ljubljana.si** Detailed information on sights and events in the capital.
ⓦ **www.burger.si** Superb interactive maps and panoramic photos.

a terminal – the local library is your best bet – expect to pay around 300SIT/hr.

Getting around

Traversing Slovenia by public transport is relatively easy and usually very scenic. Slovene Railways (Slovenske železnice; ⓦwww .slo-zeleznice.si) is smooth and efficient. **Trains** (*vlaki*) are divided into *potniški* (which stop at every halt) and *IC* (intercity). Some of the latter, colloquially known as *zeleni vlaki* ("green trains") and designated on timetables by the initials ICZV, are express services on which prior seat reservations (*rezervacije*) are obligatory. Most timetables have English notes, and timetable leaflets (*vozni red*) are sometimes available from counters; "departures" is *odhodi*, "arrivals" is *prihodi*. Eurail and InterRail are valid. The **bus** network consists of an array of local companies, but their services are well co-ordinated. Towns such as Ljubljana, Maribor and Koper have big bus stations with computerized booking facilities where you can buy your tickets hours or days in advance – recommended if you're travelling between Ljubljana and the coast in high season. Elsewhere, simply pile onto the bus and pay the driver or conductor. You'll be charged extra for cumbersome items of baggage, like a backpack, which must be stored in the hold.

Accommodation

While tourist **accommodation** is universally clean and good quality, it's not much cheaper than in neighbouring Italy or Austria – unless you opt for a private room. Apart from a couple of *fin-de-siècle* establishments in Ljubljana, Slovene **hotels** tend to be high-rise concrete affairs providing modern comforts but little atmosphere. Anything lower than two-star is very rare. Expect to pay £30/$45 upwards for a double at two-star hotels, £40/$60 upwards for a three-star. Family-run **pensions** in rural areas, especially the mountains, offer the same facilities as hotels but usually with a cosier atmosphere and a lower price. Outside alpine resorts, however, pensions tend to be well away

from town centres. **Private rooms** (*zasebne sobe*) are available throughout Slovenia, with bookings administered by the tourist office in Ljubljana or travel agents like Slovenijaturist or Kompas elsewhere (which are usually open daily 9am–7/8pm in summer). Rooms are pretty good value at about £14–20/$21–30 a double, although stays of three nights or under are invariably subject to a thirty-percent surcharge. Self-catering **apartments** (*apartmaji*) are also plentiful in the mountains and on the coast, with per-person rates working out the same as, or sometimes cheaper than, private rooms if you're travelling in a group of more than two people.

Hostels are thin on the ground, although there's a scattering of student dorms (*dijaški dom*) which open their doors to non-students over the summer and at weekends at other times of year. Advance booking is advised. Expect to pay about £8–12/$12–18 per person per night. **Campsites** are plentiful in the mountains and on the coast and tend to have good facilities, restaurants and shops. Two people travelling with a tent can expect to pay £8–10/$12–15; add another £2/$3 for a vehicle. The majority of campsites are open from May to September. Camping rough without permission is punishable by a spot fine.

Food and drink

Slovene **cuisine** draws on Austrian, Italian and Balkan influences. There's a native tradition, too, based on age-old peasant recipes, although this is gradually losing out as restaurants and cafés become increasingly international. Supermarkets and *delikatesa* are good places to stock up on **picnic** ingredients, like local cheese (*sir*) and salami (*salama*). Buy fresh fruit and vegetables from outdoor markets or roadside stalls, and bread (*kruh*) from a *pekarna* (bakery). For **breakfast** and **snacks**, *okrepčevalnice* (snack bars) and street kiosks dole out *burek*, a flaky pastry filled with cheese (*sirov burek*) or meat (*burek z mesom*). Sausages come in various forms, most commonly hot dogs, *hrenovke* (Slovene frankfurters), or *kranjska klobasa* (big spicy sausages).

Menus in a *restavracija* (restaurant) or *gostilna* (inn) are dominated by roast meats (*pečenka*) and schnitzels (*zrezek*), mostly pork (*svinjina*) and veal (*teletina*). Liver (*jetra*) and grilled or fried brains (*možgani*) are popular standbys in cheaper restaurants. Goulash (*golaž*) is found almost everywhere; *segedin* is goulash with lashings of sauerkraut. Two traditional dishes are *žlikrofi*, ravioli filled with potato, onion and bacon; and *žganci*, once the staple diet of rural Slovenes, a buckwheat or maize porridge often served with sauerkraut. *Ocvrti sir* (cheese fried in breadcrumbs) is one of the few dishes that will appease vegetarians. On the coast you'll find plenty of fish (*riba*), mussels (*žkoljke*) and squid (*kalamari*). Italian pasta dishes appear on most restaurant menus, and no Slovene high street is without at least one pizzeria. Typical **desserts** include strudel filled with apple or rhubarb; *žtruklji*, dumplings with fruit filling; *potica*, a doughy roll filled with nuts and honey; and *prekmurska gibanica*, a delicious local cheesecake.

Daytime **drinking** takes place in small café/bars, or in a *kavarna*, where a range of cakes, pastries and ice cream is usually on offer. Coffee (*kava*) is usually served black unless specified otherwise – ask for *mleko* (milk) or *smetana* (cream) – and often drunk alongside a glass of mineral water (*mineralna voda*). Tea (*čaj*) is usually served black. Evening haunts include bars or the more traditional *pivnica* (beer hall) or *vinarna* (wine cellar). Slovene **beer** (*pivo*) is usually excellent (*Laško Zlatorog* is considered the best), although most breweries also produce *temno pivo* ("dark beer"), a Guinness-like stout. The local **wine** (*vino*) is either *črno* (red) or *belo* (white) and has an international reputation: dry whites like *Lazki rizling* and *Ljutomerčan* are regularly found on Western supermarket shelves. Best of the reds are the light *Cviček* and the dark, dry *Kraški teran*. Favourite aperitifs include *slivovka* (plum brandy), *vilijemovka* (pear brandy), the fiery *sadjevec*, a brandy made from various fruits, and the gin-like *brinovec*.

Opening hours and holidays

Most **shops** open Mon–Fri 8am–7pm and Sat 8am–1pm; an increasing number open on Sun. Some shops outside major centres take lengthy lunch breaks. Museum times vary, but most are usually closed on Mon. All shops and banks are closed on **public holidays**: Jan 1 & 2; Feb 8; Easter Mon; April 27; May 1 & 2; June 25; Aug 15; Oct 31; Nov 1; Dec 25 & 26.

Emergencies

You're unlikely to have much contact with the **police** (*policija*); they're generally easy-going and likely to speak some basic English. EU citizens are entitled to free health care. **Pharmacies** (*lekarna*) follow shop hours, and a rota system covers night-time and weekend opening; details are posted in the window of each pharmacy.

Emergency numbers

Police ☎113; ambulance and fire ☎112.

SLOVENIA | Basics

26

Ljubljana

The Slovene capital **LJUBLJANA** curls under its castle-topped hill, an old centre marooned in the shapeless modernity that stretches out across the plain, a vital and self-consciously growing capital. The city's sights are only part of the picture; first and foremost Ljubljana is a place to meet people and to get involved in the nightlife – the buildings just provide the backdrop.

Arrival, information and accommodation

Your likely point of arrival (and drop-off point for buses from Brnik airport, 23km north of the city) is the main **train and bus station**, located on Trg Osvobodilne fronte, ten minutes' walk north of the centre. The main **Tourist Information Office (TIC)** is in the old town on Stritarjeva next to the Triple Bridge (daily 8/10am–6/8pm; ☏01/306-1215, ⊛www.ljubljana.si); there's also an information office at the train station (Mon–Fri 8/10am–5.30/9pm; June–Sept also Sat & Sun; ☏01/433-9475). Ljubljana's buses are cheap and frequent. You can pay on the bus – put your money in a box next to the driver (230SIT per journey) – or buy tokens (*žetoni*; 170SIT) in advance, sold at post offices and most newspaper kiosks. The TIC has a limited stock of central **private rooms** (❸), which can only be booked on the day.

Hotels

AA Lipa Celovška 264 ☏01/507-4822, ⊛aa-lipa@siol.net. Grim place poorly located 5km northwest of the centre, but one of the cheapest options going. Buses #1, #15, #16. ❸

BIT Center Litijska 57 ☏01/548-0055, ⊛www.bit-center.net. Modern, functional rooms in this sports centre 2km east of the centre; 50-percent discount on use of sporting facilities and free use of pool in summer. Buses # 5, #9 and #13. ❸

City Hotel Turist Dalmatinova 15 ☏01/234-9130, ⊛www.hotelturist.si. Decent, if a little pricey, downtown hotel just a 5min walk from stations. ❺

M Hotel Derčeva 4 ☏01/513-7000, ⊛www.m-hotel.si. Neat and bright modern hotel, 2.5km northwest of the city centre off Celovška cesta. ❺

Park Tabor 9 ☏01/433-1306, ⊛hotel.park@siol.net. High-rise located amidst a jumble of apartment buildings a few blocks east of the station with shabby, bare rooms, some with en-suite facilities. ❹

Pri Mraku Rimska 4 ☏01/421-9600, ⊛www.daj-dam.si. Perky downtown pension, with colourful, cosy rooms. 10-percent discount for stays of more than 3 nights. ❺

Hostels

Dijaški Dom Ivana Cankarja Poljanska 26 ☏01/474-8600. Student hostel, open July & Aug only. 3000SIT.

Dijaški Dom Poljane Potočnikova 3 ☏01/300-3137. Another student hostel option. July & Aug only. 3000SIT.

Dijaški Dom Tabor Vidovdanska 7 ☏01/234-8840. Most central of the student hostels. July & Aug only. 3000SIT.

Youth hostel Metelkova 9 ☏01/430-1890. By far the best budget option – a brilliant new hostel, reconstructed in a former military prison, 10min walk from the stations. 2500–4000SIT.

Campsite

Ježica ☏01/568-3913. Pleasant site 5km north. Bus #6 or #8 north along Dunajska cesta. Also has a few bungalows (❸).

The City

Ljubljana's main point of reference is **Slovenska cesta**, a busy north–south thoroughfare that slices the city down the middle. Most of the sights are within easy walking distance of here, with the Old Town straddling the River Ljubljanica to the south and east and the nineteenth-century quarter to the west, where the principal museums and galleries are to be found.

From the bus and train stations head south down Miklošičeva for ten minutes and you're on **Prešernov trg**, the hub around which everything in Ljubljana's delightful Old Town revolves. Overlooking the bustling square and the River Ljubljanica, the Baroque seventeenth-century **Franciscan Church** (daily 9am–noon & 3–7pm), blushes a sandy-red; despite its weary-looking interior, it's worth a look for Francesco

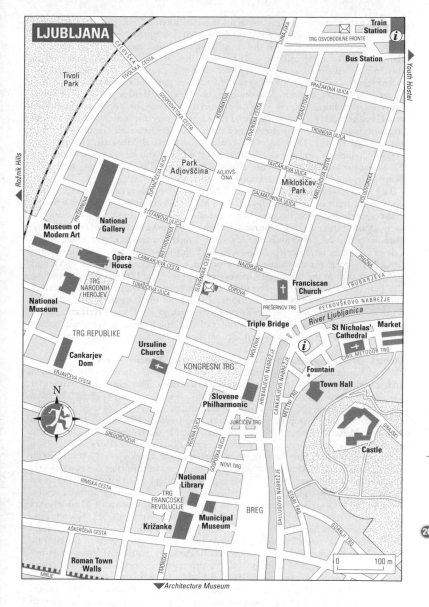

LJUBLJANA

Train Station

TRG OSVOBODILNE FRONTE

Bus Station

Youth Hostel

Tivoli Park

Rožnik Hills

Park Adjovščina

ADJOVŠČINA

Miklošičev Park

Museum of Modern Art

National Gallery

Opera House

TRG NARODNIH HEROJEV

National Museum

TRG REPUBLIKE

Cankarjev Dom

Ursuline Church

KONGRESNI TRG

Franciscan Church

PREŠERNOV TRG

Triple Bridge

River Ljubljanica

St Nicholas' Cathedral

Market

Fountain

Town Hall

CIRIL METODOR TRG

Slovene Philharmonic

JURČIČEV TRG

Castle

National Library

TRG FRANCOSKE REVOLUCIJE

NOVI TRG

BREG

Križanke

Municipal Museum

Roman Town Walls

MIRJE

Architecture Museum

0   100 m

Robba's marble high altar, richly adorned with spiral columns and plastic figurines. Robba, an Italian architect and sculptor, was brought in to remodel the city in its eighteenth-century heyday. There's more of his work across the elegant Tromostovje, or **Triple Bridge**, the most distinguished of which is a beautifully sculpted **fountain**, symbolizing the meeting of the rivers Sava, Krka and Ljubljanica. Opposite the fountain on cobbled Mestni trg is the **Town Hall** (Magistrat) – an undistinguished Baroque building, but which has some interesting sgraffiti in the courtyard. The area south of here is crammed with colourful Baroque town houses, pavement cafés and boutiques. A little east of Mestni trg, on Ciril-Metodov trg, **St Nicholas' Cathedral** (daily 6am–noon & 3–6pm) is the most sumptuous and overblown of Ljubljana's Baroque statements. Smothered with fabulous frescoes, this is the best preserved of the city's ecclesiastical buildings. Just to the west of the cathedral buildings, along the riverside, you can't fail to miss the brash, free-for-all **general market** (not Sun). Just beyond the market, take a look at the beautiful **Dragon Bridge**, each corner pylon topped with spitting dragons – the city symbol. Opposite the market, Študentovska winds up the thickly wooded hillside to the **Castle**, originally a twelfth-century construction but whose present appearance dates from the sixteenth-century following the earthquake of 1511. Within the castle is the **Virtual Museum** (10am–7pm; 700SIT), which presents the development of the city in the form of an enlightening 3D visual presentation. Climb the **clock tower** for a superlative view of the Old Town below and the magnificent Kamniške Alps to the north.

Back on the western side of the river, the broad slash of **Slovenska cesta** forms the commercial heart of Ljubljana, though it's a place to do business rather than sightsee. Further south along here, the park-like expanse of Kongresni trg slopes away from the early-eighteenth-century **Ursuline Church** (Uršulinska Cerkev), whose looming Baroque coffee-cake exterior is one of the city's most impressive. Lower down, by the side of the main university building, Vegova Ulica leads south from Kongresni trg towards Trg francoske revolucije, passing on the way the chequered pink, green and grey brickwork of the **National University Library**. The **Illyrian Monument** on Trg francoske revolucije was erected in 1930 in belated recognition of Napoleon's short-lived attempt to create a fiefdom of the same name centred on Ljubljana. Virtually next door is the seventeenth-century monastery complex of **Križanke**: originally the seat of a thirteenth-century order of Teutonic Knights, its delightful colonnaded courtyard was restored to form a permanent venue for the Summer Festival.

West of Slovenska: museums and Tivoli Park

West of Slovenska, Cankarjeva heads down towards a neatly ordered corner of town that contains the city's most important **museums**. The **National Museum** (Tues–Sun 10am–6pm, Thurs till 8pm; 500SIT; ⊛www.narmuz-lj.si), at Muzejska 1, has its permanent collection under wraps until at least 2005, but they do present an excellent rota of temporary exhibitions. The building also houses the **Natural History Museum** (same hours and ticket), notable for having the one complete mammoth skeleton found in Europe. The **National Gallery** (Tues–Sun 10am–6pm; 500SIT, free Sat pm; ⊛www.ng-slo.si) at Cankarjeva 20 is housed in the former Narodni Dom, built in the 1890s to accommodate Slovene cultural institutions in defiance of the Habsburgs. The gallery is rich in local medieval Gothic work, although most visitors gravitate towards the halls devoted to the Slovene Impressionists. Diagonally across from here the **Museum of Modern Art** at Cankarjeva 15 (Tues–Sat 10am–6/7pm, Sun 10am–1pm; 400SIT; ⊛www.mg-lj.si) carries on where the National Gallery left off, showing how the Slovene Impressionists developed more experimental styles in the early years of the twentieth century. Beyond the galleries lies **Tivoli Park**, an expanse of lawns and tree-lined walkways backed by dense woodland, perfect for a short ramble. A villa above the centre contains the most enjoyable of Ljubljana's museums, the **Museum of Modern History** (Tues–Sun 10am–6pm; 500SIT, free first Sun of the month; ⊛www.muzej-nz.si) with dioramas, video screens and period music combining to produce an evocative journey through twentieth-century Slovene history, including the Ten-Day War of Independence in 1991.

Eating, drinking and nightlife

Ljubljana boasts a tight concentration of **restaurants**, most of which offer excellent value for money. The best choice for **snacks** are the burek kiosks near the stations and the stands scattered throughout town selling hot dogs and the local *gorenjska* sausages. The **market** is on Vodnikov trg. On summer evenings the **cafés and bars** of Ljubljana's Old Town spill out onto the streets. A wander up and down the riverbanks and along Stari trg and Mestni trg will yield an interesting hostelry every 50m or so. The free English-language magazine *Ljubljana Life* (Ⓦwww.ljubljanalife .com), available from the tourist office, has excellent **bar** and **club** listings. The Cankarjev Dom, Prešernova 10, is the scene of major orchestral and theatrical events, as well as occasional folk and jazz concerts (ticket office Mon–Fri 10am–2pm & 4.30–8pm, Sat 10am–1pm; also 1hr before performance). The Slovenska Filharmonija orchestra performs at Kongresni trg 9, while the National Opera and Ballet Theatre is at Županičeva 1 (ticket office Mon–Fri 2–5pm, Sat 6–7pm; also 1hr before performance). The **International Summer Festival** (July & Aug; Ⓦwww.festival-lj.si) features orchestral concerts at major venues. The free monthly *Where To? Events* pamphlet, from the tourist office, has complete listings.

Restaurants

Casa del Papa Celovška 54a. International food in rooms decorated on an Ernest Hemingway theme (Key West room, Cuba room and so on). Closed Sun.

Emonska klet Plečnikov trg 1. Once the halls of the Ursuline convent, this capacious cellar restaurant serves up pizzas, salads and Slovenian dishes. Nightly live music and a cracking bar turns this into a bit of a party place in the evenings.

Figovec Gosposvetska 1. Charmingly old-fashioned downtown restaurant specializing in pony steaks (sic), horsemeat goulash and traditional Slovene standards.

Joe Pena's Cankarjeva 6. Bright, breezy and very popular – the city's best Mexican restaurant.

Julija Stari trg 9. A simple eatery in a lovely Old Town location, with decent salads, pastas and seafood dishes.

Pizzeria Foculus Gregorčičeva 3. Extensive range of pizzas in lively surroundings, including several vegetarian options and a generous salad buffet.

Šestica Slovenska 40. Traditional place on the main street with elegant vine-trellised interior. Slovene, meat-heavy menu. Closed Sun.

Zlata Ribica Cankarjevo Nabrežje 5. With arguably the best outdoor dining area in the city, this modest and inexpensive fish restaurant by the River Ljubljanica is delightful.

Cafés and bars

Bi-Ko-Fe Židovska steza 1. Artsy, colourful café with an imaginative range of coffees.

Čajna Hiša Stari trg 3. Bijou café serving the best teas in town, excellent sandwiches and cakes and decent breakfasts. Closed Sun.

Café Gaudi Nazorjeva 10. Delightful interior and seductive range of coffees makes this a terrific place for a coffee stop.

Cutty Sark Knafljev prehod 1. A more straightforward drinking venue, with draft beers and a more raucous atmosphere.

Le Petite Café Trg francoske revolucije 4. Wonderful place, ideal for a coffee and croissant during the day or a glass of wine in the evening.

Maček Krojaška 5. Hip café with large outdoor terrace; the place to be seen on Ljubljana's riverfront, and consequently crammed. Happy hour 4–7pm.

Pr'skelet Ključavničarska 5. Devilishly original bar – it's full of skeletons.

Ragamuffin Krojaška 4. In an alleyway just behind *Maček* (see above). Small, reggae-oriented café/bar, good for a daytime chill-out or more boisterous evening drink.

Clubs and discos

Gajo Jazz Club Beethovnova 8. Refined late-night jazz club with quality offerings by both domestic and foreign acts. See Ⓦwww.jazzclubgajo.com for programme.

Hound Dog At *M Hotel*, Derčeva 4. Animated basement bar with regular live rock music. A fifteen-minute walk northeast of the centre.

K4 Kersnikova 4. Stalwart of Ljubljana's alternative scene, offering different styles of music on different nights – including at least one gay night a week.

KUD Prešeren Karunova 14. Superb gig venue which also has regular literary events, workshops and art exhibitions.

Metelkova mesto Metelkova cesta. Ljubljana's alternative cultural Mecca, consisting of a cosmopolitan gang of clubs and bars (collectively entitled Metelkova), is located in the former army barracks near the youth hostel.

Orto Bar Grablovičeva 1. Stylish media haunt east of the train station with pumping disco tunes and frequent live-rock evenings.

SLOVENIA | Ljubljana

26

Listings

Embassies and consulates Australia, Trg republike 3 ☎01/425-4252; Canada, Miklošičeva 19 ☎01/430-3570; UK, Trg republike 3 ☎01/200-3910; US, Prešernova 31 ☎01/200-5500.
Exchange At the train station and *Menjalnica* on Pogarčarjev trg.
Hospital Bohoričeva 4 ☎01/232-3060.
Internet access Čerin, Trubarjeva 52 (closed Sat & Sun); library in train station underpass (closed Sat & Sun).
Laundry Chemo-express, Wolfova 12 (closed Sat & Sun; ☎01/251-4404).
Left luggage Train station (24hr).
Pharmacy Lekarna Miklošič, Miklošičeva 24 ☎01/231-4558 (24hr).
Post office Slovenska 32 and Trg Osvobodilne fronte 5.

The rest of Slovenia

Emphatically not to be missed while you're in Ljubljana is a visit to the **Postojna Caves** – easily managed either as a day-trip from the capital or en route south to Slovene Istria, to Croatia or to Italy. A more low-key alternative to the cave stopoff is **Lipica**, where the celebrated white Lipizzaner horses are bred, or **Predjamski Grad**, near Postojna, an atmospherically sombre castle high above a cave entrance in the midst of a dramatic landscape. Close to the Italian and Croatian borders, the towns of **Slovene Istria** have long been popular resorts, yet have still managed to retain some charm and identity. Much of this stems from their Italian character, a legacy of four hundred years of Venetian rule. The main draw is **Piran**, which, with its cobbled piazzas, shuttered houses and back alleys laden with laundry, is almost overwhelmingly pretty, while **Portorož** is Slovenia's brashest beach resort. Within easy reach northwest of Ljubljana are the mountain lakes of **Bled** and **Bohinj**. The magnificent **Soča valley**, on the western side of the Slovene alps, is much less touristed, although small towns like **Kobarid** and **Bovec** are excellent bases for hiking and adventure sports. East of Ljubljana on the main route to Hungary, **Ptuj** is Slovenia's oldest town and one of its most attractive.

Postojna and Predjamski Grad

POSTOJNA is on the main rail route south, 65km from Ljubljana, but as the walk to the caves from Postojna train station is further than from the bus stop, most people go by one of the regular buses. Once in the town, signs direct you to the **caves** (daily 9/10am–4/6pm; tours every 1–2hr, last tour 1hr before closing; 2600SIT, ⓦwww.postojna-cave.com). Inside, a railway whizzes you through 2km of preliminary systems before the guided tour starts. The vast and fantastic jungles of rock formations are quite breathtaking. Your best bet for **accommodation** in Postojna are private rooms (❷), arranged by Kompas in the town centre at Titov trg 2a (Mon–Fri 8am–7pm, Sat 9am–1pm; ☎05/726-4281, ✉info@kompas-postojna.si); they're also the best source of information on the town and the caves. The *Kras* **hotel**, in the centre at Tržaška 1 (☎05/726-4071; ❹), is extremely drab. There's a **campsite**, the *Pivka Jama* (☎05/726-5382), 4km beyond the cave entrance en route to Predjamski Grad, which also has four-person bungalows for about £12/$18 per person. *Pizzeria Minutka*, at Ljubljankska 14, is a pleasant alternative to the tourist eateries by the caves.

Well signposted 7km northwest of the caves, but not served by public transport (it's a pleasant walk) is **Predjamski Grad** (daily 9/10am–4/7pm; 600SIT). Pushed up high against a cave entrance in the midst of karst landscape, this sixteenth-century castle is an impressive sight and affords excellent views of the surrounding countryside. Its damp and rather melancholy interior is less rewarding, though there are a few interesting exhibits from this and an earlier castle that stood nearby. There are **guided tours** of the cave below the castle (May–Sept daily 11am, 1pm, 3pm & 5pm; 800SIT).

Lipica

Located 7km west of the drab railway-junction town of Divača near the Italian border, **LIPICA** gave its name to the Lipizzaner horses associated with Vienna's Spanish Riding School. There are three hundred horses here, the results of fastidious breeding that can be dated back to 1580, when the Austrian Archduke Charles established the farm in order to add Spanish and Arab blood to the Lipizzaner strain that was first used by the Romans for chariot races. Tours are given round the **stud farm** (daily 9/11am–3/6pm; 1300SIT; ⊚www.lipica.org), and the horses give the elegant displays for which they're famous (April Fri & Sun 3pm; May–Oct Tues, Fri & Sun 3pm; 2500SIT). Guided group rides (3700SIT) are also possible. Public transport is poor: a few **buses** run from Sežana, 5km north of Lipica, on weekday mornings, but you have little time to look around before catching the last bus back. The alternatives include spending a (expensive) night here in one of the hotels – the *Klub* or *Maestoso* (both ☎05/739-1580; ❺), walking or hitching.

The coast: Portorož and Piran

Easily reached by bus from the coastal town of Koper, **PORTOROŽ** ("Port of Roses") sprawls at the end of a long, tapering peninsula that projects like a lizard's tail north into the Adriatic. Known as early as the end of the nineteenth century for its mild climate and the health-inducing properties of its salty mud baths, the resort is now a vibrant strip of hotels and (largely concrete) beaches. Combining Portorož's modernity with the charm of Piran (a short bus ride or forty-minute walk away; see below) is the key to enjoying this brash, consumption-oriented place. The **tourist office** is on the main coastal strip, Obala Maršala Tita, just down from the bus terminal (July & Aug 9am–1.30pm & 3–9pm; rest of year 10am–5pm; ☎05/674-0231, ⊚www.portoroz.si), with **private rooms** (❷) available from Maona, just opposite.

    PIRAN, at the tip of the peninsula 4km from Portorož's bus station, couldn't be more different. Its web of arched alleys, tightly packed ranks of houses and little Italianate squares are simply delightful. The centre, 200m around the harbour from where the buses stop, is **Tartinijev trg**, named after the eighteenth-century Italian violinist and composer Giuseppe Tartini, who was born in a house on the square and is commemorated by a bronze statue in the centre. With its striking oval-shaped interior, it's one of the loveliest squares on this coast, fringed by a mix of Venetian palaces and a grand-looking Austrian town hall. Across the harbour, in the Gabrielli Palace, the **Maritime Museum** (Tues–Sun 9am–noon & 3/6–6/9pm; 500SIT) houses a collection of fine model ships, along with an interesting display on Piran's salt industry. Follow Ulica IX Korpusa uphill from the square to the barnlike Baroque **Church of Sv Jurij**, crowning a commanding spot on the far side of Piran's peninsula. Five minutes' walk further up, the town's formidable sixteenth-century **walls** stagger across the hill, the remaining towers providing excellent views of the town and the Adriatic. Piran's **tourist office** is on Tartinijev trg (July & Aug daily 9am–1.30pm & 3–9pm; rest of year Mon–Fri 9am–4pm, Sat 10am–2pm; ☎05/673-0220). **Rooms** can be booked through Maona, between the bus station and the square at Cankarjevo nabrežje 7 (☎05/673-4520). The **HI hostel**, *Val*, in the old town at Gregorčičeva 38 (☎05/673-2555, ⊚www.hostel-val.com; ❸), has excellent facilities, as well as a delightful restaurant. The Fiesa **campsite** is 1km away – follow the trail from the church. For **eating**, the main square offers a couple of good possibilities; *Batana,* on Kidričevo Nabrežje, is a stylish pizzeria with pleasant terrace, and *Mario,* up a flight of steps from Tartinijev trg, has good-value fish and meat dishes. Numerous more expensive seafood restaurants line the seafront. *Kavana Galerija Tartini,* on Tartinijev trg, is the most relaxing place for a daytime or evening **drink**. Liveliest of the **bars** is *Da Noi,* a cellar-like space next to the *Pavel* restaurant on the seafront.

26

Bled and Bohinj

Some 50km northwest of Ljubljana, towards Austria and at the eastern end of the Julian Alps, are the mountain lakes of **Bled** and **Bohinj**, Slovenia's premier tourist attractions. Whilst Bled is more popular, Bohinj, encircled by a majestic shaft of mountains, is far more stunning. If you're interested in serious **hiking**, good maps are essential: your best bets are the 1:50,000 *Triglav National Park*, the 1:25,000 *Mount Triglav* and the 1:25,000 *Bled and environs* – all published by the Slovene alpine association. Pick them up in Ljubljana bookshops or from the tourist offices in Bled and Ribčev Laz. **Buses** are the easiest way to get here (hourly from Ljubljana; 1hr 15min to Bled, 2hr to Bohinj). **Rail** access to the region is either via the main northbound line from Ljubljana, which calls at Bled-Lesce 3km southeast of Bled (and linked to Bled by a regular bus), or a branch line which leaves the main Ljubljana–Villach route at Jesenice and crosses the mountains towards Italy and the coast, calling at Bled-Jezero and Bohinjska Bistrica. The trip from Jesenice, chugging steadily through the mountains and karst, is wonderful. A **steam train** is laid on in summer months, at considerable additional expense (8000SIT).

Bled

There's no denying that the lake resort of **BLED** has all the right ingredients for a memorable visit – a placid mirror lake with a romantic island, a fairy-tale castle high on a bluff, leafy lanes and a backdrop of snow-tipped mountains. In summer, the lake, fed by warm-water springs that take the water temperature up to 26°C, forms the setting for a whole host of water sports – major rowing contests are held here throughout summer – and in winter the surface becomes a giant skating rink. During the day a constant relay of stretched gondolas leaves from below the *Park Hotel*, the *Pension Mlino*, and the bathing resort below the castle, ferrying tourists back and forth to Bled's picturesque **island** (1800SIT return). With an early start (and by renting your own rowing boat from *Mlino*) you can beat them to it. Crowning the island, the Baroque-decorated **Church of Sv Marika Božja** is the last in a line of churches on a spot that's long held religious significance: under the present building are remains of early graves and, below the north chapel, a pre-Roman temple. In summer months it's feasible to swim from the western end of the lake to the island; during winter, under the snug muffle of alpine snow, you can walk or skate across. From the bathing resort, a couple of paths run uphill to **Bled Castle** (daily 8am–5/8pm; 700SIT), originally an eleventh-century fortification but whose present appearance dates from the seventeenth; the museum, containing local artefacts, is pretty dull, but the lovely chapel decorated with frescoes is worth a look, and the views across the lake and towards the Alps are terrific. The main attraction in the outlying hills is the **Vintgar Gorge** (May–Oct daily 8am–8pm; 600SIT), 5km north of town, an impressive defile accessed by a wooden walkway. To get there, head northwest out of Bled on the Vintgar road (just up from the bus station), turning right on the outskirts of town towards the villages of Gmajna and Zasip. Head uphill through Zasip to the hilltop chapel of Sv Katarina before picking up a path through the forest to the gorge entrance. Alternatively you can get there by bus (mid-June to Sept daily at 10am) from the bus station.

Bled's **tourist office**, down below the *Park Hotel* at Cesta svobode 15 (July & Aug daily 8am–10pm; rest of year Mon–Sat 8am–5/8pm, Sun 10am/noon–5/6pm; ☎04/574-1122, ⊛www.bled.si). **Private rooms** are available through Kompas, in the shopping centre at Ljubljanska 4 (☎04/574-1515, ⊛www.kompas-bled.si). There's an outstanding **HI hostel** (☎04/574-5250, ⊛www.mlino.si; 4000SIT) just above the bus station at Grajska 17, and some reasonable **pensions** scattered around the lake, such as the smallish *Pletna* at Cesta svobode 37 (☎04/574-3702; ❸), and the *Mlino*, 200m further along at no. 45 (☎04/574-1404; ❸). Bled **campsite** (☎04/575-2000) is beautifully located at the western end of the lake amid the pines; catch a bus towards Bohinj and ask to be set down near the access road. The best places for **eating** are in the hillside area between Bled's bus station and castle. *Gostilna Pri Planincu*, Grajska 8, offers solid Slovene home cooking; *Pizzeria Portobello* on Rikljeva is probably the best of the Italian places; and the hostel restaurant is pretty decent too.

Lake Bohinj

It's 30km from Bled to Lake Bohinj; buses run hourly through the Sava Bohinjka Valley – dense, verdant and often laden with mist and low cloud. In appearance and character **Lake Bohinj** is utterly different from Bled: the lake crooks a narrow finger under the wild mountains, woods slope gently down to the water, and a lazy stillness hangs over all. **RIBČEV LAZ** (often referred to as **JEZERO** on bus timetables), at the eastern end of the lake, is where most facilities are based, including the **tourist office** (July & Aug daily 8am–8pm; rest of year Mon–Sat 8am–6pm, Sun 9am–3pm; ☎04/572-3370, ⊛www.bohinj.si), which offers rooms (❷) and apartments around Ribčev Laz and in the idyllic villages of **STARA FUŽINA** and **STUDOR**, 1km and 2.5km north respectively. The main attraction in Ribčev Laz is the **Church of Sv Janez** (July & Aug daily 9am–noon & 5–8pm; other times contact the tourist office), a chunky-looking structure whose nave and extraordinary frescoes date back to the fourteenth century. **Walking trails** lead round both sides of the lake, or north onto the eastern shoulders of the Triglav range. One route leads north from Stara Fužina into the Voje valley, passing through the dramatic **Mostrica Canyon**, a popular local beauty spot. About 5km from Ribčev Laz at the western end of the lake is the hamlet of **UKANC** (sometimes referred to as Zlatorog), site of the Kravji Bal or "Cow Dance", a mass booze-up which celebrates the return of the cattle from alpine pastures; this usually takes place in the second or third week of September. There are several private rooms (❷) and apartments here too, which you can book through the tourist office in Ribčev Laz. The campsite (☎04/572-3483), just east of the bus stop, occupies an idyllic lakeside position. An easy walk back east takes you to the **cable car** (daily 8am–6pm every 30min; closed Nov; 1600SIT return) at the foot of **Mt Vogel** (1540m). If the Alps look dramatic from the lakeside, from Vogel's summit they're breathtaking. An hour's walk north from Ukanc are the photogenic **Savica Waterfalls** (April to Oct 8am–6pm; 300SIT). The falls themselves mark the start of one of the most popular hiking routes up Mount Triglav, which zigzags up the mountain wall to the north before bearing northwest into the **Valley of the Seven Lakes** – an area strewn with eerie boulders and hardy firs – before continuing to the summit of Triglav itself. It's not a hike of great technical difficulty, though it's steep in parts and good maps and careful planning are required. The Seven Lakes can be treated as a day-long hiking expedition from Bohinj, but the assault on Triglav itself necessitates at least one night in a mountain hut. The tourist office in Ribčev Laz will supply details and book you a place, although huts on Triglav are only open from late June to late September – the upper stretches of the mountain shouldn't be tackled outside these times.

The Soča valley

On the other, less-touristed side of the mountains from Bohinj, the river **Soča** cuts through the western spur of the Julian Alps, running parallel with the Italian border. During World War I, the Soča marked the front line between the Italian and Austro-Hungarian armies; memorial chapels and abandoned fortifications abound, located incongruously amidst awesome alpine scenery. The valley is also a major centre for activity-based tourism, with the foaming river itself providing the ideal venue for **rafting** and **kayaking** throughout the spring and summer. The main tourist centres are Kobarid and Bovec, both small towns with a range of **walking** possibilities right on their doorstep. The 1:50,000 *Posočje* map covers trails in the region: it's best to pick it up in Ljubljana if you can, as not all local shops have it.

Although both places are served by four daily buses from Ljubljana, transport connections with the rest of Slovenia are patchy. Approaching the Soča valley from the Bled-Bohinj area involves catching one of six daily trains from Bled-Jezero or Bohinjska Bistrica to **Most na Soči**, where five buses daily run onwards up the valley. Getting here from the coast entails catching buses plying the Koper-Sežana-Nova Gorica-Tolmin-Kobarid route (min. 4hr, depending on connections), although you might have to change at each stage of the journey.

It was at the little alpine town of **KOBARID** that German and Austrian troops finally broke through Italian lines in 1917, almost knocking Italy out of World War I in the process. Ernest Hemingway, then a volunteer ambulance driver on the Italian side, took part in the chaotic retreat that followed – an experience which resurfaced in his novel *A Farewell to Arms*. A processional way leads up from Kobarid's main square to a monumental, three-tiered **Italian War Memorial** officially opened by Benito Mussolini in 1938, and a fitting place from which to enjoy views of the surrounding alps and ponder Kobarid's violent past. Back in town, the **Kobarid museum** at Gregorčičeva 10 (Mon–Fri 9/10am–5/6pm, Sat & Sun 9am–6/7pm; 600SIT; ⊛www.kobariski-muzej.si) presents a thoughtful and balanced record of the war with a gripping collection of photographs, maps and mementoes. Continue past the museum, head downhill and take the Drežnica road across the river Soča to pick up trails to the **Kozjak waterfall** (50min), less impressive for its height than for the cavern-like space which it has carved out of the surrounding rock. Numerous paths branch off from here into the wooded hills, passing trench systems dug by the Italians during the war. The staff in the museum can furnish you with **tourist information** (same hours; ☎05/389-9200, ⊛www.kobarid.si); they also have a limited number of **private rooms** (❷) in Kobarid and surrounding villages. The chic rooms at the *Hvala* **hotel** on the main square (☎05/389-9300, ⊛www.topli-val-sp.si; ❺) are remarkably good value for the level of comfort on offer. There's also a **campsite**, the *Koren* (☎05/388-5312), about 500m out of town on the way towards the Kozjak waterfall. As for **eating**, there's nowhere cheap in town save for *Pizzeria pri Vitku*, hidden away in a residential district at Pri Malnik 41 (take the road south out of town and follow the signs). If you fancy a splurge, head to *Kotlar*, Trg svobode 11, one of the best seafood restaurants in Slovenia. The main **rafting** company is X-Point (☎05/388-5308, ✉x.point@siol.net), just north of Trg svobode at Stresova 1; they also organize a range of other outdoor activities. Expect to pay around £20/$30 for a rafting trip.

Some 25km up the valley from Kobarid, the village of **BOVEC** straggles between imperious mountain ridges. A useful base for the Soča Valley, it has more accommodation than Kobarid because of its status as a winter ski resort. It's also the location of most of the rafting and adventure sport companies, and is the departure point for alpine walks. The quickest route into the mountains is provided by the **gondola** (July & Aug Sat & Sun; 2400SIT return) at the southern entrance to the village, which ascends to the pasture-cloaked Mt Kanin over to the west. The **tourist office** is in the Bovec Community Centre at Trg golobarskih žrtev 8 (July & Aug daily 9am–8pm; rest of year Mon–Fri 9am–5pm, Sat & Sun 9am–noon; ☎05/384-1919, ⊛www.bovec.si). Private **rooms** (❷) and apartments are available from either *Gotour*, at Trg golobarskih žrtev 50 (☎05/389-6366, ⊛www.gotourbovec.com), or *Avrigo*, at no. 47 (☎05/384-1150). The nearest **campsite** is *Polovnik*, Ledina 8 (☎05/388-6069); follow the road north out of the village and it's signed to the right after 500m. There are a couple of places to **eat** and **drink** around the main square, the best of which is *Stari Kovač*, Rupa 3, which has a long list of inexpensive pizzas alongside the usual schnitzels. Soča Rafting (☎05/389-6200, ⊛www.arctur.si/soca_rafting), in the Sports Centre, up the road from the tourist office, is the biggest of many companies offering **rafting** trips (with prices much the same as in Kobarid). It also organizes kayaking and canyoning and rents out mountain bikes.

Ptuj

Located 120km northeast of Ljubljana, **PTUJ** is the oldest town in Slovenia and about the most attractive as well, rising up from the Drava Valley in a flutter of red roofs and topped by a friendly looking castle. But the best thing is its streets, with scaled-down mansions standing shoulder to shoulder on scaled-down boulevards, medieval fantasies crumbling next to Baroque extravagances. Ptuj is on the main rail line from Ljubljana to Budapest (the Venice–Ljubljana–Budapest express passes through here once a day in both directions), and can also be reached by bus from Slovenia's second-largest city **Maribor**, which is on the Ljubljana-Vienna line. On arriving at Maribor, turn left outside the train station and head downhill – the bus station is on the other side of the crossroads.

Ptuj's attractive main street, Prešernova cesta, snakes along the base of the castle-topped hill. At its eastern end is a sixteenth-century bell tower and the **Priory Church of St George**, a building of twelfth-century origin that holds a statue of its patron nonchalantly killing a rather homely dragon, and several marvellous frescoes. From here Prešernova cesta leads to the **Archeological Museum** (mid-April to Dec daily 10am–5pm; 600SIT), housed in what was once a Dominican monastery, gutted in the eighteenth century and now hung with spidery decoration, and worth a look for the carvings and statuary around its likeably dishevelled cloisters. A path opposite the monastery winds up to the **Castle** (daily 9am–5/6pm; July & Aug Sat & Sun till 8pm; 600SIT). There's been a castle of sorts here for as long as there's been a town, since Ptuj was the only bridging point across the Drava for miles around, holding the defences against the tribes of the north. An agglomeration of styles from the fourteenth to the eighteenth centuries, the castle was home to a succession of noble families. Most prominent were the Herbersteins, Austro–Slovene aristocrats who made their fortune in the Habsburg Empire's wars against the Turks. Their portraits hang on the walls of the castle's **museum**, containing period rooms with original tapestries and wallpaper. The most interesting part of the museum, however, is the exhibition on the *Kurenti*, an extravagant and unusual Shrovetide (late Feb/early March) carnival which celebrates the rite of spring.

Ptuj's **train station** is 500m northeast of the centre on Osojnikova cesta, the **bus station** 100m nearer town on the same road. From both points, walk down Osojnikova to its junction with ul Heroja Lacka: a right turn here lands you straight in the centre. The **tourist office** in the clocktower opposite the church (July & Aug Mon–Fri 8am–6pm, Sat 8am–4pm, Sun 10am–3pm; rest of the year closed Sun; ☎02/779-6011, ⊛www.ptuj.si) has **private rooms** in the town itself and in local farmhouses (**❷**). The superb **hostel** is located midway between the stations and the town centre at Osojnikova 9 (☎02/780-5540; **❸**). There are two reasonably priced **hotels** in the centre: the *Mitra*, Prešernova 6 (☎02/774-2101, ⊛www .hotel-mitra-fm.si; **❹**); and the *Poetovio*, near the bus station at Trstenjakova 13 (☎02/779-8201; **❸**). The **campsite** is 2km across the river at Pot v Toplice 9 (☎02/782-7821, ⊜terme.ptuj@siol.net). The best places to **eat**, both very affordable, are *Amadeus*, near the Archeological Museum at Prešernova 36, serving Slovene standards; and *Ribič*, a delightful fish restaurant down by the riverside at Dravska ulica 9. By far the liveliest venue for a **drink**, by day or night, is *Café Europa*, on Slovenski trg, though *Café Bo* and *Café Orfei* on Prešernova are equally enjoyable places.

Travel details

Trains

Bohinjska Bistrica to: Most na Soči (6 daily; 45min).

Ljubljana to: Divača (hourly; 1hr 30min); Koper (5 daily; 2hr 30min); Maribor (hourly; 2hr 20min–3hr 20min); Postojna (hourly; 1hr); Ptuj (7 daily; 2hr 30min).

Buses

Kobarid to: Bovec (5 daily; 40min); Ljubljana (3 daily; 4hr); Nova Gorica (3 daily; 1hr 15min).
Koper to: Bled (1 daily; 3hr 30min); Piran (every 20min; 40min); Portorož (every 20min; 30min); Trieste (Mon–Sat hourly; 1hr).

Ljubljana to: Bled (hourly; 1hr 15min); Bohinj (hourly; 2hr); Bovec (4 daily; 4hr 45min); Divača (10 daily; 1hr 30min); Kobarid (4 daily; 4hr); Koper (9 daily; 2hr); Maribor (7 daily; 3hr 45min); Piran (6 daily; 2hr 40min); Portorož (6 daily; 2hr 30 min); Postojna (hourly; 1hr).
Maribor to: Ptuj (every 30min; 40min).

27

Spain

Plymouth Paris Toulouse

A Coruña
Santiago de Compostela
Vigo
Oviedo
Santander
San Sebastián
Bilbao
FRANCE
Paris & Geneva
León
Pamplona
Jaca
ANDORRA
Palencia
Zaragoza
Barcelona
Oporto
Salamanca
Segovia
Ávila
El Escorial
MADRID
Cuenca
Balearic Islands
Cáceres
Toledo
Alcázar de San Juan
Valencia
Mérida
Ciudad Real
LISBON
Alicante
Córdoba
Seville
Bobadilla
Huelva
Ronda
Málaga
Granada
Almería
Cádiz
Marbella
Estepona
Algeciras
Gibráltar
Tangier
Ceuta
MOROCCO

PORTUGAL

N

0   100 km

ATLANTIC OCEAN

MEDITERRANEAN SEA

Mallorca   Menorca
Palma
Ibiza   *Balearic Islands*
Formentera

SPAIN

27

Spain highlights

* **Madrid** Party late, party hard. See p.838

* **Plaza Mayor, Salamanca** The finest square in a beautiful town. See p.844

* **Guggenheim Museum, Bilbao** The architecture is as big an attraction as the art. See p.850

* **Santiago de Compostela** The end-point of Europe's most famous pilgrim trail. See p.852

* **The Pyrenees** Trek through these little-visited mountains. See p.853

* **Pamplona** Run with the bulls. See p.854

* **Dalí museums, Costa Brava** Get into the mind of the master. See p.860

* **Barcelona** Perhaps Europe's most alluring city. See p.861

* **Ibiza** The continent's trendiest clubs. See p.870

* **Alhambra, Granada** Evocative Moorish palace atop this charming Andalucian city. See p.878

Introduction and basics

Spain might appear from the brochures to be no more than a clichéd whirl of bullfights and crowded beaches, castles and Moorish palaces. Travel for any length of time, however, and the sheer variety of this huge country, which in the north looks like Ireland and in the south like Morocco, cannot fail to impress. The separate kingdoms that made up the original Spanish nation remain very much in evidence, in a diversity of language, culture and traditions.

Modern Spain – the country of world-renowned architecture, music festivals, museums and chic city-life – is a modern phenomenon. Since 1992, when Barcelona hosted the Olympics, Seville the World Fair, and Madrid was official Cultural Capital of Europe, Spain hasn't looked back and has seen an ever-more impressed selection of tourists come to explore every corner.

In the **cities** there's always something happening – in clubs, on the streets, in fashion, in politics – and even in the most out-of-the-way places there's nightlife, music and entertainment, not to mention the more traditional fiestas. In the **countryside** you can still find villages that have been decaying since Columbus set sail: rural areas are more and more depopulated as the young head for the cities. Yet this is one of the few countries in the world where, at certain times of the year, you can ski in the morning and laze on the beach in the afternoon. Spain is as mountainous a nation as any in Europe: the *sierras* have always formed formidable barriers to centralization.

It's almost impossible to summarize Spain as a single country. Of the regions, **Catalonia** (Catalunya) in the northeast is vibrant and go-ahead; **Galicia** in the northwest a verdant rural idyll; the **Basque country** around Bilbao a remarkable contrast between post-industrial depression and unbridled optimism; **Castile** and the south still, somehow, quintessentially "Spanish".

There are definite highlights: the three great cities of **Barcelona**, **Madrid** and **Seville**; the Moorish monuments of **Andalucía** in the south and the Christian ones of **Old Castile** in the west; beach-life on the island of **Ibiza** or on the more deserted sands around **Cádiz**; and, for some of the best trekking in Europe, the **Pyrenees**.

Information & maps

The **Spanish National Tourist Office** (*Información* or *Oficina de turismo*) has a branch in virtually every major town, giving away maps and accommodation lists. There are also provincial or municipal **Turismos**, while some of the more go-ahead regions such as Catalonia and the Basque Country have their own network of offices. Both types are usually open Mon–Fri 9/10am–1pm & 4–7/8pm, Sat 9am–1/2pm. Good **maps** are published by Editorial Telstar (ⓦ www.distrimapas-telstar.es) and Editorial Almax (ⓦ www.almax-editores.com). Serious **trekkers** should look for topographical maps issued by the IGN or SGE; in the north, Editorial Alpina is more practical.

Money and banks

Currency is the **euro** (€). **Banks** and *cajas de ahorro* (equivalent to a building

Basics

SPAIN | Basics

27

Spain on the net

ⓦ **www.tourspain.es** Comprehensive information in English.
ⓦ **www.guiadelocio.com** Nationwide restaurant and entertainment listings, updated weekly.
ⓦ **www.elpais.es** English version of the main national newspaper.
ⓦ **www.gospain.org** Very useful links directory.
ⓦ **www.soccer-spain.com** English news from the Spanish football league.

society/savings and loan) have branches in all but the smallest towns, open Mon–Fri 8.30am–2pm, also Sat in low season. You can usually change cash at larger hotels (bad rates, but low commission), at travel agents, and at most El Corte Inglés department stores, which have surprisingly reasonable rates. In tourist areas you'll also find **casas de cambio**, with more convenient hours, but worse exchange rates. ATMs are widespread. Many sites offer student discounts.

Communications

Post offices (*correos*) open Mon–Fri 8.30am–2pm, Sat 9am–noon; big branches in cities open later. Stamps are also sold at tobacconists (*estancos*). Poste restante should be addressed to "Lista de Correos", followed by the name of the town and province. American Express in Madrid and Barcelona will hold mail for a month for cardholders. You can make international calls from almost any public **phone**. The various discount cards for domestic and overseas calls are the cheapest way to pay (available from tobacconists, *locutorios* and many Internet cafés). Most phone boxes accept coins as well as cards. The operator is on ☎1003 domestic, ☎025 international. Within Spain, dial all nine digits. **Internet** access is widely available – at cafés, computer shops and phone centres. Hourly rates can be €0.90 in cities, €3.60 in smaller towns, and €9 at bus and train station kiosks.

Getting around

Most of Spain is well covered by both bus and rail networks; for journeys between major towns there's often little to choose between the two in cost or speed. **RENFE** (ⓦwww.renfe.es) operates **train** services, divided into three: *Cercanías* (red) are local commuter trains in the major cities; *Regionales* (orange) run between cities, and are equivalent to buses in speed and cost – *regional exprés* and *delta* trains can cover longer distances; and *Largo recorrido* express trains (grey) come as – in ascending

order of luxury – *Diurno*, *Intercity (IC)*, *Estrella (*)*, *Talgo*, *Talgo Pendular*, *Talgo 200 (T200)*, and *Trenhotel*. Anything above Intercity can cost twice as much as standard second class. There are also private high-speed trains (white) from Madrid, such as *AVE* to Seville, *Alaris* to Valencia, and *Euromed* and *Altaria* to Alicante. A good way to avoid queuing at stations is to buy tickets at travel agents that display the RENFE sign – they can also make seat reservations (€3, the same as at the station), which are obligatory on *largo recorrido* trains. Most larger towns also have a RENFE office in the centre. You can also book on ☎902 240 202 (24hr). InterRail and Eurail are valid on all RENFE trains and also on *EuroMed*; supplements are charged on the fastest trains, as well as a reservation fee.

Many smaller villages are accessible only by **bus**, almost always leaving from the capital of their province. Service varies in quality, but buses are often faster than trains and are usually as reliable and comfortable, with prices pretty standard at around €6 per 100km. Buses may leave from a variety of places. Services are drastically reduced on Sundays and holidays – it's best to avoid travelling to out-of-the-way places on these days.

Accommodation

Simple, reasonably priced rooms are widely available in rural Spain, and in most towns you'll be able to get a double for around €26, €15 a single – more in major resorts and big cities. Prices in popular areas drop in the off season. Most places also have rooms with three or four beds for not a great deal more than the double-room rate. Tourist offices always have lists of places to stay, but often miss the cheaper deals. **Hotels** go by various names. Cheapest of all are *fondas* (identifiable by a square blue sign with a white F on it), closely followed by *casas de huéspedes* (CH) and *pensiones* (P), though these days distinctions between them are rather blurred. Slightly more expensive, but far more common, are *hostales* (marked Hs) and *hostal-residencias* (HsR), categorized from one- to three-stars, though prices vary enormously according to location. Finally, **hoteles** (H) are again star-graded, with one-stars costing no more than three-star *hostales* – sometimes they're actually cheaper. Near the top end of this scale there are also state-run **paradores**: beautiful places, often converted from castles, monasteries and other minor Spanish monuments. You'll also sometimes see **camas** (beds) and **habitaciones** (rooms) advertised in private houses or above bars, often with the phrase "*camas y comidas*" (beds and meals) – these can be the cheapest of all options.

HI **hostels** (*albergues juveniles*; ⓦwww.reaj.com) are rarely very practical. In most of the country, few stay open all year, and in towns and cities they're often inconveniently located, suffer from curfews and are often block-reserved by school groups. At around €10–25 per person, usually including breakfast, you can often pay more to stay in a hostel than to share a cheap double room in a *fonda* or *casa de huéspedes*. On the other hand some cities, including Barcelona, have a growing network of centrally located **backpacker** hostels with good facilities, no curfews and the prospect of meeting like-minded travellers. Beds are €15–21, membership not required. ⓦwww.hostelspain.com lists budget hotels and hostels. Nationwide, **agroturismo** and **casa rural** programmes offer excellent cheap accommodation in rural areas, usually in beautifully preserved and well-maintained private houses. Tourist offices have full lists. There are hundreds of **campsites**, mostly on the coast, charging about €3 per person plus the same for a tent. The National Tourist Board has the free *Mapa de Campings* and the complete *Guía de Campings* (€6); or see ⓦwww.vayacamping.net. **Camping rough** is not a good idea; you can be fined for camping near a tourist beach or campsite.

Food and drink

There are two ways to **eat**: you can go to a *restaurante* or *comedor* (dining room) and have a full meal, or you can have a succession of tapas (small snacks) or *raciones* (larger ones) at one or more bars. Note that sitting at the bar is the cheapest way to eat, a table costs almost twice as much, and a seat outside even more. Bars and cafés are best for **breakfast**, which can consist of a brioche/croissant, *churros con chocolate* – long tubular doughnuts with thick drinking chocolate – *tostadas* (toasted bread) with oil (*con aceite*) or butter and jam (*con mantequilla y mermelada*), or *tortilla* (omelette). **Coffee** and **pastries** are available at the many excellent *pastelerías* and *confiterías,* while sandwiches (*bocadillos*), filled with sliced meats, cheese or *tortilla*, are available everywhere. *Tabernas*, *tascas*, *bodegas*, *cervecerias* and bars all serve **tapas** or *pinchos*: mini portions of meat, fish, tortilla or salad for €1.20–2.80 a plate. Their big brothers, **raciones** (€3–9), make a sufficient meal in themselves. Two- or three-course main meals (*cubierto*, *menú del día* or *menú de la casa*) with wine are served at **comedores** or **cafeterías** (€6–9). *Cafeterías* serve rather bland *platos combinados* such as egg and fries or *calamares* and salad, with bread and a drink included (€4.50–8). At a **restaurant**, the cheapest full meal plus wine costs €6–10 – but prices can escalate rapidly unless you opt for the *menu del día*, a well-priced daily special. **Fish and seafood** are fresh and excellent, particularly regional specialities such as Galician fish stews (*zarzuelas*) and Valencian paellas (which also contain meat). Restaurants serving exclusively fish and seafood are called **marisquerías**. The big cities, notably Madrid, Barcelona and Valencia, but including many others, are fab for **vegetarians**, with scores of veggie restaurants plus fusion cuisine and Asian specialities widely available. Elsewhere, though, you may find that veggie staples such as salads come with tuna or egg, while beans and lentil dishes may be cooked with bacon.

Wine, either *tinto* (red), *blanco* (white) or *rosado/clarete* (rosé), is usually very good. Best red is Rioja, where you're very unlikely to go wrong; also look out for Ribera del Duero from Castilla or Somontano from Aragón. Catalonia produces the best whites, especially Penèdes or Peralada; alternatively, try the refreshing Galician Albariño or the more economical Ribeiro. *Vino de Jerez*, Andalucian **sherry**, is served chilled and either *fino/jerez seco* (dry), *amontillado* (medium), or *oloroso/jerez dulce* (sweet). *Cerveza*, lager-type **beer**, is more expensive than wine but also good – local brands, such as Cruzcampo in Sevilla or Alhambra in Granada, are usually the best. **Sangría**, a wine-and-fruit punch, and **sidra**, a dry farmhouse cider most typical in the Basque Country and Asturias, are worth sampling. Spaniards often take a *copa* of **liqueur** with their coffee; the best are *anís* (like Pernod) or *coñac*, local vanilla-flavoured brandy. There are cheaper Spanish equivalents (*nacional*) of most **spirits**, so specify if you are on a tight budget. **Coffee** is invariably espresso, unless you specify *cortado* (with a drop of milk), *con leche* (a more generous dollop) or *americano* (weaker black coffee). **Tea** is drunk black. If you want milk, ask afterwards: ordering *té con leche* might get you a glass of milk with a teabag floating on top. Herbal teas, such as *tila* (lime blossom), *menta* (mint) and *manzanilla* (camomile), are very good.

Opening hours and holidays

Almost everywhere closes for at least two hours in the hottest part of the day. There's a lot of variation, and certain **shops** stay open all day, especially department stores, but basic summer hours are Mon–Sat 9.30am–1.30pm & 4.30–8pm. **Museums**, with few exceptions, take a break between 1 and 4pm, and are closed Sun afternoon and all day Mon. The important **churches** oper-

ate similarly; others open only for worship in the early morning and/or evening. As well as scores of local **holidays**, national ones are: Jan 1; Jan 6; Maundy Thurs or Easter Mon; Good Fri; Easter Sun; May 1; Aug 15; Oct 12; Nov 1; Dec 6; Dec 8; Dec 25. The main regional holidays are May 2 (Madrid); Corpus Christi in early or mid-June; June 24; July 25; Sept 11 (Catalonia).

Emergencies

The paramilitary **Guardia Civil** (green uniforms and kepis) still police some rural areas, borders and most highways. In Catalonia, some of their responsibilities have devolved to the Mossos d'Esquadra, and in the Basque country to the Ertzaintza. In cities, you'll find the **Policía Nacional** (talk to them if you get robbed) and the **Policía Municipal** (traffic police), and there's a **Patrulla Rural** in some outlying areas. Petty theft can be particularly bad in some cities and during fiestas; use common sense and keep an eye (and an arm) on your things at all times. For minor **health** complaints go to a pharmacy (*farmacia*), which you'll find in almost any town. In more serious cases head to *Urgencias* at the nearest **hospital**, or get the address of an English-speaking doctor from the nearest consulate, *farmacia*, local police or tourist office.

Emergency numbers
All emergencies ☎112; ambulance ☎081.

Madrid

MADRID became Spain's capital by grace of its geography; when Philip II moved the seat of government here in 1561, his aim was to create a symbol of Spanish unification and centralization. However, the city has few natural advantages – it is 300km from the sea on a 650-metre-high plateau, freezing in winter, burning in summer – and it was only the determination of successive rulers to promote a strong central capital that ensured its success. Today, Madrid is a predominantly modern city, but the streets at her heart are a pleasant surprise, hiding odd pockets of medieval buildings and atmospheric, narrow alleys. There are admittedly few sights of great architectural interest, but it is home to some of Spain's best art: the monarchs acquired outstanding picture collections, which went on to form the basis of the Prado museum. Galleries and sights aside, you soon realize that it's the inhabitants – some 5.3 million Madrileños – that are the capital's key attraction: hanging out in the traditional cafés and *chocolaterías* or the summer *terrazas*, packing the lanes of the Sunday Rastro flea market, or playing hard and very, very late in a thousand bars, clubs, discos and *tascas*. Whatever Barcelona or San Sebastián might claim, the Madrid scene remains as it is immortalized in the movies of Pedro Almodóvar – vibrant, noisy and lots of fun.

Arrival, information and city transport

Barajas **airport** is 16km out of town and connected with the centre by metro line #8 or Airport Bus #89 to Plaza de Colon. **Trains** from the north and from Portugal arrive at the **Estación de Chamartín**, in the north of the city but connected to the centre – and all major city locations – via metro line #10. The central **Estación de Atocha** serves the south, east and west of Spain. Local trains use the Estaciónde Príncipe Pío, more widely known as **Estación del Norte**, below the central Plaza de España. **Bus terminals** are scattered throughout the city, but the largest – used by all international services – is the **Estación del Sur** (Metro Mendez Alvaró) on c/Mendez Alvaró, south of Atocha station.

The main municipal **tourist office** is at Plaza Mayor 3 (Mon–Sat 10am–8pm, Sun 10am–3pm; ☏915 881 636); there are branches at Duque de Medinaceli 2, near Plaza de las Cortes (same hours) and at the airport (daily 8am–8pm; ☏902 100 007). For details of **what's on**, check out the weekly *Guía del Ocio* (available from newsstands), the Friday and Saturday editions of *El Pais* and *El Mundo* (newspapers) and the free monthly *En Madrid*, available at tourist offices and bars.

The centre is comfortably walkable, but Madrid also has a good **metro system** that runs from 6am until 1.30am (flat fare €1.20, €5.20 for the metrobus ten-ride ticket, valid for buses too). The urban **bus network** is more comprehensive but more complicated – trust the **transport information** stand in Plaza de Cibeles before the quickly outdated handouts. Buses run from 6am to 11.30pm, but there are also several nightbus lines in the centre, from Plaza de Cibeles and Puerta del Sol (midnight–5am every 15min). Hop-on hop-off **tour bus** companies have stops at all the major sights (€10/12 for one/two days).

Accommodation

The cheapest **accommodation** is around the Estación de Atocha, though places closest to the station are rather grim, and the area can feel threatening at night. A better option is to head up c/Atocha towards Sol, to the streets surrounding the buzzing Plaza Santa Ana. Prices rise as you reach the Plaza Mayor and Puerta del Sol, but even here there are affordable options. Other promising areas include Gran Vía, where the huge old buildings hide a vast array of hotels and *hostales*, and north of here up noisy c/Fuencarral towards Chueca and Malsaña. The price at all hostels listed below includes breakfast.

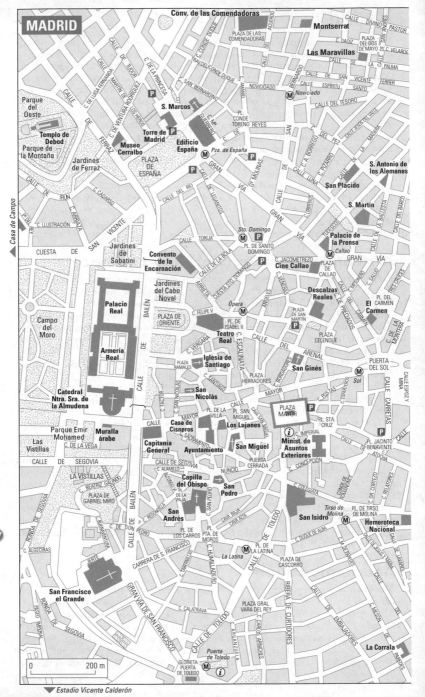

MADRID

Conv. de las Comendadoras
Montserrat
Las Maravillas

PLAZA DE LAS
COMENDADORAS

CALLE DIVINO PASTOR
PLAZA DEL DOS DE MAYO
C. VELARDE
C. DAOIZ
C. DE SAN VICENTE FERRER
CALLE DEL TESORO
C. DE SAN
CALLE DE LA PALMA

Parque del Oeste
Templo de Debod
Parque de la Montaña
Jardines de Ferraz

S. Marcos
Torre de Madrid
Museo Cerralbo
Edificio España
PLAZA DE ESPAÑA

Noviciado
Pza. de España

S. Antonio de los Alemanes
San Plácido
S. Martín

GRAN VÍA

Palacio de la Prensa
Callao
Cine Callao
PLAZA DE CALLAO
GRAN VÍA

Casa de Campo
CUESTA DE
Jardines de Sabatini

Sto. Domingo
PL. DE SANTO DOMINGO
Convento de la Encarnación
Jardines del Cabo Noval

Descalzas Reales
El Carmen
PL. DEL CARMEN

Palacio Real
PLAZA DE ORIENTE
Ópera
PLAZA DE SAN MIGUEL
Teatro Real
Iglesia de Santiago

Campo del Moro
Armería Real
Catedral Ntra. Sra. de la Almudena

PLAZA DE ISABEL II
PLAZA CELENQUE

San Ginés
PUERTA DEL SOL
Sol

Parque Emir Mohamed
Muralla árabe
Las Vistillas
San Nicolás
Casa de Cisneros
Capitanía General
Ayuntamiento

Los Lujanes
PLAZA MAYOR
PL. STA. CRUZ

San Miguel
Minist. de Asuntos Exteriores

CALLE DE SEGOVIA
LA VISTILLAS
PLAZA DE GABRIEL MIRÓ

Capilla del Obispo
San Pedro
San Andrés

PUERTA CERRADA

San Isidro
Tirso de Molina
PL. DE TIRSO DE MOLINA
Hemeroteca Nacional

San Francisco el Grande

La Latina
PLAZA DE CASCORRO

PLAZA GRAL. VARA DEL REY

La Corrala

Puerta de Toledo
GLORIETA PUERTA DE TOLEDO

CALLE DE TOLEDO

SPAIN | Madrid

27

832

0   200 m

▼ Estadio Vicente Calderón
◄ Casa de Campo

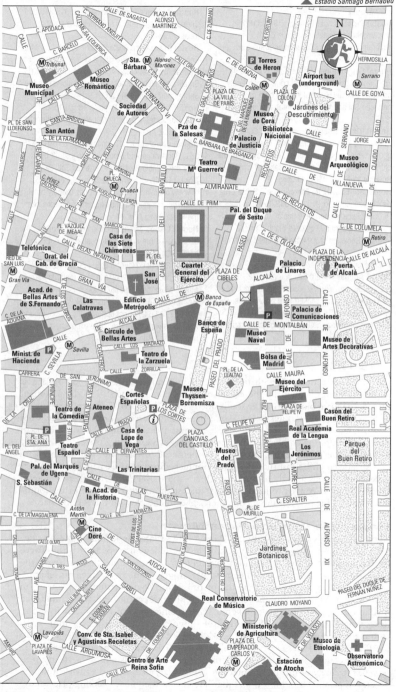

Estadio Santiágo Bernabéu

SPAIN | Madrid

27

833

Hostels

Hostal Barbieri c/Barbieri 15 ☎915 310 258, ⓦ www.barbierihostel.com. Basic dorm accommodation plus kitchen in youthful, hip Chueca. €14.

Hostal Los Amigos Campomanes 6 ☎915 471 707, ⓦ www.losamigoshostel.com. Very friendly dorm-only hostel with full kitchen on a quiet street between Sol and the Palacio Real. Metro Opera. €15.

Hostel Richard Schirmann Casa del Campo ☎914 635 699, ⓦ www.reaj.com. Friendly, comfortable and clean HI place, but way out of the city in a seedy area – taxis advisable at night. Roughly 1km from Metro El Lago. €11.

Hostel Santa Cruz de Marcenado c/Santa Cruz de Marcenado 28 ☎915 474 532. North of the Plaza de España near the Palacio Liria; reasonably pleasant, modern and quiet HI place. Curfew 1.30am. Books up fast. Metro Argüelles. €11.

Hotels

Hostal Aguilar Carrera San Jerónimo 32 ☎914 295 926, ⓦ www.hostalaguilar.com. One of several in a building packed with possibilities. ❹

Hostal Alcázar Regis Gran Vía 61 ☎915 479 317. Near the Plaza de España, deservedly popular and often full. ❹

Hostal Alonso c/Espoz y Mina 17 ☎915 315 679. Cheap and clean family-run place in a great location. ❷

Hostal Aranzazu c/Doctor Mata 1 ☎915 394 846. Centrally located near Atocha and well equipped. ❸

Hostal Armesto c/San Agustin 6 ☎914 299 031. Small, very pleasant *hostal*, well positioned for the Santa Ana area and the art galleries. ❹

Hostal Carreras c/del Principe 18 ☎915 220 036. Comfortable place in elegant old building off Plaza Santa Ana. ❹

Hostal Conchita II c/Campomanes 10 ☎915 475 061. Good value and great location just off Opera, near the Palacio Real and Puerta del Sol. ❸

Hostal Horizonte c/Atocha 28 ☎913 690 996, ⓦ www.hostalhorizonte.com. Super-friendly hotel with well-maintained and characterful rooms near the Plaza Santa Ana. ❸

Hostal Lisboa c/Ventura de la Vega 17 ☎914 299 894. Good three-star *hostal*, central but not too hectic. ❹

Hostal Riosol c/Mayor 5 ☎915 323 142. Well-priced place just off Puerta del Sol towards Plaza Mayor. Most rooms en suite. ❸

Hostal Sud-Americana Paseo del Prado 12 ☎914 292 564. Almost opposite the Prado; though standards vary, there are some excellent rooms here. Closed Aug. ❸

The City

Central **Puerta del Sol**, with its bustling crowds and traffic, is as good a place as any to start. This is officially the centre of the nation: a stone slab in the pavement outside the main building on the south side marks **Kilometre Zero**, from where six of Spain's National Routes begin, while beneath the streets, three of the city's ten metro lines converge. A statue of a bear pawing a *madroño* bush lies on the north side; this is both the emblem of the city and a favourite meeting place. Immediately north of Sol, c/de Preciados and c/del Carmen head towards the Gran Vía; both are pedestrianized and constitute the most popular **shopping area** in Madrid. West, c/del Arenal heads directly towards the Opera and Royal Palace, but there's more of interest along **c/Mayor**, one of Madrid's oldest thoroughfares, which runs south-west through the heart of the medieval city, also to end close to the Royal Palace.

Plaza de la Villa and Plaza Mayor

About two-thirds of the way along c/Mayor is the **Plaza de la Villa**, almost a case-book of Spanish architectural development. The oldest survivor here is the **Torre de los Lujanes**, a fifteenth-century building in Mudéjar style; next in age is the **Casa de Cisneros**, built by a nephew of Cardinal Cisneros in sixteenth-century Plateresque style; and to complete the picture is the **Ayuntamiento** (free tours in Spanish only, Mon at 5pm), begun in the seventeenth century, but later remodelled in Baroque mode. Baroque is taken a stage further around the corner in c/San Justo, where the church of **San Miguel** shows the unbridled imagination of its eighteenth-century Italian architects. Walking straight from the Puerta del Sol to the Plaza de la Villa, it's easy to miss altogether the **Plaza Mayor**, the most important architectural and historical landmark in Madrid. This almost perfectly preserved, extremely beautiful, seventeenth-century arcaded square, set back from the street, was planned by Philip II and Juan Herrera as the public meeting place of the new capital: *autos-da-fé* (trials of faith) were held by the Inquisition here, kings were crowned, festivals and demonstrations staged, bulls fought and gossip spread. The more important of these events would be watched by royalty from the frescoed **Casa Panadería**, named after the bakery that it replaced. Along with its popular but pricey cafés, the plaza still performs several public functions today: in summer, it's an outdoor theatre and music stage; in autumn, a book fair; and just before Christmas it becomes a bazaar for festive decorations and religious regalia. The warren of streets surrounding the Plaza Mayor are well worth exploring, housing a treasure trove of great tapas bars and restaurants.

Palacio Real

Calle del Arenal ends at the Plaza Isabel II opposite the **Teatro Real** or Opera House, which is separated from the Palacio Real by the newly renovated **Plaza de Oriente**. The chief attraction of the area is the grandiose **Palacio Real**, or Royal Palace (Mon–Fri 9/9.30am–5/6pm, Sat & Sun 9am–2/3pm; €7, free Wed to EU citizens). Built after the earlier Muslim Alcázar burned down on Christmas Day 1734, this was the principal royal residence until Alfonso XIII went into exile in 1931. The present royal family inhabits a more modest residence on the western outskirts of the city, using the Palacio Real only on state occasions. The building scores high on statistics: it claims more rooms than any other European palace; a **library** with one of the biggest collections of books, manuscripts, maps and musical scores in the world; an **armoury** with an unrivalled and often bizarre collection of weapons dating back to the fifteenth century; and an original **pharmacy**, a curious mixture of alchemist's den and early laboratory. Take your time to contemplate the extraordinary opulence of the place: acres of Flemish and Spanish tapestries, endless Rococo decoration, bejewelled clocks and pompous portraits of the monarchs. In the **Sala del Trono** (Throne Room) there's a magnificent frescoed ceiling by Tiepolo representing the glory of Spain – an extraordinary achievement for an artist by then in his seventies.

The Gran Vía

North from the palace, c/Bailén runs into the Plaza de España, longtime home of the tallest skyscrapers in the city. From here join **Gran Vía**; it was once the capital's major thoroughfare and effectively divides the old city to the south from the newer parts. Permanently crowded with shoppers and sightseers, the street is appropriately named, with splendidly quirky Art Nouveau and Art Deco facades fronting its banks, offices and apartments, and huge posters on the cinemas. At its far end, by the magnificent cylindrical **Edificio Metropolis**, it joins with c/Alcalá on the approach to Plaza de la Cibeles. Just across the junction is the majestic old **Círculo de las Bellas Artes**, a contemporary art space with a trendy café/bar (€1). On an entirely different plane, the **Monasterio de las Descalzas Reales** (Tues–Sat 10.30/11am–12.45/1.45pm & 4–5.45pm, Fri morning only, Sun 11am–1.30pm; €5), one of the hidden treasures of the city, lies just south of the Gran Vía on the Plaza de las Descalzas. This convent was founded by Juana de Austria, daughter of Carlos V, sister of Philip II and, at 19, already the widow of Prince Don Juan of Portugal. In her wake came a succession of titled ladies who brought fame and, above all, fortune. It's an amazingly rich and beautiful locale, the tranquillity within its thick walls making an extraordinary contrast to the frenzied commercialism all around. A whistle-stop guided tour takes you through the cloisters and up an overly ornate stairway to a series of chambers packed with art and treasures of every kind.

The Prado

Just across the Paseo del Prado from the Círculo de la Bellas Artes lies Madrid's **Museo del Prado** (Tues–Sat 9am–7pm, Sun 9am–2pm; €3, free Sun; ⓦwww.museoprado.mcu.es), which has been one of Europe's key art galleries ever since it opened in 1819. It houses over three thousand paintings in all, including the world's finest collections of Goya, Velázquez and Bosch. Pick up a leaflet at the entrance to find your way round. The early **Flemish masters** are displayed on the ground floor. The great triptychs of Hieronymus Bosch are familiar from countless reproductions, while the museum's collection of over 160 works of later Flemish and Dutch art has been imaginatively re-housed in a suite of twelve rooms off the main gallery on the first floor. Rubens is extensively represented – by the beautifully restored *Three Graces* among others – as are van Dyck and Jan Brueghel. The central downstairs gallery houses the **early Spanish collection**, and a dazzling array of portraits and religious paintings by El Greco, among them his mystic and hallucinatory *Crucifixion* and *Adoration of the Shepherds*. Beyond this are the Prado's **Italian** treasures: superb Titian portraits of Charles V and Philip II, as well as works by Tintoretto, Bassano, Caravaggio and Veronese. Upstairs are Goya's unmissable Black Paintings, best seen after visiting the rest of his work on the top floor. Outstanding presence among Spanish painters is **Velázquez** – among the collection are intimate portraits of the family of Felipe IV, most famously his masterpiece *Las Meninas*. The top floor of the building is devoted almost entirely to **Francisco de Goya**, whose many portraits of his patron, Charles IV, are remarkable for their lack of any attempt at flattery, while those of Queen María Luisa, whom he despised, are downright ugly. He was an enormously versatile artist: contrast the voluptuous *Majas* with the horrors depicted in *The Second of May* and *The Third of May*, on-the-spot portrayals of the rebellion against Napoleon and the subsequent reprisals.

Thyssen-Bornemisza collection

The **Colección Thyssen-Bornemisza** (Tues–Sun 10am–9pm; temporary collection €3.60, whole collection €6.60; ⊛www.museothyssen.org) occupies the old Palacio de Villahermosa, diagonally opposite the Prado. In 1993, this prestigious site played a large part in Spain's acquisition of what was perhaps the world's greatest private art collection, with important works from every major period and movement - from Duccio and Holbein, through El Greco and Caravaggio, to Schiele and Rothko; from a strong showing of nineteenth-century Americans to some very early and very late Van Goghs; and side-by-side hangings of parallel Cubist studies by Picasso, Braque and Mondrian. There's a **bar and café** in the basement and re-entry is allowed, so long as you get your hand stamped at the exit desk.

Centro de Arte Reina Sofía

The **Centro de Arte Reina Sofía** (Mon & Wed–Sat 10am–11pm, Sun 10am–2.30pm; €3, free Sat after 2.30pm & all Sun; ⊛www.museoreinasofia .mcu.es), facing Atocha station at the end of Paseo del Prado, keeps different opening hours and days from its neighbours, which is fortunate because this leading exhibition space, and permanent collection of modern Spanish art, is another essential stop on the Madrid art scene. The museum, a massive former convent and hospital, is a kind of Madrid response to the Pompidou centre in Paris. Transparent lifts shuttle visitors up the outside of the building, whose levels feature a cinema, excellent art and design bookshops, a print, music and photographic library, restaurant, bar and café, as well as the exhibition halls (top floor) and the collection of twentieth-century art (second floor). It is for **Picasso's** *Guernica* that most visitors come to the Reina Sofía, and rightly so. Superbly displayed along with its preliminary studies, this icon of twentieth-century Spanish art and politics – a response to the fascist bombing of the Basque town of Guernica in the Spanish Civil War – carries a shock that defies all familiarity. Other halls are devoted to **Dalí** and Surrealism, early-twentieth-century Spanish artists including **Miró** and post-World War II figurative art, mapping the beginning of abstraction through to Pop and avant-garde.

The Rastro

The area south of the Plaza Mayor and c/Atocha has traditionally been a tough, working-class district and in many places the old houses survive, huddled together in narrow streets. However, an influx of youthful, fashionable residents has changed the character of **La Latina** and **Lavapiés** over the last decade, making it pleasantly hip. Partly responsible for this change is the **Rastro** (Metro La Latina), which is as much part of Madrid's weekend ritual as a Mass or a *paseo*. This gargantuan, thriving, thieving shambles of a **street market** sprawls south from Metro La Latina to the Ronda de Toledo, and is particularly busy along c/Ribera de Curtidores; crowds flood through between 10am and 3pm on Sundays and holidays. Don't expect to find fabulous bargains; the serious antiques trade has mostly moved off the streets and into the shops. It's definitely worth a visit, though, if only to see the locals out in their thousands and to do as they do – recover in a selection of traditional tapas bars – after the madness had subsided. Keep a tight grip on your bags, pockets, cameras and jewellery. Afterwards head over to the bars and *terrazas* around Puerta de Moros for an *aperitivo* and to while away the afternoon.

Retiro and other parks

Madrid's many parks provide great places to escape the sightseeing for a few hours. The most central and most popular is the **Parque del Buen Retiro** behind the Prado, a stunning mix of formal gardens and wilder spaces. You can jog, row a boat, picnic, have your fortune told and, above all, promenade – on Sunday afternoon half of Madrid turns out for the *paseo*. Travelling art exhibitions are frequently housed in the beautiful **Palacio de Velázquez** and the nearby **Palacio de Cristal** (times and prices vary according to exhibition). The nearby **Jardines Botanicos** (daily 10am–sunset; €1.50; Metro Atocha), whose entrance faces the southern end of the Prado, are also delightful.

Eating and drinking

There can be few places in the world that can rival the area around Puerta del Sol in either quantity or variety of outlets for **eating and drinking**. And the feasts continue in all directions, especially towards Plaza Santa Ana and along c/de las Huertas to Atocha, but also south in the neighbourhood haunts of La Latina and Lavapiés, and north in the gay *barrio* Chueca and the alternative Malsaña. The streets between Lope de Vega, Plaza Santa Ana and c/Echegary are especially pleasant for bar-hopping. In summer, all areas of the city have pavement café/bars, where coffees are taken by day and drinks pretty much all night. The prime area is Paseo Castellana, where many of the top discos can be found. Smaller scenes are in Plaza de Chueca, Paseo Rosales del Pintor along the Parque del Oeste, the more relaxed and pleasant c/Argumosa in Lavapies/Atocha, Puerta de Moros in La Latina and Las Vistillas, on the south side of the viaduct on c/Bailén, due south of the royal palace.

Cafés and tapas bars

Café Comercial Glorieta de Bilbao. Traditional café and meeting place; linger over coffee, *coñac* or cakes.

Café Gijón Paseo de Recoletos 21, north of Plaza de Cibeles. Traditional atmospheric nineteenth-century café. Lunchtime *menú* and pricey summer terrace.

Casa Alberto c/de las Huertas 18. One of the most traditional Huertas bars: very friendly and huge portions, with a restaurant out back.

El Anciano Rey de los Vinos c/Bailén 19. Wine and sherry, some still served in the traditional manner straight from the barrel.

La Mi Venta Plaza de la Marina Española. A charming establishment, specializing in *jamón* and fish, much frequented by locals.

Las Bravas c/Espoz y Mina, Huertas. The original premises of this inexpensive Madrid institution, which now has branches throughout the city; famous for *patatas bravas*, though these days the grilled mushrooms are better.

Mejillonera El Pasaje Pasaje Matheu, off c/de Espoz y Mina, near Sol. One of many places filling this narrow street with outdoor tables – this one specializes in mussels.

Melo's c/Ave María 44. Excellent-value Galician place serving huge portions. A Lavapiés institution.

Museo del Jamón Carrera San Jerónimo 6, Puerta del Sol end. Extraordinary place where hundreds of hams hang from the ceiling, and you can sample the different (expensive) varieties over a glass or two; also has full meals and the best breakfast deals in town. Numerous other branches.

Viña P Plaza de Santa Ana 3. Friendly bar, decked out in bullfighting mementoes, serving a great range of tapas.

Mainly-for-drinking bars

Cervecería Alemána Plaza Santa Ana. One of Hemingway's favourite haunts and consequently full of Americans; good traditional atmosphere none the less.

Bodega Ángel Sierra Plaza Chueca. Great old bar right on the square, just the place for an apéritif.

Casa Antonio c/de Latoneros, near Plaza Mayor. Specializes in sherries and fine wines.

I Latina Teatro de la Latina, Plaza de la Cebada 2. Hip, modern and friendly bar in the cellar of one of Madrid's theatrical landmarks.

La Nina del Exorcista C/Fernando el Catolico 76. Horror-themed bar, where you can feed piranhas or watch horror flicks while you quaff.

Los Gabrieles c/Echegaray 17. One of the most spectacular tiled bars in Madrid, with fabulous nineteenth-century drinking scenes on the ceramic tiles, including a great version of Velázquez's *Los Borrachos* (The Drunkards).

La Luna Amor de Diós 13, off Huertas. A perennially popular dive.

Star Café c/Marqués de Valdeiglesias 5. Hip, happening gay/mixed bar. Funky grooves in the basement at weekends. Closed Sun.

La Venencia c/Echegaray 7. Marvellous old wooden bar, serving sherry only and the most basic of tapas – cheese and pressed tuna. A must.

Restaurants

Arroceria Gala c/Moratin 22. Excellent value paella restaurant with a lovely conservatory at the back.

Artemisa c/Ventura de la Vega 4. Decently priced vegetarian restaurant.

Casa Ciriaco c/Mayor 84. Good, traditional restaurant, not too expensive for the area.

Casa Eduardo Cava San Miguel, next to the market behind Plaza Mayor. Outdoor tables, Galician specialties and very cheap set *menú*.

Casa Mingo Paseo de la Florida, San Antonio de la Florida chapel. Asturian place for roast chicken washed down with cider. Good value and great fun, especially on Sun afternoon.

Creperie Ma Bretagne c/San Vicente Ferrer. Sweet little place with good pancakes.

El Estragón Plaza de la Paja 10. Good vegetarian tapas and an economical *menú del día* in an attractive plaza.

Elqui c/Buenavista 18. One of Madrid's best vegetarian restaurants. Self-service with excellent lunchtime *menú*. Closed Mon.

La Mordida c/Belén 13; c/Las Fuentes 3. Good, fresh and filling Mexican food.

Mushashi c/Conchas 4. Basic, friendly restaurant serving very tasty sushi at reasonable prices.

Sabatini c/Bailén 15, opposite Jardines Sabatini. Tasty food and significantly less expensive than you might expect.

Viuda de Vacas c/Cava Alta 23. Good-value no-frills Castilian restaurant in an area packed with great bars.

Nightlife

Madrid parties late, with **clubs** starting around 1am and staying open until well beyond dawn. For diving in and out of clubs, as Madrileños like to do, the student area of Malsaña, focused on Plaza Dos de Mayo, holds most promise and the music in the clubs here is more of a grunge scene. A key street to start off explorations is c/San Vicente Ferrer. Chueca is more exclusively (but not entirely) gay – c/Pelayo is a good point to start. The up-and-coming Lavapiés/Anton Martín area, south of Sol, is also a popular bar and club locale. The music scene in Madrid sets the pattern for the rest of the country, and the best **rock bands** either come from here or make their name here. Bigger rock concerts are usually held in one of the football stadiums or at *La Riviera* on Paseo Bajo de la Virgen del Puerto. South American music is on offer at various venues, especially during summer festivals. **Flamenco** can also be heard at its best in the summer, especially at the *noches de flamenco* in the beautiful courtyard of the old barracks on c/de Conde Duque. What's-on **listings** are detailed in the English-language magazine *En Madrid*, the quarterly *Madrid Concept*, *Guia del Ocio* and *El Pais*, while gigs are advertised on posters around Sol. In July and August the city council sponsors a **Veranos de la Villa** programme of concerts and free cinema in some attractive outside venues.

Film is a passion in Madrid, reflected in the queues outside the huge-capacity cinemas on Gran Vía. The Spanish routinely dub foreign movies, but a few cinemas specialize in original-language screenings. These include the Alphaville and Renoir theatres at c/Martín de los Heros 14 and 12, near Plaza de España, the tiny California at c/Andrés Mellado 47 (Metro Moncloa) and the Círculo de Bellas Artes, on Marqués de Casa Riera. A bargain (€1.35) programme of classic films is shown at the lovely Art Deco Filmoteca at c/Santa Isabel 3, which has a pleasant bar and, in summer, an outdoor *cine-terraza*. Cultural events in English are held from time to time at the British Institute, c/Miguel Angel 1 (℡913 337 3501, ⓦwww.britishcouncil.es; Metro Alonso Martínez), which can also be a useful point for contacts.

Music bars and clubs

Café La Palma c/La Palma 62. For a little bit of everything.

El Sol c/Jardines 3; Metro Gran Vía. For house, soul and acid jazz, plus live music.

La Ventura c/Olmo 31. Some of Madrid's top *electronica* DJs play here.

Macumba Above Chamartín station. Weekend favourite where the likes of Ministry of Sound hit the decks until 9am.

Maxim Puerta de Toledo 1; Metro Puerta de Toledo. Another biggie, hosting both underground and celebrity techno and house DJs.

Pacha c/Barcelo 11. The eternal survivor – it's exceptionally cool during the week, less so at weekends when out-of-towners take over.

Shangay Tea Dance Gran Vía 37. On Sun nights from 10pm, one of the most popular gay nights in town.

Soul Kitchen Empire, Paseo de Recoletos 16; Metro Colon. For R&B, soul and reggae.

Ya'sta c/Valverde 10. Techno, house and drum'n'bass.

Live music

Café del Mercado Mercado Puerta de Toledo. Best year-round club for South American music, with live salsa every night (not Sun).

Gruta 77 c/Nicolas Morales, s/n & c/Cucillo 6. Cool foreign indie bands often play here.

Siroco c/San Dimas 3. For fans of *electronica*.

Suristán c/de la Cruz 7. The place to head most nights for live performances of all types of world music.

Taboo c/San Vicente Ferrer 23. Often has live music by young local bands.

Flamenco

Candela Olmo 2. Legendary bar frequented by musicians, with occasional performances.

Casa Patas Cañizares 10. Authentic club with bar and restaurant. Best nights Thurs & Fri. €12.

La Soleá Cava Baja 27. Bar with spontaneous flamenco happenings – people sit around, pick up a guitar and suddenly the night takes off. See it to believe it.

Listings

Bullfights Madrid's Plaza de Toros – *Las Ventas* – hosts some of the year's most prestigious events, especially during the May/June San Isidro festivities. Tickets for all but the biggest events are available at the box office ℡913 562 200, ⓦwww.las-ventas.com.

Embassies Australia, Plaza Descubridor Diego de Ordás 3 ℡914 416 025; Canada, Nuñez de Balboa 35 ℡914 233 250; Ireland, Paseo de la Castellana 46 ℡914 364 093; New Zealand, Plaza de la Lealtad 2 ℡915 230 226; UK, c/de Fernando el Santo 16 ℡917 008 200; US, c/Serrano 75 ℡915 872 200.

Exchange Large branches of most major banks on c/Alcalá and Gran Vía. Round the clock currency exchange at the airport; Banco Central is best for

AmEx cheques.

Hospitals La Paz del Insalud, Paseo Castellana 261 ℡917 277 000 (Metro Begoñ); Hospital de Madrid, Plaza Conde del Valle de Suchil 16 ℡914 476 600 (Metro Quevedo or San Bernardo).

Laundry Onda Blue c/ Léon 3 (Metro Anton Martin) also has Internet; c/Cervantes 1 (Metro Anton Martin); c/Pelayo 44 (Metro Chueca).

Pharmacies Farmacía Atocha, c/Atocha 114 ℡915 273 415; Farmacía Lopez Vicente, c/Gran Vía, 26 ℡915 213 148; Farmacia c/ Mayor 11 ℡913 664 616 (24hr). All have a list of night pharmacies posted outside.

Post office Palacio de Comunicaciones, Plaza de las Cibeles.

Around Madrid

Surrounding the capital are some of Spain's most fascinating cities, all an easy day-trip from Madrid or a convenient stop-off on the main routes out. From **Toledo** you can turn south to Andalucía or strike west towards Extremadura. To the northwest the roads lead past **El Escorial**, from where a bus runs to Franco's tomb at **El Valle de los Caídos**, and through the dramatic scenery of the Sierra de Guadarrama to **Segovia**.

Toledo

Capital of medieval Spain until 1560, **TOLEDO** remains the seat of the Catholic primate and a city redolent of past glories. Set in a desolate landscape, it rests on a rocky mound isolated on three sides by a looping gorge of the Río Tajo (Tagus). Every available inch of this outcrop has been built on: houses, synagogues, churches and mosques are heaped upon one another in a haphazard spiral, which the cobbled lanes infiltrate as best they can. To avoid the sightseeing hordes simply slip into the back streets or stay the night; by 6pm the tour buses have all gone home. Right at the heart of the city sits the **cathedral** (daily 8am–noon & 7pm, closed Sun pm, free; museum Mon–Sat 10.30am–6pm, Sun 2–6pm, €4.95), a robust Gothic construction that took over 250 years to complete (1227–1493). Inside, at the heart of the church is the Choir (closed Sun am), with two tiers of magnificently carved wooden stalls. Directly opposite stands the gargantuan altarpiece of the Capilla Mayor, one of the triumphs of Gothic art, while directly behind the main altar is an extraordinary piece of fantasy, the Baroque *Transparente*, with marble cherubs sitting on fluffy marble clouds – it's especially magnificent when the sun reaches through the hole punched in the roof (designed specifically for that purpose). In the Capilla Mozárabe, Mass is still celebrated daily (9.30am) according to the ancient Visigothic rites. You should also see the Capilla de San Juan, housing the riches of the cathedral treasury; the Sacristía, with the cathedral's finest paintings, including works by El Greco, Velázquez and Goya; and the New Museums, with more work from El Greco, who was born in Crete but settled in Toledo in about 1577.

Toledo is physically dominated by the imposing **Alcázar** (closed for restorations until 2005), east of the cathedral. In 1936, during the Civil War, six hundred barricaded Nationalists held out against relentless Republican attack for over two months until finally relieved by one of Franco's armies. Franco's regime completely rebuilt the fortress as a monument to the endurance and glory of its defenders. An excellent collection of El Grecos can be seen to the north of here in the **Museo de Santa Cruz** (Tues–Sat 10am–6.30pm, Sun 10am–2pm; free), and the **Museo de los Concilios y de la Cultura Visigótica** (Tues–Sat 10am–2pm & 4–6.30pm, Sun 10am–2pm; free), in the Mudéjar church of **San Román**, a short way northwest of the cathedral, is also well worth a visit. The building, a delightful combination of Moorish and Christian elements, perhaps even outshines the Visigothic artefacts within. However, El Greco's masterpiece, *The Burial of the Count of Orgaz*, is housed in an annexe to the nearby church of **Santo Tomé** (daily 10am–6.45pm; €1.50). From Santo Tomé, c/de San Juan de Dios leads down to the old Jewish quarter and, on c/Reyes Católicos, the synagogue of **El Tránsito**, built along Moorish lines by Samuel Levi in 1366. The only other surviving synagogue, **Santa María la Blanca** (daily 10am–2pm & 3.30–6/7pm; €1.50), is a short way down the same street, though it looks more like a mosque. If you leave the city by the **Puerta de Cambrón** you can follow the Paseo de Recaredo, which runs alongside a stretch of Moorish walls towards the **Hospital de Tavera** (10.30am–1.30pm & 3.30–6pm; €3), a Renaissance palace with beautiful twin patios. Heading back to town, pass through the main city gate, the **Nueva Puerta de Bisagra**, marooned by a constant swirl of traffic. The main road bears to the left, but on foot you can climb towards the centre of town by a series of stepped alleyways, past the intriguing Mudéjar church of **Santiago del Arrabal** and the tiny mosque of **Santo Cristo de la Luz**, one of the oldest Moorish monuments surviving in Spain.

Practicalities

From Toledo's **train station** it's a beautiful (but uphill) twenty-minute walk to the central Plaza Zocódover (bus #5 or #6). The **bus station** is on Avenida de Castilla la Mancha in the modern, lower part of the city, a ten-minute walk from the Plaza. *Cercanía* trains run from both Atocha and Chamartín stations in Madrid (last train back to Madrid at 8.58pm); buses depart from Estación del Sur, with the last bus back to Madrid leaving Toledo at 10pm (Sun 11.30pm). The main **tourist office** (Mon–Sat 9am–6/7pm, Sun 9am–3pm; ☎925 220 843), outside the walls opposite the Puerta de Bisagra, has full accommodation lists; there's also a useful office in Plaza Ayuntamiento (daily 10.30am–2.30pm & 4.30–7pm, closed Mon pm; ☎925 254 030). In summer **rooms** can be very hard to find, so it's worth arriving early. Central and inexpensive options include *Virgen de la Estrella*, Real del Arrabal 18 (☎925 255 134; ❷); *Pension Segovia*, Recoletos 2 (☎925 211 124; ❷); *Pension Castilla*, Recoletos 6 (☎925 256 318, ❷); and *Posada del Estudiante*, hidden behind the cathedral at San Pedro 2 (☎925 210 069; ❸). The nearest **campsite**, *El Circo Romano* (☎925 220 442), is a ten-minute walk from the Puerta de Bisagra along Avda. Carlos III; *El Greco* (☎925 220 090) is better but is further out on the road to Puebla de Montalban; both enjoy good city views.

Restaurants are plentiful but relatively expensive and not always very good quality. *La Bisagra*, c/Arrabal 14, just uphill from Puerta Bisagra, and *Arrabal*, opposite, are touristy but reasonably priced; while *Casa Ludeña*, Plaza Magdalena 13, southwest of Zocódover, has a cheap set menu. Northeast of Zocódover, c/Santa Fe has several **outdoor cafés** popular with a young crowd in the evenings. Less obvious places, all with good-value lunchtime menus, include the well-hidden *Posada del Estudiante*, c/de San Pedro 2, behind the cathedral; the pricier *Restaurante Palacios*, c/Alfonso X El Sabio 3; *El Rincón*, c/San Tomé 30; and *La Estrella*, c/Airosas 1, for paella and game. At night there's not a lot of action unless you're willing to head out to the hip neighbourhood of Plaza Cuba (bus #2 or #9), but there are a couple of late **bars**, like *Taberna* on Callejón de la Sillería. For **live music**, *Picaro*, c/Cadenas 6, has a different genre every night, and *El Último*, Plaza Colegio Infantes 4, hosts regular live blues and jazz. Of the **clubs**, best is the excellent *Venta de Alma*, housed in an old farmhouse across the Puente de San Martín on Carretera de Piedrabuena.

El Escorial and El Valle de Los Caídos

Northwest of Madrid is the line of mountains formed by the Sierra de Guadarrama and the Sierra de Gredos, snow-capped and forbidding even in summer. Beyond them lies Segovia, but on the near side, in the foothills of the Guadarrama, are **SAN LORENZO DEL ESCORIAL** and the bleak monastery of **El Escorial** (Tues–Sun 10am–6/7pm; €7, free on Wed for EU citizens). Enormous and overbearing, its severe grandeur can be impressive, but all too often it's just depressing. Planned by Philip II as a monastery and mausoleum, it was the centre of his web of letters, a place from which he boasted he could "rule the world with two inches of paper". To avoid the worst of the crowds, come just before lunch, or at least visit the royal apartments – focus of all the bus tours – at that time. If you can afford to avoid coming on Wednesday, even better. The west gateway leads into the **Patio de los Reyes**, where to the left is a school, to the right the monastery, both of them still in use, and straight ahead the **church**. Back outside and around to the left are the **Sacristía** and the **Salas Capitulares** (Chapterhouses), which contain many of the monastery's religious treasures, including paintings by Titian, Velázquez and Ribera. Beside the sacristy a staircase leads down to the **Panteón de los Reyes**, the final resting place of virtually all Spanish monarchs since Charles V. Just above the entrance is the *Pudrería*, where their bodies are laid to rot for twenty years or so before the cleaned skeletons are moved. The younger Royal corpses are laid in the **Panteón de los Infantes**. Nearby are the **Library**, with probably the most valuable collection of books in Spain, and the so-called **New Museums**, where much of the Escorial's art collection – works by Bosch, Gerard David, Dürer, Titian, Zurbarán and many others – is kept in an elegant suite of rooms. Finally, there's the

Palace itself, including the spartan quarters inhabited by Philip II. Later, less ascetic monarchs enlarged and richly decorated the palace apartments, but Philip's simple rooms, with the chair that supported his gouty leg and the deathbed from which he could look down into the church where Mass was constantly celebrated, remain the most fascinating.

Some 9km north of El Escorial is **El Valle de los Caídos** (Tues–Sun 10am–6/7pm; €5, joint ticket with El Escorial €9.50, free on Wed for EU citizens). This is an equally megalomaniacal yet far more chilling monument than El Escorial: an underground basilica hewn under Franco's orders, allegedly as a monument to the Civil War dead of both sides, though in reality it's a memorial to the Generalísimo and his regime. The dictator himself lies buried behind the high altar, while the only other named tomb is that of his guru, the Falange leader José Antonio Primo de Rivera, who was shot dead by Republicans at the beginning of the war. The "other side" is present only in the fact that the complex was built by the Republican army's survivors – political prisoners on quarrying duty. Above the complex is a vast **cross**, reputedly the largest in the world, and visible for miles around.

Trains run daily from Madrid Atocha to El Escorial, though **buses** leaving from Madrid's Moncloa area are faster, slightly cheaper and take you right to the monastery. If you arrive by train, get on the connecting local bus up to the town centre; it leaves promptly and it's a long uphill walk if you miss it. From El Escorial, the local bus operated by Herranz runs from the bus station to El Valle de los Caídos (Tues–Sun at 3.15pm, returning 5.30pm). The **tourist office** is near the monastery at c/Grimaldi 2 (daily 10am–7pm; ☎918 905 313). **Accommodation** in El Escorial is useful if you're also making a trip to El Valle de los Caídos. Cheap places include *Pensión El Retiro*, c/Aulencia 17 (☎918 900 946; ❸) and *Hostal Vasco*, Plaza Santiago 11 (☎918 901 619; ❸). There's also a **campsite** (☎918 902 412), 2km out on the road to Segovia, and an HI **hostel** (☎918 905 924; €7.80), usually crowded with school groups, at c/Residencia 14. **Eating** is expensive everywhere, but try the bar just inside the gate. Otherwise, there are several inexpensive places along c/Juan de Toledo, off Plaza Virgen de Gracia, and up the hill on c/Pozas.

Segovia

For such a small city, **SEGOVIA**, 100km northwest of Madrid, has a remarkable number of outstanding architectural monuments. Most celebrated are the Roman aqueduct, the cathedral and the fairy-tale Alcázar, but the less obvious attractions – the cluster of ancient churches and the many mansions found in the lanes of the old town, all in a warm, honey-coloured stone – are what really make it worth visiting. In winter, at over 1000m, it can be very cold here.

The **cathedral** (daily 10am–2pm & 4–8pm) was the last major Gothic building in Spain and it takes that style to its logical extreme, with pinnacles and flying buttresses tacked on at every conceivable point. The treasures are almost all confined to the **museum,** which opens off the cloisters. Beside the cathedral, c/de Daoiz leads past a line of souvenir shops to the church of San Andrés and on to a small park in front of the **Alcázar** (daily 10am–6/7pm; €3.10). It's an extraordinary fantasy of a castle, which, with its narrow towers and turrets, looks like something out of Disneyland. And indeed it is a sham – originally built in the fourteenth and fifteenth centuries but almost completely destroyed by fire in 1862 and rebuilt as a hyperbolic parody of the original. The **Aqueduct**, over 800m long and at its highest point towering 30m above the Plaza de Azoguejo, stands up without a drop of mortar or cement. No one knows exactly when it was built, but it was probably around the end of the first century AD under the emperor Trajan. Segovia is an excellent city for walking, with some fine views and beautiful churches to be enjoyed just outside the boundaries. Perhaps the most interesting church is **Vera Cruz** (Tues–Sun 10.30am–1.30pm & 3.30–6/7pm; €1.50), a remarkable twelve-sided building in the valley facing the Alcázar, erected by the Knights Templar in the early thirteenth century. Inside, the nave is circular, its heart occupied by a strange two-storeyed chamber – again twelve-sided – in which the knights, as part of their initiation, stood vigil. Climb the tower for a highly photogenic vista of the city. While you're over here you could also visit the prodigiously walled **Convento de los Carmelitas** (daily 10am–1.30pm & 4–7/8pm, closed Mon am), and the rather damp, ramshackle **Monasterio del Parral** (Mon–Sat 10–11.30/12.30am & 4–6.30pm, Sun 10am–2pm & 4–8pm).

Cercanía trains run to Segovia from Atocha or Chamartín stations or there's a bus from Madrid's main bus station. The **train station** is some distance out of town; take any bus (every 30min) marked "Puente Hierro/Estación Renfe" to the central Plaza Mayor. The **main tourist office** is at Plaza del Azoguejo 1 (daily 10am–8pm; ☎921 462 906). Try one of two **pensions** – *Cubo* (☎921 460 318; ❷) or *Aragón* (☎921 460 914; ❷) – on different floors of the same building at Plaza Mayor 4; or *Hostal Juan Bravo*, at c/Juan Bravo 12 (☎921 463 413; ❹), which has comfortable, if overpriced rooms. There are other cheap possibilities in the streets behind the plaza or near the aqueduct. The **campsite**, *Camping Acueducto* (closed Oct–March), is 2km out on the road to La Granja. Calle de la Infanta Isabella, which opens off the Plaza Mayor beside the **local tourist office** (Sun–Thur 9am–8pm, Fri & Sat 9am–9pm; ☎921 460 334), is packed with noisy **bars** and cheap **restaurants**. *Mesón de Cándido*, on Plaza del Azonguejo next to the aqueduct, is one of the best, pricey, but well worth it. Other places worth a try include *José María*, c/Cronista Lecea 11; *Narízotas*, Plaza de San Martin; and, for bar food and good, filling dishes, *El Portón Bar & Grill*, c/Romero 10. For **Internet** access, there's Stars Ciber Cafe on Paseo Conde de Sepulveda.

Extremadura

The harsh environment of **Extremadura**, west of Madrid, was the cradle of the *conquistadores*, men who opened up a new world for the Spanish Empire. Remote before and forgotten since, Extremadura enjoyed a brief golden age when the heroes returned with their gold to live in a flourish of splendour. **Cáceres** preserves an entire town built with conquistador wealth, the streets crowded with the ornate mansions of returning empire builders. An even more ancient past becomes tangible in the wonders of **Mérida**, the most completely preserved Roman city in Spain.

Cáceres

Old **CÁCERES**, 350km southwest of Madrid, was largely built on the proceeds of American exploration, but today it has perhaps been over-restored. Yet it remains a rapidly growing provincial capital, which is also home to the University of Extremadura. Any visit should begin with **Plaza Mayor**, opposite the tourist office, in the old town. Almost every building here is magnificent. It features ancient walls pierced by the low **Arco de la Estrella**, the **Torre del Bujaco** – whose foundations date back to Roman times – and in the **Torre del Horno**, one of the best-preserved Moorish mud-brick structures in Spain. Another highlight, through the Estrella gate, is the **Casa de Toledo-Montezuma** to which a follower of Cortés brought back one of the New World's more exotic prizes – a daughter of the Aztec emperor as his bride. In the Casa de las Valetas, on Plaza San Mateo, is the **Museo Provincial** (Tues–Sat 9am–2.30pm & 5–8pm, Sun 10.15am–2.30pm; free), whose highlight is the cistern of the original Moorish Alcázar, with rooms of wonderful horseshoe arches. Cáceres' **train and bus stations** face each other across the Carretera Sevilla, some way out of town; bus #1 runs (every 15min) to Plaza de San Juan, a square near the centre, with signs leading on towards the Plaza Mayor and the **tourist office** (Mon–Fri 9.30am–2pm & 4–6.30/7.30pm, Sat & Sun

9.30am–2pm; ☎927 246 347, ⊛www.turismoextremadura.com). The best **places to stay** are all near Plaza Mayor – like *Pensión Carretero* at no. 23 (☎927 247 482; ❷), or *Pensión Márquez* (☎927 244 960; ❷), just off the plaza at c/Gabriel y Galán 2. Right on Plaza Mayor, *El Pato* and *El Puchero* are good **restaurant** options, as is the more expensive *El Figón*, in Plaza San Juan just off c/Pintores. For **bar-hopping**, try the Plaza Mayor or c/de Pizarro, just outside the walls on the west side of the old town.

Mérida

MÉRIDA, 70km south of Cáceres, contains one of the most remarkable concentrations of Roman monuments to be found anywhere: scattered in the midst of the modern city are remains of everything from engineering works to domestic villas. With the aid of a map and a little imagination, it's not hard to reconstruct the Roman city within the not especially attractive modern town. A **combined ticket** (€7.20) gives access to all the sites (all open daily 9.30am–1.45pm & 4/5–6.15/7.15pm). The **Teatro Romano and Anfiteatro** was a present to the city from Agrippa in around 15 BC. The stage is in a particularly good state of repair and in July it plays host to a season of classical plays. In its day the adjacent amphitheatre could accommodate up to 15,000 people – almost half Mérida's population today. Also worth seeing is the magnificent **Puente Romano**, the Roman bridge across the islet-strewn Guadiana – sixty arches long, and defended by an enormous, plain, Moorish **Alcazaba**. Nearby is the sixteenth-century **Plaza de España**, the heart of the modern town. Just across from it, the vast, red-brick bulk of the **Museo Nacional de Arte Romano** (Mon–Sat 10am–2pm & 4/5–6/7pm, Sun 10am–2pm; €2.40, free on Sat pm & Sun for EU citizens) does full justice to its high-class collection, including portrait statues of Augustus, Tiberius and Drusus, and some glorious mosaics. Of the two Roman villas in Mérida, the **Casa Romana Anfiteatro**, which lies immediately below the museum, has perhaps the best mosaics.

Mérida's **tourist office** is at the entrance to the Roman theatre site on Paseo José Saenz de Burnaga (Mon–Fri 9am–2pm & 4/5–6.30/7.15pm, Sat & Sun 9.30am–2pm; ☎924 315 353, ⊛www.turismoextramadura.com). Budget **accommodation** isn't plentiful. Try *Hostal Nueva España*, Avda. Extremadura 6 (☎924 313 356; ❸), or *Hostal Salud*, c/Vespasiano 41 (☎924 31 22 59, ⊜hsalud@blunet.com; ❸). There's a **campsite**, *Camping Merida* (☎924 303 453) not far east of town on the Madrid-Lisbon highway, and a more attractive site at Proserpina (☎924 123 055; closed Oct–May), 5km north, where you can swim in the reservoir. Mérida is a lively place for its size, and the whole area between the train station and the Plaza de España is full of **bars and restaurants**. Inexpensive food in the town is hard to come by – try *Restaurante Briz*, just off the main plaza at Félix Valverde Lillo 5.

Old Castile

The foundations of modern Spain were laid in the kingdom of **Castile**, west and north of Madrid. A land of frontier fortresses – the *castillos* from which it takes its name – it became the most powerful and centralizing force of the Reconquest, extending its domination through military gains and marriage alliances. The monarchs of this triumphant and expansionist age were enthusiastic patrons of the arts, endowing their cities with superlative monuments above which, quite literally, tower the great Gothic cathedrals of **Salamanca** and **León**.

Salamanca

SALAMANCA is probably the most graceful city in Spain, home to what was once one of the most prestigious universities in the world and still boasting an unmistakable atmosphere of erudition. It's a small place, given a gorgeous harmony by the golden sandstone from which almost the entire city seems to be constructed. Two cathedrals, one Gothic, the other Romanesque, vie for attention with Renaissance palaces; the Plaza Mayor is the finest in Spain; and the surviving university buildings are tremendous. And as if that weren't enough, Salamanca's student population ensure their town is always lively at night. Two great architectural styles were developed, and see their finest expression, in Salamanca. **Churrigueresque**, a particularly florid form of Baroque, takes its name from José Churriguera (1665–1723), the dominant member of a prodigiously creative family. **Plateresque** came earlier, a decorative technique of shallow relief and intricate detail named for its alleged resemblance to the art of the silversmith (*platero*).

A postcard-worthy overview of Salamanca is easy to attain: go to the extreme south of the city and cross its oldest surviving monument, the much-restored, 400-metre-long **Puente Romano** (Roman Bridge). To explore Salamanca from the inside, though, make for the grand **Plaza Mayor**, its bare central expanse enclosed by a four-storey building decorated with iron balconies and medallion portraits. Nowhere is the Churrigueresque variation of Baroque so refined as here, the restrained elegance of the designs heightened by the changing strength and angle of the sun. From the south side, Rua Mayor leads to the vast Baroque church of **La Clerecía**, seat of the Pontifical University (open for visits Sun 12.30pm), and the celebrated **Casa de las Conchas**, or House of Shells (Mon–Fri 9am–9pm, Sat & Sun 10am–2pm & 4–7pm; free), so called because its facades are decorated with rows of carved scallop shells, symbol of the pilgrimage to Santiago. From the Casa de las Conchas, c/Libreros leads to the **Patio de las Escuelas** and the Renaissance entrance to the **University** (Mon–Sat 9.30am–1pm & 4–7pm, Sun 10am–1pm; €4, free Mon morning). The ultimate achievement of Plateresque art, this reflects the tremendous reputation of Salamanca in the early sixteenth century, when it was one of Europe's greatest universities.

As a further declaration of Salamanca's standing, the Gothic **Catedral Nueva** (daily 9am–8pm; free) was begun in 1512, and acted as a buttress for the Old Cathedral, which was in danger of collapsing. Alberto Churriguera and his brother Joaquín both worked here – the former on the choir stalls, the latter on the dome. Entry to the **Catedral Vieja** (daily 10am–7.30pm; €3) is through the first chapel on the right. Tiny by comparison and a stylistic hotch-potch of Romanesque and Gothic, its most striking feature is the huge fifteenth-century retable. Another faultless example of Plateresque art, the **Convento de San Esteban** (Sat & Sun 9am–1pm & 4–8pm; €1.50), is a short walk down c/del Tostado from the Plaza de Anaya at the side of the Catedral Nueva. The monastery's cloisters, through which you enter, are magnificent, but the most beautiful cloisters in the city stand across the road in the **Convento de las Dueñas** (daily 10.30am–1pm & 4.30–7pm; €1.50). Built on an irregular pentagonal plan, its upper-storey capitals are wildly carved with writhing demons and human skulls. The latest jewel in Salamanca's crown is no less spectacular. The **Museo Casa Lis** (Tues–Fri 11am–2pm & 4/5–7/9pm, Sat & Sun 11am–8/9pm; €2.10; ⓦwww.museocasalis.org) near the Roman Bridge, at c/Gilbratar 14, houses a spectacular collection of Art Nouveau and Art Deco furniture, ornaments and glass; the building itself – with its extravagant use of stained glass and light – is an extra treat.

Practicalities

The **bus and train stations** are on opposite sides of the city, each about fifteen minutes' walk from the centre. The municipal **tourist office** is at Plaza Mayor 14 (daily 9am–2pm & 4.30–6.30pm; ☎923 218 342), and the regional office at Casa de las Conchas (daily 9am–2pm & 5–8pm; ☎923 268 571). **Accommodation** is reasonably priced, but can be hard to find in high season – especially at fiesta time in September, and touts tend to be out in force at the train station in summer. Plaza Mayor is the best place to look – the small, cobbled streets around house scores of small *fondas* and *hostales*, most of a high standard: *Pensión Estefania*, c/Jesus 3 (☎923 217 372; ❷), and *pensiones Lisboa* (☎923 214 333; ❷) and *Barez* (☎923 217 495; ❷), at c/Melendez 1 and 19 respectively, are particularly good. There's also a friendly HI **hostel** at c/Escoto 13–15 (☎923 269 141, ⓦwww.alberguesalamanca.com; €11.90), just off Plaza Mayor, with six-bed dorms and excellent facilities. There are several **campsites** nearby, the least expensive being *Don Quijote* (☎923 209 052) at Cabrerizos, 4km out but served by bus #2 from Gran Vía.

The **cafés** in Plaza Mayor are pricey, but worth it for the splendour and atmosphere of the square. Close by in Plaza del Mercado (by the **market**, itself a good source of provisions), there's a row of lively **tapas bars**, while the university area has loads of good-value bars and **restaurants** catering to student budgets. Good-value places include *Cervecería del Comercio*, c/Poco Amarillo 23, and *El Bardo*, c/Compañía 8, selling vegetarian food and alcohol. About the cheapest *menús del día* are at *Restaurante Bar Llamas*, c/Pavel 9, which also has outdoor seating and good sandwiches, and at places along the streets around the market and towards the bus station. Late-night **bars** abound in the Gran Vía area; among the most popular are *El Corrillo*, c/Melendez, for jazz, and *El Callejón*, Gran Vía 68, for folk. The most popular **clubs** include *El Cum Laude*, on c/Prior off Plaza Mayor, which attracts mainly teenagers at weekends; *Potemkin*, off Gran Vía, which is open until sunrise, and *El Puerto de Chus*, on Plaza de San Julián.

León

The stained glass in the cathedral of **LEÓN** and the Romanesque wall paintings in its Royal Pantheon are reason enough for many people to visit the city, but León is also – unusually for this part of the country – as attractive and enjoyable in its modern quarters as it is in those areas that remain from its heyday. The city has a rich history: in 914, as the Reconquest edged its way south from Asturias, this became the Christian capital, and along with its territories it grew so rapidly that by 1035 the county of Castile had matured into a fully fledged kingdom. For the next two centuries León and Castile jointly spearheaded the war against the Moors, but by the thirteenth century Castile's power had eclipsed that of even her mother territory.

León's **cathedral** (daily 8.30am–1.30pm & 4–7/8pm) dates from the city's final years of greatness. It is said to be a miracle that it's still standing: it has the largest proportion of glass to stone of any Gothic cathedral. The kaleidoscopic stained-glass windows present one of the most magical and harmonious spectacles in Spain, and the colours used – reds, golds and yellows – could only be Spanish; the bewildering sensation of refracting light was further enhanced by the addition last century of a glass screen, allowing a clear view up to the altar. The west facade, dominated by a massive rose window, is also magnificent. The city's other great attraction is the **Real Colegiata de San Isidoro**, which houses the bodies of the early kings of León and Castile. Ferdinand I, who united the two kingdoms in 1037, commissioned the complex as a shrine for the bones of St Isidore, which lie in a reliquary on the high altar, and a mausoleum for himself and his successors. The **pantheon** (Mon–Sat 10am–1.30pm & 4–6.30pm, Sun 10am–1.30pm; €3, free Thurs pm), a pair of small crypt-like chambers, is in front of the west facade. One of the earliest Romanesque buildings in Spain (1054–1063), it was decorated towards the end of the twelfth century with some of the most imaginative and impressive paintings of Romanesque art. They are extraordinarily well preserved and their biblical and everyday themes are perfectly adapted to the architecture of the vaults. Also worth seeing is the opulent **Monasterio de San Marcos**, built in 1168 for the Knights of Santiago, one of several chivalric orders founded in the twelfth century both to protect pilgrims on their way to Santiago de Compostela and to lead the Reconquest. Fittingly, it has been converted into a *parador*, where the guests enjoy the luxury of a magnificent church of their own, the **Iglesia San Marcos**. The church can be visited by non-patrons too; its sacristy houses a small **museum** (Tues–Sat 10am–2pm & 4/5–7/8pm, Sun 10am–2pm; €1.20) of priceless exhibits, housed in a room separated from the hotel lobby by a thick pane of glass.

The train and bus stations are both just south of the river: the **train station** at the end of Avenida de Palencia, the bridge across into town, and the **bus station** on Paseo Ingeniero Saenz de Miera – from here, turn left onto the Paseo to reach the bridge. From the roundabout, just across the river at Glorieta Guzmán El Bueno, you can see straight down Avenida de Ordoño II and across the Plaza de Santo Domingo to the cathedral. Directly opposite the cathedral's west facade stands the friendly **tourist office** (Mon–Fri 9am–2pm & 5–7pm, Sat & Sun 10am–2pm & 5–8pm; ☎987 237 082, ⊛www.jcyl.es/turismo). There are plenty of **places to stay**, particularly on the main roads leading off the Glorieta, Avda. de Roma and Avda. Ordoño II. Good budget options include: *Hostal Oviedo* at Avda. de Roma 26 (☎987 222 236; ❷); *Hostal Bayon* at Alcazar de Toledo 6 (☎987 31 446; ❷); *Pensión Suarez*, right next to the cathedral at c/Ancha 7-2° (☎987 254 288; ❷); and *Pensión Puerta del Sol* (☎987 211 966; ❷), overlooking the Plaza Mayor. There's a summer-only HI **hostel** with a pool at c/de la Corredera 4 (☎987 203 414; ❶) – follow Avda. de Independencia from Plaza de Santo Domingo – and another at c/Campos Góticos 3 (☎897 261 174; ❶), about twenty minutes' walk from the cathedral and stations, by the bullring. For sheer enjoyment, the best time of year to be in León is for the **fiesta** of St Peter in the last week of June. The rest of the year, the liveliest places tend to be the **bars and restaurants** in the small square of San Martín, behind Plaza Mayor, and the dark narrow streets that surround it. You'll find good food at the *Restaurante Fornos*, c/Cid 8, and a surprisingly tasty, cheap menu at *Parada de Postas*, in the bus station.

Spain's north coast

Spain's **north coast** veers wildly from the typical conception of the country, with a rocky, indented coastline full of cove beaches and fjord-like *rías*. It's an immensely beautiful region – mountainous, green and thickly forested, with frequent rains often shrouding the countryside in a fine mist. The summers are temperately warm and, if you don't mind the occasional shower, provide a glorious escape from the unrelenting heat of the south. In the east, butting against France, is **Euskadi** – the **Basque Country** – which, despite some of the heaviest industrialization on the peninsula, remains remarkably unspoiled: neat and quiet inland, rugged and enclosed along the coast, with easy, efficient transport connections. **San Sebastián** is the big seaside attraction, a major resort with superb but crowded beaches, but there are any number of lesser-known, equally attractive coastal villages all the way to **Bilbao** and beyond. Note that the Basque language, Euskera, bears almost no relation to Spanish (we've given the alternative Basque names where popularly used) – it's perhaps the most obvious sign of Spain's strongest separatist movement. To the west lies **Cantabria**, centred on the port of **Santander**, with more good beaches and superb trekking in the mountains of the **Picos de Europa**. The mountains extend into **Asturias**, the one part of Spain never conquered by the Moors. Its high, remote valleys are mining country, providing the raw materials for the heavy industry of the three cities: Gijón, Avilés and Oviedo. In the far west, **Galicia** looks like Ireland, and there are further parallels in its climate, culture and – despite its fertile appearance – its history of famine and poverty. While right-wing Galicia may not share the radical traditions of the Basque country or Asturias it does treasure its independence, and Gallego is still spoken by around 85 percent of the population – again, we've given Gallego place names in parentheses. For travellers, the obvious highlight is **Santiago de Compostela**, the greatest goal for pilgrims in medieval Europe.

If you're not in a great hurry, you may want to make use of the independent **FEVE rail line** (☎902 100 818, ✆www.feve.es; rail passes not valid). The rail line begins at Bilbao and follows the coast, with inland branches to Oviedo and León, all the way to El Ferrol in Galicia. Despite recent major repairs and upgrading, it's still slow but it's cheap and a terrific journey, skirting beaches, crossing rivers and snaking through a succession of limestone gorges.

San Sebastián

The undisputed queen of Basque resorts, **SAN SEBASTIÁN** (Donostia), just an hour by road from Bilbao, is a picturesque – though expensive – town with excellent beaches, restaurants and bars. Along with Santander, it has always been the most fashionable place to escape the heat of the southern summers, and in July and August it's packed with well-to-do-families. Set around the deep, still bay of La Concha and enclosed by rolling low hills, San Sebastián is beautifully situated; the old town sits on the eastern promontory at the wooded slopes of Monte Urgull, while newer development has spread inland along the banks of the River Urumea and around the edge of the bay to the foot of Monte Igüeldo.

The **old quarter**'s cramped and noisy streets are where crowds congregate in the evenings to wander among the small bars and shops or sample the shellfish from the traders down by the fishing harbour. Here too are the town's chief sights: the gaudy Baroque facade of the church of **Santa María**, and the more elegantly restrained sixteenth-century **San Vicente**. The centre of the old part is the Plaza de la Constitución, known locally as "La Consti"; the numbers on the balconies of the buildings around the square refer to the days when it was used as a bullring. Just behind San Vicente, the excellent **Museo de San Telmo** (Tues–Sat 10.30am–1.30pm & 4–8pm, Sun 10.30am–2pm; free) is a fascinating jumble of Basque folklore, funerary relics and assorted artworks. Behind this, **Monte Urgull** is criss-crossed by winding footpaths to the top. From the mammoth figure of Christ on its summit there are great views out to sea and back across the bay to the town. Still better views across the bay can be had from the top of **Monte Igüeldo**; take bus #16 or walk around the bay to its base, from where a **funicular** (daily

11am–8pm, closed Wed in winter; €1.50 return) will carry you to the summit, the home of a **funfair** (€1.10). **La Concha** beach is the most central and the most celebrated, a wide crescent of yellow sand stretching round the bay from the town. Out in La Concha bay is a small island, **Isla de Santa Clara**, which makes a good spot for picnics; a boat leaves from the Paseo Mollaberria (summer 10am–8.30pm, every 30min; €2.30). **Ondaretta**, considered the best beach for swimming and never quite as packed as La Concha, is a continuation of the same strand beyond the rocky outcrop that supports the **Palacio Miramar** (gardens open 9/10am–sunset; free), once a summer home of Spain's royal family. The atmosphere here is rather more staid – it's known as *La Diplomática* for the number of Madrid's "best" families who holiday here. Far less crowded, and popular with surfers, **Playa de Zurriola** and the adjacent **Playa de Gros** have had breakwaters added to shield them from dangerous currents. Should you tire of sun and antiquity, head for the sparkling conference and cultural centre, the **Palacio Kursaal** (guided tours Mon–Fri at 1.30pm, Sat & Sun 11.30am, 12.30pm & 1.30pm; €3) on Avenida de Zurriola. Designed by Rafael Moneo, and set on the banks of the River Urmuea by Playa de Zurriola, the building consists of two translucent glass cubes not dissimilar to Japanese lanterns – an elegant sight at night.

Practicalities

National **buses** use the terminal at Plaza Pío XII (the ticket office is round the corner on Avda. de Sancha el Sabio), twenty minutes' walk inland along the river, while regional ones go from Plaza de Guipúzcoa. The main-line **train station** is across the River Urumea on Paseo de Francia, although local lines to Hendaye and Bilbao (rail passes not valid) have their terminus on c/Easo. The **tourist office**, at c/Reina Regente 3 in the old town (Mon–Sat 8/9am–1.30pm & 3.30–7/8pm, Sun 10am–2pm; ☎943 481 166, ⊛www.sansebastianturismo.com), is very helpful in finding a place to stay, or use the **online reservations service** at ⊛www.paisvasco.com/centralreservas.

    Accommodation, though plentiful, is not cheap and can be very hard to come by in season and at weekends. In the old town, look around La Consti and c/San Jerónimo; in the central district there's better value around the cathedral, especially calles Easo, San Martín and San Bartolomé; or on the other side of the river try behind the Plaza de Cataluña, where you'll also find excellent tapas bars. Places to try in the old part include *Pensión San Jerómino*, c/San Jerómino 25 (☎943 427 525; ❹) and *Pensión Anne*, c/Esterlines 15 (☎943 421 438, ⊛www.pensionanne.es.org; ❸). Around the cathedral, try *Pensión La Perla*, c/Loyola 10 (☎943 428 123; ❸) or the more expensive *Pensión San Martín*, c/San Martín 10 (☎943 428 714; ❹), where all the rooms are en suite. The **hostel** (☎943 310 268; €13.40), known as *La Sirena*, is on Paseo de Igüeldo, just a few minutes' walk back from the end of Ondarreta beach, but away from the centre.

    San Sebastián has some of the best **restaurants** in the country. Prices reflect the popularity of the area, especially in the waterside restaurants, but it's no hardship to survive on the delicious **tapas**, which are laid out in all but the fanciest bars – check the prices first, but around €1.20 per *pintxo* is the norm. Or you can try the fixed menus at places near the cathedral, such as *Ardandegi*, c/Reyes Católicos 7, the highly recommended *La Barranquesa*, c/Larramendi 21, or, in the old quarter, *Morgan Jatetxea* on c/Narrika Kalea. Alternatively, order some well-priced *raciones* at either *Gaztelu*, c/31 de Agosto 22, or *Beti-Jai*, on c/Narrika, in the old town. The fanciest **bars and clubs** are along the promenade by the beach, Paseo de la Concha, where you'll pay €12–18 to get in; the cheaper places are mostly in the old town where people normally start the evening off – later everyone heads to the area along c/Reyes Católicos behind the cathedral or c/San Bartolomé. For late nights, head for *Etxekalte* at c/Mari Kalea 11, overlooking the port and beach, where a young clientele groove to jazz, urban soul and hip-hop (free entry). A recent addition to San Sebastián's night scene are "growshops", a blend of

27

Amsterdam café, art gallery and bar – Soma *107*, on c/Larramendi 4, is one of the best. Many summer **festivals** involve Basque sports, like the annual rowing races between the villages along the coast. The **International Jazz Festival** (third week July; ☻www.jazzaldia.com), at different locations throughout the town, invariably attracts top performers as well as hordes of people on their way home from the fiesta in Pamplona.

Bilbao

Although traditionally an industrial city, **BILBAO** (Bilbo) has given itself a makeover and is now a priority destination on any Spanish tour. And no surprise: a state-of-the-art metro (designed by Norman Foster) links the city's widespread attractions; the breathtaking Guggenheim Museum by Frank Gehry – along with Jeff Koons' puppy sculpture in flowers – is a major draw; the airport and one of the many dramatic river bridges are Calatrava-designed; and there are various bids to further develop the riverfront with university buildings and public parks. Coupled with a vibrant, friendly atmosphere, lots of elegant green spaces and some of the best cafés, restaurants and bars in Euskadi, these all make Bilbao a city that's here to stay. The **Casco Viejo**, the old quarter on the east bank of the river, is focused on the beautiful **Teatro Arriaga**, the elegantly arcaded **Plaza Nueva**, the Gothic **Catedral de Santiago** (Tues–Sat 10am–1.30pm & 4–7pm, Sun 10.30am–1.30pm; free), and the interesting **Basque Museum** on Plaza Miguel de Unamuno, 4 (Tues–Sat 11am–5pm, Sun 11am–2pm; €3). However, it is along the Río Nervión that a whole number of exciting new buildings has appeared. A good route leads from the Casco Viejo down the river past the Campo Volantin footbridge and the more imposing Zubizuri bridge to the sensual, billowing titanium curves of the **Guggenheim Museum** (Tues–Sun 10am–8pm; €7), described as "the greatest building of our time". The building and exterior sculptures are arguably more of an attraction than most of the art inside: the permanent collection, which includes works by Kandinsky, Klee, Mondrian, Picasso, Chagall and Warhol, to name a few, is housed in traditional galleries; temporary exhibitions and individual artists' collections are displayed in the huge sculpted spaces nearer the river. Further along from the Guggenheim, on the edge of the Parque de Doña Casilda de Hurriza, is the **Museo de Bellas Artes** (Tues–Sat 10am–8pm, Sun 10am–2pm; €4.50, free on Wed), which houses works by Goya and El Greco and some fine temporary exhibitions.

The FEVE and RENFE **train stations** are located just over the river from the Casco Viejo, while most **buses** arrive some way out of the centre at San Mamés – from here, catch the metro to the centre. Buses from Barcelona and Madrid arrive on c/Autonomía, a twenty-minute walk via Plaza de Zabálburu from the old town. From the **airport,** a bus (daily 6am–10pm, every 30min–1hr; €1) runs to Plaza Moyua in the centre. The **tourist office** is at c/Rodriguez Arias (Mon–Fri 9am–2pm & 4–7.30pm, Sat 9am–2pm, Sun 10am–2pm; ☎944 795 760, ☻www.bilbao.net, and there's another branch just outside the Guggenheim (Tues–Fri 11am–2.30pm & 3.30–6pm, Sat 11am–3pm & 4–7pm, Sun 11am–2pm). **Accommodation** is best in the Casco Viejo – especially along and around the streets leading off c/Bidebarrieta, which leads from Plaza Arriaga to the cathedral. In summer and at weekends, booking ahead is advisable. Good possibilities are the *Hostal Gurea*, c/Bidebarrieta 14 (☎944 163 299; ❸); the superb *pensiones Ladero*, c/Lotería 1 (☎944 150 932; ❸), and *Mendez*, c/Santa Maria 13 (☎944 160 364; ❸), where some rooms have balconies; *Pensión Serantes*, c/Somera 14 (☎944 151 557; ❷); and *Hostal Roquefer*, c/Lotería 2 (☎944 150 755; ❸). **Internet** access is available at Laser, c/Sendaja 31. **Eating and drinking** are also best in the Casco Viejo, although there are few regular restaurants – this is one of those cities where the most enjoyable way to eat is to move from bar to bar, snacking on tapas: Plaza Nueva and the area known as the *siete calles* have numerous options. For breakfast try the excellent *Café Boulevard* on Paseo del Arenal, and for a mid-afternoon coffee you can't beat the Arabic-style *Café Iruña* across the river at c/Jardines de Albia 5. For a sit-down meal, there's the highly recommended Basque restaurant *Bar Rio-Oja*, c/Perro 4, just west of the cathedral, and there are other good restaurants and bars along the same street. Bilbao can be very lively indeed at **night** – and totally wild during the August **fiesta**, La Semana Grande (from first Sat after Aug 15), with scores of open-air bars, live music and impromptu dancing. Head for the streets around c/Licenciado Poza and c/Ledesma.

Santander

Long a favourite summer resort of Madrileños, **SANTANDER** has an elegant, reserved, almost French feel. Some people find it a clean, restful base for a short stay; for others it is dull and snobbish. On a brief visit, the balance is tipped in its favour by its excellent beaches and the sheer style of its setting. The narrow **Bahía de Santander** is dramatic, with the city and port on one side in clear view of open countryside and high mountains on the other; it's a great first view of Spain if you're arriving on the ferry from England. Santander was severely damaged by fire in 1941 and what's left of the city divides into two parts: the **town and port**, clumsily reconstructed on the old grid around a mundane cathedral; and the beach suburb of **El Sardinero**, a twenty-minute walk (or bus #1, #3, #4, #7 or #9) from the centre, more if you follow the coast around the wooded headland of **La Magdalena**. There are few real sights to distract you, and it's for the glorious beaches that most people come. The first of these, **Playa de la Magdalena**, begins on the near side of the headland. The beautiful yellow strand, sheltered by cliffs and flanked by a summer windsurfing school, is deservedly popular, as is El Sardinero itself. If you find these beaches too crowded, head for the long stretches of dunes across the bay at **Somo** (which has windsurfing boards for rent and a summer campsite) or **Pedreña**; jump on a *lancha*, a cheap taxi-ferry (every 15min, €2.95 return) from the central Puerto Chico dock.

The RENFE and FEVE **train and bus stations** are centrally located, side by side near the waterfront at Plaza Porticada. There are three **tourist offices**: the best is in the Jardines de la Pereda (July–Sept daily 9am–9pm; rest of the year Mon–Fri 9.30am–1.30pm & 4–7pm, Sat 9.30am–1.30pm; ☏942 203 000). Good places to look for **rooms** are c/de Rodríguez in front of the station – *San Miguel* at no. 9 (☏942 220 363; ❸) is an option, as is *Botín* (☏942 210 094; ❸), at nearby c/Isabel Segundo 1. c/El Sardinero also has some budget options, such as *Pension Soledad* at no. 17 (☏942 270 936; ❸), and there's a **campsite** (☏942 391 542) on Cabo Mayor. There's also a summer-only **hostel**, *Albaicin*, at c/Francisco Palazuelos, 21–23 (☏942 217 753; ❷). **Food** options are plentiful around the main square and station, along c/San Simón and – for great tapas and a good **drinking** scene – c/Río de la Pila, above Plaza de Velarde. For seafood, wander down to the fishing port (*puerto pesquero*), to the east of the ferry port and stations; there's no shortage of places along c/Marqués de la Ensanada, but check prices before ordering – *Casa José* on nearby c/Mocejón is more reasonably priced than most.

Picos de Europa National Park

The **Picos de Europa** offer some of the finest hiking, canoeing and other mountain activities in Spain. The densely forested national park boasts two glacial lakes, a series of peaks over 2400m high, and wildlife ranging from otters to bears. From Santander, about 80km to the east, the park is reached by passing through San Vicente de la Barquera, Unquera and Cares; alternative access is from Oviedo in the south, a spectacular drive of 80km along winding, narrow roads. There's a helpful **tourist office** (June–Sept daily 10am–10pm; Oct–May Mon–Sat 10am–2pm & 4–7pm; ☏985 848 005, ✆www.picosdeeuropa.com) in **CANGAS DE ONÍS**, a major gateway to the park. There's **accommodation** in Cangas de Onís at *Hospedaje Torreón* (☏985 848 211, ✆www.iespana.es/pensiontorreon; ❸). There's also a **campsite** at Soto de Cangas, 3.5km west (☎985 940 097), and a private **hostel**, *Albergue La Posada del Monasterio* (☎985 848 553, ⊛www.posadadelmonasterio.com; €13.50), in an old monastery in La Vega-Villanueva, 2km northwest of Cangas de Onís; the management organizes canoeing, hiking and other activities in the park. You can also stay at **COVADONGA** in the park at the *Hospedería del Peregrino* (☎985 846 047, ⊛www.picosdeeuropa.com/incatur/elperegrino; ❸).

Santiago de Compostela

SANTIAGO DE COMPOSTELA, built in a warm golden granite, is one of the most beautiful of all Spanish cities. The whole of this medieval place has been declared a national monument and it remains remarkably uniform in its charm, the more so for being almost wholly pedestrianized. The **pilgrimage to Santiago** (see box) captured the imagination of medieval Christian Europe on an unprecedented scale; during the eleventh and twelfth centuries, when the city was at the height of its popularity, it received half a million pilgrims each year. People of all social backgrounds came to visit the supposed shrine of St James the Apostle (Santiago to the Spanish), making this the third-holiest site in Christendom, after Jerusalem and Rome. These days, tourists are as likely to be attracted by art and history as by religion, but the all-round atmosphere of the place must not be dissimilar to that of the pilgrim days. Once host to kings and all manner of society, Santiago is by no means a dead city now – it's the seat of Galicia's regional government, and houses a great contemporary art gallery and a large student population. It's also a manageable size – fifteen minutes' walk from the centre, you're in open countryside.

All roads lead to the **cathedral** (daily 7.30am–9pm, visits allowed outside Mass), whose sheer grandeur you first appreciate upon venturing into the vast expanse of the Praza de Obradoiro. Directly ahead stands a fantastic Baroque pyramid of granite, flanked by immense bell towers and everywhere adorned with statues of St James in his familiar pilgrim guise with staff, broad hat and scallop-shell badge. This Obradoiro facade was built in the mid-eighteenth century by an obscure Santiago-born architect, Fernando Casas y Novoa, and no other work of Spanish Baroque can compare with it. The building's highlight is the **Pórtico de Gloria**, the original west front, which now stands inside the cathedral behind the Obradoiro. So many millions have pressed their fingers into the roots of the *Tree of Jesse* below the saint that five deep and shiny holes have been worn into the solid marble. The spiritual climax of the pilgrimage was the approach to the **High Altar**. This remains a peculiar experience: you climb steps behind the altar, embrace the Most Sacred Image of Santiago, kiss his bejewelled cape, and are handed, by way of certification, a document in Latin called a *Compostela*. The statue has stood there for seven centuries and

The Camino de Santiago

The most famous Christian pilgrimage in the world, the **Camino de Santiago** – or Way of St James – traces routes through France and Spain to Santiago de Compostela. If you're travelling in this part of the world, you will doubtless see many pilgrims, identified – mainly to each other – by the coquille St Jacques, a large effigy of a scallop shell, that they wear attached to their backpack. "Santiago de Compostela" comes from the Latin meaning "St James of the Field of Stars"; it's named after a peasant who had a vision in a field of stars near where the town now lies; soon after, the Catholic Church miraculously discovered that the disciple James had been buried in that very spot. There are those that scoff at the notion that James was ever in Spain, never mind buried here; some see it as an early church PR exercise to garner some enthusiasm against the Moors. Whether you believe or not, the reality is that millions *do* – if not in the legend, at least in the physical and mental challenge of a pilgrimage on foot. Should you be interested in walking, cycling or taking the train, check ⊛www.caminosantiago.com.

the procedure is quite unchanged. The elaborate pulley system in front of the altar is for moving the immense incense-burner – *El Botafumeiro* – which, operated by eight priests, is swung in a vast ceiling-to-ceiling arc across the transept. It is stunning to watch, but it takes place only during certain festival services – check with the tourist office. You can also visit the treasury, archeological museum, cloisters and crypt (Mon–Sat 10am–1.30pm & 4–6.30pm, Sun 10am–1.30pm; €5).

The enormous Benedictine **San Martín** stands close to the cathedral, the vast altarpiece in its church depicting its patron riding alongside St James. Nearby is **San Francisco**, reputedly founded by the saint himself during his pilgrimage to Santiago. In the north of the city are Baroque **Santa Clara**, with a unique curving facade, and a little beyond it, **Santo Domingo**. This last is perhaps the most interesting of the buildings, featuring a magnificent seventeenth-century triple stairway, each spiral leading to a different storey of a single tower, and a fascinating museum of Gallego crafts and traditions, the **Museo do Pobo Gallego** (Mon–Sat 10am–2pm & 4–8pm; free). A symbol of Santiago's enduring creativity and charm lies just next door, in the **Centro Galego de Arte Contemporánea** (Tues–Sun 11am–8pm; free), a beautiful gallery designed by Portuguese architect Álvaro Siza and host to a revolving triumvirate of challenging visiting exhibitions.

Practicalities

Arriving at Santiago **bus station** you're 1km or so north of the town centre; bus #10 runs to Plaza de Galicia at the southern edge of the old city. The **train station** is a walkable distance south of the plaza along c/del Horreo. The **tourist office** is at Rúa do Vilar 63 (daily: summer 9am–9pm; winter 10am–3pm & 5–8pm; ☎981 555 129, ⓦwww.santiagoturismo.com), and can provide complete lists of accommodation. There is **Internet access** at Cibernova, c/Rúa Nova 50. You should have no difficulty finding an inexpensive **room**, though note that *pensiones* here are often called *hospedajes*. The biggest concentration of places is on the three parallel streets leading down from the cathedral: Rúa Nueva, Rúa do Vilar and c/del Franco. *Hospedaje Santa Cruz*, Rúa do Vilar 42 (☎981 582 362; ❷), has very friendly English-speaking owners whilst *Hostal Barbantes II*, c/del Franco 1 (☎981 581 077; ❸), has a lively bar and restaurant. *Residencia La Estela*, Avda. Raxoi 1 (☎981 582 796; ❸), is a little more expensive, but very well located on the corner of Praza Obradoiro. A cheaper option is *Hospedaje Viño* at Praza de Mazarelos 7 (☎981 585 185; ❷) – the indomitable owner also has dozens of other rooms across town. There's a summer-only **pilgrim refuge** at Avda. Quiroga Palacios (☎981 589 200; €3) and a **hostel** with good facilities 3km out of town at Monte de Gozo (☎981 558 942; ❶) – take bus #C1 or #6 from Praza de Galicia. The **campsite**, *Camping As Cancelas* (☎981 580 266), 2.5km north of the cathedral, is excellent; take city bus #4 or #6. Thanks, perhaps, to the students, there are plenty of cheap **restaurants** and excellent bars; it's also the best place in Galicia to hear local Breton-style music, played on *gaitas* (bagpipes). Seafood and fish are good at *Bodegón de Xulio*, Rúa Franco 24, and there are good **tapas bars** nearby, such as *Tacita de Juan* at Rúa Hórreo 31, and the gorgeous green-tiled and mirrored *Cafetería Paradiso*, Rúa do Vilar 29, where you'll even get a few tapas for free. Good **bars** include the inebriated *El Retablo* at Rúa Nova 13, the alternative *Bar Tolo* on Fonte de San Miguel, or the popular *A Reixa* at Tras de Salomé 3.

The Pyrenees

With the singular exception of **Pamplona** at the time of its bull-running fiesta, the area around the Spanish Pyrenees is little visited – most people who come here at all travel straight through. In doing so they miss out on some of the most wonderful scenery in Spain, and some of the country's most attractive trekking. You'll also be struck by the slower pace of life, especially in **Navarra** (in the west, a partly Basque

27

region) and **Aragón** (in the centre); the Catalan Pyrenees (for which, see p.858) are more developed. There are few cities here – Pamplona itself and **Zaragoza**, with its fine Moorish architecture, are the only large centres – but there are plenty of attractive small towns and, of course, the mountains themselves, with several beautiful **national parks** as a focus for exploration.

Pamplona

PAMPLONA (Iruña) has been the capital of Navarra since the ninth century, and long before that was a powerful fortress town defending the northern approaches to Spain. Even now it has something of the appearance of a garrison city, with its hefty walls and elaborate pentagonal citadel. The compact and lively streets of the old town offer plenty to look at – the elaborately restored **cathedral** with its magnificent cloister and interesting **Museo Diocesano** (Mon–Fri 10am–1.30pm & 4–7pm, Sat 10am–1.30pm; €3.80), the colossal **city walls** and **citadel**, the display of regional archeology, history and art in the **Museo de Navarra** (Tues–Sat 10am–2pm & 5–7pm, Sun 11am–2pm; €1.80, free Sat pm & all Sun), and much more – but most visitors come here for just one thing: the thrilling week of the Fiesta of San Fermín (see box).

The **train station** is a long way from the old part of town, but bus #9 runs every twenty minutes to the end of Paseo de Sarasate, a few minutes' walk from the central Plaza del Castillo – there is a RENFE ticket office at c/Estella 8. The **bus station** is on c/Conde Oliveto in front of the citadel, while the **tourist office** (summer Mon–Sat 10am–2pm & 4–7pm, Sun 10am–2pm; ☎948 206 540, ⓦwww.cfnavarra.es/turismonavarra) is at c/Eslava 1 on Plaza San Francisco. There's a cluster of cheap **hostales** on noisy c/San Nicolás and its continuation c/San Gregorio, off Plaza del Castillo. Rooms are in short supply during summer, and at fiesta time you've virtually no chance of a place without booking – and most at least double their prices. Good places to try include *La Montañesa*, c/San Gregorio 2 (☎948 224 380; ❷), and *Casa García*, c/San Gregorio 12 (☎948 223 893; ❹). Right next to Plaza del Castillo, the more upmarket *Hostal Arriazu*, c/Comedias 14 (☎948 210 202; ❺) is not cheap but is good value. Otherwise, try nearer the cathedral – *Santa Cecilia*, c/Navarrería 17 (☎948 222 230; ❸), is atmospheric and good.

There's a **campsite**, *Ezcaba* (☎948 330 315; bus #4), 7km out of town on the road to France; again it fills several days before the fiesta. If you end up **sleeping rough**, remember that there is safety in numbers – head for one of the many parks such as Vuelta del Castillo or Media Luna and bring a sleeping bag, as the nights are cool. To clean off, there are **public baths** at c/Eslava (Tues–Sat 8.30am–8pm, Sun 8.30am–1pm), where you can have a hot shower/bath.

Pamplona's nightlife scene is one of the most boisterously cheerful in Spain; best **bars** are on and around c/San Nicolás, and during San Fermín on c/Jarauta and c/San Lorenzo too, as well as a number of grungy late-night dives on Calderia S. Augustín on the other side of the square. **Food** is expensive in Pamplona and you'll be hard pressed to find a set menu for less than €8 – about the cheapest option is *Catachu*, c/Indatxikia 16, parallel to Paseo de Sarasate. Alternatively, try the streets around c/Mayor, in particular *Erburu* at c/San Lorenzo 19, something of a local institution, or *Bar la Campana* on c/de la Campana, which offers a combination of *bocadillos* and a good menu. C/San Nicolás also has several reasonable restaurants including *Dom Luis* and the excellent vegetarian *Sarasate*. Hundred-year-old *Café Roch* on c/ Comedias is great for tapas or, to get away from the crowds, go to the elegant *Bar Meson Caballo Blanco* on c/Redin up above the ramparts behind the cathedral. The elegant *Café Iruña*, on Plaza del Castillo, is the place to sit over a leisurely coffee.

Zaragoza

ZARAGOZA is the capital of Aragón, and easily its largest and liveliest city, with over half the province's one million people and the majority of its industry. There are some excellent bars and restaurants tucked in among its remarkable monuments, and it's also a handy transport centre, with good connections into the Pyrenees and east towards Barcelona. Try and be here for **Semana Santa** – the week before Easter – for the spectacular street processions. Zaragoza's highlight, which you should see even if you plan to do no more than change trains or buses, is the city's only surviving legacy from Moorish times. From the tenth to the eleventh century this was the centre of an independent dynasty, the Beni Kasim. Their palace, the **Aljafería** (Mon–Wed & Sat 10am–2pm & 4–6.30/8pm, Thurs 10am–2pm, Fri 4.30–6.30/8pm, Sun 10am–2pm; €3), was built in the heyday of their rule in the mid-eleventh century, and thus predates the Alhambra in Granada as well as Seville's Alcázar. From the original design the foremost relic is a tiny and beautiful mosque adjacent to the ticket office. Further on is an intricately decorated court, the Patio de Santa Isabella. Crossing from here, the Grand Staircase (added in 1492) leads to a succession of rooms remarkable chiefly for their carved ceilings. The most imposing of the city's churches, majestically fronting the Río Ebro, is the **Basilica de Nuestra Señora del Pilar** (daily 5.45am–8.30/9.30pm), one of Zaragoza's two cathedrals. It takes its name from the column that the Virgin is said to have brought from Jerusalem during her lifetime to found the first Marian chapel in Christendom. Topped by a diminutive image of the Virgin, the pillar forms the centrepiece in the Holy Chapel and is the focal point for pilgrims, who line up to kiss an exposed section encased in a silver sheath. However, in terms of beauty the basilica can't compare with the nearby Gothic-Mudéjar old cathedral, **La Seo** (Tues–Fri 10am–2pm & 4–6/7pm, Sat & Sun 10am–noon/1pm & 4/5–6/7pm; €1.50), at the far end of the pigeon-thronged Plaza del Pilar. Just south of the cathedral, at c/Espoz y Mina 23, lies the wonderful **Museo Camón Aznar** (Tues–Fri 9am–2.15pm & 6–9pm, Sat 10am–2pm & 6–9pm, Sun 11am–2pm; €0.60) – an absolute must for Goya fans. The city has recently been bringing to light its Roman past in several underground excavations: the **Forum** and **river port** (just off the Plaza del Pilar) and the **Roman Baths** (all Tues–Sat 10am–2pm & 5–8pm, Sun 10am–2pm; €1.90 each, or €3.80 combined ticket from the Forum). You can also see the remains of the **amphitheatre** in c/Veronica, where a new museum is being built around the site. Following the semicircle of c/Coso and c/Cesar Augusto, the **Roman walls** are steadily being excavated; best place to view them is at c/Echegaray at the junction with c/Coso, where remains of towers and ramparts can be seen.

Practicalities

From El Portillo **train station**, walk down c/General Mayandia, turn right onto Paseo María Agustín and take bus #22 to Plaza España – or walk it in about twenty minutes. Most local and national **bus** services use the Agreda terminal at Paseo María Agustín 7 (right from the train station). The main **tourist office** is in Plaza del Pilar (daily 10am–8pm; ☎976 393 537, ⓦ www.turismozaragoza.com), with another at the Torreón de la Zuda (same times; ☎976 201 200) – part of the city fortifications overlooking the river. There are **rooms** – and some cheap restaurants – close to the train station, along c/Madre Sacramento, parallel to Paseo María Agustín. *Pensión Miramar*, c/Capitán Casado 17 (☎976 281 094;❸), is better than most. However, there's more atmosphere in the area known as **El Tubo**, between c/de Alfonso I and c/Don Jaime I, close to Plaza del Pilar. There are upwards of a dozen cheap *pensiones* here: try *Pensión Peñafiel*, c/Méndez Núñez 38 (☎976 299 712;❷), or *El Borjano* at c/Estébanes 4 (☎976 394 875;❷). Other places to try include the HI **hostel** (☎976 306 692; €11), out of the centre but near the train station on c/Franco y Lopez 4, and the private hostel, *Ambos Mundos* (☎976 299 704; €23), located right in the centre at Plaza Pilar 16. You can **camp** at the barren *Camping Casablanca* (☎976 753 870), 2km west of the city on Paseo de Canal – take bus #36 or #24 from the train station or Plaza de España. For food in El Tubo, try *Casa Lac* on c/Mártires, supposedly the oldest **restaurant** in Spain, which is atmospheric and not too costly, or *La Tasquilla de Pedro*, c/Cinegio 3 for tapas. Alternatives include *El Fuelle* on c/Mayor near Plaza de Pilar and, for over 200 types of tapas, *Casa Dominó* on Plaza Santa Marta.

Jaca

Heading towards the Pyrenees from Zaragoza, **JACA** is the northernmost town of any size in Aragón. It's also a place of considerable interest – an early capital of the kingdom of Aragón that lay astride one of the main medieval pilgrim routes to Santiago. Accordingly, a magnificent **cathedral** (daily 9am–1.30pm & 4–8pm), the first in Spain to be built in the Romanesque style, dominates the centre of town from its position at the north edge of the old quarter. It remains impressive despite much internal remodelling over the centuries, and there's a powerful added attraction in its **Museo Diocesano** (daily 10/11am–1.30/2pm & 4–7/9pm; winter closed Mon; €1.80). The dark cloisters are home to a collection of beautiful twelfth- to fifteenth-century frescoes, gathered from village churches in the area and from higher up in the Pyrenees. Although barely 800m up, Jaca ranks as a Pyrenean resort, becoming crowded in August; even at other times of the year accommodation prices tend to be pushed up by the ski- and cross-border trade. But Jaca is foremost an army town, with a mass of conscripts attending the local mountain warfare academy. The military connection is nothing new: the **Ciudadela**, a sixteenth-century fort built to the stellar ground plan in vogue at the time, still offers good views of surrounding peaks. You can visit the interior (daily 11am–12.30pm & 5–6.30pm; €1.80 including guided tour), but it's hardly worth it, as the outside, with slumbering deer in the dry moat, is by far the most interesting part.

Arriving in Jaca by **train**, you'll find yourself 1km or so out of town; move quickly and take the connecting city bus. The **bus station** is on Avda. Jacetania, 200m northwest of the cathedral. The **tourist office** (Mon–Fri 9am–1.30/2pm & 4.30–7/8pm, Sat 9/10am–1.30pm & 5–7/8pm; summer also Sun 10am–1.30pm; ☎974 360 098, ⓦ www.jaca.com) – worth a browse for its noticeboards offering all sorts of sport- and mountaineering-related services – is on Avda. Regimiento Galicia, just downhill from the Ciudadela. All of Jaca's budget **accommodation** is on the northeast edge of the old town, with two good, quiet choices being *Hostal París* by the cathedral, Plaza de San Pedro 5 (℡974 361 020, ✉hostalparisjaca@terra.es; ❷), and, a bit closer to the action, *Hostal Residencia El Abeto*, c/Bellido 15 (℡974 361 642; ❸). There's also a **hostel** (℡974 360 536; €9.60) on Avda. Perimetral, next to the ice rink at the southern end of town, and two **campsites** – the closer but more basic *Victoria* (℡974 360 323) is 1km west of town on the Pamplona road, the wooded *Peña Oroel* (℡974 360 215) is 3km down the Sabiñanigo road. Good-value **eating** is found in the same part of the old district: carnivores will appreciate *La Fragua*, at c/Gil Berges 4 (closed Wed), while *La Cadiera* at c/Domingo Miral 19 and *Mesón Corbacho*, c/Ramiro I 2, both offer cheap but filling set menus.

The Aragonese Pyrenees

If you're not a keen trekker or skier, then the foothill villages of **ANSÓ** and **ECHO** (sometimes "Hecho") set in their beautiful namesake valleys are perhaps your best target in the **Aragonese Pyrenees**: they're noted for their distinctive, imposing architecture, and are accessible by a bus from Jaca (Mon–Sat 6.30pm), returning early in the morning (Ansó 6am; Echo 6.45am). There are summer-only **tourist offices** in both villages: on c/Santa Bárbara in Ansó (℡974 370 210), and Plaza Conde Xiquena 1, Echo (℡974 375 329). Echo, to the east, is more visited and inevitably more expensive for **accommodation and food**: try *De La Val*, Cruz Alta 1 (℡974 375 028; ❸), and the *comedor* at the *Fonda Lo Foratón* (℡974 375 247; ❷). There's also a delightful **campsite**, *Valle de Echo* (℡974 375 361). In the westerly valley, less-frequented Ansó offers several reasonable places to stay and eat, including *Hostal Aisa* (℡974 370 009; ❶) on Plaza Domingo Miral.

Worthwhile targets for a winter visit to alpine Aragón are the adjacent ski resorts of **ASTÚN-CANDANCHU**, north of Jaca, which are easily reached by bus. If your budget is limited and/or you're primarily interested in skiing, then either of the two year-round *albergues* should suit you nicely: the highly rated *El Aguila* (℡974 373 291; ✉www.infobide.com/elaguila; ❸), or *Valle de Aragón* (℡974 373 222; ❸).

For summertime walking, there's no better destination than the **Parque Nacional de Ordesa**, centred on a vast, trough-like valley flanked by imposingly striated limestone palisades. An *Alosa* bus (Mon–Sat 10.15am) from Jaca serves **Sabiñanigo**, from where there's a *Hudebus* bus (11am, also 6.30pm in high season) to Torla, the best base for the park (see below). Approaching Sabiñanigo by bus or train from Zaragoza, you'll need departures before 8.30am and 7.15am respectively to make the connection. Vehicle **entrance to the park** lies 5km beyond Torla, but trekkers should opt instead for the lovely trail (1hr 30min) on the far side of the river, well marked as part of the Pyrenean GR (long-distance path) system. Further **treks** can be as gentle or as strenuous as you like, the most popular outing being the all-day trip to the **Circo de Soaso** waterfalls. For detailed information on all activities offered in the park, head first for the **Oficina del Parque Nacional**, Ctra. de Ordesa, s/n (℡974 486 472; ✉pnomp.torla@terra.es) in Torla.

TORLA itself, a formerly sleepy, stone-built village, has been overwhelmed in its contemporary role as gateway to the park; the older corners though are still visually attractive. Don't hope for a **room** or refuge bed from late July to late August, however, without reserving well in advance – even the three **campsites**, *San Antón* (℡974 486 063, ✉www.ordesa.net/camping-sananton), *Río Ara* (℡974 486 248, ✉www.ordesa.net/camping-rioara) and *Valle de Bujaruelo* (℡974 486 348, ✉www.ordesa.net/camping-valledebujaruelo), strung out between 2km and 5km north, can often fill up. The last one also has a refuge with bunks (€9.25). At other times of the year you can usually find space at the central *Hotel Villa de Torla* (℡974 486 156; ✉www.ordesa.net/hotel-villadetorla; ❹); or try the 43-bunk *Refugio Lucien Briet* (℡974 486 221, ✉www.ordesa.net/refugio-lucienbriet; €8) or the smaller *Refugio L'Atalaya* (℡974 486 022, ✉www.ordesa.net/refugio-atalaya; €8). Both the hotel and the *Bar Brecha*, serve good-value **meals**.

BENASQUE – several valleys east of Torla, and cradled between the two highest summits in the Pyrenees – serves as another favourite jump-off point for mountain rambles. There is a daily bus service from Jaca (at 3pm, change at Huesca), and there's a marginally better chance of finding a bed here during high season, although hotels usually ask for a minimum five-night stay. The **tourist office** is at c/San Sebastián 5 (☎974 551 289, ⓦwww.turismobenasque.com). For **accommodation** try *Pensión Vescelia*, c/Mayor 5 (☎974 551 654; ❷), the budget standby – they also serve cheap meals; or *Hostal Valero* (☎974 551 061; ⓦwww.hoteles-valero .com; ❹), on c/Ctra. Anciles. Decent **food** is to be had at *Restaurante Pilar*, Ctra. de Francia, and *La Sidrería*, c/Los Huertos.

Catalonia (Catalunya)

With its own language, culture and, to a degree, government, **Catalonia** (Cataluña in Castilian Spanish, Catalunya in Catalan) has a unique identity. **Barcelona**, the capital, is very much the main event, one of the most vibrant and exciting cities in Europe. Inland, the monastery of **Montserrat**, Catalonia's main "sight", is perched on one of the most unusual rock formations in Spain, while the **Catalan Pyrenees**, though more developed than their western neighbours, are easier to access and breathtaking nonetheless. The coast immediately either side of Barcelona is rather plain, with the exception of the Modernist buildings and gay nightlife of **Sitges**, a thirty-minute train ride southwest. Further north, the rugged **Costa Brava** is shedding its erstwhile unfortunate image and boasts the best beaches in the region. Since the use of the Catalan language is so widespread, we've used Catalan spellings, with Castilian equivalents in parentheses. **Hostels** can be booked online or by a central reservations phone service (☎934 838 363, ⓦwww.tujuca.com).

The Catalan Pyrenees

The **Catalan Pyrenees**, every bit as spectacular as their Aragonese neighbours, have been exploited for far longer. While this has resulted in numerous less-than-aesthetic ski resorts and hydroelectric projects, it also means good public transport and a well-developed tourism infrastructure. In the less frequented corners, such as the westerly **Parc Nacional**, the scenery is the equal of any in Europe, while even the touristy train ride up to **Núria** to the east rarely fails to impress.

The Parc Nacional

After Ordesa, the most popular target of trekkers in the Pyrenees is the **Parc Nacional d'Aigüestortes i Estany de Sant Maurici**, covering nearly 200 square kilometres of forest, lakes and cirques, presided over by 3000m snow-capped peaks. For the less adventurous, there are lower-altitude tracks through fine scenery and visits to several villages around the park. No activity that may pollute the water is allowed in the park – and that includes all watersports. However, there is ample opportunity for hiking, climbing, potholing and paragliding: for more information about **outdoor activities**, contact the visitors' centres at Plaça del Treio 3 in Boí (9am–1pm & 3.30–7pm, closed Sun pm in winter; ☎973 696 189), or Prat del Guarda 4 in Espot (same hours; ☎973 624 036). The main access town is **Pobla de Segur**, reached by train from Barcelona. The best bases, however, are Boí and Espot, both 60km north of Pobla and, west and east of the park boundaries respectively, with Capdella to the south a less busy alternative; all are set in their own gorgeous valleys. **BOÍ** is on the main road up to the Viella tunnel, served by daily bus from Pobla via Pont de Suert. In the town itself, the tiny old quarter is dwarfed by modern construction, and tourism facilities are expensive. Exceptions include a few nameless *habitaciones* (❸), in the old quarter, or try *Pensión Pascual* (☎973 696 014;

②). *Casa Higinio*, 200m up the road to Taüll, is a good place to **eat**. If you draw a blank here, head for the more handsome neighbouring village of **TAÜLL**, 3km uphill to the east. It has a couple of decent *pensiones* – *Sant Climent*, c/Les Feixes 8 (☏973 696 052; **③**), and *La Coma*, c/Únic (☏973 696 025; **③**) – and an attractive **campsite** (☏973 696 174). **Within the park** itself, camping is forbidden and accommodation is limited to four **mountain refuges** (**②**). Trails are well marked, and you rarely have to walk for more than four hours between huts.

Núria and beyond

For a beautiful but easy way to see the Pyrenees, look no further than the rack-and-pinion rail line up to the cirque and shrine at **NÚRIA**. After a leisurely start from Ribes de Freser (see below), the tiny two-carriage train lurches up into the mountains, following a river between great crags. Once through a final tunnel, the train emerges alongside a small lake (dry in summer), at the other side of which is the one giant building that constitutes Núria. A severe stone structure, it combines church, café, ski centre and **hotel** all in one. The *Hotel Vall de Núria* (☏972 732 000; **⑦**, half-board) is expensive in summer, but the price plummets in winter. There are also several dorm-style **refuges** around, though they are often full of groups, in which case you'll have to use the **campsite** behind the hotel (pay in advance at the tourist office; ☏972 732 020) or the **hostel**, *Pic de l'Aliga* (☏972 732 048; €15.50), at the end of the cable car. You'll need good equipment, even in summer, since it gets cold at night. There are hot **snacks** or breakfast at the *Bar Finestrelles*, a **self-service** place for lunch or an evening meal, or the more expensive *El Racó de la Vall*, which serves tasty local cooking; the hotel dining room is another possibility. The privately owned **Núria train** (🖥www.valldenuria.com) runs year round (except Nov), from Ribes-Enllaç, via the towns of Ribes de Freser and Queralbs, where there are also places to stay. Trains from Barcelona connect with the Núria train at Ribes-Enllaç. Mainline trains continue to Puigcerdà, on the French frontier, astride the only surviving rail link over the Pyrenees to France. Four trains a day currently leave for La Tour de Carol, 3km over the border, but if you miss them it's easy enough to walk a slightly shorter distance east to Bourg-Madame, the actual border town. **PUIGCERDÀ** is a lot cheaper than anywhere in France, should schedules compel an overnight stay: try the reasonably priced and very comfortable *Hotel El Prado*, Ctra. De Llivia 1 (☏972 880 400; **④**, including breakfast), or *Pensió Maria Victoria*, c/Querol 7 (☏972 880 300; **③**). Restaurant prices are slightly inflated by the cross-border trade, but good bets include *La Cantonada*, c/Major 46 (beyond the bell tower), and *Bar-Restaurant Kennedy*, Pl. Héroes 2.

The Costa Brava

Stretching for 145km from the French border to the town of Blanes, the **Costa Brava** (Rugged Coast) boasts wooded coves, high cliffs, pretty beaches and deep blue water. Struggling under its image as the first developed package-tour coast in Spain, it is very determinedly rediscovering itself by revitalizing its local essence and shifting away from mass tourism. Broadly, the coast is split into three areas: the southern tip, clustered around brash **Lloret de Mar**, which most closely resembles the area's once-popular image; the stylish central area between **Palamós** and **Pals**, popular with the chic Barcelona crowd; and the more rugged northern part, dominated by the spectacular **Cap de Creus** headland and park, and the bohemian **Cadaqués**, which attracts an arty crowd paying tribute to Salvador Dalí. Inland are the twin hubs of **Girona**, the beautiful medieval capital of the region, and **Figueres**, Dalí's birthplace and home to his outrageous museum. **Buses** in the region are almost all operated by SARFA, with an office in every town. To visit the smaller, and subsequently lovelier, coves, a car or bike would make life easier, or you could walk the fabulous **camí de ronda** necklace of footpaths running along the coastline.

Figueres and Cadaqués

The northernmost parts of the Costa Brava are reached via **FIGUERES**, a provincial Catalan town with a lively Rambla and plenty of cheap food and accommodation. The place would pass almost unnoticed, however, were it not for the most visited museum in Spain after the Prado: the **Museu Dalí** (daily: July–Sept 9am–7.45pm; Oct–May 10.30am–5.45pm; ✪www.dali-estate.org; €9). Dalí was born in Figueres and, on January, 23, 1989, died there; his body now lies in a stone sarcophagus inside the museum. Installed by the artist in a building as surreal as the exhibits, the Museu Dalí is a treat, appealing to everyone's innate love of fantasy, absurdity and participation. To make your way into the middle of town, simply follow the "Museu Dalí" signs from the **train station**. The **tourist office** (summer Mon–Sat 9am–9pm, Sun 9am–3pm; rest of the year Mon–Fri 8.30am–3pm, Sat 10am–1.30pm & 3.30–6.30pm; ☎972 503 155) is in front of the post office building by the Plaça del Sol. For a comfortable **room** try the *Pensió Isabel II*, c/Isabel II 16 (☎972 504 735; ❸); the town **hostel**, c/Anicet Pagès 2 (☎972 501 213; €15.50), is behind the tourist office. There's a gaggle of cheap tourist **restaurants** in the narrow streets around the Dalí museum and, although a little more expensive, some nice pavement cafés lining the Rambla.

The beautiful fishing village of **CADAQUÉS**, an hour by bus from Figueres, was the artist's home from 1930 until his death, and has attracted an arty crowd ever since. The stunning **Casa–Museu Dalí** (daily: June–Sept 10.30am–9pm; rest of the year 10.30am–6pm; closed Jan & Feb; booking required ☎972 251 015; €8), the museum set up in his jumble of a home, lies 1km northeast in the tiny Portlligat cove and offers an enthralling glimpse into his private life. Cadaqués itself is a whitewashed village with tiny beaches and narrow cobbled streets straddling a hill topped by an imposing church. There are comfortable rooms at *Hostal Cristina*, c/Riera 5 (☎972 258 138; ❹), near the seafront. For a **drink** or a **meal**, the areas around c/Miguel Rosset and below the church are the liveliest.

Girona and around

GIRONA, 37km south of Figueres, is one of Spain's loveliest unsung cities, with alleyways winding around its compact old town, the **Barri Vell**, through the atmospheric streets of **El Call**, the beautifully preserved medieval Jewish quarter. Fought over every century since the Romans first set foot here, and dominated by its towering cathedral, Girona's eclectic past is tangible in its enchanting **Banys Arabs** (Arab Baths) and the medieval walls, which provide a great afternoon's walk. On the Rambla, the helpful **tourist office** (Mon–Fri 8am–8pm, Sat 8am–2pm & 4–8pm, Sun 9am–2pm; ✪www.ajuntament.gi) dispenses maps and there's also an information stand at the train station. Best places to **stay** are the *Pensió Viladomat*, c/Ciutadans 5 (☎972 203 176; ❹) or the neighbouring **hostel** at no. 9 (☎972 218 003; €18.50), both on a relatively quiet street in the heart of the Barri Vell. The Rambla is fine for a relaxing **drink**, but it's best to go into the Barri Vell or the area around Plaça Independència to find more interesting places to **eat** or for a drink at night.

Regular buses serve the central coast, where your best bet is to head for **BEGUR**, a hill town nestling around a seventeenth-century church in the lee of its ruined medieval castle. Its five small beaches are all served by bus from Pl. Forgas. Favoured by an affluent Barcelona crowd, it's commensurately pricey, but serves as a good base for trips up and down the coast. Best-value **accommodation** is the friendly *Hotel Rosa*, c/Pi i Ralló 11 (☎972 623015; ❺) in a lovely old building, and you're never far from good **restaurants** or from a sophisticated **bar** scene centred on the streets around the church. From Begur you're within striking distance of **EMPÚRIES** (daily 10am–6/8pm; €2.50), one of the most interesting archeological sites in Spain. It started life in 550 BC as Greek *Emporion* (literally "Trading Station") and for three centuries conducted a vigorous trade throughout the Mediterranean. Later a splendid Roman city with an amphitheatre, fine villas and a broad marketplace grew up above the old Greek town. The remains of the original

Greek colony occupy the lower ground, where remains of temples, the town gate, agora and several streets can easily be made out, along with a mass of house foundations (some with mosaics). The site lies behind a sandy bay about 2km north of **L'ESCALA**. A very good **hostel**, *Empúries*, c/Les Coves 41 (☎972 771 200; €18.50) offers a tranquil base, but you'll either need your own transport or be willing to walk the two kilometres into neighbouring L'Escala to catch a SARFA bus to get around with any ease.

Barcelona

BARCELONA, the self-confident and progressive capital of Catalonia, is a tremendous place to be. Though it boasts outstanding Gothic and Art Nouveau buildings, and some great museums – most notably those dedicated to Picasso, Miró and Catalan art – its main appeal lies in getting lost in the narrow side streets, stopping in at bars and cafés, rising, eating and drinking late, and soaking up the atmosphere. A thriving port and the most prosperous commercial centre in Spain, it has a sophistication and cultural dynamism way ahead of the rest of the country. But Barcelona has also evolved an individual and eclectic cultural identity, most perfectly and eccentrically expressed in the architecture of **Antoni Gaudí**. As in any large city, be aware that there are problems with pickpockets – some areas around the Ramblas are pretty seedy. Don't be conspicuous with expensive cameras, leave passports and tickets locked up in your hotel, and keep bags zipped up.

Arrival, information and city transport

The **airport**, 12km southwest, is linked by train (daily 6am–10pm, every 30min; €2.50) to the main train station, Estació de Sants, from where you can take the metro to the city centre (line #3 to Liceu for the Ramblas). Many trains from the airport also run on to Plaça de Catalunya, a more direct way of reaching the Barri Gòtic. Alternatively, the Airbus (5.30/6am–midnight, every 15min; €3.50) runs into the centre via Plaça d'Espanya, Gran Vía and Plaça de Catalunya. A taxi to the centre will cost around €20. **Estacío de Sants** is the city's main **train** station, for national and some international arrivals – many national buses also stop here; metro line #3 takes you directly to the Ramblas. **Estació de França**, next to the Parc de la Ciutadella, is the terminal for long-distance Spanish and European express and intercity trains. Leaving França you can take the metro (line #4) from nearby Barceloneta, or simply walk (5min) into the Barri Gòtic, up Vía Laietana and into c/Jaume. The main **bus** terminal is the **Estació del Nord** (three blocks north of Parc de la Ciutadella; Metro Arc de Triomf). Arriving by **ferry** from the Balearics, you'll dock at the **Estació Marítima** at the bottom of the Ramblas on Moll de Barcelona.

The best **tourist office** is beneath Plaça de Catalunya (daily 9am–9pm; ☎906 301 282, ✆www.barcelonaturisme.com). Other branches can be found at Plaça de Sant Jaume (Mon–Fri 9am–8pm, Sat 10am–8pm, Sun 10am–2pm), and at the airport (daily 9am–9pm). The Plaça de Catalunya branch books accommodation for personal callers only. The quickest way of getting around is by **metro** (5/6am–11pm/midnight, 2am at weekends); stations are marked by a red diamond sign. **Bus** routes (6.30am–10pm) are far more complicated, but every bus stop displays a comprehensive route map. A limited number of yellow **night buses** (10.30/11.30pm–3.30/4.30am) run from, or pass through, Plaça de Catalunya. For more information on both go to ✆www.tmb.net. There's a flat **fare** on both metro and buses (€1.05; night buses cost a little more). If you're staying a couple of days or more it's better to buy a **targeta** (ticket strip; T-10, €5.80), available at any metro station, which covers the metro, buses, and some regional train lines within the city (passes are also available for outlying zones). Similarly, there are **daily passes** (T-Dia, from €4.40/one day to €17.30/five days), which offer unlimited travel. The **Bus Turístic** links 27 of Barcelona's major sights, at which you can hop off and on

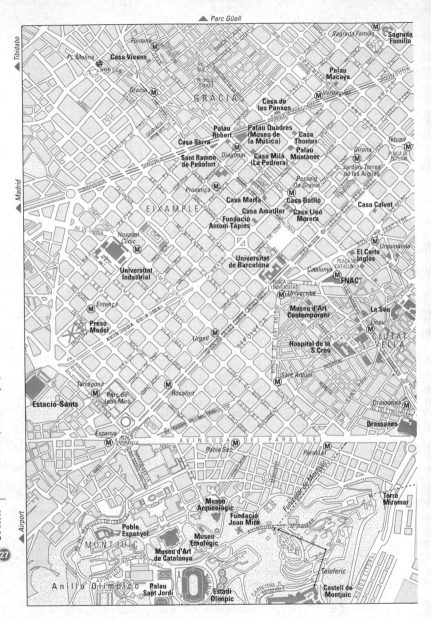

at your leisure (€15/day, €19/two days); tickets are available at tourist offices or on the bus itself and include discount coupons for museums, shops and restaurants. Black and yellow **taxis** are inexpensive, plentiful and very useful late at night. There's a minimum charge of €1.15, €1.30 after 10pm, and after that it's around €0.75/km, depending on the time of day.

BARCELONA

SANT MARTÍ

VILA OLÍMPICA

Girona

Els
Encants

Glòries

PLAÇA DE LA
HISPANITAT

DIAGONAL

Llacuna

Marina

Estació
del Nord

Bogatell

Arc De Triomf

Palau de
Justícia

Arc de
Triomf

PASSEIG DE
LLUÍS COMPANYS

Parc
de la
Ciutadella

Museu de
Zoologia

Parlement de
Catalunya

Hivernacle

Museu
Geologia

Clutadella

Mercat
del Born

Parc
Zoòlogic

Globo
Turístic

Hotel
Arts

Museu
Picasso

Estació de
França

Port
Olímpic

Santa
Maria
del Mar

Barceloneta

Jaume I

Barceloneta

PLAÇA
D'ANTONI
LÓPEZ

BARCELONETA

ADMIRALL

Platja de la

PLAÇA
PORTAL
DE LA PAU

MEDITERRANEAN SEA

MOLL DE BARCELONA

Teleferic

Torre Sant
Sebastià

Torre Jaume I

N

MOLL DE PONENT

0   500 m

Accommodation

Accommodation in Barcelona is among the most expensive in Spain and you'll be hard pushed to find a double room for under €35. The tourist office at Plaça de Catalunya can help, or you can use **Barcelona Online** (☎933 437 993, ⒲www.barcelona-on-line.es). A walk through the old town reveals heavy concentrations of hotels and *hostales*, with much of the cheapest accommodation to be found in the side streets off and around the Ramblas. The further down towards the port you get, the less salubrious and noisier the surroundings: as a general rule, anything above c/Escudellers tends to be all right. Perhaps the best hunting ground for cheap rooms is between the Ramblas and Plaça de Sant Jaume, in the area bordered by c/Escudellers and c/de la Boqueria near Plaça Reial. Visitors are strongly advised to book at least the first two nights of accommodation as far ahead as possible. There's one HI and several backpacker **hostels** in Barcelona (consult the online hostel and hotel reservation service ⓦwww.hostelbarcelona.com), and hundreds of **campsites** on the coast in either direction, but none less than 11km from the city.

Hostels

Alberg Kabul Pl. Reial 17, Barri Gòtic ☏933 185 190, ⓦwww.kabul-hostel.com. Grotty dorms but a great atmosphere and lots of facilities, overlooking a beautiful square. €16.

Albergue Mare de Déu de Montserrat Pg. Mare de Déu del Coll 41–51, Horta ☏932 105 151. A beautiful HI hostel a little more than half an hour from the city centre. Breakfast included. Metro Vallcarca. €23.

Barcelona Mar c/Sant Pau 80, Raval ☏933 248 530, ⓦwww.youthostel-barcelona.com. New hostel with laundry and Internet access, close to MACBA and the Ramblas. €21.

Center Ramblès c/Hospital 63, Raval ☏934 124 069. Large, modern hostel just off the Ramblas, with lots of facilities and no curfew. €15.50.

Gothic Point Hostel c/Vigatans 5–9, La Ribera ☏932 687 808, ⓦwwww.gothicpoint.com. Lively place with big dorms and good facilities. Very popular with younger travellers and, hence, noisy. Breakfast included. €21.

Itaca Hostel c/Ripoll 21, Barri Gòtic ☏933 019 751, ⓦwww.itacahostel.com. Extremely popular and pleasant new hostel near the cathedral, with Internet access, café, dining room and book exchange. €17.

Hotels

Hostal Centric c/Casanova 13, Eixample ☏934 267 573, ⓦwww.hostalcentric.com. Good value rooms in a quiet street that's close to the action nonetheless. ❹

Hostal Gat Raval c/Joaquím Costa 44, Raval ☏934 816 670, ⓦwww.gataccommodation.com. Sleek minimalist design and helpful, friendly staff in this refreshingly clean, bright and youthful hotel in the hip environs of MACBA. ❺

Hostería Grau c/Ramelleres 27, Raval ☏933 018 135, ⓦwww.intercom.es/grau. Bright *pensión* with a lovely café/bar in an unbeatable location just off Plaça Catalunya. ❹

Hotel La Terrassa c/Junta del Comerç 11, Raval ☏933 025 174. Clean and atmospheric budget favourite, with plain singles, doubles and triples, some en suite, and a pleasant terrace. ❸

Pension Bahia c/Canuda 2, Barri Gòtic ☏933 026 153, ⓦwww.pensionbahia.com. Cheap and serviceable but up lots of stairs, in a great location just off the Ramblas and Plaça Catalunya. ❸

The City

Scattered as Barcelona's main sights may be, the greatest area of interest is the **old town** (*la ciutat vella*). These cramped streets above the harbour are easily manageable, and far more enjoyable, on foot; at their heart are the twisting alleys of the **Barri Gòtic**. Bisecting the old town, at the western edge of the Barri Gòtic, are the famous **Ramblas**, the city's main thoroughfare. At the Ramblas' northern end is **Plaça de Catalunya**; at the southern end is the harbour and **Port Vell** (old port). West of the Ramblas lies the warren-like **Barrio Chino**, or Chinatown (officially named **El Raval**). Medieval streets continue either side of the Ramblas, reaching northeast through **La Ribera** and southwest to the fortress-topped hill of **Montjuïc**. A cable-car connects Montjuïc with **Barceloneta**, the waterfront district east of the harbour. Beyond Plaça de Catalunya stretches the modern commercial area, known as the **Eixample**, within which lies some extraordinary architecture, including Gaudí's Sagrada Familia.

Around the Ramblas

Only in Barcelona could a street – or, strictly, streets – be a highlight. But the **Ramblas** are not just any street – here you will find everything from flower markets to fire eaters, performers to pet shops, and in the evening, all of Barcelona out taking a stroll. Heading down from Plaça de Catalunya, you gradually leave the opulent facades of the banks and department stores for a seedier area towards the port, where the Ramblas cut right through the heart of the notorious red-light district. However, this harbour end is much less threatening than it once was: the transformation of the Port Vell area has meant new hip bars and clubs now rub shoulders with sleazy old ones.

Don't miss the glorious **La Boqueria**, the city's main food market (Mon–Sat 8am–8pm), a splendid gallery of sights and smells with several excellent snack bars

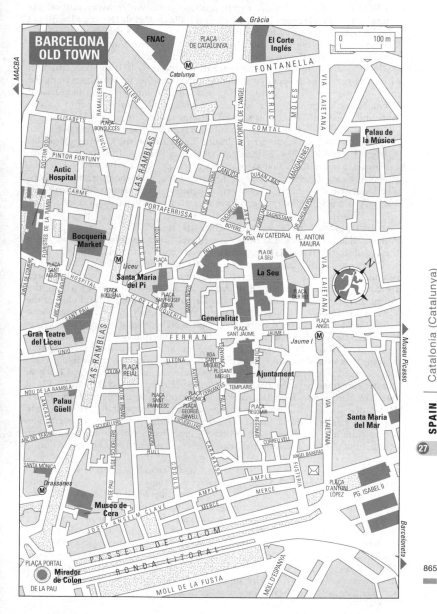

and a restaurant at the back selling market-fresh dishes. Almost adjacent is the majestic **Liceu**, Barcelona's celebrated opera house now renovated after it went up in smoke in January 1994. More or less opposite is the famous *Café de l'Ópera*, an opulent high-society meeting place – though not as expensive as you might imagine. A few minutes' walk north of here is the stunning **Museu d'Art Contemporani** or MACBA (Mon & Wed–Fri 11am–7.30pm, Sat 10am–8pm, Sun 10am–3pm; €7) with exciting displays by international and national artists.

A little way down from the Liceu, hidden behind an archway just off the Ramblas, lies the elegant nineteenth-century **Plaça Reial**. Decorated with tall palm trees and iron lamps (designed by the young Gaudí), it's the haunt of crusties, Catalan eccentrics, the odd drunk and hundreds of alfresco diners and drinkers. Gaudí's magnificent **Palau Güell** (Mon–Sat 10am–2pm & 4–7.30pm; €3) stands just off the Ramblas, towards the bottom, at c/Nou de la Rambla 3. Much of Gaudí's early career was spent constructing elaborate follies for wealthy patrons, the most important of whom was Don Eusebio Güell, a shipowner and industrialist. Wrought iron supports blend magnificently with granite, marble, ceramics, woodwork and stained and etched glass. Don't miss the roof.

Right at the harbour end of the Ramblas, Columbus stands pointing out to sea from the top of a tall, grandiose column, the **Mirador de Colom** (Mon–Fri 9/10am–1.30pm & 3.30–6.30/8.30pm, Sat & Sun 10am–6.30/8.30pm; €2). Take the lift to his head for a fine view of the city. Opposite, to the west side of the Ramblas, are the Drassanes, medieval shipyards dating from the thirteenth century. The impressive stone-vaulted buildings are home to a fine **Museu Marítim** (daily 10am–7pm, €5.40), whose star exhibit is a sixteenth-century Royal Galley.

The Barri Gòtic, La Ribera and Ciutadella

A remarkable concentration of beautiful medieval Gothic buildings just blocks from the Ramblas, the **Barri Gòtic** forms the very heart of the old city. Today's old town dates principally from the fourteenth and fifteenth centuries, when Catalonia reached the height of its commercial prosperity. The quarter is centred on **Plaça de Sant Jaume**, on one side of which stands the restored town hall, the **Ajuntament**. Across the square rises the **Palau de la Generalitat**, home of the Catalan government; restored during the sixteenth century in Renaissance style, it has a beautiful cloister on the first floor with superb coffered ceilings. Just behind the square **La Seu**, Barcelona's cathedral (daily 10am–1pm & 4/5–6.30pm), is one of the great Gothic buildings of Spain. The magnificent **cloisters** (9am–1pm & 4–7pm) look over a lush tropical garden with soaring palm trees and white geese.

The cathedral and its associated buildings aside, the most concentrated batch of historic monuments in the Barri Gòtic is the grouping around the nearby **Plaça del Rei**. Barcelona's finest Roman remains were uncovered beneath the **Palau Reial** (the former palace of the counts of Barcelona), which now houses the **Museu d'Història de la Ciutat** (Tues–Sat 9/10am–2pm & 4–8/11.30pm, Sun 10am–2pm; July also Mon 9–11.30pm; €4, free first Sat of month). Here, both Roman and Visigothic remains have been preserved where they were found during building work in the 1930s.

Heading east from Plaça de Sant Jaume, you'll cross Vía Laietana into the **La Ribera** neighbourhood and reach the Carrer de Montcada, crowded with beautifully restored old buildings. One of these houses the **Museu Picasso** (Tues–Sat 10am–8pm, Sun 10am–3pm; €5, free first Sun of month), one of the most important collections of Picasso's work in the world and the only one of any significance in his native country, although it's rather selective and contains none of his best-known work. Continue down the street and you'll come out opposite the great basilica of **Santa María del Mar** (daily 9am–1.30pm & 4.30–8pm; Sun choral Mass at 1pm), built on what was the seashore in the fourteenth century. Its soaring lines were the symbol of Catalan supremacy in Mediterranean commerce and it's still much dearer to the heart of the average local than the cathedral.

For a quick respite from the city centre, nip into the greenery and relative peace of **Parc de la Ciutadella**, which is within easy walking distance of Santa Maria. Its attractions include the meeting place of the Catalan parliament, a lake, Gaudí's monumental fountain and the city **zoo** (daily 10am–5/7.30pm; €11.50, €6.50 after 5pm in summer).

Port Vell, Barceloneta and Port Olímpic

The whole **Port Vell** area has been revitalized, notably by the vast **Maremagnum** complex, reached from near the Mirador de Colom via a dramatic wooden walkway. The city planners' desire to refocus attention on the sea has provided an upmarket shopping mall, a hugely overpriced aquarium, cinema, IMAX theatre and a multitude of bars and pricey restaurants. This lies on the fringe of the **Barceloneta** district, home to Barcelona's cleaned-up beaches and seafood restaurants. A cable car (*telefèrics*) runs from here to Montjuïc (11am–5.30/7/8pm; €3.40 one way, €4.80 return). Walk 1km east along the beach and you'll find **Port Olímpic** with its myriad bars and restaurants. At night the tables are stacked up, dance floors emerge and the area hosts one of the city's most vibrant dance scenes. Dozens of bars pump out a pulsating mix of salsa, house and techno to an uptown clientele.

Antoni Gaudí and the Sagrada Família

Barcelona offers – above all through the work of **Antoni Gaudí** (1852–1926) – some of the most fantastic and exciting modern architecture to be found anywhere in the world. Without doubt his most famous creation is the incomplete **Temple Expiatori de la Sagrada Família** (daily 9am–6/8pm; €8, lift €1.50; Metro Sagrada Família), a good way northeast of Plaça de Catalunya. With construction still ongoing, the interior is a giant building site, but it's fascinating to watch Gaudí's last-known plans being slowly realized. The size alone is startling, with eight spires rising to over 100m. For Gaudí these were metaphors for the Twelve Apostles; he planned to build four more above the main facade and to add a 180m tower topped with a gallery over the transept, itself to be surrounded by four smaller towers symbolizing the Evangelists. Take the lift, or climb up one of the towers, and you can enjoy a dizzy view down over the whole complex and clamber still further round the walls and into the towers. Inside, a small **Gaudí museum** traces the career of the architect and the history of the building. The tourist office also issues a handy leaflet describing all Gaudí's works, with a map of their locations. Above all, check out **Parc Güell** (daily 10am–6/9pm; free), his most ambitious project after the Sagrada Família. This almost hallucinatory experience, with giant decorative lizards and a vast Hall of Columns, contains another small **museum** (daily 10am–6/7.45pm; €3) with some of the furniture Gaudí designed. To get there, take the metro to Lesseps or bus #24 from the Plaça de Catalunya to Travesera de Dalt, from where it's a half-kilometre walk to the main gates on c/d'Olot.

Montjuïc

The hill of **Montjuïc** has yet more varied attractions – five museums, the "Spanish Village", the Olympic arena and a castle with grand views of the city. The most obvious way to approach is to take the metro to Plaça d'Espanya and walk from there up the imposing Avda. de la Reina María Cristina, past the 1929 International Fair buildings and the rows of fountains. If you'd rather start with the castle, take the **funicular railway** (daily 9am–10pm every 10min; €2.10 return), which runs from Parallel metro station to the start of the cable car (summer only), which in turn leads to the castle; or take bus #50 along Plaça Universitat and Gran Vía up to Parc Montjuïc.

If you tackle the stiff climb from the Plaça d'Espanya you'll arrive at the **Palau Nacional**, centrepiece of Barcelona's 1929 International Fair and now home to one of Spain's great museums, the **Museu Nacional d'Art de Catalunya**

(Tues–Sat 10am–7pm, Sun 10am–2.30pm; €6, free first Thurs of month). Its enormous collection includes a Romanesque collection that is the best of its kind in the world: 35 rooms of eleventh- and twelfth-century frescoes, meticulously removed from a series of small Pyrenean churches and beautifully displayed. There is also a substantial collection of Baroque and Renaissance works. Barcelona's important **Museu d'Arqueologia de Catalunya** (Tues–Sat 9.30am–7pm, Sun 10am–2.30pm; €2.40) containing exhibits mostly from the Roman period, but also Carthaginian and Etruscan relics, stands to the east of the Palau Nacional, lower down the hill. Nearby is the **Fundació Joan Miró** (Tues–Sat 10am–7pm, Thurs till 9.30pm, Sun closes 2.30pm; €7.20), the most adventurous of Barcelona's art museums, devoted to one of the greatest Catalan artists. A beautiful white building houses a permanent collection of paintings, graphics, tapestries and sculptures donated by Miró himself and covering the period from 1914 to 1978.

A short walk over to the other side of the Palau Nacional brings you to the **Poble Espanyol** or "Spanish Village" (Mon 9am–8pm, Tues–Sat 9am–2/4am, Sun 9am–midnight; €7), consisting of replicas of famous or characteristic buildings from all over Spain, and with a lively club scene at night. Prices, especially for products of the "genuine Spanish workshops" (and in the bars), are exorbitant. From the Poble Espanyol, the main road climbs around the hill to what was the principal **Olympic arena** in 1992. The Olympic Stadium itself, the **Estadi Olimpic** (daily 10am–6/8pm; free), built originally for the 1929 Exhibition, was completely refitted to accommodate the 1992 opening and closing ceremonies. The **Galeria Olímpica**, on Passeig Olímpic (Mon–Fri 10am–1/2pm & 4–6/7pm; €2.50), is a hands-on affair covering the staging of the Games in the city. Far above this complex of museums and sports arenas, and offering magnificent views across the city, stands the eighteenth-century **Castell de Montjuïc**, built on seventeenth-century ruins.

Eating, drinking and nightlife

There's a huge variety of **restaurants** in Barcelona and even low-budget travellers can do well for themselves. Be aware that a lot of places close on Sundays and throughout August, and that the *menú del día* is only available at lunchtime. For picnic material, head for the La Boqueria covered **market**, off the Ramblas. There are hundreds of excellent **bars** and **cafés** in the city centre, including the lively **tapas** places in the Barri Gòtic. Around the Museu Picasso is a particularly good area: the Passeig del Born, the square at the end of c/Montcada behind Santa María del Mar, is crowded with popular bars. Gràcia, north of the centre, is the most studenty area in Barcelona, great for a drink around the main Plaça del Sol. Barcelona's **nightlife** is some of Europe's most exciting, though it's not cheap - in the most exclusive places even a beer is going to cost you roughly ten times what it costs in the bar next door. Music bars close at 3am, the discos at 4/5am, and some clubs open between 5am and 9am at weekends. Among the more expensive, trendier places are the hi-tech theme palaces concentrated mainly in the Eixample, or in the rich kids' stamping ground bordered by c/Ganduxer, Avda. Diagonal and Vía Augusta, west of Gràcia. Laid back and/or alternative places can be found in the small streets around MACBA and south, while the waterfront Port Olimpic area is in favour with wealthy and bored youth, although weekdays out of summer are dead. For **listings**, buy a copy of the weekly *Guía del Ocio* from any newsstand or check Ⓦwww.guiadelociobcn.com. There's a thriving **gay scene** in Barcelona: *SexTienda*, at c/Rauric 11 (very near Plaça Reial), supplies free maps of gay Barcelona with a list of bars, clubs and contacts.

Tapas bars

Amaya Rambla Santa Mónica 20–24. Busy, smoke-filled tapas bar on one side, with a mid-range restaurant on the other. Serves Basque specialities, but the tapas are best.

El Xampanyet c/de Montcada 22, Barri Gòtic. Terrific blue-tiled champagne bar with seafood tapas, *cava* by the glass and local *sidra*. Closed Sun, Mon & all Aug.

Euskal Etxea Placeta Montcada 1–3, Barri Gòtic.

A Basque restaurant specializing in mouthwatering tapas. Closed Mon.

Jai-Ca c/Ginebra 13, Barceloneta. Small, cornerside bar with some of the best tapas in town.

Restaurants

Can Ros c/l'Almirall Aixada 7, Barceloneta. Unbeatable fish and seafood straight from the harbour. Closed Wed & Sun eve.

Casa de Madrid c/Ausias Marc 37, Eixample ☏ 932 656 723. Great neighbourhood find offering a cheap menu and dishes from the Spanish regions. Booking advised.

Comme-Bio & Comme-Bio II Via Laietana, La Ribera; and Gran Vía 603, corner Rambla de Catalunya, Eixample, Metro Catalunya. Sibling vegetarian restaurants that double as health-food stores.

La Fonda c/Escudellers 10, Barri Gòtic. Hugely popular place with good Mediterranean cuisine and tables on two levels and outdoors. The lunchtime menu is a steal. They don't take bookings, so be prepared to queue.

La Vaca Paca Pg. de Gràcia 21, Eixample. The mother of all stuff-yourself-silly buffets, for the rock-bottom price of €6.90.

Illa de Gràcia c/Sant Doménec 19, Gràcia. Bright vegetarian restaurant serving decent salads, pasta, rice dishes, omelettes and crepes. *Menú del día* for €12.

Llar del Filador c/Cortines 13, La Ribera. Tucked away in a dark lane, this renovated workshop is the place to enjoy meat, cheese and dessert fondues in a subdued and romantic atmosphere.

Perú Pg de Bourbó 10, Barceloneta. Great range of seafood. Good value *menú del día*.

Pitarra c/d'Avinyó 56, Barri Gòtic. A Catalan cookery in operation since 1890, lined with paintings and serving good, reasonably priced food. Closed Sun.

PK2 c/Mallorca 197, Eixample. Cheap, tasty and filling Uruguayan food in a friendly, rustic atmosphere, with temporary art exhibitions on the walls. Closed Sun.

Pollo Rico c/Sant Pau 31, Barri Xines. Spit-roasted chicken, fries and a glass of *cava* for under €5 make this one of the area's most popular budget spots. Closed Wed.

Silenus c/Angeles 8, Raval. Just round the corner from the MACBA and with a decidedly hip clientele, this billowing white space of an eatery serves reasonably priced, delicious and health-conscious fare.

Cafés and bars

Café de l'Òpera Ramblas 74. Elegant *fin-de-siècle* café-bar with fine coffee and a range of cakes and snacks.

Café del Sol Pl. del Sol 29, Gràcia. Trendy hangout, just one of several similar places in this square.

Casa Almirall c/Joaquím Costa 33, Raval. The oldest functioning bar in Barcelona, this place makes judicious use of wood, comfy sofas and a very cool neighbourhood.

El Café Que Pone Muebles Navarro c/Riera Alta 4–6, Raval. Gorgeously laid-back café/bar with big, comfy sofas and big, strong drinks. Popular with a gay crowd.

Els Quatre Gats c/Montsió 5, Barri Gòtic. *Modernista*-designed haunt of Picasso and his contemporaries, still an interesting and arty place for a drink and nibble. Closed Sun lunch.

London Bar c/Nou de la Rambla 34, Barri Xines. Laid-back 1920s bar with live music daily – mainly jazz and blues. Cabaret after midnight Thurs & Sun.

Mojito Bar Port Vell, Maremagnum. Perfect *mojitos*, daily salsa classes and live music until late on weekends make this the perfect place to finish off an exhausting shopping trip.

Parnasse c/Gignás 21, Barri Gòtic. Laid-back, friendly atmosphere in this hip bar. Listen to jazz, and drink modestly priced single-malt whiskies or the legendary absinthe, *à la française*. Closed Sun & Mon.

Téxtil Café c/Montcada 12, La Ribera. In the atmospheric medieval courtyard of the textile museum, with braziers in winter, although fairly pricey drinks keep out the art students. Closed Mon.

Clubs and live music venues

Apolo c/Nou de la Rambla 113, Barri Xines. Trip-hop and techno for a gay/straight crowd, old-town location. Metro Parallel.

Club Nitsa c/Nou de la Rambla 113, Barri Xines. Biggish names and burgeoning stars play live, from the worlds of alternative rock, *electronica* and techno. Metro Parallel.

La Cova de Drac c/Vallmajor 33, Eixample. One of the city's hippest locations for both jazz and dance. Metro Muntaner.

KGB c/Alegre de Dalt 55, Gracia. Multifarious club with good alternative rock and pop acts. Metro Joanic.

Metro c/Sepúlveda 185, Eixample. The original Barcelona gay club has seen everyone from Marc Almond to Jean Paul Gaultier through its doors, and it's still pulling in the crowds. Metro Universitat.

Moog c/Arc del Teatre 3, Barri Xines. Techno temple. Regular appearances from top UK and Euro DJs. Best on Wed & Sun. Metro Drassanes.

Razz Club c/Almogavers 122, Poble Nou. Underground rock and punk. Metro Bogatell.

The Loft c/Pamplona 88, Poble Nou. The place to go for hard, fast house. Metro Bogatell.

Listings

Consulates Australia, Gran Vía Carles III 98 ☎933 309 496; Canada, c/Elisenda de Pinós 10 ☎932 042 700; Ireland, Gran Vía Carles III 94 ☎934 915 021; New Zealand, Trav. de Gràcia 64 ☎932 090 399; UK, Avda. Diagonal 477 ☎933 666 200; US, Passeig de la Reina Elisenda 23 ☎932 802 227.

Exchange Most banks located in Pl. de Catalunya and Pg. de Gràcia. Money exchange at the airport and Estacío de Sants; Viajes Marsans, Ramblas 134; Caixa Catalunya in the tourist office at Pl. Catalunya; and at *casas de cambio* throughout the centre.

Hospitals Hospital de la Creu Roja, c/Dos de Maig 301 ☎935 072 700; Policlínica Barcelona,

c/Guillem Tell 4, Gràcia ☎934 161 616; Centro Médico Cruz Blanco, c/Pelai 40, Ciutat Vella ☎934 121 212.

Internet access easyEverything, Ronda de l'Universitat.

Laundry Martin, c/Carme 65, Raval.

Left luggage Lockers at all the stations.

Pharmacies Farmacia Ivarez, Pg. Gràcia 26, Eixample ☎933 021 124; Farmacia Clapés Antoja, Ramblas 98, Ciutat Vella ☎933 012 843.

Police Turisme Attention, Ramblas 43 ☎933 019 060.

Post office Correus, Pl. Antoni Lòpez, at the bottom of Vía Laietana.

The Balearic islands

The four chief **Balearic islands** – Ibiza, Formentera, Mallorca and Menorca – maintain a character distinct from the mainland and from each other. **Ibiza**, firmly established among Europe's trendiest resorts, has an intense, outrageous street life and a floating summer population that seems to include every club-going Spaniard from Seville to Barcelona. It can be fun, if this sounds like your idea of island activity, and above all if you're gay – Ibiza has a particularly good scene. Neighbouring **Formentera** is small and windswept with some gloriously undeveloped beaches. **Mallorca**, the largest of the Balearics, battles with its image, popularly reckoned as little more than sun, booze and beach parties. In reality you'll find all the clichés crammed into the mega-resorts of the Bay of Palma, with large areas that simply don't fit this image: mountains, lively fishing ports, some beautiful coves and the Balearics' one real city, **Palma**. To the east, **Menorca** – more conservative in its development, more modest in its clientele - is, after the others, a little dull.

Ferries from mainland Spain (and Marseille) are severely overpriced considering the distances involved; likewise, monopolies keep rates high for inter-island ferries. It can be cheaper to fly, even from elsewhere in Spain; the catch here is that in midseason flights are often booked out – the solution is to get up before dawn, head for the nearest airport and get yourself on a waiting list for the first flight. As "holiday islands", each with a buoyant international tourist trade, the Balearics charge considerably above mainland prices for **rooms** – which from mid-June to mid-September are in very short supply. It's sensible to try to fix up some kind of reservation in advance.

Ibiza

IBIZA (Eivissa in Catalan) is an island of excess. Beautiful and indented with scores of barely accessible coves, it's nevertheless the islanders and their visitors who make it special. However outrageous you may want to be (and outrageousness is the norm), the locals have seen it all before. For years it was the European hippy escape, but nowadays it is as synonymous with the European club scene as with its 1960s denizens, who keep coming back.

In physical as well as atmospheric terms, **IBIZA TOWN** is the most attractive place on the island. Most people stay in rented apartments or small *pensiones*, which means fewer hotels to ruin the skyline and no package incursions. Approach by sea and you'll get the full effect of the old town's walls rising like a natural extension of the rocky cliffs that protect the port. Within the walls, the ancient quarter is topped by a sturdy cathedral, whose illuminated clock shines out across the harbour throughout the night. From the **ferry terminal**, the old streets of the Sa Peña quarter lead straight ahead towards the walls of the ancient city. The **airport** is 6km out; there's a regular bus from here (7.30am–10.30pm), or you can take a taxi (€14). There's an efficient **tourist office** at the airport (May–Oct Mon–Sat 9am–2pm & 4–9pm, Sun 9am–2pm), but the main office is directly opposite the ferry building, at c/Antomi Riquer 2 (Mon–Fri 9.30am–1.30pm & 5–7.30pm, Sat 10.30am–1.30pm; ☎971 301 900, ⓦwww.visitbalears.com). **Internet** cafés in Ibiza Town include Surf@net, c/Riambau 4. Most of the cheaper **hotels** are around Paseo Vara del Rey. A starter possibility is *Hostal Sol y Brisa*, Avda. Bartomeu Vicent Ramon 15 (☎971 310 818; ❸), near the port in the street parallel to Vara de Rey. In the same area, *Hostal Ripoll*, c/Vicente Cuervo 14 (☎971 314 275; ❸), is good value, while a little further out is *Ebusitania*, c/Obispo Huix 17 (☎971 300 050; ❷). Near the port and right in the heart of things is *La Marina*, c/Olozaga 7 (☎971 310 172; ❹), where all rooms are en suite. Another notch up is *Hostal Parque*, c/Vicente Cuervo 4 (☎971 301 358; ❹). There are four **campsites** on the island, the nearest to Ibiza Town the inland *Camping Cala Bassa* (☎971 344 599), 13km away near Sant Josep.

The cheaper places **to eat** are found in the Sa Peña quarter. One of the best bets is smoky *C'an Costa* at c/Creu 19; along the road on the corner *La Victoria*,

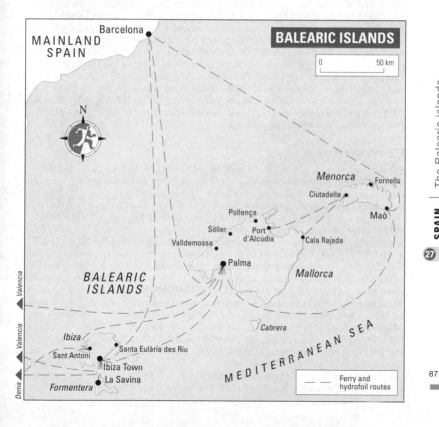

c/Riambau 1, also has cheap main meals. The *Croissant Show*, Mercat Vell, only clos-es between five and seven in the morning, and there are several other options on Plaza del Parque. The bulk of the **bars** in which to begin your night are in the port area, though some can be overpriced even during happy hour. *Dome*, Alfonso XII 5, between the port and the old town, is an old favourite with a mixed crowd; *Mike and Claire's Diner*, Avda. Andenes, has a 24-hour drinks licence; while *The Soap Café*, Manuel Sora 4, serves good food day and night.

As for **clubs**, some highlights are: the luxurious *Pacha*; *Space*, with its legendary ter-race; the wildly extravagant *Privilege*; and the cavernous *Amnesia*. None of them really gets going before 1am, and the dancing goes on until dawn. The **Discobus** links them with the centre and runs through the night (€2 single fare). The clubbing sea-son lasts from May to September, with the best time to party being the first and last two weeks. Be prepared to spend a lot of money, with entrance fees upwards of €27 and astronomical bar prices. Watch out for the free invites distributed in the streets each night. Ibiza has one of the best **gay scenes** in Europe, with the action centred on the sometimes notorious c/Virgen. *Teatro*, at no. 83, remains a popular bar, as does *Capricho* at no. 42. There's only one dedicated gay club (men only): *Anfora*, c/San Carlos 7, in the old town, but many of the island's big-name clubs hold a gay night once a week; most popular is at *Amnesia* (Wed). For the free **full-moon beach-par-ties**, try asking around in the hippy markets in Es Canar, Las Dalias or Santa Eularia.

Around Ibiza

Nowhere else can compare to the capital, certainly not the second city, San Antonio Abad, which is a highly avoidable package-resort nightmare, though it can be quite pleasant out of season. **SANTA EULALIA**, the only other real town, retains a cer-tain charm in its hilltop church looking down over the sprawling old town and modern seafront, while close by the persistent can find a number of relatively empty beaches. The same holds true for most of the rest of the coast – plenty of golden sands, but a good deal of effort required to reach them. The one major exception is the northern bay of **Portinatx**, connected by a relatively major road and, despite hotel development, with a number of clean, not overly populated beaches. **Inland** there's little to divert you – a few villages and holiday homes. There's a good **bus service** between Ibiza Town, San Antonio Abad, Santa Eulalia, Portinatx and a few of the larger beaches.

Formentera

For a complete contrast with Ibiza's hedonism, **FORMENTERA** makes for a relax-ing day-trip. Just three nautical miles south of its neighbour and smallest of the inhab-ited islands, its uncrowded beaches are a haven for anyone seeking escape with little in the way of sophistication. **Boats** (30min–1hr; €18, €27 by catamaran) dock at the tiny harbour of **LA SAVINA**, where you can rent mopeds or bicycles, while the island's only **tourist office** is by the quay (Mon–Fri 10am–2pm & 5–7pm; ☎971 322 057, ⊛www.illadeformentera.com). The whitewashed capital, **SANT FRANCESC DE FORMENTERA**, is 2km from La Savina, along a narrow road that continues from Sant Francesc to the easternmost point at La Mola. Along it, or just off it, are almost all of the island's settlements and most of its beaches. To the north, the slowly burgeoning package-tour industry is alighting on **SANT FERRAN**, which nonetheless is still a beautiful white-sand and pine coast, while to the west, a thin spur of undeveloped land straddling two tranquil beaches has been designated a nature reserve. **Platja de Migjorn**, to the south, is a five-kilometre stretch of sand broken only by the occasion-al bar or hotel, and is also an area popular with nude sunbathers. *Hostal La Sabina,* near the port at Avda. Mediterranea 22–40 (☎971 322 279; ➎), backs onto a tranquil lagoon specked with yachts. Sant Ferran has a number of other possibilities, one of the best being *Hostal Pepe*, c/Major 68–76 (☎971 328 033; ➌), where all rooms are en suite and breakfast is included; the pleasant *Pension Bon Sol*, c/Major 84–76 (☎971 328

882;❷), is one of the cheapest places to stay. **Camping** is illegal. For a **meal** or **drink**, hippy favourite *Fonda Pepe* (opposite *Hostal Pepe*) is something of a local institution, and don't miss the fantastic *Blue Bar*, at the end of a dirt track on Platja de Migjorn, signed off the main Sant Ferran to La Mola road.

Mallorca (Majorca)

MALLORCA (Majorca in English) has a split identity. A popular place that pulls in an estimated three million tourists a year, there are sections of its coast where high-rise hotels and shopping centres are continuous, broken only by a dual carriageway leading to more of the same. But the spread of development, even after thirty years, is surprisingly limited: the high-rises occupy only the **Bay of Palma**, a forty-kilometre strip flanking the island capital. Beyond, to the north and east, things are very different. Not only are there good cove beaches, but there's a really startling variety and physical beauty to the land itself, which makes the island many people's favourite in the Balearics.

Palma

You may arrive by boat from Menorca at Puerto de Alcúdia in the north of the island, but the odds are you'll find yourself in **PALMA DE MALLORCA**, the capital. The port is by far the largest in the Balearics, the evening *paseo* the most ingrained, and, in the evenings at least, you feel the city has only passing relevance to the tourist enclaves around its bay. Arriving by sea, it's beautiful and impressive, with the grand limestone bulk of the cathedral towering above the old town and the remnants of medieval walls. The **ferry** port is 3.5km west of the city centre, connected to Palma by bus #1; Palma **airport**, 9km east of the city, is served by bus #25 (every 20min) to the Passeig Mallorca. Around the cathedral, containing Gaudí features, is the **Portela quarter**, "Old" Palma, a cluster of alleyways and lanes that become more spacious and ordered as you move towards the zigzag of avenues built beside or in place of the city walls. Cutting up from the sea, beside the cathedral, is **Paseo Borne**, garden promenade as well as boulevard, and way up the hill to the northeast lies the **Plaza Mayor**, target for most of the day-tripping tourists. The **tourist office** is at Plaça de la Reina 2 (daily 9am–8pm; ☎971 712 216, ⓦ www.visitbalears.com). The best areas to try for **accommodation** are around the Passeig Mallorca, on c/Apuntadores or c/San Felio running west from Paseo Borne (cheaper), and on c/San Jaime at the top of the Paseo Borne (mid-range). Some to try include *Hostal Apuntadores*, c/Apuntadores 8 (☎971 713 491; ❷), the neighbouring *Hostal Ritzi* (☎971 714 610; ❸), and *Hostal Pons*, c/Vi 8, in an old Palma house (☎971 722 658; ❷). There's also a **hostel** at c/Costa Brava 13 in El Arenal (☎971 260 892; €18), but it's often booked by school groups; take bus #15 from Plaza de España or Plaza de la Reina. There are no official **campsites** on the island. For **Internet** access head to Big Byte Palma, c/Apuntadores 6.

Eating in Palma can be cheaper than anywhere in the Balearics. There are plenty of touristy places along Passeig des Borns, but better fare is available nearby in the Barrio de Llotja between c/Apuntados and the seafront. Here you'll find several lower-priced restaurants, including *Vecchio Giovani*, c/San Juan 3. Head up the Passeig des Borns for the quirky but fantastic *El Pilon,* on the tiny alley, c/Cifre 4 – bags of local atmosphere and great tapas from €4.50. **Nightlife** is picking up influences from its neighbours. You might want to start the evening in the Barrio de Llotja, then move on to the waterfront venue *Pacha*, Avda. Gabriel Roca 42, which has guest DJs from Ibiza. *Tito's*, Placa Gomila 3, is another hardy perennial of the Palma scene.

Around Mallorca

When you feel you've exhausted the city's possibilities head north to **SÓLLER**, **DEIÁ**, **PUERTO POLLENSA**, **PUERTO DE ALCÚDIA** or to one of the small towns around **PORTO CRISTO** on the southeast coast. Accommodation is reasonable in each of these towns, though in July or August it'll be almost impossible to find. Mallorca's **bus service** is good, but for a real treat you need to take the delightful hour-and-a-quarter **train** ride from Palma to Sóller (5 daily; €2.60 one-way). Built in 1911 to carry fruit to Palma, the line rattles and rolls in wooden carriages through the dusty outskirts of the capital before a cross-country climb into mountain passes and tunnels, passing almond groves, unruffled lakes and craggy peaks topping a thousand metres. For a different route back to Palma, catch one of the five buses a day from Plaça America in Sóller, which wends its way along the coast to Deià, where Robert Graves is buried in the tiny churchyard. You can hop off, but check bus times for the next one before leaving Sóller. Next stop is **Son Marroig** (Mon–Sat 9.30am–2pm & 3–5pm; €2.30), a clifftop mansion that once belonged to Archduke Ludwig Salvator and which is remarkable for its gardens and the headland below. Cutting inland, the route takes in **Valldemossa**, where George Sand and Chopin stayed for four months in the 1830s at the Real Cartuja de Jesús de Nazaret monastery (Mon–Sat 9.30am–4.30/6pm, Sun 10am–1pm; €8), before heading across the plain to Palma. Without stops the bus ride from Sóller to Palma takes fifty minutes.

Valencia and the east coast

Much of Valencia's coast is a landscape of over-development, a land of villas and vacation homes linked by the southbound highway. But the area still has its attractions: the stretch of coast between Jávea and Altea has escaped the worst excesses, and the cities – vibrant **Valencia**, with its a strong nightlife scene, and relaxed **Alicante** – are well worth a visit.

Valencia

VALENCIA may not approach the vitality of Barcelona or the cultural variety of Madrid, but it does have lively nightlife, and its clothes and furniture designers are renowned throughout Spain. The city is sprawling and confused, marred by thoughtless modernization, but there are some exquisite corners away from the crowds, a few really fine buildings and a couple of excellent museums. The most interesting area for wandering is undoubtedly the maze-like **Barrio del Carmen**, the oldest part of town, roughly between c/de Caballeros and the Río Turia around the Puerta de Serranos. Among Valencia's renowned **fiestas** is Las Fallas de San José (early March) when dozens of giant wooden caricatures are displayed and then ceremoniously burned amidst a riot of fireworks that explode on the final night of the festival.

The distinctive feature of Valencian architecture is its wealth of elaborate Baroque facades – you'll see them on almost every old building in town, but none so extraordinary or rich as the **Palacio del Marqués de Dos Aguas**, a short walk north of the train station. Hipólito Rovira, who designed its amazing alabaster doorway, died insane in 1740, which should come as no surprise to anyone who's seen it. Inside is the **Museo Nacional de Cerámica** (Tues–Sat 10am–2pm & 4–8pm, Sun 10am–2pm; €3), with a vast collection of ceramics from all over Spain. Nearby, in the Plaza Patriarca, is the Neoclassical former university – with its beautiful cloisters and a series of classical concerts in July – and the beautiful Renaissance **Colegio del Patriarca**, whose small art museum (daily 11am–1.30pm; €1.20) includes excellent works by El Greco, Morales and Ribalta. It's not far from here, up c/de la Paz, to the **Plaza Zaragoza**, which is dominated by two octagonal towers, the florid spire of the church of Santa Catalina and the **Miguelete**, the unfinished bell-tower of the **cathedral**. You can make the long climb up to its roof (daily 10.30am–1pm & 4.30–6pm; €1.20) for a fantastic view over the city and its blue-domed churches, while in the **museum** (daily

10.30am–1pm & 4.30–6pm; €1.20) is a gold and agate cup (the Santo Cáliz) said to be the one used by Christ at the Last Supper – the Holy Grail itself. Other museums worth visiting include **IVAM**, the modern art museum at c/Guillém de Castro 118 (Tues–Sun 10am–8pm; €2.10), and the **Museo de Bellas Artes** on c/San Pío V (Tues–Sun 10am–8pm; free). A real curiosity is the city's old riverbed. The **Río Turia** was diverted after serious flooding in 1956, which damaged much of the old city, and is now no more than a trickle – with a huge park being landscaped in the riverbed. On one bank stands the **Palau de la Música**, a futuristic glass-structure venue for concerts, and the **City of Arts and Sciences** (daily 10am–8pm; €25.85 for two-day pass), Santiago

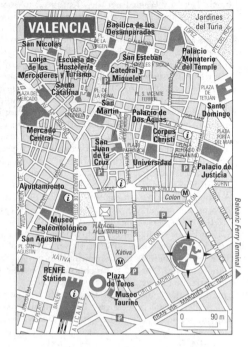

Calatrava's award-winning steel and glass pavilions, housing more concert halls, a science museum, and a giant oceanographic theme park. Five minutes' walk from the cathedral is the enormous **Mercado Central**, a huge iron and glass structure housing one of the biggest markets in Europe, full of amazing local fruit, fish and vegetables; it closes around 2pm every day.

Practicalities

Valencia's **train station** is reasonably central: head straight out, keeping the bullring to your right, along Avda. Marqués de Sotelo for the main Plaza del Ayuntamiento, beyond which lie the old parts of the city. The **bus station** is further out, at Avda. Menéndez Pidal 13, on the far bank of the dried-up river; take local bus #8 into the centre or allow twenty minutes if you walk. The **Balearic ferry terminal** is connected to Plaza del Ayuntamiento by bus #19. This square is also home to the main **tourist office** (Mon–Fri 8.30am–2.15pm & 4.15–6.15pm, Sat 9.15am–12.45pm; ☎963 510 417); there's also a branch inside the train station (Mon–Fri 9am–6.30pm). For what's on information, buy one of the two weekly **listings guides**, *Qué y Dónde* and *Turia* – or pick up the free English-language *24-7 Valencia* from the tourist office. Most of the cheaper **places to stay** are very near the train station, on c/Bailén and c/Pelayo, which run parallel to the tracks off c/Játiva. This area, however, is pretty sleazy; you may feel more comfortable paying a little more for somewhere in the centre, or staying much further out near the beach. Worth trying near the station is the friendly *Hostal-Residencia Lyon*, c/Xátiva 10 (☎963 517 247; ❷). Other options in the streets off Plaza del Ayuntamiento are the pleasant *Pensión Paris*, c/Salva 12 (☎963 526 766; ❷); the friendly if oddly partitioned *Hostal Universal*, c/Barcas 5 (☎963 515 384; ❷), and the basic *Hostal San Jose*, c/Transits 5 (963 940 152; ❷). Further north, near Plaza del Mercado, is the excellently sited and very good value *Hostal El Rincón*, c/Carda 11 (☎963 916 083; ❷); while out near the

27

beach, *Hotel La Pepica*, Paseo de Neptuno 2 (☎963 714 111; ❷), offers good-value rooms with bath, and an excellent restaurant. There are two **hostels** in the centre: the friendly, family-run *Hostal Moratin*, c/Moratin 15 (☎963 521 220; €18) is near the bar area and can get noisy, while the outwardly ramshackle but modernized *Home Youth Hostel*, c/Lonja 4 (☎963 916 229) is in the heart of the museum area.

The quality of **restaurant** food in Valencia can be poor, especially considering that this is the home of paella. However, there are decent mid-range possibilities, including *Los Toneles*, at c/Ribera 17, and *Bar Cánovas*, Gran Vía Marqués del Turia 76, one of the city's best tapas bars. For bistros and cheap restaurants the best area is Barrio del Carmen around c/Caballeros. A traditional place to go for *mejillones* (mussels) is the *Bar Pilar* on the corner of c/Moro Zeit, off Plaza del Esparto. For **paella**, try Malvarossa's *La Pepica,* Paseo Neptuno 6. Valencia can seem dead at night, but only because the action is widely dispersed. The best of the city-centre **nightlife** is centred on the Barrio del Carmen (c/Caballeros and c/Quart). *Café Sant Jaume* is a central place to start; there's also good bar-hopping on the adjoining c/Alta. The *Radio City Bar*, c/Santa Teresa 19, has a mainly young ex-pat clientele. Another area to try is near the Gran Vía de Fernando el Católico, along c/Juan Llorens and c/Calixto, where the *Café Carioca*, c/Juan Llorens 52, plays funk and R&B. The university area, around Avda. Blasco Ibáñez, is also popular: the *Rocafull Cafe* at Plaza Xuquer 14 is an old student favourite. For salsa head for *Café Bachata*, c/Jesús 36, or the bars on Juan Llorens. Many of the **discos** are in the university area – they include the perennially popular *Salamandra*, Eduardo Boscá 27. Otherwise, head for the big techno club *The Face*, Camino Montares 141, with its summertime terrace, and *Le Club*, Ctra. Fuente en Corts 36; both a ten-minute taxi ride from the centre. If this is a stretch, try the three-floor *Carmen Sui Generis*, c/Caballeros 38. The best **gay bars and discos** are in and around c/Quart; for dancing try *Venial*, c/Quart 26, or *La Goulue*, a few doors down.

Listings

Consulates UK, c/Colon 22, Valencia ☎963 520 710, or Plaza Calvo Sotelo 1–2, Alicante ☎965 216 022; US, c/Romagosa 1, Valencia ☎963 516 973.

Exchange Main branches of banks are around Pl. del Ayuntamiento or along c/Játiva 24. Outside banking hours, try: *Caja de Ahorros*, c/Játiva 14, to the left as you come out of the train station.

Hospitals Avda. Cid, at the Tres Cruces junction ☎963 862 900.

Internet access Confederation, c/Ribera 8, near the train station.

Laundry Pl. del Mercado 12, by the Mercado Central.

Left luggage At the train station.

Pharmacy Pl. del Mercado 37; at corner of Pl. del Ayuntamiento and c/Periodista Azzati.

Police Gran Vía Ramón y Cajal 40 ☎963 539 539.

Post office Pl. del Ayuntamiento 24.

The Costa Blanca

South of Valencia stretches the **Costa Blanca**, a long strip of country with, between Gandía and Benidorm, some of the best beaches on this coast. Much of it, though, suffers from the worst excesses of package tourism and in the summer it's hard to get a room anywhere – in August virtually impossible. Campers have it somewhat easier – there are hundreds of campsites. A rattling narrow-gauge **rail line** (FGV) runs hourly down the coast from Alicante to Benidorm and Denia. Beneath the wooded capes beyond, bypassed by the main road, stretch probably the most beautiful beaches on this coastline, centred on Javea – but you'll need a car to get to any of them, and even if you have a vehicle there's barely a cheap room to be found.

Alicante

Despite being a package-holiday destination, **ALICANTE** is a living, thoroughly Spanish city. There are good beaches nearby, lively nightlife in season and plenty of cheap places to stay and to eat. Wide esplanades give the town an elegant air, and around the Plaza de Luceros and along the seafront *paseo* you can relax in style at terrace cafés – paying a bit extra for the palm-tree setting, of course. Links between Alicante and Algeria have always been strong, and boats depart from here for Oran twice a week. If you can, time your visit to coincide with the **Fogueres de Sant Joan**, an elaborate, month-long extravaganza of processions, fire and fireworks which culminates in an orgy of burning on the feast night of St John the Baptist, towards the end of June. The towering **Castillo de Santa Bárbara** (daily 9am–7pm; €2.50 for the lift), on the bare rock behind the town beach, is Alicante's only real "sight" – with a tremendous view from the top. Access it from Playa Postiguet via a tunnel, then a lift shaft – cut straight up through the rock. For the best local **beaches** head for San Juan de Alicante, 6km out, reached either by bus from the Plaza del Mar or the FGV rail line. Better still, take a trip to the **island of Tabarca** to the south; boats leave from Puerto on the Esplanada de España, weather permitting (summer only; €13).

The main **train station** is on Avda. Salamanca, but trains on the private **FGV** line to Benidorm and Denia leave from the small station at the far end of the Playa del Postiguet. The **bus station** for local and international services is in c/Portugal. The **airport**, 12km west, is connected with the centre by a special bus service #C6, which stops at the central Avda. Rambla Mendez Nuñez. Nearby, at Esplanada de España 2, you'll find the very helpful **tourist office** (Mon–Sat 10am–7/8pm; ☎965 200 000); there are also offices at the train and bus stations and the airport. Except towards the end of June and in August, you should have little problem finding **accommodation**, with the bulk of the possibilities concentrated at the lower end of the old town, above the Esplanada de España – especially on c/San Fernando, c/Jorge Juan and c/Castaño. Options include the friendly *Hostal Ventura*, c/San Fernando 10 (☎965 208 337; ❷), and *Hostal San Fernando*, at no. 34 (☎965 213 656; ❷); note, though that there are several nightclubs nearby. There are cheaper places on c/San Francisco, but many are pretty seedy and not advisable for women travelling alone. On a quieter street is *Hostal Mayor*, c/Mayor 5 (☎965 201 383; ❷), while the air-conditioned *Hostal Metidja,* c/Méndez Núñez 26 (☎965 143 617; ❸) is a comfortable option. More upmarket, but a bargain out of season, when prices drop a code, is the beautiful *Les Monges*, c/San Agustin 4 (☎965 215 046; ❸). There are several **campsites**, including *El Molino* at Playa de San Juan to the north (connected by FGV train and bus #21) and *La Marina*, south of town in woods on a good beach and connected by Costa Azul buses.

Cheap **restaurants** are clustered around the Ayuntamiento, including a couple of places where you can eat couscous on c/Miguel Soler; there are other cheap eateries on c/Mayor. For **tapas**, try the atmospheric *Mesón de Labradores* near the cathedral at c/Labradores 19. For **bars** and the best **nightlife**, head into the Barrio Santa Cruz, whose narrow streets lie roughly between the cathedral, Plaza Carmen and Plaza San Cristóbal. An excellent starting point is *Desden*, c/Labradores 22, which plays jazz in the afternoon and house, dance and funk through the night till 4am. Several other clubs are concentrated on c/San Fernando, while the bars along the Playa de San Juan are a popular summertime haunt. For **Internet** access there's Zipposbar, c/Labradores 1, or Yazzgo Internet, Esplanada de España 3.

Andalucía

The southern region of Andalucía is likely to both meet your pre-conceptions of Spain, and defy them. Everywhere there is evidence of this passionate, parched country at its most exuberant: it is the home of flamenco and the bullfight, tradition and fierce pride. But it's also much more than the cliché. Evidence of the Moors' sophistication remains visible to this day in **Córdoba**, in **Seville** and, particularly, in **Granada**'s Alhambra. On the coast you could despair. Extending to either side

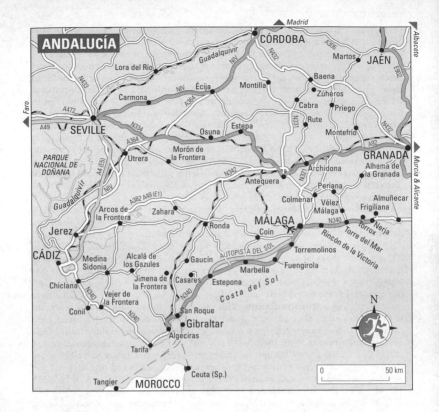

of **Málaga** is the **Costa del Sol**, Europe's most developed resort area, with its beaches hidden behind a remorseless curtain of concrete. But there is life beyond the Costa del Sol, especially the beaches of the Costa de la Luz. Here, **Tarifa** sits on the most southerly tip of Europe, its exposed position drawing swarms of windsurfers. Andalucía is also where Europe stops and Africa begins; in places the mountains of that great continent appear almost close enough to touch, in reality they are just half an hour away by ferry.

Granada

If you see only one town in Spain it should be **GRANADA**, with its wonderful backdrop of the Sierra Nevada. For here stands the Alhambra – the spectacular and serene climax of Moorish art in Spain. Granada was established as an independent kingdom in 1238 by **Ibn Ahmar**, a prince of the Arab Nasrid tribe, who had been driven south from Zaragoza. The Moors of Granada maintained their autonomy for two and a half centuries, but by 1490 only the city itself remained in Muslim hands. **Boabdil**, the last Moorish king, appealed in vain for help from his fellow Muslims in Morocco, Egypt and Turkey, and in the following year Ferdinand and Isabella marched on Granada with an army said to total 150,000 troops. For seven months, through the winter of 1491, they laid siege to the city. On January 2, 1492, Boabdil surrendered: the Christian Reconquest of Spain was complete.

There are three distinct groups of buildings on the **Alhambra** hill: the **Palacios Reales** (Royal Palace), the palace gardens of the **Generalife**, and the **Alcazaba**, from whose reddish walls the hilltop took its name: *al-Hamra* in Arabic means "the red". Ibn Ahmar rebuilt the Alcazaba and within the walls he began a palace, which he supplied with running water by diverting the River Darro; water is an integral part of the Alhambra and this engineering feat was Ibn Ahmar's greatest contribution. After their conquest of the city, Ferdinand and Isabella lived for a while in the Alcazaba, while their grandson, Charles V, demolished a whole wing to build yet another grandiose Renaissance palace. By the eighteenth century the Royal Palace was in use as a prison. In 1812 it was taken and occupied by Napoleon's forces, who looted and damaged whole sections of the palace, and on their retreat from the city tried (but fortunately failed) to blow up the entire complex.

Arrival, information and accommodation

The **train station** is 1km out of town on Avda. de Andaluces, and is connected to the centre by buses #3, #6, #9 and #11. The main **bus station**, on Carretera de Jaén, is a bit further out; bus #3 runs into town. A bus also connects the **airport** with Gran Vía de Colón (8am–6pm, up to 7 daily; €3). Details and timetables of all buses and trains are posted on the walls of the **tourist office**, which is within the beautiful Corral del Carbon on c/Mariana Pineda, off c/Reyes Católicos (Mon–Sat 9am–7pm, Sun 10am–2pm; ☎958 225 990). The **Gran Vía** is Granada's main street, cutting through the middle of town. It forms a "T" at its end with c/Reyes Católicos, which runs east to the Plaza Nueva and west to the Puerta Real, the city's two main squares. Finding **accommodation** in this area is easy, except at the very height of the season. Try the streets to either side of the Gran Vía, at the back of the Plaza Nueva, around the Puerta Real and Plaza del Carmen (particularly c/de Navas), the Plaza de la Trinidad, or along the Cuesta de Gomérez, which leads up from the Plaza Nueva towards the Alhambra.

Hostels

Albergue Juvenil Granada Avda. Ramón y Cajal 2 ☎902 510 000. Handy for the train station: turn left onto c/del Halcón, then first left across the railway line. Lots of facilities, including a pool, but very institutional. ②

Pension Doña Lupe Avda. del Generalife, Alhambra ☎958 221 473. On the road leading up to the cemetery, this is the cheapest option up here. It also has a summertime terrace offering fantastic views. Book ahead. ②

Hotels

Hostal Antares c/Cetti Meriem 10 ☎958 228 313. Good, central location just off the Gran Vía, near the cathedral. Clean and airy, some rooms en suite. ②

Hostal Atenas Gran Vía de Colón 38 ☎958 278 750, ✉hatenas@moebius.es. Large, if characterless place. Some rooms en suite. ③

Hostal Olimpia c/Alvaro de Bazán 6 ☎958 278

238. Central, good-value place off the Gran Vía. ②

Pension Los Montes c/Arteaga 3 ☎958 277 930. Just off the Gran Vía, pleasant rooms, some with baths. ②

Pension Romero c/Silleria de Mesones 1 ☎958 266 079. Just off Plaza de la Trinidad. Quite basic, some rooms overlook the square. ②

Pension Zacatin c/Ermita 11, signed off Plaza Bib-Rambla ☎958 221 155. Atmospheric place, through a tiny alleyway crammed during the day with leather goods. Run by a pleasant couple. ②

Pension Zurita Plaza de la Trinidad 7 ☎958 275 020. Airy, family-run place right on the square. Some rooms with bath, and a good café downstairs. ③

Campsite

Camping Sierra Nevada Avda. de Madrid 107 ☎958 150 062. A surprisingly leafy and relatively central site, within easy walking distance of the train station. Closed Nov–Feb.

The City

The standard approach to the **Alhambra** (daily 8.30am–8pm; €7) is along the Cuest de Gomérez, the road that climbs uphill from Plaza Nueva. You need to book in advance or at least arrive early: buy your ticket from the booth at the entrance; from any Banco BBVA in Spain (including the one in town at Plaza Isabel la Católica); by phone (☎902 224 460; credit cards only; €0.88 booking fee); or online (☎www.alhambratickets.com). A hot tip is to buy a *bono turistico Granada* (tourist voucher; €18, ask the tourist office), which lets you jump the lengthy queues and gets you into a range of museums and sights throughout the city, as well

GRANADA

SACROMONTE

ALBAICÍN

Casa del Chapiz

Iglesia del Salvador

PL. DE OYTEGAS

Mirador de San Nicolás

S. Juan de los Reyes

San Bartolomé

Arco de las Pesas

PL. DE S. NICOLÁS

Cvto. de la Concepción

PLAZA LARGA

N

San Cristóbal

MIRADOR DE ROLANDO

CARRETERA

Palacio de Dar-al-Horra

Casa de Porras

Cvto. de Sta. Isabel la Real

Murallas de Albaycín

Mirador del Carril de la Lona

San José

San Gregorio Bético

Hospital Real

Iglesia de San Ildefonso

PL. DE LA MERCED

Arco o Puerta de Elvira

PLAZA DEL TRIUNFO

AV. CAP MORENO

CAPUCHINOS

PL. DE LOS NARANJOS

ELVIRA

GRAN VÍA DE COLÓN

GRAN VÍA DE COLÓN

Fuente Del Triunfo

AVDA. DE LA CONSTITUCIÓN

SAN JUAN DE DIOS

MENDOZA

MANO DE HIERRO

PL. DE S. AGUSTÍN

Catedral

ACERA DEL TRIUNFO

ARRIOLA

Igl. de los Santos Justo y Pastor

SAN JERÓNIMO

Colegio de Niñas Nobles

S. Felipe Neri

Hospital e Iglesia de San Juan de Dios

Colegio de San Bartolomé y Santiago

Universidad

DUQUESA

PLAZA DE LA TRINIDAD

CONDE INFANTES

Monasterio e Iglesia de San Jerónimo

FÁBRICA VIEJA

RECTOR

PLAZA LOBOS

POLÍG. UNIVERSITARIO

BUENSUCESO

Guadix & Murcia

Jaén, Madrid & Bus Station

Train Station, Airport & Seville

Antequera & Málaga

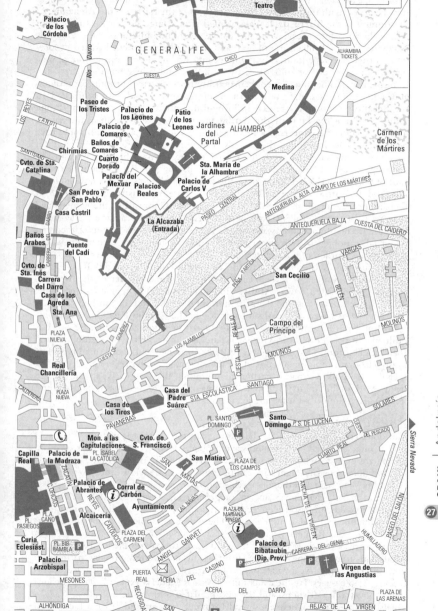

Camino del Sacromonte

PASEO DE LAS ADELFAS

Teatro

0   100 m

Palacio
de los
Córdoba

GENERALIFE

DEL   REY

CHICO

ALHAMBRA
TICKETS

CUESTA

Medina

Paseo de
los Tristes

Palacio de
los Leones

Pátio
de los
Leones

Jardínes
del
Partal

ALHAMBRA

Carmen
de los
Mártires

Palacio de
Comares

Baños de
Comares

Chirimías

Cuarto
Dorado

Palacio del
Mexuar

Palacios
Reales

Sta. María de
la Alhambra

Cvto. de Sta.
Catalina

San Pedro y
San Pablo

Palacio de
Carlos V

CAMPO DE LOS MÁRTIRES

Casa Castril

La Alcazaba
(Entrada)

ANTEQUERUELA ALTA

PASEO   CENTRAL

Baños
Arabes

ANTEQUERUELA BAJA

CUESTA DEL CAIDERO

Puente
del Cadí

Cvto. de
Sta. Inés

PEÑA PARTIDA

Carrera
del Darro

VARGAS

Casa de los
Agreda

San Cecilio

BELÉN

Sta. Ana

MOLINOS

PLAZA
NUEVA

Campo del
Príncipe

CUESTA DE GOMÉREZ

LOS ALAMILLOS

CUESTA   DEL   REALEJO

MOLINOS

Real
Chancillería

SANTIAGO

PLAZA
NUEVA

SOLARES

CALDERERÍA

Casa del
Padre
Suárez

STA. ESCOLÁSTICA

P.º DE LUCENA

DEL PESCADO

Casa de
los Tiros

PAVANERAS

PL. SANTO
DOMINGO

Santo
Domingo

P

CUARTO REAL

Mon. a las
Capitulaciones

Cvto. de
S. Francisco

Capilla
Real

Palacio de
la Madraza

PL. ISABEL
LA CATÓLICA

San Matías

SAN

PLAZA DE
LOS CAMPOS

ANCHA DE LA VIRGEN

PASEO DEL SALÓN

Palacio de
Abrantes

Corral de
Carbón

MATÍAS

Alcaicería

Ayuntamiento

LAS NAVAS

PLAZA DE
MARIANA
PINEDA

Curia
Eclesiást.

PL. A.
CANO

PL.
PASIEGOS

REYES

CATÓLICOS

PLAZA DEL
CARMEN

GANIVET

Palacio
Arzobispal

PL. BIB-
RAMBLA

P

ANGEL

CASINO

Palacio de
Bibataubín
(Dip. Prov.)

P

CARRERA   DEL   GENIL

P

HUMILLADERO

Virgen de
las Angustias

MESONES

PUERTA
REAL

ACERA

DEL

ALHÓNDIGA

ACERA

DEL

DARRO

PLAZA DE
LAS ARENAS

RECOGIDAS

SAN

ANTÓN

SAN

REJAS   DE   LA   VIRGEN

PUENTEZUELAS

ISIDRO

Purchil & Motril

C

i

i

SPAIN | Andalucía

Sierra Nevada

27

881

as allowing ten bus trips. Tickets are timed for the Palacio Nazaries; if you get the choice, opt for later in the day, after most tour groups have left. Ideally you should start your visit with the earliest, most ruined, part of the fortress – the **Alcazaba**. At the summit is the **Torre de la Vela**, named after a huge bell on its turret, from where there's a fine overview of the whole area. The buildings in the **Palacios Nazaries** show a brilliant use of light and space with ornamental stucco decoration, in rhythmic repetitions of supreme beauty. Arabic inscriptions feature prominently: some are poetic eulogies of the buildings and rulers, but most are taken from the Koran. The sultans used the **Mexuar**, the first series of rooms, for business and judicial purposes, and this is as far as most people would have penetrated. In the **Serallo**, beyond, they received distinguished guests: here is the royal throne room, known as the **Hall of the Ambassadors**, the largest room of the palace. The last section, the **Harem**, formed their private living quarters and would have been entered by no one but their family or servants. These are the most beautiful rooms of the palace, and include the **Court of the Lions**, which has become the archetypal image of Granada. You can exit the Palacios Nazaries through the courtyard of the **Charles V's Palace**, once the scene of bullfights, which now houses a museum and, although wilfully out of place here, is a distinguished piece of Renaissance design. A short walk takes you to the **Generalife,** the gardens and summer palace of the sultans. Paradise is described in the Koran as a shaded, leafy garden refreshed by running water where the "fortunate ones" may take their rest under tall canopies. It is an image that perfectly describes the Generalife, whose name means "garden of the architect".

From just below the entrance to the Generalife the **Cuesta del Rey Chico** winds down towards the River Darro and the old Arab quarter of the Albaicín. Here the little-visited **Baños Árabes** (Tues–Sat 10am–2pm; free) at Corredera del Darro 31 are marvellous, and the plaza in front of the church of San Nicolás offers probably the best view of the Alhambra in town. The **Capilla Real** in the city centre (Mon–Sat 10.30am–1pm & 4–7pm, Sun 10am–noon & 4–8pm; €2.50) was built in the first decades of Christian rule as a mausoleum for Ferdinand and Isabella. Their tombs are as simple as could be imagined, but above them is a fabulously elaborate monument erected by their grandson, Charles V. For all its stark Renaissance bulk, Granada's **cathedral**, adjoining the Capilla Real and entered from the door beside it (Mon–Sat 10.30am–1.30pm & 4–6.30pm, Sun 4–7pm; €2.50), has a simple but imposing grandeur.

Eating, drinking and nightlife

You don't come to Granada for the cuisine, but the centre has plenty of animated bars serving good, cheap food and staying open late. The open-air **cafés** on Plaza Nueva are great to while away some time, but pricey if you eat. Better-value dining, and numerous late-night bars, can be found in "Little Morocco", the warren of streets between here and the Gran Vía: good-value choices here include the *Nueva Bodega* at c/Cetti Merién 3, and its neighbour *Cafetería-Restaurante La Riviera*. Another nucleus of reasonable eateries is the area around Plaza del Carmen (near the Ayuntamiento) and along c/Navas. There's great people-watching in the bars around Plaza Bib-Rambla, while the tiny *Café Bar Soria* and *Cafetería Guerrero,* both on the nearby Plaza de la Trinidad, are good places to soak up the local atmosphere. Moroccan-style teashops, known as **teterías**, are increasingly popular, particularly with students, and serve a wide choice of herb teas (*infusiones*), accompanied by traditional Arab pastries. Try the delightful *As-Sirat* at Calderia Nueva 7, on an intriguing alleyway of craft shops, and the cheap falafels and real lemonade at *Cadillos Baraka* on the corner. There are several **Internet** cafés around c/Santa Escolastica, including Net Internet, Plaza de los Girones 3.

Nightlife is focused on c/Elvira, with its large number of bars; one of the most atmospheric is *Bodegas Castañeda*, at the junction with c/Almireceros. Another good area for drinking is around the university, on c/Gran Capitán and c/Pedro Antonio de Alarcón. In term-time, students also gather in **pubs** near the bus station around the Campo del Príncipe, a square on the southern slopes of the Alhambra, where you'll often find great tapas. At the weekend, the best **disco** in town is *El Camborio* inside the caves at the end of Camino del Sacramento. Granada is also one of the best places in Spain to hear **flamenco**, though finding the real thing can be difficult. There are numerous – and mostly lame – *espectaculares* for the tourists around Sacromonto, but you're better off going to the Albaicín district and searching the bars around Plaza Larga, west of the Iglesia del Salvador, where the gypsies play spontaneously. Be aware though that this area has seen a rise in the number of thefts from tourists; take the usual precautions and keep to the more populated streets.

Córdoba

CÓRDOBA is a minor provincial capital which once formed the largest city of Roman Spain, and for three centuries it was the heart of the great medieval caliphate of the Moors. It's an engaging, atmospheric city, easily explored and with some excellent budget accommodation. For visitors, its main attraction comes down to a single building: La Mezquita – the grandest and most beautiful mosque ever constructed by the Moors. This stands right in the centre of the city, surrounded by the labyrinthine Jewish and Moorish quarters, and is a building of extraordinary mystical and aesthetic power.

Córdoba's domination of Moorish Spain began thirty years after the conquest, in 756 AD, when the city was placed under **Abd ar-Rahman I**, who established control over all but the north of Spain. It was he who commenced the building of the Great Mosque – in Spanish, **La Mezquita** (Mon–Sat 10am–7.30pm, Sun am for worship & 2–7.30pm; €6.50) – which is approached through the Patio de los Naranjos, a classic Islamic court which preserves both its orange trees and fountains for ritual purification before prayer. Inside, nearly a thousand twin-layered red and white pillars combine to mesmeric effect, the harmony culminating only at the foot of the beautiful Mihrab (prayer niche). North of La Mezquita lies the **Judería**, Córdoba's old Jewish quarter, a fascinating network of lanes that are more atmospheric and less commercialized than Seville's. Near the heart of the quarter, at c/Maimonides 18, is a tiny **synagogue** (Tues–Sat 10am–1.30pm & 3.30–5.30pm, Sun 10am–1.30pm; €0.30), one of only three in Spain that survived the Jewish expulsion of 1492. East of the Judería, the **Museo Arqueológico** (Tues 3–8pm, Wed–Sat 9am–8pm, Sun 9am–3pm; €1.50) occupies a small Renaissance mansion in which Roman foundations have been incorporated into an imaginative and enjoyable display.

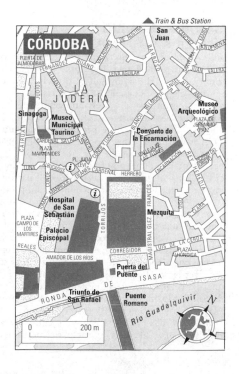

Close to the **train and bus stations**, the broad Avda. del Gran Capitán leads down to the old quarters and La Mezquita – a 25-minute walk, or short ride on bus #3. The **tourist office** is at the Palacio de Congresos y Exposiciones, c/Torrijos 10, alongside La Mezquita (Mon–Fri 9.30am–6pm, Sat 10am–6pm, Sun 10am–2pm; ☎957 471 235, ⊛www.ayuncordoba.es). The best **places to stay** are concentrated in the maze of streets northeast of La Mezquita, many with beautifully tiled courtyards. Amongst the most atmospheric is *Hostal Deanes*, c/ Deanes 6 (☎957 293 744; ❸). Calle Rey Heredia also has some good places, including the pleasant Hostal *Rey Heredia* at no. 26 (☎957 474 182; ❸). Less savoury, but likely to have room, are the cheap, run-down *fondas* in the ramshackle Plaza de la Corredera: *Fonda Corredera* (☎957 470 581; ❷), at the corner of the plaza and c/Rodríguez Marin, is clean and friendly. You pay a little more at *Hostal Maestre*, c/Romero Barros 16 (☎957 475 395; ❸), where you'll get an en-suite room, and at *Hotel-Restaurante Los Patios*, Caredenal Herrero 14 (☎957 478 340; ❸) which offers very pleasant accommodation beside La Mezquita. There's also an **HI hostel** in the Judería, a few minutes' walk from La Mezquita, at Plaza Juda Levi (☎957 290 166; ❷). Córdoba's main **campsite**, *Campamento Municipal El Brillante* (☎957 282 165; bus #10 or #11), is 2km north on the road to Villaviciosa.

Bars and **restaurants** are on the whole reasonably priced, save for the touristy places around La Mezquita. Loads of alternatives can be found not too far away in the Judería and in the old quarters off to the east, above Paseo de la Ribera: try *El Extremeño* at Plaza Agrupación de Cofradías, just north of the Mezquita. *Cafeteria Juda Levi*, opposite the hostel, does main courses from €6. For **Internet** access, head for Ch@t-is, at Claudio Marcelo 15, near Plaza Tendillas. The local barrelled **wine** is mainly *Montilla* or *Moriles* – both are magnificent, resembling mellow, dry sherries. For samples, head for *Taberna San Miguel*, Plaza San Miguel 1, a Córdoba institution affectionately known as *El Pisto*. **Flamenco** performances take place at *La Bulería*, c/Pedro López 3 (from 10.30pm), but it's poor fare compared to what you can see in Seville or Granada.

Seville (Sevilla)

SEVILLE (Sevilla) is the great city of the Spanish south, intensely hot in summer and with an abiding reputation for theatricality and intensity. It has three important monuments – the Giralda tower, the cathedral and the Alcázar – and an illustrious history, but it's the living self of this city of Carmen, Don Juan and Figaro that remains the great attraction. It is expressed on a phenomenally grand scale at the city's two great festivals – **Semana Santa**, during the week before Easter, and the **April Feria**, which lasts a week at the end of the month. Seville is also Spain's second most important centre for **bullfighting** after Madrid. It remains a poor city and petty crime is a big problem, especially in the form of bag-snatching. On a more positive note, as the site of the Expo 92 world fair, Seville has added an upbeat modern dimension to its buildings and infrastructure, though the soul of the city still lies in its historic latticework of narrow streets, patios and plazas, where minarets jostle for space among cupolas and palms.

Arrival, information and accommodation

The San Justa **train station** is a fair way out of the centre on Avda. Kansas City, which is also the airport road; bus #C1 connects it to the centre and to the San Sebastián bus station. There is an hourly bus service (6.15am–9.30pm; €2.10) connecting the **airport** to the town. The main **bus station** is at Plaza de Armas, beside the river by the Puente del Cachorro, but buses for destinations within Andalucía (plus Barcelona, Alicante and Valencia) leave from the more central terminal at Plaza de San Sebastián. Bus #C4 connects the two terminals. The **tourist office** is at Avda. de la Constitución 21 (Mon–Fri 9am–7pm, Sat 10am–2pm & 3–7pm, Sun 10am–2pm; ☎954 221 404, ⊛www.turismo.sevilla.org). The most attractive area to **stay** is the maze-like Barrio Santa Cruz, near the cathedral, although this is generally reflected in the prices you have to pay. Rooms anywhere are almost impossible to find during the big festivals, and prices double during Easter week and the April fair. If you can't find anything in the Barrio, try its periphery or slightly further out beyond Plaza Nueva, over towards the river and the Plaza de Armas bus station.

Hostel

Albergue Juvenil Sevilla c/Isaac Peral 2 ☏955 056 500. HI hostel some way out in the university district; can get crowded. Bus #34 from Puerta de Jerez or Plaza Nueva. ❶

Hotels

Hostal Arizona c/Pedro del Torro 14 ☏954 216 042. Near the Plaza de Armas bus station, basic rooms, with and without bath, gets busy so arrive early or phone ahead. ❷

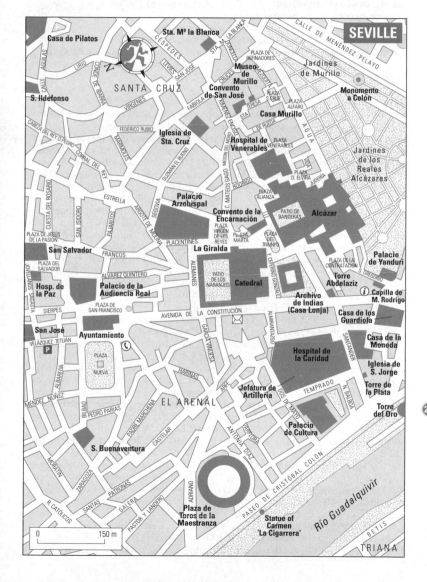

SPAIN | Andalucía

㉗

Hostal Bienvenido c/Archeros 14, Barrio Santa Cruz ☎954 413 655. Small rooms with nice roof terrace. ❸
Hostal Buen Dormir c/Farnesio 8, Barrio Santa Cruz ☎954 217 492. Good value, friendly place, with a roof patio, in a street with several possibilities. ❷
Hostal Capitol c/Zaragoza 66 ☎954 212 441. Just off Plaza Nueva – a range of rooms and prices, so look first. ❸
Hostal El Giraldill c/Gravina 23 ☎954 224 275. Has some airy rooms with tiny balconies. Also some with baths. ❸
Hostal Gala c/Gravina 52 ☎954 214 503. One of several clustered on this street near Plaza de Armas bus station. Functional, with some en-suite rooms. ❸

Hostal Gravina c/Gravina 46 ☎954 216 414. Basic but cheap and clean. The owner also runs three other places nearby. ❸
Hostal Monreal c/Rodrigo Caro 8, Barrio Santa Cruz ☎954 214 166. Great location, and plenty of rooms in a newly converted town house. Tiled courtyard café downstairs. ❷
Hostal Van Gogh c/Miguel de Manara 1 ☎954 563 727. Wonderfully situated beside the cathedral, with en-suite rooms. Has a sister hostal *Picasso* nearby. ❸

Campsite
Camping Sevilla ☎954 514 379. By the airport, with its own pool; minibus connects the site to central Seville three times a day.

The City

Seville was one of the earliest Moorish conquests (in 712 AD) and, as part of the Caliphate of Córdoba, became the second city of al-Andalus. When the caliphate broke up in the early eleventh century it was the most powerful of the independent states to emerge, and under the Almohad dynasty became the capital of the last real Moorish empire in Spain from 1170 until 1212. The Almohads rebuilt the Alcázar, enlarged the principal mosque and erected a new and brilliant minaret – the **Giralda** (Mon–Sat 11am–5pm, Sun 2.30–6pm; €6, including entrance to cathedral, free Sun) – topped with four copper spheres. It still dominates the skyline today and you can ascend the minaret for a remarkable view of the city, but most impressive of all is the tower's inner construction: a series of 35 gentle ramps wide enough to allow two mounted guards to pass. The Giralda was so venerated by the Moors that they wanted to destroy it before the Christian conquest of the city. Instead in 1402 it became the bell tower of the **cathedral** (same hours as Giralda), the largest Gothic church in the world by cubic capacity. Its centre is dominated by a vast Gothic retable composed of 45 carved scenes from the life of Christ, the lifetime's work of a single craftsman, Pierre Dancart, and the largest altarpiece in the world. Across Plaza del Triunfo from the cathedral lies the **Alcázar** (Tues–Sat 9.30am–7pm, Sun 9.30am–2.30/6pm; €5), a site that rulers of Seville have occupied from the time of the Romans. Under the Almohads, the complex was turned into an enormous citadel, forming the heart of the town's fortifications. Parts of the walls survive, but the palace was rebuilt in the Christian period by Pedro the Cruel (1350–1369). His works, some of the best surviving examples of Mudéjar architecture, form the nucleus of the Alcázar today. Later additions include a wing in which early expeditions to the Americas were planned, and the huge Renaissance apartments of Charles V. Don't miss the beautiful and rambling **Alcázar gardens**, the confused but enticing product of several eras. Ten minutes' walk south of the cathedral, **Plaza de España** and adjoining **María Luisa Park** are an ideal place to spend the middle part of the day. En route you pass the **Fábrica de Tabacos**, the old tobacco factory that was the setting for Bizet's *Carmen*. Nowadays it's part of the university. Towards the end of the María Luisa Park, some grand pavilions house museums. The furthest contains the city's **archeology** collections (Tues 3–8pm, Wed–Sat 9am–8pm, Sun 9am–2pm; €1.50), and opposite is the **Popular Arts Museum** (Tues 3–8pm, Wed–Sat 9am–8pm, Sun 9am–2pm; €1.50), with interesting displays relating to the April *feria*.

A further twenty minutes' walk northwest along the river, the Río Guadalquivir, takes you to the twelve-sided **Torre del Oro**, built in 1220 as part of the Alcázar fortifications. The tower later stored the gold brought back to Seville from the

Americas – hence its name. One block away is the **Hospital de la Caridad** (Mon–Sat 9am–1.30pm & 3.30–6.30pm, Sun 9am–1pm; €3) founded in 1676 by Don Miguel de Manara, the inspiration for Byron's Don Juan, who repented his youthful excesses and set up this hospital for the relief of the dying and destitute. There are some magnificent paintings by Murillo and Valdés Leal inside. There's more art further along at the **Museo de Bellas Artes** on Plaza del Museo (Tues 3–8pm, Wed–Sat 9am–8pm, Sun 9am–2pm; free for EU citizens), housed in a beautiful former convent. Outstanding are the paintings by Murillo, as well Zurbarán's Carthusian monks at supper and El Greco's portrait of his son.

Across the river lies the **Triana** *barrio* that was once home to the city's gypsy community and is still a lively and atmospheric place. At Triana's northern edge lies **La Cartuja** (Tues–Fri 10am–8pm, Sat 11am–8pm, Sun 10am–3pm; €1.80), a fourteenth-century former Carthusian monastery. Part of the complex is now given over to the **Museo del Arte Contemporáneo** (Tues–Sat 10am–8pm, Sun 10am–3pm; €1.80), which, in addition to work by local artists, frequently stages important exhibitions by international artists.

Eating, drinking and nightlife

Seville is a tremendously atmospheric place, and the city is packed with lively bars and restaurants, but it can be expensive, particularly in the Barrio Santa Cruz. Calle Santa María La Blanca has several reasonable **restaurants** – notably the *Alta Mira* – as does c/Mateus Gago opposite La Giralda – try the *Alcazaba* or the *Café Bar Campanario*, where two large bulls' heads will watch you eat. *Casa Vivda* on the corner of c/General Polavieja has tasty *ensaimadas* for breakfast. Other central areas to try are the streets around Plaza Nueva. On c/Albareda in the atmospheric *Cassa la Vidan* you can get a tasty breakfast for a few euros and cheap eats later on; just off the south of the square on c/Zaragoza, *Café Bar Vina* offers a set menu for €5. There are similar bargains to be had on c/Jimios nearby. *Habanita* is a pleasant **vegetarian** Cuban restaurant on c/Golfo, just off c/Pérez Galdos, in the Alfalfa area.

For straight drinking and occasional tapas there are **bars** all over town – a high concentration of them with barrelled sherries from nearby Jerez and Sanlúcar (the locals drink the cold, dry *fino*). In the centre of Santa Cruz one of the liveliest places is *Las Teresas* in c/Ximénez de Enciso (expensive tapas), but perhaps the best **tapas bar** in the city is the *Bar Modesto* at c/Cano y Cuento 5, up at the north corner of the quarter by Avda. Menéndez Pelayo. The innocuous-looking *Bodeguita* at c/Arfe 5, south of Plaza Nueva, is also worth searching out and less expensive, while *Bar Giralda* at c/Mateus Gago is excellent, as is the *Bodega Santa Cuiz* on c/Rodrigo Caro just off c/Mateus Gago.

The Alfalfa area just north of the cathedral is a lively area at night with loud **music** in many of the bars: *Bar Nao* and *Sopa de Ganso* in c/Pérez Galdos are both worth a look. The other main area for nightlife, popular with the substantial foreign student population, is just across the river on c/Betis. **Flamenco** – or more accurately *Sevillanas* – music and dance are offered at dozens of places in the city, some of them extremely tacky and expensive. An alternative are the regular performances at a museum in the heart of the old city: the **Casa de la Memoria de Al-Andalus**, c/Ximenez de Enciso 28 (☏954 560 670; nightly in the summer at 9pm; €11), which aims to preserve traditional flamenco. You'll get a very different experience in the bars – an excellent place to try is *La Carbonería* at c/Levías 18, just northeast of the Iglesia de San Juan, which often has spontaneous *Sevillanas* and other theatrical and artistic offerings.

Listings

Bullfighting The season starts with the April *feria* and continues until Sept, with most *corridas* held on Sun evenings. Tickets from the Maestranza bullring, Paseo de Colón 12 (☏954 501 382), which also

houses a museum; from as little as €10.

Consulates Australia, Federico Rubio 14 ☏954 220 971; Ireland, Plaza de Santa Cruz 6 ☏954 216 361; UK, PO Box 143 ☏954 155 018; US,

Paseo de las Delicias 7 ☎954 231 885.
Exchange Banks and *cambios* can be found
around the tourist office on Avda. de la
Constitución.
Hospital Hospital Universitario, Avda. Dr. Fedriani
3 ☎954 557 400. Also, emergency clinic just
behind the Alcázar, at corner of Menendez Pelayo
and Avda. de Cádiz.

Internet Sevilla Internet, Avda. de la Constitución,
opposite the cathedral; and c/Almirantazgo.
Laundry c/Castelar 2.
Left luggage At the train station (24hr).
Pharmacy Opposite the cathedral on Avda. de la
Constitución; in the Barrio de Santa Cruz, on the
corner of c/Mateos Gago and c/Rodrigo Caro.
Police Plaza de la Gavidia ☎954 228 840.
Post office Avda. de la Constitución 32.

Jerez de la Frontera

JEREZ DE LA FRONTERA, 100km west of Seville, is the home and heartland of **sherry** – and also, less known but equally important, of Spanish brandy. Outside the two big festivals – the May Horse Fair and the celebration of the vintage towards the end of September – you're unlikely to want to make more than a quick visit, as the town itself is not particularly distinctive. However, the tours of the sherry and brandy **bodegas** can be interesting, and you get to taste the product. Many were founded by British Catholic refugees, who even now form a kind of Anglo-Andalucian aristocracy. Most bodegas close in August, though one exception is the central **González Byass**, next to the ruins of the Moorish Alcázar on c/Manuel Maria González (tours Mon–Sat hourly 11.30am–5.30pm; ☎956 357 016; €7). Most of the other bodegas are on the outskirts of town; pick up a plan from the tourist office. The **train and bus stations** are close to each other, eight blocks east of the González bodega and the central Plaza de los Reyes Católicos. The **tourist office** is on Plaza del Arenal (Mon–Fri 9.30am–3pm & 4.30–6.30pm; Sat 9am–2.30pm; ☎956 359 654, ⊛www.webjerez.com). For **accommodation**, try the *San Miguel* in Plaza Miguel (☎956 348 562; ❷), or the *Nuevo Hotel* at c/Caballeros 23 (☎956 331 600; ❷). Other alternatives are found on c/Higueras, off c/Medina (left out of the bus station and three blocks along), or c/Morenos, off the parallel c/Arcos. There's also a **hostel** at Avda. Carrero Blanco 30 (☎956 143 901; ❷).

Cádiz

CÁDIZ is among the oldest settlements in Spain and has long been one of the country's principal ports. Its heyday was the eighteenth century, when it enjoyed a virtual monopoly on the Spanish-American trade in gold and silver. Central Cádiz, built on a peninsula-island, remains much as it must have looked in those days, with its grand open squares, sailors' alleyways and high, turreted houses. It's also the spiritual home of flamenco, and you get a sense of that to this day; the city, crumbling from the effect of sea air on soft limestone, has a tremendous atmosphere – slightly seedy, definitely in decline, but still full of mystique. Cádiz's big party time is its annual **carnival**, normally held in February and early March; expect frenzied celebrations, masked processions and satirical digs at the local big shots.

With its blind alleys, back streets and cafés, Cádiz is fascinating to wander around. To understand the city's layout, climb the **Torre Tavira**, Marques del Real Tesoro 10 (daily 10am–6pm; €3), tallest of the 160 lookout towers in the city, with an excellent camera obscura. Some specific sites to check out are the huge **Catedral Nueva** (Tues–Fri 10am–1pm & 4.30–7.30pm, Sat & Sun 10am–1pm; €3) – an unusually successful blend of High Baroque and Neoclassical styles, decorated entirely in stone. The oval, eighteenth-century chapel of **Santa Cueva,** c/Rosario (Tues–Fri 10am–1pm & 4.30–7.30pm, Sat & Sun 10am–1pm; €1.50), has eight magnificent arches decorated with frescoes by Goya.

Arriving by **train** you'll have journeyed through field upon field of sunflowers, before finding yourself on the periphery of the old town, close to the Plaza de San Juan de Dios, the busiest of the squares. This is home to the local **tourist office**

(Mon–Fri 9am–2pm & 4–6pm; ☎956 241 001, ⊛www.cadizayto.es) and an information kiosk nearby. By **bus** you'll be dropped a few blocks further north, along the water. Note that the ferry route from Cádiz to Tangier doesn't operate any more; to get **to Morocco** you'll have to go either to Algeciras or Tarifa. There's plenty of budget **accommodation** in the dense (and sometimes noisy) network of alleys around Plaza de San Juan de Dios, protruding across the neck of the peninsula from the port. The best bets are the lovely tiled *Pension Colon*, c/Marques de Cadiz 6 (☎956 285 351; ❷), which has a roof terrace, and *Pension Fantoni*, c/Flamenco 5 (☎956 282 704; ❸). A few doors down *Hostal España*, c/Marquez de Cádiz 9 (☎956 285 500; ❷), is also worth a try. There's a privately run **hostel** *Quo Qádis* at c/Diego Arias 1 (☎956 221 939; ❶), ten minutes' walk from the train station. Plaza de San Juan de Dios has several **cafés** and cheap **restaurants**, notably *La Caleta*, whose interior is built like the bow of a ship.

Tarifa

If there is one thing that defines **TARIFA**, it is the wind. This is the most southerly point in Europe and in the summer the prevailing, massively powerful, levant has made it one of the world's most popular **windsurfing** destinations. The elements aside, there's a good feel to the place – with its funky, laid-back atmosphere and maze of narrow streets. Africa feels very close, too, with the Rif Mountains clearly visible. The ten-kilometre white, sandy beaches, **Playa de los Lances** and **Playa Valdevaqueros**, are the places to head for wind- and kite-surfing. In summer they're connected to the town by a shuttle bus. Just to the east of town, nearer and often missed by tourists, are the rocky coves of **La Caleta**. If you're not an experienced surfer, remember these winds can reach storm force ten: be sure to join a course such as the one run by *Tarifa Spinout* (☎956 236 352; from €49/2hr). You can also **whale- and dolphin-watch** from Tarifa: book in advance through one of the two, non-profit-making organizations: Whale Watch España, Avda. de la Constitución 6 (☎639 476 544; €36), or Tarifa, Pedro Cortez 4 (☎956 627 008; €36).

Buses drop off at the stop on the main Cádiz-Algeciras road, Batalla del Salado; there is no train station. Head downhill for the ancient archway into the old town. EU citizens can also make the **ferry crossing to Morocco**; boats sail to Tangier (summer 4 daily; winter 5 weekly; €22.50 one-way). The **tourist office** is on the fringes of the old town at Paseo de la Alameda (Mon–Sat 10am–2pm & 6–8pm, Sun 10am–2pm; ☎956 680 993). In the summer finding **accommodation** can be tricky, making it advisable to book in advance. Your best bet is *Hostal Africa*, c/Maria Antonia Toledo 12 (☎956 680 220; ❷), in the old town: great value and a fantastic view of Africa from its large roof terrace. Also in the old town, near San Mateo church, is the lovely *Pension Correo*, c/Coronel Moscardo 8 (☎956 680 206; ❸). There are several **campsites** near the main windsurfing beaches: *Tarifa* (☎956 684 778), *Paloma* (☎956 684 203), or *Torre de la Pena* (☎956 684 903). A kiosk on the central Plaza de Oviedo by the church sells *bocadillos*, falafal and kebabs, while *Café Central* is a cosmopolitan hangout on the same square; just off it *La Capricciosa*, c/San Francisco 6, does great pizza. There are plenty of **bars** – in the old town one of the best is *La Ruina*, c/ Trinidad, which has a roof that comes off in the summer. Away from the centre, **clubs** include *Far Out Club*, which plays house, trance and funk, and the seasonal *Jungle Playa* and *La Jaima*; to get there look out for the free night buses.

Málaga and the Costa del Sol

Perhaps the outstanding feature of the **Costa del Sol**, the richest and fastest-growing resort area in the Mediterranean, is its ease of access. Hundreds of charter flights arrive here every week, which means that it's often possible to get an absurdly cheap ticket from London. Málaga airport is positioned midway between **Málaga**, the main city

27

on the coast, and **Torremolinos**, its most grotesque resort. A train (every 30min) runs along the coast between Málaga and Fuengirola, while Granada, Córdoba and Sevilla are all within easy reach, as are Ronda and the white villages (*pueblos blancos*). In some ways then, this coast's enormous popularity isn't surprising: what is surprising is that the **beaches** are generally grit-grey rather than golden and the sea is none too clean.

MÁLAGA is the second city of the south after Seville, and also one of the poorest. Yet though the clusters of high-rises look pretty grim as you approach, it can be a surprisingly attractive place. Around the old fishing villages of El Palo and Pedregalejo, now absorbed into the suburbs, are a series of small beaches and an avenue, or *paseo*, lined with some of the best fish and seafood cafés in the province. Overlooking the town and port are the Moorish citadels of the **Alcazaba** (Tues–Sun 9.30am–6/8pm; €1.80), where the lengthy excavation of a **Roman amphitheatre** continues; and the **Gibralfaro castle** (daily 9am–6/8pm; €1.80), just fifteen minutes' walk from the train or bus stations, and visible from most central points. The city is justly proud of its connection with Picasso, who was born here in 1881. Buses #5 and #18 connect the main **train and bus stations** to the centre. The **tourist office** is at Plaza de la Marina (Mon–Fri 8am–1.30pm & 4.30–7pm, Sat & Sun 9.30am–1.30pm; ☎952 122 020, ✉info@malagaturismo.com), supplemented by two kiosks (one at the bus station and the other on the Puente de Tetuan) and yellow-jacketed information officers who roam the main tourist drags. Arriving at the **airport**, catch the electric train (every 30min) to the main train station, or continue another stop to Málaga Centro: Alameda for the city centre. Málaga has a number of reasonably priced **rooms**, especially in streets north and south of the Alameda. Try *Hostal La Palma*, c/Martínez 7 (☎952 226 772; ❷), and *Hostal Castilla*, c/Córdoba 7 (☎952 218 635; ❷). Slighty more upmarket is *Hotel Lis*, c/Córdoba 7 (☎952 227 300; ❷). The closest **campsite** (☎952 382 602) is at Torremolinos on Ctra. National; take the Málaga-Torremolinos bus from the train station. Málaga's cuisine – fried fish and sweet Málaga wine – can be enjoyed at a vast choice of **tapas bars and restaurants**. One of the most atmospheric spit 'n' sawdust style bodegas is *Antigua Casa de Guardia,* Alameda Principal 16, the oldest bar in town, with wine served straight from the barrel. *Restaurante Los Pueblos* at c/Atarazanas 15 is also worth a try. You'll find plenty of other bars in the area between Plaza de la Merced and Plaza de los Martires, which is buzzing till late at the weekend. However, for the very best fish restaurants you need to head out to the suburbs of Pedregalejo and El Palo.

Approached in the right kind of spirit it's possible to have fun in **TORRE-MOLINOS**, a resort so over-the-top it's magnificent, and with furious competition keeping prices down. The concrete is a little less in evidence in the suburb of **Carihuela**, fifteen minutes' walk west of Torremolinos station. For **accommodation**, try *Hostal Flor Blanco*, Paseo Maritimo La Carihuela 4 (☎952 382 071; ❷). A good time costs more in chic **MARBELLA**, where there are bars and nightclubs galore alongside a surprisingly well-preserved old village and some wonderfully conspicuous consumption. At **ESTEPONA** there's a **campsite** and a number of **hostales**, including the *Vista al Mar*, c/Real 154 (☎952 803 247; ❷). Just south of here, **SAN PEDRO DE ALCANTARA** provides something of a haven amid the sea of development, with its pleasant Plaza de la Iglesia. For **accommodation**, try *Dona Catalina*, Avda. Oriental 14 (☎952 853 120; ❸), offering en-suite rooms with little balconies, or *Hostal La Colonia*, Avda. Oriental 18 (☎952 783 765; ❸). There's inexpensive food at *Maccherone* Italian **restaurant** on Avda. Oriental or the *Café Bar Picasso* on Avd.a Pablo Ruiz Picasso, near the church on the plaza, which also offers **Internet** facilities.

Ronda

Andalucía is dotted with small, brilliantly whitewashed settlements known as the **pueblos blancos** or "white villages", most often straggling up hillsides towards a castle or towered church. The most spectacular lie in a roughly triangular area between

Málaga, Algeciras and Seville, at whose centre is the startling town of **RONDA**, connected by a scenic road and rail line from Algeciras, the latter a wonderful ride. Built on an isolated ridge of the sierra, and ringed by dark, angular mountains, Ronda is split in half by a gaping river gorge with a sheer drop, spanned by an eighteenth-century arched bridge. The town itself is fascinating to wander around and has sacrificed surprisingly little of its character to the flow of day-trippers from the coast. Crossing the Puente Nuevo from Plaza de España takes you from the modern **Mercadillo** quarter to the old Moorish town, the **Ciudad**, centred on the church of **Santa María la Mayor**, originally the mosque. Turning off the main street to the left takes you steeply down to the old bridges – the **Puente Viejo** of 1616 and the Roman single-span **Puente Arabe**. Nearby, on the southeast bank of the river, are the distinctive **Baños Árabes** (Tues 9.30am–1.30pm & 4–6pm, Wed–Sat 9.30am–3.30pm; free). Crossing the old bridge takes you back to the modern town via the **Jardín de la Mina**, which ascends the gorge in a series of stepped terraces with superb views of the river, new bridge and remarkable stairway of the **Casa del Rey Moro** (daily 10am–7pm; €4), an early eighteenth-century mansion built on Moorish foundations. Don't miss the delightful, tiled garden of the **Casa Don Bosco** (daily 10am-7pm; €1) at Calle San Juan de Lefran 20. Behind the church is the **Palacio de Mondragón** (Mon–Fri 10am–6/7pm, Sat & Sun 10am–3pm; €2), probably the palace of the Moorish kings and now home to the Museo Municipal – a steep path descends to the river from here. The principal gate of the town, through which the Christian conquerors passed, stands at the entrance to the suburb of San Francisco, beside the ruins of the **Alcázar**, destroyed by the French in 1809. Back in the Mercadillo quarter is the **bullring** (daily 10am–8pm; €4, including museum) – one of the most prestigious in Spain – and the beautiful clifftop *paseo*, facing the open valley and the dramatic mountains of the Serrenía de Ronda.

Ronda's **tourist office** is opposite the entrance to the bullring at Plaza de Toros (Mon–Fri 9.30am–7.30pm, Sat & Sun 10am–2pm & 5.30–6.30pm; ☎952 187 119, ⓦwww.ronda.net). The regional tourist office is at Plaza de España (Mon–Fri 9am–7pm, Sat & Sun 10am–2pm; ☎952 871 272, ⓦwww.andalucia.org*)*. All the **places to stay** are in the Mercadillo quarter. Calle Almendra (a continuation of c/Lorenzo Borrego) has several options including the basic but cheap *Hostal Ronda Sol* at no. 11 (☎952 874 497; ❶); a few doors up at no. 7 is *Pension Hostal Biarritz* (☎952 872 910; ❶), which has some rooms with baths. Also worth a try, on nearby c/Sevilla, is *La Purisma* at no. 10 (☎952 871 050; ❷). In the same area you'll find en-suite rooms at the pleasant *Hotel Macias* at c/Pedro Romero 3 (☎952 874 238; ❸), and the more upmarket *Hotel Virgen de los Reyes*, c/Lorenzo Borrego 13 (☎952 871 140; ❸), where all rooms are en suite. There are three **campsites**, the best *El Sur* (☎952 875 939), 1.5km down the Algeciras road.

Most of the budget **restaurants** are grouped round the far end of Plaza del Socorro as you leave it on c/Almendra. *El Brillante* on c/Sevilla is friendly and cheap, as is *Pizzeria Michel Angelo* on c/Lorenzo Borrego. Slightly more expensive – but worth the extra few euros – is *Taberna de Santo Domingo*, on the road of the same name, just across the Puente Nuevo into the old town. On Plaza de Espana, *Hotel-Restaurante Don Miguel* offers great views of the gorge. You can combine pastries, coffee and **Internet** at Planet Adventure, just off the Plaza del Socorro on c/Molino. At the weekend, Ronda's **nightlife** kicks off along c/Niño and c/Jerez, and around Plaza de C. Abela. For the energetic, Pangea Active Nature, c/Dolores Ibarruri 4 (☎952 873 496, ⓦwww.pangea-ronda.com), arranges **hiking**, **mountain-biking** and **kayaking** through the spectacular local scenery; a half-day bike-trip costs €27, half-day kayaking €29.

Algeciras

The main reason to visit **ALGECIRAS**, a bus ride along the coast from Cádiz, is for the **ferry to Morocco**, though it has some pleasant plazas and parks hidden away in the old town. The crossings are to Tangier (10 daily; 1hr 30min; €23 one-way) and tickets are available at scores of travel agents along the waterside on Avda. Virgen del Carmen and on most approach roads. Wait till Tangier before buying any Moroccan currency. The number of people passing through guarantees plenty of inexpensive **rooms**. Try the family-run *Pension Tetuan* at Duque de Almodovar 9 (☎956 652 854; ❷), or *Hostal Levante* along the street at no. 21 (☎956 651 505; ❷). If you have trouble finding space, check out the list in the **tourist office** near the port on Avda. Villa Nueva (Mon–Fri 9am–2pm; ☎956 572 636). A good bet for cheap **restaurants** is c/Emilio Castelar in the centre.

Gibraltar

As one of Britain's last remaining colonies **GIBRALTAR** combines curiosity value with the sheer physicality of the Rock. Buses from Algeciras (40min) and Málaga (3hr) run to the border town of **La Línea**, from where you must cross the frontier on foot. The local currency is the Gibraltar pound (same value as the pound sterling). A **cable car** (Mon–Sat 9.30am–6pm; £4.90 return) from the town takes you to the summit of the Rock, with mischievous Barbary apes and views to Africa, while other attractions are the old **Moorish Castle** and **Gibraltar Museum** (Mon–Fri 10am–6pm, Sat 10am–2pm; £2). The main **tourist office** (same hours; ☎956 774 805) is on Cathedral Square. **Accommodation** can be difficult, and the only budget beds are at the *Toc H Hostel*, 36a Line Wall Rd (☎956 773 431; ❷); *Seruya's Guest House*, 92 Irish Town (☎956 773 220; ❷); and *Emile Youth Hostel* at Montagu Bastion on Line Wall Rd (☎956 751 106; ❷). **Food and drink** are not cheap, though pub snacks and fish and chips are available on Main St and King St.

Travel details

Trains

Algeciras to: Córdoba (2 daily; 2hr 50min); Granada (1 daily; 4hr); Ronda (6 daily; 1hr 40min).
Barcelona to: Bilbao (2 daily; 9hr–10hr 20min); Girona (hourly; 1hr 30min–2hr); Puigcerdà (6 daily; 3hr); Valencia (14 daily; 3–5hr); Zaragoza (15 daily; 3hr 40min–4hr 30min).
Bilbao to: León (1 daily; 4hr 40min); Madrid (1–2 daily; 5hr 30min–8hr 30min); San Sebastián (every 30min; 2hr 30min); Santander (3 daily; 2hr 20min).
Córdoba to: Madrid (28 daily; 1hr 40min–5hr); Málaga (10 daily; 2hr 10min); Seville (4–6 daily; 1hr–1hr 30min).
Granada to: Madrid (2 daily; 5hr 50min); Ronda (1 daily; 4hr 20min); Valencia (1–2 daily; 8hr 20min).
León to: Barcelona (3–4 daily; 9hr 30min–11hr 40min); Madrid (5–7 daily; 4hr–6hr 20min); Oviedo (5 daily; 2hr); Salamanca (6 daily; 3–5hr); San Sebastián (1 daily; 5hr); Santiago (1 daily; 5hr 40min).
Madrid to: Algeciras (2 daily; 5hr 50min–10hr 20min); Alicante (6–7 daily; 3hr 45min–4hr); Barcelona (6–7 daily; 6hr 45min–9hr); Bilbao(1–2 daily; 5hr 35min–8hr 45min); Cáceres (5–6 daily; 3hr 25min–5hr); Cádiz (2 daily; 5hr); Córdoba (17–22 daily; 1hr 40min–2hr 25min); Granada (2 daily; 6hr); Jaca (1 daily; 7hr); León (5–7 daily; 3hr 50min–5hr 55min); Málaga (6 daily; 4hr); Mérida (4–5 daily; 4hr 20min–7hr 30min); Oviedo (2–3 daily; 5hr 45min–8hr 10min); Pamplona (1–2 daily; 4hr 20min); Salamanca (5 daily; 2hr 30min); San Sebastián (4 daily; 6–8hr); Santander (2–4 daily; 5hr 30min–9hr); Santiago (2 daily; 7hr 20min–9hr); Segovia (7–9 daily; 2hr); Seville (18 daily; 2hr 30min); Toledo (7–10 daily; 1hr); Valencia (11 daily; 3hr 30min); Zaragoza (13 daily; 3–4hr).
Málaga to: Córdoba (10 daily; 2hr 30min–3hr 30min); Madrid (9 daily; 4–7hr); Ronda (1 daily; 2hr); Seville (6 daily; 3hr).
San Sebastián to: Madrid (2–3 daily; 6–9hr); Pamplona (1–2 daily; 2hr); Salamanca (2–3 daily; 6–7hr); Valencia (1 weekly; 10hr); Zaragoza (1–2 daily; 4hr–5hr 10min).
Santiago to: León (1 daily; 6hr); Madrid (2 daily; 7hr 30min–9hr 15min).
Zaragoza to: Barcelona (14–16 daily; 3–6hr); Canfranc (2 daily; 3hr 30min); Jaca (3 daily; 3hr 10min); Madrid (13 daily; 3hr–4hr 30min); Pamplona (5 daily; 1hr 45min–2hr 40min).

Buses

Alicante to: Barcelona (7 daily; 8hr); Granada (5 daily; 5hr); Madrid (9 daily; 8hr); Málaga (5 daily; 8hr); Valencia (hourly; 4hr).

Barcelona to: Alicante (7 daily; 8hr); Madrid (15 daily; 7hr 30min); Valencia (14–17 daily; 4hr 15min–5hr); the Vall d'Aran (1 daily; 6hr 30min); Zaragoza (22–25 daily; 3hr 30min–5hr).

Bilbao to: San Sebastián (1–2 hourly; 1hr 10min); Santander (18 daily; 1hr 30min); Santiago de Compostela (3 daily; 11–12hr).

Córdoba to: Granada (7 daily; 3hr); Madrid (4 daily; 4hr 30min); Málaga (5 daily; 3hr–3hr 30min); Seville (10 daily; 2hr 30min).

Figueres to: Barcelona (3–6 daily; 2hr 15min); Cadaqués (3 daily; 1hr); L'Escala (5 daily; 45min); Palafrugell (4 daily; 1hr 30min).

Girona to: Barcelona (3–6 daily; 2hr 15min); Cadaqués (3 daily; 1hr 50min); Begur (4 daily; 1hr 30min).

Granada to: Alicante (3 daily; 5hr); Cádiz (2 daily; 6hr); Córdoba (7 daily; 3hr); Madrid (6–9 daily; 6hr); Seville (7–9 daily; 4hr 30min); Valencia (3 daily; 7hr).

León to: Oviedo (8 daily; 1hr 30min); Salamanca (2 daily; 2hr); Santander (1 daily; 5hr).

Madrid to: Algeciras (4 daily; 8hr 30min); Alicante (7–9 daily; 4–6hr); Barcelona (7 daily; 7hr 30min); Bilbao (11 daily; 4hr 45min); Cáceres (7–10 daily; 4hr); Cádiz (6 daily; 7hr); Córdoba (6 daily; 4hr 30min); Granada (9 daily; 6hr); León (11 daily; 4hr); Málaga (7 daily; 7hr); Oviedo (12 daily; 5hr 30min); Pamplona (4 daily; 6hr); Salamanca (16 daily; 2hr 30min); San Sebastián (9 daily; 6hr); Santander (8 daily; 6hr); Santiago (5–7 daily; 8–9hr); Segovia (every 30min; 1hr 30min); Seville

(11 daily; 6hr); Toledo (every 30min; 1hr); Valencia (14 daily; 4hr).

Málaga to: Algeciras (10 daily; 3hr); Córdoba (5 daily; 3hr); Granada (14 daily; 2hr); Ronda (6 daily; 3hr); Seville (11 daily; 3hr); Torremolinos (every 30min; 30min).

Salamanca to: Mérida (5 daily; 4hr 30min); Santander (2 daily; 5hr); Seville (5 daily; 8hr).

San Sebastián to: Bilbao (1–2 hourly; 1hr 10min); Madrid (8 daily; 6hr 30min); Pamplona (13 daily; 2hr).

Santander to: Oviedo (7–9 daily; 2hr 30min–3hr); Pamplona (2 daily; 3hr 45min).

Santiago to: Porto (2 weekly; 3hr).

Seville to: Cádiz (11 daily; 2hr); Córdoba (10 daily; 2hr 30min); Granada (9 daily; 3hr 30min–4hr 30min); Madrid (11 daily; 8hr).

Valencia to: Alicante (hourly; 4hr); Barcelona (14–17 daily; 4–5hr); Madrid (13 daily; 4hr); Seville (3 daily; 11hr).

Zaragoza to: Barcelona (15 daily; 3hr 30min–5hr); Madrid (15 daily; 3hr 30min); Pamplona (7–8 daily; 2hr–2hr 45min).

Ferries

Barcelona to: Ibiza (4–6 weekly; 9hr 30min); Mahón (3–8 weekly; 9hr); Palma (2–4 daily; 8hr 30min).

Ibiza to: Formentera (6–9 daily; 40min–1hr 30min); Palma (1–3 weekly; 6hr 30min); Valencia (1–6 weekly; 9hr).

Palma to: Ibiza (1–3 weekly; 6hr 30min); Mahón (1 weekly; 6hr 30min).

Valencia to: Ibiza (1–6 weekly; 7hr); Palma (6–13 weekly; 9hr).

SPAIN | Travel details

Sweden

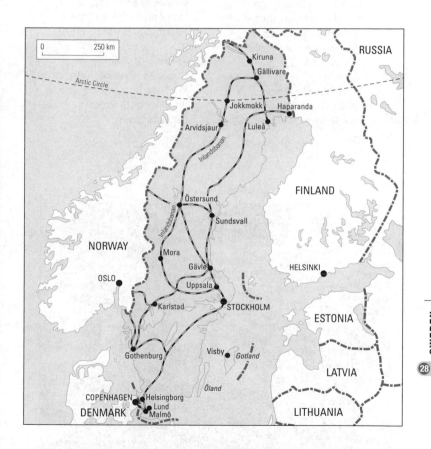

Sweden highlights

* **Gamla Stan, Stockholm**
One of Europe's most
elegant and best pre-
served medieval centres.
See p.902

* **Lilla Torg, Malmö** This
beautiful cobbled square
in the city centre is a fine
place to down a beer or
two and chill. See p.911

* **Inlandsbanan** Single
track rail line that winds
its way through virgin

forest and past crystal-
clear streams en route to
Lapland. See p.913

* **Orsa Grönklitt bear
park, Dalarna** A rare
chance to come face to
face with the King of the
Forest. See p.913

* **Jokkmokk, Arctic
Circle** An excellent base
from which to explore
the wilds of Swedish
Lapland. See p.914

Introduction and basics

Sweden is a large, geographically varied and strangely little-known country whose sense of space is one of its best features. Away from the relatively densely populated south, travelling without seeing a soul is not uncommon.

The south and southwest of the country are gently undulating, picturesque holiday lands, long-disputed Danish territory, and fringed with some of Europe's finest beaches. The west coast harbours a host of historic ports – **Gothenburg**, **Helsingborg** and **Malmö**, which is now linked by bridge to Copenhagen – but it is **Stockholm**, the capital, that is the country's supreme attraction, a bundle of islands housing monumental architecture, fine museums and the country's most active culture and nightlife. The two university towns, **Lund** and **Uppsala**, demand a visit too, while, moving northwards, **Östersund** and **Gällivare** both make justified demands on your time. This area, central and northern Sweden, is the country of tourist brochures: great swathes of forest, inexhaustible lakes (some 96,000 of them) and some of the best wilderness hiking in Europe. Two **train routes** link it with the south. The eastern run, close to the Bothnian coast, passes old wood-built towns and planned new ones such as likeable **Sundsvall**. In the centre, the trains of the **Inlandsbanan** strike off through lakelands and mountains, clearing reindeer off the track as they go. The routes meet in Sweden's far north – home of the Sámi, the oldest indigenous Scandinavian people.

Information & maps

Almost all towns have a **tourist office**, giving out maps and timetables, and usually able to book private rooms, rent bikes and change money. Some also sell discount cards in summer, giving discounts and freebies. The best **map** is the Motormännens *Sveriges Atlas*.

Money and banks

Currency is the **krona** (plural kronor), made up of 100 öre. There are coins of 50öre, 1kr, 5kr and 10kr; and notes of 20kr, 50kr, 100kr, 500kr, 1000kr and 10,000kr. **Banks** are open Mon–Fri 9.30am–3pm, Thurs also 4–5.30pm. Outside hours you can **change money** at airports and ferry terminals, and in post offices (look for the "Växel" sign), as well as at Forex offices, which usually offer the best rates (minimum 30kr commission). *Bankomat* ATMs accept most cards.

Communications

Post offices open Mon–Fri 9am–6pm, Sat 10am–1pm. You can buy stamps at post offices, supermarkets, newspaper kiosks, tobacconists and hotels. Public **phones** take cards (*telefonkort*), buyable from newsagents and kiosks. You can also use credit cards in payphones marked "CCC". Directory enquiries is on ☎118 118 (domestic), ☎118 119 (international). **Internet cafés** are surprisingly rare, though you should find at least one in the larger towns (40–60kr/hr). Access is free in local libraries.

Basics

SWEDEN |

28

Sweden on the net

ⓦ **www.cityguide.se** Up-to-date guide to events and entertainment in the main Swedish cities.

ⓦ **www.sunet.se** In-depth regional information.

ⓦ **www.sverigeturism.se** The largest single source of information in English on Sweden, its provinces, nature, culture and society.

ⓦ **www.meravsverige.nu** Tips and ideas on where to visit in Sweden.

Getting around

Swedish State Railways (SJ; @www.sj.se) has an extensive **train** network, running as far north as Sundsvall and Östersund. Tickets are good value: you'll rarely have to pay the full rate. InterRail and Eurail are valid, as is the ScanRail pass (see "Basics"). The famous Inlandsbanan line operates from late June to early August only. The *SJ Tågtider* timetable, from any station, lists many useful train services (not the Inlandsbanan or Pågatågen line, on both of which InterRail is valid). It's a good idea to reserve your seat – on some trains (marked as "IC") this costs 30kr; on the high-speed X2000 trains and most national routes reservations are mandatory, though the fee is included in the ticket price. If you're travelling on a pass, you must reserve seats separately before your journey (30kr). For all train travel north of the line between Sundsvall and Östersund, above the Arctic Circle and on into Norway, service is provided by Connex (@www.connex.se). SJ will not book tickets on Connex lines or give out information.

Complementing the rail system are **long-distance buses** (*Expressbussar*), operated by Swebus and Svenska Buss. Services tend to be cheaper and slower than the equivalent train ride. In the north, buses are more frequent since they carry mail to isolated regions. There are few domestic **ferry** services. The most comprehensive network is within the Stockholm archipelago, for which you can buy an island-hopping boat pass.

Accommodation

Sweden has 280 **hostels** operated by STF (@www.meravsverige.nu). There are usually singles and doubles as well as dorms, and virtually all have self-catering kitchens and serve a buffet breakfast. Prices are low (120–200kr); non-HI members pay about an extra 50kr a night. There's also many non-STF hostels, mostly run by SVIF (@www.svif.se).

Hotels come cheaper than you'd think, especially in Stockholm and the bigger towns during the summer, when hotels slash their prices. Reduced summer prices are identical to prices charged at weekends during the rest of the year: an average for an en-suite double room is 600kr. All hotels include breakfast in the price. Package deals in Malmö, Stockholm and Gothenburg, bookable through the tourist office, get you a hotel bed for one night, breakfast and a city discount card from 400–500kr per person (mid-June to mid-Aug & weekends year-round). In larger towns you can book a **private room** through the tourist office for about the same as a hostel bed, though they're often located out of the centre.

Practically every village has at least one **campsite**, generally of a high standard. Pitching a tent costs 80–160kr in July & Aug (plus a 10–20kr fee per person), a little less at other times. Most sites are open June to Sept, some year-round; all are listed in the book *Camping Sverige*, available at larger sites and bookshops. At most sites you'll need a camping card (60kr from your first stop). Many sites have **cabins**, usually with bunk beds and kitchen equipment but not sheets, for 350–450kr for a four-bedded affair.

Food and drink

Eating and drinking is nothing like as expensive as it used to be. Swedish **food** is largely meat-, fish- and potato-based – varied and generally tasty. **Breakfast** (*frukost*) is invariably a help-yourself buffet of juice, cereals, bread, boiled eggs, jams, salami, tea and coffee (hostels 50kr, hotels free). **Coffee** is usually filter and can be bitter; it's often free after the first cup. **Tea** is weak but costs the same (15–20kr). For **snacks**, a *Gatukök* (street kitchen) or *Korvstånd* (hot-dog stall) will serve hot dogs, burgers, chips and the like for around 40kr. A hefty burger-and-fries meal costs 50–55kr. Coffee shops always display a range of freshly baked pastries (coffee and cake can be pricey, at 40–60kr), and also serve *smörgåsar*, **open sandwiches** piled high with toppings for 30–40kr. Eating in a **restaurant** is great value at lunchtime (11am–2pm), when most places offer a set meal (*Dagens Rätt*) of a main dish with bread and salad, sometimes a drink, and coffee, at 60–70kr – the best way to sample real Swedish cooking. Specialities include northern Swedish delicacies – reindeer and elk meat, and wild berries – and herring in many different guises. More expensive are restaurants and hotels that put out the **smörgåsbord** at lunchtime for 150–200kr, where you help yourself to unlimited portions of herring, smoked and fresh salmon, hot and cold meats, potatoes, salad, cheese and fruit. Otherwise meals in restaurants, especially at **dinner** (*middag*), can be expensive: 200–250kr for three courses, plus 30–50kr for a beer. Better value are pizzerias: large pizzas cost 40–60kr lunch or dinner, usually with free salad and bread. Chinese restaurants nearly always offer a set lunch for around 60kr.

Drinking costs the same as in most European capitals. You'll pay 35–50kr for half a litre of lager-type **beer** – a *storstark*. Unless you specify, it will be *starköl*, the strongest Class III beer, or the slightly weaker *mellanöl*; *folköl* is the Class II and cheaper and weaker brew; cheapest (around half the price) is *lättöl*, a Class I concoction that is virtually nonalcoholic. Classes I and II are available in supermarkets; Class III is only on sale in state-licensed liquor stores (*Systembolaget*), where it's around a third of the price you'll pay in a bar. A glass of **wine** in a bar or restaurant costs around 40–50kr, while you can buy a whole bottle for a little more in a state bottle shop. One local firewater is **akvavit**, served ice-cold in tiny shots and washed down with beer. Bars and pubs close around midnight, a little later in Malmö, Gothenburg and Stockholm.

Opening hours and holidays

Shops open Mon–Fri 9am–6pm, Sat 9am–1/4pm. Some larger stores stay open until 8/10pm, and open Sun noon–4pm. Banks, offices and shops close on **public holidays** (and may close early on the preceding day): Jan 1; Jan 6; Good Fri; Easter Sun & Mon; May 1; Ascension; Whit Sun & Mon; June 20 & 21; Nov 1; Dec 24, 25, 26 & 31.

Emergencies

The **police** are courteous and fluent in English. In case of **health problems** go to a hospital with your passport (there is no GP system), where for a maximum of 240kr you'll receive treatment; if you have to stay it costs an extra 80kr per day. A **pharmacist** (*Apotek*) opens shop hours (Stockholm has a 24-hour pharmacy); larger towns operate a rota system, with the address of the nearest late-opener posted on each pharmacy's door.

Emergency numbers

All emergencies ☎112.

Basics

SWEDEN

28

Stockholm

STOCKHOLM comes lauded as Sweden's most beautiful city, and largely lives up to it – it's delightful, not least as a contrast to the apparently endless lakes and forests of the rest of the country. It's also a remarkably disparate capital, one whose tracts of water and range of monumental buildings give it an ageing, lived-in feel, quite at odds with its status as Sweden's most forward-looking city. Built on fourteen islands, Stockholm was a natural site for the fortifications, erected in 1255, that grew into the current city. In the sixteenth century, the city fell to King Gustav Vasa, a century later becoming the centre of the Swedish trading empire that covered present-day Scandinavia and beyond. Following the waning of Swedish power it only rose to prominence again in the nineteenth century when industrialization took off.

Arrival, information and accommodation

By **train**, you arrive at **Central Station**, a cavernous structure on Vasagatan in Norrmalm. All branches of the Tunnelbana, Stockholm's metro, meet at T-Centralen, the station directly below Central Station. **Cityterminalen**, adjacent, handles all **bus** services, both domestic and international. Viking Line **ferries** arrive at **Tegelvikshamnen** in Södermalm, in the south of the city, a thirty-minute walk from the centre, or connected by bus to Slussen and then by Tunnelbana to T-Centralen. The Silja Line terminal is in the northeastern reaches of the city, a short walk from Gärdet or Ropsten underground stations. The useful **tourist office** (Mon–Fri 9am–6pm, Sat & Sun 10am–3pm; ☎08/789 24 90, ⓦwww.stockholm-town.com) is on the lower level of Kulturhuset in Sergels Torg square, and sells the **Stockholm Card** (220/380/540kr for one/two/three days), which gives unlimited city transport (except on direct airport buses) and free museum entry and boat tours.

The best way to explore is to **walk** – it takes about 25 minutes to cross central Stockholm on foot. Storstockholms Lokaltrafik (SL) operates buses and trains (underground and local). Quickest is the **Tunnelbana** (T-bana) metro, based on three main lines. **Buses** can be less direct. **Ferries** also link some of the central islands: Djurgården is connected with Nybroplan in Norrmalm (summer only) and Skeppsbron in Gamla Stan (all year). Ferry trips cost 20kr one way, while land transport costs 20kr within one zone, so you're normally better off investing in a **pass**. Do not confuse the Stockholm Card (see above) with the more limited **24-hour** and **72-hour cards** (80/150kr), which give unlimited travel on public transport within Stockholm county. Alternatively, you can buy a strip of twenty transferable SL **ticket coupons** (*Rabattkuponger*, 110kr); you'll need two coupons for any single journey in the centre. You can hail **taxis** in the street, or book on ☎08/15 00 00. A daytime trip across the city centre costs 120–160kr; women get a 5–10 percent discount at weekends.

There's plenty of **accommodation**, but booking in advance is always a good idea. The cheapest choices lie north of Cityterminalen, in the streets west of Adolf Fredriks Kyrka. **Hotellcentralen**, a booking service on the lower level of Central Station (daily 8/9am–6/8pm; ☎08/789 24 90, ⓔhotels@svb.stockholm.se), charges a fee of 50kr per room, 20kr for a hostel if you go in person, but is free over the phone. Hotelltjänst, Vasagatan 15–17 (☎08/10 44 67), can fix you up with a double **private room** for around 500kr.

Hostels

Af Chapman Skeppsholmen ☎08/463 22 66, ⓦwww.stfchapman.com. Official hostel on a ship moored at Skeppsholmen. Without a reservation, the chances of a bed in summer are negligible. 155kr.

City Backpackers Upplandsgatan 2A, Norra Bantorget ☎08/20 69 20, ⓦwww.citybackpackers .se. Curfewless non-STF hostel with four-bed

rooms and cheaper eight-bed dorms. 180kr.

Långholmen Kronohäktet, Långholmen ☎08/720 85 00, ⓦwww.langholmen.com. Stockholm's grandest official hostel, in an old prison on Långholmen island, with ordinary doubles in summer as well as hostel beds. T-bana to Hornstull. Turn left and follow the signs. 185kr.

M/S Rygerfjord Söder Mälarstrand-Kaj 12 ☎08/84 08 30, ⓦwww.rygerfjord.se. Homely hostel-ship moored on Södermalm close to Slussen T-bana station. 180kr.

Zinkensdamm Zinkens väg 20, Södermalm ☎08/616 81 00, ⓦwww.zinkensdamm.com. Huge official hostel with kitchen facilities. Nicely situated by the water. T-bana Zinkensdamm. 165kr.

Hotels and pensions

Haga Hagagatan 29 ☎08/545 473 00, ⓦwww.hagahotel.se. Modern, good-value rooms within easy walking distance of the northern edge of the city centre. T-bana Odenplan. ❼

Pensionat Oden City Kammarkargatan 62 ☎08/796 96 00, ⓦwww.pensionat.nu. Superb location right in the city centre and at a good price. ❻

Tre små rum Högbergsgatan 81 ☎08/641 23 71, ⓦwww.tresmarum.se. T-bana Mariatorget. Seven

bright modern non-smoking rooms in the heart of Södermalm. No en-suites. ❻

Campsites

Ängby ☎08/37 04 20. West of the city on Lake Mälaren and near the beach. T-bana to Ängbyplan, then a 300-metre walk. Book in advance in winter (Sept–April).

Bredäng ☎08/97 70 71. Pricey place with a hostel and restaurant on site. Ten kilometres southwest of the centre and also by Lake Mälaren. Take T-bana to Bredäng from where it's a 700-metre walk. Closed Nov to mid-April.

Östermalms Citycamping Fiskartorpsvägen 2 ☎08/411 70 20. Stockholm's most centrally located campsite at the Östermalm sports ground surrounded by woodland. Mid-June to early Aug only.

The City

The **Stadshuset**, Hantverkargatan 1 (guided tours 10am & noon; June–Sept 2pm; 50kr; T-Centralen), at the water's edge near Central Station, and in particular its

gently-tapering 106-metre high red-brick **tower** (May–Sept daily 10am–4.30pm; 15kr), has the best fix on the city's layout. The building itself, a flagship of the National Romantic movement in the 1910s and 1920s, draws heavily on Swedish materials and themes, exemplified in the cavernous Blue Room, where the Nobel prize-givings are held, and the Golden Room, where a précis of Swedish history covers the walls in a gilt mosaic.

The Old Town: Gamla Stan

Three islands – Riddarholmen, Staden and Helgeandsholmen – make up **Gamla Stan** or **Old Stockholm**, a clutter of seventeenth- and eighteenth-century Renaissance buildings, hairline medieval alleys and tall, dark houses whose intricate doorways still bear the arms of the wealthy merchants who once dwelled within. In front of the Swedish parliament building, Riksdagshuset, accessible by a set of steps leading down from Norrbro, the **Medeltidsmuseum** (Tues–Sun 11am–4/6pm; 40kr; T-Gamla Stan) is the best city-related historical collection in Stockholm. Ruins of medieval tunnels and walls were discovered during excavations under the parliament building, and they've been incorporated into a walk-through underground exhibition here. Over a second set of bridges is the most distinctive monumental building in Stockholm, the **Kungliga Slottet** (Royal Palace; T-Gamla Stan), a beautiful Renaissance successor to the original castle of Stockholm. Finished in 1760, it's a striking achievement, outside sombre, inside a magnificent Baroque and Rococo swirl. The **Apartments** (mid-May to Aug daily 10am–4pm; rest of year Tues–Sun noon–3pm; 70kr) form a relentlessly linear collection of furniture and tapestries; the **Treasury** (same times as apartments; 70kr) has ranks of jewel-studded crowns, the oldest that of Karl X (1650). Also worth catching is **Livrustkammaren**, the Royal Armoury (June–Aug daily 10am–5pm, rest of the year Tues–Sun 11am–5pm, Thurs until 8pm; 65kr), less to do with weapons than with ceremony – suits of armour, costumes and horse-drawn coaches from the sixteenth century onwards, most notably the stuffed horse and mud-spattered garments of King Gustav II Adolf, who died in the Battle of Lützen in 1632.

Beyond the palace lies Gamla Stan proper, where the streets suddenly narrow and darken. The first major building is the **Storkyrkan** (daily 9am–4/6pm; 10kr, free in winter), consecrated in 1306 and technically Stockholm's cathedral – the monarchs of Sweden are married and crowned here. The Baroque interior is marvellous, with an animated fifteenth-century sculpture of *St George and the Dragon*, the royal pews, more like golden billowing thrones, and a monumental black and silver altarpiece. **Stortorget**, Gamla Stan's main square, is handsomely proportioned and crowded with eighteenth-century buildings. The surrounding narrow streets house a succession of arts and craft shops, restaurants and discreet fast-food outlets, clogged by summer buskers and evening strollers. Keep right on as far as the handsome Baroque **Riddarhuset** (Mon–Fri 11.30am–12.30pm; 40kr), in whose Great Hall the Swedish aristocracy met during the seventeenth-century Parliament of the Four Estates. Their coats of arms – around 2500 of them – are splattered across the walls. From here it's a matter of seconds across the bridge onto **Riddarholmen** ("Island of the Knights"), and to **Riddarholms Kyrkan** (mid-May–Sept daily 10am–4pm; 20kr), originally a Franciscan monastery and long the burial place of Swedish royalty. You'll find the unfortunate Gustav II Adolf in the green marble sarcophagus.

Skeppsholmen, Norrmalm and Östermalm

Off Gamla Stan's eastern reaches, but not connected by bridge from the old town, the island of **Skeppsholmen** is home to the **National Art Museum** (Tues–Sun 11am–5/8pm; 75kr; T-Kungsträdgården), an impressive collection of applied art – beds slept in by kings, cabinets used by queens, alongside Art Nouveau coffee pots and vases and examples of Swedish furniture design. Upstairs there is a plethora of European sculpture, mesmerizing sixteenth- and seventeenth-century Russian Orthodox icons, and a quality selection of paintings. Skeppsholmen's **Moderna**

Muséet, a superb collection of modern art, is due to reopen in 2004 – check with the tourist office for the latest details.

Modern Stockholm lies immediately north of Gamla Stan. It's split into two distinct sections: the central **Norrmalm** and the classier, residential streets of **Östermalm** to the east – though there's not much apart from a couple of specialist museums to draw you here. On the waterfront, at the foot of Norrbro, is **Gustav Adolfs Torg**, more a traffic island than a square, with the eighteenth-century **Opera House** its proudest and most notable building. It was at a masked ball here in 1792 that King Gustav III was shot; you'll find Gustav's ball costume, as well as the assassin's pistols and mask, displayed in the palace armoury in Gamla Stan. Norrmalm's eastern boundary is marked by **Kungsträdgården**, the most fashionable and central of the city's numerous parks – once royal gardens and now Stockholm's main meeting place, especially in summer when there's almost always something going on. On the opposite side of Norrmalm in Östermalm is the **Historiska Muséet** (Tues–Sun 11am–5/8pm; 60kr; T-Karlaplan). Ground-floor highlights include a Stone Age household and a mass of Viking weapons, coins and boats, while upstairs there's a worthy collection of medieval church art and architecture, evocatively housed in massive vaulted rooms, including some rare reassembled bits of stave churches uncovered on the Baltic island of Gotland.

Djurgården

A former royal hunting ground, **Djurgården** is Stockholm's nearest large expanse of park. You could walk to the park from Central Station, but it's quite a hike: you can take the bus instead – #44 from Karlaplan or #47 from Nybroplan – or in summer, the ferry from Nybroplan, or year round from Slussen. In the northeast of the park you can get excellent views from 155-metre-high **Kaknäs TV tower** (daily 10am–9pm; 25kr), one of Scandinavia's tallest structures. South over Djurgårdsbron are numerous museums. Palatial **Nordiska Muséet** (Tues–Sun 10am–5pm; 60kr) is a good attempt to represent Swedish cultural history in an accessible fashion, with a particularly interesting Sámi section. Close by, the **Vasa Muséet** (daily 10am–5/8pm; 70kr) is an essential stop, displaying the *Vasa* warship which sank in Stockholm harbour after just twenty minutes of its maiden voyage in 1628. Preserved in mud, the ship was raised along with 12,000 objects in 1961. Walkways bring you nose to nose with the cannon hatches and restored decorative relief, exhibition halls display the retrieved bits and pieces, while films and videos explain the social and political life of the period – all with excellent English notes and regular English-language **guided tours**.

Eating, drinking and nightlife

The three main areas for decent **eating**, day or night, are Norrmalm, Gamla Stan and Södermalm – the island south of Slussen. The Hötorgshallen in Hötorget is a cheap and varied indoor **market**, awash with small cafés and ethnic snacks. Outside is an excellent daily fruit and veg market too. Many cafés, restaurants and bars offer food during the day and entertainment in the evening. As well as the weekend, Wednesday night is an active time, with usually plenty going on and queues at the more popular **nightlife** haunts. Live music venues charge 60–100kr admission. The city's main **gay** centre is *TipTop*, Sveavägen 57 (℡08/736 02 12; T-bana Rådmansgatan), which has a bookshop, meeting facilities and a bar/restaurant. On the floor above is the HQ of Sweden's gay rights group RFSL (🌐www.rfsl.se), which has an excellent free paper, *Kom Ut*. Also pick up the widely available *QX* paper from gay venues.

Cafés and restaurants

Babs Kök & Bar Birger Jarlsgatan 37. Lively, young and laid-back atmosphere at this quirky restaurant/bar. Interesting eats such as duck terrine with pear and raisin. Mostly meat dishes.

Blå Lotus Katrina Bangata 21. The hangout of the alternative crowd – always has an intellectual buzz.

Café Art Västerlånggatan 60–62, Gamla Stan. A

fifteenth-century arty cellar-café with sandwiches, good coffee and cakes.

Chokladkoppen Stortorget 18, Gamla Stan. Overlooking the grand old square, this is a fabulous café specializing in rich chocolate tart.

Collage Smålandsgatan 2, Norrmalm. Fill up on huge portions from the short meat and fish menu. Try the delicious Africana pork with bananas, peanuts and mandarins.

Cosmic Café Wollmar Yxkullsgatan 5B, Södermalm, opposite Mariatorget T-bana. A tiny, fun, wholefood vegetarian café with very good-value salads, pastas and great fresh fruit milkshakes.

Creperie Fyra Knop Svartensgatan 4. Excellent-value crepes served in this dark, evocative restaurant which is fashionably tatty and plays the likes of Leonard Cohen.

Hannas Café Hornsgatan 156, Södermalm. Small, gay-friendly café serving cheap coffee. Also hosts regular art exhibitions.

Hermitage Stora Nygatan 11. Excellent, vegetarian place with delicious fresh salads and breads.

Lasse i Parken Högalidsgatan 56, Södermalm. Beautiful daytime café in an eighteenth-century house with a pleasant garden. Summer daily 11am–5pm. T-bana Hornstull.

String Café Nytorgsgatan 38, Södermalm. Ultra laid-back retro café full of young studenty types who love the mirror. Lots of big, cheapish coffees with muffins, brownies and the like.

Bars, brasseries and pubs

Fenix Götgatan 40, Södermalm. Trendy and lively American-style bar. Good selection of beers and cheapish food.

Gråmunken Västerlånggatan 18, Gamla Stan. Cosy café with live jazz several nights a week.

Mushrooms Nybroplan 6. Always full to bursting with loud, happy beer-drinkers.

O'Learys Götgatan 11, Södermalm. A good bar/restaurant for watching sport on the widescreen TV.

Sloppy's Hamngatan 2. A popular bar and nightclub open until 5am; serves food, too. Sat is *Propaganda*, a gay disco.

Söders Hjärta Bellmansgatan 22, Södermalm. Swanky restaurant with a less intimidating and friendly bar on the mezzanine floor.

Live music

Engelen Kornhamnstorg 59, Gamla Stan. Jazz, rock and blues nightly.

Fasching Kungsgatan 63, Norrmalm. Stockholm's premier jazz venue, with local acts and big names.

Kaos Stora Nygatan 21, Gamla Stan. Good live music from 9pm nightly; rock bands on Fri and Sat in the cellar and reasonable late-night food.

Nalen Regeringsgatan 74. The place to go for boogie, R&B, swing and rock & roll bands playing regularly.

Stampen Stora Nygatan 5, Gamla Stan. Long-established and rowdy jazz club.

Discos and clubs

Collage Smålandsgatan 2, Norrmalm. Upstairs from the restaurant is a lively bar and dance floor with a noisy young crowd. Black jack is also played. Open Wed–Sat only.

La Isla Fridhemsplan. Latin platters into the small hours, as well as salsa dancing. Underground in the Fridhemsplan T-bana station complex.

Sture Compagniet Sturegatan 4, Norrmalm. Terrific light show with house and techno sounds blaring on three floors of bars.

Gay venues

Bitch Girl Club Kolingsborg, Slussen. Scandinavia's biggest lesbian club. Every other Fri in summer & Sat rest of year.

Häktet Hornsgatan 82; Zinkensdamm T-bana. A friendly neighbourhood bar always packed out. Summer terrace with decent food. Open Wed (mostly women) & Fri.

Regnbågsrummet Sturecompagniet, Stureplan. Currently the hippest spot – hence long queues. Fri & Sat.

Patricia Stadsgårdskajen; Slussen T-bana. Drag shows, dancing and comedy on what was the Queen Mother's royal yacht. Also an excellent restaurant on the upper deck. Gay on Sun only.

TipTop Sveavägen 57 (see above). Gay centre that's particularly popular on Fri & Sat.

Torget Mälartorget 13, Gamla Stan. A superbly elegant and fun place to drink at any time of the evening – and always packed with beauties.

Listings

Doctor Medical Care Information ☎08/32 01 00.

Embassies Australia, Sergels Torg 12 ☎08/613 29 00; Ireland, Östermalmsgatan 97 ☎08/661 80 05; UK, Skarpögatan 6–8 ☎08/671 30 00; Canada, Tegelbacken 4 ☎08/453 30 00; US, Dag Hammarskjöldsväg 31 ☎08/783 53 00.

Exchange At Arlanda airport; Forex offices at Central Station and Cityterminalen.

Left luggage Lockers in Central Station.

Pharmacy C.W. Scheele, Klarabergsgatan 64 ☎08/454 81 30 (24hr).

Post office Central Station (Mon-Fri 7am-10pm, Sat & Sun 10am-7pm).

Millesgården and Drottningholm

Just a short way northeast of Stockholm city centre, on the mainly residential island of **Lindingö**, the **Millesgården** (May–Sept daily 10am–5pm; Oct–April Tues–Sun noon–4pm; 75kr) is the outdoor sculpture garden of Carl Milles (1875–1955), one of Sweden's greatest sculptors. Arranged on a number of garden terraces carved from the steep cliffs, this is one of the most enticing visual attractions within easy reach of central Stockholm – to get there, take the T-bana to Ropsten and then go on by train one stop to Torvikstorg before walking down Herserudsvägen. Try also to visit the harmonious royal palace of **Drottningholm** (daily 10am/noon–3.30/4.30pm; guided tours noon, 1pm & 2pm; 60kr), beautifully located on the shores of leafy Lovön island, 11km west of the centre. It's a lovely fifty-minute boat trip there (85kr return); ferries leave every thirty minutes from Stadshusbron to coincide with the opening times. You could also take the T-bana to Brommaplan and then bus #177, #301–323, #336 or #338 – a less thrilling ride, but free with the Stockholm Card. Modelled in a thoroughly French style, Drottningholm is perhaps the greatest achievement of the architects Tessin – father and son – and was begun in 1662 on the orders of King Karl X's widow, Eleonora. Good English notes are available to help you sort out the riot of Rococo decoration.

Uppsala

Forty minutes' train ride north of Stockholm, **UPPSALA** is regarded as the historical and religious centre of Sweden. It's a tranquil daytime alternative to the capital, with a delightful river-cut centre, not to mention an active student-geared nightlife. At the centre of the medieval town, a ten-minute walk from the train station, is the great **Domkyrkan** (daily 8am–6pm; free), Scandinavia's largest cathedral. The echoing interior remains impressive, particularly the French Gothic ambulatory, with its tiny chapels, one of which contains a lively set of restored fourteenth-century wall paintings that tell the legend of St Erik, Sweden's patron saint, while another contains his relics. Poke around and you'll also find the tombs of Reformation rebel monarch Gustav Vasa and his son Johan III, and that of the great botanist Carl Von Linné (self styled as Carolus Linnaeus), who lived in Uppsala. Opposite the cathedral is the **Gustavianum** (daily 11am–4pm; mid-Sept to mid-May closed Mon; 40kr), built in 1625 as part of the university, and much touted for its tidily preserved anatomical theatre. The same building houses a couple of small collections of Egyptian, Classical and Nordic antiquities and the **Uppsala University Museum**, which contains the glorious Augsburg Art Cabinet, an ebony treasure chest presented to Gustav II Adolf. The **Castle** (June–Aug English guided tours at 1pm & 3pm; 60kr) has recently been made open to the public – a 1702 fire that destroyed three-quarters of the city did away with all but one side and two towers of this opulent palace. Now you can wander around the excavations and peruse the waxworks in authentic costumes.

Uppsala's **train** and **bus stations** are beside each other, not far from the **tourist office**, Fyris Torg 8 (Mon–Fri 10am–6pm, Sat 10am–3pm; late June to early Aug also Sun noon–4pm; ☎018/27 48 00, ⓦwww.res.till.uppland.nu), which has an English map and handout. The beautifully sited HI **hostel** is 6km south at Sunnerstavägen 24 (☎018/32 42 20; ❸) – take bus #20, #25 or #50 from Stora Torget. For a central **hotel** try *Basic*, Kungsgatan 27 (☎018/480 50 00, ⓦwww.basichotel.com; ❹), with bright, clean rooms and weekend reductions. It's difficult to beat **lunch** at *Sten Sture & Co.*, a large wooden house immediately below the castle off Nedre Slottsgatan, with a good range of meat-based dishes during the day and live bands in the evening. The best **cafés** are *Ofvandahls*, Sysslomansgatan 5, a student classic, but only fun for smokers; *Güntherska*, Östra Ågatan 31, another favourite and strictly non-smoking; and *Wayne's Coffee*, Smedsgränd 4, with vast windows looking out onto the street. *Svenssons krog/bakficka*, Sysslomansgatan 15, the best **restaurant** for traditional fare. During the summer, the outdoor café/bar *Lilla Helgonet*, right by the river at Eriks Torg, is a popular spot.

Gamla Uppsala

About 5km north of town, three huge **barrows**, atmospheric royal burial mounds dating back to the sixth century, mark the original site of Uppsala, **GAMLA UPP-SALA** – reached on frequent buses #2, #24 or #54 from Stora Torget. This was a pagan settlement and a place of ancient sacrificial rites: every ninth year a festival demanded the death of nine men, hanged from a nearby tree until their corpses rotted. The pagan temple where this took place is marked by the Christian **Gamla Uppsala Kyrka** (daily 9am–4/6pm), built when the Swedish kings first took baptism in the new faith. Look in for the faded wall paintings and the tomb of Celsius. The worthwhile **Historical Centre** (mid-April to Sept daily 10am–4/5pm, closed Mon mid-April to mid-May and mid-Aug–Sept; Oct–Dec Sat & Sun noon–3pm; 50kr) explains the origin of local myths from Roman times and Uppsala's era of greatness until the thirteenth century.

Southern Sweden

Southern Sweden is a nest of coastal provinces, extensive lake and forest regions, gracefully ageing cities and superb beaches. Much of the area, especially the southwest coast, is the target of Swedish holidaymakers, with a wealth of campsites and cycle tracks, yet retaining a sense of space and tranquillity as well as plenty of historical and cultural high points. The grandest coastal city is charming **Gothenburg**, well deserving exploration. South of here, **Helsingborg**, a stone's throw from Denmark, and **Malmö**, still sixteenth-century at its core, are both worth a day or two. **Lund**, a medieval cathedral and university town, lies conveniently between the two.

Gothenburg (Göteborg)

Although **GOTHENBURG** is Scandinavia's largest port, shipbuilding has long since taken a back seat to ferry arrivals – those from Newcastle (England) alongside the dock-strewn river, and those from Denmark right in the centre of the port and shipyards. Beyond the shipyards, Gothenburg is the prettiest of Sweden's cities, with broad avenues split and ringed by an elegant seventeenth-century, Dutch-designed canal system.

Arrival, information and accommodation

DFDS **ferries** from England dock at Frihamnen, opposite the Opera House. Trams #2, #4 and #5 will trundle you from here to the centre in around ten minutes. Other arrival points are strung out along the docks. Stena Line ferries from Frederikshavn in Denmark dock within twenty minutes' walk of the centre, the Kiel ferries another ten minutes away (3km from the centre in all). Trams #3, #9 and #11 run past both to the centre. **Trains** arrive at Central Station on Drottningtorget. **Buses** from all destinations use Nils Ericsonsplatsen bus terminal. Gothenburg has two **tourist offices**: a kiosk in Nordstan, the shopping centre next to Central Station (Mon–Fri 9.30am–6pm, Sat 10am–4pm, Sun noon–3pm) and a main office on the canal front at Kungsportsplatsen 2 (June–Aug daily 9am–6/8pm; rest of year Mon–Sat 9/10am–2/5pm; ⓦwww.goteborg.com). They sell the **Gothenburg Pass** (175/295kr for 24/48hr), giving unlimited bus and tram travel, free or half-price museum entry and concessions including a free boat trip to Elfsborgs fortress and fifty-percent discount on a day trip to Frederikshavn in Denmark. Gothenburg is the most attractive Swedish city around which to **walk**, though you may well use the **public transport** system of trams and buses. Each city journey costs 20kr for adults, though it's cheaper to buy a ten-trip

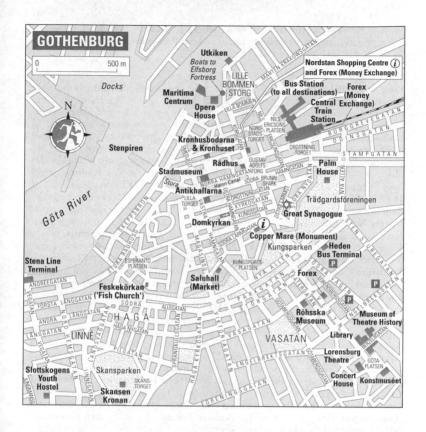

GOTHENBURG

0 — 500 m

Docks

N

Göta River

Stena Line
Terminal

Stenpiren

Utkiken

Boats to
Elfsborg
Fortress

Maritima
Centrum

Opera
House

LILLE
BOMMEN-
STORG

Nordstan Shopping Centre ⓘ
and Forex (Money Exchange)

Bus Station
(to all destinations)

Forex
(Money
Exchange)

Central
Train
Station

Forex
(Money)

Kronhusbodarna
& Kronhuset

NORD-
STADS-
TORGET

NILS
ERICSONS-
PLATSEN

BURGGREVEGATAN

ODINSGATAN

Stadmuseum

Rådhus

GUSTAV
ADOLFS

DROTTNING-
TORGET

STAMPGATAN

Palm
House

Trädgårdsföreningen

Antikhallarna

Stora

NORRA HAMNGATAN

Hamn Canal

SÖDRA BRUNN

SPARK

SÖDRA HAMNGATAN

NYA ALLÉN

LILLA
TORGET

DROTTNINGGATAN

KYRKOGATAN

KUNGSGATAN

Great Synagogue

Domkyrkan ⓘ

Copper Mare (Monument)

Kungsparken

Heden
Bus Terminal
P

Stena Line
Terminal

ESPERANTO
PLATSEN

KUNGSPORTS-
PLATSEN

NYA ALLÉN

Forex

ANDREEGATAN

Feskekörkan
('Fish Church')

SÖDRA

ALLÉGATAN

Saluhall
(Market)

P

FÖRSTA LÅNGGATAN

ANDRA

LÅNGGATAN

NORDHEMSGATAN

HAGA

HAGA NYGATAN

LINNÉ

PILGATAN

Röhsska
Museum

VASATAN

Library

Museum of
Theatre History

Slottskogens
Youth
Hostel

Skansparken

SKANS-
TORGET

Skansen
Kronan

Lorensburg
Theatre

Concert
House

GÖTA-
PLATSEN

Konstmuséet

"Hundrakort" for 100kr. Tickets can be bought from the driver, but are cheaper
from *Tidpunkten* and *Pressbyrån* kiosks around the city. Just get on and punch "2" for
city rides and "BYTE" if you are continuing on another bus or tram. **Night**
bus/tram tickets are double the daytime rates. **Taxi** rides (☎031/65 00 00) within
the city centre cost around 70kr, and there are twenty-percent discounts for women
travelling at night, but check with the driver first.

Of the **hostels**, the most central and best appointed is the excellent *Slottsskogen*,
Vegagatan 21 (☎031/42 65 20, ⑩www.hostel.nu; 140kr), two minutes' walk from
Linnégatan – take tram #1 or #2 to Olivedalsgatan. Another fine option, and well
placed for ferries to Denmark, is *Stigbergsliden*, Stigbergsliden 10 (☎031/24 16 20,
⑩www.hostel-gothenburg.com; 120kr). If you want something a little more peaceful try *Kvibergs*, Kvibergsvägen 5 (☎031/43 50 55, ⑩www.vandrarhem.se; 140kr),
housed in an old barracks building and close to Gothenburg's largest weekend fleamarket – take tram #6, #7 and #11 to Kviberg. The tourist office's **Gothenburg
package** (from 485kr/person) gets you a room in a central hotel, with breakfast
and a free Gothenburg Pass. The tourist office can book **private rooms** for around
175kr a head. Alternatively, try the friendly *Lilton*, Föreningsgatan 9 (☎031/82 88
08, ⑩www.hotellilton.com; ⑥), in a charming old house tucked away close to the
Haga area and offering a cosy atmosphere. For character and great location, opt for
the 1907 sailing ship *Barken Viking* (☎031/63 58 00, ⑩www.liseberg.se; ④), moored
on Gullbergskajen outside the Opera House on the river and very comfortable. The

all-year *Kärralund* **campsite** (🌐www.liseberg.se; 165kr/pitch) is 4km out on Olbergsgatan (tram #5 to Welandergatan) and has four-bed cabins from 600kr and an attached **hostel** (☎031/84 02 00; ➋).

The City

King Gustav II Adolf, looking for western trade, founded Gothenburg in the early seventeenth century as a response to the high tolls charged by the Danes for using the narrow sound between the two countries. As a Calvinist and businessman, Gustav much admired Dutch merchants, inviting them to trade and live in Gothenburg, and it's their influence that shaped the city, parts of which have an oddly Dutch feel. The area defined by the central canal represents what's left of old Gothenburg, centring on **Gustav Adolfs Torg**, a windswept square flanked by the nineteenth-century **Börshuset** (Exchange Building), and the fine **Rådhus**, originally built in 1672. Around the corner, the **Kronhuset**, off Kronhusgatan, built in 1643, is a typical seventeenth-century Dutch construction, and looks like the backdrop to a Vermeer. The cobbled courtyard outside is flanked by the mid-eighteenth-century **Kronhusbodarna** (Mon–Fri 11am–4pm, Sat 11am–2pm), now togged up as period craft shops selling sweets and souvenirs. The **Stadsmuseum**, Norra Hamngatan 12 (daily 10am–5/8pm; closed Mon Sept-Apr; 40kr), is worth a visit for its rich collection of archeological, cultural and industrial exhibits. Close by, the **Maritima Centrum** (March–Nov daily 10am–4/9pm; 60kr) allows you to clamber aboard a destroyer and submarine moored at the quayside. It is worth coming down here just to look at the shipyards beyond, like a rusting Meccano set put into sharp perspective by the striking **Opera House** (daily noon–6pm; ☎031/13 13 00; tickets from 50kr), a graceful and imaginative ship-like structure. Crossing the canal from Kungsportsplatsen and running all the way up to Götaplatsen, Kungsportsavenyn is Gothenburg's showiest thoroughfare. Known simply as **Avenyn**, this wide strip was once flanked by private houses fronted by gardens and is now lined with overpriced, posey yet popular pavement restaurants and brasseries. About halfway down, the excellent **Röhsska Museum of Arts and Crafts** at Vasagatan 37–39 (Tues–Sun noon–5pm, Tues till 9pm; 40kr), celebrates Swedish design through the ages, among other things. At the top end, **Götaplatsen** is the modern cultural centre of Gothenburg, home to a concert hall, theatre and **Art Museum** (daily 11am–5/6pm, Wed till 9pm; 40kr), whose enormous collections include a good selection of Impressionist paintings, Pop Art and – most impressively – superb Swedish work in the Furstenburg galleries on the sixth floor. Just a few minutes' walk to the west from Avenyn, the old working-class district of **Haga** is now a picturesque area of gentrified chic with plenty of daytime cafés and boutiques, while **Linnégatan**, a few steps further, is a more charismatic and cosmopolitan version of Avenyn with the most diverse places to eat, drink and stroll. Just five minutes' walk southeast of Götaplatsen, on the edge of the centre, is **Liseberg**, a surprisingly aesthetic amusement park (mid-April to late Aug daily noon/3–11pm; Sept Sat 1–11pm, Sun noon–8pm; 50kr) with some high-profile rides and acres of gardens, restaurants and fast food. In the opposite direction, great views of the harbour and surrounding area can be had from the excursion boats that run from Lilla Bommen to the **Nya Elfsborg Fortress** (early May to Aug daily 9.30am–4pm; 85kr, including guided tour of fortress), a seventeenth-century island defence guarding the harbour entrance, whose surviving buildings have been turned into a museum and café.

Eating and drinking

There's no shortage of places to **eat**; the city's range of ethnic restaurants is particularly good, reflecting its trading past. For **picnic food**, Saluhallen, the indoor market in Kungstorget, is tempting beyond words, and houses the two cheapest snack bars in town. In Linné, *Saluhall Briggen*, Tredje Långgatan, is smaller but brimming with mouthwatering fish, cheeses and cheap cafés. Many of the glitziest places to eat flank Avenyn, though with the exception of *Jungans Café* at no. 37 – a Gothenburg institution – they are generally samey, packed and overpriced; less obvious, and usually cheaper, places can be found in the streets clustered on Haga Nygatan: the cheapest, offering filling lunches, is *Café Kringlan*, Haga Nygatan 13. For friendly, laid-back atmosphere try *Café Engelen* and *Tintin Café*, just a few steps from each other on Engelbrektsgatan, off Avenyn – both are open round the clock. Another good choice is *Cyrano*, Prinsgatan 7 (℡031/14 31 10), an authentic Provençal bistro. For **vegetarian** and vegan meals, the classic place is *Solrosen*, Kaponjärgatan 4 in Haga district, which turns into a lively drinking venue at night. There's an excellent choice of places to **drink**, some staying open well into the small hours. Avenyn is the focal point of much of night-time Gothenburg. At the junction of Avenyn and Kristinelundsgatan, *Java Café,* at Vasagatan 23, is a studeny coffee house with a Parisian feel. *Napoleon* at Vasagatan 11 has a lovely, mellow interior and is set in a fabulous old house with exterior wall paintings. *Greta's*, Drottninggatan 35, is a stylish yet casual bar/restaurant, very popular as a **gay** venue and also serving good food. There's live music at the *The Dubliner* at Östra Hamngatan 50b, which claims to have been established in 1870 and serves Guinness and whisky. *Nefertiti*, Hvitfeldtsplatsen 6, is one of the best places to see live jazz and world **music**. The city's large student community means lots of local **live bands**. The best place to hear them is at *Kompaniet*, Kungsgatan, which has a bar on the top floor and dancing downstairs.

Helsingborg

At **HELSINGBORG** only a narrow sound separates Sweden from Denmark; indeed, Helsingborg was Danish for most of the Middle Ages, with a castle controlling the southern regions of what is now Sweden. The town's enormously important strategic position meant that it bore the brunt of repeated attacks and rebellions, the Swedes conquering the town on six separate occasions, only to lose it back to the Danes each time. Finally, in 1710, a terrible battle saw off the Danes for the last time, and the battered town lay dormant for almost two hundred years, depopulated and abandoned. Only in the nineteenth century, when the harbour was expanded and the railway constructed, did Helsingborg find new prosperity. Today, the dramatically redeveloped harbour area has breathed new life into this likeable, relaxed town. Directly south of the North Harbour café/bars, the strikingly designed **Henry Dunker Cultural House**, named after the city's foremost industrialist benefactor, is due to open as we go to press, and aims to provide a full vision of the city's history in context. East from Hamntorget and the harbours, the massive, neo-Gothic **Rådhus** marks the bottom of **Stortorget**, the long thin square sloping up to the lower battlements of what's left of Helsingborg's castle, the **kärnan** or keep (daily: April–Sept 9/10am–4/7pm; Oct–March 10am–2pm; 15kr), a fourteenth-century brick tower, the only survivor from the original fortress. The views from the top are worth the entrance fee although you don't miss much from the lower (free) battlements. Off Stortorget, **Norra Storgatan** contains Helsingborg's oldest buildings, attractive seventeenth- and eighteenth-century merchants' houses with quiet courtyards.

Apart from the Sundbussarna passenger ferry from Helsingør (Denmark), which pulls up across an arm of the docks, all **ferries**, **trains** and **buses** arrive at Knutpunkten, the harbourside **central terminal**. It's just a couple of minutes' walk from here to the **tourist office** inside the Rådhus at the corner of Stortorget and Järnvägsgatan (Mon–Fri 9am–6/8pm, Sat 9/10am–2/5pm; May–Aug also Sun 9/10am–2/5pm; ℡042/10 43 50, ⓦwww.helsingborgsguiden.com), which has free city maps and masses of brochures. The cheapest of the central **hotels** is *Linnéa*, Prästgatan 4 (℡042/37 24 00; ❻), which drops prices in summer and at weekends. The official **hostel** (℡042/13 11 30, ⓦwww.stfvandrarhem.helsingborg.nu; 160kr)is at Planteringsvägen 69-71 (bus #1) whereas, alternatively, the *Villa Thalassa*

hostel (℡042/38 06 60, ⊛www.villathalassa.com; 160kr; bus #219) is 4km north along Drottninggatan. For **camping**, try the waterfront site at Kustgatan Råå, 5km southeast; bus #1 from outside the Rådhus. Daytime **cafés** include the classic *Fahlmans* on Stortorget and the charismatic *Ebba's Fik*, Bruksgatan 20, decked out with authentic 1950s memorabilia. There are plenty of harbour-front bars. The cheapest **restaurant** is the unglamorous *Graffitti* on the first floor at Knutpunkten. The best **club** is the justifiably popular, and noisy, *Tivoli* club, Hamntorget 11, where you can get down to the very latest sounds for a 65kr entrance.

Lund

Forty minutes south of Helsingborg and fifteen minutes from Malmö, **LUND** is the most obvious target for a trip, a beautiful university town with a picturesque medieval centre and a unique buzz thanks to the student population. This does mean, though, that the life drains out of the place during the summer when the students are on vacation. Its weather-beaten **Domkyrkan** (Mon–Fri 8am–6pm, Sat & Sun 9.30am–6pm), consecrated in 1145, is considered by many to be Scandinavia's finest medieval building. Its plain interior culminates in a delicate, semicircular apse with a gleaming fifteenth-century altarpiece and a mosaic of Christ surrounded by angels – although what draws most attention is a fourteenth-century astronomical clock, revealing an ecclesiastical Punch and Judy show (Mon–Sat noon & 3pm, Sun 1pm & 3pm). Outside the cathedral, **Kyrkogatan**, lined with staunch, solid, nineteenth-century civic buildings, leads into the main square, **Stortorget**, off which **Kattesund** is home to a glassed-in set of excavated medieval walls. Adjacent at Kattesund 6 is the **Drottens museum** (Tues–Fri 9am–4pm, Sat & Sun noon–4pm; 20kr), the remains of a medieval church in the basement of another modern building, but the real interest is in the powerful atmosphere of the old streets behind the Domkyrkan. In this web of streets, **Kulturen** (daily 11am/noon–4/5pm; Oct to mid-April closed Mon; 40kr) is a village in itself of indoor and open-air collections of southern Swedish art, silverware, ceramics, musical instruments, etc. Finish off your meanderings with a visit to the **Botaniska Trädgård** (daily 6am–8pm) just beyond, an extensive botanical garden.

    Trains arrive on the western edge of town, an easy walk from the centre. The **tourist office** is opposite the Domkyrkan at Kyrkogatan 11, and is well signposted from the train station (June–Aug Mon–Fri 10am–6pm, Sat & Sun 10am–2pm; rest of year Mon–Fri 10am–5pm, May & Sept also Sat 10am-2pm; ℡046/ 35 50 40, ⊛www.lund.se). **Internet access** is available at the city library, St Petri Kyrkogata 6. Lund makes an appealing alternative stopover to Malmö or Helsingborg by virtue of private rooms which the tourist office can book for 200kr (50kr booking fee). Its unusual **hostel**, Tåget, Vävaregatan 22 (℡046/14 28 20; ❶), packs you into three-tiered sleeping compartments of six 1940s carriages parked on a branch line behind the train station; turn right and follow the signs. For a good-value central **hotel**, check into *Ahlström*, Skomakaregatan 3 (℡046/211 01 74; ❺; closed mid-June to mid-Aug), or *Hotel Överliggaren*, Bytaregatan 14 (℡046/15 72 30; ❺). There are plenty of cheap places to **eat**. *Café Ariman*, attached to the Nordic Law Department at Kungsgatan 2, has been updated, but maintains its shabby, left-wing coffee house appeal with good, cheap, light food; while *Conditori Lundagård*, Kyrkogatan 17, is the classic student café. *Fellini*, opposite the train station at Bangatan 6, is a popular Italian eatery. *Tegnérs*, next to the student union at Sandgatan 2, serves really fine food at student prices. Lund's most popular meeting place is the *Stortorget* on Stortorget with a bar, restaurant and club. The best **club** is *Basilika*, Stora Södergatan 13, just south of Stortorget – minimum age 22.

Malmö

MALMÖ, won back for Sweden from Denmark by Karl X in the seventeenth century, was a handsome city then and is now, with a cobbled medieval core that has a lived-in, workaday feel, worlds apart from the museum-piece quality of most other Swedish town centres. With the new **Øresund Link**, a sensational seventeen-kilometre-long road and rail bridge, Malmö really is the Swedish gateway from continental Europe, and after years in the doldrums, it is enjoying an economic revival. Few places in Sweden are more enjoyable – or more conducive to a leisurely stroll – than Malmö, with its canals, parks and largely pedestrianized streets and squares. Most of the medieval centre was taken apart in the early sixteenth century to make way for **Stortorget**, a vast market square. It's as impressive today as it must have been when it first appeared, flanked on one side by the **Rådhus**, built in 1546 and covered with statuary and spiky accoutrements; there are tours of the well-preserved interior (check with the tourist office for times). **Södergatan**, Malmö's main pedestrianized shopping street, runs south from here towards the canal. Behind the Rådhus stands the **St Petri Kyrka** (daily 8/10am–6pm), a fine Gothic church with an impressively decorative pulpit and a four-tiered altarpiece. **Lilla Torg** is everyone's favourite part of the city – indeed, it's been voted the most popular square in Sweden. It's a late-sixteenth-century spin-off from an overcrowded Stortorget, usually full and doing a roaring trade from jewellery stalls and summer buskers. The southern side of the square is formed by a row of mid-nineteenth-century brick and timber warehouses; the shops around here sell books, antiques and gifts, though the best place to drop into is the nearby **Saluhallen**, an excellent indoor market. Further west still lie the **Kungsparken** and the **Malmöhus** (daily 10am/noon–4pm; 40kr), a low fortified castle defended by a wide moat, two circular keeps and grassy ramparts, raised by Danish king Christian III in 1536. For a time a prison (Bothwell, third husband of Mary, Queen of Scots, was the most notable inmate), the castle and its outbuildings now constitute a series of exhibitions including Malmö's main **museum**, though unfortunately with no information in English. The grounds, peppered with small lakes and an old windmill, are good for a stroll.

Trains arrive at Central Station, including the local Pågatåg services (to and from Helsingborg and Lund; rail passes valid). The train station also has showers (20kr) and beds (5.30am–11pm; 25kr/hour). The main **bus terminal** is outside Central Station, in Centralplan. The **tourist office** is inside the station (Mon–Fri 9am–5/8pm, Sat 9/10am–2/5pm; June–Aug also Sun 10am–5pm; ☎040/34 12 00, ⓦwww.malmo.se/turist). It stocks the handy *Malmö This Month* and sells the **Malmö Card** (120kr/day, 150kr/two days, 180kr/three days), which gives free museum entry, free travel on city buses, free car parking in public places and a free sightseeing tour by bus. For **Internet** use, head for *Surfer's Paradise*, Amiralsgatan 14, or *Cyber Space*, Engelbrektsgatan 13a. Malmö is one of the easier places in the south to find good, cheap **accommodation**. A good choice of **hotel** is *Comfort Hotel Malmö* (☎040/33 04 50, ⓦwww.choicehotels.se; ➎) at Carlsgatan 10C. There is just one HI **hostel**, the inconveniently placed *STF Vandrarhem*, Backavägen 18 (☎040/822 20; ➌; closed Christmas and New Year), 5km out – take bus #21 from Central Station. A better bet is *Bosses Gästvåningar*, Södra Förstadsgatan 110B (☎040/32 62 50; ➋), a comfortable **B&B**, twenty minutes' walk south from the station or bus #15 or #20 to Södervärn. The nearest **campsite** is *Sibbarps Camping* (☎040/15 51 65) on Strandgatan; bus #12B from Central Station.

The Saluhall on Landbygatan by Lilla Torget stocks a marvellous array of picnic supplies. For **lunch**, a delightful option is the quirky *Café Siesta*, Ostindiefararegatan – turn right at the western end of Landbygatan off Lilla Torg – a fun café serving filling sandwiches and home-made apple cake. *Bageri Café* at Saluhall is excellent for filled baguettes and bagels. *Spot* **restaurant**, Stora Nygatan 33 (Mon–Fri 9am–6pm, Sat 10am–5pm), is a chic Italian and very good for cheese, fish and meat. A fabulous restaurant is *Krua Thai*, Möllevångstorget, which serves tasty Thai mains from an unbelievable 50kr. For **drinking**, Lilla Torg is the premiere choice and swarms with bustling venues through the evening. *Gustav Adolf*, Gustav Adolfs Torg, is popular at weekends. The best place for occasional **live music** is *Matssons Musikpub*, Göran Olsgatan 1, behind the Rådhus. A

28

twenty-minute walk south from the docks is Möllevångtsorget, where *Nyhavn* is one of the more appealing of the bar/pubs that are springing up all across the south city's trendy immigrant quarter. The unforgetably named *Vonk* is the **gay club** of choice at Adelgatan 2, however, it's also worth looking out the bar/club *Indigo* at Monbijougatan 15.

Central and northern Sweden

The long wedge of land that comprises **central and northern Sweden** – from the northern shores of Lake Vänern to the Finnish border – is Sweden as seen in the brochures: lakes, holiday cottages, forests and reindeer. On the eastern side, Sweden's coast forms one edge of the **Gulf of Bothnia**. With its jumble of erstwhile fishing towns and squeaky-clean contemporary urban planning, this corridor of land together with its regional town, **Sundsvall**, is worth stopping off in if you're travelling north or have just arrived from Finland by ferry. Though the weather isn't as reliable as further south, you are guaranteed clean beaches, crystal-clear waters and fine hiking. To the west, folklorish **Dalarna** county is the most picturesque region, with sweeping green countryside and inhabitants who maintain a cultural heritage (echoed in contemporary handicrafts and traditions) that goes back to the Middle Ages. This is *the* place to spend midsummer, particularly Midsummer's Night when the whole region erupts in celebration. The **Inlandsbanan**, the great Inland Railway, cuts right through this area from Lake Siljan through the modern lakeside town of **Östersund** to **Gällivare** above the Arctic Circle. An enthralling 1300-kilometre, two-day ride, it ranks with the best European train journeys.

Sundsvall

Known as the "Stone City", **SUNDSVALL** is immediately and obviously different. Once home to a rapidly expanding nineteenth-century sawmill industry, the whole city burned down in 1888 and a new centre built completely of stone emerged within ten years. The result is a living document of early-twentieth-century urban architecture, designed by architects who were engaged in rebuilding Stockholm's residential areas at the same time. The materials are limestone and brick, the style simple and the size often overwhelming. The **Esplanaden**, a wide central avenue, cuts the grid in two, itself crossed by **Storgatan**, the widest street. The area around **Stortorget** is still the roomy commercial centre that was envisaged. Behind the mock-Baroque exterior of the **Sundsvall Museum** (Mon–Fri 10am–6pm, Sat & Sun 10am–4pm; June–Aug 20kr, otherwise free), four late nineteenth-century warehouses have been developed into a cultural complex called Kulturmagasinet devoted to art exhibits and city history. The **Gustav Adolfs Kyrkan** (daily 11am–2/4pm) – a soaring red-brick structure whose interior looks like a large Lego set – marks one end of the new town. To get the best perspective on the city's plan, climb to the heights of **Gaffelbyn** and the **Norra Bergets Hantverksmuseum** (Mon–Fri 9am–4pm; June–Aug also Sat & Sun 11am–4pm; free), an open-air crafts museum down Storgatan and over the main bridge. From the **train station** the centre is five minutes' walk away, with the **tourist office** in the main Stortorget (Mon–Fri 10am–6pm, Sat 10am–2pm; ☎060/61 04 50, ✆info@sundsvallturism.com). The **bus station** is at the bottom of Esplanaden. The renovated **hostel** (☎060/61 21 19; 4–6pm; 160kr) at Norra Berget takes about half an hour to walk to from the centre. The tourist office will help book accommodation for a 20kr fee, but does not book private rooms; otherwise, *Svea Hotel*, Rådhusgatan 11 (☎060/61 16 05; ❹), has the cheapest doubles in town. For **eating**, Storgatan is lined with restaurants, most offering daily lunch menus, while *La Spezia*, Sjögatan 6, has bargain pizzas from 35kr.

Dalarna

The **Dalarna** region holds a special, misty-eyed place in the Swedish heart and should certainly be seen, though not to the exclusion of points further north. **Lake Siljan**, at the heart of the province, is the major draw, its gentle surroundings, traditions and local handicrafts weaving a subtle spell. If you've only got time to see part of the lake, **MORA** is as good a place as any, and a starting point for the Inlandsbanan rail route (see below). At the northwestern corner of Lake Siljan, the little town is a showcase for the work of Anders Zorn, the Swedish painter who lived in Mora and whose work is exhibited in the **Zorn Museum**, Vasagatan 36 (Mon–Sat 9am/noon–5pm, Sun 11am/1–5pm; 35kr), along with his small but well-chosen personal collection. Zorn's oils reflect a passion for Dalarna's pastoral lifestyle, but it's his earlier watercolours of southern Europe and North Africa that really stand out. The **tourist office** (Mon–Fri 10am–5pm; mid-June to mid-Aug Mon–Fri until 7pm, Sat & Sun 10am–5pm; ☏0250/56 76 00, ✉mora@stab.se) is at Mora station, and the HI **hostel** at Fredsgatan 6 (☏0250/381 96, ✉info@maalkullann.se; 150kr). **LEKSAND** is perhaps the most popular and traditional of the Dalarna villages and certainly worth making the effort to reach at midsummer, when the festivals recall age-old maypole dances, the celebrations culminating in the **church boat races**, an aquatic procession of decorated longboats which the locals once rowed to church every Sunday. The **tourist office** in the train station building (Mon–Fri 10am–4pm; mid-June to mid-Aug Mon–Fri until 7pm, Sat & Sun 10am–5pm; ☏0247/79 61 30, ✉leksand@stab.se) has lots of information on the area, as does the **hostel** (☏0247/152 50; 150kr), 2km south of the centre at Parkgården.

The Inlandsbanan

The **Inlandsbanan** (Inland Railway; ☏0771/53 53 53, ☒www.inlandsbanan.se), linking central Sweden with Gällivare 1300km further north, is the most charismatic of Scandinavian rail routes, the trip everyone wants to make. Long under threat of closure, the line has been privatized and looks like surviving for the moment, but only operates between late June and early August. InterRail pass holders under the age of 26 travel for free. With a ScanRail Pass there is a 25-percent discount off an Inland Railway Card which otherwise costs 995kr and which offers unlimited travel on the line for fourteen days. The full fare, travelling second class from Mora to Östersund (7hr), costs from 300kr, plus an optional 50kr seat reservation.

Mora to the Arctic Circle

The Inlandsbanan begins in Mora, making its first stop at **ORSA**, fifteen minutes up the line, where the nearby **Grönklitt bear park** (mid-May to mid-Sept daily 10am–3/6pm; 85kr) provides the best chance to see the bears that roam the countryside. The **hostel** at the park (☏0250/462 00; 160kr) has fine facilities. Several hours north of here, the line's halfway point is marked by **ÖSTERSUND**. It's a welcoming place, and its **Storsjön** – or Great Lake – gives it a holiday atmosphere unusual this far north. The lake is also alleged to be the home of a Loch Ness-style monster. In summer, you can make a tour of the lake on a **steamboat cruise**, stopping off on the small island of Verkön (check with tourist office for times; 95kr). Otherwise, the main thing to do in town is to visit **Jamtli** (June to Aug daily 11am–5pm; rest of year closed Mon; 90kr), an impressive open-air museum fifteen minutes' walk north from the centre along Rådhusgatan, full of volunteers milling around in traditional country costume encouraging visitors to join in baking, tree-felling and grass-cutting. On the way in, the **museum** (June to Aug daily 11am–5pm; rest of year closed Mon; entry covered by the Jamtli ticket) proudly shows off the ninth-century **Överhogdal tapestries**, whose simple handwoven patterns of horses, dogs and other beasts is quite breathtaking. It's also home to a small collection of monster-catching gear from the nineteenth century. Back in the centre, the town slopes steeply down to the water, and it's tiring work strolling the pedestrianized streets that run around Stortorget. From the **harbour** you can take the bridge over the lake to **Frösön** island, site of the original Viking settlement here. The **tourist office** is at Rådhusgatan 44 (Mon–Fri 9am–5/9pm; June–Aug also Sat & Sun 9am–7/9pm; ☎063/14 40 01, ☻www.turist.ostersund.se) and sells the *Östersundskortet*, valid nine days (June to mid-Aug; 120kr), giving free access to the town's sights, half-price round-trip bus journeys and half-price on the steamboat cruise. For a central **hotel**, try either *Hotell Aston*, Köpmangatan 40 (☎063/51 08 51; ❹), or the *Hotell Jemtlandia*, close to the train station at Storgatan 64 (☎063/51 73 35; ❺). The STF **hostel** in Östersund (☎063/13 91 00; 160kr) is a ten-minute walk from the train station at Södra Gröngatan 36 in the town centre. More atmospheric is the **hostel** at Jamtli (☎063/12 20 60; 140kr; take bus #2 to the end of the line) – although slightly more expensive, staying there saves on entrance fees to the museum. **Campers** can stay at either *Östersunds Camping*, 2km down Rådhusgatan (☎063/14 46 15), or on Frösön island at *Fröső Camping* (☎063/432 54; June to early Aug only; bus #3 or #4 from the centre). For **food**, try the young and trendy *Brunkullans* restaurant with its outdoor garden at Postgränd 5, or the daily specials at the Australian *Captain Cook,* Hamngatan 9 – cheaper than *Brunkullans*, with live entertainment on Wed & Sat, and very popular for **drinking** too.

Further north, **ARVIDSJAUR** contains Sweden's oldest surviving Sámi village, **Lappstaden** (daily tours in July at 5pm; 25kr, otherwise just walk in), dating from the late eighteenth century, a huddle of houses that was once the centre of a great winter market. They were not meant to be permanent homes, but rather a meeting place during festivals, and the last weekend in August is still taken up by a great celebratory shindig. There's a cosy private **hostel** at Västra Skolgatan 9 (☎0960/124 13; 130kr), and *Camp Gielas*, beside one of the lakes 1km south of the station, has cabins from 400kr. The **tourist office** (Mon–Fri 8am–5pm; June to mid-Aug daily 10am–6.30pm; ☎0960/175 00; ☻www.arvidsjaurturism.se) is at Östra Skolgatan 18C. Three and a half hours north of Arvidsjaur, the Inlandsbanan finally crosses the **Arctic Circle**, signalled by a bout of whistle-blowing as the train pulls up. Painted white rocks curve away over the hilly ground, a crude but popular representation of the Circle.

Jokkmokk

In the midst of remote, densely forested, marshy country, **JOKKMOKK** is a welcome oasis. Once wintertime Sámi quarters, the town is today a renowned handicraft centre, with a Sámi educational college keeping the language and culture alive. The **Ájtte Museum** (Mon–Fri 9/10–4/6pm, Sat & Sun 9am/noon–4/6pm; Oct–April closed Sat; 50kr) on Kyrkegatan is the place to see some of the intricate work. Have a glance, too, at the so-called **Lapp Kyrka**, enclosed by a wide wooden fence, in which corpses were interned during winter, waiting for the thaw when the Sámi could go out and dig graves. The great **winter market** still survives, now nearly 400 years old, held on the first Thursday, Friday and Saturday of each February, when 30,000 people gather in town. It's the best time to be in Jokkmokk, and staying means booking accommodation a good six months in advance. A smaller, less traditional autumn fair at the end of August is an easier though poorer option. The **tourist office** is at Stortorget 4 (mid-June to mid-Aug daily 9am–6pm; rest of year Mon–Fri 8.30am–4pm; ☎0971 222 50, ☻www.turism.jokkmokk.se). In summer there should be no problem getting a place at the HI **hostel** at Åsgatan 20 (☎0971/559 77; 165kr); just follow the signs from the station. The **campsite** is 3km east on route 97.

Gällivare

GÄLLIVARE, at the junction of the Inlandsbanan and the main line from Stockholm, is one of Europe's most important sources of iron ore, while Europe's largest open-cast copper mine sears the landscape 20km to the south. The tourist office ferries trips to the **iron ore mines** (June to Aug once daily; 200kr) and **copper mine** (June–Aug once daily; 160kr). Astounding statistics – 300 tonnes of high explosives are used for each blast – pepper the tour, which also takes in **Kåkstan**, a rebuilt shantytown on the site of the original iron ore mine; and you stop long enough to sample local delicacies like reindeer, salmon and lingonberry juice, all for 75kr at the teetotal *Café Endast för Nyktra*. Little remains of the seventeenth-century Sámi village, and the river and surrounding mountains are really the nicest feature of the town itself. You can walk up to **Björnfällän**, a four-kilometre hike on a well-marked path – the views are magnificent. Buses make the journey (150kr return) to the summit 3km north beyond Björnfällan to see the Midnight Sun daily between mid-June and mid-July. Departures are from the train station at 11pm, returning at 1am. The **tourist office** is at Storgatan 16 (Mon–Fri 9am–4/6pm; June to mid-Aug also Sat & Sun 9am–6pm; ☎0970/166 60, ⓦwww.gellivare.se). Its long summer hours are aimed at late Inlandsbanan arrivals, and the office has a museum upstairs dealing with Sámi history. The **hostel** (☎0970/143 80; 165kr) is at Barnhemsvägen 2, behind the train station, and offers accommodation in small two-person cabins (no bed linen provided), though there are a few three- and four-bed cabins too. There's also a **hotel**, the *Hotell Dundret*, Per Högströmsgatan 1 (☎0970/550 40; ❺), close to the station. The **campsite** (☎0970/100 10) is by the river; for **snacks** or an evening coffee and cakes by the river, make for the *Strandcaféet* near the campsite at Malmbergsvägen 2. Otherwise a good choice is *Restaurang Peking* at Storgatan 21B, which dishes up the usual array of Chinese food, or try the tasty Indian dishes at *New Delhi* at no. 19.

Travel details

Trains

Gällivare to: Narvik (2 daily; 4hr 40min).
Gothenburg to: Copenhagen (2–3 daily; 4hr 20min); Helsingborg (6–9 daily; 2hr 40min); Kalmar (3–5 daily; 4hr 40min); Lund (6–9 daily; 3hr 30min); Malmö (8–12 daily; 3hr by X2000, 3hr 45min InterCity); Oslo (4 daily; 4hr 40min).
Malmö to: Helsingborg (at least hourly; 50min); Lund (at least hourly; 15min); Ystad (Mon–Fri hourly, Sat & Sun 4–6 daily; 50min).
Stockholm to: Gällivare (2 daily; 16hr); Gävle (hourly; 1hr 20min); Gothenburg (21 daily; 3hr 10min by X2000, 4hr 30min InterCity); Helsingborg (14 daily; 5hr by X2000, 6hr 30min InterCity); Kalmar, change at Alvesta (8 Mon–Sat, 3 Sun; 6hr); Lund (6 daily; 4hr 40min); Malmö (11 daily; 4hr 30 min by X2000); Mora (11 daily; 3hr 30min by X2000); Narvik (2 daily; 20hr); Östersund (6 daily; 6hr); Sundsvall (9 daily; 3hr 30min by X2000); Uppsala (half hourly; 40min).
Sundsvall to: Gävle (8 daily; 2hr 30min); Östersund (5 daily; 2hr 15min).
Uppsala to: Gävle (hourly; 40 min); Mora (11 daily; 2hr 15min by X2000).

Buses

Gothenburg to: Gävle (1–2 daily; 10hr); Kalmar (1 Fri, 1 Sun; 6hr 30min); Malmö (3 Fri, 3 Sun; 4hr 40min); Oslo (3–4 daily; 4hr 50min); Uppsala (1 Fri, 1 Sun; 8hr).
Stockholm to: Gävle (3 Fri, 1 Sat, 4 Sun; 2hr 20min); Gothenburg (2–5 daily; 4hr 30min, or 7hr 20min via Jönköping); Helsingborg (1 daily, 2 Fri & Sun; 8hr); Kalmar (2–5 daily; 6hr 30min); Malmö (1 Fri, 1 Sun; 10hr 20min); Nynäshamn (3 daily; 1hr); Oskarshamn (2–5 daily; 4hr 30min); Oslo (1 Fri, 1 Sun; 9hr); Sundsvall (3 Fri, 1 Sat, 4 Sun; 6hr); Uppsala (3 Fri, 1 Sat, 4 Sun; 1hr).

International ferries

Gothenburg to: Frederikshavn (4–8 daily; 3hr 15min); Newcastle (4 weekly; 24hr); Kiel (1 daily; 14hr).
Helsingborg to: Helsingor (3 hourly; 25min).
Malmö to: Copenhagen (every 30min; 40min).
Stockholm to: Helsinki (Helsingfors), Finland (2 daily; 15hr); Tallinn (summer 1 daily plus 1 every 2 days; 15hr); Turku (Åbo), Finland (4 daily; 13hr).
Trelleborg to: Rostock (3 daily; 6hr); Travemünde (2 daily; 7–9hr).

Switzerland

and Liechtenstein

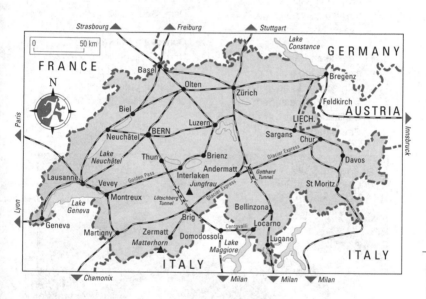

Switzerland highlights

✳ **Lausanne** Geneva's unsung neighbour, with bags of style, sass and lakeside charm. See p.930

✳ **Lake Luzern** Take a cruise on Switzerland's most scenic lake, nestling between high peaks. See p.935

✳ **Interlaken** Base for exploring the high Alps, with access to adventure sports plus the superb Schilthorn cable-car ride. See p.938

✳ **The Matterhorn** World-famous mountain peak, with guaranteed skiing and snowboarding year-round. See p.941

✳ **World's highest bungee jump** A death-defying 220m off the Verzasca Dam. See p.943

✳ **Centovalli railway** Narrow-gauge line offering a scenic and dramatic detour on a journey to or from Milan. See p.943

Introduction and basics

Switzerland is one of Europe's most visited countries, but one of its least understood. Pass through for a day or two and you'll get all the quaint stereotypes – cheese, chocolate and clocks – but not much else. Stay a bit longer and another Switzerland will emerge, which can be an infinitely more rewarding place to explore. Sights are breathtaking, transport links are excellent and costs are no higher than in Britain or Germany. Almost everyone speaks some English along with at least one of the official languages (German, French, Italian, and, in the southeast, Romansh).

Notoriously placid these days, Switzerland spent the first 500 years of its existence rent by conflict. The Swiss Confederation (abbreviated to "CH") dates back to 1291, when Alpine peasants formed an alliance to defend themselves against the Habsburgs. By the early 1500s, it had grown into a military superpower. The Swiss reputation for neutrality emerged with the Reformation and persisted right through to the boom years after World War II. In the 1990s, exposés uncovered Swiss banks' wartime collusion with the Nazis. Public soul-searching in the aftermath of the scandal heralded Switzerland's entry into the UN, and its first steps towards joining the EU.

The most visited Alpine area is the central **Bernese Oberland**, which has the highest concentration of picturesque peaks and mountainside villages; the loftiest Alps are further south, where **Zermatt** provides access to the Toblerone-peaked **Matterhorn**. In the southeast, forested mountain slopes surround the chic resort of **St Moritz**. Of the northern German-speaking cities, **Zürich** has a wealth of sightseeing and nightlife possibilities and provides easy access to the tiny principality of **Liechtenstein** on the Rhine. **Basel** and the capital **Bern** are quieter, each with an attractive historic core, while **Luzern** lies in an appealing setting close to lakes and mountains. In the French-speaking west, the cities lining the northern shore of Lake Geneva – notably **Geneva** and **Lausanne** – make up the heart of **Suisse-Romande**. South of the Alps, sunny, Italian-speaking **Ticino** can seem a world apart, particularly the palm-fringed lakeside resorts of **Lugano** and **Locarno**, with their Mediterranean atmosphere.

Information & maps

All towns have a **tourist office** (*Verkehrsverein* or *Tourismus*; *Office du Tourisme*; *Ente Turistico*), invariably located near the train station and always extremely useful. Most staff speak English, but **opening hours** in smaller towns allow for a long lunch and can be limited at weekends and in the off-season. All have accommodation and transport lists and **maps**. *Swiss Backpacker News* (ⓦwww .backpacker.ch) is an excellent free paper widely available. ⓦwww.swisstopo.ch has 1:50,000 and 1:25,000 walkers' maps.

Money and banks

Currency in Switzerland and Liechtenstein is the **Swiss franc** (CHF or Fr.), divided into 100 Rappen (Rp), centimes or centisimi (c). There are coins of 5c, 10c, 20c, 50c, Fr.1, Fr.2 and Fr.5, and notes of Fr.10, Fr.20, Fr.50, Fr.100,

---

Switzerland and Liechtenstein on the net

ⓦ**www.myswitzerland.com** Tourist office site – vast, detailed and authoritative.
ⓦ**www.rail.ch** Comprehensive travel information, with online timetables.
ⓦ**www.postbus.ch** Details of the postbus network, including Alpine routes.
ⓦ**www.museums.ch** Information on museums nationwide.
ⓦ**www.swissinfo.org** News database in English, with good links.
ⓦ**www.tourismus.li** The Liechtenstein tourist board.

Fr.200 and Fr.1000. Train stations are the best places for **changing money** – almost all have a commission-free change counter open long hours. **Banks** usually open Mon–Fri 8.30am–4.30pm; some in cities and resorts also open Sat 9am–4pm. Post offices give a similar exchange rate to banks, and **ATMs** are everywhere. Many shops, especially in tourist hubs, accept euros.

Communications

Main **post offices** tend to open Mon–Fri 7.30am–noon & 1.30–6.30pm, Sat 8–11am. Most public **phones** take phonecards (*taxcards*), available from post offices, newsagents and vending machines (Fr.5, Fr.10 or Fr.20), as well as credit cards. Kiosks also sell good-value cards from companies such as diAx for calling internationally. The expensive **operator** is on ☎111 (domestic) or ☎1141 (international). There are **Internet cafés** in all towns (Fr.8–20/hr).

Getting around

Public transport is comprehensive. Services depart on the dot, and train timetables are well integrated with those of the rural postbuses. Main stations keep a public copy of the national timetable, which covers all rail, bus, boat and cable-car services. Travelling by **train** is invariably comfortable, hassle-free and extremely scenic, with many mountain routes an attraction in their own right. The main network, run by SBB-CFF-FFS, covers much of the country, but many routes, especially Alpine lines, are operated by smaller

companies. **Buses** take over where train track runs out – generally yellow postbuses, which depart from train-station forecourts. **InterRail** and **Eurail** are vaild on SBB and most smaller lines, but the discounts they bring are patchy on boats, cable cars and mountain railways (specified in the text as "**IR**" for InterRail and "**ER**" for Eurail). Postbuses are free with all Swiss passes (see "Basics"; specified as "**SP**") – although Alpine routes command a Fr.6–12 supplement, along with seat reservation – but not to Eurail and InterRail pass-holders. Most lake **ferries** run only in summer (June–Sept), and duplicate routes which can be covered more cheaply and quickly by rail. But if you have the time, cruising through the Alpine foothills to Interlaken or along Lake Geneva beats the equivalent train journeys hands down.

Accommodation

Accommodation isn't as expensive as you might think, and is nearly always excellent. Tourist offices can often book rooms for free in their area; they normally have a display-board on the street (or at the train station) with details of every hotel, often with a courtesy phone. When you check in, ask for a guest card, which can give substantial discounts on local attractions and transport. A **hostel** (*Jugendherberge*; *Auberge de Jeunesse*; *Albergo/Ostello per la Gioventù*) represents great value for money (always book ahead June–Sept). **HI hostels** (☽www.youthhostel.ch) are of a universally high standard, with doubles as well as small dorms (average Fr.25 for a dorm bed inc. breakfast and bedding). Non-HI members

---

Adventure sports

With its landscape of mountains, glaciers, deep gorges and fast-flowing rivers, Switzerland is ideal territory for **adventure sports**. Dozens of companies, based in all the main resorts (Interlaken and Luzern are two popular centres), offer activities through the summer, such as **canyoning** (Fr.100/half-day), **river-rafting** (Fr.100/half-day), **bungee-jumping** (Fr.80 for 100m; Fr.220 for 180m), **zorbing** (where you're strapped inside a giant plastic sphere and rolled down a mountainside; Fr.50), **house-running** (where you hook a rope round yourself and run full-tilt down the side of a tall building; Fr.70), and **flying fox** (where you glide down a vertical cliff on a rope; Fr.75). **Hang-gliding** (Fr.130), **paragliding** (Fr.170) and **skydiving** from 4000m (Fr.400) can all be done alone or in tandem with an instructor. Tourist offices and ☽www.myswitzerland.com have full details.

pay Fr.5 extra. Meals, where available, are around Fr.10. A rival group known as **Swiss Backpackers** (ⓦwww.backpacker.ch) has lively hostels that are less institutional, often in prime town-centre locations, and priced to compete; they're specified in the text as "**SB**". **Campsites** are clean and well equipped; the higher the altitude the more limited the opening times – many close Oct–May. Prices are about Fr.8 per person plus Fr.8–12 per pitch and per vehicle. Many sites require an international camping carnet. Camping outside official sites is illegal. **Hotels** are everywhere, invariably excellent, and not expensive. Shared-bath doubles start at Fr.85 (average Fr.110), en suites around Fr.135.

Food and drink

Eating can punch a hole in your budget if you're not careful, although by combining a judicious choice of eateries with forays into picnicking and self-catering you can survive on a tight budget without any compromise on nutrition. Burgers, pizza slices, kebabs and falafels are universal **snack** standbys, and you'll find various kinds of **sausage**; the most popular are pork *Bratwürste*. **Dairy products** find their way into most Swiss dishes. Cheese **fondue** – a pot of wine-laced molten cheese into which you dip cubes of bread or potato – is the national dish. It's usually priced as a two-person (or more) meal, or as an all-you-can-eat deal (*fondue à discrétion* or *à gogo*). Another speciality is **raclette** – piquant molten cheese spread on a plate and scooped up with bread or potato. A Swiss-German staple is **Rösti**, grated potatoes fried to a golden-brown hash and topped with cheese, chopped ham or a fried egg. All but a handful of places offer **vegetarian** set menus. Alternative diners, many in squats in the major towns, offer budget veggie and vegan meals as standard. **Cafés** and **restaurants** usually serve meals at set times (noon–2pm & 6–10pm), with only snacks available in between. To get the best value, make lunch your main meal, and always plump for the dish of the day (*Tagesmenu, Tagesteller, Tageshit; plat/assiette du jour; piatto del giorno*) – substantial nosh for Fr.15 or less.

The same meal in the evening, or choosing *à la carte* anytime, can cost double. **Department stores** including Manor and Co-op have surprisingly good self-service diners attached, where pick-and-choose meals are great value: you pay, say, Fr.6/10 for a small/large plate, with no limit on the quantity of fresh salad or hot daily special you can pile onto it. Some offer a twenty-percent discount to students. Cafés are open from breakfast till midnight/1am and often sell alcohol; **bars** and **pubs** tend to open their doors for late-afternoon and evening business only. **Beers** are invariably excellent, at Fr.3–4 for a glass (*e'Schtange, une pression, una birra*). Even the simplest places have **wine**, most affordably as *Offene Wein, vin ouvert, vino aperto* – a handful of house reds and whites chalked up on a board (small glass Fr.3–5). Look out for local **spirits** (*Schnapps, eau-de-vie, aquavite*), including cherry Kirsch, aromatic pear Williamine, and Ticinese grappa.

Opening hours and holidays

Shop hours are Mon–Fri 9am–6.30pm, Sat 8.30am–4pm, often with a lunch-break and earlier closing in smaller towns. All shops within train stations are open later, and on Sun. Most big-city stations also have 24-hour vending machines dispensing bread, cheese and milk. **Museums** and attractions generally close on Mon. Almost everything is closed on **public holidays**: Jan 1; Good Fri & Easter Mon; Ascension Day; Whit Mon; Dec 25 & 26. In Switzerland, shops and banks close for all or part of the national holiday (Aug 1) and on a range of local holidays. Liechtenstein keeps May 1 as a public holiday, and Aug 15 as the national holiday.

The **Swiss Museum Passport** (ⓦwww.museums.ch/pass) gives free entry to over 300 attractions nationwide for a month. It costs Fr.30 (students Fr.25) from tourist offices or member museums, and can easily pay for itself in a weekend of gallery-hopping.

Emergencies

Swiss **police** – who may not speak English – are courteous enough to white people, less so to everyone else. Form E111 gives EU citizens discounted medical care in Switzerland and Liechtenstein; everyone else must have private insurance. You'll have to pay **hospital** (*Spital*, *hôpital*, *ospedale*) bills upfront and claim expenses back later. Every district has a rota system with one local **pharmacy** (*Apotheke*, *pharmacie*, *farmacia*) open outside hours; each pharmacy has a sign telling you where the nearest open one is.

Emergency numbers

Police ☎117; fire ☎118; ambulance ☎144.

Zürich

Not so long ago, **ZÜRICH** was famed for being the cleanest, most icily efficient city in Europe: apocryphal stories abound from the 1970s of tourists embarking on efforts to find a cigarette butt or food wrapper discarded on the streets – and drawing a blank every time. But there's a lot more to Zürich these days than its obsessive cleanliness: this most beautiful of cities, astride a river and turned towards a crystal-clear lake and distant snowy peaks, has plenty to recommend it, not least bars and clubs as hip and varied as those in more celebrated European cities. The steep, cobbled alleys of the Old Town are great to wander around, and with an engaging café culture and a wealth of nightlife, you could easily spend days here.

Arrival, information and accommodation

Zürich main station, the giant **Hauptbahnhof** (HB), is served by trains from all over Europe, and from the **airport**, 11km northeast. The building extends three storeys below ground, taking in a shopping mall, supermarket and some good eateries. The international **bus station** is 50m north on Sihlquai. The **tourist office** on the station concourse (Mon–Sat 8/8.30am–7/8.30pm, Sun 8.30/9am–6.30pm; ☏01 215 40 00, ⑩www.zuerich.com) will book rooms for free, and sells the **Zürich Card** (Fr.15/30 one/three days), which entitles you to free rides on public transport and free entry to museums. They also have the useful **listings** booklet *Zürich News* (⑩www.zuerich.ch). You can cover most sights by walking, but the **tram and bus** system is easy to use. The most important hubs are the city squares of Bahnhofplatz and, on the east side of the river, Central and Bellevue. Buy tickets from machines at every stop: choose between the green button (24hr; Fr.7.20); blue button (1hr; Fr.3.60); or yellow button (short one-way hop; Fr.2.10). All tickets are valid on trams, buses, some boats and local city trains (not to/from the airport).

Hostels

City Backpacker (SB) Niederdorfstr. 5 ☏01 251 90 15, ⑩www.city-backpacker.ch. Good atmosphere and central location, plus free kitchen use, laundry and Internet (though a Fr.20 key deposit). Dorms Fr.31. Rooms ❹

Jugendherberge (HI) Mutschellenstr. 114 ☏01 482 35 44, ⑩www.youthhostel.ch. Way out in a southwestern suburb. Tram #7 (direction Wollishofen) to Morgental, then walk 5min. Dorms Fr.32. Rooms ❹

Hotels

Etap Technoparkstr. 2 ☏01 276 20 00, ⑩www.etaphotel.com. Generic, functional hotel out west in the old industrial quarter, behind the trendy Schiffbau arts centre. ❹

Limmat Limmatstr. 118 ☏01 448 15 95, ⑩www.x-tra.ch/hotel. Postmodern-styled rooms above the lively *X-tra* bar and nightclub, northwest of the centre. ❺

Limmathof Limmatquai 142 ☏01 261 42 20. Central riverside cheapie with tiny rooms. ❺

Martahaus Zähringerstr. 36 ☏01 251 45 50, ⑩www.martahaus.ch. Clean, safe Old Town budget hotel with dorms and rooms, plus a women-only annexe. ❹

Otter Oberdorfstr. 7 ☏01 251 22 07, ⑩www.wueste.ch. Relaxed, friendly Old Town joint with a clientele of students and artists. Rooms are decked in murals, drapes and plants. Also dreamy top-floor apartment. ❹

Villette Kruggasse 4 ☏01 251 23 35. Simple rooms above a good city-centre fondue restaurant. ❹

Campsite

Seebucht Seestr. 559 ☏01 482 16 12, ⑩www.camping-zurich.ch. On the lakeside, 2km south of the centre. Bus #161 or #165 from Bürkliplatz to Stadtgrenze. Closed Nov–April.

The City

Across the River Limmat from the station, the narrow lanes of the medieval **Niederdorf** district stretch south, tranquil during the day and bustling after dark. The waterfront is lined with fine Baroque *Zunfthäuser* (guildhalls), arcaded lower storeys fronting the quayside, their extravagantly decorated dining-rooms now

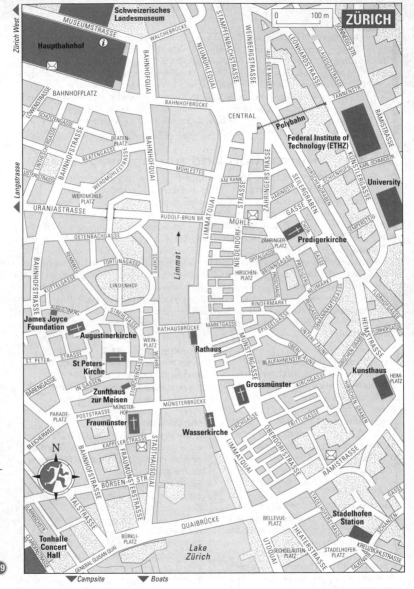

mostly upmarket restaurants. One block in is **Niederdorfstrasse**, initially tacky, but offering plenty of opportunities to explore atmospheric cobbled side-alleys and secluded courtyards: Lenin lived at Spiegelgasse 14 in 1917 (pre-Revolution), while a pub at Spiegelgasse 1 once housed the *Cabaret Voltaire*, birthplace of the Dada art movement. Just south is Zürich's trademark **Grossmünster** (Great Minster; Mon–Sat 9/10am–5/6pm), where Huldrych Zwingli, father of Swiss Protestantism, began preaching in 1519. Its exterior is largely fifteenth-century, while its twin towers were topped with distinctive octagonal domes in the seventeenth century. The interior is austere but for the intensely coloured choir windows (1933) by Augusto Giacometti and the Romanesque crypt which contains an oversized fifteenth-century statue of Charlemagne, popularly associated with the foundation of the church in the ninth century. A door, to the right on exiting, gives into the atmospheric cloister. Alleys behind the church lead up the hill to Switzerland's best gallery, the **Kunsthaus** (Tues–Thurs 10am–9pm, Fri–Sun 10am–5pm; Fr.10, free on Wed; ⓦwww.kunsthaus.ch). Some fascinating late-Gothic paintings, a roomful of Venetian masters and fine Flemish work are fleshed out by Swiss artists, among them Füssli, whose macabre fantasies contrast with the restrained classicism of his compatriot Angelika Kauffmann. The collection of twentieth-century art is stunning: works by Miró, Dalí and De Chirico head a wonderful Surrealist overview; Picasso, Chagall, Klee and Kandinsky all have rooms to themselves; there are two of Monet's most beautiful waterlily canvases, plenty of Warhols, an array of Giacometti's sculpture, and the largest Munch collection outside Scandinavia.

The **west bank** is the site of most business and commercial activity. Leading south from the station, **Bahnhofstrasse** is one of the most prestigious shopping streets in Europe. This is the gateway into the modern city, and is where all of Zürich strolls, to browse at the inexpensive department stores that crowd the first third of the street, or to sign away Fr.25,000 on a Rolex watch or a Vuitton bag at the understated super-chic boutiques further south. Two-thirds of the way down is **Paradeplatz**, a tram-packed little square offering some of the best people-watching in the city. The narrow lanes between Bahnhofstrasse and the river lead up to the **Lindenhof**, site of a Roman fortress and customs post. James Joyce wrote *Ulysses* in Zürich (1915–19), and the **Joyce Foundation**, nearby at Augustinergasse 9 (Tues–Fri 10am–5pm; free), can point you to his various hangouts, and his grave. Steps away is **St Peters-Kirche** (Mon–Fri 8am–6pm, Sat 9am–4pm), renowned for its enormous sixteenth-century clock face – the largest in Europe. Immediately south rises the slender-spired Gothic **Fraumünster** (Mon–Sat 9/10am–4/6pm), which began life as a convent in the ninth century; its spectacular stained glass by Marc Chagall is unmissable.

A tasty diversion heads south to the Lindt & Sprüngli **chocolate factory**, Seestrasse 204, Kilchberg (Wed–Fri 10am–noon & 1–4pm; free). Frustratingly, the company refuses to let anyone near the production line; instead, you're diverted to a small museum, shown a video and then let loose to sample the company's wares for free. Kilchberg is 6km south along the lake's western shore from Bürkliplatz by bus #165 or boat, also reachable by S-Bahn suburban train from Zürich.

Eating, drinking and nightlife

A wander through the Niederdorf district will turn up dozens of **eating** options – falafel, sausage, noodle and french-fry stands, plus beerhalls serving daily specials for about Fr.13. Supplementing its lively **music** venues, Zürich's **club** scene has skyrocketed recently, and you'll find dance floors heaving. The hip quarter around Langstrasse, west of the centre, is full of DJ-bars, and the industrial quarter to the northwest is where the best clubs hide themselves. August sees the **Street Parade** (ⓦwww.street-parade.ch), a hedonistic weekend of techno street-dancing second only to Berlin's Love Parade. **Listings** are in *ZüriTipp* (ⓦwww.zueritipp.ch), available at the tourist office.

Snack meals

Nordsee Train station concourse. Good-value fish meals, eat in or take away.

Suan Long Train station lower level. Cheap, filling stir-fries, veggie and not.

Wave International At Jelmoli dept store on Uraniastr. Swiss, Asian, Turkish and Arabic nosh.

Cafés and restaurants

Bodega Española Münstergasse 15. Atmospheric tapas bar and paella restaurant.

Hiltl Sihlstr. 28. Top-quality vegetarian buffet, with budget prices for takeaway.

Lily's Stomach Supply Langstr. 197. Clean, modern place in a multicultural district just west of the centre, churning out fresh-cooked Asian specialities (from Fr.10). The German menu marks dishes that are extra-spicy *!!!* and those that are an acquired taste *****.

Manora 5th floor of Manor store, Bahnhofstr. 75. Good, varied self-service meals for under Fr.13.

Pinte Vaudoise In *Hotel Villette*, Kruggasse 4. Traditional place serving what's been voted the best fondue in Zürich. Closed Sat in summer, & Sun.

Santa Lucia Marktgasse 21. Wide selection of good-value pasta and pizza. Serves until 2am.

Schlauch Upstairs at Münstergasse 20. Health food (Fr.12–17) served in a quiet atmosphere.

Schober Napfgasse 4. Don't leave Zürich without sampling a mug of hot chocolate here.

Zähringer Zähringerplatz 11. Co-operative-run café/bar with an alternative-minded clientele and cheap food.

Bars

Babalu Schmidgasse 6. Tiny, chic DJ-bar.

James Joyce Pelikanstr. 8. Original nineteenth-century interior, transported piece by piece from Dublin. Closed Sat from 7pm & all Sun.

Kaufleuten Pelikanstr. 18. Modish venue for mixing with designers, musicians and the idle rich.

Nelson Beatengasse 11. Massive, noisy pub near the station; cheap beer & late opening.

Noble Dubliner Talacker 43/Talstr. 82. Good beer, good service and a talkative atmosphere.

Oliver Twist Rindermarkt 6. Small English pub on an Old Town lane.

Pigalle Marktgasse 14. Legendary little bar filled with the elegantly wasted.

Rheinfelder Bierhalle Niederdorfstr. 76. Best of the hearty beerhalls. Closed Sun.

Wüste Oberdorfstr. 7. Mellow, comfortable den near the Grossmünster.

Clubs and music venues

Abart Manessestr. 170. Regular choice of local and foreign bands.

Casa Bar Münstergasse 20. Live jazz nightly in the Old Town.

Dynamo Wasserwerkstr. 21. Alternative, punkish bands and dance nights.

Labyrinth Pfingstweidstr. 70. Hard house at this mixed gay/straight venue.

Oxa Andreasstr. 70. Techno and house; famed after-hours parties (Sun 5am–noon).

Rote Fabrik Seestr. 395. Alternative bands, big-name DJs, cheap food and a great riverside bar.

Toni Molkerei Förrlibuckstr. 109. Eclectic dance club in a vast industrial space.

X-tra Limmatstr. 118. Hugely popular multipurpose venue.

Listings

Bike rental Free (photo-ID & Fr.20 deposit) from "Velogate", next to platform 18 of the station (daily 7.30am–9.30pm).

Consulates Ireland, Claridenstrasse 25 ☎01 289 25 15; UK, Minervastrasse 117 ☎01 383 65 60; USA, Dufourstrasse 101 ☎01 422 25 66.

Embassies in Bern.

Hospital Permanence Medical Centre, Bahnhofplatz 15 ☎01 215 44 44.

Laundry Mühlegasse 11, Niederdorf.

Pharmacy Bellevue, Theaterstrasse 14 (24hr).

Post office Kasernenstrasse, beside the station.

The Rhine falls

A great fine-weather excursion from Zürich is the half-day trip north to the **Rhine falls** (⊕www.rhinefalls.com), Europe's largest waterfalls, which tumble 3km west of **SCHAFFHAUSEN**. They are truly magnificent, not so much for their height (a mere 23m) as for their impressive breadth (150m) and the sheer drama of the place, with spray rising in a cloud of rainbows above the forested banks. The turreted castle **Schloss Laufen** on the south bank completes the spectacle. Be here on August 1, Switzerland's national day, for a famous fireworks display. Damp steps lead down from the castle souvenir shop to platforms at the water's edge (Fr.1), where the falls roar inches from your nose. In summer, the best views are from daredevil boats, which scurry about in the spray (Fr.5–7). Take a **train** from Zürich either to Winterthur, from where hourly trains serve Schloss Laufen's own little station (April–Oct only), or to Schaffhausen, from where you can walk (20min) or take bus #1 or #6 to Neuhausen Zentrum, 5min from the falls.

SWITZERLAND | Zürich

29

Lake Geneva

French-speaking Switzerland, or Suisse Romande, occupies the western third of the country, comprising the shores of **Lake Geneva** (Lac Léman in French; ⓦ www.lake-geneva-region.ch) and the hills and lakes leading north almost to Basel. The ambience here is thoroughly Gallic: historical animosity between Geneva and France has nowadays given way to a yearning on the part of most francophone Swiss to abandon their bumpkin compatriots in the east and embrace the EU. **Geneva**, at the southwestern tip of the lake, was once a haven for free-thinkers from all over Europe; now it's a city of diplomats and big business. Halfway around the lake, **Lausanne** is full of young people, a cultured, energetic town acclaimed as the skateboarding capital of Europe. Further east, the shore features vineyards and opulent villas – **Montreux** is particularly chic – and the stunning medieval **Château de Chillon**, which drew Byron and the Romantic poets. Mont Blanc, western Europe's highest mountain (4807m), is visible from Geneva city centre, while Montreux and neighbouring **Vevey** have breathtaking views across the water to the French Alps. On a sunny day, the train ride around the beautiful northern shore is memorably scenic, but the lake's excellent **boat** service (IR no discount; ER & SP free; ⓦ www.cgn.ch) helps bring home the full grandeur of the setting.

Geneva (Genève)

The Puritanism of **GENEVA** (Genève) is inextricably linked with the city's struggle for independence. Long ruled by the dukes of Savoy, sixteenth-century Genevans saw the Reformation as a useful aid in their struggle to rid themselves of Savoyard influence. By the time the city's independence was won in 1602, its religious zeal had painted it as the "Protestant Rome". Geneva remained outside the Swiss Confederation until 1815 (the Catholic cantons opposed its entry), and acquired a reputation for joylessness which it still struggles to shake off. Today, it's a working city, sharply focused on its prominent role in international diplomacy and big business. It's all very pretty, but – unlike its neighbour, Lausanne – you need time to penetrate the facade of money and power.

Arrival, information and accommodation

The main **train station**, Gare de Cornavin, lies at the head of Rue du Mont-Blanc in the city centre. Expresses from Paris, Lyon and Grenoble arrive in a separate French section (passport control), while local French trains from Annecy/Chamonix terminate at Gare des Eaux-Vives on the east side of town (tram #12 or #16 into the centre). From the **airport**, 5km northwest, trains and bus #10 run into the city. The international **bus station** (Gare Routière) is on Place Dorcière in the centre. **Boats** dock at several central quays. The **tourist office** is in the main post office at 18 Rue du Mont-Blanc (Mon–Sat 9am–6pm; July & Aug also Sun 9am–6pm; ☎022 909 70 00, ⓦ www.genevatourism.ch), and there's also a desk within the municipality's information office, on the Pont de la Machine (Mon noon–6pm, Tues–Fri 9am–6pm, Sat 10am–5pm; ☎022 311 99 70, ⓦ www.ville-ge.ch). Both have stacks of material in English, including the useful *Young People* brochure listing budget hotels and ideas. During the summer, a bus parked at the station end of Rue du Mont-Blanc houses the "CAR" info-centre (mid-June to early Sept daily 9am–11pm; ☎022 731 46 47).

Hostels

Auberge de Jeunesse (HI) 30 Rue Rothschild ☎022 732 62 60, ⓦ www.youthhostel.ch & ⓦ www.yh-geneva.ch. Big, bustling, well-maintained 330-bed hostel in a central location, with cheap meals. Bus #1 to Wilson. Fr.25.

Cité Universitaire 46 Av Miremont ☎022 839 22 22, ⓦ www.unige.ch/cite-uni. Huge place 3km south (bus #3), with dorm beds for Fr.20 in July & Aug (dorms Sept–June groups only). Plenty of cut-price singles, doubles and studios year-round. Breakfast extra. ❸

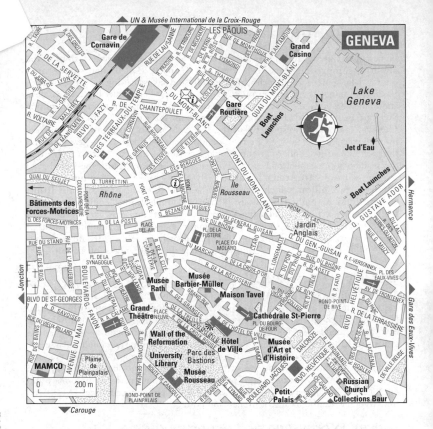

Map labels:

UN & Musée International de la Croix-Rouge

LES PÂQUIS

GENEVA

Gare de Cornavin

Grand Casino

Lake Geneva

Gare Routière

N

Boat Launches

Jet d'Eau

Boat Launches

Hermance

Rhône

Bâtiments des Forces-Motrices

Île Rousseau

Jardin Anglais

Gustave Ador

Gare des Eaux-Vives

Jonction

Musée Rath

Musée Barbier-Müller

Maison Tavel

Grand-Théâtre

Cathédrale St-Pierre

Wall of the Reformation

Hôtel de Ville

Musée d'Art et d'Histoire

MAMCO

Plaine de Plainpalais

University Library

Parc des Bastions

Musée Rousseau

Russian Church

Petit-Palais

Collections Baur

0   200 m

Carouge

SWITZERLAND | Lake Geneva

29

928

City Hostel (SB) 2 Rue Ferrier ☎022 901 15 00, ⓦwww.cityhostel.ch. Excellent backpacker place near the HI hostel, with plenty of services (including laundry), plus dorms and rooms. Bus #4 to Prieuré. Dorms Fr.24. Rooms ❸

Home St-Pierre 4 Cour St-Pierre ☎022 310 37 07, ⓦwww.homestpierre.ch. In the heart of the Old Town next to the cathedral, with two dorms (one of them women-only) plus single and double rooms (all women-only); breakfast extra. Dorms Fr.23. Rooms ❸

Hotels

At Home 16 Rue de Fribourg ☎022 906 19 00, ⓦwww.kis.ch/at-home. Clean, modern Pâquis-district rooms, with discounts for students, though a bit small and soulless. ❺

De la Cloche 6 Rue de la Cloche ☎022 732 94 81, ⓦwww.tbh-ge.ch/cloche. Eight charcterful, high-ceilinged rooms in a quiet area of the Pâquis 50m from the lake. Regularly full. ❹

Luserna 12 Av de Luserna ☎022 345 45 45, ⓦwww.hotel-luserna.ch. Quiet and friendly, family-run place north of the centre (ask for the attic), with great breakfasts. Bus #3, #9 or #10 to Servette, then walk via Avenue Wendt. ❹

Campsite

Pointe-à-la-Bise ☎022 752 12 96, ⓦwww.tcs.ch. 7km northeast in Vésanaz; bus #E. April–Oct.

The City

Orientation centres on the Rhône, which flows from the lake west into France. The **Rive Gauche**, on the south bank, takes in a grid of waterfront streets which comprise the main shopping and business districts and the adjacent high ground of the Old Town. Further south lies **Carouge**, characterized by artisans' shops, picturesque Italianate architecture and a lively, independent spirit. Behind the grand hotels lining the northern **Rive Droite** waterfront is the main station and the cosmopolitan (and sometimes sleazy) Les Pâquis district, filled with cheap restaurants. Further north are the offices of the dozens of international organizations headquartered in Geneva, including the UN.

On the Rive Gauche, beyond the ornamental flowerbeds of the **Jardin Anglais**, erupts the roaring 140-metre-high plume of Geneva's trademark **Jet d'Eau**. Nearby is the main thoroughfare of the Old Town, the cobbled, steeply ascending **Grande Rue**. Here, among the secondhand bookshops and galleries, you'll find the atmospheric seventeenth-century **Hôtel de Ville** and the arcaded **armoury**, backed by a lovely terrace with the longest wooden bench in the world (126m). A block away is the huge late-Romanesque **Cathédrale St-Pierre** (Mon–Sat 9/10am–5/7pm, Sun 11am–5/7pm), with an incongruous eighteenth-century portal and a plain, soaring interior. The frescoes of the internal Chapelle des Macchabées, with their intricate floral patterns and lute-strumming angels, are modern versions of the faded fifteenth-century originals now in Geneva's main museum. Round the corner is the hub of the Old Town, **Place du Bourg-de-Four**, a picturesque split-level square perched on the hillside and ringed by cafés. Alleys wind down from here to the university park and its austere **Wall of the Reformation** (1909–17) alongside busy Place Neuve. A stroll east of the Old Town is the gigantic **Musée d'Art et d'Histoire**, 2 Rue Charles Galland (Tues–Sun 10am–5pm; free; ®mah.ville-ge.ch). Upstairs are three stunning sculptures – a graceful *Venus and Adonis* by Canova and two powerful pieces by Rodin. The fine-art collection is crowned by Konrad Witz's famous altarpiece, made for the cathedral in 1444, showing Christ and the fishermen transposed onto Lake Geneva. Other highlights are by local artist Félix Vallotton; Cézanne, Renoir and Modigliani; and some striking blue Swiss landscapes by Bern-born Symbolist Ferdinand Hodler. The basement holds the massive archeological collection, including Egyptian mummies and Greek and Roman statuary. Nearby are the **Collections Baur**, 8 Rue Munier-Romilly (Tues–Sun 2–6pm; Fr.5), the country's premier collection of East Asian art, featuring luminescent yellow Yongzhang ceramics and spectacular porcelain and jade. Make time also for **MAMCO**, a top-quality museum of modern and contemporary art housed in an old factory west of the Old Town at 10 Rue des Vieux-Grenadiers (Tues–Sun noon–6pm; Fr.8).

About 1km north of the station, opposite the UN complex on Avenue de la Paix, is the thought-provoking **Musée International de la Croix-Rouge** (Mon & Wed–Sun 10am–5pm; Fr.10; ®www.micr.ch; bus #8 or #F to Appia), which documents the origins, growth and achievements of the Red Cross without resorting to self-congratulation. Carefully chosen audiovisual material combines with quietly dramatic exhibits – such as the 34 footprints in a tiny cell-space where a delegate found 17 people crammed together – to leave a powerful impression.

Twenty minutes south of the centre by tram #12 or #13 lies the late-Baroque suburb of **Carouge**, built by the king of Sardinia in the eighteenth century as a separate town. Its low Italianate houses and leafy streets are now largely occupied by fashion designers and small galleries, and the area's reputation as an outpost of tolerance and hedonism beyond Geneva's jurisdiction lives on in its numerous cafés and music bars. Carouge hosts a colourful **market** (Wed & Sat); the flea market at Plainpalais, near Geneva's Old Town, is also worth a browse (same days).

Eating and drinking

Cafés and bars

Bains des Pâquis 30 Quai du Mont-Blanc. Popular café-bar attached to the lakefront swimming area. Summer only.

Bar du Nord 66 Rue Ancienne, Carouge. Dark, chic, designer bar.

La Bretelle 15 Rue des Etuves. Kitsch, campy tavern, with live accordion and/or drag cabaret Thurs–Sat.

Café de l'Usine In L'Usine squat, Place des Volontaires. Graffitied upstairs café-bar, serving meals for around Fr.10. Closed Sun & Mon.

Cave à Bière 19 Rue Ancienne, Carouge. Bar with almost 400 beers from around the world. Closed

Sun & Mon.
Le Chat Noir 13 Rue Vautier, Carouge ⊛ www.chatnoir.ch. Bar and cellar venue with live music and DJ-ing. Nightly until 4am.
Le 2e (Deuxième) Bureau 9 Rue du Stand. Sleek bar thumping with deep beats.
Mr Pickwick 80 Rue de Lausanne. Homely English pub with TV football.

Restaurants

Al-Amir 12 Rue des Alpes. Excellent Lebanese kebabs and falafel from Fr.8.
Au Petit Chalet 6 Rue Chaponnière. Unpretentious place for Swiss fondues and rösti. Closed Mon.

Café Zara 25 Rue de Lausanne. Simple little Eritrean/Ethiopian café-restaurant near the station.
Jeck's Place 14 Rue de Neuchâtel. Affordable Thai food, with lunches from Fr.15. Closed Sat lunch.
Manora 4 Rue de Cornavin. Excellent self-service nosh, with plentiful veggie selections and meals from Fr.12.
Le Pain Quotidien 21 Boulevard Helvétique. No-nonsense café with superb breakfasts (Fr.7 or Fr.12) and lavish weekend brunches (Fr.28). Closed Tues eve.
Teranga 38bis Rue de Zurich. Tiny backstreet Senegalese place, with good service and great food. Closed Sat lunch & Sun.

Listings

Consulates Australia, 2 Chemin des Fins ☎ 022 799 91 00; Canada, 5 Ave de l'Ariana ☎ 022 919 92 00; New Zealand, 2 Chemin des Fins ☎ 022 929 03 50; UK, 37 Rue de Vermont ☎ 022 918 24 00; USA, 7 Rue Versonnex ☎ 022 840 51 60.

Embassies are in Bern.
Hospital Hôpital Cantonal, 24 Rue Micheli-du-Crest ☎ 022 372 3311.
Laundry Lavseul, 29 Rue de Monthoux.
Post office 18 Rue du Mont-Blanc.

Lausanne

Geneva's neighbour **LAUSANNE** is interesting, attractive, worldly and well aware of how to have a good time – in short, Switzerland's sexiest city. It's tiered above the lake on a succession of south-facing terraces, with the Old Town at the top, the train station and commercial districts in the middle, and the one-time fishing village of **Ouchy**, now prime territory for waterfront café-lounging and strolling, at the bottom. The hills are incredibly steep; copy the locals and catch a bus into the Joret forests above the city, and then blade or **skateboard** your way down to Ouchy: aficionados have been clocked doing 90kph through the streets. Switzerland's biggest university aids the youthful spirit, and a wealth of international student programmes feeds an unusually diverse, multi-ethnic makeup.

To get to the central **Place St-François** from the train station, either walk up the steep Rue du Petit-Chêne, or take the metro to Flon; from the metro platforms, lifts shuttle you up to the level of the giant **Grand Pont**, between Place Bel-Air on the left and St François on the right. Glitzy **Rue de Bourg** entices shoppers uphill from St François; beside it, Rue St-François drops down into the valley and up the other side to the cobbled **Place de la Palud**, an ancient, fountained square flanked by the arcades of the Renaissance town hall. From here the medieval **Escaliers du Marché** lead up to the **Cathedral** (daily 8am–7pm), a fine Romanesque-Gothic jumble, its clean lines only peripherally adorned with memorials and fifteenth-century frescoes. Opposite, in the former bishop's palace, is the **Musée Historique** (Tues–Thurs 11am–6pm, Fri–Sun 11am–5pm; Fr.4), which houses a model of old Lausanne – invaluable for grasping the city's confusing topography. Lausanne suffered from many medieval fires, and is the last city in Europe to keep alive the tradition of the nightwatch: every night, on the hour (10pm–2am), a sonorous-voiced civil servant calls out from the cathedral tower "*C'est le guet; il a sonné l'heure*" ("This is the nightwatch; the hour has struck"), assuring the lovers and assorted drunks below that all is well. West of the cathedral hill is **Place de la Riponne**, an arid expanse of concrete dominated by the splendidly ostentatious Palais de Rumine, housing the university library and various museums. Save your francs for the outstanding **Collection de l'Art Brut**, 11 Ave des Bergières (Tues–Sun 11am–6pm; Fr.6; ⊛ www.artbrut.ch), ten minutes' walk northwest of Riponne on Ave Vinet, or bus #2 or #3 to Jomini. This unique gallery is devoted to "outsider art", the creative output of ordinary people with no artistic training at all – often loners, psychotics or the criminally insane – who for some reason suddenly began making their own art. It's utterly absorbing. In a park on the Ouchy waterfront sits Lausanne's flagship **Olympic Museum** (daily 9am–6pm, Thurs until 8pm; Oct–April closed Mon; Fr.14), a vacuous and expensive place that trumpets the Olympic ideal by means of archive footage, stirring music and Cathy Freeman's old running shoes. Bypass it for the **Musée de l'Elysée**, an excellent museum of photography in the same park (daily 11am–6pm; Fr.8; free on 1st Sat of month).

Practicalities

Lausanne has two **tourist offices**, one in the train station (daily 9am–7pm; ☏021 613 73 73, ⓦwww.lausanne-tourisme.ch), and the other beside Ouchy metro station (daily 9am–8pm; Oct–March closes 6pm). Both have stacks of information on the whole lake region; their best buy is the **Lausanne Card** (2 days; Fr.15), which gives free transport as well as city discounts. Ouchy's waterfront hosts regular free **music** events all summer, and people come down here to do a spot of café sunbathing or blade-cruising (rent blades or skates from beside Ouchy metro). Lausanne's big party is the **Festival de la Cité** in early July (ⓦwww.lausanne.ch), featuring music, dance, drama and mime on several open-air stages in the old town. Also check out July's big-name **Paleo Rock Festival** in nearby Nyon (ⓦwww.paleo.ch).

Accommodation

Pension Bienvenue 2 Rue du Simplon ☏021 616 29 86, ⓦwww.pension-bienvenue.ch. Respectable women-only guesthouse behind the station. ❹

Jeunotel (HI) 36 Chemin du Bois-de-Vaux ☏021 626 02 22, ⓦwww.youthhostel.ch. Huge place beside *Vidy* campsite with four-bed dorms and rooms. Dorms Fr.27. Rooms ❹

Lausanne Guest House (SB) 4 Epinettes ☏021 601 80 00, ⓦwww.lausanne-guesthouse.ch. Quality no-smoking hostel with lake views, four-bedded dorms and rooms. Closed Jan & Feb. Dorms Fr.34. Rooms ❹

Du Marché 42 Rue Pré-du-Marché ☏021 647 99 00, ⓦwww.hotel-du-marche.com. Plain and comfortable small hotel near Riponne. ❹

Old Inn 11 Av de la Gare ☏021 323 62 21, ⓔold _inn@bluewin.ch. Quiet, spartan little pension. ❹

Vidy ☏021 622 50 00, ⓦwww.campinglausannevidy.ch. Bus #1 to Maladière and walk 5min to this campsite.

Restaurants and cafés

Au Couscous 2 Rue Enning. Couscous and tajine (from Fr.22), mezze (Fr.25), plus veggie and macrobiotic dishes. Closed Sat & Sun lunchtimes.

Bleu Lézard 10 Rue Enning. Fashionable, lively café-bar on a busy corner.

La Bossette 4 Pl du Nord. Friendly local café on a patch of green beneath the château, serving speciality beers plus excellent food.

Café de l'Évêché 4 Rue Curtat. Haunt of talkative students and local old-timers, just below the cathedral.

Laxmi 5 Escaliers du Marché. Indian/veggie. All-you-can-eat lunches are Fr.15, or Fr.11 for veggies, or Fr.10 for cold dishes; evening *menus* cost no more. Student discount. Closed Mon lunch & Sun.

Ma Jong 3 Escaliers du Grand-Pont. Just down from *Manora*, with freshly wok-fried meals for Fr.14. Sushi too. Closed Sun.

Manora 17 Pl St-François. Self-service place with a wide range of cheap food.

Café Romand Pl St-François (under *Pizza Hut*). Bustling, heartwarming place with cosy alcoves for beer, coffee or heavy Swiss fare.

Bars and nightlife

Au Château 1 Pl du Tunnel. Bar with funky music and flavourful home-brewed beers.

D! Pl Centrale. Happening basement club playing house and jungle. Closed Mon–Wed.

Lecaféthéâtre 10 Rue de Genève. Café/bar with live entertainment most nights. Closed Sun & Mon.

Le Loft 1 Escaliers Bel-Air. Techno club with free entry on Fri.

MAD (Moulin à Danse) 23 Rue de Genève. Cutting-edge dance club with adjoining theatre, art galleries and alternative-style café.

VO Le Jazz Café 11 Pl du Tunnel. Café/bar and live venue with regular DJ nights.

Vevey, Montreux and Chillon

East of Lausanne, trains meander through steep vineyards to **VEVEY**, a small market town looking over to the French Alps. It holds a Street Artists' Festival in late

August, jugglers, acrobats and mime artists performing on the lakeside. Vevey's charm centres on the huge lakeside **Grande Place**, a few minutes' walk southeast of the station – known also as Place du Marché and packed with market stalls (Tues & Sat) – and the narrow streets which lead off into the old town to the east. Vevey's excellent fine-art museum, **Musée Jenisch** on Rue de la Gare (Tues–Sun 11am–5.30pm; Fr.12), has Europe's largest collection of Rembrandt lithographs, as well as graphic works by Dürer, Corot, Le Corbusier and others. East of Place du Marché is a statue of Charlie Chaplin, "The Tramp", who moved to Vevey from the US in the 1950s to escape McCarthyism. To head on to Montreux and Chillon, ditch the train in favour of bus #1, which plies the coast road every 10min. If you have time, walk the floral lakeside path. **MONTREUX**, 6km east of Vevey, is a snooty place, full of money and not particularly exciting, but it enjoys spectacular views of the Dents-du-Midi peaks opposite and hosts a colourful Friday market. The whole town is protected from chill northerly winds by a wall of mountains and so basks in its own microclimate, nurturing lakeside palm trees and exotic flowers. The zigzagging streets of the old quarter above the train station provide more interest than the Grand-Rue below (head 100m left out of the station and cut down the stairs between buildings), although you should make time for the statue of one-time resident **Freddie Mercury** silently serenading the swans on the lakefront. The star-studded **Montreux Jazz Festival** (ⓦwww.montreuxjazz.com), packs the town out in early July; check online for tickets (Fr.40–120) or just join the street parties and free entertainment on the lake.

The climax of a journey around Lake Geneva is the stunning thirteenth-century **Château de Chillon** (daily 9/10am–5/6pm; Fr.7; ⓦwww.chillon.ch), one of the best-preserved medieval castles in Europe. Whether you opt for the 45-minute shoreline walk east from Montreux, or bus #1 from Vevey or Montreux, or a local train, a bike, or, best of all, a lake steamer, your first glimpse of the castle is unforgettable – an elegant, turreted pile jutting out into the water, framed by trees and craggy mountains. At the gate you'll get a follow-the-numbers pamphlet, which starts you off in the dungeons where the dukes of Savoy imprisoned François Bonivard, a Genevan priest, from 1530 to 1536 (he was manacled to the fifth pillar along); Lord Byron, after a sailing trip here with Shelley in 1816, was so affected by the story that he spent the next day in his Ouchy hotel room writing his poem *The Prisoner of Chillon*. Byron's signature, scratched on the dungeon's third pillar, probably isn't genuine. As you look out onto the lake from the castle, it's sobering to realize how sheer the rock is: just below the castle walls yawns 300m of cold water, enough to swallow the Eiffel Tower without a trace. Upstairs you'll find more wonders: gloriously grand knights' halls, secret twisting passages between lavish bedchambers, Gothic windows with dreamy views and a frescoed chapel.

The **tourist offices** of Vevey and Montreux have the same information: Vevey's is in the pillared Grenette building on Grande-Place (June–Sept Mon–Fri 9am–6pm, Sat 9am–4pm; rest of year Mon–Fri 8.30am–12.30pm & 1.30–6pm, Sat 8.30am–noon; ☎0848 868 484, ⓦwww.montreux-vevey.com); Montreux's is beside the ferry landing-stage (June–Sept daily 9.30am–6pm; Oct–May Mon–Fri 9am–12.30pm & 1.30–6pm). Their brochure *On The Trail of Hemingway* pinpoints local sites with famous-name associations. The pristine *Riviera Lodge* SB **hostel**, 5 Grande-Place in Vevey (☎021 923 80 40, ⓦwww.rivieralodge.ch; dorms Fr.26; ❹) is better-value than the HI hostel at 8 Passage de l'Auberge, beside Territet station 1500m east of Montreux (☎021 963 49 34, ⓦwww.youthhostel.ch; dorms Fr.30; ❹). Of the **hotels**, go for *Les Négociants*, 27 Rue du Conseil in Vevey (☎021 922 70 11, ⓦwww.hotelnegociants.ch; ❺), or *Elite*, 25 Ave du Casino in Montreux (☎021 966 03 03; ❽). Lakeside *La Pichette* **campsite** (☎021 921 09 97) is 2km west of Vevey. Vevey has a self-service *Manora* **restaurant** in the St Antoine mall outside the station, and plenty of pavement cafés in the centre. The food at *Hôtel des Négociants* is good. Montreux has plenty of eateries outside the station on Ave des Alpes, including some with lakeview terraces.

Into the mountains: the Golden Pass line

Montreux's station is the terminus of two narrow-gauge lines operated by MOB (ⓦwww.mob.ch) that offer spectacular viewpoints, excellent hill walking and panoramic rides towards the high Alps. The smaller line coils up to the rugged **Rochers-de-Naye** summit at 2045m (ER not valid, IR half-price), with hiking trails and incredible views over the lake. Other trains climb through the hills on the memorable **Golden Pass** route, which is well worth incorporating into an east-ward journey (ER, IR & SP free; optional reservations in panoramic carriages Fr.4–8; ⓦwww.goldenpass.ch); they switchback up to a series of tunnels beneath the prominent Dent de Jaman peak before meandering on a single track through beautiful countryside to the exclusive Alpine resort of **Gstaad**, and then on to **Zweisimmen**, from where connections continue to Spiez, Bern, Interlaken and Luzern.

The Swiss heartland

The Mittelland – the populated countryside between Lake Geneva and Zürich, flanked by the Jura range to the north and the high Alps to the south – is a region of gentle hills, lakes and some high peaks, though ones by no means as grandiose as the heights further south. There's a wealth of cultural and historical interest in the German-speaking cities of **Basel**, **Luzern** and the federal capital, **Bern**. Wherever you base yourself, the mountains are never more than a couple of hours away by train.

Basel (Bâle)

With both a gigantic river-port on the Rhine – Switzerland's only outlet to the sea – and the research HQs of several pharmaceutical multinationals, **BASEL** (Bâle in French) nurtures a reputation as Switzerland's wealthiest city. Its medieval past is endowed with some of the greatest minds of European history, including Erasmus, Zwingli, and later Nietzsche and Hesse, and its long-standing patronage of the arts has resulted in some first-rate museums and galleries. However, it's almost as if the citizens lost the plot when it came to defining their city for today. You might expect Basel, situated exactly where Switzerland, Germany and France touch noses, to hum with pan-European energy, but the close proximity of foreign languages and cultures has introverted the city rather than energized it: it's a curiously measured place, where equilibrium is everything. Even the city's massive February **carnival** (ⓦwww.fasnacht.ch) is a rigorously organized set-piece; the famous masked parades and musical festivities begin at 4am on the Monday after Mardi Gras and last for three full days.

The River **Rhine** describes a right-angled curve through the centre of Basel, flowing from east to north. On the south/west bank (1km north of the main station) is the historic Old Town, which is centred on the photogenic main square **Barfüsserplatz**, ringed by higgledy-piggledy medieval buildings. The city's cultural pre-eminence in the fifteenth and sixteenth centuries is amply demonstrated in the splendid Barfüsserkirche, now home to the **Historisches Museum** (Mon & Wed–Sun 10am–5pm; Fr.7); don't miss the sumptuous medieval tapestries, hidden behind protective blinds. Shop-lined Gerbergasse and Freiestrasse run north from the square to Marktplatz, dominated by the elaborate scarlet facade of the **Rathaus**, the central section of which is sixteenth-century. Just beyond Marktplatz is **Schifflände**, site of the main tourist office and from where **boats** depart regularly for trips along the Rhine. Alongside is the **Mittlere Brücke**, which for many centuries was the only bridge across the Rhine between its source and the sea. The working-class quarter across the river, known as Kleinbasel, was traditionally the object of scorn for the cosmopolitan merchants of the city centre: their **Lällekönig** bust still faces down the bridge, sticking out its tongue at the Kleinbaslers. Sixteenth-century lanes lead up behind Barfüsserplatz to Basel's cathedral, the impressive

Münster (Mon–Sat 10/11am–4/5pm, Sun 1/2–4/5pm). Medieval stone carving above the main portal shows the cathedral's founder, Emperor Heinrich II, holding a model of the church; beside him is a Foolish Virgin. Inside, in the north aisle, is the tomb of the Renaissance humanist Erasmus, who lived in Basel from 1521 until his death in 1536. From Barfüsserplatz, Steinenberg climbs east past a sputtering Jean Tinguely fountain and the contemporary-art **Kunsthalle** (Tues–Sun 11am–5pm, Wed until 8.30pm; Fr.9); at the top of the hill, St Alban-Graben heads northeast to the river. The venerable **Antikenmuseum** is at no. 5 (Tues–Sun 10am–5pm; Fr.7), with superb Greek and Etruscan pottery and Egyptian antiquities. Opposite at no. 16 is the absorbing **Kunstmuseum** (Tues–Sun 10am–5pm; Fr.10, includes entry to Museum für Gegenwartskunst; free on 1st Sun of month); a dazzling array of twentieth-century art is surpassed by a medieval collection featuring roomfuls of works by the prolific Holbein family. Down to the river, then right, is the **Museum für Gegenwartskunst** (Tues–Sun 11am–5pm; joint admission with Kunstmuseum), with installations by Frank Stella and Joseph Beuys sharing space with video art. A stroll away, at St Alban-Tal 37, is the restored **Basler Papiermühle** (Papermill), housing the wonderful Museum of Paper, Writing and Printing (Tues–Sun 2–5pm; Fr.9), where you can make your own paper, from pulp to final product.

A walk away on the north bank, in Solitude Park, is the beautifully designed **Museum Jean Tinguely** (Wed–Sun 11am–7pm; Fr.7; ⊛www.tinguely.ch), dedicated to one of Switzerland's best-loved artists. Tinguely used scrap metal, plastic and bits of everyday junk to create room-sized Monty-Pythonesque machines that – with the touch of a foot-button – judder into life, squeaking, clanking and scraping in a parody of the slickness of our performance-driven world. Basel's finest gallery is **Fondation Beyeler** (daily 10am–6pm, Wed until 8pm; Fr.12; tram #6 to Riehen Dorf; ⊛www.beyeler.com), sympathetically designed by Renzo Piano, architect of Paris's Pompidou Centre. A small but exceptionally high-quality collection features some of the best works by Picasso, Giacometti, Rothko, Rodin, Bacon, Miró and others. Sink into a huge white sofa opposite a giant Monet, to indulge in dreamy contemplation both of the waterlilies in front of you and the watery gardens outside.

Practicalities

Basel has two **train stations** straddling three countries. Basel SBB is the main one, most of it in Switzerland, although the section entitled Bâle SNCF is in French territory, receiving trains from Paris and Strasbourg (passport control); trams #8 and #11 shuttle to Barfüsserplatz. Some trains from Germany terminate at Basel Badischer Bahnhof (Basel Bad. for short), in a German enclave on the north side of the river (passport control); tram #6 runs to Barfüsserplatz. The main **tourist office** is in the city centre on Barfüsserplatz (Mon–Fri 8.30am–6.30pm, Sat & Sun 10am–4.15pm; ☏061 268 68 68, ⊛www.baseltourismus.ch), with a branch office inside the main SBB train station (June–Sept Mon–Fri 8.30am–7pm, Sat 8.30am–12.30pm & 1.30–6pm, Sun 10am–2pm; Oct–May Mon–Fri 8.30am–6pm, Sat 8.30am–noon). Best buy is the **Basel Card** (Fr.25/33/45 for 24/48/72 hours), which covers free museum entry, free transport, discounts at restaurants, bars and clubs, and more – but if you stay overnight you're automatically entitled to a **Mobility Card**, giving free city transport; the card is available from your hotel at check-in. Booking a room through the tourist office costs Fr.10; Basel thrives on conference business, so accommodation prices drop at weekends.

Accommodation

Au Violon Im Lohnhof 4 ☏061 269 87 11, ⊛www.au-violon.com. Comfortable, stylish hotel above a quiet Old Town courtyard. **6**

Basel Backpack Dornacherstr. 192 ☏061 333 00 37, ⊛www.baselbackpack.ch. Friendly hostel just behind the station. Dorms Fr.29. Rooms **4**

Hecht am Rhein Rheingasse 8 ☏061 691 22 20. Friendly, unfussy hotel with pricier riverside rooms. **5**

Jugendherberge (HI) St Alban-Kirchrain 10 ☏061 272 05 72, ⊛www.youthhostel.ch. Quiet, well-run hostel on the river. Dorms Fr.30. Rooms **4**

Cafés and restaurants

Manora Greifengasse. Good self-service meals.

Mr Wong Steinenvorstadt 3. Popular Asian fast-food joint just off Barfüsserplatz.

Pfalz Münsterberg 11. Fresh juices and a salad buffet. Closed Sat & Sun.

Parterre Klybeckstr. 1. Friendly place serving excellent food. Closed Sun.

Zum Isaak Münsterplatz 16. Tranquil tea-drinkers' café. Serves snacks and full meals. Closed Mon.

Zum Roten Engel Andreasplatz. Pleasant vegetarian café with snacks, full meals and fresh juices.

Bars, clubs and music venues

Atlantis Klosterberg 10. Club-bar with regular music and dance.

Bird's Eye Kohlenberg 20. Lively jazz club.

Fischerstube Rheingasse 45. Atmospheric backstreet beerhall with a hearty clientele.

Hirscheneck Lindenberg 23. Co-op owned budget café/bar/restaurant. Loud music and generous portions of simple food.

Kaserne Klybeckstr. 1. Alternative hangout offering veggie food. Mutates on Tues into Basel's premier gay/lesbian meeting-point.

Luzern (Lucerne)

An hour south of Basel and Zürich is beautiful **LUZERN** (Lucerne), offering captivating mountain views, lake cruises and a picturesque medieval quarter. The giant Mount Pilatus rears up behind the town, which is split by the River Reuss, flowing rapidly out of the northwestern end of the oddly shaped **Vierwaldstättersee** ("Lake of the Four Forest Cantons" or plain Lake Luzern). In the Middle Ages, the communities dotted around the lake guarded the approaches to the Gotthard Pass, the main route between northern and southern Europe. When Habsburg overlords tried to encroach on their privileges, the communities formed an alliance at the lakeside **Rütli Meadow** (in 1291), which was to prove the beginning of the Swiss Confederation. Luzern was drawn into the bond shortly after. About this time in Altdorf, just around the lake, **William Tell** shot the apple from his son's head; the Tell legend lies at the core of Swiss national identity, and the semi-mystical Vierwaldstättersee is the spiritual as well as the geographical centre of the country. But Luzern is no museum piece; the city's large population of young people love their café culture, and at midnight on a weekend night, the main Pilatusstrasse boulevard has the buzz of any European capital.

In 1993, fire almost destroyed the fourteenth-century **Kapellbrücke**, a covered wooden bridge angled around the squat mid-river **Wasserturm**; it was reconstructed with facsimiles of the triangular paintings fixed to its roof-beams (although a few charred originals remain) – check out no. 31's William Tell. The **Spreuerbrücke** downstream is also worth a look for its macabre "Dance of Death" paintings. The north bank is home to a compact cluster of medieval houses, with Mühlenplatz, Weinmarkt, Hirschenplatz and Kornmarkt forming an ensemble of cobbled, fountained squares ringed by colourful facades. Next to the Renaissance town hall on Kornmarkt is the small **Picasso Museum** (daily 10/11am–4/6pm; Fr.6), Furrengasse 21, displaying photographs of the artist's later years. Northeast of the Old Town is Löwenplatz, dominated by a glass building housing the diverting **Bourbaki Panorama** (daily 9am–6pm; Fr.7), a 110m-by-10m circular mural depicting a scene in the 1870–71 Franco-Prussian War. Just off the square is the moving **Löwendenkmal**, a dying lion hewn out of a cliff-face to commemorate 700 Swiss mercenaries killed by French revolutionaries in 1792. From the station, busy Pilatusstrasse storms southwest away from the river. About 100m along, a stroll south of the Kapellbrücke, is the absorbing **Sammlung Rosengart** gallery (daily 10/11am–4/6pm; Fr.14) with a superb collection of twentieth-century art. The ground floor is devoted to Picasso, the basement to Paul Klee, and the upper floor to Chagall, Monet, Renoir and others. A big reason to visit Luzern is the **Verkehrshaus**, 2km east at Lidostrasse 5 (daily 9/10am–5/6pm; Fr.21; www.verkehrshaus.org); if you're not taking the boat, hop on bus #6 or #8, or else it's a pleasant lakeside stroll. The complex, inadequately translated as "Transport Museum", is a vast area that could keep you amused all day. It's packed with original space capsules, railway locomotives (including a walk-through account of the digging of the Gotthard tunnel, dramatized with slides and soundtrack), aeroplanes, cable cars and more. An incongruous highlight is an excellent museum housing the whimsical and attractive works of the little-known Swiss artist **Hans Erni**. Adjoining the complex is an **IMAX cinema**, with shows throughout the day (Fr.16, or Fr.31 joint admission with museum; ⓦwww.imax.ch).

Practicalities

Luzern's **train station** is on the south bank, across from the Kapellbrücke and beside a stunning Convention Centre designed by French architect Jean Nouvel. The **tourist office** is on platform 3 (Mon–Fri 8.30am–6/8.30pm, Sat & Sun 9am–6/8.30pm; ☎041 227 17 17, ⓦwww.luzern.org). The HI **hostel** is 1km northwest of town by Lake Rotsee, Sedelstr. 12 (☎041 420 88 00, ⓦwww .youthhostel.ch; bus #18 to Jugendherberge; dorms Fr.32, rooms ❹); there's also the friendly SB *Backpackers*, Alpenquai 42 (☎041 360 04 20, ⓦwww .backpacker.ch; bus #6/7/8 to Weinbergli, then cut left; dorms Fr.27, rooms ❹). Of the **hotels**, the central *Tourist Hotel*, St Karliquai 12 (☎041 410 24 74, ⓦwww.touristhotel.ch; ❻), also has dorms for around Fr.35. *Löwengraben*, in the Old Town at Löwengraben 18 (☎041 417 12 12, ⓦwww.loewengraben.ch; ❽), was Luzern's prison from 1862 to 1998: now you can bed down in the comfortably refurbished cells; it also has dorms for Fr.30, as does the *Lido* **campsite**, Lidostr. 8 (☎041 370 21 46, ⓦwww.camping-international.ch). A stamped **visitors' card** grants plenty of discounts around town. Luzern is a major centre for **adventure sports**; the main operator is Outventure (☎041 611 14 41, ⓦwww.outventure.ch), which offers canyoning, bungee-jumping and more. **Eating** and **drinking** venues crowd the waterfront and the Old Town squares. *Manora* has a rooftop terrace at Weggisgasse 11; *Hug* is a great café on Mühlenplatz for breakfast or lunch; *Hofgarten*, Stadthofstr. 14, has excellent veggie food; relaxed *Parterre*, Mythenstr. 7, is another good option. Top **bars** include the buzzing *Jazz Kantine*, Grabenstr. 8, with DJs and live bands downstairs; *Wärchhof*, Werkhofstr. 11, with women-only nights (Mon); chic *Löwengraben* (see above); and frenetic *Schüür*, Tribschenstr. 1, with excellent music and cheap weekday lunches. Luzern's raucous **Carnival**, ending on Ash Wednesday, is the biggest and best in Switzerland, a six-day round of drinking, dancing and partying.

The Vierwaldstättersee (Lake Luzern)

You shouldn't leave Luzern without taking a trip on the **lake** (ferry routings at ⓦwww.lakelucerne.ch; ER & SP free, IR half-price; tourist info at ⓦwww .lakeluzern.ch), Switzerland's most beautiful and dramatic by far, the thickly wooded slopes rising sheer from the water. Of the lakeside towns, **VITZNAU** (1hr from Luzern) is the base-station of the oldest rack-railway in the world, serving the majestic **Mount Rigi** (SP, IR & ER 25-percent discount; ⓦwww.rigi.ch); and **KEHRSITEN** (35min) has a funicular up to **Bürgenstock**, from where a twenty-minute clifftop walk brings you to Europe's fastest outdoor lift, swishing you in seconds to the Hammetschwand summit. From **ALPNACHSTAD** (1hr 40min), the steepest rack-railway in the world climbs to the top of **Mount Pilatus** (ER 35-percent discount; SP 25-percent discount; IR no discount; ⓦwww.pilatus.com). Taking a leisurely boat ride to the far point of the lake at **FLÜELEN** (2hr 50min) connects with mainline trains running west to Luzern and Basel, north to Zürich and south to Lugano and Milan.

Bern

Of all Swiss cities, **BERN** is the most immediately charming. Crammed onto a steep-sided peninsula in a crook of the fast-flowing River Aare, the city's quiet, cobbled lanes, lined with sandstone arcaded buildings, have changed little in over five hundred years. The hills all around, and the steep banks of the river, are still liberally wooded. It's sometimes hard to remember that this quiet, attractive town of just 130,000 people is the nation's capital. Bern's old centre is best explored from the focal east–west **Spitalgasse**. As it leads away from the train station, Spitalgasse becomes Marktgasse, Kramgasse, and then Gerechtigkeitsgasse, but all the way down is lined with seventeenth- and eighteenth-century houses, fountains and arcaded shops. Some 200m east of the station, the street crosses **Bärenplatz**, scene of much outdoor daytime drinking and a lively Saturday-morning market; to the right of it is the domed **Bundeshaus** or Federal Parliament Building. Beyond Bärenplatz, Marktgasse continues under the **Käfigturm** (prisoners' tower), a thirteenth-century town gate. Further along is an eleventh-century gate that was converted in the sixteenth century into the **Zytglogge** – a distinctively top-heavy clocktower adorned with brightly coloured figures that judder into movement four minutes before each hour. (To the left, in Kornhausplatz, is the most famous of Bern's many ornate fountains, the horrific **Kindlifresserbrunnen**, depicting an ogre devouring a struggling baby.) Münstergasse, one block south, leads to the fifteenth-century Gothic **Münster** (Tues–Sat 10am–4/5pm, Sun 11.30am–2/5pm), noted for the magnificently gilded high-relief *Last Judgement* above the main entrance and the elegant buttressed terrace on its south side. Its 254-stepped **tower** (closes 30min earlier; Fr.4), the tallest in Switzerland, offers terrific views of the city and distant mountains. At the eastern end of the centre, the Nydeggbrücke crosses the river to the **Bärengraben** (daily 8/9am–4/6pm), Bern's famed bear-pits, which have housed generations of morose shaggies since the early sixteenth century. Legend has it that the town's founder Berchtold V of Zähringen named Bern after killing one of the beasts during a hunt; the bear has remained a symbol of the town ever since. Bern's **Kunstmuseum**, near the station at Hodlerstrasse 8–12 (Tues 10am–9pm, Wed–Sun 10am–5pm; Fr.7), is especially strong on twentieth-century art, with works by Matisse, Kandinsky, Braque and Picasso, and whole rooms devoted to Paul Klee, who was born in Bern and who returned here from Germany after the rise of Nazism. More museums are grouped around **Helvetiaplatz**, south of the river: the **Alpine Museum** (Mon 2–5pm, Tues–Sun 10am–5pm; Fr.7) houses interesting displays exploring mountain culture, and you could spend hours in the fascinating seven-floored **Historisches Museum** (Tues–Sun 10am–5pm, Wed until 8pm; Fr.8); check out the "Dance of Death" sequence in the basement, and the fine late-medieval Flemish tapestries and weaponry.

Practicalities

Bern's main **train station** is at the western end of the old centre; cross Bahnhofplatz and turn left to reach Spitalgasse. The **tourist office** is in the station (Mon–Sat 9am–6.30/8.30pm, Sun 9/10am–5/8.30pm; ☎031 328 12 12, ⊛www.bernetourism .ch). The riverside HI **hostel**, Weihergasse 4 (☎031 311 63 16, ⊛www.jugibern.ch; dorms Fr.29, rooms ❹), is below the Bundeshaus; the pleasant SB *Landhaus*, Altenbergstr. 4 (☎031 331 41 66, ⊛www.backpacker.ch; dorms Fr.30, rooms ❹), is near the Bärengraben; while the SB *Bern Backpackers/Hotel Glocke* is very central at Rathausgasse 75 (☎031 311 37 71, ⊛www.chilisbackpackers.com; dorms Fr.27, rooms ❺). *Eichholz* **campsite** is at Strandweg 49 (☎031 961 26 02, ⊛www .campingeichholz.ch; April–Sept; tram #9 to Gurten). For **eating**, *Manora*, just off Bahnhofplatz, has filling cheap food; the popular *Reitschule*, a dilapidated squat-cum-arts centre beside the tracks northeast of the station, offers a Fr.5 meal daily along with its cheap beer and liberal dope-smoking policy; cosy *Brasserie Lorraine*, Quartiergasse 17, has a top Sunday brunch; and *Anker* tavern, Kornhausplatz 16, serves fondue and *Rösti*. There's no shortage of good **café/bars**, including *Café des Pyrénées*, a jovial hangout on Kornhausplatz for artists, alcoholics and others with loud voices; the colourful *Art'Café*, Gurtengasse 3; and *Altes Tramdepot*, a sociable microbrewery beside the Bärengraben. The *Reitschule* (see above) and *Dampfzentrale*, Marzilistr. 47, are the premier venues for **live music** and clubbing. Bern hosts a carnival in February, a major jazz festival in May and a huge open-air rock event in July.

Embassies Australia, embassy in Berlin ☎004930/880 0880, consulate in Geneva ☎022 799 91 00; Canada, Kirchenfeldstr. 88, Bern ☎031 357 32 00; Ireland, Kirchenfeldstr. 68, Bern ☎031 352 14 42; New Zealand, embassy in Berlin ☎004930/20 6210, consulate in Geneva ☎022

929 03 50; UK, Thunstr. 50, Bern ☎031 359 77 70; USA, Jubiläumstr. 93, Bern ☎031 357 70 11. **Hospital** Inselspital, Freiburgstr. ☎031 632 21 11. **Laundry** Jet Wash, Dammweg 43. **Pharmacy** Hörning, in the station. **Post office** Schanzenstr., behind the station.

The Swiss Alps

South of Bern and Luzern, and east of Montreux, lies the grand Alpine heart of Switzerland, a massively impressive region of classic Swiss scenery – high peaks, sheer valleys and cool lakes – that makes for great hiking and gentle walking, not to mention world-class winter sports. The Bernese Oberland, centred on the **Jungfrau Region**, is the most accessible and touristed area, but beyond this first great wall of peaks is another even more daunting range in which the **Matterhorn**, marking the Italian border, is star attraction. The wild summits and remote valleys in the south-eastern corner of Switzerland shelter the world-famous mountain resort of **St Moritz**. Note that very little happens in the mountains in the **low seasons** (April, May, Oct & Nov); shops and hotels may be shut at these times, cable cars closed for renovations, and smaller resorts virtually deserted.

The Jungfrau Region

The most spectacular part of the Bernese Oberland is the **Jungfrau Region**, named after a grand triple-peaked ridge – the Eiger, Mönch and Jungfrau – which crests 4000m. The excursion endlessly touted hereabouts is the rack-railway up to the **Jungfraujoch**, the highest train station in Europe at 3454m. The cable-car ride up the **Schilthorn** (2970m) gets second billing, and is rejected by most visitors, but is in fact quicker, cheaper, offers a more scenic ride up, and has better views: a round-trip from Interlaken takes six hours to the Jungfraujoch, four hours to the Schilthorn (both including an hour at the summit). Setting off on the first train of the day (6.35am) brings discounts on both routes. Most beautiful part of the region's countryside is the **Lauterbrunnen valley**, overlooked by the resort of **Mürren**, which provides an excellent base for winter skiing and summer hiking, as does **Grindelwald**, in its own valley slightly east. **Interlaken** is the main transport hub for the region, but the sheer volume of tourist traffic passing through the town can make it a less-than-restful place to stay.

Interlaken

INTERLAKEN isn't much more than its long main street, Höheweg, with a train station at each end. It has little to amuse the trippers passing through on their way to the mountains, save the cafés and hotel bars lining this main drag. The town lies on a neck of land between two of Switzerland's most attractive lakes, and the best way to arrive is by boat. **Interlaken Ost** is the terminus of mainline trains and the departure point for branch lines into the mountains (see below); boats also dock here from Brienz, on the Luzern rail line. Trains from the Bern/Zürich direction pass first through **Interlaken West** (docking point for boats from Thun), and this station is nearer to the **tourist office**, which sits beneath the town's tallest building at Höheweg 37 (Mon–Fri 8am–6/6.30pm, Sat 8/9am–noon; July–Sept Sat until 5pm, Sun 10am–noon & 4–6pm; ☎033 826 53 00, ⊛www.interlakentourism.ch). Interlaken is a hub for **adventure sports**: Alpin Raft (☎033 823 41 00, ⊛www.alpinraft.ch) is the local leader, with loads of daily activities from skydiving to horse trekking. **Accommodation** fills up quickly in the summer and winter high

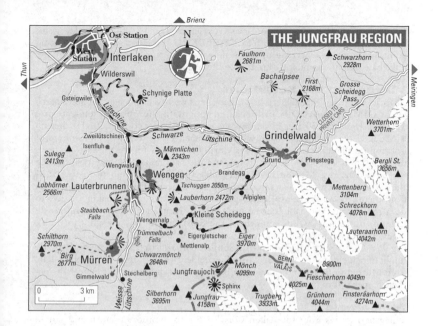

seasons; there are hotel lists and courtesy phones at both stations. The HI **hostel** is 2km east (bus #1), at Aareweg 21 in Bönigen (☎033 822 43 53, ⊛www.youthhostel .ch; dorms Fr.28, rooms ❹); you'd do better joining the backpacker crowd at the excellent SB *Balmer's Herberge*, fifteen minutes south of town at Hauptstr. 23, Matten (☎033 822 19 61, ⊛www.balmers.com; dorms Fr.22, rooms ❸). There are quieter places in town, pick of which is the excellent SB *Backpackers Villa Sonnenhof*, Alpenstr. 16 (☎033 826 71 71, ⊛www.villa.ch; dorms Fr.29, rooms ❹). SB *Happy Inn*, Rosenstr. 17 (☎033 822 32 25, ⊛www.happy-inn.com; ❹), is a backup option. The nearest **campsite** is *Sackgut* behind Ost station (☎033 822 44 34, ⊛www.campingin-terlaken.ch; May–Oct). For budget **food**, *Migros* opposite West station has self-service staples (closed Sun); *PizPaz* on Centralstr. does pizza, pasta and fish dishes (closed Mon); *El Azteca*, Jungfraustr. 30, has Mexican set-meals from Fr.14. *Café Runft* opposite West station is a tearoom, snackerie and **bar** open until 3am; *Positiv Einfach*, Centralstr. 11, is a hip music bar; and *Balmer's* hostel has cheap beer.

Lauterbrunnen and beyond

It's hard to overstate just how stunning the **Lauterbrunnen valley** is. An immense U-shaped cleft with bluffs on either side rising 1000m sheer, doused by some 72 waterfalls, it is utterly spectacular. The **Staubbach falls**, the highest in Switzerland at nearly 300m, tumble just beyond the village of **LAUTERBRUNNEN** at the valley entrance, whose train station is opposite both the funicular station for Mürren and the **tourist office** (Mon–Fri 8am–5/7pm; June–Sept also Sat & Sun 9am–12.30pm & 1.30–4/5pm; ☎033 856 85 68, ⊛www.lauterbrunnen.ch). **Accommodation** is down by the tracks at the cosy SB *Valley Hostel* (☎033 855 20 08, ⊛www.valleyhostel.ch; dorms Fr.22), while both **campsites** – *Jungfrau* (☎033 856 20 10, ⊛www.camping-jungfrau.ch) and quieter *Schützenbach* (☎033 855 12 68, ⊛www.schutzenbach-retreat.ch) – have dorms (Fr.15–20) and rooms (❸).

From Lauterbrunnen, it's a scenic half-hour walk, or an hourly postbus, 3km up the valley to the spectacular **Trümmelbach falls** (April–Nov daily 8.30/9am–5/6pm; Fr.10), a series of thunderous waterfalls – the runoff from the mountain glaciers – which have carved corkscrew channels into the valley walls. The postbus continues 1.5km to **STECHELBERG** at the end of the road, starting point for the **cable-car ride** up to Gimmelwald, Mürren and the Schilthorn; the huge base station complex is 1km before the hamlet.

Mürren and the Schilthorn

The cable car from Stechelberg leaps the valley's west wall to reach the quiet hamlet of **GIMMELWALD**, a little-visited spot with the popular self-catering *Mountain Hostel* (☎033 855 17 04, ⓦwww.mountainhostel.com; Fr.20). Further up is **MÜRREN**, a car-free village which has managed to retain its atmosphere of isolation (in the off season at least). It's worth the journey for the views: from here, the valley floor is 800m straight down, and the panorama of snowy peaks filling the sky is dazzling. Mürren is also accessible from Lauterbrunnen on the BLM Bergbahn – a steep funicular to Grütschalp and a spectacular little cliff-edge **train** from there (IR no discount; ER 25-percent discount; SP free), making it easy to do a round-trip. The cable car continues from Mürren on a breathtaking ride (20min) up to the 2970m summit of the **Schilthorn** (ⓦwww.schilthorn.ch), where you can enjoy exceptional panoramic views and sip cocktails in the revolving *Piz Gloria* summit restaurant. Schilthornbahn prices, compared to the Jungfraujoch ride, are a bargain. From Stechelberg to the top is Fr.94 round-trip, from Mürren Fr.63 (IR no discount; ER 25-percent discount; SP free to Mürren, then 25-percent discount).

Grindelwald

Valley-floor trains from Interlaken Ost also run to the more popular and visited holiday centre of **GRINDELWALD**, nestling under the craggy trio of the Wetterhorn, Mettenberg and Eiger. Numerous trails around **Pfingstegg** and especially **First** – both at the end of gondola lines from Grindelwald – provide excellent hiking. The **tourist office** (Mon–Fri 8am–6/7pm, Sat 8am–5/6pm, Sun 9–11am & 3–5pm; ☎033 854 12 12, ⓦwww.grindelwald.ch) is 200m east of the station, alongside the **Bergsteigerzentrum** (Mountaineering Centre; ☎033 854 12 80, ⓦwww.gomountain.ch), which offers bungee jumps, canyon leaps and guided ascents. Tandem Flights (ⓦwww.paragliding-grindelwald.ch) arranges accompanied **paragliding** jumps from Fr.150. A steep fifteen-minute walk will get you to Terrassenweg, a quiet lane running above the village, where there's an excellent HI **hostel** (☎033 853 10 09, ⓦwww.youthhostel.ch; dorms Fr.30, rooms ❹) and a less studenty *Naturfreundehaus* (☎033 853 13 33; dorms Fr.38, rooms ❹). SB *Mountain Hostel* (☎033 853 39 00, ⓦwww.mountainhostel.ch; dorms Fr.34, rooms ❹) is on the valley floor beside Grindelwald-Grund station. (Trains from Grindelwald pass through Grund on their way up to Kleine Scheidegg.) You can **camp** at *Aspen* (☎033 853 11 24, ⓦwww.aspen.ch; March–Oct).

To the Jungfraujoch

Switzerland's most popular (and expensive) mountain railway trundles through lush countryside south from Interlaken before coiling spectacularly up across mountain pastures, breaking the treeline and tunnelling clean through the Eiger to emerge at the **JUNGFRAUJOCH** (3454m), an icy, windswept col just beneath the Jungfrau summit. The journey up – touted endlessly under the shoutline "Top of Europe" – is scenic in parts, but very long (two-and-a-half hours from Interlaken, with the last 40min climbing in a pitch-dark tunnel), and the top station, inevitably, is a tourist circus of ice sculptures, husky sleigh rides, canteen restaurants and a post office, all overflowing with tour-groups. Nonetheless, on a clear day and with time to spare, it's worth the expense. Panoramic views from the Sphinx Terrace (3571m) to Germany's Black Forest in one direction and across a gleaming wasteland to the Italian Alps in the other are heart-thumping – as is the thin air up here. Don't forget your sunglasses.

There are two **routes** to the top. Trains head southwest from Interlaken Ost along the valley floor to Lauterbrunnen, from where you pick up the mountain line which climbs through Wengen; trains also head southeast from Interlaken Ost to Grindelwald, where you change for the climb, arriving from the other direction. All trains terminate at the spectacularly located hamlet of Kleine Scheidegg, where you must change for the final pull to Jungfraujoch; the popular practice is to go up one way and down the other. The adult round-trip **fare** from Interlaken is a budget-crunching Fr.163 (IR no discount; ER 25-percent discount; SP free to Wengen or Grindelwald then 25-percent discount); the discounted **Good Morning ticket**, valid if you travel up on the first train of the day (6.35am) and leave the summit by noon, is Fr.126.

Walking some sections, up or down, is perfectly feasible in summer, and can also save plenty. The Good Morning ticket from Lauterbrunnen is Fr.109 (7.05am train), from Grindelwald Fr.108 (7.20am), from Wengen Fr.97 (7.25am) and from Kleine Scheidegg Fr.62 (8.02am). Excellent transport networks and vista-rich footpaths linking all stations mean that with a hiking map and timetable you can see and do a great deal in a day and still get back to Interlaken, or even Bern or Zürich, by bedtime.

Zermatt and the Matterhorn

The shark's-tooth **Matterhorn** (4478m) is the most famous of Switzerland's peaks, and no other natural or human structure in the whole country is so immediately recognizable: in most people's minds, the Matterhorn stands for Switzerland like the Eiffel Tower stands for France. One reason it's so famous is that it stands alone, its impossibly pointy shape sticking up from an otherwise uncrowded horizon above **ZERMATT** village; another is that the quintessential Swiss chocolate, Toblerone, was modelled on it. The only way to reach Zermatt is on the spectacular narrow-gauge BVZ train line (ER no discount, IR half-price, SP free; ⊛ www.bvz.ch), accessed from junctions at **Brig** and **Visp**; BVZ trains depart on tracks laid in the road outside both stations. Brig and Visp are stops for fast trains from Bern and Geneva to Milan; coming from Zürich, head for Göschenen, where you switch onto the FO Furka-Oberalp line to reach Brig (ER & SP free; IR half-price). The most celebrated way to arrive is on the long east–west St Moritz-to-Zermatt **Glacier Express**, which takes in some of Switzerland's finest scenery in a day-long journey by panoramic train (reserve at any train station; ER & SP free; IR half-price; ⊛ www.glacierexpress.ch).

Zermatt's main street throngs year-round with an odd mixture of professional climbers, tour-groups, backpackers and fur-clad socialites. Electric minibuses ferry people between the train station at the northern end of the village and the cable-car terminus 1km south. Opposite the station, GGB Gornergrat-Bahn trains (ER no discount, IR half-price, SP free) climb above the village, giving spectacular Matterhorn views (sit on the right) all the way up to the **Gornergrat**, a vantage point with a magnificent Alpine panorama including Switzerland's highest peak, the Dufourspitze (4634m). In summer, GGB trains leave Zermatt once-weekly at dawn to arrive in time for a breathtaking Alpine sunrise. At the south end of Zermatt village a cable car heads up via Furi to the **Schwarzsee** (2583m), the most popular point from which to view the peak and, in summer, the trailhead for a zigzag walk (2hr) to the Berghaus Matterhorn inn (3260m), right below the mountain. All of Zermatt's cable cars and trains bring you to trailheads and spectacular views, while lifts to **Trockener Steg** give access to 21km of ski runs and a snowboard half-pipe that are open all **summer** long (day-pass Fr.60).

There's a hotel list and courtesy phone in Zermatt station; otherwise consult the helpful **tourist office** nearby (Mon–Sat 8.30am–5/6pm; June–Sept & Dec–April also Sun 9.30am–noon & 4–6pm; ☎027 966 81 00, ⊛ www.zermatt.ch). **Alpin Center** (☎027 966 24 60), on the main street, runs extreme sports such as canyoning, ice-climbing, snowshoeing and guided climbs. The excellent HI **hostel** is on the east side of the village (℡027 967 23 20, Ⓦwww.youthhostel.ch; dorms Fr.48 half-board, rooms ❺); nearby is the SB *Matterhorn Hostel* (℡027 968 19 19, Ⓦwww.matterhornhostel.com; dorms Fr.29, rooms ❹), and a *Naturfreunde-Hotel* (℡027 967 27 88, Ⓦwww.naturfreunde.ch; ❹). The *Matterhorn* **campsite** is north of the station (℡027 967 39 21; June–Sept). **Hotel** *Mischabel*, down by the river, is quiet and characterful (℡027 967 11 31, Ⓦwww.zermatt.ch/mischabel; ❼). There are plenty of places to **eat** all along Zermatt's main drag: *Hotel Post* has budget pizza/pasta, as does the lively *North Wall* bar, on the other side of the river. Pleasant *Café du Pont*, just past the church, serves affordable fondues.

St Moritz

ST MORITZ is all you expect and more – a brassy, in-your-face reminder of the hotshot world beyond the wild and beautiful Engadine Valley that runs for 100km along the south side of the Alps. For a century or more, it's been the prime winter retreat of social high-flyers, minor European royalty and the international jetset, who've sparked the arrival of Vuitton, Cartier and Armani amidst this stunningly romantic setting of forest, lake and mountains; when the tourist office trumpets St Moritz's "champagne climate", they don't necessarily mean the sparkling sunshine (although there's an amazing average of 322 days of that a year). The town spans two villages, St Moritz-Bad on the lake and St Moritz-Dorf on the hillside 2km above, linked by the main Via dal Bagn. Dorf is the upmarket one, while Bad – site of a Roman spa – is more down-to-earth. The area boasts legendary bob and toboggan courses, including the death-defying 1.2km **Cresta Run** (end-Dec to Feb; Fr.450/five rides; no credit cards; booking not possible; Ⓦwww.cresta-run.com). You can rent wooden sleds for the famous winter **Preda–Bergün toboggan run** (daily 10am–5pm; Fr.4/hr or Fr.10/day; Ⓦwww.berguen.ch), starting from Preda train station and taking a zigzag 5km down through the scenic Albula valley to Bergün, where trains cart you back to the beginning; the course is floodlit at night (not Mon).

Via Serlas winds up from the **train station** below Dorf to a central square, from where the **tourist office** is 100m east at Via Maistra 12 (Mon–Sat 9am–6pm, Sun 4–6pm; April–June, Oct & Nov Sat closes noon, closed Sun; ℡081 837 33 33, Ⓦwww.stmoritz.ch). The HI **hostel** *Stille*, Via Surpunt 60 (℡081 833 39 69, Ⓦwww.youthhostel.ch; dorms Fr.46 half board, rooms ❺), is a twenty-minute walk around the lake next to the *Stille* sports **hotel** (℡081 833 69 48, Ⓦwww.hotel-stille.ch; ❽) and near the *Olympiaschanze* **campsite** (℡081 833 40 90; June–Sept). *Hotel Bellaval* (℡081 833 32 45; ❼) is beside the station. Most **restaurants** are ridiculously expensive; affordable ones include *Boccalino* pizzeria, Via dal Bagn 6, but with this kind of scenery all around, you'd do better to picnic. Best bet for a **drink** is *Bobby's Pub*, Via dal Bagn 52. From St Moritz, the **Glacier Express** panoramic train (Ⓦwww.glacierexpress.ch) links to Zermatt; the lovely **Bernina Express** train-and-bus combination (Ⓦwww.rhb.ch) crosses a high pass into Italy, then runs alongside Lake Como to Lugano; and the **Palm Express** bus (Ⓦwww.postbus.ch) runs daily on a different route to Lugano.

㉙

Ticino

The Italian-speaking region of **Ticino** (*Tessin* in German and French) occupies the balmy, lake-laced southern foothills of the Alps. It's radically different from the rest of Switzerland in almost every way: culture, food, architecture, attitude and driving style owe more to Milan than Zürich, and the glamour of the place – its lushly wooded hills, azure lakes and palm trees – often seems to blind outsiders with romance. Switzerland has controlled the area since the early 1500s, when it secured the southern approaches of the St Gotthard Pass against the dukes of Milan. It's a cruel irony that the patriotic Ticinesi now suffer the country's highest unemployment rates, even while service industries thrive, staffed by Italian guest-workers and paid for by thousands of Swiss-German tourists and second-home-owners. The main attractions are the lakeside resorts of **Locarno** and **Lugano**, where mountain scenery merges with the subtropical flora encouraged by the warm climate.

Unless you approach from Italy, there's only one train line in – through the 16km **Gotthard Tunnel**. The track's spiralling contortions on the approach climb south of Lake Luzern are famous: trains pass the onion-domed church at Wassen three times, first far above you, then on a level, and finally far below, before entering the tunnel.

Locarno

Mainline trains speed south to Lugano and Milan, while a branch line heads west from Bellinzona to Lake Maggiore and its principal Swiss resort, **LOCARNO**, a characterful old town on a broad sweeping bay, its piazzas overlooked by subtropical gardens of palms, camellias, bougainvillea, cypress, oleanders and magnolias. It can get overrun with the rich and wannabe-famous on summer weekends yet manages to retain its sun-drenched cool. The focus of town is **Piazza Grande**, just off the palm-fringed lakefront, where on warm summer nights exquisitely groomed locals parade to and fro. The sixteenth- and seventeenth-century **Old Town** is ranged on gently rising ground behind the piazza: wandering through the alleys with an ice cream is the best way to blend in with Locarno life. The church of **Madonna del Sasso** (daily 6.30am–7pm) is an impressive ochre vision floating above the town on a wooded crag, consecrated in 1487. The walk up (or down) through a wooded ravine and past decaying shrines is glorious; or take the funicular from just west of the station to Ticino's greatest photo-op, looking down on the church and lake. From the top station, an ear-poppingly steep cable car climbs to **Cardada**, set amidst fragrant pine woods, with walking routes and a spectacular, silent chairlift whisking you up to **Cimetta**, where the restaurant terrace offers a view you won't forget in a hurry. A short bus-ride east of Locarno is **Valle Verzasca**, where deathwish freaks can re-enact the opening scene of the James Bond film *Goldeneye*, by **bungee-jumping** a world-record 220m off the Verzasca Dam (April–Oct daily; Fr.255; book on ☎0848 808 007, ⊛www.trekking.ch) – in June, July & August, you can jump by moonlight; see the website.

Locarno's **train station** is 150m northeast of Piazza Grande. Between the two is the landing-stage; summer boats run to nearby Swiss lakeside resorts such as Ascona, and way south to Italian ones such as Stresa. The **tourist office** is in the Casino complex opposite the landing-stage (Mon–Fri 9am–6pm; April–Oct also Sat 9am–5pm, Sun 10am–noon & 1–3pm; ☎091 791 00 91, ⊛www.maggiore.ch). Stay at the HI **hostel**, *Ostello Palagiovani*, Via Varenna 18 (☎091 756 15 00, ⊛www.youthhostel.ch; ④; dorms Fr.32; bus #31/36 to Cinque Vie); central *Città Vecchia*, Via Torretta 13 (☎091 751 45 54, ⊛www.cittavecchia.ch; dorms Fr.27, rooms ⑤; March–Oct); or *Delta* **campsite** (☎091 751 60 81, ⊛www.campingdelta.com; March–Oct), a 15min walk south along the lakeshore. *Manora* has good self-service food across from the train station, open late and Sundays, and Piazza Grande is full of cafés and pizzerias buzzing from morning until after midnight. In the alleys, *Cittadella*, Via Cittadella 18, serves affordable pizzas and fish dishes; friendly *Bar del Pozzo* is on Piazza Sant'Antonio; *Cantina Canetti* off Piazza Grande has plain local cooking and live accordion on weekend nights. Early August's **Locarno International Film Festival** (⊛www.pardo.ch) is stealing a march on Cannes for star-appeal; catch nightly offerings on Europe's largest movie screen, set up in Piazza Grande.

The Centovalli railway

Locarno is the eastern terminus of the dramatic **Centovalli railway** (ER, IR & SP free), well worth the detour. Ferrovie Autolinee Regionali Ticinesi – unfortunately abbreviated to FART – operate little trains from platforms beneath Locarno's station west into the thickly wooded Centovalli (so named for its "hundred" side-valleys), most of the time sidewinding above ravine-like depths; sit on the left for the best views. After the border at **Camedo** (passport needed), trains roll on through rustic villages amid spectacular scenery before easing down into the Italian town of **DOMODOSSOLA**, from where Swiss trains speed west to Brig, Geneva and Bern, and Italian ones head south to Milan.

Lugano

With its compact cluster of Italianate piazzas and extensive tree-lined promenades, **LUGANO** is the most alluring of Ticino's lake resorts, less touristic than Locarno but with, if anything, double the chic. Centre of town is **Piazza della Riforma**, a huge café-lined square metres from the exceptionally beautiful Lago di Lugano. Through the maze of steep lanes northwest of Riforma, Via Cattedrale dog-legs up to **Cattedrale San Lorenzo**, characterized by a fine Renaissance portal, fragments of interior frescoes, and spectacular views from its terrace. Also from Riforma, narrow Via Nassa – home of big-name designer boutiques – heads southwest to the medieval church of **Santa Maria degli Angioli**, containing a stunning wall-sized fresco of the Crucifixion. A little further south is the **Museo d'Arte Moderna**, Riva Caccia 5 (Tues–Sun 9am–7pm; entry varies), with world-class exhibitions; and a little further still is the modestly named district of **Paradiso**, from where a funicular rises to **San Salvatore**, a rugged rock pinnacle offering fine views of the lake and surrounding countryside. The best of the lake is behind (south of) San Salvatore on the Ceresio peninsula, accessed by boats or postbuses. Here you'll find tiny **Montagnola**, where the writer Hermann Hesse lived for 43 years; his first house, Casa Camuzzi, is now a small museum (March–Oct Tues–Sun 10am–12.30pm & 2–6.30pm; Nov–Feb Sat & Sun same hours; Fr.6), with an excellent 45-minute English film on Hesse's life in Ticino. Jewel of the lake is **Morcote** on the gorgeous southern tip of the peninsula; tranquil stepped lanes lead up to its photogenic church of Santa Maria del Sasso, and several walks explore the lush woodlands, including a trail back to San Salvatore (2hr 30min).

Lugano's **train station** overlooks the town from the west, linked to the centre by a short funicular or by steps down to Via Cattedrale. The **tourist office** is in Palazzo Civico, off Riforma (Mon–Fri 9am–5.30/6.30pm; April–Oct also Sat 9am–12.30pm & 1.30–5pm, Sun 10am–3pm; ☎091 913 32 32, ⊛www.lugano-tourism.ch); **boats** around the lake (IR & ER no discount, SP free) depart from directly opposite. An excellent HI **hostel** (with swimming pool) is at Via Cantonale 13, Savosa (☎091 966 27 28, ⊛www.youthhostel.ch; dorms Fr.31, rooms ❸; March–Nov; bus #5 to Crocifisso from the stop 200m left out of the train station). There's another HI hostel in Figino village nearby (☎091 995 11 51; dorms Fr.27, rooms ❸; March–Oct; postbus from tourist office to Casoro). The SB *Montarina* is behind the station, Via Montarina 1 (☎091 966 72 72, ⊛www.montarina.ch; dorms Fr.25, rooms ❹). *La Piodella* (☎091 994 77 88) is one of several lakeside **campsites** in Agno, a short train-ride west. For **eating**, central Piazza Cioccaro is home to a big *Manora* and *Sayonara* serving inexpensive staples; *La Tinèra*, off Via dei Gorini, behind Riforma, has tasty Ticinese chicken stews. The many cafés around Riforma are packed with evening **drinkers**, while in the warren of the Quartiere Maghetti nearby is *Etnic*, with Mediterranean-style food, beer, cocktails and a cosy studentish atmosphere. From Lugano, the **Palm Express** bus (⊛www.postbus.ch) runs daily on a lovely route up to St Moritz.

Liechtenstein

Only slightly larger than Manhattan island, **Liechtenstein** is the world's fourth-smallest country. It's an unassuming place squashed between Switzerland and Austria, ruled over by His Serene Highness Prince Hans Adam II, and has made a mint from nursing some Fr.90 billion in its numbered bank accounts, a living that has inevitably laid it open to accusations of dubious practice. The main reason to visit is the novelty value – at less than two hours from Zürich, you can see the whole country in a day. Swiss francs are legal tender, but the phone system is separate (country code ☎423).

From **Sargans** train station on the Zürich–Chur line, bus #1 shuttles over the Rhine (no border controls) in half-an-hour to **VADUZ**, labouring under the weight of being capital of a historical oddity: the tiny town bulges with glass-plated banks and squadrons of aimless whistle-stop visitors. Central hub is the post office, where all buses stop, midway between the two parallel main streets, Äulestrasse and pedestrianized Städtle. Facing it is the sleek **Kunstmuseum** (Tues–Sun 10am–5pm, Thurs till 8pm; Fr.5), displaying modern works as well as the world-famous private art collection inherited – and added to – by the prince, which includes exquisite works by Rubens and Rembrandt. Perched on the forested hillside above is the prince's restored sixteenth-century **castle** (no public access). The **tourist office**, Städtle 37 (Mon–Fri 8am–noon & 1.30–5pm; April–Oct also Sat 9/10am–noon & 1.30–5pm; May–Sept also Sun 9/10am–noon & 1.30–5pm; ☎232 14 43, ◍www.tourismus.li), will bang a stamp into your passport as a memento (Fr.2). There's an **HI hostel** at Untere Rüttigasse 6, beside Mühleholz bus stop in Schaan, 2km north (☎232 50 22; dorms Fr.29, rooms ❹; March–Oct); *Mittagsspitze* **campsite** (☎392 36 77) is 5km south in the countryside near Triesen. *Cesare*, Städtle 15 (closed Sat & Sun), has good Italian **food**; and stand-up deli *Eredi Florini*, Herrengasse 9 (closed Sun), has delicious point-and-choose meals.

Postbuses from Vaduz serve all points in Liechtenstein – if you have time to spare, catch bus #10 to the mountain resort of **MALBUN**, a blissfully quiet retreat up at 1602m. Buses also serve **Feldkirch** just across the border in Austria (passport needed), from where trains run on to Bregenz, Innsbruck and Vienna.

Travel details

Trains

Basel to: Bern (hourly; 1hr); Geneva (hourly; 2hr 50min); Interlaken Ost (hourly; 2hr 10min); Lausanne (hourly; 2hr 30min); Lugano (hourly; 3hr 50min); Luzern (hourly; 1hr 5min); Zürich (every 30min; 1hr).
Bern to: Basel (hourly; 1hr); Geneva (every 30min; 1hr 45min); Interlaken Ost (hourly; 45min); Lausanne (every 30min; 1hr 10min); Luzern (every 2hr; 1hr 20min); Zürich (every 30min; 1hr 10min).
Geneva to: Basel (hourly; 2hr 50min); Bern (hourly; 1hr 45min; 20min); Lausanne (3 hourly; 35min); Montreux (hourly; 1hr 5min); Vevey (hourly; 1hr); Zürich (every 30min; 3hr).
Interlaken Ost to: Bern (hourly; 50min); Grindelwald (hourly; 40min); Jungfraujoch (hourly; 2hr 30min – change at Grindelwald or Lauterbrunnen, then Kleine Scheidegg); Lauterbrunnen (hourly; 20min); Luzern (hourly; 1hr 55min); Zürich (hourly; 2hr 15min).
Lausanne to: Basel (hourly; 2hr 30min); Bern (every 30min; 1hr 10min); Geneva (3 hourly; 35min); Montreux (every 20min; 25min); Vevey (every 20min; 15min); Zürich (every 30min; 2hr 30min).

Lugano to: Luzern (hourly; 2hr 50min); Zürich (hourly; 3hr 10min).
Luzern to: Basel (hourly; 1hr 15min); Bern (every 2hr; 1hr 20min); Interlaken Ost (hourly; 1hr 55min); Lugano (hourly; 2hr 50min); Zürich (every 30min; 45min).
Montreux to: Geneva (twice hourly; 1hr 20min); Interlaken (every 2hr; 3hr – change at Zweisimmen & Spiez); Lausanne (every 20min; 25min); Vevey (3 hourly; 10min).
Vevey to: Geneva (twice hourly; 1hr 10min); Lausanne (every 20min; 15min); Montreux (3 hourly; 10min).
Zürich to: Basel (every 30min; 1hr); Bern (every 30min; 1hr 10min); Geneva (every 30min; 3hr); Interlaken Ost (hourly; 2hr 15min); Lausanne (every 30min; 2hr 30min); Lugano (hourly; 3hr 10min); Luzern (hourly; 50min); Sargans (hourly; 1hr 10min).

Buses

Lugano to: St Moritz (twice daily; 4hr).
Sargans to: Vaduz (every 20min; 30min).
Vaduz to: Malbun (hourly; 30min).

29

Boats

The following times are for May–Sept only; very few boats run outside these months.

Geneva to: Lausanne (3 daily; 3hr 30min); Montreux (3 daily; 5hr); Vevey (3 daily; 4hr 30min).

Lausanne to: Geneva (3 daily; 3hr 30min); Montreux (5 daily; 1hr 30min); Vevey (5 daily; 1hr).
Luzern to: Alpnachstad (6 daily; 1hr 40min); Flüelen (8 daily; 2hr 50min); Kehrsiten (hourly; 35min); Vitznau (hourly; 1hr).

Turkey

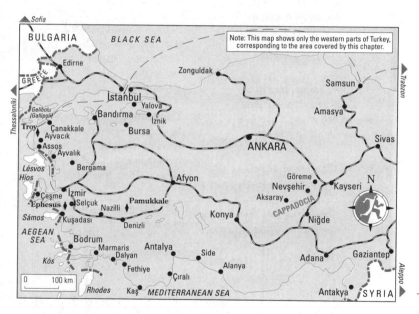

Turkey highlights

✱ **Aya Sofya, İstanbul**
Stunning sixth-century
cathedral. A fascinating
glimpse into the city's
Byzantine past. See
p.955

✱ **Covered Bazaar,
İstanbul** With over 3000
shops, stalls and work-
shops, and the ubiqui-
tous haggling, this is one
of the world's great mar-
kets. See p.958

✱ **Turkish bath, İstanbul**
Soak away the sightsee-
ing aches and pains in a
hamam. See p.960

✱ **World War I sites,
Gelibolu** The moving
cemeteries and monu-
ments of Gallipoli attract
thousands every ANZAC
Day (April 25). See p.962

✱ **Ephesus** The best
archeological site in
Turkey. See p.970

✱ **Fethiye** A great base for
beaches, ancient sites,
abandoned villages and
Lycian Way trekking.
See p.974

✱ **Cappadocia** A lunar
landscape, replete with
eerie caves, rock
dwellings and under-
ground cities. See p.982

Introduction and basics

Turkey has multiple identities, poised uneasily between East and West. The only NATO member in the Middle East region, the country has recently been accepted as a candidate for EU membership. Yet although in some respects Western, Turkey retains its contradictions: mosques coexist with churches, and Roman remnants crumble alongside ancient Hittite sites. Politically, modern Turkey was almost entirely the creation of one man, **Mustafa Kemal Atatürk**. Turkey is an explicitly secular republic, though the majority of its people are Muslim. It's a vast country and, though there are large disparities in levels of development, it's an immensely rewarding place to travel, not least because of the people, whose reputation for friendliness and hospitality is richly deserved.

Western Turkey is the most visited and economically developed part of the country. **İstanbul**, straddling the Bosphorus straits and the Marmara coast, is a heady mix of the European and Oriental. It's the country's cultural and commercial centre and also visibly the old imperial capital. Flanking İstanbul on opposite sides of the Sea of Marmara are the two earlier Ottoman capitals, **Bursa** and **Edirne**, and the former Byzantine capital of **İznik**, with, just beyond, the World War I battlefields of the **Gelibolu** peninsula (**Gallipoli**). Moving south, on the Aegean Coast small country towns such as **Ayvalık** are swathed in olive groves, while the area is littered with ancient sites, including **Assos**, **Pergamon** and **Ephesus**, which have been a magnet for travellers since the eighteenth century. Beyond the functional city of **İzmir**, the Aegean coast is Turkey at its most developed, with large numbers drawn to resorts such as **Çeşme**, **Bodrum** and **Marmaris**. There are remnants of the Lycians at **Xanthos**, and more resorts, such as **Fethiye**, along the aptly named "Turquoise Coast".

On the Mediterranean coast, **Antalya** is one of Turkey's fastest-growing cities, a useful starting-point on the stretch towards the Syrian border, featuring extensive sands and archeological sites – most notably at **Perge** – until castle-topped **Alanya**, after which the tourist numbers begin to diminish. It's worth heading inland from here for the spectacular attractions of **Cappadocia**, with its famous rock churches, subterranean cities and landscape studded with cave dwellings, as well as the Selçuk architecture and dervish associations of **Konya**. Further north, **Ankara**, Turkey's capital, is a planned city whose contrived Western feel gives some indication of the priorities of the modern Turkish Republic.

Information & maps

Most towns of any size have a **tourist office** (*Turizm Danišma Bürosu*) generally open Mon–Fri 8.30am–12.30pm & 1.30–5.30pm, with extended evening and weekend hours in cities and resorts, and during the summer. Staff may not speak English, but they often have good brochures and maps, and should be able to help you with accommodation. The best **maps** are by Geo Centre/RV ("Turkey West" and "Turkey East"). City tourist offices normally stock reasonable street plans.

Basics

TURKEY

Money and banks

Currency is the **Turkish lira** (TL). There are coins of 25,000, 50,000 (written on the coin as "50 bin"), 100,000, and 250,000 and notes of 250,000, 500,000, 1,000,000, 5,000,000, 10,000,000 and 20,000,000. Bear in mind that the 10,000,000 note looks very similar to the 1,000,000 one. Rates for foreign currency are always better inside Turkey, and because of the lira's constant devaluation you should change money only as you need it. Many pensions and hotels, particularly in the popular destinations, also quote prices in US dollars and/or euros; you can pay in either. **Banks** open Mon–Fri 8.30am–noon & 1.30–5pm; some, notably Garanti Bankasi, open at lunchtimes and on Sat. Most charge a commission of about US$2.50 for travellers' cheques. Some of the **exchange booths** run by banks in coastal resorts, airports and ferry docks charge a small commission. Private exchange offices have competitive rates and no commission. Almost all banks have **ATMs**, but it's wise to use them during banking hours in case your card is swallowed; avoid stand-alone ATMs. Post offices in sizeable towns also sometimes change cash and cheques, for a one-percent commission.

Communications

Most **post offices** (PTT) open Mon–Sat 8.30am–5.30pm, with main branches opening till 7/8pm and on Sun. Use the *yurtdışı* (overseas) slot on postboxes. **Phone calls** can be made from Turk Telecom booths and the PTT. Post offices and kiosks sell phonecards (30, 60 and 100 units) and also have metered phones. Some payphones accept credit cards. Numerous private **phone shops** (*Köntürlü telefon*) offer metered calls at dubious, unofficial rates. The international operator is on ☎115. There are **Internet** cafés in most towns, charging $0.50–1.50/hr.

Getting around

Public transport is easy and inexpensive. The **train** system, run by TCDD, is limited. The most useful services are the expresses between İstanbul and Ankara, and other long-distance links to main provincial cities such as Edirne, Konya, Denizli and İzmir. Most routes are very slow and wonderfully scenic. Cheap sleeper cabins are available on overnight services. Reservations for most journeys can be made in İstanbul, İzmir or Ankara, though they're only necessary at weekends or on national holidays. An ISIC card gets a twenty-percent discount. InterRail is valid, Eurail isn't.

Long-distance bus is the best way of getting around. Most routes are covered by several competing firms, which all have ticket booths at the bus station (*otogar* or *terminal*) from which they operate, as well as an office in the town centre. There's no such thing as a timetable. Fares vary only slightly between companies: as a broad guideline, expect to pay $3/100km. An ISIC card gets a small discount with some firms. Top companies (such as Kamil Koç, Pamukkale, Uludag and Varan) are worth the bit extra in comfort, punctuality, service and safety. From Oct to April, the bigger companies may stop running buses altogether along routes that are popular with summer visitors, in which case you may have to make do with local minibus services. For short hops you're most likely to use a **dolmuş**, a car or minibus that follows a set route, picking up and dropping off along the way. Sometimes the destination will be posted on a sign at the kerbside, and sometimes within the *dolmuş* itself, though you'll generally have to ask. On busy urban routes it's better to take the *dolmuş* from the start of its run; otherwise, hail it like a taxi to stop it in the street. Fares are very low.

Nearly all **ferries** are run by *Türkiye Denizcilik İşletmesi* (TDİ), who operate everything from inner-city shuttles and inter-island lines to international routings. Overnight services are popular, and you should buy tickets in advance through authorized TDİ agents. As an example, a third-class double cabin from İstanbul to İzmir costs about $60 per person. Students aged 28 or under get a thirty-percent discount with an ISIC card.

Accommodation

Finding **accommodation** is generally no problem, except in high season at the busier coastal resorts and in the larger towns. A double room in a one-star **hotel** costs $15–30 in season, with breakfast sometimes included. Basic ungraded hotels or **pensions** (*pansiyons*) may offer spartan rooms, with or without bathroom, for as low as $10. A new type of "bijou" hotel/pension, often in historic buildings, offers high levels of comfort, sometimes at surprisingly reasonable prices. There's also a well-established network of **backpacker hotels/pensions**. In the coastal resorts and other tourist targets, touts acting for these places meet incoming transport. Rooms tend to be sparse but clean, at $5–10 for a dorm bed, $10–20 for an en-suite double. Where places are open during low season (Nov–April), prices drop; however, most resort-based places close in winter, so it's wise to call ahead or check with the local tourist office.

There's a small chain of **hostels** under the banner "Turkish YHA", but of these only one is actually HI-affiliated (the *Interyouth* hostel in İstanbul). Hostels differ little in price and facilities from backpacker-oriented hotels and pensions. **Campsites** are common only on the coast and in national parks; tourist offices stock a map of them all. Per-person charges run from $2 to $10, plus $3–4 per tent. Campsites often rent out tents or provide **chalet accommodation** for $10–20. Camping rough is not illegal, but hardly anybody does it except when trekking in the mountains.

Food and drink

At its finest, Turkish **food** is one of the world's great cuisines, yet prices are on the whole affordable. Unadventurous travellers are prone to get stuck in a kebab rut, but everyone apart from the most dedicated vegetarians should find enough variety to keep meals interesting. **Breakfast** (*kahvaltı*) served at hotels and *pansiyons* is usually a buffet, offering bread or toast along with butter, cheese, jam, honey, olives and tea or coffee. Many workers start the morning with a *börek* or a *poça*, pastries filled with meat, cheese or potato that are sold at a tiny *büfe* (stall/café) or at street carts. Others make do with a simple *simit* (sesame-seed bread ring). **Snack** vendors hawk *lahmacun*, small "pizzas" with meat-based toppings, and, in coastal cities, *midye tava* (deep-fried mussels). Another option is *pide*, or Turkish pizza – flat bread with various toppings – served at a *pideci* or *pide salonu*. Another snack speciality is *mantı*, meat-filled ravioli drenched in yoghurt and oil. **Restaurants** (*lokanta*) serve more substantial hot dishes, which include a number of vegetable dishes, though they're invariably prepared with meat-based stock. Meat dishes include several variations on the kebab *(kebap)* – such as İskender kebap (slices of meat on *pide*, with spicy tomato sauce, yoghurt and salad), *köfte* (meatballs), *šiš* (grilled meat chunks) and *çöp šiš* (small bits of lamb). Fish and seafood are good, if usually pricey, and sold by weight more often than by item. Budget mainstays include freshly grilled *sardalya* (sardines), *palamut* (bonito), *ıskumru* (mackerel), *kalkan* (turbot) and *kefal* (grey mullet). Most budget restaurants are alcohol-free; some places marked *içkili* (licensed) may be more expensive. A useful exception is a *meyhane* (tavern), which usually serves **mezes** – an extensive array of cold appetizers – as well as grilled kebabs and fish. *Mezes* come in all shapes and sizes, the most common being *dolma* (peppers or vine leaves stuffed with rice), *patlıcan salata* (aubergine in tomato sauce), and *acılı* (a mixture of tomato paste, onion, chilli and parsley). For **dessert**, there's every imaginable concoction at a *pastane* (sweet-shop): best are the honey-soaked *baklava*, and a variety of milk puddings, most commonly *sütlaç* (rice pudding), which is available in restaurants, too. Other sweets include *ašure* (Noah's pudding), a sort of rosewater jelly laced with pulses, raisins and nuts, and *lokum* or **Turkish delight** – solidified sugar and pectin, flavoured with rosewater or pistachios, and sprinkled with powdered sugar.

Tea (*çay*) is the national drink, served in tiny tulip-shaped glasses, with sugar on the side but no milk. **Turkish coffee** (*kahve*) is served in tiny cups; don't drink the last mouthful (it's the grounds). Instant coffee is losing ground to fresh filter coffee in trendier cafés. **Fruit juices** *(meyva suyu)* can be excellent but are usually sweetened. **Mineral water**, either still *(su)* or fizzy *(maden suyu)*, is found at the tableside in most restaurants. You'll also come across *ayran*, watered-down yoghurt, which makes a refreshing drink. **Alcoholic drinks** *(içkiler)* are available without restriction in resorts and in most other places, though you may have some thirsty moments in smaller interior towns in the east. The main locally brewed brands of **beer** *(bira)* are Efes Pilsen and Tuborg; imported beers are available, but at a horrendous mark-up. The national aperitif is anis-flavoured **rakı** – stronger than Greek ouzo, it's usually drunk with ice and topped up with water.

Opening hours and holidays

Shops are generally open Mon–Sat 9am–7/8pm, and possibly Sun, depending on the owner. The two **religious holidays** are Kurban Bayram (the Feast of the Sacrifice) (in 2004: Feb 22–25) and the Şeker Bayram (Sugar Holiday), which marks the end of the Muslim fasting month of Ramadan (in 2004: Oct 16). If either falls midweek, the government may choose to extend the holiday period to as much as nine days, announcing this only a couple of weeks beforehand. In big resorts, museums generally stay open but in smaller towns they may close. Many shops and restaurants also close as their owners return to their home towns for the holiday. Banks and public

offices are closed on the **secular holidays**: Jan 1; April 23; May 19; Aug 30; Oct 29.

Emergencies

There's a thriving trade in **stolen British passports** in Turkey, and it seems that British Asians are at particular risk of being robbed; several people have gone missing, and there's been at least one murder. Exercise caution, particularly in İstanbul, and particularly if you're travelling alone.

Street crime is uncommon, theft is rare and the authorities usually treat tourists with courtesy. All **police** wear dark blue uniforms with baseball caps, with their division – *trafik*, *narkotik*, etc – clearly marked. In rural areas, you'll find the camouflage-clad *Jandarma*, a division of the regular army. For minor health complaints head for the nearest **pharmacy** *(eczane)*. Night-duty pharmacists are known as **nöbet(ci)**; the current rota is posted in every pharmacy's front window. For more serious ailments, your consulate or the tourist office may be able to provide you with the address of an English-speaking doctor. Otherwise go to a **hospital** *(klinik)* – either public *(Devlet Hastane* or *SSK Hastanesi)*, or the much higher-quality and cleaner private *(Özel Hastane)*.

Emergency numbers

Police ☏155; Ambulance ☏112; Fire ☏110.

İstanbul

Arriving in **İSTANBUL** can come as a shock. Most visitors head for the old city in and around Sultanahmet, where back streets teem with traders pushing handcarts, stevedores carrying burdens twice their size, and omnipresent shoeshine boys. Men still monopolize the public bars and teahouses, while many women cover their heads. Yet this is merely one aspect of modern İstanbul; only a couple of kilometres to the north you'll find the former European quarter of Beyoğlu, with its trendy bars and cutting-edge dance clubs, while north again are the pavement cafés and restaurants of Ortaköy and a series of swish Bosphorus suburbs.

İstanbul is the only city in the world to have played capital to consecutive Christian and Islamic empires, and retains features of both. **Byzantium**, as the city was formerly known, was an important trading centre, but only gained power in the fourth century AD, when Constantine chose it as the new capital of the **Roman Empire**. Later, as **Constantinople**, the city became increasingly dissociated from Rome, adopting the Greek language and Christianity and becoming the capital of an independent empire. In 1203 the city was sacked by the Crusaders. As the Byzantines declined, the **Ottoman Empire** prospered, and in 1453 the city was captured by Mehmet the Conqueror. In the following century, the victory was reinforced by the great military achievements of Selim the Grim and by the reign of Süleyman the Magnificent. By the nineteenth century, however, the glory days of Ottoman domination were firmly over. Defeat in World War I was followed by the **War of Independence**, after which Atatürk created a new capital in Ankara – although İstanbul retained its importance as a centre of trade and commerce. In recent years, the population of the city has reached twelve million, almost a fifth of the country's total, and is still on the rise, adding further to the cacophony and congestion.

The city is divided in two by the **Bosphorus**, which runs between the Black Sea and the Sea of Marmara, dividing Europe from Asia. At right angles to it, the inlet of the **Golden Horn** cuts the European side in two. The old centre of **Sultanahmet**, occupying the tip of the peninsula south of the Golden Horn, is home to the city's main sightseeing attractions: the cathedral of Aya Sofya, Topkapı Palace and the Blue Mosque. Annoying hustlers mean first impressions can be negative, but tourist police will respond quickly to any problems you may have. Further west, near the **city walls,** lies the **Kariye Camii**, which contains the city's finest surviving Byzantine mosaics and frescoes. Across the Golden Horn to the north, the **Galata Tower** offers superb panoramic views over the city.

Arrival, information and accommodation

İstanbul's **airport** is 24km west of the city. Buses run to Taksim Square northeast of Beyoğlu ($4). Taxis taking the direct route along the seafront road (Sahil Yolu) cost $10–15 – make sure they use the meter. The airport metro runs to the city centre at Aksaray, but for Sultanahmet it's best to change onto the tramway at Zeytinburnu; this entire journey costs only a little over a dollar. Trains from Europe terminate at **Sirkeci station**, linked to Sultanahmet by a short tram ride; trains from Asia end at **Haydarpaşa station** on the east bank of the Bosphorus, from where you can get a ferry to Eminönü and a tram from there to Sultanahmet. From İstanbul's **bus station** at Esenler, 15km northwest, the better bus companies run courtesy minibuses to various points in the city, although if you're heading for Sultanahmet it's often quicker to take the **metro** (actually an express tramway; $0.60) to Aksaray and change to the Eminönü-bound tram line which passes through Sultanahmet and Sirkeci. Some buses also stop at the Harem bus station on the Asian side, from where there are regular *dolmuşes* to Haydarpaşa station. The most central **tourist office** is in Sultanahmet near the Hippodrome on Divanyolu Cad (daily 9am–5pm; ☏0212/518 8754); there are branches at the airport (24hr) and the two train stations.

İSTANBUL CITY
EUROPE
ASIA

YILDIZ
YILDIZ PARKI
ORTAKÖY
BEŞİKTAŞ ÇIRAĞAN
Cumhuriyet Cad
Dolmabahçe Saray
TAKSİM
KABATAŞ
Bosphorus
BEYLERBEYİ
KUZGUNCUK
Golden Horn
KARAKÖY
Galata Bridge
Sirkeci
EMİNÖNÜ
SULTANAHMET
KUMKAPI
ÜSKÜDAR
SALACAK
BAĞLARBAŞI
HAREM
SELİMİYE
Ahirkapi
Lighthouse
N
Haydarpaşa
HAYDARPAŞA
KADIKÖY
SEA OF MARMARA
0   2 km

Two **bus services** operate on the same city routes, either the private Halk Otobus service (pay conductor on entry; $0.60) or the more common municipality buses (marked IETT), for which you have to buy tickets ($0.60) in advance from bus stations, newspaper kiosks or fast-food booths; some longer routes, usually served by double-deckers, require two advance tickets (look for the sign *iki bilet geçerlidir*). There are route maps at main bus stops. The European side has two **tram** lines, one running from Eminönü through Sultanahmet to Topkapı and outlying suburbs, the other running along İstiklâl Caddesi from Beyoğlu to Taksim using antique trams; buy tokens (*jetons*; $0.60) from a booth before you enter the platform. There's also a **municipal train** network running along the Marmara shore – west from Sirkeci station on the European side, and east from Haydarpaşa on the Asian (allow at least an hour to get to the Asian station from the centre). On the European side you buy a token ($0.60) to let you through the turnstile onto the platform, while on the Asian side you buy a ticket (same price). There are also **dolmuşes**, which have their point of departure and destination displayed somewhere about the windscreen. **Ferries** run between Eminönü and Karaköy on the European side, and Üsküdar, Kadiköy and Haydarpaşa in Asia; buy your ticket ($0.60) from the dockside kiosks. There are special **sightseeing boats** along the Bosphorus throughout the year from Eminönü ($10; 1hr 30min) but you'll see many of the same sights on the regular ferry to Anadolu Kavağı for less than half the price ($4 return). Last return boat from Anadolu Kavağı in summer is at 5pm, after which you must resort to a bus or *dolmuş*.

Finding **accommodation** is rarely a problem, but in high season anything up to a week's advance booking is advisable. Some of the city's best small hotels and *pansiyons* are situated in **Sultanahmet**, particularly around Yerebatan Caddesi and the back streets between the Blue Mosque and the sea. It's worth shopping around for a good deal; most hotels include breakfast in the price and some offer air-con and cable TV, while some hostels offer inclusive deals and free Internet access. **Taksim** is also a convenient base, and comes into its own at night as a centre of cultural and culinary activity; take bus #T4 from Sultanahmet, which runs via Karaköy. From Eminönü and Aksaray, many buses pass through either Karaköy or Taksim, or both.

Sultanahmet

Alp Guesthouse Adliye Sok 4 ☎0212/517 9570, @reservation@alpguesthouse.com. Friendly place with pleasant, if slightly pricey, rooms. Breakfast on the roof terrace included. ❸

And Yerebatan Cad, Cami Cikmazi 36–40 ☎0212/512 0207. Central hotel near Aya Sofya. Rooms a little past their best, but stunning rooftop views. ❹

Antique Küçük Ayasofya Cad, Oğul Sok 17 ☎0212/516 4936, @www.hotelantique.com. Quiet, comfortable hotel – the top rooms and rooftop terrace have sea views. ❸

Buhara Küçük Ayasofya Cad, Yeğen Sok 11 ☎0212/517 3427. Pleasant but basic hotel with outstanding views from its rooftop terrace. ❷

Fehmi Bey Üçler Sok 15 ☎0212/638 9083. Friendly bijou hotel with period furniture, en-suite rooms with cable TV, air-con and some with balconies. ❼

Interyouth Hostel Caferiye Sok 6/1 ☎0212/513 6150, @www.yucelthostel.com. Large, well-managed HI hostel with friendly staff, located next to Aya Sofya. Café, terrace, laundry, travel agent and Internet. Dorms $5, rooms ❶

İstanbul Hostel Kutlugün Sok 35 ☎0212/516

9380, ⓦwww.istanbul-hostel.com. Friendly hostel, with Internet access. Dorms $6, rooms ❶

Mavi Guesthouse İshak Paşa Cad, Kutlugün Sok 3 ⓣ0212/516 5878, ⓦwww.maviguesthouse.com. Backpacker-friendly place just round the corner from the *Alp*. Dorms $7, rooms ❶

Merih Alemdar Cad 20 ⓣ0212/526 9708, ⓔmerihotel@superonline.com. Friendly hotel with dorms and a few dingy doubles, just down from Aya Sofya; front rooms can be noisy. Dorms $6, rooms ❷

Orient International Youth Hostel Akbıyık Cad 13 ⓣ0212/518 0789, ⓦwww.hostels.com/orienthostel. Long-established hostel with Internet access. Dorms $7, rooms ❷

Sıde Hotel and Pansiyon Utangaç Sok 20 ⓣ0212/517 6590, ⓦwww.sidehotel.com. Welcoming staff, with clean rooms ranging from basic to well equipped and excellent sea views from the terrace. ❸, better rooms ❹

Beyoğlu and Taksim

Büyük Londra Oteli Meşrutiyet Cad 117, Tepebaşi ⓣ0212/249 1025. Century-old Italian-built hotel, full of character, with spacious, well-furnished rooms. Bargaining could halve the price. ❻

Cihangir Arslanyatağı Sok 33, Taksim ⓣ0212/251 5317, ⓦwww.cihangirhotel.com. Smart hotel on quiet back street with air-con rooms, some with balconies enjoying outstanding Bosphorus views. ❼

Dünya Meşrutiyet Cad 79, Tepebaşi ⓣ0212/244 0940. Run-down and distinctly seedy, but with clean, bargain en-suite rooms with TV. ❷

The City

The old imperial centre of İstanbul stretches from the Sultanahmet district – home to the **Aya Sofya**, **Topkapı Palace** and the **Blue Mosque** – northwest to the **Süleymaniye** mosque complex, the **Covered Bazaar** and, much further out, the remains of the **city walls**. To the north, across the Galata Bridge, the old Levantine area of Galata, now **Karaköy**, is home to one of the city's most famous landmarks, the Galata Tower. Close by is the entrance to the **Tünel**, an underground funicular railway running from Karaköy up to the start of İstiklâl Caddesi. This is the main street of **Beyoğlu**, home to many of the city's restaurants and much of the nightlife, beyond which lies **Taksim Square**, the heart of modern İstanbul.

Aya Sofya

The former Byzantine cathedral of **Aya Sofya** (Tues–Sun 9.15am–4.30/6pm; $10), readily visible thanks to its massive domed structure, is perhaps the single most compelling sight in the city. Commissioned in the sixth century by the Emperor Justinian, it was converted into a mosque in 1453, after which the minarets were added; it's been a museum since 1934. For centuries this was the largest enclosed space in the world, and the interior – filled with shafts of light from the high windows around the dome – is still profoundly impressive. Scaffolding currently obscures part of the dome's interior, but nevertheless helps bring home the scale of the place. Between the four great piers that hold up the dome, columns of green marble support the galleries. There are a few features left over from its time as a mosque – a *mihrab* (niche indicating the direction of Mecca), a *mimber* (pulpit) and the enormous wooden plaques which bear sacred names of God, the prophet Muhammad and the first four caliphs. The balconies, pediments and capitals are of white marble, many bearing the monograms of Justinian and his wife Theodora. Upstairs in the western gallery (closes one hour before museum) a large circle of green Thessalian marble marks the position of the throne of the empress. There are also remains of abstract and figurative **mosaics**. Two of the most beautiful can be seen upstairs, where the figures of Christ and Virgin with Child, as depicted on countless posters and postcards, can be found.

Topkapı Palace

Immediately north of Aya Sofya, **Topkapı Palace** (Wed–Mon 9am–5pm; $8) is the other unmissable sight. Ongoing restoration work means parts of the museum and some less important palace rooms are often closed, but this is unlikely to spoil your visit – there's still plenty to see. Built between 1459 and 1465, the palace was the

TURKEY | istanbul

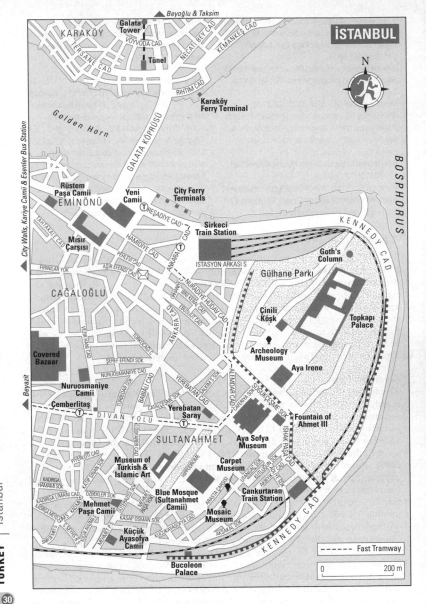

Beyoğlu & Taksim

KARAKÖY

Galata
Tower

VOYVODA CAD

Tünel

RIHTIM CAD

ERSANE CAD

NECATİ BEY CAD

KEMANKEŞ CAD

Karaköy
Ferry Terminal

N

BOSPHORUS

Golden Horn

GALATA KÖPRÜSÜ

City Walls, Kariye Camii & Esenler Bus Station

Rüstem
Paşa Camii

EMİNÖNÜ

Yeni
Camii

REŞADİYE CAD

City Ferry
Terminals

KENNEDY CAD

Sirkeci
Train Station

Mısır
Çarşısı

HAMIDIYE CAD

PEYKIYMI CAD

AŞIR EFENDİ CAD

ANKARA CAD

ISTASYON ARKASI S

Goth's
Column

FIRINILAR YOK

Gülhane Parkı

CAĞALOĞLU

NURADİYE HÜDAV CAD

İBNİ KEMAL CAD

EBUSUT CAD

Çinili
Köşk

Topkapı
Palace

ANKARA CAD

TÜRKOCAĞI Ç

Archeology
Museum

Covered
Bazaar

VEZİR HAN CAD

ŞEREF EFENDİ SOK

Aya Irene

Beyazıt

NURUOSMANIYE CAD

TÜRBEDAR SOK

BABIALİ CAD

YEREBATAN CAD

SALKIM SÖ. SOK

ALEMDAR CAD

CAFERİYA SOK

SOĞUKÇEŞME SOK

Nuruosmaniye
Camii

Çemberlitaş

ÇATALÇEŞME SOK

Fountain of
Ahmet III

DIVAN YOLU

Yerebatan
Saray

KLODFARER CAD

İSHAK PAŞA CAD

SULTANAHMET

Aya Sofya
Museum

PİYERLOTİ CAD

Museum of
Turkish &
Islamic Art

HİPPODROME

Carpet
Museum

UTANGAÇ SOK

ARASTA ÇARŞISI

KABASAKAL CAD

AKBIYIK DEĞ. SOK

Cankurtaran
Train Station

KADIRGA
HAMAMI SOK

KATİP SİNAN SOK

ÖZBEKLER SOK

Blue Mosque
(Sultanahmet
Camii)

Mosaic
Museum

KADIRGA LİMANI CAD

SULTANAHMET

KADIRGA MEYDANI

Mehmet
Paşa Camii

KASAP OSMAN SOK

KÜÇÜKAYASOFYA SOK

AKSAKAL SOK

MEHMET

Küçük
Ayasofya
Camii

KENNEDY CAD

Bucoleon
Palace

- - - - - Fast Tramway

0   200 m

centre of the Ottoman Empire for nearly four centuries. The **ticket office** is in the first courtyard, with the second courtyard the site of the beautifully restored **Divan**, containing the Imperial Council Hall and the couch that gave the institution its name. The **Divan tower** is a useful landmark, visible from many vantage points across the city. In the **Inner Treasury** there's an exhibition of arms and armour, while across the courtyard are the **palace kitchens**, with their magnificent rows of chimneys. Around the corner is the **Harem**, well worth the obligatory guided tour (9am–noon & 1–4pm, every 30min; $6.50; buy your ticket at least 15min in advance). The only men once allowed in here were eunuchs and the imperial guardsmen, who were only employed at certain hours and even then blinkered. Many rooms have never been opened to the public and are awaiting restoration, but the tour takes in a good part of the 400-room complex, including the **Hünkar Sofası** (Imperial Hall) where the sultan entertained his visitors, and the bedchamber of Murat III, covered in sixteenth-century İznık tiles and kitted out with a marble fountain and bronze fireplace. Back in the main body of the palace, in the third courtyard, the **throne room** was where the sultan awaited the outcome of sessions of the Divan in order to give his assent or otherwise to their proposals. Nearby, the **Pavilion of the Conqueror** (9am–5pm; $6.50) houses the Topkapı treasury, where you can see such famous items as the Topkapı Dagger, decorated with three enormous emeralds, and the Spoonmaker's Diamond, the fifth largest in the world. In the **Pavilion of the Holy Mantle** are the holy relics brought home by Selim the Grim after his conquest of Egypt in 1517. The fourth courtyard consists of gardens graced with various pavilions, including the **circumcision room** and the sumptuously decorated **Mecidiye Köşkü**, which commands the best view of any of the Topkapı pavilions.

Just north of Topkapı, **Gülhane Parkı**, once the palace gardens, now houses three museums all covered by one $5 ticket. In the **Archeological Museum** (Tues–Sun 9am–5pm) is a superb collection of sarcophagi, sculptures and other remains of past civilizations. The adjacent **Çinili Köşk** is the oldest secular building in İstanbul, now a **Museum of Ceramics** (Tues–Sun 9.30am–5pm), housing a select collection of İznık ware and Seljuk tiles. Nearby, the **Museum of the Ancient Orient** (Wed–Sun 9.30am–5pm) contains a small but dazzling collection of Anatolian, Egyptian and Mesopotamian artefacts.

The Blue Mosque and around

With its six minarets, the Sultanahmet Camii, or **Blue Mosque** (daily 9am–7pm; closed prayer times), is instantly recognizable; inside, its four "elephant foot" pillars obscure parts of the building and dwarf the dome they support. It's the 20,000-odd blue tiles inside the mosque that lend the mosque its name - fine examples of late-sixteenth-century İznık ware, they include flower and tree panels as well as more abstract designs. Outside the precinct wall is the **Tomb of Sultan Ahmet** (daily 8.30am–5pm), where the sultan is buried along with his wife and three of his sons. Behind the mosque is the **Vakıf Carpet Museum** (Tues–Sat 9am–4pm; $2), which houses antique carpets and kilims from all over Turkey.

West of the Blue Mosque the **Hippodrome** arena was constructed by Septimus Severus in 200 AD. The **Egyptian Obelisk** at its southern end was originally 60m tall, but only the upper third survived shipment from Egypt in the fourth century. The scenes carved on the base record its erection in Constantinople under the direction of Theodosius I. Nearby, the **Serpentine Column** comes from the Temple of Apollo at Delphi and was brought here by Constantine.

On the west side of the Hippodrome, the former palace of İbrahim Paşa, completed in 1524 for the grand vizier of Süleyman the Magnificent, is a fitting home for the **Museum of Turkish and Islamic Art** (Tues–Sun 9am–5pm; $2), containing the best-exhibited collection of Islamic artefacts in the world. İbrahim Paşa's magnificent audience hall is devoted to a collection of Turkish carpets, while on the ground floor, in rooms off the central courtyard, is an exhibition of the folk art of the Yörük tribes of Anatolia.

To the north, on the corner of Yerebatan Caddesi, the **Yerebatan Saray** or "Sunken Palace" (daily 9am–4.30/5.30pm; $5) is one of several underground cisterns that riddle the foundations of the city. Probably built by Constantine and enlarged by Justinian, the cistern is thought to have supplied water to the Great Palace of the Byzantine emperors. Raised pathways allow you to walk through the cistern's forest of columns, and gaze upon the monumental Medusa heads that support two of them. On the other side of the Blue Mosque, the **Mosaic Museum** (Tues–Sun 9.15am–4.30pm; $3), on Torun Sokak, displays some of the magnificent mosaics that once decorated the floors of the Great Palace, a vast complex which once stretched from the Hippodrome down to the sea walls.

Covered Bazaar, Sülemaniye Camii and Spice Bazaar

West of Sultanahmet, continue along busy Divan Yolu to **Cemberlitaş**, or the Column of Constantine, erected in 330 AD to mark the city's dedication as capital of the Roman Empire. Off the main street to the right lies the district of Beyazıt, centred on the **Kapalı Çarşı**, or Covered Bazaar (Mon–Sat 8.30am–6.30/7.30pm; ⨁www.kapali-carsi.com), a huge web of passageways housing over 4000 shops. It has long since spilled out of the covered area, sprawling into the streets that lead down to the Golden Horn. There are carpet shops everywhere catering for all budgets, shops selling leather goods around Kurkçular Kapı and Perdahçılar Caddesi, and gold jewellery on Kuyumcular Caddesi. Don't forget to haggle. When you need a break, the *Fes Café* on Halıcılar Caddesi is a comfortable spot to gloat over your booty.

West of the bazaar, peek into the **Beyazit Camii**, the oldest surviving imperial mosque in the city (1506), with a beautiful courtyard full of richly coloured marble. Beyond the Covered Bazaar, in a pleasant area of shady courtyards behind the university, stands one of the finest of all the Ottoman mosque complexes, the **Süleymaniye Camii**. The cemetery here (Wed–Sun 9.30am–6.30pm) holds the tomb of Süleyman the Magnificent and of Roxelana, his powerful wife. Süleyman's tomb is particularly impressive, with doors inlaid with ebony and ivory, silver and jade. The rest of the complex is made up of the famous **Süleymaniye Library**, and the **Tomb of Mimar Sinan**, a simple tomb for the master imperial architect except for a magnificent carved turban.

The area sloping down to the river behind the Covered Bazaar is known as **Eminönü**, where, on the waterfront, is the last of İstanbul's imperial mosques, **Yeni Camii**. Next door, the **Mısır Çarşısı** (Egyptian Bazaar), also known as the **Spice Bazaar**, sells everything from saffron to aphrodisiacs. A short walk west, the **Rüştem Paşa Camii** is one of the most attractive of İstanbul's smaller mosques, with tiles from the finest period of İznik tile production. On the waterfront, the most prominent landmark is the **Galata Bridge**, a modern two-tier structure that provides access to the opposite bank of the Golden Horn.

Kariye Camii and the city walls

West of Beyazit, İstanbul becomes tattier and more intimate, almost like a collection of villages intersected by major roads. **Kariye Camii** (9.30am–4.30pm, closed Wed; $5), the former church of St Saviour in Chora, was built in the early twelfth century and has some superbly preserved fourteenth-century frescoes and mosaics. It can be reached by taking the metro to Topkapı (a western district, not the city-centre palace) and walking north beside the city walls as far as the Edirnekapa gate, from where it's signposted.

Over 6km long, İstanbul's western **city walls** are among the most fascinating Byzantine remains in Turkey; they barred the peninsula to attackers for 800 years. First raised by the Emperor Theodosius II, they are the result of a hasty rebuilding to repel Attila the Hun's forces in 447 AD; an ancient edict was brought into effect whereby all citizens, regardless of rank, were required to help, and 16,000 men finished the project in just two months. Most of the outer wall and its 96 towers are still standing, and although long sections have been rebuilt and closed off, untouched sections can still be examined in detail if you're willing to clamber in the dirt and brick dust. Do pay attention to your personal security here, especially in the evening.

Plenty of **buses** run this way from Eminönü and Sultanahmet, including bus #80 to Yedikule, #84 to Topkapı and #86 to Edirnekapı, while the **tram** line runs west from Aksaray to the Topkapı gate. However, the best way to get here is to take the scenic **train** ride along the coast from Eminönü to **Yedıküle**, a district lying at the southern end of the walls in the attractive former Greek quarter of Samatya. This also has a few reasonable restaurants and cafés where you can stop before setting off on your exploration of the walls. The **Ottoman fortress of Yedıküle** (9.30am–4.30pm, closed Wed; $3), off Yedıküle Caddesi, encompasses one of the best-preserved sections, including the legendary **Golden Gate**.

Across the Golden Horn: Karaköy and Beyoğlu

Across the Galata Bridge from the old centre is **Karaköy** (formerly Galata). In 1261 Galata became a Genoese trading colony, and during the early centuries of Ottoman rule it functioned as the capital's "European" quarter, home to Jewish, Greek and Armenian minorities. Overcrowding during the subsequent centuries saw the Europeans gradually spread from Galata into neighbouring **Beyoğlu**, but after the exodus of much of the Greek population from Beyoğlu in the 1960s the area began to lose its cosmopolitan flavour, becoming home to brothels, pick-up joints and sex cinemas. It has since undergone a metamorphosis and now plays host to trendy café-bars, restaurants and clubs, coexisting alongside a seedy red light district.

The **Galata Tower** (daily 9am–8pm; $4), built in 1348, is the area's most obvious landmark; its viewing galleries, café and ridiculously expensive restaurant offer the best panoramas of the city. Up towards **İstiklâl Caddesi**, Beyoğlu's main boulevard, an unassuming doorway leads to the courtyard of the **Galata Mevlevihane** (9am–4.30pm, closed Wed; $2), a former monastery and ceremonial hall of the **Whirling Dervishes**, a sect founded in the thirteenth century. Exhibits include instruments and dervish costumes, and the building itself has been beautifully restored to late eighteenth-century splendour. Staged dervish ceremonies take place most Sundays throughout the year (information on ☎0212/245 4141). The best way to continue along İstiklâl Caddesi is to hop on the **antique tram** which trundles for 1km or so to **Taksim Square**, taking in the sumptuous *fin-de-siècle* architecture along the way.

Eating, drinking and nightlife

Sultanahmet has some decent **restaurants**, although the principal concentrations are in Beyoğlu and Taksim. The **Balık Pazar**, particularly, behind the Çiçek Pasajı (off İstiklâl Cad) is a great area for *mezes*, kebabs and fish, while **Çiçek Pasajı** itself offers similar fare but is overpriced and touristy. **Snacks** include the dubious fish sandwiches served off boats in Kadıköy, Karaköy and Eminönü; *kokoreç* (skeins of sheep's innards) sold from booths in less salubrious areas; and delicious corn on the cob sold by vendors everywhere. Western-style **bars and clubs** – invariably trendy and expensive – have all but taken over the city, packed with young revellers, although **traditional music** is making something of a comeback, with some laid-back bar-restaurants serving food accompanied by an ever-changing crowd of musicians. Venues tend to be around Taksim and in nearby suburbs, and along the Bosphorus (particularly the district of Ortaköy, just beyond Beşıktaş), although there's a collection of backpacker-oriented bars on Akbıyık Caddesi in Sultanahmet.

Sultanahmet and around

Baran Büfe Divan Yolu Cad 7. Good spot to watch the world go by whilst enjoying some cheap tasty eats or a *nargile*. Open 24hr.

Cennet Divan Yolu Cad 90. Famous for two dishes: *gözleme* and *mantı*, consumed from floor cushions to traditional music. Immense fun, reasonably priced.

Darüzziyafe Şifahane Cad 33. Reasonably priced Ottoman cuisine next to Süleymaniye mosque. Live traditional music most evenings.

Doy Doy Şifa Hamamı Sok 13, off Küçükayasofya Cad, Hippodrome end. Good, cheap kebabs, *pide* and stews.

Dubb Indian Restaurant İncili Çavuş Sok 10. Reasonable Indian food in a small, restored Ottoman house.

Şehzade Mehmet Efendi Şehzade Camii, Şehzadebaşı Cad. Wonderfully atmospheric restaurant located in the *medrese* of the Şehzade mosque. Excellent value *pide*, kebabs and stews.

Türkistan Aşevi Tavukhane Sok 36, behind the Blue Mosque. Central Asian cuisine with a good set menu. You'll be asked to take off your shoes.

Beyoğlu

Afacan İstiklâl Cad 331. Inexpensive lunch stop with some of the best stews in town.

Alem Nevizade Sok, İstiklâl Cad. *Mezes*, fish and kebabs; outside tables available.

Boncuk Nevizade Sok, İstiklâl Cad. Traditional restaurant serving some of the best food on this street.

Çatı, A. Apaydın Sok 20, Baro Han, 7th floor, İstiklâl Cad. Mixed Turkish and international cuisine, with good views of the city lights; also live music. Closed Sun.

Hacı Abdullah Sakızağa Cad 19. A local legend - stunning home cooking at reasonable prices. No alcohol.

Köşebaşı İstiklâl Cad 405. Trendy, tasty, ultra-modern take on traditional Turkish dishes.

Nature and Peace Büyükparmakkapı Sok 21, İstiklâl Cad. Vegetarian place three blocks away from Taksim, offering lentil *köfte* and other veggie favourites.

Nizam Pide Büyükparmakkapı Sok; and Kalyoncu Kulluğu Sok. Two branches serving excellent *pide*, beans and rice. Cheap and very popular, especially after the bars close. No alcohol.

Bars

Cheers Bar Akbıyık Cad 20, Sultanahmet. Loud music, cheap beer and a backpackerish clientele.

Gizli Bahçe Nevizade Sok 27, İstiklâl Cad, Beyoğlu. Cutting-edge dance music in a dilapidated Ottoman townhouse bar. Very young crowd, and deliciously illicit atmosphere.

Hayal Kahvesi Büyükparmakkapı Sok 19, İstiklâl Cad, Beyoğlu. Upmarket café-bar with live jazz and blues.

Line Bar Büyükparmakkapı Sok 14, İstiklâl Cad, Beyoğlu. Hi-tech rock venue with live music every night; $5 cover charge after 9pm on Fri & Sat. Closes 4am.

Madrid Bar İpek Sok 20, Beyoğlu. Cheap bar popular with students and impecunious ex-pats alike.

Pano Şaraphanesi Hamalbaşı Cad 26, Beyoğlu. Tapas-bar-like drinking den, also offering Turkish and international cuisine. Packed at weekends.

Sal Bar Büyükparmakkapı Sok 18, İstiklâl Cad, Beyoğlu. Traditional Turkish music and beer. For more of the same try *Ekin* and *Barabar* on the same street.

Clubs

Babylon Şeyhbender Sok 3, Asmalımescit, Tünel. Regular stints by foreign bands and DJs. Expensive, but occasionally has special offers.

Mojo Büyükparmakkapı Sok, İstiklâl Cad, Beyoğlu. Trendy basement dive with live bands most nights. Closes 4am.

People Muallin Nacı Cad, Kuruçeşme, Ortaköy. Outdoor dance club overlooking the Bosphorus – popular but pricey. Closed Oct–May.

Roxy Arslanyatağı Sok 113, Siraselviler Cad, Taksim. DJs and regular live bands in a pricey, yuppy-oriented bar/disco.

Shaft Merşrutiyet Cad 81, Tepebaşı. Live blues and jazz club. Closes 2am, except Fri & Sat (4am) when there's a $5 cover charge.

Switch Muammer Karaca Çıkmazı, İstiklal Cad, Taksim. Underground dance club with local and foreign DJs.

Listings

Consulates Australia, Tepecik Yolu 58, Etiler ☎0212/257 7050; Canada, İstiklal Cad 373/5, Beyoğlu ☎0212/251 9838; Ireland, Cumhuriyet Cad 26a, Elmadağ ☎0212/246 6025; New Zealand, İnönü Cad 92/93, Taksim ☎0212/244 0272; UK, Meşrutiyet Cad 34, Tepebaşı, Beyoğlu ☎0212/293 7540; US, Meşrutiyet Cad 104–108, Tepebaşı, Beyoğlu ☎0212/251 3602.

Hospitals American Hospital, Güzelbahçe Sok 20, Nişantaşı ☎0212/231 4050; International Hospital, İstanbul Cad 82, Yeşilköy ☎0212/663 3000.

Internet Internet Café, 2nd floor, İncili Çavuş Sok 31, Divan Yolu; Blue Internet Café, Yerbatan Cad 54; Yağmur, Şeyh Bender Sok 18, Tünel, Beyoğlu.

Laundry Active, Dr Eminpasa Sok 14, off Divan Yolu.

Left luggage Sirkeci and Haydarpaşa train stations.

Police Tourist Police, Yerebatan Cad, Sultanahmet ☎0212/527 4503.

Post office Yeni Posthane Cad, Sirkeci.

Turkish baths The most central, and most frequented by tourists, are the 400-year-old Çemberlitaş Hamam on Divan Yolu (daily 6am–midnight; $10–30), and Cağaoğlu Hamam, Hilali Ahmed Cad 34 (daily: men 7am–10pm; women 8am–8pm; $10–30). Outside the main tourist areas *hamams* are much cheaper; the 500-year-old Tophane Hamam on the Bosphorus at Tophane costs only $4 (daily 7am–10pm).

Around the Sea of Marmara

Despite their proximity to İstanbul, the shores and hinterland of the **Sea of Marmara** are relatively neglected by foreign travellers. The border town of **Edirne** was once the Ottoman capital. To the east the quaint country town of **İznik** was briefly the Byzantine capital and boasts extensive ruins, while nearby **Bursa** – on many routes towards the Aegean coast – was the first Ottoman capital. Many visitors also stop off at the extensive World War I battlefields and cemeteries of the **Gelibolu peninsula** (Gallipoli), using either the port of **Gelibolu** as a base, or, more commonly, **Çanakkale** – from where it's also easy to visit the ruins of ancient **Troy**.

Edirne

EDİRNE boasts an impressive number of elegant monuments and makes for an easily digestible introduction to Turkey. On the borders with both Greece and Bulgaria it's a lively place, albeit somewhat seedy thanks to vast numbers of truck drivers and traders who pass through. The city springs to life for the week-long **oil wrestling festival** of Kırkpınar (end of June).

You can see the sights on foot in a day. The best starting point is the **Eski Camii** bang in the centre, the oldest mosque in town, begun in 1403. Just across the way, the **Bedesten** was Edirne's first covered market, though the plastic goods it now touts are no match for the building itself. Nearby, the **Semiz Ali Paşa Çarşısı** is the other main bazaar, while a short way north of here is the beautiful **Üç Şerefeli Camii**, dating from 1447; its name means "three-balconied", derived from the presence of three galleries for the muezzin on the tallest of four idiosyncratic minarets. A little way west, the masterly **Selimiye Camii** was designed by Minar Sinan. Its four slender minarets, among the tallest in the world, also have three balconies; the interior is most impressive, its dome planned to surpass that of Aya Sofya in İstanbul. Next door, the **Museum of Turkish and Islamic Arts** (Tues–Sun 8.30am–noon & 1–5.30pm; $1) houses assorted wooden, ceramic and martial knick-knacks from the province. The main **Archeological Museum** (Tues–Sun 8.30am–noon & 1–5.30pm; $1), just east of the mosque, contains an assortment of Greco-Roman fragments, some Neolithic finds and an ethnographic section that focuses on local crafts.

The **bus station** is 9km southeast of the centre, from where there are frequent *dolmuşes* and city buses into town. The **train station** is 3km southeast of the centre. There are two **tourist offices** (both daily 8.30am–5.30pm; ☎0284/213 9208), both on Talat Paşa Caddesi, the main one about 500m west towards the Gazi Mihal bridge at no. 76a, and a helpful annexe up near Hürriyet Meydanı by the traffic signals. Edirne's few budget **hotels** are either grim dosshouses or booked solid by truck drivers. Best and least seedy of the cheapies is *Saray* (☎0284/212 1457; ❶), though it's worth paying the extra for the relative comfort of *Şaban Açikgöz*, Çilingirler Cad 9 (☎0284/213 0313; ❷), or *Efe*, Maarif Cad 13 (☎0284/213 6080, ⓦwww.efehotel.com; ❸), which also offers air-conditioning. The *Rüstem Paşa Kervanseray*, just off the main Hürriyet Meydanı on İki Kapılı Han Cad (☎0284/225 2195, ⓔk.saray@netone.com; ❻), offers overpriced rooms in a restored Ottoman *karavanserai*; bargaining is recommended. For **snacks**, look out for the tiny *ciğerci* shops serving the city speciality, deep-fried liver. The lower end of Saraçlar Caddesi offers some reasonable **cafés and restaurants**: the licensed *Café London* has a daily special plus Western fast-food and sandwiches, and is also the only place in town to get a decent filter coffee; *Urfa-Gaziantep Kepapcisi* at no. 33 has good-value kebabs and an upstairs dining room for women; *Balkan Piliç* at no. 14 offers various chicken options; while all along the street you'll find stalls packed with every kind of Turkish pudding and sweet. **Internet** is at Eska Internet Café, İlk Kapalıhan Cad 5.

Çanakkale

Although celebrated for its setting on the Dardanelles, **ÇANAKKALE** has little to detain you. However, it is a useful base for visiting the Gelibolu (Gallipoli) sites and the sparse ruins of Troy. Almost everything of interest in town – park, naval museum and archeological museum - is within walking distance of the **ferry docks**, close to the start of the main Demircioğlu Caddesi. The **bus station** is out on the coastal highway, Atatürk Caddesi, a fifteen-minute walk from the waterfront; if you're arriving on the bus from İstanbul, get off at the ferry rather than going out to the bus station. At the **tourist office** beside the ferry docks (daily 8am–noon & 1–5/8pm; ☎0286/217 1187) pick up a free map of the Gallipoli battlefields.

Except for a crowded couple of weeks during the **Çanakkale/Troy Festival** (mid-Aug), or on **ANZAC Day** (April 25), when the town is inundated with Antipodeans, you'll have little trouble finding budget **accommodation**. *Anzac House*, Cumhuriyet Meydanı 61 (☎0286/213 5969, ⓦwww.anzachouse.com; dorms \$5, rooms ❶), has small but neat rooms and Internet access. The clean and airy *Yellow Rose*, Yeni Sok 5 (☎0286/217 3343, ⓦwww.yellowrose.4mg.com; dorms \$7, rooms ❷), is a similar option, while *Kervanseray*, just round the corner at Fetvahane Sok 13 (☎0286/217 8192; ❶) is a quiet place in a dilapidated old mansion. More upmarket, the *Anafartalar*, overlooking the ferry landing (☎0286/217 4454; ❹), offers en-suite doubles (breakfast included) with fabulous views over the straits. There are several local **campsites** – at Güzelyalı, Dardanos and Kepez – all accessible by minibus. On the quayside south of the ferry jetty, the *Rıhtim* **restaurant** isn't cheap but offers great fish and scenic views. *Özel 2*, Fetvahane Sok, serves up tasty soups and kebabs, whilst further along the street the female-run *Köy Ev* offers a taste of real Turkish home cooking. There's a burgeoning café- and **bar-scene** on Yalı Caddesi and Fetvahane Sokak, with the latter boasting the current top spot, *Depo*. The *TNT* bar on Saat Kule Meydanı is popular with the Anzac crowd.

The Gelibolu (Gallipoli) peninsula

Though endowed with splendid scenery and beaches, the slender **Gelibolu (Gallipoli) peninsula**, which forms the northwest side of the Dardanelles, is known chiefly for its grim military history. In April 1915 it was the site of a plan, devised by Winston Churchill, to land Allied troops, many of them Australian and New Zealand units, with a view to putting Turkey out of the war. It failed miserably, with massive casualties. Nevertheless, this was the first time Australian and New Zealand soldiers had seen action under their own commanders; the date of the first landings, April 25, is celebrated as **ANZAC Day**. The battlefields and cemeteries have no admission fees or restricted hours, but since there's little public transport you have to take a tour unless you have your own vehicle. Various local companies offer **battlefield tours** (around \$20 per person, including lunch), the best operated by *TJ's* hostel based in Eceabat (see below). For a group of four or five renting a car and doing it yourself would work out cheaper.

The World War I battlefields and Allied cemeteries are by turns moving and numbing in the sheer multiplicity of graves, memorials and obelisks. However, it's difficult now to imagine the bare desolation of 1915 given the lush landscape of much of the area. The first stop on most tours is the **Kabatepe Orientation Centre and Museum** (daily 8am–6pm; \$1), beyond which are the **Beach**, **Shrapnel Valley** and **Shell Green** cemeteries, followed by **Anzac Cove** and **Arıburnu**, site of the ANZAC landing. Beyond Arıburnu, a left fork leads towards the beaches and salt lake at **Cape Suvla**, today renamed Kemikli Burnu; most tourists bear right for Büyük Anafartalar village and **Çonkbayırı Hill**, where there's a massive New Zealand memorial and a Turkish memorial detailing Atatürk's words and deeds. Working your way back down towards the orientation centre, you pass **The Nek**, **Walker's Ridge** and **Quinn's Post**, where the trenches of the opposing forces lay within a few metres of each other: the modern road corresponds to no-man's-land. From here the perilous supply line ran down-valley to the present location of **Beach Cemetery**.

Eceabat and Gelibolu

ECEABAT – a short hop over the Dardanelles from Çanakkale – makes a convenient base from which to explore the battle sites. The hourly **ferry** from Çanakkale arrives at the jetty in the centre of town, near to where **buses** pick-up and drop-off. Cheap, comfortable **accommodation** is offered by *Ece Hotel* (☎0286/814 1210; **❶**), *Hotel Eceabat* (☎0286/814 2458; **❷**), and *TJ's* (☎0286/814 3121, ⊛www.anzacgallipollitours.com; dorms $5, rooms **❶**). *TJ's* also has daily screenings of Peter Weir's *Gallipoli* and can organise hiking and snorkelling trips alongside the regular tours. Best place to eat is *Gul Restaurant* on the seafront; Internet access is at Gina Café Bar opposite *TJ's*. Some 45km east of Eceabat, **GELIBOLU**, the peninsula's principal town, is less convenient for visiting the sites but more picturesque, with a colourful harbour ringed by cafés and restaurants. The jetty is right at the inner harbour entrance, and the bus terminal on the coast road, 1km west of town. *Hotel Yılmaz*, Liman Cad 6 (☎0286/566 1256; **❶**), is the backpacker stopover, but the friendly *Hotel Oya*, Miralay Şeflik Aker Cad 7 (☎0286/566 0392; **❶**), is quieter, with pleasant en-suite rooms. There's a municipal **campsite** on the beach to the west of town. Waterfront **restaurants** include *İmren*, *İlhan* and the *Yelkenci*, all of which are licensed and offer the local speciality, sardines.

Troy

Although not the most spectacular archeological site in Turkey, **TROY** (Truva) is probably the most celebrated, thanks to its key role in Homer's *Iliad*. The ruins of the ancient city, just west of the main road around 20km south of Çanakkale, are on a much smaller scale than other sites, consisting mainly of defensive walls, a small theatre and the remains of a temple. Some come away disappointed, but it's worth remembering that the settlement dates back to the late Bronze Age, making Troy far older than most other classical cities. The oldest layer of remains, Troy I, dates back to about 3600 BC, while the final development, Troy IX, was built between 300 BC and 300 AD, during the heyday of the Roman Empire. Çanakkale is the most sensible base: take one of the frequent *dolmuşes* ($1), which run from its minibus station direct to the site, rather than forking out $10–12 to join an organized tour. At the **site** (daily 8am–5/7pm; $7) entrance, a road leads to a giant wooden horse. Just beyond is the ruined city itself, a craggy outcrop overlooking the plain, which stretches about 8km to the sea. It's a fantastic view, and despite the sparseness of the remains, as you stand on what's left of the ramparts and look out across the plain, it's not too difficult to imagine a besieging army camped out below.

İznik

Tucked away at the eastern end of the lake that bears its name, the sleepy little town of **İZNİK** boasts extensive, well-preserved ruins. Originally the ancient Greek city of Nicaea, it became the Byzantine capital when İstanbul fell to the Crusaders in 1204. Under the Ottomans, the city became a centre for ceramic production, an art that has recently been revived. You're free to wander the length of the Byzantine city walls that enclose almost everything of interest. In the centre sits the **Aya Sofya Museum** (daily 8am–noon & 1–5pm; $1.50), the remains of a Byzantine church originally founded by Justinian. To the northeast lies the fourteenth-century **Nilüfer Hatun İmareti**, a religious hostel that nowadays houses İznik's **Archeological Museum** (daily 8am–noon & 1–5pm; $1.50), displaying some fabulous examples of Ottoman İznik ceramics. The **İznik Foundation** (Mon–Fri 9am–7pm; ⊛www.iznik.com) has restarted local ceramic production using original materials and techniques, to great success. Given that each tile takes seventy days to make, it's no wonder that they cost around $150 each; you can see the painstaking process on the free tour, and if you want to spend more time here there are eight well-furnished, if expensive, rooms (☎0224/757 6025; **❼**). The factory, located amidst olive groves near the lake, southwest of the old city walls, is signposted as *İznık Vakfı* from Sahil Yolu.

Buses arrive at İznik's bus station, southeast of the centre, from where everything is within walking distance. The **tourist office** is near the Aya Sofya, at Kılıçaslan Cad 130 (Mon–Fri 8.30am–noon & 1–5.30pm; ☎0224/757 1933). In summer, what **accommodation** there is tends to fill up fast, so reserve in advance. *Kaynarca Pansiyon*, Gündem Sok 1 (☎0224/757 1723; ☻www.kaynarca.s5.com; dorms $5, rooms **❶**), is backpacker-friendly and provides a useful map; there's satellite TV in every room and an attached Internet café. For views over the lake, try the *Çamlık Motel* (☎0224/757 1631; **❷**), or *Cem Pansiyon* (☎0224/757 1687; **❷**). The fish **restaurants** on the coast road, Sahil Yolu, are so-so, but try the *Sahil Restaurant*, which also serves grills and *mezes*. There's a row of cheap restaurants behind Aya Sofya, including the funky old *Konat Barbeku Izgara*, which has good stews and *pide*.

Bursa

Draped along the leafy lower slopes of Uludağ, which towers more than 2000m above, **BURSA** – first capital of the Ottoman Empire and the burial place of several sultans – does more justice to its setting than any other Turkish city besides İstanbul. Gathered here are some of the finest early Ottoman monuments in Turkey, in a tidy and appealing city centre.

Flanked by the busy Atatürk Caddesi, the compact **Koza Parkı**, with its fountains, benches and cafés, is the real heart of Bursa. On the far side looms the fourteenth century **Ulu Camii**, whose interior is dominated by a huge *şadırvan* pool for ritual ablutions. Close by is Bursa's covered market, the **Bedesten**, given over to the sale of jewellery and precious metals, and the **Koza Hanı**, flanking the park, still entirely occupied by silk and brocade merchants. Across the river to the east, the **Yeşil Camii** (daily 8am–8.30pm) is easily the most spectacular of Bursa's imperial mosques. The hundreds of green tiles inside give the mosque its name. The nearby hexagonal **Yeşil Türbe** (daily 8am–noon & 1–7pm) contains the sarcophagus of Çelebi Mehmet I and assorted offspring. The immediate environs of the mosque are a busy tangle of cafés and souvenir shops. The *medrese*, the largest surviving dependency of the mosque, now houses Bursa's **Museum of Turkish and Islamic Art** (Tues–Sun 8.30am–noon & 1–5.30pm; $1), with İznik ware, Çanakkale ceramics, glass items and a mock-up of an Ottoman circumcision chamber. West of the centre, the **Hisar** ("citadel") district was Bursa's original nucleus. Narrow lanes wind up past dilapidated Ottoman houses, while walkways clinging to the rock face offer fabulous views. The best-preserved dwellings are a little way west in medieval **Muradiye**, where the **Muradiye Külliyesi** mosque and *medrese* complex was begun in 1424. This is the last imperial foundation in Bursa, although it's most famous for its tombs, set in lovingly tended gardens. Out beyond the Kültür Parkı, the **Yeni Kaplıca** (daily 9am–11pm; $6) are the nearest of Bursa's baths, a faded reminder of the days when the town was patronized as a spa.

Bursa's **bus terminal** is 5km north on the main road to İstanbul, from where bus #38 (every 15min) runs to Koza Parkı, at one corner of which is Bursa's **tourist office** (Mon–Fri 8.30am–5.30pm; ☎0224/220 1848). Avoid the few grim **hotels** around the old bus station, now the main *dolmuş* garage: better options lie in the centre and the leafy spa suburb of Çekirge, a *dolmuş* ride to the north. In the centre, *Hotel Dikmen*, Maksem Cad 78 (☎0224/224 1840; **❸**), is clean and friendly and has cable TV in all rooms; or there's the female-run *Çeşmeli* at Heykel Gümüşçeken Cad 6 (☎0224/224 1512; **❸**), which has great views from the upper rooms. *Hotel Efehan*, Heykel Gümüşçeken Cad 34 (☎0224/225 2260, ☻www.efehan.com.tr; **❸**), also has comfortable rooms. In Çekirge, the *Demirci Otel*, Hammamlar Cad 33 (☎0224/236 5104; **❷**), is unpretentious, as is the *Özha Yat Hotel* over the road at no. 31 (☎0224/236 5105; ❶). Both have their own *hamams* and there are plenty of reasonable restaurants nearby. The rather touristy *Hunkar Kebap* next to the *Yeşil Camii* offers good **kebabs** with views over the valley. In the central Heykel district, *İskender*, Unlu Cad 7, is one of a number of **restaurants** offering Bursa's speciality, *İskender kebap*; another to try on the same street is *Hacibey*, or if you've had one kebab too many, *Liberty's* serves up a decent pizza. Close to the tourist office at Belediye Cad 15, the more elegant *Çiçek Izgara* offers a decent take on many Ottoman dishes. The old fish market on Sakarya Caddesi, at the foot of the citadel, is dominated by lively **fish restaurants**, of which *Arap Şükrü*, at no. 6, is reasonably priced. This street also boasts a number of reasonable **bars**, including *Barantico*, *Cevriye* and *Piccolo*.

Turkey's Aegean coast

The **Aegean coast** is, in many ways, Turkey's most enticing destination, home to some of the best of its classical antiquities and the most appealing resorts. Tiny **Assos** with its ancient ruins is one of the gems of the coast. **Ayvalık**, the north's longest-established resort, makes an excellent place to stop for a few days, with good beaches and easy access to the ruins of **Bergama**, 70km to the southeast. Further south, the city of **İzmir** serves as a base for day-trips to adjacent sights and beaches. The territory to the south is home to the best concentration of classical, Hellenistic and Roman ruins, notably **Ephesus** and the remains inland at **Hierapolis** – although the latter is more often visited for the pools and rock formations of adjacent **Pamukkale**. The coast itself is better down south, too, and although the larger resorts, including **Kuşadası** and **Marmaris**, are beginning to be lost to the developers, **Bodrum** and **Çeşme** still have a certain charm.

Assos

ASSOS, 70km south of Çanakkale, is a tiny stone village built on a hill around the ruins of the ancient town, founded in the sixth century BC and once home to Aristotle. The old-town ruins (daily 8.30am–5/7pm; $3) are for the most part blissfully quiet; the **Temple of Athena** has had its Doric columns re-erected, and there are breathtaking views from here to the Greek island of Lésvos. The only transport is a **minibus** from Ayvacik, 25km to the north, which passes through both the upper village of Assos and its twin settlement downhill around the fishing harbour; it runs according to demand, so out of season you may have a long wait. **Pensions** in the upper village are all in restored stone houses and include the delightful *Timur Pansiyon* (☎0286/721 7449, ⊛www.hitit.co.uk/timur; ❷), which offers doubles with shared facilities, and *Dolunay* (☎0286/721 7172; ❶), which has en-suite doubles. Down on the shore are several beautiful but expensive stone-built **hotels**, which can generally be bargained down in midweek and also offer half-board; for something cheaper try *Antik Pansiyon* (☎0286/721 7101; ❷). Further along the shore are several small **campsites** including *Çakır* (☎0286/721 7048), which also has several shacks for rent (❷). On summer weekends, finding a room anywhere may be tricky, and prices will be double or triple those of midweek.

Ayvalık

AYVALIK, 2km west of the main coast road, is a small fishing port that also makes a living from olive-oil production and low-key tourism. The town lost its mainly Greek inhabitants during the exchange of populations that followed the Greek–Turkish war of 1920–1922. There's not a great deal to see, though its tangle of central streets, lined with terraces of sumptuous Greek houses and clattering with speeding horse carts, is worth a wander, and there are some decent nearby beaches.

The centre is focused on the small square İskele Meydanı, 1.5km south of the main **bus station**. The **tourist office** (May–Sept daily 9am–1am & 2–7pm; ☎0266/312 2122) is in a kiosk on the seafront in İskele Meydanı. There's a wealth of **pensions** in Ayvalık's old houses, the best by far being the beautiful *Taksiyarhis* (☎0266/312 1494, ⓦwww.taksiyarhis.com; ②), behind the Taksiyarhis church, signposted inland and uphill from the seafront – the breakfast terrace and some rooms offer delightful views of the town and sea. Alternatives are *Yalı* (☎0266/312 2423; ②), housed in a lovely old seafront mansion, and, also signposted from the seafront, *Chez Beliz*, Fethiye Mahallesi, Marezal Çakmak Cad 28 (☎0266/312 4897; ②; closed Oct–April). **Eating** possibilities include *Osmanlı Mutfağı* on Talatpaşa Caddesi, which offers well-priced superior Turkish dishes; *Kardeşler Pide Salonu*, opposite the PTT on İnönü Caddesi, with a good choice of kebabs; and *Canlı Balık* on the seafront, specializing in fish and *mezes*. There's a clutch of **drinking** dens between the main street, Edremit Caddesi and the parallel İnönü Caddesi, plus *Circus Bar*, on Gümrük Sokak. **Internet** access is offered by a number of places around Cumhuriyet Meydanı. You can take a **boat tour** of the smaller islands with set intervals for a swim, using one of the many boat companies along the seafront. **Ferry tickets** to the Greek island of Lésvos are available at Jale Tour, Gümrük Cad 24 (departures June–Sept daily; Oct–May twice weekly; $40 one-way, $50 open return; ☎0266/312 2740).

Bergama

Frequently touted as a day-trip from Ayvalık, **BERGAMA** is the site of the Hellenistic – and later Roman – city of Pergamon, ruled for several centuries by a powerful local dynasty. Excavations were completed here in 1886, but unfortunately much of what was found has since been carted off to Germany. However, the acropolis of Eumenes II remains a major attraction, and there are a host of lesser sights and an old quarter of ramshackle charm. The old town lies at the foot of the acropolis, about ten minutes' walk from the bus station. Its foremost attraction is the **Kızıl Avlu** (daily 8.30am–5.30pm; $3), a huge edifice on the river not far from the acropolis, originally built as a temple to the Egyptian god Osiris and converted to a basilica by the early Christians, when it was one of the Seven Churches of Asia Minor addressed by St John in the Book of Revelation. South along the main street is the **Archeological Museum** (Tues–Sun 8.30am–6pm; $2.50), which has a large collection of locally unearthed booty, including busts of Zeus and Socrates along with a model of the Zeus altar. Bergama has a particularly good **hamam**, the *Haci Hekim*, Bankalar Cad 32 (from $5). **Pergamon**, the ancient city of kings, is set on top of a rocky bluff towering over modern Bergama. Taking a short cut through the old town still means an uphill walk of around half an hour. By taxi, the ride costs $6 or more; a taxi-tour around all Bergama's sights costs about $15-20. The first attraction is the **acropolis** (daily 9am–5/7pm; $6.50) is the huge horseshoe-shaped **Altar of Zeus**, built during the reign of Eumenes II to commemorate his father's victory over the Gauls. North of the Zeus altar lie the sparse remains of a **Temple of Athena**, above which loom the restored columns of the **Temple of Trajan**, where the deified Roman emperor and his successor Hadrian were revered in the imperial era. From the Temple of Athena a narrow staircase leads down to the theatre, the most spectacular part of the ruined acropolis, capable of seating 10,000 spectators, and a **Temple of Dionysos**, just off-stage to the northwest.

Bergama's **bus station** is on the main road, 500m from the town centre, and within fifteen minutes' walk of most accommodation. The **tourist office** (daily 8.30am–noon & 1–5.30pm; ☎0232/633 1862) is further along the same road. Many of the budget **hotels** are located in the old town; *Athena*, Barbaros Mahallı, İmam Çıkmazı 5 (☎0232/633 3420, ⓦwww.athenapension.8m.com; ①), has elegant rooms in a nineteenth-century mansion, plus en-suite rooms in a newer annexe. Over the bridge, the family-run *Nike Pansiyon* (☎0232/633 3901, Ⓔfikretnike @yahoo.com; ①) has clean rooms around a garden with shared bathrooms. *Pergamon*

Pansiyon (☎0232/633 2395; ❶) occupies an atmospheric old stone house in the town centre. If you're on a day-trip from Ayvalık, don't feel obliged to eat at the restaurant stop: cheaper and better options abound. The **restaurant** in the *Pergamon Pansiyon*'s courtyard has excellent home cooking; while *Sağlam*, Hükümet Meydanı 29, has a good range of traditional Turkish food and a shady courtyard.

İzmir

İZMİR – ancient Smyrna – is home to nearly three million people. Mostly burned down in the Turkish-Greek war of 1922, İzmir has been built pretty much from scratch and is nowadays booming and cosmopolitan. Its hot climate is offset by its location, straddling a (heavily polluted) 50km-long gulf fed by several streams and flanked by mountains on all sides. Despite an illustrious history, much of the city is relentlessly modern. Orientation can be confusing – many streets are unmarked – but most points of interest lie near each other and walking is the most enjoyable way of exploring. İzmir cannot be said to have a single centre, although **Konak**, the busy park, bus terminal and shopping centre on the waterfront, is where visitors spend most time. It's marked by the ornate **Saat Kulesi** (clock tower), the city's official symbol, and the **Konak Camii**, distinguished by its facade of enamelled tiles. Southwest of here, the **Archeological Museum** (Tues–Sun 8.30am–5.30pm; $2.50) features an excellent collection of finds from all over İzmir province, including some stunning marble statues and sarcophagi. Immediately east of Konak is İzmir's **bazaar**. The main drag, Anafartalar Caddesi, is lined with clothing, jewellery and shoe shops; Fevzipaşa Bulvarı and the alleys just south are strong on leather garments. Worth seeking out is the handsome **Kızılara Gazi Kervanseray** on 871 Sok, which has antique and carpet shops and houses a popular café. East, across Gaziosmanpaşa Bulvarı, the **Agora** (daily 8.30am–5.30pm; $2), commercial centre of the classical city, dates back to the early second century BC. Above this is the **Kadifekale**, an irregularly shaped fortress dating from Byzantine and Ottoman times that gives great views over the city from its pine-shaded tea garden (daily 9am–9pm). The less energetic can take a red-and-white city bus #33 from Konak, but it's worth walking up from the agora, threading through once-elegant narrow streets.

Ferries anchor at the **Alsancak terminal**, 2km north of the centre, where there's also a Turkish Maritime Lines office selling onward boat tickets; a taxi into town costs $3 or you could walk 250m south and pick up bus #2 (blue-and-white) from Alsancak train station. Intercity trains pull in at **Basmane station**, 1km from the

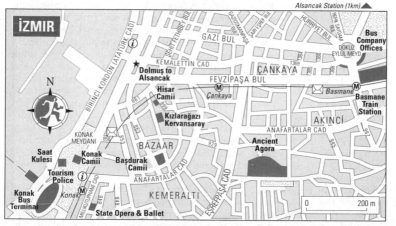

seafront at the eastern end of Fevzipaşa Bulvarı. From the **airport**, there's a shuttle train to Alsancak train station, although you'd be better off taking a Havaş bus (which runs according to flight arrivals) to the THY office at the central *Efes Hotel*. The **bus station** is way out on the east side of the city, from where buses #50, #51 and #54 run to Basmane station and Konak. Buses to and from Çeşme depart from the Uçkuyular bus station; bus #169 from Konak. There's also a **metro** system ($0.65) that passes through Basmane, Çankaya and Konak. The **tourist office** is at Akdeniz Mah., 1344 Sok 2, off Cumhuriyet Bulvari (daily 8.30am–noon & 1–5.30pm; ☎0232/483 5117). The main areas for budget **hotels** are Çankaya and Akinci, immediately west and southwest of Basmane station, or around Fevzipaşa Bulvarı and Anafartalar Caddesi. In Çankaya, there's *Hotel Zeybek* (☎0232/489 6694; ❷) and *Nil Otel*, Fevzipaşa Bul 155 (☎0232/483 5228; ❷), though rooms at the front here can be noisy. Cheapest of the lot is *Ova*, 1369 Sok 59 (☎0232/483 1267; ❶), and *Güzel İzmir*, 1368 Sok 8 (☎0232/483 5069; ❷), is also worth a try. In Akinci, *Hikmet Otel*, 945 Sok 25 (☎0232/484 2672; ❶), is a friendly place in a characterful, if ramshackle neighbourhood.

Biz Bize, Vali Kazim Dirik Cad 14, near the *Hilton*, serves delicious soups and **kebabs**, while *Bolulu Hasan Usta*, 853 Sok 13/B, does the best pudding and ice cream in town – but nothing else. In Alsancak, **restaurants** abound on the Birinci Kordon, and around the pedestrianized Kıbrıs Şehit Caddesi – try *La Sera*, Birinci Kordon 190a, with kebabs, fish and desserts plus live music in the evenings, or *Café Reci* on 398 Sok, serving salads, crêpes and ice cream. Pricey *Kemal'ın Yeri*, 1453 Sok 20/A, is famous for its seafood, while for the budget-conscious the *Kurçiçeği* at Kıbrıs Şehit Cad 75 is the place to go. Best-value **bar** is *Eko*, on the corner of Pilevne Bul and Cumhuriyet Cad, which also serves kebabs and chips. Further along on 1482 Sok, *Kahve Bahane* and *Kaos* are inexpensive student hangouts housed in a row of dilapidated old Greek merchants' houses. Splendid views of the bay are offered by the *Pagos Café*, just in front of the castle at 5250 Sok 3a. There are several **Internet** cafés around Alsancak, including Internet House, 1378 Sok 26b.

Çeşme

A once-attractive town of old Greek houses wrapped around a castle, **ÇEŞME** these days is little more than İzmir on holiday, and a convenient stopover on the way to the Greek island of Híos. The town's two main streets are İnkilap Caddesi, the main bazaar thoroughfare, and its continuation Çarşı Caddesi, which saunters south along the waterfront. The sights comprise the town's thirteenth-century Genoese **castle** (daily 8.30am–noon & 1–5.30pm; $2), with a museum containing finds from the nearby site of Erythrae, and the **Kervanseray**, a few paces south, dating from the reign of Süleyman the Magnificent but now a hotel. **Ferries** from Híos in Greece (Chios in Turkish) arrive at the small jetty in front of the castle. By **bus** from İzmir you'll probably arrive at the station 1km south, although some services stop at the top of İnkilap Caddesi. **Dolmuşes** to Dalyan leave from the roundabout at the northeast end of İnkilap Caddesi; those to other nearby attractions depart from next to the harbourside **tourist office** (daily 8.30am–noon & 1–5.30pm; ☎0232/712 6653). There is a clutch of **pensions** on the right-hand side of the castle as it faces the sea. *Avrupalı* (☎0232/712 7039; ❷) has a picturesque garden and well-appointed rooms including suites with kitchenettes, while *Özge* (☎0232/712 7021; ❷) is immaculately kept and comfortable. Away from the harbour, past the local *hamam*, is the friendly, clean and basic *Aras Apartments* (☎0232/712 7375; ❶), which offers rooms with balconies, while a ten-minute walk beyond the harbour is *Kerman Otel* (☎0232/712 7112, ✉kermanotel @hotmail.com; ❹), overlooking the beach. Among Çeşme's better **restaurants** are the *Rıhtım* and *Marina*, both overlooking the fishing harbour, though *Körfez*, on the marina, is the most elegant, serving up excellent, expensive, charcoal-grilled fish. Best-value is the *Kordon Pide* next to the post office. *Rumeli Pastanesi*, İnkilap Cad

44, serves some of the best ice cream on the Aegean, and specializes in desserts and jams made from the sap of gum trees. **Internet** access is at Emre Internet Café, Kutludal Sok 11.

Kuşadası

KUŞADASI is Turkey's most bloated resort, a brash coastal playground that extends along several kilometres of seafront. In just three decades its population has swelled from 6000 to around 50,000. The town is many people's introduction to the country: ferry services link it with the Greek island of Sámos, while the resort is a port of call for Aegean cruise ships, which disgorge vast numbers in summer. Liman Caddesi runs from the ferry port up to Atatürk Bulvarı, the main harbour esplanade, from which pedestrianized Barbaros Hayrettin Bulvarı ascends the hill. To the left of here, the **Kale** district, huddled inside the town walls, is the oldest and most appealing part of town, with a mosque and some fine traditional houses. Kuşadası's most famous beach, **Kadınlar Denizi**, 3km southwest of town, is a popular strand, usually too crowded for its own good in season. **Güvercin island**, closer to the centre, is mostly landscaped terraces dotted with tea gardens and snack bars. For the closest sandy beach, head 500m further south, just before **Yılancı Burnu**, or alternatively try **Tusan** beach 7km north of town, served by all Kuşadası–Selçuk *dolmuşes*, as well as more frequent ones labelled *Şehir İçi*. Much the best beach in the area is **Pamucak**, at the mouth of the Kücük Menderes River, 15km north, an exposed 4km stretch of sand that is as yet little developed; it's served by regular *dolmuşes* from both Kuşadası and Selçuk in season.

The **tourist office** (Mon–Fri 8am–6pm; summer also Sat & Sun; ☎0256/614 1103) is right by the ferry port. The combined **dolmuş** and long-distance **bus station** is around 2km out, past the end of Kahramanlar Caddesi on the ring road to Söke, while the *dolmuş* stop is closer to the centre on Adnan Menderes Bulvarı. **Ferries to Samos** ($30 single, $35 day return, $55 open return) are subject to demand; there are no scheduled services in winter and up to three boats a day in high summer. Diana on Kıbrıs Cad (☎0256/614 3859) runs up to two boats daily in summer; the morning Turkish boat is handled by Azim, on Liman Cad, Yayla Pasajı (☎0256/614 1553). There's plenty of **accommodation**, though some hotels and pensions, especially in areas favoured by backpackers, are used by prostitutes and their unsavoury minders. Most of the good pensions, as well as some to be avoided, are just south of the core of the town, uphill from Barbaros Hayrettin Bulvarı. *Sezgin Hotel*, Aslanar Cad 68 (☎0256/614 4225, ❻www.sezginhotel.com; ❶), has comfortable en-suite rooms and a swimming pool, while lively *Sammy's Palace*, Kıbriş Cad 14 (☎0256/612 2588, ❻www.hotelsammyspalace.com; dorms $5, rooms ❶), is firmly on the ANZAC network. *Golden Bed*, Aslanlar Cad, Uğurlu Çıkmazı 4 (☎0256/614 8708, ❻www.kusadasihotels.com/goldenbed; ❷), is a bit more characterful and has en-suite rooms. Behind the tourist office at Buyral Sok 4 is *Hotel Liman* (☎0256/614 7770, ❻hasandegirmenci@usa.net; ❷), which has air-conditioned rooms with sea views. *Turyat* **campsite** at Tusan beach is well-appointed but expensive; *Önder* and *Yat,* both behind the yacht marina, are marginally cheaper, well-kept and popular. For **food**, *Öz Urfa*, in the Kale district on Cephane Sok, has excellent-value *lahmacun* and *pide*; while the *Avlu*, also on Cephane Sok, has a wide range of kebab and steam-tray food and an outdoor courtyard. If you want to eat by the water without emptying your wallet, try *Ada Restaurant-Plaj-Café*, on Güvercin Adası. *She* **bar** is on the corner of Bahar and Sakarya sokaks, with half-a-dozen more in the adjacent streets.

Selçuk

SELÇUK has been catapulted into the limelight of premier-league tourism by its proximity to the ruins of Ephesus. The flavour of tourism here, though, is different from that at nearby Kuşadası, its location and ecclesiastical connections making it a haven for a disparate mix of backpackers and Bible-bashers from every corner of the globe. The beaches in and around Kuşadası are easily accessible on a short *dolmuş* ride. **Ayasoluk hill** (daily 8.30am–6pm; $2.50), the traditional burial place of St John the Evangelist, who died here around 100 AD, boasts the remains of a basilica built by Justinian that was one of the largest Byzantine churches in existence; various colonnades and walls have been re-erected, giving a hint of the building's magnificence. The tomb of the evangelist is marked by a slab at the former site of the altar; beside the nave is the baptistry, where religious tourists pose in the act of dunking as friends' cameras click. Just behind the tourist office, the **Archeological Museum** (Tues–Sun 8.30am–6pm; $2.50) has galleries of finds from Ephesus, while beyond the museum, 600m along the road toward Ephesus, are the scanty remains of the **Artemision** or sanctuary of Artemis. This massive Hellenistic structure was considered one of the Seven Wonders of the Ancient World, though this is hard to believe today. Some 8km southwest of Selçuk lies **Meryemana** (daily dawn–dusk; $3), a tiny Greek chapel (Mass, summer daily 7.15am, Sun also 10.30am) where some Orthodox theologians believe the Virgin Mary passed her last years, having travelled to the region with St John the Evangelist. Evidence of Mary's residence is somewhat circumstantial but that doesn't stop coach tours to Ephesus making the detour.

At the base of the castle hill in town, a pedestrian precinct leads east to the **train station**. Following the main highway a bit further south brings you to the **bus** and **dolmuş** terminal, opposite which is the **tourist office** (Mon–Fri 8.30am–noon & 1–5pm; summer also Sat & Sun; ☎0232/892 6945). Most **pensions and hotels** will pick you up from the bus station if you call on arrival, and many arrange free lifts to Ephesus and other local sights. *Pension Karahan,* 11 Ataturk Mah, Siegburg Cad (☎0232/892 2575, ✉pensionkarahan@hotmail.com; ❶) is a delightfully hospitable place run by a local family, only too willing to help out. Also recommended is *Kiwi Pension,* Ataturk Mah. 1038 Sok 26 (☎0232/892 4892, ⊛www.kiwipension.com; dorms $5, rooms ❶), which runs free trips to their swimming pool 3km away. The large *Artemis Guest House ("Jimmy's Place"),* 1012 Sok 2 (☎0232/892 1982, ⊛www.artemisguesthouse.com; dorms $4, room ❷), has Internet access, a travel library and a cosy restaurant (serving some veggie food) with patio. *Otel Ürkmez,* Namık Kemal Cad 20 (☎0232/892 6312, ⊛www.urkmez.8m.com; ❶), near the *hamam,* has a roof terrace, while more upmarket is the beautifully furnished, female-run *Nilya,* Atatürk Mah, 1051 Sok 7 (☎0232/892 9081, ✉nilya_ephesus@hotmail.com; ❹), which has splendid views over the Artemision. Selçuk's **campsite**, *Garden,* lies just beyond the İsa Bey mosque; alternatively, *Mavi Ay,* 9km west at Pamucak Beach, is served by Selçuk–Kuşadası *dolmuşes. Kalenin Prensi,* Kale Alti, is a **restaurant** owned by the family of Sagturk, the famous Turkish ballet dancer, offering ancient Roman and Turkish dishes. *Köşk Pide* on Zigberg Cad, and *Ephesus* on Namik Kemal Cad, are worth a try, as is the licensed *Old House* restaurant on Cengiz Topel Cad. Enjoy apple tea in the beautiful garden of *Karamese* **café**, Tarihi İsa Bey Camii Onu, opposite the mosque. **Internet** facilities are at Nutuk Internet Café, Ataturk Mah, 1040 Sok 6. The **hamam** (men Sat–Thurs 7am–11pm, women Fri noon–5pm; full treatment $10, plus small tip for masseur), next to the main police station, offers a cheap introduction to a good Turkish scrub and massage.

To stay outside Selçuk in the countryside, take one of the hourly minibuses to **ŞIRINCE**, a 600-year-old Greek stone village whose wine-making tradition, against the odds, has been continued by Muslim Turks who settled here in the 1920s. You can sleep overnight in one of the beautifully restored village houses which make up *Şirince Evler* (☎0232/898 3209; ❺).

Ephesus

With the exception of Pompeii, **EPHESUS** (Efes in Turkish) is the largest and best-preserved ancient city around the Mediterranean. Not surprisingly, the ruins are busy in summer, although with a little planning it's possible to tour the site in relative peace. Certainly, it's a place you should not miss. You'll need at least three partly shady hours, and a water bottle. Originally situated close to a temple devoted to the goddess Artemis, Ephesus' location by a fine harbour was the secret of its success in ancient times, eventually making it the wealthy capital of Roman Asia, ornamented with magnificent public buildings. During the Byzantine era the city went into decline, owing to the abandoning of Artemis worship, Arab raids, and (worst of all) the final silting up of the harbour, leading the population to move to the nearby hill crowned by the tomb and church of St John, future nucleus of the town of Selçuk.

Approaching from Kuşadası, get the *dolmuş* to drop you at the *Tusan Motel* junction, 1km from the gate. From Selçuk, it's a 3km walk. In the centre of the **site** (daily 8am–6pm; $10) is the **Arcadian Way**, which was once lined with hundreds of shops and illuminated at night. The nearby **theatre** has been partly restored to allow its use for open-air concerts and occasional summer festivals; it's worth the climb to the top for the views over the surrounding countryside. **Marble Street** passes the main **agora**, and a **Temple of Serapis** where the city's Egyptian merchants would have worshipped. About halfway along is a footprint, a female head and a heart etched into the rock – an alleged signpost for a **brothel**. On the side of the terraced hill, the **Slope Houses** were once the preserve of the rich and are still being excavated, not due to open to the public until 2005. Across the intersection looms the **Library of Celsus**, erected by the consul Gaius Julius Aquila between 110 and 135 AD as a memorial to his father Celsus Polemaeanus. The elegant, two-storey facade was fitted with niches for statues of the four personified intellectual virtues, today filled with copies (the originals are in Vienna). Just uphill, a **Byzantine fountain** looks across the Street of the Curetes to the **public latrines**, a favourite with visitors. Continuing along, you'll come to the so-called **Temple of Hadrian**, behind which sprawl the **Baths of Scholastica**, named after a fifth-century Byzantine woman whose headless statue adorns the entrance. On the far side of the street from the Hadrian shrine lies a huge pattern **mosaic**, which once fronted a series of shops. Further up Street of the Curetes you pass the **Temple of Domitian**, the lower floor of which houses a mildly interesting **Museum of Inscriptions**, on the way to the large, overgrown **upper agora**, fringed by a colonnade to the north, and a restored *odeion* and *prytaneum* or civic office.

Bodrum

In the eyes of its devotees, **BODRUM** – ancient Halicarnassos – with its white-washed houses and subtropical gardens, is the most attractive Turkish resort, a quality outfit in comparison to its upstart Aegean rivals. And it is a pleasant town in most senses, despite having no real beach, although development has proceeded apace over the last couple of decades. The centrepiece is the **Castle of St Peter** (Tues–Sun 9am–noon & 1–5pm; $7), built by the Knights of St John over a Selçuk fortress between 1437 and 1522. Inside, the various towers house a **Museum of Underwater Archeology**, which includes coin and jewellery rooms, classical and Hellenistic statuary, and Byzantine relics retrieved from two wrecks, alongside a diorama explaining salvage techniques. The **Carian princess hall** ($2.50 extra) displays the skeleton and sarcophagus of a fourth-century BC noblewoman unearthed in 1989. There is also the **Glass Wreck Hall** ($2.50 extra) containing the wreck and cargo of an ancient Byzantine ship, which sank near Marmaris. Immediately north of the castle lies the **bazaar**, from where you can stroll up Türkkuyusu Caddesi and turn left to the town's other main sight, the **Mausoleum** (daily 8am–5pm; $2). This is the burial place of Mausolus, who ruled Halicarnassos in the fourth century BC, greatly increasing its power and wealth. His tomb (from which we derive the word "mausoleum") was regarded as one of the Seven Wonders of the Ancient World, but the bulk of it is now in London's British Museum. The town's ancient **amphitheatre**, just above the main highway to the north, was begun by Mausolus and was modified in the Roman era; it's used during the annual September festival.

Ferries dock at the jetty west of the castle, close to the **tourist office** on İskele Meydanı (Mon–Fri 8.30am–5.30pm; summer also Sat & Sun). The **bus station** is 500m up Cevat Şakir Caddesi, which divides the town roughly in two. Bodrum Ferryboat Association (☎0252/316 0882) handles **ferries to Kos** ($20 one-way, $25 day return, $30 open return), as well as domestic services to Datça, while Bodrum Express Lines (☎0252/316 1087) handles **hydrofoils to Kos** ($30 one-way, $35 day return, $40 open return), **Rhodes** ($50 one-way, $60 day return, $70 open return) and domestic services to Marmaris. There's a port tax ($10), payable on arrival in Greece if you're not returning the same day. Some of the best **accommodation** is southeast of the bus station in Kumbahçe. *Emiko Pansiyon*, Atatürk Cad, Uslu Sok 11 (☎0252/316 5560, ✉emiko@turk.net; ❷), has a pleasant courtyard and quiet rooms. *Durak*, Rasthane Sok 8 (☎0252/316 1564; ❶), has some with balconies, as does the friendly *Uğur*, across the road at no. 13 (☎0252/316 2106; ❷). West of the bus station, *Melis*, Türkkuyusu Cad 50 (☎0252/316 0560; ❷), has en-suite rooms and attractive courtyards. The nearby *Dönen* (☎0252/316 4017; ❷) is a quiet family-run operation with a garden. *Dolmuşes* from the bus station head to nearby Akyarlar, which offers the best sandy beach around, some quiet *pansiyons* and restaurants, and a **campsite**.

You don't come to Bodrum to save money, and **eating out** is no exception. Best of the budget places is *Zetaş Ocakbaşı* on Atatürk Cad, which offers good *pide* and meat dishes. *Gemibaşı*, opposite the yacht harbour, on the corner of Firkayten Sok and Neyzen Tevfik, is good for a no-nonsense meat meal and also serves fish. The *Karadeniz* cake shop on Dr Alim Bey Cad does wonderful fruit and cream cakes. The same street boasts many of the town's fast-changing **bars** – current hot-spots include *Robin Hood* and the *White House*. *Halikarnas* at the east end of Cumhuriyet Cad is the most famous **club** on the Aegean, while the *M&M Marine Club* is reputedly the biggest floating disco in the world; it sets sail at 2am when the onshore establishments close. **Internet** access is at Hakim's Internet on Atatürk Cad.

Marmaris

MARMARIS rivals Kuşadası as the largest and most developed Aegean resort. Its huge marina and proximity to Dalaman airport mean that tourists pour in more or less non-stop during the warmer months. According to legend, the place was named when Süleyman the Magnificent, not finding the castle here to his liking, was heard to mutter *Miman as* ("Hang the architect") – a command which should perhaps still apply to the designers of the seemingly endless high-rises. Ulusal Egemenlik Bulvarı cuts Marmaris in half, and the maze of narrow streets east of it is home to most things of interest, though little is left of the sleepy fishing village that Marmaris was a mere two decades ago. Only the **Kaleiçi** district, the warren of streets at the base of the tiny castle, offers a pleasant wander, and the **castle museum** (Tues–Sun 8am–noon & 1–5.30pm; $1) has a worthwhile archeology and ethnography collection.

From the **bus station**, 1.5km south of the centre, pick up a *dolmuş* to take you into town. Many of the bus companies also offer a free transfer minibus to the centre. The **ferry** dock abuts İskele Meydanı, on one side of which stands the helpful **tourist office** (Mon–Fri 8.30am–noon & 1–5/7pm; summer also Sat & Sun). **Ferries to Rhodes** ($40 one-way, $57 open return) run daily in high season, weekly in winter. Agents include Yeşil Marmaris, Barbaros Cad 13 (☎0252/412 2290), and Engin Turizm, 3rd floor, G. Mustafa Cad 16 (☎0252/412 6944). Package tourism ensures that **hotels** here are expensive, and welcoming *pansiyons* few and far between, but the tourist office is tuned in to the needs of backpackers and can help out. The cheapest option is the *Interyouth Hostel* at Tepe Mahallesi 42, Sok 45, in the bazaar close to the Atatürk statue (☎0252/412 3687, ✉interyouth@turk.net; dorms $5, rooms ❶), with a lively rooftop café, Internet access and a competitively priced travel service. Behind the huge Tansaş shopping centre is the *Nadir*

(☎0252/412 1167; ❷) which has en-suite rooms with air-conditioning. Another good budget pension is the *Yeşim*, west of the centre towards Uzunyalı beach at Atatürk Cad 60, Sok 3 (☎0252/412 3001; ❶). More upmarket is the great-value *Marina* motel (☎0252/412 6598, ◍www.turquaz-guide.net; ❷), which has clean en-suite rooms and a breakfast terrace. The fabulous *Kırçiçeği* on Kübilay Alpagün Cad behind the bazaar offers excellent traditional Turkish **food** at reasonable prices. In the bazaar area, *Marmaris* and *Liman* are both acceptable and frequented by the locals. To the west, Uzunyali harbours various pizza joints and a reasonable Turkish restaurant, *Turhan*, at Uzunyali 26. For **drinking**, *Panorama*, up on the castle hill, offers great views, and the nearby Hacı Mustafa Sokaği contains a wealth of other drinking venues, such as *Davy Jones' Locker* and *Casablanca*.

Pamukkale and Hierapolis

The rock formations of **PAMUKKALE** (literally "Cotton Castle"), 140km northeast of Marmaris, are the most-visited attraction in this part of Turkey, a series of white terraces saturated with dissolved calcium bicarbonate, bubbling up from the feet of the Çal Dağı Mountains beyond. As the water surges over the edge of the plateau and cools, carbon dioxide is given off and calcium carbonate precipitated as hard chalk or travertine. The spring emerges in what was once the ancient city of Hierapolis, the ruins of which would merit a stop even if they weren't coupled with the natural phenomenon. The **travertine terraces** (daily 24hr; $3) are deservedly the first item on most visitors' agenda, but you should bear in mind the fragility of this natural phenomenon. Nowadays most of the pools are very shallow and closed off, with tourists confined to walking on specially marked routes, though this is, thankfully, having a positive effect, as the travertines slowly return to their former pristine whiteness, now enhanced by night-time **illumination** (8–11pm). Up on the plateau is what is spuriously billed as the **sacred pool** (daily 8am–8pm; $10) of the ancients, open for bathing in the 35°C mineral water. In reality, though, it's little more than a few big lumps of carved marble submerged in a concrete pool.

The archeological zone of **HIERAPOLIS** lies west of the village of Pamukkale Köyü, via a narrow road winding up past the *Turism Motel*. Its main features include a **Temple of Apollo** and the adjacent **Plutonium** – the latter a cavern emitting a toxic mixture of sulphur dioxide and carbon dioxide, capable of killing man and beast alike. There's also a restored **Roman theatre** dating from the second century AD, with most of the stage buildings and their elaborate reliefs intact. Arguably the most interesting part of the city, though, is the **colonnaded street** which once extended for almost 1km, terminating in monumental portals a few paces outside the walls – of which only the most northerly, a triple arch, still stands. Just south of the arch is the elaborate tomb of Flavius Zeuxis – the first of more than a thousand tombs constituting the **necropolis**, the largest in Asia Minor. There's also a **museum** (Tues–Sun 9am–12.30pm & 1.30–6.15pm; $1.50), housed in the restored, second-century baths, but the collection of statuary, sarcophagi and masonry fragments is disappointing.

There's no shortage of accommodation in the village of **PAMUKKALE KÖYÜ**, though touts at the bus stand can be particularly aggressive. One of the best and friendliest of over forty **pensions** is the air-conditioned *Koray* (☎0258/272 2222, ◍www.korayhotel.com; ❷), which has a pleasant garden and buffet meals. *Meltem Guest House* (☎0258/272 3134; ❶) and *Meltem Motel Backpacker's Inn* (☎0258/272 2413, ✉meltemmotel@superonline.com.tr; ❶) both have en-suite doubles and Internet access. Up the hill, the family-owned *Kervanseray* (☎0258/272 2209, ◍www.geocities.com/kervanseray2.tr; ❷) also has similar facilities. Most **restaurants** are attached to hotels, like the *Mustafa*, which offers vegetarian dishes cooked to order, but you'd probably do best eating at your *pansiyon*.

Turkey's Mediterranean coast

The first stretch of Turkey's **Mediterranean Coast**, dominated by the Arkdağ and Bey mountain ranges of the Taurus chain and known as the "**Turquoise Coast**", is its most popular, famed for its pine-studded shore, minor ruins and beautiful scenery. Most of this is connected by Highway 400, which winds precipitously above the sea from Marmaris to Antalya. In the west of the region, **Fethiye**, along with the nearby lagoon of **Ölüdeniz**, give good access to the pick of the region's Lycian ruins, such as **Xanthos**. The scenery becomes increasingly spectacular as you head towards the site of **Olympos**. Further along, past the port and major city of **Antalya**, the landscape is less dramatic but is home to yet more ruins, notably those of the old Pamphylian cities of **Perge** and **Sıde**, the latter better known as a tourist resort. Finally, the former pirate refuge of **Alanya** is set on a spectacular headland topped by a stunning Selçuk citadel.

Fethiye and around

FETHİYE is well sited for access to some of the region's ancient sites, many of which date from the time when this area was the independent kingdom of Lycia. The best beaches, around the Ölüdeniz lagoon, are now much too crowded for comfort, but Fethiye is still a real market town and has been able to spread to accommodate increased tourist traffic. Fethiye itself occupies the site of the Lycian city of **Telmessos**, little of which remains other than the impressive ancient theatre, which was only unearthed in 1992, and a number of Lycian rock tombs on the hillside above the bus station. You can also visit the remains of the medieval fortress, on the hillside behind the harbour area of town. In the centre of town, off Atatürk Caddesi, the small **museum** (Tues–Sun 8.30am–5.30pm; $2) has some fascinating exhibits from local sites and a good ethnographic section.

One of the most dramatic sights in the area is the ghost village of **KAYA KÖYÜ** (Levissi), 7km out of town, served by *dolmuşes* from the old bus station. The village was abandoned in 1923, when its Anatolian-Greek population was relocated, and all you see now is a hillside covered with more than two thousand ruined cottages and an attractive basilica. **Ölüdeniz** is about two hours on foot from Kaya Köyü – through the village, over the hill and down to the lagoon – or a *dolmuş* ride from Fethiye. The warm waters of this lagoon make for pleasant swimming, if you don't mind paying the small entrance fee, although the crowds can reach saturation level in high season – in which case the nearby beaches of Belceğiz and Kidrak are better bets. Ölüdeniz is also the starting point for the **Lycian Way**, Turkey's only marked trekking route, which starts from near the Montana Holiday Village on the Fethiye–Ölüdeniz road and winds along the coast almost as far as Antalya.

East of Fethiye lies the heartland of **ancient Lycia**, home to a number of important archeological sites. The closest is the **LETOÖN**, accessible by *dolmuş* from Fethiye to Kumluova, the site lying 4km off the main highway. The Letoön (daily 7am–7.30pm; $2.50) was the official sanctuary of the Lycian Federation, and the extensive remains bear witness to its importance. The low ruins of three **temples** occupy the centre of the site, and there is also a large, well-preserved **theatre**, entered through a vaulted passage. On the other side of the valley, the remains of the hilltop city of **XANTHOS** are perhaps the most fascinating of the Lycian sites, though the most important relic discovered at the site, the fourth-century Nereid Monument, is now in the British Museum. Buses between Fethiye and Patara drop you off in Kanak, from where it's a ten-minute walk up to the **ruins** (daily 7am–7.30pm; $2.50). West of the car park are the acropolis, agora and a Roman theatre, beside which are two Lycian tombs – the so-called **Harpy Tomb**, decorated with pairs of bird-woman figures carrying children in their arms, and a **sarcophagus** standing on a pillar tomb. Northeast of the agora looms a structure known popularly as the **Xanthian obelisk** – in fact the remains of a pillar tomb covered on all four sides by the longest-known Lycian inscription.

Practicalities

Fethiye's **bus station** is 2km east of the centre; *dolmuşes* to and from Ölüdeniz, Çalış beach and Kaya Köyü use the old station, east of the central market. The **tourist office** is close to the theatre, near the harbour at İskele Meydanı 1 (daily 8.30am–5.30/7.30pm; ☎0252/612 1527). There are two main concentrations of **hotels** – in the downtown area and in the quieter suburb of Karagözler, overlooking the marina to the west (there are direct *dolmuşes* to Karagözler from the bus station). Downtown, the *Ülgen Pansiyon* (☎0252/614 3491; ❶), up the stairs beyond Paspatir Cad, has simple en suites. Southeast of the centre and handiest for the bus station is *Sinderella*, Merdivenli Geçit 3 (☎0252/614 2288; ❶). In Karagözler, *Horizon* (☎0252/612 3153; ❷) is a long hike up above the marina but boasts great views, while *Pinara*, Fevzi Çakmak Cad 39 (☎0252/614 2151; ❶), is slightly noisier but friendly. Before you reach the *Horizon*, the *Ideal* (☎0252/614 1981, ⊛www10.brinkster.com/idealp/; ❶) is popular with backpackers, and has Internet access and a great terrace. For **camping**, one of the best sites is the *Ölüdeniz*, which has its own beach and restaurant; it's just past the entrance to Ölüdeniz lagoon on the left. *Sedir*, Tütün Sok 3, offers excellent, reasonably priced *pide* and home-cooked stews. Also reasonable is *Birlik Lokanta* opposite the PTT on Atatürk Cad, for traditional Turkish cooking and ice cream. The outdoor seafront **cafés** are nice places for a drink, while the hillside above the tourist office offers the garish *Yasmin*, specializing in live Turkish music. *Mango Bar* and *Car Cemetery Bar*, both on Paspartu Sok, vie for being the hottest joint in town.

Olympos and Çıralı

There's another Lycian site, **OLYMPOS**, 50km before Antalya, located on a beautiful sandy bay and the banks of a largely dry river. It's an idyllic site ($6 when someone is manning the ticket office), featuring some recently excavated tombs, the walls of a Byzantine church, and a theatre, most of whose seats have gone. On the north side of the river are more striking ruins, including a well-preserved marble temple entrance. Beyond is a Byzantine bath house with mosaic floors, and a Byzantine canal which would have carried water to the heart of the city. A pleasant 1.5km walk away is the village of **ÇIRALI**. About an hour's well-marked stroll above the village's citrus groves flickers the dramatic **Chimaera** (open 24hr; $1), a series of eternal flames issuing from cracks in the bare rock – you can put them out, but they will always re-ignite. The fire has been burning since antiquity, and inspired the Lycians to worship the god Hephaestos (or Vulcan to the Romans). The mountain was also associated with a fire-breathing monster, also known as the Chimaera, with a lion's head, a goat's rear and a snake for a tail.

There are one or two **minibuses** a day from Antalya to Çıralı in season; otherwise you'll have to take a taxi ($10) from the main road. To get directly to Olympos, catch any Kaş–Antalya bus to the minibus stop on the main highway, 8km up from the shore; there are hourly minibuses from there to Olympos in season. Çıralı boasts around forty **pensions**, ranging from the fairly basic to the frankly luxurious, all hidden in the citrus groves behind the beach – but the area is a national park and nesting turtles mean that camping on the beach, and night access in general, is forbidden. Best of the budget options is *Baris Pansiyon* (☎0212/825 7080; ❷), set around a pretty garden. *Yavuz* (☎0242/825 7021; ❷) is a moderately priced two-storey place tucked inside a grove of poplars. More upmarket *Blue and White* (☎0242/825 7006, ⊛www.bluewhite-otel.com; ❹) offers spotless air-conditioned en-suite bungalows. Back along the beach and ranged along the road behind the ruins are a group of backpacker **"tree-house" camps**, including *Kadir* (☎0242/892 1250, ⊛www.olympostreehouse.com; dorm $8, rooms ❷) and *Bayram's* (☎0242/892 1243, ⊛www.bayrams.com; ❶); both of these places are half-board and offer a variety of huts and Internet access, but can get fairly rowdy. There are a handful of pleasant, if pricey beach **restaurants** – *Karakas* does a good line in *mezes* and kebabs – but on the whole you'd do better eating in your pension/hotel. Note, too, that there are no **banks** or ATMs in Olympos or Çıralı, so make sure you have enough cash before arriving.

Antalya

ANTALYA is blessed with an ideal climate and a stunning setting. Despite the grim appearance of its concrete sprawl, it's an agreeable place, although the main area of interest for visitors is confined to the relatively small old quarter; its beaches don't rate much consideration. The city also makes a good base for visiting the nearby ancient site of Perge. The intersection of Cumhuriyet Caddesi and Sarampol is dominated by the **Yivli Minare** or "Fluted Minaret", erected in the thirteenth century. Downhill from here is the **old harbour**, recently restored and site of the evening promenade. North is the disappointing bazaar, while south, beyond the Saat Kalesi (clock tower), lies **Kaleiçi** or the old town, with every house being redone as a carpet shop, café or pension. On the far side, on Atatürk Caddesi, the triple-arched **Hadrian's Gate** recalls a visit by the emperor in 130 AD, while Hesapçı Sokak leads south past the **Kesik Minare** to a number of tea gardens and the **Hıdırlık Kulesi**, of indisputable Roman vintage but ambiguous function – it could have been a lighthouse, bastion or tomb. The one thing you shouldn't miss is the **Archeological Museum** (Tues–Sun 9am–6.30pm; $10), one of the top five archeological collections in the country; it's on the western edge of town at the far end of Kenan Evren Bulvarı, easily reachable by a tram that departs from the clock tower in Kaleiçi. Highlights include an array of Bronze Age urn burials, second-century statuary, an adjoining sarcophagus wing, and a number of mosaics, not to mention an ethnography section with ceramics, household implements, weapons and embroidery.

Antalya's main **bus station** is 8km north of town, although regular *dolmuşes* and city buses run from here to a terminal at the top of Kazım Özalp Caddesi (still known by its old name of Sarampol), which runs for just under 1km down to the clock tower on the fringe of the old town. About 5km west of the centre is the **ferry dock**, connected to the centre by *dolmuş*. The **airport** is 10km northeast; Havaş buses into town depart from the domestic terminal, five minutes' walk from the international terminal, while city-centre-bound *dolmuşes* pass nearby. The main **tourist office** is a fifteen-minute walk west from the clock tower on Cumhuriyet Cad (daily 8am–6/7pm; ☎0242/241 1747). Most travellers stay in the atmospheric old town, where almost every other building is a *pansiyon*, although there's also a nucleus of **hotels** between the bus station and the bazaar. *Sabah Pansiyon*, Hesapçı Sok 60/A (☎0242/247 5345, ⊛www.sabahpansiyon.8m.com; ❶), is clean, well-run and the owner speaks English; book ahead in season. Near the Hadarlak Kulesi, the ageing *Hadrianus*, Zeytin Sok 4/A (☎0242/244 0030; ❶), has a wonderful garden and recently renovated rooms. There are unparalleled rooftop sea views from both *Keskin 1*, Hadarlak Sok 35 (☎0242/244 0135; ❶), and the family-run *Senem*, Zeytingeçidi Sok 9 (☎0242/247 1752; ❷). *Keskin 2*, Hadarlak Sok 37 (☎0242/242 3941; ❶), has no views but a nice orange garden in which to breakfast. *Antique Pansiyon*, Tuzcular Mah, Paşa Camii Sok 28 (☎0242/242 4615, ⊜antique@ixir.com; ❷), is housed in a characterful old Ottoman house, albeit with erratic plumbing, and has an English-speaking owner. *Bambus* **camping**, 3km south of town on the Lara road, is expensive but has its own rocky cove for swimming.

Many Kaleiçi *pansiyons* have their own **restaurant**. For elegant dining, *Antique Pansiyon's* evening menu is particularly good; otherwise, the licensed *Parlak*, on Kazım Ozalp Cad, serves delicious grilled chicken, while *Sim*, Kaledibi Sok 7, offers reasonably priced home cooking. Cumhuriyet Caddesi is the location of a number of eating-places with terraces offering excellent views of the harbour; good for leisurely breakfasts. The covered pedestrian precinct, Eski Sebzeciler İçi Sokak, has a small number of restaurants serving the local speciality *tandır kebap* (mutton roasted in a clay pot). The *Gaziantep* eatery, at the edge of the bazaar through the *pasaj* at

İsmet Paşa Cad 3, is excellent. Two other quality choices are *Kebabistan* on Recep Peker Cad, which offers a good take on standard *pide* fare, and *Ol Gunegliler*, just north of the clock tower, serving southeastern specialities. **Nightlife** is mostly located around the harbour. The popular *Café İskele* has tables grouped around a fountain, while the nearby *Cece* often has live music. *Club 29*, an expensive disco, boasts a terrace with pool and a restaurant. A little inland in the Kale district, *İçi Karatayhan Pansiyon* features the laidback *Gizli Bahçe* bar. Further out, the *Olympos* disco, beside *Falez Hotel* near the archeological museum, is a popular late-night dance venue. There's an **Internet** café on Recep Peker Sok near Hadrian's Gate.

The Pamphylian cities

East of Antalya lies an area known in ancient times as **Pamphylia**, a remote region that was home to four great cities – Perge, Sillyon, Aspendos and Sıde – of which the first and last are the ones to see if time is limited. **PERGE**, 15km east of Antalya, can be reached by taking a *dolmuş* to the village of Aksu on the main east-bound road, from where it's a fifteen-minute walk to the site (daily 8.30am–7pm; $6, stadium free). It was founded around 1000 BC and is an enticing spot, the ruins expansive and impressive. Just beyond the site entrance, the theatre was originally constructed by the Greeks, but substantially altered by the Romans in the second century AD; built into the side of a hill, it could accommodate 14,000 people on 42 seating levels. Northeast of here is Perge's massive horseshoe-shaped stadium, the largest in Asia Minor, while east of the stadium is the city proper, marked by a cluster of souvenir and soft drinks stands. You'll see a Byzantine basilica, fourth-century AD agora, and some Roman baths, a couple of whose pools have been exposed. At the northwest corner of the agora is Perge's Hellenistic Gate, with its two mighty circular towers, behind which is a 300m-long colonnaded street, with a water channel running down the middle.

About 40km east of Perge, **SIDE**, a one-time port and trysting place of Antony and Cleopatra, was the foremost of the Pamphylian cities. The ruins of the ancient port just about survive; over the last ten years or so, the development of various hotel complexes has obliterated areas of real archeological interest. The **beaches** are superb, but if you're more interested in the ruins, try and visit out of season. The **city walls** are particularly well preserved, with a number of towers still in place, and the agora is today fringed with the stumps of many remaining columns. Opposite the agora is the site of the former Roman baths, now restored to house a **museum** (Tues–Sun 9am–noon & 12.30–6.30pm; $3) with a cross-section of locally unearthed objects – mainly Roman statuary, reliefs and sarcophagi. South of here, a still-intact monumental gateway serves as an entrance to the modern resort and to Sıde's 15,000-seat **theatre** ($6), the largest in Pamphylia. At the back of the theatre is a row of ancient toilets, complete with niches for statues facing the cubicles. To the west of town, the beach stretches for about 10km, lined by hotels and beach clubs, though the crowds can be heavy during high season. To the east the sands are emptier and stretch all the way to Alanya, though there's less in the way of facilities. Buses from Antalya most often drop off at Manavgat, 10km east of Sıde; **dolmuşes** from the street behind Manavgat's station will take you to Sıde's bus station, around 1km from the central waterfront, close to the monumental gateway. From here you can either walk, take a taxi or a tractor-drawn "tourist train" into the centre. Travelling on from Sıde, the best bus connections are from Manavgat.

Alanya

Now one of the Mediterranean coast's major resorts, **ALANYA** is a booming place that has fortunately managed to hold on to much of its character. It's much less crowded than Sıde, even in midsummer. Most of the old town lies on the great rocky promontory that juts out into the sea, the bulk of which is occupied by the

castle – an hour's winding climb or a short ride on an hourly bus from the tourist office. At the end of the road is the **İç Kale**, or inner fortress (daily 8am–sunset; $3), built in 1226 and virtually intact, with the shell of a Byzantine church, decorated with fading frescoes, in the centre. A platform in a corner of the fortress gives fine views of the western beaches and the mountains, though this originally served as a springboard from which prisoners were thrown to their deaths on the rocks below. On the opposite side of the promontory, the **Kızılkule** is a 35m-high defensive tower that today houses an **Ethnographic Museum** (Tues–Sun 8.30am–6pm; $1), and has a roof terrace that overlooks the town's eastern harbour. On the western side of the promontory, the **Alanya Museum** (daily 9am–noon & 1.30–6.30pm; $1) is filled with local archeological finds and ethnological ephemera, its garden a former Ottoman graveyard. Nearby, the **Damlataş** (daily 6–10am; $1), is a stalactite- and stalagmite-filled cavern with a moist, warm atmosphere said to ease asthma; it's accessible from behind the *Damlataş* restaurant. Alanya's **beaches**, though not particularly clean, are extensive, stretching 3km west and 8km east.

Alanya's **bus station** is a twenty-minute walk from the centre, but if you come in by local bus from Sıde or Manavgat you'll probably arrive at the *dolmuş* terminal, five minutes north of the centre. The **tourist office** is at Çarşı Mahallesi, Kalearkası (daily 8.30am–6pm; ☎0242/513 1240), opposite the town museum. In summer, **accommodation** soon fills up and prices can be high, although there's a concentration of *pansiyons* in the grid of streets between the bus station and the seafront. *Oba*, Meteoroloji Sok 8 (☎0242/513 2675; ❷), is a good budget choice, as is *Üstün Pansiyon* on the same street (☎0242/513 2262; ❷). Nearer the centre, behind Damlataş Cad, *Pension Best*, Alaaddinoğlu Sok 23 (☎0242/513 0446; ❶), has immaculately clean rooms and apartments. Another central alternative is *Hotel Carina*, Nergis Sok 4 (☎0242/513 1897; ❷). The small streets running between Gazipaşa and Hükümet caddesis have lots of cheap *pide* and **kebab places**. *Tuna Lokantasi*, Müftüler Cad, Kalgadam Sok 7, and *Buhara* and *Gülistan* on Kuyular Önü Sok offer excellent steam-tray, *pide* and grilled food at reasonable prices. *Kale*, overlooking the harbour, has good food and views, but at a price. There are **Internet** cafés on İskele Cad.

Central Turkey

When the first Turkish nomads arrived in **Anatolia** during the tenth and eleventh centuries, the landscape must have been strongly reminiscent of their Central Asian homeland. The terrain that so pleased the tent-dwelling herdsmen of a thousand years ago, however, has few attractions for modern visitors: monotonous, rolling vistas of stone-strewn grassland, dotted with rocky outcrops, hospitable only to sheep. In winter it can be numbingly cold, while in summer, temperatures can rise to unbearable levels. It seems appropriate that the heart of original Turkish settlement should be home to the political and social centre of modern Turkey – **Ankara**, a modern European-style capital, symbol of Atatürk's dream of a secular Turkish republic. The south-central part of the country draws more visitors, not least for **Cappadocia** in the far east of the region, where water and wind have created a land of fantastic forms from the soft tufa rock, including forests of cones, table mountains and canyon-like valleys. Further south still, **Konya** is best known as the birthplace of the mystical **Sufi** sect and is a good place to stop over between Cappadocia and the coast.

Ankara

Modern **ANKARA** is really two cities, a double identity that is due to the break-neck pace at which it has developed since being declared capital of the Turkish Republic in 1923. Until then Ankara – known as Angora – had been a small

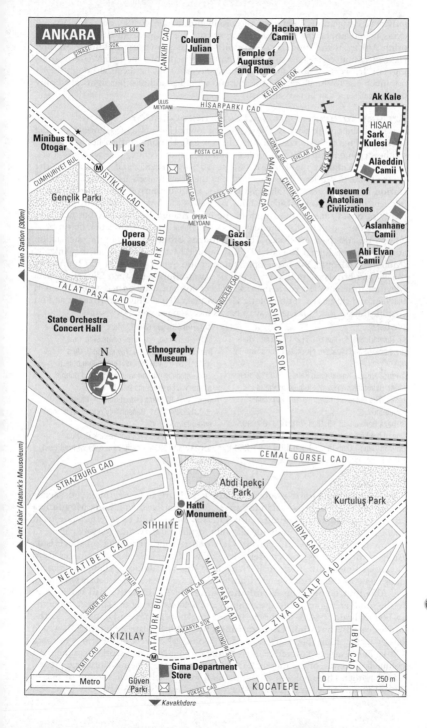

ANKARA

NEŞE SOK

ÇANKIRI CAD

Column of
Julian

Hacıbayram
Camii

Temple of
Augustus
and Rome

SINASI SOK

KEVGIRLI SOK

ULUS MEYDANI

HİSARPARKI CAD

Ak Kale

SÜSAM CAD

KONYA SOK

HISAR
Sark
Kulesi

Minibus to
Otogar

★

ULUS

POSTA CAD

ISIKLAR CAD

Alâeddin
Camii

CUMHURIYET BUL

M

İSTİKLÂL CAD

SANAYİ CAD

ÇERKES SOK

ANAFARTALAR CAD

ÇIKRIKÇILAR SOK

Museum of
Anatolian
Civilizations

Gençlik Parkı

OPERA
MEYDANI

Opera
House

Gazi
Lisesi

Aslanhane
Camii

ATATÜRK BUL

DENIZCILER CAD

Ahi Elvan
Camii

TALAT PAŞA CAD

State Orchestra
Concert Hall

HASIR CILAR SOK

N

Ethnography
Museum

Train Station (300m)

Anıt Kabir (Atatürk's Mausoleum)

CEMAL GÜRSEL CAD

STRAZBURG CAD

Abdi İpekçi
Park

Kurtuluş Park

Hatti
Monument

M

SIHHIYE

LIBYA CAD

NECATIBEY CAD

İZMİR CAD

ATATÜRK BUL

MITHAT PAŞA CAD

ZIYA GÖKALP CAD

LIBYA CAD

SÜMER SOK

TUNA CAD

KIZILAY

İZMİR CAD

SAKARYA SOK

BAYINDIR SOK

M

Gima Department
Store

- - - Metro

Güven
Parkı

YÜKSEL CAD

KOCATEPE

0   250 m

Kavaklıdere

provincial city, famous chiefly for the production of soft goat's wool. This city still exists, in and around the old citadel that was the site of the original settlement. The other Ankara is the modern metropolis that has grown up around a carefully planned attempt to create a seat of government worthy of a modern, Western-looking state. It's worth visiting just to see how successful this has been, although there's not much else to the place, and the museums and handful of other sights need only detain you for a day or two at most.

Arrival, information and accommodation

Ankara's Esenboğa **airport** is 33km north of town. Havaş buses ($4) meet incoming Turkish Airlines flights; a taxi will set you back $30. The **bus station** lies 8km to the southeast; some companies run service minibuses to the centre, otherwise take a *dolmuş* or the **Ankaray** rapid transit system ($0.50) to Kızılay and change onto the **metro** (same ticket) for Ulus, where most of the budget hotels are located. The **train station** is at the corner of Talat Paşa Caddesi and Cumhuriyet Bulvarı, from where frequent buses run to Kızılay and Ulus. As well as the Ankaray and metro there are plenty of **buses** running the length of the main Atatürk Bulvarı. Buy bus tickets in advance from kiosks next to the main bus stops (it's a good idea to stock up on tickets, as some areas have no kiosks). There's a **tourist office** across from the train station at Gazi Mustafa Kemal Bulvarı 121, just outside Maletepe station on the Ankaray (Mon–Fri 9am–5pm, Sat 10am–5pm; summer also Sun; ☎0312/231 5572). Most of the cheaper **hotels** are in the streets east of Atatürk Bulvarı between Ulus and Opera Meydanı; there are a few more upmarket places north of Ulus, on and around Çankırı Caddesi, and clusters of options along Gazi Mustafa Kemal Bulvarı in Maltepe and on Atatürk Bulvarı south of Kızılay, with prices increasing as you move south.

Hotels

As Rüzgarlı Sok 4, Ulus ☎0312/310 3998. Well-priced clean and pleasant en-suite rooms with TV. ➋

Angora House Kalekapası, Kaleiçi ☎0312/309 8380. Beautifully renovated house in the old castle. The hosts are attentive and the rooms sumptuous. ➎

Buhara Sanayi Cad 13, Ulus ☎0312/310 7999. One of the better choices in Ulus, with en suites. ➋

Devran Sanayi Cad, Tavus Sok 8, Ulus ☎0312/311 0485. Bright, clean en-suite rooms. ➋

Güleryüz Sanayı Cad 37, Ulus. Comfortable, if a little overpriced, en-suite rooms with TV. ➋

Mithat İtfaiye Meydanı, Tavus Sok 2, Ulus ☎0312/311 5410, ®www.otelmithat.com.tr. Professionally run, offering single and double rooms with bathrooms and TV. ➋

Olimpiyat Rüzgarlı Eşdost Sok 14, Ulus ☎0312/324 3331. Reasonably priced with good en-suite rooms. ➋

Yavuz Anafartalar Cad, Konya Sok 6, Ulus ☎0312/324 3255. Cheap as it gets without being too shabby. ➊

The City

The city is bisected north–south by **Atatürk Bulvarı**, and everything you need is in easy reach of this broad and busy street. At the northern end, **Ulus Meydanı**, a large square and an important traffic intersection marked by a huge equestrian Atatürk statue, is the best jumping-off point for the old part of the city - a village of narrow cobbled streets and ramshackle wooden houses centring on the **Hisar**, Ankara's old fortress and citadel. Most of what can be seen today dates from Byzantine times, with substantial Selçuk and Ottoman additions. There are tremendous views of the rest of the city from inside, as well as a twelfth-century mosque, the **Alâeddin Camii**. The **Aslanhane Camii** and **Ali Elvan Camii** bazaar areas to the south are more impressive, built by the Selçuks during the thirteenth century. Follow Kadife Sokak from here towards the modern city and you come to **the Museum of Anatolian Civilizations** (Tues–Sun 8.30am–5.30pm; $3), which boasts an incomparable collection of archeological objects housed in a restored Ottoman *bedesten*, or covered market. Hittite carving and relief work form the most compelling section of the museum, mostly taken from Carchemish, near the present Syrian border. There are also Neolithic finds from Çatal Höyük, the site of one of Anatolia's oldest settlements and widely regarded as the world's first "city".

TURKEY | Central Turkey

30

North of Ulus Meydanı is what's left of Roman Ankara, namely the **Column of Julian** on Hükümet Meydanı. Close by, the **Hacıbayram Camii**, built in 1400, was erected on the ruins of the **Temple of Augustus and Rome**, built by the Phrygians during the second century BC in honour of Cybele. South down Atatürk Bulvarı, **Gençlik Parkı** was built on the orders of Atatürk to provide a recreational spot for the hard-working citizens of his model metropolis; it features an artificial lake, funfair, cafés and an **Opera House** near the entrance. Further down Atatürk Bulvarı, the **Ethnography Museum** (Tues–Sun 8.30am–5.30pm; $1) boasts rooms used as an office by the great man, as well as the usual collection of folk costumes and Ottoman art and artefacts.

Across the main west–east rail line lies **Sıhhıye Meydanı** and the real heart of modern Ankara, which focuses on the large square of Kızılay, the main transport hub of the city. A few streets east rise the four minarets of the **Kocatepe Camii**, a modern mosque built in Ottoman-style that ranks as one of the biggest in the world. Beyond lies Turkey's parliament building, a strip of embassies, and the **Presidential Palace** (Çankaya Köşku; guided tours Sun 1.30–5pm; free) Atatürk's Ankara residence, whose grounds are home to the Çankaya Atatürk Museum (same times and ticket). Northeast of here, **Anıt Kabir** is the site of **Atatürk's mausoleum** (daily 9am–4/5pm; free; bus #265 from Ulus and near Tandoğan Ankaray station), at the end of a long colonnaded avenue lined by Hittite lions. It's almost bare inside except for the forty-tonne sarcophagus and the guards. At the south-eastern end of the courtyard is a **museum** (Sun 1.30–4.30pm) containing various pieces of Atatürk memorabilia, including a number of Lincoln limousines, which served as his official transport.

Eating and drinking

Standard *pide* and kebab places can be found on just about every street in Ankara and there's an abundance of good sweet and cake shops, though really good **restaurants** are surprisingly rare. Ulus, particularly along Çankırı Caddesi, is the place to look for cheap lunchtime venues, although most night-time eating and drinking takes place in the modern centre around Kızılay, where Sakarya, Selanik and Bayindir soks harbours a range of possibilities. Or try further south in the well-heeled district of Kavaklıdere. There are some **bars and cafés** in the more affluent parts of town towards the southern end of Atatürk Bulvarı, while there are a number of decent watering holes in the streets around Sakarya Caddesi in Kızılay. Ankara's citizens are proud of the **Opera House** at Opera Meydanı, which is great value: admission is usually $5 or under for lively and well-attended performances of works such as *Madame Butterfly* and *La Bohème*. **Clubs** can be found at *Kashmere* and *Complex*, both on Farabi Sok, Çankaya.

Cafés and restaurants

Altin Şiş Karanfil Sok 17, Kızılay. A reasonably priced kebab place, which also does good puddings.

Bosna Çankırı Cad 11, Ulus. Tasty soups, grilled chicken, kebabs, *lahmacun* and desserts.

Çiçek Lokantası Çankırı Cad 12A, Ulus. One of Ankara's mainstays, serving traditional dishes in regal splendour, albeit at a price.

Gaziantepli Fethi Bey Kebab Sanaycilar Cad 35, Ulus. Good variations on standard southeastern specialities.

Hisar Kule On the left inside the entrance to the Kule. One of several old-citadel restaurants in restored houses. Wonderful views from the terrace.

Hünkar kebap Selanik Sok 16, Kızılay. Excellent place to savour *İskender kebap*.

Kebabıstan Corner of Karanfil Sok and Yüksel Cad, Kızılay. Plush kebab restaurant, offering all kinds of kebab, including excellent mushroom *şiş*.

Samsun & Bafra Selanik Cad 6, Kızılay. Great *pide* and friendly staff.

Bars

London Pub Arjantin Cad 40, Kavaklıdere. Popular with richer students and professionals, and packed at the weekends.

Salata Bar Reşit Galip Cad 57/A, Gaziosmanpaşa. A café/bar student hangout with live music in the evening and some snack food.

Listings

Cappadocia

A land created by the complex interaction of natural and human forces over vast spans of time, **CAPPADOCIA**, around 150km southeast of Ankara, is initially a disturbing place, the great expanses of bizarrely eroded volcanic rock giving an impression of barrenness. It is in fact an exceedingly fertile region, and one whose weird formations of soft, dusty rock have been adapted over millennia by many cultures, from Hittites to later Christians hiding away from Arab marauders. There are more than a thousand rock-churches in Cappadocia, dating from the earliest days of Christianity to the thirteenth century, and some caves are still inhabited. It's a popular area with tourists, and getting more so, but the crowds are largely confined to a few areas. For breathtaking perspective on this complex geological wonderland you could splash out on a **hot air balloon** ride: Goreme Balloons (☎0384/341 5662, ⓦwww.goremeballoons.com) have offices in Göreme and Ürgüp and fly every morning between April and November.

The best-known sites are located within the triangle delineated by the roads connecting Nevşehir, Avanos and Ürgüp. Within this region are the valleys of **fairy chimneys**, formed when patches of hard lava settled on top of the soft greyish bedrock (composed of compacted volcanic ash); the areas topped by lava chunks resisted erosion, eventually forming 50m-high cones which dot the landscape. Also here are the rock-cut churches of the **Göreme Open-Air Museum**, with their amazing selection of frescoes, and the **Zelve** monastery, a complex of troglodyte dwellings and churches hewn out of the rock. **Nevşehir** itself isn't much of a town, but it's an important travel centre whilst **Göreme** and **Ürgüp** make more attractive bases to tour the area, though are less well served by public transport. Outside the triangle to the south are the underground cities of **Derinkuyu** and **Kaymaklı**, fascinating warrens attesting to the ingenuity of the ancient inhabitants.

Nevşehir

Though said to be Turkey's richest town, **NEVŞEHİR**, at the very heart of the region, can hardly be accused of ostentatious wealth. Nevertheless, frequent bus services all over Cappadocia run from here, and you'll probably find yourself detouring through when

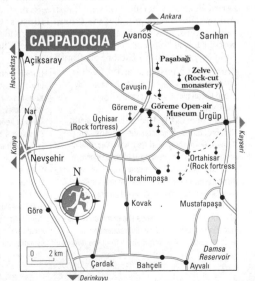

travelling between other neighbouring towns. The **Ottoman castle** at the heart of the old city, southwest of the modern centre, is a good landmark. The new city below is divided by two main streets, Atatürk Bulvarı, on which are situated most of the hotels and restaurants, and Lale Caddesi, turning into Gülzehir Caddesi to the north, where you'll find the main **dolmuş station**. The remains of the citadel are no big deal but the views are good. On the side of the hill, the impressive eighteenth-century **Damat İbrahim Paşa Camii** is set in a large precinct surrounded by narrow streets, and has a cool, dark interior enhanced by small decorative details. Opposite, the **Damat İbrahim Paşa Hamamı** (daily 5am–midnight: women only Sat 10am–4pm, men only at other times; $3 or $10 with massage, scrub, tea and *nargile*) is also in good working order and well run. The **tourist office** is on Atatürk Bulvarı, on the right as you head downhill towards Ürgüp (Mon–Fri 9am–5/5.30pm; summer also Sat & Sun; ☎0384/213 3659). **Pensions** in Nevşehir are neither as cheap nor as good as elsewhere in Cappadocia, and best value in town goes to *Hotel Viva* (☎0384/213 1326; ❶); more upmarket and just round the corner is the friendly and equally clean *Hotel Seven Brothers* (☎0384/213 4979; ❷). The nicest of the **campsites** in the region, the *Koru Mocamp*, is signposted off to the right as you turn from Nevşehir into Üçhisar. For **food**, the *Aspava Restaurant*, Atatürk Bulvarı 29, serves well-prepared dishes, and the *Sölen*, just before *Hotel Şems* on Atatürk Bulvarı, has good kebabs. The *Park-Bostan*, in gardens just off Atatürk Bulvarı, is more pricey but licensed.

Derinkuyu and Kaymaklı

Among the most extraordinary phenomena of the Cappadocia region are the remains of a number of **underground settlements**, some of them large enough to have accommodated up to 30,000 people. The cities are thought to date back to Hittite times, though the complexes were later enlarged by Christian communities, who added missionary schools, churches and wine cellars. A total of forty such settlements have been discovered, and the most thoroughly excavated is **DERİNKUYU** (daily 8am–5.30pm; $6.50), 29km from Nevşehir and accessible by *dolmuş*. The city is well lit and the original ventilation system still functions remarkably well, but some of the passages are small and cramped. The excavated area (only a quarter of the total) consists of eight floors and includes stables, wine presses and a dining hall or schoolroom with two long, rock-cut tables, plus living quarters, churches, armouries, a cruciform church, meeting hall and dungeon. Some 10km north of Derinkuyu is **KAYMAKLI** (daily 8am–5.30pm; $6.50), where only five of its underground levels have been excavated to date. The layout is very similar to Derinkuyu, with networks of streets with small living spaces leading off into underground plazas with various functions, the more obvious of which are stables, smoke-blackened kitchens, storage spaces and wine presses.

Göreme

The small town of **GÖREME** is the best known of the few remaining Cappadocian villages whose rock-cut houses and fairy chimneys are still inhabited. In the last few years these ancient living quarters have slowly been destroyed by development, which has led to a "Save Göreme" campaign. However, it is still possible to get away from what is now essentially a holiday village, and the tufa landscapes are just a short stroll away. When buying your bus ticket to Göreme be sure to check the end destination, as some bus firms may sell you a ticket there but will actually drop you off in Nevşehir, from where you'll have to continue by local bus or *dolmuş* (the last of which leaves Nevşehir at about 6pm).

There are two churches in the hills above the village, the **Durmuş kadir kilisesi**, clearly visible across the vineyard next to a cave-house with rock-cut steps, and the double-domed **Karşıbucak yusuf koç kilisesi**, which houses frescoes in very good condition. About 2km outside the village, the **Göreme Open-Air Museum** (daily 8am–5/6pm; $7.50) is the site of over thirty other churches, mainly dating from the ninth to the end of the eleventh century and containing some of the best of all the frescoes in Cappadocia. Most are barely discernible from the outside, apart from a few small holes serving as windows or air shafts. But inside, the churches re-create many of the features of Byzantine buildings, with domes, barrel-vaulted ceilings and cruciform plans supported by mock pillars, capitals and pendentives. The best-preserved church is the **Tokalı kilise** ($2.50 extra), located away from the others on the opposite side of the road, about 50m back towards the village. It's in fact two churches, both frescoed, an old church, dating from 920 AD, and a new church, whose frescoes represent some of the finest examples of tenth-century Byzantine art. The most famous of the churches in the main complex are the **Elmalı kilise**, the **Karanlık kilise** whose frescoes have recently been restored, and the **Carıklı kilise** – all eleventh-century churches heavily influenced by Byzantine forms and painted with superb skill. Look, too, at the church of **St Barbara**, named after the depiction of the saint on the north wall.

Göreme's **tourist office** (daily 5am–9pm) in the **bus station** has a useful accommodation list and maps of the local area. Cheapest of the **pensions** is the *Tuna Caves* (☎0384/271 2681; dorms $3, rooms ❶), which has cave rooms and a pleasant terrace, while the *Blue Moon*, just east of the bus station (☎0384/271 2433; ❷), has immaculate en-suite rooms. Friendly *Paradise* towards the Open-Air Museum (☎0384/271 2248, ⊛www.hitit.co.uk/paradise; ❶) has constant hot water, some cave rooms and a cave bar, while nearby *L'Elysee Pension* (☎0384/271 2244, ⓔelyseegoreme@yahoo.tr; ❷), has clean simple rooms. *Local Pansiyon* (☎0384/271 2171; ⊛www.localcavehouse.com; ❷) enjoys good views from its poolside terrace perched a little higher up the valley. For more luxury try *Göreme House* (☎0384/271 2668; ❷), just up a cobbled road behind the mosque, which has excellent en-suite rooms, central heating and some rooms with jacuzzis (❹). There are several **campsites** on the fringes of Göreme, best being *Panorama*, 1km out on the Üçhısar road, and *Dilek,* on the Ürgüp road, which is more sheltered and has a nice little restaurant; both have swimming pools. *Hotel Ataman* has the best **restaurant**, serving everything from local specialities to French soufflés; the *Ottoman House* is the place to sample traditional cuisine. Among the handful of overpriced restaurants on the main road, *Sultan* serves vegetarian food and pasta, though *Sedef* is livelier. There's **Internet** access at the Neşe Café in the town centre, not far from the Ürgüp road.

Ürgüp

There is also plenty of accommodation in **ÜRGÜP**, a pretty old town with its own cave dwellings 5km east of Göreme. In some ways, this can make a more sophisticated alternative to Göreme as it has managed to accommodate tourism much better and still allows access to the more traditional aspects of Turkish life. Ürgüp's **tourist office** (Mon–Fri 8am–5/7pm; summer also Sat & Sun; ☎0384/341 4059) on the main shopping street, Kayseri Cad, maintains an up-to-date price list of **hotels and pensions**. *Hotel Hitit* (☎0384 341 4481, ⊛www.hitithotel.com; ❸) has decent rooms, as well as a lovely rose garden and cave bar; *Asia Minor* (☎0384/341 4645; ⊛www.cappadociahouse.com; ❸), with its courtyard, is one of Ürgüp's most attractive buildings; the *Otel Melis*, out of the centre on the Nevşehir road (☎0384/341 2495, ⊛www.melishotel.com; ❸), has a variety of pleasant en-suite rooms ranged around a swimming pool; *Sun Pansiyon*, behind the *hamam* on İstiklâl Cad (☎0384/341 4493; ❷), has a few cave rooms reputed to be a thousand years old; and the *Yıldız Hotel*, just past the police station on the Kayseri road (☎0384/341 4610; ❷), has basic, spacious en suites. There are numerous **tour operators** in Ürgüp; try Magic Valley, next to the bus station at Güllüce Cad 7 (☎0384/341 2145). Eftelya, near the bus station, offers **Internet** access. **Eating** options include *Cirahan Restaurant*, in the central square, Cumhuriyet Meydani, beside the *hamam*, which serves traditional Turkish dishes. Also in the square is *Şömine,* serving well-prepared specialities. Another excellent, affordable choice is the

Kervan courtyard restaurant, for quality home cooking. *Kardeşler 2* dishes up an excellent vegetarian casserole (*güveç*), while *Kent* serves excellent *saç kavurma* (fried beef). The *Prokopi* Bar, Istikal Cad 46, provides an atmospheric place for a drink.

Konya

Roughly midway between Antalya and Nevşehir, **KONYA** is a place of pilgrimage for the Muslim world – the home of Celalledin Rumi or the **Mevlâna** ("Our Master"), the mystic who founded the Mevlevî or **Whirling Dervish** sect, and the centre of **Sufic** mystical practice and teaching. It was also a capital during the Selçuk era, many of the buildings from which are still standing, along with examples of their highly distinctive crafts and applied arts, now on display in Konya's museums. The **Mevlâna Müzesi** (Mon 10am–5pm, Tues–Sun 9am–5pm; $2.50) is housed in the first lodge (*tekke*) of the Mevlevî dervish sect, at the eastern end of Mevlâna Bulvarı, easily recognizable by its distinctive fluted turquoise dome. The main building of the museum holds the mausoleum containing the tombs of the Mevlâna, his father and other notables – as with mosques, shoes must be left at the door, women must cover their heads, and whether you're male or female, if you're wearing shorts you'll be given a skirt-like affair to cover your legs. You can take photographs of the mausoleum, but remember to be respectful; it is an extremely holy site. The original *semahane* (ceremonial hall) exhibits some of the musical instruments of the first dervishes, the original illuminated poetical work of the Mevlâna, and a 500-year-old silk carpet from Selçuk Persia that is supposedly the finest ever woven. In the adjoining room, a casket containing hairs from the beard of the Prophet Muhammad is displayed alongside illuminated medieval Korans. A separate building houses an exhibition of dervish memorabilia and some bizarre waxwork figures.

Konya's **bus station** is 10km out of town, from where the Konak *dolmuş* and tramway connects with the town centre; the **train station** is 2km out of the centre at the far end of İstasyon Caddesi, connected to the centre by regular *dolmuşes*. The **tourist office** is at Mevlâna Cad 21 (Mon–Fri 8am–5pm; ☎0332/351 1074). Konya's better **hotels** are on or just north of Mevlâna Caddesi; outside the annual Mevlâna festival (Dec) rates can usually be bargained down. *Otel Bey,* Ayanbey Sok 25 (☎0332/352 0173; ❷) is the best of the budget options; for a little less, *Otel Tur,* Esarizade Sok 13 (☎0332/351 9825; ❷), is quiet, comfortable and friendly. Similarly priced is the *Otel Çeşme*, Akifpaşa Sok 21, off İstanbul Cad (☎0322/351 2426; ❷), where some of the slightly stuffy rooms have baths. If you have a little more to spend the *Yeni Köşk*, Kadılar Sok 28 (☎0332/352 0671; ❸), is a cut above the rest. As for **eating**, the *Şifa Lokantası*, Mevlâna Cad 29, is reasonably priced, and nearby *Sema* offers tasty soups and kebabs. *Tilsum Restaurant*, west of the centre on Meram

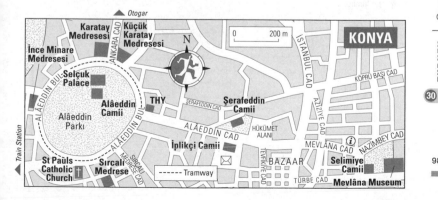

Cad, also serves excellent kebabs. For good views over the museum and a range of reasonably priced Turkish dishes try *Gulbahçesi*, whilst the *Köşk* next to the Mevlâna museum, serves local Konya kebab specialities and has live music. Express Internet, Alâeddin Bulvarı 21, is one of a number of **Internet** places southwest of Alâeddin Tepesi.

Travel details

Trains

Ankara to: İzmir (2 daily; 14–15hr).
İstanbul to: Ankara (6 daily; 8–9hr 30min); Edirne (1 daily; 6hr 30min); Denizli (1 daily; 14hr 30min); İzmir (2 daily; 11hr); Konya (3 daily; 14hr).
İzmir to: Selçuk (6 daily; 2hr).

Buses and dolmuşes

Ankara to: Antalya (12 daily; 10hr); Bodrum (10 daily; 12hr); Bursa (hourly; 7hr); Fethiye (2 daily; 12hr); İstanbul (every 30min; 6hr); İzmir (hourly; 9hr); Konya (14 daily; 3hr 30min); Marmaris (14 daily; 13hr); Nevşehir (12 daily; 4hr 30min).
Antalya to: Alanya (hourly; 2hr); Antakya (1 daily; 12hr); Denizli (6 daily; 5hr 30min); Fethiye, by inland route (3 daily; 4hr); İzmir (6 daily; 9hr 30min); Konya (6 daily; 6hr); Sıde (3 hourly; 1hr 15min); Nevşehir (1 daily; 11hr).
Ayvalık to: Bergama (8 daily; 1hr); Bursa (10 daily; 4hr 30min); Çanakkale (hourly; 3hr).
Bodrum to: Fethiye (6 daily; 4hr 30min); Kuşadası (3 daily; 3hr); Marmaris (8 daily; 3hr 15min); Selçuk (hourly; 3hr).
Bursa to: Çanakkale (hourly; 5hr).
Denizli to: Bodrum (2–3 daily; 4hr 30min);Fethiye (5 daily; 4hr); Konya (several daily; 7hr 15min); Marmaris (6 daily; 4hr).
Edirne to: Çanakkale (4 daily; 4hr 30min);
Fethiye to: Marmaris (10 daily; 3hr); Patara (10 daily; 1hr 30min).

İstanbul to: Alanya (hourly; 14hr); Antalya (4 daily; 12hr); Ayvalık (4 daily; 9hr); Bodrum (4 daily; 12hr); Bursa (hourly; 5hr); Çanakkale (hourly; 5hr 30min); Datça (1 daily; 17hr); Denizli (hourly; 15hr); Edirne (hourly; 3hr); Fethiye (hourly; 15hr); İzmir (hourly; 10hr); Göreme (5 daily; 12hr 30min); Kuşadası (3 daily; 11hr); Marmaris (4 daily; 13hr); Nevşehir (3 daily; 12hr); Sıde (1 daily; 13hr); Ürgüp (5 daily; 12hr 30min); Konya (7 daily; 11hr).
İzmir to: Ayvalık (every 30min; 2hr 30min); Bergama (hourly; 2hr); Bodrum (hourly; 4hr); Bursa (6 daily; 7hr); Çanakkale (4 daily; 5hr 30min); Çeşme (every 15–20min; 1hr 30min); Datça (hourly; 7hr); Denizli (hourly; 4hr); Fethiye (12–18 daily; 7hr); Kuşadası (every 30min; 1hr 40min); Marmaris (hourly; 5hr); Nevşehir (1 daily; 12hr); Selçuk (hourly; 1hr).
Kuşadası to: Pamukkale (12 daily; 3hr 30min).
Marmaris to: Dalaman (hourly; 1hr 30min); Nevşehir (1 daily; 14hr).
Nevşehir to: Konya (4 daily; 3hr).

Domestic ferries

Bodrum to: Datça (April–Oct 2 daily; 2hr); Marmaris (April–Oct 1 daily; 1hr30min).
Çanakkale to: Eceabat (hourly; 20min).
Gelibolu to: Lapseki (15 daily; 20min).
İstanbul to: İzmir (1 weekly; 19hr); Yalova (for Bursa or İznik, 7daily; 1hr).
Kilitbahir to: Çanakkale (hourly; 10min).

Language

Language

Language

I f you're making a general tour of Europe you can't hope always to speak the language of the country you're travelling in, and in any case in Germany, Scandinavia, and especially the Netherlands and Switzerland, many people, particularly the young, speak reasonable English. That said, it is polite to know at least a few very basic words and phrases wherever you happen to be, which is why we've included the chart on the following pages, and a smattering of French, German or Russian is handy everywhere as a common language if English fails.

Rough Guides phrasebooks are now available for Czech, Dutch, French, German, Greek, Hungarian, Italian, Polish, Portuguese, Russian, Spanish and Turkish, and there's also a European Languages phrasebook. Pocket **dictionaries** can easily be bought for most European languages in the countries where they are spoken, and usually at home too. If you want to get to grips further with any of the languages, Routledge's "Colloquial" series is the best place you could start.

Bulgarian, Croatian and Czech

	Bulgarian	Croatian	Czech
Yes	Da	Da	Ano
No	Ne	Ne	Ne
Please	Molya	Molim	Prosím
Thank you	Blagodarya	Hvala	Děkuju
Hello/Good day	Dobâr den	Bog/Dobar dan	Dobý, den/ahoj
Goodbye	Dovizhdane	Bog/Do vidjenja	Na shledanou
Excuse me	Izvinyavaïte	Izvinite	Promiňte
Where	Kude	Gdje	Kde
When	Koga	Kada	Kdy
How	Kak	Kako	Jak
Left	Lyavo	Lijevo	Vlevo
Right	Dyasno	Desno	Vpravo
Large	Golyama	Veliko	Velký
Small	Malko	Malo	Malý
Good	Dobro	Dobro	Dobrý
Bad	Plosho	Loše	Spatný
Near	Blizo	Blizu	Blízko
Far	Daleche	Daleko	Daleko
Cheap	Eftino	Jeftino	Levný
Expensive	Skupo	Skupo	Drahý
Open	Otvoreno	Otvoreno	Oteřueno
Closed	Zatvoreno	Zatvoreno	Zavřeno
Today	Dnes	Danas	Dnes
Yesterday	Vechera	Juče	Včera
Tomorrow	Utre	Sutra	Zítra

	Bulgarian	Croatian	Czech
Day	Den	Dan	Den
Week	Sedmitza	Tjedan	Týden
Month	Mesetz	Mjesec	Měsíc
Year	Godina	Godina	Rok
How much is...?	Kolko stroova?	Koliko stoji...?	Kolík stojí...?
What time is it?	Kolko e chasut?	Koliko je sati?	Kolík je hodin?
Where is...?	Kude e...?	Gdje je...?	Kde je...?
I don't understand	Ne razbiram	Ne razumijem	Nerozumím
Do you speak English?	Govorite li Angliski?	Govorite li engleski?	Miuvíte Anglicky?
Please write it down	Molya napishete go	Našiyite ga molim	Prosím, napište to
One	Edin/edna	Jedan	Jeden
Two	Dve	Dva	Dva
Three	Tri	Tri	Tři
Four	Chetiri	Četiri	Čtyři
Five	Pet	Pet	Pět
Six	Shest	Šest	Šest
Seven	Sedem	Sedam	Sedm
Eight	Osem	Osam	Osum
Nine	Devet	Devet	Devět
Ten	Deset	Deset	Deset

Danish, Dutch and Estonian

	Danish	Dutch	Estonian
Yes	Ja	Ja	Jah
No	Nej	Nee	Ei
Please	Vaer så venlig	Alstublieft	Palun
Thank you	Tak	Dank u/Bedankt	Aitäh/tänan
Hello/Good day	Goddag	Hallo	Tere
Goodbye	Farvel	Dag/Tot ziens	Head aega
Excuse me	Undskyld	Pardon	Vabandage
Where	Hvor	Waar	Kus
When	Hvornår	Wanneer	Millal
How	Hvordan	Hoe	Kuidas
Left	Venstre	Links	Vasak
Right	Højre	Rechts	Parem
Large	Stor	Groot	Suur
Small	Lille	Klein	Väike
Good	God	Goed	Hea
Bad	Dårlig	Slecht	Halb
Near	Naer	Dichtbij	Lähedal
Far	Fjern	Ver	Kaugel
Cheap	Billig	Goedkoop	Odav
Expensive	Dyr	Duur	Kallis
Open	Åben	Open	Avatud
Closed	Lukket	Dicht	Suletud

	Danish	Dutch	Estonian
Today	I dag	Vandaag	Täna
Yesterday	I går	Gisteren	Eile
Tomorrow	I morgen	Morgen	Homme
Day	Dag	Dag	Päev
Week	Uge	Week	Nädal
Month	Måned	Maand	Kuu
Year	År	Jaar	Aasta
How much is....?	Hvor meget koster...?	Wat kost...?	Kui palju maksab...?
What time is it?	Hvad er klokken?	Hoe laat is het?	Mis kell praegu on?
Where is...?	Hvor er...?	Waar is...?	Kus on...?
I don't understand	Jeg forstår ikke	Ik begrijp het niet	Ma ei saa aru
Do you speak English?	Taler de Engelsk?	Spreekt u Engels?	Kas te räägite inglise keelt?
Please write it down	Vaer venlig at skrive det	Wilt u het opschrijven, alstublieft	Palun kirjutage see üles
One	En	Een	Uks
Two	To	Twee	Tkaks
Three	Tre	Drie	Kolm
Four	Fire	Vier	Neli
Five	Fem	Vijf	Viis
Six	Seks	Zes	Kuus
Seven	Syv	Zeven	Seitse
Eight	Otte	Acht	Kaheksa
Nine	Ni	Negen	Uheksa
Ten	Ti	Tien	Kümme

Finnish, French and German

	Finnish	French	German
Yes	Kyllä	Oui	Ja
No	Ei	Non	Nein
Please	Olkaa hyvä	S'il vous plaît	Bitte
Thank you	Kiitos	Merci	Danke
Hello/Good day	Hyvää	Bonjour	Güten Tag
Goodbye	Hyvästi	Au revoir/à bientôt	Auf Wiedersehen
Excuse me	Anteeksi	Pardon	Entschuldigen Sie, bitte
Where	Missä	Où	Wo
When	Milloin	Quand	Wann
How	Kuinka	Comment	Wie
Left	Vasen	Gauche	Links
Right	Oikea	Droit	Rechts
Large	Suuri	Grand	Gross
Small	Pieni	Petit	Klein
Good	Hyvä	Bon	Gut
Bad	Paha	Mauvais	Schlecht
Near	Lähellä	Près	Nah
Far	Kaukana	Loin	Weit

	Finnish	French	German
Cheap	Halpa	Bon marché	Billig
Expensive	Kallis	Cher	Teuer
Open	Avoin	Ouvert	Offen
Closed	Suljettu	Fermé	Geschlossen
Today	Tänään	Aujourd'hui	Heute
Yesterday	Eilen	Hier	Gestern
Tomorrow	Huomenna	Demain	Morgen
Day	Päivä	Jour	Tag
Week	Viikko	Semaine	Woche
Month	Kuukausi	Mois	Monat
Year	Vuosi	Année	Jahr
How much is....?	Kuinka paljon on...?	Combien coûte...?	Wieviel kostet...?
What time is it?	Paljonko kello on?	Quelle heure est-il?	Wieviel Uhr ist es?
Where is...?	Missä on...?	Où est...?	Wo ist...?
I don't understand	En ymmärrä	Je ne comprends pas	Ich verstehe nicht
Do you speak English?	Puhutteko Englantia?	Parlez-vous anglais?	Sprechen Sie Englisch?
Please write it down	Olkaa hyvä ja kiarjoittakaa se	Veuillez me l'écrire	Bitte schreiben Sie es
One	Yksi	Un	Eins
Two	Kaksi	Deux	Zwei
Three	Kolme	Trois	Drei
Four	Neljä	Quatre	Vier
Five	Viisi	Cinq	Fünf
Six	Kuusi	Six	Sechs
Seven	Seitsemän	Sept	Sieben
Eight	Kahdeksan	Huit	Acht
Nine	Yhdeksän	Neuf	Neun
Ten	Kymmenen	Dix	Zehn

Greek, Hungarian and Italian

	Greek	Hungarian	Italian
Yes	Néh	Igen	Sì
No	Óhi	Nem	No
Please	Parakaló	Kérem	Per favore
Thank you	Efharistó	Köszönöm	Grazie
Hello/Good day	Yássas/hérete	Jó napot	Ciao/buon giorno
Goodbye	Adío	Viszontlátásra	Ciao/arrivederci
Excuse me	Signómi	Bocsánat	Mi scusi/prego
Where	Pou	Hol	Dove
When	Póte	Mikor	Quando
How	Pos	Hogyan	Come
Left	Aristerá	Balra	Sinistra
Right	Dheksiá	Jobbra	Destra
Large	Megálo	Nagy	Grande
Small	Mikró	Kicsi	Piccolo

	Greek	Hungarian	Italian
Good	Kaló	Jó	Buono
Bad	Kakó	Rossz	Cattivo
Near	Kondá	Közel	Vicino
Far	Makriá	Távol	Lontano
Cheap	Fthinós	Olcsó	Buon mercato
Expensive	Akrivós	Drága	Caro
Open	Aniktós	Nyitva	Aperto
Closed	Klistós	Zárva	Chiuso
Today	Símera	Ma	Oggi
Yesterday	Khthés	Tegnap	Ieri
Tomorrow	Ávrio	Holnap	Domani
Day	Méra	Nap	Giorno
Week	Iméra	Hét	Settimana
Month	Evdomáda	Hónap	Mese
Year	Chrónos	Év	Anno
How much is....?	Póso káni...?	Mennyibe kerül...?	Quanto è...?
What time is it?	Ti óra inai...?	Hány óra?	Che ore sono?
Where is...?	Pou íne...?	Hol van?	Dov'è...?
I don't understand	Dhen katalavéno	Nem értem	Non ho capito
Do you speak English?	Ksérite Angliká?	Beszél Angolul?	Parla Inglese?
Please write it down	Parakaló grápiste to	Legyen szíves, írja le	Lo scriva, per favore
One	Éna/mía	Egy	Uno
Two	Dhío	Kettö	Due
Three	Tría	Három	Tre
Four	Tésera	Négy	Quattro
Five	Pénde	Öt	Cinque
Six	Éksi	Hat	Sei
Seven	Eftá	Hét	Sette
Eight	Októ	Nyolc	Otto
Nine	Enyá	Kilenc	Nove
Ten	Dhéka	Tíz	Dieci

Latvian, Lithuanian and Norwegian

	Latvian	Lithuanian	Norwegian
Yes	Jā	Taip	Ja
No	Nē	Ne	Nei
Please	Lodzu	Prašau	Vaer så god
Thank you	Paldies	Ačiu	Takk
Hello/Good day	Labdien	Labas	God dag
Goodbye	Uz redzēšanos	Viso gero	Adjø
Excuse me	Atvainojiet	Atsiprašau	Unnskyld
Where	Kur	Kur	Hvor
When	Kad	Kada	Når
How	Cik	Kaip	Hvordan
Left	Kreisi	Kairė	Venstre

	Latvian	Lithuanian	Norwegian
Right	Labi	Deyinė	Høyre
Large	Liels	Didelis	Stor
Small	Mazs	Mažas	Liten
Good	Labs	Geras	God
Bad	Slikts	Blogas	Dårlig
Near	Tuvs	Artimas	I naerheten
Far	Tāls	Tolimas	Langt Borte
Cheap	Lēts	Pigus	Billig
Expensive	Dārgs	Brangus	Dyr
Open	Atvērts	Atidarytas	Åpen
Closed	Slēgts	Uždarytas	Lukket
Today	Yodien	Šiandien	I dag
Yesterday	Vakar	Vakar	I går
Tomorrow	Rīt	Rytdiena	I morgen
Day	Diena	Diena	Dag
Week	Nedela	Savaitė	Uke
Month	Menesis	Mėnuo	Måned
Year	Gads	Metai	År
How much is....?	Cik tas maksā...?	Kiek kainuoja ...?	Hvor mye er...?
What time is it?	Cik ir pulkstenis?	Kiek valandų?	Hvor mange er klokken?
Where is...?	Kur ir...?	Kur yra...?	Hvor er...?
I don't understand	Es nesaprotu	Nesuprantu	Jeg forstår ikke
Do you speak English?	Vai jūs runājat Angliski?	Ar jųs kalbate angliškai?	Snakker de Englesk?
Please write it down	Lūdzu uzrakstiet	Prašau užrašyti	Vennligst skriv det ned
One	Viens	Vienas	En
Two	Divi	Du/dvi	To
Three	Trīs	Trys	Tre
Four	Četri	Keturi	Fire
Five	Pieci	Penki	Fem
Six	Seyi	Šeši	Seks
Seven	Septiņi	Septyni	Sju
Eight	Astoņi	Aštuoni	Åtte
Nine	Deviņi	Devyni	Ni
Ten	Desmit	Dešimt	Ti

Polish, Portuguese and Romanian

	Polish	Portuguese	Romanian
Yes	Tak	Sim	Da
No	Nie	Não	Nu
Please	Proszę	Por favor	Vă rog
Thank you	Dzęlkuję	Obrigado	Mulţumesc
Hello/Good day	Dzień dobry	Olá	Salut/buna ziua
Goodbye	Do widzenia	Adeus	La revedere
Excuse me	Przepraszam	Desculpe	Permitemi-mi

L

	Polish	Portuguese	Romanian
Where	Gdzie	Onde	Unde
When	Kiedy	Quando	Când
How	Jak	Como	Cum
Left	Na lewo	Esquerda	Stânga
Right	Na prawo	Direita	Dreapta
Large	Duży	Grande	Mare
Small	Mały	Pequeno	Mic
Good	Dobry	Bom	Bun/bine
Bad	Zły	Mau	Rău
Near	Bliski	Perto	Apropriat
Far	Daleko	Longe	Departe
Cheap	Tani	Barato	Ieftin
Expensive	Drogi	Caro	Scump
Open	Otwarty	Aberto	Închis
Closed	Zamknięty	Fechado	Deschis
Today	Dziś	Hoje	Azi
Yesterday	Wczoraj	Ontem	Ieri
Tomorrow	Jutro	Amanhã	Mâine
Day	Dzień	Dia	Zi
Week	Tydzień	Semana	Săptămână
Month	Miesiąc	Mês	Lund
Year	Rok	Ano	An
How much is....?	Ile kosztuje...?	Quanto é... ?	Cât costa...?
What time is it?	Która godzina?	Que horas são?	Ce ora este?
Where is...?	Gdzie jest...?	Onde é...?	Unde este...?
I don't understand	Nie rozemiem	Não comprendo	Nu înțeleg
Do you speak English?	Pan(i) mówi po Angielsku?	Fala Inglés?	Vorbiți Englezește?
Please write it down	Proszę to napisać	Escreva-mo, por favor	Vă rog scriemi
One	Jeden	Um	Unu
Two	Dwa	Dois	Doi
Three	Trzy	Três	Trei
Four	Cztery	Quatro	Patru
Five	Pięć	Cinco	Cinci
Six	Sześć	Seis	Șase
Seven	Siedem	Sete	Șapte
Eight	Osiem	Oito	Opt
Nine	Dziewięć	Nove	Noua
Ten	Dziesięć	Dez	Zece

Russian, Slovene and Spanish

	Russian	Slovene	Spanish
Yes	Da	Ja	Sí
No	Net	Ne	No
Please	Pozháluysta	Prosim	Por favor
Thank you	Spasíbo	Hvala	Gracias

	Russian	Slovene	Spanish
Hello/Good day	Zdrávstvuyte	Živjo/dober dan	Hola
Goodbye	Do svidániya	Nasvidenje	Adiós
Excuse me	Izvinite	Oprostite	Con permiso
Where	Gde	Kje	¿Dónde?
When	Kogdá	Kdaj	¿Cuándo?
How	Kak	Kako	¿Cómo?
Left	Nalévo	Levo	Izquierda
Right	Naprávo	Desno	Derecha
Large	Bolshóy	Veliko	Gran
Small	Málenkiy	Majhno	Pequeño
Good	Khoróshiy	Dobro	Buen
Bad	Plokhóy	Slabo	Mal
Near	Bleezkiy	Blizu	Próximo
Far	Da-lyiko	Daleč	Lejos
Cheap	Dyi-shovee	Poceni	Barato
Expensive	Daragoy	Drago	Caro
Open	Otkryto	Odprto	Abierto
Closed	Zakryto	Zaprto	Cerrado
Today	Syivódnya	Danes	Hoy
Yesterday	Vcherá	Včeraj	Ayer
Tomorrow	Závtra	Jutri	Mañana
Day	Dyen	Dan	Día
Week	Nyi-dyel-ya	Teden	Semana
Month	Mye-syats	Mesec	Mes
Year	God	Leto	Año
How much is....?	Skólko stóit?	Koliko stane?	¿Cuánto cuesta...?
What time is it?	Katoree chass?	Koliko je ura?	¿Tiene la hora?
Where is...?	Gde...?	Kje je…?	¿Dónde está...?
I don't understand	Ya ne ponimáyu	Ne razumem	No entiendo
Do you speak English?	Vy govoríte po-anglíyski?	Govorite angleško?	¿Habla inglés?
Please write it down	Zapishíte éto pozháluysta	Prosim, če mi napišete	Escríbamelo, por favor
One	Odín	Ena	Un/Una
Two	Dva	Dve	Dos
Three	Tri	Tri	Tres
Four	Chetyre	Ytiri	Cuatro
Five	Pyat	Pet	Cinco
Six	Shest	Yest	Seis
Seven	Sem	Sedem	Siete
Eight	Vósem	Osem	Ocho
Nine	Dévyat	Devet	Nueve
Ten	Désyat	Deset	Diez

Swedish and Turkish

	Swedish	Turkish
Yes	Ja	Evet
No	Nej	Hayır/yok
Please	Var så god	Lütfen
Thank you	Tack	Teşkküler/mersi/sağol
Hello/Good day	Hej	Merhaba
Goodbye	Adjö	hoşça kalın
Excuse me	Ursäkta mig	Pardon
Where	Var	...nereye
When	När	Ne zaman
How	Hur	Nasfl
Left	Vänster	Sol
Right	Höger	Sağ
Large	Stor	Büyuk
Small	Liten	Kücük
Good	Bra	İyi
Bad	Dalig	Kötü
Near	Nära	Yakın
Far	Avlägsen	Uzak
Cheap	Billig	Ucuz
Expensive	Dyr	Pahalı
Open	Öppen	Açık
Closed	Stängd	Kapalf
Today	I dag	Bugün
Yesterday	I går	Dün
Tomorrow	I morgon	Yarın
Day	Dag	Gün
Week	Vecka	Hafta
Month	Månad	Ay
Year	Är	Sene
How much is....?	Vad kostar det...?	Ne kadar...?
What time is it?	Hur mycket är klockan?	Saatınız var mi?
Where is...?	Var är...?	Nerede...?
I don't understand	Jag förstår int	Anlamıyorum
Do you speak English?	Talar ni Engelska?	Biliyormusunuz?
Please write it down	Skulle ni kunna skriva det?	Lütfen yazar mısınız
One	Ett	Bir
Two	Två	İki
Three	Tre	Uç
Four	Fyra	Dört
Five	Fem	Beş
Six	Sex	Altf
Seven	Sju	Yedi
Eight	Ätta	Sekiz
Nine	Nio	Dokuz
Ten	Tio	On

LANGUAGE | Swedish and Turkish

L

Index

and small print

Index

Map entries are in colour

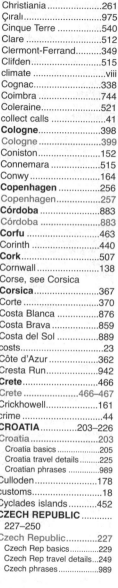

INDEX

1005

Z

X

W

Y

INDEX

A Rough Guide to Rough Guides

In the summer of 1981, Mark Ellingham, a recent graduate from Bristol University, was travelling round Greece and couldn't find a guidebook that really met his needs. On the one hand there were the student guides, insistent on saving every last cent, and on the other the heavyweight cultural tomes whose authors seemed to have spent more time in a research library than lounging away the afternoon at a taverna or on the beach.

In a bid to avoid getting a job, Mark and a small group of writers set about creating their own guidebook. It was a guide to Greece that aimed to combine a journalistic approach to description with a thoroughly practical approach to travellers' needs – a guide that would incorporate culture, history and contemporary insights with a critical edge, together with up-to-date, value-for-money listings. Back in London, Mark and the team finished their Rough Guide, as they called it, and talked Routledge into publishing the book.

That first *Rough Guide to Greece*, published in 1982, was a student scheme that became a publishing phenomenon. The immediate success of the book – with numerous reprints and a Thomas Cook prize shortlisting – spawned a series that rapidly covered dozens of destinations. Rough Guides had a ready market among low-budget backpackers, but soon also acquired a much broader and older readership that relished Rough Guides' wit and inquisitiveness as much as their enthusiastic, critical approach. Everyone wants value for money, but not at any price.

Rough Guides soon began supplementing the "rougher" information about hostels and low-budget listings with the kind of detail on restaurants and quality hotels that independent-minded visitors on any budget might expect, whether on business in New York or trekking in Thailand.

These days the guides – distributed worldwide by the Penguin group – offer recommendations from shoestring to luxury and cover more than 200 destinations around the globe, including almost every country in the Americas and Europe, more than half of Africa and most of Asia and Australasia. Our ever-growing team of authors and photographers is spread all over the world, particularly in Europe, the USA and Australia.

In 1994, we published the *Rough Guide to World Music* and *Rough Guide to Classical Music*; and a year later the *Rough Guide to the Internet*. All three books have become benchmark titles in their fields – which encouraged us to expand into other areas of publishing, mainly around popular culture. Rough Guides now publish:

- Travel guides to more than 200 worldwide destinations
- Dictionary phrasebooks to 22 major languages
- History guides ranging from Ireland to Islam
- Maps printed on rip-proof and waterproof Polyart™ paper
- Music guides running the gamut from Opera to Elvis
- Restaurant guides to London, New York and San Francisco
- Reference books on topics as diverse as the Weather and Shakespeare
- Sports guides from Formula 1 to Man Utd
- Pop culture books from Lord of the Rings to Cult TV
- World Music CDs in association with World Music Network.

Visit **www.roughguides.com** to see our latest publications.

Rough Guide credits

Text editor: Matthew Teller and Jules Brown
Managing Director: Kevin Fitzgerald
Series editor: Mark Ellingham
Editorial: Martin Dunford, Jonathan Buckley, Kate Berens, Ann-Marie Shaw, Helena Smith, Olivia Swift, Ruth Blackmore, Geoff Howard, Claire Saunders, Gavin Thomas, Alexander Mark Rogers, Polly Thomas, Joe Staines, Richard Lim, Duncan Clark, Peter Buckley, Lucy Ratcliffe, Clifton Wilkinson, Alison Murchie, Matthew Teller, Andrew Dickson, Fran Sandham, Sally Schafer, Matthew Milton, Karoline Densley (UK); Andrew Rosenberg, Yuki Takagaki, Richard Koss, Hunter Slaton (US)
Design & Layout: Link Hall, Helen Prior, Julia Bovis, Katie Pringle, Rachel Holmes, Andy Turner, Dan May, Tanya Hall, John McKay, Sophie Hewat (UK); Madhulita Mohapatra,

Umesh Aggarwal, Sunil Sharma (India)
Cartography: Maxine Repath, Ed Wright, Katie Lloyd-Jones (UK); Manish Chandra, Rajesh Chhibber, Jai Prakash Mishra (India)
Cover art direction: Louise Boulton
Picture research: Sharon Martins, Mark Thomas
Online: Kelly Martinez, Anja Mutic-Blessing, Jennifer Gold, Audra Epstein, Suzanne Welles, Cree Lawson (US); Manik Chauhan, Amarjyoti Dutta, Narender Kumar (India)
Finance: Gary Singh
Marketing & Publicity: Richard Trillo, Niki Smith, David Wearn, Chloë Roberts, Demelza Dallow, Claire Southern (UK); Geoff Colquitt, David Wechsler, Megan Kennedy (US)
Administration: Julie Sanderson
RG India: Punita Singh

Publishing information

This tenth edition published November 2003 by
Rough Guides Ltd,
80 Strand, London WC2R 0RL.
345 Hudson St, 4th Floor,
New York, NY 10014, USA.
Distributed by the Penguin Group
Penguin Books Ltd,
80 Strand, London WC2R 0RL
Penguin Putnam, Inc.
375 Hudson Street, NY 10014, USA
Penguin Books Australia Ltd,
487 Maroondah Highway, PO Box 257,
Ringwood, Victoria 3134, Australia
Penguin Books Canada Ltd,
10 Alcorn Avenue, Toronto, Ontario,
Canada M4V 1E4
Penguin Books (NZ) Ltd,
182–190 Wairau Road, Auckland 10,
New Zealand
Typeset in Bembo and Helvetica to an original design by Henry Iles.
Printed in Italy by LegoPrint S.p.A

© Jonathan Buckley and Martin Dunford 2003

No part of this book may be reproduced in any form without permission from the publisher except for the quotation of brief passages in reviews.

1064pp includes index
A catalogue record for this book is available from the British Library

ISBN 1-84353-108-9

The publishers and authors have done their best to ensure the accuracy and currency of all the information in **The Rough Guide to Europe**, however, they can accept no responsibility for any loss, injury, or inconvenience sustained by any traveller as a result of information or advice contained in the guide.

1 3 5 7 9 8 6 4 2

Help us update

We've gone to a lot of effort to ensure that the 10th edition of **The Rough Guide to Europe** is accurate and up to date. However, things change – places get "discovered", opening hours are notoriously fickle, restaurants and rooms raise prices or lower standards. If you feel we've got it wrong or left something out, we'd like to know, and if you can remember the address, the price, the time, the phone number, so much the better.

We'll credit all contributions, and send a copy of the next edition (or any other Rough Guide if you prefer) for the best letters. Everyone who writes to us and isn't already a subscriber will receive a copy of our full-colour thrice-yearly newsletter. Please mark letters: "**Rough Guide Europe Update**" and send to: Rough Guides, 80 Strand, London WC2R 0RL, or Rough Guides, 4th Floor, 345 Hudson St, New York, NY 10014. Or send an email to **mail@roughguides.com**
Have your questions answered and tell others about your trip at **www.roughguides.atinfopop.com**

Acknowledgements

The editor thanks everyone who updated this edition (in alphabetical order): Dave Abram (France), Rob Andrews (Britain, Italy), Jon Bousfield (Croatia, Estonia, Latvia, Lithuania), Lance Chilton (Greece), Belinda Dixon (Austria), Marc Dubin (France, Greece), Nick Edwards (Greece), John Fisher (Greece), Simon Foster (Spain, Turkey), Paul Gray (Britain), Patrick Graham (Poland), Lucia Graves (Italy), Rob Humphreys (Britain), Daniel Jacobs (Basics, Morocco), Fran Kellett (Germany), Phil Lee (Belgium & Luxembourg, Norway), Chris Lloyd (France, Spain), Norm Longley (Slovenia), Lucy Mallows (Hungary, Portugal), James McConnachie (France), Patrick McConnell (Spain), Jose Navarro (France), Catherine Phillips (Russia), James Proctor (Finland, Sweden), Donald Reid (Britain), Paul Sentobe (Germany), Laura Stone (Denmark, Netherlands, Romania), Matthew Teller (Switzerland), Sam Thorne (Bulgaria, Czech Republic, Slovakia), Geoff Wallis (Ireland), Greg Ward (France) and Paul Whitfield (Britain). Also to Jules Brown for stepping in with invaluable editing; Lucy Ratcliffe for tidying the odds and ends; Dan May for typesetting; Jennifer Bailey at PC Graphics and Katie Lloyd-Jones for cartography; Louise Boulton, Sharon Martins and Mark Thomas for photo research; Amanda Jones for proofreading; Matthew Teller for indexing; and Claire Saunders for overseeing the whole affair.

Readers' letters and emails

Thanks to all those who sent in their comments on the 2003 edition of this book (apologies if we've misspelled anyone's name):

Chris Beech, Miss Deepa Bhardwaj, Chris Booth, Shawn Brace, Per Bro, William Clark, Rebecca Crisp, Francine van de Duin, Jonathan Fauver, Stuart George, Pieter Gericke, B. Gordon, Heghi Maria Hajnal, Ms Khurshid A.G. Hanif, Bianca Hein, Nathan Higgins, Kevin B. Hubbard, Michael Humphreys, Davida Jordan, Ruth King, Mette Korsholm, Irene Martin, Lester May, Meredoc McMinn, Mark Meadows, Dwight Newman, Lucy Owen, Richard De Ritter, R. Saffy, Grainne Sheehan, Kai Shen, Alexander Smeitz and Esther Cohen, Alex Smith, Sarah Stevens, Juliet Sutcliffe, Marthe Tanguay, Andrew Thompson, Monika Tischer, Ann Wilks.

Photo credits

Colour Introduction

Winter festival in Davos, Switzerland © The Photographers Library
Santoríni, Greece © Roger Rowland/Travel Ink
Coffee © Neil Setchfield
Trevi Fountain, Rome © Rober
Vineyards and farm house near Jonjieux, France © Michael Busselle/Robert Harding
Running of the bulls, Pamplona, Spain. © Roberto Arakaki/Robert Harding
Hot-air balloon festival, Chateau d'Oex, Switzerland © Neil Egerton/Travel Ink

Things not to miss

Carnival, Venice, Italy © Simon Harris/Robert Harding
Mezquita, Cordoba, Spain © Peter Wilson
Edinburgh Festival, Britain © F. Good/Trip
Ljubljana, Slovenia © C Bowman
Oktoberfest, Bavaria © Robert Harding
Cappadocia, Turkey © M Jenkin/TRIP
Belgian chocolates © Nigel Francis/Robert Harding
Dubrovnik, Croatia © Ken Gillham/Robert Harding
Pont St-Benezet and Petit Palais, Avignon France © Charles Bowman
Paragliding at the Matterhorn © Valais Tourism
Houses of Parliament, Britain © Robert Harding
Brouwersgracht, Amsterdam, The Netherlands © R. Rainford/Robert Harding
The Kremlin, Moscow, Russia © Dominic Harcourt Webster/Robert Harding
Café Central, Vienna, Austria © Robert Harding
Mykonos Town, Greece © Ellen Rooney/Robert Harding
Nyhavn, Copenhagen, Denmark © Dean Miculinic/Travel Ink
Els Quatre Gats restaurant, Barcelona, Spain © Neil Setchfield

Surfing © B. Slater/Trip
The Creation of Adam in the Sistine Chapel
© Roy Rainford/Robert Harding
Golden Statue on Trocadero and Eiffel Tower,
Paris, France © Robert Harding
Atlas Mountains, Morocco © M. Jelliffe/Trip
Cheeseboard, France © Adam
Woolfitt/Robert Harding
View of the Acropolis, Greece © Neil
Setchfield
April Feria, Sevilla, Spain © K.
Gillham/Robert Harding
Reindeers grazing, Lapland © Leo F.
Postl/Travel Ink
Charles Bridge, Prague, The Czech Republic
© Greg Evans
Rynek Glowny, Krakow, Poland © Gregory
Wrona
Clubbing, Ibiza © Leelu Morris/PYMCA
Kiraly Baths, Budapest, Hungary © Adam
Woolfitt/Robert Harding
Pub sign, Cork, Ireland © Michael
Jenner/Robert Harding
Aurora Borealis, Lapland © C. Gibson/Trip
Tatra Mountains, Poland © K. Gillham/Robert
Harding

Black and whites
Schönbrunn Palace, Vienna © Gavin
Hellier/Robert Harding (p.56)
Moules frites © Simon Reddy/Travel Ink
(p.82)
Brighton Pier © H. Rogers/Trip (p.108)
Aleksandâr Nevski Cathedral, Sofia, Bulgaria
© Kyle Clapham (p.182)
City walls, Dubrovnik © Ken Gillham/Robert
Harding (p.204)
Prague Castle, The Czech Republic © John
Probert (p.228)
Skagen, Denmark © Bob Krist/Corbis (p.252)
Alexander Nevsky Cathedral, Tallinn
© Robert Harding (p.274)

Reindeer running, Finland © James Proctor
(p.290)
Chenonceau, Loire Valley © Chris Coe/Axiom
(p.306)
Oktoberfest © Neil Setchfield (p.374)
The Acropolis, Athens © Robert Harding
(p.428)
Communist Statue Park, Budapest © C.
Garnham/Trip (p.474)
Bushmills Distillery Co barrels, Antrim ©
Andy Lovell/Travel Ink (p.494)
The Palio, Siena © Loirat Ly/Robert
Harding/Explorer (p.526)
Freedom Monument, Rīga © Robert Harding
(p.604)
Trakai Castle, Lithuania © G.R.
Richardson/Robert Harding (p.616)
Town walls, Essaouira © Hamish Brown
(p.630)
Amsterdam Canal © Dominic Beddow
(p.656)
The Scream by Edvard Munch © Burstein
Collection/Corbis/DACS (p.682)
Main Square, Old Town, Krakow © K
Gillham/Robert Harding (p.706)
Bacalhau shop © Peter Wilson (p.728)
Carpathian Mountains, Romania © W.
Jacobs/Trip (p.758)
The Kremlin, Moscow © Dominic Harcourt-
Webster (p.774)
Tratas Mountains, Slovakia © N.
McDiarmid/Trip (p.794)
Mestni Trg Fountain, Ljubljana © Phil
Robinson/Robert Harding (p.810)
Paella © Neil Setchfield (p.826)
Gamla Stan, Stockholm © Paul van
Riel/Robert Harding (p.896)
View of Gornergrat above Zermatt,
Switzerland © Matthew Teller (p.918)
Sultan Ahmet (Blue Mosque), İstanbul © A.
Bedding/Travel Ink (p.948)

Rough Guides travel

key   ✪ map   ⊞ phrasebook   ⊙ cd

Rough Guides publishes new books every month:

Rough Guides music & reference

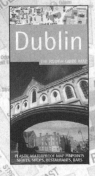

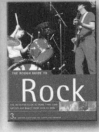

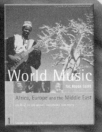

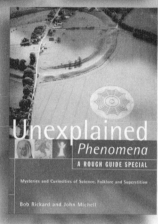

Pocket History Series

"Solidly written, immaculately researched, Rough Guides
are as near as modern guides get to essential"
Sunday Times, London

Rough Guide Reference

NOTES

NOTES

NOTES

NOTES

NOTES

NOTES

NOTES

NOTES

NOTES

NOTES

NOTES

STAYOKAY HOSTELS

Stayokay is a chain of 30 hostels located throughout the Netherlands. You will find our hostels at surprisingly lovely places: in the dunes, the woods, along the waterside and in the city. The Stayokay hostels are housed in different unique buildings, ranging from modern facilities to castles or country houses. The same informal, relaxed atmosphere can be found at all Stayokay hostels, where friendly, helpful staff awaits your arrival!

WE OFFER YOU...

• beds on comfortable 2-, 4-, 6- and 8- bedded rooms and dormitories, most with private sanitary facilities • comfortable double bunks, bedside lights, table and chairs and private cupboards • breakfast included • bedsheets included • restaurant • TV lounge • internet facilities • luggage lockers • laundry facilities (at most hostels) • discounted tickets for local attractions • and more...

HOSTELLING INTERNATIONAL

Stayokay is part of the Hostelling International network, comprising over 4.000 hostels worldwide. HI members receive € 2,50 discount per night.

RESERVATIONS

You can reserve directly at the hostel or at **www.stayokay.com**. Alternatively you can make a reservation via the Hostelling International IBN network.

OUR HOSTELS IN THE CENTRE OF AMSTERDAM

Stayokay Amsterdam Vondelpark

Zandpad 5
1054 GA Amsterdam
tel +31 (0)20 589 89 96
fax +31 (0)20 589 89 55

Diverse, exciting and comfortable Stayokay Amsterdam Vondelpark is one of Europe's largest and most modern hostels. Located in the centre of Amsterdam, in the beautiful Vondelpark.

Stayokay Amsterdam Stadsdoelen

Kloveniersburgwal 97
1011 KB Amsterdam
tel +31 (0)20 624 68 32
fax +31 (0)20 639 10 35

Downtown Amsterdam, international, exciting Stayokay Amsterdam Stadsdoelen is located in a stately canal house in the city centre.

EXPERIENCE HOLLAND, AMSTERDAM INCLUDED!
Visit our website at **www.stayokay.com** to find out more information about our other hostels. Some of them are at very short distance from Amsterdam and are in interesting areas with easy access by public transport. This way you allow yourself to see much more of Holland!

HISTORIC ROYAL PALACES

Your invitation to experience 900 years of royal history

Tower of London

Visit the Tower and discover some of Britain's most extraordinary history.
Admire the breathtaking Crown Jewels and hear tales aplenty
on a Yeoman Warder 'Beefeater' tour.

⊖ Nearest tube Tower Hill

Hampton Court Palace

Explore the Tudor and Stuart splendours of Britain's greatest palace,
set in stunning gardens by the River Thames.

⇌ 30 minute direct train from Waterloo Station

Kensington Palace

Discover royal lifestyles, from the rooms where Queen Victoria spent
her childhood to the Royal Ceremonial Dress Collection and
dresses worn by Diana, Princess of Wales.

⊖ Nearest tube: High Street Kensington or Queensway

R.S.V.P

Tower of London
For advance tickets
call 0870 756 7070
in the UK or visit
www.tower-of-london.co.uk

Hampton Court Palace
For advance tickets
call 0870 753 7777
in the UK or visit
www.hampton-court-palace.co.uk

Kensington Palace
For advance tickets
call 0870 751 5180
in the UK or visit
www.kensington-palace-org.uk

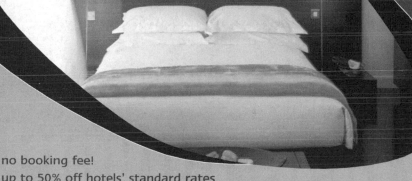